S0-AZM-621

WORLDMARK YEARBOOK 2001

ISSN 1527-6503

WORLDMARK YEARBOOK 2001

Volume 2
H–Q

Mary Rose Bonk, Editor

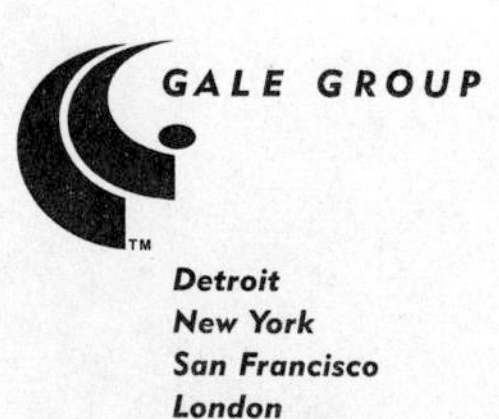

Detroit
New York
San Francisco
London
Boston
Woodbridge, CT

British Library Cataloguing in Publication Data. A Catalogue record of this book is available from the British Library.

ISBN 0–7876–5090–0 (3-Volume set)
ISBN 0–7876–5091–9 (Volume 1)
ISBN 0–7876–5092–7 (Volume 2)
ISBN 0–7876–5093–5 (Volume 3)
ISSN 1527–6503

Printed in the United States of America

10 9 8 7 6 5 4 3 2 1

CONTENTS

FOREWORD

A NEW, YEARLY REFERENCE FOR A NEW ERA

A new member of the Worldmark family, *Worldmark Yearbook* presents to users a comprehensive profile of the world's nations and territories and their current events. Information often scattered throughout books, articles, and various agencies is compiled here in an easy to use reference. It complements other Worldmark publications by presenting the most current information on countries around the world. The Worldmark line already provides you with an in-depth historical account for these countries in *Worldmark Encyclopedia of the Nations*. With the introduction of the *Worldmark Yearbook*, you can be kept up-to-date with the latest developments.

EXPANDED TO COVER MORE OF THE WORLD

Nine new countries and territories have been added to the *Yearbook*'s coverage. Spanning northern Europe to the South Pacific, these additions provide users with added breadth of coverage. Users can also now rely on the *Yearbook* for greater depth of material. Content for the 2001 edition was expanded to include five new categories in the Directory—Broadcast Media, Colleges and Universities, Newspapers and Magazines, Publishers, and Religious Organizations. It is presented here for easy reference.

THE YEAR IN REVIEW

Worldmark Yearbook begins with a look at the year in review. From Tokyo to Berlin, and from Moscow to Auckland and Pretoria, major events from the past year are highlighted and placed in an international perspective. The main focus of the *Yearbook* is on national events, so the Year in Review provides a broader look at how national issues can affect regional neighbors and the world.

WHERE IN THE WORLD?

Each country is accompanied by a map that places it within its area of the world and which details major cities and landmarks. Geography often plays an important role in a nation's politics and economy. The expansive maps can help *Yearbook* users better understand how geography may affect what goes on within a nation. In addition, in a world increasingly referred to as a "global village," national events often spill over into neighboring states. To easily identify neighbors, color regional maps are on hand for reference.

NATIONAL SYMBOLS

An added feature of the *Worldmark Yearbook* is the color illustration of national symbols, including flags and official insignia. Each country's official flag is represented and a brief description is included in each entry. A country's official insignia, such as an emblem or seal, is also represented.

PROFILES

A national profile highlights basic information for each country. The national capital, monetary unit, anthem, and climate are a few examples of the data available at the beginning of each entry.

BACKGROUND CHECK

A yearbook of current events would be of little use without a context in which to put those events. *Worldmark Yearbook*'s introductory survey provides users with this context. Recent history from the mid-twentieth century onward is outlined to provide background in and support for the events of the past year. But history itself does not present a comprehensive picture of how a nation operates. Do you want to know how a country's government is set up? Who can participate in it? How the economy operates? What are the major industrial and economic developments of the past few years? The answers to these questions, and more, can be found in the introductory survey.

ANALYZING THE YEAR'S EVENTS

A timeline is included in each entry and lists chronologically the events of the past year. Selecting the most significant of these events, an analysis explains them in greater depth and pulls together the threads of politics, economy, and culture to create a cohesive picture of a distinct nation. Economic struggles, cultural revivals, political triumphs: The analysis paints a more personal picture of each country, which can not be as easily portrayed through the simple listing of facts or statistics.

WHO'S WHO?

Who's been running the country while these events have taken place? To find out, users can reference the *Yearbook*'s directory, which, when possible, includes information on how to contact an individual or group. Main government functionaries, including the heads and ministers of state, are listed, as are political organizations active within the country and its major judicial courts. Outside of government, the directory provides information on broadcast media within a country, as well as colleges and universities, newspapers and magazines, publishing, and religious organizations. In this "global village," knowing one's neighbors is important, and maintaining official contact with them is a vital part of government operations. In this light, users will find a comprehensive listing of diplomatic representation for each country.

JUST THE FACTS

If hard data is what you're looking for, you can find it in the statistical survey. Population size and growth, economic output and development, major industrial production, and more can be located in the statistical survey. Statistics complement the analysis by explaining numerically much of what's going on in a country's society and economy. It creates a numerative picture that can be easily compared with that of other nations.

WANT MORE?

Check out the Further Reading section for sources of additional information on statistics, current events, and historical background. You can also refer to the International Organizations listing. It provides contact information and a brief description of over 1,800 international organizations that are involved in a variety of global concerns.

AT YOUR FINGERTIPS

Are you looking for something specific? A glance at the *Yearbook*'s comprehensive index will help you find your way. The user-friendly index covers personal names, subjects, and geographies and can refer you quickly to the information you need.

A COMPREHENSIVE TOOL TO TODAY'S WORLD

The *Worldmark Yearbook* pulls together the many components that make up a government and a society to give users a well-balanced, comprehensive, and illustrative source of information on the world's nations. Its many headers make quick reference points to easily locate information. The *Worldmark Yearbook* will enhance the libraries of all reference users. It offers the world.

We encourage you to contact us with comments or suggestions. Tell us what you want to see in the *Yearbook* and how we can better meet your needs. Comments and suggestions can be sent to: The Editors, *Worldmark Yearbook*, The Gale Group, 27500 Drake Road, Farmington Hills, MI 48331. Or, call toll free at 1-800-877-4253.

ACKNOWLEDGEMENTS

For editorial and technical assistance that helped keep this project on track and on time, the editors are extremely grateful to the following Gale Group contributors:

Dean Ackerman, senior programmer/analyst, **Laura L. Brandau**, assistant editor, **Pamela A. Dear**, associate editor, **Kathy Droste**, editor, **Grant Eldridge**, editor, **Jolen Gedridge**, editor, **William H. Harmer**, editor, and **Rebecca Parks**, editor.

For editorial and textual contributions to the *Worldmark Yearbook*, the editors are indebted to the following:

Michael Dawson, Carlsbad, California, **Eastword Publications Development**, Cleveland, Ohio, **Editorial Code and Data, Inc. (ECDI)**, Southfield, Michigan, **GGS Information Services**, York, Pennsylvania, **Richard Clay Hanes**, Eugene, Oregon, **Monica Langley**, Charleston, South Carolina, **Devon Marie Trevarrow**, and **Christy Wood**, Hamtramck, Michigan.

For permission to take material from personal or published sources, use of images, and for other courtesies extended during the preparation of this edition, the editors are grateful to the following sources:

Carib Media Marketing and Consultancy, N.V., **Eastword Publications Development**, **The Flag Institute Enterprises**, **International Monetary Fund**, Publications Services Unit, **Internet Caribbean Unlimited**, **Maryland Cartographics**, **Phil Nelson**, **One Mile Up**, **UNESCO (United Nations Education, Scientific and Cultural Organization)**, **UNIDO (United Nations Industrial Development Organization)**, **United Nations Conference of Trade and Development**, **United Nations Publications**, author of original material, **Oxford University Press, Inc.**, **Frederick Warne**, **World Bank**, **World Tourism Organization**, and **XNR Productions**.

KEY TO ABBREVIATIONS

ABEDA: Arab Bank for Economic Development in Africa

ACC: Arab Cooperation Council

ACCT: Agence de Cooperation Culturelle et Technique; see Agency for Cultural and Technical Cooperation

ACP: African, Caribbean, and Pacific Countries

AfDB: African Development Bank

AFESD: Arab Fund for Economic and Social Development

AG: Andean Group

AL: Arab League

ALADI: Asociacion Latinamericana de Intergracion; see Latin American Integration Association (LAIA)

AMF: Arab Monetary Fund

AMU: Arab Maghreb Fund

ANZUS: Australia-New Zealand-United States Security Trust

AO: Arctic Oscillation

APEC: Asia Pacific Economic Cooperation

AsDB: Asian Development Bank

ASEAN: Association of Southeast Asian Nations

BAD: Banque Africaine de Developpement; see African Development Bank (AfDB)

BADEA: Banque Arabe de Developpement Economique en Afrique; see Arab Bank for Economic Development in Africa (ABEDA)

BCIE: Banco Centroamericano de Integracion Economico; see Central American Bank for Economic Integration (BCIE)

BDEAC: Banque de Development des Etats de l'Afrique Centrale; see Central African States Development Bank

Benelux: Benelux Economic Union

BID: Banco Interamericano de Desarrollo; see Inter-American Development Bank (IADB)

BIS: Bank for International Settlements

BOAD: Banque Ouest-Africaine de Developpement; see West African Development Bank (WADB)

BSEC: Black Sea Economic Coorperation Zone

C: Commonwealth

CACM: Central American Common Market

CAEU: Council of Arab Economic Unity

CARICOM: Caribbean Community and Common Market

CBSS: Council of Baltic Sea States

CCC: Customs Cooperation Council

CDB: Caribbean Development Bank

CE: Council of Europe

CEAO: Communaute Economique de l'Afrique de l'Ouest; see West African Economic Community (CEAO)

CEEAC: Communaute Economique des Etats de l' Afrique Centrale; see Economic Community of Central African States (CEEAC)

CEI: Central European Initiative

CEMA: Council for Mutual Economic Assistance; also known as CMEA or Comecon

CEPGL: Communaute Economique de Pays des Grands Lacs; see Economic Community of the Great Lakes Countries (CEPGL)

CERN: Conseil European pour la Recherche Nucleaire; see European Organization for Nuclear Research (CERN)

CG: Contadora Group

CIS: Commonwealth of Independent States

CMEA: Council for Mutual Economic Assistance (CEMA); also known as Comeecon

COCOM: Coordinating Committee on Export Controls

Comecon: Council for Mutual Economic Assistance (CEMA); also known as CMEA

CP: Colombo Plan

CSCE: Conference on Security and Cooperation in Europe

DC: Developed country

EADB: East African Development Bank

EBRD: European Bank for Reconstruction and Development

EC: European Community; see European Union (EU)

ECA: Economic Commission for Africa

ECAFE: Economic Commission for Asia and the Far East; see Economic and Social Commission for Asia and the Pacific (ESCAP)

ECE: Economic Commission for Europe

ECLA: Economic Commission for Latin America; see Economic Commission for Latin America and the Caribbean (ECLAC)

ECLAC: Economic Commission for Latin America and the Caribbean

ECO: Economic Cooperation Organization

ECOSOC: Economic and Social Council

ECOWAS: Economic Community of West African States

ECSC: European Coal and Steel Community

ECWA: Economic Commission for Western Asia; see Economic and Social Council for Western Asia (ESCWA)

EEC: European Economic Community

EFTA: European Free Trade Association

EIB: European Investment Bank

Entente: Council of the Entente

ESA: European Space Agency

ESCAP: Economic and Social Commission for Asia and the Pacific

ESCWA: Economic and Social Commission for Western Asia

EU: European Union

Euratom: European Atomic Energy Community

FAO: Food and Agriculture Organization

FLS: Front Line States

FZ: Franc Zone

G-2: Group of 2

G-3: Group of 3

G-5: Group of 5

G-6: Group of 6

G-7: Group of 7

G-8: Group of 8

G-9: Group of 9

G-10: Group of 10

G-11: Group of 11

G-15: Group of 15

G-19: Group of 19

G-24: Group of 24

G-30: Group or 30

G-33: Group of 33

G-77: Group of 77

GATT: General Agreement on Tariff and Trade

Habitat: Commission on Human Settlements

IADB: Inter-American Development Bank

IAEA: International Atomic Energy Agency

IBEC: International Bank for Economic Cooperation

IBRD: International Bank for Reconstruction and Development

ICAO: International Civil Aviation Organization

ICC: International Chamber of Commerce

ICEM: Intergovernmental Committee for European Migration; see International Organization for Migration (IOM)

ICFTU: International Confederation of Free Trade Unions

ICJ: International Court of Justice

ICM: Intergovernmental Committee for Migration; see International Organization for Migration (IOM)

ICRC: International Committee of the Red Cross

ICRM: International Red Cross and Red Crescent Movement

IDA: International Development Association

IDB: Islamic Development Bank

IEA: International Energy Agency

IFAD: International Fund for Agriculture Development

IFC: International Finance Corporation

IFCTU: International Federation of Christian Trade Unions

IFRCS: International Federation of Red Cross and Red Crescent Societies

IGADD: Inter-Governmental Authority on Drought and Development

IIB: International Investment Bank

ILO: International Labor Organization

IMCO: Intergovernmental Maritime Consultative Organization; see International Maritime Organization (IMO)

IMF: International Monetary Fund

IMO: International Maritime Fund

INMARSAT: International Maritime Satelite Organization

INTELSAT: International Telecommunications Satellite Organization

INTERPOL: International Criminal Police Organization

IOC: International Olympic Committee

IOM: International Organization for Migration

ISO: International Organization for Standardization

ITU: International Telecommunications Union

LAES: Latin American Economic System

LAIA: Latin American Integration Association

LAS: League of Arab States; see Arab League (AL)

LDC: Less developed country

LLDC: Least developed country

LORCS: League of Red Cross and Red Crescent Societies

MERCOSUR: Mercado Commun del Cono Sur; see Southern Cone Common Market

MINURSO: United Nations Mission for the Referendum in Western Sahara

MTCR: Missile Technology Control Regime

NACC: North Atlantic Cooperation Council

NAM: Nonaligned Movement

NATO: North Atlantic Treaty Organization

NC: Nordic Council

NEA: Nuclear Energy Agency

NIB: Nordic Investment Bank

NIC: Newly industrializing country; see newly industrializing economy (NIE)

NIE: Newly industrializing economy

NSG: Nuclear Suppliers Group

OAPEC: Organization of Arab Petroleum Exporting Countries

OAS: Organization of American States

OAU: Organization of African Unity

OECD: Organization for Economic Cooperation and Development

OECS: Organization of Eastern Caribbean States

OIC: Organization of the Islamic Conference

ONUSAL: United Nations Observer Mission in El Salvador

OPANAL: Organismo para la Proscripcion de las Armas Nuclearea en la America Latina y el Caribe; see Agency for the Prohibition of Nuclear Weapons in Latin America and the Caribbean

OPEC: Organization of Petroleum Exporting Countries

OSCE: Organization on Security and Cooperation in Europe

PCA: Permanent Court of Arbitration

PLO: Palestinian Liberation Organization

PPP: Partnership for Peace

RG: Rio Group

SAARC: South Asian Association for Regional Cooperation

SACU: South African Customs Union

SADC: South African Development Community

SADCC: South African Development Coordination Conference

SAR: Hong Kong Special Administrative Region

SELA: Sistema Economico Latinamericana; see Latin American Economic System (LAES)

SPARTECA: South Pacific Regional Trade and Economic Cooperation Agreement

SPC: South Pacific Commission

SPF: South Pacific Forum

UDEAC: Union Douaniere et Economique de l'Afrique Centrale; see Central African Customs and Economic Union (UDEAC)

UN: United Nations

UNAVEM II: United Nations Angola Verification Mission

UNAMIR: United Nations Assistance Mission for Rwands

UNCTAD: United Nations Conference on Trade and Development

UNDOF: United Nations Disengagement Observer Force

UNDP: United Nations Development Program

UNEP: United Nations Environment Program

UNESCO: United Nations Educational, Scientific, and Cultural Organization

UNFICYP: United Nations Forces in Cyprus

UNFPA: United Nations Fund for Population Activities; see UN Population Fund (UNFPA)

UNHCR: United Nations Office of the High Commissioner for Refugees

UNICEF: United Nations Children's Fund

UNIDO: United Nations Industrial Development Organization

UNIFIL: United Nations Interim Force in Lebanon

UNIKOM: United Nations Iraq-Kuwait Observation Mission

UNITAR: United Nations Institute for Training and Research

UNMIH: United Nations Mission in Haiti

UNMOGIP: United Nations Military Observer Group in India and Pakistan

UNOMIG: United Nations Observer Mission in Georgia

UNOMIL: United Nations Observer Mission in Liberia

UNOMOZ: United Nations Operation in Mozambique

UNOMUR: United Nations Observer Mission Uganda-Rwanda

UNOSOM: United Nations Operation in Somalia

UNPROFOR: United Nations Protection Force

UNRISD: United Nations Research Institute for Social Development

UNRWA: United Nations Relief and Works Agency for Palestine Refugees in the Near East

UNTAC: United Nations Transitional Authority in Cambodia

UNTSO: United Nations Truce Supervision Organization

UNU: United Nations University

UPU: Universal Postal Union

USSR/EE: USSR/Eastern Europe

WADB: West African Development Bank

WCL: World Confederation of Labor

WEU: Western European Union

WFC: World Food Council

WFP: World Food Program

WFTU: World Federation of Trade Unions

WHO: World Health Organization

WIPO: World Intellectual Property Organization

WMO: World Meteorological Organization

WP: Warsaw Pact

WTO: World Trade Organization

WtoO: World Tourism Organization

ZC: Zangger Committee

IMPERIAL/METRIC CONVERSION KEY

WHEN YOU KNOW	MULTIPLY BY	TO FIND
Length		
Millimeters (mm)	0.04	inches (in)
Centimeters (cm)	0.4	inches (in)
Meters (m)	3.3	feet (ft)
Meters (m)	1.1	yards (yd)
Kilometers (km)	0.6	miles (mi)
Area		
sq. centimeters (cm^2)	0.155	sq. inches (in^2)
sq. meters (m^2)	10.76	sq. feet (ft^2)
sq. meters (m^2)	1.2	sq. yards (yd^2)
sq. kilometers (km^2)	0.4	sq. miles (mi^2)
hectares (ha)	2.5	acres
Weight		
grams (g)	0.035	ounces (oz)
kilograms (km)	2.2	pounds (lbs)
metric tons (t)	1.1	short tons (2,000 lbs)
Volume		
milliliters (ml)	0.03	fluid ounces (fl oz)
liters (L)	2.1	pints (pt)
liters (L)	1.06	quarts (qt)
liters (L)	0.26	gallons (gal)
cubic meters (m^3)	35.0	cubic feet (ft^3)
cubic meters (m^3)	1.3	cubic yards (yd^3)
Temperature		
Celsius (°C)	9/5 +32	Fahrenheit (°F)

WHEN YOU KNOW	MULTIPLY BY	TO FIND
Length		
inches (in)	25.4	millimeters
inches (in)	2.54	centimeters (cm)
feet (ft)	30.5	centimeters (cm)
yards (yd)	0.9	meters (m)
miles (m)	1.1	kilometers (km)
Area		
sq. inches (in^2)	6.45	sq. centimeters (cm^2)
sq. feet (ft^2)	0.09	sq. meters (m^2)
sq. yards (yd^2)	0.84	sq. meters (m^2)
sq. miles (mi^2)	0.4	sq. kilometers (km^2)
acres	0.4	hectares (ha)
Weight		
ounces (oz)	28.0	grams (g)
pounds (lbs)	0.45	kilograms (kg)
short tons (2,000 lbs)	0.9	metric tons (t)
Volume		
fluid ounces (fl oz)	30.0	milliliters (ml)
pints (pt)	0.47	liters (L)
quarts (qt)	0.95	liters (L)
gallons (gal)	3.8	liters (L)
cubic feet (ft^3)	0.03	cubic meters (m^3)
cubic yards (yd^3)	0.76	cubic meters (m^3)
Temperature		
Fahrenheit (°F)	5/9 −32	Celsius (°C)

STATUS OF NATIONS

COUNTRY NAME: SYSTEM OF GOVERNMENT

Afghanistan: transitional government

Aland Islands: self-governing, autonomous province of Finland

Albania: emerging democracy

Algeria: republic

American Samoa: unincorporated territory of the United States

Andorra: parliamentary democracy

Angola: transitional government, nominally a multiparty democracy with a strong presidential system

Anguilla: British crown colony

Antarctica: territory claimed by 9 countries; administered by the Antarctica Treaty, which has 44 member nations (28 voting, 16 non-voting)

Antigua and Barbuda: constitutional parliamentary monarchy

Argentina: republic

Armenia: republic

Aruba: parliamentary democracy

Australia: democratic, federal-state system recognizing the British monarch as sovereign

Austria: federal republic

Azerbaijan: republic

Bahamas, The: constitutional parliamentary democracy

Bahrain: traditional monarchy

Bangladesh: republic

Barbados: parliamentary democracy

Belarus: republic

Belgium: federal parliamentary democracy under a constitutional monarch

Belize: parliamentary democracy

Benin: republic under multiparty democratic rule

Bermuda: British crown colony

Bhutan: monarchy

Bolivia: republic

Bosnia and Herzegovina: emerging democracy

Botswana: parliamentary republic

Brazil: federal republic

British Virgin Islands: British crown colony

Brunei: constitutional sultanate

Bulgaria: parliamentary republic

Burkina Faso: parliamentary

Burundi: republic

Cambodia: multiparty liberal democracy under a constitutional monarchy

Cameroon: unitary republic; multiparty presidential regime (opposition parties legalized in 1990)

Canada: constitutional monarchy, federation, and democracy

Cape Verde: republic

Cayman Islands: British crown colony

Central African Republic: republic

Chad: republic

Chile: republic

China: Communist state

Christmas Island: territory of Australia

Cocos Islands: territory of Australia

Colombia: republic; executive branch dominates government structure

Comoros: independent republic

Congo, Democratic Republic of: dictatorship; presumably undergoing a transition to representative government

Congo, Republic of: republic

Cook Islands: self-governing parliamentary democracy

Costa Rica: democratic republic

Cote d'Ivoire: republic

Croatia: presidential/parliamentary democracy

Cuba: Communist state

Cyprus: republic

Czech Republic: parliamentary democracy

Denmark: constitutional monarchy

Djibouti: republic

Dominica: parliamentary democracy

Dominican Republic: representative democracy

Ecuador: republic

Egypt: republic

El Salvador: republic

Equatorial Guinea: republic in transition to multiparty democracy

Eritrea: transitional government

Estonia: parliamentary democracy

Ethiopia: federal republic

Falkland Islands: British crown colony

Faroe Islands: part of the Kingdom of Denmark; self-governing overseas administrative division of Denmark since 1948

Fiji: republic

Finland: republic

France: republic

French Guiana: French overseas department

French Polynesia: territory of France

Gabon: republic; multiparty presidential regime

Gambia, The: republic under multiparty democratic rule

Georgia: republic

Germany: federal republic

Ghana: constitutional democracy

Gibraltar: British crown colony

Greece: parliamentary republic

Greenland: part of the Kingdom of Denmark; self-governing overseas administrative division of Denmark since 1979

Grenada: constitutional parliamentary monarchy

Guadeloupe: overseas department and administrative region of France

Guam: unincorporated territory of the United States

Guatemala: constitutional democratic republic

Guernsey: dependency of the British crown

Guinea: republic

Guinea-Bissau: republic

Guyana: republic

Haiti: republic

Honduras: constitutional democratic republic

Hong Kong: Special Administrative Region (SAR) of China

Hungary: parliamentary democracy

Iceland: constitutional republic

India: federal republic

Indonesia: republic

Iran: theocratic republic

Iraq: republic

Ireland: republic

Israel: parliamentary democracy

Italy: republic

Jamaica: constitutional parliamentary democracy

Japan: constitutional monarchy

Jersey: dependency of the British crown

Jordan: constitutional monarchy

Kazakstan: republic

Kenya: republic

Kiribati: republic

Korea, North: authoritarian socialist; one-man dictatorship

Korea, South: republic

Kuwait: nominal constitutional monarchy

Kyrgyzstan: republic

Laos: Communist state

Latvia: parliamentary democracy

Lebanon: republic

Lesotho: parliamentary constitutional monarchy

Liberia: republic

Libya: Jamahiriya (a state of the masses) in theory, governed by the populace through local councils; in fact, a military dictatorship

Liechtenstein: hereditary constitutional monarchy

Lithuania: parliamentary democracy

Luxembourg: constitutional monarchy

Macau: Special Administrative Region (SAR) of China

Macedonia: emerging democracy

Madagascar: republic

Malawi: multiparty democracy

Malaysia: constitutional monarchy

Maldives: republic

Mali: republic

Malta: parliamentary democracy

Man, Isle of: British crown dependency

Marshall Islands: constitutional government in free association with the US

Martinique: overseas department and administrative region of France

Mauritania: republic

Mauritius: parliamentary democracy

Mayotte: territory of France

Mexico: federal republic operating under a centralized government

Micronesia, Federated States of: constitutional government in free association with the US

Midway Islands: territory of the United States

Moldova: republic

Monaco: constitutional monarchy

Mongolia: republic

Montenegro: republic

Montserrat: British crown colony

Morocco: constitutional monarchy

Mozambique: republic

Myanmar: military regime

Namibia: republic

Nauru: republic

Nepal: parliamentary democracy

Netherlands: constitutional monarchy

Netherlands Antilles: parliamentary

New Caledonia: territory of France

New Zealand: parliamentary democracy

Nicaragua: republic

Niger: republic

Nigeria: republic transitioning from military to civilian rule

Niue: self-governing parliamentary democracy

Norfolk Island: territory of Australia

Northern Mariana Islands: self-governing commonwealth in political with United States

Norway: constitutional monarchy

Oman: monarchy

Pakistan: federal republic

Palau: constitutional government in free association with the US

Palestinian Authority: transitional government

Panama: constitutional democracy

Papua New Guinea: parliamentary democracy

Paraguay: constitutional republic

Peru: constitutional republic

Philippines: republic

Pitcairn Islands: territory of the United Kingdom

Poland: republic

Portugal: parliamentary democracy

Puerto Rico: commonwealth

Qatar: traditional monarchy

Reunion: overseas department of France

Romania: republic

Russia: federation

Rwanda: republic; presidential multi-party

Saint Helena: British crown colony

Saint Kitts and Nevis: constitutional parliamentary monarchy

Saint Lucia: parliamentary democracy

Saint Pierre and Miquelon: French territorial collectivity

Saint Vincent and the Grenadines: constitutional monarchy

Samoa: constitutional monarchy under native chief

San Marino: republic

Sao Tome and Principe: republic

Saudi Arabia: monarchy

Senegal: republic under multiparty democratic rule

Serbia: republic

Seychelles: republic

Sierra Leone: constitutional democracy

Singapore: parliamentary republic

Slovakia: parliamentary democracy

Slovenia: parliamentary democratic republic

Solomon Islands: parliamentary democracy

Somalia: none

South Africa: republic

Spain: parliamentary monarchy

Spanish North Africa: territory of Spain

Sri Lanka: republic

Sudan: transitional

Suriname: constitutional democracy

Svalbard: territory of Norway

Swaziland: monarchy

Sweden: constitutional monarchy

Switzerland: federal republic

Syria: republic under military regime since March 1963

Taiwan: multiparty democratic regime headed by popularly elected president

Tajikistan: republic

Tanzania: republic

Thailand: constitutional monarchy

Togo: republic under transition to multiparty democratic rule

Tokelau: territory of New Zealand; currently drafting a constitution and working toward self-government

Tonga: hereditary constitutional monarchy

Trinidad and Tobago: parliamentary democracy

Tunisia: republic

Turkey: republican parliamentary democracy

Turkmenistan: republic

Turks and Caicos: British dependency

Tuvalu: constitutional monarchy with a parliamentary democracy

Uganda: republic

Ukraine: republic

United Arab Emirates: federation with specified powers delegated to the UAE federal government and other powers reserved to member emirates

United Kingdom: constitutional monarchy

United States: federal republic; strong democratic tradition

Uruguay: republic

Uzbekistan: republic; effectively authoritarian presidential rule, with little power outside the executive branch; executive power concentrated in the presidency

Vanuatu: republic

Vatican City: monarchical-sacerdotal state

Venezuela: federal republic

Vietnam: Communist state

Virgin Islands: territory of the United States

Wallis and Futuna: French overseas territory

Yemen: republic

Zambia: republic

Zimbabwe: parliamentary democracy

SOURCES OF STATISTICS

BALANCE OF PAYMENTS

SOURCE. United Nations Conference on Trade and Development, *UNCTAD Handbook of Statistics 2000*, CD-ROM available in January 2001. Data were taken from all three tables that make up the Balance of Payments portion of Section IV. Reprinted with permission.

NOTES.

The following explanatory notes are intended to provide a brief description of the balance of payments categories presented. In actual practice, there are many exceptions to the definitions of categories, and for these the reader should refer to the country notes in the *Balance of Payments Yearbook.*

Exports of goods (f.o.b.)—The export figure here differs from that reported in the trade returns because of adjustments for coverage, valuation, timing, inland freight, etc. Such adjustments to the reported export and import figures are necessary in order to make the trade statistics compatible with the concepts employed in the balance of payments. In particular, valuation adjustments are required in those cases in which the market price at which goods have been sold differs from the price used for customs' purposes. This problem in valuation is probably more important for imports than for exports and is likely to be a factor whenever there is a long delay between the date of sale and the date at which an import duty becomes payable.

The coverage of goods has been expanded here to include (a) the value of goods (on a gross basis) received/sent for processing and their subsequent export/import in the form of processed goods; (b) the value of repairs on goods; and (c) the value of goods procured in ports by carriers.

Imports of goods (f.o.b.)—Adjustments for coverage, valuation, timing, etc., are made to imports reported in trade returns, as described in the notes above. In addition, an adjustment is made to convert imports from a c.i.f. to an f.o.b. basis for those countries reporting imports c.i.f. The import figures reported here include imports of non-monetary gold.

Trade Balance—This is sometimes referred to as the Balance of Goods and is measured on an f.o.b./f.o.b. basis. It includes transactions in monetary gold.

Services and income - debit—Total payments for services and income. In general, the concept of income covers investment income plus all forms of compensation of employees.

Services and income - credit (total)—Counterpart to service and income - debit (total).

Government transfers - net—Current transfers are classified, according to the sector of the compiling economy, into two main categories: general government and other sectors. General government transfers comprise current international cooperation, which covers current transfers—in cash or in kind—between governments of different economies or between governments and international organizations.

Private transfers - net—Current transfers between other sectors of an economy and non-residents comprise those occurring between individuals, between non-governmental institutions or organizations (or between the two groups), or between non-resident governmental institutions and individuals or non-governmental institutions.

Overall balance of the current account—Covered in the current account are all transactions (other than those in financial items) that involve economic values and occur between resident and non-resident entities. Also covered are offsets to current economic values provided or acquired without a quid pro quo. Specifically, the major classifications are goods and services, income, and current transfers.

f.o.b.—Free on board, i.e., the value of goods does not include insurance and freight charges.

c.i.f.—Customs, insurance and freight, i.e., the value of goods is presented inclusive of insurance and freight charges.

FOOTNOTES.

NA—Data are not available.

-—Data are nil or negligible.

CRIME

SOURCE. Crime Prevention and Criminal Justice Division, United Nations Criminal Justice Information Network (UNCJIN), *The Fifth United Nations Survey of Crime Trends and Operations of Criminal Justice Systems* [Online], Available: http://www/ifs.univie.ac.at/~uncjin/wcs.html [October 1999]. Reprinted with permission.

NOTES.

The major goal of the Fifth United Nations Survey is to collect data on the incidence of reported crime and the operations of criminal justice systems with a view to improving the dissemination of that information globally. To that end, the Survey should facilitate an overview of trends and interrelationships between various parts of the criminal justice system so as to promote informed decision making in its administration, nationally and cross-nationally.

As with data collected for the Fourth United Nations Survey, these data demonstrate the difficulty of comparing crime data internationally. One difficulty is that the vast majority of incidents that become known to the police come from reports by victims. Thus, credibility becomes a statistical determinant. Another difficulty is that comparison is severely undermined by differences in legal definitions and by administrative procedures regarding counting, classification, and disclosure. The researcher should be aware of these shortcomings when using these data.

NA—Data are not available.

DAILY NEWSPAPERS

SOURCE. United Nations Education, Scientific, and Cultural Organization and Bernan Press, *UNESCO 1999 Statistical Yearbook*, pp. IV/106-IV/133. Reprinted with permission.

NOTES.

Data presented are for the year 1996.

Newspapers—Newspapers are periodic publications intended for the general public and mainly designed to be a primary source of written information on current events connected with public affairs, international questions, politics, etc. A newspaper thus defined and issued at least four times a week is considered to be a daily newspaper.

Circulation—These figures show the average circulation, or the average circulation per issue. The figures include the number of copies (a) sold directly, (b) sold by subscription, and (c) distributed free of charge both inside the country and abroad.

FOOTNOTES.

1—Daily and non-daily newspapers are combined in this figure.

NA—Data are not available.

DEMOGRAPHICS—A

SOURCE. U.S. Bureau of the Census, *International Database* [Online], Available: http://www.census.gov:80/ipc/www/idbnew.html [May 2000].

NOTES.

Data presented for all years later than 1998 are estimates produced by the U.S. Bureau of the Census and based on historical data, not all of which is presented here.

NA—Data are not available.

DEMOGRAPHICS—B

SOURCE. U.S. Central Intelligence Agency (CIA), *The World Factbook 2000* [Online], Available: http://www.cia.gov/cia/publications/factbook/index.html [September 2000].

ECONOMIC INDICATORS

SOURCE. U.S. Central Intelligence Agency (CIA), *The World Factbook 2000* [Online], Available: http://www.cia.gov/cia/publications/factbook/index.html [September 2000].

U.S. Department of Commerce, Bureau of the Census, *Statistical Abstract of the United States 1999*, page 842.

NOTES.

Following are CIA definitions of acronyms and terms used in these tables.

est.—Estimate.

External debt—The amount of debt owed to foreign entities by the given country.

GDP—Gross domestic product: the value of all goods and services produced within a nation in a given year. Methodology: GDP dollar estimates for all countries are derived from purchasing power parity (PPP) calculations rather than from conversions at official currency exchange rates. The PPP method involves the use of international dollar price weights, which are applied to the quantities of goods and services produced in a given economy. The data derived from the PPP method provide a better comparison of economic well-being between countries. The division of a GDP estimate in domestic currency by the corresponding PPP estimate in dollars gives the PPP conversion rate. When priced in PPPs, $1,000 will buy the same market basket of goods in any country. Whereas PPP estimates for OECD countries are quite reliable, PPP estimates for developing countries are often rough approximations.

Most of the GDP estimates are based on extrapolation of numbers published by the UN International Comparison Program and by Professors Robert Summers and Alan Heston of the University of Pennsylvania and their colleagues. Note: the numbers for GDP and other economic data can not be chained together from successive volumes of the *Factbook* because of changes in the U.S. dollar measuring rod, revisions of data by statistical agencies, use of new or different sources of information, and changes in national statistical methods and practices.

Inflation rate—An increase in prices unrelated to value.

National product—The total output of goods and services in a given country. (See gross domestic product).

NA—Data are not available.

EDUCATIONAL ATTAINMENT—A

SOURCE. United Nations Education, Scientific, and Cultural Organization and Bernan Press, *UNESCO 1999 Statistical Yearbook*, pp. 51-64. Reprinted with permission.

NOTES.

These tables present the percentage distribution of the population aged 25 years and over according to the highest level of education attained. This reflects both the outcomes of participation in education in the past and the educational composition of the population. These data have been collected mainly during national population censuses and sample surveys. The six levels of educational attainment presented here are based on the International Standard Classification of Education (ISCED) and are defined as follows:

No schooling—Refers to persons who have completed less than one year of primary education.

Primary education incomplete—Includes all persons who have completed at least one grade of primary education but who did not complete the final grade of this level of education.

Primary education completed—Refers to all persons who have completed the final grade of primary education but did not enter secondary education.

Attended lower secondary education—Comprises all persons who have attended lower secondary education but not (upper) secondary education.

Attended upper secondary education—Includes all persons who have attended (upper) secondary education but not post-secondary education.

Post-secondary education—Refers to all persons who have completed secondary education and attended post-secondary education.

FOOTNOTES.

1—Not including persons with no schooling or less than one year of primary education.

2—The category "No Schooling" comprises illiterates.

3—"Completed primary education" refers to the last two years of primary education.

4—Persons who can read and write have been counted with "incomplete primary."

5—Not including population attending and never attended school.

6—Data refer only to persons who have attended school but left school.

7—Based on a sample survey of 35,502 persons.

8—Not including persons still in school.

9—Based on a sample survey of 51,372 persons.

10—Post-secondary education refers to universities only.

11—Not including transients and residents of former canal zone.

12—The category "No schooling" refers to those who have attended less than one grade of primary education.

13—Not including armed forces stationed in the area.

14—Lower secondary education refers to "intermedio" level of education. (Upper) secondary education refers to "Media," "Tecnica," and "Normal" education.

15—Not including rural population of Northern Brazil.

16—Not including persons whose level of education is unknown.

17—Not including Jammu and Kashmir.

18—Not including persons still attending school for whom the level is unknown.

19—Household survey results based on a sample of 6,393 households. The category of "No schooling" includes illiterates.

20—(Upper) secondary education includes 'polytechnic'; post-secondary education refers to universities only.

21—Data are based on a sample of 8,619 households (5,563 urban and 3,056 rural) from the 1993 Demographic and Health Survey.

22—"Incomplete primary education" refers to grades 1 to 4 and "Complete primary education" refers to grades 5 to 8.

23—Not including expatriate workers and their families.

24—The category "No schooling" includes persons who are still in school.

25—The category "No schooling" comprises persons who did not state their level of education.

26—Based on a 20% sample of census returns.

NA—Data are not available.

EDUCATIONAL ATTAINMENT—B

SOURCE. International Bank of Reconstruction and Development / THE WORLD BANK, *2000 World Development Indicators CD-ROM*, Summary education profiles tables. Reprinted with permission.

NOTES.

NA—Data are not available.

ENERGY CONSUMPTION

SOURCE. U.S. Central Intelligence Agency (CIA), *The World Factbook 2000* [Online], Available: http://www.cia.gov/cia/publications/factbook/index.html [September 2000].

U.S. Department of Energy, Energy Information Administration, *International Energy Annual 1998*, published in January 2000, pp. 3-4.

FOOTNOTES.

kW—Kilowatt.

kWh—Kilowatt hour.

NA—Data are not available.

ENERGY PRODUCTION

SOURCE. U.S. Central Intelligence Agency (CIA), *The World Factbook 2000* [Online], Available: http://www.cia.gov/cia/publications/factbook/index .html [September 2000].

U.S. Department of Energy, Energy Information Administration, *International Energy Annual 1998*, published in January 2000, pp. 23-24.

FOOTNOTES.

kW—Kilowatt.

kWh—Kilowatt hour.

NA—Data are not available.

ETHNIC DIVISION

SOURCE. U.S. Central Intelligence Agency (CIA), *The World Factbook 2000* [Online], Available: http://www.cia.gov/cia/publications/factbook/index .html [September 2000].

NOTES.

Tables show the major ethnic divisions of peoples in the given country for the most recent year available. When available, the distribution is shown in percent.

NA—Data are not available.

EXCHANGE RATES

SOURCE. U.S. Central Intelligence Agency (CIA), *The World Factbook 2000* [Online], Available: http://www.cia.gov/cia/publications/factbook/index .html [September 2000].

NOTES.

Following are CIA definitions of acronyms and terms used in these tables.

Exchange rate—The official value of a nation's monetary unit, at a given date or over a given period of time, as expressed in units of local currency per U.S. dollar and as determined by international market forces or official fiat. These often have little relation to domestic output. In developing countries with weak currencies, the exchange rate estimate in GDP (gross domestic product) in dollars is typically one-fourth to one-half the PPP (purchasing power parity) estimate. Although exchange rates may suddenly go up or down by 10% or more, real output may have remained unchanged. On January 12, 1994, for example, the 14 countries of the African Financial Community (whose currencies are tied to the French franc) devalued their currencies by 50%. This move, of course, did not cut the real output of their countries by half.

BMR—Black market rate.

NA—Data are not available.

FOREIGN AID

SOURCE. U.S. Central Intelligence Agency (CIA), *The World Factbook 2000* [Online], Available: http://www.cia.gov/cia/publications/factbook/index .html [September 2000].

NOTES.

Following are CIA definitions of terms used in these tables.

Donor—Country that pledges official economic aid to another country.

NA—Data are not available.

ODA—Official development assistance. ODA refers to financial assistance which is concessional in characters, has the main objective of promoting economic development and welfare in less developed countries (LDCs), and contains a grant element of at least 25%.

OOF—Other official flows. OOF also refers to official government assistance, but with a main objective other than development and with a grant element less than 25%. Transactions include official export credits (such as Export-Import Bank credits), official equity and portfolio investment, and debt reorganization by the official sector that does not meet concessional terms. Aid is considered to have been committed when the parties involved initial agreements constituting a formal declaration of intent.

Recipient—Country that receives official economic aid from another country.

GDP & MANUFACTURING SUMMARY—A

SOURCE. United Nations Industrial Development Organization (UNIDO), *Industry and Development Global Report 1998*, pp. 129-243. Reprinted with permission.

NOTES.

Gross domestic product (GDP)—All economic activity in a given country, including activity engaged in by foreign nationals. For example, assets of a General Motors plant in Mexico would contribute to Mexico's GDP. *Real GDP* measures economic activity in constant prices, that is, after adjustments for inflation.

Manufacturing value added (MVA)—The value of output minus the cost of raw materials and other inputs.

FOOTNOTES.

1—Value originating from the National Accounts Statistics.

2—In 1990 constant prices.

3—The data presented here are for activities in the former Federal Republic of Germany and do not include those of the former Democratic Republic of Germany, even after unification in 1990.

e—Figures estimated by UNIDO, Research and Publication Division, Research and Studies Branch.

NA—Data are not available.

-—Value is less than half a unit.

GDP & MANUFACTURING SUMMARY—B

SOURCE. United Nations Industrial Development Organization (UNIDO), *Industry and Development Global Report 1998*, pp. 244-254. Reprinted with permission.

NOTES.

Gross domestic product (GDP)—All economic activity in a given country, including activity engaged in by foreign nationals. For example, assets of a General Motors plant in Mexico would contribute to Mexico's GDP. *Real GDP* measures economic activity in constant prices, that is, after adjustments for inflation.

Manufacturing value added (MVA)—The value of output minus the cost of raw materials and other inputs.

FOOTNOTES.

e—Figures estimated by UNIDO, Research and Publication Division, Research and Studies Branch.

NA—Date are not available.

-—Value is less than half a unit.

GDP & MANUFACTURING SUMMARY—C

SOURCE. U.S. Central Intelligence Agency (CIA), *The World Factbook 2000* [Online], Available: http://www.cia.gov/cia/publications/factbook/index.html [September 2000].

NOTES.

Gross domestic product (GDP)—All economic activity in a given country, including activity engaged in by foreign nationals.

Manufacturing value added (MVA)—The value of output minus the cost of raw materials and other inputs.

NA—Data are not available.

PPP—Purchasing power parity.

GEOGRAPHY

SOURCE. U.S. Central Intelligence Agency (CIA), *The World Factbook 2000* [Online], Available: http://www.cia.gov/cia/publications/factbook/index.html [September 2000].

NOTES.

Comparative area—Based on total area equivalents. Most entities are compared with the entire United States or one of the 50 states. The smaller entities are compared with Washington, D.C. (178 square km, 69 square miles), or The Mall in Washington, D.C. (0.59 square km, 0.23 square miles, 146 acres).

Land area—Aggregate of all surfaces delimited by international boundaries and/or coastlines, excluding inland water bodies (lakes, reservoirs, rivers).

Land use—Human use of the land surface is categorized as *arable land* —land cultivated for crops that are replanted after each harvest (wheat, maize, rice); *permanent crops* —land cultivated for crops that are not replanted after each harvest (citrus, coffee, rubber); *meadows and pastures* —land permanently used for herbaceous forage crops; *forest and woodland* —land under dense or open stands of trees; and *other* —any land type not specifically mentioned above (urban areas, roads, deserts).

Total area—Sum of all land and water area delimited by international boundaries and/or coastlines.

GOVERNMENT BUDGETS—A

SOURCE. International Monetary Fund (IMF), *Government Finance Statistics Yearbook 1998*, pp. 6 and 7.

NOTES.

IMF data were obtained primarily by means of a detailed questionnaire distribution to government finance statistics correspondents, who are usually located in each country's respective ministry of finance or central bank. Three of the six categories of central government expenditure shown in the IMF tables are comprised of subcategories, whose subtotals have been summed.

FOOTNOTES.

f—Forecast.

p—Preliminary / provisional.

NA—Data are not available.

0—Zero or less than half a significant digit.

GOVERNMENT BUDGET—B

SOURCE. U.S. Central Intelligence Agency (CIA), *The World Factbook 2000* [Online], Available: http://www.cia.gov/cia/publications/factbook/index.html [September 2000].

FOOTNOTES.

est.—Estimate.

f—Forecast.

p—Preliminary / provisional.

NA—Data are not available.

0—Zero or less than half a significant digit.

HEALTH INDICATORS

SOURCE. International Bank of Reconstruction and Development / THE WORLD BANK, *World Development Indicators 2000*, pp. 94-109. Reprinted with permission.

United Nations Development Program (UNDP) and Oxford University Press, *Human Development Report 2000*, pp. 169-171, 190-193, 237-240. Reprinted with permission.

NOTES.

World data are presented with each country's data by way of providing points of reference.

People with Access to Safe Water.—This is the share of the population with reasonable access to an adequate amount of safe water (including treated surface water and untreated but uncontaminated water, such as from springs, sanitary wells, and protected boreholes). In urban areas the source may be a public fountain or standpipe located not more than 200 meters away. In rural areas the definition implies that members of a household do not have to spend a disproportionate part of the day fetching water. An adequate amount of safe water is that needed to satisfy metabolic, hygienic, and domestic requirements—usually about 20 liters a person a day. The definition of safe water has changed over time. Data are provided for the most recent year available within the range stated.

People with Access to Sanitation.—This is the share of the population with at least adequate excreta disposal facilities that can effectively prevent human, animal, and insect contact with excreta. Suitable facilities range from simple but protected pit latrines to flush toilets with sewerage. To be effective, all facilities must be correctly constructed and properly maintained. Data are provided for the most recent year available within the range stated.

People living with HIV/AIDS—This is the percentage of people aged 15-49 years who are infected with human immunodeficiency virus (HIV).

FOOTNOTES.

a—Data are for most recent year available.

b—Official estimate.

c—UNICEF-WHO estimate based on statistical modeling.

d—Indirect estimate based on a sample survey.

e—Based on a survey covering 30 provinces.

f—Based on a sample survey.

NA—Data are not available.

HEALTH PERSONNEL

SOURCE. International Bank of Reconstruction and Development / THE WORLD BANK, *World Development Indicators 2000*, pp. 90-92. Reprinted with permission.

United Nations Development Program (UNDP) and Oxford University Press, *Human Development Report 2000*, pp. 190-193. Reprinted with permission.

NOTES.

Public Health Expenditure—This category consists of recurrent and capital spending from government (central and local) budgets, external borrowings and grants (including donations from international agencies and nongovernmental organizations), and social (or compulsory) health insurance funds.

Private Health Expenditure—This category includes direct household (out-of-pocket) spending, private insurance, charitable donations, and direct service payments by private corporations.

FOOTNOTES.

a—Data are for the most recent year available.

b—Data may not sum to totals because of rounding.

NA—Data are not available.

IMPORT AND EXPORT COMMODITIES

SOURCE. U.S. Central Intelligence Agency (CIA), *The World Factbook 2000* [Online], Available: http://www.cia.gov/cia/publications/factbook/index.html [September 2000].

NOTES.

Presented here are the commodities imported and exported by a particular country. For corresponding information about where exports are sent and from where imports are purchased, see the *Top Import Origins* and *Top Export Destinations* rubrics.

When available, commodities are distributed in percent.

INFANTS & MALNUTRITION

SOURCE. United Nations Children's Fund (UNICEF), *The State of the World's Children 2000*, pp. 83, 92-95.

International Bank of Reconstruction and Development / THE WORLD BANK, *World Development Indicators 2000*, pp. 98-100, 102-104. Reprinted with permission.

NOTES.

Under-five mortality rate—Probability of dying between birth and exactly five years of age expressed per 1,000 live births.

Low birthweight—Weights at birth that are less than 2,500 grams.

TB—Tuberculosis

DPT—Diphtheria, pertussis (whooping cough) and tetanus.

FOOTNOTES.

NA—Data are not available.

1—Data are for the most recent year available within the range listed.

2—Indicates data that refer to years other than those specified, differ from the standard definitions, or refer to only part of a country.

LABOR FORCE BY OCCUPATION

SOURCE. U.S. Central Intelligence Agency (CIA), *The World Factbook 2000* [Online], Available: http://www.cia.gov/cia/publications/factbook/index.html [September 2000].

NOTES.

Data show the number of persons in the labor force for the most recent year available.

NA—Data are not available.

LIBRARIES

SOURCE. United Nations Education, Scientific, and Cultural Organization and Bernan Press, *UNESCO 1999 Statistical Yearbook*, pp. IV/18-IV/55. Reprinted with permission.

NOTES.

National Libraries—National libraries are libraries which, irrespective of their title, are responsible for acquiring and conserving copies of all significant publications produced in a country and functioning as a *deposit* library, either by law or other arrangement, and normally compile a national bibliography. In countries where the national library has an appreciable number of service points, it can be assumed that it has other functions in additional to those described above and also as a public library, which often confirmed by the fact that the number of users is unusually high.

Public Libraries—Public (or popular) libraries are those which serve the population of a community or region free of charge or for a nominal fee; they may serve the general public or special categories of users such as children, members of the armed forces, hospital patients, prisoners, workers and employees.

FOOTNOTES.

NA—Data are not available.

LITERACY RATES—A

SOURCE. United Nations Education and Culture Organization (UNESCO), *Compendium of Statistics on Illiteracy* (1995 Edition), pp. 40-49. Reprinted with permission.

NOTES.

Literacy statistics are concerned with the stock of persons who have successfully acquired the basic reading, writing and numerical skills essential for personal growth and cohesion within contemporary societies. Levels of literacy within a population constitute on the one hand a reflection of the level of development and accomplishments of the education systems, and on the other hand a pointer on the potential for human input into further economic, social and cultural development. Literacy rate has therefore been widely used as a key common indicator for monitoring and assessing progress in the current world thrusts of Education for All and Human Resources Development, and has been regularly incorporated into various reports and publications.

As the national statistics on literacy made available to UNESCO are collected during population censuses that usually take place once every ten years, estimations and projections are carried out to fill the data gaps for the years between two censuses, as well as to provide projections showing likely progress in literacy for the future.

Literacy continues to progress in the world. Adult literacy rate, or the percentage of literates within the adult population aged 15 years and over, has been steadily growing in all countries. Entering the 1990s, over three-quarters (75.3 percent) of the world's adult population have become literate—increasing from 69.5 percent in 1980. Based on the past trends, it is estimated that the overall literacy rate in the world has further improved to 77.4 percent in 1995, and is projected to reach 80 percent at the beginning of the 21st century.

The literate adult population in the world has undergone phenomenal expansion during the past fifteen years from 1980 to 1995, and is projected to further increase in the future. In absolute numbers, the adult literate population in the world rose from 2 billion in 1980 to an estimated 3 billion in 1995, i.e. by 1 billion persons. If the current rate of progress can be maintained, the number of adult literates in the world may reach 3.4 billions in the year 2000, and 4.2 billion in 2010.

Despite these signs of positive progress in both literacy rates and number of literates, one may notice that there remains a large illiterate population in the world of today - numbering some 885 million adults aged 15 years and over—and that this illiterate population increased from an estimated 877 million in 1980. The expansion of the world's illiterate population seems to have reached its turning point during the first half of the 1990s. The projections show that if the past trend were to continue, this world total would gradually decrease to some 881 million by the year 2000. But the huge mass of more than 880 million illiterates shall continue to constitute major challenges to education in the future.

Literate—A person is literate who can with understanding both read and write a short simple statement on his everyday life.

Illiterate—A person is illiterate who cannot with understanding both read and write a short simple statement on his everyday life.

Adult—Refers to persons aged 15 years or older.

LITERACY RATES—B

SOURCE. United Nations Children's Fund (UNICEF), *The State of the World's Children 2000*, pp. 96-99.

NOTES.

World data are presented with each country's data by way of providing points of reference.

Adult Literacy Rate—Percentage of persons aged 15 years and over who can read and write.

NA—Data are not available.

1—Indicates data that refer to years or periods other than those specified, differ from the standard definitions, or refer to only part of a country.

LITERACY RATES—C

SOURCE. International Bank of Reconstruction and Development / THE WORLD BANK, *2000 World Development Indicators CD-ROM*, Summary education profiles tables. Reprinted with permission.

NOTES.

NA—Data are not available.

MAJOR LANGUAGES

SOURCE. U.S. Central Intelligence Agency (CIA), *The World Factbook 2000* [Online], Available: http://www.cia.gov/cia/publications/factbook/index.html [September 2000].

NOTES.

Tables show major language(s) spoken by inhabitants of the given country for the most recent year available. When available, the distribution is shown in percent.

NA—Data are not available.

MILITARY AFFAIRS—A

SOURCE. U.S. Arms Control and Disarmament Agency, *World Military Expenditures and Arms Transfers 1998* (WMEAT), (April 2000), pp. 69-112 and 121-164.

NOTES.

World data are presented with each country's data by way of providing points of reference. However, because of the complexity of collecting and counting these data, discussed in the notes that follow, comparisons across countries must be made carefully.

Military Expenditures

For NATO countries, military expenditures are from NATO publications and are based on the NATO definition. In this definition, (a) civilian-type expenditures of the defense ministry are excluded and military-type expenditures of other ministries are included; (b) grant military assistance is included in the expenditures of the donor country; and (c) purchases of military equipment for credit are included at the time the debt is incurred, not at the time of payment.

For other non-communist countries, data are generally the expenditures of the ministry of defense. When these are known to include the costs of internal security, an attempt is made to remove these expenditures. A wide variety of data sources is used for these countries, including the publications and data resources of other U.S. government agencies, standardized reporting to the United Nations by country, and other international sources.

It should be recognized by users of the statistical tables that the military expenditure data are of uneven accuracy and completeness. For example, there are indications or reasons to believe that the military expenditures reported by some countries consist mainly or entirely of recurring or operating expenditures and omit all or most capital expenditures, including arms purchases.

In some cases it is believed that a better estimate of total military expenditures is obtained by adding to nominal military expenditures the value of arms imports. It must be cautioned, however, that this method may over- or underestimate the actual expenditures in a given year due to the fact that payment for arms may not coincide in time with deliveries. Also, arms acquisitions in some cases may be financed by, or consist of grants from, other countries.

For countries that have major clandestine nuclear or other military weapons development programs, such as Iraq, estimation of military expenditures is extremely difficult and especially subject to errors of underestimation.

Further information in the quality of the military expenditure data presented for countries throughout the world will be difficult to achieve without better reporting by the countries themselves. Among the mechanisms commonly used to obscure such expenditures are: double-bookkeeping budget categories, military assistance, and manipulation or foreign exchange.

Particular problems arise in estimating the military expenditures of communist countries due to the exceptional scarcity and ambiguity of released information. As in past editions of this publication, data on the military expenditures of the Soviet Union are based on Central Intelligence Agency (CIA) estimates. For most of the series, these are estimates of what it would cost in the United States in dollars to develop, procure, staff, and operate a military force similar to that of the Soviet Union. Estimates of this type—that is, those based entirely on one country's price pattern—generally overstate the relative size of the second country's expenditures in intercountry comparisons. Also, such estimates are not consistent with the methods used here for converting other countries' expenditures into dollars.

Nevertheless, the basic CIA estimates are the best available for present purposes; in fact, there are no alternative estimates that can inspire confidence and have the capability to detect relatively small changes over time, such as the slowdown and decline in Soviet military spending that the CIA estimates have indicated.

For Russia, estimated military spending trends in rubles are used in conjunction with dollar estimates for earlier years to make rough estimates of spending in dollars.

Estimates for the former Warsaw Pact countries other than the Soviet Union, in 1990 and 1991 are based on total military spending in national currency as reported by the respective governments to the UN (in most cases) or the IMF. These expenditures in toto are converted to dollars at the Alton GNP conversion rates for 1989 as adjusted to 1991 by the respective U.S. and national GNP deflators (per the World Bank), without estimating personnel compensation separately at U.S. dollar rates, as was done for earlier years. The resulting military conversion rates (in national currency per dollar) are substantially lower than the 1991 market rate, and approximately the same as the implied rate for GNP.

Estimates for the newly independent states of the former Soviet Union, Yugoslavia, and Czechoslovakia and other former Warsaw Pact countries present difficulties due to scarcity of reliable data in national currencies and to problems in converting to dollars. The basic method employed for most of these countries was to establish the ratio of military expenditures to GNP in national currency and then to multiply this ratio by the World Bank's estimate of GNP in dollars as converted to international dollars by estimate PPPs and reported in the *World Bank Atlas 1997.* This method implicitly converts military spending at the GNP-wide PPP, which, as with conversion by exchange rates, preserves the same ME/GNP ratio in dollars as obtains in national currency.

Data for China are based on U.S. Government estimates of the yuan costs of Chinese forces, weapons, programs, and activities. Cost in yuan are here converted to dollars using the same estimated conversion rate as used for GNP. Due to the exceptional difficulties in both estimating yuan costs and converting them to dollars, comparisons of Chinese military spending with other data should be treated as having a wide margin of error.

Other published sources used include the *Government Finance Statistics Yearbook,* issued by the International Monetary Fund; *The World Factbook,* produced annually the Central Intelligence Agency; *The Military Balance,* issued by the International Institute for Strategic Studies (London); and the *SIPRI Yearbook: World Armaments and Disarmament,* issued by the Stockholm International Peach Research Institute.

Gross National Product (GNP)

GNP represents the total output of goods and services produced by residents of a country, valued at market prices. The source of GNP data for most non-communist countries is the International Bank for Reconstruction and Development (World Bank).

For a number of countries whose GNP is dominated by oil exports (Bahrain, Kuwait, Libya, Oman, Qatar, Saudi Arabia, and the United Arab Emirates), the World Bank's estimate of deflated (or constant price) GNP in domestic currency tends to understate increases in the monetary value of oil exports, and thus of GNP, resulting from oil price increases. These World Bank estimates are designed to measure real (or physical) product. An alternative estimate of constant-price GNP was therefore obtained using the implicit price deflator for U.S. GNP (for lack of a better national deflator). This considered appropriate because a large share of the GNP of these countries is realized in U.S. dollars.

GNP estimates of the Soviet Union are by the CIA, as published in its *Handbook of Economic Statistics 1990* and updated. GNP estimates for other Warsaw Pact countries through 1989 are from "East European Military Expenditures, 1965-1978," by Thad P. Alton and others, *op. cit.,* as updated and substantially revised by the authors. These estimates through 1989 have been extended to 1990 and 1991 on the basis of estimates for those years in the CIA's *Handbook of Economic Statistics, 1992.*

Estimates of GNP in 1992-1994 for successor states to the Soviet Union, Yugoslavia, and Czechoslovakia are based on World Bank estimates of GNP per capita employing PPPs and population, as published in the *World Bank Atlas 1997.*

GNP data for China are based on World Bank estimates in yuan. These are in line with estimates of GDP in Western accounting terms made by Chinese authorities. Converting estimates in yuan to dollars is highly problematic, however, due to the inappropriateness of the official exchange rate and lack of sufficient yuan price information by which to reliably estimate PPPs. The conversion rate used here is based on a PPP estimated for 1981 and moved by respective U.S. and China implicit GNP deflators to 1994.

GNP estimates for a few non-communist countries are from the CIA's *Handbook of Economic Statistics* cited above. Estimates for the other communist countries are rough approximations.

Military Expenditures-to-GNP Ratio

It should be noted that the meaning of the ratio of military expenditures to GNP differs somewhat between most communist (or previously communist) and other countries. For non-communist countries, both military expenditures and GNP are converted from the national currency unit to dollars at the same exchange rate; consequently, the ratio of military expenditures to GNP is the same in dollars as in the national currency and reflects national relative prices. For communist countries, however, military expenditures and GNP are converted differently. Soviet military expenditures, as already noted, are estimated in a way designed to show the cost of the Soviet armed forces in U.S. prices, as if purchased in this country. On the other hand, the Soviet GNP estimates used here are designed to show average relative size when both U.S. and Soviet GNP are valued and compared at both dollar and ruble prices. The Soviet ratio of military expenditures to GNP in ruble terms, the preferred method of comparison, is estimated to have been 15-18% in that country's latest years.

For Eastern European countries before 1992, the ratios of military expenditures to GNP in dollars were about twice the ratios that would obtain in domestic currencies. However, since official military budgets in these countries probably substantially understated their actual military expenditures, the larger ratios on dollar estimates are believed to be the better approximations of the actual ratios.

Central Government Expenditures (CGE)

These expenditures include current and capital (developmental) expenditures plus net lending to the government enterprises by central (or federal) governments. A major source is the International Monetary Fund's *Government Finance Statistics Yearbook.* The category used here is "Total Expenditures and Lending minus Repayment, Consolidated Central Government."

Other sources for these data are the International Monetary Fund, *International Financial Statistics* (monthly); OECD, *Economics Surveys;* and CIA, *The World Factbook* (annual). Data for Warsaw Pact countries are from national publications and are supplied by Thad P. Alton and others. For all Warsaw Pact countries and China, conversion to dollars is at the implicit rates used for calculating dollar estimates of GNP.

For all countries, with the same exceptions as noted above for the military expenditures-to-GNP ratio, military expenditures and central government expenditures are converted to dollars at the same rate; the ratio of the two variables is thus the same in dollars as in national currency.

It should be noted that for China, Iran, Jordan, and possibly others, the ratio of military expenditures to central government expenditures may be overstated, inasmuch as the estimate for military expenditures is obtained at least in part independently of nominal budget or government expenditure data, and it is possible that not all estimated military expenditures pass through the nominal central government budget.

Population

Population estimates are for midyear and are made available to ACDA by the U.S. Bureau of the Census.

Armed Forces

Armed forces refer to active-duty military personnel, including paramilitary forces if those forces resemble regular units in their organization, equipment, training, or mission. Reserve forces are not included unless specifically noted.

Figures for the United States and all other North American Treaty Organization (NATO) countries are as reported by NATO. Estimates of the number of personnel under arms for other countries are provided by U.S. Government sources. The armed forces series for the Soviet Union includes all special forces judged to have national security missions (e.g., KGB border guards) and excludes uniformed forces primarily performing noncombatant services (construction, railroad, civil defense, and internal security troops).

Arms Transfers

Arms transfers (arms imports and exports) represent the international transfer (under terms of grant, credit, barter, or cash) of military equipment, usually referred to as "conventional," including weapons of war, parts thereof, ammunition, support equipment, and other commodities designed for military use. Among the items included are tactical guided missiles use. Among the items included are tactical guided missiles and rockets, military aircraft, naval vessels, armored and nonarmored military vehicles, communications and electronic equipment, artillery, infantry weapons, small arms, ammunition, other ordinance, parachutes, and uniforms. Dual use equipment, which can have application in both military and civilian sectors, is included when its primary mission is identified as military. The building of defense production facilities and licensing fees paid as royalties for the production of military equipment are included when they are contained in military transfer agreements. There have been no international transfers of purely strategic weaponry. Military services such as training, supply operations, equipment repair, technical assistance, and construction are included where data are available. Excluded are foodstuffs, medical equipment, petroleum products and other supplies.

U.S. Arms Exports include both government-to-government transfers under the Foreign Military Sales (FMS), Military Assistance Program (MAP), and other programs administered by the Department of Defense, and commercial exports (enterprise-to-government or enterprise) licensed by the Department of State under International Traffic in Arms Regulations.

Beginning with the previous edition, both the material and the military services components of FMS and other government-to-government sales (such as the International Military Education and Training Program—IMET) are included in total U.S. arms exports as reported here. The commercial sales category, covering both material and military services, was included in its entirety.

The omission of FMS and other military services prior to the previous edition had been intended to improve comparability with available estimates of the arms exports of other countries, which tended to contain a much smaller services component and/or were subject to significant underestimation (services being less easily observed). The increasing importance of these services and the desire to present a full picture of U.S. arms exports consistent with other sources prompted the change to inclusion. Users should be aware, however, of both the lower true share of services in other countries' arms exports and the tendency to underestimate them. It should also be noted that a portion of the IMET program is devoted to programs that promote improved civil-military relations.

The change in scope of U.S. arms exports increased their overall volume by amounts ranging over the last decade from $2.3 billion (current dollars) to

$3.7 billion for deliveries and $2.3 billion to $7.3 billion for agreements.

The statistics contained herein are estimates of the value of goods actually delivered during the reference year, in contrast both to payments and the value of programs, agreements, contracts, or orders concluded during the period, which are expected to result in future deliveries.

U.S. arms imports data are obtained from the Department of Commerce, Bureau of Economic Analysis (BEA), and include (a) imports of military-type goods, as complied by the Bureau of the Census, and (b) Department of Defense direct expenditures abroad for major equipment, as compiled from DOD data by BEA. The goods in (a) include: complete military aircraft, all types; engines and turbines for military aircraft; military trucks, armored vehicles, etc.: military (naval) ships and boats; tanks, artillery, missiles, guns, and ammunition; military apparel and footwear; and other military goods, equipment, and parts.

Data on countries other than the United States are estimates by U.S. Government sources. Arms transfer data for the Soviet Union and other former communist countries are approximations based on limited information.

It should be noted that the arms transfer estimates for the most recent year, and to a lesser extent for several preceding years, tend to a lesser extent for several preceding years, tend to be understated. This applies to both foreign and U.S. arms exports. In former case, information on transfers comes from a variety of sources and is sometimes acquired and processed with a considerable time lag. In the U.S. case, commercial arms transfer licenses are now valued for three years, causing a delay in the reporting of deliveries made on them to statistical agencies.

Close comparisons between the estimated values shown for arms transfers and for GNP and military expenditures are not warranted. Frequently, weapons prices do not reflect true production costs. Furthermore, much of the international arms trade involves offset or barter arrangements, multiyear loans, discounted prices, third party payments, and partial debt forgiveness. Acquisitions of armaments thus may not [necessarily] impose the burden on an economy, whether in the same or in other years, that is implied by the estimated equivalent U.S. dollar value of the shipment. Therefore, the value of arms imports should be compared to other categories of data with care.

Total Imports and Exports

The values for imports and exports cover merchandise transactions and come mainly from International Financial Statistics published by the IMF. The trade figures for presently and formerly communist countries and from the CIA's *Handbook of Economic Statistics*.

FOOTNOTES.

e—Estimate based on partial or uncertain data.

NA—Data are not available.

p—Estimate based on purchasing power parities.

r—Rough estimate.

0—Nil or negligible.

1—Estimated by adding arms imports to data on military expenditures, which are believed to exclude arms purchases. However, it should be noted that the value of arms deliveries in a given year may differ significantly from actual expenditures on arms imports in that year.

2—This ratio is calculated from the dollar values shown in previous columns. In most cases it also is equal to the ratio that could be calculated from national currency values, since both numerator and denominator are usually converted into dollars by the same exchange rate or other conversion factor. In the case of this country, however, the two variables are converted at different rates, yielding a different ratio than would obtain in national currency. The ratio for Russia in rubles terms, for example, is believed to be less than 10 percent in 1995.

3—This series or entry is believed to omit a major share of total military expenditures, probably including most expenditures on arms procurement.

4—Germany, (The Federal Republic of), was known as West Germany through 1990. Thereafter, Germany refers to the unified Germany.

5—In order to reduce distortions in the trend for worked, region, and organization totals caused by data gaps for individual countries and years, rough approximations for all gaps are included in the totals.

6—To avoid the appearance of excessive accuracy, arms transfer data by country are rounded, with greater severity for larger amounts. All country group totals for arms exports and arms imports shown here are the sums of rounded country data. Consequently, world totals for arms imports and arms exports will not be equal.

7—Total imports and exports usually are as reported by individual countries and the extent to which arms transfers are included is often uncertain. Imports are reported "cif" (including cost of shipping, insurance, and freight) and exports are reported "fob" (excluding these costs). For these reasons and because of divergent sources, world totals for imports and exports are not equal.

8—Because some countries exclude arms imports or exports from their trade statistics and their "total" imports and exports are therefore understated, and because arms transfers may be estimated independently for trade data, the resulting ratios of arms to total imports or exports may be overstated and may even exceed 100 percent.

9—Some part of estimated total military expenditures may not be included in announced central budget expenditures. The ratio of ME to CGE therefore may be overstated.

10—Included major equipment purchased by the U.S. Army Corps of Engineers for use in military construction projects in Saudi Arabia, recorded in U.S. accounts as U.S. imports.

11—U.S. arms imports data shown here is revised upward substantially form reports before 1993.

12—Little data are available because of an ongoing civil war.

MILITARY AFFAIRS—B

SOURCE. U.S. Central Intelligence Agency (CIA), *The World Factbook 2000* [Online], Available: http://www.cia.gov/cia/publications/factbook/index.html [September 2000].

FOOTNOTES.

e—Estimate based on partial or uncertain data.

NA—Date are not available.

0—Nil or negligible.

POLITICAL PARTIES

SOURCE. U.S. Central Intelligence Agency (CIA), *The World Factbook 2000* [Online], Available: http://www.cia.gov/cia/publications/factbook/index.html [September 2000].

Facts About The Aland Islands, Retrieved from the internet in January 2001, http://www.aland.fin/virtual/eng/innehall.html.

NOTES.

When available, political party representation is shown for the lower house of the legislative branch of government. The lower house was chosen in order to present, in most cases, a picture of the electoral results of voting by the general public. The name of this legislative body is shown in the legend of the given table.

When available, election results are shown as a percent distribution of votes in the most recent election. Otherwise, percent distribution of seats, or number of seats, by political party is shown. If there are no political parties or there is one-party rule, this information is provided in place of tabular data.

Wherever possible, political party names have been presented in English translation.

PUBLIC EDUCATION EXPENDITURES

SOURCE. International Bank of Reconstruction and Development / THE WORLD BANK, *World Development Indicators 2000*, pp. 70-73. Reprinted with permission.

NOTES.

The data on education spending refer solely to public spending—that is, government spending on public education plus subsidies for private education. The data generally exclude foreign aid for education. They also may exclude religious schools, which play a significant role in many developing countries.

The percentage of GNP devoted to education can be interpreted as reflecting a country's effort in education. Often it bears a weak relationship to measures of output of the education system, as reflected in educational attainment. The pattern suggests wide variations across countries in the efficiency with which the government's resources are translated into education outcomes.

Public Expenditures of Education.—This is the percentage of GNP accounted for by public spending on public education plus subsidies to private education at the primary, secondary, and tertiary levels.

World data are provided at the bottom of these tables in order to offer points of reference.

FOOTNOTES.

1—Excludes expenditure on preprimary and secondary.

2—Excludes expenditure on tertiary.

RELIGION

SOURCE. U.S. Central Intelligence Agency (CIA), *The World Factbook 2000* [Online], Available: http://www.cia.gov/cia/publications/factbook/index.html [September 2000].

NOTES.

Tables show major religious denominations of the peoples of the given country for the most recent year available. When available, the distribution is shown in percent.

NA—Data are not available.

TELECOMMUNICATIONS

SOURCE. U.S. Central Intelligence Agency (CIA), *The World Factbook 2000* [Online], Available: http://www.cia.gov/cia/publications/factbook/index.html [September 2000].

NOTES.

Following are CIA definitions of terms used in these tables.

Telephone system—This entry includes a brief characterization of the system with details on the domestic and international components.

Africa ONE—a fiber-optic submarine cable link encircling the continent of Africa.

Arabsat—Arab Satellite Communications Organization (Riyadh, Saudi Arabia).

Autodin—Automatic Digital Network (US Department of Defense).

CB—citizen's band mobile radio communications.

cellular telephone system—the telephones in this system are radio transceivers, with each instrument having its own private radio frequency and sufficient radiated power to reach the booster station in its area (cell), from which the telephone signal is fed to a regular telephone exchange.

Central American Microwave System—a trunk microwave radio relay system that links the countries of Central America and Mexico with each other.

coaxial cable—a multi-channel communication cable consisting of a central conducting wire, surrounded by and insulated from a cylindrical conducting shell; a large number of telephone channels can be made available within the insulated space by the use of a large number of carrier frequencies.

Comsat—Communications Satellite Corporation (US).

DSN—Defense Switched Network (formerly Automatic Voice Network or Autovon); basic general-purpose, switched voice network of the Defense Communications System (US Department of Defense).

Eutelsat—European Telecommunications Satellite Organization (Paris).

fiber-optic cable—a multi-channel communications cable using a thread of optical glass fibers as a transmission medium in which the signal (voice, video, etc.) is in the form of a coded pulse of light.

GSM—a global system for mobile (cellular) communications devised by the Groupe Special Mobile of the pan-European standardization organization, Conference Europeanne des Posts et Telecommunications (CEPT) in 1982.

HF—high-frequency; any radio frequency in the 3,000- to 30,000-kHz range.

Inmarsat—International Mobile Satellite Organization (London); provider of global mobile satellite communications for commercial, distress, and safety applications at sea, in the air, and on land.

Intelsat—International Telecommunications Satellite Organization (Washington, DC).

Intersputnik—International Organization of Space Communications (Moscow); first established in the former Soviet Union and the East European countries, it is now marketing its services worldwide with earth stations in North America, Africa, and East Asia.

landline—communication wire or cable of any sort that is installed on poles or buried in the ground,

Marecs—Maritime European Communications Satellite used in the Inmarsat system on lease from the European Space Agency.

Marisat—satellites of the Comsat Corporation that participate in the Inmarsat system.

Medarabtel—the Middle East Telecommunications Project of the International Telecommunications Union (ITU) providing a modern telecommunications network, primarily by microwave radio relay, linking Algeria, Djibouti, Egypt, Jordan, Libya, Morocco, Saudi Arabia, Somalia, Sudan, Syria, Tunisia, and Yemen; it was initially started in Morocco in 1970 by the Arab Telecommunications Union (ATU) and was known at that time as the Middle East Mediterranean Telecommunications Network.

microwave radio relay—transmission of long distance telephone calls and television programs by highly directional radio microwaves that are received and sent on from one booster station to another on an optical path.

NMT—Nordic Mobile Telephone; an analog cellular telephone system that was developed jointly by the national telecommunications authorities of the Nordic countries (Denmark, Finland, Iceland, Norway, and Sweden).

Orbita—a Russian television service; also the trade name of a packet-switched digital telephone network.

radiotelephone communications—the two-way transmission and reception of sounds by broadcast radio on authorized frequencies using telephone handsets.

PanAmSat—PanAmSat Corporation (Greenwich, CT).

satellite communication system—a communication system consisting of two or more earth stations and at least one satellite that provides long distance transmission of voice, data, and television; the system usually serves as a trunk connection between telephone exchanges; if the earth stations are in the same country, it is a domestic system.

satellite earth station—a communications facility with a microwave radio transmitting and receiving antenna and required receiving and transmitting equipment for communicating with satellites.

satellite link—a radio connection between a satellite and an earth station permitting communication between them, either one-way (down link from satellite to earth station - television receive-only transmission) or two-way (telephone channels).

SHF—super-high-frequency; any radio frequency in the 3,000- to 30,000-MHz range.

shortwave—radio frequencies (from 1.605 to 30 MHz) that fall above the commercial broadcast band and are used for communication over long distances.

Solidaridad—geosynchronous satellites in Mexico's system of international telecommunications in the Western Hemisphere.

Statsionar—Russia's geostationary system for satellite telecommunications.

submarine cable—a cable designed for service under water.

TAT—Trans-Atlantic Telephone; any of a number of high-capacity submarine coaxial telephone cables linking Europe with North America.

telefax—facsimile service between subscriber stations via the public switched telephone network or the international Datel network.

telegraph—a telecommunications system designed for unmodulated electric impulse transmission.

telex—a communication service involving teletypewriters connected by wire through automatic exchanges.

tropospheric scatter—a form of microwave radio transmission in which the troposphere is used to scatter and reflect a fraction of the incident radio waves back to earth; powerful, highly directional antennas are used to transmit and receive the microwave signals; reliable over-the-horizon communications are realized for distances up to 600 miles in a single hop; additional hops can extend the range of this system for very long distances.

trunk network—a network of switching centers, connected by multichannel trunk lines.

UHF—ultra-high-frequency; any radio frequency in the 300- to 3,000-MHz range.

VHF—very-high-frequency; any radio frequency in the 30- to 300-MHz range.

Telephones - main lines in use—This entry gives the total number of main telephone lines in use.

Telephones - mobile cellular—This entry gives the total number of mobile cellular telephones in use.

Television - broadcast stations—This entry gives the total number of separate broadcast stations plus any repeater stations.

Televisions—This entry gives the total number of television sets.

TOP AGRICULTURAL PRODUCTS

SOURCE. U.S. Central Intelligence Agency (CIA), *The World Factbook 2000* [Online], Available: http://www.cia.gov/cia/publications/factbook/index.html [September 2000].

NOTES.

GDP—Gross Domestic Product: the value of all goods and services produced within a nation in a given year.

TOP EXPORT DESTINATIONS

SOURCE. U.S. Central Intelligence Agency (CIA), *The World Factbook 2000* [Online], Available: http://www.cia.gov/cia/publications/factbook/index.html [September 2000].

NOTES.

Top export destinations are distributed in percent when data are available.

Following are CIA definitions of the acronyms and terms used in these tables.

BLEU—Belgium-Luxembourg Economic Union.

Caricom—Caribbean Community and Common Market.

CEMA—Council for Mutual Economic Assistance; also known as *CEMA* or *Comecon.*

c.i.f.—Cost, insurance, freight.

CIS—Commonwealth of Independent States.

CMEA—Council for Mutual Economic Assistance; also known as *CEMA* or *Comecon.*

ECOWAS—Economic Community of West African States.

EFTA—European Free Trade Association.

est.—Estimate.

EU—European Union.

f.o.b.—Free on board.

FSU—Former Soviet Union.

NA—Data are not available.

OECD—Organization for Economic Cooperation and Development.

OECS—Organization of Eastern Caribbean States.

OPEC—Organization of Petroleum Exporting Countries.

SACU—South African Customs Union.

UAE—United Arab Emirates.

UK—United Kingdom.

U.S.—United States.

U.S.S.R.—Union of Soviet Socialist Republics (Soviet Union).

FOOTNOTES.

NA—Data are not available.

-—Data are nil or negligible.

TOP IMPORT ORIGINS

SOURCE. U.S. Central Intelligence Agency (CIA), *The World Factbook 2000* [Online], Available: http://www.cia.gov/cia/publications/factbook/index.html [September 2000].

NOTES.

Top import origins are distributed in percent when data are available.

For a list of the CIA definitions of the acronyms and terms used please see the list provided in the above note, the explanatory note for the "Top Export Destinations" tables.

FOOTNOTES.

NA—Data are not available.

-—Data are nil or negligible.

TOP MINING PRODUCTS—A

SOURCE. U.S. Geographic Survey, *Minerals Yearbook*, published in February 2000, [Online], Available: http://minerals.usgs/minerals/pubs/commodity. Data were drawn from individual commodity tables.

NOTES.

Commodities covered in this section are: aluminum, coal, copper, gold, iron ore, lead, nickel, salt, silver, tin, uranium, and zinc. For any particular country only commodities mined in that country are presented.

FOOTNOTES.

kg—Kilograms.

mt—Metric tons.

TOTAL MINING PRODUCTS—B

SOURCE. U.S. Central Intelligence Agency (CIA), *The World Factbook 2000* [Online], Available: http://www.cia.gov/cia/publications/factbook/index.html [September 2000].

NOTES.

Data show a list of mineral resources in the country. Whenever possible information about how the listed resources are exploited is also provided.

TOTAL LABOR FORCE—A

SOURCE. U.S. Central Intelligence Agency (CIA), *The World Factbook 2000* [Online], Available: http://www.cia.gov/cia/publications/factbook/index.html [September 2000].

Data show the number of persons in the labor force for the most recent year available.

NA—Data are not available.

TOTAL LABOR FORCE—B

SOURCE. International Bank of Reconstruction and Development / THE WORLD BANK, *World Development Report 2000/2001*, pp. 278-279. Reprinted with permission.

TRANSPORTATION

SOURCE. U.S. Central Intelligence Agency (CIA), *The World Factbook 2000* [Online], Available: http://www.cia.gov/cia/publications/factbook/index.html [September 2000].

NOTES.

Following are CIA definitions of terms used in these tables.

Airports—Only airports with usable runways are included in this listing. Not all airports have facilities for refueling, maintenance, or air traffic control. Paved runways have concrete or asphalt surfaces; unpaved runways have grass, dirt, sand, or gravel surfaces.

DWT—Deadweight tons.

GRT—Gross register tons.

km—Kilometers.

m—Meters

Merchant marine—All ships engaged in the carriage of goods. All commercial vessels (as opposed to all nonmilitary ships), which excludes tugs, fishing vessels, offshore oil rigs, etc. Also, a grouping of merchant ships by nationality or register.

NA—Data are not available.

UNEMPLOYMENT RATE

SOURCE. U.S. Central Intelligence Agency (CIA), *The World Factbook 2000* [Online], Available: http://www.cia.gov/cia/publications/factbook/index.html [September 2000].

NOTES.

Data show the rate of unemployment in percent for the most recent year available.

HAITI

CAPITAL: Port-au-Prince.

FLAG: The upper half is blue, the lower half red.

ANTHEM: *La Dessalinienne (Song of Dessalines).*

MONETARY UNIT: The gourde (G) is a paper currency of 100 centimes. There are coins of 5, 10, 20, and 50 centimes and notes of 1, 2, 5, 10, 50, 100, 250, and 500 gourdes. Silver (5, 10, and 25 gourdes) and gold (20, 50, 100, 200, 1,000 gourdes) coins have also been minted. G1 = $0.20 (or $1 = G5).

WEIGHTS AND MEASURES: The metric system is official for customs purposes.

HOLIDAYS: Independence and New Year's Day, 1 January; Forefathers Day, 2 January; Pan American Day, 14 April; Labor Day, 1 May; Flag and University Day, 18 May; National Sovereignty Day, 22 May; Assumption, 15 August; Anniversary of the Death of Dessalines, 17 October; UN Day, 24 October; All Saints' Day, 1 November; Commemoration of the Battle of Vertières and Armed Forces Day, 18 November; Discovery of Haiti, 5 December; Christmas, 25 December. Movable religious holidays include Carnival (three days before Ash Wednesday) and Good Friday.

TIME: 7 AM = noon GMT.

LOCATION AND SIZE: Haiti occupies the western third of the island of Hispaniola (the Dominican Republic occupies the eastern two thirds). Haiti has an area of 27,750 square kilometers (10,714 square miles) including the islands of Tortuga, Gonâve (Ile de la Gonâve), Les Cayemites, and Vache (Ile Á Vache). Haiti has a total boundary length of 2,046 kilometers (1,269 miles). Haiti's capital city, Port-au-Prince.

CLIMATE: The climate is tropical, with some variation depending on altitude. Temperatures in Port-au-Prince range from 20°–31°C (68°–88°F) in January to an average maximum of 23–34°C (73–93°F) in July. Port-au-Prince receives an average annual rainfall of 137 centimeters (54 inches).

Republic of Haiti
République d'Haïti

INTRODUCTORY SURVEY

RECENT HISTORY

Haiti is one of the poorest and least developed countries in the Western Hemisphere. It has been plagued by political violence and unrest most of its history.

After World War II (1939-1945) a period of instability led to a coup d'etat in 1950 that brought General Paul Magloire to power. Magloire's economic policies led to a serious depression, and he was forced from office in 1956.

In a September 1957 election François Duvalier, a middle-class black physician known to his followers as Papa Doc, became president. He began to rule by decree in 1958, and in 1964 he had himself formally elected president for life. Despite several attempted revolts, he strengthened his position, ruling largely through his security force, the Tontons Macoutes.

Papa Doc died in 1971 and his son Jean-Claude Duvalier, at the age of nineteen, became president for life. The younger Duvalier (known as Baby Doc) tried to ease political tensions and contributed to the beginnings of an economic revival. However, political arrests continued and severe economic problems persisted through the 1970s.

Tensions mounted and civil disorder broke out in the mid-1980s. In February 1986 Jean-Claude and his family fled to France. The National Governing Council (Conseil National de Gouvernement-CNG), led by Lieutenant-General Henri Namphy, seized power. A new constitution was

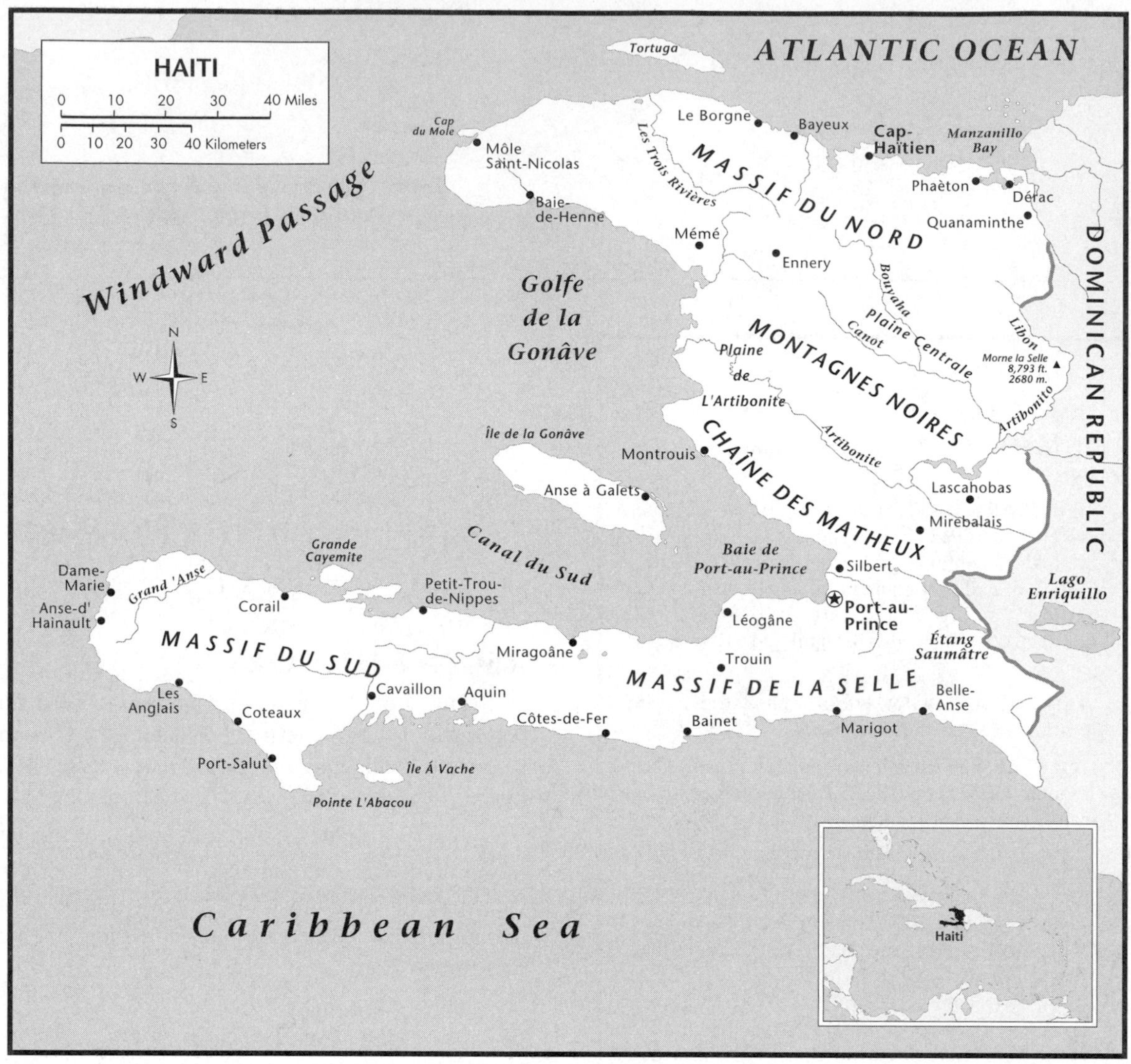

approved by referendum in March 1987. In December 1990, a Roman Catholic priest, Jean-Bertrand Aristide, was elected president.

Upset by Aristide's popularity and his foreign policy, the military, under General Raoul Cédras, ousted him in October 1991. The UN and the Organization of American States (OAS) forged an agreement between Cédras and Aristide that was to return Aristide to the presidency in October 1993, but the military stalled and remained in power. Aristide appealed to the United States that responded with sanctions against the Haitian regime.

With war seemingly imminent, a special U.S. delegation reached an agreement with Cédras and war was averted. American forces peacefully took control of the country and, in October 1994, restored Aristide to power. In December 1995 René Préval was elected to the presidency with 90 percent of the vote. He was Haiti's second democratically elected president in the country's 191-year history. In July 1997 Haiti became a member of the Caribbean Community (CARiCOM). Haiti's economic and security problems proved overwhelming. The International Monetary Fund (IMF) demanded privatization of state-owned enterprises. The former popular president Aristide resisted this move and formed a new political grouping, Préval, dissolved parliament in 1999 after failing three times to win approval for prime minister nominees and repeatedly postponed new legislative elections leaving Haiti without a fully operating government. It was predicted that Aristide would run and win in the presidential election scheduled for December 2000. Haiti's presidential elections have historically been accompanied by increase demonstrations and violence.

GOVERNMENT

The constitution adopted in March 1987 established a president elected to a five-year term as head of state. The prime minister, appointed by the president and ratified by the congress, is head of government. The prime minister in consultation with the president chooses the cabinet.

The bicameral legislative branch consists of the 27-seat National Assembly, or Senate, and the 83-seat Chamber of Deputies. The Assembly members are elected, one-third every two years, to serve six-year terms. The Deputies are elected by popular vote to serve four-year terms. Suffrage is universal at age eighteen. President Preval postponed legislative elections until early 2000.

Judiciary

The judiciary consists of four levels: the Supreme Court or Court of Cassation, courts of appeal, civil courts, and magistrates' courts. There are also land, labor, and children's courts. The 1987 constitution was put into force in 1995. All judges have been appointed and removed at the will of the government since 1986, even though the constitution calls for an independent judiciary. Military courts function in both military and civilian cases when the constitution is suspended.

Political Parties

By 1995, the dominant political force was the Lavalas Political Organization, an alliance of Aristide's Lavalas Political Organization (OPL) and the Movement for the Organization of the Country (MOP). Backed by Aristide, René Préval was elected president in December 1995. In the mid-1995 legislative elections, Lavalas candidates won the majority in both houses.

In 1997 the former president Aristide formally registered a new party, called the Lavalas Family (FL) movement, which was expected to challenge the existing Lavalas government party in the next elections.

DEFENSE

In 1994, a civilian administration replaced the military government. That year, the military government's armed forces and police of 7,400 personnel were disbanded and the air force was disbanded in 1995. Security is currently entrusted to the Haitian National Police (HNP) that has an estimated 5,300 members. The defense budget was estimated at $48 million or 2.4 percent of GDP in 1998.

ECONOMIC AFFAIRS

Haiti is one of the world's poorest countries with 80 percent of the population living in abject poverty. About three-quarters of the population work in small-scale subsistence farming. The official unemployment rate in 1999 was 70 percent. Failure to reach agreements with international sponsors deny Haiti desperately needed budget and development assistance

Public Finance

The U.S. CIA estimates that in 1997-98 government revenues totaled approximately $323 million and expenditures $363 million. External debt is estimated at $1 billion in 1997.

Income

In 1999 Haiti's gross domestic product (GDP) was $9.2 billion, or about $1,340 per capita. The estimated 1999 real growth rate of GDP was 2.4 percent and inflation 9 percent.

Industry

Industry is primarily devoted to the processing of agricultural such as sugar refining and flour milling, forestry products, and more recently construction. Other industries produce aluminum, enamelware, garments and hats, essential oils, plastics, soap, pharmaceuticals, paint, and textiles. Haitian plants also assemble U.S.-made components to create electronic devices, toys, and leather goods. A cement factory was undergoing restructuring in 1999.

Banking and Finance

The national bank of the Republic of Haiti (Banque Nationale de la République d'Haïti-BRH) is the sole bank of issue and government depository. It also serves as the nation's principle commercial bank. In 1999 eleven other commercial banks were in operation.

There is no securities exchange in Haiti. Haitian corporations that make public offerings of bonds or equities trade on the New York over-the-counter market.

Economic Development

Although its annual national revenue covers basic necessities, the government supports development programs by encouraging loans and by requiring private enterprises to finance development projects. Aided by the U.S. and various international aid organizations, the government has supported the construction of tourist facilities, public works, and irrigation and the creation of monopolies in cement, sugar marketing, tobacco and lumbering.

Macroeconomic stability, structural and institutional reforms, and poverty alleviation are still the main objectives in Haiti's agenda for the future. Haiti has attempted to work with international organizations to coordinate efforts toward these goals but political difficulties in 1999 undermined most plans for furthering economic development.

SOCIAL WELFARE

Public social insurance programs are limited, but there is a widespread tradition of self-help and personal charity. The national lottery is the principal source of welfare funds, while an employer tax provides workers' compensation for occupational accidents to the relatively small number of industrial workers. Old-age, disability, and survivor benefits are funded by taxes on employees and employers.

Healthcare

Medical facilities are scarce and sub-standard, and the level of community sanitation is low. In 1997 there were approximately one doctor per 10,000 people. Half of the doctors were in Port-au-Prince and one-fourth in other principle towns. In 1995 there were eight hospital beds per 1,000 people. The rural population has a minimum of medical services.

Tuberculosis and gastrointestinal diseases have long been a serious health problem. Malnutrition is widespread. Haiti has one of the highest HIV infection rates in the Americas. In 2000 average life expectancy was estimated to be forty-nine years.

Housing

Although housing projects have been constructed in cities such as Port-au-Prince and in Cap-Haïtien, there is an increasing shortage of low-cost housing. Outside the capital and some other cities, housing facilities are generally primitive and almost universally without sanitation. There is no official low-cost housing program.

EDUCATION

The adult literacy rate is estimated at 51.4 percent in 2000. Although education is compulsory between the ages of six and twelve, the majority of children do not attend school. Eighty percent of students speak only Creole but education programs are generally conducted in French. The sole university, the Université d'État d'Haïti, is at Port-au-Prince.

2000 KEY EVENTS TIMELINE

April

- Jean Léopold Dominique, Haiti's best-known radio journalist, is shot dead. His murder is only one of many in the wake of political violence stemming from overdue elections.

May

- International observers criticize Haiti's parliamentary and municipal elections for favoring former President Jean Bertrand Aristide's Lavalas Party. The ex-president is widely expected to win the November elections.

July

- Elections stall as Leon Manus leaves the presidency of the Provisional Electoral Council (CEP), fleeing to the United States in fear for his life. Ernst Merville takes his place.
- Runoff elections attract low attendance because the Lavalas bloc, the party of former President Jean-Bertrand Aristide, has already won by questionable means.

August

- The United States shuts down a training program for Haiti's police force because of rigged election results on August 3.

September

- On September 1 the government announces plan to raise the price of fuel to bring them in line with international prices, an increase of about 44 percent.
- The United States announces on September 5 its refusal to send observers or financial aid for the presidential election in November.

November

- Presidential and Senate elections are held November 26. President Jean-Bertrand Aristide, the country's first democratically elected president, is reelected after a five-year hiatus. Opposition parties boycott the elections, and several bombs explode at Port-Au-Prince prior to polling.

ANALYSIS OF EVENTS: 2000

BUSINESS AND THE ECONOMY

Without aid from the international community, Haiti could not survive. Already the poorest nation in the Western Hemisphere, Haiti must convince the international community that it is strengthening democratic institutions if it is continue to receive economic aid. After the November election of Jean-Bertrand Aristide, it remained unclear whether other nations were willing to work with Aristide. The United States questioned the elections and expected some kind of compromise between Aristide and the opposition before any aid was directly released to his government. By the end of 2000 U.S. officials said they would consider releasing aid through nongovernmental agencies. By then the cost of food had risen by 50–60 percent while the salaries of Haitians remained the same, at about $400 per year.

GOVERNMENT AND POLITICS

In 1990 Jean-Bertrand Aristide became Haiti's first democratically elected President, but once elected, Aristide's fiery rhetoric began to divide the nation. In 1991 he was deposed and fled the country. In 1994, 20,000 U.S. troops invaded Haiti, and with international support, Aristide returned to power.

The Haitian Constitution does not allow a president to run for a second consecutive term, so Aristide was forced to watch his friend and political colleague, René Preval, gain the presidency in the 1995 election, but Preval was unable to work with the opposition, and announced he was dissolving Parliament in January 1999. Politically and socially the country continued to spin out of control leading to the May 2000 local and parliamentary elections. By then, the Aristide's Lavalas Party even controlled the electoral commission that oversaw elections.

"Responsibility for remedying electoral flaws still resides with the Haitian authorities," Philip T. Reeker, deputy U.S. State Department spokesman, told the *New York Times* after the May election. "Low voter turnout and pre-election violence are strong indicators of the need for reconciliation among all sectors of Haitian society. We urge all Haitians to respect the rule of law and to work together to strengthen democracy and improve the well-being of the Haitian people."

The May vote was questioned and criticized by the Organization of American States (OAS) and other nations as well. The Lavalas Party won seventeen of eighteen seats in the Senate and 80 percent of the seats in the lower chamber. U.S. officials said aid would continue to flow to Haiti, but refused to work directly with the Haitian government until it addressed lingering electoral issues. Lavalas had gained control of the Senate with a disputed vote-counting method that angered the opposition. With presidential elections in November 2000 all major opposition parties decided to support a boycott, saying there were no guarantees for a fair contest. The Lavalas Party pressed ahead while Aristide remained silent. He made almost no campaign appearances and said very little leading to the election. The opposition remained on the sidelines. Opponents said Aristide's election was assured following years of political intimidation, violence, and fraud. In October barely a month before the vote for president was taken, the electoral commission was forced to publish the names of six unknown presidential candidates. As expected Aristide was announced the winner with 92 percent of the vote in the November election. The electoral commission said a little over 60 percent of eligible voters participated, a number that was quickly questioned by the opposition and international observers. Apathy and intimidation, including the explosion of several pipe bombs just prior to the election, had kept voters away, critics said. Aristide had promised "Peace in the head, peace in the belly." But considering the 2000 political developments, it remained unclear whether he could deliver on his promises after his inauguration, scheduled for February 7, 2001.

In a post-election press conference, Aristide attempted to assuage the fears of the opposition, saying he would not allow Haiti to return to a dictatorship. According to the *New York Times,* Aristide said "It is clear the government will have to reflect openness of mind if we want peace for Haiti, for all Haitians without distinction. We want to build Haiti with Haitians who want to devote themselves to human growth."

CULTURE AND SOCIETY

Is Jean-Bertrand Aristide a unifying force in Haiti? That was the question that many Haitians asked during the 2000 presidential campaign. Critics said Aristide's Lavalas Party continued to exacerbate social differences, often accusing the wealthier classes of Haiti for the nation's problems. Aristide's base of support came from some of the poorest neighborhoods in the nation. It was from there that he rose to power. Class and race divisions have been two of the most powerful forces that have shaped the country. As of the end of 2000 those divisions continued to be pronounced.

DIRECTORY

CENTRAL GOVERNMENT

Head of State

President
René G. Préval, Office of the President, National Palace, Champ de Mars, Port-au-Prince, Haiti
PHONE: +509 2223024; 2231646; 2232923

Prime Minister
Jacques Edouard Alexis, Office of the Prime Minister, Villa d'Accueil, Delmas 60, Musseau, Port-au-Prince, Haiti
PHONE: +509 2450007; 2450025
FAX: +509 2451624

Ministers

Minister of Agriculture, Natural Resources and Rural Development
François Séverin, Ministry of Agriculture, Natural Resources and Rural Development, Rte. Nationale 1, Damien, Haiti
PHONE: +509 2223595; 2223594; 2223596

Minister of Commerce and Industry
Gérald Germain, Ministry of Commerce and Industry, 26 Rue Légitime, Port-au-Prince, Haiti
PHONE: +509 2225674; 2231628; 2224152

Minister of Culture
Jean-Robert Vaval, Ministry of Culture, 31, Rue Roy, Port-au-Prince, Haiti
PHONE: +509 2228603; 2232382; 2227357

Minister of the Environment
Yves Cadet, Ministry of the Environment, Haut Turgeau, Port-au-Prince, Haiti
PHONE: +509 2457572; 2492737; 2228231

Minister of Finance and Economy
Fred Joseph, Ministry of Finance and Economy, Palais des Ministères, Port-au-Prince, Haiti
PHONE: +509 2220724; 2222822; 2223436

Minister of Foreign Affairs and Worship
Longchamp Emmanuel Fritz, Ministry of Foreign Affairs and Worship, Blvd. Harry Truman, Cité de l'Exposition, Port-au-Prince, Haiti
PHONE: +509 2221243; 2229937; 2228482

Minister of Haitians Living Abroad
Jean Généus, Ministry of Haitians Living Abroad, 37, Rue Duncombe, Port-au-Prince, Haiti
PHONE: +509 2450287; 2457006; 2451116

Minister of the Interior
Jacques Edouard Alexis, Ministry of the Interior, Palais des Ministères, Port-au-Prince, Haiti
PHONE: +509 2226490; 2225533; 2228603

Minister of Justice and Public Safety
Camille Leblanc, Ministry of Justice and Public Safety, 19 Ave. Charles Sumner, Port-au-Prince, Haiti
PHONE: +509 2455856; 2451646; 2451626

Minister of National Education, Youth and Sports
Paul Antoine Bien-Aimé, Ministry of National Education, Youth and Sports, Rue Dr. Audain, Port-au-Prince, Haiti
PHONE: +509 2221037; 2221036; 2342100

Minister of Planning and External Cooperation
Anthony Dessources, Ministry of Planning and External Cooperation, Palais des Ministères, Port-au-Prince, Haiti
PHONE: +509 2234222; 2220700; 2224148

Minister of Public Health
Michaëlle Amédée Gédéon, Ministry of Public Health, Palais des Ministères, Port-au-Prince, Haiti
PHONE: +509 2222725; 2221583; 2222728

POLITICAL ORGANIZATIONS

Front National pour le Changement et la Démocratie-FNCD (National Front for Change and Democracy)

NAME: Evans Paul

Initiatives Démocratiques (Democratic Initiatives)

NAME: Guy Alexandre; Françoise Boucard

Konfederasyon Inite Demokratik-KID (Confederation for Democratic Unity)

NAME: Evans Paul

Mobilisation pour le Devellopement National (Mobilization for National Development)

NAME: Hubert DeRonceray

Mouvement Démocratique pour la Libération d'Haïti-MODELH (Democratic Movement for the Liberation of Haiti)

NAME: François Latortue

Mouvement pour l'Instauration de la Démocratie en Haïti-MIDH (Movement for the Instauration of Democracy in Haiti)

NAME: Marc Bazin

Mouvman Konbit Nasyonal-MKN (National Cooperative Action Movement)

NAME: Volvick Rémy Joseph

Mouvement Nationale et Patriotique du 28 Novembre-MNP-28 (National Patriotic Movement of November 28)

NAME: Déjean Bélizaire

Mouvement pour l'Organisation du Pays-MOP (Movement for the Organization of the Country)

NAME: Gesner Comeau, Jean Molière

Mouvement de la Reconstruction Nationale-MRN (Movement for National Reconstruction)

NAME: René Théodore

Organisation du Peuple en Lutte-OPL (Struggling People's Organization)

NAME: Gérard Pierre-Charles

PARADIS (Haitian Party of God)

NAME: Vladimir Jeanty

Parti Agricole et Industrie National-PAIN (National Agricultural and Industrial Party)

NAME: Louis Dejoie II

Parti des Démocrates Haïtiens-PADEMH (Party of Haitian Democrats)

NAME: Jean-Jacques Clark Parent

Parti Démocratique et Chrétien d'Haïti-PDCH (Haitian Christian Democratic Party)

NAME: Fritz Pierre

Parti pour un Développement Alternatif-PADH (Alternative Party for Development)

NAME: Gérard Dalvius

Parti National Progressiste et Révolutionnaire-PANPRA (National Progressive Revolutionary Party)

NAME: Serge Gilles

Parti National des Travailleurs-PNT (National Labor Party)

NAME: Thomas Desulmé

Parti Social Chrétien d'Haïti-PSCH (Haitian Social Christian Party)

NAME: Grégoire Eugène

Pati Louvri Barye-PLB (Open the Gate Party)

NAME: Renaud Bernardin

Rassemblement des Démocrates Chrétiens-RDC (Assembly of Christian Democrats)

NAME: Eddy Volel

Rassemblement des Démocrates Nationalistes et Progressistes-RDNP (Assembly of Progressive National Democrats)

NAME: Leslie Manigat

Pouvoir Rassemblement des Organisations Populaires-PROP (Powerful Assembly of Popular Organizations)

Union des Démocrates Patriotiques-UDP (Union of Patriotic Democrats)

NAME: Rockefeller Guerre

DIPLOMATIC REPRESENTATION

Embassies in Haiti

United States
5 Harry Truman Boulevard, Port-au-Prince, Haiti
PHONE: +509 220354; 220368; 220200
FAX: +509 231641

JUDICIAL SYSTEM

Court of Cassation

BROADCAST MEDIA

Conseil National des Telecomunications (CONATEL)

BP 2002, Cité de l'Exposition 16, Port-au-Prince, Haiti
PHONE: +509 220300
FAX: +509 220579
TITLE: Chief Service Gestion des Frequences
CONTACT: Alfredo Estriplet

Radio France Internationale (RFI-Haiti)

BP 1126, Port-au-Prince, Haiti
PHONE: +509 224724; 228310
FAX: +509 229140
E-MAIL: ablanc@acn2.net
TITLE: Director
CONTACT: Marie-Christine Mourral Bussenius
TYPE: Private

Radio Vision 2000

184, Avenue John Brown, Lalue, Port-au-Prince, Haiti
PHONE: +509 454914; 453262
E-MAIL: info@radiovision2000.com
WEBSITE: www.radiovision2000.com
TITLE: Rédacteur en Chef
CONTACT: Daly Valet

Télévision Nationale d'Haiti (TNH)

PO Box 13400, Delmas 33, Port-au-Prince, Haiti
PHONE: +509 (1) 63324; 64049
FAX: +509 2460693
E-MAIL: info@intermonde.org
WEBSITE: www.haiticulture.net/tnh/
CONTACT: Jacqueline André
CHANNEL: A8, A10, A12
TYPE: Cultural, Government

Télé Haiti S. A.

BP 1126, Port-au-Prince, Haiti
PHONE: +509 (1) 23000
TITLE: Director
CONTACT: Walter Bussenius
BROADCASTS: 24 hours/day
TYPE: Commercial

COLLEGES AND UNIVERSITIES

State University of Haiti

1, Rue De Houx, BP 2279, Port-au-Prince, Haiti
PHONE: +509 2223210
FAX: +509 2238912

NEWSPAPERS AND MAGAZINES

Le Matin

Le Matin, PO Box 367, Port-au-Prince, Haiti
PHONE: +509 2221313
FAX: +509 8262931; 2232551
TITLE: Ad Manager
CONTACT: Linda Basilick
CIRCULATION: 15,000

Le Nouvelliste

BP 1013, Port-au-Prince, Haiti
CIRCULATION: 5,500

PUBLISHERS

Editions Caraiibes SA

Lalue, BP 2013, Port-au-Prince, Haiti
PHONE: +509 23179
CONTACT: Pierre J. Elie
SUBJECTS: Agriculture, Business, English as a Second Language, History, Marketing, Physics

Deschamps Imprimerie

Grand Rue, BP 164, Port-au-Prince, Haiti
PHONE: +509 232215
FAX: +509 234975
TITLE: Editorial Director
CONTACT: Mael Fouchard
SUBJECTS: Education, Fiction, Literature, Literary Criticism, Essays, Religion

Editions du Soleil

Rue du Centre, No. 102, BP1471, Port-au-Prince, Haiti
PHONE: +509 123147
CONTACT: Edouard A. Tardieu
SUBJECTS: Education

RELIGIOUS ORGANIZATIONS

Protestant

Eglise Adventiste de l'Auditorium de la Bible
37, Rue Capois, Champ de Mars, Port-au-Prince, Haiti
PHONE: +509 2229213

WEBSITE: http://www.tagnet.org/advenhaiti.aud/C.htm
TITLE: Pastor
NAME: Leon Nicolas

FURTHER READING

Articles

Fauriol, Georges A. "Aristide Flourishes, with U.S. Help, but Haitians Don't." *Wall Street Journal,* March 17, 2000, p. A19.

Gonzales, David. "U.S. to Withhold Money for Haiti's Presidential Election." *New York Times,* September 6, 2000, p.A10.

"Haiti Court Convicts 16, Many Ex-Soldiers, in '94 Killings." *New York Times,* November 12, 2000, p.11.

"Haiti to Raise Fuel Prices." *New York Times,* September 2, 2000, p. A5.

"Haiti's Downward Spiral," *The Economist,* April 2000.

"New Provisional Counsul President, Vice President Elected," *BBC,* July 19, 2000.

"US Warns Haiti it Could Lose Foreign Aid Over Tainted Elections," *Reuters,* July 14, 2000.

Books

Aristide, Jean-Bertrand. *Eyes of the Heart: Seeking a Path for the Poor in the Age of Globalization.* Monroe, ME: Common Courage Press, 2000.

Dash, Michael. *Culture and Customs of Haiti.* Westport, CT: Greenwood Press, 2000.

Dixon, Chris. *African America and Haiti: Emigration and Black Nationalism in the Nineteenth Century.* Westport, CT: Greenwood Press, 2000.

HAITI: STATISTICAL DATA

For sources and notes see "Sources of Statistics" at the front of each volume.

GEOGRAPHY

Geography

Area:

Total: 27,750 sq km.

Land: 27,560 sq km.

Land boundaries:

Total: 275 km.

Border countries: Dominican Republic 275 km.

Coastline: 1,771 km.

Climate: tropical; semiarid where mountains in east cut off trade winds.

Terrain: mostly rough and mountainous.

Natural resources: bauxite, copper, calcium carbonate, gold, marble, hydropower.

Land use:

Arable land: 20%

Permanent crops: 13%

Permanent pastures: 18%

Forests and woodland: 5%

Other: 44% (1993 est.).

HUMAN FACTORS

Demographics (A)

	1990	1995	1998	2000	2010	2020	2030	2040	2050
Population	6,028	6,423	6,683	6,868	7,950	9,072	9,997	10,908	11,852
Life expectancy - males	46.3	46.6	47.1	47.5	49.9	53.5	58.4	64.1	69.5
Life expectancy - females	49.2	50.6	50.8	51.1	53.2	57.3	62.8	69.2	75.1
Birth rate (per 1,000)	39.9	33.8	32.6	32.0	29.0	23.3	19.2	17.4	15.5
Death rate (per 1,000)	18.2	16.1	15.4	15.1	13.9	12.3	10.4	8.8	7.8
Women of reproductive age (15-49 yrs.)	1,373	1,464	1,577	1,668	2,083	2,454	2,820	2,958	3,063
Fertility rate	5.7	4.9	4.7	4.5	3.5	2.7	2.3	2.1	2.0

Except as noted, values for vital statistics are in thousands; life expectancy is in years.

Health Personnel

	National Data	World Data (wtd ave)
Total health expenditure as a percentage of GDP, 1990-1998[a]		
Public sector	1.3	2.5
Private sector	2.1	2.9
Total[b]	3.4	5.5
Health expenditure per capita in U.S. dollars, 1990-1998[a]		
Purchasing power parity	47	561
Total	37	483
Availability of health care facilities per 100,000 people		
Hospital beds 1990-1998[a]	70	330
Doctors 1992-1995[a]	16	122
Nurses 1992-1995[a]	13	248

Health Indicators

	National Data	World Data
Life expectancy at birth (years)		
1980	51	61
1998	54	67
Daily per capita supply of calories		
1970	1,944	2,358
1997	1,869	2,791
Daily per capital supply of protein		
1997 (grams)	41	74
Total fertility rate (births per woman)		
1980	5.9	3.7
1998	4.3	2.7
Population with access (%)		
To safe water (1990-96)	28	NA
To sanitation (1990-96)	24	NA
People living with (1997)		
Tuberculosis (cases per 100,000)	136.8	60.4
HIV/AIDS (% aged 15 - 49 years)	5.17	0.99

Infants and Malnutrition

	National Data	World Data (wtd ave)
Under 5 mortality rate (1989)	130	NA
% of infants with low birthweight (1992-98)[1]	15	17
Births attended by skilled health staff (% of total births 1996-98)	21	52
% fully immunized at 1 year of age (1995-98)[1]		
TB	28	82
DPT	22	77
Polio	20	77
Measles	22	74
Prevalence of child malnutrition (1992-98)[1] (based on weight for age, % of children under 5 years)	28	30

Ethnic Division

Black 95%

Mulatto plus white 5%

Religion

Roman Catholic 80%

Protestant 16%

Baptist 10%

Pentecostal 4%

Adventist 1%

Other 1%

None 1%

Other 3%

Data for 1982. Roughly one-half of the population also practices Voodoo.

Major Languages

French (official), Creole (official).

EDUCATION

Public Education Expenditures

	1980	1997
Public expenditures on education as % of GNP	1.5	NA
Expenditures per student as % of GNP per capita		
Primary & Secondary	5.9[2]	NA
Tertiary	130.0	NA
Teachers' compensation as % of total current education expenditures	66.9	NA
Pupils per teacher at the primary level	NA	NA
Duration of primary education in years	NA	6

World data for comparison

Public expenditures on education as % of GNP (mean)	3.9	4.8
Pupils per teacher at the primary level (wtd ave)	NA	33
Duration of primary education in years (mean)	NA	9

Educational Attainment (A)

Age group (1986) .... 25+

Population of this age group 2,229,501

Highest level attained (%)

- No schooling 59.5
- First level
  - Not completed 30.5
  - Completed .... NA
- Entered second level 9.3
- Entered post-secondary 0.7

(Continued on next page.)

GOVERNMENT & LAW

Military Affairs (A)

	1990	1992	1995	1996	1997
Military expenditures					
Current dollars (mil.)	54[e]	47[e]	NA	NA	NA
1997 constant dollars (mil.)	64[e]	53[e]	NA	NA	NA
Armed forces (000)	8	8	0	0	0
Gross national product (GNP)					
Current dollars (mil.)	3,230	3,090	3,100	3,250	3,340
1997 constant dollars (mil.)	3,780	3,430	3,210	3,300	3,340
Central government expenditures (CGE)					
1997 constant dollars (mil.)	460	359	350	288	348
People (mil.)	6	6.2	6.5	6.6	6.7
Military expenditure as % of GNP	1.7	1.5	NA	NA	NA
World data on military expenditure as % of GNP	4.5	3.4	2.7	2.6	2.6
Military expenditure as % of CGE	13.8	14.7	NA	NA	NA
World data on military expenditure as % of CGE	17.0	12.5	10.5	10.3	10.2
Military expenditure per capita (1997 $)	11	8	NA	NA	NA
World data on military expenditure per capita (1997 $)	242	173	146	143	145
Armed forces per 1,000 people (soldiers)	1.3	1.3	0	0	0
World data on armed forces per 1,000 people (soldiers)	5.3	4.5	4.1	3.9	3.8
GNP per capita (1997 $)	626	552	495	502	500
Arms imports[6]					
Current dollars (mil.)	0	0	40	0	5
1997 constant dollars (mil.)	0	0	41	0	5
Total imports[7]					
Current dollars (mil.)	332	278	653	665	648
1997 constant dollars (mil.)	389	308	676	676	648
Total exports[7]					
Current dollars (mil.)	160	73	110	90	175
1997 constant dollars (mil.)	187	81	114	92	175
Arms as percent of total imports[8]	0	0	6.1	0	0.8
Arms as percent of total exports[8]	0	0	0	0	0

(Continued on next page.)

EDUCATION (cont.)

Literacy Rates (A)

In thousands and percent	1990	1995	2000	2010
Illiterate population (15+ yrs.)	2,289	2,360	2,422	2,553
Literacy rate - total adult pop. (%)	41.0	45.0	49.4	57.7
Literacy rate - males (%)	44.2	48.0	52.1	59.7
Literacy rate - females (%)	37.9	42.2	46.9	55.7

GOVERNMENT & LAW (cont.)

Political Parties

National Assembly	no. of seats
Senate	
Struggling People's Organization (OPL)	7
Lavalas Family-leaning (FL-leaning)	7
Independents	3
Vacant	10
Chamber of Deputies	
Struggling People's Organization (OPL)	32
Antineoliberal bloc	24
Minor parties and independents	22
Vacant	5

Senate elections were last held 25 June 1995, with reruns on 13 August and runoffs on 17 September, and an election for nine seats 6 April 1997 but results were disputed; next election for two-thirds of Senate postponed until May 2000; Chamber of Deputies elections were last held 25 June 1995, with reruns on 13 August and runoffs on 17 September (next Senate and Chamber of Deputies elections postponed until May 2000).

Government Budgets (B)

Revenues . . . .$323 million
Expenditures . . . .$363 million

Data for FY97/98 est.

LABOR FORCE

Total Labor Force (A)

3.6 million. There is a shortage of skilled labor, unskilled labor abundant. (1998)

Labor Force by Occupation

Agriculture 66%
Services 25%
Industry 9%

Unemployment Rate

70%; widespread underemployment; more than two-thirds of the labor force do not have formal jobs (1999).

PRODUCTION SECTOR

Energy Production

Production . . . . .728 million kWh
Production by source
Fossil fuel 55.63%
Hydro 41.62%
Nuclear 0%
Other 2.75%
Exports . . . . .0 kWh

Data for 1998.

Energy Consumption

Consumption . . . . .677 million kWh
Imports . . . . .0 kWh

Data for 1998.

(Continued on next page.)

MANUFACTURING SECTOR

GDP & Manufacturing Summary (B)

	1980	1985	1990	1993	1994	1995
Gross Domestic Product						
Millions of 1990 dollars	2,381	2,270	2,281	1,829	1,588	1,657
Growth rate in percent	7.39	0.59	−0.14	−5.24	−13.19	4.38
Per capita (in 1990 dollars)	445	387	352	267	227	233
Manufacturing Value Added						
Millions of 1990 dollars	506	429	417	250	191	203[e]
Growth rate in percent	14.81	−0.84	2.41	−6.39	−23.61	5.99[e]
Manufacturing share in percent of current prices	19.1	17.6	19.5	10.8	10.8[e]	NA

PRODUCTION SECTOR (cont.)

Transportation

Highways:

Total: 4,160 km.

Paved: 1,011 km.

Unpaved: 3,149 km (1996 est.).

Waterways: negligible; less than 100 km navigable.

Merchant marine: none (1999 est.).

Airports: 13 (1999 est.).

Airports - with unpaved runways: 10.

Top Agriculture Products

Coffee, mangoes, sugarcane, rice, corn, sorghum; wood.

Top Mining Products (B)

Mineral resources include: bauxite, copper, calcium carbonate, gold, marble.

COMMUNICATIONS

Daily Newspapers

	National Data	World Data for Comparison
Daily Newspapers		
Number of Dailies	4	8,391
Total Circulation (000)	20	548,000
Circulation per 1,000 inhabitants	2.5	96

Telecommunications

Telephones - main lines in use: 60,000 (1995).

Telephones - mobile cellular: 0 (1995).

Telephone system: domestic facilities barely adequate; international facilities slightly better.

Domestic: coaxial cable and microwave radio relay trunk service.

International: satellite earth station - 1 Intelsat (Atlantic Ocean).

Radio broadcast stations: AM 41, FM 26, shortwave 0 (1999).

Radios: 415,000 (1997).

Television broadcast stations: 2 (plus a cable TV service) (1997).

Televisions: 38,000 (1997).

Internet Service Providers (ISPs): 6 (1999).

FINANCE, ECONOMICS, & TRADE

Economic Indicators

National product: GDP—purchasing power parity—$9.2 billion (1999 est.).

National product real growth rate: 2.4% (1999 est.).

National product per capita: $1,340 (1999 est.).

Inflation rate—consumer price index: 9% (1999 est.).

Exchange Rates

Exchange rates:

Gourdes (G) per US$1

January 2000	18.262
1999	17.965
1998	16.505
1997	17.311
1996	15.093
1995	16.160

Top Import Origins

$762 million (c.i.f., 1999)

Origins (1998)

United States	60%
EU	12%

FINANCE, ECONOMICS, & TRADE

Balance of Payments

	1994	1995	1996	1997	1998
Exports of goods (f.o.b.)	60	88	83	205	299
Imports of goods (f.o.b.)	−171	−517	−499	−560	−641
Trade balance	−111	−429	−416	−354	−341
Services - debits	−64	−285	−283	−332	−381
Services - credits	7	104	109	174	180
Private transfers (net)	43	109	152	256	293
Government transfers (net)	113	444	311	222	223
Overall balance	−23	−87	−138	−48	−38

Top Export Destinations

$322 million (f.o.b., 1999)

Destinations (1998)

United States	86%
EU	11%

Foreign Aid

Recipient: $730.6 million (1995).

Import/Export Commodities

Import Commodities	Export Commodities
Food	Manufactures
Machinery and transport equipment	Coffee
	Oils
Fuels	Mangoes

HONDURAS

Republic of Honduras
República de Honduras

CAPITAL: Tegucigalpa.

FLAG: The national flag consists of a white horizontal stripe between two blue horizontal stripes, with five blue stars on the white stripe representing the five members of the former union of Central American provinces.

ANTHEM: *Himno Nacional,* beginning "Tu bandera es un lampo de cielo" ("Thy flag is a heavenly light").

MONETARY UNIT: The lempira (L), also known as the peso, is a paper currency of 100 centavos. There are coins of 1, 2, 5, 10, 20, and 50 centavos, and notes of 1, 2, 5, 10, 20, 50, and 100 lempiras. L1 = $0.10638 (or $1 = L9.4).

WEIGHTS AND MEASURES: The metric system is the legal standard; some old Spanish measures are still used.

HOLIDAYS: New Year's Day, 1 January; Day of the Americas, 14 April; Labor Day, 1 May; Independence Day, 15 September; Birthday of Francisco Morazán, 3 October; Columbus Day, 12 October; Army Day, 21 October; Christmas, 25 December. Movable religious holidays include Holy Thursday, Good Friday, and Holy Saturday.

TIME: 6 AM = noon GMT.

LOCATION AND SIZE: Situated in Central America, Honduras has a total area of 112,090 square kilometers (43,278 square miles), slightly larger than the state of Tennessee. It has a total boundary length of 2,170 kilometers (1,349 miles).

The capital city of Honduras, Tegucigalpa, is located in the south central part of the country.

CLIMATE: The northern Caribbean area and the southern coastal plain have a wet, tropical climate, but the interior is drier and cooler. Temperatures vary from a mean of 31°C (88°F) in the coastal lowlands to 23°C (73°F) at the highest altitudes. Average annual rainfall varies from over 240 centimeters (95 inches) along the northern coast to about 84 centimeters (33 inches) in the south. The northwest coast is vulnerable to hurricanes.

INTRODUCTORY SURVEY

RECENT HISTORY

U.S. corporate interests, especially the United Fruit Co. (now United Brands), and military dictators dominated Honduran political and economic life during the first half of the twentieth century. The conservative General Tiburcio Carías Andino (1932-1948) dominated Honduran politics. In the 1950s and early 1960s several different governments ruled resulting from military coups in 1956 and 1963. A conservative coalition of military, Nationalist Party, and Liberal Party leaders under an air force officer, Colonel Oswaldo López Arellano, seized power. Two years later an elected national assembly adopted a new constitution and proclaimed López president in June 1965.

A bitter and destructive four-day war broke out in July 1969 between Honduras and El Salvador based largely on a long-standing border dispute and migration of some 300,000 Salvadorans in search of land. In June 1970 the two nations accepted a peace plan creating a demilitarized zone along their common frontier.

López and the military continued to dominate Honduran politics until López was overthrown in April 1974 by a group of lieutenant colonels. Two more military governments followed between 1975 and 1983. This period saw strong economic growth and a gradual movement toward democracy.

Under a 1982 constitution Roberto Suazo Córdova of the Liberal Party became president, and the military continued to grow in response to do-

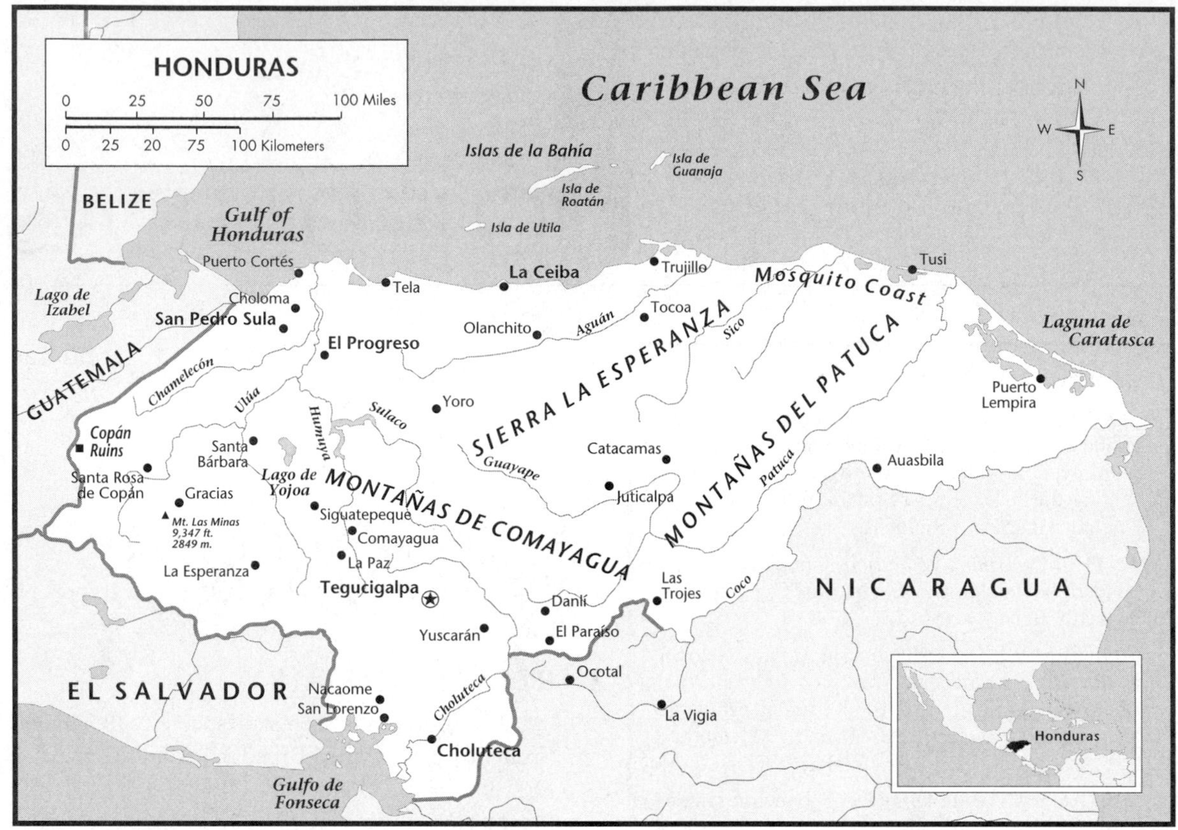

mestic unrest and the fighting in neighboring Nicaragua and El Salvador.

By 1983 several thousand anti-Sandinista guerrillas (popularly known as "contras") in Honduras were working for the overthrow of Nicaragua's Marxist Sandinista government, while the Honduran army, backed by the United States, was helping Salvadoran government forces in their fight against leftist guerrillas. The CIA used Honduras during that time as a base for covert activities against the Sandinista regime. In exchange, the United States sent large amounts of economic aid to Honduras.

In November 1985 Hondurans elected José Simón Azcona Hoyo to the presidency in the first peaceful transfer of power between elected executives in half a century. He was followed in 1989 Rafael Leonardo Callejas of the National (conservative) Party who focused on domestic issues, especially reducing the deficit. In 1993 the Liberal Party returned to power in the person of Carlos Roberto Reina. The struggle to improve economic conditions continued through 1996, with the government caught in the middle of the international financial community demanding tough structural reforms and a beleaguered population unwilling to tolerate the sacrifices entailed by such programs. In 1997 Carlos Roberto Flores of the Liberal Party won the presidency. But the fury of Hurricane Mitch destroyed Honduras' economy and placed a heavy burden on the Flores administration. The economic crisis of 1999 further worsened making Honduras the worst economic performing nation in Latin America.

GOVERNMENT

The constitution of 1982, amended in 1995, defines Honduras as a democratic republic headed by a president who is both chief of state and head of government. The president is elected by direct popular vote for a four-year term. The executive branch also includes a cabinet of twelve ministers appointed by the president. The 1982 constitution provides for the popular election of deputies to the single-chamber National Assembly, consisting of 128 deputies. All men and women 18 years of age and older are eligible to vote.

Judiciary

Judicial power is exercised by the nine-member Supreme Court and ten courts of appeal, as well as by sixty-seven courts of first instance and 325 justice of the peace courts. The Supreme Court has the power to declare laws unconstitutional. Owing to the lack of funds and corruption, the outcome of legal disputes in courts is often the product of influence and political pressure. There is a military court of first instance from which appeals can be taken to the civilian judicial system.

Political Parties

The two major parties in Honduras are the Liberal Party (Partido Liberal-PL) and the National Party (Partido Nacional-PN). The National Party is generally the more conservative.

Two minor parties occupy mildly leftist positions: the Christian Democratic Party (PDC), the National Innovation and Unity Party, and Social Democratic Party (PI NU-SD). Neither takes more than a couple of seats in the Assembly.

DEFENSE

The Honduran military forces consisted of 8,300 personnel in 2000; there were 5,500 in the army, 1,800 in the air force, and 1,000 in the navy. Police forces numbered 6,000 personnel. The defense budget in 1998 was $33 million, or 0.6 percent of GDP.

ECONOMIC AFFAIRS

Honduras is by most measures the poorest nation on the mainland of the Americas. Agriculture is key to its economy accounting for 27 percent of GDP and over 40 percent of the workforce in 1998. Coffee and bananas account for 65 percent of total Honduran export revenues. With its economy heavily dependent on coffee and banana production, the country is vulnerable to crop and world market price variations.

Hurricane Mitch destroyed 20 percent to 80 percent of the 1998 coffee and banana crops, destroyed infrastructure, and killed 5,000 people. The economy shrank 3 percent with increasing fiscal deficits in 1999. Honduras was scheduled to receive billions in international aide and in 2000 should see recovery with reconstruction projects and a recovering agricultural sector. Under the Highly Indebted Poor Countries (HIPC) initiative Honduras may get relief from its $4.4 billion external debt.

Public Finance

The U.S. CIA estimated that in 1998 government revenues totaled approximately $980 million and expenditures $1.15 billion. External debt totaled $4.4 billion in 1999.

Income

In 1999 Honduras' gross domestic product (GDP) was estimated at $14.1 billion, or about $2,050 per capita. The 1999 estimated growth rate of GDP was a decline of 3 percent and inflation was estimated at 14 percent for 1999. The 1998 estimated GDP contribution by sector was agriculture 20 percent, industry 25 percent, and services 55 percent.

Industry

Industry as a whole has continually supplied almost 25 percent of Honduras' GDP with small scale, light manufacturing accounting for 15 percent of the total.

The country has an established apparel assembly industry that employed 110,000 in 1999. Light manufacturing included matches, cigars, cigarettes, cement, food and beverage processing, shoes, candles, plastics, furniture, leather, and wood and paper products. Coffee and sugar also contribute to the industrial sector.

Banking and Finance

In 1950, the Central Bank of Honduras (Banco Central de Honduras), the sole bank of issue, was established to centralize national financial operations. In 1999 there were twenty-three commercial banks and some 150 non-bank financial institutions, many of them associated with the major banks. The Banco Atlántida, the most important commercial bank, holds over one-half of the total assets of private banks. U.S. banks play a significant role in the commercial system.

The government-controlled banks, including the National Development Bank, the National Agricultural Development Bank, and the Municipal Bank, provide credit for development projects. The National Development Bank extends agricultural and other credit-mainly to the tobacco, coffee, and livestock industries-and furnishes technical and financial assistance and other services to national economic interests. The Municipal Bank gives assistance at the local level.

In 1990 a stock exchange opened in San Pedro Sula to raise short-term bond finance for local businesses.

Economic Development

The November 1993 elections gave birth to a new political era in Honduras. President Reina of the Liberal Party was expected to slow down the pace of market-oriented reforms but to continue privatization. Continued strong growth in nontraditional exports and the prospects for moderate improvement in coffee prices brought an improvement in the current account deficit. For this reason, the continuation of official aid and the promotion of foreign investment are expected to play an increasing role in financing Honduras external gap.

By 1998 reforms were focused on alleviating the lot of the poorest citizens and improving international competitiveness. Hurricane Mitch caused major setbacks but by 1999 the economy was heading toward more stability.

SOCIAL WELFARE

The present Honduran Social Insurance Law covers accidents, illness, maternity, old age, occupational disease, unemployment, disability, death, and other circumstances affecting the capacity to work and maintain oneself and one's family. Actual coverage, however, has been limited mainly to maternity, sickness, and workers' compensation. These programs exclude domestic and agricultural workers. In 2000 the government committed 32 percent of its budget to public education and health care.

Traditional attitudes prevent women from obtaining full access to educational and economic opportunities guaranteed by the law.

Healthcare

Health conditions in Honduras are among the worst in the Western Hemisphere, and health care remains inadequate. In the mid-1990s there were 1,266 people per physician and 1.1 hospital beds per 1,000 people. In 1993 62 percent of the population had access to health care services.

Major causes of illness are diseases of the digestive tract, intestinal parasites, influenza, pneumonia, cancer, and infant diseases. Malnutrition, impure water, poor sewage disposal, and inadequate housing are the major causes of health problems. In 2000 life expectancy was an average of seventy years.

Housing

Many urban dwellings and most rural dwellings lack running water, electricity, and indoor plumbing. Estimates of the shortage in housing units grew to 500,000 in 1985.

EDUCATION

The rate of illiteracy among adults in 2000 was estimated at 27.8 percent. Public education is free and compulsory for children ages of seven to thirteen in primary school and ages fourteen to nineteen in secondary school. As of 1998 there were one million students in primary schools and 169,430 enrolled in secondary schools.

In 1994 total university enrollment was 54,106 with 4,078 teaching staff. The major university is the National Autonomous University of Honduras.

2000 KEY EVENTS TIMELINE

March

- Pirates attack a Dutch family of three off the Honduran coast; the attack leaves the thirteen-year old son paralyzed.

April

- Honduras defeats the United States two-to-one in under-twenty-three men's soccer.

May

- Archaeologists study the ancient Mayan city of El Pajaral.

July

- The government delays the sale of its stake in the country's telephone company, Empresas Hondurena de Telocomunicaciones.

November

- The World Bank approves a $66.5 million International Development Association loan November 7 to repair roads damaged by Hurricane Mitch in 1998.
- U.N. official Jeffrey Avina states November 24 that the United Nations will sponsor a complete audit of Honduran military firms, that have recently been accused of corruption.

December

- The Inter-American Development Bank (IDB) approves three loans totaling $37.6 million. A reported $23 million will be devoted to support education in rural areas; other funds will go toward updating Congress and to studies of the economy.
- The World Bank and International Monetary Fund (IMF) announce on December 23 that the United States, Canada, Japan, and nations of Europe will provide debt relief for twenty-two of the world's poorest nations, including Benin, Bo-

livia, Burkina Faso, Cameroon, The Gambia, Guinea, Guinea-Bissau, Guyana, Honduras, Nicaragua, Madagascar, Malawi, Mali, Mauritania, Mozambique, Niger, Rwanda, São Tomé and Príncipe, Senegal, Tanzania, Uganda, and Zambia.

ANALYSIS OF EVENTS: 2000

BUSINESS AND THE ECONOMY

In July the World Bank and the International Monetary Fund (IMF) announced they would restructure Honduras's foreign debt, for savings of $556 million over the next two decades. The plan was part of a project to reduce the debt of some of the world's poorest nations. Despite Hurricane Mitch, which devastated the country in October 1998, Honduras has been slowly recovering on the economic front. In 1999 inflation was 11 percent, well below the 23 percent registered in 1990. Yet the country continued to feel the effects of Mitch, with some communities unable to grow food on land destroyed by mudslides. In April 2000 government officials had to bring food to eighteen indigenous communities suffering from famine in the southeastern part of the country. Their farmlands had been washed over with rocks, pebbles, and sand.

A border dispute with Nicaragua practically closed that country's markets to Honduran products. While a free-trade agreement existed between the neighbors, Nicaragua imposed a 35 percent tariff on Honduran products as retaliation against Honduras for its recognition of Colombia's claims to more than 100,000 square kilometers in the Caribbean. While the two countries continued to negotiate over the dispute, Honduras attempted to find new markets for its products, including striking economic agreements with Colombia. Honduras and Nicaragua have argued their cases in front of international tribunals. Top business leaders also pressured Honduran President Carlos Flores to withdraw from all trade agreements with other Central American countries for their indifference to the trade problem.

GOVERNMENT AND POLITICS

A dispute over the waters of the Caribbean nearly brought Honduras and Nicaragua to war. Relations between the two countries became strained after the Honduran Congress ratified an agreement that claimed 130,000 square kilometers of the Caribbean for Honduras and Colombia. Nicaragua has historical claims to the territory, whose waters are rich in fisheries and natural resources, possibly including oil. With international intervention, both countries agreed to reduce the number of troops at the border, and allowed the dispute to be heard by the United Nations. By mid-2000 the presidents of both nations said they wanted to reach a peaceful agreement, and vowed to press forward with negotiations.

In October the assassination of a prominent legislator underscored a serious crime problem affecting the country. Several heavily armed men kidnapped Justo Jiménez, a legislator for the governing Liberal Party. He was found dead with several gunshots to his body. Prominent national leaders addressed the nation asking for help to curtail growing crime in the country, where the society has been undermined by poverty, unemployment, and continuing severe social problems in the wake of Hurricane Mitch, which devastated the country in late 1998.

The country appeared to be on the verge of an electoral crisis when the National Party threatened to withdraw from the December 2000 primary election and the 2001 general election if its presidential candidate was not allowed to participate. The National Party said the governing Liberal Party, through the national election commission, was trying to invalidate the candidacy of Ricardo Maduro, claiming he was not born in Honduras. Maduro, an economist who graduated from Stanford University, admitted he was born in Panama, but claimed he had Honduran citizenship through his mother, who was born in Guatemala but whose mother (his grandmother) was born in Honduras. According to the Honduran Constitution, only Hondurans who were born in the country are allowed to run for office. But the children of Hondurans who were born outside the country also are eligible to run for office. Maduro already has held elected positions in Honduras, and his citizenship had not been questioned. In national polls, Maduro was favored by more than 50 percent of the electorate, placing him as the favorite for the presidency in the 2001 elections, when hundreds of offices will be up for a vote.

CULTURE AND SOCIETY

During February forty Honduran children were arrested in Canada for allegedly selling illegal drugs in the streets of Vancouver, B.C. The arrests underscored a growing concern for the Central American country, where 15 percent of the workforce was made up of children. A nonprofit organization said it had documented the illegal removal of 500 children from Honduras in the last twenty years. They were forcibly taken from their mothers, given up for adoption, and in many cases, were sexually exploited. Honduran officials said they would seek to repatriate about 200 Honduran children living illegally in Vancouver. Honduran authorities said drug gangs have been using the young Hondurans to sell illegal substances both in Canada and the United States. Most children arrived illegally to these countries. Honduras was one of several Central American countries where prostitution among children has been growing. In Honduras a U.S. citizen was convicted and jailed for running a prostitution ring for tourists seeking to have sex with young children. Yet prostitution is only part of the problem. In Honduras where about 80 percent of the nation's 6.3 million people live in poverty, child labor remained important for families trying to make a living. And children, unprotected by the law, end up doing some of the nastiest work, according to nonprofit agencies that have attempted to protect the young.

In 1999 Honduran officials found dozens of graves at the *El Aguacate* air base in eastern Honduras. The United States built the base for Nicaraguan Contra rebels fighting the leftist government of that country. In September 2000 the Organization of American States said it would search and destroy any mines at the air base to ease the search for the bodies of up to 184 people who disappeared in Honduras during the 1980s. As of late 2000 officials had been able to pinpoint forty-eight graves, some believed to hold multiple remains.

DIRECTORY

CENTRAL GOVERNMENT

Head of State

President
Carlos Roberto Flores Facussé, Office of the President
PHONE: +504 2344922
FAX: +504 2378521

Ministers

Minister of Agriculture and Livestock
Guillermo Alvarado, Ministry of Agriculture and Livestock, Avenida La Paz, Edificio Atala, Tegucigalpa, M.D.C., Honduras, C.A.
PHONE: +504 2328851
FAX: +504 2325375

Minister of Culture, Arts, and Sports
Herman Allan Padgett, Ministry of Culture, Arts, and Sports, Avenida La Paz, Edificio Atala, Tegucigalpa, M.C.D., Honduras, C.A.
PHONE: +504 2369643
FAX: +504 2369532

Minister of Defense
Edgardo Dumas, Ministry of Defense

Minister of Education
Ramon Calix, Ministry of Education, 1era Calle, 2-3 Avenida, Comayaguela, M.D.C., Honduras, C.A.
PHONE: +504 2228571
FAX: +504 2374192

Minister of Finance
Gabriela Nunez, Ministry of Finance

Minister of Foreign Relations
Roberto Flores Bermúdez, Ministry of Foreign Relations, Antigua Casa Presidencial Boulevard Fuerzas Armadas, Tegucigalpa, Honduras C.A.
PHONE: +504 2341922; 2345411; 2341178
FAX: +504 2341484
E-MAIL: rfloresb@sre.hn

Ministers

Minister of Government and Justice
Enrique Flores, Ministry of Government and Justice

Minister of Industry and Commerce
Oscar Kafati, Ministry of Industry and Commerce

Minister of Labor
Rosa America Miranda, Ministry of Labor

Minister of Natural Resources and Environment
Xiomara Gomez, Ministry of Natural Resources and Environment
PHONE: +504 2327718
FAX: +504 2375725

Minister of Presidency
Gustavo Adolfo Alfaro Zelaya, Ministry of Presidency

Minister of Public Health

Plutarco Castellanos, Ministry of Public Health

Minister of Public Works, Transportation, and Housing

Tomas Lozano Reyes, Ministry of Public Works, Transportation, and Housing, Barrio La Bolsa, Apartado Postal No 976, Comayaguela, M.D.C., Honduras, C.A.
PHONE: +504 2337690
FAX: +504 2339227

Minister of Tourism

Ana del Socorro Abarca, Ministry of Tourism

POLITICAL ORGANIZATIONS

Partido de Inovación y Unidad-Social Democracia (National Innovation and Unity Party)

Apdo 105, 29 Avenida de Comayagüela 912, Tegucigalpa, Honduras
PHONE: +504 371357; 371178
FAX: +504 374245
TITLE: President
NAME: Olban Valladares

Partido Liberal de Honduras (Liberal Party of Honduras)

Colonia Miramonte Atrás del Supermercado La Colonia No.1, Tegucigalpa, Honduras
PHONE: +504 320520; 324850
FAX: +504 320797
TITLE: President
NAME: Jorge Reina

Partido Nacional (National Party)

Paseo el Obelisco, Comayagüela M.D.C., Tegucigalpa, Honduras
PHONE: +504 377310; 377413
FAX: +504 377365
TITLE: President
NAME: Porfirio Lobo

DIPLOMATIC REPRESENTATION

Embassies in Honduras

Peru

Reformation Colony, Stroll The Reformation 2618, Tegucigalpa, Honduras, P.O. Box 3171
PHONE: +504 2210596; 2210604
FAX: +504 2366070
E-MAIL: embaperu@netsys.hn
TITLE: Ambassador
NAME: Víctor Yamamoto Miyakawa

United States

Avenido La Paz, Apartado Postal No. 3453, AMEMB Honduras, APO AA 34022
PHONE: +504 385114
FAX: +504 369037

JUDICIAL SYSTEM

Supreme Court of Justice

BROADCAST MEDIA

Asociacion Nacional de Radiodifusores de Honduras (ANARH)

Ap. 4039, Tegucigalpa, Honduras
PHONE: +504 391992

Empresa Hondurena de Telecomunicaciones (HONDUTEL)

Ap. 1794, Tegucigalpa, Honduras
PHONE: +504 222101
TITLE: Director
CONTACT: Camilo A. Pon Z. Jefe

Power FM

E-MAIL: dj@powerfm.hn
WEBSITE: http://www.powerfm.hn/
TITLE: General Manager
CONTACT: Xavier Sierra

COLLEGES AND UNIVERSITIES

National Autonomous University Honduras

Ciudad Universitaria, Apdo. Postal 8778, Tegucigalpa, Honduras
PHONE: +504 2312110
FAX: +504 2314601
E-MAIL: webmaster@unah.hn
WEBSITE: http://www.unah.hn

NEWSPAPERS AND MAGAZINES

La Prensa

Organizacion Publicitiaria, S.A., 3a. Avenida N.O., No. 34, Apdo 134, San Pedro Sula, Honduras
PHONE: +504 533101
FAX: +504 533949; 530778; 534020
E-MAIL: laprensa@simon.intertel.hn
WEBSITE: http://www.laprenseahn.com

TITLE: Editor
CONTACT: Nelson Fernandez
CIRCULATION: 52,000

Tiempo

Editora Honduras S.A. de C.V., 1a Calle 5ta. Ave. NE, 102 B, Santa Anita, Apdo 450, San Pedro Sula, Honduras
PHONE: +504 533388
FAX: +504 534590
E-MAIL: tiempo@simon.intertel.hn; fcordon@intertel.hn
WEBSITE: http://www.tiempo.hn
TITLE: Editor
CONTACT: Manuel Gamero
CIRCULATION: 60,000

La Tribuna

Periodicos y Revistas S.A. de C.V. (PYRSA), Col. Santa Barbara, Carrera al primer, Batillon de Infanteria, Tegucigalpa, Honduras
PHONE: +504 331138; 331516; 2831283
FAX: +504 331188; 343050
E-MAIL: tribune@david.intertel.hn
WEBSITE: http://www.latribuna.hn
TITLE: Editor
CONTACT: Salatiel Gonzales
CIRCULATION: 40,000

PUBLISHERS

Editorial Guaymuras

Apdo 1843, Tegucigalpa, Honduras
PHONE: + 504 2375433
FAX: + 504 2384578
E-MAIL: editoria@guaymura.sdnhon.org.hn
TITLE: Director
CONTACT: Isolda Arita Melzer
SUBJECTS: Anthropology, Education, Environmental Studies, Ethnicity, Political Science, History, Language Arts, Linguistics, Social Sciences
TOTAL PUBLISHED: 3 print

Editorial Nuevo Continente

Ave. Cervantes, Tegucigalpa, Honduras
PHONE: + 504 225073
TITLE: Director
CONTACT: Leticia Oyuela

Editorial Universitaria

c/o Universidad de Honduras, Tegucigalpa, Honduras
PHONE: + 504 312110

RELIGIOUS ORGANIZATIONS

Mormon

San Pedro Sula Mission
L.D.S. Chapel, The Willows, Finglas Road, Glasnevin, Dublin 7, Ireland
WEBSITE: http://www.mission.net/honduras/san-pedro-sula/
TITLE: Bishop
NAME: Bernard C. O'Farrell

FURTHER READING

Articles

Adams, David. "Burnt Forest Reveals lost Mayan City." *The Times* (London), May 20, 2000, World News Features.

Oyama, David I. "Honduras Delays Sale of Telephone Stake." *Wall Street Journal,* July 25, 2000, p. A14.

Shipley, Amy, "O. Suazo Strikes Twice in Upset, Honduras 2, U.S. Men 1." *Washington Post,* May 1, 2000, p. D2.

Books

Binns, Jack R. *The United States in Honduras, 1980–1981: An Ambassador's Memoir.* Jefferson, NC: McFarland & Co., 2000.

Government Publications

Investment Treaty with Honduras. Washington: G.P.O., 2000.

Internet

ABC News, "Around-the-World Adventure Ends with Pirate Attack.", April 7, 2000 [Online] Available http://abcnews.go.com/onair/2020/2020_000412_pirates_feature.html

HONDURAS: STATISTICAL DATA

For sources and notes see "Sources of Statistics" at the front of each volume.

GEOGRAPHY

Geography

Area:

Total: 112,090 sq km.

Land: 111,890 sq km.

Land boundaries:

Total: 1,520 km.

Border countries: Guatemala 256 km, El Salvador 342 km, Nicaragua 922 km.

Coastline: 820 km.

Climate: subtropical in lowlands, temperate in mountains.

Terrain: mostly mountains in interior, narrow coastal plains.

Natural resources: timber, gold, silver, copper, lead, zinc, iron ore, antimony, coal, fish, hydropower.

Land use:

Arable land: 15%

Permanent crops: 3%

Permanent pastures: 14%

Forests and woodland: 54%

Other: 14% (1993 est.).

HUMAN FACTORS

Demographics (A)

	1990	1995	1998	2000	2010	2020	2030	2040	2050
Population	4,772	5,494	5,965	6,250	7,683	8,826	9,849	10,852	11,862
Life expectancy - males	68.0	68.8	56.3	67.9	62.1	64.4	68.4	73.2	77.6
Life expectancy - females	72.0	73.2	61.3	72.1	65.2	67.9	72.5	78.0	82.9
Birth rate (per 1,000)	38.6	36.1	34.0	32.7	25.8	21.4	18.6	16.2	14.6
Death rate (per 1,000)	5.6	5.2	10.4	5.3	8.0	7.9	7.3	6.5	6.1
Women of reproductive age (15-49 yrs.)	1,073	1,267	1,401	1,488	1,945	2,362	2,660	2,851	2,938
Fertility rate	5.4	4.8	4.5	4.3	3.2	2.5	2.2	2.1	2.0

Except as noted, values for vital statistics are in thousands; life expectancy is in years.

Health Personnel

	National Data	World Data (wtd ave)
Total health expenditure as a percentage of GDP, 1990-1998[a]		
Public sector	2.7	2.5
Private sector	5.6	2.9
Total[b]	8.3	5.5
Health expenditure per capita in U.S. dollars, 1990-1998[a]		
Purchasing power parity	202	561
Total	72	483
Availability of health care facilities per 100,000 people		
Hospital beds 1990-1998[a]	110	330
Doctors 1992-1995[a]	22	122
Nurses 1992-1995[a]	17	248

Health Indicators

	National Data	World Data
Life expectancy at birth (years)		
1980	60	61
1998	69	67
Daily per capita supply of calories		
1970	2,155	2,358
1997	2,403	2,791
Daily per capital supply of protein		
1997 (grams)	58	74
Total fertility rate (births per woman)		
1980	6.5	3.7
1998	4.2	2.7
Population with access (%)		
To safe water (1990-96)	65	NA
To sanitation (1990-96)	65	NA
People living with (1997)		
Tuberculosis (cases per 100,000)	67.4	60.4
Malaria (cases per 100,000)	1,101.2	42.2
HIV/AIDS (% aged 15 - 49 years)	1.46	0.99

Infants and Malnutrition

	National Data	World Data (wtd ave)
Under 5 mortality rate (1989)	44	NA
% of infants with low birthweight (1992-98)[1]	9	17
Births attended by skilled health staff (% of total births 1996-98)	47	52
% fully immunized at 1 year of age (1995-98)[1]		
TB	96	82
DPT	97	77
Polio	98	77
Measles	99	74
Prevalence of child malnutrition (1992-98)[1] (based on weight for age, % of children under 5 years)	25	30

Ethnic Division

Mestizo 90%

Amerindian 7%

Black 2%

White 1%

People of Mestizo ethnicity have mixed Amerindian and European ancestry.

Religion

Roman Catholic 97%

Protestant minority . . . . .NA

Major Languages

Spanish, Amerindian dialects.

EDUCATION

Public Education Expenditures

	1980	1997
Public expenditures on education as % of GNP	3.2	3.6
Expenditures per student as % of GNP per capita		
Primary & Secondary	10.7[2]	9.0
Tertiary	7.4	68.7
Teachers' compensation as % of total current education expenditures	71.1	67.8
Pupils per teacher at the primary level	NA	35
Duration of primary education in years	NA	6
World data for comparison		
Public expenditures on education as % of GNP (mean)	3.9	4.8
Pupils per teacher at the primary level (wtd ave)	NA	33

Duration of primary education in years (mean)	NA	9

Educational Attainment (A)

Age group (1983)[9] .... 25+

Population of this age group .... NA

Highest level attained (%)

No schooling 33.5

First level

Not completed 51.3

Completed .... NA

Entered second level

Lower Secondary 4.3

Upper Secondary 7.6

Entered post-secondary 3.3

(Continued on next page.)

GOVERNMENT & LAW

Military Affairs (A)

	1990	1992	1995	1996	1997
Military expenditures					
Current dollars (mil.)	64	47	52	NA	NA
1997 constant dollars (mil.)	75	52	54	NA	NA
Armed forces (000)	18	17	17	10	10
Gross national product (GNP)					
Current dollars (mil.)	2,940	3,320	4,030	4,220	4,570
1997 constant dollars (mil.)	3,440	3,680	4,170	4,290	4,570
Central government expenditures (CGE)					
1997 constant dollars (mil.)	750	956	961	919	950
People (mil.)	4.7	5.0	5.4	5.6	5.7
Military expenditure as % of GNP	2.2	1.4	1.3	NA	NA
World data on military expenditure as % of GNP	4.5	3.4	2.7	2.6	2.6
Military expenditure as % of CGE	9.9	5.5	5.6	NA	NA
World data on military expenditure as % of CGE	17.0	12.5	10.5	10.3	10.2
Military expenditure per capita (1997 $)	16	10	10	NA	NA
World data on military expenditure per capita (1997 $)	242	173	146	143	145
Armed forces per 1,000 people (soldiers)	3.8	3.4	3.1	1.8	1.7
World data on armed forces per 1,000 people (soldiers)	5.3	4.5	4.1	3.9	3.8
GNP per capita (1997 $)	725	734	766	768	798
Arms imports[6]					
Current dollars (mil.)	40	30	20	30	10
1997 constant dollars (mil.)	47	33	21	31	10
Total imports[7]					
Current dollars (mil.)	935	1,037	1,643	1,840	2,149
1997 constant dollars (mil.)	1,095	1,150	1,701	1,871	2,149
Total exports[7]					
Current dollars (mil.)	831	802	1,220	1,321	1,447
1997 constant dollars (mil.)	973	889	1,263	1,343	1,447
Arms as percent of total imports[8]	4.3	2.9	1.2	1.6	0.5
Arms as percent of total exports[8]	0	0	0	0	0

(Continued on next page.)

EDUCATION (cont.)

Literacy Rates (A)

In thousands and percent	1990	1995	2000	2010
Illiterate population (15+ yrs.)	817	869	925	1,013
Literacy rate - total adult pop. (%)	69.4	72.7	75.6	80.7
Literacy rate - males (%)	69.9	72.6	75.1	79.4
Literacy rate - females (%)	68.9	72.7	76.0	82.0

GOVERNMENT & LAW (cont.)

Political Parties

National Congress (Congreso Nacional)	% of vote	no. of seats
Liberal Party (PL)	46%	67
National Party of Honduras (PN)	38%	55
National Innovation and Unity Party-Social Democratic Party (PINU-SD)	4%	3
Christian Democratic Party (PDC)	2%	2
Democratic Unification Party (PUD)	2%	1

Elections were last held on 30 November 1997 (next to be held 30 November 2001).

Government Budgets (B)

Revenues . . . . $980.00 million

Expenditures . . . . $1.15 billion

Data for 1998 est.

LABOR FORCE

Total Labor Force (A)

2.3 million (1997 est.).

Labor Force by Occupation

Agriculture 29%

Industry 21%

Services 60%

Data for 1998 est.

Unemployment Rate

12% (1999); underemployed 30% (1997 est.).

PRODUCTION SECTOR

Energy Production

Production .2.904 billion kWh

Production by source

Fossil fuel 34.44%

Hydro 65.56%

Nuclear 0%

Other 0%

Exports . . . . .16 million kWh

Data for 1998.

Energy Consumption

Consumption . . . . .2.742 billion kWh

Imports . . . . .57.000 million kWh

Data for 1998.

Transportation

Highways:

Total: 15,400 km.

Paved: 3,126 km.

Unpaved: 12,274 km (1999 est.).

Waterways: 465 km navigable by small craft.

Merchant marine:

Total: 306 ships (1,000 GRT or over) totaling 848,150 GRT/980,995 DWT.

Ships by type: bulk 26, cargo 187, chemical tanker 5, container 7, livestock carrier 1, passenger 2, passenger/cargo 4, petroleum tanker 43, refrigerated cargo 15, roll-on/roll-off 9, short-sea passenger 5, vehicle carrier 2 (1999 est.)

Note: a flag of convenience registry; Russia owns 6 ships, Vietnam 1, Singapore 3, North Korea 1 (1998 est.).

Airports: 119 (1999 est.).

Airports - with paved runways: 12.

Airports - with unpaved runways: 107.

Top Agriculture Products

Bananas, coffee, citrus; beef; timber; shrimp.

Top Mining Products (B)

Mineral resources include: gold, silver, copper, lead, zinc, iron ore, antimony, coal.

MANUFACTURING SECTOR

GDP & Manufacturing Summary (A)

	1980	1985	1990	1995
GDP ($-1990 mil.)[1]	2,476	2,617	3,049	3,632
Per capita ($-1990)[1]	694	625	625	642
Manufacturing share (%) (current prices)[1]	15.1	15.1	16.3	15.2[e]
Manufacturing				
Value added ($-1990 mil.)[1]	336	353	443	532[e]
Industrial production index	50	64	100	258
Value added ($ mil.)	289[e]	498	466	577[e]
Gross output ($ mil.)	1,205[i]	1,618	1,651	2,092[e]
Employment (000)	58	64	79	140[e]
Profitability (% of gross output)				
Intermediate input (%)	72[e]	69	72	72[e]
Wages and salaries inc. supplements (%)	11[e]	13	11	12[e]
Gross operating surplus	17[e]	18	18	16[e]
Productivity ($)				
Gross output per worker	16,916[e]	25,279	20,996	11,947[e]
Value added per worker	4,840[e]	7,785	5,926	3,328[e]
Average wage (inc. supplements)	2,015[e]	3,219	2,239	1,747[e]
Value added ($ mil.)				
Food products	75[e]	130	128	166[e]
Beverages	53[e]	78	59	87[e]
Tobacco products	20e	42	34	32e
Textiles	13e	14	16	13e
Wearing apparel	9e	17	20	82e
Leather and fur products	3e	2	3	3e
Footwear	3e	2	2	3e
Wood and wood products	22e	30	20	27e
Furniture and fixtures	5e	8	8	9e
Paper and paper products	5e	9	12	16e
Printing and publishing	7[e]	13	10	13[e]
Industrial chemicals	1[e]	2	2	3[e]
Other chemical products	12[e]	20	20	22[e]
Petroleum refineries	13[e]	38	39	1[e]
Rubber products	5[e]	8	7	6[e]
Plastic products	9[e]	18	16	16[e]
Other non-metal mineral products	15[e]	24	26	38[e]
Iron and steel	1[e]	2	4	3[e]
Non-ferrous metals	1[e]	1	1	1[e]
Metal products	12[e]	21	21	20[e]
Non-electrical machinery	1[e]	3	4	4[e]
Electrical machinery	4[e]	8	7	6[e]
Transport equipment	NA	2	2	1[e]
Prof. and scientific equipment	NA	1	1	1[e]
Other manufacturing	2[e]	5	6	4[e]

COMMUNICATIONS

Daily Newspapers

	National Data	World Data for Comparison
Daily Newspapers		
Number of Dailies	7	8,391
Total Circulation (000)	320	548,000
Circulation per 1,000 inhabitants	55	96

Telecommunications

Telephones - main lines in use: 190,200 (1996).

Telephones - mobile cellular: 0 (1995).

Telephone system: inadequate system.

Domestic: NA

International: satellite earth stations - 2 Intelsat (Atlantic Ocean); connected to Central American Microwave System.

Radio broadcast stations: AM 241, FM 53, shortwave 12 (1998).

Radios: 2.45 million (1997).

Television broadcast stations: 11 (plus 17 repeaters) (1997).

Televisions: 570,000 (1997).

Internet Service Providers (ISPs): 14 (1999).

FINANCE, ECONOMICS, & TRADE

Economic Indicators

National product: GDP—purchasing power parity—$14.1 billion (1999 est.).

National product real growth rate: -3% (1999 est.).

National product per capita: $2,050 (1999 est.).

Inflation rate—consumer price index: 14% (1999 est.).

Exchange Rates

Exchange rates:

Lempiras (L) per US$1

January 2000	14.5744
1999	14.5039
1998	13.8076
1997	13.0942
1996	12.8694
1995	10.3432

Top Import Origins

$2.7 billion (f.o.b., 1999 est.)

Origins (1998)

United States	60%
Guatemala	5%
Netherlands Antilles	NA
Japan	NA
Germany	NA
Mexico	NA
El Salvador	NA

Top Export Destinations

$1.6 billion (f.o.b., 1999 est.)

Destinations (1998)

United States	73%
Japan	4%
Germany	4%
Belgium	NA
Spain	NA

Foreign Aid

Recipient: $557.8 million (1999).

Import/Export Commodities

Import Commodities	Export Commodities
Machinery and transport equipment	Coffee
	Bananas
Industrial raw materials	Shrimp
Chemical products	Lobster
Fuels	Meat
Foodstuffs	Zinc
	Lumber

Balance of Payments

	1994	1995	1996	1997	1998
Exports of goods (f.o.b.)	1,102	1,377	1,638	1,857	2,017
Imports of goods (f.o.b.)	−1,351	−1,519	−1,926	−2,150	−2,340
Trade balance	−250	−141	−287	−294	−323
Services - debits	−311	−334	−328	−361	−396
Services - credits	242	258	283	335	370
Private transfers (net)	94	128	148	182	269
Government transfers (net)	96	115	123	124	174
Overall balance	−343	−201	−335	−272	−158

HONG KONG

CAPITAL: Victoria

FLAG: A red flag with a stylized, white, five-petal bauhinia flower in the center.

ANTHEM: *China National Anthem*

MONETARY UNIT: The Hong Kong dollar (HK$) is a paper currency of 100 cent.

WEIGHTS AND MEASURES: The metric system is the legal standard.

HOLIDAYS: National Day, October 1-2. Also, July 1 (1997) is celebrated as Hong Kong Special Administrative Region Establishment Day.

TIME: 8 PM = noon GMT.

LOCATION AND SIZE: Hong Kong is located on the southeastern coast of China, bordering the South China Sea. Geographic coordinates are 22 15 N, 114 10 E. The Special Administrative Unit consists of a portion of the mainland of China and a number of islands. Total land area is approximately 1,092 square kilometers.

CLIMATE: The climate is tropical monsoon, cool and humid in the winter, hot and rainy from spring through summer, and warm and sunny in the fall.

Hong Kong Special
Administrative Region
Xianggang Tebiew Xingzhengqu

INTRODUCTORY SURVEY

RECENT HISTORY

On July 1, 1997, the British Crown Colony of Hong Kong ended 155 years of English rule and became the Hong Kong Special Administrative Region (SAR) of China. At this time, China implemented a "one country, two systems" formula whereby China continues its socialist economic system while Hong Kong maintains autonomy and pursues capitalism.

Hong Kong is technically an island, and its physical relationship to the mainland encloses one of the best natural sea ports in the world. Hong Kong was occupied by the United Kingdom in 1841, during the First Opium War. The Treaty of Nanking provided that China cede the territory to Britain in 1842. The results of the second Opium War changed the situation for Hong Kong somewhat, with the occupation of Hong Kong changing into a 99-year lease in 1898. The end of that lease in 1997 brought Hong Kong back to Chinese control.

Hong Kong since World War II has been a model of the capitalist economy. Inexpensive labor, free trade laws, and excellent port facilities propelled Hong Kong into becoming a manufacturing center for Asia. Hong Kong also became a major banking center. Tourism brought additional monies to the territory. While the United States and other western nations isolated communist China into the 1970s, Hong Kong became the portal for the communist regime's relations with western nations.

After the communist Chinese government on the mainland opened relations with the United States and the rest of the world, the focus on Hong Kong shifted to the question of what to do with the territory when the British lease expired. Negotiations centered on the desire of the citizens of Hong Kong to maintain their economy, freedoms, and lifestyle. Realizing the value of the strong Hong Kong economy to the rest of China, the mainland Chinese government agreed to The Basic Law, a "mini-constitution" that guarantees Hong Kong's rights as a free trade and free economic area with local control of its government.

GOVERNMENT

Hong Kong is a Special Administrative Region of the People's Republic of China. Its status was established by the Sino-British Joint Declaration of 1984 and The Basic Law. The Basic Law, or mini-

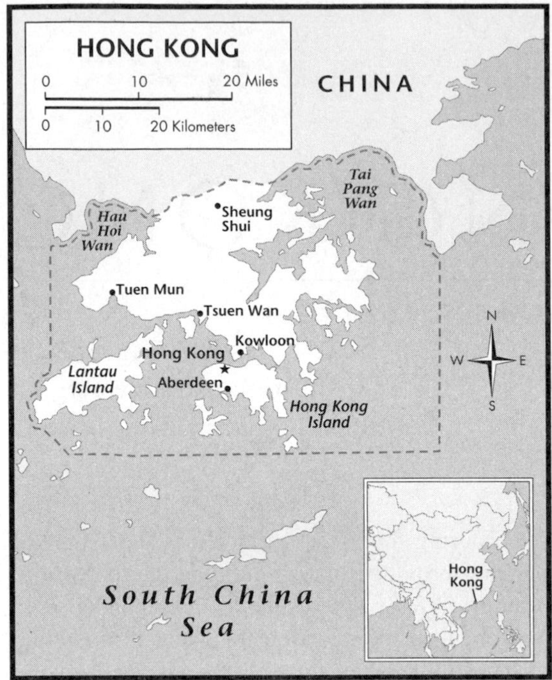

constitution, was approved by China's National People's Congress in 1990. Under the Basic Law, Hong Kong's chief of state is the president of China. A chief executive for Hong Kong is elected by a 800-member Selection Committee appointed by China. Legislative authority rests with a freely elected Legislative Council. The sixty seat council is elected to four year terms, with twenty elected by popular vote, thirty elected by functional (occupational) constituencies, and ten elected by the Selection Committee.

After control of Hong Kong reverted to the mainland, the first elections in the region were held in 1998, and they were seen as free and fair. Universal suffrage applies for all permanent residents for the past seven years who are at least 18 years of age. Since the unification with China, the Civil Service has maintained its independence, quality, and neutrality, with no discernible direction from China.

Judiciary

The Hong Kong legal system is based on English common law. The highest court is the Court of Final Appeal in the Hong Kong Special Administrative Region.

Political Parties

Multiple parties are active in Hong Kong along the British tradition. Some of the more prominent parties are the Association for Democracy and People's Livelihood; Citizens Party; Democratic Alliance for the Betterment of Hong Kong; Democratic Party; Frontier Party; Hong Kong Progressive Alliance; and Liberal Party. There are also a number of political pressure groups, including a variety of unions, the Chinese Manufacturer's Association of Hong Kong, and the Chinese General Chamber of Commerce.

DEFENSE

Defense is the responsibility of the People's Republic of China.

ECONOMIC AFFAIRS

Hong Kong is a free market economy. Natural resources are limited, and food, raw materials, fuel, and power are imported. The economy thrives on international trade. Manufacturing is a major element of the economy, and includes textiles, clothing, footwear, electronics, plastics, toys, watches, and clocks. Tourism is another large component, as is banking, insurance, and international trade.

Public Finance

The Hong Kong government spent $25.1 billion in fiscal year 1998/1999, with revenues of $23.1 billion. Hong Kong carries an external debt of about $48.1 billion. It receives no economic aid.

Income

Hong Kong's gross domestic product (GDP) was estimated for 1999 at $158.2 billion. Real growth rate in the GDP was estimated for that year at 1.8 percent. On a per capita basis, the GDP was estimated at $23,100.

Industry

Major industries are textiles, clothing, tourism, electronics, plastics, toys, watches, clocks, banking, and insurance. Hong Kong is a flag registry of convenience for ships.

Banking and Finance

The monetary system is based on the Hong Kong Dollar. Hong Kong has an active banking and insurance industry and is a center for foreign banking concerns. The Hong Kong stock exchange is very active, trading in stock, futures, and currencies.

Economic Development

Hong Kong is one of the more industrialized regions in Asia, with a strong economy and entrepreneurial spirit. The manufacturing sector remains strong. Future growth is expected primarily in the service sector, with shipping, tourism, and various financial services leading the way.

SOCIAL WELFARE

Social security in Hong Kong is limited to emergency relief. There are some allowances for unemployment, old age, and disabilities. Hong Kong's population is aging, however, and expenditures on social programs is increasing.

Healthcare

Healthcare in Hong Kong is generally good. Hospitals fall into three categories: government, government-assisted, and private. The government is aggressive toward preventive medicine and personal health services. Clinics are taken by boat to outlying villages. Government operated clinics supplement other services.

The overall life expectancy of Hong Kong residents is 79.6 years. Infant morality is 3.2 per 1,000. Health indices are improving, and a downward trend in the occurrence of major communicable diseases indicate the improving quality of health care.

Housing

Housing has been a major problem in Hong Kong. Heavy immigration in the post World War II era placed great pressure on the housing markets. A general lack of planning exacerbated the problems. Public housing has reduced the numbers of those living in shantytowns and in squatter's villages so that currently nearly half of the population lives in public housing. Land prices, however, are extremely high and the juxtaposition of opulence and poverty in Hong Kong is striking.

EDUCATION

The majoirty of education in Hong Kong is fund privately, about sixty percent, with the remainder receiving public or government subsidies. Education is compulsory between the ages of six and fifteen. Literacy rates are high, at ninety-two percent. Post-secondary schools are mostly subsidized. Two universities, the University of Hong Kong and the Chinese University of Hong Kong, operate along with numerous vocational, technical, and industrial training institutions.

2000 KEY EVENTS TIMELINE

January

- The first day of 2000 arrives with few signs of the "Y2K" computer bug. Although many had predicted software failures due to inadequate programming when the year 2000 began, nothing of consequence occurs in Hong Kong businesses.

March

- Hong Kong Chief Executive Tung Chee Hwa announces plans to travel to Washington, D.C., and lobby the United States government to grant China full member status in the club of trading nations. Mr. Tung also intends to promote trade with Hong Kong.

April

- The Hong Kong Journalists Association and the pro-democracy Frontier group are warned by a Beijing official not to support or advocate independence for Taiwan. The Journalists Association reacts angrily, while a dozen members of the Frontier group protest at government headquarters.

May

- Protestors disrupt an auction of Chinese antiques and art treasures. Some of the items sold were looted from an imperial palace in Beijing one hundred forty years ago. The auction house Christie's Hong Kong conducts the sale, and chairman Anthony Lin defends it. Protestors believe the items should be returned to China and the Chinese people.
- The Chinese Army announces it will remove British names from local military structures and replace them with politically neutral names.
- Activists demonstrate to commemorate the military crackdown that ended the Tiananmen Square democracy demonstrations in 1988. The demonstrations recalled the attempt at gaining democracy in China—an attempt that was put down with tanks and the jailing of organizers in 1989.

June

- Remembrances of the anniversary of the June 4, 1989, Tiananmen Square incident continue. However, the number of participants is less than half that gathered in 1999.

July

- Under Hong Kong's Basic Law, the first election is held by an elite group of voters to elect a committee that will select Hong Kong's future lawmakers. Protestors label the election "undemocratic," as only 177,000 of 3.1 million registered voters are eligible to choose the 800-member Election Committee. The Committee will then select six of the 60-seat legislature in September.

- The *Far Eastern Economic Review* reports Hong Kong's average household income has reached HK240,000 per year.

August

- Protestors set fire to the Honk Kong Immigration Office. Assembled to request residency permits, the group of mainland Chinese immigrants become enraged when told their time for filling out forms has passed. Fifty people suffer burns; six immigrants are listed in critical condition, and one immigration officer dies due to burns received in the incident.
- Toys distributed by the American restaurant chain McDonald's are revealed to have been made at a mainland Chinese sweatshops that illegally employ child labor. McDonald's denies responsibility but says it will investigate.

September

- Scandals mar the administration of Hong Kong Chief Executive Tung Chee Hwa. Protestors demonstrate against Tung's policies and leadership style. In support of Tung, who is pro-Beijing, the Beijing media use the events in Hong Kong to label the protestors as anti-China.
- Hong Kong's legislative elections are held. The opposition party wins twelve seats.

October

- Hong Kong scientists win the *Far Eastern Economic Review* Bronze Asian Innovation Awards.
- A Hong Kong company pays HK$1 million for a state-run Internet site in China. The Chinese government limits foreign ownership in Web firms, but Internet firms are still moving ahead in China.
- Two members of the religious group Falun Gong disappear on the mainland under unusual circumstances. The two had been detained by Chinese authorities.
- Twenty-six illegal immigrants from mainland China are found in a shipping container bound for the United States. The group is found by authorities investigating the route of previous illegal immigrants.

December

- Hong Kong investment banks and stock brokers raise record funds in the year 2000. Although twenty percent below the record high set in March, the Hang Seng Index of market activities sets records, raising HK$459.5 billion.
- Forty-seven new companies are listed on the Hong Kong stock exchange in 2000.

ANALYSIS OF EVENTS: 2000

BUSINESS AND THE ECONOMY

Following several years of poor performance in the Asian economy, the Hong Kong stock market rebounded well in 2000 and the economy surged. In the first year of mainland Chinese authority over the region, both family income and stock market performance reached new highs and helped allay fears that Beijing would negatively interfere with Hong Kong affairs.

The telecommunications industry in Hong Kong did now fair as well as the overall economy. Both China Mobile and China Unicom saw their ratings on the Hong Kong stock exchange fall between two and four percent in 2000. In October, Pacific Century CyberWorks, an Internet and telecommunications company, saw an 8.9 percent decrease in its standing on the stock exchange, continuing an industry trend for the year.

GOVERNMENT AND POLITICS

The experiment begun in 1997 of merging Hong Kong back into mainland China while maintaining autonomy and free markets continued to be a struggle in 2000. The government of Hong Kong was carefully crafted by negotiations between the British, who had previously controlled the region, and Beijing, but growing pains were evident in the first elections. Tung Chee Hwa, Hong Kong's chief executive, experienced a low point in his popularity in the territory. Several of the reforms he initiated were unpopular, especially with the civil service, and met with public outcry. It was also rumored that Mr. Tung's deputy, Anson Chan, disagrees with his stewardship. In an unusual, Beijing publicly called on the members of Hong Kong's government to give more support to its hand-picked leader.

Legislative elections in September resulted in low voter turnout, with slightly over forty percent of voters participating. Voter turnout in previous years has surpassed fifty percent. Hong Kong's Democratic Party retained its twelve seats in the Legislative Council, but it faces a stronger opposition from the pro-Beijing party, the Democratic Alliance for the Betterment of Hong Kong, which grabbed eleven seats.

CULTURE AND SOCIETY

Protestors brought publicity to a Christie's auction of Chinese antiques and art treasures in May. The items, many looted from an imperial palace in Beijing one hundred forty years ago, were sold despite protests that the artifacts should be returned to China. The demonstrations were punctuated by the removal of British names from military and government buildings.

Also in May, the government was faced with angry protestors after Beijing announced its reinterpretation of Hong Kong immigration law. The law, as interpreted by the Hong Kong Court of Final Appeal, would allow any mainland Chinese to immigrate to Hong Kong if one of their parents was a citizen of the territory. The government asked Beijing to review the case, amidst fear that more than one million new residents would flood the border. Beijing declared that Hong Kong residency could only be granted if an individual's parents had permanent residency at the time of the individual's birth. This announcement set off a series of protests in Hong Kong. The public, ever concerned about Beijing encroaching on Hong Kong's autonomy, questioned why the Hong Kong government did not implement the final ruling of its Court of Final Appeal.

DIRECTORY

CENTRAL GOVERNMENT

Head of State

Office of the Chief Executive
Tung Chee Hwa, 5/F, Central Government Offices, Main Wing, Lower Albert Road, Hong Kong
PHONE: +852 28783300
FAX: +852 25090577
E-MAIL: ceo@ceo.gov.hk

Ministers

Civil Service Bureau
Civil Service Bureau, 10/F, Central Government Offices West Wing, Central, Hong Kong
FAX: +852 28685069

Constitutional Affairs Bureau
Michael My Suen, Constitutional Affairs Bureau, Constitutional Affairs Bureau, Government Secretariat, 3rd Floor, Main Wing, Central Government Offices, Lower Albert Road, Hong Kong

Commerce and Industry Bureau
Chau Tak Hay, Commerce and Industry Bureau, Level 29, One Pacific Place, 88 Queensway, Hong Kong
PHONE: +852 29187500
FAX: +852 28401621
E-MAIL: cibenq@cib.gov.hk

Economic Services Bureau
Sandra Lee, Economic Services Bureau, Secretary for Economic Services, Room 267, 2/F., East Wing, Central Government Offices, Lower Albert Road, Central, Hong Kong
PHONE: +852 28102762
FAX: +852 25231973

Education and Manpower Bureau
Fanny Law, Education and Manpower Bureau, 9/F, Central Government Offices (West Wing), 11 Ice House Street, Central, Hong Kong
PHONE: +852 28102631
FAX: +852 28685916
E-MAIL: embhome@emb.gcn.gov.hk

Environment and Food Bureau
Lily Yam, Environment and Food Bureau

Finance Bureau
Denise Yue, Finance Bureau, Finance Bureau, 4/F Central Government Offices East Wing, Lower Albert Road, Central, Hong Kong
PHONE: +852 28103824
FAX: +852 28694531

Financial Services Bureau
Financial Services Bureau, 18/F, Tower I, Admiralty Centre, 18 Harcourt Road, Hong Kong
E-MAIL: fsbenq@fsb.gcn.gov.hk

Heatlth and Welfare Bureau
E. K. Yeoh, Health and Welfare Bureau, 19/F, Murray Building, Garden Road, Hong Kong
PHONE: +852 25413352; 28400467

Home Affairs Bureau
W.K. Lam, Home Affairs Bureau, 31/F, Southorn Centre, 130 Hennessy Road, Wan Chi, Hong Kong
PHONE: +852 28351388
E-MAIL: hab1@hab.gcn.gov.hk

Housing Bureau
Dominic S. W. Wong, Housing Bureau
PHONE: +852 25090282
E-MAIL: hbenq@hb.gcn.gov.hk

Information Technology and Broadcasting Bureau
Carrie Yau, Information Technology and Broadcasting Bureau, 1/F–2/F Murray Building, Garden Road, Central, Hong Kong
PHONE: +852 21892222
FAX: +852 28276646
E-MAIL: itbbenq@itbb.gcn.gov.hk

Planning and Lands Bureau
Gordon Siu, Planning and Lands Bureau
FAX: +852 28453489

Security Bureau
Regina IP, JP, Security Bureau, 6/F, Central Government Offices (East Wing), Central, Hong Kong
PHONE: +852 28103017
FAX: +852 25303502
E-MAIL: sbenq@sb.gcn.gov.hk

Transport Bureau
Nicholas NG, Transport Bureau, 15/F and 16/F, Murray Building, Garden Road, Hong Kong
PHONE: +852 21892189
FAX: +852 28684643
E-MAIL: tbenq@tb.gcn.gov.hk

Works Bureau
S.S. Lee
E-MAIL: wbgr@wb.gov.hk

POLITICAL ORGANIZATIONS

Democratic Party of Hong Kong

4th Floor Hanley House, 776–778 Nathan Rd., Kowloon, Hong Kong
TITLE: Chairman
NAME: Martin Ming Chu Lee

Democratic Alliance for the Betterment of Hong Kong

12/F., SUP Tower, 83 King's Road, North Point, Hong Kong
TITLE: Chairman
NAME: Tsang Yok Sing

Hong Kong Progressive Alliance

Liberal Party

Citizens Party

Rm319 2/F 88 Commercial Building, 28–34 Wing Lok Street, Sheung Wan, Hong Kong
TITLE: former Chair
NAME: Christine Loh

DIPLOMATIC REPRESENTATION

Embassies in Hong Kong

Belgium
St. John's Building, 9th Floor, 33 Garden Road, Central, Hong Kong S.A.R.
PHONE: +852 25243111
FAX: +852 28685997
E-MAIL: consulhk@netvigator.com

Chile
Suite 1408, Great Eagle Centre, 23 Harbour Road, Wanchai, Hong Kong
PHONE: +852 28271826
FAX: +852 28272060
E-MAIL: online@cgchile@org.hk

Denmark
Suite 2402 B, Great Eagle Centre, 23 Harbour Road, Wanchai, Hong Kong
PHONE: +852 28278101
FAX: +852 28274555
E-MAIL: danconhk@netvigator.com

Europe
19/F St. John's Building, 33 Garden Road, Central Hong Kong, China
PHONE: +852 25376083
FAX: +852 25221302
E-MAIL: webeu@www.ust.hk

France
Admiralty Centre, Tower II, 25/F, 18, Harcourt Road, Hong Kong
PHONE: +852 25294322
FAX: 852 28610019

India
16-D United Centre, 95 Queensway, Hong Kong
PHONE: +822 25284028; 25272275
FAX: +822 28654617

Israel
Room 701, Admiralty Centre, Tower 2, Hong Kong
PHONE: +852 25296091

FAX: +822 28650220
E-MAIL: isrcons@asiaonline.net

Italy

Room 805-810, 8/F Hutchison House, 10 Harcourt Road, Central Hong Kong
PHONE: +852 25220033
FAX: +852 28459678
E-MAIL: itconshk@netvigator.com

Japan

46th & 47th floors, One Exchange Square, 8 Connaught Place, Central, Hong Kong
PHONE: +852 252211848
FAX: +852 28680156

United States

26 Garden Road, Hong Kong
PHONE: +852 25239011
FAX: +852 28451598

JUDICIAL SYSTEM

Court of Final Appeal:

1 Battery Path, Central, Hong Kong
PHONE: +852 21230123
FAX: +852 21210300

High Court

38 Queensway, Hong Kong
PHONE: +852 28690869
FAX: +852 28690640

BROADCAST MEDIA

Hong Kong Commercial Broadcasting Co. Ltd

3 Broadcast Drive, KCPO Box 73000, Hong Kong
PHONE: +852 23365111
FAX: +852 23380021
E-MAIL: comradio@crhk.com.hk
WEBSITE: http://www.crhk.com.hk
TITLE: Director
CONTACT: G. Ho Man

Metro Broadcast Corporation Ltd.

Site 11, Basement 1 Whampoa Gardens Hunghom, Kowloon, Hong Kong
PHONE: +852 23649333
FAX: +852 23646577
E-MAIL: tech@metroradio.com.hk
WEBSITE: www.metroradio.com.hk

Radio Television Hong Kong (RTHK)

30 Broadcast Drive, PO Box 70200, Kowloon, Hong Kong
FAX: +852 23369314
E-MAIL: webmaster@rthk.org.hk
WEBSITE: www.rthk.org.hk

Asia Television Limited

81 Broadcast Drive, Kowloon, Hong Kong
PHONE: +852 29928888
FAX: +852 23380438
E-MAIL: atv@khatv.com
WEBSITE: http://www.khatv.com
TITLE: CEO
CONTACT: Mark Lee
CHANNEL: E23 and E27
WATTAGE: 10kW

Satellite Television Asian Region Ltd-STAR TV

8th Floor, One Harbourfront, 18 Tak Fung Street, Hunghom, Kowloon, Hong Kong
PHONE: +852 26218888
FAX: +852 26218000
WEBSITE: http://www.startv.com

Television Broadcasts Ltd (TVB)

TV City, Clearwater Bay Road, Kowloon, Hong Kong
PHONE: +852 23589122
FAX: +852 23581300
E-MAIL: tvbpr@tvb.com.hk
WEBSITE: www.tvb.com
TITLE: Managing Director
CONTACT: Louise Page
CHANNEL: E21 and E25
WATTAGE: 10kW

COLLEGES AND UNIVERSITIES

Asia UBS Consultant University

Rm 813, Workingbond Commercial Center, 162-164 Prince Edward Road West, Kowloon, Hong Kong
PHONE: +852 23982561
FAX: +852 23982261

Chinese University of Hong Kong

Shatin, New Terrritories, Hong Kong
PHONE: +852 26097000; 26096000
FAX: +852 26035544
E-MAIL: ugadmoff@slp.msmail.cuhk.edu.hk
WEBSITE: http://www.cuhk.hk

City University of Hong Kong

83 Tat Chee Avenue, Kowloon, Hong Kong
PHONE: +852 27887654
FAX: +852 27881167
E-MAIL: webmaster@cityu.edu.hk
WEBSITE: http://www.cityu.edu.hk

Clayton University

7th floor, Manulife Building, 169 Electric Road, North Point, Hong Kong
FAX: +852 22345620
E-MAIL: learn@culhk.com
WEBSITE: http://www.culhk.com

Hong Kong Academy for Performing Arts

1 Gloucester Road, Wanchai, Hong Kong
PHONE: +852 25848500
FAX: +852 28024372
E-MAIL: PR@hkapa.edu
WEBSITE: http://www.hkapa.edu

Hong Kong Baptist University

Kowloon Tong, Hong Kong
PHONE: +852 23397400
WEBSITE: http://www.hkbu.edu.hk

Hong Kong Institute of Education

10 Lo Ping Road, Tai Po, New Territories, Hong Kong
PHONE: +852 29488888
FAX: +852 29486000
E-MAIL: arsadmin@reg.ied.edu.hk
WEBSITE: http://www.ied.edu.hk

Hong Kong Polytechnic University

Hung Hom, Kowloon, Hong Kong
PHONE: +852 27665111
FAX: +852 27643374
E-MAIL: paadmin@internet.polyu.edu.hk
WEBSITE: http://www.polyu.edu.hk

Hong Kong University of Science and Technology

Clear Water Bay, Kowloon, Hong Kong
PHONE: +852 23586000
FAX: +852 23580537
WEBSITE: http://www.ust.hk

Lingnan University

Tuen Mun, Hong Kong
PHONE: +852 26168888
FAX: +852 24638363
WEBSITE: http://www.ln.edu.hk

Open University of Hong Kong

30 Good Shepherd Street, Homantin, Kowloon, Hong Kong
PHONE: +852 27112100
E-MAIL: aau@ouhk.edu.hk
WEBSITE: http://www.ouhk.edu.hk

University of Hong Kong

Pokfulam Road, Hong Kong
PHONE: +852 28592111
FAX: +852 28582549
E-MAIL: afss@reg.hku.hk
WEBSITE: http://www.hku.hk

NEWSPAPERS AND MAGAZINES

South China Morning Post

3/F, 1 Leighton Rd., Causeway Bay, Hong Kong
PHONE: +852 31215100
FAX: +852 26656706
TITLE: Editor
CONTACT: Robert Keatley
E-MAIL: Info@scmp.com
WEBSITE: http;//www.scmp.com

Hong Kong Voice of Democracy

7/F, 57, Peking Rd., Tsimshatsui, Hong Kong, China
PHONE: +852 92676489; 72295543
FAX: +852 27915081

Hong Kong Standard

Hong Kong Standard Newspapers Ltd., 4/F, Sing Tao Bldg., 1 Wang Kwong Rd., Kowloon Bay, Kowloon, Hong Kong
PHONE: +852 27892798; 27982647
FAX: +852 27583579; 27953009; 27957330
E-MAIL: standard@hkstandard.com; advertise@hkstandard.com
WEBSITE: http://www.hkstandard.com
TITLE: Editor-in-Chief
CONTACT: David Wong
CIRCULATION: 44,000-52,000

The Sunday Standard

Hong Kong Standard Newspapers Ltd., 4/F, Sing Tao Bldg., 1 Wang Kwong Rd., Kowloon Bay, Kowloon, Hong Kong
PHONE: +852 27892798
FAX: +852 27583579; 27953009; 27957330
TITLE: Editor-in-Chief
CONTACT: David Wong
CIRCULATION: 30,488

PUBLISHERS

The Chinese University Press

Shatin, New Territories, Hong Kong
PHONE: +852 (2) 6096508
FAX: +852 (2) 6036692
E-MAIL: cup@cuhk.edu.hk
WEBSITE: http://www.cuhk.edu.hk/cupress.wl.htm
TITLE: Director
CONTACT: Steven K. Luk
SUBJECTS: Art, Asian Studies, Business, Child Care, Education, Political Science, History, Journalism, Language Arts, Law, Literature, Philosophy, Social Sciences

Chung Hwa Book Co. (HK) Ltd.

Second Floor, 5B Ma Hang Chung Rd., Tokwawan, Kowloon, Hong Kong
PHONE: +852 (2) 7150176
FAX: +852 (2) 7138202
E-MAIL: info@chunghwabook.com.hk
TITLE: Man. Director & Editor-in-Chief
CONTACT: Kwok-fai Chan
SUBJECTS: Art, Asian Studies, Business, Career Development, Computer Science, English as a Second Language, History, Literature, Buddhism, Social Sciences

Electronic Technology Publishing Co. Ltd.

Rm 1, 9/F, Shing Win Ind Bldg., 15-17 Shing Yip St., Kwun Tong, Hong Kong
PHONE: +852 (2) 3428297
FAX: +852 (2) 3414247
E-MAIL: info@electronictechnology.com
WEBSITE: http://www.electronictechnology.com
TITLE: Manager
CONTACT: Peter Luk
SUBJECTS: Electronics, Electrical Engineering, How-To, Marketing, Radio, TV, Technology

Federal Publications Ltd.

Hunghom Commercial Centre, 37 Ma Tau Wai Rd., Units 903-905 Tower B, Kowloon, Hong Kong
PHONE: +852 (2) 3342421
FAX: +852 (2) 7645095
TITLE: Man. Director
CONTACT: Tom Y. L. Ng
SUBJECTS: Biblical Studies, Biological Studies, Computer Science, Geography, Geology, Health, Nutrition, Mathematics, Religion, Science (General)

Hong Kong University Press

14/F Hing Wai Centre, 7 Tin Wan Praya Road, Aberdeen, Hong Kong
PHONE: +852 (2) 5502703
FAX: +852 (2) 8750734
E-MAIL: upweb@hkucc.hku.hk
WEBSITE: http://www.hkupress.org
TITLE: Publisher, Rights & Permissions
CONTACT: Barbara Clarke
SUBJECTS: Anthropology, Architecture, Art, Asian Studies, Behavioral Sciences, Biography, Child Care, Education, English as a Second Language, Environmental Studies, Political Science, Law, Medicine, Science, Social Sciences, Technology

Joint Publishing (HK) Co. Ltd.

9/F Chung Sheung Bldg., 9 Queen Victoria St., 10F, Central Hong Kong
PHONE: +852 (2) 5230105
FAX: +852 (2) 8104201
E-MAIL: jpchk@hk.super.net
TITLE: Deputy General Manager
CONTACT: Au Kang Lam
SUBJECTS: Architecture, Art, Asian Studies, Business, Environmental Studies, Film, Health, History, Language Arts, Law, Literature, Medicine, Nursing, Dentistry

Modern Electronic & Computing Publishing Co. Ltd.

15-17 Shing Yip St., 9/F, Rm.1, Kwun Tong, Kowloon, Hong Kong
PHONE: +852 (2) 3428299
FAX: +852 (2) 3414247
E-MAIL: info@computertoday.com.hk
WEBSITE: http://www.computertoday.com.hk
TITLE: Assistant
CONTACT: Peter Lunk
SUBJECTS: Communications, Computer Science, Education, How-To, Microcomputers, Theology

Pearson Education China

18/F Cornwall House, 979 King's Road, Quarry Bay, Hong Kong
PHONE: +852 (3) 1810000
FAX: +852 (2) 5657440
E-MAIL: info@pearsoned.com.hk
WEBSITE: http://www.longman.com.hk
TITLE: Publisher
CONTACT: Gregg Schroeder
SUBJECTS: Business
TOTAL PUBLISHED: 2,532 print, 88 CD-ROM; 734 audio

RELIGIOUS ORGANIZATIONS

Christian

Western District Christian Church
PHONE: +852 (2) 5476768
E-MAIL: moseslck@glink.net.hk
WEBSITE: http://www.glink.net.hk/~moseslck/

Islamic

Hong Kong Islamic Youth Association
8/F, O.R. Sadick Islamic, 40 Oi Kwan Road, Wan Chai, Hong Kong
PHONE: +852 (2) 8920021
FAX: +852 (2) 8384337

Lutheran

Hong Kong Lutheran Social Service
PHONE: +852 (2) 3973721
FAX: +852 (2) 3973721
E-MAIL: hksynod@lutheran.org.hk
WEBSITE: http://www.lutheran.org.hk/

Taoist

Hong Kong Taoist Association
3rd Floor, Jinning Building, 176–178 Great Southern Street, Hong Kong
PHONE: +852 (2) 3964881; 3964783
FAX: +852 (2) 3912001

FURTHER READING

Internet

"26 immigrants found in shipping container." October 20, 2000. [Online] Available http://www.sptimes.com/News/102000/World and Nation/World_briefs.shtml (Accessed January 9, 2001).

Chang, Frank. "HongKong:Pro-China Party gains." September 28, 2000. [Online] Available http://www.feer.com/_0009_28/p30eoa.html (Accessed January 9, 2001).

"Hong Kong's Chief Executive Tung Chee Hwa in Washington." April 7, 2000. [Online] Available http://www.hongkong.org/press/dc_040100./htm (Accessed January 9, 2001).

"More Falun Gong members reportedly dead; two while in Chinese custody." September 27, 2000. [Online] Available http://www.cnn.com/2000/ASIANOW/east/09/27/china.bannedsect.ap/index.html (Accessed January 9, 2001).

Yoon, Suh-kyung. "Speed Reading." October 26, 2000. [Online] Available http://www.feer.com/_0010_26/p62innov.html (Accessed January 9, 2001).

HONG KONG: STATISTICAL DATA

For sources and notes see "Sources of Statistics" at the front of each volume.

GEOGRAPHY

Geography

Area:

Total: 1,092 sq km.

Land: 1,042 sq km.

Land boundaries:

Total: 30 km.

Border countries: China 30 km.

Coastline: 733 km.

Climate: tropical monsoon; cool and humid in winter, hot and rainy from spring through summer, warm and sunny in fall.

Terrain: hilly to mountainous with steep slopes; lowlands in north.

Natural resources: outstanding deepwater harbor, feldspar.

Land use:

Arable land: 6%

Permanent crops: 1%

Permanent pastures: 1%

Forests and woodland: 20%

Other: 72% (1997 est.).

HUMAN FACTORS

Demographics (A)

	1990	1995	1998	2000	2010	2020	2030	2040	2050
Population	5,688	6,247	6,813	7,116	7,981	8,661	8,700	8,352	7,756
Life expectancy - males	NA	76.4	76.7	76.9	78.1	79.0	79.8	80.4	80.9
Life expectancy - females	NA	82.1	82.3	82.4	83.7	84.8	85.6	86.2	86.7
Birth rate (per 1,000)	11.9	12.3	11.4	11.3	9.9	9.2	7.8	7.6	7.6
Death rate (per 1,000)	5.1	5.5	5.7	5.9	6.8	7.9	10.0	13.4	16.3
Women of reproductive age (15-49 yrs.)	1,534	1,829	2,045	2,125	2,113	1,894	1,662	1,469	1,329
Fertility rate	1.3	1.3	1.2	1.3	1.5	1.5	1.5	1.5	1.5

Except as noted, values for vital statistics are in thousands; life expectancy is in years.

Health Personnel

	National Data	World Data (wtd ave)
Total health expenditure as a percentage of GDP, 1990-1998[a]		
Public sector	2.1	2.5
Private sector	2.8	2.9
Total[b]	5.0	5.5
Health expenditure per capita in U.S. dollars, 1990-1998[a]		
Purchasing power parity	1,121	561
Total	1,134	483

Health Indicators

	National Data	World Data
Life expectancy at birth (years)		
1980	74	61
1998	79	67
Daily per capita supply of calories		
1970	2,912	2,358
1997	3,206	2,791
Daily per capital supply of protein		
1997 (grams)	100	74
Total fertility rate (births per woman)		
1980	2.0	3.7
1998	1.1	2.7
People living with (1997)		
Tuberculosis (cases per 100,000)	111.7	60.4
HIV/AIDS (% aged 15 - 49 years)	0.08	0.99

Ethnic Division

Chinese 95%

Other 5%

Religion

Eclectic mixture of local religions 90%

Christian 10%

Major Languages

Chinese (Cantonese), English; both are official.

EDUCATION

Public Education Expenditures

	1980	1997
Public expenditures on education as % of GNP	2.4	2.9
Expenditures per student as % of GNP per capita		
Primary	6.7[2]	7.8
Secondary	8.2	12.6
Tertiary	4.2	NA
Teachers' compensation as % of total current education expenditures	73.0	NA
Pupils per teacher at the primary level	NA	24
Duration of primary education in years	NA	9
World data for comparison		
Public expenditures on education as % of GNP (mean)	3.9	4.8
Pupils per teacher at the primary level (wtd ave)	NA	33
Duration of primary education in years (mean)	NA	9

Educational Attainment (B)

	1990	1995
Gross enrollment ratio (%)		
Primary level	102.4	94.0
Secondary level	79.6	73.0
Tertiary level	19.1	25.7
Enrollment of population aged 6-23 years (%)	69.0	NA

Literacy Rates (C)

Year	Adult Literacy Rate (Population aged 15 years and older)
1980	85.50%
1985	87.80%
1990	90.00%
1995	91.80%
1997	92.60%

Libraries

Public Libraries **1995**

Administrative Units 2

Service Points or Branches 56

Number of Volumes (000) 4,966

Registered Users (000) 1,996

Loans to Users (000) 21,497

Total Library Staff 806

GOVERNMENT & LAW

Political Parties

Legislative Council (LEGCO)	no. of seats
Democratic Party	13
Liberal Party	9
Democratic Alliance for the Betterment of Hong Kong	9
Hong Kong Progressive Alliance	5
Frontier Party	3
Citizens Party	1
Independents	20

Elections were last held 25 May 1998 (early elections scheduled to be held in September 2000).

Government Budgets (B)

Revenues . . . .$23.1 billion

Expenditures . . . .$25.1 billion

Data for FY98/99.

Military Affairs (B)

Military age 18

Availability

Males age 15-49 .2,012,203

Fit for military service

Males age 15-49 .1,516,533

Reaching military age annually

Males 46,485

Data for 2000 est. Separate budget for Hong Kong not established by China.

Crime

Crime volume (for 1998)

Crimes reported 71,962

Total persons convicted 33,174

Crimes per 100,000 population 1,076

Persons responsible for offenses

Total number suspects 40,422

Total number of female suspects 7,478

Total number of juvenile suspects 2,708

LABOR FORCE

Total Labor Force (A)

3.36 million (1998 est.).

Labor Force by Occupation

Wholesale and retail trade, restaurants, and hotels 31.9%

Social services 9.9%

Manufacturing 9.2%

Financing, insurance, and real estate 13.1%

Transport and communications 5.7%

Construction 2.6%

Other 27.6%

Data for October 1998.

Unemployment Rate

6% (1999 est.)

PRODUCTION SECTOR

Energy Production

Production . . . . .29.529 billion kWh

Production by source

Fossil fuel 100%

Hydro 0%

Nuclear 0%

Other 0%

Exports . . . . .610 million kWh

Data for 1998.

Energy Consumption

Consumption . . . . .34.612 billion kWh

Imports . . . . .7.760 billion kWh

Data for 1998.

Transportation

Highways:

Total: 1,831 km.

Paved: 1,831 km.

Unpaved: 0 km (1997).

Merchant marine:

Total: 271 ships (1,000 GRT or over) totaling 7,942,646 GRT/13,101,275 DWT.

Ships by type: barge carrier 1, bulk 157, cargo 28, chemical tanker 5, combination bulk 2, container 53, liquified gas 5, multi-functional large load carrier 2, petroleum tanker 14, short-sea passenger 1, vehicle carrier 3 (1999 est.).

Note: a flag of convenience registry; includes ships from 13 countries among which are UK 16, South Africa 3, China 9, Japan 6, Bermuda 2, Germany 3, Canada2, Cyprus 1, Belgium 1, and Norway 1 (1998 est.).

Airports: 3 (1999 est.).

Top Agriculture Products

Fresh vegetables; poultry.

Top Mining Products (B)

Mineral resources include: feldspar.

MANUFACTURING SECTOR

GDP & Manufacturing Summary (A)

	1980	1985	1990	1995
GDP ($-1990 mil.)[1]	38,887	51,057	74,686	95,619
Per capita ($-1990)[1]	7,717	9,358	13,091	15,616
Manufacturing share (%) (current prices)[1]	22.5	21.3	16.7	8.7[e]
Manufacturing				
Value added ($-1990 mil.)[1]	8,896	10,631	12,609	12,814[e]
Industrial production index	56	73	100	100
Value added ($ mil.)	7,343	6,582	12,034	12,759[e]
Gross output ($ mil.)	22,187	22,835	41,513	42,829[e]
Employment (000)	937	908	763	425[e]
Profitability (% of gross output)				
Intermediate input (%)	67	71	71	70[e]
Wages and salaries inc. supplements (%)	18[e]	19	17	15[e]
Gross operating surplus	15[e]	10	12	15[e]
Productivity ($)				
Gross output per worker	23,686	25,140	54,430	100,778[e]
Value added per worker	7,840	7,246	15,779	30,056[e]
Average wage (inc. supplements)	4,238[e]	4,808	9,161	15,314[e]
Value added ($ mil.)				
Food products	161	171	397	601[e]
Beverages	99	125	200	291[e]
Tobacco products	81	127	394	749[e]
Textiles	1,027	964	1,801	1,643[e]
Wearing apparel	1,920	1,594	2,455	1,724[e]
Leather and fur products	43	26	38	30[e]
Footwear	59	62	35	6[e]
Wood and wood products	45	32	38	34[e]
Furniture and fixtures	62	54	66	22[e]
Paper and paper products	110	90	275	299[e]
Printing and publishing	290	350	877	1,471[e]
Industrial chemicals	40	36	64	119[e]
Other chemical products	77	71	153	181[e]
Misc. petroleum and coal products	NA	NA	13	16[e]
Rubber products	29	17	16	10[e]
Plastic products	563	612	759	313[e]
Pottery, china and earthenware	5	3	6	2[e]
Glass and glass products	10	17	19	31[e]
Other non-metal mineral products	55	47	95	162[e]
Iron and steel	31	17	44	33[e]
Non-ferrous metals	35	20	40	62[e]
Metal products	638	460	716	632[e]
Non-electrical machinery	188	236	1,077	1,094[e]
Electrical machinery	987	752	1,153	1,749[e]
Transport equipment	176	157	333	523[e]
Prof. and scientific equipment	362	289	536	479[e]
Other manufacturing	250	253	432	484[e]

COMMUNICATIONS

Daily Newspapers

	National Data	World Data for Comparison
Daily Newspapers		
Number of Dailies	52	8,391
Total Circulation (000)	5,000	548,000
Circulation per 1,000 inhabitants	786	96

Telecommunications

Telephones - main lines in use: 3.708 million (1998).

Telephones - mobile cellular: 2.4 million (July 1998).

Telephone system: modern facilities provide excellent domestic and international services.

Domestic: microwave radio relay links and extensive fiber-optic network.

International: satellite earth stations - 3 Intelsat (1 Pacific Ocean and 2 Indian Ocean); coaxial cable to Guangzhou, China; access to 5 international submarine cables providing connections to ASEAN member nations, Japan, Taiwan, Australia, Middle East, and Western Europe.

Radio broadcast stations: AM 7, FM 13, shortwave 0 (1998).

Radios: 4.45 million (1997).

Television broadcast stations: 4 (plus two repeaters) (1997).

Televisions: 1.84 million (1997).

Internet Service Providers (ISPs): 49 (1999).

FINANCE, ECONOMICS, & TRADE

Economic Indicators

National product: GDP—purchasing power parity—$158.2 billion (1999 est.).

National product real growth rate: 1.8% (1999 est.).

National product per capita: $23,100 (1999 est.).

Inflation rate—consumer price index: -4% (1999 est.).

Exchange Rates

Exchange rates:

Hong Kong dollars (HK$) per US$

January 2000	7.7780
1999	7.7575
1998	7.7453
1997	7.7427
1996	7.7300
1995	7.8000

Hong Kong became a special administrative region of China on 1 July 1997; before then, linked to the US dollar at the rate of about 7.8 HK$ per 1 US$. Fiscal year: 1 April - 31 March.

Top Import Origins

$174.4 billion (c.i.f., 1999)

Origins (1998)

China	41%
Japan	13%
United States	8%
Taiwan	7%
South Korea	5%
Singapore	4%

Top Export Destinations

$169.98 billion (including reexports; f.o.b., 1999 est.)

Destinations (1998)

China	34%
United States	23%
Japan	5%
Germany	4%
United Kingdom	4%
Singapore	2%

Import/Export Commodities

Import Commodities	Export Commodities
Foodstuffs	Clothing
Transport equipment	Textiles
Raw materials	Footwear
Semimanufactures	Electrical appliances
Petroleum; a large share is reexported	Watches and clocks
	Toys

HUNGARY

Republic of Hungary
Magyar Népköztársaság

CAPITAL: Budapest.

FLAG: The national flag, adopted in 1957, is a tricolor of red, white, and green horizontal stripes.

ANTHEM: *Isten áldd meg a magyart (God Bless the Hungarians).*

MONETARY UNIT: The forint (Ft) of 100 fillérs is a paper currency with flexible rates of exchange. There are coins of 10, 20, and 50 fillérs and 1, 2, 5, 10, 20, 100, and 200 forints, and notes of 50, 100, 500, 1,000, and 5,000 forints. Ft1 = $0.0063 (or $1 = Ft158.66).

WEIGHTS AND MEASURES: The metric system is the legal standard.

HOLIDAYS: New Year's Day, 1 January; Anniversary of 1848 uprising against Austrian rule, 15 March; Labor Day, 1 May; Constitution Day, 20 August; Day of the Proclamation of the Republic, 23 October; Christmas, 25–26 December. Easter Monday is a movable holiday.

TIME: 1 PM = noon GMT.

LOCATION AND SIZE: Hungary is a landlocked country in Central Europe, with an area of 93,030 square kilometers (35,919 square miles), slightly smaller than the state of Indiana. It has a total boundary length of 2,009 kilometers (1,304 miles).

Hungary's capital city, Budapest, is located in the north central part of the country.

CLIMATE: Hungary lies at the meeting point of three climatic zones: the continental, Mediterranean, and oceanic. Yearly temperatures vary from a minimum of –14°C (7°F) to a maximum of 36°C (97°F). Rainfall varies, but the annual average is approximately 63 centimeters (25 inches)—more in the west and less in the east—with maximum rainfall during the summer months. Severe droughts often occur in the summers.

INTRODUCTORY SURVEY

RECENT HISTORY

In 1946 a republican constitution was adopted and a coalition government established. The Hungarian Workers (Communist) Party seized power in 1948. Hungarian foreign trade was oriented toward the Soviet bloc, and industry and land were taken over by the government. However resentment to Soviet influence increased. In October 1956 a popular uprising and announcement that Hungary would withdraw from the Warsaw Pact was quickly put down by a massive Soviet military intervention. Many people fled the country, and many others were executed.

Remaining a firm ally of the Soviet Union, in 1968 the New Economic Mechanism was introduced to make the economy more competitive and open to market forces. Reform measures beginning in 1979 further encouraged private enterprise. The movement toward relaxation of tensions in Europe in the 1970s was reflected in the improvement of Hungary's relations with Western countries, including reestablishment of diplomatic relations with the Federal Republic of Germany in 1973. Hungary led the movement to dissolve the Warsaw Pact. By the late 1980s the country owed $18 billion, the highest rate of debt in Europe.

In 1989 the constitution was amended to create a multiparty political system. After the 1990 general election, the first major free election to be held in more than four decades, a coalition government was formed.

Following collapse of the USSR in 1991, Hungary developed close political and economic ties to Western Europe. Under prime minister Jozsef Antall, Hungary began a privatization program to spur the economy. Hungary's liberal investment laws and comparatively well-developed industries permitted the nation to become an early leader in attracting Western investors. But many found the pace of transition too slow.

Also nationalistic intolerance of Hungary's ethnic minorities began to increase. Approximately 10 percent of the Hungarian population is non-Hungarian, including large populations of Jews and Roma (Gypsies).

In 1994 parliamentary elections voters turned overwhelmingly to the Hungarian Socialist Party (the former Communist Party), giving it an absolute majority of 54 percent. Hungary's international debt remains very high-the country ran a $936 million trade deficit for the first two months of 1994 alone-forcing new Prime Minister Gyula Horn to continue most of the same economic reform programs.

In January 1994 Hungary formally accepted the offer of a compromise on NATO membership. In September 1996 Hungary and Romania signed a treaty ending a centuries-old dispute over the status of Romania's 1.6 million ethnic Hungarians and the integrity of its borders. In July 1997 NATO agreed to grant Hungary full membership to the organization by 1999. Also in 1997 Hungary was invited to begin negotiations leading to membership in the European Union (EU). Hungary, along with the Czech Republic and Poland, formally joined NATO on March 12, 1999, and full membership in the EU was likely by 2004.

Despite improvements in the economy, the position of the Socialists was undermined by dissatisfaction among those negatively affected by the reforms, austerity measures, and finally by financial scandals in 1997. The Socialist government was toppled in national elections in May 1998 and Viktor Orban, leader of the victorious Federation of Young Democrats-Hungarian Civic Party, formed a new center-right coalition government in July.

GOVERNMENT

Hungary's constitution remains based upon the 1949 Soviet-style constitution, with major changes made in 1972 and 1988. The lack of a new constitution has left Hungary with a number of remnants of the communist era which affect civil liberties such as freedom of the press.

The present system is a multiparty republic, with a parliamentary government. There is one legislative house, the National Assembly, with 386 members elected by popular vote under a system of proportional and direct representation to serve four-year terms. The president is head of state, elected by the parliament for a five-year term. The head of the government is the prime minister, leader of the largest party seated in the parliament.

Judiciary

Cases usually receive their first hearing before provincial city courts or Budapest district courts. Appeals can be submitted to county courts or the Budapest Metropolitan Court. The Supreme Court is basically a court of appeal, although it may also hear important cases in the first instance. The Constitutional Law Council was established in April 1984 to verify the constitutionality of proposed laws.

Political Parties

Each of the last two parliaments has seated representatives of the same six political parties. However, the relative numbers of seats shifted dramatically between 1990 and 1994.

The dominant party is the Hungarian Civic Party (FIDESZ) that held 146 seats in the legislature. The Hungarian Socialist Party (MSZP)-the former Communist Party-has 135 seats in the legislature in 1999. Although it supports a market economy system, the MSZP, like the communists of the past, stresses a high amount of government spending. The Independent Smallholders' Party (FKGP) is a center-right party that seeks to ensure Hungarian interests in the context of European integration and holds forty-eight seats in 1999. The Alliance of Free Democrats (SZDSZ) holds twenty-four seats, the Hungarian Democratic Forum (MDF) seventeen seats, and Hungarian Justice and Life Party (MIEP) twelve seats. Independents hold three seats and one seat is vacant. Next elections were scheduled for 2002.

DEFENSE

Military service is compulsory. All males aged eighteen to fifty-five are eligible for induction for twelve months' service. In 2000 Hungary had an army of 23,500 men and an air force of 11,500 men. Security forces, consisting of frontier and border guards under the direction of the Ministry of the Interior, number about 14,000. The defense budget was estimated at $732.2 million or 1.4 percent of GDP in 1999.

ECONOMIC AFFAIRS

After the fall of communism in 1989, Hungary began a painful transition to a market economy. Freed to reach their own level, consumer prices rose 162 percent between 1989 and 1993. The rate of unemployment was 12.2 percent at the end of 1992. By late 1993, the private sector accounted for 35-40 percent of the domestic economy.

By 1994 Hungary was in an economic slump unknown since the reforms toward capitalism began, with high rates of inflation and unemployment. In March 1995 the government began a program that reduced its expenditures and devalued the currency in order to control inflation, and privatization of its enterprises. By the end of the twentieth century Hungary's debt was greatly reduced, its GDP was growing at least 4 percent yearly, inflation although still high at 10 percent was diminished, over 85 percent of the economy had be privatized, and it joined the EMU in 1999. Hungary continues to demonstrate a strong economy and will be able to join the EU by 2004.

Public Finance

Hungary made steady progress toward debt reduction through the 1990s in anticipation of EMU and EU memberships. The U.S. CIA estimated that in 1999 government revenues totaled approximately $13.6 billion and expenditures $15.1 billion. External debt totaled $27 billion in 1999.

Income

In 1999 the gross domestic product (GDP) was estimated at $79.4 billion, or $7,800 per capita. The estimated growth rate of the GDP in 1999 was 4 percent and inflation was 10 percent. The 1999 estimated GDP contribution by sector was agriculture 5 percent, industry 30 percent, and services 65 percent.

Industry

Industry has expanded rapidly since 1948 and provides the bulk of exports. Hungary's industries produce steel, machine tools, construction materials, buses, diesel engines and locomotives, televisions, radios, electric light bulbs and fluorescent lamps, telecommunications equipment, refrigerators, washing machines, medical and other precision engineering equipment, pharmaceuticals, and petrochemical products. Food processing, formerly the leading industry, provides a significant portion of exports. Mining of bauxite, manganese, and uranium also contribute to the industrial picture. Chemicals became a leading industry in the early 1990s. In 1992, Suzuki and Opel began to produce the first automobiles manufactured in Hungary since before World War II.

Banking and Finance

Following the 1987 reform of the banking system the National Bank of Hungary retained its central position as a bank of issue and its foreign exchange monopoly, but its credit functions were transferred to commercial banks. The main bank for the general public is the National Savings Bank. The Central Corporation of Banking Companies handles state property, performs international property transactions for individuals, and deals with the liquidation of bankrupt companies. The State Development Institution manages and controls development projects.

By 1997 Hungary had over thirty commercial banks, about ten specialized financial institutions, and 260 savings cooperatives. By 1998 around 75 percent of all banks had been privatized and 70 percent of these had foreign owners. Upon joining the OECD in 1996 Hungary agreed to cease its ban on the establishment of foreign bank branches by the beginning of 1998.

In Budapest an authentic commodity and stock exchange functioned from 1867 until 1948 when it was closed down as the country transformed into a centralized socialist economy. The reorganization of the Hungarian securities market, after a pause of some forty years, started at the beginning of the 1980s. The Exchange was founded on June 21, 1990.

Economic Development

The 1991-1995 economic program aimed to fully integrate Hungary into the world economy on a competitive basis. The program's main features were to accelerate privatization, control inflation, and institute measures to prepare the way for the convertibility of the forint. With the adoption of an IMR-backed stabilization program in 1995, Hungary exhibited consistent GDP annual growth of 4 percent in the late 1990s and continued growth was expected in 2000. Moreover Hungary has repaid its entire debt to the IMF and is a candidate for membership in the European Union by 2004. The latest economic reform measures include regional development, encouragement of small and medium-sized enterprises, and housing support.

SOCIAL WELFARE

By 1974, 99 percent of the population enjoyed the benefits of social insurance. Coverage includes relief for sickness, accidents, unemployment, and old age and incapacity, and provides maternity allowances for working women, allowances for children, and payment of funeral expenses.

Women receive their monthly average earnings during maternity leave, which lasts twenty-four weeks. An employed woman or a father raising his child alone is entitled to unpaid leave until the child is three years old.

Women have the same legal rights as men, including inheritance and property rights. They hold a large number of the positions in teaching, medicine, and the judiciary, which are all relatively low-paid professions. The Roma minority (Gypsies) that makes up 9 percent of the population continues to face discrimination.

Healthcare

By the end of 1974, 99 percent of the population was covered by social insurance and enjoyed free medical services. Free professional assistance is given to insured pregnant women and to the mothers of newborn children. Limited private medical practice is permitted. In 1990 to 1997 there was 3.4 physicians and nine hospital beds for every 1,000 people. Health expenditures comprised 5 percent of GDP in 1997.

Hungary has a declining population which is aging rapidly. Arteriosclerosis is a major cause of death, and there is a high incidence of cardiovascular disease. Contributing factors include work-related stress, together with smoking and dietary factors. In 2000 average life expectancy was seventy-one years.

Housing

Construction has struggled to keep pace with the needs of Hungary's growing urban population and to renovate its many old structures built before 1945, a sizable number before 1900. As of 1990, 78 percent were connected to a water system, 76 percent had flush toilets, and only 44 percent were connected to public sewage systems.

EDUCATION

Practically the entire adult population is literate in 2000. Education is compulsory between ages six and sixteen. Eight years of primary and four years of secondary education are free. The state also pays most of the costs for higher education.

The educational system is under control of the Ministry of Education. Institutions of higher education had 194,607 students in 1996. Although there are university fees, many students are excused from payment or pay reduced fees.

2000 KEY EVENTS TIMELINE

February

- Hungarian colleges fight prejudices against Gypsies, Romanies, with the creation of Romany studies programs and by efforts to dispel stereotypes by encouraging pride in Romany language and culture.

March

- The Hungarian government files a lawsuit against Esmeralda Exploration Ltd., the Australian company in partnership with the Romanian government to mine gold. The accidental dumping of more than 20,000 tons of cyanide, lead and zinc when a dam burst in northern Romania on January 30 allegedly contaminated the Tisza and Danube rivers. The contamination of the Tisza, Hungary's second biggest river, is considered the worst environmental disaster since the Chernobyl nuclear leak in 1986.
- After rejecting Hungary's claim of ecological damage due to the cyanide leak in Romania as "politically motivated," Esmeralda Exploration Ltd. goes into receivership, the first step in bankruptcy proceedings.

April

- The Tisza River rises to record flood levels, and a heat wave (temperatures reaching 86°F) (30°C) makes work strenuous for the over 20,000 volunteers working to shore up the dikes. Roads and train service to several villages is cut off, and dozens of houses are under water.

May

- Gangland-style slayings encourage cooperation between Hungarian law enforcement agencies and the U.S. Justice Department. Five agents from the U.S. Federal Bureau of Investigation and Hungarian officers form a task force targeted at Russian gangs running worldwide operations out of Budapest.
- The World Committee on Disability and the Franklin and Eleanor Roosevelt Institute present Hungary with an award for improving the lives of disabled people. Disabled people are nearly 10 percent of Hungary's population of ten million.

June

- Ferenc Madl, the only candidate for president, is elected in three rounds of parliamentary voting. He is scheduled to takc office in August.

July

- New documents unearthed by the Simon Wiesenthal Center indicate that the government of Hungary notified U.S. occupation forces in Germany in 1947 that Nazi war criminal Adolf Eichmann was in the U.S. zone, but U.S. authorities did not respond to the request for his extradition for four years.

August

- Hungarian police rescue from suffocation forty-six Asian and African illegal immigrants who are locked inside a van that is stopped by a road patrol near the village of Besenyotelek, forty-four miles (seventy kilometers) east of Budapest.
- Andras Tamas, age seventy-five and the last known prisoner of World War II, arrives back in Hungary after spending fifty-three years locked away in a Russian psychiatric hospital.

September

- Six people are killed when a bus carrying twenty-seven children and adults skids and overturns in southern Hungary; firefighters have to battle frantically to free twelve children trapped inside the wreckage.
- Hungary's six main political parties reaffirm their support for membership of the European Union, possibly by the end of 2002.
- Haulers and governments in the Netherlands and Hungary reach deals to avoid more of the fuel-price protests that have caused chaos across Europe.
- Hungarian athletes win seventeen medals at Olympics 2000 in Sydney, Australia. Eight Gold,

six Silver, and three Bronze Medals are won in eleven categories: boxing, canoe/kayak, fencing, gymnastics, handball, modern pentathlon, shooting, swimming, water polo, weightlifting, and wrestling.

October

- Hungary seeks to join the European Union in 2003.
- A Hungarian member of parliament, Zoltan Szekeley, is arrested after allegedly being caught accepting a bribe. He denies the accusation claiming that he has been framed.
- The passenger aircraft of the state airline, Malev, experiences numerous breakdowns. Reports are that the Hungarian intelligence service is investigating possible acts of sabotage.

November

- Internet access is brought to Hungary. One of the world's leading broadband companies, chello broadband nv, begins service to Hungary (www.chello.hu). By 2004, the number of Internet accounts in Hungary is expected to grow by 500 percent.
- Independent Deputy Lukacs Szabo accuses the government of sponsoring organized crime in Hungary.

ANALYSIS OF EVENTS: 2000

BUSINESS AND THE ECONOMY

Among the former communist countries Hungary was considered to be closest to establishing a successful market economy and a fully functioning democracy. However Hungary was still functioning as a two-tier economy as of 2000. There was a booming foreign-owned sector and a struggling locally owned sector. Although in 2000 the banking sector was also stronger than other former communist Eastern European countries, the planned consolidation of the still-existing forty banks was predicted to increase profitability.

Hungary invested to achieve a business-friendly environment that included good telecommunications, positive investment climate, a new airport, an improving highway system, attractive tax rates, relatively low wages and a trainable skilled labor force, easy access to European markets, and a good environmental climate. These factors enable the country to attract high levels of foreign direct investment. However, barely fifty multinational firms were contributing the major portion of the gross national product (GNP). This economic growth did not extend into minor and/or local ventures. Regional differences further highlighted these two-tiered disparities in growth, with the eastern areas of the country lagging even further behind. Hungary's annual growth rate in the late 1990s had been 4–5 percent, but was projected to exceed that rate in 2000.

The accidental spill of more than 20,000 tons of cyanide, lead, and zinc that contaminated the Tiza and Danube rivers was an economic and environmental disaster. The Environment Minister reported an estimated 110 tons of fish had died as a result of the toxic spill. The Hungarian government filed a lawsuit against the Romanian parties, including the Australian company Esmeralda Exploration Ltd. that was managing the mining project in partnership with the government of Romania.

GOVERNMENT AND POLITICS

Hungary, along with Poland and Czechoslovakia, acted to shorten the period of military conscription (to nine months in Hungary). Military service was branded as damaging to careers; as many as one-fourth of the eligible men were excused military service on medical grounds, with the more affluent less likely to serve. In Hungary when meningitis swept through an army barracks 70 percent of the populace said they wanted conscription to end. In addition, conscript training was considered too basic to train troops for battle, thereby leaving little justification for it.

Hungarian law provides for the state media supervisory boards to be made up of at least eight member drawn equally from government and opposition parties. In 2000 authorization of appointees to the state media supervisory boards evolved into a dispute. The governing center-right coalition approved a four-member, pro-government, control body for Duna TV. No opposition candidates were approved. In March and in 1999 Hungarian Radio and national television, MTV (Magyar Televizio) were similarly taken under the ruling coalition's influence. Meanwhile Hungary's broadcast industry grew as ratings increased. Subsequently, ad rates increased.

CULTURE AND SOCIETY

To mark the one-thousandth anniversary of the Hungarian state, the Holy Crown of the eleventh century Hungarian King, Stephen the First, was delivered to Parliament. Parliament restored the crown to its former role as the symbol of the Hungarian state. Opposition politicians criticized the glorification of a medieval Christian relic as belonging in a museum, not the Parliament.

A Budapest daily newspaper raised the issue of increasing anti-Semitism in Hungary, noting the increase of racist and xenophobic sites on the Internet.

With the fall of communism Hungary experienced an influx of criminals. Russian gangs ran worldwide operations out of Budapest, and Hungarian police made little headway. A joint task force with the U.S. Federal Bureau of Investigation under the command of the Hungarian national police was formed.

DIRECTORY

CENTRAL GOVERNMENT

Head of State

President
Ferenc Madl, Office of the President, V. Kossuth L.ter 1-3, H-1055 Budapest, Hungary
PHONE: +36 (1) 2684000
FAX: +36 (1) 2684800

Ministers

Prime Minister
Viktor Orban, Office of the Prime Minister, V. Kossuth L.ter 1/3, H-1055 Budapest, Hungary
PHONE: +36 (1) 2683000
FAX: +36 (1) 1533322
E-MAIL: horn@mehp.meh.hu

Minister Without Portfolio in Charge of Prime Minister's Office
Istvan Stumpf, Ministry Without Portfolio in Charge of Prime Minister's Office

Minister Without Portfolio in Charge of Civilian National Security Services
Ervin Demeter, Ministry Without Portfolio in Charge of Civilian National Security Services

Minister of Transport and Water Management
Janos Fonagy, Ministry of Transport and Water Management

Minister of Social and Family Affairs
Peter Harrach, Ministry of Social and Family Affairs

Minister for National Cultural Heritage
Jozsef Hamori, Ministry for National Cultural Heritage

Minister of Justice
David Ibolya, Ministry of Justice

Minister of Interior
Sandor Pinter, Ministry of Interior

Minister of Health
Istvan Mikola, Ministry of Health

Minister of Finance
Mihaly Varga, Ministry of Finance

Minister of Environmental Protection
Bela Turi-Kovacs, Ministry of Environmental Protection

Minister of Education
Zoltan Pokorni, Ministry of Education

Minister of Agriculture and Regional Development
Jozsef Torgyan, Ministry of Agriculture and Regional Development

Minister of Sports and Youth
Tamas Deutsch, Ministry of Sports and Youth

Minister of Economic Affairs
Gyorgy Matolcsy, Ministry of Economic Affairs, V. Honved utca 13-15, H-1880 Budapest, Hungary
PHONE: +36 (1) 3022355
FAX: +36 (1) 3022394
E-MAIL: webmaster@gm.hu

Minister of Defense
Janos Szabo, Ministry of Defense, V. ker., Balaton u. 7-11, H-1055 Budapest, Hungary
PHONE: +36 (1) 2365111
FAX: +36 (1) 4741110
E-MAIL: modpress@hm.gov.hu

Minister of Foreign Affairs
Janos Martonyi, Ministry of Foreign Affairs, Bem rkp. 47, H-1027 Budapest, Hungary
PHONE: +36 (1) 4581000

POLITICAL ORGANIZATIONS

Munkaspart-MP (Workers' Party)

TITLE: Chairman
NAME: Gyula Thurmer

Magyar Demokrata Neppart-MDNP (Hungarian Democratic People's Party)

TITLE: Chairman
NAME: Erzsebet Pusztai

Nemzeti Demokrata Part-NDP (National Democratic Party)

Fuggetlen Kisgazda, Foldmunkas es Polgari Part-FKgP (Independent Smallholders, Argarian Workers and Citizens)

TITLE: President
NAME: Jozsef Torgyan

Magyar Igazsag es Elet Partja-MIEP (Hungarian Justice and Life Party)

TITLE: Chairman
NAME: Istvan Csurka

Magyar Demokrata Forum-MDF (Hungarian Democratic Forum)

TITLE: Chairman
NAME: Ibolya David

Fiatal Demokratak Szovetsege-FiDeSz (Federation of Young Democrats)

TITLE: Chairman
NAME: Viktor Orban

Keresztenydemokrata Neppart-KDNP (Christian Democratic People's Party)

TITLE: President
NAME: Gyorgy Giczy

Szabad Demokratak Szovetsege (Alliance of Free Democrats)

Gizella ut 36, H-1143 Budapest, Hungary
PHONE: +36 (1) 2232050
E-MAIL: szdsz@szdsz.hu
TITLE: Chairman
NAME: Balint Magyar

Magyar Szocialista Part-MSZP (Hungarian Socialist Party)

Koztarsasag ter 26, H-1081 Budapest, Hungary
PHONE: +36 (1) 2100046; 2100078
FAX: +36 (1) 2100081
E-MAIL: info@mszp.hu
TITLE: Chairman
NAME: Laszlo Kovacs

DIPLOMATIC REPRESENTATION

Embassies in Hungary

Egypt

Berc u. 16, H-1016 Budapest, Hungary
PHONE: +36 (1) 4665080; 4668060
FAX: +36 (1) 2092638

Japan

Zalai ut 7, H-1125 Budapest, Hungary
PHONE: +36 (1) 2751275
FAX: +36 (1) 2751281
E-MAIL: infocons@japan-embassy.hu

United States

Szabadsag ter 12, H-1054 Budapest, Hungary
PHONE: +36 (1) 2674400; 2699331; 2699339
FAX: +36 (1) 2699326
TITLE: Ambassador
NAME: Peter F. Tufo

JUDICIAL SYSTEM

Supreme Court of the Republic of Hungary

BROADCAST MEDIA

Danubius Radio

H-1138 Budapest, Vaci u. 141, Hungary
PHONE: +36 (1) 4526100
FAX: +36 (1) 4526180
E-MAIL: info@danubius.hu
WEBSITE: http://www.danubius.hu
TITLE: Managing Director
CONTACT: Istvan Sandor
BROADCASTS: 24 hours/day
TYPE: Commercial

Helyi Rádiók Országos Egyesülete (Hungarian Local Radios Association)

H-6000 Kecskemét Deák, ferenc tér 3, Budapest, Hungary
PHONE: +36 (76) 480880
FAX: +36 (76) 480880

Juventus Rádió (Music Radio Juventis)

WEBSITE: http://www.juventus.hu/

Magyar Rádió

Bródy Sándor U. 5–7, H-1800 Budapest, Hungary
PHONE: +36 (1) 1388388; 2691993
FAX: +36 (1) 1388910; 1388943

WEBSITE: http://www.kossuth.enet.hu; www.petofi.enet.hu/
TITLE: President
CONTACT: Istvan Hajdu
TYPE: Government, Semi-Commercial

Orszagos Rádió és Televísió Testület (ORTT) (National Radio and TV Commission)

PO Box 59, H-1461 Budapest, Hungary
PHONE: +36 (1) 2672590; 2672612
FAX: +36 (1) 2672612
E-MAIL: mtl@ortt.hu
TITLE: Chairman
CONTACT: Mihaly T. Revesz

Szabad Rádiók Magyaroszági Szervezete (SZARÁMASZTER) (Organization of Free Hungarian Radio Stations)

1066 Budapest Ó utca 11. I-6, Hingary
PHONE: +36 (1) 3111855
FAX: +36 (1) 3111855
CONTACT: Peterfi Ferenc

Radio Budapest

Bródy Sándor u 5-7, H-1800 Budapest, Hungary
PHONE: +36 (1) 3288320; 3287339
FAX: +36 (1) 3288517; 3287339
WEBSITE: http://www.kaf.radio.hu/index.html
TITLE: President
CONTACT: István Hajdu
LANGUAGE: Croatian, English, German, Hungarian, Romanian, Russian, Serbian, Slovak, Ukranian

A3 (Pest-Buda TV)

Rona utca 140, 1147 Budapest, Hungary
PHONE: +36 (1) 2514749
TITLE: General Director
CONTACT: Adam Namenyi
TYPE: Local

Magyar Televfzi (MTV1 and MTV2)

Szabadság ter 17, H-1810 Budapest, 5 Hungary
PHONE: +36 (1) 1114059
FAX: +36 (1) 11574979
TITLE: President
CONTACT: Gyula Berecky
CHANNEL: 1, 2

Nap TV

Angol utca 13, H-1149 Budapest, Hungary
PHONE: +36 (1) 2510490
FAX: +36 (1) 2513372
TITLE: Chairman
CONTACT: Tamas Gyarfas
CHANNEL: 1

Sio Televisio

Fo ter 2, H-8600 Siofok, Hungary
PHONE: +36 (84) 31711
FAX: +36 (84) 310887
TYPE: Local

TV3 Budapest

Budakeszi utcal 51, H-1021 Budapest, Hungary
PHONE: +36 (1) 2751800
FAX: +36 (1) 2751801
TITLE: Director
CONTACT: Peter Kolin
TYPE: Local

Antenna Hungária Magyar Verzio

Petzvál József u. 31-33, "A" building, ground floor, H-1119 Budapest, Hungary
E-MAIL: ugyfelszolgalat@ahrt.hu
WEBSITE: http://www.ahrt.hu/
TITLE: Chief Executive Officer
CONTACT: Géza László

COLLEGES AND UNIVERSITIES

Eoetvoes Lorand Tudomanyegyete

Kun Bela Ter 2, Budapest, Hungary

Central European University

Nador Ut 9, H-1051 Budapest, Hungary

Magyar Kepzomuveszeti Foiskola

Andrassy Ut 69-71, H-1062 Budapest, Hungary

Liszt Ferenc Zenemuveszeti Foiskola

Bartok Bela Zenemueveszeti, Szakkoezepiskola, Nagymezoe U 1, H-1065 Budapest, Hungary

Allatorvostudomanyi Egyetem

Istvan Ut 2, H-1078 Budapest, Hungary

Szinhaz - Es Filmmueveszeti Foiskala

Vas U 2c, H-1088 Budapest, Hungary

Semmelweis Orvostudomanyi Egyetem

Institute of Organic Chemistry, H-1092 Budapest, Hungary

Koezgazdasagtudomanyi Egyetem

Foevam Ter 8, H-1093 Budapest, Hungary

Kerteszeti Elelmiszeripari Egyetem

Villanyi Ut 35-43, H-1118 Budapest, Hungary

Magyar Iparmuveszeti Foiskola

Zugligeti Ut 9-25, H-1121 Budapest, Hungary

Magyar Testnevelesi Foiskola

Magyar Testnevelesi Egyetem, Alkotas U 44, H-1123 Budapest, Hungary

Haynal Imre Egeszsegtudomanyi

Szabolcs-U 35 - POB 112, H-1135 Budapest, Hungary

Magyar Tancmueveszeti

POB 439, H-1372 Budapest, Hungary

Budapesti Mueszaki Egyetem

Muegyetem-Rkp 3, H-1521 Budapest, Hungary

Goedoelloe Agrartudomanyi Egyetem

Takarmanyozasi Intezet, Baromfitak 0, H-2101 Goedoello, Hungary

Miskolci Egyetem

Egyetemvaros, H-3515 Miskolc, Hungary

Kossuth Lajos Tudomanyegyetem

Egyetem Ter 1, H-4010 Debrecen, Hungary

Debreceni Orvostudomanyi Egyetem

Debreceni Orvostudomanyi Egyetem, Nagyerdei Korut 98, H-4012 Debrecen, Hungary

Debreceni Agrartudomanyi Egyetem

POB 36, H-4015 Debrecen, Hungary

Szegedi Orvostudomanyi Egyetem

Dugonics Ter 13, H-6700 Szeged, Hungary

Jozsef Attila Tudomanyegyetem

Beke Epulet, H-6701 Szeged, Hungary

Pecsi Tudomanyegyetem

Rakoczi Ut 80, H-7622 Pecs, Hungary

Pollack Mihalymuezaki Foiskola

Boszorkany U 2, H-7624 Pecs, Hungary

Pecsi Orvostudomanyi Egyetem

Anatomy Histology Dept., Szigeti Ut 12, H-7643 Pecs, Hungary

Veszpremi Vegyipari Egyetem

Egyetem U 10, H-8200 Veszprem, Hungary

Pannon Agrartudomanyi Egyetem

Deak Ferenc U 16, H-8361 Keszthely, Hungary

Mosonmagyarovar Agrar Fac

Var 2, H-9200 Mosonmagyarovar, Hungary

Erdeszeti es Faipari Egyetem

Bajcsy-Zsilinszky U 4, H-9400 Sopron, Hungary

NEWSPAPERS AND MAGAZINES

Magyar Hirlap

Magyar Hirlap Konyves Lapkiadia Ltd, Kerepesl ut 29/B, H-1097 Budapest, Hungary
PHONE: +36 (1) 2103765; 3334154; 3139439
FAX: +36 (1) 3340712; 2102143
E-MAIL: levelek@mahirlap.hu
WEBSITE: http://www.mhirlap.hu
TITLE: Editor
CONTACT: Llona Kocsi
CIRCULATION: 55,000

Mai Nap

Magyar Hirlap Konyves Lapkiadia Ltd., Kerepesi ut 27/A, H-1087 Budapest, Hungary
PHONE: +36 (1) 2102142; 3039671; 3039672
FAX: +36 (1) 2102143
E-MAIL: info@mainap.hu
WEBSITE: http://www.mainap.hu
TITLE: Editor
CONTACT: Ferenc Koszegi
CIRCULATION: 300,000

Nemzeti Sport

Nemzeti Sport Media BT, Pf. 566, H-1374 Budapest, Hungary
PHONE: +36 (1) 3121234; 3320384
FAX: +36 (1) 3121234; 3320384
TITLE: Ad Manager
CONTACT: Tibor Csifari
CIRCULATION: 120,000-150,000

Nepszabadsag

Nepszabsfdsag Kiado es Nyomdaipari Rt., Becsi ut 122-124, H-1034 Budapest, Hungary
PHONE: +36 (1) 2501680; 3687627
FAX: +36 (1) 2500250; 3689857; 3889567
E-MAIL: igaz@nepszabadsag.hu
WEBSITE: http://www.nepszabadsag.hu
TITLE: Editor
CONTACT: Pal Eotvos
CIRCULATION: 246,782

Nepszabadsag Magazin

Nepszabadsag Kiado es Nyomdaipari Rt., Besci ut. 122-124, H-1034 Budapest, Hungary
PHONE: +36 (1) 2501680
FAX: +36 (1) 2501640; 3689098
E-MAIL: marketing@nepszabadsag.hu
WEBSITE: http://www.nepszabadsag.hu
TITLE: Editor
CONTACT: Vera Volgyl
CIRCULATION: 314,600

Nepszava

Egyesult Kiadol Holding Kft., Torokvesz ut 30/A, H-1022 Budapest, Hungary
PHONE: +36 (1) 3268252; 3268272
FAX: +36 (1) 3268267; 3268260
E-MAIL: kulpol@nepszava.hu
WEBSITE: http://www.nepszava.hu
TITLE: Editor-in-Chief
CONTACT: Laszio H. Biro
CIRCULATION: 66,000

Vasarnapi News

EKH Kft., Torokvesv ut 30/A, H-1022 Budapest, Hungary
PHONE: +36 (1) 3268252; 3268272
FAX: +36 (1) 3268267; 3268260
TITLE: Editor
CONTACT: Csaba Puskas
CIRCULATION: 106,000

Metro

MTG Metro Gratis Kft., Feher ut 10, H-1106 Budapest, Hungary
PHONE: +36 (1) 4316400
FAX: +36 (1) 4316401
E-MAIL: hirdetes@metro.hu
TITLE: Editor
CONTACT: Gabor Izbeki
CIRCULATION: 160,000

Reader's Digest Valogatas

Reader's Digest Kiado Kft., Obudal - Sziget 132, H-1033 Budapest, Hungary
PHONE: +36 (1) 4571100
FAX: +36 (1) 4571122
TITLE: Editor
CONTACT: Peter Keresztes
CIRCULATION: 204466

HVG: Heti Vilaggazdasag

HVG Kiadoi RT, Pf 20, H-1300 Budapest 3, Hungary
PHONE: +36 (1) 4362020
FAX: +36 (1) 4362010; 4362009
E-MAIL: hirdet@hvg.hu
WEBSITE: http://www.hvg.hu
TITLE: Editor
CONTACT: Ivan Liovecz
CIRCULATION: 126,469
TYPE: Economic and political news

kepes Ujsag

Factum Kft. Pf. 249, H-1391 Budapest 62, Hungary
PHONE: +36 (1) 3530756
FAX: +36 (1) 3531969
TITLE: Editor-in-Chief
CONTACT: Mihaly Kovacs
CIRCULATION: 50,000
TYPE: Official Journal of the People's Patriotic Front

Reform

Globex Press, Victor Hugo u. 18-22, H-1132 Budapest, Hungary
PHONE: +36 (1) 1497999; 1490145
FAX: +36 (1) 1497184; 2700552
CIRCULATION: 80,000
TYPE: Political news

PUBLISHERS

Akademiai Kiado

Prielle K u. 4, H-1117 Budapest, Hungary
PHONE: + 36 (1) 4648230
FAX: +36 (1) 4648285
E-MAIL: barna.beata@akkrt.hu
TITLE: Man. Director
CONTACT: Zsolt Bucsi Szabo
SUBJECTS: Archaeology, Art, Biological Sciences, Earth Sciences, Economics, Engineering, Political Science, History, Law,

Literature, Medicine, Philosophy, Social Science, Science (General)
TOTAL PUBLISHED: 150 print

Aranyhal Konyvkiado Goldfish Publishing

Dolmany u 5-7, H-1131 Budapest, Hungary
PHONE: + 36 (1) 2396721
FAX: +36 (1) 2391851
E-MAIL: sprinter@com.kibernet.hu
TITLE: Owner & Manager
CONTACT: Gandor Radvan
SUBJECTS: Children's books, Animals, Child Care, Cookery, Crafts, Hobbies, Education, Humor, Language Arts, Literature, Nonfiction (General), Outdoor Recreation
TOTAL PUBLISHED: 70 print; 2 CD-ROM

Balassi Kiado Kft.

Attila u 79, H-1012 Budapest, Hungary
PHONE: + 36 (1) 1755064
FAX: +36 (1) 1162885
E-MAIL: balassi@mail.datanet.hu
TITLE: Director
CONTACT: Peter Koeszeghy
SUBJECTS: Art, History, Language Arts, Linguistics, Literature, Literary Criticism, Essays, Nonfiction (General), Philosophy, Social Sciences
TOTAL PUBLISHED: 533 print; 1 CD-ROM

Central European University Press

PO Box 519/2, H-1397 Budapest, Hungary
PHONE: + 36 (1) 3273014
FAX: +36 (1) 3273183
E-MAIL: ceupress@osi.hu
WEBSITE: http://www.ceupress.com
TITLE: Director and Editor
CONTACT: Klara Takacsi-Nagy
SUBJECTS: Economics, Political Science, History, Literature, Literary Criticism, Essays, Social Sciences, Cultural Studies, Medieval History
TOTAL PUBLISHED: 56 print; 1 online

Kijarat Kiado

Bogdani ut 8/C, H-1033 Budapest, Hungary
PHONE: + 36 (1) 888832
FAX: +36 (1) 3886312
TITLE: Manager
CONTACT: Gyorgy Palinkas
SUBJECTS: Architecture, Interior Design, Literature, Literary Criticism, Essays, Philosophy
TOTAL PUBLISHED: 69 print

KJK-Kerszov

pf 101, H-1518 Budapest, Hungary
PHONE: + 36 (1) 4645656
FAX: +36 (1) 4645657
E-MAIL: complex@kjk-kerszov.hu
WEBSITE: http://www.kjk.hu
TITLE: Man. Director
CONTACT: David G. Young
SUBJECTS: Business Economics, Education, Political Science, Journalism, Law, Marketing, Psychology, Psychiatry, Social Sciences
TOTAL PUBLISHED: 500 print; 10 CD-ROM; 5 online; 5 internet

Magyar Tudomanyos Akademia Koezponti Fizikai Kutato Intezet Koenyvtara

pf 49, H-1525 Budapest, Hungary
PHONE: + 36 (1) 1699499
FAX: +36 (1) 3922583
E-MAIL: kolcs@sunserv.kfki.hu
TITLE: Head
CONTACT: Erika Eory
SUBJECTS: Chemistry, Chemical Engineering, Computer Science, Electronics, Electrical Engineering, Mathematics, Microcomputers, Physical Sciences, Physics
TOTAL PUBLISHED: 5-10 per year

Kossuth Kiado RT

PO Box 55, H-1327 Budapest, Hungary
PHONE: + 36 (1) 3700607
FAX: +36 (1) 3700602
E-MAIL: rt@kossute.hu
WEBSITE: http://www.kossuth.hu
TITLE: Man. Director
CONTACT: Andreas Sandor Kocsis
SUBJECTS: Business, Child Care, Communications, Education, Geography, Geology, Health, Nutrition, Natural History, Psychology, Psychiatry, Catholicism, Travel, Wine & Spirits
TOTAL PUBLISHED: 80 print; 15 CD-ROM

Kulturtrade

Margit krt 64/b, H-1027 Budapest, Hungary
PHONE: + 36 (1) 3757288
FAX: +36 (1) 2027145
E-MAIL: hl2618vin@ella.hu
TITLE: Publisher & General Manager
CONTACT: Gabor Vince

SUBJECTS: Art, Health, Nutrition, How-To, Physical Sciences

Mueszaki Koenyvkiado Ltd.

Szentendrei ut 89-93, H-1033 Budapest, Hungary
PHONE: + 36 (1) 4372405
FAX: +36 (1) 4372404
E-MAIL: lakatosz@muszakikiado.hu
TITLE: Man. Director
CONTACT: Sandor Berczi
SUBJECTS: Architecture, Interior Design, Career Development, Chemistry, Engineering, Computer Science, Electronics, Mathematics, Physics, Science (General)

Mult es Jovo Kiado

Huvosvolgyi ut 50, H-1021 Budapest, Hungary
PHONE: + 36 (1) 2742260
FAX: +36 (1) 3167019
E-MAIL: mandj@mail.c3.hu
WEBSITE: http://www.c3.hu
CONTACT: Janos Kobanyai
SUBJECTS: History, Literature, Literary Criticism, Essays, Social Sciences, Sociology, Jewish Literature, History & Culture

Nemzeti Tankoenyvkiado

pf 20, H-1363 Budapest, Hungary
PHONE: + 36 (1) 1291496; 1530600
FAX: +36 (1) 3632423
E-MAIL: nk@mail.datanet.hu
TITLE: Man. Director
CONTACT: Abraham Istvan
SUBJECTS: Biological Sciences, Education, Geography, Geology, History, Language Arts, Literature, Law, Mathematics, Marketing, Philosophy Music, Dance

Novorg Kiado

pf 101, H-1518 Budapest, Hungary
PHONE: + 36 (1) 1603790; 1603596; 1602300
FAX: +36 (1) 145581
E-MAIL: novorged@kjk.hu
TITLE: Manager
CONTACT: P. Boris
SUBJECTS: Business, Cookery, Economics, Finance, How-To, Law, Management, Marketing, Public Administration, Real Estate

Panem

Zoldmali lejo 12/a, H-1025 Budapest, Hungary
PHONE: + 36 (1) 1208303
FAX: +36 (1) 3443923
E-MAIL: panem@mail.datanet.hu
TITLE: Director
CONTACT: Zsuzsa Tarr
SUBJECTS: Computer Science, Economics, Engineering (General), Science (General)

Park Konyvkiado (Park Publishers)

Sallei u 31, H-1136 Budapest, Hungary
PHONE: + 36 (1) 1315767
FAX: +36 (1) 2124363
E-MAIL: park@mail.matav.hu
TITLE: Manager
CONTACT: Andras Rochlitz
SUBJECTS: Art, Child Care & Development, Gardening, Plants, History, House & Home, Management, Nonfiction (General), Self Help
TOTAL PUBLISHED: 110 print

Typotex Kft Elektronikus Kiado

Batthyany u 14, H-1015 Budapest, Hungary
PHONE: + 36 (1) 2013317
FAX: +36 (1) 3163759
E-MAIL: typotex@euroweb.hu
WEBSITE: http://www.vision.euroweb.hu/typotex
TITLE: Director
CONTACT: Zsuzsa Votisky
SUBJECTS: Mathematics, Philosophy, Physics
TOTAL PUBLISHED: 100 print

Zenemukiado Vallalat

PB 322, H-1051 Budapest, Hungary
PHONE: + 36 (1) 1176222
E-MAIL: musicpubl@emb.hu
TITLE: Man. Director
CONTACT: Istvan Homolya
SUBJECTS: Biography, Music, Dance

RELIGIOUS ORGANIZATIONS

Buddhist

Budapest Zen Center
Arpád u. 8 VI. 156, Budapest, H-1215, Hungary
PHONE: +36 (1) 2761309
FAX: +36 (1) 2751219
E-MAIL: robi@zen.hu
NAME: Antal Dobosy

Buddhist Mission (BM)
Postafiok 952, H-1386 Budapest, Hungary
PHONE: +36 (1) 3852098
FAX: +36 (1) 3852098
E-MAIL: lilavajra@t-online.de
TITLE: CEO
NAME: Ven. Dr. Lajos Pressing

Catholic

Diocese of Esztergom-Budapest
Úri u. 62, H-1014 Budapest, Hungary
PHONE: +36 (1) 2025611
FAX: +36 (1) 2025458
WEBSITE: : http://www.katolikus.hu/esztergom/index_ang.html
TITLE: Diocesan Bishop, Archbishop of Esztergom-Budapest
NAME: Dr. Paskai László

Diocese of Pécs
István tér 23, H-7624 Pécs Szent, Hungary
PHONE: +36 (72) 314224; 326821
FAX: +36 (72) 326821
TITLE: Diocesan Bishop
NAME: Mayer Mihály

Diocese of Székesfehérvár
Városhaz tér 5, H-8000 Székesfehérvár, Hunagry
PHONE: +36 (22) 311490; 315270
FAX: +36 (22) 315055
TITLE: Diocesan Bishop
NAME: Dr. Takács Nándor

The Hungarian Catholic Bishops' Conference
Pf 79 Városligeti fasor 45, H-1406 Budapest, Hungary
PHONE: +36 (1) 3426959
FAX: +36 (1) 3426959
WEBSITE: : http://www.katolikus.hu/bcs_ang.html
TITLE: President, Archbishop of Eger
NAME: Dr. Seregély István

Military Ordinate
Szabadság tér 3, H-1054 Budapest, Hungary
PHONE: +36 (1) 1129200
FAX: +36 (1) 2694191
TITLE: Bishop
NAME: Dr. Ladocsi Gáspár

Protestant

Baptist Union of Hungary (BUH)

Magyarorszagi Baptista Egyhaz (MBE)
Aradi utca 48, H-1062 Budapest 6, Hungary
PHONE: +36 (1) 3322332
FAX: +36 (1) 1310194
TITLE: President
NAME: Dr. Rev. Mihaly Almasi

Dianetila Mission Paks
Kodaly Zoltan UT 3. FSZ. O., H-7030 Paks, Hungary
PHONE: +36 (75) 313589
FAX: +36 (75) 313589
E-MAIL: missions@smi.org

Evangelical-Lutheran Church in Hungary-National Church Presidency
Üllöi út 24, H-1085 Budapest, Hungary
PHONE: +36 (1) 3175567; 3175496
FAX: +36 (1) 3170872
E-MAIL: webmater@lutheran.hu
WEBSITE: : http://www.lutheran.hu.index_e.htm
TITLE: Presiding Bishop
NAME: D. Dr. Harmati Béla

Evangelical-Lutheran Church in Hungary-North District
Szilágyi Erzsébet fasor 24, H-1125 Budapest, Hungary
PHONE: +36 (1) 3942448; 3942335
FAX: +36 (1) 3942440
E-MAIL: north.district@lutheran.hu
WEBSITE: : http://www.lutheran.hu/nevtar/inst_re.php?did=28101
TITLE: Bishop
NAME: D. Szebik Imre

Evangelical-Lutheran Church in Hungary-South District
Puskin u. 12, H-1088 Budapest, Hungary
PHONE: +36 (1) 3382302; 3382360
FAX: +36 (1) 3382302
E-MAIL: south_district@lutheran.hu
WEBSITE: : http://www.lutheran.hu/nevtar/inst_re.php?did=28001
TITLE: Bishop
NAME: D. Dr. Harmati Béla

Scientology

Church of Scientology Mission od Nyiregyhaza
Rakoczi U. 3 I/1, H-4400 Nyiregyhaza, Hungary
PHONE: +36 (42) 409419
FAX: +36 (42) 314230
E-MAIL: missions@smi.org

Church of Scientology M. S. E. Miskolc Mission
Széchenyi u. 34.I.em, H-3530 Miskolc, Hungary
PHONE: +36 (46) 323124
E-MAIL: missions@smi.org

FURTHER READING

Articles

"Crime Busters: With the Arrival of a New Task Force in Hungary the FBI Steps Up Its Fight Against Organized Crime." *Time International,* May 8, 2000, p. 33.

"Hungarian Educators Try to Get Gypsies into the Mainstream—and into College." *Chronicle of Higher Education,* February 18, 2000, p. A68.

"Hungary Aims Pollution Suit at Romania." *American Metalmarket,* March 22, 2000, p. 7.

"Hungary: New President." *New York Times,* June 7, 2000, p. A15.

Books

Andor, Laszls. *Hungary on the Road to the European Union: Transition in Blue.* Westport, CT: Praeger, 2000.

Hupchick, Dennis P. and R. William Weisberger, editors. *Hungary's Historical Legacies: Studies in Honor of Steven Bila Vardy.* Boulder, CO: East European Monographs; distributed by Columbia University Press, 2000.

Internet

"500 People Evacuated From Three Regions in Hungary." *Deutsche Presse Agentur,* April 10, 2000. [Online] Available http://www.reliefweb.int/ (accessed 10 July 2000).

HUNGARY: STATISTICAL DATA

For sources and notes see "Sources of Statistics" at the front of each volume.

GEOGRAPHY

Geography

Area:

Total: 93,030 sq km.

Land: 92,340 sq km.

Land boundaries:

Total: 2,009 km.

Border countries: Austria 366 km, Croatia 329 km, Romania 443 km, Serbia and Montenegro 151 km (all with Serbia), Slovakia 515 km, Slovenia 102 km, Ukraine 103 km.

Coastline: 0 km (landlocked).

Climate: temperate; cold, cloudy, humid winters; warm summers.

Terrain: mostly flat to rolling plains; hills and low mountains on the Slovakian border.

Natural resources: bauxite, coal, natural gas, fertile soils, arable land.

Land use:

Arable land: 51%

Permanent crops: 3.6%

Permanent pastures: 12.4%

Forests and woodland: 19%

Other: 14% (1999).

HUMAN FACTORS

Demographics (A)

	1990	1995	1998	2000	2010	2020	2030	2040	2050
Population	10,372	10,296	10,211	10,139	9,831	9,484	9,034	8,463	7,837
Life expectancy - males	65.1	65.3	66.4	67.0	69.8	72.1	74.2	75.8	77.2
Life expectancy - females	73.8	74.7	75.3	76.1	78.5	80.6	82.3	83.6	84.7
Birth rate (per 1,000)	12.1	10.9	9.5	9.3	8.9	8.3	7.6	7.6	7.7
Death rate (per 1,000)	14.0	14.1	13.8	13.3	12.9	12.9	13.8	15.1	15.9
Women of reproductive age (15-49 yrs.)	2,543	2,610	2,597	2,562	2,375	2,205	1,834	1,581	1,372
Fertility rate	1.9	1.5	1.3	1.3	1.3	1.4	1.4	1.5	1.6

Except as noted, values for vital statistics are in thousands; life expectancy is in years.

Health Personnel

	National Data	World Data (wtd ave)
Total health expenditure as a percentage of GDP, 1990-1998[a]		
Public sector	4.1	2.5
Private sector	2.0	2.9
Total[b]	6.4	5.5
Health expenditure per capita in U.S. dollars, 1990-1998[a]		
Purchasing power parity	638	561
Total	290	483
Availability of health care facilities per 100,000 people		
Hospital beds 1990-1998[a]	910	330
Doctors 1992-1995[a]	337	122
Nurses 1992-1995[a]	NA	248

Health Indicators

	National Data	World Data
Life expectancy at birth (years)		
1980	70	61
1998	71	67
Daily per capita supply of calories		
1970	3,331	2,358
1997	3,313	2,791
Daily per capital supply of protein		
1997 (grams)	85	74
Total fertility rate (births per woman)		
1980	1.9	3.7
1998	1.3	2.7
Population with access (%)		
To safe water (1990-96)	NA	NA
To sanitation (1990-96)	94	NA
People living with (1997)		
Tuberculosis (cases per 100,000)	42.4	60.4
HIV/AIDS (% aged 15 - 49 years)	0.04	0.99

Infants and Malnutrition

	National Data	World Data (wtd ave)
Under 5 mortality rate (1989)	11	NA
% of infants with low birthweight (1992-98)[1]	9	17
Births attended by skilled health staff (% of total births 1996-98)	96	52
% fully immunized at 1 year of age (1995-98)[1]		
TB	100	82
DPT	100	77
Polio	100	77
Measles	100	74
Prevalence of child malnutrition (1992-98)[1] (based on weight for age, % of children under 5 years)	NA	30

Ethnic Division

Hungarian 89.9%
Roma 4.0%
German 2.6%
Serb 2.0%
Slovak 0.8%
Romanian 0.7%

Religion

Roman Catholic 67.5%
Calvinist 20.0%
Lutheran 5.0%
Atheist and other 7.5%

Major Languages

Hungarian 98.2%
Other 1.8%

EDUCATION

Public Education Expenditures

	1980	1997
Public expenditures on education as % of GNP	4.7	4.6
Expenditures per student as % of GNP per capita		
Primary	14.0	20.6
Secondary	NA	20.2
Tertiary	85.3	47.0
Teachers' compensation as % of total current education expenditures	45.2	NA
Pupils per teacher at the primary level	NA	11
Duration of primary education in years	NA	10

	1980	1997
World data for comparison		
Public expenditures on education as % of GNP (mean)	3.9	4.8
Pupils per teacher at the primary level (wtd ave)	NA	33
Duration of primary education in years (mean)	NA	9

Educational Attainment (A)

Age group (1990)[8] . . . . .25+
Population of this age group 6,798,765
Highest level attained (%)
No schooling 1.3
First level
Not completed 24.3
Completed 33.6

(Continued on next page.)

GOVERNMENT & LAW

Military Affairs (A)

	1990	1992	1995	1996	1997
Military expenditures					
Current dollars (mil.)	1,280e	1,230	935	1,090	1,320
1997 constant dollars (mil.)	1,500e	1,370	968	1,110	1,320
Armed forces (000)	94	78	60	50	50
Gross national product (GNP)					
Current dollars (mil.)	62,400	57,500	63,800	66,400	70,800
1997 constant dollars (mil.)	73,100	63,800	66,000	67,500	70,800
Central government expenditures (CGE)					
1997 constant dollars (mil.)	36,700	36,500	33,700	31,600	30,700
People (mil.)	10.4	10.3	10.3	10.3	10.2
Military expenditure as % of GNP	2.0	2.1	1.5	1.6	1.9
World data on military expenditure as % of GNP	4.5	3.4	2.7	2.6	2.6
Military expenditure as % of CGE	4.1	3.8	2.9	3.5	4.3
World data on military expenditure as % of CGE	17.0	12.5	10.5	10.3	10.2
Military expenditure per capita (1997 $)	144	132	94	109	129
World data on military expenditure per capita (1997 $)	242	173	146	143	145
Armed forces per 1,000 people (soldiers)	9.1	7.5	5.8	4.9	4.9
World data on armed forces per 1,000 people (soldiers)	5.3	4.5	4.1	3.9	3.8
GNP per capita (1997 $)	7,060	6,170	6,420	6,580	6,920
Arms imports[6]					
Current dollars (mil.)	0	0	30	100	100
1997 constant dollars (mil.)	0	0	31	102	100
Arms exports[6]					
Current dollars (mil.)	130	40	20	10	5
1997 constant dollars (mil.)	132	44	21	10	5
Total imports[7]					
Current dollars (mil.)	8,621	11,120	15,070	15,900	20,760
1997 constant dollars (mil.)	10,100	12,330	15,610	16,160	20,760
Total exports[7]					
Current dollars (mil.)	9,730	10,680	12,540	12,690	18,730
1997 constant dollars (mil.)	11,390	11,840	12,980	12,900	18,730
Arms as percent of total imports[8]	0	0	0.2	0.6	0.5
Arms as percent of total exports[8]	1.3	0.4	0.2	0.1	0

(Continued on next page.)

EDUCATION (cont.)

Educational Attainment (A) (cont.)

Entered second level 30.7

Entered post-secondary .10.1

Literacy Rates (B)

	National Data	World Data
Adult literacy rate		
1980		
Male	99[1]	75
Female	99[1]	58
1995		
Male	99	81
Female	99	65

Libraries

National Libraries 1997

Administrative Units 1

Service Points or Branches .3

Number of Volumes (000) 2,771

Registered Users (000) 30

Loans to Users (000) . . . . .NA

Total Library Staff 540

Public Libraries 1997

Administrative Units .2,883

Service Points or Branches 3,518

Number of Volumes (000) 43,377

Registered Users (000) 1,344

Loans to Users (000) 36,724

Total Library Staff 3,881

GOVERNMENT & LAW (cont.)

Political Parties

National Assembly (Orszaggyules)	% of vote	no. of seats
Hungarian Socialist Party (MSZP)	32.0%	134
Hungarian Civic Party (FIDESZ)	28.2%	148
Independent Smallholders (FKGP)	13.8%	48
Alliance of Free Democrats (SZDSZ)	7.9%	24
Hungarian Justice and Life Party (MIEP)	5.5%	14
Hungarian Workers Party (MMP)	4.1%	
Hungarian Democratic Forum (MDF)	2.8%	17
Christian Democratic People's Party (KDNP)	2.3%	
Hungarian Democratic People's Party (MDNP)	1.5%	
Independent		1

Elections were last held on 10 and 24 May 1998 (next to be held May/June 2002).

Government Budgets (A)

Year: 1998

Total Expenditures: 4,449.5 Billions of Forint

Expenditures as a percentage of the total by function:

General public services and public order 8.91

Defense 2.29

Education 8.57

Health 5.96

Social Security and Welfare 29.87

Housing and community amenities 1.55

Recreational, cultural, and religious affairs 1.79

Fuel and energy 0.05

Agriculture, forestry, fishing, and hunting 3.53

Mining, manufacturing, and construction 0.19

Transportation and communication 4.15

Other economic affairs and services 2.42

Crime

Crime volume (for 1998)

Crimes reported 600,621

Total persons convicted 326,738

Crimes per 100,000 population 5,926

Persons responsible for offenses

Total number suspects 140,083

Total number of female suspects 17,791

Total number of juvenile suspects 12,888

LABOR FORCE

Total Labor Force (A)

4.2 million (1997).

Labor Force by Occupation

Services 65%

Industry 27%

Agriculture 8%

Data for 1996.

Unemployment Rate

10% (1999 est.)

PRODUCTION SECTOR

Energy Production

Production ....35.104 billion kWh

Production by source

- Fossil fuel 61%
- Hydro 1%
- Nuclear 38%
- Other 0%

Exports ....3.3 billion kWh

Data for 1998.

Energy Consumption

Consumption ....33.317 billion kWh

Imports ....3.970 billion kWh

Data for 1998.

Transportation

Highways:

Total: 188,203 km.

Paved: 81,680 km (including 438 km of expressways).

Unpaved: 106,523 km (1998 est.).

Waterways: 1,373 km permanently navigable (1997).

Pipelines: crude oil 1,204 km; natural gas 4,387 km (1991).

Merchant marine:

Total: 2 ships (1,000 GRT or over) totaling 12,949 GRT/14,550 DWT.

Ships by type: cargo 2 (1999 est.).

Airports: 43 (1999 est.).

Airports - with paved runways: 16.

Airports - with unpaved runways: 27.

Top Agriculture Products

Wheat, corn, sunflower seed, potatoes, sugar beets; pigs, cattle, poultry, dairy products.

Top Mining Products (B)

Mineral resources include: bauxite, coal.

MANUFACTURING SECTOR

GDP & Manufacturing Summary (A)

	1980	1985	1990	1995
GDP ($-1990 mil.)[1]	29,517	32,206	33,055	29,270
Per capita ($-1990)[1]	2,757	3,044	3,189	2,896
Manufacturing share (%) (current prices)[1]	33.8	34.0	20.9	NA
Manufacturing				
Value added ($-1990 mil.)[1]	6,236	7,562	6,906	7,049
Industrial production index	98	108	100	89
Value added ($ mil.)	5,907	5,356	7,744[e]	8,487[e]
Gross output ($ mil.)	24,898	21,690	25,081	25,006[e]
Employment (000)	1,384	1,278	1,117	741[e]
Profitability (% of gross output)				
Intermediate input (%)	76	75	69[e]	66[e]
Wages and salaries inc. supplements (%)	8	8	11	12[e]
Gross operating surplus	16	16	20[e]	22[e]
Productivity ($)				
Gross output per worker	17,990	16,972	22,454	33,713[e]
Value added per worker	4,268	4,191	6,933[e]	11,484[e]
Average wage (inc. supplements)	1,437	1,403	2,495	4,065[e]
Value added ($ mil.)				
Food products	555	281	812[e]	1,320[e]
Beverages	83	107	170[e]	353[e]
Tobacco products	27	28	44[e]	53[e]
Textiles	353	325	320[e]	259[e]
Wearing apparel	194	158	233[e]	299[e]
Leather and fur products	48	39	40[e]	32[e]
Footwear	79	85	92[e]	109[e]
Wood and wood products	81	42	102[e]	133[e]
Furniture and fixtures	101	92	133[e]	130[e]
Paper and paper products	94	106	141[e]	138[e]
Printing and publishing	83	94	204[e]	380[e]
Industrial chemicals	418	320	441[e]	266[e]
Other chemical products	242	303	478[e]	651[e]
Petroleum refineries	153[e]	193[e]	590[e]	1,242[e]

	1980	1985	1990	1995
Misc. petroleum and coal products	2[e]	2[e]	5[e]	8[e]
Rubber products	55	71	92[e]	41[e]
Plastic products	61	80	165[e]	213[e]
Pottery, china and earthenware	57	46	59[e]	67[e]
Glass and glass products	70	71	89[e]	94[e]
Other non-metal mineral products	204	161	216[e]	219[e]
Iron and steel	370	200	368[e]	202[e]
Non-ferrous metals	215	54	274[e]	97[e]
Metal products	214	215	297[e]	361[e]
Non-electrical machinery	497	569	819[e]	572[e]
Electrical machinery	655	758	711[e]	563[e]
Transport equipment	486	507	420[e]	445[e]
Prof. and scientific equipment	272	287	316[e]	192[e]
Other manufacturing	237	164	112[e]	50[e]

COMMUNICATIONS

Daily Newspapers

	National Data	World Data for Comparison
Daily Newspapers		
Number of Dailies	40	8,391
Total Circulation (000)	1,895	548,000
Circulation per 1,000 inhabitants	186	96

Telecommunications

Telephones - main lines in use: 1.893 million (1995).

Telephones - mobile cellular: 1.269 million (1995).

Telephone system: the telephone system has been modernized and is capable of satisfying all requests for telecommunication service.

Domestic: the system is digitalized and highly automated; trunk services are carried by fiber-optic cable and digital microwave radio relay; a program for fiber-optic subscriber connections was initiated in 1996; heavy use is made of mobile cellular telephones.

International: Hungary has fiber-optic cable connections with all neighboring countries; the international switch is in Budapest; satellite earth stations - 2 Intelsat (Atlantic Ocean and Indian Ocean regions), 1 Inmarsat, 1 very small aperture terminal (VSAT) system of ground terminals.

Radio broadcast stations: AM 17, FM 57, shortwave 3 (1998).

Radios: 7.01 million (1997).

Television broadcast stations: 39 (plus several low-power stations) (1997).

Televisions: 4.42 million (1997).

Internet Service Providers (ISPs): 13 (1999).

FINANCE, ECONOMICS, & TRADE

Economic Indicators

National product: GDP—purchasing power parity—$79.4 billion (1999 est.).

National product real growth rate: 4% (1999 est.).

National product per capita: $7,800 (1999 est.).

Inflation rate—consumer price index: 10% (1999 est.).

Balance of Payments

	1994	1995	1996	1997	1998
Exports of goods (f.o.b.)	7,648	12,864	14,184	19,640	20,747
Imports of goods (f.o.b.)	−11,364	−15,297	−16,836	−21,372	−22,869
Trade balance	−3,716	−2,433	−2,652	−1,732	−2,123
Services - debits	−2,958	−3,629	−3,506	−3,695	−4,231
Services - credits	3,117	4,271	5,004	4,874	4,910
Private transfers (net)	2,789	3,513	2,310	2,420	2,000
Government transfers (net)	13	13	−15	−5	−45
Overall balance	−4,054	−2,535	−1,689	−982	−2,304

Exchange Rates

Exchange rates:

Forints per US$1

January 2000	251.150
1999	237.146
1998	214.402
1997	186.789
1996	152.647
1995	125.681

Top Import Origins

$25.1 billion (f.o.b., 1999)

Origins (1998)

Germany	28%
Austria	10%
Italy	8%
Russia	7%

Top Export Destinations

$22.6 billion (f.o.b., 1999)

Destinations (1998)

Germany	37.0%
Austria	11.0%
Italy	6.0%
Netherlands	5.0%

Foreign Aid

Recipient: $122.7 million (1995).

Import/Export Commodities

Import Commodities	Export Commodities
Machinery and equipment 46.5%	Machinery and equipment 51.9%
Other manufactures 40.2%	Other manufactures 32.7%
Fuels and electricity 6.6%	Agricultural and food products 10.5%
Agricultural and food products 3.7%	Raw materials 2.9%
Raw materials 3.0%	Fuels and electricity 1.9%

ICELAND

CAPITAL: Reykjavík.

FLAG: The national flag, introduced in 1916, consists of a red cross (with an extended right horizontal), bordered in white, on a blue field.

ANTHEM: *O Gu vors lands (O God of Our Land).*

MONETARY UNIT: The new króna (K), introduced 1 January 1981 and equivalent to 100 old krónur, is a paper currency of 100 aurar. There are coins of 5, 10, and 50 aurar and 1, 10 and 50 krónur, and notes of 10, 50, 100, 500, 1,000 and 5,000 krónur. K1 = $0.0139 (or $1 = K71.690).

WEIGHTS AND MEASURES: The metric system is used.

HOLIDAYS: New Year's Day, 1 January; First Day of Summer, April; Labor Day, 1 May; National Holiday, 17 June; Bank Holiday, August; Christmas, 25–26 December. Movable religious holidays include Holy Thursday, Good Friday, Easter Monday, Ascension, and Whitmonday. Half-holidays are observed on Christmas Eve, 24 December, and New Year's Eve, 31 December.

TIME: GMT.

LOCATION AND SIZE: Iceland, the westernmost country of Europe, is an island in the North Atlantic Ocean, just below the Arctic Circle. It has an area of 103,000 square kilometers (39,769 square miles), slightly smaller than the state of Kentucky. The total length of its coastline is about 4,970 kilometers (3,090 miles). The republic includes many smaller islands, of which the chief are the Westman Islands (Vestmannaeyjar) off the southern coast.

Iceland's capital city, Reykjavík, is located on the country's southwest coast.

CLIMATE: Despite Iceland's northern latitude, its climate is fairly mild because of the Gulf Stream current in the Atlantic Ocean. Temperatures at Reykjavík average from 11.2°C (52.5°F) in July to −0.4°C (31.3°F) in January, with an annual mean of about 4°C (39°F). Humidity is high, and there is much fog in the east. Annual rainfall in the north ranges from 30 to 70 centimeters (12–28 inches); in the south, 80–130 centimeters (31–51 inches); and in the mountains, up to 225 centimeters (89 inches).

Republic of Iceland
Lveldi Í-and

INTRODUCTORY SURVEY

RECENT HISTORY

Cut off from Denmark during World War II (1939-1945) by the German occupation of that country, Iceland established diplomatic relations with the United Kingdom and the United States. British forces, which took over the protection of the island in 1940, were replaced the following year by U.S. troops, who remained until early 1947. In May 1944 more than 97 percent of those participating voted to end the union with the king of Denmark and on June 17, 1944, Iceland became an independent republic.

In 1946 Iceland was admitted to United Nations membership, and three years later, it became a party to the North Atlantic Treaty Organization (NATO). In March 1970 Iceland joined the European Free Trade Association (EFTA) and a trade agreement was reached with the European Community in February 1973. To protect its fishing industry Iceland extended its fishing zone in 1958, 1972, and 1975 provoking conflict with the United Kingdom and other countries.

In 1985 parliament voted to declare Iceland nuclear-free. By 2000 Iceland's economy was strong and residents enjoyed long-life, literacy, strong incomes, and social cohesion.

GOVERNMENT

Iceland is a constitutional republic. Executive power is vested in the president elected by universal voting for a four-year term and the prime minister appointed by the president and enjoying the

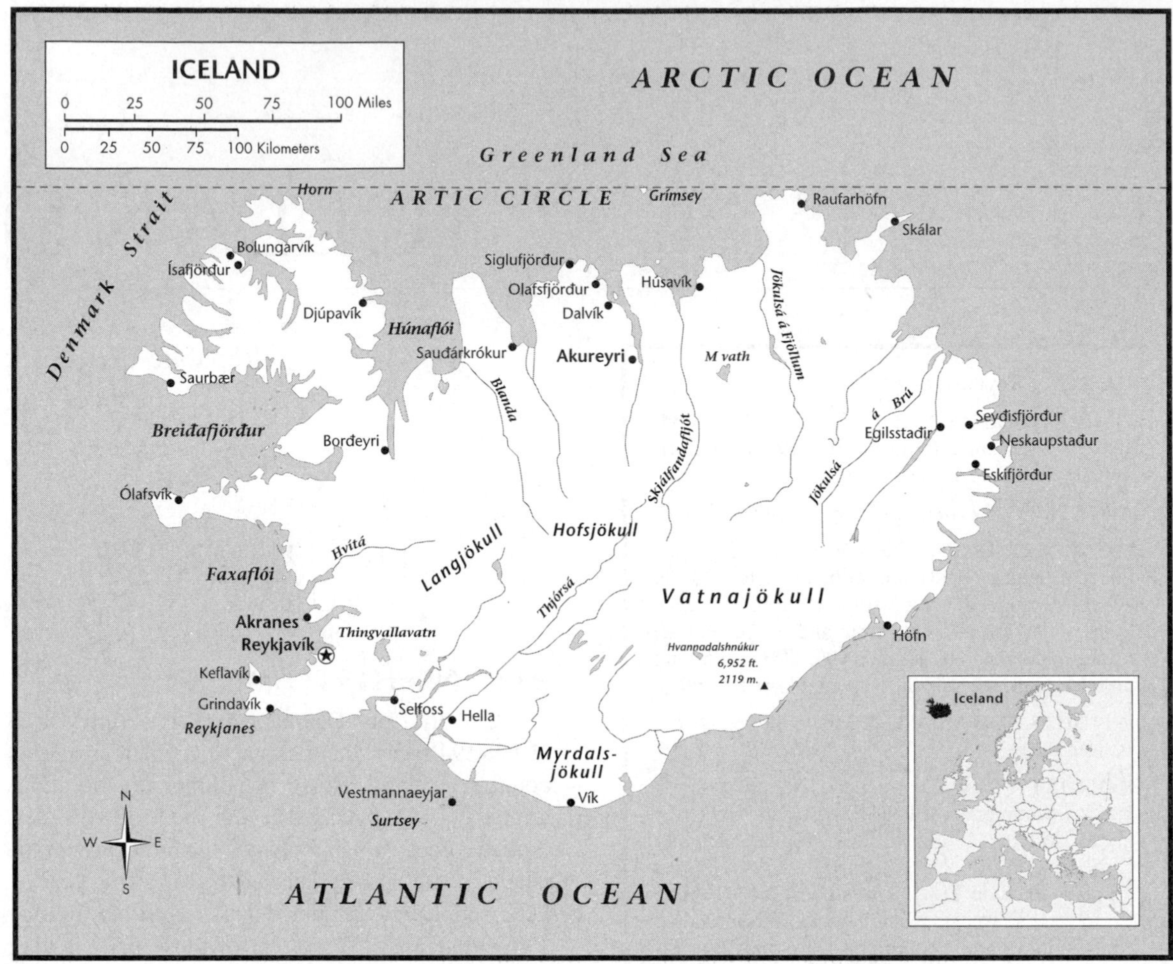

confidence of the parliament. The president appoints the cabinet.

The legislative branch consists of the unicameral 63-seat parliament, or *Althing*. Members are elected by popular vote to serve four-year terms. Suffrage is universal at age eighteen.

Judiciary

The district magistrates *(sslumenn)* and the town magistrates *(bæjarfógetar)* administer justice on a local level in twenty-six lower courts. Appeals are heard by the Supreme Court, consisting of eight justices (all appointed for life by the president), who elect one of their number as chief justice for a two-year term. There are special courts for maritime cases, labor disputes, and other types of cases.

Political Parties

No one major party in recent years has been able to command a majority of the votes, and coalition governments have been the rule. Daví Oddson formed a new coalition government following the 1995 elections between the Independence Party (IP) and the Progressive Party (PP). This coalition remained after the 1999 elections in which the IP increased its share of the popular vote while the Progressives polled more poorly. Two new parties gained representation in the Althing in 1999, the environmental Left-Green Party and the Liberal Party.

DEFENSE

Iceland is the only NATO member with no military force of its own, although the government does maintain armed fishery protection vessels and planes manned by 130 personnel. The U.S.-manned Icelandic Defense Force (IDF) headquartered at Keflavik provides Iceland's defense.

ECONOMIC AFFAIRS

Iceland's economy, once primarily agricultural, heavily depends on the fish processing industry that provides 70 percent of export earnings and employs 12 percent of the workforce. Other exports include aluminum and ferrosilicon. Iceland's economy is vulnerable to changing world commodities prices. A demand in Europe and the United States for Icelandic fish rebounded through the 1990s. This factor along with government austerity measures, diversification of the economy into tourism, biotechnology, software production, liberalization of financial services, and control of inflation have all contributed to a robust GDP growth of approximately 5 percent annually through the last half of the 1990s. Growth may slow in 2000 but still was predicted to be at 3.5 percent. Unemployment was very low at 2 percent. Iceland has remained opposed to European Union (EU) membership for fear of losing control over their fishing resources.

Public Finance

Since 1984 Iceland's budget has shown a deficit averaging nearly 2 percent of GDP raising its net indebtedness relative to GDP to almost 30 percent in 1994. Government attempts to balance the budget were frustrated by the economic downturn from 1987 to 1993 and by fiscal concessions to expedite wage settlements. The U.S. CIA estimated that in 1996 government revenues totaled approximately $1.9 billion and expenditures $2.1 billion, including capital expenditures of $146 million. External debt totaled $2.6 billion in 1999.

Income

In 1999 Iceland's gross domestic product (GDP) was estimated at $6.42 billion, or about $23,500 per capita. The estimated GDP growth rate for 1999 was 4.5 percent and inflation 1.9 percent. The contribution to the GDP by sector was estimated in 1998 at agriculture 15 percent (includes fishing at 13 percent), industry 21 percent, and services 64 percent.

Industry

Fish processing is the most important industry. Facilities for freezing, salting, sun-curing, and reducing fish to oil or fish meal are flexible enough to allow shifting from one process to another based on demand. Other industries include aluminum smelting, ferrosilicon production, geothermal power, and tourism. Small scale industries designed to meet local needs are clothing, fertilizer, cement, household items, dairy, confectionary, and beer.

Banking and Finance

In March 1961 the Central Bank of Iceland was founded to issue notes and assume other central bank functions previously exercised by the National Bank of Iceland, a wholly state-owned bank established in 1885.

In 1997 there were four commercial banks, two of which are still state owned. The country's two other banks, Islandsbanki and Sparisjodabanki, are privately owned.

The whole basis on which the financial system is supervised and regulated, however, has been transformed by Iceland's accession to the European Economic Area (EEA) agreement in 1994. Under the agreement, Iceland has been required to implement into national law the common minimum standards for the supervision of financial institutions-banks, insurance companies, and securities firms-developed at EU level.

As of 1998 the Icelandic Stock Exchange had sixty-seven companies listed.

Economic Development

In 2000 the government continued strategies that have reinvigorated the Icelandic economy. The government continues its austerity program to trim welfare costs and thereby reduce the budge, deficits, and the need for foreign borrowing. The retirement age was raised and Icelanders were being asked to pay for a greater portion of social services out of their own pockets. Liberalization of many sectors of the economy, such as telecomes and banking services, required by the European Economic Area's (EEA) agreement with the European Union (EU) in exchange for greater access to the EU market has reduced public expenditures and positively affected government finances. The government was also containing inflation, revising agricultural and fishing policies, diversifying the economy into areas such as tourism, software production, and biotechnology, and privatizing state-owned enterprises.

SOCIAL WELFARE

The national health insurance scheme, administered under the State Social Insurance Institution, includes insurance against sickness, accident, and unemployment; pensions for the aged and disabled; and a health service that provides treatment and care of the sick.

Studies show that women earn about 30 percent less than men in comparable jobs but are well represented in the government with twenty-two of sixty-three members of parliament in 1999.

Healthcare

The Director of Public Health is responsible for health matters. More than 90 percent of all health bills were paid by public insurance. Public expenditures on health were among the highest in industrialized countries. In 1992 Iceland had 2.8 doctors per 1,000 inhabitants and an estimated fifty-three hospitals with 3,985 beds. The incidence of tuberculosis, once widespread, has been greatly reduced. In 2000 life expectancy was seventy-nine years, among the highest in the world.

Housing

The total number of dwellings in the mid-1990s was 95,800. Wooden houses replaced traditional turf houses long ago. In the 1980s and 1990s most new housing was concrete. Virtually all dwellings have electricity, piped water, and central heating.

EDUCATION

Literacy was at 99.9 percent by 1997 estimates. There is practically no adult illiteracy. Education is compulsory for children aged six to sixteen. In 1997 there were 29,342 students at primary schools, approximately 31,000 in secondary schools, and 7,908 students at post-secondary institutions. The University of Iceland in Reykjavík, founded in 1911, is comprehensive offering law, medicine, and engineering.

2000 KEY EVENTS TIMELINE

February

- For the first time since 1991 Iceland's most active volcano, Mount Hekla, erupts February 26. Posing no danger the lava flow is estimated to be 4.5 miles (7 km) long. Considered as one of the gates to purgatory in Icelandic folklore, Mount Hekla has erupted more than twenty times since the eleventh century.

March

- The killer whale, Keiko, star of the film *Free Willy,* is freed in the remote Klettsvik Bay off the south coast of Iceland. After two decades in captivity Keiko's reintroduction to the wild is in graduated stages as he is familiarized with his new surroundings.

June

- A controversy arises over a license to a private company, deCode Genetics, by the Icelandic government. deCode Genetics plans to cross-reference healthcare records of Icelanders with genealogical and genetic databases. Since all Icelanders descend from a small group of Norse and Celtic settlers, some opponents believe privacy and doctor-patient relationships are compromised.
- On June 21 a tremor measuring 6.6 on the Richter scale is the second earthquake in four days to hit Iceland. The quake is considered the largest to hit Iceland since 1912.

July

- The *Islendingur,* a 22.5-meter (80-foot) replica of a Viking ship, sets sail for Newfoundland to commemorate the 1,000-year anniversary of the arrival of the Vikings, the first Europeans to reach North America.

August

- The popular performing artist, Bjork, wins MTV's Special Effects category for her breakthrough video, "All is Full of Love."

September

- The supermarket war between Safeway and Tesco heats up. Employees from both supermarket chains "invade" the competitor's stores by placing stickers on products and freezers claiming that their own prices are cheaper. The Iceland government's Trading Standards intervenes to have the stickers removed, but the competition shifts to the customer loyalty cards.
- Iceland's Vala Flofadottir wins the Bronze Medal in the Olympic 2000's track and field category for women's pole vault.

October

- In 2000 Iceland's foreign debt increases by around IKR9 billion (US$103 million) due to the weakening of the Icelandic krona. The debt currently stands at IKR137 billion (US$1.6 billion).

November

- The National Bureau of Statistics reports a trend that Icelandic employers are hiring more foreign workers. The Bureau reports a 37 percent increase in the number of foreign workers hired during August to October over the same period in 1999.
- Paloma Pictures buys the film rights to "The Journey Home," a new novel by Icelandic author, Olaf Olafsson. It is the story of an Icelandic

woman who returns to her home country after spending twenty years in England.

- Iceland is declared the country with the highest concentration of cellular phones in a report issued November 22, with a rate of 75.8 percent.

December

- Iceland celebrates December 1 as its Independence Day, the day in 1918 that it was proclaimed a free and independent country.
- The ban by nine countries within the European Union on the use of fishmeal in animal fodder will prove very expensive for Iceland if it goes through. Icelandic spokesmen note that nothing proved that the use of fish meal in animal fodder could cause Creutzfeldt-Jakob disease (popularly referred to as "Mad Cow" disease) and therefore no scientific facts support the expansion of the ban from beef and animal bones to include the use of fish meal.

ANALYSIS OF EVENTS: 2000

BUSINESS AND THE ECONOMY

Foreign trade has played an important role in Iceland's economy. Iceland's trade deficit continued to grow as a percentage of gross domestic product (GDP). Traditionally, marine products accounted for over 70 percent of Iceland's total export earnings. However Iceland's economy has been slowly diversifying away from fish. In 2000 marine exports were projected to decrease by about 2 percent. Increases in other important exports, aluminum—ferro-silicon, and equipment and electronic machinery for fishing and fish processing—were expected. The fastest-growing sectors of the economy were technology and service.

As Iceland's economy continued to modernize, the issue of joining the European Union became more prominent in 2000, with the Icelandic Federation of Labor considering the pros and cons of joining the European Union from the workers' perspective. Another issue in their changing economy in 2000 is Iceland's foreign workforce. In 2000 foreigners accounted for 3–3.5 percent of the Icelandic work force.

While Iceland is at the vanguard of a movement to legalize commercial whale hunting, the whale known as Keiko, star of the feature film, "Free Willy," was returned to the wild Icelandic waters from which he was taken more than twenty years ago.

GOVERNMENT AND POLITICS

Two pieces of legislation passed in 2000—the Act on Maternity/Paternity Leave and Parental Leave and the Act on the Equal Status and Equal Rights of Women and Men—were generous and liberal socioeconomic policies. The aim of the Maternity/Paternity Act was to ensure children's access to both their mothers and fathers and to provide the means for men and women to coordinate life and work outside the home. The aim of the Equal Status Act was to promote gender equality in all spheres of society while implementing and maintaining equal status and equal opportunities for women and men. Combined with the 1997 Parliamentary Resolution "On the creation of a public family policy and measures to reinforce the status of the family," Iceland's social and family legislation provided a consistent and comprehensive social safety net.

CULTURE AND SOCIETY

As a close-knit society Iceland perpetuated family and social values both legislatively and traditionally. The Icelandic language has remained relatively unchanged since AD 1100. Over 90 percent of the population has maintained membership in either the state church, the Evangelical Lutheran Church, or other Lutheran churches. Law has required the system of patronymy, the adoption of the father's first given name. Sons and daughters of a man named Peter (Petur) maintained the surname of Petersson (Petursson) and Petersdaughter (Petursdottir), respectively. The daughter's children claimed their father's first given name as their surname. Women customarily kept their original surname after marriage. With little immigration in the last 1000 years, Iceland's bio-social homogeneity was further highlighted by a license granted to the U.S. firm, deCode Genetics, to set up a genetic catalogue based on the medical records of the population of Iceland.

Growing forces for the nontraditional in Iceland were tourism and the entertainment sectors. Iceland's popular award-winning performer, Bjork, along with heavy tourist promotion and the spectacular scenery, attracted celebrity visitors in 2000. Reykjavik's thriving music scene was another strong attraction, especially after it was named one of the nine "European Cities of Culture." On the art scene it was reported that over 900 paintings had been forged in the name of deceased Icelandic painters. Polar explorer, Haraldur Örn Ólafsson, and his trekking partner, Ingthór Bjarnason, set out March 10 on skis for the North Pole. Ólafsson reached the North Pole on May 10, completing a journey of over 800 kilometers that began at Resolute Island. In 1998 Ólafsson trekked to the South Pole.

DIRECTORY

CENTRAL GOVERNMENT

Head of State

President
Olafur Ragnar Grimsson, Office of the President, Soleyjargotu 1, IS-150 Reykjavik, Iceland
PHONE: +354 5404400
FAX: +354 5624802

Prime Minister
David Oddsson, Office of the Prime Minister, Stjornarraoshusinu, IS-150 Reykjavik, Iceland
PHONE: +354 5609400
FAX: +354 5628626
E-MAIL: postur@for.stjr.is

Ministers

Minister of Foreign Affairs and External Trade
Halldor Asgrimsson, Ministry of Foreign Affairs and External Trade, Rauoararstig 25, IS-150 Reykjavik, Iceland
PHONE: +354 5609900
FAX: +354 5622373
E-MAIL: external@utn.stjr.is

Minister of Finance
Geir II. Haardc, Ministry of Finance, Arnarhvali, IS-150 Reykjavik, Iceland
PHONE: +354 5609200
FAX: +354 5628280
E-MAIL: postur@fjr.stjr.is

Minister of Culture and Education
Bjorn Bjarnason, Ministry of Culture and Education, Solvholsgotu 4, IS-150 Reykjavik, Iceland
PHONE: +354 5609504
FAX: +354 5623068
E-MAIL: postur@mrn.stjr.is

Minister of Justice
Solveig Petursdottir, Ministry of Justice, Arnarhvali, IS-150 Reykjavik, Iceland
PHONE: +354 5609010
FAX: +354 5527340
E-MAIL: postur@dkm.stjr.is

Minister of Fisheries
Arni M. Mathiesen, Ministry of Fisheries, Skulagotu 4, IS-150 Reykjavik, Iceland
PHONE: +354 5609670
FAX: +354 5621853
E-MAIL: postur@sjr.stjr.is

Minister of Communications
Sturla Boovarsson, Ministry of Communications, Hafnarhusinu v/Tryggvagotu, IS-150 Reykjavik, Iceland
PHONE: +354 5609630
FAX: +354 5621702
E-MAIL: postur@sam.stjr.is

Minister of Agriculture
Gudni Agustsson, Ministry of Agriculture, Rauoararstig 25, IS-150 Reykjavik, Iceland
PHONE: +354 5609750
FAX: +354 5521160
E-MAIL: postur@lan.stjr.is

Minister of the Environment
Siv Frioleifsdottir, Ministry of the Environment, Vonarstraeti 4, IS-150 Reykjavik, Iceland
PHONE: +354 5609600
FAX: +354 5624566
E-MAIL: postur@umh.stjr.is

Minister of Trade and Industry
Finnur Ingolfsson, Ministry of Trade and Industry, Arnarhvali, IS-150 Reykjavik, Iceland
PHONE: +354 5609070
FAX: +354 5621289
E-MAIL: postur@ivr.stjr.is

Minister of Health and Social Security
Ingibjorg Palmadottir, Ministry of Health and Social Security, Laugavegi 116, IS-150 Reykjavik, Iceland
PHONE: +354 5609700
FAX: +354 5519165
E-MAIL: postur@htr.stjr.is

Minister of Social Affairs
Pall Petursson, Ministry of Social Affairs, Hafnarhusinu v/Tryggvagotu, IS-150 Reykjavik, Iceland

PHONE: +354 5609100
FAX: +354 5524804
E-MAIL: postur@fel.stjr.is

POLITICAL ORGANIZATIONS

Sjalfstaedisflokkurinn-IP (Independence Party)

Haaleitisbraut 1, IS-105 Reykjavik, Iceland
PHONE: +354 5682900
FAX: +354 5692927
TITLE: Chairman
NAME: David Oddsson

Althdubandalagid-PA (People's Alliance)

Laugavegi 3, IS-101 Reykjavik, Iceland
PHONE: +354 5517500
FAX: +354 5517599
TITLE: Chairwoman
NAME: Margret Frimannsdottir

Thjodvaki (People's Movement)

c/o Althing, Reykjavik, Iceland

Framsoknarflokkurinn-PP (Progressive Party)

Hafnarstraeti 20, IS-101 Reykjavik, Iceland
PHONE: +354 5624480
FAX: +354 5623325
TITLE: Chair
NAME: Halldor Asgrimsson

Althyduflokkurinn-SDP (Social Democratic Party)

Hverfisgatu 8-10, IS-101 Reykjavik, Iceland
PHONE: +354 5529244
FAX: +354 5629155
TITLE: Chair
NAME: Sighvatur Bjorgvinsson

Samtok um Kvennalista-WA (Women's Party)

Laugavegi 17, IS-101 Reykjavik, Iceland
PHONE: +354 5513725
FAX: +354 5527560
TITLE: Chair
NAME: Kristin Astgeirsdottir

DIPLOMATIC REPRESENTATION

Embassies in Iceland

Denmark
Hverfsgata 29, IS-101 Reykjavik, Iceland
PHONE: +354 5621230
FAX: +354 5623316
TITLE: Ambassador
NAME: Klaus Otto Kappel

Germany
Laufasvegur 3 POB 400, IS-121 Reykjavik, Iceland
PHONE: +354 5301100
FAX: +354 5301101
TITLE: Ambassador
NAME: Reinhart W. Ehni

United Kingdom
Laufasvegur 31, IS-101 Reykjavik, Iceland
PHONE: +354 5505100
FAX: +354 5505104
TITLE: Ambassador
NAME: James McCulloch

United States
Laufasvegur 21, IS-101 Reykjavik, Iceland
PHONE: +354 5629100
FAX: +354 5629118
TITLE: Ambassador
NAME: Day Olin Mount

JUDICIAL SYSTEM

Supreme Court

Domshusinu vio Arnarhol, IS-150 Reykjavik, Iceland
PHONE: +354 5103030
FAX: +354 5623995

BROADCAST MEDIA

Ríkisútvarpid (RUV Radio 1 and RUV Radio 2) (Icelandic National Broadcasting Service)

Efstaleitu 1, IS-150 Reykjavik, Iceland
PHONE: +354 5153000
FAX: +354 5153010
E-MAIL: isradio@ruv.is
WEBSITE: http://www.ruv.is
TITLE: Managing Dorector
CONTACT: Markús Örh Antonsson
LANGUAGE: English, Icelandic

Navy Broadcasting Service

Officer in Charge, NAVMEDIACEN Broadcasting Det Keflavík, PSC 1003, PO Box 25, FPO, AE 09728-0325, USA
TITLE: Senior Manager
CONTACT: E. C. Zeigler
LANGUAGE: English
BROADCASTS: 24 hours/day
TYPE: U.S. Military

Radio Alpha & Omega

Omega Television, Grensasvegur 8, IS-108 Reykjavík, Iceland
PHONE: +354 5683131; 5682777
FAX: +354 5683741
TITLE: Director
CONTACT: Erik Sigurbjoernsson
LANGUAGE: English
TYPE: Religious

Ice TV Channel 3

c/o Laufey Gudjonsdottir, Kringlan 7, IS-103 Reykjavik, Iceland
PHONE: +354 5335633
FAX: +354 335966

Ríkisútvarpid-Sjónvarp (RUV Sjónvarp) (Icelandic National Television)

Laugavegur 176, IS-150 Reykjavik, Iceland
PHONE: +354 5153900
FAX: +354 5153008
WEBSITE: http://sta.ruv.is
TITLE: Managing Director
CONTACT: Petur Gudfinnsson

Omega

Grensasvegur 8, IS-108 Reykjavik, Iceland
PHONE: +354 5683131
FAX: +354 5683741
CONTACT: Erik Eriksson
TYPE: Religious

COLLEGES AND UNIVERSITIES

University of Iceland

Vid Sudurgata, IS-101 Reykjavik, Iceland
PHONE: +354 5254000
FAX: +354 5521331
E-MAIL: ask@hi.is
WEBSITE: http://www.hi.is

Reykjavik College of Music

Skipholti 33, IS-105 Reykjavik, Iceland
PHONE: +354 5530625
FAX: +354 5539240
E-MAIL: tono@issmennt.is
WEBSITE: http://www.ismennt.is/vefir/tono/

Technical College of Iceland

Hoefdabakka 9, IS-112 Reykjavik, Iceland
PHONE: +354 5771400
FAX: +354 5771401
E-MAIL: ti@ti.is
WEBSITE: http://www.ti.is

Agricultural College Hvanneyri

Hvanneyri, IS-311 Borgarnes, Iceland
PHONE: +354 4370000
FAX: +354 4370048
E-MAIL: ibh@hvanneyri.is
WEBSITE: http://www.hvanneyri.is

NEWSPAPERS AND MAGAZINES

Dv-Dagbladid/ Visir

Independent Media Inc., PO Box 3040, IS-103 Reykjavik, Iceland
PHONE: +354 5505000
FAX: +354 5505999; 5505727
E-MAIL: dvritst@ff.is; pall@ff.is
WEBSITE: http://www.visir.is,
CONTACT: Jonas Kristjansson, Ossur Skarpheoinsson
TITLE: Editors-in-Chief
CIRCULATION: 39,000-46,000

Morgunbladid

Arvakur Ltd., PO Box 3040, IS-103 Reykjavik, Iceland
PHONE: +354 5691100
FAX: +354 5691110
E-MAIL: mbl@centrum.is; angl@mbl.is
WEBSITE: http://www.strengur.is/mbl; http://www.mbl.is
TITLE: Editors
CONTACT: Styrmir Gunnarsson, Matthias Johannessen
CIRCULATION: 53,213

Mannlif

Frodi Ltd., Seijavegur 2, IS-101 Reykjavik, Iceland
PHONE: +354 5155500
FAX: +354 5155599
E-MAIL: mannlif@frodi.is

TITLE: Editors
CONTACT: Hrafn Jokulsson, Gudrun Kristjansdottir
CIRCULATION: 15,000
TYPE: General Interest

Sed & Heyrt

Frodi Ltd., Seijavegur 2, IS-101 Reykjavik, Iceland
PHONE: +354 5155652
FAX: +354 5155599
TITLE: Editors
CONTACT: Bjarni Brynjolfsson, Kristjan Thorvaldsson
CIRCULATION: 17,000-20,000

PUBLISHERS

Forlagid

Laugavegur 18, IS-101 Reykjavik, Iceland
PHONE: +354 5152519
FAX: +354 5152505
E-MAIL: forlag@mm.is
WEBSITE: http://www.malogmenning.is
TITLE: Man. Director
CONTACT: Kristjan B. Jonasson
SUBJECTS: Fiction, Nonfiction (General), Travel
TOTAL PUBLISHED: 20 print

Frodi Ltd.

Seljavegi, IS-101 Reykjavik, Iceland
PHONE: +354 5155500
FAX: +354 5155599
E-MAIL: frodi@frodi.is
WEBSITE: http://www.frodi.is
TITLE: International Contact
CONTACT: Halldora Viktorsdottir
SUBJECTS: Biography, Cookery, Fiction, Mysteries, Romance, Sports, Athletics
TOTAL PUBLISHED: 400 print

Hid Islenzka Bokmenntafelag

Sidumuli 21, IS-108 Reykjavik, Iceland
PHONE: +354 5889060
FAX: +354 5889095
E-MAIL: hib@islandia.is
WEBSITE: http://www.arctic.is/hib
TITLE: President
CONTACT: Sigurdur Lindal
SUBJECTS: Art, Political Science, History, Language Arts, Linguistics, Literature, Essays, Natural History, Psychology, Psychiatry, Social Sciences
TOTAL PUBLISHED: 10-14 yearly print

Iceland Review

Sudurlandsbraut 12, IS-108 Reykjavik, Iceland
PHONE: +354 5503000
FAX: +354 5503033
E-MAIL: iceland@icenews.is
TITLE: Publishing Manager
CONTACT: Petur Melr Dlafsson
SUBJECTS: Art, Literature, Literary Criticism, Essays, Regional Interests

Idunn

Seljavegur 1, IS-101 Reykjavik, Iceland
PHONE: +354 5528555
FAX: +354 5528380
E-MAIL: vilhj@idunn.is
CONTACT: Vilhjalmur Sigurjonsson
SUBJECTS: Art, Child Care & Development, Fiction, Health, Nutrition, History, Nonfiction (General), Poetry, Self-Help

Mal og menning

Laugavegur 18, PO Box 392, IS-121 Reykjavik, Iceland
PHONE: +354 5152500
FAX: +354 5152505
E-MAIL: holmfridur@mm.is
WEBSITE: http://www.mm.is
TITLE: Man. Director
CONTACT: Sigurdur Svavarsson
SUBJECTS: Education, Fiction, Literature, Literary Criticism, Essays, Nonfiction (General), Poetry, Travel

Namsgagnastofnun

Laugavegur 166, PO Box 5195, IS-125 Reykjavik, Iceland
PHONE: +354 5528088
FAX: +354 5624137
E-MAIL: simi@nams.is
TITLE: Director
CONTACT: Asgeir Gudmundsson
SUBJECTS: Disability, Special Needs, Education

Stofnun Arna Magnussonar a Islandi

Arnagardur vid Sudurgotu, IS-101 Reykjavik, Iceland
PHONE: +354 5354010
FAX: +354 5254035
E-MAIL: rosat@hi.is
CONTACT: Vesteinn Olason
SUBJECTS: History, Language Arts, Linguistics, Literature, Essays, Folklore, Music, Dance,

Philology, Paleography, Old Norse, Old Icelandic, Conservation, Preservation
TOTAL PUBLISHED: 62 print

RELIGIOUS ORGANIZATIONS

Protestant

The Pentecostal Movement in Iceland
E-MAIL: framkv@gospel.is
WEBSITE: : http://gospel.is/english/
TITLE: Executive Director
NAME: G. Theodor Birgisson

Other Organizations

Icelandic Church Aid

Hjalparstofnun Kirkjunnar
Tjarnargata 10, IS-150 Reykjavik, Iceland
PHONE: +354 5624400
FAX: +354 5624495
E-MAIL: iceaid@islandia.is
WEBSITE: http:/home.islandia.is/hjalparstofnun
TITLE: Director
NAME: Jonas Thorisson

FURTHER READING

Articles

Dearborn, Keri. "Althing The World's Oldest Parliament." *Faces: People, Places, and Cultures,* May 2000, vol. 16, no. 9, p. 26.

Latour, Almar and Edward Harris. "Who Needs Fish? Villagers in Iceland Cast Bets on the Net." *Wall Street Journal,* August 1, 2000, p. A18.

"Tempest in Iceland's Gene Pool: Controversy over a Private Company's Plan to Compile the Genetic History of an Entire Population," *The Christian Science Monitor,* June 30, 2000, p. 6.

Karlsson, Gunnar. *The History of Iceland.* Minneapolis, MN: University of Minnesota Press, 2000.

Government Reports

Trade Policy Review: Iceland. Geneva, Switzerland: World Trade Organization; Lanham, MD: Bernan Associates, 2000.

ICELAND: STATISTICAL DATA

For sources and notes see "Sources of Statistics" at the front of each volume.

GEOGRAPHY

Geography

Area:

Total: 103,000 sq km.

Land: 100,250 sq km.

Land boundaries: 0 km.

Coastline: 4,988 km.

Climate: temperate; moderated by North Atlantic Current; mild, windy winters; damp, cool summers.

Terrain: mostly plateau interspersed with mountain peaks, icefields; coast deeply indented by bays and fiords.

Natural resources: fish, hydropower, geothermal power, diatomite.

Land use:

Arable land: 0%

Permanent crops: 0%

Permanent pastures: 23%

Forests and woodland: 1%

Other: 76% (1993 est.).

HUMAN FACTORS

Demographics (A)

	1990	1995	1998	2000	2010	2020	2030	2040	2050
Population	254.7	267.5	273.2	276.4	289.0	297.3	301.0	297.5	289.6
Life expectancy - males	76.1	75.9	76.9	77.2	78.3	79.2	79.9	80.5	81.0
Life expectancy - females	80.5	80.1	81.8	81.8	83.2	84.4	85.3	86.0	86.6
Birth rate (per 1,000)	18.7	16.0	15.1	14.9	12.9	11.9	10.6	9.8	9.6
Death rate (per 1,000)	6.8	7.2	6.8	6.9	7.3	8.1	9.6	11.4	12.6
Women of reproductive age (15-49 yrs.)	65.1	68.5	69.9	70.2	70.2	67.5	64.3	61.1	56.7
Fertility rate	2.3	2.1	2.0	2.0	1.9	1.8	1.8	1.7	1.7

Except as noted, values for vital statistics are in thousands; life expectancy is in years.

Health Indicators

	National Data	World Data
Life expectancy at birth (years)		
1970-1975	74.3	59.9
1995-2000	79.0	66.7
Daily per capita supply of calories		
1970	3,016	2,358
1997	3,117	2,791
Daily per capital supply of protein		
1997 (grams)	113	74
People living with (1997)		
Tuberculosis (cases per 100,000)	3.6	60.4
Malaria (cases per 100,000)	200	42.2
HIV/AIDS (% aged 15 - 49 years)	0.14	0.99

Ethnic Division

Homogeneous mixture of descendants of Norwegians and Celts.

Religion

Evangelical Lutheran 91%
Other Protestant and Roman Catholic . . . . .NA
None . . . . .NA
Data for 1997.

Major Languages

Icelandic.

EDUCATION

Libraries

National Libraries **1997**
Administrative Units 1
Service Points or Branches .6
Number of Volumes (000) 521
Registered Users (000) 6.9
Loans to Users (000) 33
Total Library Staff 39
Public Libraries **1997**
Administrative Units 187
Service Points or Branches 194
Number of Volumes (000) 1,901
Registered Users (000) . . . . .NA
Loans to Users (000) .1,923
Total Library Staff 295

GOVERNMENT & LAW

Military Affairs (A)

	1990	1992	1995	1996	1997
Gross national product (GNP)					
Current dollars (mil.)	5,530	5,780	6,510	7,020	7,400
1997 constant dollars (mil.)	6,470	6,410	6,750	7,140	7,400
Central government expenditures (CGE)					
1997 constant dollars (mil.)	2,150	2,230	2,400	2,340	2,160
People (mil.)	0.3	0.3	0.3	0.3	0.3
GNP per capita (1997 $)	25,400	24,700	25,200	26,600	27,400
Arms imports[6]					
Current dollars (mil.)	0	40	20	10	10
1997 constant dollars (mil.)	0	44	21	10	10
Total imports[7]					
Current dollars (mil.)	1,680	1,684	1,756	2,032	1,992
1997 constant dollars (mil.)	1,967	1,867	1,818	2,066	1,992
Total exports[7]					
Current dollars (mil.)	1,592	1,528	1,804	1,898	1,852
1997 constant dollars (mil.)	1,864	1,694	1,868	1,930	1,852
Arms as percent of total imports[8]	0	2.4	1.1	0.5	0.5
Arms as percent of total exports[8]	0	0	0	0	0

(Continued on next page.)

Political Parties

The Parliament or Althing consists of 63 seats. Members are elected by popular vote to serve four-year terms. Elections were last held on 8 May 1999 (next to be held by April 2003). No election results are available. The following are political parties in Iceland: Independence Party, National Awakening (People's Revival Party), People's Alliance, People's Movement, Progressive Party, Social Democratic Party, and the Women's Party.

Government Budgets (A)

Year: 1997

Total Expenditures: 60,225 Millions of Kronur

Expenditures as a percentage of the total by function:

General public services and public order 10.28
Defense 0
Education 10.15
Health 24.13
Social Security and Welfare 23.57
Housing and community amenities 0.71
Recreational, cultural, and religious affairs 3.00
Fuel and energy 0.74
Agriculture, forestry, fishing, and hunting 5.83
Mining, manufacturing, and construction 0.54
Transportation and communication 7.58
Other economic affairs and services 1.72

Crime

Crime volume (for 1998)

Crimes reported 40,538
Total persons convicted . . . . . . NA
Crimes per 100,000 population 14,727

LABOR FORCE

Total Labor Force (A)

131,000 (1999).

Labor Force by Occupation

Manufacturing 12.9%
Fishing and fish processing 11.8%
Construction 10.7%
Other services 59.5%
Agriculture 5.1%

Data for 1999.

Unemployment Rate

2.4% (1999 est.)

PRODUCTION SECTOR

Energy Production

Production . . . . . . 6.187 billion kWh
Production by source
Fossil fuel 0.06%
Hydro 89.88%
Nuclear 0%
Other 10.06%
Exports . . . . . . 0 kWh

Data for 1998.

Energy Consumption

Consumption . . . . . . 5.754 billion kWh
Imports . . . . . . 0 kWh

Data for 1998.

Transportation

Highways:

Total: 12,689 km.

Paved: 3,439 km.

Unpaved: 9,250 km (1998 est.).

Merchant marine:

Total: 3 ships (1,000 GRT or over) totaling 13,085 GRT/16,938 DWT.

Ships by type: chemical tanker 1, container 1, petroleum tanker 1 (1999 est.).

Airports: 86 (1999 est.).

Airports - with paved runways: 12.

Airports - with unpaved runways: 74.

Top Agriculture Products

Potatoes, turnips; cattle, sheep; fish.

Top Mining Products (B)

Mineral resources include: diatomite.

MANUFACTURING SECTOR

GDP & Manufacturing Summary (A)

	1980	1985	1990	1995
GDP ($-1990 mil.)[1]	4,640	5,201	6,080	6,347
Per capita ($-1990)[1]	20,349	21,581	23,844	23,595
Manufacturing share (%) (current prices)[1]	19.3	18.3	16.1	NA

(Continued on next page.)

	1980	1985	1990	1995
Manufacturing				
Value added ($-1990 mil.)[1]	816	825	819	787[e]
Industrial production index	107	108	100	96[e]
Value added ($ mil.)	518	429	755	869[e]
Gross output ($ mil.)	1,676	1,471	2,602	2,708[e]
Employment (000)	28	30	22	21[e]
Profitability (% of gross output)				
Intermediate input (%)	69	71	71	68[e]
Wages and salaries inc. supplements (%)	25	22	22	21[e]
Gross operating surplus	6	7	7	11[e]
Productivity ($)				
Gross output per worker	61,052	51,071	111,991	128,743[e]
Value added per worker	18,864	14,907	32,498	41,835[e]
Average wage (inc. supplements)	15,021	11,345	25,775	29,327[e]
Value added ($ mil.)				
Food products	188	175	285	427[e]
Beverages	11	10	21	19[e]
Textiles	23	17	21	15[e]
Wearing apparel	15	10	10	13[e]
Leather and fur products	6	6	5	7[e]
Footwear	1	1	1	NA
Wood and wood products	NA	NA	1	2[e]
Furniture and fixtures	45	29	40	37[e]
Paper and paper products	4	4	9	11[e]
Printing and publishing	35	36	84	86[e]
Industrial chemicals	8	7	17	13[e]
Other chemical products	7	8	15	22[e]
Plastic products	11	11	27	30[e]
Pottery, china and earthenware	1	NA	1	1[e]
Glass and glass products	3	3	4	4[e]
Other non-metal mineral products	23	21	37	33[e]
Iron and steel	6	11	9	15[e]
Non-ferrous metals	39	13	36	18[e]
Metal products	62	44	85	64[e]
Transport equipment	21	13	20	19[e]
Other manufacturing	10	11	27	33[e]

COMMUNICATIONS

Daily Newspapers

	National Data	World Data for Comparison
Daily Newspapers		
Number of Dailies	5	8,391
Total Circulation (000)	145	548,000
Circulation per 1,000 inhabitants	535	96

Telecommunications

Telephones - main lines in use: 162,310 (1997).

Telephones - mobile cellular: 65,746 (1997).

Telephone system: adequate domestic service.

Domestic: the trunk network consists of coaxial and fiber-optic cables and microwave radio relay links.

International: satellite earth stations - 2 Intelsat (Atlantic Ocean), 1 Inmarsat (Atlantic and Indian Ocean regions) Note: Iceland shares the Inmarsat earth station with the other Nordic countries (Denmark, Finland, Norway, and Sweden).

Radio broadcast stations: AM 3, FM about 70 (including repeaters), shortwave 1 (1998).

Radios: 260,000 (1997).

Television broadcast stations: 14 (plus 156 low-power repeaters) (1997).

Televisions: 98,000 (1997).

Internet Service Providers (ISPs): 14 (1999).

FINANCE, ECONOMICS, & TRADE

Economic Indicators

National product: GDP—purchasing power parity—$6.42 billion (1999 est.).

National product real growth rate: 4.5% (1999 est.).

National product per capita: $23,500 (1999 est.).

Inflation rate—consumer price index: 1.9% (1999 est.).

Exchange Rates

Exchange rates:

Icelandic kronur (IKr) per US$1

January 2000	72.334
1999	72.352
1998	70.958
1997	70.904
1996	66.500
1995	64.692

Top Import Origins

$2.4 billion (f.o.b., 1998)

Origins (1998)

EU	56%
Germany	12%
United Kingdom	10%
Norway	9%
Denmark	8%
Sweden	6%
United States	11%

Top Export Destinations

$1.9 billion (f.o.b., 1998)

Destinations (1998)

EU	65%
United Kingdom	19%
Germany	15%
France	7%
Denmark	6%
United States	13%
Japan	5%

Import/Export Commodities

Import Commodities	Export Commodities
Machinery and equipment	Fish and fish products 70%
Petroleum products	Animal products
Foodstuffs	Aluminum
Textiles	Diatomite and ferrosilicon

Balance of Payments

	1994	1995	1996	1997	1998
Exports of goods (f.o.b.)	1,561	1,804	1,890	1,854	1,927
Imports of goods (f.o.b.)	−1,288	−1,598	−1,871	−1,851	−2,278
Trade balance	273	206	19	3	−351
Services - debits	−577	−641	−737	−799	−965
Services - credits	603	689	767	843	947
Private transfers (net)	12	15	10	17	4
Government transfers (net)	−7	−10	−9	−11	−10
Overall balance	97	57	−117	−104	−469

INDIA

CAPITAL: New Delhi.

FLAG: The national flag, adopted in 1947, is a tricolor of deep saffron, white, and green horizontal stripes. In the center of the white stripe is a blue wheel representing the wheel (chakra) that appears on the abacus of Asoka's lion capital (c. 250 BC) at Sarnath, Uttar Pradesh.

ANTHEM: *Jana gana mana (Thou Art the Ruler of the Minds of All People)*. A national song of equal status is *Vande Mataram (I Bow to Thee, Mother)*.

MONETARY UNIT: The rupee (R) is a paper currency of 100 paise. There are coins of 5, 10, 20, 25, and 50 paise, and 1, 2, and 5 rupees, and notes of 2, 5, 10, 20, 50, 100, and 500 rupees. R1 = 0.02803 (or $1 = R35.68).

WEIGHTS AND MEASURES: Metric weights and measures, introduced in 1958, replaced the British and local systems. Indian numerical units still in use include the lakh (equal to 100,000) and the crore (equal to 10 million).

HOLIDAYS: Republic Day, 26 January; Independence Day, 15 August; Gandhi Jayanti, 2 October. Annual events. The more important include Shivarati in February; and Raksha Bandhan in August. Movable religious holidays include Holi, Ganesh Chaturthi, Durga Puja, Dussehra, 'Id al-Fitr, Dewali; and Christmas, 25 December.

TIME: 5:30 PM = noon GMT.

LOCATION AND SIZE: The Republic of India fills the major part of the South Asian subcontinent (which it shares with Pakistan, Nepal, Bhutan, and Bangladesh) and includes the Andaman and Nicobar Islands in the Bay of Bengal and Lakshadweep in the Arabian Sea. India's total area is 3.3 million square kilometers (1.3 million square miles). The total boundary length is 17,723 kilometers (11,013 miles).

CLIMATE: The monsoon is the dominant feature of India's climate and helps to divide the year into four seasons: rainy (June–September); moist (October–November); dry cool (December–March); and hot (April–May).

Republic of India
Bharat Ganarajya

INTRODUCTORY SURVEY

RECENT HISTORY

The end of World War II in 1945 led to renewed negotiations on independence between Britain and the Hindu and Muslim leaders. In mid-August 1947, with Hindu-Muslim tensions rising, British India was divided into the two self-governing dominions of India and Pakistan. Known as Partition, this division caused a mass movement of Hindus, Muslims, and Sikhs who found themselves on the "wrong" side of new international boundaries. As many as twenty million people moved, and three million were killed in bloodletting on the new international frontier. Gandhi, who opposed Partition and worked untiringly for Hindu-Muslim cooperation, became a casualty of the inflamed feelings of the period. A Hindu extremist assassinated him by five months after Partition.

Among the unresolved legacies of Partition was the fate of the independent state of Jammu and Kashmir, bordering both new nations. A Muslim-majority state with a Hindu maharaja, Kashmir has been the site of periodic Indian-Pakistani clashes since 1948. Pakistan governs its portion of the former princely state as Azad ("free") Kashmir. The Indian portion is governed as Jammu and Kashmir, a state in the Indian Union. Indian and Pakistan issues remained unresolved in 1999.

Also unresolved is the Himalayan border between India and China since the Chinese occupation of Tibet in 1959. Clashes have periodically erupted between Indian and Chinese troops at a number of locations along the disputed border.

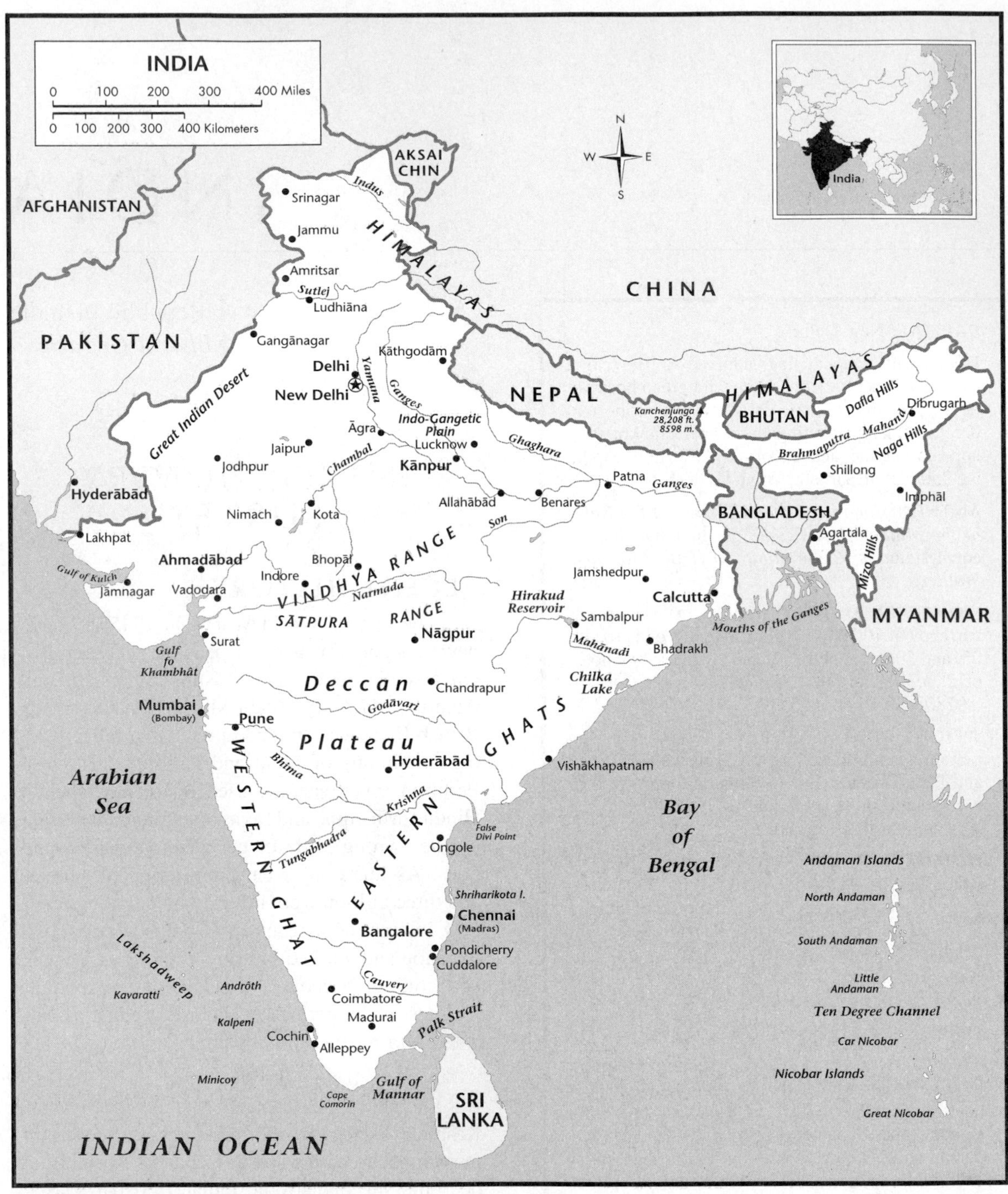

Tensions eased with an accord signed by the two countries in 1993.

The death of India's first prime minister, Jawaharlal Nehru, in 1964 led to his daughter Indira Gandhi succeeding him. India went to war with Pakistan in 1971 to support East Pakistan in its civil war with West Pakistan. Indian forces tipped the balance in favor of the separatists, which ultimately led to the creation of Bangladesh from the former East Pakistan.

Following a 1975 conviction on minor election law violations, Gandhi was embroiled in political controversy and lost her position, but regained it in 1980. In 1983 Sikh discontent led to widespread violence by Sikh separatist militants in Punjab and to the imposition of direct rule in that state. A year later, with the Sikh separatist violence unchecked, Gandhi herself became a victim-assassinated by Sikh members of her own guard.

Rajiv Gandhi immediately followed his mother as prime minister but economic and political turmoil persisted. During the election campaign in the spring of 1991, a disgruntled Sri Lankan Tamil assassinated Rajiv Gandhi. P.V. Narasimha Rao, a former minister under both Rajiv and Indira Gandhi, formed a minority government. As prime minister, Rao introduced new economic reforms, opening India to foreign investors and market economics. Between May 1996 and April 1997 political instability caused India to change its government four times. In March 1998 Hindu nationalist Atal Bihari Vajpayee became prime minister.

In May 1998 India conducted several underground nuclear test explosions, prompting international clamor. Pakistan responded with its own nuclear testing, raising concerns that India and Pakistan would begin a nuclear arms race. India and Pakistan conducted tests of medium-range missiles in April 1999.

That month Vajpayee's coalition government fell and Congress Party leader Sonia Gandhi (widow of Rajiv Gandhi) failed to form a new government. In elections that followed Sonia won a seat in Parliament but the Gandhi name failed to halt the decline of the Congress Party. The party won only 112 seats in the People's Assembly and with its allies controlled only 135 seats. The Bharatiya Janata Party (BJP) claimed 182 seats and once again A.B. Vajpayee put together a coalition government.

GOVERNMENT

India is an independent socialist democratic republic, with no religious ties to the government. Its constitution that became effective in January 1950 provides for a parliamentary form of government. The constitution also contains an extensive set of guidelines similar to the United States Bill of Rights.

The president, elected by an electoral college for five-year terms, is chief of state. The head of government is the prime minister elected by parliamentary members of the majority party following legislative elections. The president appoints the cabinet, the Council of Ministers, on the recommendation of the prime minister.

The legislative branch is a bicameral Parliament or Sansad consisting of the Council of States and the 545-seat People's Assembly. The Council of States may not have more than 250 members. The president appoints up to twelve members and the elected members of the state and territorial assemblies chooses the remainder. Members serve six-year terms. The members of the People's Assembly are elected by popular vote except for two who are appointed by the president and serve five-year terms.

Suffrage is universal at age eighteen.

Judiciary

The laws and judicial system of British India were continued after independence with only slight modifications. The Supreme Court's duties include interpreting the constitution, handling disputes between the states, and judging appeals from lower courts.

In addition, each state's judicial system is headed by a high court. Judgments from these courts may be appealed to the Supreme Court.

Personal law is administered through the civil court system. Islamic law (Shari'a) governs many noncriminal matters involving Muslims, including family law, inheritance, and divorce.

Political Parties

In various forms, the Indian National Congress has controlled the government for most of the years since independence in 1947. Founded in 1885 the Indian National Congress, known after 1947 as the Congress Party (CP), was the most powerful mass movement fighting for independence in British India. It became the ruling party of free India due to its national popularity and because most leaders of the independence movement were among its members, including India's first prime minister, Jawaharlal Nehru and the Gandhi family.

With the decline of the Congress Party as a national party, there has been a rise in the number of single state, linguistic, ethnic, and regional parties capable of governing only at the state level but available for coalition building at the national level. The Bharatiya Janata Party (BJP) emerged as the dominant national party in 1999.

DEFENSE

In 2000 armed forces members totaled 1.2 million. The army had 980,000 members; the navy (including the naval air force) had 53,000 members; the air force had 140,000 members; and the coast guard had 5,500 members.

Budgeted defense expenditures in 2000 were $10.055 billion, or 2.5 percent of GDP.

ECONOMIC AFFAIRS

The Indian economy is the fifth largest in the world when measured by GDP. Agriculture provides the livelihood for 67 percent of the population. These agricultural workers produce 25 percent of the gross domestic product (GDP). The country is rich in mineral, forest, and power resources, and its ample reserves of iron ore and coal provide a substantial base for heavy industry.

The domestic economy grew at an annual rate of about 6 percent during 1993–1996. By 1997 the GDP growth slowed to 4.6 percent and a steep rise in imports signaled that reforms were needed in order to keep up the economic recovery. Booming exports in software services bolstered the GDP growth rate back to around 6 percent in 1998 and 1999 but was accompanied by a 14 percent inflation rate.

The budget for 1999–2000 focused on opening foreign trade and encouraging foreign investment. India's international payments position remained strong in 1999. Strong demand for high technology exports will support growth in 2000.

Public Finance

The executive branch has considerable control over public finance. Thus, while parliament can oversee and investigate public expenditures and may reduce the budget, it cannot expand the budget, and checks exist that prevent the parliament from delaying passage.

Budgets in recent decades have reflected the needs of rapid economic development under rising expenditures of the five-year plans. Insufficient government receipts for financing this development have led to yearly deficits and a resulting increase of new tax measures and deficit financing.

The budget for 2000 included a 30 percent increase on defense due to the Pakistani conflict. Some observers were chagrined that the 2000 budget did not address India's substandard infrastructure.

The U.S. CIA estimated that in 1998–1999 government revenues totaled approximately $35.8 billion and expenditures $66.3 billion including capital expenditures of $15.9 billion. External debt totaled $98 billion in 1999

Income

In 1998 India's gross domestic product (GDP) was $1.805 billion, or $1,800 per capita. The 1999 estimated growth rate was 5.5 percent and inflation was 6.7 percent. The GDP contribution by sector in 1997 was agriculture 25 percent, industry 30 percent, and services 45 percent.

Industry

Textile production dominates the industrial field accounting for more than one-third of total export earnings in 1998–1999. About 64.2 million cottage workers throughout the country handloom cotton, wool, silk, and rayon.

In 1998–99 seven integrated and 180 mini steel plants produced approximately thirty million tons of finished steel. The metallurgical sector produced 640 million tons of aluminum products. Vehicle production in 1998–99 included bicycles, motorcycles and scooters, passenger vehicles, tractors, and railroad cars.

The production of computers and a wide range of consumer electronics have been boosted by the recent liberalization of imports of component parts. The information technology sector grew at an annual rate of over 50 percent during the late 1990s.

Heavy machinery production, oil refining, cement production, nitrogen fertilizer production, and refined sugar were all major components of the industrial sector.

Banking and Finance

A well-established banking system exists in India. The Reserve Bank of India, founded in 1935 and nationalized in 1949, is the central banking and note-issuing authority. At the end of 1995 there were 62,300 branches of public sector and commercial banks. The largest public-sector bank is the State Bank of India, which, at the end of 1996, accounted for one-third of income.

In an attempt to regulate lending practices and interest rates, the government has encouraged the formation of cooperative credit societies.

Of India's twenty-three stock exchanges, the Mumbai (formerly Bombay) Stock Exchange (BSE) and National Stock Exchange (NSE) are the most important. Major efforts have been made to strengthen the stock market institutionally and make it less like a casino. The Security and Exchange Board of India (SEBI), regulates the stock market.

Economic Development

Under a series of five-year plans through 1990, the government became a participant in many industrial fields and increased its regulation of existing private commerce and industry. Long the owner-operator of most railway facilities, all radio broadcasting, post, and telegraph facilities, arms and ammunition factories, and river development programs, the government reserved for itself the right to nationalize any industries it deemed necessary. Yet the government's socialist approach was pragmatic, not doctrinaire; agriculture and large segments of trade, finance, and industry remained in private hands. Planning is supervised by an eight-member Planning Commission, established in 1950 and chaired by the prime minister.

The eighth development plan (for 1992–97) most analysts proclaimed a success; economic growth averaged 6 percent a year, employment rose, poverty was reduced, exports increased, and inflation declined. The ninth development plan (1997–2002) focused on redistribution of wealth and alleviation of widespread poverty, the further privatization of the economy, and attraction of foreign investment, and reduction of the deficit.

SOCIAL WELFARE

India's governments have established an extensive social welfare system. Programs for children include supplementary nutrition for expectant mothers and for children under 7 years of age, immunization and health programs, vacation camps for low-income families, and prevocational training for adolescents. Programs for women include welfare grants, women's adult education, and working women's hostels. There are also services for the blind, deaf, mentally retarded, and orthopedically handicapped. A limited state health insurance scheme applies to some workers as do old age, disability pensions, and survivor benefits.

Special measures are aimed at rehabilitating juvenile delinquents, prostitutes, and convicts. Laws in most states and localities forbids begging in public places. Other social welfare programs cover displaced persons; family planning and maternity care; rural community development; emergency relief programs for drought, flood, earthquake, and other disasters; untouchability (the *Harijans*); and underdeveloped tribal peoples.

Below the highest political levels, and especially in rural India, the position of women remains inferior to that of men. Laws aimed at preventing employment discrimination, female bondage and prostitution, and the *sati* (the burning of widows) are often not enforced. A National Commission for Women was established in 1992 to investigate abuses against women. Despite laws against it, child marriages are still arranged in many parts of India.

In 1995 there were an estimated 500,000 children living and working on the streets. Child prostitution is widespread.

Healthcare

The government is paying increased attention to integrated health, maternity, and childcare in rural areas. Through a network of over 150,000 primary health centers, sub-centers, and health guides. There are in addition to nearly 40,000 hospitals and dispensaries in urban areas. In the mid-1990s India had nearly 400,000 physicians and 700,000 hospital beds. There are also some 278,000 registered health care providers following the Ayurvedic (ancient Hindu) and Unani systems.

Average life expectancy has increased from forty-eight years in 1971 to an estimated 62.5 in 2000. However malaria, leprosy, tuberculosis, and cataracts remain problematic as do deficiency diseases such as goiter, malnutrition (due to lack of protein), rickets, and beriberi.

Housing

Progress has been made toward improving the generally primitive housing in which most Indians live. The 1990–1995 five-year plan called for an investment of $40 billion in housing. The government's goal is to provide 8 million new housing units between 1990 and the year 2000, 2 million to meet the existing need and 6 million to meet the needs that will be created by population growth.

EDUCATION

According to 2000 estimates the population of India is 56 percent literate. In 1988 a national literacy mission was begun following which some states achieved 100 percent literacy. In 1992 the second program of action on education was introduced to reaffirm the 1986 policy with plans to achieve total literacy and free education for all children up to grade eight by the year 2000.

Free and compulsory elementary education is a guiding principle of the constitution. In 1997 there were 598,354 primary level schools with 1.8 million teachers and 110.4 million pupils. In general secondary schools there were 68.9 million pupils the same year.

India's system of higher education is still basically British in structure and approach. The university system is second only to that of the United

States in size with 150 universities and over 5,000 colleges and higher-level institutions.

2000 KEY EVENTS TIMELINE

January

- Arundhati Roy, Booker-Prize winner for *The God of Small Things,* is among those arrested for protesting against the construction of a dam in central India.
- A strike for higher wages by nearly 100,000 dock workers hits eleven port cities. This is the first nationwide strike in a decade.
- On January 5 Ugyen Trinley Dorje, the Karmapa Lama, the fourteen-year-old Buddhist leader flees Tibet for Dharmsala.
- On January 6 India charges Pakistani involvement in December 1999 hijacking.
- On January 19 the United States and India agree to the creation of a joint anti-terrorism group.

February

- Relations are strained between two rival Buddhist factions over who is the real Karmapa. In March 1994, Trinley Thaye Dorje was named Karmapa in New Delhi and Ugyen Trinley Dorje, newly arrived from Tibet, also claims the title and has the support of the Dalai Lama, Buddhism most revered leader.
- On February 29 India announces a 28 percent increase in defense spending for the next fiscal year.

March

- U.S. President Bill Clinton arrives in New Delhi on March 19.
- Over thirty Sikh villagers are killed in a massacre March 20 in Kashmir.

May

- On May 20 a UN conference on nuclear non-proliferation announces its intention to involve non-signatories, such as India, in the movement.
- India offers to evacuate Sri Lankan government troops from Jaffna on May 23.

July

- A monsoon, triggering landslides, hits the area around Mumbai (Bombay). The death toll from the storm is estimated at 135, with over seventy people buried when their shantytown is buried by mud and boulders.
- The Cabinet rejects a bid for greater autonomy for Kashmir, which would have allowed a separate president, prime minister, and courts.
- Kashmiri rebels of the Hizbul Mujahedeen announce a cease-fire July 24 in order to negotiate with the Indian government. By July 26 the Multihadda Jihad Council had rejected the cease-fire and suspended the Hizbul Mujahedeen.
- Three government ministers resign July 19, protesting the arrest of the leader of their hard-line Hindu party Shiv Sena, Bal Thackeray.
- Outlaw Veerappan kidnaps famous movie star Rajkumar on July 29.

August

- Flooding kills 120 and leaves more than 2.5 million homeless in the eastern provinces on August 7.
- A bomb kills ten in Kashmir on August 10.
- Violence in Kashmir on India's Independence Day, August 13, kills sixteen, and wounds many others.
- Thousands of protesters hold a "cyberprotest" by sending e-mails outside of the abandoned toxic Union Carbide factory at Bhopal on August 15, calling for water decontamination.
- Hundreds of Christians demonstrate in Calcutta on August 15, protesting a series of attacks on Christians during the year.
- Eight people are killed and eighteen injured in anti-India violence on August 16. Twelve more are killed in Jammu on August 21.
- Flooding in the southern state of Andhra Pradesh forces tens of thousands of people to flee on August 29. Four-hundred were reported dead in flooding on August 25 as well, in Bihar, Andhra Pradesh, and Himachal Pradesh.

September

- The Indian version of "Who Wants to Be a Millionaire?" ("Kaun Banega Crorepati") becomes extremely popular.
- Indian helicopter gunships and commandos raid what they suspect to be a separatist guerrilla base in Indian-controlled Kashmir.

- The first census in two decades in India's insurgency-wracked Jammu-Kashmir state is derailed by rebels.

October

- Former Prime Minister P. V. Narasimha Rao is sentenced on October 12 to three years in prison for bribing members of parliament to vote for his government.

November

- Three new states are formed: Chhattisgarh (November 1), Uttaranchal (November 8), and Jharkhand (November 15).
- Indian outlaw Veerappan releases movie star Rajkumar November 17 in exchange for greater Tamil cultural recognition.
- Twelve people are killed and twenty people are wounded in Kashmir violence at the start of a unilateral ceasefire by India on November 28.

December

- A freight train collides with a passenger train in Punjab, killing forty-six people.

ANALYSIS OF EVENTS: 2000

BUSINESS AND THE ECONOMY

India continued to liberalize its economy through 2000. On March 31 the government removed import licensing restrictions on 715 products. This continued a process of allowing foreign goods to enter the Indian market that was begun in 1991. Import licensing restrictions are expected to be removed from all products by April 1, 2001, which will make India a completely open economy for the first time since it became independent in 1947.

As imports rise India also has increased its exports, particularly in software. Software exports have been growing 40 percent to 50 percent a year, and were expected to reach $5 billion to $7 billion in 2000. Economists predict that 2.2 million Indians will be working in software jobs and that the industry will produce $87 billion in revenue by 2008. In addition the country deregulated its long-distance telecommunications industry on August 15, the anniversary of its independence. The deregulation measure allows multinational firms to bid for licenses and for Internet service providers to negotiate to use the undersea cables that link India to the rest of the world.

The global growth of information technology also has produced new jobs in cosmopolitan cities such as Bombay, New Delhi and Bangalore. U.S. companies are hiring information-technology workers in India and other developing countries where English is widely spoken to offer customer-service via the Internet. Indian workers process credit card payments for customers around the world, transcribe medical reports for doctors in the United States, and soothe unhappy customers who might live twelve time zones away. The high-tech service industry is expected to generate one million jobs in India and revenue of $18 billion.

Many members of India's 250 million strong middle-class see these jobs as a path to prosperity. They regard the opening of India's economy as creating a vibrant, "anything-is-possible" atmosphere. Raghav Narsalay, an economic consultant for the Third World activist group Focus on the Global South, tells a different story. He notes that Indians are hired for these jobs because they are willing to work for a much lower wage than professionals in the West. In addition such an industry only helps a small group of Indians. Lower middle-class Indians, poor urban laborers and farmers who live in villages that still lack electricity are "totally unaware" that such a revolution is taking place, Narsalav says. In addition, because the jobs are tied to the whims of a global economy, many fear that they may be here today, and gone tomorrow.

Economic benefits for the middle class often come at the expense of the poor, particularly those in rural areas. While the gross domestic product (GDP) grew by 6 percent in the 1990s, income per person rose only 4 percent. In addition, predominantly rural states such as Bihar per capita income actually declined over the past decade. Although the gap between urban rich and rural poor has long been an issue in independent India, government policies increasingly either turn a deaf ear to rural concerns or try to quash those who attempt to raise awareness of the down side of development.

In June and July several rare white tigers died of a sleeping sickness at the Nandankanan Zoo in eastern India. This issue also is tied to India's focus on participating in the global information technology economy and not on its own infrastructure. Efforts to build up the country's industrial and high-technology base have helped create a shortage of habitat for wildlife. Zoos such as Nandankanan try to ease this problem by providing a home for rare animals. But the government provides few resources to support the zoos. So, even though Nandankanan Zoo houses the world's largest collection of white tigers, its strapped budget makes it hard for it to keep the rare animals alive.

GOVERNMENT AND POLITICS

India rang in 2000 with news that produced an international sigh of relief. On December 31, 1999, as worldwide millennium gala events unfolded, India announced that the passengers on an Indian Airlines flight that had been hijacked December 24 were free. The hijacking occurred on a flight between Kathmandu, Nepal, and New Delhi. The hijackers ordered the pilot to crisscross air space over South Asia, and eventually allowed the plane to land in Afghanistan. News of the release was a particular relief because the incident not only involved two nations with nuclear capabilities—India and Pakistan—but also Islamic militants believed to be backed by Pakistan and Afghanistan's Taliban.

The relief, however, was short-lived. Soon after the hostages were freed, India began blaming Pakistan for the incident and Islamic militant leader Maulana Masood Azhar began calling for a *jihad,* or holy war, against India. India had released Azhar from prison and allowed him to return to his home in Pakistan as a condition for obtaining the hijacked passengers' freedom. As Azhar's rhetoric began drawing crowds in Pakistan, India feared that it would become the target of Islamic terrorism. The country's political leadership proposed a 10 percent hike in military spending, and began searching out sources of terrorism within India. That effort led to the arrest of students at the highly regarded Aligarh Muslim University. It also provoked a crackdown on peaceful trade relationships between India and Nepal because India claimed Islamic terrorists had found a haven in the border regions between India and Nepal where citizens of each of these countries have been able to travel without passports since 1950.

Such a concern with terrorism also shadowed the most significant world event in India this year: U.S. President Bill Clinton's visit in March. The visit was the first by an American president since Jimmy Carter's trip in 1978. In many ways, it represented a triumph for Indian prime minister Atal Behari Vajpayee and his efforts to raise the international profile of India and the Bharathiya Janata Party (BJP) which he leads. Clinton received a warm welcome: children showered him with flower petals as he traveled from one site to another, and business people lavished attention upon him as he surveyed India's efforts to develop itself as a high-tech powerhouse.

Clinton returned the warmth he received in India by welcoming Vajpayee to the United States in September. Clinton honored the Indian leader with a party that included 700 guests, the largest official dinner Clinton had ever hosted for a single visiting dignitary. Clinton praised Vajpayee for forging a new friendship and called for the most powerful (United States) and most populous (India) democracies to work together.

Vajpayee leads a coalition government known as the National Democratic Alliance (NDA). In 2000 it consisted of twenty-three parties, the most influential of which was the BJP. Coalition governments in India have been fragile in recent years, but the NDA was stable in 2000. Many credited this achievement to Vajpayee and his leadership of the BJP. Under Vajpayee, the BJP portrayed itself as an all-inclusive political party that supports a free-market global economy. Its anti-corruption image was bolstered by the September 29 conviction of former Congress Party Prime Minister P.V. Narasimha Rao on vote-rigging charges. The BJP also welcomed international investment. BJP has been able to stay in power because it has worked with other parties in the NDA coalition to shape a political message that appealed to a broad array of Indians. But the BJP also was linked to a reactionary religious ideological movement that wants to transform India into a nation guided by Hindu beliefs and values. In addition, many of the party's top leaders, including Vajpayee, had ties to the Rashtriya Swayamsevak Sangh (RSS), a paramilitary organization that openly advocates a Hindu India and exerted enormous control over BJP policies. The BJP recognized India's cultural, ethnic, and religious diversity, but it also promoted Hindu fundamentalist policies and did little in 2000 to stop increasing violence against Christians.

Over the past two years more than 200 attacks on Christians have occurred and at least thirty churches have suffered damage. Vajpayee condemned these incidents, but the BJP did little to punish the attackers. At the same time, the party passed a measure in the state of Gujarat, where many of the anti-Christian attacks have occurred, that allowed government employees to participate in RSS activities. The RSS platform is strongly anti-Muslim. Although attacks against Muslims tapered off in the past year, legitimizing the RSS in such a way raised fears of new violence.

The tension between promoting a pluralist, people-oriented India and a hard line Hindu one that characterized BJP policies also was seen in Kashmir. Control of the Himalayan state is divided between India and Pakistan, but both nations claimed Kashmir as theirs. This has caused a long-running conflict in which more than 50,000 people have died, and nearly escalated into war in 1999 when Islamic militants backed by Pakistan crossed into Indian territory. Many Kashmiris who are tired of the fighting wished to be independent from both nations. As a result, the Kashmir legislature submitted a request to the Indian national government in June, seeking autonomy. Vajpayee said he would consider the request, but a week later, the central government rejected it as inadequate.

Kashmir's situation was made more difficult by the international view of it. Most world leaders feared that tensions in the province between India and Pakistan might lead to nuclear war. Because of this, they insisted the two nations resolve the issue and payed little attention to the wishes of Kashmiris themselves. Both India and Pakistan indicated in 1999 that they would like Clinton to mediate the dispute, and many hoped the U.S. president's visit would lead to a peace agreement. However, Clinton refused to take on the role of mediator, despite his willingness to intervene in disputes in the Middle East and Korean peninsula. Clinton urged India and Pakistan to put anger over the 1999 conflict behind them and start talking about Kashmir. But neither nation would—or perhaps could—make the first move.

CULTURE AND SOCIETY

Besides Kashmir India faced numerous calls for autonomy from regional political groups, including the Asom Gana Parishad in Assam, the Akali Dal in Punjab, and a Dravidian-based political party in Tamil Nadu. The India of 2000 was perhaps the world's most diverse nation. It had seventeen official languages and nearly 600 other languages and dialects. Every major world religion claimed hundreds of thousands—if not millions—of believers in India. Nearly every state had tribal groups who continued to practice traditional land uses, despite encroaching development. Although India was proud of this multicultural heritage, the internal dissent and the increasingly violent means that police and troops used to suppress it suggested the multicultural ideal India promoted doesn't produce a harmonious reality.

Alan de Lastic, the late archbishop of Delhi and India's most prominent Catholic, criticized the government shortly before his death this year for being unwilling to promote peace and justice. Criminal gangs and bandits roamed the countryside, bearing weapons that the development of an international arms-trafficking market had helped them acquire. The threat that these gangs posed to the internal stability of India was illustrated in late July when a gang led by the bandit Veerappan kidnapped a former film star, his son-in-law, and two other people. Veerappan lived in the sandalwood forests of the South Indian state of Karnataka, and portrayed himself as a champion of tea and coffee plantation worker rights. He often kidnapped wealthy Indians, and demanded cash payment for their release. He had been wanted by police since the late 1980s, but the kidnappings continued.

Democracy in India coexists with a belief that the poor are expendable. When the country officially declared its population had passed the one billion mark in mid-May, Vajpayee established a National Population Stabilization Fund to promote family-planning. Population experts said such a policy targeted the poor and, in doing so, missed the point: poorer families in India would be willing to have fewer children, but they cannot afford to do so. Despite India's profile as a fledgling high-tech hotbed, two-thirds of the nation's people still worked in agriculture, and nearly half of the country's population lived on less than $1 a day, the gauge of dire poverty as defined by the United Nations Development Fund. However, a push to open up India's economy to outside trade forced many farmers to engage in multi-cropping, a practice in which several crops are raised primarily for export. This practice often put farmers in debt, depleted the land of nutrients, and produced droughts even in years with a good monsoon season such as 2000. As a result, agricultural families struggled with debt and faced declines in agricultural productivity. In such a situation, having a large family helped. Children, upon reaching adulthood, can be sent to find work in urban areas of India, or in many of the overseas nations—ranging from the Persian Gulf states to England, Canada, and the United States—that seek migrant workers. Rather than address the needs of the poorer Indian families directly, many said programs such as the fund Vajpayee established blames the victims.

DIRECTORY

CENTRAL GOVERNMENT

Head of State

President
Kocheril Raman Narayanan, Office of the President, Rashtrapati Bhavan, New Delhi 110 004, India

Vice President
Krishan Kant, Office of the Vice President

Prime Minister
Atal Bihari Vajpayee, Office of the Prime Minister, 3 Race Course Road, New Delhi 110 001, India
PHONE: +91 (11) 3018939

Ministers

Minister of Agriculture
Nitish Kumar, Ministry of Agriculture

Minister of Chemicals and Fertilizers
Sukhdev Singh Dhindsa, Ministry of Chemicals and Fertilizers

Minister of Civil Aviation
Sharad Yadav, Ministry of Civil Aviation

Minister of Commerce and Industry
Murasoli Maran, Ministry of Commerce and Industry

Minister of Communications
Ram Vilas Paswan, Ministry of Communications

Minister of Consumer Affairs and Public Distribution
Shanta Kumar, Ministry of Consumer Affairs and Public Distribution

Minister of Culture, Youth Affairs and Sports
Uma Bharati, Ministry of Culture, Youth Affairs and Sports

Minister of Defense
George Fernandex, Ministry of Defense

Minister of Environment and Forests
T.R. Baalu, Ministry of Environment and Forests

Minister of External Affairs
Jaswant Singh, Ministry of External Affairs

Minister of Finance
Yashwant Sinha, Ministry of Finance

Minister of Food Processing
Syed Hussain, Ministry of Food Processing

Minister of Health and Family Welfare with Independent Charge
C.P. Thakur, Ministry of Health and Family Welfare with Independent Charge

Minister of Heavy Industry and Public Enterprises
Manohar Gajanan Joshi, Ministry of Heavy Industry and Public Enterprises

Minister of Home Affairs
Lal Krishna Advani, Ministry of Home Affairs

Minister of Human Resources Development
Murli Manohar Joshi, Ministry of Human Resources Development

Minister of Information and Broadcasting
Sushma Swaraj, Ministry of Information and Broadcasting

Minister of Mines and Minerals
Rita Verma, Ministry of Mines and Minerals

Minister of Non-Conventional Energy Sources
Arun Jaitley, Ministry of Non-Conventional Energy Sources

Minister of Labour and Employment
Satyanarayan Jatiya, Ministry of Labour and Employment

Minister of Law, Justice and Company Affairs
Arun Jaitlye, Ministry of Law, Justice and Company Affairs

Minister of State Parliamentary Affairs
Pramod Mahajan, Minister for Parliamentary Affairs

Minister of State
Faggan Singh Kuleste, Ministry of Parliamentary Affairs

Minister of Petroleum
Ram Naik, Ministry of Petroleum, Shastri Bhawan, New Delhi 110 001, India

Minister of Planning and Program Implementation
Bangaru Laxman, Ministry of Planning and Program Implementation

Minister of Power
Suresh Prabhu, Ministry of Power

Minister of Railways
Mamata Banerjee, Ministry of Railways

Minister of Rural Development
Venkaiah Naidu, Ministry of Rural Development

Minister of Science and Technology and Parliamentary Affairs
Pramod Mahajan, Ministry of Science and Technology and Parliamentary Affairs

Minister of Surface Transportation
Rajnath Singh, Ministry of Surface Transportation

Minister of Steel and Parliamentary Affairs
B.K. Tripath, Ministry of Steel and Parliamentary Affairs

Minister of Small Scale Industries, Agro and Rural Industries
Raje Vasundhara, Ministry of Small Scale Industries, Agro and Rural Industries

Minister of Textiles
Kanshi Ram Rana, Ministry of Textiles

Minister of Tourism
Ananth Kumar, Ministry of Tourism

Minister of Urban Development
Bandaru Dattatreya, Ministry of Urban Development

Minister of Social Justice and Empowerment
Maneka Gandhi, Ministry of Social Justice and Empowerment, A-4, Maharani Bagh, New Delhi 110 065, India
PHONE: +91 (11) 6840402
FAX: +91 (11) 6823144

Minister of Water Resources
Bijoya Chakravarty, Ministry of Water Resources

Secretary of Agriculture and Cooperation
Bhaskar Barua, Department of Agriculture and Cooperation
PHONE: +91 (11) 3382651
FAX: +91 (11) 3386004

Minister of Atomic Energy and Animal Husbandry
Atal Behari Vajpayee, Ministry of Atomic Energy and Animal Husbandry

Minister of Chemicals and Fertilizers and Food and Consumer Affairs
Sukhdev Singh Dhindsa, Ministry of Chemicals and Fertilizers and Food and Consumer Affairs

Minister of Civil Aviation
Sharad Yadav, Ministry of Civil Aviation

Minister of Chemicals and Fertilizers
Sukhdev Singh Dhindsa, Ministry of Chemicals and Fertilizers, Tughlak Road, New Delhi 110 001, India
PHONE: +91 (11) 3017105; 3017106
FAX: +91 (11) 3017102
E-MAIL: commerce@hub.nic.in

Minister of Civil Aviation
Sharad Yadav, Ministry of Civil Aviation, 16 Sati, 3rd Main Vyalikaval, Bangalore 560003, India
PHONE: +91 (80) 3310139
FAX: +91 (80) 3310070
E-MAIL: commerce@hub.nic.in

Minister of Commerce and Industry
Murasoli Maran, Ministry of Commerce and Industry, Udyog Bhavan, New Delhi 110 011, India
PHONE: +91 (11) 3015299; 3016917
FAX: +91 (11) 3014418
E-MAIL: commerce@hub.nic.in

Minister of Communications
Ram Vilas Paswan, Ministry of Communications

Minister of Consumer Affairs and Public Distribution
Kumar Shanta, Ministry of Consumer Affairs and Public Distribution

Minister of Culture, Youth Affairs and Sports
Pon Radhakrishnan, Ministry of Culture, Youth Affairs and Sports, Shastri Bhawan, Dr. Rajendra Prasad Road, New Delhi 110 001, India
PHONE: +91 (11) 3382897
FAX: +91 (11) 3387418

Minister of Defense
George Fernandes, Ministry of Defense, Krishna Menon Marg, New Delhi 110 011, India
PHONE: +91 (11) 3017172; 3016035
FAX: +91 (11) 3793397
E-MAIL: Ramesh@dhs.unv.ernet.in

Minister of Environment and Forests
T. R. Baalu, Ministry of Environment and Forests, Paryavaran Bhavan, CGO Complex, Lodhi Road, New Delhi 110 003, India
PHONE: +91 (11) 4361896
FAX: +91 (11) 3014418
E-MAIL: secy@envfor.delhi.nic.in

Minister of External Affairs with additional charge of Department of Electronics
Jaswant Singh, Ministry of External Affairs with additional charge of Department of Electronics

Minister of Finance
Yashwant Sinha, Ministry of Finance

Minister of Family Welfare
Ministry of Family Welfare, Nirman Bhawan, New Delhi 110 011, India
E-MAIL: cdireifw@mohfw.delhi.nic.in

Minister of Food Processing Industries
Ministry of Food Processing Industries, Panchseel Bhawan, August Kranti Marg, New Delhi 110 049, India
PHONE: +91 (11) 6493012; 6492476; 6492475
FAX: +91 (11) 6493228
E-MAIL: mofpi@hub.nic.in

Minister of Heavy Industries and Public Enterprises
Manohar Joshi, Ministry of Heavy Industries and Public Enterprises

Minister of Home Affairs
Lal Krishna Advani, Ministry of Home Affairs, North Block, Central Secretariat, New Delhi 110 001, India
PHONE: +91 (11) 3011011; 3010161
FAX: +91 (11) 3015750; 3017763

Minister of Human Resource Development
Murli Manohar Joshi, Ministry of Human Resource Development, Technology Bhawan, New Mehrauli Road, New Delhi 110 016, India

Minister of Information and Broadcasting with additional charge of Food Processing Industries
Sushma Swaraj, Ministry of Information and Broadcasting with additional charge of Food Processing Industries, Panchsheel Bhawan, August Kranti Marg, New Delhi 110 049, India
PHONE: +91 (11) 6493012; 6492476; 6492475
FAX: +91 (11) 6493228
E-MAIL: mofpi@hub.nic.in

Minister of Law, Justice and Company Affairs
Arun Jaitlye, Ministry of Law, Justice and Company Affairs, 4th Floor, A-Wing, Shastri Bhavan, New Delhi 110 001, India
PHONE: +91 (11) 3387557; 3384777; 3384617
FAX: +91 (11) 3384241; 3387259; 3382733
E-MAIL: lawmin@caselaw.delhi.nic.in

Minister of Labour
Satyanarayan Jatia, Ministry of Labour, Shram Shakti Bhawan, Rafi Marg, New Delhi 110 001, India
PHONE: +91 (11) 3001425
E-MAIL: labour@lisd.delhi.nic.in

Minister of Mines and Minerals
Sunder Lal Patwa, Ministry of Mines and Minerals

Minister of Petroleum and Natural Gas
Ram Naik, Ministry of Petroleum and Natural Gas, Government of India, New Delhi, 110 001, India
PHONE: +91 (11) 3381462

Minister of Power and Non-Conventional Energy Sources
Suresh Prabhu, Ministry of Power and Non-Conventional Energy Sources, Block-14, C.G.O. Complex, Lodhi Road, New Delhi 110 003, India
PHONE: +91 (11) 4361604
FAX: +91 (11) 4361604
E-MAIL: dirmnes@ren02.nic.in

Minister of Railways
Mamta Bannerjeeb, Ministry of Railways

Minister of Rural Development
Venkaiah Naidu, Ministry of Rural Development

Minister of Surface Transportation
Rajnath Singh, Ministry of Surface Transportation

Minister of Steel and Mines
B.K. Tripath, Ministry of Steel and Mines

Minister of Textiles
Kashiram Rana, Ministry of Textiles, Udyog Bhavan, New Delhi 110 011, India
PHONE: +91 (11) 3014069
FAX: +91 (11) 3013711/3013681
E-MAIL: dirmnes@ren02.nic.in

Minister of Tourism
Ministry of Tourism, 88 Janpath, New Delhi 110 011, India
PHONE: +91 (11) 3320342; 3320005; 3320109
FAX: +91 (11) 3320342
E-MAIL: newdelhi@tourisminindia.com

Minister of Tribal Affairs
Jual Oram, Ministry of Tribal Affairs

Minister of Urban Development
Bandaru Dattatreya, Ministry of Urban Development, Nirman Bhawan, Maulana Azad Road, New Delhi 110 011, India
PHONE: +91 (11) 3018495; 3019162; 3018998
FAX: +91 (11) 3019089
E-MAIL: secyurban@alpha.nic.in

Minister of Urban Unemployment and Poverty Alleviation
Satya Narayan Jatiya, Ministry of Urban Unemployment and Poverty Alleviation

Minister of Water Resources and Parliamentary Affairs
Pramod Mahajan, Ministry of Water Resources and Parliamentary Affairs, Arjun Charan Sethi, New Delhi 110 011, India
PHONE: +91 (11) 3717129
FAX: +91 (11) 3710253
E-MAIL: mowr@hub.nic.in

POLITICAL ORGANIZATIONS

Bharatiya Janata Party-BJP (Indian People's Party)

11 Ashoka Road, New Delhi 110 001, India
PHONE: +91 (11) 3382234; 3382235
FAX: +91 (11) 3782163
E-MAIL: bjpco@bjp.org
TITLE: Party President
NAME: Kushabhau Thakre

Ajeya Bharat Party

D-56 South Extension, New Delhi 110 001, India
PHONE: +91 (11) 4697410
E-MAIL: members@ajeyabharat.com
TITLE: Party President
NAME: Santosh Singh

Shiromani Akali Dal-SAD (Akali Religious Party)

All-India Anna Dravida Munnetra Kazagham-ADMK (All-India Anna Diravida Progressive Foundation)

275 Aavai Shanmugam Road, Chennai 600 014, India
TITLE: General Secretary
NAME: Jayaram Jayalalitha

Congress Party

TITLE: President
NAME: Sonia Gandhi

Dravida Munnetra Kazhagam (DMK)

Biju Janta Dal (BJD)

Samata Party-SAP (Equality Party)

NAME: George Fernandes

Haryana Vikas Party (HVP)

Lok Shakti (LS)

Marumalarchi Dravida Munnetra Kazhhagam (MDMK)

Pattali Makkal Katchi (PMK)

Shiva Sena (SS)

Mumbai 400 051, India
TITLE: General Secretary
NAME: Shivsenapramukh Balasaheb Thackeray

Trinamool Congress (TC)

Indian Union Muslim League (IUML)

Kerala Congress-Mani (KC-M)

NAME: K. M. Mani

Republican Party of India (RPI)

National Front/Left Front/United Front (NF)

All India Forward Block (AIFB)

TITLE: Chairman
NAME: Prem Dutta Paliwal

Asom Gana Parishad-AGP (Assam People's Council)

Bhartiya Kissan Kamagar Party

Communist Party of India (CPI)

NAME: Vinod Mishra

Communist Party of India (Marxist)

A. K. Gopalan Bhawan, 27-29 Bhai Vir Singh Marg, New Delhi 110 001, India
PHONE: +91 (11) 3344918
FAX: +91 (11) 3747483
E-MAIL: cpim@vsnl.com
TITLE: General Secretary
NAME: Harkishan Singh Surjeet

Communist Party of India Liberation

AU-90 Shakarpur, New Delhi 110 092, India
PHONE: +91 (11) 2221067
FAX: +91 (11) 2218248
E-MAIL: cpim@vsnl.com
TITLE: General Secretary
NAME: Dipankar Bhattacharya

Dravida Munnetra Kazhagam-DMK (Dravida Progressive Federation)

NAME: M. Karunanidhi

Humanist Party of India

Jammu and Kashmir National Conference (JKNC)

Janata Dal-JD (People's Party)

NAME: Laloo Prasad Yadav

People's Party, Ajit Singh faction

NAME: Ajit Singh

Revolutionary Socialist Party (RSP)

NAME: Tridip Chowdhury

Samajwadi Party-SP (Socialist Party)

18 Coppernicus Lane, New Delhi 110 001, India
PHONE: +91 (11) 3386842
FAX: +91 (11) 3382430
TITLE: President
NAME: Mulayam Singh Yadav

Tamil Maanila Congress (TMC)

8 Kalakshetra Avenue, Thiruvanmiyur, India
PHONE: +91 (44) 8583945; 8583940
E-MAIL: icmcomp@md2.vsnl.net.in
TITLE: President
NAME: G. K. Moopanar

Telugu Desam-TD (Telugu Land)

NAME: Chandrababu Naidu

Rashtriya Janata Dal-RJD (National People's Party)

Victory of India Party (VIP)

DIPLOMATIC REPRESENTATION

Embassies in India

Algeria
E-12/4, Vasant Vihar, New Delhi 110 001, India
PHONE: +91 (11) 6882014; 6883910; 6112249
FAX: +91 (11) 6882289

Australia
1/50-G Shantipath, Chanakyapuri, New Delhi 110 021, India
PHONE: +91 (11) 6888223; 6885556; 6885637
FAX: +91 (11) 6885199; 6887366; 6872228

Austria
EP-13 Chandergupta Marg, Chanakyapuri, New Delhi 110 021, India
PHONE: +91 (11) 6882014; 6883910; 6112249
FAX: +91 (11) 6886929

Bangladesh
56 Ring Road, Lajpat Nagar, New Delhi 110 024, India
PHONE: +91 (11) 6834668; 6839209; 6834065
FAX: +91 (11) 6839237; 6840596

Belgium
50 N Shanti Path, Chanakyapuri, New Delhi 110 021, India
PHONE: +91 (11) 608295; 608067; 607957
FAX: +91 (11) 6885821; 6889115

Brazil
8 Aurangazeb Road, New Delhi 110 011, India
PHONE: +91 (11) 3017301
FAX: +91 (11) 3793684

Brunei Darussalam
A-42 Vasant Vihar, Vasant Marg, New Delhi 110 059, India
PHONE: +91 (11) 6888341; 6881545
FAX: +91 (11) 6881808

Bulgaria
EP 16-17 Chandragupta Marg, Chanakyapuri, New Delhi 110 021, India
PHONE: +91 (11) 607413; 607716; 608048
FAX: +91 (11) 6876190

Canada
7/8 Shantipath, Chanakyapuri, New Delhi 110 021, India
PHONE: +91 (11) 6876500
FAX: +91 (11) 6870031; 6875387; 6876579

China
50-D Shantipath, Chanakyapuri, New Delhi 110 021, India
PHONE: +91 (11) 6871585; 6871586; 6871587
FAX: +91 (11) 6885486

Colombia
82-D Malacha Marg, Chanakyapuri, New Delhi 110 021, India
PHONE: +91 (11) 3012771; 3012773
FAX: +91 (11) 3792485

Democratic Republic of Congo
C-56 Panchsheel Enclave, New Delhi 110 017, India
PHONE: +91 (11) 6222796
FAX: +91 (11) 6227226

Croatia
70 Ring Road, Lajpat Nagar-III, New Delhi 110 024, India
PHONE: +91 (11) 6924761; 6924762
FAX: +91 (11) 4924763

Cyprus
106 Jor Bagh, New Delhi 110 003, India
PHONE: +91 (11) 4697503; 4697508
FAX: +91 (11) 4628828

Czech Republic
50-M Niti Marg, Chanakyapuri, New Delhi 110 021, India
PHONE: +91 (11) 6110205; 6110318; 6110382
FAX: +91 (11) 6886221

Denmark
11 Aurangzeb Road, New Delhi 110 011, India
PHONE: +91 (11) 3010900
FAX: +91 (11) 3010961; 3011502

Egypt
1/50-M Niti Marg, Chanakyapuri, New Delhi 110 021, India
PHONE: +91 (11) 6114096; 6114097
FAX: +91 (11) 6885355

Ethiopia
7/50-G Satya Marg, Chanakyapuri, New Delhi 110 021, India
PHONE: +91 (11) 6119513; 6119514; 6884931

European Community
65 Golf Links, New Delhi 110 003, India
PHONE: +91 (11) 4629237; 4629238
FAX: +91 (11) 4629206; 6875731

Finland
E-3 Nyaya Marg, Chanakyapuri, New Delhi 110 021, India
PHONE: +91 (11) 6115258; 6118096
FAX: +91 (11) 6886713; 6885380

France
2/50-E Shantipath, Chanakyapuri, New Delhi 110 021, India
PHONE: +91 (11) 6118790
FAX: +91 (11) 6872305; 6872306

Germany
No. 6 Block 50-G, Shantipath, Chanakyapuri, New Delhi 110 021, India
PHONE: +91 (11) 6873117

Ghana
50-N Satya Marg, Chanakyapuri, New Delhi 110 021, India
PHONE: +91 (11) 6883315; 6883298
FAX: +91 (11) 6883202

Greece
6 Sundar Nagar, Chanakyapuri, New Delhi 110 021, India
PHONE: +91 (11) 4617800
FAX: +91 (11) 4601363

Hungary
2/50-M Niti Marg, Chanakyapuri 110 021, India
PHONE: +91 (11) 4617800
FAX: +91 (11) 6886742

Indonesia
50-A, Chanakyapuri, New Delhi 110 021, India
PHONE: +91 (11) 6118642; 6118643; 6118644
FAX: +91 (11) 6874402; 6886763

Iran
5 Barakhamba Road, New Delhi 110 001, India
PHONE: +91 (11) 4617800
FAX: +91 (11) 3325493

Iraq
169-171 Jor Bagh, New Delhi 110 003, India
PHONE: +91 (11) 4618011; 4618012
FAX: +91 (11) 4631547

Ireland
230 Jor Bagh, New Delhi 110 003, India
PHONE: +91 (11) 4626733; 4626741; 4626743
FAX: +91 (11) 4697053

Israel
3 Aurangzeb Road, New Delhi 110 011, India
PHONE: +91 (11) 3013238
FAX: +91 (11) 3014298

Italy
50-E Chandragupta Marg, Chanakyapuri, New Delhi 110 021, India
PHONE: +91 (11) 6114355; 6114359; 6114353
FAX: +91 (11) 6873889

Japan
50-G Shantipath, Chanakyapuri, New Delhi 110 021, India
PHONE: +91 (11) 6876581; 6876582; 6876564
FAX: +91 (11) 6885587

Jordan
1/21 ShantiNiketan, New Delhi 110 021, India
PHONE: +91 (11) 6889857; 6889733
FAX: +91 (11) 6883763

Kazakhstan
EP 16-17 Chandragupta Marg, Chanakyapuri, New Delhi 110 021, India
PHONE: +91 (11) 6888252; 6881461
FAX: +91 (11) 6888464

Kenya
66 Vasant Marg, Vasant Vihar, New Delhi 110 057, India
PHONE: +91 (11) 6876538; 6876539; 6876540
FAX: +91 (11) 6876550

North Korea
H-1 Maharani Bagh, New Delhi 110 065, India
PHONE: +91 (11) 6829644; 6829645; 6466357
FAX: +91 (11) 6466357

Kuwait
5-A Shantipath, Chanakyapuri, New Delhi 110 021, India
PHONE: +91 (11) 600791; 600972
FAX: +91 (11) 6873516

Lebanon
10 Sardar patel Marg, New Delhi 110 021, India
PHONE: +91 (11) 3013174; 3013637
FAX: +91 (11) 3015555

Libya
22 Golf Links, New Delhi 110 003, India
PHONE: +91 (11) 4697717; 4697771; 4698027
FAX: +91 (11) 4633005

Malaysia
50-M Satya Marg, Chanakyapuri, New Delhi 110 021, India
PHONE: +91 (11) 601291; 601292; 601296
FAX: +91 (11) 6881538

Mauritius
5 Kautilya Marg, Chanakyapuri, New Delhi 110 021, India
FAX: +91 (11) 3019925

Mexico
10 Jor Bagh, New Delhi 110 003, India
PHONE: +91 (11) 4697991; 4697992; 4615128
FAX: +91 (11) 4692360

Myanmar
3/50F Nyaya Marg, Chanakyapuri, New Delhi 110 021, India
PHONE: +91 (11) 6889007; 6889008
FAX: +91 (11) 6877942

Namibia
D-6/ 24, Vasant Vihar, New Delhi 110 003, India
PHONE: +91 (11) 6110389; 6110309; 6114772
FAX: +91 (11) 6116120

Nepal
Barakhamba Road, New Delhi 110 001, India
PHONE: +91 (11) 3329969; 3327361; 3329218
FAX: +91 (11) 3326857

Netherlands
6/50 F Shantipath, Chanakyapuri, New Delhi 110 021, India
PHONE: +91 (11) 6884951; 6884952; 6884953
FAX: +91 (11) 6884956

New Zealand
50-N Nyaya Marg, Chanakyapuri, New Delhi 110 021, India
PHONE: +91 (11) 6883170
FAX: +91 (11) 6872317

Norway
5 Shantipath, Chanakyapuri, New Delhi 110 021, India
PHONE: +91 (11) 6110389; 6110309; 6114772
FAX: +91 (11) 6873814

Oman
16 Olof Palam Marg, Vasant Vihar, New Delhi 110 057, India
PHONE: +91 (11) 670215; 674798; 671704
FAX: +91 (11) 6876478

Pakistan
2/50-G Shantipath, Chanakyapuri, New Delhi 110 021, India
PHONE: +91 (11) 600601; 600603; 600604
FAX: +91 (11) 687239

Philippines
50-N Nyaya Marg, Chanakyapuri, New Delhi 110 021, India
PHONE: +91 (11) 601120
FAX: +91 (11) 6866401

Poland
550-M Shantipath, Chanakyapuri, New Delhi 110 021, India
PHONE: +91 (11) 6889211; 608321
FAX: +91 (11) 6871914; 686604

Portugal
13 Sundar Nagar, New Delhi 110 003, India
PHONE: +91 (11) 4601262
FAX: +91 (11) 4601252

Qatar
G-5 Anand Niketan, New Delhi 110 021, India
PHONE: +91 (11) 6117241; 6117240
FAX: +91 (11) 6886080; 6882184

Romania
A-52 Vasant Marg, Vasant Vihar, New Delhi 110 057, India
PHONE: +91 (11) 6870447; 6870611; 6870700
FAX: +91 (11) 6870611

Russia
Shantipath, Chanakyapuri, New Delhi 110 021, India
PHONE: +91 (11) 6873799; 6873800; 6873802
FAX: +91 (11) 6886080; 6882184

Saudi Arabia
D-12 New Delhi South Extn., Chanakyapuri, New Delhi 110 049, India
PHONE: +91 (11) 6442471; 6445419
FAX: +91 (11) 6222790

Serbia
3/50 G Niti Marg, Chanakyapuri, New Delhi 110 021, India
PHONE: +91 (11) 6872073; 6873661
FAX: +91 (11) 6885535

Singapore
E-6 Chandergupta Marg, Chanakyapuri, New Delhi 110 021, India
PHONE: +91 (11) 6885659; 6886506; 6877939
FAX: +91 (11) 6886798

Slovakia
50-M Niti Marg, Chanakyapuri, New Delhi 110 021, India
PHONE: +91 (11) 6889071; 6885340; 6111075
FAX: +91 (11) 6877941

South Africa
B-18 Vasant Marg, Vasant Vihar, New Delhi 110 057, India
PHONE: +91 (11) 6119411; 6113505

Spain
512 Prithiviraj Road, New Delhi 110 011, India
PHONE: +91 (11) 63792085; 3792082; 3792074
FAX: +91 (11) 3753375

Sri Lanka
527 Kautilya Marg, Chanakyapuri, New Delhi 110 021, India
PHONE: +91 (11) 3010201; 3010202; 3010203
FAX: +91 (11) 3015295

Sweden
Nyaya Marg, Chanakyapuri, New Delhi 110 021, India
PHONE: +91 (11) 6875760; 608135
FAX: +91 (11) 6885401

Switzerland
28 Vasant Marg, Vasant Vihar, New Delhi 110 057, India
PHONE: +91 (11) 6878372; 6878373; 6878374
FAX: +91 (11) 6873093; 6112220

Syria
28 Vasant Vihar, New Delhi 110 057, India
PHONE: +91 (11) 670233; 670285
FAX: +91 (11) 6873107

Thailand
56-N Nyaya Marg, Chanakyapuri, New Delhi 110 021, India
PHONE: +91 (11) 605679; 6118103; 6118104
FAX: +91 (11) 6872029

Trinidad and Tobago
131 Jor Bagh, New Delhi 110 003, India
PHONE: +91 (11) 4618187
FAX: +91 (11) 4624581

Turkey
N-50 Nyaya Marg, Chanakyapuri, New Delhi 110 021, India
PHONE: +91 (11) 601921; 6889053; 6889054
FAX: +91 (11) 6881409

Uganda
B-3/26 Vasant Vihar, New Delhi 110 057, India
PHONE: +91 (11) 6874412; 6885817
FAX: +91 (11) 6874405

Ukraine
176 Jor Bagh, New Delhi 110 003, India
PHONE: +91 (11) 4616019; 4616086
FAX: +91 (11) 4616085; 4616087

United Arab Amirates
EP-12 Chandragupta Marg, Chanakyapuri, New Delhi 110 021, India
PHONE: +91 (11) 670830; 670945; 6872822
FAX: +91 (11) 6873272

United Kingdom
Shantipath, Chanakyapuri, New Delhi 110 021, India
PHONE: +91 (11) 6872161
FAX: +91 (11) 6872882

United States
Shantipath, Chanakyapuri, New Delhi 110 021, India
PHONE: +91 (11) 6889033
FAX: +91 (11) 6113933

Uzbekistan
D-4/6 Vasant Vihar, New Delhi 110 057, India
PHONE: +91 (11) 6119035; 6119036
FAX: +91 (11) 6873246

Zambia
F-8/22 Vasant Vihar, New Delhi 110 057, India
PHONE: +91 (11) 6877681; 6877848; 6877862
FAX: +91 (11) 6877928

JUDICIAL SYSTEM

Supreme Court

BROADCAST MEDIA

Prasar Bharati (All India Radio)

Directorate General of All India Radio, Akashvani Bhawan, I Sansad Marg, New Delhi 110 001, India
PHONE: +91 (11) 3715411; 3710006
FAX: +91 (11) 3711956
E-MAIL: air@kode.net, airlive@air.org.in
WEBSITE: http://www.air.kode.net
TITLE: Directorate General
CONTACT: O.P. Kejriwal
TYPE: Government, Commercial

Minstry of Information & Broadcasting

Main Secreteriat, A-Wing, Shastri Bhawan, New Delhi 110 001, India
TITLE: Minister for Information and Broadcasting
CONTACT: K. P. Singh Deo
TYPE: Information

Prasar Bharati Corporation of India

Mandi House, Copernicus Marg, New Delhi 110 001, India
PHONE: +91 (11) 3382094; 3382099
FAX: +91 (11) 3386507
TITLE: Chief Executive Officer
CONTACT: Surindar Singh Gill
TYPE: Public

Doordarshan India

Doordarshan Bhavan, Mandi House, Copernicus Marg, New Delhi 110 001, India
PHONE: +91 (11) 3382094; 3386507
FAX: +91 (11) 3386507
E-MAIL: Info@ddindia.net
WEBSITE: http://www.ddindia.net/
TITLE: Chief Executive Officer
CONTACT: Rajeeva Ratna Shah
TYPE: Commercial, Government

COLLEGES AND UNIVERSITIES

University of Delhi

Delhi 110 007, DH, India
PHONE: +91 (11) 7277011
FAX: +91 (11) 7257049
WEBSITE: http://www.du.ac.in

Jawaharlal Nehru University

New Mehrauli Rd., New Delhi 110 067, DH, India
PHONE: +91 (11) 6167557
FAX: +91 (11) 6198234
E-MAIL: adatta@jnuniv.ernet.in
WEBSITE: http://www.jnu.ac.in

Indira Gandhi National Open University

Maidan Garhi, New Delhi 110 068, DH, India
PHONE: +91 (11) 6865923
FAX: +91 (11) 6862312
E-MAIL: ignou@giasdl01.usnl.net.in
WEBSITE: http://www.india.edu

All India Institute of Medical Sciences

Ansari Nagar, New Delhi 110 029, DH, India
PHONE: +91 (11) 6864851
FAX: +91 (11) 6862663
E-MAIL: ragu@aiims.ac.in
WEBSITE: http://www.aiims.ac.in

Punjabi University

Patiala 147 002, PJ, India
PHONE: +91 (175) 822461
FAX: +91 (175) 822881
E-MAIL: reg.pup@pbi.ernet.in
WEBSITE: http://www.pbi.ernet.in

Chandra Shekhar Azad University

Nawabanj, Kanpur 208 002, UP, India

Kanpur University

Kalyanpur, Kanpur 208 024, UP, India

University of Lucknow

Canning College, University of Lucknow, Badshahbagh, Lucknow 226 001, UP, India

University of Bombay

University Rd., Fort City, Mumbai 400 032, MH, India

Nagpur University

Rabindranath Tagore Marg, Nagpur 440 001, MH, India

Barkatullah University

Hoshangabad Rd., Bhopal 462026, MP, India
PHONE: +91 (755) 782072
FAX: +91 (755) 581835
WEBSITE: http://www.bubhopal.org

Telugu University

Lalithakala Kshetram, Saroobagh, Public Gardens, Hyderabad, AP, India

Osmania University

Hyderabad 500 001, AP, India
PHONE: +91 (40) 7018951
FAX: +91 (40) 7019020
E-MAIL: osmanian@hdl.vsnl.net.in
WEBSITE: http://www.osmanian@hdl.vsnl.net.in

Jawaharlal Nehru Technological University

Hyderabad, Mahaveer Marg 500 028, AP, India
PHONE: +91 (40) 3391442
FAX: +91 (40) 3397648
WEBSITE: http://www.aselk.udel.edu/~jayanthi/jntu/jntu.html

Andhra Pradesh Agricultural University

Rajendranagar, Hyderabad 500 030, AP, India

University of Hyderabad

Central University P O, Hyderabad 500 046, AP, India
PHONE: +91 (40) 3010500
FAX: +91 (40) 3010145
E-MAIL: username@uohyd.ernet.in
WEBSITE: http://www.uohyd.ernet.in

Bangalore University

Jnana Bharathi, Bangalore 560 056, KA, India

Indian Institute of Science

Bangalore 560 012, KA, India
PHONE: +91 (80) 3344411
FAX: +91 (80) 3341683
E-MAIL: regr@admin.iisc.ernet.in
WEBSITE: http://www.iisc.ernet.in

University of Agricultural Sciences

G K V K Campus, Bangalore 560 065, KA, India
PHONE: +91 (80) 3332442
FAX: +91 (80) 3330277
E-MAIL: vc@uasbir.kar.nic.in
WEBSITE: http://apollo.ahabs.wisc.edu/individuals/students/dasika/uas.html

University of Mysore

Maharajas College, Mysore 570 005, KA, India
PHONE: +91 (821) 420677
FAX: +91 (821) 421263
E-MAIL: mul@nictos.ernet.in
WEBSITE: http://www.cs.purdue.edu/homes/sundaram/mysore.homepage/welcome.ht

University of Madras

University Centenary Building, Chepauk, Triplicane P O, Chennai 600 005, TN, India
PHONE: +91 (44) 568778
FAX: +91 (44) 566693
E-MAIL: regmu@unimad.ernet.in
WEBSITE: http://www.universityofmadras.edu

Anna University

Sardar Patel Rd., Guindy, Madras 600 025, TN, India
PHONE: +91 (44) 2351445
FAX: +91 (44) 2350397
E-MAIL: annalib@sirnetm-ernet.in
WEBSITE: http://www.annauniv.org

Jadavpur University

Calcutta 700 032, WB, India
PHONE: +91 (33) 4735508
FAX: +91 (33) 4736236
E-MAIL: bhaswati@tifrc3.tifr.res.in
WEBSITE: http://www.civeng.carleton.ca/~abagchi/ju/

Rabindra Bharati University

Emerald Bower Campus, 56-A Barrackpore Trunk Rd., Calcutta 700 050, WB, India

University of Calcutta

1 Senate House, 87 College St., Calcutta 700 073, WB, India

Gujarat University

Navrangpura, Ahmadabad 380 009, GJ, India
PHONE: +91 (79) 440341
FAX: +91 (79) 441654

NEWSPAPERS AND MAGAZINES

Ananda Bazar Patrika

Bappaditya Ray, 6 Prafulla Sarker St., Calcutta, West Bengal 700 001, India
PHONE: +91 (33) 274880; 278000
FAX: +91 (33) 303240; 303241
TITLE: Editor
CONTACT: K.L. Sarkar
CIRCULATION: 393,400

The Hindu

Kasturi & Sons Limited, Kasturi Blds, 859-860, Anna Salai, Chennai Tamil Nadu, 600 002, India
PHONE: +91 (44) 8413344

FAX: +91 (44) 8535325
E-MAIL: inetads@thehindu.co.in; thehindu@vsnl.com
WEBSITE: http://www.hinduonline.com/today
TITLE: Editor
CONTACT: N. Ravi
CIRCULATION: 682,118

Business Standard

Business Standard Ltd., 5, Pratap Bhavan, Bahadur Shah Zafar Marg., New Delhi 110 002, India
PHONE: +91 (11) 3720202; 3739840
FAX: +91 (11) 3720201
E-MAIL: editor@business-standard.com; advt@business-standard.com
WEBSITE: http://www.business-standard.com
TITLE: Editor
CONTACT: T.N. Ninan
CIRCULATION: 70,729

The Economic Times

Bennett Coleman & Co. Ltd., The Times of India Bldg., Dr. Dadabhoy Naoroji Rd., Mumbai Maharashtra 400 001, India
PHONE: +91 (22) 2620085; 2693916
FAX: +91 (22) 2659248; 2673145
E-MAIL: int.times@timesgroup.com; mala.biswas@timesgroup.com
WEBSITE: http://www.economictimes.com
TITLE: Editor
CONTACT: Swaminathan Aiyar
CIRCULATION: 336,059

The Financial Express

Indian Express Newspapers (Bombay) Ltd., Expres Towers, Znariman Pint, Mumbai Maharashtra 400 021, India
PHONE: +91 (22) 2022627
FAX: +91 (22) 2022139; 2044654
E-MAIL: oe.iemumbai@express.india.co.in
WEBSITE: http://www.expressindia.com
TITLE: Executive Editor
CONTACT: R. Jagannathan
CIRCULATION: 185,000

The Indian Express

Indian Express Newspapers (Bombay) Ltd., Expres Towers, Znariman Pint, Mumbai Maharashtra 400 021, India
PHONE: +91 (22) 2022627
FAX: +91 (22) 2022139; 2044654
E-MAIL: oe.iemumbai@express.india.co.in
WEBSITE: http://www.expressindia.com
TITLE: Editor
CONTACT: Shekhar Gupta
CIRCULATION: 667,706

Navbharat Times

Bennett Coleman & Co. Ltd., The Times of India Bldg., Dr. Dadabhoy Naoroji Rd., Mumbai Maharashtra 400 001, India
PHONE: +91 (22) 2620085; 2693916
FAX: +91 (22) 2659248; 2673145
E-MAIL: int.times@timesgroup.com; mala.biswas@timesgroup.com
TITLE: Editor
CONTACT: Vishwanath Sachdev
CIRCULATION: 418,461

The Times of India

Bennett Coleman & Co. Ltd., The Times of India Bldg., Dr. Dadabhoy Naoroji Rd., Mumbai Maharashtra 400 001, India
PHONE: +91 (22) 2620085; 2693916
FAX: +91 (22) 2659248; 2673145
E-MAIL: int.times@timesgroup.com; mala.biswas@timesgroup.com
WEBSITE: http://www.timesofindia.com
TITLE: Editor
CONTACT: Dileep Padgaonkar
CIRCULATION: 1,264,979

Hindustan

The Hindustan Times Ltd., Hindustan Times House, 18/20 kasturba, Gandhi Marg. New Dehli, 110 001, India
PHONE: +91 (11) 3318201
FAX: +91 (11) 3321189; 3313997
E-MAIL: htedo@giasi01.vsnl.net.in
WEBSITE: http://www.hindustantimes.com
TITLE: Editor
CONTACT: Alok Mehta
CIRCULATION: 255,284

The Hindustan Times

The Hindustan Times Ltd., Hindustan Times House, 18/20 Kasturba, Gandhi Marg. New Dehli, 110 001, India
PHONE: +91 (11) 3704590; 3710598
FAX: +91 (11) 3704551
E-MAIL: imd@hindustantimes.com
WEBSITE: http://www.hindustantimes.com
TITLE: Editor
CONTACT: V.N. Narayanan
CIRCULATION: 545,444

Delhi Punjab Kesari

The Hindu Samachar Ltd., Plot No. 2, Printing Press Complex, Near Wairpur DTC Depot, Delhi 110 052, India
PHONE: +91 (11) 7181133; 7187248; 7184619
FAX: +91 (11) 7182958; 7187700
TITLE: Editors
CONTACT: Vijay Kumar Chopra, Aninash Chopra
CIRCULATION: 318,446 (Daily); 498,174 (Sun)

The India Magazine

Business India Group, Wadia Bldg. 17/19 Dalal St., Fort, Mumbai 400 001, India
PHONE: +91 (22) 2674161; 2820179
FAX: +91 (22) 2673074; 2041974
TITLE: Editor
CONTACT: Kai Friese
CIRCULATION: 15,000
TYPE: Art and Culture

India Today Plus

Living Media India Ltd., 28 A&B, Jolly Maker Chambers II, Nariman Point, Mumbai 400 001, India
PHONE: +91 (22) 2026152
FAX: +91 (22) 2817397
E-MAIL: itgo@indi-today.com
WEBSITE: http://www.india-today.com
TITLE: Editor
CONTACT: Dilip Bobb
CIRCULATION: 82,384
TYPE: General Interest

Kadambini

The Hindustan Times Ltd., 18-20, Kasturba Gandhi Marg, New Delhi 110 001, India
PHONE: +91 (11) 3318201
FAX: +91 (11) 3321189; 3313997; 3351260
E-MAIL: execpres.di@thtl.springrpgemes.vsnl.net.in
TITLE: Editor
CONTACT: Rajendra Awasthy
CIRCULATION: 89,755
TYPE: General Interest

Kumudam

Kumudam Publications Pvt Ltd, 151, Purasawalkam High Rd., Post Box 1008, Madras Tamil Nadu 600 010, India
PHONE: +91 (44) 6422146; 6425516
FAX: +91 (44) 6425041
E-MAIL: kumudam@giasmd01.vsnl.net.in
WEBSITE: http://www.kumudam.com
TITLE: Editor
CONTACT: Jawahar Palaniappan
CIRCULATION: 495,472

Reader's Digest

RDI Print & Publishing Pte. Ltd., Orient House, Adi Marzban Path, Ballard Estate, Mumbai 400 001, India
PHONE: +91 (22) 2617291
FAX: +91 (22) 2613347
TITLE: Editor
CONTACT: Ashok Mahadevan
CIRCULATION: 379,000
TYPE: Compilation of articles

Chitralekha Gujarati

Chitralekha Group, 62, Vaju Kotak Marg, Fort, Mumbai 400 001, India
PHONE: +91 (22) 2614730
FAX: +91 (22) 2615895
E-MAIL: advertise@chitralekha.com
WEBSITE: http://www.chitralkha.com
TITLE: Editor
CONTACT: Madhuri Kotak
CIRCULATION: 296,721
TYPE: News Magazine

Chitralekha International

Chitralekha Group, 62, Vaju Kotak Marg, Fort, Mumbai 400 001, India
PHONE: +91 (22) 2614730
FAX: +91 (22) 2615895
E-MAIL: advertise@chitralekha.com
WEBSITE: http://www.chitralkha.com
TITLE: Editor
CONTACT: Madhuri Kotak
CIRCULATION: 25,000
TYPE: News Magazine

Chitralekha Marathi

Chitralekha Group, 62, Vaju Kotak Marg, Fort, Mumbai 400 001, India
PHONE: +91 (22) 2614730
FAX: +91 (22) 2615895
E-MAIL: advertise@chitralekha.com
WEBSITE: http://www.chitralkha.com
TITLE: Editor
CONTACT: Madhuri Kotak
CIRCULATION: 99,691
TYPE: News Magazine

India Today

Lioving Media Ltd., 28 A&B, Jolly Maker Chambers II, Nariman Point, Mumbai 400 021, India
PHONE: +91 (22) 2026152
FAX: +91 (22) 2817397
E-MAIL: itgo@india-today.com
WEBSITE: http://www.india-today.com
TITLE: Editor
CONTACT: Prabhu Chawla
CIRCULATION: 414,293
TYPE: News Magazine

India Today Gujurati

Lioving Media Ltd., 28 A&B, Jolly Maker Chambers II, Nariman Point, Mumbai 400 021, India
PHONE: +91 (22) 2026152
FAX: +91 (22) 2817397
E-MAIL: itgo@india-today.com
WEBSITE: http://www.india-today.com
TITLE: Editor
CONTACT: Aroon Purie
CIRCULATION: 85,269
TYPE: News Magazine

India Today Hindi

Lioving Media Ltd., 28 A&B, Jolly Maker Chambers II, Nariman Point, Mumbai 400 021, India
PHONE: +91 (22) 2026152
FAX: +91 (22) 2817397
E-MAIL: itgo@india-today.com
WEBSITE: http://www.india-today.com
TITLE: Editor
CONTACT: Prabhu Chawla
CIRCULATION: 281,353
TYPE: News Magazine

India Today Malayalam

Lioving Media Ltd., 28 A&B, Jolly Maker Chambers II, Nariman Point, Mumbai 400 021, India
PHONE: +91 (22) 2026152
FAX: +91 (22) 2817397
E-MAIL: itgo@india-today.com
WEBSITE: http://www.india-today.com
TITLE: Editor
CONTACT: Prabhu Chawla
CIRCULATION: 93,958
TYPE: News Magazine

India Today Tamil

Lioving Media Ltd., 28 A&B, Jolly Maker Chambers II, Nariman Point, Mumbai 400 021, India
PHONE: +91 (22) 2026152
FAX: +91 (22) 2817397
E-MAIL: itgo@india-today.com
WEBSITE: http://www.india-today.com
TITLE: Editor
CONTACT: Prabhu Chawla
CIRCULATION: 95,341
TYPE: News Magazine

India Today Telugu

Lioving Media Ltd., 28 A&B, Jolly Maker Chambers II, Nariman Point, Mumbai 400 021, India
PHONE: +91 (22) 2026152
FAX: +91 (22) 2817397
E-MAIL: itgo@india-today.com
WEBSITE: http://www.india-today.com
TITLE: Editor
CONTACT: Prabhu Chawla
CIRCULATION: 80,651
TYPE: News Magazine

PUBLISHERS

Addison-Wesley (Singapore) Pte. Ltd., India Liaison Office

90 New Raidhani Enclave, Ground Fl., New Delhi 110 092, India
PHONE: +91 (11) 2059850
FAX: +91 (11) 2059852
E-MAIL: awindia@del2.vsnl.net.in
WEBSITE: http://www.pearsonedindia.com
TITLE: General Manager
CONTACT: Subroto Mozumdar
SUBJECTS: Biological Sciences, Chemistry, Business, Computer Science, Electronics, Engineering, English as a Second Language, Mathematics, Physics, Social Sciences
TOTAL PUBLISHED: 303 print

Affiliated East West Press Pvt. Ltd.

104 Nirmal Tower, 26 Barakhamba Rd., New Delhi 110 001, India
PHONE: +91 (11) 3315398; 3279113
FAX: +91 (11) 3260538
E-MAIL: aewp.newdel@axcess.net.in
TITLE: Man. Director
CONTACT: Kamil Malik
SUBJECTS: Aeronautics, Agriculture, Anthropology, Biological Sciences, Chemistry,

Engineering, Economics, Electronics, Mathematics, Physics, Women's Studies

Allied Publishers Pvt. Ltd.

13/14 Asaf Ali Rd., New Delhi 110 002, India
PHONE: +91 (11) 275001
FAX: +91 (11) 270366
E-MAIL: allied@delhi.axcess.net.in
TITLE: Man. Director
CONTACT: S. M. Sachdev
SUBJECTS: Agriculture, Economics, Education, Energy, Political Science, Government, Management

APH Publishing Corp.

5 Ansari Rd., Daryaganj, New Delhi 110 002, India
PHONE: +91 (11) 5100581; 5410924; 3285807
FAX: +91 (11) 3274050
TITLE: International Rights
CONTACT: S. B. Nangia
SUBJECTS: Agriculture, Archaeology, Architecture, Biography, Business, Engineering, Criminology, Education, Energy, Environmental Sciences, Fiction, Political Science, Health, History, Labor, Law, Philosophy, Science, Hinduism, Islam, Social Sciences
TOTAL PUBLISHED: 1,200 print

Asian Educational Services

31 Hauz Khas Village, PO Box 4534, New Delhi 110 016, India
PHONE: +91 (11) 6560187; 6568594
FAX: +91 (11) 6852805; 6855499
E-MAIL: asianeds@nda.vsnl.net.in
WEBSITE: http://www.aes-books.com
TITLE: Publisher
CONTACT: Jagdish Jetley
SUBJECTS: Anthropology, Archaeology, Art, Folklore, History, Comparative Religions, Hinduism, Buddhism, Mythology, Philosophy, Numismatics, Travels & Exploration
TOTAL PUBLISHED: 100 print

S. Chand & Co. Ltd.

Ram Nagar, PO Box 5733, New Delhi 110 055, India
PHONE: +91 (11) 7772080
FAX: +91 (11) 7777446
E-MAIL: schand@schand.com
TITLE: Man. Director, Editorial & Publishing
CONTACT: Rajendra Kumar Gupta
SUBJECTS: Art, Business, Economics, Political Science, Medicine, Nursing, Dentistry, Philosophy, Science (General), Social Sciences, Technology

Chowkhamba Sanskrit Series Office

K-37/99 Gopal Mandir Lane, PO Box 1008, Varanasi 221 001, India
PHONE: +91 (542) 335020
TITLE: Man. Director, Publicity
CONTACT: Brajmohan Das Gupta
SUBJECTS: Anthropology, Archaeology, Architecture, Art, Asian Studies, Occult, Biography, Economics, Geography, Health, History, Philosophy, Religion
TOTAL PUBLISHED: 330 print

Cosmo Publications

24-B Ansari Rd. Daryaganj, New Delhi 110002, India
PHONE: +91 (11) 3278779; 3280455
FAX: +91 (11) 3274597
E-MAIL: genesis.cosmo@axcess.net.in
TITLE: Chief Editor & Sales Director
CONTACT: Subodh Kapoor
SUBJECTS: Agriculture, Anthropology, Archaeology, Art, Asian Studies, Occult, Business, Education, History, Language Arts, Literature, Hinduism, Islam, Social Sciences, Science (General)
TOTAL PUBLISHED: 850 print

DK Print World (P) Ltd.

H-12 Bali Nagar, New Delhi 110 015, India
PHONE: +91 (11) 5453975; 5466019
FAX: +91 (11) 5465926
E-MAIL: dkprint@4mis.com
TITLE: Director
CONTACT: Susheel K. Mittal
SUBJECTS: Archaeology, Art, Asian Studies, Theater, History, Dance, Music, Philosophy, Buddhism, Hinduism, Islam
TOTAL PUBLISHED: 105 print

Eastern Book Co.

34 Lalbagh, Lucknow 226001, India
PHONE: +91 (552) 214218
FAX: +91 (11) 224328
E-MAIL: ebc@poboxes.com
WEBSITE: http://www.ebcindia.com
TITLE: Chief Executive
CONTACT: P. L. Malik
SUBJECTS: Law
TOTAL PUBLISHED: 1,200 print; 1 CD-ROM

Indian Council of Social Science Research (ICSSR)

35 Feroz Shah Rd., New Delhi 110 001, India
PHONE: +91 (11) 3385959
FAX: +91 (11) 3381571
E-MAIL: nassdoc@delnet.ernet.in
TITLE: Chief Executive
CONTACT: R. Barman
SUBJECTS: Social Science, Sociology
TOTAL PUBLISHED: 500 print

Indus Publishing Co.

FS-5 Tagore Garden, New Delhi 110 027, India
PHONE: +91 (11) 5151333
FAX: +91 (11) 5449682
E-MAIL: indusbuk@del3.vsnl.net.in
CONTACT: M. L. Gidwani
SUBJECTS: Environmental Studies, History, Natural History, Buddhism, Hinduism, Social Sciences, Travel, Himalayan Studies, Mountaineering
TOTAL PUBLISHED: 200 print

Jaico Publishing House

121-125 Mahatma Gandhi Rd., Bombay 400 023, India
PHONE: +91 (22) 2676702; 2676802
FAX: +91 (11) 2041673
E-MAIL: jaicopub@giosbm01.vsnl.net.in
TITLE: Man. Director
CONTACT: Ashwin J. Shah
SUBJECTS: Occult, Behavioral Sciences, Biography, Cookery, Criminology, Economics, Engineering (General), Political Science, Health, Law, Philosophy, Religion, Self-Help

B. Jain Publishers (P) Ltd.

1921 10th St., Chuna Mandi, Pahar Ganj, New Delhi 110 055
PHONE: +91 (11) 7770430; 7770572; 7536418
FAX: +91 (11) 7510471; 7536420
E-MAIL: bjain@giasdlol.vsnl.net.in
WEBSITE: http://www.bjain.com
TITLE: Man. Director
CONTACT: Premnath Jain
SUBJECTS: Health, Nutrition, Medicine, Nursing, Dentistry, Buddhism, Hinduism
TOTAL PUBLISHED: 1, 175 print

Marg Publications

3rd Floor, Army & Navy Bldg., 148 Mahatma Gandhi Rd., Bombay 400 023, India
PHONE: +91 (22) 2821151
FAX: +91 (22) 2047102
E-MAIL: margpub@bom5.vsnl.net.in
WEBSITE: http://www.tata.com/marg
TITLE: Publisher
CONTACT: J. J. Bhabha
SUBJECTS: Indian art, paintings, sculpture, dance & architecture
TOTAL PUBLISHED: 285 print

Munshiram Manoharlal Publishers Pvt. Ltd.

54 Rani Jhansi Rd., PO Box 5715, New Delhi 110 055, India
PHONE: +91 (11) 7773650
FAX: +91 (11) 7512745
E-MAIL: mrmlpub.mrml@axcess.net.in
TITLE: Editorial Director
CONTACT: Devendra Jain
SUBJECTS: Anthropology, Archaeology, Architecture, Art, Asian Studies, Occult, Theater, History, Language Arts, Music, Dance, Philosophy, Islam, Hinduism

Orient Longman Ltd.

3-6-172 Himayat Nagar, Nadhra Pradesh, Hyderabad 500 029, India
PHONE: +91 (40) 3224305; 3224294; 3220306; 3220389; 3224391; 3225297
FAX: +91 (11) 3222900
E-MAIL: orlongco@hd2.dot.net.in
TITLE: Working Director
CONTACT: Nandini Rao
SUBJECTS: Biography, Business, Child Care, Engineering, Sciences, Computer Sciences, Cookery, Electronics, Environmental Studies, Fiction, English as a Second Language, History, Literature, Medicine, Nonfiction (General), Philosophy, Hinduism
TOTAL PUBLISHED: 4,000 print

Orient Paperbacks

1590 Madarsa Rd. Cashmere Gate, New Delhi 110 006, India
PHONE: +91 (11) 2962267; 2962201
FAX: +91 (11) 2962935
E-MAIL: orientpbk@ndb.vsnl.in
TITLE: Man. Director
CONTACT: Vishwa Nath
SUBJECTS: Occult, Business, Career Development, Cookery, Games, Theater, Fiction, Health, Nutrition, How-To, Humor, Nonfiction (General), Self-Help, Sports
TOTAL PUBLISHED: 500 print

Oxford University Press

2/11 Ansari Rd., Daryaganj, PO Box 7035, New Delhi 110 002, India
PHONE: +91 (11) 2021029; 2021198; 2021396
FAX: +91 (11) 3732312; 3360897
E-MAIL: ibho@oup.wiprobt.ems.vsnl.net.in
TITLE: Man. Director
CONTACT: Manzar Khan
SUBJECTS: Biography, Business, Developing Countries, Economics, History, Literature, Essays, Natural History, Philosophy, Hinduism, Politics, Ecology, Science, Medicine

Pointer Publishers

1-Gha-22 Jawahar Nagar, Jaipur 302 004, India
PHONE: +91 (141) 568159
FAX: +91 (141) 362000
TITLE: Manager
CONTACT: Vipin Jain
SUBJECTS: Agriculture, Business, Biological Sciences, Child Care, Education, Environmental Studies, Political Science, Literature, Social Sciences, Women's Studies
TOTAL PUBLISHED: 200 print

Pustak Mahal

10-B, Netaji Subhash Marg, Daryaganj, New Delhi 110 002, India
PHONE: +91 (11) 3276539; 3272783; 3272784
FAX: +91 (11) 3260518; 2924673
E-MAIL: delaad37@giasd101.vsnl.net.in
TITLE: Marketing & Publishing Director
CONTACT: Vikas Gupta
SUBJECTS: Architecture, Occult, Biography, Computer Science, Cookery, Crafts, Games, Health, History, House & Home, Language Arts, Music, Dance, Medicine, Science (General)

Regency Publications

20/36-G Old Market, West Patel Nagar, New Delhi 110 008, India
PHONE: +91 (11) 5712539; 5740038
FAX: +91 (11) 5783571
E-MAIL: info@regencypublications.com
WEBSITE: regencypublications.com
TITLE: Owner
CONTACT: Arun Verma
SUBJECTS: Agriculture, Archaeology, Art, Fiction, History, Religion, Social Sciences, Sports, Athletics, Women's Studies
TOTAL PUBLISHED: 110 print

Reliance Publishing House

3026/7-H Ranjit Nagar, New Delhi 110 008, India
PHONE: +91 (11) 5722605; 5786889
FAX: +91 (11) 5737377; 5772748
E-MAIL: S. K. Bhatia
TITLE: Man. Director
CONTACT: Dr. S. K. Bhatia
SUBJECTS: Agriculture, Business, Anthropology, Architecture, Asian Studies, Behavioral Science, Child Care, Criminology, Special Needs, Education, Energy, Environmental Studies, Political Science, Journalism, Literature, Science, Buddhism, Women's Studies, Technology
TOTAL PUBLISHED: 375 print; 4 online; 4 internet

Roli Books Pvt. Ltd.

M-75 Greater Kailash - 2 Market, New Delhi 110 048, India
PHONE: +91 (11) 6460886; 6462782; 6442271
FAX: +91 (11) 6467185; 6213978
E-MAIL: roli@vsnl.com
WEBSITE: http://www.rolibooks.com
CONTACT: Pramod Kapoor
SUBJECTS: Animals, Pets, Cookery, Fiction, History, Travel
TOTAL PUBLISHED: 122 print; 122 online; 4 audio

SABDA

Sri Aurobindo Ashram, Pondicherry 605 002, India
PHONE: +91 (413) 342376
FAX: +91 (11) 223328
E-MAIL: sabda@auroville.org.in
WEBSITE: http://www.miraura.org/sabda
TITLE: Manager
CONTACT: Mira Gupta
SUBJECTS: Education, Political Science, Literature, Literary Criticism, Essays, Philosophy, Poetry, Psychology, Psychiatry, Social Sciences
TOTAL PUBLISHED: 700 print

Sage Publications Pvt. Ltd.

32 M-Block Market, Greater Kailash-I, PO Box 4215, New Delhi 110 006, India
PHONE: +91 (11) 6485884; 6444958; 6453915
FAX: +91 (11) 6472426
E-MAIL: sageind@nda.vsnl.net.in
TITLE: Man. Director
CONTACT: Tejeshwar Singh

SUBJECTS: Anthropology, Asian Studies, Behavioral Sciences, Business, Communications, Developing Countries, Economics, Environmental Studies, Political Science, Social Sciences, Women's Studies
TOTAL PUBLISHED: 500 print

Scientific Publishers

Maan Bhawan, Ratanda Rd., Jodhpur 342 001, India
PHONE: +91 (986) 30712; 33323
FAX: +91 (986) 613480
E-MAIL: amrish@jpl.dot.net.in
TITLE: Man. Director, Editorial
CONTACT: Pawan Kumar
SUBJECTS: Agriculture, Biological Sciences, Engineering (General), Natural History, Social Sciences, Sociology
TOTAL PUBLISHED: 325 print

Sita Publications

308 Arjun Centre, Bombay 400 088, India
PHONE: +91 (22) 5555589
FAX: +91 (22) 5561622
E-MAIL: ssrao@bom5.vsnl.net.in
CONTACT: S. S. Rao
SUBJECTS: Aeronautics, Business, Agriculture, Architecture, Automotive, Biology, Chemistry, Engineering, Child Care, Education, Electronics, Energy, Environmental Studies, Labor, Literature, Mathematics, Technology, Science

Somaiya Publications Pvt. Ltd.

Bank Baroda Bldg., 6th Fl., Parliament St., New Delhi 110 001, India
PHONE: +91 (11) 440030; 3324939; 3324973
FAX: +91 (11) 3723351
E-MAIL: mridughar@bol.net.in
WEBSITE: www.somaiya.com
TITLE: Chairman
CONTACT: S. K. Somaiya
SUBJECTS: Agriculture, Anthropology, Asian Studies, Occult, Behavioral Sciences, Business, Communications, Special Needs, Education, Engineering, Fiction, History, Journalism, Political Science, Nonfiction (General), Hinduism, Technology
TOTAL PUBLISHED: 300 print

Star Publications

4/5B Asaf Ali Rd., New Delhi 110 002, India
PHONE: +91 (11) 3268651; 3261696
FAX: +91 (11) 3273335; 6481565
E-MAIL: del.starpub@axcess.net.in
TITLE: Director
CONTACT: Sunil Varma
SUBJECTS: Crafts, Games, Hobbies, English as a Second Language, Language Arts, Linguistics, Hinduism
TOTAL PUBLISHED: 600 print; 50 audio

Theosophical Publishing House

Adyar c/o Theosophical Society, Madras 600 020, India
PHONE: +91 (44) 4911338
FAX: +91 (44) 4901399; 4902706
E-MAIL: para.vidya@gems.vsnl.net.in
TITLE: Manager
CONTACT: D. K. Govindaraj
SUBJECTS: Biography, History, Human Relations, Mysteries, Parapsychology, Philosophy, Science (General), Religion, Theology
TOTAL PUBLISHED: 291 print

Vision Books Pvt. Ltd.

24 Feroze Gandhi Rd., Lajpat Nagar-III, New Delhi 110 024, India
PHONE: +91 (11) 2962267; 2962201
FAX: +91 (11) 2962935
E-MAIL: orienpbk@ndb.vsnl.net.in
TITLE: Man. Director
CONTACT: Sudhir Malhotra
SUBJECTS: Anthropology, Cookery, Education, Fiction, Health, Nutrition, History, How-To, Management, Medicine, Military Science, Religion, Travel, Career Guides
TOTAL PUBLISHED: 600 print

RELIGIOUS ORGANIZATIONS

Baha'I

National Spiritual Assembly-India
Baha'I House, 6 Canning Rd., PO Box 19, New Dehli 110 001, Delhi, India
PHONE: +91 (11) 3386458
FAX: +91 (11) 3782178
TITLE: Executive Secretary
NAME: A. K. Merchant

Buddhist

All Assam Buddhist Association
Desangpani Buddhist Temple, Sibsagar, Assam, India

Bhikkhu Sangha's United Buddist Mission
Sarvodaya Buddha Vihar, Opp, Kurla, Kurla Railway Terminus, Tilak Nagar Chembur Bombay 400089, India
PHONE: +91 (22) 5220738

FAX: +91 (22) 5220738
E-MAIL: rahulbodhi@hotmail.com
WEBSITE: http://www.chembur.com/bodhi/
TITLE: Chief Monk
NAME: Ven. Bhadant Rahula Bodhi Maha Thera, B. com, M.A.

Bir Sakya Lama's School
PO Chowgan, Via Bir, Mandi District, Himachal Pradesh
TITLE: Abbot
NAME: HH The Sakya Trizin

Daijokyo Japanese Monastery
Bodhgaya, India
PHONE: +91 (631) 400747

The Friends of the Western Buddhist Order (FWBO)-Bombay
TBMSG, 25 Bhimprarana, Tapodan Nagar, Bandra (E), Bombay 40051, India
PHONE: +91 (22) 6441156

The Friends of the Western Buddhist Order (FWBO)-Poona

Bhaja Retreat Centre
TBMSG, Dhammachakra Pravartana Mahavira, Raja Harishchandra Road, Dapodi, Poona 411012, Maharashtra, India

The International Meditation Centre
BPO Bodh-Gaya 82423I, Gaya District, Bihar, India
TITLE: Abbot
NAME: Ven. Dr. Rastrapal, Mahathera

Mahabodi International Meditation Centre (MIMC)-Dehli
A-116, 2nd Floor, Arjun Nagar, Safdarjung Enclave, New Delhi, 110001, India
PHONE: +91 (11) 6165017
FAX: +91 (11) 6162978; 6164444
E-MAIL: mahabodhi@geocities.com
WEBSITE: http://www.geocities.com/Tokyo/Harbor/5613/index.html

Mahabodhi Society-Bangalore
14, Kalidasa Road, Gandhinagar, Bangalore 560009, India
PHONE: +91 (80) 2250684
FAX: +91 (80) 2264438
E-MAIL: mahabodhi@vsnl.com
WEBSITE: http://www.education.vsnl.com/mahabodhi/

Mahabodhi Society-Calcutta
4a Bankim Chatterjee Street, College Square, Calcutta 700 073, WB, India
PHONE: +91 (32) 3591

Mahabodhi Society-Delhi
Mandir Marg, New Delhi, India

Root Institute
PO Bodhgaya Gaya District, Bihar 824 321, India
PHONE: +91 (6 31) 400714
FAX: +91 (6 31) 444548
E-MAIL: simmons@del2.vsnl.net.in
WEBSITE: http://www.rootinstitute.com
TITLE: Director
NAME: Tony Simmons

Tushita Mahayana Meditation Centre-New Dehli
9 Padmini Enclave, Hauz Khas, New Delhi 110 016, India
PHONE: +91 (11) 6513400
FAX: +91 (11) 4692963
E-MAIL: renukas@del2.vsnl.net.in

Vietnam Buddhist Monastery
PO Buddha Gaya, P.C. 824231, Gaya District, Bihar, India
PHONE: +91 (63) 1400733
E-MAIL: haosen@ins.net
WEBSITE: http://www.saigon.com/-haosen

Vipassana International Academy-Dhammagiri
Dhamma Giri, PO Box 6, Igatpuri 422 403, Nasik District, Maharashtra, India
PHONE: +91 (25) 5384076; 5384086; 5384302
FAX: +91 (25) 5384176
E-MAIL: dhgiri.vri@axcess.net.in
WEBSITE: http://www.dhamma.org/india.htm

Catholic

Asian Liturgy Forum (ALF)
Kristu Joyu College, Bangalore 560 036, Mysore, India
NAME: Rev. Paul Puthanangady

Congregation of the Sisters of the Adoration of the Blessed Sacrament (SABS)
Adoration Generalate, Cenacle, Alwaye 683 102, Kerala, India
PHONE: +91 (484) 670166
FAX: +91 (484) 671166
TITLE: Superior General
NAME: Mother Theda

Hindu

Ananda Marga Pracarka Samgha
Eastern Metropolis Bypass, Tiljala, Calcutta 700 039, W. Bengal, India
PHONE: +91 (33) 3434651

FAX: +91 (33) 3434237
NAME: Acarya Mantreshvarananda Avadhuta

Ananda Marga Yoga Society (AMYS)
527 VP Nagar, Eastern Metropolis Bypass, Toljala, Calcutta 700 039, W. Bengal, India
E-MAIL: ampsentral@amps.org

Sri Ianganathaswami Temple
Srirangam, 620 006, India
WEBSITE: : http://www.srirangamtemple.org/
TITLE: Joint Commisioner, Executive Officer
NAME: Sri. R. Muthusamy

Islamic

Col. Fayazuddin Muslim Charitable Society of India
Fayazuddin, M., C.F.M.C.S.I., c/o Bhartiya Net, 253 Lekhraj Market III, Indira Nagar, Lucknow 226016, India
E-MAIL: colmf@bhartiyanet.com
TITLE: Chaiman
NAME: Colonel Mir Fayazuddin

Islamic Research Foundation
56/58 Tandel Street (North), Dongri, Mumbai, 400 009 India
PHONE: +91 (22) 3736875
FAX: +91 (22) 3730689
E-MAIL: zakir@irf.net
WEBSITE: : http://www.irf.net
NAME: Dr. Zakir Abdul-Karim Naik

Jewish

Chabad India
302 Hotel Ago Rama, 298 Main, Bazar Pahar Ganj, New Delhi 110055, India
PHONE: +91 (11) 3521413; 7529293
FAX: +91 (11) 7532795
E-MAIL: info@cabad-india.com
WEBSITE: http://www.chabad-india.com

Protestant

Lutheran World Services-India (LWSI)
84 Dr. Suresh Sarkar Roa, GPO Box 2313, Calcutta 700 014, W. Bengal, India
PHONE: +91 (33) 2440448
FAX: +91 (33) 2443062
E-MAIL: lws.cal@sml.sprintrpg.ens.vsnl.net.in
TITLE: Director
NAME: Rev. Morgens Jeppesen

Other Organizations

National Council of Churches in India
Christian Council Lodge, Civil Lines, PO Box 205, Nagpur 440 001, Maharashtra, India
PHONE: +91 (712) 531312
FAX: +91 (712) 520554
TITLE: General Secretary
NAME: Rev. Dr. Ipe Joseph

Theosophical Society (TS)
Adyar, Chennai 600 020, Tamil Nadu, India
PHONE: +91 (44) 4912815
FAX: +91 (44) 4902706
E-MAIL: para.vidya@gems.vsnl.net.in
NAME: Mrs. Radha Burnier, International

United Lodge of Theosophists-India (ULT)
Theosophy Hall, 40, New Marine Lines, Bombay 400 020, Maharashtra, India
PHONE: +91 (22) 2039024
E-MAIL: arsirkar@gems.vsnl.net.in
WEBSITE: http://www.blavatsky.net

FURTHER READING

Articles

"Carried Away: A Jungle-Dwelling Bandit Makes Off with a Beloved Indian Movie Star, Leaving His Anxious Fans Furious." *People Weekly,* October 2, 2000, vol. 54, no 14, p. 157+.

"Dam Dispute." *Newsweek International,* October 30, 2000, p. 5.

Dugger, Celia W. "Chidambaram Subramaniam, India's 'Green' Rebel, 90, Dies." *New York Times,* November 10, 2000, p. C20.

———. "India: 3 New States." *New York Times,* November 4, 2000, p. A7.

"Fatal Landslide in Bombay." *New York Times,* July 15, 2000, p. A2.

"India: National Dock Strike." *New York Times,* January 19, 2000, p. A6.

"India's Nuclear Dilemmas." *The Economist (US),* November 4, 2000, vol. 357, no. 8195, p. 45.

Books

Margolis, Eric S. *War at the Top of the World: The Struggle for Afghanistan, Kashmir, and Tibet.* New York: Routledge, 2000.

INDIA: STATISTICAL DATA

For sources and notes see "Sources of Statistics" at the front of each volume.

GEOGRAPHY

Geography

Area:

Total: 3,287,590 sq km.

Land: 2,973,190 sq km.

Land boundaries:

Total: 14,103 km.

Border countries: Bangladesh 4,053 km, Bhutan 605 km, Burma 1,463 km, China 3,380 km, Nepal 1,690 km, Pakistan 2,912 km.

Coastline: 7,000 km.

Climate: varies from tropical monsoon in south to temperate in north.

Terrain: upland plain (Deccan Plateau) in south, flat to rolling plain along the Ganges, deserts in west, Himalayas in north.

Natural resources: coal (fourth-largest reserves in the world), iron ore, manganese, mica, bauxite, titanium ore, chromite, natural gas, diamonds, petroleum, limestone, arable land.

Land use:

Arable land: 56%

Permanent crops: 1%

Permanent pastures: 4%

Forests and woodland: 23%

Other: 16% (1993 est.).

HUMAN FACTORS

Demographics (A)

	1990	1995	1998	2000	2010	2020	2030	2040	2050
Population	NA	932	982	1,014	1,168	1,312	1,437	1,540	1,620
Life expectancy - males	NA	60.1	61.2	61.9	65.2	68.1	70.7	73.0	74.9
Life expectancy - females	NA	61.0	62.3	63.1	67.1	70.8	74.0	76.8	79.1
Birth rate (per 1,000)	NA	27.5	25.8	24.8	20.7	18.0	15.7	14.4	13.4
Death rate (per 1,000)	NA	9.7	9.2	8.9	7.9	7.6	7.8	8.4	9.2
Women of reproductive age (15-49 yrs.)	NA	229.4	245.1	256.0	306.2	341.5	366.1	373.9	373.6
Fertility rate	NA	3.4	3.2	3.1	2.5	2.3	2.1	2.0	2.0

Except as noted, values for vital statistics are in millions; life expectancy is in years.

Health Personnel

	National Data	World Data (wtd ave)
Total health expenditure as a percentage of GDP, 1990-1998[a]		
Public sector	0.6	2.5
Private sector	4.1	2.9
Total[b]	5.2	5.5
Health expenditure per capita in U.S. dollars, 1990-1998[a]		
Purchasing power parity	73	561
Total	18	483
Availability of health care facilities per 100,000 people		
Hospital beds 1990-1998[a]	80	330
Doctors 1992-1995[a]	48	122
Nurses 1992-1995[a]	NA	248

Health Indicators

	National Data	World Data
Life expectancy at birth (years)		
1980	54	61
1998	63	67
Daily per capita supply of calories		
1970	2,082	2,358
1997	2,495	2,791
Daily per capital supply of protein		
1997 (grams)	59	74
Total fertility rate (births per woman)		
1980	5.0	3.7
1998	3.0	2.7
Population with access (%)		
To safe water (1990-96)	81	NA
To sanitation (1990-96)	16	NA
People living with (1997)		
Tuberculosis (cases per 100,000)	118.3	60.4
Malaria (cases per 100,000)	275.3	42.2
HIV/AIDS (% aged 15 - 49 years)	0.82	0.99

Infants and Malnutrition

	National Data	World Data (wtd ave)
Under 5 mortality rate (1989)	105	NA
% of infants with low birthweight (1992-98)[1]	33	17
Births attended by skilled health staff (% of total births 1996-98)	35	52
% fully immunized at 1 year of age (1995-98)[1]		
TB	79	82
DPT	73	77
Polio	73	77
Measles	66	74
Prevalence of child malnutrition (1992-98)[1] (based on weight for age, % of children under 5 years)	NA	30

Ethnic Division

Indo-Aryan 72%
Dravidian 25%
Mongoloid and other 3%

Religion

Hindu 80.0%
Muslim 14.0%
Christian 2.4%
Sikh 2.0%
Buddhist 0.7%
Jains 0.5%
Other 0.4%

Major Languages

English enjoys associate status but is the most important language for national, political, and commercial communication, Hindi the national language and primary tongue of 30% of the people, Bengali (official), Telugu (official), Marathi (official), Tamil (official), Urdu (official), Gujarati (official), Malayalam (official), Kannada (official), Oriya (official), Punjabi (official), Assamese (official), Kashmiri (official), Sindhi (official), Sanskrit (official), Hindustani (a popular variant of Hindi/Urdu spoken widely throughout northern India). 24 languages each spoken by a million or more persons; numerous other languages and dialects, for the most part mutually unintelligible.

EDUCATION

Public Education Expenditures

	1980	1997
Public expenditures on education as % of GNP	3.0	3.2

	1980	1997
Expenditures per student as % of GNP per capita		
Primary & Secondary	10.5[2]	11.4
Tertiary	88.2	99.8
Pupils per teacher at the primary level	NA	64
Duration of primary education in years	NA	8

World data for comparison		
Public expenditures on education as % of GNP (mean)	3.9	4.8
Pupils per teacher at the primary level (wtd ave)	NA	33
Duration of primary education in years (mean)	NA	9

(Continued on next page.)

GOVERNMENT & LAW

Military Affairs (A)

	1990	1992	1995	1996	1997
Military expenditures					
Current dollars (mil.)	6,540	6,320	7,890	10,100	10,900
1997 constant dollars (mil.)	7,650	7,010	8,170	10,300	10,900
Armed forces (000)	1,260	1,260	1,260	1,260	1,260
Gross national product (GNP)					
Current dollars (bil.)	225	251	328	360	388
1997 constant dollars (bil.)	264	278	340	366	388
Central government expenditures (CGE)					
1997 constant dollars (bil.)	58	57	65	70	76
People (mil.)	855.6	883.1	933.3	950.2	967.1
Military expenditure as % of GNP	2.9	2.5	2.4	2.8	2.8
World data on military expenditure as % of GNP	4.5	3.4	2.7	2.6	2.6
Military expenditure as % of CGE	13.2	12.4	12.7	14.7	14.3
World data on military expenditure as % of CGE	17.0	12.5	10.5	10.3	10.2
Military expenditure per capita (1997 $)	9	8	9	11	11
World data on military expenditure per capita (1997 $)	242	173	146	143	145
Armed forces per 1,000 people (soldiers)	1.5	1.4	1.4	1.3	1.3
World data on armed forces per 1,000 people (soldiers)	5.3	4.5	4.1	3.9	3.8
GNP per capita (1997 $)	308	315	364	385	401
Arms imports[6]					
Current dollars (mil.)	1,800	675	480	400	410
1997 constant dollars (mil.)	2,108	748	497	407	410
Arms exports[6]					
Current dollars (mil.)	10	0	5	5	90
1997 constant dollars (mil.)	12	0	5	5	90
Total imports[7]					
Current dollars (mil.)	23,640	23,580	34,520	37,370	41,020
1997 constant dollars (mil.)	27,690	26,140	35,750	38,000	41,020
Total exports[7]					
Current dollars (mil.)	17,970	19,560	30,760	33,050	34,240
1997 constant dollars (mil.)	21,050	21,690	31,850	33,610	34,240
Arms as percent of total imports[8]	7.6	2.9	1.4	1.1	1.0
Arms as percent of total exports[8]	0.1	0	0	0	0.3

(Continued on next page.)

EDUCATION (cont.)

Educational Attainment (A)

Age group (1991)[17] . . . . .25+

Population of this age group 368,004,483

Highest level attained (%)

No schooling 57.5

First level

Not completed 28.0

Completed . . . . .NA

Entered second level 7.2

Entered post-secondary 7.3

Literacy Rates (A)

In thousands and percent	1990	1995	2000	2010
Illiterate population (15+ yrs.)	279,610	290,705	300,833	313,647
Literacy rate - total adult pop. (%)	48.4	52.0	55.8	62.6
Literacy rate - males (%)	62.4	65.5	68.6	73.8
Literacy rate - females (%)	33.5	37.7	42.1	50.7

GOVERNMENT & LAW (cont.)

Political Parties

People's Assembly (Lok Sabha)	% of vote	no. of seats
Bharatiya Janata Party Alliance (BJP alliance)	40.8%	304
Congress alliance	33.8%	134
Other	25.4%	105

Elections for the People's Assembly were last held 5 September through 3 October 1999 (next to be held in 2004).

Government Budgets (A)

Year: 1998

Total Expenditures: 2,594.7 Billions of Rupees

Expenditures as a percentage of the total by function:

General public services and public order . . . . . . .7.20[f]

Defense . . . . .15.76[f]

Education . . . . .2.97[f]

Health . . . . .1.68[f]

Social Security and Welfare . . . . .NA

Housing and community amenities . . . . .6.40[f]

Recreational, cultural, and religious affairs . . . . . .NA

Fuel and energy . . . . .NA

Agriculture, forestry, fishing, and hunting . . . . . .5.66[f]

Mining, manufacturing, and construction . . . . . .1.91[f]

Transportation and communication . . . . .1.62[f]

Other economic affairs and services . . . . .6.76[f]

Crime

Crime rate (for 1997)

Crimes reported 6,411,300

Total persons convicted 5,353,400

Crimes per 100,000 population 675

Persons responsible for offenses

Total number of suspects 7,377,500

Total number of female suspects 317,200

Total number of juvenile suspects 14,800

LABOR FORCE

Total Labor Force (B)

439 million (1999).

Labor Force by Occupation

Agriculture 67%

Services 18%

Industry 15%

Data for 1995 est.

PRODUCTION SECTOR

Energy Production

Production .448.6 billion kWh

Production by source

Fossil fuel 80.34%

Hydro 17.08%

Nuclear 2.38%

Other 0.20%

Exports . . . . .130 million kWh

Data for FY98/99 est.

Energy Consumption

Consumption . . . . .416.346 billion kWh

Imports . . . . .1.575 billion kWh

Data for 1998.

Transportation

Highways:

Total: 3,319,644 km.

Paved: 1,517,077 km.

Unpaved: 1,802,567 km (1996 est.).

Waterways: 16,180 km; 3,631 km navigable by large vessels.

Pipelines: crude oil 3,005 km; petroleum products 2,687 km; natural gas 1,700 km (1995).

Merchant marine:

Total: 321 ships (1,000 GRT or over) totaling 6,647,268 GRT/11,074,025 DWT.

Ships by type: bulk 124, cargo 69, chemical tanker 14, combination bulk 1, combination ore/oil 4, container 15, liquified gas 10, passenger/cargo 5, petroleum tanker75, short-sea passenger 2, specialized tanker 2 (1999 est.).

Airports: 346 (1999 est.).

Airports - with paved runways: 238.

Airports - with unpaved runways: 108.

Top Agriculture Products

Rice, wheat, oilseed, cotton, jute, tea, sugarcane, potatoes; cattle, water buffalo, sheep, goats, poultry; fish.

Top Mining Products (A)

	National Production	World Production
Commodities in 1998		
Aluminium (000 mt)	542	22,100
Coal (million mt)	321.3	4,243
Copper (000 mt)	36.7	12,200
Gold (000 kg)	2.4	2,460
Iron Ore (million mt)	75	1,020
Lead (000 mt)	39.3	3,080
Salt (000 mt)	9,500	186,000
Silver (mt)	34	16,400

MANUFACTURING SECTOR

GDP & Manufacturing Summary (A)

	1980	1985	1990	1995
GDP ($-1990 mil.)[1]	174,018	226,008	304,687	376,218
Per capita ($-1990)[1]	253	294	358	405
Manufacturing share (%) (current prices)[1]	17.7	17.9	18.7	18.5
Manufacturing				
Value added ($-1990 mil.)[1]	24,608	34,472	50,174	61,111
Industrial production index	55	73	100	125
Value added ($ mil.)	13,086	15,526	25,097	34,381[e]
Gross output ($ mil.)	71,387	88,304	140,511	165,406[e]
Employment (000)	6,992	6,578	7,299	8,412[e]
Profitability (% of gross output)				
Intermediate input (%)	82	82	82	79[e]
Wages and salaries inc. supplements (%)	11[e]	10	8[e]	6[e]
Gross operating surplus	8[e]	8	10[e]	14[e]
Productivity ($)				
Gross output per worker	10,210	13,423	19,250	19,664[e]
Value added per worker	1,872	2,360	3,438	4,096
Average wage (inc. supplements)	1,083	1,298	1,592[e]	1,261[e]
Value added ($ mil.)				
Food products	899	1,436	2,212	3,127[e]
Beverages	99	135	246	314[e]
Tobacco products	196	230	489	656[e]
Textiles	2,642	2,135	3,264	3,877[e]
Wearing apparel	62	87	316	1,042[e]
Leather and fur products	48	52	123	158[e]
Footwear	37	52	104	217[e]
Wood and wood products	74	73	102	120[e]
Furniture and fixtures	8	7	8	8[e]
Paper and paper products	296	233	574	601[e]
Printing and publishing	256	280	340	674[e]
Industrial chemicals	778	1,200	1,833	3,649[e]
Other chemical products	1,062	1,146	1,647	2,698[e]
Petroleum refineries	203	344	1,072	1,576[e]
Misc. petroleum and coal products	151	152	146	355[e]
Rubber products	234	363	566	657[e]
Plastic products	93	166	297	454[e]
Pottery, china and earthenware	47	27	53	57[e]
Glass and glass products	67	101	111	142[e]

	1980	1985	1990	1995
Other non-metal mineral products	399	775	1,122	1,225[e]
Iron and steel	1,489	1,790	2,551	3,017[e]
Non-ferrous metals	81	115	654	726[e]
Metal products	421	425	614	850[e]
Non-electrical machinery	1,130	1,506	2,011	2,416[e]
Electrical machinery	1,061	1,201	2,009	2,375[e]
Transport equipment	1,088	1,231	2,374	2,664[e]
Prof. and scientific equipment	92	118	165	256[e]
Other manufacturing	72	146	92	472[e]

COMMUNICATIONS

Telecommunications

Telephones - main lines in use: 18.95 million (1999).

Telephones - mobile cellular: 1.9 million (April 1998).

Telephone system: mediocre service; local and long distance service provided throughout all regions of the country, with services primarily concentrated in the urban areas; major objective is to continue to expand and modernize long-distance network in order to keep pace with rapidly growing number of local subscriber lines; steady improvement is taking place with the recent admission of private and private-public investors, but demand for communication services is also growing rapidly.

Domestic: local service is provided by microwave radio relay and coaxial cable, with open wire and obsolete electromechanical and manual switchboard systems still in use in rural areas; starting in the 1980s, a substantial amount of digital switch gear has been introduced for local and long-distance service; long-distance traffic is carried most by coaxial cable and low-capacity microwave radio relay; since 1985 significant trunk capacity has been added in the form of fiber-optic cable and a domestic satellite system with 254 earth stations; mobile cellular service is provided in four metropolitan cities.

International: satellite earth stations - 8 Intelsat (Indian Ocean) and 1 Inmarsat (Indian Ocean region); nine gateway exchanges operating from Mumbai (Bombay), New Delhi, Calcutta, Chennai (Madras), Jalandhar, Kanpur, Gaidhinagar, Hyderabad, and Ernakulam; 4 submarine cables - LOCOM linking Chennai (Madras) to Penang; Indo-UAE-Gulf cable linking Mumbai (Bombay) to Al Fujayrah, UAE; India-SEA-ME-WE3, SEA-ME-WE-2 with landing sites at Cochin and Mumbai (Bombay); Fiber-Optic Link Around the Globe (FLAG) with landing site at Mumbai (Bombay).

Radio broadcast stations: AM 153, FM 91, shortwave 68 (1998).

Radios: 116 million (1997).

Television broadcast stations: 562 (of which 82 stations have 1 kW or greater power and 480 stations have less than 1 kW of power) (1997).

Televisions: 63 million (1997).

Internet Service Providers (ISPs): 3 (1999).

FINANCE, ECONOMICS, & TRADE

Economic Indicators

National product: GDP—purchasing power parity—$1.805 trillion (1999 est.).

National product real growth rate: 5.5% (1999 est.).

National product per capita: $1,800 (1999 est.).

Inflation rate—consumer price index: 6.7% (1999 est.).

Balance of Payments

	1994	1995	1996	1997	1998
Exports of goods (f.o.b.)	25,523	31,239	33,737	35,702	34,076
Imports of goods (f.o.b.)	−29,673	−37,957	−43,789	−45,730	−44,828
Trade balance	−4,150	−6,719	−10,052	−10,028	−10,752
Services - debits	−8,200	−10,268	−11,171	−12,443	−14,540
Services - credits	6,038	6,775	7,238	9,111	11,691
Private transfers (net)	7,779	8,070	10,928	13,531	10,079
Government transfers (net)	422	334	410	440	323
Overall balance	−1,676	−5,563	−5,956	−2,965	−6,903

Exchange Rates

Exchange rates:

Indian rupees (Rs) per US$1

January 2000	43.552
1999	43.055
1998	41.259
1997	36.313
1996	35.433
1995	32.427

Top Import Origins

$50.2 billion (f.o.b., 1999 est.)

Origins (1998)

United States	10%
Belgium	7%
United Kingdom	6%
Germany	6%
Saudi Arabia	6%
Japan	6%

Top Export Destinations

$36.3 billion (f.o.b., 1999 est.)

Destinations (1998)

United States	21%
United Kingdom	6%
Germany	6%
Hong Kong	5%
Japan	5%
UAE	4%

Foreign Aid

Recipient: $2.9 billion (FY98/99).

Import/Export Commodities

Import Commodities	Export Commodities
Crude oil and petroleum products	Textile goods
Machinery	Gems and jewelry
Gems	Engineering goods
Fertilizer	Chemicals
Chemicals	Leather manufactures

INDONESIA

CAPITAL: Jakarta.

FLAG: The national flag, adopted in 1949, consists of a red horizontal stripe above a white stripe.

ANTHEM: *Indonesia Raya (Great Indonesia).*

MONETARY UNIT: The rupiah (Rp) consists of 100 sen. There are coins of 1, 2, 5, 10, 25, 50, and 100 rupiahs, and notes of 100, 500, 1,000, 5,000, and 10,000 rupiahs. Rp1 = $0.00043 (or $1 = Rp2,348).

WEIGHTS AND MEASURES: The metric system is standard.

HOLIDAYS: New Year's Day, 1 January; Independence Day, 17 August; Christmas, 25 December. Movable religious holidays include the Prophet's Birthday, Ascension of Muhammad, Good Friday, Ascension Day of Jesus Christ, the end of Ramadan, 'Id al-Fitr, 'Id al-'Adha', and the 1st of Muharram (Muslim New Year).

TIME: Western, 7 PM = noon GMT; Central, 8 PM = noon GMT; Eastern, 9 PM = noon GMT.

LOCATION AND SIZE: The Republic of Indonesia consists of five large islands and 13,677 smaller islands (about 6,000 of which are inhabited) forming an arc between Asia and Australia. With a total area of 1,919,440 square kilometers (741,100 square miles).

The five principal islands are Sumatra, 473,606 square kilometers (182,860 square miles); Java, with an area of 132,600 square kilometers (51,200 square miles); Borneo, of which the 72 percent belonging to Indonesia is known as Kalimantan, 539,460 square kilometers (208,286 square miles); Sulawesi, formerly called Celebes, 189,216 square kilometers (73,056 square miles); and Irian Jaya (West Irian), the western portion of the island of New Guinea, 421,981 square kilometers (162,927 square miles). Indonesia's total boundary length is 57,318 kilometers (35,616 miles).

CLIMATE: Indonesia has a tropical climate characterized by heavy rainfall, high humidity, high temperature, and low winds. Rainfall in lowland areas averages 180–320 centimeters (70–125 inches) annually.

Republic of Indonesia
Republik Indonesia

INTRODUCTORY SURVEY

RECENT HISTORY

An Indonesian nationalist movement steadily gained strength under the leadership of Untung Sukarno and Mohammad Hatta leading to a proclamation of independence in August 1945. After four years of fighting and negotiations, the Dutch recognized the independence of all the former Dutch East Indies (except West New Guinea) as the Republic of the United States of Indonesia on December 27, 1949.

Sukarno became the first president of the new nation, and Hatta the vice-president. Sukarno turned increasingly authoritarian with an anti-Western policy of "guided democracy." In March 1967 the People's Consultative Assembly (Majetis Permusyawaratan Rakyat-MPR) voted unanimously to withdraw all Sukarno's governmental power and appoint the commander of the army, General Suharto, acting president. One year later, it conferred full presidential powers on Suharto.

Under Suharto's "New Order," Indonesia turned to the West and began following a conservative economic course stressing private investment. In foreign affairs, Suharto's government achieved closer ties with the United States, Japan, and Western Europe while maintaining links with the Soviet Union.

Following Portugal's withdrawal from East Timor in December 1975, Indonesia sent troops into the former Portuguese colony and gained full control of the territory, which it incorporated as an Indonesian Province. The United Nations (UN) op-

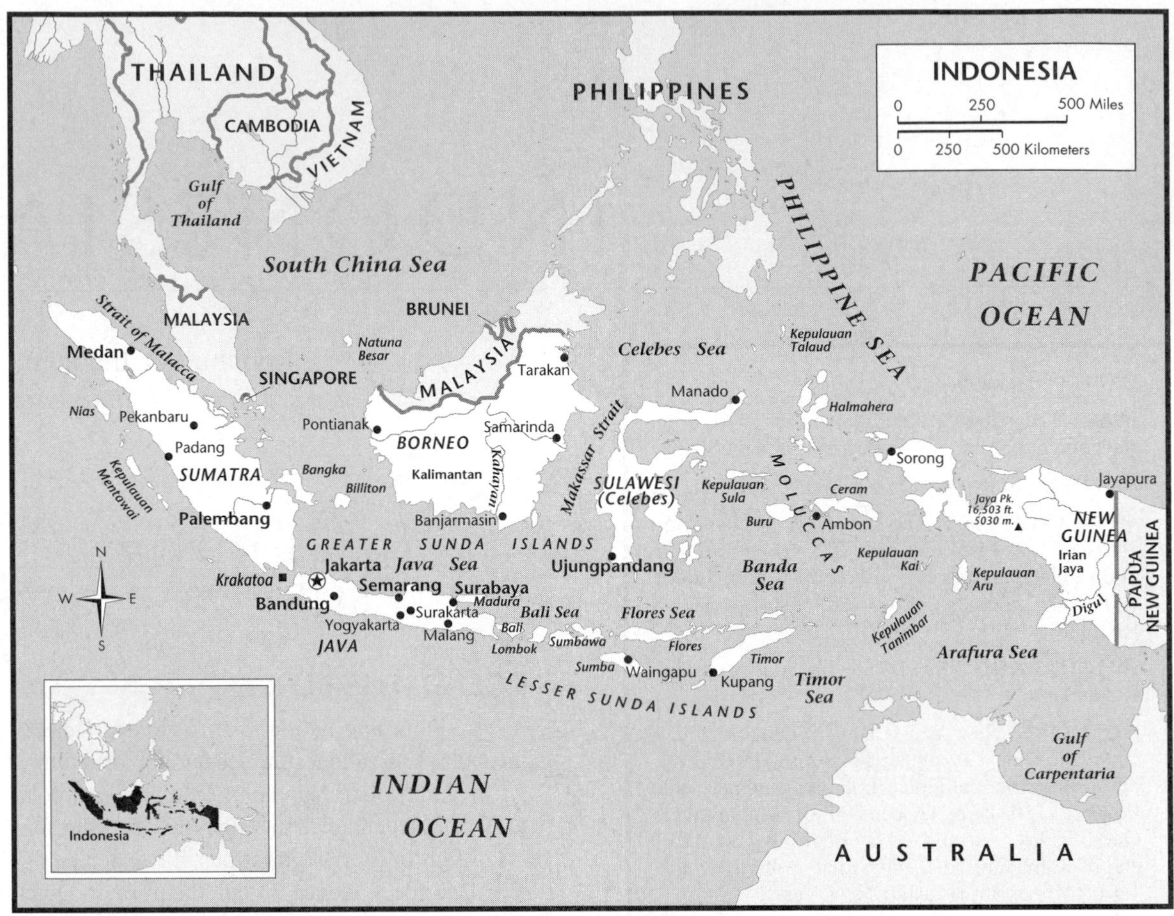

posed this action. The war continued into the 1980s, with reports of massacres by government troops and severe economic hardship among the Timorese.

By 1993 United States criticism of Indonesia's rule in East Timor increased, and a threat to revoke trade privileges was issued. A UN resolution on Indonesia's human rights violations placed the country on a rights "watch" list in 1993. Rural unrest continued in 1995–1996 in East Timor and in Kalimantan involving ethnic Chinese.

In late 1997 the value of Indonesia's currency crashed and foreign debt soared as the country was drawn into the financial crisis spreading in Asia. The government partially imposed reforms outlined by the International Monetary Fund (IMF) causing delays in assistance.

In March 1998 Suharto was elected to a seventh term as president. As the economic crisis continued political instability increased and troops were sent into the streets to deal with a growing number of demonstrations. As public defiance to Suharto and the death toll from riots increased the troubled economy stagnated and many foreigners left the country. Suharto finally resigned in May 1998.

In August 1998 Indonesia and Portugal agreed on a plan to give East Timor local autonomy and control over its own educational and cultural affairs. In August 1999 a provincial referendum for Timur independence overwhelmingly won. The Indonesia legislature approved the decision and the province was renamed again to East Timor but independence had not been officially granted. Guerilla warfare erupted in 2000 by those opposing independence. The 1999 presidential candidate Megawati Sukarnoputri opposed East Timor's independence, and East Timorese who favored integration with Indonesia took up arms against those who supported independence. Abdurrahman, a Muslim cleric, was elected president in 1999 promising democratization.

GOVERNMENT

The government operates under the 1945 constitution, suspended but restored in 1959, as a parliamentary republic. The president serves as both chief of state and head of government. The president is selected by vote of the People's Consultative Assembly for five-year terms. The cabinet is composed of twelve ministers responsible to the president. The legislative branch consists of the unicameral House of Representatives (DPR). Under the new system legislative responsibility rested with the DPR which consists of 462 members elected by popular vote and thirty-eight members appointed by military representatives. Members serve five-year terms. The People's Consultative Assembly (MPR) consists of the DPR plus 200 other selected members. The MPR meets every five years to elect a president and approve national policy. Suffrage is universal at age seventeen, except married persons eligible regardless of age.

Judiciary

The legal system is a substantially altered Roman-Dutch law infused by indigenous concepts. Government courts, each with a single judge, have jurisdiction in original civil and criminal cases. The High Court hears appeals in civil cases and reviews criminal cases. The Supreme Court, the highest court in the country, reviews lower court decisions, ministerial decrees, and regulations for conformity with the constitution but cannot review laws passed by the national assembly. Judgment in civil cases involving Muslims is based on the principles of Muslim law. Judges are appointed by the central government. Customary law *(adat)* continues in the villages unchanged.

Islamic law *(Shari'a)* governs many noncriminal matters involving Muslims, including family law, inheritance and divorce. A civil code based on Roman law is applied to Europeans. A combination of codes is applied to other groups such as ethnic Chinese and Indians.

Political Parties

Political organization is rigorously controlled. Candidates are screened and forbidden to criticize the government. For the 1971 elections the government formed Golkar (Golongan Karya), a political party. In 1975 an act fused major political organizations into two parties-the Development Unity Party (Partai Persuatan Pembangunan-PPP) and the Indonesian Democratic Party-Struggle (Partai DemoKrasi Indonesia-PDI-P). The PPP is a fusion of Muslim groups, while the PDI represents the merger of the Indonesian Nationalist Party (PNI), the Christian Party, the Roman Catholic Party, and smaller groups. In the 1999 elections, Golkar won 21 percent of the popular vote. The PPP won 11 percent of the vote, PDI 37 percent, the National Awakening Party (PKP) 17 percent, the National Mandate Party (PAN) 7 percent, and Crescent Moon and Star Party (PBB) less than 2 percent..

DEFENSE

The Indonesian armed forces consist of an army, a navy, and an air force, numbering 298,000 in 2000. The army has 230,000 personnel; the air force, 21,000; the navy, 47,000. Paramilitary forces include a 194,000-man police force and three other armed security forces, including a trained People's Security force of 1.5 million.

Indonesia spent $1 billion for defense in 1998–99, or about 1.3 percent of its gross domestic product (GDP).

ECONOMIC AFFAIRS

Production of oil, tin, timber, and rubber is central to future economic growth. However, agriculture, with rice as the chief crop, remains the main occupation of the vast majority of Indonesians. Standards of living are low, but improving. Indonesia is exceptionally rich in coal, oil, and other industrial raw materials.

Tight government monetary policies lowered inflation rates from 70 percent in 1998 to 2 percent in 1999 and the economic outlook improved for 2000 though still threatened by civil unrest. Though Indonesia's economic growth and diversification was among the most successful in the world's developing countries, drought and political unrest in 1998 led to a recession, halting economic growth.

Public Finance

Since 1952 government expenditures had outrun public income by a considerable margin each year, but after 1985 Indonesia discouraged public sector and monetary growth resulting in an overall budgetary surplus in 1991, despite a significant drop in oil revenues from falling prices. In 1998 the government deficit was over 3 percent of GDP.

The U.S. CIA estimated that in 1999–2000 government revenues totaled approximately $25.4 billion and expenditures $25.4 billion. Capital expenditures in 1998 were $12 billion. External debt was estimated at $140 billion in 1998.

Income

In 1999 Indonesia's gross domestic product (GDP) was $610 billion. Per capita GDP was $2,800 at an average inflation rate of 2 percent, resulting in a GDP real growth rate of 0 percent in 1999. Contributions to GDP by economic sector in 1999 was agriculture 21 percent, industry 35 percent, and services 44 percent.

Industry

Following World War II agriculture was foremost in the Indonesian economy until the 1990s when manufacturing took over as the dominant area. Indonesia's industries are broad-based including petroleum and natural gas production, coal, steel and chemical production, cement, paper, textiles, plywood, and large amounts of fertilizer. After a 1998 recession the government proposed increased privatization of heavy industry. The Indonesian Bank Restructuring Agency (IBRA) purchased non-performing industrial assets in 2000. The Strategic Industries (BPIS), a state-owned holding company, promotes technical development.

Banking and Finance

A 1998 national economic failure triggered a major restructuring of the banking system. The Bank of Indonesia alone had a deficit of over $4 billion in 2000. Bank Indonesia, as the central bank, is responsible for the administration and regulation of state banks and other banking operations. Bank Mandiri resulted from the merger of four state banks in 1999 and provides credits to forestry, mining, exporters, and new industries. Of the 128 commercial banks in 1998, thirty-eight were liquidated in 1999 and eight were taken over by the government.

Indonesia's stock exchange was shut down during the Japanese occupation during World War II. Not until 1977 was the Jakarta Stock Exchange (JSE) successfully launched.

Economic Development

Exceptionally rich in cola, oil, and other industrial raw materials, industrial development was slow due to chronic inefficiency and corruption of government officials. By the late 1960s, the Suharto government focused on financial stabilization relying heavily on advice and assistance from multilateral aid donors.

Efforts to restructure the economy in the 1980s resulted in increased foreign investment and steady growth in the manufacturing sector and industrial exports. However despite a broad range of reforms most of Indonesian development was still by small holders in a rural-based economy with pockets of industry, mining, and forestry. The financial system collapsed finally in 1998 and despite some recovery in 1999, faltered again in 2000 as guerilla warfare broke out and civil unrest grew. Foreign investment declined and new lending in 2000 remained low with continued concern over large outstanding debts. IMF suspended payments in late 1999 with concern over corruption.

SOCIAL WELFARE

Social programs in the Western sense do not exist, but the society is one in which family and clan relationships run strong. In addition, many orphanages, homes for the aged, youth activities, and private volunteer organizations meet special needs, some receiving government subsidies. Retirement, disability, sickness, maternity, and survivor benefits are available to some workers.

Women in Indonesia enjoy a more favorable position than is customary in Muslim societies though in practice they still often find it difficult to exercise their legal rights.

Ethnic Chinese face restrictions on the rights to own and operate businesses, to import Chinese-language publications, and to celebrate Chinese New Year. Outright violations of human rights persisted in the former Portuguese colony of East Timor.

Healthcare

Family planning is a key part of national health programs which stress small and healthy families. Elimination of contagious diseases focuses on malaria, rabies, filariasis, elephantiasis, tuberculosis, cholera, and leprosy. Overcrowded cities, poor sanitation, impure water supplies, substandard urban housing, and dietary deficiencies are contributing factors to health problems. In 1994–1995 only 63 percent of the population had access to safe water and 55 percent had adequate sanitation. The UN has contributed considerable assistance to solve Indonesia's health problems. Life expectancy was estimated in 2000 to be sixty-eight years for the total population.

In 1991 Indonesia had 1,552 hospitals, with one bed per 1,515 people in 1994. In addition there were 5,656 public health centers. In 1990–1995 only 1 percent of DP went to public health expenditures.

Housing

Housing is a serious problem in both urban and rural areas. In the 1970s approximately 20 percent of housing were one-room dwellings. Most rural housing had no electricity. In 1989, 68 percent of all households received their drinking water from wells or springs, and only 13 percent had plumbing.

Through the 1980s government began playing a larger role in stimulating new housing. In 1990 alone 210,000 new housing units were completed, and the total number of dwellings stood at almost forty-five million in the mid-1990s.

EDUCATION

Six years of primary education are free and compulsory but the number of schools and teachers are inadequate to meet the needs of the fast-growing population. The school system includes six-year primary schools, three-year junior secondary schools, three-year senior secondary schools, and higher education. In 1997 there were 29.2 million students were enrolled in 173,893 primary schools and 14.2 million secondary school students.

There are fifty-one universities, the largest of which are the University of Indonesia in Jakarta and the University of Gajah Mada in Yogyakarta. A total of 2.3 million students were enrolled in higher-level education. In 2000 adult illiteracy was estimated at 13 percent.

2000 KEY EVENTS TIMELINE

January

- During a visit by Indonesian President Abdurrahman Wahid to the strife-ridden province of Aceh, several people are killed in confrontations between Achenese separatists and security forces.

February

- Indonesia's Chinese ethnic minority is allowed public celebrations of Chinese New Year for the first time in decades.
- General Wiranto is suspended from President Wahid's cabinet on February 13 due to the General's implication in human rights violations in East Timor.
- On February 29 President Wahid visits newly independent East Timor and issues apologies for past abuses of Timorese by the Indonesian military.

March

- Forest fires on the Indonesian island of Sumatra bring air pollution to dangerous levels.

April

- Ousted President Suharto is brought in for questioning by the Attorney General regarding massive corruption during his time in power, and a close associate, timber baron Bob Hasan is arrested.

May

- Separatist rebels of the Free Aceh Movement agree to hold peace talks with the Indonesian government in Geneva, Switzerland.
- One hundred people are killed in violence between Christians and Moslems in the Moluccan Islands. Homes and a church are destroyed in the city of Ambon. Foreign aid workers are evacuated and Moslem militants arrive from Java.

June

- On the island of Sumatra, an earthquake and aftershocks kill more than 100 people, and render thousands homeless.
- Suharto is placed under house arrest in advance of his corruption trial.
- A special congress of indigenous activists in the province of West Papua, formerly Irian Jaya, declares independence from Indonesia, based on claims that the territory was illegitimately annexed in the 1960s.

July

- President Abdurrahman Wahid is the first Indonesian head of state to be summoned before Parliament on July 20, under fire for some controversial decisions made in office.
- Thousands of Indonesians protest against former President Suharto after his lawyers claim that he is too brain damaged to face trial for corruption.

August

- A bomb explodes at the Philippine ambassador's residence at Jakarta, killing three and injuring over twenty-one on August 1.
- Former President Suharto is formally charged with corruption on August 3, but the legal charge is scheduled to take place in court. He is suspected of misusing at least $150 million in donations to charitable foundations that he ran.

- President Abdurrahman Wahid hands over his daily duties to Vice President Megawati Sukarnoputri on August 9 in the wake of criticisms.
- Former President Suharto is to go to trial on August 31. The day before the trail, a car bomb explodes near the building where the case is to be tried.
- On August 31 President Suharto postpones his trial due to illness.

September

- A car bomb explodes at the Jakarta Stock Exchange September 13, killing at least thirteen people and wounding many others.
- President Abdurrahman Wahid orders the arrest of former President Suharto's son, Hutomo Mandela Putra, on September 15 in connection with recent bombings and corruption charges. Officers refuse to make the arrest for lack of evidence.
- Officials announce that tens of thousands of East Timor refugees face starvation by the end of September.
- Two hundred protesters riot near Suharto's home on September 22, calling for the former president's trial to begin.
- Indonesian officials announce on September 22 that a four-day operation is under way to disarm pro-Jakarta militias blamed for the recent deaths of three UN relief workers in West Timor.
- On September 29 Indonesian troops begin seizing militia's weapons.

October

- President Wahid appoints new armed forces chiefs in an apparent attempt to strengthen civilian control of the military.
- A court frees notorious East Timorese militia leader Eurico Guterres from police detention.
- President Abdurrahman Wahid denies pardon to the son of former President Suharto, Hutomo Mandala Putra (known as "Tommy") on October 4. Putra has been sentenced to eighteen months in prison on corruption charges, but he eludes police capture.
- More than thirty-one people are killed in Irian Jaya (West Papua) during fighting between government forces and rebels October 6 and 7.
- President Wahid appoints new chiefs of staff for the army and navy on October 9.

November

- President Wahid launches a crackdown on the independence movement in Irian Jaya sending thousands of troops to the province, and enforcing a ban on the separatist "morning star" flag.
- At least eleven people die in violence between Muslims and Christians on the Moluccan Islands November 25.
- Landslides and floods late in the month kill over 119 people on the island of Sumatra and 52 on Java.

December

- President Wahid visits Aceh for two hours, but his heavily-guarded meeting is boycotted by pro-independence leaders.
- On the thirty-ninth anniversary of Irian Jaya's independence from Dutch rule, independence activists and police clash the weekend of December 3.
- Bomb blasts occur at fifteen Christian churches in nine cities on Christmas Eve, December 24. At least fourteen people are killed and one hundred are wounded in the attacks, believed to be carried out by terrorists to intimidate the country's Christian minority (9 percent of the population).

ANALYSIS OF EVENTS: 2000

BUSINESS AND THE ECONOMY

While Indonesia's economic recovery kept in motion during 2000, foreign investors remained wary due to ongoing provincial instability and decentralization of revenue collection. President Abdurrahman Wahid's government went about its reformist plans to decrease the budget deficit by offloading state assets, trying to collect on debts, selling seized assets, and taking care of failed banks, but it was criticized for cronyism and inconsistency in economic policy. Wahid's well-entrenched economics minister, Kwik Kian Gie, was widely considered to be to blame for many of the problems. At the end of the year, most of the central bank board resigned, and Wahid immediately named a new chief for the bank. Throughout 2000 the International Monetary Fund (IMF) appeared dissatisfied with the pace and nature of reforms in the economy, but the IMF did eventually release its multimillion dollar support program loans.

The sharp rise in petroleum prices was seen as beneficial to the economy of Indonesia, an oil producer, despite public protests over the cost of fuel. Indonesia's currency, the rupiah, plunged in May and stayed weak. A high-tech development center—CyberCity, intended to encourage new industries—was making progress near Jakarta. However, a presidential decree banned foreign investments from the Internet sector, a move which struck observers as counterproductive. Efforts to privatize PT Telkom, the state owned telecommunications company, were marked by difficulties.

GOVERNMENT AND POLITICS

As in 1999 the fallout from the Suharto regime and ethnic mayhem in the provinces dominated Indonesian headlines in 2000, along with President Wahid's unpredictable leadership style.

President Wahid managed to disarm his critics in the legislature, without suppressing debate and dissent. His sense of humor and his popularity as a democratically elected leader remained robust, despite qualms about his shifting policies and seemingly haphazard governing methods. The year brought cabinet reshuffling and controversial appointments by the President. He handed over some duties to Vice President Megawati Sukarnoputri, but she remained remarkably silent and marginalized. Wahid seemed to concentrate particularly on international affairs and made constant trips overseas.

The role of the military in the government, dominant during Suharto's days, was still significant in 2000. The generals received assurances that they would keep several seats in the legislature until 2009. Concerns arose throughout the year that the military commanders were unwilling or unable to control their troops, particularly those units engaged in human rights violations connected to their security postings in areas torn by ethnic strife such as Aceh and the Malaku Islands. Low pay for the military was also seen as contributing to pervasive corruption, including involvement in questionable timber and mineral schemes. Law enforcement by local police appeared to have largely collapsed in much of the country as well, giving rise to vigilante incidents. Indonesia's coastal waters were found to be the most rife with piracyin the world according to a survey by the International Maritime Bureau.

Deposed President Suharto was called to trial on corruption charges involving the siphoning off of hundreds of millions of dollars from charity funds. Initially, the case was to be heard in September, but the court ruled the ailing Suharto unfit to stand trial; by year's end an appeals court ruled that the trial could go on without his presence. The former president's youngest son, Hutomo "Tommy Suharto" Mandala Putra, was sentenced to eighteen months in prison on fraud charges, but became a defiant fugitive. A series of bombings, some suspected to be connected to the Suharto trials, shook urban sites, including Jakarta's stock exchange.

Unrest continued in several of Indonesia's provinces, as Wahid's administration had difficulty controlling the military. Aceh was the scene of violence amid attempts to hold the military accountable for massacres and other human rights violations. President Wahid admitted that the security forces had caused the violence taking place during 2000, despite a June peace accord. Local protesters demanded a United Nations-sponsored referendum to be held on independence for Aceh.

West Timor was also the scene of bloodshed, as militia groups (backed by some elements in the Indonesian military) attacked and killed U.N. relief workers and East Timorese refugees held hostage in camps; foreign aid workers were withdrawn from the territory. The most notorious of the militia leaders, Eurico Guterres, was arrested, but later ordered released. General Wiranto, who was thought to have been responsible at the highest level for brutality in East Timor during its referendum period, was forced to resign from the cabinet by Wahid in February, and Wahid visited East Timor (then under pre-independence U.N. administration) to apologize for Indonesia's violations of human rights there.

In Irian Jaya (West Papua) the year was distinguished by strengthening of the pro-independence movement, amid clashes between security forces and independence supporters. The government banned the Papuan separatist "Morning Star" flag. The Maluku Islands continued to experience ethnic/religious violence, apparently with the government security forces siding with Muslim groups against local Christians. In Kalimantan, Indonesia's Borneo province, indigenous Dyaks and Malays fought with Madurese settlers. Other ethnic violence took place on the islands of Lombok, Sulawesi, and elsewhere in the archipelago.

Relations with the United States deteriorated somewhat over the year, due to criticisms by the U.S. ambassador in relation to West Timor, the economy, and other issues; warnings on West Timor from U.S. Secretary of Defense William Cohen; and anti-American street protests over the Middle East crisis. Within the Association of Southeast Asian Nations, Indonesia appeared to be part of a new democratic bloc with Thailand and the Philippines.

CULTURE AND SOCIETY

A new media law was established to promote a free and open press. Indonesian human rights investigators, and revered author Pramoedya Ananta Toer continued to demand that those guilty of abuses during the Suharto regime be exposed and punished. The legislature passed a constitutional human rights amendment. It was criticized for making it difficult to prosecute previously committed violations, but the government insisted that a planned tribunal on the East Timor abuses would be able to proceed. "The Year of Living Dangerously," a movie about Suharto's takeover, was finally allowed to be seen in Indonesia, at a Jakarta film festival seventeen years after its release elsewhere.

Air pollution from forest fires on Sumatra again reached severe levels in 2000. The government promised to take legal action against forty-two companies found to be setting such fires for land-clearing. An environmental crisis was revealed in Sulawesi, where uncontrolled gold miners were using mercury, which was polluting the air, water, and fish supplies.

DIRECTORY

CENTRAL GOVERNMENT

Head of State

President
Abdurrahman Wahid, Office of the President

Vice President
Megawati Sukarnoputri, Office of the Vice President

Ministers

Minister of Home Affairs
Soedirdja Surjadi, Ministry of Home Affairs, Jl. Merdeka Utara No. 7, Jakara Pusat, Indonesia
PHONE: +62 373908; 3842222
FAX: +62 360091; 372812

Minister of Foreign Affairs
Alwi Shihab, Ministry of Foreign Affairs, Jl. Pejambon No. 6, Jakarta Pusat, Indonesia
PHONE: +62 3441508
FAX: +62 360517; 380511; 363750

Minister of Defense and Security
Mohammad Mahfud, Ministry of Defense and Security, Jl. Merderka Barat No. 13-14, Jakarta Pusat, Indonesia
PHONE: +62 374408
FAX: +62 7501490; 3844500; 3804149

Minister of Justice
Ihza Mahendra Yusril, Ministry of Justice, Jl. H.R. Rasuna Said Kav. 4-5, Kuningan, Jakarta Selatan, Indonesia
PHONE: +62 513006; 513004
FAX: +62 5253095; 3104149; 5225036

Minister of Information
Yosfiah Yunus, Ministry of Information, Jl. Merdeka Barat 9, Jakarta Pusat, Indonesia
PHONE: +62 377408; 351363
FAX: +62 375953; 360113

Minister of Finance
Praptosuhardjo Prijadi, Ministry of Finance, Jl. Lapangan Banten Timur 2-4, Jakarta Pusat, Indonesia
PHONE: +62 373309; 365364
FAX: +62 375295; 375492; 353710

Minister of Industry and Trade
Luhut B. Panjaitan, Ministry of Industry and Trade, Jl. Jend. Gatot Subroto kav. 52-53, Jakarta Selatan, Indonesia
PHONE: +62 515509
FAX: +62 512720; 516458; 5201604

Minister of Agriculture
Bunngaran Saragih, Ministry of Agriculture, Jl. Harsono R.M. No. 3, Ragunan, Pasar Minggu, Jakarta Selatan, Indonesia
PHONE: +62 7806131
FAX: +62 7804237; 7800220; 7804377

Minister of Mining and Energy
Yusgiantoro Purnomo, Ministry of Mining and Energy, Jl. Merdeka Selatan No. 18, Jakarta Pusat, Indonesia

PHONE: +62 360232
FAX: +62 3847461; 5255863

Minister of Public Works
Rachmadi Bambang Sumadio, Ministry of Public Works, Jl. Pattimura No. 20, Kebayoran Baru, Jakarta Selatan, Indonesia
PHONE: +62 7395588
FAX: +62 7390769

Minister of Forestry and Plantations
Muslimin Nasution, Ministry of Forestry and Plantations, Gedung Manggala Wanabakti (Blok I), Jl. Gatot Subroto, Jakarta Selatan, Indonesia
PHONE: +62 5704503; 5733037
FAX: +62 5700226; 588732

Minister of Communications
Agum Gumelar, Ministry of Communications, Jl. Merdeka Barat No. 8, Jakarta Pusat, Indonesia
PHONE: +62 361308
FAX: +62 3107788; 451657; 5229850

Minister of Tourism, Arts, and Culture
I Gede Ardika, Ministry of Tourism, Arts, and Culture, Jl. Merdeka Barat 16-19, Jakarta 10110, Indonesia
PHONE: +62 3860822
FAX: +62 3867589; 3860828

Minister of Co-Operative and Small Enterprises
Adi Sasono, Ministry of Co-Operative and Small Enterprises, Jl. H.R. Rasuna Said Kav. 3-4-5, Jakarta Selatan, Indonesia
PHONE: +62 5240366
FAX: +62 520438

Minister of Manpower
Al Hilal Hamdi, Ministry of Manpower, Jl. Jend. Gatot Subroto Kav. 51, Jakarta Selatan, Indonesia
PHONE: +62 5255685; 5255688
FAX: +62 5255659; 5253913

Minister of Transmigration
Priyono Hendro

Minister of Education
Muhaimin Yahya, Ministry of Education, Jl. Jend. Sudirman, Senayan, Jakarta Selatan, Indonesia
PHONE: +62 5731665
FAX: +62 5736870; 5738181; 5733127

Minister of Health
Ahmad Sujudi, Ministry of Health, Jl. H.R. Rasuna Said B1 X/5 Kav. 4-9, Jakarta Selatan, Indonesia
PHONE: +62 5201590
FAX: +62 5201591; 5201588

Minister of Religious Affairs
Mohammad Tolchah, Ministry of Religious Affairs, Jl. Lapangan Banteng Barat No. 3-4, Jakarta Pusat, Indonesia
PHONE: +62 360244
FAX: +62 361720

Minister of Social Affairs
Yustika Sjarifudin Baharsjah, Ministry of Social Affairs, Jl. Salemba Raya No. 28, Jakarta, Indonesia
PHONE: +62 3103591
FAX: +62 3103783

Minister of State and State Secretary
H. Muladi, Ministry of State and State Secretary, Jl. Veteran No. 17, Jakarta Pusat, Indonesia
PHONE: +62 3847198; 3847199
FAX: +62 352685

Minister of National Development Planning
Budiono, Ministry of National Development Planning, Jl. Taman Suropati No. 2, Jakarta Pusat, Indonesia
PHONE: +62 336207; 3905650
FAX: +62 3145374; 334779

Minister of Research and Technology
A. S. Hikam, Ministry of Research and Technology, Jl. M.H. Thamrin No. 8, Jakarta Pusat, Indonesia
PHONE: +62 324714
FAX: +62 328169; 362439; 330728

Minister of Food and Horticulture
A. M. Syaifuddin, Ministry of Food and Horticulture, Jl. Gatot Subroto No. 49, Jakarta Selatan, Indonesia
PHONE: +62 510075
FAX: +62 5255306; 5255425

Minister of Population
Ida Bagus Oka, Ministry of Population, Jl. Permata No. 1, Halim Perdana Kusuma, Jakarta Timur 13650, Indonesia
PHONE: +62 8098018; 8009029
FAX: +62 8194532

Minister of Land and Agrarian Affairs
Hasan Basri, Ministry of Land and Agrarian Affairs, Jl. Sisingamangaraja No. 2, Kebayoran Baru, Jakarta Selatan, Indonesia
PHONE: +62 7222420

Minister of Housing
Erna Witoelar, Ministry of Housing, Jl. Kebon sirih No. 31, Jakarta Pusat, Indonesia
PHONE: +62 323235
FAX: +62 327430

Minister of Environment
Alexander Keraf, Ministry of Environment, Jl. Merdeka Barat No. 15, Lantai III, Jakarta Pusat, Indonesia
PHONE: +62 374627
FAX: +62 3857579; 3847075; 374371

Minister of Women's Affairs
Khofifah Indar Parawansa, Ministry of Women's Affairs, Jl. Merdeka Barat No. 15, Jakarta Pusat, Indonesia
PHONE: +62 3805540
FAX: +62 3805562

Minister of Youth and Sports
Agung Laksono, Ministry of Youth and Sports, Jl. Gerbang Pemuda No. 3, Senayan, Jakarta Selatan, Indonesia
PHONE: +62 5738310; 5738152; 5738153
FAX: +62 588313

Minister of Reform of State Apparatus
Ryaas Rasyid, Ministry of Reform of State Enterprises, Jl. Veteran III No. 2, Jakarta Pusat, Indonesia
PHONE: +62 3847028
FAX: +62 3847028

POLITICAL ORGANIZATIONS

Partai Persatuan Pembangunan-PPP (Development Unity Party)

TITLE: Chairman
NAME: Hamzah Haz

Golongan Karya-GOLKAR (Functional Groups)

Jl. Anggrek Nellymurni, Slipi Jakarta Barat 11480, Indonesia
PHONE: +62 5302222
TITLE: General Chairman
NAME: Akbar Tansung

Partai Demokrasi Indonesia-PDI (Indonesia Democracy Party)

TITLE: Chairman
NAME: Budi Hardjono

DIPLOMATIC REPRESENTATION

Embassies in Indonesia

Afghanistan
Jl. Kusumaatmaja S.H. #15, Menteng, Jakarta 10310, Indonesia
PHONE: +62 (21) 3143169
FAX: +62 (21) 335390

Algeria
Jl. H.R. Rasuna Said Kav.10, Kuningan, Jakarta 12950, Indonesia
PHONE: +62 (21) 5254719; 5254809
FAX: +62 (21) 5254654

Argentina
Menara Mulia Building, Suite 1901, 19th Floor, Jl. Jenderal Gatot Subroto, Kav. 9-11, Jakarta 12930, Indonesia
PHONE: +62 (21) 5265661
FAX: +62 (21) 5265664

Australia
Jl. H.R. Rasuna Said, Kav. C15-16, Jakarta 12940, Indonesia
PHONE: +62 (21) 5227111
FAX: +62 (21) 5227101

Austria
Jl. Diponegoro #44, Menteng, Jakarta 10310, Indonesia
PHONE: +62 (21) 338090; 338101; 3107451
FAX: +62 (21) 3904927

Bangladesh
Jl. Denpasar Raya #3, Block A-13, Kav. 10, Kuningan, Jakarta 12950, Indonesia
PHONE: +62 (21) 5251986; 5221574; 5221729
FAX: +62 (21) 5261807

Belgium
Wisma BCA Building, 16th Floor, Jl. Jenderal Sudirman Kav. 22-23, Jakarta 10310, Indonesia
PHONE: +62 (21) 3162030
FAX: +62 (21) 3162035

Brazil
Menara Mulia Building, 16th Floor, Suite 1602, Jl. Jenderal Gatot Subroto Kav. 9-11, Jakarta 12390, Indonesia
PHONE: +62 (21) 5265656; 5265660
FAX: +62 (21) 5265659

Brunei
Wisma GKBI, Suite 1901, Jl. Jenderal Sudirman # 28, Jakarta 10210, Indonesia
PHONE: +62 (21) 5741437; 5741438; 5741439
FAX: +62 (21) 5741463

Bulgaria
Jl. Imam Bonjol # 34-36, Jakarta 10310, Indonesia
PHONE: +62 (21) 3904049; 3904048

Cambodia
Panin Bank Plaza, 4th Floor, Jl. Palmerah Utara #52, Jakarta 11480, Indonesia
PHONE: +62 (21) 5484840; 5483716
FAX: +62 (21) 5483684

Canada
Wisma Metropolitan I, 5th Floor, Jl. Jenderal Sudirman Kav.29, Jakarta 12920, Indonesia
PHONE: +62 (21) 5250709
FAX: +62 (21) 5712251

Chile
Bina Mulia I Building, 7th Floor, Jl. H.R. Rasuna Said, Kav.10, Jakarta 12950, Indonesia
PHONE: +62 (21) 5201131
FAX: +62 (21) 5201955

China
Mega Kuningan No.2, Jakarta, Indonesia
PHONE: +62 (21) 5761037; 5761039
FAX: +62 (21) 5761034

Colombia
Central Plaza Building, 16th Floor, Jl. Jenderal Sudirman Kav. 47, Jakarta 12920, Indonesia
PHONE: +62 (21) 5701422
FAX: +62 (21) 5207717

Croatia
Menara Mulia Building, Suite 2101, Jl. Gatot Subroto, Kav.9-11, Jakarta 12930, Indonesia
PHONE: +62 (21) 5257822; 5257611
FAX: +62 (21) 5204073

Cuba
Villa Pejaten Mas, Block G/#4, Pejaten, Pasar Minggu, Jakarta 12520, Indonesia
PHONE: +62 (21) 7806673
FAX: +62 (21) 7807345; 7806673

Czech Republic
Jl. Gereja Theresia #20, P.O. Box 1319, Jakarta, Indonesia
PHONE: +62 (21) 3904075; 3904077
FAX: +62 (21) 336282

Denmark
Bina Mulia Building, 4th Floor, Jl. H.R. Rasuna Said, Kav.10, Jakarta 12950, Indonesia
PHONE: +62 (21) 5204350
FAX: +62 (21) 5201962

Egypt
Jl. Teuku Umar #68, Menteng, Jakarta 10350, Indonesia
PHONE: +62 (21) 3143440; 331141; 335350
FAX: +62 (21) 3145073

Finland
Bina Mulia Building I, 10th Floor, Jl. H.R. Rasuna Said, Kav.10, Kuningan, Jakarta 12950, Indonesia
PHONE: +62 (21) 5207408
FAX: +62 (21) 5252033

France
Jl. M.H. Thamrin #20, Jakarta Pusat, Indonesia
PHONE: +62 (21) 3142807
FAX: +62 (21) 3143338

Germany
Jl. M.H. Thamrin # 1, Jakarta Pusat, Indonesia
PHONE: +62 (21) 3901750
FAX: +62 (21) 3901757

Greece
Plaza 89, 12th Floor, Jl. HR. Rasuna Said Kav X-7/No.6, Kuningan, Jakarta 12950, Indonesia
PHONE: +62 (21) 5207776
FAX: +62 (21) 5207753

Hungary
Jl. H.R. Rasuna Said, Kav.X/#3, Kuningan, Jakarta 12950, Indonesia
PHONE: +62 (21) 5203459; 5203460
FAX: +62 (21) 5203461

India
Jl. H.R. Rasuna Said S-1, Kuningan, Jakarta 12950, Indonesia
PHONE: +62 (21) 5204150; 5204152; 5204157
FAX: +62 (21) 5204160

Iran
Jl. H.O.S. Cokroaminoto 110, Menteng, Jakarta Pusat, Indonesia
PHONE: +62 (21) 331391; 334637; 331378
FAX: +62 (21) 3107860

Iraq
Jl. Teuku Umar # 38, Menteng, Jakarta 10350, Indonesia
PHONE: +62 (21) 3904067
FAX: +62 (21) 3904066

Italy
Jl. Diponegoro #45, Menteng, Jakarta 10310, Indonesia
PHONE: +62 (21) 337445; 323490; 337440
FAX: +62 (21) 337422

Japan
Jl. M.H. Thamrin #24, Jakarta Pusat, Indonesia
PHONE: +62 (21) 324308
FAX: +62 (21) 325460

Jordan
Jl.Denpasar Raya Block A-13, Kav.01-02, Kuningan, Jakarta 12950, Indonesia
PHONE: +62 (21) 5204400; 5204401
FAX: +62 (21) 5202447

North Korea
Jl. H.R. Rasuna Said Kav. X-5, Kuningan, Jakarta 12950, Indonesia
PHONE: +62 (21) 5210181; 5222442; 5260066
FAX: +62 (21) 5210183

South Korea
Jl. Jenderal Gatot Subroto # 57, P.O. Box 4187 JKTM, Jakarta Selatan, Indonesia
PHONE: +62 (21) 5201915
FAX: +62 (21) 5254159

Kuwait
Jl. Denpasar Raya Block A-XII/#1, Kuningan Timur, Jakarta 12950, Indonesia
PHONE: +62 (21) 5202477; 5202478; 5202479
FAX: +62 (21) 5204359; 5224931; 5265886

Laos
Jl. Kintamani Raya C-15/#33, Jakarta 12950, Indonesia
PHONE: +62 (21) 5202673; 5229602
FAX: +62 (21) 5229601

Lebanon
Jl. YBR V/#82, Kuningan, Jakarta 12950, Indonesia
PHONE: +62 (21) 5264306; 5253074; 5207121
FAX: +62 (21) 5207121

Libya
Jl. Pekalongan #24, Menteng, Jakarta 10310, Indonesia
PHONE: +62 (21) 335308; 335754
FAX: +62 (21) 335726

Malaysia
Jl. H.R. Rasuna Said, Kav.X/6, # 1-3 Kuningan, Jakarta 12950, Indonesia
PHONE: +62 (21) 5224947
FAX: +62 (21) 5224974

Mali
Jl. Mendawai III/#18, Kebayoran Baru, Jakarta 12130, Indonesia
PHONE: +62 (21) 7208472; 7268504
FAX: +62 (21) 7229589

Mexico
Menara Mulia Building, Suite 2306, Jl. Gatot Subroto Kav. 9-11, Jakarta 12930, Indonesia
PHONE: +62 (21) 5203980
FAX: +62 (21) 5203978

Morocco
Kuningan Plaza, South Tower Suite 512, Jl. H.R. Rasuna Said, Kav.C 11-14, Kuningan, Jakarta 12950, Indonesia
PHONE: +62 (21) 5200773; 5200956
FAX: +62 (21) 5200586

Myanmar
Jl. Haji Agus Salim #109, Menteng, Jakarta Pusat, Indonesia
PHONE: +62 (21) 3140440; 327684
FAX: +62 (21) 327204

Netherlands
Jl. H.R. Rasuna Said Kav. S-3, Kuningan, Jakarta 12950, Indonesia
PHONE: +62 (21) 5251515
FAX: +62 (21) 5700734

New Zealand
BRI II Building, 23rd Floor, Jl. Jenderal Sudirman, Kav.44-46, Jakarta 10210, Indonesia
PHONE: +62 (21) 5709460; 5709470
FAX: +62 (21) 5709457; 5709471

Nigeria
Jl. Taman Patra XIV/ #11-11A, Kuningan Timur, 12950 Jakarta, Indonesia
PHONE: +62 (21) 5260922; 5260923
FAX: +62 (21) 5260924

Norway
Bina Mulia Building I, 4th Floor, Jl. H.R. Rasuna Said Kav.10, Kuningan, Jakarta 12950, Indonesia
PHONE: +62 (21) 5251990
FAX: +62 (21) 5207365

Pakistan
Jl. Teuku Umar #50, Menteng, Jakarta 10350, Indonesia
PHONE: +62 (21) 3144008; 3144009; 3144011
FAX: +62 (21) 3103947; 3103946; 3103945

Palestine
Jl. Diponogoro #59, Menteng, Jakarta 10310, Indonesia
PHONE: +62 (21) 323521; 3145444; 3108005
FAX: +62 (21) 3108011

Papua New Guinea
Panin Bank Centre, 6th Floor, Jl. Jenderal Sudirman # 1, Jakarta 10270, Indonesia

PHONE: +62 (21) 7251218
FAX: +62 (21) 7201012

Peru
Bina Mulia Building 2, 3rd Floor, Jl. H.R. Rasuna Said Kav. 11, Kuningan, Jakarta 12950, Indonesia
PHONE: +62 (21) 5201176; 5201866
FAX: +62 (21) 5201932

Philippines
Jl. Imam Bonjol # 6-8, Menteng, Jakarta 10310, Indonesia
PHONE: +62 (21) 3100302; 3149329; 3100334
FAX: +62 (21) 3159773; 3151167

Poland
Jl. Diponegoro #65, Menteng, Jakarta 10310, Indonesia
PHONE: +62 (21) 3140509
FAX: +62 (21) 327343

Qatar
Jl. Taman Ubud I/ No.5, Kuningan Timur, Jakarta 12920, Indonesia
PHONE: +62 (21) 5277751; 5277752
FAX: +62 (21) 5277754

Romania
Jl. Teuku Cik Ditiro #42A, Menteng, Jakarta Pusat, Indonesia
PHONE: +62 (21) 3106240; 3106241
FAX: +62 (21) 3907759

Russia
Jl. H.R. Rasuna Said, Kav.X-7/1-2, Kuningan, Jakarta 12950, Indonesia
PHONE: +62 (21) 5222912; 5222914; 5225195
FAX: +62 (21) 5222916; 5222915

Saudi Arabia
Jl. M.T. Haryono, Kav.27, Cawang Atas, Jakarta 13630, Indonesia
PHONE: +62 (21) 8011553; 8011537
FAX: +62 (21) 8011527

Serbia
Jl. HOS Cokroaminoto #109, Menteng, Jakarta 10310, Indonesia
PHONE: +62 (21) 3143560; 334157
FAX: +62 (21) 3143613

Singapore
Jl. H.R. Rasuna Said, Block X/4, Kav. 2, Kuningan, Jakarta 12950, Indonesia
PHONE: +62 (21) 5201489

Slovakia
Jl. Prof. Moh.Yamin, SH # 29, Menteng, Jakarta 10310, Indonesia
PHONE: +62 (21) 3101068; 3151429
FAX: +62 (21) 3101180

South Africa
Wisma GKBI, 7th Floor, Suite 705, Jl. Jenderal Sudirman #28, Jakarta 10210, Indonesia
PHONE: +62 (21) 5740660
FAX: +62 (21) 5740661

Spain
Jl. Haji Agus Salim #61, Menteng, Jakarta 10350, Indonesia
PHONE: +62 (21) 335937; 335940; 335771
FAX: +62 (21) 325996

Sri Lanka
Jl. Diponegoro # 70, Menteng, Jakarta 10310, Indonesia
PHONE: +62 (21) 3141018, 3161886; 3919364
FAX: +62 (21) 3107962

Sudan
Wisma Bank Dharmala, 7th Floor, Suite 01, Jl. Jenderal Sudirman Kav. 28, Jakarta 12910, Indonesia
PHONE: +62 (21) 5212075
FAX: +62 (21) 5212077

Sweden
Bina Mulia Building I, 7th Floor, Jl. H.R. Rasuna Said, Kav. 10, Kuningan, Jakarta 12950, Indonesia
PHONE: +62 (21) 5201551
FAX: +62 (21) 5252652

Switzerland
Jl. H.R. Rasuna Said, Block X3/2, Kuningan, Jakarta 12950, Indonesia
PHONE: +62 (21) 5256061
FAX: +62 (21) 5202289

Syria
Jl. Karang Asem I /#8, Kuningan Raya, Jakarta 12950, Indonesia
PHONE: +62 (21) 5204117; 5201641; 5255991
FAX: +62 (21) 5202511

Thailand
Jl. Imam Bonjol #74, Jakarta 10310, Indonesia
PHONE: +62 (21) 3904052; 3147925; 3915651
FAX: +62 (21) 3107469

Tunisia
Wisma Dharmala Sakti, 11th Floor, Jl. Jenderal Sudirman #32, Jakarta 10220, Indonesia
PHONE: +62 (21) 5703432; 5704220
FAX: +62 (21) 5700016

Turkey
Jl. H.R. Rasuna Said, Kav. 1, Jakarta 12950, Indonesia
PHONE: +62 (21) 5256250; 5264143; 5227440
FAX: +62 (21) 5226056; 5275673

Ukraine
Jl. Simprug Permata I / No. 39, Jakarta 12220, Indonesia
PHONE: +62 (21) 7267575; 7205356
FAX: +62 (21) 7266969

United Arab Emirates
Jl. Sisingamangaraja C-4, Kav. 16-17, Kuningan 12950, Indonesia
PHONE: +62 (21) 5206518; 5206552
FAX: +62 (21) 5206526

United Kingdom
Jl. M.H. Thamrin # 75, Jakarta Pusat, Indonesia
PHONE: +62 (21) 3156264
FAX: +62 (21) 3141824; 3902726; 3907493

United States
Jl. Medan Merdeka Selatan #5, Jakarta 10110, Indonesia
PHONE: +62 (21) 3442211
FAX: +62 (21) 3862259
TITLE: Ambassador
NAME: J. Stapleton Roy

Uzbekistan
Jl. Brawijaya Raya #7, Block P-5, Jakarta Selatan, Indonesia
PHONE: +62 (21) 7399009; 7221640; 9134212
FAX: +62 (21) 7221640

Vatican City
Jl. Medan Merdeka Timur #18, P.O. Box 4227, Jakarta Pusat, Indonesia
PHONE: +62 (21) 3841142; 3810736
FAX: +62 (21) 3841143

Venezuela
Menara Mulia, Suite 2005, 20th Floor, Jl. Jenderal Gatot Subroto Kav.9-11, Jakarta Selatan, Indonesia
PHONE: +62 (21) 5227547; 5257548
FAX: +62 (21) 5227549
E-MAIL: evenjakt@indo.net.id

Vietnam
Jl. Teuku Umar #25, Menteng, Jakarta 10350, Indonesia
PHONE: +62 (21) 9100163; 3158537; 3100358
FAX: +62 (21) 3149615

Yemen
Jl. Yusuf Adiwinata #29, Menteng, Jakarta 10350, Indonesia
PHONE: +62 (21) 3904074; 3108029; 3108035
FAX: +62 (21) 3904946

JUDICIAL SYSTEM

Supreme Court

BROADCAST MEDIA

Directorate of Radio

Department of Information, Jalan Merdeka Barat 4/5, Jakarta, Indonesia
TITLE: Deputy Director for Technical Development
CONTACT: Mr. Sunendra

Directorate General of Radio, TV & Film

Jalan Merdeka Barat 9, Jakarta, Indonesia
TITLE: Deputy Director
CONTACT: M. Arsyad Subik

Persatuan Radio Siaran Swasta Nasional Indonesia (PRSSNI) (Federation of Indonesian National Commercial Broadcasters)

Pengurus Pusat, Persatuan Radio Siaran Swasta Nasional Indonesia, Jalan K.H. Mas Mansyur 25A, Jakarta Pusat 10230, Indonesia
TITLE: Chairman
CONTACT: Siti Hardiyanti Rukmana

Radio Republik Indonesia

Jalan Merdeka Barat 4-5, PO Box 356, Jakarta, Indonesia
TYPE: Government

The Voice of Indonesia

PO Box 1157, Jakarta 10001, Indonesia
WEBSITE: http://www.rte.ie
LANGUAGE: Arabic, Chinese, English, French, German, Indonesian, Japanese, Malay, Spanish, Thai

Cakrawala Andalas Televisi (ANTEVE)

Mulia Center Building, 19th Floor, Jalan HR Rasuna Said Kav.X6 #8, Jakarta 12940, Indonesia
PHONE: +62 (21) 5222084; 5222085
FAX: +62 (21) 5222087; 5229174
WEBSITE: http://www.anteve.uninet.net.id/
TITLE: General Manager

CONTACT: Dennis M. Cabalfin
TYPE: Commercial

Cipta Televisi Pendidikan Indonesia (TPI)

Jalan Pintu II, Taman Mini Indonesia Indah, Pondok Gede, Jakarta Timur 13810, Indonesia
PHONE: +62 (21) 8412473
FAX: +62 (21) 8412470
TYPE: Commercial

Indosiar Visual Mandiri (IVM)

Jalan Damai No. 11, Daan Mogot, Jakarta 11510, Indonesia
PHONE: +62 (21) 5672222
FAX: +62 (21) 5652221
E-MAIL: webmaster@indosair.com
WEBSITE: http://www.indosiar.com/
TYPE: Commercial

Rajawali Citra Televisi Indonesia (RCTI)

Jalan Raya Perjuangan No. 3, Kebon Jeruk, Jakarta 11530, Indonesia
PHONE: +62 (21) 5303540; 5303550
FAX: +62 (21) 5493852; 5493846
E-MAIL: webmaster@rcti.co.id
TITLE: President Director
CONTACT: Muchamad Ralie Siregar

Surya Citra Televisi (SCTV)

Jalan Raya Darmo Permai Ill, Surabaya 60189, Indonesia
PHONE: +62 (31) 714567; 714033
FAX: +62 (31) 717273
WEBSITE: http://www.sctv.co.id/
CHANNEL: 11, 34, 35, 43, 44, 46
TYPE: Commercial

Televisi Pendidikan Indonesia (TPI)

Jalan Puntu II, Taman Mini Indah, Pondok Gede, Jakarta 13810
PHONE: +62 (21) 8412473
FAX: +62 (21) 8412470
WEBSITE: http://www.tpi.co.id/

Televisi Republik Indonesia (TVRI)

Jalan Jerbang, Pemuda, Senayan, Jakarta, Indonesia
PHONE: +62 (21) 5733135
FAX: +62 (21) 5732408
TITLE: Managing Director
CONTACT: Azis Husein
TYPE: Government

COLLEGES AND UNIVERSITIES

Lampung University

Universitas Pasundan Bandung

Jl. Langkong Besar No. 68, 40286 Bandung, Indonesia
PHONE: +62 (22) 4205949
FAX: +62 (22) 4217340
WEBSITE: http://www.unpas.ac.id

Universitats Merdeka Malang

Jl. Trs. Raya Dieng No. 62-64, Malang, Indonesia
PHONE: +62 (341) 568395
FAX: +62 (341) 564994
E-MAIL: ousatinfo@unmer.ac.id
WEBSITE: http://www.unmer.ac.id

Mataram University

Jl Majapahit, Mataram 83125, Nusa Tenggara, Jakarta, Indonesia

University of Indonesia - Jakarta

Jl Salemba Raya 4, Jakarta, Indonesia
E-MAIL: bapsi@makara.cso.ui.ac.id
WEBSITE: http://www.ui.ac.id

Sriwijaya University

Jl Jaksa Agung R Suprato, Palembang, Indonesia

Palangkaraya University

Kampus Unpar Tunjung Nyaho, Jl Yos Sudarso-Palangkaraya, Kalimantan, Indonesia

Trisakti University

Jl Kyai Tapa, Kampus A, Jl Kyai Tapa No. 1, 11440 Jakarta, Indonesia
PHONE: +62 (21) 5672731
FAX: +62 (21) 5655787
WEBSITE: http://www.trisakti.ac.id

Atma Jaya Catholic University, Indonesia

PO Box 2639, Jl Jendral Sudirman 51, 12930 Jakarta, Indonesia
PHONE: +62 (21) 5703306
FAX: +62 (21) 5708811
E-MAIL: webmaster@atmajaya.ac.id
WEBSITE: http://www.atmajaya.ac.id

Universitas Krishadwipayana

Jl. Raya Jati Waringin, Pondak Gede, 13077 Jakarta, Indonesia

PHONE: +62 (21) 8462229
FAX: +62(21) 8462461
WEBSITE: http://www.unkris.ac.id

Universitas Jayabaya

Jl. Pulomas Selatan Kav.23, 13210 Jakarta, Indonesia
E-MAIL: info@jayabaya.ac.id
WEBSITE: http://www.jayabaya.ac.id

Universitas Terbuk

Jalan Cabe Raya, Pondok Cabe, PO Box 6666, 15414 Pamulang Tangerang, Indonesia
PHONE: +62 (21) 7490941
FAX: +62 021 7400147
E-MAIL: info@o2m.ut.ac.id
WEBSITE: http://www.ut.ac.id

Muhammadiyak University of Jakarta

Jl. K.H. Ahmad Dahland, Cirendeu, Ciputat, 15419 Jakarta, Indonesia
PHONE: +62 (21) 7401894
E-MAIL: webmaster@umj.ac.id
WEBSITE: http://www.umj.ac.id

Universitas Pakuan

Jl. Pakuan PO Box 452, 16680 Bogor, Indonesia
PHONE: +62 251 312206
FAX: +62 251 31220
E-MAIL: unpak@indo.net.id
WEBSITE: http://www.unpak.ac.id

Universitas Islam Sumatera Utara

Campus Munawarah, Teladan, 20217 Medan, Indonesia
WEBSITE: http://www.usu.ac.id

Institut Teknologi Bandung

Jl Tamansari 64, 40132 Bandung, Indonesia
E-MAIL: webmaster@atsitb.ac.id
WEBSITE: http://www.itb.ac.id

Universitas Padjadjaran

Jl Dipati Ukur 35, 40132 Bandung, Indonesia
PHONE: +62 (22) 2503271
FAX: +62 (22) 2501977
E-MAIL: humas@unp.ed.ac.id
WEBSITE: http://gw.unpad.ac.ida:5051/

Parahyangan Catholic University

Jl. Ciumbuleuit 94, 40141 Bandung, Indonesia
PHONE: +62 (22) 2032655
FAX: +62 (22) 2031110
E-MAIL: humas@home.unpar.ac.id
WEBSITE: http://www.unpar.ac.id

Maranatha Christian University

Jalan Surya Sumantri 65, 40164 Bandung, Indonesia
PHONE: +62 (22) 212186
FAX: +62 (22) 215154
WEBSITE: http://uk.maranatha.edu/e

Universitas Islam Nusantara

Jl Soekarno-Hatta 530, PO Box 1579, 40286 Bandung, Indonesia
PHONE: +62 (22) 7531186
FAX: +62 (22) 7531163
E-MAIL: info@uninus.ac.id
WEBSITE: http://www.uninus.ac.id

Diponegoro University

Kampus Tembalang, 50239 Semarang, Indonesia
PHONE: +62 (24) 7460038
FAX: +62 (24) 7660038
WEBSITE: http://www.undip.ac.id

Gadjah Mada University

Bulaksumur, 55281 Yogyakarta, Indonesia
PHONE: +62 (274) 562011
FAX: +62 (274) 569223
E-MAIL: rektor@ugm.ac.id

Sepulah Nopember Institute of Technology

Kampus Its, Sukolilo, POB 5164, 60111 Surabaya, Indonesia
PHONE: +62 (31) 5926270
FAX: +62 (31) 5923411
E-MAIL: wwits@its.ac.id
WEBSITE: http://www.its.ac.id

Airlangga University

Jl Airlangga 4-6, 60286 Surabaya, Indonesia
PHONE: +62 (31) 5031983
FAX: +62 (31) 5032557
E-MAIL: pskua@indo.net.id
WEBSITE: http://www.unair.ac.id/tahu.html

Brawijaya University

169 Jl Mayjen Haryono, 65145 Malang, Indonesia
PHONE: +62 (341) 551611
FAX: +62 (351) 565420

E-MAIL: sakti@student.uni-magdeburg.de
WEBSITE: http://www.brawijaya.ac.id

Tanjungpura University

Jl Jenderal Achmad Yani, POB 1049, 78124 Pontianak, Indonesia
E-MAIL: webmaster@untan.ac.id
WEBSITE: http://www.untan.ac.id

Hasanuddin University

Jl Perintis Kemerdekaan, Kampus Tamalanrea, 90245 Ujungpandang, Indonesia
E-MAIL: wnhas@unhas.ac.id
WEBSITE: http://www.unhas.ac.id

NEWSPAPERS AND MAGAZINES

Indonesian Observer

Ji AM Sangaji 11, PO Box 2211, Jakarta, Java 10130, Indonesia
PHONE: +62 (21) 3500155; 384462
FAX: +62 (21) 3502417
CIRCULATION: 35,000

Kompas Morning Daily

PT Gramedia, PO Box 4612, Jakarta, Java 12046, Indonesia
PHONE: +62 (21) 5347710; 5347720; 5347730
FAX: +62 (21) 5486085
E-MAIL: kompas@kompas.com
WEBSITE: http://www.kompas.com
TITLE: Editor
CONTACT: August Parengkuan
CIRCULATION: 518,658

Amanah

Sarana Bhakti Semesta, JI Garunda No. 69, Kemayoran, Hakart Pusat, Java, Indonesia
PHONE: +62 (21) 410254
TITLE: Editor
CONTACT: Maskun Iskandar
CIRCULATION: 180,000
TYPE: News Magazine

Gatra

PT Era Media Informasi, Gedung Gatra JL. Lakibata Timur IV No. 15, Jakarta, Java 12740 Indonesia
PHONE: +62 (21) 7973535
FAX: +62 (11) 2302519
E-MAIL: gatra@gatra.com
WEBSITE: http://www.gatra.com
TITLE: Editor
CONTACT: Widi Yarmanto
CIRCULATION: 100,000/edition
TYPE: National and International News

PUBLISHERS

Alumni PT

Jln. Dr Djundjunan 190, Bandung 40163, Indonesia
PHONE: +62 (22) 50675; 58290
FAX: +62 (21) 435905
TITLE: Man. Director
CONTACT: Eddy Damian
SUBJECTS: Economics, Law Medicine, Nursing, Dentistry, Psychology, Psychiatry, Social Sciences

Andi Offset

Jln. Beo No. 38-40, Yogyakarta 55281, Indonesia
PHONE: +62 (274) 561881
FAX: +62 (274) 588282
E-MAIL: andi_pub@indo.net.id
TITLE: Director
CONTACT: J. H. Gondowijoyo
SUBJECTS: Accounting, Chemistry Chemical Engineering, Computer Science, Electronics, Electrical Engineering, Management, Marketing, Science (General), Technology

Bhratara Karya Aksara

Jl. Rawabal, Kawawan Industri Pulogadung, Jakarta, Timur 13340, Indonesia
PHONE: +62 (21) 81858
TITLE: Director
CONTACT: Adit Jayusman
SUBJECTS: Agriculture, Economics, Education, Health, Nutrition, History, Language Arts, Linguistics, Science (General), Social Sciences, Technology

Dinastindo

Jl. Tanjung Duren Raya No. 23, Jakarta, Borat 11470, Indonesia
PHONE: +62 (21) 5668702; 5662091
FAX: +62 (21) 5668703
E-MAIL: daitdr23@rad.net.id
CONTACT: Rijanto Tosin
SUBJECTS: Business, Career Development, Computer Science, Management, Self-Help

Gramedia

Jln. Palmerah, Selatan 22, Lantai 1V, Jakarta 10270, Indonesia
PHONE: +62 (21) 543008
FAX: +62 (21) 5326219
E-MAIL: elex@elexmedia.com
TITLE: Executive Manager
CONTACT: Al Adhi Mardhiyond
SUBJECTS: Accounting, Animals, Antiques, Child Care, Computer Science, Cookery, Games, Electronics, Electrical Engineering, Fiction, Gardening, How-To, Technology

Institut Teknologi Bangung

Jl. Ganesa 10, Bandung 40132, Indonesia
PHONE: +62 (22) 2504257
FAX: +62 (22) 2504257
E-MAIL: itbpress@bdg.centrin.net.id
WEBSITE: http://www.itb.ac.id
TITLE: Editor-in-Chief
CONTACT: Sofia Mansoor
SUBJECTS: Agriculture, Fine Arts, Education, Medicine, Science (General), Technology
TOTAL PUBLISHED: 280 print

Lembaga Demografi Fakultas Ekonomi Universitas Indonesia

Jl. Selemba Raya 4, Jakarta Pusat 10430, Indonesia
PHONE: +62 (21) 3900703; 336434; 336539
FAX: +62 (21) 3102457
E-MAIL: demofeui@indo.net.id
TITLE: Director
CONTACT: Haidy A. Pasay
SUBJECTS: Child Care, Developing Countries, Economics, Education, Environmental Studies, Ethnicity, Health, Labor, Library & Information Sciences, Social Sciences

Penerbit Nusa Indah

Jl. El Tari, Ende Flores 86318, Indonesia
PHONE: +62 (381) 21502
FAX: +62 (381) 21645; 22373
TITLE: Director
CONTACT: Henri Daros
SUBJECTS: Biblical Studies, Human Relations, Language Arts, Linguistics, Literature, Literary Criticism, Essays, Poetry, Catholicism, Theology
TOTAL PUBLISHED: 350 print

Pustaka Utama Grafiti, PT

Jl. Utan Kayi No. 68, E, F, G, 1292, Jakarta 13120, Indonesia
PHONE: +62 (21) 8567502; 4520747
FAX: +62 (21) 8582430
TITLE: Man. Director
CONTACT: Zulkifly Lubis
SUBJECTS: Anthropology, Art, Biography, Business, Political Science, History, Humor, Literature, Literary Criticism, Essays, Philosophy, Religion, Social Sciences

Universitas Sebelas Marat

Jln. IR Sutami 36A, Solo 57126, Indonesia
PHONE: +62 (271) 46994, ext. 341
FAX: +62 (271) 46655
E-MAIL: due-uns@slo.mega.net.id

RELIGIOUS ORGANIZATIONS

Buddhism

Bodhi Buddhist Centre Indonesia
Vihara Bodhi, Jalan. Irian Barat No. 121-123, Medan 20231 North Sumatra, Indonesia
E-MAIL: bbcid@usa.net
WEBSITE: http://welcome.to/bbcid

Indonesian Buddhist Club
E-MAIL: ben_ch@buddhist/com
WEBSITE: http://members.tripod.com/~imajinet
NAME: Chandadhammo Benny Chandra

Catholic

The Diocese of Bandung
Jl. Merdeka 12 Bandung 40117, Indonesia
WEBSITE: http://www.parokinet.org/bandung/bishop/bishop.html

Islamic

Bab-Ilm Islamic Foundation
Jalan KH. Wahid Hasyim No. 55, Jember 68137, Indonesia / Jawa Timur
PHONE: +62 (31) 483147
E-MAIL: bab_ilm@telkom.net
NAME: Jamaluddin Asymawi

Fatimah Islamic Organization

Yayasan Fatimah
Jalan Batu Ampar III No. 14 Condet, Jakarta, Timur, Indonesia
PHONE: +62 (21) 80880066
E-MAIL: yayasan_fatimah@yahoo.com
WEBSITE: http://fatimah.spancity.com
NAME: Hery

Salam alaykum-Mahdi Alcaff
Meruya ilir 18, Jakarta, Indonesia
PHONE: +62 5854771
FAX: +62 5854771

Protestant

The Salvation Army
Jalan Jawa 20, Bandung, 40017, Indonesia
PHONE: +62 (22) 4207029
FAX: +62 (22) 436754
WEBSITE: http://www.salvationarmy.or.id

Union of Indonesian Baptist Churches (UIBC)
Jalan Gunung Sahari VI 11, PO Box 2474, 10270 Jakarta, Indonesia
PHONE: +62 (21) 6399567
FAX: +62 (21) 6594638
TITLE: Executive Secretary
NAME: Guntur Subagyo

Warakas Seventh-Day Adventist Church
Jalan Warakas VII/32, Tg. Priok, Jakarta 14340, Indonesia
PHONE: +62 (21) 4366142
WEBSITE: http://www.tagnet.org/warakas/
TITLE: Pastor
NAME: S. M. Lingga

FURTHER READING

Articles

Ford, Maggie. "The Separatist Wildfires of Indonesia." *Newsweek International,* December 13, 1999, p. 51.

"Indonesia—Ready to Talk in Aceh?" *The Economist (US),* April 15, 2000, vol. 355, no. 8166, p. 38.

Landler, Mark. "Indonesian Court Rules Time Magazine Did Not Libel Suharto." *New York Times,* June 7, 2000, p. A12.

"The Month in Review: January 2000." *Current History,* March 2000, p. 141.

Sims, Calvin. "Suharto Son, Now a Fugitive, Flamboyantly Evades Capture." *New York Times,* November 13, 2000, p. A12.

Wagstaff, Jeremy. "World Bank Is Worried about Indonesia." *Wall Street Journal,* October 16, 2000, p. A30.

Books

Subritzky, John. *Confronting Sukarno: British, American, Australian and New Zealand Diplomacy in the Malaysian-Indonesian Confrontation, 1961–5* New York: St. Martin's Press, 2000.

INDONESIA: STATISTICAL DATA

For sources and notes see "Sources of Statistics" at the front of each volume.

GEOGRAPHY

Geography

Area:

Total: 1,919,440 sq km.

Land: 1,826,440 sq km.

Land boundaries:

Total: 2,602 km.

Border countries: Malaysia 1,782 km, Papua New Guinea 820 km.

Coastline: 54,716 km.

Climate: tropical; hot, humid; more moderate in highlands.

Terrain: mostly coastal lowlands; larger islands have interior mountains.

Natural resources: petroleum, tin, natural gas, nickel, timber, bauxite, copper, fertile soils, coal, gold, silver.

Land use:

Arable land: 10%

Permanent crops: 7%

Permanent pastures: 7%

Forests and woodland: 62%

Other: 14% (1993 est.).

HUMAN FACTORS

Demographics (A)

	1990	1995	1998	2000	2010	2020	2030	2040	2050
Population	188,651	206,270	217,415	224,784	259,743	288,988	312,592	329,278	337,807
Life expectancy - males	59.3	64.0	65.0	65.6	68.5	71.1	73.3	75.1	76.6
Life expectancy - females	63.2	68.6	69.7	70.4	73.7	76.5	78.9	80.9	82.5
Birth rate (per 1,000)	25.8	24.3	23.4	22.6	18.7	15.7	13.9	12.4	11.2
Death rate (per 1,000)	8.1	6.4	6.4	6.3	6.3	6.6	7.3	8.6	9.8
Women of reproductive age (15-49 yrs.)	48,968	55,657	59,737	62,254	70,227	76,372	78,483	78,425	76,636
Fertility rate	3.0	2.8	2.7	2.6	2.3	2.0	1.9	1.8	1.8

Except as noted, values for vital statistics are in thousands; life expectancy is in years.

Health Personnel

	National Data	World Data (wtd ave)
Total health expenditure as a percentage of GDP, 1990-1998[a]		
Public sector	0.6	2.5
Private sector	0.7	2.9
Total[b]	1.3	5.5
Health expenditure per capita in U.S. dollars, 1990-1998[a]		
Purchasing power parity	38	561
Total	6	483
Availability of health care facilities per 100,000 people		
Hospital beds 1990-1998[a]	70	330
Doctors 1992-1995[a]	12	122
Nurses 1992-1995[a]	67	248

Health Indicators

	National Data	World Data
Life expectancy at birth (years)		
1980	55	61
1998	65	67
Daily per capita supply of calories		
1970	1,842	2,358
1997	2,886	2,791
Daily per capital supply of protein		
1997 (grams)	67	74
Total fertility rate (births per woman)		
1980	4.3	3.7
1998	2.7	2.7
Population with access (%)		
To safe water (1990-96)	62	NA
To sanitation (1990-96)	51	NA
People living with (1997)		
Tuberculosis (cases per 100,000)	10.9	60.4
Malaria (cases per 100,000)	79.3	42.2
HIV/AIDS (% aged 15 - 49 years)	0.05	0.99

Infants and Malnutrition

	National Data	World Data (wtd ave)
Under 5 mortality rate (1989)	56	NA
% of infants with low birthweight (1992-98)[1]	11	17
Births attended by skilled health staff (% of total births 1996-98)	36	52
% fully immunized at 1 year of age (1995-98)[1]		
TB	83	82
DPT	62	77
Polio	70	77
Measles	60	74
Prevalence of child malnutrition (1992-98)[1] (based on weight for age, % of children under 5 years)	34	30

Ethnic Division

Javanese 45.0%
Sundanese 14.0%
Madurese 7.5%
Coastal Malays 7.5%
Other 26.0%

Religion

Muslim 88%
Protestant 5%
Roman Catholic 3%
Hindu 2%
Buddhist 1%
Other 1%

Data for 1998.

Major Languages

Bahasa Indonesia (official, modified form of Malay), English, Dutch, local dialects, the most widely spoken of which is Javanese.

EDUCATION

Public Education Expenditures

	1980	1997
Public expenditures on education as % of GNP	1.7	1.4
Expenditures per student as % of GNP per capita		
Primary	NA	NA
Secondary	NA	6.6
Tertiary	NA	12.9
Pupils per teacher at the primary level	NA	22
Duration of primary education in years	NA	9

World data for comparison

Public expenditures on education as % of GNP (mean)	3.9	4.8
Pupils per teacher at the primary level (wtd ave)	NA	33
Duration of primary education in years (mean)	NA	9

Educational Attainment (A)

Age group (1990) . . . . .25+

Population of this age group 78,497,680

Highest level attained (%)

No schooling 54.5

(Continued on next page.)

GOVERNMENT & LAW

Military Affairs (A)

	1990	1992	1995	1996	1997
Military expenditures					
Current dollars (mil.)	1,610	1,830	4,040[e]	4,180[e]	4,810[e]
1997 constant dollars (mil.)	1,880	2,030	4,180[e]	4,250[e]	4,810[e]
Armed forces (000)	283	283	280	280	280
Gross national product (GNP)					
Current dollars (bil.)	107	132	177	197	209
1997 constant dollars (bil.)	126	147	183	200	209
Central government expenditures (CGE)					
1997 constant dollars (bil.)	24	28	30	33	37
People (mil.)	187.7	194.0	203.5	206.6	209.8
Military expenditure as % of GNP	1.5	1.4	2.3	2.1	2.3
World data on military expenditure as % of GNP	4.5	3.4	2.7	2.6	2.6
Military expenditure as % of CGE	7.8	7.2	14.1	13.1	13.1
World data on military expenditure as % of CGE	17.0	12.5	10.5	10.3	10.2
Military expenditure per capita (1997 $)	10	10	21	21	23
World data on military expenditure per capita (1997 $)	242	173	146	143	145
Armed forces per 1,000 people (soldiers)	1.5	1.5	1.4	1.4	1.3
World data on armed forces per 1,000 people (soldiers)	5.3	4.5	4.1	3.9	3.8
GNP per capita (1997 $)	669	756	899	968	995
Arms imports[6]					
Current dollars (mil.)	300	100	430	925	410
1997 constant dollars (mil.)	351	111	445	940	410
Arms exports[6]					
Current dollars (mil.)	5	20	10	10	20
1997 constant dollars (mil.)	6	22	10	10	20
Total imports[7]					
Current dollars (mil.)	21,840	27,280	40,630	42,930	41,690
1997 constant dollars (mil.)	25,570	30,240	42,070	43,640	41,690
Total exports[7]					
Current dollars (mil.)	25,670	33,970	45,420	49,810	53,440
1997 constant dollars (mil.)	30,070	37,660	47,030	50,640	53,440
Arms as percent of total imports[8]	1.4	0.4	1.1	2.2	1.0
Arms as percent of total exports[8]	0	0.1	0	0	0

(Continued on next page.)

EDUCATION (cont.)

Educational Attainment (A) (cont.)

First level
- Not completed 26.4
- Completed .... NA

Entered second level 16.8

Entered post-secondary 2.3

Literacy Rates (A)

In thousands and percent	1990	1995	2000	2010
Illiterate population (15+ yrs.)	20,899	21,507	18,740	12,726
Literacy rate - total adult pop. (%)	81.6	83.8	87.3	92.7
Literacy rate - males (%)	88.3	89.6	92.1	95.7
Literacy rate - females (%)	75.3	78.0	82.6	89.9

GOVERNMENT & LAW (cont.)

Political Parties

House of Representatives (Dewan Perwakilan Rakyat)	% of vote	no. of seats
Indonesian Democracy Party-Struggle (PDI-P)	37.4%	154
Golkar	20.9%	120
National Awakening Party (PKB)	17.4%	51
Development Unity Party (PPP)	10.7%	58
National Mandate Party (PAN)	7.3%	35
Crescent Moon and Star Party (PBB)	1.8%	14
Other	4.5%	30

Elections were last held 7 June 1999 (next to be held June 2004).

Government Budgets (A)

Year: 1998

Total Expenditures: 168,614 Billions of Rupiah

Expenditures as a percentage of the total by function:
- General public services and public order ..... 12.47[P]
- Defense .... 5.28[P]
- Education .... 6.88[P]
- Health .... 2.29[P]
- Social Security and Welfare .... 5.01[P]
- Housing and community amenities .... 13.87[f]
- Recreational, cultural, and religious affairs ..... 2.02[P]
- Fuel and energy .... 0.62[P]
- Agriculture, forestry, fishing, and hunting ..... 6.56[P]
- Mining, manufacturing, and construction ...... 0.37[P]
- Transportation and communication .... 3.65[P]
- Other economic affairs and services .... 1.45[P]

Crime

Crime rate (for 1997)
- Crimes reported 123,700
- Total persons convicted 59,400
- Crimes per 100,000 population 61

LABOR FORCE

Total Labor Force (A)

88 million (1998).

Labor Force by Occupation

Agriculture 45%

Trade, restaurant, and hotel 19%

Manufacturing 11%

Transport and communications 5%

Construction 4%

Data for 1998.

Unemployment Rate

15%-20% (1998 est.)

PRODUCTION SECTOR

Energy Production

Production .... 73.13 billion kWh

Production by source
- Fossil fuel 88.19%
- Hydro 8.39%
- Nuclear 0%
- Other 3.42%

Exports .... 0 kWh

Data for 1998.

Energy Consumption

Consumption .... 68.011 billion kWh

Imports .... 0 kWh

Data for 1998.

Transportation

Highways:

Total: 342,700 km.

Paved: 158,670 km.

Unpaved: 184,030 km (1997 est.).

Waterways: 21,579 km total; Sumatra 5,471 km, Java and Madura 820 km, Kalimantan 10,460 km, Sulawesi (Celebes) 241 km, Irian Jaya 4,587 km.

Pipelines: crude oil 2,505 km; petroleum products 456 km; natural gas 1,703 km (1989).

Merchant marine:

Total: 586 ships (1,000 GRT or over) totaling 2,676,875 GRT/3,700,864 DWT.

Ships by type: bulk 38, cargo 346, chemical tanker 9, container 19, liquified gas 5, livestock carrier 1, passenger 7, passenger/cargo 13, petroleum tanker 114, refrigerated cargo 1, roll-on/roll-off 11, short-sea passenger 8, specialized tanker 9, vehicle carrier 5 (1999 est.).

Airports: 446 (1999 est.).

Airports - with paved runways: 127.

Airports - with unpaved runways: 319.

Top Agriculture Products

Rice, cassava (tapioca), peanuts, rubber, cocoa, coffee, palm oil, copra; poultry, beef, pork, eggs.

Top Mining Products (A)

	National Production	World Production
Commodities in 1998		
Aluminium (000 mt)	130	22,100
Coal (million mt)	61.1	4,243
Copper (000 mt)	780	12,200
Gold (000 kg)	105	2,460
Nickel (000 mt)	74	1,140
Salt (000 mt)	650	186,000
Silver (mt)	190	16,400
Tin (mt)	40,000	206,000

MANUFACTURING SECTOR

GDP & Manufacturing Summary (A)

	1980	1985	1990	1995
GDP ($-1990 mil.)[1]	61,467	78,380	106,141	149,015
Per capita ($-1990)[1]	407	468	581	755
Manufacturing share (%) (current prices)[1]	13.0	16.0	20.7	24.3
Manufacturing				
Value added ($-1990 mil.)[1]	6,916	12,718	21,115	33,861[e]
Industrial production index	55	62	100	159[e]
Value added ($ mil.)	4,372	8,104[e]	14,832	32,698[e]
Gross output ($ mil.)	11,519	21,191	38,520	83,533[e]
Employment (000)	963	1,673	2,649	4,078[e]
Profitability (% of gross output)				
Intermediate input (%)	62	62[e]	61	61[e]
Wages and salaries inc. supplements (%)	7[e]	8[e]	5	5[e]
Gross operating surplus	31[e]	30[e]	34	34[e]
Productivity ($)				
Gross output per worker	11,880	12,574	14,458	20,472[e]
Value added per worker	4,509	4,809[e]	5,567	8,067[e]
Average wage (inc. supplements)	838[e]	1,011[e]	715	1,021[e]
Value added ($ mil.)				
Food products	376	870	1,910	2,906[e]
Beverages	51	77	112	339[e]
Tobacco products	649	741	1,732	3,372[e]
Textiles	420	687	1,306	4,398[e]
Wearing apparel	15	105	458	1,251[e]
Leather and fur products	5	14	43	96[e]
Footwear	26	31	189	1,245[e]
Wood and wood products	239	612	1,382	2,551[e]
Furniture and fixtures	6	18	117	319[e]
Paper and paper products	43	110	477	1,053[e]
Printing and publishing	51	92	150	467[e]
Industrial chemicals	145	385	687	1,544[e]
Other chemical products	241	430	535	1,417[e]
Petroleum refineries	978	1,611[e]	1,174[e]	34[e]
Misc. petroleum and coal products	4[e]	6[e]	8	12[e]
Rubber products	164	328	494	643[e]
Plastic products	25	175	228	619[e]
Pottery, china and earthenware	8	24	77	322[e]

	1980	1985	1990	1995
Glass and glass products	36	98	64	151[e]
Other non-metal mineral products	200	262	374	797[e]
Iron and steel	107	420[e]	1,045	1,889[e]
Non-ferrous metals	NA	49[e]	188	319[e]
Metal products	118	278	402	1,135[e]
Non-electrical machinery	53	76	171	437[e]
Electrical machinery	180	246	403	1,303[e]
Transport equipment	217	331	1,036	3,774[e]
Prof. and scientific equipment	2	4	10	62[e]
Other manufacturing	13	24	61	242[e]

COMMUNICATIONS

Daily Newspapers

	National Data	World Data for Comparison
Daily Newspapers		
Number of Dailies	69	8,391
Total Circulation (000)	4,665	548,000
Circulation per 1,000 inhabitants	23	96

Telecommunications

Telephones - main lines in use: 3.291 million (1995).

Telephones - mobile cellular: 1.2 million (1998).

Telephone system: domestic service fair, international service good.

Domestic: interisland microwave system and HF radio police net; domestic satellite communications system.

International: satellite earth stations - 2 Intelsat (1 Indian Ocean and 1 Pacific Ocean).

Radio broadcast stations: AM 678, FM 43, shortwave 82 (1998).

Radios: 31.5 million (1997).

Television broadcast stations: 41 (1999).

Televisions: 13.75 million (1997).

Internet Service Providers (ISPs): 24 (1999).

FINANCE, ECONOMICS, & TRADE

Economic Indicators

National product: GDP—purchasing power parity—$610 billion (1999 est.).

National product real growth rate: 0% (1999 est.).

National product per capita: $2,800 (1999 est.).

Inflation rate—consumer price index: 2% (1999 est.).

Exchange Rates

Exchange rates:

Indonesian rupiahs (Rp) per US$1

January 2000	7,278.8
1999	7,855.2
1998	10,013.6
1997	2,909.4
1996	2,342.3
1995	2,248.6

Top Import Origins

$24 billion (c.i.f., 1999 est.)

Origins (1999 est.)

Japan	17%
United States	13%
Singapore	10%
Germany	9%

(Continued on next page.)

Balance of Payments

	1994	1995	1996	1997	1998
Exports of goods (f.o.b.)	40,223	47,454	50,188	56,298	50,371
Imports of goods (f.o.b.)	−32,322	−40,921	−44,240	−46,223	−31,942
Trade balance	7,901	6,533	5,948	10,075	18,429
Services - debits	−11,416	−13,540	−15,139	−16,607	−11,813
Services - credits	4,797	5,469	6,599	6,941	4,479
Private transfers (net)	449	651	796	725	710
Government transfers (net)	170	330	141	309	379
Overall balance	−2,792	−6,431	−7,663	−4,889	3,972

Top Import Origins (cont.)

Australia	6%
South Korea	5%
Taiwan	3%
China	3%

Top Export Destinations

$48 billion (f.o.b., 1999 est.)

Destinations (1999 est.)

Japan	18%
EU	15%
United States	14%
Singapore	13%
South Korea	5%
Hong Kong	4%
China	4%
Taiwan	3%

Foreign Aid

Recipient: $43 billion from IMF program and other official external financing (1997-2000).

Import/Export Commodities

Import Commodities	Export Commodities
Machinery and equipment	Oil and gas
	Plywood
Chemicals	Textiles
Fuels	Rubber
Foodstuffs	

IRAN

Islamic Republic of Iran
Jomhuri-ye Eslami-ye Iran

CAPITAL: Tehran.

FLAG: The national flag is a tricolor of green, white, and red horizontal stripes, the top and bottom stripes having the Arabic inscription *Allah Akbar* ("God Is Great") written along the edge nearest the white stripe. In the center, in red, is the coat of arms, consisting of a stylized representation of the word *Allah*.

MONETARY UNIT: The rial (R) is a paper currency of 100 dinars. There are coins of 1, 5, 10, 20, and 50 rials, and notes of 100, 200, 500, 1,000, 2,000, 5,000, and 10,000 rials. R1 = $0.00057 (or $1 = R1,749.9).

WEIGHTS AND MEASURES: The metric system is the legal standard, but local units are widely used.

HOLIDAYS: National Day, 11 February; Oil Nationalization Day, 20 March; No Ruz (New Year), 21–24 March; Islamic Republic Day, 1 April; 13th Day of No Ruz (Revolution Day), 2 April. Religious holidays (according to the lunar calendar) include Birthday of Imam Husayn; Birthday of the Twelfth Imam; Martyrdom of Imam 'Ali; Death of Imam Ja'afar Sadiq; 'Id al-Fitr; Birthday of Imam Reza; 'Id-i-Qurban; 'Id-i-Qadir; Shab-i-Miraj; Martyrdom of Imam Husayn; 40th Day after the Death of Imam Husayn; Birthday of the Prophet; Birthday of Imam 'Ali.

TIME: 3:30 PM = noon GMT.

LOCATION AND SIZE: Located in southwestern Asia, Iran covers an area of 1,648,000 square kilometers (636,296 square miles). It has a total boundary length of 8,620 kilometers (5,356 miles), and its territory includes several islands in the Persian Gulf.

Iran's capital city, Tehran, is located in the northwestern part of the country.

CLIMATE: Cold winters and hot summers are prevalent across the plateau. On the plateau, the annual rainfall does not exceed 30 centimeters (12 inches), with the deserts and the Persian Gulf area receiving less than 13 centimeters (5 inches). The Caspian Sea coastal region is warm and humid throughout the year, with annual rainfall about 100 to 150 centimeters (40–60 inches).

INTRODUCTORY SURVEY

RECENT HISTORY

Oil, the source of nearly all Iran's national wealth, quickly came to dominate post-World War II politics. Between 1947 and 1953 there were conflicts over nationalizing Iran's oil industry still dominated by the British Anglo-Iranian Oil Co. (AIOC). With Shah Muhammad Reza Pahlavi increasing his power, new arrangements between the National Iranian Oil Co. and a group of United States, United Kingdom, and Dutch oil companies were negotiated in 1954. Iran joined the Western alliance through the Baghdad Pact in 1955, later the Central Treaty Organization.

At U.S. encouragement the "white revolution" of 1962–1963 initiated land reform, political changes (including, for the first time, the right of women to hold and vote for public office), and broad economic development. With the Shah's dictatorial methods and program of rapid Westernization at the expense of Islamic tradition, the entire population turned against the Shah. Following months of demonstrations and violent army reactions, martial law was declared in Iran's major cities in September 1978. But antigovernment strikes and massive marches continued. After spending fifteen years in exile the leader of the Islamic opposition, Ayatollah Ruhollah Khomeini (the term *ayatollah* is the highest rank of the Shi'ite Muslim clergy) returned on February 1, 1979, to an enthusiastic welcome in Tehran. He quickly asserted control and appointed a provisional government.

On April 1, Khomeini declared Iran an Islamic Republic. Revolutionary groups made random arrests and illegal executions of political opponents. On November 4, 1979, militant Iranian students seized fifty-three U.S. hostages demanding the return of the Shah from the United States to stand trial in Iran. The hostages were held for 444 days. The Shah died in Egypt in July 1980.

Conflict between rival political groups within Iran continued accompanied by repeated bombings and assassinations. Iraq took advantage of Iran's political chaos and economic disorder to revive an old border dispute. Full-scale war erupted in September 1980, when Iraqi forces invaded Khuzistan in the southwest, and captured the oil refinery center of Abadan. Iran then launched its own offensive against Iraq but failed to make significant gains. When the land war became deadlocked Iraq broadened the war zone to include oil-tanker traffic in the northern Persian Gulf.

Hostilities ended in 1988 with a cease-fire. On June 3, 1989, Khomeini died of a heart attack. Over three million people attended his funeral. President Ali Khamenei succeeded him as spiritual guide.

Iran remained neutral during the Gulf War. Inflation, shortages, and unemployment—the products of revolution, war, and mismanagement—generated widespread popular discontent.

In June 1997, moderate candidate Mohammad Khatami was elected president. His election marked a move toward greater political and cultural tolerance by the Islamic government. Khatami also promised continued economic reform efforts.

GOVERNMENT

Until 1979, Iran was an absolute monarchy. The constitution of December 1979 established an Islamic theocratic republic in conformity with the principles of the Shi'ite faith. Chief of state of the republic is the country's spiritual leader *(faqih).* Ayatollah Khomeini was appointed for life in 1989. An appointed Council of Guardians consists of six religious leaders, who examine all legislation for conformity to Islamic principles, and six Muslim lawyers appointed by the Supreme Judicial Council, who rule on limited questions of constitutionality. An 86-member Assembly of Experts chooses the nation's spiritual leader. In 1998 seats were opened to non-clerics.

The executive branch consists of a president and a cabinet known as Council of Ministers. The president is elected by popular vote to a four-year term and supervises government administration. The presidency has limited power since all laws must be approved by an elite group of clerics. The president selects members of the Council of Ministers with legislative approval.

The legislative branch is a unicameral Islamic Consultative Assembly (Majles-e-Shura-ye-Eslami). The Majles consists of 290 members elected by popular vote to four-year terms. Voting is universal for those over age fifteen. The country is divided into twenty-eight administrative provinces.

Judiciary

Making Iran an Islamic state greatly changed the judicial system. In 1982 the Supreme Court invalidated all previous laws that did not conform with the dictates of Islam and all courts set up before the 1979 revolution were abolished. An Islamic system of punishment introduced in 1983 included flogging, stoning, and amputation for various crimes. There are two different court systems: civil courts and revolutionary courts.

The judicial system is under the authority of the religious leader *(faqih).* A Supreme Judicial Council responsible to the faqih oversees the Supreme Court, which has sixteen branches. The Ministry of Justice oversees law courts in the provinces. The revolutionary courts try cases involving political offenses, narcotics trafficking, and "crimes against God." The trials in revolutionary courts are rarely held in public, and there is no guarantee of access to an attorney.

Political Parties

After the overthrow of the Shah's regime in February 1979, new political parties were formed. The Islamic Republican Party (IRP) closely identified with Ayatollah Khomeini emerged as the dominant group. All parties found not to be acceptable by Islamic standards have been banned. By 2000 moderate reform organizations holding less hostile views of the West gained strength. Since the elections of May 1997 several political parties were licensed. These organizations include: Islamic Iran Solidarity Party; Islamic Partnership Front; Executives of Construction; the conservative Followers of the Imam's Line and the Leader; Islamic Coalition Association; Militant Clerics Association; and, the Second Khordad Front.

DEFENSE

Iran's regular forces include ground forces, nave, and air defense. Two years of military service is required for all males at age eighteen. In 2000 the army had 350,000 soldiers (220,000 draftees); the air force had 50,000 men; the navy 20,600 men.

The Revolutionary Guards unit *(Pasdaran)* has an estimated 100,000-man army and 20,000 sailors and marines. Complementing the *Pasdaran* are the *baseej,* radical young volunteers devoted to an Islamic Iran. Membership is estimated at 200,000. The police force numbers 150,000. The official military budget in 1998–1999 was $5.8 billion, or 2.9 percent of GDP.

ECONOMIC AFFAIRS

Following rapid economic growth during the reign of Shah Muhammad Reza Pahlavi, the economy changed drastically after 1979. The economy is a mixture of central planning, state ownership of oil and other large businesses, and village agriculture. The war with Iraq, which reduced oil exports, coupled with the decrease in the price of oil, sent oil revenues downward from $20.5 billion in 1979 to an estimated $5.3 billion in 1986.

Inflation continued to be a problem in 1998 at a 24 percent rate. GDP growth had slumped in the late 1990s. A five-year plan for 2000–2005 focused on further privatization.

Public Finance

Trade reforms implemented since 1991 have boosted economic growth and reduced budget deficits. Revenues in 1996–1997 were estimated at $34.6 billion and expenditures were $34.9 billion. External debt in 1996 was $21.9 billion. The general government deficit had fallen from 9 percent of GDP in 1988 to 2 percent in 1992 but rose again to 7 percent in 1998.

Income

In 1999 the gross domestic product (GDP) of Iran was $347.6 billion, or $5,300 per capita. Real growth rate of GDP was 1 percent and the inflation rate was 30 percent. GDP contribution by economic sector in 1997 was agriculture 21 percent, industry 34 percent, and services 45 percent.

Industry

Iran's industrial sector was setback in the 1970s by political turmoil and finally by nationalization of businesses in 1979. A privatization program was begun in 1991 leading to industrial growth of 5.3 percent from 1988 to 1998. Main industries are oil refining, petrochemicals, steel, textiles, cement, food processing such as sugar refining, and copper. Major refinery products are motor fuel, distillate fuel oil, and residual fuel oil. Oil refining capacity was 1.47 million barrels per day in 2000. With the third largest reserves in the world, the natural gas industry boomed producing 1.9 trillion cubic feet of natural gas in 1998. Industrial production growth rate was estimated in 1996 at 5.7 percent.

Banking and Finance

The Central Bank of Iran-Bank Markazil-established by the Monetary and Banking Law of 1960, issues notes, controls foreign exchange, and supervises the banking sector.

The revolutionary government nationalized all commercial banks shortly after taking office in 1979 and announced that banking practices would be brought in line with Islamic principles, which include a ban on interest payments. By 1993 there were five Islamic banks.

Despite measures to promote competition between banks, and to encourage savings within the official banking sector being introduced in the early 1990s, a basic lack of confidence in the banking system persisted.

Bank Melli, which has acted for the central bank, handles most Iranian banking operations outside the country. The requirements to abide by Islamic principles were never imposed on Bank Melli.

The Tehran Stock Exchange, known as the Bourse, was created in 1968.

Economic Development

Iran's five-year economic plan (1989–1994) authorized up to $27 billion in foreign borrowing. It aimed to increase productivity in key industrial and economic sectors and to promote the non-oil export sector. The 1994–1999 plan aimed at investing money in transport, particularly in the railroad system and in the construction of a public underground for Tehran. Other projects were aimed at revitalizing the petroleum sector. In 1995 the French company Total was contracted to develop a new oil gas site.

SOCIAL WELFARE

Traditionally Islamic *waqf* (obligatory charity) institutions supplemented the family and the tribe for the care of the infirm and the indigent. In 1974, the Ministry of Social Welfare was created to coordinate social programs. Programs include workers' compensation, disability, family, marriage, and maternity allowances, and retirement and death benefits. But in 1999 these programs only covered employed persons in specific occupations and specific areas.

Healthcare

In 2000 average life expectancy was estimated at seventy years for both women and men. In 1995 80 percent of the population had access to health care services. Tuberculosis, malaria, and smallpox are among the major health problems.

The Islamic republic has continued to provide health care programs to the rural areas. In the 1990–1997 period there were 0.3 doctors and 1.4 hospital beds per 1,000 people. Total healthcare expenditures constituted 4.2 percent of GDP.

Housing

Rapid urbanization of the 1960s and lack of construction funds after 1979 has made housing a critical problem. In 1986 43 percent of all housing units were constructed of brick with iron beams, 19 percent were adobe and wood, and 16 percent were brick with wooden beams. Electricity was available in 84 percent of all housing units, 95 percent had a water toilet, 75 percent had piped water, 54 percent had a kitchen, and 47 percent had a bath.

EDUCATION

Literacy training has been a prime concern in Iran with a literacy corps established to go to villages. In 2000 the illiteracy rate was estimated at 23.1 percent, 16.3 percent for males and 30 percent for females. In 1997 there were 9.2 million elementary school pupils, and 8.8 million secondary school students.

Education is state-financed at all levels from elementary school through university with every student required to serve the government for a number of years equivalent to those spent at the university. Since 1979 Khomeini promoted Islamization of the education system.

The country's sixteen universities, including the University of Tehran, were closed after the 1979 revolution and then reopened gradually between 1982 and 1983 with Islamic curriculums. Iran also has fifty colleges and forty technological institutes. In 1997 all higher-level institutions had 579,070 students.

2000 KEY EVENTS TIMELINE

January

- Ayatollah Ali Khamenei pardons Tehran's reformist former mayor, Gholamhossein Karbaschi.

February

- Some 500,000 citizens celebrate the twenty-first anniversary of the Islamic revolution.

March

- Votes from the February 18 legislative election are recounted, resulting in no change in the results reported earlier: supporters of the president, Mohammad Khatami, win an estimated 75 percent of the 290 seats.

April

- In an effort to clamp down on reform, Khamenei shuts down over a dozen reformist newspapers.

May

- On May 30 Khatami supporter Ayatollah Medhi Karrubi wins election as parliamentary speaker.

June

- A court closes one of the few remaining liberal newspapers, *Bayan,* challenging the Parliament's goal to loosen restrictions on freedom of the press.
- On June 21 Iran, along with other OPEC members, agrees to increase oil production.

July

- When temperatures in Abadan reach 127°F (53°C) for four days in a row, authorities cut off drinking water to preserve the supply, and violent protesters engage in vandalism.
- The Revolutionary Court convicts ten Jewish men of spying for Israel on July 1, sentencing them to prison for four to thirteen years each. Observers suspect that they were framed for their religious beliefs.
- The Minister of Education eases the dress code for elementary school students on July 18, allowing them to wear "bright, happy colors."

August

- Muslim authorities allow women to lead prayer for other women on August 1.
- The People's Mujahedeen, an outlawed opposition group positioned on the Iraqi border, kills two Iranian soldiers in a border skirmish on August 2.
- On August 6 Ayatollah Ali Khamenei orders Parliament to drop a bill for press reform that would improve free speech rights in the country.
- Officials crack down on reformers, especially authors and journalists, arresting two well-known professionals: Ibrahim Nabavi and Mohammad Qoochani, on August 14.
- On August 21 two pro-reform publishers, Faraneh Behzadi, and Fatemeh Farahmandpour, are arrested for insulting Islam and the state.
- Student riots calling for reforms occur during the entire last week of August in Khorramabad. On August 29 they accuse government troops of killing one student, and hospitalizing sixty students.

September

- Iran's parliament speaker announces that attempts are being made in the United States to lift trade sanctions against Iran after American and Iranian lawmakers met for the first time since the 1979 Islamic revolution. However, Iran's President Mohammad Khatami claims that relations between Iran and the United States will improve only if the Americans apologize for past policies in Iran.
- Iran's reformist-controlled parliament votes to investigate attacks on a student pro-democracy seminar in August that led to rioting and the death of a policeman.

- Iran invites applications from foreign banks and other financial institutions to operate in its free trade zones—the first such foreign involvement in Iran since the 1979 Islamic revolution.
- Iran's hard-line judiciary sentences twenty-four people to jail terms of one to five years for their role in several days of rioting in Khalkhal. Protests erupted in April after the hard-line Guardian Council, which oversees elections, annulled the election of reformist Keikavous Khaknejad and awarded the seat to Mottahar Kazemi, a cleric hard-liner who came in second.
- Iran's notorious Tohid prison, run by the intelligence ministry, is closed down.
- Farah Khosravi announces her intention to be the first woman to run for the presidency in Iran on September 19.
- Russia freezes a contract to sell laser equipment to Iran because of U.S. concern about technology transfers to the Islamic republic.

October

- Minister of Culture Ayatollah Mohajerani resigns October 3 due to conservative pressure. He supported a more liberal regime during his three years in office.

November

- Iranian President Mohammad Khatami meets with Japanese Prime Minister Yoshiro Mori November 1; they agree to develop the biggest untapped oil reserve in the world, found at Azadegan, Iran.
- Thousands of Iranians march in Tehran near the former U.S. embassy November 3 to celebrate the anniversary of the U.S. diplomatic departure from Iran, and the Islamic revolution, in 1979.
- President Khatami urges Muslim leaders to sever ties with Israel November 11.
- Russia notifies U.S. Secretary of State Madeleine Albright November 22 that it will begin to sell weapons to Iran after December 1. A secret agreement made between Russia and U.S. Vice President Al Gore in 1995 to halt arms sales to Iran is made public during the political campaign.

December

- Soccer fans attending a match between the countries top two teams engage in a brawl after the match in a Tehran suburb, destroying over 250 vehicles. An Iranian soccer official observes that soccer fans' behavior has become more unruly and destructive since women have been banned from attending matches.

ANALYSIS OF EVENTS: 2000

BUSINESS AND THE ECONOMY

With 80 percent of its export earnings and around half of its government revenues supplied by the petroleum industry, Iran—OPEC's second-largest oil producer—was one of the countries most buoyed by the recovery of oil prices since March 1999. By mid-2000 there were signs that the nation's economy, buffeted by the drop in world oil prices in 1998 and early 1999, was beginning to rebound. Public finances had improved, the deficit had dropped, and the trade balance and current account were expected to yield surpluses. Growth was predicted to reach 4.5 percent.

The government's latest five-year plan, which took effect in March, aimed to counter the continuing high rate of unemployment—reported at 14 percent—with still higher economic growth through structural reforms including the elimination of energy subsidies. Also planned were privatization of about 2,000 state-owned enterprises, elimination of state transport, communications, and utilities monopolies, and programs to attract increased foreign investment. In August parliament approved a bill aimed at increasing foreign investment, primarily by guaranteeing the safety of foreign assets from government seizure, as had happened following the Islamic revolution in 1979.

In spite of promising economic figures, a record-breaking drought continued to affect the lives of at least half of the country's population, spurring Iran's government to seek international aid in a plea to the United Nations.

GOVERNMENT AND POLITICS

As of 2000 the promise of sweeping political, economic, and social liberalization held out by the election of reformist president Mohammed Khatami two years earlier had yet to become a reality. Khatami's ability to effect large-scale change remained limited by the continued power of the country's clerical elite. Even the triumph of the president's liberal supporters in the February parliamentary elections, in which they won roughly 75 percent of the contested seats, failed to overcome the impasse between progressive and hard-line reactionary elements in the country's power structure. The executive and legislative branches continued to be opposed by the judiciary, which was controlled by Muslim clerics, and failed to gain real control of the country's security forces.

Khatami's political opponents countered his parliamentary victory by a concerted crackdown on the country's liberal media, shutting down about twenty newspapers and journals in the following months and jailing a number of respected journalists. The offenders were charged with violating the principles of the country's Islamic revolution, whose twenty-first anniversary had been marked by mass celebrations in February. Political tensions peaked with a parliamentary showdown early in August, when Iran's supreme religious leader, Ayatollah Ali Khamenei, issued a directive forcing legislators to reject a bill easing press censorship. Following the bill's defeat, a court closed the nation's remaining liberal newspaper and jailed four more independent journalists. However, President Khatami was not ready to concede defeat. To quell rumors of resignation, he announced in July that he would seek reelection the following May.

On the international front, there were signs of a thaw in relations with two traditional adversaries, Iraq and the United States. High-level talks between Iran and Iraq took place in September, and plans were made for Iran's foreign minister to visit Baghdad later in the year. The same month, U.S. Secretary of State Madeleine Albright and Iranian Foreign Minister Kamal Kharrazi both took part in discussions on Afghanistan at the United Nations, marking the first time in over twenty years that top officials of the two countries have participated in any talks together.

CULTURE AND SOCIETY

The widespread frustration produced by continuing barriers to political reform raised by Iran's clerical establishment found one form of expression in July, when thousands demonstrated in the capital city of Teheran. The demonstration, which united pro-democracy students and residents of Teheran's poor neighborhoods spurred by economic issues, led to violence that pitted protesters against security forces and Islamic militants. Right-wing militants and reform-minded students clashed again in August, in the western city of Khorromabad.

In spite of political and religious barriers to reform, women saw progress in a number of areas. In August, senior religious leaders issued a declaration allowing women to prayer services for women worshippers, the first time such a dispensation had been made in the history of the Shia Muslim religion. The following month brought the announcement that an Iranian woman, Farah Khosravi, intended to run for president of the country in 2001. Although she was endorsed by an established political party, as of late 2000 it was not known if in fact she would be allowed to run. The campaign to raise literacy levels countrywide, begun following the Islamic revolution, had yielded dramatic results for women. The percentage of women attending school was nearly equal to that of men, and young women accounted for 40 percent of university students, suggesting that the percentage of women in the work force—currently 12 percent—is likely to rise substantially in the future.

Iranian women also received attention internationally when *Dayereh (The Circle),* a film directed by Jafar Panahi chronicling the oppression of women in Iran, won the Golden Lion award (the top prize) at the Venice film festival in September. The same month, Iran earned international recognition at the Olympics, when weightlifter Hossein Tavakoli won an Olympic gold medal in the 105-kilogram competition.

DIRECTORY

CENTRAL GOVERNMENT

Head of State

Leader of the Islamic Revolution
Ayatollah Ali Hoseini-Khamenei, Office of the Islamic Revolution

President
Mohammad Khatami-Ardakani, Office of the President, al-Shariati Ave., Tehran, Iran
E-MAIL: iranemb@salamiran.org

Ministers

Minister of Foreign Affairs
Kamal Kharazi, Ministry of Foreign Affairs, Kushak Mersi Street, Ferdusi Ave., 11200 Tehran, Iran
FAX: +98 (21) 3116276

Minister of Agriculture and Rural Development
Mahmud Hojati, Ministry of Agriculture and Rural Development

Minister of Commerce
Mohammad Shariat-Madari, Ministry of Commerce

Minister of Reconstruction Jihad
Mohammad Saidi-Kia, Ministry of Reconstruction Jihad

Minister of Cooperatives
Morteza Haji-Qaem, Ministry of Cooperatives

Minister of Culture and Guidance
Ahmad Masjed-Jamei, Ministry of Culture and Higher Education

Minister of Defense and Armed Forces Logistics
Ali Shamkhani, Ministry of Defense and Armed Forces Logistics

Minister of Economic Affairs and Finance
Hosein Namazi, Ministry of Economic Affairs and Finance

Minister of Education and Training
Hosein Mozafar, Ministry of Education and Training

Minister of Energy
Habibollah Bitaraf, Ministry of Energy

Minister of Health, Treatment, and Medical Education
Mohammad Farhadi, Ministry of Health, Treatment, and Medical Education

Minister of Housing and Urban Development
Ali Abdol-Alizadeh, Ministry of Housing and Urban Development

Minister of Intelligence and Security
Hojjat al-Eslam Mohammad Ali Yunesi, Ministry of Intelligence and Security

Minister of Interior
Hojjat al-Eslam Abdol Vahed Musavi-Lari, Ministry of Interior

Minister of Justice
Hojjat al-Eslam Mohammad Esmail Shoshtari, Ministry of Justice

Minister of Labor and Social Affairs
Hosein Kamali, Ministry of Labor and Social Affairs

Minister of Industries & Mines
Eshaq Jahangiri, Ministry of Mines and Metals

Minister of Petroleum/Oil
Bijan Namdar-Zanganeh, Ministry of Petroleum/Oil

Minister of Post, Telegraph, and Telephone
Ahmad Motamedi, Ministry of Post, Telegraph, and Telephone

Minister of Roads and Transport
Rahman Dadman, Ministry of Roads and Transport

POLITICAL ORGANIZATIONS

Jameh-ye Ruhaniyat Mobarez-JRM (Militant Clerics Association)

NAME: Mehdi Mahdavi-Karubi

Servants of Reconstruction

Executives of Construction

Islamic Iran Solidarity Party

Islamic Partnership Front

DIPLOMATIC REPRESENTATION

Embassies in Iran

Australia
No. 11, 23rd St., Khalid Islambuli Ave., P.O. Box 15875-4334, Abbasabad, 15138 Tehran, Iran
PHONE: +98 (21) 8866153
FAX: +98 (21) 8720484

Belgium
Ave. Shahid Fayyaz Babak Street 3, Tehran, Iran
PHONE: +98 (21) 2044574
FAX: +98 (21) 2040733

Denmark
18 Dashti Street, Tehran, Iran
PHONE: +98 (21) 2030009
FAX: + 98 (21) 2030007
E-MAIL: ambadane.teheran@inet.uni2.dk
TITLE: Ambassador
NAME: Hugo Østergaard-Andersen

Ireland
Ave. Mirdamad Khiaban Razane Shomali 8, Tehran, Iran
PHONE: +98 (21) 2227672
FAX: +98 (21) 2222731

Italy
81 Ave. Neuphle le Chateau, Tehran, Iran
PHONE: +98 (21) 6496955; 6496956; 6496957
FAX: +98 (21) 6496961

New Zealand
Ave. Mirza-ye-ShiraziShahid, Ali-ye-MirzaHassani Street No. 29, Tehran, Iran
PHONE: +98 (21) 8715083; 8860336
FAX: +98 (21) 8861715; 8860336

Russia
39 Neauphle-le-Chateau, Tehran, Iran

United Kingdom
Ferdossi Ave., Tehran, Iran
TITLE: Chargé d'Affaires
NAME: J. R. James

JUDICIAL SYSTEM

Supreme Court

BROADCAST MEDIA

The Voice of the Islamic Republic of Iran

PO Box 3333, Tehran, Iran
PHONE: +98 (21) 2041051
E-MAIL: irib@dci.iran.com
WEBSITE: http://netiran.com/PersianRadio.html
LANGUAGE: 30 languages

Islamic Republic of Iran Broadcasting (IRIB)

PO Box 19395-333, Tehran, Iran
PHONE: +98 (91) 2160
FAX: +98 (21) 2045056; 2045056
E-MAIL: webmaster@irib.com
WEBSITE: http://www.irib.com
TITLE: President
CONTACT: Dr. Ali Larijani
BROADCASTS: 24 hours/day
TYPE: Government

COLLEGES AND UNIVERSITIES

Shahid Chamran University

Ahwaz, Khuzestan, Iran

University of Sistan & Baluchistan

PO Box 98135-987, Zahedan, Iran

Isfahan University

Isfahan, Iran
PHONE: +98 (31) 680069
E-MAIL: acmadi@ui.ac.ir
WEBSITE: http://www.ui.ac.ir

Payame Noor University

Lashkarak Rd., POB 19395-4697, Tehran, Iran
PHONE: +98 (21) 2442042
FAX: +98 (21) 2441511
E-MAIL: info@pnu.ac.ir
WEBSITE: http://www.pnu.ac.ir

University of Tehran

Enghelab Ave 16 Azar Street, Tehran, Iran
PHONE: +98 (21) 6462699
FAX: +98 (21) 6409348
E-MAIL: publicrel@lman.ut.ac.ir
WEBSITE: http://www.ut.ac.ir

Shiraz University

Zand Ave., Shiraz, Iran
PHONE: +98 (71) 59220
FAX: +98 (71) 332227
E-MAIL: webadmin@succ.shirazu.ar.ir
WEBSITE: http://www.shirazu.ac.ir

Ferdowsi University of Mashhad

Mashad, Iran
WEBSITE: http://www.um.ac.ir

Tehran Art University

4 Balavar St Enghlab Ave, POB 15875-1988, Tehran 15917, Iran

Shahid Beheshti University

PO Box 19395/4716, Tehran 19834, Iran
PHONE: +98 (21) 2403003
WEBSITE: http://www.sbu.ac.ir

Az-Zahra University

Vanak, Tehran 19938, Iran
PHONE: +98 (21) 8044051
FAX: +98 (21) 8035187
E-MAIL: webmaster@azzahra.ac.ir
WEBSITE: http://www.azzahra.ac.ir

Tabriz University

Tabriz 711-51664, Iran
PHONE: +98 (41) 342519
E-MAIL: administrator@ark.tabrizu.ac.ir
WEBSITE: http://www.tabrizu.ac.ir

NEWSPAPERS AND MAGAZINES

Iran Press Digest

Iran Press Digest Establishment, Hafiz Ave., 4 Kucheh Hurtab, PO Box 11365-5551, Teheran, Iran
TITLE: Editor
CONTACT: Ed. J. Behrouz

Iran Times International

2727 Wisconsin Ave. NW, Washington, DC 20007
PHONE: +(202) 6599868
FAX: +(202) 3377449
TITLE: Editor
CONTACT: Javad Khakba

Abrar

26, Shahid Danesh Kian Aley, below Zartosht. St. Vali-Asr Avenue, Tehran, Iran
PHONE: +98 (21) 8848270
FAX: +98 (21) 8849200

Alik

Jomhori Islami Ave. Allik Alley, PO Box 11365-953, 11357 Tehran, Iran
PHONE: +98 (21) 676671

Ettelaat

Ettelaat Bldg, S. Naft Ave. & Mirdamad Blvd. 11144 Tehran, Iran
PHONE: +98 (21) 3281
FAX: +98 (21) 29999
E-MAIL: bijan@ettelaat@com
WEBSITE: http://www.ettelaat.com
TITLE: International Ad Manager
CONTACT: M. Sarshar
CIRCULATION: 350,000

Hamshahri

Municipality of Tehran, 91, Motahari & Schravardi Jct., 15677 Tehran, Iran
PHONE: +98 (21) 8707755
FAX: +98 (21) 8707754
E-MAIL: advertising@hamshahri.org
WEBSITE: http://www.hamshahri.net
TITLE: Editor
CONTACT: Mohammad Atrianfar
CIRCULATION: 480,000

Jahan Eghtesad

156 Hoghooghi St., 5/F., Sharaiti Ave., 16119 Tehran, Iran
PHONE: +98 (21) 763040
FAX: +98 (21) 765400
E-MAIL: vahid@gpg.com
WEBSITE: http://www.neda.net/je
TITLE: Mng Publisher
CONTACT: Saeed Taghipour

Kayhan

Kayhan Group of Newspapers, PO Box 11365-9631, 11444 Tehran, Iran
PHONE: +98 (21) 3111127; 3112730; 3111126
FAX: +98 (21) 3906844; 3900026
E-MAIL: kayhan@istn.irost.com
WEBSITE: http://neda.net/kayhan/index.htm
TITLE: Editor
CONTACT: Husain Shariatmadri
CIRCULATION: 300,000

Tehran Times

32 Kouche Bimeh, Nejatollahi Ave., Tehran, Iran
PHONE: +98 (21) 8810293
FAX: +98 (21) 8808214
WEBSITE: http://www.tehrantimes.com

Iran News

Sokhan Gostar Co., 41 Lida St. Valie Asr. St., North of Vaak Sq., Tehran 19697, Iran
PHONE: +98 (21) 8888148
FAX: +98 (21) 8786475; 8786447
E-MAIL: irannews@www.dci.ir
WEBSITE: http://www.netiran.com
TITLE: Editor
CONTACT: Shizad Bozorgmeiir
CIRCULATION: 35,000

Iran Oil News

Petroleum Ministry, PO Box 1863, Central NIOC Bldg., Taleghani Ave., Tehran, Iran

Iranian

Box 34842, Bethesda, MD 20827-0842
E-MAIL: bulletin@iranian.com
WEBSITE: http://www.iranian.com
TITLE: Editor
CONTACT: Jahanshah Javid

PUBLISHERS

Amir Kabir Book Publishing & Distribution Co.

PO Box 1136-54191, Tehran, Iran
PHONE: +964 (021) 6463487; 390752
FAX: +964 (1) 6461931
TITLE: Director
CONTACT: H. Anwary

Scientific and Cultural Publications

Ministry of Culture & Higher Education, 64th St., Sayyed Jamal-E-Din Asad Abadi Ave., Tehran, Iran
PHONE: +964 (021) 685475
FAX: +964 (021) 686278
SUBJECTS: History, Philosophy, Religion, Science

University of Tehran Publicatons & Printing Organizations

Enghelad Ave. & 16 Azar St., Tehran, Iran
PHONE: +964 (021) 6462622
FAX: +964 (021) 6462622
WEBSITE: http://www.ut.ac.ir
TITLE: Man. Director
CONTACT: Dr. A. Rastgou

RELIGIOUS ORGANIZATIONS

Islamic

Islamic Culture Propagation Office

Daftar Nashr Farhang Islami
Ferdowsi Avenue, Tehran, Islamic Republic of Iran
PHONE: +98 (21) 3114302
E-MAIL: maleki@islamcpo.com
WEBSITE: : http://www.islamcpo.com/
TITLE: Managing Director
NAME: Abbas Maleki

Islamic Women's Institute
No. 1-275 Hedayat St., N. Saddi, Tehran, Iran
PHONE: +98 (21) 7537022
FAX: +98 (21) 7537022
E-MAIL: eghtesad@rose.ipm.ac.ir
NAME: Azam Alaie Taleghani

FURTHER READING

Articles

Drosdiak, William, "OPEC Agrees on Modest Output Increase," *Washington Post,* June 21, 2000, PM Extra.

Miller, Bill. "U.S. Judge Orders Iran to Pay $327 Million in Two Deaths." *Washington Post,* July 12, 2000, p. A5.

"The Month in Review: January 2000." *Current History,* March 2000, p. 141.

Sach, Susan. "Candidates for Reform Show Gains in Iran Tallies." *New York Times,* February 20, 2000, p. A7.

Sachs, Susan. "Iran Closes Another Paper of Reform." *New York Times,* June 26, 2000, p. A7.

Schneider, Howard. "Moderate Cleric Chosen for Iran's Speaker," *Washington Post,* May 30, 2000, PM Extra.

Internet

BBC News Online. "Iran Run-Off Goes Ahead." May 5, 2000. [Online] Available http://news6.thdo.bbc.co.uk/hi/english/world/middle_east/newsid_737000/737060.stm (accessed June 20, 2000).

IRAN: STATISTICAL DATA

For sources and notes see "Sources of Statistics" at the front of each volume.

GEOGRAPHY

Geography

Area:

Total: 1.648 million sq km

Land: 1.636 million sq km.

Land boundaries:

Total: 5,440 km.

Border countries: Afghanistan 936 km, Armenia 35 km, Azerbaijan-proper 432 km, Azerbaijan-Naxcivan exclave 179 km, Iraq 1,458 km, Pakistan 909 km, Turkey 499 km, Turkmenistan 992 km.

Coastline: 2,440 km

Note: Iran also borders the Caspian Sea (740 km).

Climate: mostly arid or semiarid, subtropical along Caspian coast.

Terrain: rugged, mountainous rim; high, central basin with deserts, mountains; small, discontinuous plains along both coasts.

Natural resources: petroleum, natural gas, coal, chromium, copper, iron ore, lead, manganese, zinc, sulfur.

Land use:

Arable land: 10%

Permanent crops: 1%

Permanent pastures: 27%

Forests and woodland: 7%

Other: 55% (1993 est.).

HUMAN FACTORS

Demographics (A)

	1990	1995	1998	2000	2010	2020	2030	2040	2050
Population	NA	NA	64,353	65,620	73,772	84,225	91,713	96,926	100,199
Life expectancy - males	NA	NA	67.8	68.3	70.9	73.1	75.0	76.5	77.8
Life expectancy - females	NA	NA	70.3	71.1	74.3	77.0	79.3	81.2	82.8
Birth rate (per 1,000)	NA	NA	20.5	18.3	19.7	16.2	12.4	12.0	10.7
Death rate (per 1,000)	NA	NA	5.6	5.4	5.3	5.2	5.9	7.3	9.1
Women of reproductive age (15-49 yrs.)	NA	NA	16,461	17,555	21,972	23,537	24,206	22,452	21,497
Fertility rate	NA	NA	2.5	2.2	2.0	1.9	1.8	1.8	1.7

Except as noted, values for vital statistics are in thousands; life expectancy is in years.

Health Personnel

	National Data	World Data (wtd ave)
Total health expenditure as a percentage of GDP, 1990-1998[a]		
Public sector	1.7	2.5
Private sector	2.5	2.9
Total[b]	4.3	5.5
Health expenditure per capita in U.S. dollars, 1990-1998[a]		
Purchasing power parity	216	561
Total	93	483
Availability of health care facilities per 100,000 people		
Hospital beds 1990-1998[a]	160	330
Doctors 1992-1995[a]	NA	122
Nurses 1992-1995[a]	NA	248

Health Indicators

	National Data	World Data
Life expectancy at birth (years)		
1980	60	61
1998	71	67
Daily per capita supply of calories		
1970	2,051	2,358
1997	2,836	2,791
Daily per capital supply of protein		
1997 (grams)	75	74
Total fertility rate (births per woman)		
1980	6.7	3.7
1998	2.7	2.7
Population with access (%)		
To safe water (1990-96)	83	NA
To sanitation (1990-96)	67	NA
People living with (1997)		
Tuberculosis (cases per 100,000)	17.7	60.4
Malaria (cases per 100,000)	59.9	42.2
HIV/AIDS (% aged 15 - 49 years)	NA	0.99

Infants and Malnutrition

	National Data	World Data (wtd ave)
Under 5 mortality rate (1989)	33	NA
% of infants with low birthweight (1992-98)[1]	10	17
Births attended by skilled health staff (% of total births 1996-98)	74	52
% fully immunized at 1 year of age (1995-98)[1]		
TB	98	82
DPT	100	77
Polio	100	77
Measles	100	74
Prevalence of child malnutrition (1992-98)[1] (based on weight for age, % of children under 5 years)	16	30

Ethnic Division

Persian 51%
Azeri 24%
Gilaki and Mazandarani 8%
Kurd 7%
Arab 3%
Lur 2%
Baloch 2%
Turkmen 2%
Other 1%

Religion

Shi'a Muslim 89%
Sunni Muslim 10%
Zoroastrian, Jewish, Christian, and Baha'i 1%

Major Languages

Persian and Persian dialects 58%
Turkic and Turkic dialects 26%
Kurdish 9%
Luri 2%
Balochi 1%
Arabic 1%
Turkish 1%
Other 2%

EDUCATION

Public Education Expenditures

	1980	1997
Public expenditures on education as % of GNP	7.5	4.0
Expenditures per student as % of GNP per capita		

	1980	1997
Primary	16.2	8.2
Secondary	NA	11.0
Tertiary	67.6	7.6
Teachers' compensation as % of total current education expenditures	NA	47.4
Pupils per teacher at the primary level	NA	31
Duration of primary education in years	NA	5

World data for comparison		
Public expenditures on education as % of GNP (mean)	3.9	4.8
Pupils per teacher at the primary level (wtd ave)	NA	33
Duration of primary education in years (mean)	NA	9

(Continued on next page.)

GOVERNMENT & LAW

Military Affairs (A)

	1990	1992	1995	1996	1997
Military expenditures					
Current dollars (mil.)	6,110	3,760	3,520	3,870	4,730
1997 constant dollars (mil.)	7,160	4,170	3,640	3,940	4,730
Armed forces (000)	440	528	530	540[e]	575[e]
Gross national product (GNP)					
Current dollars (bil.)	101	126	141	151	158
1997 constant dollars (bil.)	118	139	146	153	158
Central government expenditures (CGE)					
1997 constant dollars (bil.)	24	28	34	41	41
People (mil.)	56.9	58.9	61.5	62.6	63.5
Military expenditure as % of GNP	6.0	3.0	2.5	2.6	3.0
World data on military expenditure as % of GNP	4.5	3.4	2.7	2.6	2.6
Military expenditure as % of CGE	30.2	14.9	10.7	9.5	11.6
World data on military expenditure as % of CGE	17.0	12.5	10.5	10.3	10.2
Military expenditure per capita (1997 $)	126	71	569	63	74
World data on military expenditure per capita (1997 $)	242	173	146	143	145
Armed forces per 1,000 people (soldiers)	7.7	9.0	8.6	8.6	9.1
World data on armed forces per 1,000 people (soldiers)	5.3	4.5	4.1	3.9	3.8
GNP per capita (1997 $)	2,080	2,360	2,370	2,450	2,490
Arms imports[6]					
Current dollars (mil.)	1,900	850	330	350	850
1997 constant dollars (mil.)	2,225	942	342	356	850
Arms exports[6]					
Current dollars (mil.)	0	20	310	60	30
1997 constant dollars (mil.)	0	22	321	61	30
Total imports[7]					
Current dollars (mil.)	20,320	25,860	13,880	16,270	14,620[e]
1997 constant dollars (mil.)	23,800	28,670	14,370	16,550	14,620[e]
Total exports[7]					
Current dollars (mil.)	15,320	19,870	18,360	22,390	25,000
1997 constant dollars (mil.)	17,940	22,030	19,010	22,760	25,000
Arms as percent of total imports[8]	9.0	3.3	2.4	2.2	5.8
Arms as percent of total exports[8]	0	0.1	1.7	0.3	0.1

(Continued on next page.)

EDUCATION (cont.)

Educational Attainment (A)

Age group (1987) . . . . 10+

Population of this age group 10,628,447

Highest level attained (%)

No schooling 52.8

First level

Not completed 21.6

Completed . . . . NA

Entered second level 11.6

Entered post-secondary 4.1

Literacy Rates (C)

Year	Adult Literacy Rate (Population aged 15 years and older)
1980	50.60%
1985	56.80%
1990	64.00%
1995	70.80%
1997	73.40%

Libraries

National Libraries 1995

Administrative Units 1

Service Points or Branches 5

Number of Volumes (000) 411

Registered Users (000) 13

Loans to Users (000) 59

Total Library Staff 309

Public Libraries 1995

Administrative Units 26

Service Points or Branches 1,002

Number of Volumes (000) 15,984

Registered Users (000) 29,862

Loans to Users (000) 15,186

Total Library Staff 2,488

GOVERNMENT & LAW (cont.)

Political Parties

Islamic Consultative Assembly (Majles-e-Shura-ye-Eslami)	% of vote	no. of seats
Reformers	70%	170
Conservatives	30%	45
Independents		10

Elections were last held 18 February-April 2000 (next to be held 2004). Sixty five seats were up for runoff election in April 2000.

Government Budgets (A)

Year: 1998

Total Expenditures: 87,962 Billions of Rials

Expenditures as a percentage of the total by function:

General public services and public order . . . . . . 7.08[f]

Defense . . . . 8.50[f]

Education . . . . 15.99[f]

Health . . . . 6.43[f]

Social Security and Welfare . . . . 13.57[f]

Housing and community amenities . . . . 5.64[f]

Recreational, cultural, and religious affairs . . . . 3.14[f]

Fuel and energy . . . . 10.70[f]

Agriculture, forestry, fishing, and hunting . . . . . . 2.00[f]

Mining, manufacturing, and construction . . . . . . 0.68[f]

Transportation and communication . . . . 5.18[f]

Other economic affairs and services . . . . 11.31[f]

LABOR FORCE

Total Labor Force (A)

15.4 million. There is a shortage of skilled labor..

Labor Force by Occupation

Agriculture 33%

Industry 25%

Services 42%

Data for 1997 est.

Unemployment Rate

25% (1999 est.)

PRODUCTION SECTOR

Energy Production

Production . . . . 95.31 billion kWh

Production by source

Fossil fuel 92.33%

Hydro 7.67%

Nuclear 0%

Other 0%

Exports . . . . 0 kWh

Data for 1998.

Energy Consumption

Consumption . . . . 88.638 billion kWh

Imports . . . . .0 kWh

Data for 1998.

Transportation

Highways:

Total: 140,200 km.

Paved: 49,440 km (including 470 km of expressways).

Unpaved: 90,760 km (1998 est.).

Waterways: 904 km; the Shatt al Arab is usually navigable by maritime traffic for about 130 km; channel has been dredged to 3 m and is in use.

Pipelines: crude oil 5,900 km; petroleum products 3,900 km; natural gas 4,550 km.

Merchant marine:

Total: 138 ships (1,000 GRT or over) totaling 3,517,751 GRT/6,208,230 DWT.

Ships by type: bulk 45, cargo 36, chemical tanker 4, combination bulk 1, container 7, liquified gas 1, multi-functional large load carrier 6, petroleum tanker 26, refrigerated cargo 2, roll-on/roll-off 9, short-sea passenger 1 (1999 est.).

Airports: 288 (1999 est.).

Airports - with paved runways: 112.

Airports - with unpaved runways: 176.

Top Agriculture Products

Wheat, rice, other grains, sugar beets, fruits, nuts, cotton; dairy products, wool; caviar.

Top Mining Products (B)

Mineral resources include: coal, chromium, copper, iron ore, lead, manganese, zinc, sulfur.

MANUFACTURING SECTOR

GDP & Manufacturing Summary (A)

	1980	1985	1990	1995
GDP ($-1990 mil.)[1]	77,089	97,385	88,173	112,095
Per capita ($-1990)[1]	1,964	1,991	1,489	1,640
Manufacturing share (%) (current prices)[1]	9.1	8.5	12.3	15.0[e]
Manufacturing				
Value added ($-1990 mil.)[1]	6,234	7,920	10,621	14,196[e]
Industrial production index	79	116	100	148[e]
Value added ($ mil.)	8,186	5,374	7,994	9,147[e]
Gross output ($ mil.)	15,870	10,994	17,373	20,725[e]
Employment (000)	470	611	653	647[e]
Profitability (% of gross output)				
Intermediate input (%)	48	52	54	56[e]
Wages and salaries inc. supplements (%)	29	28	15	16[e]
Gross operating surplus	23	19	31	28[e]
Productivity ($)				
Gross output per worker	33,756	17,161	26,007	31,040[e]
Value added per worker	17,411	8,790	11,966	14,102[e]
Average wage (inc. supplements)	9,668	4,893	3,925	5,278[e]
Value added ($ mil.)				
Food products	930	553	737	1,170[e]
Beverages	145	133	152	199[e]
Tobacco products	190[e]	46	82	77[e]
Textiles	1,329	931	1,355	989[e]
Wearing apparel	78	33	85	27[e]
Leather and fur products	36	30	69	34[e]
Footwear	100	71	85	50[e]
Wood and wood products	68	52	108	64[e]
Furniture and fixtures	33	21	32	30[e]
Paper and paper products	135	115	130	152[e]
Printing and publishing	80	42	114	86[e]
Industrial chemicals	93	102	227	434[e]
Other chemical products	278	266	412	490[e]
Petroleum refineries	1,652	386[e]	31[e]	32[e]
Misc. petroleum and coal products	2	14	38	29[e]
Rubber products	93	79	116	191[e]
Plastic products	198	103	164	147[e]
Pottery, china and earthenware	45	33	41	52[e]
Glass and glass products	115	73	73	108[e]

	1980	1985	1990	1995
Other non-metal mineral products	819	601	688	703[e]
Iron and steel	367	313	893	1,393[e]
Non-ferrous metals	48	84	413	332[e]
Metal products	319	244	338	411[e]
Non-electrical machinery	208	277	724	368[e]
Electrical machinery	391	329	332	716[e]
Transport equipment	399	407	504	763[e]
Prof. and scientific equipment	24	24	23	60[e]
Other manufacturing	11	12	28	40[e]

COMMUNICATIONS

Daily Newspapers

	National Data	World Data for Comparison
Daily Newspapers		
Number of Dailies	32	8,391
Total Circulation (000)	1,651	548,000
Circulation per 1,000 inhabitants	26	96

Telecommunications

Telephones - main lines in use: 7 million (1998 est.).

Telephones - mobile cellular: 265,000 (August 1998).

Telephone system: inadequate but currently being modernized and expanded with the goal of not only improving the efficiency and increasing the volume of the urban service but also bringing telephone service to several thousand villages, not presently connected.

Domestic: as a result of heavy investing in the telephone system since 1994, the number of long distance channels in the microwave radio relay trunk has grown substantially; many villages have been brought into the net; the number of main lines in the urban systems have approximately doubled; and thousands of mobile cellular subscribers are being served; moreover, the technical level of the system has been raised by the installation of thousands of digital switches.

International: HF radio and microwave radio relay to Turkey, Azerbaijan, Pakistan, Afghanistan, Turkmenistan, Syria, Kuwait, Tajikistan, and Uzbekistan; submarine fiber-optic cable to UAE with access to Fiber-Optic Link Around the Globe (FLAG); Trans Asia Europe (TAE) fiber-optic line runs from Azerbaijan through the northern portion of Iran to Turkmenistan with expansion to Georgia and Azerbaijan; satellite earth stations - 9 Intelsat and 4 Inmarsat; Internet service available but limited to electronic mail to promote Iranian culture.

Radio broadcast stations: AM 72, FM 5, shortwave 5 (1998).

Radios: 17 million (1997).

Television broadcast stations: 28 (plus 450 low-power repeaters) (1997).

Televisions: 4.61 million (1997).

Internet Service Providers (ISPs): 1 (1999).

FINANCE, ECONOMICS, & TRADE

Economic Indicators

National product: GDP—purchasing power parity—$347.6 billion (1999 est.).

National product real growth rate: 1% (1999 est.).

National product per capita: $5,300 (1999 est.).

Inflation rate—consumer price index: 30% (1999 est.).

Balance of Payments

	1993	1994	1995	1996	1997
Exports of goods (f.o.b.)	18,080	19,434	18,360	22,391	18,381
Imports of goods (f.o.b.)	−19,287	−12,617	−12,774	−14,989	−14,123
Trade balance	−1,207	6,817	5,586	7,402	4,258
Services - debits	−5,600	−3,226	−2,339	−3,083	−3,371
Services - credits	1,084	438	593	860	1,192
Private transfers (net)	1,500	1,200	NA	471	400
Government transfers (net)	NA	−2	−4	−8	−7
Overall balance	−4,215	4,956	3,358	5,232	2,213

Exchange Rates

Exchange rates:

Iranian rials (IR) per US$1

January 2000	1,754.90
1999	1,725.93
1998	1,751.86
1997	1,752.92
1996	1,750.76
1995	1,747.93
Black market rate (December 1998)	7,000.00

As of May 1995, the "official rate" of 1,750 rials per US$1 is used for imports of essential goods and services and for oil exports, whereas the "official export rate" of 3,000 rials per US$1 is used for non-oil exports and imports not covered by the official rate. Fiscal year: 21 March - 20 March.

Top Import Origins

Imports (f.o.b., 1998 est.): $13.8 billion.

Origins: Germany, Italy, Japan, UAE, United Kingdom, Belgium.

Top Export Destinations

Exports (f.o.b., 1998 est.): $12.2 billion.

Destinations: Japan, Italy, Greece, France, Spain, South Korea.

Foreign Aid

Recipient: $116.5 million (1995).

Import/Export Commodities

Import Commodities	Export Commodities
Machinery	Petroleum 80%
Military supplies	Carpets
Metal works	Fruits
Foodstuffs	Nuts
Pharmaceuticals	Hides
Technical services	Iron
Refined oil products	Steel

IRAQ

CAPITAL: Baghdad.

FLAG: The national flag is a tricolor of red, white, and black horizontal stripes, with three five-pointed stars in green in the center of the white stripe. In 1991 the phrase *Allahu Akbar* ("God is Great") in green Arabic script was added between the stars.

ANTHEM: *Al-Salaam al-Jumhuri (Salute of the Republic).*

MONETARY UNIT: The Iraqi dinar (ID) is a paper currency of 1,000 fils. There are coins of 1, 5, 10, 25, 50, 100, and 250 fils, and notes of 250 and 500 fils and 1, 5, 10, 50, and 100 dinars. The dinar is extremely unstable, falling to $1 = ID3,000 in 1995.

WEIGHTS AND MEASURES: The metric system is the legal standard, but weights and measures in general use vary, especially in domestic transactions. The unit of land is the dunam, which is equivalent to approximately 0.25 hectare (0.62 acre).

HOLIDAYS: New Year's Day, 1 January; Army Day, 6 January; 14th Ramadan Revolution Day, 8 February; Declaration of the Republic, 14 July; and Peaceful Revolution Day, 17 July. Muslim religious holidays include 'Id al-Fitr, 'Id al-'Adha', Milad an-Nabi, and Islamic New Year.

TIME: 3 PM = noon GMT.

LOCATION AND SIZE: Iraq comprises an area of 437,072 square kilometers (168,754 square miles), slightly more than twice the size of the state of Idaho. It has a total boundary length of 3,681 kilometers (2,288 miles). Iraq's capital city, Baghdad, is located in the east central part of the country.

CLIMATE: Summers are intensely hot and dry, and during the hottest time of the day—often reaching 49°C (120°F) in the shade—people take refuge in underground shelters. Winters are damp and comparatively cold, with temperatures averaging about 10°C (50°F). With annual rainfall of less than 15.1 centimeters (5.9 inches), agriculture is dependent on irrigation.

Republic of Iraq
Al-Jumhuriyah al-'Iraqiyah

INTRODUCTORY SURVEY

RECENT HISTORY

Iraq gained independence in 1932 and was admitted to membership in the League of Nations.

On July 14, 1958, a military takeover led by General 'Abd al-Karim al-Qasim (Kassim) abolished the existing monarchy and established a republic in its place. Iraq left the anti-communist Baghdad Pact that the monarchy had joined in 1955. A farm reform law divided the great land holdings of feudal leaders and a new economic development program emphasized industrialization. Qasim ruled Iraq for over four years before another military takeover, led by Colonel 'Abd as-Salam Muhammad 'Arif, overthrew his government and executed him 1963.

In 1968 General (later Marshal) Ahmad Hasan al-Bakr, heading a section of the Ba'th Party, staged a takeover and established a new government with himself as president until July 1979 when he was followed as president by his chosen successor, Saddam Hussein (Husayn) al-Takriti.

Tensions between Iraq and Iran rose after the Iranian revolution of 1979 and the coming to power of Saddam Hussein. In September 1980 Iraq mounted a full-scale invasion of Iran. Iranian forces launched a slow but successful counterattack with major offensives aimed at the Iraqi oil port of Al Basxrah. Iraqi soldiers repelled the attacks and the war came to a stalemate with tens of thousands of casualties on each side.

The war eventually spread to Persian Gulf shipping, as both sides attacked oil tankers and

ships transporting oil, goods, and arms. It ended in August 1988 after Iran accepted a UN cease-fire proposal. Having suffered enormous casualties and physical damage, Baghdad began the postwar process of reconstruction.

With Kuwait being critical of Iraqi policies, Iraq invaded and occupied it on August 2, 1990. A devastating U.S.-led air war began in January 1991 followed by ground attack. Iraq was defeated, but not occupied. Despite vast destruction and several hundred thousand casualties, Saddam's government remained firmly in control.

Economic sanctions banned oil sales and required Iraq to submit its nonconventional weapons centers to inspection and monitoring. For humanitarian reasons in 1996 the UN agreed to let Iraq export $2 billion in oil to buy food and medical supplies. Iraq has provided inconsistent and false information to the UN Security Council regarding its possession of chemical and other weapons of mass destruction.

In January 1998 the United States sent twenty ships and 30,000 troops to the area as tension grew. UN secretary-general Kofi Annan went to Iraq in February and persuaded Hussein to comply to the inspections. But Iraqi failure to cooperate resulted in American-led air strikes in late 1998 and again in 1999 when Iraq violated the northern no-fly zone almost daily. In 1999 the oil for food program expanded. By 2000 Saddam maintained a strong hold on power despite economic hardships caused by UN sanctions.

GOVERNMENT

Since the 1968 takeover, the Ba'th Party has ruled Iraq by means of the Revolutionary Command Council, which selects the president and a cabinet composed of military and civilian leaders. The president serves as chairman of the Revolutionary Command Council, which exercises both executive and legislative powers. He is also prime minister, commander-in-chief of the armed forces, and secretary-general of the Ba'th Party. Te unicameral National Assembly of 250 members elected by popular vote has little power. Most senior officials are relatives or close associates of Saddam Hussein. Suffrage is universal at age eighteen.

Judiciary

The judiciary is not independent in Iraq. The president can override any court decision. The court system is made up of two distinct branches: security courts and a more conventional court system to handle other charges. The security courts have jurisdiction in all cases involving spying, treason, political dissent, smuggling and currency exchange violations, and drug trafficking. The ordinary civil courts have jurisdiction over civil, commercial, and criminal cases except for those that fall under the jurisdiction of the religious courts. Magistrate courts try most criminal cases in the first instance.

Shari'a (Islamic) courts rule on questions involving religious matters for every court of first instance.

Political Parties

Since 1968 the Arab Ba'th Socialist Party has been the ruling political group in Iraq. A 1991 decree greatly limits political party activity. In 1996 elections only Ba'thists or independent supporters of Saddam Hussein were allowed to run for Assembly seats. In 1999 the country's Kurdish minority had established a number of parties, most in opposition to the central government. Outside Iraq, ethnic, religious, and political opposition groups have organized a common front against Saddam Hussein, but with little effect.

DEFENSE

Iraq's military branches are the army, Republic Guard, navy, air force, Border Guard Force, and Fedayeen Saddam. The Iraqi armed forces, reduced greatly after its defeat in the Gulf War of 1991, are estimated at 429,000 men. The army has a strength of 375,000 men (100,000 recalled reservists); the navy has 2,000 men; and the air force has 35,000 men. The paramilitary forces number up to 50,000 and there are 20,000 frontier and security guards. Expenditures for defense in 1998 was estimated at $1.3 billion, or 6.8 percent of GDP.

ECONOMIC AFFAIRS

Oil is the most important sector of the economy. Petroleum production was badly hurt by the war with Iran, however, and the economy was in serious trouble in 1987. In response to the Iraqi invasion of Kuwait on August 2, 1990, the UN imposed comprehensive economic, financial, and military sanctions, totally isolating the Iraqi economy. However UN Security Council resolutions authorized the export of Iraqi crude oil worth up to $1.6 billion over a limited time to finance humanitarian imports for the Iraqi people.

Public Finance

Government budges are highly compartmentalized into various uses. Since 1980 the decline in oil exports and huge war expenditures forced Iraq to borrow and to raise funds from abroad. Iraq's invasion of Kuwait in 1990, with the consequent infrastructure damage, UN sanctions, and oil embargo, has severely diminished revenues. There are no reliable statistics on Iraq's revenues and expenditures. External debt in 1999 was $130 billion.

Income

In 1999 Iraq's gross domestic product (GDP) was $59.9 billion, or $2,700 per capita. GDP real growth rate was 13 percent and the inflation rate 135 percent. The GDP contribution by economic sector in 1993 was agriculture 6, industry 13 percent, and services 81 percent.

Industry

Main industries are oil refining, food processing, textiles, leather goods, cement and other building materials, tobacco, paper, and sulfur extraction. Iraq has ten oil refineries. In 1995 Iraq produced an estimated 200 million tons of refined petroleum products. The UN allowed limited oil sales in 1999 and 2000.

Banking and Finance

Data on the financial situation in Iraq are not generally available since the main source of official statistics, the Central Bank of Iraq, has not released figures since 1977. After 1991 six new banks were established as a result of liberalizing legislation and the opportunity for large-scale profits from currency speculation.

The Central Bank is striving to maintain the value of the dinar against the dollar through strict monetary policies. Because of the devastated state of the economy, however, it has largely failed in this attempt. In 1994 the black market value of the dinar stood at 750 to the dollar but by 1995 it had fallen to 3,000.

The stock exchange in Baghdad was inaugurated in March 1992 but few statistics are available.

Economic Development

The government both controls and participates in petroleum, agriculture, commerce, banking, and industry. The government promoted a buildup of a tanker fleet to decrease reliance on foreign oil transport companies.

Iraq has an estimated foreign debt of more than $87 billion. The imposition of sanctions against Iraq has destroyed all attempts to stabilize Iraq's payments. Iraq also faces reparation claims arising from the 1980–1988 war. Iraq is also obligated by UN resolutions to pay for various UN agency activities.

SOCIAL WELFARE

A social security law passed in 1971 provides benefits or payments for disability, maternity, old age, unemployment, sickness, and funerals. Excluded are agricultural workers and domestic servants. Although Iraq's constitution guarantees individual rights, the government sharply limits political freedoms and tolerates little public expression of dissent. The government supports equality for women, who make up about 20 percent of the work force. However women are not allowed to travel abroad unaccompanied. A 1990 decree grants immunity to men who kill female family members who have committed an "immoral act" such as adultery.

Although the constitution guarantees individual rights, Iraqis are not free to express their opposition to the government. Political offenders are subject to arbitrary arrest, imprisonment, and torture. Amputation and branding are used as a form of punishment for serious crimes.

Healthcare

During 1985-1995 93 percent of the population had access to health care services. Considerable effort has been made to expand medical facilities to small towns and more remote areas of the country. In 1990-1997 Iraq had sixty doctors per 10,000 people and 1.7 hospital beds per 1,000 inhabitants. In 2000 life expectancy was estimated at sixty-six years.

Housing

After 1980 living conditions for the vast majority of the population improved greatly. Electricity and running water are normal features of all Iraqi villages in rural areas. Brick dwellings are rapidly replacing mud huts in remote places. A trend from single-family dwellings to apartments occurred after 1985.

EDUCATION

Education in all levels including higher education is free. An estimated 42 percent of adults were illiterate in 1995, 29.3 percent of men and 55 percent of women. In 1996 2.9 million students attended 8,145 primary schools, and 1.1 million attended secondary schools. Six years of primary education is compulsory and secondary schools have a three-year intermediate course followed by a two-year course in preparation for entrance to college. There are seven universities in Iraq, the most important being the University of Baghdad. In 1988, 209,818 students were enrolled in all higher-level institutions.

2000 KEY EVENTS TIMELINE

January

- When UN Secretary General Kofi Annan nominates Rolf Ekeus as the new arms inspector for Iraq, the Iraqi press issues attacks, alleging that Annan is proposing an arms inspection system that is infiltrated by spies for the United States.
- U.S. fighter planes bomb an air defense system in northern Iraq.

February

- Iraq announces that it will bar the new UN arms inspections team from the country.

March

- Uday Hussein, president Saddam Hussein's oldest son, runs for Parliament.
- The United States claims that Iraq is funding the terrorist group Mujahedeen Khalq.
- The UN Security Council relaxes controls on Iraqi food and medical purchases and doubles the amount Iraq can spend toward oil equipment.

May

- British Conservative Party alleges the development of strong ties between Serbia and Iraq.

June

- After two people are killed when a gunman opens fire in the United Nations office in Baghdad, demanding that sanctions against Iraq be lifted, security there is tightened.

July

- The government resumes short-range missile testing; missile factories are back on line after a year and a half of reconstruction following U.S. bombings.

August

- The United States bombs a warehouse holding military equipment in southern Iraq on August 11, and two antiaircraft batteries on August 12. Iraq claims that these sites contained food supplies, and a train station, respectively.

September

- The government imposes fees on students on September 4 in the face of economic hardships due to international sanctions.
- On September 11 Iraq refuses to let independent experts into the country to assess the damage caused by economic sanctions.
- A French flight is the first to enter Baghdad on September 22 since U.N. sanctions were imposed in 1990.
- Yemen, which has joined the list of countries intending to send an aircraft to Iraq with a delegation of government officials, medicine, and other humanitarian goods, receives permission from the UN Security Council's sanctions committee.

November

- Iraqi Airlines resumes domestic flights November 5, for the first time since sanctions were imposed in 1991.
- A pipeline linking Iraq to Sudan begins pumping oil November 16 at an estimated 15,000 barrels per day.
- President Saddam Hussein asks the United Nations November 25 to send part of Iraq's food rations to Palestine.
- Iraqi Deputy Prime Minister Tareq Aziz refuses admission of U.N. weapons inspectors November 30.
- Iraq threatens to stop selling oil unless it recieves a separate fifty cents per barrel.

December

- A military parade, Al Aksa Call Parade, held December 31, is the largest since 1991 and is viewed by President Saddam Hussein, who greets units by firing rifle shots from the reviewing stand.

ANALYSIS OF EVENTS: 2000

BUSINESS AND THE ECONOMY

The Iraqi economy continued to deteriorate under the pressure of United Nations-imposed sanctions, which still blocked most imports to and exports from Iraq. The Iraqi currency, the dinar, had lost so much value that most Iraqis earned less than the equivalent of $10 a month. Agriculture, industry, and the nation's infrastructure were breaking down due to the unavailability of imported parts and materials. Many businesses had to close, unemployment increased steadily, and underemployment was rampant, as educated professionals forced out of their jobs resorted to driving taxis or working as street vendors. Public employees continued to work, but at salaries as low as $2.50 per month.

Meanwhile, Saddam Hussein was finding the funds to continue building new palaces—he had a total of nineteen as of 1996—and other grandiose projects, including what is reportedly going to be the world's largest mosque in Baghdad. His close associates continued to live in luxury as well.

GOVERNMENT AND POLITICS

As the tenth anniversary of U.N.-imposed sanctions against Iraq arrived in August 2000, international consensus was growing on the failure of the sanctions to accomplish their goal of deposing Saddam Hussein, as was dismay over the damage they continued to wreak on the Iraqi people.

Saddam Hussein's hold on the country remained as strong as ever. His likeness remained ubiquitous in public places throughout the country, and any political opposition was effectively silenced. In addition, the sixty-three-year-old Iraqi leader appeared to be preparing for an eventual succession by his eldest son, Uday, who was elected to parliament in March.

The continuation of sanctions after the UNSCOM disarmament commission disbanded in 1998 had failed to bring about a resumption of weapons monitoring, as Iraq refused to recognize the new arms control commission authorized by a U.N. Security Council resolution at the end of 1999. It was feared that the significant progress made in dismantling the country's nuclear, chemical, and biological weapons in the years between the Gulf War and 1998 would be lost, as Saddam took advantage of the impasse to disarm. Richard Butler, the former head of UNSCOM, claimed in September that Iraq could build a nuclear weapon within a year if the necessary raw materials were made available.

This possible justification of the existing sanctions was countered by their increasingly visible cost in terms of human suffering. International attention was drawn to the increasingly desperate plight of the Iraqi people by a UNICEF report alleging that the sanctions had caused the deaths of half a million children under the age of five between 1991 and 1998. The oil-for-food humanitarian program initiated in the mid-1990s was, like the sanctions themselves, widely criticized as ineffective, even as the U.N. Security Council renewed the program for another six months in June.

Ironically the three essentially autonomous Kurdish provinces in the north of the country, over which Saddam had effectively lost control, were flourishing, at least in comparison with the rest of Iraq. The oil-for-food program was working dramatically better here than in those parts of the country controlled by Saddam. Agriculture in the region was unaffected by the breakdown of irrigation networks elsewhere in the country. Sanctions also created a flourishing black market.

In September France and Russia, two countries opposed to the U.N. sanctions, seemed to challenge them implicitly by sending flights to Iraq's recently reopened international airport. Both countries claimed that in notifying the United Nations of the flights but not waiting for authorization, they were interpreting the sanctions liberally rather than violating them outright. The French flight carried doctors traveling to Iraq to provide medical assistance, and artists and athletes bound for a cultural festival. The Russians arrived with medical supplies and a delegation of politicians and oil industry executives. The Iraqis hailed both flights as signaling an impending breakdown of the sanctions.

CULTURE AND SOCIETY

As Iraq's economy and infrastructure continued to crumble under the joint pressure of U.N. sanctions and Saddam Hussein's intransigence, ordinary citizens in the formerly prosperous country tried to make do on reduced income as they coped with shortages of food and other basic commodities, contaminated water, power outages, a devastated educational system, and other difficulties. Dramatic increases in crime and prostitution had prompted institution of the death penalty for many offenses. Many educated professionals had left the country.

Two major international reports warned of a dire health crisis in Iraq. Major increases were reported in malnutrition, disease, and infant mortality as hospitals coped with shortages of such crucial commodities as sutures, disinfectant, medications, and blood supplies. Cholera, typhoid, and other diseases that had formerly been eliminated in Iraq had reappeared.

DIRECTORY

CENTRAL GOVERNMENT

Head of State

President
Saddam Hussein, Office of the President, Presidential Palace, Karadat Mariam, Baghdad, Iraq
E-MAIL: irqun@undp.org

Vice President
Taha Yasin Ramadan, Office of the Vice President

Ministers

Prime Minister
Saddam Hussein, Office of the Prime Minister

Deputy Prime Minister
Tariq Aziz, Office of the Deputy Prime Minister

Deputy Prime Minister
Hikmat Mizban Ibrahim al-Azzawi, Office of the Deputy Prime Minister

Deputy Prime Minister
Muhammad Hamza al-Zubaydi, Office of the Deputy Prime Minister

Minister of Agriculture
Abdallah Hamid Mahmud al-Salih, Ministry of Agriculture

Minister of Awqaf and Religious Affairs
Abd al-Munim Ahmad Salih, Ministry of Awqaf and Religious Affairs

Minister of Culture and Information
Humam Abd al-Khaliq Abd al-Ghafur, Ministry of Culture and Information

Minister of Defense
Hashim Ahmad al-Jabburi Tai, Ministry of Defense

Minister of Education
Fahd Salim Shaqrah, Ministry of Education

Minister of Finance
Hikmat Mizban Ibrahim al-Azzawi, Ministry of Finance

Minister of Foreign Affairs
Muhammad Said Kazim al-Sahhaf, Ministry of Foreign Affairs
PHONE: +964 (1) 8879638; 5370091
FAX: +964 (1) 5433746

Minister of Health
Umid Midhat Mubarak, Ministry of Health

Minister of Higher Education and Scientific Research
Abd al-Jabbar Tawfiq, Ministry of Higher Education and Scientific Research

Minister of Housing and Reconstruction
Maan Abdallah al-Sarsam, Ministry of Housing and Reconstruction

Minister of Industry and Minerals
Adnan Abd al-Majid Jasim al-Ani, Ministry of Industry and Minerals

Minister of Interior
Muhammad Zimam Abd al-Razzaq, Ministry of Interior

Minister of Irrigation
Mahmud Dhiyab al-Ahmad, Ministry of Irrigation

Minister of Justice
Mundhir Ibrahim al Shawi, Ministry of Justice

Minister of Labor and Social Affairs
Sadi Tumah Abbas, Ministry of Labor and Social Affairs

Minister of Oil
Amir Rashid Muhammad al-Ubaydi, Ministry of Oil

Minister of State
Abd al-Wahhab Umar Mirza al-Atrush, Ministry of State

Minister of State
Arshad Muhammad Ahmad Muhammad al-Zibari, Ministry of State

Minister of State for Military Affairs
Abd al-Jabbar Khalil Shanshal, Ministry of State for Military Affairs

Minister of Trade
Muhammad Mahdi al-Salih, Ministry of Trade

Minister of Transport and Communications
Ahmad Murtada Ahmad Khalil, Ministry of Transport and Communications

POLITICAL ORGANIZATIONS

Hizb al Baath al'Arabiyah al Ishtiraki (Socialist Arab Rebirth Party)

Assyrian Democratic Movement

Christian Union

Partiya Demokrata Kurdistane (Democratic Party of Kurdistan)

Patriotic Union of Kurdistan

Assyrian Democratic Movement Zowaa

Assyrian Progressive Nationalist Party

Constitutional Monarchy Movement

Islamic Party of Iraq

Kurdistan Communist Party

Worker Communist Party of Iraq

Ba'th Arab Socialist Party

DIPLOMATIC REPRESENTATION

Embassies in Iraq

Afghanistan
NAME: Shareh Al-Machreb

Greece
Jadriyah University Square, P.O. Box 10003, Baghdad, Iraq

PHONE: +964 (1) 7182433; 7762273; 7764360
FAX: +964 (1) 7188729

Italy
1, Zukak, 73 Mahalla 913 Hay Al-Jamiaa, Baghdad, Iraq
PHONE: +964 (1) 7765058; 7769105

Portugal
P.O. Box 2123, Alwika, Baghdad, Iraq
PHONE: +964 (1) 7187542
FAX: +964 (1) 7183508

Russia
Al Mouthanabbi 605/5/4, Baghdad, Iraq
PHONE: +964 (1) 5414749; 5414754; 5418913

JUDICIAL SYSTEM

Court of Cassation

BROADCAST MEDIA

Radio Free Iraq

E-MAIL: iraq@rferl.org
WEBSITE: www.rferl.org/bd/iq/

Radio Iraq International

PO Box 8145, Baghdad, Iraq
TITLE: Director
CONTACT: Muzaffar Abd al-Al

Republic of Iraq Radio

Iraqi Broadcasting and TV Establishment, Salihiya, Baghdad, Iraq
PHONE: +964 (1) 8844412; 8844413
TITLE: Directorate General
CONTACT: Sabah Yaseen
TYPE: Government

Iraqi Broadcasting and Television Establishment (IBTE)

Salhiya Baghdad, Iraq
PHONE: +964 (1) 8844412; 8844413
FAX: +964 (1) 5410480
TITLE: Directorate General
CONTACT: Sabah Yaseen

NEWSPAPERS AND MAGAZINES

Iraq Government Gazette

Ministry of Information, Baghdad, Iraq
CIRCULATION: 4,450

Iraq News Bulletin

Embassy of the Republic of Iraq, Press Section, 33 Golf Links, New Delhi

Iraq Oil News

Ministry of Oil, Baghdad, Iraq

PUBLISHERS

National House for Publishing, Distributing and Advertising

Al-Jumhuriyan St., PO Box 624, Bagdad, Iraq
PHONE: +964 (1) 4251846
SUBJECTS: Agriculture, Business, Economics, Education, Political Science, Science (General), Social Science

RELIGIOUS ORGANIZATIONS

With the presidency of Saddam Hussein, religious organizations became instruments of the government, handled officially by the Bureau of Islamic Affairs.

FURTHER READING

Articles

Crossette, Barbara. "Iraq: Annan Attacked." *New York Times,* January 21, 2000, p. A6.

——— "Iraq Seeks Talks with U.N. Chief on Arms-Inspection Impasse." *New York Times,* November 8, 2000, p. A8.

Kite, Melissa. "Serbia and Iraq 'In Dangerous New Alliance,'" *The Times* (London), Politics and Government.

"The Month in Review: January 2000." *Current History,* March 2000, p. 141.

Books

Arnove, Anthony. *Iraq under Siege: The Deadly Impact of Sanctions and War.* Cambridge, Mass.: South End Press, 2000.

Internet

"Iran's Unique Election." *BBC Online,* February 24, 2000. [Online] Available http://news6.thdo.bbc.co.uk/hi/english/world/middle_east/newsid_654000/654135.stm (accessed June 20, 2000).

"Reformers Are in Majority, But Not Completely in Control." *IranMania,* May 31, 2000. [Online] Available http://www.iranmania.com/news/may00/310500f.asp (accessed June 22, 2000).

IRAQ: STATISTICAL DATA

For sources and notes see "Sources of Statistics" at the front of each volume.

GEOGRAPHY

Geography

Area:

Total: 437,072 sq km.

Land: 432,162 sq km.

Land boundaries:

Total: 3,631 km.

Border countries: Iran 1,458 km, Jordan 181 km, Kuwait 242 km, Saudi Arabia 814 km, Syria 605 km, Turkey 331 km.

Coastline: 58 km.

Climate: mostly desert; mild to cool winters with dry, hot, cloudless summers; northern mountainous regions along Iranian and Turkish borders experience cold winters with occasionally heavy snows that melt in early spring, sometimes causing extensive flooding in central and southern Iraq.

Terrain: mostly broad plains; reedy marshes along Iranian border in south with large flooded areas; mountains along borders with Iran and Turkey.

Natural resources: petroleum, natural gas, phosphates, sulfur.

Land use:

Arable land: 12%

Permanent crops: 0%

Permanent pastures: 9%

Forests and woodland: 0%

Other: 79% (1993 est.).

HUMAN FACTORS

Demographics (A)

	1990	1995	1998	2000	2010	2020	2030	2040	2050
Population	18,135	19,557	21,398	22,676	29,672	36,908	43,873	50,509	56,361
Life expectancy - males	65.5	65.5	65.5	65.5	68.9	71.4	73.5	75.3	76.8
Life expectancy - females	67.6	67.6	67.6	67.6	71.7	74.8	77.5	79.7	81.6
Birth rate (per 1,000)	38.4	36.6	35.8	35.0	29.4	23.4	20.0	17.5	15.4
Death rate (per 1,000)	7.1	6.5	6.4	6.4	4.9	4.2	4.4	4.9	6.0
Women of reproductive age (15-49 yrs.)	3,915	4,491	5,084	5,490	7,563	9,780	11,761	13,109	14,092
Fertility rate	6.1	5.5	5.1	4.9	3.8	3.0	2.5	2.2	2.1

Except as noted, values for vital statistics are in thousands; life expectancy is in years.

Health Personnel

	National Data	World Data (wtd ave)
Total health expenditure as a percentage of GDP, 1990-1998[a]		
Public sector	NA	2.5
Private sector	NA	2.9
Total[b]	NA	5.5
Availability of health care facilities per 100,000 people		
Hospital beds 1990-1998[a]	150	330
Doctors 1992-1995[a]	51	122
Nurses 1992-1995[a]	64	248

Health Indicators

	National Data	World Data
Life expectancy at birth (years)		
1980	62	61
1998	59	67
Daily per capita supply of calories		
1970	2,261	2,358
1997	2,619	2,791
Daily per capital supply of protein		
1997 (grams)	56	74
Total fertility rate (births per woman)		
1980	6.4	3.7
1998	4.6	2.7
Population with access (%)		
To safe water (1990-96)	44	NA
To sanitation (1990-96)	36	NA
People living with (1997)		
Tuberculosis (cases per 100,000)	125.6	60.4
Malaria (cases per 100,000)	66.1	42.2
HIV/AIDS (% aged 15 - 49 years)	NA	0.99

Infants and Malnutrition

	National Data	World Data (wtd ave)
Under 5 mortality rate (1989)	125	NA
% of infants with low birthweight (1992-98)[1]	24	17
Births attended by skilled health staff (% of total births 1996-98)	54	52
% fully immunized at 1 year of age (1995-98)[1]		
TB	76	82
DPT	86	77
Polio	86	77
Measles	79	74
Prevalence of child malnutrition (1992-98)[1] (based on weight for age, % of children under 5 years)	12	30

Ethnic Division

Arab 75%-80%

Kurdish 15%-20%

Turkoman, Assyrian or other 5%

Religion

Muslim 97%

Shi'a 60%-65%

Sunni 32%-37%

Christian or other 3%

Major Languages

Arabic, Kurdish (official in Kurdish regions), Assyrian, Armenian.

EDUCATION

Public Education Expenditures

	1980	1997
Public expenditures on education as % of GNP	3.0	NA
Expenditures per student as % of GNP per capita		
Primary	7.0[2]	NA
Secondary	6.5	NA
Tertiary	87.5	NA
Pupils per teacher at the primary level	NA	20
Duration of primary education in years	NA	6
World data for comparison		
Public expenditures on education as % of GNP (mean)	3.9	4.8
Pupils per teacher at the primary level (wtd ave)	NA	33
Duration of primary education in years (mean)	NA	9

Educational Attainment (B)

	1990	1995
Gross enrollment ratio (%)		
Primary level	111.3	85.0
Secondary level	47.0	41.9
Tertiary level	12.6	11.2
Enrollment of population aged 6-23 years (%)	62.0	NA

Literacy Rates (A)

In thousands and percent	1990	1995	2000	2010
Illiterate population (15+ yrs.)	4,808	4,848	4,982	5,007
Literacy rate - total adult pop. (%)	52.3	58.0	63.5	73.6
Literacy rate - males (%)	66.0	70.7	74.9	82.4
Literacy rate - females (%)	38.2	45.0	51.8	64.7

GOVERNMENT & LAW

Military Affairs (A)

	1990	1992	1995	1996	1997
Military expenditures					
Current dollars (mil.)	22,500	1,800	1,260	1,230	1,250
1997 constant dollars (mil.)	26,400	2,000	1,300	1,250	1,250
Armed forces (000)	1,390	407	450	450[e]	400[e]
Gross national product (GNP)					
Current dollars (mil.)	36,700	18,600[r]	19,800[r]	20,200[r]	25,600[r]
1997 constant dollars (mil.)	43,000	20,600[r]	20,500[r]	20,500[r]	25,600[r]
People (mil.)	18.4	17.9	19.7	20.4	21.0
Military expenditure as % of GNP	61.3	9.7	6.3	6.1	4.9
World data on military expenditure as % of GNP	4.5	3.4	2.7	2.6	2.6
Military expenditure per capita (1997 $)	1,430	112	66	61	59
World data on military expenditure per capita (1997 $)	242	173	146	143	145
Armed forces per 1,000 people (soldiers)	75.4	22.7	22.8	22.1	19.0
World data on armed forces per 1,000 people (soldiers)	5.3	4.5	4.1	3.9	3.8
GNP per capita (1997 $)	2,340	1,150	1,040	1,010	1,220
Arms imports[6]					
Current dollars (mil.)	2,800	0	0	0	0
1997 constant dollars (mil.)	3,279	0	0	0	0
Arms exports[6]					
Current dollars (mil.)	30	0	0	0	0
1997 constant dollars (mil.)	35	0	0	0	0
Total imports[7]					
Current dollars (mil.)	6,526	603	616	492	766
1997 constant dollars (mil.)	7,642	668	638	501	766
Total exports[7]					
Current dollars (mil.)	10,380[e]	609[e]	424[e]	503[r]	2,309[e]
1997 constant dollars (mil.)	12,160[e]	675[e]	439[e]	511[r]	2,309[e]
Arms as percent of total imports[8]	42.9	0	0	0	0
Arms as percent of total exports[8]	0.3	0	0	0	0

Political Parties

The unicameral National Assembly or Majlis al-Watani consists of 250 seats: 30 appointed by the president to represent the three northern provinces of Dahuk, Arbil, and As Sulaymaniyah and 220 elected by popular vote. Members serve four-year terms. Elections were last held 24 March 1996 (next to be held March 2000). Election results are not available. The only political party in Iraq is the Ba'th Party.

LABOR FORCE

Total Labor Force (A)

4.4 million (1989).

PRODUCTION SECTOR

Energy Production

Production ....28.4 billion kWh

Production by source

Fossil fuel 97.89%

Hydro 2.11%

Nuclear 0%

Other 0%

Exports ....0 kWh

Data for 1998.

Energy Consumption

Consumption ....26.412 billion kWh

Imports ....0 kWh

Data for 1998.

Transportation

Highways:

Total: 45,550 km.

Paved: 38,400 km.

Unpaved: 7,150 km (1996 est.).

Waterways: 1,015 km; Shatt al Arab is usually navigable by maritime traffic for about 130 km; channel has been dredged to 3 m and is in use; Tigris and Euphrates Rivers have navigable sections for shallow-draft watercraft; Shatt al Basrah canal was navigable by shallow-draft craft before closing in 1991 because of the Gulf war.

Pipelines: crude oil 4,350 km; petroleum products 725 km; natural gas 1,360 km.

Merchant marine:

Total: 32 ships (1,000 GRT or over) totaling 606,227 GRT/1,067,770 DWT.

Ships by type: cargo 14, passenger 1, passenger/cargo 1, petroleum tanker 13, refrigerated cargo 1, roll-on/roll-off 2 (1999 est.).

Airports: 113 (1999 est.).

Airports - with paved runways: 80.

Airports - with unpaved runways: 33.

Top Agriculture Products

Wheat, barley, rice, vegetables, dates, cotton; cattle, sheep.

Top Mining Products (B)

Mineral resources include: phosphates, sulfur.

MANUFACTURING SECTOR

GDP & Manufacturing Summary (A)

	1980	1985	1990	1995
GDP ($-1990 mil.)[1]	71,810	53,524	64,898	6,761[e]
Per capita ($-1990)[1]	5,521	3,494	3,590	336[e]
Manufacturing share (%) (current prices)[1]	4.5	9.5	8.4	NA
Manufacturing				
Value added ($-1990 mil.)[1]	6,604	7,041	5,735	2,378[e]
Industrial production index	78	81	100	56[e]
Value added ($ mil.)	2,095[e]	3,676	3,623[e]	567[e]
Gross output ($ mil.)	5,182[e]	7,162	7,560[e]	1,394[e]
Employment (000)	177	174	133[e]	118[e]
Profitability (% of gross output)				
Intermediate input (%)	60[e]	49	36[e]	59[e]
Wages and salaries inc. supplements (%)	13[e]	13	64[e]	15[e]
Gross operating surplus	28[e]	39	−1[e]	25[e]
Productivity ($)				
Gross output per worker	29,252[e]	41,091	6,611[e]	11,640[e]
Value added per worker	11,827[e]	21,089	27,262[e]	4,807[e]
Average wage (inc. supplements)	3,700	5,242	3,552[e]	1,808[e]
Value added ($ mil.)				
Food products	183[e]	396	306[e]	56[e]
Beverages	90[e]	125	139[e]	19[e]

	1980	1985	1990	1995
Tobacco products	107[e]	140	125[e]	7[e]
Textiles	245[e]	248	362[e]	20[e]
Wearing apparel	42[e]	53	47[e]	7[e]
Leather and fur products	21[e]	1	1[e]	NA
Footwear	18[e]	81	70[e]	20[e]
Wood and wood products	1[e]	1	1[e]	NA
Furniture and fixtures	10[e]	13	14[e]	1[e]
Paper and paper products	49[e]	52	78[e]	20[e]
Printing and publishing	29[e]	33	50[e]	8[e]
Industrial chemicals	79[e]	151	167[e]	52[e]
Other chemical products	200[e]	389	362[e]	6[e]
Petroleum refineries	403[e]	868	836[e]	125[e]
Misc. petroleum and coal products	27[e]	40	56[e]	18[e]
Rubber products	6[e]	10	11[e]	3[e]
Plastic products	14[e]	33	28[e]	8[e]
Pottery, china and earthenware	1[e]	1	1[e]	NA
Glass and glass products	21[e]	35	31[e]	4[e]
Other non-metal mineral products	190[e]	565	557[e]	103[e]
Iron and steel	7[e]	20[e]	17[e]	23[e]
Metal products	53[e]	47	56[e]	27[e]
Non-electrical machinery	162[e]	149	111[e]	13[e]
Electrical machinery	121[e]	185	139[e]	25[e]
Transport equipment	15[e]	40	56[e]	2[e]
Prof. and scientific equipment	1[e]	NA	NA	NA
Other manufacturing	1[e]	NA	NA	NA

COMMUNICATIONS

Daily Newspapers

	National Data	World Data for Comparison
Daily Newspapers		
Number of Dailies	4	8,391
Total Circulation (000)	407	548,000
Circulation per 1,000 inhabitants	20	96

Telecommunications

Telephones - main lines in use: 675,000 (1995).

Telephones - mobile cellular: NA

Telephone system: reconstitution of damaged telecommunication facilities began after the Gulf war; most damaged facilities have been rebuilt.

Domestic: the network consists of coaxial cables and microwave radio relay links.

International: satellite earth stations - 2 Intelsat (1 Atlantic Ocean and 1 Indian Ocean), 1 Intersputnik (Atlantic Ocean region) and 1 Arabsat (inoperative); coaxial cable and microwave radio relay to Jordan, Kuwait, Syria, and Turkey; Kuwait line is probably nonoperational.

Radio broadcast stations: AM 19 (5 are inactive), FM 51, shortwave 4 (1998).

Radios: 4.85 million (1997).

Television broadcast stations: 13 (1997).

Televisions: 1.75 million (1997).

Internet Service Providers (ISPs): 1 (1999).

FINANCE, ECONOMICS, & TRADE

Economic Indicators

National product: GDP—purchasing power parity—$59.9 billion (1999 est.).

National product real growth rate: 13% (1999 est.).

National product per capita: $2,700 (1999 est.).

Inflation rate—consumer price index: 135% (1999 est.).

Exchange Rates

Exchange rates:

Iraqi dinars (ID) per US$1

Fixed official rate since 1982 . . . . .0.3109

Black market rate

December 1999 . . . . .1,900.0000

December 1998 . . . . .1,815.0000

December 1997 . . . . .1,530.0000

December 1995 . . . . .3,000.0000

Subject to wide fluctuations. Fiscal year: calendar year.

Top Import Origins

Imports (1999 est.): $8.9 billion.

Origins (1999): Russia, France, Egypt, Vietnam.

Top Export Destinations

Exports (1999 est.): $12.7 billion.

Destinations (1999): Russia, France, China.

Foreign Aid

Recipient: $327.5 million (1995).

Import/Export Commodities

Import Commodities	Export Commodities
Food	Crude oil
Medicine	
Manufactures	

IRELAND

Éire

CAPITAL: Dublin (Baile Átha Cliath).

FLAG: The national flag is a tricolor of green, white, and orange vertical stripes.

ANTHEM: *Amhrán na bhFiann (The Soldier's Song).*

MONETARY UNIT: The Irish pound (£) of 100 pence, formerly exchangeable at par with the pound sterling, has floated within the European Monetary System since 1979. Decimal coinage was introduced in February 1971 to replace the former duodecimal system, in which the Irish pound had been divided into 20 shillings of 12 pence each. There are coins of 1, 2, 5, 10, 20, and 50 pence and notes of 1, 5, 10, 20, 50, and 100 pounds. £1 = $0.63132 (or $1 = £0.613).

WEIGHTS AND MEASURES: Since 1988, Ireland has largely converted from the British system of weights and measures to the metric system.

HOLIDAYS: New Year's Day, 1 January; St. Patrick's Day, 17 March; Bank Holidays, 1st Monday in June, 1st Monday in August, and last Monday in October; Christmas Day, 25 December; St. Stephen's Day, 26 December. Movable religious holidays include Good Friday and Easter Monday.

TIME: GMT.

LOCATION AND SIZE: Ireland is an island in the eastern part of the North Atlantic Ocean, west of Britain and northwest of continental Europe. It covers an area of 84,421 square kilometers (32,595 square miles), of which 70,282 square kilometers (27,136 square miles) are in the Irish Republic (Ireland) and the remainder in Northern Ireland, a part of the United Kingdom. Comparatively, Ireland is slightly larger than the state of West Virginia.

CLIMATE: Because of its location in the Atlantic Ocean, Ireland is warmer in winter and cooler in summer than continental Europe. The mean annual temperature is 10°C (50°F), and mean monthly temperatures range from a mild 4°C (39°F) in January to 15°C (59°F) in July. Average yearly rainfall ranges from less than 76 centimeters (30 inches) in places near Dublin on the Irish Sea coast to more than 254 centimeters (100 inches) in some mountainous regions.

INTRODUCTORY SURVEY

RECENT HISTORY

Following the Easter Monday Rebellion, several years of bloodshed and political movement resulted in independence from the United Kingdom for Ireland's twenty-six southern counties. The six northern counties known as Ulster remained part of Great Britain. The Anglo-Irish Treaty was signed in 1921 establishing an Irish Free State with dominion status in the British Commonwealth.

Dominion status proved to be short-lived, and in 1948 Ireland voted itself out of the Commonwealth of Nations. On April 18, 1949, it declared itself a republic. Ireland was admitted to the UN in 1955 and became a member of the European Community (EC) in 1973.

Even after independence, sentiment in favor of a reunified Irish Republic remained strong, represented at its extreme by the terrorist activities of the Irish Republican Army (IRA). During the civil violence that disrupted Northern Ireland from the late 1960s on, the Irish government attempted to curb the "pro-visional wing" of the IRA. This part of the IRA tried to intimidate the Northern Ireland government through ongoing bombings, assassinations, and other types of terrorist means, often using Ireland as a base for attacks in the north. Despite all government efforts terrorist acts continued.

In 1997 Ireland's new prime minister, Bernie Ahern, revived the peace effort and resumed talks with the British government and with Sinn Fein

leader Gerry Adams. In April 1998 the Irish Parliament approved a peace agreement that had been authorized by the leaders of Northern Ireland a month earlier. The accord was voted on simultaneously by the people of the Irish Republic and Northern Ireland in May 1998 and approved. The accord stated that the Irish Republic would give up its territorial claim to Northern Ireland. A year after the agreement, several key provisions of the Good Friday agreement had been implemented but the peace process continued rocky despite ongoing involvements of the British and Irish prime ministers to resolve the situation in Northern Ireland.

GOVERNMENT

Ireland is a republic operating under a 1937 constitution. The chief of state is the president elected by popular vote for a seven-year term. The head of government is the prime minister nominated by the House of Representatives and appointed by the president. the president appoints the cabinet following nomination by the prime minister and approval of the House of Representatives.

The bicameral parliament (Oireachtas) consists of the sixty-seat Senate (Seanad) and 166-seat House of Representatives (Dail Eireann). Forty-three members of the Seanad are elected from candidates put forth by five vocational panels, the prime minister nominates eleven, and the universities elect six. The Dail Eireann members are elected by popular vote on the basis of proportional representation to serve five-year terms.

Judiciary

A Supreme Court, a high court with full original jurisdiction, and circuit and district courts with local and limited jurisdiction administer justice. Individual liberties are protected by the 1937 Constitution and by Supreme Court decisions. The judiciary is independent and provides a fair, efficient judicial process.

Political parties

The major political parties are Fianna Fáil, Fine Gael, the Progressive Democrats, the Democratic Left, and the Labour Party.

Fianna Fáil, the Republican party, was in power for all but six years during the period from 1932 to 1973 when it lost its majority to a Fine Gael-Labour coalition. In recent years both Fine Gael and Fianna Fáil have lost seats to the Labour Party that is now the third largest political party in Ireland. Sinn Fein, the political arm of the Provisional IRA, ended its sixty-five-year boycott of the Dáil in 1986 and won a single seat in the 1997 elections. Fianna Fáil won seventy-six of the 166 seats in the 1997 elections, Fine Gael fifty-three, Labor Party nineteen, Progressive Democrats four, Democratic Left four, the Green Alliance two, and independents seven.

DEFENSE

The army and its reserves, the air corps, and the naval service are small but well trained. In 2000 the permanent defense force numbered 11,500 and the reserve defense force 14,800. The army had 9,300 regulars, the navy 1,100, and the air force another 1,100. In 1998 the military budget was $732 million, or 0.9 percent of the GDP.

ECONOMIC AFFAIRS

Until the 1950s Ireland had a predominantly agricultural economy but now it is dwarfed by industry. Liberal trade policies and the drive for industrialization have stimulated economic expansion. Ireland's economic growth has been faster than any other European Union (EU) nation averaging a robust 9 percent in 1995 to 1999. Industry accounts for 39 percent of GDP and about 80 percent of exports and employs 28 percent of the workforce at the end of the twentieth century. Unemployment was down to 5.5 percent in 1999. Inflation was 2.2 percent in 1999.

Successes are due to a series of national economic programs implemented by the Irish government through the 1990s. Also Ireland was one of the countries launching the euro currency system in January 1999.

Public Finance

Expenditures of local authorities are principally for health, roads, housing, and social welfare.

The U.S. CIA estimated that in 1999 government revenues totaled approximately $25.3 billion and expenditures $20.9 billion including capital expenditures of $2 billion.

The annual budget deficit has remained below 3 percent since 1989, which meets the Maastricht criteria for adopting a single European currency (the Euro) in 1999. Ireland still needs, however, to reduce its $43.8 billion debt burden from its current level of over 90 percent of GDP to the Maastricht mandated level of 60 percent. The debt has generally been financed by the sale of government securities and cost the government $3.3 billion a year in debt service, which is about 9 percent of exports and 7 percent of GNP.

Income

In 1999 Ireland's gross domestic product (GDP) was estimated at $73.7 billion, or about $20,300 per capita. The real GDP growth rate was estimated at 8.4 percent in 1999 and inflation 2.2 percent. The 1998 GDP contribution by sector was agriculture 5 percent, industry 39 percent, and services 56 percent.

Industry

Today, the most important products of manufacturing are food, products, metal and engineering goods, machinery, electronics and data processing, pharmaceuticals, engineering, chemicals and chemical products, nonmetallic minerals, paper and printing, brewing, textiles, glass and crystal, and software. Industrial production continued to grow into the late 1990s posting a 15.8 percent growth in 1998.

Banking and Finance

In 1979 Ireland joined the European Monetary System, thus severing the 150-year-old tie with the British pound. The Central Bank of Ireland, established in 1942, is both the monetary authority and the bank of issue. Its role expanded considerably, particularly in monetary policy. However with advent of the European Monetary Union (EMU) in 1999, authority over monetary policy shifted to the European Central Bank.

Two main Irish-owned groups, the Bank of Ireland Group and the Allied Irish Banks Group, dominate the commercial banking sector. A number of other commercial, merchant, and industrial banks also operate. Additionally Ireland's post office operates the Post Office Savings Banks and Trustee Savings Banks.

The Irish Stock Exchange has its trading floor in Dublin. The Stock Exchange Act came into effect on December 4, 1995, and separated the Dublin Stock Exchange from the London Stock Exchange. Since that date the Central Bank of Ireland regulates the Dublin Stock Exchange.

Economic Development

Government policies are premised on private enterprise as a predominant factor in the economy. The 1987-1990 Program for National Recovery was generally credited with creating the conditions to bring government spending and the national debt under control. The 1991-1993 Program for Economic and Social Progress was designed to further reduce the national debt and budget deficit and to establish a schedule of wage increases.

A 1994-1999 national development plan called for investment of £20 billion, and aimed to achieve an average annual GDP growth rate of 3.5 percent. The government hoped to create 200,000 jobs through this plan, with funding by the state, the EC, and the private sector. Half of the money is earmarked for industry, transport, training, and energy. The Irish government has also implemented a series of national programs to curb inflation, reduce government spending, and promote foreign investment. The government has most recently concentrated on improving worker's qualifications and the educational system. Results exceeded expectations as the unemployment rate dropped to 5.5 percent in 1999 and Ireland boasted the fastest growing economy in the EU with an average of 9 percent in 1995-1999.

SOCIAL WELFARE

Since April 1974 all wage and salary earners between the ages of sixteen and sixty-eight have been covered by a compulsory social insurance program, including unemployment insurance, disability benefits, retirement and old-age pensions, widows' pensions, maternity benefits, and a death grant.

The prominence of the Roman Catholic Church has had a significant impact on social legislation. Divorce was not legalized until 1996. Contraceptives, the sale of which had been entirely prohibited, became available to married couples by prescription in the early 1980s. The need for a prescription was abolished in 1985. Also in 1985 the minimum age for marriage was raised from fourteen to eighteen for girls and from sixteen to eighteen for boys. Since then, Ireland's birth rate has plummeted and now is in line with those of most other European countries. Abortion remains illegal.

In 1990 the government established the Second Commission on the Status of Women, to help bring about the participation of women in all aspects of Irish society. Although the number of married women who hold paying jobs has increased in recent years, only a third of Irish women work outside the home. In 1998 women's weekly earnings in the industrial sector averaged only 65 percent of men's.

Healthcare

Health services are provided by the Department of Health. A comprehensive health service, with free hospitalization, treatment, and medication, is provided for low-income groups. A somewhat reduced list of services is offered free to the rest of the population. In 1990-1997 there are about two physicians for every 1,000 people.

Infant mortality has been reduced from 50.3 per 1,000 live births in 1948 to six in 1999. Tuberculosis, long a major cause of adult deaths, declined from 3,700 cases in 1947 to only twenty-one per 100,000 in 1997. Average life expectancy at birth in 2000 was seventy-seven years.

Housing

Government subsidies are given to encourage home ownership, and local authorities provide housing for those unable to house themselves adequately. In 1992 over 20,600 new private dwellings were completed.

EDUCATION

Education is compulsory for nine years. In 1997 there were 358,830 pupils in primary schools; 389,353 students were in secondary schools; 134,566 students were enrolled in higher-level institutions. Ireland has two universities, the University of Dublin (Trinity College) and the National University of Ireland. There were various vocational colleges. Literacy was at approximately 98 percent.

2000 KEY EVENTS TIMELINE

January

- On January 4 The High Court prevents the extradition of IRA member Angelo Fusco to Northern Ireland.

April

- On April 15 the government plans to investigate allegations of past police-IRA collusion.

June

- The IRA starts the process of weapons decommissioning, opening up arms dumps to international inspectors.
- Inflation rises to over 5 percent for the month, the highest it's been since August 1995, prompting speculation over ECB policy and the single monetary policy.

July

- Northern Ireland's parade commission delays a march proposed by the local Orange Order of Protestants down Garvaghy road, fearing religious conflict.
- Britain releases 86 Northern Ireland prisoners (many held for murder charges) under the Good Friday peace agreement between England and the province, bringing the total released since 1998 to 428.
- Protestant rioters attack police officers and soldiers in Belfast on July 5, demanding permission for a parade of the militant-Protestant Orange Order through a Catholic neighborhood. The parade through this section of town is officially banned on July 6, and protesters stop just short of a twenty-foot barricade on July 9, thereafter turning violent. Northern Ireland is literally pulled to a standstill for fear of violence on the streets.

- Britain releases eighty-six Northern Ireland prisoners (many held for murder charges) under the Good Friday peace agreement between England and the province, bringing the total released since 1998 to 428.
- The Royal Ulster Constabulary figures that during the first ten days of the month there were 329 attacks on militia, 305 firebomb incidents, 105 carjackings, 404 car burnings, and damage done to 174 buildings.

August

- Residents of the main Catholic neighborhood in Londonderry announce August 10 that they would allow a Protestant parade of 30,000 through their neighborhood.
- Due to violence, British troops return to the streets of Belfast on August 22 for the first time since September 1998.

September

- On September 13 the Real IRA is blamed for a bomb damaging a Royal Ulster Constabulary station at Armagh, and two bombs that are deactivated at a British Army training center at Londonderry.
- Northern Ireland Secretary Peter Mandelson announces that Britain will drop extradition requests for fugitive terrorists affiliated with paramilitary groups that are observing cease-fires. The fugitives will be free to return to Northern Ireland and apply for immediate parole under the 1998 peace agreement's early release program.

November

- Republicans in Northern Ireland, led by Sinn Fein, begin a court battle November 15 against pro-British First Minister David Trimble, who enforced sanctions against the IRA.

December

- President Clinton visits Ireland.

ANALYSIS OF EVENTS: 2000

BUSINESS AND THE ECONOMY

Gross domestic product (GDP) grew by 7–8 percent in 2000 and unemployment virtually disappeared. In the last few years annual growth rates have been approximately 9 percent. In fact a scarcity of labor has developed and many Irish emigrants are returning home. The reasons behind the country's exceptional economic performance are a highly skilled workforce and low corporate taxes. Previous governments, moreover, aggressively pursued foreign direct investments. Since 1995 25 percent of all U.S. investment in Europe has gone into the Irish economy.

Strong growth strained the employer-union partnership, which had previously produced wage restraint. In February union leadership demanded higher wages and a new agreement was signed that included wage increases for the public sector of nearly 20.5 percent. Such a wage agreement was predicted to have inflationary consequences but was still preferable, according to employers, to having no agreement at all with the trade union federation. Inflation was projected to reach 7 percent and will be more than double that of the euro zone. The Irish government had few instruments at hand to combat inflation. Interest rates are set by the European central bank and the finding ways to cool the overheating Irish economy was not a priority to the central bankers in Frankfurt, Germany. Further, the government could not easily cut spending because the country desperately needed a major overhaul of its infrastructure. Higher taxes were also out of the question. One option the government considered was to encourage the acceleration of housing construction. Housing prices have increased by 20 percent per year for the past few years, and have forced employers to offer employees cost-of-living adjustments.

In late November Irish labor unions organized a strike in the transportation, hospital, and education sectors. More than 100 labor and employer organizations signed a national agreement called "Program for Prosperity and Fairness, " which set annual levels of wage increases for three years. But many public sector unions were unhappy, considering that the inflation rate exceeded the promised wage increases and left them trailing behind private sector, high-tech pay.

GOVERNMENT AND POLITICS

The two-party minority coalition government of Fianna Fail and Progressive Democrats, elected in June 1997, was likely to serve out its full five-year term. Unprecedented prosperity and progress in the Northern Ireland peace process implied few major crises or challenges that could unseat a minority government. Bertie Ahern, forty-eight, *Taoiseach* or prime minister, is notoriously cautious and was unlikely to provoke a new election.

In February the cabinet was reshuffled after the minister of foreign affairs, David Andrews, resigned. The prime minister moved the health minister, Brian Cowen, into foreign affairs and the education minister, Michael Martin, into health.

One ongoing challenge was the steady flow of reports on political scandals. A special tribunal investigated Charles Haughey, a former prime minister, who ran complicated financial schemes and speculated in land development. Ahern was one of Haughey's assistant and signed blank checks on his boss's and party's behalf. The impression among voters, however, was that he was sloppy though not dishonest, and most of the events took place a decade ago when Ahern was young and susceptible to the charms of his mentor.

Since the 1998 signing of the Good Friday agreement, the peace process has experienced many highs and lows. Lack of confidence led to a cautious implementation of some provisions. But one major stumbling block was the manner in which the Irish Republican Army (IRA) would disarm itself. Hard-line voices in the Ulster Unionists, always suspicious of the IRA, refused to enter into any power-sharing arrangements with Sinn Fein, the political arm of the IRA, until the military branch had surrender all its weapons. Blair and Ahern kept the peace process alive and the IRA announced in May 2000 that it would allow foreign observers to inspect the contents of arms dumps to ensure that no weapons had been removed. In turn the Ulster Unionists, under considerable outside pressures, agreed to go back into government with the IRA and revived the joint government with the Catholic minority on May 29, 2000. In late June the inspection of the arms dumps took place and the team of international statesmen found a substantial amount of military material at the storage site. It appeared that the successful inspection strengthened the hand of David Trimble, the leader of the Ulster Unionists and first minister of the devolved government of Northern Ireland.

In October Trimble was under attack by hardliners for the agreeing to an inspection of weapons storage sites and for failing to demand decommissioning of IRA arms. The Ulster Unionist party has suffered a loss of electoral support at the expense of Democratic Unionists, who reject the peace agreement and who argue that in the absence of IRA decommissioning the party should pull out of the power-sharing executive. Many dissidents in the Ulster Unionist party were keen to have a showdown with their leader and destroy the shared executive. The British government has been in ongoing consultations with its Irish counterpart in late fall on whether to persevere or reverse the devolution order and reimpose direct rule from Westminster.

CULTURE AND SOCIETY

The Irish economy was the fastest growing in Western Europe in the last ten years. Economic prosperity has had important ramifications for Irish society. First, many Irish emigrants have returned to take high-paying jobs in the technology sector. The inflow of skilled labor with high spending power strained the country's infrastructure in 2000. Hospitals were overcrowded, roads were jammed, and housing was in short supply and thus expensive. The government pledged to invest $43 billion in basic services during the next seven years. But to keep the economy growing, Ireland will need some 200,000 foreign workers within five years or more than a tenth of the present workforce. In turn the flow of new workers drove up housing prices, which jumped threefold since 1989. It also stimulated the emergence of a two-track society. In 2000 there was a growing disparity between those who were employed in the traditional sector (law enforcement, teachers, public sector, administrative personnel) and the skilled foreigners who worked in the high technology area.

The presence of many young foreigners or Irish expatriates together with increased prosperity was also diluting the influence of the Catholic Church on Irish norms and behavior. Church attendance dropped dramatically, and the number of people who joined a Catholic order shrunk.

Finally, the booming Irish economy attracted asylum seekers. The influx of more than 100 new economic and political refugees a week in the early part of 2000 exhausted all of the country's emergency shelters. In response, the government scrambled to provide shelter to the rising flow of refugees. The Equal Status Act went into effect in October 2000 to protect citizens against discrimination based on gender, sexual orientation, disability, and religion as well as to protect Gypsies against bias.

DIRECTORY

CENTRAL GOVERNMENT

Head of State

President
Mary McAleese, Office of the President

Head of State

Taoiseach (Prime Minister)
Bertie Ahern, Office of the Taoiseach

Ministers

Minister for Marine and Natural Resources
Michael Woods, Ministry of Marine and Natural Resources, Leeson Lane, Dublin 2, Ireland
PHONE: +353 (1) 6199200
E-MAIL: minister@marine.irlgov.ie

Minister of Foreign Affairs
David Andrews, Ministry of Foreign Affairs, 80 St. Stephen Green, Dublin 2, Ireland
E-MAIL: library1@iveagh.irlgov.ie

Minister of Public Enterprise
Mary O'Rourke, Department of Public Enterprise, Kildare Street, Dublin 2, Ireland
PHONE: +353 (1) 6312121
FAX: +353 (1) 6312827
E-MAIL: Webmaster@entemp.irlgov.ie

Minister of Defense
Michael Smith, Ministry of Defense
E-MAIL: defence@iol.ie

Minister of Agriculture and Food
Joe Walsh, Ministry of Agriculture and Food, Kildare Street, Dublin 2, Ireland
PHONE: +353 (1) 6072000
E-MAIL: information@daff.irlgov.ie

Minister of Finance
Charlie McCreevey, Ministry of Finance, Upper Merrion Street, Dublin 2, Ireland
PHONE: +353 (1) 676571
FAX: +353 (1) 6789936
E-MAIL: wemaster@finance.irlgov.ie

Minister of Health and Children
Brian Cowen, Ministry of Health and Children, Hawkins Street, Dublin 2, Ireland
PHONE: +353 (1) 6714711
FAX: +353 (1) 6711947

Minister of the Environment and Local Government
Noel Dempsey, Ministry of the Environment and Local Government, Custom House, Dublin 1, Ireland
PHONE: +353 (1) 8882000
FAX: +353 (1) 8788640
E-MAIL: minister@environ.irlgov.ie

Minister of Social, Community and Family Affairs
Dermot Ahern, Ministry of Social, Community and Family Affairs, Store Street, Dublin 1, Ireland
PHONE: +353 (1) 6797777
E-MAIL: webweaver@welfare.eirmail400.ie

Minister of Arts, Heritage, Gaeltacht and the Islands
Sile de Valera, Ministry of Arts, Heritage, Gaeltacht and the Islands, Dun Aimhirgin, 43-49 Mespil Road, Dublin 4, Ireland
PHONE: +353 (1) 6473000
FAX: +353 (1) 6670826
E-MAIL: eolas@ealga.irlgov.ie

Minister of Justice, Equality and Law Reform
John O'Donoghue, Ministry of Justice, Equality and Law Reform, 72-76 St. Stephens Green, Dublin 2, Ireland
PHONE: +353 (1) 6028202
FAX: +353 (1) 6615461
E-MAIL: pagemaster@justice.irlgov.ie

Minister of Tourism and Trade
Jim McDaid, Ministry of Tourism and Trade

Minister of Education and Science
Micheál Martin, Ministry of Education and Science, Marlborough Street, Dublin 1, Ireland
PHONE: +353 (1) 8734700
FAX: +353 (1) 8786712

POLITICAL ORGANIZATIONS

Fianna Fáil

13 Upper Mount Street, Dublin 2, Ireland
PHONE: +353 (1) 6761551; 6613415
FAX: +353 (1) 6785690
NAME: Bertie Ahern

The Labour Party

17 Ely Place, Dublin 2, Ireland
PHONE: +353 (1) 6612615
FAX: +353 (1) 6612640
E-MAIL: ruairi_quinn@oireachtas.irlgov.ie
NAME: Ruairi Quinn

Fine Gael

51 Upper Mount Street, Dublin 2, Ireland
PHONE: +353 (1) 6198444
FAX: +353 (1) 6625046; 6627648
E-MAIL: finegael@finegael.com
NAME: John Bruton

Communist Party of Ireland

NAME: Michael O'Riordan

Sinn Féin

51/55 Falls Road, Belfast, Northern Ireland
PHONE: +44 (1232) 624421
FAX: +44 (1232) 622112
E-MAIL: sinnfein@iol.ie
NAME: Gerry Adams

Progressive Democrats

25 South Frederick Street, Dublin 2, Ireland
PHONE: +353 (1) 6794399
FAX: +353 (1) 6794757
E-MAIL: jackm@iol.ie
NAME: Mary Harney

The Workers' Party

NAME: Marion Donnelly

The Socialist Party

PHONE: +353 (1) 6772686
E-MAIL: dublinsp@clubi.ie
NAME: Joe Higgins

Green Alliance

5a Upper Fownes Street, Temple Bar, Dublin 2, Ireland
PHONE: +353 (1) 6790012
FAX: +353 (1) 6797168
E-MAIL: greenpar@iol.ie
NAME: Patricia Howard

DIPLOMATIC REPRESENTATION

Embassies in Ireland

Australia
Second Floor, Fitzwilton House, Wilton Terrace, Dublin 2, Ireland
PHONE: +353 (1) 6761517
FAX: +353 (1) 6785185
E-MAIL: austremb.dublin@dfat.gov.au

Belgium
Shrewsbury House, Shrewsbury Road, Ballsbridge, Dublin 4, Ireland
PHONE: +353 (1) 2692082
FAX: +353 (1) 2838488

France
36 Ailesbury Road, Ballsbridge, Dublin 4, Ireland
PHONE: +353 (1) 2601666
FAX: +353 (1) 2830178
E-MAIL: consul@ambafrance.ie

Israel
Carrisbrook House, 122 Pembroke Road, Dublin 4, Ireland
PHONE: +353 (1) 6680303
FAX: +353 (1) 6680418
E-MAIL: embisrael@iol.ie

Italy
63 Northumberland Road, Dublin, Ireland
PHONE: +353 (1) 6601744
FAX: +353 (1) 6682759
E-MAIL: italianembassy@tinet.ie

Netherlands
160 Merrion Road, Dublin 4, Ireland
PHONE: +353 (1) 2693444
FAX: +353 (1) 2839690
E-MAIL: nethemb@indigo.ie

New Zealand
46 Upper Mount Street, Dublin 2, Ireland
PHONE: +353 (1) 6762464
FAX: +353 (1) 6762489

Russia
186 Orwell Road, Rathgar, Dublin, Ireland
PHONE: +353 (1) 4923525; 4922048
FAX: +353 (1) 4923525

United Kingdom
29 Merrion Road Ballsbridge, Dublin 4, Ireland
PHONE: +353 (1) 2053700; 2053757
FAX: +353 (1) 2053885

JUDICIAL SYSTEM

Supreme Court

Four Courts, Inns Quay, Dublin 7, Ireland
PHONE: +353 (1) 8886000
E-MAIL: courtsinfo@justice.ie

BROADCAST MEDIA

Atlantic 252

Mornington House, Summerhill Road, Trim, Co. Meath, Ireland

PHONE: +353 (46) 36655
FAX: +353 (46) 36644
E-MAIL: programming@atlantic252.com; studio@atlantic252.com
WEBSITE: http://www.atlantic252.com/html/flash-index.htm
TITLE: Managing Director, Programme Director
CONTACT: John O'Hara
TYPE: Commercial

Radio Cork

PHONE: +353 (21) 272922
FAX: +353 (21) 273829
E-MAIL: info@rtecork.iol.ie

Radio Ireland -Today FM

Radio Ireland House, 124 Upper Abbey Street, Dublin 1, Ireland
PHONE: +353 (1) 8049000
FAX: +353 (1) 8049099
E-MAIL: admin@todayfm.com
TITLE: Managing Director
CONTACT: Dick Hill
TYPE: Commercial

Tara Television

Montrose, Donnybrook, Dublin 4, Ireland
PHONE: +44 (171) 3833330
FAX: +44 (171) 3833450
E-MAIL: info@tara-tv.co.uk
WEBSITE: http://www.taratv.net/

TV3 Television Network Limited

Westgate Business Park, Ballymount, Dublin 24, Ireland
PHONE: +353 (1) 4193333
FAX: +353 (1) 4193300
WEBSITE: http://www.irtc.ie/tv3fqs.htm; www.tv3.ie
TITLE: Chief Executive Officer, Managing Director
CONTACT: Rick Hetherington

Independent Radio & TV Commission (IRTC)

Marine House, Clanwilliam Place, Dublin 2, Ireland
PHONE: +353 (1) 6760966
FAX: +353 (1) 6760948
E-MAIL: info@irtc.ie
WEBSITE: http://www.irtc.ie
TITLE: Chairman
CONTACT: Niall Stokes

Radio Telefis Eireann (RTE)

Donnybrook, Dublin 4, Ireland
PHONE: +353 (1) 2083111; 2082601
FAX: +353 (1) 2083080; 2083034
WEBSITE: http://www.rte.ie
TITLE: Directorate General
CONTACT: Bob Collins
TYPE: Statutory

COLLEGES AND UNIVERSITIES

College of St. Patrick

Nui Maynooth, Maynooth, KL, Ireland
PHONE: +353 (45) 7083822
FAX: +353 (45) 7083822
E-MAIL: admissions@may.ie
WEBSITE: http://www.may.ie

University of Limerick

Plassey Technological Park, Limerick, LI, Ireland
PHONE: +353 (61) 333644
FAX: +353 (61) 330316
E-MAIL: admissns@tcd.ie
WEBSITE: http://www.ul.ie

National University of Ireland, Galway

Newcastle Rd., Galway, GL, Ireland
PHONE: +353 (91) 524 411
E-MAIL: registrar@nuigalway.ie
WEBSITE: http://www.nuigalway.ie

University College Cork

Cork, CK, Ireland
PHONE: +353 (21) 4903000
FAX: +353 (21) 4903456
E-MAIL: information@ucc.ie
WEBSITE: http://www.ucc.ie

Royal College of Surgeons in Ireland

123 St. Stephen's Green, Dublin 2, DU, Ireland
PHONE: +353 (1) 4022100
FAX: +353 (1) 4022458
E-MAIL: registrar@rcsi.ie
WEBSITE: http://www.rcsi.ie

Dublin Institute of Technology

Fitzwilliam House, 30 Upper Pembroke St., Dublin 2, DU, Ireland
PHONE: +353 (1) 4023445
FAX: +353 (1) 4023392
E-MAIL: admissions@dit.ie
WEBSITE: http://www.dit.ie

University of Dublin

Trinity College, Dublin 2, DU, Ireland
PHONE: +353 (1) 6772941
FAX: +353 (1) 6710037
E-MAIL: append@tcd.ie
WEBSITE: http://www.tcd.ie

Dublin Institute of Advanced Studies

10 Burlington Rd., Dublin 4, DU, Ireland
PHONE: +353 (1) 6140100
FAX: +353 (1) 6680561
E-MAIL: registrar@admin.dias.ie
WEBSITE: http://www.dias.ie

University College Dublin

Belfield, Dublin 4, DU, Ireland
PHONE: +353 (1) 7067777
FAX: +353 (1) 7061070
E-MAIL: admissions@ucd.ie
WEBSITE: http://www.ucd.ie

Milltown Institute

Milltown Park, Dublin, DU, Ireland

Dublin City University

Dcu, Dublin 9, DU, Ireland
PHONE: +353 (1) 7045000
FAX: +353 (1) 8360830
E-MAIL: registrars.office@dcu.ie
WEBSITE: http://www.dcu.ie

St. Patrick's College

Colorado of Dublin City University, Drumcondra, Dublin 9, DU, Ireland
PHONE: +353 (1) 8376191
FAX: +353 (1) 8376197
WEBSITE: http://www.spd.dcu.ie/home.htm

NEWSPAPERS AND MAGAZINES

Connaught Telegraph

Cavendish Ln., Ellison St. Castlebar Mayo, Ireland
PHONE: +353 (94) 21711
FAX: +353 (94) 24007
E-MAIL: conntel@iol.ie
WEBSITE: http://www.mayo-ireland.ie/mayo/news/conntel
TITLE: Editor
CONTACT: Tom Gillespie
CIRCULATION: 15,261

Evening Echo

Examiner Publications, PO Box 21, Cork
PHONE: +353 (21) 272722
FAX: +353 (21) 271017; 273846
E-MAIL: ray.lougheed@emaminer.ie
TITLE: Editor
CONTACT: Brian Feeney
CIRCULATION: 27,022

The Examiner

Examiner Publications, PO Box 21, Cork
PHONE: +353 (21) 272722
FAX: +353 (21) 271017; 273846
E-MAIL: anne.kearney@examiner.ie
TITLE: Editor
CONTACT: Brian Looney
CIRCULATION: 60,173

An Phoblacht/Republican News

An Phoblacht, 58 Parnell Sq., Dublin 1, Ireland
PHONE: +353 (1) 8733611; 8733839
FAX: +353 (1) 8721859; 8733074
E-MAIL: apm@irlnet.com
WEBSITE: http://www.irlnet.com/apmf
CIRCULATION: 24,000

The Echo

Tallaght Publishing Ltd., Echo House, Old Bawn Rd., Tallaght, Dublin 24, Ireland
PHONE: +353 (1) 4598513
FAX: +353 (1) 4598514; 4620710
WEBSITE: http://www.tallaght.com/theecho
TITLE: Editor
CONTACT: David Kennedy
CIRCULATION: 21,200

Evening Herald

Independent Newspapers Ltd., 90 Middle Abbey St., Dublin 1, Ireland
PHONE: +353 (1) 7055333; 8731666
FAX: +353 (1) 7055555; 8731787
TITLE: Editor
CONTACT: Paul Drury
CIRCULATION: 110,416

Ireland on Sunday

Title Media Ltd., 50 Quay City, Dublin 2, Ireland
PHONE: +353 (1) 6718255
FAX: +353 (1) 6718294
E-MAIL: adsales@ios.iol.ie
TITLE: Editor

CONTACT: Liam Hayes
CIRCULATION: 63,476

Irish Independent

Independent Newspapers Ltd., 90 Middle Abbey St., Dublin 1, Ireland
PHONE: +353 (1) 7055333; 8731666
FAX: +353 (1) 7055555; 8731787
WEBSITE: http://www.independent.ie
TITLE: Editor
CONTACT: Vincent Doyle
CIRCULATION: 162,064

The Irish Sun

News International PLC, Huguenot House, 35 St. Stephens Green, Dublin 2, Ireland
PHONE: +353 (1) 6028888
FAX: +353 (1) 6028880
E-MAIL: sidney.devine@newsint.co.uk
TITLE: Contact
CONTACT: Paddy Clancy
CIRCULATION: 77,715

The Irish Times

The Irish Times Ltd., P.O. Box 74, Dublin 2, Ireland
PHONE: +353 (1) 6792022
FAX: +353 (1) 6773241; 6716897
E-MAIL: displayad@irishtimes.ie; lholland@irish-time.ie
WEBSITE: http://www.irish-times.ie
TITLE: Editor
CONTACT: Conor Brady
CIRCULATION: 111,243

News Of The World

News International PLC, Huguenot House, 35 St. Stephens Green, Dublin 2, Ireland
PHONE: +353 (1) 6028888
FAX: +353 (1) 6028880
TITLE: Contact
CONTACT: John Moore
CIRCULATION: 161,000

The Star

The Independent Star Ltd., Star House, 62A Terenure Rd. North, Dublin 6W, Ireland
PHONE: +353 (1) 4901228
FAX: +353 (1) 4907425
TITLE: Editor
CONTACT: Gerard O' Regan
CIRCULATION: 91,849

The Sunday Business Post

Post Publications Ltd, 80 Harcourt St., Dublin 2, Ireland
PHONE: +353 (1) 6026000
FAX: +353 (1) 6796282; 6796283
E-MAIL: info@sbpost.ie
WEBSITE: http://www.sbpost.ie
TITLE: Editor
CONTACT: Damien Kiberd
CIRCULATION: 47,232

Sunday Independent

Independent Newspapers, Ltd., 90 Middle Abbey St., Dublin 1, Ireland
PHONE: +353 (1) 7055333; 8731666
FAX: +353 (1) 7055555; 8731787
TITLE: Editor
CONTACT: Aengus Fanning
CIRCULATION: 320,340

The Sunday Tribune

Tribune Publications, 15 Lower Baggot St., Dublin 2, Ireland
PHONE: +353 (1) 6615555
FAX: +353 (1) 6621581; 6614656
E-MAIL: jholland@tribune.ie
TITLE: Editor
CONTACT: Matt Cooper
CIRCULATION: 88,186

Sunday World

Sunday Newspapers Ltd., 18 Rathfamham Rd. Dublin 6, Ireland
PHONE: +353 (1) 4901980
FAX: +353 (1) 4902177
TITLE: Editor
CONTACT: Tom McGinty
CIRCULATION: 232,516

The Title

Title Media Ltd., 50 City Quay, Dublin 2, Ireland
PHONE: +353 (1) 6718255
FAX: +353 (1) 6718882; 6718294
E-MAIL: info@irelandsunday.iol.ie; adsales@ios.ie

Clare Champion

Barrack St., Ennis Clare, Ireland
PHONE: +353 (65) 28105
FAX: +353 (65) 20374
E-MAIL: editor@clarechampion.ie

WEBSITE: http://www.clarechampion.ie
TITLE: Editor
CONTACT: Gerry Collison
CIRCULATION: 20,702

Connacht Sentinel

The Connacht Tribune Ltd., 15 Market St., Galway
PHONE: +353 (91) 567251
FAX: +353 (91) 567970
E-MAIL: ctribune@iol.ie
TITLE: Editor
CONTACT: Brendan Carroll
CIRCULATION: 7,636

Connacht Tribune

The Connacht Tribune Ltd., 15 Market St., Galway
PHONE: +353 (91) 567251
FAX: +353 (91) 567970
E-MAIL: ctribune@iol.ie
WEBSITE: http://www.iol.ie/tribune
TITLE: Editor
CONTACT: John Cunningham
CIRCULATION: 29,006

Limerick Leader

The Limerick Leader Ltd., 54 O'Connell St., Limerick City, Ireland
PHONE: +353 (61) 400400
FAX: +353 (61) 401422
E-MAIL: advertising@limerick-leader.ie
WEBSITE: http;//www.limerick-leader.ie
TITLE: Editor
CONTACT: Brenden Halligan

Irish Arts Review

Irish Arts Review Ltd., PO Box 3500, Dublin 4, Ireland
PHONE: +353 (1) 6793525
FAX: +353 (1) 6793503
TITLE: Editor
CONTACT: Ann Reihill
CIRCULATION: 8,000
TYPE: Art Magazine

Hot Press

Osnovina Ltd., 13 Trinity St., Dublin 2, Ireland
PHONE: +353 (1) 6795077; 6795091
FAX: +353 (1) 6795097
WEBSITE: http://www.iol.ie/hotpress
TITLE: Editor
CONTACT: Niall Stokes
CIRCULATION: 20,810
TYPE: Muxic and fashion magazine

Image

Image Publications Ltd., 22 Crofton Rd. Dun Laoghaire Co Dublin, Ireland
PHONE: +353 (1) 2808415
FAX: +353 (1) 2808309
E-MAIL: adimagemag@tinet.ie
TITLE: Editor
CONTACT: Jane McDonnell
CIRCULATION: 24,236
TYPE: Women's fashion & lifestyle magazine

It Magazine

Smurfit Publications Ltd., 2 Clanwilliam Ct., Lower Mount St., Dublin 2, Ireland
PHONE: +353 (1) 6623158
FAX: +353 (1) 6619757
TITLE: Editor
CONTACT: Elizabeth McCormack
CIRCULATION: 21,300
TYPE: Women's magazine

U Magazine

Smurfit Publications Ltd., 2 Clanwilliam Court, Lower Mount St., Dublin 2, Ireland
PHONE: +353 (1) 6623158
FAX: +353 (1) 6619757
TITLE: Ad Manager
CONTACT: Aidan Devlin
CIRCULATION: 20,750
TYPE: Women's magazine

PUBLISHERS

Attic Press Ltd.

29 Upper Mount St., Dublin, Ireland
PHONE: +353 (1) 6616128
FAX: +353 (1) 6616176
E-MAIL: atticirl@iol.ie/atticirl
WEBSITE: ww.iol.ie/atticirl
TITLE: Publisher
CONTACT: Sara Wilbourne
SUBJECTS: Biography, Fiction, Political Science, Health, Nutrition, History, Humor, Literature, Literary Criticism, Essays, Social Sciences, Women's Studies

Ballinakella Press

Whitegate, Clare, Ireland
PHONE: +353 (61) 927030
FAX: +353 (61) 927418

E-MAIL: weir@iol.ie
TITLE: President
CONTACT: Hugh W. L. Weir
SUBJECTS: Irish historical, topographical, genealogical & biographical material
TOTAL PUBLISHED: 26 print

Clo Iar-Chonnachta Teo

Indreabhan, Conamara, County Galway, Ireland
PHONE: +353 (91) 593307
FAX: +353 (91) 593362
E-MAIL: cic@iol.ie
WEBSITE: http://www.cic.ie
TITLE: Man. Director
CONTACT: Michael O'Conghaile
SUBJECTS: Drama, Theater, Fiction, Gay & Lesbian, History, Music, Dance, Poetry, Regional Interests
TOTAL PUBLISHED: 200 print; 150 audio; 40 CD-ROM

The Collins Press

West Link Park, Doughcloyne, Wilton, Cork, Ireland
PHONE: +353 (21) 347717
FAX: +353 (21) 347720
E-MAIL: enquiries@collinspress.ie
CONTACT: Con Collins
SUBJECTS: Archaeology, Biography, History, Human Relations, Natural History, Photography, Drama, Mind, Body & Spirit
TOTAL PUBLISHED: 48 print

The Columbia Press

55A Spruce Ave., Stillorgan Industrial Park, Blackrock, Dublin, Ireland
PHONE: +353 (1) 2942556
FAX: +353 (1) 2942564
E-MAIL: sean@columbia@.ie
WEBSITE: http://www.columbia.ie
TITLE: Chief Executive & Editorial
CONTACT: Sean O'Boyle
SUBJECTS: Religion, Self-Help, Theology
TOTAL PUBLISHED: 200 print

Cork University Press

Zcrawford Business Park, Crosses Green, County Cork, Ireland
PHONE: +353 (21) 902980
FAX: +353 (21) 273553; 315329
E-MAIL: corkunip@ucc.ie
WEBSITE: http://www.ucc.ie/corkunip
TITLE: Publisher
CONTACT: Sara Wilbourne
SUBJECTS: Archaeology, Geography, Geology, History, Social Sciences, Women's Studies
TOTAL PUBLISHED: 120 print

Dominican Publications

42 Parnell Sq., Dublin 1, Ireland
PHONE: +353 (1) 8721611
FAX: +353 (1) 8731760
E-MAIL: dompubs@iol.ie
TITLE: Chief Executive
CONTACT: Austin Flannery
SUBJECTS: Catholicism, Theology
TOTAL PUBLISHED: 20 print; 2 CD-ROM

The Economic & Social Research Institute

4 Burlington Rd., Dublin 4, Ireland
PHONE: +353 (1) 6671525
FAX: +353 (1) 6686231
E-MAIL: BWJ@esri.ie
WEBSITE: http://www.esri.ie
TITLE: Director
CONTACT: Brendan J. Whalen
SUBJECTS: Economics, Education, Environmental Studies, Finance, Health, Nutrition, Social Sciences
TOTAL PUBLISHED: 300 print

The Educational Company of Ireland

Ballymount Rd., Walkinstown, Dublin 12, Ireland
PHONE: +353 (1) 4500611
FAX: +353 (1) 4500993
E-MAIL: info@edco.ie
TITLE: Executive Director
CONTACT: R. McLoughlin
SUBJECTS: Business, Career Development, Computer Science, Ethnicity, Geography, Geology, History, Mathematics, Religion, Science (General)

Four Courts Press Ltd.

Funbally Court, Lumbally Ln., Dublin 8, Ireland
PHONE: +353 (1) 4534668
FAX: +353 (1) 4534672
E-MAIL: info@four-courts-press.ie
TITLE: Man. Director
CONTACT: Michael Adams
SUBJECTS: Art, History, Literature, Literary Criticism, Essays, Philosophy, Religion, Theology, Medieval & Celtic Studies
TOTAL PUBLISHED: 450 print

Gill & Macmillan Ltd.

10 Hume Ave., Park W., Dublin 12, Ireland
PHONE: +353 (1) 5009500
FAX: +353 (1) 5009599
E-MAIL: mhgill@gillmacmillan.ie
WEBSITE: http://www.gillmacmillan.ie
TITLE: Man. Director
CONTACT: Michael Gill
SUBJECTS: Biography, Business, Child Care, Cookery, Economics, Education, Political Science, Health, Nutrition, History, Law, Psychology, Psychiatry, Regional Interests, Self-Help, Travel
TOTAL PUBLISHED: 800 print

Government Publications Ireland

Government Supplies Agency, 4-5 Harcourt Rd., Dublin 2, Ireland
PHONE: +353 (1) 6476000
FAX: +353 (1) 4752760
E-MAIL: patricia.onwumere@opw.ie
CONTACT: Patricia Onwumere
SUBJECTS: Government, Political Science

Irish Academic Press

44 Northumberland Rd., Ballsbridge, Dublin 4, Ireland
PHONE: +353 (1) 6688244
FAX: +353 (1) 6601610
E-MAIL: info@iap.ie
WEBSITE: http://www.iap.ie
TITLE: Managing Editor
CONTACT: Linda Longmore
SUBJECTS: Art, History, Literature, Literary Criticism, Essays, Military Science

Irish Management Institute

Sandyford Rd., Dublin 16, Ireland
PHONE: +353 (1) 2078400
FAX: +353 (1) 2955150
E-MAIL: 3025reception@imi.ie
TITLE: Chief Executive
CONTACT: Maureen O'Grady
SUBJECTS: Accounting, Business, Communications, Economics, Finance, Labor, Industrial Relations, Management

Irish Times Ltd.

General Services Dept., 11-15 D'Olier St., Dublin 2, Ireland
PHONE: +353 (1) 6792022
FAX: +353 (1) 6773282
E-MAIL: b.mcniff@irish-times.ie
TITLE: General Services Manager
CONTACT: Brenda McNiff
SUBJECTS: Fiction, Genealogy, Literature, Literary Criticism, Essays

Irish Youth Work Press

National Youth Federation, 20 Lower Dominick St., Dublin 1, Ireland
PHONE: +353 (1) 8729933
FAX: +353 (1) 8724183
E-MAIL: fbissett@nyf.ie
WEBSITE: http://www.lol.le/~nyt
TITLE: Services Executive
CONTACT: Fran Bissett
SUBJECTS: Child Care & Development, Education, Social Science, Sociology
TOTAL PUBLISHED: 17 print

The Lilliput Press Ltd.

62-63 Sitric Rd., Arbour Hill, Dublin 7, Ireland
PHONE: +353 (1) 6711647
FAX: +353 (1) 6711233
E-MAIL: info@lilliputpress.ie
WEBSITE: http://www.lilliputpress.ie
TITLE: Publisher
CONTACT: Anthony Farrell
SUBJECTS: Architecture, Biography, Fiction, History, Joyce Literature, Literary Criticism, Essays, Natural History, Poetry, Regional Interests
TOTAL PUBLISHED: 200 print

Mercier Press Ltd.

5 French Church St., PO Box 5, County Cork, Ireland
PHONE: +353 (21) 275040
FAX: +353 (21) 274969
E-MAIL: books@mercier.ie
TITLE: Man. Director
CONTACT: John F. Spillane
SUBJECTS: Cookery, Drama, Theater, Ethnicity, Fiction, History, Humor, Music, Dance, Catholicism

Morrigan Book Co.

Gore St., Killala, Ballina, County Mayo, Ireland
PHONE: +353 (96) 32555
FAX: +353 (1096) 2853805
E-MAIL: admin@atlanticisland.ie
WEBSITE: http://www.atlanticisland.ie
TITLE: Publisher
CONTACT: Gerald Conan Kennedy

SUBJECTS: Archaeology, Maps, Folklore, Mythology, New Age

The O'Brien Press

20 Victoria Rd., Rathgar, Dublin 6, Ireland
PHONE: +353 (1) 4923333
FAX: +353 (1) 4922777
TITLE: Man. Director
CONTACT: Michael O'Brien
SUBJECTS: Anthropology, Architecture, Interior Design, Biography, Cookery, Games, Fiction, Political Science, History, Language Arts, Linguistics, Music, Dance, Wine & Spirits

On Stream Publications Ltd.

Currabaha, Claghroe, Blarney, County Cork, Ireland
PHONE: +353 (21) 385798
FAX: +353 (21) 385798
E-MAIL: onstream@indigo.ie
TITLE: Man. Director
CONTACT: Roz Crowley
SUBJECTS: Agriculture, Behavioral Sciences, Biography, Cookery, Developing Countries, Health, Nutrition, History, How-To, Medicine, Travel, Wine & Spirits
TOTAL PUBLISHED: 30 print

Roberts Rinehart Publishers

Trinity House, Charleston Rd., Ranelagh, Dublin 6, Ireland
PHONE: +353 (1) 4976860
FAX: +353 (1) 4976861
E-MAIL: rinehart@iol.ie
TITLE: Rights Director
CONTACT: Mary Hegarty
SUBJECTS: Anthropology, Art, Biography, Environmental Studies, Ethnicity, Fiction, History, Natural History, Photography, Regional Interests, Travel

Round Hall Sweet & Maxwell

4 Upper Ormond Quay, Brehon House, Dublin 7, Ireland
PHONE: +353 (1) 8730939
FAX: +353 (1) 8720078
E-MAIL: alison.gallagher@itps.co.uk
TITLE: Marketing
CONTACT: Alison Gallagher
SUBJECTS: Criminology, Finance, Labor, Industrial Relations, Law
TOTAL PUBLISHED: 200 print

Tir Eolas

Newtownlynch, Doorus, Kinvara, County Galway, Ireland
PHONE: +353 (91) 637452
FAX: +353 (91) 637452
TITLE: Director
CONTACT: Anne Korff
SUBJECTS: Anthropology, Archaeology, Biography, Environmental Studies, History, Natural History, Outdoor Recreation
TOTAL PUBLISHED: 6 print

Tivenan Publications

Dually, New Castle West, County Limerick, Ireland
PHONE: +353 (69) 62596
FAX: +353 (69) 61168
E-MAIL: birth@indigo.ie
WEBSITE: http://www.indigo.ie/~birth
SUBJECTS: Child Care & Development, Health, Nutrition, Self-Help, Childbirth & Pregnancy
TOTAL PUBLISHED: 1 print; Internet

Town House & Country House Ltd.

Trinity House, Charleston Rd., Ranelagh, Dublin 6, Ireland
PHONE: +353 (1) 4972339
FAX: +353 (1) 4970927
E-MAIL: books@townhouse.ie
TITLE: Man. Director
CONTACT: Treasa Coady
SUBJECTS: Archaeology, Art, Biography, Fiction, Reference
TOTAL PUBLISHED: 20-30 print per year

Veritas Co. Ltd.

Veritas House, 7-8 Lower Abbey St., Dublin 1, Ireland
PHONE: +353 (1) 8788177
FAX: +353 (1) 8786507
TITLE: Director
CONTACT: Father Sean Melody
SUBJECTS: Religion, Cathechetical

Wolfhound Press

68 Mountjoy Sq., Dublin 1, Ireland
PHONE: +353 (1) 8740354
FAX: +353 (1) 8720207
WEBSITE: http://www.wolfhound.ie
TITLE: Publisher
CONTACT: Seamus Cashman
SUBJECTS: Biography, Fiction, Photography
TOTAL PUBLISHED: 300 print

RELIGIOUS ORGANIZATIONS

Buddhist

Copper Plate Zen Group of Dublin
32 Collins Avenue, Killester, Dublin 5, Ireland
NAME: Brenden Breen

Dublin Zen Dojo
10 Exchequer Street, Dublin, Ireland
PHONE: +353 (91) 529484
NAME: Alain Liebmann

Catholic

Archdiocese of Cashel and Emly
WEBSITE: http://homepage.eircom.net/~cashelemly/index.html
NAME: Most Rev. Dermot Clifford, B.Sc., Ph.D., D.D.

Archdicose of Dublin
WEBSITE: http://dublindiocese.ie/
TITLE: Archbishop
NAME: Dr. Desmond Connell

Brothers of Saint Patrick
c/o Brother James Murphy, Patrician Generalate, Tullow, Carlow, Ireland
PHONE: +353 (503) 51190
FAX: +353 (503) 51900
TITLE: Secretary General
NAME: Brother James Murphy

Mercy International Centre
64a Baggot st lr, Dublin 2, Ireland
PHONE: +353 (1) 66118061
WEBSITE: http://www.mercy-international.org/

Missionary Sisters of Our Lady of the Holy Rosary (MSHR)
c/o Sr. Monica Devine, 23 Cross Ave., Blackrock, Dublin, Ireland
PHONE: +353 (1) 2881708
FAX: +353 (1) 2836308
E-MAIL: mshrgen@indigo.ie
TITLE: Superior General
NAME: Sr. Monica Devine

Missionary Society of Saint Columban
c/o Rev. Nicholas Murray, Superior Gen., St. Columban's, Grange Road, Donaghmeme, Dublin 13, Ireland
PHONE: +353 (1) 8476647
FAX: +353 (1) 8484025
E-MAIL: 106132.1454@compuserve.com
TITLE: General Secretary
NAME: Patrick Crowley

Presentation Brothers of Mary (PB)

Fratres Presentationis Mariae (FPM)
c/o Stephen O'Gorman, Mount St. Joseph, Blarney St., Cork, Ireland
PHONE: +353 (21) 392792
FAX: +353 (21) 398200
E-MAIL: presgen@tinet.ie
NAME: Br. Stephen O'Gorman

Saint Patrick's Missionary Society (SPSFM)
St. Patrick's, Kiltegan, Wicklow, Ireland
PHONE: +353 (508) 73600
FAX: +353 (508) 73644
E-MAIL: spsgen@iol.ie
TITLE: Superior General
NAME: Very Rev. Kieran Birmingham

Sisters of Saint John of God (SSJG)
1 Summerhill Heights, Summerhill, Wexford, Ireland
PHONE: +353 (53) 42396
FAX: +353 (53) 41500
NAME: Sr. Columba Howard

Sisters of Saint Louis (SSL)

Soeurs de Saint Louis
3 Beech St., Ballinclea Road, Killiney 6, Dublin Ireland
PHONE: +353 (1) 2350304
FAX: +353 (1) 2350345
E-MAIL: sslgen@tinet.ie
TITLE: General Secretary
NAME: Sr. Margaret Healy, SSL

Jewish

Dublin Hebrew Congregation
37 Adelaide Road, Dublin, Ireland
PHONE: +353 (1) 906609; 973675; 766745

Machzekei Hadaas
77 Terenure Road North, D. Golding, Dublin, Ireland
E-MAIL: machadass@jerusalemail.com
WEBSITE: http://www.jpostmail.com/jpost/users/machadass

Mormon

Finglas Ward
L.D.S. Chapel, The Willows, Finglas Road, Glasnevin, Dublin 7, Ireland
TITLE: Bishop
NAME: Colin Guild

Orthodox

St. Colman of Oughaval Church
Stradbally Hall, Stradbally, Co. Laois, Ireland
PHONE: +353 050225160
E-MAIL: pbaulk@aol.com
TITLE: Priest
NAME: Peter Baulk

Pagan

Pagan Federation-Ireland
BM Box 7097, London WC1N 3XX, England
NAME: Moonraven

Protestant

Seventh-Day Adventist Church
47a Ranelagh Road, Ranelagh Road, Dublin 6

Scientology

Church of Scientology Mission of Dublin Ltd.
62/63 Middle Abbey Street, Dublin 1, Eire, Ireland
PHONE: +353 (1) 8720007

Other Organizations

Irish Missionary Union (IMU)
Orwell Park, Raathgar, Dublin 6, Ireland
PHONE: +353 (1) 4965433
FAX: +353 (1) 4965029
E-MAIL: imu@connect.ie
TITLE: Executive Secretary
NAME: Rev. Thomas Kiggins, SPS

Volunteer Missionary Movement-Europe (VMM)
High Park, Grace Park Road, Drumcondra, Dublin 9, Ireland
PHONE: +353 (1) 8376565
FAX: +353 (1) 8367112
E-MAIL: vmmeurgo@iol.ie
TITLE: General Coordinator
NAME: Mary Purcell

FURTHER READING

Articles

"Irish Eyes Are Smiling: Economists Forecast Continuing High Growth, But Euro Membership Brings a Danger of Overheating." *Time International,* November 29, 1999, vol. 154, no. 21, p. 38.

Kaminski, Matthew. "Sweden, Austria, Finland and Ireland remain neutral EU Bloc in Name Only." *Wall Street Journal,* March 7, 2000, p. A21.

Lavery, Brian. "Irish Economy Grows." *New York Times,* October 26, 2000, p. W1.

Underhill, William. "The Perils of Prosperity." *Newsweek International,* July 24, 2000, p. 41.

Books

Barberis, Peter, et al., editors. *Encyclopedia of British and Irish Political Organizations: Parties, Groups, and Movements of the Twentieth Century.* New York: Pinter, 2000.

Eagleton, Terry. *The truth about the Irish.* New York: St. Martin's Press, 2000

Fanning, Charles, editor. *New Perspectives on the Irish Diaspora.* Carbondale: Southern Illinois University Press, 2000.

Golway, Terry. *For the Cause of Liberty: A Thousand Years of Ireland's Heroes.* New York: Simon & Schuster, 2000.

Marwick, Arthur. *A History of the Modern British Isles, 1914–1999: Circumstances, Events, and Outcomes.* Malden, MA: Blackwell Publishers, 2000.

Selected Documents in Irish History. Armonk, NY: M.E. Sharpe, 2000.

IRELAND: STATISTICAL DATA

For sources and notes see "Sources of Statistics" at the front of each volume.

GEOGRAPHY

Geography

Area:

Total: 70,280 sq km.

Land: 68,890 sq km.

Land boundaries:

Total: 360 km.

Border countries: United Kingdom 360 km.

Coastline: 1,448 km.

Climate: temperate maritime; modified by North Atlantic Current; mild winters, cool summers; consistently humid; overcast about half the time.

Terrain: mostly level to rolling interior plain surrounded by rugged hills and low mountains; sea cliffs on west coast.

Natural resources: zinc, lead, natural gas, barite, copper, gypsum, limestone, dolomite, peat, silver.

Land use:

Arable land: 13%

Permanent crops: 0%

Permanent pastures: 68%

Forests and woodland: 5%

Other: 14% (1993 est.).

HUMAN FACTORS

Demographics (A)

	1990	1995	1998	2000	2010	2020	2030	2040	2050
Population	3,508.2	NA	3,711	3,797	4,161	4,372	4,484	4,520	4,463
Life expectancy - males	71.7	NA	73.7	74.1	75.8	77.2	78.3	79.2	79.9
Life expectancy - females	77.5	NA	79.3	79.7	81.6	83.1	84.2	85.2	85.9
Birth rate (per 1,000)	15.1	NA	14.3	14.5	14.0	11.7	11.0	10.5	9.5
Death rate (per 1,000)	9.1	NA	8.3	8.1	7.8	8.2	9.3	10.6	11.9
Women of reproductive age (15-49 yrs.)	851	NA	968	993	1,040	1,028	981	933	900
Fertility rate	2.1	NA	1.9	1.9	1.9	1.8	1.8	1.7	1.7

Except as noted, values for vital statistics are in thousands; life expectancy is in years.

Health Personnel

	National Data	World Data (wtd ave)
Total health expenditure as a percentage of GDP, 1990-1998[a]		
Public sector	4.9	2.5
Private sector	1.5	2.9
Total[b]	6.3	5.5
Health expenditure per capita in U.S. dollars, 1990-1998[a]		
Purchasing power parity	1,293	561
Total	1,333	483
Availability of health care facilities per 100,000 people		
Hospital beds 1990-1998[a]	370	330
Doctors 1992-1995[a]	167	122
Nurses 1992-1995[a]	NA	248

Health Indicators

	National Data	World Data
Life expectancy at birth (years)		
1980	73	61
1998	76	67
Daily per capita supply of calories		
1970	3,445	2,358
1997	3,565	2,791
Daily per capital supply of protein		
1997 (grams)	111	74
Total fertility rate (births per woman)		
1980	3.2	3.7
1998	1.9	2.7
People living with (1997)		
Tuberculosis (cases per 100,000)	12.0	60.4
HIV/AIDS (% aged 15 - 49 years)	0.09	0.99

Infants and Malnutrition

	National Data	World Data (wtd ave)
Under 5 mortality rate (1989)	7	NA
% of infants with low birthweight (1992-98)[1]	4	17
Births attended by skilled health staff (% of total births 1996-98)	100	52
% fully immunized at 1 year of age (1995-98)[1]		
TB	NA	82
DPT	NA	77
Polio	63[2]	77
Measles	NA	74
Prevalence of child malnutrition (1992-98)[1] (based on weight for age, % of children under 5 years)	NA	30

Ethnic Division

Celtic, English.

Religion

Roman Catholic 91.6%
Church of Ireland 2.5%
Other 5.9%

Data for 1998.

Major Languages

English is the language generally used, Irish (Gaelic) spoken mainly in areas located along the western seaboard.

EDUCATION

Public Education Expenditures

	1980	1997
Public expenditures on education as % of GNP	6.3	6.0
Expenditures per student as % of GNP per capita		
Primary	11.6	14.1
Secondary	24.3	21.9
Tertiary	60.0	36.3
Teachers' compensation as % of total current education expenditures	67.7	73.6
Pupils per teacher at the primary level	NA	22
Duration of primary education in years	NA	9
World data for comparison		
Public expenditures on education as % of GNP (mean)	3.9	4.8
Pupils per teacher at the primary level (wtd ave)	NA	33
Duration of primary education in years (mean)	NA	9

Educational Attainment (A)

Age group (1991)	25+
Population of this age group	1,983,547
Highest level attained (%)	
No schooling	0.0
First level	
Not completed	0.0
Completed	38.5
Entered second level	43.7
Entered post-secondary	14.6

Libraries

National Libraries	**1997**
Administrative Units	1
Service Points or Branches	2
Number of Volumes (000)	757
Registered Users (000)	88
Loans to Users (000)	124
Total Library Staff	56
Public Libraries	**1997**
Administrative Units	32

(Continued on next page.)

GOVERNMENT & LAW

Military Affairs (A)

	1990	1992	1995	1996	1997
Military expenditures					
Current dollars (mil.)	521	587	655	703	744
1997 constant dollars (mil.)	611	650	678	714	744
Armed forces (000)	13	13	17	17	17
Gross national product (GNP)					
Current dollars (mil.)	35,500	40,600	52,500	57,400	63,100
1997 constant dollars (mil.)	41,600	45,100	54,300	58,300	63,100
Central government expenditures (CGE)					
1997 constant dollars (mil.)	15,400	17,300	19,800	20,600	22,500
People (mil.)	3.5	3.5	3.6	3.6	3.6
Military expenditure as % of GNP	1.5	1.4	1.2	1.2	1.2
World data on military expenditure as % of GNP	4.5	3.4	2.7	2.6	2.6
Military expenditure as % of CGE	4.0	3.8	3.4	3.5	3.3
World data on military expenditure as % of CGE	17.0	12.5	10.5	10.3	10.2
Military expenditure per capita (1997 $)	174	183	189	199	206
World data on military expenditure per capita (1997 $)	242	173	146	143	145
Armed forces per 1,000 people (soldiers)	3.7	3.7	4.7	4.7	4.7
World data on armed forces per 1,000 people (soldiers)	5.3	4.5	4.1	3.9	3.8
GNP per capita (1997 $)	11,900	12,700	15,200	16,200	17,500
Arms imports[6]					
Current dollars (mil.)	5	30	0	30	30
1997 constant dollars (mil.)	6	33	0	31	30
Total imports[7]					
Current dollars (mil.)	20,670	22,480	32,640	35,870	39,300
1997 constant dollars (mil.)	24,210	24,920	33,800	36,470	39,300
Total exports[7]					
Current dollars (mil.)	23,740	28,330	44,250	48,670	53,340
1997 constant dollars (mil.)	27,810	31,410	45,820	49,480	53,340
Arms as percent of total imports[8]	0	0.1	0	0.1	0.1
Arms as percent of total exports[8]	0	0	0	0	0

(Continued on next page.)

EDUCATION (cont.)

Libraries (cont.)

Service Points or Branches 351

Number of Volumes (000) 11,212

Registered Users (000) . . . . .NA

Loans to Users (000) .12,582

Total Library Staff 1,328

GOVERNMENT & LAW (cont.)

Political Parties

Parliament (Oireachtas)	% of vote	no. of seats
Senate		
Fianna Fail	29%	NA
Fine Gael	16%	NA
Labor Party	4%	NA
Progressive Democrats	4%	NA
Others	7%	NA
House of Representatives		
Fianna Fail	NA	76
Fine Gael	NA	53
Labor Party	NA	19
Progressive Democrats	NA	4
Democratic Left	NA	4
Green Alliance	NA	2
Sinn Fein	NA	1
Independents	NA	7

Elections for the Senate were last held August 1997 (next to be held in 2002); Elections for the House of Representatives were last held 6 June 1997 (next to be held in 2002). NA stands for not available.

Government Budgets (A)

Year: 1996

Total Expenditures: 15,959 Millions of Pounds

Expenditures as a percentage of the total by function:

General public services and public order 8.96

Defense 2.89

Education 13.09

Health 15.68

Social Security and Welfare 27.05

Housing and community amenities 2.86

Recreational, cultural, and religious affairs 0.68

Fuel and energy 1.07

Agriculture, forestry, fishing, and hunting 4.75

Mining, manufacturing, and construction 3.40

Transportation and communication 3.62

Other economic affairs and services 2.84

Crime

Crime volume (for 1998)

Crimes reported 82,627

Total persons convicted 36,356

Crimes per 100,000 population 2,279

Persons responsible for offenses

Total number suspects .4,281

Total number of female suspects 557

Total number of juvenile suspects 557

LABOR FORCE

Total Labor Force (A)

1.77 million (1999 est.).

Labor Force by Occupation

Services 63%

Industry 28%

Agriculture 9%

Data for 1999 est.

Unemployment Rate

5.5% (1999)

PRODUCTION SECTOR

Energy Production

Production . . . . .19.715 billion kWh

Production by source

Fossil fuel 94.12%

Hydro 4.63%

Nuclear 0%

Other 1.25%

Exports . . . . .100 million kWh

Data for 1998.

Energy Consumption

Consumption . . . . .18.415 billion kWh

Imports .180.000 million kWh

Data for 1998.

Transportation

Highways:

Total: 92,500 km.

Paved: 87,043 km (including 115 km of expressways).

Unpaved: 5,457 km (1999 est.).

Waterways: 700 km (limited for commercial traffic) (1998).

Pipelines: natural gas 225 km (1998).

Merchant marine:

Total: 31 ships (1,000 GRT or over) totaling 100,639 GRT/115,793 DWT.

Ships by type: bulk 1, cargo 27, container 2, short-sea passenger 1 (1999 est.).

Airports: 44 (1999 est.).

Airports - with paved runways: 17.

Airports - with unpaved runways: 27.

Top Agriculture Products

Turnips, barley, potatoes, sugar beets, wheat; beef, dairy products.

Top Mining Products (B)

Mineral resources include: zinc, lead, barite, copper, gypsum, limestone, dolomite, peat, silver.

MANUFACTURING SECTOR

GDP & Manufacturing Summary (A)

	1980	1985	1990	1995
GDP ($-1990 mil.)[1]	31,870	36,144	44,930	57,942
Per capita ($-1990)[1]	9,371	10,176	12,826	16,340
Manufacturing share (%) (current prices)[1]	25.5	27.3	31.1	33.8[e]
Manufacturing				
Value added ($-1990 mil.)[1]	7,464	9,465	11,445	18,568
Industrial production index	56	69	100	161
Value added ($ mil.)	5,700	5,995	15,013	26,493[e]
Gross output ($ mil.)	15,905	15,394	33,527	55,126
Employment (000)	225	186	194	213[e]
Profitability (% of gross output)				
Intermediate input (%)	64	61	55	52[e]
Wages and salaries inc. supplements (%)	17[e]	14[e]	14[e]	11[e]
Gross operating surplus	19[e]	25[e]	31[e]	38[e]
Productivity ($)				
Gross output per worker	70,068	82,191	172,553	253,308[e]
Value added per worker	25,112	32,008	77,266	126,335[e]
Average wage (inc. supplements)	11,906[e]	11,604[e]	23,770[e]	27,250[e]
Value added ($ mil.)				
Food products	1,264	1,194	3,068	5,736[e]
Beverages	325	331	792	1,312[e]
Tobacco products	83	83	166	249[e]
Textiles	266	181	349	465[e]
Wearing apparel	147	118	207	210[e]
Leather and fur products	28	12	21	20[e]
Footwear	42	22	19	14[e]
Wood and wood products	93	66	170	280[e]
Furniture and fixtures	59	40	86	138[e]
Paper and paper products	105	75	190	273[e]
Printing and publishing	265	219	561	921[e]
Industrial chemicals	236	315	757	1,537[e]
Other chemical products	536	715	1,718	3,480[e]
Petroleum refineries	21[e]	14[e]	28[e]	46[e]
Misc. petroleum and coal products	2[e]	1[e]	2[e]	4[e]
Rubber products	52	58[e]	118	196[e]
Plastic products	113	125[e]	332	662[e]
Pottery, china and earthenware	28	13	28	32[e]
Glass and glass products	109	113	144	207[e]
Other non-metal mineral products	322	260	560	835[e]
Iron and steel	31	37	92	106[e]
Non-ferrous metals	15	8	10	8[e]
Metal products	335	216	469	663[e]
Non-electrical machinery	449	854	2,235	3,544[e]
Electrical machinery	337	512	1,840	3,884[e]
Transport equipment	190	116	309	386[e]
Prof. and scientific equipment	168	261	611	1,107[e]
Other manufacturing	79	39	132	177[e]

COMMUNICATIONS

Daily Newspapers

	National Data	World Data for Comparison
Daily Newspapers		
Number of Dailies	6	8,391
Total Circulation (000)	543	548,000
Circulation per 1,000 inhabitants	149	96

Telecommunications

Telephones - main lines in use: 1,642,541 (1999).

Telephones - mobile cellular: 941,775 (1999).

Telephone system: modern digital system using cable and microwave radio relay.

Domestic: microwave radio relay.

International: satellite earth station - 1 Intelsat (Atlantic Ocean).

Radio broadcast stations: AM 9, FM 106, shortwave 0 (1998).

Radios: 2.55 million (1997).

Television broadcast stations: 10 (plus 36 low-power repeaters) (1997).

Televisions: 1.47 million (1997).

Internet Service Providers (ISPs): 14 (1999).

FINANCE, ECONOMICS, & TRADE

Economic Indicators

National product: GDP—purchasing power parity—$73.7 billion (1999 est.).

National product real growth rate: 8.4% (1999 est.).

National product per capita: $20,300 (1999 est.).

Inflation rate—consumer price index: 2.2% (1999).

Exchange Rates

Exchange rates:

Irish pounds per US$1

January 2000	0.9865
1999	0.9374
1998	0.7014
1997	0.6588
1996	0.6248
1995	0.6235

On 1 January 1999, the European Union introduced a common currency the euro, which is now being used at a fixed rate of 0.787564 Irish pounds per euro; the euro has replaced the pound in many financial and business transactions; it will replace the local currency in consenting countries for all transactions in 2002.

Top Import Origins

$44 billion (c.i.f., 1999 est.)

Origins (1998)

EU	54%
United Kingdom	31%
Germany	6%
France	5%
United States	16%
Japan	7%
Singapore	4%

Top Export Destinations

$66 billion (f.o.b., 1999 est.)

Destinations (1998)

EU	68%
United Kingdom	22%
Germany	15%
France	8%
United States	15%

Balance of Payments

	1994	1995	1996	1997	1998
Exports of goods (f.o.b.)	33,642	44,423	49,184	55,293	65,032
Imports of goods (f.o.b.)	−24,275	−30,866	−33,430	−36,668	−41,651
Trade balance	9,366	13,557	15,754	18,625	23,381
Services - debits	−8,452	−11,303	−13,448	−15,195	−20,062
Services - credits	4,319	5,017	5,749	6,186	6,717
Private transfers (net)	2,263	2,425	2,951	2,475	2,333
Government transfers (net)	276	250	42	193	11
Overall balance	1,577	1,721	2,049	1,866	806

Foreign Aid

Donor: ODA, $240 million (1999).

Import/Export Commodities

Import Commodities	Export Commodities
Data processing equipment	Machinery and equipment
Other machinery and equipment	Computers
Chemicals	Chemicals
Petroleum and petroleum products	Pharmaceuticals
Textiles	Live animals
Clothing	Animal products

ISRAEL

CAPITAL: Jerusalem (Yerushalayim, Al-Quds).

FLAG: The flag, which was adopted at the First Zionist Congress in 1897, consists of a blue six-pointed Shield of David (Magen David) centered between two blue horizontal stripes on a white field.

ANTHEM: *Hatikvah (The Hope).*

MONETARY UNIT: The new Israeli shekel (NIS), a paper currency of 100 new agorot, replaced the shekel (IS) at a rate of 1,000 to 1 in 1985; the shekel replaced the Israeli pound (IL) in 1980 at the rate of 10 pounds per shekel. There are coins of 5, 10, and 50 agora, 1 and 5 shekels and notes of 10, 50, 100, and 200 shekels. NIS1 = $0.31008 (or $1 = NIS3.225).

WEIGHTS AND MEASURES: The metric system is the legal standard, but some local units are used, notably the dunam (equivalent to 1,000 square meters, or about 0.25 acre).

HOLIDAYS: Israel officially uses both the Gregorian and the complex Jewish lunisolar calendars, but the latter determines the occurrence of national holidays: Rosh Hashanah (New Year), September or October; Yom Kippur (Day of Atonement), September or October; Sukkot (Tabernacles), September or October; Simhat Torah (Rejoicing in the Law), September or October; Pesach (Passover), March or April; Independence Day, April or May; and Shavuot (Pentecost), May or June. All Jewish holidays, as well as the Jewish Sabbath (Friday/Saturday), begin just before sundown and end at nightfall 24 hours later. Muslim, Christian, and Druze holidays are observed by the respective minorities.

TIME: 2 PM = noon GMT.

LOCATION AND SIZE: Situated in southwestern Asia along the eastern end of the Mediterranean Sea, Israel claims an area of 20,770 square kilometers (8,019 square miles).

CLIMATE: Although climatic conditions are varied across the country, the climate is generally temperate. The coldest month is January; the hottest, August. Temperatures range from between 4° and 10°C (40°–50°F) in the hills in January to as high as 49°C (120°F) in August in Elat, in the south.

State of Israel
Arabic— *Dawlat Israel*
Hebrew— *Medinat Yisrael*

INTRODUCTORY SURVEY

RECENT HISTORY

Following World War II (1939-1945) several nations supported establishment of a Jewish state as a haven for the survivors of the Nazi Holocaust. The British government decided to relinquish their rule over Palestine and in November 1947 the UN General Assembly adopted a plan for the division of Palestine into two economically united but politically independent states, one Jewish and the other Arab.

The Arabs of Palestine immediately opposed this division but the Jews accepted the plan. On May 14, 1948, they proclaimed the formation of the State of Israel. The next day, the Arab League states-Egypt, Iraq, Jordan, Lebanon, Sa'udi Arabia, and Syria-launched a joint armed attack. Hundreds of thousands of Palestinian Arabs fled abroad leaving Israel in possession of a much larger territory than awarded under the UN plan. The Arab state failed to take shape as Jordan annexed the West Bank and Palestinian refugees resettled in camps on both banks of the Jordan River, in the Gaza Strip, in southern Lebanon, and in Syria.

Almost a half century of periodic hostilities followed and political instability in the region. In 1956 Israel with British and French support invaded Egypt and gained control of the Gaza Strip and the Sinai Peninsula only to withdraw under pressure from the United States from the occupied areas in 1957.

In June 1967 Israel attacked Egypt and its allies, Syria and Jordan scoring a decisive victory

in what was termed the Six-Day War. Israel took control of the Sinai Peninsula, the Gaza Strip, the Golan Heights, and the West Bank including Jordanian-ruled East Jerusalem.

Despite the UN Security Council calling for withdrawal of Israeli armed forces from the territories, in 1967 the Israeli government began Jewish settlement in these areas. By 1994 there were some 120,000 settlers in the occupied territories. In reaction the Palestine Liberation Organization (PLO) pursued an international campaign of terrorism, highlighted in September 1972 by the kidnap and murder of Israeli athletes at the Olympic Games in Munich, Germany. In 1973 during the Jewish high holiday of Yom Kippur, Egypt and Syria attacked Israeli-held territory in the Sinai Peninsula and the Golan Heights resulting in some territory in the Sinai returning to Egypt.

Egyptian-Israeli hostilities ended in late 1978 when Israeli Prime Minister Menachem Begin and Egyptian President Anwar al-Sadat agreed on the general framework for a peace treaty. However, agreement on Palestinian self-rule in the West Bank and the Gaza Strip was not reached and Israel continued to establish Jewish settlements in the West Bank despite Egyptian protests.

Hostilities between Israel and the PLO and Syria reached a climax in June 1982. Israel launched an invasion of southern Lebanon aimed at destroying bases from which the PLO had shelled northern Israel and initiated terrorist attacks. A multinational peacekeeping force was stationed in the Beirut area.

In December 1987 unarmed Palestinians in Gaza began a long series of stone-throwing riots against Israeli troops in the occupied territories. In this uprising (or *intifada* in Arabic) over 1,000 Palestinians were killed as well as several hundred Israelis.

In 1991 Israeli and Palestinian representatives met in Oslo, Norway developing a peace agreement transferring authority in the Gaza Strip and the West Bank city of Jericho to interim Palestinian rule. The final form of Palestinian independence was to be resolved in five years. The agreement was signed at the White House in Washington, D.C., on September 13, 1993.

Though opposed by extremists on both sides, the withdrawal of Israeli forces and establishment of Palestinian self-rule in Gaza and Jericho took place in May 1994. By 1997 six West Bank cities were under Palestinian control. In November 1995 a militant Israeli assassinated Prime Minister Yitzhak Rabin in retaliation for slowing Jewish settlement in the occupied territories.

In May 1996 Benjamin Netanyahu won Israel's first direct election for the office of prime minister. He immediately took a tougher stance on the occupied territories, increasing the construction of Jewish settlements and angering Palestinians.

In October 1998 Netanyahu, Arafat, and President Bill Clinton signed the Wye Memorandum that set a timetable for Israeli withdrawal from the West Bank. However Netanyahu faced stiff opposition to the plan at home. By the end of 1998 his government had collapsed and the Wye plan was put on hold.

In May 1999 Labor Party leader Ehud Barak defeated Netanyahu. The election was widely seen as a public rejection of the policies of Netanyahu blamed for stalling the peace process. By the end of 1999 Barak had revived the Wye plan, resumed talks with Syria, and pledged withdrawal of Israeli troops from Lebanon as of July 2000.

GOVERNMENT

Israel is a parliamentary democracy with no written constitution. The 1948 Declaration of Establishment, the Basic Laws of the parliament (Knesset), and the Israeli Citizenship law fill some of the functions of a constitution. Legislative power resides in the single-chamber Knesset (parliament), whose 120 members are elected for four-year terms by secret vote of all citizens eighteen years of age and over. Elected by the Knesset for a five-year term, the head of state is the president, who performs ceremonial duties. In 1996 a new law went into effect that allowed voters to directly elect the prime minister. The cabinet is selected by the prime minister and approved by the Knesset.

Judiciary

Magistrates' courts in all towns are the first to hear most cases and settle petty property claims and lesser criminal charges. Five district courts, serving mainly as courts of appeal, have jurisdiction over all other actions except marriage and divorce cases. These are heard, along with other personal and religious matters, in the religious courts of the Jewish (rabbinical), Muslim (Shari`ah), Druze, and Christian communities. The eleven-member Supreme Court is the court of last appeal. There is no jury system.

Political Parties

Israel's multiparty system reflects the diverse origins of the people and their long practice of party politics in Zionist organizations. The Mapai (Israel Workers Party) led the first coalition governments to rule Israel after independence. It also formed the nucleus of the present socialist Israel Labor Party, which controlled Israel's governments during 1969-1974 under Prime Minister Golda Meir and during 1974-1977 under Prime Minister Yitzhak Rabin.

In September 1973 four right-wing nationalist parties combined to form the Likud, which thus became the major opposition bloc in the Knesset (parliament). The Likud became the largest party in the Knesset by winning forty-three seats in the May 1977 elections, and its leader Menachem Begin became prime minister. The Likud and Labor parties have been Israel's two main political groupings since that time. In recent years, however, both Likud and Labor have lost seats in the Knesset as other parties, such as Shas, a religious party, and Merety, a grouping of three left-wing parties, have gained followers.

In 1999 Ehud Barak, heading a Labor-led center-left coalition called One Israel, defeated Netanyahu. In legislative elections Barak's One Israel/Israeli Labor Party Coalition won a plurality of 126 seats, followed by nineteen for the Likud.

DEFENSE

Jewish and Druze men between the ages of eighteen and twenty-six are drafted. Drafted Jewish women are trained for noncombat duties. Christians and Muslims may serve on a voluntary basis, but Muslims are rarely allowed to bear arms.

In 2000 the Israeli army had 130,000 active duty soldiers (85,000 draftees) and could mobilize as many as 530,000 more soldiers. The navy had 6,500 regulars, 2,500 draftees, and 11,500 reservists.

The air force had 37,000 regulars, 20,000 draftees, and 57,000 reserves. There are 6,000 paramilitary border police.

The Ministry of Defense's expenditure was $8.7 billion in 1999, or 9.4 percent of the gross domestic product (GDP).

ECONOMIC AFFAIRS

Israel is an advanced, technologically-strong market economy. Israel must export on a large scale to maintain its relatively high standard of living. Diamonds, high technology equipment, and agricultural products are leading exports. Israel has developed strong agricultural and industrial sectors over the past two decades. However it must import crude oil, grains, and raw materials. Israel generally posts large deficits that are covered by transfer payments from abroad and foreign loans roughly half of which come from the United States.

The average annual growth during 1990-1996 was 6 percent. Much of the economic expansion in the 1990s has come from the construction, infrastructure expansion, and capital investment brought on by the influx of thousands of well-educated Russian immigrants and the opening of new markets at the end of the Cold War.

Growth began slowing in 1996 in response to tightened fiscal and monetary policies, but inflation by 1999 was at record low levels and prospects were good for stronger GDP growth in 2000 if regional peace could be maintained.

Income

In 1999 Israel's gross domestic product (GDP) was estimated at $105.4 billion, or about $18,300 per capita. The estimated growth rate of GDP was 2.1 percent and inflation 1.3 percent. Contributions of economic sectors were estimated in 1997 to be agriculture at 2 percent, industry 17 percent, and services 81 percent.

Industry

Major expansion has taken place in textiles, machinery and transport equipment, military equipment, metallurgy, mineral processing, high technology electronics, electrical products, precision instruments, chemicals, food processing, diamond cutting and polishing, and tourism. However, industry remains handicapped by reliance on imported raw materials, relatively high wage costs, and inflation.

Public Finance

The U.S. Central Intelligence Agency (CIA) estimated that in 2000 Israel's central government took in revenues of $40 billion and had expenditures of $42.4 billion including capital expenditures of $2.9 billion.

Banking and Finance

The Bank of Israel, with headquarters in Jerusalem, began operations as the central state bank in December 1954. The bank issues currency, accepts deposits from banking institutions in Israel, extends temporary advances to the government, acts as the government's sole banking and fiscal agent, and manages the public debt. Among the largest commercial banks are the Bank Leumi, the Israel Discount Bank, and the Histadrut-controlled Bank Hapoalim. There were twenty-four licensed commercial banks in 1997; one investment bank; and nine mortgage banks. There are also numerous credit cooperatives and specialized institutions such as mortgage banks, development banks, and the Post Office Bank for Savings.

The structure of the banking industry is based on the central European model of "universal banking," whereby the banks operate as retail, wholesale, and investment banks, as well as being active in all main areas of capital market activity, brokerage, underwriting, and mutual and provident fund management.

The Tel-Aviv Stock Exchange (TASE) was formed in 1953.

Economic Development

Goals of national security, full utilization of resources, integration of immigrants, and institution of a broad welfare program dictate economic policy. Major government infrastructure projects include an expansion of the Ben-Gurion Airport, a subway for Tel-Aviv, a tunnel through Mt. Carmel, and a major new North-South highway.

By the mid-1990s the Israeli government was actively engaged in an economic liberalization program that is a stark contrast from the largely state-regulated economy of Israeli's first decades.

The government has also taken steps in the 1990s to integrate a huge influx of Russian immigrants, most of who were well educated and added to an already technologically aware workforce. As a result sectors such as medical equipment, computer hardware and software, and telecommunications, are expected to be important to Israel's economic future.

SOCIAL WELFARE

Israel has a universal social insurance system that covers all residents aged eighteen and over. Benefits include old age pensions, disability, medical care, and monthly allowances for large families. Employee-based programs include maternity benefits, workers' compensation for injuries, and unemployment benefits.

Women's rights are protected by the Equal Rights for Women Law (1951) and the Employment of Women Law (1954), which requires equal pay for equal work. In 1993, a new law barred discrimination in unemployment compensation for elderly female citizens.

International organizations cite police harassment of Arabs on the West Bank and Gaza Strip as an ongoing problem, while Israeli officials point to the threat of Arab terrorist attacks as a source of social instability.

Healthcare

In 2000 estimated life expectancy averaged 78.6 years. The Ministry of Health supervises all health matters and functions directly in the field of medical care. It also operates infant welfare clinics, nursing schools, and laboratories. The largest medical organization in the country, the Workers' Sick Fund (Kupat Holim), is the health insurance association of Histadrut. It administers hospitals, clinics, convalescent homes, and mother-child welfare stations. In 1990-1997 there were six hospital beds and 3.8 doctors per 1,000 people.

Housing

From 1960 to 1985 a total of 943,350 housing units were constructed. In 1986 94 percent of all housing units had piped water, 58.2 percent had flush toilets, and 99 percent had electric lighting. Between 1989 and 1991 a sudden rise in immigration from the former Soviet Union and Ethiopia resulted in a dramatic increase in housing demand. As of 1992 the total number of dwellings in Israel was 1.5 million.

EDUCATION

Education is compulsory for eleven years and free for all children between five and sixteen years of age. Primary education is for eight years followed by four years of secondary education. The language of instruction in Jewish schools is Hebrew; in Arab schools it is Arabic. In the period of 1988-1993 the estimated literacy rate among Israelis aged fifteen and over was 95 percent total, 97 percent for men, and 93 percent for women. In 1996 primary schools had 631,916 students and secondary level schools had 541,737 students.

Israel has eight institutions of higher learning. In 1996 the total number of students in all higher-level institutions of Israel was 198,766.

2000 KEY EVENTS TIMELINE

January

- Thousands of Christians flock to holy sites in commemoration of the millennium on the first of January.
- Israeli and Syrian delegations renew peace talks January 3–10 after a three-year hiatus.
- David Klein is nominated on January 16 to head the Bank of Israel.
- The Attorney General opens an investigation of Ehud Barak's 1999 campaign financing on January 17.
- On January 20 a criminal investigation begins against President Ezer Weizman for tax fraud.

February

- Knesset debates nuclear policy on February 2.
- On February 3 Israel withdraws its ambassador to Austria.
- The Palestinian Authority suspends peace talks with Israel on February 8.
- Controversy surrounds German President Johannes Rau's speech to the Knesset on February 16.
- On February 29 the State Archives releases a transcript of the memoirs of Nazi war criminal, German Adolph Eichman, written by Eichman while he was imprisoned in Israel in the 1960s, waiting execution. Eichman was the organizer of the trains that carried millions to their deaths during World War II, was convicted of war crimes and hanged in Israel in 1962.

March

- Israeli cabinet agrees on a pullout from its security zone in south Lebanon on March 5.
- On March 13 Prime Minister Barak wins two confidence votes
- Barak and Yasir Arafat return to the negotiating table on March 18.
- From March 20–26 Pope John Paul II visits the Holy Land
- Israeli and Palestinian delegations meet at Bolling Air Force Base near Washington, DC from March 21–28.

April

- Barak hints at the creation of an independent Palestinian state on April 16.
- On April 23 Jordan's King Abdallah meets Barak at Eilat.

May

- Iran begins the trial of thirteen Jews accused of spying for Israel on May 1.

- On May 15 Israeli and Palestinian forces engage each other during riots in the West Bank.
- Israel withdraws from south Lebanon on May 24.
- On May 28 Weizman announces he will resign effective July 10.

July

- Six cabinet members representing three nationalist parties withdraw from President Barak's coalition on July 9, protesting territorial concessions that the President may make at peace talks in the United States.
- Peace talks between Barak and Arafat begin on July 11 at Camp David, but break down on July 25, both leaders demanding control over Jerusalem.

August

- The first opposition right-wing party Likud candidate is elected president of Israel, Moshe Katsav, on August 1. Prime Minister Ehud Barak's leftist party has only 42 of 120 seats in the legislature.
- Israeli Foreign Minister David Levy resigns in the face of party opposition on August 2.

September

- Violence on the Lebanese border breaks out during the last week of September, killing seven and wounding many others.

October

- Fighting between Palestinians and Israeli's spreads into Nazareth and other towns within Israel's borders October 1.
- Lebanese guerrillas attack an Israeli military base in Lebanon October 7.
- Israel and Palestine agree to a cease-fire October 17, after more than 100 people have been killed since September 29.
- Arab League member states agree to freeze all formal diplomatic contact with Israel on October 22.
- Israeli Prime Minister Ehud Barak orders an attack on Palestinian President Yasir Arafat October 30, which is unsuccessful.

November

- The death toll rises to over 240 dead in Palestine, and 31 dead in Israel, by November 25.

December

- Barak resigns as prime minister December 10 and calls for a special election for prime minister only to be held in May 2001.
- After two deadly bomb explosions, President Barak orders the closing of the Gaza strip on December 28.
- Binyamin Kahane and his wife are killed in an ambush on December 31; Kahane is the son of Rabbi Meir Kahane who was assassinated in 1990. The Kahanes were radical right-wing settlers who advocated expulsion of all Palestinians from Israel.

ANALYSIS OF EVENTS: 2000

BUSINESS AND THE ECONOMY

Israel headed into 2000 on an upswing following a three-year economic downturn. High-tech and other exports were growing briskly, and gross domestic product (GDP) growth was expected to reach 3.5–4 percent. Thanks to low annual inflation—expected to total 3–4 percent for the year—real interest rates had fallen to 6.1 percent at mid-year. The tourism industry was thriving, with arrivals expected to total 3 million for the year. Israel also remained the world's single largest recipient of U.S. foreign aid, with an allotment of $3 billion in 2000.

The engineering and technological expertise fostered by Israel's heavy investment in defense had fueled a high-tech boom, with over 130 Israeli firms listed on stock exchanges in the United States—more than any other foreign country—and 97 on the Nasdaq.

GOVERNMENT AND POLITICS

The first year of the new millennium brought major setbacks for the government of Ehud Barak, still in its first year, and profound disillusionment with the peace process begun seven years earlier by the Oslo accords. Although Israeli prime minister Ehud Barak spent much of the year trying to negotiate a final peace agreement with the Palestinians, hopes for Middle East peace in the new millennium were dashed in the fall by the outbreak of hostilities in the West Bank, as priorities shifted from a long-term peace agreement to the prevention of immediate all-out war in the country, and possibly the region as well.

The year began with an investigation of President Ezer Weizman for tax fraud, ultimately leading to Weizman's resignation in July. During the first half of the year, Prime Minister Barak attempted to keep the Middle East peace process alive, meeting with Palestinian leader Yasir Arafat and President Clinton in an effort to work out a framework agreement for a peace deal by the end of May. Negotiations with Syria, resumed in January after a three-year hiatus, remained deadlocked. Israel honored its pledge to withdraw its forces from southern Lebanon, and this was accomplished in May.

With a final peace deal still out of reach, Barak and Arafat agreed to hold a summit meeting with President Clinton at Camp David in July. Barak arrived at the summit in a weakened negotiating position, having lost his parliamentary majority at the beginning of the month, and the fifteen-day talks ultimately broke down over the issue of East Jerusalem. Barak suffered a further political setback at the beginning of August, when his political ally, veteran political leader Shimon Peres, was defeated by the opposition Likud candidate Moshe Katzav when Israel's parliament, the Knesset, selected a new president to replace Ezer Weizman. By this point, it was widely believed that Barak would have to call new parliamentary elections within the next six months.

September arrived with all the parties involved still trying to craft a final status treaty in time to ward off the threatened unilateral declaration of a Palestinian state by Yasir Arafat. By the end of the month, however, violence had broken out on the West Bank, triggered by a September 28 visit to the Temple Mount, a prominent Arab holy site in Jerusalem, by opposition Likud leader Ariel Sharon. Rioting by Palestinians and a crackdown by the Israeli police created a seemingly unstoppable wave of escalating violence. Within the next two weeks, some 100 Arabs had been killed. Tensions were further inflamed by the kidnapping of three Israeli soldiers in Lebanon and televised scenes of the beating deaths of two Israeli soldiers by a mob in Ramallah, who then dragged their bodies through the streets. As the Israeli government retaliated with targeted bombing raids on the city and on Palestinian Authority facilities in Gaza, the terrorist bombing of a U.S. warship in a Yemeni harbor that killed 17 crew members and left 39 missing came as a reminder of the potential for Israeli-Palestinian violence to threaten the stability of the entire Middle East region.

Between October and December over 330 people—all but eight of them Arabs—had been killed in what many now regarded as a new Palestinian uprising in the occupied territories. A fragile ceasefire forged in a summit meeting in Egypt in October had not held, and violence continued in the West Bank and the Gaza Strip. Due to the escalating conflict, Barak resigned in early December, calling for an election for prime minister and looking for a mandate for his policies from the Israeli people. Barak would likely face Likud chairman Ariel Sharon in the February election. Former Prime Minister Shimon Peres also was considering running.

CULTURE AND SOCIETY

In spite of opposition from some right-wing groups, the historic visit of Pope John Paul II was welcomed by most Israelis, and many were moved by the sight of the aging pontiff praying at the Western Wall in Jerusalem and visiting the Holocaust memorial at Yad Vashem. The papal pilgrimage was seen as a milestone in the gradually thawing relations between Jews and the Catholic Church over the period since the Second Vatican Council, which in 1965 had denied that the Jews as a people had any responsibility for the death of Christ.

While Christians and Jews boasted of harmonious relations, tensions and conflicts between secular and ultra-orthodox Jews remained a central feature of Israeli life, with political ramifications that could (and sometimes did) unseat a government or affect international relations. These conflicts were highlighted by the controversy over a Supreme Court ruling in May that allowed women to lead prayer services at the Western Wall, an action considered sacrilegious by Orthodox Jews. (One legislator termed it a "desecration of a holy place.") In response, conservative members of parliament pushed through a bill that barred women from wearing traditional ritual garments or performing Torah readings at the Wall, and imposed penalties as stiff as seven years in jail for persons who violated the law. The passage of the bill triggered a wave of protest that included criticism by Jewish groups in the United States.

One social trend of the 1990s that was still going strong as the twenty-first century began was technopop culture among Israel's young people.

Like many of their counterparts in other Western countries, Israeli youth sported tattoos and body piercings, spent their nights writhing at raves, and promoted the increasingly popular drug ecstasy as a way to smooth over the tension of everyday life in Israel.

DIRECTORY

CENTRAL GOVERNMENT

Head of State

President
Moshe Katzav, Office of the President

Prime Minister and Minister of Defense
Ehud Barak, Office of the Prime Minister, 3 Kaplan St., PO Box 187, Kiryat Ben-Gurion, 91919 Jerusalem, Israel
PHONE: +972 (2) 6705555
FAX: +972 (2) 6512631

Ministers

Minister of Justice
Yossi Beilin, Ministry of Justice, 29 Salah A-din St., 91010 Jerusalem, Israel
PHONE: +972 (2) 6708511
FAX: +972 (2) 6288618

Minister of Public Security
Shlomo Ben-Ami, Ministry of Public of Security, Kiryat Hamemshala, PO Box 18182, 91181 Jerusalem, Israel
PHONE: +972 (2) 5308003
FAX: +972 (2) 5847872

Minister of Communications and Deputy Prime Minister
Benjamin Ben-Eliezer, Ministry of Communications, 23 Yaffo St., 91999 Jerusalem, Israel
PHONE: +972 (2) 6706320
FAX: +972 (2) 6706372

Minister of Health
Roni Milo, Ministry of Health, 2 Ben-Tabai St., PO Box 1176, 91010 Jerusalem, Israel
PHONE: +972 (2) 6705705
FAX: +972 (2) 6796491

Minister of Industry and Trade
Ehud Barak, Ministry of Industry and Trade, 30 Agron St., PO Box 299, 91002 Jerusalem, Israel
PHONE: +972 (2) 6220339
FAX: +972 (2) 6259274

Minister of Religious Affairs
Yossi Beilin, Ministry of Religious Affairs, 36 Yaffo St., PO Box 13059, 91130 Jerusalem, Israel
PHONE: +972 (2) 5311171
FAX: +972 (2) 5311183

Minister of the Environment
Dalia Itzik, Ministry of the Environment, 5 Kanfei Nesharim St., Givat Shaul, PO Box 34033, 95464 Jerusalem, Israel
PHONE: +972 (2) 6553777
FAX: +972 (2) 6553777

Minister of Foreign Affairs
Shlomo Ben Ami, Ministry of Foreign Affairs
PHONE: +972 (2) 5303111
FAX: +972 (2) 5303367

Minister of Construction and Housing
Binyamin Ben-Eliezer, Ministry of Construction and Housing, PO Box 18110, 91180 Jerusalem, Israel
PHONE: +972 (2) 5825501
FAX: +972 (2) 5825501

Minister of Tourism
Amnon Lipkin-Shahak, Ministry of Tourism, 24 King George St., PO Box 1018, 91009 Jerusalem, Israel
PHONE: +972 (2) 6754811
FAX: +972 (2) 6250890

Minister of Diaspora and Social Affairs
Michael Melchior, Ministry of Diaspora and Social Affairs

Minister of Transportation
Amnon Lipkin-Shahak, Ministry of Transportation, 97 Yaffo St., 91000 Jerusalem, Israel
PHONE: +972 (2) 6228211
FAX: +972 (2) 6228693

Minister of Agriculture and Rural Development
Ehud Barak, Ministry of Agriculture and Rural Development, 8 Arania St., Hakirya, 61070 Tel Aviv, Israel
PHONE: +972 (3) 6971444
FAX: +972 (3) 6968899

Minister of Regional Cooperation
Shimon Peres, Ministry of Regional Cooperation

Minister of Jerusalem Affairs
Haim Ramon, Ministry of Jerusalem Affairs

Minister of Education, Culture and Sports
Ehud Barak, Ministry of Education, Culture and Sports, 34 Shivtei Israel St., PO Box 292, 91911 Jerusalem, Israel
PHONE: +972 (2) 5602222
FAX: +972 (2) 5602752

POLITICAL ORGANIZATIONS

Likud Party

TITLE: Prime Minister
NAME: Ariel Sharon

Tzomet

NAME: Rafael Eitan

National Religious Party

NAME: Yitzhak Levi

Yisra'el Ba'Aliya

NAME: Natan Sharansky

United Jewish Torah

NAME: Meir Porush

Third Way

NAME: Avigdor Kahalani

DIPLOMATIC REPRESENTATION

Embassies in Israel

Argentina
3A, Rehov Jabotinsky, 52520 Ramat-Gan, Israel
PHONE: +972 (3) 5759170
FAX: +972 (3) 5759178

Australia
37 Shaul Hamelech Blvd., 64928 Tel Aviv, Israel
PHONE: +972 (3) 6950451
FAX: +972 (3) 6968404

Belarus
2 Rehov Kaufman, 68012 Tel Aviv, Israel
PHONE: +972 (3) 5102236
FAX: +972 (3) 5102235

Belgium
266 Rehov Hayarkon, 63504 Tel Aviv, Israel
PHONE: +972 (3) 6054164
FAX: +972 (3) 5465345

Bolivia
7A Rehov Hashalom, 90805 Mevasseret Zion, Israel
PHONE: +972 (2) 5335195
FAX: +972 (2) 5335196

Brazil
2 Rehov Kaplan, 64734 Tel Aviv, Israel
PHONE: +972 (3) 6919292
FAX: +972 (3) 6916060

Bulgaria
124 Ibn Gvirol, 62308 Tel Aviv, Israel
PHONE: +972 (3) 5241759
FAX: +972 (3) 5241798

Cameroon
79 Rehov Yehuda Hamaccabi, 62300 Tel Aviv, Israel
PHONE: +972 (3) 6043640
FAX: +972 (3) 6043639

Canada
3 Nirim Beit Hasapanut, Yad Eliyahu, 67060 Tel Aviv, Israel
PHONE: +972 (3) 6363300

China
222 Rehov Ben Yehuda, 63473 Tel Aviv, Israel
PHONE: +972 (3) 5467277
FAX: +972 (3) 5467251

Columbia
52 Rehov Pinkas, 6th floor, Apt. 26, 62261 Tel Aviv, Israel
PHONE: +972 (3) 5461434
FAX: +972 (3) 5461404

Congo
25 Rehov Leisen, PO Box 21352, 61212 Tel Aviv, Israel
PHONE: +972 (3) 6912414
FAX: +972 (3) 6952825

Costa Rica
13 Rehov Diskin, Apt. 1, PO Box 1318, 91012 Jerusalem, Israel
PHONE: +972 (2) 5666197
FAX: +972 (2) 5632591

Côte d'Ivoire
14 Rehov He Be'Iyar, Kikar HaMedina, 62093 Tel Aviv, Israel
PHONE: +972 (3) 6963727
FAX: +972 (3) 6968888

Cyprus
Top Tower, 50 Rehov Dizengoff, 64332 Tel Aviv, Israel
PHONE: +972 (3) 5250212
FAX: +972 (3) 6290535

Czech Republic
23 Zeitlin, 64955 Tel Aviv, Israel
PHONE: +972 (3) 6918282
FAX: +972 (3) 6918286

Denmark
23 Rehov Bnei Moshe, 62308 Tel Aviv, Israel
PHONE: +972 (3) 5442144
FAX: +972 (3) 5465502

Dominican Republic
4 Sderot Shaul Hamelech, 64733 Tel Aviv, Israel
PHONE: +972 (3) 6957580
FAX: +972 (3) 6962032

Egypt
PHONE: +972 (3) 5464151
FAX: +972 (3) 5441615

El Salvador
34 Rehov Rahel Imeinu, 93228 Jerusalem, Israel
PHONE: +972 (2) 5633575
FAX: +972 (2) 5638528

Equador
Asia House, 4 Rehov Weizman, 64239 Tel Aviv, Israel
PHONE: +972 (3) 6958764
FAX: +972 (3) 6969437

Ethiopia
48 Derech Petach Tikva, 66184 Tel Aviv, Israel
PHONE: +972 (3) 6397831
FAX: +972 (3) 6397837

European Community
3 Rehov Daniel Frisch, 64731 Tel Aviv, Israel
PHONE: +972 (3) 6964160
FAX: +972 (3) 6951983

Finland
Beit Eliyahu 8th Floor, 2 Rehov Ibn Gvirol, 64077 Tel Aviv, Israel
PHONE: +972 (3) 6950527
FAX: +972 (3) 6966311

France
112 Herbert Samuel, 63572 Tel Aviv, Israel
PHONE: +972 (3) 5245371
FAX: +972 (3) 5465937

Gabon
32 Rehov Jabotinsky, 52495 Ramat-Gan, Israel

Germany
3 Rehov Daniel Frisch, 64731 Tel Aviv, Israel
PHONE: +972 (3) 6931313
FAX: +972 (3) 6969217

Ghana
15 Abba Hillel Silver, 52522 Ramat-Gan, Israel

Greece
47 Rehov Bodenheimer, 62008 Tel Aviv, Israel
PHONE: +972 (3) 6055461
FAX: +972 (3) 6054374

Guatemala
74 Rehov He Be'Iyar, 62198 Tel Aviv, Israel
PHONE: +972 (3) 5467372
FAX: +972 (3) 5467317

Honduras
46 Rehov He Be'Iyar, Kikar HaMedina, 62093 Tel Aviv, Israel
PHONE: +972 (3) 5469506
FAX: +972 (3) 5469505

Hungary
18 Rehov Pinkas, 62661 Tel Aviv, Israel
PHONE: +972 (3) 5466860
FAX: +972 (3) 5468968

India
PHONE: +972 (3) 5101431
FAX: +972 (3) 5101434

Ireland
Carlton Hotel, 10 Rehov Eliezer Peri, 63573 Tel Aviv, Israel

Italy
PHONE: +972 (3) 6964223
FAX: +972 (3) 6918428

Japan
Asia House, 4 Rehov Weizman, 64239 Tel Aviv, Israel
PHONE: +972 (3) 6957292
FAX: +972 (3) 6910516

Jordan
12 Abba Hillel Silver, 52506 Ramat-Gan, Israel
PHONE: +972 (3) 7517722
FAX: +972 (3) 7517712

Kazakhstan
33 Rehov Jabotinsky, 52511 Ramat-Gan, Israel

Kenya
50 Rehov Jabotinsky, PO Box 22115, 61220 Tel Aviv, Israel
PHONE: +972 (3) 5249935
FAX: +972 (3) 5241611

Korea
38 Chen Blvd, 64166 Tel Aviv, Israel
PHONE: +972 (3) 6963244
FAX: +972 (3) 6963243

Kyrgyzstan
7 Abba Hillel Silver, 52522 Ramat-Gan, Israel
PHONE: +972 (3) 6136546
FAX: +972 (3) 6136548

Latvia
Rehov Pinkas, Apt. 51, 62261 Tel Aviv, Israel
PHONE: +972 (3) 5462438

Liberia
6 Rehov Frug, 52482 Ramat-Gan, Israel
PHONE: +972 (3) 6728532
FAX: +972 (3) 6727167

Lithuania
50 Rehov Dizengoff, Suite 1404, 64332 Tel Aviv, Israel
PHONE: +972 (3) 5288514
FAX: +972 (3) 5257265

Mauritania
18/12 Rehov He Be'Iyar, 62093 Tel Aviv, Israel

Mexico
3 Rehov Bograshov, 63808 Tel Aviv, Israel
PHONE: +972 (3) 5230367
FAX: +972 (3) 5237399

Moldova
7 Rehov Havakook, Apt. 303, 63505 Tel Aviv, Israel
PHONE: +972 (3) 6040014

Morocco
67 Rehov Weizman, Apt. 5, 62155 Tel Aviv, Israel
PHONE: +972 (3) 5464007

Myanmar
26 Hayarkon, Tel Aviv, Israel
PHONE: +972 (3) 5170760
FAX: +972 (3) 5171440

Netherlands
4 Rehov Weizman, 64239 Tel Aviv, Israel
PHONE: +972 (3) 6957377
FAX: +972 (3) 6957370

Nigeria
34 Rehov Gordon, 63414 Tel Aviv, Israel
PHONE: +972 (3) 5222144
FAX: +972 (3) 5248991

Norway
40 Hanamal, 63506 Tel Aviv, Israel
PHONE: +972 (3) 5442030
FAX: +972 (3) 5442034

Oman
79 Rehov Yehuda Hamaccabi, 62300 Tel Aviv, Israel

Panama
10 Rehov He Be'Iyar, Kikar HaMedina, 62998 Tel Aviv, Israel
PHONE: +972 (3) 6956711
FAX: +972 (3) 6910045

Paraguay
1/4 Rehov Carmel, 90805 Mevasseret Zion, Israel
PHONE: +972 (2) 5334830
FAX: +972 (2) 5333878

Peru
37 Rehov Hamarganit, 52584 Ramat-Gan, Israel
PHONE: +972 (3) 6135591
FAX: +972 (3) 7512286

Philippines
2 Rehov Kaufman, 68012 Tel Aviv, Israel
PHONE: +972 (3) 5104651
FAX: +972 (3) 5102229

Poland
16 Rehov Soutine, 64684 Tel Aviv, Israel
PHONE: +972 (3) 5240188
FAX: +972 (3) 5237806

Portugal
4 Rehov Weizman, 64585 Tel Aviv, Israel
PHONE: +972 (3) 6956372
FAX: +972 (3) 6956366

Romania
24 Rehov Adam Hacohen, 64662 Tel Aviv, Israel
PHONE: +972 (3) 5230066
FAX: +972 (3) 5247379

Russia
120 Rehov Hayarkon, Tel Aviv, Israel
PHONE: +972 (3) 5226733
FAX: +972 (3) 5226713

Rwanda
30 Rehov He Be'Iyar, Kikar Hamedina, 62093 Tel Aviv, Israel
PHONE: +972 (3) 6912319
FAX: +972 (3) 6963408

Serbia
8 Rehov Shaul Hamelech, 64776 Tel Aviv, Israel
PHONE: +972 (3) 6938412
FAX: +972 (3) 6938411

Slovakia
37 Rehov Jabotinsky, PO Box 6459, 61064 Tel Aviv, Israel
PHONE: +972 (3) 5440066
FAX: +972 (3) 5440069

Slovenia
2 Rehov Kaufman, 68012 Tel Aviv, Israel
PHONE: +972 (3) 5163425
FAX: +972 (3) 5163530

South Africa
Top Tower, Floor 16, 50 Rehov Dizengoff, 64332 Tel Aviv, Israel
PHONE: +972 (3) 5252566
FAX: +972 (3) 5253230

Spain
Dubnov Tower, Floor 16, 3 Rehov Daniel Frisch, 64731 Tel Aviv, Israel
PHONE: +972 (3) 6965218
FAX: +972 (3) 6965217

Sweden
4 Rehov Weizman, 64239 Tel Aviv, Israel
PHONE: +972 (3) 6958111
FAX: +972 (3) 6958116

Switzerland
228 Rehov Hayarkon, 63405 Tel Aviv, Israel
PHONE: +972 (3) 5464455
FAX: +972 (3) 5464408

Turkey
202 Rehov Hayarkon, 63405 Tel Aviv, Israel
PHONE: +972 (3) 5241101
FAX: +972 (3) 5240499

Ukraine
12 Rehov Striker, 62006 Tel Aviv, Israel
PHONE: +972 (3) 6040311
FAX: +972 (3) 6042512

United States
71 Rehov Hayarkon, 63903 Tel Aviv, Israel
PHONE: +972 (3) 5197575
FAX: +972 (3) 5102444

Uruguay
52 Rehov Pinkas, Apt. 10, Floor 2, 62261 Tel Aviv, Israel
PHONE: +972 (3) 6040411
FAX: +972 (3) 5441452

Uzbekistan
1 Rehov Ben Yehuda, 63801 Tel Aviv, Israel
PHONE: +972 (3) 5104684
FAX: +972 (3) 5104679

Vatican City
PO Box 150, 61001 Jaffa, Israel
PHONE: +972 (3) 6835658
FAX: +972 (3) 6835659

Venezuela
2 Rehov Kaufman, Floor 16, 61500 Tel Aviv, Israel
PHONE: +972 (3) 5176287
FAX: +972 (3) 5176210

Zaire
1 Rehov Rachel, 64584 Tel Aviv, Israel
PHONE: +972 (3) 5248306
FAX: +972 (3) 5229951

JUDICIAL SYSTEM

Supreme Court

BROADCAST MEDIA

Israel Broadcasting Authority

PO Box 28080, 97 Jaffa Road, Jerusalem 91280, Israel
PHONE: +972 (2) 240124; 291888
FAX: +972 (2) 257034; 242944
WEBSITE: http://www.iba.org.il/
TITLE: Directorate General
CONTACT: Mordechai Kirshenbaum

Galei Zahal (Israel Defense Forces Radio)

Military PO Box 01005, Israel
PHONE: +972 (3) 5694276
FAX: +972 (3) 814697
E-MAIL: galatz@glz.co.il
WEBSITE: http://www.glz.co.il
TITLE: Director
CONTACT: M. Shionsky

Israel National Radio

PHONE: +972 (2) 9972425
E-MAIL: a7@arutzsheva.org
WEBSITE: http://www.a7.org/

Palestinian Broadcasting Corporation

PO Box 4052, Gaza, Israel
PHONE: +972 (2) 910220; 921221
FAX: +972 (7) 923809
WEBSITE: http://www.bailasan.com/pinc
CONTACT: Radwan Abu Hayash
LANGUAGE: Arabic, English, Hebrew

Radio Haifa

WEBSITE: http://www.1075fm.co.il/

Kol Israel (The Voice of Israel)

Main Studios: Helini Hamalka 21, PO Box 1082, Jerusalem 91010, Israel

PHONE: +972 (2) 302222
FAX: +972 (2) 253282
WEBSITE: http://www.israel-mfa.gov.il/gov/brdcast.html
TITLE: Programme Director
CONTACT: Amnon Nadav
LANGUAGE: 16 languages

Arutz Echad

Jerusalem Studios, Romema, Jerusalem 91071
PHONE: +972 (2) 301333
FAX: +972 (2) 301345

Channel 2

97 Jaffa Street, Jerusalem 94340, Israel
PHONE: +972 (2) 242776, +972 (2) 242750
FAX: +972 (2) 242720
TITLE: Managing Director
CONTACT: Oren Tokalty
CHANNEL: E22, E27, E35

Israel Educational Television

14 Klausner Street, Tel Aviv, Israel
PHONE: +972 (3) 5434343
TITLE: General Manager
CONTACT: Y. Lorenbaum
TYPE: Educational

Israel Television

PO Box 7139, Jerusalem 91071, Israel
PHONE: +972 (2) 291888
FAX: +972 (2) 292944
TITLE: Directorate General
CONTACT: Ayre Mekel

Palestinian Broadcasting Corporation, TV

Ramallah-Um Al Sharyet, Israel
PHONE: +972 (2) 6564017; 6564019
FAX: +972 (2) 6564029
TITLE: Director
CONTACT: Radwan Abu Hayash
CHANNEL: 4, 23

COLLEGES AND UNIVERSITIES

Birzeit University

PO Box 14 Birzeit, West Bank, Israel

Open University of Israel

Tel Aviv, Israel
PHONE: +972 (3) 6404040
FAX: +972 (3) 6422016
E-MAIL: infodesk@oumail.openu.ac.il
WEBSITE: http://www.openu.ac.il

Bethlehem University

PO Box 9, Bethlehem, Israel
PHONE: +972 (2) 2741241
FAX: +972 (2) 2744440
WEBSITE: http://www.bethlehem.edu

Haifa University

Mount Carmel, 31905 Haifa, Israel
PHONE: +972 (4) 8240111
FAX: +972 (4) 8342104
WEBSITE: http://www.haifa.ac.il

Technion-Israel Institute of Technology

12 Haaliya Str. Bat-Galim, 32000 Haifa, Israel
PHONE: +972 (4) 8221513
FAX: +972 (4) 8235195
E-MAIL: gradsc@technion.ac.il
WEBSITE: http://www.technion.ac.il

Bar Ilan University

52100 Ramat Gan, Israel
PHONE: +972 (3) 5318111
WEBSITE: http://www.biu.ac.il

Shenkar College of Textile Technology

12 Anna Frank St., 52526 Ramat Gan, Israel
PHONE: +972 (3) 7521133
FAX: +972 (3) 7521299
E-MAIL: gela@mail.shenkar.ac.il
WEBSITE: http://www.shenkar.ac.il

Tel-Aviv University

Dept of Nephrology, Chaim Sheba Medical Centre, PO Box 39040, 69978 Tel Hashomer, Israel
PHONE: +972 (3) 6408639
E-MAIL: tauinfo@post.tau.ac.il
WEBSITE: http://www.tau.ac.il

Weizmann Institute of Science

PO Box 26, 76100 Rehovot, Israel
PHONE: +972 (8) 9342111
FAX: +972 (8) 9344107
E-MAIL: webmaster@www.weizman.ac.il
WEBSITE: http://www.weizman.ac.il

Ben Gurion University of the Negev

PO Box 653, 84105 Beer-Sheva, Israel
PHONE: +972 (7) 6461111
FAX: +972 (7) 6237682
E-MAIL: webmaster@bgumail.ac.il
WEBSITE: http://www.bgu.ac.il

Jerusalem College-Technology

PO Box 16031, 91160 Jerusalem, Israel
PHONE: +972 (2) 6751117
E-MAIL: pr@brachot.jct.ac.il
WEBSITE: http://www.jct.ac.il

Studium Biblicum Franciscanum

PO Box 19424, Monastery of the Flagellation, 91193 Jerusalem, Israel
PHONE: +972 (2) 6282936
FAX: +972 (2) 6264519
E-MAIL: sbfnet@netvision.net.il
WEBSITE: http://www.sbf.edu.il

Hebrew University of Jerusalem

Mount Scopus Campus, 91904 Jerusalem, Israel
PHONE: +972 (2) 5882607
WEBSITE: http://www.huji.ac.il

NEWSPAPERS AND MAGAZINES

Al Ittihad

9 Elhariri St., PO Box 104, Haifa, Israel
PHONE: +972 (4) 511296
FAX: +972 (4) 511297
TITLE: Editor
CONTACT: Mohd Youssef
CIRCULATION: 16,000
TYPE: General news

Davar

45 Shenkin St., PO Box 199, Tel-Aviv, Israel
PHONE: +972 (3) 5286141
FAX: +972 (3) 5294783
CIRCULATION: 39,000

Globes

53 Etzel St., 75706 Rishon Le-Zion, Tel-Aviv, Israel
PHONE: +972 (3) 9538659
FAX: +972 (3) 9520694
E-MAIL: gsaad@globes.co.il
WEBSITE: http://www.globes.co.il
CONTACT: Guy Saad
CIRCULATION: 45,000
TYPE: Economics and financial

Ha'Aretz Weekly Magazine

21 Salman Schocken St., PO Box 233, 61001 Tel-Aviv, Israel
PHONE: +972 (3) 5121110; 5121212
FAX: +972 (3) 6810012; 6815859
WEBSITE: http://www.haaretzdaily.com
TITLE: Publisher
CONTACT: Amos Schocken
CIRCULATION: 92,000

International Herald Tribune/Ha'Aretz

21 Salman Schocken St., PO Box 233, 61001 Tele-Aviv, Israel
PHONE: +972 (3) 5121110; 5121212
FAX: +972 (3) 6810012; 6815859
E-MAIL: kedem@haaretz.co.il
WEBSITE: http://www.haaretzdaily.com
CIRCULATION: 35,000

The Jerusalem Post

PO Box 81, 91000 Jerusalem, Israel
PHONE: +972 (2) 5315616
FAX: +972 (2) 5387408
E-MAIL: subs@jpost.co.il
WEBSITE: http://www.jpost.co.il
TITLE: Publisher
CONTACT: Tom Rose
CIRCULATION: 78,000

Kul Al-Arab

PO Box 430, 16000 Nazareth, Israel
PHONE: +972 (6) 6569619
FAX: +972 (6) 6569887
WEBSITE: http://www.sofnet.co.il/kul-alarab
TITLE: Editor
CONTACT: Samih El-Kassem
CIRCULATION: 30,000

Ma'Ariv

2 Carlebach St., PO Box 20010, 61200 Tel-Aviv, Israel
PHONE: +972 (3) 5632111
FAX: +972 (3) 5610614
TITLE: Publisher
CONTACT: Ofer Nimrody
CIRCULATION: 200,000

Al-Sinnara

PO Box 148, Nazareth, Israel
PHONE: +972 (6) 5700621; 555750
FAX: +972 (6) 578092
TITLE: Editor-in-Chief
CONTACT: Lufty Mashour
CIRCULATION: 35,000

Yediot Achronot

138 Yehuda and Noah Mosesn St., PO Box 109, 61001 Tel-Aviv, Israel
PHONE: +972 (3) 6972222
FAX: +972 (3) 6953950
TITLE: Editor
CONTACT: Moshe Vardi
CIRCULATION: 660,000

Israel Agritechnology Focus

PO Box 57179, Tel-Aviv 61571, Israel
PHONE: +972 (3) 5628512
FAX: +972 (3) 5628512
TITLE: Editor
CONTACT: Nicky Blackbum
TYPE: Agriculture, technology

Israel High-Tech & Investment Report

FAX: +972 (3) 5227799
WEBSITE: http://www.ishitech.co.il
E-MAIL: htirl@netvision.net.il
TITLE: Editor
CONTACT: Joseph Morgenstern
TYPE: Finance, investments, general

Israel Dance Quarterly

39 Shoham St., Haifa 34679, Israel
FAX: +972 (4) 8344051
TITLE: Editor
CONTACT: Giora Manor
CIRCULATION: 2,000

Israel Exploration Journal

FAX: +972 (2) 6247772
E-MAIL: les@ums.huji.ac.il
WEBSITE: http://www.huji.ac.il/ies
TITLE: Editor
CONTACT: Miriam Tadmor

Israel Diamond and Precious Stones

FAX: +972 (3) 5752201
TITLE: Editor
CONTACT: Russ Shor
CIRCULATION: 3,000
TYPE: Gemology, general

Israel Journal of Entomology

PO Box 6, Bet Dagan 50200, Israel
FAX: +972 (3) 9604180
TITLE: Editor
CONTACT: A. Friedberg

Israel Journal of Physiotherapy

93 Arlozorov St., Tel-Aviv, Israel
TITLE: Editor
CONTACT: Oded Daskal
CIRCULATION: 500

Israel Law Review

FAX: +972 (2) 5823042
E-MAIL: msiln@pluto.mscc.huji.ac.il
TITLE: Editor
CONTACT: Frances Raday
CIRCULATION: 1,500

Israel Update

PO Box 37604, Tel-Aviv 61375, Israel
FAX: +972 (3) 5252341
TITLE: Editor
CONTACT: Amit Kama
CIRCULATION: 500

Israeli Forum

PO Box 57500, Tel-Aviv 61574, Israel
FAX: +972 (3) 5759791

Israel Journal of Aquaculture

PO Box 12, Rehovot 76100, Israel
FAX: +972 (8) 9465763
E-MAIL: vanRijn@agri.huji.ac.il
TITLE: Editor
CONTACT: Jaap van Rijn

Jerusalem Fellow

PO Box 775, Jerusalem 91007, Israel
FAX: +972 (2) 6243144
WEBSITE: http://www.jerusalembookfair.com
CIRCULATION: 5,000

Jerusalem Report

FAX: +972 (2) 6291037
E-MAIL: jrep@attmail.com
WEBSITE: http://www.jreport.virtual.co.il
TITLE: Editor
CONTACT: Hirsch Goodman
TYPE: Social science, general

Journal of Chemistry

FAX: +972 (2) 65222277
E-MAIL: laserpages@netmedia.net.il
TITLE: Editor
CONTACT: H. Levanon
TYPE: Science, chemistry

Journal of Earth Sciences

FAX: +972 (2) 6522277
E-MAIL: laserpages@netmedia.net.il
CONTACT: Y. Bartov
TYPE: Environmental science, earth sciences, general

PUBLISHERS

Astrolog Publishing House

PO Box 11231, 4511 Hod Hasharon, Israel
PHONE: +972 (9) 7412044
FAX: +972 (9) 741044
E-MAIL: sarabm@netvision.net.il
TITLE: Man. Director
CONTACT: Sara Ben-Mordechai
SUBJECTS: Nonfiction (General), New Age, Alternative Medicine, Mysticism, Prediction of the Future, Awareness
TOTAL PUBLISHED: 600 print

Bar Ilan University Press

Bar Ilan University, 52900 Ramat Gan, Israel
PHONE: +972 (3) 5318401; 5318575
FAX: +972 (3) 5353446
E-MAIL: press@mail.biu.ac.il
WEBSITE: http://www.biu.ac.il/press
TITLE: General Manager
CONTACT: Margalit Avisar
SUBJECTS: Archaeology, Biblical Studies, Education, Geology, History, Language Arts, Law, Literature, Philosophy, Psychology, Psychiatry, Social Sciences
TOTAL PUBLISHED: 25 print

Ben-Zvi Institute

12 Abarbanel St., PO Box 7660, 91076 Jerusalem, Israel
PHONE: +972 (2) 5639204
FAX: +972 (2) 5638310
E-MAIL: mahonzvi@h2.hum.huji.ac.il
WEBSITE: http://www.ybz.org.il
CONTACT: Haggai Ben-Shammai
SUBJECTS: Ethnicity, Foreign Countries, History, Language Arts, Linguistics, Literature, Literary Criticism, Essays, Regional Interests, Jewish Religion
TOTAL PUBLISHED: 100 print

Breslov Research Institute

PO Box 5370, 91053 Jerusalem, Israel
PHONE: +972 (2) 5824641
FAX: +972 (2) 5825542
E-MAIL: info@breslov.org
TITLE: Executive Director
CONTACT: Rabbi Chaim Kramer
SUBJECTS: Biblical Studies, Biography, Education, Health, History, Literature, Nonfiction (General), Philosophy, Psychology, Psychiatry, Jewish Religion, Theology
TOTAL PUBLISHED: 70 print; 70 online; 70 internet

Carta, The Israel Map & Publishing Co. Ltd.

18 Ha'uman St. Industrial Area, Talpiot, 91024 Jerusalem, Israel
PHONE: +972 (2) 6783355
FAX: +972 (2) 6782373
E-MAIL: cartaben@netvision.net.il
WEBSITE: http://www.holyland-jerusalem.com
TITLE: President, Chief Executive
CONTACT: Shay Hausman
SUBJECTS: Cartography, Archaeology, Education, Health, Nutrition, History
TOTAL PUBLISHED: 300 print; 3 CD-ROM

Cordinata Ltd. (Holy Land 2000)

27 Sutin St., 64684 Tel Aviv, Israel
PHONE: +972 (3) 5226885
FAX: +972 (3) 5276661
E-MAIL: cordinata@isdn.net.il
WEBSITE: http://www.holy-land2000.com
TITLE: Gen. Manager
CONTACT: Eliezer Sacks
SUBJECTS: Books, albums, maps, videos, and calendars about the Holy Land
TOTAL PUBLISHED: 10 print; 5 CD-ROM; 5 online; 15 internet; 5 audio

DAT Publications

PO Box 27019, 61270 Jaffa, Israel
PHONE: +972 (3) 5071239
FAX: +972 (3) 5070458
E-MAIL: dat_pub@inter.net.il
WEBSITE: http://www.y-dat.co.il
TITLE: Man. Director
CONTACT: Yigal Miller
SUBJECTS: Biblical Studies, Fiction, History, Humor, Literature, Nonfiction (General), Philosophy, Jewish Religion, Self-Help, Theology
TOTAL PUBLISHED: 61 print

Dionon/Papyrus Publishing House of the Tel-Aviv

University Students Union, PO Box 39287, 61392 Tel Aviv, Israel
PHONE: +972 (3) 6410351; 6410352; 6427545
FAX: +972 (3) 6423149
TITLE: General Manager
CONTACT: Ittamar Herman
SUBJECTS: Behavioral Sciences, Business, Chemistry, Child Care, Criminology, Education, Genealogy, History, Medicine, Nonfiction (General), Social Sciences, Philosophy

Dvir Publishing Ltd.

32 Schocken St., 61001 Tel Aviv, Israel
PHONE: +972 (3) 6812244
FAX: +972 (3) 6826138
TITLE: Man. Director
CONTACT: Ohad Zmora
SUBJECTS: Literature, Literary Criticism, Essays, Poetry, Jewish Religion
TOTAL PUBLISHED: 1,500 print

The Arnold & Leona Finkler Institute of Holocaust Research

Bar-Ilan University, 52900 Ramat-Gan, Israel
PHONE: +972 (3) 5340333
FAX: +972 (3) 5351233
E-MAIL: finkshoa@mail.bio.ac.il
TITLE: Professor & Chairman
CONTACT: Dan Michman
SUBJECTS: History, Jewish Religion, Holocaust, 20th Century Jewish Religion
TOTAL PUBLISHED: 30 print

Gefen Publishing House, Ltd.

PO Box 36004, 91360 Jerusalem, Israel
PHONE: +972 (2) 5380247
FAX: +972 (2) 5388423
E-MAIL: info@gefenpublishing.com
TITLE: Publisher
CONTACT: Dror Greenfield
SUBJECTS: Archaeology, Art, Biblical Studies, Biography, Cookery, English as a Second Language, Fiction, Political Science, Health, History, How-To, Law, Medicine, Nonfiction (General), Photography, Jewish Religion, Theology, Travel

Habermann Institute for Literary Research

PO Box 383, 71101 Lod, Israel
PHONE: +972 (8) 9244569; 9234008
FAX: +972 (8) 9249466
E-MAIL: zmalachi@post.tau.ac.il
TITLE: Director
CONTACT: Michal Saraf
SUBJECTS: Ethnicity, Literature, Literary Criticism, Essays, Poetry, Jewish Religion
TOTAL PUBLISHED: 50 print

Hod-Ami, Computer Books, Ltd.

3 Bilu St., PO Box 6108, 46160 Herzliya, Israel
PHONE: +972 (9) 9564716
FAX: +972 (9) 9571582
E-MAIL: info@hod-ami.co.il
WEBSITE: http://www.hod-ami.co.il
TITLE: CEO
CONTACT: Itzhak Amihud
SUBJECTS: Computer Science
TOTAL PUBLISHED: 180 print

Intermedia Audio, Video Book Publishing Ltd.

20 Ha-hashmal St., 61367 Tel Aviv, Israel
PHONE: +972 (3) 5608501
FAX: +972 (3) 5608513
E-MAIL: freed@inter.net.il
TITLE: Man. Director
CONTACT: Arie Fried
SUBJECTS: Business, Education, English as a Second Language, Health, Journalism, Mathematics, Medicine, Philosophy, Self-Help, Alternative Medicine
TOTAL PUBLISHED: 25 print; 6 audio

The Institute for the Translation of Hebrew Literature

23 Baruch St., PO Box 10051, 10051 Ramat Gan, Israel
PHONE: +972 (3) 5796830
FAX: +972 (3) 5796832
E-MAIL: litscene@ithl.org.il
WEBSITE: http://www.ithl.org.il
TITLE: Man. Director
CONTACT: Nilli Cohen
SUBJECTS: Hebrew Literature, Literary Criticism, Essays, Fiction, Poetry, Children's Books

Israel Antiquities Authority

PO Box 568, 91004 Jerusalem, Israel
PHONE: +972 (2) 5638421
FAX: +972 (2) 6289006
E-MAIL: sussman@israntique.org.il
WEBSITE: http://www.israntique.org.il

TITLE: Editor-in-Chief
CONTACT: Ayala Sussmann
SUBJECTS: Archaeology
TOTAL PUBLISHED: 74 print

Israel Music Institute (IMI)

144 Hayarkon St., PO Box 3004, 61030 Tel Aviv, Israel
PHONE: +972 (3) 5246475
FAX: +972 (3) 5245276
E-MAIL: 035245275@doar.net
TITLE: Director
CONTACT: Paul Lindau
SUBJECTS: Music, Dance

Jabotinsky Institute in Israel

PO Box 23110, 61239 Tel Aviv, Israel
PHONE: +972 (3) 6210611; 5287320
FAX: +972 (3) 5285587
E-MAIL: jabo@actcom.co.il
WEBSITE: http://www.jabotinsky.org
SUBJECTS: Government, Political Science, History
TOTAL PUBLISHED: 2-3 yearly

Jerusalem Center for Public Affairs

13 Hai St., 92107 Jerusalem, Israel
PHONE: +972 (2) 5619281
FAX: +972 (2) 5619112
E-MAIL: jcpa@netvision.net.il
WEBSITE: http://www.jcpa.org
TITLE: Publications Coordinator
CONTACT: Mark Ami-El
SUBJECTS: Israel, Jewish communities, Jewish political tradition & federalism
TOTAL PUBLISHED: 60 print

L B Publishing Co.

PO Box 32056, 91000 Jerusalem, Israel
PHONE: +972 (2) 25664637
FAX: +972 (2) 25664637
TITLE: President
CONTACT: Lili Breziner
SUBJECTS: History, Regional Interests, Jewish Religion
TOTAL PUBLISHED: 25 print

Machbarot Lesifrut

32 Zalman Schocken St., 66556 Tel Aviv, Israel
PHONE: +972 (3) 6812244
FAX: +972 (3) 6826138
TITLE: Publisher
CONTACT: Zvi Zmora
SUBJECTS: Fiction, Political Science, History, Language Arts, Linguistics, Literature, Literary Criticism, Essays
TOTAL PUBLISHED: 250 print

Ministry of Defence Publishing House

27 David Elazar St., PO Box 7103, 67673 Tel Aviv, Israel
PHONE: +972 (3) 5655900; 6917940
FAX: +972 (3) 5655994; 6375509
TITLE: Director
CONTACT: Joseph Perlovitch
SUBJECTS: Foreign Countries, History, Military Science, History & Geography of Israel, Holocaust
TOTAL PUBLISHED: 1,500 print

Password Publishers Ltd.

61 Shalma Rd., PO Box 5138, 61051 Tel Aviv, Israel
PHONE: +972 (3) 6833566
FAX: +972 (3) 6833702
E-MAIL: pass@password.co.il
WEBSITE: password.co.il
TITLE: Man. Director
CONTACT: Ilan Kernerman
SUBJECTS: English as a Second Language, Language Arts, Linguistics
TOTAL PUBLISHED: 30 print; 2 CD-ROM

Rubin Mass Ltd.

7 Ha'Ayin Het St., PO Box 990, 91009 Jerusalem, Israel
PHONE: +972 (2) 6277863
FAX: +972 (2) 6277864
E-MAIL: rmass@inter.net.il
TITLE: Man. Director
CONTACT: Oren Mass
SUBJECTS: Biblical Studies, Biography, Education, Political Science, Medicine, Nursing, Dentistry, Philosophy, Psychiatry, Psychology, Jewish Religion
TOTAL PUBLISHED: 1,550 print

Schlesinger Institute

PO Box 3235, 91031 Jerusalem, Israel
PHONE: +972 (2) 6555266
FAX: +972 (2) 6523295
E-MAIL: medhal@szmc.org.il
WEBSITE: http://www.szmc.org.il/machon
TITLE: Assistant to Administrative Director
CONTACT: Leora Rosen
SUBJECTS: Medical Ethics, Jewish Law

TOTAL PUBLISHED: 11 print

Schocken Publishing House Ltd.

24 Nathan Yelin Mor St., PO Box 2316, 61022 Tel Aviv, Israel
PHONE: +972 (3) 5610130
FAX: +972 (3) 5622668
E-MAIL: rachely@iol.co.il
WEBSITE: http://www.schocken.co.il
TITLE: Publisher
CONTACT: Racheli Edelman
SUBJECTS: Anthropology, Behavior Sciences, Child Care, Criminology, Drama, Education, Fiction, Health, Law, Literature, Nonfiction (General), Jewish Religion, Women's Studies

Steimatzky Ltd.

11 Hakishon, PO Box 1444, 51114 Bnei-Brak, Israel
PHONE: +972 (3) 5775777
FAX: +972 (3) 5794567
E-MAIL: stmzky_2@netvision.net.il
WEBSITE: http://www.steimatzky.co.il
TITLE: Man. Director
CONTACT: Yehoshua Matzliah
SUBJECTS: Art. Biography, Fiction, Music, Dance, Religion, Social Sciences

Tel Aviv University

The Jaffee Center for Strategic Studies, PO Box 39040, 69978 Ramat Aviv, Israel
PHONE: +972 (3) 6424571; 6409200; 6426682
FAX: +972 (3) 6422404; 6408355
TITLE: Professor
CONTACT: Zeev Maoz
SUBJECTS: Foreign Countries, Political Science, Government, History, Military Science, Regional Interests, Social Sciences, Sociology

Yad Izhak Ben-Zvi Press

Ben-Zvi Institute, 12 Abrabanel St., PO Box 7660, 91076 Jerusalem, Israel
PHONE: +972 (2) 5639204
FAX: +972 (2) 5638310
E-MAIL: mahonzvi@h2.hum.huji.ac.il
TITLE: Director
CONTACT: Zvi Zameret
SUBJECTS: Geography, Geology, History, Jewish Religion, Oriental Jewish Communities
TOTAL PUBLISHED: 260 print

Yad Vashem - The Holocaust Martyrs' & Heroes' Remembrance Authority

Mount Herzl, PO Box 3477, 91034 Jerusalem, Israel
PHONE: +972 (2) 6751611
FAX: +972 (2)6433511
E-MAIL: research@yad-vashem.org.il
TITLE: Publications
CONTACT: Esther Aram
SUBJECTS: Biography, Education, History, Nonfiction (General), Holocaust Research

RELIGIOUS ORGANIZATIONS

Buddhist

Jerusalem Center of Mindfulness
Shikunei Hariel 3, Beit Hekerem, Jerusalem, Israel
PHONE: +972 (2) 6525790
FAX: +972 (2) 6583399
E-MAIL: ramban@netvision.net.il
NAME: Yael Avnon

Tel Aviv Zen Center
Shabazi 28, Neve Tsedek, Tel Aviv 65150, Israel
PHONE: +972 (3) 510 7356
E-MAIL: zendo@isdn.net.il

Catholic

Assembly of Ordinary Catholics of the Holy Land

Assemblee des Ordinaires Catholiques de Terre Sainte
Notre Dame of Jerusalem Centre, PO Box 20531, Jerusalem, Israel
PHONE: +972 (2) 288554
FAX: +972 (2) 288555
NAME: Rev. P. Pierre Grech

Jewish

Agudath Israel World Organization (AIWO)

Organisation Mondiale Agudath Israel (OMAI)
Hacherat Square, PO Box 326, 91002 Jerusalem, Isreal
PHONE: +972 (2) 5384357
FAX: +972 (2) 5383634
TITLE: Chairman
NAME: Rabbi Yeudah Meir Abramowitz

Association of Jewish Religious Professionals from the Commonwealth of Independent Stated and Eastern Europe (SHAMIR)
PO Box 5749, 6 David Yellin St., Jerusalem, Israel
PHONE: +972 (2) 5385702
FAX: +972 (2) 5385118
E-MAIL: bhtorah@netmedia.net.il
TITLE: Honorary Chm.
NAME: Herman Branover

Reunion of the Children of Noah
168 Erzel St., 76266 Rehovot, Israel
TITLE: Organizer
NAME: Yehoshua Nof

Root and Branch Association
PO Box 8672, German Colony, 91086 Jerusalem, Israel
PHONE: +972 (2) 6739013
FAX: +972 (2) 6739012
E-MAIL: rb@rb.org.il
WEBSITE: http://www.rb.org.il
TITLE: President
NAME: Aryeh Gallin

World Confederation of Jewish Community Centers (WCJCC)

Confederacion Mundial de Centros Comunitarios Judios
12 Hess St., 94185 Jerusalem, Israel
PHONE: +972 (2) 6251265
FAX: +972 (2) 6247767
TITLE: Executive Director
NAME: Sara Bogen

Orthodox

Armenian Patriarchate of St. James-Jerusalem
PO Box 14235, Jerusalem (Old City), Israel

Other Organizations

Ecumenical Institute for Theological Studies (EITS)

Institut Oecumenique de Recherches Theologiques
PO Box 19556, 91194 Jerusalem, Israel
PHONE: +972 (2) 6760911
FAX: +972 (2) 6760914:
TITLE: Rector
NAME: Rev. Dr. Thomas F. Stransky

Israel Interfaith Association (IIA)
PO Box 7739, 91077 Jerusalem, Israel
PHONE: +972 (2) 6203251
FAX: +972 (2) 6251478
TITLE: Chair of Secretariat
NAME: Dr. Michael Krupp

FURTHER READING

Articles

Kifner, John. "New Clashes in West Bank and Gaza Put Israel on Edge." *New York Times,* November 7, 2000, p. A12.

"The Month in Review: January 2000." *Current History,* March 2000, p. 141.

Pope, Hugh. "In the Mideast, Conflict Even Over a Peacekeeping Force; Arafat Favors the U.N. Role Barak Firmly Opposes; Hebron Is One Model." *Wall Street Journal,* November 10, 2000, p. A16.

"Price Tags for Peace." *World Press Review,* March 2000, vol. 47, no. 3, p. 28.

ISRAEL: STATISTICAL DATA

For sources and notes see "Sources of Statistics" at the front of each volume.

GEOGRAPHY

Geography

Area:

Total: 20,770 sq km.

Land: 20,330 sq km.

Land boundaries:

Total: 1,006 km.

Border countries: Egypt 255 km, Gaza Strip 51 km, Jordan 238 km, Lebanon 79 km, Syria 76 km, West Bank 307 km.

Coastline: 273 km.

Climate: temperate; hot and dry in southern and eastern desert areas.

Terrain: Negev desert in the south; low coastal plain; central mountains; Jordan Rift Valley.

Natural resources: copper, phosphates, bromide, potash, clay, sand, sulfur, asphalt, manganese, small amounts of natural gas and crude oil.

Land use:

Arable land: 17%

Permanent crops: 4%

Permanent pastures: 7%

Forests and woodland: 6%

Other: 66% (1993 est.).

HUMAN FACTORS

Demographics (A)

	1990	1995	1998	2000	2010	2020	2030	2040	2050
Population	4,512	5,305	5,639	5,843	6,645	7,315	7,873	8,271	8,517
Life expectancy - males	75.4	75.9	76.3	76.6	77.8	78.8	79.6	80.2	80.7
Life expectancy - females	79.1	79.7	80.3	80.7	82.3	83.7	84.7	85.5	86.2
Birth rate (per 1,000)	21.7	20.3	19.7	19.3	16.9	14.8	13.4	12.2	11.3
Death rate (per 1,000)	6.2	6.3	6.3	6.2	6.2	6.3	7.3	8.3	9.3
Women of reproductive age (15-49 yrs.)	1,098	1,334	1,415	1,462	1,626	1,784	1,853	1,875	1,853
Fertility rate	3.0	2.8	2.7	2.6	2.3	2.1	1.9	1.9	1.8

Except as noted, values for vital statistics are in thousands; life expectancy is in years.

Health Personnel

	National Data	World Data (wtd ave)
Total health expenditure as a percentage of GDP, 1990-1998[a]		
Public sector	7.0	2.5
Private sector	3.4	2.9
Total[b]	10.4	5.5
Health expenditure per capita in U.S. dollars, 1990-1998[a]		
Purchasing power parity	1,801	561
Total	1,701	483
Availability of health care facilities per 100,000 people		
Hospital beds 1990-1998[a]	600	330
Doctors 1992-1995[a]	459	122
Nurses 1992-1995[a]	671	248

Health Indicators

	National Data	World Data
Life expectancy at birth (years)		
1980	73	61
1998	78	67
Daily per capita supply of calories		
1970	3,014	2,358
1997	3,278	2,791
Daily per capital supply of protein		
1997 (grams)	105	74
Total fertility rate (births per woman)		
1980	3.2	3.7
1998	2.7	2.7
Population with access (%)		
To safe water (1990-96)	99	NA
To sanitation (1990-96)	100	NA
People living with (1997)		
Tuberculosis (cases per 100,000)	7.3	60.4
HIV/AIDS (% aged 15 - 49 years)	0.07	0.99

Infants and Malnutrition

	National Data	World Data (wtd ave)
Under 5 mortality rate (1989)	6	NA
% of infants with low birthweight (1992-98)[1]	8	17
Births attended by skilled health staff (% of total births 1996-98)	99	52
% fully immunized at 1 year of age (1995-98)[1]		
TB	NA	82
DPT	95	77
Polio	96	77
Measles	55	74
Prevalence of child malnutrition (1992-98)[1] (based on weight for age, % of children under 5 years)	NA	30

Ethnic Division

Jewish 80.1%
Europe/America-born 32.1%
Israel-born 20.8%
Africa-born 14.6%
Asia-born 12.6%
Non-Jewish (mostly Arab) 19.9%

Data for 1996 est.

Religion

Jewish 80.1%
Muslim (mostly Sunni Muslim) 14.6%
Christian 2.1%
Other 3.2%

Data for 1996 est.

Major Languages

Hebrew (official), Arabic used officially for Arab minority, English most commonly used foreign language.

EDUCATION

Public Education Expenditures

	1980	1997
Public expenditures on education as % of GNP	8.2	7.6
Expenditures per student as % of GNP per capita		
Primary & Secondary	16.0	20.6
Tertiary	75.6	37.1
Teachers' compensation as % of total current education expenditures	51.1	NA
Pupils per teacher at the primary level	NA	NA

Duration of primary education in years	NA	11
World data for comparison		
Public expenditures on education as % of GNP (mean)	3.9	4.8
Pupils per teacher at the primary level (wtd ave)	NA	33
Duration of primary education in years (mean)	NA	9

Educational Attainment (A)

Age group (1983) . . . . .25+

Population of this age group 2,043,720

Highest level attained (%)

No schooling 10.5

First level

Not completed 42.4

(Continued on next page.)

GOVERNMENT & LAW

Military Affairs (A)

	1990	1992	1995	1996	1997
Military expenditures					
Current dollars (mil.)	7,360	7,870	9,120	9,340	9,340
1997 constant dollars (mil.)	8,620	8,730	9,440	9,490	9,340
Armed forces (000)	190	181	185	185	185
Gross national product (GNP)					
Current dollars (mil.)	55,900	67,500	87,200	92,700	96,000
1997 constant dollars (mil.)	65,500	74,800	90,300	94,200	96,000
Central government expenditures (CGE)					
1997 constant dollars (mil.)	34,800	37,400	44,000	46,900	44,600
People (mil.)	4.5	4.9	5.3	5.4	5.5
Military expenditure as % of GNP	13.2	11.7	10.5	10.1	9.7
World data on military expenditure as % of GNP	4.5	3.4	2.7	2.6	2.6
Military expenditure as % of CGE	24.8	23.3	21.5	20.2	20.9
World data on military expenditure as % of CGE	17.0	12.5	10.5	10.3	10.2
Military expenditure per capita (1997 $)	1,910	1,770	1,780	1,750	1,690
World data on military expenditure per capita (1997 $)	242	173	146	143	145
Armed forces per 1,000 people (soldiers)	42.1	36.7	34.9	34.1	33.4
World data on armed forces per 1,000 people (soldiers)	5.3	4.5	4.1	3.9	3.8
GNP per capita (1997 $)	14,500	15,200	17,000	17,400	17,300
Arms imports[6]					
Current dollars (mil.)	1,400	1,600	775	925	1,100
1997 constant dollars (mil.)	1,640	1,774	802	940	1,100
Arms exports[6]					
Current dollars (mil.)	700	625	875	750	370
1997 constant dollars (mil.)	820	693	906	763	370
Total imports[7]					
Current dollars (mil.)	16,790	20,250	29,580	31,680	30,780
1997 constant dollars (mil.)	19,660	22,450	30,630	32,210	30,780
Total exports[7]					
Current dollars (mil.)	11,580	13,120	19,050	20,610	22,590
1997 constant dollars (mil.)	13,560	14,540	19,720	20,950	22,590
Arms as percent of total imports[8]	8.3	7.9	2.6	2.9	3.6
Arms as percent of total exports[8]	6.0	4.8	4.6	3.6	1.6

(Continued on next page.)

EDUCATION (cont.)

Educational Attainment (A) (cont.)

Completed . . . . .NA

Entered second level 35.9

Entered post-secondary .11.2

Literacy Rates (B)

	National Data	World Data
Adult literacy rate		
1980		
Male	95[1]	75
Female	88[1]	58
1995		
Male	97	81
Female	93	65

Libraries

National Libraries 1995

Administrative Units 1

Service Points or Branches .1

Number of Volumes (000) 3,000

Registered Users (000) 2.2

Loans to Users (000) 23

Total Library Staff 176

Public Libraries 1993

Administrative Units 271

Service Points or Branches 1,180

Number of Volumes (000) 11,242

Registered Users (000) 738

Loans to Users (000) .11,948

Total Library Staff 1,393

GOVERNMENT & LAW (cont.)

Political Parties

Knesset	% of vote	no. of seats
One Israel	20.2%	26
Likud Party	14.1%	19
Shas	13.0%	17
MERETZ	7.6%	10
Yisra'el Ba'Aliya	5.1%	4
Shinui	5.0%	6
Center Party	5.0%	6
National Religious Party	4.2%	5
United Torah Judaism	3.7%	5
United Arab List	3.4%	5
National Union	3.0%	4
Hadash	2.6%	3
Yisra'el Beiteinu	2.6%	4
Balad	1.9%	2
One Nation	1.9%	2
Democratic Movement	NA	2

Elections last held 17 May 1999 (next to be held May 2003). The Democratic Movement Party was formed after the election. Members were elected under Yisra'el Ba'Aliya list. NA stands for not available.

Government Budgets (A)

Year: 1998

Total Expenditures: 181,362 Millions of New Sheqalim

Expenditures as a percentage of the total by function:

General public services and public order 5.30

Defense 17.79

Education 13.41

Health 13.86

Social Security and Welfare 25.23

Housing and community amenities 3.32

Recreational, cultural, and religious affairs 0.89

Fuel and energy 0.26

Agriculture, forestry, fishing, and hunting 0.89

Mining, manufacturing, and construction 2.12

Transportation and communication 1.94

Other economic affairs and services 0.87

Crime

Crime volume (for 1998)

Crimes reported 302,873

Total persons convicted 89,348

Crimes per 100,000 population 5,017

Persons responsible for offenses

Total number suspects 58,821

Total number of female suspects 7,451

Total number of juvenile suspects 5,141

LABOR FORCE

Total Labor Force (A)

2.3 million (1997).

Labor Force by Occupation

Public services 31.2%

Manufacturing 20.2%

Finance and business 13.1%
Commerce 12.8%
Construction 7.5%
Personal and other services 6.4%
Transport, storage, and communications 6.2%
Agriculture, forestry, and fishing 2.6%

Data for 1996.

Unemployment Rate

9.1% (1999 est.)

PRODUCTION SECTOR

Energy Production

Production ....35.338 billion kWh

Production by source

Fossil fuel 99.9%
Hydro 0.1%
Nuclear 0%
Other 0%

Exports ....1.061 billion kWh

Data for 1998.

Energy Consumption

Consumption ....31.805 billion kWh
Imports ....2.000 million kWh

Data for 1998.

Transportation

Highways:

Total: 15,965 km.

Paved: 15,965 km (including 56 km of expressways).

Unpaved: 0 km (1998 est.).

Pipelines: crude oil 708 km; petroleum products 290 km; natural gas 89 km.

Merchant marine:

Total: 20 ships (1,000 GRT or over) totaling 711,831 GRT/823,929 DWT.

Ships by type: container 19, roll-on/roll-off 1 (1999 est.).

Airports: 58 (1999 est.).

Airports - with paved runways: 33.

Airports - with unpaved runways: 25.

Top Agriculture Products

Citrus, vegetables, cotton; beef, poultry, dairy products.

Top Mining Products (B)

Mineral resources include: copper, phosphates, bromide, potash, clay, sand, sulfur, asphalt, manganese, small amounts of crude oil.

MANUFACTURING SECTOR

GDP & Manufacturing Summary (A)

	1980	1985	1990	1995
GDP ($-1990 mil.)[1]	34,904	40,516	49,692	66,678
Per capita ($-1990)[1]	8,998	9,571	10,663	12,068
Manufacturing share (%) (current prices)[1]	16.0	22.6	23.9	13.3[e]
Manufacturing				
Value added ($-1990 mil.)[1]	6,303	7,513	8,394	12,110
Industrial production index	76	92	100	142
Value added ($ mil.)	6,490	6,655	10,193	13,521[e]
Gross output ($ mil.)	14,332	16,351	24,574	38,974[e]
Employment (000)	259	292	292	358[e]
Profitability (% of gross output)				
Intermediate input (%)	55	59	59	65[e]
Wages and salaries inc. supplements (%)	30[e]	30[e]	32[e]	24[e]
Gross operating surplus	15[e]	11[e]	10[e]	11[e]
Productivity ($)				
Gross output per worker	54,619	55,297	83,074	107,166[e]
Value added per worker	24,733	22,506	34,461	37,180[e]
Average wage (inc. supplements)	16,734[e]	16,765[e]	26,622[e]	25,780[e]
Value added ($ mil.)				
Food products	706	748	1,221	1,394[e]
Beverages	66	56	146	232[e]
Tobacco products	24	10	33	24[e]
Textiles	422	243	404	444[e]
Wearing apparel	293	229	427	608[e]
Leather and fur products	18	13	19	27[e]
Footwear	38	42	55	68[e]
Wood and wood products	112	78	116	147[e]
Furniture and fixtures	90	81	131	211[e]
Paper and paper products	150	135	241	302[e]

GDP & Manufacturing Summary (A)

	1980	1985	1990	1995
Printing and publishing	184	227	470	740[e]
Industrial chemicals	256	317	498	752[e]
Other chemical products	250	241	420	450[e]
Petroleum refineries	93	106	115	144[e]
Misc. petroleum and coal products	93	106	115	144[e]
Rubber products	104	64	76	87[e]
Plastic products	212	290	468	724[e]
Pottery, china and earthenware	26	25	30	32[e]
Glass and glass products	30	23	37	45[e]
Other non-metal mineral products	239	143	306	483[e]
Iron and steel	148	118	113	157[e]
Non-ferrous metals	61	36	61	114[e]
Metal products	1,060	967	1,228	1,623[e]
Non-electrical machinery	245	224	279	448[e]
Electrical machinery	831	1,415	2,200	3,061[e]
Transport equipment	610	522	742	705[e]
Prof. and scientific equipment	66	129	125	195[e]
Other manufacturing	63	67	120	158[e]

COMMUNICATIONS

Daily Newspapers

	National Data	World Data for Comparison
Daily Newspapers		
Number of Dailies	34	8,391
Total Circulation (000)	1,650	548,000
Circulation per 1,000 inhabitants	288	96

Telecommunications

Telephones - main lines in use: 2.8 million (1999).

Telephones - mobile cellular: 2.5 million (1999).

Telephone system: most highly developed system in the Middle East although not the largest.

Domestic: good system of coaxial cable and microwave radio relay; all systems are digital.

International: 3 submarine cables; satellite earth stations - 3 Intelsat (2 Atlantic Ocean and 1 Indian Ocean).

Radio broadcast stations: AM 23, FM 15, shortwave 2 (1998).

Radios: 3.07 million (1997).

Television broadcast stations: 24 (plus 31 low-power repeaters) (1997).

Televisions: 1.69 million (1997).

Internet Service Providers (ISPs): 23 (1999).

FINANCE, ECONOMICS, & TRADE

Economic Indicators

National product: GDP—purchasing power parity—$105.4 billion (1999 est.).

(Continued on next page.)

Balance of Payments

	1994	1995	1996	1997	1998
Exports of goods (f.o.b.)	17,198	19,268	21,241	22,650	22,972
Imports of goods (f.o.b.)	−22,753	−26,834	−28,426	−27,824	−26,197
Trade balance	−5,555	−7,566	−7,185	−5,174	−3,226
Services - debits	−7,701	−8,382	−9,271	−9,382	−9,825
Services - credits	6,579	7,759	8,093	8,418	9,049
Private transfers (net)	2,282	2,661	2,698	2,583	2,739
Government transfers (net)	3,575	3,343	3,846	3,895	3,949
Overall balance	−3,387	−5,196	−5,316	−3,398	−668

Economic Indicators (cont.)

National product real growth rate: 2.1% (1999 est.).

National product per capita: $18,300 (1999 est.).

Inflation rate—consumer price index: 1.3% (1999 est.).

Exchange Rates

Exchange rates:

New Israeli shekels (NIS) per US$1

November 1999	4.2260
1999	3.8001
1997	3.4494
1996	3.1917
1995	3.0113

Top Import Origins

$30.6 billion (f.o.b., 1999)

Origins (1997)

United States	19%
Benelux	12%
Germany	9%
United Kingdom	8%
Italy	7%
Switzerland	6%

Top Export Destinations

$23.5 billion (f.o.b., 1999)

Destinations (1997)

United States	32%
United Kingdom	NA
Hong Kong	NA
Benelux	NA
Japan	NA
Netherlands	NA

Foreign Aid

Recipient: $1.1 billion from the US (1999).

Import/Export Commodities

Import Commodities	Export Commodities
Raw materials	Machinery and equipment
Military equipment	Software
Investment goods	Cut diamonds
Rough diamonds	Chemicals
Fuels	Textiles and apparel
Consumer goods	Agricultural products

ITALY

CAPITAL: Rome (Roma).

FLAG: The national flag is a tricolor of green, white, and red vertical stripes.

ANTHEM: *Fratelli d'Italia (Brothers of Italy).*

MONETARY UNIT: The lira (L) is a paper currency of 100 centesimi. There are coins of 5, 10, 20, 50, 100, 200, 500, and 1,000 lire, and notes of 1,000, 2,000, 5,000, 10,000, 50,000, and 100,000 lire. The lira has floated freely since February 1973. L1 = $0.00066 (or $1 = L1,515.1).

WEIGHTS AND MEASURES: The metric system is the legal standard.

HOLIDAYS: New Year's Day, 1 January; Epiphany, 6 January; Liberation Day, 25 April; Labor Day, 1 May; Assumption, 15 August; All Saints' Day, 1 November; National Unity Day, 5 November; Immaculate Conception, 8 December; Christmas, 25 December; St. Stephen's Day, 26 December. Easter Monday is a movable holiday. In addition, each town has a holiday on its Saint's Day.

TIME: 1 PM = noon GMT.

LOCATION AND SIZE: Situated in southern Europe, the Italian Republic, including the major islands of Sicily and Sardinia, covers a land area of 301,230 square kilometers (116,306 square miles), slightly larger than the state of Arizona. Within the frontiers of Italy are the sovereign Republic of San Marino and the sovereign state of Vatican City.

Italy's capital city, Rome, is located in the west central part of the country.

CLIMATE: Climate varies with elevation and region. The coldest period occurs in December and January; the hottest in July and August. In the Po Plain, the average annual temperature is about 13°C (55°F); in Sicily, about 18°C (64°F); and in the coastal lowlands, about 14°C (57°F).

Italian Republic
Repubblica Italiana

INTRODUCTORY SURVEY

RECENT HISTORY

Italy joined Germany against the United States and its allies in World War II (1939-1945). Defeats in Greece and North Africa and the Allied invasion of Sicily toppled Mussolini's regime in July 1943. Soon Italy was divided into two warring zones, one controlled by the Allies in the south and the other held by the Germans. When German power collapsed Mussolini was captured and executed by Italian partisans.

In 1946 Italy became a republic by popular referendum; the following year, a new constitution was drafted. The war left Italy poverty stricken and in political chaos. By the early 1950s with foreign assistance including $1.5 billion from the United States under the Marshall Plan, Italy managed to restore its economy to prewar levels. Italy was a charter member of the North Atlantic Treaty Organization (NATO) and European Economic Community (EEC) and joined political and economic unification of Western Europe in the 1990s including adopting the euro in 1999.

Politically postwar Italy has been marked by a pattern of instability with a different coalition government coming to power on average about once a year since 1946. Left-wing terrorism plagued Italy during the 1970s and early 1980s. By the mid-1980s internal security had improved and a major effort against organized crime was under way. Corruption and scandals involving senior politicians and government officials in the early 1990s led to hundreds of investigations and arrests. The scan-

dals discredited the major parties that had governed since 1948 and boosted the popularity of new reformist groups.

GOVERNMENT

The chief of state of the Italian Republic is the president, who is elected for a seven-year term by an electoral college consisting of both houses of parliament and fifty-eight regional representatives. Presidential powers and duties include nomination of the prime minister, the head of government, who chooses a Council of Ministers (cabinet) with the approval of Parliament. Legislative power is vested in the two-chamber Parliament, consisting of the 630-member Chamber of Deputies and the 315-member Senate. Parliament is elected by universal direct vote. Of the 630 Chamber members, 475 are directly elected with 155 by regional proportional representation. Members serve five years. Of the 315 Senate seats, 232 are directly elected and eighty-three are elected by regional proportional representation, all for five-year terms.

Judiciary

Civil cases and lesser criminal cases are tried before judges called *pretori.* There are 159 tribunals each with jurisdiction over its own district; ninety assize courts, where cases are heard by juries; and twenty-six assize courts of appeal. The Court of Cassation in Rome acts as the highest level of appeal in all cases except those involving constitutional matters that are brought before the special Constitutional Court. For many years the number of civil and criminal cases has been increasing more rapidly than the judicial resources to deal with them.

Political Parties

The 1996 election saw a resurgence of the left with the Olive Tree Coalition anchored by former communists. Olive Tree took 284 seats of the 630-seat Chamber of Deputies. By 2000 Olive Tree had evolved into the Center-Left Coalition. The Freedom Alliance, a center-right coalition, took 246 seats. The separatists Northern League won fifty-nine seats, and the Communist Renewal thirty-five.

DEFENSE

Since 1949 Italy as a member of the North Atlantic Treaty Organization (NATO) has maintained large and balanced modern forces. The total strength in 2000 was 265,500 (126,100 draftees), not including 113,200 *carabinieri,* or paramilitary national police. The total reserve strength was 72,000. Mandatory military service is for 12 months for all services.

Army personnel numbered 165,600, including 95,800 draftees. Navy personnel totaled 38,000, including 11,000 draftees and 1,000 marines, and 2,500 naval commandos. The air force had a total strength of 61,900 personnel, including 19,300 draftees. Italy's military budget for 1999 was $23.3 billion, or 1.7 percent of the gross domestic product (GDP).

ECONOMIC AFFAIRS

As the Italian economy has expanded since the 1950s its structure has changed and diversified markedly. The role of agriculture has declined, while the importance of industry has increased dramatically. Precision machinery and motor vehicles have led the surge in manufacturing, and Italy has generally been a leader in European industrial design and fashion in recent decades. By 1989 Italy had the fifth largest Organization for Economic Cooperation and Development (OECD) economy. In the second half of the 1990s Italy adopted budgets compliant with the requirements of the European Monetary Union (EMU).

Unemployment has hovered around 10 percent to 12 percent for most of the 1990s. Italy's large public debt, public sector deficit, and complicated tax system are restrictions to economic growth. Italians living in the northern part of the country enjoy a substantially higher standard of living than those living in the south where unemployment runs 20 percent.

Public Finance

Reflecting both increasing economic activity and the pressures of inflation, the Italian budget has expanded continually since 1950. The U.S. CIA estimated that in 1999 government revenues totaled approximately $530 billion and expenditures $522 billion.

Income

In 1999 Italy's gross domestic product (GDP) was estimated at $1.2 trillion, or about $21,400 per capita. The 1999 estimated real growth rate of GDP was 1.3 percent and inflation 1.7 percent. The 1998 GDP contribution by sector was agriculture 2.6 percent, industry 31.6 percent, and services 65.8 percent.

Industry

With the drive toward greater European integration in full gear, Italy is liberalizing its economic and commercial legislation. These promise a marked change as mergers and foreign investment increase. Major private companies include: the Fiat automobile company; the Olivetti Company specializing in office computers and telecommunications; the Montedison chemical firm; and, Pirelli rubber. Other industries include machinery, iron and steel, food processing, textiles, footwear, and tourism.

Banking and Finance

The Bank of Italy (Banca d'Italia), the central bank, is the sole bank of issue and exercises credit control functions.

Three banks are of nationwide standing: the Bank of Rome, Credito Italiano, and the Italian Commercial Bank. At the end of 1992 there were numerous foreign banks operating in Italy.

A new banking law was passed in 1993, to bring Italy into conformity with the EU's Second Banking directive, and to introduce two major innovations that aim to move Italy toward a model of universal banking. It allows banks to hold shares in industrial concerns; and it eliminates the distinction between banks (aziende di credito) and special credit institutions (aziende di credito speciale), thus allowing all banks to perform operations previously limited to specific types of intermediary.

In January 1997 the government drafted legislation to promote restructuring and consolidation in Italy's largely inefficient and highly fragmented banking sector. The bill was the latest in a series of attempts since 1990 to rationalize the sector. Mergers are also changing the face of the Italian banking industry. In early 1999 four of the five largest Italian banks were involved in such deals.

There are ten stock exchanges in operation. The most important is that in Milan (established in 1808). Since 1974 the National Commission for Companies and the Stock Exchange have regulated the markets.

Economic Development

Priorities of the early 1990s were cutting government spending, fighting tax evasion to reduce public debt, and selling off state-owned enterprises. At the end of the decade the results of these policies were mixed. Liberalization provided the impetus for greater foreign investment while the funds generated from privatization eased the public debt. Italy qualified for the first round of European Monetary Union (EMU) and entered the euro zone in January 1999. Tax evasion remains a problem. The underground economy is still estimated at nearly 25 percent of official GDP. At the beginning of the twenty-first century Italy must work to stimulate employment, promote wage flexibility, hold down pension costs, and tackle the underground economy. The 1993 "social pact" has been credited with bringing Italy's inflation into conformity with EMU requirements and will be updated further.

SOCIAL WELFARE

Under current social insurance, all workers and their families are covered and receive old age, disability, and survivor pensions, unemployment and injury benefits, health and maternity coverage, and family allowances. In 1999 social insurance was funded by employee and employer contributions.

Women earn about 20 percent less than men, fill only about 10 percent of managerial positions, and are not well represented in professional positions.

Healthcare

A national health plan, begun in 1980, seeks to provide free health care for all citizens, but certain minimum charges remain. The shortage of medical personnel and hospital facilities in Italy's rural areas remains serious. In 1994, the government announced plans to dismantle public universal insurance. Consistent health reforms are hampered by frequent political changes in administration. Average life expectancy was estimated to be seventy-nine years for women and men in 2000.

In 1990-1997 there were 1.7 doctors and 6.4 hospital beds per 1,000 people and health expenditures were 7.6 percent of GDP.

Housing

Italy's housing and public building program was a major item in the general program of postwar reconstruction. Between 1940 and 1945 almost 20 percent of the habitable rooms in the country were destroyed. Between 1953 and 1961 a total of fifteen million rooms were constructed alleviating the nation's immediate housing problems. By the mid-1990s the total number of housing units was 24.8 million.

EDUCATION

In 2000 approximately 98.5 percent of the population were literate. Education is free and compulsory for eight years. In the academic year 1997 there were 2.8 million pupils in primary schools. Also 4.6 million students were enrolled in secondary schools.

Higher education had a total enrollment of 1.9 million in 1997. There are forty-one state universities and fifteen other universities, colleges, and higher learning institutes including the University of Bologna founded in the eleventh century and the University of Rome that is the country's largest.

2000 KEY EVENTS TIMELINE

January

- On January 4 Italy establishes diplomatic relations with North Korea.
- Ex-Prime Minister Bettino Craxi dies in Tunisia on January 19.

February

- An Italian boat qualifies on February 6 for the America's Cup.
- On February 19 Italian scientists claim to discover the particle in "dark matter."

April

- Ex-prime minister and current European Union (EU) Commission president, Romano Prodi, meets Libya's Muammar Qadafi in Cairo on April 3.
- Forza Italia/Northern League coalition wins eight of fifteen regional elections held on April 16.
- On April 19 Prime Minister Massimo D'Alema resigns.
- Giuliano Amato, head of a center-left coalition, replaces D'Alema on April 26 as prime minister.

June

- The Institute for Industrial Reconstruction (IRI), a state holding company founded under the government of Benito Mussolini, is shut down. At the peak of IRI's influence in the 1960s, it employed 600,000 people and controlled many major industries, including Alitalia Airlines and the state television station.

July

- The man who would be crowned prince of Italy, Emanuele Filiberto di Savoia, asks on July 18 to be allowed to visit Italy despite the wrongs committed by the Savoys.
- *L'Unità,* the most popular Communist Italian paper, publishes its last issue on July 28.

August

- Italy calls for an urgent meeting with its southern European neighbors over human trafficking after a ship carrying 418 migrants is intercepted off the southern Italian coast at the end of July.
- In response to the sexual assaults and slayings of two young girls, Italy's government announced it will set up a listening initiative in schools as part of a series of new efforts to detect and prosecute sex crimes against children.

September

- Floodwater and mud sweep through a campsite in southern Italy, killing ten people, some of them participants in a group of disabled campers.
- The imminent execution of a half-Italian death row prisoner in the U.S. prompts protests by the Pope and Italian Olympic athletes, as well as intense and widespread outrage in Italy, where the public largely opposes capital punishment.
- North Korean Foreign Minister Paek Nam-sun comes to Italy, September 27–28, in a rare visit to a Western country.
- Authorities declare a state of emergency in Italy's southern region of Calabria after rain triggers scattered flooding and mudslides.

October

- A week of torrential rainfall kills 25 people and displaces at least 22,000 others.

November

- The Vittoriano, a monument honoring King Victor Emanual II who died in 1878 after unifying Italy, reopens after a three-year, $4.5 million restoration. The restoration repaired mosaics and marble that make up the structure, and the thirty-three by thirty-nine-foot bronze statue of the king on horseback.
- Mudslides from heavy rains kill at least four people, and leave many homeless in the region of Liguria on November 24.

December

- The lower house of Parliament rejected a proposed change to the country's immigration law that would have allowed military border guards to use armed force in the fight against illegal immigration.

ANALYSIS OF EVENTS: 2000

BUSINESS AND THE ECONOMY

After four years of growth well below the European Union (E.U.) average, economic activity has begun to expand more rapidly. Italian economic growth averaged only 1.5 percent in the past four years, compared with an E.U. average of 2.3 percent. However, growth picked up and a rate of around 3 percent looked sustainable over the medium term. Although tax revenues increased by around 1 percent of gross domestic product (GDP) in fiscal year 1999/2000, the budget deficit was still 1.9 percent of GDP. The government had expected to raise more cash with the auction of third generation mobile phones and anticipated receiving around $28 billion in the twelve months ending July 2001 from privatizations and the sale of three G licenses. It was not clear if Italy could meet its promises to its European partners to bring down its budget deficit to less than 1 percent of GDP now that the sale of mobile phone licenses yielded less revenue than anticipated.

Italy's accumulated national debt has fallen from 122 percent of GDP to 114.7, which is still far above the Economic and Monetary Union (EMU) guidelines of 60 percent of GDP. Inflation crept up to 2.6 percent, almost twice the figure planned by the government, higher than the E.U. average and above the 2.0 percent ceiling set by the European Central Bank (ECB). Inflation was boosted in early 2000 by rising oil prices, causing the government to cut petrol taxes to keep retail prices down. The government also supported measures—like rail fares, public transport, and motorway tolls—that are still controlled by the Treasury, aimed at holding down the price of owning and operating a car.

One persistent weakness of the Italian economy was unemployment, at around 10.5 percent (down from 11.5 percent) in 2000. Unemployment was particularly serious in the south of the country and among young people. There are some areas of southern Italy where more than 50 percent of young people are reportedly unemployed. However, there was evidence that many who were officially unemployed were in fact "moonlighting" in the so-called "submerged economy." Italy's labor market is very rigid, giving employers little authority over hiring, firing, or even for moving employees from one part of the country to another. This has led to many informal hiring arrangements.

In March the Fiat group announced it would sign a joint venture with General Motors because it could no longer compete by itself in the global automotive industry. Fiat will concentrate on diversification by providing automobile financing, insurance, maintenance, and servicing.

GOVERNMENT AND POLITICS

At the end of March the Italian government was led by Massimo d'Alema. His coalition was made up of his own party, the Democrats of the left (DS), with 172 seats in the 630-member Chamber of Deputies, plus a half-dozen small groups ranging from small Catholic and non-Catholic parties of the political center to the more moderate of the two small Marxist parties. The result was a narrow majority of 316 out of 630 seats in the Chamber of Deputies, reinforced by the abstention of the eight Socialist Members of Parliament (MPs), and a more comfortable 165 out of 315 seats in the Senate. Since the coalition represented a wide range of political visions, from fundamentally conservative Catholic groups to traditional Marxists, it encountered repeated difficulties.

In opposition was the Freedom Pole, made up of Silvio Berlusconi's Forza Italia (FI) and the National Alliance (AN), plus the Northern League (NL). During the regional elections in April, the opposition formed an electoral alliance and soundly trounced the government parties. The losses for the center-left coalition were so bruising that D'Alemo felt obliged to resign. The left was able to forge a stop-gap measure and appointed Giuliano Amato prime minister, who took over from D'Alema in early May. According to many observers, the left lost mostly on the issue of illegal immigration. The flow of migrants has increased in the last two years and many voters linked high immigration with crime.

The job of prime minister was not easy because the coalition contained a discordant group of Greens, Socialists, Catholics, ex-Communists, and disciples of former Prime Minister Romano Prodi. Amato reshuffled the cabinet and promoted a few new faces to the cabinet posts of justice and public health. Referenda held on May 21 were disappointing because only 32 percent of the voters bothered to vote. The most important question on the ballot was a proposal to abandon proportional representation for parliamentary elections. Although 82 percent of the voters were in favor of abolishing proportional representation, which accounts for the election of a quarter of Italy's members of government, the low turnout invalidated the outcome. The Italian parliament was still home to forty-plus parties, which thrive thanks to direct proportional representation.

The present center-left coalition government, led by Giuliano Amato, had only a slender majority, and might not last until the April 2001 deadline for the next general election. In the fall public opinion polls gave the center-right Freedom Alliance, led by ex-premier Berlusconi, a clear lead. Berlusconi, its official leader and candidate for the premiership, controlled three of four private television networks, newspapers and magazines and vast financial resources. Many Italians felt a man in his powerful position should not be involved in politics.

In confirming a major program of tax reductions for the end of this year and 2001 (1.9 percent of 2001 GDP), the government aligned itself with the most ambitious tax reduction program of its European counterparts, Germany and France. These reductions were revised upward in the last quarter of 2000, due to two factors. First, the oil crisis magnified the scale of the decline in household purchasing power, threatened consumer spending, and therefore threatened economic growth. Second, the ruling coalition did not have a lead in opinion polls and results of the general election were close. The most important measure was a reduction in all levels of income tax—from 25.5 percent to 24 percent; from 33 percent to 32 percent; from 39.5 percent to 39 percent; and from 45 percent to 44.5 percent. The purchase of a first home was made entirely free of tax. At the same time, companies benefited from a one-point reduction in the corporate tax rate which was set at 36 percent for 2001 and 2002. These measures were well received by all social partners, including the powerful business association. Combined, the measures will have the effect of supporting consumer spending which, for this reason, was expected to increase by 2.9 percent in 2001 compared with 2.4 percent in 2000, despite a still high estimated inflation level averaging 2.5 percent in 2001 compared with 2.6 percent.

CULTURE AND SOCIETY

In spite of witnessing enormous social and economic changes in the last three decades, the family was still the center of life for most Italians. The proportion of unmarried Italian men aged up to thirty who still lived with their parents was 70 percent and higher than anywhere else in Europe. Moreover, 43 percent of all married Italians aged up to sixty-five lived within half a mile of their mothers. The close-knit family formed an extensive support system because grandparents provided childcare to working parents. Customarily, parents helped their married children buy their first house and family members tended to help one another.

Although the structure of society was still traditional, Italian society was nonetheless becoming much less ethnically and religiously homogeneous. The economic program of the current coalition received much voter approval, but the government was faulted for its softness on immigration. Many Italians worried about the future of Italian identity and culture.

DIRECTORY

CENTRAL GOVERNMENT

Head of State

President
Carlo Azeglio-Ciampi, Office of the President, Palazzo del Quirinale, I-00187 Rome, Italy
FAX: +39 (6) 46992384

Ministers

Prime Minister
Giuliano Amato, Office of the Prime Minister, Piazza Colonna 370, I-00187 Rome, Italy
FAX: +39 (6) 6783998; 6796894

Minister of Culture
Giovanna Melandri

Minister of Justice
Piero Fassino, Ministry of Justice, Via Arenula 70, I-00186 Rome, Italy
FAX: +39 (6) 5227855

Minister of Finance
Ottaviano Del Turco, Ministry of Finance, Viale Europa 242, I-00144 Rome, Italy
PHONE: +39 (6) 59971
FAX: +39 (6) 5917240; 5910993

Minister of Treasury
Vincenzo Visco, Ministry of Treasury, Via XX Settembre 97, I-00187 Rome, Italy
FAX: +39 (6) 4882146

Minister of Defense
Sergio Mattarella, Ministry of Defense, Via XX Settembre 8, I-00187 Rome, Italy
PHONE: +39 (6) 4882126
FAX: +39 (6) 4747775; 4885756

Minister of University and Scientific and Technological Research
Ortensio Zecchino, Ministry of University and Scientific and Technological Research, Piazzale Kennedy 20, I-00144 Rome, Italy
FAX: +39 (6) 5926146

Minister of Education
Tullio De Mauro, Ministry of Education, Viale Trastevere 76/A, I-00153 Rome, Italy
FAX: +39 (6) 58492057

Minister of Public Works
Nerio Nesi, Ministry of Public Works, Piazza di Porta Pia 1, I-00198 Rome, Italy
FAX: +39 (6) 44124308; 44267275

Minister of Environment
Willer Bordon, Ministry of Environment, Piazza Venezia 11, I-00187 Rome, Italy
PHONE: +39 (6) 6783331
FAX: +39 (6) 6783844

Minister of Agricultural, Food and Forestry Resources
Alfonso Pecoraro Scanio, Ministry of Agricultural, Food and Forestry Resources, Via XX Settembre 20, I-00187 Rome, Italy
FAX: +39 (6) 4746168

Minister of Transport and Merchant Marine
Pierluigi Bersani, Ministry of Transport and Merchant Marine, Piazza della Croce Rossa 1, I-00161 Rome, Italy
FAX: +39 (6) 44241539; 8540664

Minister of Communications
Salvatore Cardinale, Ministry of Communications, Viale America 201, I-00144 Rome, Italy
FAX: +39 (6) 5942274; 6780408

Minister of Industry, Commerce and Crafts
Enrico Letta, Ministry of Industry, Commerce and Crafts, Via Molise 2, I-00187 Rome, Italy
FAX: +39 (6) 47052215

Minister of Labor and Social Welfare
Cesare Salvi, Ministry of Labor and Social Welfare, Via Flavia 6, I-00187 Rome, Italy
FAX: +39 (6) 47887174; 4881087

Minister of Foreign Trade
Enrico Letta, Ministry of Foreign Trade, Viale America 341, I-00144 Rome, Italy
FAX: +39 (6) 59647507; 59647494

Minister of Health
Umberto Veronesi, Ministry of Health, Piazzale dell'Industria 20, I-00144 Rome, Italy
FAX: +39 (6) 59945328

Minister of National Patrimony
Giovanna Melandri, Ministry of National Patrimony, Via del Collegio Romeno 27, I-00186 Rome, Italy
FAX: +39 (6) 6791905; 6793156

POLITICAL ORGANIZATIONS

Forza Italia-FI (Italy Ahead)

Via dell'Umilta 48, I-00187 Rome, Italy
PHONE: +39 (6) 6731268; 6731276
FAX: +39 (6) 69941392; 69941315
NAME: Silvio Berlusconi

Partito Democratico della Sinistra (PDS)

Via delle Botteghe Oscure 4, I-00186 Rome, Italy
PHONE: +39 (6) 6711318; 6711558
FAX: +39 (6) 6792085

Partito della Rifondazione Comunista (PRC)

Via Barberini 11, I-00187 Rome, Italy
PHONE: +39 (6) 4870871
FAX: +39 (6) 4883252

Partito Popolare Italiano (PPI)

Piazza del Gesu' 46, I-00186 Rome, Italy
FAX: +39 (6) 67753951

Cristiani Democratici Uniti (CDU)

Piazza del Gesu' 46, I-00186 Rome, Italy
PHONE: +39 (6) 67751; 67753844
FAX: +39 (6) 67753951

Comitato per l'Italia che Vogliamo (Ulivo)

Largo Pietro di Brazza 26, I-00187 Rome, Italy
PHONE: +39 (6) 69920282; 69920464
FAX: +39 (6) 69920457

Centro Cristiano Democratico

Via di Ripetta 142, I-00186 Rome, Italy
PHONE: +39 (6) 68806108
FAX: +39 (6) 68806414

Alleanza Nazionale (AN)

Via della Scrofa 39, I-00186 Rome, Italy
PHONE: +39 (6) 6833769; 6872918; 6864364
FAX: +39 (6) 6879581; 4879252

Lega Nord (Northern League)

Via Carlo Bellerio 41, 20161 Milano, Italy
FAX: +39 (2) 66211298; 66202375

Federazione dei Verdi

Via Catalana 1/A, I-00186 Rome, Italy
PHONE: +39 (6) 68802879
FAX: +39 (6) 68803023

Partito Radicale

Via Uffici del Vicario 21, I-00186 Rome, Italy
PHONE: +39 (6) 6760592; 67603311; 6780804
FAX: +39 (6) 6781904; 6780804

Partito Radicale Transnazionale

PHONE: +39 (6) 689791
FAX: +39 (6) 68805396

La Rete-Movimento per la Democrazia

Lungotevere Marzio 3, I-00186 Rome, Italy
PHONE: +39 (6) 68300448; 68300447
FAX: +39 (6) 68300446

Patto Segni

Via Belsiana 100, I-00187 Rome, Italy
PHONE: +39 (6) 6786240; 6786240; 6780840
FAX: +39 (6) 6789890

Unione di Centro

Via della Stelletta 23, I-00186 Rome, Italy
PHONE: +39 (6) 6872344

Partito Repubblicano Italiano

Piazza dei Caprettari 70, I-00186 Rome, Italy
PHONE: +39 (6) 6834037; 6834038; 6834039
FAX: +39 (6) 68300903

Federazione dei Liberali Italiani

Via Frattina 89, I-00187 Rome, Italy
PHONE: +39 (6) 6783252
FAX: +39 (6) 6797102

Partito Socialista Italiano (PSI)

Via Tomacelli 146, I-00186 Rome, Italy
PHONE: +39 (6) 68604274
FAX: +39 (6) 68604282

Rinascita Socialista

Via G. De Calvi 6, I-00151 Rome, Italy
PHONE: +39 (6) 5371371
FAX: +39 (6) 538041

Alleanza Democratica

Via del Plebiscito 102, I-00186 Rome, Italy
PHONE: +39 (6) 69942200
FAX: +39 (6) 69942435

Movimento Cristiano-Sociali

Piazza Adriana 5, I-00193 Rome, Italy
PHONE: +39 (6) 68300537
FAX: +39 (6) 68300539

DIPLOMATIC REPRESENTATION

Embassies in Italy

Albania
Via Asmara 9, Rome, Italy
PHONE: +39 (6) 8380725

Argentina
Piazza Esquilino 2, Rome, Italy
PHONE: +39 (6) 4742551

Austria
Via Pergolesi 3, Rome, Italy
PHONE: +39 (6) 8558241

Belgium
Via Monti Parioli 49, Rome, Italy

Brazil
Piazza Navona 14, Rome, Italy
PHONE: +39 (6) 6838841

Bulgaria
Via Rubens 21, Rome, Italy
PHONE: +39 (6) 3224643

Canada
Via G.B. de Rossi 27, I-00161 Rome, Italy
FAX: +39 (6) 44598754

Croatia
Via SS. Cosma e Damiano 26, Rome, Italy
PHONE: +39 (6) 33250242

Czech Republic
Via Colli Farnesina 144, Rome, Italy
PHONE: +39 (6) 3296711

Denmark
Via Monti Parioli 50, Rome, Italy
PHONE: +39 (6) 3200441

Finland
Via Lisbona 3, Rome, Italy
PHONE: +39 (6) 8548329; 8848182

Germany
Via Po 25/c, Rome, Italy
PHONE: +39 (6) 884741

Greece
Via Mercadante 36, Rome, Italy
PHONE: +39 (6) 8442584

Hungary
Via Villini 12/16, Rome, Italy
PHONE: +39 (6) 4402032

Iceland
Via Donatello 21, Milan, Italy
PHONE: +39 (2) 70638515

Ireland
Largo Nazareno 3, Rome, Italy
PHONE: +39 (6) 6782541

Japan
Via Sella 60, Rome, Italy
PHONE: +39 (6) 4817151

Lithuania
Piazza Farnese 44, Rome, Italy
PHONE: +39 (6) 6865786

Luxembourg
Via Ardeatina 134, Rome, Italy
PHONE: +39 (6) 5180885

Malta
Lungotevere Marzio 12, Rome, Italy
PHONE: +39 (6) 6892687; 6879990

Monaco
Via Bertoloni 36, Rome, Italy
PHONE: +39 (6) 8077692

Netherlands
Via Mercati 8, Rome, Italy
PHONE: +39 (6) 3221141

Norway
Via Terme Deciane 79, Rome, Italy
PHONE: +39 (6) 5755853

Poland
Via Rubens 20, Rome, Italy
PHONE: +39 (2) 3224455; 3224597

Portugal
Via Pezzana 9, Rome, Italy
PHONE: +39 (6) 8073801

Romania
Via Tartaglia 36, Rome, Italy
PHONE: +39 (6) 8078807; 8084423

Russia
Via Gaeta 5, Rome, Italy
PHONE: +39 (6) 4941649

Serbia
Via Monti Parioli 20, Rome, Italy
PHONE: +39 (6) 3200805; 3200897

Slovakia
Via Colli Farnesina 144, Rome, Italy
PHONE: +39 (6) 36308617

Slovenia
Via Pisano 10, Rome, Italy
PHONE: +39 (6) 8081075

South Africa
Via Tanaro 14/16, Rome, Italy
PHONE: +39 (6) 8419794

Spain
Via Garibaldi 35, Rome, Italy
PHONE: +39 (6) 5800144

Sweden
Piazza Rio de Janeiro 3, Rome, Italy
PHONE: +39 (6) 44231459

Switzerland
Via Oriani 61, Rome, Italy
PHONE: +39 (6) 8083641

Turkey
Via Palestro 28, Rome, Italy
PHONE: +39 (6) 4469932; 4941526

Ukraine
Via Castelfidardo 50, Rome, Italy
PHONE: +39 (6) 44700172

United Kingdom
Via XX Settembre 80/a, Rome, Italy
PHONE: +39 (6) 4825441

United States
Via Veneto 119/a, I-00187 Rome, Italy
FAX: +39 (6) 4882672

JUDICIAL SYSTEM

Corte Suprema di Cassazione (Supreme Court of Cassation)

Palazzo di Giustizea, Piazza Cavour, I-00193 Rome, Italy
FAX: +39 (6) 6874170

Corte Costituzionale (Constitutional Court)

Palazzo della Consulta, Piazza del Quirinale 41, I-00187 Rome, Italy

Consiglio Superiore della Magistratura (Superior Council of the Judiciary)

Piazza dell'Indipendenza 6, I-00185 Rome, Italy

BROADCAST MEDIA

Adventist World Radio-Europe

AWR-Europe, Casiela Postale 383, I-47100 Forli, Italy
PHONE: +39 (543) 766655
FAX: +39 (543) 768198
WEBSITE: http://www.awr.org/awr-europe/
TITLE: Europe Region Director
CONTACT: Bert Smit
LANGUAGE: 19 languages
TYPE: Religious

Nexus-International Broadcasting Association

PO Box 10980, I-20110 Milan, Italy
PHONE: +39 (2) 2666971
FAX: +39 (2) 70638151
E-MAIL: info@nexus.org
WEBSITE: http://www.nexus.org/
TITLE: President
CONTACT: Alfredo Cotronea
LANGUAGE: English, French, German, Italian, Russian, Spanish
BROADCASTS: daily

RAI International

Largo Willy De Luca, I-00188 Roma, Italy
PHONE: +39 (6) 33174258
FAX: +39 (6) 33171885
WEBSITE: http://www.mix.it/raiinternational/
TITLE: Director

CONTACT: Roberto Morrione
LANGUAGE: 29 languages

Radio Italia

WEBSITE: http://www.italianetwork.it/

Radio Tirol GmbH

Postfach 26, Aichweg 4, I-39019 Dorf Toril, Italy
PHONE: +39 (473) 93656
FAX: +39 (473) 93663
TITLE: General Manager
CONTACT: Gerald Fleischmann

Rundfunk Anstalt Südtirol (RAS)

Europaaliee 164/A, I-39100 Bozen, Italy
PHONE: +39 (471) 546666
FAX: +39 (471) 200378
E-MAIL: ras@provinz.bz.it/ras
WEBSITE: http://www.provinz.bz.it
TITLE: President
CONTACT: Helmuth Hendrich
LANGUAGE: German

Southern European Broadcasting Sce.

APO New York, NY 09221, USA
TITLE: Commander, MAJ SC
CONTACT: Bernard L. Miles Public Statutory Body of the Autonomous Province of Southern Tyrol
TYPE: U.S. Military

Rundfunkanstalt Südtirol (RAS)

Europaalee 164A, I-39100 Bozen, Italy
PHONE: +39 (471) 33174258
TITLE: President
CONTACT: Helmuth Heindirch
CHANNEL: RAS1, RAS2, RAS3

Radiotelevisione Italiana

Direzione Centrale TV, Viale Mazzini 14, I-00195 Rome, Italy
PHONE: +39 (6) 38781
FAX: +39 (6) 3226070
TITLE: Chairman
CONTACT: Enzo Siciliano

Radiotelevisione Italiana (RAI)

Ciale Mazzini 14, I-00195 Rome, Italy
PHONE: +39 (6) 38781
FAX: +39 (6) 3226070
E-MAIL: webmaster@rai.it
WEBSITE: http://www.rai.it
TITLE: Chairman
CONTACT: Roberto Zaccaria
BROADCASTS: 0600–2400

COLLEGES AND UNIVERSITIES

Salesian Pontifical University

Piazza Ateneo Salesiano 1, I-00146 Rome, Italy
PHONE: +39 (6) 872901
FAX: +39 (6) 872903
E-MAIL: rettore@ups.urbe.it

University of Roma

Viale di Villa Massimo 36, I-00161 Rome, Italy
PHONE: +39 (6) 595803
FAX: +39 (6) 595804
E-MAIL: vergata@uniroma.it
WEBSITE: http://www.uniroma.it

John Cabot University

Via Della Lungara 233, I-00165 Rome, Italy
PHONE: +39 (6) 6819121
FAX: +39 (6) 6832088
E-MAIL: jcu@johncabot.edu
WEBSITE: http://www.johncabot.edu

Pontifical Urban University

Via Urbano Viii 16, I-00165 Rome, Italy
PHONE: +39 (6) 9882351
FAX: +39 (6) 9881871
E-MAIL: puusegre@pcn.net

Catholic University of the Sacred Heart - Rome

Largo Francesco Vito 1, I-00168 Rome, Italy
PHONE: +39 (6) 30151
E-MAIL: webadmin@mi.unicatt.it
WEBSITE: http://www.unicatt.it

St. Thomas Aquinas Pontifical University

Largo Angelicum 1, I-00184 Rome, Italy
PHONE: +39 (6) 67021
FAX: +39 (6) 6790407

Pontifical Gregorian University

Piazza Della Pilotta 4, I-00187 Rome, Italy
PHONE: +39 (6) 67011
FAX: +39 (6) 67015
WEBSITE: http://www.unigre.urbe.it

Free University Maria SS Assunta

Via della Traspontina 21, I-00193 Rome, Italy

PHONE: +39 (6) 6865945
FAX: +39 (6) 6878447
E-MAIL: lumsa@giannturi.caspur.it
WEBSITE: http://www.lumsa.it

Politecnico di Torino

Facolta Di Ingegneria, Politecnico Di Torino, Corso Duca Degli Abruzzi 24, I-10129 Turin, Italy
PHONE: +39 (11) 5646254
FAX: +39 (11) 5646299
E-MAIL: servstudenti@polito.it
WEBSITE: http://www.polito.it

University of Turin

Corso Unione Sovietica 218 Bis, I-10134 Turin, Italy
PHONE: +39 (11) 88021
E-MAIL: michelis@cisi.unito.it
WEBSITE: http://www.unito.it

University of Genoa

Via Balbi 5, I-16126 Genoa, Italy
PHONE: +39 (10) 20991
WEBSITE: http://www.unige.it

University of Milan

Via Gozzano 4, I-20131 Milan, Italy
PHONE: +39 (2) 58351
WEBSITE: http://www.unimi.it

University Vita-Sallute San Faffaele, Milan

Via Olgettina 58, I-20132 Milan, Italy
WEBSITE: http://www.regione.lombardia.it/aladino/dininitno

Technical University of Milano

Piazza Leonardo Da Vinci 32, I-20133 Milan, Italy
PHONE: +39 (2) 23991
FAX: +39 (2) 23992206
E-MAIL: siwa@polimi.it
WEBSITE: http://www.polimi.it

Iulm University, Milan

Via Filippo de Liscate 1.2, I-20143 Milan, Italy
PHONE: +39 (2) 582181
E-MAIL: ivana.bandirali@iulm.it
WEBSITE: http://www.iulm.it

University of Venice

Dorsoduro 3246 - Ca'foscari, I-30123 Venice, Italy
PHONE: +39 (41) 5298111
FAX: +39 (41) 5298321
WEBSITE: http://www.unive.it

University of Bologna

Viale Risorgimento 2, I-40136 Bologna, Italy
PHONE: +39 (51) 2099999
FAX: +39 (51) 2099374
E-MAIL: rettoro@ammc.unibo.it
WEBSITE: http://www.unibo.it

University of Florence

Piazza San Marco 4, I-50132 Florence, Italy
PHONE: +39 (55) 257357326
WEBSITE: http://www.unifi.it

University of Bari

Viale Ennio, I-70124 Bari, Italy
PHONE: +39 (80) 5711111
E-MAIL: rettore@uniba.it
WEBSITE: http://www.uniba.it

Technical University of Bari

Via Amendola 126, I-70126 Bari, Italy
PHONE: +39 (80) 5962559
FAX: +39 (80) 5460510
E-MAIL: gatta@polliba.it
WEBSITE: http://www.poliba.it

University of Naples Fedrico II

Corso Umberto I 41 Bis, I-80138 Naples, Italy
PHONE: +39 (81) 5477111
E-MAIL: admin@www.unina.it
WEBSITE: http://www.unina.it

University of Catania

Via Valdisavoia 5, I-95123 Catania, Italy
PHONE: +39 (95) 7307111
WEBSITE: http://www.unict.it

NEWSPAPERS AND MAGAZINES

Affari & Finanza

Piazza Indipendenza 11b, I-00185 Rome, Italy
PHONE: +39 (6) 49821
FAX: +39 (6) 49822923
WEBSITE: http://www.repubblica.it
TITLE: Editor

CONTACT: Alessandra Carini
CIRCULATION: 616,779

Avvenire

Piazza Carbonari 3, I-20125 Milan, Italy
PHONE: +39 (2) 67801
FAX: +39 (2) 6780208
WEBSITE: http://www.avvenire.it
TITLE: Editor
CONTACT: Dino Boffo
CIRCULATION: 90,834

Corriere Adriatico

Via Berti 20, I-60100 Ancona, Italy
PHONE: +39 (71) 42985/4581
FAX: +39 (71) 887141
TITLE: Editor
CONTACT: Paolo Biagi
CIRCULATION: 23,353

Sette Corriere della Sera

Via Solferino 28, I-20121 Milan, Italy
PHONE: +39 (2) 66256438
FAX: +39 (2) 66256266
TITLE: Managing editor
CONTACT: Claudio Calabi
CIRCULATION: 797,229

L'Eco di Bergamo

Viale Papa Giovanni XXIII 118, I-24121 Bergamo, Italy
PHONE: +39 (35) 386111
FAX: +39 (35) 225795
E-MAIL: sesaab@eco.bg.it
WEBSITE: http://www.eco.bg.it
TITLE: Editor
CONTACT: Sergio Borsi
CIRCULATION: 57,456

La Gazzetta del Mezzogiorno

Viale Scipione l'Africano 264, I-70124 Bari, Italy
PHONE: +39 (80) 5470312
FAX: +39 (80) 5470311
TITLE: Managing editor
CONTACT: Lino Patruno
CIRCULATION: 61,365

Gazzettino, Il

Via Torino 110, I-30172 Mestre, Venice, Italy
PHONE: +39 (41) 665111
FAX: +39 (41) 665386
E-MAIL: giulio.centro@gazzettino.it
WEBSITE: http://www.gazzettino.it
CONTACT: Giulio Giustiniani
CIRCULATION: 145,000

Il Mattino

Via Chiatamone 65, I-80121 Naples, Italy
PHONE: +39 (81) 7947111
FAX: +39 (81) 7947288
TITLE: Editor
CONTACT: Paolo Graldi
CIRCULATION: 104,885

La Nazione

Via Enrico Mattei 106, I-40138 Bologna, Italy
PHONE: +39 (51) 536111
FAX: +39 (51) 6570020
TITLE: Editor
CONTACT: Umberto Cecchi
CIRCULATION: 165,948

Il Resto del Carlino

Via Enrico Mattei 106, I-10138 Bologna, Italy
PHONE: +39 (51) 536111
FAX: +39 (51) 6570020
TITLE: Editor
CONTACT: Francesco Carrassi
CIRCULATION: 200,952

L'Unione Sarda

Viale Regina Elena 14, I-09100 Cagliari, Italy
PHONE: +39 (70) 60131
FAX: +39 (70) 6013276
E-MAIL: liori@vol.it
WEBSITE: http://www.vol.it/unione/unione.html
TITLE: Editor
CONTACT: Antonangelo Liori
CIRCULATION: 67,558

Il Venerdi

Piazza Indipendenza 11b, I-00185 Rome, Italy
PHONE: +39 (6) 49821
FAX: +39 (6) 49822923
WEBSITE: http://www.repubblica.it
TITLE: Editor
CONTACT: Ezio Mauro
CIRCULATION: 700,449

PUBLISHERS

Franco Angeli SRL

Viale Monza 106, I-50123 Milan, Italy
PHONE: +39 (2) 2827651

FAX: +39 (6) 2891515
E-MAIL: frangeb@tin.it
TITLE: Man. Director
CONTACT: Franco Angeli
SUBJECTS: Anthropology, Architecture, Business, Behavioral Sciences, Communications, Computer Science, Engineering, Political Science, Labor Relations, Mathematics, Science (General), Social Sciences, Women's Studies
TOTAL PUBLISHED: 205 print

Apostolato della Preghiera

Segretariato Nazionale Apostolato della Preghiera, Via Degli Astalli 16, I-00186 Rome, Italy
PHONE: +39 (6) 6976071
FAX: +39 (6) 6781063
E-MAIL: adp@adp.it
WEBSITE: http://www.adp.it
TITLE: Director
CONTACT: Max Taggi
SUBJECTS: Psychology, Psychiatry, Religion, Bible, Spirituality, Pastoral Activities, Prayer
TOTAL PUBLISHED: 198 print; 198 online

Casa Editrice Astrolabio-Ubaldini Editore

Via Guido d'Arezzo 16, I-00198 Rome, Italy
PHONE: +39 (6) 8552131
FAX: +39 (6) 8542245
E-MAIL: astrolabio.gana@alphacomm.it
TITLE: Chief Executive
CONTACT: Francesco Gana
SUBJECTS: Philosophy, Psychology, Psychiatry, Social Sciences, Sociology, Oriental Studies
TOTAL PUBLISHED: 820 print

Bardi Editore srl

Via Pave 7, I-00181 Rome, Italy
PHONE: +39 (6) 4817656
FAX: +39 (6) 48912514
E-MAIL: bardied@tin.it
WEBSITE: http://www.infinito.it/utento/bardieditore
TITLE: Man. Director
CONTACT: Garcia Y Laurent
SUBJECTS: Oriental Studies, Antiques, Archaeology, Architecture, Interior Design, History, Music, Dance
TOTAL PUBLISHED: 300 print

Editore Giorgio Bretschneider

Via Crescenzio 43, Casella Postale 30011, Rm. 47, I-00193 Rome, Italy
PHONE: +39 (6) 6879361
FAX: +39 (6) 6864543
E-MAIL: info@bretschneider.it
WEBSITE: http://www.bretschneider.it
TITLE: Man. Director
CONTACT: Boris Bretschneider
SUBJECTS: Archaeology, History
TOTAL PUBLISHED: 400 print

Camera dei Deputati Ufficio Pubblicazioni Informazione Parlamentare

Piazza Montecitorio, I-00186 Rome, Italy
PHONE: +39 (6) 67609328
FAX: +39 (6) 6781326
E-MAIL: rizzo_s@camera.it
WEBSITE: http://www.camera.it
TITLE: Chief Executive
CONTACT: Stefano Rizzo
SUBJECTS: Economics, History, Law
TOTAL PUBLISHED: 250 print

CIC Edizioni Internazionali

Corso Trieste 42, I-00198 Rome, Italy
PHONE: +39 (6) 8412673
FAX: +39 (6) 8412688
E-MAIL: info@gruppocic.it
WEBSITE: http://www.gruppocic.it
TITLE: Director General
CONTACT: Raffaele Salvati
SUBJECTS: Medicine, Nursing, Dentistry, Psychology, Psychiatry
TOTAL PUBLISHED: 150 print; 10 CD-ROM; 15 audio

Il Cigno Galileo Galilei-Edizioni di Arte e Scienza

San Salvatore Lauro 15, I-00186 Rome, Italy
PHONE: +39 (6) 6865493; 6873842
FAX: +39 (6) 6892109
E-MAIL: lzichic@tin.it
CONTACT: Delfina Bergamaslhi
SUBJECTS: Art, Law, Mathematics, Science (General)
TOTAL PUBLISHED: 385 print; 4 CD-ROM

Cittadella Editrice

Via Ancaiani 3, 06081 Assisi, Italy
PHONE: +39 (75) 813595
FAX: +39 (75) 813719
E-MAIL: amministrazione@cittadellaeditrice.com
WEBSITE: http://www.cittadellaeditrice.com
TITLE: Editorial Manager
CONTACT: Giuseppina Pompei

SUBJECTS: Biblical Studies, Biography, Psychology, Psychiatry, Catholicism, Social Sciences, Theology
TOTAL PUBLISHED: 466 print

CLUEB (Cooperativa Libraria Universitaria Editrice Bologna)

Via Marsala 31, I-40126 Bologna, Italy
PHONE: +39 (51) 220736
FAX: +39 (51) 237758
E-MAIL: clueb@clueb.it
WEBSITE: http://www.clueb.it
TITLE: Man. Director
CONTACT: Luigi Guardigli
SUBJECTS: Agriculture, Architecture, Art, Business, Economics, Education, History, Human Relations, Language Arts, Literature, Philosophy, Science (General)
TOTAL PUBLISHED: 150 print; 3 CD-ROM

Colonnese Editore

Via San Pietro a Majella 7, I-80138 Naples, Italy
PHONE: +39 (81) 459858; 293900
FAX: +39 (81) 455420
E-MAIL: info@colonnese.it
WEBSITE: http://www.spacee.tin.it/lettura/gacolon
TITLE: Director, Publishing & Sales
CONTACT: Gaetano Colonnese
SUBJECTS: Archaeology, Drama, Theater, Fiction, History, Humor, Language Arts, Linguistics, Literature, Literary Criticism, Photography, Women's Studies
TOTAL PUBLISHED: 300 print

Edagricole - Edizioni Agricole

Via Emilia Levante N 31/2, I-40139 Bologna, Italy
PHONE: +39 (51) 62267
FAX: +39 (51) 490200
E-MAIL: comm@calderini.agriline.it
WEBSITE: http://www.edagricole.it
TITLE: Man. Director & Editorial
CONTACT: Alberto Perdisa
SUBJECTS: Agriculture, Animals, Pets, Biological Sciences, Gardening, Plants, Health, Nutirtion, Science (General), Veterinary Science
TOTAL PUBLISHED: 2,000 print

Editrice Bibliografica SpA

Viale Vittorio Veneto 24, I-20124 Milan, Italy
PHONE: +39 (2) 29006965
FAX: +39 (2) 654624
E-MAIL: bibliografica@alice.it
WEBSITE: http://www.alice.it/eb
TITLE: Administrator
CONTACT: Michele Costa
SUBJECTS: Library & Information Sciences
TOTAL PUBLISHED: 300 print; 1 CD-ROM

Edizioni Mediterranee SRL

Via Flaminia 109, I-00196 Rome, Italy
PHONE: +39 (6) 3235433
FAX: +39 (6) 3236277
E-MAIL: info@ediz-mediterranee.com
WEBSITE: http://www.ediz-mediterranee.com
TITLE: General Manager
CONTACT: Giovanni Canonico
SUBJECTS: Archaeology, Art, Occult, Biography, Gardening, Health, How-To, Medicine, Military Science, Parapsychology, Philosophy, Psychiatry, Sports, New Age, Martial Arts, Yoga, Esotherism
TOTAL PUBLISHED: 1,500 print

Giunti (Gruppo Editoriale)

Via Bolognese 165, I-50139 Frienze, Italy
PHONE: +39 (55) 50621
FAX: +39 (55) 5062274
E-MAIL: estero@giunti.it
TITLE: Man. Director
CONTACT: Martino Montanarini
SUBJECTS: Archaeology, Art, Education, Fiction, History, Science (General), Travel
TOTAL PUBLISHED: 4,500 print; 200 CD-ROM

Gruppo Calderini Edagricole

Via Emilia Levante 31/2, I-40139 Bologna, Italy
PHONE: +39 (51) 62267
FAX: +39 (51) 490200
E-MAIL: comunica@calderini.agriline.it
WEBSITE: http://www.calderini.it
TITLE: Man. Director
CONTACT: Giovanna Villani Perdisa
SUBJECTS: Architecture, Art, Computer Science, Cookery, Education, Games, Electronics, Engineering, Science (General), Self-Help, Sports, Travel
TOTAL PUBLISHED: 988 print

Gruppo Editoriale Armenia SpA

Via Valtellina 63, I-20159 Milan, Italy
PHONE: +39 (2) 683911
FAX: +39 (2) 6684884
E-MAIL: armenia@mr-net.it
WEBSITE: http://www.armenia.it

TITLE: President
CONTACT: Giovanni Armenia
SUBJECTS: Animals, Pets, Astrology, Occult, Crafts, Hobbies, Health, Nutrition, How-To, Self-Help, New Age
TOTAL PUBLISHED: 500 print

Edizioni Guerini e Associati Spa

Viale Filippetti 28, I-20122 Milan, Italy
PHONE: +39 (2) 58298030
FAX: +39 (2) 58298030
E-MAIL: guerini@iol.it
TITLE: President
CONTACT: Angelo Guerini
SUBJECTS: Anthropology, Management, Philosophy, Psychology, Psychiatry, Literary Criticism, Architecture, Gardening
TOTAL PUBLISHED: 1,000 print

Hermes Edizioni SRL

Via Flaminia 109, I-00196 Rome, Italy
PHONE: +39 (6) 3222797
FAX: +39 (6) 3236277
E-MAIL: edimedit@flashnet.it
WEBSITE: http://www.ediz-mediterranee.com
TITLE: General Manager
CONTACT: Giovanni Canonico
SUBJECTS: Anthropology, Health, Nutrition, Medicine, Nursing, Dentistry, Parapsychology, Psychology, Psychiatry, Buddhism, Hinduism, Sports
TOTAL PUBLISHED: 300 print

Angelo Longo Editore

Via Paolo Costa 33, I-48100 Ravenna, Italy
PHONE: +39 (544) 217026
FAX: +39 (544) 217554
E-MAIL: longo-ra@linknet.it
WEBSITE: http://www.longo-editore.it
TITLE: Gen. Manager
CONTACT: Alfio Longo
SUBJECTS: Archaeology, Art, Drama, Theater, Film, Fiction, History, Language Arts, Literature, Linguistics, Music, Dance, Philosophy, Photography, Women's Studies
TOTAL PUBLISHED: 800 print; 1 CD-ROM

Manifestolibri

Via Tomacelli 146, I-00186 Rome, Italy
PHONE: +39 (6) 68719654
FAX: +39 (6) 5882839
E-MAIL: bedazione@manifestolibri.it
WEBSITE: http://www.manifestolibri.it
CONTACT: Simona Bonsignori
SUBJECTS: Political Science, Government, Philosophy, Social Sciences, Sociology, Socioeconomic Affairs
TOTAL PUBLISHED: 200 print; 2 CD-ROM; 10 audio

Editrice Massimo SAS di Crespi Cesare

Viale Bacchiglione 20A, I-20139 Milan, Italy
PHONE: +39 (2) 55210800; 55211220
FAX: +39 (2) 55211315
TITLE: Man. Director
CONTACT: Cesare Crespi
SUBJECTS: Astronomy, Biblical Studies, Biography, Theater, Fiction, History, Literature, Philosophy, Psychology, Psychiatry, Catholicism, Social Sciences, Theology
TOTAL PUBLISHED: 400 print

Arnoldo Mondadori Editore SpA

Via Mondadori, I-20090 Milan, Italy
PHONE: +39 (2) 75421
FAX: +39 (2) 75422302
E-MAIL: aallegri@mondadori.it
WEBSITE: http://www.mondadori.it
TITLE: Corporate Communications & Advertising Director
CONTACT: Andrea Zagami
SUBJECTS: Art, Biography, Education, Fiction, History, How-To, Medicine, Nursing, Dentistry, Music, Dance, Philosophy, Psychology, Psychiatry, Religion, Science (General)
TOTAL PUBLISHED: 1,200 print

Instituto Nazionale di Studi Romani

Piazza dei Cavalieri di Malta 2, I-00139 Rome, Italy
PHONE: +39 (6) 573442; 5743445
FAX: +39 (6) 5743447
E-MAIL: studiromani@mclink.it
WEBSITE: http://www.romacivica.net/studiromani
TITLE: Director
CONTACT: Fernanda Roscetti
SUBJECTS: Architecture, Interior Design, Art, History, Literature, Literary Criticism, Essays
TOTAL PUBLISHED: 826 print

Leo Olschki

Viuzzo del Pozzetto 8, I-50126 Florence, Italy
PHONE: +39 (55) 6530684
FAX: +39 (55) 6530214
E-MAIL: celso@olschki.it
WEBSITE: http://www.olschki.it

SUBJECTS: Anthropology, Archaeology, Art, Architecture, Astronomy, Biblical Studies, Political Science, History, Library & Information Sciences, Literature, Philosophy, Religion, Science (General), Social Sciences, Theology, Music, Language
TOTAL PUBLISHED: 3,000 print

SEMAR Publishers SRL

Via Arco Di Parma 18, I-00186 Rome, Italy
PHONE: +39 (6) 6876523
FAX: +39 (6) 68308601
E-MAIL: semarpublishers@altavista.net
WEBSITE: http://www.semarweb.com
TITLE: President
CONTACT: Luciano Sahlan Momo
SUBJECTS: Art, Drama, Theater, Environmental Studies, Literature, Literary Criticism, Essays, Music, Dance, Philosophy, Poetry
TOTAL PUBLISHED: 160 print; 6 CD-ROM; 176 online; 10 audio

TEA Tascabili degli Editori Associati SpA

Corso Italia 13, I-20122 Milan, Italy
PHONE: +39 (2) 8900830
FAX: +39 (2) 8900844
E-MAIL: stefano.res@tealibri.it
TITLE: Man. Director
CONTACT: Mario Spagnol
SUBJECTS: Art, Cookery, Fiction, Health, History, How-To, Humor, Nonfiction (General), Philosophy, Photography, Psychology, Psychiatry, Religion, Self-Help
TOTAL PUBLISHED: 1,100 print

Tecniche Nuove SpA

Via Menotti 14, I-20129 Milan, Italy
PHONE: +39 (2) 75701
FAX: +39 (2) 7610351
E-MAIL: libri@tecnet.it
WEBSITE: http://www.tecnet.it
TITLE: Man. Director
CONTACT: Giuseppe Nardella
SUBJECTS: Business, Computer Science, Electronics, Electrical Engineering, Energy, Health, Nutrition, Technology
TOTAL PUBLISHED: 700 print; 30 CD-ROM; 30 internet

Urbaniana University Press

Division of Pontificia Universita Urbaniana, I-Via Urbano VIII, 16, 00120 Citta Del Vaticano, Italy
PHONE: +39 (6) 69882351; 69881745; 69882182
FAX: +39 (6) 9881871
E-MAIL: uupdic@pen.net
TITLE: Chief Executive, Rights & Permissions & Publicity
CONTACT: Gaspare Mura
SUBJECTS: Anthropology, Biblical Studies, Law, Philosophy, Psychology, Psychiatry, Catholicism, Theology
TOTAL PUBLISHED: 500 print

RELIGIOUS ORGANIZATIONS

Atheist

Associazione per lo Sbattezzo
E-MAIL: papini@abanet.it
WEBSITE: http://www.abanet.it/papini/index.htm

Buddhist

Centro Italiano Zen Soto
Via Gaetana Agnesi 18, Milano I-20135, Italy
NAME: Ven. Ryusui Zensen

Centro Zen Ho Un Do
Via Garian 43a, Milano, I-20146, Italy
PHONE: +39 (2) 4264940

Centro Zen Roma
Via Adolfo Rava, 106 c/o Jinko Club, Roma, I-00142, Italy
PHONE: +39 (6) 5414635; 5414635
E-MAIL: mc0984@mclink.it
WEBSITE: http://www.geocities.com/Tokyo/3905/
NAME: Rosamaria Mariano

Roma Sangha
Via Frangipane 27, Roma, I-00184, Italy
PHONE: +39 (6) 6784469; 5819026
NAME: Tiziana Faggiani

Catholic

Apostles of the Sacred Heart
Via Arnaboldi 2, I-20149 Milan, Italy
PHONE: +39 (2) 39210152

Association of Advisors on Education and International Religious Congregations (AAEIRC)
Via della Stazione Aurelia 95, I-00165 Rome, Italy
NAME: Sr. Maryann Eckhoff

Brothers of Charity (BC)

Freres de la Charite (FC)
c/o Fr. Oscar Duym, Via G. B. Pagano 35, Casella Postale 9082, I-00167 Rome, Italy
PHONE: +39 (6) 6604901
FAX: +39 (6) 6631466
E-MAIL: fcduymsg@pcn.net
TITLE: Secretary General
NAME: Fr. Oscar Duym

Carmelite Missionaries (CM)

Carmelitane Missionarie
Via del Casaletto 115, I-00151 Rome, Italy
PHONE: +39 (6) 535472
FAX: +39 (6) 58232279
TITLE: Secretary General
NAME: Sr. Maria Pilar Miguel Garcia

Congregation of the Holy Spirit (CSSp)
Clivo di Cinna 195, I-00136 Rome, Italy
PHONE: +39 (6) 3540461
FAX: +39 (6) 35450676
E-MAIL: cssp@rm.nettuno.it
TITLE: General Secretary
NAME: James Hurley

Discalced Brothers of the Most Blessed Virgin Mary of Mount Carmel

Ordo Fratrum Excalceatorum Beatissimae Mariae Virginis de Monte Carmelo
Corso d-Italia 38, I-00198 Rome, Italy
PHONE: +39 (6) 854431
FAX: +39 (6) 85350206
TITLE: Superior General
NAME: Camilo Maccise

Divine Word Missionaries (DWM)

Societa del Verbo Divino (SVD)
Via dei Verbiti 1, I-00154 Rome, Italy
PHONE: +39 (6) 5754021
FAX: +39 (6) 5783031
E-MAIL: dwn@mwci.net
WEBSITE: http://red.vais.net/svd
TITLE: Superior General
NAME: Very Rev. Heinrich Barlage, SVD

Institute of the Brothers of the Christian Schools

Fratres Scholarum Christianarum (FSC)
c/o Brother John Johnston, Via Aurelia 476, Casella Postale 9099, Aurelio, I-00100 Rome, Italy
PHONE: +39 (6) 6638786
FAX: +39 (6) 6638821
E-MAIL: casa@lasalle.org
TITLE: Superior General
NAME: Brother John Johnston

International Association for Patristic Studies (AIEP)

Association Internationale d'Etudes Patristiques
Institutum Patristicum Augustinianum, Via Paolo VI, 25, I-00193 Rome, Italy
PHONE: +39 (6) 680069
FAX: +39 (6) 68006298
TITLE: Secretary General
NAME: Professor Angelo di Berardino

International Union of Superiors General (IUSG)

Union Internationale des Superieures (UISG)
Piazza di Ponte San Angelo 28, I-00186 Rome, Italy
PHONE: +39 (6) 6840020
FAX: +39 (6) 68400239
TITLE: Secretary General
NAME: Sr. Marguerite Latourneau

Istituto Internazionale Soure di Santa Marcellina (ISM)
Piazza Cardinal Andrea Ferrari 5, I-20122 Milan, Italy
PHONE: +39 (2) 58306661
FAX: +39 (2) 58322623
TITLE: Superior General
NAME: Sr. Maria Paola Albertario

Missionaries of the Company of Mary (SMM)
Casa Generalizia Monfortani, Viale dei Monfortani 65, I-00135 Rome, Italy
PHONE: +39 (6) 3052332
FAX: +39 (6) 35505742
E-MAIL: smm@pcn.net
TITLE: Superior General
NAME: Rev. Fr. William Considine

Order of Friars Minor (OFM)
Via Santa Maria Mediatrice 25, I-00165 Rome, Italy
PHONE: +39 (6) 68491365
FAX: +39 (6) 68491364
E-MAIL: comgen@ofm.org
WEBSITE: http://www.ofm.org
TITLE: Minster General
NAME: Fr. Giacomo Bini

Order of St. Camillus
Piazza della Maddalena 53, I-00186 Rome, Italy
PHONE: +39 (6) 6797796
FAX: +39 (6) 6789418

TITLE: Superior General
NAME: Fr. Angelo Brusco

Salesian Youth Movement (SYM)

Movimiento Juvenil Salesiano (MJS)
Via della Pisana 1111, I-00163 Rome, Italy
PHONE: +39 (6) 6561121
FAX: +39 (6) 65612556
E-MAIL: adomenech@sdb.org
WEBSITE: http://www.sdb.org
TITLE: Counselor
NAME: Antonio Domenech

School Sisters of Notre Dame (SSND)

Armen Schulschwestern conUnserer Liben Frau
c/o Sister Rosemary Howarth, SSND, Via della Stazione Aurelia 95, I-00165 Rome, Italy
PHONE: +39 (6) 66418065
FAX: +39 (6) 66411212
WEBSITE: http://www.ssnd.org/ssnd/
TITLE: General Superior
NAME: Sister Rosemary Howarth

Sisters of the Good Shepherd (SGS)

Soeur du Bon Pasteur
Via Raffaello Sardiello 20, I-00165 Rome, Italy
PHONE: +39 (6) 66418545
FAX: +39 (6) 66418864
TITLE: General Secretary
NAME: Sr. Digna Maria Rivas

Society of Saint Teresa of Jesus (STJ)

Compania de Santa Teresa de Jesus
Via Val Cannuta 134, I-00166 Rome, Italy
PHONE: +39 (6) 6636813
FAX: +39 (6) 6635750
E-MAIL: secretaria.stj@pcn.net
NAME: Sister Silvia M. Casado Alverdi

Tertiary Capuchins of Our Lady of Sorrows (TC)

Religiosos Terciarios Capuchinos de Nuestra Senora de los Dolores (TC)
c/o Fr. Pedro Acosta. Via Bernardo Blumenstihl 28-36, I-00135 Rome, Italy
PHONE: +39 (6) 3055931
FAX: +39 (6) 3057972
TITLE: Secretary
NAME: Brother Pedro Acosta

Union of Superiors General (USG)

Unione Superiori Generali
Via dei Penitenzieri 19, I-00193 Rome, Italy
PHONE: +39 (6) 6868229
FAX: +39 (6) 6874317
TITLE: Secretary General
NAME: Brother Lino Da Campo

World Christian Life Community (WCLC)

Weltgemeinschaft Christliches Lebens
CP 6139, Borgo Sant Spirito 8, I-00195 Rome, Italy
PHONE: +39 (6) 6868079
FAX: +39 (6) 6868079
E-MAIL: mcvx.wici@agora.stm.it
WEBSITE: http://maple.lemoyne.edu/jesuit/clc
TITLE: Executive Secretary
NAME: Giles Michaud

Islamic

Associazione Islamica "Ahl Al Bait"
Confalone, 7, Napoli, 80136 Italy
PHONE: +39 0815441587
E-MAIL: ilpuroislam@iol.it
WEBSITE: http://www.shia-islam.org
NAME: Ammar De Martino

Scientology

Chiesa di Scientology Missione di Milano
Via Roma, 85, 24020 Gorle (Bergamo), Italy
WEBSITE: http://www.smi.org/address/itlay.htm

Chiesa di Scientology Missione di Bologna
Via Angelo Custode 66/2, Bologna, Italy

FURTHER READING

Articles

"C'mon Let's Cruise: Italy's Wealthiest Politician Pushes Out the Boat to Launch His Campaign to Unseat the Ruling Coalition." *Time International,* April 17, 2000, vol. 155, no. 15, p. 42.

"Italy Plans Tax Cuts of $23.3 Billion, Matching Germany." *Wall Street Journal,* August 29, 2000, p. A18.

"The Month in Review: January 2000." *Current History,* March 2000, p. 141.

Stanley, Alessandra. "Italy's New Politics: The Beauty Contest." *New York Times,* October 30, 2000, p.A6.

Trofimov, Yaroslov. "Italy's Amato Forms Government." *Wall Street Journal,* April 26, 2000, p. A22.

ITALY: STATISTICAL DATA

For sources and notes see "Sources of Statistics" at the front of each volume.

GEOGRAPHY

Geography

Area:

Total: 301,230 sq km.

Land: 294,020 sq km.

Note: includes Sardinia and Sicily.

Land boundaries:

Total: 1,932.2 km.

Border countries: Austria 430 km, France 488 km, Vatican City (Holy See) 3.2 km, San Marino 39 km, Slovenia 232 km, Switzerland 740 km.

Coastline: 7,600 km.

Climate: predominantly Mediterranean; Alpine in far north; hot, dry in south.

Terrain: mostly rugged and mountainous; some plains, coastal lowlands.

Natural resources: mercury, potash, marble, sulfur, dwindling natural gas and crude oil reserves, fish, coal, arable land.

Land use:

Arable land: 31%

Permanent crops: 10%

Permanent pastures: 15%

Forests and woodland: 23%

Other: 21% (1993 est.).

HUMAN FACTORS

Demographics (A)

	1990	1995	1998	2000	2010	2020	2030	2040	2050
Population	NA	57,263	57,510	57,634	57,409	55,540	52,868	49,431	45,017
Life expectancy - males	NA	74.9	75.6	75.8	77.1	78.3	79.2	79.9	80.5
Life expectancy - females	NA	81.5	82.2	82.4	83.6	84.7	85.5	86.2	86.7
Birth rate (per 1,000)	NA	9.2	9.2	9.1	7.5	6.7	7.1	7.0	7.3
Death rate (per 1,000)	NA	9.7	9.8	10.0	11.2	12.4	13.6	15.5	17.9
Women of reproductive age (15-49 yrs.)	NA	14,486	14,308	14,157	13,308	11,481	9,560	8,388	7,336
Fertility rate	NA	1.2	1.2	1.2	1.2	1.3	1.4	1.5	1.7

Except as noted, values for vital statistics are in thousands; life expectancy is in years.

Health Personnel

	National Data	World Data (wtd ave)
Total health expenditure as a percentage of GDP, 1990-1998[a]		
Public sector	5.3	2.5
Private sector	2.3	2.9
Total[b]	7.6	5.5
Health expenditure per capita in U.S. dollars, 1990-1998[a]		
Purchasing power parity	1,536	561
Total	1,511	483
Availability of health care facilities per 100,000 people		
Hospital beds 1990-1998[a]	650	330
Doctors 1992-1995[a]	NA	122
Nurses 1992-1995[a]	NA	248

Health Indicators

	National Data	World Data
Life expectancy at birth (years)		
1980	74	61
1998	78	67
Daily per capita supply of calories		
1970	3,422	2,358
1997	3,507	2,791
Daily per capital supply of protein		
1997 (grams)	109	74
Total fertility rate (births per woman)		
1980	1.6	3.7
1998	1.2	2.7
People living with (1997)		
Tuberculosis (cases per 100,000)	8.5	60.4
HIV/AIDS (% aged 15 - 49 years)	0.31	0.99

Infants and Malnutrition

	National Data	World Data (wtd ave)
Under 5 mortality rate (1989)	6	NA
% of infants with low birthweight (1992-98)[1]	7	17
Births attended by skilled health staff (% of total births 1996-98)	100	52
% fully immunized at 1 year of age (1995-98)[1]		
TB	NA	82
DPT	95	77
Polio	96	77
Measles	55	74
Prevalence of child malnutrition (1992-98)[1] (based on weight for age, % of children under 5 years)	NA	30

Ethnic Division

Italian (includes small clusters of German-, French-, and Slovene-Italians in the north and Albanian-Italians and Greek-Italians in the south).

Religion

Predominately Roman Catholic with mature Protestant and Jewish communities and a growing Muslim immigrant community.

Major Languages

Italian (official), German (parts of Trentino-Alto Adige region are predominantly German speaking), French (small French-speaking minority in Valle d'Aosta region), Slovene (Slovene-speaking minority in the Trieste-Gorizia area).

EDUCATION

Public Education Expenditures

	1997
Public expenditures on education as % of GNP	4.9
Expenditures per student as % of GNP per capita	
Primary	22.4
Secondary	NA
Tertiary	21.2
Teachers' compensation as % of total current education expenditures	67.3
Pupils per teacher at the primary level	11
Duration of primary education in years	8
World data for comparison	
Public expenditures on education as % of GNP (mean)	4.8
Pupils per teacher at the primary level (wtd ave)	33
Duration of primary education in years (mean)	9

Educational Attainment (A)

Age group (1981) . . . . .6+

Population of this age group 53,481,852
Highest level attained (%)
No schooling[2] 2.1
First level
Not completed 12.2
Completed 32.5
Entered second level
Lower Secondary 30.7
Upper Secondary 18.6
Entered post-secondary . . . . .3.

(Continued on next page.)

GOVERNMENT & LAW

Military Affairs (A)

	1990	1992	1995	1996	1997
Military expenditures					
Current dollars (mil.)	19,400	20,000	19,300	21,500	22,700
1997 constant dollars (mil.)	22,700	22,100	20,000	21,800	22,700
Armed forces (000)	493	471	435	431	419
Gross national product (GNP)					
Current dollars (bil.)	894	957	1,070	1,100	1,130
1997 constant dollars (bil.)	1,050	1,060	1,110	1,120	1,130
Central government expenditures (CGE)					
1997 constant dollars (bil.)	522	568	560	570	557
People (mil.)	57.7	56.9	57.3	57.4	57.5
Military expenditure as % of GNP	2.2	2.1	1.8	2.0	2.0
World data on military expenditure as % of GNP	4.5	3.4	2.7	2.6	2.6
Military expenditure as % of CGE	4.4	3.9	3.6	3.8	4.1
World data on military expenditure as % of CGE	17.0	12.5	10.5	10.3	10.2
Military expenditure per capita (1997 $)	394	390	349	380	395
World data on military expenditure per capita (1997 $)	242	173	146	143	145
Armed forces per 1,000 people (soldiers)	8.5	8.3	7.6	7.5	7.3
World data on armed forces per 1,000 people (soldiers)	5.3	4.5	4.1	3.9	3.8
GNP per capita (1997 $)	18,200	18,700	19,300	19,400	19,700
Arms imports[6]					
Current dollars (mil.)	420	340	390	480	430
1997 constant dollars (mil.)	492	377	404	488	430
Arms exports[6]					
Current dollars (mil.)	200	470	220	160	700
1997 constant dollars (mil.)	234	521	228	163	700
Total imports[7]					
Current dollars (bil.)	182	189	206	208	210
1997 constant dollars (bil.)	213	209	213	212	210
Total exports[7]					
Current dollars (bil.)	171	178	223	252	240
1997 constant dollars (bil.)	200	198	242	256	240
Arms as percent of total imports[8]	0.2	0.2	0.2	0.2	0.2
Arms as percent of total exports[8]	0.1	0.3	0.1	0.1	0.3

(Continued on next page.)

EDUCATION (cont.)

Literacy Rates (B)

	National Data	World Data
Adult literacy rate		
1980		
Male	97[1]	75
Female	95[1]	58
1995		
Male	99	81
Female	98	65

Libraries

National Libraries **1997**

Administrative Units 2

Service Points or Branches 4

Number of Volumes (000) 12,804

Registered Users (000) .786

Loans to Users (000) .1,312

Total Library Staff 609

Public Libraries **1997**

Administrative Units 84

Service Points or Branches 2,155

Number of Volumes (000) 41,474

Registered Users (000) 274,425

Loans to Users (000) 257,962

Total Library Staff 23,840

GOVERNMENT & LAW (cont.)

Political Parties

Parliament (Parlamento)	no. of seats
Senate	
Olive Tree	157
Freedom Alliance	116
Northern League-Padania	27
Communist Renewal	10
Regional lists	3
Social Movement-Tricolored Flames	1
Panella Reformers	1
Chamber of Deputies	
Olive Tree	284
Freedom Alliance	246
Northern League	59
Communist Renewal	35
Southern Tyrol People's Party	3
Autonomous List	2
Other	1

Senate elections were last held 21 April 1996 (next scheduled for April 2001); Chamber of Deputies were last held 21 April 1996 (next scheduled for April 2001).

Government Budgets (B)

Revenues . . . .$530 billion

Expenditures . . . .$522 billion

Data for 1999 est.

Crime

Crime volume (for 1998)

Crimes reported 2,425,748

Total persons convicted 631,665

Crimes per 100,000 population 4,214

Persons responsible for offenses

Total number suspects 813,124

Total number of female suspects . . . . .NA

Total number of juvenile suspects 23,255

LABOR FORCE

Total Labor Force (A)

23.193 million.

Labor Force by Occupation

Services 61%

Industry 32%

Agriculture 7%

Data for 1996.

Unemployment Rate

11.5% (1999 est.)

PRODUCTION SECTOR

Energy Production

Production . . . . .243.027 billion kWh

Production by source

Fossil fuel 80.22%

Hydro 17.30%

Nuclear 0%

Other 2.48%

Exports . . . . .900 million kWh

Data for 1998.

Energy Consumption

Consumption . . . . .266.705 billion kWh

Imports . . . . .41.590 billion kWh

Data for 1998.

Transportation

Highways:

Total: 654,676 km.

Paved: 654,676 km (including 6,957 km of expressways).

Unpaved: 0 km (1998 est.).

Waterways: 2,400 km for various types of commercial traffic, although of limited overall value.

Pipelines: crude oil 1,703 km; petroleum products 2,148 km; natural gas 19,400 km.

Merchant marine:

Total: 427 ships (1,000 GRT or over) totaling 6,971,578 GRT/9,635,770 DWT.

Ships by type: bulk 41, cargo 45, chemical tanker 73, combination ore/oil 2, container 20, liquified gas 38, livestock carrier 1, multi-functional large load carrier 1, passenger 6, petroleum tanker 87, roll-on/roll-off 58, short-sea passenger 26, specialized tanker 13, vehicle carrier 16 (1999 est.).

Airports: 136 (1999 est.).

Airports - with paved runways: 97.

Airports - with unpaved runways: 39.

Top Agriculture Products

Fruits, vegetables, grapes, potatoes, sugar beets, soybeans, grain, olives; beef, dairy products; fish.

Top Mining Products (B)

Mineral resources include: mercury, potash, marble, sulfur, dwindling crude oil reserves, coal.

MANUFACTURING SECTOR

GDP & Manufacturing Summary (A)

	1980	1985	1990	1995
GDP ($-1990 bil.)[1]	880	943	1,095	1,163
Per capita ($-1990)[1]	15,588	16,610	19,205	20,324
Manufacturing share (%) (current prices)[1]	28.1	24.5	22.7	21.1[e]
Manufacturing				
Value added ($-1990 mil.)[1]	191,859	202,663	245,232	267,456
Industrial production index	90	85	100	101
Value added ($ mil.)	97,032	64,726	144,733	156,300[e]
Gross output ($ mil.)	250,912	212,913	478,032	553,812
Employment (000)	3,333	2,875	2,757	2,830[e]
Profitability (% of gross output)				
Intermediate input (%)	61	70	70	72[e]
Wages and salaries inc. supplements (%)	21[e]	18[e]	27[e]	18[e]
Gross operating surplus	18[e]	12[e]	4[e]	10[e]
Productivity ($)				
Gross output per worker	74,433	73,115	170,315	191,448[e]
Value added per worker	28,784	22,227	51,566	54,143[e]
Average wage (inc. supplements)	15,647[e]	13,630[e]	46,298[e]	35,051[e]
Value added ($ mil.)				
Food products	6,362	3,618	9,599	11,291[e]
Beverages	1,672	1,354	2,015	2,297[e]
Tobacco products	307	224	556	747[e]
Textiles	6,716	5,062	10,327	10,423[e]
Wearing apparel	3,197	2,322	4,876	6,120[e]
Leather and fur products	718	560	1,234	1,764[e]
Footwear	1,495	1,260	2,231	2,912[e]
Wood and wood products	1,318	786	1,616	1,986[e]
Furniture and fixtures	1,936	1,257	2,900	3,812[e]
Paper and paper products	2,260	1,661	3,878	4,236[e]
Printing and publishing	3,017	2,271	6,171	5,358[e]
Industrial chemicals	6,364[e]	4,217[e]	5,906	5,446[e]
Other chemical products	4,058[e]	2,473[e]	3,974	9,938[e]
Petroleum refineries	1,095[e]	899[e]	1,718	3,086[e]
Misc. petroleum and coal products	238[e]	208[e]	406	804[e]
Rubber products	1,832	1,107	2,254	2,630[e]
Plastic products	1,465	1,729	4,799	4,570[e]
Pottery, china and earthenware	1,445[e]	848[e]	2,860	731[e]

(Continued on next page.)

GDP & Manufacturing Summary (A) (Cont.)

	1980	1985	1990	1995
Glass and glass products	1,093[e]	662[e]	1,673	1,666[e]
Other non-metal mineral products	4,143[e]	2,338[e]	4,299	6,572[e]
Iron and steel	8,354	3,846	8,117	5,720[e]
Non-ferrous metals	1,315	875	1,788	2,012[e]
Metal products	5,687	3,405	8,014	11,131[e]
Non-electrical machinery	9,326	8,914	20,330	21,607[e]
Electrical machinery	8,435	5,813	14,990	12,601[e]
Transport equipment	10,280	6,172	14,550	11,798[e]
Prof. and scientific equipment	2,032	550	1,761	3,406[e]
Other manufacturing	871	297	1,890	1,626[e]

COMMUNICATIONS

Daily Newspapers

	National Data	World Data for Comparison
Daily Newspapers		
Number of Dailies	78	8,391
Total Circulation (000)	5,960	548,000
Circulation per 1,000 inhabitants	104	96

Telecommunications

Telephones - main lines in use: 25 million (1998).

Telephones - mobile cellular: 17.7 million (1998).

Telephone system: modern, well-developed, fast; fully automated telephone, telex, and data services.

Domestic: high-capacity cable and microwave radio relay trunks.

International: satellite earth stations - 3 Intelsat (with a total of 5 antennas - 3 for Atlantic Ocean and 2 for Indian Ocean), 1 Inmarsat (Atlantic Ocean region), and NA Eutelsat; 21 submarine cables.

Radio broadcast stations: AM about 100, FM about 4,600, shortwave 9 (1998).

Radios: 50.5 million (1997).

Television broadcast stations: 6,317 (of which only 117 have 2 kW or more of transmitter power) (1997).

Televisions: 30.3 million (1997).

Internet Service Providers (ISPs): 219 (1999).

FINANCE, ECONOMICS, & TRADE

Economic Indicators

National product: GDP—purchasing power parity—$1.212 trillion (1999 est.).

National product real growth rate: 1.3% (1999 est.).

National product per capita: $21,400 (1999 est.).

Inflation rate—consumer price index: 1.7% (1999 est.).

Exchange Rates

Exchange rates:

Euros per US$1

January 2000 . . . . .0.9867

1999 . . . . .0.9386

Italian lire (Lit) per US$1

January 1999 . . . . .1,688.7000

1998 . . . . .1,736.2000

(Continued on next page.)

Balance of Payments

	1994	1995	1996	1997	1998
Exports of goods (f.o.b.)	191,421	233,998	252,039	240,404	242,572
Imports of goods (f.o.b.)	−159,854	−195,269	−197,921	−200,527	−206,941
Trade balance	31,568	38,729	54,118	39,878	35,631
Services - debits	−48,238	−55,050	−57,605	−59,227	−63,379
Services - credits	53,681	61,620	65,660	66,991	67,549
Private transfers (net)	6,478	7,969	7,120	6,147	5,847
Government transfers (net)	−7,179	−5,356	−7,566	−3,399	−6,385
Overall balance	13,209	25,076	39,999	32,403	19,998

Exchange Rates (cont.)

1997	1,703.1000
1996	1,542.9000
1995	1,628.9000

On 1 January 1999, the EU introduced a common currency that is now being used for non-cash transactions in some member countries at a fixed rate of 1,936.27 lire per euro; the euro will replace the local currency in consenting countries for all transactions in 2002.

Top Import Origins

$206.9 billion (f.o.b., 1998)

Origins (1998)

EU	61.00%
Germany	18.80%
France	13.12%
United Kingdom	6.47%
Netherlands	6.20%
Belgium-Luxembourg	4.70%
United States	5.10%

Top Export Destinations

$242.6 billion (f.o.b., 1998)

Destinations (1998)

EU	56.0%
Germany	16.5%
France	12.7%
United Kingdom	7.2%
Spain	5.8%
Netherlands	2.9%
United States	8.5%

Foreign Aid

Donor: ODA, $1.3 billion (1997).

Import/Export Commodities

Import Commodities	Export Commodities
Engineering products	Engineering products
Chemicals	Textiles and clothing
Transport equipment	Production machinery
Energy products	Motor vehicles
Minerals and nonferrous metals	Transport equipment
Textiles and clothing	Chemicals
Food, beverages and tobacco	Food, beverages and tobacco
	Minerals and nonferrous metals

JAMAICA

CAPITAL: Kingston.

FLAG: Two diagonal yellow gold bars forming a saltire divide the flag into four triangular panels. The two side panels are black, and the top and bottom panels are green.

ANTHEM: First line, "Eternal father, bless our land . . . "

MONETARY UNIT: The Jamaican dollar (J$) of 100 cents was introduced on 8 September 1969. There are coins of 1, 5, 10, and 25 cents, and 1 dollar, and notes of 2, 5, 10, 20, 50, and 100 dollars. J$1 = US$0.02865 (or US$1 = J$34.909).

WEIGHTS AND MEASURES: Both metric and imperial weights and measures are used.

HOLIDAYS: New Year's Day, 1 January; Labor Day, 23 May; Independence Day, 1st Monday in August; National Heroes' Day, 3rd Monday in October; Christmas, 25 December; Boxing Day, 26 December. Movable religious holidays include Ash Wednesday, Good Friday, and Easter Monday.

TIME: 7 AM = noon GMT.

LOCATION AND SIZE: Jamaica is an island in the Caribbean Sea situated about 160 kilometers (90 miles) south of Cuba. It has a total area of 10,990 square kilometers (4,243 square miles), slightly smaller than the state of Connecticut. The total coastline is 1,022 kilometers (634 miles).

Jamaica's capital city, Kingston, is located on the country's southeastern coast.

CLIMATE: The climate ranges from tropical at sea level to temperate in the uplands; there is relatively little seasonal variation in temperature. The average annual temperature in the coastal lowlands is 27°C (81°F); for the Blue Mountains, 13°C (55°F). The island has an average annual rainfall of 198 centimeters (78 inches), with wide variations during the year between the north and south coasts. The rainy seasons are May to June and September to November.

INTRODUCTORY SURVEY

RECENT HISTORY

In 1944 Jamaica was granted self-government by England and had its first election. Jamaica became an independent state on August 6, 1962, with dominion status in the Commonwealth of Nations. The Jamaica Labour Party (JLP) became the ruling party, and its leader, Sir Alexander Bustamante, became the nation's first prime minister.

The JLP held power through the 1960s. In February 1972 the rival People's National Party (PNP) gained a majority in Parliament, and Michael Manley headed a new democratic socialist government. Manley established friendly relations with Cuba, which the United States criticized.

Deteriorating economic conditions led to violence in Kingston and elsewhere during the mid-1970s, discouraging tourism. By 1976 Jamaica was faced with declining exports and an unemployment rate estimated at 30 percent-40 percent. Tourism suffered another blow in January 1979 with three days of rioting in Kingston at the height of the tourist season.

Manley called for elections in the fall of 1980. The opposition JLP won a landslide victory, and Edward Seaga became prime minister and minister of finance. He announced a conservative economic program that brought an immediate harvest of aid from the United States and the International Monetary Fund (IMF). In October 1981 Jamaica broke off diplomatic relations with Cuba, and two years later it participated in the U.S.-led invasion of Grenada.

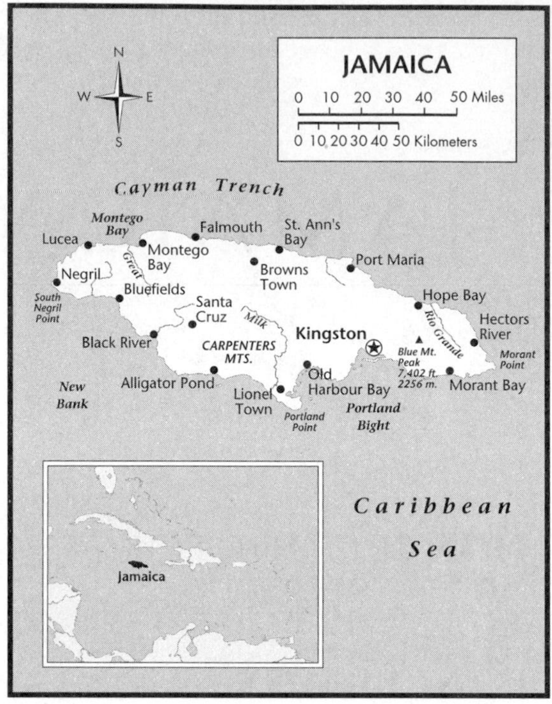

The conservative JLP under Seaga remained in power through the 1980s, but its support eroded as it carried out unpopular economic policies mandated by the IMF.

Criticizing the decline in social services under Seaga and promising to attract foreign investment, Manley and the PNP were returned to office in the 1989 elections. Manley reversed many of Seaga's policies, but by 1992 inflation was on the rise and the economy slowed. Unemployment hovered around 20 percent.

Manley retired in 1992 leaving the government to Percival J. Patterson who moved politically further to the right, encouraging more reforms.

Patterson encouraged more market-oriented reforms. Violence erupted during the campaigning of the 1995 elections, and political violence resurged again in 1996. Patterson was reelected in 1997. However Patterson and the PNP presided over an increasingly troubled country with continued economic contraction and an escalating crime wave. In the first half of 1999 alone, an estimated 500 Jamaicans had been killed n gang-related violence.

GOVERNMENT

The 1962 constitution provides a constitutional parliamentary democracy. The chief of state is the British monarch who is represented on the island by a governor general. The head of government is the prime minister. The governor general appoints both the prime minister and deputy prime minister. The governor general on the advice of the prime minister appoints the cabinet.

The bicameral parliament consists of a 21-member Senate and a 60-seat House of Representatives. The governor general appoints members of the Senate on the recommendations of the prime minister and the opposition leader. The ruling party has thirteen seats and eight are reserved for the opposition. The House members are elected by popular vote to serve five-year terms. Suffrage is universal at age eighteen.

Judiciary

Cases may be heard first before a lay magistrate (justice of the peace), a magistrate, or a judge in the Supreme Court, according to the seriousness of the offense or the amount of property involved. The Supreme Court also hears appeals. Final appeal rests with the seven-member Court of Appeals.

Political Parties

Two political parties dominate Jamaican politics. The Jamaica Labour Party (JLP), the more conservative of the two parties, held a parliamentary majority during the first ten years of independence, and again from 1980-89 under Edward Seaga. Seaga remains opposition leader.

The People's National Party (PNP), which was returned to power in 1989 under Norman W. Manley, its founder, holds to a moderate socialist program. Percival J. Patterson succeeded Manley on his retirement in 1992. Both the JLP and PNP stand for a broad program of social reform and welfare, and for economic development with the participation of foreign investment.

Bruce Golding, former leader of the JLP, formed a third political party, the National Democratic Movement (NDM), in October 1995. Tensions between the NDM and the JLP have resulted in ten political murders.

DEFENSE

The Jamaica Defense Force includes Ground Forces, Coast Guard, and Air Wing and in 2000 numbered 3,780 personnel, including 950 reserves. Jamaica also has a Jamaica constabulary force. In 1997-98, Jamaica spent $47.9 million on defense.

ECONOMIC AFFAIRS

The structure of the Jamaican economy has undergone major changes since 1945, when it was primarily dependent on tropical agricultural products. The island has since become one of the world's largest producers of bauxite. It also has developed as a major tourist center for North Americans.

Economic reforms of elimination of most price controls, streamlined tax schedules, and privatized government enterprises helped to slow inflation and stabilize the exchange rate. However contraction of the economic output impacted adversely on the employment situation, especially in the garment industry where 25 percent of employment in the industry was lost. The 1996-1999 GDP showed negative growth. Persistent problems include high interest rates, weak financial condition of businesses and of the financial sector resulting in the necessity of government bailouts, problematic exchange rate, widening trade deficit, and increased foreign competition. A mounting crime rate in 1999 was negatively affecting tourism.

Public Finance

The U.S. CIA estimated that in 1998-1999 government revenues totaled approximately $2.27 billion and expenditures $3.66 billion, including capital expenditures of $1.265 billion. External debt totaled $3.8 billion by 1998 estimates.

Income

In 1999 Jamaica's gross domestic product (GDP) was estimated at $8.8 billion, or about $3,350 per capita. The estimated 1999 real growth rate of the GDP was a decline of 0.5 percent and inflation was 9.4 percent. The 1997 estimated GDP contribution by sector was agriculture 7.4 percent, industry 42.1 percent, and services 50.5 percent.

Industry

The major industries in Jamaica are the production of bauxite and aluminum and tourism. Other industries include textiles and clothing, food processing, light manufacturing, rum, cement, metal, paper, and chemical products.

Banking and Finance

The Bank of Jamaica, the central bank, acts as the government's banker and is authorized to act as agent for the government in the management of the public debt. It also issues and redeems currency, administers Jamaica's external reserves, oversees private banks, and influences the volume and conditions of the supply of credit. In 1999 financial institutions included six commercial banks, thirteen merchant banks, three development banks, and sixty-seven credit unions.

The extent of the drain upon public finances caused by the precarious state of the financial sector became clear in mid-February 1997, when it was reported that net advances by the Bank of Jamaica to financial institutions had risen dramatically. Century National Bank, which was taken over by the government in July 1996, is still dependent upon the government to solve its liquidity problem as are several other financial institutions. In 1997 the government established the Financial Sector Adjustment Company (FINSAC) to rescue the ailing financial sector.

In September 1968 the Jamaican Stock Exchange was incorporated. Jamaica's security market merged with the stock markets in Barbados and Trinidad and Tobago in 1989.

Economic Development

Key sectors in this island economy are bauxite (aluminum and bauxite account for more than half of exports) and tourism. Since assuming office in 1992 Prime Minister Patterson has consolidated the market-oriented reforms initiated by his predecessor, Michael Manley, to make Jamaica a regional leader in economic reform. Patterson has eliminated most price controls, streamlined tax schedules, and privatized government enterprises. Tight monetary and fiscal policies under an IMF program have helped slow inflation and stabilize the exchange rate, but, as a result, economic growth has slowed down and unemployment remains high. Continued progress will depend on increased investment in the productive sectors, maintaining a competitive exchange rate, and stabilizing the labor environment and the financial sector with proper fiscal and monetary policies.

SOCIAL WELFARE

Jamaica has pioneered in social welfare in the West Indies since 1938. Government assistance is provided to those in need, and rehabilitation grants and family allowances are made. A National Insurance Scheme (NIS) came into effect in April 1966, providing benefits in the form of old-age and disability health and maternity coverage, pensions, workers' compensation, widows' and widowers' pensions, and grants.

Cultural traditions, economic discrimination, and workplace sexual harassment have prevented women from achieving full equality.

Crime is a serious social problem, with 900 reported homicides in 1996.

Healthcare

The central government provides most medical services in Jamaica through the Ministry of Health. In 1995 85 percent of the population had access to health care services. In the mid-1990s the government operated 364 primary health centers and twenty-three public hospitals. In addition there were nine small private hospitals. There were fourteen doctors per 10,000 people.

The government conducts a broad public health program, involving epidemic control, health education, industrial health protection, and campaigns against tuberculosis, venereal diseases, yaws, and malaria. Tuberculosis, hookworm, and venereal diseases remain the most prevalent diseases. Life expectancy in 2000 averaged seventy-five years.

Housing

Although middle- and upper-income housing is comparable to that in neighboring areas of North America, facilities for low-income groups are poor by any standard. The problem has been aggravated by constant migration from the rural areas to the cities, causing the growth of urban slums. Most new urban housing is built of cinder block and steel on the edges of cities. Rural housing is primarily built of wood and roofed with zinc sheeting. Squatter settlements surround the major cities of Jamaica.

EDUCATION

In 2000 Jamaica's estimated illiteracy rate was 13.3 percent. Education is compulsory for six years of primary education.

The University of the West Indies, founded in 1948, serves all British Commonwealth Caribbean territories. At the university and higher-level institutions, there were 8,434 students enrolled in 1997.

2000 KEY EVENTS TIMELINE

June

- Major aluminum companies Alcoa and Alcan suspend talks on US$500 million in expansion projects for the country's aluminum industry because of low productivity and refining capacity. Kaiser's Gramercy bauxite refinery in Louisiana, which bought a large portion of Jamaica's bauxite, is still closed due to a fire last year.
- Russia and Jamaica show interest in bilateral trade agreements, and Russia orders a shipment of aluminum.

July

- Prime Minister Percival Patterson holds peace talks from July 14–18 on the border conflict between Guyana and Surinam in Kingston. The countries fail to reach a settlement, but progress is reportedly made.

November

- Jamaican narcotics police make the largest drug bust in history on November 16, when they seize 782 kilograms of cocaine, worth approximately $5 million.

ANALYSIS OF EVENTS: 2000

BUSINESS AND THE ECONOMY

Following several consecutive years of recession, Jamaica's economy was considered one of the weakest in the Western Hemisphere. It had been a decade since strong growth was experienced. From 1990 until 1996 the economy had been flat; it had contracted every year since then. Interest rates were soaring, and the cost of imports was more than double the revenue from exports. Unemployment exceeded 18 percent and was further exacerbated by job cuts in the postal service and private plant closings, including local facilities operated by U.S.-based SaraLee/Hanes (clothing) and Cifuentes y Cia (cigars). Government economic policy, still monitored by the International Monetary Fund (IMF), called for cutting the fiscal deficit and lowering public-sector debt over the coming two years.

The major aluminum firms Alcoa and Alcan, both involved in major mergers, suspended plans to expand their facilities in Jamaica, possibly costing the country as much as $500 million in investment capital.

Tourism continued to thrive, however, with over one million visitors annually and a variety of upscale facilities, including all-inclusive resorts where a flat fee covered room, board, and a range of vacation activities. In October tourist industry heads from around the world gathered at two luxury hotels in Montego Bay for the World Travel Awards. The ceremony was broadcast on CNN.

GOVERNMENT AND POLITICS

Although Jamaica was in a state of crisis due to its faltering economy and an unprecedented crime wave, its government remained stable and democratic. One factor contributing to stability, if not necessarily to effective government, was the lack of significant ideological differences between Jamaica's two major parties, which had adopted very similar approaches to the country's economic problems. However, Prime Minister Percival J. Patterson, who had been in power since 1992, came under criticism for failing to provide the leadership necessary to pull the country out of the financial doldrums, a task made more difficult by the strength of entrenched interest groups, including labor unions and the civil service, that opposed economic liberalization. Another problem for the government was massive public-sector debt.

Contrary to opinions expressed by most observers, Prime Minister Patterson asserted that Jamaica was ready to pull out of the previous four years of stagnation. In July Patterson hosted peace talks in Kingston between Guyana and Suriname aimed at resolving a border dispute between the two countries. Progress was reported, although no final resolution was reached.

CULTURE AND SOCIETY

A shrinking economy and rampant crime created a sense of crisis among many Jamaicans. One survey found that more than half of all Jamaicans would move to the United States if they had a chance. With over 800 people murdered in 1999 out of a population of 2.6 million, Jamaica had one of the highest murder rates in the world. Between January and the latter part of November, 730 people had been killed, mostly in or around the capital city of Kingston.

Together with the rising rate of violent crime, increasing drug traffic through Jamaica added a further challenge to maintaining law and order on the island, as transshipments of cocaine from Colombia and other Latin American countries multiplied. The increased level of violence also threatened Jamaica's lucrative tourist industry.

The most high-profile criminal investigation of 2000 was probably that centering around the disappearance of twenty-nine-year-old Claudia Kirschhoch, an American travel writer who had traveled to Jamaica as part of a press junket and was last seen at the Beaches resort in late May. By fall extensive investigation by Jamaican authorities as well as by Kirshhoch's family had failed to solve the case, and tensions had been aroused in several quarters. Suggestion of irresponsible behavior by the missing woman had brought heated responses by her family and employer, and the operators of the resort, Sandals Resorts International, had countered allegations of a cover-up made on a U.S. newsmagazine program aired by ABC Broadcasting in early September.

DIRECTORY

CENTRAL GOVERNMENT

Head of State

Monarch
Elizabeth II, Queen of England

Governor-General
Howard Felix Cooke

Prime Minister
P.J. Patterson, Office of the Prime Minister, Jamaica House, Kingston 6, Jamaica
PHONE: +(876) 9279941
FAX: +(876) 9290005

Ministers

Minister without Portfolio
Maxine Henry-Wilson, Office of Minister without Portfolio, Jamaica House, Kingston 6, Jamaica
PHONE: +(876) 9279941
FAX: +(876) 9290005

Minister of State
Derrick Kellier, Ministry of State, Jamaica House, Kingston 6, Jamaica
PHONE: +(876) 9279941
FAX: +(876) 9290005

Minister of Tourism & Sports
Portia Simpson-Miller, Ministry of Tourism & Sports, 64 Knutsford Boulevard, Kingston 5, Jamaica
PHONE: +(876) 9204956
FAX: +(876) 9204944
E-MAIL: Opmt@cwjamaica.com

Minister of Foreign Affairs
Paul Robertson, Ministry of Foreign Affairs, 21 Dominica Drive, Kingston 5, Jamaica
PHONE: +(876) 9264220
FAX: +(876) 9295112
E-MAIL: Mfaftjam@cwjamaica.com

Minister of Finance and Planning
Omar Davies, Ministry of Finance and Planning, 30 National Heroes Circle, Kingston 4, Jamaica
PHONE: +(876) 9228600
FAX: +(876) 9228804
E-MAIL: Mfaftjam@cwjamaica.com

Minister of Labor, Social Security and Sports
Donald Buchanan, Ministry of Labor, Social Security and Sports, 14 National Heroes Circle, Kingston 4, Jamaica
PHONE: +(876) 9228000; 9229500; 9671900
FAX: +(876) 9226902
E-MAIL: Mfaftjam@cwjamaica.com

Minister of Mining and Energy
Robert Pickersgill, Ministry of Mining and Energy, 36 Trafaglar Road, Kingston 10, Jamaica
PHONE: +(876) 9269170
FAX: +(876) 9682082
E-MAIL: Hmme@cwjamaica.com

Minister of Industry and Investment
Phillip Paulwell, Ministry of Industry and Investment, 36 Trafaglar Road, Kingston 10, Jamaica
PHONE: +(876) 9298990
FAX: +(876) 9298196
E-MAIL: Gojmii@infochan.com

Minister of Transportation and Works
Peter Phillips, Ministry of Transportation and Works, 140 Maxfield Avenue, Kingston 10, Jamaica
PHONE: +(876) 9263110
FAX: +(876) 9292996

Minister of National Security and Justice
K.D. Knight, Ministry of National Security and Justice, 12 Ocean Bouvelard, Kingston, Jamaica
PHONE: +(876) 9220080
FAX: +(876) 9226950
E-MAIL: inform@infochan,com

Minister of Land & the Environment
Seymour Mullings, Ministry of Environment and Housing, 2 Hagley Park Road, Kingston 10, Jamaica
PHONE: +(876) 9261590; 9267008
FAX: +(876) 9262591
E-MAIL: Mehsys@hotmail.com

Minister of Education and Housing
Burchell Whiteman, Ministry of Education and Housing, 2 National Heroes Circle, Kingston 4, Jamaica
PHONE: +(876) 9221400
FAX: +(876) 9671837

Minister of Agriculture
Roger Clarke, Ministry of Agriculture, Hope Gardens, Kingston 6, Jamaica
PHONE: +(876) 9271731
FAX: +(876) 9271904

Minister of Health
John Junor, Ministry of Health, Oceana Hotel Complex, 2 King St., Kingston, Jamaica
PHONE: +(876) 9671092
FAX: +(876) 9271904

Minister of Local Government, Youth and Community Development
Arnold Bertram, Ministry of Local Government, Youth and Community Development, 85 Hagley Park, Kingston 10, Jamaica
PHONE: +(876) 7540994
FAX: +(876) 9600725

Minister of Water
Karl Blythe, Ministry of Water, 7th floor, Island Life Building, 6 St. Lucia Avenue, Kingston 5, Jamaica
PHONE: +(876) 7540973
FAX: +(876) 7540975
E-MAIL: prumow@cwjamaica.com

Minister of Commerce and Technology
Phillip Paulwell, Ministry of Commerce and Technology
PHONE: +(876) 9298990
FAX: +(876) 9601623
E-MAIL: prumow@cwjamaica.com

POLITICAL ORGANIZATIONS

People's National Party (PNP)

89 Old Hope Road, Kingston 6, Jamaica
PHONE: +(876) 9277805
FAX: +(876) 9274389
TITLE: Leader
NAME: P.J. Patterson

Jamaica Labour Party (JLP)

20 Belmont Road, Kingston 5, Jamaica
PHONE: +(876) 9290987
FAX: +(876) 9291276

TITLE: Leader
NAME: Edward Seaga

National Democratic Movement (NDM)

15A Old Hope Road, Kingston 5, Jamaica
PHONE: +(876) 9207848
FAX: +(876) 9207846
TITLE: Leader
NAME: Bruce Golding

Natural Law Party

c/o 21st Century Integrated Medical Centre Shop Of. 3, Overton Plaza, 49 Union Street, Montego Bay, Jamaica
PHONE: +(876) 9719107
FAX: +(876) 9719109
TITLE: Leader
NAME: Leo Campbell
E-MAIL: nlp@cwjamaica.com

DIPLOMATIC REPRESENTATION

Embassies in Jamaica

Canada
30-36 Knutsford Boulevard, Kingston 5, Jamaica
PHONE: +(876) 9261500
FAX: +(876) 9261702
E-MAIL: carol.hart@kngno1.x400.gc.ca
TITLE: High Commissioner
NAME: Gavin Stewart

China
8 Sea View Avenue, Kingston 10, Jamaica
PHONE: +(876) 9273871
FAX: +(876) 9276920
TITLE: Ambassador
NAME: Li Shangsheng

Germany
10 Waterloo Road, PO Box 444, Kingston 10, Jamaica
PHONE: +(876) 9266728
FAX: +(876) 9298282
TITLE: Ambassador
NAME: Wilfried Bolewski

India
4 Retreat Avenue, Kingston 6, Jamaica
PHONE: +(876) 9273114
FAX: +(876) 9782801
E-MAIL: hicomind@toj.com
TITLE: High Commissioner
NAME: Vidya Bhushan Soni

Japan
3rd Floor, 32 Trafalgar Road, Kingston 10, Jamaica
PHONE: +(876) 9273114
FAX: +(876) 9782801
TITLE: Ambassador
NAME: Motoi Okubo

Nigeria
5 Waterloo Road, Kingston 10, Jamaica
PHONE: +(876) 9266400
FAX: +(876) 9687371
TITLE: Acting High Commissioner
NAME: Baba Gana Zanna

Russia
22 Norbrook Drive, Kingston 8, Jamaica
PHONE: +(876) 9241048
FAX: +(876) 9258290
TITLE: Ambassador
NAME: Igor Iakovlev

United Kingdom
28 Trafalgar Road, Kingston 10, Jamaica
PHONE: +(876) 9269050
FAX: +(876) 9297869
E-MAIL: emjam@sysnet.net
TITLE: High Commissioner
NAME: A. Richard Thomas

United States
Mutual Life Building, 3rd Floor, 2 Oxford Road, Kingston 5, Jamaica
PHONE: +(876) 9294850
FAX: +(876) 9356000

JUDICIAL SYSTEM

Supreme Court of Jamaica

Public Building E, 134 Tower Street, Kingston, Jamaica
PHONE: +(876) 9228300; 9225606; 9674859
E-MAIL: webmaster@sc.gov.jm

Court of Appeal

BROADCAST MEDIA

Island Broadcasting Services

19 Caledonia Road, Mandeville, Jamaica
BROADCASTS: 24 hours/day

Jamaica Broadcasting Corporation

Box 100, Kingston 10, Jamaica
PHONE: +(876) 9265620; 9265629
FAX: +(876) 9291029
TITLE: Directorate General

CONTACT: Claude Robinson
BROADCASTS: 24 hours/day
TYPE: Government, Commercial

Radio Jamaica Limited (RJR)

PO Box 23, Kingston 5, Jamaica
PHONE: +(876) 9261100
FAX: +(876) 9297467
E-MAIL: rjrnews@toj.com
WEBSITE: http://www.rjr.com.jm/
TITLE: Chairman and Managing Director
CONTACT: J. A. Lester Spaulding
TYPE: Commercial

CVM Jamaica

69 Constant Sprint Road, Kingston 10, Jamaica
PHONE: +(876) 9319400
FAX: +(876) 9319417
E-MAIL: manager@cvmtv.com
WEBSITE: http://www.cvmtv.com/
TITLE: General Manager
CONTACT: Angela Patterson

Jamaica Broadcasting Corporation

Box 100, Kingston 10, Jamaica
PHONE: +(876) 9265620; 9265629
FAX: +(876) 9291029
TITLE: Directorate General
CONTACT: Claude Robinson
CHANNEL: 7, 8, 9, 10, 11, 12, 13
TYPE: Commercial

TV Jamaica (TVJ)

5-9 South Odeon Avenue, Kingston 10, Jamaica
PHONE: +(876) 9265620
FAX: +(876) 9291029
E-MAIL: tvjadmin@cwjamaica.com
WEBSITE: http://www.radiojamaica.com/tvj/

The Jamaican Broadcasting Commission

Fifth Floor, Victoria Mutual Building, 53 Knutsford Boulevard, Kingston 5, Jamaica
E-MAIL: broadcomp@toj.com

COLLEGES AND UNIVERSITIES

University of Technology

237 Old Hope Road, Kingston 6, Jamaica
PHONE: +(876) 9271680
FAX: +(876) 9774388; 9271925
WEBSITE: http://www.utech.edu.jm/

University of the West Indies, Mona

Mona, Kingston 7, Jamaica
PHONE: +(876) 9272779; 9271661; 9358287; 9358313
FAX: +(876) 9272272
E-MAIL: admissns@uwimona.edu.jm
WEBSITE: http://isis.uwimona.edu.jm/

NEWSPAPERS AND MAGAZINES

Daily Gleaner/Sunday Gleaner

PO Box 40, Kingston, Jamaica
PHONE: +(876) 922 3400
FAX: +(876) 922 2058
E-MAIL: ginredtr@infochan.com
WEBSITE: http://www.jamaica-gleaner.com
TITLE: Editor
CONTACT: Wyvolyn Gager
CIRCULATION: 103,000

Jamaica Observer

2 Fagan Ave., Kingston 2, Jamaica
PHONE: +(876) 9317825
FAX: +(876) 9317838
E-MAIL: moore@jamaicaobserver.com
WEBSITE: http://www.jamaicaobserver.com
TITLE: Editor
CONTACT: Paget de Frertas
CIRCULATION: 45,000

The Star

PO Box 40, Kingston, Jamaica
PHONE: +(876) 9223400
FAX: +(876) 9226223
WEBSITE: http://www.jamaica-gleaner.com
CIRCULATION: 69,000

Airteam Circle

Airports Authority of Jamaica, 64 Knutsford Blvd., Kingston 5, Jamaica
TITLE: Editor
CONTACT: Trevor Spence
TYPE: Aviation

Cajanus

Caribbean Food and Nutrition Institute, U.W.I. Mona Campus, PO Box 140, Kingston 7, Jamaica
FAX: +(876) 9272657
TITLE: Editor
CONTACT: Clare Forrester
CIRCULATION: 2,028
TYPE: Nutrition

Caribbean Quarterly

University of the West Indies, Box 42, Kingston 7, Jamaica
TITLE: Editor
CONTACT: Rex Nettleford
CIRCULATION: 1,500
TYPE: Scholarly journal of political science

Farmer

Jamaica Agricultural Society, North Parade, Kingston, Jamaica
TYPE: Agriculture and animal husbandry

Investor's Choice

Financial & Economic Resources Ltd., 12 Merrick Ave., Kingston 10, Jamaica
TITLE: Editor
CONTACT: John Jackson
CIRCULATION: 10,000
TYPE: Investments and securities

Jamaica Beat

Newshound Publication, PO Box 393, Kingston 10, Jamaica
TITLE: Editor
CONTACT: Eric McNish

Jamaica Vacation Guide

Creative Communications Inc., Ltd., PO Box 105, Kingston 10, Jamaica
FAX: +(876) 9775448
E-MAIL: creativecom@colis.com
TITLE: Editor
CONTACT: Odette Dixon Neath
TYPE: Travel

Jamaican Journal of Science and Technology

Scientific Research Council, PO Box 350, Kingston 6, Jamaica
FAX: +(876) 9275347
E-MAIL: infosrc@toj.com
TITLE: Editor
CONTACT: Tara P. Dasgupta
CIRCULATION: 2,500
TYPE: Scholarly publication of science and technology, illustrated

Real Estate Jamaica

Financial & Economic Resources Ltd., 12 Merrick Ave., Kingston 10, Jamaica
TITLE: Editor
CONTACT: John Jackson
TYPE: Real estate trade publication

Skywritings

Creative Communications Inc., Ltd., PO Box 105, Kingston 10, Jamaica
FAX: +(876) 9775448
E-MAIL: creativecom@colis.com
CONTACT: Odette Dixon Neath
CIRCULATION: 250,000
TYPE: Travel

West Indian Law Journal

Council of Legal Education, PO Box 231, Mona, Kingston, Jamaica
TITLE: Editor
CONTACT: H. Aubrey Fraser
CIRCULATION: 1,000
TYPE: Law

West Indian Medical Journal

University of the West Indies, Mona Campus, Kingston 7, Jamaica
FAX: +(876) 9272556
TITLE: Editor
CONTACT: Dr. W.N. Gibbs
CIRCULATION: 2,000
TYPE: Scholarly medical journal

PUBLISHERS

American Chamber of Commerce of Jamaica

77 Knutsford Blvd., Kingston 5, Jamaica
PHONE: +(876) 9297866
FAX: +(876) 9298597
TITLE: Chief Executive Officer
CONTACT: Dr. Ofe S. Dudley
SUBJECTS: Environmental Studies, Management, Marketing

Carlong Publishers (Caribbean) Ltd.

33 2nd St., PO Box 489, Newport West, Kingston 10, Jamaica
PHONE: +(876) 9237019; 9237008
FAX: +(876) 9237003
TITLE: Man. Director
CONTACT: Shirley Carby
SUBJECTS: Drama, Theater, Foreign Countries, Geography, Geology, History, Human Relations, Mathematics, Science (General), Social Sciences

Institute of Jamaica Publications

2a Suthermere Rd., Kingston 10, Jamaica
PHONE: +(876) 9265683; 9294786; 9294785
FAX: +(876) 926817
TITLE: Man. Director
CONTACT: Patricia V. Stevens
SUBJECTS: Ethnicity, Fiction, History, Natural History, Nonfiction (General), Science (General), Social Sciences

Jamaica Publishing House Ltd.

97 Church St., Kingston, Jamaica
PHONE: +(876) 9221385
FAX: +(876) 9223257
TITLE: Manager
CONTACT: Elaine R. Stennett
SUBJECTS: Biography, Education, Geography, Geology, History, House & Home, Language Arts, Linguistics, Literature, Mathematics, Social Sciences

Kingston Publishers Co.

7 Norman Rd., LOJ Complex, Bldg. 10, Kingston 5, Jamaica
PHONE: +(876) 9278899
FAX: +(876) 9285719
TITLE: Marketing Manager
CONTACT: Dawn Chambers
SUBJECTS: Cookery, Fiction, Music, Dance, Nonfiction (General), Travel

The Press - University of the West Indies

One A Aqueduct Flats, Mona, Kingston 7, Jamaica
PHONE: +(876) 9772659
FAX: +(876) 9772660
E-MAIL: salex@uwimona.edu.jm
TITLE: Director
CONTACT: Pansy Benn
SUBJECTS: Ethnicity, Government, Political Science, History

Randle Publishers Ltd.

206 Old Hope Rd., Kingston 6, Jamaica
PHONE: +(876) 9272085
FAX: +(876) 9270243
TITLE: International Rights
CONTACT: Ian Randle
SUBJECTS: Biography, Cookery, History, Sports, Athletics, Women's Studies

West Indies Publishing Ltd.

7-9 Norman Rd., Unit 33, Kingston 7, Jamaica
PHONE: +(876) 9289081
FAX: +(876) 9285269
TITLE: Man. Director
CONTACT: D. Andrew Rousseau
SUBJECTS: Cookery, Education, Fiction, Geography, Geology, History, Mathematics, Science (General)

RELIGIOUS ORGANIZATIONS

Catholic

Archdiocese of Kingston
Archbishop's Residence, 21 Hopefield Avenue, PO Box 43, Kingston 6, Jamaica
PHONE: +(876) 9279915; 9276282
WEBSITE: http://www.opus.co.tt/aec/kingston.htm
TITLE: Archbishop of Kingston in Jamaica
NAME: Most Rev. Edgerton R. Clarke

Catechetical Center
Golding Avenue, PO Box 198, Kingston 7, Jamaica
PHONE: +(876) 9772920
FAX: +(876)(876) 9772920
TITLE: SJ
NAME: Gerard McKeon

Diocese of Montego Bay
Bishop's Residence, PO Box 197, Montego Bay, St. James, Jamaica
PHONE: +(876) 9526678
FAX: +(876)(876) 9526679
E-MAIL: diosmbay@infochan.com
WEBSITE: http://www.opus.co.tt/aec/montego.htm
TITLE: Second Bishop of Montego Bay
NAME: Most Rev. Charles Dufour

Protestant

Kencot Seventh-Day Adventist Church
10-12 Osbourne Road, Kingston 10, Jamaica, West Indies
PHONE: +(876) 9292773; 062279
WEBSITE: http://www.tagnet.org/kencot/
TITLE: Pastor
NAME: Linton G. Williams

The Salvation Army
3 Waterloo Road, Kingston, 10, Jamaica
PHONE: +(876) 9296190; 9296191; 9296192
FAX: +(876)(876) 9297560
WEBSITE: http://www.salvationarmycarib.org

West Indies Union Conference of Seventh-Day Adventists
PO Box 22, 125 Manchester Road, Mandeville, Jamaica
PHONE: +(876) 9622910; 9622284
FAX: +(876)(876) 9623417
E-MAIL: wiunion@cwjamaica.com
WEBSITE: http://www.tagnet.org/wiunion/cpage.html

FURTHER READING

Articles

"President Patterson Comments on Guyana-Surinam Border Meeting." *BBC,* July 19, 2000.

"Majors Freeze Jamaican Bauxite Talks." *Financial Times,* June 2, 2000.

JAMAICA: STATISTICAL DATA

For sources and notes see "Sources of Statistics" at the front of each volume.

GEOGRAPHY

Geography

Area:

Total: 10,990 sq km

Land: 10,830 sq km.

Land boundaries: 0 km.

Coastline: 1,022 km.

Climate: tropical; hot, humid; temperate interior.

Terrain: mostly mountains, with narrow, discontinuous coastal plain.

Natural resources: bauxite, gypsum, limestone.

Land use:

Arable land: 14%

Permanent crops: 6%

Permanent pastures: 24%

Forests and woodland: 17%

Other: 39% (1993 est.).

HUMAN FACTORS

Demographics (A)

	1990	1995	1998	2000	2010	2020	2030	2040	2050
Population	2,463	2,569	2,624	2,653	2,851	3,127	3,353	3,481	3,505
Life expectancy - males	71.1	72.2	72.8	73.3	75.1	76.6	77.9	78.9	79.7
Life expectancy - females	74.6	76.0	76.7	77.3	79.5	81.4	82.9	84.1	85.1
Birth rate (per 1,000)	24.4	22.6	20.2	18.5	15.3	13.8	11.8	10.5	10.0
Death rate (per 1,000)	6.3	5.8	5.6	5.5	5.3	5.5	6.4	8.3	10.6
Women of reproductive age (15-49 yrs.)	633.3	679.2	706.1	724.3	802.4	828.6	813.4	778.1	719.9
Fertility rate	2.7	2.5	2.3	2.1	1.9	1.8	1.7	1.7	1.7

Except as noted, values for vital statistics are in thousands; life expectancy is in years.

Health Personnel

	National Data	World Data (wtd ave)
Total health expenditure as a percentage of GDP, 1990-1998[a]		
Public sector	2.3	2.5
Private sector	2.4	2.9
Total[b]	4.7	5.5
Health expenditure per capita in U.S. dollars, 1990-1998[a]		
Purchasing power parity	158	561
Total	116	483
Availability of health care facilities per 100,000 people		
Hospital beds 1990-1998[a]	210	330
Doctors 1992-1995[a]	57	122
Nurses 1992-1995[a]	69	248

Health Indicators

	National Data	World Data
Life expectancy at birth (years)		
1980	71	61
1998	75	67
Daily per capita supply of calories		
1970	2,538	2,358
1997	2,553	2,791
Daily per capital supply of protein		
1997 (grams)	63	74
Total fertility rate (births per woman)		
1980	3.7	3.7
1998	2.6	2.7
Population with access (%)		
To safe water (1990-96)	70	NA
To sanitation (1990-96)	74	NA
People living with (1997)		
Tuberculosis (cases per 100,000)	4.7	60.4
HIV/AIDS (% aged 15 - 49 years)	0.99	0.99

Infants and Malnutrition

	National Data	World Data (wtd ave)
Under 5 mortality rate (1989)	11	NA
% of infants with low birthweight (1992-98)[1]	10	17
Births attended by skilled health staff (% of total births 1996-98)	92	52
% fully immunized at 1 year of age (1995-98)[1]		
TB	90	82
DPT	88	77
Polio	88	77
Measles	88	74
Prevalence of child malnutrition (1992-98)[1] (based on weight for age, % of children under 5 years)	92	30

Ethnic Division

Black 90.9%
East Indian 1.3%
White 0.2%
Chinese 0.2%
Mixed 7.3%
Other 0.1%

Religion

Protestant 61.3%
Church of God 21.2%
Baptist 8.8%
Anglican 5.5%
Seventh-Day Adventist .9.0%
Pentecostal 7.6%
Methodist 2.7%
United Church 2.7%
Brethren 1.1%
Jehovah's Witness 1.6%
Moravian 1.1%
Roman Catholic 4.0%
Other, including some spiritual cults 34.7%

Major Languages

English, Creole.

EDUCATION

Public Education Expenditures

	1980	1997
Public expenditures on education as % of GNP	7.0	7.4
Expenditures per student as % of GNP per capita		
Primary	13.9	NA
Secondary	22.0	NA
Tertiary	202.9	NA

Teachers' compensation as % of total current education expenditures	65.6	54.5
Pupils per teacher at the primary level	NA	NA
Duration of primary education in years	NA	6
World data for comparison		
Public expenditures on education as % of GNP (mean)	3.9	4.8
Pupils per teacher at the primary level (wtd ave)	NA	33
Duration of primary education in years (mean)	NA	9

Educational Attainment (A)

Age group (1991) .25+
Population of this age group 970,086
Highest level attained (%)
No schooling .0
First level
Not completed 67.5
Completed NA
Entered second level 29.9
Entered post-secondary[10] 2.7

Literacy Rates (A)

In thousands and percent	1990	1995	2000	2010
Illiterate population (15+ yrs.)	271	254	248	221
Literacy rate - total adult pop. (%)	82.9	85.0	86.4	89.7
Literacy rate - males (%)	78.5	80.8	82.4	85.7
Literacy rate - females (%)	87.1	89.1	90.3	93.7

GOVERNMENT & LAW

Political Parties

Parliament	no. of seats
People's National Party (PNP)	50
Jamaica Labor Party (JLP)	10

Elections last held 18 December 1997 (next to be held by March 2002).

Government Budgets (B)

Revenues $2.270 billion
Expenditures $3.660 billion
Capital expenditures $1.265 billion

Data for FY98/99 est.

Crime

Crime volume (for 1998)
Crimes reported 47,763
Total persons convicted 38,210
Crimes per 100,000 population 1,871
Persons responsible for offenses
Total number suspects 38,327
Total number of female suspects NA
Total number of juvenile suspects NA

(Continued on next page.)

LABOR FORCE

Total Labor Force (A)

1.13 million (1998).

Labor Force by Occupation

Services 60%
Agriculture 21%
Industry 19%

Data for 1998.

Unemployment Rate

15.5% (1998)

PRODUCTION SECTOR

Energy Production

Production 6.386 billion kWh
Production by source
Fossil fuel 92.70%
Hydro 2.21%
Nuclear .0%
Other 5.09%
Exports .0 kWh

Data for 1998.

Energy Consumption

Consumption 5.939 billion kWh
Imports .0 kWh

Data for 1998.

Transportation

Highways:
Total: 18,700 km.
Paved: 13,100 km.
Unpaved: 5,600 km (1997 est.).
Pipelines: petroleum products 10 km.

Merchant marine:

Total: 1 ship (1,000 GRT or over) totaling 1,930 GRT/3,065 DWT.

Ships by type: petroleum tanker 1 (1999 est.).

Airports: 36 (1999 est.).

Airports - with paved runways: 11.

Airports - with unpaved runways: 25.

Top Agriculture Products

Sugarcane, bananas, coffee, citrus, potatoes, vegetables; poultry, goats, milk.

Top Mining Products (B)

Mineral resources include: bauxite, gypsum, limestone.

GOVERNMENT & LAW (cont.)

Military Affairs (A)

	1990	1992	1995	1996	1997
Military expenditures					
Current dollars (mil.)	55	50	35	31	53
1997 constant dollars (mil.)	64	56	37	31	53
Armed forces (000)	3	3	3	3	3
Gross national product (GNP)					
Current dollars (mil.)	4,690	5,170	5,850	6,080	6,040
1997 constant dollars (mil.)	5,500	5,730	6,060	6,180	6,040
Central government expenditures (CGE)					
1997 constant dollars (mil.)	1,590[e]	NA	1,540	1,750	2,200
People (mil.)	2.5	2.5	2.6	2.6	2.6
Military expenditure as % of GNP	1.2	1.0	0.6	0.5	0.9
World data on military expenditure as % of GNP	4.5	3.4	2.7	2.6	2.6
Military expenditure as % of CGE	4.0	NA	2.4	1.8	2.4
World data on military expenditure as % of CGE	17.0	12.5	10.5	10.3	10.2
Military expenditure per capita (1997 $)	26	22	14	12	20
World data on military expenditure per capita (1997 $)	242	173	146	143	145
Armed forces per 1,000 people (soldiers)	1.2	1.2	1.2	1.2	1.1
World data on armed forces per 1,000 people (soldiers)	5.3	4.5	4.1	3.9	3.8
GNP per capita (1997 $)	2,230	2,290	2,350	2,380	2,310
Arms imports[6]					
Current dollars (mil.)	10	10	10	10	5
1997 constant dollars (mil.)	12	11	10	10	5
Total imports[7]					
Current dollars (mil.)	1,859	1,668	2,757	2,927	3,026
1997 constant dollars (mil.)	2,177	1,849	2,855	2,976	3,026
Total exports[7]					
Current dollars (mil.)	1,135	1,102	1,414	1,379	1,352
1997 constant dollars (mil.)	1,329	1,222	1,464	1,402	1,352
Arms as percent of total imports[8]	0.5	0.6	0.4	0.3	0.2
Arms as percent of total exports[8]	0	0	0	0	0

MANUFACTURING SECTOR

GDP & Manufacturing Summary (A)

	1980	1985	1990	1995
GDP ($-1990 mil.)[1]	3,369	3,382	4,242	4,432
Per capita ($-1990)[1]	1,579	1,464	1,793	1,796
Manufacturing share (%) (current prices)[1]	16.1	19.3	18.2	NA
Manufacturing				
Value added ($-1990 mil.)[1]	619	658	824	739[e]
Industrial production index	137	111	100	107[e]
Value added ($ mil.)	441	363[e]	831	847[e]
Gross output ($ mil.)	1,661	1,498	2,549	3,512[e]
Employment (000)	44	54[e]	65	63[e]
Profitability (% of gross output)				
Intermediate input (%)	80	76[e]	74	76[e]
Wages and salaries inc. supplements (%)	11[e]	10[e]	10[e]	10[e]
Gross operating surplus	9[e]	14[e]	16[e]	14[e]
Productivity ($)				
Gross output per worker	48,137	27,761[e]	42,749	56,156[e]
Value added per worker	9,985[e]	6,737[e]	11,381	13,548[e]
Average wage (inc. supplements)	5,378[e]	2,783[e]	4,442[e]	5,510[e]
Value added ($ mil.)				
Food products	78	73[e]	182	223[e]
Beverages	63	43[e]	103	93[e]
Tobacco products	61	40[e]	56	50[e]
Textiles	3[e]	2[e]	4[e]	5[e]
Wearing apparel	15[e]	14[e]	29[e]	35[e]
Leather and fur products	2	2[e]	2	2[e]
Footwear	8	4[e]	7	6[e]
Wood and wood products	3	2[e]	5	2[e]
Furniture and fixtures	12	10[e]	19	15[e]
Paper and paper products	8[e]	8[e]	16[e]	15[e]
Printing and publishing	13[e]	12[e]	25[e]	23[e]
Industrial chemicals	4[e]	4[e]	11[e]	13[e]
Other chemical products	22[e]	25[e]	42[e]	48[e]
Petroleum refineries	55	50[e]	151	105[e]
Misc. petroleum and coal products	NA	NA	1[e]	2[e]
Rubber products	12[e]	4[e]	10[e]	15[e]
Plastic products	13[e]	8[e]	22[e]	28[e]
Pottery, china and earthenware	1[e]	2[e]	5[e]	7[e]
Glass and glass products	2[e]	3[e]	8[e]	10[e]
Other non-metal mineral products	8[e]	11[e]	29[e]	38[e]
Iron and steel	1[e]	2[e]	6[e]	6[e]
Metal products	10[e]	13[e]	28[e]	33[e]
Non-electrical machinery	11[e]	3[e]	6[e]	4[e]
Electrical machinery	7[e]	7[e]	17[e]	20[e]
Transport equipment	26[e]	19[e]	40[e]	47[e]
Other manufacturing	4	3[e]	6	4[e]

COMMUNICATIONS

Daily Newspapers

	National Data	World Data for Comparison
Daily Newspapers		
Number of Dailies	3	8,391
Total Circulation (000)	158	548,000
Circulation per 1,000 inhabitants	63	96

Telecommunications

Telephones - main lines in use: 292,000 (1995).

Telephones - mobile cellular: 45,178 (1995).

Telephone system: fully automatic domestic telephone network.

Domestic: NA

International: satellite earth stations - 2 Intelsat (Atlantic Ocean); 3 coaxial submarine cables.

Radio broadcast stations: AM 10, FM 13, shortwave 0 (1998).

Radios: 1.215 million (1997).

Television broadcast stations: 7 (1997).

Televisions: 460,000 (1997).

Internet Service Providers (ISPs): 6 (1999).

FINANCE, ECONOMICS, & TRADE

Economic Indicators

National product: GDP—purchasing power parity—$8.8 billion (1999 est.).

National product real growth rate: -0.5% (1999 est.).

National product per capita: $3,350 (1999 est.).

Inflation rate—consumer price index: 9.4% (1999 est.).

Exchange Rates

Exchange rates:

Jamaican dollars (J$) per US$1

- December 1999 . . . . .41.139
- 1999 . . . . .9.044
- 1998 . . . . .36.550
- 1997 . . . . .35.404
- 1996 . . . . .37.120
- 1995 . . . . .35.142

Balance of Payments

	1994	1995	1996	1997	1998
Exports of goods (f.o.b.)	1,548	1,796	1,721	1,700	1,613
Imports of goods (f.o.b.)	−2,099	−2,625	−2,715	−2,833	−2,710
Trade balance	−551	−829	−994	−1,132	−1,097
Services - debits	−961	−1,094	−1,141	−1,226	−1,260
Services - credits	1,497	1,613	1,625	1,715	1,770
Private transfers (net)	480	613	652	661	682
Government transfers (net)	19	52	50	40	46
Overall balance	93	−74	−112	−312	−255

Top Import Origins

$2.7 billion (f.o.b., 1999 est.)

Origins (1998)

- United States 50.9%
- EU (excluding United Kingdom) 9.5%
- Caricom countries 10.4%
- Latin America 6.0%

Top Export Destinations

$1.4 billion (f.o.b., 1999 est.)

Destinations (1998)

- United States 39.5%
- EU (excluding United Kingdom) 15.6%
- United Kingdom 12.1%
- Canada 11.5%

Foreign Aid

Recipient: $102.7 million (1995).

Import/Export Commodities

Import Commodities	Export Commodities
Machinery and transport equipment	Alumina
Construction materials	Bauxite
Fuel	Sugar
Food	Bananas
Chemicals	Rum
Fertilizers	

JAPAN

Nippon

CAPITAL: Tokyo.

FLAG: The Sun-flag (Hi-no-Maru) consists of a red circle on a white background.

ANTHEM: (de facto) *Kimigayo (The Reign of Our Emperor),* with words dating back to the ninth century.

MONETARY UNIT: The yen (Y) of 100 sen is issued in coins of 1, 5, 10, 50, 100, and 500 yen, and notes of 500, 1,000, 5,000, and 10,000 yen. ¥1 = $0.00897 (or $1 = ¥113.8).

WEIGHTS AND MEASURES: The metric system is the legal standard.

HOLIDAYS: New Year's Day, 1 January; Adults' Day, 15 January; Commemoration of the Founding of the Nation, 11 February; Vernal Equinox Day, 20 or 21 March; Greenery Day, 29 April; Constitution Day, 3 May; Children's Day, 5 May; Respect for the Aged Day, 15 September; Autumnal Equinox Day, 23 or 24 September; Health-Sports Day, 10 October; Culture Day, 3 November; Labor-Thanksgiving Day, 23 November; Emperor's Birthday, 23 December.

TIME: 9 PM = noon GMT.

LOCATION AND SIZE: Situated off the eastern edge of the Asian continent, the Japanese archipelago (a group of islands) has a total area of 377,835 square kilometers (145,883 square miles), slightly smaller than the state of California.

Each of Japan's five districts consists of a main island of the same name and hundreds of surrounding islands. The five districts are Honshu, 231,058 square kilometers (89,212 square miles); Hokkaido, 83,519 square kilometers (32,247 square miles); Kyushu, 42,145 square kilometers (16,272 square miles); Shikoku, 18,805 square kilometers (7,261 square miles); and Okinawa, 2,254 square kilometers (870 square miles).

CLIMATE: Throughout the year, there is fairly high humidity, with average rainfall ranging by area from 100 centimeters to over 300 centimeters (40–120 inches). There is a rainy season that moves from south to north during June and July.

INTRODUCTORY SURVEY

RECENT HISTORY

Following World War II, with economic aid from the United States and the determination of the Japanese people to rebuild their country, the Japanese economy rapidly recovered. The standard of living quickly surpassed the prewar level by a wide margin. In 1956, Japan was elected to United Nations membership.

During the 1960s Japan's remarkable economic expansion raised it to the level of a great trading power. In 1968 it surpassed the Federal Republic of Germany (FRG) to stand second after the United States among non-communist nations in total value of its gross national product (GNP). The lack of domestic petroleum resources, however, caused two separate oil crises. Another oil crisis during the 1970s led to long-range programs for energy conservation and diversification.

The yen declined in value in the early 1980s causing Japanese exports to become cheaper in overseas markets. The United States and other leading trading partners began to demand that Japan limit certain exports and remove import barriers to Japan's domestic market.

Emperor Hirohito died of cancer in January 1989 at the age of eighty-seven. He was succeeded by the Crown Prince Akihito, who was enthroned in a formal ceremony in November 1990.

The 1980s ended with a major scandal involving illegal stock trading. Scandals continued into the 1990s with stock dealings and in 1992 contribu-

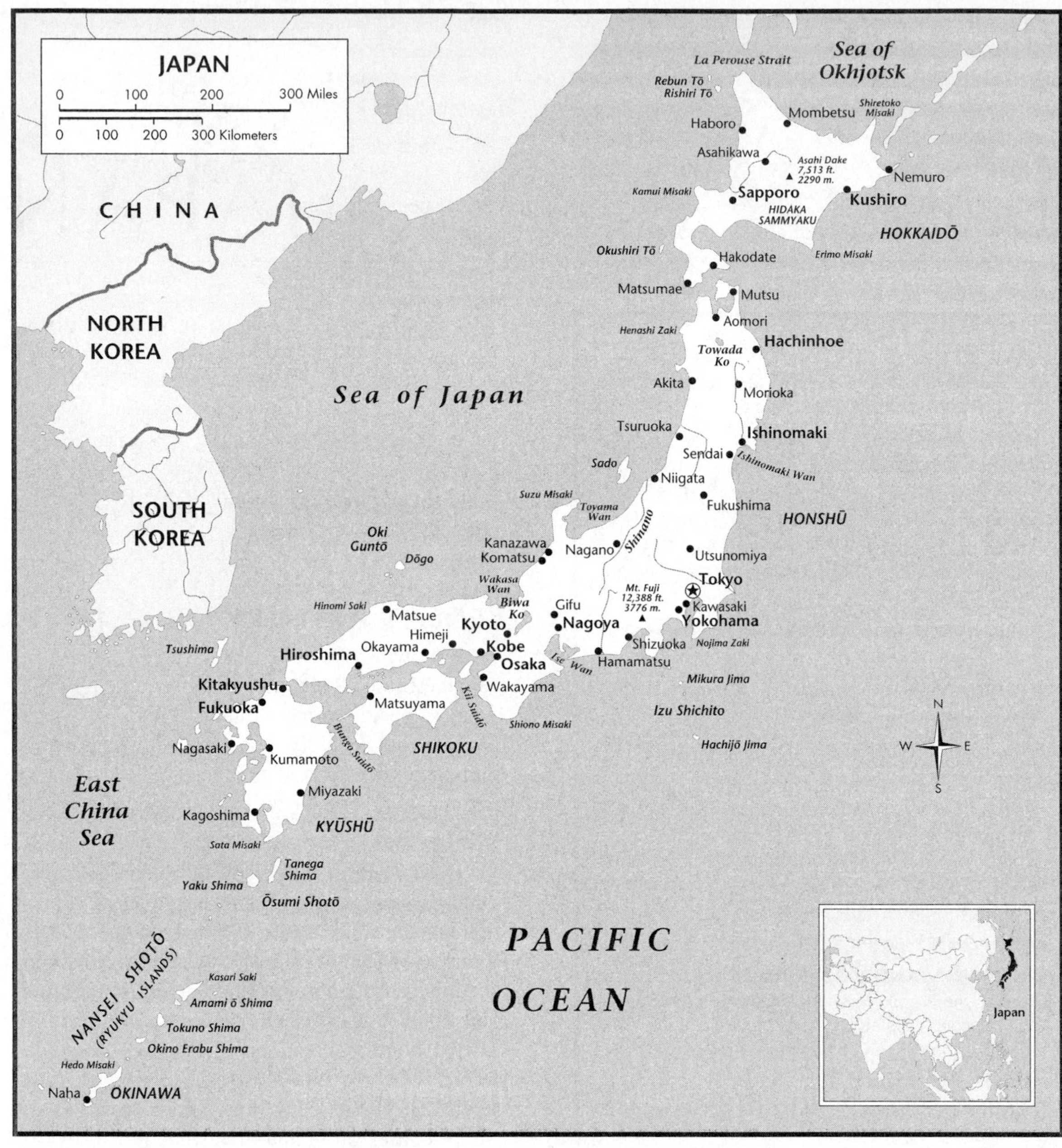

tions to politicians from a trucking company linked to organized crime. The stock market started falling in 1990. By the summer of 1992 it was at its lowest point in six years, 62 percent below the record high of 1989. By the end of 1993 Japan was amid its worst economic downturn in at least twenty years.

Against the background of scandals and economic recession, the political landscape began a major change. After the resignation of Prime Minister Noboru Takeshita in April 1989, the ruling Liberal Democratic Party (LDP) lost its majority in the upper house of the Diet (parliament), its worst defeat in thirty-four years. The new prime minister, Mirihiro Hosokawa (JNP), was chosen in July 1993 by a seven-party coalition of LDP defectors, Socialists, and conservatives. In April 1994 the LDP and the Socialist Party, traditionally opponents, allied to form a new coalition. They selected as prime minister Tomiichi Murayama, the head of the Socialist Party and the first Socialist prime minister since 1948. Ryutaro Hashimoto of the LDP became prime minister in 1996. During his administration Japan fell into its worst recession since World War II.

In July 1998 the LDP was defeated in elections for half the seats in the upper house of the Diet (although it still held more than any other party), and Hashimoto resigned. Keizo Obuchi of the LDP was confirmed as new prime minister. Obuchi suffered a stroke in April 1999. On April 2000 Yoshiro Mori was elected prime minister.

GOVERNMENT

Japan follows a parliamentary system in accordance with the constitution of 1947. The most significant change from the previous constitution of 1889 was the transfer of power from the emperor to the people. The emperor is now defined as "the symbol of the state and of the unity of the people." The constitution provides for the supremacy of the National Diet (parliament) as the legislative branch of the government; upholds the separation of legislative, executive, and judicial powers; and guarantees civil liberties.

A prime minister selected from the Diet by its membership heads the executive branch. The cabinet consists of the prime minister and twenty state ministers (as of January 1988), each heading a government ministry or agency. The prime minister appoints cabinet ministers.

The National Diet is bicameral (consisting of two chambers). The House of Representatives (the lower house) has 500 members selected by popular vote for four-year terms. The House of Councillors (the upper house) has 252 members elected by popular vote for six-year terms. Anyone age twenty or older can vote.

Judiciary

The system consists of the Supreme Court, eight regional higher courts, district courts, and a number of summary courts. In addition, there are family courts, on the same level as the district courts, to rule on family conflicts and complaints such as divisions of estates, marriage annulments, and juvenile protection cases.

The Supreme Court determines the constitutionality of any law, order, regulation, or official act that is challenged during the regular hearing of a lawsuit. The Constitution affords criminal defendants a right to a speedy and public trial by an impartial judge. There is no right to a trial by jury.

Political Parties

The Liberal Democratic Party (LDP) represents much of Japanese society, but most especially the conservative elements. Formed in 1955, this party held the reins of government from its formation until July 1993. The Japan Socialist Party (JSP), Japan's principal opposition party, drew its support mainly from the working class.

In the summer of 1993, amid economic recession and scandals involving corruption, sex, and organized crime, the old political order disintegrated as dozens of younger LDP members defected to form new parties. By December 1999 the distribution of seats in the House was: the LDP with 267; the most significant opposition coming from the Democratic Party of Japan (DPJ) with ninety-three seats; the Komeito/Reform Club with forty-eight; the Liberal Party with thirty-nine; the Japan Communist Party (JCP) with twenty-six; and, the Social Democratic Party (SDP) with fourteen. The LDP, Komeito, and Liberal Party worked closely together.

DEFENSE

There has been a heated debate over the reestablishment of Japanese defense forces since Japan's participation in World War II. Laws establishing a Defense Agency and a Self-Defense Force became effective on July 1, 1954, both under firm civilian control.

The strength of Japan's armed forces in 2000 was 236,300. The Ground Self-Defense Force had 145,900 personnel. There were also 49,000 men in the reserves. The Maritime Self-Defense Force consisted of 43,800 personnel. Air Self-Defense Force personnel numbered 45,200. Japan's forces are purely defensive in nature.

Although Japan's defense budgets-out $45.1 billion in 1996-rank high by world standards, they are small in relation to the size of the nation's economy. Japan relies for its military security on U.S. conventional and nuclear forces, and the United States has repeatedly urged Japan to shoulder more of its own conventional defense burden. The United States maintains extensive military facilities and 40,000 troops in Japan.

ECONOMIC AFFAIRS

Japan's economy is the most advanced in Asia and the second largest in the world, behind that of the United States. Japan was the first Asian country to develop a large urban middle-class industrial society. Contributing to the powerful economy is government-industry cooperation, a strong work ethic, advanced technology, and a relatively small outlay for defense.

Industry is the most important sector but is dependent on imported raw materials and fuels. The agriculture sector is much smaller but highly protected and subsidized and Japan maintains one of the largest fishing fleets. For three decades Japan saw spectacular growth. Growth slowed in the 1990s and 1997-1998 brought a severe recession. Japan had begun to recover in 1999 as government spending began to take hold and business confidence improved.

Public Finance

Japan's government deficit was 3 percent of GDP in 1994 and reached 4.3 percent of GDP in 1995, due to ongoing high levels of public sector borrowing. The government's focus on fiscal policy to compensate for a tight monetary policy has restricted spending on infrastructure.

The U.S. CIA estimated that in 2000-2001 Japanese government revenues totaled approximately $463 billion and expenditures $809 billion.

Income

In 1999 Japan's GDP was estimated to be $2.95 trillion, or about $23,400 per capita. The real growth rate estimate for 1999 of the GDP was 0.3 percent and inflation −0.8 percent. The 1999 estimated GDP by sector was agriculture 2 percent, industry 35 percent, and services 63 percent.

Industry

During the 1970s and early 1980s the rate of Japan's industrial growth surpassed that of any other non-communist industrialized country. Japanese industry is characterized by a complex system of exclusive buyer-supplier networks and alliances.

The electronics industry grew with extraordinary speed in the 1980s and now leads the world. Japan plays an increasingly important role in the computer industry. Japan is the world's leading shipbuilder. More than half the ships built are exported, including some of the world's largest oil tankers. In the early 1980s Japan became the world's leading automobile producer, topping the United States for the first time in the history of the industry. Japan's superior technology in the design of bicycles, motorcycles, buses, and high-speed trains has been another major factor in the growth of the transport industry. The chemical and petrochemicals industry has been another of the economy's key growth areas since the late 1960s. Textiles and apparel has been a steady decline from the mid-twentieth century.

Banking and Finance

Japan's highly sophisticated banking system continues to play a dominant role in financing the country's and the world's economic development. In the mid-1980s, while the U.S. was becoming a debtor nation, Japan became the world's largest creditor.

The controlling national monetary institutions are the Bank of Japan and the Ministry of Finance. The Bank of Japan, as central bank, has power over note issue and audits financial institutions to provide guidance for improving banking and management practices. Eleven city banks with branches throughout the country account for two-thirds of all commercial bank assets, the rest accruing to 131 regional banks, seven trust banks, and eighty-three foreign banks. Also many Japanese families use postal savings facilities.

Major securities exchanges are in Tokyo, Hiroshima, Fukuoka, Nagoya, and Osaka. The Tokyo Securities and Stock Exchange became the largest in the world in 1988 in terms of combined market value of outstanding shares and capitalization, while the Osaka Stock Exchange ranked third after those of Tokyo and New York.

Economic Development

Japan's phenomenal economic growth since the 1950s has been based on an efficient blend of economic tendencies. First is government activism in national planning and implementation, with guidance of the largely free economy via sophisticated and powerful monetary and fiscal policies. Second is the distinctively Japanese way of coupling largely private ownership of assets with conservative, public-spirited management. Manufacturers, suppliers, and distributors work together in groups called keiretsu. Although eroding somewhat by the late 1990s, a third feature is a guarantee of lifetime employment for substantial portion of the work force. Especially significant is the role of the Ministry of International Trade and Industry (MITI), which coordinates national industrial policies consistent with economic and social growth.

In 1988 a five-year plan was adopted to sustain real GNP growth at 3.75 percent per year, maintain low unemployment (2.5 percent per year), contain inflation, reduce the country's trade surplus, and improve the quality of life through a shorter work week and stabilized property prices. Many of these objectives were achieved or surpassed in the closing years of the decade. Since 1992, however, the economy's downturn has been compared by some analysts to the 1974 recession in its severity and length. Economic indicators have included steep declines and sluggish recovery in the stock market index since 1989, falling real estate prices, as well as a shrunken rate of GNP growth, despite surging exports. To prompt a recovery, the Ministry of Finance approved large stimulus packages for 1992 and 1993. Growth picked up to 3.9 percent in 1996 reflecting fiscal and monetary stimulative policies as well as low inflation. However in 1997-1998 Japan experienced a severe recession due primarily to financial difficulties in the banking system and real estate markets. Emerging government spending was necessary and gradually 1999 saw improvement. Since Japanese wages have been rising, wage pressures are creating a higher cost for business, which would tend to make Japan less competitive in a world that is becoming increasingly more competitive.

SOCIAL WELFARE

The social stability of Japan is due largely to the strong sense of family solidarity among the Japanese. Virtually every home has its *butsudan*, or altar of the ancestors, and most elderly people are cared for in the homes of their grown children.

The social insurance system includes national health insurance, welfare annuity insurance, maternity coverage, unemployment insurance, workers' accident compensation insurance, seamen's insurance, national government employees' mutual aid association, and day workers health insurance. It also provides pension plans designed to maintain living standards for the elderly and for families of deceased workers.

Nearly the entire population receives benefits in one form or another from the health insurance system. Those not covered at work are insured through the National Health Insurance program.

Change is evident in the fact that women now make up 40 percent of Japan's employed workers. Marriages arranged by a go-between, or *o-miai* (half of all marriages in 1966), had declined dramatically by the 1990s.

Healthcare

The Ministry of Health and Welfare has become the central administrative agency responsible for maintaining public health, welfare, and sanitation. In 1990-1997 there were sixteen hospital beds and 1.8 doctors per 1,000 people. In addition the Ministry also recognizes and authorizes practices based upon tradition Japanese health professions.

Death rates from cancer and heart disease have risen considerably and now rank among the leading causes of death, trailing cerebrovascular diseases (high blood pressure and strokes). In 1993 there were 300,000 deaths due to cardiovascular disease. Average life expectancy in 2000 was estimated to be about eighty-one years, among the highest rates in the world.

About 66 percent of Japanese men and 14 percent of Japanese women smoke. In 1995 it was estimated that smoking was the underlying cause for 12 percent of all deaths.

Housing

Construction of new housing slowed down in the 1980s, falling to between 1.1 million and 1.5 million units. This is due to a rapid rise in land and construction costs, which has put new housing out of the reach of many potential buyers. In te mid-1990s the average salaried worker could only afford a house forty kilometers outside of Tokyo. Condominiums and prefabricated homes provided much of the nation's new housing.

EDUCATION

Japan's entire educational system was reorganized and made similar to the United States system after World War II with six years of primary school, three years of lower secondary school, three years of upper secondary school-full-time, part-time or correspondence-and four years of college. Education is available to both males and females. Virtually the entire adult population is literate.

Enrollment at the compulsory elementary and junior high school levels is very high, approaching 100 percent. In 1998 7.9 million students were enrolled in the 24,376 elementary schools. In 1995 9.9 million students were enrolled in lower and upper secondary schools. In 1995 there were 3.9 million students enrolled in all higher educational institutions.

2000 KEY EVENTS TIMELINE

January

- On January 15 a U.S. marine is accused of raping a Japanese woman at a nightclub on Okinawa.

February

- Fusae Ota becomes first woman governor of a prefecture on February 6.
- A fifty-nine-year old female employee wins a judgement of 5.1 million yen (US$46,000) on February 23 in a sex discrimination suit.
- Japanese police establish links between the Aleph cult and computer software production on February 29.
- Japan makes it illegal to drive wearing platform shoes.
- The National Space Development Agency reports that a three-stage rocket carrying a satellite fails to reach its target orbit. This is the Agency's second failed attempt at a satellite launch.

March

- On March 8 two subway trains collide in Tokyo.
- Mount Usu, north of Tokyo on the island of Hokkaido, erupts on March 31 after lying dormant for twenty years. Advance warning had enabled residents of the area to evacuate.

April

- As of April 1 many Japanese hotels will no longer charge tourists the 3 percent tourism tax. The tax, applicable to hotel rooms that cost more than about US$140 per night, has been in effect for over forty years.
- Liberal Party leaders resign from the coalition on April 1.
- On April 3 dissident members of the Liberal Party quit and form the Conservative Party.
- Prime Minister Keizo Obuchi suffers a stroke on April 3.
- Japan and North Korea begin two days of talks on April 5 about normalizing relations.

May

- On May 14 Former Prime Minister Keizo Obuchi dies at age sixty-two.

June

- More than 1,000 people attend the funeral of Japan's longest-living Empress Dowager, who lived through the nation's devastating defeat in World War II and saw its ascension to economic eminence.
- On June 19 a new over-the-counter-type stock exchange opens in Japan with trading in the stock of eight companies.
- Results from the June 25 election indicate that the governing Liberal Democratic Party suffered losses, with the opposition Democratic party in the lower house of Parliament winning 127 seats, up from 95. The ruling coalition's 271 seats represent just 56 percent of the total, down from 65 percent controlled by the coalition prior to the election.
- Prime Minister Yoshiro Mori is reelected, and his Liberal Democratic Party wins legislative elections, but by a small margin.

July

- A Japanese court sentences to death two former members of the doomsday cult Aum Shinri Kyo for their roles in the deadly 1995 sarin gas attack on Tokyo's subway system.
- The Group of Eight, or G-8, summit is held in Okinawa, in southern Japan. Narrowing the global "digital divide" and addressing international fears about globalization are among the key topics addressed.
- Finance official Kimitaka Kuze, chairman of the Financial Reconstruction Agency, hands in his resignation on July 30 facing charges of accepting bribes from Mitsubishi Trust.
- Japan plans to keep pursuing research whaling despite calls by the United States, Britain and environmentalists to stop.

August

- Japan and North Korea quarrel over long-standing grievances as talks on normalizing relations begin. Japan later announces willingness to expand contacts with North Korea's communist regime.

September

- The mayor of Miyake and the governor of Tokyo prefecture issue simultaneous orders on September 1 to the 3,850 residents of Miyake Island to evacuate because of seismic and volcanic activity there.
- Efforts by Russia and Japan to sign the first peace treaty between Russia and Japan since World War II look set to fail because of continuing disagreement over ownership of four islands.

- The United States and Japan sign a $4 billion security pact to continue defense cooperation. The agreement is a five-year renewal of an existing agreement on U.S.-Japan security cooperation and calls on Japan to provide "host-nation support" for U.S. forces stationed there.
- The United States places sanctions against Japan for whaling activities on September 13; Japan remains unrepentant.
- The political rights of more than 700,000 Koreans living in Japan are one of the items leading the agenda for this month's Japan-South Korea summit.

November

- Mr. Koichi Kato, head of the Liberal Democratic Party and the coalition government of Japan, champions a vote of no confidence in Japanese Prime Minister Yoshiro Mori which fails November 20 and causes a split in his party.
- Japan enacts a measure to ban human cloning November 30.

December

- Prime Minister Mori reorganizes his cabinet to prepare for government reforms to be implemented in January 2001.

ANALYSIS OF EVENTS: 2000

BUSINESS AND THE ECONOMY

The Japanese economy continued the slow recovery from its economic slump begun the previous year. Corporate profits and private capital investment were booming, although unemployment remained at 4.8 percent—a figure that would be considered low in many other countries but was still nearly a record high for Japan, and high enough to keep consumers wary about spending. Japan's fiscal deficit was a high $6.3 trillion, or 136 percent of gross domestic product (GDP), leading economists to advocate cuts in public works spending. The national pension and health care systems were depleted financially, and experts were pushing for restructuring of these programs.

In spite of the concern raised by the serious accident at the Tokai nuclear fuel processing plant the previous year, Japan continued to rely on fifty-one nuclear power plants for over one-third of its electricity. In addition, four new plants remained under construction, with plans calling for an additional nine plants by 2010. In October following a yearlong investigation, six Tokai plant employees were arrested for negligence in connection with the accident, the worst in Japan's history.

Japanese whaling remained a controversial issue. The United States boycotted two environmental meetings held in Japan in September over opposition to Japan's whaling practices, specifically allegations that whales allegedly killed for research purposes were actually being used for food.

GOVERNMENT AND POLITICS

Japan found itself with its seventh prime minister in eight years when Yoshiro Mori, secretary-general of the ruling Liberal Democratic Party (LDP), was appointed in April to replace Keizo Obuchi, rendered comatose by a stroke. (Obuchi died the following month.) Mori, a traditional politician with a reputation as a consensus builder, was regarded by many as a caretaker whose tenure was not likely to be a long one, a view reinforced by a series of public gaffes by the new prime minister, some of which embarrassed the Japanese by evoking the nation's militaristic imperial past.

The coalition formed by Mori's predecessor lost sixty-five seats in the lower house of the Diet, Japan's parliament, in the general election at the end of June. Mori's Liberal Democratic Party (LDP) remained the most powerful party in the legislature, but with an increased reliance on its coalition partners. Support for the government, and for Mori personally, was so weak that members of Parliament held a no-confidence vote in November to oust the leader. Although he survived the vote, Mori's unpopularity continued. In the meantime, the government prepared for administrative reforms scheduled to go into effect at the beginning of 2001. The existing twenty-one ministries and agencies were to be consolidated into twelve "super ministries," and the cabinet was to be streamlined from nineteen posts to about a dozen.

In foreign affairs Mori's most high-profile task was representing Japan and lobbying for Asian interests at the Group of Eight summit meeting held in July in Okinawa. Tensions between Japan and China over incursions into Japanese waters by Chinese commercial and intelligence vessels were resolved at an August meeting between the foreign ministers of the two countries. The attitude of Russian president Vladimir Putin toward balancing military cooperation with China and economic cooperation with Japan remained an important concern in the region.

CULTURE AND SOCIETY

Popular discontent and discouragement resulting from Japan's economic downturn were cited as reasons for the "mended lives" phenomenon—a publishing trend that featured inspiring memoirs by people who had triumphed over disabilities and other obstacles. These books, popularly referred to as "encouragement stories" or "tales of mended lives," continued to top bestseller lists.

A less benign social trend was Japan's rising crime rate, which reached a thirty-year high. Of special concern was the role played by youth violence, which accounted for over half of all offenses and had focused public attention through a rash of teen killing sprees. Singled out for attention was a traditional social phenomenon—the hikikomori, or recluse. Previously considered strange but harmless misfits, these mostly male young people, who shut themselves in their rooms, sometimes for years, were now being viewed with a new level of alarm.

In 2000 pressure continued to grow for the Japanese government to pay reparations to those subjected to slave labor in mines, factories, construction sites, and other venues during World War II, including thousands of Koreans, Chinese, and other Asians, as well as Allied prisoners of war. Also included were "comfort women," who had been subjected to sexual enslavement.

With Prime Minister Keizo Obuchi felled by a stroke attributed to possible overwork, the Japanese government renewed its efforts to get industrious Japanese employees to expand their vacation time—still, on average, totaling only nine days per year—with its "Happy Mondays" program designed to give workers additional long weekends by switching some public holidays from Saturday to Monday.

The conviction of Osaka's governor in a sexual harassment case was a sign of the slow but steady progress of Japanese women in changing their traditionally subservient role in their society. However, they still had far to go. As of 2000 Japan ranked 140th internationally in participation of women in politics. In the general election held in June, women captured 35 out of 480 parliamentary seats—a small total but a significant improvement from the 23 seats previously held. By shaking up the existing power structure, the economic downturn and rising unemployment of the past decade had actually provided new opportunities for women. Nevertheless, gender discrimination and sexual harassment remain widespread, and there are few legal safeguards for women. The election of a woman to replace the ousted governor of Osaka was considered a major milestone for women. However, she was unable to perform the governor's traditional duty of awarding the prize in the sumo wrestling tournament when sumo association officials refused to allow her to set foot in the ring, and a male deputy had to carry out the task.

In February the government banned women wearing atsuzoko ("super-platform" shoes with heels up to nine inches high) from driving. The shoes, part of the trendy "girl gang" look and popularly dubbed "death boots," had already been implicated in a variety of mishaps and injuries.

DIRECTORY

CENTRAL GOVERNMENT

Head of State

Emperor
Akihito, Office of the Emperor, Imperial Household Agency, 11 Chiyoda, Chiyoda-ku, Tokyo 100, Japan

Prime Minister
Yoshiro Mori, Office of the Prime Minister, 1-6-1 Nagata-cho, Chiyoda-ku, Tokyo 100, Japan
PHONE: +81 (33) 5812361

Ministers

Minister of Agriculture, Forestry, and Fisheries
Yoichi Tani, Ministry of Agriculture, Forestry, and Fisheries, 1-2-1 Kasumigaseki, Chiyoda-ku, Tokyo 100, Japan
PHONE: +81 (33) 5028111

Minister of Construction
Chikage Ogi, Ministry of Construction, 1-2-2 Kasumigaseki, Chiyoda-ku, Tokyo 100-8972, Japan

Minister of Education
Tadamori Oshima, Ministry of Education, 3-2-2 Kasumigaseki, Chiyoda-ku, Tokyo 100, Japan
PHONE: +81 (3) 581-4211

Minister of Finance
Kiichi Miyazawa, Ministry of Finance, 3-1-1 Kasumigaseki, Chiyoda-ku, Tokyo 100, Japan
PHONE: +81 (3) 5814111

Minister of Home Affairs
Mamoru Nishida, Ministry of Home Affairs, 2-2-1 Toranomon, Minato-ku, Tokyo 105, Japan
PHONE: +81 (3) 55747111

Minister of Foreign Affairs
Yohei Kono, Ministry of Foreign Affairs, 2-2-1 Kasumigaseki, Chiyoda-ku, Tokyo 100, Japan
PHONE: +81 (3) 5803311

Minister of Health and Welfare
Yuji Tsushima, Ministry of Health and Welfare, 1-2-2 Kasumigaseki, Chiyoda-ku, Tokyo 100, Japan
PHONE: +81 (3) 5031711

Minister of International Trade and Industry
Takeo Hiranuma, Ministry of International Trade and Industry, 1-3-1 Kasumigaseki, Chiyoda-ku, Tokyo 100, Japan
PHONE: +81 (3) 5011511

Minister of Justice
Okiharu Yasuoka, Ministry of Justice, 1-1-1 Kasumigaseki, Chiyoda-ku, Tokyo 100, Japan
PHONE: +81 (3) 5804111

Minister of Labor
Yoshio Yoshikawa, Ministry of Labor, 1-2-2 Kasumigaseki, Chiyoda-ku, Tokyo 100, Japan
PHONE: +81 (3) 2117451

Minister of Education
Tadamori Oshima, Ministry of Education, 2-2-1 Kasumigaseki, Chiyoda-ku, Tokyo 100, Japan
PHONE: +81 (3) 5815271
FAX: +81 (3) 5950567

Minister of Posts and Telecommunications
Kozo Hirabayashi, Ministry of Posts and Telecommunications, 1-3-2 Kasumigaseki, Chiyoda-ku, Tokyo 100, Japan
PHONE: +81 (3) 5044798

Minister of Transport
Hajime Morita, Ministry of Transport, 2-1-3 Kasumigaseki, Chiyoda-ku, Tokyo 100, Japan
PHONE: +81 (3) 5803111

POLITICAL ORGANIZATIONS

Liberal Democratic Party (LDP)

TITLE: Secretary General
NAME: Yoshiro Mori

Shinseito-JRP (Japan Renewal Party)

Minshuto (Democratic Party)

Liberal Party

TITLE: President
NAME: Ichiro Ozawa

Komeito-CGP (Clean Government Party)

17 Minamimotomachi, Shinjuku-ku, Tokyo 151-8586, Japan
TITLE: Secretary-General
NAME: Tetsuzo Fuyushiba

Japanese Communist Party

4-26-7 Sendagaya, Shibuya-ku, Tokyo 160, Japan
TITLE: Secretariat Head
NAME: Tetsuzo Fuwa

Minshu Shakaito (Democratic Socialist Party)

Shakai Minshuto (Social Democratic Party)

8-1 Nagatacyo 1, Chiyodaku, Tokyo 100-8909, Japan
PHONE: +81 (3) 35801171
TITLE: Secretariat Head
NAME: Sadao Fuchigami

New Party Sakigake (New Harbinger Party)

TITLE: President
NAME: Masayoshi Takemura

Japan Labor Party

PHONE: +81 (3) 32951011
FAX: +81 (3) 32951004

Kaikaku Kurabu-RC (Reform Club)

Zenkokushakensha (Socialist Workers Party)

Okiyama Building, 1-17-11 Minami Ikebukuro, Toshima-ku, Tokyo, Japan
PHONE: +81 (3) 39710622
E-MAIL: swp@aqu.bekkoame.ne.jp

Niigata (New Party for People)

Jiyu Rengo (Liberal League)

PHONE: +81 (3) 35513980
FAX: +81 (3) 35516406

The Japan Wellbeing Party

PHONE: +81 (3) 59826855
FAX: +81 (3) 59826853
E-MAIL: jwp@t3.rim.or.jp

Japan Revolutionary Communist League

525-3 Waseda-tsurumaki-cho, Shinjuku-ku, Tokyo 162-0041, Japan
PHONE: +81 (3) 32071261
E-MAIL: jrcl@pop21.odn.ne.jp

DIPLOMATIC REPRESENTATION

Embassies in Japan

Afghanistan
Olympia Annex Apt. 503, 6-31-21 Jingumae, Shibuya-ku, Toyko 150, Japan
PHONE: +81 34077900
FAX: +81 34007912

Algeria
2-10-67 Mita, Meguro-ku, Toyko 153, Japan
PHONE: +81 37112661
FAX: +81 37106534

Argentina
2-14-14 Moto-Azabu, Minato-ku, Toyko 106, Japan
PHONE: +81 54207101
FAX: +81 54207109

Australia
2-1-14 Mita, Minato-ku, Toyko 108, Japan
PHONE: +81 52324111
FAX: +81 52324149

Austria
1-1-20 Moto-Azabu, Minato-ku, Toyko 106, Japan
PHONE: +81 34518281
FAX: +81 34518283

Bangladesh
4-15-15, Megro-ku, Toyko 153, Japan
PHONE: +81 57040216
FAX: +81 57041696

Belarus
Royal Court 603, 23-2 Ichiban-cho, Chiyoda-ku, Toyko 102, Japan

Belgium
5 Niban-cho, Chiyoda-ku, Toyko 102, Japan
PHONE: +81 32620191
FAX: +81 32620651

Bolivia
No. 38 Kowa Building, 8th Floor, Room 804, 4-12-24, Nishi-Azabu, Minato-ku, Toyko 106, Japan
PHONE: +81 34995441
FAX: +81 34995443

Brazil
2-11-12 Kita-Aoyama, Minato-ku, Toyko 107, Japan
PHONE: +81 34045211
FAX: +81 34055846

Brunei
6-5-2 Kitashinagawa, Shinagawa-ku, Toyko 141, Japan
PHONE: +81 34477997
FAX: +81 34479260

Bulgaria
5-36-3 Yoyogi, Shibuya-ku, Toyko 151, Japan
PHONE: +81 34651021; 34651026
FAX: +81 34651031

Burkina Faso
Hiroo Glisten Hills 3F, 3-1-17 Hiroo, Shibuya-ku, Toyko, Japan
PHONE: +81 34007919
FAX: +81 34006945

Burundi
6-5-3, Kita-Shinagawa, Shinagawa-ku, Toyko 141, Japan
PHONE: +81 34437321
FAX: +81 34437720

Cambodia
8-6-9 Akasaka, Minato-ku, Toyko 107, Japan
PHONE: +81 34780861
FAX: +81 34780865

Cameroon
3-27-16 Nozawa, Setagaya-ku, Toyko 154, Japan
PHONE: +81 54304381
FAX: +81 54306489

Canada
7-3-38 Akasaka, Minato-ku, Toyko 107, Japan
PHONE: +81 34082101; 834039176
FAX: +81 34795320

Chile
Nihon Seimei Akabanebashi Bldg., 8F, 3-1-14 Shiba, Minato-ku, Toyko 105, Japan
PHONE: +81 34527561
FAX: +81 34524457

China
3-4-33 Moto-Azabu, Minato-ku, Toyko 106, Japan

PHONE: +81 34033380
FAX: +81 34033345

Colombia
3-10-53 Kami-Osaki, Shinagawa-ku, Toyko 141, Japan
PHONE: +81 34406451
FAX: +81 34406724

Costa Rica
4-12-24 Nishi-Azabu, Minato-ku, Toyko 106, Japan
PHONE: +81 34861812
FAX: +81 34861813

Côte d'Ivoire
2-19-12 Uehara, Shibuya-ku, Toyko 151, Japan
PHONE: +81 54541401
FAX: +81 54541405

Croatia
2-8-1 Tomigaya, Shibuya-ku, Toyko 151, Japan
PHONE: +81 54788481; 54788542; 54788549
FAX: +81 54788491; 54788564

Cuba
4-11-12 Shimomeguro, Meguro-ku, Toyko 153, Japan
PHONE: +81 37163112
FAX: +81 37164334

Czech Republic
2-16-14 Hiroo, Shibuya-ku, Toyko 150, Japan
PHONE: +81 34008122
FAX: +81 34008124

Denmark
29-6, Sarugaku-cho, Shibuya-ku, Toyko 150, Japan
PHONE: +81 34963001
FAX: +81 34963440

Djibouti
9-12 Nanpeidai-cho, Shibuya-ku, Toyko 150, Japan
PHONE: +81 34966135; 34965629
FAX: +81 34968335

Dominican Republic
No. 38 Kowa Building, Room 904, 4-12-24 Nishi-Azabu, Minato-ku, Toyko 106, Japan
PHONE: +81 34996020
FAX: +81 34992627

Ecuador
No. 38 Kowa Building, Room 806, 12-24 Nishi-Azabu, Minato-ku, Toyko 106, Japan
PHONE: +81 34992800; 34983984
FAX: +81 34994400

Egypt
1-5-4, Aobadai, Meguro-ku, Toyko 153, Japan
PHONE: +81 37708022
FAX: +81 37708021

El Salvador
No. 38 Kowa Building, 8th floor, Room 803, 4-12-24 Nishi-Azabu, Minato-ku, Toyko 106, Japan
PHONE: +81 34994461
FAX: +81 34867022

Ethiopia
1-14-15, Midorigaoka, Meguro-ku, Toyko 152, Japan
PHONE: +81 37181003
FAX: +81 37180978

European Union
Europa House, 9-15 Sanban-cho, Chiyoda-ku, Toyko 102, Japan
PHONE: +81 32390441
FAX: +81 32615194

Fiji
Noa Building 14th Floor, 2-3-5 Azabudai, Minato-ku, Toyko 106, Japan
PHONE: +81 35872038
FAX: +81 35872563

Finland
3-5-39 Minami-Azabu, Minato-ku, Toyko 106, Japan
PHONE: +81 34422231
FAX: +81 34422175

France
4-11-44 Minami-Azabu, Minato-ku, Toyko 106, Japan
PHONE: +81 54208800
FAX: +81 54208847; 54208917

Gabon
1-12-11 Kami-Osaki, Shinagawa-ku, Toyko 141, Japan
PHONE: +81 34489540
FAX: +81 34481596

Germany
4-5-10 Minami-Azabu, Minato-ku, Toyko 106, Japan
PHONE: +81 3473151
FAX: +81 34734243

Ghana
6-2-4 Fukazawa, Setagaya-ku, Toyko, Japan
PHONE: +81 57063201
FAX: +81 57063205

Greece
3-16-30 Nishi-Azabu, Minato-ku, Toyko 106, Japan
PHONE: +81 34030871
FAX: +81 34024642

Guatemala
No. 38 Kowa Building, 9F, Room 905, 4-12-24 Nishi-Azabu, Minato-ku, Toyko 106, Japan
PHONE: +81 34001830
FAX: +81 34001820

Guinea
2-7-43 Shirogane, Minato-ku, Toyko 108, Japan
PHONE: +81 34438211
FAX: +81 34438213

Haiti
No. 38 Kowa Building, #906, 4-12-24 Nishi-Azabu, Minato-ku, Toyko 106, Japan
PHONE: +81 34867070; 34867096
FAX: +81 34867070

Honduras
No. 38 Kowa Building, 8F, Room 802, 4-12-24 Nishi-Azabu, Minato-ku, Toyko, Japan
PHONE: +81 34091150
FAX: +81 34090305

Hungary
2-17-14 Mita, Minato-ku, Toyko 108, Japan
PHONE: +81 37988801
FAX: +81 37988812

India
2-2-11 Kudan-Minami, Chiyoda-ku, Toyko 102, Japan
PHONE: +81 32622391
FAX: +81 32344866

Indonesia
5-2-9 Higashi-Gotanda, Shinagawa-ku, Toyko 141, Japan
PHONE: +81 34414201
FAX: +81 34471687

Iran
3-10-32 Minami-Azabu, Minato-ku, Toyko 106, Japan
PHONE: +81 34468011
FAX: +81 34469002

Iraq
8-4-7 Akasaka, Minato-ku, Toyko 107, Japan
PHONE: +81 34231727
FAX: +81 34028636

Ireland
2-10-7 Kojimachi, Ireland House, Chiyoda-ku, Toyko 102, Japan
PHONE: +81 32630695
FAX: +81 32652275

Israel
3 Niban-cho, Chiyoda-ku, Toyko 102, Japan
PHONE: +81 32640911
FAX: +81 32640832

Italy
2-5-4 Mita, Minato-ku, Toyko 108, Japan
PHONE: +81 34535291
FAX: +81 34562319

Jamaica
Daiwa Nakameguro Bldg. 7F, 4-6-1 Nakameguro, Meguro-ku, Toyko 153, Japan
PHONE: +81 57214114
FAX: +81 57214118

Jordan
Chiyoda House 4F, 2-17-8 Nagata-cho, Chiyoda-ku, Toyko, 100 Japan
PHONE: +81 35805856
FAX: +81 35939385

Kenya
3-24-3 Yakumo, Meguro-ku, Toyko 152, Japan
PHONE: +81 37234006
FAX: +81 37234488

South Korea
1-2-5 Minami-Azabu, Minato-ku, Toyko 106, Japan
PHONE: +81 34527611
FAX: +81 52326911

Kuwait
4-13-12 Mita, Minato-ku, Toyko 108, Japan
PHONE: +81 34550361
FAX: +81 34566290

Laos
3-3-22 Nishi-Azabu, Minato-ku, Toyko 106, Japan
PHONE: +81 54112291
FAX: +81 54112293

Lebanon
Chiyoda House, 5th floor, 2-17-8 Nagata-cho, Chiyoda-ku, Toyko 103, Japan
PHONE: +81 35801227; 35801206
FAX: +81 35802281

Liberia
Sugi Terrace 201, 3-13-11 Okusawa, Setagaya-ku, Toyko 158, Japan
PHONE: +81 37265711
FAX: +81 37265712

Libya
10-14 Daikanyama-cho, Shibuya-ku, Toyko 150, Japan
PHONE: +81 34770701
FAX: +81 34640420

Luxembourg
Niban-cho TS Building, 4F, 2-1 Niban-cho, Chiyoda-ku, Toyko 102, Japan
PHONE: +81 32659621
FAX: +81 32659624

Madagascar
2-3-23 Moto-Azabu, Minato-ku, Toyko 106, Japan
PHONE: +81 34467252
FAX: +81 34467078

Malawi
3-12-9 Kami-Osaki, Shinagawa-ku, Toyko 141, Japan
PHONE: +81 34493010
FAX: +81 34493220

Malaysia
20-16 Nanpeidai-cho, Shibuya-ku, Toyko 150, Japan
PHONE: +81 34763840
FAX: +81 34764971

Marshall Islands
Meiji Park Height 1F, 9-9 Minamimoto-machi, Shinjuku-ku, Toyko 106, Japan
PHONE: +81 53791701
FAX: +81 53791810

Mauritania
5-17-5 Kita-Shinagawa, Shinagawa-ku, Toyko 141, Japan
PHONE: +81 34493810
FAX: +81 34493822

Mexico
2-15-1 Nagata-cho, Chiyoda-ku, Toyko 100, Japan
PHONE: +81 35811131
FAX: +81 35814058

Micronesia
Reinanzaka Building, 2nd floor, 1-14-2 Akasaka, Minato-ku, Toyko 107, Japan
PHONE: +81 35855456
FAX: +81 35855348

Mongolia
21-4 Kamiyama-cho, Shibuya-ku, Toyko 150, Japan
PHONE: +81 34692088; 34692091
FAX: +81 34692216

Morocco
Silva Kingdom Bldg., 5th and 6th Floor, 3-16-3 Sendagaya, Shibuya-ku, Toyko 151, Japan
PHONE: +81 34783271
FAX: +81 34020898

Mozambique
33-3 Ohyama-cho, Shibuya-ku, Toyko 151, Japan
PHONE: +81 34857621
FAX: +81 34857622

Myanmar
4-8-26 Kita-Shinagawa, Shinagawa-ku, Toyko 140, Japan
PHONE: +81 34419291
FAX: +81 34477394

Nepal
7-14-9 Todoroki, Setagaya-ku, Toyko 158, Japan
PHONE: +81 37055558
FAX: +81 37058264

Netherlands
3-6-3 Shibakoen, Minato-ku, Toyko 105, Japan
PHONE: +81 54010411
FAX: +81 54010420

New Zealand
20-40 Kamiyama-cho, Shibuya-ku, Toyko 150, Japan
PHONE: +81 34672271
FAX: +81 34676843; 34672278

Nicaragua
No. 38 Kowa Building, 9th Floor, Room 903, 4-12-24 Nishi-Azabu, Minato-ku, Toyko 106, Japan
PHONE: +81 34990400
FAX: +81 34993800

Nigeria
5-11-17, Shimo-Meguro, Meguro-ku, Toyko 153, Japan
PHONE: +81 57215391
FAX: +81 57215342

Norway
5-12-2 Minami-Azabu, Minato-ku, Toyko 106, Japan
PHONE: +81 34402611
FAX: +81 34402620

Oman
2-28-11 Sendagaya, Shibuya-ku, Toyko 151, Japan
PHONE: +81 34020877; 34022122
FAX: +81 34041334

Pakistan
2-14-9 Moto-Azabu, Minato-ku, Toyko 106, Japan
PHONE: +81 34544861
FAX: +81 34570341

Panama
No. 38 Kowa Building, 9th Floor, Room 902, 4-12-24 Nishi-Azabu, Minato-ku, Toyko 106, Japan
PHONE: +81 34993741
FAX: +81 54853548

Papua New Guinea
Mita Kokusai Bldg., 3rd floor Room 313, 1-4-28 Mita, Minato-ku, Toyko 108, Japan
PHONE: +81 34547801
FAX: +81 34547275

Paraguay
Kowa 38 Bldg., 7F, Room 701, 4-12-24 Nishi-Azabu, Minato-ku, Toyko 106, Japan
PHONE: +81 54853101
FAX: +81 54853103

Peru
4-4-27 Higashi, Shibuya-ku, Toyko 150, Japan
PHONE: +81 34064240
FAX: +81 34097589

Portugal
Olympia Annex, Apt. 303, 6-31-21 Jingumae, Shibuya-ku, Toyko 150, Japan
PHONE: +81 34007907
FAX: +81 34007909

Qatar
6-8-7 Akasaka, Minato-ku, Toyko 107, Japan
PHONE: +81 32243911
FAX: +81 32243917

Romania
3-16-19 Nishi-Azabu, Minato-ku, Toyko 106, Japan
PHONE: +81 34790311
FAX: +81 34790312

Russia
2-1-1 Azabudai, Minato-ku, Toyko 106, Japan
PHONE: +81 35834224; 35828751
FAX: +81 35050593

Rwanda
No. 38, Kowa Building, Room 702, 4-12-24 Nishi-Azabu, Minato-ku, Toyko 106, Japan
PHONE: +81 34867801
FAX: +81 34092434

Saudi Arabia
1-53 Azabu Nagasaka-cho, Minato-ku, Toyko 106, Japan
PHONE: +81 35895241
FAX: +81 35895200

Senegal
1-3-4 Aobadai, Meguro-ku, Toyko 153, Japan
PHONE: +81 34648451
FAX: +81 34648452

Serbia
4-7-24 Kita-Shinagawa, Shinagawa-ku, Toyko 140, Japan
PHONE: +81 34473571
FAX: +81 34473573

Singapore
5-12-3 Roppongi, Minato-ku, Toyko 106, Japan
PHONE: +81 35869111
FAX: +81 35821085

Slovakia
2-16-14 Hiroo, Shibuya-ku, Toyko 150, Japan
PHONE: +81 34008122; 34008328
FAX: +81 34066215

Slovenia
7-5-15 Akasaka, Minato-ku, Toyko 107, Japan
PHONE: +81 55706275
FAX: +81 55706075

South Africa
4F, Zenkyoren Building, 2-7-9 Hirakawa-cho, Chiyoda-ku, Toyko 102, Japan
PHONE: +81 32653366
FAX: +81 32651108

Spain
1-3-29 Roppongi, Minato-ku, Toyko 106, Japan
PHONE: +81 35838531
FAX: +81 35828627

Sri Lanka
1-14-1 Akasaka, Minato-ku, Toyko 107, Japan
PHONE: +81 35857431
FAX: +81 35869307

Sudan
Kindai-Shisetsu Bldg., 2F and 3F, 1-13-4 Aobadai, Meguro-ku, Toyko 153, Japan
PHONE: +81 34760811
FAX: +81 34760814

Sweden
1-10-3-100 Roppongi, Minato-ku, Toyko 106, Japan
PHONE: +81 55625050
FAX: +81 55629095

Switzerland
5-9-12 Minami-Azabu, Minato-ku, Toyko 106, Japan
PHONE: +81 34730121
FAX: +81 34736090

Syria
Homat-Jade, 6-19-45 Akasaka, Minato-ku, Toyko 107, Japan
PHONE: +81 35868977
FAX: +81 35868979

Tanzania
4-21-9 Kamiyoga, Setagaya-ku, Toyko 158, Japan
PHONE: +81 34254531
FAX: +81 34257844

Thailand
3-14-6 Kami-Osaki, Shinagawa-ku, Toyko 141, Japan
PHONE: +81 34411387; 34417352
FAX: +81 34426750

Tunisia
1-18-8 Wakaba, Shinjuku-ku, Toyko 160, Japan
PHONE: +81 33534111
FAX: +81 32254387

Turkey
2-33-6, Jingumae, Shibuya-ku, 150, Toyko, Japan
PHONE: +81 34705131
FAX: +81 34705136

Uganda
39-15 Oyama-cho, Shibuya-ku, Toyko 151, Japan
PHONE: +81 34654552
FAX: +81 34654970

Ukraine
5-31-7 Shinbashi, Minato-ku, Toyko 105, Japan
PHONE: +81 34320917
FAX: +81 34320970

United Arab Emirates
9-10 Nanpeidai-cho, Shibuya-ku, Toyko 150, Japan
PHONE: +81 54890804
FAX: +81 54890813

United Kingdom
1 Ichiban-cho, Chiyoda-ku, Toyko 102, Japan
PHONE: +81 32655511
FAX: +81 52753164

United States
1-10-5, Akasaka, Minato-ku, Toyko 107, Japan
PHONE: +81 32245000
FAX: +81 35051862

Uruguay
No. 38 Kowa Building, Room 908, 4-12-24 Nishi-Azabu, Minato-ku., Toyko 106, Japan
PHONE: +81 34861888
FAX: +81 34869872

Vatican City
9-2 Sanban-cho, Chiyoda-ku, Toyko 102, Japan
PHONE: +81 32636851
FAX: +81 32636060

Venezuela
No. 38 Kowa Building, 7th Floor, Room 703, 4-12-24 Nishi-Azabu, Minato-ku, Toyko 106, Japan
PHONE: +81 34091501
FAX: +81 34091505

Vietnam
50-11, Moto-yoyogi-cho, Shibuya-ku, Toyko 151, Japan
PHONE: +81 34663311; 34663313
FAX: +81 34663312; 34663391

Yemen
No. 38 Kowa Building, 8th Floor, Room 807, 4-12-24 Nishi-Azabu, Minato-ku, Toyko 106, Japan
PHONE: +81 34997151
FAX: +81 34994577

Zambia
Harajuku Green Heights, Rm. 701, Toyko 142, Japan
PHONE: +81 34910121
FAX: +81 34910123

Zimbabwe
5-9-10 Shiroganedaiu, Minato-ku, Toyko 108, Japan
PHONE: +81 32800331
FAX: +81 32800466

JUDICIAL SYSTEM

Supreme Court

BROADCAST MEDIA

American Forces Network (AFN)

APN Tokyo, Yakota Air Base, Fussa, Tokyo
PHONE: +81 (42) 5522511 ext. 52379
E-MAIL: afn.eagle810@yakota.af.mil
WEBSITE: http://www.yakota.af.mil/afn

Broadcasting Bureau Ministry of Posts & Telecommunications

3-2 Kasumigaseki 1-chome, Chiyoda-ku, Tokyo 100-8798, Japan
PHONE: +81 (3504) 4411
WEBSITE: http://www.mpt.go.jp/outline/broad.html
TITLE: Minister
CONTACT: S. Noda

Nippon Hoso Kyokai (NHK) (The Japan Broadcasting Corporation

2-1, Jinnan 2-chome, Shibuya-ku, Tokyo 150-8001, Japan
PHONE: +81 (3) 34651111
FAX: +81 (3) 34698110
WEBSITE: http://www.nhk.or.jp
TITLE: Chairman
CONTACT: H. Suda

MusicBird

E-MAIL: mb@tfm.co.jp
WEBSITE: http://www.tfm.co.jp/MB/home2.html

Radio Tampa (Nihon Short-Wave Broadcasting Co., Ltd.)

9-15, Akasaka 1-chome, Minato-ku, Tokyo 107-8373, Japan
PHONE: +81 (3) 35838151
FAX: +81 (3) 35837441
WEBSITE: http://www.tampa.co.jp
TITLE: President
CONTACT: T. Ikeda

Radio Japan, NHK World, External Service, Foreign Service

2-1 Jinnan 2-chome, Sibuyu-ku, Tokyo 150-8001, Japan
PHONE: +81 (3) 34651111
FAX: +81 (3) 34811350
E-MAIL: info@intl.nhk.or.jp
WEBSITE: http://www.nhk.or.jp/rjnet/index.html
TITLE: Dictorate General
CONTACT: K. Irisawa

University Broadcasting Station

Hoso Daigku, 2-11, Wakaba, Mihama-ku, Chiba 261-5856, Japan
WEBSITE: http://www.u-air.ac.jp/hp
BROADCASTS: 2100–1500

Armed Forces Radio and TV Service

OLAA, AFPBS, APO San Francisco 96519, USA
CHANNEL: 8, 66
TYPE: U.S. Military

Fuji Network System (FNN)

PHONE: +81 (3) 33531111
FAX: +81 (3) 33581747
WEBSITE: http://www.fujitv.co.jp/jp/index.html

Nippon Hoso Kyokai (Japan Broadcasting Corporation)

2-2-1, Jinnan, Shibuya-ku, Tokyo 150-01, Japan
PHONE: +81 (3) 34856517; 34811362
FAX: +81 (3) 34811576
WEBSITE: http://www.nhk.or.jp
TITLE: President
CONTACT: Mikio Kawaguchi
TYPE: Non-Commercial, Non-Government

Sky PerfecTV

PHONE: +81 (3) 58025550
E-MAIL: webmaster@perfectv.co.jp
WEBSITE: http://www.skyperfectv.co.jp/main.html

The Ministry of Posts and Telecommunications

E-MAIL: feedbacke@mpt.go.jp
WEBSITE: http://www.mpt.go.jp/eng/index.html
CONTACT: Kozo Hirabayashi

The National Association of Commercial Broadcasters in Japan

3-23, Kio-cho, Chiyodaku, Tokyo 102-8577, Japan
PHONE: +81 (3) 52137700
FAX: +81 (3) 52137701
WEBSITE: http://www.nab.or.jp
TITLE: President
CONTACT: S. Ujiie

Tokyo Broadcasting System, Inc. (TBS)

5-3-6 Akasaka, Minato-ku, Tokyo 107-8006, Japan
PHONE: +81 (3) 37461111
FAX: +81 (3) 35886378
E-MAIL: www@tbs.co.jp
WEBSITE: http://www.tbs.co.jp/index.html
CONTACT: Yukio Sunahara
CHANNEL: 6

COLLEGES AND UNIVERSITIES

Sapporo International University

4-1-4-1 Kiyota, Sapporo, Hokkaido 004-8602, Japan
PHONE: +81 (11) 8118844
FAX: +81 (11) 8853370
WEBSITE: http://www.siu.ac.jp

Hokkaido Institute of Technology

4-1, 7-15 Maeda, Teine-Ku, Sapporo 006-8585, Japan
PHONE: +81 8 (11) 6812161
FAX: +818 (11) 6813622
E-MAIL: nyushi@hit.ac.jp
WEBSITE: http://www.hit.ac.jp

Hokkaido University

Kita 8 Nishi 5, Kita-Ku, Sapporo 060-0808, Japan
PHONE: +81 (11) 7062334
FAX: +81 (11) 7469488
E-MAIL: bureau@hokudai.ac.jp
WEBSITE: http://www.hokudai.ac.jp

Sapporo University

7-3-1 Nishioka, Toyohira-Ku, Sapporo, Sapporo 062-8520, Japan
PHONE: +81 (11) 852 1181
FAX: +81 (11) 856 8280
WEBSITE: http://www.sapporo-u.ac.jp

Meiji University

1-1 Kanda Surugadai, Chiyoda-Ku, Tokyo 101-8301, Japan
PHONE: +81 (3) 3296 4545
FAX: +81 (3) 3296 4360
WEBSITE: http://www.meiji.ac.jp

Senshu University

3-8-1 Kandajimbo-Cho, Chiyoda-Ku, Tokyo 101-8425, Japan
PHONE: +81 (3) 32656211
FAX: +81 (3)32653649
E-MAIL: iaffairs@acc.senshu-u.ac.jp
WEBSITE: http://www.senshu-u.ac.jp

Hosei University

2-17-1 Fujimi, Chiyoda-Ku, Tokyo 102, Japan
PHONE: +81 3 3264 9314
FAX: +813 3222 6459
E-MAIL: ic@fujimilhosei.ac.jp
WEBSITE: http://www.hosei.ac.jp

Nihon University

4-8-24 Kudan-Minami, Chiyoda-Ku, Tokyo 102-8275, Japan
PHONE: +81 (35) 2758116
FAX: +81 (35) 2758315
E-MAIL: intldiv@adm.nihon-u.ac.jp
WEBSITE: http://www.nihon-u.ac.jp

Temple University Japan

2-8-12 Minami Azabu, Minato, Tokyo 106-0047, Japan
PHONE: +81 (3) 54419800
FAX: +81 (3) 54419862
E-MAIL: tujinfo@tuj.ac.jp
WEBSITE: http://www.tuj.ac.jp

Kitasato University

5-9-1 Shirokane, Minato-Ku, Tokyo 102, Japan
PHONE: +81 (3) 34416161
FAX: +81 (3) 34442530
WEBSITE: http://www.kitasato-u.ac.jp

Keio University

2-15-45 Mita, Minato-Ku, Tokyo 108-8345, Japan
PHONE: +81 (3) 34534511
FAX: +81 (3) 37692047
E-MAIL: cc-staff@mita.cc.keio.ac.jp
WEBSITE: http://www.mita.keio.ac.jp

Hoshi University

2-4-41 Ebara, Shinagawa-Ku, Tokyo 142-8051, Japan
PHONE: +81 (3) 54985821
FAX: +81 (3) 37870036
E-MAIL: www@hoshi.ac.jp
WEBSITE: http://www.hoshi.ac.jp

Kokushikan University

4-28-1 Setagaya, Setagaya-Ku, Tokyo 154-8515, Japan
PHONE: +81 3 54813206
FAX: +81 (3) 54813210
E-MAIL: wwwadmin@kiss.kokushikan.ac.jp
WEBSITE: http://www.kokushikan.ac.jp

Komazawa University

1-23-1 Komazawa, Setagaya-Ku, Tokyo 154-8525, Japan
PHONE: +81 (3) 34189048
FAX: +81 (3) 37029721
E-MAIL: intlcent@komazawa-u.ac.jp
WEBSITE: http://www.komazawa-u.ac.jp

Musashi Institute of Technology

1-28-1 Tamazutsumi, Setagaya-Ku, Tokyo 176-8521, Japan
PHONE: +81 (3) 37033111
FAX: +81 (3) 57072222
E-MAIL: kogyokai@comm.musashi-tech.ac.jp
WEBSITE: http://www.musashi-tech.ac.jp

Kogakuin University

1-24-2 Nishi-Shinjuku, Shinjuku-Ku, Tokyo 163-8677, Japan
PHONE: +81 (3) 33421211
FAX: +81 (3) 33400135
WEBSITE: http://www.kogakuin.ac.jp

Rikkyo University

St. Paul's University, 3-34-1 Nishi-Ikebukuro, Toshima-Ku, Tokyo 171-8501, Japan
PHONE: +81 (3) 39852208
FAX: +81 (3) 39852826
WEBSITE: http://www.rikkyo.ne.jp

Gakushuin University

1-5-1 Mejiro, Toshima-Ku, Tokyo 171-8588, Japan
PHONE: +81 (3) 39860221
FAX: +81 (3) 39861005
WEBSITE: http://www.gakushuin.ac.jp

Rissho University

4-2-16 Osaki, Shinagawa-Ku, Tokyo 171-8602, Japan
PHONE: +81 (3) 34926649
FAX: +81 (3) 54873347
WEBSITE: http://www.ris.ac.jp

Seikei University

3-3-1 Kichijoji- Kitamachi, Musashino-Shi, Tokyo 180-8633, Japan
PHONE: +81 (422) 373531
FAX: +81 (422) 373883
WEBSITE: http://www.seikei.ac.jp

Kyorin University

6-20-2 Shinkawa, Mitaka-Shi, Tokyo 181-8611, Japan
PHONE: +81 (422) 493362
FAX: +81 (422) 493361
WEBSITE: http://www.kyorin-u.ac.jp

Hitotsubashi University

2-1 Naka, Kunitachi, Tokyo 186-8601, Japan
PHONE: +81 (42) 5808000
FAX: +81 (42) 5808006
E-MAIL: ishi@econ.cc.hit-u.ac.jp
WEBSITE: http://www.hit-u.ac.jp

Meisei University

2-1-1 Hodokubo, Hino-Shi, Hino-Shi, Tokyo 186-8601, Japan
PHONE: +81 (42) 5915111
FAX: +81 (42) 5918181
E-MAIL: gakumu@agora.meisei-u.ac.jp
WEBSITE: http://www.meisei-u.ac.jp

Soka University

1-236 Tangi-Cho, Hachioji-Shi, Tokyo 192-0003, Japan
PHONE: +81 (426) 912211
FAX: +81 (426) 919300
E-MAIL: intloff@j.soka.ac.jp
WEBSITE: http://www.soka.ac.jp

Chuo University

742-1 Higashinakano, Hachioji-Shi, Tokyo 192-0393, Japan
PHONE: +81 (426) 742211
FAX: +81 (426) 742214
E-MAIL: intlcent@tamajs.chuo-u.ac.jp
WEBSITE: http://www.chuo-u.ac.jp

St. Marianna Ika University

2-16-1 Sugao Miyamae-Ku, Kawasaki-Shi, Kawasaki-Shi, Kanagawa 216-8511, Japan
PHONE: +81 (44) 9778111
FAX: +81 (44) 9777939
E-MAIL: ezh00673@nifty.ne.jp
WEBSITE: http://www.marianna-u.ac.jp

Kanagawa University

3-27-1 Rokkakubashi, Kanagawa-Ku, Yokohama-Shi, Kanagawa 221-8686, Japan
PHONE: +81 (45) 4815661
FAX: +81 (45) 4917951
WEBSITE: http://www.kanagawa-u.ac.jp

Ferris University

37 Yamate-Cho, Naka-Ku, Yokohama-Shi, Kanagawa 231-8660, Japan
PHONE: +81 (45) 6815150
FAX: +81 (45) 6626102
WEBSITE: http://www.ferris.ac.jp

Nagano University

Shimonogo, Ueda-Shi, Nagano 386-1298, Japan
PHONE: +81 (268) 382350
FAX: +81 (268) 380002
E-MAIL: nucco@dma.nagano.ac.jp
WEBSITE: http://www.nagano.ac.jp

Nagoya University

Furo-Cho Chikusa-Ku, Nagoya 464-8601, Japan
PHONE: +81 (52) 7815111
FAX: +81 (52) 7892045
E-MAIL: t9985135@post.jimu.nagoya-u.ac.jp
WEBSITE: http://www.nagoya-u.ac.jp

Nagoya Institute of Technology

Gokiso-Cho, Showa-Ku, Nagoya-Shi, Aichi 466-8555, Japan
PHONE: +81 (52) 7355000
FAX: +81 (52) 7355009
WEBSITE: http://www.nitech.ac.jp

Osaka Institute of Technology

5-16-1 Omiya, Asahi-Ku, Osaka-Shi, Osaka 535-8585, Japan
PHONE: +81 (6) 69544097
FAX: +81 (6) 69539496
WEBSITE: http://www.oit.ac.jp

Osaka University

1-1 Yamadaoka, Suita, Osaka 565-0871, Japan
PHONE: +81 (6) 68775111
FAX: +81 (6) 68797039
E-MAIL: kokusai@user.center.osaka-u.ac.jp
WEBSITE: http://www.osaka-u.ac.jp

Kyoto University

Yoshida-Honmachi, Sakyo-Ku, Kyoto 606-8501, Japan
PHONE: +81 (75) 7532047
FAX: +81 (75) 7532042
E-MAIL: koryu52@mail.adm.kyoto-u.ac.jp
WEBSITE: http://www.kyoto-u.ac.jp

Kyoto Institute of Technology

Hashigami-Cho, Matsugasaki, Sakyo-Ku, Kyoto 606-8585, Japan
PHONE: +81 (75) 7247131
FAX: +816 (75) 7247120
E-MAIL: webmaster@adm.kit.ac.jp
WEBSITE: http://www.kit.ac.jp

Kobe University

1-1 Rokkodai-Cho, Nada-Ku, Kobe, Hyogo 657-8501, Japan
PHONE: +81 (78) 8811212
FAX: +81 (78) 8030059
E-MAIL: kouhou@ofc.kobe-u.ac.jp
WEBSITE: http://www.kobe-u.ac.jp

Okayama University

1-1-1 Naka, Tsushima, Okayama, Japan
PHONE: +81 86 86 252 1111
FAX: +8186 86 254 6104
E-MAIL: ryugaku@biwako.shiga-u.ac.jp
WEBSITE: http://www.okayama-u.ac.jp

Kawasaki Medical College

577 Matsushima, Kurashiki, Okiyama 701-0193, Japan
PHONE: +81 (86) 4621111
FAX: +81 (86) 4641019
E-MAIL: admin@med.kawasaki-m.ac.jp
WEBSITE: http://www.kawasaki-m.ac.jp

Hiroshima University

1-1-89 Higashisenda-Machi, Naka-Ku, Hiroshima 730, Japan
PHONE: +81 (824) 227111
FAX: +81 (824) 246020
E-MAIL: soumu-soumu@bur.hiroshima-u.ac.jp
WEBSITE: http://www.hiroshima-u.ac.jp

Hiroshima Institute of Technology

2-1-1 Miyake, Saeki-Ku, Hiroshima731-5193, Japan
PHONE: +81 (82) 9213121
FAX: +81 (82) 9221480
E-MAIL: kouhou@jim.it-hiroshima.ac.jp
WEBSITE: http://www.it-hiroshima.ac.jp

Kochi University

2-5-1-Akeboni-Cho, Kochi-Shi, Kochi 780-8520, Japan
PHONE: +81 (88) 8440111
FAX: +81 (88) 8448147
E-MAIL: nys-web@jimu.kochi-u.ac.jp
WEBSITE: http://www.kochi-u.ac.jp

Kochi University of Technology

185 Miyanokuchi, Tosayamada, Kochi 782-8502, Japan
PHONE: +81 (887) 531111
FAX: +81 (887) 572000

E-MAIL: query@jim.kochi-tech.ac.jp
WEBSITE: http://www.kochi-tech.ac.jp

Kitakyushi University

4-2-1 Kitagata Kokuraminami-Ku, Kokuraminami-Ku, Kitakyushu-Shi, Fukuoka 802-8577, Japan
PHONE: +81 (93) 9644004
FAX: +81 (93) 9644000
WEBSITE: http://www.kitakyu-u.ac.jp

Fukuoka University

+8-19-1 Nanakuma, Jonan-Ku, Fukuoka 814-0180, Japan
PHONE: +81 (92) 8716631
E-MAIL: fupr@adm.fukuoka-u.ac.jp
WEBSITE: http://www.fukuoka-u.ac.jp

Fukuoka Institute of Technology

3-30-1 Wajiro-Higashi, Higashi-Ku, Fukuoka 811-0295, Japan
PHONE: +81 (92) 6063131
FAX: +81 (92) 6068923
E-MAIL: yamasaki@fjct.fit.ac.jp
WEBSITE: http://www.fit.ac.jp

Nagasaki Institute of Applied Science

536 Aba-Machi, Nagasaki-Shi, Nagasaki 851-01, Japan
PHONE: +81 (95) 8393111
FAX: +81 (95) 8390584
E-MAIL: nyusi@office.nias.ac.jp
WEBSITE: http://www.nias.ac.jp

Nagasaki University

1-14 Bunkyo-Machi, Nagasaki 852-8521, Japan
PHONE: +81 (95) 8471111
FAX: +81 (95) 8442349
E-MAIL: tanaka@net2.nagasaki-u.ac.jp
WEBSITE: http://www.nagasaki-u.ac.jp

Okinawa University

747 Kokuba, Naha 902-8521, Japan
PHONE: +81 (98) 8323216
FAX: +81 (98) 8318650
WEBSITE: http://www.okinawa-u.ac.jp

International University of Japan

Yamato-Machi, Minami Uonuma, Nigata 949-7277, Japan
PHONE: +81 (257) 791111
FAX: +81 (257) 794441
E-MAIL: admis@iuj.ac.jp
WEBSITE: http://www.iuj.ac.jp

NEWSPAPERS AND MAGAZINES

Akita Sakigake Shimpo

1-2-6 Ohtemachi, Akita 010 Japan
CIRCULATION: 252,036

To-o-Nippo

2-2-11 Shin-machi, Aomori 030 Japan
PHONE: +81 (177) 731111
CIRCULATION: 254,155

Fukui Shimbun

1-1-14 Haruyama, Fukui 910 Japan
PHONE: +81 (776) 235111
CIRCULATION: 188,637

Fukushima Mimpo

13-17 Ohtemachi, Fukushima 960 Japan
PHONE: +81 (245) 314111
CIRCULATION: 299,319

Chugoku Shimbun

7-1 Dobaski-cho, Nakaku 730 Hiroshima, Japan
PHONE: +81 (82) 2362111
WEBSITE: http://www.hiroshima-cdas.or.jp/chugoku-np
CIRCULATION: 702.067

Fukushima Minyu

4-29 Yanagimachi, Fukushima 960 Japan
PHONE: +81 (245) 231191
CIRCULATION: 184,409

Kobe Shimbun

1-5-7 Higashi-kawasaki-cho, Chuo-ku, Kobe 650 Japan
PHONE: +81 (78) 3627081
WEBSITE: http://www.kobe-np.co.jp
CIRCULATION: 507,190

Kochi Shimbun

3-2-15 Hon-cho, Kochi 780 Japan
PHONE: +81 (888) 222111
E-MAIL: master@kochinews.co.jp
WEBSITE: http://www.kochinews.co.jp
CIRCULATION: 227,865

Kumamoto Nichi-Nichi Shimbun

2-33 Kamitori-machi, Kumamoto 860 Japan

PHONE: +81 (96) 3271111
CIRCULATION: 381,951

Kyoto Shimbun

Karasuma-dori, Ebisugawa-agaru, Nakagyo-ku, Kyoto 604 Japan
PHONE: +81 (75) 2222111
FAX: +81 (75) 2222200
E-MAIL: kpdesk@mb.kyoto-np.co.jp
WEBSITE: http://www.kyoto-np.co.jp
TITLE: Editor
CONTACT: Kenzo Matsunaga
CIRCULATION: 495,697

Jomo Shimbun

1-50-21 Furuichi-machi, Maebashi 371 Japan
PHONE: +81 (272) 514341
TITLE: Editor
CONTACT: Toyomi Suzuki
CIRCULATION: 283,008

Ehime Shimbun

1-12-1 Otemachi, Matsuyama 790-8511 Japan
PHONE: +81 (89) 9352323
FAX: +81(89) 9418111
WEBSITE: http://www.ehime-np.co.jp
TITLE: Editor
CONTACT: Ryoji Yano
CIRCULATION: 322,038

Ibaraki Shimbun

2-15 Kitami-machi, Mito 310 Japan
PHONE: +81 (292) 213121
TITLE: Editor
CONTACT: Masao Mitomi
CIRCULATION: 116,427

Iwate Nippo

3-7 Uchimaru, Morioka 020 Japan
PHONE: +81 (196) 534111
CIRCULATION: 224,422

Nagasaki Shimbun

3-1 Mori-machi, Nagasaki 852 Japan
PHONE: +81 (958) 442111
CIRCULATION: 191.016

Chunichi Shimbun

1-6-1 San-no-maru, Naka-ku, Nagoya City 460-8511 Japan
PHONE: +81 (52) 2018811
FAX: +81 (52) 2014331
WEBSITE: http://www.chunichi.co.jp
TITLE: Editor
CONTACT: Shinsuke Yoshimura
CIRCULATION: 3,341,279

Asahi Evening News

5-3-2 Tsukiji, Chuo-ku, Tokyo 104-8011 Japan
PHONE: +81 (3) 55407755
FAX: +81 (3) 55407741
WEBSITE: http://www.asahi.com
TITLE: Editor
CONTACT: Yoshio Marakami
CIRCULATION: 38,800

Asahi Shimbun

5-3-2 Tsukiji, Chuo-ku, Tokyo 104-8011 Japan
PHONE: +81 (3) 55407755
FAX: +81 (3) 55407741
WEBSITE: http://www.asahi.com
TITLE: Editor
CONTACT: Kiyofuko Chuma
CIRCULATION: 8,362,108

Asahi Weekly

5-3-2 Tsukiji, Chuo-ku, Tokyo 104-8011 Japan
PHONE: +81 (3) 55407755
FAX: +81 (3) 55407741
WEBSITE: http://www.asahi.com
CIRCULATION: 155,000

Daily Yomiuri, The

1-7-1 Otemachi, Chiyoda, Ku, Tokyo 100-55 Japan
PHONE: +81 (3) 32168932
FAX: +81 (3) 32168934
E-MAIL: ad-6-02@tokyo.yomiuri.co.jp
TITLE: Editor
CONTACT: Atsushi Kojima

Kahoku Shimpo

1-2-28 Itsutsu-bashi, Aobo-ku, Sendai 980-8660 Japan
PHONE: +81 (22) 2111111
E-MAIL: kahoku@po.kahoku.co.jp
WEBSITE: kohoku.co.jp/eng/index.html
CIRCULATION: 485,355

Nikkei Financial Daily

1-9-5 Otemachi, Chiyoda-ku, Tokyo 100-8066 Japan
PHONE: +81 (3) 32700251
FAX: +81 (3) 52552648

E-MAIL: ap-info@tokyo.nikkei.co.jp
WEBSITE: http://www.nni.nikkei.co.jp
TITLE: Editor
CONTACT: Tadamichi Kanda
CIRCULATION: 50,000

Sankei Shimbun

1-7-2 Otemachi, Chiyoda-ku, Tokyo 100-77 Japan
PHONE: +81 (3) 32317111
FAX: +81 (3) 32704580
CIRCULATION: 1,920,123

Tokyo Shimbun

2-3-13 Konan, Minato-ku, Tokyo 108 Japan
PHONE: +81 (3) 34712211
FAX: +81 (3) 37402529
WEBSITE: http://www.tokyo.np.co.jp
TITLE: Editor
CONTACT: Yukihiro Iizuka
CIRCULATION: 700,532

Tokyo Chunichi Sports

2-3-Konan, Minato-ku, Tokyo 108 Japan
PHONE: +81 (3) 34712211
FAX: +81 (3) 37402529
CIRCULATION: 3,126,570

Sports Nippon

2-1-30 Ecchujima, Koto-ku, Tokyo 135 Japan
PHONE: +81 (3) 38200700
CIRCULATION: 1,011,770

Tokyo Chunichi Sports

2-3-13 Konan, Minato-ku, Tokyo 108 Japan
PHONE: +81 (3) 34712211
FAX: +81 (3) 37402529
CIRCULATION: 3,126,570

Tokyo Shimbun

2-3-13 Konan, Minato-ku, Tokyo 108 Japan
PHONE: +81 (3) 3471221
FAX: +81 (3) 37402529; 34711851
WEBSITE: http://www.tokyo-np.co.jp
TITLE: Manager Editor
CONTACT: Yukihiro Iisuka
CIRCULATION: 700,532

To-O Nippo

The To-O Nippo Press Co Ltd, 2-2-11 Shinmachi, Aomori, Japan
PHONE: +81 (177) 731111
TITLE: Advertising Manager
CONTACT: Susumu Kudo
CIRCULATION: 188,637

Yomiuri Shimbun, The

1-7-1 Otemachi, Chiyoda-ku, Tokyo 100-8055 Japan
PHONE: +81 (3) 3242111
FAX: +81 (3) 32168749
E-MAIL: ad-1-03@tokyo.yomiuru.co.jp
WEBSITE: http://www.yomiuri.co.jp
TITLE: Publisher
CONTACT: Tsuneo Watanabe
CIRCULATION: 10,220,512

PUBLISHERS

Chinjin Shokan Co. Ltd.

15 Naka-machi, Shinjuku-ku, Tokyo 162-0835, Japan
PHONE: +81 (3) 32354422
FAX: +81 (3) 32358984
E-MAIL: KYY02177@nifty.ne.jp
WEBSITE: http://www.chijinshokan.co.jp
TITLE: Man. Director
CONTACT: Tomoaki Ogawa
SUBJECTS: Engineering (General), Medicine, Nursing, Dentistry, Physical Aciences, Science (General), Technology
TOTAL PUBLISHED: 450 print

Daiichi Shuppan Co. Ltd.

One Chome, 39 Kanda Jimbo-cho, Chiyoda-ku, Tokyo 101-0051, Japan
PHONE: +81 (3) 32914577
FAX: +81 (3) 32914579
E-MAIL: ishikawa@japan
TITLE: Prsident
CONTACT: Hideji Ishikawa
SUBJECTS: Health, Nutrition, Medicine, Nursing, Dentistry
TOTAL PUBLISHED: 150 print; 5 CD-ROM

Froebel-Kan Co. Ltd.

6-14-9 Honkomagome, Bunkyo-ku, Tokyo 113-8611, Japan
PHONE: +81 (3) 53956614
FAX: +81 (3) 53956639
E-MAIL: tada-m@froebel-kan.co
WEBSITE: http://www.froebel-kan.co.jp
TITLE: Director
CONTACT: Mitsuhiro Tada

SUBJECTS: Children's Books, Animals, Pets, Education, Fiction, Nonfiction (General)
TOTAL PUBLISHED: 1,000 print; 1 CD-ROM

Fukuinkan Shoten Publishers Inc.

6-6-3 Honkomagome, Bunkyo-ku, Tokyo 113-8686, Japan
PHONE: +81 (3) 39420032
FAX: +81 (3) 39421401
E-MAIL: mariko-o@fukuinkan.co.jp
WEBSITE: http://www.fukuinkan.co.jp
TITLE: Director, International Dept.
CONTACT: Mariko Ogawa
SUBJECTS: Fiction, Literature, Literary Criticism, Essays, Fiction, Nonfiction (General), Science (General), Science Fiction, Fantasy
TOTAL PUBLISHED: 1,000 print

Iwanami Shoten, Publishers

2-5-5 Hitosubashi, Chiyoda-ku, Tokyo 101-8002, Japan
PHONE: +81 (3) 52104000
FAX: +81 (3) 52104039
E-MAIL: noasmith@iwanami.co.jp
WEBSITE: http://www.iwanami.co.jp
TITLE: Foreign Rights Director
CONTACT: Sachiko Kagaya
SUBJECTS: Art, Biography, Economics, Electronics, Engineering, History, Philosophy, Photography, Psychology, Psychiatry, Science (general), Social Sciences
TOTAL PUBLISHED: 5,000 print; 30 CD-ROM; 10 audio

Kaitakusha

2-5-4 Kanda Jinbocho, Chiyoda-ku, Tokyo 101-0051, Japan
PHONE: +81 (3) 32657641
FAX: +81 (3) 32652989
E-MAIL: webmaster@kaitakusha.co.jp
WEBSITE: http://www.kaitakusha.co.jp
TITLE: Foreign RIghts
CONTACT: Yusuhiko Yamamoto
SUBJECTS: Education, English as a Second Language, Language Arts, Literature, Literary Criticism, Essays
TOTAL PUBLISHED: 300 print; 10 CD-ROM; 50 audio

Kinokuniya Co. Ltd. (Publishing Department)

38-1 Sakuragaoka, 5-Chome, Setagaya-ku, Tokyo, 156-0054 Japan
PHONE: +81 (3) 34390128; 54695919
FAX: +81 (3) 34393955; 54695959
E-MAIL: publish@kinokuniya.co.jp
WEBSITE: http://www.kinokuniya.co.jp
TITLE: General Manager
CONTACT: Shinjiro Kuroda
SUBJECTS: Art, Biography, Engineering (General), Political Science, History, Medicine, Music, Dance, Philosophy, Psychology, Science (General), Social Sciences
TOTAL PUBLISHED: 400 print

Kodansha

12-21 Otowa, 2-Chome, Bunyo-Ku, Tokyo 112-0013, Japan
PHONE: +81 (3) 53953419
FAX: +81 (3) 39444441
E-MAIL: e minc@kodansha.co.jp
WEBSITE: http://www.kodansha.co.jp
TITLE: Rights & Permissions
CONTACT: Takashi Kasahara
SUBJECTS: Art, Economics, Education, Fiction, History, Humor, Language Arts, Literature, Medicine, Nonfiction (General), Religion, Social Sciences

Kosei Publishing Co. Ltd.

2-7-1 Suginami-ku, Tokyo 166-8535, Japan
PHONE: +81 (3) 53852319
FAX: +81 (3) 53852331
E-MAIL: kspub@mail.kosei-shuppan.co.jp
WEBSITE: http://www.mediagalaxy.co.jp/kosei
TITLE: Director, International Publishing
CONTACT: Koichiro Yoshida
SUBJECTS: Art, Child Care, Education, History, Human Relations, History, Literature, Medicine, Music, Dance, Nonfiction (General), Buddhism Self-Help, Travel
TOTAL PUBLISHED: 481 print; 2 audio; CD-ROM

Maruzen Co. Ltd.

3-10 Nihonbashi, 2-Chome, Chuo-ku, Tokyo 103-8245, Japan
PHONE: +81 (3) 32733243
FAX: +81 (3) 32789256
E-MAIL: webmaster@maruzen.co.jp
WEBSITE: http://www.maruzen.co.jp
TITLE: Man. Director
CONTACT: Isamu Tanahashi
SUBJECTS: Architecture, Biological Sciences, Chemistry, Engineering, Computer Science, Electronics, Physics, Science (General)

Mejikaru Furendo-sha

2-4 Kudan kita, 3-Chome, Chiyada-ku, Tokyo 102-0073, Japan
PHONE: +81 (3) 32646611
FAX: +81 (3) 32616602
E-MAIL: mfhensyu@mb.infoweb.ne.jp
TITLE: President, Rights & Permissions
CONTACT: Yoshihiro Ogura
SUBJECTS: Art, Health, Nutrition, Medicine, Nursing, Dentistry

Minerva Shobo Co. Ltd.

One Tsutsumidani-cho, Hinooka, Yamashina-ku, Tokyo 607-8494, Japan
PHONE: +81 (75) 5815191
FAX: +81 (75) 5818379
E-MAIL: info@minervashobo.co.jp
WEBSITE: http://www.minervashobo.co.jp
TITLE: Foreign Rights
CONTACT: Takeo Isozaki
SUBJECTS: Child Care & Development, Special Needs, Economics, Education, Political Science, History, Philosophy, Social Sciences
TOTAL PUBLISHED: 3,010 print

The Nikkan Kogjo Shimbun Ltd.

8-10 Kudan-kita, 1-Chome, Chiyoda-ku, Tokyo 102-8181, Japan
PHONE: +81 (3) 32227011
FAX: +81 (3) 32391989
E-MAIL: webmaster@nikkan.co.jp
WEBSITE: http://www.nikkan.co.jp
TITLE: President
CONTACT: Taihei Kanno
SUBJECTS: Business, Technology

Nippon Hoso Shuppan Kyokai (NHK Publishing)

41-1 Udagawa-cho, Shibuya-ku, Tokyo 150-0042, Japan
PHONE: +81 (3) 37803356
FAX: +81 (3) 34960123
TITLE: Man. Director
CONTACT: Fumihiko Inatsugu
SUBJECTS: Astronomy, Business, Biological Sciences, Chemistry, Engineering, Cookery, Communications, Theater, Games, Education, Electronics, Environmental Studies, Fashion, Fiction, Political Science, Literature, Religion, Social Sciences

Ohmsha Ltd.

3-1 Kanda-Nishiki-cho, Chiyoda-ku, Tokyo 101-8460 Japan
PHONE: +81 (3) 32330641
FAX: +81 (3) 32336224
E-MAIL: hanbaibu@ohmsha.co.jp
WEBSITE: http://www.ohmsha.co.jp
TITLE: Director, Foreign Rights & International Rights
CONTACT: Osami Takeo
SUBJECTS: Engineering (General), Science (General)
TOTAL PUBLISHED: 2,500 print

Pearson Education (Japan)

Nishi-Shinjuku, KF Bldg., 8-14-24, Shinjuku-ku, Tokyo, Japan
PHONE: +81 (3) 33659001
FAX: +81 (3) 33659009
E-MAIL: name@pearsoned.co.jp
WEBSITE: http://www.pearsoned.co.jp
TITLE: President
CONTACT: Naoto Ono
SUBJECTS: Business, Computer Science, Economics, English as a Second Language, Medicine, Nursing, Dentistry, Microcomputers
TOTAL PUBLISHED: 400 print

Reimei-Shobo Co. Ltd.

3-6-27 Marunouchi, Naka-ku, Nagoya 460-0002, Japan
PHONE: +81 (52) 9623045
FAX: +81 (52) 9519065
E-MAIL: reimei@mui.biglobe.ne.jp
TITLE: International Rights
CONTACT: Masako Yoshikawa
SUBJECTS: Child Care & Development, Education, Psychology, Psychiatry
TOTAL PUBLISHED: 1,550 print

Rinsen Book Co. Ltd.

Imadegawa-Dori, Kawabata-Higashi-Iru, Sakyo-Ku, Tokyo 606-0000, Japan
PHONE: +81 (75) 7816166
FAX: +81 (75) 7816168
TITLE: International Rights
CONTACT: Ohashz Kyoko
SUBJECTS: Asian Studies, History, Literature, Literary Criticism, Essays, Buddhism

Sangyo-Tosho Publishing Co. Ltd.

2 Chome 11-13, Iidabashi, Chiyoda-ku, Tokyo 102-0072, Japan
PHONE: +81 (3) 36217821
FAX: +81 (3) 32392178
E-MAIL: info@san-to.co.jp
TITLE: President
CONTACT: Takehiko Ezura
SUBJECTS: Biological Sciences, Chemistry, Engineering, Electronics, Mathematics, Philosophy, Physical Sciences, Physics, Science (General), Social Sciences
TOTAL PUBLISHED: 500 print

Shobunsha Publications Inc.

2nd Seiko Bldg., 211 Kudan-kita, 4-Chome, Chiyoda-ku, Tokyo 102-0073, Japan
PHONE: +81 (3) 32622141
FAX: +81 (3) 32622147
TITLE: President
CONTACT: Toshio Kuroda
SUBJECTS: Travel
TOTAL PUBLISHED: 300 print

Shufunotomo Sha Co. Ltd.

9 Kanda Surugadai, 2-Chome, Chiyoda-ku, Tokyo 101-0062, Japan
PHONE: +81 (3) 52807588
FAX: +81 (3) 52807556
E-MAIL: international@shufunotomo.co.jp
WEBSITE: http://www.shufunotomo.co.jp
TITLE: General Manager
CONTACT: Shunichi Kamiya
SUBJECTS: Architecture, Career Development, Child Care, Cookery, Games, Hobbies, Education, Fashion, Fiction, Gardening, Health, NutritionHow-To, Nonfiction (General), Buddhism, Travel, Photography
TOTAL PUBLISHED: 1,200 print; 10 CD-ROM; 3 internet

Springer-Verlag Tokyo

EBS Hongo Bldg., 3-3-11 Hongo, 3-Chome, Tokyo 113-0033, Japan
PHONE: +81 (3) 38120757
FAX: +81 (3) 38120719
SUBJECTS: Economics
TOTAL PUBLISHED: 300 print; 15 CD-ROM

Tamagawa University Press

1-1 Tamagawa-Gakuen, 6-Chome, Machida Shi 194-0041, Japan
PHONE: +81 (427) 398935
FAX: +81 (427) 398940
E-MAIL: tup@adm.tamagawa.ac.jp
TITLE: Director & Editor
CONTACT: Kubo Kouichiro
SUBJECTS: Education, Social Sciences, Sociology

Tankosha Publishing Co. Ltd.

19-1 Shino miya-Nishi-machi, Kita-ku, Kyoto 603-8158, Japan
PHONE: +81 (75) 4325151
FAX: +81 (75) 4140273
E-MAIL: tankosha@magical.egg.or.jp
WEBSITE: http://www.tankosha.topica.ne.jp
TITLE: Executive Vice-President
CONTACT: Yoshito Naya
SUBJECTS: Antiques, Architecture, Interior Design, Arts, Crafts, Games, Hobbies, Ethnicity, History, Philosophy, Religion
TOTAL PUBLISHED: 4,000 print

Thomson Learning

Dai 5, Nomura Bldg. 3F, I-3, Kanda Jinbo-cho, Chiyoda-ku, Tokyo 102, Japan
PHONE: +81 (3) 52825180
FAX: +81 (3) 52855181
E-MAIL: yuko@tlj.co.jp
WEBSITE: http://www.tlj.co.jp
TITLE: General Manager
CONTACT: Yuko Matsuika
SUBJECTS: Communications, English as a Second Language, Language Arts, Linguistics

Kokai University Press

28-4 Tomigaya, 2-Chome, Shibuya-ku, Tokyo 151-0063, Japan
PHONE: +81 (3) 54780891 ,
FAX: +81 (3) 33411833
SUBJECTS: Art, Biological Sciences, Earth Sciences, History, Language Arts, Linguistics, Literature, Philosophy, Religion, Social Sciences, Technology

Tokyo Shoseki Co. Ltd.

2-17-1 Horifune, Kita-ku, Tokyo 114-8524, Japan
PHONE: +81 (3) 53907531
FAX: +81 (3) 53907538
E-MAIL: tfs@tokyo-shoseki.co.jp
WEBSITE: http://www.tokyo-shoseki.co.jp
TITLE: International Dept. Manager
CONTACT: Shigeki Oyama

SUBJECTS: Art, Disability, Special Needs, Education, English as a Second Language, Fiction, History, Mathematics, Buddhism, Science (General), Travel
TOTAL PUBLISHED: 1,000 print; 100 CD-ROM

Toppan Co. Ltd.

c/o Toppan Shibaura Bldg., 3-19-26 Shibaura, Minato-ku, Tokyo 108-0023, Japan
PHONE: +81 (3) 54182535
FAX: +81 (3) 54182529
E-MAIL: yuri@top.co.jp
WEBSITE: http://www.toppan-pub.topica.ne.jp
TITLE: Man. Director
CONTACT: Naomi Yoshikawa
SUBJECTS: Biological Sciences, Computer Sciences, Environmental Studies, Library & Information Sciences
TOTAL PUBLISHED: 350 print

University of Tokyo Press

3-1 Hongo, 7-Chome, Bunkyo-ku 113-0033, Japan
PHONE: +81 (3) 38151902
FAX: +81 (3) 38126958
TITLE: Man. Director
CONTACT: Tadashi Yamashita
SUBJECTS: Engineering (General), History, Medicine, Nursing, Dentistry, Philosophy, Psychiatry, Psychology, Social Sciences

The Zion Press

165-83 Arise Ikawadani-cho, Nishi-ku, Kobe 651-2113, Japan
PHONE: +81 (78) 9757373
FAX: +81 (78) 9757373
E-MAIL: mmineo@kh.vim.or.jp
TITLE: President
CONTACT: Mirei Moritani
SUBJECTS: Christianity
TOTAL PUBLISHED: 1,000 print

RELIGIOUS ORGANIZATIONS

Baha'I

National Spiritual Assembly of the Baha'is of Japan
7-2-13, Shinjuku, Shinjuku-ku, Tokyo 160, Japan
PHONE: +81 (3) 32097521
FAX: +81 (3) 32040773

Buddhist

All Japan Young Buddhist Association
c/o Baikyu-in Buddhist Temple, 1-18 Yuhigaoka-cho, Tennoji-ku, Osaka City, 543 Japan
PHONE: +81 (6) 7611667
FAX: +81 (6) 7711796

Buddhist English Academy
802 Diamond Place, 3-5-3, Nishi Shinjuku, Shinjuku-ku, Tokyo 160 Japan
PHONE: +81 (3) 3426605

Buddhist Promotion Foundation

Bukkyo Dendo Kyokai
3-4 Shiba-4 Chromes, Minato-ku, 108 Tokyo, Japan
PHONE: +81 (3) 4907868

Dhammakaya International Meditation Center
2-59-20-201 Kaneko Boulevard, Shimo, Kita-ku, Tokyo 115 Japan
PHONE: +81 (3) 39036571, +81 (3) 39036572
FAX: +81 (3) 39036573
E-MAIL: dimejpl@z2.zzz.or.jp

Dharma Center of Japan
2-21-4 Kohinata, Bunkyo-ku, Tokyo 112-0006 Japan
PHONE: +81 (3) 53951088
FAX: +81 (3) 53954257
E-MAIL: jam@dharma-japan.org
WEBSITE: http://www.dharma-japan.org
NAME: John Munroe

Dogen Sangha (Ida Ryogokudo Zazen Dojo)
5-11-20 Minami Yawata, Ichikawa City Chiba Prefecture, Japan 272
PHONE: +81 473791596
FAX: +81 473786232
E-MAIL: dsangha@gol.com
WEBSITE: http://www.windbell.com/

Honganji International Center
Higashi-naka-suji Rokujo-sagaru, Shimogyo-ku, Kyoto, Japan 600-8341
PHONE: +81 (75) 3715547
FAX: +81 (75) 3714070

International Zen Center-Kyoto

Kyoto Kokusai Zendo
c/o Tokoji Rinzai Zentempel, Hozumi Gensho Roshi, 621-0027 Kyoto-fu, Kameoka-shi, Sogabe-cho, Inukai, Japan
PHONE: +81 771231784
FAX: +81 771231784
E-MAIL: Genpo-HR-Doering@t-online.de

WEBSITE: http://www.kaiser-bischof.de/shoboji/english/kokusai/index.htm
NAME: Hozumi Gensho Roshi

International Zen Dojo
611 Tsurushima, Uenoharacho, Kita Tsura-gun, Yamanashi-ken 409-01
PHONE: +81 (5546) 2-3198
NAME: Rev. Kanemaru Roshi

Japan Vipassana Centre
c/o 92 Ginkakuji-cho, Sakyo-ku, Kyoto 606, Japan
PHONE: +81 (75) 7523685
FAX: +81 (75) 7523685
E-MAIL: jvipa@mbox.kyoto-inet.or.jp

San'un Zendo
2-16-5 Komachi, Kamakura-shi, Kangawa-ken 248, Japan
PHONE: +81 (467) 232010

Tendai Lotus Teachings
468-0069 Aichi-Ken, Nagoya-shi, Tnpaku-Ku, Omoteyama 2-2102, Yagoto Lodge A205
E-MAIL: jion@profitwatch-japan.com
WEBSITE: http://www.tendai-lotus.org
NAME: Jion Prosser

Toshoji Zen Temple
International Zen Center, 4-5-18 Yutakacho, Shinagawa-Ku, Tokyo 142-0042 Japan
PHONE: +81 (3) 37814235
FAX: +81 (3) 37816168
E-MAIL: toshoji@mb.infoweb.ne.jp
WEBSITE: http://village.infoweb.or.jp/~fwgc8522/index.htm

World Buddhist Fellowship-Japan
Buddhist Temple, 3-24-2, kabane-dai, Kita-ku, Tokyo, Japan
NAME: Rev. Fuji Nakayama

Protestant

Anglican Church in Japan

Nippon Sei Ko Kai
65, Yarai-cho, Shinjuku-ku, Tokyo 162, Japan
PHONE: +81 (3) 52283171
FAX: +81 (3) 52283175
E-MAIL: wfh@nskk.org
TITLE: General Secretary
NAME: Rev. Samuel I. Koshiishi

Asian-Pacific Christian Peace Conference (APCPC)
19-5 Udagawa-cho, Shibuya-ku, Tokyo, Japan
NAME: Rev. S. T. Hirayama

Japan Baptist Convention (JBC)
1-2-4, Minami Urawa, Urawa 336, Saitama, Japan
PHONE: +81 (48) 8831091
FAX: +81 (48) 8837092
E-MAIL: bapjo@mua.biglobe.ne.jp
TITLE: Executive Secretary
NAME: Sieya Yamashita

Japan Evangelical Lutheran Church
1-1, Sadowara-cho, Ichigaya, Shinjuku-ku, Tokyo 169, Japan
PHONE: +81 (3) 32608631
FAX: +81 (3) 32683589
TITLE: General Secretary
NAME: Rev. Isamu Aota

National Christian Council in Japan
Japan Christian Centre, 2-3-18-24, Nishi Waseda, Shinjuku-ku, Tokyo 169, Japan
PHONE: +81 (3) 32030372
FAX: +81 (3) 32049495
TITLE: General Secretary
NAME: Rev. Kenichi Otsu

Shinto

Meiji Jingu
Gaien (The Outer Garden), 9 Kasumigaoka, Shinjuku-ku, Tokyo, Japan
PHONE: +81 (3) 34010312
WEBSITE: http://www.meijijingu.or.jp

Other Organizations

Nanzan Institute for Religion and Culture
Nanzan University, 18 Yamazato-cho, Showa-ku, Nagoya 466, Japan
PHONE: +81 (52) 8323111
FAX: +81 (52) 8336157
E-MAIL: nirn@ic.nanzan-u.ac.ip
WEBSITE: http://www.ic.nanzan-u.ac.jp/SHUBUNKEN
NAME: Dr. James W. Heisig

FURTHER READING

Articles

"Catch Up If You Can." *The Economist (US),* September 23, 2000, vol. 356, no. 8189.

French, Howard W. "Governing Party in Japan Suffers Election Setback." *New York Times,* June 26, 2000, p. A1.

———. "Japan Orders Residents Out After Tremors Rock Island." *New York Times,* September 3, 2000, p. 11.

"No Warning: On the Eve of a Major International Meeting on Smoking, Japan's Lonely Anti-Cigarette Activists Wonder Why the Nation Is Still Tobacco's Best Friend." *Time International,* October 9, 2000, vol. 156, no. 14, p. 20+.

"Volcano in Japan Erupts Twice in Two Days." *New York Times,* April 1, 2000, p. A5.

JAPAN: STATISTICAL DATA

For sources and notes see "Sources of Statistics" at the front of each volume.

GEOGRAPHY

Geography

Area:

Total: 377,835 sq km.

Land: 374,744 sq km.

Note: includes Bonin Islands (Ogasawara-gunto), Daito-shoto, Minami-jima, Okino-tori-shima, Ryukyu Islands (Nansei-shoto), and Volcano Islands (Kazan-retto).

Land boundaries: 0 km.

Coastline: 29,751 km.

Climate: varies from tropical in south to cool temperate in north.

Terrain: mostly rugged and mountainous.

Natural resources: negligible mineral resources, fish.

Land use:

Arable land: 11%

Permanent crops: 1%

Permanent pastures: 2%

Forests and woodland: 67%

Other: 19% (1993 est.).

HUMAN FACTORS

Demographics (A)

	1990	1995	1998	2000	2010	2020	2030	2040	2050
Population	123,537	125,287	126,069	126,550	127,252	123,380	116,740	109,130	101,229
Life expectancy - males	76.0	76.6	77.3	77.5	78.6	79.4	80.1	80.7	81.1
Life expectancy - females	82.3	83.5	83.8	84.0	85.0	85.8	86.4	86.9	87.2
Birth rate (per 1,000)	9.9	9.5	9.8	10.0	8.9	7.7	8.1	8.1	8.0
Death rate (per 1,000)	6.7	7.4	7.8	8.1	10.2	12.4	14.3	15.3	16.0
Women of reproductive age (15-49 yrs.)	31,466	31,019	30,279	29,402	27,066	24,787	21,254	19,090	17,768
Fertility rate	1.5	1.4	1.4	1.4	1.5	1.5	1.6	1.6	1.7

Except as noted, values for vital statistics are in thousands; life expectancy is in years.

Health Personnel

	National Data	World Data (wtd ave)
Total health expenditure as a percentage of GDP, 1990-1998[a]		
Public sector	5.9	2.5
Private sector	1.4	2.9
Total[b]	7.1	5.5
Health expenditure per capita in U.S. dollars, 1990-1998[a]		
Purchasing power parity	1,757	561
Total	2,379	483
Availability of health care facilities per 100,000 people		
Hospital beds 1990-1998[a]	1,620	330
Doctors 1992-1995[a]	177	122
Nurses 1992-1995[a]	641	248

Health Indicators

	National Data	World Data
Life expectancy at birth (years)		
1980	76	61
1998	81	67
Daily per capita supply of calories		
1970	2,704	2,358
1997	2,932	2,791
Daily per capital supply of protein		
1997 (grams)	96	74
Total fertility rate (births per woman)		
1980	1.8	3.7
1998	1.4	2.7
Population with access (%)		
To safe water (1990-96)	96	NA
To sanitation (1990-96)	100	NA
People living with (1997)		
Tuberculosis (cases per 100,000)	33.6	60.4
HIV/AIDS (% aged 15 - 49 years)	0.01	0.99

Infants and Malnutrition

	National Data	World Data (wtd ave)
Under 5 mortality rate (1989)	4	NA
% of infants with low birthweight (1992-98)[1]	6	17
Births attended by skilled health staff (% of total births 1996-98)	100	52
% fully immunized at 1 year of age (1995-98)[1]		
TB	91	82
DPT	100	77
Polio	98	77
Measles	94	74
Prevalence of child malnutrition (1992-98)[1] (based on weight for age, % of children under 5 years)	NA	30

Ethnic Division

Japanese 99.4%

Other (mostly Korean) 0.6%

Religion

Observe both Shinto and Buddhist 84%

Other (including Christian 0.7%) 16%

Major Languages

Japanese.

EDUCATION

Public Education Expenditures

	1980	1997
Public expenditures on education as % of GNP	5.8	3.6
Expenditures per student as % of GNP per capita		
Primary	14.8	19.3
Secondary	16.6	19.0
Tertiary	21.0	13.9
Teachers' compensation as % of total current education expenditures	49.8	NA
Pupils per teacher at the primary level	NA	19
Duration of primary education in years	NA	9
World data for comparison		
Public expenditures on education as % of GNP (mean)	3.9	4.8
Pupils per teacher at the primary level (wtd ave)	NA	33
Duration of primary education in years (mean)	NA	9

Educational Attainment (A)

Age group (1990)[18] ....25+
Population of this age group 81,991,363
Highest level attained (%)
No schooling 0.3
First level
Not completed 33.6
Completed ....NA
Entered second level 43.7
Entered post-secondary 20.7

Literacy Rates (B)

	National Data	World Data
Adult literacy rate		
1980		
Male	100[1]	75
Female	99[1]	58
1995		
Male	NA	81
Female	NA	65

Libraries

National Libraries 1990
Administrative Units 1
Service Points or Branches 3
Number of Volumes (000) 5,528
Registered Users (000) 452
Loans to Users (000) 409
Total Library Staff ....NA
Public Libraries **1993**
Administrative Units 2,172
Service Points or Branches 3,561
Number of Volumes (000) 195,390
Registered Users (000) 24,745
Loans to Users (000) 424,107
Total Library Staff 19,339

GOVERNMENT & LAW

Political Parties

Diet (Kokkai)	no. of seats
House of Councillors	
Liberal Democratic Party (LDP)	102
Democratic Party of Japan (DPJ)	47
Japan Communist Party (JCP)	23
Komeito	22
Social Democratic Party (SDP)	13
Liberal Party	12
Independents	26
Others	7
As of December 1999	
Liberal Democratic Party (LDP)	105
Democratic Party of Japan (DPJ)	57
Komeito	24
Japan Communist Party (JCP)	23
Social Democratic Party (SDP)	13
Liberal Party	12
Independents	6
Others	12
House of Representatives	
Liberal Democratic Party (LDP)	240
New Frontier Party (NFP)	142
Democratic Party of Japan (DPJ)	52
Japan Communist Party (JCP)	26
Social Democratic Party (SDP)	15
Sun Party	10
Others	15
As of December 1999	
Liberal Democratic Party (LDP)	267
Democratic Party of Japan (DPJ)	93
Komeito/Reform Club	48
Liberal Party	39
Japan Communist Party (JCP)	26
Social Democratic Party (SDP)	14
Independents	9
Others	4

House of Councillors elections were last held 12 July 1998 (next to be held July 2001); House of Representatives elections were last held 20 October 1996 (next to be held by October 2000).

Government Budgets (A)

Year: 1993

Total Expenditures: 112,655 Billions of Yen

Expenditures as a percentage of the total by function:
General public services and public order ......3.63[P]
Defense ....4.11[P]
Education ....6.03[P]
Health ....1.60[P]
Social Security and Welfare ....36.80[P]
Housing and community amenities ....13.76[P]
Recreational, cultural, and religious affairs .....0.14[P]
Fuel and energy ....NA
Agriculture, forestry, fishing, and hunting .....1.09[P]
Mining, manufacturing, and construction ......1.64[P]
Transportation and communication ....0.30[P]
Other economic affairs and services ....0.32[P]

Military Affairs (A)

	1990	1992	1995	1996	1997
Military expenditures					
Current dollars (mil.)	30,500	33,800	37,500	39,300	40,800
1997 constant dollars (mil.)	35,700	37,500	38,800	40,000	40,800
Armed forces (000)	250	242	240	250	250
Gross national product (GNP)					
Current dollars (bil.)	3,180	3,530	3,870	4,100	4,250
1997 constant dollars (bil.)	3,720	3,910	4,000	4,170	4,250
Central government expenditures (CGE)					
1997 constant dollars (bil.)	594	594	583	620	621[e]
People (mil.)	123.5	124.4	125.2	125.4	125.7
Military expenditure as % of GNP	1	1	1	1	1
World data on military expenditure as % of GNP	4.5	3.4	2.7	2.6	2.6
Military expenditure as % of CGE	6.0	6.3	6.7	6.5	6.6
World data on military expenditure as % of CGE	17.0	12.5	10.5	10.3	10.2
Military expenditure per capita (1997 $)	289	301	310	319	325
World data on military expenditure per capita (1997 $)	242	173	146	143	145
Armed forces per 1,000 people (soldiers)	2.0	1.9	1.9	2.0	2.0
World data on armed forces per 1,000 people (soldiers)	5.3	4.5	4.1	3.9	3.8
GNP per capita (1997 $)	30,100	31,400	32,000	33,200	33,800
Arms imports[6]					
Current dollars (mil.)	1,600	2,000	1,800	2,400	2,600
1997 constant dollars (mil.)	1,874	2,217	1,864	2,440	2,600
Arms exports[6]					
Current dollars (mil.)	70	10	20	20	20
1997 constant dollars (mil.)	82	11	21	20	20
Total imports[7]					
Current dollars (bil.)	235	233	336	349	339
1997 constant dollars (bil.)	276	259	348	355	339
Total exports[7]					
Current dollars (bil.)	288	340	443	411	421
1997 constant dollars (bil.)	337	377	459	418	421
Arms as percent of total imports[8]	0.7	0.9	0.5	0.7	0.8
Arms as percent of total exports[8]	0	0	0	0	0

Crime

Crime volume (for 1998)

Crimes reported 2,113,425

Total persons convicted 851,710

Crimes per 100,000 population 1,671

Persons responsible for offenses

Total number suspects 392,102

Total number of female suspects 83,518

Total number of juvenile suspects 166,643

LABOR FORCE

Total Labor Force (A)

67.76 million (November 1999).

Labor Force by Occupation

Trade and services 65%

Industry 30%

Agriculture, forestry, and fishing 5%

Unemployment Rate

4.7% (1999 est.)

PRODUCTION SECTOR

Energy Production

Production ....995.982 billion kWh

Production by source

Fossil fuel 56.68%

Hydro 8.99%

Nuclear 31.93%

Other 2.40%

Exports ....0 kWh

Data for 1998.

Energy Consumption

Consumption ....926.263 billion kWh

Imports ....0 kWh

Data for 1998.

Transportation

Highways:

Total: 1,152,207 km.

Paved: 863,003 km (including 6,114 km of expressways).

Unpaved: 289,204 km (1997 est.).

Waterways: about 1,770 km; seagoing craft ply all coastal inland seas.

Pipelines: crude oil 84 km; petroleum products 322 km; natural gas 1,800 km.

Merchant marine:

Total: 662 ships (1,000 GRT or over) totaling 13,039,488 GRT/18,024,969 DWT.

Ships by type: bulk 146, cargo 49, chemical tanker 13, combination bulk 16, combination ore/oil 4, container 25, liquified gas 45, passenger 9, passenger/cargo 2, petroleum tanker 214, refrigerated cargo 22, roll-on/roll-off 48, short-sea passenger 9, vehicle carrier 60 (1999 est.).

Airports: 171 (1999 est.).

Airports - with paved runways: 140.

Airports - with unpaved runways: 31.

Top Agriculture Products

Rice, sugar beets, vegetables, fruit; pork, poultry, dairy products, eggs; fish.

MANUFACTURING SECTOR

GDP & Manufacturing Summary (A)

	1980	1985	1990	1995
GDP ($-1990 bil.)[1]	1,981	2,339	2,932	3,128
Per capita ($-1990)[1]	16,962	19,353	23,734	25,010
Manufacturing share (%) (current prices)[1]	28.2	28.2	27.5	25.9[e]
Manufacturing				
Value added ($-1990 mil.)[1]	530,348	673,212	852,566	867,160
Industrial production index	72	82	100	97
Value added ($ bil.)	339	413	892	1,366[e]
Gross output ($ bil.)	971	1,115	2,246	3,259
Employment (000)	10,253	10,652	11,172	10,474[e]
Profitability (% of gross output)				
Intermediate input (%)	65	63	60	58[e]
Wages and salaries inc. supplements (%)	12	13	13	15[e]
Gross operating surplus	23	24	27	27[e]
Productivity ($)				
Gross output per worker	88,443	102,310	201,017	308,627[e]
Value added per worker	30,912	37,862	79,822	132,802[e]
Average wage (inc. supplements)	11,522	13,644	26,368	46,638[e]
Value added ($ mil.)				
Food products	25,889	32,041	66,676	110,520[e]
Beverages	5,015	5,303	10,305	25,499[e]
Tobacco products	1,888	700	2,003	3,962[e]
Textiles	15,436	15,259	27,046	33,629[e]
Wearing apparel	5,156	5,622	11,921	16,459[e]
Leather and fur products	886	977	1,865	2,614[e]
Footwear	697	658	1,478	3,805[e]
Wood and wood products	8,997	6,888	14,006	20,235[e]
Furniture and fixtures	3,788	3,798	8,730	14,065[e]
Paper and paper products	9,310	9,759	22,287	38,739[e]
Printing and publishing	17,099	20,789	47,938	76,769[e]

	1980	1985	1990	1995
Industrial chemicals	13,809	16,811	38,076	54,306[e]
Other chemical products	15,471	19,758	46,764	85,315[e]
Petroleum refineries	6,620	4,595	4,841	19,146[e]
Misc. petroleum and coal products	1,063	713	1,540	2,312[e]
Rubber products	4,150	5,077	11,403	16,846[e]
Plastic products	9,478	13,570	30,796	50,978[e]
Pottery, china and earthenware	1,623	1,627	2,984	5,415[e]
Glass and glass products	2,876	4,029	8,487	11,388[e]
Other non-metal mineral products	12,565	12,321	26,652	42,670[e]
Iron and steel	26,444	25,224	48,539	57,823[e]
Non-ferrous metals	7,458	5,236	11,976	15,062[e]
Metal products	22,409	26,356	62,905	105,807[e]
Non-electrical machinery	39,270	53,576	126,563	182,363[e]
Electrical machinery	38,868	63,180	133,884	178,557[e]
Transport equipment	32,107	45,158	95,594	142,745[e]
Prof. and scientific equipment	5,685	6,972	12,798	25,331[e]
Other manufacturing	5,178	6,510	13,730	23,128[e]

COMMUNICATIONS

Daily Newspapers

	National Data	World Data for Comparison
Daily Newspapers		
Number of Dailies	122	8,391
Total Circulation (000)	72,705	548,000
Circulation per 1,000 inhabitants	578	96

Telecommunications

Telephones - main lines in use: 60.3 million (1997).

Telephones - mobile cellular: 36.5 million (1998).

Telephone system: excellent domestic and international service.

Domestic: NA

International: satellite earth stations - 5 Intelsat (4 Pacific Ocean and 1 Indian Ocean), 1 Intersputnik (Indian Ocean region), and 1 Inmarsat (Pacific and Indian Ocean regions); submarine cables to China, Philippines, Russia, and US (via Guam).

Radio broadcast stations: AM 190, FM 88, shortwave 24 (1999).

Radios: 120.5 million (1997).

Television broadcast stations: 7,108 (plus 441 repeaters; in addition, US Forces are served by 3 TV stations and 2 TV cable services) (1999).

Televisions: 86.5 million (1997).

Internet Service Providers (ISPs): 357 (1999).

FINANCE, ECONOMICS, & TRADE

Economic Indicators

National product: GDP—purchasing power parity—$2.95 trillion (1999 est.).

National product real growth rate: 0.3% (1999 est.).

National product per capita: $23,400 (1999 est.).

Inflation rate—consumer price index: -0.8% (1999 est.).

Exchange Rates

Exchange rates:

Yen per US$1

January 2000	105.16
1999	113.91
1998	130.91
1997	120.99
1996	108.78
1995	94.06

Top Import Origins

$306 billion (c.i.f., 1999 est.)

Origins (1999)

United States	22.0%
China	14.0%
South Korea	5.1%
Australia	4.2%
Taiwan	4.1%

Top Export Destinations

$413 billion (f.o.b., 1999 est.)

Destinations (1999)

United States	31.0%
Taiwan	7.0%
China	5.5%
South Korea	5.4%
Hong Kong	5.2%

Balance of Payments

	1994	1995	1996	1997	1998
Exports of goods (f.o.b.)	385,698	428,717	400,279	409,240	374,044
Imports of goods (f.o.b.)	−241,508	−296,931	−316,717	−307,640	−251,655
Trade balance	144,191	131,787	83,562	101,600	122,389
Services - debits	−106,356	−122,626	−129,962	−123,454	−111,833
Services - credits	58,297	65,274	67,724	69,302	62,412
Private transfers (net)	1,546	1,655	5,878	5,832	5,382
Government transfers (net)	−2,823	−3,279	−1,967	−2,319	−2,192
Overall balance	130,256	111,045	65,884	94,353	120,696

Foreign Aid

Donor: ODA, $9.1 billion (1999).

Import/Export Commodities

Import Commodities	Export Commodities
Fuels	Motor vehicles
Foodstuffs	Semiconductors
Chemicals	Office machinery
Textiles	Chemicals
Office machinery	

JERSEY

Bailiwick of Jersey

CAPITAL: Saint Helier.

FLAG: White with a diagonal red cross of Saint Patrick (patron saint of Ireland) extending to the corners of the flag. In the top triangular field is the seal of Jersey—a red shield with three gold lions, topped by a gold crown.

ANTHEM: God Save the Queen.

MONETARY UNIT. 1 Jersey pound (£J) = 100 pence.

WEIGHTS AND MEASURES: The imperial system is standard, but the metric and historic local measurement units are used as well.

HOLIDAYS: Liberation Day, 9 May.

TIME: Noon = noon GMT.

LOCATION AND SIZE: Jersey, a territory of England, lies about 32 km (20 miles) off the coast of France in the English Channel. 49°15′N, 2°10′W. Total area: 117 sq. km.

CLIMATE: Jersey has a mild, maritime climate, with an average rainfall of 84 cm (33 inches). February temperatures average 6°C (43°F) and August temperatures range between 16–17°C (60–63°F). The most southerly of the Channel Islands, Jersey has one of the best sunshine records in the British Isles.

INTRODUCTORY SURVEY

RECENT HISTORY

Jersey is one of a group of islands known as the Channel Islands lying from ten to thirty miles off the northwest coast of France. Once a part of the Dukedom of Normandy, the islands have belonged to the Crown of England since the twelfth century. Although belonging to the Crown, they are not part of the United Kingdom which includes England, Wales, Scotland, and Northern Ireland. The islands, including Jersey, maintain their own legislative, legal, and administrative systems.

By the fifteenth century Jersey had its own administrator called captain. The captain's position evolved into the governor and in 1854 into the lieutenant governorship. Jersey's Royal Court was created in the seventeenth century and the legislative body, the States of Jersey, in the eighteenth century. The lieutenant governorship, Royal Court, and States of Jersey continue into the twenty-first century. Although plagued by family wars through the eighteenth and nineteenth centuries, the Jersey population grew economically from fisheries, smuggling, and later from cattle, potatoes, and tourism. Jersey has long been famous for the Jersey milk cattle, a pure breed exported worldwide. Jersey, just as all of the Channel Islands, was left undefended from 1940 to 1945 during World War II and fell briefly to the Germans.

GOVERNMENT

The Bailiwick of Jersey has a unique relation with the United Kingdom. Neither a sovereign state nor part of the United Kingdom, it is a British Crown dependency. The chief of state is the British monarch. The monarch's personal representative and channel for communication between the Crown and island government is the lieutenant-governor which also serves as commander-in-chief of Jersey. Appointed by the Crown, the lieutenant-governor may attend and speak in the legislative body, the States of Jersey, but has no vote. He holds veto power over specific forms of legislation.

Jersey's unicameral legislative branch, the Assembly of the States of Jersey, is composed of the lieutenant governor, the bailiff and deputy bailiff, the Dean of Jersey, the attorney-general, the solicitor-general, and fifty-three members elected by uni-

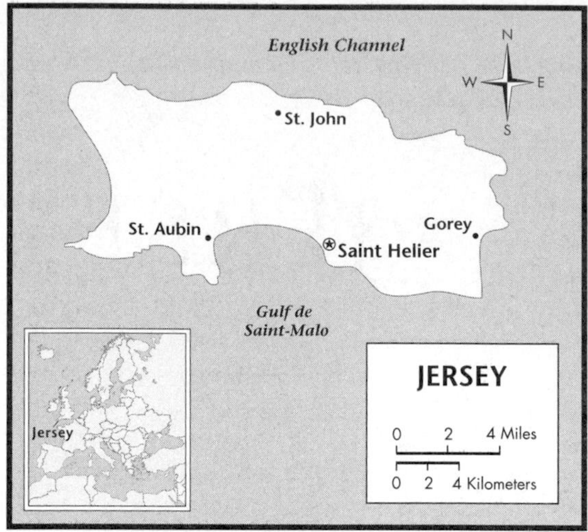

versal suffrage. Appointed by the Crown, the bailiff is president of the Assembly and has the right of dissent and one casting vote. The deputy bailiff also has a casting vote. Also appointed by the Crown, the dean, attorney general, and solicitor-general may sit and speak in the Assembly but not vote. The fifty-three elected seats include twelve senators popularly elected for six-year terms with half retiring every third year, twelve constables of the twelve parishes popularly elected triennially, and twenty-nine deputies popularly elected triennially. Except in certain instances, permanent laws passed by the Assembly require the sanction of the Queen-in-Council.

The Committees of the States, whose members are appointed by the Assembly of States of Jersey, serves as the administrative cabinet.

Judiciary

The Royal Court administers Jersey's justice system. The Royal Court is comprised of the bailiff or deputy bailiff when authorized to act for the bailiff, and twelve jurats or magistrates. Appeals proceed to the Court of Appeal consisting of the bailiff and two judges selected from a Crown-appointed panel. In specific cases, final appeal may be made to the Judicial Committee of the Privy Council in England. Minor civil and criminal cases fall within the jurisdiction of a Stipendiary Magistrate.

Political Parties

No political parties exist. All elected officials are independents.

DEFENSE

Jersey maintains its own form of self-government but the British government remains responsible for Jersey's international relations and for its defense.

ECONOMIC AFFAIRS

Financial services, tourism and agriculture are the key sectors of Jersey's economy. Of the Channel Islands, Jersey maintains the largest offshore financial centers. Jersey's commercial laws encourage merchant banks, especially subsidiaries of London banks, to locate on the island due to Jersey's ability to set low taxation rates. The finance sector contributed approximately 55 percent of Jersey's gross domestic product (GDP) in 1996 compared to only 26 percent in 1980 when the banking interests first began to expand. Tourism, with a long history as an economic mainstay, accounts for 24 percent of the GDP.

The agriculture sector concentrates on dairying and breeding of the Jersey milk cattle, which are exported worldwide. Milk products are exported chiefly to the United Kingdom and other European markets. Many small farms grow potatoes, tomatoes, cauliflower, and flowers for export primarily to the United Kingdom. Greenhouse production of flowers and vegetables contributes significantly to the total crop output.

In the 1990s the government successfully encouraged light industry to locate in Jersey. An electronics industry developed alongside the traditional manufacturing of knitted woolen jerseys.

Jersey's chief exports include light industrial and electrical goods, foodstuffs, and textiles. Exports are protected by British tariff barriers. Major imports include machinery and transport equipment, manufactured goods, foodstuffs, mineral fuels, and chemicals. Imports are free of British purchase tax. The inflation rate for 1998 was 4.7 percent.

Public Finance

In 1997 revenue amounted to 291 million pounds and expenditures were 245 million pounds. The chief revenue source is taxation.

Income

The 1999 estimated GDP was $2.2 billion, or $24,800 per capita. In 1998 inflation was 4.7 percent. In 1996 the composition of the GDP by sector was 93 percent services, 5 percent agriculture, and 2 percent industry.

Industry

Banking and finance, tourism, and dairies are Jersey's primary industries. Financial services are the largest employer, followed by distributive trades, construction, and hotels and restaurants. Principle industrial activities concentrate in light industries such as electrical goods, the traditional knitted textiles, and clothing and foodstuffs.

Banking and Finance

The Jersey Financial Services Commission serves as the financial services regulator. In 1998 seventy-nine banks were licensed in Jersey as the island maintained the largest offshore financial district of the Channel Islands. The range of financial services provided fund management, corporate banking, and company and trust formation. Concerns over investment fraud and tax evasion under the lax enforcement of banking regulations drew considerable attention of the British government through the 1990s.

SOCIAL WELFARE

The Jersey's Social Security Department administers a contributory Health Insurance Scheme. Benefits paid out by the Department are in the areas of long-term benefits, sickness, invalidity, and family allowances.

Healthcare

In 1995 five hospitals with 651 beds were located on Jersey. Ninety-five doctors practiced on Jersey. In 2000 life expectancy for the total population was 78.5 years, with males seventy-six years and females eighty-one years.

EDUCATION

In 1996 Jersey had twenty-four public primary schools and five public secondary schools. Eight private primary schools and eight private secondary schools were also available. Jersey had one higher education college.

2000 KEY EVENTS TIMELINE

June

- Under pressure from the Financial Action Task Force on Money Laundering (FATF) based in Paris, France, Jersey says it will cooperate to eliminate illegal offshore banking and money-laundering practices. Guernsey and the Isle of Man are also listed as cooperating with FATF.

August

- Jersey fishermen blockade the French ports of Saint Malo and Granville Island on August 30 in protest of rising fuel costs. No ferries can leave the blockaded ports leaving passengers stranded on both coasts.
- The Jersey Milk Marketing Board wants to control the production of milk.
- The blockade of the ports of Saint Malo and Granville Island are lifted on August 31.

September

- Jersey may be involved in an independence movement from the United Kingdom. In order to avoid prosecution from the OECD for tax-evasion schemes and money-laundering, Jersey makes a bid for independence on September 2.

October

- Jersey Treasurer Ian Black says on October 17 that public spending is too high because the people insist that the government provide so many services.
- Jersey Island announces that it wants to form a political alliance with Guernsey and other Channel Islands which would improve economic and political power.

ANALYSIS OF EVENTS: 2000

BUSINESS AND THE ECONOMY

Jersey's economy combines the traditional and the modern. Jersey farms continued to be large producers of milk. In 2000 there were protests from dairy farmers because the government wanted to limit the production of milk in order to stabilize prices. However the largest industry is the off-shore banking and financial centers. Jersey was the target—like many other small countries with lenient tax policies—of investigations by the Organization for Economic Cooperation and Development (OECD). Jersey assured OECD that it would cooperate to the fullest to eliminate money-laundering schemes. The low tax base in Jersey is attractive to many foreign companies. Tourism also played a large part in the Jersey economic picture, although

2000 saw a decline in tourism that caused government concern. There was also an effort to improve marketing and production of potatoes.

GOVERNMENT AND POLITICS

Jersey is a Crown dependency but is not part of the United Kingdom. The Jersey government handled its own internal affairs, with guidance in foreign policy matters from the United Kingdom. Like neighboring Guernsey Island, Jersey has a bailiff who serves as president. In 2000 the Bailiff was Sir Philip Martin Bailhache. The States of Jersey is the legislative branch government and it makes laws and raises taxes for the island. In recent years the government balked at increasing public expenditures, but the citizens have come to expect the government to provide most goods and services. Jersey has initiated a move to combine some services with Guernsey. The island nations—often referred to together as the Channel Islands—agreed on many issues, but neither wanted to combine their governments officially. One point on which they disagreed was independence from Great Britain. Jersey has viewed complete independence as an escape clause if the island economy were to be threatened by the Organization for Economic Cooperation and Development (OECD). Guernsey, on the other hand, had no interest in an independence movement.

CULTURE AND SOCIETY

Many people of Jersey speak a unique language that is over 1000 years old. It is a Norman-French language from the time of William the Conqueror (1066 BC). It was through this language, called Jèrrais, that the people spoke of their history and customs. As of 2000, the language was still taught in schools. Although most of the inhabitants of Jersey were of French descent, the government was concerned in 2000 about the small number of minorities suffering discrimination in housing, employment, and education. In March 2001, the planned census of population will include questions about ethnicity so that the government can provide better social services.

DIRECTORY

CENTRAL GOVERNMENT

Head of State

Lieutenant-Governor
Michael Wilkes

Bailiff of Jersey
Sir Phillip Ballhache, Bailiff's Chambers, Royal Court House, St. Heller, Jersey JE1 1DD
PHONE: +44 (1534) 502100
FAX: +44 (1534) 502199

Cabinet

Controller of the Social Security Department
A. Esterson, Social Security Department, St. Heller, Jersey JE4 8PE
PHONE: +44 (1534) 280000

Chief Executive Officer of Financial Services Department
C.A. Syvret, Financial Services Department, PO Box 267, St. Heller, Jersey JE4 8TP
PHONE: +44 (1534) 603000
FAX: +44 (1534) 89155

Chief Administrator of Health and Social Services
G. Jennings, Office of Health and Social Services, 4th Floor, Peter Crill House, St. Heller, Jersey JE2 3QS
PHONE: +44 (1534) 622291
FAX: +44 (1534) 37050

Director of Tourism
S.P. Henwood, Office of Tourism, Liberation Square, St. Heller, Jersey JE1 1BB
PHONE: +44 (1534) 507000
FAX: +44 (1534) 500899

Head of Housing Department
E.H. Le Ruez, Housing Department, PO Box 587, Hilgrove House, Hilgrove St., St. Helier, Jersey JE4 8XT
PHONE: +44 (1534) 884422
FAX: +44 (1534) 884488

Director of Education
T.W. McKeon, Office of Education, PO Box 142, St. Seviour, Jersey JE4 8QJ
PHONE: +44 (1534) 509500
FAX: +44 (1534) 509800

Chief Executive Officer of the Planning and Building Services Department
J. Young, Planning and Building Services Department, 8A South Hill, St Heller, Jersey JE2 4US
PHONE: +44 (1534) 25511
FAX: +44 (1534) 68952

Chief Officer of Agriculture and Fisheries
P. Bastion, Office of Agriculture and Fisheries, Trinity, Jersey JE4 8UF

PHONE: +44 (1534) 866200
FAX: +44 (1534) 866201

Chief Executive Officer of Public Services Department

C.J. Swinnerton, Public Services Department, PO Box 412, South Hill, St. Heller, Jersey JE4 8UY
PHONE: +44 (1534) 601690
FAX: +44 (1534) 68950

JUDICIAL SYSTEM

Royal Court

Royal Court House, St. Heller, Jersey JE1 1DD
PHONE: +44 (1534) 502100
FAX: +44 (1534) 502199

BROADCAST MEDIA

Channel 103FM

6 Tunnell Street, St. Helier, Jersey JE2 4LU
PHONE: +44 (1534) 888103
FAX: +44 (1534) 887799
WEBSITE: http://www.103fm.itl.net/
TITLE: Station Director
CONTACT: Richard Johnson

Radio Jersey 88.8FM/1026AM

BBC Radio Jersey, 18 Parade Road, St. Helier, Jersey
PHONE: +44 (1534) 870000
E-MAIL: radio.jersey@bbc.co.uk
TITLE: Editor
CONTACT: Denzil Dudley

Channel Television

WEBSITE: http://www.channeltv.co.uk/
E-MAIL: creative@channeltv.co.uk
TITLE: Managing Director
CONTACT: Michael Lucas

NEWSPAPERS AND MAGAZINES

Jersey Evening Post

PO Box 582, Jersey JE3 4DG
FAX: +44 (1) 534611622
E-MAIL: jepdaily@itl.net
CIRCULATION: 25,000

Jersey at Home

Springfield St. Helier, Jersey JE2 4LF
TITLE: Editor
CONTACT: J.W. Godfrey
CIRCULATION: 2,000

Jersey Weekly Post

PO Box 582, Jersey JE4 8XQ
FAX: +44 (1) 534611622
CIRCULATION: 1,800

RELIGIOUS ORGANIZATIONS

As a dependency of the British crown, religious affairs are generally handled through archdioceses and home organizations on the mainland of the United Kingdom.

FURTHER READING

Articles

"Ocelot International Ltd." *Oil and Gas Journal,* April 10, 2000, vol. 98, no. 15, p. 42.

Internet

BBC News Online. "Sanctions Threat to 'Tax Havens.'" June 26, 2000. [Online] Available http://news6.thdo.bbc.co.uk/hi/english/business/newsid%5F806000/806236.stm (accessed October 12, 2000).

JERSEY: STATISTICAL DATA

For sources and notes see "Sources of Statistics" at the front of each volume.

GEOGRAPHY

Geography

Area:

Total: 116 sq km.

Land: 116 sq km.

Land boundaries: 0 km.

Coastline: 70 km.

Climate: temperate; mild winters and cool summers.

Terrain: gently rolling plain with low, rugged hills along north coast.

Natural resources: arable land.

Land use:

Arable land: 66%

Permanent crops: 0%

Permanent pastures: 0%

Forests and woodland: 0%

Other: 34%

HUMAN FACTORS

Ethnic Division

UK and Norman-French descent.

Religion

Anglican, Roman Catholic, Baptist, Congregational New Church, Methodist, Presbyterian.

Major Languages

English (official), French (official), Norman-French dialect spoken in country districts.

Demographics (A)

	1990	1995	1998	2000	2010	2020	2030	2040	2050
Population	NA	86.3	87.9	88.9	91.9	93.1	92.9	89.6	84.1
Life expectancy - males	NA	75.3	75.7	76.1	77.4	78.5	79.4	80.1	80.6
Life expectancy - females	NA	80.1	80.7	81.1	82.6	83.9	84.9	85.7	86.3
Birth rate (per 1,000)	NA	13.2	12.4	11.6	8.6	9.4	9.2	8.2	8.7
Death rate (per 1,000)	NA	9.5	9.4	9.3	9.5	10.6	12.2	14.2	16.0
Women of reproductive age (15-49 yrs.)	NA	23.1	22.7	22.4	21.4	18.5	17.7	17.1	15.3
Fertility rate	NA	1.5	1.5	1.6	1.6	1.6	1.6	1.7	1.7

Except as noted, values for vital statistics are in thousands; life expectancy is in years.

GOVERNMENT & LAW

Political Parties

The unicameral Assembly of the States consists of 55 voting members: 12 senators, 12 constables or heads of parishes and 29 deputies. All are elected for six-year terms. Half are elected every third year. The bailiff and the deputy bailiff; and 3 non-voting members - the Dean of Jersey, the Attorney General and the Solicitor General all appointed by the monarch. There are no political parties. Independents won 52 seats.

Government Budgets (B)

Revenues	$666.9 million
Expenditures	$618.5 million
Capital expenditures	$128.4 million

Data for 1996 est.

LABOR FORCE

Total Labor Force (A)

57,050 (1996).

Unemployment Rate

0.7% (1998 est.)

PRODUCTION SECTOR

Energy Production

Production	266 million kWh
Production by source	
Fossil fuel	100%
Hydro	0%
Nuclear	0%
Other	0%
Exports	0 kWh

Data for 1998.

Energy Consumption

Consumption	467 million kWh
Imports	201 million kWh

Data for 1995.

Transportation

Highways:

Total: 577 km (1995).

Merchant marine: none (1999 est.).

Airports: 1 (1999 est.).

Top Agriculture Products

Potatoes, cauliflower, tomatoes; beef, dairy products.

MANUFACTURING SECTOR

GDP & Manufacturing Summary (C)

Total GDP (1999 est.)	$2.2 billion
Real growth rate	NA
Per capita (1999 est.)	$24,800
Composition by sector	
Agriculture	5%
Industry	2%
Services	93%

Values in purchasing power parity. NA stands for not available.

COMMUNICATIONS

Telecommunications

Telephones - main lines in use: NA

Telephones - mobile cellular: NA

Telephone system:

Domestic: NA

International: 3 submarine cables.

Radio broadcast stations: AM NA, FM 1, shortwave 0 (1998).

Radios: NA

Television broadcast stations: 1 (1997).

Televisions: NA

Internet Service Providers (ISPs): NA

FINANCE, ECONOMICS, & TRADE

Economic Indicators

National product: GDP—purchasing power parity—$2.2 billion (1999 est.).

National product real growth rate: NA.

National product per capita: $24,800 (1999 est.).

Inflation rate—consumer price index: 4.7% (1998).

Exchange Rates

Exchange rates:

Jersey pounds per US$1

January 2000	0.6092
1999	0.6180
1998	0.6037
1997	0.6106
1996	0.6403
1995	0.6335

The Jersey pound is at par with the British pound. Fiscal year: 1 April - 31 March.

Top Import Origins

Origins: United Kingdom.

Top Export Destinations

Destination: United Kingdom.

Import/Export Commodities

Import Commodities	Export Commodities
Machinery and transport equipment	Light industrial and electrical goods
Manufactured goods	Foodstuffs
Foodstuffs	Textiles
Mineral fuels	
Chemicals	

JORDAN

CAPITAL: ʽAmman.

FLAG: The national flag is a tricolor of black, white, and green horizontal stripes with a seven-pointed white star on a red triangle at the hoist.

ANTHEM: *As-Salam al-Maliki (Long Live the King).*

MONETARY UNIT: The Jordanian dinar (JD) is a paper currency of 1,000 fils. There are coins of 1, 5, 10, 20, 25, 50, 100, and 250 fils and notes of 1, 5, 10, and 20 dinars. JD1 = $1.41044 (or $1 = JD0.709).

WEIGHTS AND MEASURES: The metric system is the legal standard, but some local and Syrian units are still widely used, especially in the villages.

HOLIDAYS: Arbor Day, 15 January; Independence Day, 25 May; Accession of King Hussein, 11 August; King Hussein's Birthday, 14 November. Muslim religious holidays include the 1st of Muharram (Islamic New Year), ʽId al-Fitr, ʽId al-ʽAdhaʾ, and Milad an-Nabi. Christmas and Easter are observed by sizable Christian minorities.

TIME: 2 PM = noon GMT.

LOCATION AND SIZE: Situated in southwest Asia, Jordan has an area of 83,335 square kilometers (32,175 square miles), slightly smaller than the state of Indiana. It has a total boundary length of 1,645 kilometers (1,022 miles), not including the West Bank.

Jordan's capital city, ʽAmman, is located in the northwestern part of the country.

CLIMATE: The Jordan Valley has little rainfall, intense summer heat, and mild, pleasant winters. The desert regions are subject to great extremes of temperature and receive rainfall of less than 20 centimeters (8 inches) annually, while the rest of the country has an average rainfall of up to 58 centimeters (23 inches) a year.

Temperatures at ʽAmman range from about −4°C (25°F) in winter to more than 38°C (100°F) in summer.

The Hashemite Kingdom of Jordan
Al-Mamlaka al-Urdunniyya al-Hashimiyya

INTRODUCTORY SURVEY

RECENT HISTORY

Following the 1948 Arab-Israeli war King ʽAbdallah of the Hashemite Kingdom of Jordan annexed the area of Palestine now known as the West Bank. Jordan also absorbed about half of some one million Palestinian Arab refugees, mostly sheltered in UN-administered camps. In July 1951 ʽAbdallah was assassinated in Jerusalem by a Palestinian Arab, and the throne passed to his grandson Hussein I, who was formally enthroned on May 2, 1953.

As the movement for Arab unity grew in the 1950s, Jordan maintained a close association with Britain in an effort to preserve the kingdom as a separate, independent country.

While retaining Jordan's Western ties, Hussein gradually steadied his relations with other Arab states (except Syria). Terrorist raids launched from within Jordan drew strong Israeli reprisals. In addition, the activities of the Palestine Liberation Organization (PLO) often violated Jordan's borders leading Hussein in 1966 and 1967 to withdraw support for the PLO angering the Arab world.

In the 1967 Six-Day War with Israel, Israel took over the Jordanian West Bank (including all of Jerusalem). Jordan suffered heavy casualties, and over 300,000 Palestinians fled across the Jordan River to the East Bank. Jordan's refugee population swelled from 700,000 in 1966 to over 1 million, adding to the severe economic problems.

After acceptance of a cease-fire with Israel in 1970, Hussein suppressed various Palestinian guer-

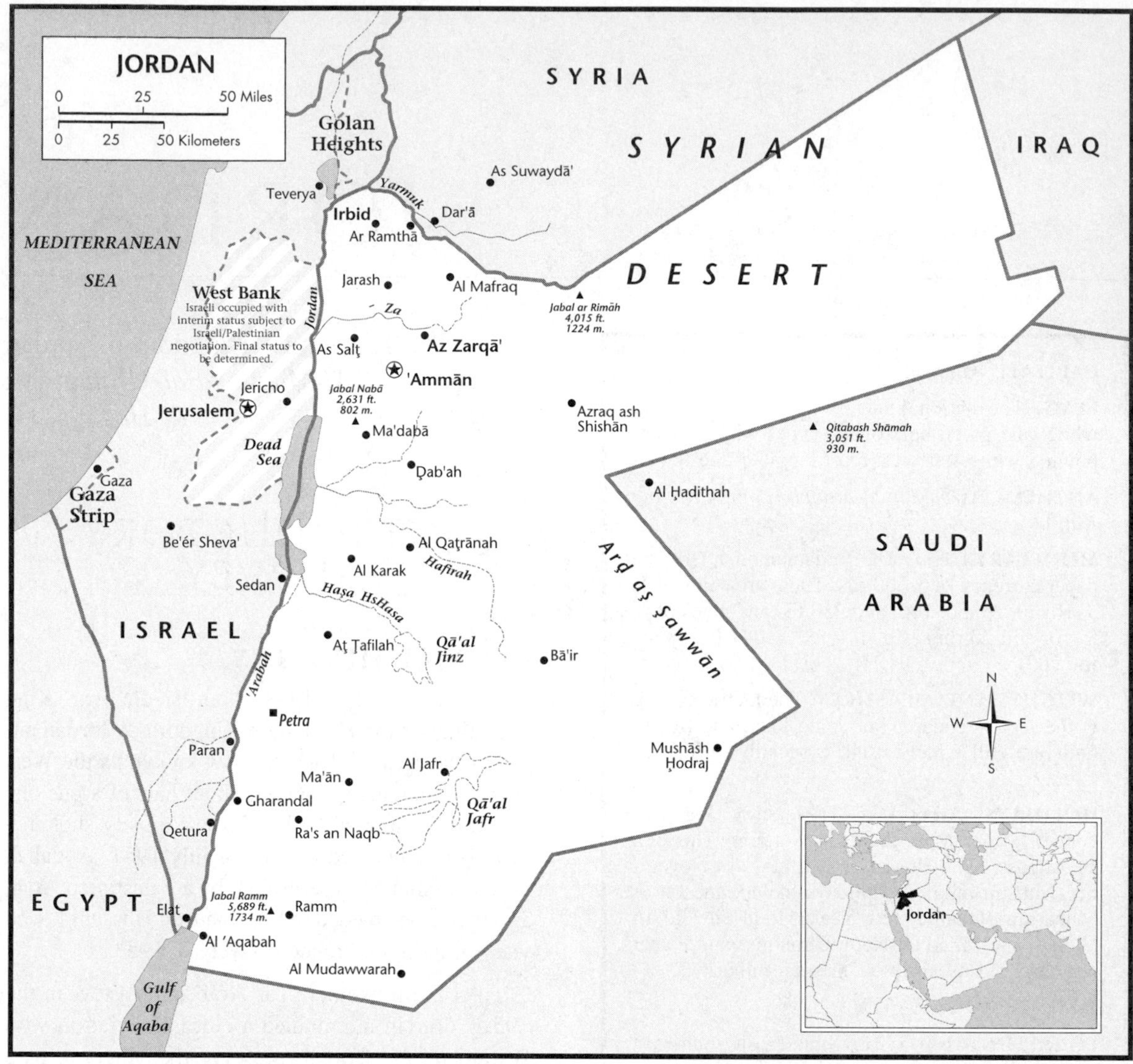

rilla organizations. Jordan did not actively participate in the "Yom Kippur War" against Israel in October 1973, but did send an armored brigade of about 2,500 men to assist Syria.

In the 1980s Hussein gradually liberalized internal politics. In 1989 Jordan held relatively free parliamentary elections for the first time since 1956. In 1988 Jordan cut its ties with the Israeli occupied West Bank.

Critical of the 1990 Gulf War, Jordan's relations with the United States and the Gulf states declined. But willingness to participate in peace talks with Israel in late 1991 helped repair Western relations. In June 1994 Jordan and Israel began meetings to work out practical steps on water, borders, and energy that would normalize relations. In July 1994, Jordan and Israel signed a peace treaty officially ending their state of war and in 1995, Israel agreed to transfer administrative control of the West Bank to the Palestinians.

On February 7, 1999, King Hussein died of cancer after a reign of forty-six years. His oldest son, Abdullah, succeeded him. In his first year he paved the way for Jordan's entry into the World Trade Organization (WTO) in January 2000. Abdullah declared his intention for administrative and educational reforms, and took a firm stance against Islamic extremists in Jordan diving the radical Hamas out of the country.

GOVERNMENT

Jordan is a constitutional monarchy. The king has wide powers over all branches of government. He appoints a prime minister and together they appoint members of the cabinet. The legislative branch is a bicameral National Assembly that consists of a forty-member Senate and eighty-member House of Representatives. Senators are appointed by the monarch from designated categories of public figures to serve four-year terms. The members of the House are elected by popular vote on the basis of proportional representation to four-year terms.

There is universal suffrage at age 18, women having received the right to vote in April 1973.

Judiciary

There are four levels of civil and criminal courts, religious courts, and tribal courts. The Supreme Court and the courts of appeals deal with appeals from lower courts. Courts of First Instance hear major civil and criminal cases. Magistrates courts deal with cases not coming within jurisdiction of Courts of First Instance. Religious courts, such as the Muslim Shari`ah courts, have authority over matters such as marriage, divorce, wills and testaments, and orphans.

Political Parties

Political parties were abolished in 1957 following an alleged attempted coup by Arab militants. In 1992 parties were again permitted and twenty were allowed to take part in elections. The main opposition group has been the Islamic Action Front, the political arm of the Moslem (Muslim) Brotherhood. In 1997 nine pro-government parties banded together to form the National Constitutional Party but were able to win only three seats.

The Islamic opposition boycotted the elections altogether. Independent pro-government candidates representing local tribal interests won sixty-two of the eighty seats, ten seats were won by nationalist and leftist candidates, and eight by independent Islamists.

DEFENSE

In 2000 the Jordanian army had some 90,000 men. The air force had 13,500 men, and the navy had only about 480 men. Reserve manpower was estimated at 35,000. Defense expenditures for 1998 were $608.9 million or 7.8 percent of GDP.

ECONOMIC AFFAIRS

Jordan's economy has been greatly affected by the Arab-Israeli conflict. The loss of the West Bank in 1967 resulted in the loss of most of Jordan's richest agricultural land and a decline in the growing tourist industry. Western economic aid, notably from the United States, Britain, and Germany, has also been important to the economy.

The start of a recession in Jordan in the mid-1980s followed by the economic collapse of 1988-89 and the Gulf War in 1991 left the country with an unemployment rate of approximately 30-35 percent and high inflation. About 25-30 percent of the population fell below the poverty line. The international embargo against Iraq caused Jordan to lose a major market for its exports and re-exports. The economy rebounded in 1992 largely due to the influx of capital repatriated by workers returning from the Gulf War. The GDP growth rate averaged 9 percent from 1992 to 1995, but slowed to a 2 percent average from 1996 to 1999. In an effort to spur growth King Abdallah undertook economic reforms including privatization and entry into the WTO in January 2000.

In 1995, the government began a program of economic reforms, which included market-oriented policies, commitment to international investment, and the signing of trade and transportation agreements with Israel.

Public Finance

Jordan has had to rely on foreign assistance for support of its budget, which has increased rapidly since the 1967 war. During the late 1980s, Jordan incurred large fiscal deficits, which led to a heavy burden of external debt. In 1992 expenditures exceeded revenues by $600 million. By 1993 the current account deficit stood at 11.4 percent of GDP. By 1994 the government's austerity measures reduced this figure to 6.7 percent, and in 1995 it had come into line with targets at 3.7 percent of GDP. The current account had a surplus of 0.4 percent of GDP in 1997 and was balanced in 1998.

The U.S. CIA estimated that in 2000 government revenues totaled approximately $2.8 billion and expenditures $3.1 billion. External debt totaled $8.4 billion by 1998 estimates.

Income

In 1999 Jordan's gross domestic product (GDP) was estimated at $16 billion or about $3,500 per capita. The estimated 1999 GDP growth rate was 2 percent and inflation 3 percent. The 1998 estimated GDP by sector was agriculture 3 percent, industry 25 percent, and services 72 percent.

Industry

Most industrial income comes from four industries: cement, oil refining, phosphates, and potash. Other industries are light manufacturing and tourism. The industrial sector grew an average of 6.7 percent annually between 1988 and 1998.

Banking and Finance

The Central Bank of Jordan, founded in 1964, is in charge of note issue, foreign exchange control, and supervision of commercial banks, in cooperation with the Economic Security Council.

Besides the Central Bank, the banking system includes thirteen commercial banks, five investment banks, two Islamic banks, one Industrial Development Bank, and several other institutions. The Arab Bank and the Housing Bank are the largest banks in Jordan.

Loans are extended by the Jordan Industrial Bank, Agricultural Credit Corporation, Jordan Cooperative Organization, and other credit institutions.

The Amman Financial Market (AFM) has been in existence since the late 1970s and had a total of 115 companies listed in 1997. In 1999 the Amman Stock Exchange with 149 listed companies was established as a privately managed institution.

Economic Development

In 1988 Jordan began working with the IMF on restructuring its economy. These plans were thrown into considerable disarray by political events in the Gulf (most notably Jordan's ill-conceived support of Iraq in the face of global opposition to that country's 1990 invasion of Kuwait), but new agreements were concluded in 1991 as Jordan began to institute democratic reforms. Foremost in the IMF plan are reductions in government spending, taming of inflation, increasing foreign exchange, and decreasing government ownership of economic enterprises. In the economic plan of 1996-1998 Jordan is expected to decrease its ownership of enterprises from 1994's level of 64 percent to 55 percent by 1998. Jordan entered the WTO in January 2000.

SOCIAL WELFARE

The social insurance system provides old age, disability, and survivor benefits, as well as workers' compensation. Public employees and workers over the age of sixteen working n companies with five or more employees are covered. The UN Relief and Works Agency (UNRWA) conducts an extensive welfare program for Palestinian refugees. Many Christian groups maintain hospitals, orphanages, and schools and are financed from foreign sources.

Women experience legal discrimination regarding pension and social security benefits, inheritance, and divorce. Under Islamic law, a female heir's inheritance is half that of a male, and in court, a woman's testimony has only half the value of a man's. However in 1992 Parliament effectively blocked Islamists from enacting further legislation discriminating against women.

Healthcare

In 1995 Jordan had 6,839 physicians, 3,118 pharmacists, 2,015 dentists, and 4,304 nurses. Total health care expenditures for 1995 were $347 million. In 1992 97 percent of the population had access to health care services. UNRWA operates its own hospitals and maternity centers for refugees. Trachoma, hepatitis, typhoid fever, intestinal parasites, acute skin inflammations, and some other conditions remain common, however. In 1990-1995 89 percent of the population had access to safe water, and 95 percent of the population had adequate sanitation. In 2000 the average life expectancy is seventy-seven years.

Housing

Jordan still lacked adequate housing in the early 1980s. During 1981-1986 some 42,300 new residential building permits were issued. According to the latest available information for 1980-1988, the total number of dwellings was 660,000 with 4.1 people per dwelling.

EDUCATION

The illiteracy rate declined from 68 percent of the population in 1961 to 13 percent in 1995, with male illiteracy estimated at 6.6 percent and female at 20.6 percent. Education is compulsory between the ages of six and fifteen. Ten years are devoted to primary education followed by two years at the secondary stage. In 1998 Jordan had 2,623 primary schools with 45,367 teachers and 1.1 million pupils. Secondary schools had a total of 155,008 pupils the same year. The UNRWA operates 208 schools in refugee camps.

In 1997 a total of 112,959 students were enrolled at all higher-level institutions. Jordan has five universities and fifty-three community colleges.

2000 KEY EVENTS TIMELINE

January

- Jordanians travel to Wadi Kharrar, the site on the banks of the Jordan River where Jesus is believed to have been baptized.

February

- Jordanian authorities indict thirteen people on terrorist conspiracy charges.

March

- Pope John Paul visits Jordan on March 21.

August

- On August 25 Foreign Minister Abdelelah al-Jatib denies Jordan's involvement in the arms trafficking of 10,000 Russian assault rifles through Peru to Colombian guerrillas.

October

- Thousands of Jordanians demonstrate against Israel on October 25, the same day that the United States and Jordan negotiate a free trade agreement.

November

- On November 19, Hard-line professional associations and unions issue a blacklist of Jordanians who have done business with Israel. An Israeli diplomat is shot and wounded at Amman on the same day.

December

- A five-member commission led by former U.S. Senator George Mitchell arrives December 12 for talks with King Abdullah II; the commission is investigating the causes of Israeli-Palestinian violence.

ANALYSIS OF EVENTS: 2000

BUSINESS AND THE ECONOMY

King Abdullah lived up to his promise to focus on the economy, setting in motion numerous initiatives as part of an economic reform and liberalization program, including a major campaign to attract foreign investment. The Economic Consultative Council (ECC), created by Abdullah at the end of 1999 and made up of members from both government and private industry, was active in carrying the king's programs forward. Significant growth was expected to come from information technology, tourism, the fertilizer industry, and special industrial zones known as QIZs. Major government initiatives on the economy by midyear included liberalization of the banking system, tariff reduction, restructuring of the nation's power distribution companies, and new legislation on stock market regulation and intellectual property protection. Additional measures slated for succeeding months included reform of the state pension system and the income tax system. In addition, Jordan and the United States finalized a free-trade agreement in the fall.

As of 2000 however Jordan's economy was still growing only about half as fast as its population. Debt repayment drained much of the nation's budget, and unemployment was officially reported at 15 percent but thought to be substantially higher. On the plus side, the budget deficit, which had been declining since 1998 was projected to fall to 7 percent of gross domestic product (GDP) in 2000, and the balance of payments had yielded a surplus of $622.4 million in 1999.

In April the European Commission pledged to provide Eur 80 million ($72.8 million) in aid to assist Jordan with economic reform.

GOVERNMENT AND POLITICS

In his second year in power, Jordan's King Abdullah continued his energetic approach to governing, largely winning positive marks from observers both at home and abroad, although Jordan still faced substantial political and economic challenges both at home and abroad. Early in the year, Jordan's parliament tried unsuccessfully to unseat Prime Minister Abdel Raouf Rawabdeh, whom opponents charged with corruption and economic mismanagement. Even after the effort failed, relations among legislators remained stormy. Abdullah maintained his support for Rawabdeh.

In international affairs King Abdullah maintained the peace his father, King Hussein, had negotiated with Israel and continued Hussein's support for the Middle East peace process, demonstrating his commitment to peace by shutting down the Jordan offices of the radical group Hamas and prosecuting thirteen alleged terrorists said to have ties to Saudi financier and provocateur Osama bin

Laden. However, he also worked to achieve a balance between Jordan's friendship with Israel and its relations with the neighboring Arab states of Syria and Lebanon. Abdullah continued to travel frequently in the Middle East, pursuing political and economic initiatives and attempting to repair rifts that had grown up between Jordan and some of its Arab neighbors during the reign of his father. In April he became the first Arab head of state to travel to Israel for meetings with Israeli prime minister Ehud Barak. The following month he made a ten-day visit to the United States.

CULTURE AND SOCIETY

A year after King Abdullah ascended the throne of Jordan, the country's people continued to enjoy the political, social, and economic stability they had known under the rule of his father, King Hussein. However, Abdullah also inherited significant economic problems, including slow economic growth that contributed to the fact that about one-third of the country's population lived below the poverty line. An estimated 40,000 Jordanians were working illegally in Israel to make ends meet; others took jobs in the Persian Gulf region or left the country permanently. Under King Abdullah, the government committed itself to the goal of doubling per capita income by 2020.

Among Abdullah's social goals was his determination to end inequities between Jordanians from the East Bank and those with Palestinian roots, who account for 60 percent of the country's population. Reflecting the government's commitment to the advancement of Palestinians in Jordanian society was the appointment of a Palestinian, All Abu Ragheb, as prime minister in June, and also the inclusion of several ministers of Palestinian origin in the cabinet.

In the area of public health the government launched a campaign to reduce smoking among Jordanians. Special attention was to be paid to young people; it was estimated that about one-quarter of all students under the age of fourteen were smokers. The campaign, which was publicized by a large antismoking demonstration in the capital city of Amman in May, was to focus on educating and persuading the public to give up smoking, but mandatory bans were also being considered in such public places as health and social agencies, universities, and airliners.

DIRECTORY

CENTRAL GOVERNMENT

Head of State

King
Abdallah ibn al-Hussein al-Hashimi, Monarch
E-MAIL: info@nic.gov.jo

Prime Minister
Abd al-Raouf al-Rawabdeh, Office of the Prime Minister, PO Box 80, Amman, Jordan

Ministers

Minister of Agriculture
Zuhair Zannouneh, Ministry of Agriculture, PO Box 2099, Amman, Jordan
PHONE: +962 686431
FAX: +962 686310

Minister of Awqaf and Islamic Affairs
Abdul Salam al-Abbadi, Ministry of Awqaf and Islamic Affairs

Minister of Culture
Mahmoud Kayed, Ministry of Culture

Minister of Communications
Ministry of Communications, PO Box 71, Amman, Jordan
PHONE: +962 624301
FAX: +962 825262

Minister of Defense
Ali Abu al-Ragheb, Ministry of Defense

Minister of Education
Khalid Touqan, Ministry of Education, PO Box 1646, Amman, Jordan
PHONE: +962 669181; 667182
FAX: +962 666019

Minister of Energy and Mineral Resources
Wael Sabri, Ministry of Energy and Mineral Resources, PO Box 140027, Amman, Jordan
PHONE: +962 863326
FAX: +962 666019

Minister of Finance
Michel Marto, Ministry of Finance

Minister of Foreign Affairs
Abdel-Elah al-Khatib, Ministry of Foreign Affairs, PO Box 1577, Amman 11511, Jordan
PHONE: +962 6644361
FAX: +962 6648825

Minister of Health
Tareq Suheimat, Ministry of Health, PO Box 86, Amman, Jordan

PHONE: +962 5665131
FAX: +962 5688373

Minister of Justice
Faris Nabulsi, Ministry of Justice, PO Box 6040, Amman, Jordan
PHONE: +962 663103
FAX: +962 680238

Minister of Transport
Mohammed Farhan Kalaldeh, Ministry of Transport, PO Box 35214, Amman, Jordan

Minister of Higher Education
Ministry of Higher Education, PO Box 138, Amman, Jordan
PHONE: +962 847671
FAX: +962 837616

Minister of Industry and Trade
Wasif Azar, Ministry of Industry and Trade, PO Box 2019, Amman, Jordan
PHONE: +962 663191
FAX: +962 603721

Minister of Information
Taleb al-Rifal, Ministry of Information, PO Box 1845, Amman, Jordan
PHONE: +962 642311
FAX: +962 648895

Minister of Interior
Khleifat Awad, Ministry of Interior

Minister of Labor
Aid al-Fayez, Ministry of Labor, PO Box 8160, Amman, Jordan
PHONE: +962 663945; 663186; 667161
FAX: +962 667193

Minister of Municipal, Rural Affairs and Environment
Abdul Rahim Akour, Ministry of Municipal, Rural Affairs and Environment, PO Box 1799, Amman, Jordan
PHONE: +962 4641393
FAX: +962 4640404

Minister of Planning
Jawad Hadid, Ministry of Planning, PO Box 555, Amman, Jordan
PHONE: +962 644466
FAX: +962 649341

Minister of Post and Telecommunications
Fawaz Hatem Zobi, Ministry of Post and Telecommunications

Minister of Public Works and Housing
Husni Abu Ghida, Ministry of Public Works and Housing

Minister of Religious Affairs
Abdelsalam Abbadi, Mininstry of Religious Affairs

Minister of Social Development
Tamam Ghoul, Ministry of Social Development, PO Box 1310, Amman, Jordan
PHONE: +962 5931391
FAX: +962 5607391

Minister of Transport
Mohammed Farhan Kalaldeh, Ministry of Transport, PO Box 35214, Amman, Jordan
PHONE: +962 641461
FAX: +962 649428

Minister of Tourism
Aqel Biltaji, Ministry of Tourism, PO Box 224, Amman, Jordan
PHONE: +962 642311
FAX: +962 648465

Minister of Youth and Sports
Said Shuqum, Ministry of Youth and Sports

Minister of Water and Irrigation
Hatim Halawani, Ministry of Water and Irrigation, PO Box 2769, Amman, Jordan
PHONE: +962 689400; 689410
FAX: +962 689916

POLITICAL ORGANIZATIONS

Al-Ahrar (Freedom Party)

TITLE: Secretary General
NAME: Ahmad Zo'bi

Arab Ba'th (Progressive Party)

TITLE: Secretary General
NAME: Mahmoud al-Ma'aytah

Doa'a (Arab Islamic Democratic Party)

TITLE: Secretary General
NAME: Yousif Abu Bakr

Arab Land Party

TITLE: Secretary General
NAME: Muhammad al-'Oran

Arab Jordanian Ansar Party

TITLE: Secretary General
NAME: Mahummad Majali

Democratic Party of the Left

TITLE: Secretary General
NAME: Musa Ma'aitah

Islamic Action Front

TITLE: Secretary General
NAME: Abd-al-Latif Arabiyat

Jordanian Arab Constitutional Front Party

TITLE: Secretary General
NAME: Milhem Tell

Jordanian Ba'th Arab Socialist Party

TITLE: Secretary General
NAME: Tayseer al-Homsi

Jordanian Communist Party

TITLE: Secretary General
NAME: Ya'acoub Zayadin

Jordanian Democratic Popular Unity Party

TITLE: Secretary General
NAME: Sa'eed Mustapha

Jordanian Labor Party

TITLE: Secretary General
NAME: Muhammad Khatayibah

Jordanian Peace Party

TITLE: Secretary General
NAME: Shaher Khreis

Jordanian People's Democratic Party

TITLE: Secretary General
NAME: Salem Nahhas

Al-Mustaqbal (Future Party)

TITLE: Secretary General
NAME: Suleiman 'Arar

Haqq (National Action Party)

TITLE: Secretary General
NAME: Muhammad Zo'bi

National Constitutional Party

TITLE: Secretary General
NAME: Abdul Hadi Majali

National Democratic Public Movement Party

TITLE: Secretary General
NAME: Muhammad al-'Amer

Progressive Party

TITLE: Secretary General
NAME: Na'el Barakat

Al-Umma (Nation Party)

TITLE: Secretary General
NAME: Ahmad Hneidi

DIPLOMATIC REPRESENTATION

Embassies in Jordan

Australia
PHONE: +962 5930246

Austria
PHONE: +962 4644635

Belgium
PHONE: +962 5675683

Brazil
PHONE: +962 4642169

Canada
PO Box 815403, Amman 11180, Jordan
PHONE: +962 6666124
FAX: +962 6689227

Chile
PHONE: +962 5924097

China
PHONE: +962 5699137

Denmark
PHONE: +962 5603703

Egypt
PHONE: +962 5605202

France
PHONE: +962 4641273

Germany
PHONE: +962 5930351

Greece
PHONE: +962 5672331

Hungary
PHONE: +962 5930836

India
PHONE: +962 4637262

Iraq
PHONE: +962 4623175

Israel
PHONE: +962 5524680

Italy
PHONE: +962 4638185

Japan
PHONE: +962 5923005

South Korea
PHONE: +962 5660745

Netherlands
PHONE: +962 4619693

Pakistan
PHONE: +962 4622787

Poland
PHONE: +962 4637153

Russia
PHONE: +962 4641158

Saudi Arabia
PHONE: +962 5924154

South Africa
PHONE: +962 5812288

Spain
PHONE: +962 4614167

Turkey
PHONE: +962 4641251

United Kingdom
PHONE: +962 5923100

United States
PO Box 354, Amman 11118, Jordan
PHONE: +962 6820101
NAME: William Joseph Burns

JUDICIAL SYSTEM

Court of Cassation

BROADCAST MEDIA

Jordan Radio

PO Box 1041 (QSL PO Box 909), Amman, Jordan
E-MAIL: rj@jrtv.gov.jo

Jordan Satellite Channel (JSC)

PO Box 1041, Amman, Jordan
E-MAIL: jsc@jrtv.gov.jo

Jordan Radio & Television Corporation (JRTV/JTV)

PO Box 1041, Amman, Jordan
PHONE: +962 (6) 77311; 77319; 4748884
FAX: +962 (6) 751503; 788115; 4779402
E-MAIL: rj@jrtv.gov.jo, eng@jrtv.gov.jo, general@jrtv.gov.jo
WEBSITE: http://www.jrtv.com
CONTACT: Ihsan Ramzi, Directorate General
LANGUAGE: Arabic, English, French
BROADCASTS: 24 hours-day
CHANNEL: 8 channels
TYPE: Government

COLLEGES AND UNIVERSITIES

Yarmouk University

PO Box 566, Irbid, Jordan
PHONE: +962 (2) 7271100
FAX: +962 (2) 7274725
WEBSITE: http://www.yu.edu.jo

University of Jordan

Amman, Jordan
PHONE: +962 (6) 843555
FAX: +962 (6) 840150; 832318
E-MAIL: admin@ju.edu.jo
WEBSITE: http://www.ju.edu.jo

Jordan University of Science and Technology

PO Box 3030, Irbid, Jordan
PHONE: +962 (2) 295111
FAX: +962 (2) 205123
E-MAIL: webmaster@just.edu.jo

Mu'tah University

PO Box 7, Mu'tah, Al Karak, Jordan
PHONE: +962 (3) 836061
FAX: +962 (3) 654061
E-MAIL: webmaster@mutah.edu.jo
WEBSITE: http://www.mutah.edu.jo

NEWSPAPERS AND MAGAZINES

Ad-Dustour

Jordan Press and Publishing, P.O. Box 591-1118, 591 Amman, Jordan
PHONE: +962 (6) 5667170; 5686121
FAX: +962 (6) 5667170; 5685810
E-MAIL: dustour@go.com.jo
WEBSITE: http://www.addustour.com

TITLE: Editor
CONTACT: Nabeel Al-Sharif
CIRCULATION: 90,500

Hadath, Al

P.O. Box 961167, 11196 Amman, Jordan
PHONE: +962 (6) 55160824; 5160820
FAX: +962 (6) 5160810
E-MAIL: hadath@access.com.jo
WEBSITE: http://accessme.com/al-hadath

Jordan Times

P.O. Box 6710, Amman, Jordan
PHONE: +962 (6) 5667171
FAX: +962 (6) 5661242
E-MAIL: jotimes@go.com.jo
WEBSITE: http://www.accessme.com/jordantimes
TITLE: Editor-in-Chief
CONTACT: George Hawatmeh
CIRCULATION: 12,000

Ra'I, Al

Jordan Press Foundation, P.O. Box 6710, 11118 Amman, Jordan
PHONE: +962 (6) 5667171
FAX: +962 (6) 5661242
E-MAIL: alrai@go.com.jo
WEBSITE: http://www.access2arabia.com/alrai
TITLE: Publisher
CONTACT: Mahmood Al-Kayed

Sawt Al-Shaab

Dar Al Shaab Press, Al-Jaminah St., P.O. Box 3037-925155, Amman, Jordan
TITLE: Editor-in-Chief
CONTACT: Hashem Khaisat
CIRCULATION: 30,000

Star, The

Media Services International, P.O. Box 9313, 11191 Amman, Jordan
PHONE: +962 (6) 465580
FAX: +962 (6) 4648298
E-MAIL: star@arabia.com
WEBSITE: http://star.arabia.com
CIRCULATION: 7,000

Jordan Today Staff

PO Box 9313, 11191 Amman, Jordan
PHONE: +962 652380
FAX: +962 648298
E-MAIL: Star@arabia.com
WEBSITE: http://corp.arabia.com/JordanToday
TITLE: Publisher
CONTACT: Osama El Sherif
TYPE: Monthly, English-language magazine on tourism, culture and entertainment

PUBLISHERS

Al-Tanwir Al Ilmi (Scientific Enlightenment Publishing House)

PO Box 4237, al-Mahatta, 11131 Amman, Jordan
PHONE: +962 (26) 4899619
FAX: +962 (26) 4899619
E-MAIL: taisir@yahoo.com
TITLE: Owner
CONTACT: Taisir Subhi Mohmoud
SUBJECTS: Education, Electronics, Electrical Engineering, Philosophy, Science (General), Social Sciences, Sociology
TOTAL PUBLISHED: 55 print

Jordan Book Centre Co. Ltd.

PO Box 301, 11941 Amman, Jordan
PHONE: +962 (6) 5151882; 5156882; 5155882
FAX: +962 (6) 602016
E-MAIL: jbc@nets.com.jo; jbc@go.com.jo
TITLE: Chief Executive
CONTACT: I. Sharbain
SUBJECTS: Art, Business, Computer Science, Economics, Education, Engineering, Fiction, History, Medicine, Nonfiction (General), Science, Technology
TOTAL PUBLISHED: 197

Jordan Distributing Agency Co. Ltd.

PO Box 375, 11118 Amman, Jordan
PHONE: +962 (6) 4630191; 4630192
FAX: +962 (6) 463152
E-MAIL: jda@go.com.jo
TITLE: General Manager
CONTACT: Raja Elissa
SUBJECTS: History
TOTAL PUBLISHED: 18 print

Jordan House for Publication

PO Box 1121, Amman, Jordan
PHONE: +962 (6) 24224
FAX: +962 (6) 51062
TITLE: Man. Director
CONTACT: Mursi El-Ashkar
SUBJECTS: Medicine, Nursing, Dentistry

RELIGIOUS ORGANIZATIONS

Islamic

Young Moslem Women's Association
Centre for Special Education, PO Box 19124, Sport City Area, Amman, Jordan
PHONE: +962 (6) 4207755
FAX: +962 (6) 4207788
E-MAIL: kareh@nets.com.jo
TITLE: Secretary
NAME: Mrs. Nojood Fawzi

FURTHER READING

Articles

"Answer to Jordan's Economic Woes May Lie in Iraq: Jordan's Transportation Minister Recently Visited Iraq, and the Prime Minister May Follow Suit." *Christian Science Monitor,* September 22, 2000, p. 7.

"Jordan Hopes the World Accepts Peace, Maybe at Half the Price." *Barron's,* June 5, 2000, vol. 80, no. 23, p. 12.

"Jordan's Warrior King." *The Economist (US),* July 8, 2000, vol. 356, no. 8178, p. 41.

Orme, William A. Jr. "Anti-U.S. Fury in Jordan's Streets Overshadows a Trade Pact." *New York Times,* October 25, 2000, p. A3.

Owen, Richard. "Baptismal Dispute Puts Pope under Pressure," *The Times* (London), March 22, 2000, Middle East.

Books

Jordan. Oakland, CA: Lonely Planet, 2000.

JORDAN: STATISTICAL DATA

For sources and notes see "Sources of Statistics" at the front of each volume.

GEOGRAPHY

Geography

Area:

Total: 89,213 sq km.

Land: 88,884 sq km.

Land boundaries:

Total: 1,619 km.

Border countries: Iraq 181 km, Israel 238 km, Saudi Arabia 728 km, Syria 375 km, West Bank 97 km.

Coastline: 26 km.

Climate: mostly arid desert; rainy season in west (November to April).

Terrain: mostly desert plateau in east, highland area in west; Great Rift Valley separates East and West Banks of the Jordan River.

Natural resources: phosphates, potash, shale oil.

Land use:

Arable land: 4%

Permanent crops: 1%

Permanent pastures: 9%

Forests and woodland: 1%

Other: 85% (1993 est.).

HUMAN FACTORS

Demographics (A)

	1990	1995	1998	2000	2010	2020	2030	2040	2050
Population	3,262	4,202	4,686	4,999	6,486	7,920	9,373	10,692	11,773
Life expectancy - males	72.0	74.0	74.6	74.9	76.5	77.8	78.8	79.6	80.2
Life expectancy - females	76.2	78.9	79.5	79.9	81.7	83.2	84.3	85.3	86.0
Birth rate (per 1,000)	35.5	32.3	28.4	26.2	19.0	17.0	15.2	13.1	12.2
Death rate (per 1,000)	3.6	2.8	2.7	2.6	2.8	3.3	4.0	5.3	7.2
Women of reproductive age (15-49 yrs.)	725	975	1,113	1,211	1,732	2,152	2,373	2,524	2,586
Fertility rate	5.4	4.4	3.8	3.4	2.3	2.0	2.0	2.0	1.9

Except as noted, values for vital statistics are in thousands; life expectancy is in years.

Health Personnel

	National Data	World Data (wtd ave)
Total health expenditure as a percentage of GDP, 1990-1998[a]		
Public sector	3.7	2.5
Private sector	4.2	2.9
Total[b]	7.9	5.5
Health expenditure per capita in U.S. dollars, 1990-1998[a]		
Purchasing power parity	215	561
Total	123	483
Availability of health care facilities per 100,000 people		
Hospital beds 1990-1998[a]	180	330
Doctors 1992-1995[a]	158	122
Nurses 1992-1995[a]	224	248

Health Indicators

	National Data	World Data
Life expectancy at birth (years)		
1980	NA	61
1998	71	67
Daily per capita supply of calories		
1970	2,418	2,358
1997	3,014	2,791
Daily per capital supply of protein		
1997 (grams)	75	74
Total fertility rate (births per woman)		
1980	6.8	3.7
1998	4.1	2.7
Population with access (%)		
To safe water (1990-96)	89	NA
To sanitation (1990-96)	95	NA
People living with (1997)		
Tuberculosis (cases per 100,000)	6.9	60.4
HIV/AIDS (% aged 15 - 49 years)	0.02	0.99

Infants and Malnutrition

	National Data	World Data (wtd ave)
Under 5 mortality rate (1989)	36	NA
% of infants with low birthweight (1992-98)[1]	2	17
Births attended by skilled health staff (% of total births 1996-98)	97	52
% fully immunized at 1 year of age (1995-98)[1]		
TB	NA	82
DPT	91	77
Polio	91	77
Measles	86	74
Prevalence of child malnutrition (1992-98)[1] (based on weight for age, % of children under 5 years)	5	30

Ethnic Division

Arab 98%

Circassian 1%

Armenian 1%

Religion

Sunni Muslim 96%

Christian 4%

Data for 1997 est.

Major Languages

Arabic (official), English widely understood among upper and middle classes.

EDUCATION

Public Education Expenditures

	1980	1997
Public expenditures on education as % of GNP	6.6	6.8
Expenditures per student as % of GNP per capita		
Secondary	24.5	112.4
Tertiary	59.9	81.0
Teachers' compensation as % of total current education expenditures	70.4	70.4
Pupils per teacher at the primary level	NA	21
Duration of primary education in years	NA	9
World data for comparison		
Public expenditures on education as % of GNP (mean)	3.9	4.8
Pupils per teacher at the primary level (wtd ave)	NA	33
Duration of primary education in years (mean)	NA	9

Educational Attainment (B)

	1995	1997
Gross enrollment ratio (%)		
Primary level	71.3	70.6
Secondary level	55.3	57.4
Tertiary level	17.4	19.4

Literacy Rates (A)

In thousands and percent	1990	1995	2000	2010
Illiterate population (15+ yrs.)	425	414	370	267
Literacy rate - total adult pop. (%)	82.1	86.6	89.8	94.8
Literacy rate - males (%)	90.9	93.4	95.1	97.5
Literacy rate - females (%)	72.7	79.4	84.2	91.9

(Continued on next page.)

GOVERNMENT & LAW

Military Affairs (A)

	1990	1992	1995	1996	1997
Military expenditures					
Current dollars (mil.)	402	424[e]	562	599	626
1997 constant dollars (mil.)	471	470[e]	581	609	626
Armed forces (000)	100	100	100	100	102
Gross national product (GNP)					
Current dollars (mil.)	3,710	4,810	6,480	6,680	6,940
1997 constant dollars (mil.)	4,340	5,340	6,710	6,790	6,940
Central government expenditures (CGE)					
1997 constant dollars (mil.)	1,710	1,720	2,190	2,410	2,500[e]
People (mil.)	3.3	3.8	4.1	4.2	4.3
Military expenditure as % of GNP	10.8	8.8	8.7	9.0	9.0
World data on military expenditure as % of GNP	4.5	3.4	2.7	2.6	2.6
Military expenditure as % of CGE	27.5	27.3	26.6	25.2	25.0
World data on military expenditure as % of CGE	17.0	12.5	10.5	10.3	10.2
Military expenditure per capita (1997 $)	144	125	142	145	145
World data on military expenditure per capita (1997 $)	242	173	146	143	145
Armed forces per 1,000 people (soldiers)	30.5	26.6	24.4	23.8	23.6
World data on armed forces per 1,000 people (soldiers)	5.3	4.5	4.1	3.9	3.8
GNP per capita (1997 $)	1,330	1,420	1,640	1,610	1,610
Arms imports[6]					
Current dollars (mil.)	150	40	80	120	130
1997 constant dollars (mil.)	176	44	83	122	130
Total imports[7]					
Current dollars (mil.)	2,601	3,255	3,698	4,428	4,095
1997 constant dollars (mil.)	3,046	3,609	3,829	4,502	4,095
Total exports[7]					
Current dollars (mil.)	1,064	1,215	1,769	1,817	1,843
1997 constant dollars (mil.)	1,246	1,347	1,832	1,847	1,843
Arms as percent of total imports[8]	5.8	1.2	2.2	2.7	3.2
Arms as percent of total exports[8]	0	0	0	0	0

(Continued on next page.)

EDUCATION (cont.)

Libraries

National Libraries	1995
Administrative Units	1
Service Points or Branches	1
Number of Volumes (000)	706
Registered Users (000)	NA
Loans to Users (000)	NA
Total Library Staff	68

GOVERNMENT & LAW (cont.)

Political Parties

House of Representatives	no. of seats
National Constitutional Party	2
Arab Land Party	1
Independents	75
Other	2

House of Representatives elections were last held 4 November 1997 (next to be held November 2001). The House of Representatives has been convened and dissolved by the monarch several times since 1974. In November 1989 the first parliamentary elections in 22 years were held.

Government Budgets (A)

Year: 1997

Total Expenditures: 1,681.9 Millions of Dinars

Expenditures as a percentage of the total by function:

General public services and public order	14.42
Defense	17.90
Education	14.58
Health	10.24
Social Security and Welfare	17.77
Housing and community amenities	2.03
Recreational, cultural, and religious affairs	2.10
Fuel and energy	0.38
Agriculture, forestry, fishing, and hunting	3.79
Mining, manufacturing, and construction	0.08
Transportation and communication	3.79
Other economic affairs and services	0.66

Crime

Crime volume (for 1998)

Crimes reported	55,647
Total persons convicted	53,783
Crimes per 100,000 population	1,170

LABOR FORCE

Total Labor Force (A)

1.15 million. In addition, at least 300,000 workers are employed abroad (1997 est.).

Labor Force by Occupation

Industry	11.4%
Commerce, restaurants, and hotels	10.5%
Construction	10.0%
Transport and communications	8.7%
Agriculture	7.4%
Other services	52.0%

Data for 1992.

Unemployment Rate

15% official rate; actual rate is 25%-30% (1999 est.).

PRODUCTION SECTOR

Energy Production

Production	6.08 billion kWh
Production by source	
Fossil fuel	99.51%
Hydro	0.49%
Nuclear	0%
Other	0%
Exports	2 million kWh

Data for 1998.

Energy Consumption

Consumption	6.102 billion kWh
Imports	450.000 million kWh

Data for 1998.

Transportation

Highways:

Total: 8,000 km.

Paved: 8,000 km.

Unpaved: 0 km (2000 est.).

Pipelines: crude oil 209 km; may not be in use.

Merchant marine:

Total: 7 ships (1,000 GRT or over) totaling 42,746 GRT/59,100 DWT.

Ships by type: bulk 2, cargo 2, container 1, livestock carrier 1, roll-on/roll-off 1 (1999 est.).

Airports: 20 (1999 est.).

Airports - with paved runways: 16.

Top Agriculture Products

Wheat, barley, citrus, tomatoes, melons, olives; sheep, goats, poultry.

Top Mining Products (B)

Mineral resources include: phosphates, potash, shale oil.

MANUFACTURING SECTOR

GDP & Manufacturing Summary (A)

	1980	1985	1990	1995
GDP ($-1990 mil.)[1]	3,058	3,940	3,934	5,281
Per capita ($-1990)[1]	1,046	1,028	924	983
Manufacturing share (%) (current prices)[1]	NA	11.6	14.6	14.4[e]
Manufacturing				
Value added ($-1990 mil.)[1]	349	477	520	641
Industrial production index	64	82	100	111
Value added ($ mil.)	406	581	583	1,046[e]
Gross output ($ mil.)	917	1,997	1,846	3,690[e]
Employment (000)	25	42	44	84[e]
Profitability (% of gross output)				
Intermediate input (%)	56	71	68	72[e]
Wages and salaries inc. supplements (%)	12	9	7	7[e]
Gross operating surplus	32	20	25	22[e]
Productivity ($)				
Gross output per worker	26,708	38,671	33,230	36,419[e]
Value added per worker	11,819	11,243	10,489	10,487[e]
Average wage (inc. supplements)	4,418	4,326	2,786	2,860[e]
Value added ($ mil.)				
Food products	24	48	58	116[e]
Beverages	20	27	28	57[e]
Tobacco products	50	92	75	136[e]
Textiles	10	14	20	28[e]
Wearing apparel	8	10	13	26[e]
Leather and fur products	2	2	4	4[e]
Footwear	8	8	3	8[e]
Wood and wood products	7	7	4	12[e]
Furniture and fixtures	11	11	14	28[e]
Paper and paper products	9	9	20	31[e]
Printing and publishing	7	11	12	23[e]
Industrial chemicals	10	14	44	51[e]
Other chemical products	20	28	42	87[e]
Petroleum refineries	53	87	55	44[e]
Rubber products	NA	NA	1	1[e]
Plastic products	12	13	17	41[e]
Pottery, china and earthenware	2	3	3	NA
Glass and glass products	2	3	3	2[e]
Other non-metal mineral products	98	123	85	184[e]
Iron and steel	11[e]	8	24	26[e]
Non-ferrous metals	5[e]	4	9	19[e]
Metal products	27[e]	31	23	48[e]
Non-electrical machinery	2[e]	4	9	20[e]
Electrical machinery	2	2	11	23[e]
Transport equipment	NA	1	1	23[e]
Prof. and scientific equipment	NA	NA	2	1[e]
Other manufacturing	7	23	2	5[e]

COMMUNICATIONS

Daily Newspapers

	National Data	World Data for Comparison
Daily Newspapers		
Number of Dailies	4	8,391
Total Circulation (000)	250	548,000
Circulation per 1,000 inhabitants	42	96

Telecommunications

Telephones - main lines in use: 402,600 (1997).

Telephones - mobile cellular: 75,000 (1999).

Telephone system: service has improved recently with the increased use of digital switching equipment, but better access to the telephone system is needed in the rural areas and easier access to pay telephones is needed by the urban public.

Domestic: microwave radio relay transmission and coaxial and fiber-optic cable are employed on trunk lines; considerable use is made of mobile cellular systems; Internet service is available.

International: satellite earth stations - 3 Intelsat, 1 Arabsat, and 29 land and maritime Inmarsat terminals; fiber-optic cable to Saudi Arabia and microwave radiorelay link with Egypt and Syria; connection to international submarine cable FLAG (Fiber-Optic Link Around the Globe); participant in MEDARABTEL; international links total about 4,000.

Radio broadcast stations: AM 6, FM 5, shortwave 1 (1999).

Radios: 1.66 million (1997).

Television broadcast stations: 8 (plus approximately 42 repeaters and 1 TV receive-only satellite link) (1999).

Televisions: 500,000 (1997).

Internet Service Providers (ISPs): 8 (1999).

FINANCE, ECONOMICS, & TRADE

Economic Indicators

National product: GDP—purchasing power parity—$16 billion (1999 est.).

National product real growth rate: 2% (1999 est.).

National product per capita: $3,500 (1999 est.).

Inflation rate—consumer price index: 3% (1999 est.).

Exchange Rates

Exchange rates:

Jordanian dinars (JD) per US$1

January 1996-2000	0.7090
1995	0.7005

Since May 1989, the dinar has been pegged to a group of currencies.

Top Import Origins

Imports (c.i.f., 1999 est.): $3.3 billion.

Origins:: Germany, Iraq, United States, Japan, United Kingdom, Italy, Turkey, Malaysia, Syria, China.

Top Export Destinations

Exports (f.o.b., 1999 est.): $1.8 billion.

Destinations: Iraq, India, Saudi Arabia, EU, Indonesia, UAE, Lebanon, Kuwait, Syria, Ethiopia.

Foreign Aid

Recipient: ODA, $850 million (1996 est.).

Import/Export Commodities

Import Commodities	Export Commodities
Crude oil	Phosphates
Machinery	Fertilizers
Transport equipment	Potash
Food	Agricultural products
Live animals	Manufactures
Manufactured goods	

Balance of Payments

	1994	1995	1996	1997	1998
Exports of goods (f.o.b.)	1,424	1,770	1,817	1,836	1,799
Imports of goods (f.o.b.)	−3,004	−3,288	−3,818	−3,649	−3,412
Trade balance	−1,579	−1,518	−2,001	−1,813	−1,613
Services - debits	−1,393	−1,615	−1,598	−1,537	−1,784
Services - credits	1,562	1,709	1,846	1,737	1,825
Private transfers (net)	1,123	1,266	1,562	1,682	1,626
Government transfers (net)	324	326	408	414	358
Overall balance	−398	−259	−222	29	3

KAZAKSTAN

Republic of Kazakstan
Kazakstan Respublikasy

CAPITAL: Astana (formerly Akmola, Tselinograd).

FLAG: Light blue with a yellow sun and soaring eagle in the center and a yellow vertical ornamentation in the hoist.

ANTHEM: *National Anthem of Kazakstan.*

MONETARY UNIT: The tenge (T), issued in 15 November 1993, is the national currency, replacing the ruble (R). There is a coin, the tyin. One hundred tyin equal one tenge. T1 = \$0.01439 (or \$1 = T69.5), but exchange rates fluctuate widely.

WEIGHTS AND MEASURES: The metric system is in force.

HOLIDAYS: New Year, 31 December–1 January; International Women's Day, 8 March; Nauryz (Kazak New Year), 28 March; Solidarity Day, 1 May; Victory Day, 9 May; Independence Day, 25 October.

TIME: 5 PM = noon GMT.

LOCATION AND SIZE: Kazakstan is located in southern Asia between Russia and Uzbekistan, bordering on the Caspian Sea and the Aral Sea, with a total area of 2,717,300 square kilometers (1,049,155 square miles). Kazakstan's boundary length totals 12,012 kilometers (7,466 miles). In mid-1998 the capital was moved from Almaty (Alma-Ata) to Astana (formerly known as Akmola and before that, Tselinograd) in the north central part of the nation.

CLIMATE: The country has a dry continental climate. In Almaty the mean temperature is 27°C (81°F) in July and –5°C (23°F) in January. Rainfall averages between 25 centimeters (9.8 inches) and 38 centimeters (15 inches).

INTRODUCTORY SURVEY

RECENT HISTORY

In World War II much Russian industry was moved to Kazakstan. From 1953 to 1965 the so-called Virgin Lands campaign converted huge tracts of Kazak grazing land to wheat and other grain production bringing thousands more Russians and other non-Kazaks to Kazakstan. As a result Kazakstan became the only Soviet republic in which the native people were not a majority of the population.

The first public nationalist protest in the Soviet Union before its breakup occurred in Kazakstan in 1986. In June 1989 more civil disturbances brought about the appointment of Nursultan Nazarbaev as republic leader. Nazarbaev, who later became president, strongly promoted Kazak participation in the formation of the Commonwealth of Independent States. Kazakstan declared its independence on December 16, 1991.

In November 1994 Kazakstan agreed to transfer bomb-grade uranium to the United States with Russia's approval. The nuclear material was poorly protected and could have been a possible source of nuclear material for other countries or arms dealers.

On June 10, 1998, the Kazak government officially transferred the country's capital from Alomaty in the south to Astana (formerly Akmola, or Tselinograd) in the north. Astana, which means "capital," is a rapidly growing city of 300,000.

In elections held on January 10, 1999, President Nazarbayev received 82 percent of the vote.

However foreign observers characterized the elections as unfair.

Current issues in Kazakstan include resolving problems resulting from an ethnically diverse population, establishing stable relations with foreign powers including Russia and China, and developing the country's vast energy and mineral resources.

GOVERNMENT

The chief of state is the president elected by popular vote for a seven-year term. The head of government is the prime minister. The president appoints the prime minister, first deputy prime minister, and cabinet, known as the Council of Ministers. President Nursultan A. Nazarbayev, first elected in 1991, by presidential decree, expanded his power to include that only he can appoint and dismiss the government, dissolve parliament, and initiate constitutional amendments.

The bicameral parliament consists of the 47-seat Senate and the seventy-seven seat Majilis. The president appoints seven senators and others are popularly elected, two from each oblast to serve six-year terms. The number of oblasts are being reduced and the Senate will eventually be reduced to thirty-seven. The members of the Majilis are popularly elected to serve five-year terms.

Suffrage is universal at age eighteen.

Judiciary

The seven-member Constitutional Council determines the constitutionality of laws adopted by the legislature. The courts are arranged in three tiers: local level, province *(oblys)* level, and Supreme Court. Local level courts provide initial hearings for less serious crimes. Oblys level courts hear more serious criminal cases and also hear cases in rural areas where no local courts have been established. Judgment of local courts may be appealed to the oblys level. The Supreme Court hears appeals from the oblys courts. The judiciary is under the control of the president and the executive branch.

Political Parties

Most parties are small, ephemeral, based on personalities, and lack detailed programs. Nine parties participated in the party list of the October 1999 Majilis elections and five won seats. Those five were: the Otan formed in 1999 from several prominent pro-Nazarbayev parties; the Civic Party formed in 1998 representing state-industrial interests; the Communist Party; the Agrarian Party; and, the People's Cooperative Party.

DEFENSE

Kazakstan's armed forces are estimated at 65,800, with approximately 46,800 in the army. There is no navy, and the air force has 19,000 personnel. Paramilitary forces consist of 2,000 republican guards, 20,000 security troops, and 12,000 border guards. The defense budget in 1999 was estimated at $322 million, or 1.5 percent of GDP.

ECONOMIC AFFAIRS

Legislation adopted since 1992 has promoted the spread of private ownership in business and housing, and the inflow of large foreign investments. Extensive foreign investment is shaping the economic development of the country, taking it from a dilapidated heavy-industrial complex to a productive market for two-way trade. Kazakstan possesses vast untapped oil and gas reserves and plentiful supplies of minerals and metals. The pipeline from the Tengiz oil fields to the Black Sea scheduled for completion in 2002 will substantially increase oil exports. The agricultural potential in livestock and grain is also enormous.

Due to slumping oil prices and a financial crisis in Russia, Kazakstan's economy took a downturn in 1998 with the GDP declining 2.5%. By 1999 the growth had turned upward with a recovery of international oil prices, a bumper grain harvest, and a well-timed devaluation of Kazakstan's currency, the tenge.

Public Finance

The U.S. Central Intelligence Agency (CIA) estimated the central government of Kazakstan in 1999 took in revenues of $3.1 billion and had expenditures of $3.6 billion. The 1999 external debt estimate stood at $7.9 billion.

Income

In 1999 Kazakstan's gross domestic product (GDP) was estimated at $54.5 billion or about $3,200 per capita. The 1999 estimated GDP growth rate was 1.7 percent and inflation 8.3%. The 1999 estimated contribution by sector was agriculture 10%, industry 30%, and services 60%.

Industry

Kazakstan's industrial sector is slowly being converted toward market-driven production. The government has required that nearly all state-owned enterprises must be sold to private companies by 2000. The industrial sector rests on extraction and processing of natural resources. Kazakstan has the largest oil and gas reserves of the Caspian Sea regional states.

Metallurgy and mining industries include coal, iron ore, manganese, chromite, lead, zinc, copper, titanium, bauxite, gold, silver, phosphates, sulfur, iron and steel, and nonferrous metal.

Textile and leather production is well developed because Kazakstan produces its own wool and hides and imports cotton from other former Soviet republics nearby. Machine building such as tractors, other agricultural machinery, and electrical motors, is also among the largest of Kazakstan's industries. Kazakstan also has vast potential n the agricultural sector with livestock and grain production.

Banking and Finance

In December 1990 the Alma-Ata branch of Gosbank (the former Soviet State Bank) was made into the Independent Kazak (National Bank of Kazakstan-NBK). In 1991, the existence of private and public financial institutions was legalized. In 1993 the parliament approved a new banking law that separated the National Bank of Kazakstan from the government, and gave the central bank the power to conduct monetary and credit policies and regulate the commercial banking sector.

In 1999 there were seventy-one commercial banks including one state bank with 3 percent of total financial sector assets, one intergovernmental bank, twenty-three banks with foreign participation, and thirteen foreign representative offices. Kazakstan's banks tend to be very small, concentrated n Almaty, and more interested in treasury bills than providing long-term credits. There remains no deposit insurance scheme and organized crime was a problem for many banks.

The Kazakstan Stock Exchange and the Central Asian Stock Exchange both operate in Kazakstan.

Economic Development

Since sovereignty was declared in 1990 Kazakstan has embarked on a process of economic restructuring, aimed at establishing a market economy. Gradual privatization of most state enterprises has been the focal point of the restructuring program and the centralized state ordering system was abolished in 1992.

In addition to price liberalization, government decrees since 1991 have mandated the gradual elimination of various subsidies to industry and other sectors, further reductions in state expenditures, and the development of a social safety net to assist households at high poverty risk. The government is also placing great emphasis on realizing the infusion of foreign capital both to the oil and gas industry as well as various other industrial subsectors, such as agro-processing, light industry and ferrous metals.

In 1996 Kazakstan signed the Caspian Pipeline Consortium agreement to build a pipeline from western Tengiz oil field to the Black Sea, promising further development of the oil sector. The scheduled completion was 2002.

SOCIAL WELFARE

Social security programs provide for old age, disability, and survivorship pensions. The government, however, is often unable to pay out benefits to citizens.

Women generally have access to higher education but are still channeled into mostly low-level, low-paid jobs.

There is some tension between ethnic Kazaks and Russians. Kazaks receive preferential treatment in housing, education, and employment.

Healthcare

In 2000 the average life expectancy was sixty-three years. In 1990-1997, there was 3.6 doctors and 10.3 hospital beds per 1,000 inhabitants.

Housing

In 1990 Kazakstan had 14.2 square meters (107 square feet) of housing space per person. As of January 1, 1991, 520,000 households were on waiting lists for housing in urban areas.

EDUCATION

The adult illiteracy rate was estimated at 2%. Both primary and secondary education is free and state funded. In 1997 there are 1.3 million primary school students and 1.9 million secondary school students. There are fifty-five institutions of higher education and three universities. Institutions of higher education had 260,043 students in 1996.

2000 KEY EVENTS TIMELINE

January

- In election results announced January 10 Nursultan Nazarbayev wins a new seven-year term as president. The elections are condemned by international observers, but the turnout is reported to be 86 percent and Nazarbayev is reported to have won 80 percent of the vote.
- A military tribunal tries two people—a military official, Bakhitzhan Yertayev, and a businessman, Alexander Petrenko—over arms sales to North Korea.

February

- On February 10 talks begin in Tashkent between Kazakstan and Uzbekistan to establish their common border.

June

- New legislation grants President Nursultan Nazarbayev a permanent seat on the Kazakh Security Council and the right to address major state agencies and the general population whenever he wishes, even after his term of office ends in 2006.

July

- Former Prime Minister Akezhan Kazhegeldin is arrested in Rome at the request of Kazakstan's INTERPOL agency on charges of money laundering and tax evasion. Kazhegeldin is politically opposed to President Nursultan Nazarbayev, and denies the charges.
- Kazhegeldin is released on July 14, after being detained for two days.
- Kazakh officials are accused of accepting bribes from western oil countries amounting to roughly one billion in Swiss bank accounts.

November

- Work is completed on a 948-mile pipeline connecting Tengiz petroleum fields in western Kazakstan to a Russian port on the Black Sea.

The pipeline is to transport an estimated 600,000 barrels of oil per day.

ANALYSIS OF EVENTS: 2000

BUSINESS AND THE ECONOMY

In 2000 the development of the Kashagan oil field in the Caspian Sea continued. Estimates of reserves in this field, site of Kazakstan's first offshore oil exploration, ranged from one billion tons to 6.8 billion tons. The governments of the United States, Russia, and Iran competed further to develop pipeline projects to deliver Kazakh oil to world markets. The United States gained only hesitant commitments from multinational petroleum companies to develop its route—through the Caucasus and Turkey to the Mediterranean Sea—because of its higher expense compared to alternate routes through Iran and Russia. The U.S. strategy revolved around establishing a new source of oil for western markets that would be shipped through a friendly country, in this case Turkey, a member of the North Atlantic Treaty Organization (NATO) and aspirant to the European Union. The routes proposed by Russia and Iran were preferred by the multinational firms, primarily due to their lower cost, and both countries hoped to gain revenue for transit fees.

The Kyoto Protocol, an accord designed to allow trading of "emissions credits," showed great promise for Kazakstan. The declining industrial output in Kazakh factories and power plants since independence has created a tradable commodity, in which the emissions that are not produced in one nation can be sold in the form of a credit to other industrial nations. The system originated at the Kyoto Summit of 1997, in which thirty-nine countries agreed to either reduce emissions or buy the unused quotas of other countries. Kazakstan was not party to that agreement, but made moves in 2000 to join. Analysts estimated that the unused element of the Kazakh quota could be worth about $800 million annually, assuming the international treaty was ratified.

Several multinational energy firms were investigated in a kickback probe related to concessions for pipelines and other major investments in Kazakstan. Included in the investigation were Belgian holding company Tractebel, as well as some giant U.K. and U.S. oil firms. Court-obtained bank records illustrated cases in which local Kazakh officials in charge of pipeline contracts and related petroleum-exploitation negotiations were paid kickbacks directly from corporate coffers. As of the end of 2000 the investigation was ongoing.

Space research was conducted by Russians teamed with German scientists from Daimler-Chrysler Aerospace. The first flight of the Inflatable Reentry and Descent Technology (IRDT) space vehicle came back to earth in the Kazakh steppe in 2000. The development project, which cost about $1.75 billion, was aimed at eliminating the waste in current rocket launch technology by reusing the upper stages of spacecraft. The IRDT had as its key element an inflatable heat shield that doubled as a parachute. In another space-related project, the Baikonur Cosmodrome, leased from Kazakstan, served as Russia's launch base to send supplies and astronauts to the International Space Station.

GOVERNMENT AND POLITICS

In election results announced January 10, Nursultan Nazarbayev won a new seven-year term as president. Government sources reported turnout at 86 percent and Nazarbayev's share of the vote as 80 percent, but international observers condemned the elections. On January 25 Uzbek border guards traversed about three miles into southern Kazakstan to unilaterally establish a new forty-eight mile stretch of border between the two countries. The section of territory, essentially annexed by Uzbekistan, was originally part of a military district established under Soviet rule, the large majority of which (except for the annexed area) lies within recognized Uzbek territory. The Kazakh government responded with only a letter of protest.

President Nazarbayev put forth a plan to increase military spending by 40 percent, to $90 million. The lack of response to the incursion by Uzbek border guards illustrated the weakness of Kazakh military forces relative to regional power Uzbekistan. New legislation passed midyear by Parliament granted President Nazarbayev a permanent seat on the Kazakh Security Council and the right to address major state agencies and the general population whenever he wished, even after his term of office officially ended in 2006.

The World Bank engaged in talks with the Kazakstan government regarding a $50 million loan for development projects. A portion of the money was earmarked for construction of a dam in the northern region of the Aral Sea, intended to preserve a remainder of the sea which has lost three-fourths of its water in forty years due to overirrigation. On the shores of the Caspian Sea about 4,000 seals died from unknown causes. A preliminary report from the Russian Fisheries Institute indicated that the seals suffered from bacterial infections, although the cause remained undetermined. Local environmentalists and politicians feared that oil and gas exploration in the vicinity played a role.

Army chief of staff Bakhitzhan Yertayev was acquitted on charges of illegally selling forty fighter planes to North Korea. A military court found businessman Alexander Petrenko guilty of participating in the sale, but he was released under an amnesty. The scandal erupted in 1999 after South Korea protested about the transaction.

CULTURE AND SOCIETY

The multicultural nature of Kazakstan was illustrated in 2000 through the viewpoints of two minorities in the country, ethnic Germans and ethnic Russians. The trend of decreasing population slowed due to the German government's end to free flights for ethnic Germans returning to Germany. From 1989 to 1999 the population of Kazakstan dropped by 1.25 million, including Russians, Ukrainians, and Tatars, in addition to German emigrants. The leaders of several Slavic organizations, together with the Communist Party, demanded that Kazakstan join the Russia-Belarus union, and called for a nationwide referendum on the issue. About five million Kazakhs are ethnically Russian.

Perhaps the best known Kazakh cultural export is Yevgeny Nabokov, rookie goalie for the San Jose Sharks hockey team. He may be the most famous Kazakh on the international scene as a result of his league-leading performance in the National Hockey League of North America.

DIRECTORY

CENTRAL GOVERNMENT

Head of State

President
Nursultan Nazarbayev, Office of the President, Republic Square, 480091 Almaty, Kazakstan
PHONE: +7 (3272) 623016

Prime Minister
Kasymzhomart Tokayev, Office of the Prime Minister, Republic Square, 480091 Almaty, Kazakstan
PHONE: +7 (3272) 623097

Ministers

First Deputy Prime Minister
Aleksandr Pavlov, Office of the First Deputy Prime Minister

Deputy Prime Minister
Daniyal Akhmetov, Office of the Deputy Prime Minister

Deputy Prime Minister
Yerzhan Utembayev, Office of the Deputy Prime Minister

Minister of Finance
Mazhit Yesenbayev, Ministry of Finance

Minister of Foreign Affairs
Yerlan Idrisov, Ministry of Foreign Affairs

Minister of Defense
Lt. Gen. Tokpakbayev, Ministry of Defense

Minister of Economy
Zhaksibek Kulekeyev, Ministry of Economy

Minister of Labor and Social Protection
Alikhan Baymenov, Ministry of Labor and Social Protection

Minister of Education and Science
Krimbek Kusherbayev, Ministry of Education and Science

Minister of Power Engineering, Industry and Trade
Vladimir Shkolnik, Ministry of Power Engineering, Industry and Trade

Minister of Interior Affairs
Lt. Gen. Suleymenov, Ministry of Interior Affairs

Minister of State Incomes
Kakimzhanov Zeinulla Khalidollovich, Ministry of State Incomes

Minister of Justice
Igor Rogov, Ministry of Justice

Minister of Culture, Information and Public Accord
Altynbek Sarsenbayev, Ministry of Culture, Information and Public Accord

Minister of Agriculture
Sauat Mynbayev, Ministry of Agriculture

Minister of Natural Resources and Environmental Protection
Serikbek Daukeyev, Ministry of Natural Resources and Environmental Protection

POLITICAL ORGANIZATIONS

People's Unity Party (PUP)

TITLE: Chairman
NAME: Akhan Bizhanov

People's Congress of Kazakstan (NKK)

TITLE: Chairman
NAME: Olzhas Suleimenov

Azamat Movement

NAME: Petr Svoik

Communist Party (KPK)

TITLE: First secretary
NAME: Serikbolsyn Abdildin

December National Democratic Party

TITLE: Chairman
NAME: Hasen Kozhakhmetov

Labor and Workers Movement

TITLE: Chairman
NAME: Madel Ismailov

Republican People's Slavic Movement

TITLE: Chairman
NAME: Aleksander Samarkin

Russian Center (RT)

TITLE: Chairwoman
NAME: Nina Sidorova

DIPLOMATIC REPRESENTATION

Embassies in Kazakstan

United States
99/97A Furmanova St., Almaty, Republic of Kazakstan 49009
PHONE: +7 (3272) 6333921; 631375; 507623
FAX: +7 (3272) 633883
TITLE: Ambassador
NAME: Richard H. Jones

JUDICIAL SYSTEM

Supreme Court

Constitutional Council

BROADCAST MEDIA

Nezavisimaya Veshatelnaya Systema (Independent Broadcasting System)

E-MAIL: nvs@nvs-tv.msk.ru

Kazak Radio

Kheltoksan Street 175 A, 480013 Almaty, Kazakhstan
PHONE: +7 (3272) 631207
WEBSITE: http://www.radio.kz/
TITLE: General Director
CONTACT: A. N. Midike
TYPE: Government

Baylanis Ministirliki

Bogenbay Batira köchesi 134, 480000 Almaty, Kazakhstan
PHONE: +7 (3272) 623194
FAX: +7 (3272) 637210
TITLE: Minister
CONTACT: Igor V. Ulyanov

Radio Almaty

Zheltoksan Street 175A, 480013 Almaty, Kazakhstan
PHONE: +7 (3272) 627694
TITLE: Editor-in-Chief
CONTACT: Nadya Usayeva
LANGUAGE: English, German, Kazakh, Korean, Russian, Tatar, Turkish

Republican TV and Radio Broadcasting Corporation of Kazakhstan

Zheltoksan Street, 175 A, 480013 Almaty, Kazakhstan
TITLE: President
CONTACT: Ashirbek Kopishev
TYPE: Government

Kazakh Television

Jeltoksan kösesi 175, 480013 Almati, Kazakhstan
PHONE: +7 (3272) 695188
FAX: +7 (3272) 631207
TYPE: Government

ORT-1 Relays

ORT, 12 Academika Korolyova Street, Moscow 12700, Russia
PHONE: +7 (95) 2177898

FAX: +7 (95) 2889542
TITLE: Directorate General
CONTACT: Sergei Blagovolin
TYPE: Public

COLLEGES AND UNIVERSITIES

Temirtau Technical University

Prospekt Lenina 34, 472300 Temirtau, Kazakhstan

Kazakh Al-Farabi State University

Al-Farabi Ave. 71, 480121 Almaty, Kazakhstan

Tomsk State University

Prospekt Lenina 36, Kazakhstan
E-MAIL: webmaster@tsu.ru
WEBSITE: http://www.tsu.ru

NEWSPAPERS AND MAGAZINES

The Almaty Herald

Ste. 304, Dostyk Ave., 85a, Almaty, Kazakstan
PHONE: + 7 (3272) 506203
FAX: +7 (3273) 633655
E-MAIL: herald@asdc.kz
WEBSITE: http://www.herald.asdc.kz
TITLE: Editor
CONTACT: Lena Savicheva

Caravan

Caravan-Press ISC, Chaikovsky St. 9/11, Almaty 480004 Kazakstan
PHONE: +7 (3272) 329342
FAX: +7 (3272) 399200
E-MAIL: advertising@caravan.kz
WEBSITE: http://www.caravan.kz
TITLE: Editor
CONTACT: Kagarova Saule
CIRCULATION: 250,000

Egmen Kazakhstan

Cabinet of Ministers, Zhibek Zholy 5, Almaty, Kazakstan
PHONE: +7 (3272) 632546
FAX: +7 (3272) 632546
TITLE: Editor
CONTACT: M. Serkhanov

The Globe

PHONE: +7 (3272) 507639
E-MAIL: ipa@kaznet.kz
CONTACT: Wallace Kaufman
CIRCULATION: 5,550

Karaganda Newspapers Weekly Review

E-MAIL: http://gazeta.inet.kz/

Kasakhstanskaja Pravda

39 Gogolya St., Almaty, Kazakstan
PHONE: +7 3273 630586
TITLE: Editor
CONTACT: Vladimir Srubnylh
CIRCULATION: 170,000

Narodniy Kongress (National Congress)

85 Vinogradov St., 2/F, Almaty, Kazakstan
PHONE: +7 (3272) 634895
TITLE: Editor
CONTACT: Gennada Tolmachev

Delovaya Nedelya

Ul. Zhybek Zholy, 64, 2 etazh, 480000 Almaty, Kazakhstan
PHONE: +7 (3272) 339148
E-MAIL: rikki@kazmail.asdc.kz
WEBSITE: http://www.dn.kz
TITLE: Editor
CONTACT: Tulegan Askarov

Panorama

WEBSITE: http://www.panorama.kz

PUBLISHERS

Gylym, Izd-Vo

Ul Puskina 111-113, 480100 Almaty, Kazakstan
PHONE: +7 (3272) 618005; 618845
FAX: +7 (3272) 618845; 618005
CONTACT: Sagin-Girey Baimenov
SUBJECTS: Biological Sciences, Chemistry, Engineering, Earth Sciences, Economics, Mathematics, Physical Sciences, Science (General), Social Sciences

Kazakh Al-Farabi State National University

Al-Farabi Ave. 71, 480078 Almaty, Kazakstan
PHONE: +7 (3272) 472517
E-MAIL: evgenyaakazgu@ksisti.alma.ata.su
SUBJECTS: Biological Sciences, Chemistry, Engineering, Economics Environmental Studies, Political Science, History, Journalism Mathematics, Philosophy, Social Sciences

Kazakhstan, Izd-Vo

Prospect Abaja 143, Dom Izdatel'stv, 480009 Almaty, Kazakstan
PHONE: +7 (3272) 422929; 428562
FAX: + (3272) 422929
TITLE: Director
CONTACT: E. H. Syzdykov
SUBJECTS: Economics, Political Science, Medicine, Nursing, Dentistry, Science (General), Social Sciences

Kramds-reklama Publishing & Advertising

Ul Mira 115, 480091 Almaty, Kazakstan
PHONE: +7 (3272) 453968
FAX: + (3272) 696753
TITLE: Director
CONTACT: Lubov Shabykina
SUBJECTS: Photography

Zazusy

Prospect Abaya 143, 48009 Almaty, Kazakstan
PHONE: +7 (3272) 422849
TITLE: Director
CONTACT: D. I. Isabekov
SUBJECTS: Literature, Literary Criticism, Essays, Poetry

RELIGIOUS ORGANIZATIONS

Jewish

The Association of Jewish Communities of Kazakhstan
66/120 Buhar-Zhirau Street, 480057 Almaty, Kazakhstan
PHONE: +7 (3272) 450043
FAX: +7 (327) 450043
E-MAIL: kazakhstan@fjc.ru
WEBSITE: : http://www.fjc.ru/topka.html

Central Synagogue and JCC of Almaty-Chabad
206-E, Raimbek Peroulok, 480061 Almaty, Kazakhstan
PHONE: +7 (3272) 439358
WEBSITE: : http://www.fjc.ru/lKazakhstanfr.htm
TITLE: Chief Rabbi of Almaty and Kazakhstan
NAME: Rabbi Yeshaya Cohen

Protestant

Almaty Sabbath Fellowship
PHONE: +7 (3272) 322280
E-MAIL: benjamin@lorton.com
WEBSITE: : http://www.tagnet.org/almaty/menu .html
TITLE: Pastor
NAME: Benjamin Anderson

Scientology

Dianetics Center of Almaty
A. B. Box 219, 480000 Almaty, Kazakhstan
PHONE: +7 (3272) 432413

FURTHER READING

Articles

"Kazakh Opposition Head Kazhegeldin Detained in Rome," *Reuters,* July 14, 2000.

"Kazakhstan—Priming the Pump." *The Economist (US),* May 27, 2000, vol. 355, no. 8172, p. 43.

"World Briefing: Kazakhstan: Former Leader Freed." *New York Times,* July 15, 2000, p. A4.

"World Briefing: Kazakhstan: President's New Powers." *New York Times,* June 28, 2000, p. A6.

KAZAKSTAN: STATISTICAL DATA

For sources and notes see "Sources of Statistics" at the front of each volume.

GEOGRAPHY

Geography

Area:

Total: 2,717,300 sq km.

Land: 2,669,800 sq km.

Land boundaries:

Total: 12,012 km.

Border countries: China 1,533 km, Kyrgyzstan 1,051 km, Russia 6,846 km, Turkmenistan 379 km, Uzbekistan 2,203 km.

Coastline: 0 km (landlocked).

Note: Kazakstan borders the Aral Sea, now split into two bodies of water (1,070 km), and the Caspian Sea (1,894 km).

Climate: continental, cold winters and hot summers, arid and semiarid.

Terrain: extends from the Volga to the Altai Mountains and from the plains in western Siberia to oases and desert in Central Asia.

Natural resources: major deposits of petroleum, natural gas, coal, iron ore, manganese, chrome ore, nickel, cobalt, copper, molybdenum, lead, zinc, bauxite, gold, uranium.

Land use:

Arable land: 12%

Permanent crops: 11%

Permanent pastures: 57%

Forests and woodland: 4%

Other: 16% (1996 est.).

HUMAN FACTORS

Demographics (A)

	1990	1995	1998	2000	2010	2020	2030	2040	2050
Population	16,708	16,943	16,779	16,733	17,276	18,542	19,538	20,488	21,028
Life expectancy - males	62.2	58.9	58.1	57.7	60.6	64.4	67.4	70.1	72.4
Life expectancy - females	71.7	70.1	69.3	68.9	71.1	74.5	77.2	79.5	81.4
Birth rate (per 1,000)	22.8	18.1	16.7	16.8	20.9	16.2	14.3	13.7	11.6
Death rate (per 1,000)	8.2	9.6	10.1	10.6	10.3	9.3	9.2	9.8	10.2
Women of reproductive age (15-49 yrs.)	4,175	4,425	4,510	4,571	4,714	4,674	4,968	4,873	4,954
Fertility rate	2.8	2.3	2.0	2.0	2.4	2.3	2.0	1.9	1.8

Except as noted, values for vital statistics are in thousands; life expectancy is in years.

Health Personnel

	National Data	World Data (wtd ave)
Total health expenditure as a percentage of GDP, 1990-1998[a]		
Public sector	2.1	2.5
Private sector	2.5	2.9
Total[b]	4.8	5.5
Health expenditure per capita in U.S. dollars, 1990-1998[a]		
Purchasing power parity	217	561
Total	68	483
Availability of health care facilities per 100,000 people		
Hospital beds 1990-1998[a]	850	330
Doctors 1992-1995[a]	360	122
Nurses 1992-1995[a]	874	248

Health Indicators

	National Data	World Data
Life expectancy at birth (years)		
1980	67	61
1998	65	67
Daily per capita supply of calories		
1970	NA	2,358
1997	3,085	2,791
Daily per capital supply of protein		
1997 (grams)	97	74
Total fertility rate (births per woman)		
1980	2.9	3.7
1998	2.0	2.7
People living with (1997)		
Tuberculosis (cases per 100,000)	101.4	60.4
HIV/AIDS (% aged 15 - 49 years)	0.03	0.99

Infants and Malnutrition

	National Data	World Data (wtd ave)
Under 5 mortality rate (1989)	43	NA
% of infants with low birthweight (1992-98)[1]	9	17
Births attended by skilled health staff (% of total births 1996-98)	NA	52
% fully immunized at 1 year of age (1995-98)[1]		
TB	99	82
DPT	100	77
Polio	100	77
Measles	100	74
Prevalence of child malnutrition (1992-98)[1] (based on weight for age, % of children under 5 years)	8	30

Ethnic Division

Kazakh (Qazaq) 46.0%
Russian 34.7%
Ukrainian 4.9%
German 3.1%
Uzbek 2.3%
Tatar 1.9%
Other 7.1%

Data for 1996.

Religion

Muslim 47%
Russian Orthodox 44%
Protestant 2%
Other 7%

Major Languages

Kazakh (Qazaq, state language) 40%
Russian (official, used in everyday business) 66%

EDUCATION

Public Education Expenditures

	1997
Public expenditures on education as % of GNP	4.4
Expenditures per student as % of GNP per capita	
Primary	NA
Secondary	NA
Tertiary	21.9
Pupils per teacher at the primary level	NA
Duration of primary education in years	11
World data for comparison	
Public expenditures on education as % of GNP (mean)	4.8
Pupils per teacher at the primary level (wtd ave)	33
Duration of primary education in years (mean)	9

Educational Attainment (A)

Age group (1989) . . . . .25+
Population of this age group 8,414,539
Highest level attained (%)
No schooling 7.7
First level
Not completed 29.2
Completed . . . . .NA
Entered second level 50.7
Entered post-secondary .12.4

Literacy Rates (B)

	National Data	World Data
Adult literacy rate		
1995		
Male	100	81
Female	99	65

GOVERNMENT & LAW

Military Affairs (A)

	1992	1995	1996	1997
Military expenditures				
Current dollars (mil.)	1,950	990[e]	NA	699
1997 constant dollars (mil.)	2,160	1,030[e]	NA	699
Armed forces (000)	NA	20	30	34
Gross national product (GNP)				
Current dollars (mil.)	66,600[e]	52,700	53,900	55,700
1997 constant dollars (mil.)	73,800[e]	54,500	54,900	55,700
Central government expenditures (CGE)				
1997 constant dollars (mil.)	NA	11,000	14,300	15,800
People (mil.)	17.0	17.0	16.9	16.9
Military expenditure as % of GNP	2.9	1.9	NA	1.3
World data on military expenditure as % of GNP	3.4	2.7	2.6	2.6
Military expenditure as % of CGE	NA	9.3	NA	4.4
World data on military expenditure as % of CGE	12.5	10.5	10.3	10.2
Military expenditure per capita (1997 $)	127	60	NA	41
World data on military expenditure per capita (1997 $)	173	146	143	145
Armed forces per 1,000 people (soldiers)	NA	1.2	1.8	2.0
World data on armed forces per 1,000 people (soldiers)	4.5	4.1	3.9	3.8
GNP per capita (1997 $)	4,350	3,220	3,240	3,300
Arms imports[6]				
Current dollars (mil.)	0	320	280	140
1997 constant dollars (mil.)	0	331	285	140
Arms exports[6]				
Current dollars (mil.)	0	40	10	0
1997 constant dollars (mil.)	0	41	10	0
Total imports[7]				
Current dollars (mil.)	4,080	3,807	4,241	4,301
1997 constant dollars (mil.)	4,523	3,942	4,312	4,301
Total exports[7]				
Current dollars (mil.)	3,166	5,250	5,911	6,497
1997 constant dollars (mil.)	3,510	5,436	6,010	6,497
Arms as percent of total imports[8]	0	8.4	6.6	3.3
Arms as percent of total exports[8]	0	0.8	0.2	0

Political Parties

Parliament	no. of seats
Majilis	
Otan	25
Civic Party	10
Communist Party	3
Agrarian Party	3
People's Cooperative Party	1
Independents	32
3 seats unaccounted for	NA

Majilis elections were last held 10 October 1999 (next to be held in 2004). Most independent candidates in the Majilis are affiliated with parastatal enterprises and other pro-government institutions.

Government Budgets (A)

Year: 1998

Total Expenditures: 318,252 Millions of Tenge

Expenditures as a percentage of the total by function:

- General public services and public order 15.19
- Defense 5.12
- Education 4.78
- Health 7.74
- Social Security and Welfare 38.12
- Housing and community amenities 0
- Recreational, cultural, and religious affairs 2.04
- Fuel and energy 0.15
- Agriculture, forestry, fishing, and hunting 1.52
- Mining, manufacturing, and construction 0.18
- Transportation and communication 3.22
- Other economic affairs and services 4.97

Crime

Crime rate (for 1997)

- Crimes reported 162,500
- Total persons convicted 101,200
- Crimes per 100,000 population 1,300

Persons responsible for offenses

- Total number of suspects 97,500
- Total number of female suspects 13,600
- Total number of juvenile suspects 6,950

LABOR FORCE

Total Labor Force (A)

8.8 million (1997).

Labor Force by Occupation

- Industry 27%
- Agriculture and forestry 23%
- Other 50%

Data for 1996.

Unemployment Rate

13.7% (1998 est.)

PRODUCTION SECTOR

Energy Production

Production ...... 49.299 billion kWh

Production by source

- Fossil fuel 87.73%
- Hydro 12.07%
- Nuclear 0.20%
- Other 0%

Exports ...... 400 million kWh

Data for 1998.

Energy Consumption

Consumption ...... 48.822 billion kWh

Imports ...... 3.374 billion kWh

Data for 1998.

Transportation

Highways:

Total: 119,390 km.

Paved: 103,272 km.

Unpaved: 16,118 km (1998 est.).

Waterways: 3,900 km on the Syrdariya (Syr Darya) and Ertis (Irtysh).

Pipelines: crude oil 2,850 km; refined products 1,500 km; natural gas 3,480 km (1992).

Airports: 10 (1997 est.).

Top Agriculture Products

Grain (mostly spring wheat), cotton; wool, livestock.

Top Mining Products (A)

	National Production	World Production
Commodities in 1998		
Copper (000 mt)	337	12,200
Gold (000 kg)	12.5	2,460
Iron Ore (million mt)	9	1,020
Lead (000 mt)	30	3,080
Nickel (000 mt)	6	1,140
Silver (mt)	470	16,400
Uranium (mt	1,250	33,932

COMMUNICATIONS

Telecommunications

Telephones - main lines in use: 1.963 million (1995).

Telephones - mobile cellular: 4,600 (1995).

Telephone system: service is poor; equipment antiquated.

Domestic: intercity by landline and microwave radio relay; mobile cellular systems are available in most of Kazakstan.

International: international traffic with other former Soviet republics and China carried by landline and microwave radio relay; with other countries by satellite and by the Trans-Asia-Europe (TAE) fiber-optic cable; satellite earth stations - 2 Intelsat.

Radio broadcast stations: AM 60, FM 17, shortwave 9 (1998).

Radios: 6.47 million (1997).

Television broadcast stations: 12 (plus nine repeaters) (1998).

Televisions: 3.88 million (1997).

Internet Service Providers (ISPs): 83 (Kazakstan and Russia) (1999).

FINANCE, ECONOMICS, & TRADE

Economic Indicators

National product: GDP—purchasing power parity—$54.5 billion (1999 est.).

National product real growth rate: 1.7% (1999 est.).

National product per capita: $3,200 (1999 est.).

Inflation rate—consumer price index: 8.3% (1999 est.).

Balance of Payments

	1995	1996	1997	1998
Exports of goods (f.o.b.)	5,440	6,292	6,899	5,839
Imports of goods (f.o.b.)	−5,326	−6,627	−7,176	−6,589
Trade balance	114	−335	−276	−750
Services - debits	−776	−928	−1,124	−1,127
Services - credits	535	674	842	897
Private transfers (net)	7	10	18	10
Government transfers (net)	73	61	73	84
Overall balance	−213	−751	−794	−1,201

Exchange Rates

Exchange rates:

Tenges per US$1

January 2000	139.02
1999	119.52
1998	78.30
1997	75.44
1996	67.30
1995	60.95

Top Import Origins

$4.8 billion (1999 est.)

Origins (1998)

Russia	39%
Ukraine	NA
United States	NA
Uzbekistan	NA
Turkey	NA
United Kingdom	NA
Germany	NA
South Korea	NA

(Continued on next page.)

MANUFACTURING SECTOR

GDP & Manufacturing Summary (B)

	1980	1985	1990	1993	1994	1995
Gross Domestic Product						
Millions of 1990 dollars	21,683	28,636	39,831	27,591	20,693	18,852
Growth rate in percent	3.76	6.15	15.53	−12.90	−25.00	−8.90
Per capita (in 1990 dollars)	1,455	1,815	2,389	1,638	1,230	1,121
Manufacturing Value Added						
Millions of 1990 dollars	3,882	5,107	5,497	4,382	3,155	2,886[e]
Growth rate in percent	NA	6.15	−3.20	−14.80	−28.00	−8.52[e]
Manufacturing share in percent of current prices	NA	NA	13.8[e]	17.0[e]	NA	NA

FINANCE, ECONOMICS, & TRADE (cont.)

Top Export Destinations

$5.2 billion (1999 est.)

Destinations (1998)

EU	32%
China	29%
Russia	29%

Foreign Aid

Recipient: $409.6 million (1995).

Import/Export Commodities

Import Commodities	Export Commodities
Machinery and parts	Oil 40%
Industrial materials	Ferrous and nonferrous metals
Oil and gas	Machinery
Vehicles	Chemicals
	Grain
	Wool
	Meat
	Coal

KENYA

Republic of Kenya
Jamhuri ya Kenya

CAPITAL: Nairobi.

FLAG: The flag is a horizontal tricolor of black, red, and green stripes separated by narrow white bars. At the center is a red shield with black and white markings superimposed on two crossed white spears.

ANTHEM: *Wimbo Wa Taifa (National Anthem),* beginning "Ee Mungu nguvu yetu, ilete baraka Kwetu" ("O God of all creation, bless this our land and nation").

MONETARY UNIT: The Kenya shilling (Sh) is a paper currency of 100 cents; the Kenya pound (K£) is a unit of account equivalent to 20 shillings. There are coins of 5, 10, and 50 cents, and 1 and 5 shillings; and notes of 5, 10, 20, 50, 100, and 200 shillings. Sh1 = $0.01796 (or $1 = Sh55.694).

WEIGHTS AND MEASURES: The metric system is used.

HOLIDAYS: New Year's Day, 1 January; Labor Day, 1 May; Madaraka Day, 1 June; Kenyatta Day, 20 October; Uhuru (Independence) Day, 12 December; Christmas, 25 December; Boxing Day, 26 December. Movable holidays include Good Friday, Easter Monday, 'Id al-Fitr, and 'Id al-'Adha'.

TIME: 3 PM = noon GMT.

LOCATION AND SIZE: Situated on the eastern coast of Africa, Kenya lies astride the equator. Its total area, including 11,230 square kilometers (4,336 square miles) of water, is 582,650 square kilometers (224,962 square miles). Comparatively, the area occupied by Kenya is slightly more than twice the size of the state of Nevada. It has a total boundary length of 3,969 kilometers (2,467 miles). Kenya's capital city, Nairobi, is located in the south-central part of the country.

CLIMATE: The climate of Kenya is as varied as its topography. The coastal temperature averages 27°C (81°F), and the temperature decreases as the altitude increases. The capital, Nairobi, at 1,661 meters (5,449 feet), has a mean annual temperature of 19°C (66°F); at 2,740 meters (9,000 feet) the average is 13°C (55°F). Seasonal variations are distinguished by amount of rainfall rather than by changes of temperature.

INTRODUCTORY SURVEY

RECENT HISTORY

The region that would become Kenya was ruled by Great Britain as a colony in the first half of the twentieth century. Many Kenyans were unhappy with British rule and struggled against it. The Mau Mau revolutionary movement led to the declaration of a state of emergency in October 1952 that lasted until late 1959. The 1960 "Macleod" constitution mandated an African-elected majority in Kenya's Legislative Council. This marked a decisive shift in the direction of African control.

In December 1963 Kenya became independent. Exactly one year later it became a republic within the Commonwealth of Nations, with Jomo Kenyatta as the country's first president. His political party, the Kenya African National Union (KANU), dominated the government. Leaders of a rival party, banned in 1969, were arrested.

Kenyatta died in August 1978 and was succeeded by his vice-president, Daniel arap Moi, who was elected president without opposition a month later. In June 1982 the National Assembly voted unanimously to make Kenya formally a one-party state. President Moi ran unopposed in the elections of September 1983. In 1986 Moi declared that KANU was above government, the parliament, and the judiciary. Critics of Moi were expelled from KANU and government repression increased. In July 1990, clashes between pro-democracy demonstrators and police left five dead. In 1991 riot police dispersed thousands of protesters.

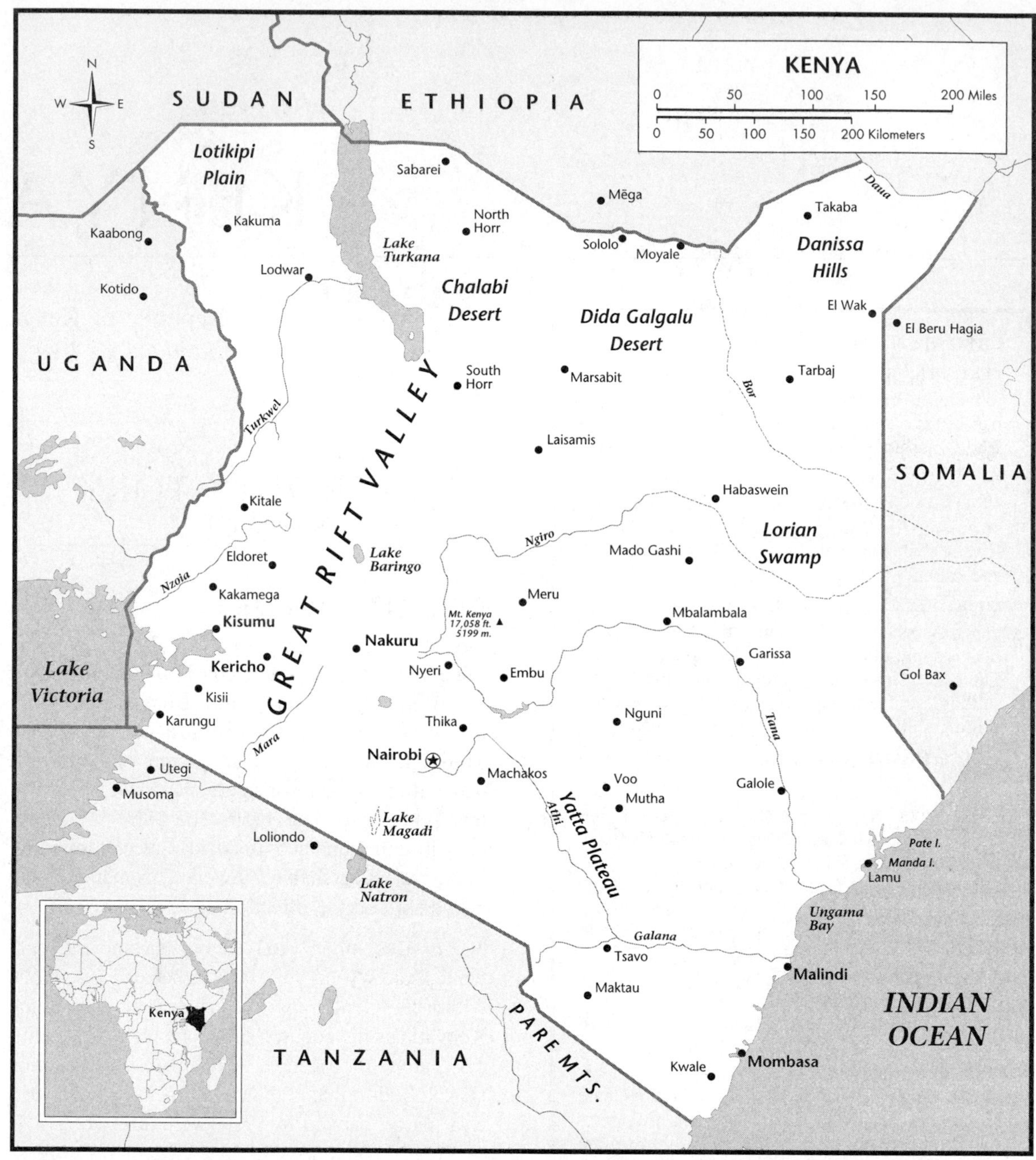

In December 1991, in response to growing pressure by the United States and other donors of foreign aid, Moi proposed dropping the 1982 constitutional amendment legalizing one-party rule. KANU agreed to it, but opposition to Moi and civil unrest continued. In Nairobi in January 1992, more than 100,000 attended the first legal anti-government rally in twenty-two years. The following year Moi delayed elections until his opposition, divided into eight parties, fell apart. In the late December elections, Moi was reelected with 37 percent of the vote. Foreign aid has been reduced as Moi continues to pressure the opposition in and out of parliament. In 1993 Africa Watch, a U.S.-based human rights group, reported that as many as 1,500 Kenyans have been killed and over 300,000 displaced as a result of ethnic violence triggered by Moi's regime. The government's security forces increased oppression of the opposition in 1994 and 1995. Civil unrest escalated through 1997 and international donors have become reluctant to offer assistance. Moi was reelected in 1997 for a fourth term in balloting rife with fraud and violence.

On August 7, 1998, U.S. embassies in Nairobi and Dar es Salaam, Tanzania were bombed killing over 200 people. It was believed that Islamist terrorists were responsible.

Moi announced he will retire in 2002 after twenty-four years in power and the quest for a successor was underway.

GOVERNMENT

According to the constitution of 1963, as later amended, a president who is chief of state, head of government, and commander-in-chief of the armed forces leads the government of Kenya. The president is elected by popular vote from among members of the National Assembly for a five-year term. The president appoints the members of the cabinet from among members of the National Assembly. The unicameral 222-seat National Assembly, or Bunge, was established when the Senate and House of Representatives were merged by constitutional amendment in 1967. Twelve members are appointed by the president and 210 members elected by popular vote to serve five-year terms. Suffrage is universal at age eighteen.

Judiciary

The judicial system consists of the Court of Appeal, which has final appellate jurisdiction, and subordinate courts. The High Court has both civil and criminal jurisdiction, serving as an appellate tribunal in some cases and a court of first instance in others. Lower courts are presided over by resident magistrates and district magistrates. Questions of Islamic law are determined by *qadis'* courts. Military courts handle courts marital of military personnel.

Political Parties

Since 1964 the Kenya African National Union (KANU) has dominated Kenyan politics. In December 1991 the Moi government decided to end KANU's monopoly on legal political activity. A grand coalition known as the Forum for the Restoration of Democracy (FORD) formed. Before the December 1992 election it fragmented into two factions-FORD-Kenya and FORD-Asili, and later into a third, FORD-People. The Democratic Party of Kenya was formed. In the 1997 election KANU took 107 seats in the national assembly, FORD-A one seat, FORD-K seventeen seats, FORD-People three seats, and DP thirty-nine. Other parties taking seats were the National Development Party (NDP) with twenty-one seats, Social Democratic party (SDP) fifteen seats, and SAFINA five seats.

DEFENSE

Military service is voluntary. In 2000 the army had 20,500 men; the navy, 1,200 men; and the air force, 2,500 men. The 5,000-member national police has general service, air, and naval paramilitary units. In 1998-1999 Kenya spent $197 million, or 1.9 percent of GDP on defense.

ECONOMIC AFFAIRS

Kenya could potentially be a growth leader in East Africa but poor management and an unorganized reform commitment have hindered economic progress. A program of economic liberalization and support from the World Bank, IMF, and other foreign donors produced a short-lived turnaround n economic performance with the GDP growing 5 percent in 1995 and 4 percent in 1996. However growth slowed in 1997-1999 with government failure to curb corruption and maintain reforms. Unemployment ran 50 percent in 1998. Political violence severely hurt the tourist industry. A new economic team with renewed efforts planned to revitalize the economy was put in place in 1999 but wary donors continued to withhold funding aid.

Public Finance

The fiscal year extends from 1 July to 30 June. The U.S. CIA estimated that in 2000 government revenues totaled approximately $2.91 billion and expenditures $2.97 billion. External debt totaled $6.5 billion in 1998.

Progress in reducing the deficit was substantial between 1993-94 and 1994-95 as the deficit fell from 6.5 percent of GDP to 0.7 percent.

Income

In 1999 Kenya's gross domestic product (GDP) was $45.1 billion, or about $1,600 per capita. The 1999 estimate of GDP growth rate was 1.5 percent and inflation 6 percent. The 1999 estimated GDP by sector was agriculture 6 percent, industry 18 percent, and services 56 percent.

Industry

The transformation of agricultural raw materials, particularly of coffee and tea, remains the principal industrial activity. Meat and fruit canning, wheat flour and cornmeal milling, and sugar refining are also important. Electronics production, vehicle assembly, publishing, soda ash processing, and small-scale consumer goods, cement, and tourism are all significant parts of the sector. Assembly of computer components began in 1987. An oil refinery is located in Mombasa and typically operates at 65 percent of capacity.

Banking and Finance

The Central Bank of Kenya (CBK) was established in May 1966, taking over the administration of exchange control. The powers of the CBK were greatly reduced in the early 1990s with the liberalization of the financial sector. Commercial banks are free to set their own exchange and interest rates.

In 1999 Kenya had forty-eight domestic and foreign commercial banks, six building societies, seven development finance companies, and the Post Office Savings Bank. The financial sector is dominated by two multinational banks, the Standard Chartered Bank and Barclays Bank of Kenya, and by the parastatal banks—Kenya Commercial Bank and National Bank of Kenya.

The reputation of the banking sector has suffered from a series of scandals. Banking sector fragility in 1999 resulted from poor management, and worsening economic conditions.

The Nairobi Stock Exchange, founded in 1965, is one of the largest in Sub-Saharan Africa with sixty-two listed companies in 1998.

Economic Development

Central to Kenyan government planning is a continuing expansion of the level of exports and diversification of cash crops. Moreover Kenya has sought the orderly introduction of large numbers of African farmers into former European agricultural areas. With the goal of full economic independence, the government continues to pursue Africanization of the private sector, particularly in commerce.

Development in Kenya now depends on the private sector and on foreign and domestic investment as the parastatal sector is dismantled. Foreign exchange earnings are key to the sixth development plan (1989-1993). Increased agricultural and industrial productivity, job creation, and diversification are also goals of current development policy. Failure to maintain a steady reform process and widespread public sector corruption has stalled economic development.

SOCIAL WELFARE

The National Social Security Fund operates a limited pension for employed persons. Disability and survivor benefits are also paid. Social welfare is largely in the hands of private and voluntary agencies that are highly developed. There are societies that care for the blind, the deaf and mute, and the physically disabled, and voluntary organizations that care for the poor and destitute. Homes and hostels have been established throughout the country for the care of orphans, young offenders, and juvenile prostitutes. Women must obtain written permission from their husbands or fathers to acquire a passport. Intertribal violence is a recurring problem.

Healthcare

The most important health insurance program in Kenya is the National Hospital Insurance Fund. Membership is compulsory for all civil servants. The government encourages the private healthcare sector.

Among Kenya's major health problems are tuberculosis and protein deficiency. Although the incidence of malaria has been reduced, it still accounted for over 20 percent of outpatient deaths in 1990. Water supply, sanitation, and sleeping sickness also pose major problems. Diseases caused by parasites are widespread in some areas. There has been a rapid spread of AIDS since the 1980s. In 1994-1995 only 49 percent of the population had access to safe water and only 43 percent had adequate sanitation. There was an average life expectancy of forty-eight years in 2000.

Housing

Housing in rural areas is privately owned. Most of these homes, built with traditional materials, fall apart in a relatively short time. An increasing number of people now build their homes with more permanent materials. The central government is responsible for all housing projects and works closely with local authorities.

EDUCATION

Primary education is free and compulsory for eight years. Children start school at the age of 5 or 6 and spend eight years at primary school, five years at secondary school, and a further four years at the university. In 1995 there were 5.5 million primary school students. In general secondary schools, there were 632,388 students. There are four major universities in Kenya. In 2000 the adult illiteracy rate was 17.5 percent, an estimated 11 percent for men and 24 percent for women.

2000 KEY EVENTS TIMELINE

January

- A Kenya Airways Airbus 310 crashes into the Atlantic Ocean moments after take-off January 30; approximately 169 people are killed.

June

- Kenya raises its VAT from 15 percent to 18 percent, cuts the civil service drastically, and sells 49 percent of the national telecoms company in an effort to tighten the national budget. Raising social tension; including the stresses of increased crime, AIDS infection, and drought; have damaged the economy.

July

- An estimated three million people need emergency food assistance as the drought continues.
- Members of Parliament vote to delete their names, and those of relatives, off of the "List of Shame" on July 19, which implicates them in the theft of hundreds of millions.

November

- Six people are charged with manslaughter November 22 after their home-brewed alcoholic beverage kills 134 people and hospitalizes hundreds of others.
- Kenya deports 137 Ugandans November 24 for fear that some may carry the deadly *Ebola* virus.

December

- Rain falls in Kenya for the first time in eighteen months, helping to end a three-year drought that has devastated the country.

ANALYSIS OF EVENTS: 2000

BUSINESS AND THE ECONOMY

The release of $198 million in International Monetary Fund (IMF) loan funds to Kenya in late July came at a crucial time for the beleaguered country. Already weakened by corruption, economic mismanagement, and low coffee prices, the country's economy had been pushed to the edge by two years of drought. Deaths from starvation had been reported, and rural areas were so decimated that tribal cattle herders were driving their cows into the capital city of Nairobi in search of water and grazing land. Some had sustained livestock losses from which it was feared they would never fully recover. In the cities, the closing of businesses pushed unemployment levels—already high—to nearly 50 percent. Economic growth had slowed to 1.4 percent.

The drought from which Kenya had suffered since the mid-1980s also aggravated problems in the electic power supply. Since the rivers were drying up, the nation's dams, the major source of electrical power, were incapacitated as a result. The unavailability of a reliable power supply had forced many businesses, especially those in the building trade, to close. Power rationing, instituted in June, limited electricity to twelve hours a day or less. Water was being rationed as well.

In addition to providing crucial immediate economic relief, the IMF funds were cause for celebration because other donors were expected to follow suit. In August the World Bank pledged an additional $150 million in loans.

GOVERNMENT AND POLITICS

As the twenty-first century began, efforts to reform Kenya's constitution remained stalled, and it was unclear whether President Daniel Arap Moi, who was slated to retire in 2002 after twenty-two years in office, would actually do so. The Kenyan government continued to be regarded as one of the most corrupt in Africa, with Moi's associates using illicit strategies of all kinds to drain the country's funds for their own personal use. However, the 1999 appointment of famed paleontologist and opposition politician Richard Leakey to clean up the nation's civil service appeared to have yielded results, at least in terms of the outside world's attitude toward the Kenyan government. The IMF, which had frozen all aid three years earlier due to the country's pervasive corruption, announced in July that it would start releasing funds to the increasingly impoverished nation.

However, the release of funds was made conditional on a set of restrictions so stringent—the toughest it had ever imposed—that the IMF would virtually control the Kenyan government. The requirements—numbering more than sixty altogether—included regular financial disclosure by public officials and their immediate family members, weekly inspection of central bank records, IMF approval of all new projects, and passage and implementation of a new anticorruption law whose provisions had already been set by the IMF. In addition, power over district finances was to be transferred from district commissioners and the president's office and turned over to a new treasury department.

CULTURE AND SOCIETY

Two years of drought and a three-year dearth of international aid had left many Kenyans in desperate straits. Commerce and industry were crippled by endemic power shortages, and unemployment had resulted in rising crime rates. As of 2000 more than half of Kenya's population was living in poverty, 10 percent more than a decade earlier. Power rationing, officially at twelve hours per day, came to as little as two hours per day in some cases, and water, also rationed, was only available at certain hours and on certain days of the week. Outrage, both local and international, over the situation was exacerbated by the knowledge that top government officials continued to enrich themselves, enjoying the fruits of the country's rampant corruption.

Although not often cited among Kenya's litany of problems, AIDS, which had long since reached epidemic proportions in sub-Saharan Africa, was an important contributor to the nation's suffering and impoverishment. One in every seven people in Kenya is HIV-positive, and on average 500 Kenyans a day die of AIDS. In addition to those directly afflicted with the illness, AIDS affected all residents of the country by producing a shortage of trained workers in crucial public service sectors such as medicine, education, and law enforcement. It was estimated that two policemen per week died of AIDS.

The ravages of AIDS also translated into economic figures. The government estimated that Kenya had already lost $10 billion in productivity to AIDS and that the illness was now costing the country as much as $2.7 million per day. And people with AIDS were victimized further by discrimination as individual businesses scrambled to cut their own losses. Employers regularly fired workers suspected of having AIDS to cut down on lost productivity and avoid paying benefits, and mortgage underwriters required medical information including blood tests from applicants. A successful public health campaign, such as those waged in Uganda and Senegal, was unlikely to occur until the nation began to recover from its economic and administrative difficulties.

DIRECTORY

CENTRAL GOVERNMENT

Head of State

President and Commander-in-Chief of the Armed Forces
D. T. Arap Moi, Office of the President, Harambee House, Harambee Ave., P.O. Box 30510, Nairobi, Kenya
PHONE: +254 (2) 227411

Vice President
George Saitoti, Office of the Vice President, Jogoo House, Harambee Ave., P.O. Box 30520, Nairobi, Kenya
PHONE: +254 (2) 228411

Ministers

Minister of State
Julius Sunkuli, Ministry of State, Harambee House, Harambee Ave., P.O. Box 30510, Nairobi, Kenya
PHONE: +254 (2) 227411

Minister of State
Marsden H. Madoka, Ministry of State, Harambee House, Harambee Ave., P.O. Box 30510, Nairobi, Kenya
PHONE: +254 (2) 227411

Minister of State
Shariff Nasir Taib, Ministry of State, Harambee House, Harambee Ave., P.O. Box 30510, Nairobi, Kenya
PHONE: +254 (2) 227411

Minister of State
William ole Ntimama, Ministry of State, Harambee House, Harambee Ave., P.O. Box 30510, Nairobi, Kenya
PHONE: +254 (2) 227411

Minister of Home Affairs, Heritage, Culture and Sport
Noah Katana Ngala, Ministry of Home Affairs, Heritage, Culture and Sport, Jogoo House, Harambee Ave., P.O. Box 30520, Nairobi, Kenya
PHONE: +254 (2) 228411

Minister of Agriculture
Chris Mogere Obure, Ministry of Agriculture, Kilimo House, Cathedral Rd., P.O. Box 30028, Nairobi, Kenya
PHONE: +254 (2) 718870

Minister of Rural Development
Hussein Maalim Mohammed, Ministry of Rural Development, Kilimo House, Cathedral Rd., P.O. Box 30028, Nairobi, Kenya
PHONE: +254 (2) 718870

Minister of Education
Stephen Kalonzo Musyoka, Ministry of Education, Jogoo House "B," Harambee Ave., P.O. Box 30040, Nairobi, Kenya
PHONE: +254 (2) 334411
E-MAIL: elimu1@africaonline.co.ke

Minister of Science and Technology
Henry Kosgey, Ministry of Science and Technology, Jogoo House "B," Harambee Ave., P.O. Box 30040, Nairobi, Kenya
PHONE: +254 (2) 334411
E-MAIL: elimu1@africaonline.co.ke

Minister of Labor
Joseph Ngutu, Ministry of Labor, Jogoo House "B," Harambee Ave., P.O. Box 30040, Nairobi, Kenya
PHONE: +254 (2) 334411
E-MAIL: elimu1@africaonline.co.ke

Minister of Energy
Yekoyada Francis Masakhalia, Ministry of Energy, Nyayo House, Kenyatta Ave., P.O. Box 30582, Nairobi, Kenya
PHONE: +254 (2) 333551

Minister of Environment
Francis Nyenz, Ministry of Environment, Kencom House, Moi Ave., P.O. Box 30126, Nairobi, Kenya
PHONE: +254 (2) 229261

Minister of Mineral Exploitation
Jackson Kalweo, Ministry of Mineral Exploitation, Kencom House, Moi Ave., P.O. Box 30126, Nairobi, Kenya
PHONE: +254 (2) 229261

Minister of Finance
Chrysanthus Okemo, Ministry of Finance, Treasury Building, Harambee Ave., P.O. Box 30007, Nairobi, Kenya
PHONE: +254 (2) 338111
E-MAIL: mof@form-net.com

Minister of Planning
Gideon Ndambuki, Ministry of Planning, Treasury Building, Harambee Ave., P.O. Box 30007, Nairobi, Kenya
PHONE: +254 (2) 338111
E-MAIL: mof@form-net.com

Minister of Foreign Affairs and International Co-operation
Bonaya Godana, Ministry of Foreign Affairs and International Co-operation, Old Treasury Building, Harambee Ave., P.O. Box 30551, Nairobi, Kenya
PHONE: +254 (2) 334433

Minister of Transport and Communications
W. Musalia Mudavadi, Ministry of Transport and Communications, Telecom House, Ngong Rd., P.O. Box 52692, Nairobi, Kenya
PHONE: +254 (2) 729200

Minister of Lands and Settlement
Joseph Nyagah, Ministry of Lands and Settlement, Ardhi House, Ngong Rd., P.O. Box 30450, Nairobi, Kenya
PHONE: +254 (2) 718050

Minister of Local Government
Joseph J. Kamotho, Ministry of Local Government, Jogoo House "A," Taifa Rd., P.O. Box 30004, Nairobi, Kenya
PHONE: +254 (2) 217475
E-MAIL: mlog@form-net.com

Minister of Public Works and Housing
Andrew C. Kiptoon, Ministry of Public Works and Housing, Ngong Rd., P.O. Box 30260, Nairobi, Kenya
PHONE: +254 (2) 723101

Minister of Tourism, Trade and Industry
Kipyator Nicholas K. Biwott, Ministry of Tourism, Trade and Industry, Utalii House, Uhuru Highway, P.O. Box 331030, Nairobi, Kenya
PHONE: +254 (2) 723101

POLITICAL ORGANIZATIONS

Kenya African National Union (KANU)

TITLE: President
NAME: Daniel Toroitich arap Moi

Democratic Party of Kenya (DP)

NAME: Mwai Kibaki

Forum for the Restoration of Democracy-Asili (FORD-A)

TITLE: Chairman
NAME: Martin Shikuku

Forum for the Restoration of Democracy-Kenya (FORD-K)

NAME: Michael Kijana Wamalwa

Forum for the Restoration of Democracy-People (FORD-People)

NAME: Raymond Matiba

National Development Party (NDP)

TITLE: President
NAME: Raila Odinga

DIPLOMATIC REPRESENTATION

Embassies in Kenya

Algeria
4th. Floor, Comcraft House, Haile Selassie Ave., P.O. Box 53902, Nairobi, Kenya
PHONE: +254 (2) 213864
FAX: +254 (2) 337286; 217477
E-MAIL: algerianembassy@form-net.com

Argentina
7th Floor, Town House, Kaunda Street, P.O. Box 30283, Nairobi, Kenya
PHONE: +254 (2) 335242; 339949
E-MAIL: argentina@form-net.com

Australia
ICIPE House, River Side Drive, P.O. Box 39341, Nairobi, Kenya
PHONE: +254 (2) 445034
FAX: +254 (2) 444617

Austria
6th Floor, Posta Sacco Plaza, P.O. Box 30560, Nairobi, Kenya
PHONE: +254 (2) 228281
FAX: +254 (2) 331972

Bangladesh
Ole Odume Rd., P.O. Box 41645, Nairobi, Kenya
PHONE: +254 (2) 562815
FAX: +254 (2) 562817

Belgium
Muthaiga, Limuru Rd., P.O. Box 30461, Nairobi, Kenya
PHONE: +254 (2) 741564
FAX: +254 (2) 741568
E-MAIL: belgianemb_ke@form-net.com

Brazil
4th Floor, Jeevan Bharati Building, Harambee Ave., P.O. Box 30754, Nairobi, Kenya
PHONE: +254 (2) 332649; 215755
FAX: +254 (2) 336245

Burundi
14th Floor, Development House, Moi Ave., P.O. Box 44439, Nairobi, Kenya
PHONE: +254 (2) 218458
FAX: +254 (2) 219005

Canada
6th Floor, Comcraft House, Haile Selassie Ave., P.O. Box 30481, Nairobi, Kenya
PHONE: +254 (2) 214804
FAX: +254 (2) 226987
E-MAIL: kenyapsudir@form-net.com

Chile
5th Floor, International House, Mama Ngina St., P.O. Box 45554, Nairobi, Kenya
PHONE: +254 (2) 337934; 331320
FAX: +254 (2) 215648
E-MAIL: echileke@form-net.com

China
Woodlands Rd., Hurlingham, P.O. Box 30508, Nairobi, Kenya
PHONE: +254 (2) 722559
FAX: +254 (2) 746402

Colombia
Muthaiga Rd., House No. 3, P.O. Box 48494, Nairobi, Kenya
PHONE: +254 (2) 765927
FAX: +254 (2) 765911
E-MAIL: embcol@form-net.com

Comoros
Nation Centre, Kimathi Street, P.O. Box 43912, Nairobi, Kenya
PHONE: +254 (2) 222964
FAX: +254 (2) 222564
E-MAIL: embcol@form-net.com

Democratic Republic of Congo
12th Fl., Electricity House, Harambee Ave., P.O. Box 48106, Nairobi, Kenya
PHONE: +254 (2) 229771-2
FAX: +254 (2) 564394

Costa Rica
Geosurvey Building, Wilson Airport, Langata Rd., P.O. Box 30750, Nairobi, Kenya
PHONE: +254 (2) 500226; 721845
FAX: +254 (2) 222564
E-MAIL: aranibarmkt@form-net.com

Côte d'Ivoire
Lonrho House, Standard Street, P.O. Box 22683, Nairobi, Kenya

PHONE: +254 (2) 220179
FAX: +254 (2) 211677; 228427

Cyprus
5th Floor, Eagle House, Kimathi Street, P.O. Box 30739, Nairobi, Kenya
PHONE: +254 (2) 220881; 441954
FAX: +254 (2) 331232

Czech Republic
Embassy House, Harambee Rd., P.O. Box 48785, Nairobi, Kenya
PHONE: +254 (2) 210494

Denmark
11th Floor, HFCK Building, Kenyatta Ave., P.O. Box 40412, Nairobi, Kenya
PHONE: +254 (2) 331088
FAX: +254 (2) 331492

Djibouti
2nd Floor, Comcraft House, Haile Selassie Ave., P.O. Box 59528, Nairobi, Kenya
PHONE: +254 (2) 339640; 336433

Egypt
7th Floor, Harambee Plaza, Haile Selassie Ave., P.O. Box 30285, Nairobi, Kenya
PHONE: +254 (2) 570360
FAX: +254 (2) 211560

Eritrea
2nd Floor, New Rehema House, Raphta Rd., P.O. Box 38651, Nairobi, Kenya
PHONE: +254 (2) 444316
FAX: +254 (2) 443165

Ethiopia
State House Ave., P.O. Box 45198, Nairobi, Kenya
PHONE: +254 (2) 723027
FAX: +254 (2) 723401

Finland
2nd Floor, International House, Mama Ngina St., P.O. Box 30379, Nairobi, Kenya
PHONE: +254 (2) 334777; 334408
FAX: +254 (2) 335986

France
9th Floor, Barclays Plaza, Loita Street, P.O. Box 41784, Nairobi, Kenya
PHONE: +254 (2) 339783; 339978
FAX: +254 (2) 339421
E-MAIL: maisonfrance@form-net.com

Gabon
Hotel Intercontinental, City Hall Way, P.O. Box 30353, Nairobi, Kenya
PHONE: +254 (2) 335550
FAX: +254 (2) 337854

Germany
4th Floor, Williamson House, Ngong Rd., P.O. Box 30180, Nairobi, Kenya
PHONE: +254 (2) 712527
FAX: +254 (2) 714886
E-MAIL: bavaria@form-net.com

Greece
13th Floor, Nation Centre, Kimathi Street, P.O. Box 30543, Nairobi, Kenya
PHONE: +254 (2) 340722
FAX: +254 (2) 216044

Hungary
Ole Odume Rd., P.O. Box 61146, Nairobi, Kenya
PHONE: +254 (2) 560060; 560453
FAX: +254 (2) 560114

Iceland
Ruaka Rd., Runda, P.O. Box 45000, Nairobi, Kenya
PHONE: +254 (2) 521487
FAX: +254 (2) 521487

India
2nd Floor, Jeevan Bharati Building, Harambee Ave., P.O. Box 30074, Nairobi, Kenya
PHONE: +254 (2) 225104; 225180
FAX: +254 (2) 334167
E-MAIL: hcindia@form-net.com

Indonesia
3rd Floor, Utalii House, Uhuru Highway, P.O. Box 48868, Nairobi, Kenya
PHONE: +254 (2) 215848
FAX: +254 (2) 340721
E-MAIL: hcindia@form-net.com

Iran
Dennis Pritt Rd., P.O. Box 49170, Nairobi, Kenya
PHONE: +254 (2) 720343; 720796
FAX: +254 (2) 339936

Iraq
Loresho Rd., P.O. Box 49213, Nairobi, Kenya
PHONE: +254 (2) 580262; 581073
FAX: +254 (2) 582880

Ireland
5th Floor, Waumini House, Chiromo Rd., P.O. Box 30659, Nairobi, Kenya
PHONE: +254 (2) 444367
FAX: +254 (2) 440897

Israel
Bishops Rd., P.O. Box 30354, Nairobi, Kenya

PHONE: +254 (2) 722182
FAX: +254 (2) 715966

Italy
9th Floor, International House, Mama Ngina Street, P.O. Box 30107, Nairobi, Kenya
PHONE: +254 (2) 337356
FAX: +254 (2) 337056
E-MAIL: afra@form-net.com

Japan
15th Floor, ICEA Building, Kenyatta Ave., P.O. Box 60202, Nairobi, Kenya
PHONE: +254 (2) 332955
FAX: +254 (2) 332955

South Korea
Anniversary Towers, University Way, P.O. Box 30455, Nairobi, Kenya
PHONE: +254 (2) 333581
FAX: +254 (2) 332839
E-MAIL: koremb@form-net.com

Kuwait
Muthaiga Rd., House No. 38, P.O. Box 42353, Nairobi, Kenya
PHONE: +254 (2) 761614
FAX: +254 (2) 762837
E-MAIL: kuwaitembassy@form-net.com

Lebanon
9th Floor, Maendeleo House, Monrovia Street, P.O. Box 30074, Nairobi, Kenya
PHONE: +254 (2) 223708; 229981
FAX: +254 (2) 340944

Lesotho
4th Floor, International House, Mama Ngina St., P.O. Box 44096, Nairobi, Kenya
PHONE: +254 (2) 224876; 217785
FAX: +254 (2) 337493

Luxembourg
8th Floor, International House, Mama Ngina St., P.O. Box 30610, Nairobi, Kenya
PHONE: +254 (2) 224318
FAX: +254 (2) 229938

Madagascar
1st Floor, Hilton Hotel, Mama Ngina Street, P.O. Box 41723, Nairobi, Kenya
PHONE: +254 (2) 226494; 225286

Malawi
Mvuli, Church Rd., Westlands, P.O. Box 30453, Nairobi, Kenya
PHONE: +254 (2) 440569
FAX: +254 (2) 440568

Malaysia
4th Floor, Eagle House, Kimathi Street, P.O. Box 45000, Nairobi, Kenya
PHONE: +254 (2) 229724
FAX: +254 (2) 521487

Mauritius
1st Floor, Union Towers, Moi Ave., P.O. Box 49326, Nairobi, Kenya
PHONE: +254 (2) 330215
FAX: +254 (2) 221006

Mexico
Kibagare Way off Loresho Ridge, P.O. Box 14145, Nairobi, Kenya
PHONE: +254 (2) 582850; 582579
FAX: +254 (2) 581500
E-MAIL: embmexke@form-net.com

Morocco
3rd Floor, Diamond Trust House, Moi Ave., P.O. Box 61093, Nairobi, Kenya
PHONE: +254 (2) 222361; 222364
FAX: +254 (2) 222364
E-MAIL: embassymorocco@form-net.com

Mozambique
4th Floor, Hughes Building, Kenyatta Ave., P.O. Box 66923, Nairobi, Kenya
PHONE: +254 (2) 221979
FAX: +254 (2) 222446

Netherlands
6th Floor, Uchumi House, Nkrumah Ave., P.O. Box 41537, Nairobi, Kenya
PHONE: +254 (2) 227111
FAX: +254 (2) 339155
E-MAIL: holland@form-net.com

Nigeria
Lenana Rd. Hurlingham, P.O. Box 30516, Nairobi, Kenya
PHONE: +254 (2) 564116
FAX: +254 (2) 564117; 562776

Norway
8th Floor, Rehani House, Kenyatta Ave., P.O. Box 46363, Nairobi, Kenya
PHONE: +254 (2) 337121
FAX: +254 (2) 216009

Pakistan
St. Michael's Rd., Westlands Ave., P.O. Box 30045, Nairobi, Kenya
PHONE: +254 (2) 443911
FAX: +254 (2) 446507

Peru
Lagutrop House, Enterprise Rd., P.O. Box 59446, Nairobi, Kenya
PHONE: +254 (2) 530156
FAX: +254 (2) 524114

Philippines
State House Rd., P.O. Box 47941, Nairobi, Kenya
PHONE: +254 (2) 721791
FAX: +254 (2) 725897

Poland
Kabarnet Rd., Woodley, P.O. Box 30086, Nairobi, Kenya
PHONE: +254 (2) 566288
FAX: +254 (2) 727701
E-MAIL: polambnairobi@form-net.com

Portugal
10th Floor, Reinsurance Plaza, Aga Khan Walk, P.O. Box 34020, Nairobi, Kenya
PHONE: +254 (2) 338990; 339853
FAX: +254 (2) 214711

Russia
Lenana Rd., P.O. Box 30049, Nairobi, Kenya
PHONE: +254 (2) 722462; 728700
FAX: +254 (2) 721888

Saudi Arabia
Muthaiga Rd., P.O. Box 58297, Nairobi, Kenya
PHONE: +254 (2) 762781

Seychelles
7th Floor, Agip House, Waiyaki Way, P.O. Box 20400, Nairobi, Kenya
PHONE: +254 (2) 440552
FAX: +254 (2) 441150

Slovakia
Milimani Rd., P.O. Box 30204, Nairobi, Kenya
PHONE: +254 (2) 721896
FAX: +254 (2) 721898

South Africa
Lonrho House, Standard Street, P.O. Box 42441, Nairobi, Kenya
PHONE: +254 (2) 215616
FAX: +254 (2) 223687

Spain
5th Floor, Bruce House, Standard Street, P.O. Box 45503, Nairobi, Kenya
PHONE: +254 (2) 335711
FAX: +254 (2) 332858

Sri Lanka
8th Floor, International House, Mama Ngina St., P.O. Box 48145, Nairobi, Kenya
PHONE: +254 (2) 227577; 227878
FAX: +254 (2) 225391

Sudan
Minet-ICDC Building, Mamlaka Rd., P.O. Box 48784, Nairobi, Kenya
PHONE: +254 (2) 720853; 721704
FAX: +254 (2) 721015

Swaziland
3rd Floor, Transnational Plaza, Mama Ngina St., P.O. Box 41887, Nairobi, Kenya
PHONE: +254 (2) 339231; 222817
FAX: +254 (2) 330540

Sweden
10th Floor, International House, Mama Ngina St., P.O. Box 30060, Nairobi, Kenya
PHONE: +254 (2) 229042
FAX: +254 (2) 218908; 220863

Switzerland
7th Floor, International House, Mama Ngina St., P.O. Box 30752, Nairobi, Kenya
PHONE: +254 (2) 228735
FAX: +254 (2) 217388
E-MAIL: sdckenya@form-net.com

Tanzania
Continental House, Uhuru Highway, P.O. Box 47790, Nairobi, Kenya
PHONE: +254 (2) 331056
FAX: +254 (2) 218269

Thailand
Ground Floor, Ambassadeur House, Rose Ave., P.O. Box 58349, Nairobi, Kenya
PHONE: +254 (2) 715800
FAX: +254 (2) 715801
E-MAIL: thainbi@form-net.com

Turkey
Gigiri Rd., P.O. Box 30785, Nairobi, Kenya
PHONE: +254 (2) 520404
FAX: +254 (2) 521237

Uganda
5th Floor, Uganda House, Kenyatta Ave., P.O. Box 60853, Nairobi, Kenya
PHONE: +254 (2) 330801; 330814
FAX: +254 (2) 330970

United Kingdom
Bruce House, Standard Street, P.O. Box 48868, Nairobi, Kenya
PHONE: +254 (2) 335944
FAX: +254 (2) 333196

United States
Moi Ave./Haile Selassie Ave., P.O. Box 30137, Nairobi, Kenya
PHONE: +254 (2) 334141
FAX: +254 (2) 340838; 340835

Vatican City
Apostolic Nuciature, Manyani Rd., Waiyaki Way, P.O. Box 14326, Nairobi, Kenya
PHONE: +254 (2) 442975
FAX: +254 (2) 446789
E-MAIL: nunciokenya@form-net.com

Venezuela
International House, Mama Ngina Street, P.O. Box 34477, Nairobi, Kenya
PHONE: +254 (2) 340134
FAX: +254 (2) 337487
E-MAIL: embavenez@form-net.com

Yemen
Ngong, Kabarnet Rd., P.O. Box 44642, Nairobi, Kenya
PHONE: +254 (2) 564379; 564517
FAX: +254 (2) 564394

Zambia
Nyerere Rd., P.O. Box 48741, Nairobi, Kenya
PHONE: +254 (2) 724850; 724796
FAX: +254 (2) 718494

Zimbabwe
6th Floor, Minet-ICDC Building, Mamlaka Rd, P.O. Box 30806, Nairobi, Kenya
PHONE: +254 (2) 721071
FAX: +254 (2) 726503

JUDICIAL SYSTEM

Court of Appeal

High Court

BROADCAST MEDIA

Capital FM

19th floor, Lohnro House, Standard Street, PO Box 74933, Nairobi, Kenya
PHONE: +254 (2) 210020
FAX: +254 (2) 332349
E-MAIL: lynxah1@users.africaonline.co.ke
TITLE: Programme Director
CONTACT: Phil Matthews

Kenya Broadcasting Corporation (KBC)

Box 30456, Harry Thuku Road, Nairobi, Kenya
PHONE: +254 (2) 334567
FAX: +254 (2) 220675

Kenya Telvision Network (KTN-TV)

PO Box 56985, Nairobi, Kenya
PHONE: +254 (2) 227122
FAX: +254 (2) 214467
WEBSITE: http://www.kenyaweb.com/ktn/ktn.html
TITLE: Chairman
CONTACT: Mwakio Sio
CHANNEL: 59, 62
TYPE: Commercial

Kenya Broadcasting Corporation (KBC)

PO Box 30456, Harry Thuku Road, Nairobi, Kenya
PHONE: +254 (2) 334567
FAX: +254 (2) 220675
WEBSITE: http://www.africaonline.co.ke/AfricaOnline/netradio.html
TITLE: Managing Director TV
CONTACT: Simeon Anabwani
TITLE: Managing Director Radio
CONTACT: Philip Okundi
LANGUAGE: English, Hindi, Somali, Swahili, other ethnic languages
CHANNEL: 2, 4, 6, 10, 11
TYPE: Commercial, Government

COLLEGES AND UNIVERSITIES

Jomo Kenyatta University of Agriculture & Technology

PO Box 62000, Nairobi, Kenya
PHONE: +254 (2) 15152711
FAX: +254 (2) 15152164
E-MAIL: jku-lib@nbnet.co.ke
WEBSITE: http://www.jkuat.ac.ke

University of Nairobi

PO Box 30197, Nairobi, Kenya
PHONE: +254 (2) 334244
FAX: +254 (2) 336885
E-MAIL: vcuon@form.net.com
WEBSITE: http://www.uonbi.ac.ke

Kenyatta University

PO Box 43844, Nairobi, Kenya
PHONE: +254 (2) 810901
FAX: +254 (2) 811575
E-MAIL: ku@nbnet.co.ke
WEBSITE: http://www.nbnet.co.ke/ku/index.html

Moi University

PO Box 3900, Eldoret, Kenya
PHONE: +254 (321) 43620

FAX: +254 (321) 43047
E-MAIL: vcmu@irmmoi.com
WEBSITE: http://www.tcol.co.uk/orgs/moi/moi .htm

Egerton University

PO Box 536, Njoro, Kenya
PHONE: +254 (37) 61276
FAX: +254 (37) 61527
E-MAIL: egerton@users.africaonline.co.ke

NEWSPAPERS AND MAGAZINES

Coastweek

Coastweek Ltd., PO Box 87270, Mombasa, Kenya
PHONE: +254 (11) 313767
FAX: +254 (11) 225003
E-MAIL: coastwk@africaonline.co.ke
WEBSITE: http://www.africaonline.co.ke/AfricaOnline/coastwk.html
TITLE: Editor
CONTACT: Adrian Grimwood
CIRCULATION: 15,000

Daily Nation/Sunday Nation

Nation Newspapers Ltd., Tom Mboya St., PO Box 49010, Nairobi, Kenya
PHONE: +254 (2) 221222
FAX: +254 (2) 213946
E-MAIL: nation@africaonline.co.ke
WEBSITE: http://www.nationaudio.com
TITLE: Editor
CONTACT: Mwangi Wangethi
CIRCULATION: 195,000

The East African

Nation Newspapers Ltd., Tom Mboya Street, PO Box 49010, Nairobi, Kenya
PHONE: +254 (2) 221222
FAX: +254 (2) 213946
E-MAIL: nation@users/africaonline.co.ke
TITLE: Editor
CONTACT: Joseph Odindo
CIRCULATION: 32,000

East African Standard

The Standard Ltd., PO Box 30080, Nairobi, Kenya
PHONE: +254 (2) 540280
FAX: +254 (2) 545794
E-MAIL: standard@formnet.com
TITLE: Editor
CONTACT: Kamau Kanyanga
CIRCULATION: 60,000

Kenya Leo

Kenya Times Media Trust, PO Box 30958, Nairobi, Kenya
PHONE: +254 (2) 337798
TITLE: Editor
CONTACT: Joram Amadi
CIRCULATION: 35,000

Kenya Times

Kenya Times Media Trust, PO Box 30958, Nairobi, Kenya
PHONE: +254 (2) 24251
TITLE: Editor
CONTACT: Phllip Ochieng
CIRCULATION: 36,000

Africa Media Review

PO Box 47495, Nairobi, Kenya
FAX: +254 (2) 216135
E-MAIL: acceb@arcc.permanet.org; acceb@form-net.com
TITLE: Editor
CONTACT: Charles Okigbo
CIRCULATION: 700
TYPE: Social science, sociology, general

Kenya Gazette

Haile Selaissie Ave., PO Box 30128, Nairobi, Kenya
CIRCULATION: 8,000
TYPE: Political science, government affairs and administration

Kenya Past and Present

c/o National Museums of Kenya, PO Box 40658, Nairobi, Kenya
TITLE: Editor
CONTACT: Edmond Martin
CIRCULATION: 2,000
TYPE: History in Africa, science, general

Kenya Record

PO Box 57881, Nairobi, Kenya
TITLE: Editor
CONTACT: Joel Mbogo
TYPE: Social science, general

Kenya Yetu

PO Box 8053, Nairobi, Kenya
TITLE: Editor
CONTACT: M. Ndavi
CIRCULATION: 10,000
TYPE: Social sciences, general

Nairobi Law Monthly

PO Box 53234, Nairobi, Kenya
TITLE: Editor
CONTACT: Gitobu I. Imanyara
TYPE: Law, general

PUBLISHERS

Academy Science Publishers

PO Box 24916, Nairobi, Kenya
PHONE: +254 (2) 884402-5
FAX: +254 (2) 884406
E-MAIL: asp@arcc.or.ke
TITLE: Publishing Manager
CONTACT: Mrs. Serah Mwanycky
SUBJECTS: Developing Countries, Environmental Studies, Science (General), Technology
TOTAL PUBLISHED: 23 print

African Centre for Technology Studies (ACTS)

PO Box 45917, Nairobi, Kenya
PHONE: +254 (2) 524000; 524700
FAX: +254 (2) 524001; 522987
E-MAIL: acts@cgiar.org
WEBSITE: http://www.acts.or.ke
TITLE: Editor
CONTACT: Charles Nyambuga
SUBJECTS: Agriculture, Biological Sciences, Developing Countries, Earth Sciences, Education, Environmental Studies, Health, Law, Science (General), Social Sciences

Camerapix Publishers International Ltd.

PO Box 45048, Nairobi, Kenya
PHONE: +254 (2) 448923; 448924; 448925
FAX: +254 (2) 448926; 448927
E-MAIL: info@camerapix.com
WEBSITE: http://www.camerapix.com
TITLE: Man. Director
CONTACT: Rukhsana Haq
SUBJECTS: Art, Regional Interests, Travel

Heinemann Kenya Limited (EAEP)

PO Box 45314, Nairobi, Kenya
PHONE: +254 (2) 222057; 222144; 228947
FAX: +254 (2) 448753; 226286
TITLE: Man. Director
CONTACT: Henry Chakava
SUBJECTS: Agriculture, Art, Business, Automotive, Cookery, Theater, Fashion, Fiction, Education, Political Science, Science, Literature, Nonfiction (General), Social Sciences, Religion

International Centre for Research in Agroforestry (ICRAF)

PO Box 30677, Nairobi, Kenya
PHONE: +254 (2) 52145; +1 (650) 8336645
FAX: +254 (2) 521001
E-MAIL: icraf@cgiar.org
WEBSITE: http://www.cgiar.org/ICRAF
TITLE: Director General
CONTACT: Dr. Pedro Sanchez
SUBJECTS: Agriculture, Environmental Studies

Kenway Publications Ltd.

PO Box 45314, Nairobi, Kenya
PHONE: +254 (2) 444700
FAX: +254 (2) 448753; 532095
E-MAIL: eaep@africaonline.co.ke
TITLE: Sales & Marketing Director
CONTACT: Winston Mutua Nzioki
SUBJECTS: Animals, Pets, Anthropology, Biography, Cookery, Music, Dance, Regional Interests, Sports, Travel
TOTAL PUBLISHED: 48 print

Kenya Literature Bureau

PO Box 30022, Nairobi, Kenya
PHONE: +254 (2) 506142; 506143; 506148
FAX: +254 (2) 505903; 601474
TITLE: Man. Director
CONTACT: S. C. Langat
SUBJECTS: Agriculture, Animals, Pets, Education, Health, Nutrition, Law, Mathematics, Medicine, Nursing, Dentistry, Science (General), Veterinary Science
TOTAL PUBLISHED: 700 print

Nairobi University Press

PO Box 30197, Nairobi, Kenya
PHONE: +254 (2) 334224 (ext. 2258)
FAX: +254 (2) 336885
SUBJECTS: Archaeology, Biological Sciences, Chemistry, Business, Engineering, Economics, Education, Electronics, Environmental Studies

Pauline Publications-Africa

PO Box 49026, Nairobi, Kenya

PHONE: +254 (2) 447202; 447203
FAX: +254 (2) 442319
E-MAIL: paulines@iconnect.co.uk
TITLE: Director
CONTACT: Sr. Teresa Marcazzan
SUBJECTS: Biblical Studies, Biography, Child Care, Communications, Education, History, Nonfiction (General), Psychology, Psychiatry, Catholicism, Women's Studies

Space Sellers Ltd.

PO Box 47186, Nairobi, Kenya
PHONE: +254 (2) 555811; 557517; 557863
FAX: +254 (2) 557815; 558847
E-MAIL: sstms@africaonline.co.ke
CONTACT: Sylvia King
SUBJECTS: Automotive, Business, Career Development, Gardening, Plants, How-To, Selp-Help, Travel

RELIGIOUS ORGANIZATIONS

Catholic

African International Movement of Catholic Students (AIMCS)

Branche Africaine de Mouvement International des Etudiants Catholiques
PO Box 62106, Nairobi, Kenya
PHONE: +254 (2) 502451
FAX: +254 (2) 502451
E-MAIL: imesafr@arcc.or.ke
TITLE: Panafrican Coordinator
NAME: Mr. Jean Lokenga

International Movement of Catholic Students-African Secretariat (IMCS-Afr.Sec.)
House No. 310, Mombasa Road, PO Box 62106, Nairobi, Kenya
PHONE: +254 (2) 502451
FAX: +254 (2) 502451
E-MAIL: imcsafr@arcc.or.ke
TITLE: Pan African Coordinator
NAME: Jean Lokenga N.

Islamic

Young Muslim Association
PO Box 48509, Nairobi, Kenya
PHONE: +254 (2) 229896
FAX: +254 (2) 229756
E-MAIL: yma@africaonline.co.ke
WEBSITE: http://www.yma.org/main_page.html

Mormon

The Church of Jesus Christ of Latter-Day Saints, Kenya Nairobi Mission
PO Box 39634, Nairobi, Kenya, East Africa
PHONE: +254 (2) 740444
WEBSITE: http://www.xmission.com/~jbowen/mission/

Protestant

All-Africa Conference of Churches (AACC)

Conference des Eglises de Toute l-Afrique (CETA)
The General Secretary, Waiyaki Way, Westlands, PO Box 14205, Nairobi, Kenya
PHONE: +254 (2) 441338
FAX: +254 (2) 443241
E-MAIL: aacc-selfood@maf.org

Association of Christian Lay Centers in Africa (ACLCA)
PO Box 14205, Nairobi, Kenya
PHONE: +254 (2) 441483
FAX: +254 (2) 443241
NAME: Rev. Jonah Katoneene

Association of Evangelicals in Africa (AEA)

Association des Evangeliques d'Afrique (AEA)
PO Box 49332, Nairobi, Kenya
PHONE: +254 (2) 722769
FAX: +254 (2) 710254
E-MAIL: aea@maf.org
TITLE: General Secretary
NAME: Dr. Tokunboh Adeyeno

Association of Member Episcopal Conferences in Eastern Africa (AMECEA)

Association des Membres des Conferences Episcopales de l'Afrique Orientale
c/o Rev. P Lwaminda, 49 Gitanga Road, PO Box 21191, Nairobi, Kenya
PHONE: +254 (2) 566506
FAX: +254 (2) 578009
E-MAIL: amacea@africaonline.co.ke
TITLE: Secretary General
NAME: Rev. P. Lwaminda

Kenya Evangelical Lutheran Church
PO Box 54128, Nairobi, Kenya

The Salvation Army
Moi Avenue, Box No. 40575, Nairobi, Kenya
PHONE: +254 (2) 227541; 227542; 227549
FAX: +254 (2) 335538

Other Organizations

Africa Church Information Service (ACIS)
PO Box 14205, Nairobi, Kenya
PHONE: +245 (2) 440224
E-MAIL: acis/aps@arcc.permenent.org
TITLE: Secretary General
NAME: Rev. P. Lwaminda

FURTHER READING

Articles

Brough, David. "Food Shortages Dire in Drought-Hit Kenya." *Reuters,* July 18, 2000.

"Kenya Budget Aims to Ease Economic Crisis." *Financial Times,* June 16, 2000.

"Kenya To Impose Half-Day Power Cuts." *Wall Street Journal,* May 24, 2000, p. A21.

"Kenyan Religious Leaders Take Charge of Constitutional Review." *America,* January 29, 2000, vol. 182, no. 3, p. 4.

"Two Kenyans Win Boston Run." *Jet,* May 8, 2000, vol. 97, no. 22, p. 48.

"Why Kenya's Clergy Got Political: In a Press Conference Last Week, Catholic Bishops Slammed the Government for Corruption and Violence. *Christian Science Monitor,* September 20, 2000, p. 6.

Books

Trade Policy Review. Kenya. Geneva: World Trade Organization, 2000.

Watson, Mary Ann, editor. *Modern Kenya: Social Issues and Perspectives.* Lanham, MD: University Press of America, 2000.

KENYA: STATISTICAL DATA

For sources and notes see "Sources of Statistics" at the front of each volume.

GEOGRAPHY

Geography

Area:

Total: 582,650 sq km.

Land: 569,250 sq km.

Land boundaries:

Total: 3,446 km.

Border countries: Ethiopia 830 km, Somalia 682 km, Sudan 232 km, Tanzania 769 km, Uganda 933 km.

Coastline: 536 km.

Climate: varies from tropical along coast to arid in interior.

Terrain: low plains rise to central highlands bisected by Great Rift Valley; fertile plateau in west.

Natural resources: gold, limestone, soda ash, salt barites, rubies, fluorspar, garnets, wildlife, hydropower.

Land use.

Arable land: 7%

Permanent crops: 1%

Permanent pastures: 37%

Forests and woodland: 30%

Other: 25% (1993 est.).

HUMAN FACTORS

Demographics (A)

	1990	1995	1998	2000	2010	2020	2030	2040	2050
Population	23,767	27,315	29,277	30,340	33,068	34,002	34,836	36,247	38,660
Life expectancy - males	56.0	50.3	48.2	46.9	43.9	46.9	52.9	62.1	71.8
Life expectancy - females	56.2	50.5	49.6	49.0	44.7	48.1	55.0	65.5	76.5
Birth rate (per 1,000)	39.0	36.8	34.1	29.4	21.9	20.2	18.1	15.9	14.9
Death rate (per 1,000)	10.3	12.9	13.7	14.1	17.9	18.1	15.2	10.7	7.5
Women of reproductive age (15-49 yrs.)	5,198	6,254	6,883	7,318	8,997	9,858	9,844	9,788	9,719
Fertility rate	5.7	4.9	4.3	3.7	2.4	2.1	2.0	2.0	2.0

Except as noted, values for vital statistics are in thousands; life expectancy is in years.

Health Personnel

	National Data	World Data (wtd ave)
Total health expenditure as a percentage of GDP, 1990-1998[a]		
Public sector	2.2	2.5
Private sector	1.0	2.9
Total[b]	1.0	5.5
Health expenditure per capita in U.S. dollars, 1990-1998[a]		
Purchasing power parity	10	561
Total	3	483
Availability of health care facilities per 100,000 people		
Hospital beds 1990-1998[a]	160	330
Doctors 1992-1995[a]	15	122
Nurses 1992-1995[a]	32	248

Health Indicators

	National Data	World Data
Life expectancy at birth (years)		
1980	55	61
1998	51	67
Daily per capita supply of calories		
1970	2,187	2,358
1997	1,976	2,791
Daily per capital supply of protein		
1997 (grams)	52	74
Total fertility rate (births per woman)		
1980	7.8	3.7
1998	4.6	2.7
Population with access (%)		
To safe water (1990-96)	53	NA
To sanitation (1990-96)	77	NA
People living with (1997)		
Tuberculosis (cases per 100,000)	139.9	60.4
HIV/AIDS (% aged 15 - 49 years)	11.64	0.99

Infants and Malnutrition

	National Data	World Data (wtd ave)
Under 5 mortality rate (1989)	117	NA
% of infants with low birthweight (1992-98)[1]	16	17
Births attended by skilled health staff (% of total births 1996-98)	45	52
% fully immunized at 1 year of age (1995-98)[1]		
TB	94	82
DPT	76	77
Polio	78	77
Measles	71	74
Prevalence of child malnutrition (1992-98)[1] (based on weight for age, % of children under 5 years)	23	30

Ethnic Division

Kikuyu 22%
Luhya 14%
Luo 13%
Kalenjin 12%
Kamba 11%
Kisii 6%
Meru 6%
Other African 15%
Non-African 1%

Non-Africans include Asian, European, and Arab.

Religion

Protestant 38%
Roman Catholic 28%
Indigenous beliefs 26%
Muslim 7%
Other 1%

Major Languages

English (official), Kiswahili (official), numerous indigenous languages.

EDUCATION

Public Education Expenditures

	1980	1997
Public expenditures on education as % of GNP	6.8	6.5
Expenditures per student as % of GNP per capita		
Primary & Secondary	15.7[2]	NA
Tertiary	928.2	NA
Pupils per teacher at the primary level	NA	30
Duration of primary education in years	NA	8
World data for comparison		
Public expenditures on education as % of GNP (mean)	3.9	4.8

	1980	1997
Pupils per teacher at the primary level (wtd ave)	NA	33
Duration of primary education in years (mean)	NA	9

Educational Attainment (A)

Age group (1979)[25] ....25+

Population of this age group 4,818,310

Highest level attained (%)

No scholing 58.6

First level

Not completed 32.2

Completed ....NA

Entered second level

Lower Secondary 7.9

Upper Secondary 1.3

Entered post-secondary ....NA

Literacy Rates (A)

In thousands and percent	1990	1995	2000	2010
Illiterate population (15+ yrs.)	3,357	3,237	2,934	2,397
Literacy rate - total adult pop. (%)	72.0	78.1	83.1	90.1
Literacy rate - males (%)	82.2	86.3	89.5	93.7
Literacy rate - females (%)	62.0	70.0	76.7	86.6

Libraries

Public Libraries **1993**

Administrative Units 2

Service Points or Branches 21

Number of Volumes (000) 603

Registered Users (000) 227

Loans to Users (000) 267

Total Library Staff 720

GOVERNMENT & LAW

Political Parties

National Assembly (Bunge)	no. of seats
Kenya African National Union (KANU)	107
Forum for the Restoration of Democracy-Asili (FORD-A)	1
Forum for the Restoration of Democracy-Kenya (FORD-K)	17
Forum for the Restoration of Democracy-People (FORD-People)	3
Democratic Party of Kenya (DP)	39
National Development Party (NDP)	21
Social Democratic Party (SDP)	15
SAFINA	5
Smaller parties	2
Appointed by the president	
Kenya African National Union (KANU)	6
Forum for the Restoration of Democracy-Kenya (FORD-K)	1
Democratic Party of Kenya (DP)	2
Social Democratic Party (SDP)	1
National Development Party (NDP)	1
SAFINA	1

Elections were last held 29 December 1997 (next to be held between 1 December 2002 and 30 April 2003).

Government Budgets (A)

Year: 1996

Total Expenditures: 152,832 Millions of Shillings

Expenditures as a percentage of the total by function:

General public services and public order 18.61

Defense 5.91

Education 20.24

Health 5.96

Social Security and Welfare 0.03

Housing and community amenities 3.43

Recreational, cultural, and religious affairs 1.97

Fuel and energy 0

Agriculture, forestry, fishing, and hunting 5.00

Mining, manufacturing, and construction 1.06

Transportation and communication 7.60

Other economic affairs and services 2.20

(Contiuned on next page.)

LABOR FORCE

Total Labor Force (A)

9.2 million (1998 est.).

Labor Force by Occupation

Agriculture 75%-80%

Unemployment Rate

50% (1998 est.)

GOVERNMENT & LAW (cont.)

Military Affairs (A)

	1990	1992	1995	1996	1997
Military expenditures					
Current dollars (mil.)	210	234	178[e]	191	206
1997 constant dollars (mil.)	246	259	184[e]	195	206
Armed forces (000)	20	24	22	24	24
Gross national product (GNP)					
Current dollars (mil.)	7,240	7,700	8,930	9,580	10,000
1997 constant dollars (mil.)	8,480	8,530	9,240	9,740	10,000
Central government expenditures (CGE)					
1997 constant dollars (mil.)	2,510	2,620	2,970	3,080	2,870
People (mil.)	23.9	25.4	26.9	27.3	27.8
Military expenditure as % of GNP	2.9	3.0	2.0	2.0	2.1
World data on military expenditure as % of GNP	4.5	3.4	2.7	2.6	2.6
Military expenditure as % of CGE	9.8	9.9	6.2	6.3	7.2
World data on military expenditure as % of CGE	17.0	12.5	10.5	10.3	10.2
Military expenditure per capita (1997 $)	10	10	7	7	7
World data on military expenditure per capita (1997 $)	242	173	146	143	145
Armed forces per 1,000 people (soldiers)	0.8	0.9	0.8	0.9	0.9
World data on armed forces per 1,000 people (soldiers)	5.3	4.5	4.1	3.9	3.8
GNP per capita (1997 $)	355	336	344	357	360
Arms imports[6]					
Current dollars (mil.)	70	20	10	20	40
1997 constant dollars (mil.)	82	22	10	20	40
Total imports[7]					
Current dollars (mil.)	2,124	1,713	2,949	2,912	3,273
1997 constant dollars (mil.)	2,487	1,899	3,054	2,961	3,273
Total exports[7]					
Current dollars (mil.)	1,031	1,399	1,878	2,067	2,054
1997 constant dollars (mil.)	1,207	1,484	1,945	2,101	2,054
Arms as percent of total imports[8]	3.3	1.2	0.3	0.7	1.2
Arms as percent of total exports[8]	0	0	0	0	0

PRODUCTION SECTOR

Energy Production

Production .4.23 billion kWh

Production by source

Fossil fuel 8.27%

Hydro 82.74%

Nuclear 0%

Other 8.99%

Exports . . . . .0 kWh

Data for 1998.

Energy Consumption

Consumption . . . . .4.078 billion kWh

Imports .144.000 million kWh

Data for 1998.

Transportation

Highways:

Total: 63,800 km.

Paved: 8,868 km.

Unpaved: 54,932 km (1996 est.).

Waterways: part of the Lake Victoria system is within the boundaries of Kenya.

Pipelines: petroleum products 483 km.

Merchant marine:

Total: 2 ships (1,000 GRT or over) totaling 4,893 GRT/6,255 DWT.

Ships by type: petroleum tanker 1, roll-on/roll-off 1 (1999 est.).

Airports: 230 (1999 est.).

Airports - with paved runways: 21.

Airports - with unpaved runways: 209.

Top Agriculture Products

Coffee, tea, corn, wheat, sugarcane, fruit, vegetables; dairy products, beef, pork, poultry, eggs.

Top Mining Products (B)

Mineral resources include: gold, limestone, soda ash, salt barites, rubies, fluorspar, garnets.

MANUFACTURING SECTOR

GDP & Manufacturing Summary (A)

	1980	1985	1990	1995
GDP ($-1990 mil.)[1]	5,726	6,488	8,532	9,351
Per capita ($-1990)[1]	344	327	363	344
Manufacturing share (%) (current prices)[1]	12.9	11.4	11.4	9.5[e]
Manufacturing				
Value added ($-1990 mil.)[1]	552	653	862	977
Industrial production index	74	79	100	109[e]
Value added ($ mil.)	744	670	921	814[e]
Gross output ($ mil.)	3,656	4,301	7,975	9,644[e]
Employment (000)	143[e]	163	188	199[e]
Profitability (% of gross output)				
Intermediate input (%)	80	84	88	92[e]
Wages and salaries inc. supplements (%)	9	7	4	3[e]
Gross operating surplus	11	9	8	6[e]
Productivity ($)				
Gross output per worker	25,544[e]	26,428	42,491	48,488[e]
Value added per worker	5,197[e]	4,115	4,907	4,025[e]
Average wage (inc. supplements)	2,269[e]	1,795	1,605	1,251[e]
Value added ($ mil.)				
Food products	177	185	252	258[e]
Beverages	65	72	90	78[e]
Tobacco products	10	13	12	12[e]
Textiles	59	40	55	47[e]
Wearing apparel	17	19	16	13[e]
Leather and fur products	6	3	4	3[e]
Footwear	9	6	13	8[e]
Wood and wood products	20	17	17	14[e]
Furniture and fixtures	9	8	11	6[e]
Paper and paper products	34	23	42	36[e]
Printing and publishing	22	19	27	19[e]
Industrial chemicals	25	16	17	15[e]
Other chemical products	39	50	67	54[e]
Petroleum refineries	15	6	7	6[e]
Rubber products	25	27	33	25[e]
Plastic products	14	13	24	27[e]
Pottery, china and earthenware	1	NA	1	1[e]
Glass and glass products	3	4	5	3[e]
Other non-metal mineral products	20	17	42	29[e]
Iron and steel	12[I,a]	6[I,a]	12[a]	14[I,a]
Metal products	44	31	64	51[e]
Non-electrical machinery	6	4	5	5[e]
Electrical machinery	40	36	44	46[e]
Transport equipment	64	43	39	28[e]
Prof. and scientific equipment	1	1	2	1[e]
Other manufacturing	6	8	18	14[e]

COMMUNICATIONS

Daily Newspapers

	National Data	World Data for Comparison
Daily Newspapers		
Number of Dailies	4	8,391
Total Circulation (000)	263	548,000
Circulation per 1,000 inhabitants	9.4	96

Telecommunications

Telephones - main lines in use: 290,000 (1998).

Telephones - mobile cellular: 6,000 (1999).

Telephone system: unreliable; little attempt to modernize.

Domestic: trunks are primarily microwave radio relay; data commonly transferred by a very small aperature terminal (VSAT).

International: satellite earth stations - 4 Intelsat.

Radio broadcast stations: AM 24, FM 8, shortwave 6 (1999).

Radios: 3.07 million (1997).

Television broadcast stations: 8 (1997).

Televisions: 730,000 (1997).

Internet Service Providers (ISPs): 7 (1999).

FINANCE, ECONOMICS, & TRADE

Economic Indicators

National product: GDP—purchasing power parity—$45.1 billion (1999 est.).

National product real growth rate: 1.5% (1999 est.).

National product per capita: $1,600 (1999 est.).

Inflation rate—consumer price index: 6% (1999 est.).

Exchange Rates

Exchange rates:

Kenyan shillings (KSh) per US$1

December 1999 . . . . .73.943
1999 . . . . .70.326
1998 . . . . .60.367
1997 . . . . .58.732
1996 . . . . .57.115
1995 . . . . .51.430

Top Import Origins

$3.3 billion (f.o.b., 1999 est.)

Origins (1998)

United Kingdom 12%
UAE 9%
United States 8%
Japan 8%
Germany 6%
India 4%

Top Export Destinations

$2.2 billion (f.o.b., 1999 est.)

Destinations (1998)

Uganda 16%
United Kingdom 13%
Tanzania 13%
Egypt 5%
Germany 5%

Foreign Aid

Recipient: $457 million (1997).

Balance of Payments

	1993	1994	1995	1996	1997
Exports of goods (f.o.b.)	1,263	1,537	1,914	2,071	2,051
Imports of goods (f.o.b.)	−1,510	−1,775	−2,652	−2,581	−2,934
Trade balance	−247	−238	−738	−510	−883
Services - debits	−569	−687	−871	−860	−837
Services - credits	1,063	1,117	1,034	956	944
Private transfers (net)	179	208	452	437	533
Government transfers (net)	94	123	91	128	98
Overall balance	71	98	−400	−74	−377

Import/Export Commodities

Import Commodities	Export Commodities
Machinery and transportation equipment	Tea
	Coffee
	Horticultural products
Petroleum products	Petroleum products
Iron and steel	

KIRIBATI

Republic of Kiribati

CAPITAL: Tarawa.

FLAG: Above a blue and white heraldic representation of Pacific waters, a golden sun rises against a red background, with a golden frigate bird at the top.

ANTHEM: *Troika kain Kiribati (Stand Kiribati).*

MONETARY UNIT: The Australian dollar (A) is the national currency. A$1 = US$0.79177 (or US$1 = A$1.263).

WEIGHTS AND MEASURES: Kiribati is in transition from imperial to metric standards.

HOLIDAYS: New Year's Day, 1 January; Independence Day, 12 July; Youth Day, 4 August; Christmas Day, 25 December; Boxing Day, 26 December. Movable holidays include Good Friday, Easter Monday, Queen's Birthday (June), Bank Holiday (August), and Prince of Wales's Birthday (November).

TIME: Midnight = noon GMT.

LOCATION AND SIZE: Kiribati (pronounced "Kiribass") consists of 33 islands in the central Pacific, situated around the point where the International Date Line intersects the equator. Scattered over more than 5 million square kilometers (2 million square miles) of ocean, Kiribati's total land area is 717 square kilometers (277 square miles), and its total coastline is 1,143 kilometers (710 miles).

Kiribati's capital city, Tarawa, is located on the small island of Tarawa (between Abaiang and Maiana).

CLIMATE: Rainfall varies from an average of 102 centimeters (40 inches) near the equator to 305 centimeters (120 inches) in the extreme north and south. Daily temperatures range from 25°C (77°F) to 32°C (90°F), with an annual mean temperature of 27°C (81°F).

INTRODUCTORY SURVEY

RECENT HISTORY

The Gilbert group of islands was declared a British colony in 1916. Japanese forces occupied the Gilbert Islands during World War II (1939-1945) until 1943 when U.S. forces drove them out. Internal self-government for the Gilberts was established in 1977. The Gilbert Islands became the independent Republic of Kiribati on July 12, 1979. Ieremia Tabai, chief minister at the time of independence, became president of the new republic in 1979 and was reelected in May 1982 and February 1983.

Kiribati began resettling more than 4,700 people on outlying atolls in August 1988 to relieve overcrowded conditions on the Tarawa atolls. In September 1988 Kiribati ratified the South Pacific Regional Fisheries Treaty that permits U.S. tuna ships to operate within its 200-mile exclusive zone. In early 1992 the House of Assembly told the government to seek payment from the United States for damage done to the country during World War II. In 1999 Kiribati joined the United Nations.

GOVERNMENT

Kiribati is a democratic republic within the Commonwealth of Nations. It has a single-chamber 41-seat legislature, the House of Assembly (Maneaba ni Maungatabu). Thirty-nine members are elected by popular vote for four-year terms. The *beretitenti* (president), who is both head of state and head of government, is elected directly by popular vote for a four-year term. The House

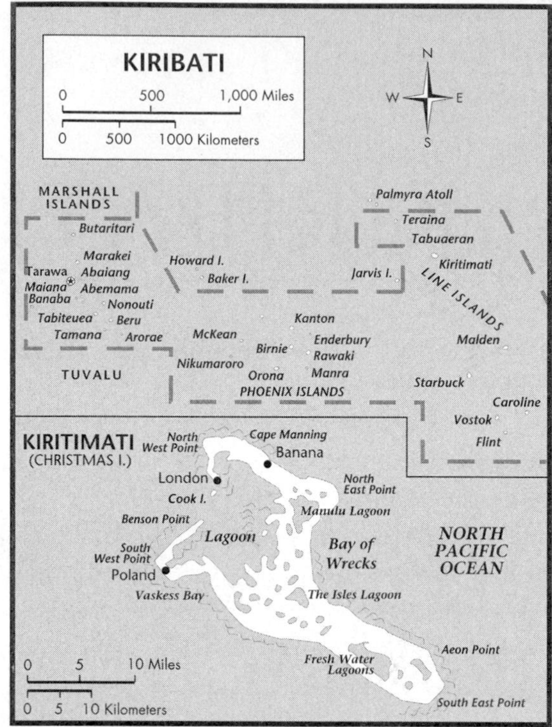

chooses the presidential candidates from among its members and then those candidates compete in a general election.

Judiciary

The 1979 constitution provides for a High Court to act as a supreme court and court of appeal. Island courts were established in 1965 to deal with civil and criminal offenses. Native land courts handle property claims.

Political Parties

There are no formal political parties in Kiribati. The parties are more like interest groups and have no formal headquarters, platforms, or structure. The groups include the Liberal party, the Maneaban Te Mauri, and the National Progressive Party.

DEFENSE

There have been no armed forces in Kiribati since legislation providing for the establishment of a defense force of 170 men was repealed in 1978. There is a small police force. Australia and New Zealand provide defense assitance.

ECONOMIC AFFAIRS

Kiribati has few natural resources. The nation relies on fishing, subsistence agriculture, and exports of copra (dried coconut meat) and is heavily dependent on aid from the United Kingdom, New Zealand, Japan, and investment from Australia. Aid supplied 25 percent to 50 percent of GDP in recent years. Remittances from workers abroad accounted for more than $5 million each year. Economic development is constrained by a shortage of skilled workers, poor infrastructure, and remoteness from markets.

Public Finance

Local revenues are derived mainly from import duties, fishing fees, and investment income from the phosphate fund. The country has been running a capital account deficit since independence. Overall, budgetary deficits have appeared in recent years, growing substantially in the mid-1990s.

The U.S. CIA estimated that in 1996 government revenues totaled approximately $33.3 million and expenditures $47.7 million. External debt totaled $7.2 million.

Income

In 1999 Kiribati's gross domestic product (GDP) was estimated at $74 million supplemented by a nearly equal amount from external sources. Per capita income was estimated at $860. The 1999 estimated real growth rate of GDP was 2.5 percent and inflation 2 percent. The 1996 estimated GDP by sector was agriculture 14 percent, industry 7 percent, and services 79 percent.

Industry

Copra and fishing are major contributors to the economy. Several small industries have been established, including a soft-drink plant, a biscuit factory, boat-building shops, construction companies, furniture plants, repair garages, and bakeries. The government also promotes local handicrafts.

Banking and Finance

The Westpac Banking Corp. (Australia) and the government of Kiribati jointly own the Bank of Kiribati in Tarawa. The Kiribati Development Bank, opened in 1987, was to take over the assets of the National Loans Board when it became fully operational.

Economic Development

The economic development plan for 1987-91 was economic self-reliance through gradual and sustainable development, with particular emphasis on the subsistence lifestyle of the outer islands. The UN Development Program is implementing an economic development plan for the northern Line Islands focusing on infrastructure, agriculture, and tourism. The financial sector is in an early state as is the expansion of private sector initiatives. Foreign financial aid is critical.

SOCIAL WELFARE

A provident fund system provides old age, disability, and survivor benefits in the form of lump sum payments only, with the worker and employer contributing through payroll.

The majority of the population still lives a traditional village life with an extended family system. This makes state welfare largely unnecessary. Problems exist mainly in the south Tarawa Island area, where cities have grown rapidly. Some juvenile delinquency has developed there.

Women are accorded the same rights as men but generally remain in traditional subordinate roles.

Healthcare

All health services are free. A nurse training school is maintained at the 160-bed Central Hospital in Tarawa. There are four medical districts, each with its own medical officer and staff. Each inhabited island has a health clinic, and there is a medical radio network linking all the islands.

Tuberculosis remains the most serious public health problem. Other widespread diseases are leprosy, filariasis, and dysentery. In 2000 average life expectancy was about sixty years.

Housing

Most Kiribatians live in small villages of ten to 150 houses. They construct their own dwellings from local materials. The use of more permanent building materials, such as concrete with corrugated aluminum roofing, is becoming common in urban areas.

EDUCATION

Education is compulsory for children between the ages of six and fifteen years. There are seven years of primary education and five years of secondary education. The estimated adult literacy rate is 93 percent.

In 1997 Kiribati had eighty-six primary schools with 17,594 students enrolled. At the secondary level, there were 215 teachers and 4,403 students. Kiribati has a teacher-training college, a technical institute, and a marine training school. Higher education courses are available at the Kiribati Extension Centre of the University of the South Pacific (Fiji) in Tarawa.

2000 KEY EVENTS TIMELINE

January

- A BBC team travels to Millennium Island, formerly known as Caroline Island, to see in the year 2000.

March

- A study reports that Kiribati has a high incidence of AIDS and is facing an AIDS crisis.
- The Environmental Ministry expresses concern that a proposed Japanese space shuttle landing strip on Christmas Island (Kiritimati) will endanger millions of seabirds.

May

- The Australian government approves an environmental study on the proposed missile launch site on Christmas Island (Kiritimati); construction is expected to begin in October 2000.

August

- A new independent newspaper, "New Star," starts publication during Media Freedom Week. A weekly paper in the Gilbertese dialect, it competes with the official government press, "Te Uekera."
- The government acquires the majority share of the Bank of Kiribati in a mutual agreement with Westpac Banking Corporation.

October

- The South Pacific Forum, with representatives from sixteen independent, self-governing nations, meets in Kiribati October 28–29, to discuss political, economic, and social issues.
- The government provides an additional $400,000 to copra societies in the outer islands, solving an existing cash flow problem for the societies.

ANALYSIS OF EVENTS: 2000

BUSINESS AND THE ECONOMY

Kiribati's promotion of Kiritimati, its most remote island, as a millennium tourist destination brought the island nation to the world's attention and proved very profitable when Norwegian Cruise

Line and its parent company, Star Cruises, paid US$1.3 million for a four-year contract giving it exclusive rights to call at Kiribati's Fanning Island. Twenty ships were to call in the first sixteen months of the contract, with the number to increase later. In addition to the revenue generated through the cruise contract, the cruise line agreed to make certain improvements to the facilities at Fanning Island. Included in these improvements were the provision of generators and supplies for the schools, guesthouse renovations, and a jetty upgrade. The government planned to encourage the local people to make handicrafts to sell to the tourists.

In February 2000 Kiribati received $6 million from the European Union for a rural electrification project that would use renewable sources of power to bring electricity to 1,500 households and meeting halls on the outer islands. The project was to be implemented by the Kiribati Solar Energy Company, and was expected to take five years.

In May 2000 New Zealand and Kiribati signed a mutual aid treaty by which New Zealand will spend US$1 million on projects in Kiribati over the next fiscal year.

GOVERNMENT AND POLITICS

The media traveled to Kiribati for millennium celebrations on Caroline Island (re-christened Millennium Island) as 2000 dawned in the South Pacific. Some citizens criticized the lavish US$605,000 festivities and said the money could have been spent instead on improving schools and medical facilities on the outer islands. President Teburoro Tito defended the expenditure, stating that the nation would benefit from it over the coming years because of the attention it would bring to Kiribati as a tourist destination. In addition the focus on Kiribati in the international celebrations brought attention to the rising sea level issue as it affected Kiribati and other low-lying Pacific island nations.

In October the Pacific Islands Forum met in Kiribati to discuss political, economic, social, and environmental issues. Kiribati and the other fifteen members of the Forum shared concerns over sea-level rise and toxic waste disposal, the latter being an issue of great concern to Kiribati, as it was among the South Pacific nations cited in a South Pacific Regional Environment Programme (SPREP) report of contamination caused by improper disposal or storage of hazardous wastes. SPREP was to offer assistance in determining proper disposal and finding funds to ship the contaminated material to treatment facilities elsewhere. Kiribati received two additional direct benefits from the Forum meeting: a commitment from Vanuatu Prime Minister Sope to pay ten-year-old compensation claims concerning the deportation of a Kiribati citizen, and a Japanese commitment to negotiate World War II compensation claims brought by the people of Kiribati.

CULTURE AND SOCIETY

Members of youth groups chanted on the beach of Kiritimati Island at daybreak on January 1, 2000, to celebrate the new millennium. Interdenominational church services were also held, followed by the unveiling of the First Daylight Millennium Monument.

A new independent newspaper, "New Star," began publication during Media Freedom Week in August 2000. A weekly paper in the Gilbertese dialect, it competed with the official government press, "Te Uekera," but planned a wider distribution than "Te Uekera."

A 2000 study by the Institute of Justice and Applied Legal Studies in Suva, Fiji, showed that Kiribati had a significant incidence of AIDS and was facing an AIDS crisis. It appeared that the disease was being spread by Kiribati men working as seamen on foreign ships; one third of the infected men were seamen and all the infected women were married to seamen. The high concentration of Kiribati's population in the Tarawa area was also thought to be conducive to the disease's spread. The report called for greater AIDS education for the wives of seamen, mandatory AIDS testing for seamen, and legal penalties for those who knowingly transmitted the disease to others.

DIRECTORY

CENTRAL GOVERNMENT

Head of State

President

Teburoro Tito, Office of the President
PHONE: +686 21183; 21342
FAX: +686 21466

Ministers

Minister of Commerce, Industry and Tourism
Tanieru Awerika, Ministry of Commerce, Industry and Tourism
PHONE: +686 21342
FAX: +686 21466

Minister of Education, Training and Technology
Willie Tokataake, Ministry of Education, Training and Technology
PHONE: +686 21342
FAX: +686 21466

Minister of Environment and Social Development
Anote Tong, Ministry of Environment and Social Development
PHONE: +686 21342
FAX: +686 21466

Minister of Finance and Economic Planning
Beniamina Tinga, Ministry of Finance and Economic Planning
PHONE: +686 21343
FAX: +686 21466

Minister of Foreign Affairs
Teburoro Tito, Ministry of Foreign Affairs
PHONE: +686 21183; 21342
FAX: +686 21466

Minister of Health and Family Planning
Kataotika Teeke, Ministry of Health and Family Planning
PHONE: +686 21342
FAX: +686 21466

Minister of Home Affairs and Rural Development
Tewareka Tentoa, Ministry of Home Affairs and Rural Development
PHONE: +686 21342
FAX: +686 21466

Minister of Information, Communication and Transport
Manraoi Kaiea, Ministry of Information, Communication and Transport
PHONE: +686 21342
FAX: +686 21466

Minister of Commerce, Industry, & Employment
Tanieru Awerika, Ministry of Commerce, Industry, & Employment
PHONE: +686 21342
FAX: +686 21466

Minister of Line and Phoenix Development
Teiraoi Tatabea, Ministry of Line and Phoenix Development
PHONE: +686 21342
FAX: +686 21466

Minister of Natural Resources and Development
Anote Tong, Ministry of Natural Resources and Development
PHONE: +686 21342
FAX: +686 21466

Minister of Works and Energy
Emile Schutz, Ministry of Works and Energy
PHONE: +686 21342
FAX: +686 21466

POLITICAL ORGANIZATIONS

Liberal Party

NAME: Tewareka Tenota

Maneaban Te Mauri Party

NAME: Teburoro Tito

National Progressive Party

NAME: Teatao Teannaki

New Movement Party

DIPLOMATIC REPRESENTATION

Embassies in Kiribati

Australia
PO Box 77, Bairiki, Tarawa, Kiribati
PHONE: +686 21184
FAX: +686 21440

New Zealand
P.O. Box 53, Tarawa, Kiribati
PHONE: +686 21400
FAX: +686 21402

JUDICIAL SYSTEM

High Court

Court of Appeal

BROADCAST MEDIA

Radio Kiribati

PO Box 78, Bairiki, Tarawa, Kiribati, Central Pacific
PHONE: +686 21187
FAX: +686 21096

TITLE: Manager
CONTACT: Bill Reiher
LANGUAGE: English, I-kiribati

Television Kiribati

PO Box 78, Bairiki, Tarawa, Kiribati
PHONE: +686 21187
FAX: +686 21096

Kiribati Broadcasting and Publications Authority

PO Box 78, Bairiki, Tarawa, Kiribati
PHONE: +686 21187
FAX: +686 21096
E-MAIL: bpa@tskl.net.ki

COLLEGES AND UNIVERSITIES

University of the South Pacific-Kiribati Extension Centre

PO Box 59, Bairiki, Kiribati
PHONE: +686 21085
FAX: +686 21419
WEBSITE: http://www.usp.ac.fj

NEWSPAPERS AND MAGAZINES

New Star

PO Box 10, Bairiki, Tarawa, Kiribati
PHONE: +686 21652
FAX: +686 21671
E-MAIL: newstar@tskl.net.ki
WEBSITE: http://www.users.bigpond.com/kiribati_newstar
TITLE: Editor-in-Chief
CONTACT: Ngauea Uatioa

Te Uekera

Kiribati Broadcasting and Publications Authority, PO Box 78, Bairiki, Tarawa, Kiribati
TITLE: Editor-in-Chief
CONTACT: Ngauea Uatioa

RELIGIOUS ORGANIZATIONS

Protestant

Christian Family Life
PO Box 79, Teaoraereke, Tarawa, Kiribati
PHONE: +686 21219
FAX: +686 21401

FURTHER READING

Articles

Feuer, A.B. "Friendly Fire in the Gilberts." *World War II,* November 1999, vol. 14, no. 4, p. 58.

Books

Dun and Bradstreet's Export Guide to Kiribati. Parsippany, NJ: Dun & Bradstreet, 1999.

KIRIBATI: STATISTICAL DATA

For sources and notes see "Sources of Statistics" at the front of each volume.

GEOGRAPHY

Geography

Area:

Total: 717 sq km.

Land: 717 sq km.

Note: includes three island groups - Gilbert Islands, Line Islands, Phoenix Islands.

Land boundaries: 0 km.

Coastline: 1,143 km.

Climate: tropical; marine, hot and humid, moderated by trade winds.

Terrain: mostly low-lying coral atolls surrounded by extensive reefs.

Natural resources: phosphate (production discontinued in 1979).

Land use:

Arable land: 0%

Permanent crops: 51%

Permanent pastures: 0%

Forests and woodland: 3%

Other: 46% (1993 est.).

HUMAN FACTORS

Ethnic Division

Micronesian.

Religion

Roman Catholic 53%

Protestant (Congregational) 41%

Seventh-Day Adventist, Baha'i, Church of God, Mormon 6%

Data for 1995 est.

Major Languages

English (official), Gilbertese.

Demographics (A)

	1990	1995	1998	2000	2010	2020	2030	2040	2050
Population	71.3	81.5	87.7	92.0	115.3	143.0	173.4	204.3	235.3
Life expectancy - males	53.2	55.0	56.1	56.9	60.5	63.9	67.0	69.7	72.1
Life expectancy - females	58.6	60.7	62.0	62.8	66.8	70.5	73.8	76.6	79.0
Birth rate (per 1,000)	38.5	35.3	33.4	32.4	30.1	27.5	24.0	21.6	19.2
Death rate (per 1,000)	10.9	9.9	9.3	9.0	7.8	6.8	6.3	6.1	6.2
Women of reproductive age (15-49 yrs.)	17.7	19.8	21.2	22.5	29.2	35.7	44.6	52.7	60.0
Fertility rate	4.8	4.6	4.5	4.4	4.0	3.5	3.1	2.8	2.5

Except as noted, values for vital statistics are in thousands; life expectancy is in years.

EDUCATION

Literacy Rates (B)

	National Data	World Data
Adult literacy rate		
1995		
Male	NA	81
Female	92[1]	65

GOVERNMENT & LAW

Political Parties

House of Assembly (Maneaba Ni Maungatabu)	no. of seats
Maneaban Te Mauri Party	14
National Progressive Party	11
Independents	14

Elections were last held 23 September 1998 (next to be held by September 2002). There is no tradition of formally organized political parties in Kiribati. They more closely resemble factions or interest groups because they have no party headquarters, formal platforms, or party structures.

Government Budgets (B)

Revenues . . . .$33.3 million

Expenditures . . . .$47.7 million

Data for 1996 est.

LABOR FORCE

Total Labor Force (A)

7,870 economically active, not including subsistence farmers (1985 est.).

Unemployment Rate

2%; underemployment 70% (1992 est.).

PRODUCTION SECTOR

Energy Production

Production . . . . .7 million kWh

Production by source

- Fossil fuel 100%
- Hydro 0%
- Nuclear 0%
- Other 0%

Exports . . . . .0 kWh

Data for 1998.

Energy Consumption

Consumption . . . . .7 million kWh

Imports . . . . .0 kWh

Data for 1998.

Transportation

Highways:

Total: 670 km (1996 est.).

Waterways: small network of canals, totaling 5 km, in Line Islands.

Merchant marine:

Total: 1 ship (1,000 GRT or over) totaling 1,291 GRT/1,295 DWT.

Ships by type: passenger/cargo 1 (1999 est.).

Airports: 21 (1999 est.).

Airports - with unpaved runways: 17.

Top Agriculture Products

Copra, taro, breadfruit, sweet potatoes, vegetables; fish.

Top Mining Products (B)

Mineral resources include: phosphate (production discontinued in 1979).

MANUFACTURING SECTOR

GDP & Manufacturing Summary (C)

Total GDP (1999 est.) . . . .$74 million

Real growth rate (1999 est.) 2.5%

Per capita (1999 est.) $860

Composition by sector

- Agriculture 14%
- Industry 7%
- Services 79%

Values in purchasing power parity. The total GDP is supplemented by a nearly equal amount from external sources.

COMMUNICATIONS

Telecommunications

Telephones - main lines in use: 2,600 (1995).

Telephones - mobile cellular: 0 (1995).

Telephone system:

Domestic: NA

International: satellite earth station - 1 Intelsat (Pacific Ocean) Note: Kiribati is being linked to the Pacific Ocean Cooperative Telecommunications Network, which should improve telephone service.

Radio broadcast stations: AM 1, FM 1, shortwave 1 (1998).

Radios: 17,000 (1997).

Television broadcast stations: 1 (1997).

Televisions: 1,000 (1997).

Internet Service Providers (ISPs): NA

FINANCE, ECONOMICS, & TRADE

Economic Indicators

National product: GDP—purchasing power parity—$74 million (1999 est.), supplemented by a nearly equal amount from external sources.

National product real growth rate: 2.5% (1999 est.).

National product per capita: $860 (1999 est.).

Inflation rate—consumer price index: 2% (1999 est.).

Exchange Rates

Exchange rates:

Australian dollars ($A) per US$1

January 2000	1.5207
1999	1.5497
1998	1.5888
1997	1.3439
1996	1.2773
1995	1.3486

Top Import Origins

$37 million (c.i.f., 1998)

Origins (1996)

Australia	46%
Fiji	NA
Japan	NA
New Zealand	NA
United States	NA

Top Export Destinations

Exports (f.o.b., 1998): $6 million.

Destinations (1996): United States, Australia, New Zealand.

Foreign Aid

Recipient: $15.5 million (1995), largely from UK and Japan.

Import/Export Commodities

Import Commodities	Export Commodities
Foodstuffs	Copra 62%
Machinery and equipment	Seaweed
Miscellaneous manufactured goods	Fish
Fuel	

Balance of Payments

	1990	1991	1992	1993	1994
Exports of goods (f.o.b.)	3	4	6	4	6
Imports of goods (f.o.b.)	−28	−26	−37	−29	−27
Trade balance	−24	−23	−32	−25	−21
Services - debits	−19	−18	−19	−19	−17
Services - credits	8	13	14	15	18
Private transfers (net)	3	3	3	3	3
Government transfers (net)	8	11	9	9	5
Overall balance	−9	4	−9	−4	1

NORTH KOREA (DPRK)

CAPITAL: P'yongyang.

FLAG: A wide horizontal red stripe is bordered on top and bottom by narrow blue stripes, separated from the red by thin white stripes. The left half of the red stripe contains a red five-pointed star on a circular white field.

ANTHEM: *The Song of General Kim Il-sung.*

MONETARY UNIT: The won (W) of 100 ch'on (or jeon) is the national currency. There are coins of 1, 5, 10, and 50 ch'on, and 1 won, and notes of 1, 5, 10, 50, and 100 won. w1 = $0.4561 (or $1 = w2.15).

WEIGHTS AND MEASURES: The metric system and native Korean units of measurement are used.

HOLIDAYS: New Year's Day, 1 January; Kim Jong Il's Birthday, 16 February; International Women's Day, 8 March; Kim Il-sung's Birthday, 15 April; May Day, 1 May; Liberation Day, 15 August; National Foundation Day, 9 September; Founding of the Korean Workers' Party, 10 October; Anniversary of the Constitution, 27 December.

TIME: 9 PM = noon GMT.

LOCATION AND SIZE: The Democratic People's Republic of Korea (DPRK), often called North Korea, occupies the northern 55 percent of the Korean Peninsula in East Asia. It has an area of 120,540 square kilometers (46,541 square miles), slightly smaller than the state of Mississippi. It has a total boundary length of 2,309 kilometers (1,435 miles).

The DPRK's capital city, P'yongyang, is located in the southwestern part of the country.

CLIMATE: The climate ranges widely on the small peninsula. The average January temperature is −17°C (1°F) on the north-central border and −8°C (18°F) at P'yongyang. In the hottest part of the summer, temperatures range only from 24°C (75°F) in P'yongyang to 21°C (70°F) along the northeast coast. Precipitation is around 50 centimeters (20 inches) along the upper reaches of the Tumen, but more than half of the peninsula receives 75–100 centimeters (30–40 inches) per year.

Democratic People's Republic of Korea
Choson Minjujuui Inmin Konghwa-guk

INTRODUCTORY SURVEY

RECENT HISTORY

After Japan surrendered on August 14, 1945, the 38th parallel was chosen as a line of demarcation in Korea between Soviet occupation forces in the North and American occupation forces in the South. The Americans set up a military government allied with conservative Korean political forces. The Soviets allied their government with leftist and communist Korean forces led by Kim Il-sung, who had been an anti-Japanese guerrilla leader in Manchuria. Unable to agree on terms for the reunification of the country, the two governments proclaimed two separate republics in 1948: the Republic of Korea (ROK) in the South and the Democratic People's Republic of Korea (DPRK) in the North.

In June 1950, the People's Army of the DPRK invaded the ROK to unify the country under communist control. Though DPRK forces advanced rapidly, U.S. and UN multinational forces came to the aid of the South Koreans and defeated the DPRK's forces.

U.S. General Douglas MacArthur then made a fateful decision to attack the North. China entered the fighting, forcing MacArthur into a costly retreat. On July 27, 1953, all parties signed a peace agreement. The war killed an estimated 415,000 South Koreans, 23,300 Americans, 3,100 UN allies, and, according to official numbers, 50,000 North Koreans and Chinese, although this number is thought to be as high as two million.

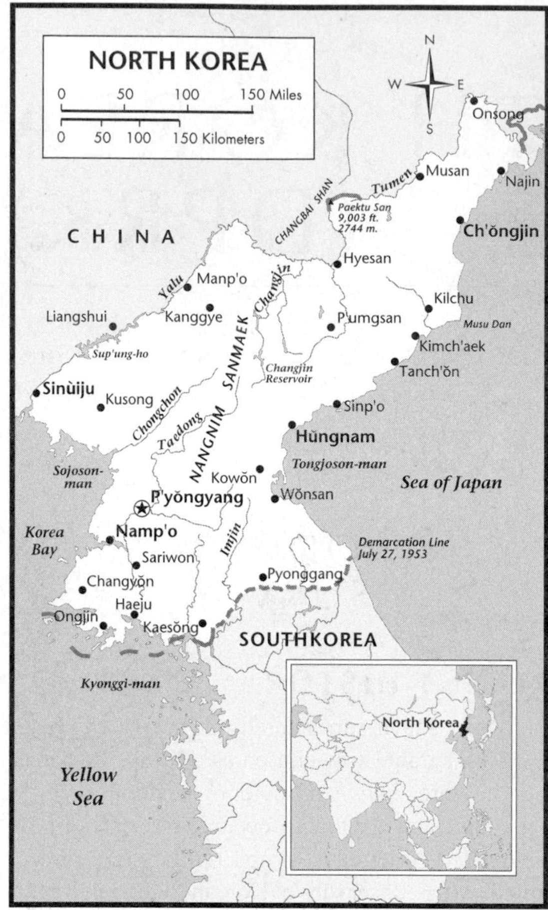

The DPRK, with the aid of China and the former Soviet Union, began to restore its war-damaged economy and Kim Il-sung had emerged as the unchallenged leader. In the 1980s, Korea's basic divisions remained unresolved, but there was some improvement in relations between the North and South.

The collapse of the Soviet Union ended an important source of economic and political support for the DPRK. Despite efforts in 1990 to establish trade with China, the DPRK found itself increasingly isolated and in severe economic difficulty.

In July 1994, President Kim Il-sung died. Kim Jong-il replaced his father as president following an election by the Supreme People's Assembly on July 11, 1994.

Widespread flooding, due in part to massive deforestation, has led to a national famine. Relief efforts have not been able to provide enough food to feed the starving population. The government's own strict authoritarian policies have made it difficult for other nations to donate food aid. By late 1997, an estimated two million North Koreans were starving. Finally in 1998 the UN-sponsored World Food Program (WPF) was able to mount a $1 billion food aid program that Korea accepted. Famine conditions continued in 1999 and 2000.

GOVERNMENT

North Korea's government is classified as authoritarian socialist, or one-man dictatorship. Kim Jong-il has been leader since 1994. Governmental control rests with the leadership of the Korean Workers' (Communist) Party.

In theory, the highest state power is the legislative branch, the Supreme People's Assembly (SPA), with 687 members in 1999. SPA members are elected every five years and meet only a few days each year to ratify decisions made by other governmental and party organs. Elections are on a single slate of Communist-approved candidates, on a yes or no basis. As part of a series of constitutional changes made by SPA in 1998, a Supreme People's Assembly Presidium was created to operate as the top governmental body between sessions of the SPA. The Presidium carries out functions that formerly belonged to the Standing Committee and the Central People's Committee.

In another 1998 reform, the executive branch post of president of the country was abolished four years after Kim Il-sung's death. His son, Kim Jong-il, who assumed power in 1994, was formally acknowledged simply as the nation's leader "rather than president" by the 1998 session of the SPA. The SPA also elected Hong Song Nam as Premier. Responsibilities of the Cabinet (Naegals), formerly called the Administrative Council, were expanded. Members are appointed by SPA.

The state ideology is self-reliance (*Chuch'e* or *Juch'e*), the Korean version of Marxism-Leninism. Suffrage extends to all men and women seventeen years of age or older.

Judiciary

The DPRK's judicial system consists of the Central Court, formerly called the Supreme Court; the courts of provinces, cities, and counties; and special courts (courts-martial and transport courts). People's courts at the city or county level try most cases first. Provincial courts try important cases and examine appeals of lower court judgments. Procedural due process, as guaranteed by Western democratic systems, is not respected. Prosecution of alleged crimes against the state is conducted in secret outside the judicial system.

Political Parties

In October 1945, the Communist Party merged with the New Democratic Party to form the Korean Workers' (Communist) Party, now the ruling party of the DPRK. The National Party Congress adopts the party program and approves the political line. Officially, there are two non-communist political parties: the Korean Social Democratic Party, and the Chondoist Chongu Party (formerly the Friends Party), founded in 1946 for adherents of the Ch'ondogyo faith.

DEFENSE

The DPRK has one of the world's largest and best-equipped armed forces. Out of an estimated one million personnel on active duty in 2000, 950,000 were in the army, 46,000 in the navy, and 86,000 in the air force. An additional 4.7 million were in the reserves, and there was a civilian militia of three to five million. Defense expenditures in 1998 totaled about $3.7 to $4.9 billion, or 25 percent to 33 percent of gross domestic product (GDP).

ECONOMIC AFFAIRS

North Korea is one of the world's most centrally planned and isolated economies. The Korean War devastated much of the DPRK's economy, but postwar reconstruction helped repair it rapidly. The communist regime has used its rich mineral resources to promote industry, especially heavy industry. Available information suggests that since the early 1990s, the country has suffered serious economic problems. Available information is limited and not reliable. The state owns almost all industries. Economic conditions appeared at a standstill at the end of the 1990s due to energy shortages, aging industrial facilities, lack of new investment, and decades of mismanagement.

The agricultural outlook remains bleak with fertilizer shortages, successive natural disasters, and marginal arable land. The country does not produce enough to meet its own minimum requirements and relies heavily on international food aid to feed its population. North Korean malnutrition rates are among the highest in the world, yet the country continues to expend resources to maintain the fifth largest army in the world.

Public Finance

The annual state budget, the leading element of the command economy, is approved at regular sessions of the SPA. In April 1995, the government failed to announce its 1995-96 budget at the annual meeting of the Supreme People's Assembly, which exacerbated the economic stagnation. Foreign aid, important after the Korean War, has not appeared as budgetary income since 1961. External debt in 1996 was about $12 billion.

In 1997, North Korea received an estimated $200 million to $300 million in humanitarian aid from the United States, South Korea, Japan, and the European Union, plus much additional aid from the UN and non-governmental organizations.

Estimates of government revenues and expenditures in the late 1990s are not available.

Income

The U.S. Central Intelligence Agency (CIA) estimated the DPRK's gross domestic product (GDP) at $22.6 billion in 1997, or $1,000 per capita. The 1999 estimates place the GDP rate of growth at 1 percent. The GDP composition by sector was: agriculture, 30 percent; industry, 42 percent; and services, 28 percent.

Industry

The communist regime has emphasized the development of manufacturing. By the late 1980s, heavy industry accounted for 50 percent of total industrial production. About 90 percent of all industry is state-owned. Industries include military products, machine building, electric power, chemicals, iron and steel manufacturing, coal and iron ore mining, oil refining, textiles and clothing, food processing, cement, and chemical fertilizers.

Banking and Finance

The Central Bank, established in 1946, is the sole recipient of national revenues and the repository for all precious metals. It supplies basic operating funds to various sectors of the economy and is subordinate to the Ministry of Finance. The Central Bank is also an administrative organ that executes the fiscal policies of the State Planning Commission. It supervises the Foreign Trade Bank and the Industrial Bank that provides loans and credits to fishing and farm cooperatives.

There are no securities exchanges in the DPRK.

Economic Development

The economy is operated on a planned basis, with priority given to the development of industry, particularly heavy industry. Statements released by the Korean Workers' Party Central Committee in late 1993 confirmed the overall failure of the last seven-year plan and announced a two to three year period of economic adjustment during which investments in agriculture, light industry, and foreign trade would be prioritized. Nonetheless, acute energy shortages, poorly maintained industrial facilities, lack of new investment, and widespread flooding in the late 1990s severely stressed the economy.

In the past, the DPRK's principal economic benefactors were the USSR and China. Soviet assistance to the North was curtailed in 1991. At the end of the 1990s international food aid was critical.

SOCIAL WELFARE

All citizens are entitled to free medical care, disability benefits, and retirement allowances. There are also programs allowing paid vacations and paid maternity leaves. Retirement pensions are roughly one-half of the annual average wages. Those who continue working after retirement age receive both their salary and their pension.

The constitution guarantees equal rights for women. The state provides nurseries and day-care centers, and large families are encouraged.

Human rights organizations are not allowed to operate. An estimated 150,000 political prisoners are held in rural camps.

The government classifies all citizens (most recently in 1996) into three groups: core, wavering, and hostile. The security rating is a mark of how much loyalty the government expects that the individual will give. The rating may be considered when the government allocates housing, employment, medical, and other benefits. Travel abroad is prohibited; travel within the country is also strictly controlled.

Healthcare

The Ministry of Public Health is responsible for all national health services, and by 1993, all of the population had access to healthcare. For the period 1990-1994, there were 2.72 doctors and 13.5 hospital beds per 1,000 people.

Western medicine is used alongside traditional Eastern medicine (*tonguihak*). Cancer is now the leading cause of death, followed by heart disease and high blood pressure. In 1999, average life expectancy was seventy-one years.

Housing

The Korean War (1950-1953) destroyed about one-third of the country's housing. A construction level of 150,000-200,000 units a year was projected for 1987-1993. Available figures for 1980-1988 show a total housing stock of 4.6 million with 4.5 people per dwelling. The government reported that heavy floods in 1995 caused 500,000 residents to become homeless.

EDUCATION

Both primary and secondary education is free and compulsory for ten years beginning at age six. Children ages one to five are cared for in nursery schools, followed by one year of kindergarten, four years of primary school, and six years of secondary school.

Kim Il-sung University is the only university. Admission to the university is by intensely competitive examination. There is also a polytechnic institute, an agricultural college, and a medical school. The adult literacy rate was estimated to be over 99 percent in 1991.

2000 KEY EVENTS TIMELINE

January

- Pyongyang establishes diplomatic relations with Italy.

February

- Pyongyang denies allegations of importing uranium from the Democratic Republic of Congo (DRC) for the manufacture of nuclear weapons in exchange for military aid to the DRC.
- Pyongyang and Russia sign a friendship and mutual cooperation treaty.

May

- The Academy of Medical Science inaugurates the Endocrine Institute in Pyongyang with financial support from overseas Koreans.

June

- Historic summit between Kim Dae Jung of South Korea (Republic of Korea or ROK) and Kim Jong-il of North Korea (Democratic People's Republic of Korea or DPRK) is held in Pyongyang, the capital. The two Kims agree to set up a military communications hotline to diffuse hostilities in case of imminent war.

July

- Committee for Demanding Compensation to Comfort Women for the Army criticizes the Japanese Diet, saying that legislation awarding payments to Korean comfort women during World War II is inadequate. The Committee demands significant enhancement of monies to be paid.

- North Korea joins the ASEAN regional forum on July 27 to discuss security interests in Asia.

August

- Three days of high-level talks with South Korea begin August 29 in Pyongyang.
- One-hundred families are reunited in Seoul on August 15 for four days, after fifty years of separation.

September

- The International Atomic Energy Agency (IAEA) criticizes the DPRK for failure to allow full inspection of its nuclear program.

November

- The United States and North Korea hold missile talks at Kuala Lumpur November 1.
- North Korea says November 18 that it will not improve relations with Japan until the country compensates for colonization.
- Two-hundred elderly people are reunited across the Korean border November 29.

ANALYSIS OF EVENTS: 2000

BUSINESS AND THE ECONOMY

The main event of the year 2000 in North Korea was an historic meeting between Kim Jong-il and Kim Dae-jung, heads of state of North and South Korea, respectively, in June. This meeting heralded the beginnings of a reconciliation between the two halves of the nation that has been divided since 1948, and opened the door for much-needed economic improvements in North Korea. North Korea's Marxist economy was hit hard by the collapse of the Soviet Union in 1991 and suffered further deterioration in the face of extended drought and other natural disasters. Agricultural output steadily declined and famine became widespread. Economic choices to put military and industrial spending first, plus an inefficient and even destructive agricultural system, contributed to the depletion of available foodstuffs.

The balanced budget for 2000 allocated a 15.4 percent increase in spending for the power sector, a 14.5 percent increase in military spending, a 12.3 percent increase for coal mining, but only 5 percent more for the agricultural sector. Despite continual "work-harder" campaigns, North Korea still faced a predicted 2.4 million-ton food shortage at the end of 2000, the worst shortage since the famine of 1996–97 that killed tens of thousands of people. In response, South Korea, the European Union (E.U.), the United States (U.S.), the United Nations (U.N.), and the International Red Cross (IRC) all agreed to send aid to the starving nation. U.N. figures for famine in North Korea were staggering: some eight million people, one-third of the population, were at risk of starvation, and over 420,000 children under the age of seven suffered from malnutrition.

North Korea's move to improve relations with South Korea and leave its previous isolation encouraged many other nations to officially recognize the state and establish political and economic ties. These ties allowed for greater trade between the countries that helped North Korea begin to recover from its economic crisis.

GOVERNMENT AND POLITICS

In politics the millennium was a watershed year for North Korea. It made great strides in the process of reconciliation with South Korea. Samsung Electronics and the Hyundai Group, both South Korean companies, reached separate agreements with North Korean officials to begin joint projects. In August the two Koreas agreed to reconstruct the railroad between the two countries that was closed in 1945. The construction will require the removal of landmines strewn across the area by both sides—a big step toward ending the state of war that has existed for half a century. To supervise this and other demilitarization efforts, North and South Korean defense ministers met in September for the first of many talks about mutual security issues.

North and South Korea also signed a four-part economic treaty in November to address trade between the two countries. The treaty, which grants reciprocal "most-favored-nation" status, among other things, will need to be approved by both countries' parliaments, a process that could take up to three years. But it sets the stage for new inter-Korean economic exchange that would help boost North Korea's failing economy.

North Korea began to establish itself as a contributing member of the international community during the year 2000. In July, North Korea for the first time in its history joined an intergovernmental security organization: the Association of Southeast Asian Nations (ASEAN) Regional Forum, or ARF. The ARF is a security dialogue group including ten ASEAN nations plus South Korea, the United States, China, Japan, Russia, Australia, Canada, New Zealand, India, and the European Union. Several nations either established full diplomatic relations with North Korea in 2000 or expressed an interest in doing so, including Italy, the Philippines, Russia, the Netherlands, Belgium, Germany, Britain, Canada, Spain, Sweden, Denmark, Finland, Austria, Portugal, Australia, and New Zealand. The United States opened talks with North Korea after more than fifty years of hostility between the two countries, and even Japan resumed negotiations that had ended bitterly in 1992. The European Union stated that it would consider opening formal ties with North Korea in 2001.

Two small but significant gestures of reconciliation gave hope to both North and South Korea for increased peace: the South canceled a veterans parade to commemorate the fiftieth anniversary of the start of the Korean War, and the North turned off its loudspeakers that had for years blasted propaganda at the South's soldiers stationed along the demilitarized zone.

CULTURE AND SOCIETY

Despite moves towards increased openness and international cooperation, North Korea remained a repressive totalitarian regime in 2000. Poverty and famine continued to be a severe problem for its people, forcing many to slip across the border into China in search of food. If caught, they were subject to imprisonment or even the death penalty. The U.N. Human Rights Commission and Amnesty International both expressed unabated concern for the denial of human rights in North Korea, citing harsh conditions in concentration camps (where many detainees died), public executions, torture, the interception and misdirection of aid from starving civilians to military and government personnel, and the sexual traffic in women and children along border areas and in detention centers. In a rather grim show of inter-Korean solidarity, both North and South Korean women participated in a mock tribunal held in Tokyo in December to publicize the issue of sexual slavery imposed on Korean women by the Japanese Imperial Army during World War II in so-called "comfort stations."

On a positive note, Kim Jong-il and Kim Dae-jung arranged reunions between long-divided family members that took place in August and December. Each reunion allowed one hundred people from each side to visit family and friends across the border. Future reunions were discussed.

DIRECTORY

CENTRAL GOVERNMENT

Head of State

Chairman of the National Defense
Kim Jong-il, Office of the President

Eternal President
Kim Il-sung (b. 1912–1994)

Premier
Hong Song-nam, Office of the Premier

Ministers

Minister of Agriculture
Yi Ha-sop, Ministry of Agriculture

Minister of Chemical Industry
Pak Pong-chu, Ministry of Chemical Industry

Minister of City Management
Chong-kon Ch'oe, Ministry of City Management

Minister of Commerce
Yong-son Yi, Ministry of Commerce

Minister of Construction and Building-Materials Industries
Yun-hui Cho, Ministry of Construction and Building-Materials Industries

Minister of Culture
Nung-su Kang, Ministry of Culture

Minister of Education
Yong-rip Pyon, Ministry of Education

Minister of Extractive Industries
Chong-ho Son, Ministry of Extractive Industries

Minister of Finance
Il-Pong Mun, Ministry of Finance

Minister of Fisheries
Song-un yi, Ministry of Fisheries

Minister of Foreign Affairs
Nam-sun Paek, Ministry of Foreign Affairs

Minister of Foreign Trade
Chong-mo Kang, Ministry of Foreign Trade

Minister of Forestry
Sang-mu Yi, Ministry of Forestry

Minister of Labor
Won-il Yi, Ministry of Labor

Minister of Land and Environment Protection
Il-Son Chang, Ministry of Land and Environment Protection

Minister of Land and Marine Transport
Yong-il Kim, Ministry of Land and Marine Transport

Minister of Light Industry
Yon-su Yi, Ministry of Light Industry

Minister of Metal and Machine-Building Industries
Sung-hun Chong, Ministry of Metal and Machine-Building Industries

Minister of Physical Culture and Sports
Myong-ch'ol Pak, Ministry of Physical Culture and Sports

Minister of Post and Telecommunications
Kum-pom Yi, Ministry of Post and Telecommunications

Minister of Power and Coal Industries
T'ae-nok Sin, Ministry of Power and Coal Industries

Minister of Procurement and Food Administration
Ch'ang-yong Paek, Ministry of Procurement and Food Administration

Minister of Public Health
Su-hak Kim, Ministry of Public Health

Minister of Public Security
Hak-nim Paek, Ministry of Public Security

Minister of Railways
Yong-sam Kim, Ministry of Railways

Minister of State Construction Control
Tal-chun Pae, Ministry of State Construction Control

Minister of State Inspection
Ui-sun Kim, Ministry of State Inspection

Minister of People's Armed Forces
Vice Marshal Il-ch'ol Kim, Ministry of People's Armed Forces

POLITICAL ORGANIZATIONS

Democratic Front for the Reunification of the Fatherland (DF)

Korean Workers' Party (KWP)

TITLE: General Secretary
NAME: Chong-il Kim

Korean Social Democratic Party

TITLE: Chairwoman
NAME: Pyong-sik Kim

Chondoist Chongu Party

TITLE: Chairwoman
NAME: Mi-yong Yu

JUDICIAL SYSTEM

Supreme Court

BROADCAST MEDIA

Korean Central Broadcasting Station

Joson Jung-ang Pangsong, Jonsung-dong, Moranbong District, Pyongyang, North Korea
PHONE: +850 (2) 812301
FAX: +850 (2) 814418
BROADCASTS: 2000–1800

Pyongyang FM Broadcasting Station

Pyangyang FM Pangsong, Pyongyang, North Korea
TYPE: Religious

The Radio and Television Broadcasting Committee of the Democratic People's Republic of Korea

Jonsung-dong, Moranbong District, Pyongyang, North Korea
PHONE: +850 (2) 816035
FAX: +850 (2) 812100
TITLE: Chairman
CONTACT: Jong Ha Chol

Radio Pyongyang

R Pyongyang, Pyongyang, North Korea
LANGUAGE: 12 languages
BROADCASTS: daily

Educational Broadcasting System (EBS)

Kyoyuk Pangsong
PHONE: +850 (2) 5211586; 5984553
FAX: +850 (2) 5210241; 5210241
E-MAIL: info@mail.ebs.co.kr
WEBSITE: http://www.ebs.co.kr/

Kaesong Television

Kaesong, North Korea
CHANNEL: 8, 9

Mansudae Television

Mansudae, Pyongyang, North Korea
CHANNEL: 5

COLLEGES AND UNIVERSITIES

Kim Chaek University Technology

Waesong District, Pyongyang, Democratic People's Republic of Korea

Kim Hyong-Jik University of Education

Pyongyang, Democratic People's Republic of Korea

Pyongyang University of Medicine

Woesong District, Pyongyang, Democratic People's Republic of Korea

Pyongyang University of Agriculture

Pyongyang, Democratic People's Republic of Korea

Kim Il Sung University

Deasong District, Pyongyang, Democratic People's Republic of Korea

NEWSPAPERS AND MAGAZINES

Choson Sinbo

E-MAIL: webmaster@korea-np.co.jp
WEBSITE: http://www.korea-np.co.jp

The People's Korea

2-4, Tsukudo Hachiman-cho Shinjuku-ku, Tokyo 162 Japan
PHONE: +81 (3) 32605881
FAX: +81 (3) 32688583

Sinboi

WEBSITE: http://www.korea-np.co.jp/sinboj/sinboj.htm

Choson Munhak

Central Committee of the Korean Writers' Union, Pyongyang, North Korea
TYPE: Literary criticism and collections

Choson Yesul

Central Committee of the General Federation of Literature and Arts of Korea, Pyongyang, North Korea
TYPE: Art, general

Korea Today

Korean Publications Exchange Association, Export Section, PO Box 222, Pyongyang, North Korea
TITLE: Editor
CONTACT: Nam-Suk Hahn
TYPE: Political science, general

Korean Nature

Korean Association for Conservation of Nature, Pyongyang, North Korea
TYPE: Environmental science

Korean Women

Korean Democratic Women's Union, Pyongyang, North Korea
TYPE: Political science, social science, general

Korea

Korea Publications Exchange Association, PO Box 222, Pyongyang, North Korea
TYPE: Travel, general

PUBLISHERS

Academy of Sciences Publishing House

Nammundung, Dir Choe Kwan Sik, Pyongyang, Democratic People's Republic of Korea
PHONE: +850 (2) 51956
SUBJECTS: Biological Science, Chemistry, Engineering, Economics, Education, Geography, Geology, History, Philosophy, Physics, Science (General)

The Foreign Language Press

Sochon-dong, Sosong District, Pyongyang, Democratic People's Republic of Korea
PHONE: +850 (2) 841342
FAX: +850 (2) 812100
TITLE: President
CONTACT: Sun Myong Hwang
SUBJECTS: Archaeology, Art, Biography, Child Care & Development, Cookery, Education, History, Philosophy

RELIGIOUS ORGANIZATIONS

Buddhist

Bul-Il Dendo International Meditation Centre
Kwang Sa Monastery, Seung Ju Kun, 543-43, Cholla Namdo, Korea
PHONE: +850 130131132

Korean Buddhists Federation
PO Box 77, Pyongyang, Democratic People's Republic of Korea
PHONE: +850 (2) 43698
TITLE: Secretary
NAME: Sim Sang Ryon

Shin Won Sa

International Zen Center
Yang Wha Ri, Kye Ryong Myon, Kong-Ju Gun, Chung-chong Namdo, 315-43 Korea

Song Kwang Sa

International Meditation Center
Seung Ju Kun, Chonnamdo, 543-43 Korea

Catholic

Korean Roman Catholic Association
Changchung 1-dong, Songyo District, Pyongyang, Democratic People's Republic of Korea
PHONE: +850 (2) 23492
TITLE: Chairman
NAME: Jang Jae Chol

FURTHER READING

Articles

French, Howard W. "North Korea Shyly Courts Capitalism." *New York Times,* April 30, 2000, p. A6.

Perlez, Jane. "Albright Greeted with a Fanfare by North Korea." *New York Times,* October 24, 2000, p. A1+.

Sims, Calvin. "2 Koreas Finish Deal to Reunite Families." *New York Times,* July 1, 2000, p. A5.

Keesings Record of World Events, February 2000.

Korea Central News Agency, January 6, February 9, May 20, and June 14, 2000.

Books

Noland, Marcus. *Avoiding the Apocalypse: The Future of the Two Koreas.* Washington, DC: Institute for International Economics, 2000.

Oh, Kongdan and Ralph C. Hassig, eds. *North Korea Through the Looking Glass.* Washington, DC: Brookings Institution Press, 2000.

Portal, Jane. *Korea: Art and Archaeology.* New York: Thames & Hudson, 2000.

NORTH KOREA: STATISTICAL DATA

For sources and notes see "Sources of Statistics" at the front of each volume.

GEOGRAPHY

Geography

Area:

Total: 120,540 sq km.

Land: 120,410 sq km.

Land boundaries:

Total: 1,673 km.

Border countries: China 1,416 km, South Korea 238 km, Russia 19 km.

Coastline: 2,495 km.

Climate: temperate with rainfall concentrated in summer.

Terrain: mostly hills and mountains separated by deep, narrow valleys; coastal plains wide in west, discontinuous in east.

Natural resources: coal, lead, tungsten, zinc, graphite, magnesite, iron ore, copper, gold, pyrites, salt, fluorspar, hydropower.

Land use:

Arable land: 14%

Permanent crops: 2%

Permanent pastures: 0%

Forests and woodland: 61%

Other: 23% (1993 est.).

HUMAN FACTORS

Demographics (A)

	1990	1995	1998	2000	2010	2020	2030	2040	2050
Population	NA	21,551	21,234	21,688	23,753	25,143	26,141	26,600	26,388
Life expectancy - males	NA	48.9	48.9	67.8	70.4	72.7	74.7	76.3	77.6
Life expectancy - females	NA	53.9	53.9	73.9	76.7	79.1	81.0	82.6	83.9
Birth rate (per 1,000)	NA	20.1	15.3	20.4	13.9	13.2	12.1	10.7	10.1
Death rate (per 1,000)	NA	16.1	15.6	6.9	7.5	8.4	9.1	10.4	11.9
Women of reproductive age (15-49 yrs.)	NA	5,664	5,717	5,848	6,395	6,200	6,051	5,852	5,612
Fertility rate	NA	2.1	1.6	2.3	1.9	1.9	1.8	1.8	1.7

Except as noted, values for vital statistics are in thousands; life expectancy is in years.

Health Indicators

	National Data	World Data
Life expectancy at birth (years)		
1980	67	61
1998	63	67
Daily per capita supply of calories		
1970	NA	2,358
1997	NA	2,791
Daily per capital supply of protein		
1997 (grams)	NA	74
Total fertility rate (births per woman)		
1980	2.8	3.7
1998	2.0	2.7
People living with (1997)		
Tuberculosis (cases per 100,000)	NA	60.4
HIV/AIDS (% aged 15 - 49 years)	NA	0.99

(Continued on next page.)

GOVERNMENT & LAW

Military Affairs (A)

	1990	1992	1995	1996	1997
Military expenditures					
Current dollars (mil.)	5,940	5,500	6,000	6,000	6,000
1997 constant dollars (mil.)	6,960	6,100	6,210	6,100	6,000
Armed forces (000)	1,200	1,200	1,100	1,100	1,100
Gross national product (GNP)					
Current dollars (mil.)	NA	22,000	21,000	21,400	21,800
1997 constant dollars (mil.)	NA	24,400	21,700	21,800	21,800
Central government expenditures (CGE)					
1997 constant dollars (mil.)	NA	21,400[r]	NA	NA	NA
People (mil.)	21.4	20.7	21.6	21.5	21.3
Military expenditure as % of GNP	NA	25.0	28.6	28.0	27.5
World data on military expenditure as % of GNP	4.5	3.4	2.7	2.6	2.6
Military expenditure as % of CGE	NA	28.5	NA	NA	NA
World data on military expenditure as % of CGE	17.0	12.5	10.5	10.3	10.2
Military expenditure per capita (1997 $)	325	294	288	284	281
World data on military expenditure per capita (1997 $)	242	173	146	143	145
Armed forces per 1,000 people (soldiers)	56.0	57.9	51.0	51.1	51.6
World data on armed forces per 1,000 people (soldiers)	5.3	4.5	4.1	3.9	3.8
GNP per capita (1997 $)	NA	1,180	1,010	1,010	1,020
Arms imports[6]					
Current dollars (mil.)	200	150	100	30	30
1997 constant dollars (mil.)	234	166	104	31	30
Arms exports[6]					
Current dollars (mil.)	210	170	60	110	70
1997 constant dollars (mil.)	246	188	62	112	70
Total imports[7]					
Current dollars (mil.)	2,620[e]	1,900[e]	1,240[e]	1,978[e]	1,447[e]
1997 constant dollars (mil.)	3,068[e]	2,106[e]	1,284[e]	2,011[e]	1,447[e]
Total exports[7]					
Current dollars (mil.)	2,020	1,300[e]	805[e]	994[e]	866[e]
1997 constant dollars (mil.)	2,366	1,441[e]	834[e]	1,011[e]	866[e]
Arms as percent of total imports[8]	7.6	7.9	8.1	1.5	2.1
Arms as percent of total exports[8]	10.4	13.1	7.5	11.1	8.1

(Continued on next page.)

HUMAN FACTORS (cont.)

Infants and Malnutrition

	National Data	World Data (wtd ave)
Under 5 mortality rate (1989)	30	NA
% of infants with low birthweight (1992-98)[1]	NA	17
Births attended by skilled health staff (% of total births 1996-98)	100	52
% fully immunized at 1 year of age (1995-98)[1]		
TB	64	82
DPT	37	77
Polio	77	77
Measles	34	74
Prevalence of child malnutrition (1992-98)[1] (based on weight for age, % of children under 5 years)	32	30

Ethnic Division

Racially homogeneous; there is a small Chinese community and a few ethnic Japanese.

Religion

Traditionally Buddhist and Confucianist, some Christian and syncretic Chondogyo (Religion of the Heavenly Way). Autonomous religious activities now almost nonexistent; government-sponsored religious groups exist to provide illusion of religious freedom.

Major Languages

Korean.

GOVERNMENT & LAW (cont.)

Political Parties

The unicameral Supreme People's Assembly or Ch'oego Inmin Hoeui consists of 687 seats. Members are elected by popular vote to serve five-year terms. Elections were last held 26 July 1998 (next to be held in 2003). The Korean Workers' Party (KWP) approves a single list of candidates who are elected without opposition. Minor parties hold a few seats. The other political parties are the Chondoist Chongu Party and Korean Social Democratic Party.

Crime

Crime rate (for 1994)

Crimes reported .1,309,326

Total persons convicted 129,259

Crimes per 100,000 population 2,945

Persons responsible for offenses

Total number of suspects 1,423,618

Total number of female suspects 183,027

Total number of juvenile suspects 6,514

LABOR FORCE

Total Labor Force (A)

9.6 million.

Labor Force by Occupation

Agricultural 36%

Nonagricultural 64%

PRODUCTION SECTOR

Energy Production

Production . . . . .31.975 billion kWh

Production by source

Fossil fuel 34.4%

Hydro 65.6%

Nuclear 0%

Other 0%

Exports . . . . .0 kWh

Data for 1998.

Energy Consumption

Consumption . . . . .29.737 billion kWh

Imports . . . . .0 kWh

Data for 1998.

Transportation

Highways:

Total: 31,200 km.

Paved: 1,997 km.

Unpaved: 29,203 km (1996 est.).

Waterways: 2,253 km; mostly navigable by small craft only.

Pipelines: crude oil 37 km; petroleum product 180 km.

Merchant marine:

Total: 107 ships (1,000 GRT or over) totaling 675,609 GRT/937,477 DWT.

Ships by type: bulk 5, cargo 91, combination bulk 1, multi-functional large load carrier 1, passenger 2, passenger/cargo 1, petroleum tanker 4, short-sea passenger 2 (1999 est.).

Airports: 49 (1994 est.).

Airports - with paved runways: 22.

Airports - with unpaved runways: 27.

Top Agriculture Products

Rice, corn, potatoes, soybeans, pulses; cattle, pigs, pork, eggs.

Top Mining Products (B)

Mineral resources include: coal, lead, tungsten, zinc, graphite, magnesite, iron ore, copper, gold, pyrites, salt, fluorspar.

COMMUNICATIONS

Daily Newspapers

	National Data	World Data for Comparison
Daily Newspapers		
Number of Dailies	3	8,391
Total Circulation (000)	4,500	548,000
Circulation per 1,000 inhabitants	199	96

Telecommunications

Telephones - main lines in use: 1.1 million (1995).

Telephones - mobile cellular: 0 (1999).

Telephone system:

International: satellite earth stations - 1 Intelsat (Indian Ocean) and 1 Russian (Indian Ocean Region); other international connections through Moscow and Beijing.

Radio broadcast stations: AM 16, FM 14, shortwave 12 (1999).

Radios: 3.36 million (1997).

Television broadcast stations: 38 (1999).

Televisions: 1.2 million (1997).

Internet Service Providers (ISPs): NA

FINANCE, ECONOMICS, & TRADE

Economic Indicators

National product: GDP—purchasing power parity—$22.6 billion (1999 est.).

National product real growth rate: 1% (1999 est.).

National product per capita: $1,000 (1999 est.).

Inflation rate—consumer price index: NA.

Exchange Rates

Exchange rates:

Official: North Korean won (Wn) per US$1

May 1994	2.15
May 1992	2.13
September 1991	2.14
January 1990	2.10
December 1989	2.30

Market: North Korean won (Wn) per US$1 . . . . 200.00

Fiscal year: calendar year.

Top Import Origins

$954 million (c.i.f., 1998 est.)

Origins (1995)

China	33%
Japan	17%
Russia	5%
South Korea	4%
Germany	3%

Top Export Destinations

$680 million (f.o.b., 1998 est.)

Destinations (1995)

Japan	28%
South Korea	21%
China	5%
Germany	4%
Russia	1%

Foreign Aid

Recipient: NA; An estimated $200 million to $300 million in humanitarian aid from US, South Korea, Japan, and EU in 1997 plus much additional aid from the UN and non-governmental organizations.

Import/Export Commodities

Import Commodities	Export Commodities
Petroleum	Minerals
Coking coal	Metallurgical products
Machinery and equipment	Manufactures (including armaments)
Consumer goods	Agricultural and fishery products
Grain	

SOUTH KOREA (ROK)

CAPITAL: Seoul.

FLAG: The flag, called the T'aegukki, shows, on a white field, a central circle divided into two parts, red on top and deep blue below, in the shape of Chinese yin and yang symbols. Broken and unbroken black bars in each of the four corners are variously arranged in sets of three, representing divination diagrams.

ANTHEM: *Aegukka (The Song of Patriotism),* officially adopted on 15 August 1948.

MONETARY UNIT: The won (w) is the national currency. There are notes of 500, 1,000, 5,000, and 10,000 won. w1 = $0.0012 (or $1 = w831.3).

WEIGHTS AND MEASURES: Both the metric system and ancient Korean units of measurement are used.

HOLIDAYS: New Year's Days, 1–3 January; Independence Movement Day, 1 March; Labor Day, 10 March; Arbor Day, 5 April; Children's Day, 5 May; Memorial Day, 6 June; Constitution Day, 17 July; Liberation Day, 15 August; Armed Forces Day, 1 October; National Foundation Day, 3 October; Han'gul (Korean Alphabet) Day, 9 October; Christmas, 25 December.

TIME: 9 PM = noon GMT.

LOCATION AND SIZE: The Republic of Korea (ROK), also known as South Korea, occupies the southern 45 percent of the Korean Peninsula in East Asia and has an area of 98,480 square kilometers (38,023 square miles), slightly larger than the state of Indiana. The ROK has a total boundary length of 1,558 kilometers (968 miles). Over 3,000 islands, most of them off the southern and western coasts, belong to the ROK.

The ROK's capital city, Seoul, is located in the northwestern part of the country.

CLIMATE: The average January temperature ranges from −5°C (23°F) at Seoul to 4°C (39°F) on Cheju Island (Cheju Do). In the hottest part of the summer, average temperatures range only from 25°C to 27°C (77°–81°F) in most lowland areas. Most of the nation receives between 75 and 100 centimeters (30 and 40 inches) of rain a year.

Republic of Korea
Taehan Min-guk

INTRODUCTORY SURVEY

RECENT HISTORY

The Republic of Korea, headed by President Syngman Rhee, was proclaimed on August 15, 1948 in the southern portion of the Korean Peninsula, which had been under U.S. military administration since 1945. Like the Democratic People's Republic of Korea (DPRK), established in the north with backing from the Soviet Union, but the ROK was recognized as the legitimate government by the UN General Assembly.

In June 1950 the People's Army of the DPRK invaded the ROK to unify the country under communist control. The DPRK forces advanced rapidly, and the destruction of the ROK seemed near. However, U.S. and UN multinational forces came to the aid of the South Koreans. A military campaign led by U.S. General Douglas MacArthur brought about the total defeat of the DPRK's forces.

After a successful counterattack into North Korea the battle line stabilized near the 38th parallel. On July 27, 1953, all parties signed a peace agreement. The war killed an estimated 415,000 South Koreans, 23,300 Americans, 3,100 United Nations allies, and, according to official numbers, 50,000 North Koreans and Chinese (although this number is thought to be as high as two million).

In 1954 the United States and the ROK signed a mutual defense treaty, under which United States troops remained in the country. Syngman Rhee ran

the government until 1960, when his authoritarian rule provoked violent student demonstrations that finally brought about his downfall. In May 1961 the short-lived Second Korean Republic that followed Rhee was overthrown in a military coup headed by Major General Park Chung-hee.

For the next eighteen years Park ruled South Korea periodically resorting to martial law in response to student demonstrations and other forms of opposition. On October 26, 1979, Park was assassinated by the director of the Korean intelligence agency (KCIA), Kim Jae-gyu, who was later executed.

Following a revision of the constitution in 1987 South Koreans enjoyed greater freedoms of expression and assembly and freedom of the press. The United States agreed to withdraw its nuclear weapons from the ROK in November 1991. And, on the last day of the year, the ROK and the DPRK signed an agreement to ban nuclear weapons from the entire Korean peninsula.

In the presidential election of December 1992 Kim Young Sam, now leader of the majority Democratic Liberal Party (a merger of the DJP with two opposition parties - DLP), was elected president. Kim cleaned up the government and business sector by arresting, firing, or publicly scolding several thousand government officials and business people.

In late 1997 Korea's debts became more than its economy could handle. Increased domestic economic instability, government corruption, and the Asian economic crisis led to a severe financial decline. The government requested the help of the International Monetary Fund, which authorized loans totaling $55 billion, the largest assistance package ever made by the institution. Kim Dae Jung was elected president in 1997.

By mid-2000 Kim Dae Jung had managed to steer Korea's economy out of the worst of its crises. In 2000 legislative elections improved the position of Kim's party, called the New Millennium Party (NMP). In an historic meeting in 2000 Kim traveled to North Korea to meet Kim Chong-il. Both promised cooperation in the future.

GOVERNMENT

Under the new constitution, which took effect in February 1988, the president, the chief of state, is elected by direct popular vote for a single term of five years. A prime minister and two deputy prime ministers head the State Council (the cabinet). The president appoints the prime minister, deputy prime minister, and cabinet. The ROK legislature is the 273-seat National Assembly (Kuk Hoe). Members are elected by popular vote to serve four-year terms. Suffrage is universal at age twenty.

Judiciary

The legal system combines elements of European civil law, Anglo-American law, and classical Chinese philosophies. The highest judicial court is the Supreme Court. Under the Supreme Court are three intermediate appeals courts, located in Seoul, Taegu, and Kwangju. Lower courts include district and family courts. Constitutional challenges go to the Constitutional Court.

The constitution provides for a presumption of innocence, protection from self-incrimination, the right to a speedy trial, protection from double jeopardy, and other due process safeguards. There are no jury trials. The constitution provides for an independent judiciary.

Political Parties

In January 2000 three political parties dominated the political scene. Kim Dae Jung reorganized his party, the National Congress for New Politics (NCNP) into the New Millennium Party (NMP). The NMP captured 115 seats in the National Assembly in the April 2000 election. The Grand National Party (GNP), formerly the New Korean Party (NKP), too 133 seats. A minority party, the United Liberal Democrats (ULD) took seventeen seats.

DEFENSE

The ROK has one of the world's largest and best-equipped armed forces. Defense spending accounted for $9.9 billion in 1998–1999, or 3.2 percent of gross domestic product (GDP). Of a total of 672,000 personnel on active duty, 560,000 were in the army; 60,000 in the navy and marines; and 52,000 in the air force. An additional 4.5 million were in the reserves. All males age nineteen must serve twenty-six to thirty months in the military.

ECONOMIC AFFAIRS

The ROK has been one of the fastest-developing countries in the post-war period, shifting from an agricultural to an industrial economy in the course of only a few decades. Much of this industrialization involves heavy industry, notably steel, construction, shipbuilding, and technologically advanced goods such as electronics. To finance industrial expansion, ROK borrowed heavily through the 1980s. By 1986 it was one of the world's four most indebted economies. Steady account surpluses allowed ROK to reduce this figure but foreign debt still reached 50 percent of GDP in 1998.

The domestic economy grew by an annual average of 9.6 percent during 1985-1990, but slowed to about 8.4 percent during the early 1990s. However, the economy grew by 9 percent in 1995 and by 7.1 percent in 1996. The Asian financial crisis of 1997-1998 exposed longstanding weaknesses in the economy including the massive foreign borrowing. RDK recovered financial stability by 1999 turning a substantial decline in 1998 to a strong growth rate of 10 percent in 1999.

Public Finance

The U.S. CIA estimated that in 1998 government revenues totaled approximately $69 billion and expenditures $82.3 billion. External debt totaled $142 billion in 1999.

Income

In 1998 Korea's gross domestic product (GDP) was estimated at $625.7 billion or about $13,300 per capita. The 1998 estimated GDP by sector was agriculture 5%, industry 45%, and services 50%.

Industry

The ROK ranks as a major Asian producer of steel, chemicals, ships, machinery, nonferrous metals, and electronic equipment. In the 1980s the manufacture of metals, machinery, electronic, and other equipment overtook textile production as the country's leading industry.

The production of passenger cars has grown steadily with RDK accounting for 5 percent of the world's production in 1995. Hyundai is the leading automotive manufacturer, followed by Kia and Daewoo. But bankruptcy had hit both Hyundai and Kia by 2000.

Samsung Electronics, LG, and Daewoo Electronics dominate in the production of high technology consumer electronics capturing 10 percent of the world's market by 2000. Samsung was the world's largest producer of computer memory chips in 1996.

Banking and Finance

The Bank of Korea, established in 1950, serves as the central bank, the bank of issue, and the depository for government funds. The Financial Supervisory Service regulates the banking system. The state-run Korea Development Bank, the Export-Import Bank of Korea, and nine state-run specialized banks provide other banking services. Eleven nationwide commercial banks, ten provincial banks, and forty-two foreign banks handled commercial banking operations in 1999.

The Korean Stock Exchange, a share-issuing private corporation, functions as the country's only stock exchange.

Economic Development

The ROK has a market economy in which both private enterprise and foreign investors play an important role. Overall economic development is guided, however, by the Economic Planning Board and since 1962 by a series of five-year plans. The revised Seventh Five-Year Economic and Social Development Plan for 1992-1996 aimed at establishing the ROK as an advanced industrialized economy by the year 2000. More specific goals included improving social and economic equity, continued liberalization, improving industrial and export competitiveness, as well as strengthening the role of the private sector while government intervention in management is reduced.

SOCIAL WELFARE

The government passed legislation in 1988 that included old age, disability, and survivors' pensions and extended these benefits to farmers, fishermen, and the rural self-employed in 1995. It passed health insurance legislation in 1989.

The wage of the average female worker is roughly half of that of the average male worker. The Amended Family Law of 1991 recognizes women as heads of households and strengthens property rights.

Healthcare

Health care has improved greatly owing to improvement of diet, the rise in living standards, and the development of health and medical programs. During 1985-1995 100 percent of the population had access to health care services. In 2000 life expectancy was 74.4 years. In 1990-1997 there were 4.4 hospital beds and 1.2 physicians for every 1,000 people.

Housing

A housing shortage continues to plague the nation especially in large cities. The government, through the Korean Housing Corporation, plans to construct 500,000 to 600,000 housing units per year from 1993 to 1998 increasing the rate of home ownership to 90%.

EDUCATION

Six-year elementary schools are free and compulsory for children between six and twelve years of age. Secondary education begins at twelve years of age and lasts for up to six years. Nearly 95 percent of children in this age group were enrolled in the secondary schools in 1995. In 1998 there were 3.8 million students in primary schools, 4.7 million in secondary schools, and 2.5 million in colleges and universities. For 2000 the estimated rate of adult illiteracy was 2.2%. In the late 1990s the government allocated approximately 17.5 percent of its total expenditure to education.

2000 KEY EVENTS TIMELINE

January

- Ruling National Congress for New Politics, led by Kim Dae Jung, shuffles cabinet and assumes a new name: New Millennium Party (NMP).
- Ministry of Information and Communication announces that ten million people now connect to the Internet.
- Justice Ministry says that illegal foreigners working in South Korea have soared 35.6 percent from one year ago to 135,300.

February

- Government announces banking reforms that prohibit *chaebol* (business conglomerates) from owning banks.
- Government announces a major subsidy to cover 30 percent of construction of stadiums in preparation for the 2002 World Cup Finals.
- Government announces measures to strengthen medical insurance by increasing its contributory share and increasing premiums deducted from workers' salaries.
- Lee Han Dong, leader of the United Liberal Democrats (ULD), ends his party's coalition with Kim's NMP but promises to cooperate on key legislative initiatives on a case-by-case basis.

April

- General elections strengthen Kim's NMP, but the party fails to capture a majority as the Grand National Party wins a plurality of 133 seats to NMP's 115.

May

- Civic groups call for Prime Minister Park Taejoon's resignation, alleging tax evasion and avoidance through the use of his private treasurer.

June

- First ever summit meeting between North Korea (Democratic People's Republic of Korea or DPRK) and South Korea (Republic of Korea or ROK) is held in Pyongyang, the capital of North Korea, with Kim Jong-il and Kim Dae Jung both promising to work actively toward unification.

- North and South Korean Red Cross officials agree to allow families from the two countries to be reunited. One hundred families from each country will travel to the other country beginning August 15 to meet for four days with relatives. This is the first cooperative action to come out of the summit meeting earlier in June.

July

- First Gay Theme Restaurant opens in Seoul challenging traditional Confucian values.
- The government proposes high-level talks with North Korea July 19 to discuss the route towards reconciliation.

August

- Activists demand the resignation of education minister Song Ja because his daughters have dual U.S. Korean citizenship and his wife has renounced Korean citizenship in favor of U.S. passport.
- Kim Dae Jung provides amnesty to 30,647 people on the 55th anniversary of liberation from Japanese rule (August 14).
- One-hundred families separated since 1950 are reunited in Seoul on August 15 for four days, while another one-hundred are sent into North Korea, in the first of three such reunions scheduled by Korean governments.

September

- Government announces a major investigation of corruption and accounting irregularities of Daewoo and its subsidiaries.
- South Korea plans to import a large amount of grain from foreign countries and loan it to hunger-stricken, communist North Korea.
- Workers begin rebuilding a railway line across the heavily armed border of the two Koreas to connect Seoul and Pyongyang for the first time in fifty years.
- During their summit meeting, Japanese Prime Minister Yoshiro Mori and South Korean President Kim Dae-jung issue a joint statement on cooperation on information technology and agree to try to forge a treaty to protect investors by the end of the year. The political rights of more than 700,000 Koreans living in Japan are another one of the items leading the agenda.
- North and South Korea agree to work to find long-lost families and exchange letters from the end of the year, and set their fourth round of ministerial talks for November 28 to December 1.
- Leaders of Green Korea United expose that U.S. military bases have been dumping oil, polluting the South Han River since 1990.

October

- Repeated medical strikes by doctors lead to patient protests as medical service delivery is paralyzed.
- President Kim Dae-jung wins the Nobel Peace Prize on October 13 for his work on the peace process with North Korea and his championship of human rights.

November

- Tens of thousands of South Korean farmers protest November 21 against government plans to ease their debt instead of completely canceling it.
- Approximately 15,000–20,000 union workers protest government-led corporate restructuring on November 19 and 26, in fear of massive layoffs.
- North and South Korea discuss plans for crossborder transit on November 28. Plans include a railway and a four-lane highway.

December

- North and South Korea hold talks December 12.

ANALYSIS OF EVENTS: 2000

BUSINESS AND THE ECONOMY

The Republic of Korea, commonly referred to as South Korea, experienced an economic slowdown during 2000, as well as scandal, strikes, and conflict over attempted reforms. President Kim Dae-jung made an effort to implement much-needed changes to the traditional *chaebol* (family-run conglomerate) system but was met with resistance from nearly all sides. A survey by the Korean Development Institute showed that 362 out of 4,800 large companies had not made enough profits in the past three years to cover their debts. To address the issue of corporate indebtedness, the government released a list on November 3 of twenty-nine companies that faced closure, but the banks refused to let the failing companies collapse and instead issued new loans or rolled over old ones. Korea's refusal to trim the dead wood from their economy discouraged foreign investors, and the stock market plunged. Even the hopes for a new economy based on high technology were dashed when the Kosdaq—the Korean technology stock market index—fell by 60 percent from January to November.

Repeated strikes also hampered economic growth. Doctors struck in protest over government health reforms; financial workers struck over proposed banking reforms; striking workers at the Lotte Hotel in Seoul engaged in a violent battle with police on June 29; workers at the National Health Insurance Corporation went on strike—in the first half of the year, a total of 138 strikes were reported. Optimistically, this was seen by some as an indication that South Korea was becoming a more open society, welcoming different opinions and viewpoints. Pessimistically, however, it was also seen as an indicator of the entrenched nature of Korean culture resisting change, even when it was clearly needed.

The economic problems were perhaps most acutely demonstrated in the collapse or near-collapse of three of South Korea's top conglomerates: Hyundai, Daewoo, and Samsung. Samsung was forced to sell 70 percent of its car manufacturing to the French company, Renault, the first foreign car company to buy into South Korea's auto industry. Daewoo was rejected by Ford Motor Company, then began negotiations with General Motors and Fiat. Hyundai Engineering and Construction was given a reprieve from bankruptcy when its restructuring plan was accepted. Fearing the effects on the larger economy if Hyundai collapsed, creditors agreed to roll over existing loans until the end of 2000. However, no new loans were granted and Hyundai was warned that the company would go into receivership if another crisis occurred.

Given their own state of insolvency, South Koreans worried about the increasing moves towards reunification with North Korea. The North Korean economy in 2000 was at most one-tenth the size of South Korea's, and to bring productivity in the North up to even half that of the South would cost trillions of dollars. Until the South Korean economy is more stable, reunification could be disastrous.

GOVERNMENT AND POLITICS

The year was one of great highs and lows for President Kim Dae-jung and his government. In June Kim Dae-jung met with North Korean "supreme leader" Kim Jong-il for the first-ever summit meeting between North and South. As a result of the meeting, 400 North and South Koreans were allowed to meet with family members on the other side of the border in two formally arranged reunions. Other steps towards reconciliation were also taken, including an agreement to reconnect the rail link between the two nations. Kim Dae-jung was awarded the Nobel Peace Prize for his efforts toward increased stability and potential reunification of the Korean peninsula. He also stepped up talks with Japan and the United States (U.S.) to improve relations with those world powers.

However Kim Dae-jung faced mounting problems at home with economic turmoil, labor unrest, scandals involving high-level government officers, and losses in the April elections that put his New Millennium Party in the minority. The continuing presence of U.S. armed forces in South Korea sparked repeated protests throughout the year, and the government was accused of both moving too fast and not moving fast enough with economic reforms. By the end of the year, President Kim Dae-jung's popularity rating had dropped below 50 percent for the first time since his election in 1997.

The U.S. military presence in South Korea became an issue on a number of levels. In the summer the U.S. military admitted to dumping toxic chemicals in the Han River that flows through Seoul. Though the United States issued an apology, South Koreans were far from satisfied. Then in December the U.S. military further angered South Koreans by finding that U.S. soldiers did not act under orders in the massacre of hundreds of Korean civilians in No Gun Ri in July 1950 but rather reacted in panic to a perceived threat. South Korea had asked for a joint commission to study the incident to avoid coming up with conflicting findings but was refused by the U.S. military, which then carried out its own investigation. South Koreans believe that the U.S. soldiers were ordered to shoot the civilians and want reparations for the victims' families, at the very least. The U.S. military's denial of any wrongdoing jeopardized the work of Kim Dae-jung to improve relations between the two countries.

CULTURE AND SOCIETY

South Koreans took the lead among Asians in their use of high technology in 2000. By the end of the year, estimates showed some 60 percent of the population used mobile phones and almost half were connected to the Internet. Nearly two-thirds of all stock trading in South Korea was done online. It was predicted that by 2002 more South Koreans than Americans or Japanese would use high-speed Internet connections.

Though worried about the economic effects of reunification with North Korea, and frustrated with the continuing presence of U.S. soldiers in their country, most South Koreans were increasingly open to international interaction in 2000. Preparations for the 2002 World Cup soccer championship that South Korea will co-host with Japan created a greater willingness on both sides to become acquainted with each other. South Korean pop music grew in popularity in Japan in 2000, and a joint symposium on relations between Japan and South Korea in December agreed to promote citizen exchanges between the two countries, particularly of young people. North and South Korean reunions marked a tremendous departure from historic tension and distrust between the two Korean neighbors, and talks began for more reunions and cooperative ventures among citizens of both Koreas.

DIRECTORY

CENTRAL GOVERNMENT

Head of State

President
Kim Dae-jung, Office of the President, 1 Sejong-no, Chongno-ku, Seoul, South Korea
FAX: +82 (2) 5037727

Ministers

Prime Minister
Kim Chong-pil, Office of the Prime Minister, 77 Sejong-ro, Chongno-gu, Seoul 110–050, South Korea
PHONE: +82 (2) 7370094
FAX: +82 (2) 7370109
E-MAIL: m_opm@opm.go.kr

Minister of Agriculture and Forestry
Kim Song-hoo, Ministry of Agriculture and Forestry, 1 Chungang-dong, Kwachon, Kyonggi-do 427–010, South Korea
PHONE: +82 (2) 5037200
FAX: +82 (2) 5037238

Minister of Budget and Planning
Chin Nyom, Ministry of Budget and Planning

Minister of Commerce, Industry and Energy
Chung Tok-ku, Ministry of Commerce, Industry and Energy, 1 Chungang-dong, Kwachon, Kyonggi-do 427–010, South Korea
PHONE: +82 (2) 5037171
FAX: +82 (2) 5033142

Minister of Construction and Transportation
Yi Kun-chun, Ministry of Construction and Transportation, 1 Chungang-dong, Kwachon, Kyonggi-do 427–010, South Korea
PHONE: +82 (2) 5049031
FAX: +82 (2) 5046825

Minister of Culture and Tourism
Pak Chi-won, Ministry of Culture and Tourism, 82–1 Sejong-ro, Chongno-gu, Seoul 110–050, South Korea
PHONE: +82 (2) 7367946
FAX: +82 (2) 7368513

Minister of Education
Kim Tok-chung, Ministry of Education, 77 Sejong-ro, Chongro-ku, Seoul 110–760, South Korea
PHONE: +82 (2) 7203400
FAX: +82 (2)7235656

Minister of Environment
Kim Myong Cha, Ministry of Environment, 1 Chungang-dong, Kwachon, Kyonggi-do 427–010, South Korea
PHONE: +82 (2) 5037171
FAX: +82 (2) 5049277

Minister of Finance and Economy
Kang Pong-kyun, Ministry of Finance and Economy, 1 Chungang-dong, Kwachon, Kyonggi-do 427–010, South Korea
PHONE: +82 (2) 5037171
FAX: +82 (2) 5020193

Minister of Foreign Affairs and Trade
Hong Soon-young, Ministry of Foreign Affairs and Trade, 77–6 Sejongro, Chongno-gu, Seoul, South Korea
PHONE: +82 (2) 7032114
FAX: +82 (2) 7202686

Minister of Government Administration and Local Autonomy
Kim Ki-chae, Ministry of Government Administration and Local Autonomy, 77–6 Sejong-ro, Chongno-gu, Seoul 110–050, South Korea
PHONE: +82 (2) 7357401
FAX: +82 (2) 7208681

Minister of Health and Welfare
Cha Hung-pong, Ministry of Health and Welfare, 1 Chungang-dong, Kwachon, Kyonggi-do 427–010, South Korea
PHONE: +82 (2) 5037505
FAX: +82 (2) 5037568

Minister of Information and Communication
Namgung Suk, Ministry of Information and Communication, 116 1-ga Shinmun-ro, Chongno-gu Seoul 110–061, South Korea
PHONE: +82 (2) 7502000
FAX: +82 (2) 7502915

Minister of Justice
Kim Chung-kil, Ministry of Justice, 1 Chungang-dong, Kwachon Kyonggi-do 427–010, South Korea
PHONE: +82 (2) 5037012
FAX: +82 (2) 5043337

Minister of Labor Affairs
Yi Sang-yong, Ministry of Labor Affairs, 1 Chungang-dong, Kwachon Kyonggi-do 427–010, South Korea
PHONE: +82 (2) 5039713
FAX: +82 (2) 5038862

Minister of Maritime Affairs and Fisheries
Chong Sang-chun, Ministry of Maritime Affairs and Fisheries, 826–14 Yoksam-dong, Kangnam-gu Seoul 135–080, South Korea
PHONE: +82 (2) 5542095
FAX: +82 (2) 5542096

Minister of National Defense
Cho Song-tae, Ministry of National Defense, 1 3-ga Yongsan-dong, Yongsan-gu, Seoul 140–023, South Korea
PHONE: +82 (2) 7950071
FAX: +82 (2) 7960369

Minister of Science and Technology
So Chong-ok, Ministry of Science and Technology, 1 Chungang-dong, Kwachon Kyonggi-do 427-010, South Korea
PHONE: +82 (2) 5037171
FAX: +82 (2) 5037673
E-MAIL: depta3@mostws.most.go.kr

Minister of Unification
Yim Tong-won, Ministry of Unification, 77-6 Sejong-ro, Chongno-gu Seoul 110-050, South Korea
PHONE: +82 (2) 7202431
FAX: +82 (2) 7202432
E-MAIL: m_unikorea@unikorea.go.kr

POLITICAL ORGANIZATIONS

National Congress for New Politics (NCNP)

14-31 Youido-dong, Yongdungpo-gu, Seoul 150-010, South Korea
PHONE: +82 (2) 7847007
FAX: +82 (2) 7846070
NAME: Dae Jung Kim

United Liberal Democratic Party (ULD)

103-4 Shinsu-dong, Mapo-gu, Seoul 121-110, South Korea
PHONE: +82 (2) 7013355
FAX: +82 (2) 7071637
NAME: Jong Pil Kim

New People's Party (NPP)

TITLE: President
NAME: Yi In-che

Grand National Party (GNP)

14-8 Youido-dong, Yongdungop-gu, Seoul 150-010, South Korea
PHONE: +82 (2) 7839811
FAX: +82 (2) 7804687
TITLE: President
NAME: Cho Sun

DIPLOMATIC REPRESENTATION

Embassies in South Korea

Algeria
2-6 Itaewon 2-dong, Yongsan-ku, Seoul, South Korea
PHONE: +82 (2) 7945034
FAX: +82 (2) 7927845
TITLE: Ambassador
NAME: Ahmed Boutache

Argentina
733-73 Hannam-dong, Yongsan-ku, Seoul 140-210, South Korea
PHONE: +82 (2) 7934062; 7970636
FAX: +82 (2) 7925820
TITLE: Ambassador
NAME: Jorge T. Lapsenson

Australia
11th Floor, Kyobo Bldg., Chongro-1-Ka, Chongro-Ku, South Korea
PHONE: +82 (2) 7306490
FAX: +82 (2) 7356601
TITLE: Ambassador
NAME: Anthony John Hely

Austria
1913 19th Fl. Kyobo Bldg., Chongro 1-Ka, Chongro-ku C.P.O. Box 10099, Seoul, South Korea
PHONE: +82 (2) 7329071
FAX: +82 (2) 7329486
TITLE: Ambassador
NAME: Ewald Jaeger

Bangladesh
1-67 1-92 Dongbinggo-dong, Yongsan-ku, Seoul, South Korea
PHONE: +82 (2) 7964056; 7956535
FAX: +82 (2) 7905313
E-MAIL: dootrok@soback.kornet21.net
TITLE: Charge d'Affaires
NAME: Nazrul Islam

Belarus
5-1005 Chunghwa Apt. 22 2, Itaewon dong, Yongsan-Ku, Seoul 140-200, South Korea
PHONE: +82 (2) 7989004
FAX: +82 (2) 7989360
TITLE: Charge d'Affaires
NAME: Igor A. Malevich

Belgium
1-94 Dongbinggo-dong, Yongsan-ku, Seoul 140-230 P.O. Box 4406, South Korea
PHONE: +82 (2) 7490381
FAX: +82 (2) 7971688
E-MAIL: Seoul@Diplobel.org
TITLE: Ambassador
NAME: Renier Nijskens

Brazil
3rd Fl., Keumjung Bldg., 192-11 Uljiro 1-ka, Chung-ku, Seoul 100-191, South Korea
PHONE: +82 (2) 7563170
FAX: +82 (2) 7522180
E-MAIL: braseul@soback.kornet21.net
TITLE: Ambassador
NAME: Sergio Serra

Brunei
1-97 Dongbinggo-dong, Yongsan-ku, Seoul 140-230, South Korea
PHONE: +82 (2) 7977679; 7985565
FAX: +82 (2) 7985564
E-MAIL: kbrunei@chollian.net
TITLE: Ambassador
NAME: Dato A. Aziz Mohammad

Bulgaria
723-42 Hannam 2-dong, Yongsan-ku, Seoul 140-212, South Korea
PHONE: +82 (2) 7948625
FAX: +82 (2) 7948627
TITLE: Ambassador
NAME: Dimiter Ikonomov

Canada
10th and 11th Fl., Kolon Bldg., 45 Mugyo-dong, Chung-ku, Seoul, South Korea
PHONE: +82 (2) 34556000
FAX: +82 (2) 7550686
TITLE: Ambassador
NAME: Arthur Perron

Chile
9th Fl., Youngpoong Bldg., 142 Nonhyun-dong, Kangnam-ku, Seoul, South Korea
PHONE: +82 (2) 5491654
FAX: +82 (2) 5491656
E-MAIL: echilekr@soback.kornet.nm.kr
TITLE: Ambassador
NAME: Ignacio Gonzalez Serrano

China
83 Myund-dong 2-ka, Chung-ku, Seoul, South Korea
PHONE: +82 (2) 3195101
FAX: +82 (2) 3195103
TITLE: Ambassador
NAME: Dawei WU

Colombia
13th Fl., Kyobo Bldg., 1 Chongro 1-ka, Chongro-ku, P.O. Box 1175, Seoul, South Korea
PHONE: +82 (2) 7201369
FAX: +82 (2) 7256959
TITLE: Ambassador
NAME: Miguel Duran

Côte d'Ivoire
2nd Fl., Chungam Bldg., 794-4 Hannam-dong, Yongsan-ku, Seoul, South Korea
PHONE: +82 (2) 37850561
FAX: +82 (2) 37850564
TITLE: Ambassador
NAME: Charles D. A. Atchimon

Czech Republic
1-121 Shinmoonro 2-ka, Chongro-ku, Seoul, South Korea
PHONE: +82 (2) 7256765; 7206453
FAX: +82 (2) 7346452
TITLE: Charge d'Affaires
NAME: Milan Hupcej

Denmark
5th Fl., Namsong Bldg., 260-199 Itaewon-dong, Yongsan-ku, Seoul 140-200, South Korea
PHONE: +82 (2) 7954187
FAX: +82 (2) 7960986

TITLE: Charge d'Affaires
NAME: Hans Jorgen Ipland

Dominican Republic
1601 Garden Tower Bldg., 98-78 Woonni-dong, Chongro-ku, Seoul, South Korea
PHONE: +82 (2) 7426867
FAX: +82 (2) 7441803
TITLE: Charge d'Affaires
NAME: Juan Dominguez

Ecuador
330-275 Sungbuk-dong, Sungbuk-ku, Seoul 136-020, South Korea
PHONE: +82 (2) 7431617
FAX: +82 (2) 7456963
E-MAIL: e26258@nuri.net
TITLE: Ambassador
NAME: Patricio Zuquilanda-Duque

Egypt
744-4 Hannam-dong, Yongsan-ku, Seoul 140-210, South Korea
PHONE: +82 (2) 7490787
FAX: +82 (2) 7952588
TITLE: Ambassador
NAME: Hussein Elfarouk Derar

El Salvador
701 Garden Tower Bldg., 98-78 Wooni-dong Chongro-ku, Seoul, South Korea
PHONE: +82 (2) 7417527; 7659726
FAX: +82 (2) 7417528
TITLE: Ambassador
NAME: Alfredo Francisco Ungo

Ethiopia
657-26 Hannam-dong, Yongsan-ku, Seoul 140-210, South Korea
PHONE: +82 (2) 7908927
FAX: +82 (2) 7908929
TITLE: Ambassador
NAME: Fekade Workneh

Finland
1602 Kyobo Bldg., Chongro 1-ka, Chongro-ku, Seoul, South Korea
PHONE: +82 (2) 7326737
FAX: +82 (2) 7234969
TITLE: Ambassador
NAME: Unto Turunen

France
30 Hap-dong, Sodaemun-ku, South Korea
PHONE: +82 (2) 3123272
FAX: +82 (2) 3936108
TITLE: Ambassador
NAME: Jean-Paul Reau

Gabon
4th Fl., Yoosung Bldg., 738-20 Hannam-dong, Yongsan-ku, Seoul, South Korea
PHONE: +82 (2) 7939575
FAX: +82 (2) 7939574
E-MAIL: amgabsel@unitel.co.kr
TITLE: Ambassador
NAME: Joseph Mamboungou

Germany
308-5 dongbinggo-dong, Yongsan-ku, Seoul 140-230, South Korea
PHONE: +82 (2) 7484114
FAX: +82 (2) 7484161
E-MAIL: germany@shinbiro.com
TITLE: Ambassador
NAME: Claus Vollers

Greece
27th Fl., Hanwha Bldg., 1 Janggyo-dong, Chung-ku, Seoul 100-797, South Korea
PHONE: +82 (2) 7291400
FAX: +82 (2) 7291402
TITLE: Ambassador
NAME: Ioannis Vavvas

Guatemala
602 Garden Tower Bldg., 98-78 Wooni-dong, Chongro-ku, Seoul I, South Korea
PHONE: +82 (2) 7653265
FAX: +82 (2) 7636010
TITLE: Ambassador
NAME: Giovanni R. Castillo Polanco

Honduras
802 Garden Tower Bldg., Woonni-dong Chongro-ku, Seoul, South Korea
PHONE: +82 (2) 7447563; 7417677
FAX: +82 (2) 7447564
TITLE: Ambassador
NAME: Gustavo E. Gamero Rosales

Hungary
1-103 Dongbinggo-dong, Yongsan-ku, Seoul 140-230, South Korea
PHONE: +82 (2) 7922103
FAX: +82 (2) 7922109
E-MAIL: huembsel@shinbiron.com
TITLE: Charge d'Affaires
NAME: Istavan Perosa

India
37-3 Hannam-dong, Yongsan-ku, Seoul, South Korea
PHONE: +82 (2) 7984257
FAX: +82 (2) 7969534
E-MAIL: eoiseoul@soback.kornet.nm.kr

TITLE: Ambassador
NAME: Santosh Kumar

Indonesia
55 Yoido-dong, Youngdeungpo-ku, Seoul, South Korea
PHONE: +82 (2) 7835675; 7835371
FAX: +82 (2) 7804280
TITLE: Ambassador
NAME: Jauhari Nataatmaja

Israel
823-21 Yeoksam-dong, Kangnam-ku, Seoul, South Korea
PHONE: +82 (2) 5643448
FAX: +82 (2) 5643449
TITLE: Ambassador
NAME: Arie Arazi

Iran
726-126 Hannam-dong, Yongsan-ku, Seoul, South Korea
PHONE: +82 (2) 7937751
FAX: +82 (2) 7927052
E-MAIL: matbuat@mfa.gov.Ir
TITLE: Ambassador
NAME: Mohsen Talaei

Ireland
15th Fl., Daehan Fire and Marine Insurance Bldg., 51-1 Namchang-dong, Chung-ku, Seoul 100-060, South Korea
PHONE: +82 (2) 7746455
FAX: +82 (2) 7746458
E-MAIL: hibernia@bora.dacom.co.kr
TITLE: Charge d'Affaires
NAME: Paul Barnwell

Italy
1-398 Hannam-dong, Yongsan-ku, South Korea
PHONE: +82 (2) 7960491
FAX: +82 (2) 7975560
TITLE: Ambassador
NAME: Carlo Trezza

Japan
18-11 Choonghak-dong, Chongro-ku, Seoul, South Korea
PHONE: +82 (2) 7335626
FAX: +82 (2) 7344528
TITLE: Ambassador
NAME: Kazuo Ogura

Kazakstan
32-15 Nonhyun-dong, Kangnam-ku, Seoul, South Korea
PHONE: +82 (2) 5481415; 5161440
FAX: +82 (2) 5481416
TITLE: Ambassador
NAME: Tulegen Zhukeyev

Kuwait
309-15 Dongbinggo-dong, Yongsan-ku, Seoul, South Korea
PHONE: +82 (2) 7493688
FAX: +82 (2) 7493687
TITLE: Ambassador
NAME: Salem Abdullah Jaber Al-Sabah

Lebanon
1-48 Dongbinggo-dong, Yongsan-lu, Seoul, South Korea
PHONE: +82 (2) 7946482
FAX: +82 (2) 7946485
TITLE: Charge d'Affaires
NAME: Salim Baddoura

Malaysia
4-1 Hannam-dong, Yongsan-ku, South Korea
PHONE: +82 (2) 7940349; 7953032
FAX: +82 (2) 7945488
TITLE: Ambassador
NAME: Dato Vyramuttu Yoogalingam

Mexico
33-6 Hannam-dong, Yongsan-ku, Seoul 140-210, South Korea
PHONE: +82 (2) 7981694
FAX: +82 (2) 7900939
TITLE: Charge d'Affaires
NAME: Armando Alvarez Reina

Mongolia
33-5 Hannam-dong, Yongsan-ku, Seoul, South Korea
PHONE: +82 (2) 7941350
FAX: +82 (2) 7947605
E-MAIL: monemb@uriel.net
TITLE: Ambassador
NAME: Lodoidamba Galbadrah

Morocco
S-15 U.N. Village, 270-3, Hannam-Dong, Yongsan-Ku, Seoul, South Korea
PHONE: +82 (2) 7936249
FAX: +82 (2) 7928178
E-MAIL: sifamase@bora.dacom.co
TITLE: Ambassador
NAME: Mohamed Bennani-Smires

Myanmar
723-1 Hannam-dong, Yongsan-ku, Seoul 140-210, South Korea
PHONE: +82 (2) 7923341; 7969858
FAX: +82 (2) 7965570
TITLE: Ambassador
NAME: U Nyi Nyi Than

Netherlands
14th Fl., Kyobo Bldg., . 1 Chongro 1-ka, Chongro-ku, P.O. Box 509, Seoul 110-714, South Korea
PHONE: +82 (2) 7379514
FAX: +82 (2) 7351321
E-MAIL: nlgovseo@bora.dacom.co.kr
TITLE: Charge d'Affaires
NAME: Gert Heijkoop

New Zealand
18th Fl., Kyobo Bldg., 1 Chongro 1-ka Chongro-ku, Seoul, South Korea
PHONE: +82 (2) 7307794
FAX: +82 (2) 7374861
TITLE: Ambassador
NAME: Roy Neil Ferguson

Nigeria
724-5 Hannam-dong, Yongsan-ku, Seoul, South Korea
PHONE: +82 (2) 7972370
FAX: +82 (2) 7961848
TITLE: Ambassador
NAME: Olanrewaju Falola

Norway
258-8 Itaewon-dong, Yongsan-ku, Seoul 140-200, South Korea
PHONE: +82 (2) 7956850
FAX: +82 (2) 7986072
E-MAIL: noram@bora.dacom.co.kr
TITLE: Ambassador
NAME: Torolf Raa

Oman
309-3, Dongbinggo-dong, Yongsan-ku, Seoul, South Korea
PHONE: +82 (2) 7902431
FAX: +82 (2) 7902430
TITLE: Ambassador
NAME: Yahya Salim Al-Wahaibi

Pakistan
258-13 Itaewon-dong, Yongsan-ku, Seoul 140-230, South Korea
PHONE: +82 (2) 7968252; 7960312
FAX: +82 (2) 7960313
TITLE: Ambassado
NAME: Tariq Osman Hyder

Panama
1101 Garden Tower Bldg., 98-78, Wooni-dong, Chongro-ku, Seoul, South Korea
PHONE: +82 (2) 7450720; 7640363
FAX: +82 (2) 7425874
TITLE: Ambassador
NAME: Alfredo Zebede Macharaviaya

Papua New Guinea
5th Fl., 36-1 Hannam 1-dong, Yongsan-ku, Seoul, South Korea
PHONE: +82 (2) 7989854
FAX: +82 (2) 7989856
TITLE: Ambassador
NAME: David Anggo

Paraguay
603 Garden Tower Bldg., 98-78 Woonni-dong Chongro-ku, Seoul, South Korea
PHONE: +82 (2) 7422190
FAX: +82 (2) 7422191
E-MAIL: pyemc@nuri.net
TITLE: Charge d'Affaires
NAME: Nilda Acosta

Peru
6th Fl., Namhan Bldg., 76-42 Hannam-dong, Yongsan-ku, Seoul 140-210, South Korea
PHONE: +82 (2) 7935810; 7905758
FAX: +82 (2) 7973736
E-MAIL: Ipruseul@uriel.net
TITLE: Ambassador
NAME: Luis Felipe Galvez Villarroel

Philippines
9th Fl. Diplomatic Center 1376-1, Seocho-dong, Seocho-ku, Seoul, South Korea
PHONE: +82 (2) 5776147; 5716147
FAX: +82 (2) 5744286
E-MAIL: Phsk@soback.Kornet.nm.kr
TITLE: Ambassador
NAME: Juanito P. Jarasa

Poland
1-72 Dongbinggo-dong, Yongsan-ku, Seoul, South Korea
PHONE: +82 (2) 7499681
FAX: +82 (2) 7499680
TITLE: Ambassador
NAME: Janusz Switkowski

Portugal
2nd Fl., Wonseo Bldg., 171 Wonseo-dong, Chongro-ku, Seoul 110-280, South Korea
PHONE: +82 (2) 36752251
FAX: +82 (2) 36752250
E-MAIL: embport@chollian.net
TITLE: Ambassador
NAME: Fernando R. Machado

Qatar
1-44 Dongbinggo-dong, Yongsan-ku, Seoul, South Korea
PHONE: +82 (2) 7901308
FAX: +82 (2) 7901027

TITLE: Ambassador
NAME: Ali Abdullateef Ahmed al-Muslemani

Romania
UN Village, 1-42 Hannam-dong, Yongsan-ku, Seoul, South Korea
PHONE: +82 (2) 7974924
FAX: +82 (2) 7943114
TITLE: Ambassador
NAME: Nicolae Ropotean

Russia
1001-13, 14 Daechi-dong, Kangnam-ku, Seoul, South Korea
PHONE: +82 (2) 5527096; 5388896
FAX: +82 (2) 5527098
TITLE: Ambassador
NAME: Evgeny V. Afannasiev

Saudi Arabia
1-112, Shinmoonro 2-ka, Chongro-ku, P.O. Box 108, Seoul, South Korea
PHONE: +82 (2) 7391631
FAX: +82 (2) 7323110
TITLE: Ambassador
NAME: Saleh Bin Mansour Al-Rajhy

Singapore
19th Fl., Taepyungno Building, 310 Taepyungno 2ka Chung-ku, Seoul 100-102, South Korea
E-MAIL: singemb@unitel.co.kr
TITLE: Ambassador
NAME: Teo Eng Cheng

Slovakia
389-1 Hannam-dong, Yongsan-ku, Seoul, South Korea
PHONE: +82 (2) 7943981
FAX: +82 (2) 7943982
TITLE: Ambassador
NAME: Peter Sopko

South Africa
1-37 Hannam-dong, Yongsan-ku, Seoul, South Korea
PHONE: +82 (2) 7924855
FAX: +82 (2) 7924856
TITLE: Ambassador
NAME: Johannes J. Spies

Spain
726-52 Hannam-dong, Yongsan-ku, Seoul, South Korea
PHONE: +82 (2) 7943581
FAX: +82 (2) 7968207
TITLE: Ambassador
NAME: Enrique Romeu

Sri Lanka
2002 Kyobo Bldg., Chongro 1-ka, Chongro-ku, Seoul 110-714, South Korea
PHONE: +82 (2) 7352966; 7222681
FAX: +82 (2) 7379577
E-MAIL: lankaemb@ktnet.co.kr
TITLE: Charge d'Affairs
NAME: Shanthi Sudusinghe Fernando

Sudan
653-24 Hannam-dong, Yongsan-ku, Seoul, South Korea
PHONE: +82 (2) 7938692; 7491090
FAX: +82 (2) 7938693
E-MAIL: sudansol/@ppp.kornet.nm.kr
TITLE: Ambassador
NAME: Abdel-Hamied Ibrahim Gibreel

Sweden
12th Fl., Hanhyo Bldg., 136 Seorin-dong, Chongro-ku, Seoul, South Korea
PHONE: +82 (2) 7380846; 7381149; 7394767
FAX: +82 (2) 7331317
E-MAIL: swedemb@sobadk.kornet.nm.kr
TITLE: Ambassador
NAME: Sture T. Stiernlof

Switzerland
32-10 Songwol-dong, Chongro-ku, Seoul 100-101, South Korea
PHONE: +82 (2) 7399511
FAX: +82 (2) 7379392
E-MAIL: swissemb@elim.net
TITLE: Ambassador
NAME: Eric N. Pfister

Thailand
653-7 Hannam-dong, Yongsan-ku, South Korea
PHONE: +82 (2) 7953098
FAX: +82 (2) 7983448
E-MAIL: rteseoul@elim.net
TITLE: Ambassador
NAME: Vichai Vannasin

Tunisia
7-13 Dongbinggo-dong, Yongsan-ku, Seoul 140-230, South Korea
PHONE: +82 (2) 7904334
FAX: +82 (2) 7904333
E-MAIL: tunseoul@att.co.kr
TITLE: Ambassador
NAME: Mondher Jemail

Turkey
4th Fl., Vivien Corporation Bldg., 4-52 Subinggo-dong, Yongsan-ku, Seoul, South Korea
PHONE: +82 (2) 7940255

FAX: +82 (2) 7978546
E-MAIL: seulbe@soback.korne21.net
TITLE: Ambassador
NAME: Halil Dag

Ukraine
901 Diplomatic Center, 1376-1 Seoch 2-dong, Seocho-ku, Seoul, South Korea
PHONE: +82 (2) 5786910; 5786911
FAX: +82 (2) 5785514
E-MAIL: ukremb@chollian.dacom.co.kr
TITLE: Ambassador
NAME: Mykhailo B. Reznik

United Arab Emirates
5-5 Hannam-Dong, Yongsan-Ku, Seoul, South Korea
PHONE: +82 (2) 7903235
FAX: +82 (2) 7903238
TITLE: Ambassador
NAME: Abdulla Mohamed Ali al-Shurafa al-Hammady

United Kingdom
PHONE: +82 (2) 7357341
FAX: +82 (2) 7251738
E-MAIL: postmaster@seoul.mail.fco.gov.uk
TITLE: Ambassador
NAME: Stephen D.R. Brown

United States
82 Sejong-ro, Chongro-ku, South Korea
PHONE: +82 (2) 3974114
TITLE: Ambassador
NAME: Stephen W. Bosworth

Uruguay
Daewoo Center Bldg., Rm. 1802 541, Namdaemoon-ro 5-ka, Chung-ku, South Korea
PHONE: +82 (2) 7537893; 7540720
FAX: +82 (2) 7774129
E-MAIL: uruseul.nuri.net
TITLE: Ambassador
NAME: Julio Giambruno

Uzbekistan
Room 701, Diplomatic Center 1376-1 Seocho 2-dong, Seocho-ku, Seoul, South Korea
PHONE: +82 (2) 5746554; 5773660
FAX: +82 (2) 5780576
TITLE: Charge d'Affaires
NAME: Vitali V. Fen

Venezuela
1801 Garden Tower Bldg., 98-78, Wooni-dong, Chongro-ku, South Korea
PHONE: +82 (2) 7410036
FAX: +82 (2) 7410046
E-MAIL: emvesel@soback.koret.nm.kr
TITLE: Charge d'Affaires
NAME: Alberto Murrillo

Vietnam
28-58 Samcheong-dong, Chongro-ku, Seoul, South Korea
PHONE: +82 (2) 7392065; 7382318
FAX: +82 (2) 7392064
TITLE: Ambassador
NAME: Nguyen Van Xuong

Yemen
657-40 Hannam-dong, Yongsan-ku, Seoul, South Korea
PHONE: +82 (2) 7929883
FAX: +82 (2) 7929885
E-MAIL: yemensel@ppp.hornet21.net
TITLE: Charge d'Affaires
NAME: Yahya A. al-Wazir

JUDICIAL SYSTEM

Supreme Court

967 Socho-dong, Socho-gu, Seoul 137-070, South Korea
PHONE: +82 (2) 34801100
FAX: +82 (2) 5331911

BROADCAST MEDIA

Armed Forces Broadcasting System

Kukkun Pangsong, San 2, Yongsan 2-ga-dong, Yongsan-Guadalcanal, Seoul, South Korea
TITLE: Programming Manager
CONTACT: Ha-Skik Chung
BROADCASTS: 24 hours/day

Buddhist Broadcasting System (BBS)

Pulgyo Pangsong, Tabo Building, 140, Map'o-dong, Map'o-gu, Seoul 121-050, South Korea
PHONE: +82 (2) 7045114
FAX: +82 (2) 7055229
WEBSITE: http://www.bbsfm.co.kr
TITLE: President
CONTACT: Nak-Seung Sung
TYPE: Religious

Christian Broadcasting System (CBS)

Kidokkyo Pangsong, 917–1, Mok-dong, Yangch'on-gu, Seoul 158–701, South Korea
PHONE: +82 (2) 6507000
WEBSITE: http://www.cbs.co.kr
TITLE: President
CONTACT: Ho-kyong Kwon
TYPE: Religious

Far East Broadcasting Corporation, Korea

Far East Broadcasting Co., PO Box 88, Map'o, Seoul 121-707, South Korea
PHONE: +82 (2) 3200114
FAX: +82 (2) 3200229
WEBSITE: http://www.febc.org/korea/korea.html
TITLE: President
CONTACT: Billy Kim
LANGUAGE: Chinese, English, Korean
TYPE: Religious

Korean Broadcasting System (KBS)

Hanguk Pangsong Kongsa, 18, Yo-ui-do-dong, Yongdungp'o-gu, Seoul 150–790, South Korea
PHONE: +82 (2) 7812410
FAX: +82 (2) 7612499
WEBSITE: http://www.kbs.co.kr
TITLE: President
CONTACT: Kwon-Sang Park
TYPE: Public

Kwangju Broadcasting Co., Ltd. (KBC)

Kwangju Pangsong, 114–14, Sp-dong, Nam-gu, Kwangju 503–010, South Korea
PHONE: +82 (62) 6503114
BROADCASTS: 24 hours/day

Kyonggi Broadcasting Co.

Kyonggi Pangsong, 332–2, Wonch'on-dong, P'aldal-gu, Suwon-shi, Kyonggi-do 442–380, South Korea
PHONE: +82 (331) 2177762
WEBSITE: http://www.kfm.co.kr
BROADCASTS: 2000–1700

Munhwa Broadcasting Corporation (MBC)

Munhwa Pangsong, 31, Yo-ui-do-dong, Yongdungp'o-gu, Seoul 150–728, South Korea
PHONE: +82 (2) 7842000
WEBSITE: http://www.mbc.co.kr
TITLE: President
CONTACT: Duk-Ryal Lee
TYPE: Commercial

Pusan Broadcasting Corp. (PSB)

Pusam Oangsong, 603–8, Yonsan-4-dong, Yonje-gu, Pusan 611–084, South Korea
PHONE: +82 (51) 8509000
WEBSITE: http://www.psb.co.kr
BROADCASTS: 24 hours/day

Radio Korea International

Radio Hanguk, 18 Yo-ui-do-dong, Yongdungp'o-gu, Seoul 150–790, South Korea
PHONE: +82 (2) 7813650
FAX: +82 (2) 7813694
E-MAIL: rki@ksbnt.kbs.co.kr
WEBSITE: http://rki.kbs
TITLE: Directorate General
CONTACT: Sun-ok Kim
LANGUAGE: 10 languages

Radio Pacis (PBC)

P'yonghwa Pangsong, 2–3, 1-ga, Ch'o-dong, Chong-gu, Seoul 100–031, South Korea
PHONE: +82 (2) 2702114
FAX: +82 (2) 2784972
WEBSITE: http://www.pcb.cp.kr
TITLE: President
CONTACT: Shin-on Park

Seoul Broadcasting System (SBS)

10–2, Yo-ui-do-dong, Yongdungp'o-gu, Seoul 150–010, South Korea
PHONE: +82 (2) 7860792
FAX: +82 (2) 7860785
WEBSITE: http://www.sbs.co.kr
TITLE: President
CONTACT: Hyok-ki Yoon
BROADCASTS: 24 hours/day

Taegu Broadcasting Corporation (TBC)

Taegu Pangsong, 201–9, Tusan-dong, Susong-gu, Taugu 760–080, South Korea
PHONE: +82 (53) 7601900
WEBSITE: http://www.tbc.co.kr

Taejon Broadcasting Co., Ltd. (TJB)

Taejon Pangsong, 122–1, Hyo-dong, Tong-gu, Taejon 300–722, South Korea
PHONE: +82 (42) 2811101
WEBSITE: http://www.tjb.co.kr
BROADCASTS: 24 hours/day

Traffic Broadcasting Network (TBN)

Kyot'ong Pangsong, 580–8, Taeyon-3-dong, Nam-gu, Pusan 608–023, South Korea
PHONE: +82 (51) 6259944
WEBSITE: http://www.kortic.or.kr/rtsa_tbn.html

Traffic Broadcasting System (TBS)

Kyot'ong Pangsong, 3–8, Yejand-dong, Chung-gu, Seoul, South Korea

PHONE: +82 (2) 3115114
WEBSITE: http://tbs.seoul.kr
TITLE: General Manager
CONTACT: In-Hwan Choi

Wonbuddhism Broadcasting System (WBS)

Wonum Pangsong, 344, Shinyong-dong, Iksan-shi, Cholla Puk-do 570–754, South Korea
PHONE: +82 (653) 8503166
WEBSITE: http://www.wbs.chonbuk.kr
BROADCASTS: 2000–1500
TYPE: Religious

Korean Broadcasting System (KBS TV 1)

18 Yoido-dong Youngdungpo-gu, Seoul 150–790, South Korea
PHONE: +82 (2) 7812001
FAX: +82 (2) 7812009
E-MAIL: pr@kbsnt.kbs.co.kr
WEBSITE: http://www.kbs.co.kr
TITLE: President
CONTACT: Too-Pyo Hong
TYPE: Public, Munhwa Broadcasting Corp., 31 Yoido-dong Youngdungpo-gu, Seoul 150–728, South Korea
PHONE: +82 (2) 7892851
FAX: +82 (2) 7823094
WEBSITE: http://www.mbc.co.kr
TITLE: President
CONTACT: Sung-Koo Kang
TYPE: Commercial

Seoul Broadcasting System

10–2 Yoido-dong Youngdungpo-gu, Seoul 150–010, South Korea
PHONE: +82 (2) 7860792
FAX: +82 (2) 7856171
TITLE: President
CONTACT: Hyuck-ki Yoon
CHANNEL: 6
TYPE: Commercial

Educational Broadcasting System (EBS)

Kyoyuk Pangsong, 92–6, Umyon-dong, Soch'o-gu, Seoul, South Korea
PHONE: +82 (2) 5725021
FAX: +82 (2) 5228020
WEBSITE: http://www.ebs.co.kr
TITLE: President
CONTACT: Heung-Soo Park
TYPE: Educational

COLLEGES AND UNIVERSITIES

Dankook University

San 8, Han Nam-Dong, Yong San-Gu, Seoul, South Korea
PHONE: +82 (2) 7092114
WEBSITE: http://www.dankook.ac.kr

Berea University of Graduate Studies

665-10 Dealim 3 Dong, Youngdeunjgpo-Gu, Seoul, South Korea
PHONE: +82 (2) 8312272
FAX: +82 (2) 8311724
E-MAIL: samshan@berea.ac.kr
WEBSITE: http://www.berea.ac.kr

Kangnam University

Kyunggi-Do, South Korea
PHONE: +82 (31) 2803500
FAX: +82 (31) 2813604
E-MAIL: master@venus.kangman.ac.kr
WEBSITE: http://www.kangnam.ac.kr

Daejin University

11-1 Sandan-Ri, Pacheon-Up, Pacheon Gun, Kyunggi-Do, South Korea
PHONE: +82 (357) 5391081
FAX: +82 (357) 5391089
E-MAIL: web@www.daejin.ac.kr
WEBSITE: http://www.daejin.ac.kr

Chodang University

419 Sungnam-Ri, Muan-Kun, Chonnam, South Korea
PHONE: +82 (636) 4534960
FAX: +822 (636) 4534969
WEBSITE: http://www.chodang.ac.kr

Howon University

727 Walha-Ri, Impi, Kunsan, Chonbuk, South Korea
PHONE: +82 (654) 4507114
FAX: +82 (654) 4507777
WEBSITE: http://www.howon.ac.kr

Daebul University

72 Samho-Ri, Samho-Myeon, Yeon Gam-Gun, Chonam, South Korea
PHONE: +82 (693) 4691114
FAX: +82 (693) 4622510
E-MAIL: webman@daebul.daebul.ac.kr
WEBSITE: http://www.daebul.ac.kr

Sogang University

CPO 1142, Seoul 100-611, South Korea
PHONE: +82 (2) 7058118
FAX: +82 (2) 7058239
WEBSITE: http://www.sogang.ac.kr

Sung Kyun Kwan University

Sung Kyun Kwan University, 53 3-Ka Myunglyun-Dong, Chongro-Ku, Seoul 110-745, South Korea
PHONE: +82 (2) 809 7600114
FAX: +82 (2) 7600810
E-MAIL: vision21@www.skku.ac.kr
WEBSITE: http://www.skku.ac.kr

Korea National Open University

Seoul 110-791, South Korea
PHONE: +82 (2) 36684191
E-MAIL: knouipsi@av9500.knou.ac.kr
WEBSITE: http://www.knou.ac.kr

Yonsei University

134 Shinchon-Dong, Sodaemoon-Ku, Seoul 120-749, South Korea
PHONE: +82 (2) 3612114
FAX: +82 (2) 3131388
E-MAIL: hjkim@bubble.yonsei.ac.kr

Hongik University, Seoul

72-1 Sangsu-Dong, Mapo-Gu, Seoul 121-791, South Korea
PHONE: +82 (2) 3201114
FAX: +82 (2) 3201122
E-MAIL: hkkuh@gayakreonet.re.kr
WEBSITE: http://www.hongik.ac.kr

Kyung Hee University

Seoul 130-701, South Korea
PHONE: +82 (2) 9610114
E-MAIL: name@nms.kyunghee.ac.kr
WEBSITE: http://www.kyunghee.ac.kr

Korea University

1, 5-Ka, Anam-Dong, Sungbuk-Ku, Seoul 136-701, South Korea
PHONE: +82 (2) 32901152
FAX: +82 (2) 9225820
E-MAIL: jk1004@korea.ac.kr
WEBSITE: http://www.korea.ac.kr

Kookmin University, Seoul

861-1 Chongnung-Dong, Songbuk-Gu, Seoul 136-702, South Korea
PHONE: +82 (2) 9104174
FAX: +82 (2) 9104179
E-MAIL: prea4172@kum.kookmin.ac.kr
WEBSITE: http://www.kookmin.ac.kr

International University, Seoul

Chongneung-Dong, Songbuk-Gu, Seoul 136-704, South Korea
PHONE: +82 (2) 9407114
FAX: +82 (2) 9190345
WEBSITE: http://www.seokyeong.ac.kr

Korean Bible University

Seoul139-791, South Korea
PHONE: +82 (2) 9505402
FAX: +82 (2) 9505408
E-MAIL: help@bible.ac.kr
WEBSITE: http://www.bible.ac.kr

Seoul National University

San 56-1, Shillm-Dong, Kwanak-Gu, Seoul 151-742, South Korea
PHONE: +82 (2) 8805114
FAX: +82 (2) 8855272
E-MAIL: engadmin@snu.ac.kr
WEBSITE: http://www.snu.ac.kr

Kangwon National University

Chunchon 200-701, South Korea
PHONE: +82 (33) 2506114
FAX: +82 (33) 2519556
WEBSITE: http://www.kangwon.ac.kr

Hallym University

1 Okchon-Dong, Chunchon, Kangwon-Do 200-702, South Korea
PHONE: +82 (361) 2401000
FAX: +82 (361) 2554650
E-MAIL: deloll@sun.hallym.ac.kr
WEBSITE: http://www.hallym.ac.kr

Kangnung National University

123 Chibyon-Dong, Kangnung, Kangwon-Do 210-702, South Korea
PHONE: +82 (391) 6417001
FAX: +82 (391) 6437110
E-MAIL: webadmin@knusun.kangnun.ac.kr
WEBSITE: http://www.kangnung.ac.kr

Taejon University

96-3 Yongun-Dong, Tong-Gu, Taejon 300-716, South Korea
PHONE: +82 (42) 2820231
FAX: +82 (42) 2838808
E-MAIL: taejon@dragon.taejon.ac.kr
WEBSITE: http://www.taejon.ac.kr

Kongju National University

San. 42-1, Hyoh Yun-Don, Kyongju, Kyongbok, Chungnam 314-701, South Korea
PHONE: +82 (551) 7705114
FAX: +82 (551) 7485553
WEBSITE: http://www.kongju.ac.kr

Chonan University

115 Abseo-Dong, Chonan, Chungnam 330-704, South Korea
PHONE: +82 (417) 5509114
FAX: +82 (417) 5509113
E-MAIL: hskim@mail.chonan.ac.kr

Hanseo University

360 Taegok-Li, Haemi-Muen, Seosan Ct, Chungnam 352-820, South Korea
PHONE: +82 (455) 6601144
FAX: +82 (455) 6601149
E-MAIL: webmaster@hanseo.ac.kr
WEBSITE: http://www.hanseo.ac.kr

Hannam University

133 Ojung-Dong, Taeduk-Gu, Taejon 356-706, South Korea
PHONE: +82 (42) 6297114
FAX: +82 (42) 6295874
E-MAIL: webmaster@eve.hannan.ac.kr
WEBSITE: http://www.hannam.ac.kr

Chongju University

36 Naedok-Dong, Sangdang-Ku, Chongju-Shi, Chungbuk 360-764, South Korea
PHONE: +82 (431) 2298114
FAX: +82 (431) 2298110
E-MAIL: webmaster@chongju.ac.kr
WEBSITE: http://www.chongju.ac.kr

Catholic University of Korea

43-1 Yokkok, 2 Don 9 Wonmi-Gu, Puchon City 420-743, South Korea
PHONE: +82 (2) 3403114
FAX: +82 (2) 3403111
E-MAIL: presiden@waw.cuk.ac.kr
WEBSITE: http://www.cuk.ac.kr

Korea Polytechnic University

Kuyggi-Do 429-450, South Korea
PHONE: +82 (345) 4968000
FAX: +82 (345) 4968179
E-MAIL: htkim@kpu.ac.kr
WEBSITE: http://www.kpu.ac.kr

Anyang University

708-113 Anyang 5-Dong, Manan-Gu, Anyang, Kyung-Gi-Du 430-714, South Korea
PHONE: +82 (343) 4670700
FAX: +82 (343) 4483870
WEBSITE: http://www.anyang.ac.kr

Chung-Ang University

221 Huksuk-Dang, Dongjak-Gu 456-756, South Korea
PHONE: +82 (2) 8205114
E-MAIL: webmaster@cau.ac.kr
WEBSITE: http://www.cau.ac.kr

Chonnam National University

300 Yongbong-Dong, Kwangju 500-757, South Korea
PHONE: +82 (62) 5300111
FAX: +82 (62) 5301189
E-MAIL: admiss@altair.chonnam.ac.kr
WEBSITE: http://www.chonnam.ac.kr

Chosun University

375 Seosuk-Dong, Dong-Gu, Kwangju 501-759, South Korea
PHONE: +82 (62) 2307114
WEBSITE: http://www.chosun.ac.kr

Honam University

59-1 Seobong-Dong, Kwangsan-Ku, Kwangju 506-714, South Korea
PHONE: +82 (62) 9405114
FAX: +82 (62) 9405005
WEBSITE: http://www.honam.honam.ac.kr

Mokpo National University

61 Toim-Ri, Chonggye-Myon, Muan-Gun, Chonnam 534-729, South Korea
PHONE: +82 (631) 4502114
FAX: +82 (631) 4524793
E-MAIL: scpark@www.mokpo.ac.kr
WEBSITE: http://www.mokpo.ac.kr

Yosu National University

96 Dunduk-Dong, Yosu Ct, Chonnam 550-749, South Korea
PHONE: +82 2 (662) 6592114
FAX: +82 (662) 6593003
WEBSITE: http://www.yosu.ac.kr

Jeonju University

1200 Hyoja 3 Ga 1200, Jeonju 560-759, South Korea
PHONE: +82 (652) 2202114
FAX: +82 (652) 2202464
E-MAIL: webmaster@jeonju.ac.kr
WEBSITE: http://www.jeonju.ac.kr

Chonbuk National University

664-14 1-Ga, Duck-Jin Dong, Chon-Ju, Chonbuk 561-756, South Korea
PHONE: +82 (652) 2702098
FAX: +82 (652) 2702099
E-MAIL: office@moak.chonbuk.ac.kr
WEBSITE: http://www.chonbuk.ac.kr

Hanil University & Presbyterian Theological Seminary

694-1 Shin-Ri, Sanggwan-Myun, Wanju-Gun, Chonbuk 565-830, South Korea
PHONE: +82 (652) 2305400
FAX: +82 (652) 2847863
WEBSITE: http://www.hanil.ac.kr

Dong-A University

Hadan-2 Dong 840, Saha-Gu, Pusan 604-714, South Korea
PHONE: +82 (51) 2006677
FAX: +82 (51) 2006419
WEBSITE: http://www.donga.ac.kr

Pukyong National University

Pusan 608-737, South Korea
PHONE: +82 (51) 6206005
FAX: +82 (51) 6287909
E-MAIL: hanyh@dolphin.pknu.ac.kr
WEBSITE: http://www.pknu.ac.kr

Dong Eui University

Kaya-Dong, Pusanjin-Gu, Pusan 614-714, South Korea
PHONE: +82 (51) 8901114
FAX: +82 (51) 8953727
WEBSITE: http://www.dongeui.ac.kr

Dongseo University

69-1 San Churye-2 Dong, Sasang-Gu, Pusan 617-716, South Korea
E-MAIL: webmaster@dongseo.ac.kr
WEBSITE: http://www.dongseo.ac.kr

Miryang National University

1025-1 Naei-Dong, Miryang, Kyongnam 627-702, South Korea
PHONE: +82 (527) 3543181
FAX: +82 (527) 3553186
E-MAIL: uadmin@kmiryang.ac.kr
WEBSITE: http://www.miryang.ac.kr

Changwon National University

9 Sarim-Dong, Changwon, Kyung-Nam 641-773, South Korea
PHONE: +82 (551) 2797000
FAX: +82 (551) 2832970
E-MAIL: webmaster@changwon.ac.kr
WEBSITE: http://www.changwon.ac.kr

Gyeongsang National University

900 Kajoa-Dong, Chinju Ct, Kyongnam 660-701, South Korea
PHONE: +82 (55) 7516114
FAX: +82 (55) 7508714
E-MAIL: webadmin@nongae.gsnu.ac.kr
WEBSITE: http://www.gsnu.ac.kr

Cheju National University

1 Ara 1-Dong, Cheju, Cheju-Do 690-756, South Korea
PHONE: +82 (64) 7542002
FAX: +82 (64) 7578583
E-MAIL: hyj@cheju.cheju.ac.kr
WEBSITE: http://www.cheju.ac.kr

Kyungpook National University

1370 Sankyuk-Dong, Puk-Gu, Taegu 702-701, South Korea
PHONE: +82 (53) 9055114
E-MAIL: www@www.kyungpook.ac.kr
WEBSITE: http://www.kyungpook.ac.kr

Catholic University of Taegu-Hyosung

330 Kumrak 1-Ri, Hayong-Up, Kyong-Shi, Kyongbuk 712-702, South Korea
PHONE: +82 (53) 8528001
FAX: +82 (53) 8528030
E-MAIL: webmaster@cuth.cataegu
WEBSITE: http://www.cataegu.ac.kr

Kaya University

Jisan-Ri, Koryong-Kun, Kyungbuk 717-800, South Korea
PHONE: +82 (54) 9563100
FAX: +82 (54) 9546094
WEBSITE: http://www.kaya.ac.kr

Kyungwoon University

San 5-1, Induck-Ri, Sandong-Myun, Kumi, Kyungbuk 730-850, South Korea
PHONE: +82 (546) 4701021
FAX: +82 (546) 4791029
E-MAIL: webmaster@kyungwoon.ac.kr
WEBSITE: http://www.kyungwoon.ac.kr

NEWSPAPERS AND MAGAZINES

Chosun Ilbo

The Chosun Ilbo Ltd., PO Box 199, Chung-gu, Seoul, South Korea
PHONE: +82 (2) 7245826
FAX: +82 (2) 7245809
WEBSITE: www.chosun.com
TITLE: Editor
CONTACT: Bo-Kil Ihn
CIRCULATION: 2,668,700

Daily Trade News

159-11 Samsong-dong, Kangnam-gu, Seoul, South Korea
PHONE: +82 (2) 5510114
TITLE: Managing Editor
CONTACT: Chong Hae-Wan
CIRCULATION: 2,150,000

The Hankook Ilbo

Kwanghwamun, PO Box 264, Seoul, South Korea
PHONE: +82 (2) 7242114
FAX: +82 (2) 7395928

Joong-Ang Ilbo

The Joong-Ang Daily News, 7 Soonhwa-dong, Chung-gu, Seoul 100-759, South Korea
PHONE: +82 (2) 7515773
FAX: +82 (2) 7515807
E-MAIL: feedback@joongang.co.kr
WEBSITE: www.joongang.co.kr
TITLE: Editor-in-Chief
CONTACT: Sang Pyong-Uk
CIRCULATION: 1,850,000

The Korean Economic Daily

4441 Chungnim-dong, Chung-gu, PO Box 960, Seoul, South Korea
PHONE: +82 (2) 3135511
FAX: +82 (2) 3924168
WEBSITE: www.ked.co.kr
TITLE: Editor
CONTACT:

Yung-Jin

CIRCULATION: 520,000

Korea Herald

Korea Herald, Inc., 1-12, 3-ga Hoehyon-dong, Chung-gu, Seoul 100-171, South Korea
PHONE: +82 (2) 7270114
FAX: +82 (2) 7270670
E-MAIL: kherald@boradacom.co.kr
WEBSITE: www.koreaherald.co.kr
TITLE: Editor
CONTACT: Choi Nam-hynn
CIRCULATION: 120,000

The Korea Times

The Hankook Ilbo Co., Ltd., 14 Chunghak-dong, Chongno-gu, Seoul 100-792, South Korea
PHONE: +82 (2) 7346872
FAX: +82 (2) 7231623
WEBSITE: www.koreatimes.co.kr
TITLE: Editor
CONTACT: Park Chang-cook
CIRCULATION: 263,000

Kyung Hyang Shinmun

22, Jeong-dong, Chung-gu, Seoul 100-702, South Korea
PHONE: +82 (2) 7305151
FAX: +82 (2) 7364985
WEBSITE: www.khan.co.kr
TITLE: Editor
CONTACT: Park Jong-Hwa
CIRCULATION: 1,478,500

Maeil Business Newspaper

1-51 Phil-Dong, Jung-gu, Seoul 100-728, South Korea
PHONE: +82 (2) 20002114
FAX: +82 (2) 22758070
E-MAIL: ind@mk.co.kr
WEBSITE: www.mk.co.kr
TITLE: Editor
CONTACT: Jin-Soo Kim
CIRCULATION: 800,000

Naeway Economic Daily

The Korea Herald - The Naeway Economic Daily, Inc., 1-12, 3-ga Hoehyon-dong, Chung-gu, Seoul 100, South Korea
PHONE: +82 (2) 7270114
FAX: +82 (2) 7564850
TITLE: Managing Editor
CONTACT: Yun Yong
CIRCULATION: 300,000

The Pusan Ilbo

Pusan Ilbo-Sa, 1-10 Sujung-Dong Dong-gu, Pusan 601-738, South Korea
PHONE: +82 (51) 4614114
FAX: +82 (51) 5642770
TITLE: Managing Editor
CONTACT: Pak Chong-In
CIRCULATION: 600,000

Seoul Kyngje Shunmun (Seoul Economic News)

The Hankook Ilbo Co., Ltd., 14 Chunghak-dong, Chongno-gu, Seoul 110-792, South Korea
PHONE: +82 (2) 7324151
FAX: +82 (2) 7395928
TITLE: Editor
CONTACT: Pak Pyong-Yun
CIRCULATION: 500,000

Seoul Shinmun

CPO Box 5204, Chung-gu, Seoul, South Korea
PHONE: +82 (2) 7357711
WEBSITE: www.seoul.co.kr
TITLE: Managing Editor
CONTACT: Kim Ho-Chun
CIRCULATION: 900,000

Chongyongnyon

c/o Korean Chamber of Commerce & Industry, 45, 4-ka Namdaemun-no, CPO Box 25, Chung-ku, Seoul, South Korea
TITLE: Editor
CONTACT: Bong-Shik Shin
CIRCULATION: 13,000
TYPE: Business and economics

Konggan

219 Wonseo-dong, Chongro-gu, Seoul 110-280, South Korea
FAX: +82 (822) 7472894
TITLE: Editor
CONTACT: Heon-Hun Kim
CIRCULATION: 5,000
TYPE: Art, architecture, general

Korea Business World

4-F, Suhgun Bldg., 107-6 Banpo-dong, Seocho-ku, Seoul 137-040, South Korea
FAX: +82 (2) 5947663
CIRCULATION: 40,200
TYPE: Business and economics, general

Korea Economic Quarterly

28-1 Yoido-dong, Yeongdungpo-ku, Seoul 150-756, South Korea
FAX: +82 (2) 7850270
WEBSITE: www.keri.com
TYPE: Business and economics

Korea Focus

526 Namdaemunno 5-ga, Chung-gu, Seoul 100-095, South Korea
FAX: +82 (2) 7572049
E-MAIL: kofo@soback.kornet.nm.kr
WEBSITE: www.kofo.kr
TITLE: Editor
CONTACT: Hong Soon-il
CIRCULATION: 10,000
TYPE: Social science, general

Korea Observer

CPO Box 3410, Seoul 100-634, South Korea
FAX: +82 (2) 5641190
TITLE: Editor
CONTACT: Myong Whai Kim
CIRCULATION: 3,500
TYPE: History, Asia

PUBLISHERS

Ahn Graphics

260-88 Songbuk 2-dong, Songbuk-gu, Seoul 136022, South Korea
PHONE: +82 (2) 7438065/6
FAX: +82 (2) 7433352
E-MAIL: webmaster@ag.co.kr
WEBSITE: http://www.ag.co.kr
TITLE: President
CONTACT: Ok-Chul Kim
SUBJECTS: Art, Computer Science

BCM Publishers Inc.

823-33 Yuksam-dong, Kangnam-gu, Seoul 135080, South Korea
PHONE: +82 (2) 5670644

FAX: +82 (2) 5529169
E-MAIL: bcmpub@nuri.net
WEBSITE: http://www.bcm.co.kr
TITLE: Chairman
CONTACT: Byoung-Chul Min
SUBJECTS: Education, English as a Second Language

BIRYONGSO Publishing

5 F Kangnam Publishing, Culture Center, Shisa-dong, Kangnam-gu, Seoul 135120, South Korea
PHONE: +82 (2) 5152000
FAX: +82 (2) 5152007
E-MAIL: michell@bora.dacom.co.kr
TITLE: Foreign Rights Manager
CONTACT: Michelle Nam
SUBJECTS: Picture books for children
TOTAL PUBLISHED: 100 print

Cheong-mun-gap Publishing Co.

486-9 Gileum 3-dong, Songbuk-gu, Seoul, 136113, South Korea
PHONE: +82 (2) 9851451; 9897423; 9897421
FAX: +82 (2) 9828679
E-MAIL: CMGbook@hitel.kol.co.kr
TITLE: International Rights
CONTACT: Han-Seung Kim
SUBJECTS: Science (General), Technology

Chung Rim Publishing Co. Ltd.

Young Bldg. 63, Nonhyn-Dong, Kangnam-gu, Seoul 135010, South Korea
PHONE: +82 (2) 5443616
FAX: +82 (2) 5468053
CONTACT: Koh Young-Soo
SUBJECTS: Art, Behavioral Sciences, Business, Biography, Career Development, Child Care, Communications, Computer Science, Education, Electronics, Fiction, History, Journalism, Literature, Law, Science, Social Sciences, Technology
TOTAL PUBLISHED: 1,300 print; 3 CD-ROM

Damoa

4F Leeseobang Bldg., 23-7, Bomun-Dong 7-ka, Songbuk-gu, Seoul 136087, South Korea
PHONE: +82 (2) 9295411
FAX: +82 (2) 9295413
E-MAIL: dongari@chollian.dacom.co.kr
CONTACT: Shin Hyum Mi
SUBJECTS: How-To, Language Arts, Linguistics, Literature, Literary Criticism, Essays, Poetry

Youl Hwa Dang Publishers

506 Shinsa-Dong, Kangnam-gu, Seoul, Korea
PHONE: +82 (2) 5153141; 5153143; 5153142
FAX: +82 (2) 5153144
E-MAIL: yhdp@hitel.net
TITLE: Editor & Foreign Rights
CONTACT: Ji-Hong Park
SUBJECTS: Antiques, Architecture, Interior Design, Art, Crafts, Hobbies, Games, Film, Video, Music, Dance, Photography, Korean Art
TOTAL PUBLISHED: 500 print

Hakgojae Publishing Inc.

70 Sogyeog-Dong, Jongro-gu, Seoul 110200, South Korea
PHONE: +82 (2) 7361713
FAX: +82 (2) 7398592
E-MAIL: hkjass@hitel.co.kr
TITLE: International Rights
CONTACT: Hyun-ki Park
SUBJECTS: Archaeology, Architecture, Interior Design, Art, Asian Studies, Foreign Countries, History, Literature, Literary Criticism, Photography, Korean Studies

Hakmun Publishing Co.

Sahak Hall, 7-2, Sajik-dong, Jongro-gu, Seoul 110054, South Korea
PHONE: +82 (2) 7385118, ext. 117
FAX: +82 (2) 7258023; 7338998
E-MAIL: hakmun@hakmun.co.kr
WEBSITE: http://www.hakmunsa.com
TITLE: President
CONTACT: Young Chul Kim
SUBJECTS: Art, Business, Child Care, Computer Science, Education, Engineering, English as a Second Language, Science (General), Social Sciences, Athletics, Study-Aids
TOTAL PUBLISHED: 3,000 print

Hanul Publishing Co.

201 Hyuam Bldg., 503-24 Changcheon-dong, Seodaemun-gu, Seoul 120-180, South Korea
PHONE: +82 (2) 3260095; 3366183
FAX: +82 (2) 3337543
E-MAIL: newhanul@nuri.net
TITLE: Director
CONTACT: Lim Hee-Kun
SUBJECTS: Asian Studies, Economics, Geography, Health, History, Law, Journalism, Literature, Medicine, Philosophy, Social Sciences, Theology, Women's Studies

TOTAL PUBLISHED: 1,200 print

Hollym Corporation Publishers

14-5 Kwancheul-Dong, Chongno-ku, Seoul 110111, South Korea
PHONE: +82 (2) 7357551; 7357554; 7357553
FAX: +82 (2) 7305149; 7308192
E-MAIL: hollym@chollian.dacom.co.kr
TITLE: Man. Director
CONTACT: Shin-Won Chu
SUBJECTS: Biography, Cookery, Fiction, Poetry, Travel

Hongik Media Plus Ltd.

1515 Hanseo River Park Bldg., 11-11, Yeoyidodong, Youngdeungpo-su, Seoul 120010, South Korea
PHONE: +82 (2) 7861016
FAX: +82 (2) 7861709
E-MAIL: hongikcb@soback.kornet.nm.kr
CONTACT: Tae-Gi Yu
SUBJECTS: Biography, Career Development, Computer Science, Education, English as a Secopnd Language

Hyein Publishing House

Usin Blg., Ste. 202, 11-2 Gusan_dong, Eunpyeoung-Gu, Seoul 122060, South Korea
PHONE: +82 (2) 3836928
FAX: +82 (2) 3836929
E-MAIL: vvh103@chollian
CONTACT: Choon-Won Cho
SUBJECTS: Education, Health, Nutrition, Science (General), Travel

Iljo-gag Publishers

9 Gongpyeuung-Dong, Jongro-gu, KPO Box 279, Seoul 110160, South Korea
PHONE: +82 (2) 733543011
FAX: +82 (2) 7385857
E-MAIL: ilchokak@hitel.co.kr
TITLE: President
CONTACT: Man-Nyun Han
SUBJECTS: Anthropology, Education, Engineering (General), History, Law, Medicine, Nursing, Dentistry, Psychology, Psychiatry, Science (General), Social Sceinces

Jigyungsa Ltd.

790-14 Yeogsam-Dong, Kangnam-gu, Seoul 135-080, South Korea
PHONE: +82 (2) 5576351
FAX: +82 (2) 5576352
E-MAIL: jigyung@nextell.net
TITLE: Director, International & Planning Dept.
CONTACT: Hyosik Kim
SUBJECTS: Fiction, Nonfiction (General)

Korea University Press

1-2 Anam-dong 5-ga, Songbug-gu, Seoul 136701, South Korea
PHONE: +82 (2) 9021720
FAX: +82 (2) 9236311
TITLE: President
CONTACT: Hie-Jip Kim
SUBJECTS: Agriculture, Earth Sciences, Education, Engineering (General), History, Language Arts, Linguistics, Literature, Philosophy, Social Sciences

Koreaone Press Inc.

9F Gyeongun Bldg. 70 Gyeongun-dong, Jongro-gu, Seoul 110310, South Korea
PHONE: +82 (2) 7391156
FAX: +82 (2) 7343512
TITLE: President
CONTACT: Nark-Cheon Kim
SUBJECTS: Biography, Business, Career Development, Education, Environmental Studies, Fiction, Literature, Nonfiction (General), Philosophy, Religion, Social Sciences

Kukmin Publishing Co. Inc.

822 Guro-dong, Guro-gu, Seoul 152050, South Korea
PHONE: +82 (2) 8582461/3
FAX: +82 (2) 8582464
TITLE: Chief Editor
CONTACT: Jung Hee Park
SUBJECTS: Religion, Theology

Literature Academy

133 Iwha-Dong, Jongro-gu, Seoul 110500, South Korea
PHONE: +82 (2) 7645057
FAX: +82 (2) 7458516
E-MAIL: munhak@munhakac.co.kr
WEBSITE: http://www.munhakac.co.kr
TITLE: Publisher
CONTACT: Je-Chun Park
SUBJECTS: Art, Language Arts, Linguistics, Literature, Literary Criticism, Essays, Poetry
TOTAL PUBLISHED: 280 print

Minumsa Publishing Co.

5F Kangnam Publishing Culture Centre, 506 Sinsa-Dong, Kangnam-gu, Seoul 110500, South Korea
PHONE: +82 (2) 5152000; 5152005
FAX: +82 (2) 5152007
E-MAIL: webmaster@minumsa.co.kr
WEBSITE: http://www.minumsa.co.kr
TITLE: Foreign Rights Manager
CONTACT: Michelle Nam
SUBJECTS: Fiction, History, Literature, Literary Criticism, Nonfiction (General), Philosophy, Science (General), Social Sciences
TOTAL PUBLISHED: 200 print

Minjisa Publishing Co.

673-3 Mia-Dong, Seoul 142105, South Korea
PHONE: +82 (2) 9806382
FAX: +82 (2) 9861531
E-MAIL: webmaster@minjisa.co.kr
WEBSITE: http://www.minjisa.co.kr
TITLE: President
CONTACT: Tai-Seung Ri
SUBJECTS: Child Care & Development, Education, Health, Nutrition, History, Literature, Essays, Literary Criticism, Psychology, Psychiatry
TOTAL PUBLISHED: 100 print

Moon Jin Media Co. Ltd.

3rd Floor Shinwoo Bldg. 5-7, Yongsan-Dong 3-Ka, Yongsan-ku, Seoul 140023, South Korea
PHONE: +82 (2) 7927611
FAX: +82 (2) 7928885
E-MAIL: mjmedia@hitel.co.kr
TITLE: International Rights
CONTACT: Jong Yeon Park
SUBJECTS: English as a Second Language

Nachimban House Publishers

5F Hanjin Bldg., 101-6, 2-ga Eeuljiro, Jungro-gu, Seoul 100192, South Korea
PHONE: +82 (2) 2670825
FAX: +82 (2) 2756003
E-MAIL: navan@chollian.net
TITLE: Editor
CONTACT: Timothy Oh
SUBJECTS: Biblical Studies, Biography, Fiction, History, Human Relations, Literature, Literary Criticism, Essays, Religion, Theology

Pearson Education (Korea)

No. 404 Sin La 2 Bldg., 137-5 Yeonhee-Dong, Seodaemun-ku, Seoul 120111, South Korea
PHONE: +82 (2) 3320841
FAX: +82 (2) 3320843
E-MAIL: info@pearsoned.co.kr
WEBSITE: http://www.awl-elt.com/longman_map
TITLE: President & Man. Director
CONTACT: Yong-Jin Oh
SUBJECTS: Computer Science, Engineering
TOTAL PUBLISHED: 500 print

St. Pauls

103-36 Mia 9-Dong, Gangbuk-gu, Seoul 142109, South Korea
PHONE: +82 (2) 9861361; 9861364
FAX: +82 (2) 9844622
E-MAIL: miari@paolo.net
WEBSITE: http://www.paolo.net
TITLE: General & Editorial Director
CONTACT: Chang-Ouk Lee
SUBJECTS: Biblical Studies, Fiction, Human Relations, Philosophy, Poetry, Catholicism, Theology
TOTAL PUBLISHED: 150 print; 30 audio

Sogang University Press

One Sinsoo-Dong, Mapo-gu, Seoul 121742, South Korea
PHONE: +82 (2) 7150141, 7150147
FAX: +82 (2) 7018962
TITLE: President
CONTACT: Hong Park
SUBJECTS: History, Language Arts, Linguistics, Literature, Literary Criticism, Essays, Science (General), Social Sciences

Suhagsa

1586-4 Seocho 3-Dong, Seocho-ku, Seoul 137073, South Korea
PHONE: +82 (2) 5844642
FAX: +82 (2) 5844642
TITLE: President
CONTACT: Youn-Ho Lee
SUBJECTS: Fashion, Health, Nutrition, House & Home
TOTAL PUBLISHED: 143 print

Woong Jin Publishing Co. Ltd.

Dongweon Bldg., Ineui-Dong 112-1, Jongro-gu, Seoul 110717, South Korea
PHONE: +82 (2) 7427941

FAX: +82 (2) 7441904
E-MAIL: wjmap@chollian.dacom.co.kr
TITLE: Foreign Rights Manager
CONTACT: Seang-Ju Hong
SUBJECTS: Business, Education, English as a Second Language, How-To, Literature, Literary Criticism, Essays, Mysteries, Nonfiction (General), Romance, Travel

Woongjin Media Corporation

28-9 Inevi-dong, Jongro-gu, Seoul 110410, South Korea
PHONE: +82 (2) 745-6712
FAX: +82 (2) 7450777
E-MAIL: wjmhky@woongjin.co.kr
TITLE: Man. Director
CONTACT: Heungsung Lee
SUBJECTS: Business, Fiction, History, Nonfiction (General), Science (General)

Yonsei University Press

134 Sinchon-dong, Seodaemun-gu, Seoul 120749, South Korea
PHONE: +82 (2) 3926201
FAX: +82 (2) 3931421
E-MAIL: ysup@bubble.yonsei.ac.kr
TITLE: Director
CONTACT: Suk-Hyun Kim
SUBJECTS: Art, History, Medicine, Nursing, Dentistry, Philosophy, Religion, Science (General), Social Sciences, Technology

RELIGIOUS ORGANIZATIONS

Buddhist

Bulguksa Temple
#15 Chinhyon-dong, Kyongja, Kyongsangbuk-do, Korea
WEBSITE: http://www.bulguksa.or.kr/bulguksa/html_english/2.htm

Chikchisa Temple at Mt. Whangak
216 Unsoodong, Daehangmyun, Kimchonsi, Kyongbuk 741-810, Korea
WEBSITE: http://www.chikchisa.or.kr/change.htm

Korean United Buddhist Association
46-19, Soosong-dong, Chongno-ku, Seoul 110-140, South Korea
PHONE: +82 (2) 7324885
TITLE: President
NAME: Song Wol-Joo

Korean Buddhist Chogye Order
45 Kyunji-dong, Chongno-ku, Seoul, South Korea 110-170
PHONE: +82 (2) 7355864
FAX: +82 (2) 7350614
E-MAIL: 1994071103@buddhism.or.kr
WEBSITE: www.buddhism.or.kr
TITLE: President
NAME: Jong Dae

Lotus Lantern International Buddhist Centre
148-5, Sokyok-dong, Chongno-ku, Seoul 110-200, South Korea
PHONE: +82 (2) 7255347
FAX: +82 (2) 7207849
E-MAIL: buddha@uriel.net
WEBSITE: http://www.buddhapia.com/mem/lotus/index.html

The Research Institute of Tripitaka Koreana
683-139 hannam2-dong youngsan-Guadalcanal Seoul, Korea 140-212
PHONE: +82 (2) 7970585
FAX: +82 (2) 7930581
E-MAIL: hederein@nuri.net
WEBSITE: http://members.iworld.net/hederein/indexeng.html

Seoul International Zen Center
487 Suyu 1 Dong, Kangbuk, Gu, Seoul, Korea 142-071
PHONE: +82 (2) 9004326
FAX: +82 (2) 9955770
E-MAIL: sizc@bora.dacom.co.kr

Songkwang-sa Temple
12 Shin pyong-ri Song Kwang-myun Sunchon-si Chonnam/540-930 Korea
PHONE: +82 06617550107-9
FAX: +82 06617550408
E-MAIL: songkwanh@www.buddhism.or.kr
WEBSITE: http://temple.buddhism.or.kr/songkwang/eng01/eng-main.html

Vipassana Korea Centre
277-39 Hing Eun 3 Dong, Soedae Moonku, Seoul 120-100
TITLE: Teacher
NAME: Bhante Cho Amarayano

Catholic

Catholic Bishops' Conference of Korea
PHONE: +82 (2) 4607500
FAX: +82 (2) 4607688
WEBSITE: http://www.cbck.or.kr/

Islamic

Ali Mola Org
Pupyung ku, Shipjung 2 dong 578-7, Inchon City, Inchon, South Korea
PHONE: +82 114175319
E-MAIL: alishahbaba@yahoo.com
NAME: Naveed Shah

Jewish

South Post Chapel
Yongsan Military Reservation, Seoul, South Korea
PHONE: +82 (2)7239915
NAME: Larry Rosenberg

Orthodox

Korean Orthodox Mission
301 Ga-ondg, Ehwa-villa, 615 Banghak 2-ondg, Seoul, Dobong 132-022, Korea
PHONE: +82 (2) 34930048
E-MAIL: fr.justin.kang@rocor,org.au
TITLE: Priest
NAME: Justin Kang

Protestant

Adventist Chaplaincy Ministries
International Serviceman's Center, 66 Hoegi Dong, PO Box 110 Chung Ryand, Seoul 130-650, Korea
PHONE: +82 (2) 9646124
E-MAIL: Adventistchaplains@compuserve.com
WEBSITE: http://www/tagnet/org/nso/
TITLE: Director
NAME: Richard O. Stenbakken

National Council of Churches in Korea
Christian Bldg., Rm. 706, 136-46, Yonchi-dong, Chongno-ku, Seoul 110, Republic of Korea
PHONE: +82 (2) 7638427
NAME: Rev. Oh Chung-Il

The Salvation Army
Central PO Box 1192, Seoul, 100-611, South Korea
PHONE: +82 (2) 7321402
FAX: +82 (2) 7200496
E-MAIL: korea@salvationarmy.org
WEBSITE: http://soback.kornet21.net/~sally

Seventh day Adventist Dangei Church
Kang Won-Do Won Ju-Si Dangei-Dong 820-13, Korea
PHONE: +82 (371) 433784
E-MAIL: eckc023@syu.ac.kr
WEBSITE: http://user.chollian.net/~sdakorea/

FURTHER READING

Articles

French, Howard W. "North Korea Shyly Courts Capitalism." *New York Times,* April 30, 2000, p. A6.

———. "South Korean President Wins Nobel Peace Prize for Efforts to Heal Rift." *New York Times,* October 14, 2000, p. A5.

"The Month in Review: January 2000." *Current History,* March 2000, p. 141.

Sims, Calvin. "2 Koreas Finish Deal to Reunite Families." *New York Times,* July 1, 2000, p. A5.

Books

Duncan, John B. *The Origins of the Choson Dynasty.* Seattle: University of Washington Press, 2000.

Kim, Samuel S., ed. *Korea's Globalization.* New York: Cambridge University Press, 2000.

Noland, Marcus. *Avoiding the Apocalypse: The Future of the Two Koreas.* Washington, DC: Institute for International Economics, 2000.

Pai, Hyung Il. *Constructing "Korean" Origins: A Critical Review of Archaeology, Historiography, and Racial Myth in Korean State-Formation Theories.* Cambridge, MA: Harvard University Asia Center, 2000.

Portal, Jane. *Korea: Art and Archaeology.* New York: Thames & Hudson, 2000

SOUTH KOREA: STATISTICAL DATA

For sources and notes see "Sources of Statistics" at the front of each volume.

GEOGRAPHY

Geography

Area:

Total: 98,480 sq km.

Land: 98,190 sq km.

Land boundaries:

Total: 238 km.

Border countries: North Korea 238 km.

Coastline: 2,413 km.

Climate: temperate, with rainfall heavier in summer than winter.

Terrain: mostly hills and mountains; wide coastal plains in west and south.

Natural resources: coal, tungsten, graphite, molybdenum, lead, hydropower potential.

Land use:

Arable land: 19%

Permanent crops: 2%

Permanent pastures: 1%

Forests and woodland: 65%

Other: 13% (1993 est.).

HUMAN FACTORS

Demographics (A)

	1990	1995	1998	2000	2010	2020	2030	2040	2050
Population	42,869	45,175	46,573	47,471	51,097	52,978	53,763	53,157	51,148
Life expectancy - males	67.2	69.6	70.3	70.8	73.0	74.9	76.4	77.7	78.7
Life expectancy - females	75.6	77.7	78.2	78.5	80.6	82.3	83.6	84.7	85.5
Birth rate (per 1,000)	15.3	16.0	15.5	15.1	12.2	10.6	10.3	9.4	9.1
Death rate (per 1,000)	5.8	5.5	5.7	5.8	6.8	8.2	9.9	12.1	13.7
Women of reproductive age (15-49 yrs.)	12,115	12,892	13,285	13,478	13,138	12,296	11,205	10,533	9,884
Fertility rate	1.6	1.7	1.7	1.7	1.7	1.7	1.7	1.7	1.7

Except as noted, values for vital statistics are in thousands; life expectancy is in years.

Health Personnel

	National Data	World Data (wtd ave)
Total health expenditure as a percentage of GDP, 1990-1998[a]		
Public sector	2.5	2.5
Private sector	3.0	2.9
Total[b]	5.6	5.5
Health expenditure per capita in U.S. dollars, 1990-1998[a]		
Purchasing power parity	824	561
Total	578	483
Availability of health care facilities per 100,000 people		
Hospital beds 1990-1998[a]	460	330
Doctors 1992-1995[a]	127	122
Nurses 1992-1995[a]	232	248

Health Indicators

	National Data	World Data
Life expectancy at birth (years)		
1980	67	61
1998	73	67
Daily per capita supply of calories		
1970	2,786	2,358
1997	3,155	2,791
Daily per capital supply of protein		
1997 (grams)	86	74
Total fertility rate (births per woman)		
1980	2.6	3.7
1998	1.6	2.7
Population with access (%)		
To safe water (1990-96)	83	NA
To sanitation (1990-96)	100	NA
People living with (1997)		
Tuberculosis (cases per 100,000)	57.3	60.4
Malaria (cases per 100,000)	3.8	42.2
HIV/AIDS (% aged 15 - 49 years)	0.01	0.99

Infants and Malnutrition

	National Data	World Data (wtd ave)
Under 5 mortality rate (1989)	5	NA
% of infants with low birthweight (1992-98)[1]	4	17
Births attended by skilled health staff (% of total births 1996-98)	98	52
% fully immunized at 1 year of age (1995-98)[1]		
TB	75	82
DPT	74	77
Polio	71	77
Measles	85	74
Prevalence of child malnutrition (1992-98)[1] (based on weight for age, % of children under 5 years)	NA	30

Ethnic Division

Homogeneous (except for about 20,000 Chinese).

Religion

Christian 49%

Buddhist 47%

Confucianist 3%

Shamanist, Chondogyo (Religion of the Heavenly Way), and other 1%

Major Languages

Korean, English widely taught in junior high and high school.

EDUCATION

Public Education Expenditures

	1980	1997
Public expenditures on education as % of GNP	3.7	3.7
Expenditures per student as % of GNP per capita		
Primary	10.6[2]	18.8
Secondary	9.3	12.9
Tertiary	16.1	6.0
Teachers' compensation as % of total current education expenditures	69.2	NA
Pupils per teacher at the primary level	NA	31
Duration of primary education in years	NA	9
World data for comparison		
Public expenditures on education as % of GNP (mean)	3.9	4.8
Pupils per teacher at the primary level (wtd ave)	NA	33
Duration of primary education in years (mean)	NA	9

Educational Attainment (A)

Age group (1995)	25+
Population of this age group	26,217,862
Highest level attained (%)	
No schooling	8.7
First level	
Not completed	0.9
Completed	17.3
Entered second level	
Lower Secondary	15.7
Upper Secondary	36.2
Entered post-secondary	21.1

Literacy Rates (A)

In thousands and percent	1990	1995	2000	2010
Illiterate population (15+ yrs.)	937	697	493	224
Literacy rate - total adult pop. (%)	97.1	98.0	98.7	99.4
Literacy rate - males (%)	99.0	99.3	99.5	99.7
Literacy rate - females (%)	95.2	96.7	97.9	99.2

(Continued on next page.)

GOVERNMENT & LAW

Military Affairs (A)

	1990	1992	1995	1996	1997
Military expenditures					
Current dollars (mil.)	9,720	10,500	12,000	14,000	15,000
1997 constant dollars (mil.)	11,400	11,700	12,400	14,300	15,000
Armed forces (000)	650	750	750	670	670
Gross national product (GNP)					
Current dollars (bil.)	233	282	377	410	437
1997 constant dollars (bil.)	273	313	390	417	437
Central government expenditures (CGE)					
1997 constant dollars (bil.)	51	59	79	90	103
People (mil.)	42.9	43.7	45.0	45.5	45.9
Military expenditure as % of GNP	4.2	3.7	3.2	3.4	3.4
World data on military expenditure as % of GNP	4.5	3.4	2.7	2.6	2.6
Military expenditure as % of CGE	22.3	19.8	15.6	15.8	14.6
World data on military expenditure as % of CGE	17.0	12.5	10.5	10.3	10.2
Military expenditure per capita (1997 $)	266	268	276	314	327
World data on military expenditure per capita (1997 $)	242	173	146	143	145
Armed forces per 1,000 people (soldiers)	15.2	17.2	16.7	14.7	14.6
World data on armed forces per 1,000 people (soldiers)	5.3	4.5	4.1	3.9	3.8
GNP per capita (1997 $)	6,370	7,160	8,670	9,160	9,520
Arms imports[6]					
Current dollars (mil.)	950	1,200	1,900	1,300	1,100
1997 constant dollars (mil.)	1,113	1,330	1,967	1,322	1,100
Arms exports[6]					
Current dollars (mil.)	140	40	50	30	30
1997 constant dollars (mil.)	164	44	52	31	30
Total imports[7]					
Current dollars (bil.)	70	82	135	150	145
1997 constant dollars (bil.)	82	91	140	153	145
Total exports[7]					
Current dollars (bil.)	65	77	125	130	136
1997 constant dollars (bil.)	76	85	130	132	136
Arms as percent of total imports[8]	1.4	1.5	1.4	0.9	0.8
Arms as percent of total exports[8]	0.2	0.1	0	0	0

(Continued on next page.)

EDUCATION (cont.)

Libraries

National Libraries **1995**

Administrative Units 1

Service Points or Branches 2

Number of Volumes (000) 2,576

Registered Users (000) 2,158

Loans to Users (000) 5,870

Total Library Staff 266

Public Libraries **1996**

Administrative Units 304

Service Points or Branches 304

Number of Volumes (000) 13,020

Registered Users (000) 40,175

Loans to Users (000) 36,465

Total Library Staff 4,776

GOVERNMENT & LAW (cont.)

Political Parties

National Assembly (Kukhoe)	no. of seats
New Korea Party (NKP)	139
National Congress for New Politics (NCNP)	79
United Liberal Democrats (ULD)	50
Democratic Party (DP)	15
Independents	16
As of January 2000	
Grand National Party (GNP)	130
Millenium Democratic Party (MDP)	103
United Liberal Democrats (ULD)	55
Independents	11

Elections were last held 11 April 1996 (next to be held 13 April 2000). Subsequent to the legislative election of April 1996 the following parties disbanded: New Korea Party (NKP) and Democratic Party (DP). On 20 January 2000, The National Congress for New Politics (NCNP) was renamed the Millennium Democratic Party (MDP).

Government Budgets (B)

Revenues . . . . $68.9 billion

Expenditures . . . . $82.3 billion

Capital expenditures . . . . $14.5 billion

Data for 1998.

Crime

Crime volume (for 1998)

Crimes reported 633,235

Total persons convicted 552,814

Crimes per 100,000 population 1,348

Persons responsible for offenses

Total number suspects 821,361

Total number of female suspects 147,106

Total number of juvenile suspects 103,245

LABOR FORCE

Total Labor Force (A)

22 million (1998).

Labor Force by Occupation

Services and other 68%

Mining and manufacturing 20%

Agriculture, fishing, forestry 12%

Data for 1998.

Unemployment Rate

6.3% (1999 est.)

PRODUCTION SECTOR

Energy Production

Production . . . . 221.258 billion kWh

Production by source

Fossil fuel 59.56%

Hydro 1.91%

Nuclear 38.51%

Other 0.02%

Exports . . . . 0 kWh

Data for 1998.

Energy Consumption

Consumption . . . . 205.77 billion kWh

Imports . . . . 0 kWh

Data for 1998.

Transportation

Highways:

Total: 86,990 km.

Paved: 64,808 km (including 1,996 km of expressways).

Unpaved: 22,182 km (1998 est.).

Waterways: 1,609 km; use restricted to small native craft.

Pipelines: petroleum products 455 km; additionally, there is a parallel petroleum, oils, and lubricants (POL) pipeline being completed.

Merchant marine:

Total: 461 ships (1,000 GRT or over) totaling 5,093,620 GRT/8,100,634 DWT.

Ships by type: bulk 98, cargo 149, chemical tanker 39, combination bulk 4, container 53, liquified gas 13, multi-functional large load carrier 1, passenger 3, petroleum tanker 61, refrigerated cargo 26, roll-on/roll-off 4, specialized tanker 4, vehicle carrier 6 (1999 est.).

Airports: 103 (1999 est.).

Airports - with paved runways: 67.

Airports - with unpaved runways: 36.

Top Agriculture Products

Rice, root crops, barley, vegetables, fruit; cattle, pigs, chickens, milk, eggs; fish.

Top Mining Products (B)

Mineral resources include: coal, tungsten, graphite, molybdonum, lead.

MANUFACTURING SECTOR

GDP & Manufacturing Summary (A)

	1980	1985	1990	1995
GDP ($-1990 mil.)	104,146	155,956	253,672	363,191
Per capita ($-1990)	2,732	3,822	5,917	8,087
Manufacturing share (%) (current prices)	28.6	29.7	29.2	26.1[e]
Manufacturing				
Value added ($-1990 mil.)	24,133	41,035	73,967	109,785\
Industrial production index	36	60	100	152
Value added ($ mil.)	19,520	30,731	100,209	196,400[e]
Gross output ($ mil.)	59,725	88,541	250,519	448,198[e]
Employment (000)	2,015	2,395	2,958	2,985[e]
Profitability (% of gross output)				
Intermediate input (%)	67	65	60	56[e]
Wages and salaries inc. supplements (%)	10	9	11	11[e]
Gross operating surplus	23	25	29	33[e]
Productivity ($)				
Gross output per worker	29,206	36,314	82,959	146,227[e]
Value added per worker	9,545	12,604	33,184	64,077[e]
Average wage (inc. supplements)	2,837	3,476	9,353	16,435[e]
Value added ($ mil.)				
Food products	1,526	2,048	6,047	11,726[e]
Beverages	571	764	1,889	3,456[e]
Tobacco products	1,143	1,442	2,794	3,020[e]
Textiles	2,640	3,295	6,833	12,479[e]
Wearing apparel	905	1,293	3,401	6,339[e]
Leather and fur products	138	270	1,144	1,811[e]
Footwear	112	211	594	1,891[e]
Wood and wood products	239	262	876	1,774[e]
Furniture and fixtures	100	203	972	2,441[e]
Paper and paper products	426	682	2,123	4,631[e]
Printing and publishing	440	732	2,531	5,329[e]
Industrial chemicals	998	1,275	4,181	6,129[e]
Other chemical products	1,016	1,422	4,926	8,702[e]
Petroleum refineries	757	1,079	2,865	5,855[e]
Misc. petroleum and coal products	211	291	517	623[e]
Rubber products	657	910	3,036	2,033[e]
Plastic products	359	709	2,734	8,774[e]
Pottery, china and earthenware	89	107	275	500[e]
Glass and glass products	198	307	991	1,979[e]
Other non-metal mineral products	838	1,065	3,697	6,872[e]
Iron and steel	1,256	2,040	6,187	11,239[e]
Non-ferrous metals	265	335	1,201	2,203[e]
Metal products	635	1,237	5,145	11,258[e]
Non-electrical machinery	672	1,453	7,004	16,853[e]
Electrical machinery	1,587	3,621	15,066	31,789[e]
Transport equipment	1,152	2,790	10,242	22,602[e]
Prof. and scientific equipment	214	290	1,144	1,756[e]
Other manufacturing	367	598	1,769	2,335[e]

COMMUNICATIONS

Daily Newspapers

	National Data	World Data for Comparison
Daily Newspapers		
Number of Dailies	60	8,391
Total Circulation (000)	17,700	548,000
Circulation per 1,000 inhabitants	394	96

Telecommunications

Telephones - main lines in use: 23.1 million (1998).

Telephones - mobile cellular: 8.6 million (1998).

Telephone system: excellent domestic and international services.

Domestic: NA

International: fiber-optic submarine cable to China; the Russia-Korea-Japan submarine cable; satellite earth stations - 3 Intelsat (2 Pacific Ocean and 1 Indian Ocean) and 1 Inmarsat (Pacific Ocean region).

Radio broadcast stations: AM 106, FM 97, shortwave 6 (1999).

Radios: 47.5 million (1997).

Television broadcast stations: 121 (plus 850 repeater stations and the eight-channel American Forces Korea Network) (1999).

Televisions: 15.9 million (1997).

Internet Service Providers (ISPs): 11 (1999).

FINANCE, ECONOMICS, & TRADE

Economic Indicators

National product: GDP—purchasing power parity—$625.7 billion (1999 est.).

National product real growth rate: 10% (1999 est.).

National product per capita: $13,300 (1999 est.).

Inflation rate—consumer price index: 0.8% (1999 est.).

Exchange Rates

Exchange rates:

South Korean won (W) per US$1

January 2000 . . . . 1,130.32
1999 . . . . 1,188.82
1998 . . . . 1,401.44
1997 . . . . 951.29
1996 . . . . 804.45
1995 . . . . 771.27

Top Import Origins

$116 billion (c.i.f., 1999)

Origins (1998)

United States 22%
Japan 18%
China 7%
Australia 5%
Saudi Arabia 5%

Top Export Destinations

$144 billion (f.o.b., 1999)

Destinations (1998)

United States 17%
Japan 9%
China 9%
Hong Kong 7%
Taiwan 4%

Import/Export Commodities

Import Commodities	Export Commodities
Machinery	Electronic products
Electronics and electronic equipment	Machinery and equipment
Oil	Motor vehicles
Steel	Steel
Transport equipment	Ships
Textiles	Textiles
Organic chemicals	Clothing
Grains	Footwear
	Fish

Balance of Payments

	1994	1995	1996	1997	1998
Exports of goods (f.o.b.)	94,964	124,632	129,968	138,619	132,122
Imports of goods (f.o.b.)	−97,824	−129,076	−144,933	−141,798	−90,495
Trade balance	−2,860	−4,444	−14,965	−3,179	41,627
Services - debits	−18,606	−25,806	−29,592	−29,502	−23,951
Services - credits	16,805	22,827	23,412	26,301	24,580
Private transfers (net)	3,583	4,014	4,247	5,241	6,694
Government transfers (net)	−228	−259	−371	−375	−403
Overall balance	−3,867	−8,507	−23,006	−8,167	40,552

KUWAIT

CAPITAL: Kuwait (Al-Kuwayt).

FLAG: The flag, adopted in 1961, is a rectangle divided equally into green, white, and red horizontal stripes, with a black trapezoid whose longer base is against the staff and is equal to the breadth of the flag, and whose shorter base is equal to the breadth of the white stripe.

ANTHEM: National Anthem, melody only; no words.

MONETARY UNIT: The Kuwaiti dinar (KD) has 1,000 fils. There are coins of 1, 5, 10, 20, 50, and 100 fils, and notes of 250 and 500 fils and of 1, 5, 10, and 20 Kuwaiti dinars. KD1 = $3.34448 (or $1 = KD0.299).

WEIGHTS AND MEASURES: The metric system is the legal standard, but imperial weights and measures also are in use, and some U.S. measures are recognized.

HOLIDAYS: New Year's Day, 1 January; Emir's Accession Day, 25 February. Movable religious holidays include Muslim New Year (1st of Muharram); Laylat al-Miraj; Milad an-Nabi; 'Id al-Fitr; and 'Id al-'Adha'.

TIME: 3 PM = noon GMT.

LOCATION AND SIZE: Kuwait is situated at the western head of the Persian Gulf. Its area is estimated at about 17,820 square kilometers (6,880 square miles), slightly smaller than the state of New Jersey. Of the islands that form part of Kuwait, only Faylakah is inhabited. Kuwait has a total boundary length of 963 kilometers (602 miles).

Kuwait's capital, Kuwait city, is located on the Persian Gulf coast.

CLIMATE: Between November and April, the climate is pleasant, with cool nights and warm sunny days. In December and January, night temperatures occasionally reach the freezing point. Summer temperatures range from 29°C (84°F) in the morning to more than 49°C (120°F) in the shade at noon. Annual rainfall, which averages less than 10 centimeters (4 inches), comes in the form of showers or storms between October and April.

State of Kuwait
Dawlat al-Kuwayt

INTRODUCTORY SURVEY

RECENT HISTORY

At the end of the nineteenth century Sheikh Mubarak as-Sabah, fearing the territorial ambitions of the Ottoman Turks, asked to be taken under British protection. The British were concerned also by the activities of Russia and Germany in the area. In 1899 Sheikh Mubarak agreed not to open any of his territory to foreign control. In return the British offered their services as well as an annual subsidy to support the sheikh and his heirs.

In June 1961 the protective treaty with the United Kingdom was terminated by mutual consent, and Kuwait declared itself fully independent. By this time the sheikhdom had already become a major oil producer. Iraq refused to recognize Kuwait's independence asserting it had inherited the Ottoman claim to the territory. Baghdad's threat of an invasion was foiled by British troops and later by the support of the Arab League. Iraq then appeared to agree to Kuwait's sovereignty, although border issues were never definitely resolved. During the next two decades Kuwait succeeded in establishing an open and prosperous economy, based in large part on foreign, especially Palestinian and Egyptian, labor.

During the Iran-Iraq War (1980-1988), Kuwait, although technically neutral, provided important aid to Baghdad, including shipment of goods and over $6 billion in loans. In 1987 Iranian attacks on Persian Gulf shipping led Kuwait to request U.S. protection for its supertankers.

With the end of the war Iraq-Kuwait relations were stable until 1990 when Saddam Hussein, president of Iraq, accused his neighbor of illegally pumping oil from the shared Rumailia field. On August 2, 1990, Iraqi forces invaded Kuwait asserting that they were rightfully reclaiming their own territory. Kuwaiti defense forces offered little resistance and most senior officials fled the country.

The United States led an international coalition of Arab and other nations to demand the withdrawal of Iraqi forces. After a lengthy buildup of forces Iraq was assaulted by massive air and land forces; after six weeks its defenses collapsed and Kuwait was liberated in February 1991. Kuwait's leaders returned to find a hostile population that resented their abandonment and demanded greater political participation. Enormous physical damage had been inflicted on the country, including over 700 oil well fires that did serious ecological damage before being extinguished after almost nine months' effort.

The regime and many Kuwaitis turned harshly against those suspected of collaboration with Iraq, and many from the large Palestinian community were ejected from the country. Relations with Iraq remained tense. Kuwait's vulnerability to possible attack from Iraq or Iran drew the nation closer to the United States, which has been willing to offer enhanced security collaboration.

In October 1994 Iraq began moving 60,000 troops to within thirty-two kilometers (twenty miles) of the Kuwaiti border. The United Nations Security Council condemned Iraq's actions. Kuwait then agreed to let the United States station a squadron of warplanes there. On November 10, 1994, Iraq agreed to recognize the independence and borders of Kuwait. The United Nations renewed its multinational force of border observers to oversee the demilitarized zone that separates Kuwait from Iraq. As of 2000 the border area remained tense.

Political matters awaiting parliamentary consideration included a controversial decree by the amir that would allow women to vote and run for office by the next election, scheduled for 2003.

GOVERNMENT

Kuwait is an independent, sovereign Arab state, under a constitutional monarch, the amir. Executive power is vested in the amir, who exercises it through a prime minister and Council of Ministers. The amir appoints the prime minister and deputy prime ministers. The prime minister in consultation with the amir appoints the council members. The legislative branch, the National Assembly (*Majlis*), consists of fifty elected representatives and twenty-five appointed members. Suffrage extends to only 10 percent of the population.

Judiciary

A Tribunal of First Instance has jurisdiction over matters involving personal status, civil and commercial cases, and criminal cases, except those of a religious nature. The Court of Appeals, the highest in the land, has jurisdiction over appeals involving personal status and civil cases, as well as those involving commercial and criminal cases. Ordinary criminal cases may be appealed to the High Court of Appeals. State security court decisions may be appealed to the Court of Cassation. A military court handles offenses committed by members of the security forces. Religious courts, Sunni and Shi'ite, decide family law matters according to Muslim law.

Political Parties

Political parties are prohibited but opposition groups are active in the nation's political life. Muslim fundamentalists held seventeen of fifty seats in the National Assembly in 1996.

DEFENSE

Kuwait's rebuilt armed forces totaled 15,300 volunteers in 2000. The army had 11,000 men and 200 tanks; the air force, 2,500 men and seventy-six combat aircrafts; and the navy, 1,800 men and two patrol crafts. There is a 5,000-member National Guard. United Nations observers and advisors number 149. Estimated defense expenditures in 1998-1999 were $2.7 billion, or 2.7 percent of GDP.

ECONOMIC AFFAIRS

The Kuwaiti standard of living was among the highest in the Middle East and in the world by the early 1980s. The government has used its oil revenues to build ports, roads, an international airport, a seawater distillation plant, and modern government and office buildings. Oil extraction and processing accounts for about 50 percent of GDP, 90 percent of export earnings, and 75 percent of government revenues.

Kuwait's economy suffered enormously from the effects of the Gulf War and the Iraqi occupation that ended in February 1991 with the destruction of much of Kuwait's oil production capacity and other economic infrastructure. The damage inflicted on the economy is estimated at $20 billion. After the war the gross domestic product (GDP) increased by 22.4 percent in 1993, 1.3 percent in 1994, and 2.9 percent in 1995. Although lower oil prices caused a decline in the GDP for 1998, by 1999 prices rebounded and helped reduce the budget deficit from $5.5 billion to $3 billion in 1999. Oil prices were expected to remain strong throughout 2000.

Public Finance

The U.S. Central Intelligence Agency estimated that in 1999 government revenues totaled approximately $10 billion and expenditures $13 billion. Much of the recent improvement in public finances is the result of higher oil prices and production rather than government reforms. In 1994 the Kuwaiti government began to consider various austerity measures, which became a source of debate in parliament. Several plans in discussion call for reductions in government subsidies and welfare benefits, increases in taxes, privatization of state-owned businesses, and banking sector reforms. Subsidies are one of the most contentious and politicized austerity measures; in 1995 the Ministry of Finance stated that the country annually spends $1.8 billion on utility subsidies and free health care. The Kuwaiti cabinet passed a reform package in 1999 including a reduction in subsidies and increasing taxes on luxury goods.

Income

In 1999 the gross domestic product (GDP) was $44.8 billion or about $22,500 per capita. The real growth rate estimated for the GDP in 1999 was 1.1 percent and inflation 2 percent. The 1996 GDP contribution by sector was agriculture 0 percent, industry 55 percent, and services 45 percent.

Industry

Although oil extraction continues to be the economic mainstay, Kuwait has diversified its industry to give manufacturing a larger role. Small-scale manufacturing plants produce ammonia, fertilizer, paper products, processed foods, and other consumer goods. Major refinery products were fuel oil, gas oil, naphtha, kerosene, and diesel fuel. Industrial products include desalinated water, chemical detergents, chlorine, caustic soda, urea, concrete pipes, soap, cleansers, asbestos, and bricks. The construction industry is highly developed.

Banking and Finance

The Central Bank of Kuwait, established in 1969, formulates and implements the nation's monetary policy, regulates the currency, and controls the banking system. There are seven commercial banks with ninety-six branches in Kuwait, of which one is a single-branch operation belonging to a joint-venture bank (the Bank of Bahrain and Kuwait). Apart from this special case, foreign banks are not permitted to operate within Kuwait or to own shares in Kuwaiti banks. Kuwaiti bank shares are typically closely held, either by the government and its agencies or by the merchant families who founded them. The pre-eminent bank is the National Bank of Kuwait that at the end of 1995 accounted for one-third of all Kuwaiti bank branches.

There are three specialized banks, one of which, Kuwait Finance House, operates as a commercial bank restricted to Islamic financial transactions. The other two, Industrial Bank of Kuwait and Kuwait Real Estate Bank, were created to provide long-term credit and function like a U.S. investment bank. The idea of establishing more Islamic banks has been welcomed.

Kuwait's official securities exchange, the Kuwait Stock Exchange (KSE), was founded in 1977 and handles only government bonds and securities of Kuwaiti companies. All trading operations of the KSE were suspended with the Iraqi invasion of Kuwait in August 1990. The KSE recommenced trading in September 1992. On the exchange 1995 was a banner year. The combined effect of rapidly expanding credit and privatization resulted in a 36 percent increase in the stock price index and a 226 percent increase in trading volume.

Economic Development

Since the mid-1970s, Kuwait has restrained its spending on economic development and has fostered a policy of controlled growth. From 1977 to 1982, allocations for development projects remained steady at $1.7-2.5 billion annually, of which 76 percent was spent on public works, electric power plants, and desalination and irrigation projects. Development plans for the 1980s, stressing industrial diversification, included the expansion of local oil refineries and major projects in petrochemicals, electricity, water supply, highway construction, and telecommunications. Overseas, refining and marketing operations were stepped up.

Post-war economic planning was hampered by the expulsion of the mainly Palestinian middle-ranking civil servants in various government departments. The Industrial Bank of Kuwait has played a major role in the industrial redevelopment of the emirate following the war. In 1994 the World Bank urged Kuwait to begin privatization (including the oil industry). The Kuwait Investment Authority sold nearly $1 billion of its foreign assets in 1995. In March 1996 Kuwait National Petroleum Co. announced that it would sell off one-third of its 90 gasoline stations as a preliminary move in divesting 80 percent of its retail assets.

In December 1961 Kuwait established the Kuwait Fund for Arab Economic Development, patterned after Western and international lending agencies, to issue loans at low rates of interest for Arab economic development. By the end of 1985 Kuwait had extended loans to developing countries amounting to $4.3 billion. The Kuwait-based Arab Fund for Economic and Social Development also has contributed to various development institutions. However in 1990 the AFESD transferred its operations to Bahrain. Since Iraq's invasion most of Kuwait's aid commitments have taken the form of government-to-government agreements. Within the Arab world the overwhelming share of Kuwaiti aid goes to Egypt and Syria.

SOCIAL WELFARE

Kuwait has a widespread system of social welfare, financed by government oil revenues. It offers welfare services for the poor, provides free medical service and education to all residents, and spends heavily for waterworks, public gardens, and other public facilities. Social insurance legislation provides for old age, disability, and survivor pensions.

Women are denied equal rights and legal protection under Kuwaiti law. They are not permitted to vote. The government began a counseling service in 1995 for women suffering from male violence.

Abusive treatment of foreign domestic servants is also an ongoing social problem. Bedouins (Bedu) are not entitled to citizenship and are unable to legally work or enroll their children in schools.

Healthcare

Kuwait has a highly advanced public health service that is extended to all Kuwait residents, citizens and non-citizens alike. Between 1990 and 1995 7 percent of GDP went to healthcare services. In 2000 life expectancy was seventy-six years. In 1993 100 percent of the population had access to health care services. In 1999 100 percent of the population had access to safe water and adequate sanitation.

Housing

According to the 1995 census there were 251,682 dwellings in Kuwait. About 50 percent of all housing units were apartments, 19 percent detached homes, 15 percent traditional dwellings (mostly small cottages and mud huts), 10 percent annexes, and 4 percent shacks.

EDUCATION

Kuwait offers its students free education, including free food, clothing, books, stationery, and transportation, from kindergarten through the fourth year of college. In 1998 142,308 students were enrolled in primary school and 224,293 in secondary schools.

In 1995 Kuwait University had a student enrollment of 12,712. The estimated literacy rate in 1995 was 78.6 percent (male 82.2 percent and female 74.9 percent).

2000 KEY EVENTS TIMELINE

January

- Colonel Alaa Hussein Ali, who headed the government installed by Iran after its invasion of Kuwait in 1990, is arrested in Kuwait when he arrives on a flight from Norway.

May

- Kuwait is alarmed by Iranian gas drilling in the Dorra field, an offshore area east of the Saudi Arabia-Kuwait Neutral Zone. Iran's actions in an area near Iran, but still undelineated between Saudi Arabia and Kuwait, raises memories of the Iraqi occupation of Kuwait and other sensitive unresolved border disputes in the region.

June

- Kuwaiti and Saudi officials meet to discuss the maritime borders disputed with Iran in the Dorra offshore gas field. The talks will continue.
- A decision over Kuwait's claim of reparations for US$21.5 billion in damages for oil destroyed by Iraq is delayed by the UN Compensation Commission.

July

- Elections to the fifty-seat assembly turned out almost 80 percent of the eligible voters—men over twenty-one years of age among Kuwaiti nationals. Members of the armed forces and Kuwaitis naturalized after 1966, and women are excluded from voting. Women will be allowed to vote and run for office in 2003.
- The Kuwaiti foreign minister rules out setting up political parties. Comparing society to a single family, he believes that political parties would disrupt that unity.

August

- Ten years after the Iraqi invasion of Kuwait (August 2, 1990), Kuwaitis struggle with Kuwait's identity. Islamic conservatives and tribal traditionalists are critical of the increasing influence of the United States as a force for Westernization. Kuwait's security is maintained by the U.S. military presence. However, Kuwait's financial recovery is bolstered by its petroleum reserves. Psychological counseling remains available for the almost 2,000 new cases a year who suffer from post-traumatic stress.

September

- Iraq accuses Kuwait on September 19 of stealing at least 300,000 barrels of oil a day from oilfields at the border.
- The Gulf Co-operation Council (GCC)—made up of Kuwait, Bahrain, Oman, Qatar, Saudi Arabia and the United Arab Emirates (UAE)—meets to study Qatar's suggestion to lift sanctions imposed on Iraq for its invasion of Kuwait.
- Kuwait wins a Bronze Medal in the Olympics 2000 in the shooting category for the men's double trap event.

October

- Thousands of U.S. troops in Kuwait are ordered October 31 to upgrade security measures following the bombing of the U.S.S. *Cole.*
- Kuwait and Iran agree to coordinate efforts in the fight against drug trafficking and organized crime. Iran faces a very real threat from drugs produced in neighboring Afghanistan.
- Five Palestinians wounded in clashes with Israeli troops arrive in Kuwait for treatment. Their ages range from fifteen to thirty-eight and all have serious injuries. Kuwait invests in a fund, Al-Aqsa Fund, to assist them.

November

- Kuwait seizes an Iranian ship suspected of smuggling a cargo of Iraqi dates on November 22; the smugglers are arrested for breaking U.N. sanctions.
- Kuwait lifts its ban on the recruitment of labor from Bangladesh.
- Kuwait announces the arrest of three of its nationals alleged to be linked with the Islamist dissident Osama Bin Laden. A fourth suspect is said to still be at large. The seizure of a cache of explosives—293 pounds of powerful explosives, 5 hand grenades, and about 1,450 detonators—linked with the suspects is also announced.

December

- The Japanese-Kuwaiti Friendship Society is inaugurated in Japan.
- After 3,784 days, over 600 Kuwaiti and other nationals are still held in Iraqi detention camps. Iraq refuses to disclose details about these POWs who were snatched by the invading Iraqi forces on August 2, 1990.

ANALYSIS OF EVENTS: 2000

BUSINESS AND THE ECONOMY

Privatization was the key concern of Kuwait's economic planning and policies in 2000. Privatization of the oil sector was to occur only if it did not jeopardize the presence of a national work force.

A major work force issue surrounded a "freeze" the Kuwaiti government placed on Bangladesh labor. Kuwait's strong Bangladeshi community numbered about 200,000 in addition to nearly 5,000 strong Bangladeshi troops stationed in Kuwait who were deployed for mine-clearing and other missions in Kuwait since the 1991 Gulf War. The ban, which was lifted in November, had been instituted in 1999 after a Bangladeshi worker strangled his ninety-year-old employer, stole his money, and fled home to Bangladesh. He was awaiting trial in Bangladesh, but Kuwait did not have an extradition treaty with Bangladesh.

Another immigration issue related to the Bedouin peoples numbering over 100,000 in Kuwait. In May the Kuwaiti parliament approved a law to grant citizenship to 2,000 adults and their families each year. The law cleared the way for some 35,000 Bedouins to qualify for Kuwaiti citizenship, which would be granted only after exhaustive tests. In October the Kuwaiti government provisionally agreed to grant citizenship to a thousand stateless Bedouins and their families.

In September the United Nations (U.N.) Security Council approved a claim for $15.9 billion compensation made against Iraq by Kuwait. The Kuwait Petroleum Corporation instituted the claim for lost oil production during Iraq's August 1990 invasion and its seven-month occupation of the emirate. Iraq has only been able to sell oil legally through the U.N.'s "oil-for-food" program. The UN Compensation Commission adopted a 25 percent compensation figure allowing Iraq to pay off the Kuwaiti claim and others over a longer period of time.

GOVERNMENT AND POLITICS

In 1990 Iraq invaded Kuwait. The U.N. passed a resolution to eject Iraq. In 1991 in the Second Gulf War, Iraq invaded Kuwait again. A U.N. coalition of forces was assembled and the bombing of Iraq started in Operation Desert Storm. Within a month Iraqi forces retreated from Kuwait.

Ten years after Kuwait was invaded private and public places have been re-built or renovated. The more than 600 Kuwaiti oil wells that were torched were repaired and were productive again. Although Kuwait's infrastructure was renovated the Kuwaiti people still suffer from invasion trauma—depression, anxiety attacks, drug and alcohol abuse, and other symptoms of post-traumatic stress disorder. There was an increasing incidence of behavioral problems among young people that was attributed to the effects of torture and imprisonment (experiencing it, or observing it). Kuwaiti still expressed fear of Iraq and some are still awaiting news of their "Missing" loved ones. The political and economic devastation of this internecine warfare has become social and extended intergenerationally.

Heightened security was a major government concern. Kuwait increased its surveillance and security against smuggling of drugs and organized crime. In 2000 Kuwait reported the arrests of an estimated fourteen hundred smugglers and addicts, including eight hundred Kuwaitis. In 2000 Kuwait seized twenty-five ships that were smuggling oil and other products out of Iraq. These vessels broke the comprehensive economic sanctions imposed by the United Nations when Iraq invaded Kuwait in 1990. The goods were sold at auction and the crewmembers were detained, fined and deported to their home countries. An example of one of these seizures occurred in December. Kuwait seized five ships on suspicion of breaking the economic embargo against Iraq. The fifty-one crewmembers among the ships were arrested. The cargo (520 goats, 402 sheep, 872 tons of Iraqi dates, and an unspecified amount of lentils) was auctioned off. Kuwait also announced the seizure of explosives and the arrest of three of its nationals alleged to be linked with the Islamist dissident Osama bin Laden. In the desert Kuwaiti authorities uncovered a large arms cache, including missiles, explosives, and mines.

CULTURE AND SOCIETY

The government reinforced the conservative and traditional aspects of Kuwaiti society. A conservative Kuwaiti parliamentarian urged Kuwaiti national television to take certain women's events at the Olympics in Sydney, Australia, off the air as "too sexy." Western standards of modesty did not provide the protection that Islam provides for a woman's body. His complaint included events such as women's beach volleyball, diving, and synchronized swimming. In his view the Olympics was more about sex than sport. He has also campaigned against music concerts, Valentine's Day, and Kuwait's annual shopping festival. Music concerts in Kuwait attended by men and women were banned after one of his campaigns. This same parliamentarian criticized a British Broadcasting Corporation (BBC) radio broadcast about extramarital affairs. The BBC defended the program as part of a series on sex and reproductive health.

DIRECTORY

CENTRAL GOVERNMENT

Head of State

Amir
Jabir al-Ahmad al-Jabir al-Sabah, Monarch

Crown Prince and Prime Minister
Sheikh Saad al-Abdullah al-Salem al-Sabah, Office of the Prime Minister, Amir Sheikh, Amiri Diwan, P.O. Box 799, 13008 Safat, Kuwait
PHONE: +965 5398888
FAX: +965 5393069

Ministers

Minister of Foreign Affairs
Sabah al-Ahmed al-Jaber al-Sabah, Ministry of Foreign Affairs, P.O. Box 3, Safat 13001, Kuwait
PHONE: +965 2425141
FAX: +965 2412169

Minister of Defense
Sheikh Salem al-Sabah, P.O. Box 1170, Safat 13012, Kuwait
PHONE: +965 48483009
FAX: +965 4837244

Minister of Cabinet Affairs
Muhammad Dayfallah al-Sharar, Ministry of Cabinet Affairs

Minister of Finance and Communication
Sheik Ahmed Abdallah al-Ahmed al-Sabah, Ministry of Finance and Communication

Minister of Justice
Saad Jassem Youssef al-Hashel, Ministry of Justice, Ministries Complex, Block 4, Safat, Kuwait
PHONE: +965 2486232
FAX: +965 2460290
E-MAIL: webmaster@mail.moj.gov.kw

Minister of Information
Saad Muhammad al-Tiflah, Ministry of Information, P.O. Box 193, Safat 13002, Kuwait
PHONE: +965 2415301
FAX: +965 2419642

Minister of Oil
Saud Nasser al-Sabah, Ministry of Oil

Minister of Foreign Affairs
Suleiman Majed al-Shaheen, Ministry of Foreign Affairs

Minister of State Housing Affairs and Minister of Awqaf and Islamic Affairs
Adel Khaled al-Sebeih, Ministry of State Housing Affairs and Ministry of Awqaf and Islamic Affairs

Minister of Trade and Industry and Minister of Labour and Societal Affairs
Abdel Wahab Mohammed al-Wazzan, Ministry of Trade and Industry and Ministry of Labour and Societal Affairs, P.O. Box 2944, Safat 13030, Kuwait
PHONE: +965 2463600
FAX: +965 2436832; 2411089

Minister of Public Works
Eid Hathal Saud al-Rashidi, Ministry of Public Works

Minister of Planning and Administrative Development Affairs
Mohammed Bteihan al-Dweihees, Ministry of Planning and Administrative Development Affairs

Minister of Health
Mohammed Ahmed al-Jarallah, Ministry of Health

Minister of the Interior
Sheik Mohammed Khaled al-Hamad al-Sabah, Ministry of the Interior

Minister of Education and Higher Education
Youssef Hamad al-Ibrahim, P.O. Box 7, Safat 13001, Kuwait
PHONE: +965 4836800
FAX: +965 4837829

POLITICAL ORGANIZATIONS

None.

DIPLOMATIC REPRESENTATION

Embassies in Kuwait

Austria
P.O. Box 33259, Rawdha 73453, Kuwait
PHONE: +965 2552532; 2532761
FAX: +965 2563052

Brazil
P.O. Box 21370, Safat 13074, Kuwait
PHONE: +965 2561029
FAX: +965 2562153

Canada
P.O. Box 25281, Safat 13113, Kuwait
PHONE: +965 2563025; 2561456
FAX: +965 2564167

China
P.O. Box 2346, Safat 13024, Kuwait
PHONE: +965 5333340
FAX: +965 5333341

France
P.O. Box 1037, Safat 13011, Kuwait
PHONE: +965 2571062
FAX: +965 2571058

Germany
P.O. Box 805, Safat 13009, Kuwait
PHONE: +965 2520857
FAX: +965 2520763

India
P.O. Box 1450, Safat 13015, Kuwait
PHONE: +965 2530600
FAX: +965 2525811

Italy
P.O. Box 4453, Safat 13043, Kuwait
PHONE: +965 4817400
FAX: +965 4817244

Japan
P.O. Box 2304, Safat 13024, Kuwait
PHONE: +965 5312870
FAX: +965 5326168

Russia
P.O. Box 1765, Safat 13018, Kuwait
PHONE: +965 2560427
FAX: +965 2524969

Spain
P.O. Box 22207, Safat 13083, Kuwait
PHONE: +965 5325827
FAX: +965 5325826

Turkey
P.O. Box 20627, Safat 13067, Kuwait
PHONE: +965 2531785; 2531466
FAX: +965 2560673

United Kingdom
P.O. Box 2, Safat 13001, Kuwait
PHONE: +965 2403336
FAX: +965 2407395; 2426799

United States
P.O. Box 77, Safat 13001, Kuwait
PHONE: +965 2424151
FAX: +965 2442855

JUDICIAL SYSTEM

High Court of Appeal

BROADCAST MEDIA

Radio Kuwait

E-MAIL: radiokuwait@radiokuwait.org
WEBSITE: http://www.radiokuwait.org/

Radio of the State of Kuwait

PO Box 397, Safat 13004, Kuwait
PHONE: +965 2423774
FAX: +965 2456660
E-MAIL: kwtfreq@ncc.moc.kw
WEBSITE: http://www.radiokuwait.org
TITLE: Minister
CONTACT: Saud Nasir Al-Saud Al-Sabah
LANGUAGE: Arabic, English
TYPE: Government

Voice of America Relay Station

330 Independence Avenue, SW, Washington, DC 20547, USA
PHONE: +(202) 6192538
FAX: +(202) 6191241
E-MAIL: pubaff@voa.gov; letters@voa.gov
WEBSITE: http://www.voa.gov
TITLE: Director
CONTACT: Sanford Ungar

Kuwait Television

Ministry of Information, PO Box 193, Safat 13002, Kuwait
PHONE: +965 (24) 150301
FAX: +965 (24) 34511
TITLE: Minister
CONTACT: Saud Nasir Al-Saud Al-Sabah
CHANNEL: 8, 9, 10, 11, 24, 26, 38, 39, 45, 47
TYPE: Government

COLLEGES AND UNIVERSITIES

Kuwait University

PO Box 5969, Safat 13060, Kuwait
PHONE: + 965 4831965
FAX: +965 4839146
E-MAIL: OFVPAA@kuc01.kuniv.edu.kw
WEBSITE: http://www.kuniv.edu.kw

NEWSPAPERS AND MAGAZINES

Kuwait Times

Kuwait Times Publishing House, PO Box 1301, Safat 13014, Kuwait
PHONE: +965 4835616
FAX: +965 4835620
E-MAIL: kwtimes@qualitynet.net
TITLE: Publisher, Editor-in-Chief
CONTACT: Yousuf S. Alyan
CIRCULATION: 35,000

Al-Rai Al-Aam (Voice of the People)

Dar Al-Rai El Aam Press, PO Box 695, Shuwaikh, Safat 13007, Kuwait
PHONE: +965 4813133
FAX: +965 4831462
TITLE: Editor
CONTACT: Hamad Jasim Al-Saied
CIRCULATION: 88,740

Al-Watan

Dar Al Watan Press, Printing and Publishing, PO Box 1142, Safat 13012, Kuwait
PHONE: +965 4840950
FAX: +965 4834388
E-MAIL: watan@watan.com
WEBSITE: http://www.watan.com
TITLE: Editor
CONTACT: Jasem Al-Mutawa'a
CIRCULATION: 59,940

Kuwait Al-Youm

PO Box 748, Safat 13002, Kuwait
FAX: +965 4831044
CIRCULATION: 5,000
TYPE: Political science, public affairs and administration

Kuwaiti Digest

PO Box 9758, Ahmadi, 61008 Ahmadi, Kuwait
FAX: +965 3983661
TITLE: Editor
CONTACT: Ali H. Murad
CIRCULATION: 7,000
TYPE: Social science, general

PUBLISHERS

Kuwait Publishing House

PO Box 5209, Safat 13053, Kuwait City, Kuwait
PHONE: +965 2414697
TITLE: Director
CONTACT: Amin Hamadeh

Ministry of Information

PO Box 193, Safat 13002, Kuwait City, Kuwait
PHONE: +965 2415300
FAX: +965 2421926
SUBJECTS: Art, Education, Geography, Geology, Histoy, Language Arts, Linguistics, Literature, Literary Criticism, Essays, Mathematics, Physics, Social Sciences, Sociology

Press Agency

Fahd al-Salim St., PO Box 1019, Kuwait
PHONE: +965 432269; 411495
FAX: +965 411495
TITLE: Managing Director
CONTACT: Abdullah M N Harami

RELIGIOUS ORGANIZATIONS

Islamic

Husainiyat Al-Yasseen
Block 4, street 14, Building 13, Al-Mansouriyah, Kuwait
PHONE: +965 2541718
E-MAIL: 4fp1alhamada@vms.csd.mu.edu
WEBSITE: http://www.karbala.com
NAME: Ali Ibn Bu'Ayish

International Islamic Federation of Student Organizations (IIFSO)

Federacion Islamica Internacional de Organizaciones
PO Box 8631, Salmimiyah 22057, Kuwait
PHONE: +965 2443548
FAX: +965 2443549
E-MAIL: sou.tahan@usa.net
TITLE: Executive Director
NAME: Mustafa Mohammed Tahan

Shi'a Association of Kuwait
PO Box 25628, Safat 13117, Kuwait
PHONE: +965 5398395; 2443408
NAME: Sajod A. Rizvi

FURTHER READING

Articles

Farivar, Masood. "Unease in Two Gulfs Sends Crude to 10-Year High." *Wall Street Journal,* September 18, 2000, p. C17.

"Kuwait:Iraq-Backed Leader Held." *New York Times,* January 15, 2000, p. A6.

"U.S., Britain Seek to Gain U.N. Accord for Kuwait Oil Claim." *Wall Street Journal,* September 26, 2000, p. A21.

Books

Robison, Gordon. *Bahrain, Kuwait & Qatar.* London: Lonely Planet, 2000.

KUWAIT: STATISTICAL DATA

For sources and notes see "Sources of Statistics" at the front of each volume.

GEOGRAPHY

Geography

Area:

Total: 17,820 sq km.

Land: 17,820 sq km.

Land boundaries:

Total: 464 km.

Border countries: Iraq 242 km, Saudi Arabia 222 km.

Coastline: 499 km.

Climate: dry desert; intensely hot summers; short, cool winters.

Terrain: flat to slightly undulating desert plain.

Natural resources: petroleum, fish, shrimp, natural gas.

Land use:

Arable land: 0%

Permanent crops: 0%

Permanent pastures: 8%

Forests and woodland: 0%

Other: 92% (1993 est.).

HUMAN FACTORS

Demographics (A)

	1990	1995	1998	2000	2010	2020	2030	2040	2050
Population	2,142	1,621	1,836	1,974	2,788	3,741	4,604	5,488	6,375
Life expectancy - males	72.8	74.4	75.1	75.3	76.6	77.7	78.6	79.5	80.2
Life expectancy - females	74.3	75.4	76.3	76.9	79.2	81.0	82.4	83.6	84.6
Birth rate (per 1,000)	18.9	25.4	23.6	22.0	21.7	19.3	18.0	17.3	16.6
Death rate (per 1,000)	2.2	2.3	2.4	2.5	2.3	2.2	2.3	2.3	2.4
Women of reproductive age (15-49 yrs.)	485	363	404	434	632	848	1,062	1,271	1,452
Fertility rate	2.5	3.7	3.5	3.3	2.7	2.3	2.2	2.0	2.0

Except as noted, values for vital statistics are in thousands; life expectancy is in years.

Health Personnel

	National Data	World Data (wtd ave)
Total health expenditure as a percentage of GDP, 1990-1998[a]		
Public sector	2.9	2.5
Private sector	0.4	2.9
Total[b]	3.3	5.5
Health expenditure per capita in U.S. dollars, 1990-1998[a]		
Purchasing power parity	NA	561
Total	551	483
Availability of health care facilities per 100,000 people		
Hospital beds 1990-1998[a]	280	330
Doctors 1992-1995[a]	178	122
Nurses 1992-1995[a]	468	248

Health Indicators

	National Data	World Data
Life expectancy at birth (years)		
1980	71	61
1998	77	67
Daily per capita supply of calories		
1970	2,607	2,358
1997	3,096	2,791
Daily per capital supply of protein		
1997 (grams)	97	74
Total fertility rate (births per woman)		
1980	5.3	3.7
1998	2.8	2.7
Population with access (%)		
To safe water (1990-96)	100	NA
To sanitation (1990-96)	100	NA
People living with (1997)		
Tuberculosis (cases per 100,000)	30.5	60.4
HIV/AIDS (% aged 15 - 49 years)	0.12	0.99

Infants and Malnutrition

	National Data	World Data (wtd ave)
Under 5 mortality rate (1989)	13	NA
% of infants with low birthweight (1992-98)[1]	6	17
Births attended by skilled health staff (% of total births 1996-98)	98	52
% fully immunized at 1 year of age (1995-98)[1]		
TB	NA	82
DPT	93	77
Polio	94	77
Measles	100	74
Prevalence of child malnutrition (1992-98)[1] (based on weight for age, % of children under 5 years)	2	30

Ethnic Division

Kuwaiti 45%
Other Arab 35%
South Asian 9%
Iranian 4%
Other 7%

Religion

Muslim 85%
Sunni 45%
Shi'a 40%
Christian, Hindu, Parsi, and other 15%

Major Languages

Arabic (official), English widely spoken.

EDUCATION

Public Education Expenditures

	1980	1997
Public expenditures on education as % of GNP	2.4	5.0
Expenditures per student as % of GNP per capita		
Primary	14.8	39.6
Secondary	NA	5.5
Tertiary	37.5	87.9
Teachers' compensation as % of total current education expenditures	46.5	NA
Pupils per teacher at the primary level	NA	14
Duration of primary education in years	NA	8
World data for comparison		
Public expenditures on education as % of GNP (mean)	3.9	4.8
Pupils per teacher at the primary level (wtd ave)	NA	33
Duration of primary education in years (mean)	NA	9

Educational Attainment (A)

Age group (1988) . . . . .10+
Population of this age group 1,409,065
Highest level attained (%)
No schooling 17.6
First level
Not completed 18.4
Completed . . . . .NA
Entered second level
Lower Secondary 22.7
Upper Secondary 14.6
Entered post-secondary .11.1

Literacy Rates (A)

In thousands and percent	1990	1995	2000	2010
Illiterate population (15+ yrs.)	330	200	222	231
Literacy rate - total adult pop. (%)	75.7	78.6	81.5	86.0
Literacy rate - males (%)	78.5	82.2	84.1	87.4
Literacy rate - females (%)	71.6	74.9	78.6	84.4

Libraries

Public Libraries 1992
Administrative Units 1
Service Points or Branches 18
Number of Volumes (000) 272
Registered Users (000) . . . . .NA
Loans to Users (000) 890
Total Library Staff 99

GOVERNMENT & LAW

Political Parties

The unicameral National Assembly or Majlis al-Umma consists of 50 seats. Members are elected by popular vote to serve four-year terms. Elections were last held 3 July 1999 (next to be held in 2003). There are no political parties, therefore independents won all 50 seats.

Government Budgets (A)

Year: 1998
Total Expenditures: 3,509 Millions of Dinars
Expenditures as a percentage of the total by function:
General public services and public order 19.29
Defense 20.26
Education 11.94
Health 7.41
Social Security and Welfare 18.61
Housing and community amenities 3.33
Recreational, cultural, and religious affairs 3.56
Fuel and energy 9.95
Agriculture, forestry, fishing, and hunting 0
Mining, manufacturing, and construction 0
Transportation and communication 0.97
Other economic affairs and services 0

Crime

Crime volume (for 1998)
Crimes reported 27,277
Total persons convicted . . . . .NA
Crimes per 100,000 population 1,346
Persons responsible for offenses
Total number suspects 17,157
Total number of female suspects 1,716
Total number of juvenile suspects . . . . .NA

(Continued on next page.)

LABOR FORCE

Total Labor Force (A)

1.3 million. 68% of the population in the 15-64 age group is non-national (July 1998).

Labor Force by Occupation

Government and social services 50%
Services 40%
Industry and agriculture .10%

Data for 1996 est.

Unemployment Rate

1.8% (official 1996 est.).

PRODUCTION SECTOR

Energy Production

Production . . . . .26.995 billion kWh
Production by source
Fossil fuel 100%
Hydro 0%
Nuclear 0%
Other 0%
Exports . . . . .0 kWh

Data for 1998.

Energy Consumption

Consumption ....25.105 billion kWh

Imports ....0 kWh

Data for 1998.

Transportation

Highways:

Total: 4,450 km.

Paved: 3,590 km.

Unpaved: 860 km (1999 est.).

Pipelines: crude oil 877 km; petroleum products 40 km; natural gas 165 km.

Merchant marine:

Total: 48 ships (1,000 GRT or over) totaling 2,506,448 GRT/4,040,921 DWT.

Ships by type: bulk 1, cargo 9, container 6, liquified gas 7, livestock carrier 4, petroleum tanker 21 (1999 est.).

Airports: 7 (1999 est.).

Top Agriculture Products

Practically no crops; fish.

GOVERNMENT & LAW (cont.)

Military Affairs (A)

	1990	1992	1995	1996	1997
Military expenditures					
Current dollars (mil.)	13,000[e]	18,700[e]	3,430	3,830	2,760
1997 constant dollars (mil.)	15,200[e]	20,700[e]	3,550	3,900	2,760
Armed forces (000)	7	12	20	22	28[e]
Gross national product (GNP)					
Current dollars (mil.)	24,400	24,300	30,900	35,800	36,600
1997 constant dollars (mil.)	28,600	26,900	32,000	36,400	36,600
Central government expenditures (CGE)					
1997 constant dollars (mil.)	11,300	21,500	12,700	10,600	10,300
People (mil.)	2.1	1.4	1.7	1.8	1.8
Military expenditure as % of GNP	53.1	77.0	11.1	10.7	7.5
World data on military expenditure as % of GNP	4.5	3.4	2.7	2.6	2.6
Military expenditure as % of CGE	134	96.3	27.9	36.7	26.8
World data on military expenditure as % of CGE	17.0	12.5	10.5	10.3	10.2
Military expenditure per capita (1997 $)	7,130	14,800	2,120	2,220	1,510
World data on military expenditure per capita (1997 $)	242	173	146	143	145
Armed forces per 1,000 people (soldiers)	3.3	8.6	12.0	12.5	15.3
World data on armed forces per 1,000 people (soldiers)	5.3	4.5	4.1	3.9	3.8
GNP per capita (1997 $)	13,400	19,300	19,100	20,700	20,000
Arms imports[6]					
Current dollars (mil.)	270	1,000	1,300	1,700	2,000
1997 constant dollars (mil.)	316	1,109	1,346	1,728	2,000
Arms exports[6]					
Current dollars (mil.)	0	10	0	0	0
1997 constant dollars (mil.)	0	11	0	0	0
Total imports[7]					
Current dollars (mil.)	3,972	7,261	7,784	8,374	8,247
1997 constant dollars (mil.)	4,652	8,050	8,060	8,514	8,247
Total exports[7]					
Current dollars (mil.)	7,042	6,660	12,930	14,860	13,950
1997 constant dollars (mil.)	8,247	7,383	13,390	15,110	13,950
Arms as percent of total imports[8]	6.8	13.8	16.7	20.3	24.3
Arms as percent of total exports[8]	0	0.2	0	0	0

MANUFACTURING SECTOR

GDP & Manufacturing Summary (A)

	1980	1985	1990	1995
GDP ($-1990 mil.)[1]	31,087	24,187	17,969	22,798
Per capita ($-1990)[1]	22,608	14,062	8,385	13,482
Manufacturing share (%) (current prices)[1]	5.6	5.9	11.9	10.3[e]
Manufacturing				
Value added ($-1990 mil.)[1]	1,608	1,717	2,151	4,733[e]
Industrial production index	103	122	100	103[e]
Value added ($ mil.)	1,752	1,275	2,179	3,168[e]
Gross output ($ mil.)	6,218	7,435	5,531	7,106[e]
Employment (000)	43	46	56	62[e]
Profitability (% of gross output)				
Intermediate input (%)	72	83	61	55[e]
Wages and salaries inc. supplements (%)	7[e]	8	8[e]	10[e]
Gross operating surplus	21[e]	9	31[e]	34[e]
Productivity ($)				
Gross output per worker	144,813	151,542	94,963	111,264[e]
Value added per worker	40,798	25,988	37,394	49,619[e]
Average wage (inc. supplements)	9,789[e]	13,000	8,062[e]	11,615[e]
Value added ($ mil.)				
Food products	96	101	69	143[e]
Beverages	20	31	21	46[e]
Textiles	7	8	16	24[e]
Wearing apparel	84	75	54	125[e]
Leather and fur products	NA	NA	NA	4[e] 1[e]
Wood and wood products	40	14	10	15[e]
Furniture and fixtures	41	31	30	50[e]
Paper and paper products	5	12	31	31[e]
Printing and publishing	40	52	5	28[e]
Industrial chemicals	118	56	43	102[e]
Other chemical products	13	16	15	24[e]
Petroleum refineries	915	561	1,652	2,010[e]
Misc. petroleum and coal products	1	1	NA	7[e]
Rubber products	5	7	2	3[e]
Plastic products	24	24	16	55[e]
Glass and glass products	2	4	12	17[e]
Other non-metal mineral products	143	115	72	168[e]
Iron and steel	7	14	11	33[e]
Metal products	99	88	54	120[e]
Non-electrical machinery	10	30	19	71[e]
Electrical machinery	22	15	27	43[e]
Transport equipment	45	12	2	27[e]
Prof. and scientific equipment	5	2	1[e]	NA
Other manufacturing	7	5	17	20[e]

COMMUNICATIONS

Daily Newspapers

	National Data	World Data for Comparison
Daily Newspapers		
Number of Dailies	8	8,391
Total Circulation (000)	635	548,000
Circulation per 1,000 inhabitants	377	96

Telecommunications

Telephones - main lines in use: 411,600 (1997).

Telephones - mobile cellular: 150,000 (1996).

Telephone system: the civil network suffered some damage as a result of the Gulf war, but most of the telephone exchanges were left intact and, by the end of 1994, domestic and international telecommunications had been restored to normal operation.

Domestic: new telephone exchanges provide a large capacity for new subscribers; trunk traffic is carried by microwave radio relay, coaxial cable, open wire and fiber-optic cable; a cellular telephone system operates throughout Kuwait, and the country is well supplied with pay telephones; approximately 15,000 Internet subscribers in 1996.

International: coaxial cable and microwave radio relay to Saudi Arabia; linked to Bahrain, Qatar, UAE via the Fiber-Optic Gulf (FOG) cable; satellite earth stations - 3 Intelsat (1 Atlantic Ocean, 2 Indian Ocean), 1 Inmarsat (Atlantic Ocean), and 2 Arabsat.

Radio broadcast stations: AM 6, FM 11, shortwave 1 (1998).

Radios: 1.175 million (1997).

Television broadcast stations: 13 (plus several satellite channels) (1997).

Televisions: 875,000 (1997).

Internet Service Providers (ISPs): 2 (1999).

FINANCE, ECONOMICS, & TRADE

Economic Indicators

National product: GDP—purchasing power parity—$44.8 billion (1999 est.).

National product real growth rate: 1.1% (1999 est.).

National product per capita: $22,500 (1999 est.).

Inflation rate—consumer price index: 2% (1999 est.).

Exchange Rates

Exchange rates:

Kuwaiti dinars (KD) per US$1

January 2000	0.3042
1999	0.3044
1998	0.3047
1997	0.3033
1996	0.2994
1995	0.2984

Top Import Origins

$8.1 billion (f.o.b., 1999 est.)

Origins (1997)

United States	22%
Japan	15%
United Kingdom	13%
Germany	8%
Italy	6%

Top Export Destinations

$13.5 billion (f.o.b., 1999 est.)

Destinations (1997)

Japan	24%
India	16%
United States	13%
South Korea	11%
Singapore	8%

Foreign Aid

Recipient: $27.6 million (1995).

Import/Export Commodities

Import Commodities	Export Commodities
Food	Oil and refined products
Construction materials	Fertilizers
Vehicles and parts	
Clothing	

Balance of Payments

	1994	1995	1996	1997	1998
Exports of goods (f.o.b.)	11,284	12,833	14,946	14,281	9,614
Imports of goods (f.o.b.)	−6,616	−7,254	−7,949	−7,747	−7,714
Trade balance	4,669	5,579	6,997	6,534	1,900
Services - debits	−4,531	−5,381	−5,100	−5,129	−5,483
Services - credits	1,415	1,401	1,520	1,760	1,762
Private transfers (net)	NA	NA	NA	NA	NA
Government transfers (net)	−145	−90	−83	−99	−118
Overall balance	3,227	5,016	7,107	7,935	2,527

KYRGYZSTAN

Kyrgyz Republic
Kyrgyz Respublikasy

CAPITAL: Bishkek.

FLAG: Red field with a yellow sun in the center; in the center of the sun is a red ring crossed by two sets of three lines, a stylized representation of the vent in a Kyrgyz yurt.

ANTHEM: *Kyrgyz National Anthem.*

MONETARY UNIT: The som was established in May 1993; som1 = $0.08264 (or $1 = som12.1).

WEIGHTS AND MEASURES: The metric system is in force.

HOLIDAYS: Constitution Day, 5 May; Independence Day, 31 August; National Day, 2 December.

TIME: 5 PM = noon GMT.

LOCATION AND SIZE: Kyrgyzstan is located in southern Asia, between China and Kazakstan. Comparatively, it is slightly smaller than the state of South Dakota, with a total area of 198,500 square kilometers (76,641 square miles). The country's boundary length totals 3,878 kilometers (2,410 miles), and its capital city, Bishkek, is located in the north central part of the country.

CLIMATE: The country's climate ranges from continental to polar in the Tian Shan Mountains. In the valley the average temperature is 28°C (82°F) in July and in January is −21°C (−5°F).

INTRODUCTORY SURVEY

RECENT HISTORY

As Bolshevik power was consolidated, Kyrgyzstan was first made an autonomous province (*oblast*) of the Russian Federation in 1924, then upgraded in 1926 to an autonomous republic, but still within Russia. It did not become a full Soviet Republic until 1936.

The republic was regarded as one of the least developed of the Soviet states, politically and economically, making it a great surprise when, in October 1990, Kyrgyzstan became the first Soviet republic to select its own non-communist leader, Askar Akayev. Akayev and his supporters began an ambitious program of disengaging the republic from the Communist Party. Kyrgyzstan declared its independence on August 31, 1991.

On October 12, 1991, Akayev's presidency was confirmed by direct popular election. A constitution was adopted in May 1993. Akayev's presidency was reaffirmed by a popular referendum of support conducted in January 1994. Akayev was reelected to the presidency in December 1995 in the first official elections held by Kyrgyzstan. In July 1998 Akayev hailed a Constitutional Court decision permitting him to run for a third term in 2000.

GOVERNMENT

Kyrgyzstan operates under a 1993 constitution, amended in 1996. The chief of state is the president, elected by popular vote for a five-year term. The head of government is the prime minister appointed by the president. The president on the recommendation of the prime minister appoints the Cabinet of Ministers.

The bicameral Supreme Council consists of the Assembly of People's Representatives with seventy members elected by popular vote to serve five-year terms and the Legislative Assembly with thirty-five members also elected by popular vote for five-year terms.

Judiciary

The 1993 constitution instituted a Western-type judicial system. However, the judicial system still operates mostly under former-Soviet laws and

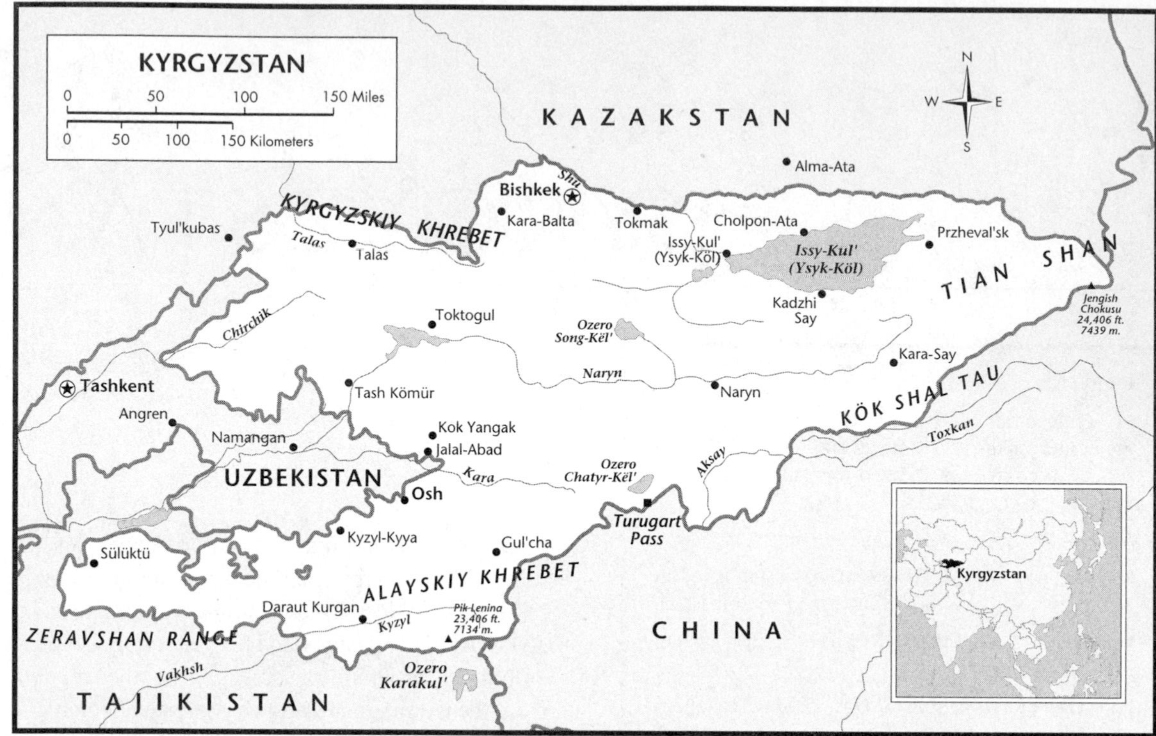

procedures. There are three levels of criminal courts: local courts that handle petty crimes; provincial courts that consider most categories of crime; and, the appellate Supreme Court. A Constitutional Court authorized to review legislation and administrative acts for consistency with the constitution. It also considers cases on appeal involving individual rights and liberties of citizens. Constitutional Court decisions are final.

Political Parties

The Communist Party of Kyrgyzia, which was the only legal political party during the Soviet years, was abolished at the time of independence. Over two-dozen parties are legally registered in 2000, though all are small and some inactive. Fewer than one-half of legislators claim party affiliation. Pro-Akayev parties include the Birimdik (Unity) Party and the Adilet (Justice Party). The main "constructive opposition" party is the People's Party.

DEFENSE

Active armed forces are estimated at 9,200 personnel with 57,000 reserves. The army has 6,800 personnel. The air force has 2,400 and relies on aircraft left at the former Soviet Air Force training school. There is a paramilitary force of 3,000. Defense expenditures in 1999 were $12 million, or 1 percent of GDP.

ECONOMIC AFFAIRS

Kyrgyzstan is among the poorest of the post-Soviet countries with a per person income estimated to be roughly half that of Russia. Although coal, gold, mercury, and uranium deposits are considerable, the country boasts few of the oil and gas reserves that promise a badly needed economic windfall to other Central Asian republics. The country's post-Soviet economy remains dominated by agriculture.

Under the presidency of Askar Akaev the transition to a free market economy has outpaced that of most other post-Soviet republics. By 1999 most state-owned enterprises had been privatized or converted to a joint stock company. The government began a tight monetary policy that reduced inflation from 23 percent per month in 1993 to 2.3 percent by 1995. But inflation was up again to 37% in 1999. However the GDP grew that same year by 3.4%.

Public Finance

In 1992 parliament agreed to a further tightening of fiscal policy (including decreased expenditures and the elimination of transfers to inefficient state enterprises) due to the virtual termination of in-flowing subsidies caused by the demise of the Soviet Union. The som, currency introduced by the government in May 1993, has proven fairly stable, and monthly inflation has slowed from 40 percent to about 10%.

The U.S. Central Intelligence Agency (CIA) estimated that in 1996 Kyrgyzstan's central government took in revenues of approximately $225 million and had expenditures of $308 million, including capital expenditures of $11 million. External debt in 1999 was $1.1 billion.

Income

In 1999 Kyrgyzstan's gross domestic product (GDP) was estimated at $10.3 billion, or about $2,300 per capita. The 1999 estimated GDP growth rate was 3.4 percent and inflation was 37%. The 1999 estimated GDP contribution by sector was agriculture 45%, industry 20%, and services 35%.

Industry

Nearly all of Kyrgyzstan's industrial output comes from Bishkek and surrounding areas. Mechanical and electrical engineering (vehicle assembly, washing machines, electrical appliances, electronics), light industry (mainly textiles and wool processing), and food processing make up close to 75 percent of the country's industrial production and 80 percent of its industrial exports. Other important industries include chemicals, leather goods, and construction materials.

Banking and Finance

The central bank of Kyrgyzstan is the National Bank of the Kyrgyz Republic and began to operate independently in 1991. It heads all eighteen banks in the system, the savings bank, three former specialized state banks that have been converted into joint-stock commercial banks, two foreign joint-venture banks, and newly established, and as of 1996 still very small, commercial banks. The specialized banks still dominate the allocation of credit and the taking of deposits, although some smaller banks are starting to challenge the major banks. However, nine of the country's commercial banks had only one office at the beginning of 1995. The larger banks have bad loan portfolios; Promstroybank (Construction Bank) had 80 percent of its loans overdue at the end of 1994. Bank failures and bank consolidation were common during the late 1990s.

The government has stuck with a tight monetary policy through the 1990s. The currency unit was initially the ruble following independence; however, with IMF support, the government introduced a new currency, the som, in May 1993 in order to stabilize the economy, avoid the inflation of the ruble, and attract foreign investment.

The country has a small stock exchange, opened in May 1995. As of January 1996, 298 companies issued securities, with 7 trading on the stock exchange.

Economic Development

Kyrgyzstan declared its independence in 1991. Since then the Kyrgyzstan government faced the task of sustaining a viable national economy despite the sudden cessation of transfers from the central government, the country's critical dependence on oil and gas imports, and its landlocked geographic position that has hampered development of trading ties outside the economically troubled former Soviet Union. Reforms have aimed at making the transition to a market-oriented economy.

Kyrgyzstan experienced declines in gross domestic product (GDP) from 1991-1994. Both per capita income and overall output fell to well below the 1990 level. Agricultural output fell by an estimated 20%, and industrial output, by 42%. By 1996 however Kyrgyzstan had begun to show progress, especially when compared to the other former Soviet republics, in the areas of privatizing state enterprises, ending the state ordering system, lifting price controls, and converting military enterprises to civilian uses. Prime Minister Apas Jumagulov reported in 1995 that the economic crises had eased, and the rates of decline were slowing.

Foreign assistance played a significant role in the country's economic turnaround in 1996-1997. In May 1996 President Akayev negotiated an aid package from the Asian Development Bank that included $60 million in loans to finance privatization of agriculture and to renovate power and heating facilities in Bishkek. In support of the government's efforts to evolve the country's agriculture from large communes to private farms, the Asian Development Bank also offered loans to small farmers. In July 1996 the International Finance Corporation promised $40 million to finance a project to mine for gold near Issy-Kul', a large lake in the northeast. In November 1996 the World Bank moved to support programs to reform the Kyrgyzstan banking system and to modernize the electric power generating system.

Overall through the 1990s Kyrgyzstan was one of the most progressive countries of the former Soviet Union in carrying out market reforms. Much of the government's stock in enterprises was sold. Reforms continue to combat excessive external debt, inflation, and inadequate revenue collection.

SOCIAL WELFARE

Social security laws were introduced in 1990, and amended in 1992 and 1994. All employees and members of cooperatives and collective farms are eligible for old age, disability, and survivors' pensions. A universal medical care system exists for all residents. Workers' compensation, unemployment benefits, and family allowances are also provided. The government, however, is often unable to pay pension benefits.

Women have equal status under the law and are well represented in the work force in urban areas.

In 1993 parliament narrowly rejected a law to legalize polygamy (having multiple spouses). Polygyny (one man with multiple wives) is most common, and each wife must be provided with her own household. In order for a woman to have multiple husbands (polyandry), she must have substantial wealth or influence.

Healthcare

In 1990-1997 Kyrgyzstan had three physicians and 8.8 hospital beds per 1,000 inhabitants. In 2000 life expectancy was 63.4 years. The incidence of tuberculosis and diphtheria increased in the early 1990s, reflecting economic hardship and the deterioration of health care.

Housing

In 1989 42.7 percent of all privately owned urban housing had running water, 32.4 percent had sewer lines, 14 percent had central heating, and 1.4 percent had hot water. In 1990 Kyrgyzstan had 12.1 square meters (130 square feet) of housing space per person. In 1991 18.6 percent of households were on waiting lists for housing in urban areas.

EDUCATION

The adult illiteracy rate was estimated at 3%. In 1996, 473,077 students were enrolled in primary schools and 530,854 students were enrolled in secondary schools. During 1996, 42,286 students were enrolled at institutions of higher learning, including the State University of Kyrgyzstan.

2000 KEY EVENTS TIMELINE

February

- The Communists emerge as the largest party in parliament with 28 percent of the vote while their main opponents, the Union of Democratic Forces, finish second with 18 percent; foreign observers cite pre-election irregularities.

April

- U.S. Secretary of State Madeleine Albright visits Kyrgyzstan.

May

- President Askar Akaev travels to Minsk to meet Belarus's Alexandr Lukashenka.

August

- On August 13 the government claims that over ten of its soldiers and more than thirty rebel gunmen have been killed over the weekend at Batken.

September

- The interior ministers of eleven former Soviet states meet in Kyrgyzstan on September 8, agreeing to work together to combat militant Islamic groups.
- Islamic rebels fire grenades on government troops on Kyrgyzstan's southern border on September 15.

October

- Kyrgyz security forces remain vigilant against incursions of Islamic gunmen in remote mountainous area in the south, where 120 rebels have been killed and 200 more injured.
- Leaders from Kyrgyzstan and five other former Soviet republics (Armenia, Belarus, Kazakstan, Russia, and Tajikistan) agree to pool military resources in face of the increasing might of Taliban regime in neighboring Afghanistan.
- In national elections, Kyrgyz president Askar Akayev wins third term in office; international observers charge that the vote is undemocratic.

ANALYSIS OF EVENTS: 2000

BUSINESS AND THE ECONOMY

Kyrgyzstan, unlike its counterparts among the central Asian republics, remained a country without significant oil reserves. Therefore the highlights of the economy in 2000 were not the development of natural resources, but rather, the development of trade and transport integration with its giant neighbor to the east, China. Kyrgyz Ambassador Omar Sultanov signed a bilateral agreement with China regarding its accession to the World Trade Organization (WTO). The agreement was expected to promote trade and economic relations between the two countries. Prospects for foreign trade likewise improved with the development of transport links in neighboring China. The road from Osh in Kyrgyzstan to the newly opened extension of the Chinese rail system in Kashgar, China, received substantial improvement. A possible rail link between Osh and Kashgar was also surveyed.

GOVERNMENT AND POLITICS

Kyrgyzstan, formerly known as the most democratic nation in the region, lost its good reputation following the presidential election in October and the parliamentary elections earlier in the year. President Ali Akayev was sworn in for a third term as President on December 9. Although the Constitution limits the president to two terms, the Constitutional Court had ruled that Akayev's first term didn't count because he had run for office unopposed the first time. In the elections for Parliament, the Communists emerged from elections as the largest party in Parliament with 27 percent of the vote. Their main opponents, the Union of Democratic Forces, finished second with 18 percent as foreign observers noted pre-election irregularities. Both the parliamentary and presidential election were criticized by the Organization for Security and Cooperation in Europe (OSCE) for failing to meet international standards. The OSCE expressed concern about the campaign after the government Elections Committee excluded more than half of the thirty political parties, and several popular opposition politicians complained of intimidation by security and intelligence officials. Three major opposition parties were barred from the contest on technicalities, including the popular opposition party Democratic Movement of Kyrgyzstan, which claimed it was unfairly disqualified from the race. A total of 545 candidates ran for 105 seats, but some seats required another round of voting scheduled for March 2001. The public reaction to the official results of the election were tumultuous. In the capital Bishkek, citizens protested the fact that not a single opposition candidate received a seat in the parliament. A crowd occupied the Constitutional Courthouse and hundreds more marched on the main government buildings. Riot police were eventually called in to disperse the protest. Leaders of the protest met with a delegation from the OSCE, led by General-Secretary Jan Kubish, that happened to be in Bishkek for scheduled talks when the protest developed.

Kyrgyzstan's most important foreign policy issue involved the potential destabilizing effect of violence between Muslim fundamentalists and government forces. Security officials from Kyrgyzstan met with their counterparts from Uzbekistan and Tajikistan in August in response to clashes between Islamist rebels and government soldiers near the southern Kyrgyz town of Batken. Military sources reported five soldiers were wounded in the battle against about forty rebels, who were traversing the southern Kyrgyz region on their way from Afghanistan to Uzbekistan. The rebels reportedly were members of the Islamic Movement of Uzbekistan, led by Dzhuma Namangoni. As part of the efforts to mitigate such violence, delegates from Kyrgyzstan attended the Islamic Conference of Foreign Ministers in Kuala Lumpur, Malaysia. The delegates took part in discussions focusing on conflicts involving Muslims and also the plight of Muslim minorities. Kyrgyzstan's importance as a democratic outpost and ally in the region was bolstered by the visit of U.S. Secretary of State Madeleine Albright.

CULTURE AND SOCIETY

Efforts to promote tourism in Kyrgyzstan were set back after two incidents in which foreign visitors were kidnapped. Eight German mountain climbers held hostage for four days by Islamist rebels were freed. The climbers had been training in the mountains on the Kyrgyz-Tajik border when they were encountered and captured by a traveling group of rebels. Four adventurers, on a trip sponsored by a U.S. sporting goods company, escaped after being held by militant Uzbek kidnappers for six days in Kyrgyzstan. After pushing one of their captors over a cliff, the group hiked twenty-nine kilometers to freedom. In May the uninhabited mountain region of Chon-Keminsky, about thirty-six miles east of the town of Batken, experienced an earthquake measuring 6.5 on the Richter scale. No casualties or significant damage was reported.

DIRECTORY

CENTRAL GOVERNMENT

Head of State

President
Askar Akaev, Office of the President, Ulitsa Kirova 205, Bishkek, Kyrgyzstan

Ministers

Prime Minister
Amangeldi Muraliev, Office of the Prime Minister, Zhorgorku Kenesh, Bishkek, Kyrgyzstan

First Deputy Prime Minister
Boris Silaev, Office of the First Deputy Prime Minister

Deputy Prime Minister, Minister of Industry and Foreign Trade
Esengul Omuraliev, Ministry of of Industry and Foreign Trade

Minister of Foreign Affairs
Muratbek Imanaliyev, Ministry of Foreign Affairs

Minister of Economics and Finance
Sultan Mederov, Ministry of Economics and Finance

Minister for Social Welfare
Imankadyr Rysaliev, Ministry of Social Welfare

Minister of Agriculture and Water Resources
Alexander Kostyuk, Ministry of Agriculture and Water Resources

Minister of Environmental Protection
Tynybek Alykulov, Ministry of Environmental Protection

Minister of National Security
Tashtemir AItbayev, Ministry of National Security

Minister of the Interior
Omurbek Kutuyev, Ministry of the Interior

Minister of Defense
Lt. Gen. Esen Topoyev, Ministry of Defense

Minister of Health
Tilekbek Meymanaliyev, Ministry of Health

Minister of Justice
Nellya Beyshenaliyeva, Ministry of Justice

Minister of Communications and Transportation
Jantoro Satybaldiyev, Ministry of Communications and Transportation

Minister of Emergencies and Civil Defense
Sultan Urmanayev, Ministry of Emergencies and Civil Defense

Minister of Education, Science and Culture
Tursunbek Bekbolotov, Ministry of Education, Science and Culture

POLITICAL ORGANIZATIONS

Alta Mekel (Fatherland)

NAME: Omurbek Tekebayev

Argrarian Party of Kyrgyzstan

NAME: A. Aliyev

Ashar (Mutual Help Movement)

NAME: Zhumagazy Usupov

Banner National Revival Party (ASABA)

NAME: Chaprashty Bazarbay

Democratic Movement of Kyrgyzstan (DDK)

TITLE: Chairman
NAME: Jypar Jeksheyev

Communist Party of Kyrgyzstan (PKK)

TITLE: Chairman
NAME: Absamat Masaliyev

Kyrgyzstan Erkin-ErK (Democratic Movement of Free Kyrgyzstan)

NAME: Tursunbay Bakir Uulu

Movement for the People's Salvation

NAME: Djumgalbek Amambayev

Republican Popular Party of Kyrgyzstan

NAME: Zh. Sharshenaliyev

Social Democratic Party (PSD)

NAME: J. Ibramov

JUDICIAL SYSTEM

Supreme Court

Constitutional Court

Higher Court of Arbitration

BROADCAST MEDIA

Kyrgyz Radio

Jash Gvardiya Boulevard 68, 720300 Bishkek, Kyrgyzstan
PHONE: +996 (3312) 253404
FAX: +996 (3312) 257930
TITLE: General Director
CONTACT: Tugelbay Kazakov
LANGUAGE: English, German, Russian
TYPE: Government

Radio Free Europe/Radio Liberty—Kyrgyz Service

PHONE: +996 (4202) 21122383
FAX: +996 (4202) 21122399
E-MAIL: carlsonc@rferl.org
WEBSITE: http://www.rferl.org/bd/ky/
TITLE: Director
CONTACT: Charles Carlson

Kyrgyz Television

pr. Molodoj Gvardii 63, 720885 Bishkek, Kyrgyzstan
PHONE: +996 (3312) 253404
FAX: +996 (3312) 257930
TITLE: General Director
CONTACT: Tugelbay Kazakov
TYPE: Government

Kyrgyzstan State Radio and TV Broadcasting Co.

Jash Gvardiya Boulevard 63, 720300 Bishkek, Kyrgyzstan
TYPE: Government

COLLEGES AND UNIVERSITIES

Kyrgyz State University

Ul Frunze 537, 720024 Bishkek, Kyrgyzstan

NEWSPAPERS AND MAGAZINES

Bishkek Shami

ul. Pravdi 24, 720000 Bishkek, Kyrgyzstan
PHONE: +996 (3312) 725780
CONTACT: Abdidjapar Sootbekov

Central Asian Post

E-MAIL: webmaster@elcat.kg
WEBSITE: www.elcat.kg

Kabar - Kyrgyz National News Agency

Sovietskaya 175, 720337 Bishkek, Kyrgyzstan
PHONE: +996 (3312) 226739; 224611
FAX: +996 (3312) 661467
E-MAIL: webmaster@kabar.gov.kg
WEBSITE: www.kabar.gov.kg

Kirgis Tuuschu

ul. Abdymomynova 193, 720000 Bishkek, Kyrgyzstan
PHONE: +996 (3312) 224509
CONTACT: A. Matisakov
CIRCULATION: 70,000

Respublica

ul. Belinskovo 28, 720000 Bishkek, Kyrgyzstan
PHONE: +996 (3312) 219733
CONTACT: Zamira Sidikova

Slovo Kirgizstana

ul. Abdymomynova 193, 72000 Bishkek
PHONE: +996 (3312) 225392
CONTACT: Alexander Malevany

Vecherny Bishkek

Joint-Stock Company, Usenbaeva 2, 720021 Bishkek, Kyrgyzstan
PHONE: +996 (3312) 284597
FAX: +996 (3312) 680268
E-MAIL: webmaster@vb.kyrnet.kg
WEBSITE: http://vb.kyrnet.kg
TITLE: Editor
CONTACT: Alexander Kim
CIRCULATION: 35,000 (Mon-Thu); 90,000 (Fri)

Delo N

WEBSITE: www.delo.elcat.kg/

Echo Science Magazine

WEBSITE: www.echo.online.kg

RELIGIOUS ORGANIZATIONS

Jewish

The Jewish Community of Kyrgyzstan-Bishkek
159 Moskowskaya St., 720013 Bishkek, Kyrgyzstan
E-MAIL: kyrgyzstan@fjc.ru
WEBSITE: http://fjc.ru/topky.html
TITLE: President
NAME: Roza Fish

FURTHER READING

Articles

"Caution Issued on Kyrgyz Travel." *Travel Weekly,* September 4, 2000, vol. 59, no. 71, p. 10.

Frantz, Douglas. "Kyrgyzstan: President Re-Elected." *New York Times,* October 31, 2000, p. A6.

"Kirgizstan—And the Winner Is . . . " *The Economist (US),* November 4, 2000, vol. 357, no. 8195, p. 47.

"Kyrgyzstan, Uzbekistan: Defense Pact." *New York Times,* September 28, 2000, p. A10.

LeVine, Steve. "In Kyrgyzstan, Flawed Election Portends a Shift to Autocracy." *The Wall Street Journal,* October 30, 2000, p. A26.

———. "A Shocking Verdict." *Newsweek International,* August 21, 2000, p. 41.

"Mein Herr of Kirgizstan." *The Economist (US),* January 15, 2000, vol. 354, no. 8153, p. 40.

"A Worrying Vote," *The Economist,* February 26, 2000, p. 51.

KYRGYZSTAN: STATISTICAL DATA

For sources and notes see "Sources of Statistics" at the front of each volume.

GEOGRAPHY

Geography

Area:

Total: 198,500 sq km.

Land: 191,300 sq km

Land boundaries:

Total: 3,878 km.

Border countries: China 858 km, Kazakhstan 1,051 km, Tajikistan 870 km, Uzbekistan 1,099 km.

Coastline: 0 km (landlocked).

Climate: dry continental to polar in high Tien Shan; subtropical in southwest (Fergana Valley); temperate in northern foothill zone.

Terrain: peaks of Tien Shan and associated valleys and basins encompass entire nation.

Natural resources: abundant hydropower; significant deposits of gold and rare earth metals; locally exploitable coal, oil, and natural gas; other deposits of nepheline, mercury, bismuth, lead, and zinc.

Land use:

Arable land: 7%

Permanent crops: 0%

Permanent pastures: 44%

Forests and woodland: 4%

Other: 45% (1993 est.).

Note: Kyrgyzstan has the world's largest natural growth walnut forest.

HUMAN FACTORS

Demographics (A)

	1990	1995	1998	2000	2010	2020	2030	2040	2050
Population	4,390	4,535	4,581	4,685	5,444	6,344	7,267	8,192	9,041
Life expectancy - males	62.2	60.3	59.4	59.1	61.8	65.4	68.3	70.9	73.1
Life expectancy - females	70.9	69.1	68.3	67.9	70.2	73.7	76.6	79.0	80.9
Birth rate (per 1,000)	30.5	27.3	26.6	26.3	25.6	21.8	19.4	17.9	16.2
Death rate (per 1,000)	8.1	8.6	9.0	9.1	8.4	7.0	6.6	6.9	7.4
Women of reproductive age (15-49 yrs.)	1,028	1,109	1,151	1,199	1,455	1,674	1,910	2,049	2,197
Fertility rate	3.8	3.4	3.3	3.2	2.9	2.7	2.5	2.3	2.3

Except as noted, values for vital statistics are in thousands; life expectancy is in years.

Health Personnel

	National Data	World Data (wtd ave)
Total health expenditure as a percentage of GDP, 1990-1998[a]		
Public sector	2.7	2.5
Private sector	0.4	2.9
Total[b]	3.1	5.5
Health expenditure per capita in U.S. dollars, 1990-1998[a]		
Purchasing power parity	71	561
Total	11	483
Availability of health care facilities per 100,000 people		
Hospital beds 1990-1998[a]	950	330
Doctors 1992-1995[a]	310	122
Nurses 1992-1995[a]	879	248

Health Indicators

	National Data	World Data
Life expectancy at birth (years)		
1980	65	61
1998	67	67
Daily per capita supply of calories		
1970	NA	2,358
1997	2,447	2,791
Daily per capital supply of protein		
1997 (grams)	82	74
Total fertility rate (births per woman)		
1980	4.1	3.7
1998	2.8	2.7
Population with access (%)		
To safe water (1990-96)	81	NA
To sanitation (1990-96)	NA	NA
People living with (1997)		
Tuberculosis (cases per 100,000)	119.3	60.4
HIV/AIDS (% aged 15 - 49 years)	NA	0.99

Infants and Malnutrition

	National Data	World Data (wtd ave)
Under 5 mortality rate (1989)	66	NA
% of infants with low birthweight (1992-98)[1]	6	17
Births attended by skilled health staff (% of total births 1996-98)	98	52
% fully immunized at 1 year of age (1995-98)[1]		
TB	94	82
DPT	97	77
Polio	97	77
Measles	98	74
Prevalence of child malnutrition (1992-98)[1] (based on weight for age, % of children under 5 years)	11	30

Ethnic Division

Kirghiz 52.4%
Russian 18.4%
Uzbek 12.9%
Ukrainian 2.5%
German 2.4%
Other 11.8%

Religion

Muslim 75%
Russian Orthodox 20%
Other 5%

Major Languages

Kirghiz (Kyrgyz) - official language, Russian - official language. In March 1996, the Kyrgyzstani legislature amended the constitution to make Russian an official language, along with Kirghiz, in territories and workplaces where Russian-speaking citizens

EDUCATION

Public Education Expenditures

	1980	1997
Public expenditures on education as % of GNP	NA	5.3
Expenditures per student as % of GNP per capita		
Primary & Secondary	NA	NA
Tertiary	NA	48.8
Pupils per teacher at the primary level	NA	20
Duration of primary education in years	NA	10
World data for comparison		
Public expenditures on education as % of GNP (mean)	3.9	4.8
Pupils per teacher at the primary level (wtd ave)	NA	33
Duration of primary education in years (mean)	NA	9

Literacy Rates (B)

	National Data	World Data
Adult literacy rate		
1995		
Male	99	81
Female	95	65

GOVERNMENT & LAW

Government Budgets (A)

Year: 1998

Total Expenditures: NA

Expenditures as a percentage of the total by function:

General public services and public order 19.06
Defense 6.52
Education 22.33
Health 12.77
Social Security and Welfare 13.03
Housing and community amenities . . . . .NA
Recreational, cultural, and religious affairs . . . . . .NA
Fuel and energy . . . . .NA
Agriculture, forestry, fishing, and hunting . . . . . . .NA
Mining, manufacturing, and construction . . . . . . .NA
Transportation and communication . . . . .NA
Other economic affairs and services . . . . .NA

Crime

Crime rate (for 1997)

Crimes reported 39,600
Total persons convicted 22,700
Crimes per 100,000 population 850

Persons responsible for offenses

Total number of suspects 23,400
Total number of female suspects 2,600
Total number of juvenile suspects 1,650

(Continued on next page.)

LABOR FORCE

Total Labor Force (A)

1.7 million.

Labor Force by Occupation

Agriculture and forestry 55%
Industry 15%
Services 30%

Data for 1999 est.

Unemployment Rate

6% (1998 est.)

PRODUCTION SECTOR

Energy Production

Production . . . . .12.206 billion kWh

Production by source

Fossil fuel 10.78%
Hydro 89.22%
Nuclear 0%
Other 0%

Exports . . . . .1.1 billion kWh

Data for 1998.

Energy Consumption

Consumption . . . . .11.102 billion kWh
Imports .850.000 million kWh

Data for 1998.

Transportation

Highways:

Total: 18,500 km.

Paved: 16,854 km (including 140 km of expressways).

Unpaved: 1,646 km (1996 est.).

Waterways: 600 km (1990).

Pipelines: natural gas 200 km.

Airports: 54 (1994 est.).

Airports - with paved runways: 14.

Airports - with unpaved runways: 40.

Top Agriculture Products

Tobacco, cotton, potatoes, vegetables, grapes, fruits and berries; sheep, goats, cattle, wool.

Top Mining Products (B)

Mineral resources include: significant deposits of gold and rare earth metals; locally exploitable coal, oil, and natural gas; other deposits of nepheline, mercury, bismuth, lead, and zinc.

COMMUNICATIONS

Telecommunications

Telephones - main lines in use: 357,000 (1995).

Telephones - mobile cellular: NA

Telephone system: poorly developed; about 100,000 unsatisfied applications for household telephones.

Domestic: principally microwave radio relay; one cellular provider, probably limited to Bishkek region.

International: connections with other CIS countries by landline or microwave radio relay and with other countries by leased connections with Moscow international gateway switch and by satellite; satellite earth stations - 1 Intersputnik and 1 Intelsat; connected internationally by the Trans-Asia-Europe (TAE) fiber-optic line.

Radio broadcast stations: AM 12 (plus 10 repeater stations), FM 14, shortwave 2 (1998).

Radios: 520,000 (1997).

Television broadcast stations: NA (repeater stations throughout the country relay programs from Russia, Uzbekistan, Kazakstan, and Turkey) (1997).

Televisions: 210,000 (1997).

Internet Service Providers (ISPs): NA

GOVERNMENT & LAW (cont.)

Military Affairs (A)

	1992	1994	1995	1996	1997
Military expenditures					
Current dollars (mil.)	NA	79[e]	127	118	159
1997 constant dollars (mil.)	NA	83[e]	132	120	159
Armed forces (000)	12	13	13	13	14
Gross national product (GNP)					
Current dollars (mil.)	12,200[e]	8,850[e]	8,570	9,270	10,200
1997 constant dollars (mil.)	13,600[e]	9,360[e]	8,880	9,430	10,200
Central government expenditures (CGE)					
1997 constant dollars (mil.)	NA	2,230	2,570	2,140	2,240
People (mil.)	4.5	4.5	4.5	4.6	4.6
Military expenditure as % of GNP	NA	0.9	1.5	1.3	1.6
World data on military expenditure as % of GNP	4.5	3.4	2.7	2.6	2.6
Military expenditure as % of CGE	NA	3.7	5.1	5.6	7.1
World data on military expenditure as % of CGE	17.0	12.5	10.5	10.3	10.2
Military expenditure per capita (1997 $)	NA	18	29	26	34
World data on military expenditure per capita (1997 $)	242	173	146	143	145
Armed forces per 1,000 people (soldiers)	2.6	2.9	2.9	2.8	3.0
World data on armed forces per 1,000 people (soldiers)	5.3	4.5	4.1	3.9	3.8
GNP per capita (1997 $)	2,990	2,060	1,960	2,060	2,210
Arms exports[6]					
Current dollars (mil.)	0	10	30	0	0
1997 constant dollars (mil.)	0	11	31	0	0
Total imports[7]					
Current dollars (mil.)	419	316	522	839	710
1997 constant dollars (mil.)	465	334	541	853	710
Total exports[7]					
Current dollars (mil.)	316	361	409	505	604
1997 constant dollars (mil.)	350	0	423	514	604
Arms as percent of total imports[8]	0	2	0	0	0
Arms as percent of total exports[8]	0	2.9	7.3	0	0

FINANCE, ECONOMICS, & TRADE

Economic Indicators

National product: GDP—purchasing power parity—$10.3 billion (1999 est.).

National product real growth rate: 3.4% (1999 est.).

National product per capita: $2,300 (1999 est.).

Inflation rate—consumer price index: 37% (1999 est.).

Exchange Rates

Exchange rates:

Soms (KGS) per US$1

January 2000	46.235
1999	39.008
1998	20.838
1997	17.362
1996	12.810
1995	10.822

Top Import Origins

$590 million (1999 est.)

Origins (1998)

Russia	24%
Uzbekistan	14%
Kazakstan	9%
Germany	6%
China	5%

Top Export Destinations

$515 million (1999 est.)

Destinations (1998)

Germany	37%
Kazakstan	17%
Russia	16%
Uzbekistan	8%
China	3%

Foreign Aid

Recipient: $329.4 million (1995).

Import/Export Commodities

Import Commodities	Export Commodities
Oil and gas	Cotton
Machinery and equipment	Wool
Foodstuffs	Meat
	Tobacco
	Gold
	Mercury
	Uranium
	Hydropower
	Machinery
	Shoes

Balance of Payments

	1994	1995	1996	1997	1998
Exports of goods (f.o.b.)	340	409	531	631	535
Imports of goods (f.o.b.)	−426	−531	−783	−646	−756
Trade balance	−86	−122	−252	−15	−221
Services - debits	−71	−195	−249	−171	−180
Services - credits	33	39	31	45	63
Private transfers (net)	1	1	2	3	2
Government transfers (net)	62	78	82	65	47
Overall balance	−84	−235	−425	−139	−371

LAOS

CAPITAL: Vientiane (Viangchan).

FLAG: The national flag, officially adopted in 1975, is the former flag of the Pathet Lao, consisting of three horizontal stripes of red, dark blue, and red, with a white disk, representing the full moon, at the center.

ANTHEM: *Pheng Sat Lao (Hymn of the Lao People).*

MONETARY UNIT: The new kip (K) is a paper currency of 100 at (cents). There are notes of 10, 20, 50, 200, and 500 new kip. K1 = $0.0011 (or $1 = K920).

WEIGHTS AND MEASURES: The metric system is the legal standard, but local units are also used.

HOLIDAYS: Anniversary of the Founding of the Lao People's Democratic Republic, 2 December. To maintain production, the government generally reschedules on weekends such traditional festivals as the Lao New Year (April); Boun Bang-fai (Rocket Festival), the celebration of the birth, enlightenment, and death of the Buddha (May); Boun Khao Watsa, the beginning of a period of fasting and meditation lasting through the rainy season (July); Boun Ok Watsa (Water Holiday), a celebration of the end of the period of fasting and meditation (October); and That Luang, a pagoda pilgrimage holiday (November).

TIME: 7 PM = noon GMT.

LOCATION AND SIZE: Laos is a landlocked Southeast Asian country on the Indochinese peninsula. The Indochinese peninsula includes Vietnam, Cambodia, and Thailand. It occupies an area of 236,800 square kilometers (91,429 square miles), slightly larger than the state of Utah. It has a total boundary length of 4,513 kilometers (2,804 miles). The capital, Vientiane, is on the western border.

CLIMATE: From May through September, rainfall averages 28 to 30 centimeters (11–12 inches) a month, but from November through March the monthly average is only about 1.3 centimeters (0.5 inches). Humidity is high throughout the year, even during the season of drought. Average daily temperatures in Vientiane range from 14° to 28°C (57–82°F) in January, the coolest month, and from 23° to 34°C (73–93°F) in April, the hottest.

Lao People's Democratic Republic
Sathalanalat Paxathipatai Paxaxon Lao

INTRODUCTORY SURVEY

RECENT HISTORY

During World War II (1939-1945) Laos was occupied by Japan. After the war French forces reoccupied Laos and established Sisavang Vong, the king of Louangphrabang, as king of Laos under French domination. In May 1947 the king established a constitution providing for a democratic government and by 1953 Laos had achieved full sovereignty.

In the meantime Vietnamese communist (Viet-Minh) forces had invaded Laos in the spring of 1953. A Laotian communist movement, the Pathet Lao (Lao State), collaborated with the Viet-Minh during its Laotian offensive. Under the terms of a 1954 cease-fire the Pathet Lao pulled back to two northern provinces, but the group was to continue fighting for control of Laos until it finally prevailed some twenty years later.

In the 1960s Laos was steadily drawn into the role of a main theater in the escalating Vietnam War. The Laotian segment of the so-called Ho Chi Minh trail, vital for troop movement from North Vietnam to the south, was the target for heavy United States bombing raids. While the Vientiane (capital city of Laos) government was heavily bolstered by United States military and economic support, the Pathet Lao received key support from the Democratic Republic of Vietnam in the north.

By the end of the war the Pathet Lao controlled over three-fourths of Laos. Following the fall of the U.S.-backed regimes in Vietnam and Cambodia in April 1975, the Laotian communists embarked on a

campaign to achieve complete military and political supremacy in Laos. On August 23 Vientiane was declared "liberated," and on December 2, 1975, the Lao People's Democratic Republic (LPDR) was established with Prince Souphanouvong as president. King Savang Vatthana abdicated his throne, ending the monarchy that had survived in Laos for 622 years.

During the late 1970s the communists moved to consolidate their control and socialize the economy. Private trade was banned, factories were nationalized, and forcible collectivization of agriculture was initiated. "Reeducation" camps for an estimated 40,000 former royalists and military leaders were established in remote areas.

However with the economy near collapse in 1979 in part because of severe drought followed by flooding, the Laotian government slowed the process of socialization and announced a return to private enterprise and a readiness to accept aid from the non-communist world.

In April 1994 the first international bridge, the Mittaphap (Friendship) Bridge, linking Laos and Thailand across the Mekong River, was opened. The 1,174-meter (3,852-foot) bridge, built and paid for by Australia, is part of a plan for an Asian super-highway to facilitate travel from Singapore to Shanghai. The most immediate benefits are anticipated by the tourism industry and as a spur to real estate investment.

The U.S. Department of State notes that despite constitutional guarantees, freedom of speech, assembly, and religion are restricted, and political killings have accompanied continued rebellion, primarily among Hmong tribesmen.

GOVERNMENT

Under a new constitution adopted in 1991, the executive branch consists of the president, prime minister and two deputy prime ministers, and the Council of Ministers (cabinet). The president is elected by the National Assembly for a five-year term. The prime minister, deputy prime minister, and Council are all appointed by the president with the approval of the National Assembly. The legislative branch is the 99-seat National Assembly whose members are elected by universal suffrage for a period of five years. The judicial branch is the Supreme People's Court Leaders. The constitution calls for a strong legislature elected by secret ballot, but most political power continues to rest with the party-dominated council of ministers.

Judiciary

The government is now in the process of developing a codified body of laws. The constitution contains provisions designed to guarantee the independence of judges and prosecutors, but in practice the courts appear to be subject to influence of other government agencies. There are provincial courts, appellate courts, and a Central Supreme Court in Vientiane. In 1993 the government began publishing an official gazette in which all laws and regulations are disseminated.

Political Parties

The only legal political party was the communist Lao People's Revolutionary Party (LPRP) that includes the Lao Front for National Construction (LFNC).

DEFENSE

In 2000 the armed forces in Laos numbered 29,100, with 18 months of military service compulsory for all males. A total of 25,000 Laotians served in the army. The navy, equipped with sixteen patrol craft and boats, enlisted 600. The air force, with 3,500 men, was equipped with antiaircraft missiles and twenty-six combat aircraft. The village self-defense force numbers 100,000. There are also about 2,000 rebels from the United Lao National Liberation Front (ULNLF) in Laos ready to confront the armed forces. Defense expenditures in 1996-1997 were 4.2 percent of GDP.

ECONOMIC AFFAIRS

One of the world's poorest and least-developed nations, Laos is overwhelmingly agricultural, with about 80 percent of the population engaged in subsistence farming, which accounts for about 56 percent of the gross domestic product (GDP). Because industrialization is minimal, Laos imports nearly all the manufactured products it requires.

The hostilities of the 1960s and 1970s badly disrupted the economy, forcing the country to depend on imports from Thailand to supplement its daily rice requirements. The third five-year plan (1991-1995) emphasized improvement of communications and transportation networks, export growth, and development of domestic industry to decrease reliance on imports.

By 1997 there was more than $5 billion in foreign investment, as Laos had opened up its economy. However, inflations and problems with tax collection have contributed to increasing budget deficits.

Laos was damaged by the Asian financial crisis. From June 1997 to 1999 the Lao kip lost 87%. The currency stabilized but 140 percent inflation persisted in 1999. The economy continued to depend on foreign aid for the foreseeable future.

Public Finance

The civil war rendered normal budgetary procedures impossible, the budget being covered largely by U.S. aid and monetary inflation. Deficit financing continued in the 1970s and 1980s, covered mostly by foreign aid from communist nations. With the collapse of this support, however, Laos has increasingly looked to foreign investment capital and Western lending agencies for financial support. Beginning in 1994 the IMF initiated an annual program of loans to assist the country with a structural adjustment program. It lent Laos $17 million in 1995. Still 31 percent of the 1995 budget was international aid.

The U.S. Central Intelligence Agency estimated that in 1997-1998 government revenues totaled approximately $202.7 million and expenditures $385.1 million. External debt totaled $2.32 billion.

Income

In 1999 Laos's gross domestic product (GDP) was estimated at $7 billion, or about $1,300 per capita. The estimated GDP for 1999 was 5.2 percent and inflation was 140%. The estimated 1999 GDP contribution by sector was agriculture 51%, industry 22%, and services 27%.

Industry

Industrial development is rudimentary. Manufacturing is largely confined to the processing of agricultural products, forestry products including two-dozen sawmills, and garments and fabric production. There are some mining operations including tin and gypsum mining, charcoal ovens, a cement plant, a few brick works, carpenter shops, a tobacco factory, rice mills, and some furniture factories. Handicrafts account for an important part of the income of many Laotians.

New resource development is focused on hydroelectric power. Hydroelectric production accounted for more than 15 percent of GDP.

Banking and Finance

The central bank, the Bank of the Laotian People's Democratic Republic, regulates a rapidly expanding sector comprising thirteen national and foreign-owned banks under the terms of the Commercial Bank and Financial Institutions Act of January 1992. Most of the wholly foreign-owned banks are Thai (such as the Thai Military Bank and Siam Commercial) and Thai financiers back many of the joint-venture banks such as the Joint Development Bank. The central bank continues to receive technical assistance from multilateral lending agencies, and is gradually strengthening the potential framework. The banks are now believed to be more efficient. The largest commercial bank, established in 1953, is the Bank of Indochina.

All banks now provide basic business services and offer a range of deposit and credit facilities. Interest rates are increasingly responsive to market conditions but tend to remain close to rates set by the central bank. Public confidence in the banking system is still low.

The system suffered severe liquidity problems in 1990-91 when the "privatization" of former state-owned enterprises was at its peak: old debts were not repaid and new capital arriving as a result of the opening of the economy to foreign investors was coming in too slowly. Laos was badly hit in 1997 by the Asian financial crisis, leading to further liquidity problems in 1998.

Economic Development

A series of five-year plans begun in 1981 continued into the 1990s. The third Five Year Plan (1991-1995) continued previous policies of infrastructure improvement, export growth, import substitution, tax reform, decentralized decision-making, market-determined prices, and encouragement of foreign investment. Four sectors are considered as areas of future income for Laos: mining and energy; agriculture and forestry; tourism; and service, as a way station and service center between China, Viet Nam, and Cambodia. Laos has untapped mineral resources and proven reserves of gold, gemstones and iron ore. In 1993 three western oil companies, Enterprise Oil and Monument Oil, both from the UK, and Hunt Oil of Dallas, engaged in exploration for oil and gas in Laos. The potential for finding hydrocarbons in Laos is largely unknown and exploration risks are considerable, including inadequate geological maps, unexploded ordinance, tough terrain, encounters with the remnants of the anti-communist insurgency movement, tropical and dietary illness, and the expense of drilling and pipeline construction for transport to the Vietnamese coast. Two major hydroelectric projects, the Nam Thuen Dam on a tributary of the Mekong in Khammouan province, and the Xeset dam in southern Laos produce electricity sold to Thailand. In the area of forestry pulp and paper tree plantations would be substituted for the export of timber and agricultural products to serve the Thai market. The opening of the Mittaphap (Friendship) Bridge over the Mekong between Laos and Thailand (1994) is an opportunity for both trade and tourism. A second bridge was approved in 1996.

At the sixth party congress, held in March 1996, Laotian officials debated the country's slow pace of opening up to the international investment community. By that year, the country had allowed more than 500 foreign investors, in a variety of sectors, to either establish or buy (in whole or in part) Laotian businesses. The majority of $5 billion (75%) was invested in hydroelectric power.

For the foreseeable future the economy will depend largely on aid from the IMF and international sources. Japan is currently Laos' largest donor. Aid from the former USSR/Eastern Europe has been cut sharply. In the 1990s the U.S. suspended aid and preferential treatment based on Laos' failure to assist the suppression of drug traffic, but reversed this decision following renewed co-operation by Laos.

SOCIAL WELFARE

Government-sponsored social welfare programs are virtually nonexistent. Laos is one of the world's most impoverished nations. Food intake does not meet basic requirements, and contamination of drinking water is widespread. In 1980 the government indicated that it regarded the nation's population as too low. Family planning programs were disbanded and the use of contraceptives banned. The Laotian population increased by 2.4 percent per year during 1980-1990.

Almost no families own cars, and bicycles and radios are considered luxuries. In general, the lowland Lao have the highest living standards, with lower standards prevailing among the upland tribes.

Women in Laos have traditionally been subservient to men and have generally been discouraged from obtaining an education.

Healthcare

The use of Western medicine has improved health generally but many problems remain. In parts of Laos, malaria-the most serious health threat-is known to affect the majority of children. Other health problems are acute upper respiratory infections (including pneumonia and influenza), diarrhea and dysentery, parasites, yaws, skin ailments, various childhood diseases, hepatitis, venereal disease, and tuberculosis.

In 1995 only 51 percent of the population had access to safe water, and only 32 percent had adequate sanitation. In 1990-1997 there were 0.2 doctors and 2.6 hospital beds per 1,000 people. For the same time period total healthcare expenditures were 2.6 percent of GDP. In 2000 average life expectancy was fifty-three years.

Housing

The traditional Laotian dwelling is rectangular, built entirely of wooden planks and bamboo, with a thatched roof, and raised off the ground on wooden pilings one to two meters (three to six feet) high. There is a critical housing shortage in the towns and many dwellings are substandard. As of 1990, 47 percent of urban and 25 percent of rural dwellers had access to a public water supply while 30 percent of urban and 8 percent of rural dwellers had access to sanitation services.

EDUCATION

Education in Laos is compulsory for eight years. In 1997 there were 7,896 primary schools with 25,831 teachers and 786,335 students. In 1996 all secondary schools enrolled 169,691 students. Sisavongvong University is located in Vientiane. These are also regional technical colleges and sixty-three teacher-training colleges. In 1997 there were 1,369 teaching faculty and 12,732 students enrolled at all higher-level institutions. For 2000 the illiteracy rate was 38.2 percent (males 26.4 percent and females 49.5%).

2000 KEY EVENTS TIMELINE

March

- The Laotian government blames terrorists for a March 30 grenade explosion in a restaurant.

April

- A delegation including Laotian evangelical leaders is sent to Beijing by the Laotian government to learn from the example of China's state-sanctioned churches.

May

- Several people are killed when a bomb explodes in a goldsmith's shop in a crowded Vientiane marketplace.

June

- Two people die in an explosion at a bus station in Vientiane. No group claims responsibility for the wave of bombings in the capital city.

July

- On July 3 a group of royalist Laotian rebels cross into Laos from Thailand and fight a battle with government soldiers in the town of Wang Tao.
- A bomb is found in the capital city of Vientiane's airport on July 30.
- A bomb explodes at the main post office of the capital city of Vientiane on July 31, injuring several people.

August

- A bomb is defused at the Vietnamese embassy at Vientiane on August 1.

September

- Flooding of the Mekong River kills at least nine people in Laos and damages tens of thousands of acres of rice fields.
- Khamsat Souphanouvong, a cabinet minister, is reported to have been missing overseas since July.

October

- A Lao Aviation flight crashes in northeast Laos, killing several passengers.

November

- A bomb explodes at the airport in Vientiane on November 9, injuring at least three people. The blast precedes a visit by Chinese President Jiang Zemin, November 11–13, that strengthens bilateral cooperation between the two countries.
- The Ganga-Mekong Swarnabhuhmi Project is begun in Vientiane November 9 during a conference between Indian and Southeast Asian leaders.
- Chinese President Jiang Zemin visits Laos and discusses economic links.

December

- The Association of Southeast Asian Nations and the European Union hold their joint meeting in Vientiane, an occasion marred by controversy over ASEAN member Myanmar's inclusion in the talks.
- A foreign-owned sapphire mining company is seized by the government, and its Autralian head of security is detained.

ANALYSIS OF EVENTS: 2000

BUSINESS AND THE ECONOMY

The chronically stagnant economy of Laos showed little improvement in 2000. Laos remained one of the world's poorest countries, with most Laotians eking out a living as subsistence farmers. Corruption and inefficiency hampered attempts at growing a free market economy under the auspices of the authoritarian, secretive Communist/military regime.

The Laotian currency, the kip, which spent 1999 in near free-fall, appeared to stabilize at around 7,500 to the dollar in 2000. Government austerity measures put the brakes on inflation, but growth remained slow. The World Bank planned to make its loans to Laos conditional on political reform, seeming to put in jeopardy the controversial Nam Theun II hydroelectric dam project which would need World Bank guarantees for its financing. The dam, a Thai energy project, had been criticized for environmental reasons.

Record autumnal flooding of the Mekong River damaged farmland and disrupted transport in Laos, although the damage was not as severe as in the downstream neighboring countries of Cambodia and Vietnam, and the death toll in Laos was relatively low. Laos continued to depend heavily on foreign aid, but international lenders were impatient with lack of reforms. Thai and Chinese investments were key to the Laotian economy, with China providing sorely needed infrastructure assistance. The United States suspended normal trading relations to pressure Laos regarding two ethnic Hmong dissidents (naturalized U.S. citizens) who disappeared after infiltrating into Laos in April.

A "Visit Laos Year" tourism promotion campaign was marred by bombings near some sites frequented by foreigners. Northern Laos became popular with young travelers, many of whom were seeking narcotics such as locally-grown opium, that were easily available in that region.

GOVERNMENT AND POLITICS

Stirrings of discontent, suddenly revealed by a brief prodemocracy academic demonstration in October 1999, turned shockingly violent in 2000. Unknown elements planted a series of bombs in the capital, Vientiane, and elsewhere, killing several people and creating a sense of unease in the normally somnolent city. Additionally, the Hmong insurgency which dates back to the Indochina War of the 1970s revived in the form of raids and harassment by guerrilla bands. The Hmong rebels were reportedly inspired by millennial prophecies.

Another armed rebel group, apparently loyal to the Laotian royal family deposed by the ruling Communists, staged a daring incursion from Thailand in July. These violent episodes were quickly suppressed, and there were no overt signs of discord or of liberalization from within the politburo. But exiled members of the royal family, notably Paris-based Prince Soulivong Savang, the grandson of Laos's last deposed king, garnered support from the overseas Laotian community. The thirty-seven-year-old prince held meetings with exiled Hmong resistance leaders, and called on the United States to actively broker a transition to democracy for Laos.

In the former royal capital, Luang Prabang, there were subtle signs of monarchist-revival sentiment. Surreptitiously posted prodemocracy stickers began to appear in public places around Vientiane, apparently distributed through clandestine student networks. But despite 2000's obvious manifestations of discontent, any prodemocracy movement inside of Laos was operating strictly underground, with no group coming out in the open to non-violently challenge the regime. Thongpaseuth Keuakhone, a university lecturer arrested at the October 1999 demonstration, may be expected to assume a leadership role if such a movement does emerge.

Relations with Thailand were strained by the cross border raid, with the Laotian government accusing Thailand of willingly harboring its enemies. There were reports (denied by the Laotian government) of Vietnamese military assistance, including ground troops, for suppressing insurgency. Unsubstantiated rumors circulated of conflict within the government between "pro-Vietnam" and "pro-China" factions.

Participation in the Association of Southeast Asian Nations (ASEAN) continued to be an important international forum for Laos, which was perceived as voting in an authoritarian bloc with Vietnam and Myanmar (Burma) in the organization. A joint European Union and ASEAN conference planned to be held in Laos was put in jeopardy by the E.U.'s objections to the Myanmar regime's participation. The U.S. State Department noted Laos's lack of basic political freedoms.

CULTURE AND SOCIETY

A new cultural center, promoting traditional performing arts, was opened in Vientiane. Laos sent a team to the 2000 Olympics in Sydney, Australia. An official delegation was sent to China to study the "official church" method of regulating Christianity.

Media and the arts were heavily censored, but the pop-culture influence of Thai radio and television broadcasts was strong. HIV/AIDS infection continued to rise in Laos, particularly due to intravenous drug abuse. In addition to Golden Triangle heroin addiction, the use of cheap amphetamines (manufactured in Myanmar and smuggled through Laos to Thailand) spread at alarming rates among young people in Laos.

Deforestation by lucrative logging operations, often illegal but with military participation, continued to decimate the environment of the Laotian highlands, and contributed to the ferocity of the Mekong floods. Endemic bureaucratic corruption, rising street crime, and violent business disputes combined with a new atmosphere of political desperation to tarnish Laos's serene, Buddhist self-image.

DIRECTORY

CENTRAL GOVERNMENT

Head of State

President
Khamtay Siphandone, Office of the President

Prime Minister
Sisavath Keobounphanh, Office of the Prime Minister

Ministers

Minister of Foreign Affairs
Somsavat Lengsavad, Ministry of Foreign Affairs, Thatluang Road, Vientiane, Laos
PHONE: +856 414031

Minister of Interior
Asang Laoly, Ministry of Interior

Minister of Education
Phimmasone Leuangkhamma, Ministry of Education

Minister of Information and Culture
Sileua Bounkham, Ministry of Information and Culture

Minister of Labor and Social Welfare
Somphanh Phengkhammy, Ministry of Labor and Social Welfare

Minister of Commerce
Phoumy Thipphavone, Ministry of Commerce

Minister of Industry and Handicrafts
Soulivong Daravong, Ministry of Industry and Handicrafts

Minister of Communications, Transport, Posts and Construction
Phao Bounnaphol, Ministry of Communications, Transport, Posts and Construction

Minister of Public Health
Ponemek Daraloy, Ministry of Public Health

Minister of Justice
Kham Ouane Boupha, Ministry of Justice

Minister of Agriculture and Forestry
Siene Saphangthong, Ministry of Agriculture and Forestry

POLITICAL ORGANIZATIONS

Laos People's Revolutionary Party (LPRP)

TITLE: President
NAME: Khamtai Siphandon

DIPLOMATIC REPRESENTATION

Embassies in Laos

Australia
Nehru St., Vientiane, Laos
PHONE: +856 413610; 413805; 413602

Bulgaria
Sisangvonh area, Vientiane, Laos
PHONE: +856 412110

Cambodia
Thanon Saphan Thong Neua, Vientiane, Laos
PHONE: +856 314952; 312584

Czech Republic
The Deua Rd, Km 4, Vientiane, Laos
PHONE: +856 315291; 215899

China
Wat Nak St., Vientiane, Laos
PHONE: +856 315100; 315101; 315103

Cuba
Ban Saphanthong Nua, Vientiane, Laos
PHONE: +856 314902

France
Sethathirath St., Vientiane, Laos
PHONE: +856 215258; 215259
FAX: +856 215255

Germany
26 Thanon Sok Pa Luang, Vientiane, Laos
PHONE: +856 312110; 312111

India
That Luang Road, Vientiane, Laos
PHONE: +856 413802

Indonesia
Phon Kheng Road, P.O. Box 277, Vientiane, Laos
PHONE: +856 413907; 413909; 413910

Japan
Sisangvone Road, Vientiane, Laos
PHONE: +856 212623; 414400; 414406
FAX: +856 414403

North Korea
Wat Nak Road, Sisattanak, Vientiane, Laos
PHONE: +856 315260; 351261

Malaysia
That Luang Road, Vientiane, Laos
PHONE: +856 414205

Mongolia
Tha Deua Road Km 2, Vientiane, Laos
PHONE: +856 315220

Myanmar
Sokphaluand Road, Vientiane, Laos
PHONE: +856 312439; 314910

Palestine
The Deua Road Km 2.5, Vientiane, Laos
PHONE: +856 315252

Poland
The Deua Road, Km 3, Vientiane, Laos
PHONE: +856 313940; 312085

Russia
Thaphalanxay area, Vientiane, Laos
PHONE: +856 312219; 212222

Slovakia
Tha Deua Rd., Km 4, Vientiane, Laos
PHONE: +856 315291; 215899

Sweden
Wat Nak, Vientiane, Laos
PHONE: +856 313772; 315000; 315018

Thailand
Thanon Phon Kheng, Vientiane, Laos
PHONE: +856 214582; 214583; 214585

United States
Thanon Bartholomie, Vientiane, Laos
PHONE: +856 212580; 312609
FAX: +856 212584

JUDICIAL SYSTEM

Supreme People's Court

BROADCAST MEDIA

Radio Nationale Lao

PO Box 310, Vientiane, Laos
PHONE: +856 212432
FAX: +856 212430
TITLE: Directorate General
CONTACT: Bounthan Inthaxay
TYPE: Government

Voice of America—Lao

VOA—Lao Service, 330 Independence Avenue SW, Room 2702, Washington D.C. 20237, USA
PHONE: +(202) 6193787
FAX: +(202) 6191840
WEBSITE: http://www.voa.gov/lao/
TITLE: Service Chief
CONTACT: Linthong Noinala

Lao National Television (TVNL)

PO Box 310 Vientiane, Laos
PHONE: +856 212432
FAX: +856 212430
TITLE: Directorate General
CONTACT: Khekkeo Soisaya
CHANNEL: 9, 12, 23
TYPE: Government

COLLEGES AND UNIVERSITIES

National University of Laos

PO Box 7322, Vientiane, Laos
PHONE: +856 413631
FAX: +856 412381
E-MAIL: kongsy@pa-laos.net.la
WEBSITE: http://www.canpub.com/nuol

NEWSPAPERS AND MAGAZINES

Khaosan Pathet Lao (News Agency)

WEBSITE: http://asean.kplnet.net/lao_news_agency.html

Viangchan Mai

Viangchan Thurakit-Sang Khom

Vientiane Times

Ministry of Information and Cultures, PO Box 5723, Pangkham ST, Vientiane, Laos
PHONE: +856 216364
FAX: +856 216365
WEBSITE: http://www.vientianetimes.com

Valasan Pathet Lao

80 rue Sethathirath, BP 989, Vientiane, Laos
CIRCULATION: 2,000
TYPE: Political science, general

PUBLISHERS

Lao-phanit

Vientiane Ministere de l'Education nationale, Bureau des manuels, scolaires, Vientiane, Laos
SUBJECTS: Art, Cookery, Economics, Education, Fiction, Geography, Geology, History, Music, Dance, Physics, Social Sciences

RELIGIOUS ORGANIZATIONS

Communist as late as 1978, "re-education" centers specialized in eradicating religious influences from the country. Although Laos has generally made progress toward a more free, democratic system of government, religion has been slow in reorganizing after the purges of the 1970s. Most Laotians are Buddhist; some mountainous regions of the country claim more animists than Buddhist influences.

FURTHER READING

Articles

"Armed Protest in Laos." *The Economist (US),* July 8, 2000, vol. 356, no. 8178, p. 38.

"Laos: Remains Returned to U.S." *New York Times,* October 31, 2000, p. A6.

Swarts, Will. "Not Quite Neighborly." *World Press Review,* September 2000, vol. 47, no. 9, p. 27.

Books

Mansfield, Stephen. *Lao Hill Tribes: Traditions and Patterns of Existence.* New York: Oxford University Press, 2000.

Quincy, Keith. *Harvesting Pa Chay's Wheat: The Hmong and America's Secret War in Laos.* Spokane, WA: Eastern Washington University Press, 2000.

LAOS: STATISTICAL DATA

For sources and notes see "Sources of Statistics" at the front of each volume.

GEOGRAPHY

Geography

Area:

Total: 236,800 sq km.

Land: 230,800 sq km.

Land boundaries:

Total: 5,083 km.

Border countries: Burma 235 km, Cambodia 541 km, China 423 km, Thailand 1,754 km, Vietnam 2,130 km.

Coastline: 0 km (landlocked).

Climate: tropical monsoon; rainy season (May to November); dry season (December to April).

Terrain: mostly rugged mountains; some plains and plateaus.

Natural resources: timber, hydropower, gypsum, tin, gold, gemstones.

Land use:

Arable land: 3%

Permanent crops: 0%

Permanent pastures: 3%

Forests and woodland: 54%

Other: 40% (1993 est.).

HUMAN FACTORS

Demographics (A)

	1990	1995	1998	2000	2010	2020	2030	2040	2050
Population	NA	4,846	5,229	5,498	6,993	8,637	10,249	11,832	13,171
Life expectancy - males	NA	49.4	50.5	51.2	54.9	58.6	62.1	65.4	68.3
Life expectancy - females	NA	52.9	54.2	55.0	59.3	63.5	67.5	71.1	74.3
Birth rate (per 1,000)	NA	40.6	39.2	38.3	33.4	27.7	23.3	19.9	15.9
Death rate (per 1,000)	NA	15.1	14.0	13.4	10.5	8.6	7.6	7.2	7.2
Women of reproductive age (15-49 yrs.)	NA	1,119	1,225	1,304	1,733	2,250	2,780	3,214	3,528
Fertility rate	NA	5.7	5.4	5.2	4.3	3.4	2.8	2.4	2.0

Except as noted, values for vital statistics are in thousands; life expectancy is in years.

Health Personnel

	National Data	World Data (wtd ave)
Total health expenditure as a percentage of GDP, 1990-1998[a]		
Public sector	1.2	2.5
Private sector	1.3	2.9
Total[b]	2.6	5.5
Health expenditure per capita in U.S. dollars, 1990-1998[a]		
Purchasing power parity	34	561
Total	6	483
Availability of health care facilities per 100,000 people		
Hospital beds 1990-1998[a]	260	330
Doctors 1992-1995[a]	NA	122
Nurses 1992-1995[a]	NA	248

Health Indicators

	National Data	World Data
Life expectancy at birth (years)		
1980	45	61
1998	54	67
Daily per capita supply of calories		
1970	2,093	2,358
1997	2,108	2,791
Daily per capital supply of protein		
1997 (grams)	52	74
Total fertility rate (births per woman)		
1980	6.7	3.7
1998	5.5	2.7
Population with access (%)		
To safe water (1990-96)	39	NA
To sanitation (1990-96)	24	NA
People living with (1997)		
Tuberculosis (cases per 100,000)	37.0	60.4
Malaria (cases per 100,000)	1,075.8	42.2
HIV/AIDS (% aged 15 - 49 years)	0.04	0.99

Infants and Malnutrition

	National Data	World Data (wtd ave)
Under 5 mortality rate (1989)	116	NA
% of infants with low birthweight (1992-98)[1]	18	17
Births attended by skilled health staff (% of total births 1996-98)	30	52
% fully immunized at 1 year of age (1995-98)[1]		
TB	56	82
DPT	55	77
Polio	67	77
Measles	71	74
Prevalence of child malnutrition (1992-98)[1] (based on weight for age, % of children under 5 years)	40	30

Ethnic Division

Lao Loum (lowland) 68%

Lao Theung (upland) 22%

Lao Soung (highland) 9%

Ethnic Vietnamese/Chinese 1%

The Lao Soung includes the Hmong ("Meo") and the Yao (Mien).

Religion

Buddhist 60%

Animist and other 40%

In October 1999, the regime proposed a constitutional amendment making Buddhism the state religion; the National Assembly is expected to vote on the amendment sometime in 2000.

Major Languages

Lao (official), French, English, and various ethnic languages.

EDUCATION

Public Education Expenditures

	1997
Public expenditures on education as % of GNP	2.1
Expenditures per student as % of GNP per capita	
Primary	6.4
Secondary	13.8
Tertiary	60.6
Teachers' compensation as % of total current education expenditures	67.2
Pupils per teacher at the primary level	30
Duration of primary education in years	5
World data for comparison	
Public expenditures on education as % of GNP (mean)	4.8

Pupils per teacher at the primary level (wtd ave) . . .33

Duration of primary education in years (mean) 9

Educational Attainment (B)

	1995	1997
Gross enrollment ratio (%)		
Primary level	111.6	111.9
Secondary level	26.8	28.5
Tertiary level	3.0	2.8

Literacy Rates (A)

In thousands and percent	1990	1995	2000	2010
Illiterate population (15+ yrs.)	1,149	1,170	1,190	1,225
Literacy rate - total adult pop. (%)	51.5	56.6	61.7	71.3
Literacy rate - males (%)	65.1	69.4	73.5	80.7
Literacy rate - females (%)	38.6	44.4	50.4	62.2

GOVERNMENT & LAW

Military Affairs (A)

	1990	1992	1995	1996	1997
Military expenditures					
Current dollars (mil.)	NA	110	72	67	60
1997 constant dollars (mil.)	NA	122	75	68	60
Armed forces (000)	55	37	50	50	50
Gross national product (GNP)					
Current dollars (mil.)	947	1,130	1,480	1,610	1,750
1997 constant dollars (mil.)	1,110	1,250	1,540	1,640	1,750
Central government expenditures (CGE)					
1997 constant dollars (mil.)	NA	NA	325	353	342
People (mil.)	4.2	4.4	4.8	5.0	5.1
Military expenditure as % of GNP	NA	9.8	4.9	4.1	3.4
World data on military expenditure as % of GNP	4.5	3.4	2.7	2.6	2.6
Military expenditure as % of CGE	NA	NA	22.9	19.3	17.5
World data on military expenditure as % of CGE	17.0	12.5	10.5	10.3	10.2
Military expenditure per capita (1997 $)	NA	27	15	14	12
World data on military expenditure per capita (1997 $)	242	173	146	143	145
Armed forces per 1,000 people (soldiers)	13.1	8.3	10.3	10	9.8
World data on armed forces per 1,000 people (soldiers)	5.3	4.5	4.1	3.9	3.8
GNP per capita (1997 $)	265	281	318	330	343
Arms imports[6]					
Current dollars (mil.)	40	10	0	0	10
1997 constant dollars (mil.)	47	11	0	0	10
Total imports[7]					
Current dollars (mil.)	185[e]	432	589	690	706
1997 constant dollars (mil.)	217[e]	479	610	702	706
Total exports[7]					
Current dollars (mil.)	61[e]	133	311	328	359
1997 constant dollars (mil.)	71[e]	147	322	328	359
Arms as percent of total imports[8]	21.6	2.3	0	0	1.4
Arms as percent of total exports[8]	0	0	0	0	0

Political Parties

The unicameral National Assembly consists of 99 seats. Members are elected by popular vote to serve five-year terms. By presidential decree, on 27 October 1997, the number of seats increased from 85 to 99. Elections were last held 21 December 1997 (next to be held in 2002). All 99 seats were won by the Lao People's Revolutionary Party (LPPR) or LPRP-approved (independent, non-party member) candidates.

Government Budgets (B)

Revenues . . . .$202.7 million

Expenditures . . . .$385.1 million

Data for FY97/98 est.

LABOR FORCE

Total Labor Force (A)

1 million - 1.5 million.

Labor Force by Occupation

Agriculture 80%

Data for 1997 est.

Unemployment Rate

5.7% (1997 est.)

PRODUCTION SECTOR

Energy Production

Production . . . . .1.34 billion kWh

Production by source

Fossil fuel 2.99%

Hydro 97.01%

Nuclear 0%

Other 0%

Exports . . . . .782 million kWh

Data for 1998.

Energy Consumption

Consumption . . . . .514 million kWh

Imports . . . . .50 million kWh

Data for 1998.

Transportation

Highways:

Total: 21,716 km.

Paved: 9,673.5 km.

Unpaved: 12,042.5 km (1998 est.).

Waterways: about 4,587 km, primarily Mekong and tributaries; 2,897 additional km are sectionally navigable by craft drawing less than 0.5 m.

Pipelines: petroleum products 136 km.

Merchant marine:

Total: 1 ship (1,000 GRT or over) totaling 2,370 GRT/3,000 DWT.

Ships by type: cargo 1 (1999 est.).

Airports: 52 (1999 est.).

Airports - with unpaved runways: 43.

Top Agriculture Products

Sweet potatoes, vegetables, corn, coffee, sugarcane, tobacco, cotton; tea, peanuts, rice; water buffalo, pigs, cattle, poultry.

Top Mining Products (B)

Mineral resources include: gypsum, tin, gold, gemstones.

MANUFACTURING SECTOR

GDP & Manufacturing Summary (B)

	1980	1985	1990	1993	1994	1995
Gross Domestic Product						
Millions of 1990 dollars	515	705	869	1,035	1,122	1,201
Growth rate in percent	1.70	5.06	7.61	6.00	8.40	7.04
Per capita (in 1990 dollars)	161	196	207	225	237	246
Manufacturing Value Added						
Millions of 1990 dollars	23	31	37	49	53[e]	57[e]
Growth rate in percent	7.94	3.85	9.96	8.10	8.50[e]	7.66[e]
Manufacturing share in percent of current prices	NA	NA	NA	13.4	13.4[e]	NA

COMMUNICATIONS

Daily Newspapers

	National Data	World Data for Comparison
Daily Newspapers		
Number of Dailies	3	8,391
Total Circulation (000)	18	548,000
Circulation per 1,000 inhabitants	3.7	96

Telecommunications

Telephones - main lines in use: 20,000 (1995).

Telephones - mobile cellular: 1,600 (1997).

Telephone system: service to general public is poor but improving, with over 20,000 telephones currently in service and an additional 48,000 expected by 2001; the government relies on a radiotelephone network to communicate with remote areas.

Domestic: radiotelephone communications.

International: satellite earth station - 1 Intersputnik (Indian Ocean region).

Radio broadcast stations: AM 12, FM 1, shortwave 4 (1998).

Radios: 730,000 (1997).

Television broadcast stations: 4 (1999).

Televisions: 52,000 (1997).

Internet Service Providers (ISPs): NA

FINANCE, ECONOMICS, & TRADE

Economic Indicators

National product: GDP—purchasing power parity—$7 billion (1999 est.).

National product real growth rate: 5.2% (1999 est.).

National product per capita: $1,300 (1999 est.).

Inflation rate—consumer price index: 140% (1999 est.).

Exchange Rates

Exchange rates:

New kips (NK) per US$1

January 2000	7,674.00
1999	7,102.03
1998	3,298.33
1997	1,259.98
1996	921.02
1995	804.69

As of September 1995, a floating exchange rate policy was adopted.

Top Import Origins

Imports (f.o.b., 1999 est.): $497 million.

Origins: Thailand, Japan, Vietnam, China, Singapore, Hong Kong.

Top Export Destinations

Exports (f.o.b., 1999 est.): $271 million.

Destinations: Vietnam, Thailand, Germany, France, Belgium.

Foreign Aid

Recipient: $345 million (1999 est.).

Import/Export Commodities

Import Commodities	Export Commodities
Machinery and equipment	Wood products
Vehicles	Garments
Fuel	Electricity
	Coffee
	Tin

Balance of Payments

	1994	1995	1996	1997	1998
Exports of goods (f.o.b.)	306	311	323	318	342
Imports of goods (f.o.b.)	−519	−627	−644	−601	−507
Trade balance	−214	−316	−321	−283	−165
Services - debits	−152	−122	−126	−111	−96
Services - credits	87	97	104	106	145
Private transfers (net)	NA	NA	NA	NA	NA
Government transfers (net)	121	110	82	100	74
Overall balance	−160	−237	−265	−206	−77

LATVIA

Republic of Latvia
Latvijas Republika

CAPITAL: Riga

FLAG: The flag consists of a single white horizontal stripe on a maroon field.

ANTHEM: *Dievs, sveti Latviju! (God bless Latvia!)*

MONETARY UNIT: The lat (Ls) was introduced as the official currency in May 1993; $1 = Ls0.33.

WEIGHTS AND MEASURES: The metric system is in force.

HOLIDAYS: New Year's Day, 1 January; Good Friday (movable); Midsummer Festival, 23–24 June; National Day, Proclamation of the Republic, 18 November; Christmas, 25–26 December; New Year's Eve, 31 December.

TIME: 2 PM = noon GMT.

LOCATION AND SIZE: Latvia is located in northeastern Europe, bordering the Baltic Sea, between Sweden and Russia. Comparatively, Latvia is slightly larger than the state of West Virginia, with a total area of 64,100 square kilometers (24,749 square miles). Latvia's boundary length totals 1,150 kilometers (715 miles). Latvia's capital city, Riga, is located in the northern part of the country along the Baltic Sea coast.

CLIMATE: The mean temperature is between 16.8° and 17.6°C (62–64°F) in July and between −6.6° and 2.6 °C (20–27 °F) in January. Mean annual rainfall is between 60–65 centimeters (24–26 inches).

INTRODUCTORY SURVEY

RECENT HISTORY

Germans, Poles, Swedes, and Russians competed for influence in what is now Latvia from the Middle Ages until the eighteenth century when it was incorporated into the Russian Empire. During the nineteenth century a Latvian nationalist movement occurred and on November 18, 1918, the independent Republic of Latvia was proclaimed. It was recognized by Moscow ten years later. However the 1939 Nazi-Soviet pact placed Latvia under Soviet influence. Soviet forces invaded Latvia on June 17, 1940, and incorporated it into the Soviet Union. The Germans seized Latvia in July 1941 when Hitler launched his attack on the Soviet Union, but was recaptured by Soviet forces in 1944.

In the 1980s Soviet President Mikhail Gorbachev's liberal policies allowed Latvians to voice their long-suppressed desire for national self-determination. The Latvian Popular Front (LPF) gained a majority in the elections for the Latvian Supreme Council in the spring of 1990. In August 1991-shortly after the failed coup against Gorbachev-Latvia once again proclaimed its independence.

In April 1994 the Latvian and Russian governments agreed to a schedule that withdrew all Russian troops from Latvia by August 31, 1994. The agreement did not include 599 soldiers at the Skrunda Radar Station that Russia was allowed to operate until August 1998 and dismantle by February 2000. In June 1995 Latvia signed an accord with the European Union that could possibly lead to full membership.

In 1995 Andrise Shkele became prime minister. Shkele balanced the budget and sped up economic reform although his leadership style alienated many and a new government coalition formed in late 1998 opted to exclude him. Latvia elected its first female president in 1999, Vaira Vike-Freiberga, known for strongly promoting Latvian culture. Moscow remains concerned for the status of Russians in Latvia, which constitute 30 percent of the population.

In October 1999 the European Union (EU) announced that Latvia would be a candidate for membership as early as 2003.

GOVERNMENT

Latvia is a parliamentary democracy operating under a 1991 Constitutional Law that supplements the 1922 constitution. The chief of state is the president elected by parliament for a four-year term. The head of government is the prime minister appointed by the president. The cabinet, the Council of Ministers, is nominated by the prime minister and appointed by parliament.

The legislative branch is the unicameral 100-seat parliament, or Salima. Members are elected by direct popular vote to serve four-year terms. Suffrage is universal for Latvian citizens at eighteen years of age.

Judiciary

The courts are being reorganized along democratic lines. Regional courts were added in 1995 to hear appeals of lower court decisions. There is also a Supreme Court and a Constitutional Court.

Political Parties

In the October 1998 elections, six parties gained representation in the parliament (Saeima). The People's Party won the most seats, at twenty-four. The Latvia's Way (LC) took twenty-one seats, National Harmony Party (TSP) took sixteen, a merger of For Fatherland and Freedom with Latvian National Conservative party (TB/LNNK) won seventeen, the Social Democrats won fourteen, and New Party won eight.

DEFENSE

The Latvian armed forces total 5,730, including 1,300 National Guard personnel for border and coastal defense with only one battalion ready for mobile warfare. The 14,500-man militia serves as a reserve. The army has 2,550 personnel, the navy 840, and the air force 210.

ECONOMIC AFFAIRS

Latvia has a relatively well-developed transport and communications network and a variety of industries. The growth rate of the gross domestic product (GDP) increased from −33.5 percent in 1992 to 2.1 percent in 1996. The inflation rate declined from 960 percent to 3.2 percent in 1999. The Latvian economic growth slowed somewhat in 1999 due to the Russian crisis the previous year. Nonetheless Latvia was continuing with its privatization program in hope of qualifying for EU membership in 2003.

Public Finance

A stabilization program was commenced in 1992 (with IMF support), and a new currency (the lat) was issued in May 1993. Tight fiscal and monetary policy helped minimize public finance deterioration and curb inflation. The U.S. Central Intelligence Agency (CIA) estimated that in 1998 Latvia's government took in revenues of approximately $1.33 billion and had expenditures of $1.27 billion, including capital expenditures of $157 million. External debt totaled $1.58 billion.

Income

In 1999 the gross domestic product (GDP) was estimated at $9.8 billion, or $4,200 per capita. The 1999 estimated GDP growth rate was 0 percent and inflation 3.2%. The GDP contribution by sector in 1998 was agriculture 8%, industry 29%, and services 63%.

Industry

Latvia has mainly heavy industries such as chemicals and petrochemicals, metalworking, and machine building. Other industries include synthetic fibers, agricultural machinery, fertilizers, radios, electronics, pharmaceuticals, processed foods, and textiles. Major manufactured items include street and railroad cars, buses and vans, mopeds, washing machines, and telephone systems.

Banking and Finance

In 1991 banking matters were transferred to the Bank of Latvia from Soviet bank officials. The central bank had the authority to issue Latvian rubles and regulate the commercial banking sector. There are many banks in Latvia including the Baltic Transit Bank, Banka Atmoda, Latgale Stocj Commercial Bank, Latvian Credit Bank, Investment Bank of Latvia, and the Latvian Land Bank.

Latvia effectively exited the ruble zone on July 20, 1992. By early 1993 the Bank of Latvia introduced a national currency, the lat. The lat is now fully convertible for capital- and current-account purposes.

Latvia's banking sector has proved one of the country's most successful industries and also its most controversial. Riga has developed into an offshore financial center, offering numbered accounts and related services, and drawing in a substantial chunk of flight capital from other former Soviet republics. Owing to fairly liberal banking laws in the early 1990s, a large number of banks (fifty-four as of May 1995) had been established. Subsequently, capital and other requirements have been progressively tightened.

In February 1997 the Bank of Latvia gave its approval to the proposed merger between the Latvian Savings Bank and the United Baltic Bank of Riga. As a result of the merger, the state now owns 75 percent of shares in the Latvian Savings Bank. The government's plans are to privatize the newly merged entity.

There is a stock exchange in Riga.

Economic Development

The government began introducing economic reforms in 1990 to effect the transition to a market-driven economy. Individual and family-owned businesses, cooperatives, and privately- and publicly-held companies are now permitted. The privatization process was simplified with a 1994 law that created the Privatization Agency (PA) and the State Property Fund.

By mid-1994 450 state enterprises had been transferred for privatization. Large-scale privatization began in 1996. Privatization of large state-owned utilities faced delays in 1999 but was expected to accelerate in the next two years.

Latvia officially joined the World Trade Organization in 1999. Latvia projected 3.5 percent GDP growth, 3 percent inflation, and a 2 percent fiscal deficit by 2000. Preparing for EU membership by 2003 was the top foreign priority.

SOCIAL WELFARE

Laws passed in 1995, 1996, and 1998 on social insurance established old age, disability, and survivorship pensions for all wage and salary earners, self-employed persons, active military personnel, and persons in various other categories. Sickness and maternity benefits are provided to all permanent residents. A universal program of family allowances exists as well as workers' compensation and unemployment programs.

Although employment discrimination based on sex is illegal, women are barred from certain occupations considered dangerous. Some employers hesitate to hire women because they are legally required to pay childbirth benefits to female employees.

Healthcare

Life expectancy in 2000 was 68.4 years. In 1990-1997 there were three physicians for every 1,000 people. During that same period public health expenditures equaled 3.5 percent of GDP. Heart disease is the cause of death for 40% of all Latvians over age sixty-five.

Housing

Housing construction lags behind demand. At the beginning of 1990 165,000 families (one out of five) were registered for new housing.

EDUCATION

Compulsory education lasts for nine years beginning at the age of seven. Primary education lasts for four years followed by eight years of secondary education. Latvia has two major universities: the University of Latvia and the Riga Technical University. In 1997 there were 56,187 students in institutes of higher learning. The literacy rate was 100%.

2000 KEY EVENTS TIMELINE

January

- Along with Baltic neighbors Estonia and Lithuania, Latvia signs the Charter of Partnership with NATO.

February

- In a change of policy, the European Union (EU) announces that Latvia, one of the "second-wave" EU candidate countries, can proceed to accession negotiations.

April

- Andris Skele resigns as prime minister on April 12 after his three-party centrist coalition falls apart over a privatization issue and charges of pedophilia. Andris Berzins becomes prime minister at the head of a center-right coalition.

August

- Lawmakers ease a rule requiring use of the Latvian language in most situations on August 23, bowing to the demands of Russian-speaking Latvians and anti-discrimination standards.

November

- The leaders of Latvia's four major religions boycott Independence Day services November 18 due to political corruption and immorality.
- Prime Minister Andris Berzins announces November 29 the biggest campaign ever to fight corruption in Latvia.

ANALYSIS OF EVENTS: 2000

BUSINESS AND THE ECONOMY

The generally healthy state of Latvia's economy in the wake of a 1995 banking crisis and Russia's 1999 economic crisis was largely credited to austerity measures adhered to by outgoing prime minister Andris Skele, as well as effective management of the nation's central bank. Upon taking office the country's new prime minister, Andris Berzins, voiced his intention of continuing the tight economic policies of his predecessor to further reduce Latvia's budget deficit and attract foreign investment.

One area in which Latvia's progress had been slow was privatization, where the country lagged behind neighboring Estonia and other former Soviet-bloc countries. The small number of major enterprises that had been sold off by the government was considered to account at least in part for Latvia's comparatively low level of foreign investment. Prime Minister Berzins announced that he would support the cash sale of state-owned companies.

Compliance with the international standards and laws needed for admission to the European Union (E.U.) was a top priority of Latvia's new government. In February the E.U. announced that Latvia, in spite of its status as a "second-wave" candidate, could proceed to accession negotiations. Formal membership talks were opened the same month in talks that also included representatives of Romania, Bulgaria, Slovakia, Lithuania, and Malta.

GOVERNMENT AND POLITICS

Latvia's ninth government of the past decade's post-Soviet era collapsed in April with the withdrawal of one of its coalition partners, the Fatherland Party, following a controversy over the privatization of the state-owned power utility, as well as the implication of government officials in a pedophilia scandal. On April 12 Prime Minister Andris Skele announced his resignation—the third time he had resigned the office of prime minister four years. A new four-party center-right coalition headed by former Riga mayor Andris Berzins took over the reigns of government the following month. Given the revolving-door nature of Latvia's governments, it was considered possible that Berzins's government might not even last until the next scheduled elections, in the fall of 2002.

The new government, like its predecessors, faced the difficult task of balancing its aspirations to join the E.U. and North Atlantic Treaty Organization (NATO) with its close historical, economic, and geographic ties to Russia. Latvia's president, Vaira Vike-Freiberga, voiced concern over the assertive foreign-policy stance of Russian president Vladimir Putin. Russia, for its part, expressed a strong negative reaction to official confirmations of Latvia's status as a viable candidate for NATO membership. Relations with Russia were further complicated by the second-class citizenship of Latvia's large Russian-speaking population and the ongoing and controversial prosecution of former Soviet officers for war crimes committed during World War II.

CULTURE AND SOCIETY

The status of Latvia's Russian speakers, who made up almost 40 percent of the nation's population, remained an inflammatory issue. International pressure had ended the blatant discrimination that characterized the early years of the post-Soviet era, but ethnic Russians were still required to pass exams to attain citizenship, without which they were barred from public-sector jobs. The sensitivity of the matter was evident in the response produced by amendments to a new language requirement law requiring ethnic Russians to use the Latvian language in certain situations. Russia, backed by the OSCE, had condemned the law as discriminatory while Latvian nationalist groups attacked it as too liberal. The amendments governed language certification requirements.

Contributing to tensions between Latvia's major ethnic groups were a series of trials such as that of Vasily Kononov, charged with crimes against humanity for his Nazi resistance activities as a member of the Russian partisans during World War II. The seventy-seven-year-old Kononov was held responsible for the deaths of nine civilians in a raid on a Latvian village. Russia charged that by prosecuting former Soviet partisans more vigorously than Nazi sympathizers, the Latvian government was discriminating against ethnic Russians and implicitly showing support for Naziism.

The sex scandal that helped topple the government of Prime Minister Andris Skele brought renewed attention to Latvia's alleged status as a major transit point for the sex trade in eastern Europe. The scandal—in which directors of a modeling agency and beauty pageant were arrested for procurement and sale of pornographic videos—rocked the nation when hearings produced allegations of ties to top government officials including Prime Minister Skele and Justice Minister Valdis Birkavs. Although both leaders vigorously attacked the accusations as political motivated, the resulting taint was sufficient to bring down an already weakened government, and some feared the matter could endanger Latvia's all-important relationships with the E.U. and NATO. In the aftermath of the affair, the Latvian government banned children under the age of eighteen from modeling or entering beauty contests.

DIRECTORY

CENTRAL GOVERNMENT

Head of State

President
Vaira Vike-Freiberga, Office of the President,
Pils Laukums 3, LV-1900 Riga, Latvia
PHONE: +371 (34) 7377548
FAX: +371 (34) 7325800
E-MAIL: chancery@president.lv

Ministers

Prime Minister
Andris Ðíçle, Office of the Prime Minister,
Brîvîbas Blvd. 36, LV-1395 Riga, Latvia
PHONE: +371 (34) 7332232
FAX: +371 (34) 7286598

Minister of Defense
Ìirts Valdis Kristovskis, Ministry of Defense

Minister of Foreign Affairs
Indulis Bçrziòð, Ministry of Foreign Affairs, Brivibas Blvd. 36, LV-1395 Riga, Latvia
PHONE: +371 (34) 7016210
FAX: +371 (34) 7828121; 7282882
E-MAIL: info@mfa.gov.lv

Minister of Finance
Gundars Berzins, Ministry of Finance

Minister of Economy
Edmunds Krastiòð, Ministry of Economy

Minister of Interior
Mareks Segliòð, Ministry of Interior

Minister of Education and Science
Karlis Greiskalns, Ministry of Education and Science, Vaïòu Iela 2, LV-1050 Rîga, Latvia
PHONE: +371 (34) 7222415
FAX: +371 (34) 7213992
E-MAIL: izm@izm.gov.lv

Minister of Special Assignments for Public and Municipal Reform Affairs
Jânis Bunkðs, Ministry of Special Assignments for Public and Municipal Reform Affairs

Minister of Co-Operation with International Financial Institutions
Roberts Zîle, Ministry of Co-Operation with International Financial Institutions

Minister of Culture
Karina Pçtersone, Ministry of Culture

Minister of Welfare
Andrejs Pozarnovs, Ministry of Welfare

Minister of Transport
Anatolijs Gorbunovs, Ministry of Transport

Minister of Justice
Ingrida Labucka, Ministry of Justice

Minister of Environmental Protection and Regional Development
Vladimirs Makarovs, Ministry of Environmental Protection and Regional Development, Peldu iela 25, LV-1494 Riga, Latvia
PHONE: +371 (34) 7026470
FAX: +371 (34) 7820442

Minister of Agriculture
Atis Slakteris, Ministry of Agriculture

POLITICAL ORGANIZATIONS

Demokratiska Partija Saimnieks-DPS (Democratic Party Master)

TITLE: Chairman
NAME: Ziedonis Cevers

Latvijas Zemnieku Savienîba (Latvian Farmer's Union)

Jçkaba 16-309, LV-1001 Rîga, Latvia
PHONE: +371 (34) 7087270
FAX: +371 (34) 7087262
E-MAIL: lzs@lzs.lv
TITLE: Chairman
NAME: Laimonis Strujevics

Latvijas Zemnieku Savieniba-LZS (Latvian Farmers Union)

TITLE: Chairmen
NAME: Laimonis Strujevics; Talavs Jundzis

Savieniba Latvijas Celš-LC (Latvia's Way)

TITLE: Chairman
NAME: Andrei Pantelejevs

Latvian Social-Democratic Workers Party (LSDA)

NAME: Janis Bojars

Latvijas Socialistiska Partija-LSP (Latvian Socialist Party)

NAME: Sergejs Diamanis

Latvijas Vienibas Partija-LVP (Latvian Unity Party)

NAME: A. Kauls

Tautas Saskadias Partija (National Harmony Party)

NAME: Janis Jurkans

Jauna Partija (New Party)

NAME: Raimonds Pauls

Tautas Kustibas Latvijai-TKL (People's Movement for Latvia)

NAME: Joachim Siegerist

Tautas Partija-TP (People's Party)

Dzirnavu iela 68, LV-1050 Rîga, Latvia
PHONE: +371 (34) 7286441
FAX: +371 (34) 7286405
E-MAIL: koord1@tautaspartija.lv
TITLE: Chairman
NAME: Andris Ðîçle

Tevzemei un Brivibai-TB (Fatherland and Freedom)

NAME: Maris Grinblats; Anna Seile; Andrejs Krastins

Latvian Green Party (LSZ)

NAME: Olegs Batarevsk

Savienîba "Latvijas cels" (LC)

DIPLOMATIC REPRESENTATION

Embassies in Latvia

Austria
Basteja bulvaris 14, LV-1050 Riga, Latvia
PHONE: +371 (34) 7216125
FAX: +371 (34) 7216126
TITLE: Ambassador
NAME: Anton Kozusnik

Canada
Doma laukums 4, LV-1977 Riga, Latvia
PHONE: +371 (34) 7226315; 7221822; 7830141
FAX: +371 (34) 7830140
TITLE: Ambassador
NAME: Peter P.L. McKellar

China
Ganibu dambis 5, LV-1045 Riga, Latvia
PHONE: +371 (34) 7357023; 7357024
FAX: +371 (34) 7357025; 9350502
TITLE: Ambassador
NAME: Yao Peisheng

France
Raina bulvaris 9, LV-1050 Riga, Latvia
PHONE: +371 (34) 7820135; 7213972
FAX: +371 (34) 7820131
TITLE: Ambassador
NAME: Louise Avon

Germany
Raina bulvaris 13, LV-1050 Riga, Latvia
PHONE: +371 (34) 7229096
FAX: +371 (34) 7820223
TITLE: Ambassador
NAME: Reinhart Kraus

Italy
Teatra iela 9, 4th floor, LV-1050 Riga, Latvia
PHONE: +371 (34) 7216069; 7211507; 7211517
FAX: +371 (34) 7216084
E-MAIL: ambitalia.riga@apollo.lv
TITLE: Ambassador
NAME: Alessandro Pietromarchi

Russia
Antonijas iela 2, LV-1010 Riga, Latvia
PHONE: +371 (34) 7220693; 7332151
FAX: +371 (34) 7830209
E-MAIL: rusembas@junik.lv
TITLE: Ambassador
NAME: Alexander Udaltsov

United Kingdom
J. Alunana iela 5, LV-1010 Riga, Latvia
PHONE: +371 (34) 7338126
FAX: +371 (34) 7338132
E-MAIL: british.embassy@apollo.lv
TITLE: Ambassador
NAME: Stephen Thomas Nash

United States
Raina bulvaris 7, LV-1510 Riga, Latvia
PHONE: +371 (34) 7210005; 7222349
FAX: +371 (34) 7820047
TITLE: Ambassador
NAME: James H. Holmes

JUDICIAL SYSTEM

Supreme Court

BROADCAST MEDIA

Latvijas Radio

Doma Iaukuma 8, LV-1505 Riga, Latvia
PHONE: +371 (34) 206722
FAX: +371 (34) 206709
E-MAIL: radio@radio.org.lv
WEBSITE: http://www.radio.org.lv/
TITLE: Directorate General
CONTACT: Dzintris Kolats
TYPE: Government

Radio Latvia

PO Box 266, LV-1098, Riga, Latvia
PHONE: +371 (34) 206735
FAX: +371 (34) 206709
WEBSITE: http://www.radio.org.lv
TITLE: Director
CONTACT: Jogita Cinkus
LANGUAGE: English, Latvian, Russian

Lavijas Neatkarariga Televizija (LNT)

PHONE: +371 (34) 333034
TYPE: Government

Latvijas Televizija (LTV)

Zakusalas krastmala 3, Riga LV-1509, Latvia
PHONE: +371 (34) 200314

FAX: +371 (34) 200025
TITLE: Director of Television
CONTACT: Imants-Rakins
TYPE: Government

Latvijas Valsts Radio un Televizijas Centrs (Latvian State Radio and Television Center)

Erglu iela 7, LV-1012 Riga, Latvia
PHONE: +371 (34) 108704
FAX: +371 (34) 333886
E-MAIL: lvtrc@lvtrc.lv
WEBSITE: http://www.lvrtc.lv
TITLE: Director
CONTACT: Maris Pauders
TYPE: Government

Nacionala Radio un Televizijas Padome (National Radio and Television Council)

Smilsu iela 1/3, LV-1939 Riga, Latvia
PHONE: +371 (34) 221848
FAX: +371 (34) 220448
TITLE: Chairman
CONTACT: Ojars Rubenis
TYPE: Public

COLLEGES AND UNIVERSITIES

Latvijas Universitate

Bulvar Rainisa 19, Riga LV-1586, Latvia
PHONE: +371 (34) 7229076
FAX: +371 (34) 7820113
E-MAIL: lu@lanet.lv
WEBSITE: http://www.lu.lv

Riga Technical University

Kalku Iela 1a, Riga LV-1658, Latvia
PHONE: +371 (34) 7225885
FAX: +371 (34) 7820094
E-MAIL: rtu@adm.tru.lv
WEBSITE: http://www.rtu.lv

NEWSPAPERS AND MAGAZINES

Biznes-Shans (Business Chance)

Dizhe Ltd., Balasta Dambis 3-065, Riga LV-1081 Latvia
PHONE: +371 (34) 468169
FAX: +371 (34) 468074
TITLE: Editor
CONTACT: Lucy Pribylskaya
CIRCULATION: 12,600

Diena (The Day)

Joint Stock Co. Diena, Mukusalas 41, Riga, Latvia
PHONE: +371 (34) 7063120
FAX: +371 (34) 7063197
E-MAIL: diena@diena.lv
WEBSITE: http://www.diena.lv
TITLE: Editor-in-Chief
CONTACT: Samite Elerte
CIRCULATION: 60,000

Dienas Bizness (Business Day)

PO Box 2, Riga LV-1081 Latvia
PHONE: +371 (34) 464690
FAX: +371 (34) 464719
TITLE: Editor-in-Chief
CONTACT: Juris Paiders
CIRCULATION: 18,000

Patvijas Zeme/Latviyskaya Zemlya (The Land of Latvia)

Republikas Laukuma 2, Riga LV-1068 Latvia
PHONE: +371 (34) 327923
FAX: +371 (34) 325638
TITLE: Editor-in-Chief
CONTACT: Ksenija Zagorarska
CIRCULATION: 46,000

Lauku Avize

Lauku Avize Ltd., Dzirnavu iela 21, Riga LV-1010 Latvia
PHONE: +371 (34) 7096698
FAX: +371 (34) 7096697
E-MAIL: lavize@mail.bkc.lv
WEBSITE: http://www.news.lv/lavize
TITLE: Editor-in-Chief
CONTACT: Viesturs Serdans
CIRCULATION: 105,000

Nakts (The Night)

Nedelraksts Nakts, Kr. Barona 5, Riga LV-1011 Latvia
CIRCULATION: 20,000

Neatkariga Rita Avize

NC Ltd., Balasta Dambis 3 ak 34, Riga LV-1081 Latvia
PHONE: +371 (34) 462496
FAX: +371 (34) 462291
E-MAIL: al@nra.v
WEBSITE: http://www.nra.lv
TITLE: Publisher, Editor-in-Chief

CONTACT: Andris Jakubans
CIRCULATION: 12,000

Panorama Latvii (View of Latvia)

Panorama Latvii Ltd., Balasta Dambis 3, Riga LV-1081 Latvia
PHONE: +371 (34) 463366
FAX: +371 (34) 465381
TITLE: Editor-in-Chief
CONTACT: Vladimir Fabers
CIRCULATION: 30,000

Rigas Blass (Voice of Riga)

Baltic News Ltd., Balasta Dambis 3, Riga LV-1081 Latvia
PHONE: +371 (34) 7286284
FAX: +371 (34) 7860070
TITLE: Editor-in-Chief
CONTACT: Balda Krumina
CIRCULATION: 38,000

Rigas Santims

Petits Ltd., Balasta Dambis 3, Riga LV-1081 Latvia
PHONE: +371 (34) 466148
FAX: +371 (34) 467782

Rigas Vilni

Latvijas TV, Zakusalas krastmala, Riga LV-1081 Latvia
PHONE: +371 (34) 7200558
FAX: +371 (34) 7200832
TITLE: Editor-in-Chief
CONTACT: Anita Spruksta

Vakara Zinas (Evening News)

BMMC Ltd., Bezdeligu 12, Riga LV-1047 Latvia
PHONE: +371 (34) 7619641
FAX: +371 (34) 7612383
TITLE: Editor
CONTACT: Ainis Saulitis
CIRCULATION: 76,000

Baltic IT Review

Raina Blvd., 29, LV-1459 Riga, Latvia
FAX: +371 (34) 7242397
E-MAIL: maraj@dtmedia.lv
TITLE: Editor
CONTACT: Mara Jakobsone
TYPE: Education, library and information science

Baltiiskie Shakhmaty

PO Box 241, 226050 Riga, Latvia
TITLE: Editor
CONTACT: Nikolai Zhuravlev
CIRCULATION: 10,000
TYPE: Sports and recreation, general

Latvijas Ekonomist

Elizabetes, 45-47, ofis 317, Riga, Latvia
FAX: +371 (34) 7222861
TITLE: Editor
CONTACT: E. Ogurok
TYPE: Business and economics, general

Latvijas Kimijas Zurnals

Turgeneva iela, 19, Riga LV-1530 Latvia
TITLE: Editor
CONTACT: T. Millers
TYPE: Science, chemistry, general

PUBLISHERS

Artava Ltd.

Bezdeligu 12, LV-1007 Riga, Latvia
PHONE: +371 (34) 7830254
FAX: +371 (34) 7830254
E-MAIL: artava@bmmc.lv
TITLE: Director
CONTACT: Vladis Spare
SUBJECTS: Biography, Fiction, How-To, Poetry, Romance, Science Fiction, Fantasy, Self-Help

Bibliography Institute of the National Library of Latvia

Anglikanu iela 5, 1816 Riga, Latvia
PHONE: +371 (34) 7225135
FAX: +371 (34) 7224587
E-MAIL: anitag@lbi.lnb.lv
WEBSITE: http://www.vip.latnet.lv/lnb
TITLE: Deputy Director
CONTACT: Anita Goldberg
SUBJECTS: Publishing & Book Trade Reference, Library & Information Sciences
TOTAL PUBLISHED: 3 print; 3 online

Egmont Latvia Ltd.

3 Balasta Dambis, PO Box 30, LV-1081 Riga, Latvia
PHONE: +371 (34) 2468671
FAX: +371 (34) 7860049
E-MAIL: janis@egmont.lv
TITLE: General Manager
CONTACT: Janis Blums

SUBJECTS: Advertising, Fiction, Film, Video, Sports, Athletics, Western Fiction, Children's Literature

Lielvards Apgads

Gaismas iela, 5070 Lielvarde Ogresraj, Latvia
PHONE: +371 (25) 53824
FAX: +371 (25) 54310
E-MAIL: lvards@lanet.lv
SUBJECTS: Biological Sciences, Chemistry, Engineering, Computer Science, Geography, Geology, Health, Nutrition, History, Physics, Social Sciences

Nordik/Tapals Publishers Ltd.

Daugavgrivas 36-9, LV-1007 Riga, Latvia
PHONE: +371 (34) 7602672; 7602617
FAX: +371 (34) 7602818
E-MAIL: nordik@nordik.lv
WEBSITE: http://www.nordik.lv
TITLE: Director
CONTACT: Janis Juska
SUBJECTS: Animals, Communications, Criminology, Environmental Studies, Fiction, History, Law, Literature, Nonfiction (General), Science, Religion, Music
TOTAL PUBLISHED: 60 print

Patmos

Baznicas iela 12a, LV-1010 Riga, Latvia
PHONE: +371 (34) 7289674
FAX: +371 (34) 7820437
E-MAIL: bauc@mail.bkc.lv
TITLE: Publishing Director
CONTACT: Zigurds Laudurgs
SUBJECTS: Biblical Studies, Health, Nutrition, Religion, Theology

Preses Nams

Balasta dambis 3, LV-1081 Riga, Latvia
PHONE: +371 (34) 465732
FAX: +371 (34) 465624
TITLE: Director, Publishing House
CONTACT: Mara Caune
SUBJECTS: Agriculture, Animals, Art, Occult, Behavioral Sciences, Biography, Business, Child Care, Education, Engineering, Science, Environmental Studies, Fiction, History, Health, Literature, Sports, Women's Studies
TOTAL PUBLISHED: 600 print

S/A Tiesiskas informacijas cerfus

Baznicas icla 27/29, LV-1010 Riga, Latvia
PHONE: +371 (34) 7220422
FAX: +371 (34) 7213854
E-MAIL: mariss@date.lv
TITLE: Director
CONTACT: Signe Terihova
SUBJECTS: Law

Zvaigzne ABC Publishers Ltd.

105 K Valdemara iela, LV-1013 Riga, Latvia
PHONE: +371 (34) 372396
FAX: +371 (34) 7828431
E-MAIL: zvaigzne@latnet.com.lv
TITLE: Foreign Rights & Sales Manager
CONTACT: Ruta Keisa
SUBJECTS: Education, English as a Second Language, Nonfiction (General)
TOTAL PUBLISHED: 1,700 print

RELIGIOUS ORGANIZATIONS

Buddhist

Riga Zen Center
Stabu 6-4, Riga, LV-1010 Latvia
E-MAIL: kolo@mailbox.riga.lv
NAME: Wu Bong

Jewish

Chabad Lubaitch of Latvia
PO Box 96, Riga LV-1047, Latvia
PHONE: +371 (34) 7338221
E-MAIL: chabad@mailbox.riga.lv
WEBSITE: http://www.glasnet.ru/~jns/english/cis/latvia/latvia.htm
NAME: Rabbi Mordechai Glazman

Orthodox

Great Martyr Barbara Church
Krasta iela 99, Riga LV-1063, Latvia
PHONE: +371 (34) 2256219
TITLE: Abbot Constantine
NAME: Maslov

Protestant

Consistory of the Evangelical Lutheran Church of Latvia
Pils iela 4, Riga, LV-1050, Latvia
PHONE: +371 (34) 7226057
FAX: +371 (34) 7820041
E-MAIL: konsistorija@parks.lv
WEBSITE: http://www.lutheran.lv
TITLE: Archbishop
NAME: Dr. Janis Vanags

Latvian Conference of Seventh-Day Adventists Church
Baznicas Street 12a, Riga LV-1010, Latvia
PHONE: +371 (34) 7240121
FAX: +371 (34) 7240013
E-MAIL: lds@mail.bkc.lv
WEBSITE: http://www.tagnet.org/latvia/en/

Scientology

Dianetics Center of Riga
Laspesa Street 27 of 4, Riga LV-1011, Latvia
PHONE: +371 (34) 280195

FURTHER READING

Articles

"Andris Berzins, a Hard-Pressed Latvian." *The Economist (US),* June 24, 2000, vol. 355, no. 8176, p. 62.

"Latvia's Language Tremors." *Christian Science Monitor,* September 19, 2000, p. 13.

Books

Noble, John. *Estonia, Latvia, and Lithuania.* 2nd ed. London: Lonely Planet, 2000.

Press, Bernhard. *The Murder of the Jews in Latvia: 1941–1945.* Evanston, IL: Northwestern University Press, 2000.

LATVIA: STATISTICAL DATA

For sources and notes see "Sources of Statistics" at the front of each volume.

GEOGRAPHY

Geography

Area:

Total: 64,589 sq km.

Land: 64,589 sq km.

Land boundaries:

Total: 1,150 km.

Border countries: Belarus 141 km, Estonia 339 km, Lithuania 453 km, Russia 217 km.

Coastline: 531 km.

Climate: maritime; wet, moderate winters.

Terrain: low plain.

Natural resources: minimal; amber, peat, limestone, dolomite, hydropower, arable land.

Land use:

Arable land: 27%

Permanent crops: 0%

Permanent pastures: 13%

Forests and woodland: 46%

Other: 14% (1993 est.).

HUMAN FACTORS

Demographics (A)

	1990	1995	1998	2000	2010	2020	2030	2040	2050
Population	2,672	2,523	2,447	2,405	2,252	2,151	2,019	1,894	1,755
Life expectancy - males	64.0	60.8	61.8	62.5	65.7	68.6	71.2	73.3	75.2
Life expectancy - females	74.2	73.1	74.0	74.6	77.3	79.6	81.4	82.9	84.2
Birth rate (per 1,000)	14.2	8.5	7.5	7.8	10.7	8.9	7.8	8.5	7.5
Death rate (per 1,000)	13.1	15.4	15.1	14.9	14.6	14.2	14.3	15.1	16.0
Women of reproductive age (15-49 yrs.)	648.4	610.5	607.4	606.4	570.8	486.9	439.2	357.2	327.7
Fertility rate	2.0	1.3	1.1	1.1	1.4	1.6	1.5	1.5	1.5

Except as noted, values for vital statistics are in thousands; life expectancy is in years.

Health Personnel

	National Data	World Data (wtd ave)
Total health expenditure as a percentage of GDP, 1990-1998[a]		
Public sector	4.0	2.5
Private sector	2.4	2.9
Total[b]	6.4	5.5
Health expenditure per capita in U.S. dollars, 1990-1998[a]		
Purchasing power parity	366	561
Total	168	483
Availability of health care facilities per 100,000 people		
Hospital beds 1990-1998[a]	1,030	330
Doctors 1992-1995[a]	303	122
Nurses 1992-1995[a]	628	248

Health Indicators

	National Data	World Data
Life expectancy at birth (years)		
1980	69	61
1998	70	67
Daily per capita supply of calories		
1970	NA	2,358
1997	2,864	2,791
Daily per capital supply of protein		
1997 (grams)	79	74
Total fertility rate (births per woman)		
1980	2.0	3.7
1998	1.1	2.7
People living with (1997)		
Tuberculosis (cases per 100,000)	81.0	60.4
HIV/AIDS (% aged 15 - 49 years)	0.01	0.99

Infants and Malnutrition

	National Data	World Data (wtd ave)
Under 5 mortality rate (1989)	22	NA
% of infants with low birthweight (1992-98)[1]	4	17
Births attended by skilled health staff (% of total births 1996-98)	100	52
% fully immunized at 1 year of age (1995-98)[1]		
TB	100	82
DPT	94	77
Polio	94	77
Measles	97	74
Prevalence of child malnutrition (1992-98)[1] (based on weight for age, % of children under 5 years)	NA	30

Ethnic Division

Latvian 56.5%

Russian 30.4%

Byelorussian 4.3%

Ukrainian 2.8%

Polish 2.6%

Other 3.4%

Religion

Lutheran, Roman Catholic, Russian Orthodox.

Major Languages

Lettish (official), Lithuanian, Russian, other.

EDUCATION

Public Education Expenditures

	1980	1997
Public expenditures on education as % of GNP	3.3	6.3
Expenditures per student as % of GNP per capita		
Secondary	NA	37.1
Tertiary	19.1	32.9
Teachers' compensation as % of total current education expenditures	NA	40.5
Pupils per teacher at the primary level	NA	13
Duration of primary education in years	NA	NA
World data for comparison		
Public expenditures on education as % of GNP (mean)	3.9	4.8
Pupils per teacher at the primary level (wtd ave)	NA	33
Duration of primary education in years (mean)	NA	9

Educational Attainment (A)

Age group (1989) ....25+
Population of this age group 1,725,639
Highest level attained (%)
No schooling 0.6
First level
Not completed 18.5
Completed 21.2
Entered second level 46.3
Entered post-secondary 13.4

Literacy Rates (B)

	National Data	World Data
Adult literacy rate		
1980		
Male	100	75
Female	98	58
1995		
Male	100	81
Female	100	65

(Continued on next page.)

GOVERNMENT & LAW

Military Affairs (A)

	1992	1995	1996	1997
Military expenditures				
Current dollars (mil.)	160	84	87	97
1997 constant dollars (mil.)	177	87	88	97
Armed forces (000)	5	7	7	5
Gross national product (GNP)				
Current dollars (mil.)	10,300[e]	9,420[e]	9,960	10,800
1997 constant dollars (mil.)	11,400[e]	9,760[e]	10,100	10,800
Central government expenditures (CGE)				
1997 constant dollars (mil.)	NA	3,180	3,260	3,840
People (mil.)	2.6	2.5	2.5	2.4
Military expenditure as % of GNP	1.6	0.9	0.9	0.9
World data on military expenditure as % of GNP	3.4	2.7	2.6	2.6
Military expenditure as % of CGE	NA	2.7	2.7	2.5
World data on military expenditure as % of CGE	12.5	10.5	10.3	10.2
Military expenditure per capita (1997 $)	67	35	36	40
World data on military expenditure per capita (1997 $)	173	146	143	145
Armed forces per 1,000 people (soldiers)	1.9	2.8	2.8	2.1
World data on armed forces per 1,000 people (soldiers)	4.5	4.1	3.9	3.8
GNP per capita (1997 $)	4,350	3,900	4,110	4,460
Arms imports[6]				
Current dollars (mil.)	0	10	10	0
1997 constant dollars (mil.)	0	10	10	0
Total imports[7]				
Current dollars (mil.)	944	1,810	2,311	2,718
1997 constant dollars (mil.)	1,047	1,874	2,350	2,718
Total exports[7]				
Current dollars (mil.)	825	1,283	1,424	1,664
1997 constant dollars (mil.)	915	1,328	1,448	1,664
Arms as percent of total imports[8]	0	0.6	0.4	0
Arms as percent of total exports[8]	0	0	0	0

(Continued on next page.)

EDUCATION (cont.)

Libraries

National Libraries **1997**
- Administrative Units 1
- Service Points or Branches 1
- Number of Volumes (000) 2,414
- Registered Users (000) 80
- Loans to Users (000) 1,039
- Total Library Staff 423

Public Libraries **1997**
- Administrative Units 998
- Service Points or Branches . . . . NA
- Number of Volumes (000) 14,948
- Registered Users (000) 508
- Loans to Users (000) 17,806
- Total Library Staff 2,315

GOVERNMENT & LAW (cont.)

Political Parties

Parliament (Saeima)	% of vote	no. of seats
People's Party	21%	24
Latvia's Way (LC)	18%	21
National Harmony Party (TSP)	14%	16
For Fatherland and Freedom/Latvian National Conservative Party (TB/LNNK)	14%	17
Social Democrats	13%	14
New Party	8%	8

Elections last held 3 October 1998 (next to be held October 2002).

Government Budgets (A)

Year: 1998

Total Expenditures: 1,246.48 Millions of Lats

Expenditures as a percentage of the total by function:
- General public services and public order 13.29
- Defense 2.60
- Education 5.35
- Health 11.02
- Social Security and Welfare 40.84
- Housing and community amenities 1.38
- Recreational, cultural, and religious affairs 1.83
- Fuel and energy 0.03
- Agriculture, forestry, fishing, and hunting 5.37
- Mining, manufacturing, and construction 0.05
- Transportation and communication 6.30
- Other economic affairs and services 1.04

Crime

Crime volume (for 1998)
- Crimes reported 36,674
- Total persons convicted 20,757
- Crimes per 100,000 population 1,492

Persons responsible for offenses
- Total number suspects 17,476
- Total number of female suspects 1,765
- Total number of juvenile suspects 3,023

LABOR FORCE

Total Labor Force (A)

1.4 million (1997).

Labor Force by Occupation

- Agriculture and forestry 16%
- Industry 41%
- Services 43%

Data for 1990.

Unemployment Rate

9.6% (1999 est.)

PRODUCTION SECTOR

Energy Production

Production . . . . 4.766 billion kWh

Production by source
- Fossil fuel 29.58%
- Hydro 70.42%
- Nuclear 0%
- Other 0%

Exports . . . . 400 million kWh

Data for 1998.

Energy Consumption

Consumption . . . . 4.882 billion kWh

Imports . . . . 850.000 million kWh

Data for 1998.

Transportation

Highways:

Total: 59,178 km.

Paved: 22,843 km.

Unpaved: 36,335 km (1998 est.).

Waterways: 300 km perennially navigable.

Pipelines: crude oil 750 km; refined products 780 km; natural gas 560 km (1992).

Merchant marine:

Total: 14 ships (1,000 GRT or over) totaling 58,699 GRT/64,043 DWT.

Ships by type: cargo 4, petroleum tanker 4, refrigerated cargo 6 (1999 est.).

Airports: 50 (1994 est.).

Airports - with paved runways: 36.

Airports - with unpaved runways: 14.

Top Agriculture Products

Grain, sugar beets, potatoes, vegetables; beef, milk, eggs; fish.

Top Mining Products (B)

Mineral resources include: amber, peat, limestone, dolomite.

MANUFACTURING SECTOR

GDP & Manufacturing Summary (A)

	1980	1985	1990	1995
GDP ($-1990 mil.)[1]	5,617	6,632	7,805	3,836
Per capita ($-1990)[1]	2,217	2,538	2,923	1,513
Manufacturing share (%) (current prices)[1]	46.0	37.1	34.5	18.1
Manufacturing				
Value added ($-1990 mil.)[1]	2,100	2,429	2,690	740[e]
Industrial production index	NA	NA	NA	NA
Value added ($ mil.)	NA	NA	NA	828
Gross output ($ mil.)	12,055[e]	10,779[e]	6,362	1,851
Employment (000)	531[e]	422[e]	346	154
Productivity ($)				
Gross output per worker	22,632[e]	25,490[e]	18,413	12,035
Value added per worker	NA	NA	NA	5,383
Average wage (inc. supplements)	2,713[e]	3,001[e]	2,330[e]	1,357[e]
Value added ($ mil.)				
Food products	NA	NA	NA	214
Beverages	NA	NA	NA	109
Tobacco products	NA	NA	NA	6
Textiles	NA	NA	NA	40
Wearing apparel	NA	NA	NA	26
Leather and fur products	NA	NA	NA	3
Footwear	NA	NA	NA	7
Wood and wood products	NA	NA	NA	79
Furniture and fixtures	NA	NA	NA	20
Paper and paper products	NA	NA	NA	3
Printing and publishing	NA	NA	NA	44
Industrial chemicals	NA	NA	NA	18
Other chemical products	NA	NA	NA	31
Petroleum refineries	NA	NA	NA	1
Rubber products	NA	NA	NA	1
Plastic products	NA	NA	NA	7
Pottery, china and earthenware	NA	NA	NA	3
Glass and glass products	NA	NA	NA	3
Other non-metal mineral products	NA	NA	NA	17
Iron and steel	NA	NA	NA	12
Non-ferrous metals	NA	NA	NA	1
Metal products	NA	NA	NA	20
Non-electrical machinery	NA	NA	NA	55
Electrical machinery	NA	NA	NA	32
Transport equipment	NA	NA	NA	64
Prof. and scientific equipment	NA	NA	NA	5
Other manufacturing	NA	NA	NA	9

COMMUNICATIONS

Daily Newspapers

	National Data	World Data for Comparison
Daily Newspapers		
Number of Dailies	24	8,391
Total Circulation (000)	616	548,000
Circulation per 1,000 inhabitants	247	96

Telecommunications

Telephones - main lines in use: 748,000 (1997).

Telephones - mobile cellular: 175,348 (1999).

Telephone system: inadequate but is being modernized to provide an international capability independent of the Moscow international switch; more facilities are being installed for individual use.

Domestic: expansion underway in intercity trunk line connections, rural exchanges, and mobile systems; still many unsatisfied subscriber applications.

International: international connections are now available via cable and a satellite earth station at Riga, enabling direct connections for most calls (1998).

Radio broadcast stations: AM 8, FM 56, shortwave 1 (1998).

Radios: 1.76 million (1997).

Television broadcast stations: 74 (1998).

Televisions: 1.22 million (1997).

Internet Service Providers (ISPs): 11 (1999).

FINANCE, ECONOMICS, & TRADE

Economic Indicators

National product: GDP—purchasing power parity—$9.8 billion (1999 est.).

National product real growth rate: 0% (1999 est.).

National product per capita: $4,200 (1999 est.).

Inflation rate—consumer price index: 3.2% (1999 est.).

Exchange Rates

Exchange rates:

Lats (LVL) per US$1

January 2000	0.583
1999	0.585
1998	0.590
1997	0.581
1996	0.551
1995	0.528

Top Import Origins

$2.8 billion (f.o.b., 1998)

Origins (1998)

Germany	17%
Russia	12%
Finland	10%
Sweden	7%

Top Export Destinations

$1.9 billion (f.o.b., 1999)

Destinations (1998)

Germany	16%
United Kingdom	14%
Russia	12%
Sweden	10%

Foreign Aid

Recipient: $96.2 million (1995).

Import/Export Commodities

Import Commodities	Export Commodities
Machinery and equipment	Wood and wood products
Chemicals	Machinery and equipment
Fuels	Metals
	Textiles
	Foodstuffs

Balance of Payments

	1994	1995	1996	1997	1998
Exports of goods (f.o.b.)	1,022	1,368	1,488	1,838	2,011
Imports of goods (f.o.b.)	−1,322	−1,947	−2,286	−2,686	−3,141
Trade balance	−301	−580	−798	−848	−1,130
Services - debits	−297	−246	−742	−662	−761
Services - credits	657	720	1,126	1,033	1,040
Private transfers (net)	26	36	42	54	50
Government transfers (net)	107	35	51	33	42
Overall balance	201	−16	−280	−345	−714

LEBANON

Republic of Lebanon
Al-Jumhuriyah al-Lubnaniyah

CAPITAL: Beirut (Bayrut).

FLAG: The national flag, introduced in 1943, consists of two horizontal red stripes separated by a white stripe which is twice as wide; at the center, in green and brown, is a cedar tree.

ANTHEM: *Kulluna lil watan lil'ula lil'alam (All of Us for the Country, Glory, Flag).*

MONETARY UNIT: The Lebanese pound, or livre libanaise (LL), is a paper currency of 100 piasters. There are coins of 1, 2, 5, 10, 25, and 50 piasters and 1 Lebanese pound, and notes of 1, 5, 10, 25, 50, 100, 250, 1,000 and 10,000 Lebanese pounds. LL1 = $0.00064 (or $1 = LL1,556.0).

WEIGHTS AND MEASURES: The metric system is the legal standard, but traditional weights and measures are still used.

HOLIDAYS: New Year's Day, 1 January; Arab League Day, 22 March; Independence Day, 22 November; Evacuation Day, 31 December. Christian religious holidays include Feast of St. Maron, 9 February; Good Friday; Easter Monday; Ascension; Assumption, 15 August; All Saints' Day, 1 November; and Christmas, 25 December. Muslim religious holidays include 'Id al-Fitr, 'Id al-'Adha', and Milad an-Nabi.

TIME: 2 PM = noon GMT.

LOCATION AND SIZE: Situated on the eastern coast of the Mediterranean Sea, Lebanon has an area of 10,400 square kilometers (4,015 square miles), about three-fourths the size of the state of Connecticut, and a total boundary length of 656 kilometers (407 miles). Lebanon's capital city, Beirut, is located on the Mediterranean coast.

CLIMATE: Lebanon has an extraordinarily varied climate: within 45 minutes' drive in winter, spring, and fall, both skiing and swimming are possible. Rainfall averages about 90 centimeters (35 inches) yearly along the coast, about 125 centimeters (50 inches) on the western slopes of the mountains, and less than 38 centimeters (15 inches) in the Bekaa Valley. The average annual temperature in Beirut is 21°C (70°F), with a range from 13°C (55°F) in winter to 28°C (82°F) in summer.

INTRODUCTORY SURVEY

RECENT HISTORY

Following World War II Lebanon gained complete independence in 1946. The 1950s and 1960s were generally characterized by economic and political stability. With an influx of Western commercial personnel and growing oil royalties, Lebanon seemed the calmest part of the Middle East taking little part in the Arab-Israeli war of 1948 and no action in the wars of 1967 and 1973.

However, by the early 1970s Lebanon's role began changing. Well-armed members of the Palestinian Liberation Organization (the PLO) moved into Lebanon fighting Israel for an independent homeland. Clashes grew between the PLO and Lebanon's army. Fearing a civil war, Lebanon signed the so-called Cairo Accord in 1969 with the PLO making the terrorist organization practically a separate state within Lebanon. The PLO could establish military bases and launch cross-border raids into Israel.

PLO activities inflamed tensions between Christians and Muslims and by 1975 led to a civil war. The war pitted Maronite Christians against Muslims and other Christian sects and rightist militants against Palestinian guerrillas and other leftist Arab forces. At least 100,000 people were killed and some 600,000 persons displaced during eighteen months of fighting. A cease-fire arranged through the mediation of Sa'udi Arabia and other Arab countries enabled a peacekeeping force to end hostilities in October 1976.

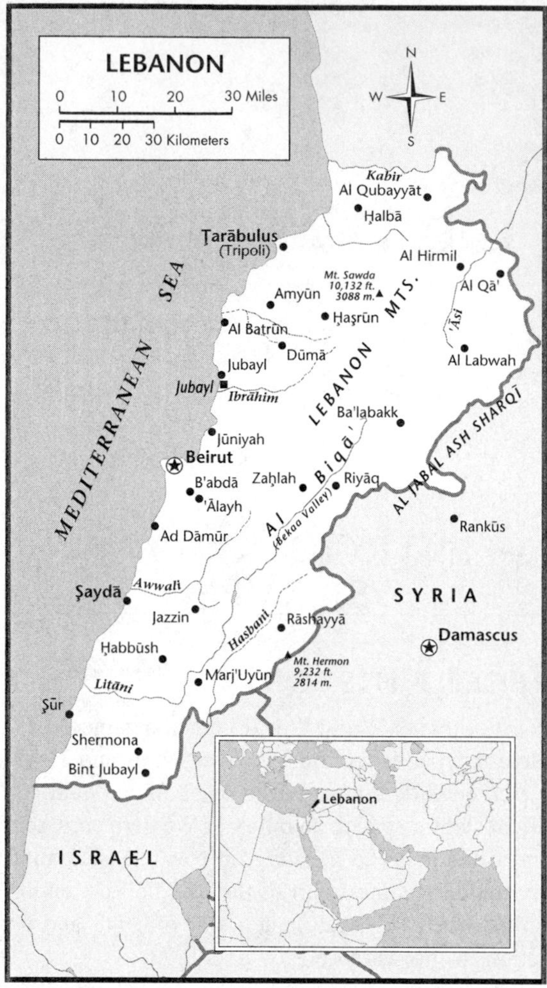

The conflict devastated Lebanon economically and weakened the central government. The Syrians, the Palestinians, and militias of some thirty factions controlled different parts of the country.

In March 1978, the Israeli army invaded southern Lebanon destroying PLO bases. It withdrew and a United Nations (UN) force was assigned to keep the peace.

However, the PLO continued rocket attacks on northern Israel prompting Israel to launch a full-scale invasion of Lebanon in June 1982. Following a two-month Israeli siege of West Beirut where the Palestinians were encamped, Israel, the PLO, and Syria reached a truce. A multinational peacekeeping force composed of British, French, and Italian soldiers and U.S. marines was stationed in the Beirut area in early September. Despite the truce the violence continued. In 1983, Israeli and Syrian troops still occupying large portions of Lebanon became targets of attack by Muslim and Druze forces. The American embassy in Beirut was bombed in April 1983 and on October 23 a truck-bomb explosion killed 241 marines in the U.S. barracks at Beirut airport.

With the country badly divided, Christian Army Commander Michel Aoun asserted himself as prime minister, giving Lebanon two governments, a Muslim one in West Beirut and a Christian one in East Beirut. In September 1989, a committee appointed by the Arab League arrived at a seven-point ceasefire called the Ta'if Accord.

Under the Ta'if Accord, almost all militias were dissolved, and Palestinian militants were repressed in Sayda (Sidon). Internally, the poor economy aggravated political instability, but the appointment of Prime Minister Rafiq al-Hariri in November 1992 promised a serious effort at reconstruction. Al-Hariri, who became a self-made billionaire in Sa'udi Arabia, had a long history of making charitable donations to help rebuild Beirut. His efforts to reunite the country generally won public approval and al-Hariri was reelected in 1996.

Southern Lebanon, occupied by Israeli forces, still witnessed political violence. In 1996, 255 people including twenty-seven Israeli soldiers were killed. In November 1998, Emile Lahoud was sworn in as Lebanon's eleventh president. Salim al-Hurr became prime minister following al-Hariri who resigned. In May 2000, Israeli troops withdrew from southern Lebanon however the exact border between Lebanon and Israel remained unsettled.

GOVERNMENT

As defined by the constitution of 1926 and subsequent amendments, Lebanon is an independent republic. Executive power is vested in a president, elected by the National Assembly for six years, and a prime minister and cabinet, chosen by the president but responsible to the National Assembly. By custom the president is a Maronite Christian, the prime minister is a Sunni Muslim, and the speaker of the legislature is a Shi'a Muslim. Legislative power is exercised by a 128-member National Assembly elected for a four-year term by universal adult suffrage. The Taif Accord of 1989 set the Christian-Muslim balance in parliament at 50–50, but the failure of Christians to participate in the elections of 1992 and 1996 gave Muslim groups the largest number of seats in the Chamber.

Judiciary

Ultimate supervisory power rests with the minister of justice, who appoints the magistrates. Courts of first instance, of which there are 56, give cases their first hearing; they are presided over by a single judge and deal with both civil and criminal cases. Appeals may be taken to 11 courts of appeal, each made up of three judges. Of the four Courts of Cassation, three hear civil cases and one hears criminal cases. A Council of State handles administrative cases.

Religious courts-Islamic, Christian, and Jewish-deal with marriages, deaths, inheritances, and other matters of personal status in their respective faiths. In the Palestinian refugee camps, rival factions try opponents without any semblance of due process.

Political Parties

Principal political groups are organized along largely sectarian lines. The National Liberal Party and the Phalangist Party have mainly Christian membership. There are various parties of the left, including the Progressive Socialist Party (of mostly Druze membership), the Ba'th Party, and the Lebanese Communist Party.

The various Palestinian groups, allied under the Palestine Liberation Organization, have played an important role in the political life of Lebanon since the late 1960s. Amal, a conservative grouping, and Hezbollah, more militant, represent the Shi'ite Muslim community.

DEFENSE

In 2000, the regular Lebanese army numbered 65,000 men. There was a small navy of 1,200 and an air force of 1,700 personnel, neither well armed.

Although many of the militias have disbanded, the Muslim Hezbollah with 3,000 personnel is the only significant communal army remaining. The South Lebanese Army, mostly Christian, numbers 2,500 and receives Israeli support for its border patrol duties.

ECONOMIC AFFAIRS

Lebanon is traditionally a trading country with a relatively large agricultural sector and small but well-developed industry. Until the 1975–1976 civil war it had always figured prominently as a center of tourist trade. The war caused an estimated $5 billion in property damage and reduced economic activities to about 50 percent of the prewar level.

After the 1989 Taif Accord for National Reconciliation ended hostilities, the economy began to recover. Peace enabled the central government to restore control in Beiruit and begin tax collection, allow the banking system to revive, and the resilient manufacturers start up. Economic activity surged in 1991 and in 1993 the al-Hariri government was able to stabilize the economy and launch a program to reconstruct the country's transportation and communication networks. Between 1992 and 1998 annual economic growth has averaged about 4 percent and inflation fell from 100 percent to 5%. A rising budget deficit may threaten further reforms.

Public Finance

The annual budget of the central government must be approved by the National Assembly. The Lebanese government annually faces the formidable problem of financing a massive deficit resulting from heavy financial obligations and huge shortfalls in revenues. To reduce the deficit the government has tried to increase revenues by raising taxes and tightening the budget. The government relies heavily on grants and loans from multilateral agencies, Arab governments, and the French to cover the deficit.

In 1999, government revenues totaled approximately $4.9 billion and expenditures $8.36 billion. External debt totaled $8.8 billion in 1999.

Income

In 1999, the gross domestic product (GDP) was $16.2 billion, or $4,500 per capita. The estimated 1999 GDP growth rate was 1 percent and inflation was 4.5%. The 1998 estimate of GDP by sector was agriculture 12%, industry 27%, and services 61%.

Industry

The civil war caused tremendous damage to the industrial sector. By 1993 it was estimated that the Lebanese industry suffered losses of $1.5 billion. Inadequate transport and communications networks and a shortage of skilled labor are major obstacles in the process of rehabilitation. In 1998 industry accounted for 27 percent of the gross domestic product. Major industrial products are clothing, metal, food, marble and sanitary equipment, cement, jewelry, furniture, paper, beverages, plastic, mineral and chemical products, and metal fabricating. Banking had again become a chief industry by 2000.

Banking and Finance

The Bank of Lebanon, established in April 1964, is now the sole bank of issue. Its powers to regulate and control commercial banks and other institutions and to implement monetary policy were expanded by amendments to the Code of Money and Credit promulgated in October 1973. Before the civil war Lebanon was an important banking center. Many organizations moved their headquarters from Cairo to Beirut after the 1952 Egyptian revolution. After 1973 Lebanese banks handled additional oil revenue from the Gulf. The system of free exchange and strict secrecy laws attracted money from across the world.

Legislation to permit a banking free zone in Beirut to encourage foreign banks became effective in 1977. However the banking sector was an early casualty of the civil war between 1975 and 1991 with money and institutions leaving the capital. The firm Solidere set about rebuilding Beirut's business district in the mid-1990s. The banking sector began to revive. In the late 1990s banking underwent a period of expansion and consolidation. By 1998 over seventy banks were operating in Lebanon.

In September 1995, the Beirut Stock Exchange reopened after a 12-year closure and trading began in January 1996. From early 1997 the Beirut exchange began to cross-list shares with exchanges in Kuwait and Egypt.

Economic Development

Since World War II, Lebanon has followed free enterprise and free-trade policies. The country's favorable geographical position as a transit point and the traditional importance of the trading and banking sectors of the economy helped make Lebanon prosperous by the early 1970s. Lebanon became a center of trade, finance, and tourism by means of a stable currency backed largely with gold, by a conservative fiscal policy, by various incentives for foreign investors, and by minimization of banking regulations.

The 1975 to 1991 civil war all but destroyed Lebanon's economy. The national output was cut in half and its financial banking hub all but ended.

Under the leadership of Prime Minister Rafiq al-Hariri, Lebanon embarked on the Horizon 2000 program in 1993. Areas of major activity targeted by the plan are the rehabilitation of telecommunications, electricity grids, highways, sewage, waste management, water networks, renovation of the Beirut International Airport, harbor, education, and housing. The plan also calls for investment in commercial facilities that will reestablish Beirut as an international business center in competition with Hong Kong and Singapore. Although in 1997 the government reset the target date to 2007, the plan had been scheduled for completion by 2000. The total cost is estimated at over $18 billion.

Great progress was made in reducing inflation from 100 percent in 1992 to 5 percent in 1998. Increased capital inflows generated foreign payments and surpluses. Reducing the government budget deficit is a major goal. Progress has also been made in rebuilding the physical and financial infrastructure. The firm Solidere is overseeing the reconstruction of Beirut's business district and the stock market reopened in January 1996. International banks and insurance companies are returning.

In the late 1990s, a widening gap between rich and poor caused grassroots dissatisfaction and the government had to focus on improving living contitions.

SOCIAL WELFARE

A government social security plan, not fully implemented, is intended to provide sickness and maternity insurance, accident and disability insurance, family allowances, and end of service indemnity payments, retirement, disability, and survivor benefits.

Many of the religious laws governing family and personal status discriminate against women. Careers in government, the professions, and business are open to women but social pressures often prevent them from taking full advantage of employment opportunities.

Healthcare

In 1994, 100 percent of the population had access to safe water and 95% had access to health care services. In 1990–1997 there were 1.9 physicians and 3.1 hospital beds per 1,000 population. In 2000 average life expectancy was seventy-one years.

The Lebanese Ministry of Health reported the major health problems as hypertension, diabetes, asthma, eye and ear diseases, and cardiac conditions. The major cause of death between 1987 and 1991 was war violence. Many children suffer from post-traumatic stress disorders.

Housing

The civil war and subsequent fighting, in which half of the country's real estate was severely damaged or destroyed, aggravated a housing shortage in the early 1970s. According to the latest available information for 1980–1988 total housing units numbered 820,000 with 3.3 people per dwelling. Housing needs until 2000 have been estimated at 400,000 units. With the return of stability a boom in construction is underway in Beirut.

EDUCATION

Lebanon's illiteracy rate is relatively low for the Middle East. In 2000 an estimated 13.9 percent (7.7 percent of adult males and 19.6 percent of adult females) cannot read and write. Free primary education was introduced in 1960 but about two-thirds of all students attend private schools. In 1997 there were 382,309 primary school pupils and 347,850 general secondary school students. In 1996 the total enrollment for all higher-level institutions was 81,588. Leading universities include the American University in Beirut, St. Joseph University, and the Lebanese (State) University.

2000 KEY EVENTS TIMELINE

January

- Pro-Chechen demonstrators attack Russian embassy in Beirut.

March

- The Lebanese government deports four members of the Japanese Red Army terrorist group to Japan.

May

- Israeli troops, occupying a strip of southern Lebanon since 1982, abruptly stage a pullout, about six weeks ahead of the announced July 7 planned deadline.

August

- Lebanese security forces occupy the southern portion of Lebanon for the first time in twenty-two years on August 9, but leave the border on Israel to U.N. forces.

September

- Former Prime Minister Rafik Hariri and his supporters win a powerful majority in Parliamentary elections, according to official election results released September 5.

October

- Israeli warplanes conduct drills over southern Lebanon on October 10 and 13.
- President Émile Lahoud names former Prime Minister Rafik Hariri prime minister on October 23.

November

- Lebanese soldiers kill an Israeli soldier, and a bomb explodes on the Israel-Lebanon border injuring Israeli soldiers on November 26.
- Palestinians in Lebanese refugee camps and Lebanese students protest against Israel and the United States on November 29.

ANALYSIS OF EVENTS: 2000

BUSINESS AND THE ECONOMY

The sweeping parliamentary election victory that returned multibillionaire businessman Rafik Hariri to the post of prime minister was largely imputed to the nation's dire need for economic rescue. Lebanon's new government faced the serious challenge of bringing the nation's economy out of a six-year downturn. During this period, growth slid from 8 percent to 1 percent as the nation slipped into recession. At $21 billion, the nation's debt equaled a massive 140 percent of gross domestic product (GDP). Adding to Lebanon's problems were a crumbling infrastructure, high interest rates, and the scarce availability of long-term bank financing.

A major factor in the recovery equation was foreign aid. In April Lebanon had received an aid package worth Eur50 million (US$47.9 million) from the European Union (E.U.). Further grants for economic and social development (Eur25 million; US$24 million), industrial modernization (Eur11 million; US$10.5 million), and the establishment of a value-added tax (Eur2 million; US$1.9 million) were expected to be made later in the year.

Lebanese government officials met with representatives of donor countries and international agencies in July to request funding for projects totaling US$6.5 billion. Of this total, the government proposed to allocate US$260 million for emergency infrastructure rehabilitation and humanitarian aid and US$1.3 billion for development of southern Lebanon, including a US$100 million irrigation project. The World Bank had already authorized about US$30 million in emergency funding for southern Lebanon.

GOVERNMENT AND POLITICS

In 2000 the political outlook in Lebanon was changed by two events that had the potential to increase the country's freedom from foreign influence. In May Israeli troops ended two decades of occupation in southern Lebanon. Responding to a series of attacks by Islamist Hezbollah militants, Israel pulled out of the area six weeks before a July deadline agreed to by Prime Minister Ehud Barak. Lebanese security forces moved into the area in August to coordinate their efforts with those of some 400 United Nations peacekeepers stationed along the border with Israel.

The June death of Syrian leader Hafez el-Assad also figured prominently in Lebanon's future, as Syria has effectively controlled Lebanon since the mid-1970s. Syria's new president, Bashar Assad—son of the deceased leader—demonstrated greater flexibility in dealing with Lebanon than his father had, and some observers hailed the transfer of power in Syria as heralding a new era of autonomy for Lebanon. However, others noted that the major contenders to become prime minister following parliamentary elections in August and September were all supporters of Syria, which still maintained 35,000 troops in the country.

The elections yielded a dramatic victory for parliamentary supporters of Rafik Hariri, a multibillionaire developer who had served as prime minister from 1992 to 1998. Pro-Hariri candidates won almost three-fourths of 128 contested seats in parliament, and Hariri was virtually assured of regaining the prime minister's post.

The stability of Lebanon, like that of the Middle East as a whole, was called into question in late September and October with the outbreak of Israeli-Palestine hostilities in the West Bank and the Gaza Strip. In October Lebanon was drawn into the tumult engulfing the region when the Hezbollah guerilla group took four Israeli prisoners. The first three were soldiers captured on the Lebanese border; the fourth was an alleged Israeli spy whom Hezbollah claimed to have lured into the country in an intricate sting operation.

CULTURE AND SOCIETY

Although hailed internationally, the Israeli pullout from south Lebanon didn't change the daily lives of most Lebanese, who had been largely unaffected by either the Israeli military presence in the south or the ongoing low-grade resistance by Muslim guerrillas, except when Israel launched retaliatory aid raids. The majority of Lebanese continued to struggle under the burden of an ailing economy and hoped that reinvigorated political leadership on the throne and in parliament would provide positive change.

Among those hoping most fervently for change were the Palestinian refugees in Lebanon, living in dire poverty and still facing an uncertain future. Thought to number somewhere between 200,000 and 375,000, they were not regarded as permanent residents of Lebanon and thus barred from most professions and ineligible for social services. Although officially the Palestinians continued to demand repatriation to their original homes within the state of Israel, it was likely that the ultimate resolution of their situation would involve resettlement of at least some refugees in the West Bank and Gaza and in other countries.

Despite security concerns raised by two weeks of regional violence and the holding of four Israeli hostages by Hezbollah guerrillas, the opening of the twelve-nation Asian Cup soccer tournament in Beirut took place as scheduled on October 12.

DIRECTORY

CENTRAL GOVERNMENT

Head of State

President
Emile Lahoud, Office of the President

Prime Minister
Rafiq Hariri, Office of the Prime Minister

Ministers

Minister of Agriculture
Ali Abdallah, Ministry of Agriculture
PHONE: +961 (1) 423525; 455630; 455631

Minister of Cultural and Higher Education Affairs
Ghassan Salameh, Ministry of Cultural and Higher Education Affairs

Minister of Displaced Persons
Marwan Hamadeh, Ministry of Displaced Persons

Minister of Economy and Trade
NAME: Basil Flayhan, Ministry of Economy and Trade, Artois Street, Hamra, Beirut, Lebanon
PHONE: +961 (1) 340503
FAX: +961 (1) 354640
E-MAIL: PostMaster@Economy.gov.lb

Minister of Environment
Michel Moussa, Ministry of Environment
PHONE: +961 (1) 522222
E-MAIL: info@moe.gov.lb

Minister of Finance
Fuad Siniora, Ministry of Finance

Minister of Foreign Affairs
Mahmud Hammud, Ministry of Foreign Affairs

Minister of Housing and Cooperatives
Mahmud Abu Hamdan, Ministry of Housing and Cooperatives

Minister of Industry and Oil
George Frem, Ministry of Industry and Oil

Minister of Information
Ghazi Aridi, Ministry of Information

Minister of Interior
Elias Murr, Ministry of Interior

Minister of Justice
Samir Al-Jisr, Ministry of Justice

Minister of Labor
Ali Qanso, Ministry of Labor

Minister of Municipal and Rural Affairs
Michel al-Murr, Ministry of Municipal and Rural Affairs

Minister of National Defense
Khalil Hrawi, Ministry of National Defense

Minister of National Economy and Trade
Basil Flayhan, Ministry of National Economy and Trade

Minister of Youth and Sports
Sebouh Hovnanian, Ministry of Youth and Sports

Minister of Post and Telecommunications
Jean Louis Cordahi, Ministry of Post and Telecommunications, Badaro, Sami El-Solh Street, 3rd Floor, Beirut, Lebanon
PHONE: +961 (1) 424400; 422404
FAX: +961 (1) 888310
E-MAIL: PK@mpt.gov.lb

Minister of Public Health
Karam Karam, Ministry of Public Health

Minister of Public Works
Najib Mikati, Ministry of Public Works, Damascus Road, Beirut, Lebanon
PHONE: +961 (1) 458975; 458980

Minister of Social Affairs
Asad Diab, Ministry of Social Affairs

Minister of State
Talal Arslam, Ministry of State

Minister of State
Nazih Baydun, Ministry of State

Minister of State
Pierre Helu, Ministry of State

Minister of State
Bishara Merhej, Ministry of State

Minister of State
Michel Pharaon, Ministry of State

Minister of State
Bahej Tabbarah, Ministry of State

Minister of Administrative Reform Affairs
Fuad Saad, Ministry of Administrative Reform Affairs

Minister of Tourism
Karam Karam, Ministry of Tourism
E-MAIL: mot@lebanon-tourism.gov.lb

Minister of Transportation
Najib Mikati, Ministry of Transportation

Minister of Vocational and Technical Education
Mohammed Yousef Beydoun, Ministry of Vocational and Technical Education

POLITICAL ORGANIZATIONS

Amal Movement

TITLE: President
NAME: Nabih Berri

Arab Democratic Party

TITLE: President
NAME: Ali Eid

Baath Arab Socialist Party

TITLE: Regional Secretary
NAME: Ghazi Seifeddin

Christian Democratic Party

TITLE: President
NAME: George Jabre

Communist Party

TITLE: General Secretary
NAME: Farouk Dahrouj

Congress Party

TITLE: President
NAME: Hassan Hachem

Democratic Socialist Party

TITLE: President
NAME: Kamel al-Assaad

Federation of Popular Leagues and Committees

TITLE: General Coordinator
NAME: Maan Bashour

Guardians of the Cedars

TITLE: President
NAME: Etienne Sakr

Henchak Party

TITLE: President
NAME: Vahrij Jerijian

Hizbollah

E-MAIL: hizbollahmedia@hizbollah.org
TITLE: General Secretary
NAME: Hassan Nasrallah

Islamic Amal Movement

TITLE: President
NAME: Hussein Moussawi

Islamic Charitable Projects Association

TITLE: President
NAME: Hussam Karakira

Islamic Group

TITLE: General Secretary
NAME: Faysal Mawlawi

Kataeb Party

TITLE: President
NAME: George Saadeh

Lebanese Democratic Movement

TITLE: President
NAME: Jacques Tamer

Lebanese Movement

TITLE: President
NAME: Nabil Mchantaf

Lebanese People's Front

TITLE: President
NAME: Joseph Haddad

Lebanese Popular Congress

TITLE: President
NAME: Kamal Shatila

Lebanese Republican Party

TITLE: President
NAME: Imad Jaara

Marada Institution

TITLE: President
NAME: Sleiman Frangieh

Maronite League

TITLE: President
NAME: Pierre Helou

Movement of Change

TITLE: President
NAME: Elie Mahfoud

Najjadeh Party

TITLE: President
NAME: Mostafa Al-Hakim

Nasserite Unification Movement

NAME: Samir Sabbagh

National Bloc

TITLE: General Secretary
NAME: Ibrahim Estefan

National Liberal Party

TITLE: President
NAME: Dory Chamoun

Popular Nasserite Organization

TITLE: President
NAME: Mustafa Saad

Progressive Socialist Party

TITLE: President
NAME: Walid Joumblatt

Ramgavar Party

TITLE: President
NAME: Hovsep Amirian

Socialist Arab Union

TITLE: President
NAME: Mounir As-Sayyad

Solidarity Party

TITLE: President
NAME: Emile Rahmeh

Syrian National Social Party

TITLE: President
NAME: Inaam Raad

Tahcnak Party

TITLE: General Secretary
NAME: Sebouh Hovnanian

Union Party

TITLE: President
NAME: Omar Harb

Waad Party

TITLE: President
NAME: Elias Hobeika

Workers League

TITLE: President
NAME: Zaher al-Khatib

DIPLOMATIC REPRESENTATION

Embassies in Lebanon

Italy
Rue de Rome Immobiliere 209, Hamra, BP 11–4128, Beirut, Lebanon
PHONE: +961 (1) 749801
FAX: +961 (1) 749804
E-MAIL: istitlib@inco.com.lb

United States
Awkar, P.O. Box 70–840, Beirut, Lebanon
PHONE: +961 (1) 542600; 543600
FAX: +961 (1) 544136

JUDICIAL SYSTEM

Courts of Cassation

Constitutional Council

Supreme Council

BROADCAST MEDIA

Radio Liban

Ministry of Information, Beirut, Lebanon
PHONE: +961 (1) 346880
TITLE: Director
CONTACT: M. Sobhi Eid
LANGUAGE: Arabic, Armenian, English, French
TYPE: Government

Voice of Hope

PO Box 3379, Limassol, Cyprus
PHONE: +972 (6) 959174
E-MAIL: voh@broadcast
WEBSITE: http://www.highadventure.org/voh_midd.html
TITLE: Manager
CONTACT: Gary Hull
LANGUAGE: Arabic, English, Farsi, French, Russian, Turkish
TYPE: Religious

Future Television

White House, Spears Street, Sanayeh, PO Box 13–6052, Beirut, Lebanon
PHONE: +961 (1) 355355
FAX: +961 (1) 6023111
E-MAIL: future@future.com.lb; future@dm.net.lb
WEBSITE: http://www.future.com.lb
CHANNEL: 28, 37, 46, 52

Lebanese Broadcasting Corp. International

PO Box 16–5853 Beirut, Lebanon
PHONE: +961 (9) 938938
FAX: +961 (9) 937916
E-MAIL: lbci@lbci.com.lb
WEBSITE: http://www.lbci.com.lb
TITLE: Station Manager
CONTACT: Pierre Al Daher
CHANNEL: 5H, 9H, 10H, 12H, 33H
TYPE: Commercial

Middle East Television

PO Box 5689, Nicosia, Cyprus
TITLE: General Manager
CONTACT: Wes Hylton
CHANNEL: E5, E12
TYPE: Commercial

Murr Television (MTV)

Fouad Chehab Avenue, PO Box 166000, Fassouh, MTV Building, Lebanon

PHONE: +961 (1) 217000
FAX: +961 (1) 423121
E-MAIL: mtv@dm.net.lb
WEBSITE: http://www.dm.net.lb/mtv/
TITLE: President
CONTACT: Michel El Murr
CHANNEL: 28, 38, 48, 68
TYPE: Commercial

Télé-Liban

BP 115054, Hazmieh, Beirut, Lebanon
PHONE: +961 (1) 405100
FAX: +961 (1) 457253
WEBSITE: http://158.222.24.64/tl/index.html
TITLE: Directorate General
CONTACT: Jean-Claude Boulos
TYPE: Government

COLLEGES AND UNIVERSITIES

Beirut Arab University

PO Box 115020, Beirut, Lebanon
PHONE: +961 (1) 300110
FAX: +961 (1) 818402
E-MAIL: bau@inco.com.lb
WEBSITE: http://www.bau.edu.lb

Lebanese University

BP 14-6573, Place du Musee, Beirut, Lebanon
PHONE: +961 (1) 612618
FAX: +961 (1) 612621
E-MAIL: secretaire_generale:sgu@ul.edu.lb
WEBSITE: http://www.ul.edu.lb/

University of the Holy Spirit

PO Box 446, Jounieh, Lebanon
PHONE: +961 (9) 640664
FAX: +961 (9) 642333

St. Joseph University

Rue De Damas, Beirut, Lebanon
PHONE: +961 (1) 426456
FAX: +961 (1) 423369
E-MAIL: rectorat@usj.edu.lb
WEBSITE: http://www.usj.edu.lb

NEWSPAPERS AND MAGAZINES

Al-Amal

rue Liberateur, PO Box 959, Beirut, Lebanon
PHONE: +961 (1) 382992
TITLE: Editor
CONTACT: Georges Oumayra
CIRCULATION: 35,000

The Daily Star

The Daily Star Co., PO Box 11-987, Achrafieh, Beirut, Lebanon
PHONE: +961 (1) 587277
FAX: +961 (1) 561333
E-MAIL: letterbox@dailystar.com.lb
WEBSITE: http://www.dailystar.com.lb
TITLE: Editor
CONTACT: Ed Blanche
CIRCULATION: 10,800

An-Nahar (The Day)

An-Nahar S.A.L., Cooperative de Presse Bldg, Bque du Liban, St. Hamra, 11-226 Beirut, Lebanon
PHONE: +961 (1) 340960
FAX: +961 (1) 340557
E-MAIL: annahar@annahar.com.lb
WEBSITE: http://www.annahar.com.lb
TITLE: Editor-in-Chief
CONTACT: Ounsi El-Hajj
CIRCULATION: 65,000

L'Orient-Le Jour

Accaoui, PO Box 166495, Beirut, Lebanon
PHONE: +961 (1) 561406
FAX: +961 (1) 561412
E-MAIL: oj@lorient-lejour.com.lb
WEBSITE: http://www.lorient-lejour.com.lb
TITLE: Editor
CONTACT: Issa Ghoraieb
CIRCULATION: 18,450

Arab Film and Television Center News

Box 3434, Beirut, Lebanon
CIRCULATION: 3,000
TYPE: Performing arts, film, technology, television and video

Arab World

PO Box 567, Jounieh, Lebanon
FAX: +961 (9) 935096
TITLE: Editor
CONTACT: Naji Naaman
TYPE: Political science, international relations

Lebanon Report

Tayyar Bldg., Mkalles, Sin al-Fil, Beirut, Lebanon

FAX: +961 (1) 601787
TITLE: Editor
CONTACT: Michael Bacos Young
TYPE: Political science, business and economics, history

PUBLISHERS

Arab Scientific Publishers BP

Reem Bldg., Ein El-Tineh, Sakiet el-Janzeer Str., PO Box 13-5574, Beirut, Lebanon
PHONE: +961 (1) 785107; 785108; 786233
FAX: +961 (1) 786230
E-MAIL: asp@asp.com.lb
WEBSITE: http://www.asp.com.lb
TITLE: President
CONTACT: Bassam Chebaro
SUBJECTS: Automotive, Biological Sciences, Computer Science, Cookery, Travel, Health & Beauty, Management
TOTAL PUBLISHED: 300 print; 10 CD-ROM; 15 internet

Darl el-Machreq Sarl

PO Box 11-0946, Raid el-Solh, Beirut, Lebanon
PHONE: +961 (1) 202423; 202424
FAX: +961 (1) 329348
E-MAIL: machreq@cyberia.net.lb
TITLE: Man. Director, Rights & Permissions
CONTACT: Camille Hechaiime
SUBJECTS: Biblical Studies, History, Language Arts, Linguistics, Literature, Literary Criticism, Essays, Philosophy, Catholicism, Islam, Theology, Children's Books
TOTAL PUBLISHED: 538

Institute for Palestine Studies, Publishing & Research Organization (IPS)

PO Box 11-07164, Beirut, Lebanon
PHONE: +961 (1) 868387
FAX: +961 (1) 868387
TITLE: Executive Secretary
CONTACT: Walid Khalidi
SUBJECTS: Government, Political Science, Social Sciences

Librairie du Liban

Riad Al-Solh Sq., PP Box 11945, Beirut, Lebanon
PHONE: +961 (357) 862957
FAX: +961 (357) 9512906
TITLE: Man. Director, Rights & Permissions
CONTACT: Khilil Sayegh
SUBJECTS: Fiction, Language Arts, Linguistics, Literature, Literary Criticism, Essays, Travel

Librairie Orientale sal

Sin el-Fil, Jisr el-Wati, PO Box 55206, Beirut, Lebanon
PHONE: +961 (1) 485793; 485794; 485795
FAX: +961 (1) 485796
E-MAIL: libor@cyberia.net.lb
TITLE: Chief Executive Officer
CONTACT: Maroun Nehme
SUBJECTS: Archaeology, Education, English as a Second Language, History, How-To, Language Arts, Literature, Nonfiction (General), Philosophy, Regional Interests, Catholicism
TOTAL PUBLISHED: 1,000 print

Naufal Group Sarl

Naufal Bldg., Mamaris St., PO Box 11-2161, Beirut, Lebanon
PHONE: +961 (1) 317018; 354898
FAX: +961 (1) 317018
TITLE: Man. Dorector, Rights & Permissions
CONTACT: Tony P. Naufel
SUBJECTS: Fiction, History, Law, Literature, Literary Criticism, Essays

World Book Publishing

282 Rue Emile Edde, PO Box 11-3176, Beirut, Lebanon
PHONE: +961 (1) 349370; 743357; 743358
FAX: +961 (1) 351226
E-MAIL: info@arabook.com
WEBSITE: http://www.arabook.com
TITLE: Director-General
CONTACT: El Zein Said-Mohamed
SUBJECTS: Education, Literature, Literary Criticism, Essays, Philosophy, Poetry, Islam
TOTAL PUBLISHED: 3,000 print; 1,000 online

RELIGIOUS ORGANIZATIONS

Islamic

Editions Africaines
PO Box 3176, Beirut, Lebanon
E-MAIL: wbookpub@inco.com.lb
WEBSITE: http://www.arabook.com/arabook/editions/edmain.htm
NAME: Mohamed El-Zein

Protestant

Evangelical Lutheran Contact and Resource Center
PO Box 113-5216, Beirut, Lebanon

FURTHER READING

Articles

Kifner, John. "Lebanese Businessman Is Once Again Premier." *New York Times,* October 24, 2000, p. A10.

———. "Lebanon Challenger Takes on Syria, Too." *New York Times,* September 3, 2000, p. A10.

———. "Opposition Leader Scores Upset in Lebanon Elections." *New York Times,* September 4, 2000, p. A4.

"The Month in Review: January 2000." *Current History,* March 2000, p. 141.

Books

Dagher, Carole. *Bring Down the Walls: Lebanon's Postwar Challenge.* New York: St. Martin's Press, 2000.

El-Khazen, Farid. *The Breakdown of the State in Lebanon, 1967–1976.* Cambridge: Harvard University Press, 2000.

LEBANON: STATISTICAL DATA

For sources and notes see "Sources of Statistics" at the front of each volume.

GEOGRAPHY

Geography

Area:

Total: 10,400 sq km.

Land: 10,230 sq km.

Land boundaries:

Total: 454 km.

Border countries: Israel 79 km, Syria 375 km.

Coastline: 225 km.

Climate: Mediterranean; mild to cool, wet winters with hot, dry summers; Lebanon mountains experience heavy winter snows.

Terrain: narrow coastal plain; Al Biqa' (Bekaa Valley) separates Lebanon and Anti-Lebanon Mountains.

Natural resources: limestone, iron ore, salt, water-surplus state in a water-deficit region, arable land.

Land use:

Arable land: 21%

Permanent crops: 9%

Permanent pastures: 1%

Forests and woodland: 8%

Other: 61% (1993 est.).

HUMAN FACTORS

Demographics (A)

	1990	1995	1998	2000	2010	2020	2030	2040	2050
Population	3,147	3,335	3,479	3,578	4,056	4,417	4,701	4,906	4,941
Life expectancy - males	66.0	67.5	68.3	68.9	71.4	73.5	75.3	76.8	78.0
Life expectancy - females	70.5	72.2	73.1	73.7	76.6	79.0	80.9	82.5	83.8
Birth rate (per 1,000)	21.5	20.7	20.6	20.3	16.6	13.0	12.1	10.8	9.7
Death rate (per 1,000)	7.1	6.7	6.5	6.4	6.1	6.0	6.6	8.1	10.9
Women of reproductive age (15-49 yrs.)	813	946	1,016	1,053	1,177	1,235	1,148	1,086	1,036
Fertility rate	2.8	2.3	2.2	2.1	1.8	1.7	1.7	1.7	1.7

Except as noted, values for vital statistics are in thousands; life expectancy is in years.

Health Personnel

	National Data	World Data (wtd ave)
Total health expenditure as a percentage of GDP, 1990-1998[a]		
Public sector	3.0	2.5
Private sector	7.0	2.9
Total[b]	10.0	5.5
Health expenditure per capita in U.S. dollars, 1990-1998[a]		
Purchasing power parity	594	561
Total	361	483
Availability of health care facilities per 100,000 people		
Hospital beds 1990-1998[a]	270	330
Doctors 1992-1995[a]	191	122
Nurses 1992-1995[a]	122	248

Health Indicators

	National Data	World Data
Life expectancy at birth (years)		
1980	65	61
1998	70	67
Daily per capita supply of calories		
1970	2,336	2,358
1997	3,277	2,791
Daily per capital supply of protein		
1997 (grams)	85	74
Total fertility rate (births per woman)		
1980	4.0	3.7
1998	2.4	2.7
People living with (1997)		
Tuberculosis (cases per 100,000)	22.3	60.4
HIV/AIDS (% aged 15 - 49 years)	0.09	0.99

Infants and Malnutrition

	National Data	World Data (wtd ave)
Under 5 mortality rate (1989)	35	NA
% of infants with low birthweight (1992-98)[1]	19	17
Births attended by skilled health staff (% of total births 1996-98)	89	52
% fully immunized at 1 year of age (1995-98)[1]		
TB	NA	82
DPT	96	77
Polio	96	77
Measles	91	74
Prevalence of child malnutrition (1992-98)[1] (based on weight for age, % of children under 5 years)	3	30

Ethnic Division

Arab 95%
Armenian 4%
Other 1%

Religion

Muslim 70%
Christian 30%
Jewish . . . . .NEGL%

There are 5 legally recognized Islamic groups - Shi'a, Sunni, Druze, Isma'ilite, Alawite or Nusayri. There are 11 legally recognized Christian groups - 4 Orthodox Christian, 6 Catholic, 1 Protestant. NEGL stands for negligible.

Major Languages

Arabic (official), French, English, Armenian widely understood.

EDUCATION

Public Education Expenditures

	1997
Public expenditures on education as % of GNP	2.5
Expenditures per student as % of GNP per capita	
Primary	18.5[1]
Secondary	NA
Tertiary	22.3
Pupils per teacher at the primary level	NA
Duration of primary education in years	9
World data for comparison	
Public expenditures on education as % of GNP (mean)	4.8
Pupils per teacher at the primary level (wtd ave)	33
Duration of primary education in years (mean)	9

Educational Attainment (B)

	1995	1997
Gross enrollment ratio (%)		
Primary level	109.3	110.7
Secondary level	80.6	81.0
Tertiary level	27.0	27.1

Literacy Rates (A)

In thousands and percent	1990	1995	2000	2010
Illiterate population (15+ yrs.)	154	151	138	115
Literacy rate - total adult pop. (%)	90.8	92.4	93.7	95.8
Literacy rate - males (%)	93.6	94.7	95.6	96.9
Literacy rate - females (%)	88.2	90.3	92.0	94.7

GOVERNMENT & LAW

Political Parties

The unicameral National Assembly or Majlis Alnuwab (Arabic) or Assemblee Nationale (French) consists of 128 seats. Members are elected by popular vote on the basis of sectarian proportional representation to serve four-year terms. Elections were last held 18 August–15 September 1996 (next to be held in 2000). One half of the seats are Christian and the other half, Muslim. Political party activity is organized along largely sectarian lines. Numerous political groupings exist, consisting of individual political figures and followers motivated by religious, clan, and economic considerations.

Military Affairs (A)

	1990	1992	1995	1996	1997
Military expenditures					
Current dollars (mil.)	316[e]	425	537	552	465
1997 constant dollars (mil.)	370[e]	471	556	561	465
Armed forces (000)	36	37	55	55	57
Gross national product (GNP)					
Current dollars (mil.)	7,800	10,500	13,900	14,500	15,300
1997 constant dollars (mil.)	9,140	11,700	14,300	14,700	15,300
Central government expenditures (CGE)					
1997 constant dollars (mil.)	2,640[e]	2,550	4,860	5,440	5,540[e]
People (mil.)	3.4	3.2	3.3	3.4	3.4
Military expenditure as % of GNP	4.1	4.0	3.9	3.8	3.0
World data on military expenditure as % of GNP	4.5	3.4	2.7	2.6	2.6
Military expenditure as % of CGE	14.0	18.5	11.4	10.3	8.4
World data on military expenditure as % of CGE	17.0	12.5	10.5	10.3	10.2
Military expenditure per capita (1997 $)	110	147	166	165	135
World data on military expenditure per capita (1997 $)	242	173	146	143	145
Armed forces per 1,000 people (soldiers)	10.7	11.5	16.5	16.2	16.5
World data on armed forces per 1,000 people (soldiers)	5.3	4.5	4.1	3.9	3.8
GNP per capita (1997 $)	2,710	3,630	4,300	4,330	4,450
Arms imports[6]					
Current dollars (mil.)	0	0	50	40	40
1997 constant dollars (mil.)	0	0	52	41	40
Total imports[7]					
Current dollars (mil.)	2,525	4,202	7,278	7,582	7,500[e]
1997 constant dollars (mil.)	2,957	4,658	7,536	7,708	7,500[e]
Total exports[7]					
Current dollars (mil.)	489	560	825	1,017	NA
1997 constant dollars (mil.)	573	621	854	1,034	NA
Arms as percent of total imports[8]	0	0	0.7	0.5	0.5
Arms as percent of total exports[8]	0	0	0	0	0

Government Budgets (A)

Year: 1998

Total Expenditures: 8,385.46 Billions of Pounds

Expenditures as a percentage of the total by function:

General public services and public order	17.10
Defense	9.66
Education	8.30
Health	2.63
Social Security and Welfare	6.40
Housing and community amenities	2.08
Recreational, cultural, and religious affairs	0.78
Fuel and energy	0.02
Agriculture, forestry, fishing, and hunting	0.65
Mining, manufacturing, and construction	5.75
Transportation and communication	3.62
Other economic affairs and services	2.31

Crime

Crime volume (for 1998)

Crimes reported	108,513
Total persons convicted	NA
Crimes per 100,000 population	2,713

Persons responsible for offenses

Total number suspects	107,400
Total number of female suspects	NA
Total number of juvenile suspects	NA

LABOR FORCE

Total Labor Force (A)

1.3 million. In addition, there are as many as 1 million foreign workers (1997 est.).

Labor Force by Occupation

Services	62%
Industry	31%
Agriculture	7%

Data for 1997 est.

Unemployment Rate

18% (1997 est.)

PRODUCTION SECTOR

Energy Production

Production	9.7 billion kWh

Production by source

Fossil fuel	90.72%
Hydro	9.28%
Nuclear	0%
Other	0%
Exports	0 kWh

Data for 1998.

Energy Consumption

Consumption	9.629 billion kWh
Imports	608.000 million kWh

Data for 1998.

Transportation

Highways:

Total: 7,300 km.

Paved: 6,200 km.

Unpaved: 1,100 km (1999 est.).

Pipelines: crude oil 72 km (none in operation).

Merchant marine:

Total: 68 ships (1,000 GRT or over) totaling 346,029 GRT/536,861 DWT.

Ships by type: bulk 8, cargo 44, chemical tanker 1, combination bulk 1, combination ore/oil 1, container 4, livestock carrier 4, roll-on/roll-off 2, vehicle carrier 3 (1999 est.).

Airports: 9 (1999 est.).

Top Agriculture Products

Citrus, grapes, tomatoes, apples, vegetables, potatoes, olives, tobacco; sheep, goats.

Top Mining Products (B)

Mineral resources include: limestone, iron ore, salt.

MANUFACTURING SECTOR

GDP & Manufacturing Summary (C)

Total GDP (1999 est.)	$16.2 billion
Real growth rate (1999 est.)	1%
Per capita (1999 est.)	$4,500

Composition by sector

Agriculture	12%
Industry	27%
Services	61%

Values in purchasing power parity.

COMMUNICATIONS

Daily Newspapers

	National Data	World Data for Comparison
Daily Newspapers		
Number of Dailies	15	8,391
Total Circulation (000)	435	548,000
Circulation per 1,000 inhabitants	141	96

Telecommunications

Telephones - main lines in use: 330,000 (1995).

Telephones - mobile cellular: 120,000 (1995).

Telephone system: telecommunications system severely damaged by civil war; rebuilding well underway.

Domestic: primarily microwave radio relay and cable.

International: satellite earth stations - 2 Intelsat (1 Indian Ocean and 1 Atlantic Ocean) (erratic operations); coaxial cable to Syria; microwave radio relay to Syria but inoperable beyond Syria to Jordan; 3 submarine coaxial cables.

Radio broadcast stations: AM 20, FM 22, shortwave 4 (1998).

Radios: 2.85 million (1997).

Television broadcast stations: 28 (1997).

Televisions: 1.18 million (1997).

Internet Service Providers (ISPs): 19 (1999).

FINANCE, ECONOMICS, & TRADE

Economic Indicators

National product: GDP—purchasing power parity—$16.2 billion (1999 est.).

National product real growth rate: 1% (1999 est.).

National product per capita: $4,500 (1999 est.).

Inflation rate—consumer price index: 4.5% (1999 est.).

Exchange Rates

Exchange rates:

Lebanese pounds per US$1

January 2000 . . . . 1,507.5
1999 . . . . 1,507.8
1998 . . . . 1,516.1
1997 . . . . 1,539.5
1996 . . . . 1,571.4
1995 . . . . 1,621.4

Top Import Origins

$5.7 billion (f.o.b., 1999 est.)

Origins (1998)

Italy 12%
France 10%
United States 9%
Germany 9%
Switzerland 6%
Japan . . . . NA
United Kingdom . . . . NA
Syria . . . . NA

Top Export Destinations

$866 million (f.o.b., 1999 est.)

Destinations (1998)

Saudi Arabia 12%
UAE 10%
France 9%
Syria 7%
United States 7%
Kuwait 4%
Jordan . . . . NA
Turkey . . . . NA

Foreign Aid

Recipient: $3.5 billion (pledges 1997-2001).

Import/Export Commodities

Import Commodities	Export Commodities
Foodstuffs	Foodstuffs and tobacco
Machinery and transport equipment	Textiles
Consumer goods	Chemicals
Chemicals	Metal and metal products
Textiles	Electrical equipment and products
Metals	Jewelry
Fuels	Paper and paper products
Agricultural foods	

LESOTHO

CAPITAL: Maseru.

FLAG: The flag is divided diagonally from the lower hoist side corner; the upper half is white bearing the brown silhouette of a large shield with crossed spear and club; the lower half is a diagonal blue band with a green triangle in the corner.

ANTHEM: *Lesotho Fatse La Bo-nata Rona (Lesotho, the Country of Our Fathers).*

MONETARY UNIT: Lesotho is part of the South African monetary area; the maloti of 100 lisente, introduced in 1980, is on a par with the South African rand (R), which is also legal tender. There are coins of 1, 2, 5, 10, 25, and 50 lisente, and notes of 2, 5, 10, 20, and 50 maloti (M). M1 = $0.21268 (or $1 = M4.702).

WEIGHTS AND MEASURES: British and metric weights and measures are in general use.

HOLIDAYS: New Year's Day, 1 January; Moshoeshoe's Day, 12 March; Family Day, 1st Monday in July; King's Birthday, 17 July; Independence Day, 4 October; National Sports Day, 6 October; Christmas, 25 December; Boxing Day, 26 December. Movable Christian holidays include Good Friday, Easter Monday, and Ascension.

TIME: 2 PM = noon GMT.

LOCATION AND SIZE: Lesotho is located entirely within the borders of the Republic of South Africa, with an area of 30,350 square kilometers (11,718 square miles), slightly larger than the state of Maryland. Lesotho's capital city, Maseru, is located on the country's northwest border.

CLIMATE: Temperatures vary widely from one geographical zone to another, and frequently within zones, depending on the altitude. In the lowlands, temperatures reach 32°C (90°F) or more in the summer and rarely fall below −7°C (19°F) in the winter. The range in the highlands is greater; temperatures sometimes fall below −18°C (0°F), and frost and hail are frequent hazards. Rainfall, which is mostly concentrated in the months from October to April, averages 71 centimeters (28 inches) annually.

Kingdom of Lesotho
Muso oa Lesotho

INTRODUCTORY SURVEY

RECENT HISTORY

Under indirect British rule, local chiefs governed through the 1950s. A new constitution in 1960 created an indirectly elected legislative body, the Basutoland National Counci. A pre-independence constitution became effective in 1965.

The United Kingdom granted independence to the newly named Kingdom of Lesotho on October 4, 1966. Moshoeshoe II was proclaimed king. During general elections in 1970, Prime Minister Leabua Jonathan declared a state of emergency and suspended the constitution. King Moshoeshoe II was placed under house arrest.

Through the early 1980s the Lesotho Liberation Army (LLA) struggled for control against the Jonathan government. They claimed responsibility for periodic bombings in Maseru, ambushes of government officials, and attacks on police stations. The Lesotho government charged that South Africa was allowing the LLA to use its territory as a base of operations.

As relations with South Africa deteriorated a military coup led by Major General Justin Metsing Lekhanya overthrew the government. All political activity was banned. There was widespread skepticism about the military government and its links to South Africa. In November 1990 Moshoeshoe's son, King Letsie III, was elected king by an assembly of chiefs. In April 1991 rebel army officers staged a bloodless coup forcing Lekhanya to resign.

Finally on March 27, 1993, in the first democratic elections in twenty-three years, the Basotho Congress Party (BCP) won all sixty-five seats in the Assembly. The BCP formed a new government under Prime Minister Dr. Ntsu Mokhehle. After three weeks of sporadic fighting, opposing factions within the military agreed to new negotiations.

In September 1994 the king and Prime Minister Mokhehle signed an agreement reestablishing democratic rule and removing King Letsie III from the throne and returning his father, the exiled King Moshoeshoe II. In 1996 King Moshoeshoe II was killed in a car crash and his son was returned to power. The move alarmed supporters of democracy because Letsie had suspended parliament when he earlier held power.

In the 1998 elections opposition parties claimed fraud and staged a coup. Southern African Development Community (SADC) forces intervened to restore order and set up the Interim Political Authority to create a new electoral system and conduct new elections.

GOVERNMENT

According to the 1965 constitution and its 1993 replacement the Kingdom of Lesotho is a parliamentary constitutional monarchy. The bicameral parliament consists of a National Assembly of eighty members and a Senate with thirty-three members. A coup after the 1998 legislative election resulted in an Interim Political Authority set temporarily in power.

Until 1993 the king was official chief of state *(motlotlehi)*. The 1993 constitution, however, clearly defines the king's role as ceremonial with no executive or legislative powers. Under traditional law the college of chiefs has the power to determine who is next in line of succession and may even dispose the monarch.

Judiciary

The judicial system consists of the High Court, the Court of Appeal, subordinate courts including magistrate courts, commissioner's courts, central and local courts, and the Judicial Service Commission (JSC). The High Court hears appeals from subordinate courts, but also has unlimited original jurisdiction over civil and criminal matters. Chiefs administer customary and tribal law. There is no trial by jury.

Political Parties

As Lesotho entered into the twenty-first century, the dominant political party was the ruling Lestho Congress for Democracy (LCD) under the leadership of Dr. Pakaltha Mosisili who was the prime minister. The major opposition party was the Basotho National Party (BNP).

DEFENSE

A 2,000-member army has eight combat companies armed with United States and United Kingdom weapons and one air squadron.

ECONOMIC AFFAIRS

Lesotho is an agricultural country based on subsistence agriculture and livestock. Lesotho's only important natural resource is water. Completed in January 1998 a major hydropower facility allows Lesotho to sell water to Africa. Another source of income, although a declining one, is remittances from Lesotho mine workers employed in South Africa.

Civil disorder in September 1998 destroyed most of the commercial infrastructure. The challenge in 1999 and 2000 was to rebuild businesses. In 1998 output dropped 10 percent but recovery had begun slowly in 1999.

Public Finance

Proceeds from membership in a common customs union with South Africa account for the majority of government revenue. The government has posted budget surpluses since 1992. The U.S. Central Intelligence Agency estimated that in 1996-1997 government revenues totaled approximately $507 million and expenditures $487 million including capital expenditures of $170 million. The 1996 surplus was expected to be about 1 percent of GDP. External debt totaled $675 million in 1998.

Income

In 1998 Lesotho's gross domestic product (GDP) was estimated at $4.7 billion, or about $2,240 per capita. The 1998 estimated growth rate of GDP was a decline of 10 percent. Inflation was estimated at 8 percent in 1998. In 1997 the estimated GDP by sector was agriculture 14 percent, industry 42 percent, and services 44 percent.

Industry

Lesotho has a wide variety of light industries, which include, food and beverages, tire retreading, tapestry weaving, diamond processing, and the production of textiles, electric lighting, candles, ceramics, explosives, furniture, and fertilizers. Manufacturing depends largely on agricultural inputs to support milling, canning, leather, and jute industries.

Banking and Finance

Lesotho is a member of the Common Monetary Area. The 1974 agreement, revised in 1986, provides access to the South African capital market for the Lesotho banking system. Lesotho is now responsible for its own monetary policy and controls its own financial institutions, but management of the rand currency and the gold and foreign exchange reserves of the rand area remains the sole responsibility of South Africa.

Demand for credit to the private sector has been strong in the 1990s in response to growth in the manufacturing, services and construction sectors. In contrast claims on central government have been sharply reduced as a result of the IMF-supported Structural Adjustment Program; in fact, the government has been a net saver with the domestic banking system since 1992.

The commercial bank sector is dominated by the government-owned Lesotho Bank and the South African-owned Stambic Bank that has recently acquired Barclays Bank's interest in Lesotho. The Lesotho Building Finance Corporation merged with Lesotho Bank in April 1993 to facilitate an increase in the scale of domestic mortgage lending. The Lesotho Agricultural Development Bank (LADB) serves to mobilize rural savings and provide agricultural credit.

No securities exchange was in operation in Lesotho as of 1997.

Economic Development

The Lesotho government's development objectives are based on a food-security policy approach built around small-scale irrigated agriculture projects and improved rural water supplies. Donors supported the fourth five-year plan (1988-1991) with pledges of $390 million. Lesotho receives development assistance from the United Kingdom, South Africa, Canada, Taiwan, the World Bank, and various United Nations agencies. Political reforms in South Africa in 1994 should have a beneficial impact on the Lesotho economy.

Completion of a major hydropower facility in January 1998 permits Lesotho to sell water to South Africa generating royalties that will be an important source of income for Lesotho.

Following the 1998 civil disorder the government focused on rebuilding the commercial infrastructure that was 80 percent destroyed.

SOCIAL WELFARE

The Ministry of Health administers the Social Welfare Department. The Homemakers' Association, an organization long active in social welfare, has given family-management courses in remote areas under a grant from the Oxford Committee for Famine Relief (Oxfam).

Law and tradition limits the roles of women, although a few women serve in important government roles.

Healthcare

Major health problems include pellagra, kwashiorkor, and other diseases that stem from poor nutrition and inadequate hygiene. In 1989-1995 21 percent of children under five years of age were considered malnourished. Famines have resulted from periodic droughts. Tuberculosis and venereal diseases are also serious problems.

In 1990-1997 there were 0.1 doctors and 1.4 hospital beds per 1,000 people. In 1995 approximately 80 percent of the population had access to health care service. In 2000 estimated life expectancy was fifty-one years.

Housing

The Lesotho Housing Corp. builds new housing for sale and rent, and a government-supported development program is building low-cost housing.

EDUCATION

A by-product of the long history of missionary activity in Lesotho was the relatively comprehensive development of education. Education is compulsory between the ages of six and thirteen.

In 1996 Lesotho had 1,249 primary schools. That year, there were 374,628 primary school pupils taught by 7,898 teachers, and 68,132 general secondary school students taught by 2,878 teachers. In 1992 1,590 students were enrolled in vocational training.

The University of Lesotho, at Botswana and Swaziland, was renamed the National University of Lesotho in 1975 by Prime Minister Leabua Jonathan. In 1997 all higher-level institutions totaled 4,614 pupils and 574 teaching staff.

The projected adult illiteracy rate for 2000 was 16.1 percent (males 26.4 percent and females 6.4 percent).

2000 KEY EVENTS TIMELINE

January

- Minister of Foreign Affairs, Tom Thabane, says the government will demand tougher sentences for criminals who commit brutal crimes such as murder.

February

- King Letsie III, Africa's last bachelor king marries Karabo Motsoeneng in ceremonies held in Maseru, the capital.

April

- Government announces establishment of a commission to exam the political unrest that occurred after the May 1998 general elections which required South African troops to restore order.

June

- The Director of Aon Holdings B.V. Corporation, which acquired a large minority share of Lesotho Bank in a privatization bid, promises that workers will not be laid off.

July

- The European Union announces major foreign aid to commence phase two of measles immunization to take place in the fall.

August

- Students and staff protest at the University of Lesotho, demanding the resignation of Vice Chancellor Moletsane.

September

- Media exposes Chinese forgery of international trademarks in Maseru, the capital. Despite government intervention, numerous fake goods bearing international trademarks still exist.

October

- Lesotho Network for Conflict Resolution (LNCR) warns that decentralization will lead to conflict between traditional and modern authorities.

November

- Police use tear gas to disperse a student rally for the opposition party November 16.
- The Lesotho Youth Movement demands November 28 fingerprint identification during voting for the following year.

ANALYSIS OF EVENTS: 2000

BUSINESS AND THE ECONOMY

Lesotho was still recovering from the damage wrought by civil unrest in 1998, which destroyed commercial facilities in Maseru and two of the country's other major towns. Agricultural production was reduced by drought, and remittances from miners employed in South Africa continued to decline. Despite privatization efforts, the private sector remained small.

Lesotho was a founding member of the Southern Africa Free Trade Zone, formed in September by the Southern African Development Community (SADC). It was hoped that the alliance would eventually create a single market encompassing some 200 million people in fourteen countries. Its goals included lowering and ultimately eliminating tariffs, increasing trade among members to 35 percent of all trade by 2004, and facilitating foreign trade with the region as a whole.

The European Union announced it would provide major assistance for the second phase of measles immunization in the fall.

GOVERNMENT AND POLITICS

Lesotho enjoyed a long-awaited event when its thirty-six-year-old bachelor king, Letsie III, married in February. It was hoped that the celebrations surrounding the marriage would help bring unity to a country riven by deep political divisions following civil unrest in 1998. King Letsie's bride, and Lesotho's new queen, was Karabo Motsoeneng, a twenty-three-year-old commoner with a science degree. The wedding ceremony, held in the national sports stadium in the capital city of Maseru, was witnessed by a crowd of 40,000, and many more were turned away. The country spent a total of $1.5 million on three days of wedding festivities.

In April the government appointed a commission to investigate the political unrest following the 1998 elections, which had required military intervention by South African troops, authorized by the Southern Africa Development Community (SADC).

Controversy continued to swirl around the Lesotho Highlands Development Project, recently inaugurated to supply water to South Africa and thus capitalize on Lesotho's chief natural resource, its water power, popularly referred to as "white gold." The project's former chief executive officer was charged with bribery and corruption in a case pending before the nation's high court. Other problems had been generated by the relocation of hundreds of people to make way for the project and opposition by environmental groups. The World Bank, who provided assistance for the $8 million project, pledged to aid in further corruption investigations.

In November Metsing Lekhanya, leader of the opposition Basotho National Party, called on Prime Minister Pakalitha Mosisili to resign as head of the ruling Lesotho Congress for Democracy. A planned protest march was barred by the country's defense forces.

In March Lesotho supplied cargo planes for the delivery of relief aid to flood-stricken Mozambique. In May a settlement was reached regarding expenses incurred by South Africa when its defense forces entered Lesotho in 1998 to quell an insurrection in Maseru, at the request of Lesotho's government. South Africa had initially demanded payment of expenses involved in the operation, but ultimately it was agreed that each country would pay its own expenses.

Ireland's prime minister, Bertie Ahern, visited Lesotho as part of a trip to promote trade between his country and southern Africa.

CULTURE AND SOCIETY

Addressing Parliament at its opening session in August, King Letsie III listed the country's major social problems as poverty, crime, unemployment, and HIV/AIDS. The country's poverty had been exacerbated in recent years by droughts that had depressed agricultural production, as well as reductions in the number of Basotho miners employed in South Africa. The government announced a major poverty-reduction program with the broad goals of expanding the private sector, improving education, and encouraging economic growth.

The Lesotho Association of Non Formal Educational (LANFE), an alliance of public and private-sector groups dedicated to reducing illiteracy, celebrated its twenty-first anniversary.

The government announced that the Danish government was to provide aid for the Lesotho Environment Education Support Project, whose goal was the integration of environmental education into the public school curriculum at both the primary and secondary levels.

In December Lesotho was scheduled to host a conference on implementation of the Southern African Development Community's policies on violence against women and children.

The second Morija Arts and Cultural Festival was held in September and featured traditional song, dance, and drama as well as equestrian arts. Entitled the Peace and Unity Festival, the three-day festival began with an AIDS awareness event.

DIRECTORY

CENTRAL GOVERNMENT

Head of State

King

Letsie III, Monarch, Royal Palace, Maseru, Lesotho

Ministers

Prime Minister
Pakalitha Mosisili, Office of the Prime Minister, c/o The Government Secretary, PO Box 527, Maseru 100, Lesotho

Deputy Prime Minister and Minister of Finance and Development Planning
Kelebone Albert Maope, Ministry of Finance and Development Planning

Minister of Agriculture, Cooperatives, and Land Reclamation
Vova Bulane, Ministry of Agriculture, Cooperatives, and Land Reclamation

Minister of Communications Information, Broadcasting, Posts and Telecommunications
Qnyane Mphafi, Ministry of Communications Information, Broadcasting, Posts and Telecommunications

Minister of Defense
Pakalitha Mosisili, Ministry of Defense

Minister of Education
Lesao Archibald Lehohla, Ministry of Education

Minister of Employment and Labor
Nots'i Victor Molopo, Ministry of Employment and Labor

Minister of Environment, Gender, and Youth Affairs
Mathabiso Lepono, Ministry of Environment, Gender, and Youth Affairs

Minister of Foreign Affairs
Motsoahae Thomas Thabane, Ministry of Foreign Affairs

Minister of Health and Social Welfare
Tefo Mabote, Ministry of Health and Social Welfare

Minister of Industry, Trade, and Marketing
Mpho Meli Malie, Ministry of Industry, Trade, and Marketing

Minister of Justice, Human Rights, Law and Constitutional Affairs
Shakane Mokhehle, Ministry of Justice, Human Rights, Law and Constitutional Affairs

Minister of Local Government and Home Affairs
Mopshatla Mabitle, Ministry of Local Government and Home Affairs

Minister of Natural Resources
Monyane Moleleki, Ministry of Natural Resources

Minister of Public Works and Transport
Mofelehetsi Moerane, Ministry of Public Works and Transport

Minister of Tourism, Sports, and Culture
Mlalele Motaung, Ministry of Tourism, Sports, and Culture

POLITICAL ORGANIZATIONS

Basotho Congress Party (BCP)

NAME: Molapo Qhobela

Basotho National Party (BNP)

NAME: Evaristus Sekhonyana

DIPLOMATIC REPRESENTATION

Embassies in Lesotho

United States
254 Kingsway, PO Box 333, Maseru 100, Lesotho
PHONE: +266 312666
FAX: +266 310116

JUDICIAL SYSTEM

High Court

Court of Appeal

Magistrate's Court

BROADCAST MEDIA

Mnet

E-MAIL: webmaster@mnet.co.za
WEBSITE: http://www.mnet.co.za/

Lesotho National Broadcasting Service

PO Box 552, Maseru 100, Lesotho
PHONE: +266 323561
FAX: +266 310003
TITLE: Principal Secretary
CONTACT: Mpine Tente
LANGUAGE: English, SeSotho
TYPE: Government

COLLEGES AND UNIVERSITIES

National University of Lesotho

PO Roma 180, Maseru, Lesotho
PHONE: +266 340601

FAX: +266 340000
E-MAIL: info@nul.ls
WEBSITE: http://www.nul.ls

NEWSPAPERS AND MAGAZINES

Leselinyana la Lesotho

PO Box 7, Morija 190, Lesotho
FAX: +266 360005
TITLE: Editor
CONTACT: Aaron B. Thoahlane
CIRCULATION: 7,500

Mopheme

PHONE: +266 311670
E-MAIL: lawrence@mopheme.co.ls
WEBSITE: http://www.lesoff.co.za/mopheme

Lentsoe la Basotho

PO Box 36, Maseru 100, Lesotho
FAX: +266 310003
TITLE: Editor
CONTACT: Khaliso Lesenya
CIRCULATION: 7,000
TYPE: Social science, general

Leseli Ka Sepolesa

PO Box 13, Maseru 100, Lesotho
TITLE: Editor
CONTACT: Serabele Sekoateng
CIRCULATION: 2,500
TYPE: Social science, general

Lesotho Law Journal

PO Roma 180, Maseru, Lesotho
FAX: +266 340000
TITLE: Editor
CONTACT: Kenneth Asamoa Acheampong
CIRCULATION: 500
TYPE: Law, general, political science, civil rights, public affairs and administration

PUBLISHERS

Government Printer

PO Box 527, Maseru 100, Lesotho

Longman Lesotho (Pty) Ltd.

104 Christie House, Orpen Rd., PO Box 1174, Maseru, Lesotho
PHONE: +266 317340
FAX: +266 310118
TITLE: Manager
CONTACT: Leomile Putosa

Mazenod Book Centre

PO Box 39, Mazenrod 160, Lesotho
PHONE: +266 350224
TITLE: Manager
CONTACT: B. Mohlalisi
SUBJECTS: History, Literature, Literary Criticism, Essays, Regional Interests, Religion

Saint Michael's Mission

Roma The Social Centre, PO Box 25, Roma, Lesotho
TITLE: Man. Director
CONTACT: M. Ferrange
SUBJECTS: Anthropology, Biography, History, Regional Interests, Religion, Social Sciences

RELIGIOUS ORGANIZATIONS

Recent turmoil in the government has forced most religious groups into hiding or nonexistence; due to colonial influences from the Dutch in the nineteenth century, most Lesothoans superimpose Christian beliefs on earlier indigenous religious practices of tribal origin.

FURTHER READING

Articles

Corry, John. "Wedding in Maseru." *The American Spectator,* July–August 2000, p. 32+.

Keesing's Record of World Events, April 2000.

Mopheme (The Survivor), January 4, June 20, and July 11, 2000. 2000.

Books

Dun and Bradstreet's Export Guide to Lesotho. Parsippany, NJ: Dun & Bradstreet, 1999.

Murray, Jon. *South Africa, Lesotho & Swaziland.* 4th ed., London: Lonely Planet, 2000.

LESOTHO: STATISTICAL DATA

For sources and notes see "Sources of Statistics" at the front of each volume.

GEOGRAPHY

Geography

Area:

Total: 30,355 sq km.

Land: 30,355 sq km.

Land boundaries:

Total: 909 km.

Border countries: South Africa 909 km.

Coastline: 0 km (landlocked).

Climate: temperate; cool to cold, dry winters; hot, wet summers.

Terrain: mostly highland with plateaus, hills, and mountains.

Natural resources: water, agricultural and grazing land, some diamonds and other minerals.

Land use:

Arable land: 11%

Permanent crops: 0%

Permanent pastures: 66%

Forests and woodland: 0%

Other: 23% (1993 est.).

HUMAN FACTORS

Demographics (A)

	1990	1995	1998	2000	2010	2020	2030	2040	2050
Population	1,732	1,945	2,069	2,143	2,339	2,382	2,459	2,602	2,849
Life expectancy - males	55.2	55.1	51.8	49.8	36.4	39.4	45.8	56.3	68.5
Life expectancy - females	59.9	59.9	54.8	51.8	39.0	42.3	49.6	61.2	74.4
Birth rate (per 1,000)	36.8	34.3	32.8	31.7	27.0	24.9	22.6	20.1	18.1
Death rate (per 1,000)	11.8	11.4	13.3	14.6	24.6	22.4	18.5	12.8	7.5
Women of reproductive age (15-49 yrs.)	409.8	475.1	512.3	534.2	587.9	620.9	665.6	721.8	782.2
Fertility rate	4.9	4.5	4.3	4.2	3.5	2.9	2.5	2.3	2.2

Except as noted, values for vital statistics are in thousands; life expectancy is in years.

Health Personnel

	National Data	World Data (wtd ave)
Total health expenditure as a percentage of GDP, 1990-1998[a]		
Public sector	3.7	2.5
Private sector	2.4	2.9
Total[b]	NA	5.5
Availability of health care facilities per 100,000 people		
Hospital beds 1990-1998[a]	NA	330
Doctors 1992-1995[a]	5	122
Nurses 1992-1995[a]	33	248

Health Indicators

	National Data	World Data
Life expectancy at birth (years)		
1980	53	61
1998	55	67
Daily per capita supply of calories		
1970	1,986	2,358
1997	2,243	2,791
Daily per capital supply of protein		
1997 (grams)	64	74
Total fertility rate (births per woman)		
1980	5.5	3.7
1998	4.6	2.7
Population with access (%)		
To safe water (1990-96)	52	NA
To sanitation (1990-96)	6	NA
People living with (1997)		
Tuberculosis (cases per 100,000)	257.2	60.4
HIV/AIDS (% aged 15 - 49 years)	8.35	0.99

Infants and Malnutrition

	National Data	World Data (wtd ave)
Under 5 mortality rate (1989)	136	NA
% of infants with low birthweight (1992-98)[1]	11	17
Births attended by skilled health staff (% of total births 1996-98)	50	52
% fully immunized at 1 year of age (1995-98)[1]		
TB	46	82
DPT	50	77
Polio	48	77
Measles	49	74
Prevalence of child malnutrition (1992-98)[1] (based on weight for age, % of children under 5 years)	16	30

Ethnic Division

Sotho 99.7%

Europeans, Asians, and other 0.3%

Religion

Christian 80%

Indigenous beliefs 20%

Major Languages

Sesotho (southern Sotho), English (official), Zulu, Xhosa.

EDUCATION

Public Education Expenditures

	1980	1997
Public expenditures on education as % of GNP	5.1	8.4
Expenditures per student as % of GNP per capita		
Primary	8.6	13.8
Secondary	72.5	53.7
Tertiary	1,003.6	779.3
Teachers' compensation as % of total current education expenditures	60.9	57.6
Pupils per teacher at the primary level	NA	47
Duration of primary education in years	NA	7
World data for comparison		
Public expenditures on education as % of GNP (mean)	3.9	4.8
Pupils per teacher at the primary level (wtd ave)	NA	33
Duration of primary education in years (mean)	NA	9

Educational Attainment (B)

	1995	1997
Gross enrollment ratio (%)		
Primary level	110.9	107.7
Secondary level	30.8	30.7
Tertiary level	2.3	2.4

Literacy Rates (A)

In thousands and percent	1990	1995	2000	2010
Illiterate population (15+ yrs.)	341	340	338	326
Literacy rate - total adult pop. (%)	66.7	71.3	75.5	82.4
Literacy rate - males (%)	77.7	81.1	83.9	88.4
Literacy rate - females (%)	56.6	62.3	67.6	76.6

GOVERNMENT & LAW

Political Parties

Parliament	% of vote	no. of seats
Lesotho Congress for Democracy (LCD)	61%	79
Basotho National Party (BNP)		1

Elections were last held 23 May 1998 (next to be held in 2000; date to be determined by Interim Political Authority). Election results were contested. Opposition parties claimed the election was fraudulent and staged a coup. Southern African Development Community (SADC) forces intervened in September 1998 and restored order. The Interim Political Authority (IPA) was set up in December 1998 to create a new electoral system and conduct new elections within 18 months.

Military Affairs (A)

	1990	1992	1995	1996	1997
Military expenditures					
Current dollars (mil.)	44[e]	31	23	28	32
1997 constant dollars (mil.)	51[e]	34	24	28	32
Armed forces (000)	2	2	2	2	2
Gross national product (GNP)					
Current dollars (mil.)	117	850	1,050	1,200	1,270
1997 constant dollars (mil.)	956	943	1,080	1,220	1,270
Central government expenditures (CGE)					
1997 constant dollars (mil.)	299	323	412	466	530
People (mil.)	1.7	1.8	2.0	2.0	2.0
Military expenditure as % of GNP	5.3	3.6	2.2	2.3	2.5
World data on military expenditure as % of GNP	4.5	3.4	2.7	2.6	2.6
Military expenditure as % of CGE	17.1	10.5	5.9	6.0	6.1
World data on military expenditure as % of CGE	17.0	12.5	10.5	10.3	10.2
Military expenditure per capita (1997 $)	29	18	12	14	16
World data on military expenditure per capita (1997 $)	242	173	146	143	145
Armed forces per 1,000 people (soldiers)	1.2	1.1	1.0	1.0	1.0
World data on armed forces per 1,000 people (soldiers)	5.3	4.5	4.1	3.9	3.8
GNP per capita (1997 $)	551	514	552	606	620
Total imports[7]					
Current dollars (mil.)	640	900	986	1,001	1,102
1997 constant dollars (mil.)	750	997	1,021	1,018	1,102
Total exports[7]					
Current dollars (mil.)	59	109	160	189	195
1997 constant dollars (mil.)	70	121	166	192	195
Arms as percent of total imports[8]	0	0	0	0	0
Arms as percent of total exports[8]	0	0	0	0	0

Government Budgets (A)

Year: 1998

Total Expenditures: 2,443 Millions of Maloti

Expenditures as a percentage of the total by function:

- General public services and public order . . . . .27.68[p]
- Defense . . . . .6.54[p]
- Education . . . . .26.71[p]
- Health . . . . .9.31[p]
- Social Security and Welfare . . . . .NA
- Housing and community amenities . . . . .NA
- Recreational, cultural, and religious affairs . . . . . .NA
- Fuel and energy . . . . .NA
- Agriculture, forestry, fishing, and hunting . . . . .5.13[p]
- Mining, manufacturing, and construction . . . . .13.41[p]
- Transportation and communication . . . . .0.73[p]
- Other economic affairs and services . . . . .2.02[p]

Crime

Crime rate (for 1997)

- Crimes reported 445,000
- Total persons convicted 93,500
- Crimes per 100,000 population 26,200

Persons responsible for offenses

- Total number of suspects 26,900
- Total number of female suspects 17,000
- Total number of juvenile suspects 18,000

LABOR FORCE

Total Labor Force (A)

689,000 economically active.

Labor Force by Occupation

86% of resident population engaged in subsistence agriculture; roughly 35% of the active male wage earners work in South Africa.

Unemployment Rate

Substantial unemployment and underemployment affecting more than half of the labor force (1999 est.).

PRODUCTION SECTOR

Energy Production

Production . . . . .0 kWh

Production by source

- Fossil fuel 0%
- Hydro 0%
- Nuclear 0%
- Other 0%

Exports . . . . .0 kWh

Data for 1998.

Energy Consumption

Consumption . . . . .209 million kWh

Imports . . . . .209 million kWh

Data for 1998.

Transportation

Highways:

Total: 4,955 km.

Paved: 887 km.

Unpaved: 4,068 km (1996 est.).

Airports: 29 (1999 est.).

Airports - with unpaved runways: 25.

Top Agriculture Products

Corn, wheat, pulses, sorghum, barley; livestock.

Top Mining Products (B)

Mineral resources include: some diamonds and other minerals.

MANUFACTURING SECTOR

GDP & Manufacturing Summary (A)

	1980	1985	1990	1995
GDP ($-1990 mil.)[1]	383	411	584	695[e]
Per capita ($-1990)[1]	280	263	327	343[e]
Manufacturing share (%) (current prices)[1]	6.3	10.4	13.1	NA
Manufacturing				
Value added ($-1990 mil.)[1]	20	36	64	93[e]
Industrial production index	27[e]	63	100[e]	149[e]
Value added ($ mil.)	14[e]	22[e]	68[e]	134[e]
Gross output ($ mil.)	57[e]	66[e]	189[e]	378[e]
Employment (000)	4[e]	7[e]	19[e]	18[e]
Profitability (% of gross output)				
Intermediate input (%)	75	67	65	67[e]
Wages and salaries inc. supplements (%)	6[e]	9[e]	6[e]	6[e]
Gross operating surplus	18[e]	24[e]	28[e]	28[e]

Productivity ($)				
Gross output per worker	13,616[e]	9,778	10,162[e]	20,697[e]
Value added per worker	3,372[e]	3,234	3,659[e]	7,521[e]
Average wage (inc. supplements)	949[e]	1,039[e]	1,360[e]	3,391[e]
Value added ($ mil.)				
Food products	6[e]	9[e]	29[e]	58[e]
Beverages	5[e]	6[e]	20[e]	38[e]
Textiles	1[e]	2[e]	7[e]	14[e]
Wearing apparel	NA	1[e]	2[e]	4[e]
Leather and fur products	NA	NA	NA	1[e]
Footwear	NA	NA	1[e]	2[e]
Furniture and fixtures	NA	NA	1[e]	1[e]
Printing and publishing	NA	NA	1[e]	2[e]
Other chemical products	1	1	4[e]	9[e]
Other non-metal mineral products	NA	NA	1[e]	1[e]
Metal products	1	1	2[e]	4[e]

COMMUNICATIONS

Daily Newspapers

	National Data	World Data for Comparison
Daily Newspapers		
Number of Dailies	2	8,391
Total Circulation (000)	15	548,000
Circulation per 1,000 inhabitants	7.6	96

Telecommunications

Telephones - main lines in use: 18,000 (1995).

Telephones - mobile cellular: 0 (1995).

Telephone system: rudimentary system.

Domestic: consists of a few landlines, a small microwave radio relay system, and a minor radiotelephone communication system.

International: satellite earth station - 1 Intelsat (Atlantic Ocean).

Radio broadcast stations: AM 1, FM 2, shortwave 1 (1998).

Radios: 104,000 (1997).

Television broadcast stations: 1 (2000).

Televisions: 54,000 (1997).

Internet Service Providers (ISPs): 1 (1999).

FINANCE, ECONOMICS, & TRADE

Economic Indicators

National product: GDP—purchasing power parity—$4.7 billion (1998 est.).

National product real growth rate: -10% (1998 est.).

National product per capita: $2,240 (1998 est.).

Inflation rate—consumer price index: 8% (1998 est.).

Exchange Rates

Exchange rates:

Maloti (M) per US$1

January 2000	6.12439
1999	6.10948
1998	5.52828
1997	4.60796
1996	4.29935
1995	3.62709

The Basotho loti is at par with the South African rand. Fiscal year: 1 April - 31 March.

Balance of Payments

	1994	1995	1996	1997	1998
Exports of goods (f.o.b.)	143	160	187	196	193
Imports of goods (f.o.b.)	−810	−985	−999	−1,024	−866
Trade balance	−667	−825	−812	−828	−673
Services - debits	−64	−61	−56	−68	−52
Services - credits	38	39	43	87	54
Private transfers (net)	13	4	3	2	3
Government transfers (net)	459	207	186	200	154
Overall balance	108	−323	−303	−269	−280

Top Import Origins

$700 million (f.o.b., 1998 est.)

Origins (1997)

South African Customs Union	90%
Asia	7%

Top Export Destinations

$235 million (f.o.b., 1998 est.)

Destinations (1998)

South African Customs Union	65%
North America	34%

Foreign Aid

Recipient: $123.7 million (1995).

Import/Export Commodities

Import Commodities	Export Commodities
Food	Manufactures 75% (clothing, footwear, road vehicles)
Building materials	Wool and mohair
Vehicles	Food and live animals
Machinery	
Medicines	
Petroleum products	

LIBERIA

Republic of Liberia

CAPITAL: Monrovia.

FLAG: The national flag, dating from 1847, consists of 11 horizontal stripes, alternately red (6) and white (5), with a single five-pointed white star on a square blue field 5 stripes deep in the upper left corner.

ANTHEM: *All Hail, Liberia, Hail.*

MONETARY UNIT: The Liberian dollar (L$) of 100 cents is established by law as equivalent to the U.S. dollar. There are no Liberian notes. U.S. notes in the denominations of 5, 10, 20, 50, and 100 dollars are in circulation and are legal tender. Both U.S. and Liberian coins of 1, 5, 10, 25, and 50 cents, and 1 dollar are in circulation; in 1982, a $5 Liberian coin was issued.

WEIGHTS AND MEASURES: U.S. and UK weights and measures are used.

HOLIDAYS: New Year's Day, 1 January; Armed Forces Day, 11 February; Decoration Day, 2d Wednesday in March; Birthday of J. J. Roberts (first president), 15 March; Fast and Prayer Day, 2d Friday in April; National Redemption Day, 12 April; Unification Day, 14 May; Independence Day, 26 July; Flag Day, 24 August; Thanksgiving Day, 1st Thursday in November; Anniversary of 1985 Coup Attempt, 12 November; President Tubman's Birthday, 29 November; Christmas, 25 December. Good Friday and Easter Monday are movable religious holidays.

TIME: GMT.

LOCATION AND SIZE: Located on the west coast of Africa, Liberia has an area of about 111,370 square kilometers (43,000 square miles), slightly larger than the state of Tennessee. Liberia's capital city, Monrovia, is located on the Atlantic coast.

CLIMATE: The climate is tropical with a mean temperature of 27°C (81°F). Yearly rainfall is as high as 510 centimeters (200 inches) on the coast. Most of the rainfall occurs between late April and mid-November. Between December and March, a dust-laden wind known as the harmattan blows from the Sahara Desert.

INTRODUCTORY SURVEY

RECENT HISTORY

The establishment of a United States airbase in Liberia during World War II (1939-1945) and the building of an artificial harbor at Monrovia stimulated the country's development. William V. S. Tubman, elected president in 1944 and reelected for five additional terms, sought to unify the descendants of the original American ex-slaves and the tribal peoples of the interior. Upon Tubman's death in 1971 Vice-President William R. Tolbert, Jr., succeeded to the presidency. Having been elected without opposition in October 1975, Tolbert was inaugurated for an eight-year term in January 1976.

Tolbert and at least twenty-six supporters were killed in the fighting during a military coup on April 12, 1980. Thirteen officials were publicly executed ten days later. Sergeant Samuel K. Doe, who became head of state, led the People's Redemption Council (PRC), formed to rule the country. The constitution was suspended but a return to civilian rule was promised for 1985. In the elections held in October 1985 Doe was elected president with 51 percent of the vote. Foreign observers declared that the elections were rigged, and most of the opposition candidates who were elected refused to take their seats.

Since late December 1989 Liberia has fallen into chaos. Insurgents (people who revolt against authority) led by Charles Taylor began a campaign to overthrow the Doe regime. Gunmen on both sides massacred thousands of civilians. Hundreds

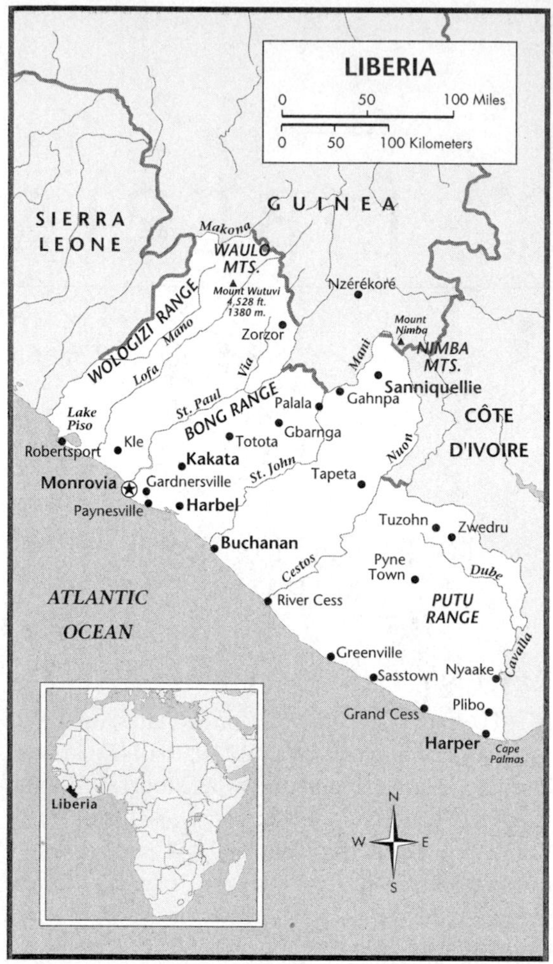

of thousands fled their homes. By June 1990 Doe was besieged in Monrovia. In an effort to stop the killing a regional peacekeeping force, known as ECOMOG, entered the country and installed an interim government. Most of the ECOMOG force was supplied by Nigeria. However on September 9, 1990, rebel forces shot their way into ECOMOG's headquarters and executed Doe. On two occasions since entering the country the ECOMOG forces prevented Charles Taylor's forces from capturing the capital, Monrovia.

The interim government was able to establish authority over most of Monrovia, but the rest of Liberia was in the hands of various factions. Despite three major peace agreements since 1990, fighting continued. Finally in August 1995 all sides agreed to a cease-fire and set up a council of state to govern the country until elections could be held. The cease-fire only held until the year's end, when fighting resumed. In early 1996 roving gangs of heavily armed teenagers recklessly shot up Monrovia. International relief organizations became the targets of looting, since seven years of war had left the country empty of anything worth stealing.

Liberia's four main militias approved a peace plan in May 1996. In August 1996 West African leaders put together a new cease-fire agreement between the warring factions and selected an interim government. Elections were finally held in July 1997 and were overseen by ECOMOG forces. ECOMOG's presence in Liberia was an important factor in ending the civil war that had killed more than 150,000 people over seven years. Charles Taylor, the man who had initially started the uprising, was elected with 75 percent of the vote. Although insecurity prevailed in parts of Liberia, the last ECOMOG troops began leaving in October 1999. In 2000 Taylor held strong executive power with no real political opposition.

GOVERNMENT

Under the constitution approved on July 3, 1984, Liberia is a republic modeled after the United States. Its constitution provides for a president and vice-president elected jointly by universal vote for a six-year term with a limit of two consecutive terms. The legislature is divided into a 26-member Senate and a 64-member House of Representatives. Senators are elected by popular vote for nine-year terms. Representatives are elected by popular vote for six-year terms.

Judiciary

Since the civil war the legal system has not functioned in most of Liberia. In theory most cases originate in magistrates' courts and may be taken for appeal to one of ten circuit courts or to the highest court. More serious cases originate in the circuit courts. Traditional courts are presided over by tribal chiefs. The 1984 constitution provides for the establishment of a Supreme Court consisting of a chief justice and four associate justices.

Since 1997 donors have trained paralegals and human rights monitors to protect citizens. The U.S. Department of Justice has rebuilt magistrate courts, compiled thirty years of Supreme Court decisions, and published the Liberian Code so that judges and lawyers have recourse to legal reference works. In May 2000 assistance was contemplated for the Grimes Law School in Monrovia.

Political Parties

Charles Taylor's National Patriotic Party (NPP) gained influence since his election to the presidency in 1997 and holds forty-nine of sixty-four House seats and twenty-one of twenty-six Senate seats. The Unity Party (UP) held seven House seats and three Senate seats. The All Liberia Coalition Party held three House seats and two Senate seats. Three other parties held the remaining House seats.

DEFENSE

The regular armed forces (5,000 personnel) and police are active only in parts of Monrovia. Liberia no longer has air or naval capabilities. The rebel National Patriotic Forces of Liberia number 15,000. A six-nation African peacekeeping force numbers around 6,000. As of 2000 a military reorganization plan calls for a newly reunited armed forces including an army, navy, and air force.

ECONOMIC AFFAIRS

Liberia's economy, which is primarily agricultural due to an abundance of water and a favorable climate, is in turmoil as a result. Even prior to the civil war, however, Liberia faced serious financial problems. In 1988 the World Bank closed its offices in Monrovia. In March of 1990 the International Monetary Fund (IMF) threatened to expel Liberia for nonpayment of its debt.

The civil war left most of Liberia's infrastructure in shambles. Businessmen and capital left the country and continuing turmoil prevented normal economic life. The Taylor government, elected in 1997, inherited massive international debt and relies almost solely on revenues from its maritime (ship) registry to provide foreign exchange income. Although there are no official statistics it was estimated that 85 percent of the population was unemployed in 1999.

Public Finance

Government budgets, roughly in balance up to the mid-1970s, had since run heavily into deficit. Since civil war erupted in 1989 Liberia's fiscal management collapsed. The U.S. Central Intelligence Agency estimated that in 1994 government revenues totaled approximately $225 million and expenditures $285 million. External debt totaled $3 billion by 1999 estimates.

Income

Liberia's gross domestic product (GDP) in 1999 was estimated at $2.85 billion, or about $1,000 per capita. The 1999 estimated GDP growth rate was 0.5 percent and inflation was 3 percent by 1998 estimates. The 1999 estimated GDP by sector was agriculture 50 percent, industry 15 percent, and services 35 percent.

Industry

Before the civil war, Liberia's industrial sector was dominated by processing plants associated with its key agricultural outputs: rubber, palm oil, and lumber. Liberia also produced cement, plastics, shoes, recycled steel, and refined petroleum products. Liberia was a leading purveyor of transportation for the world's merchant fleet but its position has declined rapidly. The port of Monrovia was not even operational in 1999.

During 1990-1996 faction leaders and traders exploited the industrial wealth of Liberia. They used forced labor and stolen goods and fuel. The method of manufacture often harmed the environment or the ability to produce in the future. Profits from these enterprises were used to buy more weapons.

Banking and Finance

In 1974 the government established the National Bank of Liberia. It became the exclusive banker and fiscal agent of the government. Banks operating in 1999 included the International Trust Company of Liberia, the Liberia Bank for Development and Investment (LBDI), the National Bank of Liberia, the National House and Savings Bank (NHSB), and the Tradevco Bank. Banks were only available as a repository for funds, and did not pay interest or make loans. The only currency in circulation in 1999 was the Liberia $5 piece.

Economic Development

The civil war and international financial obligations dim the prospects of economic development. While refugee resettlement looms as an early postwar priority, future economic development, restoration of infrastructure, and the raising of incomes depend on reestablishing international confidence in Liberia's financial management and thereby attracting foreign investment.

SOCIAL WELFARE

In 1976 the National Social Security and Welfare Corp. was established to administer pensions, sickness benefits, and welfare funds. Before the civil war the Liberian Red Cross was active in childcare and welfare as were the Antoinette Tubman Welfare Foundation and the Catherine Mills Rehabilitation Center. By 2000 virtually no social services were functioning within the country.

Women participate in politics but most remain largely subordinate in both public and private life.

Healthcare

In 2000 Liberia has an average life expectancy of only fifty-one years. In 1992 there were an estimated eleven doctors per 100,000 people, and only about 39 percent of the population had access to health care services. The major causes of death are malaria and gastrointestinal disease. The World Health Organization (WHO) estimates that about one million people in sub-Saharan Africa are HIV positive.

Housing

The typical dwelling of the tribal people in the Liberian interior is the rondavel, a circular, one-room mud-and-wattle thatch-roofed hut, windowless and with a single low door. These rondavels are being replaced by large rectangular huts, also of mud and wattle, subdivided into two or more rooms and equipped with windows. Many of the older corrugated-iron structures in Monrovia have also been replaced with more modern dwellings.

EDUCATION

Although education is compulsory from ages six to sixteen, probably fewer than half of all children are in school. Projected adult illiteracy rate for 2000 was 46.6 percent. There are three institutions of higher learning: the government-operated University of Liberia in Monrovia (established in 1862); Cuttington University College at Monrovia, an Episcopalian institution; and a three-year engineering school, the William V. S. Tubman College of Technology.

2000 KEY EVENTS TIMELINE

January

- Armed men thought to be members of the former NPFL, Taylor's rebel army, rob President Charles Taylor's residence in Gbarnga, central Liberia, taking a generator and other valuables.
- The capacity of Liberian diplomatic missions to function is being severely affected by nearly US$30 million in arrears. The debt, accumulated over a decade, is symptomatic of huge arrears and has resulted in enforcement of the Brooke Amendment, cutting off U.S. foreign aid to the government of Liberia.

February

- President Charles Taylor proposes recruitment of teenagers into his National Patriotic Party (NPP) to ensure that party membership is sustained. Taylor plans to indoctrinate the youngsters to prepare them for future responsibility.

March

- Independent Star radio, set up in July 1997 to promote democracy in post-war Liberia, is closed by the government. Radio Veritas of the Catholic Church is also closed.
- Liberia's Information Ministry lifts the suspension of the Roman Catholic station Radio Veritas. The Ministry urges the media to "operate within the statutory laws of Liberia."

April

- Acute water shortage in Monrovia forces people to go to other parts of the town to obtain water. The areas worst hit include Clara Town and Doe Community on Bushrod Island.

May

- President Taylor urges the Revolutionary United Front (RUF) rebels to stop hostilities in Sierra Leone immediately and to abandon any planned invasion of Freetown. Taylor has been accused of supporting the RUF with weapons in exchange for diamonds.
- Liberia welcomes the removal of rebel leader Foday Sankoh from Sierra Leone to another country. A local trial is thought to exacerbate the hostilities in the neighboring country of Sierra Leone.

June

- Members of the ECOWAS committee of the Mediation and Security Council meet with President Taylor in Monrovia to discuss the crisis in Sierra Leone. The delegation appeals to Taylor for help in releasing Indian UN peacekeepers still under detention by the Revolutionary United Front.
- Liberian dissidents in Sierra Leone are planning to attack their country because of the support Monrovia is alleged to be giving to RUF rebels in Sierra Leone. The dissidents are reportedly two former Liberian rebel factions, ULIMO-K and ULIMO-J.

July

- President Taylor names Moses Blah as his vice president. Blah has been Liberian ambassador to Libya and was Taylor's confidant in the National Patriotic Front.
- U.S. Undersecretary of State Thomas warns President Taylor Pickering to stop trading diamonds and arms with rebels in Sierra Leone.

August

- The Taylor government announces that it will use all force at its disposal to flush rebels out of Lofa County. The government says the rebels are backed by Guinea.
- Yellow fever claims four lives and infect at least eighty people in the counties of Margibi, Nimba, Montserrado, Grand Bassa and Grand Cape Mount.
- A British television crew accused of spying is freed on August 25, in exchange for an apology.

September

- Taylor calls a halt to diamond prospecting in a field in a suburb of Monrovia. Up to 3,000 people began digging without permits following rumors that a diamond-rich area had been discovered.
- Liberia calls on Guinea to support joint monitoring of their common border by their security forces to prevent incursions by dissidents seeking cross border refuge.

October

- Fighting in Liberia's northern Lofa County displaces thousands of people, many of whom need health care. Rebels step up attacks in the northern border area.
- The U.S. Carter Center closes its doors in Liberia after a decade of promoting human rights and democracy. President Carter accuses President Taylor of "making it difficult for the center and others to be effective in supporting democracy, human rights, and the rule of law."

November

- A mob of some 100 persons attacks former interim President Amos Sawyer and former youth and sports minister, Commany Wesseh, during a raid at their office in Monrovia.

December

- Liberia and five other West African states—The Gambia, Ghana, Guinea, Nigeria, and Sierra Leone—decide to create a West African Monetary Zone. The six countries belong to the fifteen-member state Economic Community of West African States (ECOWAS), and may eventually join together with members of the CFA franc zone to form a common monetary union.

ANALYSIS OF EVENTS: 2000

BUSINESS AND THE ECONOMY

Although it has improved since 1997, the business and economic picture for Liberia remains gloomy. According to data released by the government, government revenue increased by 22 percent in 1999. The government also reported gains in revenue amounting to US$66 million—the result of better property, motor vehicle, and individual and business incomes tax collection. It also reported productivity increases in agriculture due to improved extension services, higher-yielding varieties, and improved harvesting practices. The government plans to introduce more capital-intensive technologies and larger scale production. It also prepared a new mining code with three main classes of licensing from rapid assessment to exploitation of a discovered deposit. Areas under rice and cassava production reached 70 percent and 9 percent respectively of pre-war levels.

However gains were offset by the loss of shipping registry business to a Caribbean flag of convenience, and a reduced levy on rice imports. The shipping registry formerly provided significant revenues to government coffers for a minimal administration cost. Foreign fishing went under- or unreported due to lack of patrols, and gold and other precious metals were mined illicitly and smuggled out of the country. According to 1997 data, one European country reported nearly US$289 million in value from Liberian diamonds, while the government's records showed nothing.

Ostentatious lifestyles and overt corruption also discouraged entrepreneurship. The administration failed to restore public institutions, monopolized import/export sub-sectors, and drove business underground through intimidation by police and the armed forces. Although President Charles Taylor sacked three government ministers for stealing international airline fees, his warlord style of government did little to give investors and business people confidence.

President Taylor meanwhile blamed bi- and multilateral creditors for failing to offer debt relief. The government owes 50 percent of its debt to multilateral donors, 29 percent to bilateral donors, and 7 percent to domestic creditors. However, Taylor has hurt Liberia's cause by failing to meet minimum debt payments. His unwillingness to cooperate with the West resulted in sanctions imposed by the United States effective July 29. These sanctions proscribe any U.S. assistance to a branch of the Liberian government.

In 2001 it is predicted that business and investments will suffer from the uncertainty and high risks. The International Monetary Fund (IMF) was unlikely to argue against the U.S. position. Indeed, U.S. assistance fell from US$36 million in 1998 to US$14 million in 2000. World Bank loans were put on hold in September, and the European Union suspended a US$47 million aid package. Apparently, Libya is asking Liberia to settle its US$1 million debt incurred during the war. Unless a compromise is reached, the financial and political impasse between Taylor and the West was likely to stymie the Liberian economy for the foreseeable future.

GOVERNMENT AND POLITICS

The year was marred by tensions between the government of President Charles Taylor and the international community, and by a growing domestic skepticism concerning President Taylor's campaign promises. The United States and the United Kingdom were at the fore of accusing Taylor of buying and selling "blood" diamonds from Sierra Leone, and supplying the Revolutionary United Front (RUF) with arms. The RUF has not abandoned its nine-year fight to overthrow the Sierra Leone government. While Taylor denied the allegations, and demanded that his accusers produce proof of his mischief, the White House imposed visa restrictions on Taylor and senior members of his government and their close associates. U.S. non-essential personnel were placed on "ordered departure" status in September.

Taylor's government also fell out this year with Guinea over cross-border attacks. Both countries accused the other of harboring rebels, and of conducting the attacks. It was not clear who was responsible for organizing the attacks, but hundreds of civilians, including women and children, were killed in villages along the border and entire villages were burned. The outbreak of fighting in Lofa County (in the northwest) was such that Taylor had to declare a state of emergency in July. Analysts credited Liberians United for Reconciliation and Democracy (LURD) with resistance to the Liberian army; LURD had elements of all the defunct civil war factions.

Taylor's leadership style has been erratic, intolerant, and punitive. He sacked three ministers without explanation, and accused nine soldiers of conspiring to overthrow the government. Four of them were found guilty of sedition and sentenced to ten years in jail with hard labor. In March the government closed Radio Veritas temporarily, and shut down Star Radio, the only independent broadcast media in the country. Since the end of the civil war, the government has failed to commit itself to political, economic, and social recovery. Monrovia, the capital, is still without electricity, and parts of the city have no running water.

Human rights abuses have also risen. Reports indicated that human rights violations include extra-judicial killings, torture, harassment by armed forces, arbitrary arrests, and detention. The November raid on the office of former transition head of state, Amos Sawyer, appeared to be organized thuggery and sent a signal that no democrats in Liberia would be safe. Given the power of the Executive, there was little recourse to justice, either in the courts or in the legislature, which is little more than a rubber stamp.

In response to this bleak outlook, a coalition of eleven opposition parties calling themselves Collaborating Political Parties (CPP) called upon Liberians to prevent the country from sliding into a major crisis, and to sustain efforts to build democracy. Similarly, in the United States and Europe, Liberians began to mobilize themselves to lobby against the Taylor regime and to organize a credible political movement for the 2003 presidential and legislative elections. Within Liberia Archbishop Michael Francis stood up to Taylor and refused to allow him to close Radio Veritas, the FM and short-wave media outlet of the Catholic Diocese.

Former presidential candidate, Ellen Sirleaf-Johnson, called on the Liberian House of Representatives to investigate the "blood" diamonds charge with the aim of impeaching Taylor. The National Patriotic Party (NPP), fearful of Taylor's wrath, was unlikely to allow such a process to proceed. However, if the political outlook for Liberia was to improve in 2001, allegations of government support to the RUF must be investigated and if proven, the trade in "blood" diamonds must be stopped.

CULTURE AND SOCIETY

While Liberian nongovernmental organizations (NGOs) and their donor partners have rebuilt many of the hospitals, dispensaries, and schools looted and destroyed during the war, many professionals who fled the country have not returned. It was estimated that as many as 500,000 Liberians have not returned to their homes from neighboring countries since the official end of the war. Others who left permanently have become part of the so-called "brain drain." It was estimated that only eighty–one hundred Liberian doctors remained in the country.

The lack of health professionals has led to one of the worst health records in the world. Maternal mortality was at 780 per 100,000, and poor health was aggravated by food insecurity, and by an estimated 80 percent of the population living below the poverty line.

High population mobility, the presence of troops, sex slavery, and prostitution during and since the war have increased the incidence of HIV/AIDS. Government analysts, civil society leaders, and donor technicians conceded that the rate of infection would accelerate and could explode over the next few years. To reduce the spread of AIDS by 15 percent over the next three years, the country needed at least US$6.5 million. The Health Minister recommended that HIV/AIDS be placed at the top of the development agenda, and development partners were being engaged in the fight.

DIRECTORY

CENTRAL GOVERNMENT

Head of State

President
Charles Ghanky Taylor, Office of the President, PO Box 10-9001, Capitol Hill, 1000 Monrovia 10, Liberia
PHONE: +231 226737; 224467

Vice President
Moses Zeh Blah, Office of the Vice President, Executive Mansion, PO Box 10-9001, Capitol Hill 1000 Monrovia 10, Liberia
E-MAIL: EMansion@liberia.net

Ministers

Minister of Agriculture
Roland Massaquoi, Ministry of Agriculture, Tubmand Blvd, PO Box 10-9010, 1000 Monrovia 10, Liberia

Minister of Commerce and Industry
Amelia Ward, Ministry of Commerce and Industry, Ashmun Street, PO Box 10-9014, 1000 Monrovia 10, Liberia

Minister of Information, Culture and Tourism
Joe Mulbah, Ministry of Information, Culture and Tourism, PO Box 10-9021, Capitol Hill, 1000 Monrovia 10, Liberia

Minister of Defense
Peter D. Chea, Ministry of Defense, Benson Street, PO Box 10-9007, 1000 Monrovia 10, Liberia

Minister of Education
Evelyn White Kandakai, Ministry of Education, Broad Street, PO Box 10-1545, 1000 Monrovia 10, Liberia

Minister of Finance
Nathaniel Barnes, Ministry of Finance, Broad Street, PO Box 10-9013, 1000 Monrovia 10, Liberia

Minister of Foreign Affairs
Monie Captan, Ministry of Foreign Affairs, PO Box 10-9002, Mamba Point, 1000 Monrovia 10, Liberia
PHONE: +231 227857
FAX: +231 226076

Minister of Health and Social Welfare
Peter Coleman, Ministry of Health and Social Welfare, PO Box 10-9004, Sinkor, 1000 Monrovia 10, Liberia

Minister of Internal Affairs
Maxwell Poe, Ministry of Internal Affairs, Corner of Warren and Benson Streets, PO Box 10-9008, 1000 Monrovia 10, Liberia

Minister of Justice
Eddington Vamah, Ministry of Justice, Ashmun Street, PO Box 10-9006, 1000 Monrovia 10, Liberia

Minister of Labour
Christian Neufville, Ministry of Labour, Mechlin Street, PO Box 10-9040, 1000 Monrovia 10, Liberia

Minister of Lands, Mines and Energy
Jenkins Dunbar, Ministry of Lands, Mines and Energy, Capitol Hill, PO Box 10-9024, 1000 Monrovia 10, Liberia

Minister of National Security
Philip Kamah, Ministry of National Security

Minister of Planning and Economic Affairs
Larmie Kawah, Ministry of Planning and Economic Affairs, Broad Street, PO Box 10-9016, 1000 Monrovia 10, Liberia

Minister of Posts and Telecommunications
John Bright, Ministry of Posts and Telecommunications, Carey Street, Monrovia, Liberia

Minister of State for Presidential Affairs
Jonathan Taylor, Ministry of State for Presidential Affairs, Executive Mansion, Capitol Hill, Monrovia, Liberia

Minister of Public Works
Emmett Taylor, Ministry of Public Works, Lynch Street, PO Box 10-9011, 1000 Monrovia 10, Liberia

Minister of Rural Development
Hezekiah Bowen, Ministry of Rural Development, PO Box 10-9030, 1000 Monrovia 10, Liberia

Minister of Transport
Francis Carbah, Ministry of Transport

Minister of Youth and Sports
Francois Massaquoi, Ministry of Youth and Sports, Sinkor, PO Box 10-9040, 1000 Monrovia 10, Liberia

POLITICAL ORGANIZATIONS

National Patriotic Party (NPP)

TITLE: Leader
NAME: Charles Ghanky Taylor

All Liberia Coalition Party (ALCOP)

TITLE: Chairman
NAME: Lusinee Kamara

Free Democratic Party (FDP)

TITLE: Chairman
NAME: Fayah Gbollie

Liberian Action Party (LAP)

TITLE: Chairman
NAME: Cletis Wotorson

Liberian National Union (LINU)

TITLE: Chairman
NAME: Harry Moniba

Liberian Peoples Party (LPP)

TITLE: Chairman
NAME: Togba-Nah Tipoteh

Liberian Unification Party (LUP)

TITLE: Chairman
NAME: Laveli Supuwood

National Democratic Party of Liberia (NDPL)

TITLE: Chairman
NAME: Isaac Dakinah

National Reformation Party (NRP)

TITLE: Chairman
NAME: Martin Sherif

People's Democratic Party of Liberia (PDPL)

TITLE: Chairman
NAME: George Toe Washington

People's Progressive Party (PPP)

TITLE: Chairman
NAME: Chea Cheapoo

Reformation Alliance Party (RAP)

TITLE: Chairman
NAME: Henry Boimah Fahnbulleh

True Whig Party (TWP)

TITLE: Chairman
NAME: Rudolph Sherman

Unity Party (UP)

TITLE: Chairman
NAME: Charles Clarke

United People's Party (UPP)

TITLE: Chairman
NAME: Gabriel Baccus Matthews

DIPLOMATIC REPRESENTATION

Embassies in Liberia

Nigeria
Box 366, Monrovia, Liberia

Poland
PO Box 860, Gardener Avenue, Monrovia, Liberia
PHONE: +231 261113

United States
111 United Nations Drive, PO Box 100098, Mamba Point, Monrovia, Liberia
PHONE: +231 226370
FAX: +231 226148
NAME: Bismarck Myrick

JUDICIAL SYSTEM

Supreme Court

BROADCAST MEDIA

D.C. 101.1 FM

Ducor Broadc. Corp., PO Box 1312, Monrovia, Liberia
PHONE: +231 226464
TITLE: President
CONTACT: Fred Bass-Golokeh
BROADCASTS: 0600–2400
TYPE: Community

Radio Liberia International

PO Box 1103, 1000 Monrovia 10, Liberia
PHONE: +231 226963
FAX: +231 226003
WEBSITE: http://www.africanetwork.fr/afric/liberia/liberia.html
TITLE: Deputy Manager
CONTACT: James Kasoyen
LANGUAGE: English

Radio Monrovia 98 FM

PO Box 10–3501, Monrovia, Liberia
PHONE: +231 225301
FAX: +231 222743
TITLE: President
CONTACT: Charles A. Snetter, Jr.
BROADCASTS: 0600–2400
TYPE: Commercial

Radio Veritas

PO Box 3569, Monrovia, Liberia
PHONE: +231 221658
BROADCASTS: 0500–1100, 1800–2300
TYPE: Religious

Star Radio

PHONE: +231 221658
BROADCASTS: 0500–1100, 1800–2300
TYPE: Religious

Liberia Broadcasting System

PO Box 10–594, 1000 Monrovia 10, Liberia
PHONE: +231 224984
FAX: +231 228042
TITLE: Directorate General
CONTACT: James Wolo
TYPE: Government

Liberia Communication Network

PO Box 1103, 1000 Monrovia 10, Liberia
PHONE: +231 226963
FAX: +231 226003
WEBSITE: http://www.afric-network.fr/afric/liberia/liberia.html
TITLE: Deputy Manager
CONTACT: James Kassoyen
LANGUAGE: English

Liberian Broadcasting Corporation

PO Box 10–594, Monrovia, Liberia
PHONE: +231 271250
TITLE: Directorate General
CONTACT: Jesse B. Karnlet
CHANNEL: E6
TYPE: Commercial, Government

COLLEGES AND UNIVERSITIES

Cuttington University College

PO Box 10-0277, 1000 Monrovia 10, Liberia
PHONE: +231 227519
FAX: +231 227519
E-MAIL: cuc@libnet.net
WEBSITE: http://www.cuttington.org/

NEWSPAPERS AND MAGAZINES

Daily Listener

Johnson & Carey St., PO Box 35, Monrovia, Liberia
CIRCULATION: 3,500

Liberian Age

True Whig Party, Carey St., Monrovia, Liberia
TITLE: Editor
CONTACT: Stanton B. Peabody
CIRCULATION: 4,000

Liberian Star

Republic Press Inc., PO Box 691, Monrovia, Liberia
TITLE: Editor
CONTACT: Henry B. Cole
CIRCULATION: 3,500

Sunday Digest

Johnson & Carey S., PO Box 35, Monrovia, Liberia
CIRCULATION: 5,000

African Labour News

PO Box 415, Monrovia, Liberia
TITLE: Editor
CONTACT: Gab Atitsogbui
TYPE: Political science, labor and industrial relations

Liberia: Political, Economics and Social Monthly

Monrovia, Liberia
TITLE: Editor
CONTACT: Bill Frank
TYPE: Social science, general

Liberian Economic and Management Review

University of Liberia, Monrovia, Liberia
TYPE: Business and economics, general

RELIGIOUS ORGANIZATIONS

Protestant

Lutheran Church in Liberia
PO Box 10-1046, 1000 Monrovia, Liberia

The Salvation Army Territorial Headquarters
17th Street, Sinkor, Monrovia, Liberia
PHONE: +231 226349
FAX: +231 226349

FURTHER READING

Articles

Harden, Blaine. "2 African Nations Said to Break U.N. Diamond Embargo." *New York Times,* August 1, 2000, p. A3.

Books

Dunn, D. Elwood, Amos J. Beyan, and Carl Patrick Burrowes. *Historical Dictionary of Liberia.* 2d ed. Lanham, Md.: Scarecrow, 2000.

Lyons, Terrence. *Voting for Peace: Postconflict Elections in Liberia.* Washington, D.C.: Brookings Institution Press, 1999.

Internet

BBC News Online. "Sanctions Threat to 'Tax Havens.'" June 26, 2000. [Online] Available http://news6.thdo.bbc.co.uk/hi/english/business/newsid%5F806000/806236.stm (accessed October 12, 2000).

LIBERIA: STATISTICAL DATA

For sources and notes see "Sources of Statistics" at the front of each volume.

GEOGRAPHY

Geography

Area:

Total: 111,370 sq km.

Land: 96,320 sq km.

Land boundaries:

Total: 1,585 km.

Border countries: Guinea 563 km, Cote d'Ivoire 716 km, Sierra Leone 306 km.

Coastline: 579 km.

Climate: tropical; hot, humid; dry winters with hot days and cool to cold nights; wet, cloudy summers with frequent heavy showers.

Terrain: mostly flat to rolling coastal plains rising to rolling plateau and low mountains in northeast.

Natural resources: iron ore, timber, diamonds, gold, hydropower.

Land use:

Arable land: 1%

Permanent crops: 3%

Permanent pastures: 59%

Forests and woodland: 18%

Other: 19% (1993 est.).

HUMAN FACTORS

Ethnic Division

Indigenous African tribes	95.0%
Americo-Liberians	2.5%
Congo People	2.5%

The indigenous African tribes include Kpelle Bassa, Gio, Kru, Grebo, Mano, Krahn, Gola, Gbandi, Loma, Kissi, Vai, and Bella. The Americo-Liberians are descendants of immigrants from the US who had been slaves. The Congo People are descendants of immigrants from the Caribbean who had been slaves.

Demographics (A)

	1990	1995	1998	2000	2010	2020	2030	2040	2050
Population	2,190	1,983	2,663	3,164	4,073	5,294	6,745	8,344	10,000
Life expectancy - males	31.1	31.1	48.9	49.6	53.3	57.0	60.6	64.0	67.1
Life expectancy - females	50.3	50.3	51.6	52.5	56.8	61.0	65.1	69.0	72.4
Birth rate (per 1,000)	46.2	44.2	48.6	47.2	40.8	36.2	31.9	27.3	23.5
Death rate (per 1,000)	24.6	23.3	17.2	16.6	13.5	11.0	9.1	7.7	6.9
Women of reproductive age (15-49 yrs.)	489	477	636	749	926	1,266	1,671	2,130	2,634
Fertility rate	6.6	5.9	6.6	6.4	5.7	4.9	4.1	3.5	2.9

Except as noted, values for vital statistics are in thousands; life expectancy is in years.

Religion

Indigenous beliefs 40%

Christian 40%

Muslim 20%

Major Languages

English 20% (official), some 20 ethnic group languages, of which a few can be written and are used in correspondence.

EDUCATION

Educational Attainment (B)

	1980	1985
Gross enrollment ratio (%)		
Primary level	48.1	39.8
Secondary level	22.0	17.4
Tertiary level	2.4	2.4
Enrollment of population aged 6-23 years (%)	27.0	NA

Literacy Rates (A)

In thousands and percent	1990	1995	2000	2010
Illiterate population (15+ yrs.)	937	1,104	1,094	1,255
Literacy rate - total adult pop. (%)	33.5	38.3	43.2	53.7
Literacy rate - males (%)	48.7	53.9	58.8	68.2
Literacy rate - females (%)	18.1	22.4	27.4	39.0

GOVERNMENT & LAW

Political Parties

National Assembly	no. of seats
Senate	
National Patriotic Party (NPP)	21
Unity Party (UP)	3
All Liberia Coalition Party (ALCOP)	2
House of Representatives	
National Patriotic Party (NPP)	49
Unity Party (UP)	7
All Liberia Coalition Party (ALCOP)	3
Alliance of Political Parties	2
United People's Party (UPP)	2
Liberian People's Party (LPP)	1

Elections for the Senate were last held 19 July 1997 (next to be held in 2006); House of Representatives elections were last held 19 July 1997 (next to be held in 2003). The Alliance of Political Parties was a coalition of the Liberation Action Party (LAP) and the Liberia Unification Party (LUP).

(Continued on next page.)

LABOR FORCE

Labor Force by Occupation

Agriculture 70%

Industry 8%

Services 22%

Data for 1999 est.

Unemployment Rate

70%

PRODUCTION SECTOR

Energy Production

Production .490 million kWh

Production by source

- Fossil fuel 62.24%
- Hydro 37.76%
- Nuclear 0%
- Other 0%

Exports . . . . .0 kWh

Data for 1998.

Energy Consumption

Consumption . . . . .456 million kWh

Imports . . . . .0 kWh

Data for 1998.

Transportation

Highways:

Total: 10,600 km (there is major deterioration on all highways due to heavy rains and lack of maintenance).

Paved: 657 km.

Unpaved: 9,943 km (1996 est.).

Merchant marine:

Total: 1,593 ships (1,000 GRT or over) totaling 54,513,479 GRT/85,495,576 DWT.

Ships by type: barge carrier 3, bulk 360, cargo 109, chemical tanker 185, combination bulk 22, combination ore/oil 50, container 225, liquified gas 91, multi-functional large load carrier 1, passenger 40, petroleum tanker 351, refrigerated cargo 76, roll-on/roll-off 16, short-sea passenger 3, specialized tanker 15, vehicle carrier 46 (1999 est.).

Note: a flag of convenience registry; includes ships from 54 countries among which are Germany 186, US 161, Norway 142, Greece 144, Japan 124, Hong Kong 100, China 53, UK 32, Singapore 39, and Monaco 38 (1998 est.).

Airports: 45 (1999 est.).

Airports - with unpaved runways: 43.

Top Agriculture Products

Rubber, coffee, cocoa, rice, cassava (tapioca), palm oil, sugarcane, bananas; sheep, goats; timber.

Top Mining Products (B)

Mineral resources include: iron ore, diamonds, gold.

COMMUNICATIONS

Daily Newspapers

	National Data	World Data for Comparison
Daily Newspapers		
Number of Dailies	6	8,391
Total Circulation (000)	35	548,000
Circulation per 1,000 inhabitants	16	96

Telecommunications

Telephones - main lines in use: 5,000 (1995).

Telephones - mobile cellular: 0 (1995).

Telephone system: telephone and telegraph service via microwave radio relay network; main center is Monrovia.

Domestic: NA

International: satellite earth station - 1 Intelsat (Atlantic Ocean).

Radio broadcast stations: AM 0, FM 6, shortwave 4 (1999).

Radios: 790,000 (1997).

Television broadcast stations: 2 (plus four low-power repeaters) (2000).

Televisions: 70,000 (1997).

Internet Service Providers (ISPs): NA

FINANCE, ECONOMICS, & TRADE

Economic Indicators

National product: GDP—purchasing power parity—$2.85 billion (1999 est.).

National product real growth rate: 0.5% (1999 est.).

National product per capita: $1,000 (1999 est.).

Inflation rate—consumer price index: 3% (1998 est.).

(Continued on next page.)

GOVERNMENT & LAW (cont.)

Military Affairs (A)

	1990	1992	1995	1996	1997
Armed forces (000)	8	2	NA	NA	NA
People (mil.)	2.3	2.1	2.3	2.4	2.6
Armed forces per 1,000 people (soldiers)	3.5	0.9	NA	NA	NA
World data on armed forces per 1,000 people (soldiers)	5.3	4.5	4.1	3.9	3.8
GNP per capita (1997 $)	NA	NA	NA	NA	111
Arms imports[6]					
Current dollars (mil.)	10	0	0	10	0
1997 constant dollars (mil.)	12	0	0	10	0
Arms exports[6]					
Current dollars (mil.)	0	0	0	0	0
1997 constant dollars (mil.)	0	0	0	0	0
Total exports[7]					
Current dollars (mil.)	1,941[e]	780[e]	952[e]	1,082[e]	949[e]
1997 constant dollars (mil.)	2,273[e]	865[e]	986[e]	1,100[e]	949[e]
Arms as percent of total imports[8]	NA	0	0	NA	0
Arms as percent of total exports[8]	0	0	0	0	0

MANUFACTURING SECTOR

GDP & Manufacturing Summary (B)

	1980	1985	1990	1993	1994	1995
Gross Domestic Product						
Millions of 1990 dollars	846	779	805	824	824	824
Growth rate in percent	−6.29	−2.02	−1.99	0.00	0.00	0.00
Per capita (in 1990 dollars)	451	354	313	372	389	388
Manufacturing Value Added						
Millions of 1990 dollars	57	55	59	64	66	67[e]
Growth rate in percent	−21.21	−1.61	−2.98	2.01	3.60	1.76[e]
Manufacturing share in percent of current prices	9.5	6.6	7.9	NA	NA	NA

FINANCE, ECONOMICS, & TRADE (cont.)

Exchange Rates

Exchange rates:

Liberian dollars (L$) per US$1

Official fixed rate since 1940 . . . . .1.0000

Market exchange rate

December 1998 . . . . .40.0000

October 1995 . . . . .50.0000

Market rate floats against the US dollar. Fiscal year: calendar year.

Top Import Origins

$142 million (f.o.b., 1998 est.)

Origins (1997)

South Korea 38%

Japan 14%

Italy 11%

Singapore 9%

Top Export Destinations

$39 million (f.o.b., 1998 est.)

Destinations (1997)

Benelux 36%

Norway 18%

Ukraine 15%

Singapore 9%

Foreign Aid

Recipient: $200 million pledged (1998).

Import/Export Commodities

Import Commodities	Export Commodities
Fuels	Diamonds
Chemicals	Iron ore
Machinery	Rubber
Transportation equipment	Timber
Manufactured goods	Coffee
Rice and other foodstuffs	Cocoa

Balance of Payments

	1983	1984	1985	1986	1987
Exports of goods (f.o.b.)	421	447	430	408	375
Imports of goods (f.o.b.)	−375	−325	−264	−259	−312
Trade balance	46	121	167	149	63
Services - debits	−109	−93	−80	−81	−74
Services - credits	39	37	35	57	53
Private transfers (net)	31	36	37	32	30
Government transfers (net)	114	104	92	63	18
Overall balance	−103	−1	57	−18	−145

LIBYA

CAPITAL: Tripoli (Tarabulus).

FLAG: The national flag is plain green.

ANTHEM: *Almighty God.*

MONETARY UNIT: The Libyan dinar (LD) of 1,000 dirhams is a paper currency. There are coins of 1, 5, 10, 20, 50, and 100 dirhams, and notes of 1, 5, and 10 dinars. LD1 = $2.75482 (or $1 = LD0.363).

WEIGHTS AND MEASURES: The metric system is the legal standard, but some local weights and measures are used.

HOLIDAYS: UK Evacuation Day, 28 March; U.S. Evacuation Day, 11 June; Anniversary of the Revolution, 1 September; Constitution Day, 7 October. Muslim religious holidays include 'Id al-Fitr, 'Id al-'Adha', the 1st of Muharram, and Milad an-Nabi.

TIME: 2 PM = noon GMT.

LOCATION AND SIZE: Situated on the coast of North Africa, Libya is the fourth-largest country on the continent, with an area of 1,759,540 square kilometers (679,362 square miles), slightly larger than the state of Alaska. Libya's capital city, Tripoli, is located on the Mediterranean coast.

CLIMATE: The climate has marked seasonal variations influenced by both the Mediterranean Sea and the desert. Summer temperatures range between 27–46°C (81–115°F). The ghibli, a hot, dry desert wind, can change temperatures by 17–22°C (30–40°F) in both summer and winter. Rain falls generally in a short winter period and frequently causes floods. Evaporation is high, and severe droughts are common. The Sahara Desert has less than 5 centimeters (2 inches) of rain a year.

Socialist People's Libyan
Arab Jamahiriya
Al-Jamahiriyah al-'Arabiyah al-Libiyah ash-Sha'biyah al-Ishtirakiyah

INTRODUCTORY SURVEY

RECENT HISTORY

In September 1911 the Italians invaded Libya meeting fierce resistance from both Turks and indigenous Libyans. The Italian struggle for control of the region continued until 1932 when its conquest was completed. In World War II (1939-1945) Libya became a main battleground for Allied and Axis forces until it was occupied by victorious British and Free French troops. The Treaty of 1947 between Italy and the Allies ended Italian rule in Libya. When the Allies could not decide upon the country's future Libya's fate was left to the United Nations. On November 21, 1949, the United Nations General Assembly voted that Libya should become an independent state. On December 24, 1951, Libya gained independence, with Muhammad Idris al-Mahdi as-Sanusi as king.

In September 1969 a secret army organization, the Free Unionist Officers, staged a coup and took power with Col. Muammar Abu Minyar al-Qadhafi as their leader. Qadhafi has sought to make Libya the axis of a unified Arab nation, but relations with many Arab nations, including Egypt and Tunisia, have often been tense. Qadhafi has been equally active in Africa, annexing the disputed Aouzou Strip from Chad in 1973, and supporting the failing regimes of Uganda's Idi Amin in 1979, and Chad's Goukouni Oueddei in 1980. Qadhafi has also been accused of supporting subversive plots in such countries as Morocco, Niger, Sudan, and Egypt. He has also been accused of providing material support to

the Irish Republican Army, the Muslim rebels in the Philippines, and to Japanese and German terrorists.

A combination of socialism and Islam, Qadhafi's political system was called the Third International Theory. The revolutionary Qadhafi used oil funds from the 1970s and 1980s to espouse his ideology throughout the world supporting terrorists abroad to bring an end to capitalism and Marxism.

In 1982 the United States charged Qadhafi with supporting international terrorism. In January 1986 the United States ordered all Americans to leave Libya and cut off all economic ties. On April 15 following a West Berlin bomb attack in which United States servicemen were victims, United States warplanes bombed targets in Tripoli and Banghazi.

Qadhafi has survived several reported assassination and coup attempts (1984 and 1993). Opposition from Islamic groups prompted him to crack down on militants in 1993. His most serious challenge has been the tough sanctions imposed on

Libya by the United Nations Security Council. These sanctions were imposed after he refused to surrender two men suspected in the terrorist bombing of a Pan American passenger jet over Lockerbie, Scotland, in 1988.

In September 1995 Libya began deporting thousands of Palestinian, Sudanese, and Egyptian workers. Qadhafi claimed the foreigners were being deported to create jobs for Libyans. However Qadhafi stated that many of those being deported were Islamic militant "infiltrators" pretending to be migrant workers.

In 1996 it was believed that Libya was almost finished building the world's largest underground chemical weapons plant at Tarhunah near Tripoli. Intelligence officials from the United States claimed that the facility is capable of producing tons of poison gas per day. The Libyan government claimed that the building was a water irrigation system.

In 1999 UN sanctions were lifted with the extradition of the Pan Am bombing suspects.

GOVERNMENT

The people theoretically exercise their authority through a system of people's committees (the executive cabinet - General People's Committee) and congresses (the legislative branch - General People's Congress - GPC). Qadhafi, as "Leader of the Revolution," however, is the de facto head of state. He also is the commander of the armed forces and virtually all power is concentrated in him and his close advisers.

Judiciary

The Libyan legal system largely follows Egyptian codes and precedents. All cases relating to personal status are dealt with according to Muslim law. A sitting judge in each village and town may hear minor civil and commercial cases. Courts of first instance initially hear other cases, and appeals may be taken to provincial courts of appeal. There is also a Supreme Court consisting of a president and judges appointed by the GPC. In 1981 the private practice of law was abolished and all lawyers became employees of the secretariat of justice. Since 1981 revolutionary committees have been encouraged to conduct public trials without legal safeguards.

Political Parties

Political parties have not played an effective role in Libya's history. In 1971 the RCC (Revolutionary Command Council) founded the Libyan Arab Socialist Union as an alternative to political parties. It was viewed as an organization to promote national unity but has functioned in a minor capacity since 1977. Seven exiled opposition groups agreed in Cairo in 1987 to form a joint working group but have had no impact on political conditions in Libya.

DEFENSE

In 2000 the army had 35,000 personnel about half armored, half infantry. Armaments included 1,600 tanks, all made in the former Soviet Union. The navy had 8,000 personnel and sixty vessels, including four Russian submarines. The air force had 22,000 personnel, with 420 combat aircraft and fifty-two combat helicopters. The military budget was estimated at $1.4 billion in 1995, or 7 percent of the gross domestic product (GDP).

ECONOMIC AFFAIRS

Until the late 1950s Libya was one of the poorest countries in the world. But with the discovery of the Zaltan oil field in 1959, the economic horizons of the country were dramatically enlarged. Production has fallen since 1970 but its value has increased, and Libya remains one of the world's leading oil producers. Until the late 1950s about 80 percent of the population was engaged in agriculture and animal farming. In 1999, however, only 18 percent of the labor force was engaged in agricultural pursuits and agriculture, forestry, and fishing represented only 5 percent of GDP.

A massive water pipeline project, called the Great Manmade River (GMR) project, began in the early 1990s. The GMR will carry water in a huge 267-mile-long pipeline from 225 underground wells to irrigate 1.2 million acres of land used to grow cereal crops. The public works project is expected to cost $25 billion. There is concern among United States intelligence officials that the GMR might be used for military reasons.

Since the 1992 UN-imposed air embargo, many large projects have been postponed because of budget restrictions. Libya's isolation has slowed the pace of oil exploration through the absence of major foreign oil companies. Lack of outlets is limiting the development of refineries, petrochemicals, and gas facilities. Nevertheless the oil sector accounts for almost all export earnings and about 25 percent of GDP. Oil revenues give Libya one of the highest per capita GDP in Africa but little income reaches most of the people who periodically suffer through shortages of basic goods and food. With little arable land Libya must import 75 percent of its foodstuffs. Approximately 20 percent of GDP comes from iron, steel, aluminum, and various petrochemicals.

Higher oil prices in 1999 stimulated the economy. With the lifting of UN sanctions that same year, Libya has been eager to encourage foreign oil investors.

Public Finance

Since 1974, the fiscal year has followed the calendar year. There are two budgets, one for ordinary expenses and the other and larger one for development. By law, 15 percent of oil revenues is put aside yearly into the country's reserves while 70 percent of the remainder goes to development expenditures. All non-oil revenues are assigned to cover ordinary expenditures, and any shortfall is made up by transferring petroleum revenues from the development budget.

If funds from petroleum revenues are not sufficient to cover development expenses, some planned projects are postponed. Although Libya has used part of its oil revenue to finance internal development (new schools, hospitals, roads) much has been wasted. Limited privatization continued in 1993 involving the sale of some parastatal assets.

The U.S. Central Intelligence Agency estimated that in 1998 government revenues totaled approximately $3.6 billion and expenditures $5.1 billion. External debt totaled $4.0 billion.

Income

In 1999 Libya's gross domestic product (GDP) was estimated at 39.3 billion, or $7,900 per capita. The estimated 1999 GDP growth rate was 2 percent and inflation was 18 percent. The 1997 estimated GDP by sector was agriculture 7 percent, industry 47 percent, and services 46 percent.

Industry

Libyan manufacturing industries had been developing significantly since the early 1960s, but have fallen far behind the petroleum sector of the economy. Libya has six major refineries and reserves are expected to last another fifty years.

A large methanol, ammonia, and urea plant is at Marsa al-Burayqah, and a major plant producing ethylene, propylene, and butane was opened in 1987. The $6 billion iron and steel complex at Misratah began operations in 1990. Libya's other manufacturing industries are small, lightly capitalized and devoted primarily to the processing of local agricultural products and to textiles, building materials, and basic consumer items. Handicraft products include carpets, silver jewelry, glassware, and leather goods.

Banking and Finance

The Central Bank of Libya, established in 1956, supervises the national banking system, regulates credit and interest, and issues bank notes. It also regulates the volume of currency in circulation, acts as a banker to the government, provides clearinghouse facilities for the country's commercial banks, and administers exchange control. Since 5 August 1962, the bank has been vested with a monopoly in the import of fine gold.

Libya formerly had branches of many Arab, Italian, and British commercial banks; they were nationalized in 1969. The government ruled that 51 percent of the capital of each should be taken over by the government, which paid the value of this share. Thus the Banco di Roma became Umma Bank, Barclays Bank eventually became Jamahiriya Bank, and the Banco di Sicilia became the Sahara Bank. The commercial department of the Central Bank was merged with two small banks to form the National Commercial Bank. In 1972 a reorganization of the commercial banks left the Jamahiriya and Umma banks owned by the Central Bank of Libya. The Central Bank and private interests jointly owned two other institutions, the Sahara Bank and the Wahda Bank.

The National Agricultural Bank provides loans and guidance on agricultural problems. The Savings and Real Estate Bank and the Development Bank makes loans for building, food-processing, chemical, and traditional industries. The Libyan Arab Foreign Investment Co. makes foreign investments.

In 1997, in addition to the central bank, there were eight other banks in Libya: the Agricultural Bank, Jamahiriya Bank, Libyan Arab Foreign Bank, National Commercial Bank, Sahara Bank, Savings and Real Estate Investment Bank, Umma Bank, and Wahda Bank.

There are no securities exchanges in Libya.

Economic Development

Beginning in 1963 Libya put forth a series of five-year development plans. Of the government's oil revenues, 70 percent were earmarked for development. These monies were allocated for public works, agriculture, communications, education, public health, and industry. The plan for 2001 to 2005 foresees $35 billion total of investments, mostly in hydrocarbons, power, and water.

The Libyan Arab Foreign Investment Company has invested extensively in Arab companies and also has significant holdings in African countries.

With the 1999 lifting of UN sanctions Libya is encouraging foreign investment to further develop its large oil reserves.

SOCIAL WELFARE

By law all employees are entitled to sickness, invalid, disability, death, and maternity benefits, unemployment payments, and pensions. Profit sharing, free medical care and education, and subsidized food are other social welfare benefits.

Women were granted full legal rights in 1969, but few women work outside the home.

Under Libyan law an individual may be arrested and detained without a specific charge. Political dissenters are imprisoned. Citizens do not have the right to legal counsel or to fair public trials.

Healthcare

Virtually 100 percent of Libya's population has access to healthcare services. Widespread diseases include typhoid, venereal diseases, and infectious hepatitis. With the assistance of the World Health Organization (WHO), Libya has eradicated malaria, once a major problem. In 2000 the average life expectancy was 75.5 years.

Housing

Increasing urbanization has created slum conditions in the major cities. There have been slum clearance and building projects since 1954 but the housing deficit has not yet been met. Real estate was the main area of private investment until 1978 when most tenants were made owners of their residences.

EDUCATION

The government has invested heavily in education that is free at all levels. School is compulsory from the age of six until fifteen. Illiteracy was estimated at 24 percent in 1995 (males, 12.1 percent and females, 37 percent). In 1994 primary schools had 1.4 million pupils. Secondary schools had 310,556 pupils in 1992.

In 1976 the University of Libya at Tripoli was renamed Al-Fatah University, and the University of Libya at Banghazi was renamed the University of Garyounis. The Bright Star University of Technology at Marsa al-Brega was founded in 1981. Total enrollment at all higher-level institutions was 72,899 in 1992.

2000 KEY EVENTS TIMELINE

January

- British customs agents confirm that, in November 1999, thirty-two crates of missile parts were discovered on a British Airways flight headed for Libya.

February

- Britain protests against Libyan smuggling of missile parts through London.

March

- United States and Libyan officials hold their first official meeting in Tripoli since relations were broken off in 1981. The U.S. embassy in Libya was burnt down by rioting students in 1979.
- Muammar Qadhafi scraps most of the country's ministries, devolving their power to "people's assemblies;" excepting the ministries of justice, security, foreign affairs, economics, and information.

May

- The trial of two Libyans accused of the 1988 bombing of a Pan Am 747 over Lockerbie Scotland begins on the May 3 in the Netherlands.

August

- Abu Sayyaf, a Muslim group, is working to free hostages held in the Philippines. Libya is helping to raise the $12 million ransom demanded by the kidnappers in exchange for release of the remaining Western hostages. It has been reported that Libya has pledged $25 million in development aid to the Muslim region of the Philippines. When the hostages are released in Tripoli, Libya, officials from several European nations praise Qadhafi.

September

- Abdul Majid, a Libyan double agent, testifies at the trial of Lamen Khalifa Fhimah and Ali Mohmen al-Megrahi. The two are charged in the 1988 bombing of Pan Am Flight 103 over Lockerbie, Scotland.

October

- Colonel Muammar Qadhafi visits Jordan.
- During the first week of October at least 150 people are killed, mostly Africans, in the wake of anti-foreigner violence. Hundreds of thousands of black migrants are exported to Niger and Chad.
- Libya officially withdraws its ambassador, Ali Mahmud Mariya, from Beirut October 23 because Lebanon neglects to invite him to the opening session of the Lebanese Chamber of Deputies.

December

- A letter from Colonel Muammar Qadhafi to President Hugo Chavez of Venezuela, is released to the world news media. In the letter Qadhafi urges all oil-producing nations to consider halting oil production for a year or two to prevent worldwide oil prices from falling.

ANALYSIS OF EVENTS: 2000

BUSINESS AND THE ECONOMY

More than $10 billion per year continued to pour into Libya from production of 1.4 million barrels of oil per day. Dramatically improved current account figures for 1999 were released in August. High energy prices were expected to keep the country in a strong position externally, with export revenues forecast at $12 billion, assuming oil prices remained steady. Following a period of stagnation, gross domestic product (GDP) was expected to rise 5 percent in both 2000 and 2001, compared with 2 percent in 1999. It was hoped that increased growth would help lower the country's high unemployment rate, estimated at 30–40 percent. In spite of the country's healthy oil revenues, Libya was planning to reduce its dependence on oil by raising investment in other sectors, including mining, agriculture, fisheries, and tourism.

The best economic news for Libya in 2000 was the previous year's lifting of United Nations-sponsored economic sanctions, which was followed by a flurry of interest in investment by Europe's business community, including Italian, British, and German companies. A pipeline deal was signed with ENI, the leading Italian oil and gas company, and Libyan Airlines ordered twenty-four wide-bodied jets from Airbus Industries. Libya's improved political situation also brightened the prospects of its oil industry even further. A report from the United Kingdom rated Libya as one of the top countries in the world for oil exploration and development, as the country set a new production goal of 2 million barrels per day.

GOVERNMENT AND POLITICS

In 2000 Libya continued to emerge from the decade of international isolation that had followed the 1988 bombing of Pan Am Flight 747 over Lockerbie, Scotland. The previous year, Libyan leader Muammar Qadhafi had abandoned his long-time refusal to turn over two Libyans accused in the bombing, thus ending seven years of economic sanctions by both the United Nations and United Kingdom. The United States—home of the majority of those killed in the disaster—did not lift its own sanctions against Libya but still backed the lifting of U.N. sanctions, and there were other signs of a thaw in its attitude toward the north African nations. U.S. and Libyan officials met officially for the first time since 1981. The U.S. State Department considered lifting its ban on travel to Libya, and four U.S. oil firms were allowed to survey possible drilling sites in the country.

Meanwhile the trial of the two bombing suspects opened in a Dutch courtroom in May. A verdict in the case was not anticipated until sometime in 2001, and it was considered likely in some quarters that the evidence—most of it circumstantial—would not be sufficient to win a conviction.

Another step in Qadhafi's attempted journey from terrorism sponsor to statesman came with his role in brokering a deal to win the release of twenty-eight hostages held by the separatist Islamic group Abu Sayyaf in the Philippines. The agreement, which included a grant of $25 million in Libyan aid to the Pacific region, was concluded in August.

Although said to enjoy popular support within his own country, Qadhafi remained a repressive ruler who crushed dissent by banning political parties and unions and persecuting political opponents. He also appeared to be planning an eventual transfer of power to one or more of his five sons. In March Qadhafi closed most of the country's ministries, whose powers were transferred to "people's assemblies."

CULTURE AND SOCIETY

Although the Libyan government has spent billions of dollars on infrastructure and on grandiose projects like Qadhafi's projected "Manmade River" irrigation project, many of Libya's average citizens still enjoy little of the country's vast oil wealth. In 2000 the average teacher earned the equivalent of $1,200 per year, and many Libyans sought health care across the border in Tunisia. The youthful makeup of the country's population (70 percent under age twenty) sends thousands of young people every year into a job market not large enough to accommodate them, and even a swollen public sector can't provide enough jobs.

Although Qadhafi has tried to position himself as a leading figure in African politics, there has been significant resistance to his attempts at integrating immigrants from sub-Saharan countries into Libyan society, with established residents blaming the newcomers for crime, AIDS, and other social ills.

Libya's reentry into the international community was visible in areas besides politics and the economy. The first soccer match between Libya and Britain took place in May, inaugurating a new stadium in the capital city of Tripoli. The Libyan players beat the visiting Middlesbrough team by a score of one to zero.

DIRECTORY

CENTRAL GOVERNMENT

Head of State

Leader of the Revolution, De facto Head of State
Mu'ammar al-Qadhafi, Office of the President

General People's Committee

Secretary of the General People's Congress
Mohammad al-Zenati, General People's Congress

Assistant Secretary of the General People's Congress
Ahmad Mohamed Ibrahim, General People's Congress

Secretary of the General People's Committee
Mubarak Abdullah Al-Shamikh, General People's Committee

Secretary of Agriculture
Ali Yousif Juma, Department of Agriculture

Secretary of Animal Wealth
Mas'oud Abul-So'oud, Department of Animal Wealth

Secretary of Communications and Transport
Izz al-Deen al-Hinsheeri, Department of Communications and Transport

Secretary of Culture
Jum'a al-Fazzani, Department of Culture

Secretary of Economy and Trade
Abd al-Hafeedh al-Zleetni, Department of Economy and Trade

Secretary of Education and Vocational Training
Ma'touq Mohammad Ma'touq, Department of Education and Vocational Training

Secretary of Energy
Abdallah Salim al-Badri, Department of Energy

Secretary of Finance
Mohammad Bayt al-Mal, Department of Finance

Secretary of Health and Social Security
Ehtaywish Faraj Ehtaywish, Department of Health and Social Security

Secretary of Housing and Utilities
Embarak el-Shamikh, Department of Housing and Utilities

Secretary of Industry and Mines
Muftah Ezouzah, Department of Industry and Mines

Secretary of Information, Culture, and Mass Mobilization
Fawziyah Shalabi, Department of Information, Culture, and Mass Mobilization

Secretary of Justice and Public Security
Mohammad Bel-Qasim al-Zuwayy, Department of Justice and Public Security

Secretary of Marine Resources
Basheer Ramadan Abu-Jinah, Department of Marine Resources

Secretary of People's Control and Follow-up
Mahmoud Badi, Department of People's Control and Follow-up

Secretary of People's External Liaison and International Cooperation Bureau
Omar Mustafa al-Muntassir, Department of People's External Liaison and International Cooperation Bureau

Secretary of Planning
Jadallah 'Azzouz al-Talhi, Department of Planning

Secretary of Tourism
Al-Bokhari Salem Hauda, Department of Tourism

Secretary of Youth and Sport
Mohammad Mahmoud al-Hijazi, Department of Youth and Sport

Governor of the Central Bank
Tahir al-Jehaimi, Department of the Central Bank

POLITICAL ORGANIZATIONS

Attajamoa al-Watani al-Leebi (Libyan National Group)

Al-Haraka al-Wataniya ad-Dimokratia al-Leebiya (Libyan Democratic National Movement)

At-Tajamoa al-Watani ad-Dimokrati al-Leebi (Libyan Democratic National Group)

Al-Haraka al-Wataniya al-Leebiya (Libyan National Movement)

Aj-Jamaa al-Islamiya "Libya" (Islamic Group Libya)

Al-Haraka al-Islamiya "Libya" (Islamic Movement Libya)

Aj-Jabha al-Leebiya al-Wataniya ad-Dimokratiya (Democratic National Libyan Front)

Aj-Jabha al-Wataniya Li-Inqad Libya (National Front For The Salvation Of Libya)

Jaish al-Inqad al-Watani al-Leebi (Libyan National Salvation Army)

Harakat al-Kifah al-Watani al-Leebi (Libyan National Struggle Movement)

Monathamat Jaish al-Inqad al-Watani al-Leebi (Libyan National Salvation Army Organization)

Al-Haraka al-Leebiya Lil-Taghyieer Wal-Islah (Libyan Movement For Change)

Monathamat Tahreer Libya (Organization For Free Libya)

Attantheem Alwatani Alleebi (Libyan National Group)

Al-Haiaa al-Libiya Lil-Kalas al-Watani (Libyan Authority For National Salvation)

Monathamat al-Burkan al-Leebi (Libyan Volcano Group)

Al-Ittihad ad-Dostouri al-Leebi (Libyan Constitutional Union)

Hizb at-Tahreer (Freedom Party)

Jabhat al-Wataniyeen al-Libi-Yeen (National Libyans Front)

Harakat al-Nidal Ash-Shaabi al-Leebi (Libyan People's Struggle Movement)

Al-Hizb ad-Dimokrati al-Leebi (Libyan Democratic Party)

Hizb al-Umma (Nation's Party)

Attahalof al-Watani al-Leebi (Libyan National Union)

Al-Motamar ad-Dimokrati al-Leebi (Libyan Democratic Conference)

Hai-At at-Tanseeq ad-Dimokratiya al-Leebiya (Libyan Democratic Authority)

Aj-Jamaa al-Islamiya al-Mokatila (Fighting Islamic Group)

Hizb al-Mohafi-Deen al-Leebi (Libyan Conservatives Party)

DIPLOMATIC REPRESENTATION

Embassies in Libya

Brazil
Shara Ben Ashur, PO Box 2270, Tripoli, Libya
PHONE: +218 (21) 3607747
FAX: +218 (21) 607970
E-MAIL: 100125.52@compuserve.com
TITLE: Trade Attache
NAME: Jose Marcos Viana

British Interests Section, c/o Italian Embassy
Sharia Uahran 1, PO Box 4206, Tripoli, Libya
PHONE: +218 (21) 3331191
FAX: +218 (21) 4445753

India
16/18 Shara Mahmoud Shaltout, Garden City, PO Box 3150, Tripoli, Libya
PHONE: +218 (21) 41835
FAX: +218 (21) 37560

Italy
Shara Uaharan, 1, Tripoli, Libya
PHONE: +218 (21) 3334131
FAX: +218 (21) 3331673

Japan

Organization of African Unity Road, Dhat al-Imad, Tower No.4, Halls No.13 and 14, PO Box 3265, Tripoli, Libya
PHONE: +218 (21) 3350056; 3350057
FAX: +218 (21) 3350055

Nigeria

PO Box 4417, Tripoli, Libya
PHONE: +218 (21) 43036

Russia

10 Mustafa Kamel Street, Tripoli, Libya
PHONE: +218 (21) 30545; 30546
FAX: +218 (21) 21821

JUDICIAL SYSTEM

Supreme Court

BROADCAST MEDIA

Libyan Jamahiriya Broadcasting

PO Box 9333, Soug al Jama, Tripoli, Libya
PHONE: +218 (21) 603191; 603195

Libyan Television

PO Box 9333, Soug al Jama, Tripoli, Libya
PHONE: +218 (21) 603191
TYPE: Government

People's Revolution Broadcasting TV

PO Box 333, Tripoli, Libya
TITLE: Director
CONTACT: Youssif Debri
TYPE: Government

COLLEGES AND UNIVERSITIES

7th April University

PO Box 16418, Zawia, Libya

Al-Arab Medical University

PO Box 18251, Benghazi, Libya
PHONE: +218 (61) 25007; 21152
FAX: +218 (61) 22195

Al-Fateh University

PO Box 13040, Tripoli, Libya

Omar Elmukhtar University for Agriculture

PO Box 919, Al Bayda, Libya
PHONE: +218 (21) 3610719

Sebha University

PO Box 18758, Sebha, Libya
PHONE: +218 (71) 21575
FAX: +218 (71) 29201

University of Garyounis

PO Box 1308, Benghazi, Libya
PHONE: +218 (61) 25007
FAX: +218 (61) 20051

NEWSPAPERS AND MAGAZINES

Libya Daily

WEBSITE: http://www.libyadaily.com

Mahatta

WEBSITE: http://www.libyanet.com

Shu'un Libiyah (Libyan Affairs)

E-MAIL: jla97@aol.com
WEBSITE: http://www.libyanaffairs.com
TITLE: Managing Editor
CONTACT: Breik A. Swessi

Libya Antiqua

Via Cassiodoro 19, PO Box 6192, 00193 Rome, Italy
E-MAIL: erma@sysin.it
WEBSITE: http://www.sysin.it/erma
TITLE: Director
CONTACT: Abdullah Shaibub
TYPE: History, Middle East and Africa

Libyan Journal of Sciences

PO Box 13040, Tripoli, Libya
TITLE: Editor
CONTACT: M. J. Salem
CIRCULATION: 500
TYPE: Science, general

PUBLISHERS

Al-Fatah University, General Administration of Libraries, Printing & Publication

PO Box 13543, Tripoli, Libya
PHONE: +218 (21) 621988

RELIGIOUS ORGANIZATIONS

Colonel Mu'ammar al-Qadhafi has declared all religious practices besides Islam illegal and punishable by exile or death, and eliminated independent religious organizations outside the jurisdiction of the ruling party, the Revolutionary Command Council.

FURTHER READING

Articles

Cockburn, Andres. "Libya." *National Geographic,* vol. 198, no. 5, November 2000, p. 2–31.

"Gadhafi Returns to 'People Power," *Financial Times,* March 4, 2000.

"Hostages in Philippines Best Shot: Help from Libya." *Christian Science Monitor,* August 24, 2000, p. 7.

"Jordan: Qaddafi Comes Calling." *New York Times,* October 5, 2000, p. A12.

"Libya—Qaddafi, Floating Like a Butterfly." *The Economist (US),* September 2, 2000, vol. 356, no. 8186, p. 41.

"Libya Smuggling Scud Missile Part, Britain Says." *New York Times,* January 10, 2000, p. A4.

McNeil, Donald G. Jr. "Libyan Double Agent Testifies in Lockerbie Bomb Trial." *New York Times,* September 27, 2000, p. A3.

"Philippines: Libya Increases Ransom." *New York Times,* August 23, 2000, p. A10.

Books

St. John, Ronald Bruce. *Historical Dictionary of Libya.* [computer file] Boulder, CO: netLibrary, Inc., 2000.

LIBYA: STATISTICAL DATA

For sources and notes see "Sources of Statistics" at the front of each volume.

GEOGRAPHY

Geography

Area:

Total: 1,759,540 sq km.

Land: 1,759,540 sq km.

Land boundaries:

Total: 4,383 km.

Border countries: Algeria 982 km, Chad 1,055 km, Egypt 1,150 km, Niger 354 km, Sudan 383 km, Tunisia 459 km.

Coastline: 1,770 km.

Climate: Mediterranean along coast; dry, extreme desert interior.

Terrain: mostly barren, flat to undulating plains, plateaus, depressions.

Natural resources: petroleum, natural gas, gypsum.

Land use:

Arable land: 1%

Permanent crops: 0%

Permanent pastures: 8%

Forests and woodland: 0%

Other: 91% (1993 est.).

HUMAN FACTORS

Demographics (A)

	1990	1995	1998	2000	2010	2020	2030	2040	2050
Population	4,140	4,654	4,875	5,116	6,447	7,740	8,880	9,951	10,817
Life expectancy - males	70.6	72.3	72.9	73.3	75.2	76.7	77.9	78.9	79.7
Life expectancy - females	74.5	76.4	77.1	77.7	79.9	81.7	83.1	84.3	85.2
Birth rate (per 1,000)	31.4	26.2	27.5	27.7	24.6	19.1	16.5	15.4	13.6
Death rate (per 1,000)	4.2	3.6	3.5	3.5	3.5	3.6	4.2	5.3	7.0
Women of reproductive age (15-49 yrs.)	904	1,115	1,235	1,326	1,739	2,046	2,286	2,407	2,519
Fertility rate	5.0	4.1	3.9	3.7	3.0	2.5	2.2	2.1	2.0

Except as noted, values for vital statistics are in thousands; life expectancy is in years.

Health Personnel

	National Data	World Data (wtd ave)
Total health expenditure as a percentage of GDP, 1990-1998[a]		
Public sector	NA	2.5
Private sector	NA	2.9
Total[b]	NA	5.5
Availability of health care facilities per 100,000 people		
Hospital beds 1990-1998[a]	430	330
Doctors 1992-1995[a]	219	122
Nurses 1992-1995[a]	334	248

Health Indicators

	National Data	World Data
Life expectancy at birth (years)		
1980	60	61
1998	70	67
Daily per capita supply of calories		
1970	2,453	2,358
1997	3,289	2,791
Daily per capital supply of protein		
1997 (grams)	78	74
Total fertility rate (births per woman)		
1980	7.3	3.7
1998	3.7	2.7
Population with access (%)		
To safe water (1990-96)	90	NA
To sanitation (1990-96)	86	NA
People living with (1997)		
Tuberculosis (cases per 100,000)	22.9[1]	60.4
HIV/AIDS (% aged 15 - 49 years)	0.05	0.99

Infants and Malnutrition

	National Data	World Data (wtd ave)
Under 5 mortality rate (1989)	24	NA
% of infants with low birthweight (1992-98)[1]	5	17
Births attended by skilled health staff (% of total births 1996-98)	94	52
% fully immunized at 1 year of age (1995-98)[1]		
TB	100	82
DPT	97	77
Polio	95	77
Measles	92	74
Prevalence of child malnutrition (1992-98)[1] (based on weight for age, % of children under 5 years)	5	30

Ethnic Division

Berber and Arab 97%
Greeks . . . . .NA
Maltese . . . . .NA
Italians . . . . .NA
Egyptians . . . . .NA
Pakistanis . . . . .NA
Turks . . . . .NA
Indians . . . . .NA
Tunisians . . . . .NA

Religion

Sunni Muslim 97%

Major Languages

Arabic, Italian, English, all are widely understood in the major cities.

EDUCATION

Public Education Expenditures

	1980	1997
Public expenditures on education as % of GNP	3.4	NA
Expenditures per student as % of GNP per capita		
Primary & Secondary	NA	NA
Tertiary	58.2	NA
Pupils per teacher at the primary level	NA	NA
Duration of primary education in years	NA	9
World data for comparison		
Public expenditures on education as % of GNP (mean)	3.9	4.8
Pupils per teacher at the primary level (wtd ave)	NA	33
Duration of primary education in years (mean)	NA	9

Educational Attainment (A)

Age group (1984)[4] .25+
Population of this age group .996,774
Highest level attained (%)
No schooling .59.7
First level
Not completed .15.4
Completed .8.5
Entered second level
Lower Secondary .5.2
Upper Secondary .8.5
Entered post-secondary .2.7

Literacy Rates (A)

In thousands and percent	1990	1995	2000	2010
Illiterate population (15+ yrs.)	741	702	649	514
Literacy rate - total adult pop. (%)	69.9	76.2	81.6	89.8
Literacy rate - males (%)	83.9	87.9	91.2	96.0
Literacy rate - females (%)	53.6	63.0	71.0	83.1

GOVERNMENT & LAW

Political Parties

The unicameral General People's Congress members are elected indirectly through a hierarchy of people's committees. There are no political parties.

Government Budgets (B)

Revenues .$3.6 billion
Expenditures .$5.1 billion

Data for 1998 est.

Crime

Crime volume (for 1998)
Crimes reported .48,300
Total persons convicted .NA
Crimes per 100,000 population .966
Persons responsible for offenses
Total number suspects .50,879
Total number of female suspects .2,798
Total number of juvenile suspects .1,170

(Continued on next page.)

LABOR FORCE

Total Labor Force (A)

1.2 million (1997 est.).

Labor Force by Occupation

Services and government .54%
Industry .29%
Agriculture .17%

Data for 1997 est.

Unemployment Rate

30% (1998 est.)

PRODUCTION SECTOR

Energy Production

Production .16.92 billion kWh
Production by source
Fossil fuel .100%
Hydro .0%
Nuclear .0%
Other .0%
Exports .0 kWh

Data for 1998.

Energy Consumption

Consumption .15.736 billion kWh
Imports .0 kWh

Data for 1998.

Transportation

Highways:

Total: 83,200 km.

Paved: 47,590 km.

Unpaved: 35,610 km (1996 est.).

Waterways: none.

Pipelines: crude oil 4,383 km; petroleum products 443 km (includes liquefied petroleum gas or LPG 256 km); natural gas 1,947 km.

Merchant marine:

Total: 27 ships (1,000 GRT or over) totaling 401,303 GRT/656,632 DWT.

Ships by type: cargo 9, chemical tanker 1, liquified gas 3, petroleum tanker 6, roll-on/roll-off 4, short-sea passenger 4 (1999 est.).

Airports: 142 (1999 est.).

Airports - with paved runways: 59.

Airports - with unpaved runways: 83.

Top Agriculture Products

Wheat, barley, olives, dates, citrus, vegetables, peanuts; beef, eggs.

Top Mining Products (B)

Mineral resources include: gypsum.

GOVERNMENT & LAW (cont.)

Military Affairs (A)

	1990	1992	1995	1996	1997
Military expenditures					
Current dollars (mil.)	NA	1,810	1,810	NA	NA
1997 constant dollars (mil.)	NA	2,010	1,880	NA	NA
Armed forces (000)	86	85	76	76	70[e]
Gross national product (GNP)					
Current dollars (mil.)	22,300[e]	23,900[e]	29,600	34,400	37,400[e]
1997 constant dollars (mil.)	26,200	26,500	30,600	34,900	37,400
Central government expenditures (CGE)					
1997 constant dollars (mil.)	NA	NA	9,520	12,400	13,500
People (mil.)	4.4	4.4	4.7	4.7	4.8
Military expenditure as % of GNP	NA	7.6	6.1	NA	NA
World data on military expenditure as % of GNP	4.5	3.4	2.7	2.6	2.6
Military expenditure as % of CGE	NA	NA	19.7	NA	NA
World data on military expenditure as % of CGE	17.0	12.5	10.5	10.3	10.2
Military expenditure per capita (1997 $)	NA	461	403	NA	NA
World data on military expenditure per capita (1997 $)	242	173	146	143	145
Armed forces per 1,000 people (soldiers)	19.7	19.5	16.3	16.2	14.7
World data on armed forces per 1,000 people (soldiers)	5.3	4.5	4.1	3.9	3.8
GNP per capita (1997 $)	6,010	6,070	6,580	7,450	7,860
Arms imports[6]					
Current dollars (mil.)	370	90	0	20	5
1997 constant dollars (mil.)	433	100	0	20	5
Arms exports[6]					
Current dollars (mil.)	60	10	0	0	0
1997 constant dollars (mil.)	70	11	0	0	0
Total imports[7]					
Current dollars (mil.)	5,336	5,161	4,903	5,136	6,900[e]
1997 constant dollars (mil.)	6,249	5,722	5,076	5,222	6,900[e]
Total exports[7]					
Current dollars (mil.)	13,200	9,948[e]	8,483[e]	10,100[e]	9,816[e]
1997 constant dollars (mil.)	15,490	11,030[e]	8,784[e]	10,270[e]	9,816[e]
Arms as percent of total imports[8]	6.9	1.7	0	0.4	0.1
Arms as percent of total exports[8]	0.5	0.1	0	0	0

MANUFACTURING SECTOR

GDP & Manufacturing Summary (A)

	1980	1985	1990	1995
GDP ($-1990 mil.)[1]	31,992	26,663	26,078	27,664
Per capita ($-1990)[1]	10,513	7,043	5,738	5,116
Manufacturing share (%) (current prices)[1]	1.9	4.5	8.3[e]	NA
Manufacturing				
Value added ($-1990 mil.)[1]	937	1,821	2,185	3,276[e]
Industrial production index	62	87[e]	100	150[e]
Value added ($ mil.)	358	541[e]	693[e]	857[e]
Gross output ($ mil.)	1,177	1,726[e]	2,301[e]	2,761[e]
Employment (000)	18	23[e]	26[e]	33[e]
Profitability (% of gross output)				
Intermediate input (%)	70	69[e]	70[e]	69[e]
Wages and salaries inc. supplements (%)	13	13[e]	12[e]	12[e]
Gross operating surplus	17	19[e]	18[e]	19[e]
Productivity ($)				
Gross output per worker	64,186[e]	75,484[e]	85,187[e]	80,602[e]
Value added per worker	19,577[e]	24,557[e]	27,763[e]	27,641[e]
Average wage (inc. supplements)	8,327[e]	9,620[e]	10,187[e]	9,856[e]
Value added ($ mil.)				
Food products	35	37[e]	38[e]	37[e]
Beverages	17	18[e]	21[e]	19[e]
Tobacco products	55	73[e]	79[e]	81[e]
Textiles	14	22[e]	26[e]	32[e]
Wearing apparel	5[e]	8[e]	15[e]	28[e]
Leather and fur products	7[e]	15[e]	20[e]	29[e]
Footwear	14	25[e]	32[e]	44[e]
Wood and wood products	3[e]	4[e]	3[e]	3[e]
Furniture and fixtures	2[e]	2[e]	2[e]	2[e]
Paper and paper products	3	3[e]	3[e]	3[e]
Printing and publishing	NA	8[e]	9[e]	9[e]
Industrial chemicals	35	41[e]	52[e]	60[e]
Other chemical products	21	33[e]	31[e]	45[e]
Petroleum refineries	81	124[e]	198[e]	234[e]
Rubber products	NA	NA	1[e]	1[e]
Plastic products	2	4[e]	5[e]	7[e]
Pottery, china and earthenware	1	2[e]	2[e]	2[e]
Other non-metal mineral products	51	99	131[e]	187[e]
Non-ferrous metals	3	5	4	4
Electrical machinery	3	5[e]	4[e]	4[e]
Transport equipment	NA	NA	NA	NA
Other manufacturing	9	18[e]	23[e]	34[e]

COMMUNICATIONS

Daily Newspapers

	National Data	World Data for Comparison
Daily Newspapers		
Number of Dailies	4	8,391
Total Circulation (000)	71	548,000
Circulation per 1,000 inhabitants	14	96

Telecommunications

Telephones - main lines in use: 318,000 (1995).

Telephones - mobile cellular: NA

Telephone system: telecommunications system is being modernized; mobile cellular telephone system became operational in 1996.

Domestic: microwave radio relay, coaxial cable, cellular, tropospheric scatter, and a domestic satellite system with 14 earth stations.

International: satellite earth stations - 4 Intelsat, NA Arabsat, and NA Intersputnik; submarine cables to France and Italy; microwave radio relay to Tunisia and Egypt; tropospheric scatter to Greece; participant in Medarabtel (1999).

Radio broadcast stations: AM 17, FM 4, shortwave 3 (1998).

Radios: 1.35 million (1997).

Television broadcast stations: 12 (plus one low-power repeater) (1997).

Televisions: 730,000 (1997).

Internet Service Providers (ISPs): NA

FINANCE, ECONOMICS, & TRADE

Economic Indicators

National product: GDP—purchasing power parity—$39.3 billion (1999 est.).

National product real growth rate: 2% (1999 est.).

National product per capita: $7,900 (1999 est.).

Inflation rate—consumer price index: 18% (1999 est.).

Exchange Rates

Exchange rates:

Libyan dinars (LD) per US$1

January 2000	0.4687
1999	0.4616
1998	0.3785
1997	0.3891
1996	0.3651
1995	0.3532
Official rate	
December 1998	0.4500

Fiscal year: calendar year.

Top Import Origins

$7 billion (f.o.b., 1998 est.)

Origins (1997)

Italy	23%
Germany	12%
United Kingdom	9%
France	7%
Tunisia	5%
Belgium	4%

Top Export Destinations

$6.6 billion (f.o.b., 1998 est.)

Destinations (1997)

Italy	40%
Germany	17%
Spain	12%
France	4%
Sudan	4%
United Kingdom	3%

Foreign Aid

Recipient: $8.4 million (1995).

Import/Export Commodities

Import Commodities	Export Commodities
Machinery	Crude oil
Transport equipment	Refined petroleum products
Food	Natural gas
Manufactured goods	

Balance of Payments

	1986	1987	1988	1989	1990
Exports of goods (f.o.b.)	6,186	5,821	5,653	7,274	11,352
Imports of goods (f.o.b.)	−4,718	−5,384	−5,762	−6,509	−7,575
Trade balance	1,468	437	−109	765	3,777
Services - debits	−1,114	−1,436	−1,637	−1,481	−1,385
Services - credits	87	114	128	117	117
Private transfers (net)	NA	NA	NA	NA	NA
Government transfers (net)	−39	−56	−37	−16	−35
Overall balance	−166	−1,043	−1,826	−1,026	2,201

LIECHTENSTEIN

CAPITAL: Vaduz.

FLAG: The national flag is divided into two horizontal rectangles, blue above red. On the blue rectangle, near the hoist, is the princely crown in gold.

ANTHEM: *Oben am jungen Rhein (On the Banks of the Young Rhine).*

MONETARY UNIT: The Swiss franc (SwFr) of 100 centimes, or rappen, has been in use since February 1921. There are coins of 1, 5, 10, 20, and 50 centimes and 1, 2, and 5 francs, and notes of 10, 20, 50, 100, 500, and 1,000 francs. SwFr1 = $0.7092 (or $1 = SwFr1.41).

WEIGHTS AND MEASURES: The metric system is the legal standard.

HOLIDAYS: New Year's Day, 1 January; Epiphany, 6 January; Candlemas, 2 February; St. Joseph's Day, 19 March; Labor Day, 1 May; Assumption, 15 August; Nativity of Our Lady, 8 September; All Saints' Day, 1 November; Immaculate Conception, 8 December; Christmas, 25 December; St. Stephen's Day, 26 December. Movable religious holidays include Good Friday, Easter Monday, Ascension, Whitmonday, and Corpus Christi.

TIME: 1 PM = noon GMT.

LOCATION AND SIZE: Liechtenstein is a landlocked country in the Rhine (Rhein) River Valley. The fourth-smallest country in Europe, the principality has an area of 160 square kilometers (61.8 square miles), about 0.9 times the size of Washington, D.C. Liechtenstein's capital city, Vaduz, is located in the western part of the country.

CLIMATE: The annual lowland temperature varies between −4.5°C (24°F) in January and 19.9°C (68°F) in July. Late frost and prolonged dry periods are rare. Average annual precipitation is 105 centimeters (41 inches).

Principality of Liechtenstein
Fürstentum Liechtenstein

INTRODUCTORY SURVEY

RECENT HISTORY

From 1852 to the end of World War I (1914-1918) Liechtenstein was closely tied economically to Austria. After Austria's devastating defeat in the war, Liechtenstein sought closer ties with its other neighbor, Switzerland. A treaty concluded in 1923 provided for a customs union and the use of Swiss currency.

Liechtenstein, like Switzerland, remained neutral in World War II as it had in World War I. The postwar decades have been marked by political stability and outstanding economic growth, spurred by the country's low taxes. In August 1984 Franz Josef II, who succeeded his granduncle Franz I in 1938, handed over executive authority to his eldest son and heir, Crown Prince Hans Adam.

Liechtenstein has sought further integration into the world community. The country was admitted to the United Nations in September 1991. In 1995 Liechtenstein became a member of the European Economic Area (an organization associated with the European Union).

In 1999 Liechtenstein ranked as one of the world's most prosperous countries with one of the world's highest living standards. However in June 2000 an international task force revealed Liechtenstein banking laws make money laundering possible.

GOVERNMENT

Liechtenstein is a constitutional monarchy ruled by the hereditary princes of the house of

Liechtenstein. The constitution provides for a single-chamber parliament (Diet or Landtag) of twenty-five members elected by direct popular vote under proportional representation to serve four years. The prince appoints the head of government and deputy head of government on the recommendation of the Diet. The leader of the majority part in the Diet is usually appointed the head of government and leader of the largest minority part of the Diet is generally appointed deputy head.

Judiciary

Courts that function under sole Liechtenstein jurisdiction are the County Court (Landgericht), which decides minor civil cases and criminal offenses; the juvenile court; and the Schöffengericht, a court for misdemeanors. The remaining courts have a mixed composition of judges from Liechtenstein, Switzerland, and Austria. The criminal court (Kriminalgericht) is for major crimes. Other courts of mixed jurisdiction are the assize court, the superior court, and a supreme court. An administration court of appeals hears appeals from government actions, and the State Court determines the constitutionality of laws.

Political Parties

The two principal parties are the Fatherland Union (Vaterländische Union-VU) and the Progressive Citizens' Party (Fortschrittliche Bürgerpartei-FBPL). The other party holding seats in the Diet in 2000 is the Free List (FL).

DEFENSE

Since 1868 no military forces have been maintained in Liechtenstein. Defense is the responsibility of Switzerland.

ECONOMIC AFFAIRS

Despite its small size and limited national resources, Liechtenstein has developed since the 1940s from a mainly agricultural to an industrialized country and a prosperous center of trade, finance, and tourism. Its standard of living is on par with the large prosperous European countries. About 73,700 companies taking advantage of low business taxes and easy incorporation rules have established nominal offices in Liechtenstein and provide 30 percent of state revenues. Liechtenstein's currency is the Swiss franc and it participates with Switzerland in a customs union. It has been a member of the European Economic Area since 1995.

Public Finance

The U.S. Central Intelligence Agency estimated that in 1998 government revenues totaled approximately $424.2 million and expenditures $414.1 million. Liechtenstein has no public debt.

Income

In 1998 Liechtenstein's gross domestic product (GDP) was estimated at $730 million, or $23,000 per capita. The inflation rate was estimated in 1997 to be 0.5 percent.

Industry

The industry of Liechtenstein, limited by shortages of raw materials, is primarily devoted to small-scale production of high technology precision items. The output includes optical lenses, high-vacuum pumps, heating equipment, electron microscopes, and electronic measuring and control devices and small machinery. Other industries include textiles, ceramics, pharmaceuticals, food processing, and tourism.

Banking and Finance

Although there is a national bank the duties of the central bank are performed by the Swiss National Bank, a consequence of the currency union with Switzerland. Liechtenstein's banks form an important part of the economy, and they have experienced significant growth in the 1990s. As of 1994 the banking sector employs an estimated 4 percent of the work force.

The National Bank of Liechtenstein (Liechtensteinische Landesbank), founded in 1861, is the state bank of issue; in addition, it deals in real estate mortgages and ordinary banking operations. Liechtenstein Global Trust (LGT), the country's biggest financial institution (owned by the royal family), and the Private Trust Bank Corp., founded in 1956, play an important role in the finance and credit spheres of Liechtenstein's economy. Banking is linked with the Swiss banking system, as is securities trading. Liechtenstein's banks contributed over 12 percent to the country's national income in terms of taxes and dividends paid in 1996.

Because of Liechtenstein's strict bank secrecy, several thousand foreign businesses are nominally headquartered there. The secrecy laws are, however, waived in the case of criminal intent. There are at present no restrictions on foreign investors' access to financing in Liechtenstein. New laws to combat insider trading and money laundering have recently tightened fiduciary regulations.

Economic Development

The government generally encourages the increasing diversification of industry and the development of tourism. The principality's low taxes and highly secret banking system are attractive to foreign corporations wanting to safeguard patents and trademarks and to individuals who want to protect their wealth for the future. Thousands of corporations have established nominal headquarters in Liechtenstein.

Liechtenstein is working to integrate its economy into the more unified European economy.

SOCIAL WELFARE

Accident, old age, and survivors' insurance are compulsory, as are unemployment and health insurance. Family allowances have been granted since 1958. A 1992 constitutional amendment guarantees women equality under the law. A new equal opportunity law passed in 1999 addresses workplace discrimination and sexual harassment.

Healthcare

In 2000 average life expectancy was about seventy-nine years. In the mid-1990s Liechtenstein had an estimated 2.5 physicians and 8.3 hospital beds per 1,000 population. Regular examinations are provided for children up to the age of ten.

Housing

Liechtenstein does not have a significant housing problem.

EDUCATION

While there are no universities in Liechtenstein, many students continue their studies at universities in Switzerland, Austria, and Germany. Education is conducted on Roman Catholic principles and is under government supervision. School attendance is compulsory for five years beginning at the age of seven. Education is offered from kindergarten to the upper school. Literacy is 100 percent.

2000 KEY EVENTS TIMELINE

January

- The German press reveals that illegal contributions to former Chancellor Helmut Kohl's slush funds were funneled through Liechtenstein.

June

- Police raid the royal-owned LGT Bank.
- Liechtenstein is among the top fifteen countries named by an international task force investigating countries whose banking laws make money laundering possible.

August

- The government reports evidence of money laundering; possibly by Colombia drug cartels, a Sicilian mafia group, and Russian criminal gangs in the country on August 31.

December

- Latvia adopts amendments to its free trade agreements with members of the European Free Trade Assocation (EFTA)—Iceland, Liechtenstein, Switzerland, and Norway.
- The government announces plans to create a panel of historians to study allegations that

Liechtenstein helped the Nazis during World War II.

- The Liechtenstein Global Trust, a financial concern, reorganizes its operations into five new business units: Private Banking Europe, Private Banking Asia, Capital Management, Alternative Investments, and Operations and Technology.

ANALYSIS OF EVENTS: 2000

BUSINESS AND THE ECONOMY

Liechtenstein's economy—40 percent of which was made up by banking and financial services—found itself under threat from censure of its banking industry and threatened sanctions by two international organizations. The principality's easy rules of incorporation and loose reporting requirements were cited as magnets for shady business operations. Some 80,000 "letter-box" holding companies registered in Liechtenstein occupied only nominal office space in the country but enjoyed its low 18 percent corporate tax rate, and Liechtenstein was host to numerous anonymous bank accounts, trusts, and foundations.

In June the country's failure to adopt stricter banking laws placed it on lists drawn up by the Organization for Economic Cooperation and Development (OECD) and the G77. The OECD placed Liechtenstein among thirty-five "tax havens" whose financial policies were likely to attract depositors seeking to evade taxes or launder money. All of the listed countries faced possible sanctions unless reforms were begun within a year and completed by 2005. The G7's Financial Action Task Force on Money Laundering (FATF) listed Liechtenstein as one of fifteen countries it claimed were soft on money laundering, allowing deposits of illegally obtained money to remain hidden from authorities through lax reporting laws and an absence of provisions for information sharing across its borders.

In July Liechtenstein's banks agreed to ban accounts opened anonymously through intermediaries, requiring the identity of all depositors to be known.

Liechtenstein participated in a customs union with Switzerland and used the Swiss franc as its national currency. It has been a member of the European Economic Area (an organization serving as a bridge between the European Free Trade Association and the European Union) since May 1995.

GOVERNMENT AND POLITICS

The top story dominating both politics and finance in 2000 was an international crackdown on banking practices, in both Liechtenstein and other top financial centers, to cut down on money laundering and tax evasion. The country's banks had already come under fire in a German intelligence report alleging that Liechtenstein was one of several countries whose banks were used by gangs and drug cartels to launder money. This charge was followed by press reports in January 2000 stating that illegal political contributions to former German chancellor Helmut Kohl had been channeled into slush funds through accounts in Liechtenstein. Later the principality's banks were linked to deposits of bribe payments made to German politicians by the French oil company Elf Aquitaine.

As the year progressed Liechtenstein's own government was drawn into the banking scandals. In May the principality, with the assistance of Austrian police, arrested four officials including a legislator and a brother of the deputy Prime Minister on charges of fraud and money laundering. The following month Liechtenstein police raided the offices of the Liechtenstein Global Trust (LGT) bank, controlled by the country's ruling family, seizing account information related to charges of money laundering. The brother of Liechtenstein's ruler, Prince Hans Adam II, was a top official at the bank.

In response to the bank scandals, as well as inclusion in embarrassing blacklists in June by two international organizations, Liechtenstein's Parliament passed a series of laws tightening bank reporting requirements and facilitating cooperation with international authorities to fight money laundering. Provisions were also made for the hiring of new justice department personnel with experience in fighting white-collar crime.

In addition to new laws to counter money laundering, Liechtenstein's government continued to work both for reform of the Constitution to modify the power of the ruling family, and toward harmonization of its policies to accord with European economic integration.

CULTURE AND SOCIETY

Liechtenstein continued to have high living standards, comparable to those in major urban areas of other Western European countries. Its population was estimated at 32,307 in July 2000. Prince Hans Adam II opened his castle residence to all citizens on the country's national holiday August 15 for a celebration, as he does each year. Of the total population, 71 percent were fifteen to sixty-four years of age, 18 percent were fourteen and under, and 11 percent were sixty-five or over. The average life expectancy was close to seventy-nine years, and the net rate of migration was 5.03 per 1,000 population. The literacy rate was 100 percent.

DIRECTORY

CENTRAL GOVERNMENT

Head of State

Prince
Hans-Adam II, Schloss, FL-9490 Vaduz, Liechtenstein

Head of Government
Mario Frick, Office of the Head of Government, Regierungsgebaeude, FL-9490 Vaduz, Liechtenstein

Ministers

Deputy Head of Government
Michael Ritter, Office of the Deputy Head of Government

Member of the Government in Charge of Foreign Affairs, Family and Equal Rights, Culture and Sports
Andrea Willi, Office of Foreign Affairs, Family and Equal Rights, Culture and Sports

Member of the Government in Charge of Justice
Heinz Frommelt, Office of Justice

POLITICAL ORGANIZATIONS

Vaterlandische Union-VU (Fatherland Union)

NAME: Oswald Krantz

Fortschrittliche Burgerpartei-FBP (Progressive Citizens' Party)

Aeulestrasse 56, FL-9490 Vaduz, Liechtenstein
PHONE: +41 (75) 2377940
FAX: +41 (75) 2377949
TITLE: Party Secretary
NAME: Norbert Seeger

Freie Liste-FL (The Free List)

Im Bretscha 4, Postfach 177, FL-9494 Schaan, Liechtenstein
PHONE: +41 (75) 2377940
FAX: +41 (75) 2377949
E-MAIL: FListe@lie-net.li
TITLE: Party Secretary
NAME: Norbert Seeger

JUDICIAL SYSTEM

Oberster Gerichtshof (Supreme Court)

Obergericht (Superior Court)

BROADCAST MEDIA

Radio L

Dorfstr. 24, 9495 Triesen, Fürstentum, Liechtenstein
PHONE: +41 (75) 3661313
FAX: +41 (75) 3991399
E-MAIL: radiol@radiol.li
WEBSITE: http://www.radiol.li
TITLE: Program Manager
CONTACT: Dani Sigel
TYPE: Commercial

COLLEGES AND UNIVERSITIES

Liechtensteinische Musikschule

St. Florinsgasse 1, FL-9490 Vaduz, Liechtenstein
PHONE: +41 (75) 2324620
FAX: +41 (75) 2324642
E-MAIL: emu@pingnet.li

NEWSPAPERS AND MAGAZINES

Liechtensteiner Vaterland

Fuerst Franz Josef Str. 13, FL-9490 Vaduz, Liechtenstein
PHONE: +41 (75) 2361616
FAX: +41 (75) 2361617
E-MAIL: redaktion@vaterland.li
WEBSITE: http://www.vaterland.li
TITLE: Editor-in-Chief
CONTACT: Guenther Fritz
CIRCULATION: 16,440

Liechtensteiner Volksblatt

Presseverein Liechtensteiner Volksblatt, Postfach 193, FL-9494 Schaan, Liechtenstein
PHONE: +41 (75) 2375151
FAX: +41 (75) 2375155

E-MAIL: flvobla@flvobla.lol.lo
WEBSITE: http://www.lol.lo/volksblatt
CIRCULATION: 14,500

Liechtenstein Politische Schriften

Am Schraegen Weg 2, Postfach 44, FL-9490 Vaduz, Liechtenstein
FAX: +41 (75) 2322837
TITLE: Editor
CONTACT: Gerard Batliner
CIRCULATION: 520
TYPE: Political science, general

Liechtenstein - Principality in the Heart of Europe

Government Palace, FL-9490 Vaduz, Liechtenstein
FAX: +41 (75) 2366460
E-MAIL: pafl@sda-ats.ch
CIRCULATION: 30,000
TYPE: History, Europe, general

Liechtensteiner Bau- und Hauszeitung

Postfach 983, FL-9490 Vaduz, Liechtenstein
FAX: +41 (75) 2375601
TITLE: Editor
CONTACT: Norman Kaufmann
CIRCULATION: 2,000
TYPE: Technology, construction

PUBLISHERS

Botanisch-Zooloogische Gelellschaft

Liechtenstein-Sargans-Werdenberg, Im Bretscha 22, FL-9494 Schaan, Liechtenstein
PHONE: +41 (75) 2324819
FAX: +41 (75) 2332819
E-MAIL: renat@pingnet.li
CONTACT: Georg Willi
SUBJECTS: Animals, Pets, Earth Sciences, Gardening, Plants, Physical Sciences

Frank P van Eck Publishers

Haldenweg, FL-9495 Triesen, Liechtenstein
PHONE: +41 (75) 29557
FAX: +41 (75) 29557
TITLE: Manager
CONTACT: Elizabeth van Eck-Schaedler
SUBJECTS: Art, Sports, Athletics

Liechtenstein Verlag AG

Schwefelstr 33, PO Box 133, FL-9490 Vaduz, Liechtenstein
PHONE: +41 (75) 22414; 23925
FAX: +41 (75) 2324340
E-MAIL: flbooks@verlag_ag.lo.li
TITLE: Man. Director
CONTACT: Albart Piet Schiks
SUBJECTS: Finance, Government, Political Science, History, Law

Lichtensteinische Staatliche Kunstsammlung Vaduz

Staedtle 37, PO Box 370, FL-9490 Vaduz, Liechtenstein
PHONE: +41 (75) 2322341
FAX: +41 (75) 2327864
E-MAIL: lsk@firstlink.li ,
WEBSITE: http://www.firstlink.li/lsk
SUBJECTS: 19th Century Art
TOTAL PUBLISHED: 24 print

Verlag der Liechtensteinischen Akademischen Gesellschaft

Amschragenweg 2, FL-9490 Vaduz, Liechtenstein
PHONE: +41 (75) 22424
FAX: +41 (75) 2320542
E-MAIL: gkieber@interadvice.li
CONTACT: Georg Kieber
SUBJECTS: Government, Political Science, Law
TOTAL PUBLISHED: 3 print

Megatrade AG

Landstrasse 36, FL-9490 Vaduz, Liechtenstein
PHONE: +41 (75) 2375252
FAX: +41 (75) 2375253
E-MAIL: wanger@wanger.net
WEBSITE: http://www.wanger.net
CONTACT: Dr. Markus Wanger
SUBJECTS: Art, Business, Economics, Law
TOTAL PUBLISHED: 29 print

Rheintal Handelsgesellschaft Anstalt

PO Box 444, FL-9495 Triesen, Liechtenstein
PHONE: +41 (75) 921882; 8442786
FAX: +41 (75) 39236464; 8442806
E-MAIL: vetsch.p@bluewin.ch
TITLE: International Rights
CONTACT: Nick U. Schweinfurth
SUBJECTS: Career Development, Education, Interactive AudioCourses in CD-ROM

Topos Verlag AG

Industriestrasse 105, PO Box 551, FL-9491 Ruggell, Liechtenstein

PHONE: +41 (75) 3771111
FAX: +41 (75) 3771119
E-MAIL: topos@lie-net.li
WEBSITE: http://www.topos.li
TITLE: Man. Director
CONTACT: Graham A.P. Smith
SUBJECTS: Economics, Education, Law, Social Sciences, Sociology

RELIGIOUS ORGANIZATIONS

Buddhist

Zen Group Vaduz AZI
Pradafant 30, FL-9490 Vaduz, Liechtenstein
NAME: Gerhard Reuteler

FURTHER READING

Articles

"Cleanup Time: A Lot of European Tax Havens Are Under Increasing International Pressure To Change Rules That Foster Money Laundering." *Time,* September 25, 2000, vol. 156, no. 13, p. B15.

Olsen, Elizabeth. "Liechtenstein Is Found Lax in Monitoring of Bank Deals." *New York Times,* September 1, 2000, p. A4.

Internet

BBC News Online. "Sanctions Threat to 'Tax Havens.'" June 26, 2000. [Online] Available http://news6.thdo.bbc.co.uk/hi/english/business/newsid%5F806000/806236.stm (accessed October 12, 2000).

LIECHTENSTEIN: STATISTICAL DATA

For sources and notes see "Sources of Statistics" at the front of each volume.

GEOGRAPHY

Geography

Area:

Total: 160 sq km.

Land: 160 sq km.

Land boundaries:

Total: 76 km.

Border countries: Austria 35 km, Switzerland 41 km.

Coastline: 0 km (landlocked).

Climate: continental; cold, cloudy winters with frequent snow or rain; cool to moderately warm, cloudy, humid summers.

Terrain: mostly mountainous (Alps) with Rhine Valley in western third.

Natural resources: hydroelectric potential, arable land.

Land use:

Arable land: 24%

Permanent crops: 0%

Permanent pastures: 16%

Forests and woodland: 35%

Other: 25% (1993 est.).

HUMAN FACTORS

Ethnic Division

Alemannic	87.5%
Italian, Turkish, and other	12.5%

Religion

Roman Catholic	80.0%
Protestant	7.4%
Unknown	7.7%
Other	4.9%

Data for 1996.

Demographics (A)

	1990	1995	1998	2000	2010	2020	2030	2040	2050
Population	NA	30.9	31.5	32.2	35.0	36.9	37.8	37.3	35.8
Life expectancy - males	NA	73.8	74.2	75.2	76.7	77.9	78.9	79.7	80.3
Life expectancy - females	NA	79.3	81.9	82.5	83.8	84.8	85.6	86.3	86.8
Birth rate (per 1,000)	NA	13.8	12.4	11.8	9.7	9.9	9.6	9.0	9.3
Death rate (per 1,000)	NA	7.3	6.8	6.7	7.6	9.0	11.3	13.1	14.4
Women of reproductive age (15-49 yrs.)	NA	8.6	8.5	8.6	8.5	8.0	7.8	7.5	6.9
Fertility rate	NA	1.6	1.5	1.5	1.5	1.6	1.6	1.6	1.7

Except as noted, values for vital statistics are in thousands; life expectancy is in years.

Major Languages

German (official), Alemannic dialect.

EDUCATION

Literacy Rates (B)

	National Data	World Data
Adult literacy rate		
1995		
Male	100[1]	81
Female	100[1]	65

Libraries

National Libraries **1997**

Administrative Units 1

Service Points or Branches 2

Number of Volumes (000) 168

Registered Users (000) . . . . NA

Loans to Users (000) 59

Total Library Staff 10

Public Libraries **1997**

Administrative Units 3

Service Points or Branches 3

Number of Volumes (000) 24

Registered Users (000) 135

Loans to Users (000) 75

Total Library Staff 5

GOVERNMENT & LAW

Political Parties

Diet (Landtag)	% of vote	no. of seats
Fatherland Union (VU)	50.1%	13
Progressive Citizens' Party (FBPL)	41.3%	10
The Free List (FL)	8.5%	2

Elections were last held on 2 February 1997 (next to be held by 2001).

Government Budgets (B)

Revenues . . . . $424.2 million

Expenditures . . . . $414.1 million

Data for 1998 est.

LABOR FORCE

Total Labor Force (A)

22,891 of which 13,847 are foreigners; 8,231 commute from Austria and Switzerland to work each day.

Labor Force by Occupation

Industry, trade, and building 45%

Services 53%

Agriculture, fishing, forestry, and horticulture 2%

Data for 1997 est.

Unemployment Rate

1.8% (February 1999)

PRODUCTION SECTOR

Energy Production

Production . . . . 150 million kWh

Data for 1995.

Transportation

Highways:

Total: 250 km.

Paved: 250 km.

Unpaved: 0 km.

Airports: none.

Top Agriculture Products

Wheat, barley, corn, potatoes; livestock, dairy products.

MANUFACTURING SECTOR

GDP & Manufacturing Summary (C)

Total GDP (1998 est.) . . . . $730 million

Per capita (1998 est.) $23,000

Values in purchasing power parity.

COMMUNICATIONS

Daily Newspapers

	National Data	World Data for Comparison
Daily Newspapers		
Number of Dailies	2	8,391
Total Circulation (000)	19	548,000
Circulation per 1,000 inhabitants	602	96

Telecommunications

Telephones - main lines in use: 19,000 (1995).

Telephones - mobile cellular: NA

Telephone system: automatic telephone system.

Domestic: NA

International: linked to Swiss networks by cable and microwave radio relay.

Radio broadcast stations: AM 0, FM 4, shortwave 0 (1998).

Radios: 21,000 (1997).

Television broadcast stations: NA (linked to Swiss networks) (1997).

Televisions: 12,000 (1997).

Internet Service Providers (ISPs): 115 (Liechtenstein and Switzerland) (1999).

FINANCE, ECONOMICS, & TRADE

Economic Indicators

National product: GDP—purchasing power parity—$730 million (1998 est.).

National product real growth rate: NA.

National product per capita: $23,000 (1998 est.).

Inflation rate—consumer price index: 0.5% (1997 est.).

Exchange Rates

Exchange rates:

Swiss francs, franken, or franchi (SFR) per US$1

January 2000	1.5878
1999	1.5022
1998	1.4498
1997	1.4513
1996	1.2360
1995	1.1825

Top Import Origins

Imports (1996): $917.3 million.

Origins (1996): EU countries, Switzerland .

Top Export Destinations

$2.47 billion (1996)

Destinations (1995)

EU and EFTA countries	60.57%
Switzerland	15.70%

Import/Export Commodities

Import Commodities	Export Commodities
Machinery	Small specialty machinery
Metal goods	Dental products
Textiles	Stamps
Foodstuffs	Hardware
Motor vehicles	Pottery

LITHUANIA

Republic of Lithuania
Lietuvos Respublika

CAPITAL: Vilnius.

FLAG: Three equal horizontal bands of yellow (top), green, and red.

ANTHEM: *Tautika Giesme (The National Song).*

MONETARY UNIT: The Lithuanian lita of 100 cents has replaced the transitional system of coupons (talonas) which had been in force since October 1992, when the Soviet ruble was demonetized. There are coins of 1, 2, 5, 10, 20, and 50 cents and 1, 2, and 5 litas, and notes of 10, 20, 50, and 100 litas; litas 1 = $0.25 (or $1 = litas 4.0).

WEIGHTS AND MEASURES: The metric system is in force.

HOLIDAYS: New Year's Day, 1 January; Day of the Restoration of the Lithuanian State, 16 February; Good Friday (movable); Anniversary of the Coronation of Grand Duke Mindaugas of Lithuania, 6 July; National Day of Hope and Mourning, 1 November; Christmas, 25–26 December.

TIME: 2 PM = noon GMT.

LOCATION AND SIZE: Lithuania is located in eastern Europe, bordering the Baltic Sea, between Latvia and Russia. With a total area of 65,200 square kilometers (25,174 square miles), it is slightly larger than the state of West Virginia. Lithuania's boundary length totals 1,372 kilometers (853 miles).

Lithuania's capital city, Vilnius, is located in the southeastern part of the country.

CLIMATE: Lithuania's climate is transitional between maritime and continental. Yearly, the mean temperature is 6.1°C (43°F). The mean temperature in July is 17.1°C (63°F). Rainfall averages from 54 centimeters (21 inches) to 93 centimeters (37 inches), depending on location.

INTRODUCTORY SURVEY

RECENT HISTORY

From the fourteenth to the eighteenth centuries the Grand Duchy of Lithuania was linked to the Kingdom of Poland. What is now Lithuania was annexed to the Russian Empire in 1795. During the nineteenth century a Lithuanian nationalist movement arose.

On February 16, 1918, Lithuania proclaimed its independence. The new Bolshevik government in Moscow (Russia) attempted to seize power in Lithuania, but failed. In July 1920 Moscow recognized Lithuanian independence. However the 1939 Nazi-Soviet pact assigned Lithuania to Soviet control and Soviet forces were stationed on its territory. After proclaiming Lithuania a Soviet Socialist Republic in July 1940, Moscow lost control of the area to Germany in June 1941 but recaptured it in 1944.

Soviet president Mikhail Gorbachev's unrestricted policies allowed Lithuanians to once again seek national self-determination. Lithuanian independence was proclaimed on March 11, 1990, but was not generally recognized until August 1991.

In February 1993 former communist Algirdas Brazauskas was elected president in a general election, but conservatives took back the parliament in 1996 amid growing concerns of corruption. Valdas Adamkus, who had lived in the United States over thirty years after World War II, was elected president in 1998. President Adamkus dedicated to continuing his country's efforts to gain admission to

both the European Union (EU) and the North Atlantic Treaty Organization (NATO). In October 1999 the EU announced Lithuania would be considered for EU membership by 2003.

GOVERNMENT

Lithuania is a parliamentary democracy operating under a 1992 constitution. The chief of state is the president who is elected by popular vote for a five-year term. The head of government is the premier appointed by the president with the approval of parliament. The president on the nomination of the premier appoints the cabinet, called the Council of Ministers.

The legislative branch consists of a unicameral parliament or Seimas. Of the 141 members of Seimas, seventy-one are directly elected by popular vote, and seventy are elected by proportional representation. Members serve four-year terms. Suffrage is universal at eighteen.

Judiciary

The legal system is being transformed from that of the old Soviet regime to a democratic model. A new civil and criminal procedure code and a court reform law were enacted in 1995. The system now consists of a constitutional court and a Supreme Court, a Court of Appeals that hears appellate cases from the district courts, and district and local courts. The judiciary is independent.

Political Parties

The majority party in the Seimas since the 1996 parliamentary elections has been the conservative Homeland Union Party (TS) that won seventy out of 141 seats. The other party of the right wing, the Christian Democrat Party (LKDP) took sixteen seats and entered into a coalition government with TS and the Lithuanian Center Union (LCS) that won thirteen seats.

The Democratic Labor Party (LLDP) composed of mostly ex-communists won twelve seats. Other parties with parliamentary representation included the Lithuanian Social Democratic Party (LSDP) ten seats, and the Lithuanian Democratic Party (DP) two seats.

DEFENSE

The army numbers 7,840. There is a small navy of 1,320 personnel and an air force with 970 members but no combat aircraft. The paramilitary has 3,500 border guards and coast guard of 400. The defense budget for 1999 was $181 million, or 1.5 percent of GDP.

ECONOMIC AFFAIRS

Historically Lithuania's economy was agricultural but during the Soviet dominance a large if somewhat inefficient industrial base grew and accounted for 32 percent of the country's economy by 1998. That same year inflation had been pulled down to 5 percent and the GDP grew at 4.5 percent. However an economic crisis occurred in 1999 due in part to the Russian financial crisis of 1998.

The GDP registered a 3 percent negative growth rate, unemployment increased to 10 percent, and the budget deficit was 8 percent to 9 percent of GDP. Premier Andrius Kubilius took the reigns in November 1999 and committed to an austere 2000 budget to stabilize the economy. Privatization, especially of the energy sector, continued as did attempts to reduce the deficit. EU assession talks were scheduled for early 2000.

Public Finance

The U.S. Central Intelligence Agency (CIA) estimated in 1997 the central government took in $1.5 billion in revenues and had $1.7 billion of expenditures. The 1999 unemployment rate was 10 percent, highest since independence in 1991. The budget deficit was estimated at between 8 percent and 9 percent of GDP.

Income

In 1999 the gross domestic product (GDP) was estimated at $17.3.billion, or about $4,800 per capita. The GDP was estimated to decline by 3 percent in 1999, and inflation was 0.3 percent. The 1998 estimated GDP contribution by sector was agriculture 10 percent, industry 32 percent, and services 58 percent.

Industry

Lithuania underwent rapid industrialization during the Soviet era. Major industries include machine building and metalworking, textiles, leather, and agro-processing. The country's diverse industrial base also includes electric motors, television sets, refrigerators and freezers, petroleum refining, shipbuilding, furniture, fertilizers, agricultural machinery, optical equipment, electronic components, and computers. Due to a rapid program of privatization, about 65 percent of the industrial sector is privately owned.

Banking and Finance

Since 1991 Lithuania has reorganized its banking sector numerous times. On July 3, 1992 the government adopted a new currency unit, the lita, to replace the ruble. As of April 1996 there were twenty-seven registered banks of which eleven were fully operational including one investment bank and three partly state-owned institutions. Lithuania has had its share of banking crises although not on the level experienced in Estonia and more recently Latvia. Between 1992 and 1995 six banks lost their licenses and two were merged. As of mid-1996 sixteen were either suspended or facing bankruptcy procedures. The first serious crisis centered on Aurasbankas, the eighth largest bank in the country, and the deposit bank for many ministries. The Bank of Lithuania suspended Aurasbankas's operations in mid-1995 because of liquidity problems caused by bad lending and deposit-taking practices. Operations at Lithuania's largest bank, the Joint-Stock Innovation Bank, were suspended on December 20, 1995, and those of the Litimpeks bank, the country's second largest, two days later. The two were in the process of merging to create the Lithuania United Bank and the fraud was uncovered during pre-merger audits. Due to rumors of a devaluation of the currency, a shortage of foreign exchange throughout the whole banking sector was created.

By May 1999 only five commercial banks remained. Moreover foreign investment by Sweden helped keep several of the banks operating.

In 1997, a key feature of the new economic framework in Lithuania was the pegging of the lita to a currency basket composed of the dollar and the D-mark. In 1999 the Bank of Lithuania announced its intention to peg the lita to the euro in 2001.

The National Stock Exchange, which opened in September 1993, is the most active in the region, with 245 listed companies.

Economic Development

In 1990 the Lithuanian government began a comprehensive economic reform program aimed at effecting the transformation to a market-driven economy. Reform measures include price reform, trade reform, and privatization. By mid-1993 92 percent of housing and roughly 60 percent of businesses slated for privatization had been privatized. By 1996 about 36 percent of state enterprises and about 83 percent of all state property had been privatized. International aid agencies committed about $765 million of assistance between 1992 and1995. Most international aid goes either to infrastructure construction or loan credits to business.

In 1999 Lithuania, which had conducted the most trade with Russia of any of the Baltic states, faced an economic and financial crisis partly based on the Russian 1998 financial crisis. In November 1999 the Lithuanian government committed to an austere 2000 budget and focused on fiscal restraint, economic stabilization, and accelerated reforms.

Lithuania was scheduled to begin EU assession talks in early 2000.

SOCIAL WELFARE

A national system of social insurance covers all of Lithuania's residents. Old age, sickness, disability, and unemployment benefits are paid on an earnings-related basis. Women receive maternity and day-care benefits. The state also pays universal pensions and other benefits to those not covered through employment.

Healthcare

In 2000 life expectancy was about sixty-nine years. In 1990-1997 there were four physicians for every 1,000 people and public health expenditures were 5 percent of GDP. One side effect of the breakup of the Soviet Union was the dramatic spread of diphtheria. There was a 13 percent increase in diphtheria cases during 1994-1995.

Housing

At the end of 1989 housing floor space totaled 70.8 million square meters (761.8 million square feet). A total of 142,000 families (18 percent of all families) were on waiting lists for housing.

EDUCATION

In 2000 the adult illiteracy rate is estimated at 0.5 percent. Education is free and compulsory for all children between the ages of six and sixteen years. In 1997 primary schools enrolled 225,701 students and secondary enrolled 378,754. At the postsecondary level institutions, over 83,645 pupils were enrolled in 1997. Universities include Kaunas University of Technology; Vilnius Technical University; Vilnius University; and Vytautas Magnus University.

2000 KEY EVENTS TIMELINE

January

- Along with Baltic neighbors Estonia and Latvia, Lithuania signs the Charter of Partnership with NATO.

April

- Lithuania's Roman Catholic Church apologizes for its failure to oppose more openly the Holocaust.
- Lithuania begins exporting power to its neighbor, Estonia.

June

- Russia arrests a Lithuanian that it claims is spying for the United States.
- Lithuanian parliament signs legislation seeking retribution from fifty years of Russian abuse; payments could cost Russia billions.

July

- The United States calls for closure of Lithuania's Chernobyl-style nuclear power plant, Ignalina, which supplies more than 70 percent of the country's electrical needs.

October

- Parliamentary elections take place October 9; the Social Democrat Coalition wins forty-nine seats and the New Union and Liberal Union gain twenty-eight seats each. They are expected to form a coalition government.
- The chairman of the Lithuanian Liberal Union, Rolandas Paksas, is elected prime minister of the coalition government on October 26.

November

- It is announced on November 23 that state radio and television may cease broadcasting on December 4 because of unpaid electricity bills.

ANALYSIS OF EVENTS: 2000

BUSINESS AND THE ECONOMY

Economic reform remained a key priority of President Valdas Adamkus, who stated in his April 20, 2000, state of the union address that the delay of free-market initiatives such as antitrust programs and energy industry restructuring had contributed significantly to the economic difficulties Lithuania experienced in the wake of Russia's 1998 economic crisis. He also criticized the government for failing to cut the nation's large budget deficit. As of 2000 unemployment in Lithuania was at a post-Soviet record of 11 percent.

Energy figured prominently in the health of the Lithuanian economy. The government itself was facing power cuts as of July because it owed the country's main energy company $18 million. However, the greatest energy-related controversy surrounded plans to close one of two power units at the Ignalina nuclear plant by 2005. Under pressure from the European Union (E.U.), Lithuania's parliament passed a bill in May ordering shutdown of the unit, whose design had been described as unsafe by E.U. officials. The decision was highly unpopular within the country, as the plant supplies 80 percent of Lithuania's energy needs, and its closing will force Lithuanians to meet most of their energy needs with imports. In a related story, Kazakhstan agreed to increase oil exports to Lithuania following disputes with Russia, the country's major oil supplier.

GOVERNMENT AND POLITICS

In March Lithuania marked the tenth anniversary of its declaration of independence from the Soviet Union, which set in motion the chain of events that ultimately led to the demise of the U.S.S.R. The occasion was celebrated with a special session of parliament, speeches by President Valdas Adamkus and former nationalist leader Vytautas Landsbergis, and a flag-raising ceremony on Independence Square.

A decade into its existence as an independent state, Lithuania was working toward gaining membership in the E.U. and the North Atlantic Treaty Organization (NATO), while maintaining its historical and geographic ties to Russia. At the end of 1999, Lithuania had been one of seven countries tapped for E.U. membership as early as 2003, but observers claimed that 2007 would be a more realistic target. President Adamkus, a strong supporter of Lithuanian participation in European integration, mentioned 2002 as a target date for NATO membership.

Following inconclusive parliamentary elections in October, four Lithuanian centrist parties formed a coalition government headed by the center-right Liberal Union Party and the center-left New Union. The formation of the new government was supported by President Adamkus.

Lithuanians with past ties to the KGB—the Soviet secret police—came forward in large numbers in early August to beat the deadline for taking advantage of an amnesty law under which they would be guaranteed confidentiality in exchange for confessions, although the confidentiality would not apply if they chose to run for public office or work in non-elective public-sector jobs. Former KGB agents who did not voluntarily confess would, if identified through other means, have their names made public and be forbidden to work for the government for ten years. Leaders of the political opposition vigorously opposed the law, charging that it was a tool for the country's nationalist government to eliminate its left-leaning opponents from the political arena through intimidation. They were planning to challenge the law on grounds of human rights violation.

CULTURE AND SOCIETY

Hundreds of Lithuanians crowded into Independence Square in the capital city of Vilnius to observe the tenth anniversary of their nation's independence and celebrate a decade of progress toward a democratic society and economic recovery.

Efforts to halt illegal westward immigration at Lithuania's border with Belarus served as a reminder that many in Asia were still striving for freedom and decent living conditions. Border guards reported that new surveillance equipment supplied by the E.U. had contributed significantly in cutting down on the number of persons entering the country clandestinely.

In April the Roman Catholic Church in Lithuania issued a formal apology for failing to oppose the Nazi Holocaust more vigorously.

Publicity was garnered by the right-wing Young Lithuania party a month before the October general elections when parliamentary candidate and former Olympic swimmer Birute Uzkuraityte-Statkeviciene swam 500 meters across a lake in her home district with both her hands and feet bound together. The forty-seven-year-old candidate relied on a "seal-like" motion to carry her across the water and, she hoped, into office. In other sports news, Lithuania's national basketball team mounted the strongest challenge yet by foreign players to a U.S. "dream team" made up of National Basketball Association (NBA) players (final score 85–76) and became the first to achieve a second-half lead against such a team.

DIRECTORY

CENTRAL GOVERNMENT

Head of State

President
Valdas Adamkus, Office of the President, Simono Daukanto a. 3, LT-2008 Vilnius, Lithuania
PHONE: +370 (2) 625542
FAX: +370 (2) 225382
E-MAIL: info@president.lt

Prime Minister
Rolandas Paksas, Office of the Prime Minister, Gedimino ave. 11, 2039 Vilnius, Lithuania
PHONE: +370 (2) 622101
FAX: +370 (2) 225382
E-MAIL: info@president.lt

Ministers

Minister of Agriculture
Kestutis Kristinatis, Ministry of Agriculture, Gedimino 19 (Lelevelio 6), LT-2025 Vilnius, Lithuania
PHONE: +370 (2) 621681
FAX: +370 (2) 619953
E-MAIL: zum@zum.lt

Minister of Culture
Gintautas Kevisas, Ministry of Culture, Basanavièiaus g. 5, LT-2600 Vilnius, Lithuania
PHONE: +370 (2) 619486
FAX: +370 (2) 623120
E-MAIL: el.paðtas culture@muza.lt

Minister of Economy
Eugenijus Maldeikis, Ministry of Economy, Gedimino av. 38/2, LT-2600 Vilnius, Lithuania
PHONE: +370 (2) 622416
FAX: +370 (2) 623974

Minister of Education and Science
Algirdas Monkevicius, Ministry of Education and Science, A. Volano g. 2/7, LT-2600 Vilnius, Lithuania
PHONE: +370 (2) 622483
FAX: +370 (2) 612077
E-MAIL: smmin@smm.lt

Minister of Environment
Danius Lygis, Ministry of Environment, A. Jaksto 4/9, 2694 Vilnius, Lithuania
PHONE: +370 (2) 610558
FAX: +370 (2) 616515; 220847
E-MAIL: Danius.Lygis@aplinkuma.lt

Minister of Finance
Jonas Lionginas, Ministry of Finance, J. Tumo-Vaizganto 8a/2, LT-2600 Vilnius, Lithuania
PHONE: +370 (2) 390005; 390100
FAX: +370 (2) 226387
E-MAIL: finmin@finmin.lt

Minister of Foreign Affairs
Antanas Valionis, Ministry of Foreign Affairs, J.Tumo-Vaiþganto g. 2, LT-2600 Vilnius, Lithuania
PHONE: +370 (2) 390005; 390100
FAX: +370 (2)620752; 618689; 221287

Minister of Justice
Gintautas Bartkus, Ministry of Justice, Gedimino pr. 30/1, LT-2600 Vilnius, Lithuania
PHONE: +370 (2) 226615
FAX: +370 (2) 625940

Minister of Defense
Linas Linkevicius, Ministry of Defense, Totoriø 25/3, 2001 Vilnius, Lithuania
PHONE: +370 (2) 618700
FAX: +370 (2) 226082

Minister of Administration Reforms and Municipal Affairs
Jonas Rudalevicius, Ministry of Administration Reforms and Municipal Affairs, Gedimino av. 11, LT-2039 Vilnius, Lithuania
PHONE: +370 (2) 628518
FAX: +370 (2) 226935
E-MAIL: administ@vrsrm.lt

Minister of Social Security and Labor
Vilija Blinkeviciute, Ministry of Social Security and Labor, A. Vivulskio 11, 2693 Vilnius, Lithuania
PHONE: +370 (2) 652283
FAX: +370 (2) 652463
E-MAIL: post@socmin.lt

Minister of Transport and Communications
Striaukas Gintaras, Ministry of Transport and Communications, Gedimino av. 17, 2679 Vilnius, Lithuania
PHONE: +370 (2) 393911
FAX: +370 (2) 224335
E-MAIL: transp@transp.lt

POLITICAL ORGANIZATIONS

Lietuvos Centro Sajunga-LCJ (Center Union of Lithuania)

TITLE: Chairman
NAME: Romualdas Ozolas

Lietuvos Demokratine Darbo Partija-LDDP (Democratic Labor Party of Lithuania)

TITLE: Chairman
NAME: Ceslovas Jursenas

Lietuvos Lenku Rinkimu Akcija-LLRA (Election Action of Lithuania's Poles)

TITLE: Chairman
NAME: Rinkimu Akcija

Tevynes sajunga/Lietuvos konservatoriai-TS-LK (Homeland Union/Conservative Party)

TITLE: Chairman
NAME: Vytautas Landsbergis

Lietuviu Krikšsioniu Demokratu Partija-LKDP (Lithuanian Christian Democratic Party)

TITLE: Chairman
NAME: Algirdas Saudargas

Lietuvos Demokratu Partija-LDP (Lithuanian Democratic Party)

TITLE: President
NAME: Lydie Wurth-Polfer

Lietuvos Tautininku Sajunga-LTS (Lithuanian Nationalist Union)

TITLE: Chairman
NAME: Rimantas Smetona

Lietuvos Socialdemokratu Partija-LSDP (Lithuanian Social Democratic Party)

TITLE: Chairman
NAME: Aloyzas Sakalas

DIPLOMATIC REPRESENTATION

Embassies in Lithuania

Canada
Gedimino pr. 64, 2001 Vilnius, Lithuania
PHONE: +370 (2) 220898
FAX: +370 (2) 220884

China
Algirdo 36, 2006 Vilnius, Lithuania
PHONE: +370 (2) 262861; 262862
FAX: +370 (2) 262682; 290237

France
Didzioji 1, LT-2600 Vilnius, Lithuania
PHONE: +370 (2) 222858; 222979; 222484
FAX: +370 (2) 223530

Germany
Sierakausko 24/8, LT-2600 Vilnius, Lithuania
PHONE: +370 (2) 650272; 263627; 650182
FAX: +370 (2) 231813

Italy
Tauro g. 12, Vilnius, Lithuania
PHONE: +370 (2) 220620; 220621; 220622
FAX: +370 (2) 220405

Russia
Latviu 53, LT-2600 Vilnius, Lithuania
PHONE: +370 (2) 721763
FAX: +370 (2) 723877

JUDICIAL SYSTEM

Supreme Court

Constitutional Court

Gedimino av. 36, LT-2600 Vilnius, Lithuania
PHONE: +370 (2) 226043
FAX: +370 (2) 227975
E-MAIL: mailbox@ConstCourtLt.omnitel.net

Court of Appeals

BROADCAST MEDIA

Lietuvos Radijas

S. Konarskio 49, LT-2600 Vilnius, Lithuania
PHONE: +370 (2) 334471
FAX: +370 (2) 235333
WEBSITE: http://www.lrtv.lt/lr.htm
TITLE: Director
CONTACT: Laima Grumadiené
LANGUAGE: Byelorussian, Lithuanian, Russian, Tartar, Yiddish
TYPE: Public

Radio Vilnius

kor naskio 49, LT-2674 Vilnius, Lithuania
PHONE: +370 (2) 233526; 236627
FAX: +370 (2) 233526
E-MAIL: ravil@rtv.lrtv.ot.lt
WEBSITE: http://www.lrtv.lt/lr.htm
TITLE: Managing Director
CONTACT: Laima Grumadiene
LANGUAGE: English, Lithuanian

Kedainiu Krasto TV

Kedainiu TV, Valdybos Culturos Contras, Radvilu 5, LT-5030 Kedainiai, Lithuania
PHONE: +370 (57) 53947
FAX: +370 (57) 65894
TITLE: Director
CONTACT: Vytoldas Burneika
CHANNEL: 35, R9
TYPE: Municipal

Klaipédos TV

Klaipédos municipaliné televizijos studijas, Vilties 12, LT-Klaipéda, Lithuania
PHONE: +370 (61) 11701
TITLE: Director
CONTACT: Vytautas Peckus
CHANNEL: R12
TYPE: Municipal

Marijampolés Televizija

Kauno 13, LT-4520 Marijampolé, Lithuania
PHONE: +370 (43) 51687
FAX: +370 (43) 50606
TITLE: Director
CONTACT: Stasys Baublys BOTH
TYPE: Municipal

Lietuvos Radijas ir Televizija

Konarskio 43, LT-2674, Vilnius MTP, Lithuania
PHONE: +370 (2) 633182
FAX: +370 (2) 263282
WEBSITE: http://www.lrtv.lt
TITLE: Directorate General
CONTACT: Arvydas Ilginis
TYPE: Government

COLLEGES AND UNIVERSITIES

Vilnius Gediminas Technological University

Sauletekio Aleja 11, LT-2040 Vilnius, Lithuania
PHONE: +370 (2) 763760
FAX: +370 (2) 700112
E-MAIL: vtu.rector@vtu.lt
WEBSITE: http://www.vtu.lt

Vilnius University

Universiteto 3, LT-2734 Vilnius, Lithuania
PHONE: 370 (2) 687001
FAX: 370 (2) 687096
E-MAIL: info@vu.lt
WEBSITE: http://www.vu.lt

Vytautas Magnus University

Daukanto 28, LT-3000 Kaunas, Lithuania
PHONE: 370 (7) 222739
FAX: +370 (7) 203858

Kaunas University of Technology

K. Donelaicio st.73, LT-3006 Kaunas, Lithuania
PHONE: +370 (7) 300000; 300099; 324140
FAX: +370 (7) 324144
E-MAIL: rastine@cr.ktu.lt
WEBSITE: http://www.ktu.lt

NEWSPAPERS AND MAGAZINES

Akistata

UAB Kriminalistika, 16 Zemales Str., Kaunas, Lithuania
PHONE: +370 (7) 251272
FAX: +370 (7) 251382
TITLE: Editor-in-Chief
CONTACT: V. Zutautas

Diena (The Day)

UAP Tiesa, Laisves pr. 60, LT-2056 Vilnius, Lithuania
PHONE: +370 (2) 429933
FAX: +370 (2) 421790
TITLE: Editor-in-Chief
CONTACT: Domas Sniukas
CIRCULATION: 35,000

Echo Litvy

Laisves pr. 60, LT-2600 Vilnius, Lithuania
PHONE: +370 (2) 428463
FAX: +370 (2) 428636
E-MAIL: echo.litvy@mail.iti.lt
TITLE: Editor
CONTACT: Vasilij Jemeljanov
CIRCULATION: 55,000

Kauno Diena

UAB Kauno Diena, 27 Vytauto pr., LT-3687 Kaunas, Lithuania
PHONE: +370 (7) 741971
FAX: +370 (7) 227404
E-MAIL: redakcija@kaunodiena.lt
WEBSITE: http://www.kaunodiena.lt
TITLE: Editor-in-Chief
CONTACT: Tekle Maciuliene

Klaipeda Daily

LT-5800, Šauliu 21, Klaipeda, Lithuania
E-MAIL: office@klaipeda.daily.lt
WEBSITE: http://www.klaipeda.daily.lt

Kurier Wilenski (Vilnius Express)

Liasves pr. 60, LT-2056 Vilnius, Lithuania
PHONE: +370 (2) 426963
FAX: +370 (2) 427265
TITLE: Editor-in-Chief
CONTACT: Czeslaw Malewski
CIRCULATION: 31,710

Laikinoki Sostine

Joint Stock Co. Lietuvos Rytas, 7 Laisves al., LT-3000 Kaunas, Lithuania
PHONE: +370 (7) 220388
FAX: +370 (7) 203242
E-MAIL: daily@lrytas.ot.it
TITLE: Editor
CONTACT: V. Rachlevicius

Lietuvos Aidas (Echos of Lithuania)

Kestucio g. 54, LT-3000 Kaunas, Lithuania
PHONE: +370 (7) 209900
TITLE: Editor-in-Chief
CONTACT: Roma Grinbergiene
CIRCULATION: 79,500

Lietuvos Rytos (Lithuania's Morning)

Lietuvos Rytas Co., Gedimino 12A, LT-2001 Vilnius, Lithuania
PHONE: +370 (2) 226389
FAX: +370 (2) 227656
E-MAIL: daily@lrytas.lt
WEBSITE: http://www.lrytas.lt
TITLE: Editor-in-Chief
CONTACT: Gedvydas Vainauskas
CIRCULATION: 75,000

Lietuvos Sportas

Odminits Str. 9, LT-2600 Vilnius, Lithuania
FAX: +370 (2) 616757
TITLE: Editor
CONTACT: Bronius Cekanauskas
CIRCULATION: 8,000
TYPE: Sports and recreation, general

Lithuanian Weekly

PO Box 53, LT-2024 Vilnius, Lithuania
PHONE: +370 (2) 224283
FAX: +370 (2) 223730
TITLE: Editor-in-Chief
CONTACT: Vitas Katilius
CIRCULATION: 15,000

Panevezio Rytas

15 Ramygalos Str., LT-5319 Panevezys, Lithuania
PHONE: +370 (5) 434134
FAX: +370 (5) 437232
TITLE: Editor-in-Chief
CONTACT: Liuda Jonusiene

Respublika

UAB Dienrastis Respublika, A. Smetonos Str. 2, LT-2600 Vilnius, Lithuania
PHONE: +370 (2) 223112
FAX: +370 (2) 223538
E-MAIL: respublika@mail.tipas.lt
WEBSITE: http://www.randburg.com/li/respublika.html
TITLE: Editor-in-Chief
CONTACT: Vitas Tomkus
CIRCULATION: 70,000

Valstieciu laikrastis

UAB Valstieciu Iaikrastis, 60 Laisves pr., LT-2056 Vilnius, Lithuania
PHONE: +370 (2) 421281
FAX: +370 (2) 427564
E-MAIL: valst@taka.lt
TITLE: Editor-in-Chief
CONTACT: Jonas Svoba
CIRCULATION: 91,000

Verslo Zinios

CJ-V "Verslo Zinios", Gostauto St. 129, LT-2000 Vilnius
PHONE: +370 (2) 613104
FAX: +370 (2) 613196
E-MAIL: vzinios@vzinios.com
WEBSITE: http://www.vzinios.com
TITLE: Editor
CONTACT: Rolandas Barysas
CIRCULATION: 10,000

Balistica

Universiteto 3, LT-2734 Vilnius, Lithuania
FAX: +370 (2) 221754
E-MAIL: baltistica@flf.vu.lt
TITLE: Editor
CONTACT: Bonifacas Stundzia
CIRCULATION: 500
TYPE: Language arts, linguistics

Karalius KNK

PO Box 114, LT-3005 Kaunas, Lithuania
E-MAIL: jo@socl.klp.osf.lt
WEBSITE: http://www.soften.ktu.lt/~kaleck/KoksNorsKelias
TITLE: Editor
CONTACT: Jonas Oskinis
TYPE: Music, general

Karys

Pamenkalnio ul., 13, LT-2600 Vilnius, Lithuania
FAX: +370 (2) 613410
TITLE: Editor
CONTACT: M. Barkauskas
CIRCULATION: 1,300
TYPE: History, military, general

Kataliku Pasaulis

Pranciskonu 3-6, LT-2001 Vilnius, Lithuania
TITLE: Editor
CONTACT: Ausvydas Belickas
CIRCULATION: 13,000
TYPE: Religion, Roman Catholicism

Literatura ir Menas

Universiteto 4, LT-2600 Vilnius, Lithuania
FAX: +370 (2) 610831
TITLE: Editor
CONTACT: A. Slepikas
CIRCULATION: 7,600
TYPE: Political science, general

Lietuviu Kalbotyros Klausimai

Antakalnio 6, LT-2055 Vilnius, Lithuania
FAX: +370 (2) 226573
TITLE: Editor
CONTACT: Kazys Morkunas
CIRCULATION: 500
TYPE: Language arts, linguistics

Lietuvos Fizikos Zhurnalas

A. Gostauto 12, LT-2600 Vilnius, Lithuania
FAX: +370 (2) 618464
E-MAIL: shileika@uj.pfi.lt
TITLE: Editor
CONTACT: Algirdas Shileika
CIRCULATION: 600
TYPE: Science, physics, optics

Lithuania Infoservice

PO Box 673, LT-5815 Klaipeda Lithuania
FAX: +370 (6) 229879
TITLE: Editor
CONTACT: Igor Balenko
CIRCULATION: 10,000
TYPE: Social science, general

PUBLISHERS

Algarve

Rinktines 3/11, LT-2600 Vilnius, Lithuania
PHONE: +370 (2) 725910; 721635
FAX: +370 (2) 721462
TITLE: Publisher
CONTACT: Algimantas Matulevicius
SUBJECTS: Advertising, Fiction, Health, Nutrition, Science (General), Esoteric, Applied Health Education Literature
TOTAL PUBLISHED: 40 print

Alma Littera

Sermuksniu 3, LT-2600 Vilnius, Lithuania
PHONE: +370 (2) 617927; 624695
FAX: +370 (2) 617927
E-MAIL: post@almali.lt
WEBSITE: http://www.almali.lt
TITLE: Director
CONTACT: Arvydas Andrijauskas
SUBJECTS: English as a Second Languages
TOTAL PUBLISHED: 600 print; 8 audio

Klaipedos Universiteto Leidykla

H Manto 84, LT-5800 Klaipeda, Lithuania
PHONE: +370 (6) 398900
FAX: +370 (6) 398902

E-MAIL: rektorius@reut.ku.lt
WEBSITE: http://www.ku.lt
TITLE: Manager
CONTACT: Lolita Zemliene
SUBJECTS: Biological Sciences, Education, History, Maritime, Mathematics, Science (General), Social Sciences
TOTAL PUBLISHED: 300 print

Lietus Ltd.

A Jakto 8/10, LT-2600 Vilnius, Lithuania
PHONE: +370 (2) 312298
FAX: +370 (2) 312298
TITLE: International Rights
CONTACT: Agne Kudirkaite
SUBJECTS: Education, Fiction, Nonfiction (General)
TOTAL PUBLISHED: 70 print

Lietuvos Rasytoju Sajungos Leidykla (Lithuanian Writers' Union Publishers)

K Sirvydo 6, LT-2600 Vilnius, Lithuania
PHONE: +370 (2) 221433
FAX: +370 (2) 628945
E-MAIL: rsleidykla@is.lt
WEBSITE: http://www.rsleidykla.lt
TITLE: Director
CONTACT: Giedre Soriene
SUBJECTS: Fiction, Literature, Literary Criticism, Essays, Poetry
TOTAL PUBLISHED: 45 print

Mokslo ir enciklopediju leidybos institutas

23 L Asanaviciutes St., LT-2050 Vilnius, Lithuania
PHONE: +370 (2) 458526; 457980; 458528
FAX: +370 (2) 458537
E-MAIL: meli@meli.taide.lt
TITLE: Director
CONTACT: Rimantas Kareckas
SUBJECTS: Agriculture, Biological Sciences, History, Language Arts, Literature, Mathematics, Medicine, Nursing, Dentistry, Physics, Social Sciences

Sviesa Publishers

Vytauto Ave. 25, LT-3000 Kaunas, Lithuania
PHONE: +370 (7) 341834
FAX: +370 (7) 342032
E-MAIL: sviesa@balt.net
WEBSITE: http://www.sviesa.lt
TITLE: Director
CONTACT: Jonas Barcys
SUBJECTS: Education
TOTAL PUBLISHED: 360

Svietimo ir mokslo ministerijos Leidybos centras

Gelezinio vilko 12, LT-2600 Vilnius, Lithuania
PHONE: +370 (2) 617480; 611060; 616081
FAX: +370 (2) 617480
E-MAIL: office@smmlc.elnet.lt
TITLE: Director
CONTACT: Kareckas Rimantas
SUBJECTS: English as a Second Language, Education, History, Mathematics, Music, Dance, Religion

Tyto Alba Publishers

J Jasinskio 10, LT-2001 Vilnius, Lithuania
PHONE: +370 (2) 625602
FAX: +370 (2) 625602
E-MAIL: tytoalba@taide.lt
TITLE: Director
CONTACT: Lolita Varanaviciene
SUBJECTS: Art, Business, Fiction, Nonfiction (General), Philosophy
TOTAL PUBLISHED: 200 print

Vaga Ltd.

Gedimino pr 50, LT-2600 Vilnius, Lithuania
PHONE: +370 (2) 626443; 616002; 613448
FAX: +370 (2) 616902
E-MAIL: vaga@post.omnitel.net
TITLE: Director
CONTACT: Arturas Mickevicius
SUBJECTS: Art, Biography, Fiction, Literature, Literary Criticism, Essays, Religion

RELIGIOUS ORGANIZATIONS

Buddhist

Kaunas Zen Group
Box 609, LT-3021 Kaunas, Lithuania
PHONE: +370 9822063
FAX: +370 (7) 268572
E-MAIL: muailit@takas.lt
TITLE: Teacher
NAME: Myong Oh Sunim

Ko Bing Sa-Vilnius Zen Center
Rulikii 19, LT-2016 Vilnius, Lithuania
PHONE: +370 345746
E-MAIL: hubertasagne@takas
WEBSITE: http://www.zen.lt/
NAME: Hubertas Petrus

Catholic

Lithuanian Caritas Federation
Aukstaiciu 10, LT-3005 Kaunas, Lithuania
PHONE: +370 (7) 323548
FAX: +370 (7) 205549
TITLE: General Director
NAME: Rev. Robertas Grigas

Jewish

Central Synagogue of Vilnius-Chabad
12 Saltiniu g. Street, LT-2006 Vilnius, Lithuania
PHONE: +370 (2) 250387
E-MAIL: office@chabad.osf.lt
WEBSITE: http://www.fjc.ru/lithuania.htm
TITLE: Chief Rabbi
NAME: Rabbi Sholom Ber Krinsky

Protestant

Evangelical Lutheran Church of Lithuania
Bretkuno Street 13, LT-5900 Taurage, Lithuania

Mission of Adventist Church
Lithuanian Mission Field of Seventh-Day Adventists, Pašiles 122, LT-3031 Kaunas, Lithuania
PHONE: +370 7798619
FAX: +370 7351754
WEBSITE: http://www.tagnet.org/bauc/en

Scientology

Vilniaus Centras Dianetika
a/d 42, LT-2000 Vilnius, Lithuania
PHONE: +370 610961; 619973

FURTHER READING

Articles

"Lithuania: Leftists Win, But Fail." *New York Times,* October 10, 2000, p. A6.

"Lithuania to Seek Damages," *Reuters,* June 28, 2000.

"Lithuania—Small Wonder. *The Economist (US),* October 14, 2000, vol. 357, no. 8192, p. 61.

"US Calls for Closure of Lithuania Nuclear Plant," *Reuters* July 20, 2000.

Books

Noble, John, et al., eds. *Estonia, Latvia, and Lithuania.* 2nd ed. London: Lonely Planet, 2000.

LITHUANIA: STATISTICAL DATA

For sources and notes see "Sources of Statistics" at the front of each volume.

GEOGRAPHY

Geography

Area:

Total: 65,200 sq km.

Land: 65,200 sq km.

Land boundaries:

Total: 1,273 km.

Border countries: Belarus 502 km, Latvia 453 km, Poland 91 km, Russia (Kaliningrad) 227 km.

Coastline: 99 km.

Climate: transitional, between maritime and continental; wet, moderate winters and summers.

Terrain: lowland, many scattered small lakes, fertile soil.

Natural resources: peat, arable land.

Land use:

Arable land: 35%

Permanent crops: 12%

Permanent pastures: 7%

Forests and woodland: 31%

Other: 15% (1993 est.).

HUMAN FACTORS

Demographics (A)

	1990	1995	1998	2000	2010	2020	2030	2040	2050
Population	3,703	3,673	3,642	3,621	3,560	3,557	3,470	3,365	3,214
Life expectancy - males	66.4	61.9	62.8	63.1	65.8	68.7	71.3	73.4	75.2
Life expectancy - females	76.2	74.8	75.2	75.4	77.2	79.5	81.4	82.9	84.1
Birth rate (per 1,000)	15.3	10.9	9.9	9.8	12.5	10.9	9.5	9.7	8.5
Death rate (per 1,000)	10.8	13.2	12.9	12.9	12.9	12.3	12.4	13.2	14.2
Women of reproductive age (15-49 yrs.)	923.2	917.2	927.3	933.1	917.4	819.1	772.4	691.4	648.9
Fertility rate	2.0	1.5	1.4	1.3	1.7	1.8	1.7	1.6	1.5

Except as noted, values for vital statistics are in thousands; life expectancy is in years.

Health Personnel

	National Data	World Data (wtd ave)
Total health expenditure as a percentage of GDP, 1990-1998[a]		
Public sector	7.2	2.5
Private sector	1.0	2.9
Total[b]	8.3	5.5
Health expenditure per capita in U.S. dollars, 1990-1998[a]		
Purchasing power parity	533	561
Total	240	483
Availability of health care facilities per 100,000 people		
Hospital beds 1990-1998[a]	960	330
Doctors 1992-1995[a]	137	122
Nurses 1992-1995[a]	366	248

Health Indicators

	National Data	World Data
Life expectancy at birth (years)		
1980	71	61
1998	72	67
Daily per capita supply of calories		
1970	NA	2,358
1997	3,261	2,791
Daily per capital supply of protein		
1997 (grams)	98	74
Total fertility rate (births per woman)		
1980	2.0	3.7
1998	1.4	2.7
People living with (1997)		
Tuberculosis (cases per 100,000)	78.7	60.4
HIV/AIDS (% aged 15 - 49 years)	0.01	0.99

Infants and Malnutrition

	National Data	World Data (wtd ave)
Under 5 mortality rate (1989)	23	NA
% of infants with low birthweight (1992-98)[1]	4	17
Births attended by skilled health staff (% of total births 1996-98)	100	52
% fully immunized at 1 year of age (1995-98)[1]		
TB	99	82
DPT	93	77
Polio	88	77
Measles	97	74
Prevalence of child malnutrition (1992-98)[1] (based on weight for age, % of children under 5 years)	NA	30

Ethnic Division

Lithuanian 80.6%
Russian 8.7%
Polish 7.0%
Byelorussian 1.6%
Other 2.1%

Religion

Roman Catholic (primarily), Lutheran, Russian Orthodox, Protestant, evangelical Christian Baptist, Muslim, Jewish.

Major Languages

Lithuanian (official), Polish, Russian.

EDUCATION

Public Education Expenditures

	1997
Public expenditures on education as % of GNP	5.4
Expenditures per student as % of GNP per capita	
Primary	NA
Secondary	28.5
Tertiary	42.1
Pupils per teacher at the primary level	16
Duration of primary education in years	9
World data for comparison	
Public expenditures on education as % of GNP (mean)	4.8
Pupils per teacher at the primary level (wtd ave)	33
Duration of primary education in years (mean)	9

Educational Attainment (B)

	1995	1997
Gross enrollment ratio (%)		
Primary level	95.9	98.0
Secondary level	84.2	86.3
Tertiary level	28.2	31.4

Literacy Rates (B)

	National Data	World Data
Adult literacy rate		
1980		
Male	98	75
Female	95	58
1995		
Male	100	81
Female	99	65

Libraries

National Libraries **1997**
Administrative Units 1
Service Points or Branches 15
Number of Volumes (000) 5,878
Registered Users (000) 23
Loans to Users (000) 35
Total Library Staff 596

Public Libraries **1997**
Administrative Units 61
Service Points or Branches 1,478
Number of Volumes (000) 23,168
Registered Users (000) .779
Loans to Users (000) .20,942
Total Library Staff 4,089

GOVERNMENT & LAW

Military Affairs (A)

	1990	1995	1996	1997
Military expenditures				
Current dollars (mil.)	NA	73[e]	80	127
1997 constant dollars (mil.)	NA	76[e]	81	127
Armed forces (000)	10	12	12	12
Gross national product (GNP)				
Current dollars (mil.)	16,700[e]	13,900[e]	14,800	15,600
1997 constant dollars (mil.)	18,500[e]	14,400[e]	15,000	15,600
Central government expenditures (CGE)				
1997 constant dollars (mil.)	NA	4,080[e]	3,980	4,560
People (mil.)	3.7	3.7	3.6	3.6
Military expenditure as % of GNP	NA	0.5	0.5	0.8
World data on military expenditure as % of GNP	4.5	2.7	2.6	2.6
Military expenditure as % of CGE	NA	1.9	2.1	2.8
World data on military expenditure as % of CGE	17.0	10.5	10.3	10.2
Military expenditure per capita (1997 $)	NA	21	22	35
World data on military expenditure per capita (1997 $)	242	146	143	145
Armed forces per 1,000 people (soldiers)	2.6	3.3	3.3	3.3
World data on armed forces per 1,000 people (soldiers)	5.3	4.1	3.9	3.8
GNP per capita (1997 $)	4,990	3,940	4,140	4,330
Arms imports[6]				
Current dollars (mil.)	0	5	20	5
1997 constant dollars (mil.)	0	5	20	5
Total imports[7]				
Current dollars (mil.)	1,084	3,649	4,468	5,644
1997 constant dollars (mil.)	1,202	3,778	4,542	5,644
Total exports[7]				
Current dollars (mil.)	1,145	2,705	3,335	3,860
1997 constant dollars (mil.)	1,269	2,801	3,391	3,860
Arms as percent of total imports[8]	0	0.1	0.4	0.1
Arms as percent of total exports[8]	0	0	0	0

Political Parties

Parliament (Seimas)	no. of seats
Homeland Union/Conservative Party (TS)	69
Christian Democratic Party (LKDP)	15
Lithuanian Center Union (LCS)	15
Democratic Labor Party of Lithuania (LDDP)	12
Lithuanian Social Democratic Party (LSDP)	10
Democratic Party (DP)	2
Independents	12
Others	6

Elections were last held 20 October and 10 November 1996 (next to be held in October 2000).

Government Budgets (A)

Year: 1998

Total Expenditures: 13,037.6 Millions of Litai

Expenditures as a percentage of the total by function:

General public services and public order	12.46
Defense	3.10
Education	6.05
Health	15.46
Social Security and Welfare	32.25
Housing and community amenities	0
Recreational, cultural, and religious affairs	2.24
Fuel and energy	0.24
Agriculture, forestry, fishing, and hunting	4.93
Mining, manufacturing, and construction	0.61
Transportation and communication	5.89
Other economic affairs and services	0.51

Crime

Crime volume (for 1998)

Crimes reported	78,149
Total persons convicted	31,650
Crimes per 100,000 population	2,057

Persons responsible for offenses

Total number suspects	25,373
Total number of female suspects	3,428
Total number of juvenile suspects	3,720

LABOR FORCE

Total Labor Force (A)

1.8 million.

Labor Force by Occupation

Industry	30%
Agriculture	20%
Services	50%

Data for 1997 est.

Unemployment Rate

10% (1999)

PRODUCTION SECTOR

Energy Production

Production	15.58 billion kWh
Production by source	
Fossil fuel	13.09%
Hydro	4.30%
Nuclear	82.61%
Other	0%
Exports	7 billion kWh

Data for 1998.

Energy Consumption

Consumption	7.829 billion kWh
Imports	340.000 million kWh

Data for 1998.

Transportation

Highways:

Total: 71,375 km.

Paved: 64,951 km (including 417 km of expressways).

Unpaved: 6,424 km (1998 est.).

Waterways: 600 km perennially navigable.

Pipelines: crude oil, 105 km; natural gas 760 km (1992).

Merchant marine:

Total: 52 ships (1,000 GRT or over) totaling 316,319 GRT/351,700 DWT.

Ships by type: cargo 23, combination bulk 11, petroleum tanker 2, rail car carrier 1, refrigerated cargo 11, roll-on/roll-off 1, short-sea passenger 3 (1999 est.).

Airports: 96 (1994 est.).

Airports - with paved runways: 25.

Airports - with unpaved runways: 71.

Top Agriculture Products

Grain, potatoes, sugar beets, flax, vegetables; beef, milk, eggs; fish.

Top Mining Products (B)

Mineral resources include: peat.

COMMUNICATIONS

Daily Newspapers

	National Data	World Data for Comparison
Daily Newspapers		
Number of Dailies	19	8,391
Total Circulation (000)	344	548,000
Circulation per 1,000 inhabitants	93	96

Telecommunications

Telephones - main lines in use: 1.048 million (1997).

Telephones - mobile cellular: 297,500 (1998).

Telephone system: inadequate but is being modernized to provide an improved international capability and better residential access.

Domestic: a national fiber-optic cable interurban trunk system is nearing completion; rural exchanges are being improved and expanded; mobile cellular systems are being installed; access to the Internet is available; still many unsatisfied telephone subscriber applications.

International: landline connections to Latvia and Poland; major international connections are to Denmark, Sweden, and Norway by submarine cable for further transmission by satellite.

Radio broadcast stations: AM 3, FM 112, shortwave 1 (1998).

Radios: 1.9 million (1997).

Television broadcast stations: 82 (mainly repeater stations) (1998).

Televisions: 1.7 million (1997).

Internet Service Providers (ISPs): 10 (1999).

FINANCE, ECONOMICS, & TRADE

Economic Indicators

National product: GDP—purchasing power parity—$17.3 billion (1999 est.).

National product real growth rate: -3% (1999 est.).

National product per capita: $4,800 (1999 est.).

Inflation rate—consumer price index: 0.3% (1999 est.).

Exchange Rates

Exchange rates:

Litai per US$1 . . . . .4.000

Fixed rate since 1 May 1994.

Top Import Origins

$4.5 billion (f.o.b., 1999)

Origins (1999)

Russia	20.4%
Germany	16.5%
Denmark	3.8%
Belarus	2.2%
Latvia	2.0%

Top Export Destinations

$3.3 billion (f.o.b., 1999)

Destinations (1999)

Russia	17.4%
Germany	15.8%
Latvia	12.7%
Denmark	5.9%
Belarus	5.2%

(Continued on next page.)

MANUFACTURING SECTOR

GDP & Manufacturing Summary (B)

	1980	1985	1990	1993	1994	1995
Gross Domestic Product						
Millions of 1990 dollars	6,892	8,497	12,179	5,476	5,530	5,694
Growth rate in percent	NA	0.00	5.74	−17.14	0.99	2.97
Per capita (in 1990 dollars)	2,008	2,369	3,282	1,460	1,477	1,524
Manufacturing Value Added						
Millions of 1990 dollars	NA	NA	4,490	2,446	2,470	2,522[e]
Growth rate in percent	NA	NA	NA	−16.98	0.99	2.10[e]
Manufacturing share in percent of current prices	37.8	35.2	35.4	46.8[e]	NA	NA

FINANCE, ECONOMICS, & TRADE (cont.)

Foreign Aid

Recipient: $228.5 million (1995).

Import/Export Commodities

Import Commodities	Export Commodities
Machinery and equipment 30%	Machinery and equipment 19%
Mineral products 16%	Mineral products 19%
Chemicals 9%	Textiles and clothing 19%
Textiles and clothing 9%	Chemicals 10%
Foodstuffs	Foodstuffs

Balance of Payments

	1994	1995	1996	1997	1998
Exports of goods (f.o.b.)	2,029	2,706	3,413	4,192	3,962
Imports of goods (f.o.b.)	−2,234	−3,404	−4,309	−5,340	−5,480
Trade balance	−205	−698	−896	−1,147	−1,518
Services - debits	−376	−498	−677	−897	−868
Services - credits	322	485	798	1,032	1,109
Private transfers (net)	39	49	72	131	133
Government transfers (net)	118	61	73	100	103
Overall balance	−94	−614	−723	−981	−1,298

LUXEMBOURG

CAPITAL: Luxembourg.

FLAG: The flag is a tricolor of red, white, and blue horizontal stripes.

ANTHEM: *Ons Hémecht (Our Homeland).*

MONETARY UNIT: The Luxembourg franc (LFr) of 100 centimes is a paper currency equal in value to the Belgian franc. There are coins of 25 and 50 centimes and 1, 5, 10, and 20 francs, and notes of 50 and 100 francs. Belgian currency is legal tender in Luxembourg, and bills of 500, 1,000, and 5,000 Belgian francs are regularly circulated. LFr1 = $0.03204 (or $1 = LFr31.21).

WEIGHTS AND MEASURES: The metric system is the legal standard.

HOLIDAYS: New Year's Day, 1 January; Labor Day, 1 May; public celebration of the Grand Duke's Birthday, 23 June; Assumption, 15 August; All Saints' Day, 1 November; Christmas, 25–26 December. Movable religious holidays include Shrove Monday, Easter Monday, Ascension, and Pentecost Monday.

TIME: 1 PM = noon GMT.

LOCATION AND SIZE: A landlocked country in Western Europe, Luxembourg has an area of 2,586 square kilometers (998 square miles), slightly smaller than the state of Rhode Island. It has a total boundary length of 356 kilometers (221 miles). Luxembourg's capital city, also named Luxembourg, is located in the southcentral part of the country.

CLIMATE: Summers are generally cool, with a mean temperature of about 17°C (63°F); winters are seldom severe, average temperature being about 0°C (32°F). Precipitation throughout the country averages about 74 centimeters (29 inches) annually.

Grand Duchy of Luxembourg
French— *Grand-Duché de Luxembourg*
German— *Grossherzogtum Luxemburg*

INTRODUCTORY SURVEY

RECENT HISTORY

After World War II the government agreed to form an economic union with Belgium and the Netherlands. The first phase, the Benelux Customs Union, took effect in 1948. In February 1958 representatives of the three countries signed a treaty of economic union. During the postwar decades Luxembourg also became an active member of the North Atlantic Treaty Organization (NATO) and became one of the six founding countries of the European Economic Community that later became the European Union.

In April 1963 Luxembourg celebrated its 1,000th anniversary as an independent state. On November 12, 1964, Grand Duchess Charlotte abdicated in favor of her son, Jean, who became grand duke and who remained so as of 1994. His reign was marked by continued prosperity as Luxembourg's economy shifted from dependence on steel to an emphasis on services, notably international banking. In January 1999 Luxembourg joined the European Monetary Union in launching the euro.

In December 1999 the Grand Duke Jean announced he would abdicate in favor of his eldest son Prince Henri in September 2000.

GOVERNMENT

Luxembourg is a constitutional monarchy, with hereditary power passed down through the house of Nassau-Weilbourg. Legislative power is vested in the Chamber of Deputies with the sixty members elected by popular vote for five-year

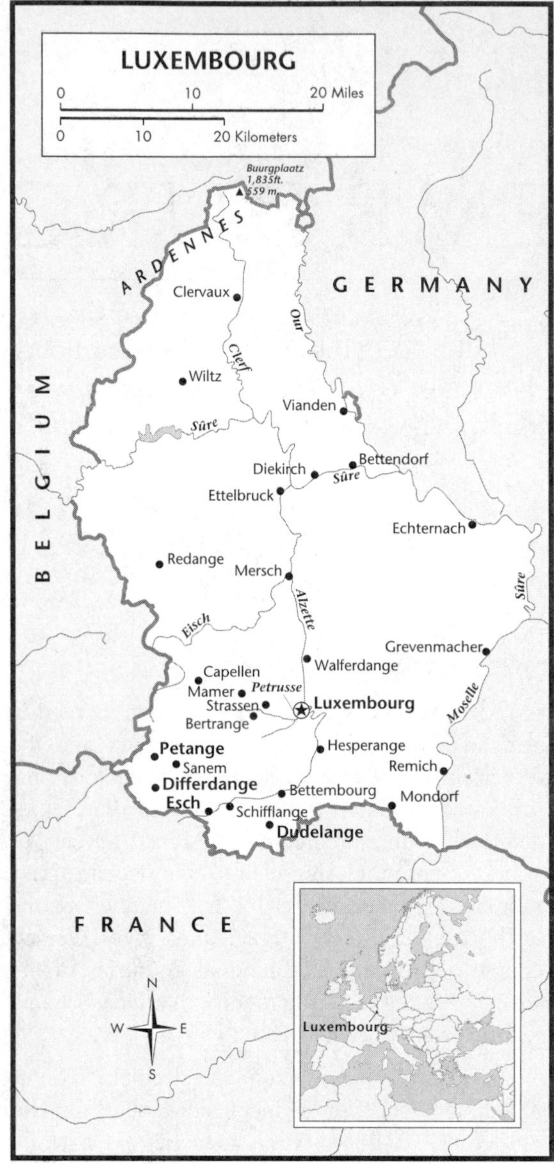

terms. In addition, the Council of State, composed of 21 members appointed for life by the sovereign, acts as a consulting body in legislative, administrative, and judicial matters and has the right of suspensive veto.

Executive power rests jointly in the monarch, the chief of state, who may initiate legislation and a prime minister, president of the government, who is appointed by the monarch and who in turn selects a cabinet, the Council of Ministers. Voting is compulsory and eligibility begins at age eighteen.

Judiciary

Minor cases generally come before a justice of the peace. On a higher level are the two district courts, one in the city of Luxembourg and the other in Diekirch. The Superior Court of Justice acts as a court of appeal. The Court of Assizes, within the jurisdiction of the Superior Court, deals with criminal cases. Luxembourg is the site of the European Court of Justice.

Political Parties

Since 1947 the country has been governed by shifting coalitions among the three largest parties, The Christian Social People's Party (Parti Chrétien Social-CSV) which favors progressive labor legislation and protection for farmers and small business; the Luxembourg Socialist Workers' Party (LSAP) which supports expanding social welfare programs; and, the Democratic Party (DP) which favors minimal government activity in the economy. Two other parties that secured seats in the Chamber of Deputies in 1999 were the Green Party and the Marxist and Reformed Communist Party DEI LENK (the Left).

DEFENSE

In 1967 Luxembourg abolished conscription and created a volunteer military force that is part of the North Atlantic Treaty Organization (NATO). In 2000 its army consisted of one infantry battalion of 768 and a police force of 612. Luxembourg has no air force or navy. Budgeted defense expenditures in 1998 were $142 million, or 0.8 percent of GDP.

ECONOMIC AFFAIRS

In relation to its size and population, Luxembourg is one of the most highly industrialized countries in the world with stable economy, low inflation, and low unemployment. Its standard of living rivals that of any country in Europe. Steel production, once the dominant industry, has declined since the 1970s. Aiming for diversification, plastics, rubber, chemicals, and other light industries have been developed. Banking and other service industries are a major part of the economy and have more than made up for a decline in steel.

The gross domestic product increased by 4.2 percent in 1999. The unemployment rate was 2.7 percent in mid-1997. Luxembourg has close trade and financial ties to Belgium and the Netherlands, and has all the open market and advantages of belonging to the European Union. It joined the euro in January 1999.

Public Finance

The budget of the Luxembourg government is presented to the Chamber of Deputies late in each calendar year and becomes effective the following year. Government budgets showed steady surpluses from 1984 to 1990. The 1990 surplus, amounting to 3.4 percent of GDP, enabled the government to channel additional monies into investment funds and into a budget reserve exceeding LFr6 billion ($160 million). That a budget reserve exists at all reflects the conservatively healthy management of Luxembourg's public finances.

Continued funding of the government's investment program largely caused deficits in 1991 and 1992. To fund the program the government draws from accumulated surpluses and raises capital in financial markets.

The U.S. Central Intelligence Agency estimated that in 2000 government revenues totaled approximately $4.73 billion and expenditures $4.71 billion.

The government's budget balance in 1996 amounted to 0.8 percent of GDP; government gross debt came to 5.9 percent of GDP that year.

Income

In 1999 Luxembourg's gross domestic product (GDP) was estimated at $14.7 billion, or $34,200 per capita. The 1999 estimated GDP growth rate was 4.2 percent and inflation was 1.1 percent. The 1999 estimated GDP composition by sector was agriculture 1 percent, industry 23 percent, and services 76 percent.

Industry

Massive reorganization of the steel industry and continuing diversification of industries characterized the 1980s. In 1997 steel was responsible for 29 percent of all exports. Chemicals, rubber, metal processing, glass, aluminum, engineering, and food processing gained importance.

Banking and Finance

Banking has been gaining in importance since the 1970s. By 1980 the sector accounted for 18 percent of the GDP. The principal bank and the sole bank of issue is the International Bank of Luxembourg (Banque Internationale à Luxembourg), founded in 1856. The Belgium-Luxembourg monetary agreement, as renewed for 10 years in 1991, provided for the establishment of the Luxembourg Monetary Institute to represent the nation at international monetary conferences and institutions. The banking sector has benefitted from favorable laws governing holding companies. The European Investment Bank (an institution of the European Union) and the European Monetary Fund are headquartered in Luxembourg. As a financial center Luxembourg has the advantages of strict banking secrecy, a trained multilingual workforce, and a government that is sympathetic to the sector's needs. These last two factors are proving attractive to the developing cross-border insurance business.

Faced with the impossibility of raising capital through its steel industry alone, Luxembourg has always been open to the financial world. But its current success in the field owes more to legislation in neighboring countries and external economic factors than to any deliberate policy on the part of the government.

The Euro-markets have made Luxembourg the home of Cedel Bank, one of the two international clearing and settlement depositories, and has also had a positive effect on issues in Luxembourgish francs. In 1995 these represented 3.4 percent of world issues in terms of value.

Luxembourg controls about 90 percent of Europe's offshore investment funds, making it the fourth largest world market.

The Luxembourg Bourse (stock exchange), founded in 1929 in the city of Luxembourg, primarily handles stocks and bonds issued by domestic companies, although it also lists Belgian securities.

Economic Development

The keystone of the economic system is free enterprise, and the government has attempted to promote the well-being of private industry by every means short of direct interference. The full-employment policy pursued by every postwar government has produced a high ratio of economically active, highly skilled, population to total population. The government encourages the diversification of industry by tax concessions and remains supportive of the financial sector. Adopting the euro in 1999 will further its ties with a more integrated European economy.

SOCIAL WELFARE

A broad system of social insurance covers practically all employees and their families. In the late 1980s Luxembourg ranked second in the world after Sweden in spending on social security and housing as a percentage of the national budget.

Sickness, maternity, old age, disability, and survivors' benefits are paid. Birth, maternity, child, and education allowances are also provided to all residents.

Although women are legally entitled to equal pay for equal work, their salaries on average are 9 percent to 25 percent lower than men's earnings.

Healthcare

Luxembourg has an advanced national health service supervised by the Ministry of Public Health. Public health facilities are available to physicians, and treatment of patients is on a private basis. Hospitals are operated either by the state or by the Roman Catholic Church. Public health facilities are available to physicians, and treatment of patients is on a private basis. In 1995 there were 780 physicians (two per 1,000 inhabitants) and 217 dentists. In 1994 there were thirty-four hospitals with 4,560 beds (11.3 per 1,000 inhabitants).

The average life expectancy is seventy-seven years. Leading causes of death in 1992 were circulatory/heart diseases (1,686); cancer (996); road accidents (76); and suicides (59). There were 107 cases of AIDS in 1996.

Housing

The immediate post-World War II housing shortage has been relieved by large-scale construction of private homes and apartment buildings.

EDUCATION

There is practically no adult illiteracy. School attendance is compulsory between the ages of six and fifteen. Pupils attend primary schools for six years and then enter secondary schools for a period of up to seven years. In 1997 school enrollment included 28,437 elementary pupils with 1,844 teachers. In 1997 there were 28,796 pupils in secondary schools with 2,836 teachers. Post-secondary institutions include the Central University of Luxembourg, Superior Institute of Technology, and teacher training schools. The most advanced students attend institutions of higher learning in Belgium and France.

2000 KEY EVENTS TIMELINE

March

- It is reported that nearly two-thirds of all offshore funds are registered in Luxembourg.

June

- A gunman takes a nursery school by storm, holding twenty-five children and three teachers hostage for thirty hours. A policeman shoots the gunman in the head; no one else was injured.
- The OECD classifies Luxembourg as a tax haven, calling for stricter regulation.

September

- The coronation of Crown Prince Henri, is postponed on September 19 until October 7 due to the poor health of his younger brother, Prince Guillaume, who remains in a coma from a car crash in Paris.
- Emergency fuel talks are held September 21 in Luxembourg in an attempt to halt European protests.

October

- Grand Duke Jean retires, leaving the duchy to his son Henri on October 7.
- Luxembourg banks are forced to mitigate secrecy rules October 27 as U.S. authorities study bank accounts for tax evasion.

November

- On November 1 Luxembourg Prime Minister Jean-Claude Juncker warns against hasty eastward E.U. expansion.

ANALYSIS OF EVENTS: 2000

BUSINESS AND THE ECONOMY

Luxembourg is Europe's fifth most-prosperous state. Gross domestic product (GDP) rose by 4.6 percent in 2000 while the unemployment rate stood at 2.6 percent of the labor force. The general government budget recorded a comfortable surplus of 2.4 percent of GDP. Its strong growth rate led to an increase of cross-border workers, as Luxembourg's own economy cannot supply enough workers to the labor market. The large flow of cross-border workers strained Luxembourg's pension funds. Although employees pay social security contributions, they retire abroad, meaning that the Grand Duchy exported an ever-larger proportion of its pension payments.

Employment in the financial service sector continued to grow by 7 percent in 2000 and 213 banks operate in the country. Luxembourg's investment fund sector was the largest in Europe. The government actively encouraged the expansion of financial services. To that effect, the government passed laws to make the Grand Duchy a center for cross-border pensions and mortgage-backed bonds. It hoped to create the right environment for the sale of private pensions funds. Fund managers could then manage the pension assets for multinational companies on behalf of their employees.

There was good reason to focus on the development of pension fund management since pressures by the United States and the European Union (E.U.) were forcing the government to relax its rules on banking confidentiality. In October 2000 Parliament passed a law to provide legal help to the U.S. federal government in criminal cases that could include tax fraud. This law marked a significant weakening of Luxembourg's banking secrecy. Moreover, the E.U. planned to introduce rules on taxing non-residents' savings, which were currently not taxed in Luxembourg. The new tax rule would force Luxembourg to revise its banking secrecy principle with regard to accounts held by E.U. citizens.

GOVERNMENT AND POLITICS

Since 1994 Jean-Claude Juncker has been Luxembourg's prime minister. His party, the Christian Social People's party, has held nineteen seats in Parliament since the June 1999 general election, when it formed a coalition with the liberal Democratic Party, which held fifteen seats. Government policy has continued essentially unchanged for the past few years. Fiscal prudence and bolstering Luxembourg's competitiveness through diversification continued to be the priorities.

The government faced two hot issues: pensions and education. In 1999 the previous coalition government revamped the public sector pension system by cutting pensions from 83 percent of final salary to 72 percent. This reform damaged the previous coalition's popularity and especially hurt the Socialist Party, but more reform was necessary. Education was more complex. Critics said the existing educational system was old-fashioned and inflexible, leading to high dropout rates. Some of the problems with the educational system, however, can be traced to the fact that nearly half of the school population was of foreign origin, and many students struggled with the two languages of instruction—German and Luxembourgish. The education issue was also linked to Luxembourg's goal of economic diversification. Partly to offset its dependence on financial services, the government and private sector have made efforts to position Luxembourg as one of Europe's main communication centers. Internet companies and media conglomerates already operated in Luxembourg. The government has pledged to increase funding and to reform the school curriculum to endow future labor force entrants with the appropriate skills.

Luxembourg's long-standing enthusiasm for closer cooperation with its European neighbors has been tempered by the prospect of institutional changes which would lessen its voting weight in the European Parliament and EU Council of Ministers. The future expansion of the E.U. to twenty-five or perhaps thirty members would diminish Luxembourg's role.

The next election was scheduled for June 2004.

CULTURE AND SOCIETY

Grand Duke Jean, age seventy-nine, was supposed to step down after a thirty-six-year reign in favor of his son, Prince Henri, forty-five, in late September. The event was to be a gala occasion. But the injury of thirty-seven-year-old prince Guillaume in a serious car accident on September 10 forced the Grand Duke to postpone the festivities. The country has prepared for Prince Henri's rise to throne since 1998 when the Grand Duke vested his oldest son with the powers to sign legislation. The Duke also decided in 1998 that Luxembourg's quota of euro coins to be entered into circulation in 2002 should have Henri's head and not his own.

Luxembourg's strong growth attracted not only cross-border workers but also immigrants from further afield. The immigrant population constituted 35 percent of the total populace in 2000. If current trends continued, then the total population would double by the year 2025 and reach 700,000. Such a rapid increase in population growth brought scores of new problems. It meant that Luxembourg must invest in roads, infrastructure, schools, and hospitals. The key, according to many observers, was to focus on high value-added industries that do not rely on much labor power.

DIRECTORY

CENTRAL GOVERNMENT

Head of State

Grand Duke
Henri, Grand Ducal Palace, L-2013 Luxembourg

President of the Government, Prime Minister, Minister of Labour and Employment, Finance and the Treasury
Jean-Claude Juncker, Office of the Prime Minister and Ministry of State, Hotel de Bourgogne, 4 rue de la Congrégation, L-2910 Luxembourg
FAX: +352 461720

Ministers

Vice-Prime Minister
Lydie Polfer, Vice-Prime Minister, 5 rue Notre Dame, L-2940 Luxembourg
FAX: +352 223144

Minister of Agriculture, Viticulture and Rural Development
Fernand Boden, Ministry of Agriculture, Viticulture and Rural Development, 4 rue de la Congrégation, L-2913 Luxembourg
FAX: +352 464027

Minister of Justice, Budget, European Union and Monetary Union, Relations with Parliament
Luc Frieden, Ministry of Justice, 16 boulevard Royal, L-2934 Luxembourg
FAX: +352 227661

Minister of the Family, Women's Affairs and the Handicapped
Marie-Josée Jacobs, Ministry of the Family, 12–14 avenue Emile Reuter, L-2919 Luxembourg
FAX: +352 4786570

Minister of Educational and Vocational Training, Minister of Culture and Religion
Erna Hennicot-Schoepges, Ministry of Cultural and Religious Affairs, 20 montée de la Petrusse, L-2912 Luxembourg
FAX: +352 402427

Minister of Interior, Civil Service and Administrative Reform
Michel Wolter, Ministry of the Interior, 15 rue Beaumont, L-2933 Luxembourg

Minister of Economy, Public Works and Energy
Henri Grethen, Ministry of Economy and Trade, 6 boulevard Royal, L-2914 Luxembourg
FAX: +352 460448

Minister of Health, Physical Education and Sports
Carlo Wagner, Ministry of Health, 57 boulevard de la Petrusse, L-2935 Luxembourg
FAX: +352 491337

Minister of Environment
Charles Goerens, Ministry of Environment, Plateau de St. Esprit, L-2915 Luxembourg
FAX: +352 462682

Minister of Social Security
Carlo Wagner, Ministry of Social Security, 26 rue Zithe, L-2936 Luxembourg
FAX: +352 4786328

State Secretary for Foreign Affairs, Foreign Trade and Cooperation
Lydie Polfer, Chambré des Députés, 9 rue du Saint-Esprit, L-1475 Luxembourg
PHONE: +352 466966
FAX: +352 220203

POLITICAL ORGANIZATIONS

Parti Chrétien Social-PCS (Christian Social People's Party)

4 rue de l'Eau, L-1449 Luxembourg
PHONE: +352 225731
FAX: +352 472716
E-MAIL: csv@chd.lu
TITLE: President
NAME: Erna Hennicot-Schoepges

Parti Ourvier Socialiste Luxembourgeois-POSL (Socialst Workers' Party of Luxembourg)

16 rue de Crécy, L-1364 Luxembourg
PHONE: +352 455991
FAX: +352 456575
E-MAIL: lasp@chd.lu
TITLE: President
NAME: Jean Asselborn

Parti Democratique-PD (Democratic Party)

46 Grand rue, L-1669 Luxembourg
PHONE: +352 455991
FAX: +352 541620
E-MAIL: groupdp@chd.lu

TITLE: President
NAME: Lydie Würth-Polfer

Comité d'Action pour la Démocratie et la Justice-CADJ (Action Committee for Democracy and Justice)

9 rue de la Loge, L-1945 Luxembourg
PHONE: +352 463742
FAX: +352 463745
E-MAIL: adr@chd.lu
TITLE: President
NAME: Roby Mehlen

Déi Gréng (The Greens)

BP 454, L-2014 Luxembourg
PHONE: +352 463740
FAX: +352 463743
E-MAIL: greng@greng.lu
TITLE: Secretary
NAME: Jean Huss

Parti Communiste Luxembourgeois (Communist Party)

16 rue Christophe Plantin, L-2339 Luxembourg-Gasperich
PHONE: +352 492095
FAX: +352 496920
TITLE: President
NAME: Andre Hoffman

Déi Lénk (The Left)

BP 1228, L-1012 Luxembourg
PHONE: +352 426193
FAX: +352 426193
E-MAIL: info@dei-lenk.lu

DIPLOMATIC REPRESENTATION

Embassies in Luxembourg

Belgium
4 rue de Girondins, L-1626 Luxembourg
PHONE: +352 442746
FAX: +352 454182
TITLE: Ambasssador
NAME: Willy de Valck

Czech Republic
5 rue Notre Dame, L-2240 Luxembourg

France
8 blvd. Joseph 2, L-1840 Luxembourg
PHONE: +352 457271
FAX: +352 403016
TITLE: Ambasssador
NAME: Jane Debenest

Germany
20–22 avenue Emile Reuter, L-2420 Luxembourg
PHONE: +352 4534451
FAX: +352 455604
TITLE: Ambasssador
NAME: Horst Pakowski

Netherlands
5 rue C.M. Spoo, L-2546 Luxembourg
PHONE: +352 227570
FAX: +352 403016
TITLE: Ambasssador
NAME: J.S.L. Gualthérie van Weezel

Poland
5 rue Notre Dame, L-2240 Luxembourg

Slovakia
5 rue Notre Dame, L-2240 Luxembourg

United Kingdom
14 blvd Roosevelt, L-2450 Luxembourg
PHONE: +352 229864
FAX: +352 229867
TITLE: Ambasssador
NAME: John Nicholas Elam

United States
22 blvd E. Servais, L-2535 Luxembourg
PHONE: +352 460123
FAX: +352 461401
TITLE: Ambasssador
NAME: Clay Constatinou

JUDICIAL SYSTEM

High Court of Justice

Palais du Justice, 12 Côte D'Eich, L-1450 Luxembourg
PHONE: +352 475981

BROADCAST MEDIA

CLT-UFA

45 Boulevard, Pierre Frieden, L-2850 Luxembourg
PHONE: +352 421422175
FAX: +352 421422756
WEBSITE: http://www.clt-ufa.com
TITLE: President
CONTACT: Alain Berwick
TYPE: Commercial

CLT Multi Media

45 Boulevard, Pierre Frieden, L-1543 Luxembourg-Kirchberg, Luxembourg
PHONE: +352 421421
FAX: +352 421422760
WEBSITE: http://www.cltmulti.com
TITLE: Managing Director
CONTACT: Rémy Sautter
CHANNEL: 7, 21, 24, 27, 41

RTL

177 rue de Luxembourg, L-8077 Bertrange, Luxembourg
PHONE: +352 2527251
FAX: +352 252725431
WEBSITE: http://www.rtl.lu
TYPE: Local

COLLEGES AND UNIVERSITIES

Superior Institute of Technology

6 Rue Coudenhoue - Kalergi, L-1359 Luxembourg - Kirchberg, Luxembourg
PHONE: +352 420101
FAX: + 352 432124
E-MAIL: admin@ist.lu
WEBSITE: http://www.ist.lu

Conservatoire de Musique

33 Rue Charles Martel, L-2134 Luxembourg, Luxembourg

Fachhochschule - Abt Trier - Luxembourg

52 Boulevard De La Petrusse, L-2320 Luxembourg, Luxembourg

Centre Universitaire de Luxembourg

162A Avenue de la Faiencerie, L-1511 Luxembourg, Luxembourg
PHONE: +352 466644-1
FAX: +352 466644-506
E-MAIL: informations_academiques@cu.lu
WEBSITE: http://www.cu.lu

Sacred Heart University at Luxembourg

25 B Boulevard Royal, L-2449 Luxembourg, Luxembourg
PHONE: +352 227613
FAX: +352 227623
E-MAIL: shulacad@pt.lu
WEBSITE: http://www.shu.lu

NEWSPAPERS AND MAGAZINES

L'Avenir du Luxembourg

Editions de l'Avenir, rue des Deportes 38, L-6700 Arlon, Belgium
PHONE: +32 (63) 231020
FAX: +32 (63) 234289
TITLE: Editor-in-Chief
CONTACT: Jean-Luc Henquinet
CIRCULATION: 33,500

Le Jeudi

WEBSITE: http://www.le-jeudi.lu
TITLE: Editor-in-Chief
CONTACT: Jean Portante
CIRCULATION: 5,040

Journal des 3 Frontieres

E-MAIL: 3frontieres@pi.be

Letzebuerger Journal

Editions Letzebuerger Journal S.A., rue Adolphe Fischer 123, BP 2101, L-1021 Luxembourg, Luxembourg
PHONE: +352 4930331
FAX: +352 492065
E-MAIL: journal@logic.lu
WEBSITE: http://www.journal.lu
TITLE: Editor
CONTACT: Rob Roemen
CIRCULATION: 13,000

Luxemburger Wort/La Voix du Luxembourg

Imprimerie Saint Paul S.A., rue Christophe Plantin 2, BP 1908, L-2339 Luxembourg, Luxembourg
E-MAIL: publicite@isp.lu; wort@isp.lu
WEBSITE: http://www.wort.lu
TITLE: Editor
CONTACT: Leon Zeches
CIRCULATION: 87,777

LW Annonceblad

Imprimerie Saint Paul S.A., rue Christophe Plantin 2, BP 1908, L-2339 Luxembourg, Luxembourg
FAX: +352 491078
E-MAIL: christian.stoehr@isp.lu
WEBSITE: http://www.isp.lu

Tageblatt

Editpress Luxembourg S.A., 44 rue du Canal, L-4050 Esch-sur-Alzette, Luxembourg
PHONE: +352 5471311
FAX: +352 541761
E-MAIL: annonces@tabeblatt.lu
WEBSITE: http://www.tageblatt.lu
TITLE: Editor
CONTACT: Alvid Sold
CIRCULATION: 30,028

Zeitung vum Letzeburger Vollek

Cooperative Ouvriere de Presse ed d'Edition, rue Christophe Plantin 16, BP 2106, L-1021 Luxembourg, Luxembourg
PHONE: +352 492101
FAX: +352 496920
TITLE: Editor
CONTACT: Ali Ruckert
CIRCULATION: 8,000

Carriere

BP 2535, L-1025 Luxembourg, Luxembourg
FAX: +352 573282
TITLE: Editor-in-Chief
CONTACT: Monique Mathieu
TYPE: Women's general interest

Letzebuerger Gemengen

24, rue Michel Rodange, L-4660 Differdange, Luxembourg
PHONE: +352 584546
FAX: +352 584919
E-MAIL: admin@sud-zeitung.lu
WEBSITE: http://www.sud-zeitung.lu
TYPE: Social science, business and economics, general

Luxembourg Business

25 rue Philippe II, L-2340 Luxembourg, Luxembourg
FAX: +352 470056
E-MAIL: e-mail@business.lu
WEBSITE: http://www.business.lu
TITLE: Editor
CONTACT: Simon Gray
CIRCULATION: 5,200
TYPE: Business and economics, general

Luxembourg News

25 rue Philippe II, L-2340 Luxembourg, Luxembourg
FAX: +352 470056
E-MAIL: email@news.lu
WEBSITE: http://www.news.lu
TITLE: Editor
CONTACT: Duncan Roberts
CIRCULATION: 4,500
TYPE: Social science, general

PUBLISHERS

Editions APESS ASBL

17 rue Muller-Fromes, L-9261 Diekirch, Luxembourg
PHONE: +352 808358
FAX: +352 802813
E-MAIL: apess@ci.educ.lu
CONTACT: Carlo Felten
SUBJECTS: Art, Education, History, Literature, Literary Criticism, Essays, Philosophy, Poetry, Science (General)
TOTAL PUBLISHED: 35 print

Eiffes Romain

293 Avenue de Luxembourg, L-4940 Bascharage, Luxembourg
PHONE: +352 651052
E-MAIL: rend@pt.lu
CONTACT: Romain Eiffes
SUBJECTS: English as a Second Language, Music, Dance, Poetry
TOTAL PUBLISHED: 3 print

Editions Objectif Lune

One rue de Schoenfels, L-8151 Bridel, Luxembourg
PHONE: +352 335233
FAX: +352 335230
E-MAIL: j-p.kieffer@objectif-lune.lu
WEBSITE: http://www.objectif-lune.lu
TITLE: President
CONTACT: Jean-Paul Kieffer
SUBJECTS: Drama, Theater, Film, Photography

Op der Lay

19 rue d'Eschdorf, L-9650 Esch-Sure, Luxembourg
PHONE: +352 839742
FAX: +352 899350
E-MAIL: opderlay@pt.lu
WEBSITE: http://www.webplaza.pt.lu/public/opderlay
CONTACT: Robert Gollo Steffen
SUBJECTS: Music, Dance, Poetry, Travel
TOTAL PUBLISHED: 7 audio

Editions Phi

PO Box 66, L-6401 Echternach, Luxembourg
PHONE: +352 728006
FAX: +352 728325
E-MAIL: phi@phi.lu
TITLE: Man. Director
CONTACT: Van Francis Maele
SUBJECTS: Art, Drama, Theater, Literature, Literary Criticism, Essays
TOTAL PUBLISHED: 320 print

Editions Promoculture

14 rue Duchscher, L-1424 Luxembourg
PHONE: +352 480691
FAX: +352 400950
E-MAIL: promoculture@ibm.net
CONTACT: Albert Daming
SUBJECTS: Accounting, Economics, Education, Finance, Law, Mathematics, Regional Interests

Service Central de la Statistique et des Etudes Economiques (STATEC)

BP304, L-2013 Luxembourg
E-MAIL: statec.post@statec.etat.lu
TITLE: Director
CONTACT: Robert Weides
SUBJECTS: Agriculture, Business, Economics, Finance, Labor, Industrial Relations, Library & Information Sciences, Public Administration, Social Sciences

Service Central des Imprimes et des Fournitures de Bureau de l'Etat

22 rue des Bruyeres, L-1274 Howald, Luxembourg
PHONE: +352 498811916
FAX: +352 400881
E-MAIL: claude.schaber@scie.etat.lu
CONTACT: Claude Schaber
SUBJECTS: Archaeology, Art, Law, Natural History, Public Administration
TOTAL PUBLISHED: 973

RELIGIOUS ORGANIZATIONS

Atheist

La Libre Pensée Luxembourgeoise
Letzeburger Freidenkenbond, BP 198, L-2011 Luxembourg, Luxembourg
PHONE: +352 329110

Liberté de Conscience (LIBCO)
BP 18, L-5801 Hesperange, Luxembourg
E-MAIL: theodore.pescatore@sip.etat.lu
WEBSITE: http://members.forfree.at/~libco/

Catholic

Action Catholique des Femmes du Luxembourg (ACFL)
5, Marie-Therese, BP 313, L-2013 Luxembourg, Luxembourg
PHONE: +352 44743255
FAX: +352 44743257
TITLE: President
NAME: Gisele Kirsch-Toussing

Orthodox

SS Peter and Paul Russion Orthodox Church
c/o Priest Sergei Poukh,10, Rue J. p. Probst, L-2352 Luxembourg, Luxembourg
PHONE: +352 453383
TITLE: Priest
NAME: Sergei Poukh

FURTHER READING

Articles

"Police Sniper Ends Siege at Luxembourg Nursery School." *Financial Times,* June 2, 2000.

Books

Dun and Bradstreet's Export Guide to Luxembourg. Parsippany, NJ: Dun & Bradstreet, 1999.

LUXEMBOURG: STATISTICAL DATA

For sources and notes see "Sources of Statistics" at the front of each volume.

GEOGRAPHY

Geography

Area:

Total: 2,586 sq km.

Land: 2,586 sq km.

Land boundaries:

Total: 359 km.

Border countries: Belgium 148 km, France 73 km, Germany 138 km.

Coastline: 0 km (landlocked).

Climate: modified continental with mild winters, cool summers.

Terrain: mostly gently rolling uplands with broad, shallow valleys; uplands to slightly mountainous in the north; steep slope down to Moselle flood plain in the southeast.

Natural resources: iron ore (no longer exploited), arable land.

Land use:

Arable land: 24%

Permanent crops: 1%

Permanent pastures: 20%

Forests and woodland: 21%

Other: 34%

HUMAN FACTORS

Ethnic Division

Celtic base (with French and German blend), Portuguese, Italian, and European (guest and worker residents).

Religion

Roman Catholic	97%
Protestant and Jewish	3%

Demographics (A)

	1990	1995	1998	2000	2010	2020	2030	2040	2050
Population	NA	409.8	426.5	437.4	492.6	542.4	580.0	597.4	594.1
Life expectancy - males	NA	72.9	73.6	73.8	75.6	77.0	78.2	79.1	79.9
Life expectancy - females	NA	80.2	79.7	80.6	82.3	83.6	84.7	85.5	86.2
Birth rate (per 1,000)	NA	13.2	12.8	12.4	11.5	11.5	10.8	10.1	9.7
Death rate (per 1,000)	NA	9.3	9.2	8.9	8.8	8.9	9.5	10.7	11.9
Women of reproductive age (15-49 yrs.)	NA	104.2	107.8	109.9	120.6	125.3	129.3	128.5	120.8
Fertility rate	NA	1.7	1.7	1.7	1.7	1.7	1.7	1.7	1.7

Except as noted, values for vital statistics are in thousands; life expectancy is in years.

Major Languages

Luxembourgian, German, French, English.

EDUCATION

Educational Attainment (A)

Age group (1991) . . . . .25+
Population of this age group 262,628
Highest level attained (%)
No schooling . . . . .NA
First level
Not completed 39.7
Completed . . . . .NA
Entered second level 40.3
Entered post-secondary 10.8

Libraries

National Libraries 1997
Administrative Units 1
Service Points or Branches 2
Number of Volumes (000) 607
Registered Users (000) .9.1
Loans to Users (000) 128
Total Library Staff 37
Public Libraries 1997
Administrative Units 2
Service Points or Branches 5
Number of Volumes (000) 528
Registered Users (000) 1,772
Loans to Users (000) 1,990
Total Library Staff 153

GOVERNMENT & LAW

Political Parties

Chamber of Deputies	% of vote	no. of seats
Christian Social People's Party (CSV)	29.79%	19
Democratic Party (DP)	21.58%	15
Luxembourg Socialist Workers' Party (LSAP)	23.75%	13
Action Committee for Democracy and Pension Rights (ADR)	10.36%	6
Green Party	9.09%	2
Marxist and Reformed Communist Party DEI LENK (the Left)	3.77%	2

Elections were last held 13 June 1999 (next to be held by June 2004).

Government Budgets (B)

Revenues . . . .$4.73 billion
Expenditures . . . .$4.71 billion
Data for 2000 est.

Crime

Crime volume (for 1998)
Crimes reported 27,155
Total persons convicted 10,759
Crimes per 100,000 population 6,409
Persons responsible for offenses
Total number suspects 13,162
Total number of female suspects 1,618
Total number of juvenile suspects 1,114

(Continued on next page.)

LABOR FORCE

Total Labor Force (A)

236,400 (one-third of labor force is foreign workers, mostly from Portugal, Italy, France, Belgium, and Germany) (1998 est.).

Labor Force by Occupation

Services 83.2%
Industry 14.3%
Agriculture 2.5%
Data for 1998 est.

Unemployment Rate

2.7% (1999 est.)

PRODUCTION SECTOR

Energy Production

Production .382 million kWh
Production by source
Fossil fuel 60.73%
Hydro 24.86%
Nuclear 0%
Other 14.41%
Exports . . . . .900 million kWh
Data for 1998.

Energy Consumption

Consumption . . . . .5.856 billion kWh
Imports . . . . .6.400 billion kWh
Data for 1998.

Transportation

Highways:

Total: 5,166 km.

Paved: 5,166 km (including 118 km of expressways).

Unpaved: 0 km (1998 est.).

Waterways: 37 km; Moselle.

Pipelines: petroleum products 48 km.

Merchant marine:

Total: 48 ships (1,000 GRT or over) totaling 1,283,738 GRT/1,872,071 DWT.

Ships by type: bulk 2, chemical tanker 10, container 1, liquified gas 18, passenger 4, petroleum tanker 6, roll-on/roll-off 7 (1999 est.).

Airports: 2 (1999 est.).

Top Agriculture Products

Barley, oats, potatoes, wheat, fruits, wine grapes; livestock products.

Top Mining Products (B)

Mineral resources include: iron ore (no longer exploited).

GOVERNMENT & LAW (cont.)

Military Affairs (A)

	1990	1992	1995	1996	1997
Military expenditures					
Current dollars (mil.)	89	109	116	124	134
1997 constant dollars (mil.)	104	121	120	126	134
Armed forces (000)	1	1	1	1	1
Gross national product (GNP)					
Current dollars (mil.)	12,200	13,700	15,200	15,900	16,600
1997 constant dollars (mil.)	14,200	15,200	15,700	16,200	16,600
Central government expenditures (CGE)					
1997 constant dollars (mil.)	4,580	5,460	6,090	6,410	NA
People (mil.)	0.4	0.4	0.4	0.4	0.4
Military expenditure as % of GNP	0.7	0.8	0.8	0.8	0.8
World data on military expenditure as % of GNP	4.5	3.4	2.7	2.6	2.6
Military expenditure as % of CGE	2.3	2.2	2.0	2.0	NA
World data on military expenditure as % of CGE	17.0	12.5	10.5	10.3	10.2
Military expenditure per capita (1997 $)	273	309	294	303	319
World data on military expenditure per capita (1997 $)	242	173	146	143	145
Armed forces per 1,000 people (soldiers)	2.6	2.6	2.4	2.4	2.4
World data on armed forces per 1,000 people (soldiers)	5.3	4.5	4.1	3.9	3.8
GNP per capita (1997 $)	37,300	38,800	38,400	39,000	39,600
Arms imports[6]					
Current dollars (mil.)	30	30	140	100	60
1997 constant dollars (mil.)	35	33	145	102	60
Total imports[7]					
Current dollars (mil.)	7,596	8,221	9,938	9,515	9,323
1997 constant dollars (mil.)	8,895	9,114	12,290	9,674	9,323
Total exports[7]					
Current dollars (mil.)	7,041	6,691	7,815	7,210	6,971
1997 constant dollars (mil.)	8,246	7,418	8,092	7,330	6,971
Arms as percent of total imports[8]	0.4	0.4	1.4	1.1	0.6
Arms as percent of total exports[8]	0	0	0	0	0

MANUFACTURING SECTOR

GDP & Manufacturing Summary (A)

	1980	1985	1990	1995
GDP ($-1990 mil.)[1]	6,329	7,164	8,898	10,033[e]
Per capita ($-1990)[1]	17,386	19,520	23,594	24,650[e]
Manufacturing share (%) (current prices)[1]	25.1	24.0	21.9	19.9[e]
Manufacturing				
Value added ($-1990 mil.)[1]	1,670	1,946	2,316	2,340
Industrial production index	69	84	100	102
Value added ($ mil.)	1,168	944	2,130	2,459[e]
Gross output ($ mil.)	3,269	2,916	6,057	7,272
Employment (000)	38	37	36	34[e]
Profitability (% of gross output)				
Intermediate input (%)	71	73	73	72[e]
Wages and salaries inc. supplements (%)	26[e]	18[e]	18[e]	18[e]
Gross operating surplus	3[e]	9[e]	9[e]	10[e]
Productivity ($)				
Gross output per worker	92,439	84,771	196,286	213,982[e]
Value added per worker	29,294	24,952	57,389	67,558[e]
Average wage (inc. supplements)	23,530[e]	15,415[e]	34,185[e]	41,841[e]
Value added ($ mil.)				
Food products	31	33	67	118[e]
Beverages	33[e]	24[e]	58[e]	75[e]
Tobacco products	9[e]	6[e]	15[e]	19[e]
Textiles	24	15[e]	88[e]	171[e]
Wearing apparel	5	3[e]	8[e]	15[e]
Wood and wood products	2[e]	3[e]	6[e]	8[e]
Furniture and fixtures	2[e]	3[e]	8[e]	12[e]
Paper and paper products	21[e]	21[e]	56[e]	90[e]
Printing and publishing	11[e]	11[e]	31[e]	52[e]
Industrial chemicals	15[e]	16[e]	62[e]	91[e]
Other chemical products	3	8	28	117[e]
Misc. petroleum and coal products	2[e]	1[e]	5[e]	6[e]
Rubber products	145[e]	127[e]	249[e]	261[e]
Plastic products	11[e]	11[e]	39[e]	56[e]
Pottery, china and earthenware	11[e]	6[e]	15[e]	12[e]
Glass and glass products	10[e]	14[e]	66[e]	85[e]
Other non-metal mineral products	50[e]	40[e]	154[e]	184[e]
Iron and steel	592	405	623	391[e]
Non-ferrous metals	32	26	62	86[e]
Metal products	24	78	210	300[e]
Non-electrical machinery	98	63	158	178[e]
Electrical machinery	19	19[e]	71[e]	77[e]
Transport equipment	7	4	19	16[e]
Prof. and scientific equipment	10	7[e]	32[e]	37[e]
Other manufacturing	NA	NA	1[e]	2[e]

COMMUNICATIONS

Daily Newspapers

	National Data	World Data for Comparison
Daily Newspapers		
Number of Dailies	5	8,391
Total Circulation (000)	135	548,000
Circulation per 1,000 inhabitants	328	96

Telecommunications

Telephones - main lines in use: 314,700 (1999).

Telephones - mobile cellular: 95,400 (1999).

Telephone system: highly developed, completely automated and efficient system, mainly buried cables.

Domestic: nationwide cellular telephone system; buried cable.

International: 3 channels leased on TAT-6 coaxial submarine cable (Europe to North America).

Radio broadcast stations: AM 2, FM 9, shortwave 2 (1999).

Radios: 285,000 (1997).

Television broadcast stations: 8 (1999).

Televisions: 285,000 (1998 est.).

Internet Service Providers (ISPs): 13 (1999).

FINANCE, ECONOMICS, & TRADE

Economic Indicators

National product: GDP—purchasing power parity—$14.7 billion (1999 est.).

National product real growth rate: 4.2% (1999 est.).

National product per capita: $34,200 (1999 est.).

Inflation rate—consumer price index: 1.1% (1999 est.).

Exchange Rates

Exchange rates:

Euros per US$1

January 2000	0.9867
1999	0.9386

Luxembourg francs (LuxF) per US$1

January 1999	34.7700
1998	36.2990
1997	35.7740
1996	30.9620
1995	29.4800

The Luxembourg franc is at par with the Belgian franc, which circulates freely in Luxembourg. On 1 January 1999, the EU introduced a common currency that is now being used by financial institutions in some member countries at a fixed rate of 40.3399 francs per euro; the euro will replace the local currency in consenting countries for all transactions in 2002.

Top Import Origins

$9.6 billion (c.i.f., 1998)

Origins (1998)

Belgium	36%
Germany	27%
France	12%
Netherlands	5%
United States	4%

Top Export Destinations

$7.5 billion (f.o.b., 1998)

Destinations (1998)

Germany	33%
France	20%
Belgium	12%
United Kingdom	6%
United States	5%
Netherlands	4%

Foreign Aid

Donor: ODA, $160 million (1999).

Import/Export Commodities

Import Commodities	Export Commodities
Minerals	Finished steel products
Metals	Chemicals
Foodstuffs	Rubber products
Quality consumer goods	Glass
	Aluminum
	Other industrial products

MACAU

CAPITAL: Macau.

FLAG: The flag is light green with a white lotus flower above a stylized bridge and water and beneath an arc of five stars—one large and four smaller ones as on the flag of China.

ANTHEM: Chinese national anthem is used.

MONETARY UNIT: 1 pataca (P) = 100 avos.

WEIGHTS AND MEASURES: The metric system is used.

HOLIDAYS: New Year's Day, 1 January; Labor Day, 1 May; National Days, 1 and 2 October; Chinese New Year, three-day festival in January or February, depending on the year.

TIME: 8 PM = noon GMT.

LOCATION AND SIZE: Macau (Macao) is situated on the south coast of China, at the mouth of the Pearl (Zhu) River, almost directly opposite Hong Kong, which is about 65 km (40 mi.) away. Located at 22°6′ to 22°13′N and 113°33′ to 113°37′E, Macau consists of a peninsula, about 5 km (3 mi.) long and 1.6 km (1 mi.) wide, and two small islands, Taipa and Coloane. The total area is about 16 sq. km (6 sq. mi.), and the total coastline is 41 km (25 mi.).

CLIMATE: The climate is subtropical, with high humidity from April to October, when Macau receives most of its rainfall. Daily maximum temperatures average 29°C (84°F) during the summer; normal daily temperatures are less than 20°C (68°F) during the winter months.

INTRODUCTORY SURVEY

RECENT HISTORY

Macau is the oldest European settlement in the Far East. The first Portuguese attempts to establish relations with China were made in the early sixteenth century. In 1557 the Chinese authorities agreed to Portuguese settlement of Macau with leaseholder rights. The Portuguese however treated Macau as their possession and established a municipal government in the form of a senate of the local inhabitants. Disputes concerning jurisdiction and administration developed. In 1833 Macau became an overseas province of Portugal under the control of the governor-general of Goa, and in 1849 Portugal succeeded in having Macau declared a free port. On March 26, 1887, China confirmed perpetual occupation and governance of Macau and its dependencies by Portugal, but the question of the delimitation of the boundaries was left unsettled.

As the only neutral port on the South China Sea during World War II, Macau enjoyed a modicum of prosperity. In 1949 the government of the People Republic of China (PRC) renounced the "unequal treaty" granting Portuguese suzerainty over Macau. Civil disturbances in late 1966 between Macau police and Chinese leftist groups resulted in concessions to the territory's pro-China elements. The 1974 military coup in Portugal led to a constitutional change in Macau's status from a Portuguese province to a "special territory." In January 1976 Portugal's remaining few hundred troops were withdrawn from Macau. PRC and Portugal established diplomatic ties in 1980. In March 1987 the PRC and Portugal reached an agreement for the return of Macau to the PRC in 1999. The PRC guaranteed not to interfere in Macau's capitalist economy and way of life for a period of fifty years.

GOVERNMENT

After being returned to China, Macau became the Macau Special Administrative Region and comes under the "one-country, two systems" formula implemented by China in 1997 when it re-

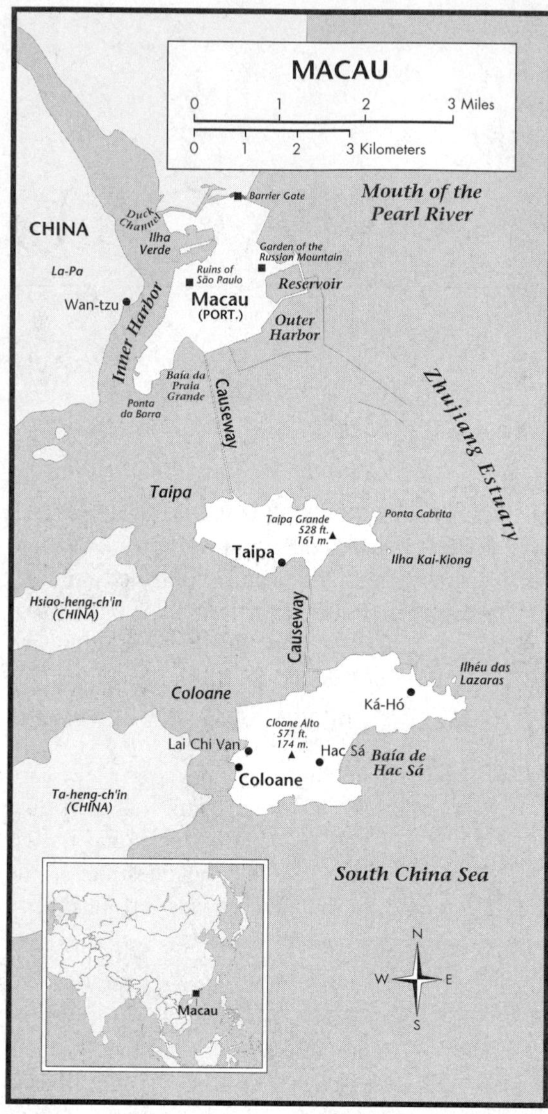

gained control of Hong Kong. Macau continues to exercise local autonomy; however, its chief of state is the president of China. Edmund Ho Hau-Wah, a member of a prominent Macanese family, was made the region's first chief executive in May 1999 and is assisted by the Executive Council consisting of all five government secretaries, three legislators, and two businessman.

The legislative branch is a unicameral 23-seat Legislative Council (LEGCO). Eight members are elected by popular vote, eight by indirect vote, and seven appointed by the chief executive. All serve four-year terms.

Judiciary

For most of 1999 the laws of Portugal ruled Macau as applied through the Portuguese judicial system. Since ownership of Macau reverted to the People's Republic of China on December 20, 1999, its judicial system became subject to the Basic Law of the Macau Special Administrative Region of the People's Republic of China. The Basic Law was adopted earlier in the 1990s by the National People's Congress in China to serve as the area's constitutional law under the "one country, two systems" policy. The appeals court is the Court of Final Appeal in the Macau Special Administrative Region.

Political Parties

Since Macau's transition back to Chinese rule it has no formal political parties. Instead civic associations are used. There are six civic associations holding seats in the LEGCO.

DEFENSE

The Macau garrison of China's People's Liberation Army (PLA) includes about 500 troops. Defense is the responsibility of China as of December 1999.

ECONOMIC AFFAIRS

Macau's economic mainstays are tourism including gambling, textiles, and fireworks manufacturing. Tourism accounts for 25 percent of GDP and gambling 40 percent of GDP. The clothing industry provided about three-fourths of export earnings. China supplies most food, fresh water and energy while Japan and Hong Kong are the main suppliers of raw materials and capital goods. The GDP growth rate declined 4 percent in 1998 and remained weak in 1999. A dark spot on the economy was gang violence that would probably decrease in 2000 due to tightened measures and thereby benefit the tourist sector.

Public Finance

The unit of currency is the Macau pataca (P). Corporate taxes and import duties are important sources of revenue; major expenditures are for finance, security, education, and health and welfare. The U.S. Central Intelligence Agency (CIA) estimates Macau's 1998 revenues at $1.34 billion and expenditures of $1.34 billion including capital expenditures of $260 million.

Income

The CIA estimated the GDP for 1998 at $7.65 billion or $17,500 per capita. The 1998 estimated GDP growth rate was a decline of 4 percent and inflation was estimated in 1999 at −3 percent. The

1997 contribution by sector was agriculture 1 percent, industry 40 percent, and services 59 percent.

Industry

Macau's economy is consumer-oriented. There is little agriculture, and the territory is heavily dependent on imports from China for food, fresh water, and electricity. Important economic sectors are commerce, tourism, gambling, fishing, and light industry. There are small- or medium-scale enterprises concerned especially with the finishing of imported semi-manufactured goods, in particular the manufacture of clothing, fireworks, ceramics, electronic equipment, footwear, toys, and, and the printing and dyeing of cloth and yarn. Gambling and tourism are important industries in Macau.

Banking and Finance

The territory has its own currency-issuing bank, 12 commercial banks, and 10 foreign banks.

Economic Development

Macau's historic role has been that of a gateway for southern China. It has close trade relations with neighboring Hong Kong, another free port, which serves as a point of transshipment for Macau's exports and imports. Gold trading, formerly a major facet in Macau's economy, virtually came to a halt in 1974-1975 following Hong Kong's decision to lift its own restrictions on gold trading. Exports in 1995 were estimated at $1.9 billion, shipped mainly to the U.S., EU, Hong Kong, and China. The principal exports are textiles, clothing, fireworks, artificial flowers, ceramics, optical equipment, electronic goods, leatherwork, toys, and fish. Textiles alone accounted for an estimated 76.9 percent of exports in 1994. The principal imports for domestic use are food, fuel, machinery, iron and steel, and automobiles. Total imports in 1997 were valued at just over $2 billion of which Hong Kong provided 25 percent, China 29 percent, Japan 9 percent, and the EU 12.4 percent. Transit trade still dominates the flow in and out of Macau.

With its picturesque seaport and varied gambling facilities, tourism provides about 25 percent of GDP, and the gambling industry accounts for about 40 percent of GDP. Before reassuring control of Macau in 1999 the Chinese government stated its intentions of reducing Macau's dependence on the gambling industry by diversifying its economy. Many hoped that this would also help reduce crime in the region. Other than diversification China intends to leave Macau's economy alone.

In 1991 there were 1,695,453 visitors to Macau with over 80 percent from Hong Kong. Of those classed as tourists 88,331 came from Japan, 7,209 from the UK, and 9,800 from the U.S. and Canada.

Healthcare

The Medical and Health Department, although critically understaffed, operates a 400-bed hospital. The 800-bed Kiang Vu Hospital has a largely China-trained staff.

EDUCATION

Government schools are operated mainly for the children of civil servants and wealthier families, while poor Chinese students are educated in schools indirectly supported by China. Macau's University of East Asia opened in 1981.

2000 KEY EVENTS TIMELINE

January

- Edmund Ho becomes first minister of Macau after Portugal cedes Macau to China. Ho, who received his education in Ontario, Canada, promises to clean up crime and gambling. He plans a trip to Las Vegas, Nevada, to learn about the casino business.
- China unveils its plans for Macau, where 42 percent of the revenue comes from gambling in its offshore casinos. Macau will seek to improve its infrastructure and rebuild bridges and roads. The Chinese government will launch investigations into Macau's triads, or crime gangs, and music piracy operations. China may apply Hong Kong-style anti-piracy rules in Macau.

July

- For sixty years Macau's gambling casinos, the dominant industry, have been run by a monopoly. After studying American and Australian gambling casinos, Chief Executive Edmund Ho plans to issue new licenses to competing companies.

December

- A battle for control of gambling casinos is heating up one year after Macau was handed over to

China. The casinos are controlled by Stanley Ho, a private individual, and his partners. Under the Chinese government, competition for casino business is growing.

ANALYSIS OF EVENTS: 2000

BUSINESS AND THE ECONOMY

Macau has no natural resources, so tourism and taxes on gambling are the main sources of revenue. Annually, close to ten million tourists came to Macau from China and Japan. Over 900,000 came in August 2000 alone.

Gambling continued to bring in enormous sums of money, much of it from Hong Kong residents who spent weekends gambling in Macau's casinos. The industry was so central to Macau's economy that Chief Executive Edmund Ho had even traveled to Las Vegas to study how American casinos are run. However, gambling had also attracted the powerful Asian crime syndicates called triads, and the Chinese had voiced fears that organized crime activities could endanger the tourism sector.

Macau's gambling industry had been controlled since 1962 by Stanley Ho Hung-sun, whose $3 billion conglomerate, STDM, was involved not only in the lucrative casino business but also in greyhound and horse racing, hotels, and high-speed ferries between Hong Kong and Macau. The company's activities supplied about one-third of Macau's gross domestic product (GDP) and generated the funds for roughly half of the government's annual budget. However, Ho's monopoly over gambling was due to end in 2001, when the government was planning to open up the sector. In one form or another, gambling in Macau had been run by monopolies since 1937.

Macau also operated a lottery called "Macau Welcomes You," in which contestants entered their passport numbers, and the winner received thousands of dollars and expensive items as prizes. Auto racing, including the Grand Prix of Macau, also contributed to the economy.

GOVERNMENT AND POLITICS

The changeover from Portuguese domination to Chinese control on December 20, 1999, had significant implications for the future of Macau. Like Hong Kong, Macau was to be governed under the "one country, two systems" policy, allowing it to retain its capitalist economy for another fifty years (although it remained to be seen whether China would honor this pledge). Macau was designated a Special Administrative Region of China, with its own political system, legislative assembly, and political parties. Canadian-educated Edmund Ho served as Chief Executive of Macau.

There was speculation that the transfer of Macau to China might discourage music piracy because the Chinese have strict laws regulating the copyrighting of music.

CULTURE AND SOCIETY

Of Macau's population of 450,000, 93 percent were Chinese and 5 percent were Portuguese. Cantonese Chinese was the major spoken language, followed by Portuguese and English.

Within the past fifteen years a large influx of immigrants seeking work has come to Macau, mostly from mainland China and the Philippines. The presence of these immigrants, who work for low wages, has aroused criticism and even provoked demonstrations among the native population. However Chief Executive Edmund Ho says that Macau's economy needs the imported labor.

Macau's Grand Prix auto race attracted some 70,000 visitors, with over 220 million viewers watching the race on television.

Spectators at a soccer match between Macau and Hong Kong were astonished when Macau's referee, provoked by a Hong Kong player, repeatedly struck the player in the head. Players from both teams eventually separated the dueling duo; Hong Kong won the match 1-0.

In 2000 Macau's Institute for Tourism Studies received certification by the World Tourism Organization (WTO) for meeting global standards for education and training in the tourism industry.

DIRECTORY

For most of 1999 Macau was administered under Portuguese authority. On December 19, 1999, it reverted to the People's Republic of China. Macau's administration since December 19 has changed to reflect this shift in sovereignty.

CENTRAL GOVERNMENT

Head of State

Chief Executive
Edmund Ho

Governor General
Vasco Joachim Rocha Viera, Office of the Governor, Government Palace, Ave. da Praia Grande, Macau
PHONE: +853 565555
FAX: +853 563377

Cabinet

Secretary for Administration and Justice
Florinda da Rosa Silva Chan

Secretary for Economy and Finance
Francis Tam Pak Un

Secretary for Security
Cheong Kuoc Va

Secretary for Social Affairs and Culture
Fernando Chui Sai On

Secretary for Transports and Public Works
Ao Man Long

POLITICAL ORGANIZATIONS

Macau has no formal political parties.

BROADCAST MEDIA

Teledifusao de Macau, Sarl

Avenida Dr. Rodrigo Rodrigues, No. 223-225, Edif. "Nam kwong" 7 Andar, Macau
PHONE: +853 522978; 335888
FAX: +853 343199
LANGUAGE: Cantonese, Portuguese
BROADCASTS: 24 hours/day
TYPE: Commercial, Private

Teledifusão de Macau (TDM Sarl)

PO Box 446, Macau
PHONE: +853 520204; 520206
FAX: +853 520208
TITLE: Chairman
CONTACT: Stanley Ho
CHANNEL: 30, 32

COLLEGES AND UNIVERSITIES

Asia International Open University

PO Box 1266, Macau
PHONE: +853 781698
FAX: +853 781691
E-MAIL: genoffice@aiou.edu
WEBSITE: http://www.aiou.edu

Institute for Tourism Studies

Colina de Mong-Há, Macau
PHONE: +853 561252
FAX: +853 519058
E-MAIL: iftpr@ift.edu.mo
WEBSITE: http://www.ift.edu.mo

Inter-University Institute of Macau

NAPE, Lote 18, Rua de Londres-P, Edf. Tak Ip Plaza, R/C-3, Macau
E-MAIL: adm@iium.edu.mo
WEBSITE: http://www.iium.edu.mo

Macau Polytechnic Institute

Avenida de Luis Gonzaga Gomes, Edificio do Antigo Liceu de Macau, Macau
WEBSITE: http://www.ipm.edu.mo

University of Macau

PO Box 3001, Macau
PHONE: +853 841661
FAX: +853 831694
E-MAIL: registry@umac.mo
WEBSITE: http://www.umac.mo

NEWSPAPERS AND MAGAZINES

Futuro Macao

E-MAIL: futuromacau@hotmail.com
TITLE: Editor
CONTACT: Luis A. de Sá

Jornal Tribuna de Macao

E-MAIL: tribuna@macau.ctm.net
WEBSITE: http://www.jtm.com.mo/news/hoje

Jornal Va Kio

E-MAIL: vakiopou@macau.ctm.net
WEBSITE: http://www.vakiodaily.com

Macao Daily News

E-MAIL: guyu_macau@hotmail.com
WEBSITE: http://www.macaodaily.com

PUBLISHERS

Livros Do Oriente

Av. Amizada 876-12 C, Macau
PHONE: +853 518063

FAX: +853 518064
TITLE: Editor
CONTACT: Rogerio Coelho
SUBJECTS: Anthropology, Biography, Photography, Romance, Social Sciences, Sociology, Travel

Museu Maritimo

Largo do Pagode da Barra, n 1, Macau
PHONE: +853 595481; 595483
FAX: +853 512160
E-MAIL: museu@macau.ctm.net
WEBSITE: http://www.museumaritimo.gov.mo
SUBJECTS: Asian Studies, History, Maritime, Technology, Transportation
TOTAL PUBLISHED: 44 print

Instituto Portugues Oriente

Av. Cons Ferreira de Almeida, 95 G, Macau
PHONE: +853 370642
FAX: +853 305426
E-MAIL: ipor@macau.ctm.net
TITLE: President
CONTACT: Ana Paula Laborinho
SUBJECTS: Asian Studies, History, Language Arts. Linguistics

Universidadede de Macau, Centro de Publicacoes

Av. Padre Tomas Perreira, S.J., Taipa, Macau
PHONE: +853 831622; 3974505
FAX: +853 831694
SUBJECTS: Art, Economics, Education, Political Science, History, Literature, Management, Public Administration, Social Sciences

RELIGIOUS ORGANIZATIONS

Macau is a territory of the People's Republic of China, although Chinese authorities have promised to not interfere in the functioning of the country for 50 years. Colonized by the Portugese, Macau is 50 percent Buddhist, 15 percent Roman Catholic, and 35 percent indigenous or atheist.

FURTHER READING

Baird, David. "From Canadian Roots: Beijing's New Man in Macau Is an Ontario-Educated Pragmatist." *Maclean's,* January 1, 2000, p. 224.

"Ho's Macau Gaming Empire Threatened." *Wall Street Journal,* July 19, 2000, p. A16.

Books

Dun and Bradstreet's Export Guide to Macau. Parsippany, NJ: Dun & Bradstreet, 1999.

McGivering, Jill. *Macao Remembers.* New York: Oxford University Press, 1999.

MACAU: STATISTICAL DATA

For sources and notes see "Sources of Statistics" at the front of each volume.

GEOGRAPHY

Geography

Area:

Total: 21 sq km.

Land: 21 sq km.

Land boundaries:

Total: 0.34 km.

Border countries: China 0.34 km.

Coastline: 40 km.

Climate: subtropical; marine with cool winters, warm summers.

Terrain: generally flat.

Natural resources: negligible.

Land use:

Arable land: 0%

Permanent crops: 2%

Permanent pastures: 0%

Forests and woodland: 0%

Other: 98% (1998 est.).

HUMAN FACTORS

Demographics (A)

	1990	1995	1998	2000	2010	2020	2030	2040	2050
Population	NA	404.2	429.2	445.6	527.3	615.3	695.6	763.4	828.1
Life expectancy - males	NA	77.8	78.6	78.8	79.6	80.3	80.8	81.2	81.5
Life expectancy - females	NA	85.7	84.3	84.6	85.4	86.1	86.6	87.0	87.4
Birth rate (per 1,000)	NA	14.5	12.9	12.5	12.5	12.6	11.2	11.5	12.0
Death rate (per 1,000)	NA	3.3	3.5	3.6	4.4	5.2	6.7	8.5	9.2
Women of reproductive age (15-49 yrs.)	NA	126.1	135.4	141.8	162.0	166.7	178.8	183.4	192.2
Fertility rate	NA	1.4	1.3	1.3	1.4	1.5	1.5	1.6	1.7

Except as noted, values for vital statistics are in thousands; life expectancy is in years.

Ethnic Division

Chinese 95%
Macanese . . . . .NA
Portuguese . . . . .NA
Other . . . . .NA

The Macanese have mixed Portuguese and Asian ancestry.

Religion

Buddhist 50%
Roman Catholic 15%
None and other 35%

Data for 1997 est.

Major Languages

Portuguese, Chinese (Cantonese).

GOVERNMENT & LAW

Political Parties

Legislative Council	no. of seats
Associaco Promotora para a Economia de Macau (APPEM)	2
Uniao Promotora para o Progresso (UNIPRO)	2
Convergenia para o Desenvolvimento (CODEM)	1
Uniao Geral para o Desenvolvimento (UDM)	1
Uniao para o Desenvolvimento (UPD)	1
Associacao de Novo Macau Democratico (ANMD)	1

Elections were last held 22 September 1996 (next to be held by 15 October 2001). There are no formal political parties, but civic associations are used instead.

Government Budgets (B)

Revenues . . . .$1.34 billion
Expenditures . . . .$1.34 billion
Capital expenditures . . . .$260.00 million

Data for 1998 est.

Military Affairs (B)

Availability
Males age 15-49 123,581
Fit for military service
Males age 15-49 67,974

Data for 2000 est.

Crime

Crime volume (for 1998)
Crimes reported 8,488
Total persons convicted . . . . .NA
Crimes per 100,000 population 1,698

LABOR FORCE

Total Labor Force (A)

281,117 (1998).

Labor Force by Occupation

Industry 31%
Restaurants and hotels 28%
Other services 41%

Unemployment Rate

6.9% (1999)

PRODUCTION SECTOR

Energy Production

Production . . . . .1.34 billion kWh
Production by source
Fossil fuel 100%
Hydro 0%
Nuclear 0%
Other 0%
Exports . . . . .1 million kWh

Data for 1998.

Energy Consumption

Consumption . . . . .1.42 billion kWh
Imports . . . . .175.00 million kWh

Data for 1998.

Transportation

Highways:

Total: 50 km.

Paved: 50 km.

Unpaved: 0 km (1996 est.).

Merchant marine: none (1999 est.).

Airports: 1 (1999 est.).

Top Agriculture Products

Rice, vegetables.

MANUFACTURING SECTOR

GDP & Manufacturing Summary (A)

	1980	1985	1990	1995
GDP ($-1990 mil.)[1]	NA	2,502	3,731	4,887
Per capita ($-1990)[1]	NA	8,176	10,029	11,364
Manufacturing share (%) (current prices)[1]	NA	NA	NA	NA

Manufacturing				
Value added ($-1990 mil.)[1]	NA	NA	NA	NA
Industrial production index	76[e]	66[e]	100	59[e]
Value added ($ mil.)	127	225	470	450[e]
Gross output ($ mil.)	NA	759	1,625	1,718[e]
Employment (000)	46	59	63	44[e]
Profitability (% of gross output)				
Intermediate input (%)	NA	70	71	74[e]
Wages and salaries inc. supplements (%)	NA	17	16	15[e]
Gross operating surplus	NA	13	13	11[e]
Productivity ($)				
Gross output per worker	NA	12,557	25,099	37,966[e]
Value added per worker	2,693	3,723	7,263	9,932[e]
Average wage (inc. supplements)	NA	2,113	4,155	5,901[e]
Value added ($ mil.)				
Food products	1	3	6	11[e]
Beverages	1	1	4	3[e]
Tobacco products	NA	NA	NA	2[e]
Textiles	31	43	92	82[e]
Wearing apparel	71	99	231	227[e]
Leather and fur products	2	4	8	2[e]
Footwear	NA	1	5	10[e]
Wood and wood products	1	1	2	1[e]
Furniture and fixtures	1	2	5	3[e]
Paper and paper products	1	2	4	2[e]
Printing and publishing	4	3	9	16[e]
Other chemical products	NA	1	6	4[e]
Petroleum refineries	NA	NA	NA	NA
Plastic products	2	1	3	2[e]
Pottery, china and earthenware	NA	2	3	1[e]
Other non-metal mineral products	NA	NA	NA	23[e]
Iron and steel	NA	NA	NA	NA
Metal products	1	1	8	9[e]
Non-electrical machinery	NA	NA	1	1[e]
Electrical machinery	2	8	7	11[e]
Transport equipment	1	2	4	3[e]
Prof. and scientific equipment	1	3	4	2[e]
Other manufacturing	6	46	68	34[e]

COMMUNICATIONS

Daily Newspapers

	National Data	World Data for Comparison
Daily Newspapers		
Number of Dailies	10	8,391
Total Circulation (000)	200	548,000
Circulation per 1,000 inhabitants	455	96

Telecommunications

Telephones - main lines in use: 222,500 (1997).

Telephones - mobile cellular: 55,000 (1998).

Telephone system: fairly modern communication facilities maintained for domestic and international services.

Domestic: NA

International: HF radiotelephone communication facility; access to international communications carriers provided via Hong Kong and China; satellite earth station - 1 Intelsat (Indian Ocean).

Radio broadcast stations: AM 0, FM 2, shortwave 0 (1998).

Radios: 160,000 (1997).

Television broadcast stations: 0 (receives Hong Kong broadcasts) (1997).

Televisions: 49,000 (1997).

Internet Service Providers (ISPs): NA

FINANCE, ECONOMICS, & TRADE

Economic Indicators

National product: GDP—purchasing power parity—$7.65 billion (1998 est.).

National product real growth rate: -4% (1998 est.).

National product per capita: $17,500 (1998 est.).

Inflation rate—consumer price index: -3% (1999 est.).

Exchange Rates

Exchange rates:

Patacas (P) per US$1

January 2000	8.010
1999	7.990
1998	7.980
1997	7.990
1996	7.962
1993-95	8.034

Linked to the Hong Kong dollar at the rate of 1.03 patacas per Hong Kong dollar. Fiscal year: calendar year.

Top Import Origins

$1.5 billion (c.i.f., 1999)

Origins (1998)

China	33%
Hong Kong	24%
EU	11%
Taiwan	10%
Japan	8%

Top Export Destinations

$1.7 billion (f.o.b., 1999)

Destinations (1998)

United States	48%
EU	31%
Hong Kong	8%
China	7%

Import/Export Commodities

Import Commodities	Export Commodities
Raw materials	Textiles
Foodstuffs	Clothing
Capital goods	Toys
Fuels	Electronics
Consumer goods	Cement
	Footwear
	Machinery

MACEDONIA

CAPITAL: Skopje.

FLAG: The flag consists of a gold sun with eight rays on a red field.

ANTHEM: *Denec Nad Makedonija (Today over Macedonia)*

MONETARY UNIT: The currency in use is the denar (Den). Denominations from smallest to largest are fifty deni, one denar, two denari, and five denari. In 1995, US$1 = Den38.8 (Den1 = US$0.0256), but exchange rates are likely to fluctuate.

WEIGHTS AND MEASURES: The metric system is in effect in Macedonia.

HOLIDAYS: Orthodox Christmas, 7 January; national holiday, 2 August; Day of Referendum, 8 September.

TIME: 1 PM = noon GMT.

LOCATION AND SIZE: Macedonia is a landlocked nation located in southeastern Europe. With a total area of 25,333 square kilometers (9,781 square miles), Macedonia is slightly larger than the state of Vermont. It has a total boundary length of 748 kilometers (465 miles). Macedonia's capital city, Skopje, is located in the northwestern part of the country.

CLIMATE: Macedonia's climate features hot summers and cold winters. The mean temperature is between 20 and 23°C (68 and 73°F) in July and between −20 and 0°C (4 and 32°F) in January. Rainfall averages 48 centimeters (19 inches) a year. Snowfalls can be heavy in winter.

Former Yugoslav Republic of Macedonia
Republika Makedonija

INTRODUCTORY SURVEY

RECENT HISTORY

World War II (1939–1945) Macedonia became one of the co-equal republics of the Federal Socialist Yugoslavia under the communist regime of Marshal Tito. The Macedonian language became its official language and was used as the language of instruction in schools.

All the republics of the former Federal Socialist Republic of Yugoslavia share a common history between 1945 and 1991, the year of Yugoslavia's break-up. A conflict erupted between Tito and the Russian leader Joseph Stalin in 1948 and Yugoslavia was expelled from the Soviet Bloc. Yugoslavia developed its own brand of Marxist economy based on workers' councils and self-management of enterprises and institutions and became the leader of the nonaligned group of nations.

Being more open than the Soviet bloc to Western influences, the Yugoslav Communist regime relaxed its central controls and the 1974 constitution shifted much of the decision-making power from the federal level to the republics.

Following Tito's death in 1980 an economic crisis loomed. Severe inflation and inability to pay the nation's foreign debts led to tensions between the different republics. Demands for a reorganization of the Yugoslav federation into a confederation of sovereign states and a market economy grew stronger. By 1990 the non-communists won majorities in multiparty elections in Slovenia and Croatia ending the era of Communist Party monopoly of power.

In the wake of developments in Slovenia and Croatia, Macedonia held its first multiparty elections in late 1990 with the participation of over twenty political parties. In January 1991 the Macedonian Assembly passed a declaration of sovereignty.

With the dissolution of Yugoslavia by 1991 Macedonia refused to join Serbia and Montenegro

opting for independence on November 20, 1991. In April 1993 Macedonia gained membership in the United Nations but only under the name of "Former Yugoslav Republic of Macedonia."

Greece refused to recognize the newly independent Macedonia for fear of unrest among Slav Macedonians in Northern Greece and proclaimed a trade embargo against Macedonia in 1994. In the fall of 1995 a preliminary agreement was reached and Greece lifted its blockade and assumed diplomatic relations with Macedonia. Macedonia agreed to restrict the use of certain national symbols in its flag and currency.

As tensions between majority Albanians and minority Serbs in the neighboring Yugoslav province of Kosovo heated up from 1997 to 1999 fear mounted that full scale fighting would spread to Macedonia. Ethnic violence erupted in July 1997 in the town of Gostivar as tensions between ethnic Albanians and Macedonians in the country increased.

The war in Kosovo and the movement of hundreds of thousands of Kosovar Albanian refugees into Macedonia brought problems in 1999. International pressure forced Macedonia to keep its borders open to refugees despite fears that the large numbers of Kosovar Albanian refugees would someday join with Macedonia's ethnic Albanian population to separate from Macedonia itself.

GOVERNMENT

Macedonia became independent of the former Yugoslavia on November 20, 1991, having adopted its constitution on November 17, 1991. Macedonia is considered to be an emerging democracy.

The chief of state is the president elected by popular vote for a five-year term. The head of government is the prime minister appointed by the president. The cabinet, known as the Council of Ministers, is the elected by the majority vote of all the deputies in the Assembly.

The legislative branch is the unicameral Assembly or Sobranje. Eighty-five members are elected by popular vote and thirty-five come from lists of candidates submitted by parties based on the percentage that parties gain from the overall vote. All serve four-year terms. Suffrage is universal at age eighteen.

Judiciary

The judicial system is comprised of three levels: municipal courts, district courts, and the Supreme Court. A Constitutional Court handles issues of constitutional interpretation, including protection of individual rights.

Political Parties

Following the 1998 elections party representation in the Sobranje was as follows: the Internal Macedonian Revolutionary Organization-Democratic Party for Macedonian National Unity (VMRO-DPMNE) with forty-nine seats; Social Democratic Alliance of Macedonia (SDSM), that is the former Communist Party, with twenty-seven seats; Party for Democratic Property (PDP) with fourteen seats; Democratic Alternative (DA) thirteen seats; Democratic Party for Albanians (DPA) eleven seats; Liberal Democratic Party (LDP) four seats; Socialist Party one seat; and, Roma Party one seat.

DEFENSE

In January 1992 the Macedonian Assembly approved the formation of a standing army of 25,000-30,000 troops. However the actual size of the military is estimated to be 16,000 regular soldiers. Reservists total 102,000. Defense spending amounted to $77 million in 1999, or 2.5 percent of GDP.

ECONOMIC AFFAIRS

Although the poorest of the six former Yugoslav republics, Macedonia is capable of meeting its food and energy needs using its own agricultural and coal resources but much depends on outside sources for its oil, gas, and modern machinery parts. Due to the shortage of fertile land in the Vardar River Valley and other valleys in the west, the employment of Macedonians in Serbia and Germany has become more common.

In August 1992, because it resented the use of "Macedonia" as the republic's name, Greece imposed a partial blockade on Macedonia. This blockade, combined with the United Nations sanctions on Serbia and Montenegro, cost the Macedonian economy some $2 billion by the end of 1994. Greece ended the embargo in 1995 after the European Union threatened to take legal action. The Kosovo crisis of 1999 and resulting regional economic dislocations severely disrupted the Macedonian economy and held growth down.

Public Finance

Regional conflict, sanctions against Serbia and Montenegro, and a transition to a market economy severely disrupted the government's ability to account for public revenues and expenditures. The U.S. Central Intelligence Agency estimated that 1996 revenues were $1.06 billion and expenditures were $1 billion including capital expenditures of $107 million. External debt in 1998 stood at $1.7 billion.

Income

In 1999 Macedonia's gross domestic product (GDP) was estimated to be $7.6 billion, or about $3,800 per capita. In 1999 the inflation rate was 1 percent, and the real growth rate in the domestic economy was 2.5 percent. In 1998 mining and industry accounted for 13 percent of the domestic economy; agriculture and fishing 32 percent; and services and trade 55 percent.

Industry

Steel and chemical production, along with textiles, furniture, and ceramics are important industries. Other industries include coal, metallic chromium, lead, zinc, ferronickel, wood products, tobacco, and food and beverages. Industry suffers from low levels of technology and overstaffing.

Banking and Finance

In 1992 the National Bank of Macedonia was created to issue currency, conduct monetary polices, and regulate the banking sector of the country.

Commercial banks in Macedonia include the Komercijalna Banka and Scopanska Banka, both in Skopje. The currency unit is the Macedonia denar (Den) introduced on May 10, 1993. There are no security exchanges in the country.

Under a five-year stabilization program agreed with the IMF, the government is focusing on reducing inflation, overhauling the financial system and launching structural reforms.

Economic Development

In 1995 net resource flows from international financial institutions consisted of $43 million from the World Bank, $37 million from the IMF, and $16 million from other institutions. The government began privatizing its largest state-owned industries. A total of 1,200 enterprises were to be privatized, 65 percent of them classified as small (fewer than fifty employees).

Continued recovery in 2000 depended on Macedonia's ability to attract investment, to revive trade ties with Greece, Serbia, and Montenegro, to maintain its focus on economic liberalization, and to deal with the influx of Kosovar refugees that flooded across the border disrupting trade routes.

SOCIAL WELFARE

Macedonia, historically the poorest of the former Yugoslav republics, suffered further from the imposition of international sanctions against its trading partner Serbia, the rising tide of refugees, and increasing unemployment. Many of the state's social welfare programs for children have been inoperative due to the region's political and economic crises.

Although women have the same legal rights as men, the traditional cultures of both Christian and Muslim communities have limited their advancement in society.

Healthcare

In 2000 life expectancy was estimated at seventy-four years. Physicians are adequately trained, but there is a shortage of medicines and medical equipment. Patients who are seriously ill must often go to another country for medical help.

Housing

During the years of the former Yugoslav SFR there was a chronic shortage of housing. Since independence the ability to find apartment or condominium housing had improved. Bank loans are now available to finance building new housing.

EDUCATION

Education at the elementary level is free and compulsory for eight years between the ages of seven and fifteen. In 1997 there were 260,917 students enrolled in primary schools and 83,746 secondary students. At the postsecondary level there are two universities: Bitola University founded in 1979 and the University of Skopje founded in 1949. In 1997 institutions of higher learning had a combined enrollment of 30,754 students.

2000 KEY EVENTS TIMELINE

March

- On March 17 the NATO commander in charge of forces in Macedonia requests more U.S. troops.
- The World Bank and International Monetary Fund pledge US$2.3 billion in aid to the Balkans, including Macedonia, on March 30.

April

- On April 13 U.S. troops are arrested for rowdy behavior.

May

- Macedonia is among eight eastern European countries seeking to join NATO on May 20.

July

- Brush fires erupt due to record heat during the middle of July. High temperatures kill several Macedonians.

August

- The International Organization for Migration announces August 10 that more than 600,000 women have been brought illegally from Eastern European countries into Macedonia to be sold into slavery.

September

- Local elections take place September 10, although the results are criticized by international observers because of violence and ballot-box destruction. First-round results are withheld, and both opposing parties claim victory.
- The former Yugoslav Republic of Macedonia competes for the first time in the Olympics, winning a bronze medal in freestyle wrestling, September 31.

October

- Yugoslav ambassador to Macedonia Zoran Janackovic decries an anti-Yugoslav campaign in Macedonia that is predominantly aimed against Serbs.

November

- Macedonians throw stones at the Bulgarian embassy November 4, following a spate of anti-Bulgarian propaganda on Macedonian television.
- European Union leaders offer financial aid and the prospect of E.U. membership to Macedonia November 24.
- Approximately 500 ethnic Albanian refugees cross the border into Macedonia from Serbia on November 27, fleeing from fighting between Serb police and Albanian guerillas.

ANALYSIS OF EVENTS: 2000

BUSINESS AND THE ECONOMY

Macedonia's economic indicators remained largely positive, but the nation's poverty level and high unemployment remained a problem. Its per capita gross domestic product (GDP) of $1,600–$1,700 remained far below those of the former Yugoslav republics of Slovenia and Croatia, which were $10,000 and $5,000 respectively.

Following a dip due to the Kosovo crisis of 1999, foreign investment, which had totaled $175 million in 1998, resumed its upward path. Privatization of small and medium-sized companies had essentially been accomplished, although mostly through management or employee buyouts, which had limited the amount of new capital investment in the firms. Privatization of the agricultural sector, which accounted for roughly 10 percent of GDP, had also been carried out. However, divestiture of larger state-owned companies was proceeding more slowly, partly for fear that the resulting layoffs would raise the country's already high unemployment rate of 30–35 percent. (Around 10,000 people were employed by the twelve large companies slated for eventual privatization.) By 2000 the private sector accounted for 55–60 percent of the country's GDP, and privatization plans were going ahead for the sell-off of Makedonska Telekommunikacil, the company's public telecommunications firm. President Trajkovski's major economic goals included increasing exports and attracted additional foreign investment.

Stabilization of Macedonia's relations with Greece after an extended sovereignty dispute that lasted up to the mid-1990s contributed to the country's economic progress. The National Bank of Greece paid $55 million to acquire a majority stake in Stopanska Banka, Macedonia's largest bank, and Greeks made other major investments in the country. Smaller stakes in Stopanska Banka were bought by the European Bank for Reconstruction & Development (EBRD) and the International Finance Corporation, which was affiliated with the World Bank. Although major restructuring had taken place in Macedonia's banking sector since 1991, the country's population and the size of its economy were still considered too small to support the twenty-four commercial banks still operating.

Macedonia was among the recipients of $2.3 billion in aid to the Balkans pledged by the World Bank and the International Monetary Fund in March.

GOVERNMENT AND POLITICS

Municipal elections held throughout the country in the fall were considered crucial to the survival of Macedonia's center-right government, embattled over its economic policies and over the status of the country's ethnic Albanian minority. Prime Minister Ljupco Georgievski had stated that a poor showing in the polling for mayors and town councils would lead to early general elections before the year was out. Initial voting in September was not considered conclusive due to irregularities that led the Organization for Security and Cooperation in Europe (OSCE) to rule that the elections did not meet its democratic standard. The OSCE cited election-related violence and intimidation, primarily in western Macedonia—home to most of the nation's ethnic Albanians—where shootings injured four people. Also criticized was election coverage by Macedonia's state-run television network, which was reported to have provided six times as much airtime to government views than to those of the opposition bloc. Further irregularities, including the destruction of fourteen ballot boxes, were reported following a second round of voting later in September, and a third round of municipal elections took place in October.

Ethnic differences took center stage in the controversy over a law passed in July authorizing the establishment of a privately funded Albanian-language university, which would replace an illegal facility that had been in operation since 1994. Opponents of the new institution claimed it would further the de facto ethnic partition of the country. The university was to be funded jointly by Western governments, the Council of Europe, and the Soros Foundation.

Although nearly one-third of Macedonia's population was made up of ethnic Albanians, Macedonia managed to emerge from the Kosovo crisis of the previous year without being pulled into the fighting. However, the country was strongly affected by it socially, politically, and economically. President Boris Trajkovski continued to pursue stability in the region by maintaining friendly relations with Greece, the Federal Republic of Yugoslavia, and other neighboring states. He also maintained his advocacy of European integration and support for Macedonia's eventual entry into both the European Union (E.U.) and the World Trade Organization (WTO). A Stabilization and Association Agreement with the E.U. was expected to be signed by year's end. At an international conference held in Florence in May, Foreign Minister Aleksandar Dimitrov reiterated Macedonia's request to join the North Atlantic Treaty Organization (NATO) by 2002 as one of nine new applicants from Eastern European.

In the spring, sporadic incidents were reported at Macedonia's border with Kosovo. In April four Macedonian soldiers were kidnapped but later released. In June two soldiers were wounded by sniper fire, and gunmen fired on two border checkpoints.

CULTURE AND SOCIETY

Macedonians were among those sweltering in temperatures that topped 44°C (111°F) during a major heat wave that struck the Balkans in July. Heat-related deaths were reported in nearby Croatia and Bulgaria.

The International Organization for Migration reported that Macedonia had become a major center for international trafficking in women, and that the country was harboring thousands of women who had been abducted from Romania, Bulgaria, Ukraine, and other nations in the region and forced into prostitution. Authorities said that traffickers had been attracted by the foreign currency brought into Macedonia in the wake of the Kosovo crisis.

In September Macedonian athletes competed in their first Olympic games, in Sydney, Australia. Freestyle wrestler Mogamed Ibragimov won the country its first medal by taking home the bronze in the eighty-five-kilogram competition.

DIRECTORY

CENTRAL GOVERNMENT

Head of State

President
Boris Trajkovski, Office of the President, 11 Oktomvrii b.b., 91000 Skopje, Macedonia
PHONE: +389 (91) 112255
FAX: +389 (91) 237947

Prime Minister
Ljubco Georgievski, Office of the Prime Minister, Ilindenska b.b., 91000 Skopje, Macedonia
PHONE: +389 (91) 115389
FAX: +389 (91) 119561

Vice President
Dosta Dimovska, Office of the Vice President

Vice President
Radmila Kiprijanova Radovanovic, Office of the Vice President

Vice President
Bedredin Ibrahimi, Office of the Vice President

Ministers

Minister of Defense
Ljuben Paunovski, Ministry of Defense, Orce Nikolov Street b.b., 91000 Skopje, Macedonia
PHONE: +389 (91) 230928
E-MAIL: info@morm.gov.mk

Minister of Justice
Xhevdet Nasufi, Ministry of Justice, Veljko Vlahovich b.b., Skopje, Macedonia
PHONE: +389 (91) 230732; 226975

Minister of Finance
Nikola Gruevski, Ministry of Finance, Dane Gruev 14, Skopje, Macedonia
PHONE: +389 (91) 116012; 117280

Minister of Development
Milijana B. Danevska, Ministry of Development, Bote Bocevski 9, Skopje, Macedonia
PHONE: +389 (91) 112766; 112799

Minister of Labour and Social Welfare
Bedredin Ibrahimi, Ministry of Labour and Social Welfare, Dame Gruev 14, Skopje, Macedonia
PHONE: +389 (91) 117787; 220408

Minister of Traffic and Communications
Ljubco Balkovski, Ministry of Traffic and Communications, Ilendenska b.b., Skopje, Macedonia
PHONE: +389 (91) 123292

Minister of Education & Science
Nenad Novkovski, Ministry of Education & Science, Ilendenska b.b., Skopje, Macedonia
PHONE: +389 (91) 238610; 235573

Minister of Culture
Ganka Samoilova-Cvetanova, Ministry of Culture, Ilendenska b.b., Skopje, Macedonia
PHONE: +389 (91) 127136; 127112

Minister of Information
Redzep Zlatku, Ministry of Information, Guro Gakovik 64, 91000 Skopje, Macedonia
PHONE: +389 (91) 116476
FAX: +389 (91) 11486

Minister of Environment
Marjan Dodovski, Ministry of Environment, Drezdenska 52, 91000 Skopje, Macedonia
PHONE: +389 (91) 366930
FAX: +389 (91) 366931
E-MAIL: info@moe.gov.mk

Minister of Sports and Youth
Georgi Boev, Ministry of Sports and Youth, Drezdenska 52, 91000 Skopje, Macedonia
PHONE: +389 (91) 117268; 117631

Minister of Interior
Dosta Dimovska, Ministry of Interior, Dimche Mirchev b.b., 91000 Skopje, Macedonia
PHONE: +389 (91) 221972; 112468

Minister of Foreign Affairs
Srgjan Kerim, Ministry of Foreign Affairs, Dame Gruev 6, 91000 Skopje, Macedonia
PHONE: +389 (91) 110333
FAX: +389 (91) 115790
E-MAIL: mailmnr@mnr.gov.mk

Minister of Economy
Besnik Fetai, Ministry of Economy, Samoilova 10, Skopje, Macedonia
PHONE: +389 (91) 119628; 111541

Minister of Urban Planning, Construction and Environment
Marjan Dodovski, Ministry of Urban Planning, Construction and Environment, Dame Gruev 14, 91000 Skopje, Macedonia
PHONE: +389 (91) 117288
FAX: +389 (91) 117163
E-MAIL: gjorgeva@unet.com.mk

Minister of Agriculture, Forestry and Water Economy
Marjan Gjorcev, Ministry of Agriculture, Forestry and Water Economy, Vasil Gjorgov b.b., Skopje, Macedonia
PHONE: +389 (91) 113045; 211997

Minister of Education
Nenad Novkovski, Ministry of Education, Dimitrija Cuposki No 9, 91000 Skopje, Macedonia
PHONE: +389 (91) 117277
FAX: +389 (91) 117163
E-MAIL: mofk@mofk.gov.mk

Minister of Health
Dragan Danilovski, Ministry of Health, 50 Divizija b.b., Skopje, Macedonia
PHONE: +389 (91) 113429; 113014

Minister of Immigration
Martin Trenevski, Ministry of Immigration
PHONE: +389 (91) 117443

Minister of Trade
Nikola Gruevski, Ministry of Trade
PHONE: +389 (91) 127178

Minister of Local Self-Government
Xhemail Saiti, Ministry of Local Self-Government
PHONE: +389 (91) 128059

POLITICAL ORGANIZATIONS

Liberalno-Demokratska Partija-LDP (Liberal-Democratic Party)

NAME: Risto Penov

Democratic Alternative

NAME: Vasil Tupukovski
PHONE: +389 (91) 362713; 364130
FAX: +389 (91) 363089

Social Democratic League of Macedonia

Bihachska 8, Skopje, Macedonia
PHONE: +389 (91) 231371; 221071
TITLE: Leader
NAME: Branko Tsrvenkovski

Liberal Party

Ilindenska b.b., Skopje, Macedonia
PHONE: +389 (91) 288944; 228004
TITLE: Leader
NAME: Stojan Andov

Socialist Party of Macedonia

Oktomvri 17, Skopje 11, Macedonia
PHONE: +389 (91) 228015; 231255; 220075
TITLE: Leader
NAME: Ljubisav Ivanov

Social Democratic Party of Macedonia

ul. Kliment Ohridski 54, Skopje, Macedonia
PHONE: +389 (91) 222507; 224353
TITLE: Leader
NAME: Aleksandar Donev

Democratic Party

Partizanski odredi 89, Skopje, Macedonia
PHONE: +389 (91) 363099
TITLE: Leader
NAME: Petar Goshev

Democratic Party of Macedonia

Tetovo, Bazaar 3, Macedonia
PHONE: +389 (91) 20826; 20006; 20776
TITLE: Leader
NAME: Tomislav Stojanovski

Movement of Pan-Macedonian Action (MAAK)

Maksim Gorki 18/III, Skopje, Macedonia
PHONE: +389 (91) 116540
TITLE: Leader
NAME: Strasho Angelovski

Democratic Party for Macedonian National Unity

ul. "Makedonija" 17a, PF 903, 91000 Skopje, Macedonia
PHONE: +389 (91) 124244
FAX: +389 (91) 124366
E-MAIL: vmro_dpmne@vmro-dpmne.org.mk
TITLE: Leader
NAME: Ljupcho Georgievski

Fatherland Party

Marko Krale 34b, Skopje, Macedonia
PHONE: +389 (91) 23369
TITLE: Leader
NAME: Dimitar Tsrnomarov

Democratic Party

ul. Jane Sandanski 116/3–24, Skopje, Macedonia
PHONE: +389 (91) 419036
TITLE: Leader
NAME: Vladimir Golubovski

Macedonian National Democratic League

Sava Kovachevich 12, Skopje, Macedonia
PHONE: +389 (91) 781758
TITLE: Leader
NAME: Tomislav Stefkovski

United Party

Gemidzhiska 65, Skopje, Macedonia
TITLE: Leader
NAME: Atanas Aleksovski

Party for Democratic Prosperity of Macedonia

Karaorman 62, Tetovo, Macedonia
PHONE: +389 (91) 25709; 20435
TITLE: Leader
NAME: Abdurahman Haliti

National Democratic Party

Kiro Ristevski-Dane 23, Tetovo, Macedonia
PHONE: +389 (91) 31190
TITLE: Leader
NAME: Ilijaz Halimi

Demokratic Party of the Turks in Macedonia

ul. Krste Misirkov 67, Skopje, Macedonia
PHONE: +389 (91) 114696
TITLE: Leader
NAME: Erdogan Sarach

Party for Complete Emancipation of the Romanies in Macedonia

Shuto Orizari b.b., Skopje, Macedonia
PHONE: +389 (91) 612726
TITLE: Leader
NAME: Bajram Berat

Democratic Progressive Party of the Romanies in Macedonia

Demirhisarska 44, Skopje, Macedonia
PHONE: +389 (91) 266939
TITLE: Leader
NAME: Arif Bekir

Democratic Party of the Serbs in Macedonia

27 Mart 11, Skopje, Macedonia
PHONE: +389 (91) 254274; 722959; 222005
TITLE: Leader
NAME: Dragisha Miletich

Workers' Party

GTC Kula II, kat VIII, Skopje, Macedonia
PHONE: +389 (91) 236064; 232692
TITLE: Leader
NAME: Krste Jankovski

Communist League of Macedonia

ul. Marks i Engels 1/3–15, Skopje, Macedonia
TITLE: Leader
NAME: Milan Panchevski

Communist Party of Macedonia

Kozle 109, Skopje, Macedonia
TITLE: Leader
NAME: Todor Pelivanov

Macedonian National Front

Dimo Narednikot 53, Prilep, Macedonia
PHONE: +389 (91) 24911
TITLE: Leader
NAME: Ivan Spirkoski

Party for Democratic Action-Islamic Way

Ilindenska 191, Tetovo, Macedonia
PHONE: +389 (91) 32113
TITLE: Leader
NAME: Mazlam Kenan

Macedonian National Party

ul. 110 br. 8, Skopje, Macedonia
PHONE: +389 (91) 32113; 225246
TITLE: Leader
NAME: Vladimir Stefanovski

Civil Liberal Party

Venjamin Machukovski 5/2–11, Skopje, Macedonia
PHONE: +389 (91) 415490
TITLE: Leader
NAME: Boris Gegaj

Party for Democratic Movement of the Egyptians of Macedonia

Solunska 3, Struga, Macedonia
TITLE: Leader
NAME: Sinan Naser

Party for Democratic Action of Macedonia

Dzhon Kenedi 25–5–1, Skopje, Macedonia
PHONE: +389 (91) 415490
TITLE: Leader
NAME: Avdija Pepich

Albanian Democratic League-Liberal Party

Gale Hristov k. 3–6, Skopje, Macedonia
PHONE: +389 (91) 263523
TITLE: Leader
NAME: Dzhem Idrizi

Party for Democratic Prosperity-Party for National Union in Macedonia

Vtora makedonsko-albanska brigada 15–4, Skopje, Macedonia
PHONE: +389 (91) 31443
TITLE: Leader
NAME: Nevzat Halili

Party for Democratic Prosperity of the Albanians in Macedonia

Marshal Tito 2, Tetovo, Macedonia
PHONE: +389 (91) 31534
TITLE: Leader
NAME: Arben Dzhaferi

Party for Democratic Action-Civil League

Gjorgi Hristov 1/1–11, Skopje, Macedonia
PHONE: +389 (91) 266408; 238540
TITLE: Leader
NAME: Sadrija Hasanovich

Democratic Party for the Complete Emancipation of the Romanies in Macedonia

Ilindenska b.b., Kumanovo, Macedonia
PHONE: +389 (91) 112077
TITLE: Leader
NAME: Sevdzhan Sulejmanovski

Vnatrešno-Makedonska Revolucionerna Organizacija (Internal Macedonian Revolutionary Organization)

TITLE: President
NAME: Ljupco Georgievski

DIPLOMATIC REPRESENTATION

Embassies in Macedonia

Austria
Vasil Stefanovski 7, 91000 Skopje, Macedonia
PHONE: +389 (91) 109550
FAX: +389 (91) 130237
E-MAIL: austra@unet.com.mk
TITLE: Ambassador
NAME: Harald W. Kotschy

Canada
12-ta Udarna Brigada 2A, 91000 Skopje, Macedonia
PHONE: +389 (91) 125228; 122680
FAX: +389 (91) 122681
E-MAIL: dfaitmk@unet.com.mk
TITLE: Ambassador
NAME: Raphael Girard

China
Salvador Aljende 73, 91000 Skopje, Macedonia
PHONE: +389 (91) 176670; 176675
FAX: +389 (91) 133554
E-MAIL: embroc@unet.com.mk
TITLE: Charge d'Affaires
NAME: Cheng Po-chiu

France
Salvador Aljende 73, PO Box 557, 91000 Skopje, Macedonia
PHONE: +389 (91) 118749; 117574
FAX: +389 (91) 117760
E-MAIL: franamba@nic.mpt.com.mk
TITLE: Ambassador
NAME: Jacques Huntzinger

Germany
Dimitrija Chupovski 26, 91000 Skopje, Macedonia
PHONE: +389 (91) 110507
FAX: +389 (91) 117713
TITLE: Ambassador
NAME: Werner Burkart

Greece
Borka Talevski 6, 91000 Skopje, Macedonia
PHONE: +389 (91) 130198; 130208
FAX: +389 (91) 115718
TITLE: Ambassador
NAME: George Kaklikis

Italy
Osma Udarna brigada 22, 91000 Skopje, Macedonia
PHONE: +389 (91) 117430
FAX: +389 (91) 117087

E-MAIL: itl-emb@unet.com.mk
TITLE: Ambassador
NAME: Antonio Tarelli

Japan
Ul. Ilinden 9, 91000 Skopje, Macedonia
PHONE: +389 (91) 118731
FAX: +389 (91) 117087
TITLE: Ambassador
NAME: Yushu Takashima

Netherlands
Leninova 69–71, 91000 Skopje, Macedonia
PHONE: +389 (91) 129319; 109250
FAX: +389 (91) 129309
TITLE: Ambassador
NAME: Hendrik Heijnen

Russia
Pirinska 44, 91000 Skopje, Macedonia
PHONE: +389 (91) 117160
FAX: +389 (91) 117808
TITLE: Ambassador
NAME: Piotr Dobroserdov

Serbia
Pitu Guli 8, 91000 Skopje, Macedonia
PHONE: +389 (91) 129289; 131299; 128422
FAX: +389 (91) 129427
TITLE: Ambassador
NAME: Zoran Janackovic

Turkey
Slavej Planina bb, 91000 Skopje, Macedonia
PHONE: +389 (91) 113270; 112173
FAX: +389 (91) 117024
TITLE: Ambassador
NAME: Mustafa Fazli Kesmir

United Kingdom
Veljko Vlahovic 26, 91000 Skopje, Macedonia
PHONE: +389 (91) 117555; 117005
FAX: +389 (91) 117024
TITLE: Ambassador
NAME: Mark Dickinson

United States
Ul. Ilinden bb, 91000 Skopje, Macedonia
PHONE: +389 (91) 116180
FAX: +389 (91) 117103
TITLE: Ambassador
NAME: Michael Enik

JUDICIAL SYSTEM

Constitutional Court

Judicial Court of the Republic

BROADCAST MEDIA

American Forces Network

TYPE: U.S. Military

Makedonska Radiodefuzija

Goce Delcev bb, 91000 Skopje, Macedonia
PHONE: +389 (91) 117301
FAX: +389 (91) 225520
TITLE: Directorate General
CONTACT: T. Ilievski
TYPE: Government

Republika Macedonija Sovet za Radiodifuzija

Ilindenska No. 9, 91000 Skopje, Macedonia
PHONE: +389 91129084; 129226
FAX: +389 91130211
E-MAIL: sovetrd@lotus.mot.com.mk
TITLE: Technical Coordinator
CONTACT: Ljupcho Manchevski
TYPE: Private

Televizija Makedonije

Dolno Nerezi bb, 91000 Skopje, Macedonia
PHONE: +38 (91) 258230

COLLEGES AND UNIVERSITIES

Sts. Cyril and Methodius University

Bul. Krste Misirkov bb, 91000 Skopje, Macedonia
PHONE: +389 (91) 118155
FAX: +389 (91) 116370
E-MAIL: webmaster@marnet.mk
WEBSITE: http://www.ukim.edu.mk

Univerzitet Sv. Kliment Ohridski

Bul. 1 Maj bb, 97000 Bitola, Macedonia
PHONE: +389 (97) 23788; 23192
FAX: +389 (97) 23594
WEBSITE: http://www.uklo.edu.mk

NEWSPAPERS AND MAGAZINES

Delo

Pind Vrmem, 26 Petar Drapsin St., 91000 Skopje, Macedonia
PHONE: +389 (91) 231949
FAX: +389 231949
TITLE: Managing Editor
CONTACT: Bratislav Tashovski

Dnevnik

Nikola Vapcarov 2/4, Skopje, Macedonia
PHONE: +389 (91) 127037
FAX: +389 (91) 127037
E-MAIL: dnevnik@soros.org.mk
WEBSITE: http://www.dnevnik.com.mk
TITLE: Editor
CONTACT: Branko Geroski
CIRCULATION: 50,000

Flaka E Vallazerimit

Nip Nova Makedonija, M.II. Jasmin B.B., 91000 Skopje, Macedonia
PHONE: +389 (91) 228632
FAX: +389 (91) 224829
TITLE: Editor-in-Chief
CONTACT: Abdulahadi Zulfikjari

Fokus

PIND Step de Fokus, Debarca 56, 91000 Skopje, Macedonia
PHONE: +389 (91) 111327
FAX: +389 (91) 115458
E-MAIL: info@focus.com.mk
WEBSITE: http://www.focus.com.mk
TITLE: Editor
CONTACT: Nikola Miadenov
CIRCULATION: 15,000

Nova Makedonija (New Macedonia)

Nip Nove Makedonija, M.H. Jasmin B.B., 91000 Skopje, Macedonia
PHONE: +389 (91) 237455
FAX: +389 (91) 118238
WEBSITE: http://www.novamakedonija.com.mk
TITLE: Editor-in-Chief
CONTACT: Georgi Ajanovski
CIRCULATION: 25,000

Oglasnik M

Nip M, PO Box 441, 91000 Skopje, Macedonia
PHONE: +389 (91) 238808
WEBSITE: http://www.oglasnik.com.mk
TITLE: Editor
CONTACT: P. Ancevski
CIRCULATION: 10,000

Puls

Nip Nova Makedonija, M.H. Jasmin B.B., 91000 Skopje, Macedonia
PHONE: +389 (91) 117124
FAX: +389 (91) 118024
E-MAIL: contact@puls.com.mk
WEBSITE: http://www.puls.com.mk
TITLE: Editor-in-Chief
CONTACT: Vasil Mickovski
CIRCULATION: 4,000

Start

WEBSITE: http://www.start.com.mk

Vecer

Nip Nova Makedonija, M.H. Jasmin B.B., 91000 Skopje, Macedonia
PHONE: +389 (91) 111537
FAX: +389 (91) 238327
E-MAIL: vecer@lotus.mpt.com.mk
WEBSITE: http://www.vecer.com.mk
TITLE: Editor-in-Chief
CONTACT: Goran Mihailovski
CIRCULATION: 50,000

Balkan Forum

Ul. Mito Hadzivasilev B.B., PO Box 556, Skopje, Macedonia
TITLE: Editor
CONTACT: Risto Lazarov
TYPE: Political science, general

Macedonian Review

Ruzveltova, 6, PO Box 85, 91001 Skopje, Macedonia
TITLE: Editor
CONTACT: Boris Vishinski
TYPE: Literary criticism and collections, art, social science, general

Makedonsko Sonce

Redakcija "Makedonsko sonce" ul. "Leninova" br.79, MK 1000 Skopje, Macedonia
PHONE: +389 (91) 130137
FAX: +389 (91) 130137
E-MAIL: urednik@makedonskosonce.com
WEBSITE: http://www.makedonskosonce.com
TYPE: Social science, general

PUBLISHERS

Medis, Skopje

M. Hadzhivasilev 36/1-2, 1000 Skopje, Macedonia
PHONE: +389 (91) 118104
FAX: +389 (91) 272253
E-MAIL: medis@informa.mk
WEBSITE: http://www.medis.com.mk

TITLE: President
CONTACT: Mirko Spiroski
SUBJECTS: Biological Sciences, Communications, Computer Science, Education, Electronics, Mathematics, Medicine, Nursing, Dentistry, Microcomputers

Menora Publishing House

Bul Jane Sandanski 36-4/13, 1000 Skopje, Macedonia
PHONE: +389 (91) 418872
FAX: +389 (91) 418872
E-MAIL: menora@unet.com.mk
WEBSITE: http://www.members.xoom.com/menora
TITLE: Director
CONTACT: Jordan Pop-Atanazov
SUBJECTS: Science

Mi-An Knigoizdatelstvo

ul. Vasil Gjorgov 39, baraka 7, 1000 Skopje, Macedonia
PHONE: +389 (91) 121182
FAX: +389 (91) 121182
E-MAIL: mian@mian.com.mk
CONTACT: Katerina Milchevska
SUBJECTS: Journalism, Literature, Literary Criticism, Essays, Poetry, Publishing & Book Trade Reference

Nov svet (New World)

Briselska 1, 1000 Skopje, Macedonia
PHONE: +389 (91) 378662
CONTACT: Jozo T. Boskovski
SUBJECTS: Art, Journalism, Literature, Literary Criticism, Essays, Philosophy, Poetry, Science (General)
TOTAL PUBLISHED: 2,000 print

Seizmoloska Opservatorija

PO Box 422, 1000 Skopje, Macedonia
PHONE: +389 (91) 231953
FAX: +389 (91) 114042
E-MAIL: ljupco@iunona.pmf.ukim.edu.mk
TITLE: Editor, International Rights
CONTACT: Vera Cejkovska
SUBJECTS: Computer Science, Earth Sciences, Electronics, Electrical Engineering, Geography, Geology

St. Clement of Ohrid National And University Library

Bul Goce Delcev 6, 1000 Skopje, Macedonia
PHONE: +389 (91) 115177; 133418
FAX: +389 (91) 226846
E-MAIL: kliment@nubsk.edu.mk
WEBSITE: http://www.nubsk.edu.mk
TITLE: Director & Chief Executive
CONTACT: Vera Kalajlievska
SUBJECTS: Library & Information Sciences

Zumpres Publishing Firm

ul. Vanjamin Macukovski 6, P Fah 363, 1000 Skopje, Macedonia
PHONE: +389 (91) 163539; 425175
FAX: +389 (91) 425176; 429196
E-MAIL: zumpres@yahoo.com
SUBJECTS: Anthropology, Archaeology, Astrology, Behavioral Sciences, Biography, Biblical Studies, Computer Science, Fiction, History, Literature, Philosophy

RELIGIOUS ORGANIZATIONS

As a former Communist republic and member of the Yugoslav federation, religious organizations in Macedonia were generally eradicated or forced into hiding. Nearly 70 percent belong to the Orthodox Church, 30 percent Muslim, and 3 percent Roman Catholic.

FURTHER READING

Articles

"Macedonia: NATO Sued Over Bees." *New York Times,* September 15, 2000, p. A6.

Perry, Duncan. "Macedonia's Quest for Security and Stability." *Current History,* March 2000, vol. 99, no. 635, p. 129+.

Books

Ackermann, Alice. *Making Peace Prevail: Preventing Violent Conflict in Macedonia.* Syracuse, NY: Syracuse University Press, 2000.

Poulton, Hugh. *Who Are the Macedonians?* 2nd ed. Bloomington: Indiana University Press, 2000.

MACEDONIA, THE FORMER YUGOSLAV REPUBLIC OF: STATISTICAL DATA

For sources and notes see "Sources of Statistics" at the front of each volume.

GEOGRAPHY

Geography

Area:

Total: 25,333 sq km.

Land: 24,856 sq km.

Land boundaries:

Total: 748 km.

Border countries: Albania 151 km, Bulgaria 148 km, Greece 228 km, Serbia and Montenegro 221 km (all with Serbia).

Coastline: 0 km (landlocked).

Climate: warm, dry summers and autumns and relatively cold winters with heavy snowfall.

Terrain: mountainous territory covered with deep basins and valleys; three large lakes, each divided by a frontier line; country bisected by the Vardar River.

Natural resources: chromium, lead, zinc, manganese, tungsten, nickel, low-grade iron ore, asbestos, sulfur, timber, arable land.

Land use:

Arable land: 24%

Permanent crops: 2%

Permanent pastures: 25%

Forests and woodland: 39%

Other: 10% (1993 est.).

HUMAN FACTORS

Demographics (A)

	1990	1995	1998	2000	2010	2020	2030	2040	2050
Population	NA	1,986	2,015	2,042	2,115	2,171	2,187	2,161	2,108
Life expectancy - males	NA	69.7	70.5	71.6	73.7	75.5	76.9	78.1	79.0
Life expectancy - females	NA	74.0	75.0	76.2	78.6	80.7	82.3	83.7	84.7
Birth rate (per 1,000)	NA	16.2	14.4	13.7	12.9	11.8	10.2	9.8	9.4
Death rate (per 1,000)	NA	8.2	8.1	7.7	8.3	8.9	9.8	11.3	12.5
Women of reproductive age (15-49 yrs.)	NA	506.0	519.4	527.4	536.7	516.8	486.4	443.2	408.7
Fertility rate	NA	2.1	1.9	1.8	1.7	1.7	1.7	1.7	1.7

Except as noted, values for vital statistics are in thousands; life expectancy is in years.

Health Personnel

	National Data	World Data (wtd ave)
Total health expenditure as a percentage of GDP, 1990-1998[a]		
Public sector	7.8	2.5
Private sector	0.8	2.9
Total[b]	7.5	5.5
Health expenditure per capita in U.S. dollars, 1990-1998[a]		
Purchasing power parity	NA	561
Total	171	483
Availability of health care facilities per 100,000 people		
Hospital beds 1990-1998[a]	520	330
Doctors 1992-1995[a]	213	122
Nurses 1992-1995[a]	NA	248

Health Indicators

	National Data	World Data
Life expectancy at birth (years)		
1980	NA	61
1998	73	67
Daily per capita supply of calories		
1970	NA	2,358
1997	2,664	2,791
Daily per capital supply of protein		
1997 (grams)	69	74
Total fertility rate (births per woman)		
1980	2.5	3.7
1998	1.8	2.7
People living with (1997)		
Tuberculosis (cases per 100,000)	31.6	60.4
HIV/AIDS (% aged 15 - 49 years)	0.01	0.99

Infants and Malnutrition

	National Data	World Data (wtd ave)
Under 5 mortality rate (1989)	27	NA
% of infants with low birthweight (1992-98)[1]	8	17
Births attended by skilled health staff (% of total births 1996-98)	95	52
% fully immunized at 1 year of age (1995-98)[1]		
TB	97	82
DPT	97	77
Polio	97	77
Measles	98	74
Prevalence of child malnutrition (1992-98)[1] (based on weight for age, % of children under 5 years)	NA	30

Ethnic Division

Macedonian 66.6%
Albanian 22.7%
Turkish 4.0%
Roma 2.2%
Serb 2.1%
Other 2.4%

Data for 1994.

Religion

Macedonian Orthodox 67%
Muslim 30%
Other 3%

Major Languages

Macedonian 70%
Albanian 21%
Turkish 3%
Serbo-Croatian 3%
Other 3%

EDUCATION

Public Education Expenditures

	1997
Public expenditures on education as % of GNP	5.1
Expenditures per student as % of GNP per capita	
Primary	20.2
Secondary	27.3
Tertiary	69.5
Pupils per teacher at the primary level	19
Duration of primary education in years	8
World data for comparison	
Public expenditures on education as % of GNP (mean)	4.8
Pupils per teacher at the primary level (wtd ave)	33
Duration of primary education in years (mean)	9

Educational Attainment (A)

Age group (1994)	15+
Population of this age group	1,136,2492
Highest level attained (%)	
No schooling	28.0
First level	
Not completed	28.2
Completed	NA
Entered second level	30.6
Entered post-secondary	6.7

Libraries

National Libraries	**1995**
Administrative Units	1
Service Points or Branches	1
Number of Volumes (000)	2,317
Registered Users (000)	158
Loans to Users (000)	1.42
Total Library Staff	154
Public Libraries	**1992**
Administrative Units	62
Service Points or Branches	122
Number of Volumes (000)	2,729
Registered Users (000)	987
Loans to Users (000)	NA
Total Library Staff	389

GOVERNMENT & LAW

Political Parties

Assembly (Sobranje)	no. of seats
Internal Macedonian Revolutionary Organization-Democratic Party for Macedonian National Unity (VMRO-DPMNE)	49
Social-Democratic Alliance of Macedonia (SDSM)	27
Party for Democratic Prosperity (PDP)	14
Democratic Alternative (DA)	13
Democratic Party for Albanians (DPA)	11
Liberal Democratic Party (LDP)	4
Socialist Party	1
Roma Party	1

Elections were last held 18 October and 1 November 1998 (next to be held in 2002). The SDSM is the former Communist Party.

Government Budgets (B)

Revenues	$1.06 billion
Expenditures	$1.00 billion
Capital expenditures	$107.00 million

Data for 1996 est.

Military Affairs (A)

	1995	1996	1997
Military expenditures			
Current dollars (mil.)	90[e]	107	83
1997 constant dollars (mil.)	93[e]	109	83
Armed forces (000)	16	15	15
Gross national product (GNP)			
Current dollars (mil.)	3,110	3,190	3,290
1997 constant dollars (mil.)	3,220	3,250	3,290
Central government expenditures (CGE)			
1997 constant dollars (mil.)	809	825	816
People (mil.)	2.0	2.0	2.0
Military expenditure as % of GNP	2.9	3.3	2.5
World data on military expediture as % of GNP	2.7	2.6	2.6
Military expenditure as % of CGE	11.5	13.2	10.2
World data on military expediture as % of CGE	10.5	10.3	10.2
Military expenditure per capita (1995 $)	47	55	42
World data on military expediture per capita (1997 $)	146	143	145
Armed forces per 1,000 people (soldiers)	8.1	7.6	7.5
World data on armed forces per 1,000 people (soldiers)	4.1	3.9	3.8
GNP per capita (1997 $)	1,640	1,640	1,650
Total imports[7]			
Current dollars (mil.)	1,719	1,464[e]	1,600[e]
1997 constant dollars (mil.)	1,780	14,880[e]	1,600[e]
Total exports[7]			
Current dollars (mil.)	1,205	1,147	1,200[e]
1997 constant dollars (mil.)	1,248	1,166	1,200[e]
Arms as percent of total imports[8]	0	0	0
Arms as percent of total exports[8]	0	0	0

Crime

Crime volume (for 1998)

Crimes reported 22,123

Total persons convicted 14,446

Crimes per 100,000 population 1,102

Persons responsible for offenses

Total number suspects 21,967

Total number of female suspects . . . . .NA

Total number of juvenile suspects 6,546

LABOR FORCE

Total Labor Force (A)

673,000 (1995 est.).

Unemployment Rate

35% (1999 est.)

PRODUCTION SECTOR

Energy Production

Production .6.664 billion kWh

Production by source

Fossil fuel 85.37%

Hydro 14.63%

Nuclear 0%

Other 0%

Exports . . . . .0 kWh

Data for 1998.

Energy Consumption

Consumption . . . . .6.198 billion kWh

Imports . . . . .0 kWh

Data for 1998.

Transportation

Highways:

Total: 8,684 km.

Paved: 5,540 km (including 133 km of expressways).

Unpaved: 3,144 km (1997 est.).

Waterways: none, lake transport only.

Pipelines: 10 km.

Airports: 16 (1999 est.).

Airports - with paved runways: 10.

Top Agriculture Products

Rice, tobacco, wheat, corn, millet, cotton, sesame, mulberry leaves, citrus, vegetables; beef, pork, poultry, mutton.

Top Mining Products (B)

Mineral resources include: chromium, lead, zinc, manganese, tungsten, nickel, low-grade iron ore, asbestos, sulfur.

MANUFACTURING SECTOR

GDP & Manufacturing Summary (A)

	1980	1985	1990	1995
GDP ($-1990 mil.)	2,673	2,748	2,590	1,550
Per capita ($-1990)	1,489	1,429	1,266	719
Manufacturing share (%) (current prices)	NA	NA	NA	NA
Manufacturing				
Value added ($-1990 mil.)	1,478	1,892	1,822	906e
Industrial production index	NA	NA	NA	NA
Value added ($ mil.)	1,459e	959e	929	909
Gross output ($ mil.)	5,217e	2,881e	2,206	2,044
Employment (000)	230e	199e	185	127
Profitability (% of gross output)				
Intermediate input (%)	72	67e	58	56
Wages and salaries inc. supplements (%)	8e	10e	20e	21
Gross operating surplus	20e	24e	22e	23
Productivity ($)				
Gross output per worker	22,677e	14,482e	11,911	16,097
Value added per worker	6,422e	4,844e	5,016	7,157
Average wage (inc. supplements)	1,861e	1,416e	2,389e	3,415
Value added ($ mil.)				
Food products	132e	82e	80	137
Beverages	33e	23e	24	81
Tobacco products	134e	83e	82	89
Textiles	108e	102e	82	43
Wearing apparel	232e	141e	106	96
Leather and fur products	34e	22	20	21
Footwear	43e	27	37	7
Wood and wood products	5e	3e	5	6

	National Data		World Data for Comparison	
Furniture and fixtures	23^e	22^e	31	23
Paper and paper products	13^e	9^e	7	14
Printing and publishing	24^e	15^e	22	22
Industrial chemicals	89^e	55^e	46	61
Other chemical products	15^e	12^e	37	33
Petroleum refineries	56^e	36^e	42	34
Rubber products	2^e	2^e	NA	1
Plastic products	29^e	15^e	9	17
Pottery, china and earthenware	44^e	16^e	16	6
Glass and glass products	4^e	3^e	1	4
Other non-metal mineral products	17^e	11^e	8	5
Iron and steel	169^e	63^e	83	30
Non-ferrous metals	5^e	3^e	8	4
Metal products	69^e	58^e	45	48
Non-electrical machinery	19^e	18^e	6	14
Electrical machinery	69^e	62^e	69	62
Transport equipment	80^e	66^e	52	41
Prof. and scientific equipment	1^e	1^e	1	3
Other manufacturing	11^e	9^e	9	9

COMMUNICATIONS

Daily Newspapers

	National Data	World Data for Comparison
Daily Newspapers		
Number of Dailies	3	8,391
Total Circulation (000)	41	548,000
Circulation per 1,000 inhabitants	21	96

Telecommunications

Telephones - main lines in use: 407,000 (1997).

Telephones - mobile cellular: NA

Telephone system:

Domestic: NA

International: NA

Radio broadcast stations: AM 29, FM 20, shortwave 0 (1998).

Radios: 410,000 (1997).

Television broadcast stations: 136 (1997).

Televisions: 510,000 (1997).

Internet Service Providers (ISPs): 6 (1999).

FINANCE, ECONOMICS, & TRADE

Economic Indicators

National product: GDP—purchasing power parity—$7.6 billion (1999 est.).

National product real growth rate: 2.5% (1999 est.).

National product per capita: $3,800 (1999 est.).

Inflation rate—consumer price index: 1% (1999 est.).

Balance of Payments

	1996	1997	1998
Exports of goods (f.o.b.)	1,147	1,201	1,318
Imports of goods (f.o.b.)	−1,464	−1,589	−1,715
Trade balance	−317	−388	−398
Services - debits	−309	−273	−304
Services - credits	154	128	131
Private transfers (net)	422	528	665
Government transfers (net)	52	7	28
Overall balance	−288	−275	−288

Exchange Rates

Exchange rates:

Denars per US$1

January 2000 .... 59.773
1999 .... 56.902
1998 .... 54.462
1997 .... 50.004
1996 .... 39.981
1995 .... 37.882

Top Import Origins

$1.56 billion (f.o.b., 1999 est.)

Origins (1998)

Germany 13%
Serbia and Montenegro 13%
Slovenia 8%
Ukraine 6%
Italy 6%

Top Export Destinations

$1.2 billion (f.o.b., 1999 est.)

Destinations (1998)

Germany	21%
Serbia and Montenegro	18%
United States	13%
Greece	7%
Italy	6%

Foreign Aid

Recipient: Taiwan $10.5 million; EU $100 million to be split with Albania (1999).

Import/Export Commodities

Import Commodities	Export Commodities
Machinery and equipment	Food
Chemicals	Beverages
Fuels	Tobacco
Food products	Miscellaneous manufactures
	Iron and steel

MADAGASCAR

CAPITAL: Antananarivo.

FLAG: The flag consists of a white vertical stripe at the hoist flanked at the right by two horizontal stripes, the upper in red, the lower in green.

ANTHEM: *Ry Tanindrazanay Malala O (Our Beloved Country).*

MONETARY UNIT: The Malagasy franc (FMG) is a paper currency. There are coins of 1, 2, 5, 10, 20, 25, 50, 100, and 250 Malagasy francs and notes of 50, 100, 500, 1,000, 2,500 5,000, 10,000 and 25,000 Malagasy francs. FMG1 = $0.00025 (or $1 = FMG3,999.4).

WEIGHTS AND MEASURES: The metric system is generally used.

HOLIDAYS: New Year's Day, 1 January; Commemoration of 1947 Rebellion, 29 March; Labor Day, 1 May; Independence and National Day, 26 June; All Saints' Day, 1 November; Christmas, 25 December; Anniversary of the Democratic Republic of Madagascar, 30 December. Movable religious holidays include Good Friday, Easter Monday, Ascension, and Pentecost Monday.

TIME: 3 PM = noon GMT.

LOCATION AND SIZE: Situated off the southeast coast of Africa, Madagascar is the fourth-largest island in the world, with an area of 587,040 square kilometers (226,657 square miles), slightly less than twice the size of Arizona. It is separated from the coast of Africa by the Mozambique Channel, where it claims a number of small islands covering about 28 square kilometers (11 square miles), which are administered by France. The coastline of Madagascar is 4,828 kilometers (3,000 miles). Madagascar's capital city, Antananarivo, is located near the center of the island.

CLIMATE: The climate of the eastern and northwestern coasts is dominated by heavy rains from May to September, and from which the central plateau, the western coast, and the southern part of the island are sheltered. The central plateau enjoys a tropical mountain climate with well-differentiated seasons. Generally speaking, the climate throughout the island is moderated by altitude, with the coast being hotter (average temperatures 21–27°C, or 70–80°F) and wetter than the plateau (average temperatures 13–19°C, or 55–67°F).

Democratic Republic of Madagascar
République Démocratique de Madagascar
Repoblika Demokratika n'i Madagaskar

INTRODUCTORY SURVEY

RECENT HISTORY

Once an independent kingdom, Madagascar became a French colony in 1886. During World War II (1939-1945) Madagascar was occupied by British troops to prevent its naval facilities from being used by the Japanese. In 1943 French administration was restored under General Charles de Gaulle's Free French government. Madagascar became a French overseas territory in 1946.

The Malagasy Republic became an independent nation on June 26, 1960, and on September 20, 1960, was elected to United Nations membership.

The constitution that was adopted in October 1958 and amended in June 1960 provided Madagascar with a strong presidential form of government. The president, Philibert Tsiranana, remained in power until May 1972 when political protests throughout Madagascar led to the fall of his government. General Gabriel Ramanantsoa was immediately asked to form a nonpolitical "government of national unity." Ramanantsoa raised the minimum wage, provided strike pay, prosecuted corrupt officials, and introduced price and currency controls. The new government also broke diplomatic ties with South Africa, established relations with the Communist countries, and arranged for the withdrawal of French military forces under new cooperation agreements with France.

In December 1975 the Second Malagasy Republic, to be called the Democratic Republic of Madagascar, was proclaimed, and Admiral Didier

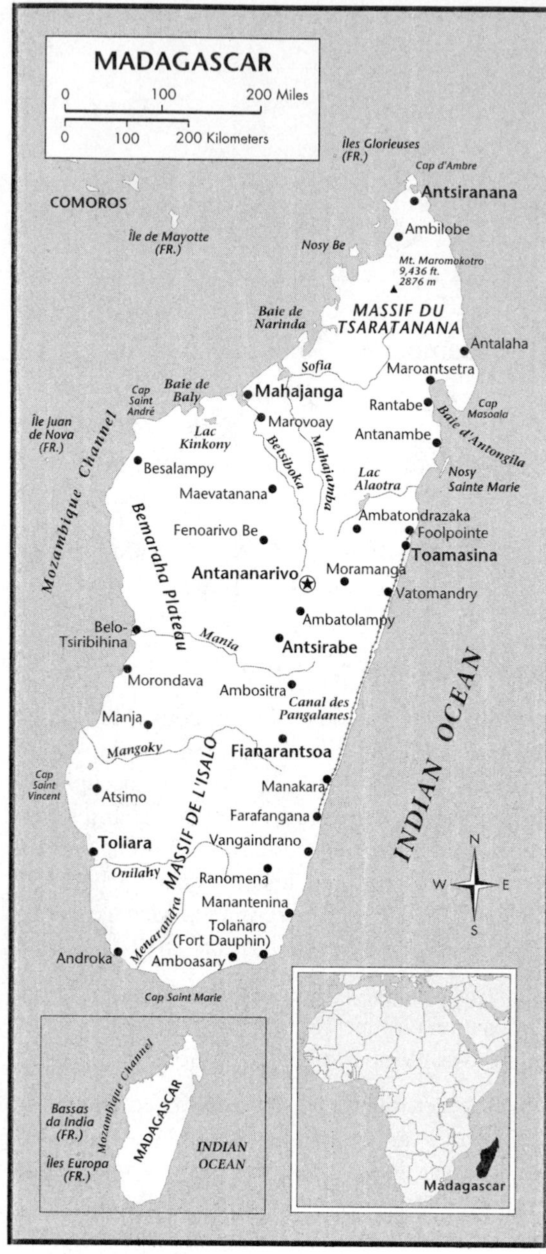

Ratsiraka was installed as president on January 4, 1976. The new regime accelerated growing state control of the economy and Madagascar turned to the former Soviet Union and the Democratic People's Republic of Korea for military aid. By 1979, however, growing economic difficulties forced Ratsiraka to develop closer ties with the West. Ratsiraka was elected to a new term as president on November 7, 1982. By early 1987 the governing coalition appeared to be unraveling. On May Day four of the parties called for the resignation of the government and early elections. By November Ratsiraka agreed to share power with a transitional government headed by Albert Zafy, his main rival. Ratsiraka's Revolutionary Supreme Council stepped down from power.

On August 19, 1992, a new constitution was approved by national referendum. During 1992-1993 free presidential and National Assembly elections were held ending seventeen years of single party rule. Territorial elections, the first step in the creation of the senate, were held in November 1995.

President Zafy was impeached in September 1995, and Ratsiraka defeated Zafy in a runoff election that December. Ratsiraka became the second African head of state to have lost and then reclaimed the presidency through competitive elections.

A March 1998 constitutional referendum approved extensive revisions of the 1992 Constitution. The revised constitution significantly strengthened the presidency at the expense of the National Assembly.

GOVERNMENT

The first government of the Third Republic was formed in late August 1993 and operates under a 1992 constitution. The chief of state is the president who is elected by popular vote for a five-year term. The head of government is the prime minister appointed by the president from a list of candidates nominated by the National Assembly. The prime minister appoints the cabinet, called the Council of Ministers.

Its August 1992 constitution provides for a two-chamber legislature—a 150-deputy National Assembly and a Senate. Electors representing geographical areas and various economic and social sectors of the population indirectly choose two-thirds of the senators, and the president appoints one-third. The legislature is scheduled to become bicameral with the establishment of the Senate. Suffrage is universal at age eighteen.

Judiciary

At the top of the judicial system is the Supreme Court in Antananarivo. Other courts include the Court of Appeal, also in Antananarivo; courts for first trials of civil and criminal cases; ordinary and special criminal courts; and military courts. There are also a High Court of Justice to try high officials and a High Constitutional Court. Military courts presided over by civilian magistrates hear cases involving national security.

The traditional courts *(dina)* continue to handle some civil disputes and recently have been used in criminal cases because of inconvenience and inadequacy of the formal court system.

Political Parties

In the elections of 1998 the association for the Rebirth of Madagascar (AREMA) took sixty-three seats; Economic Liberalism and Democratic Action for National Recovery (LEADER/Fanilo) took sixteen seats; Judged by Your Work (AVI) took fourteen seats; Action, Truth, Development, and Harmony took six; and, four other parties and independents winning the remainder of the seats.

DEFENSE

The armed forces of Madagascar were composed in 2000 of about 21,000 personnel, including an army of 20,000, a navy of 500 (100 marines), and an air force of 500. Manpower is provided by conscription of all men from twenty to fifty for 18-month periods, but most servicemen are volunteers.

The paramilitary Gendarmerie National that had a strength of 7,500 in 2000 is the main force for the maintenance of public order and internal security. Military spending was estimated at $49 million in 1995.

ECONOMIC AFFAIRS

Madagascar is a poor country with over 70 percent of the population falling below the poverty level. Its agricultural-based economy supports a majority of the labor force. The agricultural sector accounted for 34 percent of GDP in 1998. Important export crops are coffee, vanilla, and cloves. There are substantial mineral deposits but poor infrastructure had made it impossible to exploit them profitably. Industry that accounted for 12 percent of GDP in 1998 is centered on food processing and textiles. Important investments have been made in tourism.

Huge obstacles stand in the way of Madagascar's economic growth. Government reforms are erratic, corruption and political instability continues, and the population continues to grow rapidly while malnutrition is chronic. Growth potential depends on reforms, outside financial aid and foreign investment.

Public Finance

Madagascar's budget has been consistently in deficit. Wages and salaries are the largest component of government expenditure. In 1998 the budget deficit amounted to 4 percent of GDP. In order to gain funds the government increased the tax rate to over 10 percent of GDP in 1998 and in 1999 to 2000 it was forecast to approach 11 percent of the GDP.

The U.S. Central Intelligence Agency estimated that 1998 government revenues totaled approximately $553 million and expenditures $735 million. External debt totaled $4.1 billion in 1997.

Income

In 1997 Madagascar's gross domestic product (GDP) was estimated at $11.5 billion, or about $780 per capita. The 1999 estimated GDP was 4.5 percent and the inflation rate was 9.5 percent. The estimated 1997 GDP contribution by sector was agriculture 34 percent, industry 12 percent, and services 54 percent.

Industry

Industrialization has been severely hampered by inadequate internal transportation and a restricted local market. The majority of industrial enterprises process agricultural products: rice, sugar, flour, tobacco, tapioca, and sisal. In addition there are some meat-packing plants. Urea- and ammonia-based fertilizers are produced in a plant that opened in 1985. Other industrial enterprises include two cement plants, a paper pulp factory, cotton spinning and weaving mills, and three automobile assembly plants. Additional industries are petroleum, tourism, soap, breweries, tanneries, and glassware.

Banking and Finance

Upon leaving the franc zone in June 1973 the government established the Central Bank of the Malagasy Republic (Banque Centrale de la République Magache).

In 1989 the Banque Nationale de Paris was the first French bank to open a private bank, the BMOI, since 1975 when the Ratsiraka government nationalized all private financial institutions. Financial sector liberalization has been a key condition of adjustment support through the 1990s. In early 1993 the privatization of the three state banks was still incomplete although from January it became possible for foreigners to buy shares in the Bankin'ry Tantsaha Mpamokatra (BTM) controlled by the Bank of Africa. A new bank, the Union Commercial Bank (UCB), incorporated in Mauritius, began operations in February 1993.

In 1999 there were six commercial banks in Madagascar including the BMOI and BNI-Credit Lyonnais (BNI-CL), both controlled by European banking institutions; the UCB and State Bank of Mauritiús (SBM), both controlled by Mauritián companies; the BTM; and, the Bank of New York (BFV/SG).

There are no securities exchanges in Madagascar.

Economic Development

Anti-government strikes, corruption, and a lack of commitment limited progress on the reforms through the 1990s. In 1997 a World Bank structural adjustment credit of $70 million was approved and in 1999 a $100 million credit plus $40 million from the IMF. The GDP growth rate increased steadily after these credits were allocated to Madagascar. However external debt remained at $4 billion throughout the 1990s although the inflation rate decreased from 45 percent in 1993 to 6.2 percent in 1998.

Growth should be in the 5 percent range for 2000-2001.

SOCIAL WELFARE

There is a National Social Security Fund that provides family allowances and workers' compensation for wage earners. Old age, disability, and survivors' pensions were introduced in 1969. The Labor Code requires employers to provide sick leave and maternity leave.

Women in urban areas enjoy a highly visible and influential-although secondary-position in society. Women hold many posts in business and government. Rural women face greater hardships, engaging in subsistence labor while raising a family.

Healthcare

All medical services in Madagascar are free. Each province has a central hospital, and local clinics, dispensaries, and mobile health units supplement maternity-care centers. Approximately 65 percent of the population has access to health care services. In 1996 there was one doctor for every 8,380 people. The most widespread diseases are malaria, leprosy, schistosomiasis, and tuberculosis. In 1994-1995 32 percent of the population had access to safe water and only 17 percent had adequate sanitation. The average life expectancy was fifty-five years in 2000.

Housing

Malagasy houses, although constructed of varying materials in different parts of the island (brick and wood in the plateau, thatch and leaves in the west, and often on stilts in the east), are always rectangular, sited north-south, with the doorway opening to the west. The rapid growth of towns after the end of World War II in 1945 created grave housing and sanitation problems, especially in Antananarivo.

EDUCATION

Although education is free and compulsory between the ages of six and twelve, there is still a considerable degree of illiteracy, estimated at 20 percent. In 1996 there were 1.6 million pupils attending 13,325 primary schools, secondary school enrollment was 302,035 pupils, and there were 26,715 students enrolled in higher education. The University of Madagascar in Antananarivo has several campuses. Also in Antananarivo are the Rural College of Ambatobe and the National Institute of Telecommunications and Posts.

2000 KEY EVENTS TIMELINE

March

- Cyclones and flooding cut major road links seriously endangering food security, access to medical care, and shelter for more than 600,000 people.
- The World Food Program (WFP) organizes an airlift of food and basic necessities for thousands of flood-trapped victims.

April

- Madagascar urges the United Nations to make an urgent appeal for US$15.7 million from donors to provide humanitarian assistance for cyclone and flood victims.

June

- The Food and Agricultural Organization (FAO) and WFP predict that food and seed stocks will be very tight throughout 2000 and 2001 in flood-stricken regions. The cyclones are expected to cause a serious decline in nutritional status in children under five, pregnant women, and the elderly. Export crops also are affected by the flooding.

August

- The IMF indicates that continued progress on economic reforms will permit Madagascar to qualify for the Heavily Indebted Poor Countries (HIPC) relief program.

November

- Doctors make an urgent appeal for medicines to treat a new outbreak of cholera that has killed four and hospitalized another eleven in Fianarantsoa. It is estimated that the country's supply of medicine is sufficient to treat just 300 people, which may not be enough.

December

- Only 25–35 percent of the voters turn out to vote in the local elections in Madagascar. Opposition parties and religious leaders call for a boycott saying that politicians failed to explain the importance of these elections aimed at increasing autonomy in Madagascar's six provinces.
- The World Bank and International Monetary Fund (IMF) announce on December 23 that the United States, Canada, Japan, and nations of Europe will provide debt relief for twenty-two of the world's poorest nations, including Benin, Bolivia, Burkina Faso, Cameroon, The Gambia, Guinea, Guinea-Bissau, Guyana, Honduras, Madagascar, Malawi, Mali, Mauritania, Mozambique, Nicaragua, Niger, Rwanda, São Tomé and Príncipe, Senegal, Tanzania, Uganda, and Zambia.

ANALYSIS OF EVENTS: 2000

BUSINESS AND THE ECONOMY

The bad news this year for Madagascar was the devastating floods, the huge costs they inflicted on human life, and the extensive damage they caused to property, infrastructure, and livelihood. The World Bank estimated that the floods resulted in $137 million of damage to infrastructure, and wreaked far greater havoc on businesses and cash crops. It was estimated that $77 million was lost in coffee, vanilla, and cloves. Analysts calculated that it would take four years for the coffee sector—where quality had been falling off steadily—to recover. As for staples some 150,000 hectares of rice, representing 20 percent of the total area under rice cultivation, were lost. Replacement imports were expected to reach 120,000 tons of rice at a cost of $26.6 million.

The response from the Bretton Woods institutions was quick. The World Bank offered a $24 million soft loan package with $18 million coming from the World Bank, $3 million from the government, and about $3 million from local communities. The International Monetary Fund (IMF) readjusted long-term support and relaxed repayment schedules. However, they pressured the government to give more policy attention to poverty reduction. The government was in the process of drafting a strategy that, along with tighter fiscal management, should free up resources for social spending when debt relief from the heavily indebted poor countries (HIPC) initiative was approved as expected near the end of 2000.

Independent of the flood damage, Madagascar's per capita income fell over the past three years by nearly 50 percent. In four years the franc fell against the dollar from 5,000:1 to 7,500:1. In 2000 real gross domestic product (GDP) improved slightly to 4.8 percent over 4.7 percent 1999, and given recovery, was expected to reach 5.6 percent in 2001. Inflation was projected to reach 10 percent, down from 14.4 percent in December 1999.

GOVERNMENT AND POLITICS

Malagasy politics revolved around three issues in 2000: keeping the military in the barracks, cleaning up the public sector, and campaigning for the December provincial elections. In June and July rumors of three coup plots hit the streets, implicating parliamentarians, ministers, soldiers, private sector executives, foreigners, and even Albert Zafy, the former president. Observers discounted the likelihood of a coup given no deep ethnic, regional, or military divisiveness. In August grievances within the military were aired, and the willingness by the officer corps to discuss grievances indicated the presence of a safety valve for avoiding unrest in the military.

One major accomplishment by the government was the establishment of a central corruption agency. In June the government began inspecting the ministries of public works, social welfare, and the national public administration school. The president has the authority to order inspections. It remained to be seen whether he will challenge vested interests and patronage networks.

The conduct of the provincial and local elections on December 3 marked a milestone in Madagascar's long and complicated autonomous province (AT) scheme. The scheme called for elections to six new provincial councils on a proportional representation list system. The councilors in each province select their governor. Several key rules—such as the exact powers of the governors, the relationship between the governors and the central government representatives at the provincial level, and constituency boundaries—had not been clearly set forth. It was also unclear to many Malagasy to what extent the central government was delegating authority to the provinces to legislate, manage their budgets, raise taxes, and deliver services.

Based on the lack of information, the radical opposition and many civil society groups boycotted the elections. Voter turnout was only 25–35 percent of the electorate. Early returns showed the moderate AVI party headed for a victory in Antananarivo with 55 percent of the vote. The ruling party, Arema, however, which was represented throughout the country, was thought to lead overall. Arema put up former Prime Minister Pascal Rakotomavo for governor of Antananarivo. He faced the AVI party's candidate, Norbert Ratsirahonana, a former prime minister as well. The final results were expected in January.

CULTURE AND SOCIETY

The Malagasy were hit hard in February, March, and April by the worst floods and cyclone damage in memory. Authorities estimated that more than 200 people were killed, and one million people affected, with some 400,000 of them requiring emergency aid. Thousands of homes were destroyed, along with 1,727 primary schools, 173 secondary schools, 82 primary health centers, and 86 district health centers. Irrigation systems were also damaged. Initially, the government estimated it would require emergency relief, excluding air transportation costs, estimated at US$3.7 million, but the United Nations (U.N.) revised the figures to US$15 million. Once emergency and humanitarian needs had been met, it was estimated that the costs of reconstruction were likely to reach US$120 million.

Prior to the cyclones, 70 percent of the population was at risk due to poverty. These figures were likely to be adjusted upwards as the full extent of the damage became known in 2001. The United Nations Development Program (UNDP) ranked Madagascar 141 of 174 countries on its Human Development Index scale (1998 data). Malagasy had a life expectancy at birth of 57.9 years, and adult literacy rate of 64.9 percent, a school enrollment of 40 percent, and a gross domestic product (GDP) per capita of $756. The Malagasy were among the most literate Africans, but they were also among the poorest people in the world.

DIRECTORY

CENTRAL GOVERNMENT

Head of State

President
Didier Ratsiraka, Office of the President, Ambohitsirohitra 101, Antananarivo, Madagascar
PHONE: +261 (2) 33444

Prime Minister
Tantely Andrianarivo, Office of the Prime Minister, Palais de Mahazoarivo, Antananarivo, Madagascar

Ministers

Minister of Foreign Affairs
Ministry of Foreign Affairs, BP 836, Anosy, Antananarivo 101, Madagascar
PHONE: +261 (2) 2234397; 2221198
FAX: +261 (2) 2234484

Minister of the Environment
Alphonse Randrianambinina, Ministry of the Environment, B.P. 651 Anosy, Antananarivo 101, Madagascar
PHONE: +261 (2) 24710

Vice Prime Minister of Budget and Development of Autonomous Provinces
Pierrot Jocelyn Rajaonarivelo, Ministry of Budget and Development of Autonomous Provinces

Minister of Agriculture
Marcel Theophile Raveloarijaona, Ministry of Agriculture

Minister of Armed Forces
Marcel Ranjeva, Ministry of the Armed Forces

Minister of the Civil Service, Labor, and Social Laws
Alice Razafinakanga, Ministry of the Civil Service, Labor, and Social Laws

Minister of Commerce and Consumer Affairs
Alphonse Randrianambinina, Ministry Minister of Commerce and Consumer Affairs

Minister of Economy and Finance
Tantely Andrianarivo, Ministry of Economy and Finance

Minister of Energy and Mines
Charles Rasoza, Ministry of Energy and Mines

POLITICAL ORGANIZATIONS

Committee of Living Forces (CFV)

TITLE: President
NAME: Emmanuel Rakotovahiny

Support Committee for Democracy and Development in Madagascar (CSDDM)

TITLE: President
NAME: Francisque Ravony

Action and Reflection Group for the Development of Madagascar (GRAD)

Congress Party for Madagascar Independence and Renewal (AKFM-Fanavaozana)

TITLE: President
NAME: Richard Andriamanjato

Association of United Malagasys (Famima)

TITLE: Leader
NAME: Didier Ratsiraka

Confederation of Civil Societies for Development (CSCD)

NAME: Guy Willy Razanamasy

Militant Party for the Development of Madagascar (PMDM)

NAME: Manandafy Rakotonirina

Rally for Social Democracy (RPSD)

TITLE: President
NAME: Evariste Marson

DIPLOMATIC REPRESENTATION

Embassies in Madagascar

United States
14–16, rue Rainitovo, Antsahavola, BP 620, Antananarivo, Madagascar
PHONE: +261 (2) 20089; 21257
FAX: +261 (2) 34539
TITLE: Charge d'Affaires
NAME: Howard T. Perlow

JUDICIAL SYSTEM

Supreme Court

High Constitutional Court

BROADCAST MEDIA

Radio Nederland Wereldomrop (RNW) (Radio Netherlands Relay Station)

PO Box 222, 1200 JG Hilversum, Netherlands
PHONE: +31 356724211
FAX: +31 356724207; 356724239
E-MAIL: letters@rnw.nl
WEBSITE: http://www.rnw.nl
BROADCASTS: Daily

Radio Television Analamanga

BP 7547, Ampesiloha, Madagascar
PHONE: +261 (2) 62804
TITLE: Owner
CONTACT: Ottacio Ermini
BROADCASTS: 25 hours/day
TYPE: Private

Tsioka Vao

BP 315, Tana, Madagascar
PHONE: +261 (2) 21749
TITLE: Director
CONTACT: Detkou Dedonnais
BROADCASTS: 0300–1900
TYPE: Private

Radio-Television Malagasy

PO Box 442, Antananarivo, Madagascar
PHONE: +261 (2) 21784
TITLE: Director
CONTACT: M. Rabesahala
CHANNEL: 5
TYPE: Government

COLLEGES AND UNIVERSITIES

University of Antananarivo

D'Ankatso BP 566, Antananarivo 101, Madagascar
PHONE: +261 (2) 24114
FAX: +261 (2) 22304

Institut Supérieur de Technologie d'Antananarivo

Route de Toamasina, Ampasampito BP 8122, Antananarivo 101, Madagascar
PHONE: +261 (2) 40542
FAX: +261 (2) 40543

Institut Supérieur de Technologie d'Antsiranana

BP 453, Antsiranana 201, Madagascar
PHONE: +261 (82) 22431
FAX: +261 (82) 39425

NEWSPAPERS AND MAGAZINES

Imongo Vaovao

Societe Imongo Vaovao, II-K-4 bis-Andravoahangy, 101 Antananarivo, Madagascar
PHONE: +261 (2) 2232879

Madagascar Tribune

Societe Malgache d'Edition, BP 659, 101 Antananarivo, Madagascar
PHONE: +261 (2) 2222635
FAX: +261 (2) 2222254
E-MAIL: tribune@bow.dts.mg
WEBSITE: http://www.madonline.com/tribune/index.htm
TITLE: Editor
CONTACT: Franck Raharison
CIRCULATION: 6,415

Midi Madagasikara

Ialana Ravoninahitriniarivo, BP 1414, Ankorondrano, 101 Antananarivo, Madagascar
PHONE: +261 (2) 2269779
FAX: +261 (2) 2227351
E-MAIL: midi@dts.mg
WEBSITE: http://www.dta.dta.mg/midi
TITLE: Editor
CONTACT: Stephane Jacob
CIRCULATION: 16,500

Madagascar Renouveou

BP 271, Antananarivo, Madagascar
TYPE: Social science, general

PUBLISHERS

Editions Ambozontany

c/o Librairie St. Paul Ambatomena, BP 1170, Fianarantsoa 301, Madagascar
PHONE: +261 (7) 50027; 51441
TITLE: Man. Director
CONTACT: Justin Bethaz
SUBJECTS: Ethnicity, History, Religion, Social Sciences

Maison d'Editions Protestante ANTSO

19 Lalana Venance Manifatra, Antananarivo 101, Madagascar
PHONE: +261 (2) 20886
FAX: +261 (2) 26372
TITLE: Man. Director
CONTACT: Hans Andriamampianina
SUBJECTS: Economics, Government, Political Science, Religion, Social Sciences, Sociology

Madagascar Printing & Press Company

rue Rabesahala, BP 953, Antananarivo 101, Madagascar
PHONE: +261 (2) 2222536
FAX: +261 (2) 2234534
E-MAIL: roi@dts.mg
TITLE: Man. Director, Editorial
CONTACT: Georges Ranaivosoa
SUBJECTS: History, Literature, Literary Criticism, Essays
TOTAL PUBLISHED: 24 print

Societe Malgache d'Edition

BP 659, Ankorondrano 101, Madagascar
PHONE: +261 (2) 2222635
FAX: +261 (2) 2222254
E-MAIL: tribune@bow.dts.mg
TITLE: Man. Director
CONTACT: Rahaga Ramaholimihaso
SUBJECTS: Communications, Economics, Education, Finance, Journalism, Law
TOTAL PUBLISHED: 4 print

Musee d'Art et d'Archaeologie

17 rue Dr. Villette Isoraka, PB 564, Antananarivo 101, Madagascar
PHONE: +261 (2) 21047
FAX: +261 (2) 28218
E-MAIL: musedar@syfed.refer.mg
TITLE: Director
CONTACT: J. A. Rakotoarisoa
SUBJECTS: Travel

Trano Printy Fiangonana Loterana Malagasy (TPFLM)-(Imprimerie Lutherienne)

9 ave. Grandidier Isoraka, PB 538, Antananarivo 101, Madagascar
PHONE: +261 (2) 223340
FAX: +261 (2) 262643
E-MAIL: impluth@dts.mg
TITLE: Man. Director

CONTACT: Raymond Randrianatoandro
SUBJECTS: Fiction, Relgion
TOTAL PUBLISHED: 100 print

RELIGIOUS ORGANIZATIONS

Mormon

Madagascar Mission
BP 5094, Antananarivo 101, Madagascar
WEBSITE: http://www.intelcities.com/Frolic_Freeway/madamission/madagascar.html

Protestant

Malagasy Lutheran Church
BP 1741, Antananarivo 101, Madagascar

FURTHER READING

Articles

Hubbard, Kim. "For the Love of Lemurs." *Audubon,* September 2000, vol. 102, no. 5, p. 60.

"Madagascar, Still Reeling after the Cyclones." *The Economist (US),* March 18, 2000, vol. 354, no. 8162, p. 43.

Naik, Gautum. "Vacationing with the Vermin." *Wall Street Journal,* September 8, 2000, p. W6.

Books

Covell, Maureen. *Historical Dictionary of Madagascar.* [computer file] Boulder, CO: netLibrary, Inc., 2000.

Oluonye, Mary N. *Madagascar.* Minneapolis, MN: Carolrhoda Books, 2000. [juvenile]

MADAGASCAR: STATISTICAL DATA

For sources and notes see "Sources of Statistics" at the front of each volume.

GEOGRAPHY

Geography

Area:

Total: 587,040 sq km.

Land: 581,540 sq km.

Land boundaries: 0 km.

Coastline: 4,828 km.

Climate: tropical along coast, temperate inland, arid in south.

Terrain: narrow coastal plain, high plateau and mountains in center.

Natural resources: graphite, chromite, coal, bauxite, salt, quartz, tar sands, semiprecious stones, mica, fish, hydropower.

Land use:

Arable land: 4%

Permanent crops: 1%

Permanent pastures: 41%

Forests and woodland: 40%

Other: 14% (1993 est.).

HUMAN FACTORS

Demographics (A)

	1990	1995	1998	2000	2010	2020	2030	2040	2050
Population	11,522	13,340	14,598	15,507	20,993	28,405	38,140	50,439	65,460
Life expectancy - males	49.6	50.9	52.0	52.7	56.4	60.0	63.5	66.6	69.4
Life expectancy - females	52.6	55.1	56.4	57.3	61.5	65.6	69.4	72.8	75.8
Birth rate (per 1,000)	44.3	43.9	43.4	42.9	40.5	38.2	35.5	32.7	30.0
Death rate (per 1,000)	15.4	14.1	13.3	12.7	10.1	8.1	6.7	5.7	5.0
Women of reproductive age (15-49 yrs.)	2,595	3,034	3,328	3,539	4,843	6,647	9,078	12,238	16,133
Fertility rate	6.2	6.0	5.9	5.8	5.5	5.1	4.7	4.3	3.9

Except as noted, values for vital statistics are in thousands; life expectancy is in years.

Health Personnel

	National Data	World Data (wtd ave)
Total health expenditure as a percentage of GDP, 1990-1998[a]		
Public sector	1.1	2.5
Private sector	1.0	2.9
Total[b]	2.1	5.5
Health expenditure per capita in U.S. dollars, 1990-1998[a]		
Purchasing power parity	NA	561
Total	5	483
Availability of health care facilities per 100,000 people		
Hospital beds 1990-1998[a]	90	330
Doctors 1992-1995[a]	24	122
Nurses 1992-1995[a]	55	248

Health Indicators

	National Data	World Data
Life expectancy at birth (years)		
1980	51	61
1998	58	67
Daily per capita supply of calories		
1970	2,424	2,358
1997	2,021	2,791
Daily per capital supply of protein		
1997 (grams)	46	74
Total fertility rate (births per woman)		
1980	6.6	3.7
1998	5.7	2.7
Population with access (%)		
To safe water (1990-96)	29	NA
To sanitation (1990-96)	15	NA
People living with (1997)		
Tuberculosis (cases per 100,000)	82.8[1]	60.4
HIV/AIDS (% aged 15 - 49 years)	0.12	0.99

Infants and Malnutrition

	National Data	World Data (wtd ave)
Under 5 mortality rate (1989)	157	NA
% of infants with low birthweight (1992-98)[1]	15	17
Births attended by skilled health staff (% of total births 1996-98)	57	52
% fully immunized at 1 year of age (1995-98)[1]		
TB	80	82
DPT	68	77
Polio	68	77
Measles	65	74
Prevalence of child malnutrition (1992-98)[1] (based on weight for age, % of children under 5 years)	40	30

Ethnic Division

Malayo-Indonesian (Merina and related Betsileo), Cotiers (mixed African, Malayo-Indonesian, and Arab ancestry - Betsimisaraka, Tsimihety, Antaisaka, Sakalava), French, Indian, Creole, Comoran.

Religion

Indigenous beliefs 52%
Christian 41%
Muslim 7%

Major Languages

French (official), Malagasy (official).

EDUCATION

Public Education Expenditures

	1980	1997
Public expenditures on education as % of GNP	4.4	1.9
Expenditures per student as % of GNP per capita		
Primary & Secondary	9.1[2]	NA
Tertiary	402.5	NA
Teachers' compensation as % of total current education expenditures	81.8	NA
Pupils per teacher at the primary level	NA	37
Duration of primary education in years	NA	6
World data for comparison		
Public expenditures on education as % of GNP (mean)	3.9	4.8
Pupils per teacher at the primary level (wtd ave)	NA	33
Duration of primary education in years (mean)	NA	9

Educational Attainment (B)

	1990	1995
Gross enrollment ratio (%)		
Primary level	102.9	91.6
Secondary level	18.0	15.6
Tertiary level	3.1	2.1
Enrollment of population aged 6-23 years (%)	40.0	NA

Literacy Rates (B)

	National Data	World Data
Adult literacy rate		
1980		
Male	56[1]	75
Female	43[1]	58
1995		
Male	60	81
Female	32	65

GOVERNMENT & LAW

Military Affairs (A)

	1990	1992	1995	1996	1997
Military expenditures					
Current dollars (mil.)	34	31	29	42	53
1997 constant dollars (mil.)	40	35	30	42	53
Armed forces (000)	21	21	21	21	21
Gross national product (GNP)					
Current dollars (mil.)	2,780	2,770	3,070	3,230	3,440
1997 constant dollars (mil.)	3,250	3,080	3,180	3,290	3,440
Central government expenditures (CGE)					
1997 constant dollars (mil.)	572	648	592	606	616
People (mil.)	11.5	12.2	13.3	13.7	14.1
Military expenditure as % of GNP	1.2	1.1	0.9	1.3	1.5
World data on military expenditure as % of GNP	4.5	3.4	2.7	2.6	2.6
Military expenditure as % of CGE	6.9	5.4	5.0	7.0	8.5
World data on military expenditure as % of CGE	17.0	12.5	10.5	10.3	10.2
Military expenditure per capita (1997 $)	3	3	2	3	4
World data on military expenditure per capita (1997 $)	242	173	146	143	145
Armed forces per 1,000 people (soldiers)	1.8	1.7	1.6	1.5	1.5
World data on armed forces per 1,000 people (soldiers)	5.3	4.5	4.1	3.9	3.8
GNP per capita (1997 $)	282	252	239	241	245
Arms imports[6]					
Current dollars (mil.)	10	0	5	0	0
1997 constant dollars (mil.)	12	0	5	0	0
Total imports[7]					
Current dollars (mil.)	571	448	499	507	478
1997 constant dollars (mil.)	669	497	517	515	478
Total exports[7]					
Current dollars (mil.)	319	277	368	299	224
1997 constant dollars (mil.)	374	307	381	304	224
Arms as percent of total imports[8]	1.8	0	1.0	0	0
Arms as percent of total exports[8]	0	0	0	0	0

Political Parties

National Assembly (Assemblee Nationale)	no. of seats
Association for the Rebirth of Madagascar (AREMA)	63
Economic Liberation and Democratic Action for National Recovery (LEADER/Fanilo)	16
Judged by Your Work (AVI)	14
Renewal of the Social Democratic Party (RPSD)	11
Action, Truth, Development and Harmony (AFFA)	6
Movement for the Progress of Madagascar (MFM)	3
Congress Party for Malagasy Independence (AKFM/Fanavaozana)	3
Group of Reflection and Action for the Development of Madagascar (GRAD/Iloafo)	1
Fihaonana Rally (Fihaonana)	1
Independents	32

Elections for the National Assembly were last held 17 May 1998 (next to be held in 2002).

Government Budgets (A)

Year: 1996

Total Expenditures: 2,799.1 Billions of Francs

Expenditures as a percentage of the total by function:

General public services and public order	19.73
Defense	5.40
Education	9.13
Health	6.83
Social Security and Welfare	0.93
Housing and community amenities	NA
Recreational, cultural, and religious affairs	0.24
Fuel and energy	NA
Agriculture, forestry, fishing, and hunting	10.21
Mining, manufacturing, and construction	NA
Transportation and communication	1.29
Other economic affairs and services	2.70

Crime

Crime rate (for 1994)

Crimes reported	10,752
Total persons convicted	NA
Crimes per 100,000 population	75

Persons responsible for offenses

Total number of suspects	6,150
Total number of female suspects	781
Total number of juvenile suspects	30

LABOR FORCE

Total Labor Force (A)

7 million (1995).

PRODUCTION SECTOR

Energy Production

Production	750 million kWh
Production by source	
Fossil fuel	33.33%
Hydro	66.67%
Nuclear	0%
Other	0%
Exports	0 kWh

Data for 1998.

Energy Consumption

Consumption	698 million kWh
Imports	0 kWh

Data for 1998.

Transportation

Highways:

Total: 49,837 km.

Paved: 5,781 km.

Unpaved: 44,056 km (1996 est.).

Waterways: of local importance only; isolated streams and small portions of Lakandranon' Ampangalana (Canal des Pangalanes).

Merchant marine:

Total: 13 ships (1,000 GRT or over) totaling 24,819 GRT/34,173 DWT.

Ships by type: cargo 7, chemical tanker 1, liquified gas 1, petroleum tanker 2, roll-on/roll-off 2 (1999 est.).

Airports: 133 (1999 est.).

Airports - with paved runways: 29.

Airports - with unpaved runways: 104.

Top Agriculture Products

Coffee, vanilla, sugarcane, cloves, cocoa, rice, cassava (tapioca), beans, bananas, peanuts; livestock products.

Top Mining Products (B)

Mineral resources include: graphite, chromite, coal, bauxite, salt, quartz, tar sands, semiprecious stones, mica.

MANUFACTURING SECTOR

GDP & Manufacturing Summary (A)

	1980	1985	1990	1995
GDP ($-1990 mil.)	2,211	2,089	2,376	2,339
Per capita ($-1990)	244	196	188	157
Manufacturing share (%) (current prices)	19.0	16.9	19.8	15.0[e]
Manufacturing				
Value added ($-1990 mil.)	627	420	453	466[e]
Industrial production index	121	87	100	76[e]
Value added ($ mil.)	221	132	142[e]	127[e]
Gross output ($ mil.)	569	328	343[e]	316[e]
Employment (000)	41	47	46[e]	50[e]
Profitability (% of gross output)				
Intermediate input (%)	61	60	59[e]	60[e]
Wages and salaries inc. supplements (%)	15	16	13[e]	13[e]
Gross operating surplus	24	25	28[e]	27[e]
Productivity ($)				
Gross output per worker	14,005	6,872	7,456[e]	6,339[e]
Value added per worker	5,460	2,790	3,105[e]	2,562[e]
Average wage (inc. supplements)	2,083	1,099	988[e]	837[e]
Value added ($ mil.)				
Food products	23	45	19[e]	19[e]
Beverages	34	16	16[e]	15[e]
Tobacco products	3	3	2[e]	1[e]
Textiles	67	16	58[e]	45[e]
Wearing apparel	19	6	3[e]	4[e]
Leather and fur products	3	1	1[e]	1[e]
Footwear	8	5	3[e]	2[e]
Wood and wood products	2	1	1[e]	1[e]
Furniture and fixtures	2	NA	1[e]	1[e]
Paper and paper products	4	3	5[e]	5[e]
Printing and publishing	6	2	2	2[e]
Industrial chemicals	1	1	NA	NA
Other chemical products	10	11	8[e]	8[e]
Petroleum refineries	11[e]	7[e]	9[e]	10[e]
Rubber products	1	1	1[e]	1[e]
Plastic products	3	2	1[e]	1[e]
Glass and glass products	2	NA	1[e]	NA
Other non-metal mineral products	2	1	2[e]	3[e]
Metal products	9	5	4[e]	4[e]
Non-electrical machinery	9	8	4[e]	4[e]
Electrical machinery	3	3	3[e]	3[e]
Transport equipment	7	2[e]	1[e]	1[e]
Other manufacturing	2	1	NA	NA

COMMUNICATIONS

Daily Newspapers

	National Data	World Data for Comparison
Daily Newspapers		
Number of Dailies	5	8,391
Total Circulation (000)	66	548,000
Circulation per 1,000 inhabitants	4.6	96

Telecommunications

Telephones - main lines in use: 33,000 (1995).

Telephones - mobile cellular: 0 (1995).

Telephone system: system is above average for the region.

Domestic: open-wire lines, coaxial cables, microwave radio relay, and tropospheric scatter links.

International: submarine cable to Bahrain; satellite earth stations - 1 Intelsat (Indian Ocean) and 1 Intersputnik (Atlantic Ocean region).

Radio broadcast stations: AM 2 (plus 8 repeater stations), FM 7, shortwave 5 (1998).

Radios: 3.05 million (1997).

Television broadcast stations: 1 (plus 36 repeaters) (1997).

Televisions: 325,000 (1997).

Internet Service Providers (ISPs): 3 (1999).

FINANCE, ECONOMICS, & TRADE

Economic Indicators

National product: GDP—purchasing power parity—$11.5 billion (1999 est.).

National product real growth rate: 4.5% (1999 est.).

National product per capita: $780 (1999 est.).

Inflation rate—consumer price index: 9.5% (1999 est.).

Exchange Rates

Exchange rates:

Malagasy francs (FMG) per US$1

October 1999	6,302.90
1999	5,877.81
1998	5,441.40
1997	5,090.90
1996	4,061.30
1995	4,265.60

Top Import Origins

$881 million (c.i.f., 1998 est.)

Origins (1997)

France	39%
Hong Kong	5%
Japan	5%
China	
Singapore	

Top Export Destinations

$600 million (f.o.b., 1998 est.)

Destinations (1997)

France	40%
United States	9%
Germany	8%
Japan	6%
United Kingdom	6%

Foreign Aid

Recipient: $838 million (1997).

Import/Export Commodities

Import Commodities	Export Commodities
Intermediate manufactures 30%	Coffee 45%
Capital goods 28%	Vanilla 20%
Petroleum 15%	Cloves
Consumer goods 14%	Shellfish
Food 13%	Sugar
	Petroleum products

Balance of Payments

	1992	1993	1994	1995	1996
Exports of goods (f.o.b.)	327	335	450	507	509
Imports of goods (f.o.b.)	−471	−514	−546	−628	−629
Trade balance	−144	−180	−96	−122	−120
Services - debits	−260	−302	−328	−359	−373
Services - credits	174	187	206	242	293
Private transfers (net)	108	113	49	78	94
Government transfers (net)	79	81	56	61	137
Overall balance	−198	−258	−277	−276	−153

MALAWI

Republic of Malawi

CAPITAL: Lilongwe.

FLAG: The national flag is a horizontal tricolor of black, red, and green, with a red rising sun in the center of the black stripe.

ANTHEM: Begins "O God, Bless Our Land of Malawi."

MONETARY UNIT: The kwacha (K) of 100 tambala (t) is the national currency; it replaced the Malawi pound (M£) on 28 August 1970 and was linked with the pound sterling until November 1973. There are coins of 1, 2, 5, 10, and 20 tambala, and notes of 50 tambala and 1, 5, 10, 20, and 50 kwacha. K1 = $0.06536 (or $1 = K15.3).

WEIGHTS AND MEASURES: The metric system is the legal standard.

HOLIDAYS: New Year's Day, 1 January; Martyrs' Day, 3 March; Kamuzu Day, 14 May; Republic or National Day, 6 July; Mothers' Day, 17 October; National Tree Planting Day, 21 December; Christmas, 25 December; Boxing Day, 26 December. Movable holidays include Good Friday and Easter Monday.

TIME: 2 PM = noon GMT.

LOCATION AND SIZE: A landlocked country in southeastern Africa, Malawi (formerly Nyasaland) has an area of 118,480 square kilometers (45,745 square miles), slightly larger than the state of Pennsylvania, with a total boundary length of 2,768 kilometers (1,720 miles). Malawi's capital city, Lilongwe, is located in the southwestern part of the country.

CLIMATE: Precipitation is heaviest along the northern coast of Lake Malawi, where the average is more than 163 centimeters (64 inches) per year. The average daily minimum and maximum temperatures in November, the hottest month, are 17°C (63°F) and 29°C (84°F); those in July, the coolest month, are 7°C (45°F) and 23°C (73°F).

INTRODUCTORY SURVEY

RECENT HISTORY

Between World Wars I (1914-1918) and II (1939-1945) Nyasaland seemed headed for eventual independence. In 1953, however, it was joined with the two Rhodesias—Northern Rhodesia (now Zambia) and Southern Rhodesia (now Zimbabwe)—in the Central African Federation.

When African citizens expressed angry opposition to the federation in 1959 a state of emergency was declared. In 1960 the Malawi Congress Party (MCP) headed by Dr. Hastings Kamuzu Banda stepped up the campaign against federation rule. At a constitutional conference held in London in November 1962, it was agreed that Nyasaland should become fully self-governing early in 1963 and that Banda who headed the MCP should become prime minister.

On July 6, 1964, Nyasaland became a fully independent member of the British Commonwealth of Nations, and adopted the name Malawi. On July 6, 1966, Banda assumed the presidency. During the first decade of Banda's presidency, Malawi's relations with its neighbors were sometimes stormy. In addition to claiming extensive territories outside the present boundaries of Malawi, Malawi became the first black African country to establish diplomatic relations with white-ruled South Africa; moreover, Banda became the first black African head of state to be officially received in South Africa that supplied arms and development funds to Malawi.

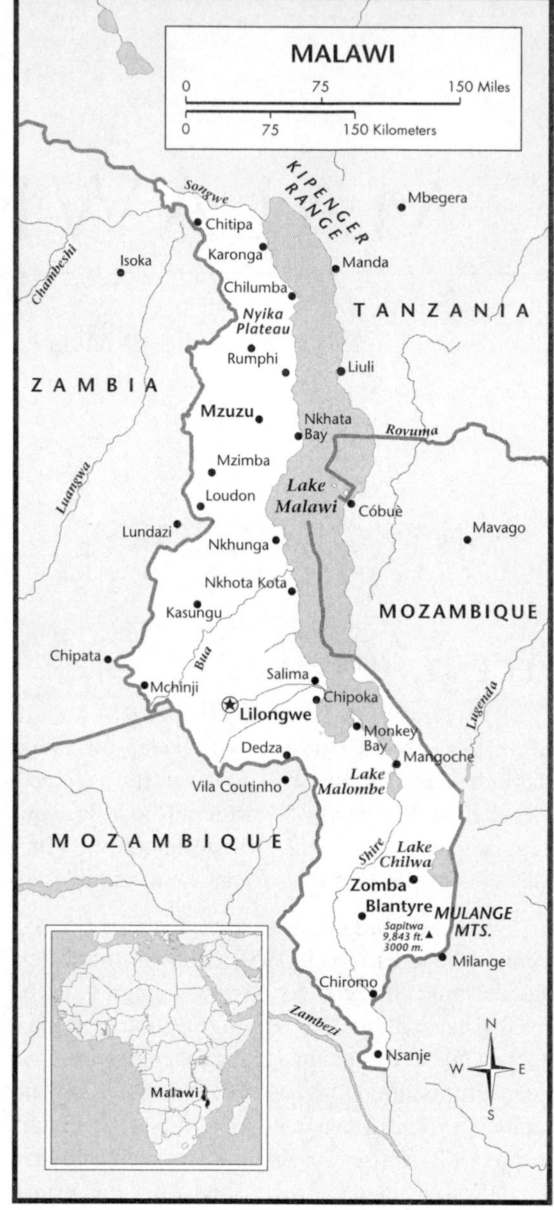

Banda continued to rule Malawi with an iron hand through the 1970s and into the late 1980s. During his rule his opponents were treated severely. Several thousand people were imprisoned for political offenses at one time or another, and leaders of the opposition groups were persecuted.

Opposition to Banda's harsh rule strengthened and Banda's grip on the country began to weaken. Under mounting pressure, Banda agreed to hold a referendum early in 1993 on whether Malawi should remain a one-party state. On 14 June 1993, 63 percent of those voting favored adopting multiparty democracy. Banda agreed to hold elections in 1994 and to draft a new constitution. Parliament adopted laws ending one-party rule and imprisonment without trial, and allowing dissidents to return home.

In the May 17, 1994, multiparty elections were held under the provisional constitution. Bakili Muluzi, a former cabinet minister, was elected president over Banda and two other candidates. Muluzi immediately ordered the release of political prisoners and the closing of the most notorious jails. The transition of power was fairly smooth, and an atmosphere of relative tolerance prevails. The new constitution took effect in May 1995.

GOVERNMENT

Malawi officially became a republic on July 6, 1966. The new constitution took effect on May 18, 1995. The president is the head of state and supreme executive authority. He is elected by popular vote for a five-year term. There is a 28-member cabinet named by the president. Legislative power is vested in the single-chamber 193-seat National Assembly whose members are elected by popular vote. Suffrage is universal at age eighteen. Parliamentary elections are to occur every five years unless the president dissolves the National Assembly before then. In March 1995 the National Assembly voted to establish a second chamber of parliament (a senate of eighty seats) in 1999.

Judiciary

The constitution provides for an independent judiciary and the government respects this provision. Defendants have the right to public trial, to have an attorney, to challenge evidence and witnesses, and to an appeal. There are numerous local courts throughout Malawi with a chain of appeals from the local courts up to a Supreme Court of Appeal.

In 1993 the attorney general suspended the operation of regional and national level traditional courts. Traditional courts at the local level may survive the recent reforms and continue to hear cases involving small claims and customary law.

Political Parties

Malawi was officially a one-party state from October 1973 until July 1993. The Malawi Congress Party (MCP) was the national party and Hastings Kamuzu Banda was its president for life. In a 1993 referendum voters rejected single-party rule by a margin of 63 percent to 35 percent and opposition parties and coalitions blossomed. Elections were held in May 1994 with seven parties participating.

Three parties took most of the seats: the United Democratic Front (UDF) with ninety-three seats; the MCP with sixty-six seats; and, the Alliance for Democracy (AFORD) with twenty-nine seats.

DEFENSE

In 2000 Malawi had an army of 5,000 men, organized into three infantry battalions and one support battalion. The air wing had eighty men and six transports. A 220-member naval force had one lake patrol craft. In 1996-97 Malawi spent $17 million or 0.8 percent of GDP on defense.

ECONOMIC AFFAIRS

Malawi is one of the world's least developed countries. In 1999 the agricultural sector employed an estimated 86 percent of Malawi's population and accounted for 45 percent of GDP. Over 90 percent of the population lives in rural areas.

Major agricultural exports include tobacco, tea, peanuts, coffee, and sugar. Malawi's agricultural economy has been troubled in recent years by drought and financial instability.

The economy also depends on international financial aid from individual donor nations, the IMF, and the World Bank. International aid donors, concerned about human rights abuses in Malawi, have tied future support to human rights reforms. During 1999 aid from international organizations, and bilateral aid from other countries amounted to over $500 million.

The fledgling mining sector in Malawi is slowly growing with the support of international financing. The government continues to privatize public enterprises although the wealth of the country resides in the hands of a small elite.

Public Finance

Government current revenues derive from import duties, income taxes on companies and individuals, income from government enterprises, excise duties, licenses, and value added tax. Education, health, and agriculture were the three biggest items on the budget for 2000. The U.S. Central Intelligence Agency estimated that in 1999-2000 government revenues totaled approximately $490 million and expenditures $523 million. External debt totaled $2.3 billion.

Income

In 1999 Malawi's gross domestic product (GDP) was $9.4 billion, or $940 per person. The 1999 estimated GDP growth rate was 4.2 percent and inflation was 45 percent. The 1998 estimated GDP contribution by sector was agriculture 37 percent, industry 29 percent, and services 43 percent.

Industry

Malawi's manufacturing sector is diverse. The processing of tea, tobacco, sugar, coffee, and cotton accounts for most of its output. Factories manufacture soap, detergents, cigarettes, furniture, cookies, bread, blankets and rugs, clothing, mineral waters plus other various consumer goods. Other operations include a gin distillery, a cotton mill, two textile plants, sawmills, brick making, roofing, tile manufacturing, radio assembly, tire retreading, and metal products.

Banking and Finance

The Reserve Bank of Malawi was established in Blantyre in 1964. It took over, by stages, the functions in Malawi of the former Bank of Rhodesia and Nyasaland until that bank wound up its affairs in June 1965. The main duties of the Reserve Bank are to maintain currency stability and to act as banker to the government and to the commercial banks. The Reserve Bank administers exchange control and acts as registrar for local registered stock. The Reserve Bank also handles the issue of treasury bills on behalf of the government.

Malawi's financial services are unsophisticated and basic. Aside from the central bank, there are five licensed commercial banks that are dominated by the two leading banks, the National Bank of Malawi and the Commercial Bank of Malawi with branches or agencies throughout the country. The Investment and Development Bank of Malawi (Indebank), formed in 1972 with foreign and local participation, provides medium- and long-term credit. The sole mortgage finance institution is the new Building Society. Other financial institutions include two savings banks, four development finance institutions, four leasing and finance companies, and seven insurance companies.

The Malawi Stock Exchange (MSE) was established in December 1994 along with Stockbrokers Malawi to deal with listed company shares and to act as a broker in government and other securities approved by the Reserve Bank of Malawi (RBM). The stock exchange had no listings until November 1996 when shares in NICO were put up for sale. Since November 1994 the RBM has marketed Treasury bills of varying maturities in an attempt to encourage greater participation by the private sector.

Economic Development

Malawi's public investment program is revised annually to take account of changing needs and the expected availability of resources. The development program continues to be financed largely from external sources.

During the first decades of independence, agricultural development was emphasized. More recently improvements in the transportation infrastructure, especially in roads, have been emphasized. In the manufacturing sector the government has stressed diversification. With major constraints on its foreign exchange, Malawi aims to reduce the trade gap, encourage exports, and reduce government expenditures. The government also faces challenges to improve educational and health facilities, to control the radical spread of HIV/AIDS, and to deal with environmental problems of deforestation and erosion.

The United Kingdom is Malawi's principal aid donor. South Africa has been a significant source of aid as well, especially in financing construction in the capital at Lilongwe and the railway extension from Lilongwe to Mchinji. Other significant aid donors have included the European Community, France, Canada, Germany, Japan, the United States, Denmark, the African Development Bank, and the World Bank/IDA.

SOCIAL WELFARE

The Ministry of Community Services is responsible for social welfare generally. Pension systems exist for public employees only. Employers are required to obtain private workers' injury insurance. Workers' compensation is administered under a 1990s law and includes both disability and survivor benefits. Government hospitals and clinics provide some medical services to residents without charge.

Beginning in 1992 a gradual improvement in Malawi's human rights record was evident. However the use of excessive force and mistreatment of prisoners are still reported. Vigilante killings (executions conducted by a group of citizens that have taken the law into their own hands) are increasing.

Healthcare

Health services, which rank among the poorest in Africa, are under supervision of the Ministry of Health and are provided to Africans free of charge. In the mid-1990s 80 percent of the population had access to healthcare services. However there was only one physician per 50,400 inhabitants.

The major health threats are malnutrition, malaria, and tuberculosis. In addition there are thousands of acquired immune deficiency syndrome (AIDS) cases in Malawi. In 1997 an estimated 15 percent of all adults were infected with HIV, the virus that causes AIDS. There were 43,067 new cases of AIDS reported in 1996. In 2000 life expectancy averaged 37.6 years.

Housing

Government-built houses are either rented or sold. The Malawi Housing Corp. has also developed housing plots in order to relocate urban squatters. Nearly half of all dwellings did not have flush toilets nor bathing facilities of any kind.

EDUCATION

School attendance is compulsory for eight years at the primary level. Secondary education lasts for four years. In excess of 90 percent of children attend primary school but only 2 percent of the relevant age group enrolled in secondary school in the mid-1990s. Children in remote areas do not attend school. The University of Malawi has three campuses. In 1996 there were 531 teachers and 5,561 pupils at all higher level institutions.

2000 KEY EVENTS TIMELINE

February

- President Bakili Muluzi dismisses cabinet after sustained criticism regarding irregularities in the 1999 general election.

March

- President Muluzi announces the formation of a new cabinet with heavy criticism for favoring Southern politicians.

June

- Laborers working for Indian and Pakistani businessmen reach an agreement for a 100 percent increase in salary according to the Asian Workers Association, ending a peaceful protest.

July

- The Malawi Censorship Board blames the influx of violent and pornographic films for the increase in violent youth crimes.

- Businessman Kwacha Ghambi, serving a three year sentence for obtaining a passport under false pretenses, dies after being tortured by police.

August

- Twenty-nine members of parliament (MPs) have died from AIDS during 1994–99. Discussion takes place to build temporary homes for legislators in the Lilongwe, the capital, so families can accompany them there.

September

- The law commission begins review of criminal statutes and seeks to make it a national crime for those who willingly and knowingly transmit the HIV virus.

October

- The government announces major effort to curb illegal migration.

November

- President Bakili Muluzi dissolves his cabinet and appoints a new one November 1.
- The ruling United Democratic Front wins local government elections held on November 22.
- The Malawi government increases the minimum wage by 100 percent on November 29.

December

- The World Bank and International Monetary Fund (IMF) announce on December 23 that the United States, Canada, Japan, and nations of Europe will provide debt relief for twenty-two of the world's poorest nations, including Benin, Bolivia, Burkina Faso, Cameroon, The Gambia, Guinea, Guinea-Bissau, Guyana, Honduras, Madagascar, Malawi, Mali, Mauritania, Mozambique, Nicaragua, Niger, Rwanda, São Tomé and Príncipe, Senegal, Tanzania, Uganda, and Zambia.

ANALYSIS OF EVENTS: 2000

BUSINESS AND THE ECONOMY

The tobacco industry, under siege by anti-smoking campaigns and falling global prices, remained Malawi's prime export earner, accounting for 70 percent of foreign exchange earnings. Trade reform meant that most of the country's industries faced stiffer competition from imports, and a 60 percent devaluation of the nation's currency against the currency of the United States, the dollar, added to their troubles. Adding to the country's industrial stagnation was a series of taxes and levies imposed in recent years. The most recent was a levy amounting to 2 percent of payroll annually to fund employee training. The measure was vigorously opposed by the nation's employers, who warned that it would lead to widespread layoffs.

The World Bank announced in December that it would forgive about half of Malawi's $2.5 billion in foreign debt in response to the poverty reduction program outlined by the government.

A crucial stretch of rail line between Blantyre and a Mozambican port city reopened for the first time in nearly twenty years, restoring Malawi's shortest route to the sea. It was estimated that the renewed availability of this route would save the country as much as $700 million per year in transport costs.

GOVERNMENT AND POLITICS

Corruption charges continued to plague Malawi's government in 2000. In February President Bakili Muluzi dismissed his entire cabinet following complaints about irregularities in the 1999 election. His selection of new cabinet members, however, was criticized from the outset for favoring politicians from the southern part of the country, and complaints intensified following publication of a report in July implicating top government officials in alleged corruption and fraud linked to government contracts and to the embezzlement of more than $2 million. At first Muluzi had claimed there was insufficient evidence to justify any dismissals. However when the IMF and donor nations including Britain complained, he was forced to take action. In November he once again dismissed his cabinet and named yet another one, managing along the way to eliminate two potential rivals for the presidency.

The major political opposition remained the Malawi Congress Party formerly led by the late president Hastings Banda and ousted by Muluzi's United Democratic Front in 1994. The Congress Party was defeated again in the 1999 elections, a defeat it had challenged in court. In May the challenge, which alleged that the United Democratic Front's margin of victory was too small to be conclusive, was denied. In addition to the legal challenge, Gwanda Chakuamba, the leader of the

Congress Party, had boycotted sessions of parliament since the election to protest Muluzi's victory. In June Chakuamba was banned from parliament and charged that the action was an attempt to eliminate his party. By August opposition members had split among themselves, and held two competing conventions, one loyal to Chakuamba and one backing his deputy and chief rival, John Tembo. Reports indicated that most Congress Party members favored Tembo over Chakuamba.

Malawi's first multiparty local elections were held in November. Low voter turnout was attributed to disenchantment with both the ruling United Democratic Front and the opposition Malawi Congress Party. Polling was conducted to choose two thousand local council representatives for thirty-nine local assemblies.

Donors including the United States (U.S.), Norway, Canada, the United Nations (U.N.), and the European Union (E.U.) pledged $109 million to help with Malawi's five-year campaign, begun the year before, against AIDS. With an estimated 14 percent of the population infected with the HIV virus, and about 400,000 children already orphaned by AIDS, a legal commission considered proposals making it a crime to knowingly risk transmitting HIV to one's sexual partner. In addition, the government implemented a crackdown on prostitution, arresting both prostitutes and their clients.

CULTURE AND SOCIETY

Most of Malawi's population continued to suffer chronic poverty. In the all-important tobacco sector, farmers could not get by without the free labor provided by their children. Very young children were reported being put to work on both tobacco and tea plantations. The practice drew a threat of possible sanctions by the International Labor Organization (ILO).

Malawi's anti-abortion law continued to have profound effects on a society where one-third of all pregnant women were HIV positive. One high-profile case involved a woman arrested for having an abortion three months after being raped by two burglars in her home.

Malawi's Rastafarian population, now free to openly sport dreadlocks and practice their faith after the persecution suffered during the years under former president Banda, agitated for legalization of marijuana, arguing that consumption of the weed was integral to their religious doctrine.

DIRECTORY

CENTRAL GOVERNMENT

Head of State

President
Bakili Muluzi, Office of the President

Vice President and Minister of Privatisation
Justin Malewezi, Office of the Vice President

Ministers

Minister of Agriculture and Irrigation Development
Leonard Mangulama, Ministry of Agriculture and Irrigation Development

Minister of Defense
Rodwell Munyenyembe, Ministry of Defense

Minister of Natural Resources and Environmental Affairs
Harry Thomson, Ministry of Natural Resources and Environmental Affairs

Minister of Foreign Affairs and International Cooperation
Lilian Patel, Ministry of Foreign Affairs and International Cooperation

Minister of Justice and Attorney General
Peter Fatchi, Ministry of Justice and Attorney General

Minister of Finance
Mathews Chikaonda, Ministry of Finance, PO Box 30049, Capital City, Lilongwe 3, Malawi
PHONE: +265 782199
FAX: +265 781679

Minister of Home Affairs and Internal Security
Mangeza Maloza, Ministry of Home Affairs and Internal Security

Minister of State for Presidential Affairs
Ken Lipenga, Ministry of State for Presidential Affairs

Minister of Tourism, National Parks and Wildlife
George Mtafu, Ministry of Tourism, National Parks and Wildlife

Minister of Commerce and Industry
Kaliyoma Phumisa, Ministry of Commerce and Industry

Minister of Health
Aleke Banda, Ministry of Health

Minister of Transport and Public Works
Brown Mpinganjira, Ministry of Transport and Public Works

Minister of Lands, Housing and Physical Planning
Thengo Maloya, Ministry of Lands, Housing and Physical Planning

Minister in the President's Office Responsible for District and Local Government Administration
Patrick Mbewe, Ministry of District and Local Government Administration

Minister of Education, Science and Technology
Cassim Chilumpha, Ministry of Education, Science and Technology

Minister in the President's Office Responsible for Statutory Corporations
Bob Khamisa, Ministry of Statutory Corporations

Minister of Water Development
Yusufu Mwawa, Ministry of Water Development

Minister of Information
Clement Stambuli, Ministry of Information

Minister of Women, Children and Community Affairs
Mary Banda, Ministry of Women, Children and Community Affairs

Ministry of Labour and Vocational Training
Peter Chupa, Ministry of Labour and Vocational Training

POLITICAL ORGANIZATIONS

Democratic Front (UDF)

NAME: Bakili Muluzi

Congress Party (MCP)

TITLE: Secretary General
NAME: Gwanda Chakuamba

Alliance for Democracy (AFORD)

TITLE: Secretary General
NAME: Chakufwa Chihana

Socialist League of Malawi (LESOMA)

TITLE: Secretary General
NAME: Kapote Mwakusula

Malawi Democratic Union (MDU)

NAME: Harry Bwanausi

Congress for the Second Republic (CSR)

NAME: Kanyama Chiume

Malawi Socialist Labor Party (MSLP)

NAME: Stanford Sambanemanja

DIPLOMATIC REPRESENTATION

Embassies in Malawi

Canada
Accord Centre, PO Box 51902, Lilongwe 3, Malawi
PHONE: +265 645441
FAX: +265 645004

China
PO Box 30221, Lilongwe 3, Malawi
PHONE: +265 783611; 781527

Egypt
Area 10, Plot No. 247, Tsoka Road, PO Box 30451, Lilongwe 3, Malawi
PHONE: +265 730300

France
Area 40, Road No. 8, Capital City, PO Box 30054, Lilongwe 3, Malawi
PHONE: +265 783577; 783732; 783520
FAX: +265 780438

Italy
PO Box 40, Lilongwe 3, Malawi
PHONE: +265 720266; 720481
FAX: +265 723350

Netherlands
PO Box 5096, Lilongwe 3, Malawi
PHONE: +265 651171

South Africa
Mpico Building, City Centre, PO Box 30043, Lilongwe 3, Malawi
PHONE: +265 783722
FAX: +265 782571; 781042

United Kingdom
Capital City, PO Box 782, Lilongwe 3, Malawi
PHONE: +265 782400
FAX: +265 782657

United States
Area 40, Plot No. 24, PO Box 30016, Lilongwe 3, Malawi
PHONE: +265 783166; 783342
FAX: +265 780471
TITLE: Ambassador
NAME: Michael T. F. Pistor

JUDICIAL SYSTEM

Supreme Court of Appeal

High Court

Magistrate's Courts

BROADCAST MEDIA

Malawi Broadcasting Corporation (MBC)

PO Box 30133, Chichiri, Blantyre 3, Malawi
PHONE: +265 671222
FAX: +265 671257; 671353
E-MAIL: dgmbc@malawi.net
TITLE: Acting Directorate General
CONTACT: Sam Gunde
LANGUAGE: Chichewa, English
BROADCASTS: 24 hours/day
TYPE: Commercial

COLLEGES AND UNIVERSITIES

University of Malawi

Chancellor College, University of Malawi, PO Box 280, Zomba, Malawi
PHONE: +265 522622
FAX: +265 522760
E-MAIL: university.office@unima.wn.apc.org

NEWSPAPERS AND MAGAZINES

Africa News Online - Malawi

WEBSITE: http://www.africaonline.com/malawi/

The Daily Times

Blantyre Newspapers Ltd., Private Bag 39, Blantyre, Malawi
PHONE: +265 671566
FAX: +265 671114
TITLE: Editor
CONTACT: Ken Lipanje
CIRCULATION: 11,500

Malawian

PO Box 30087, Lilongwe 3, Malawi
TITLE: Editor
CONTACT: C.G. Mputahelo

Malawi News

Blantyre Newspapers Ltd., Private Bag 39, Ginnery Corner, Blantyre, Malawi
PHONE: +265 671566
FAX: +265 671114
TITLE: Editor
CONTACT: Ken Lipanje
CIRCULATION: 20,000

Malawi Economic Report

PO Box 37, Zomba, Malawi
TYPE: Business and economics

Malawi News

PO Box 39, Ginnery Corner, Malawi
TITLE: Editor
CONTACT: K. Lipenga
CIRCULATION: 13,500
TYPE: Social science, general

PUBLISHERS

Central Africana Ltd.

PO Box 631, Blantyre, Malawi
PHONE: +265 623227
FAX: +265 622236
E-MAIL: africana@sdwp.org.mw
TITLE: Chairman & Publisher
CONTACT: Frank M. I. Johnston
SUBJECTS: History, Travel
TOTAL PUBLISHED: 15 print

Christian Literature Association in Malawi

PO Box 503, Blantyre, Malawi
PHONE: +265 620839
TITLE: General Manager
CONTACT: J. T. Matenje
SUBJECTS: Biography, Fiction, History, Poetry, Regional Interests, Religion

Dzuka Publishing Company Ltd.

Private Bag 39, Blantyre, Malawi
PHONE: +265 670855; 670880
FAX: +265 670021
CONTACT: Egidio Mpanga
SUBJECTS: Agriculture, Education, Fiction, Geography, Geology, History, Mathematics

Government Printer (Imprimerie Nationale)

Government Printing Department, Ministry of Finance, PO Box 37, Zomba, Malawi
PHONE: +265 523155
FAX: +265 523133

Popular Publications

PO Box 5592, Limbe, Malawi
PHONE: +265 651833

FAX: +265 651171
TITLE: General Manager
CONTACT: Vales Machila
SUBJECTS: Biblical Studies, Fiction

RELIGIOUS ORGANIZATIONS

Officially Muslim, a small minority of exiles from the north of the country (former northern Rhodesia) cause general discord within the country during elections, often razing mosques and churches to the ground. As they are the first target, most religious organizations are careful about giving their locations and information to the general public.

FURTHER READING

Articles

Keesing's Record of World Events, February 2000.

"Malawi: 2 Top Aides Dropped." *New York Times,* November 7, 2000, p. A6.

Panafrican News Agency, June 27 and July 13, 2000.

Books

Briggs, Philip. *The Bradt Travel Guide: Malawi.* 2d ed. Old Saybrook, CT: Globe Pequot Press, 1999.

Dun and Bradstreet's Export Guide to Malawi. Parsippany, NJ: Dun & Bradstreet, 1999.

MALAWI: STATISTICAL DATA

For sources and notes see "Sources of Statistics" at the front of each volume.

GEOGRAPHY

Geography

Area:

Total: 118,480 sq km.

Land: 94,080 sq km.

Land boundaries:

Total: 2,881 km.

Border countries: Mozambique 1,569 km, Tanzania 475 km, Zambia 837 km.

Coastline: 0 km (landlocked).

Climate: sub-tropical; rainy season (November to May); dry season (May to November).

Terrain: narrow elongated plateau with rolling plains, rounded hills, some mountains.

Natural resources: limestone, arable land, hydropower, unexploited deposits of uranium, coal, and bauxite.

Land use:

Arable land: 34%

Permanent crops: 0%

Permanent pastures: 20%

Forests and woodland: 39%

Other: 7% (1993 est.).

HUMAN FACTORS

Demographics (A)

	1990	1995	1998	2000	2010	2020	2030	2040	2050
Population	9,219	9,536	10,042	10,386	11,621	12,318	12,817	13,551	14,729
Life expectancy - males	41.3	37.6	37.4	37.2	35.6	38.8	44.8	53.9	64.4
Life expectancy - females	42.4	40.2	38.8	38.0	35.9	39.5	46.6	57.5	69.9
Birth rate (per 1,000)	48.0	42.1	39.9	38.5	31.8	26.2	22.2	19.5	17.2
Death rate (per 1,000)	21.5	22.2	22.2	22.4	24.1	22.0	18.0	12.5	7.9
Women of reproductive age (15-49 yrs.)	2,086	2,144	2,292	2,402	2,920	3,325	3,634	3,868	4,067
Fertility rate	6.9	6.1	5.6	5.3	3.9	3.0	2.4	2.2	2.1

Except as noted, values for vital statistics are in thousands; life expectancy is in years.

Health Personnel

	National Data	World Data (wtd ave)
Total health expenditure as a percentage of GDP, 1990-1998[a]		
Public sector	2.8	2.5
Private sector	0.4	2.9
Total[b]	3.3	5.5
Health expenditure per capita in U.S. dollars, 1990-1998[a]		
Purchasing power parity	20	561
Total	5	483
Availability of health care facilities per 100,000 people		
Hospital beds 1990-1998[a]	130	330
Doctors 1992-1995[a]	2	122
Nurses 1992-1995[a]	6	248

Health Indicators

	National Data	World Data
Life expectancy at birth (years)		
1980	44	61
1998	42	67
Daily per capita supply of calories		
1970	2,359	2,358
1997	2,043	2,791
Daily per capital supply of protein		
1997 (grams)	54	74
Total fertility rate (births per woman)		
1980	7.6	3.7
1998	6.4	2.7
Population with access (%)		
To safe water (1990-96)	45	NA
To sanitation (1990-96)	53	NA
People living with (1997)		
Tuberculosis (cases per 100,000)	205.0	60.4
HIV/AIDS (% aged 15 - 49 years)	14.92	0.99

Infants and Malnutrition

	National Data	World Data (wtd ave)
Under 5 mortality rate (1989)	213	NA
% of infants with low birthweight (1992-98)[1]	20	17
Births attended by skilled health staff (% of total births 1996-98)	55	52
% fully immunized at 1 year of age (1995-98)[1]		
TB	100	82
DPT	96	77
Polio	93	77
Measles	90	74
Prevalence of child malnutrition (1992-98)[1] (based on weight for age, % of children under 5 years)	30	30

Ethnic Division

Chewa, Nyanja, Tumbuko, Yao, Lomwe, Sena, Tonga, Ngoni, Ngonde, Asian, European.

Religion

Protestant 55%
Roman Catholic 20%
Muslim 20%
Indigenous beliefs . . . . .NA

Major Languages

English (official), Chichewa (official), other languages important regionally.

EDUCATION

Public Education Expenditures

	1980	1997
Public expenditures on education as % of GNP	3.4	5.4
Expenditures per student as % of GNP per capita		
Primary & Secondary	7.6	8.8
Tertiary	1,839.9	1,593.7
Teachers' compensation as % of total current education expenditures	43.4	NA
Pupils per teacher at the primary level	NA	59
Duration of primary education in years	NA	8
World data for comparison		
Public expenditures on education as % of GNP (mean)	3.9	4.8
Pupils per teacher at the primary level (wtd ave)	NA	33
Duration of primary education in years (mean)	NA	9

Educational Attainment (A)

Age group (1987) . . . . .25+
Population of this age group 2,859,826
Highest level attained (%)
No schooling 55.0

First level

Not completed 31.8

Completed 8.0

Entered second level

Lower Secondary 2.7

Upper Secondary 2.1

Entered post-secondary 0.4

Literacy Rates (A)

In thousands and percent	1990	1995	2000	2010
Illiterate population (15+ yrs.)	2,366	2,587	2,587	2,732
Literacy rate - total adult pop. (%)	52.3	56.4	60.4	68.1
Literacy rate - males (%)	69.2	71.9	74.6	79.5
Literacy rate - females (%)	36.9	41.8	46.8	57.0

Libraries

Public Libraries **1992**

Administrative Units 1

Service Points or Branches 7

Number of Volumes (000) 237

Registered Users (000) 37

Loans to Users (000) 294

Total Library Staff 96

GOVERNMENT & LAW

Military Affairs (A)

	1990	1992	1995	1996	1997
Military expenditures					
Current dollars (mil.)	20	19[e]	16	23	26[e]
1997 constant dollars (mil.)	24	21[e]	17	23	26[e]
Armed forces (000)	7	10	10	8	8
Gross national product (GNP)					
Current dollars (mil.)	1,590	1,690	2,020	2,320	2,480
1997 constant dollars (mil.)	1,860	1,880	2,100	2,360	2,480
Central government expenditures (CGE)					
1997 constant dollars (mil.)	505	530[e]	761	603	894
People (mil.)	9.1	8.6	9.4	9.5	9.7
Military expenditure as % of GNP	1.3	1.1	0.8	1.0	1.0
World data on military expenditure as % of GNP	4.5	3.4	2.7	2.6	2.6
Military expenditure as % of CGE	4.8	3.9	2.2	3.9	2.9
World data on military expenditure as % of CGE	17.0	12.5	10.5	10.3	10.2
Military expenditure per capita (1997 $)	3	2	2	2	3
World data on military expenditure per capita (1997 $)	242	173	146	143	145
Armed forces per 1,000 people (soldiers)	0.8	1.2	1.0	0.8	0.8
World data on armed forces per 1,000 people (soldiers)	5.3	4.5	4.1	3.9	3.8
GNP per capita (1997 $)	203	219	224	248	256
Total imports[7]					
Current dollars (mil.)	581	718	475	624	667[e]
1997 constant dollars (mil.)	680	796	492	634	667[e]
Total exports[7]					
Current dollars (mil.)	417	383	405	481	537
1997 constant dollars (mil.)	488	425	419	489	537
Arms as percent of total imports[8]	0	0	0	0	0
Arms as percent of total exports[8]	0	0	0	0	0

Political Parties

National Assembly	% of vote	no. of seats
United Democratic Front (UDF)	48%	93
Malawi Democratic Party (MCP)	34%	66
Alliance for Democracy (AFORD)	15%	29
Others	3%	4
Vacancy		1

Elections were last held 15 June 1999 (next to be held in 2004).

Government Budgets (B)

Revenues . . . .$490 million

Expenditures . . . .$523 million

Data for FY99/00 est.

(Continued on next page.)

LABOR FORCE

Total Labor Force (A)

3.5 million.

Labor Force by Occupation

Agriculture 86%

Wage earners 14%

Data for 1990 est.

PRODUCTION SECTOR

Energy Production

Production . . . . .922 million kWh

Production by source

Fossil fuel 2.39%

Hydro 97.61%

Nuclear 0%

Other 0%

Exports . . . . .0 kWh

Data for 1998.

Energy Consumption

Consumption . . . . .857 million kWh

Imports . . . . .0 kWh

Data for 1998.

Transportation

Highways:

Total: 28,400 km.

Paved: 5,254 km.

Unpaved: 23,146 km (1996 est.).

Waterways: Lake Nyasa (Lake Malawi); Shire River, 144 km.

Airports: 44 (1999 est.).

Airports - with unpaved runways: 39.

Top Agriculture Products

Tobacco, sugarcane, cotton, tea, corn, potatoes, cassava (tapioca), sorghum, pulses; cattle, goats.

Top Mining Products (B)

Mineral resources include: limestone, unexploited deposits of uranium, coal, and bauxite.

MANUFACTURING SECTOR

GDP & Manufacturing Summary (A)

	1980	1985	1990	1995
GDP ($-1990 mil.)[1]	1,636	1,853	2,145	2,283
Per capita ($-1990)[1]	265	256	230	236
Manufacturing share (%) (current prices)[1]	17.6	17.5	16.6	NA
Manufacturing				
Value added ($-1990 mil.)[1]	220	236	315	335
Industrial production index	58	69	100	97
Value added ($ mil.)	123	90	193[e]	153[e]
Gross output ($ mil.)	340	330	623[e]	487[e]
Employment (000)	39	31	25[e]	28[e]
Profitability (% of gross output)				
Intermediate input (%)	64	73	69[e]	69[e]
Wages and salaries inc. supplements (%)	12	10	9[e]	9[e]
Gross operating surplus	24	18	21[e]	22[e]
Productivity ($)				
Gross output per worker	8,783	10,745	23,908[e]	16,833
Value added per worker	3,174	2,923	7,349[e]	5,251[e]
Average wage (inc. supplements)	1,046	1,035	2,318[e]	1,627[e]
Value added ($ mil.)				
Food products	54	14	72[e]	54[e]

Beverages	8	7	13[e]	9[e]
Tobacco products	9	5	3[e]	2[e]
Textiles	12	14	16[e]	12[e]
Wearing apparel	2	1	−1[e]	NA
Footwear	1[e]	3	NA	NA
Wood and wood products	2	2	3[e]	2
Furniture and fixtures	1	1	1[e]	NA
Paper and paper products	2	2	3[e]	3[e]
Printing and publishing	8	6	10[e]	8[e]
Industrial chemicals	2	8	13[e]	12[e]
Other chemical products	5	14	19[e]	15[e]
Rubber products	1	1	1[e]	1[e]
Plastic products	2	2	5[e]	5[e]
Other non-metal mineral products	3	1	2[e]	2[e]
Metal products	6	6	11[e]	9[e]
Non-electrical machinery	NA	1	6[e]	7[e]
Electrical machinery	5	1	3[e]	2[e]
Transport equipment	1[e]	1	1[e]	1[e]
Other manufacturing	NA	NA	11[e]	9[e]

COMMUNICATIONS

Daily Newspapers

	National Data	World Data for Comparison
Daily Newspapers		
Number of Dailies	5	8,391
Total Circulation (000)	NA	548,000
Circulation per 1,000 inhabitants	NA	96

Telecommunications

Telephones - main lines in use: 34,000 (1995).

Telephones - mobile cellular: 382 (1995).

Telephone system:

Domestic: fair system of open-wire lines, microwave radio relay links, and radiotelephone communications stations.

International: satellite earth stations - 2 Intelsat (1 Indian Ocean and 1 Atlantic Ocean).

Radio broadcast stations: AM 9, FM 4 (plus 15 repeater stations), shortwave 3 (1998).

Radios: 2.6 million (1997).

Television broadcast stations: 1 (1999).

Televisions: 0 (1999).

Internet Service Providers (ISPs): 1 (1999).

FINANCE, ECONOMICS, & TRADE

Economic Indicators

National product: GDP—purchasing power parity—$9.4 billion (1999 est.).

National product real growth rate: 4.2% (1999 est.).

National product per capita: $940 (1999 est.).

Inflation rate—consumer price index: 45% (1999).

Exchange Rates

Exchange rates:

Malawian kwachas (MK) per US$1

December 1999	46.3494
1999	44.0881
1998	31.0727
1997	16.4442
1996	15.3085
1995	15.2837

Top Import Origins

$512 million (f.o.b., 1999)

Origins (1998)

South Africa	38%
Zimbabwe	18%
Zambia	8%
Japan	4%
United States	NA
United Kingdom	NA
Germany	NA

Top Export Destinations

$510 million (f.o.b., 1999)

Destinations (1998)

South Africa	15%
United States	9%
Germany	9%
Netherlands	7%
Japan	NA

Foreign Aid

Recipient: $416.5 million (1995).

Import/Export Commodities

Import Commodities	Export Commodities
Food	Tobacco
Petroleum products	Tea
Semimanufactures	Sugar
Consumer goods	Cotton
Transportation equipment	Coffee
	Peanuts
	Wood products

Balance of Payments

	1990	1991	1992	1993	1994
Exports of goods (f.o.b.)	406	476	400	317	363
Imports of goods (f.o.b.)	−280	−416	−415	−340	−639
Trade balance	126	60	−15	−23	−276
Services - debits	−268	−356	−339	−260	−234
Services - credits	37	39	29	30	22
Private transfers (net)	59	96	102	82	37
Government transfers (net)	78	66	57	90	106
Overall balance	−86	−228	−285	−166	−450

MALAYSIA

CAPITAL: Kuala Lumpur.

FLAG: The national flag consists of 14 alternating horizontal stripes, of which 7 are red and 7 white; a gold 14-pointed star and crescent appear on a blue field in the upper left corner.

ANTHEM: *Negara Ku (My Country).*

MONETARY UNIT: The Malaysian ringgit (M$), or dollar, is divided into 100 sen, or cents. There are coins of 1, 5, 10, 20, and 50 sens and 1 ringgit, and notes of 1, 5, 10, 20, 100, 500, and 1,000 ringgits. M$1 = US$0.3741 (or US$1 = M$2.6730).

WEIGHTS AND MEASURES: The metric system became the legal standard in 1982, but some British weights and measures and local units are also in use.

HOLIDAYS: National Day, 31 August; Christmas, 25 December. Movable holidays include Vesak Day, Birthday of His Majesty the Yang di-Pertuan Agong, Hari Raya Puasa, Hari Raya Haji, the 1st of Muharram (Muslim New Year), Milad an-Nabi, Dewali, Thaipusam, and the Chinese New Year. Individual states celebrate the birthdays of their rulers and other holidays observed by native ethnic groups.

TIME: 7 PM = noon GMT.

LOCATION AND SIZE: Situated in Southeast Asia, Malaysia, with an area of 329,750 square kilometers (127,581 square miles), consists of two separate, nonadjoining areas: Peninsular Malaysia on the Asian mainland, and the states of Sarawak and Sabah, known together as East Malaysia, on the island of Borneo. Comparatively, the area occupied by Malaysia is slightly larger than the state of New Mexico.

CLIMATE: The climate of Peninsular Malaysia is characterized by fairly high but uniform temperatures (ranging from 23° to 31°C/73° to 88°F throughout the year), high humidity, and heavy rainfall, averaging about 250 centimeters (100 inches) annually. There are seasonal variations in rainfall, with the heaviest rains from October to December or January. The nights are usually cool because of the nearby seas. The climate of East Malaysia is relatively cool for an area so near the equator.

INTRODUCTORY SURVEY

RECENT HISTORY

Japanese forces invaded Malaya and the Borneo territories in December 1941 and occupied them throughout World War II (1939–1945). Within a year after the Japanese surrender in September 1945 the British formed the Malayan Union that was succeeded by the Federation of Malaya in February 1948. Over the next decade Malaya progressed toward self-government. On August 31, 1957, the Federation of Malaya became an independent member of the Commonwealth of Nations.

In September 1963 the Federation of Malaya, the State of Singapore, and the newly independent British colonies of Sarawak and Sabah merged to form the Federation of Malaysia, but by 1965 Singapore seceded from the Federation and established an independent republic. Internal disorders stemming from hostilities between Chinese and Malay communities in Kuala Lumpur disrupted the 1969 national elections and prompted the declaration of a state of emergency lasting from mid-1969 to February 1971. Successive governments managed to sustain political stability until 1987 when racial tensions between Chinese and Malay increased over a government plan to assign non-Mandarin-speaking administrators to Chinese-language schools.

The rise of Dayak nationalism in Sarawak was also considered a threat to political stability after the 1987 state elections, but it had been diffused by the 1991 elections, when The Sarawak Native People's Party (PBDS, Parti Bansa Dayak Sarawak) retained only seven of the fifteen seats it had won in

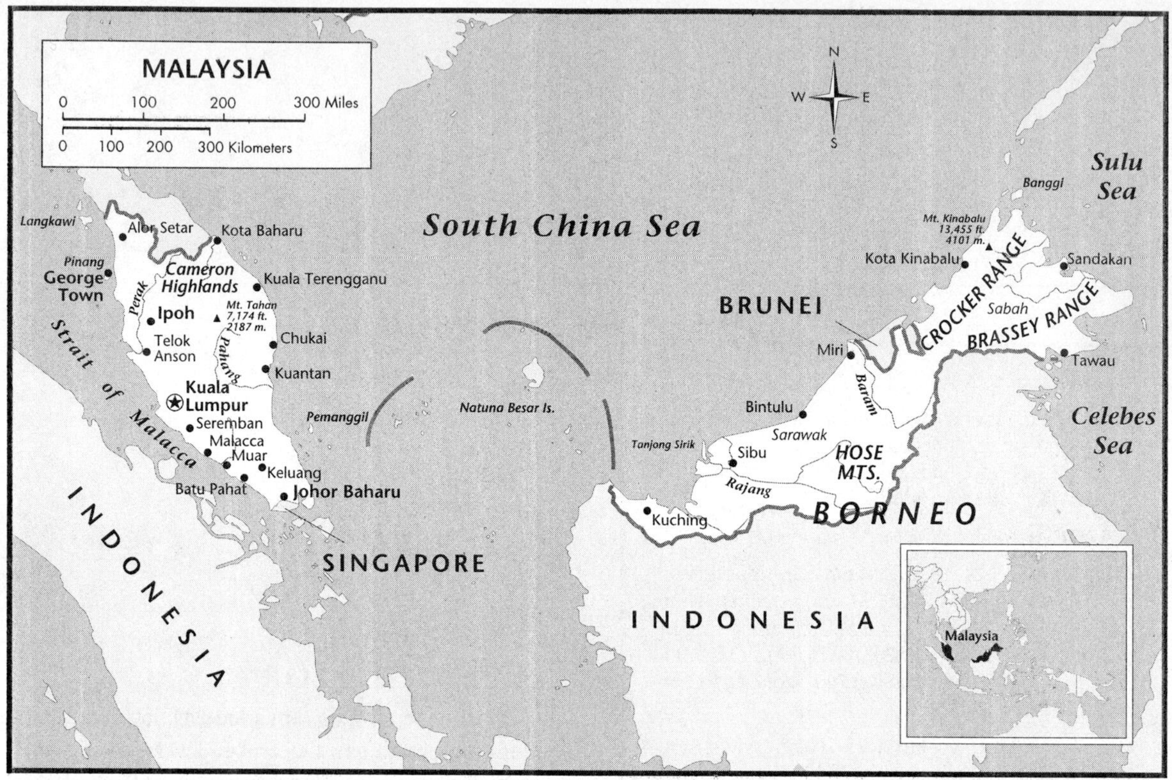

1987. In 1991 Malaysia's ruling party, the United Malays National Organization (UMNO) raised the issue of the alleged abuse of privilege by Malaysia's nine hereditary rulers, and in January 1993 proposed Constitutional amendments that passed limiting their powers and removing their immunity from legal prosecution. In 1994 the government moved to ban the Islamic sect, Al-Arqam.

The Asian economic crisis of 1997 affected both the economy and the political landscape in Malaysia. However by the end of 1998 the economy began to recover and the government officially announced the revision was over by August 1999. Sato' Sei Dr. Mahathir Mohamid, who had served as prime minister since 1981, was able to stay in power when his party, the UMNO led a coalition that took a two-thirds majority in parliament in 1999.

GOVERNMENT

Malaysia is a constitutional monarchy consisting of 13 states. The constitution of 1957, subsequently amended, provides for the election of a royal head of state, the yang di-pertuan agong (or "paramount ruler"), for a single term of five years and a deputy paramount ruler. Both are elected by the Conference of Rulers, nine hereditary sultans whose consent must be obtained for any law that alters state boundaries; affects the rulers' privileges or honors; or extends any religious observances or ceremonies to the country as a whole.

The yang di-pertuan agong, who must be one of the hereditary sultans, is commander-in-chief of the armed forces and has the power to designate judges for the Federal Court and the High Courts on the advice of the prime minister, whom he appoints.

Executive power rests with the cabinet, chosen by the prime minister, who is the leader of the majority party or coalition of the House of Representatives (Dewan Rakyat), the lower house of Parliament. The 193 members of the House of Representatives must be at least twenty-one years old; they are elected by universal adult vote. Their term is five years unless the House is dissolved earlier.

The 69-member Senate (Dewan Negara) consists of twenty-six members appointed by the state legislatures (two from each state) and forty-three members appointed by the paramount ruler on the basis of distinguished public service or their eligibility to represent an ethnic minority. Senators, who serve six-year terms, must be at least thirty years old.

Of the thirteen Malaysian states sultans head nine and the federally appointed governors head the other four. Suffrage is universal at twenty-one years of age.

Judiciary

Most cases come before magistrates and sessions courts. Religious courts decide questions of Islamic law and custom. The Federal Court, the highest court in Malaysia, reviews decisions referred from the High Court of Peninsular Malaysia, the High Court of Sabah and Sarawak, the Court of Appeals, and subordinate courts. The magistrates' courts hear criminal cases in which the maximum sentence does not exceed twelve months. The sessions courts hear cases involving landlord-tenant disputes and car accidents. High courts have jurisdiction over all serious criminal cases and most civil cases. The Court of Appeals has jurisdiction over high court and sessions court decisions. The Federal Court, of which the *yang di-pertuan agong* (paramount ruler) is lord president, has original jurisdiction in disputes among states or between a state and the federal government.

Political Parties

As of 1999 there were more than thirty registered parties, thirteen of which are represented in the federal parliament. Some of the main parties are: the Barisan Nasional (National Front), a broad coalition comprising the United Malays National Organization (UMNO) and twelve other parties, most ethnically based; the Chinese-based Democratic Action Party (DAD); Parti Se-Islam Malaysia (PAS); the National Justice Party (NJP); Parti Bersatu Sabah (PBS); the Malaysian Chinese Association (MCA); and Semangat '46. In the election held in November 1999, of the 193 seats the results were National Front winning 148 seats, PAS twenty-seven seats, DAP ten, NJP five, and PBS three.

DEFENSE

In 1995, the all-volunteer armed forces numbered 105,000. The total strength of the army was 80,000. Contingents of the Malaysian army patrol the Malaysia-Thailand border against communist guerrillas and provide four United Nations observer teams.

The navy and air force each had 12,500 personnel and seventy-nine combat aircraft. Paramilitary forces numbered 20,100, and the People's Volunteer Corps had 240,000. There are 40,600 reserves. Malaysian arms and equipment are a mixture of domestic, United Kingdom, and United States material. Expenditures on defense amounted to $2.1 billion in 1998 or 2.1 percent of the gross domestic product.

ECONOMIC AFFAIRS

Malaysia is one of the most prosperous nations in Southeast Asia. Until the 1970s Malaysia's economy was based chiefly on its plantation and mining activities, with rubber and tin the principal exports. Since then, however, Malaysia has added palm oil, tropical hardwoods, petroleum, natural gas, and manufactured items to its export list. Malaysia is the world's third largest producer of semiconductors (after the United States and Japan).

In 1985–1986 Malaysia's long period of high growth abruptly halted as oil and palm oil prices were halved. Recovery began in 1987 with growth spurred by foreign demand for exports. Growth rates continued on the average in the 8 percent to 9 percent range from 1987 to 1992. As of 1997 the economy had annually grown by an average of nearly 9 percent for eight years. The Asia economic crisis of 1997 adversely affected the economy but Malaysia made a quick recovery with the GDP growing 5 percent in 1999 responding to a robust export sector. The healthy export sector enabled the country to build up its already large financial reserves. The economy stabilized and both inflation and unemployment were very low at 3 percent or less. Forecasters predicted the GDP to grow from 5 percent to 6 percent in 2000.

Sarawak's basic economy is based on agriculture, supplemented by petroleum production and refining, the collection of forest produce, fishing, and the cultivation of cash crops, primarily rubber, timber and pepper. Sabah's economy rests on logging, petroleum production, rubber, pepper, and timber.

Public Finance

The U.S. Central Intelligence Agency estimated that in 1999 government revenues totaled approximately $23.2 billion and expenditures $27.6 billion. External debt totaled $43.6 billion by 1999 estimates.

Income

In 1999 Malaysia's gross domestic product (GDP) was estimated at $229.1 billion, or $10,700 per capita. The 1999 estimated GDP was 5 percent and inflation 2.8 percent. The 1998 GDP's contribution by sector was agriculture 12 percent, industry 46 percent, and services 42 percent.

Industry

In 1998 the leading manufacturing industries include rubber processing, light manufacturing, electronics, palm oil processing, tin smelting, and timber processing. Other manufactured goods include cement, cigarettes, and appliances; textiles, clothing and footwear; chemicals and petroleum products; other machinery and transport equipment; and iron and steel products. Malaysia is also a leading exporter of semiconductor devices.

A top industrial priority in 2000 is the development of what Malaysia calls the "multimedia super corridor" (MSC), an area it hopes will become a world-class research and development site for industry. The MSC is composed of several projects: the completion of the Petronas Twin Towers in Kuala Lumpur (the tallest building in the world); the building of an $8 billion city and technology center; a $3.6 billion international airport; and, a massive fiber-optic telecommunications system linking them all.

Banking and Finance

In 1958 the Bank Negara Tanah Melayu, later renamed the Bank Negara Malaysia in 1963, was created as the central banking institution. At the end of 1997 Malaysia had thirty-five licensed commercial banks, through 1,714 offices. A total of thirty-six foreign banks have offices in Malaysia, but their banking privileges are restricted. Other financial institutions include twelve merchant banks, twenty-five finance companies, seven discount houses, and a national savings bank. Specialized credit institutions include the Federal Land Development Authority (FELDA), the Agricultural Bank of Malaysia (Bank Pertanian Malaysia), and Bank Rakyat, serving rural credit cooperative societies. International trade is financed mainly by the commercial banks.

As an alternative system Malaysia offers Islamic banking that is based on the concept of profit sharing as opposed to the use of interest in the conventional banking system. The sole Islamic bank is Bank Islam Malaysia Berhad.

The central bank has embarked on a plan to develop Malaysia as a regional Islamic financial center. Toward this end, the central bank formed a consultative committee on Islamic banking in January 1996 to serve as a think-tank group to develop strategies and proposals to map out the future direction of Islamic banking. Although Islamic operations are still only a small proportion of total business, Malaysia has achieved more than most other Islamic countries in this respect, and its developments are regarded as models by them.

The principal market for securities is the Kuala Lumpur Stock Exchange (KLSE), which separated from the joint Stock Exchange of Malaysia and Singapore in 1973. A second, smaller exchange has operated since 1970 to serve indigenous Malay interests.

Economic Development

Recent economic planning has stressed a "look East" policy with Malaysia attempting to emulate the economic successes of Japan and the Republic of Korea by importing technology from those countries. In response to deteriorating prices for oil and other exports, the Fifth Malaysia Plan (1986–1990) has aimed at promoting foreign investment particularly in export industries.

The year 1990 marked the culmination of several economic development plans: the Fifth Malaysia Plan (FMP) 1986–90); the conclusion of the First Outline Perspective Plan (OPP1) 1971–1990; and the completion of the New Economic Policy (NEP) 1971–90. A post-1990 NEP defined Malaysian economic strategy for full development by 2020. Three ten-year Outline Perspective Plans that include a New Development Plan and six five-year plans make up the NEP. A Second Outline Perspective Plan (OPP2) 1991–2000 aims to sustain growth momentum and to achieve a more balanced development of the economy. The Sixth Malaysia Plan calls for an average annual growth rate of 7.5 percent, and expenditures on infrastructure are included to ensure prospects for further development. Development trends are toward privatization, encouraging the spread of industry throughout the country, increasing manufacturing in the free trade zones, and providing financing for industry through the establishment of specialized financing institutions.

The five-year development plan beginning in May 1996 forecasted average growth of 8 percent a year for 1996 to 2000. But it also tackled issues that bother skeptics of the Malaysian economy: Low rises in productivity, a skills shortage, and a gaping current-account deficit. In 1997 and 1998 these issues, along with a global financial crisis based in Asia caused the downturn that skeptics expected. Prospects for continuation of the Second Industrial Master Plan from 1996 through 2005 seemed grim although the economy began to rebound in 1999. Massive capital and infrastructure projects have attracted foreign investment and international respect.

SOCIAL WELFARE

Public financial assistance is provided within the framework of Malaysian society's highly developed sense of family and clan responsibility. The government has generally encouraged volunteer social welfare activities and has subsidized programs of private groups. The government's program of public assistance takes the form of cash, commodities, and institutional care. Since 1951 a provident fund has provided lump-sum benefits for old age, disability, and death.

Children's services, begun in 1952, provide casework services and administer children's homes. A probation service provides care and assistance for juvenile delinquents and dependents, and a handicapped persons' service aids the deaf, mute, and blind. In addition, care is provided for the aged and chronically ill.

Women make up more than 40 percent of the nation's total labor force, but except in teaching and nursing are underrepresented in professional occupations. In family and religious matters, Muslim women are subject to Islamic law that allows polygamy (multiple wives) and favors men in matters of inheritance.

Healthcare

Malaysia enjoys a comparatively high standard of health, due to the government's long-established health and medical services. The country has improved its health care and social conditions, and is considering a national health insurance plan. As of 1990, the government paid for three-fourths of health care expenses. About 80 percent of the population had access to health care facilities in 1993. In 1990–1997 hospital beds totaled two per 1,000 people. For that same period total healthcare expenditures were 2.9 percent of GDP.

In 1994–1995 90 percent of the population had access to safe water and 94 percent had adequate sanitation. In 1989–1995 23 percent of children less than five years of age were considered malnourished. Life expectancy was seventy-one years in 2000.

Housing

The need for urban housing is acute: an estimated 24 percent of Kuala Lumpur's population consists of recently arrived squatters living in overcrowded shantytowns with few urban amenities. The total number of housing units is about 3.4 million units: 92 percent of all housing units are detached houses, 7 percent are apartments, and 1 percent are single rooms.

EDUCATION

Six years of free primary education is followed by three years of comprehensive general and prevocational education. A two-year pre-university course prepares students for admission to the universities. Malay is the language of instruction in primary and secondary schools with English a compulsory second language.

School enrollment in Malaysia in 1997 was 2.8 million pupils instructed by 148,000 teachers. In all secondary schools there were 102,139 teachers and 1.9 million pupils. In 1996 210,724 students were enrolled in institutions of higher education, which include the University Kebangsaan Malaysia (the National University of Malaysia), the University of Malaya, and the Technological University of Malaysia, all in or near Kuala Lumpur, and the University of Science Malaysia.

For 2000 an estimated 12.5 percent of the adult population (males 8.5 percent; females 16.4 percent) was illiterate.

2000 KEY EVENTS TIMELINE

January

- Opposition figures including Marina Yusoff of the Keadilan party, and Karpal Singh of the Democratic Action Party (lawyer for former Deputy Prime Minister Anwar Ibrahim) are arrested for sedition, January 12–13.
- Eleven demonstrators are arrested on January 25, as Anwar Ibrahim's trial on sodomy charges resumes.

February

- Malaysia's stock exchange breaks the 1,000 mark.

March

- *Harakah,* an opposition bi-weekly newspaper, has its permit revoked by the government and is put on a limited publication schedule. The government withdraws permission to publish from *Detik* magazine, which shifts to an Internet-only edition.
- Ethnic Chinese representatives demand compensation from Japan for mistreatment during World War II in Malaysia.

April

- The High Court judge presiding over Anwar Ibrahim's sodomy trial rules that the defense's calling Prime Minister Mahathir Mohamad to testify is not necessary.
- Leaders of the opposition party Keadilan are arrested following a demonstration in Kuala Lumpur on April 14.

May

- Ms. Zeti Akhtar Aziz becomes head of Malaysia's central bank, Bank Negara.
- A report, "Justice in Jeopardy: Malaysia in 2000" by three international legal organizations expresses concerns about the independence of Malaysia's judiciary.

June

- In a June 17 speech, Prime Minister Mahathir Mohamad comments that his successor could be from a non-Malay ethnic minority, in what is interpreted as an attempt to keep his ruling coalition together.

July

- Members of Al-Ma'unah, an Islamic sect, seize weapons from a Malaysian army camp in the state of Perak and kill two hostages before being captured and charged with treason.

August

- Former Deputy Prime Minister Anwar Ibrahim, already serving a prison term for corruption, is sentenced on August 8 to an additional nine years on sodomy charges with a former driver of the family, Azizan Abu Bakar. It is rumored that Prime Minister Mahathir used his influence to convict Ibrahim because of differences of opinion.

September

- Prime Minister Mahathir Mohamad announces on September 11 that he will shift some governing duties to his deputy prime minister, in order to concentrate on rebuilding support for his political party, the United Malays National Organization.
- Malaysia's first satellite, named Tiung Sat, is launched by a Russian rocket.

October

- The government bans video arcades as promoters of "unhealthy activities" for young people.
- Steven Gan, editor of the news website *Malaysiakini,* wins an International Press Freedom Award from the Committee to Protect Journalists.

November

- Malaysian firm Genting Bhd announces November 15 that it will build the world's biggest hotel (with 6,300 rooms) in Kuala Lumpur.
- Twelve people die and at least 8,000 are left homeless after monsoon rains hit the northern state of Terengganu November 24.
- The United States and North Korea hold missile reduction talks in Malaysia's capital, Kuala Lumpur.

December

- Former national police chief Abdul Rahim, convicted of beating Anwar Ibrahim in prison, has his two-month assault sentence upheld in court.
- Dr. Mahathir declares that he will resign as prime minister before the next general election, which is to be held by November 2004.

ANALYSIS OF EVENTS: 2000

BUSINESS AND THE ECONOMY

Malaysia's Central Bank had predicted higher inflation for 2000, but that increase did not occur. Malaysia's inflation rate was minimal during 2000, despite the significant rise in the price of gasoline. The government increased petrol prices by 9 percent in October to save some $78 million in government oil subsidies. The leap in oil prices on the international market was basically favorable for Malaysia, a petroleum-exporting nation.

Unlike the markets of several Southeast Asian neighbors, Malaysia's stock market performance did not go into serious decline in 2000. In February the market broke the 1,000 mark, but the government cautioned against "over-optimism." The upward trend had been due to expectations of Malaysian stocks being included again in global market indexes. But later in the year the market did level off. A marked lack of investor confidence leading to the exit of overseas capital was the main factor keeping the Malaysian stock exchange weak. In a more hopeful sign of recovery, Malaysia's gross domestic product (GDP) continued to grow in double digits, with particular strength in the manufacturing sector.

Malaysia's first communications satellite was launched by a Russian rocket in September after some delays. Zeti Akhtar Aziz was named Governor of the Central Bank in May, becoming the first woman to hold that post.

Malaysia requested that the World Trade Organization (WTO) rule the United States in violation of WTO mandates, regarding a U.S. regulation banning shrimp imports from nations whose fishing fleets kill endangered sea turtles.

GOVERNMENT AND POLITICS

Former Deputy Prime Minister Anwar Ibrahim, already serving a six-year sentence for corruption, was tried and convicted again, this time on sodomy charges for which he received an additional nine years in prison. Malaysian protesters and international observers decried the verdict as excessive and politically motivated by government rivalries. Anwar himself filed a $25 million defamation lawsuit against Prime Minister Mahathir Mohamad. Supporters of Anwar Ibrahim and his wife Wan Azizah Ismail's Keadilan Party were harassed and arrested. A large pro-democracy and pro-Anwar street protest led by prominent opposition figures was broken up by riot police in November, as all antigovernment demonstrations were banned.

Malaysians were shocked by a July 2 attack on an army base in the northern province of Perak by members of al-Ma'unah, a Muslim sect, in which several soldiers and sect members were killed. Twenty-nine captured al-Ma'unah members were to be put on trial for treason. Some observers believed that the incident was exploited, or even staged, by the Prime Minister's United Malays National Organization (UMNO) for political gains against the rival Islamic Party of Malaysia.

During 2000 there were efforts to pressure the political opposition by severing state contracts with non-UMNO professionals. UMNO itself experienced internal problems relating to the erosion of ethnic Malay support during the Anwar Ibrahim trials. UMNO had to perform a delicate balancing act involving its traditional Muslim Malay power base and coalition-building Chinese and indigenous peoples' political groups. In September Dr. Mahathir announced that he would hand over some of his duties to his deputy prime minister in order to concentrate on revitalizing UMNO.

International lawyers' groups criticized Malaysia's judicial system for lack of political impartiality. Human Rights Watch released a report detailing abuse of Muslim refugees from Myanmar.

Islamic extremists from the Philippines seized several Malay and foreign staff and tourists from a resort island off Malaysian Borneo, and held them hostage in the Philippines. The hostages were eventually released, but the incidents strained relations between Malaysia and the Philippines.

Malaysia's relations with the United States had their usual ups and downs. The United States declared that improvements in relations with Malaysia would be contingent on improvements in Malaysia's human rights record. U.S. President Bill Clinton drew attention to Malaysia's press restrictions. Dr. Mahathir reacted strongly to a resolution in the U.S. House of Representatives that called for a new trial for Anwar Ibrahim. On the positive side, groundbreaking talks between the United States and North Korea were hosted in Malaysia's capital, Kuala Lumpur.

Control and preservation of natural resources continued to be a source of conflict, particularly in Malaysia's Borneo states of Sarawak and Sabah. Starting in August several communities of Penan indigenous people barricaded roads in Sarawak to block the access of logging trucks to rain forest lands.

CULTURE AND SOCIETY

UMNO used press restrictions against rival party publications and Dr. Mahathir attempted to crack down on non-Malay (Chinese and Indian) influence on satellite television programming. The government banned video game arcades, claiming that they promoted "unhealthy activities" for youths.

The government did hold to its promise to keep its hands off Internet content, and an alternative media grew on the Web. For instance, *Detik,* a magazine that had its permission to publish revoked, went from a print format to a Web edition. Steven Gan, the editor of *Malaysiakini,* a popular on-line Malaysian newsmagazine, won an International Press Freedom Award from the Committee to Protect Journalists.

DIRECTORY

CENTRAL GOVERNMENT

Head of State

Paramount Ruler
Tuanku Ja'afar ibni al-Marhum Tuanku Abdul Rahman, Istana Negara, Jalan Istana, 50500 Kuala Lumpur, Malaysia
PHONE: +60 (3) 2388311

Deputy Paramount Ruler
Tunku Salahuddin Abdul Aziz Shah ibni al-Marhum Sultan Hisammuddin Alam Shah, Office of the Deputy Paramount Ruler

Ministers

Prime Minister
Mahathir bin Mohamad, Prime Minster's Department, Jalan Dato'Onn, 50502 Kuala Lumpur, Malaysia
PHONE: +60 (3) 2321957
FAX: +60 (3) 2329227

Deputy Prime Minister
Abdullah bin Ahmad Badawi, Prime Minsters Department, Jalan Dato'Onn, 50502 Kuala Lumpur, Malaysia
PHONE: +60 (3) 2321957
FAX: +60 (3) 2329227

Minister of Special Functions in the Department of the Prime Minister
Daim Zainuddin, Ministry of Special Functions in the Department of the Prime Minister

Minister of Agriculture
Mohamed Effendi Norwawi, Ministry of Agriculture, Wisma Tani, Jalan Sultan Salahuddin, 50624 Kuala Lumpur, Malaysia
E-MAIL: menteri@smtp.moa.my

Minister of Culture, Arts, and Tourism
Abdul Kadir bin Sheik Fadzir, Ministry of Culture, Arts, and Tourism

Minister of Defense
Mohamed Najib bin Abdul Razak, Ministry of Defense, Kementerian Pertahanan, Jalan Padang Tembak, 50634 Kuala Lumpur, Malaysia
PHONE: +60 (3) 2314891
FAX: +60 (3) 2914163
E-MAIL: cpa@mod.gov.my

Minister of Domestic Trade and Consumer Affairs
Muhyiddin bin Mohamed Yassin, Ministry of Domestic Trade and Consumer Affairs, Tingkat 33, Menara Dayabumi, Jalan Sultan Hishamuddin, 50623 Kuala Lumpur
PHONE: +60 (3) 2743983
FAX: +60 (3) 2744520
E-MAIL: mjunid@kpdnhq.gov.my

Minister of Education
Musa Mohamad, Ministry of Education
E-MAIL: najib@moe.gov.my

Minister of Energy, Communications, and Multimedia
Leo Moggie Anak Irok, Ministry of Energy, Communications and Multimedia, 1st Floor, Wisma Damansara, Jalan Semantan, 50668 Kuala Lumpur, Malaysia
PHONE: +60 (3) 2575000
FAX: +60 (3) 2533485
E-MAIL: Webmaster@ktkm.gov.my

Minister of Entrepreneur Development
Mohamed Nazri bin Abdul Aziz, Ministry of Entrepreneur Development, Tingkat 14–16 and 22–26, Medan Mara, Jalan Raja Laut, 50652 Kuala Lumpur, Malaysia
PHONE: +60 (3) 2985022
FAX: +60 (3) 2917623

Minister of Finance
Tun Dato' Daim bin Zainuddin, Ministry of Finance, Perbendaharaan Malaysia, Block 9, Kompleks Kerajaan Jalan Duta, 50592 Kuala Lumpur, Malaysia
PHONE: +60 (3) 2582000
FAX: +60 (3) 2556264
E-MAIL: webmaster@treasury.gov.my

Minister of Foreign Affairs
Syed Hamid bin Syed Jaafar Albar, Ministry of Foreign Affairs, Wisma Putra, 50602 Kuala Lumpur, Malaysia
PHONE: +60 (3) 2488088
FAX: +60 (3) 2424551
E-MAIL: webmaster@kln.gov.my

Minister of Health
Chua Jui Meng, Ministry of Health, Block E, Jalan Dungun, Buit Damansara, 54200 Kuala Lumpur, Malaysia
PHONE: +60 (3) 2540088
FAX: +60 (3) 2561566
E-MAIL: zainal@dph.gov.my

Minister of Home Affairs
Abdullah bin Ahmad Badawi, Ministry of Home Affairs, Jalan Dato' Onn, 50546 Kuala Lumpur, Malaysia
PHONE: +60 (3) 2309344

FAX: +60 (3) 2936122
E-MAIL: irg@kdn.gov.my

Minister of Housing and Local Government
Ong Kah Ting, Ministry of Housing and Local Government

Minister of Human Resources
Fong Chan Ong, Ministry of Human Resources, Level 2–4, Block B North, Jalan Damanlela, Pusat Bandar, Damansara, 50530 Kuala Lumpur, Malaysia
PHONE: +60 (3) 2557200
FAX: +60 (3) 2554700
E-MAIL: mhr@po.jaring.my

Minister of Information
Khalil Yaakob, Ministry of Information

Minister of International Trade and Industry
Rafidah binti Abdul Aziz, Ministry of International Trade and Industry

Minister of Land and Cooperative Development
Kasitah bin Gaddam, Ministry of Land and Cooperative Development

Minister of National Unity and Social Development
Siti Zaharah binti Sulaiman, Ministry of National Unity and Social Development, Tingkat 20/21, Wisma Bumi Raya, Jalan Raja Laut, 50562 Kuala Lumpur, Malaysia
PHONE: +60 (3) 2925022
FAX: +60 (3) 2937353
E-MAIL: zaleha@kempadu.gov.my

Minister of Primary Industries
Lim Keng Yaik, Ministry of Primary Industries, Tingkat 6–8, Menara Dayabumi, Jalan Sultan Hishamuddin, 50654 Kuala Lumpur, Malaysia
PHONE: +60 (3) 22747511
FAX: +60 (3) 22745014
E-MAIL: samilhah@kpu.gov.my

Minister of Rural Development
Azmi bin Khalid, Ministry of Rural Development

Minister of Science, Technology, and Environment
Law Hieng Ding, Ministry of Science, Technology, and Environment, Tingkat 14, Wisma Sime Darby, Jalan Raja Laut, 50662 Kuala Lumpur, Malaysia
PHONE: +60 (3) 2938955
FAX: +60 (3) 2936006
E-MAIL: lhd@mastic.gov.my

Minister of Transport
Ling Liong Sik, Ministry of Transportation, Level 3, Wisma Perdana, Jalan Dungun, Damansara Height, 50616 Kuala Lumpur, Malaysia
PHONE: +60 (3) 2548122
FAX: +60 (3) 2557041
E-MAIL: info@jpj.gov.my

Minister of Works
S. Samy Vellu, Ministry of Works

Minister of Youth and Sports
Hishammuddin bin Hussein, Ministry of Youth and Sports, Level 6, Block K, Pusat Bandar Damansara, 50570 Kuala Lumpur, Malaysia
PHONE: +60 (3) 2552255
FAX: +60 (3) 2537877

POLITICAL ORGANIZATIONS

Democratic Action Party (DAP)

24 Jalan 20/9, Petaling Jaya, 46300 Selangor, Malaysia
PHONE: +60 (3) 7578022
FAX: +60 (3) 757571
E-MAIL: dap.malaysia@pobox.com
TITLE: National Chairman
NAME: Lim Kit Siang

Malaysian Chinese Association

8th Floor, Wisma MCA, 163, Jalan Ampang, 50450 Kuala Lumpur, Malaysia
PHONE: +60 (3) 2618044
FAX: +60 (3) 2619772
E-MAIL: info@mca.org.my
TITLE: President
NAME: Datuk Seri Dr Ling Liong Sik

Menara Manickavasagam Congress (Malaysian Indian Congress)

Tingkat 6, 1 Jalan Rahmat, Kuala Lumpur, Malaysia
E-MAIL: mic.malaysia.org
TITLE: President
NAME: Dato' Seri S. Samy Vellu

Parti Gerakan Rakyat Malaysia (Malaysian People's Movement Party)

Level 5, Menara PGRM, 8 Jalan Pudu Ulu, Cheras, 56100 Kuala Lumpur, Malaysia
PHONE: +60 (3) 9876868
FAX: +60 (3) 9878866
E-MAIL: pgrmhq@pgrmhq.po.my

TITLE: President
NAME: Datuk Seri Dr Lim Keng Yaik

Parti Islam Se Malaysia (Pan Malaysian Islamic Party)

Lrg Hj Hassan, Tmn Melewar, Batu Caves, 68100 Selangor, Malaysia
PHONE: +60 (3) 6895612
FAX: +60 (3) 6889520
E-MAIL: webmaster@parti-pas.org

Parti Progresif Penduduk Malaysia (People's Progressive Party Of Malaysia)

Jalan Maharajarela, 29A, 50150 Kuala Lumpur, Malaysia
PHONE: +60 (3) 2441922
FAX: +60 (3) 2442041
TITLE: President
NAME: Datuk M. Kayveas

Sabah Progressive Party

2nd Floor, Lot 23, Bornion Centre, Luyang, 88300 Kota Kinabalu, Sabah, Malaysia
PHONE: +60 (88) 242107
FAX: +60 (88) 249188
E-MAIL: sapp@po.jaring.my

United Malay National Organisation

DIPLOMATIC REPRESENTATION

Embassies in Malaysia

Australia
No 6, Jalan Yap Kwan Seng, 50450 Kuala Lumpur, Malaysia
PHONE: +60 (3) 2465555
FAX: +60 (3) 2415773
E-MAIL: pa@austhc.po.my
TITLE: High Commissioner
NAME: Bob Cotton

Canada
7th floor, Plaza MBF, 172 Jalan Ampang, 50540 Kuala Lumpur, Malaysia
PHONE: +60 2612000
FAX: +60 2613428

Chile
8th Floor, West Block, Wisma Selangor Dredging, 142-C, Jalan Ampang, 50450 Kuala Lumpur, Malaysia
PHONE: +60 (3) 2616203
FAX: +60 (3) 2622219
E-MAIL: prochile@ppp.nasionet.net

Denmark
Wisma Denmark, 22nd Floor, 86 Jalan Ampang, 50450 Kuala Lumpur, Malaysia
PHONE: +60 (3) 2022001
FAX: +60 (3) 2022012
E-MAIL: denmark@rdembsy.po.my
TITLE: Ambassador
NAME: Lasse Reimann

Japan
No. 11, Pesiaran Stonor, off Jalan Tun Razak, 50450 Kuala Lumpur, Malaysia
PHONE: +60 (3) 2427044
FAX: +60 (3) 2672314
TITLE: Ambassador
NAME: Hideki Harashima

Singapore
209 Jalan Tun Razak, 50400 Kuala Lumpur, Malaysia
PHONE: +60 (3) 2616277
FAX: +60 (3) 2616343
E-MAIL: shckl@pd.jaring.my
TITLE: High Commissioner
NAME: Krishnasamy Kesavapany

United Kingdom
185 Jalan Semantan Ampang, 50450 Kuala Lumpur, Malaysia
TITLE: D. J. Moss

United States
376 Jalan Tun Razak, PO Box 10035, 50700 Kuala Lumpur, Malaysia
PHONE: +60 (3) 2685000
FAX: +60 (3) 2422207
TITLE: Ambassador
NAME: B. Lynn Pascoe

JUDICIAL SYSTEM

Federal Court of Malaysia

Bangunan Sultan Abdul Samad, Jalan Raja, 50506 Kuala Lumpur, Malaysia
PHONE: +60 (3) 293901

Court of Appeal

Bangunan Sultan Abdul Samad, Jalan Raja, 50506 Kuala Lumpur, Malaysia
PHONE: +60 (3) 2929011

BROADCAST MEDIA

Best 104

PO Box 1, Tamam Seri Terbrau, Johore Bharu, Malaysia

PHONE: +60 (7) 311011
BROADCASTS: 2200–1700
TYPE: Commercial

Radio Penerangan (Information Radio)

BROADCASTS: 18 hours/day
TYPE: Government

Radio Muzik

Tingkat 2, Wisma Radio Angkasapuri, Kuala Lumpur 50740, Malaysia
PHONE: +60 (3) 2857288

Time Highway Radio (THR)

20th Floor, Plaza Berjaya, 12 Jalan Imbi, 55100 Kuala Lumpur, Malaysia
PHONE: +60 (3) 2433088
E-MAIL: thr.time.com.my
TITLE: Chief Executive
CONTACT: Hisham Rahman
BROADCASTS: 24 hours/day
TYPE: Commercial

Saura Malaysia (Voice of Malaysia)

PO Box 11272, 50740 Kuala Lumpur, Malaysia
PHONE: +60 (3) 2825333
FAX: +60 (3) 2847594
WEBSITE: http://www.asiaconnect.com.my/rtm-net/
TITLE: Controller
CONTACT: Stephen Sipaun
LANGUAGE: Arabic, Bahasa Malaysia, English, Indonesian, Mandarin, Myanmar, Tagalog

Metrovision

33 Jalan Delima 1/3 Subang, Hi-Tec Industrial Park 40000, Shahalam, Malaysia
PHONE: +60 (3) 7328000
FAX: +60 (3) 7328932
TITLE: General Manager
CONTACT: Tunku Yahaya

System Malaysia Berhad (TV3)

Sri Pentas No. 3, Persiaran Banjar Utama, Petaling Jaya, 47800, Selangor Darul Ehsan, Malaysia
PHONE: +60 (3) 7166333
FAX: +60 (3) 716133
TITLE: Managing Director
CONTACT: Khalid Hj Ahmad
CHANNEL: 11, 12, 23, 26, 27, 29, 41

TV Malaysia Sabah and Sarawak

PO Box 1016, 88614 Kota Kinabalu, Malaysia
PHONE: +60 (88) 52711
TITLE: Program Controller
CONTACT: M. A. Mahmood
TYPE: Government

Radio Television Malaysia (RTM)

Department of Broadcasting, Angkasapuri, Kuala Lumpur 50614, Malaysia
PHONE: +60 (3) 2825333, +60 (3) 2823140
FAX: +60 (3) 2824735
WEBSITE: http://www.asiaconnect.com.my
TITLE: Directorate General
CONTACT: Dato' Jaafar Kamin
TYPE: Government

Radio Telvision Malaysia-Kota Kinabalu

2.4km, Tuaran Road, Beg Berkunci 2022, 88614 Kota Kinabalu, Malaysia
PHONE: +60 (88) 213444
FAX: +60 (88) 223493
TITLE: Director of Broadcasting
CONTACT: Angrick Saguman
TYPE: Government

Radio Television Malaysia-Sarawak

Broadcasting House, Jalan P. Ramlee, 93614 Kuching, Malaysia
PHONE: +60 (82) 248422
FAX: +60 (82) 241914
TYPE: Government

COLLEGES AND UNIVERSITIES

Northern University of Malaysia

Sintok Jitra, 06010 Kedah, Malaysia
PHONE: +60 (3) 89250001
E-MAIL: ncukc@pkrisc.cc.ukm.my
WEBSITE: http://www.ukm.my

University of Science - Malaysia

Minden, 11800 Penang, Malaysia
PHONE: +60 (4) 6577888
FAX: +60 (4) 6571526
E-MAIL: vc@usm.my
WEBSITE: http://www.usm.my

University of Agriculture Malaysia

UPM Serdang, 43400 Selangor, Malaysia
PHONE: +60 (3) 89486101
FAX: +60 (3) 89486304
E-MAIL: cans@admin.upm.edu.my
WEBSITE: http://www.upm.edu.my

National University of Malaysia

UKM Bangi, 43600 Selangor, Malaysia
PHONE: +60 (3) 89250001
FAX: +60 (3) 8256484
E-MAIL: kpppro@pkrisc.cc.ukm.my
WEBSITE: http://www.ukm.my

International Islamic University - Selangor

PO Box 70 Jalan Sultan, Petaling Jaya, 46700 Selangor, Malaysia
PHONE: +60 (3) 20564000
FAX: +60 (3) 20564858
E-MAIL: rector@iiu.edu.my
WEBSITE: http://www.iiu.my

University of Malaya

Pantai Valley, 50603 Kuala Lumpur, Malaysia
PHONE: +60 (3) 79593273
FAX: +60 (3) 79560027
E-MAIL: pro@um.edu.my
WEBSITE: http://www.um.edu.my

University of Technology Malaysia

UTM Skudai, 81310 Johor, Malaysia
PHONE: +60 (7) 5502388
FAX: +60 (7) 5579376
E-MAIL: mc@utmjb.utm.my
WEBSITE: http://www.utm.my

University Malaysia Sarawak

Kota Samarhan, 94300 Sarawak, Malaysia
PHONE: +60 (82) 671000
FAX: +60 (82) 672411
E-MAIL: zawawi@adm.unimas.my
WEBSITE: http://www.unimas.my

NEWSPAPERS AND MAGAZINES

Berita Harian

The New Straits Times Press (Malaysia) Berhad, Balai Berita, 31 Jalan Riong, Selangor, 59100 Kuala Lumpur, Malaysia
PHONE: +60 (3) 2822328
FAX: +60 (3) 2821428
WEBSITE: http://www.jaring.my/bharian
CIRCULATION: 350,000

Borneo Post

Borneo Post Sdn Bhd, PO Box 20, Sarawak, 96007 Sibu, Malaysia
PHONE: +60 (84) 331714
FAX: +60 (84) 321255
TITLE: Editor
CONTACT: Nguoi How Yieng
CIRCULATION: 40,603

Business Times

Financial Publications Sdn. Bhd., 31 Jalan Riong, 59100 Kuala Lumpur, Malaysia
TITLE: Editor
CONTACT: Henry Chang
CIRCULATION: 12,000

Daily Express

Sabah Publishing House Sdn Bhd, PO Box 10139, Sabah, 88801 Kota Kinabalu, Malaysia
PHONE: +60 (88) 52343
FAX: +60 (88) 238611
E-MAIL: sph@tm.net.my
WEBSITE: http://www.infosabah.com.my
TITLE: Publisher
CONTACT: Clement Yah
TITLE: General Manager
CONTACT: Yeh Mei Tze
CIRCULATION: 30,000

Hwa Chiaw Jit Pao (Overseas Chinese Daily News)

Sabah Publishing House Sdn Bhd, PO Box 10139, Sabah, 88801 Kota Kinabalu, Malaysia
PHONE: +60 (88) 52343
FAX: +60 (88) 238611
CONTACT: Yeh Mei Tze

International Times

International Times Sdn Bhd, Lot 2215, Section 66, Off Jalan Utama, Sarawak, 93450 Kuching, Malaysia
PHONE: +60 (82) 482215
FAX: +60 (82) 340034
E-MAIL: kcb@pc.jaring.my
TITLE: Editor
CONTACT: Lee Fook Onn
CIRCULATION: 34,517

Kwong Wah Yit Poh

Kwong Wah Yit Poh Press Bhd, 19 Presgrave St., PO Box 31, Penang, 10300 George Town, Malaysia
PHONE: +60 2612312
FAX: +60 2628540
E-MAIL: kwyp@tm.net.my
WEBSITE: http://www.kwongwah.com.my
CONTACT: Tan Aye Choo
CIRCULATION: 69,092

Malaysia Daily News

PO Box 237, Sarawak, 96000 Sibu, Malaysia
CONTACT: Wong Seng Kwong
CIRCULATION: 27,000

Mingguan Malaysia

11A, The Right Angle, Jl 14/22, Selangor, 46100 Petaling Jaya, Malaysia
PHONE: +60 (3) 7563355
FAX: +60 (3) 7577755
CONTACT: Abjul Rashid Jamil
CIRCULATION: 541,174

Nanyang Siang Pau

Nanyang Press (M) Bhd, 1, Jalan SS 7/2, Selangor, 47301 Petaling Jaya, Malaysia
PHONE: +60 (3) 7776000
FAX: +60 (3) 7776850
E-MAIL: advert@nanyang.com.my
WEBSITE: http://www.nanyang.com; www.malaysia-net.com
CONTACT: Wong Kam Hor
CIRCULATION: 814,279

New Life Post

Life Publishers Bhd, 2 Jl 19/1 Selangor, 47300 Petaling Jaya, Malaysia
PHONE: +60 (3) 7562400
FAX: +60 (3) 7570262
CONTACT: Peter Chong
CIRCULATION: 136,457

Sarawak Tribune/Utusan Sarawak

Sarawak Press Sdn Bhd, PO Box 138, Sarawak, 93700 Kuching, Malaysia
PHONE: +60 (8) 226496
FAX: +60 (8) 2420358
E-MAIL: tribune@po.jaring.my
WEBSITE: http://www.jaring.my/tribune
CIRCULATION: 37,768

Sin Chew Jit Poh

Pemandangan Sinar Sdn Bhd, No. 19, Jalan Semangat, Selangor, 46200 Petaling Jaya, Malaysia
PHONE: +60 (3) 7582888
FAX: +60 (3) 7575135
E-MAIL: editorial@mail.sinchew.com.my
WEBSITE: http://www.rhmedia.com/sinchew
TITLE: Editor-in-Chief
CONTACT: C.C. Liew
CIRCULATION: 241,638

Star/Sunday Star

Star Publications (Malaysia) Berhad, 13 Jalan 13/16, Selangor, 46200 Petaling Jaya, Malaysia
PHONE: +60 (3) 7578811
FAX: +60 (3) 7554039
E-MAIL: ping@thestar.com.my
WEBSITE: http://www.jaring.my/~star; www.thestar.com.my
CIRCULATION: 192,059 (daily); 232,790 (Sun)

Dewan Masyarakat

Jalan Wisma Putra, PO Box 10803, 50926 Kuala Lumpur, Malaysia
TITLE: Editor
CONTACT: Nik Zainal Abidin Hassan
CIRCULATION: 65,000
TYPE: Social science, general

Dewan Pelajar

Jalan Wisma Putra, PO Box 10803, 50926 Kuala Lumpur, Malaysia
TITLE: Editor
CONTACT: Zaleha Hashim
CIRCULATION: 71,000
TYPE: Juvenile fiction/non-fiction

Dewan Perintis

Box 1390, Kuching, Sarawak, Malaysia
TITLE: Editors
CONTACT: Hamzah Hamdoni and Yeop Johari Yaakob
CIRCULATION: 6,000
TYPE: Juvenile fiction/non-fiction

Dharma

Batu 6, Jalan Puchong, Jalan Kelang Lama, 58200 Kuala Lumpur, Malaysia
FAX: +60 (3) 7928303
TITLE: Editor
CONTACT: Mother A. Mangalam
CIRCULATION: 3,000
TYPE: Religion, philosophy

Malay Literature

Box 10803, 50926 Kuala Lumpur, Malaysia
FAX: +60 (3) 2482726
TITLE: Editor
CONTACT: S. Jaafar Husin
CIRCULATION: 3,000
TYPE: Literature

New Life Post

80M Jalan SS21-39, Damansara Utama, 47400 Petaling Jaya, Selangor, Malaysia
FAX: +60 (3) 7172163
TITLE: Editor
CONTACT: Low Beng Chee
CIRCULATION: 160,000
TYPE: Social science

PUBLISHERS

S. Abdul Majeed & Co.

7 Jalan Bangsar Utama TIGA, Bangsar, PO Box 12393, 50100 Kuala Lumpur, Malaysia
PHONE: +60 (3) 2832230
FAX: +60 (3) 2825670
E-MAIL: peer@pc.jaring.my
TITLE: Man. Partner
CONTACT: Peer Mohamed Majid
SUBJECTS: Asian Studies, Child Care, Cookery, English as a Second Language, Health, Nutrition, Management, Marketing, Islam, Travel

Dewan Bahasa dan Pustaka

Jalan Dewan Bahasa, PO Box 10803, 50926 Kuala Lumpur, Malaysia
PHONE: +60 (3) 2481011; 2424310
FAX: +60 (3) 2482726; 2444460; 2445727
E-MAIL: aziz@dbp.gov.my
WEBSITE: http://www.dbp.gov.my
TITLE: Director General
CONTACT: Haji A. Aziz
SUBJECTS: Malay language, linguistics, literature & culture
TOTAL PUBLISHED: 500 print

Federal Publications Sdn Bhd

Times Subang, Lot 46, Subang Hi-Tech Industrial Park, Batu Tiga, 40000 Shah Alam, Selangor, Malaysia
PHONE: +60 (3) 7351511
FAX: +60 (3) 7364620
E-MAIL: kesoon@po.jaring.my
TITLE: Vice President & General Manager
CONTACT: Stephen Lim
SUBJECTS: Astronomy, Career Development, Child Care, Computer Science, Education, English as a Second Language, Gardening, Mathematics, Science (General), Sports
TOTAL PUBLISHED: 500 print

Forum Publications

11 Jalan 11-4E, 46200 Petaling Jaya, Selangor, Malaysia
PHONE: +60 (3) 7554007
FAX: +60 (3) 7561879
E-MAIL: g2jomo@umcsd.um.edu.my
TITLE: President
CONTACT: Abdul Karim Hassan
SUBJECTS: Anthropology, Developing Countries, Economics, Political Science, History, Labor, Industrial Relations, Regional Interests, Islam

IBS Buku Sdn Bhd

24 Jaylan 20/16A, 4633 Petaling Jaya, Schanger Darul Ehsan, Malaysia
PHONE: +60 (3) 7751763; 7751566; 7760514
FAX: +60 (3) 7765551
E-MAIL: ibsbuku@po.jaring.my
TITLE: Man. Director, Rights & Permissions
CONTACT: M. N. Meera
SUBJECTS: Career Development

International Law Book Services

Lot 4.1 (4th floor) Wisma Shen 149, Jalan Masjid India, PO Box 11664, 50752 Kuala Lumpur, Malaysia
PHONE: +60 (3) 26939862; 26939864
FAX: +60 (3) 26928035
E-MAIL: order@bookgold.com
WEBSITE: http://www.bookgold.com
TITLE: Sole Proprietor
CONTACT: Syed Ibrahim
SUBJECTS: Law
TOTAL PUBLISHED: 925 print; 1 CD-ROM

Mahir Publications Sdn Bhd

Stadium Shah Alam 1 Quadran B Seksyen 13, 40000 Shah Alam, Selangor, Malaysia
PHONE: +60 (3) 5501826; 5501442; 5501755
FAX: +60 (3) 5501826
TITLE: Man. Director
CONTACT: Ahmad Mahir Kamaruddin
SUBJECTS: English as a Second Language

MDC Publishers Printers

MDC Building, 2718 Jalan Permata 4, Taman Permata, Hulu Kelang, 53300 Kuala Lumpur, Malaysia
PHONE: +60 (3) 4086600
FAX: +60 (3) 4081506
E-MAIL: mdcpp@2mws.com.my
WEBSITE: http://www.2mws.com.my/mdc

TITLE: Director
CONTACT: Tajuddin Husain
SUBJECTS: Law, Management
TOTAL PUBLISHED: 300 print

Mecron Sdn Bhd

15 Lengkongan Vethavanam, BT 3 1/2 mile, Jalan Ipoh, 51100 Kuala Lumpur, Malaysia
PHONE: +60 (3) 6269326
FAX: +60 (3) 6219869
TITLE: Director
CONTACT: Zaliha B. Samsudeen
SUBJECTS: Children's boks

Pearson Education Malaysia Sdn Bhd

Lot 2, Jalan 215, Off Japan Templer, 46050 Petaling Jaya, Selangor Darul Ehsan, Malaysia
PHONE: +60 (3) 77820466
FAX: +60 (3) 77818005
E-MAIL: inquiry@pearsoned.com.my
TITLE: General Manager/Director
CONTACT: Wong Mei Mei
SUBJECTS: Literature, Literary Criticism, Essays, Mathematics, Physics, Science (General)
TOTAL PUBLISHED: 2,000 print

Pelanduk Publications (M) Sdn Bhd

12 Jalan SS 13/3E, Subang Jaya Industrial Estate, 47500 Petaling Jaya, Selangor Darul Ehsan, Malaysia
PHONE: +60 (3) 7386885
FAX: +60 (3) 7336575
E-MAIL: pelpub@tm.net.my
WEBSITE: http://www.pelanduk.com
CONTACT: M. H. Chong
SUBJECTS: Biography, Business, Economics, Language Arts, Linguistics, Management, Islam, Social Science, Sociology
TOTAL PUBLISHED: 600 print

Penerbit Jayatinta Sdn Bhd

No 18 Jalan 51A/223, 46100 Petaling Jaya, Selangor Darul Ehsan, Malaysia
PHONE: +60 (3) 7764036
TITLE: Man. Director
CONTACT: Lim Swee Sing
SUBJECTS: Economics, English as a Second Language, Environmental Studies, Geography, Geology, History, Philosophy, Islam, Science (General)

Penerbit Universiti Sains Malaysia

d/a Perpustakaan Universiti Sains Malaysia, Minden, 11800 Pulau Pinang, Malaysia
PHONE: +60 (4) 6577888
FAX: +60 (4) 6571526
E-MAIL: chieflib@usm.my
WEBSITE: http://www.lib.usm.my/press
TITLE: Chairman
CONTACT: Salleh Yaapar
SUBJECTS: Biological Sciences, Chemistry, Engineering, Computer Science, Education, Electronics, Management, Mathematics, Social Sciences, Humanities
TOTAL PUBLISHED: 260 print

Pustaka Cipta Sdn Bhd

58 C Jalan Kampung Attap, 50460 Kuala Lumpur, Malaysia
PHONE: +60 (3) 2744593
FAX: +60 (3) 2749588
E-MAIL: rrapc@po.jaring.my
TITLE: Publication Direction
CONTACT: Rosihan Juara Baharuddin
SUBJECTS: Art, Biography, Communications, Computer Science, Education, Fiction, Literature, Nonfiction (General), Islam, Technology, Travel, Women's Studies

Syarikat Cultural Supplies Sdn Bhd

306 Block C Glomac Business Centre, 10 Jalan 217, Petalina, Jaya, 47301 Selangor Darul Ehsan, Malaysia
PHONE: +60 (3) 7046628; 7554103; 7925729
FAX: +60 (3) 7046629
E-MAIL: malian@po.jaring.my
CONTACT: Kow Ching Chuan
SUBJECTS: Education
TOTAL PUBLISHED: 200 print

Tropical Press Sdn Bhd

66-2 Jalan Maarof, Bangsar Baru, 59100 Kuala Lumpur, Malaysia
PHONE: +60 (3) 2825138; 2825338
FAX: +60 (3) 2823526
E-MAIL: feedback@tpress.po.my
TITLE: Man. Director
CONTACT: Winston Ee
SUBJECTS: Child Care & Development, Mathematics, Mathematics, Natural History, Physical Sciences, Science (General), Technology
TOTAL PUBLISHED: 55 print

University of Malaya, Department of Publications

Lembah Pantai, 59100 Kuala Lumpur, Malaysia
PHONE: +60 (3) 7574361
FAX: +60 (3) 7574473
E-MAIL: a8sidin@cc.um.edu.my
TITLE: Head, Rights & Permissions
CONTACT: Sidin Ahmad Ishak
SUBJECTS: Economics, Fiction, Foreign Countries, Political Science, History, Medicine, Nursing, Dentistry, Science (General), Social Sciences
TOTAL PUBLISHED: 21 print

RELIGIOUS ORGANIZATIONS

Baha'I

Spiritual Assembly of the Baha'is of Malaysia
4 Lorong Titiwangsa 5, Jalan Pahang, 53200 Kuala Lumpur, Malaysia
PHONE: +60 (3) 4235183
FAX: +60 (3) 4226277

Buddhist

Balik Palau Buddhist Hermitage
c/o 21 Jalan Hilir Sungai Burung, 11000 Balik Palau, Malaysia
PHONE: +60 (4) 8669827
E-MAIL: bpbh@po.jaring.my
WEBSITE: http://www.buddhist.org.my/buddhist/

Buddha Dhamma Society
82, 2nd Floor, Jalan Pending, 93450 Kuching, Sarawak, Malaysia
PHONE: +60 (8) 2333232
E-MAIL: buddhadhamma@hotmail.com
WEBSITE: http://bdc.faithweb.com
NAME: Wendy Francis

Hoeh Beng Zen Center
18-A Jalan Raja Bot, Kuala Lumpur, 50300 Malaysia
PHONE: +60 (3) 2929839
FAX: +60 (3) 2929839
TITLE: Teacher
NAME: Dae Bong

Mahindarama Buddhist Temple
2, Kampar Road, 10460 Pulau Penang, Malaysia
PHONE: +60 (4) 2822534
FAX: +60 (4) 2825944
E-MAIL: msps@mol.net.my
WEBSITE: http://www.focus-asia.com/home/mits/
TITLE: Abbot
NAME: Maha Thero E. Indaratana

Malaysian Buddhist Association
182 Burmah Road, 10050 Penang, Malaysia
PHONE: +60 (4) 2262690
FAX: +60 (4) 2263024
E-MAIL: mbapg@po.jaring.my

Malaysian Buddhist Meditation Centre
355 Jalan Mesjid Negeri, Penang, 11600, Malaysia
PHONE: +60 (4) 2822534
E-MAIL: mbmc@tm.net.my
WEBSITE: http://www.karensoft.net.my/mbmc
TITLE: Honorary Secretary
NAME: Tan Ah Huat

Moek
Jalan Saga, Kuala Lumpur, 52200, Malaysia
PHONE: +60 6334463
FAX: +60 6334463
E-MAIL: moek@setec.com.my
TITLE: Teacher
NAME: Moek

Young Buddhists Association of Malaysia
YBAM HG Secretariat, 10 Jalan SS2/75, 47300 Petaling Jaya, Selangor, Malaysia
PHONE: +60 (3) 7764591
FAX: +60 (3) 7762770
E-MAIL: ybamhq@ybamhq.po.my
WEBSITE: http://www.founder.net.my/ybam

Catholic

Catholic Bishops' Conference of Malaysia, Singapore, and Brunei
c/o Catholic Bishops' Conference, Xavier Hall, Jalam Gasing, 46000 Petaling Jaya, Malaysia
PHONE: +60 (3) 7581371
FAX: +60 (3) 7581371
E-MAIL: cbcmsb@jaring.my
TITLE: President
NAME: Archbishop Peter Chung Hoan Ting

Diocese of Kota Kinabalu
Catholic Diocesan Center, PO Box 10225, 88802-Kota Kinabalu, Sabah, Malaysia
PHONE: +60 (88) 712297; 715017
FAX: +60 (88) 711954
WEBSITE: http://www.rc.net/malaysia/kotakinabalu/

Miri Diocese
Diocesan Center, PO Box 392, 98007 Miri, Sarawak, Malaysia
PHONE: +60 (85) 410560
WEBSITE: http://www.rc.net/malaysia/miri/

Islamic

Children Islamic Center
PHONE: +60 (3) 5713251, +60 (1) 23257208
E-MAIL: childrenislamic@hotmail.com
WEBSITE: http://skybusiness.com/children/index.html
TITLE: Advisor
NAME: Ustaz Azizi Ahmad
TITLE: Director
NAME: Hjh Qutreen Nada Ahmad

Al-Jam'iyah Al-Khairiyah
7, Pesiaran Lidcol, Jalan Yap Kwan Seng, Kuala Lumpur, Wilayah Persekutuan, Malaysia
PHONE: +60 (3) 4511803
NAME: Mr. Alatas

Islamic Development Department of Malaysia
Menara Pusat Islam, 50519 Jalan Perdana, Kuala Lumpur Malaysia
PHONE: +60 (3) 22749333
WEBSITE: http://www.islam.gov.my/english/

Regional Islamic Da'wah Council of Southeast Asia and the Pacific

Majlis Sa'wah Islamiah Serantau Asia Teaggara san Pasifik
Perkim Bldg., 5th Fl., Jalan Ipoh, 51200 Kuala Lumpur, Malaysia
PHONE: +60 (3) 4428166
FAX: +60 (3) 4410655
E-MAIL: riscap@asiapac.net
WEBSITE: http://ngo.asiapac.net/riseap/index.html
TITLE: Honorable Secretary General
NAME: Dato Ahmad Nordin

Protestant

Council of Churches of Malaysia
26 Jalan University, 46200 Petaling Jaya, Malaysia
PHONE: +60 (3) 7567092
FAX: +60 (3) 7560353
E-MAIL: cchurchm@tm.net.my
TITLE: General Secretary
NAME: Rev. Dr. Hermen Shastri

Johor Bahru Seventh-Day Adventist Church
No. 3, Jalan Dato Mentri, 80100 Johor Bahru, Johor, Malaysia
PHONE: +60 (7) 2249598
WEBSITE: http://www.tagnet.org/sdajb/
TITLE: Pastor
NAME: Joshua Gan

Methodist Church in Malaysia
23 Jalan Mayang, 50450 Kuala Lumpur
PHONE: +60 (3) 7541811
FAX: +60 (3) 7541787
NAME: Dr. Peter Chin Sing Ching

Petaling Jaya English Seventh-Day Adventist Church
No. 1 Jalan 6/6, 46000 Petaling Jaya, Selangor, Malaysia
WEBSITE: http://www.tagnet.org/pjchurch/

Presbyterian Church in Malaysia
Joyful Grace Church, Jalan Alsagoff, 82000 Pontian, Malaysia
PHONE: +60 (7) 711390
FAX: +60 (7) 324384

FURTHER READING

Articles

Arnold, Wayne. "A Reviving Malaysia Gives Foreign Investors New Jitters; Banking Reform in Starts, Stops and Starts." *New York Times,* September 14, 2000, p. C4.

"Crunch Time for Malaysian Banking." *Business Week,* March 13, 2000, no. 3672, p. 140E6.

Lopez, Leslie and Neil King Jr. "Malaysian Verdict Deprives Opposition of Crucial Leader." *Wall Street Journal,* August 9, 2000, p. A18.

"Malaysia: Mahathir Goes On And On . . . " *The Economist (US),* January 8, 2000, vol. 354, no. 8152, p. 39.

Mydans, Seth. "Malaysia: Opposition Members Jailed." *New York Times,* November 10, 2000, p. A6.

Books

Dun and Bradstreet's Export Guide to Malaysia. Parsippany, NJ: Dun & Bradstreet, 1999.

Eliot, Joshua, et al., eds. *Malaysia Handbook: The Travel Guide.* 3d ed. Bath: Footprint, 2000.

Gomez, Edmund Terence. *Malaysia's Political Economy: Politics, Patronage and Profits.* 2d ed. New York: Cambridge University Press, 1999.

Gunn, Geoffrey C. *New World Hegemony in the Malay World.* Trenton, NJ: Red Sea Press, 2000.

Lucas, Robert E. B. *Restructuring the Malaysian Economy: Development and Human Resources.* New York: St. Martin's Press, 1999.

MALAYSIA: STATISTICAL DATA

For sources and notes see "Sources of Statistics" at the front of each volume.

GEOGRAPHY

Geography

Area:

Total: 329,750 sq km.

Land: 328,550 sq km.

Land boundaries:

Total: 2,669 km.

Border countries: Brunei 381 km, Indonesia 1,782 km, Thailand 506 km.

Coastline: 4,675 km (Peninsular Malaysia 2,068 km, East Malaysia 2,607 km).

Climate: tropical; annual southwest (April to October) and northeast (October to February) monsoons.

Terrain: coastal plains rising to hills and mountains.

Natural resources: tin, petroleum, timber, copper, iron ore, natural gas, bauxite.

Land use:

Arable land: 3%

Permanent crops: 12%

Permanent pastures: 0%

Forests and woodland: 68%

Other: 17% (1993 est.).

HUMAN FACTORS

Demographics (A)

	1990	1995	1998	2000	2010	2020	2030	2040	2050
Population	17,504	19,611	20,912	21,793	26,144	30,740	35,306	39,411	43,122
Life expectancy - males	65.3	66.8	67.6	68.2	70.8	73.0	74.9	76.5	77.7
Life expectancy - females	70.3	72.0	73.0	73.6	76.5	78.9	80.9	82.5	83.8
Birth rate (per 1,000)	29.0	27.6	26.6	25.3	22.1	20.5	18.1	16.4	15.4
Death rate (per 1,000)	6.1	5.6	5.4	5.3	5.1	5.3	5.8	6.5	7.2
Women of reproductive age (15-49 yrs.)	4,517	5,037	5,383	5,625	6,749	7,727	8,720	9,508	10,052
Fertility rate	3.5	3.4	3.4	3.3	2.9	2.7	2.5	2.3	2.2

Except as noted, values for vital statistics are in thousands; life expectancy is in years.

Health Personnel

	National Data	World Data (wtd ave)
Total health expenditure as a percentage of GDP, 1990-1998[a]		
Public sector	1.3	2.5
Private sector	1.0	2.9
Total[b]	2.4	5.5
Health expenditure per capita in U.S. dollars, 1990-1998[a]		
Purchasing power parity	180	561
Total	78	483
Availability of health care facilities per 100,000 people		
Hospital beds 1990-1998[a]	200	330
Doctors 1992-1995[a]	43	122
Nurses 1992-1995[a]	160	248

Health Indicators

	National Data	World Data
Life expectancy at birth (years)		
1980	67	61
1998	72	67
Daily per capita supply of calories		
1970	2,560	2,358
1997	2,977	2,791
Daily per capital supply of protein		
1997 (grams)	75	74
Total fertility rate (births per woman)		
1980	4.2	3.7
1998	3.1	2.7
Population with access (%)		
To safe water (1990-96)	89	NA
To sanitation (1990-96)	94	NA
People living with (1997)		
Tuberculosis (cases per 100,000)	64.4	60.4
Malaria (cases per 100,000)	127.0	42.2
HIV/AIDS (% aged 15 - 49 years)	0.62	0.99

Infants and Malnutrition

	National Data	World Data (wtd ave)
Under 5 mortality rate (1989)	10	NA
% of infants with low birthweight (1992-98)[1]	8	17
Births attended by skilled health staff (% of total births 1996-98)	98	52
% fully immunized at 1 year of age (1995-98)[1]		
TB	100	82
DPT	95	77
Polio	94	77
Measles	86	74
Prevalence of child malnutrition (1992-98)[1] (based on weight for age, % of children under 5 years)	20	30

Ethnic Division

Malay and other indigenous 58%

Chinese 26%

Indian 7%

Others 9%

Religion

Islam, Buddhism, Daoism, Hinduism, Christianity, Sikhism. Note: in addition, Shamanism is practiced in East Malaysia.

Major Languages

Bahasa Melayu (official), English, Chinese dialects (Cantonese, Mandarin, Hokkien, Hakka, Hainan, Foochow), Tamil, Telugu, Malayalam, Panjabi, Thai; in addition, in East Malaysia several indigenous languages are spoken, the largest of which are Iban and Kadazan.

EDUCATION

Public Education Expenditures

	1980	1997
Public expenditures on education as % of GNP	6.0	4.9
Expenditures per student as % of GNP per capita		
Primary & Secondary	12.0[2]	11.1
Tertiary	148.9	57.3
Teachers' compensation as % of total current education expenditures	57.5	58.6
Pupils per teacher at the primary level	NA	20
Duration of primary education in years	NA	NA
World data for comparison		
Public expenditures on education as % of GNP (mean)	3.9	4.8

Pupils per teacher at the primary level (wtd ave)	NA	33
Duration of primary education in years (mean)	NA	9

Educational Attainment (A)

Age group (1996) ....25+

Population of this age group 9,654,600

Highest level attained (%)

No schooling 16.7

First level

Not completed 13.0

Completed 20.7

Entered second level

Lower Secondary 19.4

Upper Secondary 23.6

Entered post-secondary 6.9

Literacy Rates (A)

In thousands and percent	1990	1995	2000	2010
Illiterate population (15+ yrs.)	2,190	2,057	1,891	1,490
Literacy rate - total adult pop. (%)	80.2	83.5	86.9	92.0
Literacy rate - males (%)	86.9	89.1	91.2	94.2
Literacy rate - females (%)	73.6	78.1	82.6	89.8

Libraries

National Libraries **1995**

Administrative Units 1

Service Points or Branches 9

Number of Volumes (000) 1,108

Registered Users (000) 176

Loans to Users (000) 264

Total Library Staff 248

Public Libraries **1995**

Administrative Units 14

Service Points or Branches 471

Number of Volumes (000) 10,895

Registered Users (000) 1,920

Loans to Users (000) 6,991

Total Library Staff 1,979

GOVERNMENT & LAW

Political Parties

House of Representatives	% of vote	no. of seats
National Front (NF)	56%	148
Parti Islam SeMalaysia (PAS)		27
Democratic Action Party (DAP)		10
National Justice Party (NJP)		5
United Sabah Party (PBS)		3
Other	44%	

Elections for the House of Representatives were last held 29 November 1999 (next to be held 3 November 2004).

Government Budgets (A)

Year: 1997

Total Expenditures: 55,481 Millions of Ringgit

Expenditures as a percentage of the total by function:

General public services and public order ......16.30[f]

Defense ....11.14[f]

Education ....22.80[f]

Health ....6.26[f]

Social Security and Welfare ....7.20[f]

Housing and community amenities ....7.31[f]

Recreational, cultural, and religious affairs ......NA

Fuel and energy ....NA

Agriculture, forestry, fishing, and hunting ......4.65[f]

Mining, manufacturing, and construction ....NA

Transportation and communication ....9.89[f]

Other economic affairs and services ....7.07[f]

Crime

Crime volume (for 1998)

Crimes reported 133,924

Total persons convicted 43,525

Crimes per 100,000 population 604

Persons responsible for offenses

Total number suspects 33,984

Total number of female suspects 109

Total number of juvenile suspects 2,715

(Continued on next page.)

LABOR FORCE

Total Labor Force (A)

9.3 million (1999 est.).

Labor Force by Occupation

Manufacturing 27%

Agriculture, forestry, and fisheries 16%
Local trade and tourism 17%
Services 15%
Government 10%
Construction 9%

Data for 1999 est.

Unemployment Rate

3% (1999 est.)

PRODUCTION SECTOR

Energy Production

Production . . . . .57.435 billion kWh
Production by source
Fossil fuel 94.78%
Hydro 5.22%
Nuclear 0%
Other 0%
Exports . . . . .75 million kWh

Data for 1998.

(Continued on next page.)

GOVERNMENT & LAW (cont.)

Military Affairs (A)

	1990	1992	1995	1996	1997
Military expenditures					
Current dollars (mil.)	1,260	1,790	2,280	2,190	2,090
1997 constant dollars (mil.)	1,480	1,980	2,360	2,230	2,090
Armed forces (000)	130	128	122	128	110
Gross national product (GNP)					
Current dollars (mil.)	45,800	55,900	77,500	85,600	93,500
1997 constant dollars (mil.)	53,600	61,900	80,300	87,000	93,500
Central government expenditures (CGE)					
1997 constant dollars (mil.)	16,400	19,200	19,000	21,000	21,000
People (mil.)	17.5	18.3	19.6	20.1	20.5
Military expenditure as % of GNP	2.8	3.2	2.9	2.6	2.2
World data on military expenditure as % of GNP	4.5	3.4	2.7	2.6	2.6
Military expenditure as % of CGE	9.0	10.3	12.4	10.6	9.9
World data on military expenditure as % of CGE	17.0	12.5	10.5	10.3	10.2
Military expenditure per capita (1997 $)	84	108	120	111	102
World data on military expenditure per capita (1997 $)	242	173	146	143	145
Armed forces per 1,000 people (soldiers)	7.4	7.0	6.2	6.4	5.4
World data on armed forces per 1,000 people (soldiers)	5.3	4.5	4.1	3.9	3.8
GNP per capita (1997 $)	3,060	3,380	4,090	4,340	4,560
Arms imports[6]					
Current dollars (mil.)	70	250	825	200	725
1997 constant dollars (mil.)	82	277	854	203	725
Arms exports[6]					
Current dollars (mil.)	0	0	40	5	5
1997 constant dollars (mil.)	0	0	41	5	5
Total imports[7]					
Current dollars (mil.)	29,260	39,930	77,750	78,420	79,030
1997 constant dollars (mil.)	34,260	44,260	80,510	79,730	79,030
Total exports[7]					
Current dollars (mil.)	29,420	40,710	74,040	78,330	78,740
1997 constant dollars (mil.)	34,450	45,130	76,660	79,630	78,740
Arms as percent of total imports[8]	0.2	0.6	1.1	0.3	0.9
Arms as percent of total exports[8]	0	0	0.1	0	0

PRODUCTION SECTOR (cont.)

Energy Consumption

Consumption ....53.423 billion kWh

Imports ....83.000 million kWh

Data for 1998.

Transportation

Highways:

Total: 94,500 km.

Paved: 70,970 km (including 580 km of expressways).

Unpaved: 23,530 km (1996 est.).

Waterways: 7,296 km (Peninsular Malaysia 3,209 km, Sabah 1,569 km, Sarawak 2,518 km).

Pipelines: crude oil 1,307 km; natural gas 379 km.

Merchant marine:

Total: 361 ships (1,000 GRT or over) totaling 5,000,706 GRT/7,393,915 DWT.

Ships by type: bulk 61, cargo 119, chemical tanker 34, container 55, liquified gas 19, livestock carrier 1, passenger 2, petroleum tanker 57, refrigerated cargo 1,roll-on/roll-off 6, specialized tanker 1, vehicle carrier 5 (1999 est.).

Airports: 115 (1999 est.).

Airports - with paved runways: 32.

Airports - with unpaved runways: 83.

Top Agriculture Products

Peninsular Malaysia - rubber, palm oil, rice; Sabah - subsistence crops, rubber, timber, coconuts, rice; Sarawak - rubber, pepper; timber.

Top Mining Products (B)

Mineral resources include: tin, copper, iron ore, bauxite.

MANUFACTURING SECTOR

GDP & Manufacturing Summary (A)

	1980	1985	1990	1995
GDP ($-1990 mil.)[1]	23,989	30,784	42,822	64,688
Per capita ($-1990)[1]	1,743	1,964	2,393	3,212
Manufacturing share (%) (current prices)[1]	21.2	19.9	26.5	32.5
Manufacturing				
Value added ($-1990 mil.)[1]	4,707	6,064	11,493	21,186
Industrial production index	46	53	100	200
Value added ($ mil.)	3,624	4,879	9,068	23,831[e]
Gross output ($ mil.)	13,550[e]	18,539	35,422	92,809[e]
Employment (000)	456[e]	473	831	1,299[e]
Profitability (% of gross output)				
Intermediate input (%)	73[e]	73	74	74[e]
Wages and salaries inc. supplements (%)	8[e]	9	8	7[e]
Gross operating surplus	19[e]	18	18	19[e]
Productivity ($)				
Gross output per worker	29,370[e]	38,561	42,503	71,398[e]
Value added per worker	8,067[e]	10,249	10,881	18,475[e]
Average wage (inc. supplements)	2,247[e]	3,375	3,240	4,903[e]
Value added ($ mil.)				
Food products	667[e]	703	865	1,790[e]
Beverages	106[e]	122	201	206[e]
Tobacco products	94[e]	205	127	217[e]
Textiles	185[e]	133	297	774[e]
Wearing apparel	67[e]	100	280	478[e]
Leather and fur products	6[e]	2	6	32[e]
Footwear	11[e]	5	4	13[e]
Wood and wood products	388[e]	263[e]	584	1,551[e]
Furniture and fixtures	34[e]	40	70	314[e]
Paper and paper products	34[e]	55	155	401[e]
Printing and publishing	145[e]	197	266	638[e]
Industrial chemicals	79[e]	616	748	1,298[e]
Other chemical products	117[e]	153	232	525[e]
Petroleum refineries	115[e]	136	199	589[e]
Misc. petroleum and coal products	2[e]	21	32	115[e]
Rubber products	295[e]	250	528	977[e]
Plastic products	69[e]	92	261	922[e]
Pottery, china and earthenware	10[e]	13	36	77[e]
Glass and glass products	24[e]	23	73	180[e]
Other non-metal mineral products	169[e]	297	441	1,120[e]
Iron and steel	79[e]	153	287	448[e]

(Continued on next page.)

	1980	1985	1990	1995
Non-ferrous metals	39[e]	35	63	204[e]
Metal products	139[e]	147	316	976[e]
Non-electrical machinery	117[e]	99	348	1,097[e]
Electrical machinery	434[e]	738	1,945	7,219[e]
Transport equipment	153[e]	211	494	1,156[e]
Prof. and scientific equipment	25[e]	30	97	302[e]
Other manufacturing	23[e]	39	111	211[e]

COMMUNICATIONS

Daily Newspapers

	National Data	World Data for Comparison
Daily Newspapers		
Number of Dailies	42	8,391
Total Circulation (000)	3,345	548,000
Circulation per 1,000 inhabitants	163	96

Telecommunications

Telephones - main lines in use: 4.4 million (1998).

Telephones - mobile cellular: 2.17 million (1998).

Telephone system: international service good.

Domestic: good intercity service provided on Peninsular Malaysia mainly by microwave radio relay; adequate intercity microwave radio relay network between Sabahand Sarawak via Brunei; domestic satellite system with 2 earth stations.

International: submarine cables to India, Hong Kong, and Singapore; satellite earth stations - 2 Intelsat (1 Indian Ocean and 1 Pacific Ocean).

Radio broadcast stations: AM 56, FM 31 (plus 13 repeater stations), shortwave 5 (1999).

Radios: 9.1 million (1997).

Television broadcast stations: 27 (plus 15 high-power repeaters) (1999).

Televisions: 3.6 million (1997).

Internet Service Providers (ISPs): 8 (1999).

FINANCE, ECONOMICS, & TRADE

Economic Indicators

National product: GDP—purchasing power parity—$229.1 billion (1999 est.).

National product real growth rate: 5% (1999 est.).

National product per capita: $10,700 (1999 est.).

Inflation rate—consumer price index: 2.8% (1999).

Exchange Rates

Exchange rates:

Ringgits (M$) per US$1

January 2000	3.8000
1999	3.8000
1998	3.9244
1997	2.8133
1996	2.5159
1995	2.5044

Top Import Origins

$61.5 billion (1999 est.)

Origins (1999 est.)

Japan	21%
United States	18%
Singapore	14%
Taiwan	5%
South Korea	5%
Thailand	4%
China	3%

Balance of Payments

	1993	1994	1995	1996	1997
Exports of goods (f.o.b.)	46,238	56,897	71,767	76,881	77,881
Imports of goods (f.o.b.)	−43,201	−55,320	−71,871	−73,055	−74,005
Trade balance	3,037	1,577	−103	3,826	3,876
Services - debits	−9,516	−12,052	−14,981	−17,308	−17,516
Services - credits	6,412	9,320	11,602	14,510	15,016
Private transfers (net)	388	336	600	693	717
Government transfers (net)	57	51	54	−14	4
Overall balance	−2,991	−4,520	−8,469	−4,596	−4,792

Top Export Destinations

$83.5 billion (1999 est.)

Destinations (1999 est.)

United States	23%
Singapore	16%
Japan	11%
Hong Kong	5%
Netherlands	5%
Taiwan	5%
Thailand	3%

Import/Export Commodities

Import Commodities	Export Commodities
Machinery and equipment	Electronic equipment
Chemicals	Petroleum and liquefied natural gas
Food	Chemicals
Fuel and lubricants	Palm oil
	Wood and wood products
	Rubber
	Textiles

MALDIVES

Republic of Maldives
Dhivehi Raajjeyge Jumhooriyyaa

CAPITAL: Malé.

FLAG: The national flag consists of a white crescent at the center of a green field which, in turn, is at the center of a red field.

MONETARY UNIT: The Maldivian rupee, or rufiyaa (MR), is a paper currency of 100 laris. There are notes of 1/2, 1, 2, 5, 10, 50, and 100 rufiyaa. The dollar circulates freely and is the only currency accepted at some resorts. MR1 = $0.08496 (or $1 = MR11.770).

WEIGHTS AND MEASURES: The metric system has been adopted, but some local units remain in use.

HOLIDAYS: National Day, 7 January; Independence Day, 26 July; Republic Day, 11 November; Fishermen's Day, 10 December. 'Id al-Fitr, 'Id al-'Adha', and Milad an-Nabi are some of the Muslim religious holidays observed.

TIME: 5 PM = noon GMT.

LOCATION AND SIZE: The smallest country in Asia, the Republic of Maldives consists of an archipelago (a large group of islands) of nearly 1,200 coral islands and sand banks in the Indian Ocean, about 200 of which are inhabited. The area occupied by Maldives is slightly more than 1.5 times the size of Washington, D.C.

Maldives' capital, Malé, is situated on the largest island in the entire chain, in the Malé Atoll.

CLIMATE: The Maldives' equatorial climate is generally hot and humid, with a mean temperature of about 27°C (81°F). Annual rainfall in the south averages about 380 centimeters (150 inches); in the north, 250 centimeters (100 inches).

INTRODUCTORY SURVEY

RECENT HISTORY

Although it gained independence from the United Kingdom in 1948, the Maldives remained under the protection of Great Britain. In 1959 government forces crushed rebellions in two of the southernmost atolls. The Sultanate of the Maldive Islands achieved complete independence in July 1965. A new republican constitution came into force in November 1968 establishing the Republic of Maldives. Britain left the Gan airbase on December 31, 1975, and the United Kingdom-Maldivian protection accord was formally terminated the following year.

Maumoon Abdul Gayoon was confirmed in a popular referendum as president in 1978. In November 1988 President Gayoom successfully resisted an attempt to overthrow him by hired soldiers from Sri Lanka. He was helped by an Indian military contingent flown to the Maldives at his request. Gayoom was reelected for a fifth term as president in 1998/99.

GOVERNMENT

Under the 1968 constitution, the president is elected to a five-year term by the Majlis (parliament) but must be confirmed in office by popular referendum. The president is both chief of state and head of government. The president appoints the cabinet. The Majlis, or People's Council, has fifty members, forty-two directly elected and eight appointed by the president. All serve for five-year terms.

Judiciary

Justice is carried out according to traditional Islamic law *(Shari'a)* by the High Court and lower courts appointed for that purpose by the president. Civil law is also applied but remains subordinate to Shari'a.

On the capital island, Malé, there is a High Court and four lower courts. The High Court hears

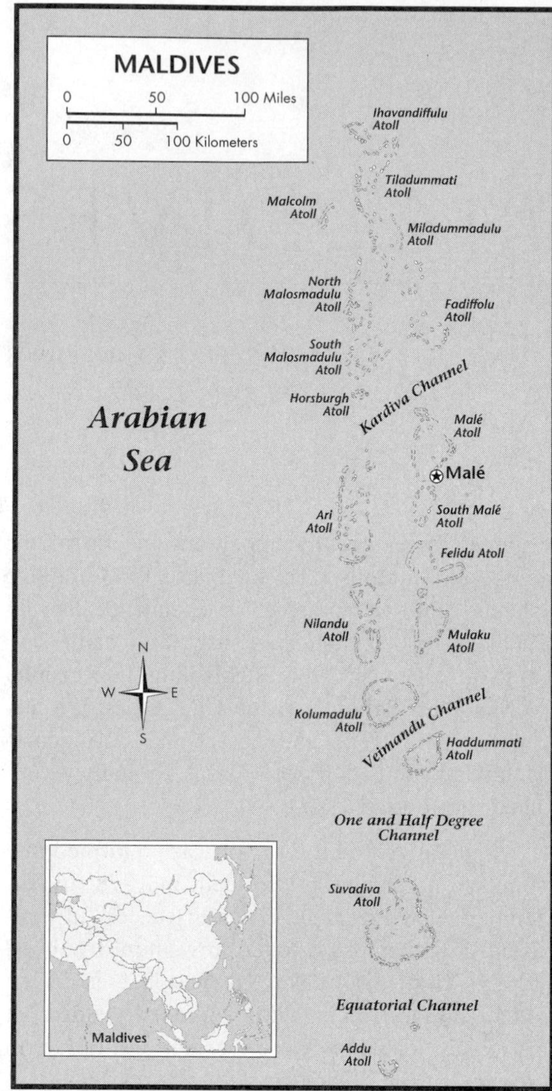

a range of cases as a court of first instance and also serves as a court of appeal. The four lower courts deal with a specific area such as theft or family law. The On the other islands, there is one all-purpose lower court, and complex cases are referred to the appropriate specialized court in Malé. There are 204 general courts on the islands.

Political Parties

There are no organized political parties. Candidates run for election as independents and campaign based on their personal and family reputations.

DEFENSE

The armed forces of the Maldives consist of a paramilitary National Security Service and Militia of only a few hundred. Armed boats patrol the territorial waters to protect the local fishing industry. Defense spending may reach $1.8 million a year.

ECONOMIC AFFAIRS

The Maldives is among the least developed countries in the world. Yet economic progress has been steady. Since the early 1990s the country's GDP growth rate has been estimated at 6 percent to 7 percent per year. Tourism, fishing, and shipping are the mainstays of the economy. Over 90 percent of government revenues come from tourism-related taxes and import duties. Tourism accounts for 20 percent of GDP. The government is seeking to diversify the economy through further promotion of tourism, processing industries, and garment production.

Agriculture and manufacturing continue to play a minor role and most foodstuffs must be imported. Authorities are concerned about the impact of erosion and possible global warming on their low-lying country.

Public Finance

Public enterprises, including the State Trading Organization, the state shipping line, and public utilities, account for nearly half of government revenues; customs and tourist receipts make up most of the rest.

The U.S. Central Intelligence Agency estimated that in 1999 government revenues totaled approximately $166 million and expenditures $192 million including capital expenditures of $80 million. External debt totaled $188 million by 1998 estimates..

Income

In 1997 Maldives's gross domestic product (GDP) was estimated at $540 million, or about $1,800 per capita. The 1999 estimated GDP growth rate was 7 percent and inflation was 3 percent. The 1999 estimated GDP by sector was agriculture 20 percent, industry 18 percent, and services 62 percent.

Industry

After the tourism and fishing industry, important traditional industries in the Maldives include the manufacture of coir (a rope made from dried coconut fibers) and lacemaking. Other industries include shipping, boat building, coconut processing, garments, woven mats, handicrafts, and coral and sand mining.

Banking and Finance

The Maldives Monetary Authority, established July 1, 1981, issues currency, advises the government on banking and monetary matters, supervises commercial banks, and manages exchange rates and exchange assets. The Bank of Maldives (created in 1982) and branches of the Bank of India, Habib Bank Ltd. of Pakistan, and the Bank of Ceylon provides other banking services. There is no securities exchange.

Economic Development

The government has implemented a series of development programs to improve and expand fishing and related industries, textile manufacturing, food processing, tourism, communications, and health and education services. Part of the economic thrust has been to lessen the reliance on fishing and to diversify the economy. In 1986 Malé's new commercial harbor was opened considerably speeding up cargo handling from 200-300 tons to 1,500 tons a day. As part of an economic reform program in 1989, import quotas were lifted and export laws were liberalized. More foreign investment was encouraged with liberalized regulation.

Malé's international airport was upgraded in the late 1980s, comprising a critical factor in the growth of the country's tourism sector. Given the growing wealth in the country in recent years, the government is considering bolstering government development revenues by instituting a personal income tax, though concerns remain that enforcement may prove difficult. Continued expansion of tourism has been particularly targeted in government development plans for the immediate future, along with facilitating a spread of economic activity to outlying island groups. Water taxis and scheduled sea vessel and light aircraft transportation services were developing in the late 1990s for this purpose.

SOCIAL WELFARE

There is no organized social welfare system. Assistance is traditionally provided through the extended family. In spite of traditional Islamic restrictions on women, they have increased their participation in public life.

Healthcare

In 1993 the Maldives had fifteen physicians and six midwives. There is an 86-bed hospital in Malé, backed by a 12-bed regional hospital and medical rescue services in the outlying atolls. In 2000 life expectancy was 62.2 years.

Housing

Most houses have coral or coconut-wood walls; the roofs are tiled or made of corrugated galvanized iron. The poorer houses are walled from the street with mats, called *cadjan,* or palm leaves. In 1999 the government announced a ban on coral mining for construction to encourage use of other materials.

EDUCATION

An estimated 3.7 percent of the adult population was illiterate in 2000. Primary level education is for five years and secondary education is in two stages, five years at a lower level and two years at a higher level. Education is not compulsory. In 1998 there were 48,895 students in primary schools and secondary schools had 36,905 students. Maldivians must go abroad for higher education.

2000 KEY EVENTS TIMELINE

March

- Maldavian Foreign Minister Fathulla Jameel visits India March 6 to attend the fourth meeting of the Indo-Maldives Joint Commission on Economic and Technical Cooperation.

May

- The Czech and Maldives defense ministers meet in order to discuss open, bilateral cooperation. Maldives has no standing army, and only 900 policemen.
- Most of Maldives' islands are in danger of sinking into the sea, despite the Great Wall of Male which keeps the waters out of the capital city.

July

- Maldives is among the thirty-five places designated as "tax havens" by the Organization for Economic Cooperation and Development (OECD). The OECD asks that tax reforms be developed by the end of 2000 and implemented by the end of 2005, and threatens sanctions if the places fail to comply.

August

- U.K. Deputy Prime Minister John Prescott, speaking on August 25 to representatives of seventy-seven of the world's developing countries, said that industrialized nations must develop programs to reduce greenhouse gases. Some scientists believe that greenhouse gases are contributing to global warming and rising sea levels worldwide.

November

- Testifying at the international meeting on climate change in The Hague, Netherlands, on November 22, Maldives representative Siwad Saeed warns that with just a one-meter rise in sea levels, his country would disappear under the sea.

ANALYSIS OF EVENTS: 2000

BUSINESS AND THE ECONOMY

Maldives's primary economic sector, tourism, remained threatened by the rising sea levels that were sweeping away the alluring beaches that drew visitors to the country. In an attempt to diversify the economy, the government was trying to attract investment in the emerging fishing industry, but that sector was nowhere near the point where it could replace tourism in maintaining current living standards on the islands.

Maldives's foreign minister Fathulla Jameel, traveled to India in March for the fourth meeting of the Indo-Maldives Joint Commission on Economic and Technical Cooperation.

GOVERNMENT AND POLITICS

President Abdul Gayoum, in the midst of his fifth consecutive term in office, continued to preside over a corrupt and repressive regime. As Asia's longest-serving ruler Gayoum had been unopposed in the polling in which he was reelected two years earlier, and he maintained tight control of the media. Political parties had been barred from participating in parliamentary elections the previous November, a move that critics charged had helped the government target and persecute its opponents. In January the human rights organization Amnesty International charged that three opposition candidates detained since shortly before the election had been tortured by police, and that their health and safety were still in jeopardy. One man had been placed under house arrest in October after arguing publicly with a government-supported parliamentary candidate and later moved to a prison facility. The other two had been arrested in November. The Maldives government denied the charges of human rights violations, asserting that it held no political prisoners. However, Amnesty International also claimed that about 100 more people had been detained since the election.

Maldives was one of thirty-five countries and territories around the world identified in June by the Organization for Economic Cooperation and Development (OECD) as "tax havens" that allegedly tried to attract deposits or investments by people seeking to launder money or avoid paying taxes. The international organization announced that it would initiate some form of sanctions against those entities that failed to institute tax reform. Governments on the list were asked to announce their intention of cooperating on reform by the end of the year, and of completing the reform process by the end of 2005. Other locations on the OECD list included Monaco, Panama, Andorra, and various overseas possessions of the United States, the United Kingdom, and the Netherlands. The action was described as an attempt to eliminate unfair tax competition. The nature of the proposed sanctions was not specified.

Maldives has no standing army and fewer than one thousand policeman, but it does have a defense minister, and he met with his counterpart from the Czech Republic in May to discuss bilateral cooperation between the two nations.

CULTURE AND SOCIETY

Maldives has attempted to preserve its nearly thousand-year-old Islamic culture by keeping most of its population from interacting with tourists. However, tourism—and the fate of the islands themselves—may be endangered by the rising sea levels that threaten the more than one thousand coral islands, both inhabited and uninhabited, that make up the country. With terrain averaging less than one meter above sea level, the islands stand to be destroyed by the three-quarter-of-a-meter rise in water level that many experts predict will take place take place during the twenty-first century, caused by greenhouse gases resulting from air pollution. Global warming also threatens the islands in other ways, including damage to coral caused by the absorption of carbon dioxide from the air into the water, and warmer water temperatures that have discolored or destroyed much of the coral in some parts of the islands. It is also thought that rising temperatures could contribute to the frequency and severity of tropical storms.

In addition to speaking out on the problem of global warming, the Maldives government has partially surrounded the capital city of Male with a six-foot-high concrete barrier, popularly called the Great Wall. It is also considering consolidating the country's population on only a few larger islands, which would be protected by sea walls, although such a measure would detract from the charm and sense of community found on the many small islands of the Maldives. Along similar lines, the government has claimed to be building an artificial island on higher ground that could afford shelter to about half the country's population if necessary.

DIRECTORY

CENTRAL GOVERNMENT

Head of State

President
Maumoon Abdul Gayooom, Office of the President
PHONE: +960 323701
FAX: +960 325500

Ministers

Minister of Atolls Administration
Abdulla Hameed, Ministry of Atolls Administration, Faashanaa Building, Boduthakurufaanu Magu, Male, 20 05, Republic of Maldives
PHONE: +960 323070
FAX: +960 327750

Minister of Construction and Public Works
Umar Zahir, Ministry of Construction and Public Works, Izzuddeen Magu, Male, 20 01, Republic of Maldives
PHONE: +960 323234
FAX: +960 326637
E-MAIL: mcpw@dhivehinet.net.mv

Minister of Defense and National Security
Maumoon Abdul Gayoom, Ministry of Defense and National Security, Bandaara Koshi, Ameer Ahmed Magu, Male, 20 05, Republic of Maldives
PHONE: +960 322607
FAX: +960 325525

Minister of Education
Mohammed Latheef, Ministry of Education, Ghaazee Building, Ameer Ahmed Magu, Male, 20 05, Republic of Maldives
PHONE: +960 323262
FAX: +960 321201
E-MAIL: educator@dhivehinet.net.mv

Minister of Finance and Treasury
Maumoon Abdul Gayoom, Ministry of Finance and Treasury, Ameenee Magu, Male, 20 04, Republic of Maldives
PHONE: +960 322269
FAX: +960 324432
E-MAIL: educator@dhivehinet.net.mv

Minister of Fisheries, Agriculture and Marine Resources
Abdul Rasheed Hussain, Ministry of Fisheries, Agriculture and Marine Resources, Ghaazee Building, Ameer Ahmed Magu, Male, 20 05, Republic of Maldives
PHONE: +960 322625
FAX: +960 326558
E-MAIL: fishagri@dhivehinet.net.mv

Minister of Foreign Affairs
Fathulla Jameel, Ministry of Foreign Affairs, Boduthakurufaanu Magu, Male, 20 05, Republic of Maldives
PHONE: +960 323400
FAX: +960 323841
E-MAIL: admin@foreign.gov.mv

Minister of Health
Ahmed Abdulla, Ministry of Health, Ghaazee Building, Ameer Ahmed Magu, Male, 20 05, Republic of Maldives
PHONE: +960 328887
FAX: +960 328889
E-MAIL: moh@dhivehinet.net.mv

Minister of Home Affairs, Housing and Environment
Ismail Shafeeu, Ministry of Home Affairs, Housing and Environment, Huravee Building, Ameer Ahmed Magu, Male, 20 05, Republic of Maldives
PHONE: +960 323820
FAX: +960 324739

Minister of Human Resources, Employment and Labour
Abdulla Kamaludheen, Ministry of Human Resources, Employment and Labour

Minister of Information, Arts and Culture
Ibrahim Manik, Ministry of Information, Arts and Culture, Buruzu Magu, Male, 20 04, Republic of Maldives
PHONE: +960 323838
FAX: +960 326211
E-MAIL: informat@dhivehinet.net.mv

Minister of Justice
Ahmed Zahir, Ministry of Justice, Justice Building, Orchid Magu, Male, 20 02, Republic of Maldives
PHONE: +960 322303
FAX: +960 324103
E-MAIL: informat@dhivehinet.net.mv

Minister of Planning and National Development
Ibrahim Hussain Zaki, Ministry of Planning and National Development, Ghaazee Building, Ameer Ahmed Magu, Male, 20 05, Republic of Maldives
PHONE: +960 323919
FAX: +960 327351
E-MAIL: mpre@dhivehinet.net.mv

Minister of Tourism
Hassan Sabir, Ministry of Tourism, Boduthakurufaanu Magu, Male, 20 05, Republic of Maldives
PHONE: +960 323224
FAX: +960 322512
E-MAIL: tourism@dhivehinet.net.mv

Minister of Trade and Industries
Abdulla Yameen, Ministry of Trade and Industries, Ghaazee Building, Ameer Ahmed Magu, Male, 20 05, Republic of Maldives
PHONE: +960 323668
FAX: +960 323840

Minister of Transport and Civil Aviation
Ilyas Ibrahim, Ministry of Transport and Civil Aviation, Ghaazee Building, Ameer Ahmed Magu, Male, 20 05, Republic of Maldives
PHONE: +960 323991/323344
FAX: +960 323994

Minister of Women's Affairs and Social Security
Rashida Yoosuf, Ministry of Women's Affairs and Social Security, Umar Shopping Arcade, 2nd Floor, Chaandhanee Magu, Male, 20 05, Republic of Maldives
PHONE: +960 317165
FAX: +960 316237
E-MAIL: kamana@dhivehinet.net.mv

Minister of Youth and Sports
Mohammed Zahir Hussain, Ministry of Youth and Sports, Ghaazee Building, Ameer Ahmed Magu, Male, 20 05, Republic of Maldives
PHONE: +960 326986
FAX: +960 327162
E-MAIL: mys@dhivehinet.net.mv

DIPLOMATIC REPRESENTATION

Embassies in Maldives

Denmark
25 Boduthakurufaanu Magu, Male 20 05, Maldives
PHONE: +960 322451
FAX: +960 323523

JUDICIAL SYSTEM

High Court of Maldives

Moonlight Hingun, Male, 20 06, Republic of Maldives
PHONE: +960 323082
FAX: +960 316371

Civil Court

Justice Building, Orchid Magu, Male, 20 02, Republic of Maldives
PHONE: +960 323682
FAX: +960 323986

Criminal Court

Justice Building, Orchid Magu, Male, 20 02, Republic of Maldives
PHONE: +960 323268
FAX: +960 322304

BROADCAST MEDIA

Voice of Maldives

"Moonlight Higun," Male 20 06, Maldives
PHONE: +960 325577
FAX: +960 328357
TITLE: Directorate General of Broadcasting
CONTACT: Ibrahim Manik
TYPE: Government

Television Maldives

Buruzu Magu, 20 04 Malé, Maldives
PHONE: +960 323105; 324105
FAX: +960 325083
TITLE: Directorate General
CONTACT: Hussain Mohamed

NEWSPAPERS AND MAGAZINES

Haveeru Daily

PO Box 20103, Male 20 02 Maldives
PHONE: +960 32567
FAX: +960 323103

E-MAIL: haveeru@dhivehinet.net.mv
WEBSITE: http://www.haveeru.com
TITLE: Editor
CONTACT: Ali Rafeeq
CIRCULATION: 4,500

Miadhu News

WEBSITE: http://www.miadhu.com

PUBLISHERS

Non-Formal Education Centre

Salahuddeen Building, Male 20 03, Maldives
PHONE: + 960 328772; 324622
TITLE: Deputy Director
CONTACT: Abdul Raheem Hasan
SUBJECTS: Agriculture, Child Care, Education, English as a Second Language, Environmental Studies, Health, Islam, Social Sciences, Sports

Novelty Printers & Publishers

Maafannu Varey Villa, Dhilbahaaru Higun Male 20 01, Maldives
PHONE: + 960 322474
FAX: +960 322490
TITLE: Man. Director
CONTACT: Ali Hussain
SUBJECTS: Animals, Pets, Foreign Countries, Regional Interests, Travel

RELIGIOUS ORGANIZATIONS

Until 1975, the Maldives were a territory of the British Empire. Most Christian religious organizations have not yet had time to establish a presence independent of the main organizations on the British mainland.

FURTHER READING

Articles

"Czech, Maldives Defense Ministers Discuss Cooperation," *BBC,* May 30, 2000.

"Maldivian Foreign Minister to Pay Two-Day Visit Beginning 6 March," *PVI,* March 3, 2000.

"Not Sinking but Drowning," *The Economist,* May 13, 2000.

Books

Lyon, James. *Maldives.* 4th ed. London: Lonely Planet, 2000.

Subritzky, John. *Confronting Sukarno: British, American, Australian and New Zealand Diplomacy in the Malaysian-Indonesian Confrontation, 1961–5.* New York: St. Martin's Press, 2000.

Internet

BBC News Online. "Sanctions Threat to 'Tax Havens.'" June 26, 2000. [Onine] Available http://news6.thdo.bbc.co.uk/hi/english/business/newsid%5F806000/806236.stm (accessed October 12, 2000).

MALDIVES: STATISTICAL DATA

For sources and notes see "Sources of Statistics" at the front of each volume.

GEOGRAPHY

Geography

Area:

Total: 300 sq km.

Land: 300 sq km.

Land boundaries: 0 km.

Coastline: 644 km.

Climate: tropical; hot, humid; dry, northeast monsoon (November to March); rainy, southwest monsoon (June to August).

Terrain: flat, with white sandy beaches.

Natural resources: fish.

Land use:

Arable land: 10%

Permanent crops: 0%

Permanent pastures: 3%

Forests and woodland: 3%

Other: 84% (1993 est.).

HUMAN FACTORS

Demographics (A)

	1990	1995	1998	2000	2010	2020	2030	2040	2050
Population	216.4	256.9	283.3	301.5	399.8	508.3	618.2	721.3	815.0
Life expectancy - males	57.5	59.3	60.3	61.0	64.4	67.4	70.1	72.5	74.4
Life expectancy - females	59.2	61.3	62.6	63.4	67.4	71.0	74.2	77.0	79.3
Birth rate (per 1,000)	46.3	43.1	40.5	39.0	32.5	27.0	22.0	18.7	16.5
Death rate (per 1,000)	11.2	9.7	8.8	8.3	6.4	5.2	4.7	5.1	5.6
Women of reproductive age (15-49 yrs.)	47.2	54.9	61.3	66.6	96.4	128.6	163.6	192.4	210.1
Fertility rate	6.6	6.2	5.8	5.6	4.4	3.4	2.7	2.3	2.2

Except as noted, values for vital statistics are in thousands; life expectancy is in years.

Health Indicators

	National Data	World Data
Life expectancy at birth (years)		
1970-1975	51.4	59.9
1995-2000	64.5	66.7
Daily per capita supply of calories		
1970	1,607	2,358
1997	2,584	2,791
Daily per capital supply of protein		
1997 (grams)	88	74
Population with access (%)		
To safe water (1990-96)	60	NA
To sanitation (1990-96)	44	NA
People living with (1997)		
Tuberculosis (cases per 100,000)	63.4	60.4
Malaria (cases per 100,000)	3.8	42.2
HIV/AIDS (% aged 15 - 49 years)	0.05	0.99

Ethnic Division

South Indians, Sinhalese, Arabs.

Religion

Sunni Muslim.

Major Languages

Maldivian Dhivehi (dialect of Sinhala, script derived from Arabic), English spoken by most government officials.

EDUCATION

Educational Attainment (B)

	1995	1997
Gross enrollment ratio (%)		
Primary level	131.9	128.3
Secondary level	55.7	69.1
Tertiary level	NA	NA

Literacy Rates (A)

In thousands and percent	1990	1995	2000	2010
Illiterate population (15+ yrs.)	9	9	10	10
Literacy rate - total adult pop. (%)	92.2	93.2	94.0	95.5
Literacy rate - males (%)	92.5	93.3	94.0	95.3
Literacy rate - females (%)	91.9	93.0	94.1	95.7

GOVERNMENT & LAW

Political Parties

The unicameral People's Council (Majlis) consists of 50 seats: 42 elected by popular vote and 8 appointed by the president. Members serve five-year terms. Elections were last held 20 November 1999 (next to be held in November 2004). Independents won all 42 seats. Although political parties are not banned, none exist.

Government Budgets (A)

Year: 1998

Total Expenditures: 2,216.3 Millions of Rufiyaa

Expenditures as a percentage of the total by function:

General public services and public order	NA
Defense	NA
Education	19.00
Health	10.05
Social Security and Welfare	2.79
Housing and community amenities	10.46
Recreational, cultural, and religious affairs	0
Fuel and energy	1.60
Agriculture, forestry, fishing, and hunting	0.57
Mining, manufacturing, and construction	0
Transportation and communication	9.48
Other economic affairs and services	1.02

Military Affairs (B)

Availability

Males age 15-49 68,940

Fit for military service

Males age 15-49 38,402

Data for 2000 est.

Crime

Crime rate (for 1997)

Crimes reported	6,950
Total persons convicted	4,100
Crimes per 100,000 population	2,800

Persons responsible for offenses

Total number of suspects	3,250
Total number of female suspects	175
Total number of juvenile suspects	400

LABOR FORCE

Total Labor Force (A)

67,000 (1995).

Labor Force by Occupation

Agriculture	22%
Industry	18%

Services 60%

Data for 1995.

Unemployment Rate

Negligible.

PRODUCTION SECTOR

Energy Production

Production . . . . .85 million kWh

Production by source

Fossil fuel 100%

Hydro 0%

Nuclear 0%

Other 0%

Exports . . . . .0 kWh

Data for 1998.

Energy Consumption

Consumption .79 million kWh

Imports . . . . .0 kWh

Data for 1998.

Transportation

Highways:

Total: NA

Paved: NA

Unpaved: NA; Male has 9.6 km of coral highways within the city (1988 est.).

Merchant marine:

Total: 20 ships (1,000 GRT or over) totaling 69,599 GRT/105,599 DWT.

Ships by type: cargo 17, container 1, petroleum tanker 1, short-sea passenger 1 (1999 est.).

Airports: 5 (1999 est.).

Top Agriculture Products

Coconuts, corn, sweet potatoes; fish.

MANUFACTURING SECTOR

GDP & Manufacturing Summary (C)

Total GDP (1999 est.) . . . .$540 million

Real growth rate (1999 est.) 7%

Per capita (1999 est.) $1,800

Composition by sector

Agriculture 20%

Industry 18%

Services 62%

Values in purchasing power parity.

COMMUNICATIONS

Daily Newspapers

	National Data	World Data for Comparison
Daily Newspapers		
Number of Dailies	2	8,391
Total Circulation (000)	5	548,000
Circulation per 1,000 inhabitants	19	96

Telecommunications

Telephones - main lines in use: 21,000 (1999).

Telephones - mobile cellular: 300 (1999).

Telephone system: minimal domestic and international facilities.

Domestic: interatoll communication through microwave links; all inhabited islands are connected with telephone and fax service.

International: satellite earth station - 3 Intelsat (Indian Ocean).

Radio broadcast stations: AM 1, FM 1, shortwave 1 (1998).

Radios: 35,000 (1999).

Television broadcast stations: 1 (1997).

Televisions: 10,000 (1999).

Internet Service Providers (ISPs): NA

FINANCE, ECONOMICS, & TRADE

Balance of Payments

	1993	1994	1995	1996	1997
Exports of goods (f.o.b.)	39	75	85	92	108
Imports of goods (f.o.b.)	−178	−195	−236	−266	−307
Trade balance	−139	−120	−151	−174	−199
Services - debits	−56	−63	−77	−79	−87
Services - credits	178	197	233	289	310
Private transfers (net)	NA	NA	NA	NA	NA
Government transfers (net)	8	16	23	26	17
Overall balance	−48	−11	−18	10	−16

Economic Indicators

National product: GDP—purchasing power parity—$540 million (1999 est.).

National product real growth rate: 7% (1999 est.).

National product per capita: $1,800 (1999 est.).

Inflation rate—consumer price index: 3% (1999 est.).

Exchange Rates

Exchange rates:

Rufiyaa (Rf) per US$1 .11.770

Fixed rate since 1995.

Top Import Origins

Imports (f.o.b., 1998): $312 million.

Origins: Singapore, India, Sri Lanka, Japan, Canada.

Top Export Destinations

Exports (f.o.b., 1998): $98 million.

Destinations: United States, United Kingdom, Sri Lanka, Japan.

Import/Export Commodities

Import Commodities	Export Commodities
Consumer goods	Fish
Intermediate and capital goods	Clothing
Petroleum products	

MALI

CAPITAL: Bamako.

FLAG: The flag is a tricolor of green, yellow, and red vertical stripes.

ANTHEM: National Anthem begins "At thy call, O Mali."

MONETARY UNIT: The Malian franc (MF), a paper currency that had been floating with the French franc, was replaced in June 1984 by the French Community Franc (CFA Fr) at a ratio of MF2 = CFA Fr1. There are coins of 1, 2, 5, 10, 25, 50, and 100 CFA francs and notes of 50, 100, 500, 1,000, 5,000, and 10,000 CFA francs. CFA Fr1 = \$0.0018 (or \$1 = CFA Fr571).

WEIGHTS AND MEASURES: The metric system is the legal standard.

HOLIDAYS: New Year's Day, 1 January; Armed Forces Day, 20 January; Democracy Day, 26 March; Labor Day, 1 May; Africa Day, 25 May; Independence Day, 22 September; Christmas, 25 December. Movable religious holidays include 'Id al-Fitr, 'Id al-'Adha', Milad an-Nabi, and Easter Monday.

TIME: GMT.

LOCATION AND SIZE: A landlocked country in West Africa, Mali has an area of about 1.2 million square kilometers (479,000 square miles), slightly less than twice the size of the state of Texas. Its total boundary length is 7,501 kilometers (4,661 miles). Mali's capital city, Bamako, is located in the southwestern part of the country.

CLIMATE: Southern and western Mali, the Sudanese zone, has a climate with a short rainy season when rainfall averages 140 centimeters (55 inches). To the north is the Sahelian zone, a semiarid region along the southern border of the Sahara, with about 23 centimeters (9 inches) of rainfall a year. Continuing north, one gradually enters into a Saharan climate, marked by the virtual absence of rain and an extremely dry atmosphere.

The year is divided into three main seasons varying in length according to latitude: a cool and dry season; a hot and dry season; and a season of rains characterized by lower temperatures and an increase in humidity.

Republic of Mali
République du Mali

INTRODUCTORY SURVEY

RECENT HISTORY

Around 1880 the French began their advance into what was to become the Republic of Mali. Under French administration, the area became known as French Sudan (Soudan Français) and was a part of French West Africa. In 1946 the Sudanese became French citizens, with representation in the French parliament. In 1958 under the constitution of the Fifth French Republic, French Sudan became an autonomous republic, called the Sudanese Republic, within the French Community. Achievements under French rule included the building of a railway, and development of the Niger River delta.

In June 1960 the new Mali Federation, consisting of the Sudanese Republic and Senegal, became a sovereign state. However, disagreements soon arose. On September 22, 1960, the Sudan declared itself independent as the Republic of Mali and all ties between Senegal and Mali were soon severed as well.

The one-party dictatorship led by President Modibo Keita evolved into a socialist regime modeled on that of the People's Republic of China. However by 1968 economic problems and discontent became severe. On November 19 Keita was overthrown in a bloodless coup led by Lieutenant (later General) Moussa Traoré. The 1960 constitution was abolished, and a 14-member Military Committee for National Liberation took command. Lieutenant Traoré became president in 1969. The military regime's efforts to improve the economic situation in Mali were frustrated by the prolonged

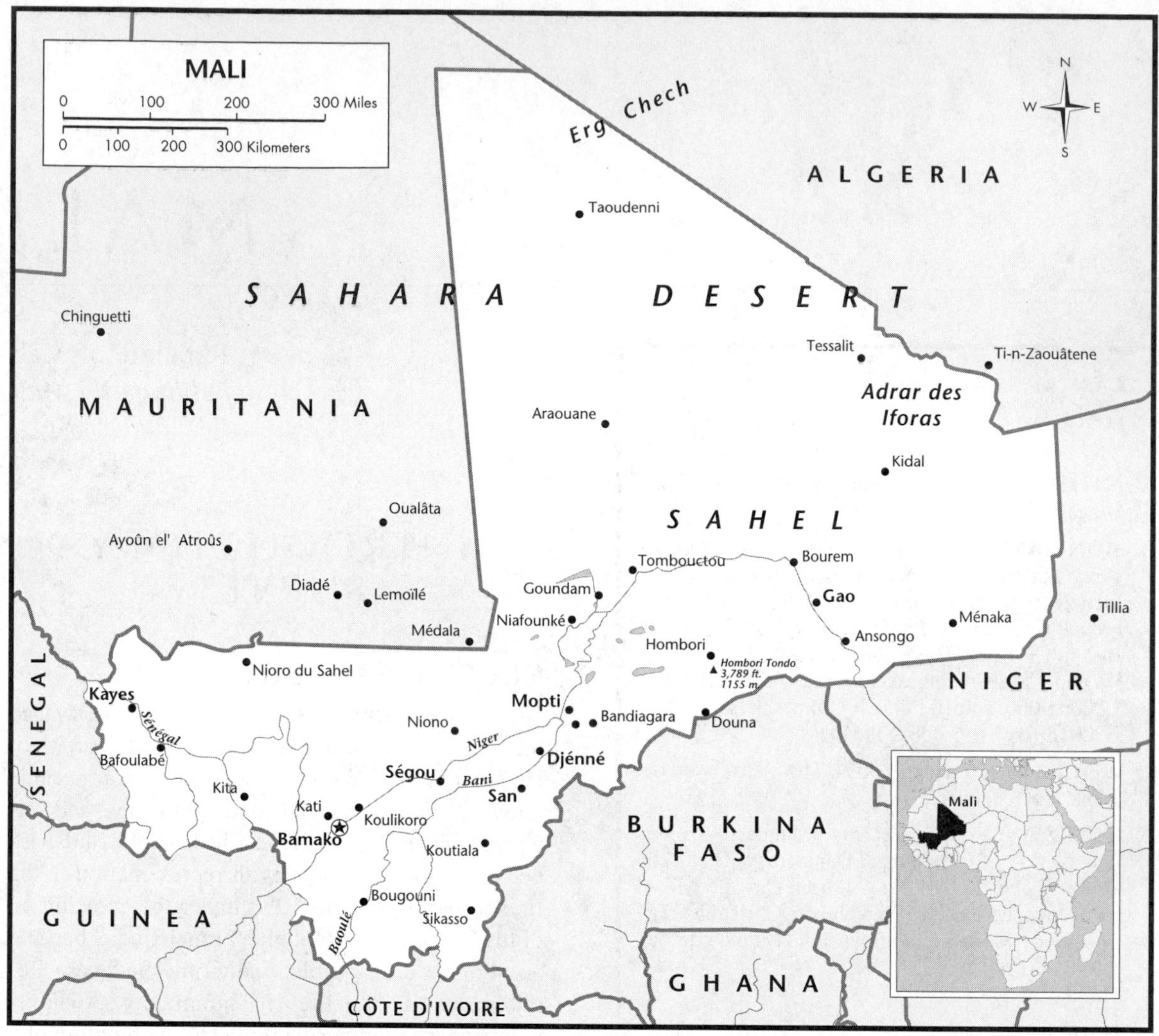

period of drought that began in 1968 and peaked in 1973.

Traoré was elected president in 1979 under a new constitution, which also confirmed Mali as a one-party state. He was reelected in 1985. However on March 26, 1991, Lieutenant Colonel Amadou Toumani Touré engineered a coup that toppled the Traoré government.

After the coup a National Conference drafted new electoral rules, party statutes and a new constitution. The new constitution was adopted by referendum in January 1992. It established an agenda for the transition to a multi-party state. New elections were held and in April 1992 Dr. Alpha Oumar Konaré, the leader of the Alliance for Democracy in Mali (ADEMA), became Mali's first democratically elected president with 69 percent of the vote, and The Third Republic was launched.

One of the last acts of the Touré transitional government was to negotiate (with Algerian mediation) a peace treaty in April 1992 with rebel members of the ethnic Tuaregs in the north. The government acknowledged the northerners' special status, and the Tuaregs renounced their claims to independence. Thousands of Tuareg returned home to Mali. The mid-1990s were marked by student unrest. Students were disgruntled over the economy, high unemployment, and the negative effects of government, structural reforms.

In 1999 President Konaré took steps toward healing the nation. Successful rural community elections wee held. Konaré announced a new national government with a new ministerial lineup. Konaré also planned a relaunch of the economy. Government overall became more responsive because of press freedoms exercised in Mali.

GOVERNMENT

The 1979 constitution was replaced by a new constitution adopted by referendum in January 1992. The chief of state is the president elected by popular vote to serve a five-year term. The head of government is the prime minister appointed by the president. The prime minister appoints the cabinet, known as the Council of Ministers. The unicameral National Assembly has 147 members elected by popular vote for five-year terms.

Judiciary

A Supreme Court was established in Bamako in 1969. It is made up of nineteen members, nominated for five years. The judicial section has three civil chambers and one criminal chamber. The administrative section deals with appeals and fundamental rulings. The Court of Appeal is also in Bamako. There are two magistrate courts of first instance, courts for labor disputes, and a special court of state security. The 1992 Constitution established a separate constitutional court and a High Court of Justice charged with responsibility for trying senior government officials accused of treason.

Political Parties

The Democratic Union of Malian People (Union Démocratique de Peuple Malien-UDPM) was created as the sole legal political party in 1979. Shortly after the military coup in March 1991, some forty-eight parties were functioning of which twenty-three contested the 1992 elections. The Alliance for Democracy in Mali (ADEMA) is the majority party with 130 seats in the National Assembly in 1997. Four other parties hold seats: the Party for National Renewal (PARENA) with eight seats; the Democratic and Social Convention (CDS) with four seats; the Union for Democracy and Development (UDD) with three seats; and, the Party for Democracy and Progress (PDP) with two seats.

DEFENSE

Armed forces' strength was 7,350 in 2000: 6,900 were in the ground forces, fifty in the marine forces, and 400 in the air forces, (all considered part of the army). In 1995 Mali spent $56 million on defense, or 2.5 percent of the gross domestic product (GDP). Paramilitary forces numbered 4,800.

ECONOMIC AFFAIRS

Economic activity in Mali centers on domestic agricultural and livestock production. Approximately 80 percent of the labor force engages in farming; 10 percent is nomadic with livestock herds. Industry concentrates on processing agricultural commodities. The main export is cotton. Vast stretches of Sahara desert limit Mali's agricultural potential and subject the country to severe, prolonged, recurrent drought (1968-1974, 1982-1985). In periods of adequate rainfall, Mali approaches food self-sufficiency. The GDP has gone from a high of 12.5 percent in 1989 when rainfall was good to negative growth (0.5 percent) in dry years.

In January 1994 France devalued the CFA franc, cutting its value in half overnight. Mali did not benefit very much from the devaluation because it has few exports. Inflation reached 35 percent after the devaluation but dropped off to 3 percent in 1999. Gold mining operations were expected to strengthen the economy in 1999. The growth rate for 2000-2001 was estimated at 5 percent.

Mali is highly dependent on foreign aid and will likely remain so for the foreseeable future. In 1999 the EU and the Western African Development Bank provided $82 million for roads and bridges.

Public Finance

The U.S. Central Intelligence Agency estimated that in 1997 government revenues totaled approximately $730 million and expenditures $770 million. External debt totaled $3.1 billion in 1998. Foreign assistance accounts for about 20 percent of Mali's national budget in 1999.

Income

In 1997 Mali's gross domestic product (GDP) was estimated at $8.5 billion, or about $820 per capita. The 1999 GDP growth rate estimate was 5 percent and inflation 3 percent. The 1998 GDP by sector was agriculture 46 percent, industry 21 percent, and services 33 percent.

Industry

Mali has a very small industrial sector, mostly government-owned plants for producing textiles, consumer goods, and for food processing. Textiles account for about 50 percent of the industrial output's value. Ground nut (peanut) oil, rice polishing, fruit preserving, sugar distilling, tea, and cottonseed oil and cottonseed cake plants are in operation, as are three slaughterhouses. Other industrial facilities include a vinegar factory, a cigarette factory, a soft-drink plant, a flourmill, a shoe factory, a tannery, and two textile plants. There are a few construction related facilities, including a cement works, a brick factory, and a ceramics factory. Salt mining provides an average of 5,000 tons each year. Mining includes silver, phosphates, and rapidly expanding gold extraction.

Banking and Finance

In 1959 the Central Bank of the West African States (Banque Centrale des États de l'Afrique de l'Ouest-BCEAO) succeeded the Currency Board of French West Africa and Togo as the bank of issue for the former French West African territories, known now as the franc zone: Benin, Burkina Faso, Côte d'Ivoire, Mali, Niger, Senegal, and Togo. Foreign exchange receipts of the member states went into the franc zone's exchange pool, which in turn covered their foreign exchange requirements. In July 1962, however, Mali withdrew from the BCEAO and West African Monetary Union and established a bank of its own, the Bank of the Republic of Mali, which issued a new currency, the Malian franc.

In 1967 Mali returned to the franc zone, with its franc set at half the value of the CFA franc. In March 1968 the banking system was reorganized, and the Central Bank of Mali was established as the central issuing bank. In December 1982 Mali's application to rejoin the West African Monetary Union was rejected, as Upper Volta (now Burkina Faso), which had a border dispute with Mali, continued to oppose Mali's re-admission until 1983. In 1984 it rejoined the BCEAO and the monetary union.

In addition to the Central Bank, commercial banks in 1997 included: the Bank of Africa, Banque Commerciale de Sahel, Banque Malienne de Crédit et du Depots, and the Financial Bank Mali. Development banks in Mali include the Banque de Développment du Mali, and the Banque Nationale de Développment Agricole.

Economic Development

Fiscal management reform and continued dependence on foreign aid into the foreseeable future are the hallmarks of the economic development effort in the coming years. The 1994 devaluation of the CFA franc resulted in increased exports of cotton, livestock, gold, and other products. However, the agricultural sector is still highly vulnerable to drought and worldwide commodity price fluctuations.

In 1997 the government continued IMF-recommended structured adjustments that have helped the economy grow, diversify, and attract foreign investment. Several multinational corporations have invested in gold mining operations. Mali's infrastructure has been improving due to IMF and West African Development Bank loans.

SOCIAL WELFARE

Social welfare is available, mainly in urban areas and is an extension of the labor code, which includes provisions for medical care, workers' compensation, and retirement benefits. A system of family allowances for wage earners provides small maternity and children's allowances, along with classes in prenatal and infant care. Traditionally the individual's basic welfare needs were cared for by the tribal organization. This system, however, is breaking down as the country develops. Social and cultural factors still sharply limit educational and economic opportunities for most women.

Healthcare

Most health care is provided by the public medical services. Lack of organization and misappropriation of money has impaired the effectiveness of the health system. The number of private doctors and well-equipped medical institutions is small. In 1993 the population per physician was about 18,376. From 1985 to 1995 only 30 percent of the population had access to health care services.

The principal diseases are malaria, leprosy, tuberculosis, enteritis and other intestinal diseases, cholera, pneumonia, and infectious and parasite-related diseases, such as schistosomiasis, onchocerciasis, and trypanosomiasis. Anemia, malnutrition, and tetanus are also widespread. In 1990-1995 only 37 percent of the population had access to safe water and 31 percent had adequate sanitation. In 2000 the average life expectancy was 46.7 years.

Housing

Housing structures in Bamako are mainly like those of a European city. Elsewhere housing ranges from typical urban structures to the tents of Tuareg nomads, the circular mud huts with thatched roofs characteristic of native African villages, and traditional Sudanese architecture whose buildings resemble those in North Africa and the Middle East.

Since World War II (1939-1945) the growth of Bamako and other towns has been rapid, with government activity largely concentrated on improvement of urban housing and sanitation. The Real Estate Trust, a public corporation established in 1949, provides housing loans to persons wishing to build on their own land.

EDUCATION

The Malian school system begins with an initial primary cycle of six years, followed by a six-year cycle of secondary schooling. In 1995 69 percent of the adult population of Mali was illiterate (60.6 percent of males and 76.9 percent of females). In 1998 there were 2,511 primary schools with 10,853 teachers and 862,875 pupils. In the general secondary schools there were 188,109 pupils.

Located in Koulikoro is the Rural Polytechnic Institute of Katibougou. There are schools of business, administration, engineering, medicine and dentistry, and education in Bamako. All higher level institutions had a total of 13,847 pupils and approximately 800 teachers in 1998.

2000 KEY EVENTS TIMELINE

January

- President Alpha Konaré appoints seven colonels to serve in the ministries of Mines and Energy, Rural Development and Water, Economy, Interior, Health, Public Works and Transport and Communications. The appointments are made to stave off mutinies connected with demands for pay for peacekeeping assignments in Africa.
- One person is wounded when bandits ambush two U.S. Agency for International Development (USAID) vehicles in northern Mali some forty-five kilometers south of Timbuctou.

February

- High water levels in December are responsible for higher fish catches in the Niger River.
- President Alpha Konaré announces the formation of a new national government led by Prime Minister Mandé Sidibé.

March

- Some fifty Malian children working on plantations in neighboring Côte d'Ivoire are repatriated. It is estimated that over 100 Ivorian plantations employ child labor.

May

- Liberian President Charles Taylor visits Bamako for talks with President Konaré, who is also the current chairman of the Economic Community of West African States (ECOWAS). The leaders discuss Sierra Leone, including Liberia's role in securing the release of United Nations (UN) hostages detained by the rebel RUF.

June

- The interior ministers of Mali and Mauritania estimate that CFA Fr2 billion (about US$2.9 million) will be needed to demarcate their common border. They note the existence of persistent pockets of insecurity near their borders with Algeria where armed bands of Tuaregs operate.
- Interior ministers from Mali and Mauritania announce on June 23 that they are seeking funding of US$29 million to map their common border in a project to begin in 2001.

July

- Parliament passes a law that will grant political parties 0.25 percent of total tax earnings. Approximately 40 percent will go to those with seats in parliament while 20 percent will go to others meeting the requirements under the law. An additional 40 percent will be given to municipal councilors.
- Mali's anti-corruption commission alleges that state-owned companies such as the National Tobacco and Match Company, the state pension funds, the Interior Ministry and public hospitals in the capital have embezzled billions of CFA. Since President Alpha Konare launched the anti-corruption drive last year, some fifteen senior officials have been arrested.

August

- Former president Moussa Traore, who has been serving a life sentence since being overthrown in 1991, returns home after receiving medical treatment in Algeria for back problems.

September

- The World Bank and IMF declare Mali eligible to receive $870 million in debt relief under the Highly Indebted Poor Country (HIPC) program due to progress made in economic and social reforms.

December

- Representatives of Scandinavian countries meet in Stockholm with Mali's foreign minister, as well as the foreign ministers of eight other African nations (Benin, Botswana, Ghana, Mozambique, Nigeria, Senegal, South Africa, and Tanzania) to discuss arms control, the role of arms embargoes, and ways of combating the illicit traffic in small arms. A report on U.N. peacekeeping operations in Africa and cooperation between the United Nations, African organizations, and the European Union was also presented during the two-day meeting.

- The World Bank and International Monetary Fund (IMF) announce on December 23 that the United States, Canada, Japan, and nations of Europe will provide debt relief for twenty-two of the world's poorest nations, including Benin, Bolivia, Burkina Faso, Cameroon, The Gambia, Guinea, Guinea-Bissau, Guyana, Honduras, Madagascar, Malawi, Mali, Mauritania, Mozambique, Nicaragua, Niger, Rwanda, São Tomé and Príncipe, Senegal, Tanzania, Uganda, and Zambia.

ANALYSIS OF EVENTS: 2000

BUSINESS AND THE ECONOMY

Performance of the economy in 1999 and 2000 was mixed. While there were sizeable trade losses and serious problems in the cotton and electricity sectors, gold improved, and international demand on the spot market for cotton increased. Analysts at the International Monetary Fund (IMF) reported satisfaction with macroeconomic performance, although some key structural reforms were delayed. In May a combined IMF-World Bank team approved the national budget, which ensured continued disbursements under the 1999–2000 Enhanced Structural Adjustment Facility (ESAF).

The economy continued to expand and inflation declined, staying under 1 percent for the year. Cereal production expanded and strong mining investment was expected to produce 4.8 percent real gross domestic product (GDP) for 2000. The government succeeded in keeping spending under control, particularly on wages, and implemented important fiscal reform measures. Investors were expected to be attracted by steady progress in privatization, although many parastatals required upgrading before they would be saleable. Investors were also predicted to be more bullish on energy with a hydroelectric dam on the Senegal River scheduled to open in 2002.

A critical weakness in the economy was the external debt. At the end of 1998 debt amounted to US$2.8 billion, 120 percent of the gross national product (GNP). Debt service devoured US$82 million, nearly 13 percent of total exports. This drain on national revenue was offset by donor inflows in grants and loans totaling some US$100 million, Heavily Indebted Poor Countries (HIPC) assistance, and expected improvements in the euro against the dollar. Together, these developments could put Mali's account balance in the black in 2001.

GOVERNMENT AND POLITICS

Political parties began serious posturing for the 2002 presidential elections. Alliance for Democracy (ADEMA), the ruling party, has the inside track even though President Alpha Konaré will no longer be eligible to run. Ibrahima Boubacar Keita, former Prime Minister, resigned his post in February to devote himself full-time to lead ADEMA. However, Konaré's warmth for former head of state, General Amadou Toumani Touré, threatens Keita's chances. Touré maintained a high profile on the speaking circuit, and presented a formidable challenge to Keita. He led the popular revolt against Traoré in 1991, and if he allied himself with the Mouvement Patriotique pour le Renouveau (MPR), he could be unstoppable.

The opposition alliance, COPPO, announced that it would contest the 2002 elections, but the key issue was whether the alliance would be able to field a common candidate, and if so, could that candidate be General Touré? A second issue was whether ADEMA's coalition could hold. The coalition lost the Parti pour la Renaissance Nationale (Parena) in February. Analysts questioned whether it could withstand attacks in the press and a general public disenchantment with a pattern of corruption. Public companies such as the water and electric utilities have been wracked by cronyism, and failed to provide adequate service. To his credit Konaré initiated an anti-corruption committee in October 1999, and in February he purged the cabinet. The outgoing ministers' personal wealth, visible by their homes and vehicles, far outstripped their government salaries. Nevertheless, critics wondered why it took Konaré seven years to get tough on corruption.

In the meantime Konaré positioned himself to retire as African statesman. He appointed seven women to ministerial posts, he served as Economic Community of West African States (ECOWAS) chair this year, and next year assumes the chair of Union Economique et Monetaire Ouest Africaine (UEMOA), the economic and monetary union of the CFA franc zone. As ECOWAS president, he mediated regional conflicts and was a possible successor to Organization of African Unity (OAU) chairman, Salim Ahmed Salim.

President Konaré's success in institutionalizing democracy will come under scrutiny in 2001. Mali had a dysfunctional national electoral commission (CENI) that botched the 1997 election, and pushed many parties into boycotting the elections. However, under Ousman Sy, the Ministry of Territorial Administration organized and conducted successful municipal elections last year. With the presidency at stake in 2002, Malians will be monitoring the updating of voter rolls and other preparations to see whether they will be undertaken with the same equanimity and transparency as they were in 1999.

CULTURE AND SOCIETY

One of the preoccupying issues facing Mali was the sustainability of its environment. A study showed that each Malian uses an average of 1.5 kilograms of firewood per day, or about 6.5 million metric tons each year among the country's nearly twelve million people. That means more than 464,285 hectares of the land would have to be reforested each year to control soil erosion and the deterioration of Sahelian catchment basins. In 2000 the Malian government continued to develop regulations for taxing commercial users under its decentralization program. The Malian Parliament adopted several laws governing forest exploitation, but monitoring the wood trade was difficult.

An additional concern has been the proliferation of small arms in the country. Mali's chairman of a national commission for the control of the proliferation of light weapons, Colonel Sirakoro Sangare, has taken the lead in the region to involve the Malian public, leaders of other countries in the region, and international organizations and donors in the control of light weapons. The Tuareg rebellion that erupted in Mali in 1990 and the ousting of President Moussa Traoré following a popular uprising in 1991 contributed to the large number of weapons in the country.

Some of these weapons have fallen into the hands of bandits, and the southern Sahara region between Mali, Niger, and Chad has been plagued by banditry in this and recent years. The bandits were thought to be former rebels who fought the Malian and Niger armies until peace deals were reached in 1995. In Niger rebellion broke out again in 1997, and ended in 1998. In northern Chad a new rebellion began in late 1998. Mali was a fairly homogeneous society as of 2000, but the presence of these armed bandits has stirred old fears that parts of the country remained susceptible to threats from ethnic Tuaregs and rebels.

DIRECTORY

CENTRAL GOVERNMENT

Head of State

President
Alpha Oumar Konaré, Office of the President, Koulouba, Bamako, Mali

Prime Minister
Mande Sidibe, Office of the Prime Minister, Primature, Quartier du Fleuve BPE 790, Bamako, Mali
PHONE: +223 225534
FAX: +223 228583

Ministers

Minister of Foreign Affairs and Malians Abroad
Modibo Sidibe, Ministry of Foreign Affairs and Malians Abroad, Koulouba, Bamako, Mali
PHONE: +223 225226
FAX: +223 225634

Minister of Health, Solidarity, and the Elderly
Traore Fatoumata Nafo, Ministry of Health, Solidarity, and the Elderly, Koulouba BP 232, Bamako, Mali
PHONE: +223 225302
FAX: +223 230203

Minister of Industry, Commerce and Transport
Toure Alimata Traore, Ministry of Industry, Commerce and Transport, Quartier du Fleuve BP 1759, Bamako, Mali
PHONE: +223 228058
FAX: +223 230267

Minister of Youth and Sports
Adama Kone, Ministry of Youth and Sports, Route de Koulouba BP 91, Bamako, Mali
PHONE: +223 223153
FAX: +223 231087

Minister of Armed Forces and War Veterans
Soumeylou Boubeye Maiga, Ministry of Armed Forces and War Veterans, Route de Koulouba BP 2083, Bamako, Mali
PHONE: +223 225021
FAX: +223 232318

Minister of Employment, Civil Service, and Labor
Makan Moussa Sissoko, Ministry of Employment, Civil Service, and Labor, Route de Koulouba BP 80, Bamako, Mali
PHONE: +223 223431
FAX: +223 223431

Minister of Rural Development
Ahmed el Madani Diallo, Ministry of Rural Development, Quartier du Fleuve, Bamako, Mali
PHONE: +223 222979
FAX: +223 220295

Minister of Environment
Soumailia Cisse, Ministry of Environment

Minister of Education
Moustapha Dicko, Ministry of Education, Bagadadji BP 2468, Bamako, Mali
PHONE: +223 225530
FAX: +223 228297

Minister of Territorial Administration and Local Communities
Ousmane Sy, Ministry of Territorial Administration and Local Communities, Face Direction de la RCFM, Bamako, Mali
PHONE: +223 224212

Minister of Justice and Keeper of Seals
Abdoulaye Ogotembely Poudiougou, Ministry of Justice and Keeper of Seals, Quartier du Fleuve BP 97, Bamako, Mali
PHONE: +223 222651
FAX: +223 230063

Minister of Culture and Communication
Pascal Baba Coulibaly, Ministry of Culture and Communication, Quartier du Fleuve BP 116, Bamako, Mali
PHONE: +223 222647
FAX: +223 228319

Minister of Mining Industry and Hydraulics
Aboubacary Coulibaly, Ministry of Mining Industry and Hydraulics, Quartier duFleuve BP 1909, Bamako, Mali
PHONE: +223 224184
FAX: +223 222160

POLITICAL ORGANIZATIONS

Alliance pour la Démocratie en Mali-ADEMA (Alliance for Democracy in Mali)

NAME: Ibrahim N'diaye

Democratic and Social Convention-CDS

NAME: Mamadou Bakary Sangare

Congres Nationale pour la Initiative Démocratie-CNIS (National Congress for Democratic Initiative)

NAME: Mountaga Tall

Parti pour la Démocratie et le Progrès-PDP (Party for Democracy and Progress)

NAME: Idrissa Traore

Party for National Renewal (PARENA)

Mouvement Populaire pour la Développement et la République Unie de l'Afrique de l'Ouest-MPD (Popular Movement for the Development of the Republic of West Africa)

Union Soudanaise-US (Sudanese Union)

NAME: Mamadou Bamou Toure

Union pour Démocratie et Développement-UDD (Union for Democracy and Development)

NAME: Moussa Balla Coulibaly

DIPLOMATIC REPRESENTATION

Embassies in Mali

Algeria
Daoudabougou, route aéroport, Bamako, Mali
PHONE: +223 225176
FAX: +223 229374

Burkina Faso
Hippodrome, rue 224 BP 9022, Bamako, Mali
PHONE: +223 223171
FAX: +223 229266

Canada
Hippodrome, route de Koulikoro BP 198, Bamako, Mali
PHONE: +223 222236
FAX: +223 224362

China
Hippodrome, route de Koulikoro BP 112, Bamako, Mali
PHONE: +223 223597
FAX: +223 223597

Cuba
PHONE: +223 222844

Egypt
Badala est avenue de l'OUA BP 44, Bamako, Mali
PHONE: +223 223565
FAX: +223 220891

France
Square Patrice Lumumba BP 17, Bamako, Mali
PHONE: +223 222951
FAX: +223 226697

Germany
Badala est, rue de l'OUA BP 100, Bamako, Mali
PHONE: +223 223299
FAX: +223 229650

Guinea
Immeuble Saybou Maïga, Quartier du fleuve BP 118, Bamako, Mali
PHONE: +223 222975; 230897

Iran
Hippodrome BP 2136, Bamako, Mali
PHONE: +223 223593
FAX: +223 220731

Iraq
Badala est BP 2512, Bamako, Mali
PHONE: +223 223860
FAX: +223 222416

Korea
Sogoniko, face autocars sise Sotelma BP 76, Bamako, Mali
PHONE: +223 225183
FAX: +223 225183

Libya
Ngolonina Immeuble Nimaga BP 1670, Bamako, Mali
PHONE: +223 222518
FAX: +223 226697

Malaysia
PHONE: +223 222783

Mauritania
Hippodrome route de Koulikoro BP 135, Bamako, Mali
PHONE: +223 224815
FAX: +223 224908

Morocco
Badala est avenue de l'OUA BP 2013, Bamako, Mali
PHONE: +223 222123; 222423
FAX: +223 227787

Nigeria
Badala est BP 57, Bamako, Mali
PHONE: +223 225771
FAX: +223 225284

Netherlands
Hippodrome angle de la rue 437 route de Koulikoro BP 2220, Bamako, Mali
PHONE: +223 229582; 229572

Saudi Arabia
Sogoniko, route de l'aéroport, Bamako, Mali
PHONE: +223 222528; 223910
FAX: +223 225074

Senegal
Quartier du fleuve BP 42, Bamako, Mali
PHONE: +223 228274

United States
Avenue Mohamed V, rue de Rochester BP 34, Bamako, Mali
PHONE: +223 225470; 225663
FAX: +223 223712
TITLE: Ambassador
NAME: David Rawson

JUDICIAL SYSTEM

Supreme Court

Court of Appeal

High Court of Justice

BROADCAST MEDIA

Office de Radiodifusion Télévision du Mali (ORTM)

BP 171, Bamako, Mali
PHONE: +223 212019; 212474
FAX: +223 214205
E-MAIL: ortm@spider.toolnet.org
TITLE: Directorate General
CONTACT: Sidiki Konate

Radiodiffusion Télévision de Mali

BP 171, Bamako, Mali
PHONE: +223 222019; 224308
CONTACT: Abdoulaye Sidibe, Directorate General
CHANNEL: 5

COLLEGES AND UNIVERSITIES

Institut Pedagogique National du Mali

BP 1583, Bamako, Mali
PHONE: +223 224262
FAX: +223 227767

National Centre for Scientific and Technological Research (CNRST)

BP 1576, Bamako, Mali

Universite du Mali

BP E 2526, Bamako, Mali
PHONE: + 223 221933; 229302; 229252
FAX: +223 221932

NEWSPAPERS AND MAGAZINES

Les Echos

Cooperative Culturelle Jamana, PO Box 2043, Bamako, Mali
PHONE: +223 226289
FAX: +223 227639
E-MAIL: jamana@malinet.ml
WEBSITE: http://www.mali.ml
TITLE: Publisher
CONTACT: S. Berthe
CIRCULATION: 30,000

L'Essor

Sauare Lumumba, Bomoko Mali, Bamako, Mali
PHONE: +223 223683
TITLE: Editor-in-Chief
CONTACT: S. Drabo
CIRCULATION: 4,000

PUBLISHERS

EDIM SA

642 av. Mardiagne, BP 2412, Bamako, Mali
PHONE: +223 225522
FAX: +223 238503
TITLE: Man. Director
CONTACT: Aliou Tomota
SUBJECTS: Biography, Fiction, History, Nonfiction (General), Poetry, Religion, Social Sciences

RELIGIOUS ORGANIZATIONS

The Alliance for Democracy in Mali, the sole and ruling party in the country, along with turmoil in the country, have made circumstances difficult for organized religion within the country. Due to technology and communications issues, very little information outside the country is available at this time.

FURTHER READING

Articles

"Mali, Turkey, Three Arab States Subject of State Dept. Updates." *Travel Weekly,* October 12, 2000, vol. 59, no. 82, p. 4.

Onishi, Norimitsu. "Undependable Rains Bring Seasonal Exodus." *New York Times,* January 4, 2000, p. A4.

Books

Celati, Gianni. *Adventures in Africa.* Chicago: University of Chicago Press, 2000.

Dun and Bradstreet's Export Guide to Mali. Parsippany, NJ: Dun & Bradstreet, 1999.

Imperato, Pascal J. *Historical Dictionary of Mali.* [computer file] Boulder, CO: netLibrary, Inc., 2000.

MALI: STATISTICAL DATA

For sources and notes see "Sources of Statistics" at the front of each volume.

GEOGRAPHY

Geography

Area:

Total: 1.24 million sq km.

Land: 1.22 million sq km.

Land boundaries:

Total: 7,243 km.

Border countries: Algeria 1,376 km, Burkina Faso 1,000 km, Guinea 858 km, Cote d'Ivoire 532 km, Mauritania 2,237 km, Niger 821 km, Senegal 419 km.

Coastline: 0 km (landlocked).

Climate: subtropical to arid; hot and dry February to June; rainy, humid, and mild June to November; cool and dry November to February.

Terrain: mostly flat to rolling northern plains covered by sand; savanna in south, rugged hills in northeast.

Natural resources: gold, phosphates, kaolin, salt, limestone, uranium, hydropower.

Note: bauxite, iron ore, manganese, tin, and copper deposits are known but not exploited.

Land use:

Arable land: 2%

Permanent crops: 0%

Permanent pastures: 25%

Forests and woodland: 6%

Other: 67% (1993 est.).

HUMAN FACTORS

Demographics (A)

	1990	1995	1998	2000	2010	2020	2030	2040	2050
Population	8,228	9,160	10,065	10,686	14,349	18,984	24,412	30,322	36,359
Life expectancy - males	42.2	43.8	44.8	45.5	49.0	52.7	56.4	60.0	63.4
Life expectancy - females	44.1	45.9	47.1	47.8	51.9	56.2	60.5	64.6	68.5
Birth rate (per 1,000)	51.3	51.1	50.0	49.2	44.6	39.1	33.2	28.0	23.8
Death rate (per 1,000)	23.1	21.1	19.9	19.1	15.3	12.1	9.6	8.0	7.1
Women of reproductive age (15-49 yrs.)	1,844	2,055	2,261	2,400	3,277	4,539	6,114	7,922	9,745
Fertility rate	7.3	7.2	7.0	6.9	6.1	5.1	4.2	3.4	2.9

Except as noted, values for vital statistics are in thousands; life expectancy is in years.

Health Personnel

	National Data	World Data (wtd ave)
Total health expenditure as a percentage of GDP, 1990-1998[a]		
Public sector	2.0	2.5
Private sector	1.8	2.9
Total[b]	3.8	5.5
Health expenditure per capita in U.S. dollars, 1990-1998[a]		
Purchasing power parity	28	561
Total	10	483
Availability of health care facilities per 100,000 people		
Hospital beds 1990-1998[a]	20	330
Doctors 1992-1995[a]	4	122
Nurses 1992-1995[a]	9	248

Health Indicators

	National Data	World Data
Life expectancy at birth (years)		
1980	42	61
1998	50	67
Daily per capita supply of calories		
1970	2,195	2,358
1997	2,029	2,791
Daily per capital supply of protein		
1997 (grams)	61	74
Total fertility rate (births per woman)		
1980	7.1	3.7
1998	6.5	2.7
Population with access (%)		
To safe water (1990-96)	37	NA
To sanitation (1990-96)	31	NA
People living with (1997)		
Tuberculosis (cases per 100,000)	43.7	60.4
Malaria (cases per 100,000)	3,688.3	42.2
HIV/AIDS (% aged 15 - 49 years)	1.67	0.99

Infants and Malnutrition

	National Data	World Data (wtd ave)
Under 5 mortality rate (1989)	237	NA
% of infants with low birthweight (1992-98)[1]	17	17
Births attended by skilled health staff (% of total births 1996-98)	24	52
% fully immunized at 1 year of age (1995-98)[1]		
TB	84	82
DPT	52	77
Polio	52	77
Measles	57	74
Prevalence of child malnutrition (1992-98)[1] (based on weight for age, % of children under 5 years)	27	30

Ethnic Division

Mande (Bambara, Malinke, Soninke) 50%
Peul 17%
Voltaic 12%
Songhai 6%
Tuareg and Moor 10%
Other 5%

Religion

Muslim 90%
Indigenous beliefs 9%
Christian 1%

Major Languages

French (official), Bambara 80%, numerous African languages.

EDUCATION

Public Education Expenditures

	1980	1997
Public expenditures on education as % of GNP	3.7	2.2
Expenditures per student as % of GNP per capita		
Primary & Secondary	31.7	13.8
Tertiary	3,631.4	382.7
Teachers' compensation as % of total current education expenditures	51.0	NA
Pupils per teacher at the primary level	NA	80
Duration of primary education in years	NA	9
World data for comparison		
Public expenditures on education as % of GNP (mean)	3.9	4.8

Pupils per teacher at the primary level (wtd ave)	NA	33
Duration of primary education in years (mean)	NA	9

Educational Attainment (B)

	1995	1997
Gross enrollment ratio (%)		
Primary level	40.5	48.9
Secondary level	10.7	12.6
Tertiary level	0.8	1.0

Literacy Rates (A)

In thousands and percent	1990	1995	2000	2010
Illiterate population (15+ yrs.)	3,686	3,917	4,111	4,355
Literacy rate - total adult pop. (%)	24.6	31.0	38.0	52.9
Literacy rate - males (%)	32.5	39.4	46.5	60.8
Literacy rate - females (%)	17.3	23.1	29.8	45.4

GOVERNMENT & LAW

Military Affairs (A)

	1990	1992	1995	1996	1997
Military expenditures					
Current dollars (mil.)	NA	44[e]	38[e]	43	43
1997 constant dollars (mil.)	NA	49[e]	39[e]	44	43
Armed forces (000)	13	12	12	10	10
Gross national product (GNP)					
Current dollars (mil.)	1,670	1,900	2,130	2,260	2,450
1997 constant dollars (mil.)	1,950	2,100	2,210	2,300	2,450
Central government expenditures (CGE)					
1997 constant dollars (mil.)	NA	522[e]	529	544	591
People (mil.)	8.2	9.7	9.2	9.5	9.8
Military expenditure as % of GNP	NA	2.3	1.8	1.9	1.7
World data on military expenditure as % of GNP	4.5	3.4	2.7	2.6	2.6
Military expenditure as % of CGE	NA	9.4	7.4	8.1	7.2
World data on military expenditure as % of CGE	17.0	12.5	10.5	10.3	10.2
Military expenditure per capita (1997 $)	NA	5	4	5	4
World data on military expenditure per capita (1997 $)	242	173	146	143	145
Armed forces per 1,000 people (soldiers)	1.6	1.2	1.3	1.1	1.0
World data on armed forces per 1,000 people (soldiers)	5.3	4.5	4.1	3.9	3.8
GNP per capita (1997 $)	237	216	240	243	251
Arms imports[6]					
Current dollars (mil.)	10	0	0	5	10
1997 constant dollars (mil.)	12	0	0	5	10
Total imports[7]					
Current dollars (mil.)	601	606	770	766	689
1997 constant dollars (mil.)	704	672	797	779	689
Total exports[7]					
Current dollars (mil.)	359	343	457	439	560
1997 constant dollars (mil.)	420	380	0	446	560
Arms as percent of total imports[8]	1.7	0	0	0.7	1.5
Arms as percent of total exports[8]	0	0	0	0	0

Political Parties

National Assembly (Assemblee Nationale)	no. of seats
Alliance for Democracy (ADEMA)	130
Party for National Renewal (PARENA)	8
Democratic and Social Convention (CDS)	4
Union for Democracy and Development (UDD)	3
Party for Democracy and Progress (PDP)	2

Elections were last held 20 July and 3 August 1997 (next to be held in two rounds in 2002); Much of the opposition boycotted the election.

Government Budgets (B)

Revenues . . . .$730 million

Expenditures . . . .$770 million

Capital expenditures . . . .$320 million

Data for 1997 est.

Crime

Crime volume (for 1998)

Crimes reported 1,103

Total persons convicted 122

Crimes per 100,000 population 10.03

Persons responsible for offenses

Total number suspects .1,775

Total number of female suspects . . . . .NA

Total number of juvenile suspects . . . . .NA

LABOR FORCE

Total Labor Force (B)

5 million (1999).

Labor Force by Occupation

Agriculture and fishing 80%

Data for 1998 est.

PRODUCTION SECTOR

Energy Production

Production .310 million kWh

Production by source

Fossil fuel 38.71%

Hydro 61.29%

Nuclear 0%

Other 0%

Exports . . . . .0 kWh

Data for 1998.

Energy Consumption

Consumption . . . . .288 million kWh

Imports . . . . .0 kWh

Data for 1998.

Transportation

Highways:

Total: 15,100 km.

Paved: 1,827 km.

Unpaved: 13,273 km (1996 est.).

Waterways: 1,815 km navigable.

Airports: 28 (1999 est.).

Airports - with unpaved runways: 22.

Top Agriculture Products

Cotton, millet, rice, corn, vegetables, peanuts; cattle, sheep, goats.

Top Mining Products (B)

Mineral resources include: gold, phosphates, kaolin, salt, limestone, uranium.

Note: bauxite, iron ore, manganese, tin, and copper deposits are known but not exploited.

MANUFACTURING SECTOR

GDP & Manufacturing Summary (B)

	1980	1985	1990	1993	1994	1995
Gross Domestic Product						
Millions of 1990 dollars	1,748	2,006	2,510	2,853	2,921	3,097
Growth rate in percent	4.01	8.50	2.41	3.83	2.40	6.00
Per capita (in 1990 dollars)	255	253	272	282	279	287
Manufacturing Value Added						
Millions of 1990 dollars	86	160	196	222	233	248[e]
Growth rate in percent	1.58	4.37	−2.35	6.38	4.70	6.46[e]
Manufacturing share in percent of current prices	4.9	7.5	8.2	9.2[e]	8.8[e]	NA

COMMUNICATIONS

Daily Newspapers

	National Data	World Data for Comparison
Daily Newspapers		
Number of Dailies	3	8,391
Total Circulation (000)	12	548,000
Circulation per 1,000 inhabitants	1.2	96

Telecommunications

Telephones - main lines in use: 17,000 (1995).

Telephones - mobile cellular: 0 (1995).

Telephone system: domestic system poor but improving; provides only minimal service.

Domestic: network consists of microwave radio relay, open wire, and radiotelephone communications stations; expansion of microwave radio relay in progress.

International: satellite earth stations - 2 Intelsat (1 Atlantic Ocean and 1 Indian Ocean).

Radio broadcast stations: AM 1, FM 14, shortwave 7 (1998).

Radios: 570,000 (1997).

Television broadcast stations: 1 (plus two repeaters) (1997).

Televisions: 45,000 (1997).

Internet Service Providers (ISPs): 1 (1999).

FINANCE, ECONOMICS, & TRADE

Economic Indicators

National product: GDP—purchasing power parity—$8.5 billion (1999 est.).

National product real growth rate: 5% (1999 est.).

National product per capita: $820 (1999 est.).

Inflation rate—consumer price index: 3% (1999 est.).

Exchange Rates

Exchange rates:

Communaute Financiere Africaine francs (CFAF) per US$1

January 2000	647.25
1999	615.70
1998	589.95
1997	583.67
1996	511.55
1995	499.15

Since 1 January 1999, the CFAF is pegged to the euro at a rate of 655.957 CFA francs per euro. Fiscal year: calendar year.

Top Import Origins

$650 million (f.o.b., 1999 est.)

Origins (1997)

Cote d'Ivoire	19%
France	17%
Other Franc Zone and EU countries	NA

Top Export Destinations

$640 million (f.o.b., 1999 est.)

Destinations (1997)

Thailand	20%
Italy	20%
China	9%
Brazil	5%
Franc Zone	NA

Foreign Aid

Recipient: $596.4 million (1995).

Import/Export Commodities

Import Commodities	Export Commodities
Machinery and equipment	Cotton 50%
Construction materials	Gold
Petroleum	Livestock
Foodstuffs	
Textiles	

Balance of Payments

	1993	1994	1995	1996	1997
Exports of goods (f.o.b.)	371	334	441	433	560
Imports of goods (f.o.b.)	−491	−448	−556	−550	−551
Trade balance	−120	−114	−115	−118	10
Services - debits	−360	−316	−434	−382	−345
Services - credits	75	69	87	87	82
Private transfers (net)	152	123	140	136	112
Government transfers (net)	137	155	123	106	54
Overall balance	−188	−162	−283	−273	−178

COLOR FLAGS, SEALS AND REGIONAL MAPS

Seals for Antarctica, French Polynesia, Niue, and Palestinian Authority are not availale at this time. No flag is presented for Antarctica as what exists is only a number of proposed, symbolic flags. Where published color standards for seals are lacking, they are shown in black and white.

Afghanistan

Aland Islands

Albania

Algeria

American Samoa

Andorra

Angola

Anguilla

Antigua and Barbuda

Argentina

Armenia

Aruba

Australia

Austria

Azerbaijan

Bahamas

Bahrain

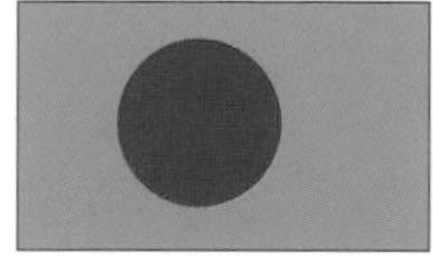

Bangladesh

Barbados

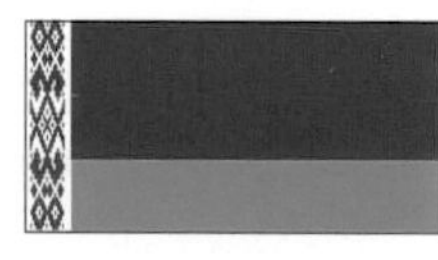

Belarus

Belgium

Belize

Benin

Bermuda

Bhutan

Bolivia

Bosnia and Herzegovina

Botswana

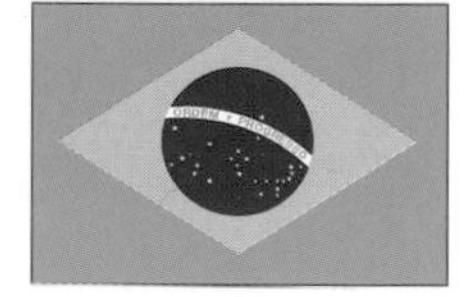

Brazil

British Virgin Islands

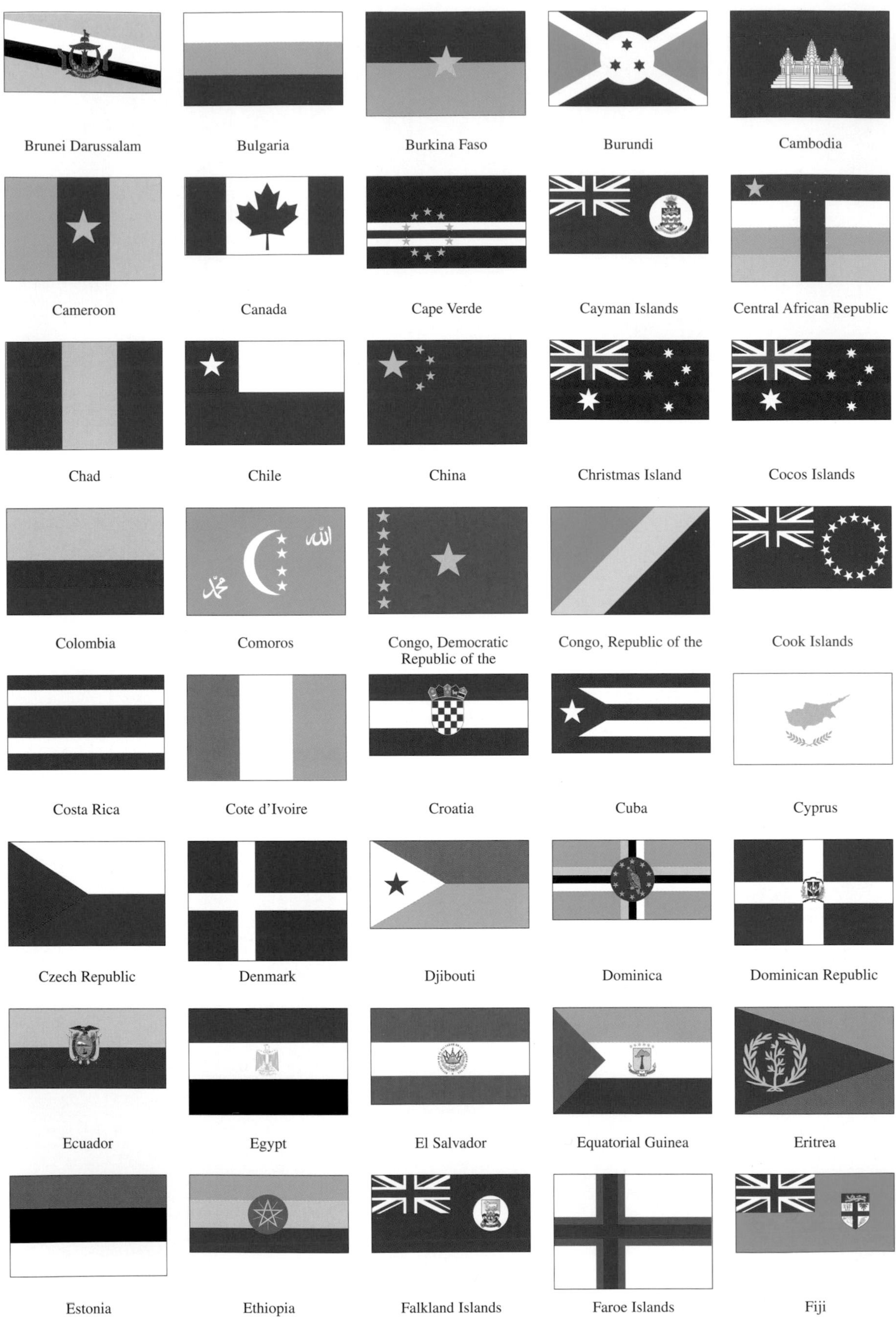
Brunei Darussalam
Bulgaria
Burkina Faso
Burundi
Cambodia
Cameroon
Canada
Cape Verde
Cayman Islands
Central African Republic
Chad
Chile
China
Christmas Island
Cocos Islands
Colombia
Comoros
Congo, Democratic Republic of the
Congo, Republic of the
Cook Islands
Costa Rica
Cote d'Ivoire
Croatia
Cuba
Cyprus
Czech Republic
Denmark
Djibouti
Dominica
Dominican Republic
Ecuador
Egypt
El Salvador
Equatorial Guinea
Eritrea
Estonia
Ethiopia
Falkland Islands
Faroe Islands
Fiji

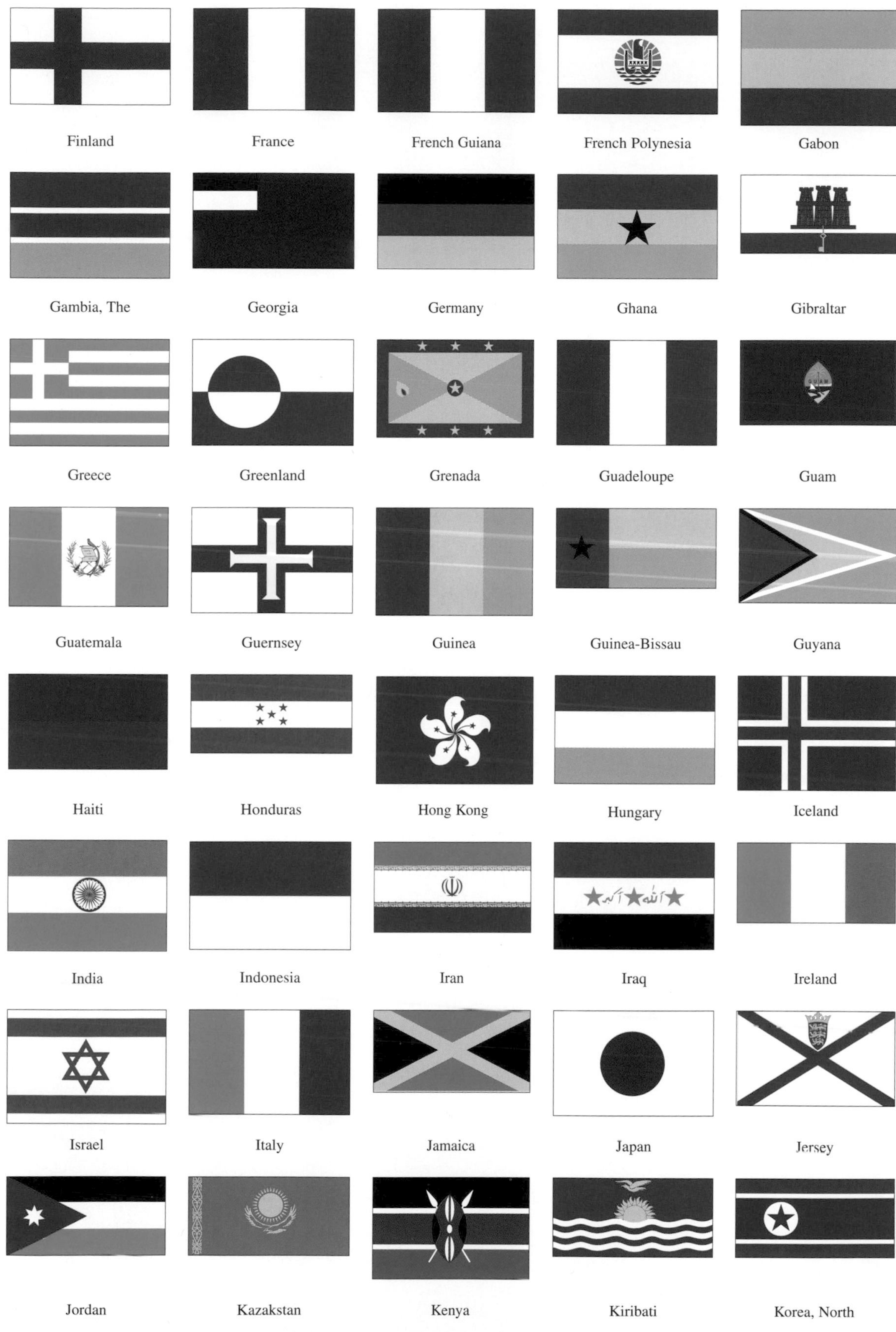
Finland
France
French Guiana
French Polynesia
Gabon
Gambia, The
Georgia
Germany
Ghana
Gibraltar
Greece
Greenland
Grenada
Guadeloupe
Guam
Guatemala
Guernsey
Guinea
Guinea-Bissau
Guyana
Haiti
Honduras
Hong Kong
Hungary
Iceland
India
Indonesia
Iran
Iraq
Ireland
Israel
Italy
Jamaica
Japan
Jersey
Jordan
Kazakstan
Kenya
Kiribati
Korea, North

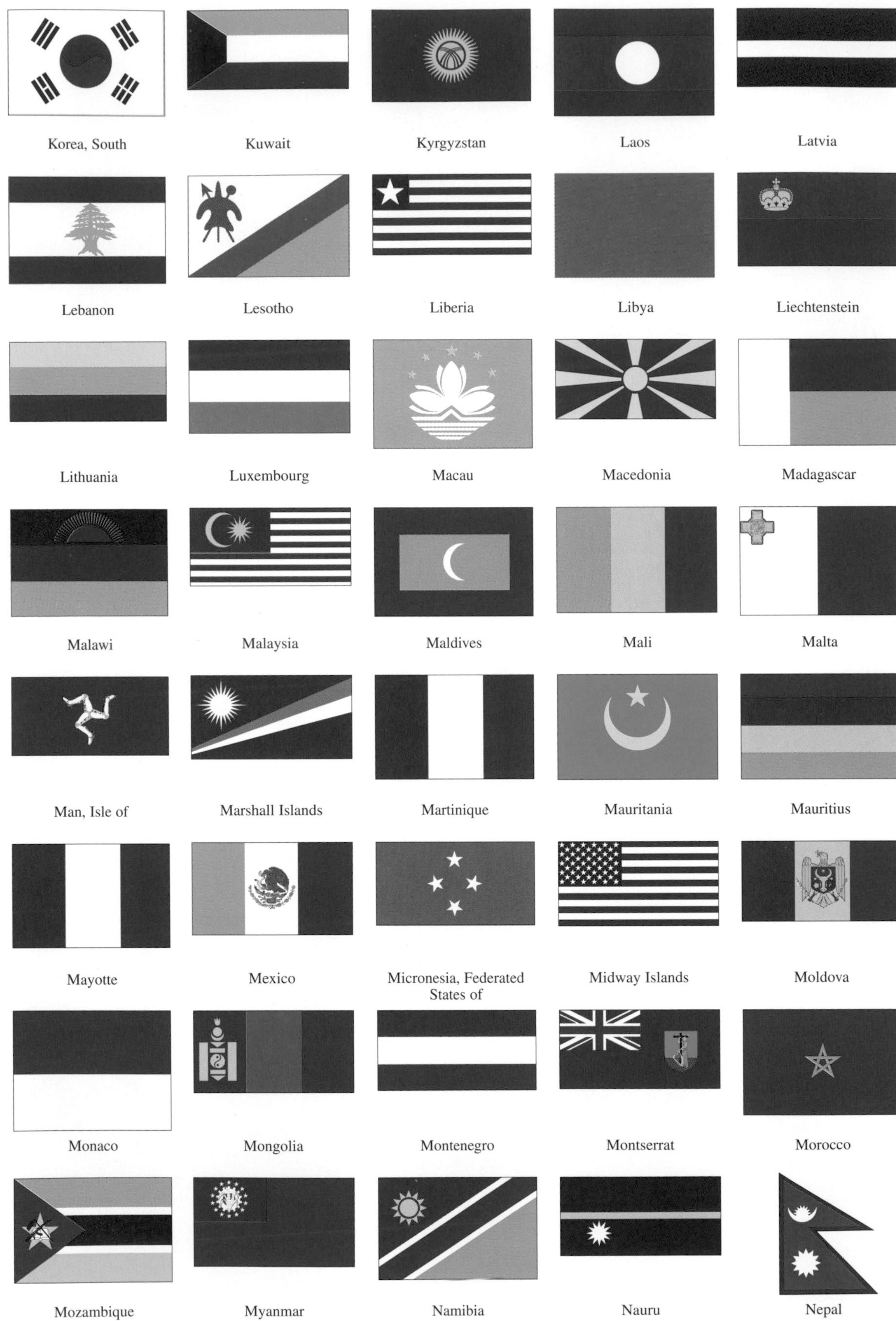
Korea, South
Kuwait
Kyrgyzstan
Laos
Latvia
Lebanon
Lesotho
Liberia
Libya
Liechtenstein
Lithuania
Luxembourg
Macau
Macedonia
Madagascar
Malawi
Malaysia
Maldives
Mali
Malta
Man, Isle of
Marshall Islands
Martinique
Mauritania
Mauritius
Mayotte
Mexico
Micronesia, Federated States of
Midway Islands
Moldova
Monaco
Mongolia
Montenegro
Montserrat
Morocco
Mozambique
Myanmar
Namibia
Nauru
Nepal

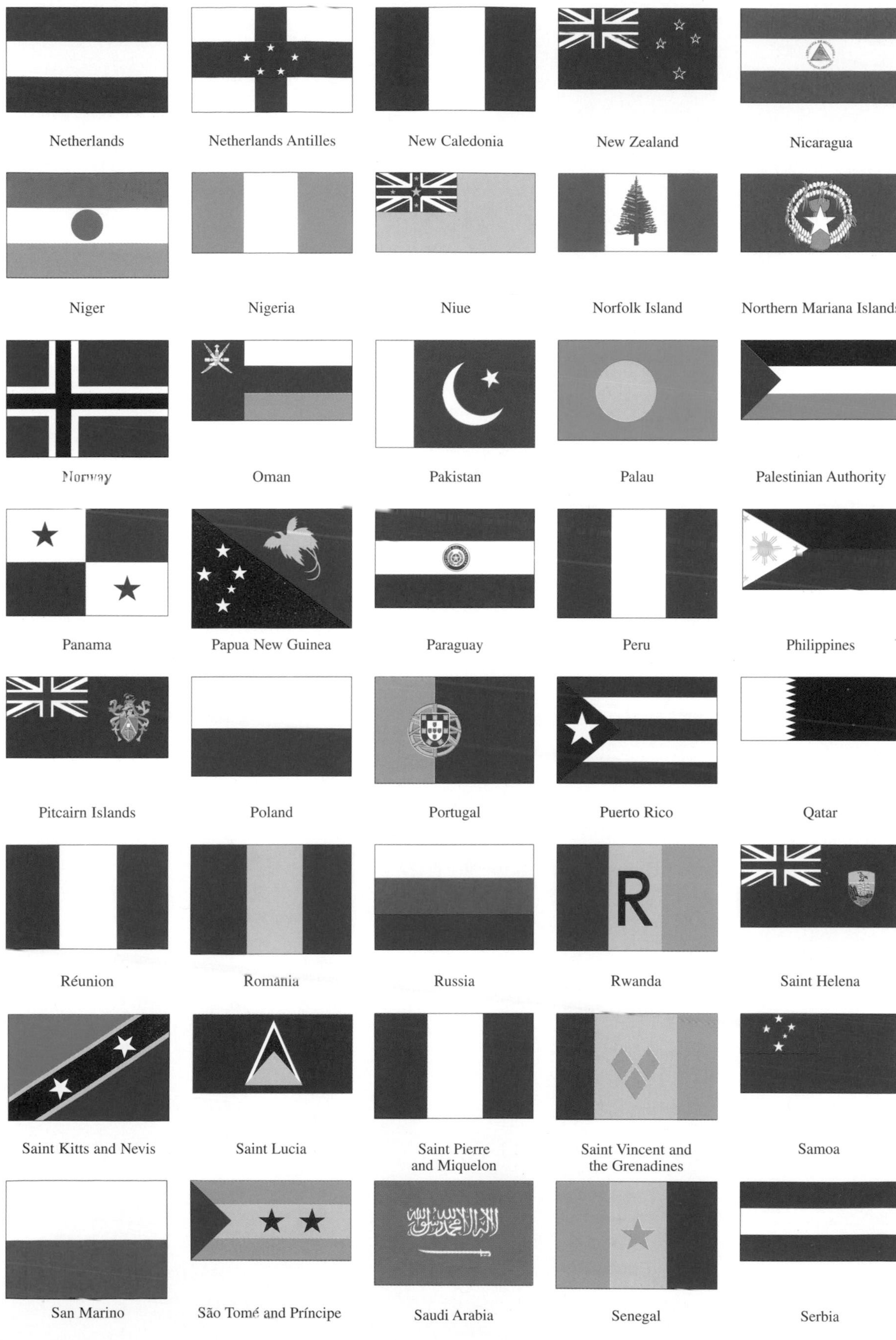

Netherlands
Netherlands Antilles
New Caledonia
New Zealand
Nicaragua
Niger
Nigeria
Niue
Norfolk Island
Northern Mariana Islands
Norway
Oman
Pakistan
Palau
Palestinian Authority
Panama
Papua New Guinea
Paraguay
Peru
Philippines
Pitcairn Islands
Poland
Portugal
Puerto Rico
Qatar
Réunion
Romania
Russia
Rwanda
R
Saint Helena
Saint Kitts and Nevis
Saint Lucia
Saint Pierre and Miquelon
Saint Vincent and the Grenadines
Samoa
San Marino
São Tomé and Príncipe
Saudi Arabia
Senegal
Serbia

Seychelles
Sierra Leone
Singapore
Slovakia
Slovenia
Solomon Islands
Somalia
South Africa
Spain
Spanish North Africa
Sri Lanka
Sudan
Suriname
Svalbard
Swaziland
Sweden
Switzerland
Syria
Taiwan
Tajikistan
Tanzania
Thailand
Togo
Tokelau
Tonga
Trinidad and Tobago
Tunisia
Turkey
Turkmenistan
Turks and Caicos Islands
Tuvalu
Uganda
Ukraine
United Arab Emirates
United Kingdom
United States
Uruguay
Uzbekistan
Vanuatu
Vatican City

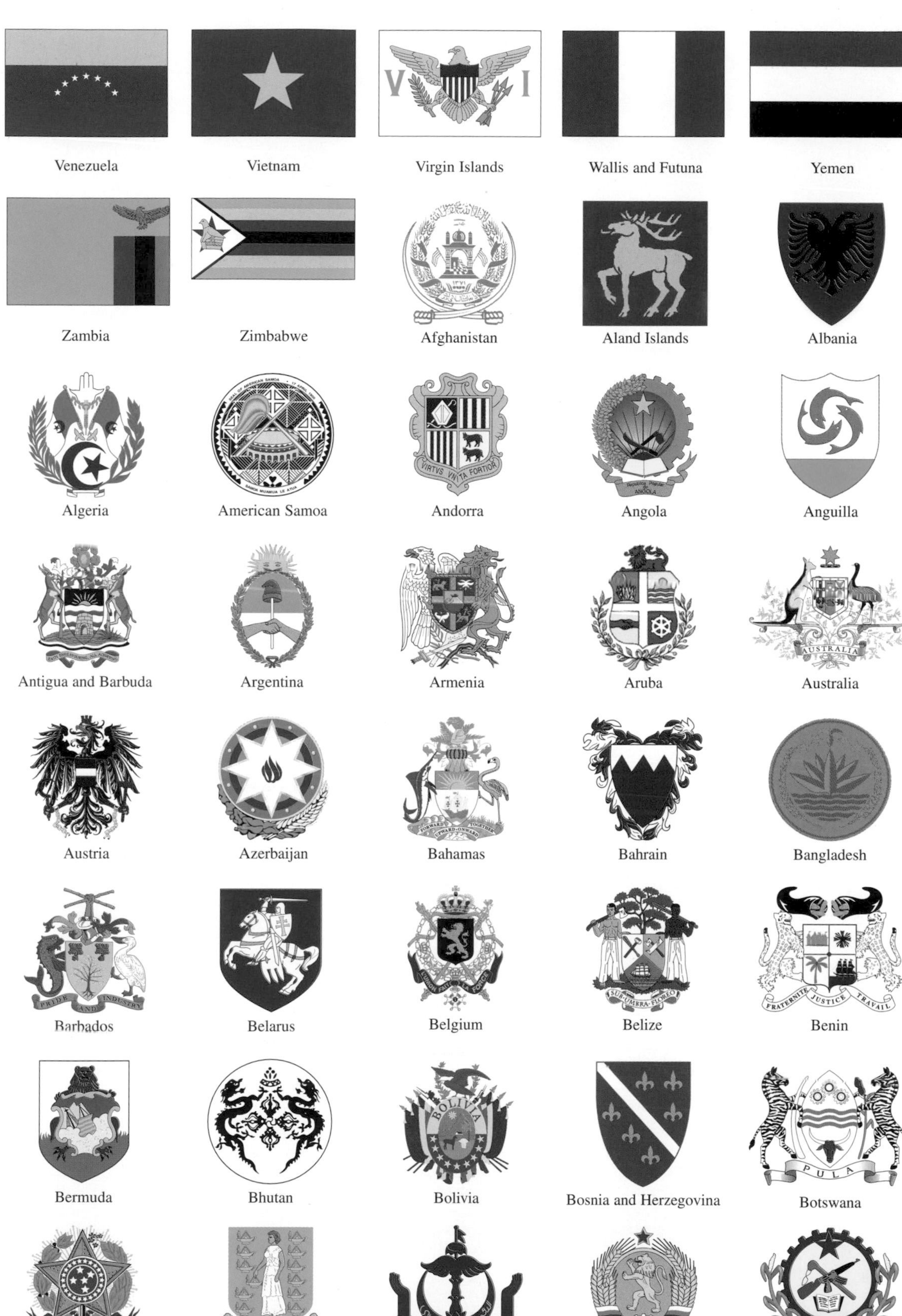

Venezuela | Vietnam | Virgin Islands | Wallis and Futuna | Yemen

Zambia | Zimbabwe | Afghanistan | Aland Islands | Albania

Algeria | American Samoa | Andorra | Angola | Anguilla

Antigua and Barbuda | Argentina | Armenia | Aruba | Australia

Austria | Azerbaijan | Bahamas | Bahrain | Bangladesh

Barbados | Belarus | Belgium | Belize | Benin

Bermuda | Bhutan | Bolivia | Bosnia and Herzegovina | Botswana

Brazil | British Virgin Islands | Brunei Darussalam | Bulgaria | Burkina Faso

Burundi

Cambodia

Cameroon

Canada

Cape Verde

Cayman Islands

Central African Republic

Chad

Chile

China

Christmas Island; Cocos Islands

Colombia

Comoros

Congo, Democratic Republic of the

Congo, Republic of the

Cook Islands

Costa Rica

Cote d'Ivoire

Croatia

Cuba

Cyprus

Czech Republic

Denmark

Djibouti

Dominica

Dominican Republic

Ecuador

Egypt

El Salvador

Equatorial Guinea

Eritrea

Estonia

Ethiopia

Falkland Islands

Faroe Islands

Fiji

Finland

France

French Guiana

Gabon

Gambia, The | Georgia | Germany | Ghana | Gibraltar

Greece | Greenland | Grenada | Guadeloupe | Guam

Guatemala | Guernsey | Guinea | Guinea-Bissau | Guyana

Haiti | Honduras | Hong Kong | Hungary | Iceland

India | Indonesia | Iran | Iraq | Ireland

Israel | Italy | Jamaica | Japan | Jersey

Jordan | Kazakstan | Kenya | Kiribati | Korea, North

Korea, South | Kuwait | Kyrgyzstan | Laos | Latvia

Lebanon, Lesotho, Liberia, Libya, Liechtenstein

Lithuania, Luxembourg, Macau, Macedonia, Madagascar

Malawi, Malaysia, Maldives, Mali, Malta

Man, Isle of, Marshall Islands, Martinique, Mauritania, Mauritius

Mayotte, Mexico, Micronesia, Federated States of, Midway Islands, Moldova

Monaco, Mongolia, Montenegro, Montserrat, Morocco

Mozambique, Myanmar, Namibia, Nauru, Nepal

Netherlands, Netherlands Antilles, New Caledonia, New Zealand, Nicaragua

Niger | Nigeria | Norfolk Island | Northern Mariana Islands | Norway

Oman | Pakistan | Palau | Panama | Papua New Guinea

Paraguay | Peru | Philippines | Pitcairn Islands | Poland

Portugal | Puerto Rico | Qatar | Réunion | Romania

Russia | Rwanda | Saint Helena | Saint Kitts and Nevis | Saint Lucia

Saint Pierre and Miquelon | Saint Vincent and the Grenadines | Samoa | San Marino | São Tomé and Príncipe

Saudi Arabia | Senegal | Serbia | Seychelles | Sierra Leone

Singapore | Slovakia | Slovenia | Solomon Islands | Somalia

South Africa

Spain

Spanish North Africa

Sri Lanka

Sudan

Suriname

Svalbard

Swaziland

Sweden

Switzerland

Syria

Taiwan

Tajikistan

Tanzania

Thailand

Togo

Tokelau

Tonga

Trinidad and Tobago

Tunisia

Turkey

Turkmenistan

Turks and Caicos Islands

Tuvalu

Uganda

Ukraine

United Arab Emirates

United Kingdom

United States

Uruguay

Uzbekistan

Vanuatu

Vatican City

Venezuela

Vietnam

Virgin Islands

Wallis and Futuna

Yemen

Zambia

Zimbabwe

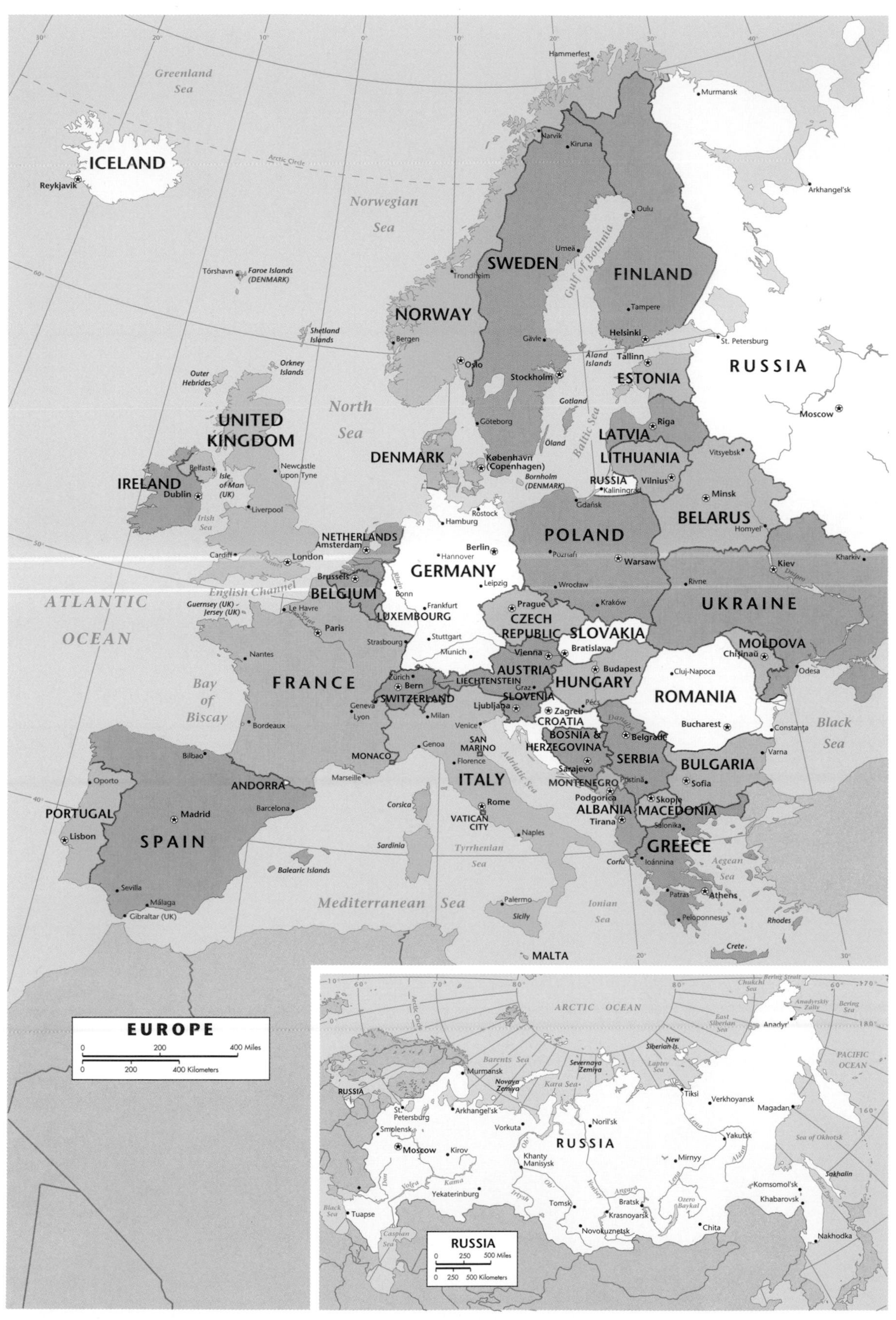
EUROPE
0 200 400 Miles
0 200 400 Kilometers
Greenland Sea
ICELAND
Reykjavík
Arctic Circle
Norwegian Sea
Tórshavn
Faroe Islands (DENMARK)
Shetland Islands
Orkney Islands
Outer Hebrides
UNITED KINGDOM
IRELAND
Dublin
Belfast
Isle of Man (UK)
Newcastle upon Tyne
Liverpool
Irish Sea
Cardiff
London
North Sea
NORWAY
Bergen
Oslo
Trondheim
Hammerfest
Narvik
Kiruna
SWEDEN
Umeå
Gävle
Stockholm
Göteborg
Gotland
Öland
FINLAND
Oulu
Tampere
Helsinki
Gulf of Bothnia
Åland Islands
Tallinn
ESTONIA
Baltic Sea
LATVIA
Riga
LITHUANIA
Vilnius
RUSSIA
Kaliningrad
Murmansk
Arkhangel'sk
St. Petersburg
Moscow
DENMARK
København (Copenhagen)
Bornholm (DENMARK)
Gdańsk
Vitsyebsk
Minsk
BELARUS
Homyel'
POLAND
Poznań
Warsaw
Wrocław
Kraków
Rostock
Hamburg
Berlin
Hannover
GERMANY
Leipzig
Bonn
Frankfurt
Stuttgart
Munich
Rhein
NETHERLANDS
Amsterdam
Brussels
BELGIUM
LUXEMBOURG
English Channel
Guernsey (UK)
Jersey (UK)
Le Havre
Seine
Paris
Strasbourg
ATLANTIC OCEAN
Nantes
FRANCE
Bay of Biscay
Bordeaux
Lyon
Geneva
Zürich
Bern
SWITZERLAND
LIECHTENSTEIN
Milan
Genoa
MONACO
Marseille
Prague
CZECH REPUBLIC
SLOVAKIA
Bratislava
Vienna
AUSTRIA
Graz
Budapest
HUNGARY
Pécs
SLOVENIA
Ljubljana
Zagreb
CROATIA
Danube
BOSNIA & HERZEGOVINA
Sarajevo
Belgrade
SERBIA
MONTENEGRO
Podgorica
Priština
ALBANIA
Tirana
Skopje
MACEDONIA
Sofia
BULGARIA
Varna
Kiev
Kharkiv
Rivne
UKRAINE
Dnipro
MOLDOVA
Chişinău
Odesa
Cluj-Napoca
ROMANIA
Bucharest
Constanța
Black Sea
Venice
SAN MARINO
Florence
Adriatic Sea
ITALY
Rome
VATICAN CITY
Naples
Corsica
Sardinia
Tyrrhenian Sea
Palermo
Sicily
MALTA
Mediterranean Sea
Ionian Sea
Bilbao
Oporto
ANDORRA
Barcelona
PORTUGAL
Lisbon
Madrid
SPAIN
Balearic Islands
Sevilla
Málaga
Gibraltar (UK)
Corfu
Ioánnina
Salonika
GREECE
Aegean Sea
Patras
Athens
Peloponnesus
Rhodes
Crete
ARCTIC OCEAN
Barents Sea
Kara Sea
Laptev Sea
East Siberian Sea
Chukchi Sea
Bering Strait
Bering Sea
PACIFIC OCEAN
Sea of Okhotsk
Novaya Zemlya
Severnaya Zemlya
New Siberian Is.
Anadyr'
Murmansk
Arkhangel'sk
St. Petersburg
Smolensk
Moscow
Kirov
Vorkuta
Noril'sk
Tiksi
Verkhoyansk
Magadan
Yakutsk
Mirnyy
RUSSIA
Khanty Mansiysk
Yekaterinburg
Volga
Kama
Don
Ob
Irtysh
Yenisey
Angara
Lena
Aldan
Tomsk
Bratsk
Krasnoyarsk
Novokuznetsk
Ozero Baykal
Chita
Komsomol'sk
Khabarovsk
Sakhalin
Nakhodka
Tuapse
Caspian Sea
RUSSIA
0 250 500 Miles
0 250 500 Kilometers

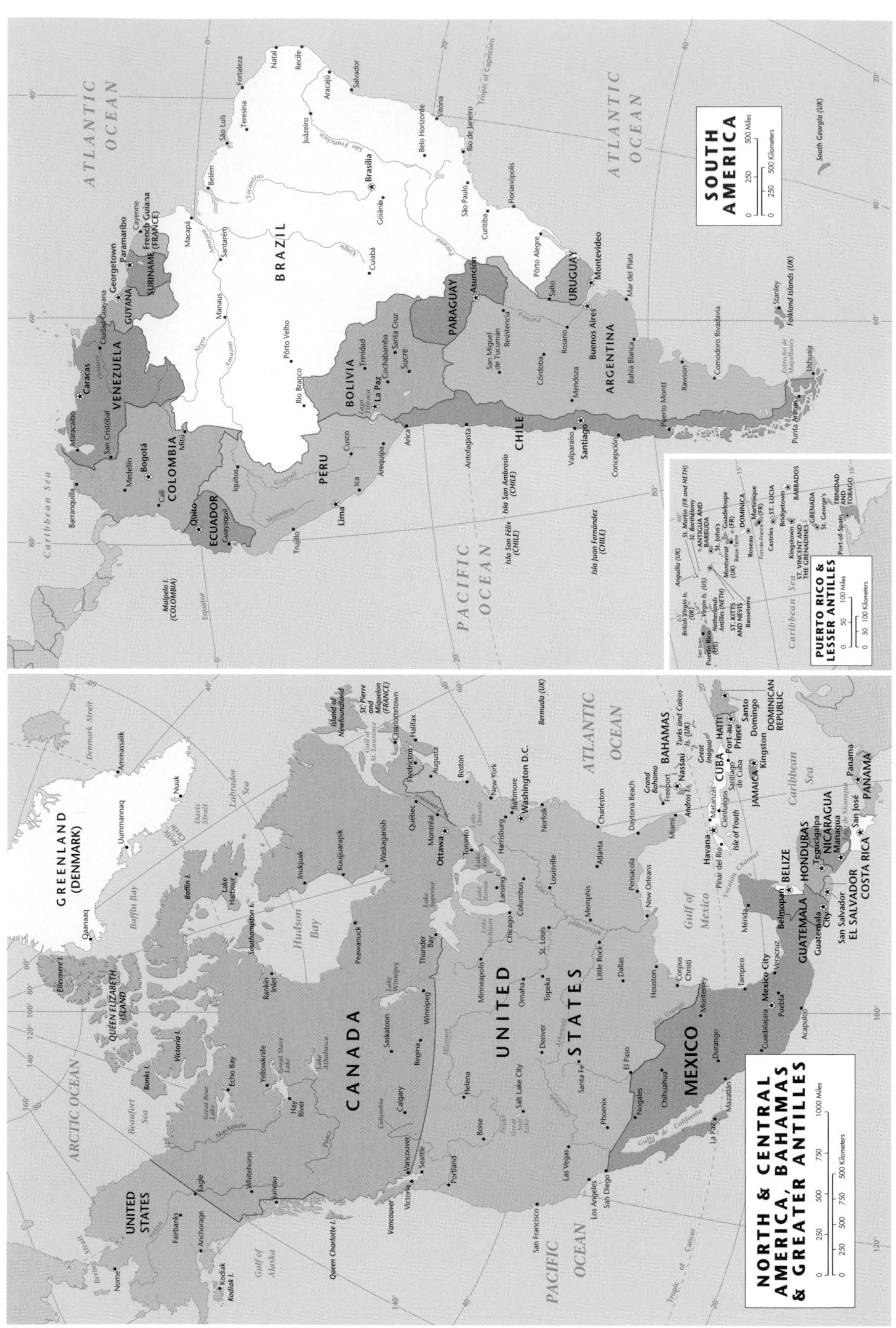
NORTH & CENTRAL AMERICA, BAHAMAS & GREATER ANTILLES
SOUTH AMERICA
PUERTO RICO & LESSER ANTILLES

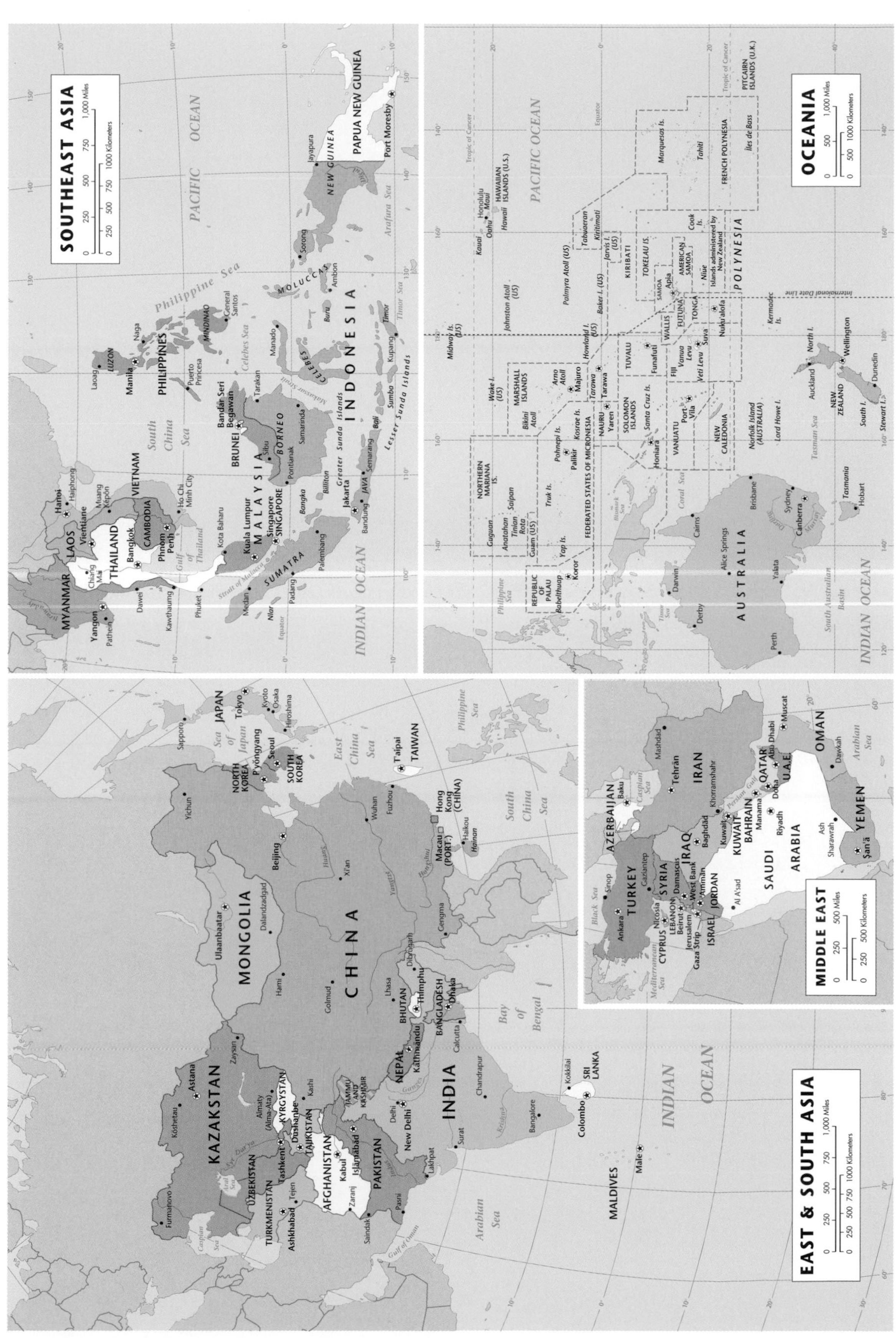
SOUTHEAST ASIA
OCEANIA
EAST & SOUTH ASIA
MIDDLE EAST
PACIFIC OCEAN
INDIAN OCEAN
MYANMAR
LAOS
THAILAND
CAMBODIA
VIETNAM
PHILIPPINES
MALAYSIA
BRUNEI
SINGAPORE
INDONESIA
PAPUA NEW GUINEA
AUSTRALIA
NEW ZEALAND
KAZAKHSTAN
MONGOLIA
CHINA
INDIA
PAKISTAN
AFGHANISTAN
NEPAL
BHUTAN
BANGLADESH
SRI LANKA
MALDIVES
JAPAN
TAIWAN
TURKEY
SYRIA
IRAQ
IRAN
SAUDI ARABIA
YEMEN
OMAN

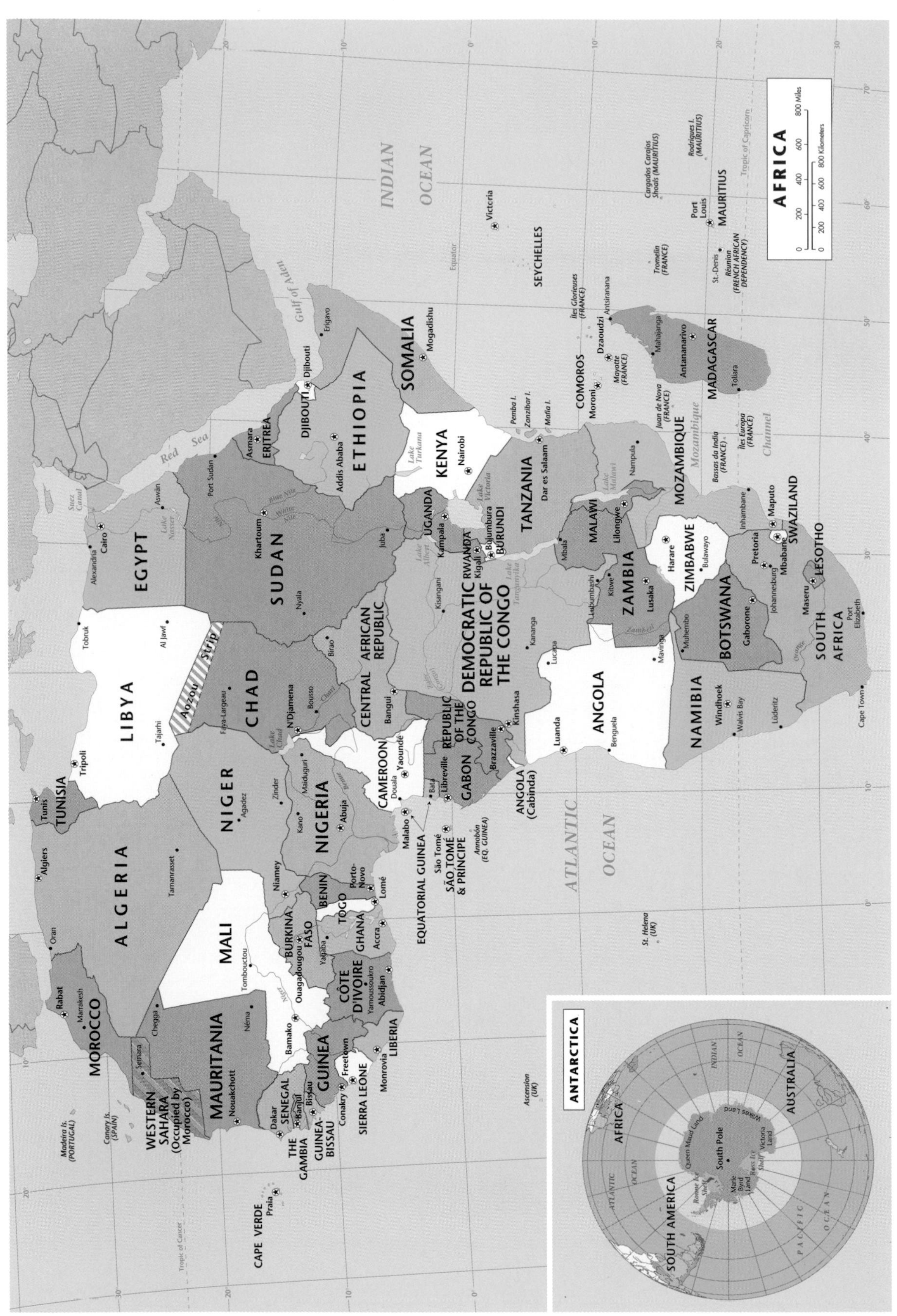
AFRICA
ANTARCTICA
INDIAN OCEAN
ATLANTIC OCEAN
MOROCCO
ALGERIA
TUNISIA
LIBYA
EGYPT
WESTERN SAHARA (Occupied by Morocco)
MAURITANIA
MALI
NIGER
CHAD
SUDAN
ERITREA
DJIBOUTI
ETHIOPIA
SOMALIA
SENEGAL
THE GAMBIA
GUINEA-BISSAU
GUINEA
SIERRA LEONE
LIBERIA
CÔTE D'IVOIRE
BURKINA FASO
GHANA
TOGO
BENIN
NIGERIA
CAMEROON
CENTRAL AFRICAN REPUBLIC
EQUATORIAL GUINEA
SÃO TOMÉ & PRÍNCIPE
GABON
REPUBLIC OF THE CONGO
DEMOCRATIC REPUBLIC OF THE CONGO
UGANDA
KENYA
RWANDA
BURUNDI
TANZANIA
ANGOLA
ANGOLA (Cabinda)
ZAMBIA
MALAWI
MOZAMBIQUE
ZIMBABWE
NAMIBIA
BOTSWANA
SOUTH AFRICA
LESOTHO
SWAZILAND
MADAGASCAR
COMOROS
SEYCHELLES
MAURITIUS
CAPE VERDE
Aozou Strip
Red Sea
Gulf of Aden
Mozambique Channel
Tropic of Cancer
Tropic of Capricorn
Equator
Madeira Is. (PORTUGAL)
Canary Is. (SPAIN)
St. Helena (UK)
Ascension (UK)
Annobón (EQ. GUINEA)
Réunion (FRENCH AFRICAN DEPENDENCY)
Tromelin (FRANCE)
Cargados Carajos Shoals (MAURITIUS)
Rodrigues I. (MAURITIUS)
Mayotte (FRANCE)
Juan de Nova (FRANCE)
Bassas da India (FRANCE)
Îles Europa (FRANCE)
Îles Glorieuses (FRANCE)
SOUTH AMERICA
AUSTRALIA
South Pole
0 200 400 600 800 Miles
0 200 400 600 800 Kilometers

MALTA

CAPITAL: Valletta.

FLAG: The national flag consists of two equal vertical stripes, white at the hoist and red at the fly, with a representation of the Maltese Cross, edged with red, in the canton of the white stripe.

ANTHEM: *L'Innu Malti (The Maltese Hymn).*

MONETARY UNIT: The Maltese lira (LM) consists of 100 cents, with each cent divided into 10 mils. There are coins of 2, 3, and 5 mils and of 1, 2, 5, 10, 25, and 50 cents, and notes of 2, 5, 10, and 20 lira. Gold and silver coins of 1, 2, 4, 5, 10, 20, 25, 50, and 100 lira are also in circulation. LM1 = $0.357 (or $1 = LM2.80112).

WEIGHTS AND MEASURES: The metric system is the legal standard, but some local measures are still in use.

HOLIDAYS: New Year's Day, 1 January; National Day, 31 March; May Day, 1 May; Assumption, 15 August; Republic Day, 13 December; Christmas, 25 December. Movable holidays include Good Friday.

TIME: 1 PM = noon GMT.

LOCATION AND SIZE: Malta lies in the central Mediterranean Sea. There are three main islands—Malta, Gozo, and Comino—as well as two small uninhabited islands, Cominotto and Filfla. Malta's total area is 320 square kilometers (124 square miles), slightly less than twice the size of Washington, D.C. The total coastline of the inhabited islands is 140 kilometers (87 miles).

Malta's capital city, Valletta, is located on the east coast of the island of Malta.

CLIMATE: The climate is typically Mediterranean. The average winter temperature is 9°C (48°F); the average summer temperature, 31°C (88°F). Rainfall averages about 64 centimeters (25 inches) per year.

The Republic of Malta
Repubblika Ta' Malta

INTRODUCTORY SURVEY

RECENT HISTORY

During almost the entire nineteenth century, a British military governor ruled the colony. The Maltese remained loyal to Britain in World War I (1914-1918) and World War II (1939-1945). For gallantry under heavy fire during the German-Italian siege (1940-1943) the entire population was awarded the George Cross.

Although the Maltese enjoyed a great degree of self-government, they wanted complete independence except in matters of defense and foreign affairs. Malta became a sovereign and independent nation within the British Commonwealth of Nations on September 21, 1964. At the same time mutual defense and financial agreements were signed with the United Kingdom.

On December 13, 1974, Malta formally adopted a republican form of government, and the former governor-general, Sir Anthony Mamo, became the first president. Dom Mintoff, leader of the Malta Labour Party and prime minister from 1971 through 1984, adopted socialist measures domestically and initiated a nonaligned policy in foreign affairs. The Nationalists under Eddie Fenech Adami have been in power since 1987. Vincent Tabone was elected president in 1989.

Maltese politics has revolved around foreign policy issues, in particular Malta's relationship with Europe. The Nationalist Party government has been a strong advocate of European Union membership. Malta has applied for full membership in

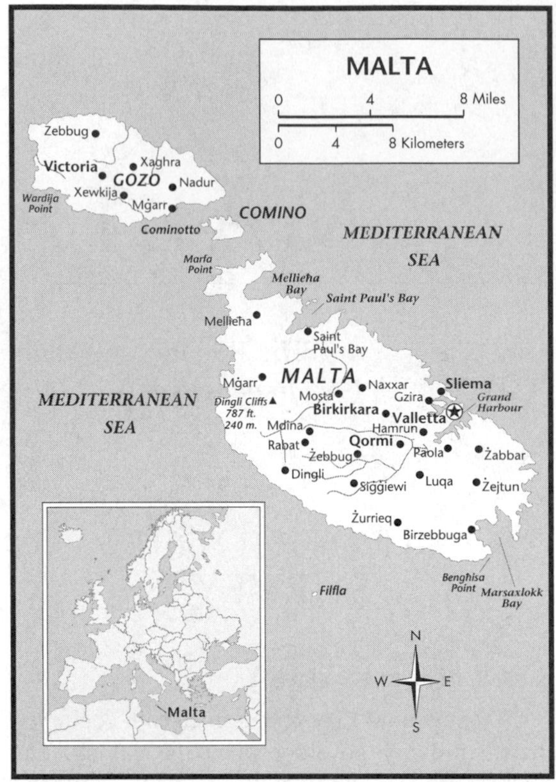

the European Union. However since the Labor Party won the 1996 elections, the government's stance has shifted towards maintaining neutrality. Alfred Sant became prime minister. The government began to renegotiate Malta's relationship with the European Union but did not withdraw its application.

The Labor Party adopted economic policies such as raising utility rates that alienated both the electorate and elements within the party itself. New elections were called for ahead of schedule in September 1998. The Nationalist Party won a majority in a vote seen at least partly as a referendum on the European Union (EU) membership question. In March 1999 the House of Representatives elected Guido de Marco of the nationalist Party president and Adami regained the post of prime minister. Adami moved to reactivate Malta's EU membership application and adopted policies, such as the reimposition of a controversial value-added tax-intended to pave the way for membership approval that was seen as possible by 2003.

GOVERNMENT

The single-chamber parliament, the House of Representatives, consists of sixty-five members elected on the basis of proportional representation for a five-year term by universal adult suffrage gained at eighteen years of age. The House elects the chief of state, called the president of the republic for a five-year term. The president appoints the prime minister for a five-year term. The individual selected for prime minister is usually the leader of the majority party or majority coalition following legislative elections.

Judiciary

The superior courts consist of the Constitutional Court (with the power to review laws and executive acts), the court of appeal, the court of criminal appeal, two civil courts, the criminal court, and the commercial court.

Political Parties

There are two major political parties, the Nationalist Party (PN) and the Malta Labour Party (MLP), which have alternated in political power. The Nationalist Party favors association with the EU. The Labor Party opposed to membership in the EU and sought to end Malta's associate membership with NATO, and sought closer ties with Libya. In September 1998 the Nationalist Party won a majority and its leadership took steps to reactivate Malta's application for EU membership.

DEFENSE

The volunteer army of 1,900 composes the armed forces that include land forces, an air squadron, a maritime squadron, and the Revenue Security Corps. There is also the Maltese Police Force. Malta spent $201 million on defense in 1998-1999.

ECONOMIC AFFAIRS

Until 1964 the dominant factor in the economy was the presence of British military forces. With withdrawal of UK military personnel by 1979, the dockyards were converted to commercial use. By 2000 Malta's economy depended on: foreign trade and with its strategic location a major freight transshipment point; tourism with over a million visitors in 1999; a financial center; and, manufacturing, especially electronics and textiles. Most food, industrial raw materials, and all energy must be imported. Although divided over the question of EU membership Malta remains an official candidate for membership.

Public Finance

The principal sources of recurrent revenues are income taxes, and customs and excise taxes.

The U.S. Central Intelligence Agency estimated that in 1998 government revenues totaled approximately $1.32 billion and expenditures $1.76 billion. External debt totaled $103 million in 1997.

Income

In 1999 Malta's gross domestic product (GDP) was estimated at $513 billion or about $13,800 per capita. The estimated GDP for 1999 was 4 percent and inflation was 1.8 percent. The 1999 estimated GDP contribution by sector was agriculture 3 percent, industry 26 percent, and services 71 percent.

Industry

Malta's principal industries are tourism, electronics, shipbuilding and maintenance, construction, textiles, food and beverages, and tobacco.

Banking and Finance

In June 1968 activities of the Currency Board were transferred to the new Central Bank of Malta. The Central Bank is responsible for the regulation of the banking system, the money supply, the issue of currency, and the administration of exchange control. The Central Bank manages the official external reserves and advises the Minister of Finance regarding the exchange rate of the Maltese lira. The Maltese lira is calculated on the basis of a currency basket that currently consists of the ECU, pound sterling, and U.S. dollar. There are four commercial banks—the Bank of Valletta, Mid-Med Bank, Lombard Bank Malta, and APS Bank—as well as the National Savings Bank.

In November 1995 Midland Bank (UK) became the first foreign bank to be granted a license to operate in the domestic market. Six international banking institutions are established in Malta: Turkiye Garanti Bankas, First Austrian Bank Malta, First International Merchant Bank, Izola Bank, Bank of Valletta International, and Mid-Med Bank Overseas.

A stock exchange was founded in 1992.

In 1994 the Malta International Business Authority became the Malta Financial Services Center (MFSC), responsible for the regulation and registration of financial services provided in and from Malta.

Economic Development

Under the LM123-million development plan for 1973-1980, manufacturing, shipbuilding, and tourism expanded rapidly. The new Marsa shipyard and a 300,000-ton dock were completed by 1980; the Marsaxlokk harbor complex was to be developed into a free port.

Legislation adopted in 1988 provides for the establishment of offshore businesses and trusts. The Malta Development Corp. is a public agency that encourages new investment in industry. As of 1996 leading incentives for investment in industrial projects included: a ten-year tax holiday to new industries that export 95 percent of their products; an investment allowance of up to 30 percent on capital equipment and 15 percent on industrial buildings; accelerated depreciation rates; duty-free imports of plant machinery; and subsidized rent for factory space.

In the late 1990s the Nationalist government's primary aim is to have Malta's economy in line to meet EU standards in time for the next round of enlargement. The elimination of trade barriers, deficit reduction, and more efficient tax collection comprise the most significant elements of the government's EU-harmonization plan.

SOCIAL WELFARE

The National Insurance Act of 1956, as amended in 1987, provides benefits for sickness, unemployment, old age, widowhood, orphanhood, disability, and industrial injuries. Further legislation provides for family allowances and maternity benefits. A constitutional amendment in 1993 requires government protection of all groups against economic, social, and political discrimination.

Healthcare

Free health services are administered by the government-run Polyclinics. In 2000 average life expectancy was 77.9 years.

Housing

Malta has approximately 111,700 dwellings.

EDUCATION

Free primary and secondary education is compulsory between the ages of five and sixteen. Maltese law requires that the teachings of the Roman Catholic Church be included in the public school curriculum. In 1997 there were 35,375 students in primary schools, 34,211 in secondary schools, and 8,260 enrolled in higher-level institutions. Institutes of higher learning include the University of Malta and a law and art school. In 2000 adult illiteracy was estimated to be 7.9 percent.

2000 KEY EVENTS TIMELINE

May

- Gunter Verheugen, the enlargement commissioner for the European Union (EU), declares that he will wait until later during 2000 to decide on Malta's accession to the EU.

June

- Malta is criticized as one of Europe's centers for money laundering; an illegal tax haven.

July

- The Lockerbie trial in the Netherlands confirms suspicions that the suspects flew to Malta, where they loaded a bomb onto the flight from an Air Malta jet.

October

- Prosecutors in the trial of the Lockerbie, Scotland, bombing suspects (taking place in The Netherlands) rest their case after claiming defendants were secret agents working in Malta; they also charge that the defendants sent the suitcase bomb on the Pan Am flight from Malta to London in a December 21, 1988, terrorism attack that killed 270 people.
- British doctors operate to separate conjoined infant twins, "Jodie" and "Mary," daughters of unidentified Roman Catholic parents from Malta. The event makes international headlines as the court-ordered surgery raises key questions about medical ethics.

ANALYSIS OF EVENTS: 2000

BUSINESS AND THE ECONOMY

As in 1999 manufacturing was the major component of the 2000 gross domestic product (GDP), followed by the contributions made by the banking, insurance, and real estate sector. Income in the government enterprises sector of the economy decreased, in part due to rising oil prices.

Malta agreed to cooperate with international efforts to end unfair banking practices that provide tax havens for international investors, at a cost to their home national economies.

GOVERNMENT AND POLITICS

In December 2000, the fifteen-member European Union (E.U.) met in Nice, France, to discuss an expansion plan that would nearly double the group's size. Having applied for E.U. membership in 1998, Malta was one of twelve nations whose potential member status was under consideration. Criteria for membership included a functioning market economy capable of withstanding competitive pressure, and a functioning democratic government with demonstrated respect for minorities and human rights. Because of its strong market economy, it was expected that Malta would be accepted into the E.U., but issues dealing with work permits and land ownership could make it part of the second wave of expansion rather than the first wave group. Because of the complexity of the membership talks and the ratification process, Malta could not expect to join before 2004.

The E.U. discussion on expansion included the issue of national veto rights, which some feared would bring a larger assembly to frequent stalemate. Another point of contention was the demand of larger members for a greater say in decision making, in proportion to their populations. The E.U. endorsed the Commission's Enlargement Strategy Document in mid-December. A Maltese government press release stated that Malta welcomed the agreements reached on enhanced cooperation and the extension of majority decision in non-sensitive areas of debate, with the retention of the requirement for unanimous decisions in areas such as foreign policy and defense matters.

Malta's Prime Minister, the Honorable Dr. E. Fenech Adami, traveled to Libya in April for a friendly visit aimed at developing the relations between the two nations. The two sides emphasized the need for support and cooperation among the Mediterranean states, and pledged to make the Mediterranean a "sea of peace." The Maltese contingent expressed its appreciation for Colonel Muammar Qadhafi and the support he has given the Maltese people. In turn the Libyans stated their appreciation of the support Malta provided during the sanctions period.

Malta was among the first nations to sign the United Nations International Convention for the Suppression of the Financing of Terrorism. The 2000 Convention called upon member nations to take all steps possible to prevent illegal activities related to the financing of terrorism. In March Malta refused to extradite Egyptian murder suspect

Mohammed Abdul Abbas Aly to Turkey because Turkey still had the death sentence. The suspect confessed to killing British tourist Edgar Fernandes, but later retracted his confession.

CULTURE AND SOCIETY

In June a Dutch doctor announced plans to outfit a ship as a floating abortion clinic, to be harbored just outside the waters of countries that prohibit abortion. Rumors pointed to Malta as one of its first stops.

A woman from Gozo gave birth to conjoined daughters (popularly referred to as "Siamese twins") in Manchester, England in August. It was determined that one of the babies was drawing life from the other, and that if they remained joined, both would die, probably within a few months. In September the British courts ruled that the conjoined babies, known as Mary and Jodie, should be separated; the parents decided not to contest the judgment, although it went against their personal religious beliefs. In November they were separated, and, as expected, the weaker baby died as a result of the surgery.

DIRECTORY

CENTRAL GOVERNMENT

Head of State

President
Guido de Marco, Office of the President, The Palace, Valletta CMR 02, Malta
PHONE: +356 221221; 238156
FAX: +356 241241

Ministers

Prime Minister
Eddie Fenech Adami, Office of the Prime Minister, Auberge de Castille, Valletta CMR 02, Malta
PHONE: +356 242560
FAX: +356 249888

Deputy Prime Minister
Joseph Borg, Office of the Deputy Prime Minister

Minister of Social Policy
Lawrence Gonzi, Ministry of Social Policy, Palazzo Ferreria, Republic Street, Valletta CMR 02, Malta
PHONE: +356 225709
FAX: +356 243017

Minister of Education
Louis Galea, Ministry of Education, Great Siege Road, Floriana CMR 02, Malta
PHONE: +356 221401
FAX: +356 221634

Minister of Finance
John Dalli, Ministry of Finance, 158, Old Mint Street, Valletta CMR 02, Malta
PHONE: +356 249640
FAX: +356 224667

Minister of Environment, Drainage, Public Cleansing and Waste, Capital Construction Projects, Works
Francis Zammit Dimech, Ministry of Environment, Drainage, Public Cleansing and Waste, Capital Construction Projects, Works, Block B, Floriana CMR 02, Malta
PHONE: +356 222378; 224501
FAX: +356 243306

Minister of Tourism
Michael A. Refalo, Ministry of Tourism, Palazzo Spinola, St. Julians CMR 02, Malta
PHONE: +356 383847
FAX: +356 383834

Minister of Transport and Communications
Censu Galea, Ministry of Transport and Communications, House of Four Winds, Hastings Gardens, Valletta CMR 02, Malta
PHONE: +356 225200; 220604
FAX: +356 248937; 233970

Minister of Economic Services
Josef Bonnici, Ministry of Economic Services, Auberge d'Aragon, Independence Square, Valletta CMR 02, Malta
PHONE: +356 226263
FAX: +356 226261

Minister of Home Affairs
Tonio Borg, Ministry of Home Affairs, Casa Leoni, St. Joseph High Road, Santa Venera CMR 02, Malta
PHONE: +356 485100
FAX: +356 485800

Minister of Agriculture and Fisheries
Ninu Zammit, Ministry of Agriculture and Fisheries, Barriera Wharf, Valletta CMR 02, Malta
PHONE: +356 225236
FAX: +356 231294

Minister of Gozo
Giovanna Debono, Ministry of Gozo, St. Francis Square, Victoria Gozo, Malta
PHONE: +356 563202; 559482
FAX: +356 561755

Minister of Health
Louis Deguara, Ministry of Health, Palazzo Castellania, Merchants Stree, Valletta CMR 02, Malta
PHONE: +356 224071
FAX: +356 252574

Minister of Foreign Affairs
Joe Borg, Ministry of Foreign Affairs, Palazzo Parisio, Merchants Street, Malta
PHONE: +356 242853
FAX: +356 237822

Minister of Justice and Local Government
Austin Gat, Ministry of Justice and Local Government, Auberge de Castille, Valletta CMR 02, Malta
PHONE: +356 226808
FAX: +356 250700

POLITICAL ORGANIZATIONS

Malta Labour Party (MLP)

National Labour Centre, Mile End Street, Hamrun, HMR 02, Malta
PHONE: +356 252001
TITLE: Leader
NAME: Alfred Sant

DIPLOMATIC REPRESENTATION

Embassies in Malta

Costa Rica
PHONE: +356 2201602
FAX: +356 2203738
TITLE: Consul Honorario
NAME: David Reuben

Delegation of the European Commission
Villa "The Vines," 51 Ta'Xbiex Sea Front, Ta'Xbiex, MSD 11, Malta
PHONE: +356 344891
FAX: +356 344897

United States
Development House, 3rd Floor, Anne Street, Floriana, Malta
PHONE: +356 235960
FAX: +356 243229
TITLE: Consul
NAME: James M. Perez

JUDICIAL SYSTEM

Constitutional Court

Court of Appeal

BROADCAST MEDIA

Malta Broadcasting Authority

Mile-end Road, Hamrun, Malta
PHONE: +356 247908; 221281
FAX: +356 240855
TITLE: Chief Executive
CONTACT: Antoine J. Ellul

Public Broadcasting Services Ltd.

Box 82, Valletta, Malta
PHONE: +356 225051
FAX: +356 244601
TITLE: Head of Radio
CONTACT: J. Inguanez

Radio Melita (Voice of the Mediterranean)

PO Box 143, Valletta CMR 01, Malta
PHONE: +356 248080; 240421
FAX: +356 241501
WEBSITE: http://www.woden.com/~falcon/schedule.html
TITLE: Managing Director
CONTACT: Richard Vella Laurenti
LANGUAGE: Arabic, English, French, German, Japanese, Maltese
TYPE: Government

Public Broadcasting Services Ltd.

PO Box 70, Msida 01, Malta
PHONE: +356 225051
FAX: +356 244601
TITLE: Chairman
CONTACT: J. J. Cremona
CHANNEL: E10

Super One TV

CHANNEL: 29

COLLEGES AND UNIVERSITIES

University of Malta

Msida MSD 06, Malta
PHONE: +356 333903
FAX: +356 336450
E-MAIL: intoff@um.edu.mt
WEBSITE: http://www.um.edu.mt

NEWSPAPERS AND MAGAZINES

Alternattiva Direct

E-MAIL: alternattiva@usa.net

In-Nazzjon Toghna

Independent Print, Triq Herbert Ganado St., Jamrun HMR 08, Malta
PHONE: +356 243641
FAX: +356 242886
E-MAIL: nazzjon@vol.net.mt
WEBSITE: http://www.vol.net.mt
TITLE: Editor-in-Chief
CONTACT: Joseph Zahra
CIRCULATION: 22,000

It-Torca (The Torch)

A41 Industrial Estate, Marsa, Malta
PHONE: +356 247687
FAX: +356 238484
TITLE: Editor-in-Chief
CONTACT: Alfred Briffa
CIRCULATION: 30,000

Kullhadd

Ufficyu Editorjali, Centru Nazzjonali Laburista, Hamrun HMR 102, Malta
E-MAIL: kullhadd@keyworld.net
WEBSITE: http://www.keyworld.net/kullhadd

The Malta Business Weekly

Standard Publications Ltd., Standard House, Birkirkara Hill, St. Julians STJ 09, Malta
PHONE: +356 345888
FAX: +356 344884
E-MAIL: tmbw@mail.independent.com.mt
WEBSITE: http://www.business-line.com/business-weekly

The Malta Independent

Standard Publications Ltd., Standard House, Birkikiara Hill, St. Julians STJ 09, Malta
PHONE: +356 345888
FAX: +356 346062
E-MAIL: spltd@maltanet.net
TITLE: Editor
CONTACT: Andy Round

The Malta Independent on Sunday

Standard Publications Ltd., Standard House, Birkikara Hill, St. Julians STJ 09, Malta
PHONE: +356 345888
FAX: +356 346062
E-MAIL: spltd@maltanet.net
TITLE: Editor
CONTACT: Anthony Manduca

L'Orrizant

A41 Industrial Estate, Marsa, Malta
PHONE: +356 247687
FAX: +356 238484
TITLE: Editor-in-Chief
CONTACT: Francis Ghirxi
CIRCULATION: 20,000

The People

People Enterprises Ltd., Headlines House, Bone Alley, Mriehel BKR 14, Malta
PHONE: +356 445455
FAX: +356 445563

Times/Sunday Times

Allied Newspapers Ltd., 341 St. Paul St., Box 328, Vallette CMR01, Malta
PHONE: +356 241464
FAX: +356 240806
TITLE: Editors
CONTACT: Victor Aquilina (Times), Lawrence Grech (Sunday Times)
CIRCULATION: 36,000

Malta Today

Network Publications, Vjal Ir-Rihan, San Gwann SGN 07, Malta
PHONE: +356 382741
E-MAIL: editorial@networkpublications.com.mt
WEBSITE: http://www.maltamag.com
TITLE: Editor-in-Chief
CONTACT: Saviour Balzan
TYPE: Social science, business and economics, general

PUBLISHERS

Gaulitana

2, Triq Gedrin, Rabat, Gozo, VCT 104, Malta
PHONE: +356 554212
FAX: +356 554212
E-MAIL: joseph.bezzina@magnet.mt
SUBJECTS: History, Catholicism, Travel

Gozo Press

Mgarr Rd., Victoria, VCT 103, Gozo, Malta
PHONE: +356 551534; 564395
FAX: +356 560857

E-MAIL: gozopress@orbit.net.mt
WEBSITE: http://www.homestead.com.cauchy/Index2.html
TITLE: Director
CONTACT: Achilles F. Cauchi
SUBJECTS: Crafts, Hobbies, Games, History, Literature, Literary Criticism, Essays, Religion
TOTAL PUBLISHED: 24 print

Media Centre

National Rd., Blata I-Bajda, HMR 02, Malta
PHONE: +356 249005; 223047, 247460
FAX: +356 243508
E-MAIL: joseborg@keyworld.net
TITLE: President
CONTACT: Joseph Borg
SUBJECTS: Biblical Studies, Communications, Education, Catholicism, Social Sciences

Patrimonju Publishing Ltd.

115 Triq it-Teatru 1 Qadim, Valletta, VLT 07, Malta
PHONE: +356 231515
FAX: +356 250118
E-MAIL: patrimonju@keyworld.net
WEBSITE: http://www.patrimonju.org.mt
TITLE: Executive
CONTACT: Peter Calascione
SUBJECTS: Antiques, Archaeology, Art, Biography
TOTAL PUBLISHED: 12 print

Progress Press Co. Ltd.

Strickland House, 341 St. Paul St., Valetta, VTL 01, Malta
PHONE: +356 241464
FAX: +356 241411
TITLE: Man Director
CONTACT: W. B. Asciak
SUBJECTS: Literature, Literary Criticism, Essays
TOTAL PUBLISHED: 46 print

Publishers' Enterprises Group (PEG) Ltd.

PEG Bldg., UB7 Industrial Estate, San Gwann, SGN 09, Malta
PHONE: +356 440083; 448539
FAX: +356 488908
E-MAIL: pegltd@global.net.mt
WEBSITE: http://www.peg.com.mt
TITLE: Man. Director, Rights & Permissions
CONTACT: Emanuel Debattista
SUBJECTS: Children's Books, Cookery, Fiction, History, Education
TOTAL PUBLISHED: 300 print

The University of Malta Publications Section

Administration Bldg., Msida, MSD 06, Malta
PHONE: +356 343572
FAX: +356 344879
SUBJECTS: Ethnicity, Language Arts, Linguistics, Law, Natural History, Regional Interests

RELIGIOUS ORGANIZATIONS

Malta is 98 percent Roman Catholic with a small Protestant minority.

FURTHER READING

Articles

"EU Applicants Await Entry Dispute," *Financial Times,* May 12, 2000.

"Safety Testimony at Lockerbie Trial," *AP,* July 14, 2000.

Books

Dun and Bradstreet's Export Guide to Malta. Parsippany, NJ: Dun & Bradstreet, 1999.

Wilson, Neil. *Malta.* London: Lonely Planet, 2000.

MALTA: STATISTICAL DATA

For sources and notes see "Sources of Statistics" at the front of each volume.

GEOGRAPHY

Geography

Area:

Total: 316 sq km.

Land: 316 sq km.

Land boundaries: 0 km.

Coastline: 140 km.

Climate: Mediterranean with mild, rainy winters and hot, dry summers.

Terrain: mostly low, rocky, flat to dissected plains; many coastal cliffs.

Natural resources: limestone, salt, arable land.

Land use:

Arable land: 38%

Permanent crops: 3%

Permanent pastures: 0%

Forests and woodland: 0%

Other: 59% (1993 est.).

HUMAN FACTORS

Health Indicators

	National Data	World Data
Life expectancy at birth (years)		
1970-1975	70.6	59.9
1995-2000	77.2	66.7
Daily per capita supply of calories		
1970	3,147	2,358
1997	3,398	2,791
Daily per capital supply of protein		
1997 (grams)	110	74
People living with (1997)		
Tuberculosis (cases per 100,000)	3.0	60.4
Malaria (cases per 100,000)	NA	42.2
HIV/AIDS (% aged 15 - 49 years)	0.11	0.99

Demographics (A)

	1990	1995	1998	2000	2010	2020	2030	2040	2050
Population	NA	NA	385.8	391.7	420.3	441.5	448.5	443.6	431.6
Life expectancy - males	NA	NA	75.1	75.5	76.9	78.1	79.1	79.8	80.4
Life expectancy - females	NA	NA	80.3	80.6	82.3	83.6	84.7	85.5	86.2
Birth rate (per 1,000)	NA	NA	12.8	12.7	12.5	11.1	10.1	9.9	9.3
Death rate (per 1,000)	NA	NA	7.7	7.7	8.3	9.5	11.1	12.4	12.8
Women of reproductive age (15-49 yrs.)	NA	NA	95.8	95.7	94.7	94.6	92.7	87.8	83.8
Fertility rate	NA	NA	1.9	1.9	1.9	1.8	1.8	1.7	1.7

Except as noted, values for vital statistics are in thousands; life expectancy is in years.

Ethnic Division

Maltese (descendants of ancient Carthaginians and Phoenicians, with strong elements of Italian and other Mediterranean stock).

Religion

Roman Catholic 91%

Major Languages

Maltese (official), English (official).

EDUCATION

Educational Attainment (B)

	1995	1997
Gross enrollment ratio (%)		
Primary level	106.7	107.5
	1995	**1997**
Secondary level	84.1	84.4
Tertiary level	26.0	29.0

Literacy Rates (B)

	National Data	World Data
Adult literacy rate		
1980		
Male	83	75
Female	84	58
1995		
Male	90	81
Female	91	65

Libraries

National Libraries 1992

Administrative Units 1

Service Points or Branches .1

Number of Volumes (000) 373

Registered Users (000) . . . . .NA

Loans to Users (000) . . . . .NA

Total Library Staff 43

Public Libraries 1995

Administrative Units 2

Service Points or Branches .3

Number of Volumes (000) 526

Registered Users (000) .216

Loans to Users (000) 833

Total Library Staff . . . . .NA

GOVERNMENT & LAW

Political Parties

House of Representatives	% of vote	no. of seats
Nationalist Party (PN)	51.8%	35
Malta Labor Party (MLP)	46.9%	30
Alternativa Demokratika/Alliance for Social Justice (AD)	1.2%	

Elections were last held 5 September 1998 (next to be held by September 2003).

Government Budgets (A)

Year: 1997

Total Expenditures: 535.42 Millions of Liri

Expenditures as a percentage of the total by function:

General public services and public order 11.88

Defense 2.09

Education 12.18

Health 9.93

Social Security and Welfare 34.43

Housing and community amenities 9.45

Recreational, cultural, and religious affairs 2.15

Fuel and energy 0.16

Agriculture, forestry, fishing, and hunting 1.34

Mining, manufacturing, and construction 2.67

Transportation and communication 4.71

Other economic affairs and services 2.61

Crime

Crime rate (for 1997)

Crimes reported 13,300

Total persons convicted .NA

Crimes per 100,000 population 3,500

(Continued on next page.)

LABOR FORCE

Total Labor Force (A)

143,700 (October 1997).

Labor Force by Occupation

Industry 24%

Services 71%

Agriculture 5%

Data for 1999 est.

Unemployment Rate

5.5% (September 1999)

PRODUCTION SECTOR

Energy Production

Production ....1.62 billion kWh

Production by source

Fossil fuel 100%

Hydro 0%

Nuclear 0%

Other 0%

Exports ....0 kWh

Data for 1998.

Energy Consumption

Consumption ....1.507 billion kWh

Imports ....0 kWh

Data for 1998.

Transportation

Highways:

Total: 1,742 km.

Paved: 1,677 km.

Unpaved: 65 km (1997 est.).

Merchant marine:

Total: 1,484 ships (1,000 GRT or over) totaling 28,083,952 GRT/46,772,146 DWT.

Ships by type: bulk 431, cargo 424, chemical tanker 54, combination bulk 16, combination ore/oil 14, container 64, liquified gas 2, livestock carrier 3, multi-functional large load carrier 4, passenger 7, petroleum tanker 331, refrigerated cargo 44, roll-on/roll-off 48, short-sea passenger 21, specialized tanker 5, vehicle carrier 16 (1999 est.).

(Continued on next page.)

GOVERNMENT & LAW (cont.)

Military Affairs (A)

	1990	1992	1995	1996	1997
Military expenditures					
Current dollars (mil.)	18	24	30	31	31
1997 constant dollars (mil.)	21	27	31	32	31
Armed forces (000)	2	2	2	2	2
Gross national product (GNP)					
Current dollars (mil.)	2,190	2,540	3,040	3,180	3,370
1997 constant dollars (mil.)	2,570	2,810	3,150	3,230	3,370
Central government expenditures (CGE)					
1997 constant dollars (mil.)	1,060	1,030	1,190	1,330	1,490
People (mil.)	0.4	0.4	0.4	0.4	0.4
Military expenditure as % of GNP	0.8	0.9	1.0	1.0	0.9
World data on military expenditure as % of GNP	4.5	3.4	2.7	2.6	2.6
Military expenditure as % of CGE	2.0	2.6	2.6	2.4	2.0
World data on military expenditure as % of CGE	17.0	12.5	10.5	10.3	10.2
Military expenditure per capita (1997 $)	60	74	83	86	81
World data on military expenditure per capita (1997 $)	242	173	146	143	145
Armed forces per 1,000 people (soldiers)	5.6	4.2	4.0	4.0	4.0
World data on armed forces per 1,000 people (soldiers)	5.3	4.5	4.1	3.9	3.8
GNP per capita (1997 $)	7,260	7,800	8,470	8,630	8,940
Total imports[7]					
Current dollars (mil.)	1,964	2,331	2,890	2,801	2,556
1997 constant dollars (mil.)	2,300	2,584	2,992	2,848	2,556
Total exports[7]					
Current dollars (mil.)	1,133	1,540	1,861	1,736	1,642
1997 constant dollars (mil.)	1,327	1,707	1,927	1,765	1,642
Arms as percent of total imports[8]	0	0	0	0	0
Arms as percent of total exports[8]	0	0	0	0	0

PRODUCTION SECTOR (cont.)

Transportation (cont.)

Note: a flag of convenience registry; includes ships from 49 countries among which includes Greece 445, Russia 51, Switzerland 45, Italy 44, Norway 40, Croatia 26, Turkey 35, Germany 32, Georgia 23, and Monaco 24 (1998 est.).

Airports: 1 (1999 est.).

Top Agriculture Products

Potatoes, cauliflower, grapes, wheat, barley, tomatoes, citrus, cut flowers, green peppers; pork, milk, poultry, eggs.

Top Mining Products (B)

Mineral resources include: limestone, salt.

MANUFACTURING SECTOR

GDP & Manufacturing Summary (A)

	1980	1985	1990	1995
GDP ($-1990 mil.)[1]	1,577	1,715	2,318	3,000
Per capita ($-1990)[1]	4,866	4,987	6,547	8,173
Manufacturing share (%) (current prices)[1]	33.1	29.5	27.0	NA
Manufacturing				
Value added ($-1990 mil.)[1]	464	457	554	718[e]
Industrial production index	72	75	100	146[e]
Value added ($ mil.)	302	265	511	661[e]
Gross output ($ mil.)	706	650	1,637	2,611[e]
Employment (000)	29	26	27	28[e]
Profitability (% of gross output)				
Intermediate input (%)	57	59	69	75[e]
Wages and salaries inc. supplements (%)	23[e]	22	17[e]	13[e]
Gross operating surplus	20[e]	19	15[e]	13[e]
Productivity ($)				
Gross output per worker	23,265	24,271	58,341	88,220[e]
Value added per worker	9,945	9,914	18,230	23,179[e]
Average wage (inc. supplements)	5,653[e]	5,561	10,150[e]	11,943[e]
Value added ($ mil.)				
Food products	20	25	56	65[e]
Beverages	20	22	42	60[e]
Tobacco products	8	8	9	7[e]
Textiles	17	8	17	16[e]
Wearing apparel	88	65	80	91[e]
Leather and fur products	4	1	2	6[e]
Footwear	8	9	12	19[e]
Wood and wood products	2	1	2	3[e]
Furniture and fixtures	14	9	28	35[e]
Paper and paper products	2	3	7	10[e]
Printing and publishing	22	17	34	61[e]
Industrial chemicals	1	2	2	3[e]
Other chemical products	5	6	14[e]	25[e]
Rubber products	10	7	17	21[e]
Plastic products	6	4	11	17[e]
Pottery, china and earthenware	1	NA	1	1[e]
Glass and glass products	2	1	2	2[e]
Other non-metal mineral products	6	7	15	24[e]
Metal products	14	10	26	26[e]
Non-electrical machinery	5	8	8	12[e]
Electrical machinery	22	31	61	88[e]
Transport equipment	6	3	27	10[e]
Prof. and scientific equipment	12	12	19	24[e]
Other manufacturing	8	5	21	35[e]

COMMUNICATIONS

Daily Newspapers

	National Data	World Data for Comparison
Daily Newspapers		
Number of Dailies	2	8,391
Total Circulation (000)	48	548,000
Circulation per 1,000 inhabitants	127	96

Telecommunications

Telephones - main lines in use: 171,000 (1995).

Telephones - mobile cellular: 15,650 (1999).

Telephone system: automatic system satisfies normal requirements.

Domestic: submarine cable and microwave radio relay between islands.

International: 2 submarine cables; satellite earth station - 1 Intelsat (Atlantic Ocean).

Radio broadcast stations: AM 1, FM 18, shortwave 6 (1999).

Radios: 255,000 (1997).

Television broadcast stations: 6 (1999).

Televisions: 280,000 (1997).

Internet Service Providers (ISPs): 4 (1999).

FINANCE, ECONOMICS, & TRADE

Economic Indicators

National product: GDP—purchasing power parity—$5.3 billion (1999 est.).

National product real growth rate: 4% (1999 est.).

National product per capita: $13,800 (1999 est.).

Inflation rate—consumer price index: 1.8% (1999 est.).

Exchange Rates

Exchange rates:

Maltese liri (LM) per US$1

January 2000 .... 0.4086
1999 .... 0.3994
1998 .... 0.3885
1997 .... 0.3857
1996 .... 0.3604
1995 .... 0.3529

Top Import Origins

$2.7 billion (f.o.b., 1998)

Origins (1998)

Italy 19.3%
France 17.8%
United Kingdom 12.4%
Germany 10.5%
United States 8.9%

Top Export Destinations

$1.8 billion (f.o.b., 1998)

Destinations (1998)

France 20.7%
United States 18.1%
Germany 12.6%
United Kingdom 7.7%
Italy 4.8%

Import/Export Commodities

Import Commodities	Export Commodities
Machinery and transport equipment	Machinery and transport equipment
Manufactured goods	Manufactures
Food	
Drink	
Tobacco	

Balance of Payments

	1994	1995	1996	1997	1998
Exports of goods (f.o.b.)	1,618	1,948	1,773	1,663	1,822
Imports of goods (f.o.b.)	−2,221	−2,671	−2,536	−2,320	−2,415
Trade balance	−603	−723	−763	−657	−592
Services - debits	−687	−808	−820	−793	−827
Services - credits	995	1,082	1,117	1,167	1,240
Private transfers (net)	66	52	54	69	54
Government transfers (net)	32	10	57	30	28
Overall balance	−132	−358	−357	−207	−169

ISLE OF MAN

CAPITAL: Douglas.

FLAG: The flag of the Isle of Man is red with the Three Legs of Man emblem (Trinacria), in the center; the three legs are joined at the thigh and bent at the knee; in order to have the toes pointing clockwise on both sides of the flag, a two-sided emblem is used.

ANTHEM: *God Save the Queen.*

MONETARY UNIT: 1 Manx pound (£M) = 100 pence.

WEIGHTS AND MEASURES: The metric system is used.

HOLIDAYS: New Year's Day, 1 January; Good Friday; Easter Monday; May Day, first Monday in May; May Bank Holiday, last Day in May; Senior TT Race Day, Friday of the first full week in June; Tynwald Day, 5 July; August Bank Holiday, last Monday in August; Christmas Day; Boxing Day, 26 December.

TIME: Noon = noon GMT.

LOCATION AND SIZE: The islands comprising the United Kingdom of Great Britain and Northern Ireland lie off the northwest coast of the European Continent. Located in the Irish Sea between Great Britain and Ireland (54°15′N, 4°30′W), the Isle of Man comprises a total land mass of 588 sq. km.

CLIMATE: The Isle of Man experiences cool, humid summers and mild winters. Prevailing southwesterly winds make the climate temperate and equable year round. Weather patterns frequently change, but few temperature extremes occur. Temperatures range from a mean of 4.5°C (40°F) in winter to about 15.5°C (60°F) in summer. A low of −6.5°C (20°F) is sometimes reached during winter, and a high of 32°C (90°F) may infrequently occur in summer. Humidity in summer ranges from 50 percent to 80 percent. Average annual rainfall is 76–127 cm (30–50 inches), usually distributed evenly throughout the year.

INTRODUCTORY SURVEY

RECENT HISTORY

The Isle took its name from later inhabitants, the Celts, whose language, Manx, persisted until the nineteenth century. By 1828 England acquired all of the Atholl's interests in Man. The Isle became a British Crown possession and remains a dependency of the Crown. The Isle is locally self-ruling with its own legislative assemblies, system of law, and taxation systems.

GOVERNMENT

The Isle of Man is an autonomous sovereign country under the British Crown with its own legislature and judiciary. The head of state, referred to as the Lord of Mann, is the British monarch. The British monarch's personal representative on the island is the lieutenant governor, appointed by the Crown for a five-year term. The head of government known as the Chief Minister administers the island. The legislative branch elects the Chief of Minister. The Council of Ministers consists of the Chief Minister and ministers of major departments, including Treasury; Agriculture; Fisheries and Forestry; Education; Health and Social Security, Home Affairs, Local Government and the Environment; Tourism and Leisure, Trade and Industry, and Transport.

A bicameral legislature, known as Tynwald, consists of the ten-member Legislative Council and the 24-seat House of Keys. The Legislative Council is composed of the President of Tynwald, the Lord Bishop of Sodor and Man, a non-voting attorney general, and eight members selected by the House

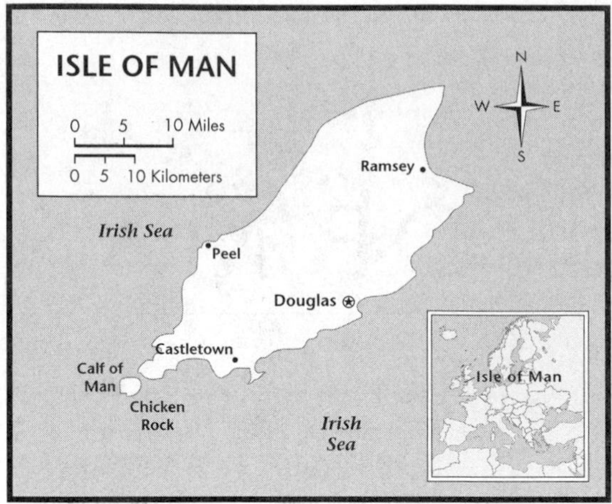

of Keys. The House of Keys, one of the most ancient legislative assemblies in the world, has twenty-four members elected by adult suffrage, twenty-four years of age and older, for five-year terms. These two branches of Tynwald sit as one body but vote separately on questions except on certain occasions.

Twenty-four local authorities are elected in the Isle. The Isle of Man is represented in neither the United Kingdom nor European parliaments.

Judiciary

The Isle of Man administers its own common and statute law that essentially parallels the law and principles of equity in English courts but modified to meet local needs. Although based on the English system the Isle's judiciary operates independently and includes the High Court of Justice and the Manx Court of Appeal. The final court of appeal for court decisions in the Isle of Man is the Judicial Committee of the Privy Council in England.

Political Parties

No political party system operates on the Isle of Man. Members of the legislature sit as independents.

DEFENSE

The defense of the Isle of Man is the responsibility of the United Kingdom. The Isle makes financial contributions to defray costs of this service.

ECONOMIC AFFAIRS

Offshore financial services, high technology manufacturing, and tourism are key sectors of the Isle of Man's economy. With the ability to set low taxation rates, the government successfully attracted high technology companies and financial institutions thereby expanding employment opportunities in high-income industries. Banking and other services contribute approximately 80 percent of the Isle's gross domestic product (GDP) while tourism accounts for 6 percent. Income from construction, transport and communication, and retail distribution is also significant.

Fishing and agriculture, once important mainstays of the economy, now account for only 2 percent of GDP. Scallops are the principle fish of the Manx fleet. The agricultural sector produces cereals and potatoes in addition to raising sheep, cattle, poultry, and pigs.

Although the Isle of Man is neither a member nor contributes funds to or receives money from the European Union (EU) trade organization, a special relationship limited to trade rights does exist between the two. The Isle enjoys free access to EU markets for trade and adopts EU's external trade policies and tariff with non-EU countries. The Isle of Man's rate of unemployment in 1999 was 0.7 percent.

Public Finance

Major revenue areas are customs duties and income tax. The standard personal income tax rate is primarily 15 percent although a 20 percent rate also exists. Business tax rate is 20 percent of taxable income. Revenue is also raised through taxes on expenditures, health and social security contributions, and fees and charges for services. Major expenditure items are social security, health services, and education.

The Isle of Man is required by law to budget for a surplus of estimated revenue over expenditure. The U.S. Central Intelligence Agency (CIA) estimated 1999 revenues at $816 million with expenditures of $504 million.

Income

The CIA estimated the 1998 GDP to be $1.2 billion, or $16,000 per capita. The inflation rate was estimated at 2 percent in 1999. The 1999 GDP contribution by sector was estimated to be agriculture 1 percent, industry 10 percent, and services 89 percent.

Industry

In 1999 banking and financial services coupled with professional and scientific services accounted for 36 percent of employment. The manufacturing, construction, transport and communication, and retail distribution industries each employed approximately 10 percent of the labor force. The tourism sector also contributes to the Isle's economy.

Banking and Finance

The Isle of Man Government Financial Supervision Commission regulates licensing authorization and supervision of banks, building societies, and investment businesses. Likewise the commission is responsible for financial intermediaries who give financial advice and those who receive clients' money for investment and management. In 1991 the Commission established a compensation fund to protect investors.

In 1998 approximately sixty-seven banks, eighty-one investment businesses, and three building societies were licensed in the Isle. The Insurance and Pensions Authority regulates the insurance industry with 200 companies licensed. The Isle of Man issues its own notes and coin. United Kingdom coins and notes are also legal tender.

SOCIAL WELFARE

Major government expenditures include social security, health services, and education. Approximately 60 percent of social security system government expenditures went to the elderly in 1997-1998. Benefits to residents include retirement pensions, unemployment benefit, sick and disablement benefit, child benefit, and supplementary benefit.

Healthcare

Since 1948 the Isle of Man's National Health Service has provided medical, dental, and ophthalmic services. The Isle has two hospitals and a third was under construction in 1999. Life expectancy for the total population in 2000 was estimated at 77.5 years, male 74.9 years, and female eighty-one years.

EDUCATION

Between the ages of five and sixteen education is compulsory. In 1998 approximately 6,300 students attended thirty-three primary schools and 4,700 attended secondary schools operated by the Department of Education. The Department also operates one college. Education is a key government expenditure.

2000 KEY EVENTS TIMELINE

May

- The Isle of Man wants to set a policy limiting immigration similar to policies in force on neighboring Guernsey and Jersey. Non-Manx workers now need a permit or green card to work on the Isle of Man. The island does not seek independence.
- British Telecom (BT) opens the world's first 3G universal mobile telecommunications system on the island.

June

- Under pressure from the Financial Action Task Force on Money Laundering (FATF) based in Paris, France, the Isle of Man says it will cooperate to eliminate illegal offshore banking and money-laundering practices. Guernsey and Jersey are also listed as cooperating with FATF.

September

- The Isle of Man sponsors the Tourist Trophy Races. These are very dangerous motorcycle, moped, and motor scooter races in which many people have died or been injured.

October

- A new Lieutenant Governor, Air Marshal Ian Macfadyen, is sworn in at Castle Rushan.
- On October 13, the Manx (Isle of Man) electric railway reports a 28 percent increase in riders due to an improved on-time record. The railway considers transporting school children.

November

- The Financial Supervisory Commission of the Organization for Economic Cooperation and Development (OECD) appoints Neil Kennedy and Paul Heckles on November 30 to head up a task force to counter money laundering on the Isle of Man.

ANALYSIS OF EVENTS: 2000

BUSINESS AND THE ECONOMY

The main source of revenue for the Isle of Man in 2000 was the banking and financial sector. The island had very low tax rates which encouraged companies to make their corporate headquarters on the island. The capital city of Douglas was home to over sixty banks. The Minister of the Treasury, the Honorable R.K. Corkill, wanted the island to remain competitive and proposed a new income tax rate that would tax corporations 10 percent and others 15 percent. Naturally, as a tax haven, the Isle of Man was targeted by the Organization for Economic Cooperation and Development (OECD) to comply with its regulations. The Isle of Man agreed, but said it would still issue economic incentives for new investors. Also the establishment of a duty free port on the island helped the manufacturing business to become highly successful. This free port also encouraged tourism.

GOVERNMENT AND POLITICS

The Isle of Man is a Crown Colony but is not part of the United Kingdom. It has a working relationship with the European Union and its governor is appointed by Queen Elizabeth II. In October the Queen appointed Ian Macfadyen as the Lieutenant Governor. Locally elected officials are in charge of internal affairs. These are conducted by the *Tynwald* or Parliament. The Isle of Man has its own tax system, which is much lower than that of the United Kingdom, and the island has no Value Added Tax (VAT), which makes it a shopper's haven. The Isle of Man's residents have no desire for political independence. They already control their own taxation and immigration laws. Workers who come to the island must have work permits and visitors have only a six month visa.

CULTURE AND SOCIETY

The heritage of the people of the Isle of Man goes back over one thousand years to the Celts and the Vikings who first colonized the island's approximately 227 square miles. The first inhabitants were Christian and probably farmed the land. In 2000, the land was not very arable and most of the citizens worked in the banking and financial sectors. Although the major language is English, Celtic and Gaelic dialects are popular. The island is known as *Ellan Vannin Veg Veen*, meaning "The Dear Little Isle of Man" in Gaelic. Although not officially a part of the United Kingdom, the Isle of Man is a Crown colony and is administered by a governor appointed by Queen Elizabeth II. The most famous resident of the Isle of Man is probably the Manx cat, which is noted for not having a tail. The Isle of Man also hosts a very famous motorcycle race called the Tourist Trophy (TT) races. These races involve mopeds, motorcycles, sidecar motorcycles, and motor scooters. Often riders are killed because these courses are so dangerous. The race moved to the Isle of Man in 1907 because Great Britain imposed strict speed limits on public highways. The TT races are run on public roads. Held in the summer, the TT races are preceded by a huge festival, which attracts a great many tourists to the island every year.

DIRECTORY

CENTRAL GOVERNMENT

Head of State

Monarch
Elizabeth II, Queen of England

Lieutenant-Governor
Timothy Daunt

Chief Minister
D. J. Gelling, Office of the Chief Minister
PHONE: +44 (1624) 685711

Ministers

Minister of Agriculture, Fisheries and Forestry
T. A. Warren, Ministry of Agriculture, Fisheries and Forestry, Murray House, Mount Havelock, Douglas, Isle of Man
PHONE: +44 (1624) 685835

Minister of Education
R. B. Cowin, Ministry of Education, Murray House, Mount Havelock, Douglas, IM1 2SG, Isle of Man
PHONE: +44 (1624) 685820
FAX: +44 (1624) 685834

Minister of Health and Social Security
Ministry of Health and Social Security, Markwell House, Market Street, Douglas, IM1 2RZ, Isle of Man
PHONE: +44 (1624) 685028

Minister of Home Affairs
M. Williams, Ministry of Home Affairs, Homefield, 88 Woodbourne Road, Douglas, IM2 3AP, Isle of Man
PHONE: +44 (1624) 623355
FAX: +44 (1624) 621298

Minister of Local Government and the Environment
R. A. Hamilton, Ministry of Local Government and the Environment, Murray House, Mount Havelock, Douglas, IM1 2SF, Isle of Man
PHONE: +44 (1624) 685954

Minister of Tourism and Leisure
T. P. Toohey, Ministry of Tourism and Leisure, Sea Terminal Building, Douglas, IM1 2RG, Isle of Man
PHONE: +44 (1624) 686801

Minister of Trade and Industry
K. B. Bawden, Ministry of Trade and Industry, Illiam Dhone House, 2 Circular Road, Douglas, IM1 1PJ, Isle of Man
PHONE: +44 (1624) 685675
FAX: +44 (1624) 685683

Minister of Transport
N. R. Cooil, Ministry of Transport, Sea Terminal Building, Douglas, Isle of Man
PHONE: +44 (1624) 686600

Minister of the Treasury
J. A. Cashen, Ministry of the Treasury, Government Office, Buck's Road, Douglas, Isle of Man
PHONE: +44 (1624) 685586

POLITICAL ORGANIZATIONS

Mec Vannin

E-MAIL: mkermode@mcb.net

JUDICIAL SYSTEM

High Court

PHONE: +44 (1624) 685242

BROADCAST MEDIA

Manx Radio

PO Box 1368, Broadcasting House, Douglas, Isle of Man, IM99 1SW
PHONE: +44 (1624) 682600
FAX: +44 (1624) 682604
E-MAIL: postbox@manxradio.com
WEBSITE: http://www.manxradio.com/

Radio TT 2000

Valicot Cottage, Glen Maye, Isle of Man, IM5 3BJ, British Isles
PHONE: +44 (1624) 843858
WEBSITE: http://www.radiott.com/
CONTACT: Roger Hurst

Manx Television

Manx Radio Buildings, Douglas, Isle of Man
PHONE: +44 (1624) 8606627
WEBSITE: http://www.manx-tv.com/

Isle of Man International Broadcasting PLC (IMIB)

PO Box 279, Ramsey, Isle of Man IM88 4HT
PHONE: +44 (1624) 818151
FAX: +44 (1624) 817094
E-MAIL: reception"longwave.radio.com
WEBSITE: http://www.279longwave.com/

COLLEGES AND UNIVERSITIES

Isle of Man College

Homefield Road, Douglas, Isle of Man IM2 6RB
PHONE: +44 (1624) 623113

NEWSPAPERS AND MAGAZINES

Isle of Man Newspapers, Ltd.: Isle of Man Examiner, Isle of Man Courier, Manx Independent

Publishing House, Peel Rd., Douglas, Isle of Man IM1 5PZ
PHONE: +44 (1624) 623451
FAX: +44 (1624) 661041
E-MAIL: lionel-cowin@isle-of-man-newspapers.com
WEBSITE: http://www.iomonline.com
TITLE: Editorial Director
CONTACT: Lionel Cowin

RELIGIOUS ORGANIZATIONS

Although locally self-ruling, the Isle of Man retains close ties with the United Kingdom, and religious organizations of significance are generally handled through London.

FURTHER READING

Articles

"Closing the Isle of Man." *The Economist (US),* May 6, 2000, vol. 355, no. 8169.

"Isle of Man." *Wall Street Journal,* March 23, 2000, p. C25.

Internet

BBC News Online. "Sanctions Threat to 'Tax Havens.'" June 26, 2000. [Online] Available http://news6.thdo.bbc.co.uk/hi/english/business/newsid%5F806000/806236.stm (accessed October 12, 2000).

ISLE OF MAN: STATISTICAL DATA

For sources and notes see "Sources of Statistics" at the front of each volume.

GEOGRAPHY

Geography

Area:

Total: 572 sq km.

Land: 572 sq km.

Land boundaries: 0 km.

Coastline: 160 km.

Climate: cool summers and mild winters; temperate; overcast about one-third of the time.

Terrain: hills in north and south bisected by central valley.

Natural resources: none.

Land use:

Arable land: 9%

Permanent crops: 0%

Permanent pastures: 46%

Forests and woodland: 6%

Other: 39% (includes 25% mountain and heathland).

HUMAN FACTORS

Ethnic Division

Manx (Norse-Celtic descent), Briton.

Religion

Anglican, Roman Catholic, Methodist, Baptist, Presbyterian, Society of Friends.

Major Languages

English, Manx, Gaelic.

Demographics (A)

	1990	1995	1998	2000	2010	2020	2030	2040	2050
Population	68.8	71.4	72.4	73.1	77.0	80.4	82.5	82.3	80.1
Life expectancy - males	72.5	73.5	73.7	74.1	75.8	77.2	78.3	79.2	79.9
Life expectancy - females	78.1	79.1	80.7	81.0	82.6	83.9	84.9	85.7	86.3
Birth rate (per 1,000)	12.9	11.9	11.7	11.6	10.7	10.4	9.9	9.4	9.2
Death rate (per 1,000)	13.8	13.7	12.3	12.0	10.8	10.5	11.2	12.0	13.2
Women of reproductive age (15-49 yrs.)	16.5	17.0	17.1	17.1	18.0	17.9	17.3	16.6	15.5
Fertility rate	1.8	1.7	1.6	1.6	1.6	1.7	1.7	1.7	1.7

Except as noted, values for vital statistics are in thousands; life expectancy is in years.

GOVERNMENT & LAW

Political Parties

The bicameral Tynwald consists of the Legislative Council (a 10-member body composed of the Lord Bishop of Sodor and Man, a nonvoting attorney general, and 8 others named by the House of Keys) and the House of Keys (24 seats; members are elected by popular vote to serve five-year terms). Elections for the House of Keys was last held 21 November 1996 (next to be held in November 2001). There is no party system. Members sit as independents.

Government Budgets (B)

Revenues	$816 million
Expenditures	$504 million

Data for FY99/00 est.

LABOR FORCE

Total Labor Force (A)

36,610 (1998).

Labor Force by Occupation

Agriculture, forestry and fishing	3%
Manufacturing	11%
Construction	10%
Transport and communication	8%
Wholesale and retail distribution	11%
Professional and scientific services	18%
Public administration	6%
Banking and finance	18%
Tourism	2%
Entertainment and catering	3%
Miscellaneous services	10%

Unemployment Rate

0.7% (July 1999)

PRODUCTION SECTOR

Energy Production

Production	329 million kWh
Production by source	
Fossil fuel	100%
Hydro	0%
Nuclear	0%
Other	0%

Data for 1999.

Energy Consumption

Consumption	287 million kWh

Data for 1999.

Transportation

Highways:

Total: 800 km.

Paved: 800 km.

Unpaved: 0 km (1999).

Merchant marine:

Total: 144 ships (1,000 GRT or over) totaling 4,333,826 GRT/7,254,867 DWT.

Ships by type: bulk 23, cargo 6, chemical tanker 13, combination bulk 3, container 20, liquified gas 13, petroleum tanker 44, refrigerated cargo 2, roll-on/roll-off 15, vehicle carrier 5 (1999 est.).

Note: a flag of convenience registry; UK owns 8 ships, Denmark 1, Sweden 1, Belgium 1, and Netherlands 1 (1998 est.).

Airports: 1 (1999 est.).

Top Agriculture Products

Cereals, vegetables; cattle, sheep, pigs, poultry.

MANUFACTURING SECTOR

GDP & Manufacturing Summary (C)

Total GDP (1998 est.)	$1.2 billion
Real growth rate	NA
Per capita (1998 est.)	$16,000
Composition by sector	
Agriculture	1%
Industry	10%
Services	89%

Values in purchasing power parity. NA stands for not available.

COMMUNICATIONS

Telecommunications

Telephones - main lines in use: 51,000 (1999).

Telephones - mobile cellular: NA

Telephone system:

Domestic: landline, telefax, mobile cellular telephone system.

International: fiber-optic cable, microwave radio relay, satellite earth station, submarine cable.

Radio broadcast stations: AM 1, FM 1, shortwave 0 (1998).

Radios: NA

Television broadcast stations: 0 (receives broadcasts from the UK and satellite) (1999).

Televisions: 27,490 (1999).

Internet Service Providers (ISPs): NA

FINANCE, ECONOMICS, & TRADE

Economic Indicators

National product: GDP—purchasing power parity—$1.2 billion (1998 est.).

National product real growth rate: NA.

National product per capita: $16,000 (1998 est.).

Inflation rate—consumer price index: 2% (1999 est.).

Exchange Rates

Exchange rates:

Manx pounds per US$1

January 2000	0.6092
1999	0.6180
1998	0.6037
1997	0.6106
1996	0.6403
1995	0.6335

The Manx pound is at par with the British pound. Fiscal year: 1 April – 31 March.

Top Import Origins

Origins: United Kingdom.

Top Export Destinations

Destination: United Kingdom.

Import/Export Commodities

Import Commodities	Export Commodities
Timber	Tweeds
Fertilizers	Herring
Fish	Processed shellfish
	Beef
	Lamb

MARSHALL ISLANDS

Republic of the Marshall Islands

CAPITAL: Majuro, Majuro Atoll.

FLAG: The flag, adopted in 1979, is blue, with two diagonal strips of orange over white; in the canton is a white star with 4 large rays and 20 shorter ones.

ANTHEM: *Ij iokwe lok aelon eo ao ijo iaar lotak ie* (I Love My Island, Where I Was Born).

MONETARY UNIT: The U.S. dollar is the official medium of exchange.

WEIGHTS AND MEASURES: British units are used, as modified by U.S. usage.

HOLIDAYS: The government has not legislated official holidays.

TIME: 11 PM = noon GMT.

LOCATION AND SIZE: The Marshall Islands is located in the central Pacific Ocean, just north of the equator. The country consists of 29 atolls (ring-shaped coral islands) and 5 islands extending over a sea area exceeding 1.9 million square kilometers (750,000 square miles), but a land area of only about 181 square kilometers (70 square miles), slightly larger than Washington, D.C.

The capital city of the Marshall Islands, Majuro, is located on the island of Majuro.

CLIMATE: The climate is hot and humid, with little seasonal temperature change. Daily variations generally range between 21° and 34°C (70° and 93°F). Rainfall averages about 30–38 centimeters (12–15 inches) per month.

INTRODUCTORY SURVEY

RECENT HISTORY

During World War II (1939–1945) after bitter fighting between United States and Japanese forces, the islands came under U.S. control. In 1947 the Marshalls became part of a United Nations trusteeship administered by the United States. The United States used Bikini and Enewetak atolls as nuclear testing sites from 1946 to 1958 exploding sixty-six atomic and nuclear tests during this period and displacing the native people.

In 1979 the Republic of the Marshall Islands became a self-governing territory and Amata Kabua was elected its first president. A Compact of Free Association with the United States providing for full self-government except for defense was ratified by the United States in 1986 and went into effect the same year.

In February 1990 the United States agreed to pay $45 million to the victims of the nuclear testing program. The Republic became an independent state and joined the United Nations in September 1991.

In the late 1990s global warming and the possibility of rising sea levels have raised concern over the long-term prospects for the low-lying islands in the middle of the Pacific Ocean.

In late 1999 and early 2000 two major political changes took place. For the first time an opposition party, the newly formed United Democratic Party (UDP), gained a majority in parliament in the November 1999 elections. Then in January 2000 Kessai Note, Speaker of the Nitijela, was elected to the presidency becoming the first president who is a commoner (not a traditional chief).

GOVERNMENT

The Marshall Islands is an independent republic operating under a 1979 constitution. The president elected by the Nitijela from among its own members for a four-year term is both chief of state and head of government. The president selects the cabinet from among members of the Nitijela.

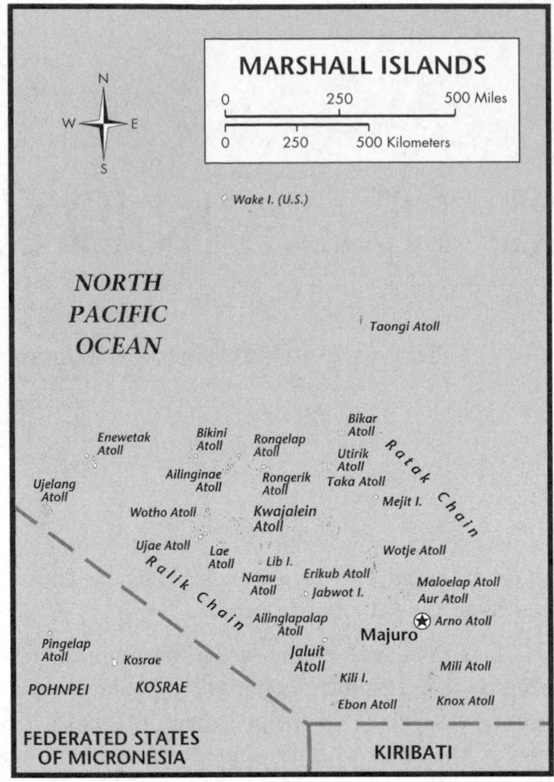

The legislative branch is a unicameral parliament known as the Nitijela that consists of thirty-three members elected from twenty-four electoral districts, each corresponding roughly to an atoll. The Council of Iroij (Chiefs) has twelve members whose main functions are to request consideration by the Nitijela of any bills affecting customary laws or practice and to advise on national matters of concern.

There are twenty-four local governments for the inhabited islands and atolls.

Judiciary

The judiciary consists of the Supreme Court, the High Court, the District Court, and twenty-two community courts. The Supreme Court has final appellate jurisdiction. Community courts in local government areas rule on civil and criminal cases.

Political Parties

Historically there have been no formally organized political parties. Instead the organizations more closely resemble interest groups. However two groups have competed in balloting for the Nitijela in recent years. They are the United Democratic Party (UDP) that gained a majority in the Nitijela in the November 1999 elections and the Kabua Party (KABUA).

DEFENSE

There are no armed forces. Under the Compact of Free Association the United States provides defense for a minimum fifteen-year period and operation of the missile range on Kwajalein Atoll for thirty years.

ECONOMIC AFFAIRS

The mainstay of this tiny island group is U.S. government assistance. Having few natural resources imports far exceed exports. The Marshall Island's closest trading partner is Hawaii located over 2,000 mile to the northeast. The U.S. government provides grants of $6.5 million annually under the Compact of Free Association that amounts to 70 percent of GDP. These funds are given in exchange for furnishing military facilities. Radioactive testing was imposed on the inhabitants in the 1950s affecting at least half of the population. Negotiations to extend terms of the aid compact were initiated in 1999.

Agricultural production is concentrated on small farms and fishing is small scale. Of those engaged in agriculture and fishing, the main activities are copra (dried coconut meat) production and the cultivation of breadfruit, taro, and pandanus. Though efforts are being made to capitalize on the Island's beaches World War II relics the tourism industry is in its infancy as radioactive fallout deters visitors.

Public Finance

Government revenues are derived from domestic sources and U.S. grants. Domestic revenues are from taxes and non-tax sources (fishing rights, philatelic sales, and user charges). The leading areas of expenditure include health services, education, public works, and transportation and communication. The U.S. Central Intelligence Agency estimated that in 1995–1996 government revenues totaled approximately $80.1 million and expenditures $77.4 million. External debt totaled $125 million by 1996–1997 estimates.

Income

In 1998 the Marshall Islands' gross domestic product (GDP) was estimated to be $105 million or $1,670 per capita. During 1997 the average annual inflation rate was 5.4 percent. The estimated growth rate of GDP in 1998 was a decline of 5 percent. The 1995 GDP contribution by sector was agriculture 15 percent, industry 13 percent, and services 72 percent.

Industry

The economy's small manufacturing sector is centered largely in Majuro. The largest industrial operation is a copra-processing mill. Other manufacturing consists of small-scale operations, such as coir making, furniture making, handicrafts, and boat making. Commercial fishing is small scale. Tourism is being encouraged. There is an embryonic offshore banking segment.

Banking and Finance

Financial services are provided by three commercial banks, the Bank of Guam, the Bank of Marshalls located in Majuro, and the Bank of Hawaii located in Ebeye. The Marshall Islands Development Loan Office in Majuro was established as an independent government corporation in 1982. There were four credit unions operated by over 2,000 members. The Marshall Islands has no stock issues or securities trading.

Economic Development

The first five-year national development plan (1986–1991), designed to meet the requirements of the Compact of Free Association with the U.S., constituted the first phase of a fifteen-year development program. The plan focused on economic development with emphasis on private-sector expansion, personnel development and employment creation, regional development, population planning and social development, and cultural and environmental preservation. Development projects include a new capitol building, docks, and causeways.

Financial aid from the United States totals over $65 million per year under terms of the Compact of Free Association due to expire in 2001. Tourism was under development in the late 1990s with the opening of a first-calls resort hotel, the first in the Marshall Islands.

SOCIAL WELFARE

The Ministry of Social Services is involved in five major areas: housing, women's and youth development, feeding programs, aging, and other community development welfare programs. A social security system provides old age, disability, and survivor benefits.

The Marshallese society has a matrilineal structure. Each person belongs to the *bwij,* or clan, of his or her mother, through whom traditional rank and property are inherited.

Healthcare

The leading causes of death after infancy are respiratory diseases, diarrhea and other intestinal diseases, diabetes, and heart disease. Alcoholism and drug abuse are common, and there is a relatively high incidence of sexually transmitted diseases. There are two hospitals: the Armer Ishoda Hospital in Majuro and a recently renovated hospital in Ebeye. In 1991 there were twenty doctors, 130 nurses, and four midwives. Health care on the outer atolls is provided through sixty-nine dispensaries staffed by health assistants. In 2000 average life expectancy was 65.5 years.

Housing

Houses in the urban centers are simple wooden or cement-block structures, with corrugated iron roofs; because of the limited land availability, houses are heavily crowded. In 1988 there were 4,943 dwellings on the Marshall Islands. The Ministry of Social Services provides housing grants, principally to low-income families.

EDUCATION

About 93 percent of the Marshallese are literate. The Ministry of Education provides for public education at the elementary, secondary, and higher education levels. The public elementary education provides eight years of basic compulsory education to those aged six to fourteen. A high school entrance exam is given to all eighth graders in order to determine the 300 or so students to be admitted to two high schools.

The Majuro campus of the College of Micronesia opened its School of Nursing and Science Center in 1986. In 1991 Marshall Islands became a member of the University of the South Pacific.

2000 KEY EVENTS TIMELINE

January

- A U.S. prototype intercontinental ballistic missile is launched from the Marshall Islands, but fails to hit its mark 140 miles above the Pacific Ocean.
- New President Kessai Note takes the oath of office in a special parliamentary session.

April

- A report by the group Geopolitical Drug Watch states that drug trafficking is flourishing because criminal organizations can easily launder their money in the Marshall Islands and other Pacific nations.

May

- The government announces plans to evacuate its citizens from Fiji, in response to the political unrest there.
- A board is appointed to address the crisis facing the country's social security system.

June

- The G7 group of major industrialized nations cites the Marshall Islands for failing to cooperate in the fight against international money laundering.
- U.S. officials, aware of attempts to mount a protest against missile testing on Kwalalein Atoll, concede that, if pressed, they could move their testing elsewhere.

July

- Education Minister Wilfred I. Kendall gives public school teachers a two-year period during which they must work towards their college degrees or lose their jobs.
- The Outrigger's Micronesian Basketball Tournament is held in Majuro, Marshall Islands. Fifteen teams from throughout the region participate. Seven women's teams are included, marking the first time women have taken part.

August

- The Marshall Islands meet the deadline for a $1.8 million payment to HMAA (Hawaii Management Alliance Association) to keep the country's health program from closing.
- The Marshall Islands are named in the South Pacific Regional Environment Program (SPREP) study of contamination caused by hazardous material storage in South Pacific island nations.

September

- Copra prices are cut 20 percent in response to declining prices worldwide. The impact on the Marshall Islanders is potentially great, as copra is the main source of income for people on the remote atolls.

October

- The Marshall Islands petitions the U.S. government for US$27 million in additional funds for compensation for injuries caused by nuclear testing, stating that the original fund of US$45 million is about to run out.
- Air Marshall Islands pilots strike October 13, due to the use of dangerously old equipment. The airline, in turn, sues German aircraft manufacturer Dornier, alleging the German company interfered with the sale of an Air Marshall Islands plane and also caused the nation's airline to make payments on planes it couldn't use.

November

- On November 29, U.S. military officials announce that the the remains of nineteen World War II Marines who perished on the Makin Atoll at the hands of Japanese soldiers have been identified.
- The Marshall Islands casts its vote at the United Nations with the United States and Israel; they are the only three countries opposed to ending the United States trade embargo against Cuba.
- Marshall Islanders who became ill after working at Bikini and Enewetak during the nuclear tests are deemed eligible for U.S. nuclear benefits under the new Department of Energy Compensation Act and the amended Radiation Exposure Compensation Act.

ANALYSIS OF EVENTS: 2000

BUSINESS AND THE ECONOMY

In June 2000 Finance Minister Mike Konelios introduced a US$29.9 million supplementary budget bill in the legislature, nearly US$20 million of which came from Taiwan. The bill called for the money from Taiwan to be spent on a variety of development projects, with US$5.7 million going to public works, US$2.8 million going to the ministry of transportation, and US$2.6 million going to education. Additional money in the supplementary budget came from the Asian Development Bank's Reform Loan (US$3 million) and a commercial bank loan (US$5 million).

The legacy of U.S. nuclear testing performed in the Marshall Islands in the 1940s lingered into the twenty-first century and influenced the Marshall Island's economic development as well as the health of its people. Tourism operators expressed interest in developing Rongelap Atoll as a diving and fishing site, but feared that the atoll might still be contaminated from the U.S. nuclear tests. In an unrelated study, scientists agreed upon a cost of $212 million for nuclear waste cleanup on three islands of the Marshall Islands. The meant cleanup was to include the use of potassium fertilizer and the removal and replacement of contaminated soil.

In September the price of copra, the main source of income for Marshall Islanders on the remote atolls, was cut 20 percent in response to declining prices worldwide.

In October the Marshall Islands petitioned the U.S. government for US$27 million additional funds for compensation for injuries caused by nuclear testing, stating that the original fund of $45 million was about to run out. In November it was announced that Marshall Islanders who worked at Bikini and Enewetak during the nuclear testing would be eligible for U.S.-provided benefits. Under the new Department of Energy (DOE) Compensation Act, workers or their survivors would be eligible for $150,000 plus health insurance. Under the amended Radiation Exposure Compensation Act, $75,000 could be paid to those who participated in on-site atmospheric testing and later developed an exposure-related disease.

GOVERNMENT AND POLITICS

Early in January 2000 newly elected President Kessai Note took the oath of office in a special parliamentary session; a new ten-member cabinet was also sworn in. President Note, the Marshall Islands' third president since 1979, said his first goal would be to get a budget introduced and passed. He also pledged to take a firm stand against corruption. Although President Note said the Marshall Islands would not break its ties with Taiwan, his government did establish a task force to investigate alleged "secret deals" between Taiwan and the government of the previous president, Imata Kabua. While it was believed that President Note might favor Beijing, People's Republic of China over Taiwan, by mid-January it was announced that the Marshall Islands would maintain its ties with Taiwan.

U.S. missile tests took place on Kwalalein Atoll in the Marshall Islands in January, but the prototype intercontinental ballistic missile failed to hit its mark 140 miles above the Pacific Ocean. U.S. officials, aware of attempts to mount a protest against missile testing on Kwalalein, conceded that if pressed, they could move their testing elsewhere.

In a November meeting of the United Nations, the Marshall Islands voted against ending the U.S. trade embargo against Cuba. The only other countries to vote against ending the embargo were the United States and Israel.

CULTURE AND SOCIETY

Malnutrition among children, especially those under one year of age, dropped in 1999–2000, but remained a serious problem in the Marshall Islands, not only in Majuro, but also on the outer islands. In 2000 the government set the goal of reducing malnutrition in the country by encouraging home gardening, breastfeeding, and education. A new program, called the "Home Gardening Project," aimed to increase the availability of locally grown food crops, using tools provided by UNICEF under the monitoring of the Community Health Council.

In July Education Minister Wilfred I. Kendall declared that public school teachers were being given a two-year period during which they must work toward getting their college degrees or lose their jobs.

Taiwan funded two projects in 2000 that would bring electricity to some underserved areas of the Marshall Islands. A $2 million project to build a dam on Wotje Atoll would provide electricity there using underground distribution lines. A second project would provide household electricity on Rong Rong Island on the western side of the Majoro Atoll.

The 2000 Outrigger's Micronesian Basketball Tournament was held in Majuro, with fifteen teams from throughout the region participating. Seven women's teams were included, marking the first time women had taken part.

DIRECTORY

CENTRAL GOVERNMENT

Head of State

President

Kessai Note, Office of the President, PO Box 1, 96960 Marshall Islands

PHONE: +692 6254022; 6252233; 6253213

FAX: +692 6254021; 6253649

Ministers

Minister of Transportation and Communication
Brenson Wase, Ministry of Transportation and Communication, PO Box 2, 96960 Marshall Islands
PHONE: +692 6252233; 6253213; 6253445
FAX: +692 6254021; 6253649

Minister of Education
Wilfred Kendall, Ministry of Education, PO Box 2, 96960 Marshall Islands
PHONE: +692 6254673; 6255262; 6256646
FAX: +692 6257735

Minister of Foreign Affairs and Trade
Alvin Jacklick, Ministry of Foreign Affairs and Trade, PO Box 2, 96960 Marshall Islands
PHONE: +692 6253181; 6253012
FAX: +692 6253685; 6254979

Minister of Finance
Michael Konelios, Ministry of Finance, PO Box 2, 96960
PHONE: +692 6258320; 6258311
FAX: +692 6253607

Minister in Assistance to the President
Gerald Zackios, Ministry in Assistance to the President, PO Box 2, 96960 Marshall Islands
PHONE: +692 6254022; 6252233; 6253213
FAX: +692 6254021; 6253649

Minister of Resources and Development
John Silk, Ministry of Resources and Development, PO Box 2, 96960 Marshall Islands
PHONE: +692 6252233; 6253213; 6253445
FAX: +692 6254021; 6253649

Minister of Internal Affairs
Nidel Lorak, Ministry of Internal Affairs, PO Box 2, 96960 Marshall Islands
PHONE: +692 6253845; 6258240; 6258225
FAX: +692 6255353

Minister of Health and Environment
Tadashi Lometo, Ministry of Health and Environment, PO Box 2, 96960 Marshall Islands
PHONE: +692 6254680; 6253480; 6255660
FAX: +692 6253432

Minister of Justice
Hemos A. Jack, Ministry of Justice, PO Box 2, 96960 Marshall Islands
PHONE: +692 6252233; 6253213; 6253445
FAX: +692 6254021; 6253649

POLITICAL ORGANIZATIONS

Our Islands Party

Ralik/Ratak Democratic Party (RRDP)

NAME: Ramsey Reimers

DIPLOMATIC REPRESENTATION

Embassies in Marshall Islands

United States
Oceanside Mejen Weto, Long Island, Majuro, Marshall Islands, 20521-4380
PHONE: +692 2474011
FAX: +692 2474012
TITLE: Ambassador
NAME: Joan M. Plaisted

JUDICIAL SYSTEM

Supreme Court

High Court

PHONE: +692 6253201; 6253279
FAX: +692 6253323

District Court

BROADCAST MEDIA

Central Pacific Network (AFRTS)

Box 23, APO San Francisco, CA 96555, USA
BROADCASTS: 24 hours/day
TYPE: U.S. Military

Marshall Islands Broadcasting Co.

Department of Interior and Outer Island Affairs, Majuro, Marshall Islands 96960
PHONE: +692 (625) 3240
FAX: +692 (625) 3413
TITLE: Chief Information Specialist
CONTACT: Billy Sawej
BROADCASTS: 1900–1000
TYPE: Commercial, Government

Micronesia Heatwave

PO Box 1, Majuro 96960, Marshall Islands
PHONE: +692 6253250
BROADCASTS: 24 hours/day
TYPE: Commercial

V7AA

PO Drawer H, Majuro 96960–1008, Marshall Islands
PHONE: +692 (625) 3141
FAX: +692 (625) 4690

AFRTS Television

PO Box 23, APO San Francisco, CA 96555, USA
TITLE: Network Manager
CONTACT: Larry Malinowski
CHANNEL: 9, 13
TYPE: Military

Marshall Islands Broadcasting Company TV (MBC-TV)

MBC, Majuro 96960, Marshall Islands
PHONE: +692 6253413

COLLEGES AND UNIVERSITIES

College of the Marshall Islands

PO Box 1258, Majuro, Marshall Islands 96960
PHONE: +692 (625) 3394; 3321; 3236
FAX: +692 (625) 7203
E-MAIL: cmi@ntamar.com
WEBSITE: http://www.geocities.com/athens/delphi/5634

NEWSPAPERS AND MAGAZINES

Marshall Islands Gazette

Marshall Islands Journal

PO Box 14, Majuro 96960, Marshall Islands
FAX: +692 625 3143
E-MAIL: journal@ntamar.com
TITLE: Editor
CONTACT: Giff Johnson
CIRCULATION: 3,300
TYPE: Social science, general

RMI Online

E-MAIL: info@rmiembassyus.org
WEBSITE: http://www.rmiembassyus.org

RELIGIOUS ORGANIZATIONS

Protestant

Majuro Seventh-Day Adventist Schools
PO Box I-SDA, Majuro, MH 96960
PHONE: +692 6253367
FAX: +692 6253367
E-MAIL: sda1@ntamar.com
WEBSITE: http://www.tagnet.org/majuro/
TITLE: Principal
NAME: Jeff Brown

FURTHER READING

Articles

Oakley, Doug. "Marshall Islands' Majuro a Diver's Paradise." *Travel Weekly,* October 12, 2000, vol. 59, no. 82, p. 39.

Woodard, Colin. "Payback Time." *Bulletin of the Atomic Scientists,* March 2000, vol. 56, no. 2, p. 11.

Internet

BBC News Online. "Sanctions Threat to 'Tax Havens.'" June 26, 2000. [Online] Available http://news6.thdo.bbc.co.uk/hi/english/business/newsid%5F806000/806236.stm (accessed October 12, 2000).

MARSHALL ISLANDS: STATISTICAL DATA

For sources and notes see "Sources of Statistics" at the front of each volume.

GEOGRAPHY

Geography

Area:

Total: 181.3 sq km.

Land: 181.3 sq km.

Note: includes the atolls of Bikini, Enewetak, and Kwajalein.

Land boundaries: 0 km.

Coastline: 370.4 km.

Climate: wet season from May to November; hot and humid; islands border typhoon belt.

Terrain: low coral limestone and sand islands.

Natural resources: phosphate deposits, marine products, deep seabed minerals.

Land use:

Arable land: 0%

Permanent crops: 60%

Permanent pastures: 0%

Forests and woodland: 0%

Other: 40%

HUMAN FACTORS

Ethnic Division

Micronesian.

Religion

Christian (mostly Protestant).

Major Languages

English (universally spoken and is the official language), two major Marshallese dialects from the Malayo-Polynesian family, Japanese.

Demographics (A)

	1990	1995	1998	2000	2010	2020	2030	2040	2050
Population	46.2	56.2	63.1	68.1	100.4	144.5	201.0	269.6	347.9
Life expectancy - males	60.3	62.1	63.0	63.7	66.8	69.6	72.0	74.1	75.8
Life expectancy - females	63.4	65.4	66.6	67.4	71.0	74.2	77.0	79.3	81.2
Birth rate (per 1,000)	48.0	46.0	45.3	45.2	42.9	38.6	34.7	30.6	26.7
Death rate (per 1,000)	8.6	7.4	6.8	6.4	4.8	3.9	3.4	3.2	3.2
Women of reproductive age (15-49 yrs.)	9.4	11.6	13.3	14.6	21.9	32.4	47.3	65.3	86.8
Fertility rate	7.1	6.9	6.7	6.6	6.0	5.3	4.6	4.0	3.4

Except as noted, values for vital statistics are in thousands; life expectancy is in years.

EDUCATION

Literacy Rates (B)

	National Data	World Data
Adult literacy rate		
1995		
Male	NA	81
Female	90[1]	65

GOVERNMENT & LAW

Political Parties

The unicameral Parliament or Nitijela consists of 33 seats. Members are elected by popular vote to serve four-year terms. Elections were last held in November 1999 (next to be held in November 2003). Election results are not available. The Council of Chiefs is a 12-member body that advises on matters affecting customary law and practice. Traditionally there have been no formally organized political parties. What has existed more closely resembles factions or interest groups because they do not have party headquarters, formal platforms, or party structures. The following two "groupings" have competed in legislative balloting in recent years: Kabua Party and United Democratic Party or UDP.

Government Budgets (B)

Revenues . . . .$80.1 million
Expenditures . . . .$77.4 million
Capital expenditures . . . .$19.5 million

Data for FY95/96 est.

Crime

Crime rate (for 1994)
Crimes reported 1,761
Total persons convicted .NA
Crimes per 100,000 population 3,261
Persons responsible for offenses
Total number of suspects 1,761
Total number of female suspects 81
Total number of juvenile suspects . . . . .NA

LABOR FORCE

Unemployment Rate

16% (1991 est.)

PRODUCTION SECTOR

Energy Production

Production . . . . .57 million kWh
Exports . . . . .0 kWh

Data for 1994.

Energy Consumption

Consumption .57 million kWh
Imports . . . . .0 kWh

Data for 1994.

Transportation

Highways:

Total: NA

Paved: NA

Unpaved: NA

Note: paved roads on major islands (Majuro, Kwajalein), otherwise stone-, coral-, or laterite-surfaced roads and tracks.

Merchant marine:

Total: 143 ships (1,000 GRT or over) totaling 6,801,336 GRT/11,785,065 DWT.

Ships by type: bulk 48, cargo 8, chemical tanker 5, combination bulk 1, container 19, liquified gas 2, multi-functional large load carrier 1, petroleum tanker 58, vehicle carrier 1 (1999 est.).

Note: a flag of convenience registry; includes the ships of Canada 1, China 1, Germany 1, Japan 1, and US 7 (1998 est.).

Airports: 16 (1999 est.).

Airports - with unpaved runways: 12.

Top Agriculture Products

Coconuts, cacao, taro, breadfruit, fruits; pigs, chickens.

Top Mining Products (B)

Mineral resources include: phosphate deposits, deep seabed minerals.

MANUFACTURING SECTOR

GDP & Manufacturing Summary (C)

Total GDP (1998 est.) . . . .$105 million
Real growth rate (1998 est.) . . . .−5%
Per capita (1998 est.) $1,670
Composition by sector
Agriculture 15%
Industry 13%
Services 72%

Values in purchasing power parity. The total GDP is supplemented by approximately $65 million annual US aid.

COMMUNICATIONS

Telecommunications

Telephones - main lines in use: 3,000 (1994).

Telephones - mobile cellular: 280 (1994).

Telephone system: telex services.

Domestic: Majuro Atoll and Ebeye and Kwajalein islands have regular, seven-digit, direct-dial telephones; other islands interconnected by shortwave radiotelephone (used mostly for government purposes).

International: satellite earth stations - 2 Intelsat (Pacific Ocean); US Government satellite communications system on Kwajalein.

Radio broadcast stations: AM 3, FM 4, shortwave 0 (1998).

Radios: NA

Television broadcast stations: 3 (of which two are US military stations) (1997).

Televisions: NA

Internet Service Providers (ISPs): NA

FINANCE, ECONOMICS, & TRADE

Economic Indicators

National product: GDP—purchasing power parity—$105 million (1998 est.), supplemented by approximately $65 million annual US aid.

National product real growth rate: −5% (1998 est.).

National product per capita: $1,670 (1998 est.).

Inflation rate—consumer price index: 5% (1997).

Exchange Rates

Exchange rates: US currency is used.

Top Import Origins

Imports (f.o.b., 1997 est.): $58 million.

Origins: United States, Japan, Australia, New Zealand, Guam, Singapore.

Top Export Destinations

Exports (f.o.b., 1997 est.): $28 million.

Destinations: United States, Japan, Australia.

Foreign Aid

Recipient: approximately $65 million annually from the US.

Import/Export Commodities

Import Commodities	Export Commodities
Foodstuffs	Fish
Machinery and equipment	Coconut oil
	Trochus shells
Fuels	
Beverages and tobacco	

MARTINIQUE

Department of Martinique
Departement de la Martinique

CAPITAL: Fort-de-France.

FLAG: The flag of France is used.

MONETARY UNIT: The currency of France is used, with 1 French franc (F) = 100 centimes. Notes are in denominations of F20, 10, 5, 2, and 1, and 50, 20, 10, and 5 centimes. As of June 1999, $1 = F6.29.

WEIGHTS AND MEASURES: The metric system is used.

HOLIDAYS: New Year's Day, I January; Labour Day, 1 May; Victory Day, 8 May; National Day, 14 July; Assumption, 15 August; All Saint's Day, 1 November; Armistice day, 11 November; Christmas Day, 25 December. Movable holidays include Carnival, Easter Monday, Ascension Day, and Whit Monday.

TIME: 8 AM = noon GMT.

LOCATION AND SIZE: Martiniques is one of the Windward islands in the Caribbean Sea north of Trinidad and Tobago. With a total area of 1,100 square kilometers, it occupies an area slightly more than 6 times the size of Washington, D.C. Its capital city, Fort-de-France, is located on the central western side of the island.

CLIMATE: The island experiences warm and humid tropical conditions throughout the year, moderated by trade winds. The main rainy season is from June through October. Showers can occur at other times of the year but they are usually brief. The temperature is cooler in the uplands. Devastating hurricanes occur every eight years on average.

INTRODUCTORY SURVEY

RECENT HISTORY

First inhabited by Carib Indians, Martinique was discovered by Columbus in 1502 and colonized by the French in 1635. Except for the periods 1762–1763, 1793–1802, and 1809–1815, the island has remained in French hands ever since.

GOVERNMENT

Martinique is an overseas department of France that operates under the 1958 French constitution. The chief of state is the president of France who appoints a prefect on the advice of the French Ministry of Interior to represent him on Martinique. The heads of government are the presidents of the legislative bodies, the General Council, and the Regional Assembly. The presidents are elected by members of their respective council.

The General Council, or Conseil General, has forty-five members and the Regional Assembly, or Conseil Regional, has forty-one members. All members of the both are popularly elected for six-year terms. Martinique also elects two seats to the French Senate and four seats to the French National Assembly.

Judiciary

The legal system is based on the French legal system and includes a Court of Appeal.

Political Parties

Political parties with representation in the legislative councils include the Martinique Progressive Party (PPM), the Rally for the Republic (RPR), the Union for French Democracy (UDF), the Martinique Independence Movement (MIM), and the Martinique Socialist Party (PMS).

DEFENSE

Martinique's defense is the responsibility of France.

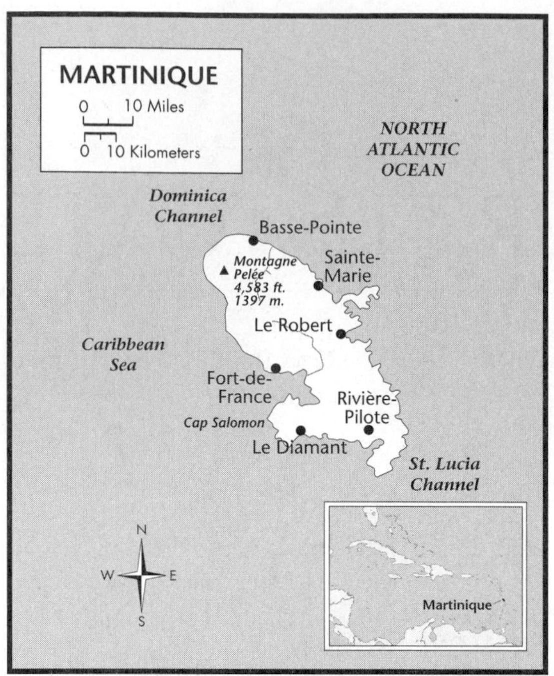

ECONOMIC AFFAIRS

Martinique's economy is based on agriculture, tourism, and light industry. Agriculture accounts for only 6 percent of GDP while industry accounts for 11 percent according to 1997 estimates. Sugarcane and bananas are the leading crops; pineapples, citrus fruit, mangoes, avocados, coffee, and cacao are also grown. Most of the sugarcane is used in rum distillation. Most foodstuffs must be imported which results in a chronic trade deficit requiring large aid transfers from France.

As a source of foreign exchange, tourism has become more important than agricultural exports. The majority of the workforce is employed in the service sector that accounted for 83 percent of GDP by 1997 estimates.

Public Finance

The U.S. Central Intelligence Agency (CIA) reports Martinique's revenues in 1996 were $900 million and expenditures were $2.5 billion including capital expenditures of $140 million.

Income

The CIA estimated in 1996 the GDP was $4.24 billion, or $10,700 per capita. The 1997 estimated GDP contribution by sector was agriculture 6 percent, industry 11 percent, and services 83 percent.

Industry

Sugar refining, rum distilling, and fruit processing are the chief industries. Bananas, petroleum products, and rum are the principal exports; foodstuffs and oil are the main imports. Martinique produced about 4.8 million barrels of refined petroleum products in 1994 from imported crude oil. Timber production was 12,000 cubic meters in 1995, and the fish catch in 1994 was 5,905 tons. In 1994 exports totaled $218.6 million; imports totaled $1,642.3 million. Trade is mainly with France which heavily subsidizes the budget. Tourism has become more important than agriculture as a source of foreign exchange.

SOCIAL WELFARE

Healthcare

Martinique has sixteen hospitals. The infant mortality rate in 1999 was estimated at 6.76 per 1,000 births, down from fourteen in 1985. Life expectancy was 78.3 years in 2000.

EDUCATION

Education is compulsory through primary and secondary levels. There is a branch of the Centre Universitaire Antilles-Guyana.

2000 KEY EVENTS TIMELINE

January

- From January through June, gas stations are attacked and robbed at gunpoint. Police suspect juvenile offenders.

March

- The French government reduces the TVA (Value Added Taxes) from 9.5 percent to 8.5 percent.

June

- The French government issues a report declaring Martinique to be fiscally sound.

July

- Poet Aimé Cesaire, age eight-six, steps down from his role as mayor of Fort de France on July 18. He does not endorse anyone for the position.

November

- In an attempt to attract more tourists, Martinique opens up a new water park called Aqualand on November 26.

ANALYSIS OF EVENTS: 2000

BUSINESS AND THE ECONOMY

The biggest sector of the economy of Martinique is tourism. Practically all cruise ships include Martinique as a port of call. Because of the French influence on the culture, independent tourists travel to the island to enjoy the magnificent climate, beaches, and the atmosphere of being in a little part of France. Carnival and an annual jazz festival also increased tourism in the spring months. Agriculture, formerly a significant portion of the economy, has dwindled, but the production of bananas is still significant.

GOVERNMENT AND POLITICS

As a French overseas department, Martinique in 2000 was administered by the elected government of France. Local elections provided leaders who decide internal affairs. The last mayor of the capital city of Fort-de-France, Aimé Cesaire, resigned at eighty-six years of age. He did not name a preferred successor, so there will be an election to choose a new mayor. A new head of the overseas departments of France, Christian Paul, replaced Jean-Jack Queyranne as of August 2000. New local taxes, such as the debarkation tax, the fuel tax, the vehicle registration tax, and the vacation taxes on hotel and villas, were expected to help the economy of Martinique. In March 2000 the French government reduced the TVA (value-added tax on goods and services) from 9.5 percent to 8.5 percent to encourage tourists to spend more time and money in Martinique.

CULTURE AND SOCIETY

Martinique's population is comprised of an ethnic mixture of French citizens, people of African descent who were initially slaves on the island, and their descendants, some of whom are the children of marriages between members of the two groups. The first wife of Emperor Napoleon I, Joséphine de Beauharnais, was perhaps Martinique's most famous resident. Many people of the French nobility came to Martinique to escape persecution during the French Revolution of 1789. Even though French is the official language as of 2000, the majority of people spoke a patois called Creole, a mixture of French and African languages. No one who only understood French could expect to understand Creole. The structure of the government and educational systems remain entirely French. Jacques Chirac, the president of France, was head of the government in 2000. Martinique is known as the "island of flowers" as it is a true tropical paradise. Main holidays include the French national independence holiday, Bastille Day on July 14, as well as local saint's day celebrations. Carnival or Mardi Gras celebrations were held during the months before Easter. Every year in July the Festival of Fort-de-France is held in the capital city. There are parades and parties. An annual international jazz festival was held in February.

DIRECTORY

CENTRAL GOVERNMENT

Head of State

Prefect
Dominique Bellion

President
Jacques Chirac, Office of the President, Palais de l'Elysée, 55, rue du faubourg Saint-Honoré, 75008 Paris, France
PHONE: +33 (1) 42928100
FAX: +33 (1) 47422465

President of the General Council
Claude Lise, Office of the President of the General Council

POLITICAL ORGANIZATIONS

Rally for the Republic (RPR)

NAME: Michel Charlone

Martinique Forces

NAME: Maurice Laouchez

Martinique Socialist Party (PPM)

NAME: Ernest Wan-Ajouhu

Movement for a Liberated Martinique

NAME: Philippe Petit

Combat Worker

NAME: Gerard Beaujour

DIPLOMATIC REPRESENTATION

Embassies in Martinique

Belgium
Pointe des Sables, 97200, Fort de France, Martinique
PHONE: +596 595051

Germany
Acajou, 97232 Le Lamentin, Martinique
PHONE: +596 503839

Italy
28, Boulevard Allegre, 97200, Fort de France, Martinique
PHONE: +596 705475

Mexico
31 Rue Moreau de Jonnes, 97200, Fort de France, Martinique
PHONE: +596 605024

Netherlands
44/46 Avenue Maurice Bishop, 97200, Fort de France, Martinique
PHONE: +596 733161

Spain
PHONE: +596 542779

Sweden
Immeuble Kerlys, 97200, Fort de France, Martinique
PHONE: +596 605454

Switzerland
Lotissement La Trompeuse, 97232, Le Lamentin, Martinique
PHONE: +596 501243

United Kingdom
Route du Phare, 97200, Fort de France, Martinique
PHONE: +596 615630

Venezuela
Rue du Prof R. Garcin, 97200, Fort de France, Martinique
PHONE: +596 633416

JUDICIAL SYSTEM

Court of Appeal

BROADCAST MEDIA

Radio Caraïbes International Martinique (RCI)

2 Boulevard de la Maren, 97200 Fort de France, Martinique
PHONE: +596 639870
FAX: +596 632659
E-MAIL: 100444.2371@compuserve.com
WEBSITE: http://www.fwinet.com/rci.htm
TITLE: Director
CONTACT: Yann Duval
BROADCASTS: 24 hours/day
TYPE: Commercial

Radio-Télévision Française d'Outre Mer (RFO)

BP 662, 97263 Fort de France, Martinique
PHONE: +596 595200
TITLE: Director
CONTACT: Fred Joujoud

ATV Antilles Television

28 rue Arawaks, 97200 Fort de France, Martinique
PHONE: +596 754444
FAX: +596 755565
CONTACT: 34, 39, 44, 52
TYPE: Commercial, Private

Canal Antilles

Centre Commercial la Galléria, 97232 Le Lamentin, Martinique
PHONE: +596 505787
CHANNEL: 25, 29, 34, 46, 50
TYPE: Commercial, Private

Société National de Radio-Télévision d'Outre Mer (RFO)

BP 662, 97263 Fort de France Cedex, Martinique
PHONE: +595 595200
TITLE: Director
CONTACT: Fred Jouhoud
CHANNEL: K4

Tele Caraibes International Martinique (TCI-Martinique)

Immeuble RCI/TCI-Zone industrielle-97232 Le Lamentin, Martinique
PHONE: +596 510606
FAX: +596 518562
TYPE: Commercial, Private

COLLEGES AND UNIVERSITIES

Universite des Antilles et de la Guyane - Martinique

Campus De Schoelcher, BP 7209, Schoelcher, Martinique
PHONE: +596 727300
FAX: +596 727302
E-MAIL: j.laviolette@martinique.univ-ag.fr
WEBSITE: http://www.martinique.univ-ag.fr

NEWSPAPERS AND MAGAZINES

Antilla

Antilla, BP 46, Lamentin, Martinique
FAX: +596 755846
E-MAIL: antilla.hebdo@wanadoo.fr

Aujourd'hui Dimanche

Presbytere de Bellevue, Fort-de-France, Martiniquc
CONTACT: Pere Gauthier
CIRCULATION: 12,000

France Antilles

Societe France Antilles et Cie, Place Francois Mitterand, BP 577, 97200 Fort-de-France, Martinique
PHONE: +596 728800
FAX: +596 602996
TITLE: Editor-in-Chief
CONTACT: Henri Mangattale
CIRCULATION: 65,000

Martinique. Institut National de la Statistique et des Etudes Economiques. Bulletin de Statistique

Institut National de la Statistique et des Etudes Economiques, Pointe de Jaham, BP 7212, 97233 Schoelcher Cedex, Martinique

Revolution Socialiste Antilles

Groupe Revolution Socialiste, BP 1031, 97200 Fort-de-France, Martinique
CIRCULATION: 2,500

PUBLISHERS

Editions Gondwana

Morne Pavillon, 97220 Trinite, Martinique
PHONE: +596 583676
FAX: +596 580014
CONTACT: Eric Leroy
SUBJECTS: Agriculture, Archaeology, Gardenig, Plants

George Lise-Huyghes des Etages

108 rue de la Republique, 97200 Fort-de-France, Martinique
PHONE: +596 736819
SUBJECTS: Behavioral Sciences, Education, Human Relations, Psychology, Psychiatry

Virlogeux Francoise-COMEDIT

Rue de la Reine-Hortense, 97229 Les Trois Ilets, Martinique
PHONE: +596 683985
FAX: +596 683423

RELIGIOUS ORGANIZATIONS

Jewish

Maison Grambin
Plateau Fofo Voie 1, Fort-De-France, Martinique 97233
PHONE: +596 603727
NAME: Andre Gabay

FURTHER READING

Articles

"Martinique: The Isle of Flowers." *Travel Weekly,* October 2, 2000, vol. 59, no. 79, p. S48.

Mooney, Carolyn J. "On Martinique, Elevating the Status of Creole." *Chronicle of Higher Education,* June 9, 2000, vol. 46, no. 40, p. B2.

Books

Dun and Bradstreet's Export Guide to Martinique. Parsippany, NJ: Dun & Bradstreet, 1999.

Martinique, Guadeloupe, Dominica & St. Lucia Alive! Edison, NJ: Hunter, 2000.

MARTINIQUE: STATISTICAL DATA

For sources and notes see "Sources of Statistics" at the front of each volume.

GEOGRAPHY

Geography

Area:

Total: 1,100 sq km.

Land: 1,060 sq km.

Land boundaries: 0 km.

Coastline: 350 km.

Climate: tropical; moderated by trade winds; rainy season (June to October); vulnerable to devastating cyclones (hurricanes) every eight years on average; average temperature 17.3 degrees C; humid.

Terrain: mountainous with indented coastline; dormant volcano.

Natural resources: coastal scenery and beaches, cultivable land.

Land use:

Arable land: 8%

Permanent crops: 8%

Permanent pastures: 17%

Forests and woodland: 44%

Other: 23% (1993 est.).

HUMAN FACTORS

Ethnic Division

African and African-White-Indian mixture 90%

White 5%

East Indian, Lebanese, Chinese less than 5%

Religion

Roman Catholic 95%

Hindu and pagan African 5%

Major Languages

French, Creole patois.

Demographics (A)

	1990	1995	1998	2000	2010	2020	2030	2040	2050
Population	373.6	394.0	406.4	414.5	447.5	469.7	486.7	490.9	478.6
Life expectancy - males	74.4	78.6	78.8	79.0	79.8	80.4	80.9	81.3	81.5
Life expectancy - females	80.0	76.2	76.9	77.5	79.7	81.6	83.0	84.2	85.2
Birth rate (per 1,000)	17.2	16.9	16.6	16.1	12.4	11.5	11.0	9.7	9.4
Death rate (per 1,000)	6.0	6.4	6.4	6.4	6.6	7.2	8.4	10.6	13.3
Women of reproductive age (15-49 yrs.)	103.7	110.0	112.0	113.2	118.2	110.6	103.1	100.7	94.9
Fertility rate	2.0	1.8	1.8	1.8	1.8	1.8	1.7	1.7	1.7

Except as noted, values for vital statistics are in thousands; life expectancy is in years.

GOVERNMENT & LAW

Political Parties

Legislature	no. of seats
General Council	NA
Regional Assembly	
Rally for the Republic-Union for French Democracy (RPR-UDF)	14
Martinique Independence Movement (MIM)	13
Martinique Progressive Party (PPM)	7
Left parties	4
Martinique Socialist Party (PMS)	3

NA stands for not available. Elections for General Council were last held in March 1994 (next to be held in 2000); Regional Assembly election were last held on 15 March 1998 (next to be held by March 2004). The Martinique Progressive Party (PPM) won a plurality in the General Council elections.

Government Budgets (B)

Revenues	$900.0 million
Expenditures	$2.5 billion
Capital expenditures	$140.0 million

Data for 1996.

LABOR FORCE

Total Labor Force (A)

170,000 (1997).

Labor Force by Occupation

Agriculture	10%
Industry	17%
Services	73%

Data for 1997.

Unemployment Rate

24% (1997)

PRODUCTION SECTOR

Energy Production

Production	1.075 billion kWh
Production by source	
Fossil fuel	100%
Hydro	0%
Nuclear	0%
Other	0%
Exports	0 kWh

Data for 1998.

Energy Consumption

Consumption	1 billion kWh
Imports	0 kWh

Data for 1998.

Transportation

Highways:

Total: 2,724 km (1994).

Merchant marine: none (1999 est.).

Airports: 2 (1999 est.).

Top Agriculture Products

Pineapples, avocados, bananas, flowers, vegetables, sugarcane.

MANUFACTURING SECTOR

GDP & Manufacturing Summary (B)

	1980	1985	1990	1993	1994	1995
Gross Domestic Product						
Millions of 1990 dollars	1,734	2,159	2,800	2,810	2,998	3,155[e]
Growth rate in percent	2.80	4.50	2.94	2.69	6.68	5.26[e]
Per capita (in 1990 dollars)	5,320	6,331	7,778	7,553	7,972	8,303[e]
Manufacturing Value Added						
Millions of 1990 dollars	113	159	256	153	167	177[e]
Growth rate in percent	−9.91	26.89	2.95	5.43	8.98	6.29[e]
Manufacturing share in percent of current prices	5.1	NA	NA	NA	NA	NA

COMMUNICATIONS

Daily Newspapers

	National Data	World Data for Comparison
Daily Newspapers		
Number of Dailies	1	8,391
Total Circulation (000)	30	548,000
Circulation per 1,000 inhabitants	78	96

Telecommunications

Telephones - main lines in use: 155,000 (1994).

Telephones - mobile cellular: NA

Telephone system: domestic facilities are adequate.

Domestic: NA

International: microwave radio relay to Guadeloupe, Dominica, and Saint Lucia; satellite earth stations - 2 Intelsat (Atlantic Ocean).

Radio broadcast stations: AM 0, FM 14, shortwave 0 (1998).

Radios: 82,000 (1997).

Television broadcast stations: 11 (plus nine repeaters) (1997).

Televisions: 66,000 (1997).

Internet Service Providers (ISPs): NA

FINANCE, ECONOMICS, & TRADE

Economic Indicators

National product: GDP—purchasing power parity—$4.24 billion (1996 est.).

National product real growth rate: NA.

National product per capita: $10,700 (1996 est.).

Inflation rate—consumer price index: 3.9% (1990).

Exchange Rates

Exchange rates:

Euros per US$1

January 2000 . . . . .0.9867

1999 . . . . .0.9386

French francs (F) per US$1

January 1999 . . . . .5.6500

1998 . . . . .5.8995

1997 . . . . .5.8367

1996 . . . . .5.1155

1995 . . . . .4.9915

Fiscal year: calendar year.

Top Import Origins

$2 billion (c.i.f., 1997)

Origins (1997)

France 62%

Venezuela 6%

Germany 4%

Italy 4%

United States 3%

Top Export Destinations

$250 million (f.o.b., 1997)

Destinations (1997)

France 45%

Guadeloupe 28%

Foreign Aid

Recipient: NA. Substantial annual aid from France.

Import/Export Commodities

Import Commodities	Export Commodities
Petroleum products	Refined petroleum products
Crude oil	Bananas
Foodstuffs	Rum
Construction materials	Pineapples
Vehicles	
Clothing and other consumer goods	

MAURITANIA

CAPITAL: Nouakchott.

FLAG: The flag consists of a gold star and crescent on a light green field.

ANTHEM: *Mauritania* (no words).

MONETARY UNIT: The ouguiya (UM), a paper currency of 5 khoums, issued by the Central Bank of Mauritania, replaced the Communauté Financière Africaine franc on 29 June 1973. There are coins of 1 khoum and 1, 5, 10, and 20 ouguiyas, and notes of 100, 200, 500, and 1,000 ouguiyas. UM1 = $0.00715 (or $1 = UM139.86).

WEIGHTS AND MEASURES: The metric system is the legal standard.

HOLIDAYS: New Year's Day, 1 January; Labor Day, 1 May; African Liberation Day, 25 May; Anniversary of the Proclamation of the Republic, 28 November. Movable religious holidays include Laylat al-Miraj, 'Id al-Fitr, 'Id al-'Adha', 1st of Muharram (Muslim New Year), and Milad an-Nabi.

TIME: GMT.

LOCATION AND SIZE: Situated in West Africa, Mauritania has an area of over 1 million square kilometers (almost 398,000 square miles), slightly larger than three times the size of the state of New Mexico. Its total estimated boundary length is 5,828 kilometers (3,622 miles). The capital city, Nouakchott, is located on the Atlantic Coast.

CLIMATE: Although conditions are generally desert like, three climatic regions can be distinguished. Southern Mauritania has one rainy season from July to October. Annual rainfall averages 66 centimeters (26 inches) in the far south; at Nouakchott the annual average is 14 centimeters (5.5 inches). The coastal region is arid, with an average maximum temperature for October of 32°C (90°F) and an average minimum of 13°C (55°F) for January. Most of Mauritania north of Atar has a desert climate with daytime temperatures exceeding 38°C (100°F) in most areas for over six months of the year.

Mauritanian Islamic Republic
Arabic— *Al-Jumhuriyah al-Islamiyah al-Muritaniyah*

INTRODUCTORY SURVEY

RECENT HISTORY

Mauritania became one of eight territories that constituted the French West Africa federation. In 1946 a Mauritanian Territorial Assembly was established with some control over internal affairs. Complete independence from France was attained on November 28, 1960. Since independence the government of Mauritania has enjoyed considerable stability. Two problems that have dominated internal politics are conflicts between regions and trade union pressures for pro-labor policies and higher wages. Mauritania joined the Arab League in 1973 but ties with Europe, especially France, and the United States remain strong. The disastrous drought that struck Mauritania and the rest of the region during 1968–1974 elicited substantial aid from the European Community (EC), the United States, Spain, France, and the Arab countries.

In April 1976 Mauritania annexed the southern third of the former Spanish Sahara, now Western Sahara. Polisario guerrillas opposed the annexation and raided the Mauritanian railway, iron mines, and coastal settlements. The raids forced Mauritania to call French and Moroccan troops to its defense. In 1979 Mauritania relinquished the annexed territory. The effects of the war weakened the government both economically and politically and in July 1978 Moktar Ould Daddah, Mauritania's president since 1961, was overthrown by a military coup. Lieutenant-Colonel Khouna Ould Haydalla became chief of state in January 1980. A military

coup on December 12, 1984, brought Colonel Moaouia Ould Sidi Mohamed Taya to power.

Many problems including an unsuccessful coup attempt in 1987 are linked to ethnic conflict. It is estimated that Moors accounts for between 60 percent and 80 percent of the population. The remainder is blacks concentrated along the Senegal River border. Mass deportations of blacks have fueled charges that Mauritania is trying to eliminate its non-Moorish population. On January 26, 1992, Taya was elected in Mauritania's first multiparty presidential election with 63 percent of the vote. A new cabinet was formed in January 1993.

Taya was reelected in 1997 but opposition leaders described the vote as a "masquerade" with widespread irregularities. Multiparty legislative elections were held for eighteen of the fifty-six Senate seats in April of 1998 and municipal elections in 1999. Despite having multiparty elections, Mauritania is far from a free society. Opposition politicians and journalists are harassed and even arrested. Since 1993 Mauritania has been denied U.S. trade privileges because of its poor human rights record. Demonstrations of opposition parties against Taya continued in 2000.

GOVERNMENT

The July 1991 constitution delegates most powers to the executive branch. The president is to be elected by universal suffrage (vote) for a six-year term. The president appoints the prime minister. Parliament is composed of a directly elected 79-seat National Assembly and an indirectly elected 56-seat Senate. Competing political parties were legalized in July 1991.

Judiciary

The 1991 Constitution completely revised the judicial system. The revised judicial system includes lower (department), middle, and upper level courts, each with specialized jurisdiction. Forty-three department-level tribunals now bridge the traditional and modern court systems. These courts are staffed by *qadis,* traditional magistrates trained in Koranic law. Ten regional courts of first instance handle general civil cases. Three regional courts of appeal hear challenges to decisions at the department level. A supreme court reviews appeals taken from decisions of the regional courts of appeal.

Political Parties

The Front for the Liberation of Africans in Mauritania (FLAM) played a major role in stirring the 1989 unrest that led to multiparty elections in 1993. Coup leader Colonel Moaouia Ould Sidi Mohamed Taya formed the Democratic and Social Republican Party (Parti Republicain et Democratique Social—PRDS). Chief among fourteen opposition parties has been the Union of Democratic Forces (UFD). The PRDS took seventy-one seats in the April 1998 Assembly elections and the Action for Change (AC) party holds one Senate seat. Independents account for the rest.

DEFENSE

The army had 15,000 men in 2000; the navy, 500 men and seventeen patrol boats; and the air force, 150 men and seven combat aircraft. Paramilitary personnel numbered 5,000.

ECONOMIC AFFAIRS

While Mauritania is an agricultural country dependent on livestock production, its significant iron ore deposits have been the backbone of the export economy in recent years accounting for almost 50 percent of exports. The droughts of the 1970s and 1980s transformed much of Mauritania as the herds died off and the population shifted to urban areas. Eighty-five percent of the population lived as nomadic herders in 1960 but that percentage had fallen to 5 percent in 1999. Leading staple agriculture crops are millet, sorghum, rice, corn, sweet potatoes, pulses, and dates. The contribution of livestock and agriculture was 25 percent of GDP and employed about half of the workforce but covered only 35 percent of the country's needs. Fish exports contributed 37 percent of exports but are declining.

Droughts have led to a build up of foreign debt leaving the country dependent on financial aid flows from international donors. The government signed an agreement with a joint World Bank-IMF mission on a $54 million enhanced structural adjustment facility (ESAF) in March 1999. Also economic objectives have been set for 1999–2002. Privatization remains one of the key issues.

Public Finance

Mauritania's budget is habitually in deficit. In 1994 the government instituted fiscal reform designed to broaden the tax base and reduce exemptions. A VAT introduced in 1995 helped increase revenues by 6.5 percent and reduced the deficit to 0.4 percent of GDP in 1995. The U.S. Central Intelligence Agency estimated that in 1996 government revenues totaled approximately $329 million and expenditures $265 million, including capital expenditures of $75 million. External debt totaled $2.5 billion in 1997.

Income

In 1999 Mauritania's gross domestic product (GDP) was estimated at $4.9 billion, or about $1,910 per capita. The 1999 estimated GDP growth rate was 3.7 percent. The average annual inflation rate was 9.8 percent in 1998.

Industry

Fish processing, the principal industrial activity, is carried out in Nouadhibou. The other major industry is iron ore mining and processing that accounted for between 30 percent and 50 percent of export earnings after the 1980s. Gypsum is another growing industry. In 1998 and 1999 the government signed exploration contracts with foreign countries to find gold, oil, phosphate, aluminum, and copper. Other small industries in 1999 included chemicals, plastics, food and beverages, metal products, building materials, and cookie factories.

Banking and Finance

Mauritania created its own currency, the ouguiya, and a national bank, the Central Bank of Mauritania (Banque Centrale de Mauritanie), which was established in 1973. In 1999 there were five commercial banks: Banque Al-Braka Mauritanie Islamique (BAMIS) of which the Saudi Al-Baraka firm owned 85 percent; Banque Mauritanie poir le Commerce Internationále (BMCI); Banque Natioñale de Mauritania (BNM); Generale de Banque de Mauritanie (GBM); and, the World Bank Representative in Mauritania. There was also one bank specializing in housing construction and three credit agencies.

A significant drawback for the Mauritanian economy partly due to the small number and low income of the population is a dearth of domestic capital. The poor reputation of the domestic banking system, notwithstanding its recent overhaul, has further discouraged local savings. Despite considerable improvement in regulation and restructuring under an ongoing World Bank-assisted program, the banking system remains fragile and further donor support will be required to consolidate good practice.

Economic Development

Until the export earning capacity of Mauritania improves, its economy will remain fragile. External deficit management dominates the public investment horizon. In 1999 Mauritania obtained financing from the World Bank and other organizations for its economic and social development projects. Funded was a mining sector capacity building project with $500,000 co-financing from the government. A $11.6 million loan was to upgrade and develop small dams. The World Bank approved a $15 million load to support access to the country's mining sector.

SOCIAL WELFARE

The National Social Security Fund administers family allowances, industrial accident benefits, insurance against occupational diseases, and old age pensions. Employers either provide medical benefits to workers on their own or through a joint program for companies. The program covers employed persons and students in trade schools but excludes agricultural workers.

Opportunities for women are severely limited by social and cultural factors. Although slavery has been abolished many times in Mauritania, there are still an estimated 90,000 full-time slaves.

Healthcare

Mauritania's public health system consists of administrative units and health facilities organized in pyramid style with some 300 basic health units in villages, 130 health posts, and fifty health centers. The only major hospital is in Nouakchott. In 1990–1997 there were ten doctors per 100,000 people. Although medical services are available free to those unable to pay, only about 63 percent of the population had access to health care services in 1985–1995. The main health problems include malaria, tuberculosis, measles, dysentery, and influenza. In 2000 the average life expectancy was 50.8 years.

Housing

The phenomenal growth of Nouakchott and the effects of rural migration, impelled by drought, have strained housing resources. As of 1990 67 percent of urban and 65 percent of rural dwellers had access to a public water supply.

EDUCATION

Education is compulsory but only a minority of school-age children attend school. In 1997 there were 312,671 students in primary schools. In 1996 51,765 students were enrolled in secondary schools. All higher-level institutions had a total of 270 teachers and 8,496 pupils in 1996. These include the National Institute of Higher Islamic Studies and the University of Nouakchott. Projected adult illiteracy rates for 2000 stood at 60.1 percent (males 49.4 percent; females 70.5 percent).

2000 KEY EVENTS TIMELINE

February

- Officials, citing "lack of proof," release Mohambedou Ould Slahi, who had been held for three weeks on suspicion that he was planning bomb attacks against the United States. U.S. authorities believe Ould Slahi has links to Osama bin Laden.

- Mauritania qualifies for debt relief under the World Bank and International Monetary Fund program for Heavily Indebted Poor Countries.

May

- Doctors Without Borders urges Mauritania and other poor countries not to accept a World Trade Organization patent law treaty that may increase medical costs.

June

- Interior ministers from Mali and Mauritania announce on June 23 that they are seeking funding of US$29 million to map their common border in a project to begin in 2001.

September

- To qualify for 40 percent reduction of foreign debt, the World Bank has challenged the government to prove that cash freed up by the debt relief will be spent on development and social service programs. Since 1980 Mauritania's foreign debt grew from $840 million to $2.6 billion.

October

- President Maaouya Ould Sid'Ahmed Taya inaugurates Mauritania's first cellular telephone network on October 4.

- The opposition Union of Democratic Forces-New Era party stages pro-Palestinian demonstrations in the nation's capital, Nouakchott, on October 31. The government bans the demonstrations, and clashes occur between police and demonstrators.

December

- The World Bank and International Monetary Fund (IMF) announce on December 23 that the United States, Canada, Japan, and nations of Europe will provide debt relief for twenty-two of the world's poorest nations, including Benin, Bolivia, Burkina Faso, Cameroon, The Gambia, Guinea, Guinea-Bissau, Guyana, Honduras, Madagascar, Malawi, Mali, Mauritania, Mozambique, Nicaragua, Niger, Rwanda, São Tomé and Príncipe, Senegal, Tanzania, Uganda, and Zambia.

ANALYSIS OF EVENTS: 2000

BUSINESS AND THE ECONOMY

The iron-ore mining company SNIM and the country's fishing industry accounted for Mauritania's entire export earnings and employed nearly two-thirds of the work force. SNIM, whose annual turnover was as large as Mauritania's entire budget, also dominated the transport industry as a road builder and operator of the country's only railroad. SNIM had also entered the tourism industry.

Mauritania entered the new millennium under a staggering burden of foreign debt, which had grown from $840 million in the 1980s to $2.6 billion at the end of the twentieth century. The country was spending six times as much per year on debt repayment as on health care for its people; 70 percent of its aid from Western donor countries went to servicing its debt. The World Bank and International Monetary Fund (IMF) agreed to grant the country debt relief in February, and the Paris Club of donor nations followed suit in March. However, in exchange for a debt reduction of 40 percent, the World Bank intended to assure through stringent oversight measures that the money saved would be spent on development and social services.

GOVERNMENT AND POLITICS

In the spring tensions between Mauritania and Senegal over the use of water from the Senegal River reached a peak. Since the revival of an old dam project on the river by the Senegalese government, Mauritania had accused its neighbor of hurting Mauritanian farmers and subverting earlier agreements over water rights on their common border. There were reports that the two countries were going to expel each other's nationals, and the tensions prompted many to cross the border to their respective homelands even without being forced. With the aid of mediation by Morocco, The Gambia, and Mali, threats of repatriation had been dropped by June 10.

In July Mauritania's president, Maaouya Ould Taya, met with Moroccan government officials to discuss the construction of a 400-meter stretch of transSaharan highway that would form a link in a proposed road linking Marrakesh with Lagos, Nigeria.

Mauritania's controversial establishment of diplomatic ties with Israel in 1999 was followed up in April with the visit of seven Israeli legislators to the country to meet with their Mauritanian counterparts. Earlier in the year a team of Israeli doctors spent a week in Mauritania working in the main hospital in Nouakchott, the capital.

The Mauritanian government continued its harassment of the country's most visible opposition leader, Ahmed Ould Daddah, head of the Union of Democratic Forces. Following multiple arrests and a trial the previous year, Daddah was arrested in April and charged with inciting violence, but released five days later. Muhambedou Ould Slahi, a suspected terrorist with possible links to Saudi financier Osama bin Laden, was detained for three weeks in February but released on lack of evidence.

CULTURE AND SOCIETY

By the close of the twentieth century about 85 percent of Mauritania's population had crowded into its cities, driven out of the countryside by drought. Poverty, overcrowding, disease, and illiteracy were widespread. Even the money allocated to social services was mismanaged: Mauritania spent two to three times as much on health care as its neighbors, Mali and Burkina Faso, without noticeable results.

In spite of official denials by the government and favorable reports by the U.S. State Department, it was alleged that the enslavement of black Mauritanians by those of Arab descent was still a firmly entrenched institution in Mauritania. The 800-year-old system of slavery, supported by tradition and even by Islamic courts, mandated that Arab *beydannes*, or masters, should do no physical labor, while their slaves, called *haratines*, performed such daily tasks as cooking, cleaning, hauling water, and doing farm work. Masters exercised complete control over their slaves, including the power to bar them from marriage, education, and other basic rights, as well as selling or loaning them to others in an informal network that defied the twenty-year-old legal ban on the practice. Critics charged that the U.S. State Department's human rights report alleging that only "vestiges" of slavery remained in Mauritania was skewed to favor a government that had renounced its ties to Saddam Hussein and initiated a diplomatic relationship with Israel.

DIRECTORY

CENTRAL GOVERNMENT

Head of State

President
Maaouya Ould Sid Ahmed Taya, Office of the President

Prime Minister
Cheikel Afia Ould Mohamed Khouna, Office of the Prime Minister

Ministers

Minister of Civil Service, Labor, Youth, and Sports
Baba Ould Sidi, Ministry of Civil Service, Labor, Youth, and Sports

Minister of Communications and Relations with Parliament
Rachid Ould Saleh, Ministry of Communications and Relations with Parliament

Minister of Culture and Islamic Orientation
Moustaph Ould sid 'El Isselmou, Ministry of Culture and Islamic Orientation

Minister of Education
Sghair Ould M'Bareck, Ministry of Education

Minister of Equipment and Transportation
Ba Amadou Racine, Ministry of Equipment and Transportation

Minister of Finance
Camara Aly Gueladio, Ministry of Finance

Minister of Fisheries and Maritime Economy
Mohamed el Moctar Ould Zamel, Ministry of Fisheries and Maritime Economy

Minister of Foreign Affairs and Cooperation
Ahmed Ould Sidi Ahmed, Ministry of Foreign Affairs and Cooperation

Minister of Health and Social Affairs
Mohamed Salem Ould Merzoug, Ministry of Health and Social Affairs

Minister of Hydraulics and Energy
Cheikh Ahmed Ould Zahaf, Ministry of Hydraulics and Energy

Minister of Interior, Post, and Telecommunications
Dahould Abdel Jelil, Ministry of Interior, Post, and Telecommunications

Minister of Justice
Sidi Mahmoud Ould Cheikh Ahmed Lemrabott, Ministry of Justice

Minister of Mines and Industry
Ishagh Ould Rajel, Ministry of Mines and Industry

Minister of National Defense
Kaba Ould Elewa, Ministry of National Defense

Minister of Planning
Mohamedou Ould Michel, Ministry of Planning

Minister of Rural Development and Environment
Ahmedy Ould Hamady, Ministry of Rural Development and Environment

Minister of Commerce, Handicrafts, and Tourism
Diop Abdoul Hamet, Ministry of Commerce, Handicrafts, and Tourism

Minister of Women's Affairs
Mintata Mint Hiddeid, Ministry of Women's Affairs

POLITICAL ORGANIZATIONS

Democratic and Social Republican Party

TITLE: President
NAME: Maaouya Ould Sid'Ahmed Taya

Union of Democratic Forces-New Era

NAME: Ahmed Ould Daddah

Assembly for Democracy and Unity

NAME: Ahmed Ould Sidi Baba

Popular Social and Democratic Union

NAME: Mohamed Mahmoud Ould Mah

Mauritanian Party for Renewal

NAME: Hameida Bouchraya

National Avant-Garde Party

NAME: Khattry Ould Jiddou

Mauritanian Party of the Democratic Center

NAME: Bamba Ould Sidi Badi

Action for Change

NAME: Messoud Ould Boulkheir

DIPLOMATIC REPRESENTATION

Embassies in Mauritania

United Kingdom
BP 2069 Nouakchott, Mauritania
TITLE: Honorary Consul

United States
Rue Abdallahi Oul Oubeid, B.P. 222, Nouakchott, Mauritania
PHONE: +222 252660; 52663
FAX: +222 251592
TITLE: Ambassador
NAME: Timberlake Foster

JUDICIAL SYSTEM

High Supreme Court

BROADCAST MEDIA

Radio Mauritanie

TYPE: Government

Televisíon du Martinique (TVM)

BP 5522, Nouakchott, Mauritania
PHONE: +222 53303
CHANNEL: E5
TYPE: Government

COLLEGES AND UNIVERSITIES

University of Nouakchott

PO Box 5026, Nouakchott, Mauritania
PHONE: +222 251382
FAX: +222 253997
WEBSITE: http://www.univ-nkc.mr/index_us.html

NEWSPAPERS AND MAGAZINES

Agence Mauritanienne d'Information

BP 467 - 371, Nouakchott, Mauritania
PHONE: +222 253856
FAX: +222 254587
E-MAIL: ami@mauritania.mr
WEBSITE: http://www.mauritania.mr/ami/

Horisons/Chaab

CIRCULATION: 3,000

AllAfrica.com - Mauritania

WEBSITE: http://www.allafrica.com/mauritania/

PUBLISHERS

Imprimerie Commerciale des Administrative de Mauritanie

BP 164, Nouakchott, Mauritania
SUBJECTS: Education

RELIGIOUS ORGANIZATIONS

Officially the Mauritanian Islamic Republic, religious organizations are inextricably linked with the government and handled internally.

FURTHER READING

Articles

"Mauritania—Life after Debt." *The Economist (US),* September 23, 2000, vol. 356, no. 8189, p. 52.

"Terrorist Suspect Is Released by Mauritania." *New York Times,* February 21, 2000, p. A6.

Teyeb, Moctar. "A Call For Freedom." *Tikkun,* July 2000, vol. 15, no. 4, p. 10.

Books

Celati, Gianni. *Adventures in Africa.* Chicago: University of Chicago Press, 2000.

Dun and Bradstreet's Export Guide to Mauritania. Parsippany, NJ: Dun & Bradstreet, 1999.

MAURITANIA: STATISTICAL DATA

For sources and notes see "Sources of Statistics" at the front of each volume.

GEOGRAPHY

Geography

Area:

Total: 1,030,700 sq km.

Land: 1,030,400 sq km.

Land boundaries:

Total: 5,074 km.

Border countries: Algeria 463 km, Mali 2,237 km, Senegal 813 km, Western Sahara 1,561 km.

Coastline: 754 km.

Climate: desert; constantly hot, dry, dusty.

Terrain: mostly barren, flat plains of the Sahara; some central hills.

Natural resources: iron ore, gypsum, fish, copper, phosphate.

Land use:

Arable land: 0%

Permanent crops: 0%

Permanent pastures: 38%

Forests and woodland: 4%

Other: 58% (1993 est.).

HUMAN FACTORS

Demographics (A)

	1990	1995	1998	2000	2010	2020	2030	2040	2050
Population	1,984	2,342	2,515	2,668	3,562	4,671	5,942	7,286	8,636
Life expectancy - males	45.2	46.9	48.0	48.7	52.4	56.1	59.7	63.1	66.3
Life expectancy - females	48.7	50.8	52.0	52.9	57.2	61.4	65.5	69.3	72.7
Birth rate (per 1,000)	45.4	45.3	44.1	43.4	39.3	34.7	29.6	25.0	21.5
Death rate (per 1,000)	17.4	15.6	14.6	14.0	11.1	8.9	7.3	6.4	6.1
Women of reproductive age (15-49 yrs.)	452	532	572	608	837	1,147	1,532	1,953	2,350
Fertility rate	6.6	6.6	6.4	6.3	5.5	4.6	3.8	3.1	2.6

Except as noted, values for vital statistics are in thousands; life expectancy is in years.

Health Personnel

	National Data	World Data (wtd ave)
Total health expenditure as a percentage of GDP, 1990-1998[a]		
Public sector	1.8	2.5
Private sector	4.1	2.9
Total[b]	5.2	5.5
Health expenditure per capita in U.S. dollars, 1990-1998[a]		
Purchasing power parity	68	561
Total	28	483
Availability of health care facilities per 100,000 people		
Hospital beds 1990-1998[a]	70	330
Doctors 1992-1995[a]	356	122
Nurses 1992-1995[a]	1,020	248

Health Indicators

	National Data	World Data
Life expectancy at birth (years)		
1980	47	61
1998	54	67
Daily per capita supply of calories		
1970	1,910	2,358
1997	2,622	2,791
Daily per capital supply of protein		
1997 (grams)	74	74
Total fertility rate (births per woman)		
1980	6.3	3.7
1998	5.4	2.7
Population with access (%)		
To safe water (1990-96)	64	NA
To sanitation (1990-96)	32	NA
People living with (1997)		
Tuberculosis (cases per 100,000)	158.4	60.4
HIV/AIDS (% aged 15 - 49 years)	0.52	0.99

Infants and Malnutrition

	National Data	World Data (wtd ave)
Under 5 mortality rate (1989)	183	NA
% of infants with low birthweight (1992-98)[1]	9	17
Births attended by skilled health staff (% of total births 1996-98)	40	52
% fully immunized at 1 year of age (1995-98)[1]		
TB	69	82
DPT	28	77
Polio	28	77
Measles	20	74
Prevalence of child malnutrition (1992-98)[1] (based on weight for age, % of children under 5 years)	23	30

Ethnic Division

Mixed Maur/black 40%

Maur 30%

Black 30%

Religion

Muslim 100%

Major Languages

Hasaniya Arabic (official), Pular, Soninke, Wolof (official), French.

EDUCATION

Public Education Expenditures

	1980	1997
Public expenditures on education as % of GNP	NA	5.1
Expenditures per student as % of GNP per capita		
Primary & Secondary	30.4	11.1
Tertiary	NA	205.9
Pupils per teacher at the primary level	NA	50
Duration of primary education in years	NA	6
World data for comparison		
Public expenditures on education as % of GNP (mean)	3.9	4.8
Pupils per teacher at the primary level (wtd ave)	NA	33
Duration of primary education in years (mean)	NA	9

Educational Attainment (A)

Age group (1988) . . . . .25+

Population of this age group 679,667

Highest level attained (%)

- No schooling 60.8
- First level
  - Not completed 34.1
  - Completed ....NA
- Entered second level 3.8
- Entered post-secondary 1.3

Literacy Rates (A)

In thousands and percent	1990	1995	2000	2010
Illiterate population (15+ yrs.)	723	806	904	1,099
Literacy rate - total adult pop. (%)	35.2	37.7	40.1	44.6
Literacy rate - males (%)	47.1	49.6	52.0	56.1
Literacy rate - females (%)	23.9	26.3	28.7	33.4

GOVERNMENT & LAW

Political Parties

Legislature	no. of seats
National Assembly	
Democratic and Social Republican Party (PRDS)	71
Action for Change (AC)	1
Independents and other	7

National Assembly elections were last held 11 and 18 October 1996 (next to be held in 2001). Parties were legalized by the constitution passed 12 July 1991, however, politics continue to be tribally based.

Government Budgets (B)

- Revenues ....$329 million
- Expenditures ....$265 million
- Capital expenditures ....$75 million

Data for 1996 est.

Crime

Crime rate (for 1997)

- Crimes reported 4,750
- Total persons convicted 3,550
- Crimes per 100,000 population 225

Persons responsible for offenses

- Total number of suspects 4,750
- Total number of female suspects ....NA
- Total number of juvenile suspects ....NA

(Continued on next page.)

LABOR FORCE

Total Labor Force (A)

465,000 (1981 est.); 45,000 wage earners (1980).

Labor Force by Occupation

- Agriculture 47%
- Services 39%
- Industry 14%

Unemployment Rate

23% (1995 est.)

PRODUCTION SECTOR

Energy Production

- Production ....152 million kWh
- Production by source
  - Fossil fuel 80.26%
  - Hydro 19.74%
  - Nuclear 0%
  - Other 0%
- Exports ....0 kWh

Data for 1998.

Energy Consumption

- Consumption ....141 million kWh
- Imports ....0 kWh

Data for 1998.

Transportation

Highways:

Total: 7,660 km.

Paved: 866 km.

Unpaved: 6,794 km (1996 est.).

Waterways: mostly ferry traffic on the Senegal River.

Merchant marine: none (1999 est.).

Airports: 26 (1999 est.).

Airports - with unpaved runways: 18.

Top Agriculture Products

Dates, millet, sorghum, root crops; cattle, sheep; fish products.

Top Mining Products (B)

Mineral resources include: iron ore, gypsum, copper, phosphate.

COMMUNICATIONS

Daily Newspapers

	National Data	World Data for Comparison
Daily Newspapers		
Number of Dailies	2	8,391
Total Circulation (000)	1	548,000
Circulation per 1,000 inhabitants	0.5	96

Telecommunications

Telephones - main lines in use: 9,000 (1995).

Telephones - mobile cellular: 0 (1995).

Telephone system: poor system of cable and open-wire lines, minor microwave radio relay links, and radiotelephone communications stations (improvements being made).

Domestic: mostly cable and open-wire lines; a recently completed domestic satellite telecommunications system links Nouakchott with regional capitals.

(Continued on next page.)

GOVERNMENT & LAW (cont.)

Military Affairs (A)

	1990	1992	1995	1996	1997
Military expenditures					
Current dollars (mil.)	28[e]	26[e]	26	25	24
1997 constant dollars (mil.)	33[e]	29[e]	27	26	24
Armed forces (000)	17	16	11	11	11
Gross national product (GNP)					
Current dollars (mil.)	670	740	921	980	1,050
1997 constant dollars (mil.)	784	820	953	996	1,050
Central government expenditures (CGE)					
1997 constant dollars (mil.)	266	216	249	257	250
People (mil.)	1.9	2.1	2.3	2.4	2.4
Military expenditure as % of GNP	4.2	3.5	2.8	2.6	2.3
World data on military expenditure as % of GNP	4.5	3.4	2.7	2.6	2.6
Military expenditure as % of CGE	12.3	13.3	10.9	10.1	9.8
World data on military expenditure as % of CGE	17.0	12.5	10.5	10.3	10.2
Military expenditure per capita (1997 $)	17	14	12	11	10
World data on military expenditure per capita (1997 $)	242	173	146	143	145
Armed forces per 1,000 people (soldiers)	8.8	7.6	4.7	4.6	4.5
World data on armed forces per 1,000 people (soldiers)	5.3	4.5	4.1	3.9	3.8
GNP per capita (1997 $)	405	388	408	417	427
Arms imports[6]					
Current dollars (mil.)	0	0	20	0	0
1997 constant dollars (mil.)	0	0	21	0	0
Total imports[7]					
Current dollars (mil.)	220	600[e]	642[e]	638[e]	613[e]
1997 constant dollars (mil.)	258	665[e]	665[e]	649[e]	613[e]
Total exports[7]					
Current dollars (mil.)	469	448[e]	557[e]	551[e]	540[e]
1997 constant dollars (mil.)	549	497[e]	577[e]	560[e]	540[e]
Arms as percent of total imports[8]	0	0	3.1	0	0
Arms as percent of total exports[8]	0	0	0	0	0

COMMUNICATIONS (cont.)

Telecommunications (cont.)

International: satellite earth stations - 1 Intelsat (Atlantic Ocean) and 2 Arabsat.

Radio broadcast stations: AM 1, FM 2, shortwave 1 (1998).

Radios: 360,000 (1997).

Television broadcast stations: 1 (1997).

Televisions: 62,000 (1997).

Internet Service Providers (ISPs): NA

FINANCE, ECONOMICS, & TRADE

Economic Indicators

National product: GDP—purchasing power parity—$4.9 billion (1999 est.).

National product real growth rate: 3.7% (1999 est.).

National product per capita: $1,910 (1999 est.).

Inflation rate—consumer price index: 9.8% (1998).

Exchange Rates

Exchange rates:

Ouguiyas (UM) per US$1

December 1999	219.560
1999	209.514
1998	188.476
1997	151.853
1996	137.222
1995	129.768

Top Import Origins

$444 million (f.o.b., 1997)

Origins (1997)

France	26%
Spain	8%
Germany	7%
Benelux	7%

Balance of Payments

	1991	1992	1993	1994	1995
Exports of goods (f.o.b.)	436	407	403	400	476
Imports of goods (f.o.b.)	−399	−461	−400	−352	−293
Trade balance	37	−55	3	47	184
Services - debits	−151	−179	−185	−181	−217
Services - credits	31	20	21	26	28
Private transfers (net)	18	59	8	12	12
Government transfers (net)	99	96	100	100	79
Overall balance	−30	−118	−174	−70	22

(Continued on next page.)

MANUFACTURING SECTOR

GDP & Manufacturing Summary (B)

	1980	1985	1990	1993	1994	1995
Gross Domestic Product						
Millions of 1990 dollars	878	875	1,052	1,161	1,215	1,271
Growth rate in percent	0.70	3.35	3.50	3.00	4.60	4.60
Per capita (in 1990 dollars)	566	495	525	537	548	559
Manufacturing Value Added						
Millions of 1990 dollars	64	103	119	150	160	170[e]
Growth rate in percent	−1.43	22.44	18.98	6.19	6.51	6.36[e]
Manufacturing share in percent of current prices	5.6	12.8	12.9	11.1[e]	NA	NA

FINANCE, ECONOMICS, & TRADE (cont.)

Top Export Destinations

$425 million (f.o.b., 1997)

Destinations (1997)

Japan	24%
Italy	17%
France	14%
Spain	8%

Foreign Aid

Recipient: $227.9 million (1995).

Import/Export Commodities

Import Commodities	Export Commodities
Machinery and equipment	Fish and fish products
Petroleum products	Iron ore
Capital goods	Gold
Foodstuffs	
Consumer goods	

MAURITIUS

Republic of Mauritius

CAPITAL: Port Louis.

FLAG: The national flag consists of four horizontal stripes of red, blue, yellow, and green.

ANTHEM: *Glory to Thee, Motherland, O Motherland of Mine.*

MONETARY UNIT: The Mauritius rupee (R) is a currency of 100 cents. There are coins of 1, 2, 5, 10, 25, and 50 cents and 1 rupee, and notes of 5, 10, 20, 50, 100, 200, 500, and 1,000 rupees. R1 = $0.05629 (or $1 = R17.764).

WEIGHTS AND MEASURES: The metric system is in general use; traditional weights and measures are also employed.

HOLIDAYS: New Year, 1–2 January; National Day, 12 March; Labor Day, 1 May. Christian, Hindu, and Muslim holidays are also observed.

TIME: 4 PM = noon GMT.

LOCATION AND SIZE: Mauritius, situated in the Indian Ocean, off the African coast, includes the island of Rodrigues, the two islands of Agelega, and the St. Brandon Group (Cargados Carajos Shoals). Comparatively, the area occupied by Mauritius is slightly less than 10.5 times the size of Washington, D.C. It has a coastline of 177 kilometers (110 miles). The capital city of Mauritius, Port Louis, is located on the island's northwest coast.

CLIMATE: The climate of Mauritius is humid, with temperatures ranging from 18° to 30°C (64–86°F) at sea level, and from 13 to 26°C (55–79°F) at an elevation of 460 meters (1,500 feet). The central plateau and windward slopes have a yearly average rainfall of over 500 centimeters (200 inches). On the coast, rainfall averages about 100 centimeters (40 inches) annually.

INTRODUCTORY SURVEY

RECENT HISTORY

When slavery was abolished in the British Empire in the 1830s, many former slaves left Mauritius for Africa causing a labor shortage. From 1837 to 1907 indentured workers were imported to Mauritius from India. About 450,000 Indians went to Mauritius under this system. Since 1948 politicians of Indian descent have dominated the government.

Mauritius became independent on March 12, 1968. Sir Seewoosagur Ramgoolam, chief minister in the colonial government, became the first prime minister after independence. Ramgoolam's Mauritius Labor Party (MLP) held power alone or in coalition with others until June 1982 when a coalition known as the Militant Socialist Movement (MSM) formed a government. Its leader, Aneerood Jugnauth, became prime minister.

Elections in August 1983 produced a clear mandate for a new coalition forged by Jugnauth that won clear-cut electoral victories in August 1987 and September 1991. The new alliance amended the constitution making Mauritius a republic within the British Commonwealth. Since March 12, 1992, a Mauritian chief of state had replaced Queen Elizabeth II.

GOVERNMENT

The Mauritian government is a parliamentary democracy operating under a 1968 constitution, amended in 1992. The chief of state is the president. The National Assembly elects the president and vice

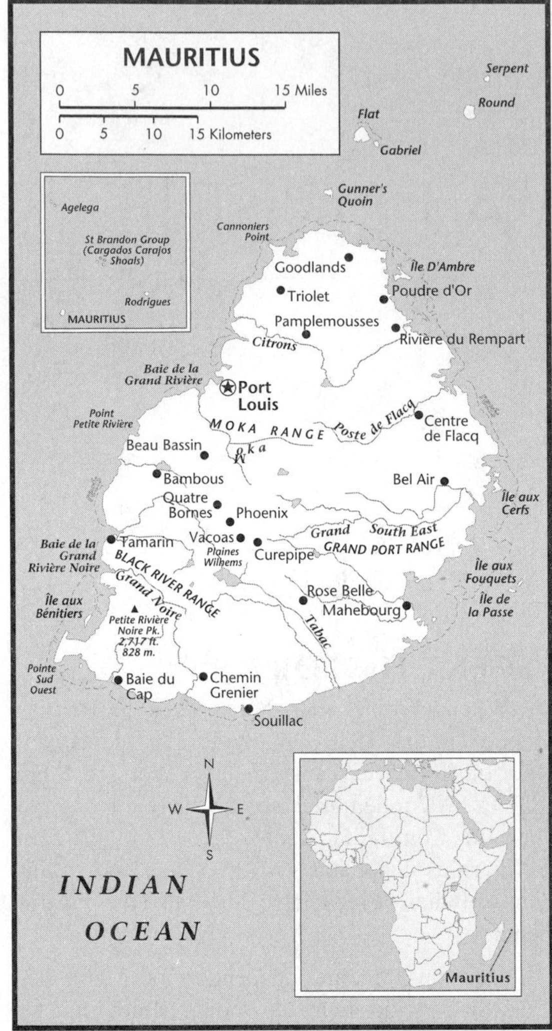

president for five-year terms. The head of government is the prime minister appointed by the president and is generally the leader of the majority party in the National Assembly. The cabinet, known as the Council of Ministers, is appointed by the president on the recommendation of the prime minister and is responsible to the National Assembly.

The legislative branch is the unicameral 66-seat National Assembly. Sixty-two members are elected by popular vote. Four are appointed by the election commission from the losing political parties to give representation to various ethnic minorities.

Suffrage is universal at age eighteen.

Judiciary

The Supreme Court has a chief justice and six other judges who also serve on the Court of Criminal Appeal, the Court of Civil Appeal, the Intermediate Court, the Industrial Court, and ten district courts. Final appeal can be made to the UK Privy Council.

Political Parties

The Mauritius Labor Party (MLP) received popular support during 1947–1982. In the 1982 elections the MMM (Mauritian Militant Movement) captured forty-two seats in parliament and joined the Mauritian Socialist Party (Parti Socialiste Mauricien—PSM) in a ruling coalition under Aneerood Jugnauth. Jugnauth's government fell apart in the early months of 1983 and he then formed the Mauritian Socialist Movement (Mouvement Socialiste Mauricien—MSM).

A newly solidified MMM/MLP coalition won sixty of sixty-six seats in the December 1995 elections.

DEFENSE

The National Police Force is responsible for defense. In 2000 it had some 1,500 members including 1,000 in the Special Mobile Force and 500 in the National Coast Guard.

ECONOMIC AFFAIRS

The Mauritius economy, diverse and conservatively managed, is based on export-oriented manufacturing (mainly clothing), sugar, tourism, and increasingly an offshore banking sector. Most production is done by private enterprise with government merely providing institutional facilities, and incentives for production. Nearly 275 garment factories were operating in the Export Processing Zone (EPZ) of Mauritius in 1999. The EPZ, where imported goods and raw materials are processed for export, is important to industrial development. In addition to textiles and clothing (80 percent), EPZ products include electrical components and diamonds. Between 1988 and 1998 the economy was estimated to have grown at an annual rate between 5 percent and 6 percent.

Sugarcane covers approximately 90 percent of cultivated land and accounted for up to 25 percent of export savings in the late 1990s. Mauritius attracted over 9,000 offshore entities aimed at commerce in India and South America. Investment in the banking sector has steadily grown.

Stable government and a positive human rights record continue to attract considerable foreign investment and have boosted Mauritius' per capita GDP to one of the highest in Africa at $10,400 by 1999 estimates.

Public Finance

In 1997 the deficit reached 4.6 percent but the government announced measures aimed at reducing the figure to 3.6 percent of GDP. The U.S. Central Intelligence Agency estimated that in 1999 government revenues totaled approximately $1.1 billion and expenditures $1.2 billion.

Income

In 1999 Mauritius's gross domestic product (GDP) was estimated at $12.3 billion, or about $10,400 per capita. The 1999 estimated growth rate of GDP was 4 percent and inflation was 8.6 percent in 1999. The 1996 GDP contribution by sector was agriculture 10 percent, industry 29 percent, and services 61 percent.

Industry

Manufacturing focuses on the processing of agricultural products, especially sugar cane and its by-products including molasses and rum and on textiles. Local tobacco is made into cigarettes and four factories are maintained to process tea. Other small industries produce goods for local consumption such as beer and soft drinks, shoes, metal products, and paints.

The Export Processing Zone (EPZ) is an important part of Mauritius's industrial development. Imported goods are processed for export in the EPZ, which gives investors special tax breaks and duty exemption. Textiles generate 80 percent of exports from the EPZ. EPZ industries also produce sunglasses, toys, nails, razor blades, tires, and audiocassettes.

Banking and Finance

The Bank of Mauritius is the central bank. The Development Bank of Mauritius was established in March 1964 to provide loans for agricultural and industrial enterprises. There were ten commercial banks operating in the country in 1997.

Locally owned banks include the Mauritius Commercial Bank Limited and the State Bank of Mauritius Limited, both of which dominate the market. Seven banks are offshore offering attractive tax rates especially to U.S. investment in India.

The country has a security exchange, the Stock Exchange of Mauritius. The number of domestic listed shares in 1997 was forty-five.

Economic Development

France has backed training for labor, a stock exchange (which opened under the Stock Exchange Act of 1988), and irrigation projects. The EU is supporting efforts at diversifying agriculture. The Mauritius plan to become an international financial center advanced as liberalized currency rules were put into effect in 1986. In 1995 Mauritius became the twelfth member of the Southern African Development Community (SADC). In 2000 Mauritius continued to successfully encourage foreign investment. Mauritius planned to invest up to $1.5 billion in infrastructure development projects from 1997 to 2007.

SOCIAL WELFARE

Mauritius has a universal system of pensions that supplements an earnings related pension system. A program of family allowances assists needy families with more than three children. Employment related sickness and maternity benefits are provided as well as workers' compensation and unemployment benefits under a 1993 law. Women do not face significant legal discrimination but most remain limited to traditional roles in the household and workplace.

Healthcare

In 2000 the average life expectancy is seventy-one years. Mauritius has seven general hospitals, and two private hospitals. There are also seventy-four maternity, child health, and family planning centers. There is one physician per 1,165 people. In 1995 100 percent of the population had access to safe water and sanitation.

Housing

There are three basic types of houses: wattle and daub (woven poles or sticks with plaster) construction with thatched roofs; galvanized sheet-iron structures; and houses constructed of wood.

EDUCATION

Education is free up to college level and is compulsory between the ages of five and twelve. The estimated adult illiteracy rate in 1995 was 17 percent. In 1997 an estimated 283 primary schools had 127,109 pupils and 6,434 teachers, and general secondary schools had 93,839 pupils.

Postsecondary institutions include the University of Mauritius, the Mauritius College of the Air, and the Mahatma Gandhi Institute. In 1997–1998 universities had 6,419 students. Many university students study in Europe, India, Australia, and the United States.

2000 KEY EVENTS TIMELINE

January

- The cabinet agrees to introduce legislation to create the University of Technology, Mauritius in response to increased demand for technical workers.

February

- Seven international firms submit tenders to acquire 40 percent of state-owned Mauritius Telecom.

April

- Government announces intent to create a Commission for Racial Equality to prevent racial conflict such as that which occurred in March 1999.

June

- The government destroys drugs with a street value of over US$400,000, sending a warning to drug traffickers by promising death sentences.

July

- Government announces a record trade deficit for the first quarter of 2000 as a result of declining sugar prices and increased fuel costs.
- Hundreds of islanders sue the British government to return to their home-island of Diego Garcia on July 17. The United States first confiscated the island for use as a military base in the 1960s, and the British later leased the island.

August

- The Mauritian rupee continues its devaluation against the British pound sterling and the U.S. dollar. In June and July, the rupee depreciated 0.5 percent.

September

- Results of the September 11 election show the opposition parties, the *Mouvement Socialiste Mauricien* and the *Mouvement Militant Mauricien* led by Sir Anerood Jugnauth, winning the national assembly elections by a landslide fifty-four seats out of sixty-two. Jugnauth is names the new prime minister.
- Air Namibia announces flights to Mauritius.
- Civil servants protest after the government announces a suspension of a 300-rupee monthly wage increase. The government (swept out of power in the election) had promised increases now rescinded by the new government on the basis that the raise would bankrupt the national treasury.

October

- Despite record profits of Delphis Bank-Mauritius, Standards Manufacturers, and Mauritius Breweries, President Cassam Ulteem states that the country's economy continues to remain weak.
- The Federation of Civil Service Unions of Mauritius goes to court October 5 against the government for revoking a 300-rupee monthly raise that was scheduled in September.

November

- Hundreds of civil servants demonstrate November 6 against a negative salary report released November 3. The president of the Civil Service Unions of Mauritius, Rashid Imrith, demands an extra 1,000 rupees monthly for workers and a reevaluation of government policy.

ANALYSIS OF EVENTS: 2000

BUSINESS AND THE ECONOMY

With its diversified economy, Mauritius had generally enjoyed economic growth well beyond that of most of its African neighbors—roughly 5–6 percent annually—and corresponding social development. However, its economy was in a weak period in spite of record profits by major companies. In April the government announced a record trade deficit for the quarter as a result of increased fuel expenses and falling sugar prices.

Mauritius was among thirty-five nations listed in June by the Organization for European Cooperation and Development (OECD) as "tax havens" whose banking practices were likely to attract depositors seeking to evade taxes or launder money. All of the listed countries faced possible sanctions unless reforms were begun within a year and completed by 2005. In a related development, officials of India's government demanded back taxes from foreign investors who had based their operations in Mauritius because of a bilateral treaty that allowed them to be taxed under Mauritian law, thus avoiding capital gains taxes.

Mauritius was a founding member of the Southern Africa Free Trade Zone, formed in September by the Southern African Development Community (SADC). It was hoped that the alliance would eventually create a single market encompassing some 200 million people in fourteen countries. Its goals included lowering and ultimately eliminating tariffs, increasing trade among members to 35 percent of all trade by 2004, and facilitating foreign trade with the overall region.

In May leaders from COMESA (Common Market for Eastern and Southern Africa) met in Mauritius to discuss proposed economic integration.

GOVERNMENT AND POLITICS

In August the Parliament of Mauritius was unexpectedly dissolved by the nation's president, Cassam Uteem, following a series of government corruption scandals. General elections were scheduled for September, several months earlier than they would normally have been held. In the elections an opposition alliance consisting of the Socialist Militant Party and the Militant Movement won control of the government in a landslide, with fifty-four of the legislative body's sixty-two seats. Under an agreement between the two parties, Socialist Militant leader Anerood Jugnath would serve for the first three years and then turn over the office to his alliance partner Paul Berenger—making Berenger the nation's first non-Hindu leader.

Corruption and ethnic rioting had helped bring down the government of outgoing prime minister Navin Ramgoolam. The new prime minister declared his intention of reinvigorating the nation's economy by boosting confidence on the part of both local and foreign investors. The new government soon faced controversy when it reversed a wage increase promised to civil servants by its predecessor, spurring protests by public-sector employees. The government claimed the raise would empty the nation's coffers.

In October Mauritius won the African seat on the United Nations Security Council, beating out Sudan by a vote of 113 to 55. Sudan's nomination for the seat had raised protests because of its tarnished human rights record, which included charges of slavery.

In response to a growing need for workers with technical skills, legislation was introduced to create a technical university in Mauritius.

CULTURE AND SOCIETY

The nation's successful transition from an agricultural to a diversified economy was reflected in its social development: life expectancy was 71 years, infant mortality had fallen to 6.7 deaths per 1,000 live births, and adult literacy was 83 percent. Per capita income at the end of 1999 was about $10,000.

Mauritius had a population of 1.3 million, of which just over half were Hindus, with the next largest groups being Creole and Muslim. Creoles, descendants of slaves brought from Africa by Dutch and French colonizers, remained marginalized by Mauritian society, with most living in poverty and subjected to serious employment discrimination, including discrimination in public employment. Social problems including substance addiction and prostitution were more widespread among Creoles than among the general population. Tensions between poor youths in the Creole slums and the country's overwhelmingly Hindu police forces sometimes erupted into violence, as they had following the detention and death of a popular Creole singer in 1998. The country's new government—which would be the first to have a non-Hindu prime minister—had promised reform of the civil service and police force to redress discrimination against Creoles. A national holiday commemorating the abolition of slavery was also planned.

Mauritius gained some publicity when Britain's Prince William traveled to the island to take part in an educational project with the Royal Geographical Society. The nature of the project was not disclosed.

DIRECTORY

CENTRAL GOVERNMENT

Head of State

President
Cassam Uteem, Office of the President,
Government House, Port Louis, Mauritius
PHONE: +230 4543021
FAX: +230 4645370
E-MAIL: statepas@intnet.mu

Ministers

Prime Minister
Anerood Jugnauth, Office of the Prime Minister, New Government Centre, 6th Floor, Port Louis, Mauritius
PHONE: +230 2011018
FAX: +230 2129393

Minister of Defense and Home Affairs
Anerood Jugnauth, Ministry of Defense and Home Affairs, 4th Floor Government Centre, Port Louis, Mauritius
PHONE: +230 2029020; 2029024
FAX: +230 2117907

Minister of External Communications and Outer Islands
Navinchandra Ramgoolam, Ministry of External Communications and Outer Islands, 5th Floor, Air Mauritius Building, Port Louis, Mauritius
PHONE: +230 2101122
FAX: +230 2117708

Minister of Foreign Affairs
Ali Gayan, Ministry of Foreign Affairs, Level Five, New Government Centre, Port Louis, Mauritius
PHONE: +230 2011416
FAX: +230 2126764

Minister of Commerce, Industry, and International Trade
Jayen Cuttaree, Ministry of Industry, Commerce, and International Trade, 7th Floor, Air Mauritius Centre, John Kennedy Street, Port Louis, Mauritius
PHONE: +230 2107100
FAX: +230 2128201
E-MAIL: minic@intnet.mu

Minister of Justice and Human Rights
Emmanuel Leung Shing, Ministry of Justice and Human Rights

Minister of Finance
Paul Berenger, Ministry of Finance, Ground Floor, Government House, Port Louis, Mauritius
PHONE: +230 2011777
FAX: +230 2087854
E-MAIL: mof@bow.intnet.mu

Minister of Education
Steve Obeegadoo, Ministry of Education, IVTB House, Pont Fer, Phoenix, Mauritius
PHONE: +230 6980464; 6977862; 6977730
FAX: +230 6982550
E-MAIL: meduhrd@bow.intnet.mu

Minister of Agriculture
Pravin Jugnauth, Ministry of Agriculture, 9th Floor, Renganaden Seeneevassen Building, Port Louis, Mauritius
PHONE: +230 2120814
FAX: +230 2124427

Minister of Labor and Industrial Relations
Showkatally Soodhun, Ministry of Labor and Industrial Relations

Minister of Civil Service Affairs and Administrative Reform
Ahmad Jeewah, Ministry of Civil Service Affairs and Administrative Reform, 6th Floor, New Government Centre, Port Louis, Mauritius
FAX: +230 2129528
E-MAIL: civser@bow.intnet.mu

Minister of Regional Administration, Urban and Rural Development
Joe Lesjongard, Ministry of Regional Administration, Urban and Rural Development

Minister of Arts and Culture
Motee Ramdass, Ministry of Arts and Culture, 7th Floor,Renganaden Seeneevassen Building, c/r Pope Hennessy and Maillard Streets, Port Louis, Mauritius
PHONE: +230 2129993
FAX: +230 2129366; 2113196
E-MAIL: culture@intnet.mu

Minister of Environment
Rajesh Bhagwan, Ministry of Environment

Minister of Public Infrastructure
Anil Baichoo, Ministry of Public Infrastructure, Treasury Building, Intendence Street, Port Louis, Mauritius
PHONE: +230 2083063; 2126071; 2121876
FAX: +230 2087149

Minister of Women, Family Welfare and Child Development
Arianne Navarre-Marie, Ministry of Women, Family Welfare and Child Development, CSK Building, Corner Remy Ollier/Emmanuel Anquetil Streets, Port Louis, Mauritius
PHONE: +230 2401377
FAX: +230 2407717
E-MAIL: mwfwcd@bow.intnet.mu

Minister of Tourism and Leisure
Nando Bodha, Ministry of Tourism and Leisure, Level 12, Air Mauritius Centre, John Kennedy Street, Port Louis, Mauritius
PHONE: +230 2101329

FAX: +230 2086776
E-MAIL: mot@intnet.mu

Minister of Health and Quality of Life
Ashok Jugnauth, Ministry of Health and Quality of Life
PHONE: +230 2011910; 2116204
E-MAIL: Keswar@intnet.mu

Minister of Housing and Lands
Mukeshwar Choonee, Ministry of Housing and Lands, 4th, 5th, 6th Floors, Sugar Industry Labor Welfare Fund Building, Edith Cavell St., Port Louis, Mauritius
PHONE: +230 2082831
FAX: +230 2129369

Minister of Telecommunications and Information Technology
Pradeep Jeeha, Ministry of Telecommunications and Information Technology, Level 9, Air Mauritius Centre, President John Kennedy Street, Port Louis, Mauritius
PHONE: +230 2100201
FAX: +230 2121673
E-MAIL: mintelit@intnet.mu

Minister of Social Security and Institutional Reform
Samioulah Lauthan, Ministry of Social Security and Institutional Reform, R. Seeneevassen Building, Jules Koenig St., Port Louis, Mauritius
PHONE: +230 2129813; 2123001
FAX: +230 2128190
E-MAIL: mssns@intnet.mu

Minister of Fisheries and Co-operatives
Sylvio Michel, Ministry of Fisheries and Co-operatives, 3rd and 4th Level, LICI Building, John Kennedy Street, Port Louis, Mauritius
PHONE: +230 2088319

Minister of Youth and Sports
Ravi Yerrigadoo, Ministry of Youth and Sports, Headquarters, 3rd Level, Emmanuel Anquetil Bldg, Port Louis, Mauritius

Minister of Public Utilities
Alan Ganoo, Ministry of Public Utilities

Minister of Cooperatives
Prem Koonjoo, Ministry of Cooperatives

POLITICAL ORGANIZATIONS

Parti Travailiste (Mauritius Labor Party)

7, Guy Rozemont Square, Port Louis, Mauritius
PHONE: +230 2126691
E-MAIL: Labor@intnet.mu
TITLE: Leader
NAME: Navinchandra Ramgoolam

Mouvement Militant Mauricien (Mauritian Militant Movement)

NAME: Paul Berenger

Organisation du Peuple Rodriguais (Organization of the People of Rodrigues)

NAME: Louis Serge Clair

Mouvement Rodriguais (Rodrigues Movement)

NAME: Nicolas Vonmally

Parti Gaetan Duval (Gaetan Duval Party)

NAME: Gaetan Duval

Hizbullah (Party of God)

NAME: Imam Mustapha Beeharry

DIPLOMATIC REPRESENTATION

Embassies in Mauritius

Australia
2nd Floor, Rogers House, Port Louis, Mauritius
PHONE: +230 2081700

Austria
PHONE: +230 2086801

Belgium
Dr Ferriere Street, Port Louis, Mauritius
PHONE: +230 2081241

Canada
King Georges Avenue, Floreal, Mauritius
PHONE: +230 6865796

China
Royal Road, Belle Rose, Mauritius
PHONE: +230 4643073

Denmark
4 Edith Cavell Street, Port Louis, Mauritius
PHONE: +230 2085051

Egypt
King George Avenue, Floreal, Mauritius
PHONE: +230 6962605

Finland
5 Pres. John Kennedy Street, Port Louis, Mauririus
PHONE: +230 2086801

France
5 bis, Rue Champ de Lort-BP 12, Port Louis, Mauritius
PHONE: +230 2087981; 2087984
FAX: +230 2088432
E-MAIL: port_louis@dree.org

Germany
60 SS Ramgoolam Street, Port Louis, Mauritius
PHONE: +230 2080666

Great Britain
Les Cascades Building, Edith Cavell Street, Port Louis, Mauritius
PHONE: +230 2111361
FAX: +230 2111369

India
Sir William Newton Street, Port Louis, Mauritius
PHONE: +230 2080666

Netherlands
Docteur Ferriere Street, Port Louis, Mauritius
PHONE: +230 2082811

Korea
Rainbow House, Port Louis, Mauritius
PHONE: +230 2083308

Malaysia
Queen Mary Avenue, Floreal, Mauritius
PHONE: +230 6865015

Norway
5 Pres. John Kennedy St., Port Louis, Mauritius
PHONE: +230 2086801

Pakistan
7th Floor, Anglo Mauritius House, Port Louis, Mauritius
PHONE: +230 2126547

Russia
Queen Mary Avenue, Floreal, Mauritius
PHONE: +230 6961545

South Africa
Pope Hennessy St., Port Louis, Mauritius
PHONE: +230 2126926

JUDICIAL SYSTEM

Supreme Court

BROADCAST MEDIA

Mauritius Broadcasting Corp.

1 Louis Pasteur Street, Forest Side, Mauritania
PHONE: +230 6755001; 6755002
FAX: +230 6757332
TITLE: Chairman
CONTACT: Denis Rivet
TYPE: Commercial

COLLEGES AND UNIVERSITIES

University of Mauritius

Reduit, Mauritius
PHONE: +230 4541041
FAX: +230 4549642
E-MAIL: goofa@uom.ac.mu
WEBSITE: http://www.uom.ac.mu

Mauritius College of the Air

Mauritius College of the Air, Reduit, Mauritius
PHONE: +230 4648854
FAX: +230 4658653
WEBSITE: http://www.saide.org.za/worldbank/countries/mauritius/coa.htm

NEWSPAPERS AND MAGAZINES

L'Express

La Sentinelle Ltd., 3, rue Brown Sequard, PO Box 247, Port Louis, Mauritius
PHONE: +230 2121826
FAX: +230 2115437
E-MAIL: sentinelle@bow.intnet.mu
WEBSITE: http://www.lexpress-net.com
TITLE: Editor-in-Chief
CONTACT: Jean Claude de L'Estrac
CIRCULATION: 36,000

Le Mauricien

Le Mauricien Ltd., 8, rue St. Georges, Port Louis, Mauritius
PHONE: +230 2087808
FAX: +230 2087059
E-MAIL: publicite@lemauricien.com
WEBSITE: http://www.lemauricien.com
TITLE: Editor
CONTACT: Gilbert Ahnee
CIRCULATION: 35,000

The New Nation

Independent Publishers Ltd., 31 Edith Cavell St., PO Box 647, Port Louis, Mauritius
CIRCULATION: 15,000

La Vie Catholique

28 Route Nicolay, Port Louis, Mauritius
PHONE: +230 2420975
FAX: +230 2423114

E-MAIL: viecatho@bow.intnet.mu
TITLE: Editor
CONTACT: Clency Lajoie
CIRCULATION: 15,000

Week-End

Le Mauricien Ltd., 8, rue St. Georges, Port Louis, Mauritius
PHONE: +230 2087808
FAX: +230 2087059
E-MAIL: publicite@lemauricien.com
WEBSITE: http://www.lemauricien.com
TITLE: Editor
CONTACT: Gerard Cateaux
CIRCULATION: 85,000

Week-End Scope

Le Mauricien Ltd., 8, rue St. Georges, Port Louis, Mauritius
PHONE: +230 2087808
FAX: +230 2087059
E-MAIL: publicite@lemauricien.com
WEBSITE: http://www.lemauricien.com
TITLE: Editor-in-Chief
CONTACT: Ahmad Salarbux
CIRCULATION: 40,000

Mauritius Times

23 Bourbon St., Port-Louis, Mauritius
FAX: +230 2121313
TITLE: Editor
CONTACT: B. Ramlallah
CIRCULATION: 15,000
TYPE: Social science, general

PROSI Magazine

Plantation House, Port Louis, Mauritius
PHONE: +230 2123302
FAX: +230 2128710
E-MAIL: prosi@bow.intnet.mu
TITLE: Editor
CONTACT: Sabina Narainen
TYPE: Agriculture

Turf Magazine

Le Mauricien Ltd., 8, rue St. Georges, Port Louis, Mauritius
PHONE: +230 2087808
FAX: +230 2087059
E-MAIL: publicite@lemauricien.com
WEBSITE: http://www.lemauricien.com

PUBLISHERS

De l'edition Bukie Banane

8 Edwin Ythier St., Rose Hill, Mauritius
PHONE: +230 4542327
TITLE: Man Director
CONTACT: Dev Virahsawmy
SUBJECTS: Drama, Theater, Poetry, Regional Interests

Government Printer (Imprimerie Nationale)

La Tour Loenig, Pointe aux Sables, Mauritius
PHONE: +230 2345284

Hemco Publications

7 Virgil Naz St., Rose Hill, Mauritius
PHONE: +230 4643141
TITLE: Editor
CONTACT: H. Gyaram
SUBJECTS: Education, Medicine, Nursing, Dentistry, Buddhism, Hinduism, Catholicism, Islam

Editions de l'Ocean Indien Ltd.

Stanley, Rose Hill, Mauritius
PHONE: +230 4646761
FAX: +230 4643445
TITLE: Assistant Publications Manager
CONTACT: S. Ramlallah

EDITIONS le Printemps

4 Club Rd., Vacoas, Mauritius
PHONE: +230 6961017
FAX: +230 6867302
E-MAIL: elp@bow.intnet.mu
TITLE: Man. Director
CONTACT: Ahmud Islam Sulliman
SUBJECTS: Biography

Vizavi Editions

29 Saint Georges St., Port Louis, Mauritius
PHONE: +230 2112435
FAX: +230 2113047
E-MAIL: vizavi@intnet.mu
TITLE: Director
CONTACT: P.M. Siew
SUBJECTS: Biography, Cookery, Political Science, History, Literature, Literary Criticism, Essays, Nonfiction (General)

RELIGIOUS ORGANIZATIONS

Hindu

International Council of Hindu Youth (ICHY)
12 Bourbon Street, Room 4, PO Box 382, Port Louis, Mauritius
PHONE: +230 2409964
FAX: +230 2409964
TITLE: Secretary General
NAME: N. Bossoondyal

Islamic

Shia Ithna Asheri Jamat of Mauritius
57, Madad ul Islam Street, Port-Louis, Mauritius
PHONE: +230 2406539
NAME: Raza Hussein Kassamally Esmael

Mormon

Church of Jesus Christ of Latter-Day Saints
67 Antelme Avenue, Quatre Bornes, Mauritius
WEBSITE: http://www.intelcities.com/Frolic_Freeway/madamission/mauritius.html

FURTHER READING

Articles

The Indian Ocean Newsletter, February 26, 2000.

"Mauritius: Opposition Victory." *New York Times,* September 13, 2000, p. A13.

Mauritius News, February and May 2000.

Panafrican News Agency, June 26 and July 11, 2000.

Books

Dun and Bradstreet's Export Guide to Mauritius. Parsippany, NJ: Dun & Bradstreet, 1999.

Government Publications

Background Notes: Mauritius. Washington, D.C.: G.P.O., 1999.

MAURITIUS: STATISTICAL DATA

For sources and notes see "Sources of Statistics" at the front of each volume.

GEOGRAPHY

Geography

Area:

Total: 1,860 sq km.

Land: 1,850 sq km.

Note: includes Agalega Islands, Cargados Carajos Shoals (Saint Brandon), and Rodrigues.

Land boundaries: 0 km.

Coastline: 177 km.

Climate: tropical, modified by southeast trade winds; warm, dry winter (May to November); hot, wet, humid summer (November to May).

Terrain: small coastal plain rising to discontinuous mountains encircling central plateau.

Natural resources: arable land, fish.

Land use:

Arable land: 49%

Permanent crops: 3%

Permanent pastures: 3%

Forests and woodland: 22%

Other: 23% (1993 est.).

HUMAN FACTORS

Demographics (A)

	1990	1995	1998	2000	2010	2020	2030	2040	2050
Population	1,074	1,129	1,160	1,179	1,280	1,371	1,433	1,457	1,451
Life expectancy - males	65.5	66.4	66.4	67.0	69.7	72.1	74.2	75.8	77.2
Life expectancy - females	73.4	74.3	74.4	75.0	77.7	79.9	81.7	83.2	84.3
Birth rate (per 1,000)	21.0	18.3	17.1	16.7	14.7	13.3	11.9	11.1	10.6
Death rate (per 1,000)	6.6	6.6	6.9	6.8	6.9	7.5	8.9	10.6	11.6
Women of reproductive age (15-49 yrs.)	295.9	319.4	331.1	333.1	341.9	338.1	335.0	327.3	311.1
Fertility rate	2.3	2.1	2.0	2.0	1.9	1.8	1.8	1.8	1.7

Except as noted, values for vital statistics are in thousands; life expectancy is in years.

Health Personnel

	National Data	World Data (wtd ave)
Total health expenditure as a percentage of GDP, 1990-1998[a]		
Public sector	1.9	2.5
Private sector	1.6	2.9
Total[b]	3.5	5.5
Health expenditure per capita in U.S. dollars, 1990-1998[a]		
Purchasing power parity	361	561
Total	120	483
Availability of health care facilities per 100,000 people		
Hospital beds 1990-1998[a]	310	330
Doctors 1992-1995[a]	11	122
Nurses 1992-1995[a]	27	248

Health Indicators

	National Data	World Data
Life expectancy at birth (years)		
1980	66	61
1998	71	67
Daily per capita supply of calories		
1970	2,355	2,358
1997	2,917	2,791
Daily per capital supply of protein		
1997 (grams)	72	74
Total fertility rate (births per woman)		
1980	2.7	3.7
1998	2.0	2.7
Population with access (%)		
To safe water (1990-96)	98	NA
To sanitation (1990-96)	100	NA
People living with (1997)		
Tuberculosis (cases per 100,000)	13.7[1]	60.4
Malaria (cases per 100,000)	5.7	42.2
HIV/AIDS (% aged 15 - 49 years)	0.08	0.99

Infants and Malnutrition

	National Data	World Data (wtd ave)
Under 5 mortality rate (1989)	23	NA
% of infants with low birthweight (1992-98)[1]	NA	17
Births attended by skilled health staff (% of total births 1996-98)	97	52
% fully immunized at 1 year of age (1995-98)[1]		
TB	87	82
DPT	90	77
Polio	90	77
Measles	85	74
Prevalence of child malnutrition (1992-98)[1] (based on weight for age, % of children under 5 years)	15	30

Ethnic Division

Indo-Mauritian 68%
Creole 27%
Sino-Mauritian 3%
Franco-Mauritian 2%

Religion

Hindu 52.0%
Christian 28.3%
Roman Catholic 26.0%
Protestant 2.3%
Muslim 16.6%
Other 3.1%

Major Languages

English (official), Creole, French, Hindi, Urdu, Hakka, Bojpoori.

EDUCATION

Public Education Expenditures

	1980	1997
Public expenditures on education as % of GNP	5.3	4.6
Expenditures per student as % of GNP per capita		
Primary & Secondary	15.8[2]	9.8
Tertiary	343.6	69.5
Teachers' compensation as % of total current education expenditures	31.4	NA
Pupils per teacher at the primary level	NA	24
Duration of primary education in years	NA	7

	1980	1997
World data for comparison		
Public expenditures on education as % of GNP (mean)	3.9	4.8
Pupils per teacher at the primary level (wtd ave)	NA	33
Duration of primary education in years (mean)	NA	9

Educational Attainment (A)

Age group (1990) . . . . .25+

Population of this age group 540,244

Highest level attained (%)

No schooling 18.3

First level

Not completed 42.6

Completed 6.1

Entered second level

Lower Secondary 7.2

Upper Secondary 23.9

Entered post secondary 1.9

Literacy Rates (C)

Year	Adult Literacy Rate (Population aged 15 years and older)
1980	74.10%
1985	77.20%
1990	79.90%
1995	82.40%
1997	83.30%

Libraries

National Libraries **1992**

Administrative Units 1

Service Points or Branches 1

Number of Volumes (000) 38

Registered Users (000) .NA

Loans to Users (000) . . . . .NA

Total Library Staff 4

GOVERNMENT & LAW

Political Parties

National Assembly	% of vote	no. of seats
Mauritian Labor Party/Mauritian Militant Movement (MLP/MMM)	65%	35/25
Militant Socialist Movement/ Mauritian Militant Renaissance (MSM/MMR)	20%	
Allies of MLP and MMM on Rodrigues Island		2
Other	15%	
Appointed seats		
Rodrigues Movement		2
Mauritian Social Democrat Party (PMSD)		1
Hizbullah		1

Elections were last held on 20 December 1995 (next to be held by December 2000).

Government Budgets (A)

Year: 1998

Total Expenditures: 21,446 Millions of Rupees

Expenditures as a percentage of the total by function:

General public services and public order 18.28

Defense 0.88

Education 16.89

Health 8.34

Social Security and Welfare 20.61

Housing and community amenities 5.85

Recreational, cultural, and religious affairs 1.55

Fuel and energy 0.05

Agriculture, forestry, fishing, and hunting 5.12

Mining, manufacturing, and construction 0.65

Transportation and communication 1.71

Other economic affairs and services 4.29

Crime

Crime volume (for 1998)

Crimes reported 37,562

Total persons convicted 19,615

Crimes per 100,000 population 3,340

Persons responsible for offenses

Total number suspects 29,515

Total number of female suspects 3,931

Total number of juvenile suspects 3,595

(Continued on next page.)

LABOR FORCE

Total Labor Force (A)

514,000 (1995).

Labor Force by Occupation

Construction and industry 36%
Services 24%
Agriculture and fishing 14%
Trade, restaurants, hotels 16%
Transportation and communication 7%
Finance 3%

Data for 1995.

Unemployment Rate

2% (1996 est.)

PRODUCTION SECTOR

Energy Production

Production ....1.225 billion kWh
Production by source
Fossil fuel 91.84%
Hydro 8.16%
Nuclear 0%
Other 0%
Exports ....0 kWh

Data for 1998.

(Continued on next page.)

GOVERNMENT & LAW (cont.)

Military Affairs (A)

	1990	1992	1995	1996	1997
Military expenditures					
Current dollars (mil.)	9	11	13	12	12
1997 constant dollars (mil.)	10	12	14	13	12
Armed forces (000)	1	1	1	1	1
Gross national product (GNP)					
Current dollars (mil.)	2,510	2,970	3,620	3,870	4,140
1997 constant dollars (mil.)	2,940	3,290	3,750	3,940	1,060
Central government expenditures (CGE)					
1997 constant dollars (mil.)	690	777	845	915	1,060
People (mil.)	1.1	1.1	1.1	1.1	1.2
Military expenditure as % of GNP	0.3	0.4	0.4	0.3	0.3
World data on military expenditure as % of GNP	4.5	3.4	2.7	2.6	2.6
Military expenditure as % of CGE	1.5	1.5	1.6	1.4	1.2
World data on military expenditure as % of CGE	17.0	12.5	10.5	10.3	10.2
Military expenditure per capita (1997 $)	10	11	12	11	11
World data on military expenditure per capita (1997 $)	242	173	146	143	145
Armed forces per 1,000 people (soldiers)	0.9	0.9	0.9	0.9	0.9
World data on armed forces per 1,000 people (soldiers)	5.3	4.5	4.1	3.9	3.8
GNP per capita (1997 $)	2,730	3,000	3,320	3,450	3,590
Arms imports[6]					
Current dollars (mil.)	5	5	0	20	10
1997 constant dollars (mil.)	6	6	0	20	10
Total imports[7]					
Current dollars (mil.)	1,618	1,630	1,976	2,278	2,242
1997 constant dollars (mil.)	1,895	1,807	2,046	2,316	2,242
Total exports[7]					
Current dollars (mil.)	1,194	1,297	1,538	1,747	1,630
1997 constant dollars (mil.)	1,398	1,438	1,593	1,776	1,630
Arms as percent of total imports[8]	0.3	0.3	0	0.9	0.4
Arms as percent of total exports[8]	0	0	0	0	0

PRODUCTION SECTOR (cont.)

Energy Consumption

Consumption . . . . .1.139 billion kWh

Imports . . . . .0 kWh

Data for 1998.

Transportation

Highways:

Total: 1,910 km.

Paved: 1,834 km (including 36 km of expressways).

Unpaved: 76 km (1998 est.).

Merchant marine:

Total: 12 ships (1,000 GRT or over) totaling 126,358 GRT/173,079 DWT.

Ships by type: cargo 3, combination bulk 2, container 4, liquified gas 1, refrigerated cargo 2 (1999 est.).

Note: a flag of convenience registry; India owns 1 ship (1998 est.).

Airports: 5 (1999 est.).

Top Agriculture Products

Sugarcane, tea, corn, potatoes, bananas, pulses; cattle, goats; fish.

COMMUNICATIONS

Daily Newspapers

	National Data	World Data for Comparison
Daily Newspapers		
Number of Dailies	6	8,391
Total Circulation (000)	85	548,000
Circulation per 1,000 inhabitants	76	96

Telecommunications

Telephones - main lines in use: 148,000 (1995).

Telephones - mobile cellular: 11,735 (1995).

Telephone system: small system with good service.

Domestic: primarily microwave radio relay.

International: satellite earth station - 1 Intelsat (Indian Ocean); new microwave link to Reunion; HF radiotelephone links to several countries.

Radio broadcast stations: AM 5, FM 9, shortwave 2 (1998).

Radios: 420,000 (1997).

Television broadcast stations: 2 (plus 11 repeaters) (1997).

Televisions: 258,000 (1997).

Internet Service Providers (ISPs): 1 (1999).

FINANCE, ECONOMICS, & TRADE

Economic Indicators

National product: GDP—purchasing power parity—$12.3 billion (1999 est.).

National product real growth rate: 4% (1999 est.).

National product per capita: $10,400 (1999 est.).

Inflation rate—consumer price index: 6.8% (1999).

Exchange Rates

Exchange rates:

Mauritian rupees (MauRs) per US$1

January 2000 . . . . .25.485

1999 . . . . .25.186

1998 . . . . .22.993

1997 . . . . .21.057

1996 . . . . .17.948

1995 . . . . .17.386

(Continued on next page.)

MANUFACTURING SECTOR

GDP & Manufacturing Summary (B)

	1980	1985	1990	1993	1994	1995
Gross Domestic Product						
Millions of 1990 dollars	1,409	1,769	2,559	2,985	3,128	3,265
Growth rate in percent	−10.06	6.88	7.15	5.50	4.80	4.39
Per capita (in 1990 dollars)	1,459	1,742	2,421	2,736	2,833	2,923
Manufacturing Value Added						
Millions of 1990 dollars	200	299	502	614	659	705[e]
Growth rate in percent	−7.03	15.27	7.72	10.00	7.29[e]	7.01[e]
Manufacturing share in percent of current prices	15.0	20.3	23.1	20.8	20.8[e]	NA

FINANCE, ECONOMICS, & TRADE (cont.)

Top Import Origins

$2.1 billion (f.o.b., 1998)

Origins (1997)

- France 19%
- South Africa 12%
- India 9%
- Hong Kong 7%
- United Kingdom 6%

Top Export Destinations

$1.7 billion (f.o.b., 1999)

Destinations (1997)

- United Kingdom 32%
- France 19%
- United States 14%
- Germany 6%
- Italy 4%

Foreign Aid

Recipient: $42 million (1997).

Import/Export Commodities

Import Commodities	Export Commodities
Manufactured goods	Clothing and textiles
Capital equipment	Sugar
Foodstuffs	Cut flowers
Petroleum products	Molasses
Chemicals	

Balance of Payments

	1994	1995	1996	1997	1998
Exports of goods (f.o.b.)	1,377	1,572	1,811	1,639	1,738
Imports of goods (f.o.b.)	−1,774	−1,812	−2,136	−2,085	−2,018
Trade balance	−397	−241	−326	−447	−280
Services - debits	−546	−641	−673	−672	−730
Services - credits	633	778	961	915	974
Private transfers (net)	118	137	174	203	190
Government transfers (net)	9	6	5	7	4
Overall balance	−232	−22	34	−91	35

MAYOTTE

CAPITAL: Mamoutzou.

FLAG: The flag of France is used.

ANTHEM: La Marseillaise.

MONETARY UNIT: 1 French franc (F) = 100 centimes.

WEIGHTS AND MEASURES: The metric system is used.

HOLIDAYS: Bastille Day, 14 July.

TIME: 3 PM = noon GMT.

LOCATION AND SIZE: Mayotte, the southernmost of four main islands in the Comoros Archipelago, with an area of 374 sq. km (144 sq. mi.), lies in the Mozambique Channel about 480 km (300 mi.) NW of Madagascar, at 12°49′S and 45°17′E. Mayotte is surrounded by a coral reef, which encloses the islets of M'Zambourou (Grand Terre) and Pamanzi. Beyond the island's coastal plain, a plateau reaches heights of 660 m (2,165 ft.).

CLIMATE: Mayotte has a warm, humid, tropical climate. There is a fresh, dry season from May through October, followed by a rather hot, humid season from November to April. Temperatures range from 24°C (75°F) in August to 27°C (81°F) in December. Annual rainfall is 500 cm (200 inches). November marks the onset of the monsoon season and the increase in temperatures. Rainfall is heaviest in January, and there are often cyclones and sometimes even waterspouts and damaging tidal waves in the summer. In the winter, temperatures drop, with the minimum average in July being 23°C (73°F).

INTRODUCTORY SURVEY

RECENT HISTORY

The island of Mayotte experienced several waves of invasion and resettlement in its early history. In the fifteenth century Arab peoples invaded Mayotte converting its inhabitants to Islam. Although visiting Mayotte as early as the sixteenth century, the French did not take colonial control over the island until 1843. The Comoro island group including Mayotte, other Comoro islands, and Madagascar became a single French Overseas Territory early in the twentieth century. Reflecting their diverse history, most people of Mayotte are of Malagasy origin and Muslim faith and are strongly influenced by French culture.

In 1975 three of the northernmost islands of the Comoro group voted for independence as the Comoro state. Choosing to remain a French dependency, Mayotte voted against independence. Since the Comoros declared independence France has administered Mayotte separately as a distinct political entity granting the island a special status of collective territoriale (territorial collectivity). Territorial collectivity is thought of as being a status midway between a French overseas territory and a French department, the higher status. Mayotte continued to reject proposals from the Comoros for reunification.

In 1979 the French National Assembly extended Mayotte's special status even though the United Nations at that time passed a resolution supporting Comoros' sovereignty and unification with Mayotte. Despite political pressure from Mayotte for full French departmental status, it has not been approved by France and Mayotte remained a territorial collectivity at the close of the twentieth century.

Under French control Mayotte's relative stability contrasted with severe political and economic upheaval in the Comoros' state. During the 1990s illegal immigration from the Comoros to Mayotte led to persistent racial tension and attacks against Comoran immigrants residing in Mayotte.

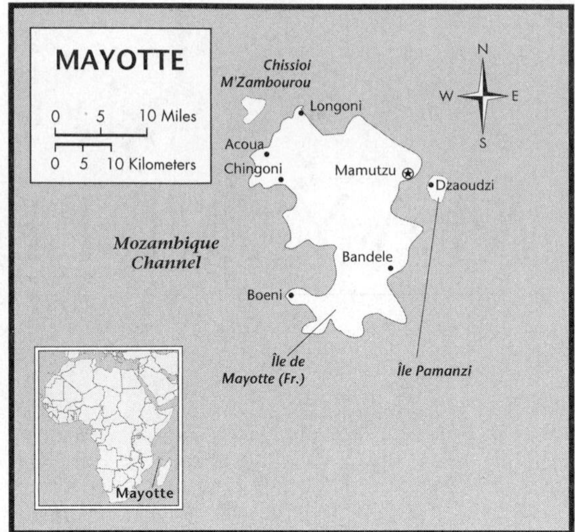

Although solidly aligned with France Mayotte's specific status remains under constant examination by commissions charged with developing a more appropriate status for the twenty-first century. The most severe problem facing Mayotte is a high birth rate resulting in 50 percent of its population being under the age of fifteen. The population increased by an annual average of 5.7 percent between 1991 and 1997. Unemployment was 41.2 percent in 1997 with half of those unemployed under twenty-five years of age.

GOVERNMENT

The chief of state is the President of France. Representing the French government is an appointed prefect. The head of government is the president of the General Council who is elected by the members of the General Council for a six-year term. The legislative branch is the unicameral General Council of nineteen members elected by universal adult suffrage, those eighteen years and older. Mayotte elects one member to the French Senate, one member to the French National Assembly, and is represented in the European Parliament.

Judiciary

Mayotte's justice system is based on French law and systems. The court of first instance, the *Tribunal de Première Instance,* and the appeal court, the *Tribunal Supérieur d'Appel,* form the court system.

Political Parties

Political parties include the Mahoran Popular Movement (MPM), Mahoran Rally for the Republic (RPR), Democratic Front (FD), Association for French Mayotte, Socialist Party (PS), and Union for French Democracy (UDF).

DEFENSE

Defense of Mayotte is the responsibility of France. A small contingent of French troops is stationed on the island. Mayotte has been used as a strategic military base on occasion. A build up French troops occurred in 1989 for possible intervention in the Comoros after the assassination of the Comoran President. Likewise in late 1990 a French build up began in response to the possibility of French participation in the Persian Gulf War in 1991.

ECONOMIC AFFAIRS

Economic activity is based predominately on the agricultural sector. Principle crops are ylang-ylang (a perfume essence), vanilla, coconuts, cinnamon, coffee, and copra. Fishing, livestock raising, and the cultivation of rice, cassava, and corn contribute to domestic needs.

Due to Mayotte's remote location, tourism has failed to develop.

Mayotte must import a large portion of its foodstuffs that accounted for 22 percent of the total value of imports in 1988. Additional imports include building materials, machinery, and transportation equipment, metals, chemicals, and clothing. France along with Africa and Southeast Asia are Mayotte's suppliers. Exports include vanilla, ylang-ylang, and copra. France is the chief recipient of exports. The Comoros and Réunion also receive Mayotte's exports.

A high trade deficit exists with the value of imports in 1996 reaching $131.5 million and exports $3.64 million. Due to increased international competition and falling prices, exports of ylang-ylang and vanilla significantly decreased in 1997–1998. The island is heavily dependent on French financial assistance. High unemployment particularly among youth persists.

Public Finance

Mayotte depends on extensive French financial assistance. French aid amounted to $107.7 million in 1995.

Income

The gross domestic product (GDP) estimate for 1998 was $85 million with French supplemental assistance. The GDP per capita by 1998 estimate was $600.

Industry

Construction of public buildings is the chief industry. A lobster and shrimp industry was created in the late 1990s with production at 1,500 tons in 1997.

Banking and Finance

Currency is the French franc. The Institut d'Émission d'Outre-mer maintains a branch bank in Mamudzou as does the Banque Française Commerciale in Dzaoudzi.

Economic Development

In the late 1980s the French government granted financial aid for construction projects in an unsuccessful attempt to develop tourism. Implementation of an Economic Development Plan to improve infrastructure continued from 1986 to 1993. For the period of 1995–1999 Mayotte signed an economic and social development plan with France for financial aid to further develop infrastructure.

SOCIAL WELFARE

Free medical services are available to the Mayotte population.

Healthcare

Mayotte has two hospitals with a total of one hundred beds. One is located at Dzaoudzi and the other at Mamoudzou. Mayotte is divided into six medical sectors each with a doctor and medical workers. Malaria, parasitic infections, and tuberculosis are major illnesses.

EDUCATION

Education is compulsory for children from six to sixteen years of age. The education system includes traditional Islamic schools and French primary and secondary schools. Students receive five years of primary and five years of secondary education. In 1997 25,805 pre-primary and primary students were enrolled. Eight secondary schools served 6,190 students. The explosive birth rate estimated at forty-six births per 1,000 population estimated in 1999 kept pressure on the education system to build more schools and hire more teachers. Vocational training is provided on Mayotte and further technical training is available on Réunion.

2000 KEY EVENTS TIMELINE

January

- The Maori population is to be an important factor in the determination of the governmental structure of Mayotte. The vote is scheduled for July.

June

- The French education minister Jack Lang is examining ways to improve both primary and secondary education in Mayotte.

September

- The French government signs a document called "The Future of Mayotte" on September 11 in which the government agrees to give Mayotte some $4 billion dollars to improve health care, roads, and schools. The economy of Mayotte is in trouble and the French government is trying to bring Mayotte up to the standards of other overseas possessions.

November

- On November 13, a governmental committee recommends changing the island from a French territory to a French department, to choose a leader to preside over the general council, and to give native Mahorais the right of self-determination and possibly independence.

ANALYSIS OF EVENTS: 2000

BUSINESS AND THE ECONOMY

Mayotte was not at all self-sufficient during 2000. France supplied both food and money to keep the island solvent. Subsistence agriculture and fishing provided people with some sustenance and France encouraged the production of the ylang-ylang flower to make perfume, which is a huge industry in France. Even though Mayotte had a paved airstrip, it was too remote to attract tourists to its shores. In September 2000 France issued a pamphlet on the "future of Mayotte" in which the French government laid out a plan to improve the economic situation by improving the port, infrastructures, the development of tourism and sports and the construction of a cultural center. Modernization of the infrastructure is of prime importance. France is planning to spend some four billion dollars to improve Mayotte.

GOVERNMENT AND POLITICS

Mayotte is considered a territorial collectivity of France. In 1843 the Comoros Islands were turned over to France by the then ruling king. In 1974 many of the islands became independent but Mayotte alone chose to remain with France. As of 2000, Mayotte's political future is still uncertain. While the Mahorais voted by a 73 percent margin to remain French (July 2000) Comoros still claims that Mayotte is part of the Federal Islamic Republic of the Comoros Islands. The United Nations still recognizes Comoros' claim to Mayotte as legitimate, but France is going with the wishes of the Mahorais and gives the island a seat in the French parliament. The local government is represented by Younoussa Bamana. The majority party is the Mouvement Populaire Mahorais (MPM), which wants to elevate Mayotte from a territorial collectivity to that of an overseas department.

CULTURE AND SOCIETY

The citizens of Mayotte, an island in the Comoros group between Mozambique and Madagascar, are mainly of Bantu, Malaysian Indonesian, Portuguese and French descent. Those people are often referred to as Mahorais. They share a common history of colonization and culture with the Comoros Islands, although the citizens of Mayotte have cast their future with the French instead of their island counterparts. The official languages are Mahroais (a type of Swahili) and French They are mainly Muslim in faith, following both French and Islamic laws. The Islamic religious code permits polygamy, which is allowed on Mayotte. The natives rely on agriculture and the cultivation of ylang-ylang flowers, which are used in the manufacture of perfume. The French refer to Mayotte as the "perfume isle." Mayotte is mainly a volcanic outgrowth, surrounded by coral reefs. Many of the native teenage boys leave home and build thatched roof houses called "bangas" in which they live until they get married. These can be found on the outskirts of town and are often elaborately decorated. The population is about 150,000 with the majority living in Mamoutzou, the capital city.

DIRECTORY

CENTRAL GOVERNMENT

Head of State

Conseil General
Office of the Conseil General
PHONE: +269 611233
FAX: +269 611018

Prefect
Philip Boisadam, Office of the Prefecture, BP 20, 97610 Dzaoudzi, Mayotte
PHONE: +269 601054
FAX: +269 601850

Ministers

Minister of Employment
Ministry of Employment, 4, place du Mariage, 97600 Mamoudzou, Mayotte
PHONE: +269 611657
FAX: +269 610337

Minister of Education
Ministry of Education, Rue du College, 97600 Mamoudzou, Mayotte
PHONE: +269 611024
FAX: +269 610987

Minister of Agriculture and Forestry
Ministry of Agriculture and Forestry, 15, rue Mariaze, 97600 Mamoudzou, Mayotte
PHONE: +269 611213
FAX: +269 611031

Minister of Youth and Sports
Ministry of Youth and Sports, 15, Rue Mariaze, 97600 Mamoudzou, Mayotte
PHONE: +269 611087
FAX: +269 610126

Minister of Sanitary and Social Affairs
Ministry of Sanitary and Social Affairs, 15, rue Mariaze, 97600 Mamoudzou, Mayotte
PHONE: +269 611225
FAX: +269 601956

POLITICAL ORGANIZATIONS

Association pour Mayotte Francaise (Association for French Mayotte)

NAME: Didier Beoutis

Democratic Front (FD)

NAME: Youssouf Moussa

Mahoran Popular Movement (MPM)

NAME: Younoussa Bamana

Mahoran Rally for the Republic (RPR)

NAME: Soibahadine Ibrahim Ramadan

Union for French Democracy (UDF)

NAME: Henri Jean-Baptiste

DIPLOMATIC REPRESENTATION

Embassies in Mayotte

None. Territorial collectivity of France.

JUDICIAL SYSTEM

Tribunal Administrator

Les Hauts des Jardeis du College, 97600
Mamoudzou, Mayotte
PHONE: +269 611095
FAX: +269 611856

BROADCAST MEDIA

Radio-Télévision Française d'Outre-Mer (RFO-Mayotte)

BP 103, F-97610 Pamandzi, Ile de Mayotte
PHONE: +269 601017
FAX: +269 601852
TITLE: Station Director
CONTACT: Robert Xavier
CHANNEL: 4H, 7H, 9H

NEWSPAPERS AND MAGAZINES

Le Journal de Mayotte

RELIGIOUS ORGANIZATIONS

As the single French Overseas Territory existing under the designation territorial collectivity, all Roman Catholic affairs are handled through France. The Muslim population is, however, the largest, with 99 percent of citizens subscribing to Islam.

FURTHER READING

Internet

BBC News Online. "Mayotte Stays with France," July 3, 2000. [Online] Available http://news.bbc.co.uk/hi/english/world/africa/newsid_816000/816428.stm (accessed November 14, 2000).

MAYOTTE: STATISTICAL DATA

For sources and notes see "Sources of Statistics" at the front of each volume.

GEOGRAPHY

Geography

Area:

Total: 374 sq km.

Land: 374 sq km.

Land boundaries: 0 km.

Coastline: 185.2 km.

Climate: tropical; marine; hot, humid, rainy season during northeastern monsoon (November to May); dry season is cooler (May to November).

Terrain: generally undulating, with deep ravines and ancient volcanic peaks.

Natural resources: negligible.

HUMAN FACTORS

Religion

Muslim 97%

Christian (mostly Roman Catholic) ....NA

Major Languages

Mahorian (a Swahili dialect), French (official language) spoken by 35% of the population.

Demographics (A)

	1990	1995	1998	2000	2010	2020	2030	2040	2050
Population	89.6	120.3	141.3	155.9	231.2	311.9	403.6	498.6	592.6
Life expectancy - males	53.7	55.6	56.7	57.4	61.0	64.3	67.4	70.1	72.4
Life expectancy - females	57.3	59.4	60.7	61.5	65.6	69.4	72.8	75.8	78.3
Birth rate (per 1,000)	51.8	49.4	46.9	45.3	38.8	33.9	28.5	24.0	20.6
Death rate (per 1,000)	12.6	10.7	9.7	9.1	7.0	5.9	5.2	5.0	5.0
Women of reproductive age (15-49 yrs.)	19.1	25.8	30.1	33.1	51.0	72.4	99.8	131.7	159.6
Fertility rate	7.0	6.7	6.5	6.3	5.4	4.4	3.5	2.9	2.5

Except as noted, values for vital statistics are in thousands; life expectancy is in years.

GOVERNMENT & LAW

Political Parties

General Council (Conseil General)	no. of seats
Mahoran Popular Movement (MPM)	8
Mahoran Rally for the Republic (RPR)	5
Socialist Party (PS)	1
Independents	5

Elections were last held 23 March 1997 (next to be held March 2000). Only nine of the 19 seats were subjected to voting in March 1997. The Socialist Party (PS) is the local branch of French Parti Socialiste.

Government Budgets (B)

Revenues	NA
Expenditures	$73 million

Data for 1991 est. NA stands for not available.

LABOR FORCE

Unemployment Rate

45% (1997)

PRODUCTION SECTOR

Transportation

Highways:

Total: 93 km.

Paved: 72 km.

Unpaved: 21 km.

Merchant marine: none (1999 est.).

Airports: 1 (1999 est.).

Top Agriculture Products

Vanilla, ylang-ylang (perfume essence), coffee, copra.

MANUFACTURING SECTOR

GDP & Manufacturing Summary (C)

Total GDP (1998 est.)	$85 million
Per capita (1998 est.)	$600

Values in purchasing power parity.

COMMUNICATIONS

Telecommunications

Telephones - main lines in use: 450 (1999).

Telephones - mobile cellular: 0 (1999).

Telephone system: small system administered by French Department of Posts and Telecommunications.

Domestic: NA

International: microwave radio relay and HF radiotelephone communications to Comoros and other international connections.

Radio broadcast stations: AM 1, FM 4, shortwave 0 (1998).

Radios: NA

Television broadcast stations: 3 (1997).

Televisions: 3,500 (1994).

Internet Service Providers (ISPs): NA

FINANCE, ECONOMICS, & TRADE

Economic Indicators

National product: GDP—purchasing power parity—$85 million (1998 est.).

National product real growth rate: NA.

National product per capita: $600 (1998 est.).

Inflation rate—consumer price index: NA.

Exchange Rates

Exchange rates:

Euros per US$1

January 2000	0.9867
1999	0.9386

French francs (F) per US$1

January 1999	5.6500
1998	5.8995
1997	5.8367
1996	5.1155
1995	4.9915

Fiscal year: calendar year.

Top Import Origins

$141.3 million (f.o.b., 1997)

Origins (1997)

France	66%
Africa	14%
Southeast Asia	11%

Top Export Destinations

$3.44 million (f.o.b., 1997)

Destinations	
France	80%
Comoros	15%
Reunion	NA

Foreign Aid

Recipient: $107.7 million (1995); Extensive French financial assistance.

Import/Export Commodities

Import Commodities	Export Commodities
Food	Ylang-ylang (perfume essence)
Machinery and equipment	Vanilla
Transportation equipment	Copra
Metals	Coconuts
Chemicals	Coffee
	Cinnamon

MEXICO

CAPITAL: Mexico City (México).

FLAG: The national flag is a tricolor of green, white, and red vertical stripes; at the center of the white stripe, in brown and green, is an eagle with a snake in its beak, perched on a cactus.

ANTHEM: *Mexicanos, al grito de guerra* (Mexicans, to the Cry of War).

MONETARY UNIT: The peso (P) is a paper currency of 100 centavos. There are coins of 1, 5, 10, 20, 50, 100, 500, 1,000 and 5,000 pesos and notes of 2,000, 5,000, 10,000, 20,000, 50,000 and 100,000 pesos. As of 1 January 1993, a new unit of currency (the new peso) was issued, worth 1,000 of the pesos that were used until 31 December 1992. P1 = $0.12425 (or $1 = P8.048).

WEIGHTS AND MEASURES: The metric system is the legal standard, but some old Spanish units are still in use.

HOLIDAYS: New Year's Day, 1 January; Constitution Day, 5 February; Birthday of Benito Juárez, 21 March; Labor Day, 1 May; Anniversary of the Battle of Puebla (1862), 5 May; Opening of Congress and Presidential Address to the Nation, 1 September; Independence Day, 16 September; Columbus Day, 12 October; Revolution Day (1910), 20 November; Christmas, 25 December. Movable religious holidays include Holy Thursday, Good Friday, and Holy Saturday. All Souls' Day, 2 November, and Our Lady of Guadalupe Day, 12 December, are not statutory holidays but are widely celebrated.

TIME: 6 AM = noon GMT.

LOCATION AND SIZE: Situated south of the United States on the North American continent, Mexico has an area of nearly 2 million square kilometers (762,000 square miles), slightly less than three times the size of the state of Texas. It has a total boundary length of 13,857 kilometers (8,610 miles), including the narrow peninsula of Baja California.

Mexico's capital city, Mexico City, is located in the south-central part of the country.

CLIMATE: The climate varies according to altitude and rainfall from 25–27°C (77–81°F) to 17°C (63°C).

United Mexican States
Estados Unidos Mexicanos

INTRODUCTORY SURVEY

RECENT HISTORY

The years since World War II (1939–1945) have been marked by political stability, economic expansion, and the rise of the middle class, but also by general neglect of the poorest segments of the population. An economic boom during the late 1970s brought about by huge oil export earnings benefited only a small percentage of the people. Declining world oil prices in 1981 led to a severe financial crisis in 1982.

A major earthquake devastated Mexico City in September 1985. The official death toll was 7,000 although unofficial estimates were as high as 20,000. In addition 300,000 were left homeless. There was widespread protest over the fact that many of the buildings destroyed had been built in violation of construction regulations and there were claims that the government mishandled foreign emergency aid.

In August 1992 formal negotiations regarding the North American Free Trade Agreement (NAFTA) were concluded whereby Mexico would join the United States and Canada in the elimination of trade barriers, the promotion of fair competition, and increased investment opportunities. NAFTA went into effect on January 1, 1994.

In January 1994 a primarily Amerindian group calling itself the Zapatista Army of National Liberation resorted to an armed uprising initially taking control of four municipalities in the state of Chiapas on the Isthmus of Tehuantepec to protest

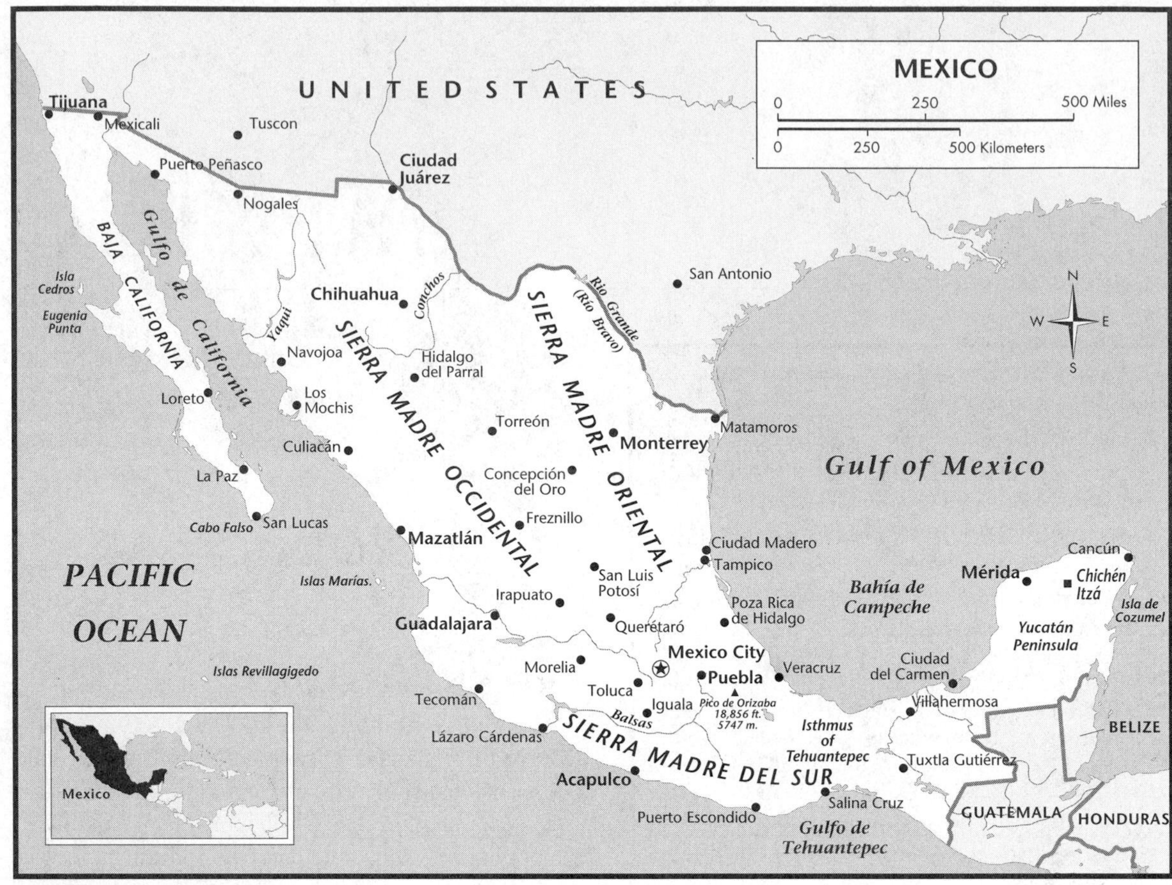

what it regarded as government failure to deal effectively with regional social and economic problems. Two months later Mexico had its first high-level assassination in over sixty years when PRI presidential candidate Luis Donaldo Colosio was murdered in Tijuana. His replacement, Ernesto Zedillo, was elected at the end of the year in a closely monitored campaign.

In December 1994 the Mexican peso was devalued. The economy went into its worst recession in over fifty years. During the first five months of 1995 over one million Mexicans lost their jobs. The United States offered a multimillion-dollar bailout to keep the economy from getting worse.

The public discontent with the economic crisis, poverty, crime, and corruption led to a rejection of the PRI. Until then the PRI had ruled in Mexico for about seventy years as a virtual one-party system. In July 1997 the PRI lost its majority in the lower house of the National Congress to the combined power of the Party of the Democratic Revolution (PRD) and the National Action Party (PAN).

In January 1998 tens of thousands of Mexicans supporting the Zapatista movement demonstrated in Mexico City against the December 1997 massacre of forty-five Indians by pro-government gunmen in Chiapas. In late 1999 the government proposed a new peace initiative in Chiapas.

In the late 1990s Mexico was facing an unprecedented crime wave that affected every facet of society. On July 2, 2000, after seven decades of PRI rule PAN candidate Vicente Fox Quesada defeated PRI candidate Francisco Labastida Ochoa for the presidency. Fox promised to tackle crime, government corruption, and economic reform.

GOVERNMENT

Mexico is a federal republic consisting of thirty-one states and the Federal District. The president, elected for a six-year term by universal adult vote beginning at age eighteen and not eligible for reelection, appoints the attorney general and a cabinet which may vary in number with consent of the Senate. There is no vice-president. If the president dies or is removed from office, Congress is constitutionally empowered to elect a provisional president.

The two-chamber Congress, also elected by direct universal suffrage, is composed of a Senate (Cámara de Senadores), made up of 128 members (4 from each state and 4 from the Federal District), and a Chamber of Deputies (Cámara de Diputados) made up of 500 members. Senators are elected for six years (half the Senate is elected every three years) and deputies for three years, and both groups are ineligible for immediate reelection.

In an effort to unite various interest groups within the government party, in 1961 President Adolfo López Mateos (1958–1964) formed a National Consultative Committee composed of living ex-presidents of Mexico.

Judiciary

Federal courts include the Supreme Court, with twenty-one magistrates; thirty-two circuit tribunals, and ninety-eight district courts. The Supreme Court has both original and appellate jurisdiction in four divisions: administrative, civil, labor, and penal. Circuit courts hear appeals from the district courts. The jury system is not commonly used in Mexico.

Political Parties

From 1929 to 1997 the majority party and the only political group to gain national importance was the Institutional Revolutionary Party (Partido Revolucionario Institucional—PRI). The PRI includes only civilians and embraces all shades of political opinion. Three large pressure groups operate within the PRI: labor, the peasantry, and the "popular" sector (such as bureaucrats, teachers, and small business people).

In the July 1997 elections the PRI failed to keep a majority of seats in the 500-member Chamber of Deputies for the first time in nearly seventy years. The Party of Democratic Revolution (PRD) won 125 seats and formed a coalition with the National Action Party (Partido de Acción Nacional—PAN), which won 122 seats. The PRI held 239 seats. The Green Ecological Party (PVEM) held six seats and the Worker's Party (PT) held seven seats.

DEFENSE

Total full-time strength of the armed forces was 178,770 in 2000. The army had 130,000 personnel. Regular army units included the presidential guard, three infantry brigades, one armored brigade, an airborne brigade, and support units. The navy including naval air force and marines had 37,000 personnel. The air force had 11,770 personnel and 125 combat aircraft. Paramilitary forces included 14,000 rural defense militia; military reserves numbered 300,000. Defense expenditures in 1999 amounted to $4 billion.

Under the required military training program, all eighteen year-old males must complete one year of part-time basic army training. In 2000 60,000 draftees were on active duty drawn by lottery.

ECONOMIC AFFAIRS

Although Mexico's economy is predominately agricultural with more than 24 percent of its economically active population employed there, commerce and industry have long been the nation's chief income earners. A great mining nation, Mexico is the world's leading producer of silver and is well endowed with sulfur, copper, manganese, iron ore, lead, and zinc.

Since 1960 there has been a gradual improvement in social and economic equality, but because of the rapid rate of population increase, many Mexicans still remain in poverty. While peasant wages remained static during the 1960s, industrial wages increased more than 80%, leading to large-scale migration from countryside to city. Mexico City's enormous population growth has been accompanied by mass poverty.

Oil discoveries of the early 1970s led to a boom with Mexico's economy becoming one of the fastest growing in the world. About three quarters of all export earnings wee brought in by crude oil. When world oil prices began falling in the early 1980s, this dependency contributed to Mexico's financial crisis of 1982. Inflation reached 100%.

In December 1987 the Pact for Stability and Economic Growth (PECE), a series of price and wage agreements between government, labor, and business went into effect. The PECE helped curb inflation to 51.6 percent in 1988 without causing a recession. Gradual recovery has seen the inflation rate fall to 15 percent in 1999.

The North American Free Trade Agreement (NAFTA), in effect as of January 1, 1994, opened the domestic market to foreign trade by eliminating trade barriers between Mexico, the United States, and Canada over the next fifteen years.

Mexico's domestic economy declined 6.9 percent in 1995. The problem began with a massive devaluation of the peso in December 1994 that brought on a financial crisis and exposed certain weak spots in the economy. Inflation and interest rates soared, which discouraged foreign investment. The United States provided $20 billion of a $50 billion assistance package but the Mexican government only used half of that amount for its recovery in 1996.

The depreciation of the peso had the effect of making Mexican goods less expensive and more competitive on world markets. In 1997 because of the increase in exports, Mexico had a GDP growth rate of 6.8%. The National Program for Development Finance (PRON AFIDE) of 1997 outlined the government's economic policy framework for the period of 1997 to 2000. It supported further privatization and deregulation of the economy. State-owned enterprises numbering about 1,000 in 1982 numbered only 200 in 1999. The government focused on privatizing and expanding seaports, railroads, telecommunications, electricity and natural gas, and airports.

Trade with the United States and Canada almost doubled since NAFTA and Mexico is working out additional trade agreements with Latin America and the EU. The economic growth rate is predicted at 4.5 percent in 2000.

Public Finance

Major sources of revenue are income taxes, a value-added tax, and public enterprise revenues. Among regular government departments education receives the largest budget allocation but outlays for debt service, subsidies to federal enterprises, and capital expenditures for highways, irrigation, and hydroelectric projects have exceeded regular departmental expenditures in recent years.

During the 1960s government revenues rose at a faster rate than GDP with revenues from income taxes including surcharges increasing by 170 percent in the 1960–1969 period. Budgets in the 1970s and early and mid-1980s continued to show current-account "surpluses," or minimal apparent deficits; the fact that borrowings and transfers are built into the budget structure masked the true magnitude of annual deficits. In the late 1970s and the early 1980s real budget deficits increased substantially reaching nearly 18 percent of the GDP by 1982. By slashing public spending the government was able to bring the deficit down to 8.9 percent of the GDP in 1983 and 7.1 percent in 1984 but the collapse of the world oil price sent it up to 16.3 percent in 1986. By the early 1990s, however, public finances were strengthening, and a surplus (on a cash basis) of P35,054 million was recorded in 1992 equivalent to 3.4 percent of GDP in 1991. Non-recurrent revenues amounted to P30,123 million, mainly derived from the sale of shares of the state-owned telephone company and bank privatization. Excluding privatization revenues the surplus in 1992 was equivalent to 1.5 percent of GDP in 1992 as opposed to a deficit of 1.5 percent in 1991. Public revenues policy in 1992 sought to widen the tax base and simplify and enforce tax administration. At the same time public expenditures have been reoriented to provide basic infrastructure and services. In 1997 and 1998 there was a current account deficit equaling 0.7 percent and 1.3%, respectively.

The U.S. Central Intelligence Agency estimated that in 1998 government revenues totaled approximately $117 billion and expenditures $123 billion. External debt totaled $155.8 billion in 1999.

Income

In 1999 Mexico's gross domestic product (GDP) was estimated at $865 billion, or about $8,500 per capita. The 1999 estimated GDP growth rate was 3.7 percent and inflation rate was 15%. The 1999 GDP contribution by sector was agriculture 5%, industry 29%, and services 66%.

Industry

Mexico is one of the leading manufacturing nations in Latin America. The principal manufacturing industries include automobile and related parts production, steel, textiles, cement and related construction materials, chemicals and petrochemicals, paper and paper products, food processing, breweries, and glass. The soft drink industry is growing. In 1995 Mexico produced 935,017 vehicles. The leading manufacturers were Ford, Chrysler, General Motors, and Volkswagen.

Maquiladoras, which are facilities engaged in what is known as re-export processing, play an important role in Mexican manufacturing. Usually located near the United States border and owned by a foreign corporation, maquiladoras assemble or process imported goods brought in from the U.S. and then re-export them duty free. In 1999 there were some 3,300 maquiladora factories employing 494,721 workers.

Banking and Finance

The Bank of Mexico (established 1925), in which the government owns 51 percent of the capital stock, is the central bank and bank of issue. Together with the National Banking and Insurance Commission and the National Securities Commission, it supervises commercial, savings, trust, mortgage, capitalization, and investment institutions. National institutions for economic development extend agricultural and long-term industrial credit and finance and develop public works, international trade, cooperatives, and the motion picture industry; they also operate savings accounts. The National Financing Agency (founded in 1934) acts as a financing and investing corporation; it also regulates the Mexican stock market and long-term credits.

In September 1982 in order to stop the flight of capital the government nationalized all fifty-seven private banks. Their combined assets were estimated at $48.7 billion. The government had consolidated the commercial banking system into nineteen financial institutions by the end of 1986. In November 1986 the government introduced a plan that would privatize eighteen of Mexico's nineteen state-owned commercial banks. The sale of the banks began in 1987. In 1990 the government began allowing foreigners to buy up to 30 percent of the state's banks. By July 1992 the banking system was completely private. The only foreign bank permitted to operate within Mexico as of 1993 was Citibank.

At the end of 1994 there were around fifty commercial banks in operation compared with just nineteen two years earlier. The newly privatized commercial banks have had problems almost from the outset. The principal cause has been poor asset quality that has manifested itself in an increasingly serious burden of non-performing loans.

Faced with the prospect of a wholesale banking collapse, the government has come up with a succession of different measures to deal with the problem of bad debts. There has been a scheme to enable bank loans to be rescheduled using index-linked *Unidades de Inversión* (UDIs) and a program of support for bank debtors (*Apoyo a Deudores,* ADE) designed to help as many as eight million people reschedule debts.

Apart from providing relief for debtors the government has also set up a program to enable banks to meet capital and loan loss provisions (*Programa Temporal de Capitalización Temporal*), as well as a fund (*Fondo Bancario de Protección de Ahorro-Fobaproa*) to take over banks' bad debts in exchange for new capital injections by shareholders. Nevertheless it has had to step in and take control of a number of institutions.

While needing to shore up the banking sector in order to get the economy going again, the government has also been aware that the financial institutions must apply U.S. General Accounting Principles from the beginning of 1997.

There are a number of state development banks, including Nacional Financiera (Nafin, mainly for small and medium-sized businesses) and Banco Nacional de Comercio Exterior (Bancomext, foreign trade).

In mid-March 1997 after two years of preparation, the government introduced measures to curb money laundering. It has been established that anywhere between $4 billion and $30 billion of drug money is laundered in Mexico every year. Starting in 1998 banks, brokerages, and large foreign exchange houses will have to report all cash transactions involving $10,000 or more to the central bank.

The National Securities Commission (founded in 1946) supervises stock transactions. The Stock Exchange of Mexico (Bolsa Mexicana de Valores), the largest stock exchange in Latin America, was organized in its present form in 1933. It lists the stocks of the most important industrial companies as well as a few mining stocks. Two smaller exchanges at Monterrey and Guadalajara were absorbed in 1976 by the Mexico City exchange.

In 1996 the recovery in the stock market strengthened as the economy began to pull out of recession, inflation and interest rates fell, and the currency held steady. As confidence grew so foreign investment flowed back into the market.

Economic Development

Modern Mexican economic policy derives in principle from the constitution of 1917 which in Article 27 proclaims national ownership of subsoil rights, provides for expropriation of property needed for national purposes, and provides for the breaking up of large estates and the establishment of village communal land holdings (ejidos). The property of foreign oil companies was expropriated in 1938 and production, refining, and distribution were placed under the government-controlled PEMEX. The government has also nationalized the railway and banking systems, owns most electric power plants, and partly owns some industrial establishments. Majority Mexican ownership was required in virtually all sectors until early 1984, when restrictions on foreign investment were relaxed somewhat.

When the exploitation of huge oil deposits began in the mid-1970s the Mexican government embarked on an expansionist economic policy that included an ambitious public-spending program financed to a great degree by foreign borrowing. A seventeen-point development program announced in 1978 created about three million new jobs by 1981 but it was not fully implemented because of the drop in world oil prices and the subsequent financial crisis. The crisis reached its climax in August 1982 when the government suspended all payments of foreign debt principal and had to resort to emergency credits to avoid default.

New credits from the IMF were conditional upon Mexico's acceptance of an austerity program that entailed reduction of the budget deficit from 17.9 percent of the GDP in 1982 to 8.5 percent in 1983. Other austerity measures included tax increases, increases in the prices of controlled commodities, such as bread and salt, and steps to decrease tax evasion and reduce inflation. The de la Madrid administration simultaneously pursued policies to reduce the inflated value of the peso and to generate massive trade surpluses; indicative of their effectiveness were the 1983 and 1984 surpluses over $13 billion in each year. The government, moreover, pursued rescheduling of its foreign debt, winning agreements in 1983 ($14 billion) and 1986 ($43.7 billion). In 1985 and 1986, however, the earthquake and the fall in world oil prices undermined the recovery; export revenues plunged, and inflation soared. The 1986 rescheduling was conditional upon Mexico's agreement to increase development of the export sector and encourage efficient import-substitution policies, as well as foreign investment.

Since Mexico joined GATT in 1986 trade barriers have been eliminated and tariffs reduced. Privatizations since 1989 include: the telephone company, Telmex; Mexico's eighteen commercial banks; the airlines, Aeromexico and Mexicana; two large copper mines, Cananea and Mexicana de Cobre; and two large steel companies, Sicartsa and AHMSA. Privatizations have produced large one-time revenues for the government, while simultaneously reducing the government's role in the economy thus garnering savings by reducing its transfers to inefficient enterprises. Furthermore these new profit-making private sector companies have widened the tax base.

The North American Free Trade Agreement (NAFTA), ratified in 1992 and implemented in 1994, culminated several years of trade liberalization efforts begun in 1986. Tariffs on most industrial and agricultural goods will be eliminated or phased out within fifteen years. NAFTA trading benefits are only given to goods produced wholly or principally in NAFTA countries. NAFTA also eliminates trade barriers and investment restrictions on participating countries autos, trucks, buses and auto parts within ten years. NAFTA also proposes to safeguard domestic agricultural production of the dairy, egg, poultry, and sugar sectors. NAFTA also opens up foreign investment possibilities in the Mexican energy sector. NAFTA also has provisions for the textiles and services sectors, banking, investment, and intellectual property rights. Labor and environmental impacts are also addressed. Trade with the United States and Canada has nearly doubled since NAFTA was implemented.

Mexico, to reduce its independence on the United States, established free trade agreements with Venezuela and Colombia as a member of the Group of Three and with several other Central American nations. Mexico also signed a free trade agreement with Chile in 1991.

SOCIAL WELFARE

Mexico's social security system includes old age pensions, disability, medical, and work injury benefits. Insured workers receive medical aid in addition to wage benefits, and the insured worker's family receives first-aid treatment. During pregnancy and childbirth and for a period thereafter, insured women receive obstetrical care, nursing aid, a cash subsidy, and a layette. A worker who has been 60 percent disabled for at least twelve months is eligible for an invalid's pension and all residents are eligible for old age pensions at age sixty. The Security and Social Services Institute for Civil Workers covers government employees.

The National Institute for Child Protection oversees programs for children including a primary-school breakfast program. The Mexican Institution for Child Welfare provides care for neglected, abandoned, or sick children.

Women have held top political and union leadership roles, have the right to file for separation or divorce, and the right to own property in their own name. Domestic violence, however, remains a problem.

Indigenous peoples have full protection under the law but in practice they face discrimination.

Healthcare

Mexico has made slow but measurable progress in public health. Average life expectancy was estimated at 71.5 years in 2000. Cholera, yellow fever, plague, and smallpox have been virtually eliminated and typhus has been controlled. Permanent campaigns are waged against malaria, poliomyelitis, skin diseases, tuberculosis, leprosy, onchocercosis, and serious childhood diseases. In 1990–1995 83 percent of the population had access to safe water and 50 percent had adequate sanitation.

In 1993 there was one doctor for every 615 people and one hospital bed per 1,704 people. That year 91 percent of the population had access to health care services.

Housing

Mexico's housing shortage was worsened by high population growth in the 1980s. The government allocated $1.93 billion in 1989 to build 250,000 low-cost housing units, and expected to receive an additional $700 million from the World Bank to build more. The 1990 National Housing Plan predicted a shortage of 6.1 million homes to be felt most severely in the outskirts of urban areas including Mexico City, Guadalajara, Monterey, and cities in the northern states. In 1992 Mexico had 15.1 million dwellings of which 49.9 percent had piped water, 51 percent had flush toilets, and 87.5 percent had electric lighting.

EDUCATION

A government literacy program helped reduce Mexico's adult illiteracy rate from 37.8 percent in 1960 to an average of about 10 percent in 1995 (males: 8.2 percent and females: 12.6%).

Primary schooling is compulsory and free. In 1997 Mexico had 524,927 teachers and 14.65 million students at the primary level. At the secondary level there were 485,059 teachers and 7.9 million students.

Major universities include the National Autonomous University (founded in 1551), the National Polytechnic Institute, and Iberoamericana University (private), all in Mexico City. There were 170,350 teachers and 1.6 million students in all higher-level institutions in 1997.

The government provides adult education through cultural and motorized missions, community development brigades, reading rooms, and special centers for workers' training, art education, social work, and primary education.

2000 KEY EVENTS TIMELINE

January

- The strike by students at the National Autonomous University, going on since April 1999, is the focus of two different votes this month. The student protesters are gauging their support with two days of voting in support of their demands for open admissions and free tuition for the needy, while the administration's counterproposal will also be put to a vote.
- January is a busy time at the border between Mexico and the United States, as thousands of Mexicans who spent the Christmas and New Year's holidays with family in Mexico attempt to cross the border illegally to return to work.

February

- Law students protest the nine-month strike at the National Autonomous University, and try to gain entry to the law school by tearing down barricades. Strikers drove the protesters away by throwing rocks.
- Federal police take over the National Autonomous University, arresting 750 protestors. In response, more than 7,000 took to the streets in a march to protest the arrests.

March

- On March 31 prominent newsman Jacobo Zabludovsky (age seventy-one), main nightly news anchor from 1971 to 1998, resigns from the country's largest broadcast company, Televisa. Two other Televisa anchors resigned on March 30 signaling a personnel and news policy change at the station, away from a policy of supporting the government to a more objective perspective.
- The U.S. Trade Representative's report criticizes Mexican trade practices.

April

- A fisherman finds the fossil remains of a mastodon on the shores of Lake Chapala, 37 miles south of Guadalajara.

June

- A clash between Zapatistas and police in the state of Chiapas leaves seven policemen dead.
- A Mexican radical offers US$10,000 for a dead U.S. border patrol agent.

July

- Elections held on July 3 put Vicente Fox Quesada of the conservative National Action Party (PAN) in the president's seat with 42.8 percent of the vote. His victory ends seventy-one years of rule by the Institutional Revolutionary Party (PRI).
- The Mexico City auditor takes out top police officials July 19 on charges of embezzlement to the tune of $121 million budgeted for police salaries.

August

- An earthquake hits Mexico City on August 9, but no real damage is reported.
- Nine people are killed and forty are wounded in political protests against the PRI in Mexico State on August 18.

September

- Mexico detains 126 Iraqi illegal immigrants in Tijuana. The immigrants were attempting to enter the United States with claims of religious persecution.

October

- President-elect Vicente Fox calls for cooperation among nations in battling drug traffickers.
- The Mexican Supreme Court, ruling in a land dispute, orders U.S. retirees to leave Baja California. The case stems from a paperwork error that occurred almost thirty years ago, when U.S. citizens were issued permits to build homes on land that the court says rightfully belongs to a Mexican company not involved in the real estate deal.
- Thousands of public employees block streets of Mexico City to demand that the traditional government bonus be paid in December.

November

- Residents in the volatile southern state of Chiapas clash with 200 federal police; authorities are prepared to arrest members of a paramilitary group believed to be involved in a 1997 massacre of Tzotzil Indians.
- Nearly 50,000 sugar workers go on strike in fifty-eight mills throughout the country, demanding salary increases and retirement benefits.
- Rioting in a working-class neighborhood of Mexico City results in police occupation. Unrest was prompted by police crackdown on street vendors; dozens are injured.

December

- Vicente Fox takes office as Mexico's president on December 1.
- The Popocatepetl volcano erupts in late December, causing several small earthquakes. Experts believe more eruptions are likely.

ANALYSIS OF EVENTS: 2000

BUSINESS AND THE ECONOMY

For seven decades the Mexican economy, like everything else in the country, has been controlled and manipulated by the nationalist Institutional Revolutionary Party (PRI). With the election of Vicente Fox Quesada on July 2, the rules were certain to change. For Mexicans the good news came early. For the first time in two decades there was no economic crisis following the presidential election. In past elections, the country's currency, the peso, usually plummeted. Investors fled the country, inflation grew at exorbitant rates, and the poor suffered the consequences of the PRI's mistakes. Yet in December 2000 outgoing President Ernesto Zedillo left his post without an economic crisis, just as he had promised. It was, in some ways, a predictable outcome. Mexico averaged 5 percent economic growth over the past four years. Zedillo's team of economists also managed to bring the economy under control. And thanks to the North American Free Trade Agreement (NAFTA), inherited by the Zedillo administration, Mexico's exports to the United States grew from $60 billion in 1995 to $100 billion by 1999. That figure was expected to rise in 2000, not only for Mexican, but for U.S. exports as well.

Yet millions of Mexicans lived at or below the poverty line, and little has changed for them. For Fox, one of his biggest challenges was to deliver on his promises to improve their lives, a daunting task that would take longer than his six years in office. That has not deterred Fox from making lofty promises. He pledged to create 1.35 million jobs per year during his presidency, to spend more money on social programs, and called for sweeping tax and fiscal reforms, which will require changes to the constitution. Tax revenue in Mexico was equal to about only 11 percent of Mexico's gross domestic product (GDP); for comparison, tax revenue in the

United States is about 30 percent of GDP. Fox also sought to create a more equitable and efficient tax collection system. He wanted wealthier Mexicans to pay their fair share, but he also wanted to collect from the poor, including vendors who made a living in the so-called informal economy. Millions made a living selling food and thousands of other products on the streets. Taxing food and medicine was one of Fox's most controversial proposals. Fox, a former Coca-Cola executive, wanted to run Mexico's government like a chief executive officer runs a successful company. But that would mean sweeping changes at all levels of government, and may mean opening up state-owned companies to foreign investment, a sensitive issue for Mexicans who can't imagine PEMEX—the state-owned oil company—run by foreigners. Changes also needed to be made in other energy sectors, especially electricity, where the state-owned monopoly was unable to keep up with the growing nation's needs. Foreign investors wanted Fox to open up the electrical sector to investments, and he might just have to do that if he was to accomplish his predicted growth rates for the country. The lack of cheap electricity forced some companies to close or made their products less competitive.

During 2000 Fox traveled throughout the Americas to lay the foundation for future trade agreements. Central American leaders have anxiously waited to see what Fox would do during his administration, and so far, he has not disappointed them. Fox wanted tighter relations with his southern neighbors, and that included South America. In December his administration began high-level talks with Chile to integrate the two nations' economies. Fox also talked at length about blurring the borders that separate Mexico, the United States, and Canada. But as of the end of the year, that remained a dream, one of many that Fox has woven for the nation.

GOVERNMENT AND POLITICS

On July 2 only hours after polls closed, President Ernesto Zedillo stunned the nation by congratulating National Action Party (PAN) candidate Vicente Fox for winning the presidency. It was an unprecedented moment for Mexico, which had been ruled by Zedillo's authoritarian PRI and its uninterrupted string of presidents for seventy-one years.

"Today we have shown for all to see that ours is a nation of free men and women who believe in the means of democracy and law to achieve progress," he told viewers. On that day Zedillo and Fox sealed their historic legacy. Zedillo likely will be remembered for pushing the PRI to accept a level playing field for its opponents, and for democratizing Mexico's institutions. During his presidency, Congress approved many of his proposed electoral reforms, including public funds for presidential candidates to pay for their campaigns. Reforms created a truly independent election office, the Federal Electoral Institute, which brought transparency and legitimacy to the electoral system. Its first major success was in 1997, when the PRI lost Mexico City's important mayoral post and its majority in the lower house of Congress, a historic defeat, in relatively clean elections. No one questioned the July 2, 2000, results either. For Mexicans and international observers, it was the freest and most fair election in the history of the country.

Yet Zedillo was not solely responsible for these historic changes. While Zedillo had cautiously pushed for democratic reforms during his presidency, it fell on countless others to push for democratic reforms for the past three decades to set the stage for the historic July 2 presidential elections. Zedillo took some bold steps to assert himself against PRI patriarchs, known as "dinosaurs" for their reluctance to embrace change. He eliminated the "dedazo" (the PRI practice of handpicking his successor), and replaced it with a primary in 1999. The relatively unknown Francisco Labastida Ochoa survived the party's first, and hostile, primary election to become its presidential candidate for the 2000 election.

By 2000 the dramatic political changes that had taken place in Mexico made for a close presidential race. Labastida was certainly not out of the running, and the PRI could still wield a great deal of influence. Cárdenas had performed well as Mexico City's mayor, but not well enough to gain any converts to his left-of-center party. Two consecutive presidential losses didn't bode well for his candidacy. Fox, the governor from the state of Guanajuato, was disliked by many of his colleagues within PAN. He was considered too brash, too outspoken, and Fox had made things worse by going outside the party to challenge for the presidency. Fox quickly gained converts with his candor and openly hostile attacks against the PRI. As a rancher wearing cowboy boots, he had charisma and appealed to large numbers of people. According to the *New York Times,* "He has little formal background in economics. By instinct and training from his days as president of Coca-Cola of Mexico, he sold himself to Mexico like a soft drink. He is a delegator, with deep faith in corporate management techniques. He is a man given to great, sometimes transitory enthusiasm, and his transition to power has been marked by a few possibly "pie-in-the-sky" fiscal policy pronouncements.

Despite his gains at the polls, many analysts believed Fox would have to strike a political compromise with Cárdenas to defeat the PRI. But that never happened. Fox relentlessly attacked Labastida as well as Cárdenas. As the presidential vote neared, Cárdenas had no chance of winning, but Fox and Labastida held similar numbers in the polls, and it was nearly impossible to project a winner.

When the polls closed, Fox had won the election with 43 percent of the vote, surprising political analysts for his margin of victory over Labastida, who finished with 36 percent. Cárdenas was a distant third with 17 percent, but his party won important seats in Congress.

Fox may have won the presidency, but he was not a clear winner. His party held 208 seats in the lower house of Congress, forty-three votes short of a majority. The PRI had 209 seats and the PRD held fifty-three seats. In the 128-seat Senate, PAN held forty-six votes, PRI held sixty and the PRD held fifteen. Clearly, Fox would be forced to negotiate with the PAN and PRI parties to make any legislative and constitutional changes. Fox acknowledged his predicament when he said the "presidency, for many years, imposed a monologue. Today, more than ever, to govern means to conduct a dialogue (with the opposition)." After his election Fox visited Labastida and Cárdenas to apologize for some of the remarks he made about the two men during the presidential campaign. The symbolic gesture of humility and fence mending signaled his willingness to negotiate with opposing parties. Yet, Fox is considered brash, often emotional and likely to lose control under pressure. Those are attributes that may become a problem if he wants the opposition to work with him. As of late 2000, it remained difficult to gauge how Cárdenas, and more importantly how PRI leaders, would react to Fox's mandate.

The PRI had its own internal problems. After his loss Labastida disappeared from view and the PRI spun out of control, with different factions trying to take over the leadership of the party. The PRI is not dead, but it is certainly fighting for its survival and relevance in Mexico's new political arena. Many analysts believe the PRI will succumb much like Communist parties faded in importance after losing state support in Eastern European countries with the fall of the Berlin Wall.

Fox already has shown a sensitive side to his country's enormous social problems. On inauguration day he had breakfast with ninety homeless children and promised to give them a better future. He also reached for Mexico's ten million underprivileged indigenous peoples, saying "Never again a Mexico without you." He said the suffering of Mexican Indians was unacceptable. A day after taking office, he made a gesture of reconciliation to the Zapatista National Liberation Army by ordering the removal of several dozen army roadblocks in Chiapas. The leader of the Indian uprising, Subcommander Marcos, welcomed Fox's gesture, and said he was willing to meet with government officials to negotiate a peace settlement sometime in February 2001.

CULTURE AND SOCIETY

The end of 2000 marked the end of the PRI era. With the election of President Fox, seventy-one years of continuous rule by the PRI political machine came to a halt. For seven decades, the PRI controlled nearly every facet of Mexico's society. As of 2000, Mexicans wondered how different life will be without the PRI. In Mexico City the mayor is a PRD member and the PAN controls the council. Mexico in 2000 may be compared with other nations such as Spain and Portugal that for decades struggled against authoritarian regimes. Stagnant in culture and economy for decades under dictatorships, both nations are vibrant after dramatic political change—but change took time, and did not come without pain. And so it might be for Mexico, a nation of dashed hopes for many generations. Fox reached out to his nation's indigenous peoples, long exploited and then neglected and left to languish in poverty. He sought to deliver on his campaign promises and to effect real change in Mexico's society and culture.

DIRECTORY

CENTRAL GOVERNMENT

Head of State

President

Quesada Vincente Fox, Office of the President, Puerta Centrale Premiere Piso, Col. San Miguel, Chapultepec, 11850 Mexico City, DF, Mexico

PHONE: +52 (5) 5157994
FAX: +52 (5) 5165762

Cabinet

Secretary of Agrarian Reform
Maria Teresa Herrera, Department of Agrarian Reform, Rio Sena No. 49, Col. Cuauhtemoc, 06500 México City, DF, Mexico
PHONE: +52 (5) 5257580

Secretary of Agriculture
Javier Usabiaga, Department of Agriculture

Secretary of Communications and Transport
Pedro Cerisola y Weber, Department of Communications and Transport, Xola Y Avenida Universidad, Cuerpo C, Piso 1 Col., Navarte, Del. Benito Juarez, 03028 Mexico City, DF, Mexico
PHONE: +52 (5) 5309203
FAX: +52 (5) 5190692

Secretary of Comptroller General
Francisco Barrio, Department of the Comptroller General, Insurgentes sur 1735, Col. Guadalupe Inn, 01020 México City, DF, Mexico
PHONE: +52 (5) 6633636

Secretary of Public Education
Reyes Tamez, Department of Public Education

Secretary of Energy
Ernesto Martens, Department of Energy, Insurgentes Sur 890, Col. Del Valle, 03100 México City, DF, México
PHONE: +52 (5) 4486000
E-MAIL: energia1@energia.gob.mx

Secretary of Environment, Natural Resources, and Fisheries
Victor Lichtinger, Department of the Environment, Natural Resources, and Fisheries, Periférico Sur 4209, Fraccionamiento Jardines en la Montaña, Delegación Tlalpan, 14210 México City, DF, Mexico
PHONE: +52 (5) 6280600

Secretary of Finance and Public Credit
Francisco Gil, Department of Finance and Public Credit

Secretary of Foreign Relations
Jorge Castaneda, Department of Foreign Relations

Secretary of Government
Santiago Creel, Department of Government

Secretary of Health
Julio Frenk, Department of Health, Lieja, 7-1er Piso, Col. Juárez, 06696 Mexico City, DF, Mexico
PHONE: +52 (5) 5536967
FAX: +52 (5) 5537917
E-MAIL: ssa@ssa.gob.mx

Secretary of Labor and Social Welfare
Carlos Abascal, Department of Labor and Social Welfare

Secretary of National Defense
Gen. Gerardo Clemente Ricardo Vega, Department of National Defense

Secretary of the Navy
Vice Adm. Marco Antonio Peyrot, Office of the Navy

Secretary of Social Development
Josefina Vazquez, Department of Social Development, Av. Constituyentes 947, Edif. B, P.A., Col. Belén de las Flores, Del. Alvaro Obregón, 01110 México City, DF, Mexico
PHONE: +52 (5) 2718481
FAX: +52 (5) 2718862

Secretary of Tourism
Leticia Navarro, Department of Tourism

Secretary of Economy
Luis Ernesto Derbez, Department of Economy

Secretary of Public Security and Justice Services
Alejandro Gertz, Department of Public Security and Justice Services

POLITICAL ORGANIZATIONS

Zapatista Front of National Liberation

Calle Zapotecos 7 bis, Colonia Obrera, Del. Cuauhtmoc, 06800 Mexico City, DF, Mexico
PHONE: +52 (5) 7614236
FAX: +52 (5) 7614236
E-MAIL: floresu@spin.com.mx

Partido Accion Nacional (National Action Party)

Angel Urraza 812, Del Valle, 03109 Mexico City, DF, Mexico
PHONE: +52 (5) 5596300
FAX: +52 (5) 5590975
E-MAIL: relaciones@cen.pan.org.mx
TITLE: Presidente Nacional
NAME: Luis Felipe Bravo Mena

Partido de la Revolucion Democratica (Democratic Revolutionary Party)

Monterrey 50, PB, Col. Roma, 06700 Mexico City, DF, Mexico
PHONE: +52 (5) 5256059
FAX: +52 (5) 2087863
TITLE: Presidente Nacional
NAME: Amalia Garcia Medina

Partido de la Revolucionario Institucional (Institutional Revolutionary Party)

NAME: Dulce Maria Sauri

Partido de Trabajo-PT (Worker's Party)

Av. Cuauhtemoc 47, Col. Roma, 06700 Mexico City, DF, Mexico
PHONE: +52 (5) 2074441
FAX: +52 (5) 5252727
E-MAIL: pt@pt.org.mx
TITLE: Dirigente Nacional
NAME: Alberto Anaya Gutirrez

Partido Verde Ecologista de Mexico (Green Ecological Party of Mexico)

Medicina 74 Col., Copilco Universidad, 04360 Mexico City, DF, Mexico
PHONE: +52 (5) 6598272
E-MAIL: pvem@pvem.org.mx
TITLE: Presidente Nacional
NAME: Jorge Gonz lez Torres

DIPLOMATIC REPRESENTATION

Embassies in Mexico

Angola
Schiller 503 Col. Polanco, 11560 México City, DF, Mexico
PHONE: +52 (5) 5455883
FAX: +52 (5) 5452733
E-MAIL: info@palanca-negra.org

Canada
Calle Schiller 529, Colonia Rincon Del Bosque, Polanco, 11560 Mexico City, DF, Mexico
PHONE: +52 (5) 7247900
FAX: +52 (5) 7247982
TITLE: Ambassador
NAME: Stanley Gooch

France
Campos Elíseos 339, Col. Polanco, 11560 Mexico City, DF, Mexico
PHONE: +52 (5) 2829700
FAX: +52 (5) 2829703
TITLE: Ambassador
NAME: Bruno Delaye

Italy
Paseo de las Palmas 1994, Col. Lomas de Chapultepec, 11000 México City, DF, Mexico
PHONE: +52 (5) 5963655
FAX: +52 (5) 5967710
E-MAIL: embitaly@data.net.mx

Japan
Domicillio Del Centro Cultural, Paseo de law Reforma 295, Piso 3, Col Cuauhtemoc, 06500 Mexico City, DF, Mexico
PHONE: +52 (5) 5144507

United Kingdom
Col. Cuauhtémoc, 06500 México City, DF, Mexico
PHONE: +52 (5) 2072089
FAX: +52 (5) 2077672
TITLE: Ambassador
NAME: Adrian Charles Thorpe

United States
Paseo de la Reforma 305, Col. Cuauhtémoc, 06500 Mexico City, DF, Mexico
PHONE: +52 (5) 2099100
FAX: +52 (5) 5119980
E-MAIL: ccs@usembassy.net.mx

JUDICIAL SYSTEM

Supreme Court

Pino Suárez No. 2, Col. Centro, 06065 México City, DF, México

BROADCAST MEDIA

Direccion General de Concesiones y Permisos de Telecomunicaciones

Departmento de Asignacíon de Frecuencias, Unidad Contel Sga-2, Avenue de las Telecomunicaciones s/n, Ixtapalapa, 09310 México, DF, Mexico
PHONE: +52 (5) 6920077
TITLE: Director
CONTACT: Sergio Cervantes

Instituto Mexicano de Televisión (IMEVISIÓN)

Avenue Periférico Sur 4121, Colonia Fuentes del Pedregal, 14141 México, DF, Mexico
PHONE: +52 (5) 5685684, +52 (5) 5681313
TITLE: Directorate General

CONTACT: Jose Antono Alvarez Lima
CHANNEL: 7, 13
TYPE: Government

Televisa, S.A.

Avenue Chapultepec 28, 06724 México, DF, Mexico
PHONE: +52 (5) 7093333
FAX: +52 (5) 7093021
TITLE: Chairman of the Administrative Council
CONTACT: R. O'Farrill Jr.
CHANNEL: 2, 4, 5, 9
TYPE: Commercial, Private

COLLEGES AND UNIVERSITIES

University Simon Bolivar, Mexico

Av. Rio Mixoac #48, col Insurgentes Mixoac, Mexico City, DF, Mexico
PHONE: +52 (5) 6299700
WEBSITE: http://bolivar.usb.mx

Autonomous Technical Institute of Mexico

Rio Hondo 1 Tizapan San Angel, 01000 Alvaro Obregon, DF, Mexico
PHONE: +52 (5) 6284000
E-MAIL: leenheer@intacad.rhon.itam.mx
WEBSITE: http://www.itam.mx

University Christopher Columbus Veracruz

Apdo. 167, 91930 Veracruz, VC, Mexico
PHONE: +52 (2) 9219674
FAX: +52 (2) 9221757
E-MAIL: promocion@aix.ver.ucc.mx
WEBSITE: http://www.ver.ucc.mx

Technological University of Mexico

Av. Marina Nacional No. 162 Colonia, 11320 Anahuac, DF, Mexico
PHONE: +52 (5) 3992000
FAX: +52 (5) 3991576
WEBSITE: http://www.unitec.mx

Autonomous University of the State of Mexico

Toluca, ME, Mexico
PHONE: +52 (72) 134732
FAX: +52 (72) 145546
E-MAIL: ugh@coatepec.uaemex.mx
WEBSITE: http://www.uaemex.mx

Instituto Tecnologico de Merida

Adpo 9-11, 97000 Merida, YU, Mexico
PHONE: +52 (99) 448197
FAX: +52 (99) 448181
E-MAIL: glaguna@labna.itmerida.mx
WEBSITE: http://www.itmerida.mx

Universidad Iberoamericana

Prol Paseo-Reforma 880 Col, Lomas De Santa Fe, 01210 Mexico City, DF, Mexico
PHONE: +52 (5) 2674000
FAX: +52 (5) 2674005
E-MAIL: enrique.gonzalez@uia.mx
WEBSITE: http://www.uia.mx

Metropolitan Autonomous University Mexico

Azcapotzalco Campus Ap 306, Av San Pablo 180 Col, Reynosa-Tamaulipas Del, 02000 Azcapotzalco, DF, Mexico
PHONE: +52 (5) 7244041
FAX: +52 (5) 3953902
E-MAIL: riebeling@tonatiuh.uam.mx
WEBSITE: http://www.uam.mx

ISEC University, Mexico

Mier y Pesafo No 227, Col. del Valle, 03100 Mexico City, DF, Mexico
PHONE: +52 (5) 5361440
FAX: +52 (5) 6827889
E-MAIL: isecuniv@mail.internet.com.mx
WEBSITE: http://www.isecuniv.edu.mx

Pan American University Mexico

Augusto Rodin 498, Col Mixcoac 03920, 03920 Mexico City, DF, Mexico
PHONE: +52 (5) 5982779
FAX: +52 (5) 6112265
E-MAIL: master@mixcoac.upmx.mx
WEBSITE: http://www.upmx.mx

Universidad Nacional Autonoma de Mexico

Ciudad Universitaria, Del Coyoacan, 04510 Mexico City, DF, Mexico
PHONE: +52 (5) 6284000
FAX: +52 (5) 6284102
E-MAIL: arturof@rectoria.rhon.tam.mx
WEBSITE: http://www.unam.mx

La Salle University Mexico

Benjamin Franklin 47, Col Condesa, 06140 Cuauhtemoc, DF, Mexico
PHONE: +52 (5) 7280500
FAX: +52 (5) 2718585
E-MAIL: ulsarec@vmulsa.ulsa.mx
WEBSITE: http://www.ulsa.mx

National Polytechnical Institute

Miguel Othon Mendizabul Sln, Col Residencial la Escalera, 07738 Mexico City, DF, Mexico
PHONE: +52 (5) 7296000
E-MAIL: webmaster@ipn.mx
WEBSITE: http://www.ipn.mx

El Colegio de Mexico A.C.

Camino Al Ajusco 20, Col. Pedregal de Santa Teresa, 10740 Mexico City, DF, Mexico
PHONE: +52 (5) 4493000
FAX: +52 (5) 6450464
WEBSITE: http://www.colmex.mx

Intercontinental University Mexico

South Av. Insurgent 4303 Sta, Ursula Xitla 14420 C.P. Tlalpan D.F., 14000 Mexico City, DF, Mexico
PHONE: +52 (5) 5738544
FAX: +52 (5) 6651543
WEBSITE: http://www.uic.edu.mx

Autonomous University of Ciudad Juarez

Av. Lopez Mateos 20, 32310 Ciudad Juarez, CH, Mexico
PHONE: +52 (16) 165778
FAX: +52 (16) 162111
E-MAIL: rlau@uacj.mx
WEBSITE: http://www.uacj.mx

Instituto Tecnologico de Ciudad Juarez

Blvd. Tecnologico 1340, Apdo 2734, 32500 Ciudad Juarez, CH, Mexico
PHONE: +52 (16) 173897
FAX: +52 (16) 173512

University of Guadalajara

Avda Juarez 975, Sector Juarez, 44100 Guadalajara, JA, Mexico
PHONE: +52 (3) 8267880
FAX: +52 (3) 8264048
E-MAIL: victor@redudg.udg.mx
WEBSITE: http://www.udg.mx

Autonomous University of Guadalajara

Apdo Postal 1-440, 44100 Guadalajara, JA, Mexico
PHONE: +52 (3) 6417051
FAX: +52 (3) 6425427
E-MAIL: uag@uag.edu
WEBSITE: http://www.uag.mx

Autonomous University of Nuevo Leon

Ciudad Universitaria, 66451 San Nicolas de los Garza, NL, Mexico
PHONE: +52 (83) 522885
FAX: +52 (83) 767757
WEBSITE: http://www.dsi.uanl.mx

Instituto Tecnologico de Nuevo Leon

Av Eloy Cavazos 2001 Junto Al Parque, La Pastora Col. Tolteca, 67170 Guadalupe, NL, Mexico
PHONE: +52 (83) 370330
FAX: +52 (83) 678834
WEBSITE: http://rodeo.itnl.edu.mx

Popular Autonomous University of the State of Puebla

21 Sur 1103, Cononia Santiago, 72000 Puebla, PU, Mexico
PHONE: +52 (22) 320266
FAX: +52 (22) 325251
E-MAIL: vpocheco@sun1.pue.upaep.mx
WEBSITE: http://www.upaep.mx

Instituto Tecnologico de Puebla

Apdo. 1145, 72220 Puebla, PU, Mexico
PHONE: +52 (22) 221354
FAX: +52 (22) 298810
WEBSITE: http://www.itpuebla.edu.mx

University of the Americas, Mexico

Santa Catarina Martir, 372 Col., 72820 Cholula, PU, Mexico
PHONE: +52 (2) 292000
FAX: +52 (2) 292018
WEBSITE: http://info.pue.udlap.mx

University of Veracruz

Zona Univ Lomas Del Estadio, 91090 Jalapa, VC, Mexico
PHONE: +52 (29) 421763
FAX: +52 (29) 176370
E-MAIL: victora@speedy.coacade.uv.mx
WEBSITE: http://www.uv.mx

Instituto Tecnologico de Veracruz

Apdo. 539, 91860 Boca del Rio, VC, Mexico
PHONE: +52 (29) 381930
FAX: +52 (29) 342279
WEBSITE: http://www.itver.edu.mx

Autonomous University of Yucatan

Apdo. 1418-3, Calles 57 y 60, 97000 Merida, YU, Mexico
PHONE: +52 (99) 248000
FAX: +52 (99)+ 282557
E-MAIL: rbello@tunku.uady.mx
WEBSITE: http://www.uady.mx

NEWSPAPERS AND MAGAZINES

La Aficion

Ignacio Mariscal 23, A.P. 64-Bis, 06030 Mexico D.F., Mexico, Mexico
PHONE: +52 (5) 5359342
E-MAIL: opino@aquila.el-universal.com.mx
WEBSITE: serpiente.dgsca.unam.mx/universal/aficion
TITLE: President, General Director
CONTACT: Juan Francisco Ealy Ortiz
CIRCULATION: 85,000

Cuestion

Libertad de Expresion, Editorial Hara, S.A., Laguna de Mayran No. 410 Anahuac, 11320 Mexico D.F., Mexico
PHONE: +52 (5) 2600499
FAX: +52 (5) 2604562
E-MAIL: cuestion@compuserve.com
TITLE: General Director
CONTACT: Alberto Gonzalez Parra
CIRCULATION: 48,000

Diario de Juarez

Editora Paso del Norte, S.A. de C.V., Paseo Triunfo de la Republica No. 3505, 32310 Juarez Chih, Mexico.
PHONE: +52 (16) 291900
FAX: +52 (16) 291992
E-MAIL: djuarez@buzon.diario.com.mx
WEBSITE: http://www.diario.online.com.mx/dcj
TITLE: Editor
CONTACT: Armando Velez
CIRCULATION: 47,797

Diario de Mexico

Editoriales de Mexico, S.A. de C.V., Chimalpopoca No. 38, Col. Obrera, 06800 Mexico D.F., Mexico
PHONE: +52 (5) 5883821
TITLE: General Director
CONTACT: Federico Bracamontes Galvez
CIRCULATION: 76,000

El Diario de Monterrey

Periodico El Diario de Monterrey S.A. de C.V., Eugenio Garza Sada 2245 Sur, Col. Roma, A.P. 3128, 64700 Monterrey N.L., Mexico
PHONE: +52 (83) 592525
FAX: +52 (83) 591414
E-MAIL: eldiario@mail.intercable.net
WEBSITE: http://www.intercable.net/diariomty
TITLE: Editor
CONTACT: Roberto Mora
CIRCULATION: 80,000

El Diario de Nuevo Laredo

Editorial Villmar, S.A. de C.V., Gonzalez #240, A.P. 101, 88000 Nuevo Laredo Tamaulipas, Mexico
PHONE: +52 (87) 128444
FAX: +52 (87) 128221
E-MAIL: eldiario@nld.bravo.net
TITLE: Editor
CONTACT: Ruperto Villareal Marroquin
CIRCULATION: 73,495

Diario de Yucatan

Cia Tipografica Yucateca SA de CV, Calle 60, No. 521, 65 y 67 Centro, 97000 Merida Yuc., Mexico
PHONE: +52 (99) 238444
FAX: +52 (99) 282850
E-MAIL: diario@sureste.com
WEBSITE: http://www.yucatan.com.mx
TITLE: Editor
CONTACT: Carlos R. Menendez Navarrete
CIRCULATION: 65,399

El Empresario

Periodico El Economista, S.A. de C.V., Avenida Coyoacan 515, Del Valle, 03100 Mexico D.F., Mexico
PHONE: +52 (5) 3265454
FAX: +52 (5) 6873821
TITLE: Editor
CONTACT: Martin Casillas de Alba
CIRCULATION: 40,000

Esto

Cia Periodistica ESTO, S.A. de C.V., Guillermo Prieto No. 7-Planta Baja, 06470 Mexico D.F., Mexico
PHONE: +52 (5) 5352722
FAX: +52 (5) 5352687
E-MAIL: mau@oem.com.mx
WEBSITE: http://www.oem.com.mx
TITLE: Editor
CONTACT: Mauricio Vazquez Ramos
CIRCULATION: 450,000

Excelsior

El Periodico de la Vida Nacional, Excelsior Cia Editorial SCL, Reforma 18 2do piso, Col. Centro, 06600 Mexico D.F., Mexico
PHONE: +52 (5) 5356552
FAX: +52 (5) 5460787
WEBSITE: http://www.excelsior.com.mx
TITLE: Director
CONTACT: Regino Diaz Redondo
CIRCULATION: 5,500,000

El Financiero

El Financiero SA de C.V., Lago Bolsena 176, Col. Anahuac, 11320 Mexico D.F., Mexico
PHONE: +52 (5) 2277600
FAX: +52 (5) 2551881
WEBSITE: http://www.elfinanciero.com.mx
TITLE: Editor
CONTACT: Alejandro Ramos
CIRCULATION: 135,000

El Heraldo de Mexico

Dr. Lucio Esq. Dr. Velasco, Col. Doctores, 06720 Mexico D.F., Mexico
PHONE: +52 (5) 5783632
FAX: +52 (5) 5789824
WEBSITE: http://www.heraldo.com.mx
TITLE: President
CONTACT: Gabriel Alarcon Valazquez
CIRCULATION: 120,000

El Informador

Union Editorial S.A., Calle Independencia Sur No. 300, A.P. 3 Bis, 44100 Guadalajara Jal., Mexico
PHONE: +52 (3) 6146340
FAX: +52 (3) 6139323
WEBSITE: http://www.informador.com.mx
TITLE: Editor
CONTACT: Jorge Alvarez del Castillo
CIRCULATION: 75,000

La Jornada

Desarrollo de Medios, S.A. de C.V., Balderas No. 68, Col. Centro, 06050 Mexico D.F., Mexico
PHONE: +52 (5) 7282900
FAX: +52 5212763
E-MAIL: jornada@condor.dqsca.unam.mx
WEBSITE: serpiente.dgsca.unam.mx/jornada/index.html
TITLE: General Director
CONTACT: Carmen Lira Saade
CIRCULATION: 106,471

Metro

Av. Mexico Coyoacan No. 40, Col. Santa Cruz Atoyac, 03310 Mexico D.F., Mexico
PHONE: +52 (5) 6287878
FAX: +52 (5) 6287550
TITLE: General Commander Director
CONTACT: Ricardo Junco
CIRCULATION: 50,000

El Mexicano

Gran Diario Regional, Carretera al Aeropuerto s/n Fracc. Alamar, A.P. 2333, 22540 Tijuana B.C., Mexico
PHONE: +52 (66) 213400
FAX: +52 (66) 212944
CONTACT: Patricia Ciccone
CIRCULATION: 200,000

El Norte

Washington 629 Ote, 64000 Monterrey N.L., Mexico
PHONE: +52 (8) 3188300
FAX: +52 (8) 3432476
E-MAIL: desplegados@elnorte.com.mx
WEBSITE: http://www.infosel.com.mx/elnorte
TITLE: Editor
CONTACT: Ramon Alberto Garza
CIRCULATION: 160,000

Novedades

Novedades Editores S.A. de C.V., Morelos 16 Primer piso, Col. Centro, 06040 Mexico D.F., Mexico
PHONE: +52 (5) 5124903
FAX: +52 (5) 2730311
E-MAIL: commentarios@novedades.com
WEBSITE: http://www.novedades.com
CIRCULATION: 43,536

El Occidental

Periodistica del Sol de Guadalajara, S.A. de C.V., Calz. Independencia Sur 324, A.P. 1-699, 44100 Guadalajara Jal., Mexico
PHONE: +52 (3) 6130660
FAX: +52 (3) 6136796
TITLE: Editor
CONTACT: Guillermo Chao Ebergenyl
CIRCULATION: 110,000

Ovaciones

Editorial Ovacione, S.A. de C.V., Lago Zirahuen 279-2o Piso Anahuac, 11320 Mexico D.F., Mexico
PHONE: +52 (5) 3280700 ext. 1417
FAX: +52 (5) 3280775
CIRCULATION: 130,000

La Prensa

Editora La Prensa, S.A. de C.V., Basilio Badillo 40, Col. Centro, 06030 Mexico D.F., Mexico
PHONE: +52 (5) 2289977
FAX: +52 (5) 2288981
WEBSITE: http://www.oem.com.mx
TITLE: Editor
CONTACT: Mauricio Ortega Camberos
CIRCULATION: 270,000

Reforma

Editora EL SOL, S.A. de C.V., Av. Mexico Coyoacan No. 40, Col. Santa Cruz Atoyac, 03310 Mexico D.F., Mexico
PHONE: +52 (5) 6287878
FAX: +52 (5) 6287550
E-MAIL: amaya@reforma.com.mx
WEBSITE: http://www.reforma.infosel.com
TITLE: Editor-in-Chief
CONTACT: Lazaro Rios
CIRCULATION: 126,000

El Sol de Guadalajara

Periodistica del Sol de Guadalajara, S.A. de C.V., Calz. Independencia Sur No. 324, A.P. 1-699, 44100 Guadalajara Jal., Mexico
PHONE: +52 (3) 6130690
FAX: +52 (3) 6136796
TITLE: Editor
CONTACT: Guillermo Chao Ebergenyl
CIRCULATION: 45,000

El Sol de Mexico

Cia. Periodistica del Sol de Mexico, S.A. de C.V., Guillermo Prieto 7, Col. San Rafael, 06470 Mexico D.F., Mexico
PHONE: +52 (5) 5356042
E-MAIL: ecobos@oem.com.mx
WEBSITE: http://www.oem.com.mx
TITLE: President
CONTACT: Mario Vazquez Rana
CIRCULATION: 76,000

El Sol de Tijuana

Editora America Latina, S.A., Rufino Tamayo No. 4 Zona Rio, 22320 Tijuana B.C., Mexico
PHONE: +52 (66) 343232
FAX: +52 (66) 342234
CIRCULATION: 50,000

El Sol

Editora El Sol, S.A. de C.V., Washington 629 Ote, 64000 Monterrey N.L., Mexico
PHONE: +52 (8) 3188300
FAX: +52 (8) 3432476
WEBSITE: http://www.infosel.com.mx
TITLE: Editor
CONTACT: Alejandro Junco de la Vega
CIRCULATION: 45,300

Ultimas Noticias

Excelsior Bldg, Paseo de la Reforma 18, Apdo 120 bis, 06600 Mexico D.F., Mexico
PHONE: +52 (5) 5662200
FAX: +52 (5) 5660223
TITLE: Director
CONTACT: Regino Diaz Redondo
CIRCULATION: 54,000

El Universal

Cia Periodistica Nal. S.A. de C.V., Bucareli No. 12, 2 piso, Col Centro, 06040 Mexico D.F., Mexico
PHONE: +52 (5) 7091313
FAX: +52 (5) 5218080
WEBSITE: http://www.el-universal.com.mx
CIRCULATION: 458,000

La Voz de la Frontera

Editora America Latina, S.A., Ave. Madero No. 1545, A.P. 946, 21100 Mexicali B.C., Mexico
PHONE: +52 (6) 5524832
FAX: +52 (6) 5536912
E-MAIL: lavoz@oem.com.mx

TITLE: President, General Director
CONTACT: Mario Vazquez Rana
CIRCULATION: 65,000

La Voz de Michoacan

La Voz de Michoacan S.A. de C.V., Av. Periodismo Jose Tocaven Lavin 1270, A.P. 121, 58190 Mexico
PHONE: +52 (4) 3273712
FAX: +52 (4) 3273728
E-MAIL: redaccion@mail.giga.com
WEBSITE: http://www.boznet.com.mx
TITLE: Publisher, Editor
CONTACT: Miguel Medina, Jr.
CIRCULATION: 50,000

Epoca

Epoca de México, S.A. de C.V., Medellín 94, Col. Roma, C.P. 06700, Mexico D.F., Mexico Conmutador
PHONE: +52 309700
FAX: +52 309701
WEBSITE: http://www.epoca.com.mx
TITLE: President/Director General
CONTACT: Guillermo Mora Tavares

Expansion

Grupo Editorial Expansion, Salamanca 35, Col. Roma, 06700 Mexico D.F., Mexico
FAX: +52 2082819
WEBSITE: http://www.expansion.com.mx
TITLE: Director General
CONTACT: Alejandro Serna Barrera
CIRCULATION: 23,516
TYPE: Economics, business, finance

Proceso

Comunicacion e Informacion, S.A. de C.V., Fresas 13, Col. del Valle, 03100 Mexico D.F., Mexico
PHONE: +56 292050
FAX: +55 595105
WEBSITE: http://www.proceso.com.mx
TITLE: President/Editor
CONTACT: Julio Scherer Garcia

La Revista Peninsular

Calle 35 No. 489-E por 54 y 52 Centro, Mérida, Yucatán, Mexico
PHONE: +52 9274101
FAX: +52 9273927
E-MAIL: redaccion@informaya.com.mx
WEBSITE: http://www.larevista.com.mx
TITLE: Director
CONTACT: Rodrigo Menéndez Cámara

PUBLISHERS

ALPHA OMEGA Grupo Editor

Tabasco 106, Col Roma, Mexico, DF 06700
PHONE: +52 (5) 5119203
FAX: +52 (5) 2077158
E-MAIL: gferreyra@spin.com.mx
TITLE: Director de Edicione
CONTACT: Ferreyra C. Gonzalo
SUBJECTS: Computer Science, Electronics, Engineering, Management, Microcomputers, Technology

Libreria y Ediciones Botas SA

Justo sierra 5Z, Mexico, DF
PHONE: +52 (5) 5223896
FAX: +52 (5) 7025403
E-MAIL: botas@mail.nextgeninter.net.mx
TITLE: Man. Director
CONTACT: Andreas Botas Hernandez
SUBJECTS: Art, Economics, Fiction, History, Law, Medicine, Nursing, Dentistry, Philosophy, Science (General)

Centro de Estudios Mexicanos y Centroamericanos

Sierra Leona No. 330, Col Lomas dr Chapultepec, Mexico, DF 11000
PHONE: +52 (5) 5405921; 5405922
FAX: +52 (5) 5405923
E-MAIL: cemca@data.net.mx
TITLE: Director
CONTACT: Martine Dauzier
SUBJECTS: Anthropology, Archaeology, Biological Sciences, Earth Sciences, Economics, Environmental Studies, Ethnicity, Foreign Countries, Political Science, History, Social Sciences
TOTAL PUBLISHED: 250 print

El Colegio de Mexico AC

Camino al Ajusco No. 20, Col Pedregal de Santa Teresa, Mexico, DF 10740
PHONE: +52 (5) 5686033, ext. 388
FAX: +52 (5) 6526233
E-MAIL: biblio@colmex.mx
TITLE: Publications Coordinator
CONTACT: Marta Lilia Prieto
SUBJECTS: Asian Studies, Economics, Environmental Studies, Political Science,

History, Language Arts, Linguistics, Literature, Social Sciences, Women's Studies

Colegio de Postgraduados en Ciencias Agricolas

Carr Mexico-Texcoco Km 35.5 Montecillo, 56230 Chapingo Edo de Mexico
PHONE: +52 (595) 584555
FAX: +52 (595) 10275
E-MAIL: difusion@colpos.colpos.mx
TITLE: Secretary
CONTACT: Alfonso Larque Saavedra
SUBJECTS: Agriculture, Biological Sciences, Economics, Education, Mathematics, Science (General), Social Sciences, Technology, Veterinary Medicine

Publicaciones Cruz O SA

Patriotismo No. 875-D, Colonia Mixcoac, Mexico, DF 03910
PHONE: +52 (5) 5637544; 5930232
FAX: +52 (5) 6806122
E-MAIL: pcosa@infosel.net.mx
TITLE: General Director
CONTACT: Oscar Rene Cruz
SUBJECTS: Biography, Economics, Law, Philosophy, Psychology, Psychiatry, Buddhism, Catholicism, Jewish Religion, Social Sciences
TOTAL PUBLISHED: 285 print

Editorial Diana SA de CV

Roberto Gayol 1219, Col Del Valle, Mexico, DF 03100
PHONE: +52 (5) 5750711
FAX: +52 (5) 5753211; 5751818
E-MAIL: editors@diana.com.mx
TITLE: President
CONTACT: Jose Luis Ramirez C
SUBJECTS: Archaeology, Animals, Business, New Age, Occult, Biography, Cookery, Child Care, Education, Fiction, Health, Literature, Journalism, Nonfiction (General), Religion, Sports, Self-Help
TOTAL PUBLISHED: 110 print

Edamex SA de CV

Heriberto Frias No. 1104, Col Del Valle, Del Benito Juarez, Mexico, DF 03100
PHONE: +52 (5) 5598588
FAX: +52 (5) 5750555; 5757035
E-MAIL: info@edamex.com
WEBSITE: http://www.edamex.com
TITLE: Director General
CONTACT: Manuel Colmenares
SUBJECTS: Architecture, Interior Design, Art, Biography, Journalism, Management, Parapsychology, Self-Help, Social Sciences, Sports, Athletics
TOTAL PUBLISHED: 120 print; 420 online; 420 internet

El Colegio de Michoacan A C

Martinez de Navarrete 505, Fraccionamiento Las Fuentes, 59699 Zamora, Michoacan, Mexico
PHONE: +52 (3) 5157100, ext. 1710
FAX: +52 (3) 5157100, ext. 1712
E-MAIL: pdelgado@colmich.edu.mx
WEBSITE: http://www.colmich.edu.mx
TITLE: Publications
CONTACT: Patricia Delgado Gonzalez
SUBJECTS: Anthropology, Archaeology, Art, Biography, Ethnicity, Political Science, History, Social Sciences
TOTAL PUBLISHED: 250 print

Editorial El Manual Moderno SA de CV

Ave. Sonora 206, Col Hipodromo Condesa, Mexico, DF 06100
PHONE: +52 (5) 5648979; 5642321
FAX: +52 (5) 2641701; 2651162
E-MAIL: mmoderno@compuserve.com.mx
TITLE: Marketing & Sales
CONTACT: Jose Pesez
SUBJECTS: Biological Sciences, Health, Nutrition, Medicine, Nursing, Dentistry, Psychology, Psychiatry, Self-Help, Veterinary Medicine

Ediciones Era SA de CV

Calle del Trabajo 31, Col La Fama Del Tlalpan, Mexico, DF 14269
PHONE: +52 (5) 5281221
FAX: +52 (5) 6062904
E-MAIL: edicionesera@laneta.apc.org
TITLE: Man. Director
CONTACT: Nieves Espresate Xirau
SUBJECTS: Art, Economics, Fiction, Political Science, History, Literature, Literary Criticism, Essays, Social Sciences
TOTAL PUBLISHED: 300 print

Fondo de Cultura Economica

Carretera Picacho-Ajusco No. 227, Col Bosques del Pedregal, Mexico, DF 1000
PHONE: +52 (5) 5242240; 5243840; 5246664
FAX: +52 (5) 2274640; 2274683
E-MAIL: fceedi@infoabc.com

TITLE: Man. Director
CONTACT: Miguel de la Madrid
SUBJECTS: Agriculture, Anthropology, Business, Archaeology, Behavior Sciences, Communications, Education, Energy, Political Science, History, Nonfiction (General)

Ibcon SA

Gutenberg 224, Col Anzures, Mexico, DF 11590
PHONE: +52 (5) 2554577
FAX: +52 (5) 2554577
E-MAIL: ibcon@infosel.net.mx
WEBSITE: http://www.ibcon.com.mx
TITLE: Editor
CONTACT: Gabriel Zaid
SUBJECTS: Business
TOTAL PUBLISHED: 17 print; CD-ROMs

Informatica Cosmos SA de CV

Cal del Hueso 122-A1, Col Ex-Hacienda Coapa, Mexico, DF 14300
PHONE: +52 (5) 6774868; 6776043
FAX: +52 (5) 6793575
E-MAIL: macazaga@cosmos.com.mx
WEBSITE: http://www.cosmos.com.mx
TITLE: Man. Director
CONTACT: Raul Macazaga
SUBJECTS: Industry guides, products, producers, suppliers of industry, chemicals, food & feed, container & packaging, rubber, plastics & resins & equipment

Editorial Limusa SA de CV

Balderas No. 95, Col Centro Dele Cuauhtemoc, Mexico, DF 06040
PHONE: +52 (5) 5212105; 5212187; 5212487
FAX: +52 (5) 5122903; 5109415
E-MAIL: limusa@noriega.com.mx
WEBSITE: http://www.noriega.com.mx
TITLE: Vice President & Editorial Director
CONTACT: Miguel Noriega Arias
SUBJECTS: Aeronautics, Agriculture, Art, Behavioral Sciences, Business, Child Care, Communications, Computer Science, Engineering, Education, Electronics, Political Science, Health, Law, Medicine, Science, Social Sciences, Religion, Sports
TOTAL PUBLISHED: 2,500 print

McGraw-Hill Interamericana de Mexico, SA de CV

Cedro No. 512, Col Atlampa, Cuahutemoc, Mexico, DF 06450
PHONE: +52 (5) 1171515
FAX: +52 (5) 6285367
E-MAIL: mcgraw-hill@infosel.net.mx
WEBSITE: http://www.mcgraw-hill.com.mx
TITLE: Man. Director
CONTACT: Carlos Rios
SUBJECTS: Business, Engineering (General), Mathematics, Public Administration, Social Science, Sociology

Instituto Nacional de Antropologia e Historia

Cordoba 45, Col Roma, Mexico, DF 06700
PHONE: +52 (5) 5335246, 5332272; 2074559
FAX: +52 (5) 2074633
E-MAIL: difusion@inah.gob.mx
TITLE: International Rights
CONTACT: Sol Levin
SUBJECTS: Anthropology, Antiques, Archaeology, Art, History, Language Arts, Music, Dance, Native American Studies, Photography, Social Sciences
TOTAL PUBLISHED: 120 print

Naves Internacional de Ediciones SA

Amores No. 135, Col Del Valle, Del Benito Juarez, Mexico, DF 03100
PHONE: +52 (5) 6690595
FAX: +52 (5) 6823728
E-MAIL: niesa@mpsnet.com.mx
CONTACT: Pablo Llaca
SUBJECTS: Advertising, Architecture, Interior Design, Art, Cookery, Photography

Editorial Pax-Mexico - Libreria Carlos Cesarman SA

Av. Cuauhtemoc No. 1434, Mexico, DF 03310
PHONE: +52 (5) 6057677
FAX: +52 (5) 6057600
E-MAIL: editorialpax@mexis.com
TITLE: Man. Director
CONTACT: Gerardo Gally
SUBJECTS: Business, Career Development, Education, Health, Nutrition, How-To, Literature, Literary Criticism, Essays, Psychology, Psychiatry

Pearson Educacion de Mexico

Calle 4, No. 25, Fraccionamiento Industrial Alce Blanco, Naucalpan, Estado de Mexico 5337
PHONE: +52 (5) 3870700
FAX: +52 (5) 3586445
E-MAIL: Martha.Millan@pearsoned.com.mx

WEBSITE: http://www.pearson.com.mx
TITLE: Man. Director
CONTACT: Guillermo Hernandez
SUBJECTS: Art, Biological Sciences, Business, Chemistry, Computer Sciences, Education, History, Economics, Mathematics, Science (General), Technology
TOTAL PUBLISHED: 76 print

Plaza y Valdes SA de CV

cedro No. 299, Col sta Maria Riviera, Mexico, DF 06400
PHONE: +52 (5) 5359851; 5664055
FAX: +52 (5) 7050030
E-MAIL: pyvedito@servidor.unam.mx
TITLE: Director General
CONTACT: Fernando Valdes
SUBJECTS: Agriculture, Anthropology, Archaeology, Communications, Public Administration, Buddhism, Social Sciences, Fantasy, Science Fiction

Editorial Progreso SA de CV

Naranjo 248, Col Santa Ma La Rivera, Mexico, DF 06400
PHONE: +52 (5) 5477304; 5471780; 5411187
FAX: +52 (5) 5415342
E-MAIL: editprogresosav@infosel.net.mx
TITLE: Director
CONTACT: Joaquin Flores Sequra
SUBJECTS: Education, Catholicism
TOTAL PUBLISHED: 300 print

Sayrols Editorial SA de CV

Mier y Pesado No. 128, Col Del Valle, Mexico, DF 03100
PHONE: +52 (5) 6874699; 6603535
FAX: +52 (5) 6874699
E-MAIL: sayrols@spin.com.mx
TITLE: General Director
CONTACT: Roberto Dav G
SUBJECTS: Astrology, Occult, Computer Science, Cookery, Crafts, Hobbies, Games, Education, Fashion

SCRIPTA - Distribucion y Servicios Editoriales SA de CV

Copilco 178 Edif 21-501, Col Copilco Universidad, Mexico, DF 04340
PHONE: +52 (5) 5481716
FAX: +52 (5) 6161496
E-MAIL: dyse@data.net.mx
CONTACT: Bertha R. Alavez Magana
SUBJECTS: Art, Business, Film, Video, History

Selector S.A. de C.V.

Dr. Erazo 120 Colonia Doctores, Mexico, DF 06720
PHONE: +52 (5) 5887272
FAX: +52 (5) 7615716
E-MAIL: info@selector.com.mx
WEBSITE: http://www.selector.com.mx
SUBJECTS: Child Care, Crafts, Games, Hobbies, English as a Second Language, Health, Nutrition, Humor, Nonfiction (General), Human Relations, Selp-Help
TOTAL PUBLISHED: 77 print

Sistemas Universales, SA

Insurgentes Centro 123, Col San Rafael, Mexico, DF 06470
PHONE: +52 (5) 7054568; 7055937
FAX: +52 (5) 7053421
CONTACT: Arturo Delgado
SUBJECTS: Accounting, Automotive, Electronics, Electrical Engineering, English as a Second Language, Microcomputers
TOTAL PUBLISHED: 290 print

Ediciones Suromex SA

General Francisco Murguia No. 7, Col Hipodromo C, Mexico, DF 06170
PHONE: +52 (5) 2770744; 2770946
FAX: +52 (5) 2710470
E-MAIL: suromex@mail.internet.com.mx
TITLE: General Manager
CONTACT: Victor Lemus Dominguez
SUBJECTS: Art, Astrology, Occult, Biography, Cookery, Earth Sciences, House & Home, Religion, Self-Help
TOTAL PUBLISHED: 350 print

Universidad Nacional Autonoma de Mexico (National University of Mexico)

Torre 11 de Humanidades P 14, Ciudad Universitaria, Mexico, DF 04510
PHONE: +52 (5) 6650584
FAX: +52 (5) 5507428
TITLE: Director
CONTACT: Mario Mendoza Castaneda
SUBJECTS: Anthropology, Archaeology, Architecture, Chemistry, Education, Engineering, Drama, History, Journalism Law, Literature, Mathematics, Medicine, Psychology, Philosophy, Social Sciences, Technology

Universidad Veracruzana Direccion General Editorial y de Publicaciones
Zamora 25, Apartado Postal 97, Codigo Postal, 91001 Xalapa, Veracruz, Mexico
PHONE: +52 (29) 2871316
FAX: +52 (29) 28174435
E-MAIL: direditaspeedy@coacade.uv.mx
CONTACT: Jaime Pasquel Brash
SUBJECTS: Anthropology, Art, Drama, Theaterm Education, Fiction, History, Music, Dance, Philosophy, Psychology, Psychiatry, Social Sciences
TOTAL PUBLISHED: 15 print

RELIGIOUS ORGANIZATIONS

Buddhist

Centro Mexicano del Buddhismo Theravada A. C.
Apartado Postal 19, Banderilla, Ver. C. P. 91300, Mexico
WEBSITE: http://www.cmbt.org/english/index.htm
TITLE: President
NAME: Jesús Valdés-Martínez

Centro Zen de la Ciudad de Mexico
221 Monte Tauro, Mexico D. F., 01100 Mexico
NAME: Mariano Ozen Barragon

Centro Zen de Mexico
Andador Epigmenio Ibarra 16-106, Col. Romero de Terreros, Mexico D. F., 04310 Mexico
PHONE: +52 (5) 5543741
TITLE: Teacher
NAME: Tesshin Sanderson

Catholic

Guadalupe Missioners (GM)

Misioneros de Guadalupe (MG)
c/o Ignacio Garza Evia, Insurgentes Sur 4120, 14090 Mexico City, DF, Mexico
PHONE: +52 (5) 5732500
FAX: +52 (5) 5731337
E-MAIL: igarzae@spin.com.mx
TITLE: Vicar General
NAME: Ignacio Garza Evia

La Iglesia Católica en Tijuana
C. 10ma. Y Ocampo 8585, 22000 Tijuana, B. C., Mexico
PHONE: +52 (6) 6848411; 6848412
FAX: +52 (6) 6847683
E-MAIL: obispado@telnor.net
WEBSITE: http://www.iglesiatijuana.org/direct .html
TITLE: Pastor
NAME: Alberto Cuevas

Missionaries of the Holy Spirit (MSpS)

Misioneros del Espiritu Santo (MSpS)
Avenida Universidad 1702, 04010 Mexico City, DF, Mexico
PHONE: +52 (5) 6587433
TITLE: Secretary General
NAME: Eugenio Sanchez Sierra

Islamic

Centro Cultural Islamico de Mexico A. C.
Avenue Col del Valle 324-7 Col Del Valle, 03100 Mexico, D. F.
PHONE: +52 (5) 5455638; 6870514
FAX: +52 (5) 6876204
E-MAIL: omarwest@planet.com.mx
WEBSITE: http://planet.com.mx/islam/
NAME: Brother Omar Weston

Jewish

Beth Israel Community Center
Virreyes 1140, Lomas, Mexico City, Mexico
PHONE: +52 (5) 5209569

Mikvah c/o Mogen David Synogogue
Presidente Masaryk and Bernard Shaw, Mexico City, Colonia Polanco, Mexico
PHONE: +52 (5) 5403492

Protestant

Federation of National Committees in the International Christian Youth Exchange

Intercambio Internacional Cristino de Jovenes
Apartado Postal 1586, 72000 Puebla, Puebla, Mexico
NAME: Alejandro Lopez

The Salvation Army
San Borja 1456, Colonia Vértiz Navarte, Mexico
PHONE: +52 (5) 5595244; 5751042
FAX: +52 (5) 5753266
E-MAIL: mexico@salvationarmy.org

Scientology

Mission of Tijuana
Calle Baldoa #19-5284, Lomaas Hipodromo, Tijuana B.C. Mexico 2248, Mexico
PHONE: +52 (5) 266811933

FURTHER READING

Articles

Dillon, Sam. "Boom Turns Borer to Speed Bump." *New York Times,* January 18, 2000, p. A4.

Macintyre, Ben. "Mexican Puts Bounty on life of US Agents." *The Times* (London), June 7, 2000, Central/South America.

Preston, Julia. "In Mexico, Top Newsman and Network Part Ways." *New York Times,* April 1, 2000, p. A5.

Thompson, Ginger. "Zedillo Says He Takes Pride in Improvements for Mexico." *New York Times,* September 2, 2000, p. A4.

Weiner, Tim. "Mexico Imprisons Two Generals, Longtime Suspects in Drug Cases." *New York Times,* September 2, 2000, p. A4.

Books

Bourbon, Fabio. *The Lost Cities of the Mayas: The Life, Art, and Discoveries of Frederick Catherwood.* New York: Abbeville, 2000.

Caistor, Nick. *Mexico City: A Literary and Cultural Companion.* New York: Interlink Books, 2000.

Carrasco, David, ed. *The Oxford Encyclopedia of Mesoamerican Cultures.* New York: Oxford University Press, 2000.

Kirkwood, Burton. *The History of Mexico.* Westport, CT: Greenwood Press, 2000.

Meyer, Michael, ed. *The Oxford History of Mexico.* New York: Oxford University Press, 2000.

Palka, Joel W. *Historical Dictionary of Ancient Mesoamerica.* Lanham, MD: Scarecrow Press, 2000.

Townsend, Richard F. *The Aztecs.* London: Thames & Hudson, 2000.

Government Publications

United States Congress. *Oversight of United States/Mexico Counternarcotics Efforts.* Washington, DC: G.P.O, 2000.

MEXICO: STATISTICAL DATA

For sources and notes see "Sources of Statistics" at the front of each volume.

GEOGRAPHY

Geography

Area:

Total: 1,972,550 sq km.

Land: 1,923,040 sq km.

Land boundaries:

Total: 4,538 km.

Border countries: Belize 250 km, Guatemala 962 km, United States 3,326 km.

Coastline: 9,330 km.

Climate: varies from tropical to desert.

Terrain: high, rugged mountains; low coastal plains; high plateaus; desert.

Natural resources: petroleum, silver, copper, gold, lead, zinc, natural gas, timber.

Land use:

Arable land: 12%

Permanent crops: 1%

Permanent pastures: 39%

Forests and woodland: 26%

Other: 22% (1993 est.).

HUMAN FACTORS

Demographics (A)

	1990	1995	1998	2000	2010	2020	2030	2040	2050
Population	84,446	92,488	97,245	100,350	114,995	128,008	139,125	147,660	153,162
Life expectancy - males	65.6	67.1	67.9	68.5	71.0	73.2	75.1	76.6	77.8
Life expectancy - females	71.5	73.1	74.0	74.7	77.3	79.6	81.5	83.0	84.2
Birth rate (per 1,000)	28.3	25.7	24.2	23.1	19.2	16.7	14.9	13.5	12.6
Death rate (per 1,000)	5.9	5.3	5.2	5.1	5.0	5.4	6.2	7.4	8.9
Women of reproductive age (15-49 yrs.)	21,546	24,537	26,254	27,332	32,047	34,642	35,137	34,805	33,949
Fertility rate	3.4	3.0	2.8	2.7	2.3	2.1	2.0	2.0	2.0

Except as noted, values for vital statistics are in thousands; life expectancy is in years.

Health Personnel

	Data	World Data (wtd ave)
Total health expenditure as a percentage of GDP, 1990-1998[a]		
Public sector	2.8	2.5
Private sector	1.9	2.9
Total[b]	4.7	5.5
Health expenditure per capita in U.S. dollars, 1990-1998[a]		
Purchasing power parity	369	561
Total	201	483
Availability of health care facilities per 100,000 people		
Hospital beds 1990-1998[a]	120	330
Doctors 1992-1995[a]	85	122
Nurses 1992-1995[a]	241	248

Health Indicators

	National Data	World Data
Life expectancy at birth (years)		
1980	67	61
1998	72	67
Daily per capita supply of calories		
1970	2,706	2,358
1997	3,097	2,791
Daily per capital supply of protein		
1997 (grams)	83	74
Total fertility rate (births per woman)		
1980	4.7	3.7
1998	2.8	2.7
Population with access (%)		
To safe water (1990-96)	83	NA
To sanitation (1990-96)	66	NA
People living with (1997)		
Tuberculosis (cases per 100,000)	25.0	60.4
Malaria (cases per 100,000)	5.4	42.2
HIV/AIDS (% aged 15 - 49 years)	0.35	0.99

Infants and Malnutrition

	National Data	World Data (wtd ave)
Under 5 mortality rate (1989)	34	NA
% of infants with low birthweight (1992-98)[1]	8	17
Births attended by skilled health staff (% of total births 1996-98)	68	52
% fully immunized at 1 year of age (1995-98)[1]		
TB	93	82
DPT	94	77
Polio	95	77
Measles	89	74
Prevalence of child malnutrition (1992-98)[1] (based on weight for age, % of children under 5 years)	NA	30

Ethnic Division

Mestizo (Amerindian-Spanish) 60%
Amerindian or predominantly Amerindian 30%
White 9%
Other 1%

Religion

Nominally Roman Catholic 89%
Protestant 6%
Other 5%

Major Languages

Spanish, various Mayan, Nahuatl, and other regional indigenous languages.

EDUCATION

Public Education Expenditures

	1980	1997
Public expenditures on education as % of GNP	4.7	4.9
Expenditures per student as % of GNP per capita		
Primary	4.4	11.8
Secondary	NA	17.9
Tertiary	26.4	46.8
Pupils per teacher at the primary level	NA	28
Duration of primary education in years	NA	6
World data for comparison		
Public expenditures on education as % of GNP (mean)	3.9	4.8
Pupils per teacher at the primary level (wtd ave)	NA	33
Duration of primary education in years (mean)	NA	9

Educational Attainment (A)

Age group (1990) . . . . .25+
Population of this age group 31,188,180
Highest level attained (%)
No schooling 18.8
First level
Not completed 28.6
Completed 19.9
Entered second level
Lower Secondary 12.7
Upper Secondary 10.7
Entered post-secondary 9.2

Literacy Rates (A)

In thousands and percent	1990	1995	2000	2010
Illiterate population (15+ yrs.)	6,162	6,246	6,015	5,086
Literacy rate - total adult pop. (%)	88.0	89.6	91.2	94.0
Literacy rate - males (%)	90.9	91.8	93.0	95.4
Literacy rate - females (%)	85.0	87.4	89.3	92.7

GOVERNMENT & LAW

Political Parties

National Congress (Congreso de la Union)	% of vote	no. of seats
Senate		
Institutional Revolutionary Party (PRI)	NA	77
National Action Party (PAN)	NA	33
Party of the Democratic Revolution (PRD)	NA	16
Mexican Green Ecological Party (PVEM)	NA	1
Workers Party (PT)	NA	1
As of October 1999		
Institutional Revolutionary Party (PRI)		75
National Action Party (PAN)		31
Party of the Democratic Revolution (PRD)		16
Workers Party (PT)		1
Independents		5
Chamber of Deputies		
Institutional Revolutionary Party (PRI)	39%	239
National Action Party (PAN)	27%	121
Party of the Democratic Revolution (PRD)	26%	125
Mexican Green Ecological Party (PVEM)		8
Workers Party (PT)		7
As of October 1999		
Institutional Revolutionary Party (PRI)		237
Party of the Democratic Revolution (PRD)		125
National Action Party (PAN)		120
Workers Party (PT)		7
Mexican Green Ecological Party (PVEM)		6
Independents		5

NA stands for not available. Elections for the Senate were last held 6 July 1997 for one-quarter of the seats; Chamber of Deputies elections were last held 6 July 1997 (the next legislative elections will coincide with the presidential election 2 July 2000).

Government Budgets (A)

Year: 1997
Total Expenditures: 516,230 Millions of New Pesos
Expenditures as a percentage of the total by function:
General public services and public order 7.92
Defense 3.55
Education 22.12
Health 3.44
Social Security and Welfare 18.06
Housing and community amenities 3.40
Recreational, cultural, and religious affairs 0.61
Fuel and energy 1.32
Agriculture, forestry, fishing, and hunting 4.68
Mining, manufacturing, and construction 0.77
Transportation and communication 7.17
Other economic affairs and services 3.63

Crime

Crime rate (for 1994)
Crimes reported . . . . .NA
Total persons convicted 116,489
Crimes per 100,000 population . . . . .NA

(Continued on next page.)

LABOR FORCE

Total Labor Force (A)

38.6 million (1999).

Labor Force by Occupation

Agriculture 24%
Industry 21%
Services 55%

Data for 1997.

Unemployment Rate

2.5% urban (1998); plus considerable underemployment.

PRODUCTION SECTOR

Energy Production

Production .... 176.055 billion kWh
Production by source
Fossil fuel 78.12%
Hydro 13.82%
Nuclear 5.00%

(Continued on next page.)

GOVERNMENT & LAW (cont.)

Military Affairs (A)

	1990	1992	1995	1996	1997
Military expenditures					
Current dollars (mil.)	1,330	1,720	2,160	2,100	4,290
1997 constant dollars (mil.)	1,560	1,910	2,240	2,130	4,290
Armed forces (000)	175	175	175	175	250
Gross national product (GNP)					
Current dollars (bil.)	274	314	329	354	390
1997 constant dollars (bil.)	321	349	341	360	390
Central government expenditures (CGE)					
1997 constant dollars (bil.)	62	52	57	61	69
People (mil.)	85.1	88.1	93.3	95.1	96.8
Military expenditure as % of GNP	0.5	0.5	0.7	0.6	1.1
World data on military expenditure as % of GNP	4.5	3.4	2.7	2.6	2.6
Military expenditure as % of CGE	2.5	3.7	3.9	3.5	6.2
World data on military expenditure as % of CGE	17.0	12.5	10.5	10.3	10.2
Military expenditure per capita (1997 $)	18	22	24	22	44
World data on military expenditure per capita (1997 $)	242	173	146	143	145
Armed forces per 1,000 people (soldiers)	2.1	2.0	1.9	1.8	2.6
World data on armed forces per 1,000 people (soldiers)	5.3	4.5	4.1	3.9	3.8
GNP per capita (1997 $)	3,770	3,950	3,660	3,790	4,030
Arms imports[6]					
Current dollars (mil.)	210	340	110	350	130
1997 constant dollars (mil.)	246	377	114	356	130
Arms exports[6]					
Current dollars (mil.)	20	20	20	10	20
1997 constant dollars (mil.)	23	22	21	10	20
Total imports[7]					
Current dollars (bil.)	44	65	76	94	115
1997 constant dollars (bil.)	51	72	79	95	115
Total exports[7]					
Current dollars (bil.)	41	46	80	96	110
1997 constant dollars (bil.)	48	51	82	98	110
Arms as percent of total imports[8]	0.5	0.5	0.1	0.4	0.1
Arms as percent of total exports[8]	0	0	0	0	0

PRODUCTION SECTOR (cont.)

Energy Production (cont.)

Other 3.06%

Exports ....11 million kWh

Data for 1998.

Energy Consumption

Consumption ....164.767 billion kWh

Imports ....1.047 billion kWh

Data for 1998.

Transportation

Highways:

Total: 323,977 km.

Paved: 96,221 km (including 6,335 km of expressways).

Unpaved: 227,756 km (1997 est.).

Waterways: 2,900 km navigable rivers and coastal canals.

Pipelines: crude oil 28,200 km; petroleum products 10,150 km; natural gas 13,254 km; petrochemical 1,400 km.

Merchant marine:

Total: 46 ships (1,000 GRT or over) totaling 633,219 GRT/970,947 DWT.

Ships by type: bulk 2, cargo 1, chemical tanker 4, liquified gas 4, petroleum tanker 29, roll-on/roll-off 3, short-sea passenger 3 (1999 est.).

Airports: 1,806 (1999 est.).

Airports - with paved runways: 233.

Airports - with unpaved runways: 1,573.

Top Agriculture Products

Corn, wheat, soybeans, rice, beans, cotton, coffee, fruit, tomatoes; beef, poultry, dairy products; wood products.

Top Mining Products (A)

	National Production	World Production
Commodities in 1998		
Aluminium (000 mt)	62	22,100
Copper (000 mt)	385	12,200
Gold (000 kg)	26	2,460
Lead (000 mt)	166	3,080
Salt (000 mt)	8,400	186,000
Silver (mt)	2,680	16,400
Tin (mt)	5	206,000
Zinc (000 mt)	395	755

MANUFACTURING SECTOR

GDP & Manufacturing Summary (A)

	1980	1985	1990	1995
GDP ($-1990 mil.)[1]	149,150	164,127	175,839	182,964
Per capita ($-1990)[1]	2,207	2,175	2,113	2,007
Manufacturing share (%) (current prices)[1]	21.9	23.1	22.2	18.3
Manufacturing				
Value added ($-1990 mil.)[1]	32,928	34,995	40,055	41,872
Industrial production index	79	86	100	104
Value added ($ mil.)	43,048	46,373[e]	41,416[e]	54,750[e]
Gross output ($ mil.)	102,047	106,972[e]	95,678[e]	129,526
Employment (000)	2,417	2,314[e]	2,145[e]	1,893[e]
Profitability (% of gross output)				
Intermediate input (%)	58	57[e]	57[e]	58[e]
Wages and salaries inc. supplements (%)	14	9[e]	9[e]	7[e]
Gross operating surplus	28	34[e]	35[e]	35[e]
Productivity ($)				
Gross output per worker	42,221	46,227[e]	44,602[e]	68,057[e]
Value added per worker	17,811	20,040[e]	19,307[e]	33,368[e]
Average wage (inc. supplements)	5,846	4,192[e]	3,872[e]	5,080[e]
Value added ($ mil.)				
Food products	6,989	7,015[e]	6,240[e]	8,405[e]
Beverages	2,723	2,589[e]	2,377[e]	3,526[e]
Tobacco products	623	740[e]	571[e]	1,017[e]
Textiles	3,133	3,099[e]	2,216[e]	2,658[e]
Wearing apparel	1,277	1,094[e]	863[e]	1,045[e]
Leather and fur products	366	397[e]	250[e]	329[e]
Footwear	845	658[e]	414[e]	463[e]
Wood and wood products	919	786[e]	609[e]	675[e]
Furniture and fixtures	784	498[e]	407[e]	459[e]
Paper and paper products	1,189	1,180[e]	1,196[e]	1,463[e]

(Continued on next page.)

	1980	1985	1990	1995
Printing and publishing	1,050	1,250[e]	1,192[e]	1,401[e]
Industrial chemicals	2,235	2,982[e]	2,738[e]	3,457[e]
Other chemical products	2,235	2,562[e]	2,972[e]	4,006[e]
Petroleum refineries	1,917	4,341[e]	3,987[e]	5,660[e]
Misc. petroleum and coal products	222	529[e]	489[e]	701[e]
Rubber products	767	1,164[e]	865[e]	789[e]
Plastic products	754	767[e]	774[e]	974[e]
Pottery, china and earthenware	383	420[e]	287[e]	401[e]
Glass and glass products	566	529[e]	511[e]	782[e]
Other non-metal mineral products	1,464	1,113[e]	752[e]	949[e]
Iron and steel	2,070	2,227[e]	1,955[e]	2,263[e]
Non-ferrous metals	562	506[e]	430[e]	595[e]
Metal products	1,961	1,849[e]	1,718[e]	2,112[e]
Non-electrical machinery	2,074	1,643[e]	1,463[e]	1,703[e]
Electrical machinery	1,900	1,635[e]	1,374[e]	1,678[e]
Transport equipment	2,980	3,621[e]	3,542[e]	5,089[e]
Prof. and scientific equipment	305	381[e]	485[e]	1,112[e]
Other manufacturing	754	708[e]	738[e]	1,040[e]

COMMUNICATIONS

Daily Newspapers

	National Data	World Data for Comparison
Daily Newspapers		
Number of Dailies	295	8,391
Total Circulation (000)	9,030	548,000
Circulation per 1,000 inhabitants	97	96

Telecommunications

Telephones - main lines in use: 9.6 million (1998).

Telephones - mobile cellular: 2.02 million (1998).

Telephone system: highly developed system with extensive microwave radio relay links; privatized in December 1990; opened to competition January 1997.

Domestic: adequate telephone service for business and government, but the population is poorly served; domestic satellite system with 120 earth stations; extensive microwave radio relay network; considerable use of fiber-optic cable, coaxial cable.

International: satellite earth stations - 32 Intelsat, 2 Solidaridad (giving Mexico improved access to South America, Central America, and much of the US as well as enhancing domestic communications), numerous Inmarsat mobile earth stations; linked to Central American Microwave System of trunk connections, high capacity Columbus-2 fiber-optic submarine cable with access to the US, Virgin Islands, Canary Islands, Morocco, Spain and Italy (1997).

Radio broadcast stations: AM 865, FM about 500, shortwave 13 (1999).

Radios: 31 million (1997).

Television broadcast stations: 236 (plus repeaters) (1997).

Televisions: 25.6 million (1997).

Internet Service Providers (ISPs): 167 (1999).

FINANCE, ECONOMICS, & TRADE

Economic Indicators

National product: GDP—purchasing power parity—$865.5 billion (1999 est.).

National product real growth rate: 3.7% (1999 est.).

National product per capita: $8,500 (1999 est.).

Inflation rate—consumer price index: 15% (1999 est.).

Exchange Rates

Exchange rates:

Mexican pesos (Mex$) per US$1

January 2000	9.4793
1999	9.5604
1998	9.1360
1997	7.9185
1996	7.5994
1995	6.4194

Top Import Origins

$142.1 billion (f.o.b., 1999)

Origins (1999 est.)

United States	74.8%
Germany	3.8%
Japan	3.5%
Canada	1.9%
South Korea	2.0%
Italy	1.3%
France	1.0%

Imports include in-bond industries (assembly plant operations with links to US companies).

Top Export Destinations

$136.8 billion (f.o.b., 1999)

Destinations (1999 est.)

United States	89.3%
Canada	1.7%
Spain	0.6%
Japan	0.5%
Venezuela	0.3%
Chile	0.3%
Brazil	0.3%

Exports include in-bond industries (assembly plant operations with links to US companies).

Foreign Aid

Recipient: $1.166 billion (1995).

Import/Export Commodities

Import Commodities	Export Commodities
Metal-working machines	Manufactured goods
Steel mill products	Oil and oil products
Agricultural machinery	Silver
Electrical equipment	Coffee
Car parts for assembly	Cotton
Repair parts for motor vehicles	
Aircraft and aircraft parts	

Balance of Payments

	1994	1995	1996	1997	1998
Exports of goods (f.o.b.)	60,882	79,542	96,000	110,431	117,500
Imports of goods (f.o.b.)	−79,346	−72,453	−89,469	−109,808	−125,243
Trade balance	−18,464	7,089	6,531	623	−7,743
Services - debits	−13,043	−9,715	−10,816	−12,616	−13,066
Services - credits	10,321	9,780	10,899	11,400	12,064
Private transfers (net)	3,720	3,896	4,473	5,174	5,947
Government transfers (net)	62	64	57	73	67
Overall balance	−29,662	−1,576	−2,328	−7,454	−15,787

MICRONESIA

Federated States of Micronesia

CAPITAL: Palikir, Pohnpei Island.

FLAG: Adopted in 1978, the flag is light blue, bearing four five-pointed stars arranged in a diamond in the center.

MONETARY UNIT: The U.S. dollar is the official medium of exchange.

WEIGHTS AND MEASURES: British units are used, as modified by U.S. usage.

HOLIDAYS: New Year's Day, 1 January; Federated States of Micronesia Day, 10 May; Independence Day, 3 November; Christmas Day, 25 December.

TIME: In Pohnpei and Kosrae, 10 PM = noon GMT; in Yap and Truk, 9 PM = noon GMT.

LOCATION AND SIZE: The Federated States of Micronesia (FSM) is located in the western Pacific Ocean within a large group of islands known as the Carolinian archipelago. The four states—Kosrae, Pohnpei, Truk, and Yap—consist of 607 islands with a total area of 7,866 square kilometers (3,037 square miles), comprising 702 square kilometers (271 square miles) of land, and 7,164 square kilometers (2,766 square miles) of lagoons. Comparatively, the area occupied by the Federated States of Micronesia is slightly less than four times the size of Washington, D.C.

The capital city of the Federated States of Micronesia, Palikir, is located on the island of Pohnpei.

CLIMATE: There is little seasonal or daily variation in temperature, which averages 27°C (80°F). The islands are subject to typhoons. Annual average rainfall ranges from 305 centimeters (120 inches) in Yap to 508 centimeters (200 inches) in Pohnpei.

INTRODUCTORY SURVEY

RECENT HISTORY

European navigators sighted the string of islands known as the Carolinian archipelago in the sixteenth century. Until the end of the nineteenth century the islands were under Spanish colonial administration.

In 1899 following the Spanish-American War Spain sold the islands to Germany. The Japanese took control at the end of World War I (1914–1918). Following the defeat of Germany and Japan by the Allies in World War II (1939–1945), the four states of the Federated States of Micronesia (FSM) came under United States administration as part of the United Nations Trust Territory of the Pacific Islands.

On May 10, 1979, a constitution drafted by a popularly elected constitutional convention went into effect. The government of the FSM and the U.S. government executed a Compact of Free Association in October 1982. In November 1986 that compact went into effect. The UN Security Council voted in December 1990 to terminate the U.S.-administered UN trusteeship. A capital, Palikir, was built in the Palikir Valley and has served the FSM since 1990. The FSM became an independent state and joined the United Nations in September 1991. Elections were held through the 1990s. In the May 1999 election Leo A. Falcam was elected president and Redley Killion was elected vice-president.

In 2000 the FSM and the United States entered negotiations prior to expiration of the Compact of

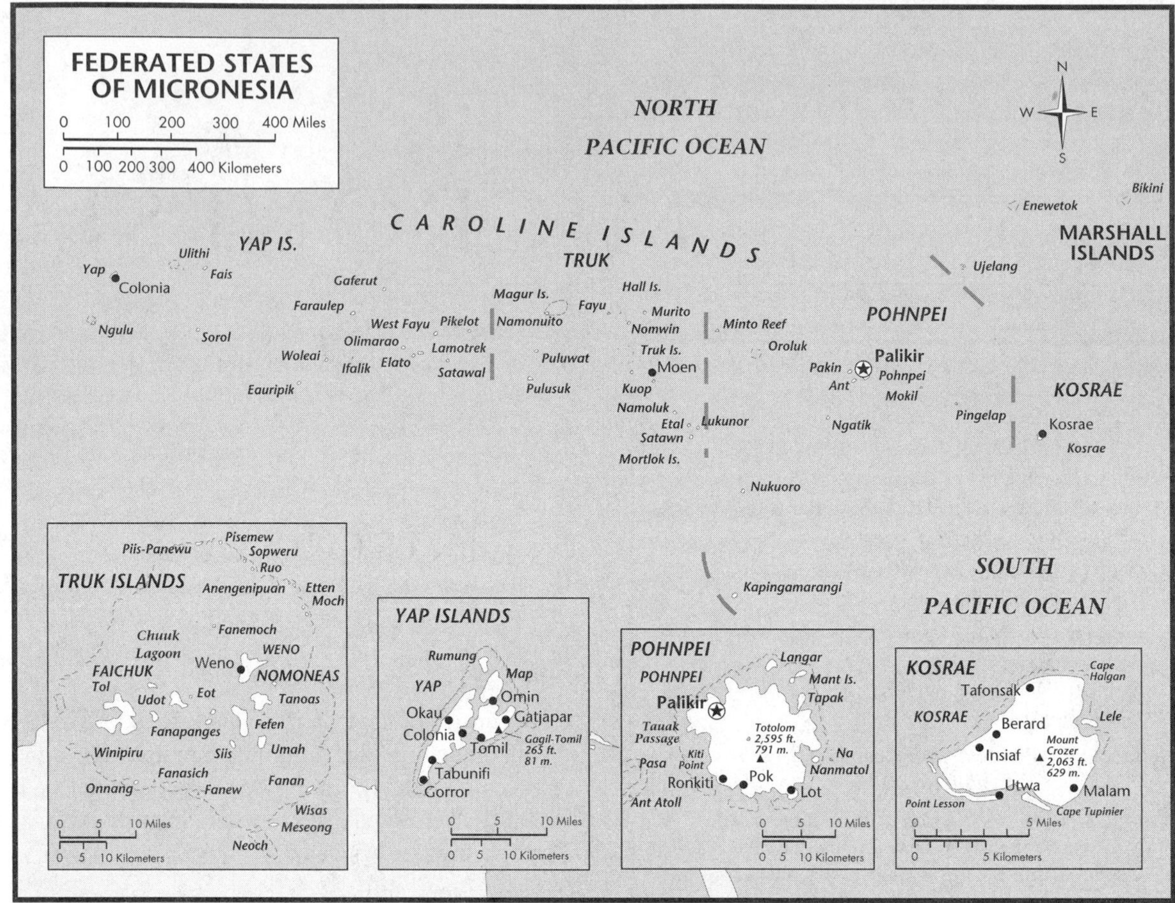

Free Association. Before the United States would consider any further assistance, it requested a full accounting of the approximately $3 billion in U.S. funding provided FSM since 1986.

GOVERNMENT

The national executive branch includes the president and vice-president, who serve four-year terms. Congress elects both from among the four senators-at-large for four-year terms. The legislature consists of a single-chamber Congress of fourteen senators. Four senators are elected-at-large from each state and then elected from single-member districts determined by population.

Each of Micronesia's four states has a legislature, governor, and lieutenant governor.

Judiciary

The national judiciary consists of a Supreme Court, headed by a chief justice, and subordinate courts established by statute. The Supreme Court applies criminal and civil laws and procedures that are similar to those of the United States. The Supreme Court has both trial and appellate divisions and reviews cases that require interpretation of the Constitution, national law, or treaties and may hear appeals from the highest state courts.

State and municipal court systems are in each state. State courts have jurisdiction over all matters not within the exclusive jurisdiction of the national courts. Municipal courts have jurisdiction over civil and criminal matters arising within their municipalities.

Political Parties

There are no formal political parties.

DEFENSE

The Federated States of Micronesia (FSM) maintains no armed forces. External security is the responsibility of the United States.

ECONOMIC AFFAIRS

FSM's economy depends largely on U.S. aid. The economy is markedly underdeveloped. Activity consists largely of subsistence farming and fishing that is thought to generate about 25 percent of GDP but statistics from the government are unreliable. The islands have few mineral deposits except high-grade phosphates, worth exploiting and potential for a tourist industry exists but the area is remote and lacks facilities. The geographical isolation and lack of infrastructure are obstacles to long-term growth.

In recent years licensing fees by foreign fishermen for tuna fishing in FSM's Exclusive Economic Zone have provided between $18 million and $24 million annually. The economy faces other serious disadvantages including shortages of technical and managerial skills.

Public Finance

Government revenues remained nearly constant during the 1990s while spending was unrestrained. However by the late 1990s the deficits had come under control. The U.S. Central Intelligence Agency (CIA) estimated that in 1995–1996 Micronesia's central government took in revenues of approximately $58 million and had expenditures of $52 million including capital expenditures of $4.7 million. External debt in 1997 was estimated at $111 million.

Income

In 1997 Micronesia's gross domestic product (GDP) was estimated to be $240 million or $2,000 per capita. The GDP 1997 estimated growth rate was 3 percent and inflation was estimated in 1996 at 4 percent. The 1996 estimated contribution by sector was agriculture 19 percent, industry 4 percent, and services 77 percent.

Industry

Handicrafts such as items from shell, wood, and pearls and small-scale processing are carried out in all states. A clothing plant in Yap is the country's largest private-sector industrial enterprise. Truk has a garment factory, a coconut-processing plant, a boat-building plant, and a breadfruit flour plant. Industry in other states includes a coconut processing and soap and oil plant, a feed mill, an ice production plant, a brick-manufacturing plant, and a wood-processing plant. In 1999 a tuna processing plant opened. Tourism remained underdeveloped.

Banking and Finance

The FSM Banking Board operates commercial banking operations. There are two foreign commercial banks, the Bank of Hawaii and the Bank of Guam. The FSM Development Bank commenced operations in 1982 to provide loans for the government's development priorities.

Economic Development

Under terms of the Compact of Free Association, the United States provided billions of dollars in grant aid from 1986 to 2001. A multi-million dollar U.S.-implemented capital improvement plan was scheduled for completion in 2001. It included new airports, docks, water and sewage systems, paved roads, and hospitals.

The first National Development Plan (1985–1989) was the initial stage of the government's fifteen-year program designed to achieve national self-sufficiency. The Second National Development Plan (1992–1996) sought to diversify Micronesia's economy and wean it from compact funds. The Asian Development Bank helped put together an economic development plan for Micronesia in 1995. Privatization, reduction of government employment, and the development of tourism and fisheries were recommended. Nevertheless little was accomplished overall. The government is downsizing and restructuring and seeking ways to encourage private sector growth. In 2000 the United States and Micronesia were in negotiations aimed at renewing some provisions of the Compact.

SOCIAL WELFARE

Rapid Westernization has resulted in increasing juvenile delinquency, drug and alcohol abuse, and crime, which are being addressed by national and state social programs. A social insurance system includes old age, disability, and survivor benefits. In spite of constitutional safeguards both sex discrimination and violence against women are serious problems. Women's roles are essentially traditional family ones, however, women face no discrimination in education.

Healthcare

There are hospitals in each state center. A community health center was established in Pohnpei in 1986. In the outer islands medical services are provided through dispensaries. Advanced medical treatment is provided through referral to Guam or Hawaii. Life expectancy was 68.6 years in 2000. The entire population has access to safe water and sanitation.

Housing

In 1980 the total housing consisted of 11,562 units. There has been a movement away from traditional construction materials toward imported lumber, plywood, and corrugated metal roofing.

EDUCATION

The state governments are responsible for the provision of education. Elementary education is compulsory up to the eighth grade or until age fifteen. Secondary education is provided through five public and five private high schools. The College of Micronesia is located in Pohnpei. FSM students are eligible for post-secondary education grants from the U.S. government and attend institutions in Guam, Hawaii, and the U.S. mainland.

2000 KEY EVENTS TIMELINE

March

- The College of Micronesia-Federated States of Micronesia (FSM) reevaluates the language instruction policy of Micronesia. A proposed National and Cultural Institute managed by the College of Micronesia would generate dictionaries, grammars and teaching materials for the eight languages so that local languages could be the first language of instruction nationwide. English, the first language of less than 2 percent of the population, is the common language. At this two-year college instruction is primarily in English preparing students to go on to four-year institutions in the United States. The FSM's eight languages (Pohnpeian, Chuukese, Yapese, Kosrean, Woleian, Satawalese, Ultithian, and Kapingamarangian) are long-neglected.

May

- As part of a renewed funding agreement for financial assistance to the FSM, the special negotiator for the U.S. Department of State is considering tying immigration restrictions to the funding. Under a Compact of Free Association the FSM enjoys free emigration to the United States. An estimated 6,000 Micronesians reside in Hawaii.

August

- Research is being done on a rare recessive disorder, achromotopsia, affecting the population of Pingelap Atoll in Micronesia. This rare recessive disorder is characterized by light sensitivity, poor vision, and a total inability to distinguish colors. All of the Pingelap people affected by this disorder can trace their ancestry to a single male survivor of a typhoon around 1775.

October

- Government health officials issue a statement October 11, claiming an end to the cholera outbreak that began in April.
- The Pacific Islands Forum—made up of Australia, Cook Islands, Federated States of Micronesia, Fiji, Kiribati, Nauru, New Zealand, Niue, Palau, Papua New Guinea, Republic of the Marshall Islands, Samoa, Solomon Islands, Tonga, Tuvalu, and Vanuatu—meets to discuss environmetnal and regional concerns, and the establishement of a Pacific Area Regional Trade Agreement (PARTA). The group establishes the Pacific Islands Forum Secretariat to be based in Suva, Fiji.

November

- Guam and the Northern Mariana Islands claim that tainted fish from Micronesia is the cause of a cholera outbreak during the first week of November.

ANALYSIS OF EVENTS: 2000

BUSINESS AND THE ECONOMY

The fiscal health of the Federated States of Micronesia (FSM) was carefully scrutinized in 2000. In February the Fourth Consultative Group of Donors heard about the FSM's economic performance and reviewed the country's economic reforms. Special attention was given to the FSM's progress for achieving self-reliance and its negotiations for a new Compact of Free Association economic assistance package with the United States, and its strategies for working with donor partners. In March an audit team from the U.S. General Accounting Office audited the FSM under a 15-year treaty whose economic provisions expire in 2001. U.S. congressional committees ordered the audits as part of a major review of the Compact of Free Association that was in the process of being renegotiated by the FSM. One report noted that this funding might depend on an assessment of the islands' strategic defense value. Also, in March the Asian Development Bank (ADB) and other aid donors for its economic reform moves praised the FSM. In May the FSM was negotiating future U.S. fiscal assistance.

In June the U.S. General Accounting Office's released a report "Better Accountability Needed over U.S. Assistance to Micronesia and the Marshall Islands." The report included a breakdown of where the money went. In July President Leo A. Falcam signed into law the Fiscal Year 2001 Budget Act, which appropriated $33,838,991. In September 2000 the FSM was adjusting to the second step-down in the U.S. Compact of Free Association financing. The International Monetary Fund mission visited the FSM and issued a statement of praise for the nation's past economic reforms and made further recommendations. The mission stressed the importance of continued progress in the areas of good governance and transparency in economic policymaking. In November the cost to the Northern Mariana Islands in subsidizing Freely Associated States (FAS) citizens was studied.

Passenger and cargo transportation was another area of concern in 2000. The Association of Pacific Islands Legislatures established an Airline Transportation Task Force to renew exploration of the feasibility of establishing a regional airline to serve Micronesia. Continental Micronesia is the main passenger and cargo airline servicing the Micronesian region. A regional airline would offer more flights and routes within and outside the region. Asia Pacific Airlines played a major role in the FSM's tuna fishing industry. It flew tons of tuna to market in Japan via Guam.

The Pacific Women's Resource Bureau (PWRB) organized a regional South Pacific Commission (SPC) workshop for handicraft producers at the Eighth Festival of Pacific Arts. Demand within and outside the Pacific for quality handicrafts stood behind the training to move the participants beyond production of handicrafts, into marketing of handicrafts. Participants looked at market research, quality control, pricing and packaging, advertising and promotion, sales techniques, and record keeping.

GOVERNMENT AND POLITICS

Although fiscal responsibility was a theme, the FSM Congress passed capital improvements bill vetoed by President Leo A. Falcam for the four states, Chuuk, Pohnpei, Kosrae, and Yap.

The United States put immigration issues on the table during economic talks. In March the Federated States of Micronesia government was put on notice that the United States planned to tighten up regulations for islanders entering the United States and its territories. The United States was concerned over the impact of large numbers of islanders from the FSM migrating to Guam, Saipan, Hawaii and the mainland. Political leaders in these areas increasingly demanded multi-million dollar annual reimbursements from the Unites States for the expense of providing social and health services to islanders who have moved there from the FSM. Under the Compact of Free Association, FSM citizens may travel without visa to the United States to live, work and study. However, in July the U.S. Department of Immigration and Naturalization Service made it easier for Micronesians and other Freely Associated States citizens to obtain employment authorization documents, commonly known as EADs. These changes cut down on the period of waiting for eligibility.

Ecological and environmental concerns predominated in the Pacific area in 2000. The twenty-two-nation South Pacific Regional Environmental Program (SPREP) surveyed wastes in thirteen Pacific countries. Already threatened by global warming and sea-level rise, the SPREP's report noted that these small nations are overwhelmed with tons of waste oil, hazardous or potentially hazardous chemicals including pesticides, polychlorinated biphenyls, general industrial chemicals, medical wastes, laboratory chemicals, oil, bitumen, timber treatment chemicals and fertilizers. Furthermore, there were more than 50 contaminated sites around the Pacific. Waste oil had been generated, mostly from power generation, motor vehicles and fishing vessels in the region for decades. Areas were severely polluted by World War II and Cold War PCB contamination. Environmentally acceptable disposal procedures needed to be enforced. The Association of Pacific Island Legislatures wanted the United States and Japan to remove unexploded ordnance that has been in their island areas since World War II.

In February a US$21 million project, the South Pacific Strategic Action Program for Protecting International Waters, was inaugurated. Fourteen Pacific Island countries were beneficiaries. The South Pacific Strategic Action Program (SAP) would enable SPREP, in close partnership with other regional organizations, to implement imperative actions earlier identified to assist the Pacific island countries to conserve and sustainably manage their coastal and watershed resources. The conservation and sustainable yield of ocean living resources in the region was another goal.

Bird conservation experts of the Guam Aquatic and Wild Life Resources Agriculture Department, and representatives from several Micronesian countries met to attempt to contain the threat to several Micronesian birds facing extinction. Seven species, including the endemic Micronesian kingfisher and the Mariana Crow, are now extinct in the wild. With limited resources cooperation was viewed as essential to conservation efforts.

The Convention on Conservation and Management of Highly Migratory Fish Stocks in the Western and Central Pacific was adopted by the FSM. This legally binding conservation and management regime ensured cooperation with distant water fishing partners, and the maintenance of a sustainable fishery for the tuna and associated fish species in the region. The Convention was five years in negotiation and represented compromises between the interests of coastal states and fishing partners.

CULTURE AND SOCIETY

Health matters relating to an outbreak of cholera predominated social concerns in 2000. In May an outbreak of cholera in the FSM spread through contaminated food, water and personal hygiene. Stringent precautions were in place for travelers from the FSM. This was the first time for a cholera epidemic to occur in Pohnpei. In 1983 Chuuk last experienced an outbreak.

The governments of the Northern Marianas, Guam, Palau, Nauru and the Marshall Islands imposed food bans on seafood from Pohnpei and other FSM states. All food (frozen, cooked, or uncooked) and other consumable products was restricted. Fish, shellfish and crustaceans were banned unless cooked and frozen to at least 32 degrees Fahrenheit, or below. The World Health Organization, according to the Department of Health, Education and Social Affairs, did not agree to the ban on food from infected areas of the FSM. Once the vibrio had been introduced only good sanitation would prevent an outbreak of cholera. Drinking only safe water, practicing good personal hygiene and preparing food safely were the recommended preventative practices. The seafood bans affected business.

To prevent recurrence of the cholera outbreak, health officials gave oral cholera vaccine to over 15,000 residents of Pohnpei state's main island, also covering the outer islands, Kosrae and Chuuk. In October Health officials declared an end to a cholera outbreak. Nineteen people died and more than three thousand others were affected. They expected that some deaths would remain unreported due to the stigma attached to cholera.

In September the FSM investigated reports alleging that an archaeology team from the University of Hawaii (UH) illegally removed artifacts from a whaling ship that sank in Pohnpei Harbor during the American Civil War. UH professor of anthropology Michael Graves, the principle investigator for the project, said no artifacts were taken from the site, other than a few pieces of "diagnostic" artifacts.

DIRECTORY

CENTRAL GOVERNMENT

Head of State

President
Leo A. Falcam, Office of the President, POB PS-53, Palikir, Pohnpei, Federated States of Micronesia 96941
PHONE: +691 3202228
FAX: +691 3202785

Vice President
Redley Killion, Office of the Vice President, POB PS-53, Palikir, Pohnpei, Federated States of Micronesia 96941
PHONE: +691 3202228
FAX: +691 3202785

Cabinet

Secretary of Foreign Affairs
Epel K. Ilon, Department of Foreign Affairs, POB PS-123, Palikir, Pohnpei, Federated States of Micronesia 96941
PHONE: +691 3202641
FAX: +691 3202933
E-MAIL: foreignaffairs@mail.fm

Secretary of Economic Affairs
Sebastian L. Anefal, Department of Economic Affairs, POB PS-12, Palikir, Pohnpei, Federated States of Micronesia 96941
PHONE: +691 3202646
FAX: +691 3205854
E-MAIL: fsmrd@mail.fm

Secretary of Transportation, Communication, and Infrastructure
Lukner Weilbacher, Department of Transportation, Communication, and

Infrastructure, POB PS-2, Palikir, Pohnpei, Federated States of Micronesia 96941
PHONE: +691 3202865
FAX: +691 3205853
E-MAIL: fsmrd@mail.fm

Secretary of Finance and Administration
John Ehsa, Department of Finance and Administration, POB PS-158, Palikir, Pohnpei, Federated States of Micronesia 96941
PHONE: +691 3202640
FAX: +691 3202380

Secretary of Health, Education, and Social Services
Eliuel K. Pretrick, Department of Health, Education, and Social Services, POB PS-70, Palikir, Pohnpei, Federated States of Micronesia 96941
PHONE: +691 3202872
FAX: +691 3205263

Secretary of Justice
Emilio Musrasrik, Department of Justice, POB PS-105, Palikir, Pohnpei, Federated States of Micronesia 96941
PHONE: +691 3202644
FAX: +691 3202234

DIPLOMATIC REPRESENTATION

Embassies in Micronesia

Australia
H and E Enterprises Bldg., P.O. Box S, Kolonia, Pohnpei, Federated States of Micronesia 96941
PHONE: +691 3205448; 3205463
FAX: +691 3205449

United States
P.O. Box 1286, Kolonia, Pohnpei, Federated States of Micronesia 96941
PHONE: +691 3202187
FAX: +691 3202186

JUDICIAL SYSTEM

Supreme Court

PS-J, Palikir Station, Pohnpei, Federated States of Micronesia 96941
PHONE: +691 3202357
FAX: +691 3202756

BROADCAST MEDIA

Federated States of Micronesia Broadcasting Service

PO Box 34, Palikir Station, Pohnpei, Federated States of Micronesia 96941
PHONE: +691 3202548; 3202092
FAX: +691 3204356
E-MAIL: jaimmy77@yahoo.com
TITLE: Special Assistant to President for Information
CONTACT: Terry Gamabruw
LANGUAGE: Yapese, Chuukese, Ponapean, Kosrean, English
BROADCASTS: 18 hours/day
TYPE: Government

V6AJ Kosrae

Office of the Governor, PO Box 147, Tofol, Kosrae, Federated States of Micronesia 96944
PHONE: +691 3703040; 3703880
TITLE: Station Manager
CONTACT: McDonald Ittu
LANGUAGE: English, Kosraen
BROADCASTS: 18 hours/day

V6AK Chuuk

PO Box 206, Weno, Chuuk, Federated States of Micronesia 96942
PHONE: +691 3302593; 3302596 (Studio)
TITLE: Station Manager
CONTACT: Joe Commor
LANGUAGE: English, Chuukese
BROADCASTS: 18 hours/day

WSZA Yap

Department of Youth and Civic Affairs, PO Box 30, Colonia, Yap, Federated States of Micronesia 96943
PHONE: +691 3502174
TITLE: Media Director
CONTACT: Peter Garamfel

WSZD Pohnpei

Kolonia, Pohnpei, Federated States of Micronesia 96941
PHONE: +691 3202296
TITLE: Station Manager
CONTACT: Francis A. Zarred

TV Station Pohnpei

KPON-TV, Central Micronesia Communications, PO Box 460, Kolonia, Pohnpei, Federated States of Micronesia 96941
PHONE: +691 3202671; 3202442
FAX: +691 3202444
TITLE: President
CONTACT: Bernard Helgenberger
CHANNEL: 4, 5, 9, A7
WATTAGE: 1kW
TYPE: Commercial

TV Station Chuuk

Weno, Chuuk, Federated States of Micronesia 96942
PHONE: +691 3304475
TITLE: President
CONTACT: Bernard Helgenberger
WATTAGE: 0.1kW
CHANNEL: A7
TYPE: Commercial

TV-Station YAP (WAAB-TV)

Department of Youth and Civic Affairs, PO Box 30, Colonia, Yap, Federated States Of Micronesia 96943
PHONE: +691 3502502
WATTAGE: 1kW
CHANNEL: A7
TYPE: Government

COLLEGES AND UNIVERSITIES

College of Micronesia - FSM

PO Box 159 Kolonia, Pohnpei, Federated States of Micronesia
PHONE: +691 3202480
FAX: +691 3202480
E-MAIL: national@comfsm.fm
WEBSITE: http://www.comfsm.fm

NEWSPAPERS AND MAGAZINES

The FSM News

FSM News Corporation, PO Box 1832, Kolonia, Pohnpei, Federated States of Micronesia 96941
PHONE: +691 3204256
FAX: +691 3204256

Micronesia Focus

KP Johnson Publishing House, PO Box 627, Kolonia, Pohnpei, Federated States of Micronesia 96941
PHONE: +691 3204672
TITLE: Publisher/Editor
CONTACT: Ketson Johnson

National Union

FSM Information Office, PO Box 490, Kolonia, Pohnpei, Federated States of Micronesia 96941
PHONE: +691 3202548
FAX: +691 3202758
TITLE: Editor
CONTACT: Terry Gamabruw
CIRCULATION: 500

RELIGIOUS ORGANIZATIONS

Catholic

Diocese of the Caroline Islands
PO Box 939, Chuuk, Federated States of Micronesia 96942
PHONE: +691 3302399
FAX: +691 3304585
E-MAIL: asamo@mail.fm, diocese@mail.fm
WEBSITE: http://www.diocesecarolines.org/
TITLE: Bishop
NAME: Most Rev. Amando Samo, D.D.

FURTHER READING

Articles

"A Small College in the Pacific Is at the Heart of a Linguistic Struggle." *The Chronicle of Higher Education,* March 31, 2000, p. A57.

Books

Galbraith, Kate. *Micronesia: Coconut Crabs and Divine Diving.* 4th ed. London: Lonely Planet, 2000.

Kiste, Robert C. and Mac Marshall, editors. *American Anthropology in Micronesia: An Assessment.* Honolulu, HI: University of Hawai'i Press, 1999.

MICRONESIA, FEDERATED STATES OF: STATISTICAL DATA

For sources and notes see "Sources of Statistics" at the front of each volume.

GEOGRAPHY

Geography

Area:

Total: 702 sq km.

Land: 702 sq km.

Note: includes Pohnpei (Ponape), Truk (Chuuk) Islands, Yap Islands, and Kosrae.

Land boundaries: 0 km.

Coastline: 6,112 km.

Climate: tropical; heavy year-round rainfall, especially in the eastern islands; located on southern edge of the typhoon belt with occasionally severe damage.

Terrain: islands vary geologically from high mountainous islands to low, coral atolls; volcanic outcroppings on Pohnpei, Kosrae, and Truk.

Natural resources: forests, marine products, deep-seabed minerals.

HUMAN FACTORS

Demographics (B)

Population (July 2000 est.)	133,144
Population growth rate	3.28%
Birth rate (births/1,000 population)	27.09
Death rate (deaths/1,000 population)	5.95
Net migration rate (migrant(s)/1,000 population)	11.65
Life expectancy at birth (years)	
total population	68.63
male	66.67
female	70.62
Total fertility rate (children born/woman)	3.83

Data for 2000 est.

Ethnic Division

Nine ethnic Micronesian and Polynesian groups.

Religion

Roman Catholic	50%
Protestant	47%
Other and none	3%

Major Languages

English (official and common language), Trukese, Pohnpeian, Yapese, Kosrean.

EDUCATION

Literacy Rates (B)

	National Data	World Data
Adult literacy rate		
1995		
Male	NA	81
Female	79[1]	65

GOVERNMENT & LAW

Political Parties

The legislative branch consists of a unicameral Congress (14 seats; members elected by popular vote; four - one elected from each state - to serve four-year terms and 10 - elected from single-member districts delineated by population - to serve two-year terms). Elections for four-year term seats last held 2 March 1999 (next to be held in March 2003); elections for two-year term seats last held March 1999 (next to be held in March 2001). Independents won all 14 seats. There are no formal parties.

Government Budgets (B)

Revenues	$58.0 million
Expenditures	$52.0 million
Capital expenditures	$4.7 million

Data for FY95/96 est.

LABOR FORCE

Labor Force by Occupation

Two-thirds are government employees.

Unemployment Rate

27% (1989)

PRODUCTION SECTOR

Transportation

Highways:

Total: 240 km.

Paved: 42 km.

Unpaved: 198 km (1996 est.).

Merchant marine: none (1999 est.).

Airports: 6 (1999 est.).

Top Agriculture Products

Black pepper, tropical fruits and vegetables, coconuts, cassava (tapioca), sweet potatoes; pigs, chickens.

Top Mining Products (B)

Mineral resources include: deep-seabed minerals.

MANUFACTURING SECTOR

GDP & Manufacturing Summary (C)

Total GDP (1997 est.)	$240 million
Real growth rate (1997 est.)	3%
Per capita (1997 est.)	$2,000
Composition by sector	
Agriculture	19%
Industry	4%
Services	77%

Values in purchasing power parity.

COMMUNICATIONS

Telecommunications

Telephones - main lines in use: 8,000 (1995).

Telephones - mobile cellular: NA

Telephone system:

Domestic: islands interconnected by shortwave radiotelephone (used mostly for government purposes).

International: satellite earth stations - 4 Intelsat (Pacific Ocean).

Radio broadcast stations: AM 5, FM 1, shortwave 0 (1998).

Radios: NA

Television broadcast stations: 2 (1997).

Televisions: NA

Internet Service Providers (ISPs): NA

FINANCE, ECONOMICS, & TRADE

Economic Indicators

National product: GDP—purchasing power parity—$240 million (1997 est.). GDP is supplemented by grant aid, averaging perhaps $100 million annually..

National product real growth rate: 3% (1997 est.).

National product per capita: $2,000 (1997 est.).

Inflation rate—consumer price index: 4% (1996 est.).

Exchange Rates

Exchange rates: US currency is used.

Top Import Origins

Imports (c.i.f., 1996 est.): $168 million.

Origins: United States, Japan, Australia.

Top Export Destinations

Exports (f.o.b., 1996 est.): $73 million.

Destinations: Japan, United States, Guam.

Foreign Aid

Recipient: $79 million (1998); Under terms of the Compact of Free Association, the US will provide $1.3 billion in grant aid during the period 1986-2001.

Import/Export Commodities

Import Commodities	Export Commodities
Food	Fish
Manufactured goods	Garments
Machinery and equipment	Bananas
Beverages	Black pepper

MIDWAY ISLANDS

CAPITAL: None; administered by Washington, D.C.

FLAG: The flag of the United States is used.

MONETARY UNIT: The U.S. dollar is the official medium of exchange.

TIME: Midnight = noon GMT.

LOCATION AND SIZE: The Midway Islands are an atoll in Oceania, part of the North Pacific Ocean, about one-third of the way (1,304 miles, or 2,098 kilometers) from Honolulu, Hawaii to Tokyo, Japan. The two main islands, with a total area of two square miles (five square kilometers), are Eastern Island and Sand Island. This represents a comparative area about nine times the size of the Mall in Washington, D.C.

CLIMATE: Although Midway is not a South Sea island, the climate is semitropical due partly to the moderating effects of the prevailing easterly winds. The weather is generally uniform throughout the year with two distinguishable seasons, summer and winter. Midway summers are warm and slightly humid, prevailing from July to October, with an average high of 78°. The highest temperature ever recorded was 92°. During the winter months of January through March, temperatures average 66°, with the lowest temperature ever recorded at 51°. In the winter the relative humidity is high as well, and winds have been known to blow quite severely at times—hard enough to blow down shallow-rooted ironwood trees and uproot shrubbery. At times it is cold enough to require space heaters. Annual rainfall is 42 inches.

INTRODUCTORY SURVEY

RECENT HISTORY

Discovered and claimed by the United States in 1859 and formally annexed in 1867, Midway became a submarine cable station early in the twentieth century and an airlines station in 1935. Made a U.S. naval base in 1941, Midway was attacked by the Japanese in December 1941 and January 1942. In one of the great battles of World War II a Japanese naval attack in June 1942 was repelled by U.S. warplanes.

In the years following World War II Midway went from a critical war outpost to Navy caretaker status. In its heyday the island held two thousand residents but by the late seventies and early eighties the population dwindled to a few hundred. In 1992 the Navy announced the closing of Midway as its outpost and it has been operationally closed since September 10, 1993. Midway at the beginning of the twenty-first century is part of the U.S. National Wildlife Refuge system and an important nesting place for seabirds.

GOVERNMENT

Midway is a U.S. unincorporated territory. In 1993 administrative control of Midway was transferred from the U.S. Department of the Navy to the U.S. Department of the Interior's Fish and Wildlife Service as part of the National Wildlife Refuge system.

DEFENSE

Military defense is the responsibility of the United States.

ECONOMIC AFFAIRS

Industry

The local economy is based on providing support services for the national wildlife refuge activities, but all food and manufactured goods have to be imported. The naval station is inactive since its closing in 1992.

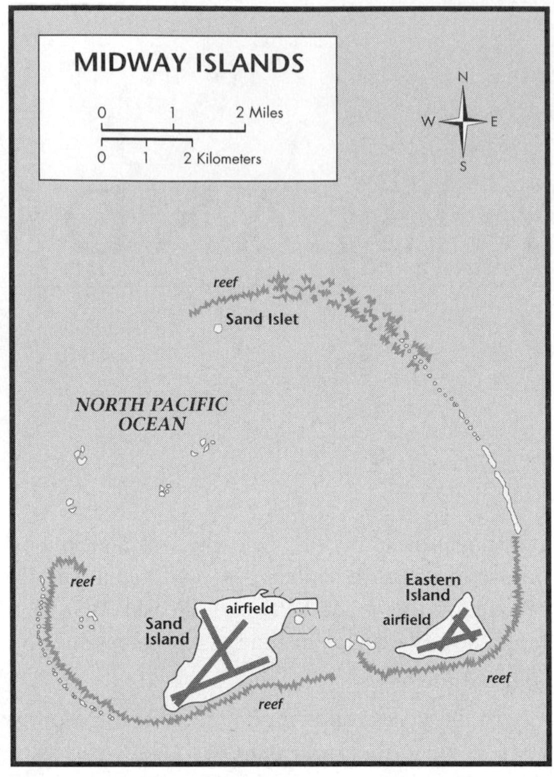

2000 KEY EVENTS TIMELINE

January

- A Bishop Museum researcher cites the increased number of Hymenoptera (stinging insects) species on Midway as resulting from the increase in travel between Midway and other islands.

February

- Aloha Airlines adds a weekly flight to Midway to its regular schedule.

June

- The U.S. Navy commemorates the fifty-eighth anniversary of the Battle of Midway with a ceremony on the island.

September

- Midway Atoll is designated a national memorial, commemorating the Battle of Midway.
- U.S. Secretary of the Interior Bruce Babbitt announces that Midway Atoll is to be a national memorial for its role in the pivotal World War II Battle of Midway.

ANALYSIS OF EVENTS: 2000

BUSINESS AND THE ECONOMY

Early in 2000, Aloha Airlines added a weekly flight to Midway to its regular schedule, making it easier for travelers to visit the island. Midway has been so isolated that a Bishop Museum researcher used it recently for a study of evolutionary processes. Because the island is so small and physically isolated, it was easier to track the arrival of new species than on a larger island or continent that might receive more frequent visitors. In results published in January 2000, researcher John Beardsley cited the increased number of *Hymenoptera* (stinging insects) species on Midway as resulting from the relative increase in travel between Midway and other islands in the last few years.

GOVERNMENT AND POLITICS

In 2000 Midway Atoll was designated a U.S. national monument in recognition of the pivotal World War II Battle of Midway, which took place between the United States and Japanese forces, June 4–6, 1942. The Fish and Wildlife Service, which had been administering the island since 1996, was ordered to form a planning committee made up of citizen group members and federal representatives to coordinate with the U.S. Navy and Marine Corps to preserve the historic buildings and artifacts. The opening ceremony was scheduled for June 2001.

CULTURE AND SOCIETY

In June 2000 the U.S. Navy commemorated the fifty-eighth anniversary of the Battle of Midway with a ceremony on Midway Island. Rear Admiral Al Harms, Commander in Chief of the U.S. Pacific Fleet, addressed an audience consisting of Midway veterans, their families, and active Navy personnel. A monument to all who have "given their lives to the defense of our nation" was dedicated on June 4, 2000.

DIRECTORY

CENTRAL GOVERNMENT

The Midway Islands are managed by the Fish and Wildlife service of the U.S. Department of the

Interior as part of the National Wildlife Refuge system. The islands are an unincorporated territory of the United States and are open to the public for wildlife-related recreation.

The islands were previously administered by the U.S. Navy, which held military operations on the island until 1993. In 1996 an executive order transferred management to the U.S. Department of the Interior.

BROADCAST MEDIA

Navy Broadcasting Service (AFRTS)

Det. 27, USNAF Box 39, San Francisco, CA 96614, USA
PHONE: (909) 4132225; (909) 4132236
FAX: (909) 4132234
E-MAIL: webadmin-afrts@dodmedia.osd.mil
WEBSITE: http://www.afrts.osd.mil
LANGUAGE: English
BROADCASTS: 24 hours/day
TYPE: Government

NEWSPAPERS AND MAGAZINES

The Midway Islands serve as a U.S. National Wildlife Refuge. No newspapers or magazines are published here.

RELIGIOUS ORGANIZATIONS

The Midway Islands, an external territory of the United States, are nearly 100 percent Christian. Due to the size and population of the islands, religious organizations are usually supported elsewhere.

FURTHER READING

Articles

Oakley, Doug. "Aloha Sets Scheduled Midway Service." *Travel Weekly,* April 13, 2000, vol. 59, no. 30, p. 17.

Government Publications

Midway Atoll National Wildlife Refuge. Washington, DC: U.S. Fish & Wildlife Service, 2000.

MIDWAY ISLANDS: STATISTICAL DATA

For sources and notes see "Sources of Statistics" at the front of each volume.

GEOGRAPHY

Geography

Area:

Total: 6.2 sq km.

Land: 6.2 sq km.

Note: includes Eastern Island, Sand Island, and Spit Island.

Land boundaries: 0 km.

Coastline: 15 km.

Climate: subtropical, but moderated by prevailing easterly winds.

Terrain: low, nearly level.

Natural resources: wildlife, terrestrial and aquatic.

Land use:

Arable land: 0%

Permanent crops: 0%

Permanent pastures: 0%

Forests and woodland: 0%

Other: 100%

HUMAN FACTORS

Demographics (B)

Population
(July 2000 est.) . . . . .No indigenous inhabitants

PRODUCTION SECTOR

Transportation

Highways:

Total: 32 km.

Pipelines: 7.8 km.

Airports: 3 (1999 est.).

MOLDOVA

Republic of Moldova
Republica Moldoveneasca

CAPITAL: Chisinau.

FLAG: Equal vertical bands of blue, yellow, and red; emblem in center of yellow stripe is Roman eagle with shield on its breast.

MONETARY UNIT: The leu is a paper currency, replacing the Russian ruble.

WEIGHTS AND MEASURES: The metric system is in force.

HOLIDAYS: Independence Day, 27 August.

TIME: 2 PM = noon GMT.

LOCATION AND SIZE: Moldova is a landlocked nation located in eastern Europe, between Ukraine and Romania. With a total area of 33,700 square kilometers (13,012 square miles), Moldova is slightly more than twice the size of the state of Hawaii. Moldova's boundary length totals 1,389 kilometers (864 miles).

Its capital city, Chisinau, is located in the south central part of the country.

CLIMATE: The climate is of the humid continental type. The mean temperature is 20 °C (68 °F) in July and −4 °C (24 °F) in January. Rainfall averages 58 centimeters (22.8 inches) a year.

INTRODUCTORY SURVEY

RECENT HISTORY

When World War II (1939-1945) broke out in Europe the 1939 Nazi-Soviet pact assigned Moldova to the Soviet area of control and Soviet forces seized it in June 1940. After the Nazi invasion of the Soviet Union, Germany helped Romania to regain Moldova that it held from 1941 until Soviet forces reconquered the area in 1944.

Moldova declared its independence from the Soviet Union on August 27, 1991. Moldova adopted a new constitution on July 28, 1994, replacing the old Soviet constitution of 1979. Russian forces, however, have remained on Moldovan territory east of the Dnister River and have supported the Russian minority (who form 30 percent of the population in this small region) in proclaiming an independent "Transdnister Republic." This move prompted fighting until Russia, Moldova, Ukraine, and Romania called a truce. The Moldova government was still trying to reach a political settlement as of 1999.

GOVERNMENT

Moldova is a republic operating under a constitution adopted in 1994. The chief of state, the president, is elected by popular vote for a four-year term. The head of government is the prime minister. The president, after consulting with parliament, will designate a candidate for the office of prime minister. Within fifteen days of the designation the prime minister-designate will request a vote of confidence from the parliament.

The legislative branch consists of the unicameral 101-seat parliament. Members are elected by popular vote to serve four-year terms. Suffrage is universal at age eighteen.

Judiciary

There are courts of first instance, an appellate court, a Supreme Court, and a Constitutional Court. The Supreme Court is divide into civil and criminal sections.

Political Parties

Although twenty-six parties or coalitions of parties participated in the February 1994 elections, only four received more than the 4 percent of the national vote required to gain seats. In 1998 elections the four parties taking seats in parliament

were: the Communist Party (PCM) with forty seats; the Democratic Convention of Moldova (CDM) with twenty-six seats; Bloc for a Democratic and Prosperous Moldova (PMDP) with twenty-four seats; and, Party of Democratic Forces (PFD) with eleven.

DEFENSE

The military is organized into the Ground Forces, Air and Air Defense Force, and the Security Forces (internal and border troops). There were about 10,650 personnel in Moldova's armed forces in 2000 including 9,600 army personnel and 1,050 air force personnel. The paramilitary consists of 2,500 internal troops and 900 riot police. Defense expenditures in 1999 were $6.3 million, or 1 percent of the GDP.

ECONOMIC AFFAIRS

In 1998 the sectors, agriculture, industry, and services, comprising the GDP were roughly equal, each contributing approximately one-third of GDP. Agriculture has long been an important sector. Favorable climate and good farmland produce a wide range of crops providing significant export revenue and employment.

Moldova has no major mineral deposits and must import all of its supplies of coal, oil, and natural gas. Since the breakup of the Soviet Union in 1991 energy shortages have contributed to sharp production declines as well as trade disruptions and droughts.

Moldovan instituted ambitious economic reforms but these efforts could not offset the impact of political and economic difficulties, both internal and external. In 1998 the Moldovan economy experienced an 8.6 percent decline due primarily to fallout from the Russian economic crisis. Continuing financial turmoil in Ukraine and Romania hurt Moldova's exports. Further isolation occurred in 1999 when the IMF halted loans following the refusal of the Moldovan parliament to carry out privatization plans. By year's end the Moldovan economy had contracted to roughly one-third of its 1989 level.

Public Finance

Moldova traditionally enjoyed a budget surplus and the fiscal position was essentially in equilibrium in 1991 as rising expenditures were covered partially by revenue measures. In 1992, however, a significant and sudden drop in revenue together with unexpected expenditures related to the Trans-Dnister conflict increased public service wage expenses and copious lending to public enterprises caused the fiscal deficit to swell to 21 percent of the GDP. As of 1992 Moldova had not yet signed an agreement with Russia concerning its liability for former Soviet debt. During the first year of its independence Moldova contracted debts of about $90 million with nations outside the former USSR. Those debts grew to a total of $550 million through 1995 and some $250 million was owed to Russia.

Moldova projected a budget of $523.2 million in 1996 with a budget deficit of approximately 3.4%. The government financed the debt with the sale of securities, national bank profits, and borrowing, but planned a budget policy and tax review to stem a long-term deficit.

The U.S. Central Intelligence Agency (CIA) estimated that in 1998 Moldova's central government took in revenue of approximately $530 million and had expenditures of $594 million. External debt in 1999 was $1,3 billion.

Income

In 1999 Moldova's gross domestic product (GDP) was estimated at $9.7 billion, or about $2,200 per capita. The 1999 estimated GDP growth rate was a decline of 4.4%, the fifth drop in a six year period. Inflation was 38 percent by 1999 estimates. The GDP contribution by sector in 1998 was agriculture 31%, industry 35%, and services 34%.

Industry

In 1998 the most prominent industries were: food processing (57%); electric energy (18%), engineering and metal processing (5%); production of construction materials (4%); light industry (5.4%); and, forestry, wood processing, and pulp and paper (3%).

Banking and Finance

Moldova's banking sector will play a key role in the country's transition from a managed economy to a market economy. The banking system was reformed in 1991. The National Bank of Moldova (NBM) is charged with implementing monetary policy and issuing currency. The bank has two policy instruments, reserve requirements which were raised progressively throughout 1994, and interest rates. State banks include the State Savings Bank with 1,000 branches, and the Bank for Foreign Economic Exchange. The currency unit is the leu introduced in late November 1993.

The banking system comprises four former Soviet banks, Agroindbank, Molindconbank, Moldotsbank, and the Savings Bank, as well as twenty-one commercial banks at the end of 1998. As in many other republics of the former Soviet Union, licensing procedures in the early 1990s were quite lax with the result that the country is now over-banked having too many small institutions and a relatively high level of non-performing loans (11 percent of total commercial bank balance sheets as of mid-1996).

The Chisinau-based Moldovan Stock Exchange opened for business in June 1995. As of mid-1996 it listed elevan shares. A commodity exchange is planned.

Economic Development

In March 1993 the Moldovan government inaugurated the Program of Activity of the Government 1992-1995 to make the transition to a market-oriented economy. The first stage focuses on stabilization including price liberalization, and the second stage concentrates on economic recovery and growth including privatization, agrarian reform, infrastructure development, social protection, and trade reform. However the government has been slow to institute privatization in the agricultural sector. Although the government has introduced stable convertible currency, backed privatization, freed prices and interest rates, and removed export controls, economic growth has been difficult. Moldova experienced a 3 percent contraction of the economy in 1995, the third straight year of negative growth. By 1998 it stood at one-third its 1989 level. In large part this decline is due to the unfavorable circumstances: the transnistrian conflict; the collapse of the Soviet Union; and, the near total loss of the grape crop in 1997.

SOCIAL WELFARE

Moldova's current social security system was enacted by law in 1990 with amendments passed in 1992 and 1993. Benefits are provided for old age, disability, survivors' pensions, and workers' compensation for injury and unemployment, and family allowances. Moldova has comprehensive legislation for the protection of children including paid maternity leave, a birth grant, and family allowances.

Although women are accorded equal rights under the law, they are under-represented in government and other leadership positions. There is also higher unemployment among women than men.

Healthcare

Moldova has been working on developing its own standards for health care among other major programs. In 2000 average life expectancy was 64.5 years. In that year, there was one doctor per eighty-one people and one hospital bed per eighty-two people. In 1995 nearly the entire urban population, 96%, but only 9 percent of the rural population had access to sanitation.

Housing

In 1989 18.2 percent of all privately owned housing had running water, 16 percent had sewer lines, and 91.3 percent had gas. As of January 1991 218,000 families (or 33.3%) were on waiting lists for urban housing. A program begun in March 1993 has privatized 80 percent of all housing units.

EDUCATION

Education is compulsory for eleven years, between the ages of six and seventeen. In 1997 primary schools enrolled 320,725 students and secondary schools had 445,501 students. In 1996 education expenditure amounted to approximately 28.1 percent of total government expenditure.

The Moldovan State University was founded in 1945. In 1997 all institutions of higher education had a combined enrollment of 93,759. For 2000 adult illiteracy was estimated at 1.1%.

2000 KEY EVENTS TIMELINE

February

- Moldova attends the first Commonwealth of Independent States (CIS) summit under the chairmanship of Russian Acting President Vladimir Putin.

May

- Moldova chooses eleven finalists to bid on the country's electric privatization.

June

- President Petru Lucinsci travels to Belarus and meets with its president, Alexandr Lukashenka, to discuss trade relations.

July

- President Petru Lucinschi vetoes a law on July 20 that would give parliament full discretion over who sits in the president's seat. He was a top Communist official during the Soviet era.

November

- A storm leaves several regions of Moldova without power November 28.

December

- Moldova's 101-seat parliament votes for a new president December 1, but bickering between supporters of Communist candidate Vladimir Voronin and Independent candidate Pavel Barbalat mars the election. Neither candidate wins a majority, causing run-off elections December 4. When the run-off fails to produce a winner, President Lucinschi says he will dissolve parliament and call new elections.
- Results of research are released indicating that the number of people infected with HIV in eastern has risen 75 percent in a year. Kazakhstan, Moldova, Russia, and Ukraine are among the countries experience the rapid spread of HIV.

ANALYSIS OF EVENTS: 2000

BUSINESS AND THE ECONOMY

There was no significant improvement in Moldova's economy in 2000; it remained one of the weakest economies in Europe. Annual per capita income was $500. Salaries averaged $30 per month, with farm labor paying as little as eighty cents a day. Agricultural exports were still reeling from the effects of the Russian economic crisis two years earlier. The major income producers were subsistence farming, remittances from Moldovans abroad, and wine sales—the latter sharply down from the days when Moldova was the primary wine producer of the Soviet Union. Adding to the country's economic woes were reductions in international aid payments by the International Monetary Fund (IMF) and other donors because of a lack of progress in privatizing state-owned enterprises.

It was estimated that half a million or more Moldovans had emigrated, seeking better opportunities in Russia or southern Europe. Unpaid bills for imported gas and electricity from Russia, Romania, and Ukraine had led to energy curtailment and shut-offs, as well as Russian threats of a railroad blockade.

In one area, though, Moldova entered the twenty-first century riding the crest of the information revolution. The country's right to the registered Internet domain name suffix ".md" yielded an arrangement with a Florida entrepreneur who sold permission to use the initials to physicians and pharmaceutical suppliers, with $20 from each sale going to the Moldovan government. The company projected a sales volume of 100,000 in 2000.

Privatization plans for Moldova's electrical distribution system went forward throughout the year. In March Union Fenosa finalized the purchase of three of the five government-owned utility companies. Sale of two distribution companies and two power stations was still pending.

GOVERNMENT AND POLITICS

Moldova entered the new millennium facing poverty, energy shortages, political disunity, and the continuing impasse over the status of the breakaway Transdniestria region, which held its own separate celebrations commemorating the tenth anniversary of post-Soviet independence in August. Russia had promised to pull some 2,000 troops out of the area by 2003. However, sentiment in favor of independence had remained strong in the eight years since tensions in the largely Russian-speaking border region had erupted into civil war, and the path toward ultimate reconciliation was unclear. The Moldovan government advocated autonomy for the region within the larger framework of Moldovan sovereignty, while the Transdniestrians continued to demand complete independence. Although Transdniestrians elected their own president, Igor Smirnov, and established a foreign ministry, they were not recognized by any foreign governments.

Moldovan politics remained fractious even aside from the stalemate in Transdniestria. In July the parliament overturned President Petru Lucinschi's veto of constitutional changes that would make the country a parliamentary democracy, with the president elected by parliament rather than directly by the people. Late in the month Lucinschi signed the changes into law, although he continued to advocate a nationwide referendum on the issue.

A small, poor nation, Moldova was particularly ill-situated to withstand the pressures that Russia continued to place on the former Soviet republics. In the case of Moldova, this included a plan for the country—consisting primarily of ethnic Romanians—to unite with the predominantly Russian Transdniestria region in a new state under Russian sponsorship. Moldova's government opposed the plan. Gas-rich Russia also holds a crucial trump card when it comes to energy, for Moldova has no energy sources of its own. In mid-2000, the country owed Russia some $900 million in gas bills.

Moldova remained a member of GUUAM, a group of five former Soviet republics that had banded together four years earlier in an attempt to establish a more effective alliance than the Commonwealth of Independent States (CIS). The group announced plans to hold regular summit meetings, establish a free-trade zone, and build energy pipelines, and its leaders met in September when they were all at United Nations headquarters in New York for the Millennium Summit. However, early in the year representatives of Moldova also attended the CIS's first meeting under the direction of Russian president Vladimir Putin.

In April Romania and Moldova signed a treaty recognizing each other's sovereignty, a move that had been complicated by concerns about the large number of Moldovans holding Romanian citizenship. In other regional diplomacy, Moldovan president Petru Lucinschi traveled to Belarus to meet with that country's president, Alexandr Lukashenka, for discussions of bilateral trade relations.

CULTURE AND SOCIETY

Government measures to end free public transportation for students in the capital city of Chisinau led to rioting in May. For the most part, however, Moldovan society was orderly and tolerant, even in the midst of some of the worst poverty in Europe.

Hit by the rising cost of aid to Kosovo, the European Union (E.U.) was planning to end humanitarian aid to Moldova at the end of 2000, a move that local aid workers warned would result in children dying of starvation. It was not uncommon for parents facing a cold, hungry winter to turn their children over to orphanages in hopes of possibly reclaiming them later, although these hopes often could not be realized. One such orphanage in Chisinau was the beneficiary of humanitarian aid from families in the United States who had adopted children there over a six-year period and became aware of the crisis conditions at the institution.

The country's ethnic divisions were evident in a dispute over the closing of eight Russian-language radio stations under legislation mandating that 65 percent of all broadcasting must be in Romanian.

DIRECTORY

CENTRAL GOVERNMENT

Head of State

President
Petru Lucinschi, Office of the President

Prime Minister
Dumitru Barghis, Office of the Prime Minister

Ministers

Deputy Prime Minister
Valeriu Cosarciuc, Office of the Deputy Prime Minister

Deputy Prime Minister
Lidia Gutu, Office of the Deputy Prime Minister

Minister of Agriculture, Food Industry, and Forestry
Ion Russu, Ministry of Agriculture, Food Industry, and Forestry, bd Stefan cel Mare 162, MD-2002 Chisinau, Moldova
PHONE: +373 (2) 233427

Minister of Culture
Gennadie Ciobanu, Ministry of Culture

Minister of Defense
Boris Gamurari, Ministry of Defense

Minister of Economy and Reform
Andrei Cucu, Ministry of Economy and Reform

Minister of Education and Sciences
Ion Gutu, Ministry of Education and Sciences

Minister of Environment
Ion Raileanu, Ministry of Environment

Minister of Finance
Mihai Manoli, Ministry of Finance

Minister of Foreign Affairs
Nicolae Tabacaru, Ministry of Foreign Affairs

Minister of Industry and Energy
Ion Lesanu, Ministry of Industry and Energy

Minister of Internal Affairs
Vladimir Turcan, Ministry of Internal Affairs

Minister of Justice
Valeria Sterbet, Ministry of Justice

Minister of Labor
Valerian Revenco, Ministry of Labor

Minister of State
Vladimir Filat, Ministry of State

Minister of Territory Development, Construction and Communal Services
Mihai Severovan, Ministry of Territory Development, Construction and Communal Services

Minister of Transportation and Communications
Afanasie Smochin, Ministry of Transportation and Communications

Minister of Health
Vasile Parasca, Ministry of Health

Minister of Cabinet
Mihai Petrache, Ministry of Cabinet

POLITICAL ORGANIZATIONS

Furnica-Speranta (Social Democratic Union)

Partidul Democrat Agrar din Moldova-PDAM (Agrarian Democratic Party)

TITLE: Chairman
NAME: Dumitru Motpan

PPSM (Party for Social Progress)

TITLE: Chairman
NAME: Eugen Sobor

Partidul Renasterii ci Concilierii din Moldova-PRCM (Party of Revival and Conciliation of Moldova)

TITLE: Chairman
NAME: Mircea Snegur

Frontul Popular Crestin si Democrat-FPCD (Christian Democratic Popular Front)

TITLE: Chairman
NAME: Iurie Rosca

Partidul Comunistilor din Moldova-PCM (Communist Party of Moldova)

TITLE: First Chairman
NAME: Vladimir Voronin

Conventia Democrata din Moldova-CDM (Democratic Convention of Moldova)

Pentru o Moldova Democrata si Prospera-PMDP (Movement for a Democratic and Prosperous Moldova)

NAME: Dumitru Diacov

Partidul Socialist-PSM (Socialist Party of Moldova)

TITLE: Co-Chairmen
NAME: Valeriu Senic; Victor Morev

Miscarea Yedinstvo (Unity Movement)

TITLE: Chairman
NAME: Vladimir Solonari

Alianta Taranilor Liberi-ATL (Alliance of Free Farmers)

Congresul Intelectualitatji-CI (Congress of Intellectuals)

CI-ATL (Peasants and Intellectuals Block)

TITLE: Chairwoman
NAME: Lidia Istrati

Partidul National Liberal-PNL (National Liberal Party)

DIPLOMATIC REPRESENTATION

Embassies in Moldova

Russia
ul. Stefan del Mare 151, Chisinau, Moldova
PHONE: +373 (2) 232600
FAX: +373 (2) 232600

JUDICIAL SYSTEM

Supreme Court

BROADCAST MEDIA

Europa Plus-Moldova

Street Alecu Russo, 1, Chisinau, Moldova
PHONE: +373 (2) 438288
FAX: +373 (2) 445398

Radio Antena C

Street V. Micle, 10, Chisinau 2012, Moldova
PHONE: +373 (2) 220488
FAX: +373 (2) 541992
E-MAIL: antenac@cni.Moldova
WEBSITE: http://www.ournet.Moldova/~antenac
TITLE: Director
CONTACT: Ion Bunduchi
LANGUAGE: Romanian, Russian
BROADCASTS: 24 hours/day
TYPE: municipal, public

Radio Contact

Street Hincesti, 53, office 501, Chisinau 2004, Moldova
PHONE: +373 (2) 737466
E-MAIL: rcontact@ch.moldpac.Moldova

Radio D'Or

Boulevard Stefan Cel Mare, 180, et 14, Chisinau 2004, Moldova
PHONE: +373 (2) 249961
FAX: +373 (2) 249961
WEBSITE: rdor.moldnet.Moldova

Radio Moldova

Street Miorita, 1, Chisinau 2028, Moldova
PHONE: +373 (2) 721388
FAX: +373 (2) 723537
LANGUAGE: Romanian, Russian, Moldavian, Ukranian
TYPE: Government

Radio Poli Disc

Hincest 59/1, Chisinau 2028, Moldova
PHONE: + 373 (2) 737446
FAX: +373 (2) 737338

Radio Pridnestrovye

NGDXM-"RP", PO Box 3297, Chisinau 2044, Moldova
PHONE: +373 (33) 35570; +373 32417
FAX: +373 (33) 32245

Radio Pro-FM

Boulevard Stefan Cel Mare, 162, et. 17, Chisinau, Moldova
PHONE: +373 (2) 213642

Canal TVC 21

Street Drumul Vilor 23/2, Chisinau, Moldova
PHONE: +373 (2) 737958
FAX: +373 (2) 737129

Catalan TV

Calea Lesilor 29A, Chisinau, Moldova
PHONE: +373 (2) 749800
FAX: +373 (2) 749800
E-MAIL: ctv@moldova.md

CIM TV

Street Stefan Cel Mare, 12, Cimislia, Moldova
PHONE: +373 (241) 22088
FAX: +373 (241) 22848

NIT

Street Hincesti, 53, Chisinau 2028, Moldova

PRO-TV Moldova

Boulevard Stefan Cel Mare, 162, et. 17, Chisinau 2004, Moldova
PHONE: +373 (2) 213645
FAX: +373 (2) 213645
E-MAIL: protv@dnt.mc

TV Moldova

Street Hincesti, 64, Chisinau 2028, Moldova
PHONE: +373 (2) 739470
FAX: +373 (2) 723537

E-MAIL: tvnewstv@cni.Moldova
WEBSITE: http://www.trm.Moldova
TYPE: public

VTV

Street Hincesti 61, Chisinau, Moldova
PHONE: +373 (2) 277028
TITLE: Director
CONTACT: F. D. Bulan
CHANNEL: 23
TYPE: Commercial, Private

COLLEGES AND UNIVERSITIES

Moldovan State University

Ulitsa Livezilor 60, Chisinau 2009, Moldova

NEWSPAPERS AND MAGAZINES

Golos Naroda

Chisinau, Kishinev, Moldova
FAX: +373 (2) 234401
TITLE: Editor
CONTACT: Georgiy Kopats
TYPE: Science/Environmental

Kishinevskie Novosti

Pushkin Str. 22, Chisinau, Moldova
FAX: +373 (2) 233918
TITLE: Editor
CONTACT: Sergey Drobot
TYPE: General

Kommersant Moldovy

Vlaiku Pyrkelab 44, Chisinau, Kishinev, Moldova
TITLE: Editor
CONTACT: Artem Varenitsa
TYPE: Business and Economics

Molodezh' Moldovy

Pushin Str. 22, Chisinau, Kishinev, Moldova
FAX: +373(2) 233708
TITLE: Editor
CONTACT: Nikolai Roshka
TYPE: Juvenile fiction and non-fiction

Trudovoi Tiraspol

United Council of Labor Collective of Tiraspol, 25 October, Tiraspol, Moldova
TYPE: Civil Rights, Labor & Industrial Relations

PUBLISHERS

Editura Hyperion

bd Stefan cel Mare 180, Chisinau, Moldova
PHONE: +373 (2) 244259
TITLE: Director
CONTACT: Valeriu Matei
SUBJECTS: Art, Fiction, Literature, Literary Criticism, Essays, Music, Dance

Izdatelstvo Katia Moldoveniaske

Prosp Lenina 180, Chisinau, Moldova
PHONE: +373 (2) 244022
TITLE: Director
CONTACT: N. N. Mumzhi
SUBJECTS: Agriculture, Economics, Government, Political Science, Human Relations, Literature, Literary Criticism, Essays, Social Sciences, Sociology

Lumina Publishing House

bd Stefan cel Mare 180, 2004, Chisinau, Moldova
PHONE: +373 (2) 246397
TITLE: Manager
CONTACT: Vladimir Chistruga
SUBJECTS: Biological Sciences, Chemistry, Chemical Engineering, Child Care and Development, Geography, Geology, History, Language Arts, Linguistics, Literature, Literary Criticism, Essays, Mathematics, Medicine, Nursing, Dentistry, Physics, Psychology, Psychiatry

RELIGIOUS ORGANIZATIONS

Jewish

JCC of Kishinev and Moldova-Chabad Lubavitch
Chabad Lubavitch 8 Street, Kishinev, Moldova
PHONE: +373 (2) 541020
E-MAIL: jcc@kishinev.org
WEBSITE: http://www.kishinev.org

Orthodox

Synzhereisky raion
Selo Bilicheny Bek., Synzhereisky Raion, Moldova
PHONE: +373 (044) 26233436
TITLE: Priest
NAME: Andrei Rudei

Scientology

Kishinev Dianetics Center
UL. Dokuchaevd 4-73, Kishinev, Moldova
PHONE: +373 (2) 708403

Other Organizations

Moldova Union Theological Seminary
Cismele Street, 8, Chisinau 2070, Moldova
PHONE: +373 (2) 734196
FAX: +373 (2) 734196
E-MAIL: yyunak@cni.md
WEBSITE: http://www.tagnet.org/moldsem

FURTHER READING

Articles

"Can Moldova Get Worse?" *The Economist (US),* July 15, 2000, vol. 356, no. 8179, p. 49.

"Russia and Its Neighbours: Frost and Friction." *The Economist (US),* September 30, 2000, vol. 356, no. 8190, p. 57.

Parker, Nicholas. "Mom, Moldova, and How a Boy Lost His Innocence." *Fortune,* May 29, 2000, vol. 141, no. 11, p. 274+.

Zachary, G. Pascal. "A Chilling Visit to a Land 6f Many Hats, Socks and Electric Radiators; Heat Is an Expensive Luxury in Moldova, as Suppliers Raise Prices and Pets Freeze." *Wall Street Journal,* January 18, 2000, p. B1.

Books

Brezianu, Andrei. *Historical Dictionary of the Republic of Moldova.* Lanham, MD: Scarecrow Press, 2000.

Dun and Bradstreet's Export Guide to Moldova. Parsippany, NJ: Dun & Bradstreet, 1999.

King, Charles. *The Moldovans: Romania, Russia, and the Politics of Culture.* Stanford, CA: Hoover Institution Press, 2000.

MOLDOVA: STATISTICAL DATA

For sources and notes see "Sources of Statistics" at the front of each volume.

GEOGRAPHY

Geography

Area:

Total: 33,843 sq km.

Land: 33,371 sq km.

Land boundaries:

Total: 1,389 km.

Border countries: Romania 450 km, Ukraine 939 km.

Coastline: 0 km (landlocked).

Climate: moderate winters, warm summers.

Terrain: rolling steppe, gradual slope south to Black Sea.

Natural resources: lignite, phosphorites, gypsum, arable land.

Land use:

Arable land: 53%

Permanent crops: 14%

Permanent pastures: 13%

Forests and woodland: 13%

Other: 7% (1993 est.).

HUMAN FACTORS

Demographics (A)

	1990	1995	1998	2000	2010	2020	2030	2040	2050
Population	4,398	4,460	4,436	4,431	4,535	4,737	4,812	4,852	4,796
Life expectancy - males	63.9	60.4	59.6	59.9	63.7	66.8	69.6	72.0	74.0
Life expectancy - females	71.0	69.4	69.3	69.2	71.7	74.8	77.5	79.7	81.6
Birth rate (per 1,000)	18.3	13.5	12.8	12.9	16.8	13.3	12.0	11.4	9.7
Death rate (per 1,000)	10.1	11.8	12.4	12.6	11.9	10.7	10.7	11.4	11.7
Women of reproductive age (15-49 yrs.)	1,108	1,160	1,200	1,210	1,211	1,172	1,180	1,088	1,073
Fertility rate	2.4	1.8	1.7	1.6	2.0	2.0	1.8	1.7	1.6

Except as noted, values for vital statistics are in thousands; life expectancy is in years,

Health Personnel

	National Data	World Data (wtd ave)
Total health expenditure as a percentage of GDP, 1990-1998[a]		
Public sector	4.8	2.5
Private sector	1.9	2.9
Total[b]	6.7	5.5
Health expenditure per capita in U.S. dollars, 1990-1998[a]		
Purchasing power parity	145	561
Total	30	483
Availability of health care facilities per 100,000 people		
Hospital beds 1990-1998[a]	1,210	330
Doctors 1992-1995[a]	107	122
Nurses 1992-1995[a]	40	248

Health Indicators

	National Data	World Data
Life expectancy at birth (years)		
1980	66	61
1998	67	67
Daily per capita supply of calories		
1970	NA	2,358
1997	2,567	2,791
Daily per capital supply of protein		
1997 (grams)	69	74
Total fertility rate (births per woman)		
1980	2.4	3.7
1998	1.7	2.7
Population with access (%)		
To safe water (1990-96)	56	NA
To sanitation (1990-96)	50	NA
People living with (1997)		
Tuberculosis (cases per 100,000)	65.4	60.4
HIV/AIDS (% aged 15 - 49 years)	0.11	0.99

Infants and Malnutrition

	National Data	World Data (wtd ave)
Under 5 mortality rate (1989)	35	NA
% of infants with low birthweight (1992-98)[1]	7	17
Births attended by skilled health staff (% of total births 1996-98)	NA	52
% fully immunized at 1 year of age (1995-98)[1]		
TB	99	82
DPT	97	77
Polio	98	77
Measles	99	74
Prevalence of child malnutrition (1992-98)[1] (based on weight for age, % of children under 5 years)	NA	30

Ethnic Division

Moldavian/Romanian .64.5%

Ukrainian .13.8%

Russian .13.0%

Gagauz .3.5%

Jewish .1.5%

Bulgarian .2.0%

Other .1.7%

Data for 1989 est. Note: internal disputes with ethnic Slavs in the Transnistrian region

Religion

Eastern Orthodox .98.5%

Jewish .1.5%

Baptist .less than 1%

Data for 1991.

Major Languages

Moldovan (official, virtually the same as the Romanian language), Russian, Gagauz (a Turkish dialect).

EDUCATION

Public Education Expenditures

	1980	1997
Public expenditures on education as % of GNP	3.4	10.6
Expenditures per student as % of GNP per capita		
Primary & Secondary	NA	NA
Tertiary	NA	63.2
Pupils per teacher at the primary level	NA	23
Duration of primary education in years	NA	11
World data for comparison		
Pupils per teacher at the primary level (wtd ave)	NA	33
Duration of primary education in years (mean)	NA	9

Educational Attainment (A)

Age group (1989) . . . . .25+
Population of this age group 2,499,613
Highest level attained (%)
No schooling 12.7
First level
Not completed 17.1
Completed . . . . .NA
Entered second level 58.9
Entered post-secondary 11.3

Literacy Rates (B)

	National Data	World Data
Adult literacy rate		
1980		
Male	96	75
Female	88	58
1995		
Male	99	81
Female	97	65

(Continued on next page.)

GOVERNMENT & LAW

Military Affairs (A)

	1992	1995	1996	1997
Military expenditures				
Current dollars (mil.)	NA	64	60	62
1997 constant dollars (mil.)	NA	67	61	62
Armed forces (000)	9	12	12	11
Gross national product (GNP)				
Current dollars (mil.)	9,650[e]	6,830	6,350	6,440
1997 constant dollars (mil.)	10,700[e]	7,070	6,460	6,440
Central government expenditures (CGE)				
1997 constant dollars (mil.)	NA	3,250	3,060	3,180
People (mil.)	4.4	4.5	4.5	4.5
Military expenditure as % of GNP	NA	0.9	0.9	1.0
World data on military expenditure as % of GNP	3.4	2.7	2.6	2.6
Military expenditure as % of CGE	NA	2.0	2.0	1.9
World data on military expenditure as % of CGE	12.5	10.5	10.3	10.2
Military expenditure per capita (1997 $)	NA	15	14	14
World data on military expenditure per capita (1997 $)	173	146	143	145
Armed forces per 1,000 people (soldiers)	2.1	2.7	2.7	2.5
World data on armed forces per 1,000 people (soldiers)	4.5	4.1	3.9	3.8
GNP per capita (1997 $)	2,410	1,580	1,450	1,440
Arms imports[6]				
Current dollars (mil.)	5	5	0	0
1997 constant dollars (mil.)	6	5	0	0
Total imports[7]				
Current dollars (mil.)	640	841	1,079	1,020[e]
1997 constant dollars (mil.)	710	871	1,097	1,020[e]
Total exports[7]				
Current dollars (mil.)	471	739	805	633[e]
1997 constant dollars (mil.)	522	765	818	633[e]
Arms as percent of total imports[8]	0.8	0.6	0	0
Arms as percent of total exports[8]	0	0	0	0

(Continued on next page.)

EDUCATION (cont.)

Libraries

National Libraries	**1995**
Administrative Units	1
Service Points or Branches	2
Number of Volumes (000)	300
Registered Users (000)	11
Loans to Users (000)	44
Total Library Staff	13
Public Libraries	**1995**
Administrative Units	1,601
Service Points or Branches	3,200
Number of Volumes (000)	18,969
Registered Users (000)	1,158
Loans to Users (000)	NA
Total Library Staff	2,671

GOVERNMENT & LAW (cont.)

Political Parties

Parliament	% of vote	no. of seats
Communist Party (PCM)	30%	40
Democratic Convention of Moldova (CDM)	19%	26
Bloc for a Democratic and Prosperous Moldova (PMDP)	18%	24
Party of Democratic Forces (PFD)	9%	11

Elections were last held 22 March 1998 (next to be held spring 2002). The comparative breakdown of seats by faction is approximate.

Government Budgets (B)

Revenues	$536 million
Expenditures	$594 million

Data for 1998 est.

Crime

Crime volume (for 1998)	
Crimes reported	36,195
Total persons convicted	23,165
Crimes per 100,000 population	957
Persons responsible for offenses	
Total number suspects	17,153
Total number of female suspects	1,870
Total number of juvenile suspects	2,521

LABOR FORCE

Total Labor Force (A)

1.7 million (1998).

Labor Force by Occupation

Agriculture	40.2%
Industry	14.3%
Other	45.5%

Data for 1998.

Unemployment Rate

2% (includes only officially registered unemployed; large numbers of underemployed workers) (September 1998).

MANUFACTURING SECTOR

GDP & Manufacturing Summary (B)

	1980	1985	1990	1993	1994	1995
Gross Domestic Product						
Millions of 1990 dollars	7,206	8,506	11,975	7,018	4,913	4,765
Growth rate in percent	1.48	−9.76	8.17	−14.80	−30.00	−3.00
Per capita (in 1990 dollars)	1,797	2,019	2,746	1,589	1,110	1,074
Manufacturing Value Added						
Millions of 1990 dollars	1,909	2,344	3,263	2,240	1,570	1,545[e]
Growth rate in percent	NA	−4.60	19.59	−10.22	−29.92	−1.55[e]
Manufacturing share in percent of current prices	NA	NA	27.2[e]	31.4[e]	31.9[e]	NA

PRODUCTION SECTOR

Energy Production

Production . . . . .5.661 billion kWh

Production by source

Fossil fuel 93%

Hydro 7%

Nuclear 0%

Other 0%

Exports . . . . .0 kWh

Data for 1998.

Energy Consumption

Consumption . . . . .7.065 billion kWh

Imports . . . . .1.800 billion kWh

Data for 1998.

Transportation

Highways:

Total: 12,300 km.

Paved: 10,738 km.

Unpaved: 1,562 km (1996 est.).

Waterways: 424 km (1994).

Pipelines: natural gas 310 km (1992).

Airports: 26 (1994 est.).

Airports - with unpaved runways: 18.

Top Agriculture Products

Vegetables, fruits, wine, grain, sugar beets, sunflower seed, tobacco; beef, milk.

Top Mining Products (B)

Mineral resources include: lignite, phosphorites, gypsum.

COMMUNICATIONS

Daily Newspapers

	National Data	World Data for Comparison
Daily Newspapers		
Number of Dailies	4	8,391
Total Circulation (000)	261	548,000
Circulation per 1,000 inhabitants	60	96

Telecommunications

Telephones - main lines in use: 566,000 (1995).

Telephones - mobile cellular: 14 (1995).

Telephone system: inadequate, outmoded, poor service outside Chisinau, some effort to modernize is under way.

Domestic: new subscribers face long wait for service; mobile cellular telephone service being introduced.

International: service through Romania and Russia via landline; satellite earth stations - Intelsat, Eutelsat, and Intersputnik.

Radio broadcast stations: AM 7, FM 50, shortwave 3 (1998).

Radios: 3.22 million (1997).

Television broadcast stations: 40 (1998).

Televisions: 1.26 million (1997).

Internet Service Providers (ISPs): 2 (1999).

FINANCE, ECONOMICS, & TRADE

Economic Indicators

National product: GDP—purchasing power parity—$9.7 billion (1999 est.).

National product real growth rate: -4.4% (1999 est.).

(Continued on next page.)

Balance of Payments

	1994	1995	1996	1997	1998
Exports of goods (f.o.b.)	618	739	823	890	644
Imports of goods (f.o.b.)	−672	−809	−1,075	−1,235	−1,043
Trade balance	−54	−70	−252	−345	−399
Services - debits	−79	−208	−178	−196	−193
Services - credits	33	145	114	134	120
Private transfers (net)	NA	44	40	50	85
Government transfers (net)	NA	21	34	42	35
Overall balance	−115	−95	−188	−268	−334

Economic Indicators (cont.)

National product per capita: $2,200 (1999 est.).

Inflation rate—consumer price index: 38% (1999 est.).

Exchange Rates

Exchange rates:

Lei (MLD) per US$1 (end of year)

January 2000	12.1408
1999	10.5158
1998	5.3707
1997	4.6236
1996	4.6045
1995	4.4958

Top Import Origins

$560 million (f.o.b., 1999)

Origins (1998)

Russia	22%
Ukraine	16%
Romania	12%
Belarus	9%
Germany	5%

Top Export Destinations

$470 million (f.o.b., 1999)

Destinations (1998)

Russia	53%
Romania	10%
Ukraine	8%
Germany	5%
Belarus	4%

Foreign Aid

Recipient: $100.8 million (1995); $547 million from the IMF and World Bank (1992-99).

Import/Export Commodities

Import Commodities	Export Commodities
Mineral products and fuel 31%	Foodstuffs
Machinery and equipment	Wine and tobacco 66%
Chemicals	Textiles and footwear
Textiles	Machinery

MONACO

Principality of Monaco
Principauté de Monaco

CAPITAL: The seat of government is at Monaco-Ville.

FLAG: The national flag consists of a red horizontal stripe above a white horizontal stripe.

ANTHEM: *Hymne Monégasque,* beginning "Principauté Monaco, ma patrie" ("Principality of Monaco, my fatherland").

MONETARY UNIT: Monaco uses the French franc (Fr), and all monetary restrictions in effect in France apply also in Monaco. Monégasque coins, on a par with French coinage, also circulate; denominations are 10, 20, and 50 centimes, and, 1, 2, 5, 10, and 50 francs. Fr1 = $0.19585 (or $1 = Fr5.106).

WEIGHTS AND MEASURES: The metric system is the legal standard.

HOLIDAYS: New Year's Day, 1 January; St. Dévôte, 27 January; Labor Day, 1 May; Assumption, 15 August; All Saints' Day, 1 November; National Day, 19 November; Immaculate Conception, 8 December; Christmas, 25 December. Movable religious holidays include Easter Monday, Ascension, Pentecost Monday, and Fête-Dieu.

TIME: 1 PM = noon GMT.

LOCATION AND SIZE: The second-smallest country in both Europe and the world after the Vatican, Monaco is situated in the southeastern part of the French administrative district of Alpes-Maritimes. Its area is 1.9 square kilometers (0.73 square miles), about three times the size of the mall in Washington, D.C. Monaco has a total boundary length of 12.7 kilometers (7.9 miles).

CLIMATE: Winters are mild, with temperatures rarely below freezing and a January average of about 8°C (46°F). Summer heat is tempered by sea breezes; the average maximum in July and August is 26°C (79°F). Rainfall averages about 77 centimeters (30 inches) a year.

INTRODUCTORY SURVEY

RECENT HISTORY

The economic development of Monaco proceeded rapidly with the opening of the railroad in 1868 and of the gambling casino. Since that time the principality has become world famous as a tourist and recreation center.

Monaco has been a constitutional monarchy since the early twentieth century. In 1956 Prince Rainier III married the popular American actress, Grace Kelly, with whom he had three children: Princess Caroline, Prince Albert (the heir to the throne), and Princess Stephanie. Princess Grace was killed in a 1982 car accident.

Monaco joined the United Nations on May 28, 1993. Gambling, operated by Société des Bains de Mer, a state controlled group, recorded a 30 percent increase in gambling receipts in 1998.

GOVERNMENT

Monaco is a constitutional monarchy ruled by the hereditary princes of the Grimaldi line. A constitution adopted on December 17, 1962, provides for a single-chamber National Council of eighteen members elected by direct popular vote every five years; it shares legislative functions with the prince who is chief of state. The head of government is the minister of state appointed by the monarch from a list of three French national candidates presented by the French Candidates.

Judiciary

A justice of the peace tries petty cases. Other courts are the Court of First Instance, the Court of Appeal, the Court of Revision, and the Criminal Court. The highest judicial authority is vested in the Supreme Tribunal.

Political Parties

Monaco does not formally have political parties, but candidates compete on the basis of various lists. The major political groups have been the National and Democratic Union (Union Nationale et Democratique-UND); Communist Action (Action Communale-AC); Èvolution Communale (EC); and the Movement of Democratic Union (MUD).

DEFENSE

France assumed responsibility for the defense of Monaco as part of the Versailles Treaty in 1919. There is no army in the principality. A private guard protects the royal family, and a police force of 390 ensures public safety.

ECONOMIC AFFAIRS

For its livelihood, Monaco depends chiefly on tourism, real estate, financial services, and light industry. A substantial part of the principality's revenue from tourist sources comes from the operations of Sea-Bathing Company (Société des Bains de Mer-SBM), in which the government owns 69 percent. The SBM operates the gambling casino at Monte Carlo as well as several luxury hotels and motion-picture theaters.

Monaco has successfully diversified into services and small, value added, non-polluting industries. Monaco thrives as a tax haven both for indidivudals and businesses since it has no income tax and low business taxes. Standard of living is high, comparable to prosperous French metropolitan areas.

Public Finance

Revenues are derived mostly from commercial and transactional taxes, income resulting from the customs agreement with France, the sale of postage stamps, and the sale of tobacco and matches. The U.S. Central Intelligence Agency estimated that in 1995 government revenues totaled approximately $578 million and expenditures $531 million.

Income

In 1996 the gross domestic product (GDP) was estimated at $870 million, or about $27,000 per capita.

Industry

The tourist industry dominates Monaco's economic life but small-scale industries produce a variety of items for domestic use and for export. About 700 small businesses make pottery and glass objects, paper and cards, jewelry, perfumes, dolls, precision instruments, plastics, chemicals and pharmaceuticals, cosmetics, machine tools, watches, leather items, and radio parts. There are also flourmills, dairies, chocolate plants, as well as textile mills and a small shipyard.

Banking and Finance

Foreign currency circulates within Monaco under the supervision of the French government. The most important local bank is Crédit Foncier de Monaco, founded in 1922. As of 1994 there were 45 banks operating in Monaco. There is no securities exchange. In 1999 Monaco's banking industry had approximately 310,000 accounts and employed 1,700 people. The vast majority of customers were nonresidents.

Economic Development

The government strenuously promotes Monaco as a tourist and convention attraction. Near the Larvotto the government has reserved a zone for the construction of residential and tourist accommodations. In the 1980s Monaco concentrated on the development of business tourism, with the construction of the Monte Carlo Convention Center and the International Conference Center.

Two major development and reclamation projects have been undertaken under Prince Rainier. These are the major landfill and reclamation project at Fontvieille, and the Monte Carlo Bord de Mer. At Fontvieille, the government financed the reclamation of 220,000 sq m (2,368,000 sq ft) of inundated shore, creating a "platform" for residential construction and new port facilities.

The Monte Carlo seashore scheme, also government-financed, involved the relocation of railroad tracks underground in order to create a manmade beach, with a boardwalk and other tourist attractions. The beach lies between two other land reclamation projects: the Larvotto, a sports complex financed by SBM, and the Portier, a entertainment complex developed by the government.

SOCIAL WELFARE

Public social welfare organizations include the Pension's Office and the Social Services Benefits Office. Social security benefits include old age and disability pensions and sickness and maternity benefits. Unemployment benefits are provided through the French system.

Both employers and employees finance social security benefits. There is a home for the aged attached to the Princess Grace Polyclinic. There is equal legal treatment of men and women who are born in Monaco.

Healthcare

In 1995 Monaco had approximately forty-two physicians, sixty-four pharmacists, and 293 nurses. There were 432 hospital beds. The entire population had access to safe water and sanitation.

Housing

In 1991 there were 12,000 principal residences in Monaco. In recent years the government has stressed the construction of luxury housing.

EDUCATION

Education is offered in Monaco from the preschool to the secondary and technical levels and is compulsory from age six to sixteen. Attendance is 90 percent, and nearly all adults are literate. In 1997 Monaco's seven public primary schools had a total of 1,919 students. The public secondary schools had 2,886 students. In the mid-1990s approximately 5.3 percent of total government expenditure was allocated to education.

2000 KEY EVENTS TIMELINE

March

- In a Nice court, Princess Stephanie's former husband, Daniel Ducruet, testifies that he was entrapped by a Belgian beauty in a scene that was filmed; the airing of the film led to break-up of the royal marriage.

June

- David Coulthard wins the famed Monaco Grand Prix.
- France issues a 400-page report criticizing Monaco's lax banking law, especially its guarantee of anonymity. France supervises Monaco's lending policies and wants to demonstrate that it is fully committed to the European Union's planned changes in banking laws to curb tax evasion. About 60 percent of 340,000 bank accounts belong to non-residents in this country of 30,000.
- Princess Caroline's husband, Ernst August, reportedly makes a spectacle of himself in public at Expo 2000 in Hanover, Germany, on June 15.

October

- France threatens October 10 to sever ties with Monaco if the country doesn't institute measures to stop money laundering.
- Monaco's Prince Rainier III threatens to demand sovereignty from France on October 31.

ANALYSIS OF EVENTS: 2000

BUSINESS AND THE ECONOMY

Fontvieille, a development of twenty-two hectares of reclaimed land to the west of the old town, has become a center for light industry and low-cost housing. The complex produced out anything from canned anchovies to cosmetics and surgical light fittings. As of 2000 gambling accounted for only 4.35 percent of total revenue while value-added taxes on hotels, banks, and industry generated 55 percent of public revenues in 1999–2000. Monaco levied the same rate of French value-added tax (V.A.T.) of 21 percent. France, however, was under pressure to bring its rate closer in harmony with European-wide rates and it was possible that French V.A.T. would be reduced by 2 percent in the near future. Such adjustments would result in a drop of 10 percent in Monaco's overall revenues. A quarter of government revenue came from tourism.

A vast new convention center was formally opened in July. Its main auditorium seats up to 1,900 delegates and was described as an opera house for businesses. Half of the building was constructed below sea level and, the building was located close to hotels and the casino.

GOVERNMENT AND POLITICS

Monaco does not have political parties as such, but candidates compete on the basis of various lists. The major political groups have been the National and Democratic Union (Union Nationale et Democratique—UND), founded in 1962; Communist Action (Action Communale—AC); Èvolution Communale (EC); and the Movement of Democratic Union (MUD).

In the general election of February 1998 the UND took all eighteen seats in the National Council.

Monaco's future in an integrated Europe has been a source of worry for the political leadership. A request to join the Council of Europe was thrown out on the grounds that Monaco did not meet the basic criteria of full sovereignty and democratic government. After all, Prince Rainier and his advisors decided everything and France had a big say over the country's affairs. Most of the advisors or ministers were appointed by France and were seconded from the French bureaucracy. In addition, more than 83 percent of the population was foreign and the Monegasques (native-born citizens) represented only five thousand of nearly 32,000 inhabitants.

Monaco has repeatedly indicated its interest in joining the euro-zone. France has blocked this request, insisting that the principality must first adopt international enforcement measures and help combat systemic tax fraud before it can join the euro-zone.

Relations with France were at their worst in the second part of 2000. Paris threatened to sever ties unless the principality revised its legal system and tackled money laundering. Monaco harbors 340,000 bank accounts of which 60 percent are held in non-residents' names. Monaco was accused of supporting tax evasion and crime-linked cash transactions. Wealthy French residents and people with business of questionable legality hid their money in Monaco's banks, which then thwarted attempts of neighboring countries to combat fraud and organized crime. French Ministers of Finance and Justice have suggested that the Monte Carlo casino, owned by the ruling Grimaldi family, should be placed under the control of French customs and that Monaco's seventy financial institutions should declare all their bank accounts. Moreover, French politicians urged the country, with the help of French input, to combat fraud and tax evasion more effectively. Failure to do so would result in France's decision to reexamine the economic, financial, and judicial arrangements between the two states. Monaco has been closely linked to France since 1918 when a treaty made between the two countries formalized France's commitment to defend Monaco and respect its sovereignty "so long as it is exercised in conformity with the political, military, naval, and economic interests of France." French officials who have complained about Monaco's tolerance for shady financial business for years were running out of patience.

CULTURE AND SOCIETY

Prince Rainier of Monaco celebrated fifty-one years on the throne during which he oversaw the development of Monaco into a prosperous territory. But he has had a difficult year. His health was poor and he underwent three major operations (repair of aneurysm in his abdominal aorta and the removal of part of a lung) in the early part of the year. His son Prince Albert, forty-one, was placed in charge, but Prince Rainier has refused to hand over the reign to his son until he is married and has a child. His family continued to cause him grief as his son-in-law, Prince Ernst-August of Hanover (husband of Princess Caroline), displayed thuggish public behavior and reportedly urinated in public. In turn, the reaction of Prince Ernst became fodder for more sensational reporting and he was in the news for several months.

Prince Rainier's youngest daughter, Princess Stephanie, age thirty-five, lost most of her inheritance in the fall of 2000 after her father cut down her bequest to 1 percent of his estate, or $11.5 million. His two remaining children will each receive $572 million. Rainier disapproved of the people with whom Princess Stephanie chose to associate, and his legal advisor warned him that her fortune could be squandered by the Princess and her more unscrupulous friends.

DIRECTORY

CENTRAL GOVERNMENT

Head of State

Prince
Rainier III, Monarch, Palais de Monaco, Boit Postal 518, 98015 Monte Carlo

Ministers

Minister of State
Patrick Leclercq, Ministry of State, Place de la Visitation, Monaco-Ville 98015, Monaco
PHONE: +37 (7) 93158000

POLITICAL ORGANIZATIONS

Union Nationale et Démocratique-UND (National and Democratic Union)

NAME: Jean-Louis Campora

Liste Campora-LC (Campora List)

NAME: Anne-Marie Campora

Liste Médecin (Medecin List)

NAME: Jean-Louis Médecin

DIPLOMATIC REPRESENTATION

Embassies in Monaco

Austria
PHONE: +37 (7) 93302300
TITLE: Consul General
NAME: Jacques de Beer de Laer

Belgium
PHONE: +37 (7) 93505989
TITLE: Consul General
NAME: André Ortmans

Brazil
PHONE: +37 (7) 93307615
TITLE: Consul General
NAME: François Ragazzoni

Cameroon
PHONE: +37 (7) 93502113
TITLE: Consul General
NAME: Jacqueline Aubery

Canada
E-MAIL: consul-canada@monte-carlo.mc

Costa Rica
PHONE: +37 (7) 92052232
TITLE: Consul General
NAME: Lucille Pellegrini

Côte d'Ivoire
PHONE: +37 (7) 93309700
TITLE: Consul General
NAME: Jean-François Cullieyrier

Cyprus
PHONE: +37 (7) 93159055
E-MAIL: consul-chypre@monte-carlo.mc
TITLE: Consul General
NAME: Lucas Haji Ioannou

Denmark
PHONE: +37 (7) 93500203
TITLE: Consul General
NAME: Kund Stefen Gam

Dominican Republic
PHONE: +37 (7) 93302914
TITLE: Consul General
NAME: Elisabeth-Anne Croesi-Notari

El Salvador
PHONE: +37 (7) 93251454
TITLE: Consul General
NAME: Laura Chatelin

Finland
PHONE: +37 (7) 93509021
TITLE: Consul General
NAME: Rainier Boisson

France
PHONE: +37 (7) 92165460
TITLE: Consul General
NAME: Jean-Bernard De Vaivre

Germany
PHONE: +37 (7) 93301949
TITLE: Consul General
NAME: Christine Esswein

Greece
PHONE: +37 (7) 93257655
TITLE: Consul General
NAME: Maria Economou

Guatemala
PHONE: +37 (7) 93506747
TITLE: Consul General
NAME: Odette Fissore

Honduras
PHONE: +37 (7) 93307059

TITLE: Consul General
NAME: Louisette Van Antwerpen

Hungary
PHONE: +37 (7) 93502018
TITLE: Consul General
NAME: Etienne Elek

Ireland
PHONE: +37 (7) 93157000
TITLE: Consul General
NAME: Michaël W.J. Smurfit

Italy
PHONE: +37 (7) 93502271
E-MAIL: ital-consul@monte-carlo.mc
TITLE: Consul General
NAME: Giovanni Andriani

Japan
PHONE: +37 (7) 92165151
TITLE: Consul General
NAME: Edmond Pastor

Jordan
PHONE: +37 (7) 93506393
TITLE: Consul General
NAME: Mohamed Tarif Al-Ayoubi

Liberia
PHONE: +37 (7) 93304030
TITLE: Consul General
NAME: Roger Richelmi

Luxembourg
PHONE: +37 (7) 93253037
TITLE: Consul General
NAME: Edmond Lecourt

Madagascar
PHONE: +37 (7) 93506237
TITLE: Consul General
NAME: Jacques Ferreyrolles

Mexico
PHONE: +37 (7) 93506647
TITLE: Consul General
NAME: Louis Orecchia

Morocco
PHONE: +37 (7) 93254026
TITLE: Consul General
NAME: Victor Pastor

Netherlands
PHONE: +37 (7) 92051502
TITLE: Consul General
NAME: Robert Smulders

Norway
PHONE: +37 (7) 93509101
FAX: +37 (7) 92161646
TITLE: Consul General
NAME: Claire Notari

Panama
PHONE: +37 (7) 93503206
TITLE: Consul General
NAME: Hubert Schurr

Peru
PHONE: +37 (7) 92165888
TITLE: Consul General
NAME: Michel Pastor

Philippines
PHONE: +37 (7) 93301010
TITLE: Consul General
NAME: Stefen Zuellig

Poland
PHONE: +37 (7) 93254312
TITLE: Consul General
NAME: Wojcieck Fibak

Portugal
PHONE: +37 (7) 93506394
TITLE: Consul General
NAME: Louis-Paul Colozier

Rwanda
PHONE: +37 (7) 92165454
TITLE: Consul General
NAME: Jean-Antoine Pastor

Senegal
PHONE: +37 (7) 93300481
TITLE: Consul General
NAME: Jacques Brillant de Boisbrillant

Seychelles
PHONE: +37 (7) 93302796
TITLE: Consul General
NAME: Michel Chiappori

Slovakia
PHONE: +37 (7) 93255006
TITLE: Consul General
NAME: Cristina Noghes-Menio

South Africa
PHONE: +37 (7) 93252426
E-MAIL: consul-afrisud@monte-carlo.mc
TITLE: Consul General
NAME: Jacques Orecchia

Spain
PHONE: +37 (7) 93302498
TITLE: Consul General
NAME: Michel Boeri

Sweden
PHONE: +37 (7) 93507560
TITLE: Consul General
NAME: François de Montseignat

Thailand
PHONE: +37 (7) 93309494
TITLE: Consul General
NAME: Jean-Claude Mourou

Turkey
PHONE: +37 (7) 93309240
TITLE: Consul General
NAME: Tuna Koprülü

United Kingdom
PHONE: +37 (7) 93509966
TITLE: Consul General
NAME: Eric Gordon Franck Blair

Uruguay
PHONE: +37 (7) 93506341
TITLE: Consul General
NAME: Ercole Canali

Venezuela
PHONE: +37 (7) 92160202
TITLE: Consul General
NAME: Mario Aletti Fabro

JUDICIAL SYSTEM

Supreme Tribunal

BROADCAST MEDIA

Radio Monte Carlo

16 Boulevard Princesse Charlotte, MC 98080, Monaco Cedex
PHONE: +377 151617; +377 151780
FAX: +377 151703
E-MAIL: rmcredacmc@rmc.mc
WEBSITE: http://www.rmc.mc

Riviera Radio

16 Boulevard Princesse Charlotte, 98000, Monaco
PHONE: +377 93254906
FAX: +377 93304245
E-MAIL: rivieraradio@monaco.mc
WEBSITE: http://www.riviera-radio.com

Tele Monte Carlo

16 Boulevard Princesse Charlotte, MC 98090, Monaco-Cedex
PHONE: +377 92165480
FAX: +377 92165481
E-MAIL: tmc@fr.multithematiques.com
WEBSITE: http://www.montecarlo-tmc.com
CHANNEL: 30, 33, 35, 39, F8
TYPE: Commercial

COLLEGES AND UNIVERSITIES

University of Southern Europe

2 Ave. Du Prince H Albert, MC-98000 Monaco, Monaco
PHONE: +377 92957057
FAX: +377 92952830
E-MAIL: use@monaco.mc
WEBSITE: http://www.riviera.fr/usehome.htm

Academie De Musique Prince Rainier

Academie De Musique, 17 Rue Princess Florestine, MC-98000 Monaco, Monaco
PHONE: +377 93152891

NEWSPAPERS AND MAGAZINES

Monte Carlo Cote d'Azur

Europa Residence, Place des Moulins, MC 98000 Monaco
FAX: +377 93257657
TITLE: Editor
CONTACT: Michel Pastor
TYPE: General

Monaco Actualite

2 rue du Gabian, MC 98000 Monaco
PHONE: +377 92057536
FAX: +377 92057534
WEBSITE: http://www.monaco.mc/actualite/

PUBLISHERS

Les Editions du Rocher

28 rue Comte Felix Gastaldi, BP 521, 98015 Monaco
PHONE: +37 (7) 93300944
FAX: +37 (7) 93507371
SUBJECTS: Antiques, Astrology, Occult, Biography, Crafts, Games, Hobbies, Drama, Theater, Fiction, Health, Nutrition, History, How-to, Literature, Literary Criticism, Essays, Military Science, Mysteries, Romance, Sports, Athletics, Western Fiction

Rondeau Giannipiero a Monaco

4 rue Langle, 98000 Monaco
PHONE: +37 (7) 93303075

FAX: +37 (7) 93257047
TITLE: President
CONTACT: S. Roudeau
SUBJECTS: Art, Fiction, History, Humor, Literature, Literary Criticism, Essays

Editions de l'Oiseau-Lyre SAM

BP 515, 98015 Monaco
PHONE: +37 (7) 93300944
FAX: +37 (7) 93301915
E-MAIL: oiseau_lyre@compuserve.com
TITLE: Managing Director
CONTACT: Moroney Davitt
SUBJECTS: Music, Dance

Victor Gadoury

57 rue, Grimaldi, Le Panorama, 98000 Monaco
PHONE: +37 (7) 93251296
FAX: +37 (7) 93501339
E-MAIL: gadoury@cyber-monaco.mc
WEBSITE: http://www.cyber-monaco.mc/gadoury

RELIGIOUS ORGANIZATIONS

Monaco is officially free to all religions, but nearly 100 percent are Roman Catholic.

FURTHER READING

Articles

Daley, Suzanne. "France Issues Tough Report on Monaco and Its Money." *New York Times,* June 25, 2000, p. 4.

"The Royal Wee: Princess Caroline's Husband, Ernst August, Makes an Exhibition of Himself." *People Weekly,* July 17, 2000, vol. 54, no. 3, p. 71.

Internet

BBC News Online. "Sanctions Threat to 'Tax Havens.'" June 26, 2000. [Online] Available http://news6.thdo.bbc.co.uk/hi/english/business/newsid%5F806000/806236.stm (accessed October 12, 2000).

MONACO: STATISTICAL DATA

For sources and notes see "Sources of Statistics" at the front of each volume.

GEOGRAPHY

Geography

Area:

Total: 1.95 sq km.

Land: 1.95 sq km.

Land boundaries:

Total: 4.4 km.

Border countries: France 4.4 km.

'Coastline: 4.1 km.

Climate: Mediterranean with mild, wet winters and hot, dry summers.

Terrain: hilly, rugged, rocky.

Natural resources: none.

Land use:

Arable land: 0%

Permanent crops: 0%

Permanent pastures: 0%

Forests and woodland: 0%

Other: 100% (urban area).

HUMAN FACTORS

Ethnic Division

French 47%
Monegasque 16%
Italian 16%
Other 21%

Religion

Roman Catholic 90%

Major Languages

French (official), English, Italian, Monegasque.

Demographics (A)

	1990	1995	1998	2000	2010	2020	2030	2040	2050
Population	30.0	30.9	31.4	31.7	33.0	34.2	34.8	34.3	33.0
Life expectancy - males	73.0	74.0	74.5	74.9	76.4	77.7	78.8	79.6	80.2
Life expectancy - females	81.5	82.3	82.7	83.0	84.2	85.1	85.9	86.5	86.9
Birth rate (per 1,000)	11.7	11.0	10.4	9.9	9.1	10.1	9.5	9.0	9.1
Death rate (per 1,000)	13.8	13.4	13.3	13.1	12.9	12.6	13.0	13.5	14.2
Women of reproductive age (15-49 yrs.)	6.9	6.8	6.7	6.7	6.9	6.8	6.8	6.8	6.2
Fertility rate	1.8	1.8	1.8	1.8	1.8	1.7	1.7	1.7	1.7

Except as noted, values for vital statistics are in thousands; life expectancy is in years.

EDUCATION

Libraries

Public Libraries	1995
Administrative Units	2
Service Points or Branches	2
Number of Volumes (000)	15
Registered Users (000)	0.8
Loans to Users (000)	479
Total Library Staff	3

GOVERNMENT & LAW

Government Budgets (B)

Revenues	$518 million
Expenditures	$531 million

Data for 1995.

Crime

Crime volume (for 1998)

Crimes reported	1,001
Total persons convicted	536
Crimes per 100,000 population	3,337

Persons responsible for offenses

Total number suspects	550
Total number of female suspects	96
Total number of juvenile suspects	57

LABOR FORCE

Total Labor Force (A)

30,540 (January 1994).

Unemployment Rate

3.1% (1998)

PRODUCTION SECTOR

Transportation

Highways:

Total: 50 km.

Paved: 50 km.

Unpaved: 0 km (1996 est.).

Merchant marine: none (1999 est.).

Airports: linked to airport in Nice, France, by helicopter service.

MANUFACTURING SECTOR

GDP & Manufacturing Summary (C)

Total GDP (1999 est.)	$870 million
Per capita (1999 est.)	$27,000

Values in purchasing power parity.

COMMUNICATIONS

Daily Newspapers

	National Data	World Data for Comparison
Daily Newspapers		
Number of Dailies	1	8,391
Total Circulation (000)	NA	548,000
Circulation per 1,000 inhabitants	NA	96

Telecommunications

Telephones - main lines in use: 31,027 (1995).

Telephones - mobile cellular: 2,560 (1994).

Telephone system: automatic telephone system.

Domestic: NA

International: no satellite earth stations; connected by cable into the French communications system.

Radio broadcast stations: AM 1, FM NA, shortwave 8 (1998).

Radios: 34,000 (1997).

Television broadcast stations: 5 (1997).

Televisions: 25,000 (1997).

Internet Service Providers (ISPs): 4 (1999).

FINANCE, ECONOMICS, & TRADE

Economic Indicators

National product: GDP—purchasing power parity—$870 million (1999 est.).

National product real growth rate: NA.

National product per capita: $27,000 (1999 est.).

Inflation rate—consumer price index: NA.

Exchange Rates

Exchange rates:

Euros per US$1

January 2000	0.9867
1999	0.9386

French francs (F) per US$1

January 1999	5.6500
1998	5.8995
1997	5.8367
1996	5.1155
1995	4.9915

Fiscal year: calendar year.

MONGOLIA

Mongol Uls

CAPITAL: Ulaanbaatar.

FLAG: The national flag, adopted in 1946, contains a light blue vertical stripe between two red stripes; in gold, on the stripe nearest the hoist, is the *soyombo,* Mongolia's independence emblem.

ANTHEM: *Bügd Nayramdah mongol ard ulsyn töriin duulal (State Anthem of the Mongolian People's Republic).*

MONETARY UNIT: The tugrik (T) of 100 mongos. There are coins of 1, 2, 5, 10, 15, 20, and 50 mongos and notes of 1, 3, 5, 10, 20, 25, 50, and 100 tugriks. T1 = $0.00163 (or $1 = T614.18).

WEIGHTS AND MEASURES: The metric system is the legal standard.

HOLIDAYS: New Year's Day, 1 January; Constitution Day, 13 January; Women's Day, 8 March; Mother and Children's Day, 1 June; Naadam Festival, 11–13 July; Mongolian Republic Day, 26 November. Movable holidays include Mongol New Year's Day, in February or March.

TIME: 8 PM = noon GMT.

LOCATION AND SIZE: Situated in east-central Asia, Mongolia has an area of 1,565,000 square kilometers (604,250 square miles), slightly larger than the state of Alaska. The largest landlocked country in the world, Mongolia has a total boundary length of 8,114 kilometers (5,042 miles).

CLIMATE: Mongolia has average January temperatures of −22° to −18°C (−8° to 0°F) and dry, practically snowless winters. Annual precipitation ranges from 25 to 38 centimeters (10 to 15 inches) in mountain areas to less than 13 centimeters (5 inches) in the Gobi Desert.

INTRODUCTORY SURVEY

RECENT HISTORY

Mongolia won its independence from China in 1921. With the support of the former Soviet Union (which formed in 1922 and broke apart in 1991) communist rule was installed. Lands of the feudal lords were confiscated starting in 1929 and those of monasteries in 1938.

On February 14, 1950, the People's Republic of China and the Soviet Union signed a treaty that guaranteed the Mongolian People's Republic's (MPR) independence. In October 1961 the MPR became a member of the United Nations. In June 1987 the MPR and the United States established diplomatic relations.

Following in the footsteps of the former Soviet Union, the MPR initiated its own policy of "openness" (*il tod*) in the late 1980s and began the transition from a centrally planned, collective economy toward a market economy. The MPRP opted for political as well as economic reforms gradually yielding its monopoly on power. The MPRP's leadership resigned in March 1990 and in May the constitution was amended to allow for new, multiparty elections which took place in July.

During 1991 the new government issued vouchers to all citizens for the purchase of state property, but economic reform was made more difficult by the economic collapse of the former Soviet Union. Elections in June 1992 created a new legislature, the State Great Hural (SGH), and in June 1993 President Punsalmaagiyn Ochirbat was elected in the first direct presidential elections. By September 1992 some 67,000 former Soviet troops (in the MPR since 1966) completed a process of withdrawal that began in 1990.

Discontent among younger voters led to the defeat of the MPRP in the 1996 parliamentary elections. The winners from the Democratic Union Coalition (DUC) were mostly political novices

who promised to intensify market reforms. The election results marked the first smooth transfer of power in Mongolia's modern history. However from 1996 through 1999 disunity and strife continuously shook the government with changes occurring annually. By August 1999 yet another DUC government had fallen and Rinchinnyamiin Amarjargal became Mongolia's third prime minister in fifteen months.

GOVERNMENT

The 1992 constitution went into effect February 12 replacing the 1960 constitution and completing Mongolia's transition from a single-party state to a multiparty, parliamentary form of government. At that time the country's official name was changed from "Mongolian People's Republic" to "Mongolia." The legislature, the State Great Hural (SGH), has seventy-six members elected by popular vote by district to four-year terms.

The president, the head of state, is selected by direct, popular vote for a four-year term. The prime minister, the head of government, is nominated by the president and confirmed by the SGH. The prime minister selects a cabinet that must be confirmed by the SGH. Suffrage is universal at eighteen years of age.

Mongolia consists of eighteen provinces (*aymag*) divided into 299 counties (*somon*) and three autonomous cities (*hot*).

Judiciary

There is a Supreme Court elected by the People's Great Hural, province and city courts elected by the corresponding assemblies of people's deputies; and local courts. Under the 1992 Constitution the Supreme Court remains the highest judicial body. There is a Constitutional Court that has sole authority for constitutional review. The local courts (peoples courts) handle most routine civil and criminal cases. Provincial courts hear more serious cases and review local court decisions. The Supreme Court hears appeals from the local and provincial courts.

Political Parties

The Mongolian People's Revolutionary Party (MPRP), the single ruling party between 1924 and 1996, legalized opposition parties in 1990. In the June 1996 elections the Democratic Union Coalition (DUC) that included the Mongolian National Democratic Party (MNDP) and the Mongolian Social Democratic Party (MSDP) plus two smaller parties defeated the MPRP, winning fifty of seventy-six seats n the SGH. The MPRP won twenty-five seats, and the remainder went to the Mongolian Conservative Party (MCP).

However in the 2000 elections MRPR candidates won seventy-two of the seventy-six seats with DUC taking three, and a nonpartisan candidate winning one.

DEFENSE

In 2000 the armed forces totaled 9,100. The army had 7,500 personnel (4,000 draftees) and a reserve strength of 140,000. Mongolia spent an estimated $20 million for defense in 1997. The air force has 800 personnel. Paramilitary forces consist of about 7,200 frontier guards and security police.

ECONOMIC AFFAIRS

After seventy years as a centrally planned economy, Mongolia has undergone a difficult transition towards a free market system since 1990. A number of factors including the sudden halt to economic aid from the former Soviet Union and allied countries, the disruption of trade with traditional trading partners, as well as a severe winter in 1990–1991, caused a steep decline in the country's economic activity. Despite these difficulties the government has continued its economic privatization program and development of oil and mineral resources as a high priority. Mongolian has extensive mineral deposits: copper, coal, molybdenum, tin, tungsten, and gold.

Animal husbandry has remained a dominant sector of the economy with live animals and processing of animal products accounting for a major share of current exports. The DUC has embraced free-market economics but the ex-communist MPRP opposes reforms.

Mongolia joined the World Trade Organization (WTO) in 1997. Economic growth picked up in that year but collapsed in 1998 and 1999 due to repercussions of the Asian financial crisis and a temporary Russian ban on exports of oil and oil products. In 1999 at the last Consultative Group Meeting in Ulaanbaatar the international donor community pledged $300 million per year.

Public Finance

The annual budget is submitted to the People's Great Hural for approval.

The U.S. Central Intelligence Agency estimated that in 1999 government revenues totaled approximately $260 million and expenditures $366 million. External debt totaled $715 million by 1997 estimates.

Income

In 1999 the gross domestic product (GDP) was estimated at $6.1 billion, or about $2,320 per capita. The 1999 estimated GDP growth rate was 3.5 percent and inflation was 9.5 percent in 1998. The 1999 estimated GDP contribution by sector was agriculture 33 percent, industry 24 percent, and services 43 percent.

Industry

Small-scale processing of livestock and agricultural products has historically been the mainstay of Mongolia's industrial sector. With establishment of the Erdenet copper plant in the late 1970s, metal processing first became important. In 1996 the leading industries included metals, accounting for 32.6 percent of industrial output; energy production, 19.1 percent; processed foods, 15.8 percent; wool and woolen apparel, 11.5 percent; mineral fuels, 6.8 percent chemicals, 6.7 percent; and, various other items, 7.5 percent.

Banking and Finance

The State Bank of Mongolia is the official bank of Mongolia and recent economic reforms have allowed the formation of a commercial banking sector. The economic reforms were brought about by the collapse of the Soviet Union.

Now Mongolia has a two-tier banking system where control of the money supply is invested in the central bank. The Bank of Mongolia has established lending rules the commercial banks must follow. Also reserve requirements are set by the national bank. In 1991 commercial functions were separated from the Mongol Bank and two commercial banks were created. In 1996 there were thirteen.

The Mongolian Securities Exchange opened in August 1995.

Economic Development

In the past Mongolia operated on the basis of a planned economy with five-year plans implemented from 1947 until 1990 receiving assistance from the former USSR and China. In 1990 with the establishment of a new consensus government, there followed a three-year plan that aimed for achieving greater efficiency in the allocation of resources and a diversified economic base by undertaking a sustained transition to a free market economy. The change was a fundamental shift, as the government relinquished its role as the primary factor in the economy and began limiting itself to policies supporting a market-oriented economy. Main components of the government's program have included privatization of state enterprises, price liberalization, changes in national law, and drafting an action plan for environmental protection. Current plans specify development of the country's energy and mining sectors, and further action in environmental protection as well as continued reforms in a number of areas including fiscal management, land tenure, and social benefit entitlements.

In 1996 the initial phase of privatization of state property was completed. According to the government, 100 percent of small- and medium-sized enterprises have been privatized as well as 97 percent of the country's livestock. In 1994 the private sector accounted for 60 percent of GDP and over 10,000 private businesses have been created since 1991. At the end of 1995, however, the government still held shares in more than 200 companies. The next phase of privatization will utilize securities market activities to replace the transitional voucher program. From 1997–1999 a series of natural disasters, declines in world prices for copper and cashmere, and the Asian oil crisis hindered development plans.

SOCIAL WELFARE

The social insurance program provides for free medical services, benefits for temporary disability, and pensions for permanent disability and old age. Although women receive equal pay for equal work, they fill almost no positions at the highest levels of government or the professions.

Healthcare

Healthcare is administered under state auspices and all medical and hospital services are free. Each province has at least two hospitals and each agricultural cooperative and state farm has a medical station. In 1990–1997 there were 2.7 physicians and 11.5 hospital beds per 1,000 population. In 1990–1995 95 percent of the population had access to health care services. Average life expectancy was an estimated sixty-seven years in 2000. Pulmonary and bronchial infections, including tuberculosis and brucellosis, are widespread but are being brought under control. Health expenditures were 4.7 percent of GDP in 1990–1997.

Housing

The standard housing of the nomadic herders, as well as of many city dwellers, is the yurt—a light, movable, dome-shaped tent consisting of a skin or felt covering stretched over a lattice frame. Large apartment-house complexes with stores, services, and cultural facilities are being built in Ulaanbaatar, as well as in various other cities and towns.

EDUCATION

Eight years of schooling is compulsory and free, starting at age eight. For 2000 adult illiteracy rates were estimated at 0.7 percent. In 1997 there were 234,193 pupils in primary schools and 195,408 in secondary schools. More than 70 percent of students from rural areas reside in dormitories adjoining the schools. The Mongolian State University in Ulaanbaatar was founded in 1942. In 1998 all institutions of higher learning had a combined enrollment of 50,961.

2000 KEY EVENTS TIMELINE

March

- Two new parties, the Mongolian New Social Democratic Party and the Civic Will Party, announce their decisions to compete in upcoming parliamentary elections.

April

- UN and various nations announce a major humanitarian mission to assist herders who have lost over two million head of livestock due to adverse weather that induced starvation.

June

- A counterfeiting operation that has produced more than US$1 million is foiled by the Ulaanbaatar Criminal Police Department.

July

- The Mongolian People's Revolutionary Party (MPRP), the former communist opposition, wins a resounding victory in parliamentary elections.

On July 2, 90 percent of the voting populace gave the MPRP seventy-three out of seventy-six open parliamentary seats.

- The Mongolian National Olympic Committee conducts its first drug tests on horses and national wrestlers.

November

- Russia and Mongolia sign a declaration of military and economic cooperation on November 14.
- Eleven coal miners are killed, twelve injured, and forty trapped in a coal mine gas explosion November 25.

ANALYSIS OF EVENTS: 2000

BUSINESS AND THE ECONOMY

The development of a free market economy, combined with high world demand for cashmere, led more Mongolians in recent years to take to the desert to raise the goats that produce the fine wool. By 2000 this trend resulted in overgrazing, and created a threat to the nomadic way of life. The fact that China offered a higher price for the product hurt the Mongolian garment industry, as the Mongolian producers preferred to sell to the Chinese over the Mongolian buyers.

GOVERNMENT AND POLITICS

Voter turnout was high when elections for Mongolia's parliament, known as the Great Hural, were held in July. The Mongolian People's Revolutionary Party (MPRP) swept back into power, winning seventy-two of the seventy-six seats up for election. In the outgoing body, the communist MPRP only held twenty-six seats.

The election of the MPRP was seen as a backlash against the political gridlock that occurred under the coalition government previously in place, and the strict austerity measures imposed by the International Monetary Fund (IMF), which had reportedly pushed many Mongolians into poverty.

MPRP leader Nambariin Enkbayar outlined plans for Mongolia's future that included reevaluating the industrial privatization program, renegotiating the terms of the financial aid provided by the IMF, providing free education, developing tourism, and widening the tax base. He stated that he would not totally roll back the country's privatization program because 20 percent of the nation's 2000 gross domestic product (GDP) came from western countries, aid agencies, the World Bank, and other international sources.

In 2000 Mongolia worked actively to strengthen its ties with its neighbors. In November Russian President Vladimir Putin visited Mongolia, in the first visit of a Russian head of state to Mongolia in twenty-six years. President Putin and Mongolian President Natsagiyn Bagabandi signed a declaration confirming a 1993 friendship agreement. In the same month China and Mongolia signed a treaty to protect the last of the world's wild camels, with the formation of a reserve spanning the border between the two nations, to allow the animals their normal migratory patterns. In June a delegation of foreign officials from China visited Mongolia, in accordance with the Protocol on Cooperation between the Ministries of External Relations in the two countries.

Mongolia's Minister of External Relations attended the first meeting of the Ministers of Foreign Affairs of Democratic Nations, held in Warsaw, Poland, in June. The goal of the organization was to develop international cooperation for strengthening democracy. Mongolia sent representatives to a meeting of international religious leaders held in Nepal in November 2000, where participants representing thirty-three nations and eleven major world religions met to discuss the world environment. Mongolian representatives pledged to reinstate the Buddhist ban on the hunting of snow leopards.

In May Wolfgang Hoffman, the Executive Secretary of the Preparatory Commission for the Comprehensive Test Ban Treaty Organization, made an official visit to Mongolia, where he met with the Minister of Enlightenment for the signing of an agreement regarding a full ban on nuclear testing. In the same month, the first of a series of meetings regarding transit traffic between Russia, China, and Mongolia took place in Ulaanbaatar, with the stated goal of improving transport, and a three-day conference on "Human Security in a Globalized World' was held, also in the capital city.

CULTURE AND SOCIETY

Nomadic herders suffered their harshest winter in thirty years. Livestock losses were high, with approximately 1.8 million animals starving or freezing to death in the first quarter of the year. The situation was made worse by the drought-related poor hay crop of the previous summer; even if animals could dig through the deep snow that blanketed the steppes, there was not much food to find.

It was estimated that one of every fifteen animals died between January and April; approximately one third of Mongolia's people depend upon their herds for their livelihood. The International Committee of the Red Cross (ICRC) projected widespread starvation unless immediate aid was found. The ICRC launched an appeal for food, stating that 412,000 people were in need of assistance. Prime Minster Renchinnyamin Amarjargal said it would cost US$10 million to restock the lost animals. The World Bank, the United States, and other nations offered aid.

DIRECTORY

CENTRAL GOVERNMENT

Head of State

President
Natsagiyn Bagabandi, Office of the President

Ministers

Prime Minister
Rinchinnyamin Amarjargal, Office of the Prime Minister

Minister of External Relations of Mongolia
Nyam-Osorin Tuya, Ministry of External Relations of Mongolia

Minister of Health and Social Welfare
Dr. Sodov Sonin, Ministry of Health and Social Welfare
PHONE: +976 (1) 321485
FAX: +976 (1) 321485
E-MAIL: mhsw@magicnet.mn

Minister of Infrastructure Development
Gavaa Batkhuu, Ministry of Infrastructure Development, Street of Unite Nation 5/2, Government Building 2, Mongolia
E-MAIL: batkhuu@mid.pmis.gov.mn

Minister of Agriculture and Industry
Choinzongiin Sodnomtseren, Ministry of Agriculture and Industry

Minister of Defense
Sharavdorjiin Tuvdendorj, Ministry of Defense

Minister of Education
A. Battur, Ministry of Education

Minister of Environment
Mendsaikhan, Ministry of Environment

Minister of Finance
Yansanjavin Ochirsukh, Ministry of Finance

Minister of Justice
Dash Ganbold, Ministry of Justice

POLITICAL ORGANIZATIONS

Mongolian People's Revolutionary Party (MPRP)

TITLE: General Secretary
NAME: N. Enkhbayar

Democratic Union Coalition (DUC)

TITLE: General secretary
NAME: Mendsaihan Enhsaihan

Mongolian Social Democratic Party (MSDP)

TITLE: Chairman
NAME: Radnaasumbereliyn Gonchigdorj

Green Party (NYAM)

Mongolian Democratic Party of Believers (MDPB)

Jargalsaihan-MCP (Mongolian Conservative Party)

Democratic Power Coalition

TITLE: Chairman
NAME: D. Byambasuren

Mongolian National Solidarity Party (MNSP)

Bourgeois Party

TITLE: Chairman
NAME: Vargalsaihan

United Heritage Party (UHP)

TITLE: Chairman
NAME: B. Jamtsai

Independence Party

Traditional United Conservative Party

Mongolian United Private Property Owners Party

Workers' Party

DIPLOMATIC REPRESENTATION

Embassies in Mongolia

Canada
P.O. Box 243-210644, Ulaanbaatar, Mongolia
PHONE: +976 (1) 328281
FAX: +976 (1) 328289

Russia
Friendship Street 6, Ulaanbaatar, Mongolia
PHONE: +976 72851; 26836; 27506

JUDICIAL SYSTEM

Supreme Court

BROADCAST MEDIA

Mongol Radio and Television

Voice of Mongolia, CPO Box 365, Ulaanbaatar 13, Mongolia
PHONE: +976 (1) 327900
FAX: +976 (1) 326663
E-MAIL: radiomongolia@magicnet.com
WEBSITE: http://www.mongol.net/vom
TITLE: Editor-in-Chief
CONTACT: Ms. Oyunchimeg
LANGUAGE: Mongolian, English, Chinese, Russian, Japanese
BROADCASTS: 8 hours/day
TYPE: Government

COLLEGES AND UNIVERSITIES

Mongolian Technical University

PO Box 46/520, Ulaanbaatar, Mongolia
PHONE: +976 1324121
E-MAIL: badarch@mtu.edu.mn
WEBSITE: http://www.mtu.edu.mn

Mongolian Agricultural University

Research Institute of Animal Husbandry, Zaisan, Ulaanbaatar, Mongolia
PHONE: +976 1344185
E-MAIL: riah@magicnet.mn
WEBSITE: http://www.mol.mn/riah

National University of Mongolia

Ikhsurguulin Gudamj 1, PO Box 46/337, Ulaanbaatar, Mongolia
PHONE: +976 1320668
E-MAIL: num@num.edu.mn
WEBSITE: http://www.num.edu.mn/

NEWSPAPERS AND MAGAZINES

Hoh Ineed

PO 46, Box 971, Ulaanbaatar, Mongolia
TITLE: Editor
CONTACT: J. Chimedtseren
TYPE: General

The Mongol Messenger

PO Box 1514, Ulaanbaatar, Mongolia
PHONE: +976 325512
FAX: +976 327857
E-MAIL: montsame@magicnet.mn
WEBSITE: http://www.mol.mn/montsame/messenger.htm

PUBLISHERS

Mongolgosknigotorg

41 Ul Lenina, Ulan-Bator, Mongolia

State Press

Ulan-Bator, Mongolia
SUBJECTS: Geography, Geology, Government, Political Science, Law

RELIGIOUS ORGANIZATIONS

Due Mongolia's former status as a Communist country, few religious organizations exist within the country.

FURTHER READING

Articles

Johnson, Ian. "Mongolia's Democrats Lose Their Grip; Coalition's Split Likely to Restore Ex-Communists." *Wall Street Journal,* June 28, 2000, p. A14.

Keesings Record of World Events, March and April 2000.

MacLeod, Calum and Leslie Pappas. "Mongolian Makeover." *Newsweek International,* July 17, 2000, p. 32.

MacLeod, Calum, Melinda Liu, and Leslie Pappas. "The Politics of the Zud." *Newsweek International,* August 21, 2000, p. 47.

Mongol Messenger, June 15, July 2, and July 10, 2000.

"State Dept.: Mongolia Violent Crime Rising." *Travel Weekly,* June 19, 2000, vol. 59, no. 49, p. 16.

Books

Dun and Bradstreet's Export Guide to Mongolia. Parsippany, NJ: Dun & Bradstreet, 1999.

Soucek, Svatopluk. *A History of Inner Asia.* New York: Cambridge University Press, 2000.

MONGOLIA: STATISTICAL DATA

For sources and notes see "Sources of Statistics" at the front of each volume.

GEOGRAPHY

Geography

Area:

Total: 1.565 million sq km.

Land: 1.565 million sq km.

Land boundaries:

Total: 8,114 km.

Border countries: China 4,673 km, Russia 3,441 km.

Coastline: 0 km (landlocked).

Climate: desert; continental (large daily and seasonal temperature ranges).

Terrain: vast semidesert and desert plains; mountains in west and southwest; Gobi Desert in southeast.

Natural resources: oil, coal, copper, molybdenum, tungsten, phosphates, tin, nickel, zinc, wolfram, fluorspar, gold.

Land use:

Arable land: 1%

Permanent crops: 0%

Permanent pastures: 80%

Forests and woodland: 9%

Other: 10% (1993 est.).

HUMAN FACTORS

Demographics (A)

	1990	1995	1998	2000	2010	2020	2030	2040	2050
Population	2,218	2,429	2,542	2,616	3,040	3,462	3,783	4,038	4,181
Life expectancy - males	58.3	60.1	61.1	61.8	65.1	68.1	70.7	72.9	74.8
Life expectancy - females	62.1	64.1	65.3	66.1	69.9	73.2	76.1	78.6	80.6
Birth rate (per 1,000)	35.9	24.6	21.7	21.8	21.6	16.8	14.6	13.4	11.6
Death rate (per 1,000)	10.0	8.0	7.4	7.2	6.5	6.3	6.9	8.3	9.6
Women of reproductive age (15-49 yrs.)	523.9	617.8	679.0	723.1	897.7	950.5	994.7	956.6	957.4
Fertility rate	4.5	2.8	2.4	2.4	2.3	2.1	2.0	1.9	1.8

Except as noted, values for vital statistics are in thousands; life expectancy is in years.

Health Personnel

	National Data	World Data (wtd ave)
Total health expenditure as a percentage of GDP, 1990-1998[a]		
Public sector	4.3	2.5
Private sector	0.4	2.9
Total[b]	4.7	5.5
Health expenditure per capita in U.S. dollars, 1990-1998[a]		
Purchasing power parity	68	561
Total	23	483
Availability of health care facilities per 100,000 people		
Hospital beds 1990-1998[a]	1,150	330
Doctors 1992-1995[a]	268	122
Nurses 1992-1995[a]	452	248

Health Indicators

	National Data	World Data
Life expectancy at birth (years)		
1980	58	61
1998	66	67
Daily per capita supply of calories		
1970	2,133	2,358
1997	1,917	2,791
Daily per capital supply of protein		
1997 (grams)	71	74
Total fertility rate (births per woman)		
1980	5.3	3.7
1998	2.5	2.7
Population with access (%)		
To safe water (1990-96)	68	NA
To sanitation (1990-96)	NA	NA
People living with (1997)		
Tuberculosis (cases per 100,000)	116.3	60.4
HIV/AIDS (% aged 15 - 49 years)	0.01	0.99

Infants and Malnutrition

	National Data	World Data (wtd ave)
Under 5 mortality rate (1989)	150	NA
% of infants with low birthweight (1992-98)[1]	10	17
Births attended by skilled health staff (% of total births 1996-98)	99	52
% fully immunized at 1 year of age (1995-98)[1]		
TB	95	82
DPT	94	77
Polio	94	77
Measles	93	74
Prevalence of child malnutrition (1992-98)[1] (based on weight for age, % of children under 5 years)	9	30

Ethnic Division

Mongol 90%

Kazakh 4%

Other 6%

Religion

Predominantly Tibetan Buddhist, Muslim 4%. Previously limited religious activity because of communist regime.

Major Languages

Khalkha Mongol 90%, Turkic, Russian.

EDUCATION

Public Education Expenditures

	1997
Public expenditures on education as % of GNP	5.7
Expenditures per student as % of GNP per capita	
Primary	NA
Secondary	46.1
Tertiary	37.7
Teachers' compensation as % of total current education expenditures	NA
Pupils per teacher at the primary level	31
Duration of primary education in years	8
World data for comparison	
Public expenditures on education as % of GNP (mean)	4.8
Pupils per teacher at the primary level (wtd ave)	33
Duration of primary education in years (mean)	9

Educational Attainment (B)

	1995	1997
Gross enrollment ratio (%)		
Primary level	88.1	88.4
Secondary level	59.2	56.2
Tertiary level	15.2	19.0

Literacy Rates (A)

In thousands and percent	1990	1995	2000	2010
Illiterate population (15+ yrs.)	259	256	250	232
Literacy rate - total adult pop. (%)	79.9	82.9	85.6	89.5
Literacy rate - males (%)	86.6	88.6	90.3	92.8
Literacy rate - females (%)	73.2	77.2	80.8	86.2

GOVERNMENT & LAW

Political Parties

State Great Hural	% of vote	no. of seats
Democratic Union Coalition (DUC)	66%	50
Mongolian National Democratic Party (MNDP)		34
Mongolian Social Democratic Party (MSDP)		13

(Continued on next page.)

Military Affairs (A)

	1990	1992	1995	1996	1997
Military expenditures					
Current dollars (mil.)	71[e]	20	20	21	19
1997 constant dollars (mil.)	84[e]	22	21	22	19
Armed forces (000)	32	21	18	20	20
Gross national product (GNP)					
Current dollars (mil.)	829	782	902	937	984
1997 constant dollars (mil.)	971	867	934	953	984
Central government expenditures (CGE)					
1997 constant dollars (mil.)	711	242	283	311	364
People (mil.)	2.2	2.3	2.5	2.5	2.5
Military expenditure as % of GNP	8.6	2.6	2.3	2.3	1.9
World data on military expenditure as % of GNP	4.5	3.4	2.7	2.6	2.6
Military expenditure as % of CGE	11.7	9.3	7.4	7.0	5.1
World data on military expenditure as % of CGE	17.0	12.5	10.5	10.3	10.2
Military expenditure per capita (1997 $)	38	10	9	9	7
World data on military expenditure per capita (1997 $)	242	173	146	143	145
Armed forces per 1,000 people (soldiers)	14.4	9.2	7.3	8.0	7.9
World data on armed forces per 1,000 people (soldiers)	5.3	4.5	4.1	3.9	3.8
GNP per capita (1997 $)	438	374	381	382	388
Total imports[7]					
Current dollars (mil.)	924	418	415	451	443
1997 constant dollars (mil.)	1,082	463	430	459	443
Total exports[7]					
Current dollars (mil.)	661	389	473	424	418
1997 constant dollars (mil.)	774	431	490	431	418
Arms as percent of total imports[8]	0	0	0	0	0
Arms as percent of total exports[8]	0	0	0	0	0

Political Parties (cont.)

State Great Hural	% of vote	no. of seats
Independents		3
Mongolian People's Revolutionary Party (MPRP)	33%	25
Mongolian Conservative Party (MCP)	1%	1

Elections were last held 30 June 1996 (next to be held in June 2000).

Government Budgets (A)

Year: 1998

Total Expenditures: 201,278 Millions of Togrogs

Expenditures as a percentage of the total by function:

- General public services and public order 12.30
- Defense 8.32
- Education 8.03
- Health 2.12
- Social Security and Welfare 25.30
- Housing and community amenities 0.72
- Recreational, cultural, and religious affairs 3.40
- Fuel and energy 4.49
- Agriculture, forestry, fishing, and hunting 2.13
- Mining, manufacturing, and construction 1.35
- Transportation and communication 3.16
- Other economic affairs and services 0.71

Crime

Crime volume (for 1998)

- Crimes reported 22,737
- Total persons convicted 19,668
- Crimes per 100,000 population 938

Persons responsible for offenses

- Total number suspects .19,632
- Total number of female suspects 1,414
- Total number of juvenile suspects 1,453

LABOR FORCE

Total Labor Force (A)

1.256 million (1998).

Labor Force by Occupation

Primarily herding/agricultural.

Unemployment Rate

4.5% (1998)

PRODUCTION SECTOR

Energy Production

Production . . . . .2.66 billion kWh

Production by source

- Fossil fuel 100%
- Hydro 0%
- Nuclear 0%
- Other 0%

Exports . . . . .0 kWh

Data for 1998.

Energy Consumption

Consumption . . . . .2.816 billion kWh

Imports .342.000 million kWh

Data for 1998.

(Continued on next page.)

MANUFACTURING SECTOR

GDP & Manufacturing Summary (B)

	1980	1985	1990	1993	1994	1995
Gross Domestic Product						
Millions of 1990 dollars	1,139	1,587	1,869	1,476	1,525	1,618
Growth rate in percent	3.43	6.19	−2.07	−1.60	3.30	6.10
Per capita (in 1990 dollars)	685	831	843	624	632	657
Manufacturing Value Added						
Millions of 1990 dollars	288	428	521	369	379	403[e]
Growth rate in percent	8.03	3.07	2.43	−4.61	2.82	6.20[e]
Manufacturing share in percent of current prices	24.2	26.6	27.9	NA	NA	NA

Transportation

Highways:

Total: 49,250 km.

Paved: 1,674 km.

Unpaved: 47,576 km (1998 est.).

Note: much of the unpaved rural road system consists of rough cross-country tracks.

Waterways: 400 km of principal routes (1999).

Airports: 34 (1994 est.).

Airports - with unpaved runways: 26.

Top Agriculture Products

Wheat, barley, potatoes, forage crops; sheep, goats, cattle, camels, horses.

Top Mining Products (B)

Mineral resources include: oil, coal, copper, molybdenum, tungsten, phosphates, tin, nickel, zinc, wolfram, fluorspar, gold.

COMMUNICATIONS

Daily Newspapers

	National Data	World Data for Comparison
Daily Newspapers		
Number of Dailies	4	8,391
Total Circulation (000)	68	548,000
Circulation per 1,000 inhabitants	27	96

Telecommunications

Telephones - main lines in use: 93,800 (1998).

Telephones - mobile cellular: NA

Telephone system:

Domestic: NA

International: satellite earth station - 1 Intersputnik (Indian Ocean Region).

Radio broadcast stations: AM 12, FM 2, shortwave 13 (1998).

Radios: 360,000 (1997).

Television broadcast stations: 1 (plus 18 provincial repeaters) (1997).

Televisions: 118,000 (1997).

Internet Service Providers (ISPs): NA

FINANCE, ECONOMICS, & TRADE

Economic Indicators

National product: GDP—purchasing power parity—$6.1 billion (1999 est.).

National product real growth rate: 3.5% (1999 est.).

National product per capita: $2,320 (1999 est.).

Inflation rate—consumer price index: 9.5% (1998).

Exchange Rates

Exchange rates:

Tughriks (Tug) per US$1

December 1999	1,070.39
1999	1,072.37
1998	840.83
1997	789.99
1996	548.40
1995	448.61

Balance of Payments

	1994	1995	1996	1997	1998
Exports of goods (f.o.b.)	367	451	423	494	434
Imports of goods (f.o.b.)	−333	−426	−460	−453	−496
Trade balance	34	25	−36	41	−62
Services - debits	−91	−95	−113	−105	−144
Services - credits	45	57	56	53	78
Private transfers (net)	NA	NA	6	4	6
Government transfers (net)	78	77	64	48	49
Overall balance	46	39	−37	28	−77

Top Import Origins

$472.4 million (f.o.b., 1998)

Origins (1998)

Russia	30.6%
China	13.3%
Japan	11.7%
South Korea	7.5%
United States	6.9%

Top Export Destinations

$316.8 million (f.o.b., 1998)

Destinations (1998)

China	30.1%
Switzerland	21.5%
Russia	12.1%
South Korea	9.7%
United States	8.1%

Foreign Aid

Recipient: $250 million (1998 est.).

Import/Export Commodities

Import Commodities	Export Commodities
Machinery and equipment	Copper
Fuels	Livestock
Food products	Animal products
Industrial consumer goods	Cashmere
Chemicals	Wool
Building materials	Hides
Sugar	Fluorspar
Tea	Other nonferrous metals

MONTENEGRO

CAPITAL: Podgorica.

FLAG: The flag is comprised of three horizontal bands of blue (top), white, and red (bottom).

MONETARY UNIT: 1 Yugoslav New Dinar (YD) = 100 paras.

HOLIDAYS: St. Vitus Day, 28 June.

TIME: 1 PM = noon GMT.

LOCATION AND SIZE: Montenegro lies in the southeastern region of Europe, bordered by the Adriatic Sea, between Albania and Bosnia-Herzegovina (44°N, 21°E). It comprises a total mass of 13,938 sq. km, including 13,724 sq. km of land and 214 sq. km of water. It shares its borders with Albania (173 km), Bosnia-Herzegovina (215 km), and Croatia (25 km). The internal boundary between Montenegro and Serbia is 211 km.

CLIMATE: Montenegro is often exposed to extremes as it is subjected to destructive earthquakes and the Adriatic climate along its coast. Its summers are hot and dry, with autumns and relatively cold winters experiencing heavy snowfall inland. There is year-round precipitation, but it is heaviest from October through December.

INTRODUCTORY SURVEY

RECENT HISTORY

Montenegro is part of the Balkan States, a group of nations located in the largely mountainous region of inland far southeastern Europe. Germany invaded the region in April of 1941 leading to later partial occupation by Italian troops. Montenegro experienced continuous fighting through World War II until 1944 when communist factions gained control. Under a 1946 Yugoslavian federal constitution, Montenegro gained recognition as one of six autonomous federated units. The socialist government ruled for over forty years under President Josip Tito who poured considerable economic investments into Montenegrin industry leading to economic stability. However as the government began to weaken in the late 1980s inter-ethnic tensions mounted. Disintegration of the Yugoslav nation came in 1991 with only Montenegro choosing to remain with Serbia in a newly constituted federation.

Disputes over political dominance and boundaries raged through the 1990s between Bosnia, Herzegovina, Serbia, Montenegro, Croatia, Macedonia, and Kosovo. Charges of extensive human rights violations by the Serbian military fighting ethnic Albanians in Kosovo in the late 1990s further spurred interests in Montenegro for independence from Serbia. By the late 1990s Montenegro more assertively challenged the validity of the federation's government, actually boycotting the federation's parliament, halting the transfer of tax revenue to the federation, and increasingly behaving as an independent nation. By late 1999 tensions mounted that Montenegro could become the next Kosovo in a struggle for independence from the Yugoslav federation. Montenegrin leaders were striving for a public referendum on independence possibly by early 2000.

GOVERNMENT

Following disintegration of communist Yugoslavia in 1991, Montenegro is a constituent republic and Serbia's junior partner in the Federal Republic of Yugoslavia. The United States denied recognition of the Republic as a continuation of the former Socialist Federal Republic of Yugoslavia.

Through much of the 1990s Montenegro operated under two governments. The new Yugoslav federation operates under a constitution adopted in 1992. Chief of state is the federation president,

which was President Slobodan Milosevic from 1997 until 2000 when he lost the election to Vojislav Kostunica. The Federal Assembly elects the president to four-year terms. The Federal Executive Council serves as cabinet. A prime minister, selected by the president and approved by parliament, manages the federation's government. The two chambers of parliament, known as the Federal Assembly, are The Chamber of the Republics composed of forty members, twenty each from Serbia and Montenegro, and the Chamber of Citizens consisting of 138 members elected by popular vote. Federal Assembly members serve four-year terms.

Though a partner with Serbia in the Yugoslav federation, Montenegro and Serbia each maintain their own republican governments. The chief of state is the President of Montenegro, which was Milo Djukanovic since January 1998. Heading Montenegrin government is a prime minister and deputy prime minister. The legislative body of Montenegro is the unicameral National Assembly composed of eighty-five members elected by popular vote. Suffrage is universal for residents over eighteen years of age and those employed over sixteen years of age.

The Federation and Montenegro enjoy little international recognition, being excluded from the UN General Assembly, the International Monetary Fund, and the World Bank. As the Federation was coming under increasing authoritarian rule with Milosevic in the late 1990s, efforts by Montenegro to become a more open democratic polity were growing.

Judiciary

Based on a civil law system, in 1997 Montenegro had two District Courts, fifteen Communal Courts, and two Economic Courts of Law. The Yugoslav Federation has a Federal Supreme Court, a Federal Constitutional Court, and military courts. Supreme Court judges and other Federal Court judges are elected by the Republic's Federal Assembly to nine-year terms.

Political Parties

Given the political instability of the region, numerous political parties are active in Montenegro and the Republic. Throughout much of the 1990s the ruling political party in Yugoslavia was the Serbian Socialist Party (SPS), the former Communist Party of the Yugoslav SFR with its leader Slobodan Milosevic. Other political organizations include the Serbian Radical Party, Serbian Renewal Movement, Yugoslav United Left, Party of Democratic Action, and the Liberal Alliance of Montenegro among others. During the 1996 Chamber of Citizens public elections, political parties winning most of the 138 seats included the Coalition of the Left, Zajedno (Together), Democratic Party of Socialists of Montenegro, and the Radical Serb Party. In the 1998 Montenegrin elections, the Coalition for a Better Life outgained the Socialist People's Party of Montenegro.

DEFENSE

Since 1997 Montenegro has assembled a fairly well armed police force of approximately 12,000 men, roughly equivalent in size to the Yugoslavian Federation troops stationed in Montenegro. NATO bombing in early 1999 primarily of Serbian targets also hit hard at Yugoslav army and navy facilities in Montenegro. Montenegro in general was spared much of the substantial destruction inflicted on Serbia. Traditionally, males over nineteen years of age were required to serve military duty in Montenegro for twelve to fifteen months.In 1999 Serbia and Montenegro spent $911 million on defense, or 6.5 percent of GDP.

ECONOMIC AFFAIRS

Highly destructive warfare since the 1991 collapse of the Yugoslav socialist federation greatly disrupted economies in the region. Output in Montenegro dropped significantly in 1992 and 1993. With many physical assets destroyed, reliance increased on other nations in the area for imports. A new currency was introduced in 1993 following a brief period of rampant inflation. Relative price stability resulted from 1995 to 1997 but ended in 1998. The Serbian emphasis on political dominance came at a cost of economic stability for the Republic and Montenegro.

Historically, Montenegro relied economically on cereal-grain farming and sheep and goat raising until the mid-20th century. In 1998 potatoes and sheep dominated agricultural activity. Following World War II Yugoslavia invested large sums into electrical power production in Montenegro to fuel steel and iron and non-ferrous-metal industries in addition to processing of agricultural products.

Exports largely to neighboring countries and Italy from Serbia and Montenegro were estimated in 1998 at $2.3 billion. Exports were primarily manufactured goods, processed foods, and raw materials. Imports constituting an estimated $3.9 million primarily came from Germany, Italy, and Russia in 1998. Famous for its Adriatic coastal resorts, a significant national debt was accumulating as war had significantly reduced Montenegro's tourist trade by late 1999.

Public Finance

Being the junior partner with Serbia in the Federation, by late 1999 Montenegro's economy amounted to only 5 percent of Serbia's shattered economy owing to international sanctions and war. By the end of the 1990s smuggling had become a key contributor to the Montenegrin economy. By 1999 the smuggling of cigarettes into Italy was estimated to be placing approximately $40 million dollars into Montenegro's economy annually and helping to address budget deficits. As part of Yugoslavia, Montenegro remains under certain economic sanctions including denial of access to funding institutions such as the World Bank and International Monetary Fund that could greatly aid economic recovery and development. By late 1999 Montenegro established a second currency, tied to the German mark, in addition to the Yugoslav dinar. External debt of Serbia and Montenegro was estimated in 1999 to be $14.1 billion.

Income

The gross domestic product (GDP) for Serbia and Montenegro estimated in 1999 was $20.6 billion at a real growth rate of 20 percent. Per capita GDP purchasing power parity was estimated at $1,800. According to 1998 estimates heavy industry was a large contributor at 50 percent with agriculture 20 percent and services 30 percent of GDP.

Industry

Industrial production in 1997 included lignite and bauxite minerals, carded cotton yarn, and heavy manufactured items. In 1999 a single large aluminum factory represented approximately half of Montenegro's gross national product. Increased privatization of industry is a goal as Montenegro seeks to become more Westernized and less tied to Serbia. Industrial growth rate for Serbia and Montenegro was estimated in 1999 to be −22 percent.

Banking and Finance

International sanctions rendered the Federation's banking system non-functional. The National Bank is the Federation's bank of issue. The larger commercial banks could still not make international transfer of funds. Foreign assets remained frozen. In 1998 the National Bank's reserves amounted to less than US$200 million.

SOCIAL WELFARE

Given the region's pervasive political turmoil, the unemployment rate was estimated in 1997 at 33 percent. The social security system of the Federation consists of sickness and maternity benefits, workers compensation, unemployment benefits, and family allowances. Survivors and dependents of veterans disabled or killed in action are eligible for benefits. Traditional gender roles keep women from enjoying equal status with me.

Healthcare

Montenegro suffers from poor nutrition and significant health problems. Infant mortality in Montenegro has consistently been high. The communist government introduced a national health insurance program following World War II and successfully fought many serious diseases that had been earlier rampant. Pregnant women, infants, and children below age sixteen receive complete health care. Life expectancy estimated in 2000 was 75.5 years for the total population with 71.5 years for males and 79.8 for females.

Housing

Yugoslavia in general suffers from crowded housing and poor sanitation services. Montenegro's more rural character alleviates some of the problems. Most villagers build their own homes.

EDUCATION

In 1997 Montenegro had 485 primary schools, forty-three secondary schools, and one high school. Twelve schools of higher learning were also available. Education in the Yugoslav republics is compulsory for eight years. The adult literacy rate in 1995 was 98 percent.

2000 KEY EVENTS TIMELINE

February

- Montenegrin President Milo Djukanovic says his republic faces the danger of attack by forces loyal to Yugoslav President Slobodan Milosevic.

March

- Serbian authorities impose severe restrictions on goods passing across the border from Montenegro to Serbia. Even items for personal use may not be allowed to be carried across the border.

June

- On June 11 results from local elections indicate that Montenegrins are almost evenly divided between those who want to declare independence from Serbia and those who wish to remain part of a united Yugoslavia. Supporters of anti-Milosevic leader Milo Djukanovic win a narrow majority.
- Montenegrin President Milo Djukanovic says his republic faces the danger of attack by forces loyal to Yugoslav President Slobodan Milosevic.

July

- Montenegro rejects constitutional changes that will pave the way for Slobodan Milosevic to extend his term of office by eight years. Montenegrin and Serbian leaders agree to work toward new terms for their union.

August

- Montenegrins plan to boycott September 24 elections because of suspicions that they are rigged. The country makes moves towards independence from Serbia.

November

- Montenegrin President Milo Djukanovic calls for independence from Yugoslavia at a Balkans summit in Croatia on November 24.

December

- President Djukanovic travels to Belgrade to attend a meeting of Yugoslavia's Supreme Defense Council convened by Vojislav Kostunica who defeated Slobodan Milosevic in the presidential election. It is Djukanovic's first visit to Belgrade in two years.

ANALYSIS OF EVENTS: 2000

BUSINESS AND THE ECONOMY

Montenegro's adoption of the deutsche mark (DM) instead of the Yugoslav dinar (YD) as its official currency in 1999 helped stabilize its economy in spite of the continuing standoff with the central bank in Belgrade, which had then cut off all transactions with the republic. (The dinar had been devalued eighteen times since 1991.)

Tourism, a traditional staple of Montenegro's economy, has been moribund for the past decade due to recurring warfare in the Balkans.

Production-sharing contracts were awarded to two British oil companies, Medusa Oil and Gas, a subsidiary of Ramco Energy, and Star Petroleum. It was considered possible that drilling might resume in 2001.

GOVERNMENT AND POLITICS

Looking ahead to possible independence from Serbia, Montenegro's government worked on strengthening its ties with neighbors in the region. Prime Minister Filip Vujanovic met early in the year with the prime ministers of Macedonia and Albania to discuss infrastructure links and control of corruption and terrorism.

Serbian opposition leader Vuk Draskovic, who had taken refuge in Montenegro in May after the government of President Slobodan Milosevic shut down his independent television station in Belgrade, survived an assassination attempt the following month. Draskovic received only minor head wounds after being shot at by two gunmen outside his residence in Montenegro.

The June local elections in Montenegro's two largest cities—Podgorica and Herceg Novi—reflected the deep political divisions in a republic still torn between independence and loyalty to Serbia, the dominant partner in what remained of the Yugoslav federation. Montenegro's pro-Western president, Milo Djukanovic, and his governing coalition won a narrow victory in Podgorica, while in

Herceg Novi, forces supportive of Milosevic won control of the local assembly.

Montenegrins were dealt a political blow by changes in the Yugoslavian constitution pushed through by Milosevic in June. The major change gave the federation president a way to renew his term in office for as long as eight more years. The new provisions also decreased Montenegro's political representation in the national government by mandating direct popular elections to the powerful upper house of the legislature. Many observers saw this move as an attempt to incite yet more warfare in the Balkans by inflaming opposition forces in Montenegro, a trademark Milosevic tactic for reviving flagging popular support. Further incitements, such as roadblocks and military exercises, took place in the weeks leading up to the September 24 national presidential election called by the Yugoslav president.

The presidential election (which was boycotted by Montenegro) resulted in a crisis when Milosevic refused to concede although his opponent, Vojislav Kostunica, appeared to have won a clear majority of the vote. Kostunica rejected the runoff election demanded by Milosevic, and a week and a half of growing protest ultimately led to the downfall of Milosevic on October 5, when opposition forces converged on Belgrade, taking over the parliament building and setting fire to the state television headquarters. Although Yugoslavia's new president, Vojislav Kostunica, called reconciliation with Montenegro a priority, Montenegro's ruling coalition declined to join Kostunica's transitional government. However, the socialist opposition accepted the invitation. A personal meeting between Kostunica and Djukanovic failed to produce a decisive understanding. Among the demands made by Montenegro were the disbanding of a Yugoslav army battalion stationed in the republic and a redefinition of the relationship between the two republics, possibly leading to looser confederation between them. Montenegro's government planned to hold a referendum by the end of June on loosening ties with Serbia.

CULTURE AND SOCIETY

Montenegro remained a politically and culturally divided republic. Although the majority claimed a distinct Montenegrin identity, about one-quarter of its population of 600,000 considered themselves Serbs, while one-third thought of themselves as Montenegrins of Serbian heritage. Over one-quarter were in favor of leaving Yugoslavia intact, while slightly fewer favored a loose confederation with Serbia, and over one-third wanted complete independence.

Holding themselves apart from Serbia, Montenegrins had begun democratic reforms even before the ouster of Slobodan Milosevic from the Yugoslav presidency, redrafting their civil and penal codes with help from the American Bar Association, privatizing industries, and cracking down on organized crime exported from nearby Italy.

DIRECTORY

CENTRAL GOVERNMENT

Montenegro and Serbia assert that together they compose a joint independent state, the Federal Republic of Yugoslavia. The United States does not formally recognize this entity as a state. Both Montenegro and Serbia have a significant amount of autonomy. Members of the governments of the Federal Republic of Yugoslavia and the Republic of Montenegro are noted here.

FEDERAL REPUBLIC OF YUGOSLAVIA

Head of State

President of the Federal Republic of Yugoslavia
Vojislav Kostunica, Office of the Federal President, Savezna Skupstina, 11000 Belgrade, Serbia, Yugoslavia

Prime Minister
Momir Bulatovic, Office of the Federal Prime Minister, Palace of Federation, Belgrade, Serbia, Yugoslavia
PHONE: +381 (11) 3117087

Ministers

Deputy Prime Minister
Vladan Kutlesic, Office of the Deputy Prime Minister

Deputy Prime Minister
Zoran Lilic, Office of the Deputy Prime Minister

Deputy Prime Minister
Nikola Sainovic, Office of the Deputy Prime Minister

Deputy Prime Minister
Danilo Vuksanovic, Office of the Deputy Prime Minister

Deputy Prime Minister
Jovan Zebic, Office of the Deputy Prime Minister

Minister of Agriculture
Nedeljko Sipovac, Ministry of Agriculture

Minister for Coordination of Relations with International Organizations
Nebojsa Maljkovic, Ministry for Coordination of Relations with International Organizations

Minister of Defense
Pavle Bulatovic, Ministry of Defense

Minister of Domestic Trade
Slobodan Nenadovic, Ministry of Domestic Trade

Minister for Economy and Industry
Rade Filipovic, Ministry for Economy and Industry

Minister of Finance
Bozidar Gazivoda, Ministry of Finance

Minister of Foreign Affairs
Zivadin Jovanovic, Ministry of Foreign Affairs

Minister of Foreign Trade
Borisa Vukovic, Ministry of Foreign Trade

Minister of Internal Affairs
Zoran Sokolovic, Ministry of Internal Affairs

Minister of Justice
Zoran Knezevic, Ministry of Justice

Minister of Labor, Health, and Social Policy
Miroslav Ivanisevic, Ministry of Labor, Health, and Social Policy

Minister of Science, Development, and Ecology
Jagos Zelenovic, Ministry of Science, Development, and Ecology

Minister of Sport
Velizar Djeric, Ministry of Sport

Minister of Telecommunication
Dojcilo Radojevic, Ministry of Telecommunication

Minister of Trade and Tourism
Djordje Siradovic, Ministry of Trade and Tourism

Minister of Transportation
Dejan Drobnjakovic, Ministry of Transportation

GOVERNMENT OF THE REPUBLIC OF MONTENEGRO

Head of State

President
Milo Djukanovic, Office of the President
E-MAIL: predsjednik@cg.yu

Ministers

Prime Minister
Filip Vujanovic, Office of the Prime Minister, Podgorica, Republic of Montenegro, Yugoslavia
E-MAIL: vlada@cg.yu

Minister of Justice
Dragan Soc, Ministry of Justice

Minister of Interior
Vukasin Maras, Ministry of Interior

Minister of Foreign Affairs
Branko Perovic, Ministry of Foreign Affairs
E-MAIL: smipdsik@eunet.yu

Minister of Finance
Bozidar Gazivoda, Ministry of Finance

Minister of Education and Science
Dragan Kujovic, Ministry of Education and Science

Minister of Culture
Budimir Dubak, Ministry of Culture

Minister of Energy, Industry and Mining
Vojin Djukanovic, Ministry of Energy, Industry and Mining

Minister of Transportation
Jusuf Kalamperovic, Ministry of Transportation

Minister of Agriculture, Forestry and Water Management
Milutin Simovic, Ministry of Agriculture, Forestry and Water Management

Minister of Tourism
Vlado Mitrovic, Ministry of Tourism

Minister of Trade
Ramo Bralic, Ministry of Trade

Minister of Urban Development
Radovan Bakic, Ministry of Urban Development

Minister of Environment Protection
Miladin Vukotic, Ministry of Environment Protection

Minister of Health
Miomir Mugosa, Ministry of Health

Minister of Labor and Social Care
Predrag Drecun, Ministry of Labor and Social Care

Minister of Religion
Slobodan Tomovic, Ministry of Religion

Minister for the Protection of National and Ethical Minorities
Ljuidj Juncaj, Ministry for the Protection of National and Ethical Minorities

Minister of Sports
Slavoljub Stijepovic, Ministry of Sports

POLITICAL ORGANIZATIONS

Democratic Party of Socialists

TITLE: President
NAME: Milo Dujkanovic

Liberal Alliance of Montenegro

TITLE: President
NAME: Slavko Perovic

Social Democratic Party

TITLE: President
NAME: Zarko Rakcevic

Albanian Democratic League

TITLE: President
NAME: Mehmed Bardhi

Albanian Democratic Union

TITLE: President
NAME: Fermat Dinaso

JUDICIAL SYSTEM

Supreme Court

Federal Court

District Court

Economic Court

BROADCAST MEDIA

Radiotelevizija Crne Gore Montenegro

Cetinjski put bb, 81000 Podogorica, Montenegro
PHONE: +381 (81) 225999
FAX: +381 (81) 225588

COLLEGES AND UNIVERSITIES

Univerzitet Crne Gore

Centinjski put bb, 81000 Podgorica, Montenegro

NEWSPAPERS AND MAGAZINES

Pobjeda

Bulevar Revolucije 11, 81000 Podgorica, Montenegro
PHONE: +381 245955
FAX: +381 244475
E-MAIL: pobjeda@cg.yu
WEBSITE: http://www.pobjeda.co.yu
TITLE: Director
CONTACT: Dragan Djurovic

Trend

Univerzitet Crne Gore, Cetinjski put bb, Postanski fah 218, 81000 Podgorica, Montenegro
PHONE: +381 224761
E-MAIL: trendpress@cg.yu
WEBSITE: http://www.trend.cg.yu
TITLE: Director
CONTACT: Goran Jevric

RELIGIOUS ORGANIZATIONS

As the former Socialist Federal Republic of Yugoslavia, religion in Montenegro has been repressed since the 1950s. Although most of the population is officially atheist, in accordance with Communist views, 65 percent ascribe to the Orthodox Church, with small minorities of Muslims, Roman Catholics, and Protestants.

FURTHER READING

Articles

Gall, Carlotta. "Blockade Is Raising Tension for Serbia's Smaller Partner." *New York Times,* April 2, 2000, p. 10.

———. "New Yugoslav Leader Tries to Calm Wary Montenegro." *New York Times,* October 18, 2000, p. A8.

"Marks Only in Montenegro." *New York Times,* November 10, 2000, p. C10.

"Plan for Yugoslav Union." *New York Times,* July 15, 2000, p. A2.

Government Publications

United States. *Continuation of National Emergency with Respect to the Federal Republic of Yugoslavia, the Bosnian Serbs, and Kosovo.* Washington, DC: G.P.O., 2000.

MONTENEGRO: STATISTICAL DATA

For sources and notes see "Sources of Statistics" at the front of each volume. The following information is for Montenegro and Serbia combined unless otherwise noted.

GEOGRAPHY

Geography (Montenegro)

Area:

Total: 13,938 sq km.

Land: 13,724 sq km.

Land boundaries:

Total: 2,246 km (includes both Serbia and Montenegro).

Border countries: Albania 173 km, Bosnia and Herzegovina 215 km, Croatia (south) 25 km,

Note: the internal boundary between Montenegro and Serbia is 211 km.

Coastline: 199 km.

Climate: in the north, continental climate (cold winters and hot, humid summers with well distributed rainfall); central portion, continental and Mediterranean climate; to the south, Adriatic climate along the coast, hot, dry summers and autumns and relatively cold winters with heavy snowfall inland.

Terrain: extremely varied; to the north, rich fertile plains; to the east, limestone ranges and basins; to the southeast, ancient mountains and hills; to the southwest, extremely high shoreline with no islands off the coast.

Natural resources: oil, gas, coal, antimony, copper, lead, zinc, nickel, gold, pyrite, chrome, hydro power.

HUMAN FACTORS

Ethnic Division

Serb	62.6%
Albanian	16.5%
Montenegrin	5.0%
Yugoslav	3.4%
Hungarian	3.3%
Other	9.2%

Data for 1991

Demographics (A) (Montenegro)

	1990	1995	1998	2000	2010	2020	2030	2040	2050
Population	NA	632.9	673.0	680.2	713.1	744.8	762.3	768.0	757.2
Life expectancy - males	NA	70.3	71.0	71.4	73.6	75.4	76.8	78.0	79.0
Life expectancy - females	NA	78.8	79.4	79.8	81.6	83.1	84.3	85.2	85.9
Birth rate (per 1,000)	NA	15.0	15.0	14.9	13.8	11.9	11.1	10.5	9.6
Death rate (per 1,000)	NA	7.8	7.8	7.9	8.5	9.0	9.6	10.9	11.9
Women of reproductive age (15-49 yrs.)	NA	161.4	175.1	176.3	173.2	172.6	167.6	158.2	153.0
Fertility rate	NA	2.0	2.0	2.0	1.9	1.9	1.8	1.8	1.7

Except as noted, values for vital statistics are in thousands; life expectancy is in years.

Religion

Orthodox	65%
Muslim	19%
Roman Catholic	4%
Protestant	1%
Other	11%

Major Languages

Serbian	95%
Albanian	5%

GOVERNMENT & LAW

Political Parties

Federal Assembly (Savezna Skupstina)	no. of seats
Chamber of Citizens	
Serbian Socialist Party/Yugoslav United Left/New Democracy (SPS/JUL/ND)	64
Zajedno coalition	22
Democratic Party of Socialists of Montenegro (DPS)	20
Serbian Radical Party (SRS)	16
People's Party of Montenegro (NS)	8
Alliance of Vojvodina Hungarians (SVM)	3
Other	5

Elections for the Chamber of Citizens were last held 3 November 1996 (next to be held in 2000).

Military Affairs (B)

Military age	19
Availability	
Males age 15-49	178,234
Fit for military service	
Males age 15-49	143,769
Reaching military age annually	
Males	5,697

Data for 2000 est.

LABOR FORCE

Total Labor Force (A)

1.6 million (1999 est.).

Unemployment Rate

30% (1999 est.)

PRODUCTION SECTOR

Energy Production

Production	38.84 billion kWh
Production by source	
Fossil fuel	67.88%
Hydro	32.12%
Nuclear	0%
Other	0%
Exports	20 million kWh

Data for 1998.

Energy Consumption

Consumption	36.141 billion kWh
Imports	40.000 million kWh

Data for 1998.

Transportation

Highways:

Total: 48,603 km.

Paved: 28,822 km (including 560 km of expressways).

Unpaved: 19,781 km (1998 est.).

Note: because of the 1999 Kosovo conflict, many road bridges were destroyed; since the end of the conflict in June 1999, Serbia has had a rapid reconstruction program to either reconstruct bridges or build by-pass routes.

Waterways: 587 km; Danube River runs through Serbia connecting Europe with the Black Sea; in early 2000 the river was obstructed at Novi Sad due to a pontoon bridge; a canal system in north Serbia is available to by-pass damage, however, lock size is limited (1999).

Pipelines: crude oil 415 km; petroleum products 130 km; natural gas 2,110 km.

Airports: 5 (1999 est.).

Airports - with paved runways: 3.

Airports - with unpaved runways: 2.

Top Agriculture Products

Cereals, fruits, vegetables, tobacco, olives; cattle, sheep, goats.

Top Mining Products (B)

Mineral resources include: oil, gas, coal, antimony, copper, lead, zinc, nickel, gold, pyrite, chrome.

MANUFACTURING SECTOR

GDP & Manufacturing Summary (C)

Total GDP (1999 est.)	$20.6 billion
Real growth rate (1999 est.)	-20%
Per capita (1999 est.)	$1,800

Composition by sector

Agriculture	20%
Industry	50%
Services	30%

Values in purchasing power parity.

COMMUNICATIONS

Telecommunications

Telephones - main lines in use: 2.017 million (1995).

Telephones - mobile cellular: 38,552 (1999).

Telephone system:

Domestic: NA

International: satellite earth station - 1 Intelsat (Atlantic Ocean).

Radio broadcast stations: AM 113, FM 194, shortwave 2 (1998).

Radios: 3.15 million (1997).

Television broadcast stations: more than 771 (including 86 strong stations and 685 low-power stations, plus 20 repeaters in the principal networks; also numerous local or private stations in Serbia and Vojvodina) (1997).

Televisions: 2.75 million (1997).

Internet Service Providers (ISPs): 6 (1999).

FINANCE, ECONOMICS, & TRADE

Economic Indicators

National product: GDP—purchasing power parity—$20.6 billion (1999 est.).

National product real growth rate: -20% (1999 est.).

National product per capita: $1,800 (1999 est.).

Inflation rate—consumer price index: 42% (1999 est.).

Exchange Rates

Exchange rates:

Yugoslav New Dinars (YD) per US $1

Official rate	
December 1998	10.00
December 1997	5.85
September 1996	5.02
early 1995	1.50
Black market rate	
December 1998	14.50
December 1997	8.90
early 1995	2 to 3

Fiscal year: calendar year.

Top Import Origins

Imports (1999): $3.3 billion.

Origins (1998): Germany, Italy, Russia, The Former Yugoslav Republic of Macedonia.

Top Export Destinations

Exports (1999): $1.5 billion.

Destinations (1998): Bosnia and Herzegovina, Italy, The Former Yugoslav Republic of Macedonia, Germany.

Import/Export Commodities

Import Commodities	Export Commodities
Machinery and transport equipment	Manufactured goods
Fuels and lubricants	Food and live animals
Manufactured goods	Raw materials
Chemicals	
Food and live animals	
Raw materials	

MONTSERRAT

CAPITAL: Plymouth.

FLAG: The flag of Montserrat is blue with the flag of the United Kingdom in the upper hoist-side quadrant and the Montserratian coat of arms centered in the outer half of the flag; the coat of arms features a woman standing beside a yellow harp with her arm around a black cross.

ANTHEM: God Save the Queen.

MONETARY UNIT: 1 EC dollar (EC$) = 100 cents.

WEIGHTS AND MEASURES: The imperial system is used.

HOLIDAYS: New Year's Day; St. Patrick's Day; Good Friday; Easter Sunday and Easter Monday; Labor Day, first Monday in May; the Queen's Birthday, early June; Whitmonday; August Bank Holiday, first Monday in August; Christmas Day; Boxing Day, 26 December; New Year's Eve.

TIME: 8 AM = noon GMT.

LOCATION AND SIZE: Situated at 16°45′N and 62°10′W, Montserrat has an area of 103 sq. km (40 sq. mi.). The island, which lies between Nevis and Guadeloupe, about 43 km (27 mi.) southeast of Antigua, has a mountainous terrain, with two peaks rising higher than 900 m (3,000 ft.). Montserrat is wholly volcanic in origin, and there are seven active volcanoes.

CLIMATE: Mean temperatures range from a minimum of 23°C (73°F) to a maximum of 31°C (88°F); June–November, the hurricane season, is the warmest time of the year, and December–March is the coolest. There is no clearly defined rainy season, although rainfall tends to be more abundant during the second half of the year; the annual average is 157 cm (62 in.).

INTRODUCTORY SURVEY

RECENT HISTORY

Christopher Columbus, upon viewing Montserrat in November 1493, gave it the name Montserrat because its rugged terrain reminded him of the site of the Abbey of Montserrat in the Spanish highlands near Barcelona. English and Irish colonists from St. Kitts settled on the island in 1632 and the first African slaves arrived thirty-two years later. Throughout the eighteenth century the British and French warred for possession of Montserrat, which was finally confirmed as a British possession by the Treaty of Versailles in 1783. By the early nienteenth century Montserrat had a plantation economy but the abolition of slavery in 1834, the elimination of the apprentice system, the declining market for sugar, and a series of natural disasters brought the downfall of the sugar estates. In the mid-nineteenth century, Joseph Sturge of Birmingham, England, organized a company that bought up the abandoned estates, planted them with limes (a product for which Montserrat is still famous), and sold plots of land to small farmers. From 1871 to 1956 Montserrat formed part of the Federation of the Leeward Islands and after two years as a separate colony it became part of the Federation of the West Indies (1958-1962).

On July 18, 1995, the Soufriere Hills volcano erupted devastating much of the island and causing residents to flee. In June 1997 a catastrophic eruption closed air and seaports. Economic and social dislocation was severe. Two-thirds of the 12,000 inhabitants fled the island. Some began to return in 1998.

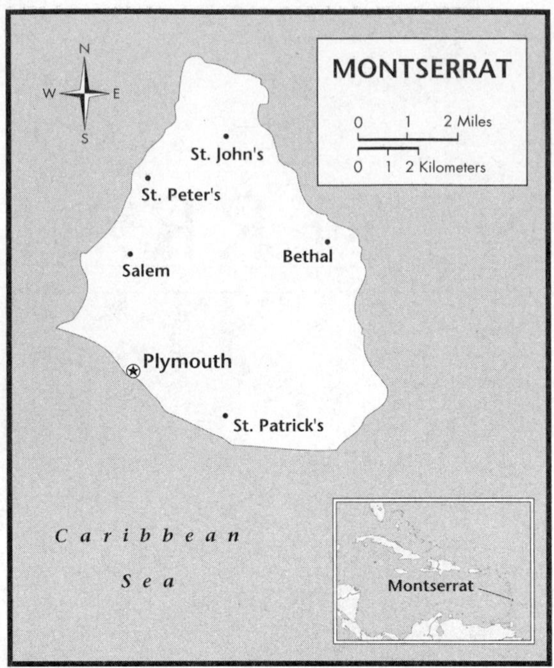

GOVERNMENT

Since the breakup of the Federation, Montserrat has been separately administered under a constitution effective January 1, 1960. The chief of state is the British monarch represented by a governor appointed by the monarch. The head of government is the chief minister who is generally the leader of the majority party following legislative elections. The cabinet, known as Executive Council, consists of the governor, the chief minister, three other ministers, the attorney general, and the finance secretary.

The eleven-seat Legislative Council includes two appointed and two ex officio members. The seven elected members of the legislature are chosen from single-member constituencies by universal adult suffrage at age nineteen. The legislators serve terms of up to five years.

Judiciary

Montserrat's judicial system consists of a magistrate's court and a Court of Summary jurisdiction. Appeals go to the Eastern Caribbean Supreme Court on St. Lucia.

Political Parties

In elections held in November 1978 the People's Liberation Movement, headed by John Osborne, swept all seven elective seats. The party was returned to power in the February 1983 general election though with a reduced majority of five seats, two having been captured by the Progressive Democratic Party.

ECONOMIC AFFAIRS

Montserrat has a small, open economy that was severely disrupted by volcanic activity on the island beginning in July 1995. Up to two-thirds of the 12,000 inhabitants fled the island in 1997 with continuing eruptions. The agriculture sector suffered destruction of crops and rendering land unsuitable for farming. Rebuilding resulted in construction being the dominant activity in 1997 and 1998. Prospects for development depend primarily on the volcano and public sector construction. The UK has committed $100 million (1996-1998) for reconstruction aid. The 1999 Country Policy Plan is a three-year plan for spending $122.8 million in British budgetary aid.

Income

In 1998 the U.S. Central Intelligence Agency (CIA) estimates the GDP at $31 million. The 1998 estimated GDP growth rate was a decline of 16 percent. Inflation in 1998 was 5 percent. The 1996 estimated GDP contribution by sector was agriculture 5.4 percent, industry 13.6 percent, and services 81 percent.

Public Finance

The CIA estimated government revenues in 1997 were $31.4 million and expenditures were $31.6 million, including capital expenditures of $8.4 million.

Industry

Tourism accounts for about one-fourth of the annual GDP. The islands had some 17,000 visitors in 1992. Important crops include hot peppers (mostly for export), limes and other orchard fruits, tomatoes, and vegetables. Exports of live cattle and leather are significant as are such light industrial exports as plastic bags, cotton garments, and electronic parts. Other industries include rum, textiles, and electronic appliances.

Banking and Finance

Montserrat uses the East Caribbean dollar.

SOCIAL WELFARE

Healthcare

The principal health facility is a 67-bed general hospital maintained by the government. Provisions for social welfare include a family planning association and an old people's welfare association. The government provides free dental care for all schoolchildren, elderly persons, and expectant or nursing mothers. In 2000 average life expectancy was seventy-eight years.

EDUCATION

Education is free and compulsory up to age fourteen. The government maintains fifteen schools; one infant school (ages five to seven), nine primary schools (ages five to twelve), two all-age schools (ages five to fifteen), and three secondary schools (ages ten to nineteen).

2000 KEY EVENTS TIMELINE

March

- Ongoing flows and ash from the Soufrière volcano, which last erupted in 1996, are destroying half of the land area of the island. Because of the ash in the atmosphere, many people are sickened by silicosis which affects the lungs. It is still too risky to rebuild or try to reclaim areas devastated by the volcano, and the British government refuses to rebuild the airport.

August

- Montserrat announces on August 24 the creation of a new media corporation that will consolidate and deliver news from the Caribbean.

September

- Chief Minister David Brandt says on September 10 that he does not want Montserratians living abroad to be able to vote in the upcoming elections on the island of Montserrat.

October

- The dome of the active volcano La Soufrière is in danger of collapse on October 29, and most of the island is uninhabitable after considerable volcanic activity.

November

- Britain announces plans on November 14 to legalize homosexuality in Montserrat (and its four other Caribbean territories—Anguilla, British Virgin Islands, Cayman Islands, and Turks and Caicos Islands) by the end of 2000. Homosexuality has been banned on Britain's Caribbean dependencies for decades. Local administrators voice their opposition to the legalization, citing moral and religious grounds.

ANALYSIS OF EVENTS: 2000

BUSINESS AND THE ECONOMY

The economy of Monserrat was formerly comprised of agriculture, with the processing and assembly of electronic components as its main exports. However, since violent volcanic eruptions began in 1995, all that is left is subsistence agriculture. The island is trying to rebuild and get basic goods and services back to normal.

GOVERNMENT AND POLITICS

Montserrat is governed by Great Britain. As of 2000 the appointed Governor was Tony Abbot who has been in office since 1997. The locally elected Chief Minister is David Brandt who has also been in office since 1997. There has been a suspension of all political activities until the island can resume normal activities when repairs to volcano damage have come under control.

CULTURE AND SOCIETY

The indigenous peoples of Montserrat were a combination of Arawak and Caribbean Indians. In 2000 the population of about 5,000 was mainly British but many have fled the island because of the continuous eruptions since 1995 of the volcano known as La Soufrière. The volcano has virtually destroyed a large part of the island along with its capital city, Plymouth.

DIRECTORY

CENTRAL GOVERNMENT

Head of State

Monarch
Elizabeth II, Queen of England

Governor
Anthony John Abbot, Governor's Office

Ministers

Prime Minister
David Brandt, Office of the Prime Minister, Old Towne, Brades, Montserrat
PHONE: +(664) 4912702
FAX: +(664) 4912711

Minister of Finance and Economic Development
David Brandt, Ministry of Finance and Economic Development
PHONE: +(664) 4913463

Minister of Education, Health, and Community Services
Adelina Tuitt, Ministry of Education, Health, and Community Services
PHONE: +(664) 4912541

Minister of Agriculture, Trade and the Environment
P. Austin Bramble, Ministry of Agriculture, Trade and the Environment
PHONE: +(664) 491 2546

Minister of Communications and Work
Rupert Weekes, Ministry of Communications and Work
PHONE: +(664) 4912521

POLITICAL ORGANIZATIONS

National Progressive Party (NPP)

NAME: Reuben T. Meade

Movement for National Reconstruction (MNR)

NAME: Percival Austin Bramble

People's Progressive Alliance (PPA)

NAME: Bertrand Osborne

National Develoment Party (NDP)

People's Liberation Movement (PLM)

NAME: Noel Tuitt

JUDICIAL SYSTEM

Magistrate's Court

Court of Summary

Eastern Caribbean Supreme Court

BROADCAST MEDIA

Radio Monteserrat

PO Box 51, Sweeneys, Montserrat
PHONE: +(664) 4912885
FAX: +(664) 4919250
E-MAIL: radmon@candw.ag
WEBSITE: mratgov.com
TITLE: Manager
CONTACT: Rose Willock
LANGUAGE: English
TYPE: Government, Commercial

Antilles TV Limited

PO Box 342, Plymouth, Montserrat
PHONE: +(664) 4912226
FAX: +(664) 4914511
TITLE: General Manager
CONTACT: K. Osborne
CHANNEL: A7
TYPE: Commercial

NEWSPAPERS AND MAGAZINES

The Montserrat Reporter

Olveston, Montserrat
PHONE: +664 4914715
FAX: +664 4912430
WEBSITE: http://www.montserratreporter.org
TITLE: Editor
CONTACT: Bennette Roach

RELIGIOUS ORGANIZATIONS

Protestant

North Caribbean Conference of Seventh-Day Adventists
PO Box 580, Christianized, St Croix 00821
PHONE: +(664) 7786589
FAX: +(664) 7786593
E-MAIL: NorthCarib@worldnet.att.net
WEBSITE: http://www.tagnet.org/ncc/html/
TITLE: Pastor
NAME: Mark Braithwaite

FURTHER READING

Articles

"Montserrat." *Travel Weekly,* September 18, 2000, vol. 59, no. 75, p. 1S54.

Internet

BBC News Online. "Sanctions Threat to 'Tax Havens.'" June 26, 2000. [Online] Available http://news6.thdo.bbc.co.uk/hi/english/business/newsid%5F806000/806236.stm (accessed October 12, 2000).

MONTSERRAT: STATISTICAL DATA

For sources and notes see "Sources of Statistics" at the front of each volume.

GEOGRAPHY

Geography

Area:

Total: 100 sq km.

Land: 100 sq km.

Land boundaries: 0 km.

Coastline: 40 km.

Climate: tropical; little daily or seasonal temperature variation.

Terrain: volcanic islands, mostly mountainous, with small coastal lowland.

Natural resources: negligible.

Land use:

Arable land: 20%

Permanent crops: 0%

Permanent pastures: 10%

Forests and woodland: 40%

Other: 30% (1993 est.).

HUMAN FACTORS

Demographics (B)

Population (July 2000 est.) 6,409

Age structure

0-14 years 24.23%

male 778

female 775

15-64 years 64.25%

male 1,969

female 2,149

65 years and over 11.52%

male 395

female 343

Population growth rate 20.53%

Birth rate (births/1,000 population) 17.48

Death rate (deaths/1,000 population) 7.49

Net migration rate (migrant(s)/1,000 population) 195.35

Demographics (A)

	1990	1995	1998	2000	2010	2020	2030	2040	2050
Population	NA	10.9	3.3	6.4	9.8	10.7	11.3	11.8	11.9
Life expectancy - males	NA	75.0	75.5	75.8	77.2	78.3	79.2	80.0	80.5
Life expectancy - females	NA	79.0	79.6	80.0	81.8	83.3	84.4	85.3	86.0
Birth rate (per 1,000)	NA	16.5	17.4	17.5	16.8	12.5	11.2	10.9	9.5
Death rate (per 1,000)	NA	8.6	7.8	7.5	6.7	6.0	6.2	7.9	10.4
Women of reproductive age (15-49 yrs.)	NA	2.8	953.0	1.9	2.9	2.9	2.8	2.5	2.4
Fertility rate	NA	1.9	1.9	1.8	1.8	1.7	1.7	1.7	1.7

Except as noted, values for vital statistics are in thousands; life expectancy is in years.

Sex ratio (male(s)/female)

at birth	1.04
under 15 years	1.00
15-64 years	0.92
65 years and over	1.15
total population	0.96
Infant mortality rate (deaths/1,000 live births)	9.10
Life expectancy at birth (years)	
total population	77.96
male	75.78
female	80.23
Total fertility rate (children born/woman)	1.85

Data for 2000 est. An estimated 8,000 refugees left the island following the resumption of volcanic activity in July 1995; some have returned.

Ethnic Division

Black, white.

Religion

Anglican, Methodist, Roman Catholic, Pentecostal, Seventh-Day Adventist, other Christian denominations.

Major Languages

English.

GOVERNMENT & LAW

Political Parties

Legislative Council	no. of seats
People's Progressive Alliance (PPA)	2
Movement for National Reconstruction (MNR)	2
National Progressive Party (NPP)	1
Independent	2

Elections were last held 11 November 1996 (next to be held by 2001).

Government Budgets (B)

Revenues	$31.4 million
Expenditures	$31.6 million
Capital expenditures	$8.4 million

Data for 1997 est.

LABOR FORCE

Total Labor Force (A)

4,521. This number was recently lowered by flight of people from volcanic activity (1992)..

Unemployment Rate

20% (1996 est.)

PRODUCTION SECTOR

Energy Production

Production	10 million kWh
Production by source	
Fossil fuel	100%
Hydro	0%
Nuclear	0%
Other	0%
Exports	0 kWh

Data for 1998.

Energy Consumption

Consumption	9 million kWh
Imports	0 kWh

Data for 1998.

Transportation

Highways:

Total: 269 km.

(Continued on next page.)

MANUFACTURING SECTOR

GDP & Manufacturing Summary (B)

	1980	1985	1990	1993	1994	1995
Gross Domestic Product						
Millions of 1990 dollars	48	54	71	72	76	81[e]
Growth rate in percent	10.22	4.61	−10.89	2.84	6.62	6.62[e]
Per capita (in 1990 dollars)	4,016	4,884	6,465	6,501	6,931	7,390[e]
Manufacturing Value Added						
Millions of 1990 dollars	3	3	4	4	5	5[e]
Growth rate in percent	10.71	−0.12	−10.48	11.78	8.07	8.04[e]
Manufacturing share in percent of current prices	5.7	5.5	4.6[e]	NA	NA	NA

PRODUCTION SECTOR (cont.)

Transportation

Paved: 203 km.

Unpaved: 66 km (1995).

Merchant marine: none (1999 est.).

Airports: 1 (1999 est.).

Top Agriculture Products

Cabbages, carrots, cucumbers, tomatoes, onions, peppers; livestock products.

COMMUNICATIONS

Telecommunications

Telephones - main lines in use: 4,000 (1992).

Telephones - mobile cellular: 70 (1994).

Telephone system:

Domestic: NA

International: NA

Radio broadcast stations: AM 1, FM 2, shortwave 0 (1998).

Radios: 7,000 (1997).

Television broadcast stations: 1 (1997).

Televisions: 3,000 (1997).

Internet Service Providers (ISPs): NA

FINANCE, ECONOMICS, & TRADE

Economic Indicators

National product: GDP—purchasing power parity—$31 million (1998 est.).

National product real growth rate: -16% (1998 est.).

National product per capita: NA.

Inflation rate—consumer price index: 5% (1998).

Exchange Rates

Exchange rates:

East Caribbean dollars (EC$) per US$1 . . . . . . .2.7000

Fixed rate since 1976.

Top Import Origins

Imports (1998): $26 million.

Origins (1993): United States, United Kingdom, Trinidad and Tobago, Japan, Canada.

Top Export Destinations

Exports (1998): $1.5 million.

Destinations (1993): United States, Antigua and Barbuda.

Foreign Aid

Recipient: $9.8 million (1995); About $100 million (1996- 98) in reconstruction aid from the UK; Country Policy Plan (1999) is a three-year program for spending $122.8 million in British budgetary assistance.

Import/Export Commodities

Import Commodities	Export Commodities
Machinery and transportation equipment	Electronic components
Foodstuffs	Plastic bags
Manufactured goods	Apparel
Fuels	Hot peppers
Lubricants and related materials	Live plants
	Cattle

Balance of Payments

	1990	1991	1992	1993	1994
Exports of goods (f.o.b.)	1	1	2	2	3
Imports of goods (f.o.b.)	−42	−34	−30	−24	−30
Trade balance	−41	−33	−28	−22	−27
Services - debits	−12	−11	−12	−11	−15
Services - credits	18	19	20	23	27
Private transfers (net)	18	11	10	9	2
Government transfers (net)	−0	−0	1	NA	1
Overall balance	−23	−21	−13	−10	−19

MOROCCO

Kingdom of Morocco
Al-Mamlakah al-Maghribiyah

CAPITAL: Rabat.

FLAG: The national flag consists of a green five-pointed star at the center of a red field.

ANTHEM: The *Hymne Chérifien* is a twentieth-century composition without words.

MONETARY UNIT: The dirham (DH) is a paper currency of 100 Moroccan centimes. There are coins of 1, 5, 10, and 20 Moroccan centimes and 1, and 5 dirhams, and notes of 5, 10, 50, 100, and 200 dirhams. DH1 = $0.11515 (or $1 = DH8.684).

WEIGHTS AND MEASURES: The metric system is the legal standard.

HOLIDAYS: New Year's Day, 1 January; Anniversary of the King's Accession, 3 March; Labor Day, 1 May; National Day, 14 August; Anniversary of the Green March, 6 November; Independence Day, 18 November. Movable religious holidays include 'Id al-Fitr, 'Id al-'Adha', 1st of Muharram (Muslim New Year), and Milad an-Nabi.

TIME: GMT.

LOCATION AND SIZE: Situated at the northwestern corner of Africa, Morocco claims a total area of 446,550 square kilometers (172,414 square miles), of which the Western Sahara comprises 252,120 square kilometers (97,344 square miles). The Western Sahara is claimed and administered by Morocco but, as of 1997, its ownership has been under dispute.

Comparatively, the area occupied by Morocco is slightly larger than the state of California. Morocco's total boundary length is 3,837 kilometers (2,389 miles). All data include Western Sahara unless otherwise noted. The capital city, Rabat, is located on the Atlantic coast.

CLIMATE: The rugged mountain ranges and the Atlantic Ocean moderate the tropical heat of Morocco. Temperatures in Casablanca range from an average minimum of 7°C (45°F) to a maximum of 17°C (63°F) in January and from a minimum of 18°C (64°F) to a maximum of 26°C (79°F) in July. Maximum annual rainfall of 75–100 centimeters (30–40 inches) occurs in the northwest, while other parts of the country receive much less.

INTRODUCTORY SURVEY

RECENT HISTORY

On March 30, 1912, the French made Morocco a protectorate under Marshal Louis Lyautey. The Moroccans sought independence first in the Rif War (1921-1926) in which they were defeated by the combined French and Spanish forces and later by forming the National Action Bloc in 1934. The Franco-Moroccan agreement of March 2, 1956, granted independence and Muhammad V became king of Morocco. Incorporated into the new nation was Tangier, formerly a British territory.

After the death of Muhammad V on February 26, 1961, his son was crowned King Hassan II and became head of government. A third constitution approved on March 1, 1972, transferred many of the king's executive and legislative powers to a parliament which was to have two-thirds of its members directly elected.

In 1975 Spain announced its intention of withdrawing from phosphate-rich Spanish Sahara (now the Western Sahara), and ceded the northern two-thirds of the region to Morocco and the southern third to Mauritania. However the guerrilla group Polisario, backed by Algeria, challenged the annexation and proclaimed Western Sahara as the Saharan Arab Democratic Republic (SADR). By the early 1980s Morocco had moved up to 100,000 soldiers into Western Sahara in a costly effort to put down the Polisario revolt.

In 1988, United Nations (UN) Secretary General Perez de Cuellar persuaded Moroccan

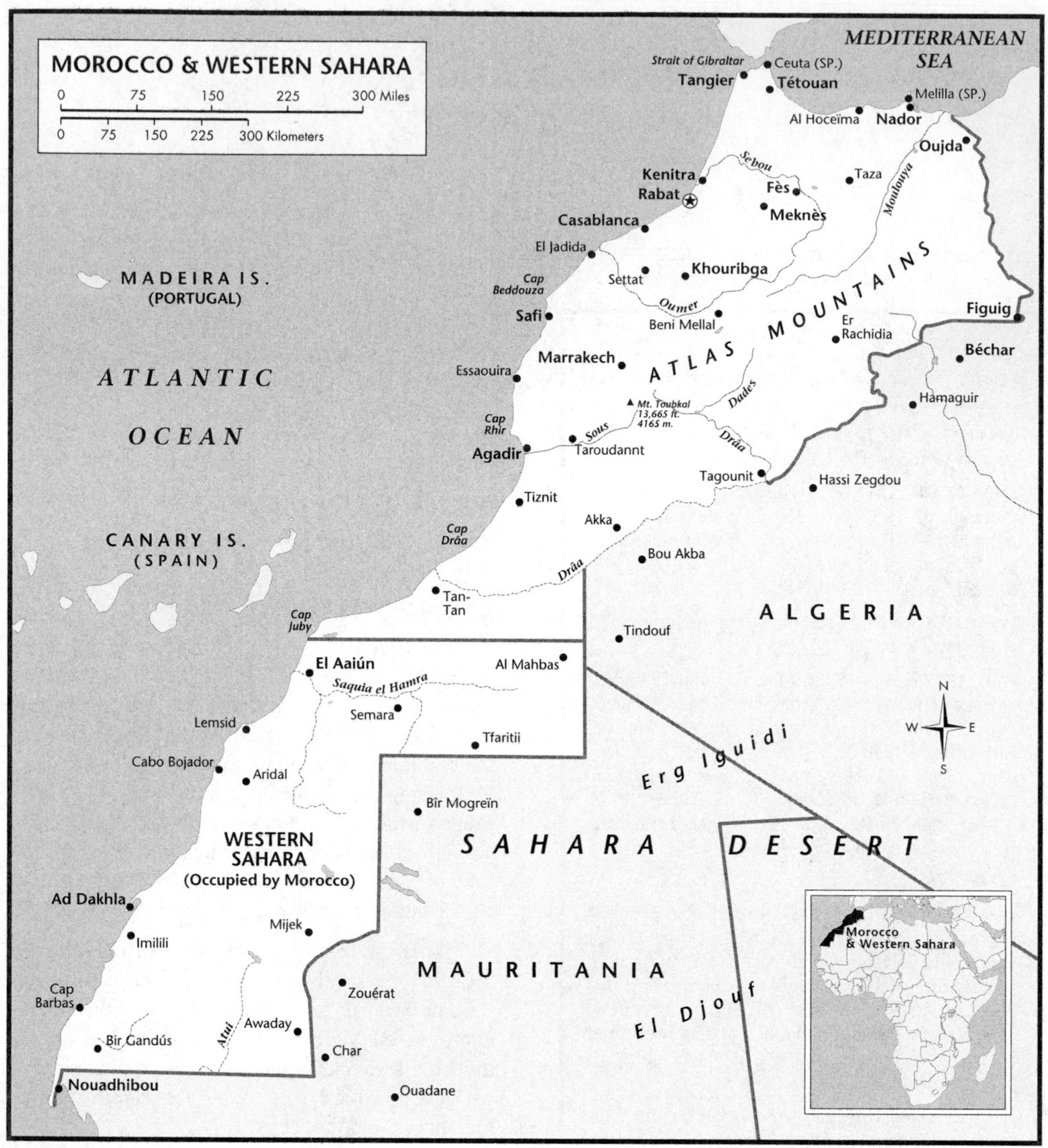

and Polisario representatives to accept a peace plan which included a cease-fire (effective in September 1991), and a referendum for the territory on independence or integration with Morocco. The status of the territory remains unresolved in 2000.

Israeli Prime Minister Yitzhak Rabin made a public visit in 1993 as King Hassan continued to play a moderate role in the search for an Arab-Israel settlement. King Hassan's government maintains close relations with Saudi Arabia and the other Gulf states and was the first Arab nation to condemn the Iraqi invasion of Kuwait.

In 1996 King Hassan proposed to make the entire parliament directly elected. Previously, one-third of the deputies were appointed, giving the king power to undermine any opposition majority. Political reforms in the 1990s under King Hassan culminated in the establishment of a bicameral legislature in 1997.

On July 23, 1999, King Hassan died of a heart attack. His eldest son succeeded him as Mohammed

VI. Like most Islamic countries of the world, Morocco's government feels under threat from an internal Islamic movement. The new king expressed that the stability of his rule will likely be based on economic success. Therefore in March 2000 he visited France to reinforce the European Union application that his father had first made in 1984. On the continuing Western Sahara conflict with the Plisario, there were no signs that Mohammed VI would change the hard line policies of his father.

GOVERNMENT

The Moroccan crown is hereditary, and the king claims descent from the Prophet Muhammad. He can dismiss the parliament (if in session) and bypass elected institutions by submitting a referendum to the people on any major issue, or whenever parliament rejects a bill he favors. He presides over the cabinet and under certain circumstances may declare a state of emergency. The constitution of 1992, approved by referendum, provides for a constitutional monarchy with increased authority for the prime minister who is appointed by the monarch following legislative elections. In 1997 King Hassan proposed revising the constitution to make the entire parliament directly elected and to create a new chamber of appointed ministers. The proposal was accepted and the 1992 constitution amended, in time for the 1997 elections.

In 2000 the legislative branch was a bicameral parliament consisting of an upper house, or Chamber of Counselors, and a 325-seat lower house, or Chamber of Representatives. The Chamber of Counselors consists of 270 members selected by indirect election. Of the 270 members, 162 would represent local authorities, eighty trade chambers, and twenty-seven employee's associations. The members of the lower house are elected by popular vote for five-year terms. Suffrage is universal at age twenty-one.

Judiciary

Morocco has a dual legal system consisting of secular courts based on French legal tradition, and Islamic courts which rule on family and inheritance cases for Moroccan Muslims. The secular system includes district courts, appellate courts, and a Supreme Court. The Islamic court system consists of only trial level courts and does not provide for appeals. Cases are decided on the basis of the Koran and derivative Shari'a.

Political Parties

Morocco's parties are formed into blocks although individual parties maintain separate candidate lists. The Democratic Block consists of Socialist Union of Popular Forces (USFP), Istiqlal (Independence Party-IP), and organization of Democratic and Popular Action (OADP). The National Entente Block consists of the conservative Popular Movement (MP), the conservative National Democratic Party (PND), and the centrist Constitutional Union (UC). The Center Block consists of the National Rally of Independents (RNI), the Democratic and Social Movement (MDS), and the National Popular Movement (MNP). In addition there are various other parties of liberal, socialist, or Islamic orientation, the latter represented by the moderate Constitutional and Democratic Popular Movement (MPCD).

The 1997 election results showed fifteen parties gaining seats in the lower house with USFP, UC, RNI, MP, MDS, and IP winning the most seats and thirteen parties obtaining seats in the upper house with RNI, MDS, UC, MP, PND, and IP at the top of the list.

DEFENSE

Total Moroccan armed strength in 2000 was 196,300. The army had 175,000 men, the navy 7,800, and the air force 13,500. Paramilitary forces totaled 42,000. An estimated 8,800 Moroccan troops were stationed in Bosnia on a peacekeeping mission. The 1997-1998 budget called for defense expenditures of $1.36 billion, or 3.8 percent of the gross domestic product (GDP).

ECONOMIC AFFAIRS

The major resources of the Moroccan economy are agriculture, phosphates, and tourism. Morocco is the world's third-largest producer of phosphates, and varying prices for phosphates on the international market greatly influence Morocco's economy. Tourism and money sent home by Moroccans working abroad have played a critical role since independence. The production of textiles and clothing is part of a growing manufacturing sector that accounted for approximately 17 percent of GDP in 1998.

The high cost of imports, especially of petroleum imports, is a major problem. Another chronic problem is unreliable rainfall, which produces drought or sudden floods. Droughts caused the GDP growth rate to decline in 1995, 1997, and 1999. However good rains result in bumper crops. Favorable rainfalls led Morocco to predict a growth of 6 percent in 2000. Morocco suffers from unemployment, inflation, a large debt, and a shortage of trained managers and administrators. The external debt in 1999 was estimated at $19.1 billion. Challenges to the nation are servicing the external debt, continuation of enterprise privatization, trade policy liberalization, attracting foreign investment, and sustaining GDP growth rates.

Public Finance

The U.S. Central Intelligence Agency estimated that in 1998-1999 government revenues totaled approximately $9.1 billion and expenditures $10 billion including $1.7 billion. External debt totaled $19.1 billion in 1999.

The Moroccan government announced plans in 1999-2000 to reduce the budget deficit by one-third in order to encourage investment and job creation. By 1998 only fifty-six of 114 companies slated for privatization had been sold and the rest had been withdrawn from sale. The government did not depend on privatization revenues for funds, rather on the ownership of phosphates industry. Nearly 50 percent of the state budget was spent on public sector salaries and 25 percent on debt servicing in 1999.

Income

In 1999 Morocco's gross domestic product (GDP) was estimated at $108 billion, or about $3,600 per capita. The 1999 estimated GDP growth rate was 0 percent and estimated inflation was 1.9 percent. The 1998 estimated GDP contribution by sector was agriculture 16 percent, industry 30 percent, and services 54 percent.

Industry

Leading industrial sectors in 1998 were phosphate rock mining and processing, food products, textiles, matches, metal and leather products, and construction. Heavy industry is largely limited to petroleum refining, chemical fertilizers, automobile and tractor assembly, foundry work (making objects by pouring metal into a mold), asphalt, and cement. Many of the processed agricultural products and consumer goods are primarily used for local consumption, but Morocco exports canned fish and fruit, wine, leather goods, and textiles, as well as such traditional Moroccan handicrafts as carpets and brass, copper, silver, and wood implements.

There are three oil refineries, several petrochemical plants, a polyvinyl chloride factory, and four phosphate-processing plants. There are four plants assembling cars and small utility vehicles: Renault Moroc, Sopriam, Somaca, and Smeia. Nine cement factories reached a total of 6.35 million tons in 1995.

Banking and Finance

The Bank of Morocco (Bank al-Maghrib), the central bank, has the sole privilege of note issue. It is required to maintain a gold or convertible currency reserve equal to one-ninth of its note issue. The Ministry of Finance is responsible for the organization of banking and the money market. In February 1996 the central bank gave clearance for banks and finance houses to issue corporate bonds. Consumer credit companies are expected to be the first to take advantage of the new ruling. Other reforms scheduled for 1996 included a secondary market in public debt, an interbank foreign exchange market, and the launch of privatization bonds and global depository receipts (GDRs). By 1997 only the interbank foreign exchange market had been implemented. From May 2 commercial banks were permitted to buy and sell foreign currency at market-determined rates where previously foreign exchange rates were fixed on a daily basis by the central bank.

Exchange control regulations are set and administered by an agency of the Ministry of Finance.

Commercial banks must have 51 percent majority ownership; some foreign banks were Moroccanized in 1975. There were fourteen commercial banks in 1996, most of which are partly owned by European banks. The largest private commercial bank is the Banque Commerciale du Maroc (BCM), which is 32 percent owned by foreign banks, including Banco Central Hispano, Credito Italiano, and Crédit Commercial de France. Public sector financial organizations specializing in development finance include the National Bank for Economic Development, Moroccan Bank for Foreign Trade, National Agricultural Credit Bank, and Deposit and Investment Fund. Also instrumental in development finance is the Bureau of Mineral Exploration and Participation, which has participatory interests in the production of all coal, petroleum, lead, and manganese. The National Bank for Economic Development, established in 1959, has been particularly active in financing manufacturing. The Agricultural Credit Bank makes loans to credit organizations, public institutions, and cooperatives. Private individuals borrow from local agricultural credit banks or from the agricultural credit and provident societies. The stock exchange (Bourse des Valeurs) at Casablanca handles mostly European and a few North African issues.

The stock exchange (Bourse des Valeurs) at Casablanca, established in 1929, handles mostly European and few North African issues.

Economic Development

Government policy stresses expansion and development of the economy, essentially through private enterprise. Morocco decided to abide by the IMF's Article VIII, thus beginning the privatization of 112 public entities-mainly manufacturing enterprises, hotels, and financial institutions. Only fifty-six had been privatized by 1998 and the process had been stopped at that time. Keeping major industries under government control, Morocco proceeded to open up investment only partially, keeping the majority of revenues from the phosphates and mining, banking, and securities industries.

Morocco has instituted a series of development plans since 1960 to modernize the economy and increase production. Plans over the last four decades have included setting growth rate targets, development and modernization of the agriculture, industrial, tourist, and energy sectors, infrastructure improvements, continued developments of phosphate processing, and creation of new jobs.

Outstanding foreign debt commitments and their servicing remained a significant obstacle to economic development. The 1999-2004 economic plan includes the creation of jobs for Morocco's youthful population, promotion of exports and tourism, resumption of privatization, and infrastructure construction. In addition to external debt long-term challenges include preparing the economy for freer trade with the EU, attracting foreign investment, improving education and living standards, and achieving sustainable economic growth in the face of intermittent drought conditions that depress the agricultural sector.

SOCIAL WELFARE

The social security system covers employees and apprentices in industrial and commercial fields and the professions, as well as in agriculture and forestry. There is also voluntary coverage for persons leaving covered employment, and voluntary complementary insurance is available. Benefits include maternity allowances, disability pensions, old age pensions, death allowances, and allowances for illness.

Women comprise about 35 percent of the work force and are employed mostly in the industrial, service, and teaching sectors. They have the right to vote and run for office (in 1993 two women were elected to parliament). However, women do not have equal status under Islamic family and estate laws. Child labor is common, particularly in the rug making and textile industries.

Healthcare

Health conditions are relatively poor, but programs of mass education in child and parent hygiene, as well as government supervised health services in schools and colleges, have helped to raise standards. Campaigns have been conducted against malaria, tuberculosis, venereal diseases, and cancer. However, gastrointestinal infections, malaria, typhoid, trachoma, and tuberculosis remain widespread. The World Health Organization (WHO) and the United Nations Children's Fund (UNICEF) have cooperated in the government's campaigns against eye disorders and venereal diseases.

The current health system is comprised of three sectors: a public sector, a semi-public sector, and a private sector.

In 1989-1995, 70 percent of the population had access to health care services. In the mid-1990s there was one physician per 2,743 people, and one hospital bed per 895 people. The average estimated life expectancy was sixty-nine in 2000.

Housing

Since the 1950s significant numbers of Moroccans (estimated at over four million) have moved from the countryside to the urban centers to escape rural unemployment. Housing and sanitation consequently have become urban problems. The government is engaged in a low-cost housing program to reduce the slum areas, called *bidonvilles,* that have formed around the large urban centers especially at Casablanca and Rabat. Loans have been available for private home construction, and builders have also received financial and technical assistance from the government to build workers' housing.

EDUCATION

In 2000, the overall illiteracy rate was an estimated 51.1 percent (38.1 percent for men and 64 percent for women). The school system includes modern secular public institutions, traditional religious schools, and private schools. Nine years of compulsory primary education was made a law in

1962. In 1997 over three million pupils were in primary school and 1.4 million in secondary school. In vocational schools there were 18,762 students. Girls leave school at a younger age than boys and are a minority in secondary as well as primary schools; they make up fewer than one-third of university students. The language of instruction in primary schools is Arabic during the first two years, and both Arabic and French are used for the next three years.

Morocco has six universities. Al-Qarawiyin University at Fès, founded in 859, is reputed to be the oldest university in the world. The first modern Moroccan university, the University of Rabat (now the Muhammad V University), was opened in 1957. Other universities are Muhammad bin ʽAbdallah (founded 1974), in Fès; Hassan II (1975), Casablanca; Cadi Ayyad (1978), Marrakech; and Muhammad I (1978), Oujda. There are about two dozen colleges and conservatories. In 1994, enrollment at all higher-level institutions was 311,743.

2000 KEY EVENTS TIMELINE

January

- Nineteen international groups bid for the construction of wind farms in Tangier and Tarfaya. The two wind parks will generate up to 200 megawatts of electricity.
- The European Union (EU)-Moroccan Association Agreement is signed January 24 by the EU Council of Foreign Ministers. A free trade area and cooperative efforts under the Euro-Mediterranean (MEDA) program are established.

March

- In Rabat government Islamist supporters march March 12. At the same time in Casablanca ten times the number of Islamists demonstrate peacefully. Islamic fundamentalism, repressed under the late King Hassan, is given new life under the civil reforms of King Mohammed VI.

June

- United Nations (UN) mediator James Baker III convenes a second round of talks between Polisario Front, rebels from the Western Sahara who favor independence for the territory, and Morocco on June 28–29 in London. The UN wants the Western Sahara, a former colony of Spain, to hold a referendum on whether to remain part of Morocco or become independent.

August

- Oil and gas deposits are discovered in the eastern region of Morocco close to the Algerian border in the Talasinnt area. Estimates are that these reserves will keep Morocco self-sufficient for thirty years.

September

- Morocco wins five medals—one Silver Medal and four Bronze Medals—in the Olympics 2000. Men win in featherweight boxing and track and field, and a woman wins a Bronze Medal in track and field for 400-meter hurdles.

October

- The government makes an offer on October 2 to hold direct talks with the opposing Polisario Front on Western Sahara.
- The Reporters Sans Frontiers group criticizes Moroccan authorities October 16 for suppressing the freedom of journalists in the country.

November

- The Moroccan Press Union calls for better working conditions for journalists.
- Long-distance runner Abdelkader Mouaziz, aged thirty-one,wins the New York marathon, becoming the first Moroccan to win the New York marathon.
- The Moroccan government revokes the accreditation of French Press Agency (AFP) bureau chief, Claude Juvenal, citing his "unethical conduct" and his "criticism and distortion" of Morocco's political and economic reforms.
- In the eleventh World Kickboxing Championship, with thirty-three countries competing in Prague, Czech Republic, the Moroccan team is victorious in both the light and full-contact categories, taking twelve medals—seven gold, two silver, and three bronze.
- Morocco closes Israel's liaison office in Rabat and Morocco's mission in Tel Aviv, Israel.
- Morocco's ambassador to Qatar returns to his post in Doha. A meeting between King Mohammed VI and the Emir of Qatar improves bilateral relations.

December

- The National AIDS Control Program (PNLS) reports that 809 AIDS cases were recorded in Morocco as of September 30.
- The government closes the country's three leading independent newspapers: French-language *Le Journal,* Arabic *Al Sahifa,* and *Demain.*
- The biggest drug seizure of the year is made in Tangier. A Spanish truck driver is caught transporting seven tons of marijuana hidden in cardboard boxes among boxes of red peppers headed for Spain. The market value of the drug is about US$740,000.
- The Polisario Front hands over 201 Moroccan soldiers captured about twenty-five years ago representatives of the Geneva-based International Committee of the Red Cross at Tindouf, in southwest Algeria.

ANALYSIS OF EVENTS: 2000

BUSINESS AND THE ECONOMY

A government study of investor experiences in Morocco reported that major problems persisted in the areas requiring state involvement: the issuance of official authorizations and licenses, taxation, and real estate. The report included related issues affecting international business, such as unfavorable labor relations, customs clearance delays under temporary import provisions, and the increasing numbers of would-be illegal emigrants stowing away on ships and long-distance trucks. Government efforts have not deterred these trespassers. Companies engaged in shipping into and out of Morocco hired private security to stop stowaways. Other emigration issues surrounded the continuous flotillas of makeshift boats, rafts, and even rubber dinghies used to attempt crossing the Straits of Gibraltar from Morocco to enter Europe via Spain. The illegal immigrants come not only from Morocco, but also from Algeria and sub-Saharan Africa. In one instance in October the Moroccan Navy arrested 443 people on board a makeshift boat, 378 of whom were Moroccans.

However, since the economy has improved slightly leading to more available employment, some predict that the drive to emigrate may subside in the next years. During the third quarter of 2000, Morocco had 1,458,000 unemployed people. This was 76,000 fewer than the 1,534,000 unemployed during the same period in 1999.

Both water and oil resources were causes for increased concern in 2000. On the eve of the 2000/2001 growing season dam water levels were at only 37.9 percent of capacity as of August 1, down from the 49.4 percent of the same time last year. These very low reserves signalled a dramatic water shortage considering that 1999 was itself a drought year.

As reported by the government, Morocco's oil bill reached US$1.3 billion in 2000, up from US$870 million in 1999, an increase of 105.4 percent. Morocco met 95 percent of its oil needs through purchases on the foreign market. These oil imports, which rose by 3 percent, accounted for 44.6 percent in the increase of total imports, due to an upsurge in oil prices on the international market. The Moroccan government's response was to increase the prices of petroleum products in the country by 4.8–10.8 percent. The prices for diesel fuel, ordinary gasoline, and high-grade motor fuel went up by 9.3 percent, 9.8 percent, and 10.8 percent respectively. The price of industrial fuel went up by 4.8 percent. Since Morocco is the only Mediterranean basin country that does not refund value-added tax (VAT) paid on commercial transport fuel, and fuel accounts for 35 percent of transportation company expenditures, strikes were threatened by merchandise and passenger transport companies. The Transport Minister averted strikes with promises to lobby for refunds on VAT passenger and merchandise transport fuel.

Since a reform of the oil exploration law in 1999 more commercial exploration for oil and gas occurred. Possible relief from international market prices for oil and gas came with the discovery of an estimated two billion barrels of oil in the northwestern Sidi Belkacem area at Talsint, some 200 kilometers from the Algerian border in Northeastern Morocco. This discovery by Lone Star Energy, the local subsidiary of a U.S. oil company known as Skidmore, represented between twenty-five and thirty years of energy consumption for Morocco. Production from these reserves, which are mainly composed of natural gas, was expected to begin in 2003.

Moroccan commercial transactions with foreign countries increased in 2000 by 9.4 percent compared to 6.4 percent in 1999, according to government report. Exports increased by 0.6 percent compared to 7.6 percent in 1999 while imports recorded a substantial increase of 15.6 percent compared to 5.5 percent the previous year. An Employers' Federation (CGEM) survey showed that as many as 69 percent of companies reported suffering from international economic factors. The worst-affected products were leather, chemicals, and clothing, although capital goods and electrical and electronic equipment benefited from the international environment.

GOVERNMENT AND POLITICS

In July King Mohammed VI of Morocco pardoned 899 prisoners to celebrate the first anniversary of his ascendancy to the throne. As part of the celebration of Revolution Day, the forty-seventh anniversary of the return from exile of his grandfather on August 20, 1953, King Mohammed VI pardoned 1,156 prisoners. He cancelled the entire sentences of 355 prisoners, reduced those of 572 others, and commuted four life sentences to lesser prison terms.

A coalition called "The United Left-wing Front of Morocco" was created by thirty member groups representing various political parties and non-governmental organizations. The coalition wishes to ensure that the Morocco's democratic transition is successful.

Morocco recalled its ambassador to Qatar to protest alleged attempts to worsen the security situation in the Maghreb. Other issues between Qatar and Morocco were Qatar's refusal to support Morocco's bid to host the 2006 football (soccer) World Cup, and the presence in Qatar of the satellite TV channel *Al Jazira. Al Jazira* had broadcast a number of programs dealing with the Sahara dispute that Morocco believes were biased in favor of the Polisario Front, an organization seeking independence of the Western Sahara from Morocco.

This issue of the independence of the Saharawi people of the Western Sahara has dragged on since 1975 when Spain ceded the Western Sahara to Morocco. The Polisario Front decided to pursue the struggle for national liberation against Morocco—a country it viewed as yet another colonial power asserting authority over Western Sahara. Eight years of deadlock over who is eligible to vote in the referendum for self-determination. (Morocco has refused to allow about 140,000 people to register to vote.) Minurso, the United Nations (U.N.) mission responsible for organizing the referendum, sought solutions from Morocco to the problems impeding the realization of the referendum on the issue of self-determination in the Western Sahara. Morocco's proposal for some form of limited autonomy for the Sahara within Morocco was considered too weak to serve as a basis for negotiation.

Another international issue Morocco faced was its refusal, since 1999, to renew the four-year fishing agreement with the European Union (E.U.). Morocco has argued that its fisheries resources were threatened with depletion due to over-exploitation. In addition, Morocco temporarily banned the fishing of cephalopods and other related species to protect high concentrations of immature octopus and conserve the coastal ecosystem.

CULTURE AND SOCIETY

Reporters Sans Frontieres (Reporters Without Borders—RSF) expressed alarm over the serious deterioration of press freedom in Morocco. According to RSF, Moroccan authorities attempted to control the press over "sensitive" subjects, such as the future of the Western Sahara, human rights violations during the reign of Hassan II, or Islamist movements. Journalists have been arrested or threatened, and newspapers have been seized, closed, or banned. The government was also drafting a law to restrict access to pornographic Internet sites.

At another level communication in Morocco improved. The Moroccan telecommunication company showed a net profit of US$115.7 million during the year up to September 1, compared to US$85.5 million during the same period in 1999. By the end of the first half of 2000 the company had nearly 2.7 million telephone subscribers including nearly 1.5 million fixed telephone subscribers, a 3 percent increase over the same period in 1999. A total of two million people subscribed to mobile phones in Morocco and 100,000 are Internet users. The Moroccan telecommunications network was fully digitized.

DIRECTORY

CENTRAL GOVERNMENT

Head of State

King

Mohammed VI, Monarch

Prime Minister
Abderrahmane Youssoufi, Office of the Prime Minister, Palais Royal, Le Mochouar, Rabat, Morocco
PHONE: +212 (7) 763804; 761763; 762425
FAX: +212 (7) 769995; 769195

Ministers

Minister of Foreign Affairs and Co-operation
Mohamed Benaissa, Ministry of Foreign Affairs and Co-operation, Avenue Roosevelt, Rabat, Morocco
PHONE: +212 (7) 762841; 761125; 762550
FAX: +212 (7) 765508; 764679
E-MAIL: ministere@maec.gov.ma

Minister of Interior
Ahmed Midaqui, Ministry of Interior, Quartier Administratif, Rabat, Morocco
PHONE: +212 (7) 761861; 760301
FAX: +212 (7) 762056

Minister of Justice
Omar Azziman, Ministry of Justice, Place Mamounia, Rabat, Morocco
PHONE: +212 (7) 732941
FAX: +212 (7) 730772

Minister of Waqf and Islamic Affairs
Abdelkabir M'Daghri Alaouim, Ministry of Waqf and Islamic Affairs, Le Méchouar, Rabat, Morocco
PHONE: +212 (7) 766801
FAX: +212 (7) 760532; 760185; 765282

Minister of Country Planning, Environment, Town Planning, and Housing
Mohamed el-Yazghi, Ministry of Country Planning, Environment, Town Planning, and Housing
PHONE: +212 (7) 763539; 764863
FAX: +212 (7) 763510

Minister of Economy and Finance
Fathallah Oualalou, Ministry of Economy and Finance, Boulevard Mohammed V, Quartier Administratif, 10000 Rabat, Morocco
PHONE: +212 (7) 765504
FAX: +212 (7) 761575
E-MAIL: ministre@mfie.gov.ma

Minister of Agriculture and Rural Development
Ismail Alaoui, Ministry of Agriculture and Rural Development, Quartier Administratif, Place Abdallah Chefchaouni, BP 607, Rabat, Morocco
PHONE: +212 (7) 760933; 760993; 760102
FAX: +212 (7) 763378

Minister of Industry, Commerce, Energy and Mines
Mustapha Mansouri, Ministry of Industry, Commerce, Energy and Mines, Quartier des Ministries, Rabat-Chellah, Morocco
PHONE: +212 (7) 761868; 761508
FAX: +212 (7) 766265
E-MAIL: ministre@mcinet.gov.ma

Minister of Employment, Vocational Training, Social Development and Solidarity
Abbas Fassi, Ministry of Employment, Vocational Training, Social Development and Solidarity
PHONE: +212 (7) 761855; 760318
FAX: +212 (7) 768881

Minister of Economic Forecast and Planning
Abdelhamid Aouad, Ministry of Economic Forecast and Planning

Minister of Health
Thami Khiari, Ministry of Health

Minister of Higher Education
Najib Zerouali, Ministry of Higher Education

Minister of Human Rights
Mohamed Oujar, Ministry of Human Rights

Minister of Youth and Sports
Ahmed Moussaoui, Ministry of Youth and Sports

POLITICAL ORGANIZATIONS

Partide l'Istiqlal (PI)

4, avenue Ibn Toumert, Bab el-Had, Rabat, Morocco
PHONE: +212 (7) 730951; 730952; 730953
FAX: +212 (7) 725354; 736129; 732183
TITLE: Secretary General
NAME: Abbas el-Fassi

Mouvement populaire (MP)

66, rue Patrice Lumumba, Rabat, Morocco
PHONE: +212 (7) 767320; 766431
FAX: +212 (7) 767537
TITLE: Secretary General
NAME: Mohamed Laensar

Union nationale des forces populaires (UNFP)

28, rue Magellan, Casablanca 01, Morocco
PHONE: +212 (2) 302023
FAX: +212 (2) 319301

TITLE: Secretary General
NAME: Abdellah Ibrahimi

Mouvement populaire democratique et constitutionnel (MPDC)

352, blvd. Mohamed V, Rabat, Morocco
PHONE: +212 (7) 734601
FAX: +212 (7) 319301
TITLE: Secretary General
NAME: Abdelkrim Khatib

Parti du progres et du socialisme

4, rue Ibn Zakour Quartier des Orangers, Rabat, Morocco
PHONE: +212 (7) 208672; 208673
FAX: +212 (7) 208674
TITLE: Secretary General
NAME: Ismail Alaoui

Union socialiste des forces popularies (USFP)

17, rue Oued Souss. Agdal, Rabat, Morocco
PHONE: +212 (7) 773902; 773903; 773905
FAX: +212 (7) 773901
TITLE: Secretary General
NAME: Abderrahmane el-Youssoufi

Rassemblement national des independants (RNI)

6, rue Laos, avenue Hassan II, Rabat, Morocco
PHONE: +212 (7) 721420; 721424
FAX: +212 (7) 733824
TITLE: President
NAME: Ahmed Osman

Parti national democrate (PND)

18, rue de Tunis-Hassan, Rabat, Morocco
PHONE: +212 (7) 732127; 730754
FAX: +212 (7) 720170
TITLE: General Secretary
NAME: Mohamed Arsalane el-Jadidi

Union constitutionelle (UC)

158, avenue des FAR, Casablanca, Morocco
PHONE: +212 (2) 313630; 312229; 441142
FAX: +212 (2) 441141
TITLE: General Secretary
NAME: Mohamed Arsalane el-Jadidi

Organisation de l'action democratique populaire (OADP)

29, avenue Lalla Yacout, Apt. N1, BP 15797, Casablanca, Morocco
PHONE: +212 (2) 278442
FAX: +212 (2) 278442
TITLE: General Secretary
NAME: Mohamed Bensaid Ait Idder

Mouvement national populaire (MNP)

avenue Imam Malik, rue el-Madani Belhoussni Souissi, Rabat, Morocco
PHONE: +212 (7) 753623
FAX: +212 (7) 759761
TITLE: General Secretary
NAME: Mahjoubi Aherdane

Parti de l'avant garde democratique et social (PAGDS)

avenue Imam Malik, rue el-Madani Belhoussni Souissi, Rabat, Morocco
PHONE: +212 (7) 200559
FAX: +212 (7) 708491
TITLE: Porte Parole
NAME: Ahmed Benjelloune

Mouvement democrate social (MDS)

avenue Imam Malik, rue el-Madani Belhoussni Souissi, Rabat, Morocco
PHONE: +212 (7) 709110; 709495
TITLE: General Secretary
NAME: Mahmoud Archane

Parti socialiste democratique (PSD)

43, rue Abou Fariss al-Marini, Rabat, Morocco
PHONE: +212 (7) 208571; 208572; 208573
FAX: +212 (7) 208573
TITLE: General Secretary
NAME: Aissa Ouardighi

Parti du front des forces democratiques (FFD)

13, blvd. Tarik Ibnou Ziad, Rabat, Morocco
PHONE: +212 (7) 661623; 661624; 661625
FAX: +212 (7) 208573
TITLE: General Secretary
NAME: Thami Khyari

Parti de l'action (PA)

113, avenue Allal Ben Abdellah, Rabat, Morocco
PHONE: +212 (7) 206661

FAX: +212 (7) 208573
TITLE: General Secretary
NAME: Mohammed el-Drissi

DIPLOMATIC REPRESENTATION

Embassies in Morocco

Algeria
46-48, rue Tarek lbn Ziad, BP 448, Rabat, Morocco
PHONE: +212 (7) 765591; 765092; 765474
FAX: +212 (7) 762237
TITLE: Ambassador
NAME: M'hamed Lakhdar Belaid

Angola
PHONE: +212 (7) 659239
FAX: +212 (7) 659238
TITLE: Ambassador
NAME: Luis José de Almeida

Argentina
12, rue Mekki Bittaouri, Souissi, Rabat, Morocco
PHONE: +212 (7) 755120; 754181
FAX: +212 (7) 755410
TITLE: Ambassador
NAME: Adolfo Enrique Nanclares

Austria
2, Zankat Tiddas, BP 135, Rabat, Morocco
PHONE: +212 (7) 764003; 761698
FAX: +212 (7) 765425
TITLE: Ambassador
NAME: Michael Fitz

Bangladesh
25, avenue Tarek Ibn Ziad, Rabat, Morocco
PHONE: +212 (7) 766731; 760963
FAX: +212 (7) 766729
TITLE: Ambassador
NAME: Muhammad Syed Hussain

Belgium
6, avenue de Marrakech, BP 163, Rabat, Morocco
PHONE: +212 (7) 764746
FAX: +212 (7) 767003
TITLE: Ambassador
NAME: André Fontaine

Brazil
3, rue Cadi Benjelloun, La Pinede, Rabat, Morocco
PHONE: +212 (7) 755151; 755219
TITLE: Ambassador
NAME: Antonio Sabino Contuaria Guimaraes

Bulgaria
4, avenue de Meknes, BP 1301, Rabat, Morocco
PHONE: +212 (7) 763201
TITLE: Ambassador
NAME: Georgi Benchev Karev

Burkina Faso
7, rue el-Bouziri-Agdal, BP 6484, 10101 Rabat, Morocco
PHONE: +212 (7) 675512; 675518
FAX: +212 (7) 675517
TITLE: Ambassador
NAME: Assimi Kouanda

Cameroon
20, rue du Rif, Souissi, BP 1790, Rabat, Morocco
PHONE: +212 (7) 754194
TITLE: Ambassador
NAME: Mahamat Paba Sale

Canada
13 bis, rue Jaafar Assadik, BP 709, Agdal, Rabat, Morocco
PHONE: +212 (7) 672880
FAX: +212 (7) 672178
TITLE: Ambassador
NAME: Mark Bailey

Central African Republic
42, Avenue Pasteur, BP 770, Agdal, Rabat, Morocco
PHONE: +212 (7) 732685; 734198
FAX: +212 (7) 672178
TITLE: Ambassador
NAME: Martin Koyou Kombele

Chile
35, av. Ahmed Balafrej, Souissi, Rabat, Morocco
PHONE: +212 (7) 636065
FAX: +212 (7) 672178

China
16, Charia Hadj Ahmed Balafrej, Souissi, Rabat, Morocco
PHONE: +212 (7) 754056
FAX: +212 (7) 757519
TITLE: Ambassador
NAME: An Guozheng

Colombia
29, av. Michlifen, Imm. Moulay Driss, 2Šme App., Agdal, Rabat, Morocco
PHONE: +212 (7) 670804; 670805
FAX: +212 (7) 670802
TITLE: Ambassador
NAME: Ximena Andrade de Casalino

Republic of Congo
34, avenue al-Nasr, Rabat, Morocco
PHONE: +212 (7) 734862

Côte d'Ivoire
21, rue de Tiddas, BP 192, Rabat, Morocco
PHONE: +212 (7) 763151
FAX: +212 (7) 762792
TITLE: Ambassador
NAME: Amadou Thiam

Croatia
73, rue Marnissa, Souissi, Rabat, Morocco
PHONE: +212 (7) 638824

Czech Republic
PHONE: +212 (7) 755421
FAX: +212 (7) 755420
TITLE: Ambassador
NAME: Marie Zajikova

Denmark
4, rue de Khemisset, BP 203, Rabat, Morocco
PHONE: +212 (7) 769293; 766986
FAX: +212 (7) 769709
TITLE: Ambassador
NAME: Troels Simon Peter Branner

Djibouti
31, rue Aljazair, Rabat, Morocco
PHONE: +212 (7) 731833; 731834
FAX: +212 (7) 706821
TITLE: Ambassador
NAME: Ahmed Amine Fathallah

Equatorial Guinea
30, avenue des Nations Unies, Agdal, Rabat, Morocco
PHONE: +212 (7) 774205; 774674

Finland
16, rue Khemisset, Rabat, Morocco
PHONE: +212 (7) 762312
FAX: +212 (7) 762352
TITLE: Charge d'Affaires
NAME: Kristi Westphalen

France
3, Zankat Sahnoun, Agdal, Rabat, Morocco
PHONE: +212 (7) 689700
TITLE: Ambassador
NAME: Michel de Bonnecorse

Gabon
PHONE: +212 (7) 751950; 751968
FAX: +212 (7) 757550
TITLE: Ambassador
NAME: Victor Afounouna

Germany
7, rue Madnine, BP 235, Rabat, Morocco
PHONE: +212 (7) 709662; 708375
FAX: +212 (7) 706851
TITLE: Ambassador
NAME: Herwing Bartels

Greece
23, rue d'Oujda, Tour Hassan, Rabat, Morocco
PHONE: +212 (7) 723839; 733446
FAX: +212 (7) 702270
TITLE: Ambassador
NAME: Kodellis Dionyssios

Guinea
15, rue Hamza, Agdal, Rabat, Morocco
PHONE: +212 (7) 674148; 673488
FAX: +212 (7) 672513
TITLE: Ambassador
NAME: Aly Kaba

Hungary
190 OLM, Souissi, BP 5026, Rabat, Morocco
PHONE: +212 (7) 750757; 757503
FAX: +212 (7) 754123
TITLE: Charge d'Affaires
NAME: Janos Terenyi

India
13, Charia Michlifen, Agdal, Rabat, Morocco
PHONE: +212 (7) 671339; 675974
FAX: +212 (7) 671269
TITLE: Ambassador
NAME: Indraht Singh Rathore

Indonesia
PHONE: +212 (7) 757860; 757861
FAX: +212 (7) 757859
TITLE: Ambassador
NAME: Iskandar Dinata

Iran
Route des Zaers, avenue Bir Kassem, Km 4,8, BP 490, Souissi, Rabat, Morocco
PHONE: +212 (7) 752167; 750353
FAX: +212 (7) 659118
TITLE: Ambassador
NAME: Jaafar Chemissane

Iraq
39, avenue Mehdi Ben Barka, Souissi, Rabat, Morocco
PHONE: +212 (7) 754466
FAX: +212 (7) 795745
TITLE: Ambassador
NAME: Abdeljabbar Omar Ghani Addouri

Israel
52, avenue Mehdi Ben Barka; Souissi, Rabat, Morocco
PHONE: +212 (7) 657680; 657682
FAX: +212 (7) 657683
TITLE: Chief of the Bureau of Liaison
NAME: David Dadon

Italy
2, avenue Driss Al Azhar, Rabat, Morocco
PHONE: +212 (7) 706597; 706792; 706912
FAX: +212 (7) 706882
TITLE: Ambassador
NAME: Emilio Franco DeStefanis

Japan
39, avenue Ahmed Balafrej, Souissi, Rabat, Morocco
PHONE: +212 (7) 631782
FAX: +212 (7) 750078
TITLE: Ambassador
NAME: Hiromi Sato

Jordan
65, Villa Ouafae, Cité OLM, Souissi II, Rabat, Morocco
PHONE: +212 (7) 751125; 759270
FAX: +212 (7) 758722
TITLE: Ambassador
NAME: Mohamed Hassan Soleimane Addaoudia

Kuwait
avenue Imam Malik, Km 4,3, Souissi, Rabat, Morocco
PHONE: +212 (7) 751775; 754588; 754623
FAX: +212 (7) 753591
TITLE: Ambassador
NAME: Souleyman Ibrahim el-Marjane

Lebanon
19, avenue de Fes, Hassan, Rabat, Morocco
PHONE: +212 (7) 761614; 760728
FAX: +212 (7) 760949
TITLE: Ambassador
NAME: Mostapha Hassan Mostapha

Liberia
Lotissement 7, Napabia, rue Oulad Frej, Souissi, Rabat, Morocco
PHONE: +212 (7) 638426

Libya
1, rue Chouaib Doukkali, Rabat, Morocco
PHONE: +212 (7) 769566
TITLE: Ambassador
NAME: Embarek Abdullah Turki

Malaysia
2, Villa Amin, avenue Marrakech, Rabat, Morocco
PHONE: +212 (7) 767389; 767423
FAX: +212 (7) 767819

Mali
56, Cité OLM, Souissi II, Rabat, Morocco
PHONE: +212 (7) 759125
FAX: +212 (7) 754742

Malta
12, rue Ghomara, Souissi, Rabat, Morocco
PHONE: +212 (7) 750897
FAX: +212 (7) 750897
TITLE: Ambassador
NAME: Claude Petiet

Mauritania
266, Quartier OLM, Rabat, Morocco
PHONE: +212 (7) 656678; 656679
FAX: +212 (7) 656680
TITLE: Ambassador
NAME: Mohamed Lamine Ould Yahya

Mexico
6, rue Kadi Mohamed Bebri, BP 1789, Souissi, Rabat, Morocco
PHONE: +212 (7) 631969
FAX: +212 (7) 768583
TITLE: Ambassador
NAME: Francisco José Cruz Gonzalez

Netherlands
40, rue de Tunis, BP 329, Rabat, Morocco
PHONE: +212 (7) 733512
FAX: +212 (7) 773333
TITLE: Ambassador
NAME: Hendrik Van Pesch

Niger
14 bis, rue Jabal al-Ayachi, Agdal, Rabat, Morocco
PHONE: +212 (7) 674615
FAX: +212 (7) 768583

Nigeria
70, avenue Omar Ibn al-Khattab, BP 347, Agdal, Rabat, Morocco
PHONE: +212 (7) 771856
TITLE: Ambassador
NAME: Mohamed Salah Abdelouahab

Norway
9, rue Khenifra, Agdal, Rabat, Morocco
PHONE: +212 (7) 764085

Oman
21, rue Hamza, Agdal, Rabat, Morocco

PHONE: +212 (7) 772788
FAX: +212 (7) 674567
TITLE: Ambassador
NAME: Mohammed Bin Salim al-Shanfari

Pakistan
11, rue Azrou, Hassan, Rabat, Morocco
PHONE: +212 (7) 766453; 762402
FAX: +212 (7) 766742
TITLE: Ambassador
NAME: Hassan Azmat

Palestine
4, rue Soussa, BP 387, Rabat, Morocco
PHONE: +212 (7) 766008; 769807
FAX: +212 (7) 767166
TITLE: Ambassador
NAME: Ouajih Hassan Ali Kacem Abou Marouane

Peru
16, rue Ifrane, Rabat, Morocco
PHONE: +212 (7) 723236; 733284
FAX: +212 (7) 702803
TITLE: Ambassador
NAME: Juan Enrique Arevalo

Poland
23, rue Oqbah, Agdal, BP 425, Rabat, Morocco
PHONE: +212 (7) 771173; 771791
FAX: +212 (7) 775320
TITLE: Ambassador
NAME: Piotr Szymanowski

Portugal
5, rue Thami Lamdouar, Souissi, Rabat, Morocco
PHONE: +212 (7) 756446
FAX: +212 (7) 756445
TITLE: Ambassador
NAME: Manuel Silva Pereira

Qatar
4, avenue Tarik Ibn Ziad, BP 1220, Rabat, Morocco
PHONE: +212 (7) 765681
FAX: +212 (7) 756445
TITLE: Ambassador
NAME: Mohamed Hassan

Romania
10, rue Ouazzane, Rabat, Morocco
PHONE: +212 (7) 738611; 724694
FAX: +212 (7) 700196
TITLE: Ambassador
NAME: Ioan Balin

Russia
Avenue Imam Malik, km 4, Rabat, Morocco
PHONE: +212 (7) 753609; 753527; 753509
FAX: +212 (7) 753590
TITLE: Ambassador
NAME: Kolotoucha Vassili Ivanovitch

Saudi Arabia
43, place de l'Unité Africaine, Rabat, Morocco
PHONE: +212 (7) 730171; 732794; 734827
FAX: +212 (7) 768587
TITLE: Ambassador
NAME: Abdelaziz Khodja

Senegal
17, rue Cadi Ben Hamadi Senhaji, Souissi, Rabat, Morocco
PHONE: +212 (7) 754171
FAX: +212 (7) 753590
TITLE: Ambassador
NAME: Doudou Diop

South Africa
34, rue des Saadiens Hassan, Rabat, Morocco
PHONE: +212 (7) 706760
FAX: +212 (7) 706756
TITLE: Charge d'Affaires
NAME: Johannes Reinhard Mostert

South Korea
41, avenue Mehdi Benbarka, Souissi, Rabat, Morocco
PHONE: +212 (7) 751767; 751966
FAX: +212 (7) 750189
TITLE: Ambassador
NAME: Dong Ho Kim

Spain
3, Zankat Madnine, Rabat, Morocco
PHONE: +212 (7) 707600; 707980
FAX: +212 (7) 707387
TITLE: Ambassador
NAME: Jorge Dezcallar Mazzaredo

Sudan
5, rue Ghomara, Souissi, Rabat, Morocco
PHONE: +212 (7) 752864; 752863
FAX: +212 (7) 752865
TITLE: Ambassador
NAME: Sadik Youssef Abou Akila

Sweden
159, avenue John Kennedy, Souissi, BP 428, Rabat, Morocco
PHONE: +212 (7) 759308; 759318; 759313
FAX: +212 (7) 758048

Switzerland
Square de Berkane, Hassan, BP 169, Rabat, Morocco
PHONE: +212 (7) 706974; 707512
FAX: +212 (7) 705749
TITLE: Ambassador
NAME: Henri Cuennet

Syria
Km 3,2, Route des Zaers, Souissi, BP 5158, Rabat, Morocco
PHONE: +212 (7) 757521; 755551
FAX: +212 (7) 757522
TITLE: Ambassador
NAME: Ali Hassan

Thailand
11, rue Tiddas, BP 4436, Rabat, Morocco
PHONE: +212 (7) 763328; 763365
FAX: +212 (7) 763920
TITLE: Ambassador
NAME: Naronk Khemayodhin

Tunisia
6, avenue de Fes, Rabat, Morocco
PHONE: +212 (7) 730636; 730576; 727866
FAX: +212 (7) 730637
TITLE: Ambassador
NAME: Mounji Bousnina

Turkey
7, avenue de Fes, Rabat, Morocco
PHONE: +212 (7) 762605; 762658
FAX: +212 (7) 704980
TITLE: Ambassador
NAME: Husein Naci Akinci

United Arab Emirates
11, blvd. al-Alaouiyine, Rabat, Morocco
PHONE: +212 (7) 730975; 730917; 730976
FAX: +212 (7) 724146; 724148
TITLE: Ambassador
NAME: Issa Hamad Abou Chihab

United Kingdom
17, boulevard de la Tour Hassan, BP 45, Rabat, Morocco
PHONE: +212 (7) 720905; 731403; 704532
FAX: +212 (7) 704531
TITLE: Ambassador
NAME: Anthony Michael Layden

United States
3, Zankat Madnine, Rabat, Morocco
PHONE: +212 (7) 758181; 762265
FAX: +212 (7) 750863
TITLE: Ambassador
NAME: Edward M. Gabriel

JUDICIAL SYSTEM

Supreme Court

Apellate Court

District Court

Islamic Court

BROADCAST MEDIA

Cope Ceuta

Sargento Mena 8, E-11701 Ceuta, Morocco
PHONE: +34 (956) 511122
FAX: +34 (956) 517603
TYPE: Commercial

OCR Convencial

Grupos Alfa 4, E-11701 Ceuta, Morocco
PHONE: +34 (956) 617886
FAX: +34 (956) 517004
TYPE: Commercial

Radio Ceuta

Ap. 180 Real 90, E-11701 Ceuta, Morocco
PHONE: + 34 (956) 511820
FAX: +34 (956) 516820
TYPE: Commercial

Radio Mediterranée Internationale

3-5 Rue Emsallah, Tangier, Morocco
PHONE: +212 (9) 936363
FAX: +212 (9) 936363
LANGUAGE: Arabic, French
TYPE: Government, Commercial

Radio Nacional de España, S.A.-Ceuta

Beatriz de Silva 12, E-11701 Ceuta, Morocco
PHONE: +34 (956) 522203
FAX: +34 (956) 519067

Radio Nacional de España, S.A.-Melilla

Ap. de Correos 222, E-29801 Melilla, Morocco
PHONE: +34 (956) 681907
FAX: +34 (956) 687332
TITLE: Director
CONTACT: Pedro A. Medina Barrenechea

Radio Sinfo Melilla

Edificio Melilla, Urbaniz Rusadir, E-29801 Melilla, Morocco
PHONE: +34 (956) 688840
FAX: +34 (956) 674317

Radiodiffusion-Télévision Marocaine

1 rue El Brihi, 10000 Rabat, Morocco
PHONE: +212 (7) 709613
FAX: +212 (7) 703208
WEBSITE: http://www.maroc.net/rc/
LANGUAGE: Arabic, English, French
TYPE: Government

R. Melilla

C/Muelle Puerto Ribera, 18, E-52005 Melilla, Morocco
PHONE: +34 (95) 2681708
FAX: +34 (95) 2681753
TITLE: Director
CONTACT: Gaspar Diaz Cerda

2M International

KM7, 300 route de Rabat, Casablanca, Morocco
PHONE: +212 (2) 354444
FAX: +212 (2) 354071
TITLE: Managing Director
CONTACT: Tawfik Bennani-Smires
TYPE: Commercial

Radiodiffusion Télévision Marocaine

1 rue Al Brihi, Rabat, Morocco
PHONE: +212 (7) 704963
FAX: +212 (7) 722047
TITLE: Directorate General
CONTACT: Mohamed Tricha
TYPE: Government

COLLEGES AND UNIVERSITIES

Ecole Nationale d'Industrie Minerale

PB 753 Adgal, Cherkaoui, Rabat, Morocco
PHONE: +212 (7) 771360
FAX: +212 (7) 771055

Universite Mohammed I Oujda

BP 524, Oujda 60000, Morocco
PHONE: +212 (68) 744785
FAX: +212 (68) 744779
E-MAIL: recteur@univ-oujda.ac.ma
WEBSITE: http://www.univ-oujda.ac.ma

NEWSPAPERS AND MAGAZINES

Al-Alam

Arrissalah, 11, Avenue Allal Ben Abdallah, BP 141, 11000 Rabat, Morocco
PHONE: +212 (7) 730237
FAX: +212 (7) 733896
TITLE: Editor-in-Chief
CONTACT: Abdelkrim Ghallab
CIRCULATION: 71,000

Al-Bayane

62, bd. De la Gironde, Casablanca, Morocco
PHONE: +212 (2) 304882
FAX: +212 (2) 308080
TITLE: General Manager
CONTACT: Mly Ismail Alaoui

L'Economiste

Ecos-Media SA, 201, Blvd. de Bordeaux, Casablanca, Morocco
PHONE: +212 (2) 271650
FAX: +212 (2) 297285
E-MAIL: leconomiste@techno.net.ma
WEBSITE: http://www.leconomiste.press.ma
TITLE: Editor-in-Chief
CONTACT: Nadia Salah
CIRCULATION: 17,000

La Gazette du Maroc

Avenue des FAR Tour des Habous, 13eme Etage, Casablanca, Morocco
PHONE: +212 (2) 313925
FAX: +212 (2) 318094
E-MAIL: info@gazette.press.ma
WEBSITE: http://www.gazette.press.ma
TITLE: Editor-in-Chief
CONTACT: Abdellah El Amvani
CIRCULATION: 15,000

Le Matin du Sahara et du Maghreb

88, bd. Mohammed V, Casablanca, Morocco
PHONE: +212 (2) 301271
FAX: +212 (2) 317535
E-MAIL: emploi@lematin.press.ma
WEBSITE: http://www.lematin.press.ma
TITLE: Editor-in-Chief
CONTACT: Boudali Stitou
CIRCULATION: 60,000

Maroc-Hebdo International

E-MAIL: mhi@maroc-hebdo.press.ma
WEBSITE: http://www.maroc-hebdo.press.ma

L'Opinion

Arrissalah, 11, Avenue Allal Ben Abdallah, BP 141, 11000 Rabat, Morocco
PHONE: +212 (7) 727812

FAX: +212 (7) 732183
TITLE: General Director
CONTACT: Mohamed Idrissi Kaitouni
CIRCULATION: 76,000

Le Quotidien du Maroc

27, rue Tata, Casablanca, Morocco
PHONE: +212 (2) 262368
FAX: +212 (2) 202210
TITLE: General Manager
CONTACT: Faycal Ghissassi

Maroc Magazine

34 rue Mohamed Smiha, Casablanca, Morocco
TITLE: Editor
CONTACT: Ahmed Alaoui
CIRCULATION: 50,000
TYPE: Business and economics, economic conditions

Maroc Business

1 Rond Point St. Exupery, Casablanca, Morocco
TITLE: Editor
CONTACT: Taieb Jamai
TYPE: Business and economics, general

PUBLISHERS

Access International Services

80 blvd. La Resistance, Casablanca, Morocco
PHONE: +212 (2) 316068
FAX: +212 (2) 304685
TITLE: President
CONTACT: Rachid Bennis
SUBJECTS: Advertising, Art, Business, Communications, Economics, How-to, Human Relations, Law, Publishing and Book Trade Reference, Religion-Islamic

Editions Al-Fourkane

8, rue Ibn Habbous, Av Yacoub El Mansour, 2, Casablanca, Morocco
PHONE: +212 (2) 983351
FAX: +212 (2) 953351
TITLE: Director
CONTACT: Dr. El Otmani Saad-Dine
SUBJECTS: Biography, Government, Political Science, Religion-Islamic, Social Sciences, Sociology

Dar El Kitab

pl de la Mosquee Habous, BP 4018, Casablanca, Morocco
PHONE: +212 (2) 304581
FAX: +212 (2) 304581
TITLE: Publicity Manager
CONTACT: Mounjedine Abdel-Ghani
SUBJECTS: History, Philosophy, Regional Interests, Science (General), Social Sciences, Sociology

Dar Nachr Al Maarifa Pour L'Edition et La Distribution

Rue Er-Rakha Quartier Industiel Cite Yacoub El Mansour, Rabat, Morocco
PHONE: +212 (7) 795702
FAX: +212 (7) 790343
TITLE: Contact
CONTACT: Zhiri M'Hamed
SUBJECTS: Economics, Education, History, Law, Literature, Literary Criticism, Essays, Mathematics, Science (General), Social Sciences, Sociology

Editions Eddif Maroc

71 ave. des Far, BP 7537, Casablanca, Morocco
PHONE: +212 (2) 442375
FAX: +212 (2) 313565
TITLE: President
CONTACT: Retnani Abdelkader
SUBJECTS: Art, Fiction, History, Literature, Literary Criticism, Essays, Social Sciences, Sociology

Editions Le Fennec

89B Boulevard d'Anfra, Casablanca, Morocco
PHONE: +212 (2) 209304
FAX: +212 (2) 264941
E-MAIL: fennec@techno.net.ma
TITLE: President, Editor
CONTACT: Layla Chaouni
SUBJECTS: Drama, Theater, Economics, Fiction, Health, Nutrition, Language Arts, Linguistics, Literature, Literary Criticism, Essays, Mysteries, Poetry, Psychology, Psychiatry, Religion-Islamic, Social Sciences, Sociology, Women Studies
TOTAL PUBLISHED: 2,000 print

Imprimerie Officielle (Government Publishing House)

ave Jean Mermoz, Rabat-Chellah, Morocco
PHONE: +212 (7) 765024
FAX: +212 (7) 765179

Editions Oum

25, rue Ibn Batouta, Casablanca, Morocco

PHONE: +212 (7) 274972
FAX: +212 (7) 208882
SUBJECTS: Art, How-to, Medicine, Nursing, Dentistry, Photography

Editions La Porte

281, ave. Mohammed-V, BP 331, Rabat, Morocco
PHONE: +212 (7) 709958
FAX: +212 (7) 709958
SUBJECTS: Economics, Government, Political Science, Language Arts, Linguistics, Law, Religion-Islamic, Religion-Other, Travel

Societe Ennewrasse Service Librairie et Imprimerie

70, ave. Okba Bnou Nafie, Agdal, Rabat, Morocco
PHONE: +212 (7) 776413
FAX: +212 (7) 776413
TITLE: Contact
CONTACT: Mohamed Ali Omar
SUBJECTS: Anthropology, Antiques, Business, Communications, Criminology, History, Human Relations, Law, Literature, Literary Criticism, Essays, Religion-Islamic, Women's Studies

RELIGIOUS ORGANIZATIONS

Buddhist

Association Zen du Maroc
55, Rue Al-Wahda, Casablanca 01, Morocco
PHONE: +212 (2) 224688

Jewish

Communauté Israélite d'Agadir
Angle Rue de la Foire et Av Moulay Abdellah, Agadir, Morocco
PHONE: +212 (8) 840341
E-MAIL: geoseb@hotmail.com
NAME: Georges Sebat

Synagogue of Casablanca
Rue Verlet Hanus, Casablanca, Morocco
PHONE: +212 (2) 270976

Orthodox

Holy Virgin Dormition Chruch
13, Rue de Blida, Casablanca, Morocco
PHONE: +212 (2) 200396

FURTHER READING

Articles

Crossette, Barbara. "Morocco: Western Sahara Talks End." *New York Times,* September 30, 2000, p. A6.

"Europe's Back Doors." *The Atlantic Monthly,* January 20, 2000, p. 26.

Homola, Victor. "Morocco: Western Sahara Talks." *New York Times,* September 29, 2000, p. A6.

"Morocco Down in the Dumps." *The Economist,* March 4, 2000, p. 48.

"Morocco King Rolls Up His Sleeves." *African Business,* January 2000, p. 31.

Newman, Barry. "Desert Wondering; Polisario's Fight Over Forgotten Land." *Wall Street Journal,* June 7, 2000, p. A1.

Rutsch, Horst. "Western Sahara." *UN Chronicle,* Spring 2000, vol. 37, no. 1, p.18.

"The United States Mission For The Referendum In Western Sahara." *Vital Speeches,* July 1, 2000, vol. 66, no. 18, p. 548.

"Western Sahara: It's a Mirage." *The Economist (US),* January 22, 2000, vol. 354, no. 8154, p. 47.

"Western Sahara: Polisario Talks." *New York Times,* June 16, 2000, p. A6.

Books

Dun and Bradstreet's Export Guide to Morocco. Parsippany, NJ: Dun & Bradstreet, 1999.

Genini, Izza. *Splendours of Morocco.* New York: Tauris Parke Books, 2000.

Gershovich, Moshe. *French Military Rule in Morocco: Colonialism and Its Consequences.* Portland, OR: F. Cass, 2000.

Penell, C. R. *Morocco Since 1830: A History.* New York: New York University Press, 1999.

Government Publications

Committee on Ways and Means, U.S. House of Representatives. *Report on Trade Mission to Czech Republic, Egypt, and Morocco.* Washington, DC: G.P.O., 2000.

MOROCCO: STATISTICAL DATA

For sources and notes see "Sources of Statistics" at the front of each volume.

GEOGRAPHY

Geography

Area:

Total: 446,550 sq km.

Land: 446,300 sq km.

Land boundaries:

Total: 2,017.9 km.

Border countries: Algeria 1,559 km, Western Sahara 443 km, Spain (Ceuta) 6.3 km, Spain (Melilla) 9.6 km.

Coastline: 1,835 km.

Climate: Mediterranean, becoming more extreme in the interior.

Terrain: northern coast and interior are mountainous with large areas of bordering plateaus, intermontane valleys, and rich coastal plains.

Natural resources: phosphates, iron ore, manganese, lead, zinc, fish, salt.

Land use:

Arable land: 21%

Permanent crops: 1%

Permanent pastures: 47%

Forests and woodland: 20%

Other: 11% (1993 est.).

HUMAN FACTORS

Demographics (A)

	1990	1995	1998	2000	2010	2020	2030	2040	2050
Population	24,686	27,447	29,066	30,122	35,301	40,266	44,665	48,238	50,872
Life expectancy - males	63.8	65.4	66.3	66.9	69.7	72.1	74.1	75.8	77.2
Life expectancy - females	67.9	69.7	70.7	71.4	74.6	77.3	79.6	81.4	82.9
Birth rate (per 1,000)	31.3	27.7	25.9	24.6	20.6	17.7	15.4	14.0	13.1
Death rate (per 1,000)	7.4	6.6	6.2	6.0	5.4	5.4	5.9	7.1	8.4
Women of reproductive age (15-49 yrs.)	5,931	6,868	7,494	7,935	9,721	10,940	11,573	11,631	11,524
Fertility rate	4.4	3.7	3.3	3.1	2.5	2.2	2.1	2.0	2.0

Except as noted, values for vital statistics are in thousands; life expectancy is in years.

Health Personnel

	National Data	World Data (wtd ave)
Total health expenditure as a percentage of GDP, 1990-1998[a]		
Public sector	1.3	2.5
Private sector	2.7	2.9
Total[b]	4.0	5.5
Health expenditure per capita in U.S. dollars, 1990-1998[a]		
Purchasing power parity	140	561
Total	49	483
Availability of health care facilities per 100,000 people		
Hospital beds 1990-1998[a]	100	330
Doctors 1992-1995[a]	34	122
Nurses 1992-1995[a]	94	248

Health Indicators

	National Data	World Data
Life expectancy at birth (years)		
1980	58	61
1998	67	67
Daily per capita supply of calories		
1970	2,468	2,358
1997	3,078	2,791
Daily per capital supply of protein		
1997 (grams)	82	74
Total fertility rate (births per woman)		
1980	5.4	3.7
1998	3.0	2.7
Population with access (%)		
To safe water (1990-96)	52	NA
To sanitation (1990-96)	40	NA
People living with (1997)		
Tuberculosis (cases per 100,000)	109.8	60.4
Malaria (cases per 100,000)	0.5	42.2
HIV/AIDS (% aged 15 - 49 years)	0.03	0.99

Infants and Malnutrition

	National Data	World Data (wtd ave)
Under 5 mortality rate (1989)	70	NA
% of infants with low birthweight (1992-98)[1]	4	17
Births attended by skilled health staff (% of total births 1996-98)	31	52
% fully immunized at 1 year of age (1995-98)[1]		
TB	90	82
DPT	93	77
Polio	93	77
Measles	91	74
Prevalence of child malnutrition (1992-98)[1] (based on weight for age, % of children under 5 years)	10	30

Ethnic Division

Arab-Berber 99.1%

Other 0.7%

Jewish 0.2%

Religion

Muslim 98.7%

Christian 1.1%

Jewish 0.2%

Major Languages

Arabic (official), Berber dialects, French often the language of business, government, and diplomacy.

EDUCATION

Public Education Expenditures

	1980	1997
Public expenditures on education as % of GNP	6.1	5.0
Expenditures per student as % of GNP per capita		
Primary	15.5[2]	14.3[2]
Secondary	54.9	NA
Tertiary	155.3	69.5
Teachers' compensation as % of total current education expenditures	NA	78.0
Pupils per teacher at the primary level	NA	28
Duration of primary education in years	NA	6
World data for comparison		
Public expenditures on education as % of GNP (mean)	3.9	4.8
Pupils per teacher at the primary level (wtd ave)	NA	33

	1980	1997
Duration of primary education in years (mean)	NA	9

Literacy Rates (A)

In thousands and percent	1990	1995	2000	2010
Illiterate population (15+ yrs.)	9,124	9,730	10,153	10,507
Literacy rate - total adult pop. (%)	38.6	43.7	48.4	57.4
Literacy rate - males (%)	52.0	56.6	60.7	68.0
Literacy rate - females (%)	25.6	31.0	36.3	47.0

Educational Attainment (B)

	1995	1997
Gross enrollment ratio (%)		
Primary level	83.7	86.0
Secondary level	38.5	39.1
Tertiary level	11.2	11.3

GOVERNMENT & LAW

Military Affairs (A)

	1990	1992	1995	1996	1997
Military expenditures					
Current dollars (mil.)	1,290	1,170	1,230	1,290	1,390
1997 constant dollars (mil.)	1,510	1,300	1,280	1,310	1,390
Armed forces (000)	195	195	195	195	195
Gross national product (GNP)					
Current dollars (mil.)	24,000	25,900	28,400	32,700	32,500
1997 constant dollars (mil.)	28,100	28,700	29,400	33,200	32,500
Central government expenditures (CGE)					
1997 constant dollars (mil.)	8,440	9,050	10,300	10,100[e]	10,700[e]
People (mil.)	26.2	25.8	27.5	28.0	28.6
Military expenditure as % of GNP	5.4	4.5	4.3	3.9	4.3
World data on military expenditure as % of GNP	4.5	3.4	2.7	2.6	2.6
Military expenditure as % of CGE	17.9	14.3	12.4	13.0	12.9
World data on military expenditure as % of CGE	17.0	12.5	10.5	10.3	10.2
Military expenditure per capita (1997 $)	58	50	46	47	49
World data on military expenditure per capita (1997 $)	242	173	146	143	145
Armed forces per 1,000 people (soldiers)	7.5	7.6	7.1	7.0	6.8
World data on armed forces per 1,000 people (soldiers)	5.3	4.5	4.1	3.9	3.8
GNP per capita (1997 $)	1,080	1,110	1,070	1,190	1,140
Arms imports[6]					
Current dollars (mil.)	230	100	60	120	180
1997 constant dollars (mil.)	269	111	62	122	180
Total imports[7]					
Current dollars (mil.)	6,800	7,348	10,020	9,704	9,525
1997 constant dollars (mil.)	7,964	8,146	10,380	9,866	9,525
Total exports[7]					
Current dollars (mil.)	4,265	3,984	6,881	6,881	7,032
1997 constant dollars (mil.)	4,995	4,417	7,125	6,996	7,032
Arms as percent of total imports[8]	3.4	1.4	0.6	1.2	1.9
Arms as percent of total exports[8]	0	0	0	0	0

Political Parties

Parliament	no. of seats
Chamber of Counselors	
National Rally of Independents (RNI)	42
Social Democratic Movement (MDS)	33
Constitutional Union (UC)	28
Popular Movement (MP)	27
National Democratic Party (PND)	21
Istiqlal Party (IP)	21
Socialist Union of Popular Forces (USFP)	16
National Popular Movement (MNP)	15
Labor Party (UT)	13
Democratic Forces Front (FFD)	12
CDT	11
UTM	8
Party of Progress and Socialism (PPS)	7
Democratic Socialist Front (PSD)	4
Democratic Party for Independence (PDI)	4
UGTM	3
UNMT	2
Other	3
Chamber of Representatives	
Socialist Union of Popular Forces (USFP)	57
Constitutional Union (UC)	50
National Rally of Independents (RNI)	46
Popular Movement (MP)	40
Social Democratic Movement (MDS)	32
Istiqlal Party (IP)	32
National Popular Movement (MNP)	19
National Democratic Party (PND)	10
Popular Constitutional and Democratic Movement (MPCD)	9
Party of Progress and Socialism (PPS)	9
Democratic Forces Front (FFD)	9
Democratic Socialist Front (PSD)	5
Organization of Democratic and Popular Action (OADP)	4
Action Party (PA)	2
Democratic Party for Independence (PDI)	1

Chamber of Counselors elections were last held 5 December 1997 (next to be held December 2000); Chamber of Representatives elections were last held 14 November 1997 (next to be held November 2002). CDT, UTM, UGTM, and UNMT are all labor unions.

Government Budgets (A)

Year: 1995

Total Expenditures: 93,889 Millions of Dirhams

Expenditures as a percentage of the total by function:

General public services and public order	17.31
Defense	13.56
Education	16.55
Health	3.12
Social Security and Welfare	6.96
Housing and community amenities	0.36
Recreational, cultural, and religious affairs	0.92
Fuel and energy	0.69
Agriculture, forestry, fishing, and hunting	4.15
Mining, manufacturing, and construction	0
Transportation and communication	4.33
Other economic affairs and services	0.77

LABOR FORCE

Total Labor Force (A)

11 million (1997 est.).

Labor Force by Occupation

Agriculture	50%
Services	35%
Industry	15%

Data for 1999 est.

Unemployment Rate

19% (1998 est.)

PRODUCTION SECTOR

Energy Production

Production	13.16 billion kWh
Production by source	
Fossil fuel	83.59%
Hydro	16.41%
Nuclear	0%
Other	0%
Exports	0 kWh

Data for 1998.

Energy Consumption

Consumption	12.363 billion kWh
Imports	124.000 million kWh

Data for 1998.

Transportation

Highways:

Total: 57,847 km.

Paved: 30,254 km (including 327 km of expressways).

Unpaved: 27,593 km (1998 est.).

Pipelines: crude oil 362 km; petroleum products 491 km (abandoned); natural gas 241 km.

Merchant marine:

Total: 40 ships (1,000 GRT or over) totaling 218,987 GRT/263,191 DWT.

Ships by type: cargo 9, chemical tanker 6, container 3, passenger 1, petroleum tanker 3, refrigerated cargo 9, roll-on/roll-off 8, short-sea passenger 1 (1999 est.).

Airports: 70 (1999 est.).

Airports - with paved runways: 26.

Airports - with unpaved runways: 44.

Top Agriculture Products

Barley, wheat, citrus, wine, vegetables, olives; livestock.

Top Mining Products (B)

Mineral resources include: phosphates, iron ore, manganese, lead, zinc, salt.

MANUFACTURING SECTOR

GDP & Manufacturing Summary (A)

	1980	1985	1990	1995
GDP ($-1990 mil.)[1]	17,776	20,900	25,826	27,027
Per capita ($-1990)[1]	917	965	1,074	1,019
Manufacturing share (%) (current prices)[1]	17.8	19.4	20.0	21.4[e]
Manufacturing				
Value added ($-1990 mil.)[1]	3,205	3,984	4,888	5,333
Industrial production index	82	88	100	107
Value added ($ mil.)	1,485	1,399[e]	3,289[e]	5,485
Gross output ($ mil.)	6,242	4,685	11,206	15,664
Employment (000)	176	227	307	454
Profitability (% of gross output)				
Intermediate input (%)	77	71[e]	72[e]	66
Wages and salaries inc. supplements (%)	13	12[e]	11[e]	12[e]
Gross operating surplus	10	17[e]	18[e]	21[e]
Productivity ($)				
Gross output per worker	33,920	19,779	35,272	33,570
Value added per worker	7,801	5,736[e]	10,011[e]	11,282
Average wage (inc. supplements)	4,363	2,434[e]	3,774[e]	4,144[e]
Value added ($ mil.)				
Food products	130	110	144	838
Beverages	62	92[e]	209[e]	292[e]
Tobacco products	38	150[e]	423[e]	677[e]
Textiles	202	172	315	488
Wearing apparel	32	42	228	385
Leather and fur products	15	30[e]	68[e]	70[e]
Footwear	24	NA	NA	NA
Wood and wood products	30	25[e]	49[e]	41[e]
Furniture and fixtures	19	16[e]	30[e]	25[e]
Paper and paper products	64	64	151	186[e]
Printing and publishing	26	19	43	52[e]
Industrial chemicals	127	166	403	743[e]
Other chemical products	97	13	30	24[e]
Petroleum refineries	114[e]	100[e]	217[e]	368[e]
Rubber products	34	35[e]	54[e]	68[e]
Plastic products	20	20[e]	45[e]	60[e]
Pottery, china and earthenware	6	6[e]	25[e]	36[e]
Glass and glass products	10	6[e]	11[e]	16[e]
Other non-metal mineral products	154	92[e]	264[e]	429[e]
Iron and steel	7[e]	1[e]	10[e]	9[e]
Non-ferrous metals	8	7[e]	71[e]	69[e]
Metal products	110	96	166	220
Non-electrical machinery	30	23[e]	49[e]	68
Electrical machinery	61	56	132	138
Transport equipment	62	49	140	172
Prof. and scientific equipment	1	3[e]	7	7
Other manufacturing	2	1	4	4

COMMUNICATIONS

Daily Newspapers

	National Data	World Data for Comparison
Daily Newspapers		
Number of Dailies	22	8,391
Total Circulation (000)	704	548,000
Circulation per 1,000 inhabitants	27	96

Telecommunications

Telephones - main lines in use: 1.391 million (1998).

Telephones - mobile cellular: 116,645 (1998).

Telephone system:

Domestic: good system composed of open-wire lines, cables, and microwave radio relay links; Internet available but expensive; principal switching centers are Casablanca and Rabat; national network nearly 100% digital using fiber-optic links; improved rural service employs microwave radio relay.

International: 7 submarine cables; satellite earth stations - 2 Intelsat (Atlantic Ocean) and 1 Arabsat; microwave radio relay to Gibraltar, Spain, and Western Sahara; coaxial cable and microwave radio relay to Algeria; participant in Medarabtel; fiber-optic cable link from Agadir to Algeria and Tunesia.

Radio broadcast stations: AM 27, FM 25, shortwave 6 (1998).

Radios: 6.64 million (1997).

Television broadcast stations: 26 (plus 35 repeaters) (1997).

Televisions: 3.1 million (1997).

Internet Service Providers (ISPs): 27 (1999).

FINANCE, ECONOMICS, & TRADE

Economic Indicators

National product: GDP—purchasing power parity—$108 billion (1999 est.).

National product real growth rate: 0% (1999 est.).

National product per capita: $3,600 (1999 est.).

Inflation rate—consumer price index: 1.9% (1999 est.).

Exchange Rates

Exchange rates:

Moroccan dirhams (DH) per US$1

January 2000	10.051
1999	9.804
1998	9.604
1997	9.527
1996	8.716
1995	8.540

Top Import Origins

$9.5 billion (f.o.b.)

Origins

France	22%
Spain	10%
United States	7%
Germany	6%
Italy	6%

Data for 1998.

Balance of Payments

	1994	1995	1996	1997	1998
Exports of goods (f.o.b.)	5,541	6,871	6,886	7,039	7,253
Imports of goods (f.o.b.)	−7,648	−9,353	−9,080	−8,903	−9,468
Trade balance	−2,107	−2,482	−2,193	−1,864	−2,215
Services - debits	−1,730	−1,890	−1,782	−1,724	−1,896
Services - credits	2,014	2,173	2,743	2,471	2,755
Private transfers (net)	2,123	2,298	2,565	2,204	2,332
Government transfers (net)	173	70	50	48	52
Overall balance	−723	−1,186	35	−87	−118

Top Export Destinations

$7.1 billion (f.o.b., 1998)

Destinations (1998)

France	27%
Spain	11%
India	7%
Japan	6%
Italy	5%

Foreign Aid

Recipient: $565.6 million (1995).

Import/Export Commodities

Import Commodities	Export Commodities
Semiprocessed goods	Phosphates and fertilizers
Machinery and equipment	Food and beverages
Food and beverages	Minerals
Consumer goods	
Fuel	

MOZAMBIQUE

CAPITAL: Maputo (formerly Lourenço Marques).

FLAG: The flag consists of broad stripes of green, black, and yellow, separated by narrow bands of white. Extending from the hoist is a red triangle; centered on the triangle is a yellow five-pointed star upon which is a white book over which are crossed the black silhouettes of a hoe and an AK47 rifle.

ANTHEM: Begins "Viva viva FRELIMO."

MONETARY UNIT: The Mozambique escudo (ME), linked until 1977 with the Portuguese escudo, was in June 1980 renamed the metical (MT); it is a paper currency of 100 centavos. There are coins of 1, 2, 5, 10, and 20 meticais, and notes of 50, 100, 500, and 1,000 meticais. MT1 = \$0.00009 (or \$1 = MT11,478.05).

WEIGHTS AND MEASURES: The metric system is in use.

HOLIDAYS: New Year's Day, 1 January; Heroes' Day, 3 February; Women's Day, 7 April; Workers' Day, 1 May; Independence Day, 25 June; Victory Day, 7 September; Day of Revolution, 25 September; Christmas, 25 December.

TIME: 2 PM = noon GMT.

LOCATION AND SIZE: Located on the southeastern coast of Africa, Mozambique (Moçambique) has an area of 801,590 square kilometers (309,496 square miles), slightly less than twice the size of the state of California. It has a total boundary length of 7,003 kilometers (4,351 miles).

CLIMATE: The wet season has monthly average temperatures between 27°C and 29°C (81°–84°F); the dry season has June and July temperatures averaging 18°–20°C (64°–68°F). The average annual rainfall is greatest, about 142 centimeters (56 inches), over the western hills and the central areas.

Republic of Mozambique
República Popular de Moçambique

INTRODUCTORY SURVEY

RECENT HISTORY

The first Europeans in the area, the Portuguese, began to settle and trade on the coast early in the sixteenth century. During the seventeenth century they set up plantations and estates. By the end of the nineteenth century Portugal had made boundary agreements with its colonial rivals, the United Kingdom and Germany, and had suppressed much of the African resistance in the interior. In 1951 Mozambique became an overseas province of Portugal.

On June 25, 1962, the Mozambique Liberation Front (FRELIMO) was formed and on September 25, 1964, began the armed struggle for independence. Samora Machel became president of FRELIMO in December 1970 after its first president, Eduardo Mondlane, was assassinated. In1974 Portuguese and FRELIMO representatives negotiated an independence agreement, and Mozambique became officially independent at midnight June 24,1975. Machel, who became the nation's first president, quickly affirmed Mozambique's support of the movement for African control of Rhodesia (now Zimbabwe), and on March 3, 1976, Mozambique closed its border with Rhodesia.

After independence, FRELIMO was transformed from a liberation movement into a Marxist-Leninist party dedicated to the creation of a Socialist state. A newly formed anti-government group opposed to FRELIMO's political stance and sympathetic to white interests, the Mozambique National Resistance (RENAMO), began to

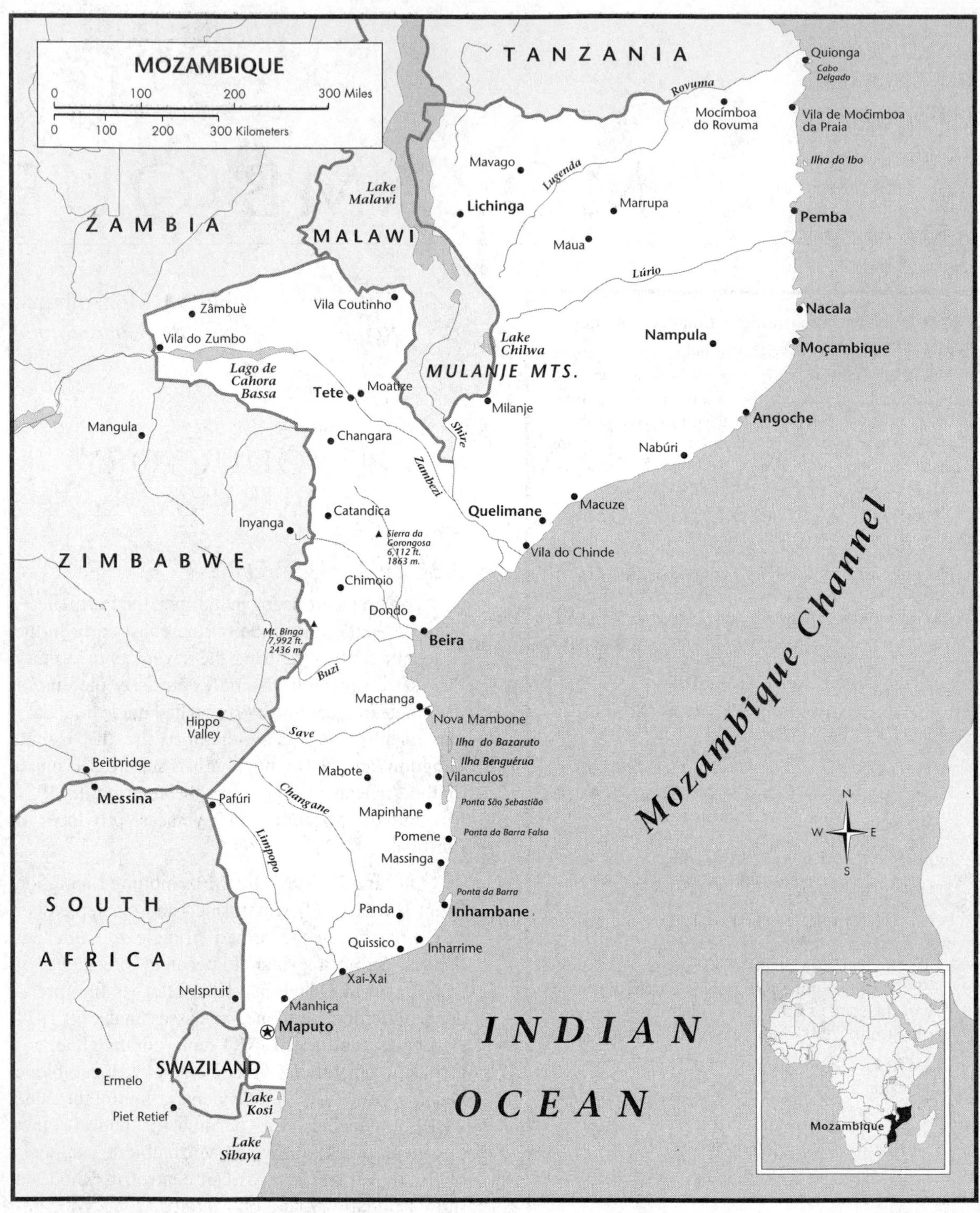

conduct a guerrilla rebellion with the backing of whites in Rhodesia. These activities continued into the 1980s and turned into a civil war. After the white government in Rhodesia fell and that country became Zimbabwe, RENAMO received substantial aid from South Africa and also had bases in Malawi.

On October 19, 1986, President Machel and thirty-three others were killed when their Soviet-built jetliner crashed inside South Africa. In August 1989 FRELIMO agreed to allow opposition parties to compete openly and legally. A peace treaty was finally signed on October 4, 1992, and a joint commission of government and RENAMO along with a small UN monitoring force were named to carry out the agreement. Democratic elections were to be held within a year. In mid-1993 the national election was postponed until October 1994. Joaquim A. Chissano, FRELIMO leader and Mozambique's foreign minister since independence, won with 53.3 percent of the vote. The elections were monitored by 2,000 international observers for fairness and agreed the elections, although less than ideal, were sufficiently accurate. In December 1999 presidential and parliamentary elections Chissano remained in power. His party, RNAMD, took 117of 250 parliament seats and FRELIMO took 133 seats.

As the late 1990s brought a semblance of normalcy to the war torn country, Mozambique attempted to repatriate millions of returning refugees. It has also engaged in wholesale privatization of formerly state-owned enterprises enticing large-scale foreign investments.

GOVERNMENT

A revised constitution with a multiparty system of government came into force on 30 November 1990. The name of the country was changed from the People's Republic to the Republic of Mozambique. According to the 1990 constitution, the president, the chief of state, is to be elected by universal adult vote for a five-year term. The president appoints the prime minister who serves as head of government. The Assembly of the Republic will replace the People's Assembly. Its 250 deputies are to be elected for five-year terms by direct popular vote.

Judiciary

The formal justice system is divided into a civil/criminal system and a separate military justice system under joint supervision of the Ministries of Defense and Justice. The Supreme Court hears appeals from both systems. Local courts, part of the civil/criminal system, handle estate, divorce, and other social and family issues. The provincial and district courts are below the Supreme Court.

Political Parties

The Mozambique Liberation Front (Frente de Libertação de Moçambique-FRELIMO) was the sole legal political party until 1991. The new constitution in force in November 1990 legalized a multiparty system. FRELIMO and the Mozambique National Resistance (RENAMO-created as an armed rebel force) have been the most popular groups. Other parties include the Mozambican National Union (UNAMO), the Democratic Party of Mozambique (PADEMO), and the Mozambique National Movement (MONAMO).

DEFENSE

The armed forces in 1996 included 4,000-5,000 army personnel and a 100-member navy, and an air force of 1,000. Mozambique spent $72 million on defense, or 4.7 percent of GDP.

ECONOMIC AFFAIRS

Mozambique is a poverty-stricken country with large debts. Civil war and droughts weakened Mozambique's economy in the 1980s leaving it heavily dependent on foreign aid. However recent shifts away from socialism and toward a market economy, as well as a resolution of the civil war, laid the foundation for an economic recovery. The economy grew by an average of 4.7 percent yearly between 1988 and 1998. International investment is increasing as stability returns, and an aggressive privatization program continues. Growth from 1997 to 1999 averaged 10 percent growth rate, one of the highest annual rates in the world. Since 1996 inflation has been low and exchange rates stable. However the country still depends on foreign aid to balance the budget. Foreign investment continues to increase. The outlook is bright as trade and transportation links to South Africa are expected to improve. However in 2000 some of the worst flooding in the history of the country killed and displaced many citizens. Long-term prospects for economic growth will depend heavily on good weather for farmers and a stable political situation.

Public Finance

The U.S. Central Intelligence Agency estimated that government revenues in 1997 totaled approximately $402 million and expenditures $799 million. External debt totaled $4.8 billion in 1999.

Income

In 1999 Mozambique's gross domestic product (GDP) was estimated at $18.7 billion, or about $1,000 per capita, ranking among the poorest in the world. The 1999 estimated GDP growth rate was 10 percent and inflation was 4 percent. The 1998 estimated GDP contribution by sector was agriculture 34 percent, industry 18 percent, and services 48 percent.

Industry

Mozambique's industrial sector is primarily centered on the processing of locally produced raw materials, especially sugar, cashews, tea, and wheat. Brewing and textile production began in the 1980s, along with cement, fertilizer, and agricultural tool manufacturing. Major investments in aluminum processing, steel production, mineral extraction, cotton and sugar production, natural gas, power generation, fishing, timber, and transportation services.

Banking and Finance

The Mozambican branch of the defunct Portuguese National Overseas Bank was nationalized without compensation. By a decree of May 23, 1975, it was reconstituted as the Bank of Mozambique (Banco de Moçambique-BM). Functioning as a central bank, it serves as the government's banker and financial adviser and as controller of monetary and credit policies. It is also an issuing bank, a commercial bank, and the state treasury; the bank manages Mozambique's external assets and acts as an intermediary in all international monetary transactions. The bank has its headquarters at Maputo. In 1978 the government nationalized four of the five remaining private commercial banks.

After 1992 the government's economic reform program began to tackle the financial sector. Foreign banks were allowed to invest in Mozambican financial institutions, in 1994 interest rates were deregulated and in 1995 the commercial activities of the central bank were assumed by a newly created institution, the Banco Comercial de Moçambique (BCM).

By 1996 the government had privatized the BCM and plans were afoot for the divestiture of the BPD (Banco Popular de Desenvolvimento), scheduled for early 1997. Portuguese interest in the BPD and other Mozambican banks has been strong.

Before 1992 Banco Standard Totta de Moçambique (BSTM) was the only private bank operating in the country. It has since been joined by Banco Português do Atlántico (BPA), Banco de Fomento e Exterior (BFE), and Banco Internacional de Moçambique (BIM), whose main shareholder is the Banco Comercial Português (BCP). By 1997 the government had privatized the BCM and BPD. In 1999 there were eight banks operating in Mozambique including BCM, BIM, and BPD.

Economic Development

In 1994 Mozambique ranked as one of the poorest countries in the world. Since then a series of reforms liberalizing the economy have been undertaken. More than 900 state enterprises have been privatized attracting foreign investments in a variety of industries, power production, agriculture, transportation services, and telecommunications. Mozambique has also focused on tax and commercial code reform. A variety of infrastructure development projects were underway in 1999 including a road and railway from Maputo to Johannesburg.

In 1999 under the Heavily Indebted Poor Country (HIPC) initiative, Mozambique's eligible debts were reduced by 90 percent by the IMF, World Bank, Paris Club, and multilateral lending agencies. The United States and United Kingdom also granted debt relief.

SOCIAL WELFARE

FRELIMO and its partner, the Organization of Mozambican Women, have widened educational and occupational opportunities for women and have pushed for a family law protecting women against desertion, abuse, and sexual harassment. Despite official policy and laws requiring equal rights for both sexes, there is still legal and social discrimination against women.

Healthcare

The government's National Health Service provides almost all healthcare services. Traditional healers continue to play a significant role. In 1985-1995 only 39 percent of the population had access to health care services. The shortage of medical supplies and trained personnel has remained severe throughout Mozambique. In 1993 there was one doctor per 36,225 people. In 2000 estimated average life expectancy was only 37.5 years.

Housing

As of 1980 63 percent of housing units were constructed of woven straw and 14 percent of cane and woodstick. Nearly 96 percent were without electricity and over half had no toilet facilities.

EDUCATION

Education is compulsory for seven years but in practice most students do not study the full compulsory period. In 1995 there were 4,149 primary schools with 24,575 teachers and 1,415,428 pupils. General secondary schools had 171,102 pupils. Eduardo Mondlane University is in Maputo with 7,143 students in 1997. The country had an estimated adult illiteracy rate of 60 percent in 1995.

2000 KEY EVENTS TIMELINE

January

- The Constitutional Court announces the results of its investigation into charges of ballot rigging in the presidential elections. The court rules that Joaquim Chissano won a second term fairly, and that his party won control of the parliament, and that the opposition party, Renamo, had failed to prove fraud.

February

- Extreme flooding wreaks havoc across the country. By the time the water recede in early March, an estimated 400 people will have died, and thousands of others will be made homeless.

March

- The United States reports that it has earmarked an additional US$2.5 million in aid to help deactivate land mines that were washed loose by the flooding in February. (The United States has spent about US$25 million since 1995 to help the country deal with land mines.)

June

- A June 3 report notes that 12,060 new cases of cholera, resulting in 161 deaths, have been recorded since January.
- International donors pledge US$530 million this year and US$560 million in 2001 to alleviate poverty and fight the spread of AIDS in Mozambique. Tanzania provides food aid for about 60,000 victims of February flooding.

August

- Government officials detain five opposition party Renamo members at Beira on August 16, claiming that they intended to incite riots.

November

- Forty-one people, including six policemen, are shot to death at an opposition Renamo party rallies November 6–10.
- Mozambique's most prominent investigative journalist, Carlos Cardosa, is murdered November 22.
- Eighty-three people are asphyxiated to death in Montepuez jail on November 22 in a cell that was holding twice its capacity. The opposition Renamo party accuses the ruling Frelimo party of causing the deaths.

December

- President Joaquim Chissano and opposition leader Afonso Dhlakama of Renamo meet for the first time since the disputed elections of December 1999, and forge an agreement to work together.
- The World Bank and International Monetary Fund (IMF) announce on December 23 that the United States, Canada, Japan, and nations of Europe will provide debt relief for twenty-two of the world's poorest nations, including Benin, Bolivia, Burkina Faso, Cameroon, The Gambia, Guinea, Guinea-Bissau, Guyana, Honduras, Madagascar, Malawi, Mali, Mauritania, Mozambique, Nicaragua, Niger, Rwanda, São Tomé and Príncipe, Senegal, Tanzania, Uganda, and Zambia.

ANALYSIS OF EVENTS: 2000

BUSINESS AND THE ECONOMY

Mozambique began the year touted as one of the great success stories of the developing world, having recorded economic growth of 10 percent or more for several years. Agriculture had grown almost 9 percent annually over the same period. Much of the country's new wealth was concentrated in the hands of an urban middle class in the area surrounding the capital, Maputo, in the south, and the majority of Mozambicans still lived in poverty, but conditions were gradually improving even for those in the countryside. In 1999 for the first time, the nation produced enough food to feed its population. Mozambique's stock market opened in October 1999, and exemplified the ruling Frelimo party's departure from its Communist past and embrace of a free-market economy, as it prepared for major expansion over the next two years.

While not completely reversing the economic gains of the previous years, the flooding—which devastated roughly 90 percent of the nation's irrigated land, destroyed a quarter of its harvest, and killed a third of its livestock—was expected to cut growth in half. It was estimated that nearly a million Mozambicans would need emergency aid of some kind. Much of the rail line connecting Mozambique to Zimbabwe, a major trade partner, had been destroyed, and over one-quarter of the country's main north-south highway had been washed away. Regional leaders in southern Africa pleaded for international debt relief for Mozambique, and in May government officials held a meeting with international aid agencies in Rome, Italy, seeking $450 million in aid to rebuild the country's homes and infrastructure and revive its agricultural sector.

Despite the devastation, many farmers were rushing back to their land by May to plant crops in the newly enriched alluvial soil, hoping for a rapid harvest within two months. The Mozal aluminum smelter continued operations virtually without a hitch, and bidding for offshore and deepwater oil concessions began in May as planned.

GOVERNMENT AND POLITICS

President Joaquim Chissano began serving his second five-year term in January, after the previous December's elections gave him a modest victory over challenger Afonso Dhlakama of the opposition Renamo party. In parliamentary polling, Chissano's ruling Frelimo party was returned to power with 133 seats to 117 for Renamo. (The small Democratic Union party lost all nine of the seats it had formerly held.) In spite of Renamo's charges of vote rigging, the elections were judged free and fair, and in January the Renamo delegates withdrew their threat to boycott the new parliament. Following sixteen years of bloody civil warfare that ended in 1992, the country's second peaceful democratic elections were cause for celebration, especially since this time the polling had been supervised internally rather than by United Nations officials.

The government still faced challenges in establishing political harmony and transparency, but its greatest challenge was one that no one could have predicted—the three weeks of catastrophic flooding that took place in February and March, threatening the dramatic economic growth that had gained international attention in recent years. By summer the government had formed a comprehensive reconstruction plan and was making efforts to resettle refugees from coastal areas on higher ground to avoid a repetition of the disaster, in which whole villages had virtually been washed away.

CULTURE AND SOCIETY

Like other disasters in Africa, Mozambique's worst flooding in fifty years which began in February took a while to attract international attention. By March television and print media throughout the world displayed dramatic scenes of Mozambicans taking refuge on rooftops, shrinking patches of high ground, and other elevated sites. Most memorably etched on the world's consciousness was the helicopter rescue of twenty-six-year-old Sophia Pedro from the treetop in which she had just given birth to her daughter, Rositha. Altogether the flooding left over a million people homeless. Within weeks the death toll had climbed over 400, and it was feared that it would ultimately number in the thousands. Some 1,000 children waited to be reunited with their parents after becoming separated during rescue efforts. The spread of malaria and other diseases, particularly in crowded refugee camps, raised the possibility that more people could die in the aftermath than during the flooding itself. There were also fears that the floodwaters had shifted some of the 1.8 million landmines estimated to have remained buried from the country's long civil war. In response the United States added an extra $2.5 million in aid to amounts already donated for deactivation of the mines.

DIRECTORY

CENTRAL GOVERNMENT

Head of State

President
Joaquim Alberto Chissano, Office of the President, Avenida Julius Nyerere 2000, Caixa Postal 285, Maputo, Mozambique
PHONE: +258 491121
FAX: +258 492068

Prime Minister
Pascoal Manuel Mocumbi, Office of the Prime Minister, Praca da Marinha Popular, Maputo, Mozambique
PHONE: +258 426861
FAX: +258 426881

Ministers

Minister of Agriculture and Fisheries
Carlos Do Rosário, Ministry of Agriculture and Fisheries, Praça dos Herois, Moçambicanos, Maputo, Mozambique
PHONE: +258 460055
FAX: +258 460055

Minister of Culture, Youth and Sports
José Mateus Katupha, Ministry of Culture, Youth and Sports, Av. Patrice Lumumba 1217, Maputo, Mozambique
PHONE: +258 420068; 493977
FAX: +258 429700; 493077

Minister of Defense
Aguiar Real Mazula, Ministry of Defense, Av. Mártires da Machava 28037, Maputo, Mozambique
PHONE: +258 493369; 492081
FAX: +258 491619

Minister of Education
Arnaldo Nhavoto, Ministry of Education, Av. 24 de Julho 167, 9° andar, Maputo, Mozambique
PHONE: +258 490830; 492829; 492006
FAX: +258 492160

Minister of Environmental Action Coordination
Bernardo Pedro Farraz, Ministry of Environmental Action Coordination, Av. Acordos de Lusaka 2115, Caixa Postal 2020, Maputo, Mozambique
PHONE: +258 466245
FAX: +258 465849
E-MAIL: micoa@ambinet.uem.mz

Minister of Foreign Affairs and Cooperation
Leonardo Santos Simão, Ministry of Foreign Affairs and Cooperation, Av. Julius Nyerere 4, Maputo, Mozambique
PHONE: +258 492258; 490222; 490223
FAX: +258 491460; 494070

Minister of Health
Aurélio Zilhão, Ministry of Health, Av. Eduardo Mondlane, Maputo, Mozambique
PHONE: +258 427131
FAX: +258 427133

Minister of Industry, Commerce, and Tourism
Oldemiro Baloi, Ministry of Industry, Commerce, and Tourism, Av. 25 de Setembro 86, Maputo, Mozambique
PHONE: +258 427204
FAX: +258 421305

Minister of the Interior
Almerino Manhenje, Ministry of the Interior, Av. Olof Palme 46/48, Maputo, Mozambique
PHONE: +258 420130
FAX: +258 420084

Minister of Justice
José Ibraimo Abudo, Ministry of Justice, Av. Julius Nyerere 33, Maputo, Mozambique
PHONE: +258 491613
FAX: +258 494264

Minister of Labor
Guilherme Luis Mavila, Ministry of Labor, Av. 24 de Julho 2351, 1° andar, Maputo, Mozambique
PHONE: +258 424400; 424072; 427051
FAX: +258 421881

Minister of Mineral Resources and Energy
John Kachamila, Ministry of Mineral Resources and Energy, Av. Fernão Magalhães 34, Maputo, Mozambique
PHONE: +258 429615; 425682
FAX: +258 427103

Minister of Planning and Finance
Tomáz Salomão, Ministry of Planning and Finance, Praça da Marinha Popular, Caixa Postal 272, Maputo, Mozambique
PHONE: +258 421303; 425071
FAX: +258 420137

Minister of Public Works and Housing
Roberto Costley-White, Ministry of Public Works and Housing, Av. Karl Marx 268, Maputo, Mozambique
PHONE: +258 420543; 430028
FAX: +258 421369

Minister of Social Action Coordination
Açucena da Costa Duarte, Ministry of Social Action Coordination, Rua de Tchamba 86, Caixa Postal 516, Maputo, Mozambique
PHONE: +258 742901; 490932
FAX: +258 490923

Minister of State Administration
Alfredo Gamito, Ministry of State Administration, Rua da Rádio Moçambique 112, Maputo, Mozambique
PHONE: +258 426666; 423335
FAX: +258 428565

Minister of Transport and Communications
Paulo Muxanga, Ministry of Transport and Communications, Av. Mártires de Inhaminga 336, Maputo, Mozambique
PHONE: +258 420223
FAX: +258 431028

POLITICAL ORGANIZATIONS

União Democrático-UD (Democratic Union)

TITLE: General Secretary
NAME: Antonio Palange

Frente da Libertação de Moçambique-FRELIMO (Front for the Liberation of Mozambique)

TITLE: Chairman
NAME: Joaquim Alberto Chissanó

Resistencia Nacional Moçambicana-RENAMO (Mozambique National Resistance)

TITLE: President
NAME: Afonso Dhlakama

DIPLOMATIC REPRESENTATION

Embassies in Mozambique

Algeria
Rua de Mukumbura, 121–125, Maputo, Mozambique
PHONE: +258 492070; 492203
FAX: +258 490582
TITLE: Ambassador
NAME: Abdelhamid Boubazine

Angola
Avenida Kenneth Kaunda, 783, Maputo, Mozambique
PHONE: +258 493691; 493139
FAX: +258 493930
TITLE: Ambassador
NAME: António José Condesse de Carvalho

Australia
Av. Julius Nyerere n° 794 9° E, Maputo, Mozambique
PHONE: +258 497329; 493072

Brazil
Av. Kenneth Kaunda n° 296, Maputo, Mozambique
PHONE: +258 492387; 492388; 492863
FAX: +258 490986
TITLE: Ambassador
NAME: Hélder Martins de Morais

Bulgaria
Av. do Zimbabwe n° 864–868, Maputo, Mozambique
PHONE: +258 491476; 490383
FAX: +258 491755

Canada
Av. Julius Nyerere, 1128, Maputo, Mozambique
PHONE: +258 492623; 492624; 492470
FAX: +258 492667
E-MAIL: canembas@ecanada.uem.mz
TITLE: Consul-General
NAME: Roberto Carr-Ribeiro

China
Av. dos Mártires da Machava n° 1309–4°, Maputo, Mozambique
PHONE: +258 491462; 491560
FAX: +258 491196
TITLE: Ambassador
NAME: Mi Shiheng

Congo
Av. Mártires da Machava, 385, Maputo, Mozambique
PHONE: +258 493779
FAX: +258 493779
NAME: Monsengo Bashwa Oshefwa

Cuba
Av. Kenneth Kaunda n° 492, Maputo, Mozambique
PHONE: +258 492444
FAX: +258 493673; 492700
TITLE: Ambassador
NAME: Evelino Dorta González

Denmark
Av. 24 de Julho n° 1500, Maputo, Mozambique
PHONE: +258 420172; 420173; 429052
FAX: +258 303526
TITLE: Consul
NAME: Peter Jul Larsen

Egypt
Av. Mao Tsé Tung n° 851 R/c, Maputo, Mozambique
PHONE: +258 491118; 491287
FAX: +258 491489
TITLE: Ambassador
NAME: Soad Mahmoud Shalaby

Finland
Av. Julius Nyerere n° 1128, Maputo, Mozambique
PHONE: +258 490518; 491663; 491660
FAX: +258 491662
TITLE: Ambassador
NAME: Ilari Rantakari

France
Av. Julius Nyerere n° 2361, Maputo, Mozambique
PHONE: +258 490444; 491693; 491694
FAX: +258 491727
E-MAIL: ambfrmoz@virconn.com
TITLE: Ambassador
NAME: Dedier Destremau

Germany
Rua Damião de Góis, 506, Maputo, Mozambique
PHONE: +258 492714; 492996; 490057
FAX: +258 492888
TITLE: Ambassador
NAME: Helmut Rau

India
Av. Kenneth Kaunda n° 167, Maputo, Mozambique
PHONE: +258 492437; 490717
FAX: +258 492364
E-MAIL: hcimpto@hcoi.uem.mz
TITLE: High Commissioner
NAME: Jaspal Singh

North Korea
Rua da Kaswende n° 167, Maputo, Mozambique
PHONE: +258 491482; 492934; 492675
TITLE: Ambassador
NAME: Ryang Gui Rak

South Africa
Av. Eduardo Mondlane no. 41-R/c, Maputo, Mozambique
PHONE: +258 490059; 490547; 490587
FAX: +258 493029; 492096
TITLE: High Commissioner
NAME: Mangisi C. Zitha

Spain
Rua Damião de Góis n° 347, Maputo, Mozambique
PHONE: +258 492025; 492027; 492030
FAX: +258 492055
TITLE: Ambassador
NAME: José Eugénio Salarich

United Kingdom
Av. Vladimir Lenine 310, Maputo, Mozambique
PHONE: +258 420111; 421695; 424635
FAX: +258 421666
TITLE: Bernard Jonathan Everett
NAME: High Commissioner

United States
Av. Kenneth Kaunda n° 193, Maputo, Mozambique
PHONE: +258 492797
FAX: +258 490114; 493695
TITLE: Ambassador
NAME: Brian Dean Curran

JUDICIAL SYSTEM

Supreme Court

Local Court

BROADCAST MEDIA

Rádio Moçambique /

CP 2000, Maputo, Mozambique
PHONE: +258 (1) 431679
FAX: +258 (1) 421816
LANGUAGE: Portuguese, Local languages
TYPE: Government

Radiotelevisao Klint (RTK)

CP 946 Avenida Agostinho Neto, Maputo, Mozambique
PHONE: +258 (1) 493311
FAX: +258 (1) 423324
TYPE: Independent

Televisão de Moçambique (TVM)

C. P. 2675, Maputo, Mozambique
PHONE: +258 (1) 744788; 471395
TITLE: Director
CONTACT: Botelho Moniz
CHANNEL: 33
TYPE: Government

COLLEGES AND UNIVERSITIES

Universidade Eduardo Mondlane

CP 257, Maputo, Mozambique
PHONE: +258 (1) 425972
FAX: +258 (1) 428128
WEBSITE: http://www.uem.mz/

NEWSPAPERS AND MAGAZINES

Domingo

Sociedade Do Noticias, SARL, 55 Rua Joachim Lapa, CP 327, Maputo, Mozambique
PHONE: +258 (1) 431026
FAX: +258 (1) 431726
TITLE: Editor
CONTACT: Jorge Matine
CIRCULATION: 40,000

Fim de Semana

Rua da Resistência, 1642, 1er Dto, Maputo, Mozambique
PHONE: +258 (1) 417012
FAX: +258 (1) 417012
E-MAIL: fsemana@teledata.mz
WEBSITE: http://www.fimdesemana.co.mz

Noticias de Mozambique

Sociedade Do Noticias, SARL, 55 Rua Joachim Lapa, CP 327, Maputo, Mozambique
PHONE: +258 (1) 431026
FAX: +258 (1) 431726
TITLE: Editor
CONTACT: Bernardo Mavanga
CIRCULATION: 15,000

Mozambique File

CP 896, Maputo, Mozambique
FAX: +258 (1) 421906
E-MAIL: aim@aimmpto.uem.mz
WEBSITE: http://www.sortmoz.com/aimnews
TITLE: Editor
CONTACT: Paul Fauvet
CIRCULATION: 1,200
TYPE: Social science, general

PUBLISHERS

Empresa Moderna Lda.

Avda 25 de Setembro, Maputo, Mozambique
PHONE: +258 424594
TITLE: Managing Director
CONTACT: Louis Galloti
SUBJECTS: Education, Fiction, History, Regional Interests

Centro De Estudos Africanos

Universidade Eduardo Mondlane, Maputo, Mozambique
PHONE: +258 490828
FAX: +258 491896
TITLE: Director
CONTACT: Doutora Teresa Cruz e Silva
SUBJECTS: Economics, Foreign Countries, Government, Political Science, History, Regional Interests

Editora Minerva Central

Rua Consiglieri Pedroso 84, Maputo, Mozambique
PHONE: +258 122092
TITLE: Managing Director
CONTACT: J. F. Carvalho
SUBJECTS: Medicine, Nursing, Dentistry, Science (General)

RELIGIOUS ORGANIZATIONS

Most Mozambicans ascribe to indigenous, former tribal beliefs, which are not well-documented or organized. A minority of Christian and Muslim exist, but as one of the poorest countries in Africa, Mozambique has little to donate to the expansion of religious organizations.

FURTHER READING

Articles

"Starting Over After the Deluge: In the Wake of Widespread Devastation and Loss of Life, the People of Mozambique Begin, Once Again, the Long Task of Recovery from National Disaster." *Time International,* March 20, 2000, vol. 155, no. 11, p. 26+.

"Mozambique Seen as Model of Recovery, But Nation's Poor Hardly Feel a Ripple." *Wall Street Journal,* February 14, 2000, p. B13.

"Mozambique: Vote Upheld." *New York Times,* January 5, 2000, p. A6.

Swarms, Rachel. "Mozambique: Flood Aftermath." *New York Times,* September 27, 2000, p. A8.

Books

Azevedo, Mario Joaquim. *Historical Dictionary of Mozambique.* Metuchen, N.J.: Scarecrow Press, 1991.

———. *Historical Dictionary of Mozambique.* [computer file] Boulder, CO: netLibrary, Inc., 2000.

Dun and Bradstreet's Export Guide to Mozambique. Parsippany, NJ: Dun & Bradstreet, 1999.

Government Publications

Investment Treaty with Mozambique. Washington, DC: G.P.O., 2000.

MOZAMBIQUE: STATISTICAL DATA

For sources and notes see "Sources of Statistics" at the front of each volume.

GEOGRAPHY

Geography

Area:

Total: 801,590 sq km.

Land: 784,090 sq km.

Land boundaries:

Total: 4,571 km.

Border countries: Malawi 1,569 km, South Africa 491 km, Swaziland 105 km, Tanzania 756 km, Zambia 419 km, Zimbabwe 1,231 km.

Coastline: 2,470 km.

Climate: tropical to subtropical.

Terrain: mostly coastal lowlands, uplands in center, high plateaus in northwest, mountains in west.

Natural resources: coal, titanium, natural gas, hydropower.

Land use:

Arable land: 4%

Permanent crops: 0%

Permanent pastures: 56%

Forests and woodland: 18%

Other: 22% (1993 est.).

HUMAN FACTORS

Health Personnel

	National Data	World Data (wtd avc)
Total health expenditure as a percentage of GDP, 1990-1998[a]		
Public sector	2.1	2.5
Private sector	NA	2.9
Total[b]	NA	5.5
Availability of health care facilities per 100,000 people		
Hospital beds 1990-1998[a]	90	330
Doctors 1992-1995[a]	NA	122
Nurses 1992-1995[a]	NA	248

Demographics (A)

	1990	1995	1998	2000	2010	2020	2030	2040	2050
Population	14,276	17,309	18,491	19,105	20,504	20,626	20,700	21,314	22,939
Life expectancy - males	44.3	43.1	40.1	38.3	32.1	35.1	41.0	50.6	62.1
Life expectancy - females	46.8	43.4	39.1	36.7	30.6	33.7	40.4	51.7	66.0
Birth rate (per 1,000)	44.7	42.2	39.7	38.0	31.1	27.0	23.3	20.4	18.2
Death rate (per 1,000)	18.4	19.3	21.7	23.3	29.9	27.0	22.3	15.3	8.9
Women of reproductive age (15-49 yrs.)	3,385	4,107	4,407	4,557	5,004	5,363	5,680	6,048	6,427
Fertility rate	5.9	5.5	5.2	4.9	3.8	3.0	2.5	2.3	2.1

Except as noted, values for vital statistics are in thousands; life expectancy is in years.

Health Indicators

	National Data	World Data
Life expectancy at birth (years)		
1980	44	61
1998	45	67
Daily per capita supply of calories		
1970	1,896	2,358
1997	1,832	2,791
Daily per capital supply of protein		
1997 (grams)	35	74
Total fertility rate (births per woman)		
1980	6.5	3.7
1998	5.2	2.7
Population with access (%)		
To safe water (1990-96)	32	NA
To sanitation (1990-96)	21	NA
People living with (1997)		
Tuberculosis (cases per 100,000)	103.2	60.4
Malaria (cases per 100,000)	NA	42.2
HIV/AIDS (% aged 15 - 49 years)	14.17	0.99

Infants and Malnutrition

	National Data	World Data (wtd ave)
Under 5 mortality rate (1989)	206	NA
% of infants with low birthweight (1992-98)[1]	20	17
Births attended by skilled health staff (% of total births 1996-98)	44	52
% fully immunized at 1 year of age (1995-98)[1]		
TB	99	82
DPT	77	77
Polio	78	77
Measles	87	74
Prevalence of child malnutrition (1992-98)[1] (based on weight for age, % of children under 5 years)	26	30

Ethnic Division

Indigenous tribal groups 99.66%

Europeans 0.06%

Euro-Africans 0.20%

Indians 0.08%

The indigenous tribal groups include Shangaan, Chokwe, Manyika, Sena, Makua, and others.

Religion

Indigenous beliefs 50%

Christian 30%

Muslim 20%

Major Languages

Portuguese (official), indigenous dialects.

EDUCATION

Public Education Expenditures

	1980	1997
Public expenditures on education as % of GNP	3.1	NA
Pupils per teacher at the primary level	NA	58
Duration of primary education in years	NA	7
World data for comparison		
Public expenditures on education as % of GNP (mean)	3.9	4.8
Pupils per teacher at the primary level (wtd ave)	NA	33
Duration of primary education in years (mean)	NA	9

Educational Attainment (A)

Age group (1980) . . . . .25+

Population of this age group 4,242,819

Highest level attained (%)

No schooling[2] 81.0

First level

Not completed 18.1

Completed . . . . .NA

Entered second level 0.8

Entered post-secondary .0.1

Literacy Rates (A)

In thousands and percent	1990	1995	2000	2010
Illiterate population (15+ yrs.)	5,158	5,298	5,700	6,040
Literacy rate - total adult pop. (%)	34.7	40.1	45.9	57.4
Literacy rate - males (%)	51.8	57.7	63.4	73.2
Literacy rate - females (%)	18.5	23.3	29.2	42.2

GOVERNMENT & LAW

Political Parties

Assembly of the Republic (Assembleia da Republica)	% of vote	no. of seats
Front for the Liberation of Mozambique (Frelimo)	48.54%	133
Mozambique National Resistance-Electoral Union (Renamo-UE)	38.81%	117

Elections were last held 3-5 December 1999 (next to be held in 2004). Renamo-UE ran as a multiparty coalition. None of the other opposition parties received the 5% required to win parliamentary seats.

Government Budgets (B)

Revenues . . . .$402 million
Expenditures . . . .$799 million

Data for 1997 est.

Military Affairs (A)

	1990	1992	1995	1996	1997
Military expenditures					
Current dollars (mil.)	120	114	67	65	73
1997 constant dollars (mil.)	140	126	69	66	73
Armed forces (000)	65	50	12	11	14
Gross national product (GNP)					
Current dollars (mil.)	1,540	1,500	2,000	2,230	2,570
1997 constant dollars (mil.)	1,810	1,660	2,070	2,270	2,570
Central government expenditures (CGE)					
1997 constant dollars (mil.)	NA	774[e]	685	638	788
People (mil.)	14.1	14.5	17.2	17.7	18.2
Military expenditure as % of GNP	7.7	7.6	3.4	2.9	2.8
World data on military expenditure as % of GNP	4.5	3.4	2.7	2.6	2.6
Military expenditure as % of CGE	NA	17.0	10.1	10.4	9.2
World data on military expenditure as % of CGE	17.0	12.5	10.5	10.3	10.2
Military expenditure per capita (1997 $)	10	9	4	4	4
World data on military expenditure per capita (1997 $)	242	173	146	143	145
Armed forces per 1,000 people (soldiers)	4.6	3.4	0.7	0.6	0.8
World data on armed forces per 1,000 people (soldiers)	5.3	4.5	4.1	3.9	3.8
GNP per capita (1997 $)	129	114	121	128	142
Arms imports[6]					
Current dollars (mil.)	140	5	5	10	0
1997 constant dollars (mil.)	164	6	5	10	0
Arms exports[6]					
Current dollars (mil.)	50	0	0	0	0
1997 constant dollars (mil.)	59	0	0	0	0
Total imports[7]					
Current dollars (mil.)	878	855	784	NA	965[e]
1997 constant dollars (mil.)	1,028	948	812	NA	965[e]
Total exports[7]					
Current dollars (mil.)	126	139	169	227[e]	269[e]
1997 constant dollars (mil.)	148	154	175	231[e]	269[e]
Arms as percent of total imports[8]	15.9	0.6	0.6	0	0
Arms as percent of total exports[8]	39.7	0	0	0	0

LABOR FORCE

Total Labor Force (B)

9 million (1999).

Labor Force by Occupation

Agriculture 81%
Industry 6%
Services 13%

Data for 1997 est.

PRODUCTION SECTOR

Energy Production

Production . . . . .1.2 billion kWh
Production by source
Fossil fuel 25%
Hydro 75%
Nuclear 0%
Other 0%
Exports . . . . .483 million kWh

Data for 1998.

Energy Consumption

Consumption . . . . .1.018 billion kWh
Imports .385.000 million kWh

Data for 1998.

Transportation

Highways:

Total: 30,400 km.

Paved: 5,685 km.

Unpaved: 24,715 km (1996 est.).

Waterways: about 3,750 km of navigable routes.

Pipelines: crude oil 306 km; petroleum products 289 km.

Note: not operating.

Merchant marine:

Total: 3 ships (1,000 GRT or over) totaling 4,125 GRT/7,024 DWT.

Ships by type: cargo 3 (1999 est.).

Airports: 170 (1999 est.).

Airports - with paved runways: 22.

Airports - with unpaved runways: 148.

Top Agriculture Products

Cotton, cashew nuts, sugarcane, tea, cassava (tapioca), corn, rice, tropical fruits; beef, poultry.

Top Mining Products (B)

Mineral resources include: coal, titanium.

COMMUNICATIONS

Daily Newspapers

	National Data	World Data for Comparison
Daily Newspapers		
Number of Dailies	2	8,391
Total Circulation (000)	49	548,000
Circulation per 1,000 inhabitants	2.7	96

Telecommunications

Telephones - main lines in use: 60,000 (1995).

Telephones - mobile cellular: NA

(Continued on next page.)

MANUFACTURING SECTOR

GDP & Manufacturing Summary (B)

	1980	1985	1990	1993	1994	1995
Gross Domestic Product						
Millions of 1990 dollars	1,386	1,102	1,318	1,501	1,576	1,647
Growth rate in percent	2.46	−8.82	1.90	8.84	5.00	4.50
Per capita (in 1990 dollars)	115	81	93	94	95	95
Manufacturing Value Added						
Millions of 1990 dollars	561	256	325	325	370	402[e]
Growth rate in percent	3.25	−13.87	−2.19	−0.11	13.84	8.75[e]
Manufacturing share in percent of current prices	33.1[e]	14.9[e]	NA	NA	NA	NA

Telecommunications (cont.)

Telephone system: fair system of tropospheric scatter, open-wire lines, and microwave radio relay.

Domestic: microwave radio relay and tropospheric scatter.

International: satellite earth stations - 5 Intelsat (2 Atlantic Ocean and 3 Indian Ocean).

Radio broadcast stations: AM 14, FM 4, shortwave 17 (1998).

Radios: 730,000 (1997).

Television broadcast stations: 1 (1997).

Televisions: 90,000 (1997).

Internet Service Providers (ISPs): 2 (1999).

FINANCE, ECONOMICS, & TRADE

Economic Indicators

National product: GDP—purchasing power parity—$18.7 billion (1999 est.).

National product real growth rate: 10% (1999 est.).

National product per capita: $1,000 (1999 est.).

Inflation rate—consumer price index: 4% (1999 est.).

Exchange Rates

Exchange rates:

Meticais (Mt) per US$1

January 2000	13,392.0
1999	12,775.1
1998	11,874.6
1997	11.543.6
1996	11,293.8
1995	9,024.3

Top Import Origins

$1.6 billion (c.i.f., 1999 est.)

Origins (1996 est.)

South Africa	55%
Zimbabwe	7%
Saudi Arabia	5%
Portugal	4%
United States	NA
Japan	NA
India	NA

Top Export Destinations

$300 million (f.o.b., 1999 est.)

Destinations (1996 est.)

Spain	17%
South Africa	16%
Portugal	12%
United States	10%
Japan	NA
Malawi	NA
India	NA
Zimbabwe	NA

Foreign Aid

Recipient: $1.115 billion (1995).

Import/Export Commodities

Import Commodities	Export Commodities
Food	Prawns 40%
Clothing	Cashews
Farm equipment	Cotton
Petroleum	Sugar
Transport equipment	Copra
	Citrus
	Coconuts
	Timber

Balance of Payments

	1992	1993	1994	1995	1996
Exports of goods (f.o.b.)	139	132	150	169	226
Imports of goods (f.o.b.)	−770	−859	−917	−705	−704
Trade balance	−630	−727	−767	−536	−478
Services - debits	−246	−271	−323	−350	−319
Services - credits	165	180	191	242	253
Private transfers (net)	NA	NA	NA	NA	NA
Government transfers (net)	499	503	565	339	283
Overall balance	−352	−446	−467	−445	−359

MYANMAR

CAPITAL: Yangon (formerly Rangoon).

FLAG: The national flag is red with a blue canton, within which 14 white stars encircle a rice stalk and an industrial wheel.

ANTHEM: *Kaba Makye* (Our Free Homeland).

MONETARY UNIT: The kyat (K) is a paper currency of 100 pyas. There are coins of 1, 5, 10, 25, and 50 pyas and 1 kyat, and notes of 1, 5, 10, 25, and 100 kyats. K1 = $0.16804 (or $1 = K5.951).

WEIGHTS AND MEASURES: Both British and metric weights and measures are in general use, but local units are also employed.

HOLIDAYS: Independence Day, 4 January; Union Day, 12 February; Peasants' Day, 2 March; Defense Services Day, 27 March; Burmese New Year, 17 April; World Workers' Day, 1 May; Martyrs' Day, 19 July; Christmas, 25 December. Movable religious holidays include Full Moon of Tabaung, February or March; Thingyan (Water Festival), April; Full Moon of Kason, April or May; Waso (Beginning of Buddhist Lent), June or July; Thadingyut (End of Buddhist Lent), October; and Tazaungdaing, November.

TIME: 6:30 PM = noon GMT.

LOCATION AND SIZE: Situated in Southeast Asia, Myanmar has an area of 678,500 square kilometers (261,970 square miles), slightly smaller than the state of Texas, and a total boundary length of 8,134 kilometers (5,055 miles).

Myanmar's capital city, Yangon (formerly Rangoon), is located in the southern part of the country.

CLIMATE: Myanmar has a largely tropical climate with three seasons. Rainfall ranges from about 76 centimeters (30 inches) in central Myanmar to more than 500 centimeters (200 inches) in upper Myanmar during the monsoon season.

The mean annual temperature is 27°C (81°F); average daily temperatures in Yangon (Rangoon) range from 18° to 32°C (64°–90°F) in January, during the cool season, and from 24° to 36°C (75°–97°F) in April, during the hot season.

Union of Myanmar
Pyidaungzu Myanma Naingngandaw

INTRODUCTORY SURVEY

RECENT HISTORY

In 1946, after the end of World War II, the sovereign Union of Burma came into being. In 1951, the nation held its first parliamentary elections. The decade of the 1950s brought an ambitious land reform program and an attempt to forge a neutral foreign policy. However the country was faced with periodic communist rebellions and an off-and-on border dispute with China.

A coup in 1962 overthrew the government, and a military regime assumed control. The Socialist Republic of Burma was proclaimed on 3 January 1974. Under a new constitution, a president was elected, but the government continued to be dominated by the military. At this time, the country's only legal political organization was the Burma Socialist Program Party (BSPP). Meanwhile, a guerrilla war in border areas of the north and east continued through the 1980s. It was fought by the underground Burmese Communist Party and rebel ethnic groups.

When the military became dissatisfied with the government and the ruling BSPP party, it staged another military coup. On September 18, 1988 the army abolished the BSPP, took over the government, and imposed military rule under the State Law and Order Restoration Council (SLORC). The SLORC was headed by the army Chief of Staff, General Saw Maung. On June 18, 1989 the Saw Maung regime renamed Burma "Myanmar," the historic ethnic Burman name for the country.

The takeover of the government by the military prompted dissent among the population. Among the most prominent dissidents was Aung San Suu Kyi. She rose to prominence by establishing a coalition party that opposed the military regime. In speeches and interviews she challenged the SLORC's record, characterizing it as one of economic and social degeneration. She also protested the SLORC's repressive laws and actions. Because of her actions, the government placed her under house arrest in 1989.

Multiparty elections were held in May 1990, but the military refused to transfer power to the winning National League for Democracy (NLD). It announced in September 1990 that it intended to remain in power for five to ten more years.

In the early 1990s, the plight of dissident Aung San Suu Kyi, who was placed under house arrest in 1989, began receiving worldwide attention. In 1991 she was awarded the 1990 Sakharov Prize for Freedom of Thought by the European Parliament. On December 10, 1991 Aung San Suu Kyi's son, Alexander, accepted the 1991 Nobel Peace Prize on her behalf.

Another type of human rights violation in Myanmar that drew international attention was forced labor. It was reported that the SLORC used forced labor on tourist projects such as the reconstruction of the gold palace in Mandalay. Of Mandalay's 500,000 residents, each family had to contribute at least three days of free labor each month. The work lasted from dawn until evening and was so strenuous that it required several days of recovery. Forced labor was also used on many building projects and to carry supplies and munitions into malaria-infested areas for the military. Prison inmates were required to work every day. Many military families could be exempted, as could any family that agreed to pay a monthly fine of $6, about a week's wages for some families. Muslim refugees who fled Myanmar said that Muslims had to pay two to three times as much as others to escape labor.

Ever since Myanmar received its independence in 1948, the government has faced ethnic minorities fighting for autonomy. However, in 1991 the 600-member Palaung State Liberation Army and the 500-member Pa-O National Army rebel group signed truce agreements with SLORC, which served as models for settlements with other rebels. The Karens, Mons, and Karenni along the Thai border began talks with the military regime in early 1994. Eventually, the junta negotiated separate peace treaties with each rebel group.

As of mid-1994 the international community was still debating the most constructive approach to dealing with Myanmar. Many Asian countries argue that maintaining relations with Myanmar is more productive than isolating it. However, the United States has stuck to its hardline isolationist policy toward Myanmar to press for advancement of democracy and human rights. The United States government still refers to Myanmar as Burma, the country's name prior to the military takeover.

In July 1995, the SLORC released dissident Aung San Suu Kyi from house arrest. She had been detained for six years. Most observers saw the SLORC's action as an attempt to gain international favor, and not as a sign that they were ready to loosen their grip on the country. Upon her release, Suu Kyi confirmed her commitment to democracy. The NLD planned to draft its own version of the constitution, and Suu Kyi planned pro-democracy rallies. Following mass student protests in December 1996, the government blamed Suu Kyi and returned her to house arrest. She was released again in July 1997. Rather than arrest her for her activities in 1998, the Myanmar military prevented her from attending opposition meetings. They did allow her to return to Myanmar after a brief visit to see her dying husband, Michael Aris, in London.

Thousands of political opponents remained in prison during 1995 and 1996. The ruling leaders also faced renewed fighting with border insurgents, particularly the Karen National Union Army.

The Myanmar government has also come under considerable international criticism for its involvement in the country's massive drug trade. Myanmar is the world's largest producer of opium and heroin, and is a major producer of methamphetamines. With the burgeoning drug production in the north, Myanmar has also developed a raging HIV/AIDS epidemic.

The late 1990s brought international economic woes to Myanmar. In June 1999 the International Labor Organization of the UN essentially expelled Myanmar for forced labor practices. In 2000 the World Bank and International Monetary Fund have been barred from lending to Myanmar.

GOVERNMENT

A military coup in September 1988 brought the State Law and Order Restoration Council (SLORC) to power. SLORC abolished the previous government and the country was placed under martial law. On September 18, 1988 the official title of the state was changed to The Union of Myanmar.

The SLORC changed its name to State Peach and Development Council (SPDC) in November 1997. The prime minister of SPDC is both chief of state and head of government. SPDC directs, supervises, and coordinates the work of the central and local government institutions.

Theoretically the legislative branch is the 485 seat People's Assembly whose members are elected by popular vote for four-year terms. The Assembly has never convened.

In a multiparty election held May 27, 1990, the National League for Democracy (NLD) received 59.9 percent of the total vote and took 396 of the 485 contested seats. However SLORC (now SPDC) refused to hand over power to the NLD, instead insisting that a new constitution be drafted and approved by SLORC prior to the transfer of power. By the late 1990s the National Convention aimed at drafting a new constitution had been suspended.

Judiciary

The British-style judicial system with which Myanmar began its independence, including a Supreme Court, was disbanded by the Revolutionary Council. Military tribunals that enforced orders issued by the State Law and Order Restoration Council (SLORC) were abolished in 1992. Ordinary courts now handle such cases with heavy military influence. The Supreme Court appoints judges after approval by the SPDC. The judiciary is not independent. Amnesty International and the United Nations have criticized the SPDC for unfair treatments and arbitrary imprisonment.

Political Parties

With the military takeover of September 1988 the ruling Burma Socialist Program Party was formally abolished and all governing authority was concentrated in the hands of the military. On September 24, 1988, the BSPP was reborn as the National Unity Party (NUP) inheriting the buildings and machinery of the old BSPP.

On September 24, 1988, the National League for Democracy (NLD), a coalition party, was formed in opposition to the military regime. The NLD won the May 1990 elections by a landslide, electing 392 candidates; the NUP took 10 seats. NLD leader Aung San Suu Kyi was placed under house arrest in July 1989 and was released in July 1995. SLORC refused to turn over power to NLD.

By March 1993 all but seven political parties had been deregistered by SLORC. SLORC changed its name to State Peace and Development Council (SPDC) in 1997.

DEFENSE

The armed forces play the major role in Myanmar's politics and administration; senior members of the government are officers who govern under martial law.

Myanmar's armed forces totaled an estimated 429,000 in 2000; military service for men and women is compulsory. The army, with 325,000 personnel, is organized in infantry battalions chiefly for internal security duties. The navy has 10,000 members, and the air force 9,000. Paramilitary forces total 85,250. Military expenditures were $3.9 billion in 1997–1998, or 2.1 percent of GDP.

ECONOMIC AFFAIRS

Myanmar remains a poor Asian country whose standard of living had not improved over the past decade of 1990–2000. Myanmar has an agriculture economy as of 1999 nearly 75 percent of the economy was in the private sector comprised chiefly of agriculture (including fish and forestry) that contributes approximately 60 percent of GDP and employs close to 63 percent of the workforce. Rice, a major export, goes to Indonesia and China. Heavy industry and energy remain largely state-controlled activities. Infrastructure is a major impediment to economic growth. Industry faces chronic power shortages, roads are poor and impassible during parts of the year, and telephone lines are lacking.

Myanmar is the world's largest supplier of illegal opiates; in 1995 its opium accounted for 60 percent of worldwide production. About 60 percent of the heroin brought into the United States comes from Myanmar. Large quantities of smuggled consumer goods are sold in Myanmar's cities, where the black market thrives. Published estimates of Myanmar's foreign trade are greatly understated because of the volume of black market trade.

Myanmar has not been able to achieve monetary and fiscal stability due to poor government planning, internal unrest, lack of foreign investment, a large trade deficit, and illegal drug production.

For all these reasons, Myanmar receives no aid from United States or European Union (EU) programs and aid from Japan is run at a maintenance level. The International Monetary Fund (IMF), the World Bank, and the Asian Development Bank (ADB) extend no credit to Myanmar.

Public Finance

The government presents its budget in March for the April 1–March 31 fiscal year. The public sector budget typically shows an overall deficit.

The U.S. Central Intelligence Agency estimated that in 1996–1997 government revenues totaled approximately $7.9 billion and expenditures $12.2 billion including capital expenditures of $5.7 billion. External debt totaled $5.9 billion in 1998–1999.

Income

In 1999 the gross domestic product (GDP) was estimated at $59.4 billion, or about $1,200 per capita. The 1999 estimated GDP growth rate was $4.6 billion and inflation was at 38 percent. The 1997 estimated GDP by sector was agriculture 59 percent, industry 11 percent, and services 30 percent.

Industry

Industry is geared largely to the processing of agricultural, mineral including copper, tin, tungsten, and iron, and wood and wood products. Principal industrial products are cement, steel, bricks and tiles, fertilizers, and processed foods. Consumer goods that were imported before 1962 and are now manufactured domestically include blankets, paper, glass products, bicycles, water pumps, and textiles and footwear. Other major consumer items manufactured are aluminum ware, jute and cotton cloth, pharmaceuticals, beverages, matches, and cigarettes. The assembly of television sets and motor vehicles is a recent development in Myanmar's industry. The petroleum and petrochemical sector is entirely state-owned.

Industrial products for 1995 included pig iron, 1,500 tons; crude steel, 25,000 tons; refined tin, 190 tons; and refined petroleum products, 5.3 million barrels.

Banking and Finance

Effective February 23, 1963, all twenty-four commercial banks in Myanmar—ten foreign and fourteen indigenously owned—were nationalized and amalgamated into 4 state banks. In addition to the Central Bank of Myanmar, Union of Burma Bank, which serves as a central bank, the other state banks were the State Agricultural Bank, the State Commercial Bank, and the Industrial Bank. After subsequent reorganizations of the banking system, these became the Myanma Investment and Commercial Bank, Myanma Economic Bank, and the Myanma Foreign Trade Bank. Agricultural credit is provided by a separate Myanmar Agricultural and Rural Development Bank. Public savings increased sharply in 1977 after the banks raised interest rates. Efforts to attract the considerable liquidity in the hands of the public into the banking sector, and thence into investment, have not had much success. In recent years the expansion of bank savings has lagged well behind inflation.

By the end of 1994 licenses to open representative offices had been issued to nineteen banks from overseas—six from Thailand, five from Singapore, three from Malaysia, and one each from France, Indonesia, Cambodia, Hong Kong, and Bangladesh. Since 1994 four private domestic banks have been permitted to conduct foreign exchange transactions for the first time. Various types of foreign exchange licenses have been issued recently to the private sector by the Central Bank. It issued seven authorized dealer licenses, three money changer licenses, 396 acceptor and holder licenses, and sixty-six FEC changer licenses in August 1994. Despite the liberalization of its economy, the country still lacks a capital market.

Economic Development

Since 1990 private investment has been encouraged as the government attempts to revitalize the economy after three decades of tight central planning. Foreign investment has been encouraged but with only moderate success.

In spite of the military government's commitment to the transformation of Myanmar's state-controlled economy to a market system, economic development has been limited by the government's failure to implement basic structural reforms. Such needed reforms include dismantling unproductive state-owned enterprises, establishing an independent state bank, making available private sector credit, controlling government spending, and adjustments to the official exchange rate. Basic infrastructure, transportation, telecommunications, and energy are inadequate. Because of the government's ongoing human rights abuses and for reasons related to its narcotics exports, Myanmar receives no financial assistance from the IMF, World Bank, or Asian Development Bank.

SOCIAL WELFARE

Although considerable advances have been made in health services, Myanmar's goal of establishing a welfare state has been limited by lack of public funds. In 1956 the government inaugurated a social security program that compensates workers for wage losses arising from sickness, injury, and maternity leave, provides free medical care, and establishes survivors' benefits. The program is funded by contributions from employers, employees, and the government. As yet Myanmar does not have unemployment insurance but workers are entitled to old age pensions.

Women have a high status in Myanmar's society and economic life. They may retain their maiden name after marriage, may obtain divorces without undue difficulty, and enjoy equal property and inheritance rights with men. However women are traditionally prevented from entering male-dominated occupations and do not always receive equal pay for equal work.

Myanmar's military government continues to engage in human rights abuses. The military uses forced labor as porters for the army. There is also widespread mistreatment of prisoners.

Healthcare

Until recent decades few people in rural areas had the benefit of modern medicine. To correct this deficiency, the country's health services were reorganized by sending more doctors to rural areas and increasing the number of rural health centers. Doctors in private practice were inducted for two years of national service.

The progress of the health services is reflected in the reduction of the physician/ population ratio from one per 15,560 in 1960 to one per 3,578 by 1986. In 1986 Myanmar had 635 hospitals with 25,839 beds. There were 12,400 doctors in 1990.

Smallpox and plague have been practically eliminated as health hazards, and programs are under way to eradicate malaria and tuberculosis. However, gastrointestinal diseases such as typhoid, dysentery, and cholera remain widespread. AIDS is a serious health risk with 350,000 to 400,000 infected persons in the north alone. In 1995 only 38 percent of the population had access to safe water. Another serious health problem is drug addiction, aggravated by the easy availability and low cost of opium. Under a drug abuse control program financed by the United States and the United Nations, a new 300-bed hospital for addicts was opened in 1982 at Thayetmyo; smaller facilities have been established in two dozen other towns.

Average life expectancy was fifty-six years in 2000. In 1990–1995 60 percent of the population had access to health care services.

Housing

Pre-World War II housing in Myanmar compared favorably with that in other Southeast Asian nations but housing conditions have deteriorated. Urban dwellings are overcrowded and often unsafe. Most houses are built with a combination of wood, bamboo, and thatch.

EDUCATION

In 1996 Myanmar had 35,752 primary schools with 5.4 million students. Secondary schools had 107,000 teachers and 1.9 million students. Primary education lasts for five years and is compulsory followed by four years of secondary education at the first stage and two years at the second stage. Observers estimated two-thirds to three-fourths of students drop out before completing the first five years.

Post-secondary institutions, including eighteen teacher-training colleges, six agricultural institutes, eight technical institutes, and thirty-five universities and colleges, enrolled a total of 245,317 students with 5,730 teaching staff in 1996.

The Mass Education Council has attempted to increase literacy through special programs. The 2000 adult illiteracy rate was estimated at 15.3 percent but international observers questioned that figure, estimating illiteracy to be much higher.

2000 KEY EVENTS TIMELINE

January

- The Myanmar government restricts Internet usage, and arrests people on charges of looking at opposition websites based overseas. Only two Internet servers, military and postal, are allowed to operate in Myanmar.
- The insurgent Karen National Union replaces longtime leader Bo Mya with veteran Saw Ba Thin as its Chairman.

February

- Buddhist monks demand dialogue between the military government and Aung San Suu Kyi's opposition National League for Democracy.

March

- The Myanmar government fails to persuade its neighbors to stay away from a closed-door diplomatic conference which takes place in South Korea. The conference seeks solutions to the impasse between the Myanmar military rulers and the opposition.

April

- Some 140 Myanmar military government figures are banned from travel to European Union (EU) countries, in a strengthening of sanctions by the EU.

May

- Myanmar hosts a conference of Association of South East Asian Nations (ASEAN) economic ministers. Japan's Trade Minister also attends, and offers aid initiatives, although three major Japanese corporations are pulling out of Myanmar.

June

- The United Nations (UN) International Labor Organization (ILO) votes to give Myanmar four months to prove it will stop using forced labor, following the ILO's major investigation of pervasive use of forced labor by Myanmar's military.
- The World Health Organization (WHO) of the UN rates Burma next to last in a survey of 191 countries for quality and availability of health care.
- The latest UN Special Envoy for Myanmar (Burma), Razali Ismail, a Malaysian government official, makes his initial visit to Myanmar on June 29, meeting with the government and opposition.

July

- The government allows colleges and universities to fully reopen July 25 after three years of closure and partial closure, due to anti-government demonstrations.

August

- General Zaw Tun, Deputy Planning and Finance Minister, is relieved of his position on August 10, following his public remarks critical of the military's handling of the economy.
- A party of sixteen members of the National League for Democracy, including Aung San Suu Kyi, are stopped by the police as they leave the capital of Yangon, August 28. In her first attempt to leave the city in two years, they hold a standoff. She remains in her car for over a week while villagers bring her food.
- Junta member Vice-Admiral Nyunt Thein gives his resignation on August 28, followed by the removal of at least seventeen naval officers.

September

- After nine days, Aung San Suu Kyi and her party end their standoff with police and return to Yangon. They are forcibly kept in their homes.
- On September 15 Aung San Suu Kyi is freed from two weeks of house arrest at Yangon.
- Epidemics of infectious diseases, including typhoid, in the Shan State are reported to have killed thousands in August–September.
- Prevented from taking a train to Mandalay from Rangoon, Aung San Suu Kyi and party members are taken from the railway station on September 21 and kept under arrest.

October

- U.N. Special Envoy Razali Ismail makes a four-day visit to Myanmar, meeting with officials and with Aung San Suu Kyi.
- British human rights activist James Mawdsley is freed and deported, after being held in a northern Burmese prison for thirteen months.
- Rajsoomer Lallah, U.N. Special Rapporteur for Burma (Myanmar), issues a report on military violence in the country, including massacres of ethnic minorities, then resigns his post.

November

- The International Labor Organization calls for sanctions against Myanmar November 17 due to widespread forced labor practices.
- The U.N. General Assembly passes a resolution condemning Myanmar's junta for a long list of human rights violations.

December

- General Maung Aye, a prominent junta member, makes an official state visit to neighboring India.
- U.S. President Bill Clinton award the Presidential Medal of Freedom to opposition leader Aung San Suu Kyi.
- Myanmar frees six pro-democracy leaders from house arrest December 1, but Aung San Suu Kyi is still in confinement at home. Following two days of talks with a representative of the European Union (E.U.) December 10–11, Myanmar's military junta agrees to free Suu Kyi at an unspecified time in the future. A delegation from the European Union will meet with Suu Kyi in January 2001.
- Amnesty International issues a report detailing Burma's pervasive use of torture.

ANALYSIS OF EVENTS: 2000

BUSINESS AND THE ECONOMY

Myanmar's economy was in a faltering condition throughout 2000. One of the generals in Myanmar's ruling State Peace and Development Council (SPDC) spoke out publicly against the military mismanagement of the economy, but he was removed from his post immediately. Foreign investment dwindled as companies pulled out under domestic political pressure or gave up on their operations because of inefficiency and corruption in Myanmar. Although a few Asian firms announced future projects, some prominent Japanese companies exited Myanmar. Myanmar's currency, the kyat, weakened to new lows during 2000.

The Supreme Court of the United States ruled that U.S. state and local sanctions against doing business with Myanmar were illegal, but federal sanctions remained in place. The European Union also maintained economic sanctions on Myanmar's regime. A lawsuit against Unocal, a California petroleum company, filed by alleged victims of its Myanmar pipeline was dismissed by a federal judge, who noted evidence that the company was aware of human rights abuses connected to its pipeline project.

In November the International Labor Organization (ILO) of the United Nations (U.N.), after years of detailed research and several waiting periods, concluded that the SPDC had not acted significantly to end its pervasive use of forced labor. The ILO called for sanctions to be imposed on Myanmar by its member states and by trade unions, a decision opposed by only a few countries. Myanmar's agricultural sector continued to struggle, despite some export of farm products. Confiscation of rice and other crops by the military was reportedly widespread. Tourism and manufacturing also slumped, although exports of garments and textiles earned foreign exchange.

GOVERNMENT AND POLITICS

This was the tenth year since national elections had given an overwhelming majority to the National League for Democracy (NLD), a result denied by the ruling military ever since. The still-popular opposition leader, Aung San Suu Kyi and her NLD experienced mounting repression throughout 2000. The government started an effort to evict the NLD from its headquarters in the capital, Rangoon, and detained many party members. When Aung San Suu Kyi left the city to visit supporters in an outlying suburb in August, her car was stopped on the road and after nine days she was forcibly returned to her home. Subsequently, in September when Aung San Suu Kyi and associates tried to take a train to Mandalay, they were seized and put under house arrest, incommunicado. The crackdown on the NLD took place as the U.N.'s Millennium Summit opened in New York, and the detention was condemned in speeches there by U.S. President Bill Clinton and United Kingdom Prime Minister Tony Blair.

One of the few people allowed to see Aung San Suu Kyi was the U.N.'s Special Envoy, Razali Ismail, a Malaysian diplomat, who also met with the Myanmar government. Throughout the year, all efforts to impel the junta to hold talks with the opposition failed, including a high level, closed door conference of international governmental representatives in Seoul, Korea, and calls by important Buddhist monks in Myanmar for dialogue. The U.N. Human Rights Commission's Special Rapporteur for Myanmar, Rajsoomer Lallah, resigned, citing lack of access to Myanmar and insufficient funding for his work. The U.N. General Assembly passed a strong resolution condemning the SPDC for violations of human rights. Large numbers of political prisoners continued to be held in Myanmar, although a British activist was released after having been kept for over a year in solitary confinement for handing out pro-democracy leaflets.

Myanmar's membership in the Association of South East Asian Nations (ASEAN) continued to be important, and Myanmar hosted a meeting of ASEAN economics ministers in May. However, within ASEAN, Thailand, the Philippines, and Indonesia sometimes expressed dissatisfaction with the regime's treatment of the opposition. An ASEAN-European Union meeting to be held in Laos was threatened by European criticism of the SPDC's treatment of the NLD. South Korea also voiced its displeasure with the regime's policies. Australia, taking a softer line than most Western countries, conducted a human rights training course for Myanmar officials and army officers. Japan continued to endorse "constructive engagement," with its first cabinet-level visit to Myanmar in seventeen years. China was engaged in business with Myanmar, and continued its weapons trade; while India edged closer to the regime at year's end with a state visit from junta member General Maung Aye. Relations with neighboring Thailand were sometimes tense due to the influx of narcotics from Myanmar, as well as refugee problems, and cross-border shelling. Bangladesh still had large numbers of refugees from Myanmar, and the situation on its border was strained by Myanmar's placement of land mines there.

Myanmar's frontier rebellion was small in scale, consisting mainly of raids by Karen and Shan guerrilla groups. Nonetheless, efforts by the SPDC to pacify and control ethnic minority areas reportedly were characterized by severe human rights violations, including widespread torture, massacres, mass rapes, village burnings, forced relocation, extortion, and forms of religious persecution.

CULTURE AND SOCIETY

Myanmar's institutions of higher learning were reopened in July after being shut down for more than three years because of the SPDC's fears of student activism. All information distribution was tightly controlled, with a new crackdown on Internet use, despite the opening of a "cyber-café" (with no email or Web access) and the announcement of government plans for promoting information technology. The SPDC's own Web site was hacked into, apparently by overseas democracy supporters.

The illicit production of narcotics such as opium, heroin, and methamphetamines continued to be the one flourishing aspect of Myanmar's economy, accompanied by money laundering for the drug trade. Most of the drug production took place in areas where ethnic former rebels honored cease-fires with the government, or in regions under direct SPDC control. Myanmar's high HIV/AIDS infection rate continued to climb, due in large part to intravenous drug abuse, prostitution, and unsafe medical practices. Myanmar was rated next to last in a World Health Organization survey of 191 countries for quality and availability of health care. Epidemics of infectious diseases swept Myanmar's Shan State, reportedly killing thousands in August and September.

DIRECTORY

CENTRAL GOVERNMENT

Head of State

Chairman of the State Peace and Development Council
Than Shwe, State Peace and Development Council

Prime Minister
Than Shwe, Office of the Prime Minister

Ministers

Minister of Agriculture and Irrigation
Nyunt Tin, Ministry of Agriculture and Irrigation
PHONE: +95 (1) 665587

Minister of Commerce
Kyaw Than, Ministry of Commerce

Minister of Communications, Post, and Telegraph
Win Tin, Ministry of Communications, Post, and Telegraph
PHONE: +95 (1) 292955

Minister of Construction
Saw Tun, Ministry of Construction
PHONE: +95 (1) 285899

Minister of Cooperatives
Aung San, Ministry of Cooperatives
PHONE: +95 (1) 277096

Minister of Culture
Win Sein, Ministry of Culture
PHONE: +95 (1) 277316

Minister of Defense
Than Shwe, Ministry of Defense

Minister of Education
Than Aung, Ministry of Education
PHONE: +95 (1) 286726

Minister of Electric Power
Tin Htut, Ministry of Electric Power

Minister of Energy
Lun Thi, Ministry of Energy
PHONE: +95 (1) 221060

Minister of Finance and Revenue
Khin Maung Thein, Ministry of Finance and Revenue
PHONE: +95 (1) 284763

Minister of Foreign Affairs
Win Aung, Ministry of Foreign Affairs
PHONE: +95 (1) 221529

Minister of Forestry
Aung Phone, Ministry of Forestry
PHONE: +95 (1) 663279

Minister of Health
Ket Sein, Ministry of Health
PHONE: +95 (1) 285896

Minister of Home Affairs
Tin Hlaing, Ministry of Home Affairs
PHONE: +95 (1) 549208

Minister of Hotels and Tourism
Saw Lwin, Ministry of Hotels and Tourism
PHONE: +95 (1) 287228; 286024; 285689; 275328

Minister of Immigration and Population
Saw Tun, Ministry of Immigration and Population

Minister of Industry No. 1
Aung Thaung, Ministry of Industry No. 1
PHONE: +95 (1) 566064

Minister of Industry No. 2
Saw Lwin, Ministry of Industry No. 2
PHONE: +95 (1) 282826

Minister of Information
Kyi Aung, Ministry of Information
PHONE: +95 (1) 294827; 294812; 294645

Minister of Labor
Tin Aye, Ministry of Labor
PHONE: +95 (1) 278320

Minister of Livestock, Breeding, and Fisheries
Maung Maung Thein, Ministry of Livestock, Breeding, and Fisheries
PHONE: +95 (1) 280398

Minister of Military Affairs
Tin Hla, Ministry of Military Affairs

Minister of Mines
Ohn Myint, Ministry of Mines
PHONE: +95 (1) 577316

Minister of National Planning and Economic Development
Soe Tha, Ministry of National Planning and Economic Development
PHONE: +95 (1) 280816

Minister of Progress of Border Areas and National Races and Development Affairs
Thein Nyunt, Ministry of Progress of Border Areas and National Races and Development Affairs
PHONE: +95 (1) 285102

Minister of Rail Transport
Pan Aung, Ministry of Rail Transport
PHONE: +95 (1) 292772

Minister of Religious Affairs
Sein Htwa, Ministry of Religious Affairs

Minister of Science and Technology
U Thaung, Ministry of Science and Technology

Minister of Social Welfare, Relief, and Resettlement
Pyei Son, Ministry of Social Welfare, Relief, and Resettlement

Minister of Sports
Sein Win, Ministry of Sports

Minister of Transport
Hla Myint Swe, Ministry of Transport

POLITICAL ORGANIZATIONS

Taingyintha Silonenyinyutye (National Unity Party)

NAME: Than Shwe

National Council of the Union of Burma (NCGUB)

Washington Office, 815 15th St. NW, Suite 910, Washington, DC 20005, USA
PHONE: +(202) 3324300
FAX: +(202) 3937343
E-MAIL: ncgub@igc.apc.org
NAME: Sein Win

DIPLOMATIC REPRESENTATION

Embassies in Myanmar

Australia
88 Strand Road, Kyauktada Tsp., Yangon, Myanmar
PHONE: +95 (1) 280965; 278307; 280234
FAX: +95 (1) 275521

China
94 Kayaybin Road, Dagon Tsp., Yangon, Myanmar
PHONE: +95 (1) 221280; 221281; 221398
FAX: +95 (1) 227019

France
102 Fydaungsu Yeiktha Road, Dagon Tsp., Yangon, Myanmar
PHONE: +95 (1) 282122; 282418; 281759
FAX: +95 (1) 287759

Germany
32 Natmauk Street, Bahan Tsp., Yangon, Myanmar
PHONE: +95 (1) 548951; 548952; 548953
FAX: +95 (1) 548899

India
545–547 Merchant Street, Kyauktada Tsp., Yangon, Myanmar
PHONE: +95 (1) 282550; 282552; 282933
FAX: +95 (1) 289562

Italy
3 Inya Myaing Road, Golden Valley, Bahan Tsp., Yangon, Myanmar
PHONE: +95 (1) 527100; 527101
FAX: +95 (1) 533670

Japan
100 Natmauk Road, Bahan Tsp., Yangon, Myanmar
PHONE: +95 (1) 549644; 549645; 549646
FAX: +95 (1) 549643

South Korea
97 University Avenue, Bahan Tsp., Yangon, Myanmar
PHONE: +95 (1) 527142; 527143; 527144
FAX: +95 (1) 532630

Russia
38 Sagawa Road, Dagon Tsp., Yangon, Myanmar
PHONE: +95 (1) 241955; 289730
FAX: +95 (1) 241953

Thailand
45 Pyay Road, 6 1/2 Mile, Hiaing Tsp., Myanmar
PHONE: +95 (1) 525670; 533082
FAX: +95 (1) 222784

United Kingdom
80 Strand Road, Kyauktada Tsp., Yangon, Myanmar
PHONE: +95 (1) 281700; 281702; 281703
FAX: +95 (1) 289566

United States
581 Merchant Street, Kyauktada Tsp., Yangon, Myanmar
PHONE: +95 (1) 282055; 282056; 282059
FAX: +95 (1) 280409

BROADCAST MEDIA

Myanma Television and Radio Department (MTRD)

426 Pyay Rd., Yangon, Myanmar

PHONE: +95 (1) 531850
LANGUAGE: Burmese, English
BROADCASTS: 12 hours/day
TYPE: Government

Myawady TV

Hmawbi Township, Yangon, Myanmar
PHONE: +95 (1) 281179; 620270
FAX: +95 (1) 289563
TYPE: Military

COLLEGES AND UNIVERSITIES

University of Yangon

University Avenue, Yangon, Myanmar
PHONE: +95 (1) 31254; 31775

Yangon Institute of Technology

Yangon-Insein Road, Yangon, Myanmar
PHONE: +95 (1) 63233; 63011

NEWSPAPERS AND MAGAZINES

Botahtaung (The Vanguard)

News & Periodicals Corp., PO Box 539, Yangon, Myanmar
PHONE: +95 (1) 74310
CIRCULATION: 96,000

The Hanthawaddy

96 Aung San St., PO Box 1025, Mandalay, Yangon, Myanmar
CONTACT: U. Win Tin
CIRCULATION: 23,000

Kyehmon (The Mirror)

Ministry of Information, c/o Publicitas Major Media, 20 Upper Circular Rd., 02-21A The Riverwalk, Singapore 058416, Singapore
PHONE: +65 5361121
FAX: +65 5361191
E-MAIL: ppm-singapore@publicitas.com
CIRCULATION: 179,200

New Light of Myanmar

Ministry of Information, c/o Publicitas Major Media, 20 Upper Circular Rd., 02-21A The Riverwalk, Singapore 058416, Singapore
PHONE: +65 5361121
FAX: +65 5361191
E-MAIL: ppn-singapore@publicitas.com
WEBSITE: http://www.myanmar.com/nlm/

Working People's Daily

News & Periodicals Corp., Working People's Daily Press, PO Box 43, Yangon, Myanmar
PHONE: +95 (1) 76220
CONTACT: U. Ko Ko Lay
CIRCULATION: 24,000

Burma Medical Journal

249 Theinbyu Rd., Yangon, Myanmar
TYPE: Medicine

Burma Research Society Journal

University Library, University Estate, Yangon, Myanmar
TYPE: Social science

Do Kyaung Tha

181-3 Sule Pagoda Rd., Yangon, Myanmar
CIRCULATION: 17,000

Myawaddy Journal

181-3 Sule Pagoda Rd., Yangon, Myanmar
CIRCULATION: 8,700

Myawaddy Magazine

181-3 Sule Pagoda Rd., Yangon, Myanmar
CIRCULATION: 4,200

Teza

181-3 Sule Pagoda Rd., Yangon, Myanmar
CIRCULATION: 29,500
TYPE: Juvenile fiction/non-fiction

Thwe-Thauk Magazine

185 48th St., Yangon, Myanmar
TYPE: Literary criticisms and collections

PUBLISHERS

Knowledge Printing and Publishing House

130 Bogyoke Aung San St., Yegyaw, Yangon, Myanmar
SUBJECTS: Art, Education, Government, Political Science, Religion-Other, Social Sciences, Sociology

Sarpay Beikman Board

529 Merchand St., Yangon, Myanmar
PHONE: +95 (1) 283611
TITLE: Chairman
CONTACT: Aung Htay

SUBJECTS: Agriculture, Biography, Ethnicity, History, Law, Literature, Literary Criticism, Essays, Science (General)

Shwepyidan Printing and Publishing House

12 A Hninban, Yegyaw Quarter, Yangon, Myanmar
SUBJECTS: Government, Political Science, Law, Religion-Other

RELIGIOUS ORGANIZATIONS

Buddhist

Chanmyay Yeiktha Meditation Centre
55a Kaba Aye Pagoda Road, Yangon, 11061 Myanmar
PHONE: +95 (1) 661479
FAX: +95 (1) 667050
WEBSITE: http://web.ukonline.co.uk/buddhism//cmyaysit.htm

Dhamma Joti Vipassana Centre
Nga Htat Gyi Pagoda Road, Bahan Township, Yangon, Myanmar
PHONE: +95 (1) 39290

Mahasi Meditation Centre
No. 16, Sasana Yeiktha Road, Bahan, Yangon, 11201 Myanmar
PHONE: +95 (1) 541974, +95 (1) 541971
FAX: +95 (1) 289960, +95 (1) 289961
WEBSITE: http://mahasi.com/

Pak Auk Forest Monastery
c/o Major U Khan Sain, 653 Lower Main Road, Mawyamyine, Mon State, Myanmar
PHONE: +95 03222132
TITLE: Teacher
NAME: Ven. Pa Auk Sayadaw

Catholic

Catholic Bishops' Conference of Myanmar
292 Py Road, Sanchaung Post Office, Yangon 11111, Myanmar
PHONE: +95 (1) 525868, +95 (1) 527198
TITLE: President
NAME: Rt. Rev. Matthias U Shwe

Protestant

Myanmar Council of Churches
Myanmar Ecumenical Sharing Centre, 601, Pyay Road, University Post Office, PO Box 1400, Yangon, Myanmar
PHONE: +95 (1) 533957
FAX: +95 (1) 296848
TITLE: General Secretary
NAME: Rt. Rev. Mahn San Si Htay

FURTHER READING

Articles

Lyall, Sarah. "Myanmar: Briton Freed." *New York Times,* October 21, 2000, p. A5.

"Myanmar: Standoff Ends." *New York Times,* September 2, 2000, p. A5.

"Myanmar: Activist Defiant." *New York Times,* September 16, 2000, p. A7.

Waldman, Peter and Phil Kuntz. "A Pipeline Project in Myanmar Puts Cheney in Spotlight." *Wall Street Journal,* October 27, 2000, p. A1.

Books

Khng, Pauline. *Myanmar.* Milwaukee, WI: Gareth Stevens Publishing, 2000. [juvenile]

Government Publications

United States. *National Emergency with Respect to Burma.* Washington, DC: G.P.O., 2000.

———. *6-Month Periodic Report on the National Emergency Declared by Executive Order 13047.* Washington, DC: G.P.O., 2000.

MYANMAR: STATISTICAL DATA

For sources and notes see "Sources of Statistics" at the front of each volume.

GEOGRAPHY

Geography

Area:

Total: 678,500 sq km.

Land: 657,740 sq km.

Land boundaries:

Total: 5,876 km.

Border countries: Bangladesh 193 km, China 2,185 km, India 1,463 km, Laos 235 km, Thailand 1,800 km.

Coastline: 1,930 km.

Climate: tropical monsoon; cloudy, rainy, hot, humid summers (southwest monsoon, June to September); less cloudy, scant rainfall, mild temperatures, lower humidity during winter (northeast monsoon, December to April).

Terrain: central lowlands ringed by steep, rugged highlands.

Natural resources: petroleum, timber, tin, antimony, zinc, copper, tungsten, lead, coal, some marble, limestone, precious stones, natural gas, hydropower.

Land use:

Arable land: 15%

Permanent crops: 1%

Permanent pastures: 1%

Forests and woodland: 49%

Other: 34% (1993 est.).

HUMAN FACTORS

Demographics (A)

	1990	1995	1998	2000	2010	2020	2030	2040	2050
Population	38,519	40,148	41,165	41,735	43,674	44,775	45,327	45,223	44,430
Life expectancy - males	51.5	52.8	53.3	53.6	55.2	58.7	62.8	67.1	71.0
Life expectancy - females	54.7	55.9	56.2	56.3	60.2	64.2	68.5	72.9	76.7
Birth rate (per 1,000)	24.1	22.7	21.5	20.6	17.0	14.4	12.7	11.6	10.8
Death rate (per 1,000)	12.8	12.3	12.3	12.4	12.0	11.5	11.4	11.7	12.4
Women of reproductive age (15-49 yrs.)	9,794	10,814	11,486	11,895	12,732	12,624	11,960	10,846	9,994
Fertility rate	3.1	2.7	2.5	2.4	1.9	1.7	1.7	1.7	1.7

Except as noted, values for vital statistics are in thousands; life expectancy is in years.

Health Personnel

	National Data	World Data (wtd ave)
Total health expenditure as a percentage of GDP, 1990-1998[a]		
Public sector	0.2	2.5
Private sector	0.8	2.9
Total[b]	1.0	5.5
Health expenditure per capita in U.S. dollars, 1990-1998[a]		
Purchasing power parity	NA	561
Total	58	483
Availability of health care facilities per 100,000 people		
Hospital beds 1990-1998[a]	60	330
Doctors 1992-1995[a]	28	122
Nurses 1992-1995[a]	43	248

Health Indicators

	National Data	World Data
Life expectancy at birth (years)		
1980	52	61
1998	60	67
Daily per capita supply of calories		
1970	2,020	2,358
1997	2,862	2,791
Daily per capital supply of protein		
1997 (grams)	72	74
Total fertility rate (births per woman)		
1980	4.9	3.7
1998	3.1	2.7
Population with access (%)		
To safe water (1990-96)	38	NA
To sanitation (1990-96)	41	NA
People living with (1997)		
Tuberculosis (cases per 100,000)	36.6	60.4
Malaria (cases per 100,000)	256.1	42.2
HIV/AIDS (% aged 15 - 49 years)	1.79	0.99

Infants and Malnutrition

	National Data	World Data (wtd ave)
Under 5 mortality rate (1989)	113	NA
% of infants with low birthweight (1992-98)[1]	16	17
Births attended by skilled health staff (% of total births 1996-98)	57	52
% fully immunized at 1 year of age (1995-98)[1]		
TB	91	82
DPT	87	77
Polio	88	77
Measles	85	74
Prevalence of child malnutrition (1992-98)[1] (based on weight for age, % of children under 5 years)	43	30

Ethnic Division

Burman 68%
Shan 9%
Karen 7%
Rakhine 4%
Chinese 3%
Mon 2%
Indian 2%
Other 5%

Religion

Buddhist 89%
Christian 4%
Baptist 3%
Roman Catholic 1%
Muslim 4%
Animist 1%
Other 2%

Major Languages

Burmese, minority ethnic groups have their own languages.

EDUCATION

Public Education Expenditures

	1980	1997
Public expenditures on education as % of GNP	1.7	1.2
Expenditures per student as % of GNP per capita		
Primary & Secondary	NA	NA
Tertiary	NA	19.0
Pupils per teacher at the primary level	NA	NA

	1980	1997
Duration of primary education in years	NA	5
World data for comparison		
Public expenditures on education as % of GNP (mean)	3.9	4.8
Pupils per teacher at the primary level (wtd ave)	NA	33
Duration of primary education in years (mean)	NA	9

Educational Attainment (B)

	1990	1995
Gross enrollment ratio (%)		
Primary level	106.5	120.9
Secondary level	22.7	29.5
Tertiary level	4.1	5.7
Enrollment of population aged 6-23 years (%)	39.0	NA

(Continued on next page.)

GOVERNMENT & LAW

Military Affairs (A)

	1990	1992	1995	1996	1997
Military expenditures					
Current dollars (mil.)	NA	3,030	4,340	3,960	NA
1997 constant dollars (mil.)	NA	3,360	4,490	4,030	NA
Armed forces (000)	230	286	322	322	322
Gross national product (GNP)					
Current dollars (mil.)	31,400	36,600	47,800	51,800	55,700
1997 constant dollars (mil.)	36,800	40,600	49,500	52,700	55,700
Central government expenditures (CGE)					
1997 constant dollars (mil.)	5,900	4,520	5,350	5,340	5,150
People (mil.)	41.1	42.6	45.0	45.7	46.5
Military expenditure as % of GNP	NA	8.3	9.1	7.6	NA
World data on military expenditure as % of GNP	4.5	3.4	2.7	2.6	2.6
Military expenditure as % of CGE	NA	74.3	84.0	75.5	NA
World data on military expenditure as % of CGE	17.0	12.5	10.5	10.3	10.2
Military expenditure per capita (1997 $)	NA	79	100	88	NA
World data on military expenditure per capita (1997 $)	242	173	146	143	145
Armed forces per 1,000 people (soldiers)	5.6	6.7	7.2	7.0	6.9
World data on armed forces per 1,000 people (soldiers)	5.3	4.5	4.1	3.9	3.8
GNP per capita (1997 $)	896	953	1,100	1,150	1,200
Arms imports[6]					
Current dollars (mil.)	110	150	140	80	80
1997 constant dollars (mil.)	129	166	145	81	81
Total imports[7]					
Current dollars (mil.)	270	651	1,335	1,358	1,358
1997 constant dollars (mil.)	316	722	1,382	1,381	1,381
Total exports[7]					
Current dollars (mil.)	325	537	846	732	732
1997 constant dollars (mil.)	381	595	876	744	744
Arms as percent of total imports[8]	40.7	23.0	10.5	5.9	5.9
Arms as percent of total exports[8]	0	0	0	0	0

(Continued on next page.)

EDUCATION (cont.)

Literacy Rates (C)

Year	Adult Literacy Rate (Population aged 15 years and older)
1980	75.70%
1985	78.30%
1990	80.80%
1995	82.90%
1997	83.70%

Libraries

National Libraries	**1996**
Administrative Units	1
Service Points or Branches	1
Number of Volumes (000)	5
Registered Users (000)	15
Loans to Users (000)	30
Total Library Staff	NA

GOVERNMENT & LAW (cont.)

Political Parties

People's Assembly	no. of seats
National League for Democracy (NLD)	396
National Unity Party (NUP)	10
Other	79

Elections were last held 27 May 1990, but the Assembly never convened.

Government Budgets (A)

Year: 1997

Total Expenditures: 98,426 Millions of Kyats

Expenditures as a percentage of the total by function:

General public services and public order	8.89
Defense	30.62
Education	9.35
Health	3.51
Social Security and Welfare	2.29
Housing and community amenities	0.37
Recreational, cultural, and religious affairs	2.29
Fuel and energy	0.01
Agriculture, forestry, fishing, and hunting	13.38
Mining, manufacturing, and construction	1.01
Transportation and communication	20.01
Other economic affairs and services	0.52

Crime

Crime volume (for 1998)	
Crimes reported	162,234
Total persons convicted	161,666
Crimes per 100,000 population	350
Persons responsible for offenses	
Total number suspects	178,078
Total number of female suspects	28,706
Total number of juvenile suspects	944

LABOR FORCE

Total Labor Force (A)

19.7 million (FY98/99 est.).

Labor Force by Occupation

Agriculture	65%
Industry	10%
Services	25%

Data for 1999 est.

Unemployment Rate

7.1% (official FY97/98 est.)

PRODUCTION SECTOR

Energy Production

Production	4.31 billion kWh
Production by source	
Fossil fuel	61.72%
Hydro	38.28%
Nuclear	0%
Other	0%
Exports	0 kWh

Data for 1998.

Energy Consumption

Consumption	4.008 billion kWh
Imports	0 kWh

Data for 1998.

Transportation

Highways:

Total: 28,200 km.

Paved: 3,440 km.

Unpaved: 24,760 km (1996 est.).

Waterways: 12,800 km; 3,200 km navigable by large commercial vessels.

Pipelines: crude oil 1,343 km; natural gas 330 km.

Merchant marine:

Total: 40 ships (1,000 GRT or over) totaling 472,284 GRT/716,533 DWT.

Ships by type: bulk 13, cargo 20, container 2, passenger/cargo 3, petroleum tanker 2 (1999 est.).

Note: a flag of convenience registry; includes ships of 2 countries: Japan owns 2 ships, US 3 (1998 est.).

Airports: 80 (1999 est.).

Airports - with paved runways: 10.

Airports - with unpaved runways: 70.

Top Agriculture Products

Paddy rice, corn, oilseed, sugarcane, pulses; hardwood.

Top Mining Products (B)

Mineral resources include: tin, antimony, zinc, copper, tungsten, lead, coal, some marble, limestone, precious stones.

COMMUNICATIONS

Daily Newspapers

	National Data	World Data for Comparison
Daily Newspapers		
Number of Dailies	5	8,391
Total Circulation (000)	449	548,000
Circulation per 1,000 inhabitants	10	96

Telecommunications

Telephones - main lines in use: 158,000 (1995).

Telephones - mobile cellular: 2,007 (1995).

Telephone system: meets minimum requirements for local and intercity service for business and government; international service is good.

Domestic: NA

International: satellite earth station - 1 Intelsat (Indian Ocean).

Radio broadcast stations: AM 2, FM 3, shortwave 3 (1998).

Radios: 4.2 million (1997).

Television broadcast stations: 2 (1998).

Televisions: 260,000 (1997).

Internet Service Providers (ISPs): 0 (1999).

FINANCE, ECONOMICS, & TRADE

Economic Indicators

National product: GDP—purchasing power parity—$59.4 billion (1999 est.).

National product real growth rate: 4.6% (1999 est.).

National product per capita: $1,200 (1999 est.).

Inflation rate—consumer price index: 38% (1999 est.).

Exchange Rates

Exchange rates:

Kyats (K) per US$1

Official rate

January 2000	6.2665
1999	6.2858
1998	6.3432
1997	6.2418
1996	5.9176
1995	5.6670
Market exchange rate (yearend 1999)	330.0000

Fiscal year: 1 April - 31 March

(Continued on next page.)

MANUFACTURING SECTOR

GDP & Manufacturing Summary (B)

	1980	1985	1990	1993	1994	1995
Gross Domestic Product						
Millions of 1990 dollars	21,156	26,701	23,969	27,889	29,789	32,701
Growth rate in percent	7.91	2.85	2.82	6.00	6.81	9.78
Per capita (in 1990 dollars)	626	711	580	640	672	725
Manufacturing Value Added						
Millions of 1990 dollars	1,733	2,275	1,865	2,176	2,371	2,637[e]
Growth rate in percent	6.86	2.92	0.11	9.75	8.94	11.21[e]
Manufacturing share in percent of current prices	9.5	9.9	7.8	7.0	7.0[e]	NA

FINANCE, ECONOMICS, & TRADE (cont.)

Top Import Origins

$2.5 billion (1998)

Origins (1998)

Singapore	31%
Japan	12%
Thailand	12%
China	9%
Malaysia	8%

Top Export Destinations

$1.2 billion (1998)

Destinations (1998)

India	13%
China	11%
Singapore	10%
Thailand	8%

Foreign Aid

Recipient: $99 million (FY98/99).

Import/Export Commodities

Import Commodities	Export Commodities
Machinery	Pulses and beans
Transport equipment	Prawns
Construction materials	Fish
Food products	Rice
	Teak
	Opiates

NAMIBIA

Republic of Namibia

CAPITAL: Windhoek.

FLAG: Top left triangle is blue, center diagonal band is red, and the bottom right triangle is green. Colors are separated by narrow white bands. On the blue triangle is a golden sun with twelve triangular rays.

ANTHEM: *Namibia Land of the Brave*, music and words by Axali Doeseb.

MONETARY UNIT: The South African rand (R) of 100 cents is in use; notes and coins are those of South Africa. R1 = $0.2874 (or $1 = R3.4795).

WEIGHTS AND MEASURES: The metric system is in use.

HOLIDAYS: New Year's Day, 1 January; Independence Day, 21 March; Easter, 1–4 April; Workers' Day, 1 May; Casinga Day, 4 May; Ascension Day, 12 May; Africa Day, 25 May; Heroes' Day, 26 August; Day of Goodwill, 7 October; Human Rights Day, 10 December; Christmas, 25–26 December.

TIME: 2 PM = noon GMT.

LOCATION AND SIZE: Namibia covers 824,290 square kilometers (318,260 square miles), slightly more than half the size of the state of Alaska. It has a total boundary length of 5,424 kilometers (3,370 miles).

Namibia's capital city, Windhoek, is in the center of the country.

CLIMATE: Namibia's climate is the driest in Africa, with sunny, warm days and cooler nights, especially during the winter months. The mean January temperature at Windhoek is 23°C (73°F). In winter, the mean temperature is 13°C (55°F). Much of Namibia experiences chronic drought. The annual rainfall, which mostly falls between December and March, generally averages only 2.5–15 centimeters (1–6 inches) in the south of the country, and some regions have gone 90 years without a drop of rain.

INTRODUCTORY SURVEY

RECENT HISTORY

After World War II (1939-1945), South Africa tried to turn Namibia into its own province. In the 1950s, senators from South-West Africa sat in the South African parliament, and Windhoek was reduced to a provincial capital. The United Nations took South Africa before the International Court of Justice but not until 1971 did the Court declare the South African occupation of Namibia illegal.

Meanwhile, in 1960, representatives of the native majority had formed the South-West Africa People's Organization (SWAPO) to seek independence and black majority rule. Beginning in 1966, but especially after 1977, SWAPO waged a guerrilla war. South Africa responded by building up its armed forces along Namibia's borders.

In 1978, South Africa accepted a Western-sponsored plan for an independent Namibia, but the plan proved difficult to implement in a way that satisfied all sides. It was not until April of 1989 that all sides finally agreed to a ceasefire and began the process of creating a new state.

Elections were held in November of 1989. SWAPO won 57 percent of the vote, the Democratic Turnahalle Alliance (DTA) received 29 percent, and a variety of ethnic-based parties received the rest. A new constitution was adopted on February 9, 1990, and Namibia became independent on March 21, 1990.

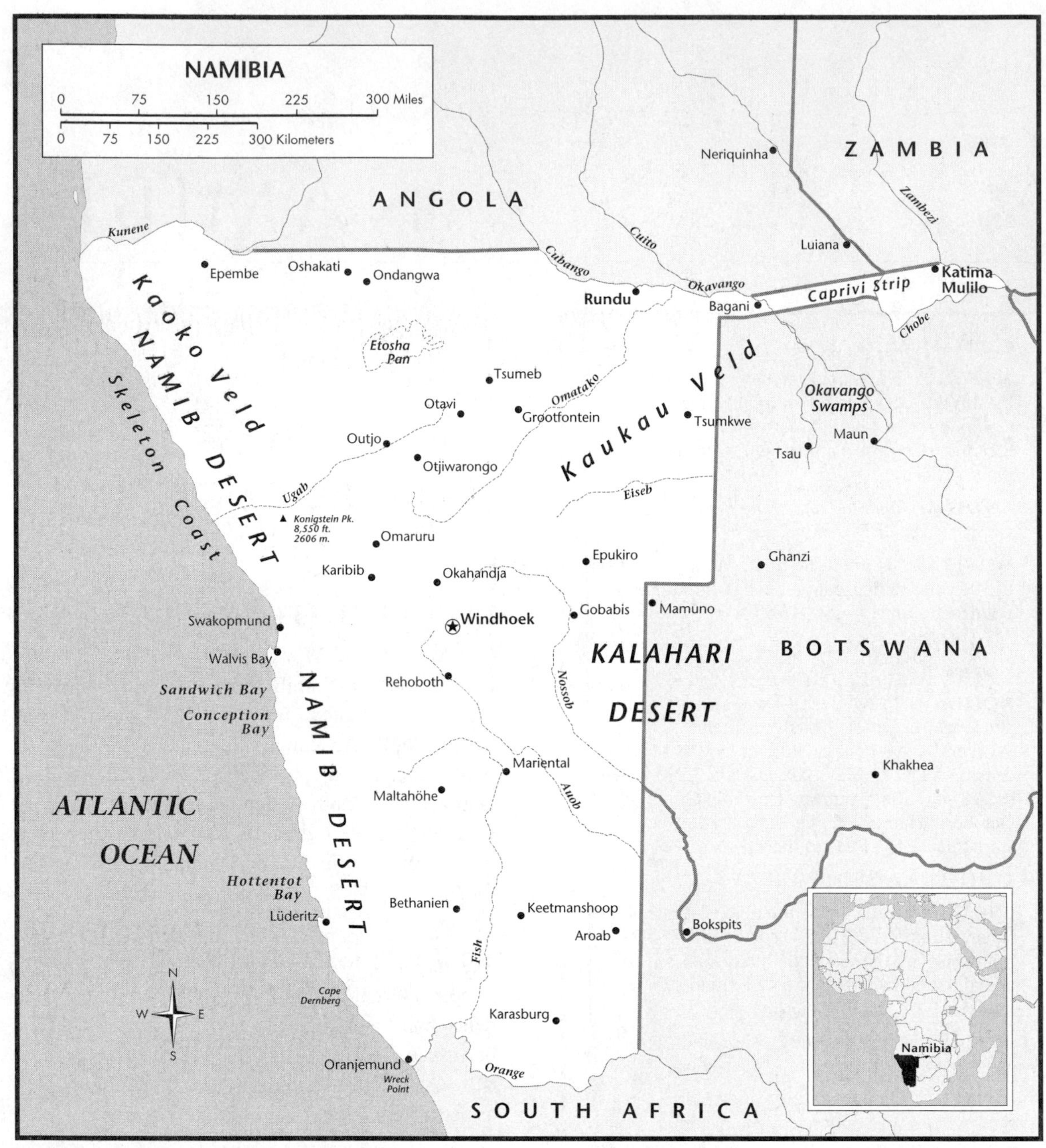

The SWAPO government (whose support comes chiefly from the Ovambo people of the north and from urban areas) has followed a policy of reconciliation with the white inhabitants and created a multiparty, nonracial democracy. In 1993, agreement was reached with South Africa to return Walvis Bay to Namibia, an act completed on March 1, 1994. Occasional border disputes with Angola disrupted the country. In mid-1994, a large section of the country's border was closed and Namibian guards had orders to shoot at any vehicles attempting to cross.

GOVERNMENT

The Namibia constitution adopted on March 21, 1990, is considered a model of democratic government. It provides for a two-chamber legislature, consisting of a 26-seat National Assembly and the National Council. The Assembly consists of seventy-two elected deputies and up to six members appointed by the president. The Council is comprised of two members chosen from each of thirteen regional councils to serve six-year terms. The National Council is a purely advisory body.

The president is elected by direct, popular vote. The president serves as chief of state, head of government, and commander-in-chief of the Defense Force. The term of office can be for no more than two five-year terms.

Judiciary

The formal court system is arranged on three levels: thirty magistrates' courts, the High Court, and the Supreme Court. The Supreme Court serves as the highest court of appeals and also exercises constitutional review of legislation. The traditional courts handle minor criminal offenses such as petty theft and violations of local customs.

Political Parties

The South-West Africa People's Organization (SWAPO) is the largest political party. Other parties include the white-led Democratic Turnhalle Alliance (DTA), the Congress of Democrats (COD), the United Democrat Front (UDF), and the Monitor Action Group (MAG).

In the 1999 National Assembly elections, SWAPO won fifty-five of seventy-two possible seats.

DEFENSE

Postwar national forces number nine thousand men in eight mixed battalions and one hundred men in naval patrol forces. There is a small national police force. Defense spending was $90 million, or 2.6 percent of GDP in 1997–1998.

ECONOMIC AFFAIRS

Namibia's economy is dependent on a few primary exports, including minerals (diamonds, uranium, copper, lead, tin, tungsten, silver), livestock (both meat and hides), and fish, which, together, account for nearly 90 percent of exports. Mining alone accounts for 20 percent of GDP.

Half of the population depends on subsistence agriculture for its livelihood. Nambia must import some foodstuffs. Even though the per capita GDP is high by African standards the majority of Nambia's population lives in poverty with 30 percent to 40 percent underemployment and unemployment, inequality of income distribution, and large portions of wealth going to foreigners.

The economy is highly integrated with that of South Africa. Years of white rule have resulted in one of the most unequal income distributions on the African continent. However, a democratically elected government is now committed to developing previously neglected regions of the country.

The economy has a superior transport and communications infrastructure, an extensive natural resource base, a small population, and a stable government committed to competitiveness in attracting investment. Large oil and gas reserves were discovered in 2000 that should be tapped by 2005. Growth should also occur in the diamond and fish sectors. For these reasons, analysts believe that Nambia's economy holds enormous potential for long-term economic growth.

Public Finance

The U.S. Central Intelligence Agency estimated that, in 1994, government revenues totaled approximately $941 million and expenditures $1.05 billion, including capital expenditures of $157 million. External debt totaled $385 million.

Income

In 1999, Namibia's gross domestic product (GDP) was estimated at $7.1 billion, or about $4,300 per capita. The 1999 estimated growth rate was 3 percent and inflation in 1999 was 8.5 percent. The 1998 estimated contribution by sector was: agriculture, 12 percent; industry, 30 percent; and services, 58 percent.

Industry

The main industry in Nambia is mining for diamonds, lead, zinc, tin, silver, tungsten, uranium, and copper.

Namibia's industry is also comprised of meat and fish processing, dairy products, and some production of basic consumer goods. There are furniture and clothing factories, metal and engineering works, assembly plants, and a cement plant. Historically, Namibia has been dependent on South African manufacturing.

Banking and Finance

Banking activities have recorded strong growth since independence in 1990, while the range of financial institutions operating in Namibia has begun to expand. Total assets of the four main commercial banks more than doubled in 1991–1995 and during 1995 bank lending to the private sector rose by 34 percent. There have been no banking failures since independence, but the regulatory regime inherited from South Africa is being brought more into line with international norms under a new banking institutions act that was due to come into effect in 1997.

First National Bank Namibia and Standard Bank Namibia have the largest branch networks and remain wholly owned subsidiaries of their South African parent banks. The Commercial Bank of Namibia (CBN), a subsidiary of the Geneva-based Société Financière pour les Pays d'outre mer (SFOM) and South Africa's NEDCOR Bank, and Bank Windhoek, in which South Africa's ABSA Bank is the main shareholder, had assets of $1 billion each. The City Savings and Investment Bank (CSIB), launched in 1994 as Namibia's first indigenously owned financial institution, had total assets of only $75 million at end-1995, and a single branch in Windhoek.

Within four years, the Namibian Stock Exchange (NSE), which started operations in October 1992, has grown to become sub-Saharan Africa's second largest in terms of market capitalization next to the Johannesburg Stock Exchange (JSE). The NSE is increasingly being used by local firms to raise capital for business expansions, while foreign investors are buying into Namibian equities through new listings and rights offers which have been mainly over-subscribed. Some 95 percent of the NSE's overall market capitalization comprises dual-listings of South African parent groups of Namibian subsidiaries, accounting for fifteen of the twenty-six listed shares in June 1996. Electronic trading began in 1998.

Economic Development

Namibia's government will continue to build and diversify its economy around its mineral reserves. Priorities include expanding the manufacturing sector, land reform, agricultural development in the populous north, and improved education and health opportunities. Transfer of Walvis Bay and twelve offshore islands to Namibia has returned to Namibia its deep-water port and 20 percent of its offshore rights.

The five-year development program started in 1994 set an annual growth rate target of 5 percent, highlighting government budget cuts and foreign investment and trade. However, actual rates hovered around 2 percent through 1998 and 3 percent in 1999. Large oil and gas reserves discovered in 2000 should start being tapped in 2005.

SOCIAL WELFARE

The constitution promotes gender, racial, and regional equality. However, discrimination against women exists in both law and tradition. Indigenous San peoples have historically faced discrimination from Namibia's other ethnic groups. Namibia's whites have a substantially higher standard of living than its blacks. There is also a big difference in the living conditions between rural and urban Namibians.

Healthcare

Medical personnel in 1990–1997 included thirty physicians per 100,000 people. Health services are provided through ethnically based government authorities, so the system is effectively segregated. In addition, most health care facilities are in the towns which are largely white. In 2000, average life expectancy is 42.5 years and 57 percent of the population has access to health care services.

Housing

There is a sharp contrast in housing standards between white and black Namibians. Most rural dwellings are self-constructed from local materials. In the 1990s, the backlog in housing units was estimated at 45,000 units.

EDUCATION

Education is compulsory for nine years between the ages of seven and sixteen. In 1998, 400,325 Namibians were in primary and 115,237 pupils were in secondary schools. There is an Academy for Tertiary Education for adult students. Projected adult illiteracy rates for 2000 stood at 17.9 percent. In 1995, there were 11,344 students in all higher-level institutions.

2000 KEY EVENTS TIMELINE

January

- Fighting near the border with Angola intensifies after Namibia agrees to allow the Angolan government to enter Namibian territory to fight rebels. Three French children are killed in an ambush by armed men engaged in the Angolan civil war.
- The government moves to alter a negative international perception about tourist security in the Caprivi region after repeated attacks and murders by UNITA guerillas from Angola.

February

- The government announces a major funding commitment of N$28 million to upgrade Walvis Bay airport terminals, runways, and warehousing.

March

- President Sam Nujoma is sworn in for his third consecutive term and promises a standard of living comparable to the developed world by 2030.

May

- The country's largest cocaine bust leads to the arrest of two South African men and a Namibian woman along with a seizure of N$1.3 million in drugs.

June

- A new stiff set of sentencing guidelines and an expanded definition for rape goes into effect.

July

- The Finnish ambassador is expelled after being critical of the Namibian government and under allegations that he assisted SWAPO dissidents in the 1970s.

August

- Namibian Army chief-of-staff, Major General Martin Shalli warns that in order to derive peace at home and abroad, discrimination against women must cease.

September

- The government bans the import of pigs from South Africa following the outbreak of foot and mouth disease in Camperdown, KwaZulu, South Africa.
- Numerous businesses oriented toward tourism in the Kavango region close due to the civil war in Angola. Statistics are published that show that over 2,260 businesses have closed as tourism continues to decline.
- Finland and Namibia share the responsibilities of presiding over the United Nations General Assembly.

October

- Namibian Breweries Ltd. enters into a joint venture with Beck's of Germany.

November

- The Osire refugee camp is declared overcrowded November 6. It holds over 17,000 Angolans, as authorities look for a new site.
- The Namibian National Defense Force kills four UNITA rebel bandits from Angola during the last week of November.

ANALYSIS OF EVENTS: 2000

BUSINESS AND THE ECONOMY

In spite of expected gross domestic product (GDP) growth of 4.5 percent in 2000, Namibia faced serious economic problems, including mounting public debt and a 35 percent unemployment rate. Each year an estimated 20,000 high school graduates competed for a mere 3,000 jobs. In addition the tourist industry had suffered a severe blow from the spillover of Angola's civil war into Namibia, which affected an area near the country's eastern border that had been prime tourism territory due to its abundant wildlife. It was reported that over 2,000 tourism-related businesses such as game lodges had been forced to close, and tour operators were reporting widespread cancellations.

With close to half of all land owned by 4,000 (mostly white) commercial farmers, Namibia also faced a land distribution crisis that could ignite if not handled effectively by the government. Thus far the government had not forced farmers to sell their land, but talk of expropriation had begun in some quarters, creating concern among farmers.

In February the government announced that it would spend $28 million to upgrade Walvis Bay airport terminals, runways, and warehousing facilities.

A new venture was launched to mine a massive deposit of sepiolite, a highly absorbent mineral in high demand, particularly in Europe, for use in cats' litter boxes. Production was eventually expected to reach 100,000 tons per year.

GOVERNMENT AND POLITICS

President Sam Nujoma was sworn in for his third term in office following elections held the previous autumn, in which both Nujoma and his ruling South West Africa Peoples' Organization (SWAPO) party won roughly three-fourths of the vote. A constitutional amendment had been required to allow the seventy-year-old Nujoma to run a third time. The festivities, attended by the president of South Africa and several other regional leaders, also marked the tenth anniversary of nationhood for the former South African-controlled South West Africa. In his inaugural address Nujoma outlined his goal of achieving a standard of living for Namibia comparable to that in the developed world by 2030. He also pledged to increase awareness of HIV/AIDS. Also sworn in was a twenty-two-member cabinet, headed by Prime Minister Hage Geingob.

The twenty-five-year-old Angolan civil war had an increasing impact on Namibia in 2000, after the government agreed that Angolan security forces could cross over the border, expanding their struggle against the UNITA rebels onto Namibian territory. Namibia also stepped up its own efforts to remove UNITA rebels fleeing Angola after a family of French tourists was attacked in the Caprivi Strip in the northeast and three children were killed. The same month Namibian forces captured eighty rebels within Namibia's borders.

After fighting in Angola intensified in July, thousands of Angolan civilians fled across the border into Namibia, spurring relief efforts by the United Nations World Food Program. By then it was estimated that about fifty Namibian civilians had been killed as a result of the spillover of the Angolan war into their country. In September the Namibian government denied reports by a human rights group that it had sent several thousand troops into Angola to help fight UNITA.

In May a Namibian woman and two South African men were arrested in Namibia's largest cocaine bust, which resulted in the seizure of $1.3 million worth of drugs.

Namibia and Finland shared responsibility for presiding over the United Nations General Assembly.

CULTURE AND SOCIETY

Namibians continued to enjoy a standard of living higher than the average for Africa, although their country was plagued by high unemployment, great inequalities in wealth, and the spread of AIDS.

Descendants of the country's Herero herders, most of whom were exterminated by German colonialists in the early 1900s, still honored the memory of their ancestors and had begun a campaign to win reparations from the German government for the extermination, which they claimed amounted to genocide. In the first decade of the twentieth century, the Herero population fell from 80,000 to 15,000. Those who survived the killings were forced to perform slave labor for German businesses, living in camps where malnutrition and disease were widespread. The tribe's case had been brought before the International Court of Justice in The Hague, Netherlands, and they were also considering a lawsuit in the German courts.

An international animal welfare group charged that seals in Namibia were being killed using prohibited and inhumane practices that forced the animals to suffer needlessly. The charges were based on secretly filmed footage of commercial seal culling in which the seals were clubbed randomly instead of according to officially approved guidelines.

DIRECTORY

CENTRAL GOVERNMENT

Head of State

President
Sam Shafiishuma Nujoma, Office of the President, Robert Mugabe Avenue, Private Bag 13339, Windhoek, Namibia
PHONE: +264 (61) 220010
FAX: +264 (61) 221780; 221770

Prime Minister
Hage Gottfried Geingob, Office of the Prime Minister, Robert Mugabe Avenue, Private Bag 13338, Windhoek, Namibia
PHONE: +264 (61) 2879111
FAX: +264 (61) 226189

Ministers

Deputy Prime Minister
Hendrik Witbooi, Office of the Deputy Prime Minister, Robert Mugabe Avenue, Windhoek, Namibia

Minister of Agriculture, Water and Rural Development
Helmut Angula, Ministry of Agriculture, Water and Rural Development, Robert Mugabe Avenue, Private Bag 13184, Windhoek, Namibia
PHONE: +264 (61) 2029111
FAX: +264 (61) 229961

Minister of Basic Education and Culture
John Mutorwa, Ministry of Basic Education and Culture, Robert Mugabe Avenue, Windhoek, Namibia

Minister of Defense
Erikki Nghimtina, Ministry of Defense, Robert Mugabe Avenue, Windhoek, Namibia

Minister of Environment and Tourism
Phillemon Malima, Ministry of Environment and Tourism, Robert Mugabe Avenue, Private Bag 13346, Windhoek, Namibia
PHONE: +264 (61) 284 91 11
FAX: +264 (61) 229 936
E-MAIL: tourism@iwwn.com.na

Minister of Finance
Nangolo Mbumba, Ministry of Finance, Robert Mugabe Avenue, Windhoek, Namibia

Minister of Fisheries and Marine Resources
Abraham Iyambo, Ministry of Fisheries and Marine Resources, Metje Behnsen Building, Private Bag 13355, Windhoek, Namibia
PHONE: +264 (61) 240201
FAX: +264 (61) 232581

Minister of Foreign Affairs
Theo-Ben Gurirab, Ministry of Foreign Affairs, Robert Mugabe Avenue, Windhoek, Namibia

Minister of Health and Social Services
Libertine Amathila, Ministry of Health and Social Services, Robert Mugabe Avenue, Windhoek, Namibia

Minister of Higher Education, Technical Training, Science and Technology
Nahas Angula, Ministry of Higher Education, Technical Training, Science and Technology, Robert Mugabe Avenue, Windhoek, Namibia

Minister of Home Affairs
Jerry Ekandjo, Ministry of Home Affairs, Robert Mugabe Avenue, Windhoek, Namibia

Minister of Justice
Ngarikutuke Tjirange, Ministry of Justice, Robert Mugabe Avenue, Windhoek, Namibia

Minister of Lands, Resettlement and Rehabilitation
Pendukeni Ithana, Ministry of Lands, Resettlement and Rehabilitation, Robert Mugabe Avenue, Windhoek, Namibia

Minister of Mines and Energy
Jesaya Nyamu, Ministry of Mines and Energy, PO Box 2895, Windhoek, Namibia
PHONE: +264 (61) 237925
FAX: +264 (61) 222638

Minister of Prisons and Correctional Services
Marco Hausiku, Ministry of Prisons and Correctional Services, Robert Mugabe Avenue, Windhoek, Namibia

Minister of Regional and Local Government and Housing
Nicky Iyambo, Ministry of Regional and Local Government and Housing, Robert Mugabe Avenue, Windhoek, Namibia

Minister of Trade and Industry
Hidipo Hamutenya, Ministry of Trade and Industry, Robert Mugabe Avenue, Private Bag 13340, Windhoek, Namibia
PHONE: +264 (61) 2849111
FAX: +264 (61) 229936

Minister of Works, Transport and Communications
Moses Amweelo, Ministry of Works, Transport and Communications, Robert Mugabe Avenue, Windhoek, Namibia

POLITICAL ORGANIZATIONS

South West Africa People's Organization of Namibia (SWAPO)

NAME: Sam Nujoma

Democratic Coalition of Namibia (DCN)

NAME: Moses K. Katjiuongua

Democratic Turnhall Alliance (DTA)

TITLE: President
NAME: Katuutire Kaura

Monitor Action Group (MAG)

NAME: Kosie Pretorius

United Democratic Front (UDF)

NAME: Justus Garoeb

DIPLOMATIC REPRESENTATION

Embassies in Namibia

Finland
P.O. Box 3649, Independence Avenue, Sanlam Centre, 5th Floor, Windhoek, Namibia
PHONE: +264 (61) 221355
FAX: +264 (61) 221349
E-MAIL: finland@iafrica.com.na
TITLE: Ambassador
NAME: Kari Karanko

United States
14 Lossen Street, Ausspannplatz, Windhoek, Namibia
PHONE: +264 (61) 221601

FAX: +264 (61) 229792
TITLE: Ambassador
NAME: George F. Ward, Jr.

JUDICIAL SYSTEM

Magistrate's Court

High Court

Supreme Court

Traditional Court

Judicial Service Commission

BROADCAST MEDIA

Namibian Broadcasting Corporation (NBC)

PO Box 321, Windhoek, Namibia
PHONE: +264 (61) 2919111; 2913111
FAX: +264 (61) 217760
WEBSITE: http://www.nbc.com.na
TITLE: Director
CONTACT: Ben Mulongeni
LANGUAGE: English, Afrikaans, Lozi, Damara/Nama, German, Oshiwambo, Otjiherero, Rukavango, Setswana
BROADCASTS: 24 hours/day
TYPE: Government

Katutura Community Radio (KCR)

PO Box 70448, Windhoek, Namibia
PHONE: +264 (61) 264768
FAX: +264 (61) 246172
E-MAIL: kcrfm@iafrica.com.na
CONTACT: Frederick Gawaseb
BROADCASTS: 10 hours/day
TYPE: Commercial

COLLEGES AND UNIVERSITIES

University of Namibia

Private Bag 13301, Windhoek, Namibia
PHONE: +264 (61) 2063111
FAX: +264 (61) 2063866
E-MAIL: vc@unam.na
WEBSITE: http://www.unam.na

NEWSPAPERS AND MAGAZINES

Namibia Economist

7 Schuster St., PO Box 49, Windhoek, Namibia
PHONE: +264 (6) 1221925
FAX: +264 (6) 1220615
E-MAIL: info@economist.com.na
WEBSITE: http://www.economist.com.na

The Namibian

PO Box 20783, Windhoek, Namibia
PHONE: +264 (61) 236970
FAX: +264 (61) 233980
E-MAIL: graham@namibian.com.na
WEBSITE: http://www.namibian.com.na
TITLE: Editor
CONTACT: Gwen Lister

Die Republikein

Democratic Media Holdings, 49 Stubel Street, Windhoek, Namibia
PHONE: +234 (61) 230331
FAX: +234 (61) 223721
E-MAIL: republikein@iafrica.com.na
WEBSITE: http://www.republikein.com.na

Namib Times

PO Box 706, Walvis Bay, Namibia
FAX: +264 6424813
TITLE: Editor
CONTACT: Paul Vincent
TYPE: Social science, general

Namibia Brief

PO Box 2123, Windhoek, Namibia
FAX: +264 06137251
TITLE: Editor
CONTACT: Cathy Blatt
TYPE: Business and economics, technology, mining

Namibiana

PO Box 67, Windhoek, Namibia
TITLE: Editor
CONTACT: K.F.R. Budack
CIRCULATION: 1,500
TYPE: History, Africa, social science, anthropology, folklore

PUBLISHERS

Desert Research Foundation of Namibia (DRFN)

PO Box 20232, Windhoek, Namibia
PHONE: +264 (61) 229855
FAX: +264 (61) 230172
E-MAIL: drfn@drfn.org.na
WEBSITE: http://www.iwwn.com.na/drfn
CONTACT: Mary Seely

SUBJECTS: Agriculture, Behavioral Sciences, Biological Sciences, Developing Countries, Earth Sciences, Education, Energy, Environmental Studies, Geography, Geology, Natural History, Physical Sciences, Regional Interests, Science (General), Botany, Zoology, Desertification Issues, Environmental Training, Water Management

Gamsberg Macmillan Publishers (Pty) Ltd.

PO Box 22830, Windhoek, Namibia
PHONE: +264 (61) 232165
FAX: +264 (61) 233538
E-MAIL: gmpubl@iafrica.com.na
WEBSITE: http://www.macmillan-africa.com/Contacts/namibia.htm
TITLE: Publishing
CONTACT: Peter Reiner
SUBJECTS: Literature, Criticism, Essays

Multi-Disciplinary Research Centre Library

University of Namibia, PB 13301, Windhoek, Namibia
PHONE: +264 (61) 2063907
FAX: +264 (61) 2063050
E-MAIL: ben@fuller.na
CONTACT: Ben Fuller
SUBJECTS: Agriculture, Developing Countries, Economics, Environmental Studies, Geography, Geology, Government, Political Science, Science (General), Social Sciences, Sociology, Gender Issues, Life Sciences

RELIGIOUS ORGANIZATIONS

Protestant

Evangelical Lutheran Church in Namibia
Private Bag 2018, Ondangwa, Namibia

Evangelical Lutheran Church in the Republic of Namibia
PO Box 5069, Windhoek 9000, Namibia

FURTHER READING

Articles

BBC News, March 21, 2000.

Cauvin, Henri E. "Namibia: French Children Slain." *New York Times,* January 5, 2000, p. A6.

"Two Preside over General Assembly." *New York Times,* September 3, 2000, p. 4.

Masland, Tom. "The Forgotten Genocide." *Newsweek International,* August 21, 2000, p. 40.

"The Month in Review: January 2000." *Current History,* March 2000, p. 142.

The Namibian, February 15, May 26, June 19, and July 13, 2000.

Panafrican News Agency, January 9, 2000.

Books

Dun and Bradstreet's Export Guide to Namibia. Parsippany, NJ: Dun & Bradstreet, 1999.

Gordon, Robert J. *The Bushman Myth: The Making of a Namibian Underclass.* 2d ed. Boulder, CO: Westview Press, 2000.

NAMIBIA: STATISTICAL DATA

For sources and notes see "Sources of Statistics" at the front of each volume.

GEOGRAPHY

Geography

Area:

Total: 825,418 sq km.

Land: 825,418 sq km.

Land boundaries:

Total: 3,824 km.

Border countries: Angola 1,376 km, Botswana 1,360 km, South Africa 855 km, Zambia 233 km.

Coastline: 1,572 km.

Climate: desert; hot, dry; rainfall sparse and erratic.

Terrain: mostly high plateau; Namib Desert along coast; Kalahari Desert in east.

Natural resources: diamonds, copper, uranium, gold, lead, tin, lithium, cadmium, zinc, salt, vanadium, natural gas, hydropower, fish.

Note: suspected deposits of oil, coal, and iron ore.

Land use:

Arable land: 1%

Permanent crops: 0%

Permanent pastures: 46%

Forests and woodland: 22%

Other: 31% (1993 est.).

HUMAN FACTORS

Demographics (A)

	1990	1995	1998	2000	2010	2020	2030	2040	2050
Population	1,409	1,604	1,711	1,771	1,909	1,956	2,033	2,182	2,465
Life expectancy - males	58.7	52.6	47.3	44.3	33.8	36.2	42.3	53.6	68.5
Life expectancy - females	61.4	53.1	44.8	40.5	31.6	34.1	40.8	53.9	71.9
Birth rate (per 1,000)	38.6	37.2	36.2	35.2	30.6	29.1	26.4	23.4	20.8
Death rate (per 1,000)	10.7	13.4	17.1	19.5	28.6	26.2	21.5	13.8	6.4
Women of reproductive age (15-49 yrs.)	321.4	375.8	404.3	418.7	443.1	479.0	521.5	589.5	678.6
Fertility rate	5.5	5.2	5.0	4.9	4.3	3.7	3.1	2.7	2.4

Except as noted, values for vital statistics are in thousands; life expectancy is in years.

Health Personnel

	National Data	World Data (wtd ave)
Total health expenditure as a percentage of GDP, 1990-1998[a]		
Public sector	3.8	2.5
Private sector	3.6	2.9
Total[b]	7.4	5.5
Health expenditure per capita in U.S. dollars, 1990-1998[a]		
Purchasing power parity	399	561
Total	150	483
Availability of health care facilities per 100,000 people		
Hospital beds 1990-1998[a]	NA	330
Doctors 1992-1995[a]	23	122
Nurses 1992-1995[a]	81	248

Health Indicators

	National Data	World Data
Life expectancy at birth (years)		
1980	53	61
1998	54	67
Daily per capita supply of calories		
1970	2,162	2,358
1997	2,183	2,791
Daily per capital supply of protein		
1997 (grams)	60	74
Total fertility rate (births per woman)		
1980	5.9	3.7
1998	4.8	2.7
Population with access (%)		
To safe water (1990-96)	57	NA
To sanitation (1990-96)	34	NA
People living with (1997)		
Tuberculosis (cases per 100,000)	372.2	60.4
Malaria (cases per 100,000)	26,216.6	42.2
HIV/AIDS (% aged 15 - 49 years)	19.94	0.99

Infants and Malnutrition

	National Data	World Data (wtd ave)
Under 5 mortality rate (1989)	74	NA
% of infants with low birthweight (1992-98)[1]	NA	17
Births attended by skilled health staff (% of total births 1996-98)	68	52
% fully immunized at 1 year of age (1995-98)[1]		
TB	85	82
DPT	74	77
Polio	74	77
Measles	63	74
Prevalence of child malnutrition (1992-98)[1] (based on weight for age, % of children under 5 years)	26	30

Ethnic Division

Black .87.5%
White .6.0%
Mixed .6.5%
Ovambo tribe .50.0%
Kavangos tribe .9.0%
Herero .7.0%
Damara .7.0%
Nama .5.0%
Caprivian .4.0%
Bushmen .3.0%
Baster .2.0%
Tswana .0.5%

Religion

Christian .80% to 90%
Lutheran .at least 50%
Indigenous beliefs .10% to 20%
Muslim .75% (predominantly Sunni)
Jewish .17%
Christian and other .8%

Major Languages

English 7% (official), Afrikaans common language of most of the population and about 60% of the white population, German 32%, indigenous languages: Oshivambo, Herero, Nama.

EDUCATION

Public Education Expenditures

	1980	1997
Public expenditures on education as % of GNP	1.5	1.9
Expenditures per student as % of GNP per capita		
Primary	NA	21.0
Secondary	NA	34.1
Tertiary	NA	101.7
Pupils per teacher at the primary level	NA	NA
Duration of primary education in years	NA	1
World data for comparison		
Public expenditures on education as % of GNP (mean)	3.9	4.8
Pupils per teacher at the primary level (wtd ave)	NA	33
Duration of primary education in years (mean)	NA	9

(Continued on next page.)

GOVERNMENT & LAW

Military Affairs (A)

	1990	1992	1995	1996	1997
Military expenditures					
Current dollars (mil.)	41	59	58	68	90
1997 constant dollars (mil.)	48	65	60	69	90
Armed forces (000)	NA	8	8	8	8
Gross national product (GNP)					
Current dollars (mil.)	2,140	2,630	3,130	3,240	3,330
1997 constant dollars (mil.)	2,510	2,910	3,240	3,300	3,330
Central government expenditures (CGE)					
1997 constant dollars (mil.)	813	1,160	1,100[e]	1,190[e]	1,240[e]
People (mil.)	1.4	1.5	1.5	1.6	1.6
Military expenditure as % of GNP	1.9	2.2	1.8	2.1	2.7
World data on military expenditure as % of GNP	4.5	3.4	2.7	2.6	2.6
Military expenditure as % of CGE	5.9	5.6	5.4	5.8	7.3
World data on military expenditure as % of CGE	17.0	12.5	10.5	10.3	10.2
Military expenditure per capita (1997 $)	34	45	39	44	57
World data on military expenditure per capita (1997 $)	242	173	146	143	145
Armed forces per 1,000 people (soldiers)	NA	5.5	5.2	5.1	5.0
World data on armed forces per 1,000 people (soldiers)	5.3	4.5	4.1	3.9	3.8
GNP per capita (1997 $)	1,780	1,990	2,100	2,100	2,090
Arms imports[6]					
Current dollars (mil.)	0	0	5	0	5
1997 constant dollars (mil.)	0	0	5	0	5
Total imports[7]					
Current dollars (mil.)	1,163	1,283	NA	1,550[e]	1,480[e]
1997 constant dollars (mil.)	1,362	1,422	NA	1,576[e]	1,480[e]
Total exports[7]					
Current dollars (mil.)	1,084	1,342	NA	1,450[e]	1,440[e]
1997 constant dollars (mil.)	1,270	1,488	NA	1,474[e]	1,440[e]
Arms as percent of total imports[8]	0	0	NA	0	0.3
Arms as percent of total exports[8]	0	0	0	0	0

(Continued on next page.)

EDUCATION (cont.)

Educational Attainment (A)

Age group (1991)[5] .... 25+
Population of this age group 340,552
Highest level attained (%)
No schooling .... NA
First level
Not completed 49.1
Completed .... NA
Entered second level 43.8
Entered post-secondary 4.0

Literacy Rates (B)

	National Data	World Data
Adult literacy rate		
1980		
Male	71	75
Female	61	58
1995		
Male	80	81
Female	77	65

GOVERNMENT & LAW (cont.)

Political Parties

Legislature	no. of seats
National Council	
South West Africa People's Organization (SWAPO)	21
Democratic Turnhalle Alliance of Namibia (DTA)	4
United Democratic Front (UDF)	1
National Assembly	
South West Africa People's Organization (SWAPO)	55
Congress of Democrats (COD)	7
Democratic Turnhalle Alliance of Namibia (DTA)	7
United Democratic Front (UDF)	2
Monitor Action Group (MAG)	1

Elections for regional councils, to determine members of the National Council were held 30 November-1 December 1998 (next to be held by December 2004). National Assembly elections were last held 30 November-1 December 1999 (next to be held by December 2004).

Government Budgets (B)

Revenues .... $883 million
Expenditures .... $950 million

Data for 1998.

Crime

Crime volume (for 1998)
Crimes reported 68,884
Total persons convicted 31,687
Crimes per 100,000 population 4,062

LABOR FORCE

Total Labor Force (A)

500,000.

Labor Force by Occupation

Agriculture 47%
Industry 25%
Services 28%

Data for 1999 est.

Unemployment Rate

30% to 40%, including underemployment (1997 est.).

PRODUCTION SECTOR

Energy Production

Production .... 1.198 billion kWh
Production by source
Fossil fuel 2%
Hydro 98%
Nuclear 0%
Other 0%
Exports .... 56 million kWh

Data for 1999.

Energy Consumption

Consumption .... 1.81 billion kWh
Imports .... 890.00 million kWh

Data for 1999.

Transportation

Highways:

Total: 63,258 km.

Paved: 5,250 km.

Unpaved: 58,008 km (1997 est.).

Merchant marine: none (1999 est.).

Airports: 135 (1999 est.).

Airports - with paved runways: 22.

Airports - with unpaved runways: 113.

Top Agriculture Products

Millet, sorghum, peanuts; livestock; fish.

Top Mining Products (B)

Mineral resources include: diamonds, copper, uranium, gold, lead, tin, lithium, cadmium, zinc, salt, vanadium.

Note: suspected deposits of oil, coal, and iron ore.

COMMUNICATIONS

Daily Newspapers

	National Data	World Data for Comparison
Daily Newspapers		
Number of Dailies	4	8,391
Total Circulation (000)	30	548,000
Circulation per 1,000 inhabitants	19	96

Telecommunications

Telephones - main lines in use: 100,848 (1997).

Telephones - mobile cellular: 20,000 (1998).

Telephone system:

Domestic: good urban services; fair rural service; microwave radio relay links major towns; connections to other populated places are by open wire; 100% digital.

International: fiber-optic cable to South Africa, microwave radio relay link to Botswana, direct links to other neighboring countries; connected to Africa ONE and South African Far East (SAFE) submarine cables through South Africa; satellite earth stations - 4 Intelsat.

Radio broadcast stations: AM 2, FM 34, shortwave 5 (1998).

Radios: 232,000 (1997).

Television broadcast stations: 8 (plus about 20 low-power repeaters) (1997).

Televisions: 60,000 (1997).

Internet Service Providers (ISPs): 4 (1999).

FINANCE, ECONOMICS, & TRADE

Economic Indicators

National product: GDP—purchasing power parity—$7.1 billion (1999 est.).

National product real growth rate: 3% (1999 est.).

National product per capita: $4,300 (1999 est.).

Inflation rate—consumer price index: 8.5% (1999).

Government transfers (net) 307 374 385 419 389

Overall balance 85 176 116 90 162

Exchange Rates

Exchange rates:

Namibian dollars (N$) per US$1

January 2000 . . . . .6.12439
1999 . . . . .6.10948
1998 . . . . .5.52828
1997 . . . . .4.60796
1996 . . . . .4.29935
1995 . . . . .3.62709

(Continued on next page.)

MANUFACTURING SECTOR

GDP & Manufacturing Summary (B)

	1980	1985	1990	1993	1994	1995
Gross Domestic Product						
Millions of 1990 dollars	1,944	1,891	2,129	2,390	2,519	2,585
Growth rate in percent	0.18	0.19	0.01	−1.53	5.41	2.62
Per capita (in 1990 dollars)	1,887	1,604	1,575	1,636	1,681	1,683
Manufacturing Value Added						
Millions of 1990 dollars	63	80	113	125	128	133[e]
Growth rate in percent	−14.65	3.72	15.63	17.17	2.10	4.27[e]
Manufacturing share in percent of current prices	4.6	4.6	6.1	8.8	8.8[e]	NA

FINANCE, ECONOMICS, & TRADE (cont.)

Top Import Origins

$1.5 billion (f.o.b., 1999 est.)

Origins (1995 est.)

South Africa	84%
Germany	NA
United States	NA
Japan	NA

Top Export Destinations

$1.4 billion (f.o.b., 1999 est.)

Destinations (1998 est.)

United Kingdom	43%
South Africa	26%
Spain	14%
France	8%
Japan	NA

Foreign Aid

Recipient: $127 million (1998).

Import/Export Commodities

Import Commodities	Export Commodities
Foodstuffs	Diamonds
Petroleum products and fuel	Copper
Machinery and equipment	Gold
Chemicals	Zinc
	Lead
	Uranium
	Cattle
	Processed fish
	Karakul skins

Balance of Payments

	1994	1995	1996	1997	1998
Exports of goods (f.o.b.)	1,320	1,418	1,404	1,343	1,278
Imports of goods (f.o.b.)	−1,406	−1,548	−1,531	−1,615	−1,451
Trade balance	−86	−130	−127	−272	−173
Services - debits	−468	−551	−581	−534	−457
Services - credits	259	315	337	380	327
Private transfers (net)	28	36	37	31	19

NAURU

Republic of Nauru
Naoero

CAPITAL: There is no formal capital. The seat of government is in the district of Yaren.

FLAG: The flag has a blue background divided horizontally by a narrow gold band, symbolizing the equator. Below the band is a white 12-pointed star, representing the island's 12 traditional tribes.

ANTHEM: *Nauru Ubwema* (Nauru, Our Homeland).

MONETARY UNIT: The Australian dollar (A$) of 100 cents is the legal currency. A$1 = US$0.7008 (or US$1 = A$1.4269).

WEIGHTS AND MEASURES: Imperial weights and measures are used.

HOLIDAYS: New Year's Day, 1 January; Independence Day, 31 January; Angam Day, 26 October (a celebration of the day on which the population of Nauru reached the pre-World War II level); Christmas Day, 25 December; and Boxing Day, 26 December.

TIME: 11:30 PM = noon GMT.

LOCATION AND SIZE: Situated in the western Pacific, Nauru is the world's smallest independent island nation, with an area of 21 square kilometers (8.1 square miles), about one-tenth the size of Washington, D.C. It lies between two island groups, the Solomons and the Gilberts and its nearest neighbor is Banaba (formerly Ocean Island, now part of Kiribati).

CLIMATE: The average annual rainfall is about 45 centimeters (18 inches), but the amount varies greatly from year to year, and long droughts have been a repeated problem. Temperatures remain steady, between 24° and 33°C (75–91°F) year round, and relative humidity is also constant at about 80%.

INTRODUCTORY SURVEY

RECENT HISTORY

Japanese bombings flattened Nauru beginning in December 1941, and all its industrial plant and housing facilities were destroyed. The Japanese occupied the island from August 1942 until the end of the war three years later. Australian forces reoccupied Nauru in September 1945.

After World War II (1939-1945), the island became a trust territory administered jointly by Australia, New Zealand, and the United Kingdom, who were to share the task of developing self-government on the island. On January 31, 1968, Nauru became the smallest independent republic in the world.

Since that time, Nauru has pursued a policy of isolation and nonalignment although it does have a role in British Commonwealth affairs. In October 1982, Queen Elizabeth II visited the island, the first British monarch to do so. Nauru filed a claim in 1989 for compensation from Australia at the International Court of Justice for the loss of nearly all its topsoil from phosphate mining during the League of Nations mandate and the United Nations trusteeship. Australia agreed to pay A$107 million (about US$73 million) in August 1993 to settle the case.

In June 1992, Nauru signed both the Climate Change and Biodiversity Conventions. In July it hosted the 24th South Pacific Forum heads of government meeting, which focused on environmental issues. In 1993, Australia, New Zealand, and the United Kingdom agreed to pay Nauru a settlement for soil damage.

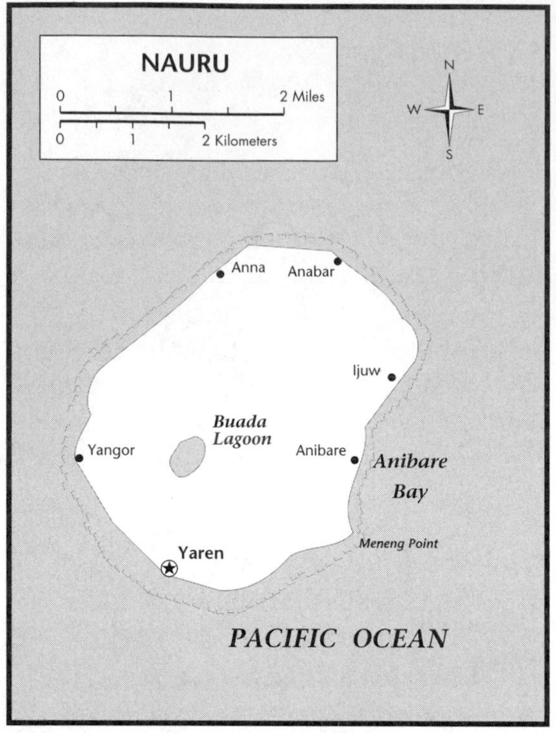

Incumbent president Bernard Dowiyogo lost his 1995 bid for reelection to Lagumot Harris. However, a series of non-confidence votes in succeeding years brought a series of changes in the presidency. It came to be known as the "revolving door" presidency. As of April 2000, Dowiyogo had returned to the office.

Nauru became a member of the Commonwealth of Nations in May 1999 and joined the United Nations in September of the same year.

GOVERNMENT

The constitution, adopted in 1968, and subsequently amended, provides that the republic shall have a parliamentary type of government. It contains provisions for the protection of fundamental rights and freedoms, a subject of particular importance, because many of the inhabitants are short-term migrants ineligible for citizenship.

The president, elected by Parliament for a three-year term, is both chief of state and head of government.

The legislative branch is the unicameral, eighteen-seat, Parliament. Members are elected by popular vote from each of the constituencies for three-year terms. Suffrage is universal and compulsory at twenty years of age.

Judiciary

The constitution provides for a Supreme Court, with a chief justice presiding. Cases are also heard in the District Court or Family Court. The Supreme Court, which has original and appellate jurisdiction, is the supreme authority on the interpretation of the constitution. Cases may be appealed further to the High Court of Australia.

Political Parties

The Democratic Party of Nauru, which aimed to curb the power of the presidency, became the only political party in Nauru in 1987. It did not play an important part in the electoral process and was no longer in existence by 1995. However, as of 1999, a new Democratic Party had been formed. Also in existence was the informal Nauru Party.

DEFENSE

Nauru has no armed forces. Although there is no formal agreement, Australia ensures its defense.

ECONOMIC AFFAIRS

The economy of Nauru has long been dependent on phosphates, which, according to recent estimates, will be exhausted by the early 2000s. By 1987, an estimated $450 million had been set aside to support the country after the phosphates run out. However, the government has borrowed from the trust since 1990 to finance fiscal deficits. In 1994, an audit revealed that $8.5 million was missing due to bad investments and corruption. By 1996, deficit spending had caused the country to default on servicing its external debt and was also creating problems in meeting government payrolls.

The replacement of phosphate income is Nauru's most pressing problem. The government has attempted to diversify the economy mainly through overseas investment. Also, Nauru has encouraged registration of offshore banks and corporations.

Aside from phosphates, Nauru has few domestic resources. Most necessities, even fresh water, and practically all consumer manufactures are imported.

Public Finance

Administrative costs in Nauru are met from the proceeds of phosphate sales, which are in decline as reserves approach exhaustion. In 1993, the governments of Nauru and Australia reached a US$73 million out-of-court settlement as restitution for Nauruan lands ruined by Australian phosphate mining. This payment assisted the government (which relies almost entirely on phosphate receipts for revenue) in facilitating economic diversification. The U.S. Central Intelligence Agency estimated that in the 1995-1996 fiscal year government revenues totaled approximately $23.4 million and expenditures $64.8 million. External debt totaled $33.3 million.

Income

The gross domestic product (GDP) of Nauru was estimated to be $100 million in 1995, or $10,000 per capita. Phosphates have given Nauruans one of the highest per person incomes in the Third World. Inflation in 1993 was −3.6%.

Industry

The phosphate industry is the major industry on the island. Financial services have been encouraged. The only other industry of note is coconut products.

Banking and Finance

The government-owned Bank of Nauru was founded in 1976. The Commonwealth Savings Bank of Australia and the Bank of New South Wales have branches in Nauru. The only commercial bank in the country is the Jefferson Bank and Trust Co. Most of the income from phosphates is invested in long-term funds overseas. There is no stock exchange.

Economic Development

Government policy is to exploit the phosphate deposits to the fullest extent for the highest returns. The government has diversified into aviation and shipping and plans to develop fishing and tourism. It has acquired the Grand Pacific Hotel on the Fijian Island of Suva and, in 1993, began work on a F$18 million renovation of the facility. In 1993, Australia agreed to provide US$73 million in compensation for pre-independence mining of phosphate to aid in restoring the extensive areas damaged by it.

In December 1998, Nauru won approval for a $5 million loan from the Asian Development Bank to aid in implementing structural reform. Reforms include reduction of over-staffed public service departments, privatization of numerous government agencies, closure of some overseas consulates, and a freezing of wages.

SOCIAL WELFARE

Medical, dental, and hospital treatment and education are free. The government provides old age and disability pensions, and widows' and sickness benefits and child endowment. Women face great social pressure to marry and raise families because Nauru's population was drastically reduced in World War II.

Healthcare

Tuberculosis, leprosy, diabetes, and vitamin deficiencies have been the main health problems, partly due to a switch to a Westernized diet. Cardiovascular disease has become a major cause of illness and death. There are two modern hospitals. One serves phosphate industry employees; the other provides free medical treatment for the rest of the population. Patients who need specialized care are flown to Australia. In 2000, average life expectancy was 60.8 years.

Housing

Nearly all houses have electricity, and newer homes have a greater number of modern features.

EDUCATION

Attendance at school is compulsory for Nauruan children from 6 to 16 years old. Two types of schools are available: those run by the government and those conducted by the Roman Catholic Church. The government provides free education. There are scholarships available for higher education overseas, mainly in Australia and a university extension center connected to the University of the South Pacific.

2000 KEY EVENTS TIMELINE

January

- Nauru announces plans to revise its banking laws to make them more consistent with international standards.

February

- The eighteen-member Parliament dissolves in preparation for general elections to be held April 8.
- Aloyious Amwano, Nauru's Acting Minister for Island Development, urges Nauru's populace to prepare for the adverse results of climate change.

April

- The new parliament reelects President Rene Harris, who resigns; Bernard Dowiyoga is elected to replace him.

May

- Nauru sues the Fiji government for seizing a historic hotel in Suva, leased by Nauru.
- The sixty-sixth Council Meeting of the Asian-Pacific Parliamentarian's Union convenes in Yaren, Nauru; attendees include delegations from Japan, Thailand, Malaysia, Vietnam and the Philippines.

June

- Air Nauru recommences flight service after a replacement engine is found for its aircraft.

August

- Australian newspapers print false reports of a coup when satellite communications problems cause a break in transmissions from Nauru.
- Nauru is named in the South Pacific Regional Environment Program (SPREP) study of contamination caused by hazardous material storage in South Pacific island nations.

September

- Nauru sends three athletes to compete in the Summer Olympics in Sydney, Australia.

October

- Nauru's government says it will renovate the Grand Pacific Hotel on Fiji, with work to begin as soon as all legalities are completed.
- Air Nauru raises all airfares 6 percent in response to the rising cost of fuel.

November

- Nauru's director of sports, Paul Coffa, resigns November 30 to organize the 2001 World Weightlifting Championships that are to be held in Nauru.

ANALYSIS OF EVENTS: 2000

BUSINESS AND THE ECONOMY

Nauru was among the thirty-five nations listed by the Organization for Economic Cooperation and Development (OECD) in 2000 as "tax havens.". These tax havens received warning to institute reforms within one year or face undefined sanctions. The OECD stated that policies in Nauru and other nations created unfair tax burdens in the wealthy nations whose citizens used banking services in the alleged tax havens. The G7 group of major industrialized nations cited Nauru for failing to cooperate in the fight against international money laundering. Early in the year then-President Rene Harris said he would not allow criminal activities in his nation's financial systems. He took action to make Nauru's banking laws obey international standards, approaching the U.S. government for help in doing so. In response a team of U.S. banking advisors was sent to Nauru in March.

A Nauru government trust took legal action in May against the Fiji government for repossessing the historic Grand Pacific Hotel in Suva, under lease to Nauru. The once majestic hotel had been closed for six years and had fallen into disrepair, and after years of trying to get it renovated, the Fiji government seized it so that it could be restored. In October President Dowiyoga flew to Fiji to meet with Fiji's Foreign Affairs Minister Kaliopate Tavola to discuss Nauru's renovation plans for the hotel.

In October Air Nauru raised all airfares 6 percent in response to the rising cost of fuel.

GOVERNMENT AND POLITICS

The year 2000 began for Nauru with a series of elections. Parliamentary elections were held on April 8. The new parliament then called for new presidential elections, and President Rene Harris, who himself had been elected in a no-confidence vote only a year earlier, was defeated by the man he had unseated, Bernard Dowiyoga. (This was the eighth government change in four years.)

President Dowiyoga soon made his voice heard in the international arena. In his opening statements before the sixty-sixth Council Meeting of the Asian-Pacific Parliamentarian's Union in May, President Dowiyoga identified the right to self-determination as a basic principle of international law, and urged the conference to support West Papua's struggle for independence. He also raised environmental concerns, and made special mention of the dangers to the region's ecosystems posed by Japan's shipping of radioactive wastes through the waters of the area. He called upon Japan and France to resolve the matter. Conference attendees included delegations from Japan, Thailand, Malaysia, Vietnam, and the Philippines.

In September President Dowiyoga spoke before the Millennium Summit of the United Nations (U.N.), where he again supported the fight of the

West Papuans for self-determination. He also asked that the United Nations recognize the Pacific states as belonging to a regional group separate from Asia, since the needs of the developing small island states were different from those of the larger Asian nations. Stating that the Pacific nations faced virtual genocide through global warming and the associated rise in sea level, Dowiyoga urged the members of the United Nations, especially those most responsible for pollution, to quickly adopt the provisions of the Kyoto Protocol. He also praised the democracy and generosity of the Republic of China (Taiwan) and urged the United Nations to reconsider that nation's international status.

Nauru attended the Pacific Islands Forum held in October in Kiribati. Nauru and the other fifteen members of the Forum shared concerns over sea-level rise and toxic waste disposal, the latter being an issue of great concern to Nauru, as it was among the South Pacific nations cited in a South Pacific Regional Environment Programme (SPREP) report of contamination caused by improper disposal or storage of hazardous wastes. SPREP was to offer assistance in determining proper disposal and finding funds to ship the contaminated material to treatment facilities elsewhere.

Australian newspapers printed false reports of a coup in Nauru when satellite communications problems in August caused a break in transmissions. Government spokesperson Helen Bogdan stated that the communications problem could have been the result of a land dispute, as the ownership of the land where the satellite was placed had been in question in the past. While rumors pointed to a coup attempt by ex-President Rene Harris, he was out of the country at the time, according to the spokesperson, and clearly not involved.

CULTURE AND SOCIETY

Global warming was an issue of great importance throughout the Pacific region. Aloyious Amwano, Nauru's Acting Minister for Island Development, urged Nauru's populace to prepare for the possible adverse results of climate change, such as drought, tidal waves, and other natural disasters. He urged the population not to be complacent, and stressed that the government would consider climate change an important factor in national planning.

Marcus Stephens became the first athlete from Nauru ever to compete in an Olympic Games when he traveled to Sydney, Australia, to enter the weightlifting competition, in which he finished eleventh.

DIRECTORY

CENTRAL GOVERNMENT

Head of State

President
Bernard Dowiyogo, Office of the President
PHONE: +674 33100

Ministers

Minister of Education and Vocational Training
Remy Namaduk, Ministry of Education and Vocational Training
PHONE: +674 4443100
FAX: +674 4443178

Minister of Foreign Affairs
Bernard Dowiyogo, Ministry of Foreign Affairs

Minister of Finance and Economic Reforms
Bernard Dowiyogo, Ministry of Finance and Economic Reforms
PHONE: +674 4443140
FAX: +674 5554477

Minister of Economic Development and Industry
Kinza Clodumar, Ministry of Economic Development and Industry

Minister of Justice
Vassal Gadoengin, Ministry of Justice
PHONE: +674 4443160
FAX: +674 4443108

Minister of Public Service
Bernard Dowiyogo, Ministry of Public Service

Minister of Works, Planning and Housing Development
Derog Gioura, Ministry of Works, Planning and Housing Development
PHONE: +674 4443177
FAX: +674 4443135

Minister of Business Development and Consumer Affairs
Kinza Clodumar, Ministry of Business Development and Consumer Affairs

Minister of Civil Aviation and Transportation
Kinza Clodumar, Ministry of Civil Aviation and Transportation

Minister of Home Affairs and Culture
Anthony Audoa, Ministry of Home Affairs and Culture

Minister of Human Resources, Development and Employment
Bernard Dowiyogo, Ministry of Human Resources, Development and Employment

Minister of Public Service
Bernard Dowiyogo, Ministry of Public Service

POLITICAL ORGANIZATIONS

Nauru Party

NAME: Bernard Dowiyogo

Democratic Party

NAME: Kennan Adeang

DIPLOMATIC REPRESENTATION

Embassies in Nauru

Australia
Civic Centre Orpo Box 6, Nauru
PHONE: +674 4443232; 4443233; 4443234
FAX: +674 4443227

China
Yaren, PO Box 294, Nauru
PHONE: +674 5554399
FAX: +674 5554594

JUDICIAL SYSTEM

Supreme Court

PHONE: +674 4443163
FAX: +674 4443140

BROADCAST MEDIA

Nauru Broadcasting Service

Information and Broadcasting Services, Chief Secretary's Department, Nauru
PHONE: +674 4443109
FAX: +674 4443195
TITLE: Station Manager
CONTACT: Rin Tsitisi
LANGUAGE: Nauruan, English
BROADCASTS: 16.5 hours/day
TYPE: Government

Nauru Television

Republic of Nauru
PHONE: +674 4443190
TYPE: Government

COLLEGES AND UNIVERSITIES

University of the South Pacific

University Centre, Private Bag, Post Office, Nauru
PHONE: +674 5556455
FAX: +675 4443774
E-MAIL: gaiyabu_m@usp.ac.fj

NEWSPAPERS AND MAGAZINES

Central Star News

PO Box 429, Nauru
PHONE: +674 (1) 444-3515
TITLE: Publisher
CONTACT: Yeru Uera

Nauru Bulletin

Dept. of Island Development and Industry, Yaren District, Nauru
PHONE: +674 (1) 444-3182
FAX: +674 (1) 444-3153
CIRCULATION: 700

RELIGIOUS ORGANIZATIONS

Nauru is 100 percent Christian, with two-thirds Protestant and one-third Catholic. Due to its close ties with Australia and its size and ability to support organizations, most religious organizations are located on the mainland of Australia.

FURTHER READING

Articles

Feizkhah, Elizabeth. "Large Load, Heavy Soil, High Spin: Nauru's Accommodating Approach to Money Launderers Lands It Between A Rock And A Hard Place." *Time International,* February 28, 2000, vol. 155, no. 8, p. 46+.

Internet

BBC News Online. "Sanctions Threat to 'Tax Havens.'" June 26, 2000. [Online] Available http://news6.thdo.bbc.co.uk/hi/english/business/newsid%5F806000/806236.stm (accessed October 12, 2000).

NAURU: STATISTICAL DATA

For sources and notes see "Sources of Statistics" at the front of each volume.

GEOGRAPHY

Geography

Area:

Total: 21 sq km.

Land: 21 sq km.

Land boundaries: 0 km.

Coastline: 30 km.

Climate: tropical; monsoonal; rainy season (November to February).

Terrain: sandy beach rises to fertile ring around raised coral reefs with phosphate plateau in center.

Natural resources: phosphates.

Land use:

Arable land: 0%

Permanent crops: 0%

Permanent pastures: 0%

Forests and woodland: 0%

Other: 100% (1993 est.).

HUMAN FACTORS

Ethnic Division

Nauruan 58%

Other Pacific Islander 26%

Chinese 8%

European 8%

Religion

Christian (two-thirds Protestant, one-third Roman Catholic).

Demographics (A)

	1990	1995	1998	2000	2010	2020	2030	2040	2050
Population	NA	10.6	11.4	11.8	14.3	16.7	19.0	20.9	22.7
Life expectancy - males	NA	55.5	56.6	57.4	60.9	64.3	67.3	70.1	72.4
Life expectancy - females	NA	62.5	63.6	64.5	68.4	71.9	75.0	77.6	79.8
Birth rate (per 1,000)	NA	30.7	28.7	27.9	23.6	20.5	17.3	15.7	14.5
Death rate (per 1,000)	NA	8.0	7.5	7.3	6.4	6.2	6.4	6.8	7.3
Women of reproductive age (15-49 yrs.)	NA	2.6	2.9	3.0	3.9	4.6	5.3	5.6	5.6
Fertility rate	NA	4.0	3.8	3.7	2.8	2.3	2.1	2.0	2.0

Except as noted, values for vital statistics are in thousands; life expectancy is in years.

Major Languages

Nauruan (official, a distinct Pacific Island language), English widely understood, spoken, and used for most government and commercial purposes.

GOVERNMENT & LAW

Political Parties

The unicameral Parliament consists of 18 seats. Members are elected by popular vote to serve three-year terms. Elections were last held 8 February 1997 (next to be held February 2000). Independents were elected to all 18 seats. There is a loose multiparty system. They have two parties: the Democratic Party and the Nauru Party.

Government Budgets (B)

Revenues	$23.4 million
Expenditures	$64.8 million

Data for FY95/96.

Military Affairs (B)

Availability	
Males age 15-49	2,945
Fit for military service	
Males age 15-49	1,620

Data for 2000 est.

LABOR FORCE

Labor Force by Occupation

Employed in mining phosphates, public administration, education, and transportation.

Unemployment Rate

0%

PRODUCTION SECTOR

Energy Production

Production	30 million kWh
Production by source	
Fossil fuel	100%
Hydro	0%
Nuclear	0%
Other	0%
Exports	0 kWh

Data for 1998.

Energy Consumption

Consumption	28 million kWh
Imports	0 kWh

Data for 1998.

Transportation

Highways:

Total: 30 km.

Paved: 24 km.

Unpaved: 6 km (1998 est.).

Merchant marine: none (1999 est.).

Airports: 1 (1999 est.).

Top Agriculture Products

Coconuts.

Top Mining Products (B)

Mineral resources include: phosphates.

MANUFACTURING SECTOR

GDP & Manufacturing Summary (C)

Total GDP (1993 est.)	$100 million
Per capita (1993 est.)	$10,000

Values in purchasing power parity.

COMMUNICATIONS

Telecommunications

Telephones - main lines in use: 2,000 (1994).

Telephones - mobile cellular: 450 (1994).

Telephone system: adequate local and international radiotelephone communications provided via Australian facilities.

Domestic: NA

International: satellite earth station - 1 Intelsat (Pacific Ocean).

Radio broadcast stations: AM 1, FM 0, shortwave 0 (1998).

Radios: 7,000 (1997).

Television broadcast stations: 1 (1997).

Televisions: 500 (1997).

Internet Service Providers (ISPs): NA

FINANCE, ECONOMICS, & TRADE

Economic Indicators

National product: GDP—purchasing power parity—$100 million (1993 est.).

National product real growth rate: NA.

National product per capita: $10,000 (1993 est.).

Inflation rate—consumer price index: -3.6% (1993).

Exchange Rates

Exchange rates:

Australian dollars ($A) per US$1

January 2000	1.5207
1999	1.5497
1998	1.5888
1997	1.3439
1996	1.2773
1995	1.3486

Top Import Origins

Imports (c.i.f., 1991): $21.1 million.

Origins: Australia, United Kingdom, New Zealand, Japan.

Top Export Destinations

Exports (f.o.b., 1991): $25.3 million.

Destinations: Australia, New Zealand.

Foreign Aid

Recipient: $2.25 million from Australia (FY96/97 est.).

Import/Export Commodities

Import Commodities	Export Commodities
Food	Phosphates
Fuel	
Manufactures	
Building materials	
Machinery	

NEPAL

CAPITAL: Kathmandu.

FLAG: The national flag consists of two red adjoining triangles, outlined in blue and merging at the center; the points are at the fly. On the upper triangle, in white, is a symbolic representation of the moon; on the lower triangle, that of the sun.

ANTHEM: The national anthem begins "May His Majesty, solemn and supremely valiant, be prosperous forever."

MONETARY UNIT: The Nepalese rupee (NR) is a paper currency of 100 paisa. There are coins of 1, 2, 5, 10, 20, 25, and 50 paisa and 1, 2, 5, 10, 20, 25, 50, and 100 rupees, and notes of 1, 2, 5, 10, 20, 50, 100, 500, and 1,000 Nepalese rupees. NR1 = \$0.01753 (or \$1 = NR57.03).

WEIGHTS AND MEASURES: The metric system is in use, but some traditional Indian standards are also employed.

HOLIDAYS: National Unity Day, 11 January; Martyrs' Day, 30 January; Rashtriya Prajatantra Divas—National Democracy Day, 18 February; Nepalese Women's Day, 8 March; Navabarsha—Nepalese New Year's Day, mid-April; UN Day, 24 October; Queen Aishworya's Birthday, 7 November; Constitution Day, 9 November; National Day (King Birendra's Birthday), 28 December. Hindu and Buddhist religious holidays are based on the lunisolar calendar. Saturday is the general day of rest.

TIME: 5:45 PM = noon GMT.

LOCATION AND SIZE: A comparatively narrow strip of territory dividing India from China, landlocked Nepal has an area of about 140,800 square kilometers (54,363 square miles), slightly larger than the state of Arkansas, with a total boundary length of 2,926 kilometers (1,818 miles).

Nepal's capital city, Kathmandu, is located in the central part of the country.

CLIMATE: Below the Kathmandu Valley, the climate is subtropical and, in the swamps and forests, extremely humid. Temperatures in Kathmandu in January range from an average minimum of 2°C (36°F) to an average maximum of 18°C (64°F). The July range is 20–29°C (68–84°F).

Kingdom of Nepal
Nepal Adhirajya

INTRODUCTORY SURVEY

RECENT HISTORY

The end of World War II (1939-1945) brought the end to British rule on the South Asian subcontinent and caused deep stirrings of change in Nepal. Resentment grew against the autocratic despotism of the Ranas. A political reform movement began in 1947 with the founding of the Nepali Congress Party.

With Indian support, rebels began operations against the Rana government. Ultimately, with the guidance of Indian Prime Minister Nehru, a political compromise was reached that ended a century of hereditary Rana family rule and restored the monarchy. By late 1951, a new government took office headed by Matrika Prasad Koirala, a founder of the Nepali Congress Party (NC).

The period after the fall of the Ranas was marked by a struggle between the government and the king for control of the country. In April 1959, King Mahendra Bir Bikram Shah proclaimed a democratic constitution providing for a constitutional monarchy, but suspended it and dissolved parliament less than eighteen months later. In April 1962, he established an indirect, non-party system of rule through a system of panchayats (councils) leading up to a National Panchayat. However, five years later, the king, under Indian pressure, began gradually liberalizing his government.

In January 1972, Mahendra died suddenly and was succeeded by his 27-year-old son, Birendra Bir Bikram Shah Dev. The young monarch, who had

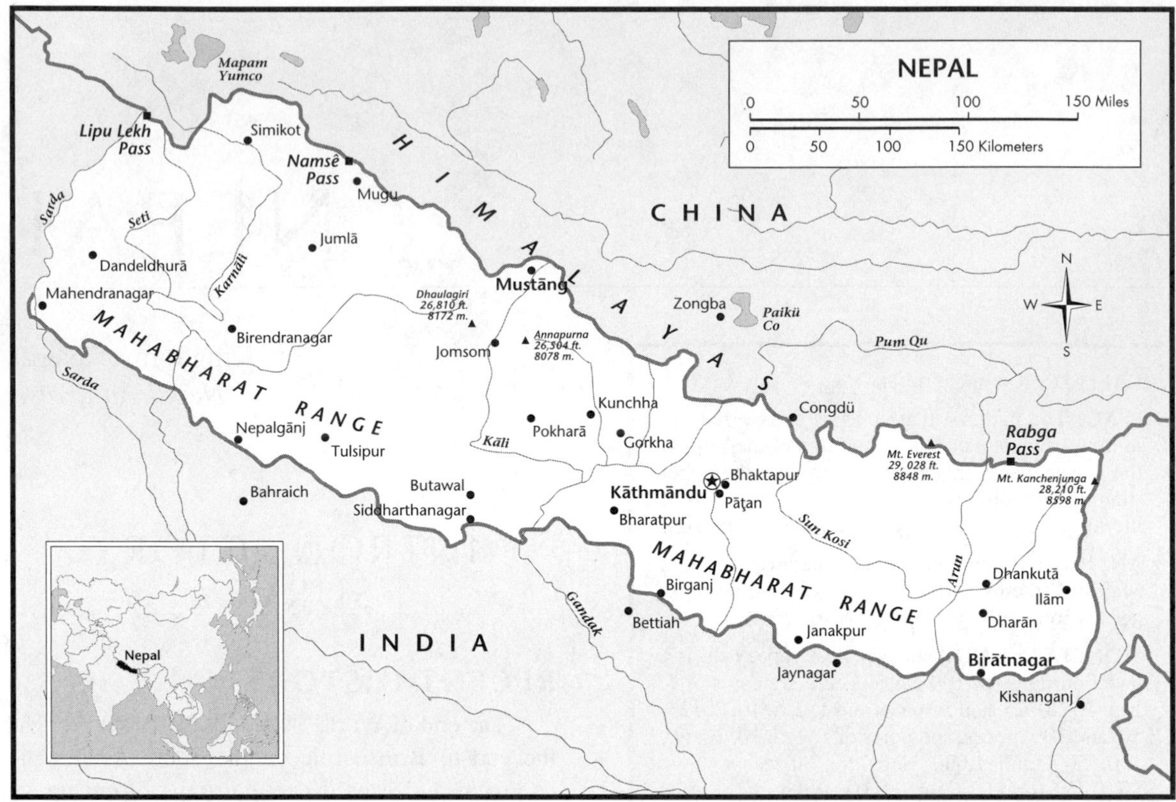

attended Harvard University in the United States, was committed to social reform. With the king promising further liberalization, the existing panchayat system was supported by 55 percent of the voters in May 1980. However, the king's failure to lift the ban on political parties angered his opposition.

Throughout the 1980s, opposition to the panchayat system, and to the ban on political parties, grew. After concessions by the king, a new constitution was adopted in November 1990. This constitution ended the panchayat era and restored multiparty democracy in a constitutional monarchy. In May 1991, the first open elections in thirty-two years were held. In the elections, the NC (Nepali Congress Party) won a majority in the new House of Representatives.

Nepal's foreign policies have remained generally neutral since World War II. It has maintained friendly relations with China and India, despite the occasional clash of policies on matters of trade. In January 1999, Nepal and India renewed their bilateral transit treaty that governs commerce across the Indo-Nepalese border and provides Nepal access to the port facilities of Calcutta. Nepal also has pursued friendly relations with the great powers and has received economic aid from India, the United States, the former Soviet Union, and the World Bank.

GOVERNMENT

Nepal, a parliamentary democracy, operates under a 1990 constitution. The chief of state is the king; the monarch is hereditary. The head of government is the prime minister. Following legislative elections, the leader of the majority party or of a majority coalition is generally appointed prime minister by the monarch. The monarch appoints the cabinet on the recommendation of the prime minister.

The legislative branch consists of a bicameral parliament that includes the sixty-seat National Council and a 205-seat House of Representatives. Of the sixty-member National Council, thirty-five are appointed by the House, ten by the king, and fifteen elected by an electoral college; one-third of the members take office every two years for six-year terms. The members of the House are elected by popular vote to serve five-year terms. Suffrage is universal at age eighteen.

Judiciary

Each district has civil and criminal courts as well as a court of appeals and fourteen zone courts.

There are five regional courts to which further appeals may be taken. At the top is the Supreme Court in Kathmandu that is empowered to issue writs of habeas corpus and decide on the constitutionality of laws. The Supreme Court is the court of last resort, but the king may grant pardons and suspend, commute, or remit sentences of any court. There are separate military courts that deal only with military personnel.

Political Parties

The main party through Nepal's modern history has been the Nepali Congress Party (NC) that opposed and finally brought down King Mahendra's panchayat system of indirect government. The Communist Party of Nepal (CPN), reorganized as the United Marxist-Leninists (UML), is a leading opposition party in the parliament. The Rastriya Prajatantra Party (RPP), also called the National Democratic Party (NDP), supports the monarchy. Most of the remaining seats in the lower house are in the hands of minor left/communist parties including the Nepal Sadbhavana Party (NSP), the Rastriya Jana Morcha, the Samyukta Janmorcha Nepal, and the Nepal Workers and Peasants Party (NWPP).

DEFENSE

Nepal maintains a small standing army of 42,800 regulars organized in eight brigades. It maintains eleven air transports and helicopters. The army is made up mostly of hill people known as gurkhas who are among the world's most renowned fighting men with extensive service in all parts of the globe in both world wars and several United Nations actions of this century. In 1995, Nepal spent an estimated $44 million on defense.

ECONOMIC AFFAIRS

Nepal remains one of the world's poorest and most underdeveloped countries, with over one-half its population living in poverty. The economy is based on agriculture, which engages about 80 percent of the labor force and accounts for 41 percent of GDP. The industrial sector is still small and dominated by traditional handicrafts, spinning and weaving, and similar occupations.

During the 1990s, the government moved forward with economic reforms, especially those encouraging trade and foreign investment. The textile and carpet industries provided 80 percent of foreign exchange earnings by the late 1990s. Tourism and the vast potential for hydroelectric development are the key areas of foreign investment. The government has been cutting expenditures by reducing subsidies, privatizing state industries, and laying off civil servants.

Political instability, together with the overall small size of the economy, technological backwardness, Nepal's remote and landlocked location, and susceptibility to natural disasters hinders economic growth.

The international aid funds play a large role in Nepal's development budget. In 1995, Nepal joined the South Asian Association for Regional Cooperation (SAARC) in the South Asian Preferential Trade Area, scheduling a free trade area by 2001.

Public Finance

For many years, government revenue was derived chiefly from privately owned land (amounting to about 30 percent of the country's area), customs duties, and forest and mining royalties. In 1955, however, because of increasing costs of development projects and administration, the government discarded the practice of adjusting the budgetary deficit by drawing on reserves and adopted a policy of raising additional revenue through taxation. Subsequently, a progressive income tax was introduced. Budget deficits grew steadily during the 1970s and 1980s, but were offset by foreign grants, domestic loans, foreign exchange borrowings, and transfers.

In 1998, government revenues totaled approximately $560 million with expenditures of $857 billion. External debt totaled $2.68 billion.

To meet revenue targets in the mid-1990s, taxes were increased on luxury items like imported liquor and cigarettes, and on petroleum and diesel fuel, with deficit financing by loans, domestic borrowing, and sales of treasury bills and development bonds.

Income

In 1999, Nepal's gross domestic product (GDP) was estimated to be $27.4 billion, or about $1,100 per person. The 1999 estimated GDP growth rate was 3.4 percent with inflation at 11.8 percent. The 1998 GDP contribution by sector was: agriculture, 41 percent; industry, 22 percent; and services, 37 percent.

Industry

Industrial activity mainly involved the processing of agricultural produce including jute, sugarcane, tobacco, oil seed, rice, and grain. Production of textiles and carpets accounted for approximately 80 percent of foreign exchange earnings in the late 1990s.

Production by heavy industries in 1995 included cement, bricks, and steel rods. Tourism is an expanding industry.

Banking and Finance

Nepal's domestic banking system consists of the Nepal Rastra (National) Bank (NRB), the central bank, with its commercial subsidiary, the Rastriya Banijya (National Commercial) Bank; the Nepal Bank, three commercial banks; and state-owned banks for industrial and agricultural development-the Nepal Industrial Development Corp. (NIDC) and the Agricultural Development Bank of Nepal (ADBN). In 1984, Nabil, or Nepal Arab Bank that is a joint venture with the UAE, was established. The French Indosuez Bank followed in 1986. Besides regulating the national currency, the NRB issues notes of various denominations and assists in preparation of the government budget. The Rastra Bank may advance loans to industry if both the government and the bank consider the loan sound.

In May 1986, the thirty-year direct link between the Nepalese and Indian rupees was ended. Since then, the Nepalese rupee has floated against a group of international currencies, including the Indian rupee.

Since 1984, the government has allowed foreign banks to open offices in Nepal. Citibank opened an office in November 1984 to deal with foreign currency loans and short-term and trade finance and to provide electronic banking facilities. Brindlays has set up a joint venture with Nepal Bank. The Bank of Dubai has set up the Nepal Arab Bank with the aim of channeling funds from Arab countries for industry, agriculture, and trade.

In the last few years, several new banks have received permission from the government to operate on a joint venture basis, and there has been rapid development of the financial sector as a result of the liberal economic policies adopted by the government. There has been a continuous increase in the number and size of banks, financial companies, and insurance companies.

The Nepal Bank of Ceylon, the biggest bank opened in the private sector through joint investments, was inaugurated at Siddharthanaga on October 14, 1996. In mid-December 1996, General Finance Ltd. went public.

The Securities Exchange Center (SEC) was set up in 1981 under the control of the NRB and the NIDC as a first step to setting up an organized stock exchange. The Nepal Stock Exchange (NSE) was established in 1984 in Kathmandu.

Economic Development

Nine development plans extending from 1955 to 1997 have slowly built up the nation's infrastructure. Through the years, the plans have focused on construction of roads, airfields, and irrigation projects, developing agriculture, expanding cottage industries, private investment, communications, electricity, creating employment opportunities, and fulfilling basic needs.

In 1991, the newly elected government reemphasized its commitment to structural adjustment through a series of reforms affecting virtually all sectors of the economy. Immediate stress was placed on tax reform, easing import restrictions, lowering tariffs, and reunifying the exchange rate market to effect a currency devaluation. To streamline government investments in economic development, a list of priority development projects was drafted and public enterprises were transferred to private ownership, freeing government revenues for other budgetary items including the social sector, drinking water, and rural infrastructure development. The government is encouraging foreign trade and investment by reducing business licenses and simplifying investment procedures. Investment in hydropower and tourism are areas of chief foreign investment interest.

Nepal's ninth five-year economic plan, in July of 1997, emphasized agriculture, liberal economic policies, hydropower projects, and privatization. Funding from the international community will continue to play a key role.

SOCIAL WELFARE

The government maintains a countrywide village development service that endeavors to meet the villagers' needs for food, clothing, shelter, health services, and education. The Employee Provident Fund administers a program of old age, disability, and death benefits for government and corporate employees.

The new Constitution has increased opportunities for women including equal pay for equal work, but few women hold formal jobs.

The abduction of young girls who are taken to India to work as prostitutes is a serious problem.

Members of lower castes suffer from widespread discrimination, and many are in positions of bonded labor.

Healthcare

Although protected by mountain barriers, Nepal is in frequent danger from epidemics, notably cholera. Common illnesses are black fever *(kala-azar)*, amoebic dysentery, eye diseases, typhoid, and venereal diseases. Malnutrition, contaminated water, and inadequate sanitation cause widespread health problems. Improved health programs in rural areas have helped control malaria, leprosy, and tuberculosis. Nepal has a large number of drug addicts. Malnutrition is a common problem of children under five years of age. In 2000, average life expectancy is about 57.8 years.

In 1994, there was one hospital bed per 4,281 inhabitants. The population per physician was 16,634 in 1993.

Housing

In the Kathmandu Valley, village houses are made of stone or mud bricks with thatched roofs and raised eaves. Elsewhere, houses are often made of bamboo and reeds. Most houses have two stories, but some contain only two rooms, a sleeping room and a room for cooking. The well-constructed houses of the Sherpas are generally built of stone and timber, roofed with wooden slats. The latest available figures for 1980-1988 show a total housing stock of nearly 3.1 million units with 5.6 people per dwelling.

EDUCATION

The number of illiterate persons is declining and was estimated in 1995 at 73 percent of adults (males, 59.1 percent; females, 86 percent). After free primary education was introduced in 1975, school enrollment for children ages six to eleven increased from about one-fourth of the total to over one-half by the mid-1980s. In 1996, there were 22,218 primary schools with 3.5 million pupils and 89,378 teachers. Secondary students numbered 1.1 million, with 36,127 teachers. In 1996, 105,694 students were enrolled in all higher-level institutions.

2000 KEY EVENTS TIMELINE

February

- After a show of no confidence for Krishna Prasad Bhattari two days earlier, eleven ministers resign February 18 from the Nepalese cabinet. The day following these resignations Maoists rebels kill fifteen policemen and injure another twenty.

March

- The prime minister of Nepal, Krishna Prasad Bhattari, resigns from office. His successor from within his party, Girija Prasad Koirala, is prime minister for his fourth time.

May

- Nepalese authorities claim success in the conservation of the one-horned rhino found only in Nepal, and the Western Indian states of Assam and West Bengal. The one-horned rhino is one of the world's most endangered species, 1,300 in India and 600 in Nepal.

June

- A law banning the employment of children under the age of fourteen in the tourism industry, i.e., trekking, mountaineering, and casino work, is enacted. Child labor in Nepal is vital to the income of poor families and similar efforts in the past have been ineffectual.

July

- A government decree frees bonded laborers, the Kamaiyas. Untrained and without promise of work it is feared that they will be a burden or be militarized.
- Over 200 women protest against the Miss Nepal beauty contest as running counter to Nepalese tradition and culture. All the protesters are arrested.

August

- On behalf of Nepal a statement on the plight of Nepalese women and young girl refugees is presented to the United Nations Sub-commission on the promotion and protection of human rights. Each year in Nepal about 5,000 women are taken across the international border to be sold into prostitution.
- Nepal is pressured (by a 4 percent duty imposed by India on imports from Nepal) to lift a six-month ban on car models made in India. Conservationists and critics point out that the Indian vehicles do not meet Nepal's emission control standards.

September

- Dragon Air is scheduled to resume flights between Kathmandu and Hong Kong.

October

- Maoists break five-day truce when they kill a policeman.
- On October 25, for the first time, the government and underground Maoists hold official talks. These talks follow meetings between the opposition Nepalese Communist Party and rebel Maoists October 22.

November

- India claims that Pakistan is using the poorly guarded Nepalese border to send troops into India.
- Maoist rebels attack a police station in western Nepal November 29, killing eleven policemen and injuring seven.
- In a controversial move, the Supreme Court in Nepal cancels pension privileges for former members of Parliament.
- Talks between Maoists rebels and the government break down.

ANALYSIS OF EVENTS: 2000

BUSINESS AND THE ECONOMY

Nepal remained among the poorest and least developed countries in the world. Nearly half of its more than twenty-four million people lived below the poverty line. Per capita income was about US$1,100 per year. Over 80 percent of the population was engaged in agriculture which accounted for about 41 percent of the gross domestic product (GDP). Industrial production involved the processing of agricultural produce: jute, sugar cane, tobacco, and grain. An estimated 80 percent of foreign exchange earnings came from the production of textiles and carpets. The international community funded more than 60 percent of Nepal's development budget.

The small size of the economy and its technological backwardness deterred prospects for foreign trade or investment. Nepal's growth remained hampered by its remoteness, landlocked geographic location containing eight of the world's ten highest peaks, and susceptibility to natural disasters, such as severe thunderstorms, flooding, landslides, drought, and famine. Widespread deforestation, soil erosion, and water pollution occurred due to Nepal's almost total dependence on wood for fuel and the expansion of agricultural land without replanting. In addition, Nepal's political instability, five different governments in recent years, strained economic reform.

Nepal acted to ban black plastic bags, colored plastic bags are unsightly and toxic, containing copper and chromium.

GOVERNMENT AND POLITICS

In March the eighth administration in ten years of Nepali democracy fell. Charges of corruption continued among state officials. Self-ascribed Maoist insurgents continued to terrorize in the name of a "people's republic," seeking an end to the monarchy and peasant ownership of land, among other demands. Tourists were not the target of their attacks, but police suffered heavy causalities.

CULTURE AND SOCIETY

A United Nations special report, "Violence Against Women" called for regional cooperation in South Asia against the trafficking of women and children. It was estimated that annually traffickers lure more than 20,000 women from the region to be sold to brothels. It was noted that the countries could not address this problem separately, and that it required cross-border cooperation.

Hepatitis was the most important water-borne disease in Nepal, due to the poor quality of the country's water supply. In Kathmandu hepatitis E virus (HEV) caused as many as 90 percent of the jaundice cases. It was also the most costly medical illness for the military. Treatment cost 20 percent of the average citizen's annual income, and resulted in lost earnings. Phase II-III clinical trials of a candidate HEV vaccine were approved by Nepal's Ministry of Health. More than 8,000 volunteered for these trials.

Nepal, as the only official Hindu state in the world, experienced record growth in its Christian population. However, to a Nepali Hindu, Christianity remained a caste-breaking foreign element destroying Nepalese culture.

DIRECTORY

CENTRAL GOVERNMENT

Head of State

King
Birendra Bir Bikram Shah Dev

Prime Minister
Koirala Girija Prasad, Office of the Prime Minister, Katmandu, Nepal
PHONE: +977 227955; 228555; 228460

Ministers

Minister of Education
Chataut Tarini Dutta, Ministry of Education, Katmandu, Nepal
PHONE: +977 414690; 411499

Minister of Local Development
Poudel Ram Chandra, Ministry of Local Development, Katmandu, Nepal
PHONE: +977 523329; 241821

Minister of Labor and Transport
Koirala Gigija Prasad, Ministry of Labor and Transport, Katmandu, Nepal
PHONE: +977 262467

Minister of Water Resources
Khadka Khum Bahadur, Ministry of Water Resources, Katmandu, Nepal
PHONE: +977 227347

Minister of Agriculture
Chakra Prasad Bastola, Ministry of Agriculture, Katmandu, Nepal
PHONE: +977 225109

Minister of Foreign Affairs
Chakra Prasad Bastola, Ministry of Foreign Affairs, Katmandu, Nepal
PHONE: +977 416001

Minister of Culture, Tourism and Civil Aviation
Tarini Dutta Chataut, Ministry of Culture, Tourism and Civil Aviation, Katmandu, Nepal
PHONE: +977 225579; 246607

Minister of Physical Planning and Works
Khum Bahadur Khadka, Ministry of Physical Planning and Works, Katmandu, Nepal
PHONE: +977 228670; 240764

Minister of Industries, Commerce and Supplies
Ram Krishna Tamrakar, Ministry of Industries, Commerce and Supplies, Katmandu, Nepal
PHONE: +977 525920

Minister of Forest and Soil Conservation
Mahantha Thakur, Ministry of Forest and Soil Conservation, Katmandu, Nepal
PHONE: +977 220160

Minister of General Administration
Girija Prasad Koirala, Ministry of General Administration, Katmandu, Nepal
PHONE: +977 524623

Minister of Home Affairs
Govinda Raj Joshi, Ministry of Home Affairs, Katmandu, Nepal
PHONE: +977 224737; 228333

Minister of Health
Ram Baran Yadav, Ministry of Health, Katmandu, Nepal
PHONE: +977 262534

Minister of Finance
Mahesh Acharya, Ministry of Finance, Katmandu, Nepal
PHONE: +977 259809; 259924

Minister of Law, Justice and Parliamentary Affairs
Mahanta Thakur, Ministry of Law, Justice and Parliamentary Affairs, Katmandu, Nepal
PHONE: +977 241577; 222874

Minister of Science and Technology
Surendra Prasad Chaudhary, Ministry of Science and Technology, Katmandu, Nepal
PHONE: +977 245434

Minister of Population and Environment
Omkar Prasad Shrestha, Ministry of Population and Environment, Katmandu, Nepal
PHONE: +977 241591

Minister of Women and Social Welfare
Girija Prasad Koirala, Ministry of Women and Social Welfare, Katmandu, Nepal
PHONE: +977 535755

Minister of Land Reform and Management
Siddha Raj Ojha, Ministry of Land Reform and Management, Katmandu, Nepal
PHONE: +977 221660

Minister of Information and Communication
Jaya Prakash Gupta, Ministry of Information and Communication, Katmandu, Nepal
PHONE: +977 242562

Minister of Defense
Girija Prasad Koirala, Ministry of Defense

POLITICAL ORGANIZATIONS

Nepal Green Party

PO Box 890, Kalikasthan, Kathmandu, Nepal
PHONE: +977 411730
FAX: +977 419497
E-MAIL: greennp@wlink.com.np
NAME: Kuber Sharma

Janawadi Morcha

PO Box 890, Indrachowk, Itumbahal, Nepal
PHONE: +977 211033
FAX: +977 412418
NAME: Piruddhin Mir

Thapa (National Democratic Party)

Naxal, Kathmandu, Nepal
PHONE: +977 437057
FAX: +977 434441
NAME: Surya Bahadur

Nepal Communist Party (ML)

Bag Bazar, Kathmandu, Nepal
PHONE: +977 223827; 252950; 231957
FAX: +977 231957
NAME: Sahana Pradhan

Nepal Communist Party (United)

Dillibazar, Kathmandu, Nepal
PHONE: +977 430869
FAX: +977 411642
NAME: Bishnu Manandhar

Nepal Rastriya Congress

Lazimpat, Kathmandu, Nepal
PHONE: +977 411090
NAME: Dilli Raman Regmi

National People's Front

Mahaboudha, Kathmandu, Nepal
PHONE: +977 224226
NAME: Chitra Bahadur

Nepal Communist Party (UML)

PO Box 5471, Madan Nagar, Balkhu, Kathmandu, Nepal
PHONE: +977 278081; 278082; 271872
FAX: +977 278084
NAME: Madhav Kumer

Nepal Communist Party (Verma)

Dillibazar, Kathmandu, Nepal
PHONE: +977 414997
NAME: Krishna Raj Venna

Nepal Sadbhawana Party

Shantinagar, New Banewhwor, Kathmandu, Nepal
PHONE: +977 488068
FAX: +977 470797
NAME: Gajendra Narayan Singh

Nepali Congress

Bhansar Tole, Teku, Kathmandu, Nepal
PHONE: +977 246248; 226761; 227748
NAME: Girija Prasad Koirala

Rastirya Janata Parishad

Dillibazar, Kathmandu, Nepal
PHONE: +977 415150
NAME: Kirti Nidhi Bista

DIPLOMATIC REPRESENTATION

Embassies in Nepal

Australia
PO Box 879, Bansbari, Kathmandu, Nepal
PHONE: +977 417566; 413076; 411578

Austria
PO Box 146, Hattisar, Kathmandu, Nepal
PHONE: +977 410891

Bangladesh
Naxal, Bhagawati Bahal, PO Box 789, Kathmandu, Nepal
PHONE: +977 414265; 414943

Belgium
Lazimpat, Kathmandu, Nepal
PHONE: +977 414760

Brazil
PO Box 2676, Kathmandu, Nepal
PHONE: +977 527223; 527261

Canada
c/o Canadian Cooperation Office, Lazimpat, Kathmandu, Nepal
PHONE: +977 415398; 415391; 415193

China
PO Box 4234, Baluwatar, Kathmandu, Nepal
PHONE: +977 415383; 411740; 411958

Cyprus
PO Box 133, Kathmandu, Nepal
PHONE: +977 225490

Denmark
Lalita Niwas Road, PO Box 6332, Kathmandu, Nepal
PHONE: +977 411409

Egypt
PO Box 792, Pulchowk, Lalitpur, Nepal
PHONE: +977 524844; 524812
FAX: +977 522975

Finland
PO Box 2126, Lazimpat, Kathmandu, Nepal
PHONE: +977 416636; 417221

France
PO Box 452, Lazimpat, Kathmandu, Nepal
PHONE: +977 413839; 412332

Germany
PO Box 226, Gyaneswor, Kathmandu, Nepal
PHONE: +977 412786; 416527
FAX: +977 416899

India
PO Box 292, Lainchour, Kathmandu, Nepal
PHONE: +977 411940; 410900; 410990
FAX: +977 413132
TITLE: Ambassador
NAME: Shri K. V. Rajan

Israel
Bishramalaya House, PO Box 371, Lazimpat, Kathmandu, Nepal
PHONE: +977 411811; 413419

Italy
PO Box 1097, Baluwatar, Kathmandu, Nepal
PHONE: +977 412280; 412743
FAX: +977 413132

Japan
PO Box 264, Maharajgunj, Kathmandu, Nepal
PHONE: +977 414083

Maldives
PO Box 324, Durbar Marg, Kathmandu, Nepal
PHONE: +977 223045

Mexico
PO Box 989, Kantipath, Kathmandu, Nepal
PHONE: +977 414343

Myanmar
PO Box 2437, Chakupath, Lalitpur, Nepal
PHONE: +977 521788
FAX: +977 523402

Netherlands
PO Box 1966, Lagankhel, Kathmandu, Nepal
PHONE: +977 522915

New Zealand
PO Box 224, Dillibazar, Kathmandu, Nepal
PHONE: +977 412436

North Korea
Jhamsikhel, Lalitpur, Nepal
PHONE: +977 521084; 521855

Norway
PO Box 1045, Lagankhel, Kathmandu, Nepal
PHONE: +977 521646

Pakistan
GPO Box 202, Panipokhari, Kathmandu, Nepal
PHONE: +977 411421

Philippines
PO Box 2640, Lazimpat, Kathmandu, Nepal
PHONE: +977 410213

Poland
Ganabahal, Kathmandu, Nepal
PHONE: +977 221101

Russia
PO Box 123, Baluwatar, Kathamandu, Nepal
PHONE: +977 411063; 412115

South Korea
PO Box 1058, Himshail, Tahachal, Red Cross Marg, Kathmandu, Nepal
PHONE: +977 270172; 270417

Spain
Batisputali, Kathmandu, Nepal
PHONE: +977 472328

Sri Lanka
PO Box 8802, Baluwatar, Kathmandu, Nepal
PHONE: +977 419289; 413623

Sweden
Khichapokhari, Kathmandu, Nepal
PHONE: +977 220939

Switzerland
Jawalakhel, Kathmandu, Nepal
PHONE: +977 523168; 523468

Thailand
PO Box 3333, Jyoti Kendra, Thapathali, Kathmandu, Nepal
PHONE: +977 213912; 213910

Turkey
Gyaneswor, Kathmandu, Nepal
PHONE: +977 412210

United Kingdom
PO Box 106, Lainchour, Kathmandu, Nepal
PHONE: +977 410583; 411281; 411590
TITLE: Ambassador
NAME: Ralph Frank

United States
PO Box 295, Panipokhari, Kathmandu, Nepal
PHONE: +977 411601; 411179; 412718
FAX: +977 419963

JUDICIAL SYSTEM

Supreme Court

BROADCAST MEDIA

Radio Nepal

Radio Broadcasting Service, PO Box 634, Singha Durbar, Nepal
PHONE: +977 (1) 233910; 225467
FAX: +977 (1) 221952
E-MAIL: radio@training.wlink.com.np; radio@engg.wlink.com.np
WEBSITE: http://www.catmando.com/news/radio-nepal/radionp.htm
TITLE: Executive Director
CONTACT: Shailendra Raj Sharma
LANGUAGE: Nepali, English
BROADCASTS: 15 hours/day
TYPE: Semi-Government, Commercial

Radio Sagarmatha

Kathmandu, Nepal
LANGUAGE: English
TYPE: Private

Nepal Television

E-MAIL: neptv@vishnu.ccsl.com.np
WEBSITE: http://www.explorenepal.com/ntv

COLLEGES AND UNIVERSITIES

Kathmandu University

Box 6250, Kathmandu, Nepal
PHONE: +977 (1) 61399
WEBSITE: http://www.nepalnet.org.np/ku

Tribhuvan University

GPO Box 8975 EPC 5703, Jamal, Kathmandu, Nepal
PHONE: +977 (1) 245798; 244047
FAX: +977 (1) 331964

NEWSPAPERS AND MAGAZINES

Arpan Weekly

Sakya & Co., PO Box 285, Kohity Bahal, Kathmandu 44601 Nepal
PHONE: +977 (1) 220531
FAX: +977 (1) 279544
E-MAIL: mrshakya@wlink.com.np
TITLE: Publisher, Editor
CONTACT: Manju Ratna Sakya
CIRCULATION: 24,000

Daily News

Sakya & Co., PO Box 285, 7/358 Kohity Bahal, Kathmandu 44601 Nepal
PHONE: +977 (1) 279147
FAX: +977 (1) 279544
E-MAIL: mrshakya@wlink.com.np
TITLE: Editor
CONTACT: Manju Ratna Sakya
CIRCULATION: 19,500

Gorkhapatra

Gorkhapatra Corp., PO Box 23, Kathmandu, Nepal
PHONE: +977 (1) 220835
FAX: +977 (1) 221748
E-MAIL: gopa@mos.com.np
WEBSITE: http://www.south-asia.com/news-ktmpost.html
TITLE: Editor-in-Chief
CONTACT: Gyan Bahadur Rai

The Kathmandu Post/Kantipur

Kantipur Publications Pvt. Ltd., PO Box 8559, Kathmandu, Nepal
PHONE: +977 (1) 480100
FAX: +977 (1) 470178
E-MAIL: kanti@kpost.mos.com.np
WEBSITE: http://www.south-asia.com/news-ktmpost.html
TITLE: Editor, The Kathmandu Post
CONTACT: Shyam Bahadur KC
TITLE: Editor, Kantipur
CONTACT: Yogesh Upadhya
CIRCULATION: 20,000 (The Kathmandu Post); 80,000 (Kantipur)

The Nepali Hindi Daily

Nepali Mudranalaya, PO Box 49, Maitidevi Phant, Kathmandu, Nepal
PHONE: +977 (1) 411374
FAX: +977 (1) 225640
TITLE: Editor-in-Chief
CONTACT: Vijay Kumar Das
CIRCULATION: 62,000

The People's Review

Samrachana Publications, PO Box 3052, Kathmandu, Nepal
PHONE: +977 (1) 417352
E-MAIL: preview@info-nepal.com
WEBSITE: http://www.info-nepal.com/p-review
TITLE: Editor-in-Chief
CONTACT: Pushpa Raj Pradhan

The Rising Nepal

Gorkhapatra Corp., PO Box 23, Kathmandu, Nepal
PHONE: +977 (1) 220835
FAX: +977 (1) 221748
E-MAIL: gopa@mos.com.np
WEBSITE: http://www.south-asia.com/news-ktmpost.html
TITLE: Editor-in-Chief
CONTACT: Gyan Bahadur Rai
CIRCULATION: 34,840

Himal South Asia

GPO Box 7251, Kathmandu, Nepal
FAX: +977 (1) 521013
TITLE: Editor
CONTACT: Kanak Mani Dixit
E-MAIL: himal@himpc.mos.com.np.
WEBSITE: http://www.south-asia.com/himal
CIRCULATION: 10,000
TYPE: Business, economics, political science

Himalayan Culture

20-136 Kamal Pokhari, Kathmandu 711000 Nepal
TYPE: History

Himalayan Economist

21-694-1 Dillibazar, Kathmandu, Nepal
CIRCULATION: 500
TYPE: Business, economics

Nepal Chronicle

Maitighar, PO Box 285, Kathmandu 44601 Nepal
TYPE: Social science

Nepal Press Digest

Lazimpat, Kathmandu, Nepal
TITLE: Editor
CONTACT: Mahesh Chandra Regmi
TYPE: Social science

Nepal Recorder

Lazimpat, Kathmandu, Nepal
TITLE: Editor
CONTACT: Mahesh Chandra Regmi
TYPE: Law, general

Nepal and the World

PO Box 269, Teku, Kathmandu, Nepal
FAX: +977 (1) 227322
E-MAIL: fincci@mos.com.np
TITLE: Editor
CONTACT: Binod H. Joshi
TYPE: Reference, general

Nepala Kanuna Paricarca

Box 1247, Kathmandu, Nepal
TITLE: Editor
CONTACT: Tope Bahadur Singh
CIRCULATION: 1,000
TYPE: Law, general

Nepalese Journal of Political Science

Tribhuvan University, Kirtipur Multiple Campus, Kathmandu, Nepal
TYPE: Political science

PUBLISHERS

International Standards Books and Periodicals

PO Box 3000, Kathmandu, Nepal
PHONE: +977 224005
FAX: +977 223036
TITLE: Chief Managing Director
CONTACT: Suindra Lall Chhipa
SUBJECTS: Agriculture, Anthropology, Archaeology, Architecture and Interior Design, Art, Business, Career Development, Chemistry, Chemical Engineering, Earth Sciences, Economics, Education, Engineering (General), Gardening, Plants, Geography, Geology, Government, Political Science, History, Human Relations, Language Arts, Linguistics, Law, Literature, Literary Criticism, Essays, Mathematics, Medicine, Nursing, Dentistry, Music, Dance, Natural History, Philosophy, Physics, Psychology, Psychiatry, Social Sciences, Sociology

Royal Nepal Academy

Kamaldi, Kathmandu, Nepal
PHONE: +977 221283
FAX: +977 221175
TITLE: Library Chief
CONTACT: T. D. Bhandari
SUBJECTS: Art, History, Literature, Literary Criticism, Essays, Science (General), Social Sciences, Sociology

Sajha Prakashan, Co-operative Publishing Organization

Pulchowk, Kathmandu, Nepal

PHONE: +977 521023
TITLE: Chairman
CONTACT: Deepak Baskota
SUBJECTS: Literature, Literary Criticism, Essays

RELIGIOUS ORGANIZATIONS

Buddhist

All Nepal Bhikku Council
Anandakuti Vihar, Swayambhu, PO Box 3007, Kathmandu, Nepal
PHONE: +977 271420
FAX: +977 227058

Buddhadharma International Foundation
c/o Ven. Dr. Dhammapiyo Bhikkhu or Mr. H. K. Awale, PO Box 8975, EPC-735, Kathmandu, Nepal
E-MAIL: dhammapiyo@wlink.com.np, dhammapiyo@buddhadharma.org
WEBSITE: http://www.buddhadharma.org
NAME: Ven. Dr. Dhammapiyo Bhikkhu

Dharmakirti Buddhist Study Circle
Dharma Kirti Vicar, Shreena, Naghal Tole, Kathmandu, Nepal
PHONE: +977 (1) 220446
FAX: +977 (1) 228028
TITLE: Teacher, Nun
NAME: Ven. Dhammawati

Himalayan Buddhist Meditation Centre
Kamaladi Ganesthan, PO Box 817 Kathmandu, Nepal
PHONE: +977 (1) 221875
FAX: +977 (1) 251409
E-MAIL: hbmc@buddha.mos.com.np
WEBSITE: http://www.south-asia.com/buddhism
TITLE: Director
NAME: Siliana Bosa

International Buddhist Society
Buddhanagar, Lumbini, PO Box 3007, Kathmandu, Nepal
PHONE: +977 (1) 227058
FAX: +977 (1) 227058
NAME: Bhikkhu Maitri

Kopan Monastery
GPO Box 817, Kathmandu, Nepal
PHONE: +977 (1) 481268
FAX: +977 (1) 481267
E-MAIL: franz@komonpc.mos.com.np
WEBSITE: http://www.kopan-monastery.com/
TITLE: Director
NAME: Geshe Lhundrup Rigsel

World Peace Temple
Bishwa Santi Vihara, Naya Baneshwana, Min Bhawon, Kathmandu, Nepal
PHONE: +977 (1) 226984; 482984
NAME: Ven. Nyanaponika Mahasthavira

FURTHER READING

Articles

Allman, T. D. "Nepal." *National Geographic,* vol. 198, no. 5, p. 96–116.

"The Church at the Top of the World." *Christianity Today,* April 3, 2000, p. 56.

"Nepal and India—The Trouble with Ghee." *The Economist,* June 17, 2000, p. 44.

"Nepal Calls the Shots in Hepatitis E Virus Vaccine Trial." *The Lancet,* May 6, 2000, p. 1623.

Books

Clorfeine, Stephen. *In the Valley of the Gods: Journals of an American Buddhist in Nepal.* Barrytown, NY: Barrytown, 2000.

Spectrum Guide to Nepal. New York: Interlink Books, 2000.

NEPAL: STATISTICAL DATA

For sources and notes see "Sources of Statistics" at the front of each volume.

GEOGRAPHY

Geography

Area:

Total: 140,800 sq km.

Land: 136,800 sq km.

Land boundaries:

Total: 2,926 km.

Border countries: China 1,236 km, India 1,690 km.

Coastline: 0 km (landlocked).

Climate: varies from cool summers and severe winters in north to subtropical summers and mild winters in south.

Terrain: Terai or flat river plain of the Ganges in south, central hill region, rugged Himalayas in north.

Natural resources: quartz, water, timber, hydropower, scenic beauty, small deposits of lignite, copper, cobalt, iron ore.

Land use:

Arable land: 17%

Permanent crops: 0%

Permanent pastures: 15%

Forests and woodland: 42%

Other: 26% (1993 est.).

HUMAN FACTORS

Demographics (A)

	1990	1995	1998	2000	2010	2020	2030	2040	2050
Population	19,325	21,907	23,560	24,702	30,758	36,925	42,840	48,384	53,294
Life expectancy - males	54.3	56.5	57.6	58.3	61.8	65.1	68.1	70.7	72.9
Life expectancy - females	53.2	55.2	56.5	57.4	61.6	65.7	69.5	72.9	75.8
Birth rate (per 1,000)	38.6	36.1	34.7	33.8	28.8	23.8	20.3	17.7	15.6
Death rate (per 1,000)	12.8	11.5	10.8	10.4	8.6	7.4	6.8	6.8	7.2
Women of reproductive age (15-49 yrs.)	4,301	4,980	5,448	5,775	7,546	9,509	11,293	12,559	13,383
Fertility rate	5.7	5.2	4.9	4.7	3.7	3.0	2.5	2.3	2.1

Except as noted, values for vital statistics are in thousands; life expectancy is in years.

Health Personnel

	National Data	World Data (wtd ave)
Total health expenditure as a percentage of GDP, 1990-1998[a]		
Public sector	1.3	2.5
Private sector	4.2	2.9
Total[b]	5.5	5.5
Health expenditure per capita in U.S. dollars, 1990-1998[a]		
Purchasing power parity	58	561
Total	11	483
Availability of health care facilities per 100,000 people		
Hospital beds 1990-1998[a]	20	330
Doctors 1992-1995[a]	5	122
Nurses 1992-1995[a]	5	248

Health Indicators

	National Data	World Data
Life expectancy at birth (years)		
1980	48	61
1998	58	67
Daily per capita supply of calories		
1970	1,959	2,358
1997	2,366	2,791
Daily per capital supply of protein		
1997 (grams)	61	74
Total fertility rate (births per woman)		
1980	6.1	3.7
1998	4.4	2.7
Population with access (%)		
To safe water (1990-96)	44	NA
To sanitation (1990-96)	6	NA
People living with (1997)		
Tuberculosis (cases per 100,000)	106.9	60.4
Malaria (cases per 100,000)	29.4	42.2
HIV/AIDS (% aged 15 - 49 years)	0.24	0.99

Infants and Malnutrition

	National Data	World Data (wtd ave)
Under 5 mortality rate (1989)	100	NA
% of infants with low birthweight (1992-98)[1]	23	17
Births attended by skilled health staff (% of total births 1996-98)	9	52
% fully immunized at 1 year of age (1995-98)[1]		
TB	86	82
DPT	76	77
Polio	70	77
Measles	73	74
Prevalence of child malnutrition (1992-98)[1] (based on weight for age, % of children under 5 years)	57	30

Ethnic Division

Newars, Indians, Tibetans, Gurungs, Magars, Tamangs, Bhotias, Rais, Limbus, Sherpas.

Religion

Hindu 90%
Buddhist 5%
Muslim 3%
Other 2%

Data for 1981. Only official Hindu state in the world.

Major Languages

Nepali (official), over 20 other languages divided into numerous dialects.

EDUCATION

Public Education Expenditures

	1980	1997
Public expenditures on education as % of GNP	1.8	3.2
Expenditures per student as % of GNP per capita		
Primary & Secondary	14.6	NA
Tertiary	27.19	115.3
Pupils per teacher at the primary level	NA	NA
Duration of primary education in years	NA	5
World data for comparison		
Public expenditures on education as % of GNP (mean)	3.9	4.8
Pupils per teacher at the primary level (wtd ave)	NA	33
Duration of primary education in years (mean)	NA	9

Educational Attainment (A)

Age group (1991)[18] . . . . .6+
Population of this age group 15,145,071
Highest level attained (%)
No schooling[2] 69.6
First level
Not completed 16.2
Completed . . . . .NA
Entered second level
Lower Secondary 8.9
Upper Secondary 2.0
Entered post-secondary .1.5

Literacy Rates (A)

In thousands and percent	1990	1995	2000	2010
Illiterate population (15+ yrs.)	8,308	9,149	10,088	12,009
Literacy rate - total adult pop. (%)	24.4	27.5	30.9	37.9
Literacy rate - males (%)	37.2	40.9	44.6	51.6
Literacy rate - females (%)	11.4	14.0	16.9	23.6

GOVERNMENT & LAW

Political Parties

House of Representatives	% of vote	no. of seats
Nepali Congress (NC)	37.3%	113
Communist Party of Nepal/United Marxist-Leninist (CPN/UML)	31.6%	69
National Democratic Party (NDP)	10.4%	11
Nepal Sadbhavana (Goodwill) Party (NSP)	3.2%	5
Rastriya Jana Morcha	1.4%	5
Samyukta Janmorcha Nepal	0.8%	1
Nepal Workers and Peasants Party (NWPP)	0.5%	1
Others	14.8%	

Elections for the House of Representatives were last held 3 and 17 May 1999 (next to be held in May 2004).

Government Budgets (A)

Year: 1998
Total Expenditures: 51,964 Millions of Rupees
Expenditures as a percentage of the total by function:
General public services and public order 9.07
Defense 4.97
Education 15.02
Health 6.01
Social Security and Welfare 1.98
Housing and community amenities 5.19
Recreational, cultural, and religious affairs 0
Fuel and energy 9.07
Agriculture, forestry, fishing, and hunting 6.11
Mining, manufacturing, and construction 136
Transportation and communication 14.27
Other economic affairs and services 6.88

Crime

Crime volume (for 1998)
Crimes reported 2,013
Total persons convicted 1,441
Crimes per 100,000 population 9.00
Persons responsible for offenses
Total number suspects .6,037
Total number of female suspects 231
Total number of juvenile suspects 56

(Continued on next page.)

LABOR FORCE

Total Labor Force (A)

10 million. There is a severe lack of skilled labor..

Labor Force by Occupation

Agriculture 81%
Services 16%
Industry 3%

Unemployment Rate

Not available; substantial underemployment (1999).

PRODUCTION SECTOR

Energy Production

Production . . . . .1.17 billion kWh
Production by source
Fossil fuel 5.13%
Hydro 94.87%
Nuclear 0%
Other 0%
Exports . . . . .72 million kWh

Data for 1998.

Energy Consumption

Consumption . . . . .1.212 billion kWh
Imports . . . . .196.000 million kWh
Data for 1998.

Transportation

Highways:
Total: 13,223 km.
Paved: 4,073 km.
Unpaved: 9,150 km (April 1999).
Airports: 45 (1999 est.).
Airports - with unpaved runways: 40.

Top Agriculture Products

Rice, corn, wheat, sugarcane, root crops; milk, water buffalo meat.

Top Mining Products (B)

Mineral resources include: quartz, small deposits of lignite, copper, cobalt, iron ore.

GOVERNMENT & LAW (cont.)

Military Affairs (A)

	1990	1992	1995	1996	1997
Military expenditures					
Current dollars (mil.)	32	35	40	41	42
1997 constant dollars (mil.)	37	39	42	41	42
Armed forces (000)	35	35	40	35	35
Gross national product (GNP)					
Current dollars (mil.)	3,090	3,620	4,430	4,740	5,020
1997 constant dollars (mil.)	3,620	4,010	4,580	4,820	5,020
Central government expenditures (CGE)					
1997 constant dollars (mil.)	605	651	780	846	829
People (mil.)	19.1	20.3	22.0	22.5	23.1
Military expenditure as % of GNP	1.0	1.0	0.9	0.9	0.8
World data on military expenditure as % of GNP	4.5	3.4	2.7	2.6	2.6
Military expenditure as % of CGE	6.1	6.0	5.4	4.9	5.1
World data on military expenditure as % of CGE	17.0	12.5	10.5	10.3	10.2
Military expenditure per capita (1997 $)	2	2	2	2	2
World data on military expenditure per capita (1997 $)	242	173	146	143	145
Armed forces per 1,000 people (soldiers)	1.8	1.7	1.8	1.6	1.5
World data on armed forces per 1,000 people (soldiers)	5.3	4.5	4.1	3.9	3.8
GNP per capita (1997 $)	190	197	209	214	217
Total imports[7]					
Current dollars (mil.)	627	776	1,330	1,442	1,716
1997 constant dollars (mil.)	734	860	1,377	1,466	1,716
Total exports[7]					
Current dollars (mil.)	210	368	345	385	402
1997 constant dollars (mil.)	246	408	357	391	402
Arms as percent of total imports[8]	1.6	0	0	0	0
Arms as percent of total exports[8]	0	0	0	0	0

MANUFACTURING SECTOR

GDP & Manufacturing Summary (A)

	1980	1985	1990	1995
GDP ($-1990 mil.)[1]	1,858	2,359	3,099	3,756
Per capita ($-1990)[1]	128	143	165	175
Manufacturing share (%) (current prices)[1]	4.3	4.8	5.6	7.5[e]
Manufacturing				
Value added ($-1990 mil.)[1]	80	114	153	235[e]
Industrial production index	60	92	100	144[e]
Value added ($ mil.)	83[e]	100[e]	269	421[e]
Gross output ($ mil.)	510[e]	473[e]	656	1,049[e]
Employment (000)	56[e]	78[e]	156	239[e]
Profitability (% of gross output)				
Intermediate input (%)	84[e]	79[e]	59	60[e]
Wages and salarics inc. supplements (%)	3[e]	4[e]	10	9[e]
Gross operating surplus	13[e]	17[e]	31	31[e]
Productivity ($)				
Gross output per worker	8,609[e]	5,737[e]	4,067	4,045[e]
Value added per worker	1,411[e]	1,274[e]	1,666	1,625[e]
Average wage (inc. supplements)	295[e]	236[e]	400	399[e]
Value added ($ mil.)				
Food products	35[e]	32[e]	38	74[e]
Beverages	1[e]	3[e]	23	31[e]
Tobacco products	14[e]	15[e]	4	41[e]
Textiles	5[e]	13[e]	54	78[e]
Wearing apparel	1[e]	4[e]	24	54[e]
Leather and fur products	1[e]	2[e]	4	4[e]
Footwear	NA	NA	1	7[e]
Wood and wood products	2[e]	2[e]	3	8[e]
Furniture and fixtures	4[e]	1[e]	2	4[e]
Paper and paper products	NA	1[e]	3	6[e]
Printing and publishing	1[e]	2[e]	2	5[e]
Other chemical products	2[e]	5[e]	13	20[e]
Rubber products	NA	NA	2	5[e]
Plastic products	NA	1[e]	3[e]	8[e]
Other non-metal mineral products	3[e]	12[e]	34	35[e]
Iron and steel	3[e]	2[e]	8	9[e]
Metal products	1[e]	32[e]	8	19[e]
Electrical machinery	1[e]	1[e]	4	12[e]
Other manufacturing	9[e]	1[e]	3	2[e]

COMMUNICATIONS

Daily Newspapers

	National Data	World Data for Comparison
Daily Newspapers		
Number of Dailies	29	8,391
Total Circulation (000)	250	548,000
Circulation per 1,000 inhabitants	11	96

Telecommunications

Telephones - main lines in use: 236,816 (January 2000).

Telephones - mobile cellular: NA

Telephone system: poor telephone and telegraph service; fair radiotelephone communication service and mobile cellular telephone network.

Domestic: NA

International: radiotelephone communications; microwave landline to India; satellite earth station - 1 Intelsat (Indian Ocean).

Radio broadcast stations: AM 6, FM 5, shortwave 1 (January 2000).

Radios: 840,000 (1997).

Television broadcast stations: 6 (1998).

Televisions: 130,000 (1997).

Internet Service Providers (ISPs): NA

FINANCE, ECONOMICS, & TRADE

Economic Indicators

National product: GDP—purchasing power parity—$27.4 billion (1999 est.).

National product real growth rate: 3.4% (1999 est.).

National product per capita: $1,100 (1999 est.).

Inflation rate—consumer price index: 11.8% (FY98/99 est.).

Exchange Rates

Exchange rates:

Nepalese rupees (NRs) per US$1

January 2000	68.784
1999	68.253
1998	65.976
1997	58.010
1996	56.692
1995	51.890

Top Import Origins

$1.2 billion (f.o.b., 1998)

Origins (FY97/98)

India	31%
China/Hong Kong	16%
Singapore	14%

Top Export Destinations

$485 million (f.o.b., 1998)

Destinations (FY97/98)

India	33%
United States	26%
Germany	25%

Exports do not include unrecorded border trade with India.

Foreign Aid

Recipient: $411 million (FY97/98).

Import/Export Commodities

Import Commodities	Export Commodities
Gold	Carpets
Machinery and equipment	Clothing
	Leather goods
Petroleum products	Jute goods
Fertilizer	Grain

Balance of Payments

	1994	1995	1996	1997	1998
Exports of goods (f.o.b.)	369	350	389	410	485
Imports of goods (f.o.b.)	−1,159	−1,311	−1,495	−1,719	−1,233
Trade balance	−790	−961	−1,106	−1,308	−748
Services - debits	−297	−313	−243	−225	−196
Services - credits	579	679	757	866	565
Private transfers (net)	80	93	94	82	139
Government transfers (net)	81	146	187	186	187
Overall balance	−352	−356	−327	−418	−58

THE NETHERLANDS

CAPITAL: Constitutional capital: Amsterdam. Seat of government: The Hague (Gravenhage; Den Haag).

FLAG: The national flag, standardized in 1937, is a tricolor of red, white, and blue horizontal stripes.

ANTHEM: *Wilhelmus van Nassouwen (William of Nassau).*

MONETARY UNIT: The guilder (gulden; abbreviated f, designating the ancient florin) of 100 cents is a paper currency with one official exchange rate. There are coins of 5, 10, and 25 cents and 1, 2, 5, 10, and 50 guilders, and notes of 5, 10, 25, 50, 100, 250, and 1,000 guilders. f1 = \$0.58962 (or \$1 = f1.696).

WEIGHTS AND MEASURES: The metric system is the legal standard.

HOLIDAYS: New Year's Day, 1 January; Queen's Day, 30 April; National Liberation Day, 5 May; Christmas, 25–26 December. Movable religious holidays include Good Friday, Holy Saturday, Easter Monday, Ascension, and Whitmonday.

TIME: 1 PM = noon GMT.

LOCATION AND SIZE: Situated in northwestern Europe, the Netherlands has a total area of 37,330 square kilometers (14,413 square miles), of which inland water accounts for more than 2,060 square kilometers (795 square miles). The land area is 33,920 square kilometers (13,097 square miles). Comparatively, the area occupied by the Netherlands is slightly less than twice the size of the state of New Jersey. The Netherlands has a total boundary length of 1,478 kilometers (918 miles).

The capital city of the Netherlands, Amsterdam, is in the western part of the country.

CLIMATE: The Netherlands has a maritime climate, with cool summers and mild winters. The average temperature is about 2°C (36°F) in January and 19°C (66°F) in July, with an annual average of about 10°C (50°F). Average annual rainfall is about 76 centimeters (30 inches).

Kingdom of the Netherlands
Koninkrijk der Nederlanden

INTRODUCTORY SURVEY

RECENT HISTORY

German forces overran The Netherlands during World War II (1939-1945). Queen Wilhelmina refused to surrender to the Germans and fled to Britain with other officials of her government. Although Dutch resistance lasted only five days, destruction was widespread. Nearly the whole of downtown Rotterdam was wiped out, and other cities suffered great damage. The Dutch withstood severe oppression until their liberation by Allied forces in May 1945. Wilhelmina gave up the throne in 1948, and was followed by her daughter, Juliana. Queen Juliana gave up the throne in 1980, in favor of her daughter, Beatrix.

The East Indies, most of which had been under Dutch rule for over 300 years, achieved independence in 1949. Suriname (formerly Dutch Guiana), controlled by the Netherlands since 1815, became an independent nation in 1975. The Netherlands Antilles and Aruba remain dependencies.

The country was a founding member of NATO and the European Community (EC) and participated in the euro's introduction in 1999. The Netherlands is a member of the European Economic and Monetary Union (EMU).

Reform of the social security system was a major political issue in the 1990s, along with efforts to reduce public spending. A number of radical social measures received parliamentary approval including conditions for administering euthanasia (causing death painlessly in terminal illnesses), le-

galization of prostitution, and laws banning discrimination.

GOVERNMENT

The Netherlands is a constitutional monarchy. Executive power is exercised by the crown and the cabinet, which must have the support of a majority in the parliament. The monarch acts as an adviser to the cabinet, may propose bills, and signs all bills approved by the legislature. The 25-member Council of State, begun in 1532, is appointed by and presided over by the crown. It considers all legislation proposed by the crown or the cabinet before it is submitted to the parliament. The prime minister is head of government, appointed by the monarch, usually being the majority party leader of the Second Chamber.

Legislative power is exercised jointly by the crown and the States-General (*Staten-Generaal*), a two-chamber parliament. The upper house (*Eerste Kamer*) consists of seventy-five members elected for four years by the provincial representative councils. The lower house (*Tweede Kamer*) has 150 members elected for four years directly by the people. All Dutch citizens who have reached the age of eighteen years and live in the Netherlands can vote.

The country is divided into twelve provinces, each governed by a representative provincial council (*Provinciale Staten*).

Judiciary

The Dutch legal system is a civil law system with an independent judiciary. There is no jury system and the state rather than the individual acts as initiator of legal proceedings. Administrative justice is separate from civil and criminal justice and not uniform in dispensation. The supreme judiciary body is the High Court of the Netherlands (Court of Cassation). Its principal task is to supervise administration of justice and to review the judgments of lower courts.

There are five courts of appeal (gerechtshoven). The nineteen district courts (arrondissementsrechtsbanken) provide first hearings of criminal cases and civil cases not handled by the sixty-two cantonal courts (kantonge-rechten) that handle petty criminal cases and civil cases involving low sums damages. There also are juvenile courts and special arbitration courts (for such institutions as the Stock Exchange Association and professional organizations).

Political Parties

Religion played an important role in political activities until the 1960s, when a trend toward political polarization led to conservative and progressive parties. Key parties winning Chamber seats was the Christian Democratic Appeal (CDA), People's Party for Freedom and Democracy (Volkspartij voor Vrijheid en Democratie-VVD), the Labor Party (Partij van de Arbeid-PvdA), and the Democrats '66 (Democraten '66-D'66). There are a number of minor parties. The Labor Party is in the political center and the conservative VVD pushes for free enterprise and separating church and state. No single party commands a majority in the States-General. The governing cabinet is made up of various party representatives according to their numerical strength.

DEFENSE

Universal military training has been in force since the beginning of the twentieth century. All able-bodied men reaching the age of twenty (about 43,000 a year) are subject to military training for twelve to fifteen months. Defense is comprised of the Royal Netherlands army, navy, and air force, and the Royal Constabulary. In 2000, there were 27,000 personnel in the army, 13,800 in the navy, and 11,980 in the air force.

The nation spent $7 billion on defense in 1998.

ECONOMIC AFFAIRS

The Netherlands is a modern industrialized nation and a large exporter of agricultural products. Having limited natural resources the Netherlands bases its economy on the importation of raw materials for processing into finished products for export. Food processing, metallurgy, chemicals, manufacturing, and oil refining are the principal industries. Because of its geographic position on the sea, outstanding harbor facilities, and numerous internal waterways, the Netherlands has traditionally been a trading, transporting, and brokerage nation. The economy, being dependent on international trade, is sharply affected by economic developments abroad-including changes in prices of primary goods-over which the Netherlands has little or no control.

Public Finance

Through the 1980s and 1990s, the country's deficit has been steadily reduced to within the 3 percent criteria for European Economic and Monetary Union (EMU) in 1999. The deficit is largely financed by government bonds. Financing is also covered by issuing Dutch Treasury Certificates, which replaced a standing credit facility for short-term deficit financing with the Netherlands Central Bank.

In 1999, government revenues totaled approximately $163 billion and expenditures $170 billion. No external debt existed.

Income

In 1999, the gross domestic product (GDP) was $365 billion, or about $23,000 per capita. GDP real growth rate was 3.4 percent and the inflation rate was 2.2 percent. Contributions to the GDP by economic sector in 1998 was agriculture 3.5 percent, industry 26.8 percent, and services 69.7 percent.

Industry

Leading industries have been mining, quarrying, manufacturing, transport, storage, and communications. The Philips Electrical Company at Eindhoven is one of the world's major exporters of electric bulbs and appliances. In 1996, Philips employed 273,000 people and had revenues of

$41 billion. The Royal Dutch/Shell Group operates one of the world's largest oil refineries at Curaçao, near Venezuela, and Rotterdam's suburb of Pernis has the largest oil refinery in Europe.

Industrial products include crude steel, pig iron, and pharmaceutical products. The Netherlands also produces cigarettes, beer, canned fish, cocoa and cocoa products, sugar, candies, biscuits, and potato flour. The industrial growth rate was estimated at 2.4 percent in 1995.

Banking and Finance

The Netherlands Bank, nationalized in 1948, is the central bank. It issues the currency and regulates its value, establishes the rates of foreign exchange, issues money permits to foreigners, and supervises the privately owned banks. Since the 1950s, the Netherlands Bank has used reserve regulations and the central bank discount rate as instruments of monetary policy. The Dutch financial services industry has a long and distinguished history and has introduced many banking innovations to the world. Since the late 1980s, a number of bank mergers and the formation of financial conglomerates of banks and insurance groups occurred. As a result, the number of dominant participants in the market has diminished to a handful. Each provides the full range of financial services. These include International Nederlanden Groep (ING), ABN-AMRO, the Dutch-Belgian Fortis group, and Rabobank.

The Netherlands has the oldest stock exchange in the world. The Amsterdam Stock Exchange (ASE), founded in the early 17th century, is one of the largest stock exchanges in operation. The issuance of new securities on the exchange is supervised by the Netherlands Bank, acting in cooperation with the commercial banks and stockbrokers. Its strong international orientation is also reflected in a large share of foreign security listings. In 1997, the Amsterdam Exchanges (AEX) was formed by the merger of the Amsterdam Stock Exchange (ASE) and the city's European Options Exchange (EDE).

Economic Development

Attempts to cope with inflation and other economic problems involved increased government control over the economy. Wage and price controls were imposed in 1970-1971, and the States-General approved a measure granting the government power to control wages, rents, dividends, health and insurance costs, and job layoffs during 1974.

Increased industrialization through incentives for private investment has been the focus of the Dutch government after World War II, but the rate of industrial development slowed in the 1990s, while the service sector expanded, and a high technology economy grew. The largest economic development projects involved land reclamation by construction of dykes and dams and the drainage of lakes. The Zuider Zee reclamation prior to World War II was followed by the Delta project inaugurated in 1986, at the cost of $2.4 billion. In addition, a bridge and tunnel were constructed across the Western Schelde estuary to improve transportation between Zeeland Flanders and the rest of the country.

SOCIAL WELFARE

A widespread system of social insurance and assistance is in effect. About two-thirds of Holland's workers are covered by the social insurance program, and the rest are covered by private insurance. Unemployment, accidents, illness, and disability are covered by insurance that is compulsory for most employees and voluntary for self-employed persons. Maternity grants and full insurance for the worker's family are also provided, as are family allowances for children. There are also widows' and orphans' funds. A state pension is granted to all persons over sixty-five. Women have equal legal status with men.

Healthcare

Under the Health Insurance Act, everyone with earned income of less than 50,900 guilders per year pays a monthly contribution in return for which, they receive medical, pharmaceutical, and dental treatment and hospitalization. The state also pays for preventive medicine including vaccinations for children, school dental services, medical research, and the training of health workers.

Most doctors and hospitals operate privately. There are numerous local and regional health centers and hospitals. The general health situation has been excellent over a long period of time, helped by a rise in the standard of living, improvements in nutrition, hygiene, housing, and working conditions, and the expansion of public health measures. In 2000, average life expectancy was estimated at 78.3 years.

There are 2.5 doctors and 11.3 hospital beds per 1,000 people. Healthcare expenditures in 1990-1997 were 8.5 percent of GDP.

Housing

During World War II, more than 25 percent of Holland's two million dwellings were damaged. From 1945 to 1985, nearly four million dwellings were built. In 1985 alone, 98,131 dwellings were built. Most of the new units were subsidized by the national government through grants to municipalities, building societies, and housing associations, which generally build low-income multiple dwellings. Over 90,000 new units were being constructed annually in the late 1990s.

EDUCATION

Illiteracy is nearly nonexistent in the Netherlands. School attendance between the ages of five and eighteen is compulsory. Secondary school is comprised of three types: general, secondary school, and pre-university. In 1997, the Netherlands had 1.2 million students enrolled in primary schools and 1.4 million in secondary schools. All schools are government-supported.

Vocational and university education is provided at the eight universities and five institutes *(Hogescholen)* which are equivalent to universities. Facilities for adult education have been opened in various municipalities. In 1997, 468,970 students attended institutions of higher learning.

2000 KEY EVENTS TIMELINE

January

- People with haemophilia are offered US$2.36 as compensation for receiving blood transfusions tainted with HIV in the 1980s.
- The Rijksmuseum celebrates 200 hundred years of existence.
- Amsterdam Exchange announces that it will revise its gold option contract to eliminate delivery and settle only in cash. It will also delist a silver option contract.

February

- The Government proposes tax reform on retirement to increase labor supply. The reform will make it harder to retire at fifty-five, which some two-thirds of the Dutch now do with full pensions. The legal retirement remains, for now, at sixty-five.
- The Netherlands records 2,961 measles cases, including three measles-related deaths. The outbreak began in June 1999 and mostly affects children who were unvaccinated because of religious beliefs.

March

- Aetna (largest U.S. health insurer) refuses a bid by Royal KPN.
- Bram Peper, interior minister in the center-left cabinet led by Wim Kok, resigns before the completion of a long-running inquiry into his expense claims. He is accused of using public money for entertainment, taxis, and expensive official cars.
- Ajax of Amsterdam, one of the Netherlands most famous soccer clubs, is 100 years old.
- World Online, the Netherlands-based internet provider, sees its share tumble to 42 percent below issue price of forty-three euros, after revelations of unusual share dealings by its founder and chairwoman Nina Brink.

April

- Endemol Entertainment sells "Big Brother" to CBS.
- Belgian, Dutch, and French stock exchanges announce a merger to be completed in September. The new exchange will have a market capitalization of 2.4 billion euro.
- Trial of the two men accused in the bombing of a Pan Am flight over Lockerbie, Scotland, finally gets underway after nearly twelve years. Scottish judges hear the case that killed 270 people.

May

- Architect Rem Koolhaas, age fifty-six, wins the Pritzker Prize for architecture. Koolhaas's office is in Rotterdam. The prize will be awarded at a ceremony in Jerusalem on May 17.
- Fireworks factory fire kills at least seventeen people and injures more than 900. The border town Enschede has to demolish 400 houses and loses four firefighters during the blaze.
- Netherlands Opera presents *Writing to Vermeer* at the Lincoln Center Festival 2000.
- Economist Intelligence Unit declares the Netherlands as the top ranking business location, displacing Hong Kong.

June

- Expected GDP growth will be above 4 percent for 2000 compared with 3.8 percent for euro zone. The jobless rate is 2.8 percent compared with 9.4 percent for the euro zone.
- Dutch parliament legalizes long-tolerated euthanasia.
- Aetna, U.S. largest health insurer, reopens merger talks with ING, the Dutch financial services group.
- Unilever, British-Dutch food maker with 255,000 employees, pays US$20.3 billion in cash to acquire Bestfoods.
- Dutch truck driver is charged with fifty-eight counts of manslaughter after his truck was found to contain the bodies of illegal Chinese immigrants in Dover.

July

- The government backs down over a controversial proposal to allow those aged from twelve to sixteen years legally to demand euthanasia without their parents' consent.
- The Dutch government auctions licenses for third-generation mobile phones and raised $2.5 billion, which was a third of the amount the finance ministry had expected.

August

- Leading Dutch newspapers fail to prevent an online news service from providing direct links to articles on newspaper websites. Kranten.com, whose site consists largely of news headlines, allows user to click on any of these to receive full text articles.
- Sara Lee U.S. food and consumer products groups is selling its U.S.-based PYA/Monarch food services unit to Royal Ahold (a Dutch supermarket chain) for $1.57 billion.
- Four Dutch citizens are accused of plotting to kill Yugoslav president Slobodan Milosevic and are in Yugoslavian jail.

September

- Legislators approve a bill on September 12 that gives same-sex partners full rights for marriage, adoption, and divorce, by a vote of 109 to 33.
- Truck drivers block two tunnels near Amsterdam and Rotterdam during rush hour on September 12, protesting high gasoline prices.
- British Airways and KLM call off their merger plans after four months of negotiations.
- The government yields on fuel duty and offers an extra rebate to truck drivers.
- The central government budget records a surplus of around one percent of gross domestic product for the first time in twenty-five years. The budget triumph is marred by the perilous conditions of the country's schools and hospitals, however.
- Dutch swimmers Inge de Bruijn and Pieter van den Hoogenband perform beyond expectation at the Olympic Games in Sidney, Australia. De Bruijn wins three and Van den Hoogenband wins two gold medals.

October

- Ruud Lubbers, former prime minister of the Netherlands, is nominated to be United Nations High Commissioner for Refugees by Secretary General Kofi Annan. Lubbers was an unsuccessful candidate for secretary general of the North Atlantic Treaty Organization (NATO) and for president of the European Commission.

November

- Parliament passes a new law that will force public companies to reveal the compensation package (salary plus any stock options) of its senior management.
- In a decision issued November 28, the Dutch High Court makes the Netherlands the first country to legalize euthanasia.

December

- Parliament and the cabinet struggle to find a compromise on proposals related to zoning and space planning in this, the most densely populated country in Europe.

ANALYSIS OF EVENTS: 2000

BUSINESS AND THE ECONOMY

Official unemployment is 2.5 percent and real gross domestic product (GDP) growth peaked at 4 percent in 2000, and was estimated to decline slightly to 3.5 percent in 2001. Real disposable income was projected to rise by 5.25 percent in 2000, representing the biggest annual gain in spending power in thirty years.

The government budget recorded a surplus of 0.5 percent of GDP for the first time in a quarter century. The public debt was forecast to fall below the 60 percent of GDP set in the Maastricht criteria on monetary union.

A labor shortage affected nearly all sectors of the economy. The tight labor market was contributing to an inflation rate of 3 percent. The labor reforms introduced in the early 1990s had apparently produced the desired outcome. Nonetheless, although there were serious shortages of skilled, technical, communications, and health workers, almost one million people are classified as disabled, with around half of this number over fifty years of age. The labor force participation rate, therefore, was more or less on par with that of neighboring countries with much higher unemployment figures.

Monetary policy was controlled by Frankfurt, Germany, and the European central bank showed little concern about the problems of an overheating Dutch economy since it is more concerned about inflationary pressure in the euro-zone generally. The Dutch government must rely on fiscal policy to slow the economy. As of 2000 it had done relatively little to relieve labor market tightness and to combat spiraling costs of office leases and housing. In the affluent Randstad, the metropolitan area that includes Amsterdam, Utrecht, and Rotterdam, prices grew by 4 percent per quarter during 1998 and 1999 and slowed down a bit in 2000. With the rise in house prices, homeowners took out second mortgages and thereby contributed to strong credit growth. For a brief period the politicians discussed restricting the Dutch system of unlimited tax deductibility on mortgage interest payments. Since voters would never elect a party that was in favor of such a move, the idea disappeared.

The current government passed a tax reform package that would go into effect in 2001, but the overall impact of the reforms was expected to create a mild economic stimulus because it mainly consisted of income tax cuts. It also replaced the wealth tax and tax on investment income with a tax of 30 percent on investment income growth.

Business reported huge profits thanks to strong consumer demand and vigorous export growth. Dutch business also earned good returns on investments in the United States. The Netherlands was one of the largest investors in the United States, where investments included insurance companies, retailing giants, semiconductor manufacturers, and vitamin producers. The earnings of these investments looked especially strong thanks to the strong dollar and weak euro.

One potential source of worry was that most Dutch companies do not have the scale to compete with those from the five largest European economies. Many companies have sought cross-border mergers, however, with modest success. In the airline industry, KLM's mergers with Italy's Alitalia and then British Airways fell apart. KPN, a telecommunication firm, could not agree on a deal with Telefonica of Spain. World Online, the Internet service provider that built a pan-European presence, just about collapsed after it was discovered that its founder lacked equity commitment to the business. Its future was in the hands of Italy's Tiscali as of late 2000.

GOVERNMENT AND POLITICS

The center-left coalition of Wim Kok, prime minister since 1994, has had some wobbly moments the last two years but has survived them unscathed. The purple coalition (consisting of an alliance of the social democrat Labor Party (PvdA), the liberal free-market People's Party for Freedom and Democracy (VVD), and the small reformist Democrats '66 (D'66)) was close to collapse in May 1999, when the junior partner resigned from the coalition after a parliamentary defeat over the use of referenda in the democratic process. A settlement was brokered and the reformist party returned to the coalition. In early 2000, another crisis erupted as the coalition was deeply divided over what to do with the 1999 budget surplus of around 0.5 percent of GDP, and future surpluses. The minister of finance, a free-market liberal, believed that the surplus should be spent on cutting taxes and reducing the level of national debt. The Prime Minister and PvdA argued that the surplus should be used to increase investments in security, health care, and education. After a lengthy debate a compromise resolved the issue of using some of the extra money for the improvement of public services. One large source of extra revenue came from the mid-year auction of third-generation mobile telephone frequencies. The coalition accord stipulated that the savings on interest payments generated by the payment could be used for extra spending. With elections scheduled for May 2002 the current coalition was under pressure to address the decline in quality of public infrastructure.

In the fall, Kok was faced by an angry blockade of Dutch truckers who protested against high gasoline prices. The transport sector in the Netherlands is crucial to a national economy based largely on distribution. The cabinet quickly offered a relief package to the trucking industry by expanding the eligibility for tax rebates on diesel fuel, formerly reserved for large trucks, to include smaller commercial vehicles. The Prime Minister refused to contemplate general reduction of gasoline taxes and insisted that any moves would be temporary.

CULTURE AND SOCIETY

The Netherlands, Europe's most densely populated country, was seeking a way to ensure the optimal use of scarce resources without causing ecological degradation. The government published a spatial planning report that would govern the usage of land until at least 2020. The demands of business cut into the living needs of the population and the government was acutely aware that Netherlands must find ways to solve the strains on its physical infrastructure and public services.

Dutch architects operated within tight rules that governed the use of space and the integrity of the design. But some new towns or suburbs have allowed planners and architects to submit bold designs to explore the boundaries of urban living. One design, which has provoked much commentary, was a seven-story building that contains twenty-eight family units with gardens, stacked one on top of another. The city council of a community comprised of man-made islands east of Amsterdam that were scheduled to house 45,000 people by 2015, was considering the adoption of this innovative concept.

Economic growth generated other strains. In the late fall Dutch family doctors went on strike to protest long hours and relatively low pay. The workload of primary care physicians has increased year after year but their pay and subsidies for hiring more staff has stagnated.

The Netherlands co-hosted with Belgium the 2000 European World Cup soccer championship. To keep order the Dutch police and specially hired security officials dealt strictly with supporters who displayed overzealous enthusiasm or hostility. One incident led to an exchange of words between prime ministers Guiliano Amato of Italy and Wim Kok. At issue was how officials at the stadium handled a group of Italy supporters and a reporting crew from state-owned RAI television.

DIRECTORY

CENTRAL GOVERNMENT

Head of State

Queen
Beatrix Wilhelmina Armgard, Monarch, Cabinet of the Queen, korte Vijver Berg 3, NL-2513 AB The Hague, Netherlands
PHONE: +31 (70) 3308888
FAX: +31 (70) 3639307

Prime Minister
Wim Kok, Office of the Prime Minister

Ministers

Minister of Agriculture, Nature Management and Fisheries
Laurens-Jan Brinkhorst, Ministry of Agriculture, Nature Management and Fisheries, Bezuidenhoutseweg 73, Postal Box 20401, NL-2500 EK The Hague, Netherlands
PHONE: +31 (70) 3793911
FAX: +31 (70) 3815153

Minister of Defence
Frank de Grave, Ministry of Defence, Plein 4, Postal Box 20701, NL-2500 ES The Hague, Netherlands
PHONE: +31 (70) 3188188
FAX: +31 (70) 3187888

Minister for Development Cooperation
Eveline Herfkens, Ministry of Foreign Affairs, Bezuidenhoutseweg 67, Postal Box 20061, NL-2500 EB The Hague, Netherlands
PHONE: +31 (70) 3486486
FAX: +31 (70) 3484848

Minister for Economic Affairs
Annemarie Jorritsma née Lebbink, Ministry of Economic Affairs, Bezuidenhoutseweg 30, Postal Box 20101, NL-2500 EC The Hague, Netherlands
PHONE: +31 (70) 3798911
FAX: +31 (70) 3474081

Minister of Education, Culture and Science
Loek Hermans, Ministry of Education, Culture and Science, Europaweg 4, Postal Box 25000, NL-2700 LZ Zoetermeer, Netherlands
PHONE: +31 (79) 3232323
FAX: +31 (79) 3232330

Minister of Finance
Gerrit Zalm, Ministry of Finance, Korte Voorhout 7, Postal Box 20201, NL-2500 EE The Hague, Netherlands
PHONE: +31 (70) 3428000
FAX: +31 (70) 3427905

Minister for Foreign Affairs
Jozias van Aartsen, Ministry of Foreign Affairs, Bezuidenhoutseweg 67, Postal Box 20061, NL-2500 EB The Hague, Netherlands
PHONE: +31 (70) 3486486
FAX: +31 (70) 3484848

Minister for General Affairs
Wim Kok, Ministry of General Affairs, Binnenhof 20, Postal Box 20001, NL-2500 EA The Hague, Netherlands
PHONE: +31 (70) 3564100
FAX: +31 (70) 3564683

Minister of Health, Welfare and Sport
Margo Vliegenhart, Ministry of Health, Welfare and Sport, Parnassusplein 5, Postal Box 20350, NL-2500 EJ The Hague, Netherlands
PHONE: +31 (70) 3407911
FAX: +31 (70) 3407834

Minister of Housing, Spatial Planning and the Environment
Jan Pronk, Ministry of Housing, Spatial Planning and the Environment, Rijnstraat 8, Postal Box 20951, NL-2500 EZ The Hague, Netherlands
PHONE: +31 (70) 3393939
FAX: +31 (70) 3391352

Minister of Home Affairs
Klaas de Vries, Ministry of Home Affairs, Schedeldoekshaven 200, Postal Box 20011, NL-2500 EA The Hague, Netherlands
PHONE: +31 (70) 3026302
FAX: +31 (70) 3639153

Minister of Justice
Benk Korthals, Ministry of Justice, Schedeldoekshaven 100, Postal Box 20301, NL-2500 EH The Hague, Netherlands
PHONE: +31 (70) 3707911
FAX: +31 (70) 3707900

Minister of Social Affairs and Employment
Willem Vermeend, Ministry of Social Affairs and Employment, Anna van Hannoverstraat 4, Postal Box 90801, NL-2509 LV The Hague, Netherlands
PHONE: +31 (70) 3334444
FAX: +31 (70) 3334040

Minister of Transport, Public Works and Water Management
Monique de Vries, Ministry of Transport, Public Works and Water Management, Plesmanweg 1, Postal Box 20901, NL-2500 EX The Hague, Netherlands
PHONE: +31 (70) 3516171
FAX: +31 (70) 3517895

Plenipotentiary Minister of the Netherlands Antilles
E. Mendes de Gouveia, Cabinet of the Plenipotentiary Minister of the Netherlands Antilles, Badhuisweg 173–175, Postal Box 90706, NL-2509 LS The Hague, Netherlands
PHONE: +31 (70) 3066111
FAX: +31 (70) 3066110

Plenipotentiary Minister of Aruba
A. Croes, Cabinet of the Plenipotentiary Minister of Aruba, R.J. Schimmelpennincklaan 1, NL-2517 JN The Hague, Netherlands
PHONE: +31 (70) 3566200
FAX: +31 (70) 3451446

POLITICAL ORGANIZATIONS

Algemeen Ouderenverbond—Unie 55+-AOV-U55+ (General Elder People's League)

Tweede Kamer Unie 55+ Fractie, Postbus 20018, NL-2500 EA, Gravenhage, Netherlands
PHONE: +31 (70) 3183825
FAX: +31 (70) 3182828
E-MAIL: unie55@pi.net

Centrumdemocraten (Centre Democrats)

Christen Democratisch Appel-CDA (Christian Democratic Appeal)

Tweede Kamer CDA-Fractie, Postbus 30805, NL-2500 GV, Gravenhage, Netherlands
PHONE: +31 (70) 3183020
FAX: +31 (70) 3182602
E-MAIL: cda@pi.net

Democraten 66 (Democrats 66)

Tweede Kamer D66-Fractie, Postbus 20018, NL-2500 EA, Gravenhage, Netherlands
PHONE: +31 (70) 3183066
FAX: +31 (70) 3183625
E-MAIL: lsd66@d66.nl

Groenen Links (Green Left)

Postbus 6192, NL-2001 HD Haarlem, Netherlands
PHONE: +31 (23) 5427370
FAX: +31 (23) 5144176
E-MAIL: info@degroenen.nl
TITLE: President
NAME: Ron van Wonderen

Natuurwetpartij Nederland (Dutch Natural Law Party)

Natuurwetpartij, Rivierenlaan 164, NL-8226 LH Lelystad, Netherlands
FAX: +31 0320258858
E-MAIL: info@natuurwetpartij.nl

Partij van de Arbeid (Labour Party)

Tweede Kamer PvdA-Fractie, Postbus 20018, NL-2500 EA, Gravenhage, Netherlands
PHONE: +31 (70) 3183025
FAX: +31 (70) 3182797
E-MAIL: tkleden@pvda.nl

Reformatorische Politieke Federatie (Reformed Political Federation)

PHONE: +31 (70) 3182930
FAX: +31 (70) 3182933

Staatkundig Gereformeerde Partij-SGP (Reformed Political League)

Socialistische Partij (Socialist Party)

Vijverhofstraat 65, NL-3032 SC Rotterdam, Netherlands
PHONE: +31 (10) 2435555
FAX: +31 (10) 2435566
E-MAIL: sp@sp.nl

Volkspartij voor Vrijheid en Democratie (People's Party for Freedom and Democracy)

VVD Afdeling Nieuwegein, Kikvorsweide 3, NL-3437 VA Nieuwegein, Netherlands
PHONE: +31 (30) 6032931
E-MAIL: vvd@pen.nl

DIPLOMATIC REPRESENTATION

Embassies in Netherlands

Algeria
Van Stolklaan 173, NL-2585 JS The Hague, Netherlands
PHONE: +31 (70) 3522954

Argentina
Javastraat 20, NL-2585 AN The Hague, Netherlands
PHONE: +31 (70) 3654836

Australia
Carnegielaan 4, NL-2517 KH The Hague, Netherlands
PHONE: +31 (70) 3108200
TITLE: Ambassador
NAME: Ted Delofski

Austria
Van Alkemadelaan 342, NL-2597 AS The Hague, Netherlands
PHONE: +31 (70) 3245470

Belgium
Lange Vijverberg 12, NL-2513 AC The Hague, Netherlands
PHONE: +31 (70) 3123456

Bolivia
Nassaulaan 5/1, NL-2514 JS The Hague, Netherlands
PHONE: +31 (70) 3616707

Bosnia and Herzegovina
Van Bleiswijkstraat 118, NL-2582 LJ The Hague, Netherlands
PHONE: +31 (70) 3588505

Brazil
Mauritskade 19, NL-2514 HD The Hague, Netherlands
PHONE: +31 (70) 3469229

Bulgaria
Duinroosweg 9, NL-2597 KJ The Hague, Netherlands
PHONE: +31 (70) 3503051

Canada
Sophialaan 7, NL-2514 JP The Hague, Netherlands
PHONE: +31 (70) 3111600

Cape Verde
Koninginnegracht 44, 2514 AD The Hague, Netherlands
PHONE: +31 (70) 3469623

Cameroon
Amaliastraat 14, NL-2514 JC The Hague, Netherlands
PHONE: +31 (70) 3469715

Chile
Mauritskade 51, NL-2514 HG The Hague, Netherlands
PHONE: +31 (70) 3642748

People's Republic of China
Adriaan Goekooplaan 7, NL-2517 JX The Hague, Netherlands
PHONE: +31 (70) 3551515

Colombia
Groot Hertoginnelaan 14, NL-2517 EG The Hague, Netherlands
PHONE: +31 (70) 3614545

Costa Rica
Laan Copes van Cattenburg 46, NL-2585 GB The Hague, Netherlands
PHONE: +31 (70) 3544675

Côte d'Ivoire
Consulate of Ivory Cost, Rivierstaete, Amsteldijk 166, NL-1079 LH Amsterdam, Netherlands
PHONE: +31 (20) 6612444

Croatia
Amaliastraat 16, NL-2514 JC The Hague, Netherlands
PHONE: +31 (70) 3633014

Cuba
Mauritskade 49, NL-2514 HG The Hague, Netherlands
PHONE: +31 (70) 3606061

Cyprus
Jan van Nassaustraat 87, NL-2596 BR The Hague, Netherlands
PHONE: +31 (70) 3284507

Czech Republic
Paleisstraat 4, NL-2514 JA The Hague, Netherlands
PHONE: +31 (70) 3469712

Denmark
Koninginnegracht 30, NL-2514 AB The Hague, Netherlands
PHONE: +31 (70) 3655830

Dominica
Consulate of Dominica, Labradordreef 18, NL-3565 AN Utrecht, Netherlands
PHONE: +31 (30) 2615095

Dominican Republic
Consulate of the Dominican Republic, Van der Veerelaan 45, NL-1181 PZ Amstelveen, Netherlands
PHONE: +31 (20) 6471062

Ecuador
Surinamestraat 11, NL-2585 GG The Hague, Netherlands
PHONE: +31 (70) 3463753

Egypt
Badhuisweg 92, NL-2587 CL The Hague, Netherlands
PHONE: +31 (70) 3542000

El Salvador
Consulate of El Salvador, Het Witte Huis, Wijnhaven 3–1, NL-3011 WG Rotterdam, Netherlands
PHONE: +31 (10) 4133304

Estonia
Consulate of Estonia, Parkstraat 15, NL-2514 JD The Hague, Netherlands
PHONE: +31 (70) 3456252

Ethiopia
Consulate of Ethiopia, Frederik Hendrikplein 1, NL-2582 AT The Hague, Netherlands
PHONE: +31 (70) 3586944

Finland
Groot Hertoginnelaan 16, NL-2517 EG The Hague, Netherlands
PHONE: +31 (70) 3469754

France
Smidsplein 1, NL-2514 BT The Hague, Netherlands
PHONE: +31 (70) 3125800

Federal Republic of Germany
Groot Hertoginnelaan 18/20, NL-2517 EG The Hague, Netherlands
PHONE: +31 (70) 3420600

Ghana
Laan Copes van Cattenburg 70, NL-2585 GD The Hague, Netherlands
PHONE: +31 (70) 3062800

Greece
Amaliastraat 1, NL-2514 JC The Hague, Netherlands
PHONE: +31 (70) 3638700

Honduras
Johan van Oldebarneveldtlaan 85, NL-2582 NK The Hague, Netherlands
PHONE: +31 (70) 3523728

Hungary
Hogeweg 14, NL-2585 JD The Hague, Netherlands
PHONE: +31 (70) 3500404

India
Buitenrustweg 2, NL-2517 KD The Hague, Netherlands
PHONE: +31 (70) 3469771

Indonesia
Tobias Asserlaan 8, NL-2517 KC The Hague, Netherlands
PHONE: +31 (70) 3108100

Iran
Duinweg 24, NL-2585 JX The Hague, Netherlands
PHONE: +31 (70) 3548483

Iraq
Johan de Witlaan 16, NL-2517 JR The Hague, Netherlands
PHONE: +31 (70) 3469683

Ireland
Dr. Kuyperstraat 9, 2514 BA The Hague, Netherlands
PHONE: +31 (70) 3630993

Israel
Buitenhof 47, NL-2513 AH The Hague, Netherlands
PHONE: +31 (70) 3760500
FAX: +31 (70) 3760555
E-MAIL: ambassade@israel.nl

Italy
Alexanderstraat 12, NL-2514 JL The Hague, Netherlands
PHONE: +31 (70) 3469249

Japan
Tobias Asserlaan 2, NL-2517 KC The Hague, Netherlands
PHONE: +31 (70) 3469544

Kenya
Nieuwe Parklaan 21, NL-2597 LA The Hague, Netherlands
PHONE: +31 (70) 3504215

South Korea
Verlengde Tolweg 8, NL-2517 JV The Hague, Netherlands
PHONE: +31 (70) 3586076

Kuwait
Carnegielaan 9, NL-2517 KH The Hague, Netherlands
PHONE: +31 (70) 3603813

Latvia
Balistraat 88, NL-2585 XX The Hague, Netherlands
PHONE: +31 (70) 3063934

Lebanon
Frederikstraat 2, NL-2514 LK The Hague, Netherlands
PHONE: +31 (70) 3658906

Lithuania
Laan van Nieuw Oost Indie 27, NL-2593 BJ The Hague, Netherlands
PHONE: +31 (70) 3855418

Luxembourg
Nassaulaan 8, NL-2514 JS The Hague, Netherlands
PHONE: +31 (70) 3607516

Malawi
Consulate of Malawi, Lange Kerkdam 91, NL-2242 BT Wassenaar, Netherlands
PHONE: +31 (70) 5114302

Malaysia
Rustenburgweg 2, NL-2517 KE The Hague, Netherlands
PHONE: +31 (70) 3506506

Malta
Consulate of Malta, Baronielaan 59, NL-4818 PC Breda, Netherlands
PHONE: +31 (76) 5209043

Mexico
Nassauplein 17, NL-2585 EB The Hague, Netherlands
PHONE: +31 (70) 3454058

Morocco
Oranjestraat 9, NL-2514 JB The Hague, Netherlands
PHONE: +31 (70) 3469617

Myanmar
Consulate of Myanmar, Baronielaan 59, NL-4818 PC Breda, Netherlands
PHONE: +31 (76) 5209054

New Zealand
Carnegielaan 10/ET4, NL-2517 KH The Hague, Netherlands
PHONE: +31 (70) 3469324

Nicaragua
Zoutmanstraat 53/E, NL-2518 GM The Hague, Netherlands
PHONE: +31 (70) 3630967

Nigeria
Wagenaarweg 5, NL-2597 LL The Hague, Netherlands
PHONE: +31 (70) 3501703

Norway
Prinsessegracht 6A, NL-2514 AN The Hague, Netherlands
PHONE: +31 (70) 3117611

Oman
Koninginnegracht 27, NL-2514 AB The Hague, Netherlands
PHONE: +31 (70) 3615800

Pakistan
Amaliastraat 8, NL-2514 JC The Hague, Netherlands
PHONE: +31 (70) 3648948

Paraguay
Consulate of Paraguay, Goudsesingel 8, 3e/3, NL-3011 KA Rotterdam, Netherlands
PHONE: +31 (10) 4045541

Peru
Nassauplein 4, NL-2585 EA The Hague, Netherlands
PHONE: +31 (70) 3653500

Philippines
Laan Copes van Cattenburch 125, NL-2585 EZ The Hague, Netherlands
PHONE: +31 (70) 3648566

Poland
Alexanderstraat 25, NL-2514 JM The Hague, Netherlands
PHONE: +31 (70) 3602806
FAX: +31 (70) 3602810
E-MAIL: ambhaga@polamb.nl
TITLE: Ambassador Extraordinary and Plenipotentiary
NAME: Maria Wodzynska-Walicka

Portugal
Bazarstraat 21, NL-2518 AG The Hague, Netherlands
PHONE: +31 (70) 3630217

Romania
Catsheuvel 55, NL-2517 KA The Hague, Netherlands
PHONE: +31 (70) 3543796

Russia
Andries Bickerweg 2, NL-2517 JP The Hague, Netherlands
PHONE: +31 (70) 3451300

Saudi Arabia
Alexanderstraat 19, NL-2514 JM The Hague, Netherlands
PHONE: +31 (70) 3614391

Serbia
Groot Hertoginnelaan 30, NL-2517 EG The Hague, Netherlands
PHONE: +31 (70) 3632397

Slovakia
Parkweg 1, NL-2585 JG The Hague, Netherlands
PHONE: +31 (70) 4167777

South Africa
Wassenaarseweg 40, NL-2596 CJ The Hague, Netherlands
PHONE: +31 (70) 3924501

Spain
Lange Voorhout 50, NL-2514 EG The Hague, Netherlands
PHONE: +31 (70) 3643814

Sri Lanka
Jakob de Graefflaan 2, NL-2517 JM The Hague, Netherlands
PHONE: +31 (70) 3655910

Sudan
Laan Copes van Cattenburch 81, NL-2585 EW The Hague, Netherlands
PHONE: +31 (70) 3605300

Suriname
Alexander Gogelweg 2, NL-2517 JH The Hague, Netherlands
PHONE: +31 (70) 3650844

Sweden
Burgemeester van Karnebeeklaan 6, NL-2585 BB The Hague, Netherlands
PHONE: +31 (70) 4120200

Switzerland
Lange Voorhout 42, NL-2514 EE The Hague, Netherlands
PHONE: +31 (70) 3642831

Syria
Consulate of Syria, Laan van Meerdervoort 53/D, NL-2517 AE The Hague, Netherlands
PHONE: +31 (70) 3469795

Tanzania
Consulate of Tanzania, Parallelweg Z 215, NL-2914 LE Nieuwerkerk aan den Ijssel, Netherlands
PHONE: +31 (70) 180320939

Thailand
Laan Copes van Cattenburch 123, NL-2585 EZ The Hague, Netherlands
PHONE: +31 (70) 3452088

Tunisia
Gentsestraat 98, NL-2587 HX The Hague, Netherlands
PHONE: +31 (70) 3512251

Turkey
Jan Evertstraat 15, NL-2514 BS The Hague, Netherlands
PHONE: +31 (70) 3604912

United Kingdom
Lange Voorhout 10, NL-2514 ED The Hague, Netherlands
PHONE: +31 (70) 4270427

United States of America
Lange Voorhout 102, NL-2514 EJ The Hague, Netherlands
PHONE: +31 (70) 3109209
FAX: +31 (70) 3614688
TITLE: Ambassador
NAME: Cynthia P. Schneider

Uruguay
Mauritskade 33, NL-2514 HD The Hague, Netherlands
PHONE: +31 (70) 3609815

Vatican City
Carnegielaan 5, NL-2517 KH The Hague, Netherlands
PHONE: +31 (70) 3503363

Venezuela
2517 KH The Hague, Netherlands, NL-2514 JS The Hague, Netherlands
PHONE: +31 (70) 3651266

Yemen
Surinamestraat 9, NL-2585 GG The Hague, Netherlands
PHONE: +31 (70) 3653936

Zaire
Violenweg 2, NL-2597 KL The Hague, Netherlands
PHONE: +31 (70) 3547904

JUDICIAL SYSTEM

Court of Cassation

Hoge Raad

Kazerngstraat 52, 2514 CV The Hague, Netherlands
PHONE: +31 (70) 3611311
FAX: +31 (70) 3617484

Gerechtshof

J. v. Stolverglaan 2, 2595 CL The Hague, Netherlands
PHONE: +31 (70) 3813131

Juvenile Court

Special Arbitration Court

BROADCAST MEDIA

American Forces Network

AFRTS Broadcast Center, 1363 Z Street, Bldg. 2730, March Air Reserve Base, CA 92518-2017
PHONE: (909) 4132236
E-MAIL: webadmin-afrts@dodmedia.osd.mil
WEBSITE: http://www.afrts.osd.mil
TYPE: Government

British Forces Broadcasting Service

BFBS Herford, BFPO 15 Herford, Germany
E-MAIL: Herford.Reception@bfbs.com

Canadian Forces Network-Brunssum

Slot 6041 PO Box 5053 STN Forces, Belleville, Ontario K8N 5W6
PHONE: +31 (45) 5262132
FAX: +31 (45) 5640097
E-MAIL: cfn@cobweb.nl
WEBSITE: http://www.cfsue.de/cfn
TITLE: Assistant Manager
CONTACT: Tara Chester

Classic FM

Naarderpoort 2, 1411 MA Naarden, Netherlands
PHONE: +31 (35) 6997999
FAX: +31 (35) 6997990
E-MAIL: classicfm@classicfm.nl
WEBSITE: http://www.classicfm.nl
TITLE: General Manager
CONTACT: Ton Lathouwers
TYPE: Commercial

Hitradio Veronica

Laapersveld 75, 1213 VB Hilversum, Netherlands
E-MAIL: veronicafm@veronica.nl
WEBSITE: http://www.veronica.nl
TYPE: Commercial

Jazz Radio

PO Box 74045, 1070 BA Amsterdam, Netherlands
PHONE: +31 (20) 515810
FAX: +31 (20) 515811
TYPE: Commercial

Nederlandse Omroep Stichting (NOS)

PO Box 26444, 1202 JJ Hilversum, Netherlands
PHONE: +31 (35) 6779222
FAX: +31 (35) 6772649
E-MAIL: postmaster@rtv.nos.nl

WEBSITE: http://www.omroep.nl/nos
TITLE: Director of Radio and Television
CONTACT: Ruud Bierman

NIKMedia Stichting

Wilhelmina Straat 21, 1211 RH Hilversum, Netherlands
PHONE: +31 (35) 6293145
FAX: +31 (35) 6293397
E-MAIL: info@nikmedia.nl
WEBSITE: http://www.omroep.nl/nikmedia.nl
CONTACT: Dick Houwaart

Radio 10 FM

PO Box 910, 1000 AX Amsterdam, Netherlands
PHONE: +31 (20) 5510333
FAX: +31 (20) 4200555
E-MAIL: info@radio10.nl
WEBSITE: http://www.radio10.nl
CONTACT: Robert Wayper
TYPE: Commercial

Radio 538

Koninginneweg 31, 1217 KR Hilversum, Netherlands
PHONE: +31 (35) 5385538
FAX: +31 (35) 6283538
WEBSITE: http://www.radio538.nl
TITLE: General Manager
CONTACT: Erik de Zwart
TYPE: Commercial

Radio Kerk Van Bloemendaal

PO Box 26, 2060 AA Bloemendaal, Netherlands
PHONE: +31 (23) 5250471
E-MAIL: cornetp@gironet.nl
WEBSITE: http://www.radiobloemendaal.nl
CONTACT: Piet Cornet
BROADCASTS: 12 hours/Sundays and Christian Holidays

Radio Nederland Wereldomroep (RNW; Radio Netherlands)

PO Box 222, 1200 JG Hilversum, Netherlands
PHONE: +31 (35) 6724222
FAX: +31 (35) 6794239
E-MAIL: letters@rnw.nl
WEBSITE: http://www.rnw.nl
CONTACT: Helma Brugma

Radio Noordzee Nationaal

PO Box 338, 1400 AH Bussum, Netherlands
PHONE: +31 (35) 6958440
FAX: +31 (35) 6946173
E-MAIL: info@nordzeefm.nl
WEBSITE: http://www.nordzeefm.nl
TITLE: Manager
CONTACT: J. Flink
TYPE: Commercial

Sky Radio

PO Box 1007, 1400 BA Bussum, Netherlands
PHONE: +31 (35) 6991007
FAX: +31 (35) 6991005
E-MAIL: info@skyradio.nl
WEBSITE: http://www.skyradio.nl
TITLE: General Manager
CONTACT: Ton Lathouwers
TYPE: Commercial

Radio and Televisie Voor Zuid - Holland Nord (RTV)

Van Vredenburchweg 71, Postbus 1220, 2280 CE Rijswijk, Netherlands
PHONE: +31 (70) 3078888
FAX: +31 (70) 3078444; 3078879
E-MAIL: west@rtvwest.nl
WEBSITE: http://www.rtvwest.nl
TITLE: Adjunct Director
CONTACT: J. T. de Jong

Nederlandse Programma Stichting (NPS)

PO Box 29000, 1202 MA Hilversum, Netherlands
PHONE: +31 (35) 6779333
FAX: +31 (35) 6774517
E-MAIL: publiek@nps.nl
WEBSITE: http://www.omroep.nl/nps
TITLE: Director
CONTACT: W. J. M. van Beusekom

COLLEGES AND UNIVERSITIES

University of Amsterdam

Spui 21, NL-1012 WX Amsterdam, Netherlands
PHONE: +31 (20) 5259111
E-MAIL: uva-info@bdu.uva.nl
WEBSITE: http://www.uva.nl

Vrije Universiteit Amsterdam

Faculteit Der Wijsbegeerte, Vrije Unversiteit Amsterdam, De Boelelaan 1105, NL-1081 Amsterdam, Netherlands

Hochschule der Kuenste Berlin - Hilversum

Burg Lambooylaan 17, NL-1217 Hilversum, Netherlands

Sweelinck Conservatorium

Hilversums Conservatorium, Hogeschool Voor De Kunsten, Snelliuslaan 10, NL-1222 Hilversum, Netherlands

Rijksuniversiteit Leiden

POB 9500, NL-2300 RA Leiden, Netherlands
PHONE: +31 (71) 5273200
FAX: +31 (71) 5273340
E-MAIL: intoff@bvdu.leidenuniv.nl
WEBSITE: http://www.leidenuniv.nl

Academy of Fine Arts

Prinsessegracht 4, NL-2514 The Hague, Netherlands
PHONE: +31 (70) 154777
FAX: +31 (70) 3154778
E-MAIL: post@kabk.nl
WEBSITE: http://www.euronet.nl/~kabk/beta/nederlands/

Universitaet Mozarteum Salzburg

Vivienstraat 64, NL-2582 The Hague, Netherlands

Delft University of Technology

Julianalaan 134, POB 5, NL-2600 AA Delft, Netherlands
WEBSITE: http://www.tudelft.nl

Erasmus Universiteit Rotterdam

Faculteit Geneeskunde En Gezondheid, Burgemeester Oudlaah 50, NL-3000 DR Rotterdam, Netherlands
PHONE: +31 (10) 4081111
FAX: +31 (10) 4525355
E-MAIL: zwet@icir.eur.nl
WEBSITE: http://www.eur.nl

Academy of Architecture

En Gehuisvestan, NL-3015 GG Rotterdam, Netherlands
PHONE: +31 (10) 241 4855
FAX: +31 (10) 241 4856
E-MAIL: j.g.t.m.tomassen@hro.nl
WEBSITE: http://www.misc.hro.nl

Universiteit Voor Humanistiek

Drift 6, Van Asch Van Wijckskade 28, POB 797, NL-3500 AT Utrecht, Netherlands
E-MAIL: info@uvh.nl
WEBSITE: http://www.uvh.nl

Universiteit Utrecht

POB 80125, NL-3508 TC Utrecht, Netherlands
PHONE: +31 (30) 2539111
FAX: +31 (30) 2533388
WEBSITE: http://www.ruu.nl

Katholieke Theologische University Utrecht

Heidelberglaan 2, NL-3584 CS Utrecht, Netherlands
PHONE: +31 (30) 2532149
FAX: +31 (30) 2533665
E-MAIL: bureau@ktu.nl
WEBSITE: http://www.kut.nl

Catholic University Brabant

POB 90153, NL-5000 LE Tilburg, Netherlands
PHONE: +31 (13) 4669111
FAX: +31 (13) 4663019
WEBSITE: http://www.kub.nl

Akademie Ind Vormgeving

Postbus 2125, NL-5600 CC Eindhoven, Netherlands

Eindhoven University of Technology

Den Dolech 2, POB 513, NL-5600 MB Eindhoven, Netherlands
PHONE: +31 (40) 2479111
WEBSITE: http://www.tue.nl

Universitaet zu Koeln

Kaldenkerkerweg 14, NL-5913 AE Venlo, Netherlands

Conservatorium Maastricht

Bonnefantenstraat 15, NL-6211 KL Maastricht, Netherlands
PHONE: +31 (43) 3466600
FAX: +31 (43) 3466609
WEBSITE: http://www.znhm.nl/twee-04.htm

Open Universiteit - Heerlen

PO Box 2960, NL-6401 Heerlen, Netherlands
PHONE: +31 (45) 5762222
E-MAIL: lilian.janssen-grootenboer@ou.ni
WEBSITE: http://www.ou.ni

Catholic University Nijmegen

Kievitshof, POB 9102, Comeniuslaan 4, NL-6500 BR Heumen, Netherlands
PHONE: +31 (24) 3612065
FAX: +31 (24) 3612757
E-MAIL: int.relations@dcm.kun.nl
WEBSITE: http://www.kun.nl

Johann Wolfgang Goethe Universitaet

Rechterslaan5, NL-6564 BC Heilig Landstichting, Netherlands

Landbouwuniversiteit Wageningen

Postbus 9101, NL-6700 HB Wageningen, Netherlands
PHONE: +31 (317) 484472
FAX: +31 (317) 484884
E-MAIL: info@wag-ur.nl
WEBSITE: http://www.wau.nl

Fachhochschule Dusseldorf - Arnhem

Prumelaan 21, NL-6284 HP Arnhem, Netherlands

Larenstein International

Postbus 9001, NL-6880 GB Velp, Netherlands
PHONE: +31 (26) 3695733
FAX: +31 (26) 3615287
E-MAIL: info@larenstein.nl
WEBSITE: http://www.larenstein.nl

Universiteit Twente

POB 217, NL-7500 AE Enschede, Netherlands
PHONE: +31 (53) 4895600
FAX: +31 (53) 4895610
E-MAIL: intoffice@disc.utwente.nl
WEBSITE: http://www.utwente.nl

Theologische Universiteit

U L C O De Vriesweg 29, NL-8084 AR T-Harde, Netherlands

Rijksuniversiteit Groningen

Broerstraats, POB 72, NL-9700 AB Groningen, Netherlands
PHONE: +31 (50) 3639111
FAX: +31 (50) 3637100
WEBSITE: http://www.rug.nl

NEWSPAPERS AND MAGAZINES

Algemeen Dagblad

PCM Landelijke Dagbladen, Postbus 8985, 3009 TE Rotterdam, the Netherlands
PHONE: +31 (10) 4066286
FAX: +31 (10) 4066958
TITLE: Editor
CONTACT: P. van Dijk
CIRCULATION: 396,900

Amersfoortse Courant

Wgener Uitgeverij Midden Nederland B.V., Postbus 5, 3990 DM Houten, the Netherlands
PHONE: +31 (30) 6399298
FAX: +31 (30) 6399460
WEBSITE: http://www.amersfoortsecourant.nl
TITLE: Editor-in-Chief
CONTACT: J.J. Lodewijks
CIRCULATION: 34,200

Brabants Dagblad

Brabant Pers B.V., Postbus 235, 5201 HB s'-Hertogenbosch, the Netherlands
PHONE: +31 (73) 6157111
FAX: +31 (73) 6137750
WEBSITE: http://www.brabantsdagblad.nl
CIRCULATION: 52,073

De Gelderlander

De Gelderlander B.V., Postbus 36, 6500 DA Nijmegen, the Netherlands
PHONE: +31 (24) 3650611
FAX: +31 (24) 3650639
WEBSITE: http://www.gelderlander.nl
CIRCULATION: 179,500

Eindhovens Dagblad

Brabant Pers B.V., Postbus 235, 5201 HB s'-Hertogenbosch, the Netherlands
PHONE: +31 (73) 6157111
FAX: +31 (73) 6137750
WEBSITE: http://www.eindhobensdagblad.nl
TITLE: Editor
CONTACT: C.J.J.M. van Houtert
CIRCULATION: 94,549

Het Financieele Dagblad

Het Financieele Dagblad B.V., Postbus 216, 1000 AE Amsterdam, the Netherlands
PHONE: +31 (20) 5928610
FAX: +31 (20) 5928600

E-MAIL: metselaar@hfd.nl
WEBSITE: http://www.hfd.nl
TITLE: Editor
CONTACT: A. Bakker
CIRCULATION: 50,129

Haagsche Courant/Dagblad het Binnenhoff

Stijhoff Pers B.V., Postbus 16050, 2500 AA The Hague, the Netherlands
PHONE: +31 (70) 3190911
FAX: +31 (70) 3906447
TITLE: Editor
CONTACT: G. Schinkelshoek
CIRCULATION: 146,300

Leeuwarder Courant/Friese Koerier

Friese Pers B.V., Postbus 394, 8901 BD Leeuwarden, the Netherlands
PHONE: +31 (58) 2845845
FAX: +31 (58) 2845509
TITLE: Editors
CONTACT: R. Mulder, P. Sijpersma, S.J. v.d. Meulen
CIRCULATION: 111,456

Nieuwsblad van het Noorden/Groninger Dagblad/De Drentse Courant

Hazewinkel Pers B.V., Postbus 60, 9700 MC Groningen, the Netherlands
PHONE: +31 (50) 5844444
FAX: +31 (50) 5844408
TITLE: Editors
CONTACT: J. de Roos, H. v.d. Velde
CIRCULATION: 192,558

Noordhollands Dagblad

Alkmaarsche edition, Ver. Noordhollandse Dagbladen B.V., Postbus 2, 1800 AA Alkmaar, the Netherlands
PHONE: +31 (72) 5196196
FAX: +31 (72) 5113295
E-MAIL: redactie@nhd.hdc.nl
WEBSITE: http://www.nhd.hdc.nl
CIRCULATION: 41,374

Noordhollands Dagblad

West Friesland edition, Ver. Noordhollandse Dagbladen B.V., Postbus 2, 1800 AA Alkmaar, the Netherlands
PHONE: +31 (72) 5196196
FAX: +31 (72) 5113295
E-MAIL: redactie@nhd.hdc.nl
WEBSITE: http://www.nhd.hdc.nl
CIRCULATION: 22,922

NRC Handelsblad

PCM Landelijke Dagbladen, Postbus 8985, 3009 TE Rotterdam, the Netherlands
PHONE: +31 (10) 4066286
FAX: +31 (10) 4066958
E-MAIL: nrc@nrc.nl
WEBSITE: http://www.nrc.nl
TITLE: Editor
CONTACT: F. Jensma
CIRCULATION: 269,667

Het Parool

Het Parool B.V., Postbus 433, 1000 AK Amsterdam, the Netherlands
PHONE: +31 (20) 5629333
FAX: +31 (20) 5622822
E-MAIL: klantenservice@perscom.nl
WEBSITE: http://www.parool.nl
TITLE: Editors
CONTACT: F. Campagne, M. v. Nieuwkerk
CIRCULATION: 90,040

Provinciale Zeeuwse Courant

Provinciale Zeeuwse Courant B.V., Postbus 18, 4380 AA Vlissingen, the Netherlands
PHONE: +31 (118) 484000
FAX: +31 (118) 470100
E-MAIL: pzcredcity1@pzc.nl
WEBSITE: http://www.pzc.nl
TITLE: Editor-in-Chief
CONTACT: A. Oosthoek
CIRCULATION: 61,990

Rotterdams Dagblad

Postbus 1162, 3000 BD Rotterdam, the Netherlands
PHONE: +31 (10) 4004397
FAX: +31 (10) 4128449
E-MAIL: digitaal@luna.nl
WEBSITE: http://www.rotterdamsdagblad.nl
TITLE: Editors
CONTACT: L. Pronk, J. Prins
CIRCULATION: 104,200

De Stem

Uitgeversmij. Zuidwest-Nederland B.V., Postbus 3229, 4800 MB Breda, the Netherlands
PHONE: +31 (76) 5312311
FAX: +31 (76) 5312310
WEBSITE: http://www.dse.nl/stem

TITLE: Editor-in-Chief
CONTACT: B. Rogmans
CIRCULATION: 47,000

De Telegraaf

B.V. Dagblad de Telegraaf, PO Box 376, 1000 EB Amsterdam, the Netherlands
PHONE: +31 (20) 5852206
FAX: +31 (20) 5852435
E-MAIL: redactie@telegraaf.nl
WEBSITE: http://www.telegraaf.nl
TITLE: Editors
CONTACT: J. Olde Kalter, E. Bos
CIRCULATION: 807,500

Trouw

PCM Landelyke Dagbladen, Postbus 859, 1000 AW Amsterdam, the Netherlands
PHONE: +31 (20) 5629444
FAX: +31 (20) 6680389
E-MAIL: klantenservice@perscom.nl
TITLE: Editors
CONTACT: F. van Exter, J. de Berg
CIRCULATION: 112,422

Utretchts Nieuwsblad

Wegener Uitgeverij Midden Nederland, Postbus 500, 3990 DM Houten, the Netherlands
PHONE: +31 (30) 6399210
FAX: +31 (30) 6399460
WEBSITE: http://www.utrechtsnieuwsblad.nl
TITLE: Editor-in-Chief
CONTACT: R. van Zanten
CIRCULATION: 90,400

De Volkskrant

Postbus 1002, 1000 BA Amsterdam, the Netherlands
PHONE: +31 (20) 5629222
FAX: +31 (20) 5626289
WEBSITE: http://www.volkskrant.nl
TITLE: Editor
CONTACT: P.J. Broertjes
CIRCULATION: 350,850

Zwolse Courant

Wegener Uitgeverij Gelderland-Overijssel B.V., Postbus 67, 8000 AB Zwolle, the Netherlands
PHONE: +31 (38) 4275275
FAX: +31 (38) 4222062
TITLE: Editor-in-Chief
CONTACT: J. Bartelds
CIRCULATION: 54,390

PUBLISHERS

Babel

Amsteldijk 44, P.O. Box 75577, 1070 AN Amsterdam, the Netherlands
FAX: +31 (20) 6792956
WEBSITE: http://www.benjamins.nl
TITLE: Editor
CONTACT: Rene Haeseryn
TYPE: Language arts, linguistics, literary criticism and collections

Cahier Vincent

Postbus 1129, 8001 BC Zwolle, the Netherlands
FAX: +31 (38) 4655989
TYPE: Art, general

Data-Info

Postbus 1310, 6501 BH Nijmegen, the Netherlands
FAX: +31 (24) 3603176
E-MAIL: redactie@marketons.nl
WEBSITE: http://www.marketons.nl
TITLE: Editor
CONTACT: Willem J. Veldkamp
CIRCULATION: 1,500
TYPE: Computers, general

Fancy

Postbus 1, 2000 MA Haarlem, the Netherlands
TITLE: Editor
CONTACT: Riek Tawfik
CIRCULATION: 115,869
TYPE: Juvenile fiction and non-fiction, music, general

Ekoland

Postbus 16, 3740 AA Baarn, the Netherlands
FAX: +31 (35) 5424119
E-MAIL: uvw@hacom.nl
TITLE: Editor
CONTACT: Harry te Walvaart
CIRCULATION: 4,150
TYPE: Agriculture, animal husbandry, environmental science

Habinjan 1183 HM Amstelveen, the Netherlands

Straat van Messina 27
TITLE: Editor
CONTACT: J.B. Sondervan
CIRCULATION: 4,000

TYPE: Religion, Judaism, social sciences, ethnic studies, general

Haven Amsterdam

Het Havengebouw, 13e etage, De Ruyterkade 7, 1013 AA Amsterdam, the Netherlands
TITLE: Editor
CONTACT: Karl O. Kolb
TYPE: Transportation, ships and shipbuilding

Herademing

Postbus 5108, 8260 GA Kampen, the Netherlands
FAX: +31 (38) 3327331
TYPE: Religion, general

Judo

Blokhoeve 5, 3438 LC Nieuwegein, the Netherlands
FAX: +31 (23) 342721
TITLE: Editor
CONTACT: Robert van der Geest
CIRCULATION: 60,000
TYPE: Sports and recreation, general

NG Magazine

Postbus Box 30435, 2500 GK The Hague, the Netherlands
FAX: +31 (70) 3469201
CIRCULATION: 29,000
TYPE: Political science, state and local government

Neerlandia

J. van Nassaustraat 109, 2596 BS The Hague, the Netherlands
FAX: +31 (70) 3246186
TITLE: Editor
CONTACT: Guido Logie
CIRCULATION: 3,000
TYPE: Political science, language arts, general

Neerslag

Postbus 70, 2280 AB Rijswijk, the Netherlands
FAX: +31 (70) 4144420
E-MAIL: nva@vewin.nl
WEBSITE: http://www.nva.net
TITLE: Editor
CONTACT: R. van Dalen
CIRCULATION: 1,900
TYPE: Nature, technology, environmental engineering

Schaaknieuws

Visserstraat 16B, 5612 BT Eindhoven, the Netherlands
FAX: +31 (40) 2439355
TITLE: Editor
CONTACT: Johan van Mil
CIRCULATION: 2,300
TYPE: Sports and recreation, general

Schaap

Postbus 4, 7000 BA Doetinchem, the Netherlands
FAX: +31 (314) 363638
TITLE: Editor
CONTACT: Wim Wisman
CIRCULATION: 9,980
TYPE: Technology, agriculture and animal husbandry

Varkens

Postbus 43, 6640 AA Beuningen, the Netherlands
FAX: +31 (24) 6779800
WEBSITE: nvs@euroneb.nl
TITLE: Editor
CONTACT: Bianca Domhof
CIRCULATION: 17,550
TYPE: Technology, agriculture and animal husbandry

Uitgeverij Ambo BV

Herengracht 435-437, 1017 BR, Amsterdam, Netherlands
PHONE: +31 (20) 5245411
FAX: +31 (20) 4200422
TITLE: Publisher
CONTACT: Eva Cossee
SUBJECTS: History, Literature, Literary Criticism, Essays, Philosophy, Psychology, Psychiatry, Religion-Other, Social Sciences, Sociology

Brill Academic Publishers

PO Box 9000, 2300 PA, Leiden, Netherlands
PHONE: +31 (71) 5353500
FAX: +31 (71) 5317532
E-MAIL: cs@brill.nl
WEBSITE: http://www.brill.nl
TITLE: Managing Director
CONTACT: R.J. Kasteleijn
SUBJECTS: Asian Studies, Biological Sciences, History, Religion-Islamic, Religion-Other
TOTAL PUBLISHED: 250 new titles per year

A.W. Bruna Uitgevers BV

Kobaltweg 23-35, Postbus 40203, 3504 AA, Utrecht, Netherlands
PHONE: +31 (30) 2470411
FAX: +31 (30) 2410018
E-MAIL: a.w.bruna@awbruna.nl
WEBSITE: http://www.awbruna.nl
TITLE: Director
CONTACT: Marian van der Beek
SUBJECTS: Computer Science, Fiction, History, Nonfiction (General), Philosophy, Psychology, Psychiatry, Science (General), Social Sciences, Sociology

Uitgeverij Ad Donker BV

Koningin Emmaplein 1, 3016 AA, Rotterdam, Netherlands
PHONE: +31 (10)4363009
FAX: +31 (10) 4362963
E-MAIL: donker@bart.nl
WEBSITE: http://users.bart.nl/~donker/home.html
TITLE: Director
CONTACT: William A. Donker
SUBJECTS: Biography, Education, Fiction, History, Psychology, Psychiatry, Social Sciences, Sociology
TOTAL PUBLISHED: 150 print

Elsevier Science BV

Sara Burgerhartstr 25, 1055 KV, Amsterdam, Netherlands
PHONE: +31 (20) 4852911
FAX: +31 (20) 4852457
E-MAIL: nlinfo-f@elsevier.nl
WEBSITE: http://www.elsevier.nl
TITLE: Chairman and CEO
CONTACT: H.P. Spruijt
SUBJECTS: Biological Sciences, Chemistry, Chemical Engineering, Computer Science, Earth Sciences, Economics, Engineering (General), Mathematics, Medicine, Nursing, Dentistry, Physics, Science (General), Technology

IOS Press BV

Nieuwe Hemweg 6B, 1013 BG, Amsterdam, Netherlands
PHONE: +31 (20) 6883355
FAX: +31 (20) 6203419
E-MAIL: market@iospress.nl
WEBSITE: http://www.iospress.nl
TITLE: Promotion Manager
CONTACT: Marcella Janmaat
SUBJECTS: Biological Sciences, Chemistry, Chemical Engineering, Computer Science, Electronics, Electrical Engineering, Environmental Studies, Health, Nutrition, Language Arts, Linguistics, Management, Mathematics, Mechanical Engineering, Medicine, Nursing, Dentistry, Physics, Technology
TOTAL PUBLISHED: 600 book titles, 55 journals

KITLV Royal Institute of Linguistics and Anthropology

Reuvensplaats 2, 2311 BE, Leiden, Netherlands
PHONE: +31 (71) 5272295
FAX: +31 (71) 5272638
E-MAIL: KITLV@kitlv.nl
WEBSITE: http://www.iias.nl/institutes/kitlv
TITLE: Director
CONTACT: G.J. Oostindie
SUBJECTS: Anthropology, Asian Studies, Economics, Environmental Studies, History, Language Arts, Linguistics, Social Sciences, Sociology, Women's Studies
TOTAL PUBLISHED: 250 print

John Benjamins BV

Postbus 75577, 1070 AN, Amsterdam, Netherlands
PHONE: +31 (20) 6762325
FAX: +31 (20) 6739773
E-MAIL: customer.services@benjamins.nl
WEBSITE: http://www.benjamins.nl
TITLE: Managing Director
CONTACT: Seline Benjamins
SUBJECTS: Art History, Linguistics, Literature, Literary Criticism, Essays, Philosophy, Psychology, Psychiatry, Social Sciences, Sociology, Applied Linguistics, Pragmatics, Translation, Cognition
TOTAL PUBLISHED: 1,300 print

Kluwer Academic Publishers

Postbus 17, 3300 AA, Dordrect, Netherlands
PHONE: +31 (78) 6392392
FAX: +31 (78) 6392254
E-MAIL: services@wkap.nl
WEBSITE: http://www.wkap.nl
TITLE: President
CONTACT: Jay Lippincot
SUBJECTS: Behavioral Sciences, Law, Medicine, Nursing, Dentistry, Science (General), Social Sciences, Sociology, Technology

Koninklijk Institut Voor de Tropen (Royal Tropical Institute)

Postbus 95001, 1090 HA, Amsterdam, Netherlands
PHONE: +31 (20) 5688711
FAX: +31 (20) 6684579
E-MAIL: pr@kit.nl
WEBSITE: http://www.kit.nl
TITLE: Managing Director
CONTACT: R. Smit
SUBJECTS: Agriculture, Anthropology, Developing Countries, Environmental Studies, Health, Nutrition, Women's Studies, International Development Corporation
TOTAL PUBLISHED: 190 print

Uitgeverij Lemma BV

Newtonlaan 57, 3584 BP, Utrecht, Netherlands
PHONE: +31 (30) 2545652
FAX: +31 (30) 2512496
E-MAIL: infodesk@lemma.nl
WEBSITE: http://www.lemma.nl
TITLE: Publisher
CONTACT: Anja Heida
SUBJECTS: Business, Communications, Economics, Education, Health, Nutrition, Labor, Industrial Relations, Law, Management, Marketing, Physical Sciences, Psychology, Psychiatry, Social Sciences, Sociology, Technology
TOTAL PUBLISHED: 230 print

Lemniscaat

Vijverlaan 48, 3062 HL, Rotterdam, Netherlands
PHONE: +31 (10) 2062929
FAX: +31 (10) 4141560
E-MAIL: info@lemniscaat.nl
WEBSITE: http://www.lemniscaat.nl
CONTACT: F.M. van den Hoek
SUBJECTS: Psychology, Psychiatry, Social Sciences, Sociology
TOTAL PUBLISHED: 380 print

J M Meulenhoff BV

Herengracht 505, 1017 BV, Amsterdam, Netherlands
PHONE: +31 (20) 5533500
FAX: +31 (20) 6258511
E-MAIL: j.m.meulenhoff@meulenhoff.nl
WEBSITE: http://www.meulenhoff.nl
TITLE: Managing Director
CONTACT: Chantal d'Aulnis
SUBJECTS: Fiction, Literature, Literary Criticism, Essays, Nonfiction (General)
TOTAL PUBLISHED: 1,000 print

Prometheus/Bert Bakker BV

Herengracht 406, 1017 BX, Amsterdam, Netherlands
PHONE: +31 (20) 6241934
FAX: +31 (20) 6225461
E-MAIL: pbo@pbo.nl
WEBSITE: http://www.pbo.nl
TITLE: Publisher/Director
CONTACT: Plien van Albada
SUBJECTS: History, Psychology, Psychiatry, Science (General), Social Sciences, Sociology, Fiction (General)
TOTAL PUBLISHED: 300 print per year

Rodopi

Tijnmuiden 7, 1046 AK, Amsterdam, Netherlands
PHONE: +31 (20) 6114821
FAX: +31 (20) 4472979
E-MAIL: orders-queries@rodopi.nl
WEBSITE: http://www.rodopi.nl
TITLE: Managing Director
CONTACT: Fred van der Zee
SUBJECTS: Antiques, History, Literature, Literary Criticism, Essays, Philosophy, Religion-Other
TOTAL PUBLISHED: 2,200 print

Uitgeverij Het Spectrum BV

Postbus 2073, 3500 GB, Utrecht, Netherlands
PHONE: +31 (20) 2650650
FAX: +31 (20) 2620850
E-MAIL: het@spectrum.nl
WEBSITE: http://www.boeknet.nl/spectrum
TITLE: Director
CONTACT: Joost C. Bloemsma
SUBJECTS: Astrology, Occult, Computer Science, Criminology, Environmental Studies, History, Literature, Literary Criticism, Essays, Management, Mysteries, Nonfiction (General), Science Fiction, Fantasy, Travel
TOTAL PUBLISHED: 800 print; 100 CD-ROM

Unieboek BV

Postbus 97, 3995 DB, Houten, Netherlands
PHONE: +31 (30) 6377660
FAX: +31 (30) 6377600
E-MAIL: info@unieboek.nl
WEBSITE: http://www.unieboek.nl
TITLE: Director

CONTACT: A.C. Akveld
SUBJECTS: Archaeology, Architecture and Interior Design, Cookery, Fiction, Government, Political Science, History, Literature, Literary Criticism, Essays, Nonfiction (General)

Van Gorcum and Comp BV

Postbus 43, 9400 AA, Assen, Netherlands
PHONE: +31 (59) 2379555
FAX: +31 (59) 2379552
E-MAIL: assen@vgorcum.nl
WEBSITE: http://www.vgorcum.nl
TITLE: Managing Director
CONTACT: L. Dykema
SUBJECTS: Anthropology, Economics, Education, Geography, Geology, History, Language Arts, Linguistics, Law, Literature, Literary Criticism, Essays, Medicine, Nursing, Dentistry, Philosophy, Psychology, Psychiatry, Religion-Other, Social Sciences, Sociology
TOTAL PUBLISHED: 125 University level text books annually

RELIGIOUS ORGANIZATIONS

Atheist

The Dutch Freethinking Association

De Vrije Gedachte
The Dutch Freethinkers Association, Vrijdenkersvereniging 'De Vrije Gedachte', Postbus 1087, 3000 BB Rotterdam, The Netherlands
PHONE: +31 (72) 5158264
FAX: +31 (10) 4250134
E-MAIL: DVG@netcetera.netcetera.nl
WEBSITE: http://www.xs4all.nl/~robbsch/

Buddhist

Buddhayana Centre Netherlands
Ehipassiko Buddhist Monastery, Veneburen 23, 8423 VH Makkinga, Netherlands
PHONE: +31 (51) 6441848
FAX: +31 (51) 6441419
E-MAIL: ehipassiko@buddhayana.nl
WEBSITE: http://www.buddhayana.nl/index2.html

The European Zen Center
Kerkstraat 408, Amsterdam, 1017 JC, Netherlands
PHONE: +31 (20) 6258884
E-MAIL: gruau@cwi.nl
TITLE: Teacher
NAME: Kosen Thibaut

The International Zen Institute
Merelstraat 176, Leiderdorp, 2352 VH, Netherlands
TITLE: Teacher
NAME: Gesshin Prabhasa Dharma

Catholic

Brothers of Our Lady, Mother of Mercy

Fraters van O.L. Vrouw, Moeder van Barmhartigheid
Gasthuisring 54, NL-5041 DT Tilburg, Netherlands
PHONE: +31 (13) 5432777
FAX: +31 (13) 5441405
E-MAIL: gb.cmm@inter.nl.net
WEBSITE: http://www.inter.nl.net/users/gbcmm
TITLE: Superior General
NAME: H. van Geene

Brothers of the Immaculate Conception of the Blessed Virgin Mary

Broeders can de Onbevlekte Ontvangenis der Heilige Maagd Maria
c/o Mr. W. Bastiaens, Brusselsestraat 38, NL-6211 PG Maastricht, Netherlands
PHONE: +31 (43) 3212114
FAX: +31 (43) 3218046
E-MAIL: gencouncil@brothers-fic.org
WEBSITE: http://www.brothers-fic.org
TITLE: Executive Secretary
NAME: W. Bastiaens

Brothers of the Immaculate Conceptions of the Mother of God (BICMG)

Congregatie Broeders van Huybergen (CFH)
c/o Brother Eduard Quint, Boomstraat 7, NL-4635 CX Huijbergen, Netherlands
PHONE: +31 (1644) 2750
FAX: +31 (1644) 2470
TITLE: Superior General
NAME: Bro. Eduard Quint

International Commission of Catholic Prison Pastoral Care (ICCPPC)

Commission Internationale des Aumoniers Generaux des Prisons (CIAGP)
c/o Rev. G. W. M. de Wit, Sperwerlaan 3, NL-3738 EH Maartensdijk, Netherlands
PHONE: +31 (346) 214220
FAX: +31 (346) 214128
E-MAIL: iccpc@pi.net
TITLE: President
NAME: Rev. L.T. Kosatka

Sisters of Charity of Saint Charles Borromeo (SCSCB)

Liefdezusters van de H. Carolus Borromeus (LCB)
Onder de Bogen, St. Servaasklooster 14, Postbus 206, NL-6200 AE Maastricht, Netherlands
PHONE: +31 (43) 3219241
FAX: +31 (43) 257262
TITLE: Superior General
NAME: Sr. Louisie Satini

Society of Jesus, Mary, and Joseph

Societe de Jesus, Marie, et Joseph
Jagerboschlaan 17, NL-5262 LS Vught, Netherlands
PHONE: +31 (73) 6561721
FAX: +31 (73) 6570249
TITLE: Superior General
NAME: Sr. Benedict Melchers, JMJ

Islamic

International Sufi Movement

Mouvement Soufi International
Banstraat 24, NL-2517 GJ The Hague, Netherlands
PHONE: +31 (70) 3461476
FAX: +31 (70) 3461476
E-MAIL: h.inayat.khan@inter.nl.net
WEBSITE: http://guess.worldweb.net/sufi/movement.html
TITLE: Vice President
NAME: Dr. H. J. Witteveen

Jewish

Liberal Jewish Union

Liberaal Joodse Gemeente
Jacob Soetendorpstraat 8, 1079 RM Amsterdam, Netherlands
PHONE: +31 (20) 6442619
E-MAIL: ljgadam@xs4all.nl
WEBSITE: http://www.xs4all.nl/~ljg
NAME: Rabbi David Lillienthal, Rabbi Mennoten Brink

Pagan

Pagan Federation International
PO Box 473, 3700 AL Zeist, The Netherlands
TITLE: National Coordinator
NAME: Lady Bara

Protestant

International Christian Esperanto Association (ICEA)

Kristana Esperantista Ligo Internacia (KELI)
Koningsmantel 4, NL-2403 HZ Alphen aan den Rijn, Netherlands
PHONE: +31 (172) 420222
NAME: Mrs. E. Van Dyk-Kuperus

The Salvation Army
Spoordreef 10, 1315 GP Almere, Netherlands
PHONE: +31 (36) 5398111
FAX: +31 (36) 5332892
WEBSITE: http://www.legerdesheils.nl/

Other Organizations

International Organization for the Study of The Old Testament (IOSOT)

Organisation Internationale pour l'Etude de l'Ancien Testament
c/o Prof. A. van der Kooij, Facilteit der Godgeleerheid, Postbus 9515, NL-2300 RA Leiden, Netherlands
PHONE: +31 (71) 5272577
FAX: +31 (71) 5272571
TITLE: General Secretary
NAME: Prof. A. van der Kooij

FURTHER READING

Articles

"Dutch Producer Prices Rose Sharply." *Wall Street Journal,* May 2, 2000, p. A18.

"Dutch Will Pay Jews for Nazi-Era Losses." *New York Times,* October 4, 2000, p. A13.

Muschamp, Herbert. "Winner Is . . . the Prize and the Architect." *New York Times,* April 17, 2000, p. B1.

Books

Vuijsje, Herman. *The Politically Correct Netherlands: Since the 1960s.* Westport, CT: Greenwood Press, 2000.

NETHERLANDS: STATISTICAL DATA

For sources and notes see "Sources of Statistics" at the front of each volume.

GEOGRAPHY

Geography

Area:

Total: 41,532 sq km.

Land: 33,889 sq km.

Land boundaries:

Total: 1,027 km.

Border countries: Belgium 450 km, Germany 577 km.

Coastline: 451 km.

Climate: temperate; marine; cool summers and mild winters.

Terrain: mostly coastal lowland and reclaimed land (polders); some hills in southeast.

Natural resources: natural gas, petroleum, arable land.

Land use:

Arable land: 25%

Permanent crops: 3%

Permanent pastures: 25%

Forests and woodland: 8%

Other: 39% (1996 est.).

HUMAN FACTORS

Demographics (A)

	1990	1995	1998	2000	2010	2020	2030	2040	2050
Population	14,952	15,459	15,705	15,892	16,617	17,085	17,327	17,153	16,721
Life expectancy - males	73.9	74.6	75.3	75.4	76.9	78.1	79.0	79.8	80.4
Life expectancy - females	80.2	80.5	80.8	81.3	82.8	84.1	85.0	85.8	86.4
Birth rate (per 1,000)	13.2	12.3	12.6	12.1	10.1	10.2	9.9	9.3	9.5
Death rate (per 1,000)	8.6	8.8	8.8	8.7	8.9	9.8	11.3	12.8	13.7
Women of reproductive age (15-49 yrs.)	3,967	4,026	3,961	3,935	3,858	3,630	3,510	3,441	3,287
Fertility rate	1.6	1.5	1.6	1.6	1.6	1.7	1.7	1.7	1.7

Except as noted, values for vital statistics are in thousands; life expectancy is in years.

Health Personnel

	National Data	World Data (wtd ave)
Total health expenditure as a percentage of GDP, 1990-1998[a]		
Public sector	6.1	2.5
Private sector	2.3	2.9
Total[b]	8.5	5.5
Health expenditure per capita in U.S. dollars, 1990-1998[a]		
Purchasing power parity	1,874	561
Total	1,988	483
Availability of health care facilities per 100,000 people		
Hospital beds 1990-1998[a]	1,130	330
Doctors 1992-1995[a]	NA	122
Nurses 1992-1995[a]	NA	248

Health Indicators

	National Data	World Data
Life expectancy at birth (years)		
1980	76	61
1998	78	67
Daily per capita supply of calories		
1970	3,024	2,358
1997	3,284	2,791
Daily per capital supply of protein		
1997 (grams)	106	74
Total fertility rate (births per woman)		
1980	1.6	3.7
1998	1.6	2.7
People living with (1997)		
Tuberculosis (cases per 100,000)	9.5	60.4
HIV/AIDS (% aged 15 - 49 years)	0.17	0.99

Infants and Malnutrition

	National Data	World Data (wtd ave)
Under 5 mortality rate (1989)	5	NA
% of infants with low birthweight (1992-98)[1]	4	17
Births attended by skilled health staff (% of total births 1996-98)	100	52
% fully immunized at 1 year of age (1995-98)[1]		
TB	NA	82
DPT	97	77
Polio	97	77
Measles	96	74
Prevalence of child malnutrition (1992-98)[1] (based on weight for age, % of children under 5 years)	NA	30

Ethnic Division

Dutch 91%

Moroccans, Turks, and other 9%

Data for 1999 est.

Religion

Roman Catholic 34%

Protestant 25%

Muslim 3%

Other 2%

Unaffiliated 36%

Data for 1991.

Major Languages

Dutch.

EDUCATION

Public Education Expenditures

	1980	1997
Public expenditures on education as % of GNP	7.7	5.1
Expenditures per student as % of GNP per capita		
Primary	13.8	NA
Secondary	23.3	21.2
Tertiary	73.3	47.3
Teachers' compensation as % of total current education expenditures	70.8	NA
Pupils per teacher at the primary level	NA	NA
Duration of primary education in years	NA	13
World data for comparison		
Public expenditures on education as % of GNP (mean)	3.9	4.8
Pupils per teacher at the primary level (wtd ave)	NA	33
Duration of primary education in years (mean)	NA	9

Educational Attainment (B)

	1995	1997
Gross enrollment ratio (%)		
Primary level	107.4	107.8
Secondary level	137.4	131.5
Tertiary level	48.6	47.0

Libraries

National Libraries **1997**
Administrative Units 1
Service Points or Branches 4
Number of Volumes (000) 2,505
Registered Users (000) 360
Loans to Users (000) 175
Total Library Staff 215
Public Libraries **1997**
Administrative Units 579
Service Points or Branches 1,130
Number of Volumes (000) 41,489
Registered Users (000) 69,797
Loans to Users (000) 158,286
Total Library Staff 8,408

GOVERNMENT & LAW

Military Affairs (A)

	1990	1992	1995	1996	1997
Military expenditures					
Current dollars (mil.)	6,800	7,040	6,570	6,780	6,840
1997 constant dollars (mil.)	7,960	7,800	6,810	6,890	6,840
Armed forces (000)	104	90	67	64	57
Gross national product (GNP)					
Current dollars (bil.)	259	285	327	346	363
1997 constant dollars (bil.)	304	316	338	352	363
Central government expenditures (CGE)					
1997 constant dollars (bil.)	110	113	121	103	107
People (mil.)	15.0	15.2	15.5	15.6	15.6
Military expenditure as % of GNP	2.6	2.5	2.0	2.0	1.9
World data on military expenditure as % of GNP	4.5	3.4	2.7	2.6	2.6
Military expenditure as % of CGE	7.3	6.9	5.6	6.7	6.4
World data on military expenditure as % of CGE	17.0	12.5	10.5	10.3	10.2
Military expenditure per capita (1997 $)	533	514	440	443	437
World data on military expenditure per capita (1997 $)	242	173	146	143	145
Armed forces per 1,000 people (soldiers)	7.0	5.9	4.3	4.1	3.6
World data on armed forces per 1,000 people (soldiers)	5.3	4.5	4.1	3.9	3.8
GNP per capita (1997 $)	20,300	20,900	21,900	22,600	23,200
Arms imports[6]					
Current dollars (mil.)	850	525	410	675	460
1997 constant dollars (mil.)	995	582	425	686	460
Arms exports[6]					
Current dollars (mil.)	200	180	340	360	500
1997 constant dollars (mil.)	234	200	352	366	500
Total imports[7]					
Current dollars (bil.)	126	135	177	181	178
1997 constant dollars (bil.)	148	149	183	184	178
Total exports[7]					
Current dollars (bil.)	132	140	196	197	195
1997 constant dollars (bil.)	154	156	203	201	195
Arms as percent of total imports[8]	0.7	0.4	0.2	0.4	0.3
Arms as percent of total exports[8]	0.2	0.1	0.2	0.2	0.3

(Continued on next page.)

Political Parties

States General (Staten Generaal)	% of vote	no. of seats
First Chamber		
Christian Democratic Appeal (CDA)	NA	20
People's Party for Freedom and Democracy (VVD)	NA	19
Labor Party (PvdA)	NA	15
Democrats '66 (D'66)	NA	4
Other	NA	17
Second Chamber		
Labor Party (PvdA)	30.0%	45
People's Party for Freedom and Democracy (VVD)	25.3%	38
Christian Democratic Appeal (CDA)	19.3%	29
Democrats '66 (D'66)	9.3%	14
Other	16.1%	24

Elections for the First Chamber were last held 25 May 1999 (next to be held in May 2003); Second Chamber elections were last held 6 May 1998 (next to be held May 2002). NA stands for not available.

Government Budgets (A)

Year: 1997

Total Expenditures: 337.62 Billions of Guilders

Expenditures as a percentage of the total by function:

General public services and public order	9.26
Defense	3.86
Education	9.97
Health	14.79
Social Security and Welfare	37.38
Housing and community amenities	1.50
Recreational, cultural, and religious affairs	0.34
Fuel and energy	0.16
Agriculture, forestry, fishing, and hunting	0.99
Mining, manufacturing, and construction	0.32
Transportation and communication	3.47
Other economic affairs and services	1.18

Crime

Crime volume (for 1998)

Crimes reported	1,222,226
Total persons convicted	195,556
Crimes per 100,000 population	7,808

Persons responsible for offenses

Total number suspects	266,853
Total number of female suspects	26,685
Total number of juvenile suspects	45,365

LABOR FORCE

Total Labor Force (A)

7 million (1998 est.).

Labor Force by Occupation

Services	73%
Industry	23%
Agriculture	4%

Data for 1998 est.

Unemployment Rate

3.5% but generous welfare benefits have prompted large numbers to drop out of the labor market (1999 est.).

PRODUCTION SECTOR

Energy Production

Production	88.736 billion kWh
Production by source	
Fossil fuel	91.32%
Hydro	0.11%
Nuclear	4.08%
Other	4.49%
Exports	400 million kWh

Data for 1998.

Energy Consumption

Consumption	94.325 billion kWh
Imports	12.200 billion kWh

Data for 1998.

Transportation

Highways:

Total: 125,575 km.

Transportation

Paved: 113,018 km (including 2,235 km of expressways).

Unpaved: 12,557 km (1998 est.).

Waterways: 5,046 km, of which 47% is usable by craft of 1,000 metric ton capacity or larger.

Pipelines: crude oil 418 km; petroleum products 965 km; natural gas 10,230 km.

Merchant marine:

Total: 563 ships (1,000 GRT or over) totaling 4,035,899 GRT/4,576,841 DWT.

Ships by type: bulk 3, cargo 343, chemical tanker 41, combination bulk 2, container 56, liquified gas 20, livestock carrier 1, multi-functional large load carrier 8, passenger 8, petroleum tanker 25, refrigerated cargo 32, roll-on/roll-off 16, short-sea passenger 3, specialized tanker 5 (1999 est.)

Note: many Dutch-owned ships are also operating under the registry of Netherlands Antilles (1998 est.).

Airports: 28 (1999 est.).

Airports - with paved runways: 19.

Top Agriculture Products

Grains, potatoes, sugar beets, fruits, vegetables; livestock.

MANUFACTURING SECTOR

GDP & Manufacturing Summary (A)

	1980	1985	1990	1995
GDP ($-1990 mil.)[1]	228,472	243,292	283,525	311,472
Per capita ($-1990)[1]	16,153	16,788	18,962	20,118
Manufacturing share (%) (current prices)[1]	19.1	18.6	20.1	18.4[e]
Manufacturing				
Value added ($-1990 mil.)[1]	42,722	46,648	53,804	56,422
Industrial production index	77	86	100	107
Value added ($ mil.)	29,080	20,595	44,818	56,417[e]
Gross output ($ mil.)	109,618	80,068	153,729	184,177
Employment (000)	944	797	780	701[e]
Profitability (% of gross output)				
Intermediate input (%)	73	74	71	69[e]
Wages and salaries inc. supplements (%)	20[e]	21[e]	19[e]	16[e]
Gross operating surplus	7[e]	5[e]	10[e]	15[e]
Productivity ($)				
Gross output per worker	110,019	87,824	157,892	260,794[e]
Value added per worker	29,285	22,782	46,329	83,229[e]
Average wage (inc. supplements)	23,135[e]	21,037[e]	37,835[e]	41,230[e]
Value added ($ mil.)				
Food products	4,562	2,896	6,037	8,344[e]
Beverages	654	737	1,500	2,252[e]
Tobacco products	282	775	1,848	2,920[e]
Textiles	734	463	1,002	1,117[e]
Wearing apparel	372	134[e]	234	217[e]
Leather and fur products	68	34[e]	70	59[e]
Footwear	118	51	72	73[e]
Wood and wood products	594	234	477	578[e]
Furniture and fixtures	418	164	362	509[e]
Paper and paper products	805	660	1,618	1,952[e]
Printing and publishing	2,480	1,446	3,217	4,656[e]
Industrial chemicals	2,263	2,436	5,592	4,826[e]
Other chemical products	913	902	1,846	3,130[e]
Petroleum refineries	533	521	1,095	1,195[e]
Misc. petroleum and coal products	101	55	131	138[e]
Rubber products	156	139	284	300[e]
Plastic products	472	466	1,305	1,865[e]
Pottery, china and earthenware	134	77	304	493[e]
Glass and glass products	245	145[e]	358	457[e]
Other non-metal mineral products	893	465[e]	1,016	1,290[e]
Iron and steel	882	793[e]	1,484[e]	1,573[e]
Non-ferrous metals	371	215[e]	341[e]	380[e]
Metal products	2,455	1,293	2,904	3,811[e]
Non-electrical machinery	2,369	1,628	3,552	4,604[e]
Electrical machinery	3,687	2,656	5,286	6,445[e]
Transport equipment	1,927	1,015	2,464	2,524[e]
Prof. and scientific equipment	237	146	308	527[e]
Other manufacturing	356	49	111	179[e]

COMMUNICATIONS

Daily Newspapers

	National Data	World Data for Comparison
Daily Newspapers		
Number of Dailies	38	8,391
Total Circulation (000)	4,753	548,000
Circulation per 1,000 inhabitants	306	96

Telecommunications

Telephones - main lines in use: 8.431 million (1996).

Telephones - mobile cellular: 1.016 million (1996).

Telephone system: highly developed and well maintained.

Domestic: the existing system of multi-conductor cables is gradually being replaced by fiber-optic cables; the density of cellular telephone traffic is rapidly increasing and further modernization of the system is expected in the year 2001, with the introduction of the third generation of the Global System for Mobile Communications (GSM).

International: 5 submarine cables; satellite earth stations - 3 Intelsat (1 Indian Ocean and 2 Atlantic Ocean), 1 Eutelsat, and 1 Inmarsat (Atlantic and Indian Ocean regions) (1996).

Radio broadcast stations: AM 4, FM 58, shortwave 3 (1998).

Radios: 15.3 million (1996).

Television broadcast stations: 15 (plus five low-power repeaters) (1997).

Televisions: 8.1 million (1997).

Internet Service Providers (ISPs): 70 (1999).

FINANCE, ECONOMICS, & TRADE

Economic Indicators

National product: GDP—purchasing power parity—$365.1 billion (1999 est.).

National product real growth rate: 3.4% (1999 est.).

National product per capita: $23,100 (1999 est.).

Inflation rate—consumer price index: 2.2% (1999 est.).

Exchange Rates

Exchange rates:

Euros per US$1

January 2000 . . . . .0.9867

1999 . . . . .0.9386

Netherlands guilders, gulden, or florins (f.) per US$1

January 1999 . . . . .1.8904

1998 . . . . .1.9837

1997 . . . . .1.9513

1996 . . . . .1.6859

1995 . . . . .1.6057

On 1 January 1999, the EU introduced a common currency that is now being used by financial institutions in some member countries at a fixed rate of 2.20371 guilders per euro; the euro will replace the local currency in consenting countries for all transactions in 2002.

Top Import Origins

$152 billion (f.o.b., 1998)

Origins (1998)

EU 61%

Germany 20%

Belgium-Luxembourg .11%

United Kingdom 10%

France 7%

United States 9%

Central and Eastern Europe . . . . .NA

Balance of Payments

	1994	1995	1996	1997	1998
Exports of goods (f.o.b.)	141,810	175,315	175,266	166,967	171,271
Imports of goods (f.o.b.)	−123,124	−153,213	−154,909	−147,974	−153,027
Trade balance	18,686	22,103	20,357	18,994	18,244
Services - debits	−41,436	−46,029	−46,130	−45,999	−47,616
Services - credits	42,847	48,290	49,965	51,755	52,818
Private transfers (net)	1,141	1,257	1,397	1,348	1,298
Government transfers (net)	−4,236	−5,292	−5,617	−4,993	−5,779
Overall balance	17,862	24,225	22,035	27,684	19,921

Top Export Destinations

$169 billion (f.o.b., 1998)

Destinations (1998)

EU	78%
Germany	27%
Belgium-Luxembourg	13%
France	11%
United Kingdom	10%
Italy	6%
Central and Eastern Europe	NA
United States	NA

Foreign Aid

Donor: ODA, $3.4 billion (1999).

Import/Export Commodities

Import Commodities	Export Commodities
Machinery and transport equipment	Machinery and equipment
Chemicals	Chemicals
Fuels	Fuels
Foodstuffs	Foodstuffs
Clothing	

NETHERLANDS ANTILLES

CAPITAL: Willemstad.

FLAG: The flag for the Netherlands Antilles is white, with a horizontal blue stripe in the center, superimposed on a vertical red band, also centered; five white-pointed stars are arranged in an oval pattern in the center of the blue band; the five stars represent the five main islands of Bonaire, Curaçao, Saba, Sint Eustatius, and Sint Maartin.

MONETARY UNIT: 1 Netherlands Antillean guilder, gulden, or florin (NAf.) = 100 cents.

WEIGHTS AND MEASURES: The metric system is used.

HOLIDAYS: New Year's Day, 1 January; Carnival Monday, 2 March; Good Friday; Easter Monday; Queen's Birthday, 30 April; Labor Day, 1 May; Ascension Day, 26 May; Flag Day, 2 July; Christmas Day, 25 December; Boxing Day, 26 December.

TIME: 8 PM = noon GMT.

LOCATION AND SIZE: The five islands of the Netherlands Antilles are divided geographically into two groups: the Leeward Islands (Benedenwindse Eilanden) and the Windward Islands (Bovenwindse Eilanden). The Windward group, off the north coast of South America, comprises the islands of Curaçao, with an area of 444 sq. km (171 sq. mi.), and Bonaire, 288 sq. km (111 sq. mi.). Aruba, another Windward island, seceded from the Netherlands Antilles in 1986. The Leeward group, more than 800 km (500 mi.) to the northeast, consists of the southern part of St. Martin (Sint Maarten), 34 sq. km (13 sq. mi.); Saba, 13 sq. km (5 sq. mi.); and Sint Eustatius, 21 sq. km (8 sq. mi.). The islands total 800 sq. km (309 sq. mi.).

CLIMATE: Temperatures rarely exceed 32°C (90°F) during the day or fall below 24°C (75°F) at night. Relative humidity averages 75 percent annually. The effect of the heat and the humidity, however, is lessened by the almost constant northeast trade winds, which are felt 10 months of the year. Rainfall averages only 56 cm (22 inches) annually, causing the island to be dusty. August, September and October are the warmest months; December, January and February are the coolest.

INTRODUCTORY SURVEY

RECENT HISTORY

A Dutch fleet captured the Windward Islands from Spanish control in 1632 and the Leeward Islands in 1634. In 1648, St. Martin was peacefully divided between the Netherlands and France, a division that still exists. During the colonial period, Curaçao was the center of the Caribbean slave trade. Under a 1954 statute, the Netherlands Antilles is a component of the Kingdom of the Netherlands, with autonomy in internal affairs.

GOVERNMENT

The Netherlands Antilles has a parliamentary form of government operating under a 1954 statute. The Netherlands' monarch is chief of state and is represented on the islands by a governor general, appointed by the monarch for six-year terms. A prime minister, usually leader of the majority party, is the head of government with a Council of Ministers as the executive body. The ministers are responsible to the Staten, a 23-member unicameral legislature (fifteen from Curaçao, three each from Bonaire and St. Martin, and one each from Saba and St. Eustatius). Members are elected by general suffrage of Dutch nationals aged eighteen or older to four-year terms.

A 1951 regulation established autonomy in local affairs for each of the then-existing island communities—Aruba, Curaçao, Bonaire, and the Leeward Islands—with responsibilities divided between an elected island council, an executive council, and a lieutenant governor. By agreements made

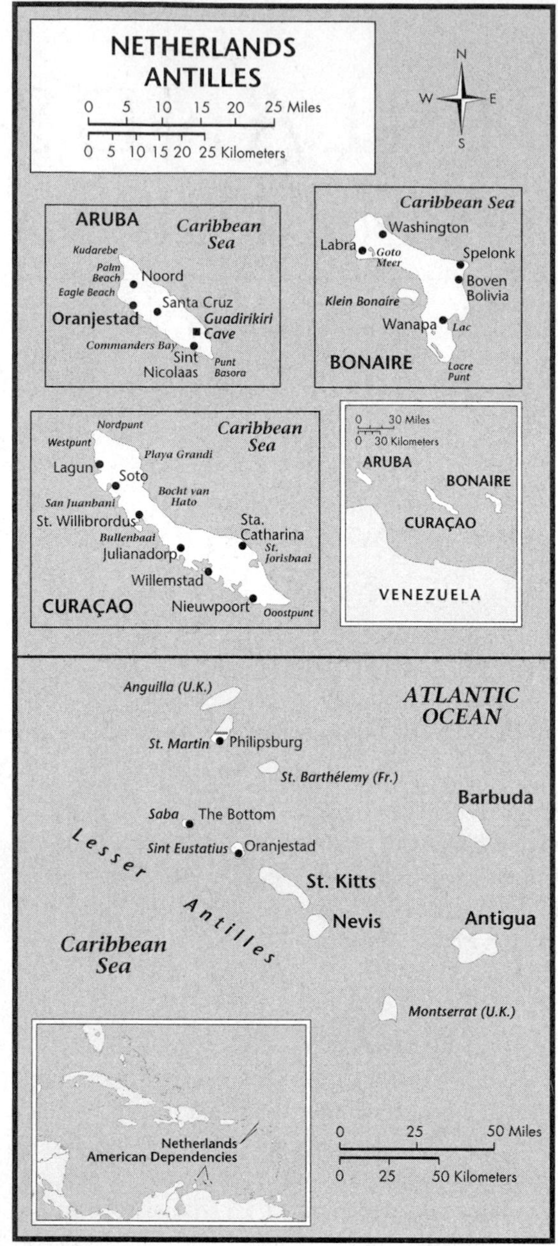

in 1983, St. Martin, Saba, and Sint Eustatius have separate representation in the Staten, elect their own separate councils, and have their own lieutenant governors and executive councils.

Judiciary

The legal system is primarily based on Dutch civil law with some English common law influence. Cases are tried in a court of first instance and on appeal in the Joint High Court of justice with justices appointed by the crown.

Political Parties

Seats in the Staten following 1998 elections were fairly evenly divided among eleven political parties. Those parties with the most seats were the Antillean Restructuring Party (PAR) with four seats, the National Peoples' Party (PNP) with three, and the Labor Party Peoples' Crusade (PLKP) with three also.

DEFENSE

Defense is the responsibility of the Netherlands. A naval contingent is permanently stationed in the islands and military service is compulsory. The Netherlands Antilles is an associate member of the European Union (EU).

ECONOMIC AFFAIRS

The prosperity of Curaçao is inseparably linked with its oil refineries. These were built there, beginning in 1918, chiefly because of the favorable location of the islands, their good natural ports and cheap labor, and the political stability of the territory. Tankers bring crude oil from Venezuela. The economic significance of the refineries is great, not only because of their output, but also because they provide employment and stimulate other economic activities, such as shipbuilding, metal industries, shipping, air traffic, and commerce in general. The government controls the price of basic foodstuffs and participates in the setting of rates to be charged for transportation and by privately owned utilities.

Public Finance

The estimated government revenue for 1997 was $710.8 million, with expenditures of $741.6 million. External debt was $1.35 billion in 1996. The Netherlands provided $97 million in aide for that year.

Income

The estimated GDP in 1998 was $2.4 billion, or $11,800 GDP per capita. The GDP real growth rate was −0.3 percent in 1998, and the annual inflation rate was 1.1 percent. The GDP composition by sector in 1996 was: agriculture, 1 percent; industry, 15 percent; and services, 84 percent.

Industry

The principal agricultural products are sorghum, orange peel, aloes, groundnuts, yams, divi-divi, and some assorted vegetables. The fish catch in 1994 was 1,100 tons. Curaçao's favorable position at the crossing of many sea-lanes has stimulated commerce since the earliest days of European settlement. Transit trade benefits from Curaçao's improved harbors; Willemstad is a free port, as are the islands of Saba and St. Eustatius. Refined petroleum products are exported to The Netherlands and other countries from a refinery on Curaçao. Petroleum shipments dominated the country's foreign trade-refined petroleum accounted for about 98 percent of exports in 1993 while crude oil made up 64 percent of imports that year.

Banking and Finance

The Bank of the Netherlands Antilles (Bank van de Nederlandse Antillen)issues currency, holds official reserves, regulates banking system, and acts as the central foreign exchange bank. There are fourteen authorized commercial banks and several savings and loan institutions that also handle financial matters. Netherlands Antilles Development Bank was created in 1981, to stimulate foreign investment in service industries. Tax treaties with the United States encouraged U.S. individuals and businesses to shelter their funds in the islands.

Economic Development

Tourism and offshore finance have diversified the economy. Annually, more than 469,000 cruise ship passengers visit the islands. Development aid from the Netherlands totals about $60 million annually. The country's infrastructure is well developed compared to other countries n the region. Poor soils and water supply inhibit agricultural development.

SOCIAL WELFARE

The unemployment rate was 14.9 percent in 1998, and 60 percent-70 percent of the work force was organized in labor unions.

Healthcare

There are six hospitals on Curaçao and four on the other islands. In 2000, life expectancy was estimated at 74.7 years.

EDUCATION

There are seventy-four nursery schools, eighty-six primary and secondary schools, one teacher-training college, and the University Institute of the Netherlands Antilles, on Curaçao (excluding Aruba). All schools are government-supported. The language of instruction is Dutch in the Leeward Islands, except in the International School, where classes are taught in English. English is also used in the Windward Islands. The literacy rate is 98 percent, although education is not compulsory.

2000 KEY EVENTS TIMELINE

January

- The government road tax goes up by 25 percent, and airport departure fees double on the heels of a sales tax increase from 2 percent to 5 percent during 1999.
- Prime Minister Pourier privatizes the bankrupt Antillean airlines Air ALM, that previously had a joint monopoly over flights between Amsterdam and the islands with KLM.

July

- European Dutch are given the rights to permanent residency in the islands without having to apply for a residence permit.

November

- The contraband drug known as ecstacy is popular in the Netherlands Antilles.

ANALYSIS OF EVENTS: 2000

BUSINESS AND THE ECONOMY

The economy of these islands was largely dependent on tourism and the shipment of petroleum products during 2000. There was no agriculture because of poor soil and most of their imports came from nearby Venezuela, the United States, and Mexico. For a small country, the infrastructure was well developed. There was an airport and in November 2000, Bonaire started its new airline. Off shore banking and financial services also attracted many new businesses to the islands.

GOVERNMENT AND POLITICS

As a Dutch dependency, the Netherlands Antilles is represented by Queen Beatrix of the Netherlands as head of state. She is represented by Governor Jaime Saleh on the islands. The elected head of the government as of 1999 was Miguel Pourier, who was also the head of the Antillean Restructuring Party (PAR). There were no international disputes. Being so close to South America, the Netherlands Antilles became a big money laundering center for drugs smuggled from South America to Europe and the United States. All governments wanted to stop these illegal practices and were working together to stop drugs from entering and leaving the country.

CULTURE AND SOCIETY

Bonaire and Curaçao are the two main islands in the Caribbean near Venezuela that are dependencies of the Netherlands. The population, which is composed of descendants of other countries' colonial populations and African slaves (85 percent), Carib-Amerinds, whites, and East Asians, has a rich and varied heritage. They speak Dutch, and, more prominently, a dialect of Portuguese called Papiamento. These two small islands are home to barely fifteen thousand people. The Netherlands Antilles is mainly known for excellent weather, which attracts tourists for diving and snorkeling. Others come for the nature preserves on nearby Klein Bonaire. This nature preserve houses sea turtles and many varieties of birds. The only mammals native to Bonaire are bats, which are popular with naturalists. Willemstad, the capital city of Curaçao, is European in design with Caribbean colors. These islands are known for being quiet and conducive to vacation relaxing. They have welcomed independent travelers as well as cruise ships. Their national holiday is Queen's Day (Queen Beatrix of the Netherlands) on April 30.

DIRECTORY

CENTRAL GOVERNMENT

Head of State

Monarch
Beatrix Wilhelmina Armgard, Queen of the Netherlands

Governor
Jaime M. Saleh, Office of the Governor

Prime Minister
Susanne Camelia-Romer, Office of the Prime Minister

Ministers

Minister of Development Corporation, Health and Humanitarian Affairs
Laurenso Abraham, Ministry of Development Corporation, Health and Humanitarian Affairs

Minister of Economic Affairs, Labor and Social Affairs
Errol Goelo, Ministry of Economic Affairs, Labor and Social Affairs

Minister of Education, Culture, Youth and Sport Affairs
Philip Nieuw, Ministry of Education, Culture, Youth and Sport Affairs

Minister of Finance
Frank Mingo, Ministry of Finance

Minister of Justice
Rutsel Martha, Ministry of Justice

Minister of Traffic and Communication
Maurice Adriaans, Ministry of Traffic and Communication

Minister of Transportation
Leo Chance, Ministry of Transportation

POLITICAL ORGANIZATIONS

Antillean Restructuring Party (PAR)

Fokkerweg 26 Unit 3, Curaçao, Netherlands Antilles
PHONE: +599 (9) 4652566; 4652610
FAX: +599 (9) 4652622
E-MAIL: omi7@ibm.net
NAME: Miguel Pourier

Democratic Party of Bonaire (PDB)

NAME: Jopi Abraham

Democratic Party of Curacao (DP)

NAME: Ephraim Jonckheer

Democratic Party of Sint Eustatius (DPSt.E)

NAME: Julian Woodley

Democratic Party of Sint Maarten (DPSt.M)

NAME: Sarah Westcott-Williams

Partido Nashonal di Pueblo-PNP (National People's Party)

TITLE: President
NAME: Suzy Romer

New Antilles Movement (MAN)

E-MAIL: dmartina@man.an
NAME: Don Dominico F. Martina

Nos Patria (NP)

NAME: Chin Behilia

Patriotic Movement of Sint Maarten (SPA)

NAME: William Marlin

Patriotic Union of Bonaire (UPB)

Saba Democratic Labor Movement (SDLM)

NAME: Steve Hassell

Saba Unity Party (SUP)

NAME: Carmen Simmonds

Serious Alternative People's Party

Socialist Independent (SI)

NAME: George Hueck; Nelson Monte

St. Eustatius Alliance (SEA)

NAME: Ingrid Whitfield

Windward Islands People's Movement (WIPM-S)

NAME: Ray Hassell

Workers' Liberation Front (FOL)

NAME: Wilson (Papa) Godett

DIPLOMATIC REPRESENTATION

Embassies in Netherlands Antilles

Belgium
Hoek Caracasbaaiweg/Schottegatweg, PO Box 3037, Netherlands Antilles
PHONE: +599 (9) 4617003; 4613094
FAX: +599 (9) 4616569
TITLE: Consul
NAME: Ivan Moreno Jr.

Bolivia
Wolkstraat 16, Kamer 11, Netherlands Antilles
PHONE: +599 (9) 4612792
TITLE: Consul
NAME: Efrain Tauber

Brazil
Concordiastraat 52, Netherlands Antilles
PHONE: +599 (9) 4615222

Canada
Plaza Jojo Correa 2–4, Netherlands Antilles
PHONE: +599 (9) 4613515
TITLE: Consul
NAME: William H.L. Fabro

Chile
Gaituweg 35, Netherlands Antilles
PHONE: +599 (9) 7374333
FAX: +599 (9) 7367747
TITLE: Consul
NAME: Ramfis Anthony Gonzalez

Colombia
Wilhelminaplein 25, Netherlands Antilles
PHONE: +599 (9) 4614663
FAX: +599 (9) 4612680
TITLE: Consul
NAME: Fabio Contreras Forero

Costa Rica
K.R. 12–3–90 nr.91.002247, Reigerweg 15, Netherlands Antilles
PHONE: +599 (9) 7378428
TITLE: Consul-Generaal
NAME: Joseph J. Frankel

Denmark
Bonam Kaya D #135, Netherlands Antilles
PHONE: +599 (9) 7366686
FAX: +599 (9) 7366686
TITLE: Consul
NAME: Ole V. Hansen

Dominica
K.B. 27–7–83 nr.84, Louise de Colignylaan 22, Netherlands Antilles
PHONE: +599 (9) 7373478
TITLE: Consul
NAME: Dennis Oscar Riviere

Dominican Republic
K.B. nr., Van Goghstraat 31, Netherlands Antilles
PHONE: +599 (9) 7378063
TITLE: Consul-Generaal
NAME: Amin Rodriguez

El Salvador
Trompetbloemweg 30, Netherlands Antilles
PHONE: +599 (9) 7375411

Finland
K.B. 17–4–86 nr. 47, Cas Coraweg 74, Netherlands Antilles
PHONE: +599 (9) 4612104
TITLE: Consul
NAME: Helga Mensing

France
Ontarioweg 8, Netherlands Antilles
PHONE: +599 (9) 4614300

FAX: +599 (9) 4614819
TITLE: Consul
NAME: Dr. Jan Hendrik R. Beaujon

Grenada
Juan Domingoweg 63, Netherlands Antilles
PHONE: +599 (9) 8681446
TITLE: Consul
NAME: Dean G. Whiteman

Guatemala
K.B. nr. Angloweg 7, Netherlands Antilles
PHONE: +599 (9) 7375011
TITLE: Consul
NAME: Beulah N. Henriquez

Guyana
Hecubaweg 4, Netherlands Antilles
PHONE: +599 (9) 7379789
TITLE: Consul
NAME: Arnold Maria Ignatius Sankies

Great Britain
Jan Sofat 215, Netherlands Antilles
PHONE: +599 (9) 8695968
FAX: +599 (9) 8695964
TITLE: Consul
NAME: Edward Wilson

Haiti
Perseusweg 1, Netherlands Antilles
PHONE: +599 (9) 4612436
FAX: +599 (9) 4658180
TITLE: Consul-Generaal
NAME: Chantal Pilie Dominique

Honduras
Schottegatweg 215 E (O), Netherlands Antilles
PHONE: +599 (9) 4615951

India
Heerenstraat 4–B, Netherlands Antilles
PHONE: +599 (9) 4612262
FAX: +599 (9) 4614345
TITLE: Consul
NAME: D. Boolchand Nandwani

Israel
Trompetbloemweg 25, Netherlands Antilles
PHONE: +599 (9) 7373533
TITLE: Consul
NAME: Dr. Paul Ackerman

Italy
Nabij van Engelen 2a, Netherlands Antilles
PHONE: +599 (9) 7371561
FAX: +599 (9) 7371582
TITLE: Consul
NAME: K.M.D. Pruneti

Jamaica
K.R. 1–1–93 nr.93.008840, Habaaiweg 68, Netherlands Antilles
PHONE: +599 (9) 4626561
TITLE: Consul
NAME: Rafaelito C. Hato

Japan
K.B.29–4–63 nr. 75, Schout bij Nacht Doormanweg 71, Netherlands Antilles
PHONE: +599 (9) 4613075
TITLE: Consul
NAME: Lionel Capriles

Lebanon
Winston Churchillweg 159, Netherlands Antilles
PHONE: +599 (9) 8684799
TITLE: Consul
NAME: Abdallah Abdul Salam Dennaoui

Liberia
K.B 23–8–74 nr. 75, Angloweg 7, Netherlands Antilles
PHONE: +599 (9) 7375011
TITLE: Consul
NAME: Heraclio M. Henriquez

Mexico
K.B. 7292/52 Scharlooweg 7, Netherlands Antilles
PHONE: +599 (9) 4613651
TITLE: Consul
NAME: Morris E. Curiel

Norway
Plaza Jojo Correa 2–4, Netherlands Antilles
PHONE: +599 (9) 4611117
TITLE: Consul
NAME: Lionel Capriles II

Panama
Maduro Plaza, Dokweg 19, Netherlands Antilles
PHONE: +599 (9) 7371566
TITLE: Consul
NAME: Mercedes Carolina Saenz Diaz

Peru
Rijkseenheid Blvd, Netherlands Antilles
PHONE: +599 (9) 4613319
TITLE: Consul

Portugal
Schottegatweg West 351, Netherlands Antilles
PHONE: +599 (9) 8688333
TITLE: Consul
NAME: Eduardo Vieira Ribeiro

Spain
Comanchestraat 4, Netherlands Antilles

PHONE: +599 (9) 7369532
FAX: +599 (9) 7369072
TITLE: Vice-Consul
NAME: Damian Leo

Suriname
ITC-gebouw, kamer TM 1.24, Netherlands Antilles
PHONE: +599 (9) 4636650
FAX: +599 (9) 4636450
TITLE: Consul Generaal
NAME: Radjendrakumar N. Sonny Hira

Sweden
Fransebloemweg 33, Netherlands Antilles
PHONE: +599 (9) 7375409
TITLE: Consul-Generaal
NAME: Henry Maduro

Trinidad and Tobago
Kaya Trinitaria #78, Netherlands Antilles
PHONE: +599 (9) 7371866
FAX: +599 (9) 7371864
TITLE: Consul
NAME: Louis C. Bergman

United States
J.B. Gorsiraweg 1, Netherlands Antilles
PHONE: +599 (9) 4612076
TITLE: Consul-Generaal
NAME: James Williams

Uruguay
Mahokstraat 7, Netherlands Antilles
PHONE: +599 (9) 4615395
FAX: +599 (9) 4615395
TITLE: Consul
NAME: Robert G. Willems

Venezuela
Handelskade 12, 2de Verdieping, Netherlands Antilles
PHONE: +599 (9) 4613100; 4613291
FAX: +599 (9) 4613179
TITLE: Consul-Generaal
NAME: Jose de Jesus Cortez Torres

JUDICIAL SYSTEM

Joint High Court of Justice

BROADCAST MEDIA

Easy 97.9 FM

Arikokweg 19A, Willemstad, Curaçao, Netherlands Antilles
PHONE: +599 (9) 4623612
FAX: +599 (9) 4628712
E-MAIL: radio@easyfm.com
WEBSITE: http://www.easyfm.com
TITLE: Director
CONTACT: Kevin Carthy
BROADCASTS: 24 hours/day

PJD-2 Radio

Plaza 21 Shopping Centre, PO Box 366, Philipsburg, St. Maarten, Netherlands Antilles
PHONE: +599 (5) 22580; 22764
FAX: +599 (5) 24905
TITLE: Director/General Manager
CONTACT: Donald R. Hughes

Radio Caribe

Willemstad, Curaçao, Netherlands Antilles
PHONE: +599 (9) 369555
FAX: +599 (9) 369569
LANGUAGE: English, Papiamento, Spanish

Radio Curom

Roodeweg 64, PO Box 2169, Willemstad, Curaçao, Netherlands Antilles
PHONE: +599 (9) 626586
FAX: +599 (9) 625796
TITLE: Director/General Manager
CONTACT: Orlando Cuales
LANGUAGE: Papiamento
BROADCASTS: 18 hours/day

Radio Hoyer 1 and 2

Plasa Hoyer 21, Willemstad, Curaçao, Netherlands Antilles
PHONE: +599 (9) 611244
FAX: +599 (9) 616528
E-MAIL: hoyer@cura.net
WEBSITE: http://www.cura.net/radiohoyer/
CONTACT: Helen Hoyer
LANGUAGE: Papiamento (Radio Hoyer 1); Dutch (Radio Hoyer 2)
TYPE: Commercial

Radio Korsou

Bataljonweg 7, PO Box 3250, Willemstad, Curaçao, Netherlands Antilles
PHONE: +599 (9) 373377
FAX: +599 (9) 372888
E-MAIL: webmaster@korsou.com
WEBSITE: http://www.korsou.com
TITLE: Program Director
CONTACT: Alan H. Evertsz
LANGUAGE: English, Dutch, Papiamento, Sranan Tongo

BROADCASTS: 24 hours/day
TYPE: Commercial

Radio Merkadeo

Generaalsweg 50, Willemstad, Curaçao, Netherlands Antilles
PHONE: +599 (9) 376115
FAX: +599 (9) 374514
TITLE: Director
CONTACT: E. Leito
LANGUAGE: Papiamento
BROADCASTS: 18 hours/day

Radio Nederland Relay Station

Kaya Gobernador Debrot 58, PO Box 45, Bonaire, Netherlands Antilles
PHONE: +599 (7) 175472
FAX: +599 (7) 175472
E-MAIL: info@rnbtech.com
WEBSITE: http://www.rnbtech.com
TITLE: General Manager
CONTACT: Leo Kool

Radio Paradise

ITC Building, PO Box 6103, Willemstad, Curaçao, Netherlands Antilles
PHONE: +599 (9) 636103
FAX: +599 (9) 636404
E-MAIL: Radiop@IBM.net
BROADCASTS: 18 hours/day

Ritmo FM

Kaya Gobernador N. Debrot 2, Kralendijk, Bonaire, Netherlands Antilles
PHONE: +599 (7) 7220
FAX: +599 (7) 8220
TITLE: Director
CONTACT: F. Piloto
LANGUAGE: Papiamento, Dutch

Trans World Radio

PO Box 388, Bonaire, Netherlands Antilles
PHONE: +599 (7) 8800
FAX: +599 (7) 8808
E-MAIL: info2@twr.org

Voz di Bonaire

PO Box 325, Kralendijk, Bonaire, Netherlands Antilles
PHONE: +599 (8) 5971
FAX: +599 (8) 5000
TITLE: Directors
CONTACT: Edsel Jesurun, Jr. and Irwin E. Halley
BROADCASTS: 24 hours/day

Tele Curaçao

PO Box 415, Willemstad, Curaçao, Netherlands Antilles
PHONE: +599 (9) 61288
FAX: +599 (9) 614138
TITLE: General Manager
CONTACT: Norbert Hendrikse
CHANNEL: A6, A8
TYPE: Commercial, Government

Leeward Broadcasting Corporation-Television

PO Box 375, Philipsburg, St. Maarten, Netherlands Antilles
CHANNEL: A7

Landsradio (Telecommunication Administration)

Schouburgweg 22, PO Box 103, Curaçao, Netherlands Antilles
PHONE: +599(9) 631111

COLLEGES AND UNIVERSITIES

University of the Netherlands Antilles

Jan Noorduynweg 111, Willemstad, Curacao, Netherlands Antilles
WEBSITE: http://www.una.net/

Saba University School of Medicine

PO Box 1000, Saba, Netherlands Antilles
PHONE: +599 (46) 3456
E-MAIL: saba@tiac.net
WEBSITE: http://www.saba.org/

NEWSPAPERS AND MAGAZINES

Beurs-En Nieuwsberichten

Extra Productions, N.V., W.I. Compagniestraat 41, PO Box 215, Willemstad Curacao, Netherlands Antilles
PHONE: +599 (9) 4624595
FAX: +599 (9) 4653411
TITLE: Editor
CONTACT: Ronny Yrausquin
CIRCULATION: 10,000

Bonaire Reporter, The

Kaya Gob. Debrot 200-6, Bonaire, Netherlands Antilles
PHONE: +599 (71) 78988
E-MAIL: reporter@bonairereporter.com
WEBSITE: http://www.bonairereporter.com

Chronicle, The

Windward Publishing Company, N.V., Arch Rd. 25, PO Box 488, Philipsburg St. Maarten, Netherlands Antilles
PHONE: +599 (5) 23919
FAX: +599 (5) 25466
E-MAIL: chronicle@megatropic.com
CIRCULATION: 3,000-3,500/daily

Dagblad Nobo

ABC Informa, N.V., Scherpenheuvel z/n, PO Box 323, Willemstad Curacao, Netherlands Antilles
PHONE: +599 (9) 7673500
FAX: +599 (9) 7672783
CIRCULATION: 12,000

Daily Herald, The

Front St. 17, PO Box 828, Philipsburg, Saint Maarten, Netherlands Antilles
PHONE: +599 (54) 25253
FAX: +599 (54) 25913
WEBSITE: http://www.thedailyherald.com

Extra

Extra Productions, N.V., Compagniestraat 41, PO Box 3011, Willemstad Curacao, Netherlands Antilles
PHONE: +599 (9) 4624595
FAX: +599 (9) 4627575
CIRCULATION: 24,500

La Prensa

Extra Productions, N.V., W.I. Compagniestraat 41, PO Box 3011, Willemstad Curacao, Netherlands Antilles
PHONE: +599 (9) 4623850
FAX: +599 (9) 4625983
TITLE: Publisher
CONTACT: R. Irausquin
CIRCULATION: 14,000

PUBLISHERS

Bredero

Reigerweg 51, Willemstad, Curacao, Netherlands Antilles
PHONE: +599 (9) 7376751
TITLE: Author
CONTACT: L.H. Bredero
SUBJECTS: Foreign Countries, History, Maritime, Nonfiction (General), Travel

De Wit Stores NV

L G Smith Blvd 110, Oranjestad, Netherlands Antilles
PHONE: +599 (9) 7823500
FAX: +599 (9) 7821575
E-MAIL: dewitstores@sctarnet.aw
TITLE: Managing Director
CONTACT: R. de Zwart
SUBJECTS: History, Language Arts, Linguistics, Regional Interests

RELIGIOUS ORGANIZATIONS

Catholic

Bishop of Willemstad
Breedestraat 31, Otroboanda, Willemstad, Curacao, Netherlands-Antilles
PHONE: +599 (9) 4625876
FAX: +599 (9) 4627347
E-MAIL: bidsomwtad@curinfo.an

Other

Curacao Council of Churches
Barenblaan 11, Willemstad, Curacao, Netherlands-Antilles
PHONE: +599 (9) 7373070
FAX: +599 (9) 73621238

FURTHER READING

Articles

"Free Entry for Dutch Approved." *The Daily Herald,* July 20, 2000.

"Government Raises Certain User Fees." *Bonaire E-News,* January 5–11, 2000.

"KLM Loses its Monopoly." *Bonaire E-News,* January 12–18, 2000.

Books

Brushaber, Susan. *The Aruba, Bonaire & Curacao Alive Guide.* [computer file] Boulder, CO: netLibrary, Inc., 2000.

Dun and Bradstreet's Export Guide to Netherlands Antilles. Parsippany, NJ: Dun & Bradstreet, 1999.

Jackson, Jack. *The Dive Sites of Aruba, Bonaire and Curacao.* Lincolnwood, IL: Passport Books, 2000.

Internet

BBC News Online. "Sanctions Threat to 'Tax Havens.'" June 26, 2000. [Online] Available http://news6.thdo.bbc.co.uk/hi/english/business/newsid%5F806000/806236.stm (accessed October 12, 2000).

NETHERLANDS ANTILLES: STATISTICAL DATA

For sources and notes see "Sources of Statistics" at the front of each volume.

GEOGRAPHY

Geography

Area:

Total: 960 sq km.

Land: 960 sq km.

Note: includes Bonaire, Curacao, Saba, Sint Eustatius, and Sint Maarten (Dutch part of the island of Saint Martin).

Land boundaries:

Total: 10.2 km.

Border countries: Guadeloupe (Saint Martin) 10.2 km.

Coastline: 364 km.

Climate: tropical; ameliorated by northeast trade winds.

Terrain: generally hilly, volcanic interiors.

Natural resources: phosphates (Curacao only), salt (Bonaire only).

Land use:

Arable land: 10%

Permanent crops: 0%

Permanent pastures: 0%

Forests and woodland: 0%

Other: 90% (1993 est.).

HUMAN FACTORS

Ethnic Division

Mixed black 85%

Carib Amerindian . . . . .NA

White . . . . .NA

East Asian . . . . .NA

Religion

Roman Catholic, Protestant, Jewish, Seventh-Day Adventist.

Demographics (A)

	1990	1995	1998	2000	2010	2020	2030	2040	2050
Population	188.8	198.9	205.8	210.1	228.4	242.9	252.8	255.6	252.6
Life expectancy - males	72.0	71.4	72.1	72.6	74.5	76.1	77.5	78.6	79.4
Life expectancy - females	76.2	75.6	76.4	77.0	79.3	81.2	82.8	84.0	85.0
Birth rate (per 1,000)	19.1	19.1	17.8	16.9	14.1	13.2	11.9	10.6	10.0
Death rate (per 1,000)	6.4	6.9	6.6	6.4	6.6	7.6	9.0	10.4	11.8
Women of reproductive age (15-49 yrs.)	55.2	56.5	57.3	57.8	59.2	57.8	56.8	55.5	52.2
Fertility rate	2.1	2.2	2.1	2.1	2.0	1.9	1.8	1.8	1.7

Except as noted, values for vital statistics are in thousands; life expectancy is in years.

Major Languages

Dutch (official), Papiamento (a Spanish-Portuguese-Dutch-English dialect) predominates, English widely spoken, Spanish.

GOVERNMENT & LAW

Political Parties

States (Staten)	no. of seats
Antillean Restructuring Party (PAR)	4
National People's Party (PNP)	3
Patriotic Movement of Sint Maarten (SPA)	1
Democratic Party of Bonaire (PDB)	2
Patriotic Union of Bonaire (UPB)	1
New Antilles Movement (MAN)	2
Labor Party People's Crusade (PLKP)	3
Windward Islands People's Movement (WIPM)	1
St. Eustatius Alliance (SEA)	1
Democratic Party of Sint Maarten (DP-St. M)	2
Liberation Front (FOL)	2

Elections were last held 30 January 1998 (next to be held by 2002). No party won enough seats to form a government. The government of Prime Minister Miguel Pourier is a coalition of several parties. Political parties are indigenous to each island.

Government Budgets (A)

Year: 1995

Total Expenditures: 655.1 Millions of Guilders

Expenditures as a percentage of the total by function:

General public services and public order	32.54
Defense	0
Education	8.98
Health	8.50
Social Security and Welfare	12.94
Housing and community amenities	2.64
Recreational, cultural, and religious affairs	0.85
Fuel and energy	0.12
Agriculture, forestry, fishing, and hunting	0
Mining, manufacturing, and construction	0
Transportation and communication	7.40
Other economic affairs and services	3.34

Military Affairs (B)

Military age	20
Availability	
Males age 15-49	53,766
Fit for military service	
Males age 15-49	30,137
Reaching military age annually	
Males	1,534

Data for 2000 est.

LABOR FORCE

Total Labor Force (A)

89,000.

Labor Force by Occupation

Agriculture	1%
Industry	13%
Services	86%

Data for 1994 est.

Unemployment Rate

14.9% (1998 est.)

PRODUCTION SECTOR

Energy Production

Production	1.02 billion kWh
Production by source	
Fossil fuel	100%
Hydro	0%
Nuclear	0%
Other	0%
Exports	0 kWh

Data for 1998.

Energy Consumption

Consumption	949 million kWh
Imports	0 kWh

Data for 1998.

Transportation

Highways:

Total: 600 km.

Paved: 300 km.

Unpaved: 300 km (1992 est.).

Merchant marine:

Total: 110 ships (1,000 GRT or over) totaling 1,028,910 GRT/1,285,837 DWT.

Ships by type: bulk 2, cargo 27, chemical tanker 2, combination ore/oil 3, container 16, liquified gas 4, multi-functional large load carrier 18, passenger 1, petroleum tanker 5, refrigerated cargo 26, roll-on/roll-off 6 (1999 est.)

Note: a flag of convenience registry; includes ships of 2 countries: Belgium owns 9 ships, Germany 1 (1998 est.).

Airports: 5 (1999 est.).

Top Agriculture Products

Aloes, sorghum, peanuts, vegetables, tropical fruit.

Top Mining Products (B)

Mineral resources include: phosphates (Curacao only), salt (Bonaire only).

MANUFACTURING SECTOR

GDP & Manufacturing Summary (C)

Total GDP (1998 est.) . . . .$2.4 billion

Real growth rate (1998 est.) . . . .-0.3%

Per capita (1998 est.) $11,800

Composition by sector

Agriculture 1%

Industry 15%

Services 84%

Values in purchasing power parity.

COMMUNICATIONS

Daily Newspapers

	National Data	World Data for Comparison
Daily Newspapers		
Number of Dailies	6	8,391
Total Circulation (000)	70	548,000
Circulation per 1,000 inhabitants	334	96

Telecommunications

Telephones - main lines in use: 75,000 (1995).

Telephones - mobile cellular: 11,727 (1995).

Telephone system: generally adequate facilities.

Domestic: extensive interisland microwave radio relay links.

International: 2 submarine cables; satellite earth stations - 2 Intelsat (Atlantic Ocean).

Radio broadcast stations: AM 9, FM 4, shortwave 0 (1998).

Radios: 217,000 (1997).

Television broadcast stations: 3 (there is also a cable service which supplies programs received from various US satellite networks and two Venezuelan channels) (1997).

Televisions: 69,000 (1997).

Internet Service Providers (ISPs): 6 (1999).

FINANCE, ECONOMICS, & TRADE

Economic Indicators

National product: GDP—purchasing power parity—$2.4 billion (1998 est.).

National product real growth rate: -0.3% (1998 est.).

National product per capita: $11,800 (1998 est.).

Inflation rate—consumer price index: 1.1% (1998).

Exchange Rates

Exchange rates:

Netherlands Antillean guilders, gulden, or florins (NAf.) per US$1 . . . . .1.790

Fixed rate since 1989.

Balance of Payments

	1991	1992	1993	1994	1995
Exports of goods (f.o.b.)	302	332	306	351	354
Imports of goods (f.o.b.)	−1,119	−1,168	−1,144	−1,272	−1,319
Trade balance	−817	−836	−838	−921	−964
Services - debits	−544	−607	−596	−671	−725
Services - credits	1,228	1,340	1,346	1,414	1,687
Private transfers (net)	58	70	83	91	86
Government transfers (net)	170	148	167	127	159
Overall balance	−6	10	1	−98	87

Top Import Origins

$1.3 billion (c.i.f., 1998)

Origins (1998)

Venezuela	35.3%
United States	21.0%
Mexico	9.8%
Italy	5.4%
Netherlands	4.8%
Brazil	3.1%

Top Export Destinations

$303 million (f.o.b., 1998)

Destinations (1998)

United States	17.5%
Guatemala	8.0%
Costa Rica	6.5%
The Bahamas	4.6%
Jamaica	4.1%
Chile	3.4%

Foreign Aid

Recipient: NA; Netherlands provided a $97 million aid package in 1996.

Import/Export Commodities

Import Commodities	Export Commodities
Crude petroleum 64%	Petroleum products 98%
Food	
Manufactures	

NEW CALEDONIA

CAPITAL: Noumea.

FLAG: The flag of France is used.

ANTHEM: La Marseillaise.

MONETARY UNIT: 1 CFP franc (CFPF) = 100 centimes.

WEIGHTS AND MEASURES: The metric system is used.

HOLIDAYS: New Year's Day, 1 January; Easter Monday; Labour Day, 1 May 1; 1945 Victory, 8 May; Ascension Day; White Sunday; National Day, 14 July; Assumption Day, 15 August; French Treaty Day, 24 September; All Saints Day, 1 November; 1918 Armistice, 11 November; Christmas Day, 25 December.

TIME: 11 PM = noon GMT.

LOCATION AND SIZE: New Caledonia (Nouvelle-Calédonie), a French overseas territory NE of Australia in the South Pacific Ocean, lies between 18° and 23°S and 162° and 169°E. The main island is about 400 km (250 mi.) long and 50 km (30 mi.) wide, with a surface area of 16,192 sq. km (6,252 sq. mi.). Mountainous and partly surrounded by coral reefs, the island is mostly forested or covered with low bush. With its dependencies and protectorates, it has an overall area of 18,576 sq. km (7,172 sq. mi.).

CLIMATE: The climate is subtropical and there is little temperature change throughout the year, averaging between 22°C and 24°C (71°F and 75°F). Average annual rainfall is about 80 inches (203 cm), and typhoons are common from December to March.

Territory of New Caledonia
and Dependencies

INTRODUCTORY SURVEY

RECENT HISTORY

New Caledonia was discovered in 1768, by Louis Antoine de Bougainville and was named by James Cook, who landed there in 1774. Local chiefs recognized France's title in 1844, and New Caledonia became a French possession in 1853. In 1946, it became a French overseas territory, and in 1958, its Assembly voted to maintain that status. An independent movement in the 1980s and early 1990s apparently dissipated after a referendum on independence was held in 1998 and voted down.

GOVERNMENT

New Caledonia operates under the 1958 French constitution as an overseas territory of France. The chief of state is the president of France, represented by a High Commissioner appointed by the French president on advice of the French Ministry of Interior. The head of government is the president of the government, elected by the members of the Territorial Congress.

The legislative branch consists of the unicameral 54-seat Territorial Congress, whose members are also members of the three Provincial Assemblies, elected by popular vote to serve five-year terms.

New Caledonia has two representatives in the French National Assembly and one in the Senate. The territory is divided into four administrative subdivisions, and there are thirty-two municipal communes.

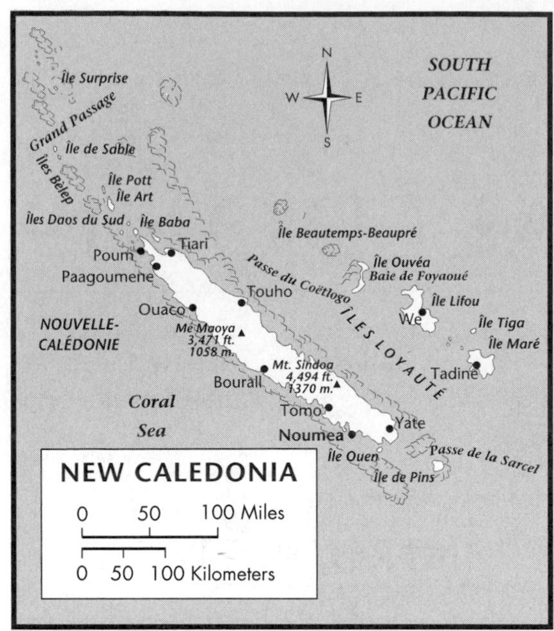

Political Parties

Of the fifty-four seats in the Territorial Congress following the 1999 elections, the Rally for Caledonia in the Republic (RPCR) held twenty-four seats, Kanak Socialist Front for National Liberation (FLNKS) held twelve, Union Nationale pour L'independence (UNI) held six, Federation des Comites de Coordination des Independantiste (FCCI) held four, National Front held four, Alliance pour la Caldonie held three, and Socialist Kanak Libeation (LKS) held one.

DEFENSE

Defense of New Caledonia is the responsibility of France.

ECONOMIC AFFAIRS

The economy is based on agriculture and mining. Coffee, copra, potatoes, cassava, corn, wheat, and fruits are the main crops, but agricultural production does not meet the domestic demand and food accounts for about 20 percent of imports. New Caledonia has more than 20 percent of the world's known nickel resources and is the fourth largest producer of ferronickel in the world after Canada, Indonesia, and Russia. Nickel mining and smelting accounted for an estimated 25 percent of GDP and 80 percent of export earnings in 1995. Recently depressed international demand for nickel has hurt the economy, but prices rebounded in 1999. Coffee, copra, and chromium make up most of the other exports. Trade is mainly with France, Australia, Japan, and the United States. In 1992, exports totaled $477 million, imports totaled $926 million.

In addition to nickel, significant aid from France and tourism are keys to the economy.

Public Finance

The U.S. Central Intelligence Agency (CIA) estimated in 1996 that government revenues were $861.3 million and expenditures were $735.3 million including capital expenditures of $52 million. By 1998 estimates the external debt was $79 million.

Income

In 1998, the CIA estimated the gross domestic product (GDP) was $3 billion, or $15,000 per capita. The 1998 estimates of GDP growth rate were 3.5 percent and inflation 1.5 percent. The 1997 estimated GDP contribution by sector was: agriculture, 40 percent; industry, 30 percent; and services, 66 percent.

Industry

Industries include nickel mining and smelting, chromium mining, coffee, copra, and fishing.

Economic Development

In 1999, large additions were made to the nickel industry capacity.

2000 KEY EVENTS TIMELINE

January

- Vice President Leopold Joredie is given a one-year suspended jail term, loss of civic rights for three years, and a fine of 55,000 French Francs for using public funds for his son's business.

August

- Local artists protest the 8th Annual Pacific Arts Festival on August 30. They state the government does little to promote regional arts and does not protect copyright laws. The festival is scheduled to begin in late October.
- Fijians who live in New Caledonia are collecting money for those affected by the coup in Fiji on May 17, 2000.

September

- The government of France appoints Christian Paul as the new minister in the Pacific on September 1. He replaces former minister Jean-Jack Queyranne. He will be in charge of the request from New Caledonia for autonomy.

- The government announces plans to raise the minimum wage to $1,000 a month on September 4. Most of the underpaid workers are domestic employees, farmers, fishermen, factory workers and retailers. Even with the new salary increase, New Caledonians still are underpaid as the cost of living in the Pacific islands is one of the highest in the world.
- The anti-independence leader of New Caledonia, Jacques Lafleur, announces he will not resign his position in the French National Assembly on September 8. Lafleur is the leader movement called the (RPCR) Rally for New Caledonia within the French Republic.
- New Caledonians march in the streets on September 25 to protest a new social pact that forces mediation in cases of strikes. Most unions in New Caledonia endorse the pact.

November

- Kanak Socialist Liberation Front Chairman Roch Wamytan is reelected President of the Union Calédonienne on November 13.
- French Prime Minister Lionel Jospin and the New Caledonian government sign an agreement in which New Caledonia can ease its way into independence within fifteen to twenty years.

December

- Gaston Flosse, his wife Tonita, and Flosse's severest critic Emile Vernaudon, are questioned for financial mismanagement on December 1.
- A law legalizing abortion is scheduled to take effect at the end of December.

ANALYSIS OF EVENTS: 2000

BUSINESS AND THE ECONOMY

The main industry in New Caledonia was the mining of nickel. About 25 percent of the world's nickel supply is mined in New Caledonia, although the declining demand for nickel in industry has taken a heavy toll on New Caledonia's economy. La Société Le Nickel (SLN) is the agency which runs the mines. There have been frequent strikes and pay disputes with the government. In April the workers settled a strike and the Doniambo smelter is now up to capacity. It produces an average rate of 56,000 tons of nickel annually. The mine workers are also affected by lung diseases typical of other mine workers. Small fisheries and local agriculture round out the economy. Trade with France, Australia, and the United States helps the economy, but France still has to subsidize a large portion of New Caledonia's annual budget. The government is trying to promote tourism as New Caledonia has an airport and there are good roads around the islands. The tourism industry is still not having much impact on the local economy. In October 2000, the government of New Caledonia signed a social pact with workers to avoid wildcat strikes and insures work will continue as the sides mediate. The workers' union, the Union of Kanak Workers (USTKE), refused to sign, creating a protest as other sides signed the agreement. The Kanak workers labeled the pact a sham.

GOVERNMENT AND POLITICS

Being an overseas territory, New Caledonia's government is that of France, with Jacques Chirac, the president of France being the head of state. New Caledonia sends representatives to the French legislature. As of May 1999 Jean Leques was governor. One of the main opposition parties is the Kanak Front for National Liberation, or the independence party (FLNKS). New Caledonia has voted to remain with France as an overseas territory as late as 1998, with a 72 percent majority approving. France has agreed to give the territory more autonomy in local affairs. In September Jacques Lafleur, the leader of the anti-independence party (RPCR), had threatened to resign his seat in the French parliament but then changed his mind. The opposition party, the National Front, was challenging him to resign. The only international disputes concerning New Caledonia in 2000 is the continuing dispute with Vanuatu over the ownership of Matthew and Hunter islands, also claimed by France. This has been an ongoing dispute and will probably not be resolved soon. Christian Paul became the new minister for overseas territories in August, 2000. He has visited New Caledonia and promised to take an interest in the autonomy issue as well as in the economy of New Caledonia. Most of the *caldoche* or European population is dead set against independence and they fear losing their political clout. The next vote on this issue is due up in 2014.

CULTURE AND SOCIETY

The *kanak* people of New Caledonia as well as other Melanesian and Polynesian groups formed the basis of the indigenous people of New Caledonia, located in the Pacific Ocean about one thousand miles east of Australia. Europeans, mainly the French who first colonized New Caledonia as a penal colony, formed the remainder of the population called *caldoche*. Even though the indigenous population was more numerous than the European population, the Europeans have been in control of business and governmental affairs since France began colonization of New Caledonia in 1853. It was made an official French Overseas Territory in 1957. French is the official language and the state-run French system of education operated the public schools. Most of the *kanak* people also speak Polynesian dialects. The *kanak* culture was composed of family alliances and membership in various clans. The families participated in life cycle ceremonies. One of the ceremonies particular to New Caledonia was the yam planting festival. The European culture has heavily influenced the main island of Grande Terre and its capital city of Nouméa. Grande Terre also contains 90 percent of the total population of New Caledonia which was about 200,000 people as of 2000. Most of the non-European people worked as domestic employees or fishermen or in the nickel mines. The government planned to raise the minimum wage and to encourage young people to get more technical training. New Caledonia was also home to rare and unusual plant species. Many botanists came from all over the world to examine and preserve these endangered species. Some of these plants were remnants from the age of dinosaurs when New Caledonia split from the Australian continent. In October New Caledonia hosted the Eighth Annual Pacific Festival of the Arts, with shows and exhibitions and recitals from twenty-eight Pacific Island countries and territories. It was a celebration of *kanak* culture and was meant to encourage pride in the indigenous peoples of the Pacific. Some *kanak* people protested the festival saying that the indigenous culture was not appreciated enough and that local artists were given very little respect. This remained a continuing problem in a country in which the minority European culture was considered insensitive to the majority language and customs.

DIRECTORY

CENTRAL GOVERNMENT

Head of State

High Commissioner
Thierry Lataste, Office of the High Commissioner, 1 avenue Foch, BP C05, 98844 Noumea, New Caledonia
PHONE: +687 266300
FAX: +687 272828

Offices

Chamber of Business
10 avenue James Cook, BP 4186, 98846 Noumea, New Caledonia
PHONE: +687 282337
FAX: +687 282729

Chamber of Agriculture
La Flottille, 3 rue A. Desmazures, BP 111, 98845 Noumea, New Caledonia
PHONE: +687 272056
FAX: +687 284587

Territorial Institute of Statistics
5 rue du General Gallieni, BP 823, 98 845 Noumea, New Caledonia
PHONE: +687 283156
FAX: +687 288148

French Office for Development
5 rue Barleux, BP J1, 98849 Noumea, New Caledonia
PHONE: +687 282088
FAX: +687 282413

Chamber of Commerce and Industry
15 rue de Verdun, BP M3, 98849 Noumea, New Caledonia
PHONE: +687 243100
FAX: +687 243131

Employment Agency
3 rue de la Somme, BP 497, 98845 Noumea, New Caledonia
PHONE: +687 281082
FAX: +687 272079

Economic and Social Committee of New Caledonia
19 avenue Marechal Foch, BP 4766, 98847 Noumea, New Caledonia
PHONE: +687 278517
FAX: +687 278509

Pacific Society
Promenade Roger Laroque, Anse-Vata, BP D5, 98848 Noumea, New Caledonia
PHONE: +687 262000
FAX: +687 263818

Consultive Customs Consul
68 avenue J.Cook, Nouville, New Caledonia
PHONE: +687 242000
FAX: 687 249320

POLITICAL ORGANIZATIONS

Progressive Melanesian Union (UPM)

NAME: Edmond Nekiriai

Kanaka Socialist National Liberation Front (FLNKS)

NAME: Rock Wamytan

Kanak Socialist Liberation (LKS)

NAME: Nidoish Naisseline

New Caledonia National Party

NAME: Georges Chateney

Rally for Caledonia in the Republic (RPCR)

NAME: Jean-Louis Mir

Liberal Caledonian Movement

NAME: Jean Leques

JUDICIAL SYSTEM

Court of Appeal

BROADCAST MEDIA

Noumea Radio Joker (NRJ 2000)

41-43 Rue de Sebastapol, BP 3260-98846, Noumea Cedex, New Caledonia
PHONE: +687 263369
FAX: +687 281627
LANGUAGE: French
BROADCASTS: 24 hours/day

Radio Alizes

BP 2557, Noumea, New Caledonia
PHONE: +687 473048

Radio Baie des Tortues

BP 241, Bourail, New Caledonia
PHONE: +687 254500

Radio Cote Est

BP 123, Poindimie, New Caledonia
PHONE: +687 273242

Radio Djiido

29 rue Mar Juin Ht. Mtga., BP 1671, Noumea, New Caledonia
PHONE: +687 253515
FAX: +687 253433
TITLE: News Editor
CONTACT: Nicole Waia
BROADCASTS: 24 hours/day

Radio Rythme Bleu (RRB)

BP 578, Noumea, New Caledonia
PHONE: +687 254646
FAX: +687 284928
BROADCASTS: 24 hours/day

Radiodiffusion Française d'Outre Mer (RFO)

BP G3 Mont Coffin, F-98848 Noumea Cedex, New Caledonia
PHONE: +687 274327
FAX: +687 281252
TITLE: Program Director
CONTACT: Louis Palmieri
LANGUAGE: French
BROADCASTS: 24 hours/day

Canal Caledonie

8 rue de Verneilh, Noumea, New Caledonia
CHANNEL: 25, 33, 43
TYPE: Commercial, Private

Radio Télévision Française d'Outre Mer (RFO-TV)

BP G3 Mont Coffin, F-98848 Noumea Cedex, New Caledonia
PHONE: +687 274327
FAX: +687 281252
TITLE: Director
CONTACT: Alain Le Garrec
CHANNEL: K4, K7, K8
TYPE: Government

COLLEGES AND UNIVERSITIES

Conservatoire National des Arts et Metiers

Noumea BP 3562, New Caledonia
PHONE: +687 283707

WEBSITE: http://slim2.emporia.edu/students/rjohnson/newcaled.htm#education

Universite Francaise du Pacifique Centre Universitaire de Nouvelle Caledonie

Noumea BP 4477, New Caledonia
PHONE: +687 254955
FAX: +687 254829
WEBSITE: http://www.univ-nc.nc

NEWSPAPERS AND MAGAZINES

Les Nouvelles Caledoniennes

Pacifique Presse Communications, 41-43 Blvd. de Sebastopol, BP 179, 98845 Noumea, New Caledonia
PHONE: +687 272584
FAX: +687 281627
E-MAIL: Inc@canl.nc
TITLE: Editor-in-Chief
CONTACT: Didier Fleaux
CIRCULATION: 18,000

Libre Expression

WEBSITE: http://www.librex.nc

The National

PO Box 6817, NCD, Port Moresby, New Caledonia
E-MAIL: national@online.net.pg
WEBSITE: http://www.wr.com.au/national

Caledonie Agricole

PO Box 111, Noumea, New Caledonia
FAX: +687 284587
TITLE: Editor
CONTACT: Roger Pene
CIRCULATION: 3,500
TYPE: Technology, agriculture and animal husbandry

PUBLISHERS

Editions du Santal

BP 3072, Noumea, New Caledonia
PHONE: +687 262533
FAX: +687 262533
E-MAIL: santal@offratel.nc
TITLE: Director
CONTACT: Paul-Jean Stahl
SUBJECTS: Art, History, Travel

Savannah Editions SARL

49 rue de la Boudeuse magenta Que mo, 98846, Noumea, New Caledonia
PHONE: +687 252919
FAX: +687 282470
SUBJECTS: How-to, Maritime, Outdoor Recreation, Sports, Athletics, Travel

RELIGIOUS ORGANIZATIONS

Protestant

Evangelical Church in New Caledonia and the Fair Islands

Eglise Evangelique en Nouvelle-Caledonie et aux Iles Loyaute
Boite Postale 277, Noumea, New Caledonia

FURTHER READING

Articles

O'Neill, Thomas. "New Caledonia." *National Geographic,* May 2000, vol. 197, no. 5, p. 54.

"Inco Ltd." *Engineering & Mining Journal,* September 2000, vol. 201, no. 9, p. 36.

Smaalders, Mark and Kim Des Rochers. "Cruising the South Lagoon." *Cruising World,* February 2000, vol. 26, no. 2, p. 60.

Books

Dun and Bradstreet's Export Guide to New Caledonia. Parsippany, NJ: Dun & Bradstreet, 1999.

NEW CALEDONIA: STATISTICAL DATA

For sources and notes see "Sources of Statistics" at the front of each volume.

GEOGRAPHY

Geography

Area:

Total: 19,060 sq km.

Land: 18,575 sq km.

Land boundaries: 0 km.

Coastline: 2,254 km.

Climate: tropical; modified by southeast trade winds; hot, humid.

Terrain: coastal plains with interior mountains.

Natural resources: nickel, chrome, iron, cobalt, manganese, silver, gold, lead, copper.

Land use:

Arable land: 0%

Permanent crops: 0%

Permanent pastures: 12%

Forests and woodland: 39%

Other: 49% (1993 est.).

HUMAN FACTORS

Ethnic Division

Melanesian	42.5%
European	37.1%
Wallisian	8.4%
Polynesian	3.8%
Indonesian	3.6%
Vietnamese	1.6%
Other	3.0%

Religion

Roman Catholic	60%
Protestant	30%
Other	10%

Major Languages

French (official), 33 Melanesian-Polynesian dialects.

Demographics (A)

	1990	1995	1998	2000	2010	2020	2030	2040	2050
Population	168.4	185.8	195.6	201.8	229.7	252.9	272.0	284.7	290.7
Life expectancy - males	68.6	68.5	69.3	69.8	72.2	74.2	75.9	77.3	78.4
Life expectancy - females	73.7	74.4	75.3	75.8	78.4	80.4	82.1	83.5	84.6
Birth rate (per 1,000)	26.0	23.0	21.8	20.8	16.7	15.0	13.1	11.5	10.7
Death rate (per 1,000)	5.5	5.8	5.7	5.6	5.8	6.4	7.3	8.3	9.8
Women of reproductive age (15-49 yrs.)	43.8	48.5	50.9	52.4	61.0	65.9	66.9	67.1	63.8
Fertility rate	3.2	2.8	2.6	2.5	2.2	1.9	1.8	1.8	1.7

Except as noted, values for vital statistics are in thousands; life expectancy is in years.

GOVERNMENT & LAW

Political Parties

Territorial Congress (Congres Territorial)	no. of seats
Rally for Caledonia in the Republic (RPCR)	24
Kanak Socialist Front for National Liberation (FLNKS)	12
Union Nationale pour l'Independance (UNI)	6
Federation des Comites de Coordination des Independantistes (FCCI)	4
National Front (FN)	4
Alliance pour la Caledonie	3
Socialist Kanak Liberation (LKS)	1

Elections were last held 9 May 1999 (next to be held in 2004).

Government Budgets (B)

Revenues . . . .$861.3 million

Expenditures . . . .$735.3 million

Capital expenditures . . . .$52.0 million

Data for 1996 est.

Military Affairs (B)

Dollar figure . . . .$192.3 million

Percent of GDP 5.3%

Data for 1996.

LABOR FORCE

Total Labor Force (A)

79,395 (including 15,018 unemployed, 1996).

Labor Force by Occupation

Agriculture 7%

Industry 23%

Services 70%

Data for 1999 est.

Unemployment Rate

15% (1994)

PRODUCTION SECTOR

Energy Production

Production . . . . .1.52 billion kWh

Production by source

Fossil fuel 65.79%

Hydro 34.21%

Nuclear 0%

Other 0%

Exports . . . . .0 kWh

Data for 1998.

Energy Consumption

Consumption . . . . .1.414 billion kWh

Imports . . . . .0 kWh

Data for 1998.

Transportation

Highways:

Total: 5,562 km.

Paved: 975 km.

Unpaved: 4,587 km (1993).

Merchant marine:

Total: 1 ship (1,000 GRT or over) totaling 1,261 GRT/1,600 DWT.

Ships by type: cargo 1 (1999 est.).

(Continued on next page.)

MANUFACTURING SECTOR

GDP & Manufacturing Summary (B)

	1980	1985	1990	1993	1994	1995
Gross Domestic Product						
Millions of 1990 dollars	1,079	1,070	1,600	1,722	1,776	1,824[e]
Growth rate in percent	−0.40	4.51	−4.27	2.02	3.11	2.71[e]
Per capita (in 1990 dollars)	7,543	6,900	9,524	9,843	9,978	10,078[e]
Manufacturing Value Added						
Millions of 1990 dollars	98	79	112	124	125	127[e]
Growth rate in percent	−4.64	−1.05	−4.27	−0.75	1.31	1.36[e]
Manufacturing share in percent of current prices	5.8	4.7	NA	NA	NA	NA

PRODUCTION SECTOR (cont.)

Transportation

Airports: 28 (1999 est.).

Airports - with unpaved runways: 23.

Top Agriculture Products

Vegetables; beef, deer, other livestock products.

Top Mining Products (B)

Mineral resources include: nickel, chrome, iron, cobalt, manganese, silver, gold, lead, copper.

COMMUNICATIONS

Daily Newspapers

	National Data	World Data for Comparison
Daily Newspapers		
Number of Dailies	3	8,391
Total Circulation (000)	24	548,000
Circulation per 1,000 inhabitants	121	96

Telecommunications

Telephones - main lines in use: 44,000 (1995).

Telephones - mobile cellular: 825 (1995).

Telephone system:

Domestic: NA

International: satellite earth station - 1 Intelsat (Pacific Ocean).

Radio broadcast stations: AM 1, FM 5, shortwave 0 (1998).

Radios: 107,000 (1997).

Television broadcast stations: 6 (plus 25 low-power repeaters) (1997).

Televisions: 52,000 (1997).

Internet Service Providers (ISPs): 1 (1999).

FINANCE, ECONOMICS, & TRADE

Economic Indicators

National product: GDP—purchasing power parity—$3 billion (1998 est.).

National product real growth rate: 3.5% (1998 est.).

National product per capita: $15,000 (1998 est.).

Inflation rate—consumer price index: 1.5% (1998 est.).

Exchange Rates

Exchange rates:

Comptoirs Francais du Pacifique francs (CFPF) per US$1

January 2000	117.67
1999	111.93
1998	107.25
1997	106.11
1996	93.00
1995	90.75

Linked at the rate of 18.18 to the French franc. Fiscal year: calendar year.

Top Import Origins

$922 million (c.i.f., 1998)

Origins (1998)

France	41%
Australia	13%
New Zealand	7%
Japan	5%

Top Export Destinations

$381 million (f.o.b., 1998)

Destinations (1997)

Japan	36%
France	30%
United States	14%
Taiwan	9%
Australia	7%

Foreign Aid

Recipient: $770 million from France (1998).

Import/Export Commodities

Import Commodities	Export Commodities
Foods	Ferronickels
Machinery and equipment	Nickel ore
Fuels	Fish
Minerals	

NEW ZEALAND

CAPITAL: Wellington.

FLAG: The flag has two main features: the red, white, and blue Union Jack in the upper left quarter and the four-star Southern Cross in the right half. On the blue state flag the stars are red outlined in white. On the red national flag, used by individuals or commercial institutions at sea, the stars are white.

ANTHEM: *God Save the Queen* and *God Defend New Zealand* have, since 1977, enjoyed equal status.

MONETARY UNIT: The New Zealand dollar (NZ$) is a paper currency of 100 cents; it replaced the New Zealand pound on 10 July 1967. There are coins of 5, 10, 20, and 50 cents and 1 and 2 dollars, and notes of 5, 10, 20, 50, and 100 dollars. NZ$1 = US$0.3982 (or US$1 = NZ$2.5113).

WEIGHTS AND MEASURES: Metric weights and measures are used.

HOLIDAYS: New Year's Day, 1 January; Waitangi Day, 6 February; Anzac Day, 25 April; Queen's Birthday, 1st Monday in June; Labor Day, 4th Monday in October; Christmas Day, 25 December; Boxing Day, 26 December. Movable holidays are Good Friday and Easter Monday. Each province has a holiday on its own anniversary day.

TIME: 12 midnight = noon GMT.

LOCATION AND SIZE: Situated in the southwest Pacific Ocean, New Zealand proper, with a total area of 268,680 square kilometers (103,738 square miles), consists of the North Island, including small islands nearby; the South Island; Stewart Island; and various minor, outlying islands. New Zealand has a total coastline of 15,134 kilometers (9,404 miles).

New Zealand's capital city, Wellington, is located on the southern tip of North Island.

CLIMATE: New Zealand has a temperate, moist ocean climate without major seasonal variations in temperature or rainfall. Mean annual temperatures at sea level range from about 15°C (59°F) in the northern part of the North Island to 12°C (54°F) in the southern part of the South Island.

INTRODUCTORY SURVEY

RECENT HISTORY

In 1907, New Zealand was made a dominion (a self-governing nation that recognizes the British monarchy) of the United Kingdom. In 1947, the New Zealand government formally claimed the complete independence available to self-governing members of the British Commonwealth. After World War II, New Zealand and U.S. foreign policies were increasingly intertwined. New Zealand was a founding member of the Southeast Asia Treaty Organization (SEATO) in 1954. New Zealand troops fought with United Nations (UN) forces in the Korea conflict and with U.S. forces in South Vietnam. The involvement in Vietnam touched off a national debate on foreign policy, however, and all New Zealand troops were withdrawn from the country by the end of 1971. New Zealand's military participation in SEATO was later terminated.

In 1984, a Labour government led by Prime Minister David Lange took office under a pledge to ban nuclear-armed vessels from New Zealand harbors. A United States request for a port visit by one of its warships was denied because of uncertainty as to whether the ship was nuclear-armed. The continuing ban put a strain on New Zealand's relations within the Australia-New Zealand-United States alliance (ANZUS) and in 1986, the United States suspended its military obligations to New Zealand under the ANZUS defense agreement. The United States also banned high-level contacts with the New Zealand government. The United

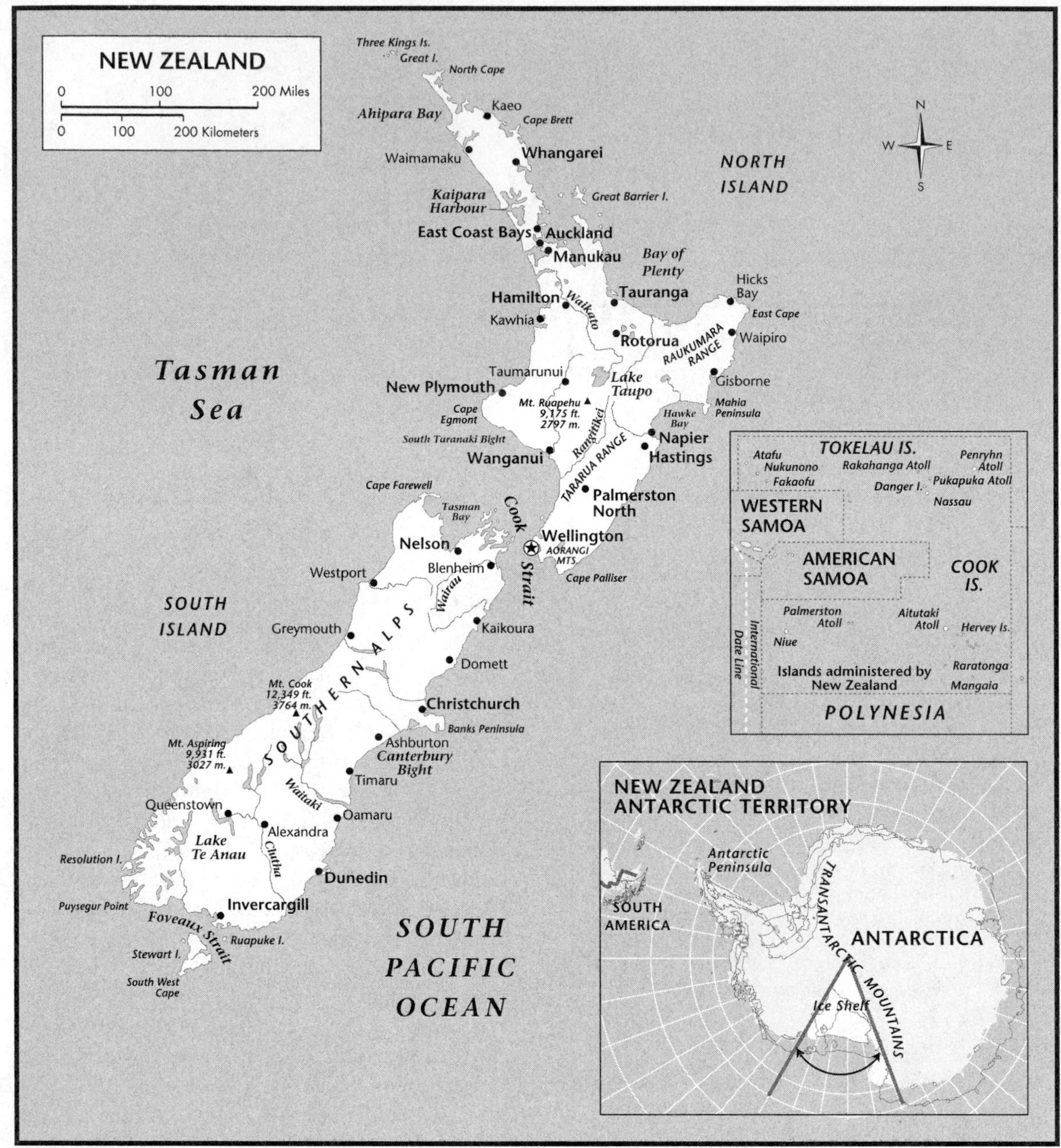

States ended its ban on high-level contacts in March 1990.

The native Maori people have claimed rights to all of the country's coastline, 70 percent of the land, and half of the fishing rights. To answer these claims a new Cabinet committee was formed in December 1989. The committee, including former Prime Minister Lange, worked with the seventeen-member Waitangi Tribunal, established in 1975 to consider complaints from Maoris. In 1996, the government settled a NZ$170 million agreement with the Waikato Tainui tribe on North Island for wrongfully taking the tribe's lands during the 1860s. Queen Elizabeth II signed the legislation, which contained an apology.

In February 1998, Auckland suffered from a power blackout that lasted for weeks, crippling commerce. In 1999, the Labour Party became the majority government over the incumbent National Party-First Party coalition. The Labour Party formed a coalition with the Alliance Party, with Helen Clark as Prime Minister. The Clark administration expressed commitment to goals aimed at benefiting all New Zealanders, closing the economic gap between the Maori and the rest of the population, and strengthening the Nuclear Free Zone in the South Pacific.

GOVERNMENT

New Zealand is an independent member of the Commonwealth of Nations. Government is parliamentary democratic and modeled on that of the United Kingdom. The chief of state, the governor-general, is the representative of the British crown. The governor-general is appointed for a five-year term.

On his appointment by the governor general, the prime minister, leader of the governing party, chooses twenty other ministers to form the cabinet. Each minister usually controls several government departments. Ministers are responsible to the House of Representatives for the operation of their departments.

The single-chamber legislature, the House of Representatives (commonly called Parliament), has ninety-seven members. Each is elected by universal adult vote for a term of three years. Although there have been coalition governments, the two-party system usually operates. The party with a majority of members elected to the House of Representatives forms the government, the other party becoming the Opposition.

The transition to a proportional voting system was introduced during the 1996 elections. Under New Zealand's proportional representation, each voter casts two votes, one for a candidate and one for a political party. Each party is awarded seats according to its share of the overall vote with a minimum set at 5 percent.

Judiciary

Most civil and criminal cases are heard first in district courts. There is the right of appeal to the High Court that is usually the court of first hearing for cases where a major crime or an important civil action is involved. Family courts were established in 1980 to hear cases involving domestic issues. The highest court, the Court of Appeal, rules on appeals only. Its decisions are final unless leave is granted to appeal to the Privy Council in London. There are also several special courts such as the Arbitration Court, the Maori Land Court, and the Children and Young Persons Court. The judicial system is based on British common law. The judiciary is independent and impartial.

Political Parties

New Zealand's major parties are the New Zealand Labour Party (NZLP), formed in 1916, and the National Party (NP), formed in 1935. In the November 1999 elections, the NZLP won forty-nine seats in the Parliament becoming the majority party. A coalition government was formed between the NZLP and the Alliance Party (a coalition of the New Labor Party, Democratic Party, New Zealand Liberal Party, and Mana Motuhake) which had taken ten seats. The National Party held thirty-nine seats. Other parties holding seats were ACT New Zealand with nine seats, Green Party with seven seats, New Zealand First Party (NZFP) with five seats, and United New Zealand (UNZ) with one seat.

DEFENSE

Service in the New Zealand regular armed forces is voluntary, but some white males (eighteen to twenty-one years of age) may be required to have military training for service in the territorial force (3,890).

In 2000, the army had a full-time regular force of 4,400 and 1,500 reserves; the navy had 2,080 regulars (350 women) and 850 reserves; and the air force had 3,050 regulars (500 women) and 1,050 reserves. The defense budget in 1997-1998 was $883 million or 1 percent of GDP.

ECONOMIC AFFAIRS

New Zealand's economy has traditionally been based on farming. The last decades, however, have seen the beginnings of heavy industry and there has been a large expansion in light industries such as plastics, textiles, and footwear, mostly to supply the home market. In recent years, there has been a trend toward the development of industries based on natural resources. The forest industry has greatly expanded. Pulp, log, and paper products are major exports.

New Zealand's heavy dependence on trade income from a restricted range of export products such as wool, meat, and dairy products makes its economy vulnerable to fluctuations in their world prices. Sharp drops in these prices, as has occurred periodically, inevitably result in the restriction of imports or a substantial trade deficit.

The economy has been subjected to two major crises in twenty years: first, the loss of a large part of the British market for New Zealand's agricultural products when the United Kingdom joined the European Community in 1973; and second, limits placed on overspending by the government in the early 1980s, which enforced a ten-year program of controls. The program helped transform New Zealand from one of the most heavily protected and regulated economies to one of the most market-oriented and open in the world capable of competing globally. Inflation remains among the lowest in the world. By the mid-1990s, the domestic economy was growing at 5-6 percent per year, there were surpluses in the government's budget, and a per capita GDP that rivaled those of the big European economies.

Public Finance

In 1994, in response to a decade of economic reforms that have opened the economy to foreign investment and triggered strong economic growth, the budget produced a surplus for the first time in fifty years. Surpluses continued through the end of the 1990s.

The U.S. Central Intelligence Agency (CIA) estimated 1997-1998 revenues at $24.9 billion and expenditures at $23.7 billion.

Income

In 1999, New Zealand's gross domestic product (GDP) was US$63.8 billion, or about US$17,400 per person. The 1999 estimated GDP growth rate was 3.1 percent and inflation was 1.3 percent. The 1998 GDP contribution by sector was: agriculture, 8 percent; industry, 23 percent; and services, 69 percent.

Industry

Industrial production has increased rapidly since the end of World War II. Plants include metal and petroleum processing, motor vehicle assembly, textiles and footwear, and a wide range of consumer appliances. The New Zealand Steel company manufactures billet slabs and ingots using domestically produced iron sands. The Tiwai Point aluminum smelter, operated by an Australian-Japanese group, has an annual capacity of 244,000 tons. Other important industries in 1999 were the manufacture of machinery and transportation equipment, banking and insurance, a diverse food processing sector, eco-tourism, and wood and paper products.

Wool-based industries have traditionally been an important part of the economy, notably wool milling, the oldest sector of the textile industry. Other significant industrial areas include electronics, tanneries, sheet glass, rubber, and plastics.

Banking and Finance

The Reserve Bank of New Zealand, established in 1933, exercises control over monetary circulation and credit. It is the bank of issue, handles all central government banking transactions, manages the public debt, and administers exchange control regulations. The Reserve Bank of New Zealand Amendment Act (1973) empowers the Bank to regulate credit from all sources and requires it to make loans (as the minister of finance may determine) in order to ensure continued full employment.

New Zealand's financial services sector is dominated by the commercial banks, leaving only a minor role for non-bank finance companies and savings institutions. In part, this reflects the impact of deregulation since the mid-1980s. The easing of regulations means that there are now only two formal categories of financial institutions: registered banks and other financial institutions. However, both can offer a wide range of financial and banking services.

To be defined as a bank, a financial institution must register with the central Reserve Bank and meet a range of eligibility criteria such as minimum capital adequacy, experience in the financial intermediation industry, and a commitment to the stability of the financial system. The number of registered banks peaked at twenty-four in 1994 and in mid-1996 there were sixteen.

A number of bank mergers have increased the concentration of total banking assets in foreign ownership. Over 95 percent of total banking assets are foreign-owned, compared with 65 percent in 1990. The New Zealand banking industry is increasingly influenced by developments in Australia, since Australian banking groups control over two-thirds of banking assets in New Zealand. This share is unlikely to increase further with the announcement in April 1996 of a conditional buy-out by Westpac Banking Corp. of Trust Bank, New Zealand's last domestically owned bank with a national branch network. The Post Office Savings Bank (established in 1865) has about 1,270 offices and agencies throughout New Zealand.

The Stock Exchange Association of New Zealand, the forerunner to the NZSE, was founded in 1915. New Zealand is advantageously placed since its trading day opens before the U.S. market closes and before the Asian and Australian markets open. The main functions of the New Zealand Stock Exchange (NZSE) are to provide an orderly market for the trading and transfer of securities, to protect investors' interests, and to ensure that the market is fully informed. As of 1992, there were thirty-eight corporate and partnership members of the NZSE.

The stock exchanges in Auckland, Wellington, Christchurch, Dunedin, and Invercargill are members of the New Zealand Stock Exchange (NZSE), with headquarters in Wellington. Official listing is granted to companies that comply with the Exchange's requirements. In 1978, a five-member Securities Commission was established to oversee law and practice relating to securities.

Economic Development

Economic policy is established and directed by the government through taxation, Reserve Bank interest rates, price and monopoly controls, and import and export licensing. Import controls, introduced early in 1958, were further tightened in 1961 and 1973 to correct deficits in the balance of payments. Since then, the government has gradually liberalized import controls; in 1981, about 79 percent of private imports to New Zealand were exempt from licensing. An industrial restructuring program, begun in the mid-1970s, focuses on certain industries (e.g., textiles, footwear, automobiles, and electronics) whose domestic prices are much higher than those of foreign substitutes, with the aim of reducing the protection granted such products.

To help maintain economic stability, the government assists and in some cases controls various economic enterprises (agricultural distribution and marketing, commercial banking, and some insurance). In June 1982, in an effort to reduce inflation, the government announced a freeze on wages, prices, rents, and dividends. The freeze was lifted in March 1984, temporarily reimposed by a new Labour government, and then terminated late in 1984. Its termination, combined with a devaluation of the dollar, led to a resumption of high inflation. The government implemented severe monetary policies to reduce inflation in order to enhance a market- and export-led recovery from the October 1987 financial markets crash. The cost was a large increase in unemployment (from 7 percent to 10.4 percent of the labor force), but by 1991, inflation had been practically eliminated (2.2 percent for the year ending September 1991).

Since 1977, the New Zealand Planning Council has been charged with advising the government on economic, social, and cultural planning and in the coordination of planning. Working independently of the Planning Council, the Economic Monitoring Group, established in 1978, produces reports on economic trends.

In 1984-1985, New Zealand contributed a total of NZ$61.4 million in technical and capital assistance and direct aid or loans to developing nations. An additional NZ$12.5 million was given in multilateral aid through the UN, the South Pacific Commission, ADB, and other organizations. The major recipients of development assistance are the nations of the South Pacific who receive about 70 percent of New Zealand's bilateral aid and about 62 percent of its total overseas aid.

SOCIAL WELFARE

By a system of monetary benefits on compulsory contributory basis and a system of medical and hospital benefits, all persons in New Zealand are now protected economically for retirement and in the event of sickness, unemployment, and widowhood. Monetary benefits under the Social Security Act are paid for retirement, unemployment, sickness, and emergencies; and to widows, orphans, families, invalids, and minors. Medical benefits include medical, hospital, and pharmaceutical payments. A 1982 plan provides compensation for all workers injured in an accident even if the injury did not occur at work.

New Zealand was the first country to grant full voting rights to women and it celebrated the 100th anniversary of that event in 1993 with conferences and other activities.

Healthcare

For over fifty years, comprehensive health services, most of them supported by the State, have been available to all New Zealanders. About 80 percent of all health costs are met by the public sector. However, the number of purchases of private health insurance has risen steadily, and by 1991, about half the population had some private insurance.

New Zealand's health care system has been undergoing a restructuring since the mid-1980s. Area health boards, formed to combine primary and hospital care facilities for each region under a single administrative unit, were established in 1985. In 1991, the government announced plans to expand health care resources for those in financial need.

In 1990-1997, there were 2.1 doctors and 7.3 hospital beds per 1,000 people. Most physicians practice under the National Health Service, established by the Social Security Act of 1938, but private practice outside the scheme is permitted.

Life expectancy at birth was seventy-eight years in 2000. The principal causes of death are heart disease, cancer, and cerebrovascular diseases. Alcoholism is a significant public health problem in New Zealand. Estimates of the number of chronic alcoholics range upward from 53,000, and another 250,000 New Zealanders may be classified as excessive drinkers.

Housing

About 18,000 houses and apartments were built in New Zealand in 1992, when New Zealand's housing stock totaled 1.2 million. More than half the total housing stock has been constructed since 1957. In recent decades, the government has introduced measures to help finance housing for contractors and private owners.

Most families own their own homes. The average private dwelling has three bedrooms, a living room, dining room, kitchen, laundry, bathroom, toilet, and garage. Most units are built of wood and have sheet-iron or tiled roofs.

EDUCATION

Education in New Zealand is compulsory for ten years for children between six and fifteen, although most children attend school from the age of five. The adult literacy rate is 99 percent. Most state schools are coeducational, but some private schools are not. New Zealand has 2,300 state primary schools and sixty privately owned schools. At the secondary level, there are 315 state-run schools and fifteen private schools.

In 1997, 357,569 students attended primary schools, 433,347 students attended secondary schools and in 1999, 63,658 students were in vocational schools. For children in isolated areas, there is a public correspondence school. In some regions there are special state primary and secondary schools for Maori children, but most Maori children attend public schools.

There are six universities: the University of Auckland, University of Waikato (at Hamilton), Massey University (at Palmerston North), Victoria University of Wellington, University of Canterbury (at Christchurch), and University of Otago (at Dunedin). All universities offer courses in the arts, social sciences, commerce, and science.

An agricultural institution, Lincoln College, is associated with the University of Canterbury. Law is offered at Auckland, Waikato, Victoria, Canterbury, and Otago, and medicine at Auckland and Otago. The Central Institute of Technology, near Wellington, is the leading institution in a network of twenty-four polytechnic institutions. There are evening classes for adults interested in continuing their education at secondary schools, institutes, and community centers. University tuition fees are low, and financial assistance is given to applicants who have passed special qualifying examinations.

2000 KEY EVENTS TIMELINE

January

- The first baby of the millennium is born at one minute past midnight on January 1 in New Zealand.
- Prime Minister Helen Clark criticizes Japan's whale hunting practices, and supports the efforts of Greenpeace to block five Japanese whaling ships currently hunting minke whales in the Antarctic.

February

- The Prime Minister says she believes it is inevitable that New Zealand will become a republic if Australia does.
- Researchers working at the University of Auckland and in the United States develop a vaccine which, when tested on rats, successfully protects their brains from the effects of stroke and epileptic seizures.
- Conservationists say the illegal cannabis growers in New Zealand are threatening local plants and wildlife, including the nation's symbol, the kiwi.

March

- Team New Zealand retains the Americas Cup championship in yachting.
- Police break up an Auckland smuggling ring that has been bringing in illegal immigrants and drugs from Asia and the Middle East.
- New Zealand wins Hong Kong Sevens Rugby Tournament, defeating the prior champion, Fiji.

April

- Hundreds of Chinese Indonesian immigrants fight to stay in New Zealand, fearing to return home to a repeat of the violence they fled in 1998.

- Prime Minister Helen Clark publicly scoffs at the suggestion that New Zealand become a state of Australia.

July

- A New Zealand soldier on duty with the U.N. peacekeeping force in East Timor is killed, the first casualty among the peacekeepers since they took control of East Timor.

August

- During an investigation of alleged people-smuggling, New Zealand police discover a possible plot to blow up a nuclear reactor in Sydney during the Olympics. The plot is thought to be the work of Afghan rebels loyal to Osama bin Laden.
- New Zealand fire fighters travel to the United States to help fight the raging forest fires in the American west.
- A banned book harshly critical of Britain's brutal treatment of the Maoris, written in 1896 by Benedictine monk Dom Felice Vaggioli, is published in New Zealand for the first time.

September

- Rower Rob Waddell wins an Olympic gold medal in the men's single scull event; New Zealand athletes also capture bronze medals in sailing and equestrian events.
- Australian Prime Minister John Howard states his nation is against the idea of a shared currency with New Zealand. The concept is popular in New Zealand, where the local dollar is worth less than its Australian counterpart.

October

- New Zealand scientists outline a possible remedy to global warming, suggesting the Southern Ocean be seeded with iron on the theory that it will increase plankton levels, which will in turn reduce the levels of carbon dioxide in the atmosphere.

November

- Prime Minister Helen Clark confirms reports that Khamsay Souphanouvong, a high-ranking Laotian government official, has been granted political asylum in New Zealand.
- The government announces November 9 that it will spend more than $28 million on programming for a Maori television station.
- Australia and New Zealand agree on open skies air travel.

December

- The World Trade Organization says the U.S. tariffs on lamb imports from New Zealand are unfair and illegal under international trade rules. This decision clears the way for a compensation claim against the United States.
- A New Zealand government minister suggests getting rid of New Zealand's combat aircraft and reducing the size of its navy, stating that the aircraft are out of date and that the money would be better spent on education and health. New Zealand's defense spending is already one of the lowest in the world—1.6 percent of the gross domestic product (GDP).
- A pod of whales is discovered stranded on Maori Beach on South Island. Despite rescuers' efforts to save them, at least twenty-two whales perish. The cause of the beaching is not known.

ANALYSIS OF EVENTS: 2000

BUSINESS AND THE ECONOMY

In 2000 the Transparency International Worldwide Corruption Perception Index once again found New Zealand to be the third least corrupt nation with which to do business, in both the government and public sectors. Only Finland and Denmark were judged to be less corrupt.

Australia and New Zealand discussed sharing a common currency, but Australia turned down the idea. The concept of a shared currency was more popular in New Zealand than it was in Australia, where the local dollar was more valuable. Australia stated it would possibly consider it in the future, but would prefer that New Zealand use the Australian currency rather than going with a new monetary system.

New Zealand asparagus growers reported that the nation's asparagus export industry was making a comeback in 2000 after a dismal few years in which production dropped considerably. New agricultural research and increased earnings were credited with the improvement. In December the World Trade Organization ruled that U.S. tariffs on lamb imports from New Zealand were unfair and illegal under international trade rules. This decision cleared the way for a compensation claim against the United States.

GOVERNMENT AND POLITICS

The year opened with New Zealand in the international spotlight when the first baby of the millennium, a boy named Tuatahi Manaakitunga Edwards, was born in New Zealand at one minute past midnight on the first day of the year. Months later world attention again focused on the nation, when a New Zealand soldier on duty with the United Nations peacekeeping force in East Timor became the first casualty among the peacekeepers since they had taken control.

People from throughout the region sought to immigrate to New Zealand. Requests from the Solomon Islands in 2000 were nearly double those received in the previous year. Hundreds of Chinese Indonesian immigrants fought for the right to stay in New Zealand, fearing to return home to a repeat of the violence they fled in 1998. In November Prime Minister Helen Clark confirmed reports that Khamsay Souphanouvong, a high-ranking Laotian government official, had been granted political asylum in New Zealand. Not all travelers came to New Zealand legally; in March police broke up an Auckland smuggling ring that was bringing in illegal immigrants and drugs from Asia and the Middle East. While investigating another instance of alleged people smuggling, New Zealand police discovered a possible plot to blow up a nuclear reactor in Sydney, Australia, during the Olympics. The plot was thought to be the work of Afghan rebels loyal to Osama bin Laden.

New Zealand statehood was an issue of discussion in 2000. In February the Prime Minister said she believed it was inevitable that New Zealand would become a republic if Australia did. She later scoffed at the idea that New Zealand might be made a province of Australia. New Zealand's foreign minister assured the people of the territory of Tokelau they would not be forced to become independent if they preferred to remain a New Zealand territory.

In April Don McKinnon, former Foreign Minister, became Secretary General of the Commonwealth. He pledged to make organization, made up of the fifty-four-member nations, more useful to the citizens of the member states.

In August Dame Silvia Cartwright was named New Zealand's next governor general. Earlier in her career, she had been the first woman to become a Chief High Court judge.

CULTURE AND SOCIETY

A book entitled *History of New Zealand and Its Inhabitants,* written by Italian Benedictine monk Dom Felice Vaggioli in 1896, was finally published in New Zealand in August. This book was so critical of the English treatment of the Maoris that it had been immediately banned in New Zealand upon publication and all copies ordered burned. No longer considered a threat to civil order, the new translation and publication were funded in part by the government.

New Zealand's scientists published important research this year. In February researchers working in the United States and New Zealand (at the University of Auckland) developed a vaccine that was shown to protect rats' brains from the effects of stroke and epileptic seizures. They hoped to develop a version that could protect people at high risk for strokes. Other New Zealand scientists outlined a possible remedy for global warming when they suggested seeding the Southern Ocean with iron. Doing so, they claimed, would increase plankton levels, which would in turn reduce the levels of carbon dioxide in the atmosphere. (High levels of carbon dioxide are linked with global warming.)

New Zealand's conservationists found much to talk about in 2000. They reported that illegal cannabis growers were threatening local plants and wildlife, including the nation's symbol—the kiwi—because they were clearing large areas of woodland and cutting down large indigenous trees. Early in the year, Prime Minister Helen Clark criticized Japan's whale hunting practices, stating that she supported the efforts of Greenpeace to block five Japanese whaling ships from hunting whales in the Antarctic.

New Zealand won many sporting honors this year. In March Team New Zealand retained the Americas Cup championship in yachting; New Zealand also won the Hong Kong Sevens Rugby Tournament, defeating the prior champion, Fiji. In September all three of New Zealand's crews advanced to the Olympic rowing finals in the Sydney Olympics: Rob Waddell came in first in the men's single event, winning a gold medal; Sonia Waddell finished sixth in the women's single event, and the coxless four rowing crew also took sixth place in its event.

DIRECTORY

CENTRAL GOVERNMENT

Head of State

Monarch
Elizabeth II, Queen of England

Governor-General
Michael Hardie Boys

Prime Minister
Helen Clark, Office of the Prime Minister, Wellington, New Zealand
PHONE: +64 (04) 4719998
FAX: +64 (04) 4737045
E-MAIL: prime.minister@ministers.govt.nz

Ministers

Minister of Foreign Affairs and Trade
Philip Goff, Ministry of Foreign Affairs and Trade, Private Mail Bag 18901, Wellington 1001, New Zealand
PHONE: +64 (04) 4728877
FAX: +64 (04) 4729596

Minister of the Environment
Marian Hobbs, Ministry of the Environment, 84 Boulcott St., PO Box 10-362, Wellington, New Zealand
PHONE: +64 (04) 4734090
FAX: +64 (04) 4710195

Minister of Commerce
Paul Swain, Ministry of Commerce, Ministry of Commerce Building, 33 Bowen Street, Wellington, New Zealand
PHONE: +64 (04) 4720030
FAX: +64 (04) 4734638
E-MAIL: enterprise@ministers.govt.nz

Minister of Health
Annette King, Ministry of Health, 133 Molesworth St., Wellington, New Zealand
PHONE: +64 (04) 4962000
FAX: +64 (04) 4962340
E-MAIL: MOH@moh.govt.nz

Minister of Biosecurity
Marian Hobbs, Ministry of Biosecurity
E-MAIL: food@ministers.govt.nz

Minister of Finance
Michael Cullen, Ministry of Finance
E-MAIL: finance@ministers.govt.nz

Minister of Social Services and Employment
Steven Maharey, Ministry of Social Services and Employment
E-MAIL: social.services@ministers.govt.nz

Minister of Maori Affairs
Dover Samuels, Ministry of Maori Affairs, Te Puni Kokiri House, 143 Lambton Quay, Wellington, New Zealand
PHONE: +64 (04) 9226000
FAX: +64 (04) 9226299
E-MAIL: maori.affairs@ministers.govt.nz

Minister of Education
Trevor Mallard, Ministry of Education, 45-47 Pipitea Street, Thorndon, Wellington, New Zealand
PHONE: +64 (04) 4735544
FAX: +64 (04) 4991327
E-MAIL: communications@minedu.govt.nz

Minister of Conservation
Sandra Lee, Ministry of Conservation
E-MAIL: vonservation@ministers.govt.nz

Minister of Accident Rehabilitation and Compensation Insurance
Michael Cullen, Ministry of Accident Rehabilitation and Compensation Insurance
E-MAIL: acc@ministers.govt.nz

Minister of Sport, Fitness and Leisure
Trevor Mallard, Ministry of Sport, Fitness and Leisure

Minister of Justice
Philip Goff, Ministry of Justice, Charles Fergusson Building, Bowen Street, Wellington, New Zealand
PHONE: +64 (04) 4949700
FAX: +64 (04) 4949701
E-MAIL: justice@ministers.govt.nz

Minister of State Owned Enterprises
Richard Burton, Ministry of State Owned Enterprises

Minister of Youth Affairs
Laila Harre, Ministry of Youth Affairs, PO Box 10-300 The Terrace, 48 Mulgrave Street, Wellington, New Zealand
PHONE: +64 (04) 4712158
FAX: +64 (04) 4712233
E-MAIL: info@youthaffairs.govt.nz

Minister of Transport
Mark Gosche, Ministry of Transport, 38-42 Waring Taylor St, Wellington, New Zealand
PHONE: +64 (04) 4721253

FAX: +64 (04) 4733697
E-MAIL: transport@ministers.govt.nz

Minister of Research, Science, and Technology
Peter Hodgson, Ministry of Research, Science, and Technology, PO Box 5336, Wellington, New Zealand
PHONE: +64 (04) 4726400
FAX: +64 (04) 4711284
E-MAIL: info@morst.govt.nz

Minister of Communications
Paul Swain, Ministry of Communications

Minister of Information Technology
Paul Swain, Ministry of Information Technology

Minister of Trade Negotiations
James Sutton, Ministry of Trade Negotiations
E-MAIL: international.trade@ministers.govt.nz

Minister of Tourism
Richard Burton, Ministry of Tourism

Minister of State Services
Trevor Mallard, Ministry of State Services
E-MAIL: state.services@ministers.govt.nz

Minister of Crown Research Initiatives
Peter Hodgson, Ministry of Crown Research Initiatives

Minister of Courts
Matt Robson, Ministry of Courts, Level 3 Vogel Building, Aitken St, Wellington, New Zealand
PHONE: +64 (04) 4948800
FAX: +64 (04) 4948820
E-MAIL: courts@ministers.govt.nz

Minister of Women's Affairs
Laila Harre, Ministry of Women's Affairs, 48 Mulgrave St., Wellington, New Zealand
PHONE: +64 (04) 4734112
FAX: +64 (04) 4720961
E-MAIL: mwa@mwa.govt.nz

Minister of Police
George Hawkins, Ministry of Police
E-MAIL: police@ministers.govt.nz

Minister of Immigration
Lianne Dalziel, Ministry of Immigration
E-MAIL: immigration@ministers.govt.nz

Minister of Pacific Island Affairs
Mark Gosche, Ministry of Pacific Island Affairs, Level 1, Charles Fergusson Bldg., Ballantrae Place, Wellington, New Zealand
PHONE: +64 (04) 4734493
FAX: +64 (04) 4734301
E-MAIL: contact@minpac.govt.nz

Minister of Senior Citizens
Lianne Dalziel, Ministry of Senior Citizens
E-MAIL: senior.citizens@ministers.govt.nz

Minister of Internal Affairs
Richard Burton, Ministry of Internal Affairs
E-MAIL: internal.affairs@ministers.govt.nz

Minister of Fisheries
Peter Hodgson, Ministry of Fisheries, 101-103 The Terrace, Wellington, New Zealand
PHONE: +64 (04) 4702600
FAX: +64 (04) 4702601
E-MAIL: info@fish.govt.nz

Minister of Agriculture
James Sutton, Ministry of Agriculture

Minister of Revenue
Michael Cullen, Ministry of Revenue

Minister of Defense
Richard Burton, Ministry of Defense, PO Box 5347, Lambton Quay, Wellington, New Zealand
PHONE: +64 (04) 4960999
FAX: +64 (04) 4960859
E-MAIL: communications@defence.govt.nz

Minister of Housing
Mark Gosche, Ministry of Housing, Level 12, Vogel Building, Aitken Street, Wellington, New Zealand
PHONE: +64 (04) 4722753
FAX: +64 (04) 4994744
E-MAIL: info@minhousing.govt.nz

Minister of Local Government
Sandra Lee, Ministry of Local Government

Minister of Statistics
Paul Swain, Ministry of Statistics

Minister of Disarmament and Arms Control
Matt Robson, Ministry of Disarmament and Arms Control

Minister of Veterans Affairs
Richard Burton, Ministry of Veterans Affairs

Minister of Corrections
Matt Robson, Ministry of Corrections

Minister of Racing
Annette King, Ministry of Racing

POLITICAL ORGANIZATIONS

New Zealand National Party

PO Box 1155, Wellington, New Zealand
PHONE: +64 (04) 4725211
FAX: +64 (04) 4781622
E-MAIL: hq@national.org.nz

NAME: Jenny Shipley

New Zealand Labor Party

PO Box 784, Wellington, New Zealand
E-MAIL: labour.party@parliament.govt.nz
TITLE: Leader
NAME: Helen Clark

New Zealand First Party

Parliament Buildings, Wellington, New Zealand
PHONE: +64 (04) 4719292
FAX: +64 (04) 4727751
E-MAIL: nzfirst@parliament.govt.nz
TITLE: Leader
NAME: Winston Peters

New Labor Party

TITLE: Leader
NAME: Jim Anderton

Green Party of Aotearoa

PO Box 11-652, Wellington, New Zealand
PHONE: +64 (04) 9388622
FAX: +64 (04) 9386251
TITLE: Co-Leaders
NAME: Jeannette Fitzsimons; Rod Donald

Mana Motuhake e Aotearoa (New Zealand Self-Government Party)

NAME: Sandra Lee

New Zealand Democratic Party

129 Onewa Road, Northcote, North Shore City, New Zealand
PHONE: +64 (09) 4800364
FAX: +64 (09) 4800438
E-MAIL: nzdemocrats@hotmail.com
TITLE: President
NAME: Peter Kane

Liberal Party

TITLE: Co-Leaders
NAME: Hanmish Macintyre; Gilbert Myles

DIPLOMATIC REPRESENTATION

Embassies in New Zealand

Argentina
PO Box 5430, Lambton Qua, Wellington, New Zealand
PHONE: +64 (04) 4728330
FAX: +64 (04) 4728331

Australia
72-78 Hobson Street, Thorndon, Wellington, New Zealand
PHONE: +64 (04) 4736411
FAX: +64 (04) 4987103

Belgium
12th Floor, Axon House, 1-3 Willeston Street, Wellington, New Zealand
PHONE: +64 (04) 4729558; 4729559
FAX: +64 (04) 4712764

Brazil
Level 9, Wool House, 10 Brandon Street, Wellington, New Zealand
PHONE: +64 (04) 4733516
FAX: +64 (04) 4733517
E-MAIL: brasemb@ihug.co.nz

Canada
61 Moleworth Street, Wellington, New Zealand
PHONE: +64 (04) 4739577
FAX: +64 (04) 4712082

Chile
19 Bolton Street, Wellington, New Zealand
PHONE: +64 (04) 4716270
FAX: +64 (04) 4725324

China
2-6 Glenmore Street, Wellington, New Zealand
PHONE: +64 (04) 4721384
FAX: +64 (04) 4990419; 4721998

Cook Islands
56 Mulgrave Street, Wellington, New Zealand
PHONE: +64 (04) 4725126; 4725127
FAX: +64 (04) 4725121

El Salvador
1/644 Manukau Road, Epsom 1003, Auckland, New Zealand
PHONE: +64 (025) 6254770
FAX: +64 (025) 6254710

Fiji
31 Pipitea Street, Thorndon, Wellington, New Zealand
PHONE: +64 (04) 4735401; 4735402

France
34-42 Manners Street, Wellington, New Zealand
PHONE: +64 (04) 3842555; 8027790; 8027791
FAX: +64 (04) 3842577; 3842579

Germany
90-92 Hobson Street, Thorndon, Wellington, New Zealand
PHONE: +64 (04) 4736063; 4736064
FAX: +64 (04) 4736069

India
10th Floor, FAI House, 180 Molesworth Street, Wellington, New Zealand
PHONE: +64 (04) 4736390; 4736391
FAX: +64 (04) 4990665

Indonesia
70 Glen Road, Kelburn, Wellington, New Zealand
PHONE: +64 (04) 4758697; 4758698; 4758699
FAX: +64 (04) 4759374

Iran
PO Box 10 249, The Terrace, Wellington, New Zealand
PHONE: +64 (04) 3862976; 3862983
FAX: +64 (04) 3863065

Israel
13th Floor, Equinox House, 111 The Terrace, Wellington, New Zealand
PHONE: +64 (04) 4722362; 4722368
FAX: +64 (04) 4990632

Italy
34-38 Grant Road, Thorndon, Wellington, New Zealand
PHONE: +64 (04) 4735339
FAX: +64 (04) 4727255

Japan
Majestic Centre, 100 Willis Street, Wellington, New Zealand
PHONE: +64 (04) 4731540
FAX: +64 (04) 4712951

Korea
Level 11, 2 Hunter Street, Wellington, New Zealand
PHONE: +64 (04) 4739073; 4739074
FAX: +64 (04) 4723865

Lithuania
28 Heather Street, Auckland, New Zealand
PHONE: +64 (025) 3796639
FAX: +64 (025) 3072911

Malaysia
10 Washington Avenue, Brooklyn, Wellington, New Zealand
PHONE: +64 (04) 3852439; 8010943
FAX: +64 (04) 3856973

Mexico
Level 8, GRE House, 111-115 Customhouse Quay, Wellington, New Zealand
PHONE: +64 (04) 4725555; 4725556
FAX: +64 (04) 4725800

Nauru
2nd Floor, 29 Union Street, Wellington, New Zealand
PHONE: +64 (04) 3091799
FAX: +64 (04) 3073113

Netherlands
Investment Center, Corner Ballance and Featherston Streets, Wellington, New Zealand
PHONE: +64 (04) 4716390
FAX: +64 (04) 4712923

Norway
61 Molesworth Street, Wellington, New Zealand
PHONE: +64 (04) 4712503
FAX: +64 (04) 4728023

Papua New Guinea
279 Willis Street, Wellington, New Zealand
PHONE: +64 (04) 3852474; 3852475; 3852476
FAX: +64 (04) 3852477

Peru
Level 8, Cigna House, 40 Mercer Street, Wellington, New Zealand
PHONE: +64 (04) 4998087
FAX: +64 (04) 4998087

Philippines
50 Hobson Street, Thorndon, Wellington, New Zealand
PHONE: +64 (04) 4729848; 4729921
FAX: +64 (04) 4725170

Poland
17 Upland Road, Kelburn, Wellington, New Zealand
PHONE: +64 (04) 4759433
FAX: +64 (04) 4759458

Portugal
Suite 1, 1st Floor, 21 Marion Street, Wellington, New Zealand
PHONE: +64 (04) 3859639
FAX: +64 (04) 3842534

Russia
57 Messines Road, Karori, Wellington, New Zealand
PHONE: +64 (04) 4766742
FAX: +64 (04) 4763843

Samoa
1A Wesley Road, Kelburn, Wellington, New Zealand
PHONE: +64 (04) 4720953; 4720954
FAX: +64 (04) 4712479

Singapore
17 Kabul Street, Khandallah, Wellington, New Zealand
PHONE: +64 (04) 4792076; 4792077
FAX: +64 (04) 4792315

South Africa
National Mutual Corporate Superannuation Services Ltd., 80 The Terrace, Wellington, New Zealand
PHONE: +64 (04) 4744953
FAX: +64 (04) 4710504

Spain
PO Box 71, Papkura, Auckland, New Zealand
PHONE: +64 (025) 2996019
FAX: +64 (025) 2989986

Sri Lanka
22 Bloomfield Terrace, Lower Hutt, New Zealand
PHONE: +64 5605817
FAX: +64 5665633

Sweden
13th Floor, Vogel Bldg., Aitken Street, Wellington, New Zealand
PHONE: +64 (04) 4999895
FAX: +64 (04) 4991464

Switzerland
Panama House, 22 Panama Street, Wellington, New Zealand
PHONE: +64 (04) 4721593; 4721594
FAX: +64 (04) 4996302

Thailand
2 Cook Street, Karori, Wellington, New Zealand
PHONE: +64 (04) 4768618; 4768619
FAX: +64 (04) 4763677

Turkey
15-17 Murphy Street, Thorndon, Wellington, New Zealand
PHONE: +64 (04) 4721292
FAX: +64 (04) 4721277

Tuvalu
PO Box 100-375, North Shore Mail Centre, Auckland, New Zealand
PHONE: +64 (025) 4106463; 2262133
FAX: +64 (025) 4106923

United Kingdom
44 Hill Street, Wellington, New Zealand
PHONE: +64 (04) 4950889
FAX: +64 (04) 4711974
TITLE: High Commissioner
NAME: Martin Williams

United States
29 Fitzherbert Terrace, Wellington, New Zealand
PHONE: +64 (04) 4722068
FAX: +64 (04) 4723537

Uruguay
7 Chisenhall Street, Karori, Wellington, New Zealand
PHONE: +64 (04) 4762275
FAX: +64 (04) 4762268

Vanuatu
50 Kelman Road, Kelston, Auckland, New Zealand
PHONE: +64 (025) 8181102

JUDICIAL SYSTEM

High Court

2 Molesworth St, PO Box 1091, Wellington, New Zealand
PHONE: +64 (04) 9158000
FAX: +64 (04) 9158434; 9158435

Court of Appeal

Cnr Molesworth and Aitken Streets, PO Box 1606, Wllington, New Zealand
PHONE: +64 (04) 9158000
FAX: +64 (04) 9158250

BROADCAST MEDIA

Community Network New Zealand

PO Box 952, Taupo, New Zealand
PHONE: +64 (7) 3783386
FAX: +64 (7) 3787295
TITLE: General Manager
CONTACT: Brian Jennings
TYPE: Private

Independent Broadcasters Association, Inc.

PO Box 3762, Auckland, New Zealand
PHONE: +64 (9) 3780788
FAX: +64 (9) 3788180
TITLE: Executive Director
CONTACT: B.G. Impey
TYPE: Private

Radio New Zealand

PO Box 123, Wellington, New Zealand
PHONE: +64 (4) 4741999
FAX: +64 (4) 4741459
E-MAIL: webmaster@awacs.co.nz

WEBSITE: http://www.rnz.co.nz; www.radionz.co.nz (text site)
TITLE: Chief Executive
CONTACT: Sharon Crosbie
BROADCASTS: 24 hours/day
TYPE: Government

Radio New Zealand International

PO Box 123, Wellington, New Zealand
PHONE: +64 (4) 4741437
FAX: +64 (4) 4741433
E-MAIL: info@rnzi.com
WEBSITE: http://www.rnzi.com
TITLE: Manager
CONTACT: Linden Clark
TYPE: Government

The Radio Network of New Zealand

PO Box 378, Auckland, New Zealand
PHONE: +64 (9) 3773097
FAX: +64 (9) 3674619
TYPE: Private

Action TV

PO Box 388-99, Wellington, New Zealand
PHONE: +64 (4) 5766999
FAX: +64 (4) 5766942
CHANNEL: 47, 48, 50, 53, 55, 56, 58

Canterbury Television (CTV)

196 Gloucester Street, Christchurch, New Zealand
CHANNEL: 48

Prime Television

PO Box 302193, North Harbor Postal Centre, Auckland, New Zealand
PHONE: +64 (9) 4153544; +64 (800) PRIMETV (774638)
FAX: +64 (9) 4153545
WEBSITE: http://www.primetv.co.nz

Sky Network Television

10 Panorama Road, Mt Wellington, Auckland, New Zealand
PHONE: +64 (9)5799999; +64 (800) SKY-SKY (759759)
FAX: +64 (9) 5790910; +64 (9) 5258355
E-MAIL: sky@skytv.co.nz
WEBSITE: http://www.skytv.co.nz
TITLE: Director of Operations
CONTACT: Greg Drummond
TYPE: Pay-TV

Television New Zealand Ltd.

100 Victoria Street, PO Box 3819, Auckland, New Zealand
PHONE: +64 (9) 9167000
FAX: +64 (9) 9167934
E-MAIL: webmaster@tvone.co.nz
WEBSITE: http://www.tvone.co.nz
TITLE: Deputy Group Executive
CONTACT: Darryl Dorrington
CHANNEL: 1, 2, 3

TV3

Private Bag 92624, Symonds Street, Auckland, New Zealand
PHONE: +64 (9) 779730
FAX: +64 (9) 3022311
WEBSITE: http://www.tv3.co.nz
TITLE: Managing Director
CONTACT: Graeme Hunter
CHANNEL: 6, 7, 10, 11
TYPE: Commercial

COLLEGES AND UNIVERSITIES

University of Canterbury

Private Bag 4800, Christchurch, New Zealand
PHONE: +64 (3) 3667001
FAX: +64 (3) 3642999
WEBSITE: http://www.canterbury.ac.nz

Otago Polytechnic

Private Bag 1919, Dunedin, New Zealand
PHONE: +64 (3) 4773014
FAX: +64 (3) 4776032
E-MAIL: info@tekotago.ac.nz
WEBSITE: http://www.tekotago.ac.nz

Telford Rural Polytechnic

Freepost 73901, Private Bag 6, Balclutha, New Zealand
PHONE: +64 (3) 4811550
FAX: +64 (3) 4183584
E-MAIL: mark.johnston@telford.ac.nz
WEBSITE: http://www.telford.ac.nz

Eastern Institute of Technology

Private Bag 92006, Auckland, New Zealand
PHONE: +64 (3) 5462483
FAX: +64 (3) 5463329
E-MAIL: info@eit.ac.nz
WEBSITE: http://www.eit.ac.nz

Aoraki Polytechnic

Private Bag 902, Timaru, New Zealand
PHONE: +64 (3) 6848240
FAX: +64 (3) 6880809
E-MAIL: study@aoraki.ac.nz
WEBSITE: http://www.aoraki.ac.nz

Whitireia Community Polytechnic

Private Bag 50910, Porirua City, Wellington, New Zealand
PHONE: +64 (4) 2373100
FAX: +64 (4) 2373101
E-MAIL: adm@whitireia.ac.nz
WEBSITE: http://www.whitireia.ac.nz

Open Polytechnic of New Zealand

Wyndrum Ave., Private Bag 31914, Lower Hutt, New Zealand
PHONE: +64 (4) 5666189
FAX: +64 (4) 5665633
E-MAIL: infocentre@mail.topnz.ac.nz
WEBSITE: http://www.topnz.ac.nz

Central Institute of Technology

Private Bag 40740, Auckland, New Zealand
PHONE: +64 (4) 9142000
FAX: +64 (4) 9142089
WEBSITE: http://www.cit.ac.nz

Wanganui Polytechnic

57 Campbell St., Private Bag 3020, Wanganui, New Zealand
PHONE: +64 (6) 3450997
FAX: +64 (6) 3452263
E-MAIL: infoline@whanganui.ac.nz
WEBSITE: http://www.whanganui.ac.nz

International Pacific College

Private Bag 11021, Palmerston North, New Zealand
PHONE: +64 (6) 3540922
FAX: +64 (6) 3540935
E-MAIL: info@ipc.ac.nz
WEBSITE: http://www.ipc.ac.nz

Massey University

Private Bag 11222, Palmerston North, New Zealand
PHONE: +64 (6) 3569099
FAX: +64 (6) 3502263
WEBSITE: http://www.massey.ac.nz

Taranaki Polytechnic

Bell St., New Plymouth, New Zealand
PHONE: +64 (6) 7573100
FAX: 64 (6) 757 6605
E-MAIL: info@taranaki.ac.nz
WEBSITE: http://www.taranaki.ac.nz

Tairawhiti Polytechnic

Private Bag 640, Gisborne, New Zealand
PHONE: +64 (6) 8688068
FAX: +64 (6) 8672186
E-MAIL: info@tairawhiti.ac.nz
WEBSITE: http://www.tairawhiti.ac.nz

Universal College of Learning

Private Bag 11022, Palmerston North, New Zealand
PHONE: +64 (6) 9527000
FAX: +64 (6) 9527002
WEBSITE: http://www.ucol.ac.nz

Waiariki Institute of Technology

Private Bag 3028, Rotorua, New Zealand
PHONE: +64 (7) 3468742
FAX: +64 (7) 3468743
E-MAIL: enquiry@waiariki.ac.nz
WEBSITE: http://www.waiariki.ac.nz

Bay of Plenty Polytechnic

Private Bag Tg12001, Tauranga, New Zealand
PHONE: +64 (7) 5440920
FAX: +64 (7) 5442386
E-MAIL: info@boppoly.ac.nz
WEBSITE: http://www.boppoly.ac.nz

Fairfield College

Private Bag 4021, Hamilton, New Zealand
PHONE: +64 (7) 8552169
FAX: +64 (7) 8552166
E-MAIL: fairfieldcollege@hotmail.com
WEBSITE: http://www.faircol.co.nz

University of Waikato

Private Bag 3105, Hamilton, New Zealand
PHONE: +64 (7) 8562889
FAX: +64 (7) 8384370
E-MAIL: hrm@waikato.ac.nz
WEBSITE: http://www.waikato.ac.nz

Whitecliffe College of Art & Design

136 Grafton Rd., Private Bag 8192, Symonds St., Auckland, New Zealand

PHONE: +64 (9) 3095970
FAX: +64 (9) 3022957
E-MAIL: webmaster@wcad.ac.nz
WEBSITE: http://www.wcad.ac.nz

Unitec Institute of Technolgy

Auckland, New Zealand
PHONE: +64 (9) 8152945
E-MAIL: jwebster@unitec.ac.nz
WEBSITE: http://www.unitec.ac.nz

Carrington Polytechnic

Private Bag, Mount Albert, Auckland, New Zealand

Auckland University of Technology

Private Bag 92006, 59-67 Wellesley St., Auckland, New Zealand
PHONE: +64 (9) 3079999
FAX: +64 (9) 3079968
E-MAIL: webchanges@aut.ac.nz
WEBSITE: http://www.aut.ac.nz

Auckland College of Education

Freepost 5454, Private Bag 5454, Symonds Street, Auckland 1035, New Zealand
PHONE: +64 (9) 6238883
FAX: +64 (9) 6238950
E-MAIL: ace contact@ace.ac.nz
WEBSITE: http://www.ace.ac.nz

Hawkes Bay Polytechnic

Taradale, Napier, New Zealand

Waikato Polytechnic

Private Bag 3036, Hamilton, New Zealand
PHONE: +64 (7) 8348877
FAX: +64 (7) 8388256
E-MAIL: info@twp.ac.nz
WEBSITE: http://www.twp.ac.nz

University of Auckland

Private Bag 92019, 1-11 Short St., Auckland 5528, New Zealand
PHONE: +64 (9) 3737528
FAX: +64 (9) 3737465
E-MAIL: postmaster@auckland.ac.nz
WEBSITE: http://www.auckland.ac.nz

Wairarapa Community Polytechnic

PO Box 698, Masterson, New Zealand
PHONE: +64 (6) 3700171
FAX: +64 (6) 3700090
E-MAIL: brodwyn-hemana@wairarapa.ac.nz
WEBSITE: http://www.wairarapa.ac.nz

Victoria University of Wellington

PO Box 600, Wellington, New Zealand
PHONE: +64 (4) 4721000
FAX: +64 (4) 4994601
E-MAIL: info-desk@vuw.ac.nz
WEBSITE: http://www.vuw.ac.nz

Hutt Valley Polytechnic

Private Bag 39803, Te Puni Mail Ctre Petone, Wellington, New Zealand
PHONE: +64 (4) 920256
FAX: +64 (4) 9292401
E-MAIL: marketing@hvp.ac.nz
WEBSITE: http://www.hvp.ac.nz

Nelson Marlborough Institute of Technology

Private Bag 19, Nelson, New Zealand
PHONE: +64 (3) 5469175
FAX: +64 (3) 5462441
E-MAIL: info@nmit.ac.nz
WEBSITE: http://www.nmit.ac.nz

Christchurch Polytechnic

PO Box 22095, Christchurch, New Zealand
PHONE: +64 (3) 3798150
FAX: +64 (3) 3666544
E-MAIL: info@chchpoly.ac.nz
WEBSITE: http://www.chchp.ac.nz

Christchurch College of Education

PO Box 31-065, Dovedale Ave., Iian, Christchurch, New Zealand
WEBSITE: http://www.cce.ac.nz

Lincoln University - Canterbury

PO Box 84, Canterbury, New Zealand
PHONE: +64 (3) 3252811
FAX: +64 (3) 3253840
E-MAIL: collinsi@lincoln.ac.nz
WEBSITE: http://www.lincoln.ac.nz

University of Otago

Otago School of Medical Sciences, University of Otago, PO Box 56, 409 Leith St., Dunedin, New Zealand
PHONE: +64 (3) 4798247
FAX: +64 (3) 4797377

E-MAIL: external-relations@otago.ac.nz
WEBSITE: http://www.otago.ac.nz

Southland Polytechnic

133 Tay St., Freepost 4 Study, Invercargill, New Zealand
PHONE: +64 (3) 2182599
FAX: +64 (3) 2144977
E-MAIL: info@sit.ac.nz
WEBSITE: http://www.sit.ac.nz

NEWSPAPERS AND MAGAZINES

Auckland City Harbour News

Suburban Newspapers Auckland, Private Bag 92815, Penrose, Auckland, New Zealand
PHONE: +64 (9) 8496060
FAX: +64 (9) 8496116
E-MAIL: corpsales@snl.co.nz
TITLE: Editor
CONTACT: Dionne Christian
CIRCULATION: 18,795

Bestbuys

Retail Media Ltd., CPO Box 3990, Auckland 0064 New Zealand
PHONE: +64 (9) 3079747
FAX: +64 (9) 3079744
E-MAIL: gscott@retailmedia.co.nx
TITLE: Publisher
CONTACT: Greg Scott
CIRCULATION: 871,050

Central Leader

Suburban Newspapers Aukland, Private Bag 92815, Penrose, Auckland, New Zealand
PHONE: +64 (9) 5250666
FAX: +64 (9) 526079
E-MAIL: corpsales@snl.co.nz
TITLE: Editor
CONTACT: Jeremy Rees
CIRCULATION: 48,662

Christchurch Star

293 Tuam St., PO Box 1467, Christchurch, New Zealand
PHONE: +64 (3) 3797100
FAX: +64 (3) 3647484
E-MAIL: star@chstar.co.nz
WEBSITE: http://www.wilsonandhorton.co.nz
TITLE: Editor
CONTACT: Michael Fletcher
CIRCULATION: 120,000

The Dominion

Wellington Newspapers Ltd., PO Box 3740, Wellington, New Zealand
PHONE: +64 (4) 4740555
FAX: +64 (4) 4740490
E-MAIL: editor@dominion.co.nz
WEBSITE: http://www.infotech.co.nz
TITLE: Editor
CONTACT: Richard Long
CIRCULATION: 69,930

East & Bays Courier

Suburban Newspapers Auckland, Private Bag 92815, Penrose, Auckland, New Zealand
PHONE: +64 (9) 5251133
FAX: +64 (9) 5253799
E-MAIL: corpsales@snl.co.nz
TITLE: Editor
CONTACT: Julie Middleton
CIRCULATION: 40,841

The Evening Post

Wellington Newspapers Ltd., PO Box 3740, Wellington, New Zealand
PHONE: +64 (4) 4740555
FAX: +64 (4) 4740490
TITLE: Editor
CONTACT: Suzanne Carty
CIRCULATION: 60,415

Manukau Courier

Suburban Newspapers Auckland, Private Bag 92815, Penrose, Auckland, New Zealand
PHONE: +64 (9) 2624700
FAX: +64 (9) 2624728
E-MAIL: corpsales@snl.co.nz
TITLE: Editor
CONTACT: David Gadd
CIRCULATION: 49,994

Manurewa Week

Community Newspapers, a division of Wilson & Horton, PO Box 12028, Penrose, Auckland, New Zealand
PHONE: +64 (9) 5258877
FAX: +64 (9) 5258887
TITLE: Group Ad Manager
CONTACT: Rikki Noonan
CIRCULATION: 19,747

National Business Review

Fourth Estate Holdings Ltd., PO Box 1734, Auckland, New Zealand
PHONE: +64 (9) 3071629
FAX: +64 (9) 3097878
E-MAIL: bcolman@liberty.co.nz
WEBSITE: http://www.nbr.co.nz
TITLE: Publisher
CONTACT: Barry Colman
CIRCULATION: 14,023

The New Zealand Herald

Wilson & Horton Newspapers Ltd., PO Box 32, Auckland, New Zealand
PHONE: +64 (9) 3795050
FAX: +64 (9) 3736420
E-MAIL: paula_blind@herald.co.nz
TITLE: Editor
CONTACT: Gavin Ellis
CIRCULATION: 226,240

North Shore Times Advertiser

Suburban Newspapers Auckland, Private Bag 92815, Penrose, Auckland, New Zealand
PHONE: +64 (9) 4894189
FAX: +64 (9) 4866700
E-MAIL: corpsales@snl.co.nz
TITLE: Editor
CONTACT: Ivan Dunn
CIRCULATION: 58,173

Papakura Courier

Suburban Newspapers Auckland, Private Bag 92815, Penrose, Auckland, New Zealand
PHONE: +64 (9) 2624700
FAX: +64 (9) 2624728
E-MAIL: corpsales@snl.co.nz
TITLE: Editor
CONTACT: David Gadd
CIRCULATION: 23,866

Papatoetoe & Otahuhu Week

Community Newspapers, a division of Wilson & Horton, PO Box 12026, Penrose, Auckland, New Zealand
PHONE: +64 (9) 5258877
FAX: +64 (9) 5258887
TITLE: Group Ad Manager
CONTACT: Rikki Noonan
CIRCULATION: 28,886

Rodney Times

Times Media Group Ltd., PO Box 91, Warkworth, New Zealand
PHONE: +64 (9) 4258169
FAX: +64 (9) 4257765
TITLE: Editor
CONTACT: Cliff Ashby
CIRCULATION: 28,382

Rural News

The Business of Farming, Rural News Ltd., PO Box 3855, Auckland, New Zealand
PHONE: +64 (9) 3070399
FAX: +64 (9) 3070122
E-MAIL: rural_news@clear.net.nz
TITLE: Publisher, Ad Manager
CONTACT: Brian Hight
CIRCULATION: 32,144

Sunday News

News Media (Auckland), PO Box 1327, Auckland, New Zealand
PHONE: +64 (9) 3021300
FAX: +64 (9) 3660095
E-MAIL: advertising@nma.co.nz
TITLE: Editor
CONTACT: Clive Nelson
CIRCULATION: 118,850

The Sunday Star Times

News Media (Auckland), PO Box 1327, Auckland 1 New Zealand
PHONE: +64 (9) 3021300
FAX: +64 (9) 3660095
E-MAIL: advertising@nma.co.nz
TITLE: Editor
CONTACT: Sue Chetwin
CIRCULATION: 195,432

The Press

Christchurch Press Co. Ltd., Private Bag 4722 adc, Christchurch, New Zealand
PHONE: +64 (3) 3790940
FAX: +64 (3) 3648487
E-MAIL: advtenquiries@press.co.nz
WEBSITE: http://www.press.co.nz
TITLE: Editor
CONTACT: T. Pankhurst
CIRCULATION: 98,071

Otago Daily Times

Allied Press Ltd., 52 Stuart St., PO Box 517, Dunedin, New Zealand
PHONE: +64 (3) 4774760
FAX: +64 (3) 4747421
TITLE: Editor
CONTACT: Robin Charteris
CIRCULATION: 49,400

The Southland Times

The Southland Times Co. Ltd., PO Box 805, Invercargill 9515 New Zealand
PHONE: +64 (3) 2181909
FAX: +64 (3) 2189239
E-MAIL: advertising@sth.co.nz
TITLE: Editor
CONTACT: Fred Tulett
CIRCULATION: 31,532

The Star

Allied Press Ltd., PO Box 517, Dunedin, New Zealand
PHONE: +64 (3) 4774760
FAX: +64 (3) 4747426

Waikato Times

Waikato & King County Press Ltd., Private Bag 3086, Hamilton, New Zealand
PHONE: +64 (7) 8496180
FAX: +64 (7) 8499587
E-MAIL: dewyn.knight@wkp.co.nz
TITLE: Editor
CONTACT: Venetia Sherson

Wairarapa Times-Age

Chapel St., Masterton, New Zealand
PHONE: +64 (6) 378 9999
FAX: + 64 (6) 378 2839
E-MAIL: keith@times-age.co.nz
WEBSITE: http://www.times-age.co.nz/

Consumer

Consumers' Institute of New Zealand, Private Bag 6996, Wellington 6030 New Zealand
PHONE: +64 (4) 3847963
FAX: +64 (4) 3858752
E-MAIL: editor@consumer.org.nz
WEBSITE: http://www.consumer.org.nz
TYPE: Consumer

Consumer Home & Garden

Consumers' Institute of New Zealand, Private Bag 6996, Wellington 6030 New Zealand
PHONE: +64 (4) 3847963
FAX: +64 (4) 3858752
E-MAIL: editor@consumer.org.nz
WEBSITE: http://www.consumer.org.nz
TYPE: Gardening, technology - construction, general reference

Discover New Zealand

PHONE: +64 (9) 3032929
E-MAIL: consult@discovernz.co.nz
WEBSITE: http://www.discovernz.co.nz
TYPE: Travel

InfoTech Weekly

WEBSITE: http://www.infotech.co.nz
TYPE: Computers, technology, business

Lava

E-MAIL: lava@lava.co.nz
WEBSITE: http://www.lava.co.nz
TYPE: Entertainment, popular culture

Meteorite

Pallasite Press, PO Box 33-1218, Takapuna, Auckland, New Zealand
PHONE: +64 (9) 4862428
FAX: +64 (9) 4896750
E-MAIL: j.schiff@auckland.ac.nz
TITLE: Editor
CONTACT: Joel Schiff
TYPE: Astronomy, science

New Zealand Adventure

PO Box 7035, Sydenham, Christchurch, New Zealand
FAX: +64 (3) 3796976
E-MAIL: sarah.moodie@xtra.co.nz
WEBSITE: http://www.xtra.co.nz
TITLE: Editor
CONTACT: Sarah Moodie
CIRCULATION: 10,000
TYPE: Travel

New Zealand NetGuide

PO Box 33084, Takapuna, Auckland, New Zealand
PHONE: +64 (9) 4888080
FAX: +64 (9) 4895090
E-MAIL: nige@netguide.co.nz

WEBSITE: http://www.netguide.co.nz
TITLE: Editor
CONTACT: Nigel Horrocks
TYPE: Consumer

New Zealand Science Monthly

PO Box 19-760, Christchurch, New Zealand
FAX: +64 (3) 845138
E-MAIL: nzsm@spis.co.nz
WEBSITE: http://www.nzsm.spis.co.nz; www.spis.co.nz
TYPE: Science

New Zealand Skeptic

E-MAIL: nzsm@spis.co.nz
WEBSITE: http://www.nzsm.spis.co.nz
TYPE: Science

Rugby News

Rugby News Ltd., PO Box 91 214, AMSC, Auckland, New Zealand
PHONE: +64 (9) 3601224
FAX: +64 (9) 3601227
E-MAIL: news@rugby.co.nz
WEBSITE: http://www.rugbynews.co.nz
TYPE: Rugby, sports

PUBLISHERS

Auckland University Press

University of Auckland, Private Bag 92019, Auckland, New Zealand
PHONE: +64 (9) 3737528
FAX: +64 (9) 3737465
E-MAIL: aup@auckland.ac.nz
WEBSITE: http://www.auckland.ac.nz/aup/
TITLE: Director
CONTACT: Elizabeth P. Caffin
SUBJECTS: Archaeology, Art, Biography, Government, Political Science, History, Literature, Literary Criticism, Essays, Poetry, Social Sciences, Sociology, Women's Studies

Bush Press Communications Ltd.

PO Box 33029, Takapuna, Auckland, New Zealand
PHONE: +64 (9) 4862667
FAX: +64 (9) 4862667
E-MAIL: bush.press@clear.net.nz
TITLE: Managing Director
CONTACT: Gordon Ell
SUBJECTS: New Zealand Non-Fiction including: Archaeology, Art, Cookery, Crafts, Games, Hobbies, Earth Sciences, Gardening, Plants, Genealogy, Geography, Geology, History, How-to, Natural History, Nonfiction (General), Outdoor Recreation, Photography, Regional Interests, Children's Non-Fiction
TOTAL PUBLISHED: 86 print

Dunmore Press Ltd.

PO Box 5115, Palmerston North, New Zealand
PHONE: +64 (6) 3587169
FAX: +64 (6) 3579242
E-MAIL: books@dunmore.co.nz
WEBSITE: http://www.dunmore.co.nz
TITLE: Owners and Managing Editors
CONTACT: Murray Gatenby and Sharmian Firth
SUBJECTS: Accounting, Business, Economics, Education, History, Philosophy, Sociology, Nonfiction (General)
TOTAL PUBLISHED: 30 new print titles in 1999

HarperCollins Publishers (New Zealand) Ltd.

31 View Rd., Glenfield, Auckland, New Zealand
PHONE: +64 (9) 4439400
FAX: +64 (9) 4439403
E-MAIL: michelle.enoka@harpercollins.co.nz
WEBSITE: http://www.harpercollins.co.nz
TITLE: Operations Manager
CONTACT: Michelle Enoka
SUBJECTS: Art, Biography, Cookery, Fiction, Gardening, Plants, History, Humor, Natural History, Regional Interests, Self-Help, Sports, Athletics, Travel
TOTAL PUBLISHED: 100 print

Hazard Press Ltd.

PO Box 2151, Christchurch, New Zealand
PHONE: +64 (3) 3770370
FAX: +64 (3) 3770390
E-MAIL: info@hazard.co.nz
WEBSITE: http://www.hazard.co.nz
TITLE: Senior Editor
CONTACT: Antoinette Wilson
SUBJECTS: Art, Cookery, Drama, Theater, Government, Political Science, Literature, Literary Criticism, Essays, Nonfiction (General), Poetry
TOTAL PUBLISHED: 180 print

Learning Media Ltd

100 Molesworth St., Box 3293, Wellington, New Zealand 6001
PHONE: +64 (4) 4725522

FAX: +64 (4) 4726444
E-MAIL: info@learningmedia.co.nz
WEBSITE: http://www.learningmedia.co.nz and www.learningmedia.com
TITLE: Chief Executive
CONTACT: Neale Pitches
SUBJECTS: Education, Nonfiction, Fiction

Legislation Direct

PO Box 12 418, Wellington, New Zealand
PHONE: +64 (4) 4965655
FAX: +64 (4) 4965698
E-MAIL: ldorders@legislationdirect.co.nz
WEBSITE: http://www.gplegislation.co.nz
TITLE: General Manager
CONTACT: Chris Eales
SUBJECTS: New Zealand Publications and All Government Legislation

New Zealand Council for Educational Research

PO Box 3237, Wellington, New Zealand
PHONE: +64 (4) 3847939
FAX: +64 (4) 3847933
E-MAIL: suzanne.hay@nzcer.org.nz
WEBSITE: http://www.nzcer.org.nz
TITLE: Chairperson
CONTACT: Ruth Mansell
SUBJECTS: Education

Reed Publishing (NZ) Ltd.

39 Rawene, Birkenhead, Auckland, New Zealand
PHONE: +64 (09) 4412960
FAX: +64 (09) 4704999
E-MAIL: kpower@reed.co.nz
WEBSITE: http://www.reed.co.nz
SUBJECTS: Biography, Cookery, Fiction, History, Natural History, Nonfiction (General), Outdoor Recreation, Regional Interests, Travel
TOTAL PUBLISHED: Over 300 print

University of Otago Press

56 Union St., Dunedin, New Zealand
PHONE: +64 (03) 4798807
FAX: +64 (03) 4798385
E-MAIL: university.press@otago.ac.nz
WEBSITE: http://www.otago.ac.nz
TITLE: Managing Editor
CONTACT: Wendy Harrex
SUBJECTS: Anthropology, Biography, Education, Environmental Studies, Fiction, Government, Political Science, History, Literature, Literary Criticism, Essays, Natural History
TOTAL PUBLISHED: 70 print

Victoria University Press

PO Box 600, Wellington, New Zealand
PHONE: +64 (04) 4636580
FAX: +64 (04) 4636581
E-MAIL: victoria-press@vuw.ac.nz
WEBSITE: http://www.vuw.ac.nz
TITLE: Publisher
CONTACT: Fergus Barrowman
SUBJECTS: Anthropology, Architecture and Interior Design, Drama, Theater, Government, Political Science, History, Language Arts, Linguistics, Law, Literature, Literary Criticism, Essays, Poetry, Social Sciences, Sociology
TOTAL PUBLISHED: 180 print

RELIGIOUS ORGANIZATIONS

Atheist

The New Zealand Association of Rationalists and Humanists, Inc.
Rationalist House, 64 Symonds Street, Aukland 1001, New Zealand
PHONE: +64 (09) 3735131
E-MAIL: heathen@nzarh.org.nz
WEBSITE: http://www.nzarh.org.nz

The Aukland University Atheists
Auklnad University Students Association, The University of Aukland, PO Box 92019, Aukland, New Zealand
PHONE: +64 (09) 3737599
E-MAIL: aua@nzarh.org.nz
WEBSITE: http://www.nzarh.org.nz/atheist/

Baha'I

National Spiritual Assembly of the Baha'is of New Zealand
PO Box 21-551, Henderson, Auckland 8, New Zealand
PHONE: +64 (09) 8374866
FAX: +64 (09) 8374898
E-MAIL: natsec@nsa.org.nz
TITLE: Chief Executive Officer
NAME: Suzanne Mahon

Buddhist

Buddha Light Buddhist Centre
Shop 8, 35 Cook Street, Howick, Auckland, New Zealand
PHONE: +64 (09) 5375558
FAX: +64 (09) 5347734
NAME: Yi Shuen

Buddhist Youth Association New Zealand
P.O. Box 82146, Highland Park, Howick, Auckland, New Zealand
PHONE: +64 (09) 5370609
E-MAIL: byanz@ihug.co.nz
WEBSITE: http://welcome.to/byanz/
NAME: Man Chung Yuen or Lai Yung Wong

Zen Institute of New Zealand
PO Box 1086, Nelson, New Zealand
PHONE: +64 (09) 5211076
FAX: +64 (09) 5211571
E-MAIL: cat@clear.net.nz
WEBSITE: http://www.zen-mtn.org/zenz/zenz.htm
NAME: Jim Jinmon Langabeer

Zen Society of New Zealand
PO Box 18-175 Glen Innes, Auckland 6, New Zealand
PHONE: +64 (09) 5211076
TITLE: Teacher
NAME: John Daido Loori

Catholic

Catholic Enquiry Centre
140 Austin Street, Wellington 6001, New Zealand
PHONE: +64 (04) 3858518
FAX: +64 (04) 3858518
TITLE: Director
NAME: Rev. Paul Shannahan S.M.

Catholic Institute of Theology-Auckland
Newman Hall, 16 Waterloo Quadrant, Auckland 1001, New Zealand
PHONE: +64 (09) 3796424
FAX: +64 (09) 3796426
E-MAIL: cit@theology.ac.nz
WEBSITE: http://catholic.org/newzealand/auckland/cit
TITLE: Principal
NAME: Rev. Neil Darragh

National Centre for Religious Studies (NCRS)
Catholic Centre, 22-30 Hill Street, PO Box 1937, Wellington 6015, New Zealand
PHONE: +64 (04) 4961761
FAX: +64 (04) 4961762
E-MAIL: ncrsnz@clear.net.nz
TITLE: Episcopal Deputy
NAME: Most Rev. Leonard Boyle D. D.

National Council for Young Catholics (NCYC)
PO Box 1937, Wellington 6015, New Zealand
PHONE: +64 (04) 04961731
E-MAIL: cduthie-jung@clear.net.nz
TITLE: Episcopal Deputy
NAME: Most Rev. John Dew D. D.

New Zealand Catholic Bishops' Conference
Catholic Centre, 22-30 Hill Street, P.O. Box 1937, Wellington, New Zealand
PHONE: +64 (04) 4961747
FAX: +64 (04) 4992519
E-MAIL: nzcbc@xtra.cd.nz
WEBSITE: http://www.catholic.org/newzealand.cathcom/bishops/bios.html
TITLE: Secretary
NAME: Most Rev. John Dew D. D.

Religious Education Centre-Auckland
Pompallier Diocesan Centre, 30 New Street, Private Bag 47904, Ponsonby, Auckland 1034, New Zealand
PHONE: +64 (09) 3784380
FAX: +64 (09) 3762829
E-MAIL: terryc@cda.org.nz
TITLE: Director
NAME: Brother Terry Costello F.M.S.

Islamic

Islamic Ahl-ul-Bayt Foundation of New Zealand
PO Box 9962, Newmarket, Aukland, New Zealand
PHONE: +64 (09) 5256533
FAX: +64 (09) 5258083
E-MAIL: ahlulbayt@xtra.co.nz
TITLE: Secretary / Trustee
NAME: Mohamed Raza Rashid

Jewish

Beth Israel-Auckland Hebrew Congregation
108 Greys Avenue, Auckland, 1001, New Zealand
PHONE: +64 (09) 3660700
E-MAIL: jay-el@ihug.co.nz
WEBSITE: http://homepages.ihug.co.nz/~jay-el
NAME: Rabbi Jeremy Lawrence

Orthodox

Community of Christ the Redeemer
447a Dominion Road, Mount Eden, Auckland 1003, New Zeland
PHONE: +64 (09) 6386048
FAX: +64 (09) 6386048
TITLE: Priest
NAME: Peter Fomin

Protestant

Baptist Churches of New Zealand
8 Puhinui Rd., Manukau City, P.O. Box 97-543, South Auckland, New Zealand
PHONE: +64 (09) 2787494
FAX: +64 (09) 2787499
E-MAIL: ianbrown@baptist.org.nz
WEBSITE: http://www.baptist.org.nz
TITLE: Executive Secretary
NAME: Reverend Ian Brown

Congregational Union of New Zealand
14 St. Catherine Crescent, West Harbour, Auckland, New Zealand
PHONE: +64 (09) 4167463
FAX: +64 (09) 3789527
TITLE: Chairman
NAME: Reine Gordon

Maori Council of Churches in New Zealand
P.O. Box 9573, Newmarket, Auckland, New Zealand
PHONE: +64 (09) 5254179
FAX: +64 (09) 5254346
TITLE: Administrator
NAME: Te Rua Gretha

Methodist Church of New Zealand
Connexional Office, P.O. Box 931, Christchurch, New Zealand
PHONE: +64 (03) 3666049
FAX: +64 (03) 3666009
E-MAIL: info@methodist.org.nz
TITLE: General Secretary
NAME: Rev. J. van de Geer

The Salvation Army
PO Box 6015, Wellington, 1, New Zealand
PHONE: +64 (04) 3845649
FAX: +64 (04) 3846277

Scientology

Church of Scientology Mission of Christchurch
71 Deepdale Street, Burnside, Christchurch, New Zealand
PHONE: +64 (03) 3572345

FURTHER READING

Articles

Clark, Helen. "New Zealand Prime Minister Helen Clark: In Search of a Nation's Soul." *Time International,* August 14, 2000, vol. 156. no. 6, p. 44+.

"New Zealand's 'New-Girl Network' At The Top." *Christian Science Monitor,* September 8, 2000, p. 7.

"New Zealand: Sir No More." *New York Times,* April 11, 2000, p. A8.

"W.T.O. Rules Against U.S." *New York Times,* October 27, 2000, p. W1.

Books

Denoon, Donald. *A History of Australia, New Zealand, and the Pacific.* Malden, MA: Blackwell, 2000.

Dun and Bradstreet's Export Guide to New Zealand. Parsippany, NJ: Dun & Bradstreet, 1999.

Jefferies, Margaret. *Adventuring in New Zealand.* 2d ed. San Francisco: Sierra Club Books, 2000.

NEW ZEALAND: STATISTICAL DATA

For sources and notes see "Sources of Statistics" at the front of each volume.

GEOGRAPHY

Geography

Area:

Total: 268,680 sq km.

Land: 268,670 sq km.

Note: includes Antipodes Islands, Auckland Islands, Bounty Islands, Campbell Island, Chatham Islands, and Kermadec Islands.

Land boundaries: 0 km.

Coastline: 15,134 km.

Climate: temperate with sharp regional contrasts.

Terrain: predominately mountainous with some large coastal plains.

Natural resources: natural gas, iron ore, sand, coal, timber, hydropower, gold, limestone.

Land use:

Arable land: 9%

Permanent crops: 5%

Permanent pastures: 50%

Forests and woodland: 28%

Other: 8% (1993 est.).

HUMAN FACTORS

Demographics (A)

	1990	1995	1998	2000	2010	2020	2030	2040	2050
Population	3,360	3,566	3,726	3,820	4,228	4,546	4,768	4,863	4,842
Life expectancy - males	72.8	73.8	74.7	74.9	76.4	77.7	78.7	79.6	80.2
Life expectancy - females	78.9	79.8	80.7	80.9	82.5	83.8	84.9	85.7	86.3
Birth rate (per 1,000)	17.9	16.2	15.2	14.3	13.2	12.3	11.1	10.3	9.8
Death rate (per 1,000)	7.9	7.8	7.5	7.6	7.5	7.9	9.0	10.1	11.4
Women of reproductive age (15-49 yrs.)	875	928	961	976	1,063	1,102	1,066	1,040	983
Fertility rate	2.3	2.1	1.9	1.8	1.8	1.8	1.7	1.7	1.7

Except as noted, values for vital statistics are in thousands; life expectancy is in years.

Health Personnel

	National Data	World Data (wtd ave)
Total health expenditure as a percentage of GDP, 1990-1998[a]		
Public sector	5.9	2.5
Private sector	1.7	2.9
Total[b]	7.6	5.5
Health expenditure per capita in U.S. dollars, 1990-1998[a]		
Purchasing power parity	1,357	561
Total	1,310	483
Availability of health care facilities per 100,000 people		
Hospital beds 1990-1998[a]	610	330
Doctors 1992-1995[a]	210	122
Nurses 1992-1995[a]	1,249	248

Health Indicators

	National Data	World Data
Life expectancy at birth (years)		
1980	73	61
1998	77	67
Daily per capita supply of calories		
1970	2,941	2,358
1997	3,395	2,791
Daily per capital supply of protein		
1997 (grams)	108	74
Total fertility rate (births per woman)		
1980	2.0	3.7
1998	1.9	2.7
People living with (1997)		
Tuberculosis (cases per 100,000)	5.0	60.4
HIV/AIDS (% aged 15 - 49 years)	0.07	0.99

Infants and Malnutrition

	National Data	World Data (wtd ave)
Under 5 mortality rate (1989)	6	NA
% of infants with low birthweight (1992-98)[1]	6	17
Births attended by skilled health staff (% of total births 1996-98)	NA	52
% fully immunized at 1 year of age (1995-98)[1]		
TB	NA	82
DPT	81	77
Polio	82	77
Measles	81	74
Prevalence of child malnutrition (1992-98)[1] (based on weight for age, % of children under 5 years)	NA	30

Ethnic Division

New Zealand European 74.5%
Maori 9.7%
Other European 4.6%
Pacific Islander 3.8%
Asian and others 7.4%

Religion

Anglican 24%
Presbyterian 18%
Roman Catholic 15%
Methodist 5%
Baptist 2%
Other Protestant 3%
Unspecified or none 33%

Data for 1986.

Major Languages

English (official), Maori.

EDUCATION

Public Education Expenditures

	1980	1997
Public expenditures on education as % of GNP	5.8	7.3
Expenditures per student as % of GNP per capita		
Primary	15.1	17.9
Secondary	13.7	23.8
Tertiary	59.9	45.7
Teachers' compensation as % of total current education expenditures	82.7	NA
Pupils per teacher at the primary level	NA	18
Duration of primary education in years	NA	10

	1980	1997
World data for comparison		
Public expenditures on education as % of GNP (mean)	3.9	4.8
Pupils per teacher at the primary level (wtd ave)	NA	33
Duration of primary education in years (mean)	NA	9

Educational Attainment (B)

	1995	1997
Gross enrollment ratio (%)		
Primary level	99.0	101.3
Secondary level	112.4	113.1
Tertiary level	60.0	63.0

GOVERNMENT & LAW

Military Affairs (A)

	1990	1992	1995	1996	1997
Military expenditures					
Current dollars (mil.)	884	721	730	717	766
1997 constant dollars (mil.)	1,040	800	756	729	766
Armed forces (000)	11	11	10	10	10
Gross national product (GNP)					
Current dollars (mil.)	42,600	45,900	55,500	57,100	58,500
1997 constant dollars (mil.)	49,900	50,800	57,500	58,000	58,500
Central government expenditures (CGE)					
1997 constant dollars (mil.)	20,500	20,100	21,800	19,100	19,400
People (mil.)	3.3	3.4	3.5	3.5	3.6
Military expenditure as % of GNP	2.1	1.6	1.3	1.3	1.3
World data on military expenditure as % of GNP	4.5	3.4	2.7	2.6	2.6
Military expenditure as % of CGE	5.0	4.0	3.5	3.8	3.9
World data on military expenditure as % of CGE	17.0	12.5	10.5	10.3	10.2
Military expenditure per capita (1997 $)	314	237	216	206	214
World data on military expenditure per capita (1997 $)	242	173	146	143	145
Armed forces per 1,000 people (soldiers)	3.3	3.3	2.9	2.8	2.8
World data on armed forces per 1,000 people (soldiers)	5.3	4.5	4.1	3.9	3.8
GNP per capita (1997 $)	15,100	15,000	16,400	16,400	16,300
Arms imports[6]					
Current dollars (mil.)	70	110	90	330	100
1997 constant dollars (mil.)	82	122	93	336	100
Arms exports[6]					
Current dollars (mil.)	0	0	5	60	0
1997 constant dollars (mil.)	0	0	5	61	0
Total imports[7]					
Current dollars (mil.)	9,501	9,202	13,960	14,720	14,520
1997 constant dollars (mil.)	11,130	10,200	14,450	14,970	14,520
Total exports[7]					
Current dollars (mil.)	9,488	9,824	13,740	14,420	14,080
1997 constant dollars (mil.)	11,110	10,890	14,230	14,660	14,080
Arms as percent of total imports[8]	0.7	1.2	0.6	2.2	0.7
Arms as percent of total exports[8]	0	0	0	0.4	0

(Continued on next page.)

Political Parties

House of Representatives (Parliament)	no. of seats
New Zealand Labor Party (NZLP)	49
National Party (NP)	39
Alliance	10
ACT New Zealand	9
Green Party	7
New Zealand First Party (NZFP)	5
United New Zealand (UNZ)	1

Elections last held 27 November 1999 (next must be called by November 2002). NZLP and Alliance formed the government coalition. The National Party became the opposition party.

Government Budgets (A)

Year: 1998

Total Expenditures: 33,005 Millions of Dollars

Expenditures as a percentage of the total by function:

General public services and public order	9.09
Defense	3.27
Education	16.18
Health	16.42
Social Security and Welfare	39.07
Housing and community amenities	0.09
Recreational, cultural, and religious affairs	0.94
Fuel and energy	0.07
Agriculture, forestry, fishing, and hunting	1.30
Mining, manufacturing, and construction	0
Transportation and communication	2.80
Other economic affairs and services	2.49

Crime

Crime rate (for 1997)

Crimes reported	473,500
Total persons convicted	176,300
Crimes per 100,000 population	12,600

Persons responsible for offenses

Total number of suspects	195,100
Total number of female suspects	36,300
Total number of juvenile suspects	44,700

LABOR FORCE

Total Labor Force (A)

1.86 million (1998).

Labor Force by Occupation

Services	65%
Industry	25%
Agriculture	10%

Data for 1995.

Unemployment Rate

7% (1999 est.)

PRODUCTION SECTOR

Energy Production

Production	35.789 billion kWh
Production by source	
Fossil fuel	27.17%
Hydro	65.82%
Nuclear	0%
Other	7.01%
Exports	0 kWh

Data for 1998.

Energy Consumption

Consumption	33.284 billion kWh
Imports	0 kWh

Data for 1998.

Transportation

Highways:

Total: 92,200 km.

Paved: 53,568 km (including at least 144 km of expressways).

Unpaved: 38,632 km (1996 est.).

Waterways: 1,609 km; of little importance to transportation.

Pipelines: petroleum products 160 km; natural gas 1,000 km; liquefied petroleum gas or LPG 150 km.

Merchant marine:

Total: 10 ships (1,000 GRT or over) totaling 102,461 GRT/133,418 DWT.

Ships by type: bulk 4, cargo 1, petroleum tanker 2, rail car carrier 1, roll-on/roll-off 2 (1999 est.).

Airports: 111 (1999 est.).

Airports - with paved runways: 44.

Airports - with unpaved runways: 67.

Top Agriculture Products

Wheat, barley, potatoes, pulses, fruits, vegetables; wool, beef, dairy products; fish.

Top Mining Products (B)

Mineral resources include: iron ore, sand, coal, gold, limestone.

MANUFACTURING SECTOR

GDP & Manufacturing Summary (A)

	1980	1985	1990	1995
GDP ($-1990 mil.)[1]	36,354	42,183	43,657	50,789
Per capita ($-1990)[1]	11,678	12,991	12,993	14,262
Manufacturing share (%) (current prices)[1]	21.7	20.7	18.2	18.9[e]
Manufacturing				
Value added ($-1990 mil.)[1]	7,068	8,335	7,636	9,283
Industrial production index	93	104	100	122
Value added ($ mil.)	4,756	4,657	6,923	9,878[e]
Gross output ($ mil.)	14,790	15,399	23,433	33,635[e]
Employment (000)	285[e]	278	212	233[e]
Profitability (% of gross output)				
Intermediate input (%)	68	70	70	71[e]
Wages and salaries inc. supplements (%)	22[e]	18[e]	18[e]	16[e]
Gross operating surplus	10[e]	12[e]	12[e]	13[e]
Productivity ($)				
Gross output per worker	51,964[e]	50,964	100,229	125,417[e]
Value added per worker	16,711[e]	15,414	29,611	37,594[e]
Average wage (inc. supplements)	11,354[e]	10,180[e]	19,410[e]	23,308[e]
Value added ($ mil.)				
Food products	1,098	1,082	1,676	2,482[e]
Beverages	110	93	216	301[e]
Tobacco products	30	19	45	57[e]
Textiles	222	193	232	284[e]
Wearing apparel	185	170	202	225[e]
Leather and fur products	45	46	54	63[e]
Footwear	55	46	41	50[e]
Wood and wood products	253	257	323	452[e]
Furniture and fixtures	92	95	126	176[e]
Paper and paper products	266	276	553	756[e]
Printing and publishing	294	326	537	775[e]
Industrial chemicals	140	134	249	357[e]
Other chemical products	155	142	211	310[e]
Petroleum refineries	26	−1	137	136[e]
Misc. petroleum and coal products	9	7	9	11[e]
Rubber products	96	70	62	74[e]
Plastic products	110	138	229	359[e]
Pottery, china and earthenware	13	11	18[e]	26[e]
Glass and glass products	44	41	70[e]	106[e]
Other non-metal mineral products	114	127	169[e]	207[e]
Iron and steel	93	71	113	180[e]
Non-ferrous metals	82	102	139	224[e]
Metal products	371	404	480	761[e]
Non-electrical machinery	235	264	340	474[e]
Electrical machinery	239	200	260	439[e]
Transport equipment	318	274	322	432[e]
Prof. and scientific equipment	14	20	24	37[e]
Other manufacturing	46	48	86	124[e]

COMMUNICATIONS

Daily Newspapers

	National Data	World Data for Comparison
Daily Newspapers		
Number of Dailies	23	8,391
Total Circulation (000)	804	548,000
Circulation per 1,000 inhabitants	216	96

Telecommunications

Telephones - main lines in use: 1.719 million (1995).

Telephones - mobile cellular: 588,000 (1998).

Telephone system: excellent international and domestic systems.

Domestic: NA

International: submarine cables to Australia and Fiji; satellite earth stations - 2 Intelsat (Pacific Ocean).

Radio broadcast stations: AM 124, FM 290, shortwave 4 (1998).

Radios: 3.75 million (1997).

Television broadcast stations: 41 (plus 52 medium-power repeaters and over 650 low-power repeaters) (1997).

Televisions: 1.926 million (1997).

Internet Service Providers (ISPs): 56 (1999).

FINANCE, ECONOMICS, & TRADE

Economic Indicators

National product: GDP—purchasing power parity—$63.8 billion (1999 est.).

National product real growth rate: 3.1% (1999 est.).

National product per capita: $17,400 (1999 est.).

Inflation rate—consumer price index: 1.3% (1999 est.).

Exchange Rates

Exchange rates:

New Zealand dollars (NZ$) per US$1

January 2000	1.9451
1999	1.8886
1998	1.8632
1997	1.5083
1996	1.4543
1995	1.5235

Top Import Origins

$11.2 billion (f.o.b., 1998 est.)

Origins (1998)

Australia	22%
United States	20%
Japan	11%
United Kingdom	5%

Top Export Destinations

$12.2 billion (f.o.b., 1998 est.)

Destinations (1998)

Australia	21%
Japan	13%
United States	13%
United Kingdom	6%

Foreign Aid

Donor: ODA, $123 million (1995).

Import/Export Commodities

Import Commodities	Export Commodities
Machinery and equipment	Dairy products
	Meat
Vehicles and aircraft	Fish
Petroleum	Wool
Consumer goods	Forestry products
Plastics	Manufactures

Balance of Payments

	1994	1995	1996	1997	1998
Exports of goods (f.o.b.)	12,176	13,478	14,257	14,123	12,156
Imports of goods (f.o.b.)	−10,769	−12,584	−13,685	−13,248	−11,242
Trade balance	1,408	895	572	875	914
Services - debits	−4,101	−4,694	−5,057	−5,031	−4,581
Services - credits	3,667	4,482	4,640	4,230	3,725
Private transfers (net)	259	275	270	257	237
Government transfers (net)	162	53	446	259	262
Overall balance	−2,384	−3,069	−4,005	−4,750	−3,217

NICARAGUA

CAPITAL: Managua.

FLAG: The national flag consists of a white horizontal stripe between two stripes of cobalt blue, with the national coat of arms centered in the white band.

ANTHEM: *Salve a ti, Nicaragua (Hail to You, Nicaragua).*

MONETARY UNIT: The gold córdoba (C$) is a paper currency of 100 centavos. There are coins of 5, 10, 25, and 50 centavos and 1 and 5 córdobas, and notes of 1, 2, 5, 10, 20, 50, 100, 500, 1,000, 5,000, 10,000, 20,000, 50,000, 100,000, 200,000, 500,000, 1,000,000, 5,000,000, and 10,000,000 córdobas. C$1 = US$0.11421 (or US$1 = C$8.756).

WEIGHTS AND MEASURES: The metric system is the legal standard, but some local units are also used.

HOLIDAYS: New Year's Day, 1 January; Labor Day, 1 May; Liberation Day (Revolution of 1979), 19 July; Battle of San Jacinto, 14 September; Independence Day, 15 September; All Saints' Day, 1 November; Christmas, 25 December. Movable religious holidays include Holy Thursday and Good Friday.

TIME: 6 AM = noon GMT.

LOCATION AND SIZE: Nicaragua, the largest of the Central American countries, has an area of 129,494 square kilometers (49,998 square miles), slightly larger than the state of New York. It has a total boundary length of 2,141 kilometers (1,330 miles).

Nicaragua's capital city, Managua, is located in the southwestern part of the country.

CLIMATE: Except in the central highlands, the climate is warm and humid. The mean temperature, varying according to altitude, is between 20° and 30°C (68° and 86°F). Average annual rainfall along the Mosquito Coast reaches 254–635 centimeters (100–250 inches). The highlands also have heavy rainfall. The Pacific coast averages over 200 centimeters (80 inches) a year.

Republic of Nicaragua
República de Nicaragua

INTRODUCTORY SURVEY

RECENT HISTORY

Except for a three-year period between 1947 and 1950, Anastasio ("Tacho") Somoza García was president for forty-two years until he was assassinated in 1956. His son, Luis Somoza Debayle, was president of congress and immediately became president under the constitution. In spite of a 1962 law attempting to limit the Somozas' hold on the government, the presidential election of February 1967 returned the Somozas to power after a four-year break. The victory for Anastasio Somoza, the younger brother of Luis, was overwhelming.

After drawing up a new constitution and declaring nine opposition parties illegal, Somoza won the 1974 elections and remained president. While Somoza consolidated his hold on Nicaragua, a rebel organization, the Sandinista National Liberation Front (Frente Sandinista de Liberación Nacional-FSLN) began to agitate against his rule. Throughout the 1970s, opposition to Somoza grew, and American support began to dissolve.

By 1979, the administration of President Jimmy Carter cut off military aid and the Sandinistas launched a final offensive. Somoza fled the country as an estimated 30,000-50,000 people died in the fighting.

The Sandinistas engaged in an ambitious program to develop Nicaragua under leftist ideals. They dissolved the National Guard, but in 1982 a number of anti-Sandinista guerrilla groups (broadly referred to as the "contras"), consisting of

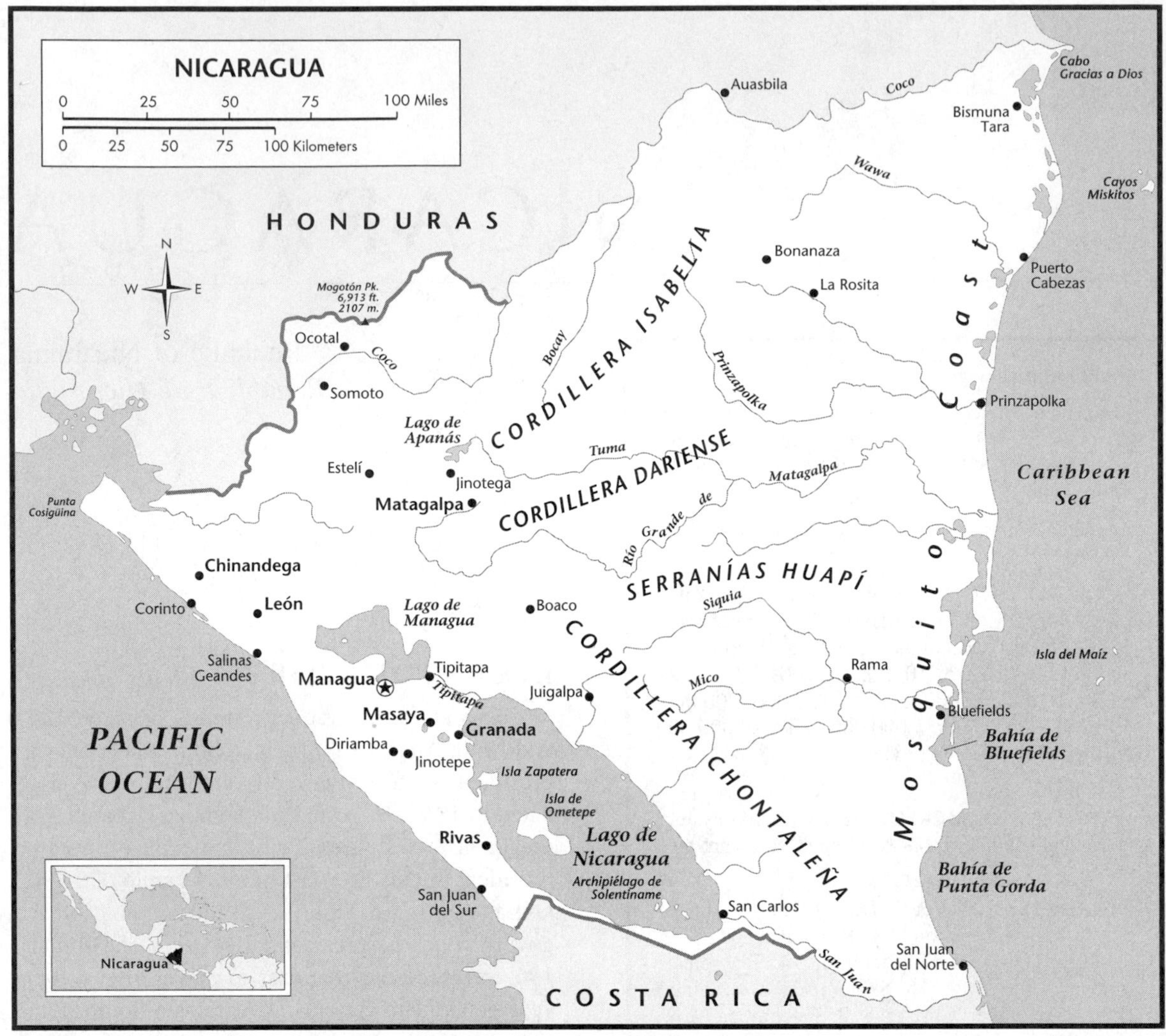

former Guard members and Somoza supporters, began operating from Honduras and Costa Rica. As antigovernment activity increased, a state of emergency, proclaimed in 1982, extended into 1987.

In 1981, the administration of President Ronald Reagan began aiding the contras with funds channeled through the Central Intelligence Agency (CIA). In 1986, it was revealed that U.S. government funds had been secretly diverting aid to the contras in violation of a U.S. congressional ban on such aid.

On the domestic scene, the Sandinistas' economic policies were ineffective. The inflation rate reached 33,000 percent in 1988, and price controls led to serious food shortages.

In August 1987, Nicaragua signed the Arias peace plan for Central America. Nicaragua promised a cease-fire with the contras, a reduction in the armed forces, and amnesty for the rebels. In exchange, the Nicaraguans were to receive guarantees of nonintervention by outside powers.

The political situation in Nicaragua remained shaky through the 1990s as international observers were called in for the 1996 elections, as they had been in 1990. Arnoldo Alemán, the conservative former mayor of Managua and leader of the Liberal Constitutionalist Party (PLC) defeated Sandinista leader Daniel Ortega in Nicaragua's first peaceful transition of power in 100 years.

Hurricane Mitch, the worst Atlantic storm in two centuries, struck Nicaragua in late October 1998. The storm left many roads impassable and seventy-one bridges either destroyed or damaged. Recovery progressed quickly and nearly all roads and bridges were in use by early 1999.

Alemán's commitment to free marketplace reforms and economic growth helped stabilize the economy. Other challenges for Alemán included land reform and land distribution, growing poverty, and migration issues.

GOVERNMENT

Nicaragua is a republic operating under a 1987 constitution with reforms in 1995 and 2000. The president, elected by popular vote for a five-year term, is both chief of state and head of government. The president appoints the cabinet, called the Council of Ministers.

Legislative power is vested in a 93-member single-chamber National Assembly elected under a system of proportional representation for six-year terms.

Judiciary

The Supreme Court in Managua, whose justices are appointed by the National Assembly for six-year terms, heads the judicial branch and has administrative, criminal, civil, and constitutional divisions. The judicial system consists of both civilian and military courts.

Political Parties

When the leftist Sandinista National Liberation Front (FSLN) came to power in July 1979, all political parties except those favoring a return to Somoza rule were permitted. Under the junta, Nicaragua's governing political coalition was the Patriotic Front for the Revolution (Frente Patriótico para la Revolución-FPR), formed in 1980.

The National Opposition Union (UNO) coalition headed by Violeta Chamorro in the early 1990s included the Conservatives and the Liberals as well as several parties formerly aligned with the Sandinistas. The three dominant parties following the 1996 elections are the Liberal Alliance (the ruling party), the left-wing Sandinista National Liberation Front (FSLN), and the left-center UNO-96 Alliance. The Liberal Alliance is a coalition of the right-leaning Liberal Constitutionalist Party (PLC) and Independent Liberal Party for National Unity (PLIUN), the center-right Neoliberal party (PALI), and the center-left Central American Unionist Party (PUCA).

DEFENSE

In 2000, the regular armed forces, a fusion of the Sandinista and Contra armies, numbered 16,000. The army had 14,000 personnel, the navy 800, and the air force 1,200 (with fifteen armed helicopters). A reorganization of the army was underway as of 1999. Nicaragua spent $26 million for defense in 1998, or 1.2 percent of GDP.

ECONOMIC AFFAIRS

When President Violeta Chamorro took office in April 1990, she inherited a country in desperate economic trouble. It had the highest per-person foreign debt in the world and inflation was climbing uncontrollably. The Chamorro administration introduced a strict economic stabilization program and worked to reestablish private enterprise (including the return of properties confiscated during the Sandinista era).

Nicaragua began free market reforms in 1991, and despite some setbacks, made dramatic progress privatizing hundreds of state enterprises, reducing inflation, and cutting foreign debt in half. As a result of the strong decline in foreign debt, the country's economy began expanding. By 1996, the annual growth rate was 5.5 percent, the best performance since 1977.

The election of Arnoldo Alemán in 1996 continued the economic reforms. Debt relief, international aid, and foreign investments have contributed to continued stabilization. Damage caused by Hurricane Mitch in 1998 reduced the GDP to 4 percent for that year, but by 1999 the GDP grew 6.3 percent while inflation remained about 12 percent and unemployment dropped, although there is considerable underemployment. The government planned to reduce taxes and further liberalize trade in 1999. Nicaragua qualified for the Highly Indebted Poor Countries (HIPC) initiative.

Public Finance

Since the mid-1960s, government spending has consistently exceeded revenues. During the Sandinista regime, detailed public finance budgets were not a priority. However, the government budget deficit shrank from 20 percent of GDP in 1990 to 4 percent in 1998. The U.S. Central Intelligence Agency estimated that in 1998 government revenues totaled approximately $527 million with expenditures of $617 million. External debt totaled $5.7 billion by 1999 estimates.

Income

In 1999, Nicaragua's gross domestic product (GDP) was estimated at $12.5 billion, or about $2,650 per capita. The 1999 estimated growth rate of the GDP was 6.3 percent and inflation was 12 percent. The 1998 GDP contribution by sector was: agriculture, 34 percent; industry, 22 percent; and services, 44 percent.

Industry

Nicaraguan industry expanded during the 1970s, but was severely disrupted by the civil war and nationalization. In 1980, the manufacturing sector began to recuperate. By 1990, all public monopolies except public utilities had been eliminated, price controls had ended, and more than 300 state enterprises had been privatized. Manufacturing is concentrated primarily in the areas of food and tobacco processing, beverages, machinery and metal products, textiles, clothing, shoes, petroleum distribution and refining, and chemicals.

Banking and Finance

The banking system, nationalized in July 1979, is under the supervision of the comptroller general. The National Bank of Nicaragua, established in 1912, has been government-owned since 1940. In 1979, the bank was reorganized to become the National Development Bank. The Central Bank of Nicaragua (Banco Central de Nicaragua), established in 1961, is the bank of issue and also handles all foreign exchange transactions. As of 1979, deposits in foreign banks were prohibited, but in May 1985, the establishment of private exchange houses was permitted. In 1990, legislation was passed that allowed for the establishment of private banks. There are no state-owned commercial banks in Nicaragua.

By 2000, there were at least eleven private banks operating. Commercial banks included the Banco Mercantil, the Banco de la Producción, the Banco de América Central, the Banco de Crédito Centroamericano, the Banco Intercontinent, the Banco de Exportación, the Banco del Café, the Banco Européo de Centroamérica, the Banco Nicaragü-se de Industria y Comercio, Banco Caley Dagnall, and Banco de Finanzas.

A small stock market began operations in the late 1990s.

Economic Development

After the 1979 revolution, the government nationalized banking, insurance, mining, fishing, forestry, and a number of industrial plans. Although the government officially favored a mixed economy, in practice the private sector took second place in a development strategy that focused on public investment and control.

In response to the macroeconomic problems that arose in 1992, a series of measures were adopted by the Chamorro administration aimed at consolidating the stabilization process, increasing the competitiveness of exports, and establishing a base for the promotion of growth.

Nicaragua now appears poised for rapid economic growth. However, long-term success is conditioned on improving governability, the openness of government financial operations, attracting investment, creating jobs, and reducing poverty, resolving the thousands of Sandinista-era property confiscation cases, and opening its economy to foreign trade.

President Alemán signed an IMF Structural Adjustment Program for Nicaragua in 1998 aimed at cutting fiscal deficit, continuing liberalization, and maintaining monetary stability. Nicaragua received at least $2.5 billion for reconstruction in the aftermath of the 1998 hurricane, debt deferral until 2001, and debt forgiveness through the Highly Indebted Poor Country (HIPC) Program.

SOCIAL WELFARE

A social insurance law enacted in 1956 provides for national compulsory coverage of employees against risks of maternity, sickness, employment injury, occupational disease, unemployment, old age, and death. Family allowance legislation enacted in 1982 provides benefits for children under the age of fifteen.

Women tend to hold traditionally low-paying jobs in the health, education, and textile sectors while occupying few management positions in the private sector. In 1995, however, Nicaragua had a female president and vice-president.

Dire economic circumstances may force many children to work to contribute to household income. Labor laws prohibit children under twelve from working and limit children ages twelve to sixteen to six-hour workdays.

Healthcare

Slow progress in health care was made from the 1960s through the 1980s. In 2000, average life expectancy was 68.7 years. However, malnutrition and anemia remained common, goiter was endemic, and intestinal parasitic infections (a leading cause of death) afflicted over 80 percent of the population.

In 1995, there were eleven hospital beds per 1,000 inhabitants. In 1997, there were about seven doctors for every 10,000 people and 83 percent of the population had access to health care services.

Housing

Both urban and rural dwellers suffer from a dire lack of adequate housing. As a result of the 1972 earthquake, approximately 53,000 residential units were destroyed or seriously damaged in the Managua area. The Sandinistas launched housing-construction programs but were hampered by a shortage of hard currency to pay for the construction equipment required.

EDUCATION

Primary and secondary education is free and compulsory between the ages of six and thirteen. In 1998, there were 783,002 pupils in 7,224 primary schools. In 1998, 287,476 students were enrolled in secondary schools.

Universities include the National Autonomous University of Nicaragua with campuses in Léon and Managua, the Central American University, and the Polytechnic University of Nicaragua. In 1997, there were 56,558 students in sixteen institutions of higher learning with 3,840 instructors.

2000 KEY EVENTS TIMELINE

April

- Colombia complains to the WTO that Nicaragua has revoked fishing licenses and imposed a 35 perent duty on previously duty-free goods. Nicaragua cites a military buildup along the Honduran border and a potential alliance between Colombia and Honduras that threaten Nicaragua's territory.

May

- A gang kills and beheads eleven family members of a former leader of a leftist group.
- Defense Minister Antonio Alvarado resigns.

June

- Heavy rains leave over 5,000 Nicaraguans homeless.
- Nicaragua reestablishes military ties with the United States.

July

- Local election observers, the Group for Ethics and Transparency, call for electoral reforms. Legislation passed by President Arnoldo Aleman purportedly guarantees that he and his party will remain in power.
- Juan Navarro (spokesman for President Arnoldo Aleman) and Noel Ramirez (President of the Central Bank) refuse HIPC debt relief for Nicaragua, calling the program a form of political blackmail.
- During June and July, armed bandits allegedly from the Andres Castro Revolutionary Front displace over 1,200 Nicaraguan citizens near the Honduran border.

August

- Approximately 100,000 landmines are estimated to exist in northern Nicaragua, remnants of the US-backed Contra Affair; the UK and the US together give $1.3 billion annually to the OAS for clean-up efforts. Hurricane Mitch displaced thousands of mines, making US maps of mine placement obsolete.
- An earthquake measuring 5.1 on the Richter scale on July 6 was followed on July 8 by a second quake measuring 4.7. The U.S. Geological Survey reports forty aftershocks, measuring from 3.0 to 4.4. Seven are dead, and over 4,500 are homeless.
- Local election observers, the Group for Ethics and Transparency, call for electoral reforms. Legislation passed by President Arnoldo Aleman purportedly guarantees that he and his party will remain in power.
- Juan Navarro (spokesman for President Arnoldo Aleman) and Noel Ramirez (President of the Central Bank) refuse HIPC debt relief for Nicaragua, calling the program a form of political blackmail.
- During June and July, armed bandits allegedly from the Andres Castro Revolutionary Front displace over 1,200 Nicaraguan citizens near the Honduran border.

August

- Approximately 100,000 landmines are estimated to exist in northern Nicaragua, remnants of the U.S.-backed Contra Affair; the United Kingdom and the United States together give $1.3 billion annually to the OAS for clean-up efforts. Hurricane Mitch displaced thousands of mines, making U.S. maps of mine placement obsolete.

October

- Hurricane Keith batters Nicaragua and neighboring Guatemala and Belize with torrential rains.

November

- Vice President Enrique Bolanos resigns from office in order to run for president in next year's election. The constitution prohibits current president, Arnoldo Aleman, from seeking reelection.
- Violence surrounds nationwide municipal elections; various conflicts involve Yatama Indian protesters, election officials, Sandanistas who charge voting fraud, and rival candidates.
- Sandinista candidate Herty Lewites wins the mayoral race in Managua, defeating Nicaragua's ruling party candidate. Leftist Sandanista candidates also win other local races; victories at municipal level could signal national comeback of the once-powerful opposition party.

December

- The World Bank and International Monetary Fund (IMF) announce on December 23 that the United States, Canada, Japan, and nations of Europe will provide debt relief for twenty-two of the world's poorest nations, including Benin, Bolivia, Burkina Faso, Cameroon, The Gambia, Guinea, Guinea-Bissau, Guyana, Honduras, Madagascar, Malawi, Mali, Mauritania, Mozambique, Nicaragua, Niger, Rwanda, São Tomé and Príncipe, Senegal, Tanzania, Uganda, and Zambia.

ANALYSIS OF EVENTS: 2000

BUSINESS AND THE ECONOMY

The administration of Alfonso Aleman continued to press the United States and other developed nations to approve the forgiveness of loans by poor debtor nations. Nicaragua, where more than 70 percent of Nicaraguans live in poverty, had a foreign debt of about $6.3 billion as of 2000. Aleman warned that his country could not move forward unless the debt was cleared and said future presidents would have to deal with the issue. Yet Nicaragua's own economic problems could snag the debt-clearing process. In November a bank declared bankruptcy, affecting more than 45,000 customers who may have lost as much as $50 million stored in savings. It was the second bank in three months to declare bunkruptcy, and the fourth in five years. There's no law that protects deposits in Nicaragua, and the government announced it would only cover some of the losses, creating uncertainty in the banking industry. To underscore the country's economic problem, an international organization delivered eight hundred tons of food to Nicaraguans suffering from hunger in August. Severe drought has destroyed farms throughout the country.

Nicaragua has strengthened economic ties with South Korea and Taiwan, which is seeking support from Central American nations for its sovereignty claims. The ties with Taiwan have been cause for concern.

In August the Nicaraguan government forced five U.S. religious leaders to leave the country after they denounced working conditions at several garment factories. The garment industry generated about 20,000 jobs with export earnings of about $200,000 annually, according to some figures.

GOVERNMENT AND POLITICS

More than a decade had passed after the leftist Frente Sandinista de Liberación Nacional (Sandinista National Liberation Front—FSLN) lost the presidency and fell out of favor with the Nicaraguan electorate. But by the late 1990s, the Sandinistas had made a strong comeback. In the November 2000 election the Sandinistas regained political control of the capital city of Managua, positioning the party for a solid shot at the presidency in 2001.

The Sandinista candidate for the Managua mayoral position, the sixty-one-year-old Herty Lewites, carried his party to major municipal victories throughout the country. The surprising surge by the Sandinistas owed much to the Liberal Party's own problems during the presidency of Alfonso Aleman. The president and his party have been tainted by several scandals, and Aleman's approval ratings have declined steadily. Many Nicaraguans felt Aleman was out of touch with the country's deep social and economic problems. Shortly before the election Aleman's administration held an exhibit near the government palace to show the country's gains during his administration.

Attacked as a political ploy to gain votes for Liberal candidates, Aleman defended the exhibit, saying it only showed what newspapers and other media refused to acknowledge about his government.

For the Sandinistas the victory at the polls was the biggest since being ousted out of power in 1990. Yet Mayor-elect Lewites moved quickly to assuage fears that he was not merely a puppet of the Sandinista party. After his election he promised to run an independent government responsive to all regardless of party affiliation. Many Nicaraguans remained cautious about Sandinista gains, even though the leftist party had cooperated, and even supported some legislature by the conservative Aleman. Former Sandinista President Raul Ortega may run again for the presidency in 2001, an unwelcome development by many of his own party colleagues. The Sandinista party itself had not agreed on a candidate, and there were several factions that began to position their own candidates within the party.

During 2000 Nicaragua had serious territorial disputes with neighbors Honduras and Costa Rica. Tensions with Honduras nearly led to violent conflict before both countries signed an agreement to prevent their border dispute from escalating into war. Meeting in Washington, D.C., the Organization of American States (OAS) helped both countries agree to freeze deployment of troops along the border. At the root of the dispute was Honduras's recognition of Colombian sovereignty over an area in the Caribbean that has been historically claimed by Nicaragua. Honduras and Nicaragua agreed to have their dispute settled by the International Court of Justice in The Hague, Netherlands. Nicaragua also eased tensions with Costa Rica after agreeing on navigation rights on a river that demarcated their border.

CULTURE AND SOCIETY

In May the government released about 100 of 300 women prisoners to mark Mother's Day. For the most part women who ended up behind bars were victims of poverty and abuse, Nicaraguan authorities have acknowledged. Most women prisoners were single mothers sentenced to jail for dealing drugs, stealing, and even murder. On the day of their release, the President's wife, María Fernanda de Aleman, greeted the women outside Managua's La Esperanza jail and gave them new clothes.

DIRECTORY

CENTRAL GOVERNMENT

Head of State

President
Arnoldo Aleman Lacayo, Office of the President, Casa de Gobierno, Apdo. 2398, Managua, Nicaragua
PHONE: +505 2282803; 2833675
FAX: +505 2786202

Ministers

Minister of Public Works, the Economy and Commerce
Noel Sacasa Cruz, Ministry of Public Works, the Economy and Commerce, Edificio Central: Km. 6 carretera Masaya, Frente a Camino de Oriente, Apartado Postal No. 8, Managua, Nicaragua
PHONE: +505 2788712; 2775556; 2670003

Minister of Agriculture and Forestry
Jose Augusto, Ministry of Agriculture and Forestry, Km 8 1/2 Carretera a Masaya, Managua, Nicaragua
PHONE: +505 2760200; 2760202; 2760203
E-MAIL: fosemag@tmx.com.ni

Minister of Defense
Jose Adan Guerra, Ministry of Defense, Del Hotel Intercontinental 2 c. al Sur, 1 c. Oeste, Managua, Nicaragua
PHONE: +505 2663580; 2681950; 2684988
E-MAIL: midef@ibw.com.ni

Minister of Education, Culture and Sports
Fernando Robleto, Ministry of Education, Culture and Sports, Centro Cívico, Managua, Nicaragua
PHONE: +505 2650046; 2650144; 2650146

Minister of Government
Jose Marenco, Ministry of Government, Edificio Silvio Mayorga, Managua, Nicaragua
PHONE: +505 2227538; 2282284; 2283678

Minister of Finance
Esteban Duque Estrada, Ministry of Finance, Frente a la Asamblea Nacional, Managua, Nicaragua
PHONE: +505 2227231; 2227232; 2227233

Minister of the Family
Rosa Aregentina Lopez, Ministry of the Family, De la distribuidora Vicky 2 1/2 c. al Oeste, Managua, Nicaragua
PHONE: +505 2781620; 2785637

Minister of Foreign Relations
Francisco Aguirre, Ministry of Foreign Relations, Barrio Altagracia Frente a Costado Sur Restaurante los Ranchos, Managua, Nicaragua
PHONE: +505 2666222; 2664097; 2664563

Minister of Health
Mariangeles Arguello, Ministry of Health, Complejo Nacional de Salud "Dra. Concepción Palacios," Semáforos de Rubenia, 500 mts. al Este, 2 c. al Sur, Managua, Nicaragua
PHONE: +505 2893482; 2893489; 2897441

Minister of Construction and Transportation
David Robleto Lang, Ministry of Construction and Transportation, Frente al Estadio Nacional, Managua, Nicaragua
PHONE: +505 2225111; 2225952; 2225955

Minister of Environment and Natural Resources
Roberto Stadthagen, Ministry of Environment and Natural Resources, Km. 12 1/2 Carretera Norte, Managua, Nicaragua
PHONE: +505 2331111; 2331113

Minister of Labor
Mario Montenegro, Ministry of Labor, Estadio Nacional 300 vs al Norte, Managua, Nicaragua
PHONE: +505 2893482; 2893489; 2897441

Minister of Foreign Cooperation
David Robleto, Ministry of Foreign Cooperation

POLITICAL ORGANIZATIONS

Partido Comunista de Nicaragua-PCdeN (Communist Party of Nicaragua)

Ciudad Jardín 0-30, Apdo. 4231, Managua, Nicaragua
NAME: Eli Altamira Pérez

Partido Liberal Independiente-PLI (Liberal Independence Party)

Ciudad Jardín, F-29 Frente a Optica Selecta, Managua, Nicaragua
NAME: Virgilio Godoy Reyes

Partido Nacional Conservador-PND (National Conservative Party)

Frente Costado Sur Galeria Internacional, Managua, Nicaragua
NAME: Silviano Matamoros Lacayo

Alianza Popular Conservadora-APC (Conservative Popular Alliance Party)

Iglesia El Carmen, 2 c. al Norte, Managua, Nicaragua
NAME: Francisco Anzoátegui Lacayo; Myriam Argüello Morales

Frente Sandinista de Liberación Nacional-FSLN (Sandinista National Liberation Front)

PHONE: +505 2660845
FAX: +505 2661560
NAME: Daniel Ortega Saavedra

Partido Liberal-Pali (Liberal Party)

Restaurante Terraza, 1 c. Abajo, Apdo J-47, Managua, Nicaragua
PHONE: +505 2663875
NAME: Andrés Zúñiga

Partido Social Cristiano Nicaragü–se-PSCN (Nicaraguan Social Christian Party)

Iglesia Larreynaga, 1 1/2c. al Lago, Apdo 4774, Managua, Nicaragua
NAME: Erick Ramírez

Partido Socialista Nicaragü–se-PSN (Nicaraguan Socialist Party)

1er Callejón, Col. Mántica de Estatua Montoya, 1 c. al Norte, Managua, Nicaragua
PHONE: +505 2662321
FAX: +505 2662936
NAME: Gustavo Tablada Zelaya

Unión Demócrata Cristiana-UDC (Christian Democratic Union)

De Iglesia Santa Ana, 2 c. Abajo, Barrio Santa Ana, Apdo 3089, Managua, Nicaragua
PHONE: +505 2662576

Partido Liberal Constitucionalista (Liberal Constitutional Party)

Alianza Liberal Nicabox 498, P.O. Box 02-5640, Miami, Florida 33102-5640
PHONE: +(505) 2651125
FAX: +(505) 2650111
TITLE: President
NAME: Arnoldo Alemán

DIPLOMATIC REPRESENTATION

Embassies in Nicaragua

Belgium
Calle 27 de Mayofrente a gasolinera, Esso Edificio Targa Industrial, Apartado Postal 3397, Managua, Nicaragua
PHONE: +505 2223202
FAX: +505 2224660

Canada
Costado oriental de la Casa Nazareth, Una Quadra Arriba, Calle Noval, Apartado Postal 25, Managua, Nicaragua
PHONE: +505 2680433
FAX: +505 2680437

Denmark
Royal Danish Embassy, De Plaza España, 1c. Abajo, 2c. Al lago, 1/2c. Abajo, Apartado Postal 4942, Managua, Nicaragua
PHONE: +505 2680250
FAX: +505 2668095
E-MAIL: denmark@ns.tmx.com.niem

France
De la Iglesia el Carmen 1 cuadra 1/2 Abajo, Managua, Nicaragua

Italy
De la Estatua de Montoya 1 cuadra al Lago, Managua, Nicaragua
PHONE: +505 2666486; 2662961
FAX: +505 2663987

Japan
Plaza Espafia 1 cuadra abajo y 1 cuadra al lago, Bolonia, Apartado Postal 1789, Managua, Nicaragua

Russia
Apartado Postal 249, Las Colinas, Calle Vista Alegre 214, Managua, Nicaragua
PHONE: +505 2799544; 2799838; 2760131
FAX: +505 2760179

Taiwan
Embassy of the Republic of China, Planes de Altamira, Lotes #19 y 20 Frente de la Cancha de Tenis, Apartado Postal 4653, Managua, Nicaragua
PHONE: +505 2706054
FAX: +505 2674025

United Kingdom
Plaza Churchill Reparto "Los Robles" Managua Apartado A-169, Managua, Nicaragua
PHONE: +505 2780014; 2780887
FAX: +505 2784085

United States
KM. 4 1/2 Carretera Sur, Managua, Nicaragua
PHONE: +505 2666010
FAX: +505 2666046

JUDICIAL SYSTEM

Supreme Court of Justice

Court of Appeals

BROADCAST MEDIA

Asociacion Nicaragüense de Radiodifusión (ANIR)

c/o Radio Ya, Apartado Postal 1787, Managua, Nicaragua
PHONE: +505 (2) 785600
TITLE: President
CONTACT: Carlos J. Guadamuz

Camara Nicaragüense de Radiodifusion

c/o Radio Corporación, Apartado Postal 2442, Managua, Nicaragua
PHONE: +505 (2) 443824
E-MAIL: rc540@ns.tmx.com.ni
WEBSITE: http://www.rc540.com.ni
TITLE: President
CONTACT: Fabio Gadia Mantilla

Dirección de Telecomunicaciones

Apartado Postal 232, Managua, Nicaragua
PHONE: +505 (2) 632171; 632181
CONTACT: Adolfo Lopez Gutiérrez

Comunicaciones Pirata, S.A. (Radio Pirata, 99.9 FM)

Apartado Postal 2777, Telcor Central, Managua, Nicaragua
PHONE: +505 (2) 784861; 707819
FAX: +505 (2) 668769
E-MAIL: pirata@ibw.com.ni
WEBSITE: http://www.pirata.com.ni
BROADCASTS: 24 hours/day
TYPE: Private, Commercial

Canal 4

Montoya 1c al Sur 1c al Este, Managua, Nicaragua
PHONE: +505 (2) 663420
FAX: + 505 (2) 663467
CHANNEL: 2

HTV Canal 23

Managua, Nicaragua
PHONE: +505 (2) 670232
FAX: +505 (2) 670170
CHANNEL: 23

NicaVision

Apartado Postal 688, Managua, Nicaragua
PHONE: +505 (2) 660691
FAX: +505 (2) 661424
CHANNEL: 12

Sistema Sandinista de Televisión

Km 31/2 Carratera Sur, Contig o Shell, Las Palmas, Managua, Nicaragua
PHONE: +505 (2) 660028; +505 (2) 660879
FAX: +505 (2) 662411
TITLE: Head of Sales
CONTACT: Miguel Chivel
CHANNEL: 1, A2, A6
TYPE: Government

Televicentro de Nicaragua

Apartado Postal 3766, Managua, Nicaragua
PHONE: +505 (2) 68222
FAX: +505 (2) 663688
E-MAIL: canal2@ibw.com.ni
WEBSITE: http://www.canal2.com.ni

COLLEGES AND UNIVERSITIES

Universidad Centroamericana

Pista De La Resistencia, Apdo 69, Managua, Nicaragua
PHONE: +505 (2) 2783923
FAX: +505 (2) 2670106
E-MAIL: comsj@ns.uca.edu.ni
WEBSITE: http://www.uca.edu.ni

Universidad Nacional Autonoma de Nicaragua

Recinto Universitario Ruben Dario, Managua, Nicaragua
WEBSITE: http://www.unan.edu.ni

Universidad Politecnica de Nicaragua

Apartado 3595, Managua, Nicaragua
PHONE: +505 (2) 2897659
FAX: +505 (2) 2499232
E-MAIL: rectoria@upoli.edu.ni
WEBSITE: http://www.upoli.edu.ni

NEWSPAPERS AND MAGAZINES

El Nuevo Diario

AP 4591, Managua, Nicaragua
PHONE: +505 (1) 2491190
FAX: +505 (1) 2490700
E-MAIL: ndiario@tmx.com.ni
WEBSITE: http://www.elnuevodiario.com.ni
TITLE: News Editor
CONTACT: Francisco Chamorro Garcia

La Prensa

Editorial La Prensa, Km 4 1/2 Carretera Norte, Apdo 192, Managua, Nicaragua
PHONE: +505 (1) 2498396
FAX: +505 (1) 2491051
E-MAIL: info@laprensa.com.ni
WEBSITE: http://www.laprensa.com.ni
TITLE: Editor
CONTACT: Pedro Xavier Solis
CIRCULATION: 75,000

Tiempos del Mundo

Apartado Postal 3525, Managua, Nicaragua
PHONE: +5050 (1) 2682945
FAX: +505 (1) 2682904
WEBSITE: http://www.tdm.com.ni
TITLE: Editor General
CONTACT: Roger Suárez

La Tribuna

A.P. 1469, Managua, Nicaragua
PHONE: +505 (1) 2-667583
E-MAIL: tribuna@latribuna.com.ni
WEBSITE: http://www.latribuna.com.ni
TITLE: News Editor
CONTACT: Joel Gutierrez

PUBLISHERS

Editorial Nueva Nicaragua

Paseo Salvador Allende, KM. 3 1/2 Carretera Sur, Apdo. Postal RP-073, Managua, Nicaragua
PHONE: +505 2666520
FAX: +505 2666520
TITLE: Director General
CONTACT: Roberto Diaz Castillo
SUBJECTS: Ethnicity, Fiction, Government, Political Science, Literature, Literary Criticism, Essays, Nonfiction (General), Poetry, Religion-Other, Social Sciences, Sociology

Universidad Centroamericana

Apdo. 69, 70352 Managua, Nicaracgua
PHONE: +505 2670106
FAX: +505 2670106
E-MAIL: comsj@ns.uca.edu.ni

RELIGIOUS ORGANIZATIONS

Ninety-five percent Roman Catholic, the former Sandinista regime and its continued albeit reduced presence have made for a difficult situation for religious organizations. Small churches exist in Nicaragua to support the population, but any large-scale religious organizations would have been targets for persecution.

FURTHER READING

Articles

Bounds, Andrew. "Nicaragua Attache for US." *Financial Times,* June 3, 2000.

"Come Rain or Shine." *The Independent—United Kingdom,* June 23, 2000.

"Nicaragua—Curious Chance." *The Economist (US),* June 3, 2000, vol. 355, no. 8173, p. 38.

Books

Investment Treaty with Nicaragua. Washington, DC: G.P.O., 2000.

Metoyer, Cynthia Chavez. *Women and the State in Post-Sandinista Nicaragua.* Boulder, CO: Lynne Rienner, 2000.

Internet

"Family Beheaded: Armed Gang Massacres 11." May 19, 2000. ABC News. [Online] more.abcnews.go.com/sections/world/dailynews/nicaragua000519_beheading.html (accessed July 10, 2000).

NICARAGUA: STATISTICAL DATA

For sources and notes see "Sources of Statistics" at the front of each volume.

GEOGRAPHY

Geography

Area:

Total: 129,494 sq km.

Land: 120,254 sq km.

Land boundaries:

Total: 1,231 km.

Border countries: Costa Rica 309 km, Honduras 922 km.

Coastline: 910 km.

Climate: tropical in lowlands, cooler in highlands.

Terrain: extensive Atlantic coastal plains rising to central interior mountains; narrow Pacific coastal plain interrupted by volcanoes.

Natural resources: gold, silver, copper, tungsten, lead, zinc, timber, fish.

Land use:

Arable land: 9%

Permanent crops: 1%

Permanent pastures: 46%

Forests and woodland: 27%

Other: 17% (1993 est.).

HUMAN FACTORS

Demographics (A)

	1990	1995	1998	2000	2010	2020	2030	2040	2050
Population	3,643	4,274	4,600	4,813	5,839	6,808	7,705	8,472	9,084
Life expectancy - males	62.0	65.3	64.7	66.8	69.6	72.0	74.1	75.8	77.2
Life expectancy - females	65.5	69.0	68.6	70.8	74.1	76.8	79.2	81.1	82.7
Birth rate (per 1,000)	36.4	32.4	30.0	28.3	22.5	19.0	16.5	14.5	13.4
Death rate (per 1,000)	6.9	5.4	5.6	4.9	4.4	4.4	5.0	6.0	7.4
Women of reproductive age (15-49 yrs.)	841	1,042	1,160	1,239	1,610	1,912	2,077	2,129	2,117
Fertility rate	4.6	3.9	3.5	3.3	2.5	2.2	2.1	2.0	2.0

Except as noted, values for vital statistics are in thousands; life expectancy is in years.

Health Personnel

	National Data	World Data (wtd ave)
Total health expenditure as a percentage of GDP, 1990-1998[a]		
Public sector	4.4	2.5
Private sector	5.3	2.9
Total[b]	9.7	5.5
Health expenditure per capita in U.S. dollars, 1990-1998[a]		
Purchasing power parity	209	561
Total	43	483
Availability of health care facilities per 100,000 people		
Hospital beds 1990-1998[a]	150	330
Doctors 1992-1995[a]	82	122
Nurses 1992-1995[a]	56	248

Health Indicators

	National Data	World Data
Life expectancy at birth (years)		
1980	59	61
1998	68	67
Daily per capita supply of calories		
1970	2,338	2,358
1997	2,186	2,791
Daily per capital supply of protein		
1997 (grams)	49	74
Total fertility rate (births per woman)		
1980	6.3	3.7
1998	3.7	2.7
Population with access (%)		
To safe water (1990-96)	81	NA
To sanitation (1990-96)	31	NA
People living with (1997)		
Tuberculosis (cases per 100,000)	64.5	60.4
Malaria (cases per 100,000)	915.2	42.2
HIV/AIDS (% aged 15 - 49 years)	0.19	0.99

Infants and Malnutrition

	National Data	World Data (wtd ave)
Under 5 mortality rate (1989)	48	NA
% of infants with low birthweight (1992-98)[1]	15	17
Births attended by skilled health staff (% of total births 1996-98)	65	52
% fully immunized at 1 year of age (1995-98)[1]		
TB	96	82
DPT	69	77
Polio	73	77
Measles	71	74
Prevalence of child malnutrition (1992-98)[1] (based on weight for age, % of children under 5 years)	12	30

Ethnic Division

Mestizo 69%

White 17%

Black 9%

Amerindian 5%

People of Mestizo ethnicity have mixed Amerindian and white ancestry.

Religion

Roman Catholic 85%

Protestant ....NA

Major Languages

Spanish (official). English and indigenous languages on Atlantic coast.

EDUCATION

Public Education Expenditures

	1980	1997
Public expenditures on education as % of GNP	3.4	3.9
Expenditures per student as % of GNP per capita		
Primary	8.2	11.4
Secondary	15.5	NA
Tertiary	25.8	NA
Teachers' compensation as % of total current education expenditures	69.7	NA
Pupils per teacher at the primary level	NA	38
Duration of primary education in years	NA	6
World data for comparison		
Public expenditures on education as % of GNP (mean)	3.9	4.8
Pupils per teacher at the primary level (wtd ave)	NA	33
Duration of primary education in years (mean)	NA	9

Educational Attainment (B)

	1995	1997
Gross enrollment ratio (%)		
Primary level	102.6	101.6
Secondary level	48.9	55.0
Tertiary level	11.0	12.0

Literacy Rates (A)

In thousands and percent	1990	1995	2000	2010
Illiterate population (15+ yrs.)	689	822	956	1,246
Literacy rate - total adult pop. (%)	64.0	65.7	67.2	69.9
Literacy rate - males (%)	63.1	64.6	65.9	68.2
Literacy rate - females (%)	64.8	66.6	68.4	71.6

GOVERNMENT & LAW

Military Affairs (A)

	1990	1992	1995	1996	1997
Military expenditures					
Current dollars (mil.)	254	36	32	27	27
1997 constant dollars (mil.)	298	40	34	28	27
Armed forces (000)	28	15	14	14	14
Gross national product (GNP)					
Current dollars (mil.)	1,210	1,160	1,450	1,610	1,860
1997 constant dollars (mil.)	1,420	1,280	1,500	1,640	1,860
Central government expenditures (CGE)					
1997 constant dollars (mil.)	504	494	547	587	605
People (mil.)	3.6	3.8	4.2	4.3	4.4
Military expenditure as % of GNP	21	3.1	2.2	1.7	1.5
World data on military expenditure as % of GNP	4.5	3.4	2.7	2.6	2.6
Military expenditure as % of CGE	59.1	8.1	6.1	4.7	4.5
World data on military expenditure as % of CGE	17.0	12.5	10.5	10.3	10.2
Military expenditure per capita (1997 $)	83	11	8	6	6
World data on military expenditure per capita (1997 $)	242	173	146	143	145
Armed forces per 1,000 people (soldiers)	7.8	3.9	3.3	3.2	3.1
World data on armed forces per 1,000 people (soldiers)	5.3	4.5	4.1	3.9	3.8
GNP per capita (1997 $)	394	336	359	379	418
Arms imports[6]					
Current dollars (mil.)	70	5	0	10	0
1997 constant dollars (mil.)	82	6	0	10	0
Arms exports[6]					
Current dollars (mil.)	0	30	40	0	0
1997 constant dollars (mil.)	0	33	41	0	0
Total imports[7]					
Current dollars (mil.)	638	855	962	1,142	1,532
1997 constant dollars (mil.)	747	948	996	1,161	1,532
Total exports[7]					
Current dollars (mil.)	331	223	526	671	704
1997 constant dollars (mil.)	388	247	545	682	74
Arms as percent of total imports[8]	11.0	0.6	0	0.9	0
Arms as percent of total exports[8]	0	13.5	7.6	0	0

(Continued on next page.)

Political Parties

National Assembly (Asamblea Nacional)	% of vote	no. of seats
Liberal Alliance (ruling party - includes PLC, PALI, PLIUN, and PUCA)	46.03%	42
Sandinista National Liberation Front (FSLN)	36.55%	36
Nicaraguan Party of the Christian Road (PCCN)	3.73%	4
Conservative Party of Nicaragua (PCN)	2.12%	3
Sandinista Renovation Movement (MRS)	1.33%	1
National Project (PRONAL)		2
Nicaraguan Resistance Party (PRN)		1
National Democratic Party (PNC)		1
Independent Liberal Party (PLI)		1
Unity Alliance (AU)		1
UNO-96 Alliance		1

Elections were last held 20 October 1996 (next to be held in 2001).

Government Budgets (A)

Year: 1994

Total Expenditures: 4,726.70 Millions of Gold Cordobas

Expenditures as a percentage of the total by function:

General public services and public order 17.61
Defense 5.82
Education 15.49
Health 13.36
Social Security and Welfare 14.70
Housing and community amenities 3.30
Recreational, cultural, and religious affairs 1.30
Fuel and energy 0.26
Agriculture, forestry, fishing, and hunting 2.70
Mining, manufacturing, and construction 0
Transportation and communication 8.02
Other economic affairs and services 0.46

Crime

Crime volume (for 1998)

Crimes reported 66,064
Total persons convicted 48,709
Crimes per 100,000 population . . . . .NA

Persons responsible for offenses

Total number suspects 37,658
Total number of female suspects 3,529
Total number of juvenile suspects 5,170

LABOR FORCE

Total Labor Force (A)

1.7 million (1999).

Labor Force by Occupation

Services 43%
Agriculture 42%
Industry 15%

Data for 1999 est.

Unemployment Rate

10.5% (1999 est.); considerable underemployment.

PRODUCTION SECTOR

Energy Production

Production .2.714 billion kWh
Production by source
Fossil fuel 53.43%
Hydro 35.34%
Nuclear 0%
Other 11.23%
Exports . . . . .99 million kWh

Data for 1998.

Energy Consumption

Consumption . . . . .2.52 billion kWh
Imports . . . . .95.00 million kWh

Data for 1998.

Transportation

Highways:
Total: 16,382 km.
Paved: 1,818 km.
Unpaved: 14,564 km (1998 est.).
Waterways: 2,220 km, including 2 large lakes.
Pipelines: crude oil 56 km.
Merchant marine: none (1999 est.).
Airports: 182 (1999 est.).
Airports - with paved runways: 11.
Airports - with unpaved runways: 171.

Top Agriculture Products

Coffee, bananas, sugarcane, cotton, rice, corn, tobacco, sesame, soya, beans; beef, veal, pork, poultry, dairy products.

Top Mining Products (B)

Mineral resources include: gold, silver, copper, tungsten, lead, zinc.

MANUFACTURING SECTOR

GDP & Manufacturing Summary (A)

	1980	1985	1990	1995
GDP ($-1990 mil.)[1]	4,788	4,951	4,232	4,563
Per capita ($-1990)[1]	1,716	1,546	1,186	1,107
Manufacturing share (%) (current prices)[1]	12.8	13.8	9.4	15.5[e]
Manufacturing				
Value added ($-1990 mil.)[1]	373	390	260	280
Industrial production index	105	107	100	108
Value added ($ mil.)	242	982	1,606[e]	700[e]
Gross output ($ mil.)	612	1,587	2,434[e]	1,052[e]
Employment (000)	34	39	47[e]	59[e]
Profitability (% of gross output)				
Intermediate input (%)	60	38	34[e]	33[e]
Wages and salaries inc. supplements (%)	12	10	11[e]	12[e]
Gross operating surplus	28	52	55[e]	55[e]
Productivity ($)				
Gross output per worker	18,017	38,009	48,250[e]	16,676[e]
Value added per worker	7,131	23,515	31,846[e]	11,101[e]
Average wage (inc. supplements)	2,078	4,152	5,750[e]	2,085[e]
Value added ($ mil.)				
Food products	52	268	392[e]	157[e]
Beverages	48	227	452[e]	200[e]
Tobacco products	28	64	118[e]	55[e]
Textiles	9	70	102[e]	42[e]
Wearing apparel	4	23	44[e]	18[e]
Leather and fur products	2	6	11[e]	4[e]
Footwear	4	27	42[e]	19[e]
Wood and wood products	3	10	13[e]	7[e]
Furniture and fixtures	1	4	4[e]	1[e]
Paper and paper products	1	3	3[e]	1[e]
Printing and publishing	4	22	36[e]	16[e]
Industrial chemicals	11	23	30[e]	15[e]
Other chemical products	14	56	100[e]	49[e]
Petroleum refineries	35	78	110[e]	49[e]
Misc. petroleum and coal products	NA	1	2[e]	1[e]
Rubber products	1	6	11[e]	5[e]
Plastic products	4	20	28[e]	13[e]
Pottery, china and earthenware	NA	2	NA	NA
Glass and glass products	NA	1	2[e]	1[e]
Other non-metal mineral products	7	17	23[e]	11[e]
Iron and steel	NA	1	2[e]	1[e]
Metal products	9	40	62[e]	28[e]
Non-electrical machinery	NA	3	4[e]	2[e]
Electrical machinery	1	5	8[e]	4[e]
Transport equipment	1	3	4[e]	2[e]
Prof. and scientific equipment	1	NA	NA	NA
Other manufacturing	NA	2	2[e]	1[e]

COMMUNICATIONS

Daily Newspapers

	National Data	World Data for Comparison
Daily Newspapers		
Number of Dailies	4	8,391
Total Circulation (000)	135	548,000
Circulation per 1,000 inhabitants	30	96

Telecommunications

Telephones - main lines in use: 140,000 (1996).

Telephones - mobile cellular: 4,400 (1995).

Telephone system: low-capacity microwave radio relay and wire system being expanded; connected to Central American Microwave System.

Domestic: wire and microwave radio relay.

International: satellite earth stations - 1 Intersputnik (Atlantic Ocean region) and 1 Intelsat (Atlantic Ocean).

Radio broadcast stations: AM 63, FM 32, shortwave 1 (1998).

Radios: 1.24 million (1997).

Television broadcast stations: 3 (plus seven low-power repeaters) (1997).

Televisions: 320,000 (1997).

Internet Service Providers (ISPs): 5 (1999).

FINANCE, ECONOMICS, & TRADE

Economic Indicators

National product: GDP—purchasing power parity—$12.5 billion (1999 est.).

National product real growth rate: 6.3% (1999 est.).

National product per capita: $2,650 (1999 est.).

Inflation rate—consumer price index: 12% (1999 est.).

Exchange Rates

Exchange rates:

Gold cordobas (C$) per US$1

December 1999	12.29
1999	11.81
1998	10.58
1997	9.45
1996	8.44
1995	7.55

Top Import Origins

$1.5 billion (c.i.f., 1999 est.)

Origins (1998)

United States	31%
Costa Rica	11%
Guatemala	8%
Venezuela	6%
El Salvador	5%
Mexico	4%

Top Export Destinations

$573 million (f.o.b., 1998 est.)

Destinations (1998)

United States	35%
Germany	13%
El Salvador	10%
Spain	4%
Costa Rica	4%
France	2%

Foreign Aid

Recipient: pledges of $1.4 billion in new aid in 1999.

Import/Export Commodities

Import Commodities	Export Commodities
Machinery and equipment	Coffee
Raw materials	Shrimp and lobster
Petroleum products	Cotton
Consumer goods	Tobacco
	Beef
	Sugar
	Bananas
	Gold

Balance of Payments

	1994	1995	1996	1997	1998
Exports of goods (f.o.b.)	364	530	674	709	579
Imports of goods (f.o.b.)	−784	−897	−1,050	−1,371	−1,384
Trade balance	−420	−367	−376	−663	−804
Services - debits	−169	−217	−249	−237	−272
Services - credits	112	118	133	158	182
Private transfers (net)	148	147	222	280	381
Government transfers (net)	148	158	135	87	65
Overall balance	−647	−520	−435	−598	−599

NIGER

CAPITAL: Niamey.

FLAG: The flag is a tricolor of orange, white, and green horizontal stripes, with an orange circle at the center of the white stripe.

ANTHEM: *La Nigérienne.*

MONETARY UNIT: The Communauté Financière Africaine franc (CFA Fr) is a paper currency with one basic official rate based on the French franc (CFA Fr = 1 French franc). There are coins of 1, 2, 5, 10, 25, 50, 100, and 500 CFA francs, and notes of 50, 100, 500, 1,000, 5,000, and 10,000 CFA francs. CFA Fr1 = $0.00196 (or $1 = CFA Fr510.65).

WEIGHTS AND MEASURES: The metric system is the legal standard.

HOLIDAYS: New Year's Day, 1 January; Anniversary of 1974 military takeover, 15 April; Labor Day, 1 May; Independence Day, 3 August; Proclamation of the Republic, 18 December; Christmas, 25 December. Movable religious holidays include 'Id al-Fitr, 'Id al-'Adha', and Milad an-Nabi.

TIME: 1 PM = noon GMT.

LOCATION AND SIZE: A landlocked country, the Republic of the Niger is the largest state in West Africa, with an area of 1,267,000 square kilometers (489,191 square miles), slightly less than twice the size of the state of Texas. It has a total boundary length of 5,621 kilometers (3,492 miles). Niger's capital city, Niamey, is located in the southwestern part of the country.

CLIMATE: Niger, one of the hottest countries in the world, has three basic climatic zones: the Sahara desert in the north, the semidesert region to the south of the desert, and the Sudan in the southwest corner stretching across Niger and Chad.

The intense heat of the Saharan zone often causes the slight rainfall to evaporate before it hits the ground. At Bilma in the east, annual rainfall is only 2 centimeters (0.79 inches), compared with 63.6 centimeters (25 inches) at Niamey in the southwest. At Niamey, the average daily temperature fluctuates from 24°C (75°F) in January to 29°C (83°F) in July.

Republic of Niger
République du Niger

INTRODUCTORY SURVEY

RECENT HISTORY

The French entered Niger at the close of the nineteenth century and pushed steadily eastward, encircling Lake Chad with military outposts by 1900. In 1901, they established Niger as a military district, part of a larger unit known as Haut-Sénégal et Niger. After putting down a Tuareg rebellion that began during World War I (1914-1918), the French made Niger a colony in 1922. It had a governor, but was administered from Paris. World War II (1939-1945) barely touched Niger, since the country was too isolated to be of use to the French anti-Nazi forces.

On December 19, 1958, Niger's Territorial Assembly voted to become an independent state within the French Community. On August 3, 1960, the Republic of the Niger was proclaimed and Hamani Diori became its first president.

Diori was able to stay in power throughout the 1960s and early 1970s. However, unrest developed as Niger suffered from the drought of the early 1970s. On April 15, 1974, the Diori government was overthrown by a military takeover led by Lieutenant Colonel Seyni Kountché, the former chief of staff. Kountché then assumed the presidency. The former president was put under house arrest from 1974 to 1980. Kountché died of a brain tumor in November 1987, and Colonel 'Ali Seybou (now Brigadier General), the army chief of staff, was appointed president.

The National Movement for the Development of Society (MNSD) was created in 1989 as Niger's

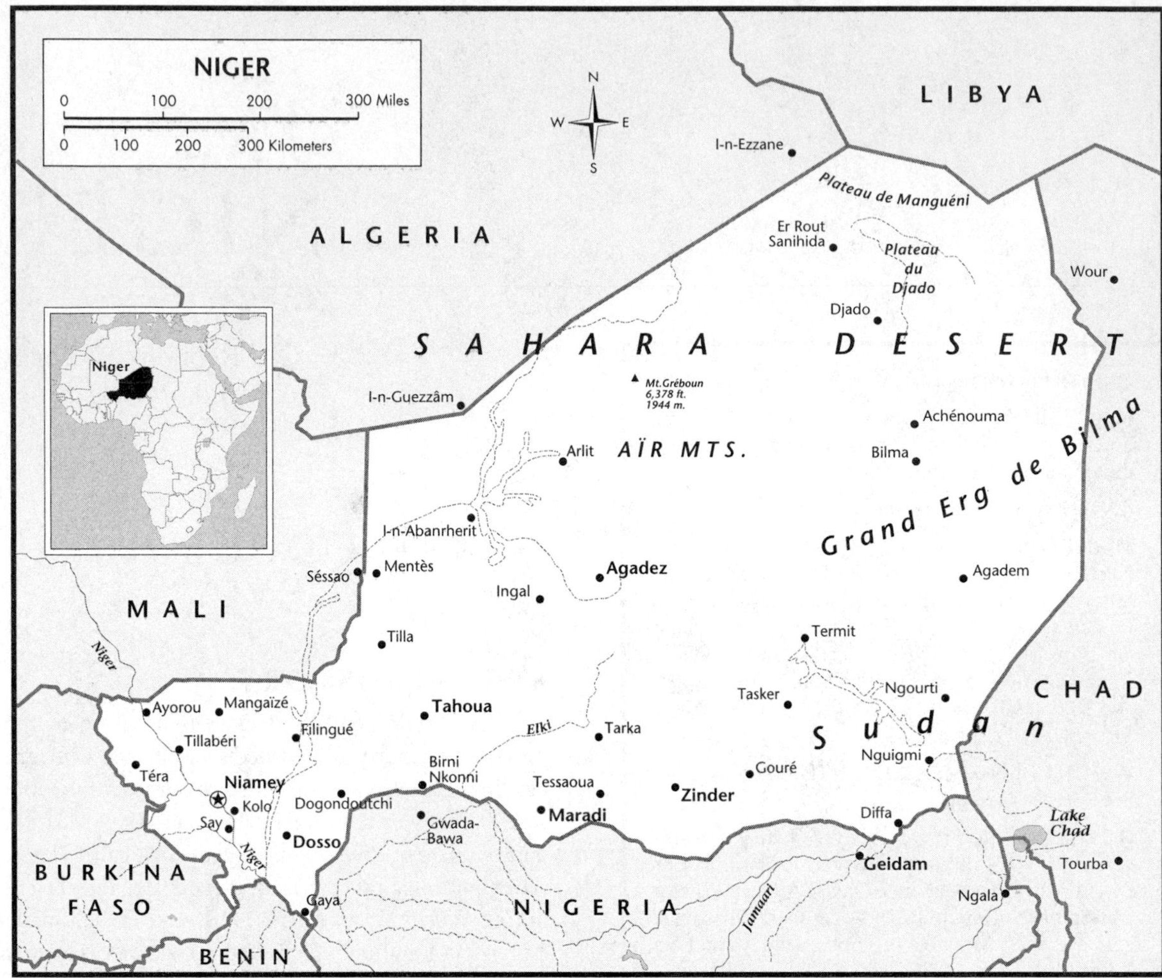

sole political party. Since then, however, there have been demands for multiparty democracy. The president agreed to the calling of a National Conference (July-October 1991) to prepare a new constitution. An interim government headed by Amadou Cheiffou was appointed. After the adoption of the new constitution in December 1992, a series of elections were held. In the elections, Mahamane Ousmane was elected president with 54 percent of the vote.

The new government has attempted to control a Tuareg rebellion in the north. It accuses Libya of encouraging the Tuaregs. Others accuse the Niger government of showing favoritism for members of the Zarma (or Djerma), one of the five major ethnic groups in Niger. High-level talks under the joint mediation of Algeria, Burkina Faso, and France were resumed and led to a peace accord in April 1995.

After the legislative elections of January 1995, there was a power struggle for the cabinet appointments of the prime minister. The president and prime minister fought over policy and power during 1995. In January 1996, Colonel Ibrahim Bare Maïnassara (known as Baré) led a military coup that removed the president and dissolved the Assembly. A civilian prime minister, Boukary Adji, was put in office within a month after the coup. In May 1996, a draft constitution was submitted for a national vote and was approved. A ban on political parties was ended and civil liberties were restored. Baré declared himself president, claiming 52 percent of the vote in July 1996. Baré was assassinated in 1999. A civilian, Mamamdou Tandja, was elected president in October 1999. Tandja promised to work for political and social stability.

GOVERNMENT

Niger operates under a 1993 constitution, revised by national referendum in May 1996 and again by referendum in July 1999. The president, elected by popular vote for a five-year term, is chief of state and head of government. There is a 24-member cabinet appointed by the president.

The legislative branch is the unicameral 83-seat National Assembly whose members are elected by popular vote for five-year terms.

Judiciary

The 1992 constitution called for an independent judiciary. The Supreme Court is now the final court of appeals. Special courts deal with civil service corruption. There are also magistrates' courts, eight labor courts, and justices of the peace in nineteen administrative districts. Traditional and customary courts hear cases involving divorce or inheritance. Customary courts are presided over by a legal practitioner with basic legal training who is advised about local tradition by a local official. There are no religious courts.

Political Parties

After the constitutional referendum of December 1992 introduced multiparty democracy, several new parties were formed.

The National Movement for the Development of Society-Nassara (MNSD-Nassara) is the largest party in the legislature (thirty-eight of eighty-three seats as of November 1999). Four other parties hold seats: Democratic and Social Convention-Rahama (CDS-Rahama); Nigerien Party for Democracy and Socialism (PNDS-Tarayya); Democratic Rally of the People-Jama'a (RDP-Jama'a); and Nigerian Alliance for Democracy and Social Progress (ANDPS-Zaman Lahiya). The MNSD and CDS formed a majority coalition. PNDS took leadership of the opposition with allies RDP and ANDPS.

DEFENSE

Niger's army numbered 5,200 in 2000. There were 100 personnel in the air force. France provides military advisers and is the chief source of military equipment. Niger spends $20 million or 1 percent of GDP on defense (1996-1997).

ECONOMIC AFFAIRS

Niger is a dry, landlocked country with much of its territory located in the Sahara desert. The economy depends mainly on bilateral and multilateral foreign aid for operating expenses and public investment, livestock raising, farming, and depends less on uranium mining, its main export since the 1970s. Uranium export earnings decreased by more than half from 1987 to 1998.

In January 1994, France suddenly devalued the CFA franc causing its value to drop by half overnight. The devaluation caused Niger's trade relationship with Nigeria to improve and it boosted revenue from exports such as livestock, cowpeas, onions, and the products of Niger's small cotton industry. However, as of 1998, Niger had yet to recover from the devaluation. Short-term economic progress relies on World Bank and IMF programs for debt relief and aid.

Public Finance

Budgets are nominally balanced, but only through the infusion of foreign loan funds and grants. Expenditures have been severely constrained because of the fall in receipts from the sale of uranium ore due to decline in world demand. The end of the uranium boom in the late 1980s left the public sector poorly equipped to adapt as public expenditures had focused on infrastructure and construction projects at the expense of agricultural development. Consequently heavy foreign debts were incurred.

The U.S. Central Intelligence Agency estimated that, in 1999, government revenues totaled approximately $377 million, with expenditures of $377 million, including capital expenditures of $105 million. External debt totaled $1.3 billion.

Income

In 1999, Niger's gross domestic product (GDP) was estimated at $9.6 billion, or about $1,000 per person. The 1999 estimated GDP growth rate was 2 percent and inflation was 4.8 percent. The 1998 GDP contribution by sector was: agriculture, 40 percent; industry, 18 percent; and services, 42 percent.

Industry

Manufacturing consists mainly of the processing of agricultural products and includes a groundnut (edible root) oil plant, rice mills, flour mills, cotton gins, and tanneries. A textile mill and cement plant are in operation and light industries produce beer and soft drinks, processed meats, baked goods, soaps and detergents, perfume, plastic and metal goods, farm equipment, and construction materials, including bricks. Although still a world leader in production of uranium, the boom times of the 1970s are over, with demand and prices for the ore on a steady decline.

Banking and Finance

The Central Bank of the West African States (Banque Centrale des États de l'Afrique de l'Ouest-

BCEAO) is the bank of issue for Niger and other West African states. Niger has a monetary committee that reports to the BCEAO and works under BCEAO general rules but possesses autonomy in internal credit matters.

Two development banks remain following the collapse of the Banque de développement de la républica du Niger (BDRN) in 1990: Crédit du Niger (CN), and the Caisse nationale du crédit agricole (CNCA). Banque Meridien-BIAO du Niger was taken over in September 1995 in a combined purchased by Banque Belgolaise of Belgium, which took 35 percent, and Cofipa, a European investment group (15 percent), the remaining 50 percent of the equity being sold to private Nigerian interests. The bank changed its name to BIAO-Niger. The Banque arabe libyenne et nigérienne pour le commerce extérieur (Balinex) was rescued in March 1992, when Libya announced a CFA Fr746 million loan to increase its capital. At least eight other commercial banks were operating in 1999, including the Nigeria International Bank Niamey owned by Citibank and the Banque Massraf Fayçal Al Islami-Niger.

Economic Development

Government development programs have had three basic aims: first, to diversify production of foodstuffs; second, to develop underground water resources; and third, to develop and improve the country's infrastructure. France is the leading bilateral aid donor. Much of Niger's short-term economic prospects depend on negotiations with the World Bank and IMF for debt relief and extended aid.

SOCIAL WELFARE

The National Fund of Social Security provides pensions, family allowances, and workers' compensation for employees in the private sector. Civil servants participate in a national insurance fund and also receive family allowances. These programs apply only to a minority of citizens formally employed. Subsistence farmers are excluded.

Women are frequently denied educational and employment opportunities and face both social and legal discrimination. Young girls have limited access to education and are often married as young as ten years of age.

Healthcare

In the 1990s, there were about three physicians per 100,000 people. There were thirty-eight medical centers throughout the country. Only 30 percent of the population had access to health care services in 1993. In 2000, the average life expectancy was forty-one years.

Housing

Most government buildings and many houses in the metropolitan centers are essentially French in style. The Tuareg nomads live in covered tents, while the Fulani live in small collapsible huts made of straw mats, the villagers in the east live in straw huts, and those in central Niger construct houses of "banco," a mixture of mud and straw.

EDUCATION

The adult illiteracy rate stood at 84.3 percent in 2000 (males: 76.5 percent and females: 91.7 percent). Schooling is compulsory for children aged seven to fifteen. In 1997-1998, there were 3,175 primary schools with 11,545 teachers and 482,065 pupils. In 1997, there were 96,675 pupils in secondary schools. Only 33 percent of secondary school students were female. In 1991, 4,513 students were enrolled in higher institutions including the National School of Administration in Niamey, the University of Niamey, and the Islamic University of West Africa at Say.

2000 KEY EVENTS TIMELINE

January

- Niger swears in a new prime minister, Hama Amadou, before the national assembly in Niamey. Amadou announces that the state coffers are empty.
- President Tandja Mamadou swears in a new cabinet that includes nine ministers from the Mouvement National pour la Société de Développement (MNSD) and eight from the Convention Démocratique et Sociale (CDS). Both parties backed Tandja in the second round of the presidential polls.

February

- Several hundred people demand an international inquiry into the assassination of former head of state, General Ibrahim Baré Mainassara.
- France offers aid worth some CFA Fr6 billion (US$9 million) that will go towards paying the

salaries of civil servants, some of whom have arrears stretching back over a year.

March

- Eleven opposition political parties organize a coalition, la Coordination des Forces Démocratiques (CFD) to promote the culture of solidarity, the defense of the rule of law, the fight against exclusion, the monitoring of government action, and good governance.

April

- The Health Ministry releases figures showing that Meningitis has killed 250 people in Niger this year and infected another 2,800. The worst affected areas are the capital, Niamey, and Birne-Konne, some 350 km due east.

June

- The national anti-narcotics center reports that Niger police have so far this year arrested at least 560 drug traffickers or users.
- Tandja says "no" to institutionalizing Islamic law and defends the secular state, citing the problems Islamic law has caused in neighboring Nigeria.

August

- The West African Development Bank grants Niger about $2.9 million towards financing water supply for the city of Tillaberi, about 120 kilometers west of Niamey.

September

- Twenty-seven people in a village 600 kilometers north of Niamey die from an unidentified disease that causes vomiting, diarrhea, fever, swelling of the stomach, convulsion and coma. No new cases of the disease are reported after health authorities treat wells with chlorine and residents with tetracycline and chloroquine.

October

- Libyan youths ransack the Nigerien embassy in Tripoli in a series of violent and bloody protests against the presence of North Africans in Libya. It is estimated that some one million Sahelians and sub-Saharan Africans have taken up residence in Libya.
- Libyans repatriate 4,000 Nigeriens, but Libyan drivers leave them stranded on the border for fear of lynching if they drive across the border. A spokesman for the Niger community in Libya claims that at least 150 of his compatriots died, 200 were injured, and 80 are missing in Libya.

November

- Islamic fundamentalists destroy houses, bars, and kiosks in protest of an international fashion festival held in Niamey. The demonstrators believe the fashion show is corrupting social mores, and encouraging prostitution, debauchery, and AIDS. Niger's interior ministry dissolves seven Islamic organizations following the protests.
- The Minister of Rural Development announces to Parliament that the country's total cereal deficit stands at 163,000 metric tons, putting at risk some four million people or 39 percent of the population. The shortfall is due to poor rainfall, which also has affected livestock adversely.

December

- The World Bank and International Monetary Fund (IMF) announce on December 23 that the United States, Canada, Japan, and nations of Europe will provide debt relief for twenty-two of the world's poorest nations, including Benin, Bolivia, Burkina Faso, Cameroon, The Gambia, Guinea, Guinea-Bissau, Guyana, Honduras, Madagascar, Malawi, Mali, Mauritania, Mozambique, Nicaragua, Niger, Rwanda, São Tomé and Príncipe, Senegal, Tanzania, Uganda, and Zambia.

ANALYSIS OF EVENTS: 2000

BUSINESS AND THE ECONOMY

The economic policy outlook for 2000 was mixed. When the administration of Mamadour Tandja was inaugurated in January, it inherited a government on the verge of bankruptcy. Strapped for cash, the government had been paying the salaries of 40,000 civil servants with foreign aid. Real growth in gross domestic product (GDP) from 1995–99 was 2.0 percent, and the current accounts balance from 1995–98 went from minus $151 million to minus $86 million. Gold reserves dropped over the five-year period, from $95 million to $39 million. The good news was that the European Union (E.U.), International Monetary Fund (IMF), and bilateral donors had already resumed aid with more expected over the coming months.

The government's economic vision was sound, but conservative. First, it planned to overhaul its public finance sector to free up domestic resources to finance a poverty eradication program. Second, it planned to cut back the civil service and accelerate privatization. Each of these measures was problematic because domestic revenues via a broadened tax base were limited, and retrenchment would be met with organized resistance from the trade unions, as would privatization. However, privatizing the telecommunications company, Sonitel, would appease donors, and Niger breathed a sigh of relief when the E.U. resumed aid without an investigation into the murder of former president Ibrahim Mainassara. In principle the E.U. no longer grants aid without conducting rule of law, human rights, and good governance assessments.

The forecast for 2001 was mixed. Analysts predicted a rosy 4.0 percent GDP growth rate despite flooding in Niamey and two of the regions and the poor rainfall elsewhere. Donor inflows were expected to offset climatic adversity. High energy and transport costs were predicted to raise inflation to 3 percent, but no higher assuming adequate food supply. In the external sector, uranium hit historic lows at $8 per pound, and gold and oil production were still years away. However thanks to abolition of customs duties through the West African Economic and Monetary Union (Union Economique et Monetaire Ouest Africaine—UEMOA), cheaper regional imports became available. Things would improve further if Niger qualified for debt relief under the Heavily Indebted Poor Countries (HIPC) initiative and met performance criteria under the next IMF facility.

GOVERNMENT AND POLITICS

President Tandja's new government under the tutelage of the prime minister survived its honeymoon this year with a disgruntled army, angry students, and obstreperous unions. Niger was still a praetorian society much as Samuel Huntington described it more than thirty years ago. Indeed this year students protested, unions threatened to strike, and the army kidnapped its members, but did not stage a coup. The government has discovered that containing social unrest while placating international donors will be a difficult balancing act.

Seven members of the national trade union umbrella, L'Union des syndicats des travalleurs du Niger, broke away from the federation to form their own syndicate in protest of civil service reform and early retirements. One of the dissenters was the teachers' union, which previously had supported the civil service reforms. All unions demanded payment for salary arrears of up to twelve months. In May student protests turned violent when police attempted to break up a stone-throwing mob with tear gas, wounding several students.

Niger's nearly 11,000-strong army also remained a political force. Officers loyal to the late General Mainassara demanded an investigation into the assassination. On June 10 a group of soldiers kidnapped the former spokesman of the military junta. Eight officers close to Mainassara were charged. The independent press picked up the story alleging that the incident was a pretext to purge troublemakers.

Led by Mahamadou Issoufou, the opposition organized a twelve-party coalition and criticized the government on a number of fronts—for failing to jumpstart the economy, for disregarding uranium miners' demands, and for using excessive force to put down student demonstrations in May. It also advocated that the investigation into the Mainassara assassination be reopened. The latter tactic was unlikely to go far given that only eight of the parliamentarians belonging to Mainassara's party voted in January to reopen the investigation. President Tandja and National Assembly President, Mahamane Ousmane, attempted to counter the opposition's Coordination des Forces Démocratiques by inviting several smaller parties to join them.

Internationally Niger stayed on good terms with Western donors, and with its main trading partner in the region, Nigeria. However despite the visit of Libyan President Muammar Qadhafi in July, and Libyan investments in Niger, relations soured over the way Nigeriens and citizens of other sub-Saharan countries were being treated in Libya.

CULTURE AND SOCIETY

The Fashion Fair fiasco in November illustrated the deep fundamentalist currents of Islamic thought and faith in Nigerien society. Ironically the Fashion Fair organizers claimed to be promoting "culture, peace, and development," and to be raising funds for the country's poverty eradication project. However hundreds of demonstrators thought otherwise, and their violent protests over what they viewed as a Western-influenced display of materialism raised the specter of deep social division, perhaps far more serious than that of the unions and student groups.

Niger has one of the steepest uphill climbs economically, politically, and socially. The United Nations Human Development Report ranks Niger 173 out of 174 countries for the third consecutive year. Only Sierra Leone is worse. Niger is last on the Human Poverty Index and the related Gender Development Index. The percentages of the population without access to safe water, health care, and sanitation were 39 percent, 70 percent, and 89 percent respectively. Thirty-five percent of the population was not expected to reach the age of forty. Per capita gross national product (GNP) was $739 in 1998, and the GNP growth rate was being outstripped by population growth.

The amount of individual wealth was miniscule, but it became still smaller given unequal distribution of national wealth. The poorest 20 percent of the population received less than 3 percent of the national income, and the richest 20 percent received more than 50 percent of the nation's wealth. This sharp disparity between the "haves" and the "have-nots" threatens to divide further Niger's fragmented society.

DIRECTORY

CENTRAL GOVERNMENT

Head of State

Head of State; Chairman of the National Reconciliation Council
Tandja Mamadou, Office of the National Reconciliation Council

Prime Minister
Hama Amadou, Office of the Prime Minister

Ministers

Minister of Animal Resources
Koroney Maoude, Ministry of Animal Resources

Minister of Mines
Yahaya Bare, Ministry of Mines

Minister of Foreign Affairs and Cooperation
Nassirou Sabo, Ministry of Foreign Affairs and Cooperation

Minister of National Defense
Sabiou Dady Gaoh, Ministry of National Defense

Minister of Higher Education, Research and Technology
Ari Ibrahim, Ministry of Higher Education, Research and Technology

Minister of Health
Assoumane Adamou, Ministry of Health

Minister of Commerce and Energy
Seyne Oumarou, Ministry of Commerce and Energy

Minister of Water Resources
Akoli Daouel, Ministry of Water Resources

Minister of Communications
Amadou Elhadj Salifou, Ministry of Communications

Minister of Environment
Issoufou Assoumane, Ministry of Environment

Minister of Finance
Ali Badjo Gamatie, Ministry of Finance

Minister of Interior
Mahamane Manzo, Ministry of Interior

Minister of Justice
Ali Sirfi, Ministry of Justice

Minister of Transportation
Abdou Labo, Ministry of Transportation

POLITICAL ORGANIZATIONS

Alliance for Democracy and Progress

TITLE: Chairman
NAME: Issoufou Bachard

Democratic and Social Convention (Rahama)

NAME: Mahamane Ousmane

Movement for Development and Pan-Africanism

TITLE: Chairman
NAME: Mai Manga Boucar

Niger Progressive Party-African Democratic Rally

NAME: Dandiko Koulodo

DIPLOMATIC REPRESENTATION

Embassies in Niger

United Kingdom
Niamey, Niger

JUDICIAL SYSTEM

Supreme Court

Court of Appeal

BROADCAST MEDIA

La Voix du Sahel

BP 309, Niamey, Niger
PHONE: +227 723155
E-MAIL: adamar@hotmail.com
TITLE: Radio Director
CONTACT: A. Khamed
LANGUAGE: French, Hausa, Djerma, Tamashek, Fulfulde, Kanouri, English
BROADCASTS: 14 hours/day
TYPE: Government

Tele-Sahel

BP 309, Niamey, Niger
PHONE: +227 723155
TYPE: Government

COLLEGES AND UNIVERSITIES

Universite de Niamey

BP 237, Niamey, Niger
PHONE: +227 732713
FAX: +227 733862

NEWSPAPERS AND MAGAZINES

Haske

Sahel Media Contact, BP 297, Niamey, Niger
PHONE: +227 741053
FAX: +227 732006
TITLE: Editor
CONTACT: Abdoulaye Seyni
CIRCULATION: 15,000

Le Republicain

BP 12015, Niamey, Niger
FAX: +227 734142
E-MAIL: nin@intenet.ne
WEBSITE: http://www.republicain-niger.com

Le Sahel Dimanche

Government Information Service, BP 368, Niamey, Niger
PHONE: +227 722020
TITLE: Editors-in-Chief
CONTACT: Emile F. Rigobert, Mamane Moustapha
CIRCULATION: 3,000

Nigerama

Agence Nigerienne de Presse, Niamey, Nigeria
TYPE: Social science, general

PUBLISHERS

Government Printer (Societe De L'Imprimerie Nationale Du Niger)

BP 61, Niamey, Niger
PHONE: +227 734798

RELIGIOUS ORGANIZATIONS

Catholic

Bishop of Niamey
BP 10270, Niamey, Nicaragua
PHONE: 733079
FAX: 741013
TITLE: Bishop
NAME: Guy Romano

FURTHER READING

Articles

Arji, Saidou. "Environment: Arab Hunters Threaten Niger's Endangered Species." *Environment Bulletin,* January 19, 2000.

"Niger Gets IMF Aid." *African Business,* November 2000, p. 6.

Books

Bell-Gam, Ruby. *Nigeria.* Santa Barbara, CA: Clio Press, 1999.

Decalo, Samuel. *Historical Dictionary of Niger,* [computer file]. Boulder, CO: netLibrary, Inc., 2000.

Dibie, Robert A. *The Military-Bureaucracy Relationship in Nigeria: Public Policy Making and Implementation.* Westport, CT: Praeger, 1999.

Dun and Bradstreet's Guide to Niger. Parsippany, NJ: Dun & Bradstreet, 1999.

Park, Mungo. *Travels in the Interior Districts of Africa.* Durham, NC: Duke University Press, 2000.

Uwadibie, Nwafejoku Okolie. *Decentralization and Economic Development in Nigeria: Agricultural Policies and Implementation.* Lanham, MD: University Press of America, 1999.

NIGER: STATISTICAL DATA

For sources and notes see "Sources of Statistics" at the front of each volume.

GEOGRAPHY

Geography

Area:

Total: 1.267 million sq km.

Land: 1,266,700 sq km.

Land boundaries:

Total: 5,697 km.

Border countries: Algeria 956 km, Benin 266 km, Burkina Faso 628 km, Chad 1,175 km, Libya 354 km, Mali 821 km, Nigeria 1,497 km.

Coastline: 0 km (landlocked).

Climate: desert; mostly hot, dry, dusty; tropical in extreme south.

Terrain: predominately desert plains and sand dunes; flat to rolling plains in south; hills in north.

Natural resources: uranium, coal, iron ore, tin, phosphates, gold, petroleum.

Land use:

Arable land: 3%

Permanent crops: 0%

Permanent pastures: 7%

Forests and woodland: 2%

Other: 88% (1993 est.).

HUMAN FACTORS

Demographics (A)

	1990	1995	1998	2000	2010	2020	2030	2040	2050
Population	7,627	8,777	9,536	10,076	13,140	16,800	20,783	24,734	28,457
Life expectancy - males	38.6	40.0	40.8	41.4	44.6	48.1	51.7	55.4	59.1
Life expectancy - females	37.6	39.5	40.5	41.1	44.6	48.4	52.5	56.8	61.1
Birth rate (per 1,000)	55.7	54.7	52.8	51.5	45.4	39.3	32.5	26.7	22.4
Death rate (per 1,000)	28.0	25.5	24.1	23.2	19.1	15.8	12.9	10.8	9.6
Women of reproductive age (15-49 yrs.)	1,746	2,006	2,160	2,269	2,997	3,989	5,176	6,500	7,654
Fertility rate	7.5	7.5	7.3	7.2	6.3	5.2	4.1	3.3	2.7

Except as noted, values for vital statistics are in thousands; life expectancy is in years.

Health Personnel

	National Data	World Data (wtd ave)
Total health expenditure as a percentage of GDP, 1990-1998[a]		
Public sector	1.3	2.5
Private sector	NA	2.9
Total[b]	NA	5.5
Availability of health care facilities per 100,000 people		
Hospital beds 1990-1998[a]	10	330
Doctors 1992-1995[a]	3	122
Nurses 1992-1995[a]	17	248

Health Indicators

	National Data	World Data
Life expectancy at birth (years)		
1980	42	61
1998	46	67
Daily per capita supply of calories		
1970	1,992	2,358
1997	2,097	2,791
Daily per capital supply of protein		
1997 (grams)	61	74
Total fertility rate (births per woman)		
1980	7.4	3.7
1998	7.3	2.7
Population with access (%)		
To safe water (1990-96)	53	NA
To sanitation (1990-96)	15	NA
People living with (1997)		
Tuberculosis (cases per 100,000)	38.9	60.4
Malaria (cases per 100,000)	10,025.6	42.2
HIV/AIDS (% aged 15 - 49 years)	1.45	0.99

Infants and Malnutrition

	National Data	World Data (wtd ave)
Under 5 mortality rate (1989)	280	NA
% of infants with low birthweight (1992-98)[1]	15	17
Births attended by skilled health staff (% of total births 1996-98)	15	52
% fully immunized at 1 year of age (1995-98)[1]		
TB	46	82
DPT	22	77
Polio	21	77
Measles	27	74
Prevalence of child malnutrition (1992-98)[1] (based on weight for age, % of children under 5 years)	50	30

Ethnic Division

Hausa 56.0%
Djerma 22.0%
Fula 8.5%
Tuareg 8.0%
Beri Beri (Kanouri) 4.3%
Arab, Toubou, and Gourmantche 1.2%
French expatriates ....less than 1%

Religion

Muslim 80%
Indigenous beliefs and Christians 20%

Major Languages

French (official), Hausa, Djerma.

EDUCATION

Public Education Expenditures

	1980	1997
Public expenditures on education as % of GNP	3.2	2.3
Expenditures per student as % of GNP per capita		
Primary	26.2	32.1[2]
Secondary	NA	82.5
Tertiary	1,538.5	NA
Teachers' compensation as % of total current education expenditures	68.2	NA
Pupils per teacher at the primary level	NA	41
Duration of primary education in years	NA	8
World data for comparison		
Public expenditures on education as % of GNP (mean)	3.9	4.8
Pupils per teacher at the primary level (wtd ave)	NA	33
Duration of primary education in years (mean)	NA	9

Educational Attainment (B)

	1995	1997
Gross enrollment ratio (%)		
Primary level	29.0	29.3
Secondary level	6.7	6.9
Tertiary level	0.7	0.6

Literacy Rates (A)

In thousands and percent	1990	1995	2000	2010
Illiterate population (15+ yrs.)	3,576	4,081	4,672	6,185
Literacy rate - total adult pop. (%)	11.6	13.6	15.9	21.4
Literacy rate - males (%)	18.2	20.9	23.8	30.5
Literacy rate - females (%)	5.2	6.6	8.3	12.7

GOVERNMENT & LAW

Political Parties

National Assembly	no. of seats
National Movement for a Developing Society-Nassara (MNSD-Nassara)	38
Democratic and Social Convention-Rahama (CDS-Rahama)	17
PNDS-Tarayya	16
Democratic Rally of the People-Jama'a (RDP-Jama'a)	8
Nigerien Alliance for Democracy and Social Progress-Zaman Lahiya (ANDPS-Zaman Lahiya)	4

Elections were last held 24 November 1999 (next to be held in 2004).

Government Budgets (B)

Revenues . . . .$377 million
Foreign sources . . . .$146 million
Expenditures . . . .$377 million
Capital expenditures . . . .$105 million

Data for 1999 est.

Crime

Crime volume (for 1998)
Crimes reported 8,918
Total persons convicted .NA
Crimes per 100,000 population 99.09

(Continued on next page.)

LABOR FORCE

Total Labor Force (A)

70,000 receive regular wages or salaries.

Labor Force by Occupation

Agriculture 90%
Industry and commerce 6%
Government 4%

PRODUCTION SECTOR

Energy Production

Production . . . . .180 million kWh
Production by source
Fossil fuel 100%
Hydro 0%
Nuclear 0%
Other 0%
Exports . . . . .0 kWh

Data for 1998.

Energy Consumption

Consumption . . . . .363 million kWh
Imports . . . . .196 million kWh

Data for 1998.

Transportation

Highways:

Total: 10,100 km.

Paved: 798 km.

Unpaved: 9,302 km (1996 est.).

Waterways: the Niger is navigable 300 km from Niamey to Gaya on the Benin frontier from mid-December through March.

Airports: 27 (1999 est.).

Airports - with unpaved runways: 18.

Top Agriculture Products

Cowpeas, cotton, peanuts, millet, sorghum, cassava (tapioca), rice; cattle, sheep, goats, camels, donkeys, horses, poultry.

Top Mining Products (B)

Mineral resources include: uranium, coal, iron ore, tin, phosphates, gold.

MANUFACTURING SECTOR

GDP & Manufacturing Summary (A)

	1980	1985	1990	1995
GDP ($-1990 mil.)[1]	2,680	2,251	2,481	2,548
Per capita ($-1990)[1]	480	341	321	278
Manufacturing share (%) (current prices)[1]	3.8	7.4	6.7	NA
Manufacturing				
Value added ($-1990 mil.)[1]	87	141	163	170[e]
Industrial production index	98	76	100	104[e]
Value added ($ mil.)	31[e]	21[e]	27[e]	21[e]
Gross output ($ mil.)	89[e]	63[e]	97	66[e]
Employment (000)	2[e]	3[e]	2[e]	2[e]
Profitability (% of gross output)				
Intermediate input (%)	65	63[e]	72[e]	61[e]
Wages and salaries inc. supplements (%)	15	14[e]	6[e]	16[e]

(Continued on next page.)

GOVERNMENT & LAW (cont.)

Military Affairs (A)

	1990	1992	1995	1996	1997
Military expenditures					
Current dollars (mil.)	NA	19[e]	20	19	20
1997 constant dollars (mil.)	NA	21[e]	20	19	20
Armed forces (000)	5	5	5	5	5
Gross national product (GNP)					
Current dollars (mil.)	1,400	1,430	1,630	1,740	1,830
1997 constant dollars (mil.)	1,640	1,580	1,690	1,740	1,830
Central government expenditures (CGE)					
1997 constant dollars (mil.)	328	269	265	231	289
People (mil.)	7.6	8.1	8.8	9.1	9.4
Military expenditure as % of GNP	NA	1.3	1.2	1.1	1.1
World data on military expenditure as % of GNP	4.5	3.4	2.7	2.6	2.6
Military expenditure as % of CGE	NA	7.9	7.7	8.4	6.9
World data on military expenditure as % of CGE	17.0	12.5	10.5	10.3	10.2
Military expenditure per capita (1997 $)	NA	3	2	2	2
World data on military expenditure per capita (1997 $)	242	173	146	143	145
Armed forces per 1,000 people (soldiers)	0.7	0.6	0.6	0.5	0.5
World data on armed forces per 1,000 people (soldiers)	5.3	4.5	4.1	3.9	3.8
GNP per capita (1997 $)	214	196	191	194	195
Arms imports[6]					
Current dollars (mil.)	5	0	0	0	5
1997 constant dollars (mil.)	6	0	0	0	5
Total imports[7]					
Current dollars (mil.)	389	479	374	387	363
1997 constant dollars (mil.)	456	531	387	393	363
Total exports[7]					
Current dollars (mil.)	283	333	287	281	270
1997 constant dollars (mil.)	331	369	297	286	270
Arms as percent of total imports[8]	1.3	0	0	0	1.4
Arms as percent of total exports[8]	0	0	0	0	0

(Continued on next page.)

MANUFACTURING SECTOR (cont.)

GDP & Manufacturing Summary (A)

	1980	1985	1990	1995
Gross operating surplus	20	23[e]	21[e]	23[e]
Productivity ($)				
Gross output per worker	43,564	22,429[e]	71,121[e]	22,621[e]
Value added per worker	15,075	8,085[e]	19,679[e]	8,177[e]
Average wage (inc. supplements)	6,537	2,996[e]	3,935[e]	2,774[e]
Value added ($ mil.)				
Food products	2	2[e]	10[a]	6[e]
Beverages	7	6[e]	NA	5[e]
Textiles	6	5[e]	8[b]	NA
Wearing apparel	1	1[e]	NA	1[e]
Paper and paper products	NA	NA	1[e]	1[e]
Printing and publishing	2	1[e]	2[e]	2[e]
Industrial chemicals	2	NA	4[e]	NA
Other chemical products	3	3[e]	NA[e]	3[e]
Other non-metal mineral products	2	1[e]	NA	1[e]
Metal products	3	1[e]	1[c]	1[e]

COMMUNICATIONS

Daily Newspapers

	National Data	World Data for Comparison
Daily Newspapers		
Number of Dailies	1	8,391
Total Circulation (000)	2	548,000
Circulation per 1,000 inhabitants	0.2	96

Telecommunications

Telephones - main lines in use: 13,000 (1995).

Telephones - mobile cellular: 0 (1995).

Telephone system: small system of wire, radiotelephone communications, and microwave radio relay links concentrated in southwestern area.

Domestic: wire, radiotelephone communications, and microwave radio relay; domestic satellite system with 3 earth stations and 1 planned.

International: satellite earth stations - 2 Intelsat (1 Atlantic Ocean and 1 Indian Ocean).

Radio broadcast stations: AM 5, FM 5, shortwave 4 (1998).

Radios: 680,000 (1997).

Television broadcast stations: 10 (plus seven low-power repeaters) (1997).

Televisions: 125,000 (1997).

Internet Service Providers (ISPs): 1 (1999).

FINANCE, ECONOMICS, & TRADE

Economic Indicators

National product: GDP—purchasing power parity—$9.6 billion (1999 est.).

National product real growth rate: 2% (1999 est.).

National product per capita: $1,000 (1999 est.).

Inflation rate—consumer price index: 4.8% (1999).

Exchange Rates

Exchange rates:

Communaute Financiere Africaine francs (CFAF) per US$1

January 2000	670.00
January 1999	560.01
1998	589.95
1997	583.67
1996	511.55
1995	499.15

Since 1 January 1999, the CFAF is pegged to the euro at a rate of 655.957 CFA francs per euro. Fiscal year: calendar year.

Top Import Origins

Imports (c.i.f., 1997): $295 million.

Origins: France, Cote d'Ivoire, United States, Benelux, Nigeria.

Top Export Destinations

Exports (f.o.b., 1997): $269 million.

Destinations: United States, Greece, Japan, France, Nigeria, Benin.

Foreign Aid

Recipient: $222 million (1995).

Import/Export Commodities

Import Commodities	Export Commodities
Consumer goods	Uranium ore 65%
Primary materials	Livestock products
Machinery	Cowpeas
Vehicles and parts	Onions
Petroleum	
Cereals	

Balance of Payments

	1991	1992	1993	1994	1995
Exports of goods (f.o.b.)	352	347	300	227	288
Imports of goods (f.o.b.)	−418	−397	−312	−271	−306
Trade balance	−66	−49	−12	−44	−18
Services - debits	−203	−201	−186	−149	−152
Services - credits	50	58	36	30	33
Private transfers (net)	13	18	14	6	6
Government transfers (net)	109	114	122	108	54
Overall balance	−176	−159	−97	−126	−152

NIGERIA

Federal Republic of Nigeria

CAPITAL: Abuja

FLAG: The national flag consists of three vertical stripes. The green outer stripes represent Nigerian agriculture. The white center stripe represents unity and peace.

ANTHEM: *Arise, All Compatriots*

MONETARY UNIT: n£) was replaced by the naira (N) of 100 kobo at a rate of N2 = N£1. There are coins of 1, 5, 10, 25, and 50 kobo and 1 naira, and notes of 5, 10, 20, and 50 naira. N1 = $0.04969 (or $1 = N20.124).

WEIGHTS AND MEASURES: As of May 1975, the metric system is the official standard, replacing the imperial measures.

HOLIDAYS: New Year's Day, 1 January; National Day, 1 October; Christmas, 25 December; Boxing Day, 26 December. Movable Christian religious holidays include Good Friday and Easter Monday; movable Muslim religious holidays include ʿId al-Fitr, ʿId al-ʿAdhaʾ, and Milad an-Nabi.

TIME: 1 PM = noon GMT.

LOCATION AND SIZE: Located at the extreme inner corner of the Gulf of Guinea on the west coast of Africa, Nigeria occupies an area of 923,770 square kilometers (356,670 square miles), slightly more than twice the size of the state of California. It has a total boundary length of 4,900 kilometers (3,045 miles). Nigeria's capital city, Abuja, is located in the center of the country.

CLIMATE: Although Nigeria lies completely within the tropical zone, its climate varies widely. Near the coast, temperatures rarely exceed 32°C (90°F). Inland, during the dry season (November to March) midday temperatures exceed 38°C (100°F). Average rainfall varies from around 130 centimeters (50 inches) over most of central Nigeria to about 430 centimeters (170 inches) in certain parts of the east. Two principal wind currents affect Nigeria: the southwest wind, and the harmattan, a hot, dry wind from the northeast that carries a reddish dust from the desert and causes high temperatures during the day.

INTRODUCTORY SURVEY

RECENT HISTORY

After World War II (1939-1945), increasing pressures for self-government resulted in a series of short-lived constitutions. In 1960, Nigeria became a fully independent member of the British Commonwealth and on October 1, 1963, it became a republic. Nnamdi Azikiwe was elected the first president of the Federal Republic of Nigeria.

Disagreements between regions led to military takeovers in 1966, bringing Lieutenant Colonel Yakubu Gowon to power as head of the military government. In 1967, Colonel Gowon announced changes in state borders throughout the country.

Rejecting the new arrangement, Eastern Region leaders formed the independent Republic of Biafra, leading to war with the federal government. By 1970, Biafra had been reduced to about one-tenth of its original area of 78,000 square kilometers (30,000 square miles), and a million or more persons had perished, many of disease and starvation.

Later, in 1975, General Gowon was overthrown and this initiated a highly unstable and often violent political climate. Change from military rule to civilian rule was blocked by crisis after crisis. Clashes between Muslims and Christians in 1991 and 1992 spread through northern cities. Hundreds were killed in the rioting and by the army seeking to control the riots.

The military denied Chief M.K.O. Abiola victory in the 1993 presidential election by annulling the election, claiming voter irregularities. Civil un-

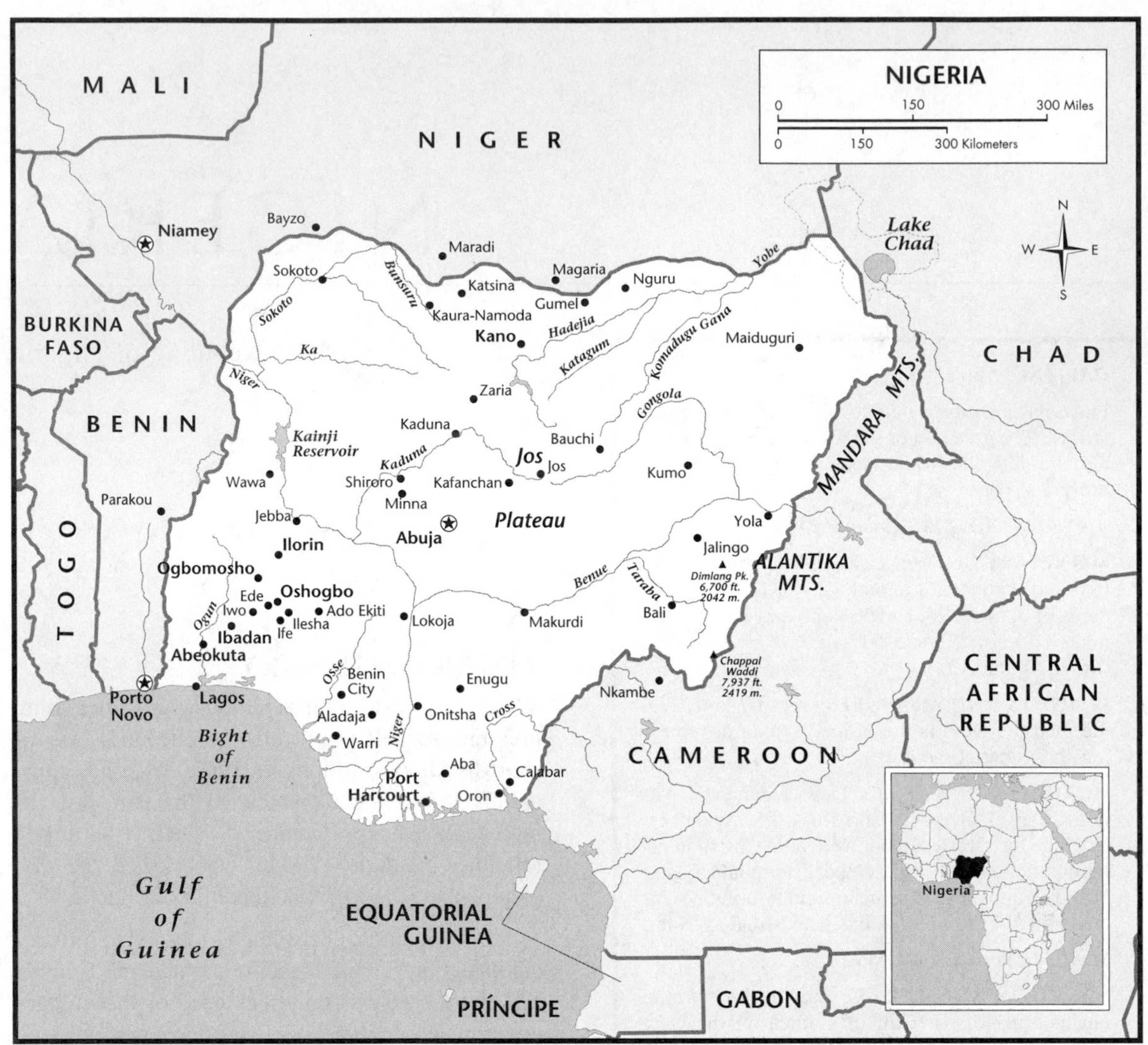

rest, especially in Lagos, followed. However, the military would not give up power. Under its latest strongman, General Sani Abacha, the corrupt military government crippled the Nigerian economy and drove the country into debt. In November 1993, Abacha took control and installed himself as head of state. He abolished all state and local governments, the national legislature, and political parties, and removed all civilians from his ruling council.

The execution of Ken Saro-Wiwa, leader of the Movement for the Survival of the Ogoni People, and eight others in November 1995 brought much criticism from the international community. Nigeria was suspended from the British Commonwealth.

In February 1998, Nigeria led the West African intervention force that helped restore the elected government of Sierra Leone. Pope John Paul II visited Nigeria in March and appealed for human rights and democracy.

In June 1998, General Abacha died of a heart attack, and General Abdulsalam Abubakar assumed control initially promoting a transition to democracy. On July 7, 1998, Abiola died of a heart attack in prison on the eve of his expected release. There was public suspicion that his death was not natural and riots broke out in Lagos, Ibadan, and Abeokuta, resulting in nineteen deaths. Public fears of ethnic division grew because Abiola was seen as a link between northern Hausas and southern Yorubas. Abubakar began releasing political prisoners and announced that the military would give up its power to an elected government in May 1999.

In February 1999, Olusegun Obasanjo won the presidential elections over Olu Falae. Obasanjo is a former general who ruled the country from 1976 to 1979 when he became the first Nigerian military ruler to return power freely to an elected civilian government. Obasanjo's agenda included restoration of law and order, fighting corruption, and unifying Nigeria's ethnically and religiously diverse people.

In 1999, Nigeria was second on Transparency International's list of the most corrupt countries. In 2000, outbreaks of fighting between Yorubas and the Hausa in the area of Lagos resulted in hundreds of deaths, as did violent clashes between Muslims and Christians in February of that year.

GOVERNMENT

The 1979 constitution established a federal system resembling that of the United States. The military government that took command after the December 1983 takeover suspended the 1979 constitution and it was still suspended after Abacha seized power on November 17, 1993. A military-dominated Provisional Ruling Council (PRC) ruled by decree and a 32-member Federal Executive Council managed government departments. In July 1998, the military government announced that it would yield power to an elected civilian government in May 1999. The elections, held in February, were monitored by international observers who found them to be fair overall.

Under the new 1999 constitution, the president, who is chief of state and head of government, is elected by popular vote for no more than two four-year terms. He chairs the cabinet, called the Federal Executive Council, which he appoints. The bicameral National Assembly consists of a 109-seat Senate and a 360-seat House of Representatives. Members of both are elected by universal suffrage (at age eighteen) to five-year terms.

Judiciary

Under the 1999 constitution the regular court system comprises federal and state trial courts, state appeals courts, the Federal Court of Appeal, the Federal Supreme Court, and Shari'ah (Islamic) and customary (traditional) courts of appeal for each state and for the federal capital territory of Abrija. Courts of the first instance include magistrate or district courts, customary or traditional courts, Shari'ah courts, and for some specified cases the state high courts.

Political Parties

In November 1993, the military rulers suspended all partisan and political activities. Abacha's regime allowed no partisan political activity but set up five political parties that it directly controlled. Under General Abubakar's transition to democracy these parties were disbanded and the people would organize their own political parties. In the 1999 elections, three parties were operating: the People's Democratic Party (PDP), which took 215 of the 360 House seats; the All People's Party (APP), seventy-five seats; and the Alliance for Democracy (AD), seventy seats.

DEFENSE

The Nigerian armed forces are the largest in sub-Saharan Africa after South Africa with 94,000 members in 2000. The army, with 79,000 members, was divided into ten brigades. The navy, with a total strength of 5,500, possessed three warships and fifty-one smaller craft. The air force, composed of 9,500 members, had ninety-one combat aircraft. Nigeria contributes observers and troops to seven different peacekeeping operations. Nigeria spent $236 million on defense in 1999.

ECONOMIC AFFAIRS

The Nigerian economy, with a wealth of natural resources, offers great potential for economic growth. However, poor economic policy, political instability, and too much reliance on oil exports have created severe problems in the economy.

In 2000, Nigeria was to restructure debt through the Paris Club and IMF who would provide a $1 billion loan, contingent on economic reforms. High world oil prices and foreign investment should boost the GDP to approximately 5 percent in 2000-2001.

Crude oil accounts for 97 percent of exports and 80 percent of government revenue in 1999. In 1996, the World Bank reported that $2 billion in oil revenues from the early 1990s had been put in a secret government bank account. There were also reports that significant amounts of oil revenue were being lost due to fraudulent practices at the country's oil terminals. By 1998, external debt had grown to $32 billion. In 1999, a newly democratic government promised to support accountability, and to stop corruption within the state.

Agriculture remains the basic economic activity for at least 54 percent of Nigerians. But this largely subsistence sector has not kept up with rapid population growth, and Nigeria, once a large net exporter of food, must import most of its food.

Public Finance

The federal government is responsible for collecting taxes on income, profits, and property, as well as import and export taxes and excise duties. The petroleum sector provides about 80 percent of budgetary revenues. A large share of these revenues is redistributed to state governments. The budget is consistently in deficit.

Public investment flourished during the oil boom years of the 1970s. When the oil market prices collapsed in the 1980s, however, the Nigerian government maintained its high level of spending thus acquiring substantial foreign debt. Although privatization efforts began in 1986, increased government spending outside the official budget since 1990 had damaged public finance reform.

The U.S. Central Intelligence Agency estimated that in 1998, government revenues totaled approximately $13.9 billion, with expenditures of $13.9 billion. External debt totaled $32 billion.

Income

In 1996, Nigeria's gross national product (GNP) was $132.7 billion at current prices, or about $1,300 per person. For the period 1985-1995, the average inflation rate was 33 percent, resulting in a real growth rate in GNP of 1.2 percent per person.

Industry

Oil has grown to a position of domination of the Nigerian economy accounting for 95 percent of foreign exchange earnings. As of 2000, Nigeria was sub-Saharan Africa's largest oil producer.

The textile industry has shown the greatest growth since independence, and the country is practically self-sufficient in printed fabrics, blankets, and towels. Other areas of expansion include cement production, tire production, and furniture assembly. Other important industries include sawmills; cigarette factories; breweries; sugar refining; rubber, paper, soap, and detergent factories; footwear factories; pharmaceutical plants; tire factories; paint factories; and assembly plants for radios, record players, and television sets. Still other industries include coal, tin, columbite, palm oil, peanuts, cotton, wood products, hides and skins, construction materials, chemicals, fertilizers, printing, ceramics, and steel. Nigeria has several state-owned motor-vehicle assembly plants.

Banking and Finance

The bank of issue is the Central Bank of Nigeria (CBN), established in 1958. The Central Bank regulates most commercial banking operations in Nigeria, but the federal Ministry of Finance has retained control of most international activities of the financial sector.

With the adoption of the Structural Adjustment Program (SAP) in 1986, the licensing of new banks was liberalized. In July 1990, the state banks were privatized. Beginning in 1990, the country allowed the establishment of foreign banks. Sixty percent of the foreign banks established in Nigeria must be held by Nigerian interests. In the same year, the government began a program to establish 500 community banks. From 1985 to 1993, the number of banks rose from forty to 120, but declined to eighty-nine in 1998. The main banks in 1999 included the Afribank, Universal Trust Bank, FSB International Bank, Diamond Bank Limited, United Bank for Africa, Union Bank of Nigeria, and First Bank of Nigeria. The government liquidated twenty-seven ailing banks in 1997, and others merged.

The Nigerian (formerly Lagos) Stock Exchange (NSE) began operations on 1 July 1961, following passage of the Lagos Stock Exchange Act. The government encourages public issues of shares by Nigerian companies in an effort to mobilize local capital for the country's development. The exchange in Lagos, with branches in Kaduna and Port Harcourt, deals in government stocks and in shares of public companies registered in Nigeria. The stock exchange is managed by the Investment Co. of Nigeria. The Securities and Exchange Commission (SEC) has a dominant say in the markets, fixing prices of all new securities and regulating the prices of those already being traded. Transactions of 50,000 shares or more are subject to SEC approval.

In a bid to encourage foreign interest in the NSE, a computerized central securities clearing system (CSCS) was installed on April 14, 1997, although it got off to a quiet start. The custodian bank for the system is Nigeria International Bank/Citibank. The benefit of the system is that trades will be settled within one week, and eventually within two days, compared with the long delays hitherto experienced in effecting share transfers after purchases and sales.

On April 21, 1997, a CBN directive lifted the restrictions on equity ownership of individual and corporate investors in Nigerian banks. Under the new legislation, it is now possible for an individual or another corporation to own up to a 100 percent share in a bank. Prior to the directive, the maximum shareholding for an individual was just 10 percent, while for companies it was 30 percent.

Economic Development

The agriculture sector has been the focus of intense development interest in recent years, with food self-sufficiency the goal. In 1990, agriculture received 28 percent of the federal budget and was the subject of a separate three-year development plan involving public and private spending targets concentrating on the family farmer. The program includes price stabilization plans and schemes to revitalize the palm oil, cocoa, and rubber subsectors.

An integrated petrochemical industry is also priority. Using the output of the nation's refineries, Nigeria produces benzene, carbon black, and polypropylene. The development of liquid natural gas facilities is expected to lead to the production of methanol, fertilizer, and domestic gas.

In the manufacturing sector, the government is backing a policy of local sourcing whereby locally produced raw materials are converted into finished products. The rehabilitation of the nation's transportation infrastructure is part of a three-year rolling investment plan begun in 1990.

By 1999, the government was more concerned about halting corruption and reigning in the state budget than economic development. In 2000, Nigeria was receiving help internationally through debt restructuring and loans. The IMF and Paris Club were major players but all hinged on political stability and continued political and economic reforms.

SOCIAL WELFARE

There are two kinds of welfare services in Nigeria-those provided by voluntary agencies and those provided by the government. Workers are protected under the Labor Code Act (1958) and the Workmen's Compensation Act, which provides protection for workers in case of industrial accidents. Most companies also provide pension plans for their employees. A national provident fund scheme, inaugurated in 1961, was the first broad social security measure in Nigeria. The scheme is contributory and designed to make financial provisions for workers when unemployment occurs due to old age or illness.

Although sex discrimination is banned under the 1999 constitution, traditional practices still deprive women of many rights. Despite gains in the workplace, women generally earn much less on average than men.

Healthcare

According to 1992 data, primary care is largely provided through approximately 4,000 health clinics scattered throughout the country. For secondary care, there are about 700 healthcare centers and 1,670 maternity centers. There are twelve university teaching hospitals with about 6,500 beds. In 1990-1997, there were twenty physicians per 100,000 people. Two-thirds of the population had access to health care services. In 2000, life expectancy was 51.5 years.

Malaria and tuberculosis are the most common diseases, but serious outbreaks of cerebrospinal meningitis still occur in the north. Just under half of all deaths are thought to be among children, who are especially vulnerable to malaria, and account for 75 percent of registered malaria deaths. Schistosomiasis, Guinea worm, trachoma, river blindness, and yaws are also widespread. Progress, however, has been made in the treatment of sleeping sickness (trypanosomiasis) and leprosy.

Housing

Housing generally has not ranked high on the scale of priorities for social spending, and state governments have tended to rely upon local authorities to meet the problem. Efforts at providing low-cost rural housing have been slight, despite the creation of the Federal Mortgage Bank of Nigeria in 1977, and shantytowns and slums are common in urban areas. The total number of housing units in 1992 was 25.7 million.

EDUCATION

The first six years of primary education were made compulsory in 1976. Recent years have seen a marked growth in educational facilities, but the overall adult illiteracy rate for the country was about 35.9 percent (males, 27.7 percent; females, 43.8 percent) in 2000.

Primary education begins in the local language but introduces English in the third year. In 1994, there were 16.2 million students in 38,649 primary schools. Secondary schools had 4.5 million students and 152,592 teachers.

There are also thirteen polytechnic colleges and four colleges of technology. In 1993-1994, all higher-level institutions combined had 12,031 teaching staff and 207,982,824 pupils.

2000 KEY EVENTS TIMELINE

January

- In Kano, the state assembly approves the introduction of Sharia, but the decision to institute Islamic law must have the governor's approval before it can be applied.
- Nigeria's National Committee on HIV/AIDS begins clinical trials to verify a Nigerian medical doctor's claim to have developed both a cure and a vaccine for AIDS and HIV.

February

- The government of Nigeria signs an agreement with neighbors Benin, Ghana, and Togo to supply them with natural gas.
- The adoption of Sharia in Gusau erupts in violent clashes between Muslims and Christians, destroying property, and leaving scores dead and wounded.

March

- The National Council of State (NCS) in Abuja suspends the implementation of Sharia law in the northern states to halt the violence.
- Three people are killed in clashes between police and protesting Muslim students who want Sharia, or Islamic law, to be declared in Sokoo and Kaduna, cities in the north.
- President Olusegun Obasanjo announces that Nigeria has spent at least 2.3 billion naira (US$22.86 million) between October 1999 and February 2000 on peacekeeping operations in Sierra Leone and on internal security relating to communal conflicts in Nigeria.
- In the Islamic state of Zamfara, an Islamic court amputates a thief's hand. The man, who is Muslim, is found guilty of stealing a cow. The sentence is carried out in a hospital in the state capital, Gusau, despite the ruling of northern governors that Sharia be suspended.
- The Ijaw National Congress accuses the federal government of favoring northern governors while neglecting the Niger River Delta's problems. The Delta area has suffered from communal and other violence spurred by oil extraction and a perceived failure on the part of the federal government to address the Delta's development needs.
- Traditional monarchs in Nigeria's southwest Osun State are trying to stop a bloody feud between the Ife and Modakeke communities. Their intervention aims to prevent more killings from recent fights related to land ownership disputes dating back some 150 years when the Modakeke people settled in Ife after being driven out of their former area in Oyo State.

April

- An arrangement introduced by President Obasanjo will provide 13 percent of Nigeria's oil revenue to the oil-producing states. The amount is far above the three per cent or less that previous regimes offered as compensation to the oil-producing states.

May

- Nigerian authorities tighten security in anticipation of new outbreaks of violence over plans by a new Biafran secessionist movement. The bloody Biafra War of succession ended thirty years ago.
- Nigeria admits to prostitution rings that send Nigerian girls to Europe and other overseas destinations under the pretense of finding them jobs in fashion and hair dressing, then selling them as sex slaves. Between January and December 1999 more than 1,000 Nigerian girls were deported from Italy alone for prostitution and invalid travel papers.

June

- Public sector workers demand higher salaries in a strike that spreads to one-third of Nigeria's thirty-six states, closing hospitals and schools.
- President Obasanjo signs into law a new bill that will create a special council to investigate corruption charges against all Nigerians.

July

- A gasoline pipeline at Oviri-Court explodes on July 10, killing at least 300 people, many of whom are schoolchildren collecting fuel to sell. Another pipeline explodes near Warri (six miles from Adeje) July 12, killing at least 100.
- Senate President Chuba Okadigbo is accused of spending $370,000, an exorbitant fee, on his home in the capital of Abuja.
- A group of armed youths take 165 hostages on two oil rigs on July 31, demanding jobs.

August

- Hostages from two oil rigs are released on August 4, with Royal Dutch/Shell representatives willing to discuss the kidnapper's demands on August 15.
- A number of northern states, including Katsina and Shariah, introduce laws at the beginning of August to implement strict Islamic law in the near future. President Olusegun Obasanjo, a Christian, faces disapproval in those regions.
- President Clinton visits Nigeria and signs a number of bilateral agreements with President Olusegun Obasanjo including commitments to intensify cooperation on military reform, to prevent the spread of HIV/AIDS and international drug trafficking, and to establish an open-skies agreement. Clinton is the second U.S. president to visit Nigeria in twenty-two years.
- Dr. Jeremiah Abalaka, who claims he has discovered a vaccine and a cure for AIDS, agrees to submit his work for verification by the international health community.

September

- The Catholic Bishops Conference of Nigeria (CBCN) urges the government to resolve the issues surrounding the imposition of Sharia in some Nigerian states, which they claim is unjustly depriving Christians of their livelihoods.
- About 4,000 women belonging to nongovernmental organizations (NGOs) march on the national assembly and presidency in Abuja to protest poverty, unequal opportunity, and the denial of female and family rights.

October

- A vigilante group in Zamfara State arms itself with swords, knives, axes, and clubs. The 2,000-strong force aims to enforce Sharia law. Eight states have declared Sharia following Zamfara's lead.
- More than 100 people are killed in Lagos when a militant Yoruba vigilante group, the Oodua People's Congress, attacks Hausas.

November

- The Gates Foundation donates $25 million dollars fight HIV/AIDS in Nigeria. The money will go to the Harvard School of Public Health and the Harvard Center for International Development.
- A man is flogged in public in the northern state of Katsina for allegedly impregnating an eighteen-year-old girl out of wedlock. He is the first to receive such punishment under Sharia law since it was adopted in August.
- Dozens of people are killed while scooping up fuel from a sabotaged pipeline near Lagos. The ruptured pipeline explodes and catches fire—one of 800 similar incidents in the country this year.

December

- Several people are injured in the southeastern town of Okigwe after heavily armed government soldiers intend to arrest Ralph Uwazurike, leader of the Movement for the Actualization of the Sovereign State of Biafra (MASSOB).
- Fifty homes are burned and several people wounded during clashes between the communities of Oku-Ibo and Ikot Offiong in the southern state of Akwa Ibom. The clashes apparently are over land.
- Nigeria and five other West African states—The Gambia, Ghana, Guinea, Liberia, and Sierra Leone—decide to create a West African Monetary Zone. The six countries belong to the fifteen-member state Economic Community of West African States (ECOWAS), and may eventually join together with members of the CFA franc zone to form a common monetary union.

ANALYSIS OF EVENTS: 2000

BUSINESS AND THE ECONOMY

The good news this year for Nigeria was the high world price of oil, which averaged $27.1 per barrel for crude oil. Strong oil prices improved Nigeria's real gross domestic product (GDP) from 2.6 percent in 1999 to 3.3 percent in 2000, and even though prices were expected to fall off to $22 per barrel in 2001, the real GDP was expected to grow to 4.1 percent next year. Export earnings reached $17.4 billion in 2000, up from $12.8 billion in 1999, and the trade balance moved from a positive $3.1 billion to $5.9 billion. The budget deficit fell from 7.2 percent of GDP in 1999 to 2.2 percent in 2000. Similarly, Nigeria benefited from a current accounts surplus of $50.6 million in 1999, or 1.2 percent of the GDP, and an increase in exports from

$12.9 billion in 1999 to $20.5 billion in 2000, which pushed the current account surplus to 11.8 percent of the GDP.

President Olusegun Obasanjo's administration pursued a policy of cautious liberalization aiming to create jobs and to reduce poverty. He discovered that hard questions remained over the pace and scope of economic reforms both within the civil service sector and in the international donor community. The political tug-of-war over raising civil service salaries or retrenching the civil service was one contentious cxample, especially given Nigeria's poverty and social unrest. The increase in oil revenue gave the administration the option to delay drawing upon the International Monetary Fund's (IMF's) US$1 billion standby facility. However, analysts believed that donors, who were insisting on debt rescheduling, will be unlikely to give in to the administration's push for debt forgiveness.

Despite its huge oil resources, the trade balance was expected to decrease in 2001 to $2.8 billion, and inflation was expected to rise from 10 percent in 2000 to 12 percent in 2001. Growth rates of 4 percent were too low to make a real dent in the grinding poverty of a country with a total population of 125 million people. Analysts believed that a real growth rate of between 8–10 percent would be needed to create the number of jobs that would outpace a population growth rate of nearly 3 percent.

One brake on economic progress this year was the political process. Debate is a hallmark of democratic procedure, but political infighting over budgets delayed passage of the 2000 budget in the first six months, resulting in gridlock—if not a deadlock—in terms of taking action on the nation's urgent development priorities.

GOVERNMENT AND POLITICS

This year's relentless and bloody violence underscored the powerful centrifugal forces tearing Nigeria apart and the fragility of its political institutions. Nine northern states declared their intention to apply Muslim Sharia law, while a group of five Igbo-speaking states from the southeast called for greater states' autonomy. The prosperity gap between these blocks of states has widened, deepening the ideological and political divide between the Muslim north and the Christian south.

Perhaps the issue attracting the most international attention this year was the struggle over Sharia. Early in the year, vigilantes from several states came by the busload to Zamfara to support Governor Sani's decision to implement Sharia law. A Muslim hardliner, Sani pushed ahead with implementation of the law, despite agreements to postpone it. Two former governors, Shehu Shagari and retired General Muhammadu Buhari backed the law, and the amputation of a hand of a Muslim man convicted of stealing a cow was indicative of their determination.

To an important extent religious differences fall along regional and ethnic lines. One of the many political factions emerging in the south is MASSOB, an Igbo secessionist group. During the year, MASSOB stepped up its campaign for the revival of the short-lived Biafra Republic, whose declaration of independence in 1967 led to a three-year-old civil war during which at least one million people were killed. Significantly, the violence upcountry this year has found its way to Lagos where several bloody clashes mainly between Hausas and Yorubas have taken place.

To bridge the religious, ethnic, and regional divides, a growing number of Nigerians called for a national conference. Proponents of a conference would like to conduct a constitutional review of states' rights, leading to a fundamental restructuring of the Nigerian state more loosely federated in the U.S. tradition. Similar issues framed the debate for the founders of the U.S. republic, who feared a tyrannical central government.

In the shadow of these events an important political process unfolded in the corridors of Nigeria's young democratic institutions of government. Obasanjo's People's Democratic Party (PDP) ran into the roadblocks of the legislative process, despite the majority it enjoys in both chambers of government. Most of the fighting occurred over budgets, which the legislature criticized for lack of detail. However, the democratic process in Nigeria (as well as elsewhere in Africa) is likely to be contentious given the executive's traditional dominance over domestic politics and new legislatures exercising their constitutional muscles.

The government made progress in combating corruption in 2000. Billions of dollars were embezzled from state coffers under military rule over the past several years. In June President Obasanjo signed into law a bill that authorized a special council to investigate charges of corruption—exempting no Nigerian. In August the president of the Senate, who had been charged with fraudulent contract awards, was impeached. However, corruption in Nigeria is endemic and will require drastic and creative measures to root it out.

On the international scene, the president made a visit to London and received a visit from U.S. President Bill Clinton in August. The United States granted Nigeria $10.6 million in military aid to refurbish transport planes and to carry out measures to continue its peacekeeping activities in the subregion and in the Congo. Nigeria is the regional powerhouse, and has become the peacekeeping proxy of the world's superpower policemen. Within the region, Nigeria improved its trading relationship with Niger, but continued to compete with neighbors Cameroon, Equatorial Guinea, and Chad over ownership of oil-rich border areas. The border dispute with Cameroon was before the International Court of Justice (ICJ), and the delimitation of international boundaries in the vicinity of Lake Chad was completed and awaited ratification by Cameroon, Chad, Niger, and Nigeria.

CULTURE AND SOCIETY

Hundreds of people were killed this year throughout the country in ethnic and religious clashes over legal, territorial, and resource issues, including access to and rights over land. The killings began on February 21 in Kaduna between Muslims and Christians during which more than five hundred died in Kaduna City. Dozens more died in clashes related to Sharia in the northern states. A week later, more than four hundred died in so-called revenge fighting in predominantly Igbo Abia State. Subsequently, scores more people died in reprisals against Hausas in Igbo states in the southeast.

The fight over resources has raised a key question among Nigerians about who was benefiting from the country's enormous oil wealth. The popular perception among southerners was that former and current government officials from the north have stolen their wealth, and the government's offer to return 13 percent of oil revenues to the producing states fell far short of the 50 percent many militants were demanding.

The Nigerian dream was evaporating for the majority of the population. Nigeria ranked in the "low human development" category of the United Nations Development Program (UNDP) Human Development Index, at 146 out of 174 countries. In 1997 life expectancy was under fifty years of age, and only 52 percent of the population could be expected to live to age sixty. While these numbers have improved over the past twenty-five years, the specter of AIDS threatened these gains. Additionally, most of the top health professionals have left for jobs in North America, Europe, the Persian Gulf states, and Southern Africa. According to the World Bank, some 20,000 Nigerian medical doctors were practicing in the United States alone, and estimates from the Nigerian Medical Association were that twice as many doctors were practicing abroad compared to a mere fourteen thousand at home.

DIRECTORY

CENTRAL GOVERNMENT

Head of State

President
Olusegun Obasanjo, Office of the President

Vice President
Atiku Abubakar, Office of the Vice President

Ministers

Minister of Commerce in Africa
Engr. Bello, Ministry of Commerce in Africa

Minister of Communications
M. Arzika, Ministry of Communications

Minister of Culture and Tourism
Tonye Grahm-Douglass, Ministry of Culture and Tourism

Minister of Defense
Yakubu Danjuma, Ministry of Defense

Minister of Education
Tande Adeniran, Ministry of Education

Minister of Environment
Alhaji Sani Zango Daura, Ministry of Environment

Minister of Health
Tim Menakaya, Ministry of Health

Minister of Information
Jerry Gana, Ministry of Information

Minister of Justice
Bola Ige, Ministry of Justice

Minister of Works and Housing
Tony Anenih, Ministry of Works and Housing

Minister of Agriculture
Hassan Adamu, Ministry of Agriculture

Minister of Aviation
Trema Achikwe, Ministry of Aviation

Minister of Finance
Malam Adamu Ciroma, Ministry of Finance

Minister of Internal Affairs
S.M. Afolabi, Ministry of Internal Affairs

Minister of Transport
Ojo Maduike, Ministry of Transport

Minister of Women and Youth
Betty Igwe, Ministry of Women and Youth

POLITICAL ORGANIZATIONS

All People's Party

NAME: Alhaji Yusuf Ali

People's Democratic Party

NAME: Soloman Lar

DIPLOMATIC REPRESENTATION

Embassies in Nigeria

Australia
2 Ozumba Mbadiwe Avenue, Victoria Island ORPO Box 2427, Lagos, Nigeria
PHONE: +234 (1) 2618875
FAX: +234 (1) 2618703

Italy
8 Eleke Crescent, Victoria Island, Lagos, Nigeria
PHONE: +234 (1) 2621046
FAX: +234 (1) 2621050

United Kingdom
11 Eleke Crescent, Victoria Island (Private Bag 12136), Lagos, Nigeria
PHONE: +234 (1) 2619531
FAX: +234 (1) 2614021

JUDICIAL SYSTEM

Supreme Court

Federal Court of Appeal

BROADCAST MEDIA

Cool FM (96.9)

Aim Plaza Plot 267 A Etim Inyang Crescent, PMB 10096, Victoria Island Annex , Lagos, Nigeria
PHONE: +234 (1) 2623051; 2623052; 2623053; 2623054
FAX: +234 (1) 2610393; 2614779
E-MAIL: Coolfm969@nova.net.ng; coolfm@hyperia.com
WEBSITE: http://www.coolfm.nu
TITLE: Managing Director
CONTACT: Amin Moussalli
BROADCASTS: 24 hours/day
TYPE: Private, Commercial

Federal Radio Corporation of Nigeria

Radio House, PMB 452, Abuja, Nigeria
PHONE: +234 (9) 2346318; 2346319; 2346487
FAX: +234 (9) 2346486
TITLE: Director General
CONTACT: Eddie Iroh
LANGUAGE: English, Yoruba, Hausa, Igbo, Izon, Efik, Tiv, Edo, Urhobo, Igala, Kanuri, Fulfulde, Nupe
TYPE: Government

National Broadcasting Commission

PO Box 55021, Lagos, Nigeria
PHONE: +234 (1) 2647867
FAX: +234 (1) 2647868
E-MAIL: info@nbc-ng.org
WEBSITE: http://www.nbc-ng.org
TITLE: Director General
CONTACT: Mallam Nasir Danladi Bako
TYPE: Government

Nigerian Telecommunications Limited

PMB 12557, Lagos, Nigeria
PHONE: +234 (9) 5235707; 5234554
FAX: +234 (9) 5234701
TITLE: Managing Director
CONTACT: Buba Bajoga
TYPE: Government

Nigerian Television Authority

Television House, PMB 120005, Victoria Island, Lagos, Nigeria
PHONE: +234 (1) 614966; 615154; 612529
FAX: +234 (1) 2610289
TITLE: Directorate General
CONTACT: Mohammed Ibrahim
TYPE: Government

COLLEGES AND UNIVERSITIES

Abubakar Tafawa Balewa University

PMB 0248, Bauchi, Nigeria

Ahmadu Bello University

Zaria, Nigeria

Bayero University

PMB 3011, Kano, Nigeria

Edo State University

PMB 14, Ekpoma, Nigeria

Enugu State University of Science & Technology

Enugu Campus, Independence Layout, PMB 01660, Enugu, Nigeria

Federal University of Technology-Akure

PMB 704, Akure, Nigeria

Federal University of Technology-Minna

PMB 65, Minna, Nigeria

Federal University of Technology-Owerri

PMB 1526, Owerri, Nigeria

Federal University of Technology-Yola

PMB 2076, Yola, Nigeria

Lagos State University

Badagry Expressway Ojo, PMB 1087, Apapa, Nigeria

Nnamdi Azikiwe University

PMB 5025, Awka, Nigeria

Obafemi Awolowo University

Ile-Ife, Nigeria

Ogun State University

PMB 2002, Ago-Iwoye, Nigeria

Ondo State University

PMB 5363, Ado-Ekiti, Nigeria

Rivers State University of Science & Technology

PMB 5080, Port Harcourt, Nigeria

University of Abuja

PMB 117, Federal Capital Territory, Abuja, Nigeria

University of Agriculture-Abeokuta

PMB 2240, Abeokuta, Nigeria

University of Agriculture-Makurdi

PMB 2373, Makurdi, Nigeria

University of Benin - Nigeria

PMB 1154, Benin City, Nigeria

University of Calabar

PMB 1115, Calabar, Nigeria

University of Ilorin

PMB 1515, Ilorin, Nigeria

University of Jos

PMB 2084, Jos, Nigeria

University of Lagos

Lagos, Nigeria

University of Maiduguri

Barma Rd., PMB 1069, Maiduguri, Nigeria

University of Port Harcourt

PMB 5323, Port Harcourt, Nigeria

Usmanu Danfodiyo University

PMB 2346, Sokoto, Nigeria

University of Ibadan

Ibadan, Nigeria
E-MAIL: library@kdl.ui.edu.ng
WEBSITE: http://www.ui.edu.ng

Abia State University

PMB 2000, Uturee, Nigeria

Federal University of Agriculture-Umudike

Umudike, PMB 7267, Umuahia, Nigeria

University of Uyo

PMB 1017, Uyo, Nigeria

University of Nigeria

Nsukka, Nigeria

NEWSPAPERS AND MAGAZINES

Daily Champion/Sunday Champion

Champion Newspapers Ltd., PO Box 2276, Oshodi, Lagos, Nigeria
WEBSITE: http://www.champion-news.com
TITLE: Editor
CONTACT: Emma Agu
CIRCULATION: 150,000

Daily Sketch/Sunday Sketch

Sketch Publishing Co. Ltd., Oba Adebimpe Rd., Pte. Mail Bag 5067, Ibadan, Nigeria
PHONE: +234 (22) 414851
CIRCULATION: 64,000 (daily); 125,000 (Sun.)

Daily Times

The Daily Times of Nigeria Ltd., PO Box 21340, Ikeja, Lagos, Nigeria
PHONE: +234 (1) 900850
TITLE: Editor
CONTACT: Farouk Umar Muhammed
CIRCULATION: 250,000

The Guardian

Guardian Newspapers Ltd., Rutam House, Isolo Expressway, Isolo PMB 1217, Oshodi, Lagos, Nigeria
PHONE: +234 (1) 524111
E-MAIL: letters@ngrguardiannews.com
WEBSITE: http://www.ngrguardiannews.com
CIRCULATION: 80,000

Irohin Yoruba

African Newspapers of Nigeria Ltd., 212 Broad St., Box 2416, Ibadan, Niberia
PHONE: +234 (1) 410886
TITLE: Editor
CONTACT: S.A. Ajibade
CIRCULATION: 85,000

Lagos Weekend

Daily Times of Nigeria Ltd., PMB 21340, Latef Jakendi Road, Ikeja, Lagos, Nigeria
PHONE: +234 (1) 4977280
FAX: +234 (1) 4977285
TITLE: Editor
CONTACT: Clement Okosun
CIRCULATION: 288,874

National Concord

Fabiyi, Moyo, Editorial Department, Isokan, Concord Press Nigeria Ltd., Concord House, 4 Concord Way, PO Box 4482, Ikeja, Lagos, Nigeria
PHONE: +234 (1) 9010109
CIRCULATION: 200,000

New Nigerian

New Nigerian Newspaper Ltd., Ahmadu Bellow Way, PO Box 254, Kaduna, Nigeria
PHONE: +234 (62) 235221
FAX: +234 (62) 235752
TITLE: Editor
CONTACT: Gausu Ahmad
CIRCULATION: 80,000

Nigerian Tribune

African Newspapers of Nigeria Ltd., Imalefalafi Street, Oke-Ado, PO Box 78, Ibadan, Nigeria
PHONE: +234 (22) 410886
CIRCULATION: 109,000

The Post Express

WEBSITE: http://www.postexpresswired.com
TITLE: Editor
CONTACT: Kelechi Onyemaobi

Vanguard

Vanguard Media Limited, Vanguard Avenue, Kirikiri, Canal, PMB 1007, Apapa, Lagos, Nigeria
PHONE: +234 (1) 5875847
E-MAIL: vanguard@linkserve.com.ng
WEBSITE: http://www.afbis.com/vanguard
TITLE: Publisher
CONTACT: Sam Amuka

African Crusader

38 Commercial Ave., Yaba, Lagos State, Nigeria
TYPE: History, Africa

African Notes

University of Ibadan, Ibadan, Nigeria
TITLE: Editor
CONTACT: Alex Iwara
CIRCULATION: 2,500
TYPE: Social sciences, ethnic studies

Nigeria Confidential

83 Palm Ave., Mushin, Lagos, Nigeria
TITLE: Editor
CONTACT: Abiodun Aloba
CIRCULATION: 1,000
TYPE: Social science, general

Nigeria Magazine

PMB 12524, Lagos, Nigeria
TITLE: Editor
CONTACT: U.N. Abalogu
CIRCULATION: 9,000
TYPE: Social science, general

Nigerian Business Journal

1 Idowu Taylor St., PO Box 109, Victoria Island, Lagos State, Nigeria
TITLE: Editor
CONTACT: S.B. Akande
CIRCULATION: 5,000
TYPE: Business and economics, commerce

PUBLISHERS

Evans Brothers (Nigeria Publishers) Ltd.

Jericho Rd., PMB 5164, Ibadan, Oyo State, Nigeria
PHONE: +234 (2) 2413708
FAX: +234 (2) 2410757
TITLE: Managing Director
CONTACT: B.O. Bolodeoku
SUBJECTS: Accounting, Agriculture, Child Care and Development, Civil Engineering, Drama, Theater, Economics, Education, Electronics, Electrical Engineering, Environmental Studies, Fiction, Geography, Geology, Government, Political Science, History, Journalism, Law, Literature, Literary Criticism, Essays, Management, Mathematics, Medicine, Nursing, Dentistry, Philosophy, Romance, Science (General), Self-Help, Social Sciences, Sociology, Sports, Athletics, Technology

RELIGIOUS ORGANIZATIONS

Islamic

Federation of Muslim Women's Association of Nigeria (FOMWAN)
No. 35 Clapperton Road, PO Boz 100, Sokoto, Nigeria
PHONE: +234 236691
NAME: Mrs. Hajoya Sa Adiya Omar

Protestant

The Salvation Army
4 Shipeolu Street, Igbobi, Shomolo, Lagos, Nigeria
PHONE: +234 (1) 8211247; 4975481
FAX: +234 (1) 5454836

Seventh-Day Adventist-West Nigeria Conference
PO Box 19, Ibadan, Nigeria
PHONE: +234 (2) 2411842; 2410136
WEBSITE: http://www.tagnet.org/westnigeria/main%20page.htm
TITLE: President
NAME: Onaolapo

Scientology

Church of Scientology Mission of Lagos
No 10 Modupe Street, Shomolu-Lagos, Nigeria, West Africa
PHONE: +234 (1) 4706759
FAX: +234 (1) 2624748

Other Organizations

Accrediting Council for Theological Education in Africa (ACTEA)

Conseil pour l'Holologation des Etablissements Theologiques en Afrique (COHETA)
Private Mail Bag 2009, Jos, Plateau, Nigeria
PHONE: +234 (73) 460880
E-MAIL: acteajos@maf.org
TITLE: Chairman
NAME: Dr. C. A. Olowola

FURTHER READING

Articles

"The Month in Review: January 2000." *Current History,* March 2000, p. 142.

"Nigerian Leader Seeks Peacemaking Role." *New York Times,* September 5, 2000, p. A10.

Onishi, Norimitsu, "Nigeria: Riots Spread." *New York Times,* October 19, 2000, p. A14.

Books

Aka, Ebenezer O. *Regional Disparities in Nigeria's Development: Lessons and Challenges for the 21st Century.* Lanham, MD: University Press of America, 2000.

Kalu, Kelechi Amihe. *Economic Development and Nigerian Foreign Policy.* Lewiston, NY: Edwin Mellen Press, 2000.

Oyewole, A. *Historical Dictionary of Nigeria.* 2nd ed. Lanham, MD: Scarecrow Press, 2000.

Peel, J. D. Y. *Religious Encounter and the Making of the Yoruba.* Bloomington: Indiana University Press, 2000.

Government Publications

United States Congress. *The Nigerian Transition and the Future of U.S. Policy.* Washington, DC: G.P.O., 2000.

NIGERIA: STATISTICAL DATA

For sources and notes see "Sources of Statistics" at the front of each volume.

GEOGRAPHY

Geography

Area:

Total: 923,768 sq km.

Land: 910,768 sq km.

Land boundaries:

Total: 4,047 km.

Border countries: Benin 773 km, Cameroon 1,690 km, Chad 87 km, Niger 1,497 km.

Coastline: 853 km.

Climate: varies; equatorial in south, tropical in center, arid in north.

Terrain: southern lowlands merge into central hills and plateaus; mountains in southeast, plains in north.

Natural resources: petroleum, tin, columbite, iron ore, coal, limestone, lead, zinc, natural gas, hydropower, arable land.

Land use:

Arable land: 33%

Permanent crops: 3%

Permanent pastures: 44%

Forests and woodland: 12%

Other: 8% (1993 est.).

HUMAN FACTORS

Demographics (A)

	1990	1995	1998	2000	2010	2020	2030	2040	2050
Population	92,483	107,210	116,788	123,338	155,588	187,437	222,313	260,853	303,587
Life expectancy - males	51.5	52.3	51.9	51.6	45.9	49.3	54.9	62.1	69.3
Life expectancy - females	53.6	54.4	52.6	51.5	48.2	52.2	58.3	66.3	74.1
Birth rate (per 1,000)	43.4	41.9	41.0	40.2	35.3	31.2	27.2	23.5	20.4
Death rate (per 1,000)	13.9	13.1	13.5	13.7	15.9	13.6	11.0	8.0	5.8
Women of reproductive age (15-49 yrs.)	20,231	24,018	26,517	28,143	36,537	46,633	58,115	70,372	82,248
Fertility rate	6.4	6.1	5.8	5.7	4.8	4.0	3.3	2.8	2.5

Except as noted, values for vital statistics are in thousands; life expectancy is in years.

Health Personnel

	National Data	World Data (wtd ave)
Total health expenditure as a percentage of GDP, 1990-1998[a]		
Public sector	0.2	2.5
Private sector	0.5	2.9
Total[b]	0.7	5.5
Health expenditure per capita in U.S. dollars, 1990-1998[a]		
Purchasing power parity	6	561
Total	9	483
Availability of health care facilities per 100,000 people		
Hospital beds 1990-1998[a]	170	330
Doctors 1992-1995[a]	21	122
Nurses 1992-1995[a]	142	248

Health Indicators

	National Data	World Data
Life expectancy at birth (years)		
1980	46	61
1998	53	67
Daily per capita supply of calories		
1970	2,392	2,358
1997	2,735	2,791
Daily per capital supply of protein		
1997 (grams)	62	74
Total fertility rate (births per woman)		
1980	6.9	3.7
1998	5.3	2.7
Population with access (%)		
To safe water (1990-96)	39	NA
To sanitation (1990-96)	36	NA
People living with (1997)		
Tuberculosis (cases per 100,000)	14.1	60.4
Malaria (cases per 100,000)	593.3	42.2
HIV/AIDS (% aged 15 - 49 years)	4.12	0.99

Infants and Malnutrition

	National Data	World Data (wtd ave)
Under 5 mortality rate (1989)	187	NA
% of infants with low birthweight (1992-98)[1]	16	17
Births attended by skilled health staff (% of total births 1996-98)	31	52
% fully immunized at 1 year of age (1995-98)[1]		
TB	27	82
DPT	21	77
Polio	22	77
Measles	26	74
Prevalence of child malnutrition (1992-98)[1] (based on weight for age, % of children under 5 years)	39	30

Ethnic Division

Hausa and Fulani 29.0%
Yoruba 21.0%
Igbo (Ibo) 18.0%
Ijaw 10.0%
Kanuri 4.0%
Ibibio 3.5%

Nigeria, which is Africa's most populous country, is composed of more than 250 ethnic groups; the following are the most populous and politically influential.

Religion

Muslim 50%
Christian 40%
Indigenous beliefs 10%

Major Languages

English (official), Hausa, Yoruba, Igbo (Ibo), Fulani.

EDUCATION

Public Education Expenditures

	1980	1997
Public expenditures on education as % of GNP	6.4	0.7
Expenditures per student as % of GNP per capita		
Primary & Secondary	4.7	NA
Tertiary	529.6	NA
Pupils per teacher at the primary level	NA	37
Duration of primary education in years	NA	6
World data for comparison		
Public expenditures on education as % of GNP (mean)	3.9	4.8

	1980	1997
Pupils per teacher at the primary level (wtd ave)	NA	33
Duration of primary education in years (mean)	NA	9

Educational Attainment (B)

	1990	1995
Gross enrollment ratio (%)		
Primary level	91.4	98.0
Secondary level	24.9	33.2
Tertiary level	4.0	4.0
Enrollment of population aged 6-23 years (%)	37.0	NA

Literacy Rates (A)

In thousands and percent	1990	1995	2000	2010
Illiterate population (15+ yrs.)	26,562	26,075	25,171	22,278
Literacy rate - total adult pop. (%)	49.4	57.1	64.5	77.1
Literacy rate - males (%)	60.8	67.3	73.3	83.2
Literacy rate - females (%)	38.6	47.3	55.9	71.1

Libraries

National Libraries **1992**
Administrative Units 1
Service Points or Branches 12
Number of Volumes (000) 865
Registered Users (000) 34
Loans to Users (000) .... NA
Total Library Staff 682
Public Libraries **1992**
Administrative Units 12
Service Points or Branches 76
Number of Volumes (000) 611
Registered Users (000) 15
Loans to Users (000) 99
Total Library Staff 1,722

GOVERNMENT & LAW

Political Parties

National Assembly	% of vote	no. of seats
Senate		
PDP	58%	65
APP	23%	24
AD	19%	20
House of Representatives		
People's Democratic Party (PDP)	58%	215
All People's Party (APP)	30%	75
Alliance for Democracy (AD)	12%	70

Elections for Senate were last held 20-24 February 1999 (next to be held in 2003); House of Representatives elections were last held 20-24 February 1999 (next to be held in 2003).

(Continued on next page.)

LABOR FORCE

Total Labor Force (A)

42.844 million.

Labor Force by Occupation

Agriculture 54%
Industry 6%
Services 40%

Data for 1999 est.

Unemployment Rate

28% (1992 est.)

PRODUCTION SECTOR

Energy Production

Production .... 14.75 billion kWh
Production by source
Fossil fuel 61.69%
Hydro 38.31%
Nuclear 0%
Other 0%
Exports .... 0 kWh

Data for 1998.

Energy Consumption

Consumption .... 13.717 billion kWh
Imports .... 0 kWh

Data for 1998.

Transportation

Highways:

Total: 194,394 km.

Paved: 60,068 km (including 1,194 km of expressways).

Unpaved: 134,326 km (1998 est.).

(Continued on next page.)

Note: many of the roads reported as paved may be graveled; because of poor maintenance and years of heavy freight traffic (in part the result of the failure of the railroad system), much of the road system is barely usable.

Waterways: 8,575 km consisting of the Niger and Benue rivers and smaller rivers and creeks.

Pipelines: crude oil 2,042 km; petroleum products 3,000 km; natural gas 500 km.

Merchant marine:

Total: 40 ships (1,000 GRT or over) totaling 360,505 GRT/644,471 DWT.

Ships by type: bulk 1, cargo 12, chemical tanker 4, petroleum tanker 22, specialized tanker 1 (1999 est.).

Airports: 71 (1999 est.).

Airports - with paved runways: 37.

Airports - with unpaved runways: 34.

Top Agriculture Products

Cocoa, peanuts, palm oil, corn, rice, sorghum, millet, cassava (tapioca), yams, rubber; cattle, sheep, goats, pigs; timber; fish.

Top Mining Products (B)

Mineral resources include: tin, columbite, iron ore, coal, limestone, lead, zinc.

GOVERNMENT & LAW (cont.)

Military Affairs (A)

	1990	1992	1995	1996	1997
Military expenditures					
Current dollars (mil.)	2,200	2,710	2,250	2,050	2,000
1997 constant dollars (mil.)	2,570	3,000	2,330	2,090	2,000
Armed forces (000)	94	76	80	80	76
Gross national product (GNP)					
Current dollars (bil.)	90	105	124	131	139
1997 constant dollars (bil.)	106	117	128	133	139
Central government expenditures (CGE)					
1997 constant dollars (bil.)	27	19	18	15	16
People (mil.)	86.5	92.1	101.0	104.1	107.3
Military expenditure as % of GNP	2.4	2.6	1.8	1.6	1.4
World data on military expenditure as % of GNP	4.5	3.4	2.7	2.6	2.6
Military expenditure as % of CGE	9.5	15.6	13.3	14.4	12.3
World data on military expenditure as % of CGE	17.0	12.5	10.5	10.3	10.2
Military expenditure per capita (1997 $)	30	33	23	20	19
World data on military expenditure per capita (1997 $)	242	173	146	143	145
Armed forces per 1,000 people (soldiers)	1.1	0.8	0.8	0.8	0.7
World data on armed forces per 1,000 people (soldiers)	5.3	4.5	4.1	3.9	3.8
GNP per capita (1997 $)	1,220	1,270	1,270	1,270	1,300
Arms imports[6]					
Current dollars (mil.)	100	160	10	10	90
1997 constant dollars (mil.)	117	177	10	10	90
Total imports[7]					
Current dollars (mil.)	5,627	8,119	10,740	8,009	12,040
1997 constant dollars (mil.)	6,590	9,001	11,120	8,143	12,040
Total exports[7]					
Current dollars (mil.)	13,670	11,890	10,640	18,610	17,670
1997 constant dollars (mil.)	16,010	13,180	11,010	18,920	17,670
Arms as percent of total imports[8]	1.8	2.0	0.1	0.1	0.7
Arms as percent of total exports[8]	0	0	0	0	0

MANUFACTURING SECTOR

GDP & Manufacturing Summary (A)

	1980	1985	1990	1995
GDP ($-1990 mil.)[1]	28,357	27,329	35,462	40,510
Per capita ($-1990)[1]	394	329	369	363
Manufacturing share (%) (current prices)[1]	8.3	8.7	6.0	NA
Manufacturing				
Value added ($-1990 mil.)[1]	1,813	1,682	2,098	2,028
Industrial production index	144	100	100	97
Value added ($ mil.)	2,422	1,726	3,682[e]	7,884[e]
Gross output ($ mil.)	4,740	3,534	6,273[e]	13,412[e]
Employment (000)	432	336	405[e]	448[e]
Profitability (% of gross output)				
Intermediate input (%)	49	51	41[e]	41[e]
Wages and salaries inc. supplements (%)	11[e]	10[e]	9[e]	10[e]
Gross operating surplus	40[e]	39[e]	50[e]	49[e]
Productivity ($)				
Gross output per worker	10,238	9,899	14,487[e]	28,365[e]
Value added per worker	5,260	4,866	8,706[e]	16,865[e]
Average wage (inc. supplements)	1,226[e]	1,014[e]	1,416[e]	2,975[e]
Value added ($ mil.)				
Food products	149	251	566[e]	1,390[e]
Beverages	267	205	390[e]	1,205[e]
Tobacco products	96	52[e]	83[e]	148[e]
Textiles	231	233	536[e]	823[e]
Wearing apparel	3	1	2[e]	5[e]
Leather and fur products	12	23	48[e]	96[e]
Footwear	12	28	61[e]	152[e]
Wood and wood products	88	14	26[e]	39[e]
Furniture and fixtures	56	14	34[e]	70[e]
Paper and paper products	38	51	121[e]	296[e]
Printing and publishing	75	45	106[e]	266[e]
Industrial chemicals	30	9	14[e]	25[e]
Other chemical products	265	213	463[e]	925[e]
Petroleum refineries	70[e]	−6[e]	9[e]	1[e]
Misc. petroleum and coal products	9[e]	−1[e]	3[e]	NA
Rubber products	26	31	66[e]	146[e]
Plastic products	98	49	108[e]	220[e]
Pottery, china and earthenware	NA	2	25[e]	2[e]
Glass and glass products	24	7	16[e]	32[e]
Other non-metal mineral products	87	106	230[e]	460[e]
Iron and steel	3	17	36[e]	81[e]
Non-ferrous metals	33	34[e]	73[e]	146[e]
Metal products	140	92	166[e]	295[e]
Non-electrical machinery	23	19	42[e]	87[e]
Electrical machinery	46	36	79[e]	160[e]
Transport equipment	526	193	388[e]	774[e]
Other manufacturing	13	6	15[e]	37[e]

COMMUNICATIONS

Daily Newspapers

	National Data	World Data for Comparison
Daily Newspapers		
Number of Dailies	25	8,391
Total Circulation (000)	2,740	548,000
Circulation per 1,000 inhabitants	27	96

Telecommunications

Telephones - main lines in use: 405,000 (1995).

Telephones - mobile cellular: 10,000 (1999).

Telephone system: an inadequate system, further limited by poor maintenance; major expansion is required and a start has been made.

Domestic: intercity traffic is carried by coaxial cable, microwave radio relay, a domestic communications satellite system with 19 earth stations, and a coastal submarine cable; mobile cellular facilities and the Internet are available.

International: satellite earth stations - 3 Intelsat (2 Atlantic Ocean and 1 Indian Ocean); coaxial submarine cable SAFE (South African Far East).

Radio broadcast stations: AM 82, FM 35, shortwave 11 (1998).

Radios: 23.5 million (1997).

Television broadcast stations: 2 government-controlled Note: in addition, in 1993, 14 licenses to operate private television stations were granted (1999).

Televisions: 6.9 million (1997).

Internet Service Providers (ISPs): 5 (1999).

FINANCE, ECONOMICS, & TRADE

Economic Indicators

National product: GDP—purchasing power parity—$110.5 billion (1999 est.).

National product real growth rate: 2.7% (1999 est.).

National product per capita: $970 (1999 est.).

Inflation rate—consumer price index: 12.5% (1999 est.).

Exchange Rates

Exchange rates:

Nairas (N) per US$1

October 1999	96.261
1999	99.000
1998	21.886
1997	21.886
1995	21.895

Top Import Origins

$10 billion (f.o.b., 1999)

Origins (1998 est.)

United Kingdom	13%
United States	12%
Germany	10%
France	9%
Netherlands	NA

Top Export Destinations

$13.1 billion (f.o.b., 1999)

Destinations (1998 est.)

United States	35%
Spain	11%
India	9%
France	6%
Italy	NA

Foreign Aid

Recipient: $39.2 million (1995).

Import/Export Commodities

Import Commodities	Export Commodities
Machinery	Petroleum and petroleum products 95%
Chemicals	Cocoa
Transport equipment	Rubber
Manufactured goods	
Food and live animals	

Balance of Payments

	1993	1994	1995	1996	1997
Exports of goods (f.o.b.)	9,910	9,459	11,734	16,117	15,207
Imports of goods (f.o.b.)	−6,662	−6,511	−8,222	−6,438	−9,501
Trade balance	3,248	2,948	3,513	9,679	5,706
Services - debits	−2,726	−3,007	−4,619	−4,827	−4,712
Services - credits	1,163	371	608	733	786
Private transfers (net)	793	550	804	947	1,920
Government transfers (net)	21	−48	NA	NA	NA
Overall balance	−780	−2,128	−2,578	3,507	552

NIUE

CAPITAL: Alofi.

FLAG: The flag of Niue is yellow with the flag of the United Kingdom in the upper hoist-side quadrant; the flag of the UK bears yellow five-pointed stars—a large one on a blue disk in the center and a smaller one on each arm of the bold red cross.

MONETARY UNIT: 1 New Zealand dollar (NZ$) = 100 cents.

WEIGHTS AND MEASURES: The metric system is used.

HOLIDAYS: Takai, first week of the year; New Year's Day, 1 January; day after New Year's Day, 2 January; Waitangi Day, first Tuesday in February; Good Friday; Easter Monday; Anzac Day; Queen's Birthday, first Monday in June; Labor Day, fourth Monday in October; Christmas Day, 25 December; Boxing Day, 26 December; Provincial Anniversary Day; Peniamina Day; Annexation Day; and Constitution Day.

TIME: 1 AM = noon GMT.

LOCATION AND SIZE: An isolated coral island, Niue is 966 km (600 mi.) northwest of the southern Cook Islands, and located at 19°02′S and 169°52′W. Nieu became a British protectorate in 1900 and was annexed to New Zealand in 1901. Although Niue forms part of the Cook Islands, because of its remoteness and cultural and linguistic differences it has been separately administered. Niue has an area of 258 sq. km (100 sq. mi.).

CLIMATE: There is little temperature change throughout the year, with mean monthly temperatures ranging from 18°C (65°F) to 29°C (85°F). Average annual rainfall is 203 cm (80 inches), but is distributed unevenly throughout the year. Most rainfall occurs during the rainy season from December to April, when temperatures and humidity are higher and typhoons occasionally strike. Droughts occur periodically, so many buildings have water catchments to provide adequate water supply.

INTRODUCTORY SURVEY

RECENT HISTORY

Archaeological research and local oral tradition indicate initial settlement of the island by Samoans around 900 followed by Tongan conquest from the west in the sixteenth century. Modern Niuean language reflects affinities to both Samoan and Tongan. European influences began in 1774, when British explorer Captain James Cook landed on the island, naming it Savage Island because of a hostile reception. British missionaries began arriving in the 1830s, but due to continued hostile receptions did not successfully settle until 1846. By 1900, Niue had become a British protectorate as part of the United Kingdom's Samoan holdings. The following year, Britain annexed Niue to New Zealand as the westernmost island of New Zealand's Cook Island properties. Although Niue forms part of the Cook Islands, because of its remoteness and cultural and linguistic differences, it has been separately administered. In 1904, Niue was given a separate political identity from the Cook Islands with its own appointed commissioner and Island Council. The first popularly elected Niuean legislature replaced the Island Council in 1960. Establishment of local governmental leadership followed in 1966. Niue inhabitants, expected to number over 2,100 in 1999, remained overwhelmingly Polynesian in character.

GOVERNMENT

A self-governing parliamentary democracy, Niue adopted a new constitution in 1974 by passing the Niue Constitution Act. Niue increased control

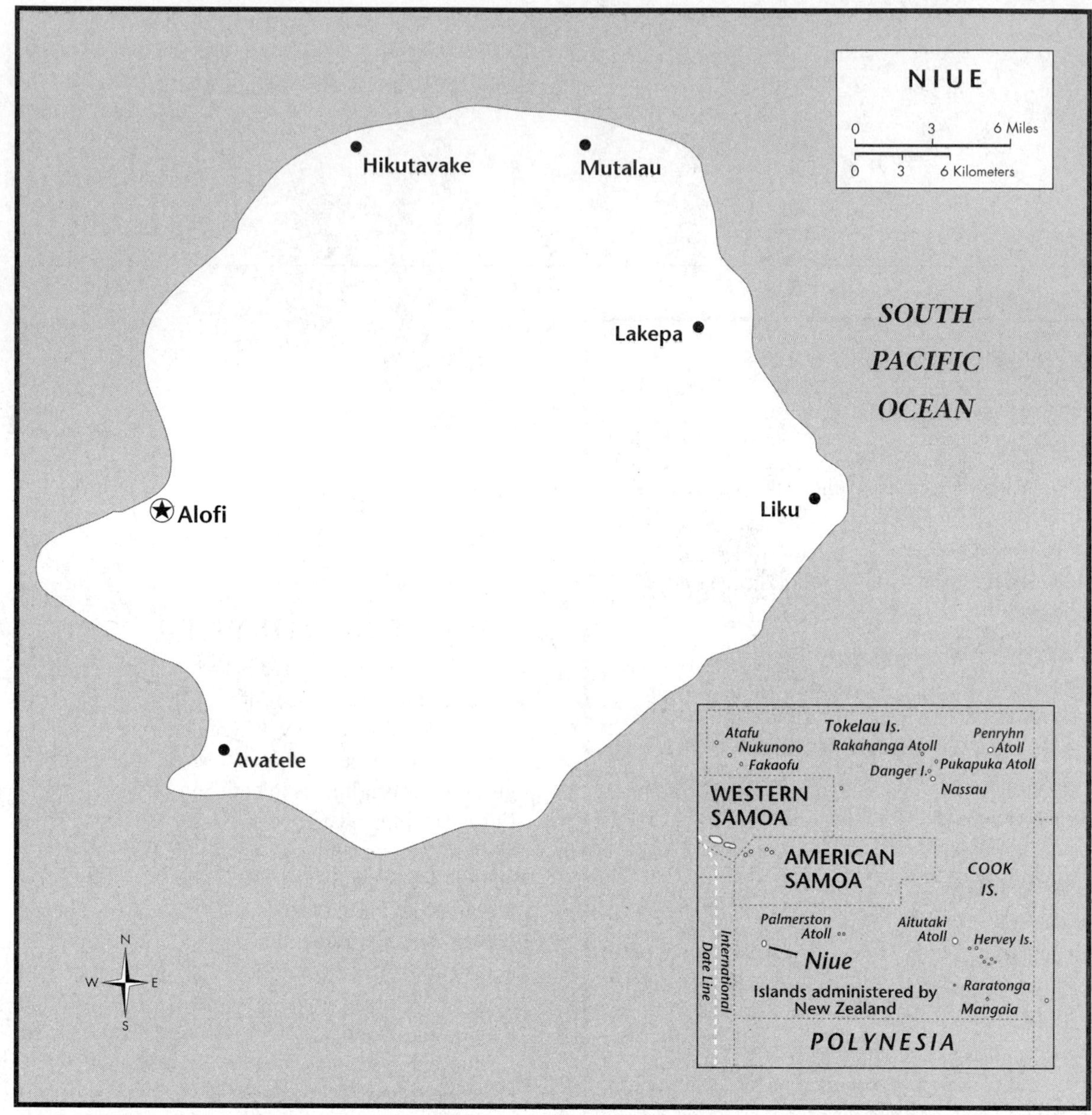

over domestic affairs, but still remained in free association with New Zealand, with Niueans enjoying New Zealand citizenship. New Zealand retains responsibility for external affairs. As a result, Niue is one of the smallest self-governing states in the world. The British monarch, which has been Queen Elizabeth II since 1952, remains chief of state. The New Zealand High Commissioner represents New Zealand and the United Kingdom in Niuean political affairs. A Premier elected by the Niuean Legislative Assembly serves three-year terms as the head of government. The first Premier, the popular Honorable Sir Robert R. Rex, served in office from 1974 to1992.

The Niuean legislative branch is the unicameral Legislative Assembly located in Alofi, the capital and administrative center of the island. The Assembly is composed of twenty members popularly elected, with qualified voters being all resident adults over eighteen years of age. Six members are elected at large and the others represent fourteen villages. Three members of the Assembly are selected by the Premier to join the Premier in a four-member cabinet. Each of the fourteen Niuean villages elects their own village council members to three-year terms. Niue is a member of the South Pacific Forum and the Pacific Community.

Judiciary

The Niuean legal system is based on English common law. Basic components are the Supreme Court of New Zealand, the Land Court, and the High Court of Niue. The Land Court hears cases involving land titles. The Chief Justice of the High Court and judge for the Land Court visit the island on a quarterly basis. In their absence, locally appointed lay justices exercise limited criminal and civil jurisdiction. A Court of Appeal, established in 1992, hears appeals of High Court rulings.

Political Parties

The island's primary political party is the Niue People's Action Party (NPP), founded in 1987 and renamed in 1995.

DEFENSE

New Zealand remains responsible for Niue defense and foreign affairs. Niue does maintain a police force.

ECONOMIC AFFAIRS

One of the largest uplifted coral islands in the world, vegetation overall is scant, despite the tropical climate. Less than a fourth of the island is capable of cultivation. Vulnerable to drought and cyclones, agriculture is primarily for local subsistence with only 8 percent of the island in permanent crops in 1993 and 4 percent in pasture. The fertile coastal strip is the primary part of the island intensively cultivated, but is still largely held in traditional family patterns inhibiting more effective development. With work largely limited to family-owned plantations, the island suffers from substantial emigration of Niueans to New Zealand. A wide range of crops and livestock are raised for subsistence purposes. Some limited cash crops include passion fruit, pawpaw, coconuts, and limes. However, a 1989 hurricane destroyed Niue's coconut plantations leading to closure of the coconut cream processing plant. Another hurricane the following year destroyed the passion fruit and lime crops. Occasional droughts have posed additional challenges. Another important revenue source is sale of postage stamps to collectors.

In 1989, exports amounted to only $117,000 whereas imports totaled $4.1 million. In 1993, the government began seeking to establish a "tax haven" to attract some foreign business. In 1996, Niue made an unsuccessful bid to join the Asian Development Bank in an effort to spur investments in the island's economy.

Tourism is still little developed though the number of hotel rooms on the island increased in the mid-1990s. Limited air service also increased in the early 1990's, and a runway at Hanan International Airport was substantially lengthened in 1995. Just over 2,000 tourists, primarily from New Zealand, were visiting the island annually in the mid-1990s. New Prime Minister Sani Lakatani, leader of the NPP elected in early 1999, vowed to make tourism development a high priority and to continue to promote a financial services industry. Overall, Niue depends on aid from New Zealand to make up the annual shortfall between revenues and expenditures.

Public Finance

With essentially no native export products, expenditures normally exceed revenues, leaving Niue almost totally dependent on economic aid. New Zealand, Niue's main trading partner, is the island's primary source of financial aid, providing almost two-thirds of Niue's revenue, or $8.3 million in economic aid in 1995. New Zealand also makes grants for capital improvements.

Income

In 1994, the gross domestic product (GDP) was estimated at $4.5 million, with a per capita of $2,250.

Industry

The extremely limited Niuean industry, following demise of the coconut, passion fruit, and lime crops, is focused on such products as honey, handicrafts, and leather goods, including footballs. Tourism is yet to become a major component of the island's economy, but continues to be encouraged as does a financial services industry.

Banking and Finance

To facilitate on-island finance, the Development Bank of Niue, known as Fale Tupe Atihake Ha Niue, began operations in 1994.

SOCIAL WELFARE

With little industry, wage work is primarily limited to government service jobs largely subsidized by New Zealand aid. Public social service expenditures are extremely limited.

Healthcare

A twenty-four-bed government-supported hospital and dental clinic are located in Alofi. Life expectancy, estimated in 1991, was 62.5 for males and sixty-five for females.

Housing

Most island residents live in small villages scattered along the coast. Following highly destructive hurricanes of 1959 and 1960, the government replaced the traditional lime-plastered, thatch-roofed houses with tin-roofed concrete-block structures. Many houses stand empty and villages only partially occupied due to the out-migration of Niueans to New Zealand and elsewhere seeking greater economic opportunities. Out of a total of nearly 17,000 Niueans, only 2,600 actually lived on the island in the late 1990s.

EDUCATION

Niue enjoys a high literacy rate of approximately 95 percent of the total population. Education, which is free of charge, is compulsory for ten years between ages five and fourteen. One primary school and one secondary school are located on the island, and the University of the South Pacific has an extension center on Niue. Approximately 10 percent of Niue's budget was dedicated to education in 1991.

2000 KEY EVENTS TIMELINE

January

- Residents on Niue are among the first to celebrate the new millennium. There is a prayer service at dawn on January 1.

June

- Rugby Union season opens.
- The Bank of Niue displays private sector goods for purchase in their annual market day.

August

- The budget department of the Niue government criticizes excessive welfare handouts on August 29. It also criticizes Premier Lakatani's travel expenses. Lakatani says these are necessary as Niue's government is in a free-association government with New Zealand.
- Sixty-four year old Sani Lakitani, the Premier of Niue, is installed as Chancellor of the University of the South Pacific on August 30.

September

- The winner of the Miss Niue Pageant on September 3 is Anna Rose Pavlihi. Her prize is a round trip ticket to New Zealand, a Cook Islands black pearl, and $500 cash.
- At least one half of the staff of Niue High School goes on strike on September 4. Some of the students are choosing to go to New Zealand to finish the high school year. The teachers are striking for a $2000 pay raise to compensate for money spent in training to qualify for New Zealand accreditation.
- The Niue government refuses to give into teachers' demands for pay increases on September 11. The high school and other schools are staffed with substitutes and parents complain. Many teachers leave to look for other jobs in nearby New Zealand.
- An earthquake of 6.3 magnitude strikes the island of Niue on September 11. The epicenter is in the Tonga Trench, 800 kilometers west of Niue.
- Members of the Niue government express concern again over Premier Lakatani's extravagant spending, citing a huge budget deficit, on September 19.

October

- Niue citizens vote to retain their sovereignty from New Zealand on October 14.

November

- On November 30, opposition leader Terry Coe announces plans to call a vote of no confidence in Premier Sani Lakatani's government in December, on charges of financial mismanagement.

December

- Opposition leader Terry Coe is escorted out of Parliament December 4 after Speaker of the House Tama Posiani blocks the vote of no confidence.
- On December 20, New Zealand's foreign minister Phil Goff encourages Niue to strive to be more self-sufficient. Only 1,700 citizens live on Niue, while 18,000 are expatriates living and working in New Zealand.

ANALYSIS OF EVENTS: 2000

BUSINESS AND THE ECONOMY

Niue received most of its revenue from tourism; the economy also received an allocation from

New Zealand. In 2000 Premier Sani Lakatani came under criticism for his handling of the country's finances. The financial report issued by Lakatani indicated that Niue had approved a NZ$20 million budget which incorporated a deficit of NZ$1.4 million dollars. Added to 1999's deficit of NZ$1.2 million dollars, this report landed Lakatani in trouble with his critics, who accused him of squandering money on phony airline schemes and spending money recklessly. (His problems extended to his personal life, where his brother reportedly rescued him from bankruptcy.) In 2000 Lakatani increased salaries of public officials by 10 percent when there were insufficient funds in the budget to pay them. Lakatani is accused of exaggerating the amount of New Zealand government financial support for Niue. Hima Takelesi, head of the Niue Public Expenditure committee, has been one of Lakatani's severest critics. In September Lakatani announced he was taking a trip to China to support the "One China" policy, in defiance of New Zealand's position on the issue. He claimed that his expenses for the trip would be paid by his hosts, but in Niue, critics are outraged that New Zealand or Niue government funds would be used for such a trip.

GOVERNMENT AND POLITICS

Aside from all the problems Premier Lakatani was having with the budget in 2000, he was being attacked for his inability to settle an ongoing teachers' strike. The strike was over a promised pay raise that did not materialize. As of 2000 many students were going to New Zealand to continue with their education. Premier Lakatani again came under attack by comparing the teacher strike to the political coup in nearby Fiji. Parents have protested as students need to take New Zealand qualifying exams at the end of the school year. Other political news included the reaffirmation in October of Niue's free association with New Zealand. The vote was 580 in favor of free association, 195 voting for full association with New Zealand, and 57 voting for full independence. Niue will keep its free association relationship for now.

CULTURE AND SOCIETY

As of 2000 there were barely 2,000 people living on the small nation island of Niue. Niue is composed of one island, about 100 square miles in size. It is often referred to as the Rock of Polynesia. The people are Polynesian (Tongan) and share a culture similar to that of the other surrounding island groups. The people continue to live in small villages, although there a few hotels and one resort accommodate vacationers who come to dive in the coral reefs. In October there were annual celebrations to commemorate Constitution Day. In June the third annual Market Day featured arts and crafts on display and for sale. Market Day was sponsored in 2000 by the Niue Development Bank. Two celebrations signifying rites of passage on the island are haircutting day ceremonies for boys who allow their hair to grow until puberty, and an ear-piercing ceremony for girls. These village gatherings are announced in the daily newspaper.

DIRECTORY

CENTRAL GOVERNMENT

Head of State

High Commissioner
Warren Searell

Premier
Sani Lakatani, Office of the Premier
PHONE: +683 4200
FAX: +683 4232

Ministers

Common Solicitor
Office of the Common Solicitor
PHONE: +683 4208
FAX: +683 4228

Minister of Planning and Development
Ministry of Planning and Development
PHONE: +683 4148
FAX: +683 4183

Minister of Administration
Ministry of Administration
PHONE: +683 4018
FAX: +683 4305

Minister of Agriculture, Forestry and Fisheries
Ministry of Agriculture, Forestry and Fisheries
PHONE: +683 4032
FAX: +683 4079

Minister of Common Affairs
Ministry of Common Affairs
PHONE: +683 4019
FAX: +683 4391

Minister of Education
Ministry of Education
PHONE: +683 4115
FAX: +683 4301

Minister of Justice and Land Titles
Ministry of Justice and Land Titles
PHONE: +683 4128
FAX: +683 4231

Minister of National Training and Development
Ministry of National Training and Development
PHONE: +683 4214
FAX: +683 4211

Minister of Police
Ministry of Police
PHONE: +683 4333
FAX: +683 4324

Minister of Telephone
Ministry of Telephone
PHONE: +683 4000
FAX: +683 4010

Minister of Treasury
Ministry of Treasury
PHONE: +683 4047
FAX: +683 4051

Minister of Public Works
Ministry of Public Works
PHONE: +683 4297
FAX: +683 4223

POLITICAL ORGANIZATIONS

Niue People's Action Party (NPP)

NAME: Young Vivian

DIPLOMATIC REPRESENTATION

Embassies in Niue

New Zealand
Tapeu Alofi, PO Box 78, Niue
PHONE: +683 4022
FAX: +683 4173

JUDICIAL SYSTEM

Supreme Court of New Zealand

High Court of Niue

BROADCAST MEDIA

Radio Sunshine

Broadcasting Corporation of Niue, PO Box 67, Alofi, Niue
PHONE: +683 4026; 4143
FAX: +683 4217
TITLE: Chairman
CONTACT: Henry Eveni

Niue TV

Broadcasting Corporation of Niue, PO Box 23, Alofi, Niue
PHONE: + 683 4026
FAX: +683 4217
TITLE: General Manager
CONTACT: Hima Douglas

COLLEGES AND UNIVERSITIES

Lord Liverpool University

George Washington School of Medicine, PO Box 173 Main Road, Alofi, Niue Island via Auckland, New Zealand
WEBSITE: http://www.lluniv.org

University of the South Pacific

University Centre, PO Box 31, Alofi, Niue
PHONE: +683 4049
FAX: +683 4315
E-MAIL: talagi_m@usp.ac.fj

NEWSPAPERS AND MAGAZINES

Niue Star

Alofi, Niue
PHONE: +683 4207
TITLE: Editor
CONTACT: Raewin Rex-Woods
CIRCULATION: 500

RELIGIOUS ORGANIZATIONS

Due to its small size and proximity to Oceania, most of the religious organizations' handling occurs on the mainland of either Australia or New Zealand.

FURTHER READING

Articles

Haxton, William. "Worth the Effort." *Cruising World,* February 2000, vol. 26, no. 2, p. 65.

Internet

BBC News Online. "Sanctions Threat to 'Tax Havens.'" June 26, 2000. [Online] Available http://news6.thdo.bbc.co.uk/hi/english/business/newsid%5F806000/806236.stm (accessed October 12, 2000).

NIUE: STATISTICAL DATA

For sources and notes see "Sources of Statistics" at the front of each volume.

GEOGRAPHY

Geography

Area:

Total: 260 sq km.

Land: 260 sq km.

Land boundaries: 0 km.

Coastline: 64 km.

Climate: tropical; modified by southeast trade winds.

Terrain: steep limestone cliffs along coast, central plateau.

Natural resources: fish, arable land.

Land use:

Arable land: 19%

Permanent crops: 8%

Permanent pastures: 4%

Forests and woodland: 19%

Other: 50% (1993 est.).

HUMAN FACTORS

Demographics (B)

Population (July 2000 est.) 2,113

Population growth rate .0.47%

Data for 2000 est.

Ethnic Division

Polynesian (with some 200 Europeans, Samoans, and Tongans).

Religion

Ekalesia Niue 75%

Latter-Day Saints 10%

Other (mostly Roman Catholic, Jehovah's Witnesses, Seventh-Day Adventist) 15%

Ekalesia Niue (Niuean Church) is a Protestant church closely related to the London Missionary Society.

Major Languages

Polynesian closely related to Tongan and Samoan, English.

EDUCATION

Literacy Rates (B)

	National Data	World Data
Adult literacy rate		
1995		
Male	NA	81
Female	99[1]	65

GOVERNMENT & LAW

Political Parties

Legislative Assembly	no. of seats
Niue People's Action Party (NPP)	9
Independents	11

Elections were last held 19 March 1999 (next to be held in March 2002).

LABOR FORCE

Total Labor Force (A)

450 (1992 est.).

Labor Force by Occupation

Most work on family plantations; paid work exists only in government service, small industry, and the Niue Development Board.

PRODUCTION SECTOR

Energy Production

Production . . . . .3 million kWh

Production by source

Fossil fuel 100%

Hydro 0%

Nuclear 0%

Other 0%

Exports . . . . .0 kWh

Data for 1998.

Energy Consumption

Consumption . . . . .3 million kWh

Imports . . . . .0 kWh

Data for 1998.

Transportation

Highways:

Total: 234 km.

Paved: 0 km.

Unpaved: 234 km.

Merchant marine: none (1999 est.).

Airports: 1 (1999 est.).

Top Agriculture Products

Coconuts, passion fruit, honey, limes, taro, yams, cassava (tapioca), sweet potatoes; pigs, poultry, beef cattle.

MANUFACTURING SECTOR

GDP & Manufacturing Summary (C)

Total GDP (1994 est.) . . . .$4.5 million

Per capita (1994 est.) $2,250

Values in purchasing power parity.

COMMUNICATIONS

Telecommunications

Telephones - main lines in use: 376 (1991).

Telephones - mobile cellular: 0 (1991).

Telephone system:

Domestic: single-line telephone system connects all villages on island.

International: NA

Radio broadcast stations: AM 1, FM 1, shortwave 0 (1998).

Radios: 1,000 (1997).

Television broadcast stations: 1 (1997).

Televisions: NA

Internet Service Providers (ISPs): NA

FINANCE, ECONOMICS, & TRADE

Economic Indicators

National product: GDP—purchasing power parity—$4.5 million (1994 est.).

National product real growth rate: NA.

National product per capita: $2,250 (1994 est.).

Inflation rate—consumer price index: 1% (1995).

Exchange Rates

Exchange rates:

New Zealand dollars (NZ$) per US$1

January 2000 . . . . .1.9451

1999 . . . . .1.8889

1998 . . . . .1.8629

1997 . . . . .1.5082

1996 . . . . .1.4543

1995 . . . . .1.5235

Top Import Origins

$4.1 million (c.i.f., 1989)

Origins

New Zealand 59%

Fiji 20%

Japan 13%

Samoa . . . . .NA

Australia . . . . .NA

United States . . . . .NA

Top Export Destinations

$117,500 (f.o.b., 1989)

Destinations

New Zealand 89%

Fiji . . . . .NA

Cook Islands . . . . .NA

Australia . . . . .NA

Foreign Aid

Recipient: $8.3 million (1995).

Import/Export Commodities

Import Commodities	Export Commodities
Food	Canned coconut cream
Live animals	Copra
Manufactured goods	Honey
Machinery	Passion fruit products
Fuels	Pawpaws
Lubricants	Root crops
Chemicals	Limes
Drugs	Footballs
	Stamps
	Handicrafts

NORFOLK ISLAND

Territory of Norfolk Island

CAPITAL: Kingston.

FLAG: The flag of Norfolk Island has three vertical bands of green (hoist side), white, and green with a large green Norfolk Island pine tree centered in the slightly wider white band.

ANTHEM: God Save the Queen.

MONETARY UNIT: 1 Australian dollar ($A) = 100 cents.

WEIGHTS AND MEASURES: The metric system is used.

HOLIDAYS: New Year's Day, 1 January; Australia Day, end of January; Good Friday; Easter Monday; Anzac Day, 25 April; Queen's Birthday, Mid-June; Christmas Day, 25 December; and Boxing Day, 26 December. In addition to these official Australian holidays, Pitcairnes, 8 June; and Thanksgiving Day, last Wednesday in November, are also celebrated.

TIME: 11 PM = noon GMT.

LOCATION AND SIZE: Norfolk Island, with an area of 36 sq. km (14 sq. mi.), is situated at 29°3′S and 167°57′E, 1,676 km (1,041 mi.) east-northeast of Sydney.

CLIMATE: Norfolk Island has a subtropical mild climate with little seasonal temperature variation.

INTRODUCTORY SURVEY

RECENT HISTORY

British explorer Captain James Cook discovered the uninhabited island in 1774, and named it for the Duke of Norfolk. The Australian colony of New South Wales claimed Norfolk in 1788, and settled it with a small party including a few convicts. The island served as a penal settlement until 1814, and later from 1825 to 1855, when the penitentiary was finally abandoned. Shortly thereafter, almost 200 descendants of the mutineers from the *HMS Bounty* and their Tahitian companions left the overcrowded Pitcairn Island and were resettled on Norfolk. The former Pitcairners established a unique society on Norfolk, and one third of residents at the end of the 20th century still claim lineal descent from these early settlers. Under the Norfolk Island Act of 1913, Norfolk became a territory of the Commonwealth of Australia, however, the exact constitutional relationship with Australia has been continually disputed.

GOVERNMENT

Norfolk Island is administered as a territory under authority of the Commonwealth of Australia. No administrative divisions exist. The chief of state is the British monarch, represented by the Governor-General of Australia. On the island, the senior government representative of the United Kingdom and Australia is the Administrator, appointed by the Australian Governor-General and responsible to the Minister for Regional Services, Territories, and Local Government.

The Norfolk Island Act of 1979 created a legislature, the Legislative Assembly, and an executive government, the Executive Council, enabling the island to govern its own internal affairs to the greatest practicable extent. The Legislative Assembly is comprised of nine members elected through an electoral process for not more than three-year terms. The Executive Council is made-up of the executive members of the Legislative Assembly. The Executive Council includes five positions: (1) the President of the Legislative Assembly and Minister for Finance and Strategic Planning; (2) the Deputy President; (3) Minister for Community and Resource Management; (4) Minister for Tourism and Commerce; and, (5) Minister for Health and

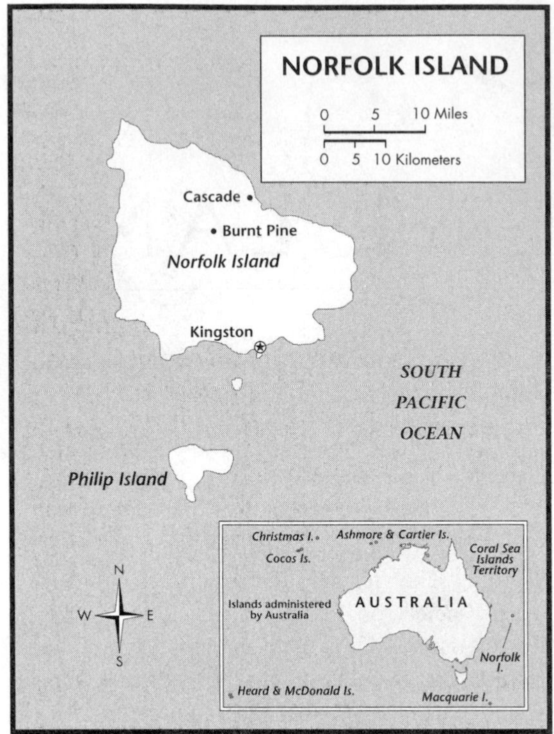

Immigration. Both bodies are lead by the Assembly President and Chief Minister who serves as head of government and is elected by the Legislative Assembly for a term of not more than three years.

The Administrator must act with the advice of the Executive Council or the Australian Minister on every law proposed by the Assembly. The Administrator may give his approval, reserve the proposed law for the Governor-General's decision, or recommend amendments.

Judiciary

Norfolk Island's judiciary system includes a Supreme Court with appeals directed to the Federal Court of Australia and the Court of Petty Sessions exercising both civil and criminal jurisdiction. The legal system is based on local ordinances and the laws of Australia. Cases not covered by local or Australian law come under English common law.

Political Parties

No formal political parties exist on Norfolk Island. All those elected in 1997 were non-partisans.

DEFENSE

The Australian military provides defense protection to Norfolk Island, backed by New Zealand and the United States through a security treaty.

ECONOMIC AFFAIRS

Since the 1960's, tourism has been Norfolk Island's predominate industry. The operation of hotels and duty-free stores employ many islanders. As many as 30,000 tourists, many from New Zealand, visit annually. Prosperity brought to the island by tourism has allowed the agricultural sector to become self-sufficient in the areas of beef, poultry, and eggs. Fishing is important locally, but expansion is severely restricted by the lack of accessible harbors. Agricultural products grown in the fertile soil include Norfolk Island pine seed, Kentia palm seeds, cereals, fruits, and vegetables. Shipped all over the world, the seed of the Norfolk Island pine is a chief export. Forestry programs strive to increase the island's resource of pines and hardwoods.

In addition to the Norfolk Island pine seeds, exports include the Kentia palm, small quantities of avocados, and postage stamps. Imports of food, fuel, and consumer goods are brought in mainly for the tourist trade. Exploitation of the gas and oil fields in the island's exclusive economic zone was a hotly debated topic at the close of the 20th century.

Public Finance

Public revenue comes from tourism, custom duties, sale of postage stamps, liquor sales (a government monopoly), and company registration and license fees. In the fiscal year ending in June of 1996, custom duties accounted for 27 percent of the total revenue. Residents are not taxed on income earning within the territory.

Industry

Tourism is the chief industry, followed by commercial cultivation of Norfolk Island pine seed and Kentia palm seed in the agricultural sector. The remainder of agricultural production is at the subsistence level with the goal of self-sufficiency.

Banking and Finance

The Commonwealth Banking Corporation and Westpac Banking Corporation Savings Bank, Ltd., both of Australia, provide banking services to the island.

SOCIAL WELFARE

The Legislative Assembly passed the Social Services Act of 1980, designed to implement a comprehensive scheme of social welfare benefits related to the scheme and benefits payable in mainland Australia.

Healthcare

Two doctors, a pharmacist and a 20-bed hospital provide medical care to the island.

Housing

Most housing is of timber construction. The island's older buildings and residences dating from the convict era are coral stone. Many larger buildings are in brick and stone.

EDUCATION

For children between the ages of six and fifteen, education is free and compulsory and run by the New South Wales Department of Education. In 1997, one state school with twenty-one full-time teachers served 328 students from pre-school to secondary levels. Scholarships and bursaries were available for students who wished to continue their education in Australia.

2000 KEY EVENTS TIMELINE

January

- The Oceania Veteran Games 2000 are held, with athletic competitions for age categories ranging from preveteran (ages thirty-five to thirty-nine) to age ninety-five and over.
- The Victoria Petroleum NL, a drilling company, is looking for evidence of oil from fossils deposited in the Paleocene and Eocene eras in the West Basin area.

March

- The Société Le Nickel (SLN) has a work stoppage by employees at a nickel mine over wages. The workers stop shipments to the smelting factory.

April

- Anzac Week is celebrated with the slogan, "Their Sacrifice Our Heritage."
- Seismic studies indicate the existence of gas extrates in the New Caledonia Basin.
- The Société Le Nickel settles its dispute with workers. The Doniambo plant smelter is now at near full capacity.

June

- Bounty Day is celebrated.
- Lyn Griffiths, director of genomics research at Griffith University in Queensland, gathers hundreds of blood samples for a study of heart disease in Norfolk Islanders.
- Robert Xowie is expected to win the upcoming election.
- The reunion of descendants of pilgrims of James Cook's discovery of Norfolk Islands is announced, scheduled for October 8-15, 2000.

September

- Rhonda Griffiths is appointed to the position of Cultural Affairs Advisor for the Secretariat of the Pacific Community (SPC) on September 3. Her duties will include developing staff skills at Pacific islands cultural institutions such as libraries and museums. She indicates that she is accepting this position.

October

- Norfolk Island is among the twenty-seven nations that sends a delegation to the Eighth Pacific Arts Festival in Noumea, New Caledonia, held from October 23–November 3.

ANALYSIS OF EVENTS: 2000

BUSINESS AND THE ECONOMY

The Norfolk Island tourism industry was expected to benefit from the increase in tourism to the South Pacific that resulted from the 2000 Millennium celebrations and publicity. Civil unrest in Fiji and the Solomon Islands also pushed tourists to find new destinations.

GOVERNMENT AND POLITICS

In February 2000, the nine-member Norfolk Legislative Assembly was elected. Members are selected by electors, and serve for a term of three years.

In September 2000, Norfolk Islander Rhonda Griffiths was appointed Cultural Affairs Advisor for the Secretariat of the Pacific Community. Her goals were to foster traditional knowledge while also aiding the emergence of contemporary forms of traditional arts.

CULTURE AND SOCIETY

In January Norfolk Island hosted the Oceania Veteran Games 2000, an athletic competition with age categories ranging from pre-veteran (ages thirty-five to thirty-nine) to age ninety-five and over.

Patriotic holidays celebrated in Norfolk Island include Anzac Day, Foundation Day, and Bounty Day. In 2000 the Norfolk Island Anzac celebration consisted of a territorial Anzac Week, under the slogan, "Their Sacrifice Our Heritage." Foundation Day festivities held in March included re-enacting the 1788 landing of the H.M.S. Supply, with its party of sixteen convicts and eight free men. In June 2000, Bounty Day was celebrated on the island to acknowledge the original mutineers and their descendants, and to re-enact the landing of the oppressed sailors.

In June 2000 Lyn Griffiths, director of genomic research at Griffith University in Queensland, began a study of heart disease in Norfolk Islanders. The location was chosen in part because of its genetic isolation. In June, she began gathering samples; the next six months were dedicated to health screening and data analysis.

DIRECTORY

CENTRAL GOVERNMENT

Head of State

Administrator
A.J. Messner

President and Chief Minister
George Charles Smith, Office of the President

Head Administrator
A.J. Messner, Office of the Head Administrator
FAX: +61 (6723) 22681
E-MAIL: Tony.Messner@dotrs.gov.au

Ministers

Minister of Finance
George Smith, Ministry of Finance

Minister of Agriculture
Ernie Friend, Ministry of Agriculture
PHONE: +61 (6723) 22609
FAX: +61 (6723) 22609

Minister of Forestry
John (Fanny) Christian, Ministry of Forestry
PHONE: +61 (6723) 23195
FAX: +61 (6723) 23317

Minister of Tourism and Commerce
James Robertson, Ministry of Tourism and Commerce

Minister of Immigration and Resource Management
Cedrick Robinson, Ministry of Immigration and Resource Management

Minister of Health
Geoff Gardner, Ministry of Health

JUDICIAL SYSTEM

Supreme Court

Supreme Court Registrar, Norfolk Island, South Pacific 2895
PHONE: +61 (6723) 23691

BROADCAST MEDIA

Norfolk Island Broadcasting SCE.

PO Box 456, Norfolk Island 2899, Australia
PHONE: + 61 (6723) 2137
FAX: + 61 (6723) 3298
TITLE: Broadcast Manager
CONTACT: Margaret Meadows
LANGUAGE: English
BROADCASTS: 24 hours/day, 15 hours/day
TYPE: Government

Norfolk Island Television SCE.

New Cascade Rd., Norfolk Island 2899, Australia
PHONE: +672 (3) 22137
FAX: +672 (3) 23298
CHANNEL: 7
WATTAGE: 0.02 kw
TYPE: Government

COLLEGES AND UNIVERSITIES

Greenwich University

Taylors Rd, Norfolk Island 2899, Australia
PHONE: +672 322834
FAX: +672 323547
E-MAIL: greenwich@university.edu.nf
WEBSITE: http://www.university.edu.nf

NEWSPAPERS AND MAGAZINES

Norfolk Island Government Gazette

Norfolk Island Administration, Kingston 2899
Norfolk Island

PHONE: +672 22001
FAX: +672 23177
TYPE: Public Affairs and Administration

The Norfolk Islander

Greenways Press, PO Box 150, Norfolk Island 2899
PHONE: +672 22159
FAX: +672 22948
TITLE: Editor
CONTACT: Tom Lloyd
CIRCULATION: 1,250

RELIGIOUS ORGANIZATIONS

The Norfolk Islands are controlled by Australia. Religious organizations are controlled through Canberra.

FURTHER READING

Articles

Davies, Michael. "A Mutineer's Paradise." *National Geographic Traveler,* September 1999, vol. 16, no. 6, p. 98+.

NORFOLK ISLAND: STATISTICAL DATA

For sources and notes see "Sources of Statistics" at the front of each volume.

GEOGRAPHY

Geography

Area:

Total: 34.6 sq km.

Land: 34.6 sq km.

Land boundaries: 0 km.

Coastline: 32 km.

Climate: subtropical, mild, little seasonal temperature variation.

Terrain: volcanic formation with mostly rolling plains.

Natural resources: fish.

Land use:

Arable land: 0%

Permanent crops: 0%

Permanent pastures: 25%

Forests and woodland: 0%

Other: 75% (1993 est.).

HUMAN FACTORS

Demographics (B)

Population (July 2000 est.)	1,892
Population growth rate	-0.68%

Data for 2000 est.

Ethnic Division

Descendants of the Bounty mutineers, Australian, New Zealander, Polynesians.

Religion

Anglican	39.0%
Roman Catholic	11.7%
Uniting Church in Australia	16.4%
Seventh-Day Adventist	4.4%
None	9.2%
Unknown	16.9%
Other	2.4%

Data for 1986.

Major Languages

English (official), Norfolk a mixture of 18th century English and ancient Tahitian.

GOVERNMENT & LAW

Political Parties

The unicameral Legislative Assembly consists of 9 seats. Members elected by electors who have nine equal votes each but only four votes can be given to any one candidate. Members serve three-year terms. Elections were last held 30 April 1997 (next to be held by May 2000). Independents won all 9 seats. There are no political parties.

Government Budgets (B)

Revenues	$4.6 million
Expenditures	$4.8 million

Data for FY92/93.

LABOR FORCE

Total Labor Force (A)

1,395 (1991 est.).

PRODUCTION SECTOR

Transportation

Highways:

Total: 80 km.

Paved: 53 km.

Unpaved: 27 km.

Merchant marine: none (1999 est.).

Airports: 1 (1999 est.).

Top Agriculture Products

Norfolk Island pine seed, Kentia palm seed, cereals, vegetables, fruit; cattle, poultry.

COMMUNICATIONS

Telecommunications

Telephones - main lines in use: 1,087 (1983).

Telephones - mobile cellular: 0 (1983).

Telephone system:

Domestic: NA

International: radiotelephone service with Sydney (Australia).

Radio broadcast stations: AM 0, FM 3, shortwave 0 (1998).

Radios: 2,500 (1996).

Television broadcast stations: 1 (local programming station plus two repeaters that bring in Australian programs by satellite) (1998).

Televisions: 1,200 (1996).

Internet Service Providers (ISPs): NA

FINANCE, ECONOMICS, & TRADE

Exchange Rates

Exchange rates:

Australian dollars ($A) per US$1

January 2000	1.5207
1999	1.5497
1998	1.5888
1997	1.3439
1996	1.2773
1995	1.3486

Top Import Origins

Imports (c.i.f., FY91/92): $17.9 million.

Origins: Australia, other Pacific island countries, New Zealand, Asia, Europe.

Top Export Destinations

Exports (f.o.b., FY91/92): $1.5 million.

Destinations: Australia, other Pacific island countries, New Zealand, Asia, Europe.

Import/Export Commodities

Import Commodities	Export Commodities
NA	Postage stamps
	Seeds of the Norfolk Island pine and Kentia palm
	Small quantities of avocados

NA stands for not available.

NORTHERN MARIANA ISLANDS

CAPITAL: Saipan.

FLAG: The flag of the Northern Mariana Islands is blue with a white five-pointed star superimposed on the gray silhouette of a latte stone (a traditional foundation stone used in building) in the center, surrounded by a wreath.

MONETARY UNIT: 1 United States dollar (US$) = 100 cents.

WEIGHTS AND MEASURES: The imperial system is used.

HOLIDAYS: New Year's Day, 1 January; Commonwealth Day, 9 January; President's Day, 3rd Monday in February; Ash Wednesday; Covenant Day, 25 March; Good Friday; Easter Monday; Memorial Day, last Monday in May; Independence Day, 4 July; Labor Day, first Monday in September; Columbus Day, 14 October; Citizenship Day, 4 November; Veterans Day, 11 November; Thanksgiving, 4th Thursday in November; Constitution Day, 9 December; Christmas Day, 25 December.

TIME: 10 PM = noon GMT.

LOCATION AND SIZE: The Northern Marianas, a U.S. commonwealth in the Western Pacific Ocean, is comprised of the Mariana Islands excluding Guam (a separate political entity). Located between 12° and 21°N and 144° and 146°E, it consists of 16 volcanic islands with a total land area of about 475 sq. km (183.5 sq. mi.). Only six of the islands are inhabited, and most of the people live on the three largest islands—Rota, 85 sq. km (33 sq. mi.); Saipan, 122 sq. km (47 sq. mi.); and Tinian, 101 sq. km (39 sq. mi.).

CLIMATE: The climate is tropical, with relatively little seasonal change; temperatures average 21–29°C (70–85°F), and relative humidity is generally high. Rainfall averages 216 cm (85 in.) per year. The southern islands, which include Rota, Saipan, and Tinian, are generally lower and covered with moderately heavy tropical vegetation. The northern islands are more rugged, reaching a high point of 959 m (3,146 ft.) on Agrihan, and are generally barren due to erosion and insufficient rainfall. Pagan and Agrihan have active volcanos, and typhoons are common from August to November.

Commonwealth of the Northern Mariana Islands

INTRODUCTORY SURVEY

RECENT HISTORY

At the outbreak of World War II (1939-1945), Japan seized Guam from the United States, but the Americans recaptured Guam and took over all of the Mariana Islands by 1944. A year later one of the islands, Tinian, served as the base for the U.S. planes that dropped the atomic bombs on Hiroshima and Nagasaki.

In 1947, the United States signed a Trustee Agreement with the United Nations to administer the Northern Mariana Islands (NMI) as a district within the Trust Territory of the Pacific Islands. The people of NMI decided in the 1970s not to seek independence, but to forge closer links with the United States. In 1975, NMI voted for status as a U.S. Commonwealth Territory. The Northern Mariana Commonwealth Covenant was signed in 1976, and in 1977, U.S. President Jimmy Carter approved the NMI constitution providing for internal self-governing. The Covenant provided for the separation of NMI from the Caroline and Marshall island group, and for the Mariana's transition to a commonwealth to be similar to the status of Puerto Rico. Elections took place in 1977 for a governor, lieutenant governor, and bicameral legislature. The United States terminated the administration of the trusteeship in 1986, when NMI was formally admitted to U.S. commonwealth status. At that time, a proclamation by U.S. President Ronald Reagan conferred U.S. citizenship on the island's residents. On November 3, 1986, the constitution of the Commonwealth of the Northern Mariana Islands came into force.

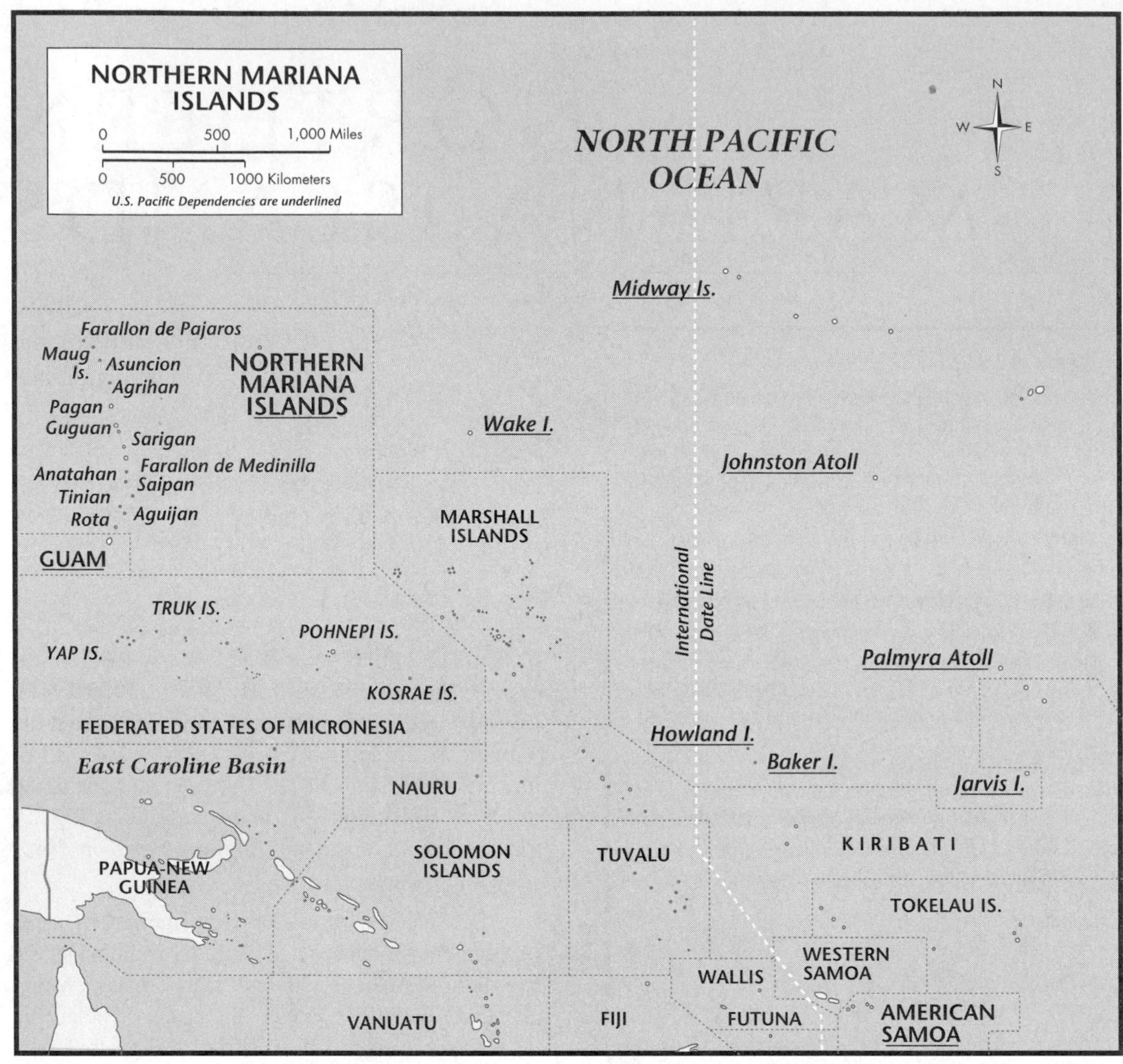

The 1980s and 1990s saw a dramatic increase in population leading to social and economic problems. Persistent problems of an inadequate minimum wage coupled with reports of improper labor practices and poor treatment of alien workers in garment factories dominated Mariana's political scene in the late 1990s.

GOVERNMENT

Northern Mariana Islands is a commonwealth in political union with the United States. The islands are divided into four municipalities-Northern Islands, Saipan, Rota, and Tinian. Although the president of the United States is the chief of state, the Commonwealth has been self-governing since 1977, and elects a governor, lieutenant governor, and bicameral legislature by popular vote. Administrative headquarters are at Chalan Kanoa in Saipan. The governor and lieutenant governor are popularly elected on the same ticket for four-year terms. Executive authority rests with the governor.

Legislative authority rests with the Northern Marianas commonwealth legislature. The bicameral legislature consists of a Senate and House of Representatives. The Senate has nine seats, three each from Saipan, Rota, and Tinian. Senators are elected by popular vote for four-year staggered terms. The House of Representatives has eighteen seats, with members elected by popular vote for two-year terms.

The Commonwealth maintains an elected official, the "resident representative," in Washington, D.C. but has no delegates in Congress.

Judiciary

The NMI judiciary includes the Commonwealth Supreme Court that hears appeals from the Superior Court, the Superior Court, and a U.S. Territorial District Court in Saipan. U.S. federal law applies to the Commonwealth except in four areas: customs, taxation, immigration, and wages. The Commonwealth is not part of U.S. Custom Territory, enacts its own taxation laws, and federal minimum wage and immigration laws do not apply. A Commonwealth court has jurisdiction over local matters.

Political Parties

The two major political parties are the Republican and Democratic parties. In 1997, the Republicans held the governor and lieutenant governorships and retained a majority of the seats in the Senate and House of Representatives.

DEFENSE

The U.S. military provides defense protection to the Northern Mariana Islands.

ECONOMIC AFFAIRS

By 1998, the Commonwealth's economy centered on tourism and garment manufacturing. The rapidly growing tourism industry employed 50 percent of the labor force and provided approximately 50 percent of the gross domestic product (GDP). Offering luxury hotels to the tourists, predominately Japanese, Korean, and American, Saipan and Rota are the main tourist centers. Large scale investment, primarily Japanese, resulted in major increases in the number of hotel rooms and tourists throughout the 1980s and 1990s. North Mariana Islands are also opening up to the gambling market with a hotel casino complex on Tinian. Tourism earned $522 million in 1995. Closely tied to tourism is the construction industry that provides employment for approximately 20 percent of the workforce building new facilities.

The lucrative garment industry rapidly expanded Commonwealth revenues in the 1990s. The garment factories, most run by Chinese or South Korean firms, operate with foreign contract workers predominately from China, Bangladesh, and the Philippines who are paid substantially less than the U.S. minimum wages. Benefiting manufacturers, the exported garments may be stamped "Made in the USA" and are free of duties and quotas applied to products made in China and Korea. In 1998, garment export shipments of $1 billion were shipped to the United States under duty and quota exemptions.

Small-scale manufacturing of handicrafts including stone, clay, and glass products provided additional employment and revenue. The agricultural sector, concentrated in small holdings and including cultivation of fruits and vegetables, and cattle and pig ranches, employed only 2.2 percent of workers in 1992.

Although declining as local government revenues increase, the United States provides considerable financial assistance. For capital development, governmental operation, and other programs the United States provided $228 million between 1986 and 1992. For the fiscal years 1993-1994 and 1995-1996 the islands received $27.7 million. From fiscal year 1996-1997 through 2002-2003, the Commonwealth with matching local funding will receive $11 million for infrastructure development.

Public Finance

Budget revenues are derived from local revenues and from United States assistance. In the fiscal year 1996, budget estimates predicted revenues of $221 million and total expenditures of $213 million.

Income

The gross domestic product (GDP) was estimated at $524 million in 1996 and reflected United States spending. The 1994 GDP per capita estimation was $9,300. Tourism and garment manufacturing are the only two major sources of income.

Industry

The predominate industrial activities include tourism, garment manufacturing, and construction. Other industries include small scale manufacturing of handicrafts and food processing.

Banking and Finance

Banking centers in Saipan include the Bank of Guam, Bank of Hawaii, Bank of Saipan, City Trust Bank, Development Bank, Hongkong and Shanghai Banking Corporation, Union Bank, and two savings and loan associations, First Savings and Loan of America and Guam Savings and Loan Bank.

SOCIAL WELFARE

Health and social welfare budgetary expenditures accounted for 18.4 percent of total government expenditure.

Healthcare

Healthcare is primarily the responsibility of the Commonwealth government and has improved substantially since 1978. In the 1990s, the Marianas operated the Commonwealth Health Center on

Saipan, a 74-bed, 110,000 square foot facility. Smaller sub-hospitals were located on Tinuan and Rota. All other inhabited islands have health dispensaries. The single greatest factor straining the health system is rapid population growth of nonresident alien workers. Tuberculosis, once the major health problem, has been controlled. In 2000, life expectancy was 75.5 years.

Housing

As a result of growth in population and the economy between 1980 and 1995, the number of housing units more than tripled to 12,058 units in 1995. In 1995, owners occupied 4,038 units and renters 5,219. Consisting of units which government and businesses provide to expatriate workers, 2,081 units were occupied without payment of rent by occupants. Persons, generally alien workers, occupying group quarters as barracks and other structures numbered 9,703 in 1995 down from the 1990 total of 11,489.

EDUCATION

School attendance for children ages eight to fourteen is compulsory. In elementary and secondary schools, instructional materials and courses offered are modeled after those in the United States, but modified to meet the unique needs and characteristics of the islands.

All inhabited islands have primary schools. Public and church-operated secondary schools are located in Saipan. Enrollment in primary and secondary schools in 1995-1996 totaled 10,634.

A public junior college, College of the Northern Marianas, was established in 1976. Students also pursue post-secondary education at the University of Guam or in various institutions in Hawaii or the continental United States.

The total literacy rate was estimated to be 97 percent in 1980. In 1995, the Mariana's government budgetary expenditure for education was 19.6 percent of total expenditures.

2000 KEY EVENTS TIMELINE

January

- The new census for the Northern Marianas reports a population of 69,216.
- Governor Pedro Tenario declares a state of emergency due to volcanic activity on Almagen Island, designating the island off-limits until further notice.

April

- U.S. Congressman Tom Davis of Virginia is seeking to have the Northern Marianas represented in the U.S. Congress. The delegate from Northern Marianas is Juan Babauta, who objects to the Marianas lack of influence in the U.S. legislature.

May

- The Northern Mariana Islands are implementing registries to track childhood immunization records.

June

- The Chamorros, indigenous people of the Northern Marianas, want to claim exclusive rights to the island, and are calling for the ouster of nonnative people.
- The Mariana Islands is accusing the United States of using the islands as a toxic waste dump during the Korean War. During the 1950s the U.S. military tested missiles in the area, but denies any wrongdoing.
- The Marianas becomes a major site for the use and sale of illegal drugs, posing a threat to all of Micronesia.
- The U.S. General Accounting Office (GAO) issues a report by U.S. Senator Daniel Akaka (D-Hawaii) that the Marianas are not doing enough to stop illegal immigration, citing lack of computer monitoring of arrivals and departures and criminal background checks. The Marianas does not require visas for entry.
- Jeffrey Schorr, a field representative for the Office of Insular Affairs on the Marianas, is accused of violations of the Hatch Act. The Hatch Act forbids the use of government offices, resources, or time on the job to promote a political campaign.

August

- The Division of Public Lands is looking to relocate cattle ranchers displaced by governmental takeover of lands.
- U.S. Vice presidential candidate Joseph Lieberman backs a bill on August 30 to prevent goods that are made in Northern Mariana Islands under

Chinese auspices to be labeled "Made in the U.S.A."

September

- Unhappy garment workers protest on September 1, calling for the release of unpaid wages due to them. About 300 Eurotex workers remain absent from work. The United States says the problem should be resolved shortly.
- Juan N. Babauta, the representative to Washington, tries to exclude the Northern Marianas from a forced hike in the minimum wage on September 20. He claims the wage increase would be an economic disaster for the islands.
- The Northern Marianas are warned on September 24 that the Commonwealth Utilities Corporation may no longer provide power, water and waste removal services as the Islands has failed to pay their bills on time.

November

- Guam and the Northern Mariana Islands claim that tainted fish from Micronesia is the cause of a cholera outbreak during the first week of November.
- Northern Marianas College reports November 10 that it is trying to collect debts totaling $2.8 million in student loans.
- The Republican Party completes its primary election November 29. Joan Babauto and Diego Benavente defeat Sablan and Villagomez to win the nomination. They will face Democratic nominees Jesus C. Borjar and Froilan C. Tenorio in the general election next year.

December

- The Northern Mariana Islands House of Representatives asks the U.S. government for $3.2 million dollars in debt relief money on December 1.
- About 300 children of alien workers born since 1986 and living in the Marianas currently have no citizenship in any country.

ANALYSIS OF EVENTS: 2000

BUSINESS AND THE ECONOMY

The Commonwealth of the Northern Mariana Islands (CNMI) received most of its 2000 income in foreign aid from the United States. About 50 percent of self-generated income came from the tourist trade. The garment industry, which came under attack from the United States for hiring workers at U.S. substandard wages, was the largest industry on the islands. The representative to Washington, Juan N. Balbauta, argued against the U.S. federal government plan to raise the minimum wage because it threatened the CNMI, which did not have nearly the standard of living enjoyed in the United States. The biggest possibility for growth in the CNMI came with the development of offshore power plants. Political unrest and deflating currencies frightened off many large power conglomerates, but the CNMI's chairman of the Commonwealth Utilities Corporation, Timothy P. Villagomez said that the CNMI could be a strong player and would encourage growth in this area.

GOVERNMENT AND POLITICS

The CNMI still had no official representative in Washington, so it could not directly air its grievances. U.S. Congressman Tom Davis of Virginia advocated that the CNMI be given a non-voting representative. The U.S. Congress was also united on preventing China from using the label "made in the USA" on garments they produced in the CNMI. As of November 2000, the governor of the CNMI was Republican Pedro P. Tenorio, and his Lt. Governor is Jesus R. Sablan. Sablan and Villagomez were defeated (November 2000) in a Republican primary election by Juan Babauto and Diego Benavente. They will face Democrats Froilan Tenorio (previously governor) and Jesus C. Borjar next November, 2001. Since illegal immigration has been a problem in the CNMI, the government worked with the Philippine government to prevent the entry of illegal workers. Most of these workers were in the garment industry.

CULTURE AND SOCIETY

The Commonwealth of the Northern Mariana Islands (CNMI) is a United States protectorate. Located in the Pacific near Guam and Japan, the CNMI is populated by various racial and religious groups. Many of the inhabitants are native Chamorros, but there are many Japanese, Chinese, and Micronesian peoples. Even though all major U.S. holidays are celebrated, the CNMI also celebrates Commonwealth Day, which is on January 8. Saipan is the capital city of the islands, which is home to about 70,000 people. Most of the people live on three of the six major islands in the group: Saipan,

Rota, and Tinian. The indigenous Chamorros would like to have the islands and its culture to themselves, but the CNMI has a very loose immigration policy. Even so, American culture has taken over, with fast food restaurants, popular music, and movies. There are currently no visas required, but in November 2000 the CNMI Border Management Systems instituted a new tracking system that recorded all comings and goings of visitors. There is also a screening system in place to track criminals and other undesirables. The system records passport information of people no matter what port of entry they use. The largest group of visitors is from Korea and Japan. United States citizens continue to have unlimited access to the islands. The health and welfare of the citizens of the CNMI is also of concern for the United States. The health system was designed for about 20,000 people and the current population of 70,000 is overtaxing that system. This has contributed to the poor screening of immigrant workers who have tuberculosis, AIDS, and HIV. The proliferation of illegal drugs is also becoming a problem. There are many immigrant garment workers who come to the CNMI but the government does not want to encourage foreign retirees to live there.

DIRECTORY

CENTRAL GOVERNMENT

Head of State

President of the United States
George W. Bush, Office of the President of the United States, The White House, 1600 Pennsylvania Ave, Washington, D.C., United States

Governor
Pedro P. Tenorio, Office of the Governor, Capitol Hill, Saipan, MP 96950, Northern Marianas Islands
PHONE: +670 6642276
FAX: +670 6642290
E-MAIL: gov.frosario@saipan.com

Lieutenant Governor
Jesus R. Sablan, Office of the Lieutenant Governor, Capitol Hill, Saipan, MP 96950, Northern Marianas Islands
PHONE: +670 6642276
FAX: +670 6642290

Ministers

Minister of Finance
Lucy Nielsen, Ministry of Finance, Governor's Cabinet, Caller Box 10007 Saipan, MP 96950, Northern Marianas Islands
PHONE: +670 6641100
FAX: +670 6641115

Minister of Labor and Immigration
Mark Zachares, Ministry of Labor and Immigration, Governor's Cabinet, Caller Box 10007 Saipan, MP 96950, Northern Marianas Islands
PHONE: +670 6643154
FAX: +670 6643153

Minister of Health Services
Joseph P. Villagomez, Ministry of Health Services, Governor's Cabinet, Caller Box 10007 Saipan, MP 96950, Northern Marianas Islands
PHONE: +670 2348950
FAX: +670 2348930

Minister of Lands and Natural Resources
Jack A. Tenorio, Ministry of Lands and Natural Resources, Governor's Cabinet, Caller Box 10007 Saipan, MP 96950, Northern Marianas Islands
PHONE: +670 3229830
FAX: +670 3222633

Minister of Community and Cultural Affairs
Thomas A. Tebuteb, Ministry of Community and Cultural Affairs, Governor's Cabinet, Caller Box 10007 Saipan, MP 96950, Northern Marianas Islands
PHONE: +670 6642571; 2333343
FAX: +670 6642570

Minister of Public Safety
Charles W. Ingram Jr., Ministry of Public Safety, Governor's Cabinet, Caller Box 10007 Saipan, MP 96950, Northern Marianas Islands
PHONE: +670 2348536
FAX: +670 2342313

Minister of Public Works
John B. Cepeda, Ministry of Public Works, Governor's Cabinet, Caller Box 10007 Saipan, MP 96950, Northern Marianas Islands
PHONE: +670 2355827
FAX: +670 2356346

Minister of Commerce
Bernadita T. Palacios, Ministry of Commerce, Governor's Cabinet, Caller Box 10007 Saipan, MP 96950, Northern Marianas Islands

PHONE: +670 6643000
FAX: +670 6643067

Minister of Administration
Jose I. De Leon Guerrero, Ministry of Administration, Governor's Cabinet, Caller Box 10007 Saipan, MP 96950, Northern Marianas Islands
PHONE: +670 6642200
FAX: +670 6642210

Minister of Programs and Legislative Review
Gloria W. Hunter, Ministry of Programs and Legislative Review, Governor's Cabinet, Caller Box 10007 Saipan, MP 96950, Northern Marianas Islands
PHONE: +670 6642286
FAX: +670 6642313

Minister of Management and Budget
Virginia C. Villagomez, Ministry of Management and Budget, Governor's Cabinet, Caller Box 10007 Saipan, MP 96950, Northern Marianas Islands
PHONE: +670 6642265
FAX: +670 6642272

Minister of Finance and Budget
Mike S. Sablan, Ministry of Finance and Budget, Governor's Cabinet, Caller Box 10007 Saipan, MP 96950, Northern Marianas Islands
PHONE: +670 6642245
FAX: +670 6642242

Minister of Public Liaison
Gregorio C. Sablan, Ministry of Public Liaison, Governor's Cabinet, Caller Box 10007 Saipan, MP 96950, Northern Marianas Islands
PHONE: +670 6642233
FAX: +670 6642390

Minister of Policy and Research
Mike Malone, Ministry of Policy and Research, Governor's Cabinet, Caller Box 10007 Saipan, MP 96950, Northern Marianas Islands
PHONE: +670 6642225
FAX: +670 6642211

Minister of Women's Affairs
Maryann Tudela, Ministry of Women's Affairs, Governor's Cabinet, Caller Box 10007 Saipan, MP 96950, Northern Marianas Islands
PHONE: +670 2884102
FAX: +670 2880845

Minister of Indigenous Affairs
Ignacio Demapan, Minister of Indigenous Affairs, Governor's Cabinet, Caller Box 10007 Saipan, MP 96950, Northern Marianas Islands
PHONE: +670 6642480
FAX: +670 2881159

POLITICAL ORGANIZATIONS

Republican Party

NAME: Benigno R. Fitial

Democratic Party

JUDICIAL SYSTEM

The Supreme Court

P.O. Box 2165 CK, Saipan, MP 96950, Northern Marianas Islands
PHONE: +670 2369715
FAX: +670 2369701
E-MAIL: supreme.court@saipan.com

The Superior Court

P.O. Box 502179, Susupe, Saipan, MP 96950, Northern Marianas Islands
PHONE: +670 2369740
FAX: +670 2369741
E-MAIL: cnmi.superior.court@gtepacifica.net

Federal District Court

BROADCAST MEDIA

Christian Science Publishing Society

KHBI Saipan, PO Box 1387, Saipan, Mariana Islands, CM 96950–1387
PHONE: +670 2346515
FAX: +670 2345452
WEBSITE: http://www.tfccs.com/GV/shortwave/shortwave_schedule.html
CONTACT: Alexander U. Igusaiar
TYPE: Religious

Far East Broadcasting Co.

Box 209, Saipan, CM 96950
PHONE: + 670 2346520 (KSAI); 3229088 (KFBS)
FAX: + 670 3223060
TITLE: Director
CONTACT: Chris Slabaugh
LANGUAGE: English
BROADCASTS: 16 hours/day
TYPE: Religious

Inter Island Communications Inc.

PO Box 914, Saipan, CM 96950
PHONE: + 670 2347239
FAX: + 670 2340447
WEBSITE: http://www.radiopacific.com/p99/
TITLE: General Manager
CONTACT: Hans W. Mickelson
LANGUAGE: English
BROADCASTS: 24 hours/day
TYPE: Commercial

Sorensen Pacific Broadcasting Inc.

PPP 415 Box 10000, Saipan 96950, Northern Mariana Islands
PHONE: +670 2357996
FAX: +670 2357998

Micronesia Broadcasting Corporation

C/o Kuam, Box 368, Agana, Guam 96920
TITLE: General Manager
CONTACT: H. Scott Kilgore

COLLEGES AND UNIVERSITIES

Northern Marianas College

PO Box 1250 Ck, Saipan, Northern Mariana Islands 96950
PHONE: +670 2343690
FAX: +670 2340759
E-MAIL: webmaster@nmcnet.edu
WEBSITE: http://www.nmcnet.edu

NEWSPAPERS AND MAGAZINES

Marianas Variety

Younis Art Studio, Inc., PO Box 231, Saipan 96950-0231 Northern Mariana Islands
PHONE: +670 2346341
FAX: +670 2349271
TITLE: Publishers
CONTACT: Abed and Paz Castro Younis
CIRCULATION: 3750

Pacific Chronicle

United Pacific Ventures, Saipan 96950 Northern Mariana Islands
PHONE: +670 2346694
FAX: +670 2340557
TITLE: Editor-in-Chief
CONTACT: Jonathan N. Navea

Saipan Shinbun

Caller Box PPP576, Saipan 96950 Northern Mariana Islands
PHONE: +670 2346096
FAX: +670 2883106
TITLE: Publisher
CONTACT: Leo Okamura
CIRCULATION: 3500

Saipan Tribune

Tan Holdings, Saipan Tribune Bldg., Middle Rd., Chalan Lau Lau, Caller Box AAA-34, Saipan 96950 Northern Mariana Islands
PHONE: +670 2352440
FAX: +670 2353733
E-MAIL: editor.tribune@saipan.com
WEBSITE: http://www.tribune.co.mp
TITLE: Editor
CONTACT: Fermin Meriang
CIRCULATION: 3500

RELIGIOUS ORGANIZATIONS

Catholic

Bishop
PO Box 745, Saipan, MP 96950, Northern Mariana Islands
PHONE: +670 (234) 3000
FAX: +670 (235) 3002
E-MAIL: bishop@cnmicatholic.org
TITLE: Bishop
NAME: Most Rev Tomas A Camacho, D.D.

Catholic Daughters of America
PO Box 745, Saipan, MP 96950, Northern Mariana Islands
PHONE: +670 (322) 3348
FAX: +670 (235) 3002
NAME: Felicidad O.T. Ogumoro

Children of God the Father
PO Box 745, Saipan, MP 96950, Northern Mariana Islands
PHONE: +670 (235) 6314
FAX: +670 (235) 3002
NAME: Mrs. Roma Diaz-Aranda

Confraternity of Christian Mothers
PO Box 745, Saipan, MP 96950, Northern Mariana Islands
PHONE: +670 (235) 0885
FAX: +670 (235) 3002
NAME: Rita C. Guerrero

Knights of Columbus
PO Box 745, Saipan, MP 96950, Northern Mariana Islands
PHONE: +670 (234) 7158
FAX: +670 (235) 3002
NAME: Bernard V. Hofschneider

Legion of Mary (San Roque)
PO Box 745, Saipan, MP 96950, Northern Mariana Islands
PHONE: +670 (234) 3000
FAX: +670 (235) 3002
NAME: Fr. Narciso Sampana

Legion of Mary (San Vincente)
PO Box 745, Saipan, MP 96950, Northern Mariana Islands
PHONE: +670 (256) 5559
FAX: +670 (235) 3002
NAME: Araceli Gipelano

Light and Salt Charismatic Community
PO Box 745, Saipan, MP 96950, Northern Mariana Islands
PHONE: +670 (234) 3000
FAX: +670 (235) 3002
NAME: Fr. Jose David

Marriage Encounter
PO Box 745, Saipan, MP 96950, Northern Mariana Islands
PHONE: +670 (234) 7361
FAX: +670 (235) 3002

FURTHER READING

Articles

"A Mutineer's Paradise." *Wall Street Journal,* March 29, 2000, p. C23.

Government Publications

United States Congress. *Northern Mariana Island Covenant Implementation Act.* Washington, DC: G.P.O, 2000.

United States General Accounting Office. *Northern Mariana Islands: Garment and Tourist Industries Play a Dominant Role in the Commonwealth's Economy.* Washington, DC: G.P.O., 2000.

NORTHERN MARIANA ISLANDS: STATISTICAL DATA

For sources and notes see "Sources of Statistics" at the front of each volume.

GEOGRAPHY

Geography

Area:

Total: 477 sq km.

Land: 477 sq km.

Note: includes 14 islands including Saipan, Rota, and Tinian.

Land boundaries: 0 km.

Coastline: 1,482 km.

Climate: tropical marine; moderated by northeast trade winds, little seasonal temperature variation; dry season December to June, rainy season July to October.

Terrain: southern islands are limestone with level terraces and fringing coral reefs; northern islands are volcanic.

Natural resources: arable land, fish.

Land use:

Arable land: 21%

Permanent crops: 0%

Permanent pastures: 19%

Forests and woodland: 0%

Other: 60%

HUMAN FACTORS

Demographics (A)

	1990	1995	1998	2000	2010	2020	2030	2040	2050
Population	44.0	58.1	66.5	71.9	98.5	122.8	142.9	156.3	161.6
Life expectancy - males	68.6	69.5	72.0	72.4	74.4	76.1	77.4	78.5	79.4
Life expectancy - females	75.5	76.2	78.4	78.8	80.8	82.4	83.8	84.8	85.6
Birth rate (per 1,000)	26.9	26.2	21.3	20.9	17.7	15.2	13.2	11.6	10.4
Death rate (per 1,000)	3.3	2.9	2.4	2.4	2.7	3.5	5.0	7.3	9.8
Women of reproductive age (15-49 yrs.)	14.4	20.5	24.0	26.2	35.3	38.0	38.8	38.3	35.6
Fertility rate	2.3	2.2	1.8	1.8	1.7	1.7	1.7	1.7	1.7

Except as noted, values for vital statistics are in thousands; life expectancy is in years.

Ethnic Division

Chamorro, Carolinians and other Micronesians, Caucasian, Japanese, Chinese, Korean.

Religion

Christian (Roman Catholic majority, although traditional beliefs and taboos may still be found).

Major Languages

English, Chamorro, Carolinian. 86% of population speaks a language other than English at home.

GOVERNMENT & LAW

Political Parties

Legislature	no. of seats
Senate	
Republican Party	8
Democratic Party	1
House of Representatives	
Republican Party	13
Democratic Party	5

Elections for the Senate and the House of Representatives were last held in November 1997 (next to be held in November 1999). The Commonwealth does not have a nonvoting delegate in the US Congress; instead, it has an elected official or "resident representative" located in Washington, DC: Juan N. Babauta of the Republican Party.

Government Budgets (B)

Revenues	$221.0 million
Expenditures	$213.0 million
Capital expenditures	$17.7 million

Data for 1996.

LABOR FORCE

Total Labor Force (A)

6,006 total indigenous labor force; 2,699 unemployed; 28,717 foreign workers (1995).

Labor Force by Occupation

Managerial	20.5%
Technical, sales	16.4%
Services	19.3%
Farming	3.1%
Precision production	13.8%
Operators, fabricators	26.9%

Unemployment Rate

14% (residents)

PRODUCTION SECTOR

Energy Production

Production by source

Fossil fuel	100%
Hydro	0%
Nuclear	0%
Other	0%

Transportation

Highways:

Total: 362 km (1991 est.).

Waterways: none.

Merchant marine: none (1999 est.).

Airports: 6 (1999 est.).

Top Agriculture Products

Coconuts, fruits, vegetables; cattle.

MANUFACTURING SECTOR

GDP & Manufacturing Summary (C)

Total GDP (1996 est.)	$524 million
Per capita (1996 est.)	$9,300

Values in purchasing power parity.

COMMUNICATIONS

Telecommunications

Telephones - main lines in use: 15,000 (1995).

Telephones - mobile cellular: 1,200 (1995).

Telephone system:

Domestic: NA

International: satellite earth stations - 2 Intelsat (Pacific Ocean).

Radio broadcast stations: AM 2, FM 3, shortwave 1 (1998).

Radios: NA

Television broadcast stations: 1 (on Saipan and one station planned for Rota; in addition, two cable services on Saipan provide varied programming from satellite networks) (1997).

Televisions: NA

Internet Service Providers (ISPs): NA

FINANCE, ECONOMICS, & TRADE

Economic Indicators

National product: GDP—purchasing power parity—$524 million (1996 est.). GDP numbers reflect US spending..

National product real growth rate: NA.

National product per capita: $9,300 (1996 est.).

Inflation rate—consumer price index: 6.5% (1994 est.).

Exchange Rates

Exchange rates: US currency is used.

Top Import Origins

Origins: United States, Japan.

Top Export Destinations

Exports (1998): $1 billion.

Destinations: United States.

Foreign Aid

Recipient: $21.1 million (1995).

Import/Export Commodities

Import Commodities	Export Commodities
Food	Garments
Construction equipment and materials	
Petroleum products	

NORWAY

CAPITAL: Oslo.

FLAG: The national flag has a red field on which appears a blue cross outlined in white.

ANTHEM: *Ja, vi elsker dette landet (Yes, We Love This Country).*

MONETARY UNIT: The krone (Kr) of 100 øre is the national currency. There are coins of 50 øre and 1, 5, and 10 kroner, and notes of 20, 50, 100, 200, 500, and 1,000 kroner. Kr1 = $0.15664 (or $1 = Kr6.384).

WEIGHTS AND MEASURES: The metric system is the legal standard.

HOLIDAYS: New Year's Day, 1 January; Labor Day, 1 May; National Independence Day, 17 May; Christmas, 25 December; Boxing Day, 26 December. Movable religious holidays include Holy Thursday, Good Friday, Easter Monday, Ascension, and Whitmonday.

TIME: 1 PM = noon GMT.

LOCATION AND SIZE: Norway occupies the western part of the Scandinavian peninsula in northern Europe, with almost one-third of the country situated north of the Arctic Circle. It has an area of 324,220 square kilometers (125,182 square miles), slightly larger than the state of New Mexico. Extending 1,752 kilometers (1,089 miles) north-northeast to south-southwest, Norway has the greatest length of any European country. It has a boundary length of 24,440 kilometers (15,273 miles).

Norway's capital city, Oslo, is in the southern part of the country.

CLIMATE: Because of the North Atlantic Drift, Norway has a mild climate for a country so far north. The north is considerably cooler than the south, while the interior is cooler than the west coast. Oslo's mean yearly temperature is 6°C (43°F) and ranges from a mean of −5°C (23°F) in January to 17°C (63°F) in July. The eastern valleys have less than 30 centimeters (12 inches) of rain yearly, whereas along the west coast the average rainfall is 330 centimeters (130 inches).

The North Cape area of Norway is the land of the midnight sun, with "white nights" from the middle of May to the end of July, during which the sun does not set.

Kingdom of Norway
Kongeriket Norge

INTRODUCTORY SURVEY

RECENT HISTORY

Despite Norway's proclaimed neutrality in World War II (1939-1945), Germany invaded in 1940, seeking control of strategically important Norwegian waters. King Haakon led the national resistance and escaped, taking the government with him. Following World War II, Norway joined the North Atlantic Treaty Organization (NATO). King Haakon died in 1957 and was succeeded by Olav V.

Economic policy has been a key national issue since the war. Especially controversial have been taxation and the degree of government involvement in private industry. Prior to the mid-1970s, the Labor Party dominated government. Economic planning has been introduced and several state-owned enterprises established.

In the November 1972 elections, Norwegians rejected Norway's entry into the European Economic Community (EEC), later known as the European Union (EU).

The Labor Party, under the leadership of Gro Harlem Brundtland, the youngest woman ever to run a modern government, found its control over the government weakened by favoring joining the EEC. The Labor Party lost control of the government to the Conservatives in 1981 elections. The Labor Party regained control in 1986, and Brundtland resumed her role as prime minister.

In January 1991, King Harald took over the throne when his father, Olav V, died.

The EU issue remained controversial. In late 1994, Norwegians again rejected EU membership despite Sweden and Finland becoming members. Those favoring membership were primarily from urban areas and engaged in business or the professions. Those opposed, from coastal areas to the north and the western rural areas, feel Norway is sufficiently strong and rich in natural resources to remain independent. Of special concern is protection of the rich fishing grounds in Norway's territorial waters.

GOVERNMENT

Norway is a constitutional monarchy. The constitution of May 17, 1814, as amended in 1884, places executive power in the king and legislative power in the Storting. The sovereign (king or queen) must be a member of the Evangelical Lutheran Church of Norway, which he or she heads. A constitutional amendment in May 1990 allows females to take the throne. Royal power is exercised through a cabinet (the Council of State) consisting of a prime minister and at least seven other ministers of state.

Since the introduction of parliamentary rule in 1884, the Storting (parliament) has become the supreme authority with complete control over finances and power to override the monarch's veto under a specified procedure. The monarch is theoretically free to choose his or her own cabinet. In practice, the Storting selects the ministers who must resign if the Storting votes no confidence. Following parliamentary elections the leader of the majority party or of a majority coalition is generally appointed the prime minister.

The Storting is made up of 165 representatives from eighteen counties. Members are elected by popular vote by proportional representation to serve four-year terms. After election, the Storting divides into two sections by choosing one-fourth of its members to form the upper chamber, Lagting, with the rest constituting the lower chamber, Odelsting. The Odelsting deals with certain types of bills (chiefly proposed new laws) after the committee stage and forwards them to the Lagting. After approving bills, the Lagting sends them to the king for the royal assent (agreement).

Judiciary

Each municipality has a conciliation council, elected by the municipal council, to mediate in lesser civil cases so as to settle them, if possible, before they go to court. Cases receive their first hearing in town courts (byrett) and rural courts (herredsrett), which try both civil and criminal cases. Their decisions may be brought before a court of appeals (lagmannsrett) that also serves as a court of first instance in more serious criminal cases; there are five such courts, at Oslo, Skien, Bergen, Trondheim, and Tromsø.

Appeals may be taken to the Supreme Court (Høyesterett) at Oslo, which consists of a chief justice and seventeen judges, of whom five sit in a single case. Special courts include a Social Insurance Court and a Labor Disputes Court that handles industrial relations disputes.

Political Parties

The present-day Conservative Party (Høyre) was established in 1885. The Liberal Party (Venstre), founded in 1885, stresses social reform. Industrial workers founded the Labor Party (Arbeiderparti) in 1887 and with the assistance of the Liberals obtained the universal vote for men in 1898, and for women in 1913.

The Agrarian (Farmers) Party, formed in 1920, changed its name to the Center Party (Senterparti) in 1958. The Christian People's Party (Kristelig Folkeparti), founded in 1933, and also known as the Christian Democratic Party, supports the principles of Christianity in public life.

The results in the 1997 elections were as follows: Labour Party (sixty-five), Center Party (eleven), Conservative Party (twenty-three), Christian People's Party (twenty-five), Socialist Left Party (nine), Progress Party (twenty-five), Liberal Party (six), and others (one).

DEFENSE

The monarch is supreme commander of the armed forces. About 16,500 draftees served in the armed forces of 31,000 officers and enlisted men in 2000. National service is required and universal, but exceptions may be made for religious reasons. Those exempted must serve for two years in the civil labor corps.

The army's total strength is 15,200 officers and men. The navy has a total of 8,200 men including 270 men in the coastal artillery. The air force consists of 6,700 officers and men with seventy-nine combat aircraft. Reservists of all services number approximately 234,000, and the home guard has 2,500 men.

Norway is the host nation for the North Atlantic Treaty Organization (NATO) Allied Forces North, and provides troops for six peacekeeping operations. The nation spent $3.2 billion on defense in 1998.

ECONOMIC AFFAIRS

Norway, with its long coastline and vast forests, was traditionally a fishing and lumbering country. Since the end of World War I, it has greatly increased its transport and manufacturing activities. The discovery since the late 1970s of major new oil reserves in the North Sea has had considerable impact on the Norwegian economy.

Foreign trade is a critical economic factor. Norway was especially sensitive to the effects of the worldwide recession of the early 1980s and is affected by variations in world prices, particularly those of oil, gas, and shipping. Since the early 1980s, Norway's exports have been dominated by petroleum and natural gas. Only Saudi Arabia exports more oil than Norway.

Norway has a mixed economy with both free market activity and government intervention. The government owns up to 50 percent of domestic businesses and controls key areas such as petroleum. The government also heavily subsidizes agriculture. The extensive social welfare system pushes public sector expenditures to more than 50 percent of GDP.

The economy grew by 2.4 percent during 1998 but only 0.8 percent during 1999 due to weak private consumption and lack of investment activity in oil and other sectors. Growth was predicted to pick up in 2000 to about 2.7 percent. In 1995, the economy grew by 3.7 percent, inflation was 2.5 percent, and unemployment was 8 percent.

Norway voted to stay out of the European Union (EU) in a 1994 referendum.

Public Finance

Norway's fiscal year coincides with the calendar year. The U.S. Central Intelligence Agency estimated that in 2000 government revenues totaled approximately $69.7 billion and expenditures $60.1 billion. Norway is a net external creditor.

Income

In 1999, Norway's gross domestic product (GDP) was $111.3 billion, or about $25,100 per capita. The 1999 estimated GDP growth was 0.8 percent and inflation was 2.8 percent. The 1998 GDP contribution by sector was: agriculture, 2.2 percent; industry, 26.3 percent; and services, 71.5 percent.

Industry

The most important export industries are oil and gas production, metalworking, shipbuilding, pulp and paper, timber, chemical products, food processing, and processed fish. Products traditionally classified as home market industries (electrical and nonelectrical machinery, casting and foundry products, textiles, paints, varnishes, rubber goods, and furniture) also make an important contribution.

Electrochemical and electrometallurgical products-aluminum, ferroalloys, steel, nickel, copper, magnesium, and fertilizers-are based mainly on Norway's low-cost electric power. Without any bauxite reserves of its own, Norway has thus been able to become a leading producer of aluminum. Industrial output is being increasingly diversified.

About half of Norway's industries are situated in the area of Oslo's fjord. In 1991, 11,532 establishments in this area employed 298,982 persons.

Banking and Finance

The Bank of Norway, acquired by the state in 1949, is the central bank and the sole note-issuing authority. The bank discounts treasury bills and some commercial paper; trades in bonds, foreign exchange, and gold and silver; and administers foreign exchange regulations. The bank also receives money for deposit on current accounts, but generally pays no interest on deposits. The head office is in Oslo and there are twenty branches.

By the mid-1990s, there were twenty commercial banks. The three largest-the Norske Creditbank, Bergen Bank, and Christiania Bank og Kreditkasse-account for more than half of the total resources of the commercial banks. In 1988, a number of small savings banks and one medium-sized commercial bank, Sunnmorsbanken, became illiquid or insolvent. Most were rescued by merging with larger banks. After a slight improvement in 1989, however, banks' positions deteriorated again in 1990 following heavy losses sustained in the securities markets. As commercial property prices continued to fall, the position of the country's second and third largest commercial banks, Christiania and Fokus, became increasingly precarious. To prevent a loss of confidence in the banking system, the government established a Government Bank Insurance Fund in 1991. Within months this was called upon to provide capital to support the country's three largest banks, two of which-Christiania and Fokus-were by then insolvent.

The banking system has gradually recovered from this crisis of the late 1980s and early 1990s.

Ten state banks and other financial institutions serve particular industries or undertakings including agriculture, fisheries, manufacturing, student loans, mortgages, and others. Although savings banks also have been merging in recent years, there were still 133 private savings banks and many credit associations in 1993.

A law of 1961 contains measures to implement the principle that banking policies are to be based on social as well as economic and financial considerations. The government appoints 25 percent of the representatives on the board of every commercial bank with funds of over Kr100 million. Guidelines for these banks are worked out cooperatively with public authorities.

The stock exchanges of Norway are at Oslo (the oldest, founded 1818), Trondheim, Bergen, Kristiansund, Drammen, Stavanger, Ålesund, Haugesund, and Fredrikstad. Amid the increasing consolidation among European stock exchanges in the late 1990s, calls increased for the Norwegian markets to merge.

Economic Development

The government holds shares in a number of large enterprises: a minority of shares in most industrial establishments and all or controlling shares in some armaments factories as well as in chemical and electrometallurgical companies, power stations, and mines. The government also participates in joint industrial undertakings with private capital. Government policy also aims at attracting foreign investment.

Rapid industrial development and exploitation of resources are major governmental goals, with special emphasis on northern Norway, where development has lagged behind that of the southern areas. The Development Fund for North Norway, established in 1952, together with a policy of tax concessions, resulted in progress there at a rate more rapid than that of the rest of the country. The exploitation of offshore oil and natural gas reserves has had a profound effect on Norway's economy in recent years. Increased oil revenues have expanded both domestic consumption and investment. The government has used oil revenues to ease taxes and increase public investment in regional development, environmental protection, social welfare, education, and communications. Although the expansion of innovative oil development projects—such as the $4.2 billion Heidrun oil project—continues, Norway is looking to produce more natural gas than oil. The $5 billion Troll gas field scheduled to begin production in 1996 is one such project.

A tax law permits industry and commerce to build up tax-free reserves for future investment, foreign sales promotion, and research. Designed to provide a flexible tool for influencing cyclical developments, the law's intent is to help ensure that total demand at any given time is sufficient to create full employment and strong economic growth.

To stimulate industry, incentives are available for undertakings in the north as well as in other economically weak regions; companies may set aside up to 25 percent of taxable income for tax-free investment. A Regional Development Fund grants low-interest, long-term loans to firms to strengthen the economy of low-income, high-unemployment areas anywhere in the country.

In 1991, the government introduced a three-year program to improve infrastructure, particularly for road and rail, and reduce unemployment.

Although Norway rejected EU membership in a 1994 referendum, Norway's economy is largely integrated with that of the EU. Norway has a free trade agreement with the EU, and its currency is kept on par with the euro. Nevertheless, Norway retains extensive control over its economic development policies.

Norway has been active in aiding developing nations under the Norwegian Agency for International Development. The leading recipients are Tanzania, Mozambique, Zambia, Bangladesh, Nicaragua, and Ethiopia.

SOCIAL WELFARE

Norway has been a pioneer in the field of social welfare and is often called a welfare state. Accident insurance for factory workers was introduced in 1894 and compulsory health insurance in 1909. Sickness benefits, family allowances during hospitalization, and grants for funeral expenses are paid. Public assistance, available in Norway since 1845, supplements the foregoing programs. Social welfare has long included maternity benefits with free prenatal clinics.

The National Insurance Act that came into effect in 1967 provides old-age pensions, rehabilitation allowances, disability pensions, widow and widower pensions, and survivor benefits to children. Workers' compensation covers both accidents and occupational diseases. Family allowance coverage, in force since 1946, is provided for children under the age of sixteen.

In spite of a 1978 law mandating equal wages for equal work by men and women, economic discrimination continues, and the average pay for women in industry is lower than that for men.

Healthcare

Since 1971, there has been a National Insurance Scheme. Hospital care is free of charge, but a minor sum is charged for medicine and primary health care.

There is a three-part system made up of regional hospitals serving parts of the country, central hospitals serving the various counties, and local hospitals also run by the counties. In 1990-1997, there were 3.1 doctors and 13.3 hospital beds per 1,000 people.

In 2000, average life expectancy, among the highest in the world, was 78.7 years. Major causes of death in 1990 were: communicable diseases and maternal/perinatal causes; noncommunicable diseases; and injuries. In 1996, there were 518 cases of AIDS.

Housing

Housing problems were complicated by the destruction caused by World War II and postwar increases in the birthrate. Norway built more dwellings per 1,000 inhabitants than any other European country completing between 31,000 and 42,000 units annually from 1967 through 1981. Construction of new dwellings has slowed in recent years, however; only 21,689 units were completed in 1991. As of 1990, Norway had a total of 1.8 million dwelling units. Since 1988, housing demand has fallen more than 50 percent. Tax reforms in 1992 contributed to the decline, making home ownership less attractive.

EDUCATION

There is practically no adult illiteracy in Norway. The Basic Education Act of 1969 introduced a nine-year system of compulsory education for all children between the ages of seven and sixteen. Local authorities generally provide school buildings and equipment, and the central government contributes funds towards teachers' salaries and covers a considerable portion of the cost of running the schools.

Secondary school for students from sixteen to nineteen may involve theoretical studies, practical training, or a combination of both. Three-year general secondary schools (gymnasiums) prepare students to go on to a university. In the 1997 academic year, 368,074 students were enrolled in the gymnasiums and other secondary schools. It is possible for students to enter a university without having passed through a gymnasium.

Since 1976, the upper secondary school system has included vocational schools. These may be operated by the state, by local authorities, or by the industrial sector.

Norway's institutions of higher education include 130 colleges and four universities, with a total enrollment of 185,320 in 1997. The largest universities include the University of Oslo, the University of Bergen, the University of Trondheim, and the University of Troms. There are also specialized institutions such as the Agricultural University of Norway (near Oslo); the Norwegian School of Economics and Business Administration (Bergen); and the Norwegian College of Veterinary Medicine (Oslo) representing fields not covered by the universities.

2000 KEY EVENTS TIMELINE

March

- The Labor Party wins the right to form a new government after toppling the coalition led by Kjell Magne Bondevik, leader of the Christian Democratic Party. The no-confidence vote comes on March 9 after Bondevik refuses to modify antipollution laws to allow construction of natural gas power plants in the country. Jens Stoltenberg becomes prime minister.

April

- Norway expresses reservations about the creation of a European Union (EU) defense force outside the North Atlantic Treaty Organization (NATO).
- Norway and Japan favor lifting restrictions on whale hunting at the meeting of the World Wide Fund for Nature.

July

- Researchers at the University of Bergen's Nansen Environmental and Remote Sensing Center predict the complete melting of the North Pole in fifty years, drastically altering the environment.

October

- Three religious leaders from Gambia and Somalia are facing charges in a Norwegian court for allegedly promoting female genital mutilation.

November

- The fifteen-mile Laerdal tunnel, one of the world's longest tunnels, opens November 27. Construction of the tunnel took over five years. It allows travel by car on a route through a mountainous area connecting Bergen on the west coast and Oslo in the east.

December

- Representatives of Scandinavian countries meet in Stockholm, Sweden, with foreign ministers from nine African nations (Benin, Botswana, Ghana, Mali, Mozambique, Nigeria, Senegal, South Africa, and Tanzania) to discuss arms control, the role of arms embargoes, and ways of combating the illicit traffic in small arms. A report on U.N. peacekeeping operations in Africa and cooperation between the United Nations, African organizations, and the European Union was also presented during the two-day meeting.

ANALYSIS OF EVENTS: 2000

BUSINESS AND THE ECONOMY

The Norwegian economy performed better in 2000 than expected. Private consumption grew by 2.7 percent and exports grew by 5 percent. Gross national product (GNP) growth rose from 0.9 percent in 1999 to 2.7 percent in 2000 (1.3 percent for non-oil-related output). Unemployment stood at 3.6 percent, and the current account had a surplus of 10 percent of gross domestic product (GDP).

The Norwegian krone (NKR) rose steadily against the euro thanks to the high price of oil. The Norwegian central bank raised interest rates several times to curb inflation, which was at a nine-year high of 3.5 percent.

Since oil discoveries on the Norwegian shelf were dwindling, Statoil wanted to explore outside its domestic market. To succeed, it needed strategic alliances and further injections of capital. Statoil's management had complained bitterly about the political infighting in the Labor Party because it feared missing out on the global consolidation in the oil industry. The most popular proposal was for Statoil to take over some of the assets of the state-owned agency, which controlled 150 offshore licenses worth about NKR200 billion, and list itself on the Oslo stock exchange. Nothing would be decided, however, until the end of the year and Statoil's privatization would not take place, if at all, until spring 2001.

GOVERNMENT AND POLITICS

In March after more than two years of political instability, the minority centrist coalition government led by Christian Democrat Kjell Magne Bondevik stepped down. The coalition made up of the Christian Democratic, Center, and Liberal parties was never anything more than a caretaker government. Much of the coalition's existence owed to the fact that the leader of the Progress Party, Carl Hagen, was determined to keep Labor out by keeping the coalition in. The issue that toppled the minority government was the pressure of Labor and Conservative majority to approve new plans to build gas-fired power stations. The coalition was not prepared to implement an environmental policy that would add to air pollution. The government stepped down on March 10, 2000.

The opposition leader, Thorborn Jagland of the Labor Party, was not much liked by the voters and he resigned in February 2000 to make way for a younger, more acceptable party leader. Jens Stoltenberg, young and photogenic, exerted much greater appeal among voters and boosted the electoral appeal of the party. After the fall of the Bondevik coalition, King Harald V asked the Labor Party to form a new (minority, since it controls only 65 seats out of 165 in parliament) government. Stoltenberg introduced his new cabinet on the March 17, 2000. During his parliamentary speech, Stoltenberg made vague promises to modernize the public sector, prioritize job creation, instigate local government reforms, and support education, research, and equal opportunities.

The first minority Labor budget was presented to parliament (Storting) in October 2000. Although the central government budget recorded a surplus of 10 percent of GDP and the Petroleum Fund, which invested in international stocks and bonds for future generations, had more than NKR300 billion stashed away, the Labor government planned to increase taxes to cover higher expenditures for healthcare and other public services. The tight budget undermined Labor's approval rate and that of its leader. It gave ammunition to the far-right Progress Party, who were advocating tax cuts and increased social spending. Carl Hagen, the veteran leader of the Progress Party and twenty-two years in opposition, claimed, contrary to Labor's program, that taxes could be cut and that spending could be increased in a non-inflationary manner. His message resonated with voters and polls showed that the Progress Party support was at 34 percent of the electorate, while the Labor party, traditionally the largest, slumped to 22 percent of the national electorate if an election would have been held in late 2000.

The Labor Party was a strong supporter of the North Atlantic Treaty Organization (NATO) and it gave generous assistance to the Baltic states. The current government sent troops (and police) to Kosovo, and volunteered 3,500 Norwegians for the planned European Union (E.U.) rapid-reaction force. Norway also handed out nearly 1 percent of its GDP in aid and humanitarian assistance.

CULTURE AND SOCIETY

In the late 1980s, unions and employers signed a solidarity pact to restore full employment while keeping inflation down. Nevertheless, the impact of the economic boom strained the pact and in late April, the trade union federation called for an indefinite strike after more than 60 percent of its members voted against a wage offer from employers. More than 80,000 members of the confederation paralyzed the hotel industry, ferry transport, construction, and private service sectors. The strike was called after employers offered unions a fifth holiday week and a 4 percent wage increase in 2000 and 2001. The rank and file rejected the offer because it was spread out over three years and because most Norwegians, already enjoying long vacations, preferred better pay. The strike cost the country NKR175 million a day and lasted six days.

DIRECTORY

CENTRAL GOVERNMENT

Head of State

King
Harald V, Monarch, Royal Palace, Det Kgl. Slott, Drammensveien 1, N-0010 Oslo, Norway
PHONE: +47 (22) 441920
FAX: +47 (22) 550880

Prime Minister
Jens Stoltenberg, Office of the Prime Minister, Akersgaten 42, PO Box 8001 Dep, N-0030 Oslo, Norway
PHONE: +47 (22) 249090
E-MAIL: odin@ft.dep.telemax.no

Ministers

Minister of Cultural Affairs
Ellen Horn, Ministry of Cultural Affairs, Akersgata 59 (R5), PO Box 8030 Dep, N-0030 Oslo, Norway
PHONE: +47 (22) 249090
FAX: +47 (22) 249550

Minister of Children and Family Affairs
Karita Bekkemellem Orheim, Ministry of Children and Family Affairs, Akersgt. 59 (R5), Postbox 8036 Dep, N-0030 Oslo, Norway
PHONE: +47 (22) 249090
FAX: +47 (22) 249515

Minister of Trade and Industry
Grete Knudsen, Ministry of Trade and Industry, Grubbegt. 8, PO Box 8148 Dep, N-0033 Oslo, Norway
PHONE: +47 (22) 243700; 249090
FAX: +47 (22) 249565

Minister of Foreign Affairs
Thorbjorn Jagland, Ministry of Foreign Affairs, 7. juni plass 1, Postbox 8114 Dep, N-0032 Oslo, Norway
PHONE: +47 (22) 243000; 243600
FAX: +47 (22) 249580; 249581

Minister of Fisheries
Otto Gregussen, Ministry of Fisheries, Grubbegt. 8, PO Box 8118 Dep, N-0032 Oslo, Norway
PHONE: +47 (22) 246400; 249090
FAX: +47 (22) 249585

Minister of Finance and Customs
Karl Eirik Schjott-Pedersen, Ministry of Finance and Customs, Akersgata 40 (blokk G), PO Box 8008 Dep, N-0030 Oslo, Norway
PHONE: +47 (22) 244100
FAX: +47 (22) 249514

Minister of Agriculture
Bjarne Hakon Hanssen, Ministry of Agriculture, Akersgata 59 (R5), Postbox 8007 Dep, N-0030 Oslo, Norway
PHONE: +47 (22) 249100
FAX: +47 (22) 249555

Minister of Defense
Bjorn Tore Godal, Ministry of Defense, Myntgata 1, PO Box 8126 Dep, N-0032 Oslo, Norway
PHONE: +47 (22) 402001
FAX: +47 (22) 402323

Minister of Justice and Police
Hanne Harlem, Ministry of Justice and Police, kersgt. 42 (blokk H), PO Box 8119 Dep, N-0032 Oslo, Norway
PHONE: +47 (22) 245100
FAX: +47 (22) 249540

Minister of Education, Research and Church Affairs
Trond Giske, Ministry of Education, Research and Church Affairs, Akersgt. 44 (blokk Y), Postbox 8119 Dep, N-0032 Oslo, Norway
PHONE: +47 (22) 247400
FAX: +47 (22) 249540

Minister of Transport and Communications
Terge Moe Gustavsen, Ministry of Transport and Communications, Akersgata 59 (R5), Postbox 8010 Dep, N-0030 Oslo, Norway
PHONE: +47 (22) 248100
FAX: +47 (22) 249570

Minister of Health
Tore Tonne, Ministry of Health, Grubbegata 10, Postbox 8011 Dep, N-0030 Oslo, Norway
PHONE: +47 (22) 248400
FAX: +47 (22) 249576

Minister of Social Affairs
Guri Ingebrigtsen, Ministry of Social Affairs

Minister of the Environment
Siri Bjerke, Ministry of the Environment, Myntgata 2, Postbox 8013 Dep, N-0030 Oslo, Norway
PHONE: +47 (22) 245700
FAX: +47 (22) 249560

Minister of Labour and Government Administration
Jorgen Kosmo, Ministry of Labour and Government Administration, Akersgata 59 (R5), Postbox 8004 Dep, N-0030 Oslo, Norway
PHONE: +47 (22) 244600
FAX: +47 (22) 242710

Minister of Local Government and Regional Development
Sylvia Brustad, Ministry of Local Government and Regional Development, Akersgata 59 (R5), Postx 8112 Dep, N-0032 Oslo, Norway
PHONE: +47 (22) 246800
FAX: +47 (22) 249545

Minister of Oil and Energy
Olav Akselsen, Ministry of Oil and Energy

Minister of Foreign Aid
Ann Kristin Sydnes, Ministry of Foreign Aid

POLITICAL ORGANIZATIONS

Det norske Arbeiderparti (Labor Party)

NAME: Thorbjorn Jagland

Hoyre (Conservative Party)

NAME: Jan Petersen

Senterpartiet (Center Party)

NAME: Johan J. Jakobsen

Kristelig Folkeparti (Christian People's Party)

NAME: Valgerd Haugland

Sosialistisk Venstreparti (Socialist Left Party)

NAME: Kristin Halvorsen

Norges Kommunistiske Parti (Norwegian Communist Party)

NAME: KareAndre Nilsen

Fremskrittspartiet (Progress Party)

TITLE: Chairman
NAME: Carl I. Hagen

Venstre (Liberal Party)

NAME: Lars Sponheim

Rod Valgallianse (Red Electoral Alliance)

NAME: Erling Folkvord

DIPLOMATIC REPRESENTATION

Embassies in Norway

Austria
Thomas Heftyesgt 19-21, N-0244 Oslo, Norway
PHONE: +47 (22) 552348
FAX: +47 (22) 554361
NAME: Harald Wiesner

Chile
Meltzersgt. 5, N-0244 Oslo, Norway
PHONE: +47 (22) 448955
FAX: +47 (22) 442421
E-MAIL: embchile@online.no
TITLE: Ambassador
NAME: Manuel Atria

Denmark
Olav Kyrres gate 7, N-0244 Oslo, Norway
PHONE: +47 (22) 540800
FAX: +47 (22) 554634
E-MAIL: anske@online.no
NAME: Ib Ritto Andreasen

Egypt
Drammensvn 90A, N-0244 Oslo, Norway
PHONE: +47 (22) 200010
FAX: +47 (22) 562268
NAME: Magdy Abdel Moneim Hefny

Finland
Thomas Heftyes gate 1, N-0244 Oslo, Norway

PHONE: +47 (22) 430400
FAX: +47 (22) 430629
E-MAIL: finland@online.no
NAME: Ole Norrback

France
Drammensvn 69, N-0244 Oslo, Norway
PHONE: +47 (22) 441820
FAX: +47 (22) 563221
NAME: Patrick Henault

Greece
Nobelsgt. 45, N-0244 Oslo, Norway
PHONE: +47 (22) 442728
FAX: +47 (22) 560072
E-MAIL: gremb@online.no
NAME: Ole Norrback

Hungary
Sophus Liesgt. 3, N-0244 Oslo, Norway
PHONE: +47 (22) 552418
FAX: +47 (22) 447693
NAME: Arpad Hargita

Indonesia
Inkognitogt. 8, N-0244 Oslo Norway
PHONE: +47 (22) 441121
FAX: +47 (22) 553444
NAME: Amiruddin Noor

Italy
Inkognitogt. 7, N-0244 Oslo, Norway
PHONE: +47 (22) 552233
FAX: +47 (22) 443436
NAME: Mario Quagliotti

Mexico
Drammensvn 108B, N-0244 Oslo, Norway
PHONE: +47 (22) 431165
FAX: +47 (22) 444352
NAME: Gustavo Iruegas Evaristo

United Kingdom
Thomas Heftyesgate 8, N-0244 Oslo, Norway
PHONE: +47 (22) 132700
FAX: +47 (22) 132741
E-MAIL: britemb@online.no
NAME: Richard Dales

United States
Drammensveien 18, N-0244 Oslo, Norway
PHONE: +47 (22) 448550
FAX: +47 (22) 430777
E-MAIL: oslo@usis.no
NAME: David B. Hermelin

JUDICIAL SYSTEM

The Supreme Court

PO Box 8016 Dep, N-0030 Oslo, Norway
PHONE: +47 (22) 035900
FAX: +47 (22) 332355

BROADCAST MEDIA

Alltid Klassisk

PHONE: +47 (23) 047882
FAX: +47 (23) 048575
LANGUAGE: Norwegian
BROADCASTS: 24 hours/day
TYPE: Classical

Alltid Nyheter

NRK, N-0342 Oslo, Norway
PHONE: +47 (23) 047000
FAX: + 47 (23) 045141
E-MAIL: alltid.nyheter@nrk.no
LANGUAGE: Norwegian during the day, English at night and on the weekends
BROADCASTS: 24 hours/day
TYPE: News

Alltid Jazz

PHONE: +47 (23) 047000
FAX: +47 (23) 047960
LANGUAGE: Norwegian
BROADCASTS: 24 hours/day
TYPE: Jazz

Europakanalen (Radio Norway International)

PHONE: + 47 (23) 048441
FAX: +47 (23) 047134
LANGUAGE: Norwegian
BROADCASTS: 24 hours/day
TYPE: News, Cultural, Youth Programming

NRK Radio P1

NRK P1, N-7005 Trondheim, Norway
PHONE: + 47 (73) 881400
FAX: +47 (73) 881549
E-MAIL: p1@nrk.no
LANGUAGE: Norwegian
BROADCASTS: 24 hours/day

NRK P2

NRK P2, N-0342 Oslo, Norway
PHONE: +47 (23) 048649
FAX: +47 (23) 047229

LANGUAGE: Norwegian
BROADCASTS: 24 hours/day
TYPE: Cultural

NRK P3

NRK P3, N-7005 Trondheim, Norway
PHONE: +47 (73) 881600
FAX: +47 (73) 881609
LANGUAGE: Norwegian
BROADCASTS: 24 hours/day
TYPE: Youth Programming

NRK P4 - Radio Helege Norge

Postboks 414, N-2603 Lillehammer, Norway
PHONE: +47 (61) 262660
FAX: +47 (61) 262920
E-MAIL: p4@p4.no
WEBSITE: http://www.p4.no
TITLE: Managing Director
CONTACT: Kalle Lisberg
LANGUAGE: Norwegian
BROADCASTS: 24 hours/day
TYPE: Commercial

Radio Norway International

N-0340 Oslo 3, Norway
PHONE: +47 (23) 048441
FAX: +47 (23) 047134
E-MAIL: info@nrk.no
WEBSITE: http://www.nrk.no/radionorway

Radio 1 Norge

Postboks 102-Grefsen, N-0409 Oslo, Norway
PHONE: +47 (22) 023300
FAX: +47 (22) 333102
WEBSITE: http://www.radio1.no
LANGUAGE: Norwegian
BROADCASTS: 24 hours/day
TYPE: Commercial

Samiradio

Postboks 183, N-9730 Karasjok, Norway
PHONE: +47 (78) 469200
FAX: +47 (78) 469223
E-MAIL: samiradio@nrk.no
TITLE: Leading Personnel
CONTACT: Nils Johan Haetta
LANGUAGE: Norwegian
TYPE: Lappish Programs

Norsk Rikskringkasting

N-0340 Oslo 3, Norway
PHONE: +47 (22) 459050
FAX: +47 (22) 457440
WEBSITE: http://www.nrk.no
TITLE: Director General
CONTACT: Einar Forde

TV-2

Postboks 2, N-5002 Bergen, Norway
PHONE: +47 (55) 908070
FAX: +47 (55) 908090
TITLE: Director of Programmers
CONTACT: Finn H Andreassen
TYPE: Private Commercial

COLLEGES AND UNIVERSITIES

Universitetet i Oslo

Postboks 1072, Blindern, N-0216 Oslo, Norway
PHONE: +47 (22) 855050
FAX: +47 (22) 854442
E-MAIL: informasjon@uio.no
WEBSITE: http://www.uio.no

Norwegian School of Veterinary Medicine

Postboks 8146 Dep, N-0033 Oslo, Norway
PHONE: +47 (22) 964500
FAX: +47 (22) 565704
E-MAIL: sekretariatet@veths.no
WEBSITE: http://www.veths.no

Oslo School of Architecture, Urbanism & Industrial Design

POB 6768 - St. Olavs Plass, N-0130 Oslo, Norway
PHONE: +47 (22) 997700
FAX: +47 (22) 111970
E-MAIL: postmottak@aho.no
WEBSITE: http://www.aho.no

National Academy of Fine Arts

St. Olavs Gate 32, N-0166 Oslo, Norway
PHONE: +47 (22) 995530
FAX: +47 (22) 995533
E-MAIL: ska_inf@khio.no
WEBSITE: http://www.statkunst.no

Oslo University College

Wergeland Sveien 27, N-0167 Oslo, Norway
PHONE: +47 (22) 452000
FAX: +47 (22) 453065
E-MAIL: postmottak@hio.no
WEBSITE: http://www.hio.no

Norwegian Lutheran School of Theology

Postboks 5144, Majorstua, N-0302 Oslo, Norway
PHONE: +47 (22) 590500
FAX: +47 (22) 691890
E-MAIL: ekspedisjon@mf.no
WEBSITE: http://www.menfak.no

Norwegian State Academy of Music

Postboks 5190, Majorstua, N-0302 Oslo, Norway
PHONE: +47 (22) 367000
FAX: +47 (22) 367001
E-MAIL: mh@nmh.no
WEBSITE: http://www.nmh.no

Diakonhjemmet College

Postboks 23, Vinderen, N-0319 Oslo, Norway
PHONE: +47 (22) 451945
FAX: +47 (22) 451950
E-MAIL: hovedstiffelsen@diakonhjemmet.no
WEBSITE: http://www.diakonhjemmet.no

Norwegian School of Management

Elias Smiths Vei 15, POB 580, N-1302 Sandvika, Norway
PHONE: +47 (67) 557000
FAX: +47 (67) 557670
E-MAIL: helle.simensen@bi.no
WEBSITE: http://web.bi.no/bihoved.nsf

Agricultural University of Norway

Postboks 5003, N-1432 Solbergskogen, Norway
PHONE: +47 (64) 947500
FAX: +47 (64) 947505
E-MAIL: info@adm.nlh.no
WEBSITE: http://www.nlh.no

Ostfold College

Remmen, N-2418 Halden, Norway
PHONE: +47 (69) 215000
FAX: +47 (69) 215002
E-MAIL: post-fa@hiof.no
WEBSITE: http://www.hiof.no

Hedmark College

Postboks 1175, N-2418 Elverum, Norway
PHONE: +47 (62) 430000
FAX: +47 (62) 430001
E-MAIL: hogskolen.hedmark@fa.hihm.no
WEBSITE: http://www.hihm.no

Lillehammer College

N-2626 Lillehammer, Norway
PHONE: +47 (61) 288000
FAX: +47 (61) 260750
E-MAIL: post@hil.no
WEBSITE: http://www.hil.no

Vestfold College

PO Box 2243, N-3103 Toensberg, Norway
PHONE: +47 (33) 031000
FAX: +47 (33) 031100
E-MAIL: bjorn.jakobsen@hive.no
WEBSITE: http://www.hive.no

Buskerud College of Higher Education

Postboks 235, N-3601 Kongberg, Norway
PHONE: +47 (32) 869500
FAX: +47 (32) 869516
E-MAIL: gunnar.aultun@hibu.no
WEBSITE: http://www.hibu.no

Telemark University College

Kjolnes Ring 56, N-3914 Porsgrunn, Norway
PHONE: +47 (35) 575000
FAX: +47 (35) 575001
E-MAIL: sentralbord@pors.hit.no
WEBSITE: http://www.hit.no

Stavanger School of Mission & Theology

Misjonsveien 34, N-4024 Stavanger, Norway
PHONE: +47 (51) 516210
FAX: +47 (51) 516225
WEBSITE: http://www.misjonshs.no

Stavanger University College

Postboks 2557, Ullandhaug, N-4300 Sandnes, Norway
PHONE: +47 (51) 831000
FAX: +47 (51) 831050
E-MAIL: postmottak@his.no
WEBSITE: http://www.his.no

Agder College

Postboks 607, N-4604 Kristiansand, Norway
PHONE: +47 (38) 141000
FAX: +47 (38) 141001
E-MAIL: svein.a.pedersen@hia.no
WEBSITE: http://www.hia.no

University of Bergen

Postboks 7800, Universitetet I Bergen, Museplass 1, N-5020 Bergen, Norway
PHONE: +47 (55) 580000
FAX: +47 (55) 589643

E-MAIL: jan.muklebust@fa.uib.no
WEBSITE: http://www.uib.no

Bergen College

Postboks 7030, N-5020 Bergen, Norway
PHONE: +47 (55) 587504
FAX: +47 (55) 587789
E-MAIL: opptak@hib.no
WEBSITE: http://www.hib.no

Bergen School of Architecture

Sandviksboder 59-61 A, N-5035 Bergen, Norway
PHONE: +47 (55) 363880
FAX: +47 (55) 363881
E-MAIL: adm@bergenarkitektskole.no
WEBSITE: http://www.bergenarkitektskole.no

Norwegian School of Economics & Business Administration

Helleveien 30, N-5045 Bergen, Norway
PHONE: +47 (55) 959000
FAX: +47 (55) 959100
E-MAIL: nhh.postmottak@nhh.no
WEBSITE: http://www.nhh.no

Stord Haugesund College

Postboks 5000, N-5409 Stord, Norway
PHONE: +47 (53) 491401
FAX: +47 (53) 191300
E-MAIL: postmottak@hsh.no
WEBSITE: http://www.hsh.no

Alesund College

Postboks 5104, Larsgarden, N-6025 Alesund, Norway
PHONE: +47 (70) 161200
FAX: +47 (70) 161300
E-MAIL: postmottak@hials.no
WEBSITE: http://www.hials.no

Volda College

Postboks 500, N-6106 Volda, Norway
PHONE: +47 (70) 075000
FAX: +47 (70) 075051
E-MAIL: gs@hivolda.no
WEBSITE: http://www.hivolda.no

Sogndal College

Postboks 133, N-6851 Sogndal, Norway
PHONE: +47 (57) 676000
FAX: +47 (57) 676100
E-MAIL: post@admin.hisf.no
WEBSITE: http://www.hisf.no

Sor-Trondelag University College

Orionveien 19, N-7004 Trondheim, Norway
PHONE: +47 (73) 559000
FAX: +47 (73) 559051
E-MAIL: postmottak@hio.no
WEBSITE: http://www.hist.no

Norwegian University of Science & Technology

Universitetet I Trondheim, N-7491 Trondheim, Norway
PHONE: +47 (73) 595000
FAX: +47 (73) 595310
E-MAIL: postmottak@adm.ntnu.no
WEBSITE: http://www.ntnu.no

Nord-Trondelag College

Kongensgt.42, Postboks 145, N-7702 Steinkjer, Norway
PHONE: +47 (74) 112000
FAX: +47 (74) 112001
E-MAIL: webmaster@hint.no
WEBSITE: http://www.hint.no

Narvik College

Postboks 385, N-8505 Narvik, Norway
PHONE: +47 (76) 966000
FAX: +47 (76) 966810
E-MAIL: postmottak@hin.no
WEBSITE: http://www.hin.no

Nesna College

N-8700 Nesna, Norway
PHONE: +47 (75) 057800
FAX: +47 (75) 057900
E-MAIL: ninfo@hinesna.no
WEBSITE: http://www.hinesna.no

Universitetet i Tromso

N-9037 Tromso, Norway
PHONE: +47 (77) 644000
E-MAIL: astrid.revhaug@adm.uit.no
WEBSITE: http://www.uit.no

Tromso University College

Central Administration, Mellomveien 110, N-9293 Tromso, Norway
PHONE: +47 (77) 660300
FAX: +47 (77) 689956

E-MAIL: postmottak@hitos.no
WEBSITE: http://www.hitos.no

Harstad College

Havnegata 5, N-9480 Harstad, Norway
PHONE: +47 (77) 058100
FAX: +47 (77) 058101
E-MAIL: postmottak@hih.no
WEBSITE: http://www.hih.no

Finnmark College

Follumsvei 31, N-9509 Alta, Norway
PHONE: +47 (78) 450500
FAX: +47 (78) 434438
E-MAIL: postmattak@hifm.no
WEBSITE: http://www.hifm.no

Sami University College

Hannoluchkka 45, N-9520 Guovdageaidnu, Norway
PHONE: +47 (78) 487700
FAX: +47 (78) 487702
E-MAIL: postmottak@samiskhr.no
WEBSITE: http://www.samiskhs.no

NEWSPAPERS AND MAGAZINES

Adresseavisen

Adresseavisen ASA, PO Box 6070, 7003 Trondheim, Norway
PHONE: +47 72500000
FAX: +47 72501754
E-MAIL: annonse@adresseavisen.no
WEBSITE: http://www.adresseavisen.no
TITLE: Editor
CONTACT: Gunnar Flikke
CIRCULATION: 95,000

Aftenposten

Schibstedgruppen A.S., PO Box 1178, Sentrum, N-0107 Oslo, Norway
PHONE: +47 22863000
FAX: +47 22426325
E-MAIL: aftenposten@aftenposten.no
WEBSITE: http://www.aftenposten.no
TITLE: Editor
CONTACT: Einar Hanseid
CIRCULATION: 280,000 daily); 223,000 Sun. morning)

Asker Og Baerums Budstikke

PO Box 133, 1361 Billingstad, Norway
PHONE: +47 66980901
FAX: +47 66770011
TITLE: Editor
CONTACT: Adreas Gjoolme
CIRCULATION: 31,900

Bergens Tidende

Bergens Tidende A/S, Nygaardsgaten 5-11, Postbox 875, 5020 Bergen, Norway
PHONE: +47 55214500
FAX: +47 55312306
E-MAIL: webmaster@bergens-tidende.no
WEBSITE: http://www.bergens-tidende.no
TITLE: Editor
CONTACT: Einar Haalien
CIRCULATION: 65,450

Dagbladet

A/S Dagbladet, PO Box 1184, Sentrum, N-0107 Oslo, Norway
PHONE: +47 22310600
FAX: +47 22310501
E-MAIL: annonse@dagbladet.no
WEBSITE: http://www.dagbladet.no
TITLE: Editor
CONTACT: Harald Stanghelle
CIRCULATION: 204,850 daily); 275,900 Sat.)

Dagens Nearingsliv

PO Box 1182, Sentrum, N-0107 Oslo, Norway
PHONE: +47 22001000
FAX: +47 22001070
E-MAIL: annonser@dn.nhst.no
WEBSITE: http://www.dn.nhst.no
TITLE: Editor-in-Chief
CONTACT: Kare Valebrokk
CIRCULATION: 60,027

Drammens Tidende/Buskeruds Blad

PO Box 7033, 3007 Drammen, Norway
PHONE: +47 32204000
FAX: +47 32204210
E-MAIL: annonser@dtbb.no
WEBSITE: http://www.dtbb.no
CIRCULATION: 45,200

Faedrelandsvennen

Faedrelandsvennen A/S, PO Box 369, Svanedamsveien 10, 4601 Kristiansand, Norway
PHONE: +47 38013000
FAX: +47 38013710
E-MAIL: fep@fedrelandsvennen.no
WEBSITE: http://www.fedrelandsvennen.no

TITLE: Editor
CONTACT: Finn Holmer-Hoven
CIRCULATION: 47,386

Haugesunds Avis

Haugesunds Avis A/S, PO Box 2024, Posttermundalen, 5501 Haugeslund, Norway
PHONE: +47 52720000
FAX: +47 52720440
E-MAIL: redaksjunen@haugesunds-avis.no
WEBSITE: http://www.haugesunds-avis.no
TITLE: Editor
CONTACT: Ragnar Larsen
CIRCULATION: 38,200

Nordlands Framtid

Storgt. 9, 8002 Bodo, Norway
PHONE: +47 75505000
FAX: +47 75505060
WEBSITE: www4.nordlands-framtid.no
TITLE: Editor
CONTACT: Thor Woje
CIRCULATION: 21,060

Oppland Arbeiderblad

PO Box 24, 2801 Gjosvik, Norway
PHONE: +47 62519500
FAX: +47 62519503
E-MAIL: annonse@ha-nett.no
WEBSITE: http://www.ha-nett.no
TITLE: Editor
CONTACT: Magne Bjornerud
CIRCULATION: 28,169

Stavanger Aftenblad

Stavanger Aftenblad ASA, PO Box 229, 4001 Stavanger, Norway
PHONE: +47 51500000
FAX: +47 51893009
E-MAIL: smimedia@pip.dk.net.dk
WEBSITE: http://www.stavanger-aftenblad.no
TITLE: Editor
CONTACT: Thor Bjrane Bore
CIRCULATION: 72,626

Sunnmorsposten

PO Box 123, 6001 Alesund, Norway
PHONE: +47 70120000
FAX: +47 70129977
E-MAIL: redaksjon@smp.no
WEBSITE: http://www.smp.no
TITLE: Editor
CONTACT: Harald H. Rise
CIRCULATION: 36,846

Tonsbergers Blad

Postboks 2003, Posttermiralen, 3103 Tonsberg, Norway
PHONE: +47 33373000
FAX: +47 33310540
WEBSITE: http://www.tonsbergs-blad.no
TITLE: Editor
CONTACT: Marit Haukom
CIRCULATION: 33,293

Vart Land

Vart Land A/S, PB 1180, Sentrum, N-0107 Oslo, Norway
PHONE: +47 22310310
FAX: +47 22310305
E-MAIL: tips@vartland.no
WEBSITE: http://www.vartland.no
TITLE: Editor
CONTACT: Helge Simonnes
CIRCULATION: 30,200

Verdens Gang - VG

Verdens Gang A/S, Postboks 1185, Sentrum, N-0107 Oslo, Norway
PHONE: +47 22000000
FAX: +47 22426780
E-MAIL: annonse@vg.no
WEBSITE: http://www.vg.no
TITLE: Editor
CONTACT: Bernt Olufsen
CIRCULATION: 364,612

Bilbransjen - Bilteknisk Fagblad

Drammensv. 97, Oslo 2, Norway
TITLE: Editor
CONTACT: Oyvind Holmvik
CIRCULATION: 5,000
TYPE: Transportation, automotive, general

Film og Kino

Dronningens gate 16, N-0152 Oslo, Norway
FAX: +47 22474698
TITLE: Editor
CONTACT: Kalle Loechen
CIRCULATION: 3,800
TYPE: Performing arts, film, general

Hjemmet

Boks 5001, Majorstua, N-0301 Oslo, Norway
TITLE: Editor

CONTACT: Roennaug Greaker
CIRCULATION: 240,000
TYPE: Social science, general

NaFo-Nytt

Postboks 7051, Homansbyen, N-0306 Oslo 3, Norway
FAX: +47 02551630
TITLE: Editor
CONTACT: Bjoerg Duve
CIRCULATION: 4,149
TYPE: Political science, labor and industrial relations, technology, agriculture and animal husbandry

Naa

Soerkedalsveien 10 A, N-0369 Oslo, Norway
FAX: +47 22961383
TITLE: Editor
CONTACT: Gunnar Holm
CIRCULATION: 83,217
TYPE: Social science, general

Sau og Geit

PO Box 2323, Solli, N-0201 Oslo 2, Norway
FAX: +47 2431660
TITLE: Editor
CONTACT: Arne Maurtvedt
CIRCULATION: 21,000
TYPE: Technology, agriculture and animal husbandry

Vaare Veger

PO Box 2476, Solli, N-0202 Oslo, Norway
FAX: +47 22947601
TITLE: Editor
CONTACT: Jarle Skoglund
TYPE: Technology, civil engineering

PUBLISHERS

Universitetsforlaget (Scandinavian University Press)

Postboks 2959, Toyen, N-0608 Oslo, Norway
PHONE: +47 22575300
FAX: +47 22575353
E-MAIL: books@scup.no; journals@scup.no
WEBSITE: http://www.scup.no
TITLE: Managing Director
CONTACT: Siri Hatlen
SUBJECTS: Behavioral Sciences, Business, Education, Language Arts, Linguistics, Law, Mechanical Engineering, Medicine, Nursing, Dentistry, Philosophy, Science (General), Modern language, Heatlhcare
TOTAL PUBLISHED: 2,000 Print; 10 CD-ROM; 35 Online; 20 Audio

Det Norske Samlaget

Postboks 4672, Sofienberg, N-0506 Oslo, Norway
PHONE: +47 22687600
FAX: +47 22687502
E-MAIL: b.nummedal@samlaget.no
TITLE: Managing Director
CONTACT: Audun Heskestad
SUBJECTS: Biography, Fiction, History, Philosophy, Poetry, Religion-Other
TOTAL PUBLISHED: (annually) 200 Print; 1 CD-ROM

Lunde Forlag og Bokhandel A/S

Sinsenveien 25, N-0572 Oslo
PHONE: +47 (22) 007350
FAX: +47 (22) 007373
E-MAIL: lunde@nlm.no
TITLE: President and Publisher
CONTACT: Asbjorn Kvalbein
SUBJECTS: Biography, Education, Fiction, Poetry, Religion-Other, Theology
TOTAL PUBLISHED: 250 Print

Pax Forlag A/S

Postboks 2336 Solli, N-0201 Oslo, Norway
PHONE: +47 22557070
FAX: +47 22554183
TITLE: Managing Director
CONTACT: Bjorn Smith Simonsen
SUBJECTS: Fiction, Nonfiction (General), Philosophy, Psychology, Psychiatry, Social Sciences, Sociology, Woman's Studies
TOTAL PUBLISHED: (annually) 60 Print

Novus Forlag

PO Box 748, Sertrum, N-0106 Oslo, Norway
PHONE: +47 22717450
FAX: +47 22718107
E-MAIL: novus@novus.no
WEBSITE: http://www.novus.no
TITLE: Publisher
CONTACT: Olav Rosset
TOTAL PUBLISHED: 200 Print

Snofugl Forlag

Postboks 95, 7084, N-7221 Melhus, Norway
PHONE: +47 72871013

FAX: +47 72871013
TITLE: Manager
CONTACT: Asmund Snofugl
SUBJECTS: Biography, Fiction, Government. Political Science, History, Literature, Literary Criticism, Essays, Nonfiction (General), Poetry
TOTAL PUBLISHED: 150 Print

NKS -Forlaget

Postboks 5853, N-0308 Oslo, Norway
PHONE: +47 225596000
FAX: +47 22596300
E-MAIL: nks-forlaget@nks.no
WEBSITE: http://www..nks.no
TITLE: Managing Director
CONTACT: Halstein Laupsa
SUBJECTS: chemistry, Chemical Engineering, Electronics, Electrical Engineering, English as a Second Language, Environmental Studies, Mathematics, Mechanical Engineering, Physics, Transportation
TOTAL PUBLISHED: 740 Print; 10 CD-ROM; 15 Audio

Gyldendal Norsk Forlag A/S

Postboks 6860, N-0130 St. Olaf, Oslo, Norway
PHONE: +47 22034100
FAX: +47 22034105
TITLE: Managing Director
CONTACT: Geri Mork
SUBJECTS: Art, Biography, Fiction, Government, Political Science, History, How-to, Music, Dance, Philosophy, Poetry, Psychology, Psychiatry, Religion-Other, Science Fiction, Fantasy, Social Sciences, Sociology

Ad-Notam Glydendal

PO Box 6730, N-0130 Oslo, Norway
PHONE: +47 22034300
FAX: +47 22034305
E-MAIL: fredrik.nissen@adnotam.no
TITLE: Managing Director
CONTACT: Fredrik Nissen
SUBJECTS: Accounting, Business, Economics, Education, Finance, Government, Political Science, Health, Nutrition, Law, Medicine, Nursing, Dentistry, Philosophy, Psychology, Psychiatry, Social Sciences, Sociology

Tano Aschehoug A/S

KR Augustsgate 7b, N-0164 Oslo, Norway
PHONE: +47 22985200
FAX: +47 22420164
E-MAIL: post@tano.no
TITLE: Director
CONTACT: Laila Stange
SUBJECTS: Behavioral Sciences, Child Care & Development, Computer Science, Education, Government, Political Science, Law, Management, Marketing, Medicine, Nursing, Dentistry, Nonfiction (General), Psychology, Psychiatry, public Administration, Social Science, Sociology

RELIGIOUS ORGANIZATIONS

Buddhist

Rinzai Zen Center Oslo
Christian Krogs gate 32 B, N-0186 Oslo, Norway
PHONE: +47 (22) 555052
E-MAIL: zen@buddhistforbundet.no
TITLE: Teacher
NAME: Herbert Koudela (Genro Seiun)

Sangha of Floating Clouds
Drivende Skyer, Oslo, Norway
PHONE: +47 (22) 687367
FAX: +47 (22) 995314
E-MAIL: bjoernph@sn.no
TITLE: Contact
NAME: Bjorn Petter Hernes

Svein Myreng
Mellombolgen 26, N-1157 Oslo, Norway
PHONE: +47 (22) 284408
E-MAIL: eevi@ifi.uio.no

Catholic

Oslo Katolske Bispedomme
Akersveien 5, N-0177 Oslo, Norway
PHONE: +47 (23) 219500
FAX: +47 (22) 204857
TITLE: Bishop
NAME: Dr. Gerhard Schwenzer, SS., CC.

Tromso Stift- Nord-Norge
Storgata 94, N-9008 Tromso, Norway
PHONE: +47 (77) 684277
FAX: +47 (77) 684414
TITLE: Biskop -prelat
NAME: Msgr. Gerhard Goebel M.S.F.

Trondheim Stift- Midt-Norge
Sverres gate 1, N-7012 Trondheim, Norway
PHONE: +47 (72) 527705
FAX: +47 (73) 528790
TITLE: Biskop
NAME: Msgr. Georg Muller SS. CC.

Jewish

The Jewish Community of Oslo
Bergstien 13, N-0172 Oslo, Norway
PHONE: +47 (22) 696570
E-MAIL: kontor@dmt.oslo.no
WEBSITE: http://www.dmt.oslo.no
TITLE: Contact
NAME: Leon Katz

Protestant

Federation of Methodist Women Norway (FMWN)

Metodistkirkens Kvinneforbund Norge (MKN)
Akersbakken 37, N-0172 Oslo, Norway
PHONE: +47 (63) 801501
FAX: +47 (63) 801501
TITLE: President
NAME: Martha Borgen

International Federation of Free Evangelical Churches (IFFEC)

Internationaler Bund Freier Evangelischer Gemeinden (IBFEG)
Linneavn 54, N-3050 Mjondalen, Norway
PHONE: +47 (32) 878850
FAX: +47 (32) 878850
E-MAIL: iffec@online.no
TITLE: Gen.Sec.
NAME: Dr. Bjorn Oyvind Fjeld

Stavanger International Church
Vaisenhusgata 41, N-4012 Stavanger, Norway
PHONE: +47 (51) 564843
FAX: +47 (51) 564670
E-MAIL: office@sic.no
TITLE: Church Administration

The Salvation Army
Box 6866, St Olavs Plass, N-0130 Oslo 1, Norway
PHONE: +47 (22) 998500
FAX: +47 (22) 208449
E-MAIL: hk@frelsesarmeen.no
WEBSITE: http://www.frelsesarmeen.no/

FURTHER READING

Articles

"Norway." *The Economist (US),* March 4, 2000, vol. 354, no. 8160, p. 106.

"Jens Stoltenberg, Norway's Cautious Prime Minister." *The Economist (US),* July 22, 2000, vol. 356, no. 8180, p. 52.

"Oslo Shake-Up After a Dispute on Pollution." *New York Times,* March 12, 2000, p. A9.

"Statoil No Longer Looks Sacred." *Business Week,* September 4, 2000, no. 3697, p. 20.

Books

DeVries, Kelly. *The Norwegian Invasion of England in 1066.* Rochester, NY: Boydell Press, 1999.

Lee, Phil. *Norway: The Rough Guide.* 2d ed. London: Rough Guides, 2000.

Moore, Tim. *Frost on My Moustache: The Arctic Exploits of a Lord and a Loafer.* New York: St. Martin's Press, 2000.

NORWAY: STATISTICAL DATA

For sources and notes see "Sources of Statistics" at the front of each volume.

GEOGRAPHY

Geography

Area:

Total: 324,220 sq km.

Land: 307,860 sq km.

Land boundaries:

Total: 2,515 km.

Border countries: Finland 729 km, Sweden 1,619 km, Russia 167 km.

Coastline: 21,925 km (includes mainland 3,419 km, large islands 2,413 km, long fjords, numerous small islands, and minor indentations 16,093 km).

Climate: temperate along coast, modified by North Atlantic Current; colder interior; rainy year-round on west coast.

Terrain: glaciated; mostly high plateaus and rugged mountains broken by fertile valleys; small, scattered plains; coastline deeply indented by fjords; arctic tundra in north.

Natural resources: petroleum, copper, natural gas, pyrites, nickel, iron ore, zinc, lead, fish, timber, hydropower.

Land use:

Arable land: 3%

Permanent crops: 0%

Permanent pastures: 0%

Forests and woodland: 27%

Other: 70% (1993 est.).

HUMAN FACTORS

Demographics (A)

	1990	1995	1998	2000	2010	2020	2030	2040	2050
Population	4,242	4,359	4,433	4,481	4,677	4,862	5,018	5,068	5,061
Life expectancy - males	73.1	74.8	75.7	75.7	77.1	78.3	79.2	79.9	80.5
Life expectancy - females	80.1	80.9	81.4	81.8	83.2	84.4	85.3	86.0	86.6
Birth rate (per 1,000)	15.0	13.8	13.1	12.8	11.1	11.3	10.7	10.0	10.0
Death rate (per 1,000)	10.9	10.4	9.9	9.9	9.4	9.4	10.5	11.6	12.3
Women of reproductive age (15-49 yrs.)	1,056	1,075	1,067	1,066	1,084	1,071	1,057	1,066	1,037
Fertility rate	2.0	1.9	1.8	1.8	1.8	1.8	1.7	1.7	1.7

Except as noted, values for vital statistics are in thousands; life expectancy is in years.

Health Personnel

	National Data	World Data (wtd ave)
Total health expenditure as a percentage of GDP, 1990-1998[a]		
Public sector	6.2	2.5
Private sector	1.3	2.9
Total[b]	7.5	5.5
Health expenditure per capita in U.S. dollars, 1990-1998[a]		
Purchasing power parity	1,996	561
Total	2,616	483
Availability of health care facilities per 100,000 people		
Hospital beds 1990-1998[a]	1,500	330
Doctors 1992-1995[a]	NA	122
Nurses 1992-1995[a]	NA	248

Health Indicators

	National Data	World Data
Life expectancy at birth (years)		
1980	76	61
1998	78	67
Daily per capita supply of calories		
1970	3,022	2,358
1997	3,357	2,791
Daily per capital supply of protein		
1997 (grams)	104	74
Total fertility rate (births per woman)		
1980	1.7	3.7
1998	1.8	2.7
Population with access (%)		
To safe water (1990-96)	100	NA
To sanitation (1990-96)	100	NA
People living with (1997)		
Tuberculosis (cases per 100,000)	4.7	60.4
HIV/AIDS (% aged 15 - 49 years)	0.06	0.99

Infants and Malnutrition

	National Data	World Data (wtd ave)
Under 5 mortality rate (1989)	4	NA
% of infants with low birthweight (1992-98)[1]	5	17
Births attended by skilled health staff (% of total births 1996-98)	100	52
% fully immunized at 1 year of age (1995-98)[1]		
TB	NA	82
DPT	92[2]	77
Polio	92[2]	77
Measles	93[2]	74
Prevalence of child malnutrition (1992-98)[1] (based on weight for age, % of children under 5 years)	NA	30

Ethnic Division

Norwegian (Nordic, Alpine, Baltic), Lapps (Sami) 20,000.

Religion

Evangelical Lutheran (state church) 86%

Other Protestant and Roman Catholic 3%

Other 1%

None and unknown 10%

Data for 1997.

Major Languages

Norwegian (official). There are small Lapp- and Finnish-speaking minorities.

EDUCATION

Public Education Expenditures

	1980	1997
Public expenditures on education as % of GNP	6.5	7.4
Expenditures per student as % of GNP per capita		
Primary	27.2[2]	31.2
Secondary	14.9	18.8
Tertiary	38.2	45.3
Pupils per teacher at the primary level	NA	NA
Duration of primary education in years	NA	9
World data for comparison		
Public expenditures on education as % of GNP (mean)	3.9	4.8

Pupils per teacher at the primary level (wtd ave)	NA	33
Duration of primary education in years (mean)	NA	9

Educational Attainment (A)

Age group (1990) . . . . .16+

Population of this age group 3,460,669

Highest level attained (%)

No schooling 0

First level

Not completed 0

Completed . . . . .NA

Entered second level

Lower Secondary 37.3

Upper Secondary 44.0

Entered post-secondary 18.7

Libraries

National Libraries **1997**

Administrative Units 2

Service Points or Branches .9

Number of Volumes (000) 2,832

Registered Users (000) .NA

Loans to Users (000) . . . . .NA

Total Library Staff 334

Public Libraries **1997**

Administrative Units 435

Service Points or Branches 1,108

Number of Volumes (000) 20,508

Registered Users (000) 19,858

Loans to Users (000) 22,204

Total Library Staff 1,870

GOVERNMENT & LAW

Political Parties

Parliament	% of vote	no. of seats
Labor Party	35.0%	65
Center Party	7.9%	11
Conservative Party	14.3%	23
Christian People's Party	13.7%	25
Socialist Left Party	6.0%	9
Progress Party	15.3%	25
Liberal Party	4.4%	6
Other parties	1.6%	1

Elections were last held 15 September 1997 (next to be held in September 2001).

Government Budgets (A)

Year: 1997

Total Expenditures: 195,412 Millions of Kroner

Expenditures as a percentage of the total by function:

General public services and public order 7.68

Defense 6.77

Education 6.93

Health 4.51

Social Security and Welfare 38.38

Housing and community amenities 0.53

Recreational, cultural, and religious affairs 1.21

Fuel and energy 0.26

Agriculture, forestry, fishing, and hunting 3.95

Mining, manufacturing, and construction 0.43

Transportation and communication 4.83

Other economic affairs and services 2.51

Crime

Crime volume (for 1998)

Crimes reported 446,672

Total persons convicted 178,669

Crimes per 100,000 population 10,048

Persons responsible for offenses

Total number suspects 70,573

Total number of female suspects 11,292

Total number of juvenile suspects 26,112

(Continued on next page.)

LABOR FORCE

Total Labor Force (A)

2.7 million (1999 est.).

Labor Force by Occupation

Services 74%

Industry 22%

Agriculture, forestry, and fishing 4%

Data for 1995.

Unemployment Rate

2.9% (1999 est.)

PRODUCTION SECTOR

Energy Production

Production ....115.485 billion kWh

Production by source

Fossil fuel 0.58%

Hydro 99.16%

Nuclear 0%

Other 0.26%

Exports ....4.4 billion kWh

Data for 1998.

Energy Consumption

Consumption ....111.001 billion kWh

Imports ....8.000 billion kWh

Data for 1998.

(Continued on next page.)

GOVERNMENT & LAW (cont.)

Military Affairs (A)

	1990	1992	1995	1996	1997
Military expenditures					
Current dollars (mil.)	2,950	3,400	3,260	3,270	3,250
1997 constant dollars (mil.)	3,460	3,770	3,370	3,320	3,250
Armed forces (000)	51	36	38	38	33
Gross national product (GNP)					
Current dollars (bil.)	97	110	134	145	152
1997 constant dollars (bil.)	114	122	139	147	152
Central government expenditures (CGE)					
1997 constant dollars (bil.)	50	59	56	55	67[e]
People (mil.)	4.2	4.3	4.4	4.4	4.4
Military expenditure as % of GNP	3.0	3.1	2.4	2.3	2.1
World data on military expenditure as % of GNP	4.5	3.4	2.7	2.6	2.6
Military expenditure as % of CGE	6.9	6.4	6.0	6.1	4.8
World data on military expenditure as % of CGE	17.0	12.5	10.5	10.3	10.2
Military expenditure per capita (1997 $)	814	880	774	759	739
World data on military expenditure per capita (1997 $)	242	173	146	143	145
Armed forces per 1,000 people (soldiers)	12.0	8.4	8.7	8.7	7.5
World data on armed forces per 1,000 people (soldiers)	5.3	4.5	4.1	3.9	3.8
GNP per capita (1997 $)	26,900	28,600	31,900	33,600	34,600
Arms imports[6]					
Current dollars (mil.)	490	430	200	290	250
1997 constant dollars (mil.)	574	477	207	295	250
Arms exports[6]					
Current dollars (mil.)	20	40	20	20	10
1997 constant dollars (mil.)	23	44	21	20	10
Total imports[7]					
Current dollars (mil.)	27,230	25,900	32,970	35,610	35,710
1997 constant dollars (mil.)	31,890	28,720	34,140	36,210	35,710
Total exports[7]					
Current dollars (mil.)	34,050	35,180	41,990	49,640	48,540
1997 constant dollars (mil.)	39,870	39,000	43,480	50,470	48,540
Arms as percent of total imports[8]	1.8	1.7	0.6	0.8	0.7
Arms as percent of total exports[8]	0.1	0.1	0	0	0

PRODUCTION SECTOR (cont.)

Transportation

Highways:

Total: 90,741 km.

Paved: 67,602 km (including 128 km of expressways).

Unpaved: 23,139 km (1998 est.).

Waterways: 1,577 km along west coast; navigable by 2.4 m draft vessels maximum.

Pipelines: refined petroleum products 53 km.

Merchant marine:

Total: 788 ships (1,000 GRT or over) totaling 21,460,260 GRT/34,178,125 DWT.

Ships by type: bulk 100, cargo 142, chemical tanker 111, combination bulk 9, combination ore/oil 35, container 18, liquified gas 86, multi-functional large load carrier 1, passenger 11, petroleum tanker 157, refrigerated cargo 11, roll-on/roll-off 48, short-sea passenger 22, vehicle carrier 37 (1999 est.)

Note: the government has created an internal register, the Norwegian International Ship register (NIS), as a subset of the Norwegian register; ships on the NIS enjoy many benefits of flags of convenience and do not have to be crewed by Norwegians.

Airports: 103 (1999 est.).

Airports - with paved runways: 67.

Airports - with unpaved runways: 36.

Top Agriculture Products

Barley, other grains, potatoes; beef, milk; fish.

Top Mining Products (A)

	National Production	World Production
Commodities in 1998		
Aluminium (000 mt)	996	22,100
Copper (000 mt)	2.7	12,200
Lead (000 mt)	1	3,080
Nickel (000 mt)	3	1,140

MANUFACTURING SECTOR

GDP & Manufacturing Summary (A)

	1980	1985	1990	1995
GDP ($-1990 mil.)[1]	83,082	97,949	105,524	125,035
Per capita ($-1990)[1]	20,333	23,585	24,882	28,863
Manufacturing share (%) (current prices)[1]	15.7	13.8	13.2	14.0
Manufacturing				
Value added ($-1990 mil.)[1]	14,041	15,028	14,437	16,092
Industrial production index	95	99	100	110
Value added ($ mil.)	9,339	7,660	13,504	16,422[e]
Gross output ($ mil.)	31,936	28,186	50,107	56,962
Employment (000)	354	312	271	255[e]
Profitability (% of gross output)				
Intermediate input (%)	71	73	73	71[e]
Wages and salaries inc. supplements (%)	21	20	19	20[e]
Gross operating surplus	8	7	8	9[e]
Productivity ($)				
Gross output per worker	89,656	89,774	184,331	216,892[e]
Value added per worker	26,217	24,397	49,677	64,116[e]
Average wage (inc. supplements)	19,129	17,852	35,540	43,972[e]
Value added ($ mil.)				
Food products	908	633	1,307	2,137[e]
Beverages	292	296	660	779[e]
Tobacco products	168	220	478	659[e]
Textiles	213	126	191	250[e]
Wearing apparel	101	59	58	67[e]
Leather and fur products	18	9	16	18[e]
Footwear	24	10	11	13[e]
Wood and wood products	587	366	619	584[e]
Furniture and fixtures	196	165	236	255[e]
Paper and paper products	452	400	787	721[e]
Printing and publishing	668	717	1,381	1,674[e]
Industrial chemicals	452	422	811	733[e]
Other chemical products	227	183	393	539[e]
Petroleum refineries	103	24	195	193[e]
Misc. petroleum and coal products	53	59	63	76[e]
Rubber products	51	39	58	25[e]
Plastic products	170	147	278	366[e]

(Continued on next page.)

GDP & Manufacturing Summary (A) (cont.)

	1980	1985	1990	1995
Pottery, china and earthenware	26	18	27	31[e]
Glass and glass products	55	50	77	91[e]
Other non-metal mineral products	281	215	361	366[e]
Iron and steel	385	276	347	396[e]
Non-ferrous metals	743	550	826	832[e]
Metal products	595	465	784	912[e]
Non-electrical machinery	933	1,079	1,590	2,121[e]
Electrical machinery	547	498	751	1,004[e]
Transport equipment	1,000	555	1,028	1,300[e]
Prof. and scientific equipment	32	39	82	148[e]
Other manufacturing	59	42	89	133[e]

COMMUNICATIONS

Daily Newspapers

	National Data	World Data for Comparison
Daily Newspapers		
Number of Dailies	83	8,391
Total Circulation (000)	2,578	548,000
Circulation per 1,000 inhabitants	590	96

Telecommunications

Telephones - main lines in use: 2,325,010 (1997).

Telephones - mobile cellular: 1,676,763 (1997).

Telephone system: high-quality domestic and international telephone, telegraph, and telex services.

Domestic: domestic satellite system.

International: 2 buried coaxial cable systems; 4 coaxial submarine cables; satellite earth stations - NA Eutelsat, NA Intelsat (Atlantic Ocean), and 1 Inmarsat (Atlantic and Indian Ocean regions) Note: Norway shares the Inmarsat earth station with the other Nordic countries (Denmark, Finland, Iceland, and Sweden).

Radio broadcast stations: AM 5, FM at least 650, shortwave 1 (1998).

Radios: 4.03 million (1997).

Television broadcast stations: 209 (1997).

Televisions: 2.03 million (1997).

Internet Service Providers (ISPs): 21 (1999).

FINANCE, ECONOMICS, & TRADE

Economic Indicators

National product: GDP—purchasing power parity—$111.3 billion (1999 est.).

National product real growth rate: 0.8% (1999 est.).

National product per capita: $25,100 (1999 est.).

Inflation rate—consumer price index: 2.8% (1999 est.).

Exchange Rates

Exchange rates:

Norwegian kroner (NKr) per US$1

January 2000	8.0129
1999	7.7992
1998	7.5451
1997	7.0734
1996	6.4498
1995	6.3352

(Continued on next page.)

Balance of Payments

	1994	1995	1996	1997	1998
Exports of goods (f.o.b.)	35,016	42,312	49,968	48,737	40,637
Imports of goods (f.o.b.)	−27,520	−33,741	−37,037	−37,585	−39,070
Trade balance	7,496	8,571	12,931	11,152	1,566
Services - debits	−12,065	−13,131	−13,545	−14,776	−15,370
Services - credits	12,247	13,347	14,171	14,624	14,132
Private transfers (net)	1,291	1,221	1,227	1,186	1,199
Government transfers (net)	−1,054	−1,200	−1,019	−985	−1,078
Overall balance	3,760	4,854	10,240	8,017	−2,161

Top Import Origins

$38.6 billion (f.o.b., 1999 est.)

Origins (1998)

- EU 69%
  - Sweden 15%
  - Germany 14%
  - United Kingdom 10%
  - Denmark 7%
- United States 7%
- Japan 4%

Top Export Destinations

$47.3 billion (f.o.b., 1999 est.)

Destinations (1998)

- EU 77%
  - United Kingdom 17%
  - Germany 12%
  - Netherlands 10%
  - Sweden 10%
  - France 8%
- United States 7%

Foreign Aid

Donor: ODA, $1.4 billion (1998).

Import/Export Commodities

Import Commodities	Export Commodities
Machinery and equipment	Petroleum and petroleum products
Chemicals	Machinery and equipment
Metals	Metals
Foodstuffs	Chemicals
	Ships
	Fish

OMAN

Sultanate of Oman
Saltanat ʿUman

CAPITAL: Muscat (Masqat).

FLAG: The flag is red with a broad stripe of white at the upper fly and green at the lower fly. In the upper left corner, white crossed swords overlay a ceremonial dagger.

ANTHEM: *Nashid as-Salaam as-Sutani (Sultan's National Anthem).*

MONETARY UNIT: The Omani riyal (RO), established in November 1972, is a paper currency of 1,000 baizas. There are coins of 2, 5, 10, 25, 50, 100, 250, and 500 baizas, and notes of 100, 250, and 500 baizas (the last two being replaced by coins) and 1, 5, 10, 20, and 50 riyals. RO1 = \$2.60417 (or \$1 = RO0.384).

WEIGHTS AND MEASURES: The metric system was adopted on 15 November 1974. The imperial and local system are also used.

HOLIDAYS: Accession of the Sultan, 23 July; National Day, 18 November; Sultan's Birthday, 19 November. Movable Muslim religious holidays include ʿId al-Fitr, ʿId al-ʿAdhaʾ, and Milad an-Nabi.

TIME: 4 PM = noon GMT. Solar time is also observed.

LOCATION AND SIZE: The Sultanate of Oman is the second-largest country on the Arabian Peninsula after Saudi Arabia, with an area officially estimated at 212,460 square kilometers (82,031 square miles), slightly smaller than the state of Kansas. The northernmost part of Oman, separated from the rest of the country by the United Arab Emirates, juts into the Strait of Hormuz. The total estimated boundary length is 3,466 kilometers (2,154 miles). The capital, Muscat, is in the northeastern part of the country.

CLIMATE: Annual rainfall varies from 10 centimeters (4 inches) in Muscat to up to 64 centimeters (25 inches) in Zufar. The climate generally is very hot, with temperatures reaching 54°C (129°F) in the hot season.

INTRODUCTORY SURVEY

RECENT HISTORY

In 1920, the Treaty of Seeb was signed between the sultan (king of a Muslim state) of Muscat and the imam (Muslim leader) of Oman. From 1920 to 1954, there was comparative peace. On the death of the imam in 1954, Saʿid bin Taymur moved to succeed him.

In that year, Saʿid concluded an agreement with the Petroleum Development (Oman) Ltd., a British-managed oil company, to maintain a small army, the Muscat and Oman Field Force (MOFF). In early 1955, MOFF together with British troops occupied all of Oman, and expelled a rebellious new imam. In 1962, the sultanate of Muscat was proclaimed an independent state. Oman joined the United Nations late in 1971.

In 1970, Qabus bin Saʿid Al Said ousted his father, changed the name of the country from Muscat and Oman to the Sultanate of Oman, and has ruled ever since. He has presided over a broad modernization program, opening the country to the outside world while preserving political and military ties with the British. Oman dominates the Strait of Hormuz that links the Gulf of Oman with the Persian Gulf. Its strategic importance drew Oman and the United States closer together during the Iran-Iraq war in the 1980s and the Gulf War in 1991. As of 1999, Oman held a middle-of-the-road stance of conciliation and compromise in Middle Eastern politics, maintaining good relations with all Middle Eastern countries.

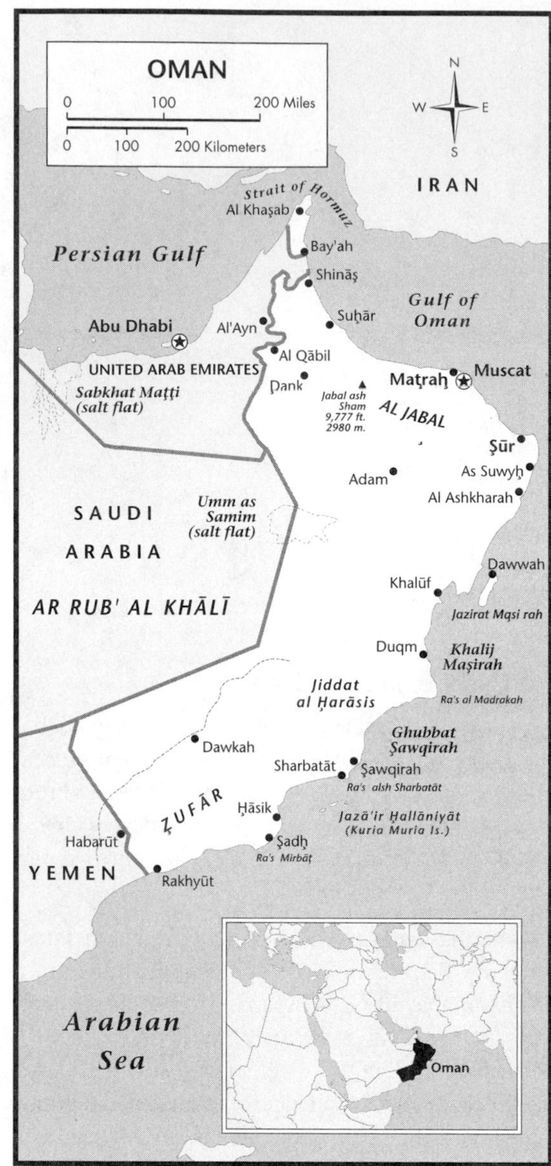

By 1959, when the last of the insurgents supporting the imam were defeated, Sa'id voided the office and declared the Treaty of Seeb terminated.

GOVERNMENT

Oman's sultan is an absolute monarch. On November 6, 1996, the sultan issued a decree providing a basic law which among other things clarifies royal succession, provides for a prime minister, establishes a bicameral legislature, and guarantees basic civil rights for Oman's citizens.

The chief of state and head of government is the monarch who holds the title of Sultan and Prime Minister. Qabus bin Said Al Said has held this position since July 1970. The monarch is assisted by a cabinet that he appoints.

The legislative branch consists of the bicameral Majlis Oman, made up of an upper chamber, the 41-seat Majlis ad-Dawla, and a lower chamber, the 82-seat Majlis ash-Shura. Members of the upper chamber are appointed by the monarch and have only advisory power. Members of the lower chamber are elected by limited suffrage. The monarch makes all final selections and can negate election results. The lower chamber has some limited power to propose legislation but otherwise has only advisory powers. Suffrage is limited to approximately 50,000 Omanis chosen by the government to vote in elections for the Majlis ash-Shura.

Judiciary

Qadis, or religious judges, appointed by the sultan, function within each region. Shari'ah courts based on Islamic law administer justice, with the Chief Court at Muscat. Appeals from the Chief Court are made to the sultan, who exercises powers of clemency (mercy or leniency in setting punishment). The magistrate court, a criminal court, rules on violations of the criminal code. Shari'ah courts equate the testimony of one man with that of two women.

In 1996, the sultan issued a basic law that recognized an independent jury. There are no jury trials.

Political Parties

There are no legal political parties nor at present is there any active opposition movement.

DEFENSE

Oman's armed forces, including foreign personnel and British advisors, numbered 43,500 in 2000. The army had 25,000 members, the air force 4,100, and the navy 4,200. Another 4,000 men are in Home Guard units in their tribal areas. In 1999, Oman spent $1.6 billion on defense, or 11.1 percent of its gross domestic product.

ECONOMIC AFFAIRS

Since the mid-1970s, most of the economy has revolved around oil. The hydrocarbons sector accounted for 75 percent of export earnings and government revenues, and 40 percent of GDP in 1999. Based on current oil production reserves should last some twenty to twenty-five years. In recent years, the production of natural gas has become a significant factor in the economy. An underwater gas pipeline to Korea, India, and Japan for the export of gas was scheduled for completion in 2000.

Public Finance

Deficits have been typical since 1982, and are financed by withdrawals from the State General Reserve Fund and external borrowing. Oman's oil resources and low foreign debt enable the government to easily borrow from abroad. Revenues expand and decline largely on the vicissitudes of the world's oil market. When oil prices fell in 1998 creating a deficit the government employed loans and drawing down the State General Reserve Fund. In anticipation of still further drops, the government increased taxes and imposed spending cuts.

The U.S. Central Intelligence Agency estimated that in 1999, government revenues totaled approximately $4 billion, and expenditures were $5.6 billion, including capital expenditures of $2.2 million. External debt was estimated in 1998 to be $4.8 billion.

Income

In 1999, Oman's gross domestic product (GDP) was estimated at $19.6 billion. The GDP averaged about $8,000 per person. The 1999 estimated GDP growth rate was 4 percent and inflation −0.07 percent.

Industry

Besides oil production and refining and natural gas production, industries include cement production, construction, mining and smelting of copper, wood and wood products, fabricated metal products, and small-scale food-processing enterprises.

Banking and Finance

The Central Bank of Oman, set up in April 1975, has powers to regulate credit and is authorized to make temporary advances to the government. The Central Bank has been encouraging banks to merge in order to cut down on the oversupply of banking services.

An Omani stock market, the Muscat Securities Market (MSM), was officially established in 1988 but trading did not begin until the following year. By 1999, there were 131 banks and companies quoted on the exchange with a combined capitalization of $4.4 billion. The MSM has now established a link with the Bahrain Stock Exchange (BSE) where shares can be cross-listed. A similar agreement with Kuwait is expected.

Economic Development

Oman's economic policy operates under five-year development plans. Oman's second five-year plan (1981-1985) suffered to some extent from the impact of declining oil prices in the early 1980s. The objectives of the third development plan (1986-1990) were to encourage the private sector to play a larger role in the economy and to expand such areas as agriculture, fishing, manufacturing, and mining. The fourth five-year development plan (1991-1995) aimed to achieve average annual GDP growth rates of just over 6 percent, and the diversification of the sources of national income in order to reduce the dependence on the oil sector. The declared aim of the fifth five-year plan (1996-2000) is to achieve a balanced budget. To meet this goal, the government plans to increase non-oil revenues, reduce public spending, enhance privatization of the economy, and encourage foreign investment. The plan also calls for growth rates in the GDP of 4.6 percent and an increase in the non-oil sector's share of the economy from 60 percent to 69 percent of GDP by the year 2000. Oman continues to liberalize its markets in an effort to gain membership in the World Trade Organization (WTO) by 2000.

A liquefied natural gas pipeline project to Korea, India, and Japan was to be completed by 2000.

SOCIAL WELFARE

Oman maintains a welfare program that provides old age pensions and disability and survivorship benefits to employed citizens between the ages of fifteen and fifty-nine. Work injury legislation in 1977 provided disability and medical benefits for injured workers.

Traditional Islamic views on the subordinate role of women in society lead most women to work exclusively inside the home. However, some progress is being made in educational opportunities and seen in the number of women entering professional areas such as medicine and communications.

Healthcare

In 1990-1997, there were 0.9 doctors per 1,000 population. In 2000, average life expectancy was 71.8 years. In 1993, 89 percent of the population had access to health care services.

Housing

In 1989, 34 percent of all housing units were traditional Arabic houses, 30 percent were modern apartments, and 36 percent were detached houses. Owners occupied 70 percent of all dwellings.

EDUCATION

The adult literacy rate is estimated at 28.1 percent for the year 2000 (males 19.6 percent; females 38.3 percent). In 1998, there were 411 primary schools with 313,516 students and 12,052 teachers. In secondary schools, there were 12,436 teachers and 217,246 students. Sultan Qabus University opened in 1986. Three teacher colleges and one agricultural college were functioning as of the mid-1980s. In 1998, all higher-level institutions had 16,032 students.

2000 KEY EVENTS TIMELINE

January

- On January 24 a brownish grey stone weighing 2.3 lbs (1,056 grams) is found in the Dhofar region of Oman. Provisionally named Dhofar 019, it is one of the few out of an estimated 20,000 known meteorites confirmed as being of Martian basalt.

April

- Members of the Gulf Cooperation Council (Oman, the United Arab Emirates (UAE), Saudi Arabia, Kuwait, Qatar, and Bahrain) meet in the Omani capital, Muscat. They express a desire to improve relations with Iran and resolve the issue of Iran's disputed takeovers of three islands that dominate the access to the Strait of Hormuz, Abu Musa, and the Greater and Lesser Tunbs.

August

- A firm is set up to oversee the multi-billion dollar Dolphin gas project designed to bring gas from Qatar's North Field to Abu Dhabi, Dubai, and Oman via an 800-km pipeline.

September

- The Gulf Co-operation Council (GCC)—made up of Oman, Bahrain, Kuwait, Qatar, Saudi Arabia and the United Arab Emirates (UAE)—meets to study Qatar's suggestion to lift sanctions imposed on Iraq for its 1990 invasion of Kuwait.

October

- Oman becomes the 139th member of the World Trade Organization (WTO) after nearly four years of negotiations. It is the eighth country in the region to join.
- Oman is awarded loans from an international consortium to finance two natural gas line projects, Sarhani and Salalah.
- Foreigners are banned from selling audio and video cassettes in a move to cut the expatriate workforce.

November

- Plans are made for Operation Swift Sword. The entire armed forces of Oman and 25,000 military personnel from Britain will participate in a six-week joint military exercise.
- Oman celebrates the thirty-year reign of Sultan Qaboos bin Said Al Said on November 20.

December

- Oman makes plans to privatize the Al-Seeb and Salalah airports. During its Sixth Plan 2001-06, Oman's economic plan is to privatize projects. Private sector management of airports is part of the government's aim to benefit from international expertise and competition in airport management.

ANALYSIS OF EVENTS: 2000

BUSINESS AND THE ECONOMY

Diversification and privatization were major economic goals for the Omani government in 2000. Since the mid-1990s Oman had been working to decrease its deficit. Variability in oil prices directly affected the deficit. Privatization of power development, transportation and telecommunications led the way. Reforms in the baking sector also progressed.

However, with the recovery in oil prices and its production levels of oil and gas Oman's economic prospects improved in 2000. Reliance on oil production still predominated as there were new oil and gas finds in the center and south of Oman. A new record for oil production was set and exports of liquefied natural gas were increasing. Oil accounted for about 35–40 percent of gross domestic product (GDP), and 80–90 percent of government revenues. Economic growth in other sectors was less encouraging due to depressed government spending. Extra revenues were used to build up reserves. Non-petroleum-based industrial growth remained less that 10 percent in 1999.

Oman worked to reduce its dependence on oil income through diversification. Its Vision 2020 plan set the oil sector's contribution to GDP at less than 20 percent. Projects aimed toward this development were to develop its gas reserves, an aluminum smelter, an oil refinery, a fertilizer plant, and to build two pipelines. Over the next 20 years the government looks to tourism as a growth sector. Development of the tourist resort on the Gulf of Oman in Al-Suwadi was one such project. Government policy also included replacing expatriate workers who number about 400,000 and made up about 25 percent of the workforce. These expatriate workers were predominantly Indians from the subcontinent.

GOVERNMENT AND POLITICS

The Gulf Cooperation Council (GCC) consisting of Oman, Saudi Arabia, Qatar, Bahrain, Kuwait, and the United Arab Emirates (UAE) condemned Iraq's obstinacy and defiance of legitimate international resolutions and of the international community.

Although some election irregularities for the Shura Council, the main consultative body, were alleged, upon investigation no corroborative evidence was found. Women could both vote and stand for election. Two women won seats and a third lost by only eight votes. Voter participation was high at about 90 percent.

CULTURE AND SOCIETY

In 2000 Omanis complained about the high cost of living. However, Oman had no income tax, health and education were free, and business was subsidized.

Oman, under Sultan Qaboos, has been undergoing a unique restoration program for its ancient forts and castles and oasis settlements. Fifty settlements were in the pilot study area. Two sites were renovated working with UNESCO, the Bahla fort, and the oasis town of Nizwa. The 2000-year-old irrigation system known as "falaj" was falling into disrepair, but was still a viable method of irrigation the government encouraged farmers to use. At Ras al-Jinz near Sur archaeologists gathered evidence to support the theory that over 3,000 years ago Oman traded with East Africa, Mesopotamia and India.

DIRECTORY

CENTRAL GOVERNMENT

Head of State

Sultan and Prime Minister
Qaboos bin Said al-Said, Office of the Prime Minister

Ministers

Deputy Prime Minister
Sayyid Fahad bin Mohamed al-Said, Office of the Deputy Prime Minister, PO Box 721, Muscat PC 113, Oman
PHONE: +968 736086
FAX: +968 738517

Minister of National Heritage and Culture
Faisal bin Ali bin Faisal al-Said, Ministry of National Heritage and Culture, PO Box 668, Muscat PC 113, Oman
PHONE: +968 602735
FAX: +968 602735

Minister of Oil and Gas
Mohammed bin Hamad bin Saif al-Ramahi, Ministry of Oil and Gas, PO Box 551, Muscat PC 113, Oman
PHONE: +968 60333
FAX: +968 696972

Minister of Higher Education
Yahya bin Mahfoudh al-Mantheri, Ministry of Higher Education, PO Box 82, Ruwi PC 112, Oman
PHONE: +968 693148
FAX: +968 513254

Minister of Interior
Sayyid Ali bin Hamoud al-Busaidi, Ministry of the Interior, PO Box 127, Ruwi PC 112, Oman
PHONE: +968 602244
FAX: +968 607145

Minister of Defense
Badr bin Saud bin Hareb al-Bu Saidi, Ministry of Defense, PO Box 113, Muscat PC 113, Oman
PHONE: +968 709199
FAX: +968 618205

Minister of Communications
Salim bin Abdullah al-Ghazali, Ministry of Communications, PO Box 648, Muscat PC 113, Oman
PHONE: +968 702233
FAX: +968 795266

Minister of Health
Ali bin Mohammed bin Moosa, Ministry of Health, PO Box 393, Muscat PC 113, Oman
PHONE: +968 602177
FAX: +968 601430

Minister of Water Resources
Hamed bin Said al-Aufi, Ministry of Water Resources, PO Box 2575, Ruwi PC 112, Oman
PHONE: +968 703552
FAX: +968 703553

Minister of Commerce and Industry
Maqbool bin Ali bin Sultan, Ministry of Commerce and Industry, PO Box 550, Muscat PC 113, Oman
PHONE: +968 799500
FAX: +968 796403

DIPLOMATIC REPRESENTATION

Embassies in Oman

Italy
Way 2411 House n.842 Qurum, Muscat, Oman
PHONE: +968 560968
FAX: +968 564846

United Kingdom
PO Box 300, Muscat PC 113, Oman
PHONE: +968 693077
FAX: +968 693087

United States
Muscat, Oman

JUDICIAL SYSTEM

Chief Court

Magistrate Court

BROADCAST MEDIA

BBC Eastern Relay Station
PO Box 6898, 112 Ruwi, Oman

Radio Sultanate of Oman
Ministry of Information, PO Box 600, 113 Muscat, Oman
PHONE: +968 603222
FAX: +968 603812
WEBSITE: http://www.oman-tv.gov.om
CONTACT: Muna Al Mandheri
LANGUAGE: Arabic and English
TYPE: Government

Sultanate of Oman Television
PO Box 600, 113 Muscat, Oman
PHONE: +968 603222
FAX: +968 602381
CONTACT: Ali Bin Abdallah Al Mujeni
TYPE: Government

COLLEGES AND UNIVERSITIES

Sultan Qaboos University
PO Box 50, Muscat 123, Oman
PHONE: +968 513333
FAX: +968 514455
WEBSITE: http://www.squ.edu.om/

NEWSPAPERS AND MAGAZINES

Oman Daily
E-MAIL: editor@omandaily.com
WEBSITE: http://www.omandaily.com

Oman Daily Observer
PO Box 974, PC 113 Muscat, Oman
FAX: +968 790524
E-MAIL: editor@omanobserver.com
WEBSITE: http://www.omanobserver.com
TITLE: Editor-in-Chief
CONTACT: Said Bin Khalfan Al-Harthy

Oman Today
Apex Publishing, PO Box 2616, Ruwi 112 Oman
PHONE: +968 799388
FAX: +968 793316
E-MAIL: apexoman@gto.net.om
TITLE: Editor
CONTACT: Emma Ventura
CIRCULATION: 40,000

Times of Oman
E-MAIL: times@omantel.net.om
WEBSITE: http://www.omantimes.com
TITLE: Editor-in-Chief
CONTACT: Essa bin Mohammed Al Zedjali
CIRCULATION: 21,000

Al Watan
PO Box 463, PC 113 Muscat, Oman
PHONE: +968 591919
FAX: +968 591280
E-MAIL: alwatan@omantel.net.com
WEBSITE: http://www.alwatan.com

TITLE: Editor-in-Chief
CONTACT: Mohammed bin Suluman Al taie

Omaniyyah

PO Box 6303, Ruwi, Muscat, Oman
TITLE: Editor
CONTACT: Saida bint Khatir al-Farisi
CIRCULATION: 11,500
TYPE: Social science, women's studies

PUBLISHERS

Apex Publishing

PO Box 2616, Way No. 2706, 112 Muscat, Oman
PHONE: +968 799388
FAX: +968 793316
WEBSITE: http://www.apexstuff.com
TITLE: President
CONTACT: Saleh M. Talib
SUBJECTS: Art, Business, Gardening, Plants, History, Outdoor Recreation, Travel

Muscat Press and Publishing House

PO Box 3112, 112 Ruwi, Oman
PHONE: +968 711953
FAX: +968 715411
TITLE: Editor-in-Chief
CONTACT: Anees Essa Mohd Al Zedjali

National Publishing and Advertising LLC

PO Box 3112, 112 Ruwi, Oman
PHONE: +968 793098
FAX: +968 708445
TITLE: Managing Director
CONTACT: Anis Issa Ai Zedjali

Oman Newspaper House

PO Box 3002, 112 Ruwi, Oman
PHONE: +968 701555
FAX: +968 790523
TITLE: Director
CONTACT: Abdul Wahab Bin Nasser Al Mantheri

RELIGIOUS ORGANIZATIONS

Oman is predominantely Muslim. Religious organizations are controlled through the government's Bureau of Islamic Affairs.

FURTHER READING

Articles

"Oman and Its Heritage." *History Today,* June 2000, p. 4.

Books

Dun and Bradstreet's Export Guide to Oman. Parsippany, NJ: Dun & Bradstreet, 1999.

Oman and the United Arab Emirates. London: Lonely Planet, 2000.

Internet

BBC News Online. "Martian Meterorite Found in Oman." May 22, 2000. [Online] Available http://news6.thdo.bbc.co.uk/hi/english/sci/tech/newsid%5F759000/759267.stm (accesssed July 20, 2000).

OMAN: STATISTICAL DATA

For sources and notes see "Sources of Statistics" at the front of each volume.

GEOGRAPHY

Geography

Area:

Total: 212,460 sq km.

Land: 212,460 sq km.

Land boundaries:

Total: 1,374 km.

Border countries: Saudi Arabia 676 km, UAE 410 km, Yemen 288 km.

Coastline: 2,092 km.

Climate: dry desert; hot, humid along coast; hot, dry interior; strong southwest summer monsoon (May to September) in far south.

Terrain: vast central desert plain, rugged mountains in north and south.

Natural resources: petroleum, copper, asbestos, some marble, limestone, chromium, gypsum, natural gas.

Land use:

Arable land: 0%

Permanent crops: 0%

Permanent pastures: 5%

Forests and woodland: 0%

Other: 95% (1993 est.).

HUMAN FACTORS

Demographics (A)

	1990	1995	1998	2000	2010	2020	2030	2040	2050
Population	NA	2,131	2,364	2,533	3,523	4,678	5,922	7,159	8,338
Life expectancy - males	NA	68.3	69.1	69.7	72.1	74.1	75.8	77.2	78.3
Life expectancy - females	NA	72.4	73.4	74.0	76.8	79.2	81.1	82.7	83.9
Birth rate (per 1,000)	NA	36.9	37.8	38.1	34.4	29.6	25.2	21.1	18.1
Death rate (per 1,000)	NA	4.6	4.3	4.2	3.7	3.7	4.0	4.3	4.3
Women of reproductive age (15-49 yrs.)	NA	402	460	497	711	1,047	1,447	1,860	2,201
Fertility rate	NA	6.2	6.1	6.1	5.4	4.3	3.3	2.6	2.3

Except as noted, values for vital statistics are in thousands; life expectancy is in years.

Health Personnel

	National Data	World Data (wtd ave)
Total health expenditure as a percentage of GDP, 1990-1998[a]		
Public sector	2.1	2.5
Private sector	NA	2.9
Total[b]	NA	5.5
Availability of health care facilities per 100,000 people		
Hospital beds 1990-1998[a]	220	330
Doctors 1992-1995[a]	120	122
Nurses 1992-1995[a]	290	248

Health Indicators

	National Data	World Data
Life expectancy at birth (years)		
1980	60	61
1998	73	67
Daily per capita supply of calories		
1970	NA	2,358
1997	NA	2,791
Daily per capital supply of protein		
1997 (grams)	NA	74
Total fertility rate (births per woman)		
1980	9.0	3.7
1998	4.6	2.7
Population with access (%)		
To safe water (1990-96)	68	NA
To sanitation (1990-96)	85	NA
People living with (1997)		
Tuberculosis (cases per 100,000)	9.8	60.4
Malaria (cases per 100,000)	44.5	42.2
HIV/AIDS (% aged 15 - 49 years)	0.11	0.99

Infants and Malnutrition

	National Data	World Data (wtd ave)
Under 5 mortality rate (1989)	18	NA
% of infants with low birthweight (1992-98)[1]	8	17
Births attended by skilled health staff (% of total births 1996-98)	91	52
% fully immunized at 1 year of age (1995-98)[1]		
TB	96	82
DPT	100	77
Polio	100	77
Measles	98	74
Prevalence of child malnutrition (1992-98)[1] (based on weight for age, % of children under 5 years)	23	30

Ethnic Division

Arab, Baluchi, South Asian (Indian, Pakistani, Sri Lankan, Bangladeshi), African.

Religion

Ibadhi Muslim 75%

Sunni Muslim, Shi'a Muslim, Hindu . . . . .NA

Major Languages

Arabic (official), English, Baluchi, Urdu, Indian dialects.

EDUCATION

Public Education Expenditures

	1980	1997
Public expenditures on education as % of GNP	2.1	4.5
Expenditures per student as % of GNP per capita		
Primary & Secondary	NA	13.1
Tertiary	NA	26.7
Teachers' compensation as % of total current education expenditures	60.3	NA
Pupils per teacher at the primary level	NA	26
Duration of primary education in years	NA	NA
World data for comparison		
Public expenditures on education as % of GNP (mean)	3.9	4.8
Pupils per teacher at the primary level (wtd ave)	NA	33
Duration of primary education in years (mean)	NA	9

Educational Attainment (B)

	1995	1997
Gross enrollment ratio (%)		
Primary level	79.2	76.0
Secondary level	66.7	66.9
Tertiary level	5.3	8.0

Literacy Rates (B)

	National Data	World Data
Adult literacy rate		
1980		
Male	52	75
Female	16	58
1995		
Male	75	81
Female	51	65

Libraries

National Libraries 1995

Administrative Units 1

Service Points or Branches .2

Number of Volumes (000) .4

Registered Users (000) 0.2

Loans to Users (000) 0.91

Total Library Staff 2

GOVERNMENT & LAW

Political Parties

The bicameral Majlis Oman consists of an upper chamber (Majlis ad-Dawla) and a lower chamber (Majlis ash-Shura) . The upper chamber has 41 seats. Its members are appointed by the monarch and it has advisory powers only. The lower chamber has 82 seats. Its members are elected by limited suffrage, however, the monarch makes final selections and can negate election results. This body has some limited power to propose legislation, but otherwise has only advisory powers. Elections were last held in October 1997 (next to be held in October 2000). Election results are not available. There are no political parties.

Government Budgets (A)

Year: 1998

Total Expenditures: 1,820.1 Millions of Rials

Expenditures as a percentage of the total by function:

General public services and public order 15.72

Defense 32.43

Education 15.58

Health 7.21

Social Security and Welfare 4.97

Housing and community amenities 6.12

Recreational, cultural, and religious affairs 1.97

Fuel and energy 5.07

Agriculture, forestry, fishing, and hunting 1.21

Mining, manufacturing, and construction 0.07

Transportation and communication 3.02

Other economic affairs and services 1.05

Crime

Crime volume (for 1998)

Crimes reported 6,609

Total persons convicted .NA

Crimes per 100,000 population 280

Persons responsible for offenses

Total number suspects 7,902

Total number of female suspects 237

Total number of juvenile suspects 948

(Continued on next page.)

LABOR FORCE

Total Labor Force (A)

850,000 (1997 est.).

PRODUCTION SECTOR

Energy Production

Production .7.36 billion kWh

Production by source

Fossil fuel 100%

Hydro 0%

Nuclear 0%

Other 0%

Exports . . . . .0 kWh

Data for 1998.

Energy Consumption

Consumption . . . . .6.845 billion kWh

Imports . . . . .0 kWh

Data for 1998.

Transportation

Highways:

Total: 32,800 km.

Paved: 9,840 km (including 550 km of expressways).

Unpaved: 22,960 km (1996 est.).

Pipelines: crude oil 1,300 km; natural gas 1,030 km.

Merchant marine:

Total: 3 ships (1,000 GRT or over) totaling 16,306 GRT/8,210 DWT.

Ships by type: cargo 1, passenger 1, passenger/cargo 1 (1999 est.).

(Continued on next page.)

PRODUCTION SECTOR (cont.)

Transportation

Airports: 142 (1999 est.).

Airports - with unpaved runways: 136.

Top Agriculture Products

Dates, limes, bananas, alfalfa, vegetables; camels, cattle; fish.

Top Mining Products (B)

Mineral resources include: copper, asbestos, some marble, limestone, chromium, gypsum.

COMMUNICATIONS

Daily Newspapers

	National Data	World Data for Comparison
Daily Newspapers		
Number of Dailies	4	8,391
Total Circulation (000)	63	548,000
Circulation per 1,000 inhabitants	28	96

(Continued on next page.)

GOVERNMENT & LAW (cont.)

Military Affairs (A)

	1990	1992	1995	1996	1997
Military expenditures					
Current dollars (mil.)	1,900	2,010	2,010	1,910	1,820
1997 constant dollars (mil.)	2,230	2,230	2,080	1,940	1,820
Armed forces (000)	32	35	36	38	38
Gross national product (GNP)					
Current dollars (mil.)	9,450	9,820	10,500	6,490	6,950
1997 constant dollars (mil.)	11,100	10,900	10,900	6,600	6,950
Central government expenditures (CGE)					
1997 constant dollars (mil.)	4,930	5,550	5,300	4,950	4,980
People (mil.)	1.8	1.9	2.1	2.2	2.3
Military expenditure as % of GNP	20.1	20.5	19.1	29.3	26.1
World data on military expenditure as % of GNP	4.5	3.4	2.7	2.6	2.6
Military expenditure as % of CGE	25.2	40.2	39.2	39.1	36.4
World data on military expenditure as % of CGE	17.0	12.5	10.5	10.3	10.2
Military expenditure per capita (1997 $)	1,270	1,160	976	878	795
World data on military expenditure per capita (1997 $)	242	173	146	143	145
Armed forces per 1,000 people (soldiers)	18.3	18.3	16.9	17.2	16.6
World data on armed forces per 1,000 people (soldiers)	5.3	4.5	4.1	3.9	3.8
GNP per capita (1997 $)	6,320	5,680	5,120	2,990	3,040
Arms imports[6]					
Current dollars (mil.)	10	10	430	370	160
1997 constant dollars (mil.)	12	11	445	376	160
Total imports[7]					
Current dollars (mil.)	2,681	3,769	4,248	4,578	5,026
1997 constant dollars (mil.)	3,140	4,178	4,399	4,654	5,026
Total exports[7]					
Current dollars (mil.)	5,501	5,425	5,962	7,339	7,630
1997 constant dollars (mil.)	6,443	6,014	6,173	7,461	7,630
Arms as percent of total imports[8]	0.4	0.3	10.1	8.1	3.2
Arms as percent of total exports[8]	0	0	0	0	0

COMMUNICATIONS (cont.)

Telecommunications

Telephones - main lines in use: 300,000 (1999).

Telephones - mobile cellular: 120,000 (1999).

Telephone system: modern system consisting of open wire, microwave, and radiotelephone communication stations; limited coaxial cable.

Domestic: open wire, microwave, radiotelephone communications, and a domestic satellite system with 8 earth stations.

International: satellite earth stations - 2 Intelsat (Indian Ocean) and 1 Arabsat.

Radio broadcast stations: AM 3, FM 9, shortwave 2 (1999).

Radios: 1.4 million (1997).

Television broadcast stations: 13 (plus 25 low-power repeaters) (1999).

Televisions: 1.6 million (1997).

Internet Service Providers (ISPs): 1 (1999).

FINANCE, ECONOMICS, & TRADE

Economic Indicators

National product: GDP—purchasing power parity—$19.6 billion (1999 est.).

National product real growth rate: 4% (1999 est.).

National product per capita: $8,000 (1999 est.).

Inflation rate—consumer price index: −0.07% (1999 est.).

Exchange Rates

Exchange rates:

Omani rials (RO) per US$1 . . . . .0.3845

Fixed rate since 1986.

Top Import Origins

$5.4 billion (f.o.b., 1999 est.)

Origins (1997)

UAE (largely reexports)	23.0%
Japan	16.0%
United Kingdom	13.0%
United States	7.5%
Germany	5.0%

Top Export Destinations

$7.2 billion (f.o.b., 1999 est.)

Destinations (1997)

Japan	21%
China	16%
Thailand	16%
South Korea	12%
United States	3%

Foreign Aid

Recipient: $76.4 million (1995).

Import/Export Commodities

Import Commodities	Export Commodities
Machinery and transport equipment	Petroleum
	Reexports
Manufactured goods	Fish
Food	Metals
Livestock	Textiles
Lubricants	

(Continued on next page.)

MANUFACTURING SECTOR

GDP & Manufacturing Summary (B)

	1980	1985	1990	1993	1994	1995
Gross Domestic Product						
Millions of 1990 dollars	4,478	8,999	10,521	12,757	12,630	13,211
Growth rate in percent	6.05	13.76	7.54	4.00	−1.00	4.60
Per capita (in 1990 dollars)	3,963	6,315	5,894	6,288	5,969	5,986
Manufacturing Value Added						
Millions of 1990 dollars	49	265	396	477	484	NA
Growth rate in percent	19.05	20.39	14.60	4.63	1.50	NA
Manufacturing share in percent of current prices	0.8	2.4	3.7	4.3[e]	NA	NA

FINANCE, ECONOMICS, & TRADE (cont.)

Balance of Payments

	1993	1994	1995	1996	1997
Exports of goods (f.o.b.)	5,365	5,542	6,065	7,339	7,631
Imports of goods (f.o.b.)	−4,030	−3,693	−4,050	−4,385	−4,649
Trade balance	1,336	1,849	2,015	2,954	2,982
Services - debits	−906	−900	−985	−975	−1,166
Services - credits	13	13	13	18	18
Private transfers (net)	39	39	39	39	39
Government transfers (net)	18	26	29	10	31
Overall balance	−1,190	−805	−801	180	−57

PAKISTAN

Islamic Republic of Pakistan
Islami Jamhooria Pakistan

CAPITAL: Islamabad.

FLAG: The national flag is dark green, with a white vertical stripe at the hoist and a white crescent and five-pointed star in the center.

ANTHEM: The opening lines of the national anthem, sung in Urdu, are "Blessed be the sacred land, Happy be the bounteous realm, Symbol of high resolve, land of Pakistan, Blessed be thou citadel of faith."

MONETARY UNIT: The rupee (R) is a paper currency of 100 paisa. There are coins of 1, 2, 5, 10, 25, and 50 paisa and of 1 rupee, and notes of 1, 2, 5, 10, 50, 100, 500, and 1,000 rupees. R1 = $0.02493 (or $1 = R40.12).

WEIGHTS AND MEASURES: The metric system was introduced in 1966 and made mandatory as of 1 January 1979.

HOLIDAYS: Pakistan Day, 23 March; May Day, 1 May; Independence Day, 14 August; Defense of Pakistan Day, 6 September; Anniversary of Death of the Quaid-e-Azam, Mohammad Ali Jinnah, 11 September; Christmas and Birthday of the Quaid-e-Azam, 25 December. Religious holidays include ʽId al-Fitr, Id al-ʿAdha', 1st of Muharram, and Milad an-Nabi.

TIME: 5 PM = noon GMT.

LOCATION AND SIZE: Situated in southern Asia, Pakistan has an area of 803,940 square kilometers (310,403 square miles), slightly less than twice the size of the state of California. The total boundary length is 7,820 kilometers (4,870 miles). Pakistan's capital city, Islamabad, is located in the northern part of the country.

CLIMATE: Pakistan's climate is dry and hot near the coast, becoming progressively cooler toward the northeastern uplands. The winter season is generally cold and dry. By the end of June the temperature may reach 49°C (120°F). Between July and September, the monsoon (very heavy rainfall) provides an average rainfall of about 38 centimeters (15 inches) in the river basins and up to about 150 centimeters (60 inches) in the northern areas.

INTRODUCTORY SURVEY

RECENT HISTORY

On August 14, 1947, British India was divided into the two self-governing dominions of India and Pakistan. Pakistan was created by combining contiguous, Muslim-majority districts of British India. This division, known as partition, resulted in a mass movement of Hindus, Muslims, and Sikhs who found themselves on the "wrong" side of new international boundaries. More than twenty million people moved, and up to three million of these were killed.

The new Pakistan was a state divided into two wings: East Pakistan (with forty-two million people crowded mainly into what had been the eastern half of India's Bengal province) and West Pakistan (with thirty-four million in a much larger territory that included the former Indian provinces of Baluchistan, Sind, the Northwest Frontier, and western Punjab). They were separated by 1600 kilometers (1000 miles) of an independent, mainly Hindu, India. Political stability proved hard to achieve despite a shared commitment to Islam.

In 1958, the Army chief, General Mohammad Ayub Khan, seized control of Pakistan, imposing martial law and banning all political activity for several years. Amid rising political tension in 1968, Ayub was forced from office and General Mohammad Yahya Khan, also opposed to greater independence for East Pakistan, assumed the presidency in 1969.

The general elections of 1970 supported greater independence for East Pakistan. However,

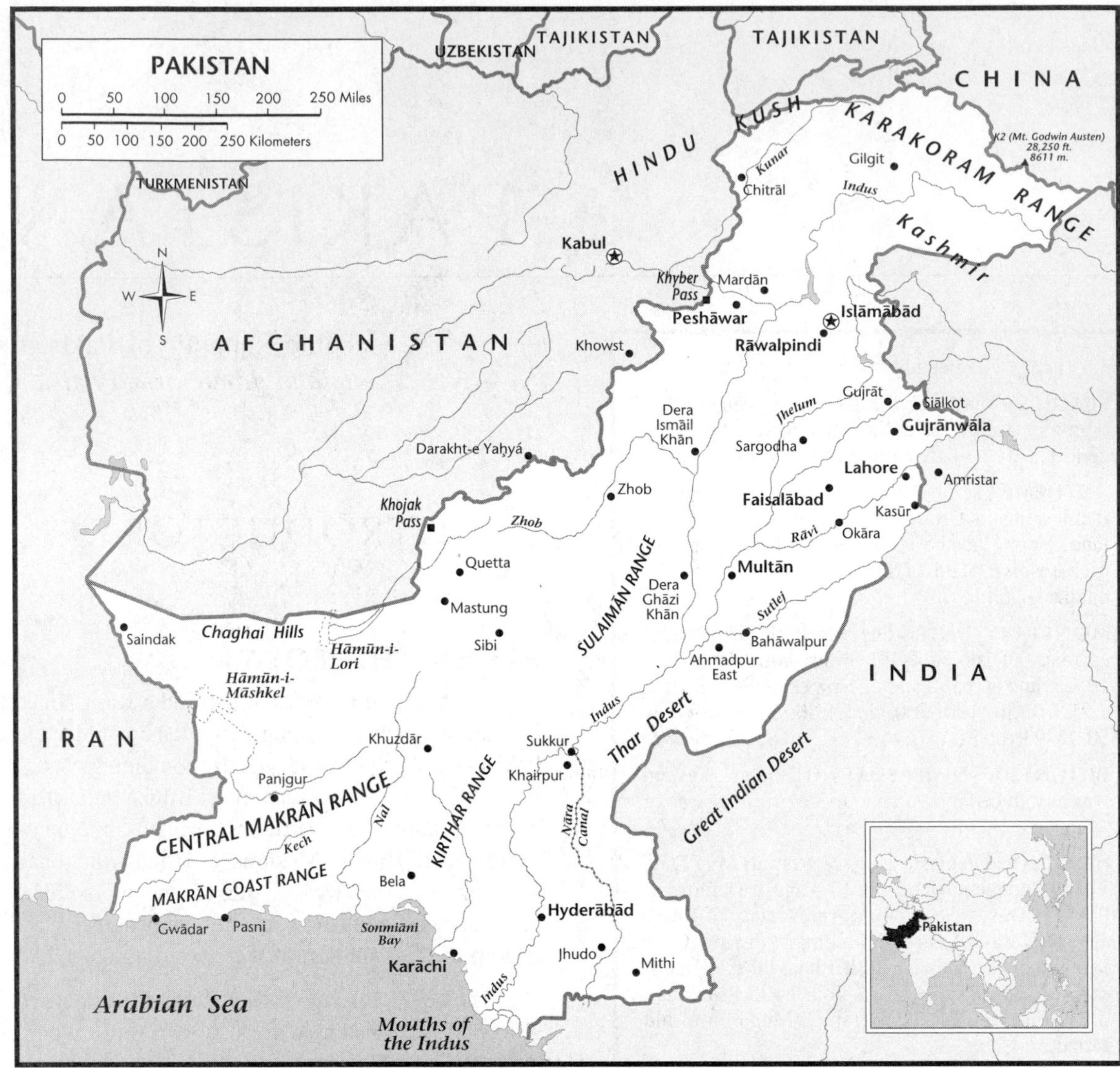

the election results were ignored, and civil unrest in East Pakistan rapidly escalated to civil war. India, with more than a million refugees pouring into its West Bengal state, joined in the conflict in support of the rebellion in November 1971, tipping the balance in favor of East Pakistan. In early 1972, the country of Bangladesh was created from the ruins of East Pakistan.

The outcome of the civil war led to the resignation of Yahya Khan and brought to the presidency Zulfikar Ali Bhutto, whose populist Pakistan Peoples Party (PPP) had won a majority of seats in West Pakistan. Bhutto quickly charted an independent course for West Pakistan that became the Islamic Republic of Pakistan. He distanced Pakistan from former close ties with the United States and Europe, seeking a much more active role in the Third World, especially in the growing international Islamic movement. Bhutto began limited land reform, nationalized banks and industries, and obtained support among all parties for a new constitution adopted in 1973, restoring a strong prime ministership that he then assumed.

In the following years, Bhutto grew more and more dictatorial until he was finally removed from office by the army on July 5, 1977. General Mohammad Zia-ul-Haq partially suspended the 1973 constitution and imposed martial law.

Zia expanded the role of Islamic values and institutions in society. He also renewed close ties with the United States to enhance Pakistan's security and improved relations with India including normalization of trade, transport, and other nonsensitive areas.

In the late 1980s, the long smoldering Kashmir dispute erupted. Kashmir bordered both India and Pakistan. India canceled election results in Kashmir and dismissed the state government. This led to the beginning of an armed rebellion against Indian rule by Muslim militants in Kashmir, an Indian province that had been split uneasily between Indian and Pakistani influence since 1949. Indian repression and Pakistani support of the Kashmir Muslim militants continue to threaten to spark new Indo-Pakistan conflict.

Zia was among eighteen officials killed in the crash of a Pakistan Air Force plane in 1988. The 1990s witnessed considerable political instability over persistent government corruption charges leading to political reforms and a shake-up of the military resulting in the dismissal and imprisonment of several high-ranking officials.

In May 1998, India conducted several underground nuclear test explosions prompting international outcry. Later that month Pakistan began its own nuclear tests intensifying global fears of a nuclear arms race between Pakistan and India. In April 1999, Pakistan and India test-fired missiles capable of carrying nuclear warheads. The economic sanctions that followed after Pakistan's nuclear tests devastated an already weak Pakistani economy. With the economic collapse crime rates soared.

The two sides made efforts to improve relations. Yet by summer of 1999 the two nations were again on the brink of war. Under intense pressure from the United States but against the Pakistani military's wishes, Sharif ordered withdrawal of Pakistani troops of the Kargil region of Kashmir. The military, under General Pervez Musharraf, arrested Sharif and took over the government. Many Pakistanis welcomed the military takeover as a change from the corruption and abuses of Sharif's rule. As of 2000, no timetable for a return to civilian government had been set.

GOVERNMENT

Pakistan is governed under the constitution of August 14, 1973, as amended, which declared Islam the state religion and provided for a president as official head of state and a prime minister as executive head of government. The parliament consists of a National Assembly of 217 members elected by popular vote for five-year terms. Ten members represent non-Muslims. The Senate has eighty-four members indirectly elected for six-year terms by the provincial assemblies and tribal councils plus three seats reserved for the federal capital area.

Following the military takeover October 12, 1999, Chief of Army Staff and Chairman of the Joint Chiefs of Staff Committee, General Pervez Musharraf suspended Pakistan's constitution and assumed the additional title of Chief Executive. He appointed an eight-member National Security Council to function as the supreme governing body of Pakistan. Musharraf dissolved both the Senate and National Assembly. No timetable was set for elections following the takeover.

Judiciary

The Supreme Court has original, appeals, and advisory jurisdictions. Each province has a high court. Below the high courts are district and session courts, and below these are subordinate courts and village courts on the civil side and magistrates on the criminal side.

Courts are subject to pressure from the executive branch partly because the president controls the appointment, transfer, and tenure of judges. The position of the judiciary has been affected by periods of military rule. A blow was dealt to the judiciary in January 2000 when Musharraf required all judges to take an oath of loyalty to his regime. The Supreme Court Chief Justice and five colleagues refused and were dismissed. This was just a week before the Court was due to hear cases challenging the legality of Musharraf's government. There are no jury trials in Pakistan.

Political Parties

The two main political parties are the Pakistan Muslim League (PML) and the Pakistan Peoples Party (PPP). Political alliances shift frequently in Pakistan. There are many local splinter groups that have been calling for the decentralization of power.

Both the PPP and the PML have competed successfully in forming governments in provincial assemblies only when they have recruited (or neutralized) strong regional parties like the Awami National Party (ANP) in the Northwest Frontier Province and the Muhajir Quami Movement (MQM) in Sindh.

DEFENSE

In 2000, Pakistan's armed forces totaled 587,000. Its army of 520,000 was the world's ninth largest. The navy has 22,000 personnel and the air force has a total strength of 45,000. Paramilitary forces, including the Pakistan rangers, the frontier corps, a maritime security agency, a national guard, and local defense units, totaled 247,000. Military service is voluntary. Defense expenditures in 1999-2000 were estimated at $2.4 billion, or 3.9 percent of gross domestic product.

ECONOMIC AFFAIRS

Pakistan is poor, over populated, racked with internal political disputes, and continues a costly confrontation with neighboring India. Despite steady expansion of industry during the 1990s, Pakistan's economy remains dominated by agriculture. In 1998, agriculture engaged 47 percent of the labor force and accounted for 24 percent of GDP as well as close to 70 percent of export revenues. Pakistan is generally poor in natural resources, although extensive reserves of natural gas and petroleum are being exploited. Iron ore, chromite, and low-quality coal are mined.

Despite strong performances in the industrial and agricultural sectors, a growing debt servicing burden, large government expenditures on public enterprises, low tax revenues, and high levels of defense spending contributed to serious financial deficits.

In 1995, the government failed to follow recommendations by the International Monetary Fund (IMF) to pursue a more market-oriented economy, so the IMF suspended a $1.5 billion loan. By 1996, the economy was in the worst recession in twenty-five years. Tax receipts and export income were down, and the government's debt increased close to the point of default. By 1999, the Musharraf government, facing a $32 billion external debt, had nearly completed rescheduling with Paris Club members and other creditors. Debt service obligations total nearly 50 percent of government expenditures, and foreign loans and grants provide 25 percent of government revenue. The IMF initiated a $1.56 billion bailout package in 1999, but it depended on the government's resolve to implement reforms of widening the tax base, privatizing public sector enterprises, and improve its balance of trade. Until the World Bank gives its positive endorsement, Pakistan may have trouble gaining foreign investment.

Public Finance

The federal government frames two separate budgets: revenue (current account) and capital. Deficits have appeared since 1971-1972, a combined result of the loss of revenues from East Pakistan, stepped-up defense expenditures, lax expenditure controls, and a low and inelastic tax base. Current expenditures (debt service, defense, administration) now consume over 70 percent of the budget; development needs (education, health, energy, and rural development) receive the remainder. Tax revenues have not kept pace with expenditure growth due to widespread evasion, corruption among tax officials, overreliance on foreign trade taxes, and a tax exemption for agricultural income that comprises 25 percent of GDP.

The U.S. Central Intelligence Agency estimated that, in 1998-1999, government revenues totaled approximately $10 billion and expenditures totaled $11.7 billion. The budget deficit was hovering at about 6.2 percent of GDP in 1995 and 1996 and was projected to reach almost 7 percent in 1997. Interest payments on the accumulated debt threatened to bankrupt thee government by mid-1997. As a condition for a $1.6 billion loan from the IMF and World Bank, the government agreed to reduce the deficit to 4 percent of GDP. To do so the government is attempting to raise revenues by expanding the tax base beyond the 1 percent of Pakistanis who currently pay income tax. Other proposals include a reduction in government payrolls, improved tax administration, and an end to the tax exemption for agricultural income. Despite the dismal financial situation, the government has yet to reduce defense spending which accounts for almost 25 percent of the budget.

Income

In 1999, Pakistan's gross domestic product (GDP) was estimated at $282 billion, or $2,000 per capita. The 1999 estimated GDP was 3.1 percent and inflation was 6 percent. The GDP contribution by sector, as estimated in 1998, was agriculture, 25.2 percent; industry, 26.6 percent; and services, 48.2 percent.

Industry

Since 1947, the government has given the highest priority to development of the industrial sector. Manufacturing grew by 5.8 percent between 1988 and 1998. Industry employs about 19 percent of the workforce and accounts for about 26.6 percent of GDP.

Cotton textile production is the most important of Pakistan's industries. Pakistan supplies its own cotton fabrics and exports substantial quantities. Factories also produce synthetic fabrics, worsted yarn, and jute textiles. In 1998-1999, the textile industry as a whole employed about 40 percent of the industrial workforce. Other important industries include food processing, chemicals and ceramics manufacture, the iron and steel industries, cement, petroleum refining, beverages, construction materials, and paper products. In 1996, Pakistan's software industry had exports of $25 million.

Banking and Finance

The central banking institution is the State Bank of Pakistan (SBP), established in 1948 at Karachi and with branches in the larger cities. The government holds 51 percent of the bank's paid-up capital; 49 percent is held by corporations, societies, and individuals. The State Bank has exclusive responsibility for the issuance of currency; it is the financial agent of the central and provincial governments, and is responsible for the flotation and management of the public debt.

As of 2000, there were forty-five commercial banks and thirty-six non-banking financial institutions in Pakistan. Of the commercial banks, four were nationalized, seventeen private, twenty foreign, and four specialized. Consumer banking is largely undeveloped and commercial banking lends primarily to corporations. Total default loans in 1998 were $2.8 billion.

There are stock exchanges at Lahore and Karachi with the latter accounting for a major share of the business. In the nine months to end-March 1996, there were thirty-three new listings on the Karachi Stock Exchange, the largest of the country's three bourses, bringing the total to 780 in 1998.

Economic Development

By the late 1980s, a number of structural factors resulted in increasingly critical fiscal and balance of payment deficits. With less than 30 percent of the budget devoted to infrastructural development and other needs in health and education, the prognosis for long-term social and economic development remained poor. In response, a medium-term structural reform program was developed under the government of Prime Minister Benazir Bhutto for implementation in 1989-1991. Aimed at correcting fiscal and external imbalances, the program targeted a reform of the tax collection system, tighter government spending controls and monetary management, the privatization of state-owned industrial enterprises, banks and utilities, the phasing out of state monopolies in the transportation, insurance, telecommunications and energy sectors, and liberalization of investment and foreign exchange regulations. Implementation of the ambitious program proceeded under the government of Nawaz Sharif, who assumed the prime minister's office in 1991. Results were uneven thus far with little effective improvements scored in the country's tax system or its fiscal and balance of payments deficits. While the rapid change of government in 1993 and ongoing political tensions appear to be dampening private investment somewhat, official assurances have been given that structural reform and privatization will continue.

Since the early 1950s through 1993, Pakistan is estimated to have received about $37 billion in aid disbursements including both long-term and medium-term loans and grants, making it one of the largest recipients in the developing world. For the Indus Valley project, Pakistan received funding of more than $1.3 billion from the IBRD, IDA, ADB, U.S., UK, and other countries. In addition to U.S. aid (a six-year commitment of $4.02 billion made in 1988 with $2.1 billion disbursed by 1990), Pakistan has also received aid from Iran and the Arab states. New economic aid from the United States was halted in 1990 under the terms of a Congressional amendment requiring certification of Pakistan's status as a nuclear weapons-free country.

Fiscal indecision and, following the 1998 nuclear tests, economic sanctions dried up foreign investments while budget and trade deficits soared in 1999. The United States lifted some sanctions, clearing the way for the IMF to negotiate a bailout package of $1.5 billion with Pakistan. Key demands included cuts in government budget deficits, further privatization, and improved tax collections. With little concessions made for these demands, Pakistan has been increasingly alienated from the World Bank and the IMF.

SOCIAL WELFARE

A social security scheme enacted in 1976 covers employees of firms with ten or more workers. Social security coverage includes old age, disability, and survivor benefits, as well as sickness and maternity payments, workers' compensation, and unemployment benefits. Since 1973, cost-of-living allowances have been paid to workers earning less than minimum wage. Disability and workers' injury benefits are provided to workers earning 3,000 rupees or less a month.

The government's Islamization program to promote social welfare in accordance with Islamic ideals was introduced in 1977. Islamic welfare taxes, the *zakat* and *ushr*, were levied to redistribute wealth. The ushr tax on landowners took effect in 1983. Islamic beliefs are taught in the public schools and reflected widely by the mass media. Laws against drinking alcoholic beverages, adultery, and lying have been strictly enforced.

The Women's Ministry, established in 1979, has sponsored some 7,000 centers in rural areas and urban slums to provide women with a basic education and to teach them such skills as livestock farming, midwifery, and secretarial work. Women face serious social and legal discrimination. Under Islamic tenets, women's testimony is not as valuable as a man's, women who have been raped may be charged with adultery, and according to a 1992 Supreme Court decision, men may divorce their wives without any notice.

The use of child labor in Pakistan is widespread. Bonded child labor is illegal but still affects hundreds of thousands of children. In bonded labor, the employer keeps the child working to pay off a long-term debt of the parent.

Healthcare

Health facilities in Pakistan are inadequate, mainly due to a lack of resources and a high population growth rate. In 1993, 85 percent of the population had access to health care. The government's goal under direction of the Federal Ministry of Health is to be able to provide healthcare to every Pakistani by 2000.

In 1992, there were 60,250 physicians and 20,000 registered homeopathic medical practitioners. Special attention has been given to the training of nurses, and several training centers are in operation. However, medical personnel ratios, though much improved, remained inadequate: one doctor per 1,923 persons and one nurse per 1,769 in 1993. The country had one hospital bed per 1,769 inhabitants that year. The vast majority of hospitals are located in urban areas.

Malaria, tuberculosis, intestinal diseases, venereal diseases, and skin diseases remain Pakistan's main public health problems. Drug addiction, especially among university students, is an increasing concern. In 2000, average life expectancy is estimated at sixty-one years.

Housing

The rapid increase in urbanization, coupled with the rising population, has added to the housing shortage in urban areas. About 25 percent of the people in large cities live in *katchi abadis* (shantytowns). The Public Works Department has built more than 8,000 units in Islamabad, Lahore, Peshawar, and Quetta. In 1987, the National Housing Authority was created to coordinate the upgrading of the existing *katchiabadis* and prevent the growth of new ones. As of 1991, 171 *abadis* had been renovated and 522 more were under development.

EDUCATION

In 2000, the illiteracy rate was 56.7 percent (males, 42.4 percent; females, 72.2 percent). By the mid-1990s, there were 15.5 million primary school pupils, 31 percent of which were female, and five million secondary school students. Girls attend separate schools at both primary and secondary levels.

In that same period, 1.7 million students were enrolled at institutions of higher learning. In 1995, there were twenty-nine colleges and universities. An agricultural university was established in 1961 at Lyallpur (now Faisalabad). Two engineering and technological universities have been founded at Lahore (1961) and Islamabad (1966). Research institutions include the Institute of Islamic Studies at Lahore, the Iqbal Academy at Lahore, and the Pakistan Institute of International Affairs at Karachi. Urdu and English are the languages of instruction.

Many adult literacy centers have been established in recent years. In addition, the People's Open University was established at Islamabad (1974) to provide mass adult education through correspondence and the communications media.

2000 KEY EVENTS TIMELINE

January

- On January 6 India accuses Pakistani involvement in a December 1999 hijacking.
- General Musharraf travels to Beijing on January 17.
- On January 26 the military government removes the chief justice of the supreme court.
- The United States threatens to classify Pakistan as a state sponsor of terrorism on January 27.

March

- On March 8 ousted Prime Minister Sharif testifies at his own trial.
- On March 10 Sharif's defense attorney is killed.
- U.S. President Bill Clinton meets Musharraff in Islamabad on March 25.

April

- Sharif is found guilty on April 6 of hijacking a commercial airliner. His sentence is life in prison, and forfeiture of all personal property. He did not take over the airplane personally (which carried 198 passengers including the current prime minister General Pervez Musharraf), but rather refused to allow it to land, even though it was low on fuel.
- On April 12 violence breaks out between Sunni and Shiite Muslims.
- On April 21 Musharraf announces a human rights campaign.

May

- On May 23 the United States warns Pakistan not to conduct more nuclear tests.
- On May 25 Musharraf promises to return to civilian rule within three years.

July

- Police arrest dozens of supporters of former Prime Minister Nawaz Sharif (who is serving a life prison sentence). They had intended to follow Kulsoom Nawaz, Nawaz Sharif's wife, on a procession to protest her husband's imprisonment. They put her under house arrest for a number of days.
- Former Prime Minister Nawaz Sharif refuses to testify before an Accountability Court, claiming it had been convened only to convict him.

August

- Ten-thousand people gather in support of Kashmiri independence from India in Karachi on August 14.

September

- A bomb explodes at a market in the capital of Islamabad, killing sixteen and wounding at least seventy-five, on September 19.

October

- October 12 marks the one-year anniversary of General Pervez Musharraf's coup. Despite the leader's efforts to shore up the economy, he faces skepticism at home and abroad. By court order his military government must return the government to civilian control in 2002.
- Foreign Minister Abdul Sattar states the nation will not allow the United States to cross Pakistani airspace in military attacks on Afghani-based Saudi terrorist Osama bin Laden.

November

- Pakistan officials close the border with Afghanistan, preventing refugees from entering the country. An estimated 30,000 arrived in Pakistan during the last month, bringing the total refugee population to more than 2.1 million.

December

- Former Prime Minister Nawaz Sharif, serving a life sentence for corruption and other charges, is released from prison December 10 after promising to stay out of politics for twenty-one years. He and his family go into exile in Saudi Arabia.
- Protests by Afghan women December 10 against the Taliban, notorious for their human rights abuses and discrimination against women, turn violent as the women begin throwing stones at a religious group shouting pro-Taliban slogans. Several women are arrested.
- Voting in local elections begins on December 31 to choose local councils. The balloting is to be held in stages and will continue through mid-2001.

ANALYSIS OF EVENTS: 2000

BUSINESS AND THE ECONOMY

Pakistan may need a miracle if the International Monetary Fund (IMF) continued its refusal to give the country a new loan before December 31, when a moratorium on interest payments on the $38 billion that Pakistan owed in foreign debt was set to expire. Without a new loan, the country would have to start making interest payments of $4.5 billion annually. Pakistan's available reserves barely total $600 million. Paying interest, let alone a staggering debt, was something it could not do.

Economic growth was expected to be near 5 percent in 2000, due largely to a bumper cotton crop and an accompanying boost in textile exports, which accounted for 60 percent of Pakistan's export earnings. In addition, the country had strong rice and wheat harvests. Industrial growth remained sluggish, however.

Pakistan has met some conditions for a new IMF loan, and most anticipated the country would be given a reprieve on interest repayments. But foreign investors did not like the idea of a military regime, such as the one installed in October 1999 by the current leader General Pervez Musharraf. Pakistan continued to invest heavily in its military establishment and in nuclear weapons. Investors and foreign leaders feared that this, coupled with the presence of Islamic militant groups and Musharraf's refusal to soften the country's stance on Kashmir, was creating a volatile world problem. Japanese Prime Minister Yoshiro Mori suggested in late August that if Pakistan would sign the Comprehensive Test Ban Treaty on nuclear weapons, foreigners would supply the money it needed. Musharraf said Pakistan would not sign the treaty unless neighboring India agreed to do so as well.

GOVERNMENT AND POLITICS

Politics in Pakistan this year centered on General Pervez Musharraf, the army leader who seized power from elected prime minister Nawaz Sharif on October 12, 1999. Musharraf took over a country that had been plagued by corruption, regional tensions, widespread poverty and illiteracy, Islamic militancy, illegal drugs and weapons smuggling, and ongoing strife with India over the status of Kashmir (whose territory both countries claimed as theirs). As he took charge, Musharraf promised to solve these problems and restore democracy within two years.

Musharraf's bold promises initially filled many Pakistanis with hope. Pakistan's Supreme Court validated the coup on May 12, and gave Musharraf the power to alter the country's constitution and carry out reforms. In doing so, the court also reiterated Pakistan's general commitment to democracy by demanding that Musharraf hold general elections no later than July 12, 2002. Awareness of Pakistan's pitiful condition also prompted many world leaders to support the military leader. U.S. President Bill Clinton expressed a willingness to work with Musharraf, as long as he stayed true to his promise to restore democracy. However, such statements of support contained a chilling caveat: Unless Pakistan curbed the power of terrorist groups within the country and softened its stance on Kashmir, it risked being isolated from the world community. "We care about their future," said U.S. National Security Adviser Sandy Berger on the eve of Clinton's one-day visit to Pakistan in March. "We don't want Pakistan to fail."

Musharraf tried to address Pakistan's problems in several ways. He traveled to Afghanistan to urge the ruling Taliban to stop sending Islamic militants into Pakistan, contending that the terrorist groups were destabilizing both countries. He cut back the number of items that could be brought into the country from Afghanistan in hopes of lessening the drugs and arms smuggling that occurs along the two countries' borders. And, he reshuffled his cabinet, removing many with ties to militant groups from power.

But these programs have come with a price. Even as Musharraf attempted to crack down on terrorism, he found he must kowtow to the country's powerful religious clergy. Mullahs and other clerical leaders posed a threat to Musharraf's authority because they could use the power of religion to incite militants within the country to action. This meant that Musharraf maintained a hard-line position on Kashmir, and repeatedly depicted India as its enemy. It also meant that he slowed social reforms opposed by the clergy. He chose not to amend a much-abused blasphemy law, and in the North West Frontier province, he allowed an appointed governor to restrict the operation of cable television networks on the belief that such programming promoted obscenity.

Musharraf's policies drew increasing opposition among those with power. Finance minister Shaukat Aziz unveiled a budget that promised a 25 percent increase in spending on social programs and poverty-reduction plans. But the budget also proposed a 15 percent income tax increase, provoking a three-week strike among traders who traditionally were exempted from paying most taxes. Although the traders eventually called off the strike, less than one-fifth have paid the tax.

Similarly, Musharraf's actions against former Prime Minister Nawaz Sharif provoked protests from Sharif's political party, the Pakistan Muslim League. Musharraf insisted that leaders such as Sharif who come from wealthy families and are backed by a landed elite have been the cause of much of the corruption and poverty that plagues Pakistan. Judges in Pakistan supported this stance by finding Sharif guilty of hijacking, terrorism, and tax evasion, and sentenced him to two life terms. None of this pleased political leaders in the Pakistan Muslim League. They joined forty other political parties in defying Musharraf's ban on protests and demanded an immediate timetable for new elections. These protests gained poignancy when police in July attempted to block a car carrying Sharif's wife, Kulsoom Nawaz, from traveling to Peshawar to collect money for drought victims. As police surrounded the car, Kulsoom Nawaz began declaring to journalists via mobile phone that the army "cannot stop us from our struggle for the restoration of democracy."

Reports such as this have made world leaders skeptical of Musharraf's commitment to democracy. Nevertheless, among the poor, Musharraf still represented a hopeful alternative. That was seen when political rallies drew not only politicians but people who hurled tomatoes and eggs in protest of the status quo the politicians want restored.

For many the question was not whether Musharraf was sincere. Rather, it was whether one man can alter Pakistan's fate. Javed Jabbar, an adviser, told the *Washington Post* that Musharraf needed to be given a chance. "He is seeking enduring change," said Jabbar. "It is a formidable task, and it takes time. How can he be expected to perform miracles overnight?"

CULTURE AND SOCIETY

A visitor to Pakistan in 2000 found cities such as Lahore, Karachi, and Islamabad clean and prosperous. People dressed stylishly, spoke English, and drove trim, foreign-made cars. However, this appearance of affluence masked the reality in which most of Pakistan's 140 million people lived. Poor housing, substandard drinking water, and widespread malnutrition plagued the country. Disease was rife, and mortality rates were high, particularly among women and children. Despite the wealth flaunted by the rich, the annual per capita income was barely $400 a year. Pakistan's adult literacy rate was 42 percent and millions of children did not attend school at all. A recent World Bank report found that 71 percent of women in Pakistan cannot read or write.

As of 2000, the official religion of Pakistan was Islam, and as an Islamic Republic, the country often was perceived as being homogenous. However, it was quite ethnically and linguistically diverse. While Punjabis made up about two-thirds of the country's population, there were also sizeable numbers of Sindhis, Pashtuns, and Baluchis. In addition, the official language of Pakistan—Urdu—was spoken only among 8 percent of its people. Other widely-spoken languages included Punjabi, Sikaiki (which is a variant of Punjabi), Sindhi, Pashto, Bali, and Baluchi. While 97 percent of its people were Muslim, there was a split between the Sunni majority and Shiites, who made up about 20 percent of the total population. The remaining 3 percent of the population practiced Christianity, Hinduism, or other faiths.

Many in Pakistan have grown disenchanted with the Punjabi ruling elite, and much of the country's internal unrest was a product of a feeling that those who hold power in Pakistan were more interested in lining their own pockets than in trying to better the country's situation as a whole. In hopes of addressing Pakistan's social problems through politics, Musharraf was developing a form of elected government that was similar to the *panchayat* (or village-level) system of government in India. Under the plan, four tiers of government would exist below the provincial level. A certain number of seats would be reserved for women, and elected leaders would be required to answer to the needs of Pakistan's ordinary people. Elections for these local assemblies were to begin in December and continue through April 2001. Musharraf called the plan a foundation for a "durable, sustainable working democracy." Critics feared that it was not only too radical but also not responsive to provincial leaders who have been most critical of the ruling elite.

DIRECTORY

CENTRAL GOVERNMENT

Head of State

Chief Executive
Pervez Musharraf, Office of the Chief Executive, Constitution Ave., Islamabad, Pakistan

Ministers

Minister of Commerce, Industries and Production
Abdul Razzaq Daud, Ministry of Commerce, Industries and Production

Minister of Communications
Lt. Gen. Javed Ashraf, Ministry of Communications

Minister of Defense
Lt. Gen. Pervez Musharraf, Ministry of Defense

Minister of Education
Zubeda Jalal, Ministry of Education

Minister of Environment, Labor and Rural Development
Omar Asghar Khan, Ministry of Environment, Labor and Rural Development

Minister of Finance
Shaukat Aziz, Ministry of Finance

Minister of Food, Agriculture and Livestock
Khair Muhammad Junejo, Ministry of Food, Agriculture and Livestock

Minister of Foreign Affairs
Abdus Sattar, Ministry of Foreign Affairs

Minister of Health
Abdul Malik Kansi, Ministry of Health

Minister of Information
Pervez Musharraf, Ministry of Information

Minister of Interior and Narcotics
Moinuddin Haider, Ministry of Interior and Narcotics

Minister of Kashmir, Northern Areas, Housing and Works
Abbas Sarfaz Khan, Ministry of Kashmir, Northern Areas, Housing and Works

Minister of Law, Human Rights and Parliamentary Affairs
Shahida Jameel, Ministry of Law, Human Rights and Parliamentary Affairs

Minister of Petroleum and Natural Resources
Usman Aminuddin, Ministry of Petroleum and Natural Resources

Minister of Privatization
Altaf Saleem, Ministry of Privatization

Minister of Railways
Javed Ashraf, Ministry of Railways

Minister of Religious Affairs
Mahmood Ghazi, Ministry of Religious Affairs

Minister of Science and Technology
Attaur Rehman, Ministry of Science and Technology

Minister of Sports, Culture, Tourism, Youth and Minorities
S.K. Tresslor, Ministry of Sports, Culture, Tourism, Youth and Minorities

POLITICAL ORGANIZATIONS

Awami National Party (ANP)

NAME: Ajmal Khan Khattak

Baluchistan National Party (BNP)

Jamiat Ulema-i-Pakistan-JUP (Islamic Movement of Pakistan)

Mansoorah, Multan Rd., Lahore 54700, Pakistan
PHONE: +92 (042) 5419520; 7844605
FAX: +92 (042)_7832194
E-MAIL: info@jamaat.org
TITLE: President
NAME: Qazi Hussain Ahmad

Mohajir Quami Mahaz-MQM (Mohajir National Movement, Altaf faction)

NAME: Altaf Hussain

National People's Party (NPP)

NAME: Ghulam Mustafa Jatoi

Pakhtun Khawa Mill Awami Party-PKMAP (Pakhtun Khwa National People's Party)

NAME: Mahmood Khan Achakzai

Pakistan Muslim League Functional Group (PML-F)

NAME: Pir Pagaro

Pakistan Muslim League Junejo faction (PML-J)

NAME: Hamid Nasir Chattha

Pakistan Muslim League Nawaz Sharif faction (PML-N)

NAME: Nawaz Sharif

Pakistan People's Party (PPP)

Zardari House-8, Street 19, Sector F-8/2, Islamabad, Pakistan
PHONE: +92 (51) 282781 282782
FAX: +92 (51) 282741
E-MAIL: info@ppp.org.pk
TITLE: Chair
NAME: Benazir Bhutto

Jamhoori Watan Party-JWP (Republican Nation Party)

NAME: Akbar Khan Bugti

DIPLOMATIC REPRESENTATION

Embassies in Pakistan

Afghanistan
8 St #90, G-6/3 Islamabad, Pakistan
PHONE: +92 826505
FAX: +92 824504

Albania
231 St #18, F-10/2, Islamabad, Pakistan
PHONE: +92 290730; 290740
FAX: +92 290750

Algeria
107 St #9, E-7 Islamabad, Pakistan
PHONE: +92 206631
FAX: +92 820912

Argentina
20 Hill Rd., F-6/3 Islamabad, Pakistan
PHONE: +92 821242
FAX: +92 825564

Australia
Diplomatic Enclave No. 2, Islamabad, Pakistan
PHONE: +92 824345

Austria
13, St #1, F-6/3 Islamabad, Pakistan
PHONE: +92 279237; 279238
FAX: +92 828366

Bangladesh
1, St #5, F-6/3, Islamabad, Pakistan
PHONE: +92 279267
FAX: +92 279266

Belgium
14 St #17, F-7/2, Islamabad, Pakistan
PHONE: +92 827091; 277753
FAX: +92 822358

Bosnia
1, School Rd., F-8/3, Islamabad, Pakistan
PHONE: +92 261041; 261003
FAX: +92 261004

Brazil
Attaturk Avenue, G-6/3 Islamabad, Pakistan
PHONE: +92 279690; 279691
FAX: +92 823034

Brunei Darussalam
16 St #21, F-6/2 Islamabad, Pakistan
PHONE: +92 823038; 823783; 823372
FAX: +92 823138

Bulgaria
6-11 Diplomatic Enclave, Islamabad, Pakistan
PHONE: +92 279196
FAX: +92 279195

Canada
Diplomatic Enclave, G-5 Islamabad, Pakistan
PHONE: +92 279100; 279102; 2791003
FAX: +92 279110

China
Diplomatic Enclave, Islamabad, Pakistan
PHONE: +92 822540; 817279
FAX: +92 821116

Croatia
70 Margala Rd., F-7/2 Islamabad, Pakistan
PHONE: +92 827662; 827649
FAX: +92 827645

Czech Republic
49, St #27, F-6/2 Islamabad, Pakistan
PHONE: +92 274304

Denmark
9, 90th St., G-6/3 Islamabad, Pakistan
PHONE: +92 824722
FAX: +92 823483

Egypt
38-51 U.N. Boulevard DE, G-5/4 Islamabad, Pakistan
PHONE: +92 279550; 820180
FAX: +92 279552

Finland
11 St #90, G-6/3 Islamabad, Pakistan
PHONE: +92 828426; 822136; 822318
FAX: +92 828426; 828427

France
Diplomatic Enclave, G-5 Islamabad, Pakistan
PHONE: +92 278730; 278731; 278932
FAX: +92 822583; 825389

Germany
Diplomatic Enclave, Ramna 5, Islamabad, Pakistan
PHONE: +92 279430
FAX: +92 279436

Greece
6 Margala Rd, F-7/3 Islamabad, Pakistan
PHONE: +92 822558; 825186
FAX: +92 825161

Hungary
12, Margala Rd., F-6/3 Islamabad, Pakistan
PHONE: +92 823352; 823353
FAX: +92 825256

India
Diplomatic Enclave, G-5, Islamabad, Pakistan
PHONE: +92 272676

Indonesia
Diplomatic Enclave 1, St#5, Islamabad, Pakistan
PHONE: +92 206656
FAX: +92 829145

Iran
222-238, St # 2, G-5/1, DE, Islamabad, Pakistan
PHONE: +92 276210
FAX: +92 8244839

Iraq
57, St #48, F-8/4 Islamabad, Pakistan
PHONE: +92 253391; 253392; 253393
FAX: +92 253394

Italy
54, Margala Rd., Shalimar 6/3, Islamabad, Pakistan
PHONE: +92 828982
FAX: +92 829026

Japan
53-70, Ramna 5/4, DE, Islamabad, Pakistan
PHONE: +92 279320; 279330
FAX: +92 279320

Jordan
131 St #14, E-7 Islamabad, Pakistan
PHONE: +92 823459; 823460
FAX: +92 823207

Kazakstan
2 St#4, F-8/3 Islamabad, Pakistan
PHONE: +92 262926; 262924
FAX: +92 262926

Kenya
10 St #9, F-7/3 Islamabad, Pakistan
PHONE: +92 279540; 279542
FAX: +92 279541

Korea
9 St #18, F-8/2 Islamabad, Pakistan
PHONE: +92 279385; 279386; 279387
FAX: +92 279391

Kuwait
1, 2 and 24, DE Islamabad, Pakistan
PHONE: +92 279413

Lebanon
6 St #27, Shalimar 6/2, Islamabad, Pakistan
PHONE: +92 278338
FAX: +92 826410

Libya
12, Margala Rd., F-8/3 Islamabad, Pakistan
PHONE: +92 255066

Malaysia
78 Margala Rd., F-6/2 Islamabad, Pakistan
PHONE: +92 279574
FAX: +92 824761

Mauritius
27, St #26, F-6/2 Islamabad, Pakistan
PHONE: +92 824657; 824658; 828985
FAX: +92 824656

Morocco
6, Gomal Rd., E-7 Islamabad, Pakistan
PHONE: +92 820565
FAX: +92 822745

Myammar
12/1 St #13, F-7/2 Islamabad, Pakistan
PHONE: +92 822460; 828818
FAX: +92 828819

Nepal
11 St #84, G-6/4 Islamabad, Pakistan
PHONE: +92 828838; 278051
FAX: +92 928839

Netherlands
2nd Floor PIA Building Blue Area, Islamabad, Pakistan
PHONE: +92 279510; 279511; 279512
FAX: +92 279512

Nigeria
6 St #22, F-6/2 Islamabad, Pakistan
PHONE: +92 823542; 823547
FAX: +92 824104

Norway
25 St #19, F-6/2 Islamabad, Pakistan
PHONE: +92 279720; 279721; 279722
FAX: +92 279729

Oman
53 St #48, F-8/4 Islamabad, Pakistan
PHONE: +92 254925; 254469
FAX: +92 255074

Palestine
486-B, St #9, F-10/2, Islamabad, Pakistan
PHONE: +92 291185
FAX: +92 294703

Philippines
8, St #60, F-7/4 Islamabad, Pakistan
PHONE: +92 824933; 822720
FAX: +92 277389

Poland
24, G-5/4, DE II, Islamabad, Pakistan
PHONE: +92 279491; 279492
FAX: +92 825442

Portugal
40 A, Main Margala Rd., F-7/2 Islamabad, Pakistan
PHONE: +92 279530; 279531
FAX: +92 279532

Qatar
20, Khayaban-e-Iqbal, F-6/3 Islamabad, Pakistan
PHONE: +92 826483; 826484
FAX: +92 820868

Romania
13, St #88, G-6/3 Islamabad, Pakistan
PHONE: +92 826514; 826515
FAX: +92 826515

Russia
Diplomatic Enclave, Ramna 4, Islamabad, Pakistan
PHONE: +92 278670; 278671
FAX: +92 826552

Saudi Arabia
14 Hill Rd., F-6/3 Islamabad, Pakistan
PHONE: +92 820156; 820150; 821056
FAX: +92 278816

Serbia
14 St #87, G-6/3 Islamabad, Pakistan
PHONE: +92 829556; 829557
FAX: +92 820956

Somalia
21 St #56, F-6/4 Islamabad, Pakistan
PHONE: +92 263383; 279789; 279790
FAX: +92 826117

South Africa
48 Margala Rd., F-8/2 Islamabad, Pakistan
PHONE: +92 262354; 262356; 250318
FAX: +92 250114

Spain
St #6, Ramna 5, DE, Islamabad, Pakistan
PHONE: +92 279480
FAX: +92 279489

Sri Lanka
St #52, F-6/4 Islamabad, Pakistan
PHONE: +92 828735
FAX: +92 828751

Sudan
7, St #1, G-6/3 Islamabad, Pakistan
PHONE: +92 827068, 828710
FAX: +92 827073

Sweden
4, St #5, F-6/3 Islamabad, Pakistan
PHONE: +92 828712; 828713; 828714
FAX: +92 825284

Switzerland
St #6, DE G-5/4 Islamabad, Pakistan
PHONE: +92 279291
FAX: +92 279286

Syria
30 Hill Rd., F-6/3 Islamabad, Pakistan
PHONE: +92 279470; 279471
FAX: +92 279472

Thailand
10, St #33, F-8/1 Islamabad, Pakistan
PHONE: +92 280586; 254697; 280909
FAX: +92 256730

Tunisia
221, St #21, E-7 Islamabad, Pakistan
PHONE: +92 827869; 827870
FAX: +92 827871

Turkey
58 Attaturk Ravenue, G-6/3 Islamabad, Pakistan
PHONE: +92 278748; 278749
FAX: +92 278752

Turkmenistan
22-A, F-7/1, Nazim-ud-Din Road, Islamabad, Pakistan
PHONE: +92 274913
FAX: +92 278799

United Arab Emirates
1-22 DE University Rd., Islamabad, Pakistan
PHONE: +92 279052; 278053; 279054

United Kingdom
PHONE: +92 822131; 822132; 822133
FAX: +92 823439

United States
Diplomatic Enclave, Ramna 5, Islamabad, Pakistan
PHONE: +92 826161; 826162; 826163
FAX: +92 276427

Uzbekistan
6 St #29, F-7/1 Islamabad, Pakistan
PHONE: +92 820779
FAX: +92 278128

Yemen
138 St #14, E-7 Islamabad, Pakistan
PHONE: +92 821146; 821147
FAX: +92 279567

JUDICIAL SYSTEM

Supreme Court

Federal Court

BROADCAST MEDIA

Azad Kashmir Radio

Muzaffarabed, Azad Kashmir, Pakistan
TITLE: Deputy Controller
CONTACT: Syed Ahmed
LANGUAGE: Urdu, English
TYPE: Government

Capital FM

BROADCASTS: 24 hours/day
TYPE: Private (music and audience participation)

Far East Broadcasting Company

FEBA Pakistan, PO Box 318, Islamabad, Pakistan
PHONE: +92 (51) 863256
FAX: +92 (51) 471747 (call first)
E-MAIL: http://febacom.isb.erum.com.pk
TYPE: Religious

Pakistan Broadcasting Corporation

Broadcasting House, Constitution Avenue, Islamabad 4400, Pakistan
PHONE: +92 (51) 9214278
FAX: +92 (51) 9223827
CONTACT: S. Anwer Mahmood
LANGUAGE: Urdu, English
TYPE: Government

Radio Pakistan

Broadcasting House, Constitution Avenue, Islamabad 4400, Pakistan
PHONE: +92 (51) 9214947
FAX: +92 (51) 9216657
CONTACT: S. Auwar Mehmood

Pakistan Television Corporation LTD.

Federal Television Complex, PO Box 1221, Islamabad, Pakistan
PHONE: +92 (51) 828723
FAX: +92 (51) 823406
CONTACT: Raana Shaikh

Shalimar Television Network (STN)

PO Box 1246, Islamabad, Pakistan
PHONE: +92 (51) 856171
FAX: +92 (51) 261225
CONTACT: M. Arshad Choundry

COLLEGES AND UNIVERSITIES

N.W.F.P. University of Engineering

N.W.F.P.University of Engineering and Technology, Peshawar University Campus Rd., PO Box 814, Peshawar 25000, Pakistan
PHONE: +92 (521) 842173
FAX: +92 (521) 841758
WEBSITE: http://www.geocities.com:0080/collegepark/quad/2406/uetface.ht

Islamia University - Bahawalpur

Islamia University-Bahawalpur, Bahawalpur, Pakistan
PHONE: +92 (11) 80331
FAX: +92 (11) 80372

Mehran University of Engineering-Technology

Jamshoro, Sindh, Pakistan
PHONE: +92 (221) 71197
FAX: +92 (221) 71633
WEBSITE: http://www.muet.edu.pk

University of Sindh

Jamshoro, District Dadu, Sindh, Pakistan
PHONE: +92 (221) 771681
FAX: +92 (221) 771372

Sindh Agricultural University

Sindh Agriculture University, Tandojam, Sindh, Pakistan
PHONE: +92 (221) 335869
FAX: +92 (221) 335300

Allama Iqbal Open University

Sector H-8, Islamabad, Pakistan
PHONE: +92 (51) 435748
FAX: +92 (51) 435766
E-MAIL: aiou@isb.comsats.net.pk
WEBSITE: http://www-icdl.open.ac.uk/cdl

Ouaid-I-Azam University

PO Box 1090, Islamabad, Pakistan
PHONE: +92 (51) 827259
FAX: +92 (51) 827259
WEBSITE: http://www.panasia.org.sg/tcdc/pakistan/

University of the Punjab-Lahore

29 Noon Ave., Muslim Town, Lahore, Pakistan
PHONE: +92 (42) 5865337
FAX: +92 (42) 5883573

WEBSITE: http://www.pgc.edu

Azad Jammu & Kashmir University

Muzaffarabad, Azad Kashmir, Pakistan
E-MAIL: yaqub@ajku.sdnpt.undp.org
WEBSITE: http://www.geocities.com/tokyo/garden/4404/uni-ajka.htm

University of Balochistan

Sariab Rd., Quetta, Balochistan, Pakistan
PHONE: +92 (81) 9211268
FAX: +92 (81) 9211277
E-MAIL: info@uob.cjb.net
WEBSITE: http://uob.cjb.net

Shah Abdul Latif Bhitai University

Khaipur, Sindh, Pakistan
PHONE: +92 (91) 7923091
FAX: +92 (91) 7923137
WEBSITE: http://www.geocities.com/tokyo/garden/4404/uni-sal.htm

Gomal University

Dera Ismail Khan, Pakistan
PHONE: +92 5299123
FAX: +92 5294673
WEBSITE: http://www.geocities.com/tokyo/garden/4404/uni-gom.htm

Ladoke Akintola University of Technology

PMB 4000, Ogbomoso, Pakistan

N.W.F.P. Agricultural University

University Campus, Peshawar, Pakistan
PHONE: +92 (91) 40230
FAX: +92 (91) 42470
WEBSITE: http://www.geocities.com/tokyo/garden/4404/uni-nwau.htm

University of Agriculture-Faisalabad

Faisalabad, Punjab 38040, Pakistan
PHONE: +92 (411) 601822
FAX: +92 (411) 647846
WEBSITE: http://www.geocities.com/tokyo/garden/4404/uni-auf.htm

International Islamic University - Islamabad

PO Box 1243, Islamabad 44000, Pakistan
PHONE: +92 (51) 850751
FAX: +92 (51) 250821
E-MAIL: iiui@paknet2.ptc.pk
WEBSITE: http://www.iiu.edu.pk/

Lahore University of Management Sciences

Opposite Sector U, Lahore Cantonment Co-Op Housing Soc., Lahore 54792, Pakistan
PHONE: +92 (42) 5722670
FAX: +92 (42) 5722591
E-MAIL: admissions@lums.edu.pk
WEBSITE: http://www.lums.edu.pk/

University of Engineering & Technology

Univ. of Engineering & Technology Lahore, Punjab, Lahore 54890, Pakistan
PHONE: +92 (42) 339205
FAX: +92 (42) 6822566
WEBSITE: http://www.uet.edu

Bahauddin Zakariya University

Multan, Punjab 60800, Pakistan
PHONE: +92 (61) 224371
FAX: +92 (61) 220091
WEBSITE: http://www.geocities.com/tokyo/garden/4404/uni-bdin.htm

University of Karachi

University Rd., Karachi 75270, Pakistan
PHONE: +92 (21) 479001
FAX: +92 (21) 4969277
E-MAIL: vc@ku.its.super.net.pk
WEBSITE: http://www.kudcs.edu.pk/

NED University of Engineering-Technology

N E D University of, Engineering & Technology, University Rd., Karachi 75270, Pakistan
PHONE: +92 (21) 4969261
FAX: +92 (21) 4961934
E-MAIL: registrar@neduet.edu.pk
WEBSITE: http://www.neduet.edu.pk

NEWSPAPERS AND MAGAZINES

Akhbar

WEBSITE: http://www.paknews.net

Business Recorder

E-MAIL: recorder@fascom.com
TITLE: Editor
CONTACT: M.A. Zuberi

Daily Jang Pakistan

E-MAIL: editorjang@jang.com.pk
WEBSITE: http://www.jang-group.com/jang/index.html

Dawn

Haroon House, Dr. Ziauddin Ahmed Road, Karachi 74200 Pakistan
FAX: +92 (21) 5683801; 5682187
E-MAIL: webmaster@dawn.com
WEBSITE: http://www.dawn.com

Daily Kawish

B/2 Civil Line Hyderabad, Sindh Pakistan
PHONE: +92 (221) 780026; 780027
FAX: +92 (221) 7800525
E-MAIL: kawish12@yahoo.com
WEBSITE: http://www.kawish.com

Millat

WEBSITE: http://www.pakpost.pair.com/urdu

Family Magazine

Nida-i-Millat (Pvt) Ltd., 4-Shara-i-Fatima Jinnah, PO Box 2059, Lahore 54000 Pakistan
PHONE: +92 (42) 6367551
FAX: +92 (42) 6367583
TITLE: Editor
CONTACT: Magid Nizami
CIRCULATION: 67,000

Herald

Pakistan Herald Publications (Pvt) Ltd., Haroon House, Dr. Ziauddin Ahmed Road, Karachi 74200 Pakistan
PHONE: +92 (21) 5670001
FAX: +92 (21) 5683801
WEBSITE: http://www.ciber.com./herald
TITLE: Editor
CONTACT: Aamer Ahmed Khan
CIRCULATION: 38,000
TYPE: Current affairs

Pakistan Archaeology

27-A Central Union Commercial Area, Shaheed-e-Millat Road, Karachi 8 Pakistan
TYPE: Archaeology

Pakistan Digest

4 Amil St., off Robson Rd., GPO Box 671, Karachi, Pakistan
CIRCULATION: 12,000
TYPE: Social science, general

Pakistan Horizon

PO Box 1447, Aiwan-e-Sadar Road, Karachi 74200 Pakistan
FAX: +92 (21) 5686069
TITLE: Editor
CONTACT: Syed Adil Hussain
CIRCULATION: 1,000
TYPE: Political science, general

Phool

Nida-i-Millat (Pvt) Ltd., 4-Shara-i-Fatima Jinnah, PO Box 2059, Lahore 54000 Pakistan
PHONE: +92 (42) 6367551
FAX: +92 (42) 6367583
TITLE: Editor
CONTACT: Magid Nizami
CIRCULATION: 41,000
TYPE: Juvenile

PUBLISHERS

Ferozsons (Pvt) Ltd.

60 Shahrah-e-Quaid-e-Azam, Lahore, Pakistan
PHONE: +92 (042) 6301196-98
FAX: +92 (042)6369204
E-MAIL: ferozsons@showroom.edunet.sdnpk.undp.org
WEBSITE: http://www.jamals.com/frsons
TITLE: Managing Director
CONTACT: A. Salam
SUBJECTS: Art, Biographies, History, Law, Literature, Medicine, Politics, Religion, Social Sciences, Travel

Sheik Ghulam Ali and Sons (Pvt) Ltd.

14-Lawrence Rd., Lahore, Pakistan
PHONE: +92 (042) 6361421
FAX: +92 (042) 6375478
E-MAIL: uzma@paknet4.ptc.pk
TITLE: Director
CONTACT: Arshad Niaz

Hamdard Foundation

Hamdard Centre, Nazimabad, Karachi, Pakistan
PHONE: +92 (021) 6616001
FAX: +92 (021) 6611175
E-MAIL: hlpak@net3.ptc.pk
TITLE: President
CONTACT: Hakim Mohommed Said
SUBJECTS: Biography, Education, History, Library and Information Sciences, Literature,

Literary Criticism, Essays, Medicine, Nursing, Dentistry, Philosophy, Religion-Islamic, Science (General), Social Sciences, Sociology

Islamic Publications (Pvt) Ltd

13-E Shahalam Market, Lahore 54000, Pakistan
PHONE: +92 (042) 7325243
FAX: +92 (042) 7658674
E-MAIL: info@ip.com.pk
WEBSITE: http://www.ip.com.pk
TITLE: Managing Director
CONTACT: Muhammed Amin Javed
SUBJECTS: Islamic Literature, Religion-Islamic
TOTAL PUBLISHED: 700 print

Islamic Research Institute

International Islamic University, Faisal Masjid, PO Box 1035, Islamabad, Pakistan
PHONE: +92 (51) 254874
FAX: +92 (51) 853360
E-MAIL: dg-iri@iri-iiu.sdnpd.undp.org
SUBJECTS: Economics, Education, History, International Relations, Philosophy, Psychiatry, Psychology, Politics, Sociology

Sheik Muhammed Ashraf Publishers

7 Aibak Road, New Anarkali, Lahore, 1, Pakistan
PHONE: +92 (4) 2353171
FAX: +92 (4) 2353489
E-MAIL: shashraf@brain.net.pk
TITLE: Publisher
CONTACT: Sh Muhammed Ashraf
SUBJECTS: Biography, Geography, Geology, Government, Political Science, History, Law, Religion-Other
TOTAL PUBLISHED: Over 250 print

Kazi Publications

121 Zulqarnain Chambers, Ganpat Rd., PO Box 1845, Lahore, Pakistan
PHONE: +92 7350805
FAX: +92 7117606
E-MAIL: kazip@brain.net.pk
WEBSITE: http://www.brain.net.pk/~kazip
TITLE: Proprietor
CONTACT: Muahmmed Ikram Siddiqi
SUBJECTS: Islamic Literature, Biography, Law, Religion-Islamic
TOTAL PUBLISHED: 200 print

Jang Publishers

13-Sir Aga Khan Road, Lahore, Pakistan
PHONE: +92 (042) 6367480-83
FAX: +92 (042) 6361026
E-MAIL: thenewslhr@jang.group.com
WEBSITE: http://www.jang-group.com
TITLE: Chief Editor
CONTACT: Shakeel ur Rehman
SUBJECTS: Cookery, Government, Political Science, History, Humor, Literature, Literary Criticism, Essays, Mysteries, Nonfiction (General), Poetry, Regional Interests, Religion-Islamic, Sports, Athletics, Travel

Malik Sirajuddin and Sons

F/1982, Kashmiri Bazar, PO Box 2250, Lahore, Pakistan
PHONE: +92 (042) 7225809
FAX: +92 (042) 7657490
E-MAIL: sirajco@brain.net.pk
TITLE: Manager
CONTACT: Malik Abdul Rauf
SUBJECTS: Law, Religion

Maqbool Academy

199 Circular Rd., Chowk Anarkali, Lahore, Pakistan
PHONE: +92 (042) 7324164
FAX: +92 (042) 7238241
E-MAIL: zmaqbool@one.net.pk
WEBSITE: http://www.maqboolacademy.com
TITLE: Proprietor
CONTACT: Maqbool Ahmed Malik
SUBJECTS: Asian Studies, Cookery, Drama, Theater, Education, Fashion, Gardening, Plants, Government, Political Science, History, Humor, Literature, Literary Criticism, Essays, Poetry, Religion-Islamic, Religion-Other, Romance, Science (General)
TOTAL PUBLISHED: 100 print

Nashiran-e-Quran Pvt Ltd.

38-Urdu Bazar, Lahore, Pakistan
PHONE: +92 (042) 58581
TITLE: Chairman
CONTACT: Abdul Hamid Khan
SUBJECTS: Literature, Literary Criticism, Essays, Religion-Islamic

National Book Foundation

6-Mauve Area, G-8/4, Talemi Chwok, PO Box 1169, Islamabad, Pakistan
PHONE: +92 (51) 9261533; 9261534
FAX: +92 (51) 264283; 9261534
E-MAIL: nbf@paknet2.ptc.pk

WEBSITE: http://www.nbf.sdnpk.org
TITLE: Managing Director
CONTACT: Ahmad Faraz
SUBJECTS: Accounting, Agriculture, Behavioral Sciences, Biological Sciences, Business, Career Development, Chemistry, Chemical Engineering, Civil Engineering, Mathematics, Psychology, Religion-Islamic
TOTAL PUBLISHED: 3,100

National Book Service

22 Urdu Bazar, Lahore, Pakistan
PHONE: +92 (042) 7355262
FAX: +92 (042) 7247323
E-MAIL: masim@brain.net.pk
WEBSITE: http://www.brain.net.pk/~masim
CONTACT: Muhammed Asim
SUBJECTS: Biology, Chemistry, Fiction, History, Literature, Mathematics, Physics, Poetry

National Language Authority

H-8/4, Pitras Bokhari Rd., Islamabad, Pakistan
PHONE: +92 (51) 446881
FAX: +92 (51) 446883
E-MAIL: nlapak@appollp.net.pk
WEBSITE: http://www.nla.gov.pk/index.html
TITLE: Chairman
CONTACT: Iftakhar H. Arif
SUBJECTS: Biology, Chemistry, Dictionaries, Language, Library Science, Mass Communication
TOTAL PUBLISHED: 200 print

Oxford University Press

5 Bangalore Town, Sharae Faisal, Karachi, Pakistan
PHONE: +92 (21) 4529025-9
FAX: +92 (21) 4547640
E-MAIL: ouppak@theoffice.net
WEBSITE: http://www.oup.com.pk
SUBJECTS: Anthropology, Art, Biography, Economics, Education, Geography, History, International Relations, Language, Linguistics, Law, Literature, Media, Philosophy, Poetry, Politics, Sociology, Sports, Travel

Publishers United Pvt Ltd.

176 Anarkali, 54000 Lahore, Pakistan
PHONE: +92 (042) 7352238
TITLE: Managing Director
CONTACT: Javed Amin
SUBJECTS: Biological Sciences, Chemistry, Chemical Engineering, Economics, Geography, Geology, History, Literature, Literary Criticism, Essays, Mathematics, Philosophy, Physics, Psychology, Psychiatry, Religion-Other, Technology

Sang-e-Meel Publications

Chowk Urdu Bazar, 25, Lower Mall, Lahore, Pakistan
PHONE: +92 (042) 7228143
FAX: +92 (042) 7245105
E-MAIL: smp@sang-e-meel.com
WEBSITE: http://www.sang-e-meel.com
TITLE: Imports and Exports
CONTACT: Afzaal Ahmad
SUBJECTS: Agriculture, Anthropology, Art, Asian Studies, Criminology, Drama, Theater, Fiction, Health, Nutrition, History, Journalism, Literature, Literary Criticism, Essays, Poetry, Travel
TOTAL PUBLISHED: 4,000 print

Vanguard Books Ltd

45 The Mall, Lahore, Pakistan
PHONE: +92 (042) 7243779
FAX: +92 (042) 7245097
E-MAIL: nasethi@lhr.comsats.net.pk
WEBSITE: http://www.vanguardbooks.com
CONTACT: Adalat Hussain Alvi
SUBJECTS: Asian Studies, Economics, Fiction, History, Law, Politics, Regional Interests, Religion-Islamic, Social Sciences
TOTAL PUBLISHED: 500 print

RELIGIOUS ORGANIZATIONS

Islamic

Ahmadiyya Society - Pakistan (ASP)
Dar-es-Salaam Colony, 5 Usman Block, New Garden Town, Lahore 54600, Pakistan
PHONE: +92 (42) 5863260
FAX: +92 (42) 5839202
TITLE: Contact
NAME: Aziz Ahmad

Jamaat-e-Islami Pakistan
Mansura, Multan Road, Lahore, Pakistan
PHONE: +92 (42) 54195204
FAX: +92 (42) 5419505
E-MAIL: info@jamaat.org
TITLE: The Secretary General

Tanzeem-e-Islami- Faisalabad
Office Tanzeem-e-Islami, P-175 Sadiq Market, Railway RD, Faisalabed, Pakistan
PHONE: +92 624290

Tanzeem-e-Islami- Gujraat
Office Tanzeem-e-Islami, Kamran Book Depot, Outside Kabuli Gate, Gujrat, Pakistan
PHONE: +92 521070

Tanzeem-e-Islami Gujranwala
Office Tanzeem-e- Islami, Sharifpura Chawk, GT Road, Gujranwala, Pakistan
PHONE: +92 53523

Tanzeem-e-Islami Hyderabad
Abdul Qadir, Hyderabad Cotton Oil Mills, Old Power House Road, Hyderabad, Pakistan
PHONE: +92 34205, +92 34235

Tanzeem-e-Islami Islamabad
House #20, St #1, Faizabad Housing Scheem, Near Fly-over Bridege, I-8/4, Islamabad, Pakistan
PHONE: +92 435430

Tanzeem-e-Islami Karachi
Anjuman Khuddam-ul-Qurab Sind., Quran Academy, DM-55, Darakhshan, Khiyaban-e-Rahat, Defence Phase 6, Karachi, Pakistan
PHONE: +92 5855219
FAX: +92 5854036

Tanzeem-e-Islami Karachi
Haq Squrae, First Floor, University Road, Gulshan Iqbal, Karachi, Pakistan
PHONE: +92 4989926

Tanzeem-e-Islami Lahore
Markaz Tanzeem-e-Islami Pakistan, 67-A, Allama Iqbal Road, Garhee Shahoo, Lahore, Pakistan
PHONE: +92 6305110

Tanzeem-e-Islami Lahore
Markazi Anjuman Khuddam-ul-Quran Lahore, Quran Academy, 36-K, Model Town, Lahore, Pakistan
PHONE: +92 5869501, +92 5869502, +92 5869503
FAX: +92 5834000
E-MAIL: anjuman@brain.net.pk

Tanzeem-e-Islami Multan
Quran Academy, 25 Officers Colony, Multan, Pakistan
PHONE: +92 521070

Tanzeem-e-Islami Peshawar
18-A, Nasir Mansion, Shuba Bazar, Railway Road No. 2, Peshwar, Pakistan
PHONE: +92 214495

Tanzeem-e-Islami Quetta
28 Syed Building, Near Bublic Health School, Jinnah Road, Quetta, Pakistan
PHONE: +92 62507

Tanzeem-e-Islami Rawalpindi
Office Tanzeem-e-Islami, 44/B/1, Hasnain Market, Near Central Hospital, Satellite Town, Rawalpindi, Pakistan
PHONE: +92 427592

Tanzeem-e-Islami Sakkar
Office Tanzeem-e-Islami Sakkar, Near Makki Masjid, Mibara Road, Sakkhar, Pakistan
PHONE: +92 24775

Tanzeem-e-Islami Sargodha
45 Farooq Colony, College Road, Sargodha, Pakistan
PHONE: +92 213557

Tanzeem-e-Islami Sialkot
Modern Book Depot, Sialkot City, Pakistan
PHONE: +92 556184

United Islamic Organization (UIO)
140 E Block 7, Gulshan Iqbal, Karachi, Pakistan
PHONE: +92 (21) 4973818

World Federation of Islamic Mission (WFIM)

Federation Mondiale des Missions Islamiques
Mission Islamic Centre, Abdul Aleem Siddiqi Rd., B Block,N. Nazimabad, Karachi 74700, Pakistan
PHONE: +92 (21) 6644156
TITLE: General Secretary
NAME: S. M. Manzar Karim

Protestant

Pakistan Adventist Seminary
Farooqabad, District Sheikhupura, 39500 Punjab, Pakistan
PHONE: +92 (0) 4945874501
FAX: +92 (0) 4945874841
E-MAIL: branko@brain.net.pk

The Salvation Army
PO Box 242, 35 Shara-e-Fatima Jinnah, Lahore, 54000 Pakistan
PHONE: +92 (42) 7581644, +92 (2) 415818
FAX: +92 (42) 7572699
E-MAIL: pakistan@salvationarmy.org

Scientology

Dr. Itqan Farouqi
A-3 Royal Avenue, First Floor, Opp:URDU College, Block 13C, Gulshan-E-Iqbal, Karachi, Pakistan
PHONE: +92 (21) 4973064
NAME: Dr. Itqan Farouqi

FURTHER READING

Articles

"The Coup That Fell to Earth." *New York Times,* April 9, 2000, p. 3.

"A General's Path to Democracy: One Year after the Coup, Pakistan's Pervez Musharraf Promises a Return to Democratic Rule in 2002." *Christian Science Monitor,* October 12, 2000, p. 6.

"The Month in Review: January 2000." *Current History,* March 2000, p. 142.

Wren, Christopher. "India and Pakistan Continue War of Words, Minus Names, Over Kashmir." *New York Times,* September 9, 2000, p. A5.

Books

Alter, Stephen. *Amritsar to Lahore: A Journey across the India-Pakistan Border.* Philadelphia: University of Pennsylvania Press, 2000.

Schofield, Victoria. *Kashmir in Conflict: India, Pakistan and the Unfinished War.* New York: I.B. Tauris, 2000.

Yong, Tan Tai. *The Aftermath of Partition in South Asia.* New York: Routledge, 2000.

Government Publications

Background Notes: Pakistan. Washington, DC: G.P.O., 2000.

United States Congress. *Crisis in Pakistan.* Washington, DC: G.P.O., 2000.

PAKISTAN: STATISTICAL DATA

For sources and notes see "Sources of Statistics" at the front of each volume.

GEOGRAPHY

Geography

Area:

Total: 803,940 sq km.

Land: 778,720 sq km.

Land boundaries:

Total: 6,774 km.

Border countries: Afghanistan 2,430 km, China 523 km, India 2,912 km, Iran 909 km.

Coastline: 1,046 km.

Climate: mostly hot, dry desert; temperate in northwest; arctic in north.

Terrain: flat Indus plain in east; mountains in north and northwest; Balochistan plateau in west.

Natural resources: land, extensive natural gas reserves, limited petroleum, poor quality coal, iron ore, copper, salt, limestone.

Land use:

Arable land: 27%

Permanent crops: 1%

Permanent pastures: 6%

Forests and woodland: 5%

Other: 61% (1993 est.).

HUMAN FACTORS

Demographics (A)

	1990	1995	1998	2000	2010	2020	2030	2040	2050
Population	113,975	126,629	135,471	141,554	171,373	199,745	226,251	249,145	267,814
Life expectancy - males	56.2	58.4	59.5	60.3	63.7	66.8	69.6	71.9	74.0
Life expectancy - females	57.1	59.7	61.0	61.9	66.0	69.7	73.1	76.0	78.5
Birth rate (per 1,000)	41.8	36.9	34.0	32.1	24.8	20.6	17.4	15.3	13.9
Death rate (per 1,000)	12.8	11.0	10.1	9.5	7.5	6.6	6.4	6.9	7.8
Women of reproductive age (15-49 yrs.)	24,864	28,129	30,692	32,696	43,891	53,861	61,056	64,213	64,130
Fertility rate	6.2	5.4	4.9	4.6	3.2	2.4	2.1	2.0	2.0

Except as noted, values for vital statistics are in thousands; life expectancy is in years.

Health Personnel

	National Data	World Data (wtd ave)
Total health expenditure as a percentage of GDP, 1990-1998[a]		
Public sector	0.9	2.5
Private sector	3.0	2.9
Total[b]	3.9	5.5
Health expenditure per capita in U.S. dollars, 1990-1998[a]		
Purchasing power parity	65	561
Total	18	483
Availability of health care facilities per 100,000 people		
Hospital beds 1990-1998[a]	70	330
Doctors 1992-1995[a]	52	122
Nurses 1992-1995[a]	32	248

Health Indicators

	National Data	World Data
Life expectancy at birth (years)		
1980	55	61
1998	62	67
Daily per capita supply of calories		
1970	2,202	2,358
1997	2,476	2,791
Daily per capital supply of protein		
1997 (grams)	61	74
Total fertility rate (births per woman)		
1980	7.0	3.7
1998	4.9	2.7
Population with access (%)		
To safe water (1990-96)	60	NA
To sanitation (1990-96)	30	NA
People living with (1997)		
Tuberculosis (cases per 100,000)	3.1[1]	60.4
Malaria (cases per 100,000)	53.8	42.2
HIV/AIDS (% aged 15 - 49 years)	0.09	0.99

Infants and Malnutrition

	National Data	World Data (wtd ave)
Under 5 mortality rate (1989)	136	NA
% of infants with low birthweight (1992-98)[1]	25	17
Births attended by skilled health staff (% of total births 1996-98)	18	52
% fully immunized at 1 year of age (1995-98)[1]		
TB	66	82
DPT	59	77
Polio	59	77
Measles	55	74
Prevalence of child malnutrition (1992-98)[1] (based on weight for age, % of children under 5 years)	38	30

Ethnic Division

Punjabi, Sindhi, Pashtun (Pathan), Baloch, Muhajir (immigrants from India at the time of partition and their descendants).

Religion

Muslim 97%
Sunni 77%
Shi'a 20%
Christian, Hindu, and other 3%

Major Languages

Punjabi 48%
Sindhi 12%
Siraiki (a Punjabi variant) 10%
Pashtu 8%
Urdu (official) 8%
Balochi 3%
Hindko 2%
Brahui 1%
English (official and lingua franca of Pakistani elite and most government ministries), Burushaski, and other 8%

EDUCATION

Public Education Expenditures

	1980	1997
Public expenditures on education as % of GNP	2.1	2.7
Expenditures per student as % of GNP per capita		
Primary	9.2[2]	NA
Secondary	NA	NA
Pupils per teacher at the primary level	NA	NA
Duration of primary education in years	NA	NA

	1980	1997
World data for comparison		
Public expenditures on education as % of GNP (mean)	3.9	4.8
Pupils per teacher at the primary level (wtd ave)	NA	33
Duration of primary education in years (mean)	NA	9

Educational Attainment (A)

Age group (1990)[19] . . . . .25+
Population of this age group . . . . .NA
Highest level attained (%)
No schooling 73.8
First level
Not completed 9.7
Completed . . . . .NA
Entered second level
Lower Secondary 5.8
Upper Secondary 8.2
Entered post-secondary .2.5

Literacy Rates (A)

In thousands and percent	1990	1995	2000	2010
Illiterate population (15+ yrs.)	44,805	48,693	53,690	64,623
Literacy rate - total adult pop. (%)	34.2	37.8	41.8	49.9
Literacy rate - males (%)	46.3	50.0	54.0	61.6
Literacy rate - females (%)	20.9	24.4	28.6	37.6

Libraries

National Libraries **1992**
Administrative Units 1
Service Points or Branches 1
Number of Volumes (000) 78
Registered Users (000) .NA
Loans to Users (000) . . . . .NA
Total Library Staff 123
Public Libraries **1992**
Administrative Units 4
Service Points or Branches 10
Number of Volumes (000) 543
Registered Users (000) 62
Loans to Users (000) 48
Total Library Staff 280

GOVERNMENT & LAW

Political Parties

Parliament (Majlis-e-Shoora)	no. of seats
Senate	
Pakistan Muslim League, Nawaz Sharif Faction (PML/N)	30
Pakistan People's Party (PPP)	17
Awami National Party (ANP)	7
Mutahida Qaumi Movement, Altaf Faction (MQM/A)	6
Jamhoori Watan Party (JWP)	5
Baluch National Party (BNP)	4
Jamiat Ulema-i-Islam, Fazlur Rehman Faction (JUI/F)	2
Pakistan Muslim League, Junejo Faction (PML/J)	2
Balochistan National Movement/Mengal Group (BNM/M)	1
Pakhtun Khwa Milli Awami Party (PKMAP)	1
Tehrik I Jafria Pakistan (TJP)	1
Independents	6
Vacant	5
National Assembly	
Pakistan Muslim League, Nawaz Sharif Faction (PML/N)	137
Pakistan People's Party (PPP)	18
Mutahida Qaumi Movement, Altaf Faction (MQM/A)	12
Awami National Party (ANP)	10
Baluch National Party (BNP)	3
Jamhoari Watan Party (JWP)	2
Jamiat Ulema-i-Islam, Fazlur Rehman Faction (JUI/F)	2
Pakistan People's Party/Shaheed Bhutto (PPP/SB)	1
National People's Party (NPP)	1
Independents	21
Minorities	10

Elections for the Senate were last held 12 March 1997; National Assembly elections were last held 3 February 1997. Gen. Pervez Musharraf dissolved Parliament following the military takeover of 12 October 1999, however, political parties have been allowed to operate. Political alliances can shift frequently.

Government Budgets (B)

Revenues . . . .$10.0 billion
Expenditures . . . .$11.7 billion

Data for FY98/99.

Military Affairs (A)

	1990	1992	1995	1996	1997
Military expenditures					
Current dollars (mil.)	2,810	3,350	3,310	3,440	3,380
1997 constant dollars (mil.)	3,290	3,710	3,430	3,500	3,380
Armed forces (000)	550	580	580	580	610
Gross national product (GNP)					
Current dollars (mil.)	37,100	45,300	54,200	58,200	59,200
1997 constant dollars (mil.)	43,500	50,300	56,100	59,200	59,200
Central government expenditures (CGE)					
1997 constant dollars (mil.)	11,300	13,300	13,600	14,800	14,000
People (mil.)	113.9	118.9	126.4	129.3	132.2
Military expenditure as % of GNP	7.6	7.4	6.1	5.9	5.7
World data on military expenditure as % of GNP	4.5	3.4	2.7	2.6	2.6
Military expenditure as % of CGE	29.1	27.9	25.3	23.7	24.2
World data on military expenditure as % of CGE	17.0	12.5	10.5	10.3	10.2
Military expenditure per capita (1997 $)	29	20	27	27	26
World data on military expenditure per capita (1997 $)	242	173	146	143	145
Armed forces per 1,000 people (soldiers)	4.8	3.1	4.6	4.5	4.6
World data on armed forces per 1,000 people (soldiers)	5.3	4.5	4.1	3.9	3.8
GNP per capita (1997 $)	382	266	444	458	448
Arms imports[6]					
Current dollars (mil.)	1,200	625	550	270	600
1997 constant dollars (mil.)	1,405	693	570	275	600
Arms exports[6]					
Current dollars (mil.)	40	30	20	0	0
1997 constant dollars (mil.)	47	33	21	0	0
Total imports[7]					
Current dollars (mil.)	7,388	9,394	11,480	12,150	11,610
1997 constant dollars (mil.)	8,652	10,410	11,890	12,350	11,610
Total exports[7]					
Current dollars (mil.)	5,589	7,317	8,005	9,336	8,731
1997 constant dollars (mil.)	6,545	8,112	8,289	9,492	8,731
Arms as percent of total imports[8]	16.2	6.7	4.8	2.2	5.2
Arms as percent of total exports[8]	0.7	0.4	0.2	0	0

Crime

Crime volume (for 1998)

Crimes reported 431,862

Total persons convicted . . . . .NA

Crimes per 100,000 population 331

LABOR FORCE

Total Labor Force (A)

38.6 million. There is an extensive export of labor, mostly to the Middle East, and use of child labor..

Labor Force by Occupation

Agriculture 44%
Industry 17%
Services 39%

Data for 1999 est.

Unemployment Rate

7% (FY98/99 est.)

PRODUCTION SECTOR

Energy Production

Production . . . . .59.262 billion kWh
Production by source
Fossil fuel 63.05%
Hydro 36.31%
Nuclear 0.64%
Other 0%
Exports . . . . .0 kWh

Data for 1998.

Energy Consumption

Consumption . . . . .55.114 billion kWh
Imports . . . . .0 kWh

Data for 1998.

Transportation

Highways:

Total: 247,811 km.

Paved: 141,252 km (including 339 km of expressways).

Unpaved: 106,559 km (1998 est.).

Pipelines: crude oil 250 km; petroleum products 885 km; natural gas 4,044 km (1987).

Merchant marine:

Total: 20 ships (1,000 GRT or over) totaling 288,249 GRT/444,451 DWT.

Ships by type: bulk 1, cargo 15, container 3, petroleum tanker 1 (1999 est.).

Airports: 118 (1999 est.).

Airports - with paved runways: 82.

Airports - with unpaved runways: 36.

Top Agriculture Products

Cotton, wheat, rice, sugarcane, fruits, vegetables; milk, beef, mutton, eggs.

Top Mining Products (B)

Mineral resources include: poor quality coal, iron ore, copper, salt, limestone.

MANUFACTURING SECTOR

GDP & Manufacturing Summary (A)

	1980	1985	1990	1995
GDP ($-1990 mil.)[1]	21,959	29,792	39,464	48,936
Per capita ($-1990)[1]	257	294	331	359
Manufacturing share (%) (current prices)[1]	13.9	15.9	17.4	17.0[e]
Manufacturing				
Value added ($-1990 mil.)[1]	2,891	4,415	6,096	8,093
Industrial production index	82	92	100	114
Value added ($ mil.)	2,423	3,236	5,114	7,550[e]
Gross output ($ mil.)	7,144	10,132	17,269	25,218[e]
Employment (000)	452	493	622	614[e]
Profitability (% of gross output)				
Intermediate input (%)	66	68	70	70[e]
Wages and salaries inc. supplements (%)	7	6	7	7[e]
Gross operating surplus	27	26	23	23[e]
Productivity ($)				
Gross output per worker	14,606	20,482	27,702	39,359[e]
Value added per worker	4,953	6,542	8,203	11,887[e]
Average wage (inc. supplements)	1,122	1,323	1,965	2,925[e]
Value added ($ mil.)				
Food products	431	580	719	1,145[e]
Beverages	45	74	72	100[e]
Tobacco products	300	372	325	534[e]
Textiles	483	562	1,407	1,412[e]
Wearing apparel	7	18	70	155[e]
Leather and fur products	41	35	56	85[e]
Footwear	4	3	23	47[e]
Wood and wood products	4	9	14	23[e]
Furniture and fixtures	3	6	8	13[e]
Paper and paper products	29	33	80	126[e]

(Continued on next page.)

GDP & Manufacturing Summary (A) (cont.)

	1980	1985	1990	1995
Printing and publishing	24	36	116	137[e]
Industrial chemicals	127	281	401	743[e]
Other chemical products	156	230	368	599[e]
Petroleum refineries	158	45	105	158[e]
Misc. petroleum and coal products	9	17	47	78[e]
Rubber products	28	41	49	65[e]
Plastic products	12	21	28	48[e]
Pottery, china and earthenware	5	8	13	20[e]
Glass and glass products	11	17	36	62[e]
Other non-metal mineral products	171	199	339	624[e]
Iron and steel	99	342	283	490[e]
Non-ferrous metals	1	1	1	2[e]
Metal products	38	33	44	64[e]
Non-electrical machinery	43	80	129	227[e]
Electrical machinery	78	98	210	344[e]
Transport equipment	97	82	132	211[e]
Prof. and scientific equipment	6	6	12	17[e]
Other manufacturing	11	11	27	22[e]

COMMUNICATIONS

Daily Newspapers

	National Data	World Data for Comparison
Daily Newspapers		
Number of Dailies	264	8,391
Total Circulation (000)	NA	548,000
Circulation per 1,000 inhabitants	NA	96

Telecommunications

Telephones - main lines in use: 2.861 million (March 1999).

Telephones - mobile cellular: 158,000 (1998).

Telephone system: the domestic system is mediocre, but improving; service is adequate for government and business use, in part because major businesses have established their own private systems; since 1988, the government has promoted investment .

Domestic: microwave radio relay, coaxial cable, fiber-optic cable, cellular, and satellite.

International: satellite earth stations - 3 Intelsat (1 Atlantic Ocean and 2 Indian Ocean); 3 operational international gateway exchanges (1 at Karachi and 2 at Islamabad); microwave radio relay to neighboring countries.

Radio broadcast stations: AM 27, FM 1, shortwave 21 (1998).

Radios: 13.5 million (1997).

Television broadcast stations: 22 (plus seven low-power repeaters) (1997).

Televisions: 3.1 million (1997).

Internet Service Providers (ISPs): 26 (1999).

FINANCE, ECONOMICS, & TRADE

Economic Indicators

National product: GDP—purchasing power parity—$282 billion (1999 est.).

National product real growth rate: 3.1% (1999 est.).

National product per capita: $2,000 (1999 est.).

Inflation rate—consumer price index: 6% (1999 est.).

Exchange Rates

Exchange rates:

Pakistani rupees (PRs) per US$1

December 1999 ....51.900
1998 ....44.550
1997 ....40.185
1996 ....35.266
1995 ....30.930

Top Import Origins

$9.8 billion (f.o.b., 1999)

Origins (FY98/99)

United States 8%
Japan 8%
Malaysia 7%
Saudi Arabia 7%
UAE 7%

Balance of Payments

	1993	1994	1995	1996	1997
Exports of goods (f.o.b.)	6,917	7,247	8,509	8,662	8,503
Imports of goods (f.o.b.)	−9,551	−9,526	−11,453	−12,386	−10,946
Trade balance	−2,634	−2,279	−2,944	−3,723	−2,443
Services - debits	−2,687	−2,576	−2,991	−3,522	−2,707
Services - credits	1,602	1,785	1,891	2,053	1,678
Private transfers (net)	2,027	2,596	2,362	2,547	3,756
Government transfers (net)	341	363	280	217	245
Overall balance	−2,953	−1,845	−3,410	−4,517	−1,792

Top Export Destinations

$8.4 billion (f.o.b., 1999)

Destinations (FY98/99)

United States 22%
Hong Kong 7%
United Kingdom 7%
Germany 7%
UAE 5%

Foreign Aid

Recipient: $2 billion (FY97/98).

Import/Export Commodities

Import Commodities	Export Commodities
Machinery	Cotton
Petroleum	Fabrics
Petroleum products	And yarn
Chemicals	Rice
Transportation equipment	Other agricultural products
Edible oils	
Grains	
Pulses	
Flour	

PALAU

Republic of Belau

CAPITAL: Koror, Koror Island.

FLAG: The flag, adopted 1 January 1981, is light blue, with a yellow disc set slightly off center toward the hoist.

ANTHEM: *Belau er Kid.*

MONETARY UNIT: The U.S. dollar is the official medium of exchange.

WEIGHTS AND MEASURES: British units are used, as modified by U.S. usage.

HOLIDAYS: New Year's Day, 1 January; Youth Day, 15 March; Senior Citizens Day, 5 May; Constitution Day, 9 July; Labor Day, 1st Monday in September; United Nations Day, 24 October; Thanksgiving Day, 4th Thursday in November; Christmas, 25 December.

TIME: 8 PM = noon GMT.

LOCATION AND SIZE: Palau (also known as Belau) consists of the Palau group of Pacific islands, in the western Caroline Islands, and four remote islands to the southwest. The country consists of more than 200 islands, with a total land area of 441 square kilometers (170.4 square miles), ranking 178 out of 192 in size among the world's nations.

CLIMATE: The annual mean temperature is 28°C (82°F) in the coolest months. There is high precipitation throughout the year—up to 380 centimeters (150 inches)—and a relatively high humidity of 82%.

INTRODUCTORY SURVEY

RECENT HISTORY

As part of the Carolinian archipelago, the islands were sighted by European navigators as early as the 16th century. In 1686, the Spanish explorer Francisco Lezcano named Yap Island (now in the Federated States of Micronesia) "La Carolina" after King Charles II of Spain. The name was later generalized to include all the islands. Spanish sovereignty was established in 1885. In 1899, after Spain's defeat in the Spanish-American War of 1898, Palau, with the rest of the Carolines, was sold to Germany. At the outbreak of World War I in 1914, the islands were taken by the Japanese. As a member of the League of Nations, Japan was given a mandate over Palau in 1920, and Koror was developed as an administrative center of Japanese possessions in the north Pacific.

In 1947, following occupation by U.S. forces in World War II, Palau became part of the United Nations (UN) Trust Territory of the Pacific Islands that was administered by the U.S. After the adoption of a constitution in 1980, Palau became a self-governing republic in 1981. Since 1982, the republic has been involved in negotiating a Compact of Free Association with the U.S. Negotiations were stalled because the 1980 constitution prohibits the placement of nuclear weapons, and the U.S. has wanted to use the islands as a military site. In June 1985, President Haruo Remelil was assassinated; Vice-President Alfonso Oiterang served as acting president until August 1985, when he was defeated by Lazarus E. Salii. President Salii committed suicide in August 1988. Kuniwo Nakamura was elected president in November 1992.

Meanwhile, a Compact of Free-Association (CPA) with the United States was approved in 1986 but was not ratified until 1993. On October 1, 1994, Palau became an independent nation, and the CPA went into force. Under the CPA, the U.S. is responsible for Palau's defense. In 1995, Palau entered into diplomatic talks with the United States, Japan and Taiwan. In February 1999, Palau opened an embassy in Tokyo, Japan.

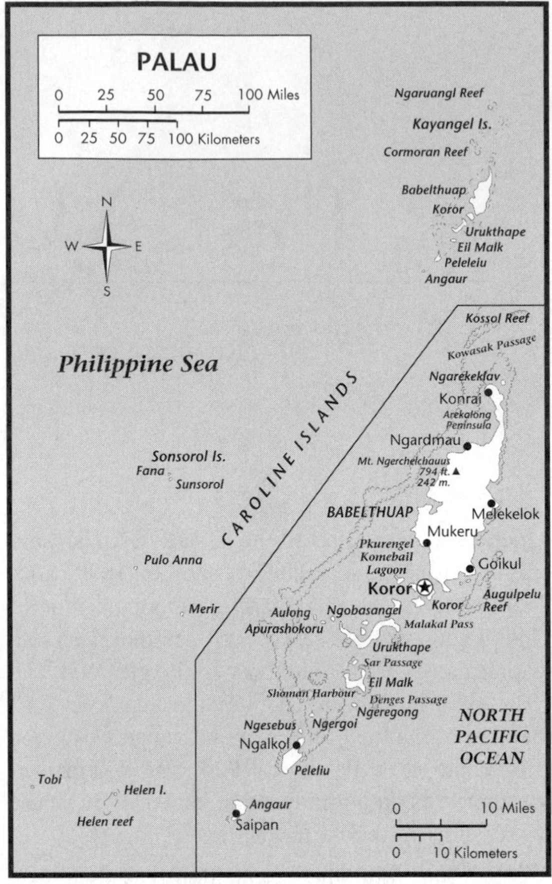

A new capital is under construction in eastern Babelthuap about twenty kilometers northeast of Koror. In October 1999, Palau hosted the 30th South Pacific Forum with more than 300 foreign delegates, observers, and media. Trade ministers of the South Pacific Forum endorsed the proposal for a Pacific Free Trade Area (FTA) that would allow goods to be traded freely in fourteen island countries with a regional market of six million people.

GOVERNMENT

The government comprises three branches: the executive, the legislative, and the judicial. The executive branch is headed by the president, who is both chief of state and head of government, and is elected by popular vote for not more than two terms of four years each. The president is assisted by a cabinet of ministers, one of whom is the vice president and is also elected by popular vote. A council of chiefs, based on Palau's clan system, advises the president on traditional and customary matters.

The legislative branch, known as the Olbiil Era Kelulau, or National Congress, is a bicameral form of legislature consisting of a fourteen-seat Senate and a sixteen-seat House of Delegates. The senators are elected by popular vote on a population basis for four-year terms. The delegates are elected from each of the sixteen states and have the same four-year term as the senators.

In March 1999, a strong movement emerged in Congress to change the existing bicameral congress to a unicameral form of government to reduce cost of government. The proposal was to be put to the people in a vote, possibly in November 2000.

Judiciary

The Supreme Court is the highest court in the land. Other courts include the National Court, which, although constitutionally mandated, was not operational as of 1987, and the lower court system consisting of the Court of Common Pleas. In October 1990, U.S. Interior Secretary Manuel Lujan issued an order granting the Interior Department in Washington the power to veto laws and reverse decisions by Palau's courts. This reassertion of legal authority by the United States was partially in response to the decade of unsuccessful negotiations concerning a plan for eventual self-government.

The Constitution provides for an independent judiciary and the government respects this provision in practice. Palau has an independent prosecutor and an independent public defender system.

Political Parties

Palau has one political party, Palau Nationalist Party.

DEFENSE

The U.S. is responsible for defense. Palau has no armed forces and does not have U.S. armed forces within its borders except for a small contingent of U.S. Navy Seabees who undertake civil action projects.

ECONOMIC AFFAIRS

The economy has a narrow production base as a result of limited natural resources and few skilled personnel. The local economy consists of primarily subsistence agriculture, livestock, and fishing. The services sector consists largely of employment in government administration and trade. Large gaps exist between government revenues and expenditures and between imports and exports. These gaps are financed largely by assistance from the U.S. The population enjoys a per capita income significantly higher than the Philippines or in much of

Micronesia. Recently, expansion of air travel in the Pacific and rising prosperity of leading East Asian countries has fueled growth of the tourist sector. Tourist arrivals were up 56 percent in 1996, while hotel accommodations are expected to double. A new airport was just completed recently.

Public Finance

Revenues include grants from the U.S. and domestic revenues from taxes and other fees. The U.S. Central Intelligence Agency estimated that in 1997, government revenues totaled approximately $52.9 million and expenditures $59.9 million. External debt was estimated to exceed $100 million.

Income

The U.S. Central Intelligence Agency (CIA) maintains statistics on gross domestic product (GDP), defined as the value of all final goods and services produced within a nation in a given year. According to CIA estimates, the GDP in 1997 was $160 million or $8,800 per capita. The 1997 estimated GDP growth rate was 10 percent.

Industry

Tourism is becoming a major industry in Palau. Other industries include construction, garment making, and craft items made of shell, wood, and pearls. A copra processing plant is located in Malakal. Concrete blocks are manufactured, utilizing imported cement, and there is a small-scale sawmill industry.

Banking and Finance

In 1993, there were five commercial banks. Two are branches of foreign banks, the Bank of Hawaii and the Bank of Guam; the other, a local bank which started in 1985, is the Bank of Palau.

Economic Development

The government's first five-year national development plan (1987-1991) was the first phase of its fifteen-year development program and it is currently entering the last years of the plan. The plan focuses on the development of a private sector production based economy, efficient public sector management, development of natural resources to earn foreign exchange, personnel development, regional development, and environmental preservation.

Long-term prospects for the tourist sector are bright, with expanded air service and rising wealth in the East Asian countries where most tourists come from.

SOCIAL WELFARE

Social organization is based on the maternal kin group, or clan. Villages ideally consist of ten clans, with the leader of the highest ranking clan serving as village chief. The society is matrilineal and women are accorded considerable respect within the clan. Sex discrimination in employment is minimal. Rapid socioeconomic change has given rise to a range of social problems for communities and social groups, particularly youth.

The United States funds most social development activities in the areas of health and education. A system of old age, disability, and survivor's pensions was first introduced in 1967. This program covers all gainfully employed persons and provides old age pensions after the age of sixty. This program is financed by 4 percent contributions from employees that are matched by an equal contribution from employers.

Healthcare

Hospital services are provided by the MacDonald Memorial Hospital in Koror that has sixty beds. The Belau Medical Clinic and the Seventh-Day Adventist Eye Clinic also provide medical services in Koror. In 1999, Palau's birth rate was 21.5 per 1,000 population and its death rate was 7.7. In 2000, the life expectancy was 68.6 years.

Housing

There were 2,501 occupied houses in 1986, of which 72 percent were located in Koror and the adjacent state of Airai. Most house walls are constructed from metal sheets, wood, or concrete blocks, and roofs are of corrugated material. About 80 percent of all houses have water and electricity. The majority of homeowners finance home construction under the traditional "ocheraol" system where clan members contribute to construction costs.

EDUCATION

Education is free and compulsory for all Palauan children aged six to fourteen. The Palau High School in Koror is the only public high school. The College of Micronesian Occupational College (MOC) in Koror provides post-secondary education. The adult literacy rate is 98 percent.

2000 KEY EVENTS TIMELINE

February

- A Japanese government team studies Palau Airport, in preparation for President Nakamura's formal request for Japanese financial assistance in developing the airport facilities.

March

- Palau's fourteen senators set an example for the country by submitting to and passing comprehensive drug tests.
- Taiwan opens an embassy in Palau.

May

- The Olympic torch makes a twenty-four-hour stopover in Palau.

June

- The Wan Smolbag Theatre of Vanuatu, a Pacific social action theater group, visits Palau to conduct two weeks of drama training, with the aim of enabling Paluans to establish a similar group.

July

- Palau and Japanese company Aoyama Planning Arts reach an agreement to introduce information technology throughout the nation with the "Palau I.N.T. Project." Project goals include computerizing education and medical care, developing non-polluting industries, and enhancing the execution of government services across the nation's widespread islands.
- A law is passed regulating radio frequencies, in response to the rapid increase in the number of radio stations, cellular phones, and paging services in use in Palau. The new law also requires radio and television stations to record all broadcasts, with the exception of prerecorded material, such as music.

August

- The first Palauan female justice, Kathleen M. Salii, is appointed to the Palau Supreme Court where she will serve as an associate justice.
- Palau is named in the South Pacific Regional Environment Program (SPREP) study of contamination caused by hazardous material storage in South Pacific island nations.

September

- Palau makes its first Olympic appearance, competing in weightlifting, athletics, and swimming at the Summer Olympics in Sydney, Australia.
- The Association of Pacific Island Legislatures meets in Palau, passing a resolution calling for the United States and Japan to remove unexploded WWII bombs and other weaponry from the Pacific islands.

November

- Vice President Tommy Esang Remengesau is narrowly elected president of Palau November 7, and is to begin his term in office in January.
- The Palau Foreign Investment Board (FIB) approves 6 new business applications, including one for an 18-hole golf course, and one for the first bowling alley on the island. An application submitted by Palau Amity Corporation for a logging business is among those not approved.

ANALYSIS OF EVENTS: 2000

BUSINESS AND THE ECONOMY

In 2000 Palau continued to develop telecommunications services across its far-flung islands. On January 31 the Palau National Communications Company (PNCC) announced that it had successfully completed its six-year project to bring universal phone service to all sixteen states of Palau, which encompass over 200 groups of islands.

In May 2000 the PNCC assumed full ownership of Island Cable Television (ICTV) after a joint agreement was signed between PNCC and United Micronesia Development Association (UMDA), which had previously held 50 percent of ICTV. Peter Sinclair, president of UMDC, stated that the transfer of ownership was in keeping with UMDA's philosophy of investing in Micronesia, developing the investment, and then turning it over to the people of the region. Officials of PNCC and ICTV stated that the merging of telephone and television service would benefit the customers through sharing of technology and the use of PNCC's widespread distribution channels.

In July Palau reached an agreement with Japanese information technology company Aoyama Planning Arts to introduce information technology throughout the nation with the "Palau I.N.T. Project". The project goals included computerizing education and medical care, developing non-polluting industries, and enhancing the execution of government services to all the scattered islands making up the nation. The tasks would be facilitated by the fact that all households in the country had already been linked by fiber optic cable.

In recognition of the growing use of high frequency and ultra-high frequency radio bands and the growing availability of pagers and cellular phones, the president signed into law a bill regulating radio frequencies, including radio and television stations. The bill included a requirement that all broadcasts, with the exception of prerecorded material, be recorded and maintained on file for at least sixty days after broadcast. The national legislature, the Olbii Era Kelulau, also appropriated $190,000 to buy and install radio equipment to extend the range of some channels.

GOVERNMENT AND POLITICS

In 2000 Palau's president Kuniwo Nakamura worked to strengthen his nation's international ties. Palau established diplomatic relations with Taiwan, becoming only the twenty-ninth nation to do so. Palau's foreign minister stated that Taiwan provided tourism revenue and had invested significantly in economic projects in Palau.

The nation of Palau also cultivated its ties with Japan; in February, the Japanese government sent a team to do an in-depth study of the condition of Palau Airport, with the intention that when the study was completed, President Nakamura would submit to Japan a formal application for financial assistance to fund the development of terminal and other airport facilities. In November the president traveled to Japan to discuss economic cooperation between the two countries.

President Nakamura took an active role at the two-day Pacific Island Leaders Conference in April, where he called for early ratification of the Kyoto protocol on reducing greenhouse gas emissions. He stated that because the Pacific island nations have fragile ecosystems, they are especially vulnerable to the changes wrought by global warming, suffering symptoms such as reduction in fish populations, loss of arable land, and coral bleaching. The possible rise in ocean level was also cited as an effect of grave concern to the small island nations.

CULTURE AND SOCIETY

The 2000 census showed that Palau's population was young and growing rapidly. A total of 3,350 households and 19,124 people were counted, an increase of 11 percent over the 1995 census. The census reported that 28.6 percent of those counted were under the age of eighteen.

In 2000 the number of women from Palau who applied to join the U.S. armed forces rose significantly. Reflecting a regional trend, the women saw military service as a way to continue their education after high school, while also receiving good benefits and a steady salary.

In January 2000 a new museum, the Etpison Museum, opened in Palau. Featuring traditional and historic Palauan artifacts, its exhibits included prehistoric tools and pottery, antique maps, beads, two full-sized canoes, and a miniature men's house, called a "bai."

The Wan Smolbag Theatre of Vanuatu, a Pacific social action theater group, visited Palau to perform dramas as well as conduct two weeks of training designed to enable Palauans to establish a similar social action drama troupe of their own. Courses offered by the visiting group included community theater management, script writing, and training for nurses and teachers in the use of drama for community education.

In August 2000 the first Palauan female justice, Kathleen M. Salii, was appointed to the Palau Supreme Court as an Associate Justice.

DIRECTORY

CENTRAL GOVERNMENT

Head of State

President
Kuniwo Nakamura, Office of the President, PO Box 100, Koror, Palau 96940

Vice President and Minister of Administration
Tommy E. Remengesau, Jr., Office of the Vice President, PO Box 100, Koror, Palau 96940

Ministers

Minister of Education
Billy G. Kuartei, Ministry of Education

Minister of Commerce and Trade
Okada Techitong, Ministry of Commerce and Trade

Minister of Health
Masao M. Ueda, Ministry of Health

POLITICAL ORGANIZATIONS

Palau Nationalist Party

NAME: Polycarp Basilius

DIPLOMATIC REPRESENTATION

Embassies in Palau

United States
PO Box 6028, Koror, Palau 96940
PHONE: +680 4882920; 4882990
FAX: +680 4882911
TITLE: Ambassador
NAME: Thomas C. Hubbard

JUDICIAL SYSTEM

The Supreme Court

PO Box 248, Koror, Palau 96940

National Court

Court of Common Pleas

BROADCAST MEDIA

KHBN

PO Box 66, Koror, Palau 96940
PHONE: +680 4882162
FAX: +680 4882163
E-MAIL: voh@broadcast.net
WEBSITE: http://www.highadventure.org/voh_china.html
CONTACT: Rolland Lau
TYPE: Religious

WSZB Broadcasting Station

Box 279, Koror State, Palau
PHONE: +680 4882417
FAX: +680 4881932
BROADCASTS: 5 hours/day

STV-TV KOROR

Koror, Palau 96940
TITLE: Manager
CONTACT: David Nolan
CHANNEL: 7
WATTAGE: 1 kw
TYPE: Commercial

NEWSPAPERS AND MAGAZINES

Tia Belau

Belau Publishing Co., PO Box 477, Koror, Palau 96940
PHONE: +680 4881461
FAX: +680 4881725
TITLE: Publisher
CONTACT: Moses Uludong

Palau Gazette

Government Media Office, PO Box 100, Koror, Palau 96940
PHONE: +680 4883257
FAX: +680 4881662
TITLE: Editor
CONTACT: Roman Yano

RELIGIOUS ORGANIZATIONS

Catholic

Jesuit Community/"Manresa Jesuit Novitiate"
PO Box 128, Koror, Palau 96940
PHONE: +680 4882392
TITLE: Director of Novices
NAME: Rev Daniel J. Mulhauser, SJ

Mercedarian Sisters' Residence
PO Box 56, Koror, Palau 96940
PHONE: +680 4882272

Vicariate Committee for Justice & Development
PO Box 1197, Koror, Palau 96940
PHONE: +680 4882253
TITLE: Chariman
NAME: Dr. Minoru Ueki

Vicariate Community House (Koror)
PO Box 128, Koror, Palau 96940
PHONE: +680 4882226
TITLE: Regional Superior, Jesuits of Micronesia
NAME: Rev. Felix Yaoch, SJ

The Vicariate of Palau
PO Box 128, Palau 96940
PHONE: +680 4881819
FAX: +680 4881725
TITLE: Vicar
NAME: Fr. John Paul Ililau

FURTHER READING

Articles

"Guardian of Paradise: Noah Idechong." *Time,* April 26, 2000, vol. 155, no. 17, p. 41.

Mahaney, Casey and Astrid Witte. "Discover the Rainbow's End: The Palauan Islands." *Skin Diver,* January 2000, vol. 49, no. 1, p. 60.

Pozzoli, Tally. "Palau—In a State of Grace." *Skin Diver,* April 2000, vol. 49, no. 4, p. 82.

Articles

Yeung, Chiu Wang. *Storage Capacity and Water Quality of Lake Ngardok, Babeldaob Island, Republic of Palau, 1996–98.* Honolulu, Hawaii: U.S. Dept. of the Interior, Denver, CO: Branch of Information Services [distributor], 1999.

PALAU: STATISTICAL DATA

For sources and notes see "Sources of Statistics" at the front of each volume.

GEOGRAPHY

Geography

Area:

Total: 458 sq km.

Land: 458 sq km.

Land boundaries: 0 km.

Coastline: 1,519 km.

Climate: wet season May to November; hot and humid.

Terrain: varying geologically from the high, mountainous main island of Babelthuap to low, coral islands usually fringed by large barrier reefs.

Natural resources: forests, minerals (especially gold), marine products, deep-seabed minerals.

HUMAN FACTORS

Ethnic Division

Palauans are Micronesian with Malayan and Melanesian admixtures.

Religion

Christian (Catholics, Seventh-Day Adventists, Jehovah's Witnesses, the Assembly of God, the Liebenzell Mission, and Latter-Day Saints), Modekngei Religion (one-third of the population observes this religion which is indigenous to Palau).

Major Languages

English and Palauan official in all states except Sonsoral (Sonsorolese and English are official), Tobi (Tobi and English are official), and Angaur (Angaur, Japanese, and English are official).

Demographics (A)

	1990	1995	1998	2000	2010	2020	2030	2040	2050
Population	15.2	17.0	18.1	18.8	21.6	23.5	25.0	26.0	26.3
Life expectancy - males	63.9	63.9	64.8	65.5	68.4	71.0	73.2	75.0	76.6
Life expectancy - females	70.2	70.2	71.2	71.9	75.0	77.6	79.8	81.6	83.1
Birth rate (per 1,000)	21.4	23.4	20.3	19.9	16.9	14.9	14.0	12.6	11.7
Death rate (per 1,000)	8.9	8.4	7.7	7.3	6.7	7.4	8.9	10.4	11.1
Women of reproductive age (15-49 yrs.)	3.6	4.4	4.8	5.0	5.5	5.5	5.6	5.9	5.9
Fertility rate	2.8	2.9	2.5	2.5	2.5	2.2	2.0	1.9	1.8

Except as noted, values for vital statistics are in thousands; life expectancy is in years.

EDUCATION

Literacy Rates (B)

	National Data	World Data
Adult literacy rate		
1995		
Male	NA	81
Female	97[1]	65

GOVERNMENT & LAW

Political Parties

The bicameral Parliament or Olbiil Era Kelulau (OEK) consists of the Senate and the House of Delegates. The Senate has 14 seats. Its members are elected by popular vote on a population basis to serve four-year terms. The House of Delegates has 16 seats, one from each state. Its members are elected by popular vote to serve four-year terms. Elections for Senate were last held 11 November 1996 (next to be held in November 2000). Elections for the House of Delegates were last held 11 November 1996 (next to be held in November 2000. Election results are not available. There is only one political party, the Palau Nationalist Party.

Government Budgets (B)

Revenues .... $52.9 million

Expenditures .... $59.9 million

Data for 1997 est.

LABOR FORCE

Unemployment Rate

7%

PRODUCTION SECTOR

Energy Production

Production .... 200 million kWh

Production by source

Fossil fuel 85%

Hydro 15%

Nuclear 0%

Other 0%

Exports .... 0 kWh

Data for 1996.

Energy Consumption

Consumption .... 200 million kWh

Imports .... 0 kWh

Data for 1996.

Transportation

Highways:

Total: 61 km.

Paved: 36 km.

Unpaved: 25 km.

Merchant marine: none (1999 est.).

Airports: 3 (1999 est.).

Top Agriculture Products

Coconuts, copra, cassava (tapioca), sweet potatoes.

Top Mining Products (B)

Mineral resources include: minerals (especially gold), deep-seabed minerals.

MANUFACTURING SECTOR

GDP & Manufacturing Summary (C)

Total GDP (1997 est.) .... $160 million

Real growth rate (1997 est.) 10%

Per capita (1997 est.) $8,800

Values in purchasing power parity.

COMMUNICATIONS

Telecommunications

Telephones - main lines in use: 1,500 (1988).

Telephones - mobile cellular: 0 (1988).

Telephone system:

Domestic: NA

International: satellite earth station - 1 Intelsat (Pacific Ocean).

Radio broadcast stations: AM 1, FM 0, shortwave 1 (1998).

Radios: 12,000 (1997).

Television broadcast stations: 1 (1997).

Televisions: 11,000 (1997).

Internet Service Providers (ISPs): NA

FINANCE, ECONOMICS, & TRADE

Economic Indicators

National product: GDP—purchasing power parity—$160 million (1997 est.). GDP numbers reflect US spending..

National product real growth rate: 10% (1997 est.).

National product per capita: $8,800 (1997 est.).

Inflation rate—consumer price index: NA.

Exchange Rates

Exchange rates: US currency is used.

Top Import Origins

Imports (f.o.b., 1996): $72.4 million.

Origins: United States.

Top Export Destinations

Exports (f.o.b., 1996): $14.3 million.

Destinations: United States, Japan.

Foreign Aid

Recipient: $155.8 million (1995); The Compact of Free Association with the US, entered into after the end of the UN trusteeship on 1 October 1994, will provide Palau with up to $700 million in US aid over 15 years in return for furnishing military facilities.

Import/Export Commodities

Import Commodities	Export Commodities
Machinery and equipment	Trochus (type of shellfish)
Fuels	Tuna
	Copra
	Handicrafts

PALESTINIAN AUTHORITY

CAPITAL: There is no official capital for the Palestinian Authority. The establishment of the Palestinian State including a capital at Jerusalem is under negotiation. The seat of government for the Palestinian Authority is nominally the city of Jericho.

FLAG: The flag of the Palestinian Authority is a triband of black (top), white (center), and green (bottom). There is a red triangle on the hoist side that points to the center of the white stripe.

ANTHEM: A national anthem has not been adopted.

MONETARY UNIT: As territories occupied by the State of Israel, the monetary system is the New Israeli Shekels (NIS) is a paper currency of 100 new agarot.

WEIGHTS AND MEASURES: The metric system is the legal standard.

HOLIDAYS: Official holidays have not been adopted. Religious holidays of the Moslem and Christian faiths are observed by Palestinians.

TIME: 2 PM = noon GMT.

LOCATION AND SIZE: Territory under the control of the Palestinian Authority in contained within areas known as the West Bank (of the Jordan River) and the Gaza Strip. The Gaza Strip is located in the Middle East, in between Israel and Egypt, with a border on the Mediterranean Sea. Geographic coordinates for the Gaza Strip are 31°25′N, 34°20′E. The land area of the Gaza Strip is approximately 360 square kilometers. The West Bank is located in the Middle East, in between Israel and Jordan, with a border on the River Jordan. Geographic coordinates for the West Bank are 32°00′N, 35°15′E. The land area of the West Bank is approximately 5,860 square kilometers.

CLIMATE: The climate of both the Gaza Strip and the West Bank are temperate with mild winters and dry, warm to hot summers. Temperature and precipitation vary with altitude.

West Bank and Gaza Strip

INTRODUCTORY SURVEY

RECENT HISTORY

The Palestinian Authority was created in 1994 as part of an ongoing peace process between the state of Israel and Palestinian refugees. The territory it controls is not technically recognized as a country, and as of October 2000, Palestinians had not declared it so. All parties involved, however, acknowledge that the intent of the Palestinian Authority's creation was to establish a governmental structure and authority that could be passed over to a recognized nation. The Palestinian Authority controls land on the West Bank of the Jordan river and an area called the Gaza Strip.

Middle Eastern political and territorial disputes are long standing, with unresolved disputes stretching back hundreds of years. The Muslim, Christian, and Jewish faiths each recognize the lands of Palestine—and especially the city of Jerusalem—as the point of origin for their religious beliefs. The sacred nature of the land and the historical significance of events and locations as they relate to religious stories and text for each religion ignite unparalleled passions. The Islamic holy shrine and mosque, Dome of the Rock, where Muhammad is believed to have risen to heaven, is built upon the ruins of the last Jewish temple. All that remains of the Jewish temple today is the Wailing Wall, and close by is the route believed to have been taken by Jesus Christ on his way to crucifixion, as related in the Christian Bible. This juxtaposition of sacred places creates unrelieved

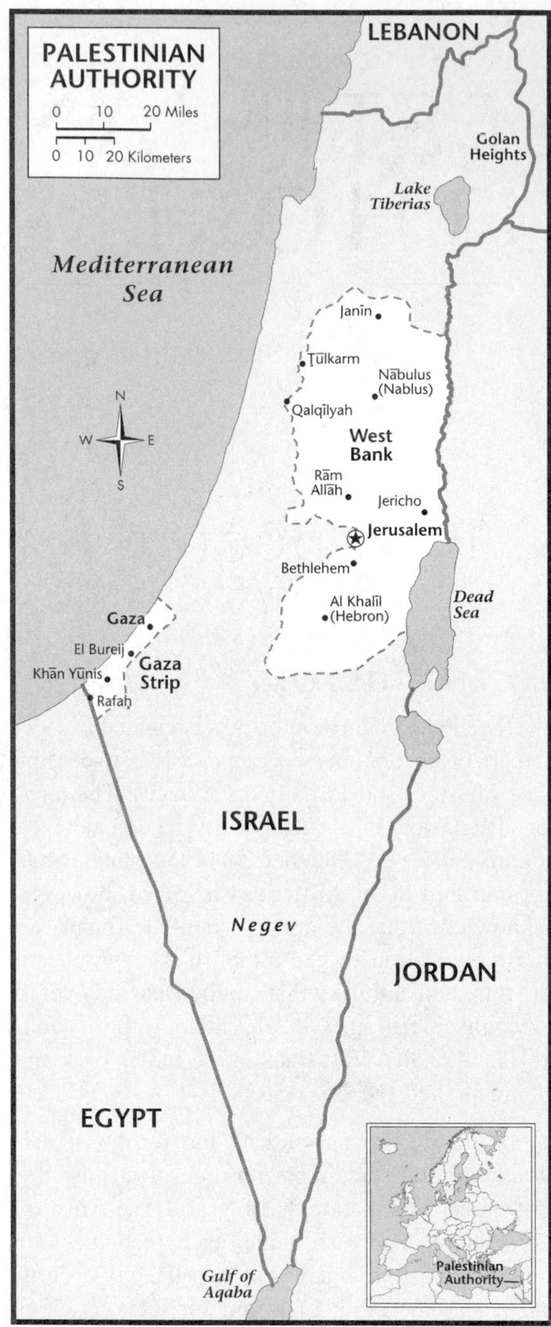

tensions between members of these three faiths, and especially between Arabic and Jewish peoples.

At the end of World War II, Jewish refugees from Europe flooded Palestine, which was under the control of the United Kingdom. Open revolt by the Jews led to the creation of the State of Israel in 1948. At the same time, Muslim Palestinians fled the Israeli lands, settling in refugee camps in neighboring countries. Armies from neighboring Arab states battled the Israeli forces until an armistice was declared under United Nations auspices in 1949. Border violence between the Israelis and Arabs continued, however. In 1956, Israel invaded the Sinai Peninsula and Gaza Strip, but withdrew in 1957.

Low-grade fighting between the Jews and Palestinians continued, until full scale war broke out again in 1967. At that time, Israel soundly defeated the Arabic states of Jordan, Syria, Lebanon, and Egypt, taking large portions of territory, including those in dispute today and over which the Palestinian Authority exercises some control. Following this war, the United Nations Security Council adopted resolutions calling for an exchange of occupied territory for peace.

Border conflicts continued. War broke out again between Israel and its neighbors in 1973 as Syria and Egypt made initial advances against Israeli forces in the occupied territories. Israel recovered, however, and the war ended with the boundaries remaining as they were. In 1977, Egyptian President Anwar Sadat and Israeli Prime Minister Menachem Begin began a peace dialogue which, with the help of United States President Jimmy Carter, culminated in an historic peace treaty in 1979. In that treaty, Israel gave the Sinai Peninsula back to Egypt in exchange for peace.

Through the 1980s conflicts continued between Israelis and Arabs along the borders of Israel. Israel invaded Lebanon to battle Palestinian Liberation Organization (PLO) forces in 1982. Israeli occupation forces withdrew from Lebanon following a non-belligerency agreement signed in 1994. Israel signed a peace treaty with Jordan later in 1994. Negotiations for peace with Syria were sporadic through the 1990s.

Throughout this period, the PLO was one of many organizations who claimed to speak for Palestinian Arabs, especially those in refugee camps. Led by Yasir Arafat, the PLO consolidated its position through the 1970s and 1980s and became the strongest representative of the Palestinian situation. In 1993, Arafat led the PLO side of negotiations with Israel, which led to the signing of a "Declaration of Principles on Interim Self-Government Arrangements" (DOP) at the White House in Washington, D.C. Preceding the declaration, Israel and the PLO exchanged letters of mutual recognition. The PLO thus solidified its position as the voice of the Palestinian Arab peoples.

In 1994, the Palestinian Authority was established to represent the Palestinian people and to provide governmental authority in selected areas. Yasir Arafat was elected the first president of the Palestinian Authority in elections held on January 20, 1996. Beginning in 1994, as agreements were reached and Israeli troops pulled out of occupied areas, the Palestinian Authority assumed all governmental duties in those areas.

Talks to arrive at a permanent peace agreement continue on a sporadic basis through the year 2000. There are still many issues to be resolved, including control over the holy city of Jerusalem and the matter of Israeli settlers living in land now controlled by the Palestinian Authority. Violence breaks out periodically as factions on both sides of the conflict jockey for position.

GOVERNMENT

The Palestinian Authority is the government of an undeclared nation for Palestinians living in the West Bank and Gaza Strip. The government is headed by a president. An 88-seat legislative council is in place to provide legislative functions. A cabinet of ministers has been appointed to control various functions in the executive branch. By law, eighty percent of the cabinet must be elected members of the legislative council.

Judiciary

A court system is being established.

Political Parties

The major political movement among the Palestinian population has been the Palestinian Liberation Organization. Hamas, a political and terrorist faction in support of a Palestinian state, did not participate in the Palestinian Authority's elections and continues to promote violence against Israel.

DEFENSE

Defense is not a function of the Palestinian Authority. There is a police force/militia that has been established to provide normal police and internal protection functions. The frequent clashes between Palestinians and Israeli troops include a mixture of the police forces and civilians.

ECONOMIC AFFAIRS

Economic affairs are chaotic and uncontrolled from a governmental perspective. As a region experiencing a mixture of occupation by Israeli troops and a new government without institutions and traditions, it is still looking for structure economically. The region has also been isolated economically from neighboring countries such as Jordan and Egypt due to years of warfare and uneasy armistice. Consequently, the economy is heavily dependent on that of Israel and on governmental decisions. Many Palestinians work in Israeli industries and service firms.

Public Finance

Palestinian Authority taxation policies and collection capabilities are not clear. Statistics and figures in this area are not available.

Income

Gross domestic product (GDP) in the Palestinian Authority was estimated for 1998 at $1.1 billion for the Gaza Strip (about $1,000 per capita) and at $3.1 billion for the West Bank (about $2,000 per capita). GDP fluctuates greatly from one year to the next depending on the status of peace in the region.

Industry

Gaza Strip industries include agricultural products such as olives, citrus, vegetables, beef, and dairy products. Small family businesses produce soap, cement, textiles, olive-wood carvings, and souvenirs.

West Bank industries also include agricultural products such as olives, citrus, vegetables, beef, and dairy products. Trade, construction, and other services dominate the West Bank. Also important is the hospitality industry, such as hotels and restaurants.

Banking and Finance

Currencies in use include the Israeli shekel, Jordanian dinar, and U.S. dollar. Banking and financial institutions are to be established or adopted from Israeli or Jordanian institutions.

Economic Development

Unemployment in the Palestinian Authority is very high, with estimates of over twenty-six percent in 1997. Development is sporadic and highly dependent on a successful peace process and an absence of armed conflict.

SOCIAL WELFARE

Social welfare programs are under development.

Healthcare

Healthcare programs are under development.

2000 KEY EVENTS TIMELINE

January

- After meeting in December 1999, Israeli and Palestinian negotiators admit failure in their attempts to come to an agreement on the next phase of the peace process.
- Israel attempts to restrict the travel of Palestinians from the occupied territories to Mecca, Saudi Arabia, for the traditional Muslim pilgrimage.
- Israel increases pressure on the Palestinians by announcing plans to annex Jewish settlements in the disputed territories, thus further muddling the peace process.

February

- The Palestinian Authority (PA) and the Israeli government fail to conclude or sign a peace accord that was, according to the schedule agreed upon at the Wye River summit, due in February.
- The Palestinian Authority accepts an Israeli plan and corresponding maps for the redeployment of Israeli troops in the disputed areas.
- Palestinian groups in opposition to Palestinian Authority president Yassir Arafat make accusations of "gangsterism" and corruption.
- On February 22, Israeli police and Palestinian demonstrators clash in Hebron. Fifteen protestors are injured.

March

- Palestinian intellectuals reassert the notion that all Palestinians have the right to resettle from refugee camps to Palestine. The United States proposes settling refugees in Iraq.
- The issue of Jerusalem and who controls it returnesto the forefront of negotiations and in public debate.
- Pope John Paul II, marking the first visit to the Holy Land by a Roman Catholic pope in centuries, visits refugee camps and al-Haram al-Sharif in Jerusalem, the Muslim world's third holiest shrine.

April

- Arafat continues to fight internal opposition, and the PA cracks down on the press.
- On April 18, the pro-Arafat Fatah attacks Gaza's Islamic University. Scores of Palestinian college students are injured in clashes.
- Arafat visits U.S. president Bill Clinton in Washington, D.C., as Israeli Prime Minister Ehud Barak appears ready to accept and recognize a Palestinian state as part of the peace negotiations.

May

- Sporadic fighting between Israeli police and soldiers and Palestinian demonstrators results in five Palestinian deaths and one thousand five hundred injured.

June

- Palestinians accuse Israeli soldiers of using chemicals in their anti-riot activities.
- The PA asks Israel to seal off Palestinian areas and limit travel in an attempt to quell violence and limit the movement of armed demonstrators.
- U.S. Secretary of State Madeline Albright makes here thirty-third visit to Palestine on June 28, in an unsuccessful effort to stop the violence and bridge the gaps between Israel and the the Palestinian Authority.

July

- Palestinian rhetoric builds as violent clashes continue between demonstrators and Israeli police and armed forces. An new *intifada* threatens to erupt.
- One thousand Palestinian refugees gather at the Lebanese-Israeli border to protest their exclusion from Palestine and the lack of resolution to their situation.
- PA President Arafat and Israeli Prime Minister Barak meet at Camp David in an attempt to come to agreement on the peace process. Israel insists on retaining full control of Jerusalem. U.S. President Bill Clinton remains involved in the process, but the talks do not produce an agreement.
- Palestinians and Jewish settlers clash in Hebron on July 23, after Israeli settlers stone a Palestinian's car.

August

- Early in August, despite stalled peace negotiations, Yassir Arafat announces his intention to make a unilateral declaration of a Palestinian State in September.
- On August 16, Israeli soldiers shoot and kill a 70-year-old Palestinian who fired on them after he mistook them for intruders in his home. Violent demonstrations ensue.

- In an attempt to calm fears of intrusion on Muslim holy ground, Israeli Prime Minister Barak reassures Palestinians that Israel will not conduct archeological excavations on the Muslim's sacred Temple Mount. Barak also publicly supports "flexibility" in negotiations over Jerusalem.

September

- Arafat backs off from his August statement to declare a Palestinian State as opposition to the declaration becomes widespread among countries from which he needs support, including the United States.
- Amnesty International, the human rights watchdog organization, accuses the Palestinian Authority of trying to silence dissent by illegally detaining critics. It also sharply criticizes the PA's record on human rights and democracy.
- Violent demonstrations continue as parties on both sides attempt to find an agreement that would quell the spiraling violence.
- On September 28, Israeli Ariel Sharon, who is considered by Palestinians to be responsible for many Palestinian deaths in previous military actions in Lebanon, enraged Palestinians and heightened tensions by making a much-publicized visit to the sacred Haram el-Sharif complex in Jerusalem.

October

- A hastily crafted cease fire fails on October 4 as violent protests rage on. As of that date, seventy Palestinian deaths and more than two thousand injuries had been tallied. Israeli police and military casualties of five dead were added to the death of one settler.

November

- The Israeli government, built on tenuous coalitions, fails and elections are scheduled for spring 2001. Palestinian violence and peace negotiations are at the forefront of the electoral debate. Peace talks are placed on hold pending the Israeli elections.

December

- Israeli Prime Minister Ehud Barak resigns, setting up a special election for prime minister in advance of the general election.
- Tourism to Israel and the occupied areas of the Palestinian Authority are announce do be down by forty percent, and normally heavy tourism to Bethlehem for Christmas never materializes.
- Violence intensified as Israel and the Palestinian Authority continued to remain deadlocked over the terms of a U.S. peace plan. Arab foreign ministers were set to meet in the beginning of January 2001 to discuss the peace plan.

ANALYSIS OF EVENTS: 2000

BUSINESS AND THE ECONOMY

The Palestinian economy suffered during the year 2000 due to the renewed violence between Palestinians and Israeli occupation forces. Consequences of this violence included strict curfews on Palestinians and the closing of borders and travel check-points, leaving many Palestinians stranded in their homes and unable to work. Border closes restricted the import and export of goods and affected many local businesses, who could not obtain supplies for production.

According to a United Nations report, Palestinians have lost US$500 million in wages and sales of goods since the level of violence flared up in September. In addition, unemployment has increased three-fold. The Palestinian economy has been tightly tied to that of Israel's for years. Palestinian workers cross the border daily to work in Israel, and over the past few years the local economy has been nurtured by the burgeoning peace process. All of this came to a halt with the increasing violence in September. Israel closed the border and the fragile Palestinian economy was strangled.

The violence has also turned away tourists, who usually flock to the area at Christmastime to visit the city of Bethlehem, located in the West Bank. In December, however, many hotels were empty. The United Nations poverty rate for the Palestinian Authority is US$2 per day. Over half of the Palestinian population in the West Bank and Gaza Strip fell below this level by the end of 2000.

GOVERNMENT AND POLITICS

A series of events prompted an increasing level of violence in clashes between Palestinians and Israelis. Former Israeli military leader Ariel Sharon's visit to a Muslim holy site in September enraged Palestinians and led to the peace-threatening violence that plagued the region for the rest of the year. Yassir Arafat was called on to quell the unrest, but he seemed unable to ease the fears and anger of the Palestinian public. At the same time, Ehud Barak's leadership was threatened within the Israeli government by calls for an election. Barak hoped to rally support for his leadership and keep the peace negotiations on track by resigning, thus prompting a special election for the position of prime minister, to occur before the general election in spring 2001.

While both Palestinian and Israeli leadership struggled to maintain control, Palestinian unrest increased in response to Israeli reactions to clashes. Israeli soldiers responded to Palestinian mobs armed with stones by shooting tear gas and rubber bullets. In many instances, real bullets were also used to injure protestors in strategic areas, such as the leg, causing permanent damage. The consistency of such injuries has led to cries of intentional cruelty by the Israeli military. Israel has denied the charges, stating that its soldiers only fire live ammunition in self defense.

CULTURE AND SOCIETY

Palestinian refugees continued to remain in refugee camps decades after the initial conflicts that placed them there. Peace in the area is dependent to a great degree on the settlement of the refugee question. Yassir Arafat and the Palestinian Authority would like refugees, scattered in various states bordering Israel and the Palestinian lands, to be allowed to return to Palestine. Many refugees would like to return to the homes they occupied prior to their dispersal. This causes problems between the PA and Israel, as many Israelis have taken over land and homes previously owned by Palestinians.

Another matter that effects both Israeli and Palestinian societies is that of Israeli settlements in the West Bank and Gaza Strip. With uneasy relations even in times of relative peace, these settlements are often the sight of open attacks and retaliations between both parties. Israel is invested in the security of the settlers, who are unwilling to leave their homes. Palestinians, however, see continuing Israeli settlements as a continuing Israeli threat. The battle over land, much of which has historical significance to both sides, extends to the city of Jerusalem—a matter on which neither Palestinians nor Israelis want to bend. Both want control of the city. These points of contention contribute to an already tense situation for both the governments and the peoples of the Palestinian Authority and Israel.

DIRECTORY

CENTRAL GOVERNMENT

Head of State

President
Yasser Arafat

Ministers

Ministry of Agriculture
Hikmat Zeid, Minister of Agriculture

Ministry of Civil Affairs
Jamil Al Tarifi, Minister of Civil Affairs

Ministry of Communication and Postal Service
Imad Al Falouji, Minister of Communication

Ministry of Economy and Commerce
Maher Al Masri, Minister of Economy and Commerce

Ministry of Environmental Affairs
PO Box 3841, Ramallah, West Bank, Palestine
PHONE: +972 (2) 2403495
FAX: +972 (2) 2403494
E-MAIL: menar@hally.net

Ministry of Finance
Mohammad Al Nashashibi, Minister of Finance

Ministry of Health
Riyad Za'anoon, Minister of Health

Ministry of Higher Education
Munther Salah, Minister of Higher Education

Ministry of Housing
Abdul Rahman Hamad, Minister of Housing

Ministry of Industry
Sadi Alkrunz, Minister of Industry, PO Box 4053, Gaza, Palestine

Ministry of Information and Culture
Yasser Abed Rabbo, Minister of Information and Culture

Ministry of Justice
Fraih Abu Meddain, Minister of Justice

Ministry of Labor
Rafiq Al-Natsheh, Minister of Labor, Gaza government center "Abu Khadra", PO Box 4021, Gaza, Palestine
PHONE: +972 (7) 2829146

FAX: +972 (2) 2822400
E-MAIL: narman@gov.ps

Ministry of Local Governance
Saeb Erekat, Minister of Local Government

Ministry of Planning and International Cooperation
Nabeel Shaath, Minister of Planning and International Cooperation
PHONE: +972 (7) 2822482

Minister of Public Works
Azzam Al Ahmad, Minister of Public Works

Ministry of Social Affairs
Intisar Al Wazeer, Minister of Social Affairs

Ministry of Supplies
AbedlAziz Ali Shahin, Minister of Supply

Ministry of Tourism and Antiquities
Mitri Abu-Eitta, Minister of Tourism and Antiquities, PO Box 534, Manger Street, Bethlehem, Palestine
PHONE: +972 (7) 2824866

Ministry of Transportation
Ali Kawasmi, Minister of Transportation

POLITICAL ORGANIZATIONS

Hamas (Islamic Resistance Movement)

TITLE: Founder
NAME: Sheikh Ahmad Yasin

The Palestine People's Party

PO Box 54224, Jerusalem, Palestine

DIPLOMATIC REPRESENTATION

There are currently no embassies or consulates with representation in the Palestinian Authority.

JUDICIAL SYSTEM

A judicial system for the Palestinian Authority is being established.

COLLEGES AND UNIVERSITIES

Al-Azhar University of Gaza

PO Box 1277, Gaza Strip, Palestine
PHONE: +972 (2) 2824020; 2824010
FAX: +972 (2) 2823180
E-MAIL: alazhar@hally.net
WEBSITE: http://www.alazhar-gaza.edu

Al-Quds University

PO Box 51000, Jerusalem, Palestine
PHONE: +972 (2) 627-4979
FAX: +972 (2) 6277166
E-MAIL: webmaster@admin.alquds.edu
WEBSITE: http://www.alquds.edu

An-Najah National University

PO Box 7, Nablus, Palestine
PHONE: +972 (9) 2376584; 2370042; 2381111
FAX: +972 (9) 2387982
WEBSITE: http://www.najah.edu

Arab American University-Jenin (AAUJ)

PO Box 240, Jenin, Palestine
PHONE: +972 (6) 2510801; 2510804
FAX: +972 (6) 2510810
E-MAIL: aramuni@planet.edu
WEBSITE: http://www.aauj.edu

Bethlehem Bible College

Hebron Road, PO Box 127, Bethlehem, Palestine
PHONE: +972 (2) 2741190
FAX: +972 (2) 2743278
E-MAIL: Bethbc@planet.edu
WEBSITE: http://www.bethlehembiblecollege.edu

Bethlehem Universtiy

PO Box 09, Bethlehem, Palestine
PHONE: +970 (2) 2741241
FAX: +970 (2) 2744440
WEBSITE: http://www.bethlehem.edu

Birzeit University

PO Box 14, Birzeit, Palestine
PHONE: +970 (2) 2982000
FAX: +970 (2) 2810656
E-MAIL: pr@birzeit.edu
WEBSITE: http://www.birzeit.edu

Hebron University

PO Box 40, Hebron, Palestine
PHONE: +972 (2) 2220995
FAX: +972 (2) 2229303
WEBSITE: http://www.hebron.edu

Ibrahimieh Community College

Mount of Olives, PO Box 19014, Jerusalem, Palestine 91190
PHONE: +972 (2) 6286361; 6264216; 6262098
E-MAIL: icc@ibrahimieh.edu
WEBSITE: http://www.ibrahimieh.edu

NEWSPAPERS AND MAGAZINES

Historic Bethlehem Newsletter

PHONE: +610 8820450
TITLE: Editor
CONTACT: Tony Hanna

Al-Massar (Palestinian Political and Cultural Bimonthly)

Al-Massar Studies Center, P.O.B 1991 Ramallah, Palestinian Authority
E-MAIL: almassar@p-ol.com
WEBSITE: http://www.almassar.com

Palestine Times

P.O. Box 10355, London NW2 3WH UK
E-MAIL: paltimes@ptimes.com
WEBSITE: http://www.ptimes.com/
TITLE: Editor-in-Chief
CONTACT: Mahmoud al-Khatib

Challenge Magazine

PO Box 4119, Jaffa 61411, Israel
E-MAIL: oda@netvision.net.il
WEBSITE: http://www.odaction.org/challenge/
TYPE: Middle Eastern affairs

Palestine Chroncile

E-MAIL: ramzy5@worldnet.att.net
WEBSITE: http://palestinechronicle.com/index.html
TYPE: Middle Eastern affairs

FURTHER READING

Internet

"Anticipation heightens for Pope John Paul II's visit to Holy Land." March 18, 2000. [Online] Available http://www.cnn.com/2000/WORLD/meast/03/18/pope.jerusalem/index.html (accessed January 9, 2001).

"Arafat and Barak reach agreement to end violence." Octover 4, 2000. [Online] Available http://www.cnn.com/2000/WORLD/meast/10/04/mideastviolence.04/ (Accessed January 9, 2001).

Assadi, Mohammed. "Little Cheer in Bethehem on Christmas Eve." December 24, 2000. [Online] Available http://dailynews.yahoo.com/h/nm/20001224/ls/mideast_christmas_dc_8.html (Accessed January 9, 2001).

Hockstader, Lee. "Barak agrees to hold new elections." November 29, 2000. [Online] Available http://www.washingtonpost.com/wp-dyn/articles/A453-2000Nov28.html (Accessed January 9, 2001).

———. "Rights group criticizes Arafat's administration." September 4, 2000. [Online] Available http://www.washingtonpost.com/wp-dyn/articles/A12425-2000Sep4.html (Accessed January 9, 2001).

"Israelis, Palestinians exchange heated rhetoric as Albright visit nears." June 26, 2000. [Online] Available http://www.cnn.com/2000/WORLD/meast/06/26/israel.palestinians/index.html (accessed January 9, 2001).

"Israeli troops, Palestinians clash after Sharon visits Jerusalem sacred site." September 28, 2000. [Online] Available http://www.cnn.com/2000/WORLD/meast/09/28/jerusalem.violence.02/ (Accessed January 9, 2001).

Reuters. "Israel's Barak submits resignation to President." December 10, 2000. [Online] Available http://dailynews.yahoo.com/h/nm/20001210/wl/mideast_leadall_dc_601.html (Accessed January 9, 2001).

Waller, Douglas. "The Peace Breakdown." August 7, 2000. [Online] Available http://www.time.com/time/europe/timetrails/israel/is000807.html (Accessed January 9, 2001).

PALESTINIAN AUTHORITY: STATISTICAL DATA

For sources and notes see "Sources of Statistics" at the front of each volume.

GEOGRAPHY

Geography

Area:

Total: 360 sq km.

Land: 360 sq km.

Land boundaries:

Total: 62 km.

Border countries: Egypt 11 km, Israel 51 km.

Coastline: 40 km.

Climate: temperate, mild winters, dry and warm to hot summers.

Terrain: flat to rolling, sand- and dune-covered coastal plain.

Natural resources: arable land.

Land use:

Arable land: 24%

Permanent crops: 39%

Permanent pastures: 0%

Forests and woodland: 11%

Other: 26% (1993 est.).

HUMAN FACTORS

Demographics (B)

Population (July 2000 est.) 1,132,063

Age structure

0-14 years 50%

male 289,954

female 275,628

15-64 years 47%

male 271,365

female 263,197

65 years and over 3%

male 13,792

female 18,127

Population growth rate 3.97%

Birth rate (births/1,000 population) 43.14

Death rate (deaths/1,000 population) 4.31

Net migration rate (migrant(s)/1,000 population) 0.83

Sex ratio (male(s)/female)

at birth 1.05

under 15 years 1.05

15-64 years 1.03

65 years and over 0.76

total population 1.03

Infant mortality rate (deaths/1,000 live births) . . .25.97

Life expectancy at birth (years)

total population 70.82

male 69.58

female 72.11

Total fertility rate (children born/woman) 6.55

Data for 2000 est. There are some 6,500 Israeli settlers in the Gaza Strip (July 2000 est.)

Health Personnel

	National Data	World Data (wtd ave)
Total health expenditure as a percentage of GDP, 1990-1998[a]		
Public sector	4.9	2.5
Private sector	3.7	2.9
Total[b]	8.6	5.5
Health expenditure per capita in U.S. dollars, 1990-1998[a]		
Purchasing power parity	NA	561
Total	81	483
Availability of health care facilities per 100,000 people		
Hospital beds 1990-1998[a]	120	330
Doctors 1992-1995[a]	NA	122
Nurses 1992-1995[a]	NA	248

Ethnic Division

Palestinian Arab and other	99.4%
Jewish	0.6%

Religion

Muslim (predominantly Sunni)	98.7%
Christian	0.7%
Jewish	0.6%

Major Languages

Arabic, Hebrew (spoken by Israeli settlers and many Palestinians), English (widely understood).

GOVERNMENT & LAW

Government Budgets (B)

Revenues	$1.6 billion
Expenditures	$1.73 billion

Data for 1999 est. Includes West Bank.

LABOR FORCE

Labor Force by Occupation

Services	66%
Industry	21%
Agriculture	13%

Data for 1996.

Unemployment Rate

14.5% (includes West Bank) (1998 est.)

PRODUCTION SECTOR

Energy Production

Production	0 kWh

Data for 1998. Electricity supplied by Israel.

Energy Consumption

Consumption	NA
Imports	NA

NA stands for not available. Electricity supplied by Israel.

Transportation

Highways: small, poorly developed road network.

Airports: 2 (1999 est.)

Note: includes Gaza International Airport that opened on 24 November 1998 as part of agreements stipulated in the September 1995 Oslo II Accord and the 23 October 1998 Wye River Memorandum.

Airports - with paved runways: 1 (1999 est.).

Airports - with unpaved runways: 1 (1999 est.).

MANUFACTURING SECTOR

GDP & Manufacturing Summary (C)

Total GDP (1999 est.)	$1.17 billion
Real growth rate (1999 est.)	4.6%
Per capita (1999 est.)	$1,060
Composition by sector	
Agriculture	33%
Industry	25%
Services	42%

Values in purchasing power parity.

COMMUNICATIONS

Telecommunications

Telephones - main lines in use: 95,729 (total for Gaza Strip and West Bank) (1997).

Telephones - mobile cellular: NA

Telephone system:

domestic: rudimentary telephone services provided by an open wire system.

international: NA

Radio broadcast stations: AM 0, FM 0, shortwave 0 (1998).

Radios: NA Note: most Palestinian households have radios (1999).

Television broadcast stations: 2 (operated by the Palestinian Broadcasting Corporation) (1997).

Televisions: NA Note: most Palestinian households have televisions (1997).

Internet Service Providers (ISPs): 3 (1999).

FINANCE, ECONOMICS, & TRADE

Economic Indicators

National product: GDP—purchasing power parity—$1.17 billion (1999 est.).

National product real growth rate: 4.6% (1999 est.).

National product per capita: $1,060 (1999 est.).

Inflation rate—consumer price index: 5% (includes West Bank) (1999 est.).

Exchange Rates

Exchange rates:

New Israeli shekels (NIS) per US$1

November 1999	4.2260
1998	3.8001
1997	3.4494
1996	3.1917
1995	3.0113

Top Import Origins

Imports (c.i.f., 1998 est.): $2.5 billion (includes West Bank).

Origins: Israel, Egypt, West Bank.

Top Export Destinations

Exports (f.o.b., 1998 est.): $682 million (Includes West Bank).

Destinations: Israel, Egypt, West Bank.

Foreign Aid

Recipient: $800 million pledged (includes West Bank) (1999).

Import/Export Commodities

Import Commodities	Export Commodities
Food	Citrus
Consumer goods	Flowers
Construction materials	

PANAMA

Republic of Panama
República de Panamá

CAPITAL: Panamá (Panama City).

FLAG: The national flag is divided into quarters. The upper quarter next to the staff is white with a blue star; the upper outer quarter is red; the lower quarter next to the staff is blue; and the lower outer quarter is white with a red star.

ANTHEM: *Himno Nacional*, beginning "Alcanzamos por fin la victoria" ("We reach victory at last").

MONETARY UNIT: The balboa (B) of 100 centésimos is the national unit of account. Panama issues no paper money, and U.S. notes are legal tender. Panama mints coins of 5, 10, 25, and 50 centésimos, and 1 and 5 balboas, which are interchangeable with U.S. coins. B1 = $1.00 (or $1 = B1.00).

WEIGHTS AND MEASURES: The metric system is official, but British, US, and old Spanish units are also used.

HOLIDAYS: New Year's Day, 1 January; Martyrs' Day, 9 January; Labor Day, 1 May; National Revolution Day, 11 October; National Anthem Day, 1 November; All Souls' Day, 2 November; Independence from Colombia, 3 November; Flag Day, 4 November; Independence Day (Colón only), 5 November; First Call of Independence, 10 November; Independence from Spain, 28 November; Mother's Day and Immaculate Conception, 8 December; Christmas, 25 December. Movable religious holidays are Shrove Tuesday and Good Friday.

TIME: 7 AM = noon GMT.

LOCATION AND SIZE: The Republic of Panama, situated on the Isthmus of Panama, has an area of 78,200 square kilometers (30,193 square miles), slightly smaller than the state of South Carolina.

CLIMATE: The annual average temperature on both coasts is 27°C (81°F), and it ranges from 10° to 19°C (50° to 66°F) at various mountain elevations. There is little seasonal change in temperature. Humidity is quite high, averaging 80%. Rainfall averages 178 centimeters (70 inches) in Panamá (Panama City) and 328 centimeters (129 inches) in Colón.

INTRODUCTORY SURVEY

RECENT HISTORY

In the decades following World War II (1939-1945), the question of sovereignty over the Canal Zone was a persistent source of conflict in Panamanian politics. In 1964, riots broke out in the Canal Zone when Panamanians protested American neglect of a 1962 joint Panama-U.S. flag-flying agreement. From then on, Panama sought sovereignty over the Canal Zone.

In October 1968, National Guard Brigadier General Omar Torrijos Herrera deposed the elected president and established a dictatorship.

Final agreement on the future of the canal and the Canal Zone came on September 7, 1977. General Torrijos and U.S. president Jimmy Carter signed the Panama Canal Treaty. The treaty recognized Panama's sovereignty over the Canal Zone, but granted the United States rights to operate, maintain, and manage the canal through December 1999. After that date ownership of the canal itself reverted to Panama.

In addition, a so-called Neutrality Treaty guaranteed the neutrality of the canal and denied the United States the right of intervention into Panamanian affairs. The treaties were ratified by popular vote in Panama on October 23, 1977. After prolonged debate the treaties were also passed by the U.S. Senate in 1978.

Torrijos resigned as head of government in 1978, but continued to rule behind the scenes as National Guard commander until his death in a

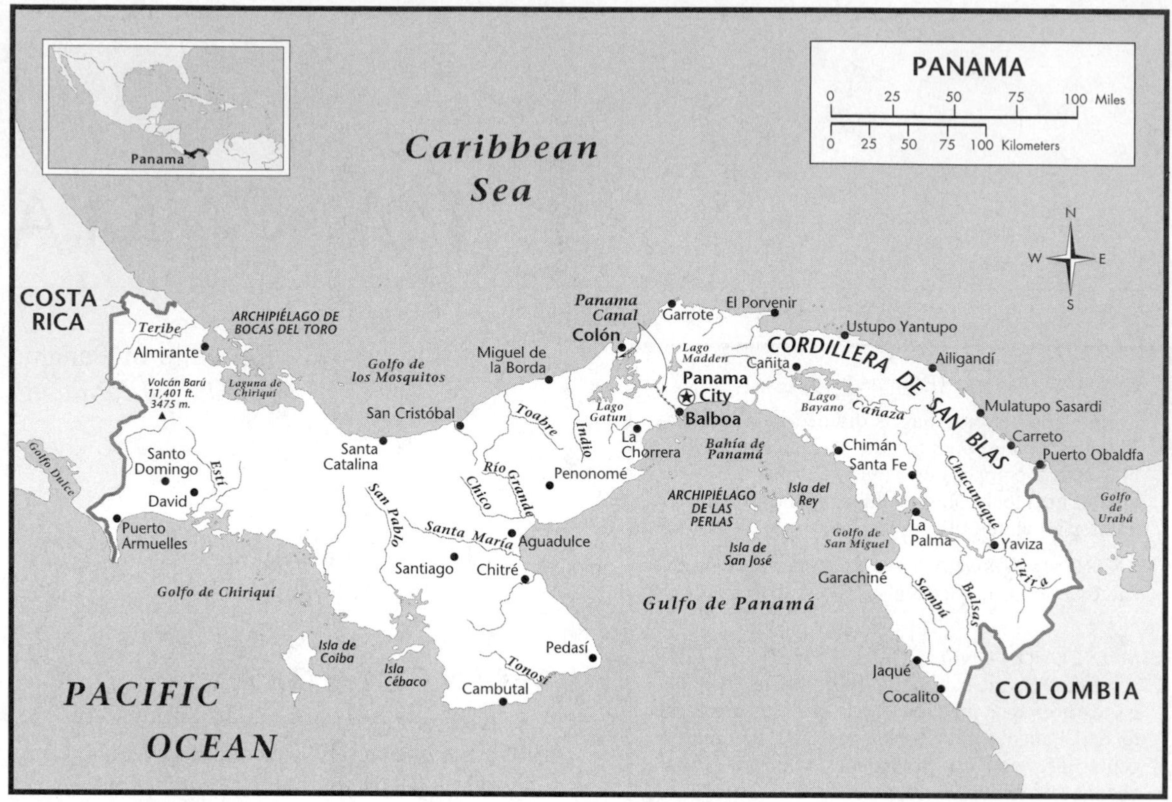

plane crash in 1981. Over the next few years, the National Guard, now renamed the Panama Defense Forces (PDF), came under the influence of General Manuel Noriega as a succession of civilian governments followed each other.

By 1987, Noriega had been accused by close associates and the United States of falsifying the 1984 election results, drug trafficking, giving aid to the Colombian and Salvadoran rebels, and providing military secrets to Cuba. The United States Senate approved legislation cutting off aid to Panama in December 1987. In February 1988, Noriega was indicted in U.S. courts for drug trafficking. Throughout 1988 and 1989, both the United States and Panamanian opposition struggled to oust Noriega who clung to power.

In December 1989, after a series of moves including a trade embargo by the United States calculated to bring down the Noriega regime, Noriega declared war on the United States and ordered attacks on U.S. military personnel. President George Bush responded quickly ordering the U.S. military into Panama. Noriega surrendered and was sent to the United States for trial.

Political instability persisted through the 1990s under the administrations of Guillermo Endara and Ernesto Pérez Balladares. Attempted economic reforms failed to produce significant improvements.

On December 31, 1999, former U.S. President Jimmy Carter signed over U.S. rule of the Panama Canal Zone

GOVERNMENT

Under the constitution of 1972, with major reforms in 1983 and 1994, Panama is a constitutional democracy in which the president, assisted by two vice-presidents and a cabinet, exercises executive power. The president and vice-presidents are elected on the same ticket by popular vote for five-year terms. Legislative power is vested in the unicameral Legislative Assembly. The seventy-two members are elected for five-year terms by direct popular vote. All Panamanians eighteen years of age or over have the right to vote.

Panama is divided into nine provinces, each subdivided into sixty-five municipal districts.

Judiciary

Judicial authority rests with the Supreme Court, which is composed of nine magistrates. There are four superior courts, eighteen circuit courts (one civil and one criminal court for each province), and at least one municipal court in each district. At the local level, two types of administrative judges, "corregidores" and "night" (or "police") judges, hear minor civil and criminal cases involving sentences under one year.

Political Parties

The coalition that came to power in 1990 consisted of President Guillermo Endara's Arnulfista Party (PA) led by Dr. Arnulfo Escalona; the National Republican Liberal Movement (MOLIRENA) led by second vice-president Guillermo Ford; and, the Christian Democratic Party (PDC) led by first vice-president Ricardo Arias. Later, Arias broke from the coalition and the PDC that controlled the Legislative Assembly.

With the election of Ernesto Pérez Balladares to the presidency in May 1994, the Democratic Revolutionary Party (PRD) returned to power. The PRD had been closely linked with the country's former military regime. In the 1999 elections, PRD took thirty-five of the seventy-two Legislative Assembly seats, and PA took eighteen. Seven other parties took eighteen seats, including MOLIRENA with three and PDC with four.

DEFENSE

The new National Police Force numbers 11,800, supported by a maritime service (400 staff, seven patrol boats) and air service (400 staff, thirty-three aircraft and helicopters). The United States maintains a garrison of 10,500 in the Canal Zone.

ECONOMIC AFFAIRS

In the early 1990s, Panama rebounded from a severe recession brought about by the United States embargo and subsequent military invasion, aimed at bringing down General Manuel Noriega, who was responsible for an increase in drug trafficking. By 1992, Panama's economic growth was among the strongest in the Western Hemisphere. In 1993, the economy continued to grow, but at a slower pace.

Panama's economy is based on well-developed service industries including the Panama Canal, banking, insurance, and government. The return of the Canal and all American bases started a construction boom. By 2000, the economy was more structurally sound and liberalized than in the 1990s. GDP growth for 2000 was projected at 3 percent to 4 percent. Key privatization reforms remain uncompleted.

Public Finance

The U.S. Central Intelligence Agency estimated that, in 1997, government revenues totaled approximately $2.4 billion and expenditures, $2.4 billion. External debt totaled $7 billion in 1999.

Income

In 1999, Panama's gross domestic product (GDP) was estimated at $21 billion, or about $7,600 per capita. The 1999 estimated GDP growth rate was 4.4 percent and inflation rate 1.5 percent. The GDP contribution by sector in 1997 was: agriculture, 8 percent; industry, 25 percent; and services, 67 percent.

Industry

Industry achieved a 7 percent growth rate during the 1990s. Construction, manufacturing, mining, and utilities together accounted for 17 percent of GDP in 1998. The construction industry was the star performer during 1998. The government and private sector invested large amounts in the construction of ports, roads, and bridges. Hence, construction activity rose 5 percent in 1998, while the production of construction-related materials rose by 23 percent and finished wood products by 38 percent.

Manufacturing of mainly non-durable goods consists principally of food-processing and alcoholic beverage production, ceramics, tropical clothing, cigarettes, hats, furniture, shoes, soap, and edible oils.

Banking and Finance

Panama was considered the most important international banking center in Latin America in the late 1980s. In 1970, only twenty-eight banks operated in Panama's international banking center. By 1987, there were 120 with assets of nearly $39 billion. The growth in Panama's offshore banking has contributed to the country's relative prosperity and accentuated the importance of the service sector in the economy.

In 1999, there were about ninety-four banks in Panama holding $36.6 billion in total assets. Fifty-seven banks hold general licenses, twenty-six held offshore licenses, twelve are foreign banks, and two government-owned. The National Bank of Panama (Banco Nacional de Panamá-BNP), founded in 1904, is the principal official (but not central) bank and also transacts general banking business. The National Banking Commission (Comisión Bancaria Nacional-CBN) supervises banking activities. Private banks include branches of U.S., Japanese, Latin American, and other foreign firms. Liberalized banking regulations and use of the dollar have made Panama one of Latin America's major offshore banking centers.

Panama's banking center has allegedly been the main money-laundering point for proceeds from international drug trafficking. In March 1994 it was decreed that persons entering Panama must declare money or financial instruments in excess of $10,000. For deposits and withdrawals in excess of this amount from local banking institutions, a form would have to be filled in providing details about the person carrying out the transaction. In 1998 a banking law was enacted in order to modernize the banking system and increase government supervision.

Panama's international stock exchange, the Bolsa de Valores de Panama, began operations in June 1990. In 1995, there were a total of 102 listed companies, of which ninety-six were local and six foreign entities. Panama's Central de Custodia de Valores (Panaclear) began operations in November 1996. A rating agency was expected to begin operations by early 1997.

Economic Development

The Panamanian economy is the most stable, and among the more prosperous in the region. But the economy is highly segmented between its dynamic, internationally oriented service sector and the domestically oriented sector that is beset with policy-induced rigidities and low productivity.

Despite Panama's relatively high per capita income, two-fifths of the population lives in poverty. Income distribution is highly skewed and has become much more regressive in the past decade. In 1979 the poorest 20 percent of the population received 4 percent of income; in 1989 that share had plunged to 2 percent leaving Panama with one of the most unequal distributions in the hemisphere. The government's strategy for mitigating poverty and inequality rests primarily on reviving sustainable growth; its economic program emphasizes reforms that will mitigate the bias against employment creation (unemployment was 13 percent in 1998), increase agricultural productivity, and reduce the high cost of the basic consumption basket.

SOCIAL WELFARE

The Social Security Fund provides medical service and hospitalization, maternity care, pensions for disability and old age, and funeral benefits. Children are cared for through a child welfare institute that operates under the Ministry of Labor and Social Welfare. The government has made efforts to integrate the Amerindian population of the eastern Caribbean coast through land grants, basic education, and improved transportation. The social security system covered more than one million persons in the mid-1980s.

While Panama has a relatively high rate of female enrollment in higher education, many female graduates are still forced to take low-paying jobs. As of 1999, women's wages were on average 20 percent lower than those of men. Women occupy only 4 percent of the country's managerial positions.

Healthcare

Public health services include free health examinations and medical care for the needy, health education, sanitation inspection, hospital and clinic construction, and nutrition services. In 1993, 82 percent of the population had access to health care services. In 1997 Panama had twelve physicians per 10,000 people and eighteen hospital beds per 1,000 inhabitants.

Malaria has been controlled and the yellow-fever mosquito practically eliminated. Today the principal causes of death are cancer, heart disease, cerebrovascular disease, pneumonia and bronchopneumonia, and enteritis and diarrhea. In some areas of Panama, poor sanitation, inadequate housing, and malnutrition still constitute health hazards. In 2000, average life expectancy was 75.5 years.

Housing

Housing in urban areas has been a permanent problem since U.S. construction in the Canal Zone brought a great influx of migrant laborers into Colón and Panamá (Panama City). In the early 1980s, the shortage of low-income housing remained acute, particularly in Colón. In 1980-1988, total housing units numbered 448,000 with 4.9 people per dwelling.

EDUCATION

In 1995, illiteracy was estimated at 9 percent of the adult population (males, 8.6 percent; females, 9.8 percent). Education is free and compulsory for children aged six through fifteen. In 1996, there were 2,849 primary schools with 371,250 students. At the secondary schools there were 221,022 students. A major school construction program began in 1999, and the percentage of students completing sixth grade was projected to rise from 78 percent in 1997 to 90 percent by 2002.

Universities include the state-run University of Panama and Santa María la Antigua. In 1996, at all institutions of higher learning, there were 4,979 teaching staff with 80,980 students enrolled.

2000 KEY EVENTS TIMELINE

January

- Panama authorities increase security as they plan for a British ship carrying radioactive material to pass through the canal.

April

- Panama rules out raising the sales tax to 7 percent or enacting recommended privatizations (of a water company and an airport), ruining its chances for an IMF credit facility.
- Panamanian authorities offer refugee protection to Colombians.

May

- Banco del Istmo and Pribanco, Panama's second and third largest banks, agree to a $3.7 billion merger.

June

- The Panamanian government announces President Moscoso's plans to visit Taiwan in July. Panama's opposition parties accuse President Mireya Moscoso of jeopardizing Panama's neutrality by recognizing Taiwan as "China" instead of the mainland.
- Trade ministers from Costa Rica, El Salvador, Guatemala, Honduras, Nicaragua, and Panama meet in Panama City to discuss a regional free trade agreement.

September

- The Colombian government's crackdown on drug trafficking and money laundering, combined with Colombia's weak economy, have caused a downturn in trading in Panama's Colon Free Zone, since Colombia is its largest customer. In addition, the Darien Gap jungle region along Panama's border with Colombia has become a dangerous zone where bands of armed guerrillas pass back and forth.

October

- Colombian rebels raid the border village of Nazaret October 15, killing one and injuring twelve others.
- Peru's former Intelligence Advisor Vladimiro Montesinos fails to find political asylum in Panama, and returns to Peru October 23.

November

- Four men, including Luis Posada Carriles, are detained November 17 in Panama for an alleged plot to kill Cuban President Fidel Castro during the Ibero-American Summit. Venezuela requests Carriles' extradition November 21, but President Mireya Moscoso wants to try the criminals.

ANALYSIS OF EVENTS: 2000

BUSINESS AND THE ECONOMY

The 1999 election of populist President Mireya Moscoso, the widow of a former three-term president of Panama, raised concerns in the business community, both at home and abroad, that growth-oriented policies would be scuttled in favor of social welfare spending. However, the country's fiscal deficit for 1999 came to only 1.2 percent of gross domestic product (GDP), as her administration proved itself able to control spending and, in addition, improve tax collection. The economy grew at 3.3 percent and inflation remained at 1 percent. Growth for 2000 was estimated at 4 percent, aided by an increase in international investment in areas that had reverted from U.S. to Panamanian control with the turnover of the canal.

While Panama, a banking and insurance center for the region, attracted business travelers, its leisure travel sector was relatively undeveloped and seen as a good potential growth area, particularly because the existence of the canal zone had left substantial undeveloped rain forest areas near its urban centers. The 340-acre Gamboa Rainforest Resort, opened in June, took advantage of the country's potential for ecotourism, offering visitors activities including birdwatching, fishing, and kayaking. Another major advance for the country's tourist industry was the inauguration in October of the Colon 2000 cruise port, with which Panama hoped to reposition itself as a cruise destination in its own right rather than merely a gateway to the Caribbean.

In May Panama's second- and third-largest banks, Banco del Istmo and Pribanco, agreed to a $3.7 million merger deal.

GOVERNMENT AND POLITICS

The new millennium brought with it ownership of the Panama Canal, turned over to Panama by the United States on December 31, 1999, under an agreement worked out by U.S. President Jimmy Carter during his term. Although a source of national pride, turnover of the canal also resulted in the withdrawal of U.S. military forces that had provided 4,000 jobs and $350 million in revenue for the government. And the legacy of the United States could still be seen in many ways, from the nation's use of the U.S. dollar as its official currency to the U.S. business franchises found in its retail centers.

The situation in neighboring Colombia concerned Panamanians in several ways. The violence and instability caused by guerrilla warfare and the country's drug trade had sent nearly 1,000 refugees fleeing over the border to Panama's Darien province. Since the fighting was not recognized internationally as a civil war, the refugees were not eligible for international aid. Guerrilla fighters had crossed the border for refuge and to procure weapons, and the region's volatility had caused trade to decline in Panama's Colon Free Zone.

In September many Panamanians were embarrassed by the decision of their government, under international pressure from powerful allies, to grant temporary refuge to Peru's former chief of intelligence, the Vladimiros Montesinos.

The hopes for a freer press raised by President Mireya Moscoso at the end of 1999, when she signed a bill repealing many of the country's "gag laws," were dashed by her actions in 2000. The government failed to implement the sweeping reforms that were supposed to follow the initial measure, and harassment of journalists continued.

In June Panama hosted a meeting of Central American trade ministers who gathered to discuss a possible regional trade agreement.

CULTURE AND SOCIETY

In spite of development in Colon's duty-free zone and in the transportation corridor between Panama City and Colon, the country's two major population centers, unequal distribution of the nation's wealth left widespread poverty in poor neighborhoods such as Panama City's San Miguelito area and among subsistence farmers in the countryside. A study by the Institute of National Economic Studies found that the wealthiest 20 percent of the population spent $30 for every dollar spent by the poorest 20 percent.

Although the primary focus on Darien had to do with threats from its Colombian border, environmentalists were concerned about the possible destructive consequences of development in the region. Since the late 1970s, large areas of rain forest had been cleared by homesteaders using slash-and-burn agriculture, and observers feared that large-scale development of the region by agribusiness and the tourism industry could devastate remaining rain forest areas and have an equally devastating effect on the indigenous communities. Even parks were not completely protected from exploitation of natural resources.

A six-year, $70.4 million project to pave an unpaved segment of the Pan-American Highway in the region was approved by the Inter-American Development Bank.

DIRECTORY

CENTRAL GOVERNMENT

Head of State

President
Mireya Moscoso, Office of the President, President's Office, 3rd Ave., near the Cathedral, Panama
PHONE: +507 (011) 2279600

Ministers

Minister of Agricultural Development
Pedro Adan, Ministry of Agriculture Development
PHONE: +507 (011) 2325043; 2325150

Minister for Canal Affairs
Ricardo Martinelli, Ministry for Canal Affairs

Minister of Commerce and Industry
Joaquin Jacome, Ministry of Commerce and Industries
PHONE: +507 (011) 2274222; 2271222

Minister of Education
Doris Rosas de Mata, Ministry of Education
PHONE: +507 (011) 2622200; 2622645

Minister of Economy and Finance
Norberto Delgado, Ministry of Economy and Finance

Minister of Foreign Relations
Jose Miguel Aleman, Ministry of Foreign Relations
PHONE: +507 (011) 2288644

Minister of Government and Justice
Winston Spadafora, Ministry of Government and Justice
PHONE: +507 (011) 2122000

Minister of Health
Jose Manuel Teran, Ministry of Health
PHONE: +507 (011) 2253540

Minister of Housing
Miguel Cardenas, Ministry of Housing
PHONE: +507 (011) 2627692; 2627222

Minister of Labor and Social Welfare
Joaquin Jose Vallarino III, Ministry of Labor and Social Welfare
PHONE: +507 (011) 2255763

Minister of Presidency
Ivonne Young, Ministry of Presidency

Minister of Public Works
Victor Nelson Juliao, Ministry of Public Works
PHONE: +507 (011) 2325333

Minister of Women, Youth, Family, and Childhood
Alba Esther Tejada de Rolla, Ministry of Women, Youth, Family, and Childhood
PHONE: +507 (011) 2610254; 2790686

POLITICAL ORGANIZATIONS

Partido Renovación Civilista-PRC (Civic Renewal Party)

NAME: Tomas Herrera

Movimiento de Renovación Nacional-MORENA (National Renovation Movement)

NAME: Pedro Vallerino

Movimiento Liberal Republicano Nacionalista-MOLIRENA (Nationalist Republican Liberal Movement)

Calle Venezuela, entre Vía España y Calle 50
Ciudad de Panamá, Panamá
NAME: Delia Cardenas
PHONE: +507 (0110 2135928; 2135929
FAX: +507 (011) 2656004
E-MAIL: molirena@hotmail.com

Partido Demócrata Cristiano-PDC (Christian Democratic Party)

NAME: Ruben Arosemena

Alianza Democrática-AD (Democratic Alliance)

Partido Arnulfista-PA (Arnulfista Party)

NAME: Mireya Moscoso de Gruber

Partido Liberal Auténtico-PLA (Authentic Liberal Party)

NAME: Arnulfo Escalona

Unión Democrática Independiente-UDI (Independent Democratic Union)

NAME: Jacinto Cardenas

Partido Liberal Nacional (National Liberal Party)

NAME: Roberto Aleman Zubieta

Movimiento Papa Egoró-MPE (Papa Egoró Movement)

NAME: Gloria Young

Pueblo Unido-PU (United People)

Partido Revolucionario Democrática-PRD (Democratic Revolutionary Party)

NAME: Gerardo Gonzalez

Partido Laborista-PALA (Labor Party)

NAME: Carlos Lopez Guevara

Partido Liberal Republicano-PLR (Liberal Republican Party)

NAME: Rodolfo Chiari

DIPLOMATIC REPRESENTATION

Embassies in Panama

Argentina
Calles 50 y 53, Urbanización Obarrio, Panamá City, Panamá
PHONE: +507 (011) 2646989

Bolvia
Calle 50, 78 Panamá City, Panamá
PHONE: +507 (011) 2690274

Brazil
Edificio El Dorado, Piso 1 Calle E Méndez, 24C Alegre, Panamá City, Panamá
PHONE: +507 (011) 2635322; 2635540

Canada
PHONE: +507 (011) 2649731; 2647115
FAX: +507 (011) 2638083

China
Edificio Grobman, Piso 6 Calle Manuel M Icaza, 12 Panamá City, Panamá
PHONE: +507 (011) 2649266
FAX: +507 (011) 2231134; 2234159

Costa Rica
Calle Gerardo Ortega, Panamá City, Panamá
PHONE: +507 (011) 2642980

Cuba
Avenidas Cuba y Ecuador, Panamá City, Panamá
PHONE: +507 (011) 2270359; 2275277
FAX: +507 (011) 2256681

Chile
Calle E Méndez y Vía España, Panamá City, Panamá
PHONE: +507 (011) 2239748

Ecuador
Calle Manuel Icaza, 12 Panamá City, Panamá
PHONE: +507 (011) 2642654
FAX: +507 (011) 2230159

El Salvador
Avenida Manuel Espinosa Batista, Panamá City, Panamá
PHONE: +507 (011) 2233020

France
Plaza de Francia, Panamá City, Panamá
PHONE: +507 (011) 2287824

Germany
Republica Federal Edificio Bancomer, Piso 6 Calles 50 y 53, Panamá City, Panamá
PHONE: +507 (011) 2637733; 2641147
FAX: +507 (011) 2236664

Greece
Consulate of Greece, Calle M Urbanizacion El Paical, Panamá City, Panamá
PHONE: +507 (011) 2602705

Japan
Edificio Sede Propia, Calles 50 y 60-E Obarrio, Panamá City, Panamá
PHONE: +507 (011) 2636155
FAX: +507 (011) 2636019

Korea
Calle 51E, Ricardo Arias, Campo Alegre, Edificio Plaza P.B., Panamá City, Panamá
PHONE: +507 (011) 2648203; 2648360
FAX: +507 (011) 2648825

Libya
Avenida Balboa y Calle 32, Panamá City, Panamá
PHONE: +507 (011) 2273342

Malta
Calle Elvira Méndez, Panamá City, Panamá
PHONE: +507 (011) 2649538

Mexico
Edificio Bancomer, Piso 5 Calle 50 y 53, Panamá City, Panamá
PHONE: +507 (011) 2635021

Nicaragua
Calle José de San Martín, 31 Panamá City, Panamá
PHONE: +507 (011) 2230981

Peru
Calles Elvira Méndez y 52, Panamá City, Panamá
PHONE: +507 (011) 2231112

Russia
Edificio Omega, Piso 7 Avenida Samuel Lewis, Panamá City, Panamá
PHONE: +507 (011) 2641408; 2641635
FAX: +507 (011) 2641558

Spain
Frente al Parque Porras Avenida 6, 44 Panamá City, Panamá
PHONE: +507 (011) 2694018
FAX: +507 (011) 2276284

Uruguay
Avenida Justo Arosemena y Calle 32, 4 Panamá City, Panamá
PHONE: +507 (011) 2259087

United States
Calle 37 y Avenida Balboa, Apartado 6959, 5 Panamá City, Panamá
PHONE: +507 (011) 2271777
FAX: +507 (011) 2271964

Venezuela
Torre Banco Union, Piso 5 Avenida Samuel Lewis, Panamá City, Panamá
PHONE: +507 (011) 2691244
FAX: +507 (011) 2691916

JUDICIAL SYSTEM

Supreme Court of Justice

Dirección de Prensa y Relaciones Públicas, Panamá City, Panamá
PHONE: +507 (011) 2627158; 2625641
FAX: +507 (011) 2625956

BROADCAST MEDIA

Asociacion Panamena De Radiodifusion

Apartado Postal 55-1326, Panama, Panama
TITLE: President
CONTACT: Fernando Eleta Casanovas

Cadena Nacional Bahia

Apartado 6-3091 El Dorado, Panama, Panama
PHONE: +507 2267381
FAX: +507 2261021
E-MAIL: info@estereobahia.com
WEBSITE: http://www.estereobahia.com
LANGUAGE: Spanish
TYPE: Private, Commercial

Direccion Nacional De Medios De Comunicacion Social

Ap. 1628, Panama 1, Panama
PHONE: +507 227300
TITLE: Director
CONTACT: Edwin Cabrera

RPC Radio

Panama, Panama
PHONE: +507 2106700
E-MAIL: rpcradio@medcom.com.pa
WEBSITE: http://www.rpcradio.com
TITLE: General Manager
CONTACT: Karen Chalmers

FETV

Apartado Postal 6-7295 El Dorado, Panama, Panama
PHONE: + 5072646555
FAX: +507 2235966
E-MAIL: comentarios@fetv.org
WEBSITE: http://www.fetv.org
TITLE: Director General
CONTACT: Fr. Manuel-Santiago Blanquer i Planells
CHANNEL: 5
TYPE: Educational

Panavision

Apartado Postal 6-2605 El-Dorado, Panama, Panama

RPC Television

Apt. 1795, Panama 1, Panama
PHONE: +507 2250160
FAX: +507 2250705
E-MAIL: webmaster@cyberimagen.com
WEBSITE: http://www.rpctv.com

Sistema de TV Educativa

Calle Jose de Fabrega, Estafeta Universitaria, Universidad de Panama, Panama
PHONE: +507 2693755; +507 2693848
FAX: +507 2236220; +507 2236251
E-MAIL: rtvel@ancon.up.ac.pa
WEBSITE: http://www.up.ac.pa/cultura
TITLE: Director General
CONTACT: I. Velasquez de Cortes
CHANNEL: 11

Telemetro

PO Box 8-116, Panama 8, Panama
PHONE: +507 2692122
FAX: +507 2692720
E-MAIL: webmaster@cyberimagen.com
WEBSITE: http://www.telemetro.com
TITLE: Director General
CONTACT: B. Marques
CHANNEL: 13

Televisora Nacional

Apartando Postal 6-3092 El Dorado, Panama, Panama
CONTACT: Alejandro Ayala V

COLLEGES AND UNIVERSITIES

University Santa Maria la Antigua

Apdo 6-1696, El Dorado, Panama City, Panama
PHONE: +507 2304011
E-MAIL: secretar@canaa.usma.ac.pa
WEBSITE: http://www.usma.ac.pa

Universidad de Panama

Estafeta Universitaria, Panama City, Panama
PHONE: +507 2636133
WEBSITE: http://www.up.ac.pa

NEWSPAPERS AND MAGAZINES

Cordialidad

Ediciones Argus S.A., PO Box 87, 1401 Panama
PHONE: +507 607043
FAX: +507 606409
TITLE: Editor
CONTACT: Cristina Nordstrom
CIRCULATION: 20,000

La Prensa

WEBSITE: http://www.sinfo.net/prensa/hoy/portada.shtml

El Siglo

E-MAIL: jpadilla@elsiglo.com
WEBSITE: http://www.elsiglo.com
TITLE: Editor
CONTACT: Jaime Padilla Beliz

PUBLISHERS

Focus Publications International SA

PO Box 63287, El Dorado, Panama
PHONE: +507 2256638
FAX: +507 2250466
E-MAIL: focusint@sinfo.net
WEBSITE: http://www.focuspublicationsint.com
TITLE: Publisher
CONTACT: Kenneth Jones
SUBJECTS: Marketing, Social Sciences, Travel

Fondo Educativo Interamericano

Edificio Eastern 6, Avda Federico Boyd y Calle 51, Apdo 6-3099, Panama
PHONE: +507 2691551
TITLE: Director
CONTACT: Alicia Chavarria

Editorial Universitaria

Urb El Cangrejo Calle Jose, Apdo Aereo Estafeta Univeristaria, Panama
PHONE: +507 2642087
FAX: +507 2692684
TITLE: Managing Director
CONTACT: Carlos M. Gasteazoro
SUBJECTS: Architecture and Interior Design, Art, Education, Geography, Geology, History, Law, Literature, Literary Criticism, Essays, Philosophy, Science (General), Social Sciences, Sociology

RELIGIOUS ORGANIZATIONS

Catholic

Chitre Diocese

Obispo de Chitre, Urbanizacion Miramar, Apartado 49, Chitre, Herrera, Panama
PHONE: +507 9967285
FAX: +507 9967284
E-MAIL: irunako@canaa.usma.ac.pa
TITLE: Excmo. Monsenor
NAME: Jose Luis Lacunza Maestrojuan, O.A.R.

Colon Diocese

Obispo de Colon, Calle 5, Amador Guerrero 5056, Apartado 2419, Cristobal, Colon, Panama
PHONE: +507 4418466
FAX: +507 4415163
TITLE: Excmo. Monsenor
NAME: Carlos Maria Ariz Bolea, C.M.F.

Conferencia Episcopal De Panama

Secretario General, Apartado 870933, Panama 7, Panama
PHONE: +507 2230075
FAX: +507 2230042
E-MAIL: cep@vasco.usma.ac.pa.

David Diocese

Obispo de David, Obispado Apartado 109, David-Chiriqui, Panama
PHONE: +507 7752916
FAX: +507 7743920
TITLE: Excmo. Monsenor

Panama (Arq.)

Arzobispo de Panama, Calle la. Sur, Carrasquilla, Apartado 6386, Zona 5, Panama, Panama
PHONE: +507 2230075
FAX: +507 2230042
TITLE: Excmo Monsenor
NAME: Jose Dimas Cedeno Delgado

Santiago De Veraguas Diocese

Obispo de Santiago de Veraguas, Obispado, Apartado 48, Santiago de Veraguas, Panama
PHONE: +507 9587085
FAX: +507 9585117
TITLE: Excmo. Monsenor
NAME: Oscar Mario Brown Jimenez

Jewish

Mikvah c/o Sociedad Israelita Shevet Ahim

Calle 44-27, Panama City, Panama
PHONE: +507 255990

FURTHER READING

Articles

Becker, Elizabeth. "Panama Steps Up Security for Ship with Atomic Waste." *New York Times,* January 15, 2000, p. A6.

"Colombia and Its Neighbours—Nervous in Darien. *The Economist (US),* October 7, 2000, vol. 357, no. 8191, p. 46.

Gonzalez, David. "Peru Closing Bribery Case of Top Aide Now an Exile." *New York Times,* September 27, 2000, p. A7.

"The Month in Review: January 2000." *Current History,* March 2000, p. 142.

"Panamanian President off to Visit Mexico, Taiwan." *Central News Agency* (Taiwan), June 28, 2000.

Books

Dun and Bradstreet's Guide to Panama. Parsippany, NJ: Dun & Bradstreet, 1999.

Sosa, Juan B. *In Defiance: The Battle against General Noriega Fought from Panama's Embassy in Washington.* Washington, DC: Francis Press, 1999.

Government Publications

United States Congress. *Background Notes: Panama.* Washington, DC: G.P.O., 2000.

———. *The Financial and Commercial Impact of the Panama Canal Treaty.* Washington, DC: G.P.O., 2000.

———. *Losing Panama: The Impact on Regional Counterdrug Capabilities.* Washington, DC: G.P.O., 2000.

———. *Security of the Panama Canal.* Washington, DC: G.P.O., 2000.

Internet

BBC News Online. "Sanctions Threat to 'Tax Havens.'" June 26, 2000. [Online] Available http://news6.thdo.bbc.co.uk/hi/english/business/newsid%5F806000/806236.stm (accessed October 12, 2000).

PANAMA: STATISTICAL DATA

For sources and notes see "Sources of Statistics" at the front of each volume.

GEOGRAPHY

Geography

Area:

Total: 78,200 sq km.

Land: 75,990 sq km.

Land boundaries:

Total: 555 km.

Border countries: Colombia 225 km, Costa Rica 330 km.

Coastline: 2,490 km.

Climate: tropical maritime; hot, humid, cloudy; prolonged rainy season (May to January), short dry season (January to May).

Terrain: interior mostly steep, rugged mountains and dissected, upland plains; coastal areas largely plains and rolling hills.

Natural resources: copper, mahogany forests, shrimp, hydropower.

Land use:

Arable land: 7%

Permanent crops: 2%

Permanent pastures: 20%

Forests and woodland: 44%

Other: 27% (1993 est.).

HUMAN FACTORS

Demographics (A)

	1990	1995	1998	2000	2010	2020	2030	2040	2050
Population	2,388	2,609	2,731	2,808	3,150	3,443	3,676	3,812	3,849
Life expectancy - males	70.2	71.6	72.3	72.7	74.7	76.3	77.6	78.6	79.5
Life expectancy - females	75.6	77.1	77.8	78.3	80.4	82.1	83.5	84.6	85.4
Birth rate (per 1,000)	26.5	22.5	20.7	19.5	15.6	13.9	12.0	10.6	10.1
Death rate (per 1,000)	5.3	5.0	5.0	4.9	5.2	5.8	6.9	8.4	10.3
Women of reproductive age (15-49 yrs.)	604.2	673.9	711.6	738.0	861.0	907.1	899.4	864.2	805.3
Fertility rate	3.1	2.6	2.5	2.3	1.9	1.8	1.7	1.7	1.7

Except as noted, values for vital statistics are in thousands; life expectancy is in years.

Health Personnel

	National Data	World Data (wtd ave)
Total health expenditure as a percentage of GDP, 1990-1998[a]		
Public sector	6.0	2.5
Private sector	1.7	2.9
Total[b]	7.6	5.5
Health expenditure per capita in U.S. dollars, 1990-1998[a]		
Purchasing power parity	402	561
Total	253	483
Availability of health care facilities per 100,000 people		
Hospital beds 1990-1998[a]	220	330
Doctors 1992-1995[a]	119	122
Nurses 1992-1995[a]	98	248

Health Indicators

	National Data	World Data
Life expectancy at birth (years)		
1980	70	61
1998	74	67
Daily per capita supply of calories		
1970	2,257	2,358
1997	2,430	2,791
Daily per capital supply of protein		
1997 (grams)	65	74
Total fertility rate (births per woman)		
1980	3.7	3.7
1998	2.6	2.7
Population with access (%)		
To safe water (1990-96)	84	NA
To sanitation (1990-96)	90	NA
People living with (1997)		
Tuberculosis (cases per 100,000)	39.2	60.4
Malaria (cases per 100,000)	18.6	42.2
HIV/AIDS (% aged 15 - 49 years)	0.61	0.99

Infants and Malnutrition

	National Data	World Data (wtd ave)
Under 5 mortality rate (1989)	20	NA
% of infants with low birthweight (1992-98)[1]	8	17
Births attended by skilled health staff (% of total births 1996-98)	84	52
% fully immunized at 1 year of age (1995-98)[1]		
TB	99	82
DPT	98	77
Polio	99	77
Measles	96	74
Prevalence of child malnutrition (1992-98)[1] (based on weight for age, % of children under 5 years)	6	30

Ethnic Division

Mestizo 70%

Amerindian and mixed (West Indian) 14%

White 10%

Amerindian 6%

People of Mestizo ethnicity have mixed Amerindian and white ancestry.

Religion

Roman Catholic 85%

Protestant 15%

Major Languages

Spanish (official), English 14%. Many Panamanians are bilingual.

EDUCATION

Public Education Expenditures

	1980	1997
Public expenditures on education as % of GNP	4.9	5.1
Expenditures per student as % of GNP per capita		
Primary	12.3[2]	NA
Secondary	11.5	NA
Tertiary	29.8	40.2
Teachers' compensation as % of total current education expenditures	65.3	51.2
Pupils per teacher at the primary level	NA	NA
Duration of primary education in years	NA	6
World data for comparison		
Public expenditures on education as % of GNP (mean)	3.9	4.8
Pupils per teacher at the primary level (wtd ave)	NA	33
Duration of primary education in years (mean)	NA	9

Educational Attainment (A)

Age group (1990)[11]	25+
Population of this age group	1,035,339
Highest level attained (%)	
No schooling	11.7
First level	
Not completed	20.2
Completed	21.8
Entered second level	
Lower Secondary	12.6
Upper Secondary	16.4
Entered post-secondary	13.2

Literacy Rates (A)

In thousands and percent	1990	1995	2000	2010
Illiterate population (15+ yrs.)	169	161	155	134
Literacy rate - total adult pop. (%)	88.8	90.8	92.1	94.4
Literacy rate - males (%)	89.4	91.4	92.7	95.0
Literacy rate - females (%)	88.3	90.2	91.5	93.8

GOVERNMENT & LAW

Military Affairs (A)

	1990	1992	1995	1996	1997
Military expenditures					
Current dollars (mil.)	74	80	96	101	114
1997 constant dollars (mil.)	87	89	100	103	114
Armed forces (000)	11	11	12	12	12
Gross national product (GNP)					
Current dollars (mil.)	5,080	6,250	7,540	7,930	8,400
1997 constant dollars (mil.)	5,950	6,930	7,810	8,060	8,400
Central government expenditures (CGE)					
1997 constant dollars (mil.)	1,430	1,570	1,900	2,240	2,400[e]
People (mil.)	2.4	2.5	2.6	2.7	2.7
Military expenditure as % of GNP	1.5	1.3	1.3	1.3	1.4
World data on military expenditure as % of GNP	4.5	3.4	2.7	2.6	2.6
Military expenditure as % of CGE	6.1	5.7	5.2	4.6	4.8
World data on military expenditure as % of CGE	17.0	12.5	10.5	10.3	10.2
Military expenditure per capita (1997 $)	36	36	38	39	42
World data on military expenditure per capita (1997 $)	242	173	146	143	145
Armed forces per 1,000 people (soldiers)	4.6	4.4	4.6	4.5	4.5
World data on armed forces per 1,000 people (soldiers)	5.3	4.5	4.1	3.9	3.8
GNP per capita (1997 $)	2,490	2,800	2,990	3,040	3,120
Arms imports[6]					
Current dollars (mil.)	10	10	10	10	10
1997 constant dollars (mil.)	12	11	10	10	10
Arms exports[6]					
Current dollars (mil.)	0	10	0	0	0
1997 constant dollars (mil.)	0	11	0	0	0
Total imports[7]					
Current dollars (mil.)	1,539	2,024	2,511	2,780	3,002
1997 constant dollars (mil.)	1,802	2,244	2,600	2,826	3,002
Total exports[7]					
Current dollars (mil.)	340	502	625	674[e]	723
1997 constant dollars (mil.)	398	557	647	685[e]	723
Arms as percent of total imports[8]	0.6	0.5	0.4	0.4	0.3
Arms as percent of total exports[8]	0	2.0	0	0	0

(Continued on next page.)

Political Parties

Legislative Assembly (Asamblea Legislativa)	no. of seats
Democratic Revolutionary Party (PRD)	35
ARmulfista Party (PA)	18
Solidarity Party (PS)	4
Christian Democratic Party (PDC)	4
Nationalist Republican Liberal Movement (MOLIRENA)	3
Civic Renewal Party (PRC)	2
National Liberal Party (PLN)	2
Democratic Change	2
National Renovation Movement (MORENA)	1

Elections were last held 2 May 1999 (next to be held in May 2004). One seat has yet to be decided.

Government Budgets (A)

Year: 1997

Total Expenditures: 2,341.3 Millions of Balboas

Expenditures as a percentage of the total by function:

General public services and public order	10.72
Defense	5.04
Education	18.33
Health	18.73
Social Security and Welfare	20.53
Housing and community amenities	5.07
Recreational, cultural, and religious affairs	0.96
Fuel and energy	0
Agriculture, forestry, fishing, and hunting	1.82
Mining, manufacturing, and construction	0.21
Transportation and communication	2.75
Other economic affairs and services	3.25

Crime

Crime volume (for 1998)

Crimes reported	11,566
Total persons convicted	3,441
Crimes per 100,000 population	419

Persons responsible for offenses

Total number suspects	4,617
Total number of female suspects	425
Total number of juvenile suspects	137

LABOR FORCE

Total Labor Force (A)

1.044 million. There is a shortage of skilled labor, but an oversupply of unskilled labor.

Labor Force by Occupation

Agriculture	18%
Industry	18%
Services	64%

Data for 1997 est.

Unemployment Rate

13.1% (1997 est.)

PRODUCTION SECTOR

Energy Production

Production	4.523 billion kWh
Production by source	
Fossil fuel	25.56%
Hydro	73.78%
Nuclear	0%
Other	0.66%
Exports	13 million kWh

Data for 1998.

Energy Consumption

Consumption	4.329 billion kWh
Imports	136.000 million kWh

Data for 1998.

Transportation

Highways:

Total: 11,258 km.

Paved: 3,783 km (including 30 km of expressways).

Unpaved: 7,475 km (1999 est.).

Waterways: 800 km navigable by shallow draft vessels; 82 km Panama Canal.

Pipelines: crude oil 130 km.

Merchant marine:

Total: 4,732 ships (1,000 GRT or over) totaling 106,054,086 GRT/159,304,019 DWT.

Ships by type: bulk 1,377, cargo 976, chemical tanker 323, combination bulk 68, combination ore/oil 15, container 525, liquified gas 184, livestock carrier 8, multi-functional large load carrier 12, passenger 46, passenger/cargo 4, petroleum tanker 496, rail car carrier 2, refrigerated cargo 313, roll-on/roll-off 106, short-sea passenger 42, specialized tanker 33, vehicle carrier 202 (1999 est.).

Note: a flag of convenience registry; includes ships from 71 countries among which are Japan 1,262, Greece 378, Hong Kong 244, South Korea 259, Taiwan 229,China 193, Singapore 103, US 116, Switzerland 78, and Indonesia 53 (1998 est.).

Airports: 105 (1999 est.).

Airports - with paved runways: 41.

Airports - with unpaved runways: 64.

Top Agriculture Products

Bananas, rice, corn, coffee, sugarcane, vegetables; livestock; shrimp.

Top Mining Products (B)

Mineral resources include: copper.

MANUFACTURING SECTOR

GDP & Manufacturing Summary (A)

	1980	1985	1990	1995
GDP ($-1990 mil.)[1]	4,672	5,383	5,009	6,699
Per capita ($-1990)[1]	2,396	2,484	2,089	2,546
Manufacturing share (%) (current prices)[1]	9.7	8.2	7.8	NA
Manufacturing				
Value added ($-1990 mil.)[1]	428	421	407	552[e]
Industrial production index	97	102	100	134
Value added ($ mil.)	477	551	591	798[e]
Gross output ($ mil.)	1,473[e]	1,765	1,703	2,338[e]
Employment (000)	31[e]	36	37	44[e]
Profitability (% of gross output)				
Intermediate input (%)	68[e]	69	65	66[e]
Wages and salaries inc. supplements (%)	9[e]	13[e]	13[e]	12[e]
Gross operating surplus	23[e]	18[e]	21[e]	22[e]
Productivity ($)				
Gross output per worker	46,753[e]	48,678	46,202	52,559[e]
Value added per worker	15,159[e]	15,183	16,040	18,045[e]
Average wage (inc. supplements)	4,241[e]	6,270[e]	6,133[e]	6,204[e]
Value added ($ mil.)				
Food products	155	171	205	289[e]
Beverages	52	53	69	86[e]
Tobacco products	26	30	27	36[e]
Textiles	4	3	6	6[e]
Wearing apparel	31	26	34	50[e]
Leather and fur products	4	1	3	4[e]
Footwear	7	9	5	7[e]
Wood and wood products	8	7	4	4[e]
Furniture and fixtures	8	11	7	9[e]
Paper and paper products	20	33	48	34[e]
Printing and publishing	22	29	29	40[e]
Industrial chemicals	4	9	6	9[e]
Other chemical products	26	42	42	49[e]
Petroleum refineries	28[e]	23[e]	17[e]	37[e]
Misc. petroleum and coal products	1[e]	NA	1[e]	2[e]
Rubber products	2[e]	2[e]	2[e]	2[e]
Plastic products	12	21	23	32[e]
Glass and glass products	1[e]	7	7	6[e]
Other non-metal mineral products	31	26	19	41[e]
Iron and steel	5	4[e]	2[e]	5[e]
Non-ferrous metals	2	3[e]	2[e]	4[e]
Metal products	19	20	17	27[e]
Non-electrical machinery	1	1	1	NA
Electrical machinery	3	4	3	5[e]
Transport equipment	4	13	6	5[e]
Prof. and scientific equipment	1	2	3	4[e]
Other manufacturing	1[e]	3[e]	2[e]	6[e]

COMMUNICATIONS

Daily Newspapers

	National Data	World Data for Comparison
Daily Newspapers		
Number of Dailies	7	8,391
Total Circulation (000)	166	548,000
Circulation per 1,000 inhabitants	62	96

Telecommunications

Telephones - main lines in use: 325,300 (1998).

Telephones - mobile cellular: 0 (1995).

Telephone system: domestic and international facilities well developed.

Domestic: NA

International: 1 coaxial submarine cable; satellite earth stations - 2 Intelsat (Atlantic Ocean); connected to the Central American Microwave System.

Radio broadcast stations: AM 80, FM 44, shortwave 0 (1998).

Radios: 815,000 (1997).

Television broadcast stations: 9 (plus 17 repeaters) (1997).

Televisions: 510,000 (1997).

Internet Service Providers (ISPs): 3 (1999).

FINANCE, ECONOMICS, & TRADE

Economic Indicators

National product: GDP—purchasing power parity—$21 billion (1999 est.).

National product real growth rate: 4.4% (1999 est.).

National product per capita: $7,600 (1999 est.).

Inflation rate—consumer price index: 1.5% (1999 est.).

Exchange Rates

Exchange rates:

Balboas (B) per US$1 .... 1.000

Fixed rate.

Top Import Origins

$6.4 billion (f.o.b., 1999 est.)

Origins (1998)

United States	40%
Central America and Caribbean	NA
Japan	NA

Top Export Destinations

$4.7 billion (f.o.b., 1999 est.)

Destinations (1998)

United States	40%
Sweden	NA
Costa Rica	NA
Spain	NA
Benelux	NA
Honduras	NA

Foreign Aid

Recipient: $197.1 million (1995).

Import/Export Commodities

Import Commodities	Export Commodities
Capital goods	Bananas
Crude oil	Shrimp
Foodstuffs	Sugar
Consumer goods	Coffee
Chemicals	

Balance of Payments

	1994	1995	1996	1997	1998
Exports of goods (f.o.b.)	6,045	6,082	5,823	6,672	6,354
Imports of goods (f.o.b.)	−6,295	−6,676	−6,475	−7,368	−7,691
Trade balance	−250	−594	−652	−696	−1,338
Services - debits	−1,064	−1,087	−1,034	−1,282	−1,210
Services - credits	1,404	1,513	1,534	1,644	1,698
Private transfers (net)	110	109	110	114	115
Government transfers (net)	67	68	64	71	83
Overall balance	9	−389	−326	−592	−1,240

PAPUA NEW GUINEA

CAPITAL: Port Moresby.

FLAG: The flag is a rectangle, divided diagonally. The upper segment is scarlet with a yellow bird of paradise; the lower segment is black with five white stars representing the Southern Cross.

ANTHEM: *O, Arise All You Sons.*

MONETARY UNIT: The kina (K) of 100 toea is linked with the Australian dollar. There are coins of 1, 2, 5, 10, 20, and 50 toea and 1 kina, and notes of 2, 5, 10, 20, and 50 kina. K1 = US$0.74906 or US$1 = K1.335.

WEIGHTS AND MEASURES: The metric system is the legal standard.

HOLIDAYS: New Year's Day, 1 January; Queen's Birthday, 1st Monday in June; Remembrance Day, 23 July; Independence Day, 16 September; Christmas, 25 December; Boxing Day, 26 December. Movable religious holidays include Good Friday and Easter Monday.

TIME: 10 PM = noon GMT.

LOCATION AND SIZE: Situated to the north of Australia, Papua New Guinea has a total land area of 461,690 square kilometers(178,259 square miles), slightly larger than the state of California. Mainland Papua New Guineaoccupies the eastern portion of the island of New Guinea, the second-largest island in the world. It shares the island with its western neighbor, a province of Indonesia. Papua New Guinea has a total boundary length of 5,972 kilometers (3,711 miles).

Papua New Guinea's capital city, Port Moresby, is located on the country's southern coast.

CLIMATE: Annual rainfall varies widely with the monsoon pattern, ranging from as little as 100 centimeters (40 inches) at Port Moresby to as much as 750 centimeters (300 inches) in other coastal regions. Most of the lowland and island areas have daily mean temperatures of about 27°C (81°F), while in the highlands temperatures may fall to 4°C (39°F) at night and rise to 32°C (90°F) in the daytime. Relative humidity is uniformly high in the lowlands at about 80 percent.

Independent State of Papua New Guinea

INTRODUCTORY SURVEY

RECENT HISTORY

British New Guinea passed to Australian control in 1902, and was renamed the Territory of Papua in 1906. German New Guinea remained intact until the outbreak of war in 1914, when Australian forces seized it. Although the territories retained their separate identities and status, they were administered jointly by Australia from headquarters at Port Moresby. In 1921, the former German New Guinea was placed under a League of Nations mandate administered by Australia; in 1947, it became the Trust Territory of New Guinea still administered by Australia, but subject to the surveillance of the UN Trusteeship Council.

Both territories were merged into the Territory of Papua and New Guinea in 1949. The Legislative Council, established in 1953, was replaced by the House of Assembly in 1964. Eight years later, the territory was renamed Papua New Guinea, and in December 1973 it was granted self-government. Separatist movements in Papua in 1973 and secessionist activities on the island of Bougainville in 1975 flared briefly and then died out, though debates over citizenship and land-reform provisions were vigorous until the passage of a constitution in 1975. Papua New Guinea achieved complete independence on September 16, 1975, with Michael Somare as prime minister of a coalition government.

Somare was voted out of office in 1980, but reelected in 1982. He put through a constitutional change giving the central government increased au-

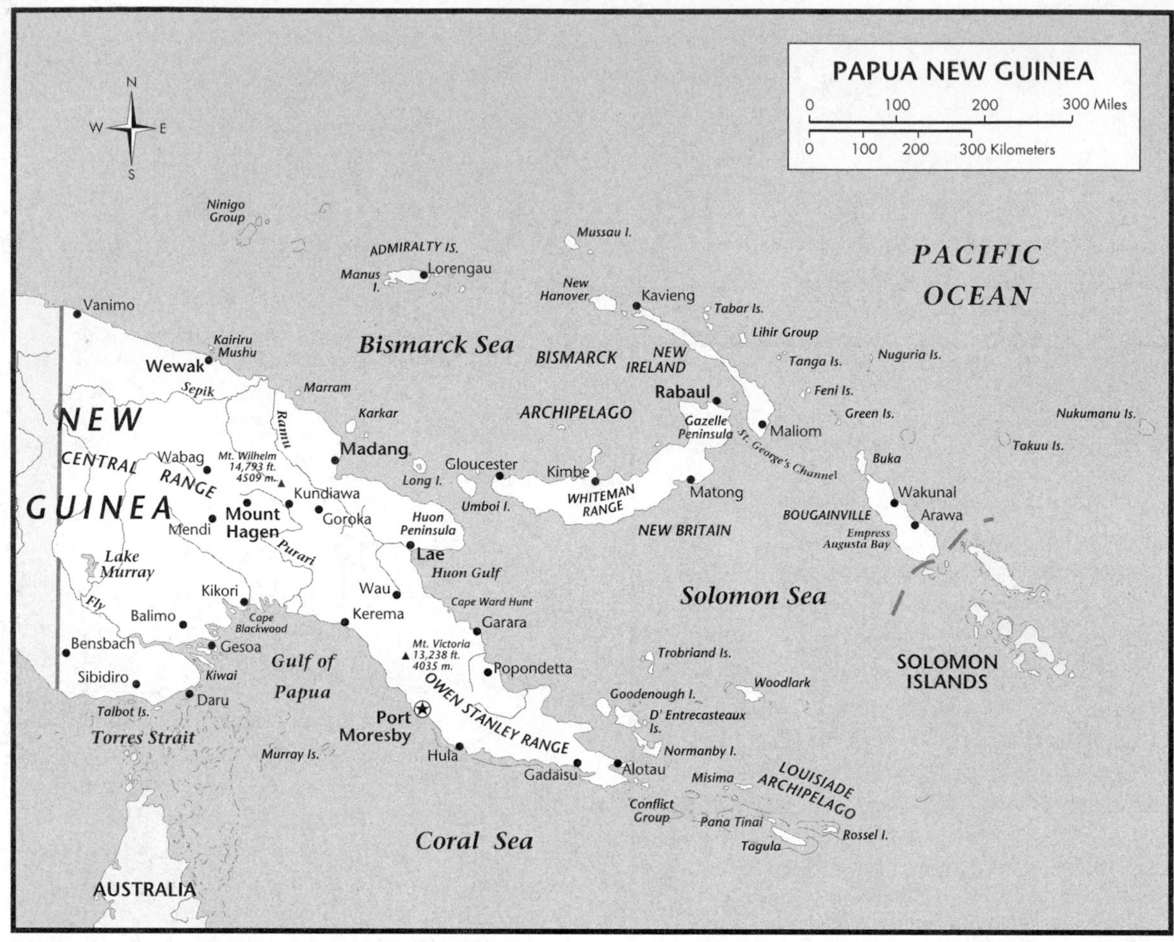

thority over the provincial governments. Soon after, he suspended three provincial administrations for financial mismanagement. Somare also had to contend with social unrest that culminated in June 1985 in a state of emergency after a prolonged wave of violent crime in Port Moresby. At the same time, his Pangu Pati was split by his deputy, Paias Wingti, who then founded a new party, the People's Democratic Movement (PDM). In November 1985, Somare was again voted out of office on a no confidence motion and Wingti formed a cabinet. Though unrest continued with serious riots in the Highlands in 1986, elections in mid-1987 returned Wingti to office at the head of a shaky five-party coalition.

Wingti's government was defeated in a no confidence vote in July 1988; a coalition government led by Rabbie Namaliu replaced the PDM government. A secessionist crisis, begun in the late 1980s on Bougainville, dominated domestic politics during much of the 1990s. Paias Wingti, the leader of the People's Democratic Movement (PDM), was reelected prime minister in July 1992 as the leader of a new coalition government with the support of the People's Progress Party and the League for National Advancement. The eight-year-old Bougainville secessionist movement continued throughout 1997 and 1998, claiming some 20,000 lives.

In 1997, members of PNG's 109-seat parliament elected reformist premier Bill Skate as governor of Port Moresby. Resolution to the Bougainville problem did not come until 1998. A permanent cease-fire agreement was signed, and reconstruction of Bougainville began. In 1999, the PNG government and rebel leaders signed the Matakana and Okatina Understanding to continue discussion of the island's political future.

Increasing crime became a major issue in PNG through the 1990s, leading to curfews and bans on alcohol sales. In July 1999, Bill Skate resigned as prime minister under allegations of corruption. The National Assembly selected Sir Mekere Morauta as prime minister. Morauta emphasized mending relations with China that had deteriorated under Skate.

GOVERNMENT

Papua New Guinea is an independent, parliamentary democracy in the Commonwealth of Nations, with a governor-general representing the British crown. Under the 1975 constitution, legislative power is vested in the National Parliament (formerly the House of Assembly) of 109 members including twenty representing provincial electorates and eighty-nine from open electorates, serving a term of up to five years. Suffrage is universal at age eighteen. The government is formed by the party, or coalition of parties that has a majority in the National Parliament, and executive power is undertaken by the National Executive Council ministers. The prime minister and deputy prime minister are appointed by the governor general for up to five years on the basis of majority support in the National Parliament. The remaining ministers are appointed by the governor general on the recommendation of the prime ministers. Papua New Guinea is divided into twenty provinces, including the National Capital District. Each province has its own government headed by a premier. In addition, there are more than 160 locally elected government councils.

Judiciary

The legal system is based on English common law. The Supreme Court is the nation's highest judicial authority and final court of appeal. Other courts are the National Court; district courts which deal with summary and nonindictable offenses; and local courts established to deal with minor offenses including matters regulated by local customs.

The Papua New Guinea government has undertaken a process of legal reform under which village courts have been established to conserve and reactivate traditional legal methods. Special tribunals deal with land titles and with cases involving minors. An Ombudsman Commission has been established to investigate and refer to the public prosecutor cases involving abuse of official authority.

The Constitution declares the judiciary independent of executive, political, or military authority. It also provides a number of procedural due process protections including the right to legal counsel for criminal defendants.

Political Parties

Political parties lack ideological conviction and rely almost exclusively on patronage politics, personalities, and regional bases. Several parties have emerged and generally party allegiances are fluid. Regional and tribal politics have had an important impact on political events. No fewer than eight parties have been founded since 1978. Major parties participating in the 1997 elections were the Pangu Pati, the People's Progress Party (PPP), the National Alliance(NA), the People's Democratic Movement (PDM), and People's National Congress(PNC).

DEFENSE

The main armed force is the Papua New Guinea Defense Force that, in 2000, had 4,300 men including 3,800 army personnel, 400 maritime forces, and an air force of 100. Australia provides a 38-member training unit to contribute to the upkeep ofthe military forces. Defense costs $42 million a year (1998) or 1 percent of gross domestic product.

ECONOMIC AFFAIRS

Economic activity is concentrated in two sectors, agriculture and mining. The subsistence sector that occupies more than two-thirds of the working population produces livestock, fruit, and vegetables for local consumption; agricultural products for export include copra, palm oil, coffee, cocoa, and tea. New mining operations have compensated for the 1989 closure of the Bougainville mine that had been a chief foreign exchange earner since the early 1970s. Currently, the main gold and silver mines are located at Ok Tedi in the Star Mountains, on Misima Island, and at Porgera. Oil and natural gas have been discovered in Southern Highlands Province. Mineral deposits including oil, copper, and gold account for 72 percent of export earnings. Forestry and fishing hold increasing importance.

A mineral and petroleum boom, centered in the Highlands region, drove double-digit economic growth in the early 1990s. Growth slowed to 3 percent in 1994,2.9 percent in 1995, and 1.6 percent in 1996 and 1997 due to an anticipated drop inproduction fromPapua New Guinea's aging mines and oil fields. Also, in 1997, droughts caused bythe El Niño weather pattern caused heavy losses to coffee, cocoa, and coconut production, agricultural mainstays of export earnings. To halt the economic decline, the government awarded a lease to private developers for the $800 million Lihir gold project. In addition, construction projects involving airports, highways, disaster rehabilitation, development of the Gobe oil field, and a petroleum refinery are planned or being implemented. These projects together contributed to a small recovery in GDP in 1998, increased to 3.6 percent in 1999 and a predicted GDP of 4.3 percent in 2000.

Public Finance

The U.S. Central Intelligence Agency (CIA) estimated that in 1998,government revenues totaled approximately $1.6 billion and expenditures $1.9 billion. External debt totaled $2.4 billion by 1999 estimates.

Income

According to CIA estimates, the GDP in 1999 was $11.6 billion or $2,500 per capita. The CIA estimated that in 1999, the inflation rate for consumer prices was 16.5 percent and that the real growth rate of GDP was 3.6 percent. The GDP contribution by sector in 1999 was: agriculture 25, percent; industry, 35 percent; and services, 40 percent.

Industry

The industrial sector is constrained by the small domestic market and the population's low purchasing power. Major industries include mining of gold, silver, and copper; food processing of copra (coconut); palm oil, cocoa and coffee exporting; plywood and wood chip production; crude oil production; and, tourism. Handicraft and cottage industries have expanded.

Banking and Finance

The Bank of Papua New Guinea, the country's central bank, was established in 1973, and the currency, the kina, was first issued in April 1975. The kina is backed by a standby arrangement with Australia and the value of the kina is tied to the Australian dollar.

The Papua New Guinea Banking Corp. was set up in 1973 to take over the savings and trading business of the former Australian government-owned bank operating in Papua New Guinea. It competes with seven other private commercial banks, three of which are subsidiaries of Australian banks. There is no securities exchange in Papua New Guinea.

Economic Development

The bulk of foreign investment is in the mining and petroleum sector. Statistics on foreign equity holdings for 1995 show that Australia was the largest investor followed by the UK and the United States. In 1995, developers RTZ and Niugini Mining were awarded a lease for the $800 million Lihir goldproject.

The Investment Promotion Authority (IPA), established in June of 1992, facilitates and certifies foreign investment. Corruption, civil unrest, and bureaucratic delays, however, frustrate the process. A number of free trade zones are in the early stages of development.

The fundamental purposes of Papua New Guinea's economic strategy have been distilled into the nation's eight aims: a rapid increase in the proportion of the economy under the control of Papua New Guineans; a more equal distribution of economic benefits; decentralization of economic activity; an emphasis on small-scale artisan, service, and business activity; a more self-reliant economy; an increasing capacity for meeting government spending from locally raised revenue; a rapid increase in the equal and active participation of women in the economy; and governmental control and involvement in those sectors where control is necessary to achieve the desired kind of development.

SOCIAL WELFARE

A social security system called the National Provident Fund was formed in 1981, and covers persons employed by firms with twenty-five or more workers, providing old age, disability, and survivor benefits. In 1995, this program was financed by 5 percent contribution of earnings from employees and 7 percent of payroll from employers. Retirement is set at age fifty-five or at any age with fifteen years of contributions. Benefits are provided as a lump sum and include total contributions plus interest. Workers' compensation is provided by employers through direct provision of benefits or insurance premiums. Rural communities traditionally assume communal obligations to those in need.

Despite a constitution guaranteeing them equal rights, women remain second-class citizens due to traditional patterns of discrimination. Village courts tend to enforce these patterns, and intertribal warfare often involves attacks on women. Polygamy is common, and the tradition of paying a bride price persists. The government is working to improve the status of women and has instituted an Office of Women's Affairs.

Healthcare

Government policy is to distribute health services widely and to provide comprehensive medical care, both preventive and curative. In 1990-1997, there were four hospital beds per 1,000 people. In 1990-1997, there were 0.1 doctors per

1,000 people.In the years between 1985 and 1995, 96 percent of the population had access to health-care services. Adequate sanitation and safe water are available to 22percent and 28 percent of the population respectively.

The main health problems are malaria, tuberculosis, leprosy, and venereal disease.Significant malnutrition occurs in some areas, and pneumonia and related respiratory infections are major risks. In 1997, there were about 250 reported cases of tuberculosis per 100,000 inhabitants. There were 66,797 cases of malaria, 5,335 cases of tuberculosis, and 6,821 measles cases in 1994. The increased incidence of malaria has been linked to importation from neighboring islands. Immunization rates for children up to one year old were fairly high in 1994: tuberculosis, 91 percent; diphtheria, pertussis, and tetanus, 66 percent; polio, 66 percent; and measles, 39 percent. While under-nutrition remains the main nutritional problem, dramatic changes have occurred in some groups with exposure to westernized diets. Diabetes in the highland populations is low, but has been documented to be as high as 16 percent in major cities of Papua New Guinea.

The country's birth rate was thirty-two per 1,000 people in 1999, with only 4 percent of married women aged fifteen to forty-nine using contraception.

The infant mortality rate decreased from 110 deaths per 1,000 live births in 1974, to fifty-six in 1999. In 1993-1996, 23 percent of all births were low birth weight babies. The general mortality rate was 9.5 per 1,000 people in 1999, and the maternal mortality rate was 370 per 100,000 live births in 1990-1997. Life expectancy was 55.8 years in 1999. Total health care expenditures in 1990 were $142 million.

Housing

Traditional housing in rural areas appears to be adequate, but in urban areas there are acute shortages because of migration. In most urban areas squatter settlements have been established. New housing (923 dwellings in 1984) has fallen far short of meeting the demand, especially for medium- and low-cost units. As of 1988, the housing stock totaled 555,000, and the number of people per dwelling averaged 5.8.

EDUCATION

Education in Papua New Guinea is not compulsory, and in the mid-1980s only one-third of the population was literate. The present government aims at upgrading and improving the quality of education. Children attend state-run community schools for primary education and provincial and national high schools for secondary education. After grade six, they are tested and screened for continuing their studies in provincial high school. After grade ten, students have to qualify through an examination to enter one of the four national senior high schools, where they attend grades eleven and twelve. After grade ten, students may enter one of the many technical or vocational schools that train them in various careers and skills depending on their interests. The adult illiteracy rate in 2000 was 24 percent (male, 16.3 percent; female, 32.3 percent). In 1995, 2,790 primary schools had a total enrollment of 516,797 students.

In addition to the National Government System, there is an international School System that ends at high school. Fees are considerably higher than the government run schools, and the curriculum is based on the British system. There are also privately run preschools and primary schools.

The University of Papua New Guinea in Port Moresby offers degrees in law, science, medicine and arts. The University of Technology in Lae offers degrees in technical subjects such as engineering, business, architecture, and forestry.

2000 KEY EVENTS TIMELINE

January

- A new undersea mineral, similar to magnesium nodules, is discovered more than three miles below the surface in the waters of Papua New Guinea.
- Papua New Guinea's only female provincial governor is ousted from office after a vote of no confidence.

February

- A medical researcher fears there are more than 10,000 undetected cases of AIDS in Papua New Guinea.

March

- Prime Minister Mekere Morauta fires three ministers after a failed cabinet attempt to mount a no-confidence motion.

- Citing environmental concerns, the World Bank advises Papua New Guinea to shut down the Ok Tedi gold and copper mine, which provides 10 percent of the nation's gross domestic product.

April

- The Bank of Papua New Guinea launches a new K5 note, made of polymer instead of paper, for protection against counterfeiting.
- The governor of Oro province demands payment for use of the Kokota Trail in the Olympic torch relay.

May

- A World Wildlife Fund for Nature report calls for a temporary halt to further logging in the forests of Papua New Guinea until allegations of bribery can be investigated and proper environmental standards enforced.

June

- Tuberculosis is reported to be on the rise in Papua New Guinea due to the introduction of AIDS into the country.

July

- An amendment to the Village Court Act makes it possible for women to be appointed village court magistrates.

August

- Teachers are offered a 15 percent pay increase.
- The Justice Department considers limiting mobility within the nation by means of requiring ID cards for everyone and enforcing the Vagrancy Act.

September

- In a speech before Parliament, Prime Minister Sir Mekere Morauta states the Papua New Guinea government will not consider allowing the Bougainville province to secede.
- Hela clanspeople rally in Port Moresby to petition the government to establish a separate homeland for them in the Southern Highlands Province. The area contains rich gas and oil fields, as well as gold, and has been the site of unrest and administrative chaos.

October

- Three suspected witches are killed, and three others injured by tribesmen in Chimbu province.
- The Papua New Guinea Copra Marketing Board announces a short-term increase in copra prices after copra growers threaten to stop production because of the falling prices.

November

- Thousands of workers strike at Port Moresby November 13 against privatization.
- Three major earthquakes hit Papua New Guinea November 16–18, killing one and leaving thousands homeless.

December

- Papua New Guinea increases border controls with the western, Indonesian province of Irian Jaya, or West Papua, after independence activists clash with police during the weekend of December 3.
- Papua New Guinea's former Prime Minister, Sir Michael Somare, is fired from his current cabinet posts of Foreign Affairs and Minister of Bougainville Affairs. His sacking brings to ten the number of ministers let go in the previous two months for alleged wrongdoing.
- A new minimum wage is announced. Over the coming three years it is to increase weekly wages from the equivalent of US$7.92 to US21.53.

ANALYSIS OF EVENTS: 2000

BUSINESS AND THE ECONOMY

In March the World Bank advised the Papua New Guinea government to shut down the Ok Tedi gold and copper mine for environmental reasons. This mine, which provides 10 percent of the nation's gross domestic product (GDP), had brought thousands of jobs to the country, but had also caused massive pollution and flooding. While the World Bank urged immediate action, the prime minister said it would take time to come up with a plan that would benefit both the local people and the national interests.

Union workers in Papua New Guinea threatened to take an unnamed "industrial action" in response to announced government plans to sell the Papua New Guinea Banking Corporation and Air New Guinea in order to alleviate the nation's debt load. The union workers stated that at least one thousand jobs would be lost if Air New Guinea were sold, and that similar losses would accompany the sale of other state enterprises.

An inquiry performed in September showed that the Papua New Guinea retirement fund, the National Provident Fund, had lost US$56 million over the previous five years. The loss was due in part to heavy speculative investment in the Highlands Gold and Highlands Pacific Limited companies.

GOVERNMENT AND POLITICS

In 2000 Papua New Guinea celebrated its twenty-fifth year of independence. In a speech given on the occasion of this anniversary, the government's Minister of Planning and Implementation expressed his grim view of the state of the nation, pointing out that the reforms started five years earlier, designed to decentralize government functions, had not succeeded in distributing services and resources throughout the nation. He noted especially that neither infant mortality nor maternal mortality rates had improved.

The year did, however, mark one gain for women in Papua New Guinea, for the Village Court Act was amended to allow women to serve as village court magistrates. Speaking in favor of the amendment, MP Sir Rabbie Nanaliu also called for women to be eligible for appointment to judgeships at the national and Supreme Court levels, and to be appointed members of parliament as well.

Hela clanspeople rallied in Port Moresby in September to petition the government to establish a separate homeland for them in the Southern Highlands Province. The area contains rich gas and oil fields, as well as gold, and has been the site of unrest and administrative chaos.

In March Prime Minister Mekere Morauta fired three ministers after a failed cabinet attempt to mount a no-confidence motion based on dissatisfaction with the economic reform program.

CULTURE AND SOCIETY

Isolated news items from 2000 showed the power of traditional beliefs in Papua New Guinea. Early in the year, the Papua New Guinea Catholic Church called for an end to the worship of the bones of the dead, a practice advocated by a group called the Kivang Association. Three men were killed and three others injured in October when local tribesmen in Chimbu province suspected them of using witchcraft. The director of the national census called to religious groups such as the Seventh Day Adventists to ask people to give safe passage to census workers after one worker was attacked with a burning log by a villager who believed him to be an agent of the devil.

While the above occurrences were unique to Papua New Guinea and its culture, others were more emblematic of world trends. In 2000 there were two thousand known cases of AIDS in the country; however, medical researchers suspected the total number of cases to be closer to ten thousand, with most occurring in the capital city, Port Moresby. Accompanying the introduction of AIDS was a resurgence of tuberculosis cases. Cigarette smoking was also seen to be on the rise, especially among the nation's young people.

At a forum on "Gender and Development in Papua New Guinea," Dr. Mattias Sapuri pointed out that girls were not provided equal education and health care, citing that girls are less likely than boys to be vaccinated against diseases. He called upon the men and women of the nation to walk together to build a stronger society.

The Papua New Guinea population and environment were threatened in March 2000 when an estimated 100 to 150 kilograms of sodium cyanide seeped into a river in the dense jungle after accidentally falling from a helicopter. As exposure to between 50 and 150 milligrams causes immediate death, villagers in the area were warned not to drink the river water, but experts feared the effects on tribal people. Environmentalists feared the monsoon rains would spread the contamination beyond the originally affected area of approximately 1250 square meters.

DIRECTORY

CENTRAL GOVERNMENT

Head of State

Queen
Elizabeth II, Monarch

Governor-General
Sir Silas Atopare, The Visitor Office,
Buckingham Palace, London SW1A 1AA,
England
PHONE: +44 (0171) 8391377
FAX: +44 (0171) 9309625

Prime Minister
Mekere Morauta, Office of the Prime Minister, PO Box 6605, Morauta House, N.C.D., Boroko, Papua New Guinea
PHONE: +675 3276792
FAX: +675 3276787
E-MAIL: primeminister@pm.gov.pg

Ministers

Deputy Prime Minister
Mao Zeming, Office of the Deputy Prime Minister, Ori Lavi Haus, Nita Street, PO Box 7354, Boroko, Papua New Guinea
PHONE: +675 3254566
FAX: +675 3251230

Minister of Agriculture and Livestock
Mao Zeming, Ministry of Agriculture and Livestock, Spring Garden Road, PO Box 417, Konedobu, Papua New Guinea
PHONE: +675 3231848
FAX: +675 3230563

Minister of Bougainville Affairs
Michael Somare, Ministry of Bougainville Affairs, PO Box 343, Waigani 131, 3rd Floor, Morauta Haus, Waigani, NCD, Papua New Guinea
PHONE: +675 3276760
FAX: +675 3258038

Minister of Defense
Muki Taranupi, Ministry of Defense, Murray Barracks FMB, Boroko 111, Papua New Guinea
PHONE: +675 3242480
FAX: +675 3256117

Minister of Education
John Waiko, Ministry of Education, PO Box 446 Waigani, P.S.A. Haus, Port Moresby, NCD, Papua New Guinea
PHONE: +675 3254648
FAX: +675 3013555

Minister of Lands and Physical Planning
John Pundari, Ministry of Lands and Physical Planning, PO Box 5665 Boroko, Aopi Centre, Tower 2, Waigani, Port Moresby, NCD, Papua New Guinea
PHONE: +675 3013116
FAX: +675 3013139

Minister of Petroleum and Energy
Fabian Pok, Ministry of Petroleum and Energy, PO Box 1993, Port Moresby, 3rd Floor, NIC Haus, Champion Parade, Port Moresby, Papua New Guinea
PHONE: +675 3201199
FAX: +675 3201141

Minister of Police
Mathias Karani, Ministry of Police, PO Box 85, Konedobu, Part Moresby, NCD, Papua New Guinea
PHONE: +675 3226100
FAX: +675 3226113

Minister of Correctional Services
Micah Wes, Ministry of Correctional Services

Minister of Provincial and Local Governments
Philemon Embel, Ministry of Provincial and Local Governments, PO Box 1287, Boroko, NCD, Papua New Guinea

Minister of Rural Development
William Ebenosi, Ministry of Rural Development, PO Box 6601, Boroko 111, Kumul Avenue, Waigani, Port Moresby, NCD, Papua New Guinea
PHONE: +675 3011607
FAX: +675 3011691

Minister of Environment and Conservation
Herowa Agiwa, Ministry of Environment and Conservation

Minister of Trade and Industry
Michael Nali, Ministry of Trade and Industry, Heduru Haus, Waigani Drive, Waigani, Papua New Guinea
PHONE: +675 3255311
FAX: +675 3254482

Minister of Transport and Civil Aviation
Bart Philemon, Ministry of Transport and Civil Aviation, Jacksons Airport PO Box 684, Boroko 111, Papua New Guinea
PHONE: +675 3244400
FAX: +675 3251919

Minister of Works
Alfred Pogo, Ministry of Works, PO Box 1489, Port Moresby 121, Port Moresby, NCD, Papua New Guinea
PHONE: +675 3222500
FAX: +675 3200236

Minister of Corporatization and Privatization
Vincent Auali, Ministry of Corporatization and Privatization

Minister of Fisheries
Ron Ganarafo, Ministry of Fisheries

Minister of Foreign Affairs
John Kaputin, Ministry of Foreign Affairs

Minister of Forests
Michael Ogio, Ministry of Forests

Minister of Housing
John Kamb, Ministry of Housing

Minister of Justice
Kilroy Genia, Ministry of Justice

Minister of Labor and Employment
Charlie Benjamin, Ministry of Labor and Employment

Minister of Culture and Tourism
Andrew Baing, Ministry of Culture and Tourism

Minister of Mining
Michael Somare, Ministry of Mining

Minister of Planning and Implementation
Moi Avei, Ministry of Planning and Implementation

Minister of Public Service
Iairo Lasaro, Ministry of Public Services

POLITICAL ORGANIZATIONS

People's Progress Party (PPP)

TITLE: National Chairman
NAME: Julius Chan

People's Democratic Movement (PDM)

TITLE: Parliamentary Leader
NAME: Paias Wingti

People's Action Party (PAP)

TITLE: Party Leader
NAME: Akoka Doi

People's National Congress

TITLE: Leader
NAME: Bill Skate

Pangu Pati (Papua New Guinea United Party)

TITLE: Party Leader
NAME: Chris Haiveta

Melanesian Alliance (MA)

TITLE: Chairman
NAME: John Momis

National Party (NP)

TITLE: Party Leader
NAME: Michael Mel

Christian-Democratic Party

Movement for Greater Autonomy

National Alliance Party (NAP)

Peoples Resources Awareness Party (PRAP)

People's Unity Party

United Party (UP)

TITLE: Party Leader
NAME: Paul Torato

DIPLOMATIC REPRESENTATION

Embassies in Papua New Guinea

United Kingdom
PHONE: +675 3251677
FAX: +675 3253547
TITLE: Ambassador
NAME: Brian B. Low

United States
Douglas Street, PO Box 1492, Port Moresby, Papua New Guinea
PHONE: +675 3211455
FAX: +675 3213423
TITLE: Ambassador
NAME: Arma Jane Karaer

JUDICIAL SYSTEM

Supreme Court

National Court

BROADCAST MEDIA

Nau FM & Yumi FM

PO Box 744, Pt. Moresby, NCD, Papua New Guinea
PHONE: +675 3201996
FAX: +675 3201995
WEBSITE: http://www.naufm.com.pg
TITLE: Chief Executive
CONTACT: Alwin Agonia
BROADCASTS: 24hours/day
TYPE: Commercial

National Broadcasting Commission (NBC-PNG)

PO Box 1359, Boroko, NCD, Papua New Guinea
PHONE: +675 3253341
FAX: +675 3255403
LANGUAGE: English, Tok Pisin
TITLE: Managing Director and Chief Executive
CONTACT: Renagi R. Lohia
TYPE: Government

EMTV

Media Niugini Pty Ltd., PO Box 443, Boroko, NCD, Papua New Guinea
PHONE: + 675 3257322
FAX: +675 3254450
E-MAIL: emtv@emtv.com.pg
WEBSITE: http://www.emtv.com.pg
TITLE: Chief Executive
CONTACT: Stephen Smith
CHANNEL: 9, 31, 68
WATTAGE: 1.1kW, 0.17kW, 0.02kW
TYPE: Commercial

COLLEGES AND UNIVERSITIES

Administrative College of Papua New Guinea

PO Box 1216, Boroko, Papua New Guinea

University of Papua New Guinea

Post Office Box 320, Port Moresby, Papua New Guinea
PHONE: +675 3267143
E-MAIL: web@upng.ac.pg
WEBSITE: http://www.upng.ac.pg

Papua New Guinea University of Technology

Private Mail Bag, Morobe Province, Lae, Papua New Guinea
PHONE: +675 4734999
FAX: +675 4757667
WEBSITE: http://www.unitech.ac.pg

PUBLISHERS

Kristen Press

PO Box 712, Madang, Papua New Guinea
PHONE: +675 8522988
FAX: +675 8523313
TITLE: Executive Director
CONTACT: Dennis T. Brown
SUBJECTS: Agriculture, Biblical Studies, Biography, Business, Education, Fiction, Health, Nutrition, Religion-Protestant, Theology, Women's Studies

The National Research Institute

PO Box 5854, Boroko, NCD, Papua New Guinea
PHONE: +675 3260300
FAX: +675 3260213
TITLE: Director
CONTACT: Wari Iamo
SUBJECTS: Anthropology, Criminology, Developing Countries, Economics, Education, Environmental Studies, Government, Political Science, Social Sciences, Sociology
TOTAL PUBLISHED: Over 200 titles

The Melanesian Institute

PO Box 571, Goroka, EHP, Papau New Guinea
PHONE: +675 7321777
FAX: +675 7321214
SUBJECTS: Anthropology, Religion-Catholic, Religion-Protestant, Religion-Other, Social Sciences, Sociology

University of Papau New Guinea Press

PO Box 320 University Post Office, Boroko, Port Moresby, Papau New Guinea
PHONE: +675 3260130
FAX: +675 3260127
E-MAIL: john.evans@upng.ac.pg
TITLE: Development Manager
CONTACT: John Evans
SUBJECTS: Books on and about Papau New Guinea in any subject area.
TOTAL PUBLISHED: 70 print

RELIGIOUS ORGANIZATIONS

Catholic

Mary Help of Christians Parish
Sabama, Papua New Guinea
E-MAIL: mhcpom@datec.com.pg

Protestant

The Salvation Army- Papua New Guinea
P.O. Box 1323, Boroko, NCD, Papua New Guinea
PHONE: +675 3255507, 3255522
FAX: +675 3233282

FURTHER READING

Articles

Brower, Kenneth and Bob Krist. "Face to Face in New Guinea." *National Geographic Traveler,* March 2000, vol. 17, no. 2, p. 82.

Gomez, Brian. "Out of Patience, BHP Wants Early Pull-Out from Ok Tedi." *American Metal Market,* July 24, 2000, vol. 108, no. 141, p. 23.

———. "Papua-New Guinea Gets $10M Mining Loan." *American Metal Market,* June 29, 2000, vol. 108, no. 125, p. 6.

"The Papua New Guinea." *Air Transport World,* March 2000, vol. 37, no. 3, p. 102.

Books

Dun and Bradstreet's Guide to Papua New Guinea. Parsippany, NJ: Dun & Bradstreet, 1999.

PAPUA NEW GUINEA: STATISTICAL DATA

For sources and notes see "Sources of Statistics" at the front of each volume.

GEOGRAPHY

Geography

Area:

Total: 462,840 sq km.

Land: 452,860 sq km.

Land boundaries:

Total: 820 km.

Border countries: Indonesia 820 km.

Coastline: 5,152 km.

Climate: tropical; northwest monsoon (December to March), southeast monsoon (May to October); slight seasonal temperature variation.

Terrain: mostly mountains with coastal lowlands and rolling foothills.

Natural resources: gold, copper, silver, natural gas, timber, oil, fisheries.

Land use:

Arable land: 0.1%

Permanent crops: 1%

Permanent pastures: 0%

Forests and woodland: 92.9%

Other: 6% (1993 est.).

HUMAN FACTORS

Demographics (A)

	1990	1995	1998	2000	2010	2020	2030	2040	2050
Population	3,825	4,345	4,688	4,927	6,171	7,400	8,593	9,707	10,670
Life expectancy - males	57.2	59.3	60.3	61.0	64.4	67.4	70.1	72.5	74.4
Life expectancy - females	60.6	63.2	64.4	65.3	69.1	72.5	75.5	78.1	80.2
Birth rate (per 1,000)	34.6	34.1	33.3	32.7	27.0	22.4	19.5	17.0	15.1
Death rate (per 1,000)	9.4	8.6	8.3	8.0	6.8	6.1	5.9	6.2	6.9
Women of reproductive age (15-49 yrs.)	864	1,021	1,108	1,169	1,524	1,939	2,265	2,534	2,683
Fertility rate	5.1	4.8	4.5	4.4	3.5	2.8	2.4	2.2	2.1

Except as noted, values for vital statistics are in thousands; life expectancy is in years.

Health Personnel

	National Data	World Data (wtd ave)
Total health expenditure as a percentage of GDP, 1990-1998[a]		
Public sector	2.6	2.5
Private sector	0.6	2.9
Total[b]	NA	5.5
Health expenditure per capita in U.S. dollars, 1990-1998[a]		
Purchasing power parity	77	561
Total	34	483
Availability of health care facilities per 100,000 people		
Hospital beds 1990-1998[a]	400	330
Doctors 1992-1995[a]	18	122
Nurses 1992-1995[a]	97	248

Ethnic Division

Melanesian, Papuan, Negrito, Micronesian, Polynesian.

Religion

Roman Catholic 22%
Lutheran 16%
Presbyterian/Methodist/London Missionary Society 8%
Anglican 5%
Evangelical Alliance 4%
Seventh-Day Adventist 1%
Other Protestant 10%
Indigenous beliefs 34%

Major Languages

English spoken by 1-2%, pidgin English widespread, Motu spoken in Papua region. There are 715 indigenous languages.

EDUCATION

Public Education Expenditures

	1980	1997
Public expenditures on education as % of GNP	NA	NA
Pupils per teacher at the primary level	NA	38
Duration of primary education in years	NA	NA
World data for comparison		
Public expenditures on education as % of GNP (mean)	3.9	4.8
Pupils per teacher at the primary level (wtd ave)	NA	33
Duration of primary education in years (mean)	NA	9

Educational Attainment (A)

Age group (1980) . . . . .25+
Population of this age group 1,135,783
Highest level attained (%)
No schooling 82.6
First level
Not completed 8.2
Completed 5.0
Entered second level
Lower Secondary 3.9
Upper Secondary 0.3
Entered post-secondary .NA

Literacy Rates (A)

In thousands and percent	1990	1995	2000	2010
Illiterate population (15+ yrs.)	731	724	710	668
Literacy rate - total adult pop. (%)	68.1	72.2	75.9	82.3
Literacy rate - males (%)	77.8	81.0	83.7	88.0
Literacy rate - females (%)	57.4	62.7	67.6	76.3

GOVERNMENT & LAW

Political Parties

National Parliament	% of vote	no. of seats
People's Progress Party (PPP)	15%	16
Papua New Guinea United Party (Pangu Pati)	14%	15
National Alliance (NA)	14%	15
People's Democratic Movement (PDM)	8%	9
People's National Congress (PNC)	6%	7
People's Action Party (PAP)	5%	5
United Party (UP)	3%	3
National Party (NP)	1%	1
People's Unity Party (PUP)	1%	1
Independents	33%	37

Elections were last held 14-28 June 1997 (next to be held June 2002). Association with political parties is very fluid.

Government Budgets (A)

Year: 1994

Total Expenditures: 1,630.23 Millions of Kina

Expenditures as a percentage of the total by function:

General public services and public order	11.69[f]
Defense	3.33[f]
Education	17.59[f]
Health	8.88[f]
Social Security and Welfare	0.66[f]
Housing and community amenities	3.54[f]
Recreational, cultural, and religious affairs	1.43[f]
Fuel and energy	3.04[f]
Agriculture, forestry, fishing, and hunting	8.19[f]
Mining, manufacturing, and construction	1.51[f]
Transportation and communication	8.60[f]
Other economic affairs and services	4.49[f]

Military Affairs (B)

Availability	
Males age 15-49	1,274,818
Fit for military service	
Males age 15-49	706,159
Dollar figure	$42 million
Percent of GDP	1%

Data for 2000 est.

LABOR FORCE

Total Labor Force (A)

1.941 million.

PRODUCTION SECTOR

Energy Production

Production	1.74 billion kWh
Production by source	
Fossil fuel	69.54%
Hydro	30.46%
Nuclear	0%
Other	0%
Exports	0 kWh

Data for 1998.

Energy Consumption

Consumption	1.618 billion kWh
Imports	0 kWh

Data for 1998.

Transportation

Highways:

total: 19,600 km.

paved: 686 km.

unpaved: 18,914 km (1996 est.).

Waterways: 10,940 km.

Merchant marine:

total: 21 ships (1,000 GRT or over) totaling 36,417 GRT/52,432 DWT.

ships by type: bulk 2, cargo 10, chemical tanker 1, combination ore/oil 1, container 1, petroleum tanker 3, roll-on/roll-off 3 (1999 est.).

Airports: 492 (1999 est.).

Airports - with paved runways: 19 (1999 est.).

Airports - with unpaved runways: 473 (1999 est.).

Top Agriculture Products

Coffee, cocoa, coconuts, palm kernels, tea, rubber, sweet potatoes, fruit, vegetables; poultry, pork.

Top Mining Products (B)

Mineral resources include: gold, copper, silver, oil.

COMMUNICATIONS

Daily Newspapers

	National Data	World Data for Comparison
Daily Newspapers		
Number of Dailies	2	8,391
Total Circulation (000)	65	548,000
Circulation per 1,000 inhabitants	15	96

Telecommunications

Telephones - main lines in use: 44,000 (1995).

Telephones - mobile cellular: 0 (1995).

Telephone system: services are adequate and being improved; facilities provide radiotelephone and telegraph, coastal radio, aeronautical radio, and international radiocommunication services.

domestic: mostly radiotelephone.

international: submarine cables to Australia and Guam; satellite earth station - 1 Intelsat (Pacific Ocean); international radio communication service.

Radio broadcast stations: AM 8, FM 19, shortwave 28 (1998).

Radios: 410,000 (1997).

Television broadcast stations: 3 (1997).

Televisions: 42,000 (1997).

Internet Service Providers (ISPs): 2 (1999).

MANUFACTURING SECTOR

GDP & Manufacturing Summary (B)

	1980	1985	1990	1993	1994	1995
Gross Domestic Product						
Millions of 1990 dollars	2,826	3,016	3,221	4,514	4,672	4,448
Growth rate in percent	−2.29	3.60	−3.00	14.44	3.50	−4.80
Per capita (in 1990 dollars)	916	876	839	1,099	1,111	1,034
Manufacturing Value Added						
Millions of 1990 dollars	411	458	388	531	589	593[e]
Growth rate in percent	−0.42	3.01	−22.77	9.34	10.94	0.58[e]
Manufacturing share in percent of current prices	7.5	11.0	12.4	8.8	8.8[e]	NA

FINANCE, ECONOMICS, & TRADE

Economic Indicators

National product: GDP—purchasing power parity—$11.6 billion (1999 est.).

National product real growth rate: 3.6% (1999 est.).

National product per capita: $2,500 (1999 est.).

Inflation rate—consumer price index: 16.5% (1999 est.).

Exchange Rates

Exchange rates:

kina (K) per US$1

November 1999	2.7624
1999	2.5200
1998	2.0580
1997	1.4340
1996	1.3180
1995	1.2760

Top Import Origins

$1 billion (f.o.b., 1999 est.)

Origins (1998)

Australia	51%
Singapore	10%
Japan	8%
United States	5%
New Zealand	5%
Malaysia	3%

Top Export Destinations

$1.9 billion (f.o.b., 1999 est.)

Destinations (1998)

Australia	20%
Japan	13%
Germany	7%
South Korea	5%
Philippines	4%
United Kingdom	3%

Balance of Payments

	1994	1995	1996	1997	1998
Exports of goods (f.o.b.)	2,651	2,670	2,530	2,160	1,773
Imports of goods (f.o.b.)	−1,325	−1,262	−1,513	−1,483	−1,078
Trade balance	1,326	1,408	1,017	677	695
Services - debits	−608	−642	−779	−924	−794
Services - credits	235	321	432	397	318
Private transfers (net)	59	67	252	70	82
Government transfers (net)	167	182	124	93	76
Overall balance	569	674	313	−99	47

Foreign Aid

Recipient: $400 million (1999 est.).

Import/Export Commodities

Import Commodities	Export Commodities
Machinery and transport equipment	Oil
	Gold
Manufactured goods	Copper ore
Food	Logs
Fuels	Palm oil
Chemicals	Coffee
	Cocoa
	Crayfish and prawns

PARAGUAY

Republic of Paraguay
República del Paraguay

CAPITAL: Asunción.

FLAG: The national flag, officially adopted in 1842, is a tricolor of red, white, and blue horizontal stripes. The national coat of arms appears in the center of the white stripe on the obverse, and the Treasury seal in the same position on the reverse.

ANTHEM: *Himno Nacional*, beginning "Paraguayos, república o muerte" ("Paraguayans, republic or death").

MONETARY UNIT: The guaraní (G) is a paper currency of 100 céntimos. There are notes of 1, 5, 10, 50, 100, 500, 1,000, 5,000, and 10,000 guaraníes. G1 = $0.00047 (or $1 = G2,110.0).

WEIGHTS AND MEASURES: The metric system is the legal standard.

HOLIDAYS: New Year's Day, 1 January; San Blas Day, 3 February; National Defense Day, 1 March; Labor Day, 1 May; Independence Days, 14–15 May; Peace Day, 12 June; Founding of Asunción, 15 August; Constitution Day, 25 August; Victory Day (Battle of Boquerón), 29 September; Columbus Day, 12 October; All Saints' Day, 1 November; Our Lady of Caacupé, 8 December; Christmas, 25 December. Movable religious holidays are Holy Thursday, Good Friday, and Corpus Christi.

TIME: 8 AM = noon GMT.

LOCATION AND SIZE: One of South America's two landlocked countries, Paraguay has a total area of 406,750 square kilometers (157,047 square miles), slightly smaller than the state of California. It has a total boundary length of 3,920 kilometers (2,436 miles). Paraguay's capital city, Asunción, is located in the southwestern part of the country.

CLIMATE: Two-thirds of Paraguay is within the temperate zone, one-third in the tropical zone. Temperatures generally range from 10° to 21°C (50° to 70°F) in autumn and winter, and 26° to 37°C (79° to 99°F) in spring and summer. Rainfall averages about 200 centimeters (80 inches) a year along the eastern frontier with Brazil, gradually diminishing toward the west to an average of 81 centimeters (32 inches) in the Chaco Boreal.

INTRODUCTORY SURVEY

RECENT HISTORY

Federico Chávez ruled from 1949 until 1954. In May 1954, General Alfredo Stroessner, commander-in-chief of the armed forces, used his cavalry to seize power. With help from the United States, he brought financial stability to an economy racked by runaway inflation, but he used terrorist methods in silencing all opposition. Stroessner won a third presidential term in February 1963, despite the constitutional stipulation that a president could be reelected only once.

Stroessner ran for reelection in 1968, 1973, 1978, 1983, and 1988, all with only token opposition permitted. On September 17, 1980, the exiled former dictator of Nicaragua, Anastasio Somoza Debayle, who had been granted asylum by the Stroessner government was assassinated in Asunción, and Paraguay broke off relations with Nicaragua.

During the 1980s, Stroessner relaxed his hold on Paraguay. The state of siege that had been renewed every three months since 1959, was allowed to lapse in April 1987. However, allegations of widespread human rights abuses continued.

On February 3, 1989, Stroessner's 35-year dictatorship came to an end at the hand of General Andrés Rodríguez, second in command of the Paraguayan military. Immediately after the coup, Rodríguez announced that elections would be held in May. With only three months to prepare, little opposition was mounted and Rodríguez won easily with 75.8 percent of the vote.

There followed an immediate easing of restrictions on free speech and organization. Labor unions were recognized, and opposition parties were allowed to operate freely. Rodríguez promised and delivered elections in 1993. In an unprecedented transfer of political power from one elected government to another, Juan Carlos Wasmosy was elected to the presidency.

Wasmosy began to push for reforms toward a market-oriented economy. The plan included the sale of state-owned enterprises. The economy, however, was slow to respond to the reforms. In 1998, Raúl Cubas Grau was elected president, marking the first time in Paraguay's history that an elected civilian succeeded another as president. Cubas claimed that corruption by the previous administration had cost the economy $2 billion since 1996. However, only a year later, Cubas had to resign after the assassination of vice-president Luis Argãna. The president of the Senate, Luis Gonzáles Macchi, was sworn in as president. It was unclear what policies Gonzáles would pursue, but many considered him a caretaker until new elections are held in 2003.

GOVERNMENT

Paraguay is a republic, operating under a 1992 constitution, with substantial powers conferred on the executive branch. The president, who is directly elected by popular vote for a five-year term, is chief of state, head of government, commander-in-chief of the military, and conducts foreign affairs. He appoints the eleven-member cabinet, most administrators, and justices of the Supreme Court. He is advised by the Council of State, consisting of the cabinet ministers, the president of the National University, the archbishop of Asunción, the president of the Central Bank, and representatives of other sectors and the military.

The legislature consists of a two-chamber congress consisting of the 45-member Chamber of Senators and the eighty-member Chamber of Deputies. Representatives must be at least twenty-five years of age and are elected for five-year terms. Voting is by secret ballot and is compulsory for all citizens between eighteen and seventy-five years of age.

Judiciary

The five-judge Supreme Court exercises both original and appeals jurisdiction. There are four appeals tribunals: civil/commercial, criminal, labor, and juvenile. There are special appeals chambers for civil and commercial cases and criminal cases. Each rural district *(partido)* has a judge, appointed by the central government, to settle local disputes and to try accused persons and sentence those found guilty.

Political Parties

Since the end of the War of the Triple Alliance, two parties have dominated politics-the National Republican Association (Asociación Nacional Republicana), generally known as the Colorado Party, and the Liberal Party, now known as the Authentic Radical Liberal Party (PLRA). Both appeared in 1887, and there has never been a recognizable ideological distinction between the Colorados and Liberals, but the two parties are similar in their disunity. They both have a history of faction splits, reemerging with a slightly different make-up through time. Also taking seats in Congress in 1998 was the National Encounter Party (PEN) formed in the late twentieth century. It consists of an alliance of several smaller parties and civic organizations, and appeals to the urban middle class.

DEFENSE

Paraguay's armed forces numbered 20,200 (12,900 draftees) in 2000, with about 14,900 in the army, 3,600 in the navy (including 900 marines), and 1,700 in the air force. Paraguay has compulsory military service of twelve to twenty-four months for all males between the ages of eighteen and twenty. Expenditures of the Ministry of Defense were $125 million in 1998.

ECONOMIC AFFAIRS

Landlocked Paraguay has a limited economy based principally on agriculture, livestock production, forestry, and the basic processing of materials. In recent years, the relative importance of agriculture has declined, and the value of services has risen; however, cattle-raising remains a key economic activity.

The large informal sector consists of the re-export of consumer goods from Asia and the United States to neighboring countries, and many small street vendors and microenterprises. Due to the importance of the informal sector in Paraguay's economy, accurate measures and statistics are difficult to gather.

During the 1970s and 1980s, Paraguay suffered from runaway inflation. An economic reform package was introduced in the early 1990s. It included judicial reform, keeping down government expenses, loosening controls over the exchange rate, and privatizing state-owned enterprises. Progress on reforms were continuing in 1996, although at a slow pace due to stiff political opposition, and reforms were all but abandoned in 1997 and 1998, resulting in the GDP declining slightly in 1998 and 1999. Political uncertainty, corruption, slowing of reforms, and lack of infrastructure all contribute to Paraguay's poor economic performance.

Public Finance

The Paraguayan government depends upon import duties for revenue, especially from the re-export trade. The government is the largest employer, and the budget represents 40 percent of GDP. The majority of the budget (80 percent) goes to public employee salaries, 15 percent to servicing the foreign debt, and 5 percent for investment. The current account balance deficit was 3.1 percent of GDP in 1998.

The U.S. Central Intelligence Agency estimates that, in 1995, government revenues totaled approximately $1.9 billion, and expenditures $2.1 billion, including capital expenditures of $700 million. External debt totaled $2.7 billion in 1999.

Income

In 1999, Paraguay's gross domestic product (GDP) was estimated at $19.9 billion, or about $3,650 per capita. The 1999 estimated GDP growth rate was a decline of 1 percent, and inflation was 5 percent. The 1999 estimated GDP contribution by sector was agriculture 28 percent, industry 21 percent, and services 51 percent.

Industry

Among Paraguay's industrial strengths are the processing of agricultural, animal, and forestry products, mainly for export, and small-scale manufacturing of consumer goods for local needs. Most manufacturing is done in the Asunción area, but some plants are located near the source of the raw material used by the particular industry.

Industries encouraged by the government include petroleum refining, foodstuffs, wood processing, and chemicals. There are two cement plants and a steel mill.

Food-processing plants include slaughterhouses, flour mills, sugar mills, oil mills for the production of cottonseed and peanut oils for domestic consumption, as well as castor, tung, coco, and palm oils for export.

Although there is a considerable textile industry, imports still run high. Products for domestic consumption include pharmaceutical and chemical goods, finished wood and furniture, brick and tiles, cigars and cigarettes, candles, shoes, matches, soap, and small metal goods.

Banking and Finance

The Central Bank of Paraguay (BCP) was founded in 1952, as a state-owned, autonomous agency charged with establishing the government's monetary credit and exchange policies. Recommendations in early 1961, by an economic mission of the IDB and IBRD, led to the establishment of the National Development Bank to provide an effective source of medium- and long-term agricultural and industrial credits. The superintendent of banks regulates savings and loan institutions. There are two state-owned banks, some locally owned banks, and nine foreign banks. Foreign-owned banks account for 82 percent of total deposits and 78 percent of all loans, and the two largest banks, Banco de Asunción and Citibank, are foreign-owned.

Paraguay's first stock market began trading in October 1993. By 1999, there were sixty local companies traded on the exchange.

Economic Development

To a considerable extent, Paraguay has a government-controlled economy; government agencies fix prices, control distribution, regulate production and exportation, and exercise monopolistic rights over much of the economy. In recent decades, and particularly since the IMF stabilization program went into effect in the late 1950s, some controls have been loosened. In the wake of the free exchange system have come moves to eliminate government subsidies, such as that for wheat. In agriculture, there is an annual plan for acreage quotas, but the principal problem has been one of meeting the quotas rather than of the surpluses. The establishment of the National Development Bank has created a source of medium- and long-term credits favorable to agriculture and industry. Price controls and marketing quotas are particularly significant to the cattle industry. Paraguay has sought to develop closer economic ties with Brazil, the United States, and Western European nations, largely to reduce the country's dependence on trade with Argentina.

Economic planning is the responsibility of the Technical Planning Secretariat for Economic and Social Development, established in 1962. Government economic reforms during the 1990s were generally promoted by opposition parties. Reforms in 1999 centered on a diversification of the economy away from the re-exportation business, and on fighting corruption that the government Comptroller office estimated to have cost $2.3 billion in 1997.

SOCIAL WELFARE

Social insurance includes free medical, surgical, and hospital care for the worker and dependents; maternity care and cash benefits; sickness and accident benefits; retirement pensions at age sixty; and funeral benefits. Unemployment insurance does not exist, but severance pay is provided. Domestic violence and workplace sexual harassment remain serious problems for women.

Healthcare

Hospital and medical facilities are generally concentrated in Asunción and other towns. In 1995, there was one hospital bed for every 762 people. In 1993, there were five doctors per 10,000 people. Approximately 60 percent of the population has access to health care services. In 1990-1996, only 42 percent of the population had access to safe water and 41 percent had adequate sanitation.

In 2000, average life expectancy was seventy-six years. The principal causes of death are bacillary dysentery and other intestinal diseases, heart disease, pneumonia, and cancer.

Housing

Between 1982 and 1988, the number of housing units rose to 755,000, with five people per dwelling. In 1973, a National Housing Bank was established to finance low-income housing development.

EDUCATION

As of 1995, the estimated illiteracy rate was 6.7 percent, 5.6 percent for males and 7.8 percent for females. Elementary education is compulsory and free between the ages of seven and fourteen. In 1997, there were 905,813 primary school students, and 327,775 students at the secondary level.

Universities include the National University of Paraguay and Nuestra Señora de la Asunción Catholic University. Total university and higher institution enrollment in 1996 was 42,302 students.

2000 KEY EVENTS TIMELINE

May

- Supporters of former army head Lino Oviedo launch a coup attempt that the government suppresses.

June

- Brazilian authorities take Oviedo to Brasilia where he awaits extradition.
- Demonstrators protesting the government's privatization program take to the streets in Asuncion.

August

- Julio César Franco, of the opposition Liberal Party, is elected to the vice presidency on August 24 after the assassination of the former vice president last year.

October

- President Luis González Macchi fires Minister of Finance Federico Zayas October 2.
- The Unification Church of the Reverend Sung Myung Moon, a sect popularly referred to as "The Moonies" acquires more than 300,000 hectares of land, including the town of Puerto Casado. The 6,000 residents there demand that control of their town be given to the local council.

December

- Pressure is growing for President Macchi to resign, making way for Julio Cesar Franco, the opposition Liberal Party vice president to take over. Macchis is criticized for corruption and mishandling of the country's economy.

ANALYSIS OF EVENTS: 2000

BUSINESS AND THE ECONOMY

Paraguay attempted to restart its economy by privatizing state-owned companies. The plan triggered protests throughout the country. In March thousands of farm workers protested in the town of Santa Rosa, pressing for more government assistance, improved credits, and higher prices for their produce. On June 10, workers and peasants took to the streets to protest against the International Monetary Fund (IMF) and the privatization process. A few days later twenty people were injured in clashes with the police in Asunción, during protests called by trade unions trying to stop privatization. The government argued that selling state companies was necessary to revive the economy. In October the Lower House of Congress, by a forty-six to twenty-one vote, approved a law authorizing the government to privatize phone, water and rail companies. The phone company has 300,000 lines, with potential demand for another 600,000. The water company provides services to about 30 percent of the population. The rail company has not functioned since the mid-1990s. Government officials believe privatizing state-owned companies is the only way to improve the five-year long economic crisis affecting the country.

Paraguay had been criticized for its slow pace of reforms. U.S. Assistant Secretary of State for Latin America, Peter Romero, told Paraguayan officials that political stability was the only way to attract investors.

GOVERNMENT AND POLITICS

Paraguay's greatest threat to its resurgent democracy in the past two years has been Lino Oviedo, a charismatic, often unbalanced former military leader with a megalomaniac thirst for power. Oviedo has been blamed several times for trying to undermine Paraguay's government since helping depose Dictator Alfredo Stroesnner in 1989, after thirty-five years in power. In 1998, Oviedo's friend and newly elected President Raúl Cúbas released him from prison. Once free, Oviedo attempted to gain control of Cúbas's Colorado Party, with eyes toward the presidency. Standing in his way was Vice President Luis María Argaña, also a Colorado party member. In March 1999 Oviedo fled the country following the assassination of Argaña, who was shot while on his way to his office in Asunción. Cúbas was forced from office, and along with Oviedo, sought political refuge abroad. While Cúbas quietly languished in Brazil, Oviedo remained defiant from exile in Argentina, calling for a coup against new President Luis González Macchi.

As former head of the Senate, and appointed president, Macchi's hold on power was precarious. Macchi was also a member of the Colorado Party, which had been unchallenged for more than fifty years. Yet, the opposition had grown stronger and more vocal as democratic reforms had taken hold. Macchi sought to bring Oviedo back to justice. Oviedo disappeared from view after his asylum in Argentina was revoked in December 1999. With his whereabouts unknown, Paraguayans braced for a possible coup. Finally on May 17 rebel soldiers and officers captured several radio stations and called for an overthrow. Tanks rolled through downtown Asunción and began to fire at the legislative palace. The coup failed within four hours, as military personnel loyal to the government pushed the rebel forces back.

In the aftermath of the coup, Macchi declared a national emergency, and ordered the arrest of dozens of Paraguayans, including high-ranking military officers. In a national address, he declared the attempted coup the"last battle" against democracy in Paraguay, and promised accelerated economic and social reforms. From his hiding place, Oviedo said he had never ordered the coup. On June 12 Oviedo was arrested by Brazilian authorities in the town of in Foz de Iguazu, on the border with Paraguay. Paraguay immediately sought his extradition. In an apparent move to make his extradition easier, a Brazilian congressional commission claimed there were clear links between Oviedo and drug trafficking. From a jail in Brazilia, he continued to influence political decisions in Paraguay.

By August the Colorado Party faced its biggest challenge in fifty-three years as voters prepared to select a new vice president to replace the assassinated Argaña. His son Felix was running mostly on his father's name. His opponent, Julio César Franco, represented the Liberal Authentic Radical Party. Franco became a symbol for change, but many loyal supporters and international observers became concerned when Oviedo endorsed him in the election. In September Franco became the first opposition candidate to be elected in fifty-three years. While it was only the vice-presidential post, many Paraguayans believed he would eventually replace Macchi, who had grown unpopular. In May the United States and the Organization of American States stood firmly in support of Macchi's government. But some Colorado Party members on Oviedo's side, and opposition members that included Franco, openly discussed a political trial against Macchi for fumbling the economy.

On October 25 a major general and two other men were sentenced to prison for their role in the assassination of Argaña. Two other men and Oviedo, who masterminded the attack, were implicated in the assassination. The two men, who escaped while in detention in Argentina, remained at large, while Oviedo awaited extradition from Brazil.

CULTURE AND SOCIETY

A tiny minority owns most land in Paraguay, and poor farmers have often resorted to violent means to acquire idle land in the past decade. In January President Macchi's government promised to give land to more than 2,000 peasants in the north of the country in exchange for an end to illegal takeover of private land. Just before the agreement three peasants were killed during clashes with police. The government also told peasants it would invest in schools, healthcare, roads and electricity for their new communities.

In October the 6,000 residents of Puerto Casado in northern Paraguay, woke up to discover their town had been sold to the Unification Church of the Reverend Sung Myung Moon. The 100-year-old town was part of a large tract of land acquired by the sect. While the purchase appeared to be legal, residents said they were not about to be displaced by the sect and asked the government for assistance. Paraguayan officials assured residents that the town would not fall in the hands of the Unification Church, which manages a newspaper in Paraguay, and owns other properties in the country. In neighboring Brazil, the sect built a community for about two thousand followers.

DIRECTORY

CENTRAL GOVERNMENT

Head of State

President, Luis Angel González Macchi, Office of the President

Ministers

Minister of Agriculture and Livestock, Enrique Zuniga

Ministry of Agriculture and Livestock
Presidente Franco 472, Asuncion, Paraguay
PHONE: +595 (21) 449614
FAX: +595 (21) 497965

Minister of Education and Worship
Nicanor Duarte Frutos, Ministry of Education and Worship, Chile 128 esq., Humaita y Piribebuy, Asuncion, Paraguay
PHONE: +595 (21) 443078
FAX: +595 (21) 443919

Minister of Finance and Economy
Francisco Oviedo, Ministry of Finance and Economy, Chile 128 esq., Palmas, Asuncion, Paraguay
PHONE: +595 (21) 440010
FAX: +595 (21) 448283

Minister of Foreign Relations
Juan Esteban Aguirre Martinez, Ministry of Foreign Relations, Juan E. O'Leary y Presidente Franco, Asuncion, Paraguay
PHONE: +595 (21) 494593
FAX: +595 (21) 493910

Minister of Industry and Commerce
Euclides Acevedo, Ministry of Industry and Commerce, Avda Espana 323, Asuncion, Paraguay
PHONE: +595 (21) 204638
FAX: +595 (21) 213529

Minister of Interior
Julio Cesar Fanego, Ministry of Interior, Estrella y Montevideo, Asuncion, Paraguay
PHONE: +595 (21) 493661
FAX: +595 (21) 448446

Minister of Justice and Labor
Silvio Ferreira, Ministry of Justice and Labor, G.R. de Francia y Estados Unidos, Asuncion, Paraguay
PHONE: +595 (21) 493515
FAX: +595 (21) 208469

Minister of National Defense
Jose Ocampos, Ministry of National Defense, Avda Mariscl Lopez y Vice-President Sanchez, Asuncion, Paraguay
PHONE: +595 (21) 204771
FAX: +595 (21) 211583

Minister of Public Health and Social Welfare
Martin Chiola, Ministry of Public Health and Social Welfare, Avda Pettirossi y Brasil, Asuncion, Paraguay
PHONE: +595 (21) 207328
FAX: +595 (21) 206700

Minister of Public Works and Communications
Walter Bower, Ministry of Public Works and Communications, Oliva y Alberdi, Asuncion, Paraguay
PHONE: +595 (21) 444411
FAX: +595 (21) 444421

POLITICAL ORGANIZATIONS

Encuentro Nacional (EN)

Senador Long 370. esquina Del Maestro, Asunción, Paraguay
PHONE: +595 (21) 610699; 610701
FAX: +595 (21) 610699

Partido Liberal Radical Auténtico-PLRA (Authentic Radical Liberal Party)

Mariscal López, 1750, Asunción, Paraguay
PHONE: +595 (21) 244867; 204869
FAX: +595 (21) 204867
NAME: Domingo Laino

Asociación Nacional Republicana Partido Colorado-ASNPC (National Republican Association Colorado Party)

Asociación Nacional Republicana Junta de Gobierno, 25 de Mayo 842, C/Tacuary, Asunción, Paraguay
PHONE: +595 (21) 444137; 498669
FAX: +595 (21) 444210
E-MAIL: anr@uninet.com.pry
TITLE: Acting President
NAME: Bader Rachid Lichi

Christian Democratic Party (PDC)

Colon 871, Casilla 1318, Asuncion, Paraguay
NAME: Miguel Montaner

Febrerista Revolutionary Party (PRF)

Casa del Pueblo, Manduvira 552, Asunción, Paraguay
PHONE: +595 (21) 94041
NAME: Carlos Maria Ljubetic

DIPLOMATIC REPRESENTATION

Embassies in Paraguay

Argentina
Dirección Av. Espana y Peru, Asuncion, Paraguay
PHONE: +595 (21) 210320; 210321; 210322
FAX: +595 (21) 211029
E-MAIL: embarpy@pla.net.py

Belgium
Belgian Consulate, Ruta II, Kur 17,5, Capiata (Asuncion), Paraguay
PHONE: +595 (21) 282081
FAX: +595 (21) 282082

Brazil
Calle Coronel Irrazabal esq. Avda. Mariscal López, Asuncion, Paraguay
PHONE: +595 (21) 214466, 214534; 214680
FAX: +595 (21) 212693

Costa Rica
San Jose 447, Casilla 1936, Asuncion, Paraguay
PHONE: +595 (21) 213535

Germany
Av. Venezuela 241, Casilla 471, Asunción, Paraguay
PHONE: +595 (21) 214009
FAX: +595 (21) 212863
E-MAIL: 100566.2610@compuserve.com

Israel
Edif. San Rafael, 8, Yegros 437, Asuncion, Paraguay
PHONE: +595 (21) 495097
FAX: +595 (21) 496355
E-MAIL: israel@quanta.com.py

Italy
Calle Luis Morales 680, Luis de Leon, Asuncion, Paraguay
PHONE: +595 (21) 207429
FAX: +595 (21) 212630
E-MAIL: ambasu@quanta.com.py

Peru
Avda Mariscal Lopez 648, Casilla 433, Asuncion, Paraguay
PHONE: +595 (21) 200949
FAX: +595 (21) 212980

Spain
Yegros 437, Asuncion, Paraguay
PHONE: +595 (21) 90686

United Kingdom
Calle Presidente Franco, 706, P.O. Box 404, Asuncion, Paraguay
PHONE: +595 (21) 444472; 496068
FAX: +595 (21) 446385

United States
1776 Mariscal Lopez Ave, Casilla Postal 402, Unit 4711 APO AA 34036 0001, Asuncion, Paraguay
PHONE: +595 (21) 213715
FAX: +595 (21) 213728

Uruguay
25 de Mayo 1894 esq. General Aquino, Asuncion, Paraguay
PHONE: +595 (21) 25391
FAX: +595 (21) 23970

Vatican City
Apostolic Nunciature, Calle Ciudad del Vaticano, entre 25 de Mayo y Caballero, Casilla 83, Asuncion, Paraguay
PHONE: +595 (21) 215139
FAX: +595 (21) 212590
E-MAIL: nunciopy@pla.net.py

Venezuela
Edif. Delime II, 1, Juan E. O'Leary esq., Eduardo Victor Haedo, Apdo 94, Asuncion, Paraguay
PHONE: +595 (21) 44242

JUDICIAL SYSTEM

The Supreme Court

Consejo de la Magistratura

BROADCAST MEDIA

Administración Nacional De Telecomunicaciones

Administración General, Casa de Correo 84, Asunción, Paraguay
PHONE: +595 (21) 44001
TITLE: President
CONTACT: Miguel Horacio Gini
LANGUAGE: Spanish

Obedira Comunicación Integra

Cdte. Gamarra esq. Isabel Barrio San Antonio, Asuncion, Paraguay

PHONE: +595 (21) 425042
FAX: +595 (21) 480048
E-MAIL: info@obedira.com.py
LANGUAGE: Spanish
TYPE: Commercial

Bruno Masi Centro de Television

Procer Carlos Aguello 1375, Asunción, Paraguay
PHONE: +595 (21) 662712; +595 (21) 662724; +595 (21) 607710
FAX: +595 (21) 609120
E-MAIL: masinformes@brunomasi.com
WEBSITE: http://www.brunomasi.com

Televisión Itapúa

Avenida Irrazabal y 25 de Mayo, Encarnación, Paraguay
PHONE: +595 (71) 204550
FAX: +595 (71) 204560
E-MAIL: duba@itacom.com.py
WEBSITE: http://www.itacom.com.py
TITLE: General Manager
CONTACT: J. Mateo
CHANNEL: 7
WATTAGE: 60 kW
TYPE: Commercial

Red Privada de Comunicación (RPC)

Calles Comendador Nicolás Bó y Guaranies de la Ciudad de Lambaré, Asunción, Paraguay
PHONE: +595 (21) 332823
FAX: +595 (21) 310399
WEBSITE: http://www.rpc.com.py
CHANNEL: 13
WATTAGE: 30kW

Sistema Nacional de Televisión (SNT)

Televisión Cerro Cora S.A., Avenida Carlos A. Lopez 572, Asunción, Paraguay
PHONE: +595 (21) 421710
FAX: +595 (21) 480230
E-MAIL: zulma@uninet.com.py
TITLE: Head of Sales
CONTACT: Hugo Montgomery
CHANNEL: 9
WATTAGE: 60kW
TYPE: Commercial

Televisión del Este

Area 5, Cd., Puerto Stroessner, Paraguay
TITLE: General Manager
CONTACT: A. Villalba
WATTAGE: 25kW

COLLEGES AND UNIVERSITIES

National University of Asuncion

Av. Espana 1098, Casilla 910, Asuncion, Paraguay
PHONE: +595 (21) 211419
FAX: +595 (21) 213734
E-MAIL: apga-una@mmail.co.py
WEBSITE: http://www.una.py

Catholic University, Asuncion

Cc 1718 Independencia Nac y Comuneros, Asuncion, Paraguay
PHONE: +595 (21) 441044
FAX: +595 (21) 445245
E-MAIL: uca@mmail.com.py
WEBSITE: http://www.uc.edu.py

Autonomous University of Asuncion

Montevideo 453, esq. Oliva, Edif. Montevideo, Asuncion, Paraguay
PHONE: +595 (21) 493873
FAX: +595 (21) 445231
E-MAIL: rrpp@uaa.edu.py
WEBSITE: http://www.uaa.edu.py

Columbia University

25 de Mayo 658 y Antequera, Asuncion, Paraguay
PHONE: +595 (21) 490811
FAX: +595 (21) 208715
E-MAIL: jbu@columbia.edu.py
WEBSITE: http://www.columbia.edu.py

NEWSPAPERS AND MAGAZINES

ABC Color

Editorial Azeta S.A., Yergo 175, Ascuncion, Paraguay
PHONE: +595 (21) 191160
FAX: +595 (21) 493059
E-MAIL: azeta@abc.una.py
TITLE: Editor
CONTACT: Aldo Zuccolillo
CIRCULATION: 65,000 (Daily); 85,000 (Sun)

El Dia

Multimedia S.A., Avda Mariscal Lopez 2948, McArthur, Asuncion, Paraguay
PHONE: +595 (21) 603400
FAX: +595 (21) 660385; 603400 (ext. 272)
E-MAIL: eldia@multimedia.com.py

WEBSITE: http://www.eldia.com.py
TITLE: Editor
CONTACT: Javier Pirovano Pena
CIRCULATION: 28,000

La Nacion

Ave. Zavala Cue y Cerro Cora, Fernando de la Mora, Asuncion, Paraguay
PHONE: +595 (21) 512520; 512535
FAX: +595 (21) 513463
E-MAIL: lanacion@conexion.com.py
WEBSITE: http://www.conexion.com.py/lanacion
TITLE: Editor
CONTACT: Osvaldo Dominquez Dibb
CIRCULATION: 26,580

Noticias

Av. Artigas y Brasilla, Asuncion, Paraguay
PHONE: +595 (21) 292721; 292724; 292717
FAX: +585 (21) 292841; 292840
E-MAIL: noticias@infonet.com.py; director@diarionoticias.com.py
WEBSITE: http://www.infonet.com.py/noticiasonline/index.html; http://www.diarionoticias.com.py
TITLE: Director
CONTACT: Hassel Aquilar Sosa
CIRCULATION: 30,000 (Daily); 35,000 (Sun.)

Popular

Multimedia S.A., Avda Mariscal Lopez 2948, Asuncion, Paraguay
PHONE: +595 (21) 603400
FAX: +595 (21) 660385
E-MAIL: popular@multimedia.com.py
WEBSITE: http://www.popular.com.py
TITLE: Editor
CONTACT: Nestor Insaurralde
CIRCULATION: 120,000

Ultima Hora

Benjamin Constant 658, Asuncion, Paraguay
PHONE: +595 (21) 496261; 496268
FAX: +595 (21) 447071
E-MAIL: uhora@supernet.com.py
WEBSITE: http://www.ultimahora.com.py
TITLE: Internatinal Ad Manager
CONTACT: Nekly Gaona de Frutos
CIRCULATION: 110,000 (Mon.); 58,600 (Tu-Sat)

Sellecionse Del Reader's Digest

RD latinoamerica, S.A., 2655 leJeune Rd., Ste. 301, Coral Gables FL 33134 USA
PHONE: (305) 4488233
FAX: (305) 4488234
TITLE: Editor
CONTACT: Audon Coria
CIRCULATION: 38,000

PUBLISHERS

Intercontinental Editora

Caballero 270, Asuncion, Paraguay
PHONE: +595 (21) 496991
FAX: +595 (21) 449738
TITLE: Director
CONTACT: Alejandro Gatti
SUBJECTS: Government, Political Science, Law, Literature, Literary Criticism, Parapsychology, Poetry

RELIGIOUS ORGANIZATIONS

Catholic

Alto Parana (Dioceses)
Obispo de Alto Parana, Ciudad del Este. Alto Parana, Paraguay
PHONE: +595 6161390
TITLE: Excmo. Monsenor
NAME: Oscar Paez Garcete

Asuncion (Arq.)
Arzobispo de Asuncion, Independencia Nacional y Mariscal Lopez 130, Casilla Correo 654, Asuncion, Paraguay
PHONE: +595 (21) 444150, +595 (21) 445551
FAX: +595 (21) 447510
TITLE: Excmo. Monsenor
NAME: Ricardo Valenzuela Rios

Concepcion (Diocese)
Obispo de Concepcion, Nuestra Senora de la Concepcion y Mariscal Lopez, Concepcion, Paraguay
PHONE: +595 312357
FAX: +595 312500 2827
TITLE: Excmo. Monsenor
NAME: Juan Bautista Gavilan Velasquez

Conferencia Episcopal De Paraguay
Calle Alberdi 782, Casilla Correo 1436, Asuncion, Paraguay
PHONE: +595 (21) 490920, 492670
FAX: +595 (21) 495115

Encarnacion (Diocese)
Obispo de Encarnacion, Dr. Juan Leon Mallorquin y General Cabanas 305, Casilla Correo 81, Encarnacion, Paraguay
PHONE: +595 713305

FAX: +595 713777
TITLE: Excmo. Monsenor
NAME: Jorge Adolfo Carlos Livieres Banks

Pilcomayo (Vic. Ap.)
Vicario Apostolico de Pilcomayo, Casilla Correo 455, Asuncion, Paraguay
PHONE: +595 (21) 606114
FAX: 595 21 60 6204
TITLE: Excmo. Monsenor
NAME: Lucio Alfert, O.M.I

San Pedro (Diocese)
Obispo de Villarrica del Espiritu Santo, Natalicio Talavera 748, Villarrica, Paraguay
PHONE: +595 5412687
TITLE: Excmo. Monsenor
NAME: Sebelio Peralta Alvarez

Orthodox

Holy Virgin Protection Church
Nuestra Senora de la Asuncion 1143, Asuncion, Paraguay
PHONE: +595 (21) 445708
FAX: +595 (541) 7685476
TITLE: Parish Administrator
NAME: Sergio Kolenko

St. Nicholas Church
General Artigas 194, Encarnacion, Paraguay
PHONE: +595 (541) 3614274
TITLE: Priest
NAME: Valentin Iwaszewicz

FURTHER READING

Articles

"A Coalition Falls, Democracy Stalls." *The Economist (US),* February 12, 2000, vol. 354, no. 8157, p. 35.

"Coup or Feint?" *World Press Review,* August 2000, vol. 47, no. 8, p. 27.

Cristaldo, Porfirio. "An IDB Plan in Paraguay Has No Room for Little Guys." *Wall Street Journal,* February 4, 2000, p. A19.

"Paraguay—Lame Ducks." *The Economist (US),* August 19, 2000, vol. 356, no. 8184, p. 30.

Books

Dun and Bradstreet's Guide to Paraguay. Parsippany, NJ: Dun & Bradstreet, 1999.

Jermyn, Leslie. *Paraguay.* New York: Marshall Cavendish, 2000. [juvenile]

Morrison, Marion. *Paraguay.* Philadelphia: Chelsea House Publishers, 2000. [juvenile]

Nickson, R. Andrew. *Paraguay.* Santa Barbara, CA: Clio Press, 1999.

PARAGUAY: STATISTICAL DATA

For sources and notes see "Sources of Statistics" at the front of each volume.

GEOGRAPHY

Geography

Area:

Total: 406,750 sq km.

Land: 397,300 sq km.

Land boundaries:

Total: 3,920 km.

Border countries: Argentina 1,880 km, Bolivia 750 km, Brazil 1,290 km.

Coastline: 0 km (landlocked).

Climate: subtropical to temperate; substantial rainfall in the eastern portions, becoming semiarid in the far west.

Terrain: grassy plains and wooded hills east of Rio Paraguay; Gran Chaco region west of Rio Paraguay mostly low, marshy plain near the river, and dry forest and thorny scrub elsewhere.

Natural resources: hydropower, timber, iron ore, manganese, limestone.

Land use:

Arable land: 6%

Permanent crops: 0%

Permanent pastures: 55%

Forests and woodland: 32%

Other: 7% (1993 est.).

HUMAN FACTORS

Demographics (A)

	1990	1995	1998	2000	2010	2020	2030	2040	2050
Population	4,236	4,878	5,296	5,586	7,162	8,938	10,842	12,766	14,636
Life expectancy - males	68.4	70.0	70.7	71.2	73.4	75.2	76.7	77.9	78.9
Life expectancy - females	72.6	74.9	75.7	76.3	78.7	80.7	82.4	83.7	84.8
Birth rate (per 1,000)	34.6	33.1	32.0	31.3	27.9	25.0	22.3	19.9	18.0
Death rate (per 1,000)	5.9	5.2	5.0	4.8	4.3	4.2	4.4	5.0	5.4
Women of reproductive age (15-49 yrs.)	1,003	1,163	1,267	1,342	1,740	2,199	2,682	3,161	3,575
Fertility rate	4.6	4.4	4.2	4.2	3.7	3.3	3.0	2.7	2.5

Except as noted, values for vital statistics are in thousands; life expectancy is in years.

Health Personnel

	National Data	World Data (wtd ave)
Total health expenditure as a percentage of GDP, 1990-1998[a]		
Public sector	2.6	2.5
Private sector	4.8	2.9
Total[b]	7.4	5.5
Health expenditure per capita in U.S. dollars, 1990-1998[a]		
Purchasing power parity	348	561
Total	122	483
Availability of health care facilities per 100,000 people		
Hospital beds 1990-1998[a]	130	330
Doctors 1992-1995[a]	67	122
Nurses 1992-1995[a]	10	248

Health Indicators

	National Data	World Data
Life expectancy at birth (years)		
1980	67	61
1998	70	67
Daily per capita supply of calories		
1970	2,589	2,358
1997	2,566	2,791
Daily per capital supply of protein		
1997 (grams)	77	74
Total fertility rate (births per woman)		
1980	5.2	3.7
1998	3.9	2.7
Population with access (%)		
To safe water (1990-96)	39	NA
To sanitation (1990-96)	32	NA
People living with (1997)		
Tuberculosis (cases per 100,000)	39.2	60.4
Malaria (cases per 100,000)	11.1	42.2
HIV/AIDS (% aged 15 - 49 years)	0.13	0.99

Infants and Malnutrition

	National Data	World Data (wtd ave)
Under 5 mortality rate (1989)	33	NA
% of infants with low birthweight (1992-98)[1]	9	17
Births attended by skilled health staff (% of total births 1996-98)	61	52
% fully immunized at 1 year of age (1995-98)[1]		
TB	83	82
DPT	81	77
Polio	81	77
Measles	NA	74
Prevalence of child malnutrition (1992-98)[1] (based on weight for age, % of children under 5 years)	NA	30

Ethnic Division

Mestizo (mixed Spanish and Amerindian) 95%

Religion

Roman Catholic 90%

Mennonite, and other Protestant ....NA

Major Languages

Spanish (official), Guarani (spoken by most of rural population).

EDUCATION

Public Education Expenditures

	1980	1997
Public expenditures on education as % of GNP	1.5	4.0
Expenditures per student as % of GNP per capita		
Primary	NA	10.9
Secondary	NA	12.0
Tertiary	NA	90.9
Pupils per teacher at the primary level	NA	21
Duration of primary education in years	NA	6
World data for comparison		
Public expenditures on education as % of GNP (mean)	3.9	4.8
Pupils per teacher at the primary level (wtd ave)	NA	33
Duration of primary education in years (mean)	NA	9

Educational Attainment (A)

Age group (1992) ....15+

Population of this age group 2,427,485

Highest level attained (%)

No schooling 7.0

First level

Not completed 38.4

Completed 22.8

Entered second level

Lower Secondary 12.8

Upper Secondary 12.2

Entered post-secondary 6.6

Literacy Rates (A)

In thousands and percent	1990	1995	2000	2010
Illiterate population (15+ yrs.)	239	235	229	213
Literacy rate - total adult pop. (%)	90.7	92.1	93.4	95.4
Literacy rate - males (%)	92.5	93.5	94.4	95.9
Literacy rate - females (%)	88.8	90.6	92.3	94.9

GOVERNMENT & LAW

Political Parties

Congress (Congreso)	no. of seats
Chamber of Senators	
Colorado Party	25
Authentic Radical Liberal Party (PLRA)	13
National Encounter (PEN)	7
Chamber of Deputies	
Colorado Party	45
Authentic Radical Liberal Party (PLRA)	26
National Encounter (PEN)	9

Elections for the Chamber of Senators and the Chamber of Deputies were last held 10 May 1998 (next to be held in May 2003).

Government Budgets (A)

Year: 1993

Total Expenditures: 1,559.4 Millions of Guaranies

Expenditures as a percentage of the total by function:

General public services and public order 20.70

Defense 10.69

Education 22.07

Health 7.33

Social Security and Welfare 16.25

Housing and community amenities 0.44

Recreational, cultural, and religious affairs 0

Fuel and energy 2.52

Agriculture, forestry, fishing, and hunting 5.39

Mining, manufacturing, and construction 0.08

Transportation and communication 8.50

Other economic affairs and services 0

Crime

Crime volume (for 1998)

Crimes reported 24,042

Total persons convicted 14,185

Crimes per 100,000 population 456

Persons responsible for offenses

Total number suspects 16,275

Total number of female suspects 3,906

Total number of juvenile suspects 651

(Continued on next page.)

LABOR FORCE

Total Labor Force (A)

1.7 million (1996).

Labor Force by Occupation

Agriculture 45%

Unemployment Rate

12% (1998 est.)

PRODUCTION SECTOR

Energy Production

Production . . . . .50.324 billion kWh

Production by source

Fossil fuel 0.12%

Hydro 99.66%

Nuclear 0%

Other 0.22%

Exports . . . . .45.307 billion kWh

Data for 1998.

Energy Consumption

Consumption . . . . .1.494 billion kWh

Imports . . . . .0 kWh

Data for 1998.

(Continued on next page.)

Transportation

Highways:

Total: 29,500 km.

Paved: 15,000 km.

Unpaved: 14,500 km (1999).

Waterways: 3,100 km.

Merchant marine:

Total: 21 ships (1,000 GRT or over) totaling 30,287 GRT/32,510 DWT.

Ships by type: cargo 15, chemical tanker 1, petroleum tanker 4, roll-on/roll-off 1 (1999 est.).

Airports: 937 (1999 est.).

Airports - with paved runways: 10.

Airports - with unpaved runways: 927.

Top Agriculture Products

Cotton, sugarcane, soybeans, corn, wheat, tobacco, cassava (tapioca), fruits, vegetables; beef, pork, eggs, milk; timber.

Top Mining Products (B)

Mineral resources include: iron ore, manganese, limestone.

GOVERNMENT & LAW (cont.)

Military Affairs (A)

	1990	1992	1995	1996	1997
Military expenditures					
Current dollars (mil.)	90	134	117	119[e]	127
1997 constant dollars (mil.)	105	149	121	121[e]	127
Armed forces (000)	16	16	16	16	16
Gross national product (GNP)					
Current dollars (mil.)	7,040	7,330	8,560	8,820	9,880
1997 constant dollars (mil.)	8,250	8,120	8,860	8,960	9,880
Central government expenditures (CGE)					
1997 constant dollars (mil.)	757	1,130	1,050	1,110	1,220
People (mil.)	4.7	4.5	4.9	5.0	5.2
Military expenditure as % of GNP	1.3	1.8	1.4	1.3	1.3
World data on military expenditure as % of GNP	4.5	3.4	2.7	2.6	2.6
Military expenditure as % of CGE	13.9	13.2	11.6	10.9	10.5
World data on military expenditure as % of CGE	17.0	12.5	10.5	10.3	10.2
Military expenditure per capita (1997 $)	23	33	25	24	25
World data on military expenditure per capita (1997 $)	242	173	146	143	145
Armed forces per 1,000 people (soldiers)	3.4	3.6	3.3	3.2	3.1
World data on armed forces per 1,000 people (soldiers)	5.3	4.5	4.1	3.9	3.8
GNP per capita (1997 $)	1,770	1,810	1,820	1,790	1,920
Arms imports[6]					
Current dollars (mil.)	5	10	10	20	5
1997 constant dollars (mil.)	6	11	10	20	5
Total imports[7]					
Current dollars (mil.)	1,352	1,422	3,144	3,204[e]	3,403
1997 constant dollars (mil.)	1,583	1,576	3,255	3,257[e]	3,403
Total exports[7]					
Current dollars (mil.)	959	657	919	1,044	1,089
1997 constant dollars (mil.)	1,123	728	952	1,061	1,089
Arms as percent of total imports[8]	0.4	0.7	0.3	0.6	0.1
Arms as percent of total exports[8]	0	0	0	0	0

MANUFACTURING SECTOR

GDP & Manufacturing Summary (A)

	1980	1985	1990	1995
GDP ($-1990 mil.)[1]	3,887	4,350	5,265	6,174
Per capita ($-1990)[1]	1,248	1,205	1,248	1,279
Manufacturing share (%) (current prices)[1]	16.5	16.2	17.3	15.6[e]
Manufacturing				
Value added ($-1990 mil.)[1]	721	761	910	1,013[e]
Industrial production index	75	83	100	84[e]
Value added ($ mil.)	575	661[e]	769[e]	904[e]
Gross output ($ mil.)	1,312	1,395	1,408	1,979[e]
Employment (000)	143[e]	129[e]	156[e]	166[e]
Productivity ($)				
Gross output per worker	9,131[e]	10,788[e]	8,911[e]	11,695[e]
Value added per worker	4,132[e]	5,134[e]	4,991[e]	5,414[e]
Average wage (inc. supplements)	NA	NA	NA	NA
Value added ($ mil.)				
Food products	170	220[e]	235[e]	277[e]
Beverages	43	56[e]	62[e]	90[e]
Tobacco products	6	7[e]	7[e]	6[e]
Textiles	44	42[e]	54[e]	67[e]
Wearing apparel	2	3[e]	3[e]	3[e]
Leather and fur products	7	14[e]	16[e]	17[e]
Footwear	18	20[e]	25[e]	31[e]
Wood and wood products	95	96[e]	106[e]	170[e]
Furniture and fixtures	6	8[e]	9[e]	16[e]
Paper and paper products	NA	1[e]	1[e]	1[e]
Printing and publishing	24	36[e]	26[e]	42[e]
Industrial chemicals	4	6[e]	6[e]	7[e]
Other chemical products	10	10[e]	8[e]	7[e]
Petroleum refineries	94	51[e]	68[e]	39[e]
Plastic products	6	16[e]	18[e]	17[e]
Glass and glass products	1	2[e]	3[e]	5[e]
Other non-metal mineral products	26	23[e]	31[e]	27[e]
Non-ferrous metals	1	4[e]	6[e]	12[e]
Metal products	9	15[e]	15[e]	11[e]
Non-electrical machinery	1	1[e]	2[e]	2[e]
Electrical machinery	NA	1[e]	1[e]	1[e]
Transport equipment	5	10[e]	8[e]	6[e]
Prof. and scientific equipment	1	1[e]	1[e]	1[e]
Other manufacturing	2	17[e]	58[e]	50[e]

COMMUNICATIONS

Daily Newspapers

	National Data	World Data for Comparison
Daily Newspapers		
Number of Dailies	5	8,391
Total Circulation (000)	213	548,000
Circulation per 1,000 inhabitants	43	96

Telecommunications

Telephones - main lines in use: 167,000 (1995).

Telephones - mobile cellular: 15,807 (1995).

Telephone system: meager telephone service; principal switching center is Asuncion.

Domestic: fair microwave radio relay network.

International: satellite earth station - 1 Intelsat (Atlantic Ocean).

Radio broadcast stations: AM 46, FM 27, shortwave 6 (three inactive) (1998).

Radios: 925,000 (1997).

Television broadcast stations: 10 (1997).

Televisions: 515,000 (1997).

Internet Service Providers (ISPs): 4 (1999).

FINANCE, ECONOMICS, & TRADE

Economic Indicators

National product: GDP—purchasing power parity—$19.9 billion (1999 est.).

National product real growth rate: -1% (1999 est.).

National product per capita: $3,650 (1999 est.).

Inflation rate—consumer price index: 5% (1999).

Balance of Payments

	1990	1991	1992	1993	1994
Exports of goods (f.o.b.)	1,382	1,121	1,082	1,500	1,871
Imports of goods (f.o.b.)	−1,636	−1,868	−1,951	−2,711	−3,148
Trade balance	−254	−747	−869	−1,211	−1,277
Services - debits	−458	−547	−542	−609	−747
Services - credits	498	904	826	987	1,267
Private transfers (net)	12	14	7	7	7
Government transfers (net)	44	59	27	35	35
Overall balance	−172	−324	−600	−834	−749

Exchange Rates

Exchange rates:

Guarani (G) per US$

January 2000 . . . . .3.332.0
1999 . . . . .3,119.1
1998 . . . . .2,726.5
1997 . . . . .2,177.9
1996 . . . . .2,056.8
1995 . . . . .1,963.0

Since early 1998, the exchange rate has operated as a managed float; prior to that, the exchange rate was determined freely in the market. Fiscal year: calendar year.

Top Import Origins

$3.2 billion (f.o.b., 1999 est.)

Origins (1998)

Brazil 34%
United States . . . . .NA
Argentina . . . . .NA
Uruguay . . . . .NA
EU . . . . .NA
Hong Kong . . . . .NA

Top Export Destinations

Exports (f.o.b., 1999 est.): $3.1 billion.

Destinations: Brazil, Argentina, EU.

Import/Export Commodities

Import Commodities	Export Commodities
Road vehicles	Soybeans
Consumer goods	Feed
Tobacco	Cotton
Petroleum products	Meat
Electrical machinery	Edible oils

PERU

Republic of Peru
República del Perú

CAPITAL: Lima.

FLAG: The national flag consists of red, white, and red vertical stripes.

ANTHEM: *Himno Nacional*, beginning "Somos libres, seámoslo siempre" ("We are free; let us remain so forever").

MONETARY UNIT: The nuevo sol (ML), a paper currency of 100 céntimos, replaced the inti on 1 July 1991 at a rate of I1,000,000 = ML1, but, in practice, both currencies are circulating. There are coins of 1, 5, 10, 20, and 50 céntimos and 1 nuevo sol, and notes of 10, 20, 50, and 100 nuevos soles and 10,000, 50,000, 100,000, 500,000, 1,000,000, and 5,000,000 intis. ML1 = $0.38911 (or $1 = ML2.57).

WEIGHTS AND MEASURES: The metric system is the legal standard.

HOLIDAYS: New Year's Day, 1 January; Labor Day, 1 May; Day of the Peasant, half-day, 24 June; Day of St. Peter and St. Paul, 29 June; Independence Days, 28–29 July; Santa Rosa de Lima (patroness of Peru), 30 August; Battle of Anzamos, 8 October; All Saints' Day, 1 November; Immaculate Conception, 8 December; Christmas, 25 December. Movable holidays include Holy Thursday and Good Friday.

TIME: 7 AM = noon GMT.

LOCATION AND SIZE: Peru is South America's third-largest country, with an area of 1,285,220 square kilometers (496,226 square miles), slightly smaller than the state of Alaska. It has a total boundary length of 9,354 kilometers (5,812 miles). Peru's capital city, Lima, is located on the Pacific coast.

CLIMATE: Average temperatures range from 21°C (70°F) in January to 15°C (59°F) in June at Lima, on the coast. At Cusco, in the mountains, the range is only from 12°C (54°F) to 9°C (48°F), while at Iquitos, in the Amazon region, the temperature averages about 32°C (90°F) all year round. In the eastern jungle, precipitation is heavy. Rainfall is often meager near the coast, but cool ocean breezes produce a sea mist called *garúa*.

INTRODUCTORY SURVEY

RECENT HISTORY

For over the next twenty years following World War II (1939-1945) Peru had a series of governments. Civilian regimes were terminated prematurely by military coups in 1948, 1962, and 1968. The 1948 coup was followed by eight years of military rule under General Manuel A. Odría. The 1968 coup inaugurated ten years of military government that implemented socialist-style economic reforms.

Peru returned to civilian government with the elections of 1980 in which former president Fernando Belaúnde Terry was returned to office. During Belaúnde's administration, a small guerrilla group, Shining Path (Sendero Luminoso) began operating openly in the Andes. The government's campaign against terrorism beginning in 1983 and continuing through 1985 resulted in the disappearance of thousands, charges of mass killings, and the granting of unlimited power to the armed forces.

The election of 1985 was historic in two ways: it was the first peaceful transfer of power in forty years and it brought into office the first president from the leftist American Popular Revolutionary Alliance (APRA) since the party's founding in 1924. The economic policies of the new president Alán García Pérez were initially successful but Peru's economic troubles persisted. After an initial boom industrial production began to sag and food shortages became common. By 1990 inflation had climbed to four-digit levels.

Meanwhile the Shining Path escalated its attacks, coming down from the mountains and striking at urban and suburban targets around Lima and Callao. In response García authorized a set of brutal counter-rebel campaigns.

By 1990 neither APRA nor the AP (the Popular Action Party of Belaúnde) had popular support. In a surprise turn of events, Alberto Fujimori, the son of Japanese immigrants, defeated conservative novelist Mario Vargas Llosa. Fujimori immediately imposed harsh economic measures designed to curb inflation. These policies caused considerable economic disruption but did reduce inflation to pre-1988 levels.

Fujimori moved aggressively to combat the Shining Path and other guerrilla groups but violence continued, human rights deteriorated, and the military became stronger. Fujimori also became more and more isolated politically shuttin down Congress and refusing to recognize any judicial decisions. A border war with Ecuador in 1995 boosted Fujimori's popularity to help him win a second term.

A two-year recession from 1997-1999 left widespread unemployment and had left one of two Peruvians living in poverty by mid-1999. Fujimori was under great international pressure to rectify undemocratic strong-arm conduct. Concerns arose about the erosion of democracy and rule of law in Peru. Though winning a third term as president in the 2000 elections Fugimori resigned under pressure in November 2000 under charges of corruption in his administration.

GOVERNMENT

Peru operates under a December 1993 constitution. The president, elected by popular vote for a five-year term, is both chief of state and head of government. The president appoints the Council of Ministers. There is a prime minister but he does not exercise executive power. This power is in the hands of the president. The legislative branch is the 120-seat unicameral Democratic Constituent Congress. Members are elected by popular vote to serve five-year terms.

Judiciary

Peru's highest judicial body, the sixteen-member Supreme Court, sits at Lima and has national jurisdiction. The nine-member Court of Constitutional Guarantees rules on human rights cases. Superior courts, sitting in the departmental capitals, hear appeals from the provincial courts of first instance that are divided into civil, penal, and special chambers.

As of 1993 approximately 70 percent of the judges and prosecutors had been appointed by President Fujimori after his seizure of all government powers in 1992, and they never were confirmed by Congress. Despite constitutional reforms many accused persons (especially those accused of drug trafficking or terrorism) may spend months or even years in prison before they are brought to trial.

Political Parties

The two major parties following April 1995 elections for the Congress were Change 90-New Majority (C90/NM) with sixty-seven seats and Union for Peru (UPP) with seventeen seats. The American Popular Revolutionary Alliance (Alianza Popular Revolucionaria Americana-APRA), founded in 1924 and legalized in 1956 and traditionally opposed to military governments, took eight seats. At least seven other parties won seats including the Popular Action Party (AP) with four seats and the rightist Popular Christian Party with three.

DEFENSE

Two years of military service are obligatory and universal, but only a limited number of men between the ages of twenty and twenty-five are drafted. There are 188,000 army reservists.

The total strength of the armed forces in 2000 was 115,000 (including 64,000 draftees). Army personnel numbered 75,000, navy 25,000 (including 3,000 marines), and air force 15,000. About 66,000 men make up the national police. In 1998 Peru spent approximately $913 million or 1.4 percent of GDP on defense.

The armed forces contend with approximately 2,000armed guerrillas of the Shining Path and 600 terrorists of the Tupac Amaru movement.

ECONOMIC AFFAIRS

Since World War II the Peruvian economy has developed rapidly exhibiting a rate of growth that has been among the highest in Latin America. The strength of Peru's economy lies in its natural resources. Silver and gold were the prized commodities of colonial Peru. In more recent times lead, copper, zinc, iron ore, and petroleum have become important exports.

In the early 1990s the Peruvian economy came out of recession as a result of an increase in foreign investment. In 1996 the economy grew by 2.8%, marking the fourth year in a row for real economic growth. The government has continued to reduce the annual rate of inflation. Annual inflation went down from 7,000 percent in 1990 to 40 percent in 1993 to 11.8 percent in 1996. The government has stressed an increasingly market-oriented economy with major privatizations in mining, electricity, and telecommunications industry. Although the Peruvian economy grew by 7.3 percent in 1997, growth slowed in 1998 and 1999 to an estimated 1.8 percent and 3.8%, respectively. A combination of El Nino weather that hurt the fishing and agricultural industries, and the Asian financial crisis that depressed metal prices, contributed to the Peruvian economic downturn. Lima did manage to complete negotiations for an Extended Fund Facility with the IMF in June 1999. The 2000 elections felt the discontent with the economic downturn pressure. Nevertheless recovery of the fishing sector and world improved commodity prices and improved the growth forecast for 2000.

Public Finance

The central government publishes an annual budget representing the government's consolidated accounts (including budgetary and extrabudgetary transactions). Indirect taxes including import and export duties constitute the major source of government revenues.

In 1990 the Fujimori administration began to pursue tighter fiscal policies and attempted to avoid domestic financing of the deficit. The consolidated public sector deficit, which in 1990 was 6.5 percent of GDP, fell to 2.5% by 1992 despite the suspension of most foreign financing after the April 5 coup. The IMF program allowed a foreign-financed deficit of 2.9 percent of GPD in 1993 for increased social sector spending and investment in infrastructure. However with lower than expected foreign financing and tax collection the deficit that could be maintained while meeting the public sector external debt obligations was only equivalent to about 2 percent of GDP. By August 1993 the government had gained $452 million through the privatization of fifteen state enterprises.

The privatization of state enterprises fattened the government coffers between 1992 and 2000. The budget deficit for 2000 was 2.5 percent of GDP due to a rise in public sector wages of 16 percent and lower than expected revenues from privatization that year.

The U.S. Central Intelligence Agency estimated that in 1996 government revenues totaled approximately $8.5 billion and expenditures $9.3 billion. External debt totaled $31 billion by 1998 estimates.

Income

In 1999 Peru's gross domestic product (GDP) was estimated at $116 billion, or about $4,420 per capita. The 1999 estimated growth rate of the GDP was 2.4 percent and inflation was down to 5.5%. The 1998 contribution by sector was agriculture 13%, industry 42%, and services 45%.

Industry

Peru's sustained economic growth has been the result of a well-diversified economic base. In 1996 the most dynamic area was agriculture with crop production rising by 7 percent due to significant increases in industrial crops like cotton, soybean, tea, and asparagus. Industries showing important growth during the late 1990s were the mining of metals, petroleum, and construction. In 1998 it was estimated that an average of eleven new oil wells would be drilled per year until 2003. Growth in construction skyrocketed by 12% with projects related to repair of damage in El Nino.

Other major industries include fishing, textiles, clothing, food processing, steel, shipbuilding, and metal fabrication.

Banking and Finance

The Central Reserve Bank, the sole bank of issue, was established in Lima in 1931 to succeed the old Reserve Bank. Also created in 1931 was the Superintendency of Banks and Insurance, an agency of the Ministry of Finance that defines procedure and obligations of banking institutions and has control of all banks. The government-owned National Bank (Banco de la Nación) not only acts as the government's tax collector and financial agent, but also is Peru's largest commercial bank. Another government agency, the Caja de Ahorros, provides secured loans to low-income borrowers. There are at least twenty-five commercial banks in Peru.

Peru's banking sector has grown rapidly as a result of the economic recovery and capital inflows into the financial system. In 1987 the president of Peru was contemplating nationalizing the entire system. Shortly after his election Mr. Fujimori decreed the abolition of the state's development and mortgage credit banks. Today only the development finance corporation, Cofide, still exists but as a second-tier bank channeling funds from other institutions and without the powers to raise financing on its own account. Along with the subsidized state development banks, a host of savings and loans cooperatives have disappeared, victims of financial mismanagement, hyperinflation, and embezzlement. With them went the savings of many lower- and middle-class Peruvians who have been left with a distrust of the financial system.

Financial operations and assets remain concentrated: four banks account for almost three-quarters of all deposits in the system. Even though deposits in the banking system have almost doubled since 1990, Peru is severely underbanked.

The privately owned Lima Stock Exchange (Bolsa de Valores de Lima-BVL) regulates the sale of listed securities. At the end of 1996 234 companies were listed on the BVL.

Economic Development

The decade of the 1990s, with an Administration in favor of a market economy, has attracted more investment into Peru's economy. With foreign capital flowing in recent years Peru was poised for economic recovery. Privatization and the rapidly growing economy are providing the government with funds to spend on infrastructure and social programs.

In August of 1990 the government began to implement an economic program based on an (1) economic stabilization plan, (2) a structural reform program and (3) a set of initiatives aimed at reintegrating the Peruvian economy into the international economic system. As a direct result economic growth in the 1990s was strong.

The economic stabilization plan focuses on achieving an inflation rate comparable to international levels and fostering an environment favorable for savings, investment and sustained economic growth. The plan is based on strict fiscal discipline in accordance with an austere monetary policy. The inflation rate was about 6 percent in 1999. Structural reforms resulted in capital amounting to $7 billion between 1991 and 1999 resulting in massive inflows of foreign investment.

The reinsertion of Peru into thc international financial system beginning in 1991 is intended to restore normal relations between the country and its international creditors. Up to the present Peru has normalized its relations with multilateral bodies and the Paris Club and is in the process of doing the same with the commercial banks.

SOCIAL WELFARE

Workers receive benefits covering disability, medical attention, hospitalization, maternity, old age, retirement, and widows' and orphans' benefits. Working mothers are entitled to maternity leave of ninety days at 100 percent pay.

Women are often kept from leadership roles in the public and private sectors by the force of tradition although they are legally equal under the constitution.

The government, Shining Path terrorists, and the Tupac Amaru Revolutionary Movement have committed human rights violations.

Healthcare

Although Peru has made significant advances toward reducing epidemic disease, improving sanitation, and expanding medical facilities, much remains to be done. Health services are concentrated around metropolitan Lima. There were eleven physicians per 10,000 people in 1997 and about 75 percent of the population had access to health care services. In 1995 there were thirteen hospital beds per 1,000 people. A General Health Law enacted in 1997 restructured and reformed the healthcare sector.

Leading causes of death in 1998 were respirators infections, intestinal infectious diseases, circulatory and cardiovascular disease, and tuberculosis. There were about 26,000 war-related deaths in Peru from 1983 to 1992. In 2000 average life expectancy is estimated at seventy years.

Housing

Successive governments since the 1950s have recognized the importance of slum clearance and public housing programs in combating disease and high mortality rates. Most housing development programs carried out by the government and by private enterprise have been in the Lima area. In rural areas a conservative estimate of the housing shortage runs to a minimum of 700,000. The total housing stock numbered 4.9 million in 1985.

EDUCATION

Education is free and compulsory for children aged six to fifteen. In 2000 the adult illiteracy rate was estimated at 10.1 percent (5.3 percent for men and 14.6 percent for women). A 1972 law established Quechua and Aymará as languages of instruction for non-Spanish-speaking Amerindians especially in the lowest grades.

In 1998 there were over four million pupils. The number of secondary school students in 1997 was almost two million with 106,614 teachers. The total higher education enrollment in 1997 reached 657,586. There is a national university in practically every major city; the oldest is the National University of San Marcos of Lima originally founded in 1551.

2000 KEY EVENTS TIMELINE

January

- Lori Berenson, a New York native jailed as a terrorist, begins a hunger strike.

April

- President Alberto Fujimori fails to receive the necessary majority in the first round of presidential voting.

May

- In second round balloting that garners international condemnation, Alberto Fujimori wins a third term with 51 percent of the vote.

June

- Presidential challenger Alejandro Toledo meets with representatives of the Organization of American States.

July

- Only two heads of state, Hugo Banzer of Bolivia and Gustavo Noboa of Ecuador, accept invitations to attend President Alberto K. Fujimori's inauguration on July 28. Riots take place on the day of his inauguration, protesting the fraudulent election.

August

- On August 29 President Alberto Fujimori's government is suspected in the smuggling of 10,000 Kalashnikov rifles from Jordan to Marxist guerrillas in Colombia in 1998.

September

- A video tape is aired on Peruvian cable television channel Canal N on September 15 that allegedly shows President Alberto K. Fujimori's party bribing a member of the opposition Peru Possible Party. Alberto Kouri (the man who was bribed) and the majority of the Peru Possible party, including president of the party Alejandro Toledo on August 8, then joined Fujimori's party just before the elections, swinging the vote to Fujimori's favor.
- President Fujimori instructs his cabinet on September 17 to begin an election process to vote in a new president due to charges of corruption. He dismantles his National Intelligence Service, and will not run for president. Rumors fly about a possible military coup, but the military claims that it will back the new elections.

October

- Former intelligence chief Vladimiro Montesinos returns to Peru under suspicion that he may plan a military coup, and Vice President Francisco Tudela resigns October 23.
- Sixty soldiers mutiny October 29 following President Alberto Fujimori's military cabinet shuffle.

November

- A judge orders Vladimiro Montesinos' arrest during the first week of November, after President Alberto Fujimori claims that Mr. Montesinos has $50 million from financial fraud stashed in a Swiss bank account.
- President Alberto Fujimori flees to Japan and resigns. Congress declares him "morally unfit" to rule, November 21. Valentin Paniagua is made interim president by the Peruvian Congress, November 22.

December

- Former President Fujimori refuses to return to Peru for trial, December 1.

ANALYSIS OF EVENTS: 2000

BUSINESS AND THE ECONOMY

Peru's ongoing political crisis—brought to a head by the resignation of President Alberto Fujimori late in 2000—shattered confidence in the economy, and forced Peruvian officials to reassure investors that its policies would remain in place despite new presidential elections scheduled for April 8, 2001. In October the United States and the agency, Standard & Poor's, showed concern about the nation's stability when the chief of intelligence and key presidential advisor, Vladimiros Montesinos, returned to Peru after temporary exile in Panama. In the meantime, President Alberto Fujimori told the Inter-American Development Bank that Peru's economic situation remained sound despite the political crisis. Fujimori's government expected a growth rate of at least 4 percent in 2000, even though a rising budget deficit remained a problem. Peru was seeking $320 million in social development loans. Fujimori's minister of economy, Carlos Boloña tried to calm falling markets by reassuring investors that economic reforms promised in August would continue. They included privatization of several state-owned enterprises. Peru hoped that a natural gas project, known as Camisea, would attract $2.5 billion in foreign investment, helping the country reverse its external deficit.

GOVERNMENT AND POLITICS

For a decade, whether he was leading the fight against leftist insurgents, quashing his political opponents, or neutralizing family members who challenged his authority, President Fujimori always appeared to be in complete control of his nation. The authoritarian Fujimori had managed to sidestep accusations of human rights violations, nepotism, government fraud, election fraud, and the derision of detractors within Peru and the international community. But by late 1999, even supportive U.S. officials had began to worry at the erosion of democracy in Peru and sent strong warnings to Fujimori to change his ways. Fujimori had managed to win two elections, but had become increasingly more authoritarian and less tolerant of dissent. Through political machinations, he engineered an unprecedented run for a third term in 2000, much to the consternation of his critics.

Yet the April 2000 elections and major political events that followed later in the year proved too damaging, even for the slippery Fujimori. Assailed from all sides, Fujimori announced in September that he would step down as president as early as July 2001, and called for early presidential elections four years ahead of schedule. The announcement stunned Peruvians, who feared a military coup would follow political instability. At the center of the maelstrom was the shadowy Vladimiro Montesinos, head of the nation's intelligence service, and Fujimori's right-hand man.

Fujimori's authoritarian hold on power began to unravel during the presidential campaign of 2000. The opposition was fractured, and no viable candidate had emerged to challenge Fujimori, who remained a popular figure among many voters. Unexpectedly, a strong candidate (much like Fujimori's own sudden appearance on the political scene ten years earlier) materialized to challenge Fujimori in the race for president. Alejandro Toledo, an Amerindian of modest means, quickly established himself as Fujimori's main opponent. Toledo's father was a bricklayer, and his mother sold fish at a street market. Despite his family's modest economic means, Toledo managed to earn scholarships to study in the United States, receiving degrees from Stanford University in California. It was an irresistible story, and his campaign managers touted Toledo's rise from shoeshine boy to official at the World Bank.

Toledo's challenge for the presidency was met by one of the dirtiest political campaigns in Peru's history. The government-controlled television stations and newspapers waged a massive campaign against Toledo, who had little access to the media. Before the April 9 elections were held, the United States and the Organization of American States (OAS) expressed concern about serious breaches in the electoral system. Before the final tally, the OAS said the election was compromised and demanded a second round. The United States warned Peru that economic sanctions would follow a Fujimori victory. After a long delay in the vote counting, the electoral board announced that Fujimori received 49.84 percent of the 50 percent majority vote needed to prevent a runoff election. Toledo received 40.31 percent. The government called for a run-off election in May. Toledo demanded to push the election date until June to fix serious electoral problems and ensure a clean election. His demands went unheard by the Fujimori administration, which insisted on the May date. One week before the election Toledo withdrew from the race, claiming conditions did not exist for a fair democratic election. In an interview with *El Pais,* an influential daily newspaper from Madrid, Spain, Toledo said Fujimori would not last a year in power if elected president.

In the May election almost half of Peruvians eligible to vote defaced their ballots or simply refused to vote. Officially the ballot gave Fujimori 50.8 percent of the vote, while Toledo, who had not been able to remove his name from the ballot, received 17.6 percent. Immediately after the tally, the United States condemned Fujimori as a threat to democracy. Later, the United States softened its stance against its long-term ally in the war on illicit drugs. Peruvians seemed resigned to another Fujimori term, but civil disorders during his inauguration showed the president remained vulnerable to growing unrest. During his acceptance speech, six Peruvians died and hundreds were injured or arrested during violent demonstrations in Lima and several other major cities.

In the end it was not the election that doomed Fujimori's presidency. It was Vladimiro Montesinos, the Rasputin of Peruvian politics. For the past decade Montesinos had lurked in the background, the real power behind Fujimori according to many analysts. Montesinos was credited with Peru's successful offensive against leftist rebels, and the country's attempt to control the drug trade. He was Fujimori's main advisor, head of the nation's intelligence service and the president's liaison to the powerful military. Over the years, serious accusations mounted against Montesinos—from protecting drug lords to ordering death-squad killings. Montesinos was the corrupter who did Fujimori's dirty work, including fixing elections and paying off legislators to support the presidency. Montesinos remained untouched by the accusations, as pressure built to neutralize his powers.

In August Montesinos was caught in a major mistake when he disclosed the break-up of an arms-smuggling ring that had acquired in 10,000 Russian rifles in Jordan and sold them to Colombian leftist rebels. But Jordanian officials said they had legally sold the weapons to the Peruvian military, an account confirmed by an unnamed U.S. official. Several military officers and Montesinos came under suspicion for the sale. Yet, the worst for Montesinos was yet to come.

On September 14 legislator Fernando Olivera released a video that allegedly showed Montesinos bribing an opposition congressman with $15,000 in cash to switch parties. The nearly one-hour video shocked Peruvians, who had always suspected that congressmen switched parties for money. Fujimori had survived serious accusations before, but the tape was too powerful to brush aside. Two days later, on September 16, Fujimori announced he would give up his office and call for early elections. He also said he would de-activate the National Intelligence Service, the domain of Montesinos. Confusing events followed, with Fujimori, Montesinos, and the armed forces caught in a power struggle. Montesinos vanished from the public eye, and Fujimori traveled to the United States seeking support for his government. After meeting with U.S. officials, Fujimori guaranteed stability and order during the transition period. Yet, Montesinos was still at large, and Peruvians believed a military coup was under preparation.

Montesinos finally appeared in Panama where he sought political asylum. Peruvians seemed relieved that Montesinos was gone, and talks about a coup diminished after the military showed public support for Fujimori. But Montesinos unexpectedly returned to Peru in late October, claiming that his life was in danger. His return forced Fujimori to hold a series of meetings with the military's top leaders. On October 25 Fujimori struck a deal with the Organization of American States to hold presidential elections by April 8, 2001. But less than a month later, Fujimori resigned from Japan, where he was visiting. On November 21, the leader of the Congress, Valentin Paniagua became interim president. Among his first actions was to appoint former U.N. Secretary-General Javier Perez de Cuellar to be prime minister and cabinet chief.

CULTURE AND SOCIETY

The U.S. explorer Geme Savoy announced he had located what appeared to be the ancient remains of the city of Cajamarquilla, one of the great cities of the Chachapoyas peoples. The twenty-five-square mile site is located in northern Peru. Archeologists said they found stone roads weaving through massive terrace cliffs, ornate stone work, and at least thirty-six burial towers.

In October the Peruvian government accused former Swedish ambassador Ulf Lewin of illegally removing archeological artifacts from the country and selling them abroad. The Peruvian government stripped Lewin of all medals and awards given to him during his tenure in the Andean nation. The Swedish government had not responded to the accusations.

DIRECTORY

CENTRAL GOVERNMENT

Head of State

President
Valentin Paniagua Corazao, Office of the President

Prime Minister
Javier Perez de Cuellar, Office of the Prime Minister

Ministers

Minister of Agriculture
Carlos Amat Y Le Chavez, Ministry of Agriculture, Pje. Zela S/N Jesús María, Lima 11, Peru
PHONE: +51 (1) 4333034; 4332271
FAX: +51 (1) 4314771
E-MAIL: postmast@oia.minag.gob.pe

Minister of Defense
Walter Ledesma Rebaza, Ministry of Defense

Minister of Economy and Finance
Javier Silva Ruete, Ministry of Economy and Finance, Jr. Junín 319, Lima 1, Peru
PHONE: +51 (1) 4273930
FAX: +51 (1) 4282509
E-MAIL: postmaster@mef.gob.pe

Minister of Education
Marcial Rubio Correa, Ministry of Education, Calle Van de Velde N° 160, San Borja, Lima, Perú
PHONE: +51 (1) 4353900
E-MAIL: postmaster@minedu.gob.pe

Minister of Energy and Mines
Carlos Herrera Descalzi, Ministry of Energy and Mines

Minister of Fisheries
Ludwig Meier Cornejo, Ministry of Fisheries, 96 Calle Uno Oeste, N° 50, Urb. Corpac, San Isidro, Lima, Peru
PHONE: +51 (1) 2243336; 2243329

Minister of Foreign Affairs
Javier Perez de Cuellar, Ministry of Foreign Affairs

Minister of Industry, Tourism, Integration, and International Trade Negotiations
Juan Inchaustegui Vargas, Ministry of Industry, Tourism, Integration, and International Trade Negotiations, Calle Uno 50, San Isidro, Lima, Peru
PHONE: +51 (1) 2243347

Minister of Interior
Ketin Vidal Herrera, Ministry of Interior

Minister of Justice
Diego Garcia Sayan, Ministry of Justice, Scipión Llona 350, Miraflores, Lima 18, Perú
PHONE: +51 (1) 4404310; 4417320
E-MAIL: webmaster@wwwminjus.gob.pe

Minister of Labor
Jaime Zavala Costa, Ministry of Labor, Av. Salaverry 655, Jesús María, Lima, Peru
PHONE: +51 (1) 4332512; 3307382
FAX: +51 (1) 4242622
E-MAIL: prodlab@mtps.gob.pe

Minister of Presidency
Emilio Navarro Castaneda, Ministry of Presidency

Minister for Promotion of Women and Human Development
Susana Villaran de la Puente, Ministry for the Promotion of Women and Human Development, Jr. Camaná 616, Lima, Peru
PHONE: +51 (1) 4289800
FAX: +51 (1) 4261665
E-MAIL: postmaster@lima.promudeh.gob.pe

Minister of Public Health
Eduardo Pretell Zarate, Ministry of Public Health, Av. Salaverry cuadra 8 S/N, Jesús María, Lima, Peru
E-MAIL: webmaster@minsa.gob.pe

Minister of Transport, Communications, Housing, and Construction
Luis Ortega Navarrete, Ministry of Transport, Communications, Housing, and Construction, Av. 28 de Julio # 800, Lima, Peru
PHONE: +51 (1) 4337800

POLITICAL ORGANIZATIONS

Unión Nacional Odriísta (UNO)

TITLE: Leader
NAME: Fernando Noriega

Renovación (National Renewal)

TITLE: Leader
NAME: Rafael Rey Rey

Renacimiento Andino (Andean Rebirth)

E-MAIL: renandino@wanka.net.pe
TITLE: Leader
NAME: Ciro Gálvez Herrera

Partido Revolucionario de los Trabajadores-PRT (Revolutionary Workers' Party)

Plaza 2 de Mayo 38, Apdo 2449, Lima 100 Peru
TITLE: Leader
NAME: Hugo Blanco

Partido Popular Cristiano-PPC (Popular Christian Party)

Avda Alfonso Ugarte 1484, Lima, Peru
PHONE: +51 (1) 4238723
FAX: +51 (1) 4236582

Partido Obrero Revolucionario Marxista-Partido Socialista de los Trabajadores (Marxist Revolutionary Workers' Party-Socialist Workers' Party)

Jirón Apurimac 465, Lima 1, Peru
PHONE: +51 (1) 4280443
TITLE: Leader
NAME: Ricardo Napuri

Partido Liberal-PL (Liberal Party)

TITLE: Leader
NAME: Miguel Cruchaga

Partido Demócrata Cristiano-PDC (Christian Democratic Party)

PHONE: +51 (1) 4238042
TITLE: Leader
NAME: Carlos Blancas Bustamante

Partido Comunista de Peru-PCP (Communist Party of Peru)

TITLE: Leader
NAME: Ruben Abimael Guzman Reinoso

Nueva Mayoría (New Majority)

TITLE: Leader
NAME: Jaime Yoshiyama Tanaka

Movimiento de Bases Hayistas-MBH (Hayist Movement)

Pasaje Velarde 180, Lima, Peru
TITLE: Leader
NAME: Andrés Townsend Ezcurra

Izquierda Unida-IU (Unified Left)

Avda Grau 184, Lima 23, Peru
TITLE: Leader
NAME: Gustavo Mohome

Izquierda Socialista (Socialist Left)

TITLE: Leader
NAME: Alfonso Barrantes Lingán

Coordinación Democrática (Democratic Coordinator)

TITLE: Leader
NAME: Jose Barba Caballero

Confluencia Socialista (Socialist Alliance)

TITLE: Leader
NAME: Jose Barba Caballero

Cambio 90 (Change 90)

TITLE: Leader
NAME: Alberto Fujimori

Alianza Popular Revolucionaria Americana-APRA (American Popular Revolutionary Alliance)

Avda Alfonso Ugarte 1012, Lima 5, Peru
PHONE: +51 (1) 4313909
TITLE: Leader
NAME: Armando Villanueva del Campo

Acción Popular-AP (Popular Action)

Paseo Colón 218, Lima 1, Peru
PHONE: +51 (14) 404907
TITLE: Leader
NAME: Fernando Belaúnde Terry

Izquierda Nacionalista (Nationalist Left)

TITLE: Leader
NAME: Pedro Reynaldo Cáceres Velásquez

DIPLOMATIC REPRESENTATION

Embassies in Peru

Argentina
Av. 28 de Julio Nro. 828, Lima 01, Peru
PHONE: +51 (1) 4339966
FAX: +51 (1) 4330769

Canada
Calle Libertad No. 130, 18-1126 Miraflores, Lima 18, Peru
PHONE: +51 (1) 4444015
FAX: +51 (1) 4444347

People's Republic of China
Jr. José Granda No. 150, Apartado Postal 395, Lima 27, Peru
PHONE: +51 (1) 4429458
FAX: +51 (1) 4429467

France
Av. Arequipa No. 3415, Apartado Postal 607, Lima 27, Peru
PHONE: +51 (1) 2217837
FAX: +51 (1) 4213693

Germany
Av. Arequipa No. 4210, Lima 18, Peru
PHONE: +51 (1) 4224919
FAX: +51 (1) 4226475

India
Magdalena del Mar, Lima 17, Perú
PHONE: +51 (1) 4602289
FAX: +51 (1) 4610374
E-MAIL: postmaster@indoperu.org.pe

Italy
Av. Gregorio Escobedo No. 298, Apartado Postal 11-0490, Lima 11, Peru
PHONE: +51 (1) 4632727
FAX: +51 (1) 4635317

Japan
Av. San Felipe Nro. 356, Apartado Postal 3708, Lima 11, Peru
PHONE: +51 (1) 4630000
FAX: +51 (1) 4630302

Russia
Av. Salaverry No. 3424, Lima 27, Peru
PHONE: +51 (1) 2640036
FAX: +51 (1) 2640130

United Kingdom
Edif. Pacífico-Washington, Natalio Sánchez No. 125, Piso 12, Apartado Postal 854, Lima 01, Peru
PHONE: +51 (1) 4334738
FAX: +51 (1) 4334735

United States
Avenida Encalada, Cuadra 17, Monterrico, P.O. Box 1995, Lima, Peru
PHONE: +51 (1) 4343000
FAX: +51 (1) 4343037
TITLE: Ambassador
NAME: Dennis C. Jett

JUDICIAL SYSTEM

Constitutional Court

Supreme Court of Justice

National Council of the Judiciary

BROADCAST MEDIA

Asociacion de Radio y Television del Peru (AR&TV)

Av. Roma 140, San Isidro, Lima 27, Peru
PHONE: +51 (1) 4703734
TITLE: President
CONTACT: Humberto Maldonado Balbin
LANGUAGE: Spanish

Cia Latinoamericana de Radiodifusion S.A.

Av. San Felipe 968, Jesus Maria, Lima 11, Peru
PHONE: +51 (1) 2191000
FAX: +51 (1) 2656660
LANGUAGE: Spanish

Instituto Nacional De Comunicacion Social

Jr. de la Union 264, Lima, Peru
CONTACT: Hernan Valdizan
LANGUAGE: Spanish

Ministerio De Transportes, Comunicaciones, Vivienday Construccion (Direccion General de Telecommunicaciones)

Av.28 de Julio 800, Lima 1, Peru
PHONE: +51 (1) 4337800
TITLE: Director of Telecommunications
CONTACT: Carlos A Romero Sanjines
LANGUAGE: Spanish

Radio La Oroya S.A.

Calle Lima 190, Tercer Piso Of. 3, Lima, Peru
PHONE: +51 (6) 4391401
FAX: +51 (6) 4391440
E-MAIL: rlofigu@net.cosapidata.com.pe

Radio Panamericana

Paseo Parodi 340, San Isidro, Lima, Peru
PHONE: +51 (1) 4226787
FAX: +51 (1) 4221182

Radio y Medios Deportivos Peruanos

Miguel Dasso 144-2A, San Isidro, Lima 27, Peru
PHONE: +51 (1) 2222353
FAX: +51 (1) 4405979

RPP Noticias

Radioprogrammes del Peru S.A., Alejandro Tirado 217, 7mo piso, Santa Beatriz, Lima, Peru
PHONE: +51 (1) 3301166
FAX: +51 (1) 4317516
LANGUAGE: Spanish

Union De Radioemisoras De Provincias Del Peru (UNRAP)

Mariano Carranza 754, Santa Beatriz, Lima 1, Peru
LANGUAGE: Spanish

Compania Latinoamericana de Radiodifusion S.A.

Av. San Felipe 968, Jesus Maria, Lima 11, Peru
PHONE: +51 (14) 707272
FAX: +51 (14) 712688

COLLEGES AND UNIVERSITIES

University Femenina-Sagrado Corazon

Av. Los Frutales S/N, La Molina Apdo. 3604, Lima, Peru

Universidad Nacional de Ucayali

Apdo. 90, Pucallpa, Peru

University Ricardo Palma, Surco

Apdo. 18-0131, Lima, Peru
PHONE: +51 (1) 2750460
FAX: +51 (1) 2750459
E-MAIL: postmaster@li.urp.edu.pe
WEBSITE: http://www.urp.edu.pe

Peruvian University Cayetano Heredia San Martin de Porres

Apdo. 5045, Lima, Peru
PHONE: +51 (1) 3190000
FAX: +51 (1) 4823435
E-MAIL: postmaster@upch.edu.pe
WEBSITE: http://www.upch.edu.pe

National University Federico Villarreal San Miguel

Stroll Federico Villarreal No. 285, San Miguel, Peru
PHONE: +51 (14) 4641424
FAX: +51 (14) 4644370
E-MAIL: postmaster@unfv-bib.edu.pe
WEBSITE: http://www.unfv-bib.edu.pe

University of San Martin de Porres, Lima

Av. Las Caladnrias S/N, Santa Anita, Lima, Peru
PHONE: +51 (1) 3620064
E-MAIL: admision@usmp.edu.pe
WEBSITE: http://www.usmp.edu.pe

University of the Pacific, Lima

Apdo. 4683, Lima 100, Peru
PHONE: +51 (1) 2190100; 4729635
E-MAIL: dri@up.edu.pe
WEBSITE: http://www.up.edu.pe

National University of San Antonio Abad, Cuzco

Apdo. 367, Cuzco, Peru
PHONE: +51 (84) 243836
E-MAIL: webmaster@unsaac.edu.pe
WEBSITE: http://www.unsaac.edu.pe

National University Hermilio Valdizan Huanuco

Jr Dos De Mayo No. 680, Apdo. 278, Huanuco, Peru
PHONE: +51 (64) 8092341
FAX: +51 (64) 8093360

National University of San Agustin Arequipa

Santa Catalina 117, Apdo. 23, Arequipa, Peru
PHONE: +51 (54) 237808
E-MAIL: sanagustin@unsa.wdu.pe
WEBSITE: http://www.unsa.edu.pe

National University of San Luis Gonzaga, Ica

Cajamarca 194, Ica, Peru
PHONE: +51 (34) 233201
FAX: +51 (34) 226036

National University Agraria La Molina

Av. the University S/N, La Molina, Apdo. 456, Lima, Peru
PHONE: +51 (1) 3495647
FAX: +51 (1) 4352260
WEBSITE: http://www.lamolina.edu.pe

National University of Callao

Ave Juan Pablo Ii S/N, Bellavista, Callao, Peru
PHONE: +51 (14) 4536387
FAX: +51 (14) 4296607
E-MAIL: vri@unac.edu.pe
WEBSITE: http://www.unac.edu.pe

Catholic University of Santa Maria

Urb. San Jose S/N Umacollo, Arequipa, Peru
PHONE: +51 (54) 251210
FAX: +51 (54) 252542
E-MAIL: ucsm@ucsm.edu.pe
WEBSITE: http://www.ucsm.edu.pe

National University of Altiplano, Puno

Avda Ejercito No. 329, Apdo 291, Puno, Peru
PHONE: +51 (54) 353471
FAX: +51 (54) 368590
E-MAIL: unap@unap.edu.pe
WEBSITE: http://www.unap.edu.pe

Private University of Tacna

Av. San Martin 361, Tacna, Peru
PHONE: +51 (54) 726881
FAX: +51 (54) 726881
E-MAIL: svorgas@heroica.upt.edu.pe
WEBSITE: http://www.upt.edu.pe

National University Jorge Basadre Grohmann, Tacna

Ave. Bolognesi/Av Pinto S/N, PO Box 316, Tacna, Peru
PHONE: +51 (54) 741405
FAX: +51 (54) 721385
WEBSITE: http://www.unjbg.edu.pe

National University of Central Peru

Calle Real 160 Casilla Postal 138, Huancayo 570, Junin, Peru

PHONE: +51 (64) 233032
WEBSITE: http://www.uncp.edu.pe

National University of Agriculture of La Selva, Tingo Maria

Apdo. 156, Tingo Maria, Huanuco, Peru
PHONE: +51 (64) 562341
FAX: +51 (64) 561156
E-MAIL: postmaster@unas.edu.pe
WEBSITE: http://www.unas.edu.pe

National University Pedro Ruiz Gallo, Lambayeque

Juan XXIII 391, Lambayeque, Peru
PHONE: +51 (74) 283281
FAX: +51 (74) 283146
E-MAIL: lsalvador22@hotmail.rcp.net.pe
WEBSITE: http://www.lampayec.rcp.net.pe/unprg

National University of Piura

Av Ramon Mugica, 131, Apdo. 333, Piura, Peru
PHONE: +51 (74) 307777
FAX: +51 (74) 308888
E-MAIL: rector@udep.edu.pe
WEBSITE: http://www.udep.edu.pe

National University of Engineering San Martin de Pores

Av. Tupac Amaru No. 210, Lima, Peru
PHONE: +51 (1) 811 035
E-MAIL: email@uni.edu.pe
WEBSITE: http://www.uni.edu.pe

National University of San Cristobal de Huamanga, Ayacucho

Portal Independencia No. 57, Apdo 220, Ayacucho, Peru
PHONE: +51 (34) 912522
FAX: +51 (34) 912510

National University of the Peruvian Amazon, Iquitos

Sargento Lores 385, Apdo 496, Iquitos, Loreto, Peru
PHONE: +51 (94) 235351
FAX: +51 (94) 233657

National University of San Martin

Martinez De Compagnon 527, Apdo 239, Tarapoto, San Martin, Peru
PHONE: +51 (94) 524253
FAX: +51 (94) 524253
E-MAIL: mleon@unsm.edu.pe
WEBSITE: http://www.unsm.edu.pe

University of Lima

Avda Javier Prado Este S/N, Monterrico Apdo. 852, Lima 100, Peru
PHONE: +51 (1) 4376767
FAX: +51 (1) 4378066
E-MAIL: duii@ulima.edu.pe
WEBSITE: http://www.ulma.edu.pe

National University of Cajamarca

Cajamarca, Peru
PHONE: +51 (44) 822346
FAX: +51 (44) 923356
WEBSITE: http://www.unc.edu.pe

Inca Private University Garcilaso de la Vega, Linee

Av. Arequipa, San Isidro, Lima 34, Peru
PHONE: +51 (1) 711421

National University of San Marcos, Lima

Av. Republica De Chile 295, Of. 506 Casilla, Lima 454, Peru
PHONE: +51 (1) 314629
E-MAIL: rrpp@unmsm.edu.pe
WEBSITE: http://www.unmsm.edu.pe

National University Jose Faustino Sanchez Carrion, Huacho

Avda Grau 592 Of. 301, Huacho 81, Peru
PHONE: +51 (14) 324 741

NEWSPAPERS AND MAGAZINES

El Comercio

Empresa Editora El Comercio S.A., R. Rivera Navarrete 737 San Isidro, Lima 1, Peru
PHONE: +51(1) 2213687; 4415800; 4415850
FAX: +51 (1) 4417070; 2213672
E-MAIL: editor@comerioperu.com.pe; gquine@comercio.com.pe
WEBSITE: http://www.rcp.net.pe/elcomercio; http://www.elcomercioperu.com.pe
TITLE: Editor
CONTACT: Eduardo Carbajal
CIRCULATION: 185,000 (Daily); 200,000 (Sun)

Expresso

Editora Nacional S.A., Jr. Libertad 117, Miraflores, Lima 18, Peru

PHONE: +51 (14) 446866; 447088; 447083
FAX: +51 (14) 446861; 447118; 447117
E-MAIL: lili@ensa.com.pe; direccion@expresso.com.pe
WEBSITE: http://www.expreso.com.pe
TITLE: Ad Manager
CONTACT: Oscar Saettone
CIRCULATION: 139,000 (Daily); 230,000 (Sun)

Gestion

Corporacion Gestion S.A., Gral. Salaverry 156, Miraflores, Lima, Peru
PHONE: +51 (14) 4479564
FAX: +51 (14) 4476763
E-MAIL: gestion@gestion.com.pe; gestion@amauta.rcp.net.pe
WEBSITE: http://www.gestion.com.pe
TITLE: Editor
CONTACT: Julio Lira
CIRCULATION: 28,000

La Republica

Cia. Impresora Peruana S.A., Jiron Camana 320-332, Cercado, Lima 1, Peru
PHONE: +51 (14) 276455; 271724
FAX: +51 (14) 262449; 265678; 263053
E-MAIL: republ@amauta.rcp.net.pe
WEBSITE: http://www.ekeko.rcp.net.pe/larepublica; http://www.larepublica.com.pe
TITLE: Editor
CONTACT: Gustavo Mohme Llona
CIRCULATION: 95,000 (Daily); 110,000 (Sun)

Sintesis

Editorial Sintesis S.A., Ave. Las Camelias 491, 7mo piso, San Isidro, Lima 27, Peru
PHONE: +51 (1) 4213426
FAX: +51 (1) 4423489; 4213426; 4210848
WEBSITE: http://www.sintesis.com.pe
TITLE: Ad Manager
CONTACT: Carlos Eslava E.
CIRCULATION: 20,000

Almanaque Mundial

Editorial Televisa, 6355 NW 36th St., Miami FL 33166 USA
PHONE: (305) 8716400
FAX: (305) 8715026
CIRCULATION: 80,000
TYPE: General Interest

Cosas

Editorial Letras e imagenes, General Recavarren, 111-Miraflores, Lima. Peru
PHONE: +51 (1) 2411178
FAX: +51 (1) 4473776
E-MAIL: cosas@amauta.rcp.net.pe
WEBSITE: http://www.cosasperu.com
TITLE: Editor
CONTACT: Elizabeth Dulanto de Miro Quesada
CIRCULATION: 20,000
TYPE: General Interest

Sellecions Del Reader's Digest

RD Latinoamerica, S.A., 2655 LeJeune Rd., Ste. 301, Coral Gables FL 33134 USA
PHONE: (305) 4488233
FAX: (305) 4488234
TITLE: Editor
CONTACT: Audon Coria
CIRCULATION: 33,000
TYPE: Compilation of articles

PUBLISHERS

Centro del la Mujer Peruana Flora Tristan

Parque Hernan Velarde 42, Lima, Peru
PHONE: +51 (1) 4332765
FAX: +51 (1) 4339500
E-MAIL: postmast@flora.org.pe
TITLE: President
CONTACT: Cecilia Olea
SUBJECTS: Essays, Health and Sexual Reproductive Rights, Nutrition, Literature, Literary Criticism, Rural Development, Science (General), Women's Rights

Instituto de Estudios Peruanos

Horacio Urteaga 694, Jesus Maria, Lima, Peru
PHONE: +51 (1) 3326194
FAX: +51 (1) 3326173
E-MAIL: libreria@iep.org.pe
TITLE: Jefa de Libreria
CONTACT: Elizabeth Andrade
SUBJECTS: Anthropology, Archaeology, Developing Countries, Economics, Education, Ethnicity, Government, Political Science, Health, Nutrition, History, Social Sciences, Sociology, Technology, Women's Studies

Instituto Frances de Estudios Andinos IFEA

Contralmirante Montero 141, Miraflores, Lima, Peru
PHONE: +51 (1) 4476070
FAX: +51 (1) 4457650
E-MAIL: postmast@ifea.org.pe
TITLE: Director
CONTACT: Jean Vaches
SUBJECTS: Agriculture, Anthropology, Archaeology, Earth Sciences, Geography, Geology, History, Language Arts, Linguistics, Social Sciences, Sociology

Universidad de Lima-Fondo de Desarollo Editorial

Av. Javier Prado Este s/n Monterrico, Lima, Peru
PHONE: +51 (1) 4376767
FAX: +51 (1) 4378066
E-MAIL: fondo_ed@lima.edu.pe
WEBSITE: http://www.ulima.edu.pe
TITLE: Executive Director
CONTACT: Jose Valdizan Ayala
SUBJECTS: Communications, Computer Science, Economics, Engineering (General), Finance, Law, Management, Marketing, Psychology, Psychiatry, Radio, TV, Science (General)
TOTAL PUBLISHED: 120 print

RELIGIOUS ORGANIZATIONS

Buddhist

Templo Japones Zionzi
San Vincente de Sanete, Lima, Peru

Catholic

Arquidiocesis de Lima
Arzobispado de Lima, Plaza Mayor s/n., Apartado 1512, Lima, Peru
PHONE: +51 (1) 4275980, 4275986
FAX: +51 (1) 4271967

Conferencia Episcopal Peruana
Estados Unidos 838, Lima 11, Peru, Apartado 310, Lima 100, Peru
PHONE: +51 (1) 4631010
FAX: +51 (1) 4636125
E-MAIL: prensa@iglesiacatolica.org.pe

Diocesis del Callao
Jr. Bolognesi 283, Bellavista, Callao, Peru
PHONE: +51 (14) 4653575
FAX: +51 (14) 4654040

FURTHER READING

Articles

Gonzalez, David. "Peru Closing Bribery Case of Top Aide Now an Exile." *New York Times,* September 27, 2000, p. A7.

Krauss, Clifford. "Intelligence Chief Returns, Sending Peru into Disarray." *New York Times,* October 24, 2000, p. A3.

Taylor, Rober. "Stressed Democracies (Peru and Bolivia). *World Press Review,* June 2000, vol. 47, no. 6, p. 27.

Books

Adorno, Rolena. *Guaman Poma: Writing and Resistance in Colonial Peru.* 2d ed. Austin: University of Texas Press, 2000.

DeAngelis, Gina. *Francisco Pizarro and the Conquest of the Inca.* Philadelphia: Chelsea House Publishers, 2000. [juvenile]

Herndon, William Lewis. *Exploration of the Valley of the Amazon, 1851–1852.* New York: Grove Press, 2000.

Klarin, Peter F. *Peru: Society and Nationhood in the Andes.* New York: Oxford University Press, 2000.

Landau, Elaine. *Peru.* New York: Children's Press, 2000. [juvenile]

Morrison, Marion. *Peru.* New York: Children's Press, 2000. [juvenile]

Worth, Richard. *Pizarro and the Conquest of the Incan Empire in World History.* Berkeley Heights, NJ: Enslow Publishers, 2000. [juvenile]

Government Publications

Background Notes: Peru. Washington, DC: G.P.O., 2000.

PERU: STATISTICAL DATA

For sources and notes see "Sources of Statistics" at the front of each volume.

GEOGRAPHY

Geography

Area:

Total: 1,285,220 sq km.

Land: 1.28 million sq km.

Land boundaries:

Total: 5,536 km.

Border countries: Bolivia 900 km, Brazil 1,560 km, Chile 160 km, Colombia 1,496 km (est.), Ecuador 1,420 km.

Coastline: 2,414 km.

Climate: varies from tropical in east to dry desert in west; temperate to frigid in Andes.

Terrain: western coastal plain (costa), high and rugged Andes in center (sierra), eastern lowland jungle of Amazon Basin (selva).

Natural resources: copper, silver, gold, petroleum, timber, fish, iron ore, coal, phosphate, potash, hydropower.

Land use:

Arable land: 3%

Permanent crops: 0%

Permanent pastures: 21%

Forests and woodland: 66%

Other: 10% (1993 est.).

HUMAN FACTORS

Demographics (A)

	1990	1995	1998	2000	2010	2020	2030	2040	2050
Population	21,989	24,556	26,049	27,013	31,472	35,566	39,253	42,198	44,393
Life expectancy - males	63.6	66.2	67.0	67.6	70.3	72.6	74.6	76.2	77.5
Life expectancy - females	68.0	70.8	71.8	72.5	75.5	78.1	80.2	81.9	83.4
Birth rate (per 1,000)	31.7	28.0	25.9	24.5	19.8	17.6	15.4	13.9	13.1
Death rate (per 1,000)	7.2	6.2	6.0	5.8	5.6	5.7	6.3	7.3	8.5
Women of reproductive age (15-49 yrs.)	5,377	6,147	6,629	6,933	8,474	9,544	10,059	10,219	10,027
Fertility rate	4.1	3.5	3.2	3.0	2.4	2.2	2.0	2.0	2.0

Except as noted, values for vital statistics are in thousands; life expectancy is in years.

Health Personnel

	National Data	World Data (wtd ave)
Total health expenditure as a percentage of GDP, 1990-1998[a]		
Public sector	2.2	2.5
Private sector	3.4	2.9
Total[b]	5.6	5.5
Health expenditure per capita in U.S. dollars, 1990-1998[a]		
Purchasing power parity	240	561
Total	141	483
Availability of health care facilities per 100,000 people		
Hospital beds 1990-1998[a]	150	330
Doctors 1992-1995[a]	73	122
Nurses 1992-1995[a]	49	248

Health Indicators

	National Data	World Data
Life expectancy at birth (years)		
1980	60	61
1998	69	67
Daily per capita supply of calories		
1970	2,198	2,358
1997	2,302	2,791
Daily per capital supply of protein		
1997 (grams)	60	74
Total fertility rate (births per woman)		
1980	4.5	3.7
1998	3.1	2.7
Population with access (%)		
To safe water (1990-96)	80	NA
To sanitation (1990-96)	44	NA
People living with (1997)		
Tuberculosis (cases per 100,000)	172.6	60.4
Malaria (cases per 100,000)	754.1	42.2
HIV/AIDS (% aged 15 - 49 years)	0.56	0.99

Infants and Malnutrition

	National Data	World Data (wtd ave)
Under 5 mortality rate (1989)	54	NA
% of infants with low birthweight (1992-98)[1]	11	17
Births attended by skilled health staff (% of total births 1996-98)	56	52
% fully immunized at 1 year of age (1995-98)[1]		
TB	96	82
DPT	99	77
Polio	99	77
Measles	90	74
Prevalence of child malnutrition (1992-98)[1] (based on weight for age, % of children under 5 years)	8	30

Ethnic Division

Amerindian 45%
Mestizo 37%
White 15%
Black, Japanese, Chinese, and other 3%

People of Mestizo ethnicity have mixed Amerindian and white ancestry.

Religion

Roman Catholic 90%

Major Languages

Spanish (official), Quechua (official), Aymara.

EDUCATION

Public Education Expenditures

	1980	1997
Public expenditures on education as % of GNP	3.1	2.9
Expenditures per student as % of GNP per capita		
Primary	7.2	NA
Secondary	11.3	6.8
Tertiary	5.2	15.4
Teachers' compensation as % of total current education expenditures	59.4	40.1
Pupils per teacher at the primary level	NA	28
Duration of primary education in years	NA	6
World data for comparison		
Public expenditures on education as % of GNP (mean)	3.9	4.8
Pupils per teacher at the primary level (wtd ave)	NA	33
Duration of primary education in years (mean)	NA	9

Educational Attainment (A)

Age group (1993) . . . . .25+
Population of this age group 9,394,681
Highest level attained (%)
No schooling 16.4
First level
Not completed 34.7
Completed . . . . .NA
Entered second level 27.2
Entered post-secondary .20.5

Literacy Rates (A)

In thousands and percent	1990	1995	2000	2010
Illiterate population (15+ yrs.)	1,847	1,736	1,627	1,286
Literacy rate - total adult pop. (%)	86.3	88.7	90.7	94.1
Literacy rate - males (%)	93.0	94.5	95.7	97.7
Literacy rate - females (%)	79.5	83.0	85.7	90.5

Libraries

National Libraries **1992**
Administrative Units 1
Service Points or Branches .1
Number of Volumes (000) 3,890
Registered Users (000) 8.7
Loans to Users (000) . . . . .NA
Total Library Staff . . . . .NA

GOVERNMENT & LAW

Military Affairs (A)

	1990	1992	1995	1996	1997
Military expenditures					
Current dollars (mil.)	623	744	970	964	1,350
1997 constant dollars (mil.)	730	825	1,000	980	1,350
Armed forces (000)	125	112	115	115	115
Gross national product (GNP)					
Current dollars (mil.)	34,000	40,400	56,000	58,500	63,800
1997 constant dollars (mil.)	39,900	44,800	57,900	59,500	63,800
Central government expenditures (CGE)					
1997 constant dollars (mil.)	6,750	7,460	9,980	8,510	10,100
People (mil.)	21.8	23.0	24.6	25.1	25.6
Military expenditure as % of GNP	1.8	1.8	1.7	1.6	2.1
World data on military expenditure as % of GNP	4.5	3.4	2.7	2.6	2.6
Military expenditure as % of CGE	10.8	11.1	10.1	11.5	13.4
World data on military expenditure as % of CGE	17.0	12.5	10.5	10.3	10.2
Military expenditure per capita (1997 $)	33	36	41	39	53
World data on military expenditure per capita (1997 $)	242	173	146	143	145
Armed forces per 1,000 people (soldiers)	5.7	4.9	4.7	4.6	4.5
World data on armed forces per 1,000 people (soldiers)	5.3	4.5	4.1	3.9	3.8
GNP per capita (1997 $)	1,820	1,950	2,360	2,370	2,490
Arms imports[6]					
Current dollars (mil.)	50	70	270	190	310
1997 constant dollars (mil.)	59	78	280	193	310
Total imports[7]					
Current dollars (mil.)	3,470	4,861	9,224	9,473	10,260
1997 constant dollars (mil.)	4,064	5,389	9,551	9,631	10,260
Total exports[7]					
Current dollars (mil.)	3,231	3,484	5,575	5,897	6,814
1997 constant dollars (mil.)	3,784	3,862	5,773	5,995	6,814
Arms as percent of total imports[8]	1.4	1.4	2.9	2.0	3.0
Arms as percent of total exports[8]	0	0	0	0	0

(Continued on next page.)

Political Parties

Democratic Constituent Congress (Congresso Constituyente Democratico)	% of vote	no. of seats
Change 90-New Majority (C90/NM)	52.1%	67
Union for Peru (UPP)	14.0%	17
American Popular Revolutionary Alliance (APRA)		8
Independent Moralizing Front (FIM)		6
Democratic Cooridinator (CODE-Pais Posible)		5
Popular Action Party (AP)		4
Popular Christian Party (PPC)		3
Renovation Party		3
United Left (IU)		2
Civic Works Movement (OBRAS)		2
Other parties	33.9%	3

Elections were last held 9 April 1995 (next to be held 9 April 2000).

Government Budgets (B)

Revenues . . . .$8.5 billion

Expenditures . . . .$9.3 billion

Capital expenditures . . . .$2.0 billion

Data for 1996 est.

Crime

Crime volume (for 1998)

Crimes reported 54,145

Total persons convicted 31,989

Crimes per 100,000 population 218

Persons responsible for offenses

Total number suspects 20,304

Total number of female suspects 1,913

Total number of juvenile suspects 1,533

LABOR FORCE

Total Labor Force (A)

7.6 million (1996 est.).

Labor Force by Occupation

Agriculture, mining and quarrying, manufacturing, construction, transport, services.

Unemployment Rate

7.7%; extensive underemployment (1997).

PRODUCTION SECTOR

Energy Production

Production .18.28 billion kWh

Production by source

Fossil fuel 24.53%

Hydro 74.79%

Nuclear 0%

Other 0.68%

Exports . . . . .0 kWh

Data for 1998.

Energy Consumption

Consumption . . . . .17.002 billion kWh

Imports . . . . .2.000 million kWh

Data for 1998.

Transportation

Highways:

Total: 72,900 km.

Paved: 8,700 km.

Unpaved: 64,200 km (1999 est.).

Waterways: 8,600 km of navigable tributaries of Amazon system and 208 km of Lago Titicaca.

Pipelines: crude oil 800 km; natural gas and natural gas liquids 64 km.

Merchant marine:

Total: 7 ships (1,000 GRT or over) totaling 65,193 GRT/100,584 DWT.

Ships by type: bulk 1, cargo 6 (1999 est.).

Airports: 234 (1999 est.).

Airports - with paved runways: 44.

Airports - with unpaved runways: 190.

Top Agriculture Products

Coffee, cotton, sugarcane, rice, wheat, potatoes, plantains, coca; poultry, beef, dairy products, wool; fish.

Top Mining Products (A)

	National Production	World Production
Commodities in 1998		
Copper (000 mt)	522	12,200
Gold (000 kg)	89	2,460
Lead (000 mt)	260	3,080
Salt (000 mt)	80	186,000
Silver (mt)	1,934	16,400
Tin (mt)	26,000	206,000
Zinc (000 mt)	869	755

MANUFACTURING SECTOR

GDP & Manufacturing Summary (A)

	1980	1985	1990	1995
GDP ($-1990 mil.)[1]	37,582	36,829	33,427	43,124
Per capita ($-1990)[1]	2,169	1,889	1,550	1,833
Manufacturing share (%) (current prices)[1]	20.2	25.3	26.7	21.7[e]
Manufacturing				
Value added ($-1990 mil.)[1]	11,958	10,758	9,745	12,861
Industrial production index	129	112	100	126
Value added ($ mil.)	4,985	3,918	7,366	7,485[e]
Gross output ($ mil.)	12,977	9,573	14,186	18,185[e]
Employment (000)	273	263	285	273[e]
Profitability (% of gross output)				
Intermediate input (%)	62	58	49	59[e]
Wages and salaries inc. supplements (%)	7[e]	6	10[e]	7[e]
Gross operating surplus	32[e]	35	42[e]	34[e]
Productivity ($)				
Gross output per worker	47,484	36,350	49,727	66,261[e]
Value added per worker	18,242	14,877	25,821	27,318[e]
Average wage (inc. supplements)	3,150[e]	2,154	4,941[e]	4,877[e]
Value added ($ mil.)				
Food products	767	402	1,077	1,109[e]
Beverages	379	303	545	991[e]
Tobacco products	84	61	59	66[e]
Textiles	466	352	647	648[e]
Wearing apparel	65	52	133	66[e]
Leather and fur products	56	20	32	18[e]
Footwear	41	20	26	27[e]
Wood and wood products	81	32	39	43[e]
Furniture and fixtures	42	19	30	40[e]
Paper and paper products	156	77	135	86[e]
Printing and publishing	100	80	151	238[e]
Industrial chemicals	215	158	237	223[e]
Other chemical products	289	193	427	577[e]
Petroleum refineries	192	1,154	1,409	1,357[e]
Misc. petroleum and coal products	6	1	5	2[e]
Rubber products	62	52	74	59[e]
Plastic products	89	90	144	181[e]
Pottery, china and earthenware	15	8	10	15[e]
Glass and glass products	47	15	37	64[e]
Other non-metal mineral products	129	113	204	300[e]
Iron and steel	192	123	177	151[e]
Non-ferrous metals	604	172	930	449[e]
Metal products	188	113	180	233[e]
Non-electrical machinery	156	58	116	116[e]
Electrical machinery	211	111	235	118[e]
Transport equipment	278	106	219	147[e]
Prof. and scientific equipment	14	10	21	23[e]
Other manufacturing	58	25	66	138[e]

COMMUNICATIONS

Daily Newspapers

	National Data	World Data for Comparison
Daily Newspapers		
Number of Dailies	74	8,391
Total Circulation (000)	2,000	548,000
Circulation per 1,000 inhabitants	84	96

Telecommunications

Telephones - main lines in use: 1.509 million (1998).

Telephones - mobile cellular: 504,995 (1998).

Telephone system: adequate for most requirements.

Domestic: nationwide microwave radio relay system and a domestic satellite system with 12 earth stations.

International: satellite earth stations - 2 Intelsat (Atlantic Ocean); Pan American submarine cable.

Radio broadcast stations: AM 472, FM 198, shortwave 189 (1999).

Radios: 6.65 million (1997).

Television broadcast stations: 13 (plus 112 repeaters) (1997).

Televisions: 3.06 million (1997).

Internet Service Providers (ISPs): 15 (1999).

FINANCE, ECONOMICS, & TRADE

Economic Indicators

National product: GDP—purchasing power parity—$116 billion (1999 est.).

National product real growth rate: 2.4% (1999 est.).

National product per capita: $4,400 (1999 est.).

Inflation rate—consumer price index: 5.5% (1999 est.).

Exchange Rates

Exchange rates:

Nuevo sol (S/.) per US$1

January 2000	3.500
1999	3.383
1998	2.930
1997	2.664
1996	2.453
1995	2.253

Top Import Origins

$8.4 billion (c.i.f., 1999 est.)

Origins (1997)

United States	19%
Colombia	6%
Venezuela	5%
Chile	4%
Brazil	4%

Top Export Destinations

$5.9 billion (f.o.b., 1999 est.)

Destinations (1997)

United States	25%
China	8%
Japan	7%
Switzerland	NA
Germany	NA
United Kingdom	NA
Brazil	NA

Foreign Aid

Recipient: $895.1 million (1995).

Import/Export Commodities

Import Commodities	Export Commodities
Machinery	Fish and fish products
Transport equipment	Copper
Foodstuffs	Zinc
Petroleum	Gold
Iron and steel	Crude petroleum and byproducts
Chemicals	Lead
Pharmaceuticals	Coffee
	Sugar
	Cotton

Balance of Payments

	1994	1995	1996	1997	1998
Exports of goods (f.o.b.)	4,598	5,588	5,899	6,832	5,735
Imports of goods (f.o.b.)	−5,596	−7,756	−7,885	−8,553	−8,200
Trade balance	−997	−2,168	−1,986	−1,721	−2,465
Services - debits	−1,565	−1,898	−2,097	−2,308	−2,294
Services - credits	1,064	1,132	1,413	1,541	1,753
Private transfers (net)	575	595	673	680	699
Government transfers (net)	62	25	17	1	−3
Overall balance	−2,662	−4,314	−3,618	−3,273	−3,794

PHILIPPINES

CAPITAL: Manila.

FLAG: The national flag consists of a white equilateral triangle at the hoist, with a blue stripe extending from its upper side and a red stripe extending from its lower side. Inside each angle of the triangle is a yellow five-pointed star, and in its center is a yellow sun with eight rays.

ANTHEM: *Bayang Magiliw (Nation Beloved).*

MONETARY UNIT: The peso (P) is divided into 100 centavos. There are coins of 1, 5, 10, 25, and 50 centavos and 1 and 2 pesos, and notes of 5, 10, 20, 50, 100, and 500 pesos. P1 = \$0.03804 (or \$1 = P26.285).

WEIGHTS AND MEASURES: The metric system is the legal standard, but some local measures are also used.

HOLIDAYS: New Year's Day, 1 January; Freedom Day, 25 February; Labor Day, 1 May; Heroes' Day, 6 May; Independence Day (from Spain), 12 June; Thanksgiving, 21 September; All Saints' Day, 1 November; Bonifacio Day, 30 November; Christmas, 25 December; Rizal Day, 30 December; Last Day of the Year, 31 December. Movable religious holidays include Holy Thursday and Good Friday.

TIME: 8 PM = noon GMT.

LOCATION AND SIZE: The Republic of the Philippines consists of a group of 7,107 islands situated southeast of mainland Asia and separated from it by the South China Sea. The total land area is approximately 300,000 square kilometers (115,831 square miles), 67 percent of which is contained within the two largest islands, Luzon and Mindanao. Comparatively, the area occupied by the Philippines is slightly larger than the state of Arizona. The Philippines has a total coastline of 36,289 kilometers (22,549 miles). The Philippines' capital city, Manila, is located on the island of Luzon.

CLIMATE: Except in the higher mountains, temperatures remain warm, the annual average ranging from about 26° to 28°C (79° to 82°F). The average annual rainfall in the Philippines exceeds 250 centimeters (100 inches). Annual normal relative humidity averages 80%. Violent tropical storms (*baguios*), or typhoons, are frequent.

Republic of the Philippines
Republika ng Pilipinas

INTRODUCTORY SURVEY

RECENT HISTORY

Beginning in December 1941, the Philippines became the site of the most bitter and decisive battles fought in the Pacific during World War II (1939-1945). By May 1942, the Japanese had achieved full possession of the islands. United States forces, led by General Douglas MacArthur, recaptured the Philippines in early 1945, following the Battle of Leyte Gulf, the largest naval engagement in history. In September 1945, Japan surrendered.

On July 4, 1946, the Republic of the Philippines was established with Manuel A. Roxas y Acuña as its first president. Casualties and damage in the Philippines from World War II were extensive, and rehabilitation was the major problem of the new state. Communist guerrillas, called Hukbalahaps, threatened the republic. Their revolutionary demands were countered by land reforms and military action.

In 1965, Ferdinand Edralin Marcos was elected president and reelected in 1969. Unable to run for a third term in 1973, President Marcos placed the entire country under martial law charging that the nation was threatened by a "full-scale armed insurrection and rebellion." Marcos arrested many of his political opponents, some of who remained in detention for years.

Throughout the 1970s, Marcos tightened his control of the government through purges of opponents, promotion of favorites, and delegation of

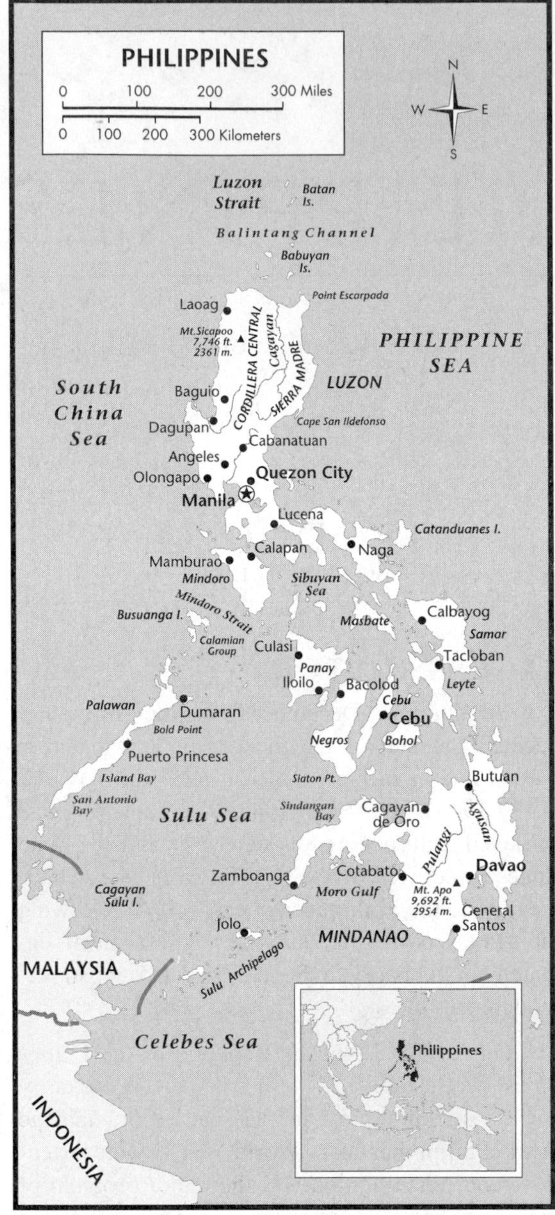

leadership of several key programs-including the governorship of metropolitan Manila-to his wife, Imelda Romualdez Marcos.

Pope John Paul II came to Manila in February 1981 and protested the violation of basic human rights. In 1983, Benigno S. Aquino, Jr., a long-time critic of Marcos, was shot at the Manila airport as he returned from self-exile in the United States to lead the political opposition in the 1984 legislative elections.

Political pressures mounted and a military revolt grew into a popular rebellion that ousted the long-time leader. United States President Ronald Reagan offered Marcos asylum, and Marcos went into exile in Hawaii.

On February 25, 1986, Corazon Aquino, widow of Benigno Aquino, assumed the presidency. In May 1987, she was elected in the first free elections in nearly two decades, held under a new constitution.

Under pressure from communist rebels, Aquino removed U.S. military bases from the Philippines in 1989. However, the Philippines was struck by three major natural disasters: (1) in July 1990, an earthquake measuring 7.7 on the Richter scale struck; (2) a super-typhoon devastated the central islands in November 1990; and, (3) in June 1991, Mount Pinatubo (in Zambales province near Olangapo) violently erupted. The Philippine economy suffered again in 1995, when a typhoon badly damaged the rice crop.

In June 1992, Fidel Ramos succeeded Corazon Aquino as president of the Philippines. Ramos, a Methodist, was the Philippines first non-Catholic president.

Internal violence by the Muslim population continued in the 1980s and 1990s. In January 1994, the government signed a ceasefire agreement with the Moro National Liberation Front, ending twenty years of guerrilla war. However, in January 1996, Philippines police uncovered a plot by Muslim terrorists to assassinate Pope John Paul II during his visit to Manila that month. Muslim rebels in Mindanao raided the town of Ipil in April 1996, killing fifty-seven people and burning the business district.

President Ramos introduced a development plan called the Philippines 2000 movement, with its major goal being making his country into an investment, trade, and tourist center of Asia and the Pacific. Progress was made on some of its economic goals, but few of its social changes were accomplished. On June 30, 1998, Joseph Ejercito Estrada was elected president.

Conflicting claims to the Spratly Islands in the South China Sea are a source of tension between the Philippines and the People's Republic of China.

GOVERNMENT

Under the constitution of February 11, 1987, the Philippines is a democratic republican state. Executive power is vested in a president elected by popular vote for a six-year term with no eligibility for reelection. A vice-president, elected for a six-year term with eligibility for one immediate reelection, and a cabinet appointed by the president, which can include the vice-president, assist the president.

Legislative power rests with a two-chamber legislature. The Senate has twenty-four members elected by popular vote for six-year terms. A 221-seat House of Representatives is elected from single-member districts for three-year terms. The president may appoint up to fifty more.

Judiciary

Under the 1973 constitution, the Supreme Court, composed of a chief justice and fourteen associate justices, was the highest judicial body of the state with supervisory authority over the lower courts. The entire court system was modified in 1981, with the creation of new regional courts of trials and of appeals. Philippine courts function without juries.

The Constitution calls for an independent judiciary, and defendants in criminal cases are afforded the right to counsel.

Political Parties

After assuming the presidency in 1986, Corazon Aquino formally organized the People's Power Movement (Lakas Ng Bayan), the successor to the party of her late husband, Benigno Aquino. In the congressional elections of May 1987, Aquino's popularity gave her party a sweep in the polls, making it the major party in the country.

In 1993, there were over a dozen recognized political organizations, and six parties organized in opposition to the government.

On August 26, 1994, President Fidel Ramos announced a new political coalition that would produce the most powerful political group in the Philippines. Ramos's Lakas-National Union of Christian Democrats (Lakas/NUCD) teamed with the Democratic Filipino Struggle (Laban ng Demokratikong Pilipino, Laban).

DEFENSE

The all-volunteer active armed forces numbered 110,000 in 2000, and reserves , 131,000. The army had 73,000 members, the navy had a total of 20,500 members (including 8,500 marines), and the coast guard had 3,500 personnel. The air force had a strength of 40,500 personnel. Several active rebel groups, ranging in membership between 500 to 8,000, operate in the Philippines. Estimated defense expenditures in 1998 were $995 million, or 1.5 percent of GDP.

ECONOMIC AFFAIRS

The Philippines is primarily an agricultural nation, raising crops for domestic use and export. It is the world's largest producer of coconuts and manila hemp *(abacá)*. Manufacturing, which has expanded and diversified since political independence, depends on imported raw materials. Mining, once centered on gold, is now diversified with chromite, copper, and iron providing important earnings. The economy is heavily dependent on foreign trade.

Throughout 1990-1992, slow economic growth plagued the Philippines. Inadequate transport and communications networks and prolonged drought reduced industrial and agricultural expansion. Widespread unemployment and underemployment characterize the Philippine labor market. High rates of labor migration abroad (686,137 in 1992) provided some relief and accounted for a substantial portion of the country's foreign exchange earnings.

Real GDP growth averaged 3 percent from 1988 to 1998, but contracted in 1998 by 0.5 percent during the Asian financial crisis. The GDP was estimated to grow 2.9 percent in 1999, and lower import levels caused a dramatic decrease in the balance of payments deficit. Semiconductors, microelectronics, and computer peripherals accounted for most of the export growth.

Since 1990, the most visible problem for the economy has been the shortage of electric power. In 1992, the water level of a lake in Mindanao fell, causing a 50 percent reduction in the power supply to Mindanao. In Manila, the industrial hub, power outages would last from four to six hours per day. Between 1993 and 1999, the Philippine government liberalized telecommunications, liberalized the foreign exchange market, deregulated transportation, privatized water, and resolved the power crisis.

Public Finance

The principal sources of revenue are income taxes, taxes on sales, and business operations, and excise duties. Infrastructural improvements, defense expenditures, and debt service continue to lead among the categories of outlays.

The government's commitment to fiscal balance resulted in a budget surplus for the first time in two decades in 1994. The surplus was achieved by higher taxes, privatization receipts, and expenditure cuts. The budget again showed a surplus in 1995, when government revenues totaled approximately $14.1 billion and expenditures $13.6 billion. In 1996, 31 percent of government revenues was spent on social services, 26.5 percent on economic services, 9 percent on defense, 17 percent on general public service, 0.5 percent on net lending, and 16 percent on interest payments.

The U.S. Central Intelligence Agency (CIA) estimated that in 1998, the Philippines central government took in revenues of approximately $14.5 billion and had expenditures of $12.6 billion, registering another surplus. In 1999, external debt was $51.9 billion.

Income

In 1999, Philippines' gross domestic product (GDP) was estimated at $282 billion, or about $3,600 per capita. The GDP growth rate estimates for 1999 were 2.9 percent, and inflation was 6.8 percent. By 1997 estimates, the GDP contribution by sector was agriculture, 20 percent; industry, 32 percent; and services, 48 percent.

Industry

The leading manufactured goods (by value) are foods, textiles, petroleum and coal, chemicals, electrical machinery, pharmaceuticals, wood products, fishing, beverages, transport equipment, basic metals, and footwear.

Exports from the electronics industry surpassed those of food products and textiles in the late 1990s. In 1999, the Philippines continued to shift from an economy earlier based on agricultural produce and sweatshop factory output to an economy anchored by the assembly of computer chips and other electronic goods, many of them computer peripherals. In a World Bank study published in 1999, the Philippines was credited with one of the world's most technologically advanced export structures.

Banking and Finance

The Philippine banking structure consists of the government-owned Central Bank of the Philippines (created in 1949) that acts as the government's fiscal agent and administers the monetary and banking system, and some fifty-three commercial banks, of which seventeen were foreign majority-owned. Other institutions include over 800 rural banks, thirty-eight private development banks, seven savings banks, ten investment houses, and two specialized government banks. The largest commercial bank, the Philippine National Bank (PNB), is a government institution with over 194 local offices and twelve overseas branches. It supplies about half the commercial credit, basically as agricultural loans. The government operates about 1,145 postal savings banks and the Development Bank of the Philippines, the Land Bank of the Philippines, and the Philippine Amanah Bank (for Mindanao). As of 1999, there are also fifteen offshore banking units in the country and twenty-six foreign bank representative offices.

Philippine stock exchanges are self-governing, although the Philippine Securities and Exchange Commission, established in 1936, has supervisory power over registrants. The country's two stock exchanges, Manila and Makati (both in the capital), were formally merged in the Philippines Stock Exchange in March 1993. A computer link-up was affected a year later, although the two retained separate trading floors until November 1995. Only 220 companies were listed as of early 1998. But the process of privatization is expected to push up listings.

Ecomomic Development

Long range planning has followed a series of economic plans, most of them covering five-year periods. Under the Aquino administration, the goals of the 1987-1992 plan were self-sufficiency in food production, decentralization of power and decision making, job creation, and rural development. Economic performance for real growth fell far short of plan targets by 25 percent or more. Structural changes to provide a better investment climate were carried out. The Foreign Investment Act of 1991 liberalized the environment for foreign investment. An Executive Order, issued in July 1991, reduced the number of tariff levels over five years and reduced the maximum duty rate from 50 percent to 30 percent. Quantitative restrictions were removed from all but a few products. The foreign exchange market was fully deregulated in 1992.

A new six-year medium-term development plan for 1993-1998 was presented by the government in May 1993. The plan stressed people empowerment and international competitiveness within the framework of sustainable development. To do this, the government planned to disperse industries to regions outside the metropolitan Manila area. The plan also called for technological upgrading of production sectors, poverty alleviation, and human/social development. The Medium Term Philippine Development Plan (MTPDP) for 1999 through 2004, focused on rural development, especially on the modernization of the agricultural sector.

In 2000, the government continued its economic reforms to help the Philippines match the pace of development in newly industrialized countries of East Asia. The government stressed improving infrastructure, overhauling the tax system to bolster government revenues, and continuing deregulation and privatization of the economy.

Another key to the Philippine economy was financial assistance, continued in 1998 and 1999 through the Asia Development Bank, World Bank, and Japan's Overseas Economic Cooperation Development Fund.

SOCIAL WELFARE

The government social program includes the settlement of landless families in new areas, building of rural roads, schools, and medical clinics, and the distribution of relief supplies to the needy.

The Social Security System (SSS) covers employees, both temporary and permanent, including domestic workers. Government employees are covered under the Government Service Insurance System (GSIS). Benefits include compensation for confinement due to injury or illness, pensions for temporary incapacity, insurance payments to families in case of death, old age pensions, and benefits to widows and orphans.

A medical care plan (Medicare) provides hospital, surgical, medicinal, and medical-expense benefits to members and their dependents. Women are eligible for paid maternity leaves of six weeks for the first four births.

Most women occupy traditional roles and occupations and, on average, earn about half as much as men.

Most, but not all, of the legal rights enjoyed by men are extended to women. A 1992 law removed restrictions on property ownership.

Healthcare

In the mid-1990s, there were 1,663 hospitals and 31,375 pphysicians. There were about 0.12 doctors per 1,000 people in 1992. Nearly 75 percent of the population had access to health care services in 1992.

Pulmonary infections (tuberculosis, pneumonia, bronchitis) are prevalent, but malaria is virtually unknown in larger cities and is being eliminated in the countryside. Malnutrition remains a health problem, despite government assistance in the form of Nutripaks, consisting of native foods such as mung beans and powdered shrimp, made available for infants, children, and pregnant women. In 2000, average life expectancy was about 67.5 years.

Housing

Tens of thousands of *barrios* (districts) are scattered throughout the Philippines, each consisting of a double row of small cottages strung out along a single road. Each cottage is generally built on stilts and has a thatched roof, veranda, and small yard. From 1984 to 1987, an annual average of about 103,150 units were built by private builders with minimal assistance from the government. The total number of dwellings in 1992 was 10.6 million.

EDUCATION

Education is free and compulsory in the primary schools and is coeducational. English is the main medium of instruction, although Filipino or the local dialect is used for instruction in the lower primary grades. In 2000, about 4.6 percent of adults were illiterate (men, 4.5 percent; women, 4.8 percent).

In 1998, 38,631 primary schools had an enrollment of 12.4 million students, and secondary schools had five million students.

The University of the Philippines is the leading institution of higher learning. In addition, there are some fifty other universities including the University of Santo Tomás, founded in 1611 and run by Dominican friars. In 1996, universities and all higher level institutions had two million students.

2000 KEY EVENTS TIMELINE

February

- Flood waters up to six feet deep sweep through parts of the southern city, Davao (population: one million). More than 7,000 people are forced to leave their homes.
- The first in a series of eruptions on the Mayon volcano in the central part of the country occurs on February 24, causing extensive damage in the surrounding area with a radius of 3.7 miles (6 kilometers). The volcano had been dormant since 1993. Seven thousand people were evacuated, but just one woman died, reportedly of a heart attack.

March

- On March 20 Muslim extremists from the group known as Abu Sayyaf seize fifty hostages from two schools. Students, teachers, and at least one priest are among those being held. Abu Sayyaf, among the groups listed by the U.S. government as a threat to U.S. citizens at home and abroad, is one of two groups engaged in a struggle to establish an independent Islamic state in Basilan in southern Philippines. Abu Sayyaf is demanding the release of Ramzi Abdel Yousef and Sheik Omar Abdel-Rahman, both being held in New York on charges of terrorism and conspiracy.

April

- During the week of April 17 terrorist members of Abu Sayyaf behead two male teachers, both of whom were among the group of hostages seized in Basilan in March. The Filipino government retaliates by launching air and artillery strikes.
- Muslim separatist rebels set off several explosions on buses aboard a ferry headed for Ozamis City in Mindanao province, killing forty-one people and injuring forty-five others.

July

- Winds of Typhoon Edeng gusting up to 140 km per hour (90 mpg) ravage the northern tip of Philippines and cause heavy rains in Manila. At least 27 people die and 40,000 people are evacuated from their homes.
- A mountain of garbage loosened by heavy rains collapses July 17 and smothers hundreds of garbage dump scavengers. Over 216 are killed, and many more are injured. President Joseph Estrata closes the dump permanently on July 20, and offers housing for those left homeless.

August

- Those who survive the garbage landslide sue those responsible on August 1.
- More than 100 people sue the United States and the Philippine government on August 18 for $103 billion. They demand reparation for deaths and illnesses caused by hazardous waste at former U.S. military bases.
- Muslim rebels kidnap a twenty-four-year-old U.S. citizen, Jeffrey Schilling, and demand a $10 million ransom.
- The kidnappers calling themselves Abu Sayyaf release five foreign hostages for a sum of $5 million paid by Libya on August 27.

September

- Muslim rebels free the last of an original twenty-one westerners September 9 for one million each, and the promise of $25 million more. Only a Filipino remains from the original number, with two French journalists, twelve Filipinos, and an American who were later taken. The rebels buy speedboats with part of the ransom money.
- Philippine forces attack rebel camps in an attempt at rescuing nineteen hostages on September 16, a day after rebels take three more hostages and several rapes of female hostages are reported. Government troops succeed in rescuing two French journalists on September 20.

October

- On October 2, government troops rescue twelve Christian evangelists that were taken hostage by the Islamic group Abu Sayyaf.
- Members of the Moro Islamic Liberation Front pledge their allegiance to President Joseph Estrada on October 5.
- Vice President Gloria Macapagal Arroyo resigns October 12, because of accusations that President Estrada has taken bribes of more than $11 million while in office. Estrada denies these charges.

November

- The House of Representatives impeaches President Estrada November 13, and the trial moves to the Senate; on November 29 thousands march in the streets calling for President Estrada's resignation.

December

- At the beginning of December, over 20,000 people protest outside of the presidential palace in Manila.
- Five bombs explode at noon on December 31, killing fourteen and injuring dozens. There were no claims of responsibility.

ANALYSIS OF EVENTS: 2000

BUSINESS AND THE ECONOMY

The Philippine economy suffered numerous setbacks in 2000. First, in January President Joseph

Estrada withdrew his proposal to change the Philippine constitution. The Constitutional Corrections for Development proposed in 1999 were designed to allow more foreign investment in an effort to bolster the struggling economy. President Estrada's decision to withdraw the proposal came after scandal erupted over his alleged involvement in illegal gambling.

Then another scandal rocked the Philippine economy when Dante Tan, the owner of BW Resources and a friend of President Estrada, was charged with insider trading and other illegal stock market activities. In protest against the way the investigation was handled, seventeen members of the Philippine Stock Exchange (PSE) resigned, leaving the PSE with no internal regulatory oversight. Foreign investors fled the market. The market plunged further in response to the scandal over President Estrada's gambling connections. The Philippine economic growth rate, at 3.4 percent in the second quarter, was much slower than many neighboring Asian countries. The unemployment rate reached 13.9 percent in April, the highest it had been in nine years.

One positive event in an otherwise difficult year was the reopening of direct flights between Taiwan and the Philippines. Flights were suspended in October 1999 when the Philippines withdrew from a 1996 agreement, claiming that Taiwan was stealing passengers from Philippine Airlines (PAL). In June 2000 after months of unproductive negotiations, Taiwan placed a ban on hiring Filipino workers. Over 100,000 Filipinos typically work in Taiwan, and by October the Philippines had lost about $300 million in earnings. When Taiwan threatened to extend the ban, the Philippine government backed down and reached an agreement setting new quotas for passengers, and flights resumed on October 8.

GOVERNMENT AND POLITICS

The Philippine government staggered under the weight of scandal, economic difficulties, and battles with Muslim insurgents in 2000. President Joseph Estrada was personally besieged with charges of corruption and calls for resignation or impeachment. His popularity rating fell sharply in the first half of the year, but then rose again after victories over the Muslim rebels. Vice-President Gloria Macapagal Arroyo, a member of the opposition party, remained highly popular with Filipinos and carefully kept her distance from Estrada's difficulties.

The biggest scandal involving President Estrada concerned charges that he received over $11 million in payoffs from illegal gambling operations. President Estrada denied all charges. However, he did suspend Bingo-2 ball gaming while its systems were investigated in light of complaints about the Bingo-2 ball contract with Philippine Amusements and Gaming Corporation (PAGCOR). Bingo-2 ball was originally instituted as a government-sponsored alternative to *jueteng,* an illegal numbers game.

The persistent conflict with Muslims in Mindanao in the southern Philippines was clearly the main preoccupation of the Philippine government in 2000. The conflict escalated sharply as the rebels kidnapped dozens of hostages in various incidents throughout the year. Two different Islamic groups were involved in the hostilities: the Abu Sayyaf ("Bearer of the Sword") and the Moro Islamic Liberation Front (MILF). A third more mainstream group, the Moro National Liberation Front (MNLF), reached an agreement with the government in 1996 and is no longer involved in guerrilla operations.

Ever since the first colonial invasion of the Philippines 400 years ago by Spain, the Muslims in Mindanao have resisted assimilation. When the MNLF made peace with the government, the MILF split off to continue fighting. Other independent groups, such as the Abu Sayyaf, have also carried on the fight. In the past thirty years alone, over 120,000 lives have been lost and more than 100,000 people driven from their homes in the battle. On July 9 government forces captured the MILF headquarters and claimed victory over the insurgents, inviting them to resume peace talks. MILF leader Hashim Salamat responded by calling for a *jihad* (holy war) against the government. Even the 1996 peace accord with the MNLF showed signs of collapsing.

In support of the peace process, North Korea assured President Estrada that it would not supply arms to the Muslim rebels. Plans continued, therefore, to establish diplomatic relations between the two countries. The Organization of Islamic Conference (OIC), a fifty-six-member international Islamic organization, also planned a fact-finding mission to the Philippines in October to investigate the implementation of the 1996 peace accords.

CULTURE AND SOCIETY

Persistent poverty was the main theme of 2000 in the Philippines. An investigation opened on January 4 into the sinking of yet another Philippine ferry on December 23, 1999. The Philippine ferry system has the reputation of being "accident prone," mostly because the ships are all very old and in need of costly repairs, but the funds are not available to fix them or buy new ships. U.S. military personnel arrived in February to begin exercises that were allowed to resume under the Visiting Forces Agreement passed in 1999. Many opposed the agreement, fearing a return of U.S. forces, but the need for military supplies persuaded the Philippine government to trade access to the islands in return for secondhand U.S. equipment.

Droughts caused by El Niño forced the government to choose between irrigating crop fields or meeting urban domestic and industrial needs for water. As in 1998 they chose to cut off irrigation water, leaving farmers even more destitute than before. Farmers had yet to receive compensation payments promised in 1998. Perhaps the worst example of Philippine poverty occurred on July 10 when a landslide at a Manila dump buried hundreds of people who lived nearby and worked as "scavengers," earning up to $5 a day selling their finds. This was not the first fatal dump avalanche in the Philippines, but the recurring disasters did not discourage poor Filipinos from returning to the dumps to survive.

DIRECTORY

CENTRAL GOVERNMENT

Head of State

President
Gloria Macapagal-Arroyo, Office of the President, Malacanang Palace, Jose P. Laurel St., Manila, Philippines
PHONE: +63 (2) 7356201
FAX: +63 (2) 7421641
E-MAIL: erap@erap.com

Departments

Executive Secretary
Renato De Villa, Office of the Executive Secretary, 2nd Floor, New Executive Bldg JP Laurel St., San Miguel 1005, Manila, Philippines
PHONE: +63 (2) 7356023; 7333608
FAX: +63 (2) 7421643

Secretary of National Defense
Eduardo Ermita, Department of National Defense, 3rd Floor, DND Building, Camp Aguinaldo, Quezon City, Philippines
PHONE: +63 (2) 9116193; 9116183
FAX: +63 (2) 9116213

Secretary of Agrarian Reform
Hernani Braganza, Department of Agrarian Reform, Rm. 209, PTS Building, Diliman 1100, Quezon City, Philippines
PHONE: +63 (2) 9283979; 9283573
FAX: +63 (2) 9283968

Secretary of Agriculture
Leonardo Montemayor, Department of Agriculture, DA Building, Eliptical Road, Diliman, Quezon City, Philippines
PHONE: +63 (2) 9262288
FAX: +63 (2) 9262288; 9288751
E-MAIL: webmaster@dfa.gov.ph

Secretary of Budget and Management
Emilia Boncodin, Department of Budget and Management, 2nd Floor, DBM Building 3, General Solano St., San Miquel, Manila, Philippines
PHONE: +63 (2) 7354887; 7354936
FAX: +63 (2) 7424173

Secretary of Education, Culture and Sports
Raul Roco, Department of Education, Culture and Sports, University of Life Building, Meralco Ave., Bo. Ugong 1600, Pasig City, Philippines
PHONE: +63 (2) 6227208; 6337228
FAX: +63 (2) 6320805

Secretary of Energy
Renato Valencia, Department of Energy, Philippine National Petroleum Center, PNCP Completx, Merritt Rd., Fort Bonifacio, Makati City, Philippines
PHONE: +63 (2) 8442850; 8178603
FAX: +63 (2) 8178603

Secretary of Environment and Natural Resources
Rey Antonio Cerilles, Department of Environment and Natural Resources, DENR Building, Visayas Ave., Quezon City, Philippines
PHONE: +63 (2) 9296633
FAX: +63 (2) 9204352

Secretary of Finance
Alberto Romulo, Department of Finance, 5th Floor, Executive Tower Building, Vito Cruz co. Mabini St., Malate 1004, Manila, Philippines
PHONE: +63 (2) 5234255; 5236051
FAX: +63 (2) 5219495

Secretary of Foreign Affairs
Lauro Baja, Department of Foreign Affairs, DFA Building, 2330 Roxas Blvd., Pasay, Metro Manila, Philippines
PHONE: +63 (2) 8318955; 8318970
FAX: +63 (2) 8321597

Secretary of Health
Antonio Lopez, Department of Health, San Lazaro Compound, Rizal Ave., Santa Cruz, Manila, Philippines
PHONE: +63 (2) 7438301
FAX: +63 (2) 7116055

Secretary of Justice
Hernando Perez, Department of Justice, Padre Faura St., Ermita, Manila, Philippines
PHONE: +63 (2) 5218344; 5213721
FAX: +63 (2) 5211614

Secretary of Interior and Local Government
Alfredo Lim, Department of Interior and Local Government, PNCC Building, EDSA Corner Reliance Street, Mandaluyong, Metro Manila, Philippines
PHONE: +63 (2) 6318777; 6318722
FAX: +63 (2) 6318831

Secretary of Labor and Employment
Patricia Santo Thomas, Department of Labor and Employment, Rm. 107, Executive Bldg., San Jose Street, Intramuros, Manila, Philippines
PHONE: +63 (2) 5272118; 5272116
FAX: +63 (2) 5273499

Secretary of Public Works and Highways
Simeon Datumanong, Department of Public Works and Highways, DPWH Bldg., Bonifacio Dr., Port Area 1002, Manila, Philippines
PHONE: +63 (2) 5274111; 5275616
FAX: +63 (2) 5275635

Secretary of Science and Technology
Filemon Urierte, Department of Science and Technology, General Santos Ave., Bicutan Taguig 1604, Metro Manila, Philippines
PHONE: +63 (2) 8372939
FAX: +63 (2) 8372937

Secretary of Social Welfare and Development
Corazon Solimon, Department of Social Welfare and Development, Constitution Hills 1100, Quezon City, Philippines
PHONE: +63 (2) 9317916; 9318068
FAX: +63 (2) 9310149

Secretary of Trade and Industry
Manuel Roxas, Department of Trade and Industry, Industry and Investment Bldg., 385 Gil J. Puyat Ave., Makati 1200, Philippines
PHONE: +63 (2) 8953515; 8976734

Secretary of Tourism
Gordon Richard, Department of Tourism, DOT Bldg., TM Kalaw St., Agrifina Circle, Rizal Park, Manila, Philippines
PHONE: +63 (2) 5241751; 5244760
FAX: +63 (2) 5217374

Secretary of Transportation and Communications
Panteleon Alvarez, Department of Transportation and Communications, Philcomcen Bldg., Ortigas Ave., Pasig 1600, Philippines
PHONE: +63 (2) 7267106; 7267125
FAX: +63 (2) 7269985

POLITICAL ORGANIZATIONS

Laban ng Masang Pilipino

Lakas ñg Edsa (People's Power)

TITLE: President
NAME: Raul Manglapus

National Union of Christian Democrats

TITLE: Secretary-General
NAME: Jose de Venecia

United Muslim Democratic Party

Nationalist People's Coalition

NAME: Eduardo Cojuangco

Partido Liberal (Liberal Party)

NAME: Raul Daza

Laban ñg Demokratikong Pilipino (Struggle for a Democratic Philippines)

NAME: Edgardo Angara

Partido ñg Demokratikong Pilipino-PDP (Philippines Democratic Party)

NAME: Jose Cojuangco

People's Reform Party

NAME: Miriam Defensor-Santiago

DIPLOMATIC REPRESENTATION

Embassies in the Philippines

Argentina
6th Floor, A.C.T. Tower Condominium, 135 Sen. Gil Puyat Avenue, Salcedo Village, Makati, Metro Manila, Philippines
PHONE: +63 (2) 8936091; 8108301
TITLE: Ambassador
NAME: Juan Luis Garibaldi

Australia
1st-5th Floors, Dona Salustiana Dee Ty Tower, 104 Paseo de Roxas, Makati, Metro Manila, Philippines
PHONE: +63 (2) 7502850
TITLE: Ambassador
NAME: John Edward Buckley

Austria
4th Floor, Prince Building, 117 Rada Street, Legaspi Village, Makati, Metro Manila, Philippines
PHONE: +63 (2) 8179191; 8174992; 8174993
TITLE: Ambassador
NAME: Wolfgang Jilly

Bangladesh
2nd Floor, Universal-Re Building, 106 Paseo de Roxas corner Perea Street, Legaspi Village, Makati, Metro Manila, Philippines
PHONE: +63 (2) 8175010; 8175001
TITLE: Ambassador
NAME: Reazul Hossain

Belgium
Multinational Bancorporation Centre, 9th Floor, 6805 Ayala Avenue, Makati, Metro Manila, Philippines
PHONE: +63 (2) 8451869; 8451874
TITLE: Ambassador
NAME: Roland Van Remoortele

Brazil
6th Floor, RCI Building, 105 Rada Street, Legaspi Village, Makati, Metro Manila, Philippines
PHONE: +63 (2) 8928181; 8928182
TITLE: Ambassador
NAME: Luiz Mattoso Maia Amado

Brunei Darussalam
11th Floor, Ayala Wing, Bank of the Philippine Islands Building, Ayala Avenue corner Paseo de Roxas, Makati, Metro Manila, Philippines
PHONE: +63 (2) 8162836
TITLE: Ambassador
NAME: Dato Paduka Haji Yahya Bin Haji Harris

Canada
9th and 11th Floors, Allied Bank Centre, 6754 Ayala Avenue, Makati, Metro Manila, Philippines
PHONE: +63 (2) 8670001
TITLE: Ambassador
NAME: John Treleaven

Chile
6th Floor, Dona Salustiana D.T. Tower, 104 Paseo de Roxas, Legaspi Village, Makati, Metro Manila, Philippines
PHONE: +63 (2) 8160395; 8103149
TITLE: Ambassador
NAME: Sergio Silva

China
4896 Pasay Road, Dasmarinas Village, Makati, Metro Manila, Philippines
PHONE: +63 (2) 8443148; 8437715
TITLE: Ambassador
NAME: Fu Ying

Colombia
18th Floor, Aurora Tower, Araneta Center, Quezon City, Metro Manila, Philippines
PHONE: +63 (2) 9113101
TITLE: Ambassador
NAME: Miguel Duran Ordonez

Cuba
101 Aguirre cor. Trasierra Streets, Cacho Gonzales Building, Penthouse, Legaspi Village, Makati, Metro Manila, Philippines
PHONE: +63 (2) 8171192
TITLE: Ambassador
NAME: Francisco Ramos

Czech Republic
1267 Acacia Road, Dasmarinas Village, Makati, Metro Manila, Philippines
PHONE: +63 (2) 8129254

Denmark
6th Floor, Salustiana D. Ty Tower, 104 Paseo de Roxas corner Perea Street, Legaspi Village, 1226 Makati, Metro Manila, Philippines
PHONE: +63 (2) 8940086
TITLE: Ambassador
NAME: Bjarne Bladbjerg

Egypt
2229 Paraiso corner Banyan Streets, Dasmarinas Village, Makati, Metro Manila, Philippines
PHONE: +63 (2) 8439220
TITLE: Ambassador
NAME: Nabil Zaki

Finland
21st Floor, Far East Bank Center, Sen. Gil Puyat Avenue, Makati, Metro Manila, Philippines
PHONE: +63 (2) 8915011
TITLE: Ambassador
NAME: Pertti Majanen

France
The Pacific Star Building, 16th Floor, Makati Avenue corner Sen. Gil Puyat Extension, Makati, Metro Manila, Philippines
PHONE: +63 (2) 8101981
TITLE: Ambassador
NAME: Gilles Chouraqui

Germany
6th Floor, Solid Bank Building, 777 Paseo de Roxas, Makati, Metro Manila, Philippines
PHONE: +63 (2) 8924906
TITLE: Ambassador
NAME: Wolfgang Gottelmann

India
2190 Paraiso Street, Dasmarinas Village, Makati, Metro Manila, Philippines
PHONE: +63 (2) 8430101; 8430102
TITLE: Ambassador
NAME: C.P. Ravindranathan

Indonesia
185 Salcedo Street, Legaspi Village, Makati, Metro Manila, Philippines
PHONE: +63 (2) 8925061
TITLE: Ambassador
NAME: Abu Hartono

Iran
4th Floor, Don Jacinto Building, Salcedo corner dela Rosa Streets, Legaspi Village, Makati, Metro Manila, Philippines
PHONE: +63 (2) 8921561
TITLE: Ambassador
NAME: Mohammad Raeisi

Iraq
2261 Avocado Street, Dasmarinas Village, Makati, Metro Manila, Philippines
PHONE: +63 (2) 8439838; 8133067
TITLE: Ambassador
NAME: Salah Nouri Hitemi al-Samarmad

Israel
23rd Floor, Trafalgar Plaza, H.V. de la Costa Street, Salcedo Village, Makati, Metro Manila, Philippines
PHONE: +63 (2) 8925329
TITLE: Ambassador
NAME: Ilan Baruch

Italy
6th Floor, Zeta Building, 191 Salcedo Street, Legaspi Village, Makati, Metro Manila, Philippines
PHONE: +63 (2) 8924531
TITLE: Ambassador
NAME: Graziella Simbolotti

Japan
2627 Roxas Boulevard, Pasay City 1300, Philippines
PHONE: +63 (2) 5515710

Korea
10th Floor, The Pacific Star Building, Makati Avenue, Makati, Metro Manila, Philippines
PHONE: +63 (2) 8116139
TITLE: Ambassador
NAME: Shin Sung-Oh

Kuwait
6th Floor, Morning Star Building, 347 Sen. Gil J. Puyat Avenue, Makati, Metro Manila, Philippines
PHONE: +63 (2) 8977751
TITLE: Ambassador
NAME: Fahd Salem al-Ajmi

Laos
34 Lapu-Lapu Street, Magallanes Village, Makati City, Philippines
PHONE: +63 (2) 8335759
TITLE: Ambassador
NAME: Sengchanh Soukhaseum

Libya
2416 Bouganvilla Street, Dasmarinas Village, Makati, Metro Manila, Philippines
PHONE: +63 (2) 8442045; 8442046
TITLE: Ambassador
NAME: Rajab Abdulaziz Azzarouq

Malaysia
107 Tordesillas Street, Salcedo Villag, Makati, Metro Manila, Philippines
PHONE: +63 (2) 8174581
TITLE: Ambassador
NAME: Abdul Aziz Mohammed

Malta
6th Floor, Cattleya Condominium, 235 Salcedo Street, Legaspi Village, Makati, Metro Manila, Philippines
PHONE: +63 (2) 8171095
TITLE: Ambassador
NAME: Enrique P. Syquia

Mexico
18th Floor, Ramon Magsaysay Center, 1680 Roxas Boulevard, Pasay, Metro Manila, Philippines
PHONE: +63 (2) 5267461
TITLE: Ambassador
NAME: Enrique Michel

Myanmar
8th Floor, Xanland Centre, 152 Amorsolo Street, Legaspi Village, Makati City, Philippines
PHONE: +63 (2) 8172372
TITLE: Ambassador
NAME: U San Thein

Netherlands
9th Floor, King's Court Building, 2129 Pasong Tamo, Makati, Metro Manila, Philippines
PHONE: +63 (2) 8125981; 8125982; 8125983
TITLE: Ambassador
NAME: George Theodore Eugene Richard Arnold

New Zealand
23rd Floor, Far East Bank Centre, Sen. Gil Puyat Avenue (near Makati Avenue), Makati, Metro Manila, Philippines
PHONE: +63 (2) 8915358
TITLE: Ambassador
NAME: Graeme Charles Waters

Nigeria
2211 Paraiso Street, Dasmarinas Village, Makati, Metro Manila, Philippines
PHONE: +63 (2) 8439866
TITLE: Ambassador
NAME: Ademola Olugbade Aderele

Norway
21st Floor, Petron Mega Plaza Building, 358 Sen. Gil Puyat Avenue, Makati, Metro Manila, Philippines
PHONE: +63 (2) 8863245
TITLE: Ambassador
NAME: Inga Magistad

Pakistan
6th Floor, Alexander House, 132 Amorsolo Street, Legaspi Village, Makati, Metro Manila, Philippines
PHONE: +63 (2) 8172776; 8172772
TITLE: Ambassador
NAME: Azmat Ghayur

Panama
Room 501, Victoria Building, 429 United Nations Avenue, Ermita, Manila, Philippines
PHONE: +63 (2) 5212790; 5211233
TITLE: Ambassador
NAME: Graciela Arauz Arias

Papua New Guinea
2280 Magnolia Street, Dasmarinas Village, Makati, Metro Manila, Philippines
PHONE: +63 (2) 8442060; 8442051
TITLE: Ambassador
NAME: Graham John Ainui

Peru
7th Floor, Unit 7-B, Country Space One Building, Sen. Gil Puyat Avenue, Makati, Metro Manila, Philippines
PHONE: +63 (2) 8138731
TITLE: Ambassador
NAME: Victor Aritomi-Shinto

Portugal
14th Floor, Unit D Trafalgar Plaza, 105 H.V. dela Costa Street, Salcedo Village, Makati City, Philippines
PHONE: +63 (2) 8483789; 8483790
TITLE: Ambassador
NAME: Joao Henrique Araujo Brito Camara

Qatar
1601 Cypress Street, Dasmarinas Village, Makati, Metro Manila, Philippines
PHONE: +63 (2) 8874944; 8874945
TITLE: Ambassador
NAME: Saleh Ibrahim al-Kuwari

Romania
1216 Acacia Road, Dasmarinas Village, Makati, Metro Manila, Philippines
PHONE: +63 (2) 8439014

Russia
1245 Acacia Road, Dasmarinas Village, Makati, Metro Manila, Philippines
PHONE: +63 (2) 8109614; 8930190
TITLE: Ambassador
NAME: Anatoli Khmelnitski

Saudi Arabia
Saudi Embassy Building, 389 Senator Gil J. Puyat Avenue Extension, Makati, Metro Manila, Philippines
PHONE: +63 (2) 8909735
TITLE: Ambassador
NAME: Saleh Mohammad al-Ghamdi

Singapore
6th Floor, ODC International Plaza, 219 Salcedo Street, Legaspi Village, Makati, Metro Manila, Philippines
PHONE: +63 (2) 8161764; 8161765
TITLE: Ambassador
NAME: Simon Tensing De Cruz

Spain
5th Floor, ACT Tower, 135 Sen. Gil Puyat Avenue, Makati, Metro Manila, Philippines
PHONE: +63 (2) 8183561; 8185526
TITLE: Ambassador
NAME: Delfin Colome

Sri Lanka
2260 Avocado Avenue, Dasmarinas Village, Makati City, Philippines
PHONE: +63 (2) 8439813; 8120335
TITLE: Ambassador
NAME: Pitiduwa Gamage Karunasiri

United States
Chancery Building, 1201 Roxas Boulevard, Manila, Philippines
PHONE: +63 (2) 5231001
TITLE: Ambassador
NAME: Thomas C. Hubbard

JUDICIAL SYSTEM

Supreme Court

BROADCAST MEDIA

CPM Broadcasting Corporation

10/F, Centrepoint Bldg., Plaridel Street, Corner Osmena Boulevard, Cebu City, Philippines
E-MAIL: dymzcebu@philexport.com

Far East Broadcasting Co.

Box 1, 0560 Valenzuela, Metro, Manila, Philippines
PHONE: +63 (2) 3611010
FAX: +63 (2) 359490
E-MAIL: febcomphil@febc.jmf.org.ph
WEBSITE: http://www.febc.org
TITLE: Managing Director
CONTACT: Efren M. Pallorina
TYPE: Religious

FBS Radio Network, Inc.

18/F Philcomcen Bldg., Ortigas Avenue, 1605 Pasig City, Philippines
PHONE: +63 (2) 635 3309
E-MAIL: lldava@philexport.com

Kapisanan NG MGA Brodkaster SA Pilipinas (KBP) (Association of Broadcasters in the Philippines)

6th Flr, LTA Bldg. 118 Perea Street, Legazpi Village, Makati, Metro-Manila, Philippines
PHONE: +63 (2) 8151990
FAX: +63 (2) 8151989
TITLE: Chairman
CONTACT: Jose E Escaner, Jr.

Melody Broadcasting Corporation (DYAC-FM)

Room 210 Dona Luisa Bldg., Fuente Osmena, Cebu City, Philippines
PHONE: +63 (2) 2535165
E-MAIL: dyaccebu@philexport.com

National Telecommunications Commission (Department of Transportation and Communications)

865 Vibal Bldg, Edsa Corner Times Street, Quezon City, Philippines
TITLE: Commissioner
CONTACT: Josefina Lichauco

Philippine Federation of Catholic Broadcasters

2307 Pedro Gil Street, Santa Ana, PO Box 3169, Manila 1099, Philippines
PHONE: +63 (2) 584828
TITLE: President
CONTACT: Jesus Y. Varela
TYPE: Religious

Primax Broadcasting Network, Inc.

Boy Scout Camp, Capitol Hills, Cebu City 6000, Philippines
PHONE: +63 (2) 2541046
FAX: +63 (2) 2539682
E-MAIL: kicebu@philexport.com
TITLE: Station Manager
CONTACT: Solitheus Noval

Radio Pilipinas

Philippine Broadcasting Sce. 4th Flr. Media Center, Visayas Ave., Diliman, Quezon City, Metro Manila 1103, Philippines
PHONE: +63 (2) 9242267
FAX: +63 (2) 9242745
TITLE: Director
CONTACT: Rafael Dante A. Cruz

Radio Veritas Asia

Philippine Radio Educational and Information Center, PO Box 2642, Quezon City 1166, Philippines
PHONE: +63 (2) 939001
FAX: +63 (2) 9381940

E-MAIL: veritas@mnl.sequel.net (programming), info@radio-veritas.org.ph (technical dept.)
WEBSITE: http://www.radio-veritas.org.ph
TITLE: Chairman
CONTACT: Jaime Cardinal Sin

Rajah Broadcasting Network, Inc.

10/F Centerpoint Hotel, Plaridel Street, Cebu City 6000, Philippines
PHONE: +63 (2) 2530300
FAX: +63 (2) 2530245
E-MAIL: dyrjcebu@philexport.com

Vimcontu Broadcasting Corporation

Quezon Memorial Circle cor. Maharlika Ave., Diliman, Quezon City, Philippines
PHONE: +63 (2) 9222575
FAX: +63 (2) 9223199
TITLE: President of the Associated Labor Union-Trade Union Congress of the Philippines [p class="2Head]National Telecommunications Commission (Department of Transportation and Communications)
CONTACT: Democrito Mendoza, 855 Vibal Bldg., Esda Corner Times Street, Quezon City, Philippines
TITLE: Commissioner
CONTACT: Josefina Lichauco

People's Television Network, Inc.

Broadcast Complex, Visayas Avenue, Quezon City 1100, Philippines
PHONE: +63 (2) 9212344
FAX: +63 (2) 9211777
TITLE: Chairman
CONTACT: Lourdes I. Ilustre
TYPE: Commercial

COLLEGES AND UNIVERSITIES

Feati University

Helios Street, Santa Cruz, Manila, Philippines

Manuel L Quezon University

916 R Hidalgo, Quiapo, Manila, Philippines

Manila Central University

Edsa, Caloocan City, Metro Manila, Philippines
E-MAIL: info@mcu.edu.ph
WEBSITE: http://www.mcu.edu.ph

Central Luzon State University

Munoz, Nueva Ecija 3120, Philippines
FAX: +63 (44) 4560107
WEBSITE: http://www2.mozcom.com/~clsu/

University of the East - Manila

2219 Claro M Recto Ave., Manila, Philippines
PHONE: +63 (2) 7355471
WEBSITE: http://www.ue.edu.ph

Centro Escolar University

9 Mendiola St., San Miguel, Manila, Philippines
PHONE: +63 (2) 7356861
FAX: +63 (2) 7356860
WEBSITE: http://www.ceu.edu.ph

University of the Philippines Open University

Manila, Philippines
PHONE: +63 2 809 033 336 0625
E-MAIL: ou_reg@laguna.net
WEBSITE: http://www.upou.edu.ph

St. Mary's University - Nueva Vizcaya

College of Arts & Sciences, Bayombong, Nueva Vizcaya 3700, Philippines
PHONE: +63 (78) 3212221; 3213650
FAX: +63 (78) 3212117
E-MAIL: smunet@smu.edu.ph
WEBSITE: http://www.smu.edu.ph

University of Mindanao

Bolton Street, Davao City, Mindanao, Philippines
PHONE: +63 2 809 227 5456
WEBSITE: http://www.umindanao.edu.ph

University of the East, Caloocan

105 Samsun Rd., Caloocan, Philippines
PHONE: +63 2 809 361 23 98
E-MAIL: webmaster@uec.edu
WEBSITE: http://www2.mozcam.com/~ue2/index.html

University of Batangas

Hilltop, Batangas City, Philippines
PHONE: +63 (43) 7230693
E-MAIL: info@ub.edu.ph
WEBSITE: http://www.ub.edu.ph

Ateneo de Naga University

Jesuit Residence, Naga City 4400, Philippines
PHONE: +63 (54) 4739934
FAX: +63 (54) 4739253

E-MAIL: aao@sili.adnu.edu.ph
WEBSITE: http://www.adnu.edu.ph

Arellano University

2600 Legarda St., Sampaloc, Manila, Philippines
WEBSITE: http://www.arellano.edu.ph

University of Pangasinan

Dagupan City, Philippines
WEBSITE: http://www.upang.edu.ph

University of Regina Carmeli

Malolos, Bulacan, Philippines
PHONE: +63 (44) 7910271; 7917188
FAX: +63 (44) 7911749
E-MAIL: infor@urc.fapenet.org
WEBSITE: http://www.urc.fapenet.org

University of Baguio

Baguio City 0220, Philippines
PHONE: +63 (74) 4423071
E-MAIL: univgo@ubaguio.fapenet.org
WEBSITE: http://www.ubaguio.fapenet.org

University of Northern Philippines

Vigan, Ilocos Sur 0401, Philippines

University of the Philippines-Manila

Taft Ave., Manila 1000, Philippines
PHONE: +63 (2) 5255689
FAX: +63 (2) 5210184
E-MAIL: info@mail.upm.edu.ph
WEBSITE: http://www.upm.edu.ph

Technical University of the Philippines

PO Box 3171, Ayala Blvd., Ermita, Manila 1000, Philippines
PHONE: +63 (2) 5244721
WEBSITE: http://www.tup.edu.ph

De La Salle University

2401 Taft Ave., Manila 1004, Philippines
PHONE: +63 (2) 5244611
FAX: +63 (2) 5219094
E-MAIL: evpciq@dlsu.edu.ph
WEBSITE: http://www.dlsu.edu.ph

Philippine Women's University

1743 Taft Ave., Manila 1004, Philippines
WEBSITE: http://www.pwu.edu

University of Santo Tomas

Espana St., Manila 1083, Philippines
PHONE: +63 (2) 7313101
E-MAIL: dcabezon@ustcc.ust.edu.ph
WEBSITE: http://www.ust.edu.ph

Ateneo de Manila University

PO Box 154, Loyola Heights, Quezon City, Manila 1108, Philippines
PHONE: +63 (2) 4266001
WEBSITE: http://www.admu.edu.ph

Isabela State University

San Fabian, Echague, Isabela, Philippines

University of Asia & the Pacific

Pearl Dr., Ortigas Center, Pasig City 1605, Philippines
PHONE: +63 (2) 6342809
FAX: +63 (2) 6343140
E-MAIL: admissions@uap.edu.ph
WEBSITE: http://www.uap.edu.ph

Tarlac State University

Romulo Blvd., San Vincente, Tarlac City 2300, Philippines
PHONE: +63 (45) 9820777
FAX: +63 (45) 5219094
E-MAIL: e_paguio@yahoo.com
WEBSITE: http://www2.mozcom.com/~tsu-ics/

St. Louis University - Baguio City

PO Box 71, A Bonifacio St., Baguio City 2600, Philippines
PHONE: +63 (74) 4423043
E-MAIL: saodean@slu.edu.ph
WEBSITE: http://www.slu.edu.ph

Benguet State University

La Trinidad, Benguet 2601, Philippines
WEBSITE: http://www.bsu.edu.ph

St. Paul University

Tugegarao City, Cagayan 3062, Philippines
E-MAIL: info@spu.edu.ph
WEBSITE: http://www.spu.edu.ph

Aquinas University

Rawis, 4500 Legazpi City, Philippines
PHONE: +63 (52) 2122123
WEBSITE: http://www.aquinas-university.edu

Central Philippine University

Lopez Jaena St., Iloilo City 5000, Philippines
PHONE: +63 (33) 3281971
FAX: +63 (33) 3203685
E-MAIL: cpuadmin@iloilo.net
WEBSITE: http://www.cpuic.edu/ccpu

University of San Jose-Recoletos

Cor. P. Lopez & Megerllanes Sts., Cebu City 6000, Philippines
E-MAIL: webmast@usjr.edu.ph
WEBSITE: http://www.usjr.edu.ph

University of San Carlos

P. Del Rosario St., Cebu City 6000, Philippines
WEBSITE: http://www.usc.edu.ph

University of Negros

Occidental Recoletos, Lizares Ave., PO Box 214, Bacolod City 6100, Philippines

Silliman University

Hibbard Ave., Dumaguete City 6200, Philippines
PHONE: +63 (35) 4426002
WEBSITE: http://www.su.edu.ph

Western Mindanao State University

Normal Rd., Baliwasan, Zamboanga City 7000, Philippines
PHONE: +63 33 809 991 1040
WEBSITE: http://www.wmsu.edu.ph

Ateneo de Davao University

PO BOX 80113, E. Jacinto St., Davao City 8000, Philippines
PHONE: +63 (82) 2212411
WEBSITE: http://www.addu.edu.ph

Liceo de Cagayan University

Rodolfo N. Palaez Blvd., Carmen, Cagayan de Oro City 9000, Philippines
PHONE: +63 (88) 8584093
E-MAIL: info@ldcu.edu.ph
WEBSITE: http://www.ldcu.edu.ph

Xavier University

Ateneo De Cagayan, Cagayan de Oro City 9000, Philippines
PHONE: +63 (88) 8583116
E-MAIL: pres@xu.edu.ph
WEBSITE: http://www.xu.edu.ph

Mindanao State University

MSUIIT, A. Bonifacio Ave., Ligan City 9200, Philippines
PHONE: +63 (63) 2214050
FAX: +63 (63) 2214056
WEBSITE: http://www.msuiit.edu.ph

Notre Dame University

Notre Dame Ave., Cotabato City 9600, Philippines
PHONE: +63 (64) 4214312
FAX: +63 (64) 4214312
WEBSITE: http://www.ndu.fapenet.org

NEWSPAPERS AND MAGAZINES

The Manila Bulletin

Manila Bulletin Publishing Co, Bulletin Bldg, Muralla St. cnr Recoletos, Intarmuros, Manila, Philippines
PHONE: +63 (2) 5277515; 5277517
FAX: +63 (2) 5277504; 5277533
E-MAIL: bulletin@mb.com.ph
WEBSITE: http://www.mb.com.ph
TITLE: Editor
CONTACT: Ben F. Rodriguez
CIRCULATION: 250,000 (Daily); 300,000 (Sun.)

The Philippine Star / The Evening Star

The Philippines Today Inc., 202 Railroad St. cnr 13th St., Port Area, Metro Manila, Philippines
PHONE: +63 (2) 5272398; 5273145
FAX: +63 (2) 5275819; 5275820
E-MAIL: info@philstar.com
WEBSITE: http://www.philstar.com
TITLE: Editor-in-Chief
CONTACT: Ramon J. Farolan
CIRCULATION: 240,000

People's Journal

Philippine Journalists, Inc., Journal Bldg, 19th St. cnr Railroad St. Port Area, Metro Manila, Philippines
PHONE: +63 (2) 5274821
FAX: +63 (2) 5274640; 5274652; 5274651
E-MAIL: jounal@skinet.net
WEBSITE: http://www.eiger.ch/eiger/pdo
TITLE: Editor-in-Chief
CONTACT: Guillermo H.A. Santos
CIRCULATION: 382,200

Panorama

Manila Bulletin Publishing Co, Bulletin Bldg, Muralla St. cnr Recoletos, Intarmuros, Manila, Philippines
PHONE: +63 (2) 5277515; 5277517; 5278121
FAX: +63 (2) 5277504; 5277533
E-MAIL: panorama@mb.com.ph
WEBSITE: http://www.mb.com.ph/PANORAMA
TITLE: Editor
CONTACT: Randy Urlanda
CIRCULATION: 300,000

The Philippine Starweek

The Philippines Today Inc., 202 Railroad St. cnr 13th St., Port Area, Metro Manila, Philippines
PHONE: +63 (2) 5272398; 5273145
FAX: +63 (2) 5275819; 5275820
E-MAIL: info@philstar.com
WEBSITE: http://www.philstar.com
TITLE: Editor
CONTACT: Doreen Yu
CIRCULATION: 271,683

The Philippine Daily Inquirer

Philippine Daily Inquirer Inc., 1098 Chino Roces Ave. cnr Mascardo and Yague Sts., Makati City, Philippines
PHONE: +63 (2) 8798808; 8448001
FAX: +63 (2) 8794793; 8794794
E-MAIL: inquirer@skinet.net
WEBSITE: http://www.inquirer.net
TITLE: Editor-in-Chief
CONTACT: Leticia Jimenez-Magsanoc
CIRCULATION: 260,000

The Manila Times

Metromedia Times Corporation, No. 30 Pioneer St., cnr EDSQ, Mandaluyong, Metro Manila, Philippines
PHONE: +63 (2) 6318971
FAX: +63 (2) 6137788
E-MAIL: manilatimes@portalinc.com
WEBSITE: http://www.portalinc.com/manilatimes; http://www.manilatimes.net
TITLE: Editor-in-Chief
CONTACT: Lourdes C. Mangahas
CIRCULATION: 194,000

People's Tonight

Philippine Journalists, Inc., Journal Bldg, 19th St. cnr Railroad St. Port Area, Metro Manila, Philippines
PHONE: +63 (2) 5274821
FAX: +63 (2) 5274640; 5274652; 5274651
WEBSITE: http://www.eiger.ch/eiger/pdo
TITLE: Editor
CONTACT: Alex Allen

Attitude

Eastgate Publishing Corp., 6/F, Emerald Bldg, Emerald Ave., Pasig, 1600 Metro Manila, Philippines
PHONE: +63 (2) 6312995; 6312929; 6312921
FAX: +63 (2) 6312992
CIRCULATION: 12,000
TYPE: General Interest

Liwayway Magazine

Liwayway Publishing Inc., 2249 Pasong Tarro St., Makati, Metro Manila, Philippines
PHONE: +63 (2) 8193130
FAX: +63 (2) 8175167
TITLE: Editor-in-Chief
CONTACT: Rodolfo Salandanan
CIRCULATION: 163,000
TYPE: General Interest

Sunday Inquirer Magazine

Philippine Inquirer, PO Box 2050, Mandaluyong, Metro Manila, Philippines
PHONE: +63 (2) 508061
FAX: +63 (2) 588948
TITLE: Editor-in-Chief
CONTACT: Leticia Magsanoc
TYPE: General Interest

Yuhum Magazine

M. Villalon Publications, Rm. 404, F&M Lopez Bldg., Legaspi Village, Makati, Metro Manila, Philippines
PHONE: +63 (2) 8151591
TITLE: Editor-in-Chief
CONTACT: Katherine Villalon
CIRCULATION: 52,584
TYPE: General Interest

PUBLISHERS

Abiva Publishing House Inc.

851 Georgio Araneta Ave., 1113 Quezon City, PO Box 2832, Manila, Philippines
PHONE: +63 (2) 7120486
FAX: +63 (2) 7320308
E-MAIL: mmrabiva@I-manila.com.ph
WEBSITE: http://www.abiva.com.ph

CONTACT: Amalia C. Villarruz
SUBJECTS: Education, History, Religion-Other, Science (General)

Anvil Publishing

2/F Team Pacific Bldg., 13 Jose Cruz St., Bo. Ugong, Pasig City, Manila, Philippines
PHONE: +63 (2) 9140155
FAX: +63 (2) 6719235
E-MAIL: anvil@fc.emc.com.ph
TITLE: General Manager
CONTACT: Cecilia R. Licauco
SUBJECTS: Cookery, Crafts, Games, Hobbies, Fiction, Gardening, Plants, Health, Nutrition, How-to, Humor, Language Arts, Linguistics, Literature, Literary Criticism, Essays, Mysteries, Religion-Catholic, Romance, Science Fiction, Fantasy, Western Fiction, Women's Studies
TOTAL PUBLISHED: 600 print

Ateneo de Manila University Press

Katipunan Rd., Bellarmine Hall, Loyola Heights, Quezon City, Philippines
PHONE: +63 (2) 4266001
FAX: +63 (2) 4265909
E-MAIL: unipress@pusit.admu.edu.ph
WEBSITE: http://www.ateneo.net
TITLE: Director
CONTACT: Esther M. Pacheco
SUBJECTS: Literature, Literary Criticism, Essays, Social Science
TOTAL PUBLISHED: 150 print

De La Salle University Press Inc.

2504 Leon Guinto St., Malate 1004, Manila, Philippines
PHONE: +63 (2) 5361761
FAX: +63 (2) 5265139
E-MAIL: inquiry@dlsupress.hypermart.net
WEBSITE: http://www.dlsupress.com
TITLE: Director
CONTACT: Elizabeth S. Reyes
SUBJECTS: Asian Studies, Business, Education, Fiction, Literature, Literary Criticism, Essays, Philosophy, Poetry, Religion-Catholic
TOTAL PUBLISHED: Over 200 print

Heritage Publishing House

33 4th Ave. corner Main Ave., Cubao, Quezon City, Philippines
PHONE: +63 (2) 7248114
FAX: +63 (2) 6471393
E-MAIL: heritage@iconn.com.ph
WEBSITE: http://www.iconn.com.ph/heritage/
TITLE: Managing Director
CONTACT: Ricardo S. Sanchez
SUBJECTS: Art, Anthropology, History, Humanities, Labor Relations, Literature, Politics, Sociology
TOTAL PUBLISHED: 10 print

National Museum of the Philippines

Museum Education Div., National Museum (Main), Padre Burgos St., Manila, Philippines
PHONE: +63 (2) 5270278; 5271215
FAX: +63 (2) 5270306
E-MAIL: nmuseum@I-next.net
WEBSITE: http://members.tripod.com/philmuseum/index
TITLE: Director
CONTACT: Gabriel Casal
SUBJECTS: Art, Anthropology, Archaeology, Botany, Conservation, Education, Geology, Zoology

New Day Publishers

11 Lands St., VASRA, Quezon City 1100, Philippines
PHONE: +63 (2) 9288046
FAX: +63 (2) 9246544
E-MAIL: newday@pworld.net.ph
TITLE: Director
CONTACT: Bezalie B. Uc-Kung
SUBJECTS: Anthropology, Asian Studies, Behavioral Studies, Biblical Studies, Biography, Business, Career Development, Communications, Cookery, Economics, Education, Ethnicity, Fiction, History, How-to, Human Relations, Humor, Labor, Industrial Relations, Literature, Literary Criticism, Essays, Management, Marketing, Nonfiction (General), Philosophy, Poetry, Religion-Catholic, Religion-Protestant, Romance, Science Fiction, Fantasy, Self-Help, Theology
TOTAL PUBLISHED: 500 print; 20 annually

SIBS Publishing House Inc.

Phoenix Bldg., 927 Quezon Ave., Quezon City 1104, Philippines
PHONE: +63 (2) 3742870
FAX: +63 (2) 3742874
E-MAIL: sibsbook@info.com.ph
WEBSITE: http://www.phoenix-sibs.com
SUBJECTS: Art, Literature, Mathematics, Religion, Science, Social Studies, Writing

RELIGIOUS ORGANIZATIONS

Buddhist

Bahay Dalangin
3194 F. Roxas, Sta. Ana, Manila, Philippines
TITLE: Contact
NAME: Sonia Punzalan

Gyoku'un Zendo
C/o 54 Stanford Street, Cubao, Quezon City, Philippines
TITLE: Contact
NAME: Mila Golez

Zen Center for Oriental Spirituality in the Philippines
85 St. Catherine Provident Village, Marikina, Manila, Philippines
TITLE: Contact
NAME: Antonio P.Perlas

Catholic

Archdiocese of Cotabato
Bishop's Residence, Sinsuat Ave, Cotabato City 9600, Philippines
PHONE: +63 (64) 4212918
FAX: +63 (64) 4290030
E-MAIL: obquev@ndu.fapenet.org
TITLE: Archbishop

Diocese of Alaminos
Bishop's Residence, Alaminos 2404, Pangasinan, Philippines
PHONE: +63 (75) 5527062
FAX: +63 (75) 5527092
E-MAIL: dzwm@gaia.psdn.org.
TITLE: Bishop
NAME: Most Rev. Jesus A. Cabrera, D.D.

Diocesis Bacolodensis
Chancery Bishop's House, Rizal St. 6100, Baclod City, P.O. Box 141 & 152, Philippines
PHONE: +63 (34) 4333310

Family Life Office
Sacred Heart Seminary Compound, Lizares St., 6100 Baclod City
PHONE: +63 (34) 25594
TITLE: Coordinator
NAME: Mrs. Rose P. Tan

Holy Rosary Major Seminary
Concepcion Pequena, Naga City 4400, Philippines

Marist Fathers
Cotabato City, Philippines
PHONE: +63 4214078
FAX: +63 4219050
E-MAIL: pat@marist.edu.ph

Notre Dame Archdiocesan Seminary
PO Box 264, Cotabato City, Philippines
PHONE: +63 (64) 4290030

Oblates of Notre Dame
P.O. Box 667, 9600 Cotabato City, Philippines
PHONE: +63 (64) 4212919
E-MAIL: ondgen@ndc.marist.edu.ph

Serra Club of Cotabato
Archdiocese of Cotabato, Cotabato City 9600, Philippines

Jewish

Beth Yaacov
110 H.V. DeLa Costa Tordesillas West 1227, Salcedo Village, Manila, Philippines
PHONE: +63 (2) 8150265
E-MAIL: jap.manila@usa.net
WEBSITE: http://www.jewishglobe.com/Member/Jewish_Philippines.html
TITLE: Contact
NAME: ShlomoAttias

Mikvah c/o Synagogue & Community Center
H.V. dela Costa & Tordesillas Sts., Manila, Salcedo Village, Philippines
PHONE: +63 (2) 8150263, 8150265

Protestant

Action International Ministries (ACTION)
PO Box 14220, Ortigas Ctr., Pasig 1605, Philippines
PHONE: +63 (2) 5310642
FAX: +63 (2) 7184904
E-MAIL: action@pacific.net.ph
TITLE: Interim Dir.
NAME: Jeff Read

Christ's Youth In Action
Unit 2, 127 Don Alejandrino Roces Ave., Quezon City, Philippines
PHONE: +63 (2) 4113146
FAX: +63 (2) 4113848

The Salvation Army
P.O. Box 3830, Manila 1099, Philippines
PHONE: +63 (2) 5240086, 5240088
FAX: +63 (2) 5216912
E-MAIL: philippines@salvationarmy.org

Women for Christ
3/F Pangarap Building, 85-C West Avenue cor. Baler St., Quezon City, Philippines
PHONE: +63 (2) 9268373

FURTHER READING

Articles

"Bungles in the Jungle: Muslim Rebels in the Southern Philippines Seize an American Hostage, Raising the Stakes in a Macabre Kidnapping Game." *Time International,* September 11, 2000, vol. 156, no. 10, p20+.

"'Enough Is Enough.'" *Newsweek International,* September 25, 2000, p. 57.

The Economist, January 8, January 15, February 19, March 4, March 25, April 15, May 6, May 13, June 24, and July 15, 2000.

Far Eastern Economic Review, July 20, and August 3, 2000.

Manila Bulletin, October 9, 2000.

The New York Times, April 24 & May 6, 2000.

Mydans, Seth. "Philippine Panel Sends Impeachment Case to Full House." *New York Times,* November 7, 2000, p. A8.

——— "Philippine Vice President Quits Cabinet, Citing Scandal." *New York Times,* October 13, 2000, p. A4.

Books

Linn, Brian McAllister. *The Philippine War, 1899–1902.* Lawrence: University Press of Kansas, 2000.

Steinberg, David Joel. *The Philippines: A Singular and a Plural Place.* 4th ed. Boulder, CO: Westview Press, 2000.

Internet

"Philippines Storm Toll Reaches 27." Reuters. July 7, 2000. [Online] Available http://www.reliefweb.int/ (accessed July 10, 2000).

"Philippine Volcano Subsides, Alert Lowered." Reuters. March 9, 2000. [Online] Available http://www.reliefweb.int/ (accessed July 10, 2000).

Philippine Center for Investigative Journalism, July–Sept 2000, vol. vi, no. 3. [Online] Available http://www.pcij.org (accessed September 30, 2000).

PHILIPPINES: STATISTICAL DATA

For sources and notes see "Sources of Statistics" at the front of each volume.

GEOGRAPHY

Geography

Area:

Total: 300,000 sq km.

Land: 298,170 sq km.

Land boundaries: 0 km.

Coastline: 36,289 km.

Climate: tropical marine; northeast monsoon (November to April); southwest monsoon (May to October).

Terrain: mostly mountains with narrow to extensive coastal lowlands.

Natural resources: timber, petroleum, nickel, cobalt, silver, gold, salt, copper.

Land use:

Arable land: 19%

Permanent crops: 12%

Permanent pastures: 4%

Forests and woodland: 46%

Other: 19% (1993 est.).

HUMAN FACTORS

Demographics (A)

	1990	1995	1998	2000	2010	2020	2030	2040	2050
Population	65,037	72,869	77,814	81,160	97,898	114,151	129,449	142,847	153,913
Life expectancy - males	61.3	63.1	64.0	64.6	67.7	70.3	72.6	74.6	76.2
Life expectancy - females	67.5	68.1	69.5	70.5	73.7	76.6	79.0	80.9	82.5
Birth rate (per 1,000)	32.3	30.3	28.8	27.8	23.3	20.1	17.6	15.7	14.3
Death rate (per 1,000)	7.3	6.8	6.4	6.1	5.5	5.4	5.7	6.4	7.3
Women of reproductive age (15-49 yrs.)	16,241	18,559	20,045	20,982	25,705	30,292	33,682	35,957	36,820
Fertility rate	4.1	3.8	3.6	3.5	2.9	2.5	2.3	2.1	2.1

Except as noted, values for vital statistics are in thousands; life expectancy is in years.

Health Personnel

	National Data	World Data (wtd ave)
Total health expenditure as a percentage of GDP, 1990-1998[a]		
Public sector	1.7	2.5
Private sector	0.1	2.9
Total[b]	3.7	5.5
Health expenditure per capita in U.S. dollars, 1990-1998[a]		
Purchasing power parity	124	561
Total	32	483
Availability of health care facilities per 100,000 people		
Hospital beds 1990-1998[a]	110	330
Doctors 1992-1995[a]	11	122
Nurses 1992-1995[a]	43	248

Health Indicators

	National Data	World Data
Life expectancy at birth (years)		
1980	61	61
1998	69	67
Daily per capita supply of calories		
1970	1,753	2,358
1997	2,366	2,791
Daily per capital supply of protein		
1997 (grams)	56	74
Total fertility rate (births per woman)		
1980	4.8	3.7
1998	3.6	2.7
Population with access (%)		
To safe water (1990-96)	83	NA
To sanitation (1990-96)	77	NA
People living with (1997)		
Tuberculosis (cases per 100,000)	294.5	60.4
Malaria (cases per 100,000)	58.8	42.2
HIV/AIDS (% aged 15 - 49 years)	0.06	0.99

Infants and Malnutrition

	National Data	World Data (wtd ave)
Under 5 mortality rate (1989)	44	NA
% of infants with low birthweight (1992-98)[1]	11	17
Births attended by skilled health staff (% of total births 1996-98)	53	52
% fully immunized at 1 year of age (1995-98)[1]		
TB	91	82
DPT	79	77
Polio	81	77
Measles	71	74
Prevalence of child malnutrition (1992-98)[1] (based on weight for age, % of children under 5 years)	30	30

Ethnic Division

Christian Malay 91.5%
Muslim Malay 4.0%
Chinese 1.5%
Other 3.0%

Religion

Roman Catholic 83%
Protestant 9%
Muslim 5%
Buddhist and other 3%

Major Languages

Pilipino (official, based on Tagalog), English (official).

EDUCATION

Public Education Expenditures

	1980	1997
Public expenditures on education as % of GNP	1.7	3.4
Expenditures per student as % of GNP per capita		
Primary	5.8[2]	9.2
Secondary	4.3	7.6
Tertiary	13.8	14.8
Pupils per teacher at the primary level	NA	35
Duration of primary education in years	NA	6
World data for comparison		
Public expenditures on education as % of GNP (mean)	3.9	4.8
Pupils per teacher at the primary level (wtd ave)	NA	33
Duration of primary education in years (mean)	NA	9

Educational Attainment (A)

Age group (1995) . . . . .15+

Population of this age group 42,700,000

Highest level attained (%)

No schooling 3.8

First level

Not completed 20.8

Completed 15.1

Entered second level

Lower Secondary 17.3

Upper Secondary 21.2

Entered post-secondary .22.0

Literacy Rates (A)

In thousands and percent	1990	1995	2000	2010
Illiterate population (15+ yrs.)	2,350	2,234	2,024	1,639
Literacy rate - total adult pop. (%)	93.6	94.6	95.7	97.3
Literacy rate - males (%)	94.0	95.0	96.0	97.4
Literacy rate - females (%)	93.2	94.3	95.5	97.1

Libraries

National Libraries **1993**

Administrative Units 1

Service Points or Branches .4

Number of Volumes (000) 902

Registered Users (000) 190

Loans to Users (000) . . . . .NA

Total Library Staff 156

GOVERNMENT & LAW

Political Parties

Congress (Kongreso)	no. of seats
Senate	
Laban Ng Masang Pilipino (Struggle of the Filipino Masses) (LAMP)	12
Lakas	5
People's Reform Party (PRP)	2
Liberal Party (LP)	1
Other	3
House of Representatives	
Laban Ng Masang Pilipino (Struggle of the Masses) (LAMP)	135
Lakas	37
Liberal Party (LP)	13
Aksyon Demokratiko	1
Other	35

Elections for the Senate and the House of Representatives were last held 11 May 1998 (next to be held 11 May 2001). The Senate now has only 23 members with one seat vacated when Gloria Macapagal-Arroyo became vice president. The seat can only be filled by election and is likely to remain open until the next regular election in 2001.

Government Budgets (A)

Year: 1997

Total Expenditures: 467,319 Millions of Pesos

Expenditures as a percentage of the total by function:

General public services and public order 17.15

Defense 7.98

Education 20.41

Health 3.21

Social Security and Welfare 2.51

Housing and community amenities 0.55

Recreational, cultural, and religious affairs 0.73

Fuel and energy 0.20

Agriculture, forestry, fishing, and hunting 6.50

Mining, manufacturing, and construction 0.04

Transportation and communication 13.64

Other economic affairs and services 1.84

Crime

Crime rate (for 1994)

Crimes reported 93,300

Total persons convicted . . . . .NA

Crimes per 100,000 population 139

(Continued on next page.)

LABOR FORCE

Total Labor Force (A)

32 million (1999 est.).

Labor Force by Occupation

Agriculture 39.8%

Government and social services 19.4%

Services 17.7%

Manufacturing 9.8%

Construction 5.8%

Other 7.5%

Data for 1998 est.

Unemployment Rate

9.6% (October 1998)

PRODUCTION SECTOR

Energy Production

Production . . . . .39.623 billion kWh

Production by source

Fossil fuel 70.12%

Hydro 10.75%

Nuclear 0%

Other 19.13%

Exports . . . . .0 kWh

Data for 1998.

Energy Consumption

Consumption . . . . .36.849 billion kWh

Imports . . . . .0 kWh

Data for 1998.

(Continued on next page.)

GOVERNMENT & LAW (cont.)

Military Affairs (A)

	1990	1992	1995	1996	1997
Military expenditures					
Current dollars (mil.)	1,230	1,160	1,040	1,260	1,270
1997 constant dollars (mil.)	1,440	1,290	1,080	1,280	1,270
Armed forces (000)	109	107	104	103	105
Gross national product (GNP)					
Current dollars (mil.)	56,400	60,800	73,300	80,100	85,700
1997 constant dollars (mil.)	66,000	67,400	75,900	81,400	85,700
Central government expenditures (CGE)					
1997 constant dollars (mil.)	13,400	12,700	13,600	14,600	16,000
People (mil.)	65.0	68.1	72.9	74.5	76.1
Military expenditure as % of GNP	2.2	1.9	1.4	1.6	1.5
World data on military expenditure as % of GNP	4.5	3.4	2.7	2.6	2.6
Military expenditure as % of CGE	10.7	10.2	7.9	8.8	7.9
World data on military expenditure as % of CGE	17.0	12.5	10.5	10.3	10.2
Military expenditure per capita (1997 $)	22	19	15	17	17
World data on military expenditure per capita (1997 $)	242	173	146	143	145
Armed forces per 1,000 people (soldiers)	1.7	1.6	1.4	1.4	1.4
World data on armed forces per 1,000 people (soldiers)	5.3	4.5	4.1	3.9	3.8
GNP per capita (1997 $)	1,020	989	1,040	1,090	1,130
Arms imports[6]					
Current dollars (mil.)	140	240	150	180	110
1997 constant dollars (mil.)	164	266	155	183	110
Total imports[7]					
Current dollars (mil.)	13,040	15,450	28,340	34,120	38,280
1997 constant dollars (mil.)	15,270	17,130	29,340	34,690	38,280
Total exports[7]					
Current dollars (mil.)	8,068	9,752	17,500	20,420	25,090
1997 constant dollars (mil.)	9,448	10,810	18,120	20,760	25,090
Arms as percent of total imports[8]	1.1	1.6	0.5	0.5	0.3
Arms as percent of total exports[8]	0	0	0	0	0

PRODUCTION SECTOR (cont.)

Transportation

Highways:

Total: 199,950 km.

Paved: 39,590 km.

Unpaved: 160,360 km (1998 est.).

Waterways: 3,219 km; limited to shallow-draft (less than 1.5 m) vessels.

Pipelines: petroleum products 357 km.

Merchant marine:

Total: 480 ships (1,000 GRT or over) totaling 5,973,024 GRT/9,025,087 DWT.

Ships by type: bulk 159, cargo 122, chemical tanker 5, combination bulk 9, container 7, liquified gas 13, livestock carrier 9, passenger 4, passenger/cargo 12, petroleum tanker 47, refrigerated cargo 20, roll-on/roll-off 19, short-sea passenger 32, specialized tanker 2, vehicle carrier 20 (1999 est.)

Note: a flag of convenience registry; Japan owns 19 ships, Hong Kong 5, Cyprus 1, Denmark 1, Greece 1, Netherlands 1, Singapore 1, and UK 1 (1998 est.).

Airports: 266 (1999 est.).

Airports - with paved runways: 76.

Airports - with unpaved runways: 190.

Top Agriculture Products

Rice, coconuts, corn, sugarcane, bananas, pineapples, mangoes; pork, eggs, beef; fish.

Top Mining Products (B)

Mineral resources include: nickel, cobalt, silver, gold, salt, copper.

MANUFACTURING SECTOR

GDP & Manufacturing Summary (A)

	1980	1985	1990	1995
GDP ($-1990 mil.)[1]	39,508	37,054	46,473	51,820
Per capita ($-1990)[1]	818	678	765	764
Manufacturing share (%) (current prices)[1]	23.7	23.5	23.7	24.8[e]
Manufacturing				
Value added ($-1990 mil.)[1]	10,067	8,605	11,003	11,951[e]
Industrial production index	34	63	100	165
Value added ($ mil.)	4,861	3,448	8,852	15,779[e]
Gross output ($ mil.)	17,369	12,081	24,321	41,069[e]
Employment (000)	949	619	1,109	997[e]
Profitability (% of gross output)				
Intermediate input (%)	72	71	64	62[e]
Wages and salaries inc. supplements (%)	6	6	8	8[e]
Gross operating surplus	22	22	28	31[e]
Productivity ($)				
Gross output per worker	16,263	19,369	19,805	40,848[e]
Value added per worker	4,552	5,528	7,209	15,771[e]
Average wage (inc. supplements)	1,127	1,257	1,802	3,151[e]
Value added ($ mil.)				
Food products	969	658	2,206	2,934[e]
Beverages	195	423	185	1,787[e]
Tobacco products	309	209	420	739[e]
Textiles	395	109	393	514[e]
Wearing apparel	205	105	509	913[e]
Leather and fur products	8	3	25	26[e]
Footwear	13	9	18	117[e]
Wood and wood products	229	86	164	180[e]
Furniture and fixtures	75	22	103	116[e]
Paper and paper products	128	97	184	264[e]
Printing and publishing	89	46	125	297[e]
Industrial chemicals	296	101	277	524[e]
Other chemical products	389	205	767	1,735[e]
Petroleum refineries	328	715	489	715[e]
Misc. petroleum and coal products	2	3	3	17[e]
Rubber products	103	34	158	269[e]
Plastic products	85	32	111	286[e]
Pottery, china and earthenware	33	9	29	67[e]
Glass and glass products	42	28	86	138[e]
Other non-metal mineral products	63	60	240	491[e]
Iron and steel	98	164	236	488[e]
Non-ferrous metals	35	28	117	343[e]

GDP & Manufacturing Summary (A)

	1980	1985	1990	1995
Metal products	127	49	156	228e
Non-electrical machinery	98	31	84	152e
Electrical machinery	260	156	775	1,607e
Transport equipment	234	35	258	614e
Prof. and scientific equipment	5	5	11	56e
Other manufacturing	49	28	93	161e

COMMUNICATIONS

Daily Newspapers

	National Data	World Data for Comparison
Daily Newspapers		
Number of Dailies	47	8,391
Total Circulation (000)	5,700	548,000
Circulation per 1,000 inhabitants	82	96

Telecommunications

Telephones - main lines in use: 1.9 million (1997).

Telephones - mobile cellular: 1.959 million (1998).

Telephone system: good international radiotelephone and submarine cable services; domestic and interisland service adequate.

Domestic: domestic satellite system with 11 earth stations.

International: 9 international gateways; satellite earth stations - 3 Intelsat (1 Indian Ocean and 2 Pacific Ocean); submarine cables to Hong Kong, Guam, Singapore, Taiwan, and Japan.

Radio broadcast stations: AM 366, FM 290, shortwave 3 (1999).

Radios: 11.5 million (1997).

Television broadcast stations: 31 (1997).

Televisions: 3.7 million (1997).

Internet Service Providers (ISPs): 93 (1999).

FINANCE, ECONOMICS, & TRADE

Economic Indicators

National product: GDP—purchasing power parity—$282 billion (1999 est.).

National product real growth rate: 2.9% (1999 est.).

National product per capita: $3,600 (1999 est.).

Inflation rate—consumer price index: 6.8% (1999).

Exchange Rates

Exchange rates:

Philippine pesos (P) per US$1

January 2000	40.427
1999	39.089
1998	40.893
1997	29.471
1996	26.216
1995	25.714

Top Import Origins

$30.7 billion (f.o.b., 1999 est.)

Origins (1998 est.)

United States	22%
Japan	20%
South Korea	8%
Singapore	6%
Taiwan	5%
Hong Kong	4%

Balance of Payments

	1994	1995	1996	1997	1998
Exports of goods (f.o.b.)	13,483	17,447	20,543	25,228	29,496
Imports of goods (f.o.b.)	−21,333	−26,391	−31,885	−36,355	−29,524
Trade balance	−7,850	−8,944	−11,342	−11,127	−28
Services - debits	−4,654	−6,926	−9,429	−14,122	−10,107
Services - credits	6,768	9,348	12,947	15,137	7,477
Private transfers (net)	969	1,070	1,108	1,619	704
Government transfers (net)	72	77	29	15	18
Overall balance	−2,950	−1,980	−3,953	−4,351	1,287

Top Export Destinations

$34.8 billion (f.o.b., 1999 est.)

Destinations (1998)

United States	34%
EU	20%
Japan	14%
Netherlands	8%
Singapore	6%
United Kingdom	6%
Hong Kong	4%

Foreign Aid

Recipient: ODA, $1.1 billion (1998).

Import/Export Commodities

Import Commodities	Export Commodities
Raw materials and intermediate goods	Electronic equipment
Capital goods	Machinery and transport equipment
Consumer goods	Garments
Fuels	Coconut products

PITCAIRN ISLANDS

Pitcairn, Henderson, Ducie, and Oeno Islands

CAPITAL: Adamstown

FLAG: A blue flag with the flag of the United Kingdom in the upper hoist-side quadrant and the Pitcairn Islander coat of arms centered on the outer half of the flag. The coat of arms is yellow, green, and light blue with a shield featuring a yellow anchor.

ANTHEM: Pitcairn does not have an anthem specific to the islands.

MONETARY UNIT: The New Zealand dollar (NZ$) is a paper currency of 100 cents.

WEIGHTS AND MEASURES: The metric system is the legal standard.

HOLIDAYS: The islands celebrate the birthday of the Queen of the United Kingdom on the second Saturday in June.

TIME: 4 AM = noon GMT

LOCATION AND SIZE: The islands are in Oceana, about one-half way between Peru and New Zealand. Geographic coordinates are 25°04′S, 130°06′W. Total land area of the islands is about 47 square kilometers, and the coastline measures about 62 kilometers.

CLIMATE: The islands' climate is tropical, hot and humid. Southeast trade winds modify the climate, and the rainy season is from November to March.

INTRODUCTORY SURVEY

RECENT HISTORY

The history of the Pitcairn Islands is short but colorful. Pitcairn and the neighboring islands of Henderson, Cuicie, and Oeno—which together form the Pitcairn Islands—were discovered in 1767, and the main island of Pitcairn was named after the midshipman who first sighted it. The islands were uninhabited until 1790, when mutineers of the British ship, the *Bounty*, and several Tahitians found the island. Led by the infamous Fletcher Christian, the mutineers scuttled and burned the *Bounty* to help avoid being spotted by passing vessels.

The mutineers and their Tahitian companions led a difficult and violent life on Pitcairn. By 1800, just ten years from their landing, only one male survived, John Adams. Adams was to live until 1829, passing away at the age of sixty-two. He was known to all islanders as "Father," as he had been the leader for well over thirty years and, for a long period, was the only adult male on the island.

Pitcairn was rediscovered by an American vessel in 1808 and again by a British vessel in 1814. Ships plying the trade routes between India and Australia to South America, or to England via Cape Horn, began to stop at Pitcairn. The ships traded extra stores and goods for provisions from the island. A few sailors returned to settle, and Adams grew increasingly concerned the island could not support its growing population. After Adams died in 1829, following his desires, the islanders moved en masse to Tahiti in March 1831.

The Pitcairn people did not fare well in Tahiti and after several died from communicable diseases, sixty-five islanders returned to Pitcairn in August 1831. Perceiving a possible need for defense, the islanders petitioned Captain Eliott of the *H.M.S. Fly* for British protection. A constitution was drawn up and signed on board the *Fly* on November 30, 1838. The islanders count their inclusion in the British empire from that date, although they were not to become a legal British settlement until the British Settlements Act of 1887.

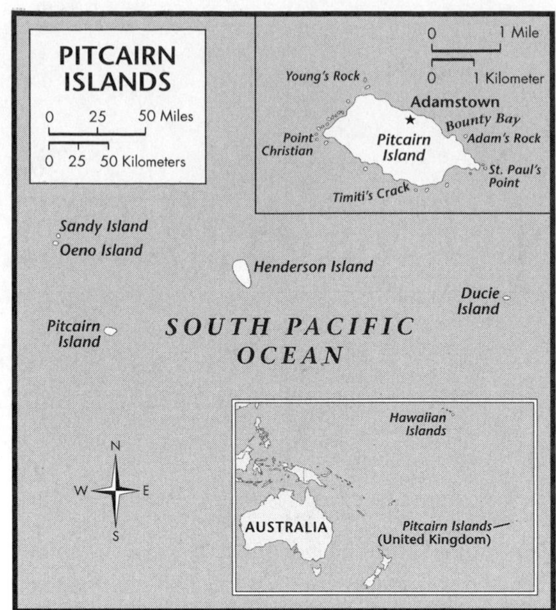

An increasing population again strained the islanders, and they left in 1856 for Norfolk Island, where ample land and farms were available. Many were unhappy at Norfolk Island, however, and sixteen returned to Pitcairn in 1858. In 1864 another group returned, and descendents of the original mutineers still occupy the island today.

GOVERNMENT

The four islands known as Pitcairn Islands are a protected territory of the United Kingdom. They are governed under a constitution established in 1964, the Local Government Ordinance. The legal system is based on local island by-laws. The islands have a governor and a commissioner appointed by the United Kingdom; the commissioner is the liaison between the UK government and the Island Council. An island magistrate and a chairman of the Island Council administer the islands.

The magistrate is elected by popular vote to a term of three years. The Island Council consists of ten members, six elected by popular vote, one appointed by those six elected members, two appointed by the governor, and one seat for the island secretary. Elections are based on universal suffrage for all who have at least three years residency and who are over the age of eighteen. Council members are elected annually.

Judiciary

The island magistrate presides over the island court.

Political Parties

There are no political parties on the Pitcairn Islands.

DEFENSE

Defense is the responsibility of the United Kingdom.

ECONOMIC AFFAIRS

The Pitcairn islanders subsist on fishing, farming, handicrafts, and postage stamps. Bartering is a normal means of exchange on the islands. Revenue is obtained by the sale of handicrafts and postage stamps to passing ships.

Public Finance

The Pitcairn Islands spent $878,199 in fiscal year 1994/1995, with revenues of $729,884. The United Kingdom spends about $6,300 per year per resident on subsistence efforts.

Income

Gross domestic product for the islands is unknown.

Industry

The islands' industries are handicrafts and postage stamps.

Banking and Finance

The currency utilized on the islands is the New Zealand dollar. There are no banks on the islands.

Economic Development

The ability to sell postage stamps is the principle source of export sales and the only new element of the economy in over one hundred years.

SOCIAL WELFARE

There are no formal social welfare programs on the islands. The islanders are a close knit community that looks out for itself.

Healthcare

There are no permanent medical care professionals on the islands. Health care practitioners in the region come to the islands for periodic visits, with some staying between two to six months.

Housing

Housing is adequate for the small population and consists primarily of wooden structures constructed from local timber and boasting thatched roofs.

EDUCATION

The islands maintain a small school for the children with one teacher. All children are required to attend.

2000 KEY EVENTS TIMELINE

January

- Electricity costs are expected to double as the year begins, due to a decrease in the island's subsidy funds.

February

- Residents on Pitcairn Island agree to an economic plan that would extend their subsidy fund, provided by the British government.
- Efforts are initiated to increase the sale of Pitcairn's stamps, long popular with philatelists around the world.

June

- After a struggle with island residents, the Pitcairn Island administration gains control over the ".pn" Internet domain name suffix.

July

- Pitcairn Island hosts an exhibition at the World Stamp Expo 2000, held in Anaheim, California, on June 7 through 16.
- The island experiences a surge in its rat population, which was previously subject to extermination in 1999. To combat the problem, cats are imported to help keep the rat population in check.

December

- Bids are being accepted for the construction of an all-weather surfacing of Pitcairn's main road, as well as for the development of a permanent water supply.

ANALYSIS OF EVENTS: 2000

BUSINESS AND THE ECONOMY

Pitcairn Island is a small territory of the United Kingdom. With fewer than one hundred inhabitants and an isolated location in the South Pacific Ocean between Panama and New Zealand, Pitcairn's economy is limited. Islanders are dependent on imports for most of their needs. In early 2000, Pitcairn Island began to develop its budding industries in dehydrated island fruits and honey.

These industries were threatened early in the year when it was revealed that the subsidy fund provided by the British government to support the island was quickly running out of money. Implications for the islanders included doubled electricity costs and runaway freight costs. The subsidy fund has helped offset costs in utilities, travel to New Zealand for medical reasons, and importing supplies to the island. To help maintain the fund, island residents agreed to a new economic plan in February 2000, which will extend the fund for another ten years. Included under the plan are efforts to promote the island's new dehydrated fruit industry and an increase in the sale of Pitcairn's stamps, which are popular with philatelic enthusiasts. A resurgence in cruise ships stopping in Pitcairn, ten scheduled in 2000, up from two or three in previous years, also gives out hope for a brighter economic situation.

Though geographically isolated from the rest of the world, Pitcairn Island has found its way onto the information superhighway. In June, the island's administration succeeded in winning from local residents the rights to the ".pn" Internet domain name suffix. The government also reserved the rights to "co.pn," "org.pn," "net.pn," and "edu.pn." While the domain name suffixes and Pitcairn's web site establish its presence on the Internet, establishing its residents with access to the Internet is more difficult. Because of its remote location, a satellite data link would have to be established with the island. This is estimated to cost more than US$25 million. Once the link has been established, use costs would also have to be lower than average to make it affordable for residents. The advantages from this access, however, include enabling residents to engage in e-commerce to sell their carved and wooden curios, dehydrated fruits, and pure honey on-line.

CULTURE AND SOCIETY

Pitcairn Island accepted bids for the construction of an all-weather surfacing of its main road, which is prone to washouts. Bids were accepted from Fiji, Tahiti, and New Zealand. The road construction will provide easier access to the village of Adamstown—a convenience for island residents living outside the village and also for visitors from the increasing number of cruise ships stopping at the island.

Discussions were also underway for the construction of an airstrip on the island. It could be used not only to bring tourists to Pitcairn, but to transport people in need of medical attention. Medical transport has previously been done by ship, travelling one thousand two hundred miles to reach the closest hospital in Papeete, Tahiti, or more than four thousand miles to New Zealand.

DIRECTORY

CENTRAL GOVERNMENT

Head of State

Queen
Elizabeth II, The Visitors Office, Buckingham Palace, London SW1A 1AA, England
PHONE: +44 8391377
FAX: +44 9309625

Prime Minister
Tony Blair, Prime Minister, Office of the Prime Minister, 10 Downing Street, London SW1A 2AA, England
PHONE: +44 (171) 8903000

Ministers

Govenor
Martin Williams, Governor

Commissioner
Leon Salt, Commissioner

Island Magistrate and Chairman of the Island Council
Jay Warren, Island Magistrate and Chairman of the Island Council, Pitcairn Island, South Pacific (via New Zealand)

DIPLOMATIC REPRESENTATION

The Pitcairn Islands are a territory of the United Kingdom. See Diplomatic Representation in the United Kingdom.

JUDICIAL SYSTEM

Island Court

Pitcairn Island, South Pacific (via) New Zealand

FURTHER READING

Articles

Clausing, Jeri. "Pacific Islands Seek Control of Internet Designations." *New York Times,* February 14, 2000, p. C1.

Ogden, Christopher. "Bounty Descendants Hunt a Future: Like Their Mutinous Ancestors, the People of Pitcairn Face Hard Times." *Time International,* October 2, 2000, vol. 39, p. 35.

PITCAIRN ISLANDS: STATISTICAL DATA

For sources and notes see "Sources of Statistics" at the front of each volume.

GEOGRAPHY

Geography

Area:

Total: 47 sq km.

Land: 47 sq km.

Land boundaries: 0 km.

Coastline: 51 km.

Climate: tropical, hot, humid; modified by southeast trade winds; rainy season (November to March).

Terrain: rugged volcanic formation; rocky coastline with cliffs.

Natural resources: miro trees (used for handicrafts), fish.

Note: manganese, iron, copper, gold, silver, and zinc have been discovered offshore.

HUMAN FACTORS

Demographics (B)

Population (July 2000 est.) .54

Population growth rate -2.06%

Data for 2000 est.

Ethnic Division

Descendants of the Bounty mutineers and their Tahitian wives.

Religion

Seventh-Day Adventist 100%

Major Languages

English (official), Pitcairnese, Tahitian, 18th century English dialect.

GOVERNMENT & LAW

Political Parties

The unicameral Island Council consists of 10 seats: 6 elected by popular vote, 1 appointed by the 6 elected members, 2 appointed by the governor, and 1 seat for the Island Secretary. Members serve one-year terms. Elections take place each December. The last was held December 1999 (next to be held in December 2000). All the seats are filled by independents. There are no political parties.

Government Budgets (B)

Revenues $729,884

Expenditures $878,119

Data for FY94/95 est.

LABOR FORCE

Total Labor Force (A)

12 able-bodied men (1997).

Labor Force by Occupation

No business community in the usual sense; some public works; subsistence farming and fishing.

PRODUCTION SECTOR

Transportation

Highways:

Total: 6.4 km.

Paved: 0 km.

Unpaved: 6.4 km.

Merchant marine: none (1999 est.).

Airports: none.

Top Agriculture Products

Wide variety of fruits and vegetables.

Top Mining Products (B)

Mineral resources include: manganese, iron, copper, gold, silver, and zinc have been discovered offshore.

COMMUNICATIONS

Telecommunications

Telephones - main lines in use: 1 (there are 17 telephones on one party line) (1997).

Telephone system: party line telephone service on the island.

Domestic: NA

International: radiotelephone.

Radio broadcast stations: AM 1, FM 0, shortwave 0 (1998).

Radios: NA

Television broadcast stations: 0 (1997).

Televisions: NA

Internet Service Providers (ISPs): NA

FINANCE, ECONOMICS, & TRADE

Exchange Rates

Exchange rates:

New Zealand dollars (NZ$) per US$1

January 2000	1.9451
1999	1.8886
1998	1.8629
1997	1.5083
1996	1.4543
1995	1.5235

Import/Export Commodities

Import Commodities	Export Commodities
Fuel oil	Fruits
Machinery	Vegetables
Building materials	Curios
Flour	Stamps
Sugar	
Other foodstuffs	

POLAND

Republic of Poland
Rzeczpospolita Polska

CAPITAL: Warsaw (Warszawa).

FLAG: The national flag consists of two horizontal stripes, the upper white and the lower red.

ANTHEM: *Jeszcze Polska nie zginela (Poland Is Not Yet Lost).*

MONETARY UNIT: The zloty (z) is a paper currency of 100 groszy. There are coins of 1, 2, 5, 10, 20, and 50 groszy and 1, 2, 5, 10, 20, 50, and 100 zlotys, and notes of 10, 20, 50, 100, 200, 500, 1,000, 2,000, and 5,000 zlotys. A currency reform on 1 January 1995 replaced 10,000 old zlotys with 1 new zloty. z1 = $0.35587 (or $1 = z2.81).

WEIGHTS AND MEASURES: The metric system is the legal standard.

HOLIDAYS: New Year's Day, 1 January; Labor Day, 1 May; National Day, 3 May; Victory Day, 9 May; All Saints' Day, 1 November; Christmas, 25–26 December. Movable holidays are Easter Monday and Corpus Christi.

TIME: 1 PM = noon GMT.

LOCATION AND SIZE: Situated in Eastern Europe, the Republic of Poland has an area of 312,680 square kilometers (120,726 square miles), slightly smaller than the state of New Mexico. Its total boundary length is 3,605 kilometers (2,240 miles). Poland's capital city, Warsaw, is located in the east central part of the country.

CLIMATE: Only the southern areas are humid. Summers are cool, and winters range from moderately cold to cold. The average mean temperature is about 7°C (45°F). Temperatures in Warsaw range, on average, from −6° to −1°C (21°–30°F) in January and from 13° to 24°C (55°–75°F) in July.

Precipitation is greatest during the summer months. Annual rainfall ranges from about 50 centimeters (20 inches) in the lowlands to 135 centimeters (53 inches) in the mountains.

INTRODUCTORY SURVEY

RECENT HISTORY

Poland suffered tremendous losses of life and property during World War II. An estimated six million Poles were killed, half of them Jews. The remaining population suffered near starvation throughout the Nazi occupation.

In 1945, Warsaw was liberated by the Soviet and Polish armies, and the Provisional Government of National Unity received formal recognition by the United States and United Kingdom. However, communist and socialist factions merged in 1948 to form the Polish United Workers' Party (PZPR) that consistently pursued a pro-Soviet policy. It shunned the Marshall Plan (plan to rebuild Europe after World War II) and renounced all dealings with the Westernpowers.

Social unrest marked communist rule through the 1950s and 1960s. Following a drought in 1969, and an exceptionally severe winter, demonstrations by shipyard workers in Gdánsk broke out in December 1970, protesting economic conditions. After widespread violence, in which at least forty-four people were killed, the government under Edward Gierek modified its economic policies and reinstated Church control over thousands of religious properties in northwestern Poland.

During the 1970s, Gierek's government vigorously pursued a policy of détente (harmony) with the West. At home, however, the economic situation kept growing worse, and Polish nationalism continued to rise. In an historic public ceremony on August

31, 1980, government officials agreed to allow workers the right to form independent trade unions and the right to strike. The independent labor movement, Solidarity, headed by Lech Walesa, the leader of the Gdánsk workers, emerged and soon claimed a membership of about ten million.

In December 1980, after union leaders in Gdánsk called for a national referendum on forming a non-communist government in Poland, General Wojciech Jaruzelski, prime minister since February, declared martial law. Almost the whole leadership of Solidarity, including Walesa, was arrested, and the union was suspended.

In the following years, martial law was gradually eased. However, continued declines in the standard of living led to waves of strikes throughout Poland in spring and fall 1988, paralyzing the nation.

By April 1989, the government agreed to establish a Senate, with the seats to be filled by open election. In addition, 35 percent of the seats in the existing parliament, the Sejm, were also made subject to direct election. In the elections of June 1989, ninety-nine of the 100 seats in the Senate went to Solidarity members. Tadeusz Mazowiecki took office in August 1989 as the first non-communist prime minister in the eastern bloc (communist nations in eastern Europe). Local elections held in May 1990 further weakened the communists' grip on power. On December 9, 1990, Walesa was elected president.

After 1990, the number of political parties grew rapidly, and a series of coalition governments without strong powers followed, giving Poland five prime ministers and four governments between 1991 and 1993.

Following the local elections in June 1994, fears of a return to communism under a new government were unfounded, as the government of Polish Peasant Party leader Waldemar Pawlak and his Democratic Left Alliance partner, Aleksander Kwasniewski, remained generally committed to democracy and economic change. In December 1995, Kwasniewski was elected president.

In 1999, the North Atlantic Treaty Organization (NATO) admitted Poland, the Czech Republic, and Hungary as members of the alliance.

GOVERNMENT

Poland's government is proceeding through a long transition period. The system combines a presidential and a parliamentary system. Poland functions on a much-amended form of its communist-era constitution with a package of amendments passed in October 1992, collectively called the "Little Constitution." A 1990 agreement made the presidency a popularly elected post rather than one of parliamentary appointment.

The president is the chief of state and directly elected for a term of five years. The cabinet is the Council of Minister responsible to the prime minister and the Sejm. Members of the Council are proposed by the prime minister, appointed by the president, and approved by the Sejm. The prime minister and deputy prime minister are the head of government, appointed by the president and confirmed by the Sejm. The presidential post includes traditional executive duties and powers, such as the duty to sign into law or veto legislation, but also retains many legislative powers, including the right to introduce bills and draft legal amendments.

The legislative branch consists of two houses: the Sejm, or lower house, with 460 seats elected through proportional representation to four-year terms; and the 100-seat Senate elected by majority vote on a provincial basis to four-year terms.

Under the communists, Poland was divided into forty-nine administrative districts called *voivods*. The 1989 Solidarity government replaced these with the *gmina*, or local authority, which chooses its own council and officials. In 1994, there were 2,383 of these local councils. Suffrage is universal at age eighteen.

Judiciary

The legal system is a combination of Napoleonic civic law and communist legal theory. The Supreme Court, the highest judicial body, functions primarily as a court of appeal. Its judges are elected by the Council of State for five-year terms. It is divided into criminal, civil, military, and labor and social insurance chambers. Supreme Court judges are appointed by the president, with recommendation of the National Council of the Judiciary, for an indefinite period of time. The Sejm selects the Constitutional Tribunal judges for nine-year terms. In addition, there are regional courts as well as special courts such as military tribunals, children's courts, and courts for cases involving social insurance.

In general, the Poles have been reluctant to remove communist-era judges, but fears about the fair-mindedness of people who served the earlier regime damage the public's belief in the judiciary. A 1993 law makes it possible for the Ministry of Justice to recall a judge determined by a disciplinary commission to have failed to exercise "court independence." Decisions may be appealed to the European Court of Justice.

Political Parties

After the restrictions of their communist past, the Poles formed a variety of political parties ranging across the full political spectrum. Sixty-nine parties participated in the 1991 parliamentary elections, of which twenty-nine gained seats, none of them with more than 14 percent of the total vote. By 1993, however, the political scene was stabilizing, and only thirty-five parties took part in that election with only five received seats.

The mid-1990s saw Poland dividing into three basic political groupings. On the right were two large coalitions made up of parties favoring a stronger role for the Catholic Church, drawing their support from Poland's rural areas.

The center is dominated by Freedom Union (UW), whose position is taken from the intellectual wing of the original Solidarity, favoring radical economic change.

The left has two major parties, the Democratic Left Alliance (SLD) and the Polish Peasant Party (PSL). Of the 460 Sejm seats in 2000, the Social Movement-Solidarity Electoral Action (RSS-AWS) held 186 seats, the pro-communist Democratic Left Alliance (SLD) held 159, and the Freedom Union (UW) held sixty. A number of parties held the remainder of seats.

DEFENSE

The conscription law of January 1959 provides for registration at eighteen and service of eighteen months at age twenty. Polish armed forces numbered 240,650, including 141,600 draftees in 2000 including 142,500 in four military districts. Navy personnel totaled 17,100. The air force had 55,300 men and 297 combat aircraft of Soviet design. The reserve had about 406,000 active members in 2000. The Ministry of Interior had 7,000 police and 13,500 border guards. Defense expenditures for 2000 amounted to $3.2 billion, or 2.1 percent of GDP.

ECONOMIC AFFAIRS

For decades, Poland had a centrally planned economy, primarily state-controlled. Since World War II, agriculture's dominant place in the economy has been shrinking. Poland, with its sizable coastline, has become a maritime nation of some importance. Poland has developed three major ports on the Baltic Sea and a greatly expanded shipbuilding industry that, in 1991, produced fifty-three ships.

Since abandoning central planning, Poland has struggled with the transformation of over 8,000 state-owned enterprises into workable private corporations. By the late 1990s, due to tight monetary policies, Poland's economy had transformed into one of the more robust of Central Europe. Hopes for an early acceptance by the European Union (EU) ran high. Privatization of many small to medium size companies and liberal laws for new firms led to a rapid growth of the private sector. The private sector became 70 percent of the domestic economy. Privatization and restructuring of large industry, including coal and steel production, had become a greater focus.

Public Finance

The U.S. Central Intelligence Agency (CIA) estimated that, in 1999, government revenues totaled approximately $31.6 billion and expenditures $34.8 billion. External debt in 1998 totaled $44 billion. The government managed to refrain from increased deficit spending. The 1996 budget deficit was only 2.5 percent of GDP, well below the 3 percent requirement for entry into the single European currency (the euro) in 1999.

Income

In 1999, the gross domestic product (GDP) was $276.5 billion, or out $7,200 per capita. The GDP real growth rate was estimated at 3.8 percent and the inflation rate, 8.4 percent. The GDP contribution by economic sector in 1998 was agriculture, 5 percent; industry, 35 percent; and services, 60 percent.

Industry

Leading industries in 1998 included food processing, fuel, metals and metal products, chemicals, coal mining, glass, shipbuilding, and textiles. With the destabilizing effects of the breakup of the bloc of communist countries in Europe and central planning, industrial production fell by 26 percent in 1990 before returning to positive growth during 1991-1998. Poland produced ten million tons of steel in the mid-1990s. Sulfur is another important industrial commodity. The industrial growth rate in 1999 was estimated at 4.5 percent.

Banking and Finance

The National Bank of Poland (Narodowy Bank Polski-NBP) is a state institution and the bank of issue. It also controls foreign transactions and prepares financial plans for the economy. On January 1, 1970, the National Bank merged with the Investment Bank and has since controlled funds for finance and investment transactions of state enterprises and organizations. The function of the Food Economy Bank and its associated cooperative banks is to supply short- and long-term credits to rural areas. The national commercial bank, Bank Handlowy w Warszawie (BH), finances foreign trade operations. The General Savings Bank (Bank Polska Kasa Opieki-PBKO), a central institution for personal savings, also handles financial transfers into Poland of persons living abroad.

A fundamental reorganization of the banking sector took place between 1990 and 1992. The NBP became only a central bank, and nine independent (so-called commercial), although state-owned, regional banks were created.

In 1993, the first of these, the Poznan-based Wielkopolski Bank Kredytowy (WBK), was privatized. A second highly controversial privatization took place in early 1994, with the sale of the Silesian Bank (Bank Slaski). Also, the Krakow-based Bank Przemyslowo-Handlowy (BPH) was disposed of at the start of 1995, and Bank Gdanski was sold in late 1995. With four major banks privatized, five remained to be sold off. Frustrated with the slow progress, the Polish government returned in 1996 to proposals for "bank consolidation" prior to privatization. By 1999, Pekao, the nation's largest commercial bank, was privatized.

In early 1991, legislation was introduced to regulate securities transactions and establish a stock exchange in Warsaw. A securities commission was formed for consumer protection. By September 1996, the Warsaw Stock Exchange had increased to sixty-three companies listed.

Economic Development

After World War II, the economy of Poland was centrally planned and almost completely under state control, especially in nonagricultural sectors.

After 1963, centralized planning and management were somewhat relaxed, and state-owned enterprises gained more freedom in the design and implementation of their programs.

Economic reform stressing decentralization of the economy was introduced in 1982, but failed to produce any significant improvements. The Economic Transformation Program, adopted in January 1990, aimed to convert Poland from a planned to a market economy. Measures were aimed at drastically reducing the large budget deficit, abolishing all trade monopolies, and selling many state-owned enterprises to private interests.

The slow pace of privatization gained some momentum in 1995, as over 500 smaller state enterprises were transferred to private National Investment Funds under the Mass Privatization Program, but large-scale industry remained largely in state hands. Desiring EU membership, the government in the late 1990s was bringing its trade economic policies in conformity with EU standards.

SOCIAL WELFARE

A social insurance institute administers social security programs through a network of branch offices, guided by new 1998 legislation. Social security, including social insurance and medical care, covers nearly the entire population.

Old age, disability, and survivors' pensions are provided, as well as family allowances, sickness benefits, maternity benefits, workers' compensation, and unemployment. Special family allowances have been a part of the social security program since 1947, and are paid for each child after the first. Maternity benefits include full wages for a total of sixteen to eighteen weeks.

Healthcare

In 1990-1997, Poland had 6.2 physicians per 1,000 people. The population per hospital bed was 161. About 54 percent of the physicians and 81 percent of the dentists were women in 1993.

Life expectancy in 2000 was estimated at seventy-three years. As with Eastern Europe in general, tuberculosis was a major health problem in 1994. Total healthcare expenditures were 5 percent of GDP in 1997.

Housing

Almost 40 percent of all urban dwelling space was destroyed during World War II. Despite increasing investment in public housing, the housing shortage remains critical. In the mid-1980s, the average wait for an apartment was about fifteen years. As of 1992, there was a shortage of 1.3 million housing units, a figure that was expected to grow to 2.4 million by 2000.

EDUCATION

Practically the entire Polish population is literate. Primary, secondary, and most university and other education is provided by the government. The centralized school system consists of an eight-year primary school, followed by either a four-year secondary general education school, five-year technical school, or basic three-year vocational training school.

In 1996, there were five million primary school students, and general secondary schools had 2.5 million students. Some 720,000 students attended institutions of higher learning.

Of the ninety-eight third-level institutions, eleven are universities; eighteen, polytechnical schools; seventeen, art schools; eleven, medical academies; and three, theological academies. Colleges include: Jagiellonian University (among the oldest in Europe), Warsaw University, the Higher Theater School (Warsaw), and the Academy of Fine Arts (Kraków). The free private university is the Roman Catholic University at Lublin. In the late 1990s, approximately 24.8 percent of government expenditures were allocated to education.

2000 KEY EVENTS TIMELINE

January

- On January 13 *The Times* of London publishes a Polish study indicating that taller men are more likely to marry and have children.
- On January 20 Poland expels nine Russian diplomats for spying.

March

- Tribesmen kidnap the Polish ambassador to Yemen on March 1.

April

- On April 4 a clash in Kosovo injures Polish soldiers.
- Warsaw hosts a clean-energy picnic on April 20 to celebrate Earth Day 2000.

- Officials call for the Prime Minister to be replaced
- The death penalty is abolished in Poland.

May

- On May 26 French Telecom and Kulcjyk Holding agree to acquire Telekomunikcja Polska.

June

- The Freedom Union withdraws from the government coalition on June 6.

August

- A Polish court clears presidential hopefuls Aleksander Kwasniewski, and former president Lech Walesa, of charges that they spied for the KGB on August 17. The charges had been brought up by Marian Krzaklewski, also running for president, who had hoped to damage the popularity of his running mates.

September

- A synagogue reopens for the first time at Auschwitz on September 12.

October

- President Aleksander Kwasniewski is elected for a second term on October 8.

ANALYSIS OF EVENTS: 2000

BUSINESS AND THE ECONOMY

Poland's economy, considered the "tiger" of Central Europe, remained one of the strongest and fastest-growing in the former Soviet bloc. Its central bank announced a medium-term goal of curbing inflation to 4 percent by 2003. Inflation control was one of two major goals for Poland cited in the most recent country report by the Organization for Economic Cooperation and Development (OECD). The other was trimming its current-account deficit, which had risen to between 6–7 percent in 1999. Unemployment, which rose to over 11 percent in 1999, posed yet another challenge. Although Poland had received $24 billion in foreign investment over the past five years, there were still barriers to overcome in attracting foreign manufacturers to Polish soil, including inadequate transport and telecommunications infrastructures and lingering doubts about the quality of items manufactured in Poland, a hold-over from the Communist era. With new laws lowering tariffs on automobile imports from European Union (E.U.) countries, several auto manufacturers, including Ford, Open, and Fiat, closed down plants in Poland because it was more cost-effective to manufacture the cars in their Western European plants and export them to Poland than to maintain a production base within the country.

The weakening of the ruling Solidarity coalition in parliament, the reelection victory of President Alexander Kwasniewski, and the expected victory of the Social Democrats in upcoming elections in 2001 suggested that the pace of economic reform would slow. Ministers of the Freedom Union party had resigned from the coalition in the spring because its traditionally labor-oriented constituency had rejected their proposed economic reforms—including budget tightening, faster privatization, lower taxes, and subsidy cuts—as too radical.

GOVERNMENT AND POLITICS

Prospects for the survival of Poland's Solidarity-led anti-communist coalition dimmed dramatically in 2000. In June the Freedom Union withdrew from the coalition because the radical economic reforms it advocated would have moved the government too far to the right for the traditional Solidarity constituency, itself an amalgam of some forty groups, among which labor unions still played an important role. The Solidarity movement was left to head a weakened minority government under the leadership of Prime Minister Jerzy Buzek.

With the reelection of Alexander Kwasniewski in October's presidential election, it appeared that Poland would soon have ex-communist leadership in both the presidency and the parliament, where the Social Democrats, or SDL, hoped to increase their representation in early elections likely to take place by the spring of 2001. Elections would be called if the Solidarity government failed to get its budget approved by the end of March. The left-leaning SDL was considered likely to curb economic reform but still work toward attaining E.U. membership as soon as possible. Kwasniewski, who won nearly 54 percent of the vote, was the first incumbent president to be reelected in Poland since the country's transition to democratic rule in 1989.

The failing fortunes of the Solidarity movement in 2000 were highlighted in ironic ways by two occurrences in the course of the year. First, the remains of World War II-era patriot and anti-communist Stanislaw Mikolajczyk, who had led the country's government-in-exile during the Nazi occupation and died in the United States in 1966, were returned to his homeland for burial in accord with the deceased leader's wishes. As it turned out, this occurred two days before the Solidarity coalition collapsed.

The other event was the withdrawal from politics by former president and Solidarity founder Lech Walesa following an unsuccessful presidential candidacy that garnered only 1 percent of the vote. The one-time national hero, who had lost the presidency narrowly to Alexander Kwasniewski in 1995, was viewed as an anachronistic candidate pushing outmoded and irrelevant campaign themes. In addition, the abrasive personal style that had led his support to dwindle while in office also alienated voters during his attempted political comeback.

Newly elected President Kwasniewski declared that the number one challenge facing him during his second term was Poland's admission to full membership in the European Union. The country had its sights set on membership by 2003, although 2005 was deemed by observers to be a more realistic goal. Negotiations on agricultural issues took place between government representatives and the European Commission in Brussels, Belgium, in June. The E.U. wanted Poland to phase out subsidies to farmers and facilitate the sale of farmland to foreigners.

Preparing for the coming enlargement, the E.U. continued to beef up security along the eastern borders of applicant countries, including Poland. Following admission, the new member states would be able to travel in Western Europe without visas but would be required to demand visas from residents of the former Soviet republics to their east. The new border security, aimed at cutting down on illegal trade, threatened to cut down on income derived from the bazaars that had grown up along these borders, including that between Poland and Ukraine.

CULTURE AND SOCIETY

The latest sign of Westernization in Poland was the stock market fever that had gripped much of the nation, luring one out of every four Poles to become an investor. An estimated $50 million per month was invested by private pension funds, and tales of overnight riches from hitting it big on the market appeared everywhere from the newspapers to the country's leading TV soap opera. Privatization had added new companies to the Polish stock market, already the largest in Eastern Europe. Led by a "hot" technology sector mimicking those in the West, the market was enjoying a boom, having risen 16 percent from January to May, and 30 percent from the previous October.

The high-profile televised wedding of an American Jewish couple at a reconstructed nineteenth-century synagogue in Wroclaw, Poland, highlighted the continuing revival of Judaism in Poland, most of whose Jewish population had perished in World War II, accounting for roughly half of the six million Jewish victims of the Holocaust. The bride and groom were both reporters who had met through their mutual interest in Jewish culture in Eastern Europe and had collaborated in the production of a documentary film on the subject. The bride, Ellen Friedland, said, "We came here as reporters, to learn about Jewish death in Poland. Today we are here to celebrate Jewish life."

DIRECTORY

CENTRAL GOVERNMENT

Head of State

President
Aleksander Kwasniewski, Office of the President, Palac Prezydencki, Krakowskie Przedmiescie 48/50, 00-071 Warsaw, Poland
PHONE: +48 (22) 6952900
E-MAIL: listy@prezydent.pl

Ministers

Prime Minister
Jerzy Buzek, Office of the Prime Minister, Aleje Ujazdowskie 1/3, 00-583 Warsaw, Poland
PHONE: +48 (22) 6946000
FAX: +48 (22) 6252637
E-MAIL: cirinfo@kprm.gov.pl

Minister of Finance
Jaroslaw Bauc, Ministry of Finance

Minister of Interior and Administration
Marek Biernacki, Ministry of Interior and Administration

Minister of Agriculture and Food Economy
Artur Balazs, Ministry of Agriculture and Food Economy, ul. Wspólna 30, 00-930 Warsaw, Poland
PHONE: +48 (22) 6231000
FAX: +48 (22) 6232750; 6232751

Minister of Culture and Arts
Andrzej Zakrzewski, Ministry of Culture and Arts, ul. Krakowskie Przedmiescie 15/17, 00-071 Warsaw, Poland
PHONE: +48 (22) 6200231
FAX: +48 (22) 8261922; 8267533
E-MAIL: mkis@warman.com.pl

Minister of Environmental Protection, Natural Resources and Forestry
Antoni Tokarczuk, Ministry of Environmental Protection, Natural Resources and Forestry, ul. Wawelska 52/54, 00-922 Warsaw, Poland
PHONE: +48 (22) 250001; 254001
FAX: +48 (22) 253332; 253972
E-MAIL: Info@Mos.Gov.Pl

Minister of Foreign Affairs
Wladyslaw Bartoszewski, Ministry of Foreign Affairs, Aleja Szucha 23, 00-580 Warsaw, Poland
PHONE: +48 (22) 6239000
FAX: +48 (22) 6290287; 6257652
E-MAIL: mszddpi@atos.warman.com.pl

Minister of Economy
Janusz Steinhoff, Ministry of Economy, Plac Trzech Krzyza 3/5, 00-950 Warsaw, Poland
PHONE: +48 (22) 6935000
FAX: +48 (22) 6286808

Minister of Health and Social Security
Grzegorz Opala, Ministry of Health and Social Security, Ul. Miodowa 15, 00-952 Warsaw, Poland
PHONE: +48 (22) 8313441
FAX: +48 (22) 8312212; 8311553
E-MAIL: mzios001@medianet.com.pl

Minister of Justice
Lech Kaczynski, Ministry of Justice, Aleje Ujazdowskie 11, 00-950 Warsaw, Poland
PHONE: +48 (22) 6284431
FAX: +48 (22) 6281692

Minister of Labor and Social Policy
Longin Komolowski, Ministry of Labor and Social Policy, Ul. Nowogrodzka 1/3, 00-513 Warsaw, Poland
PHONE: +48 (22) 6616100
FAX: +48 (22) 6284048

Minister of National Defense
Bronislaw Komorowski, Ministry of National Defense, Ul. Klonowa 1, 00-909 Warsaw, Poland
PHONE: +48 (22) 6210261; 6280031
FAX: +48 (22) 455378
E-MAIL: bpmon@mon.wp.mil.pl

Minister of Education
Edmund Wittbrodt, Ministry of Education, Aleja Szucha 25, 00-918 Warsaw, Poland
PHONE: +48 (22) 6297241; 6280461
FAX: +48 (22) 6282746
E-MAIL: root@kaliope.men.waw.pl

Minister of the Treasury
Andrzej Chronowski, Ministry of Treasury, Ul. Krucza 36, 00-522 Warsaw, Poland
PHONE: +48 (22) 6958000
FAX: +48 (22) 6251114; 6280872
E-MAIL: minister@mst.gov.pl

Minister of Communication
Maciej Srebro, Ministry of Communication, Ul. Malachowskiego 2, 00-940 Warsaw, Poland
PHONE: +48 (22) 6565000
FAX: +48 (22) 8261071

Minister of Transport and Marine Economy
Jerzy Widzyk, Ministry of Transport and Marine Economy, Ul. Chalubinskiego 4/6, 00-928 Warsaw, Poland
PHONE: +48 (22) 6244000
FAX: +48 (22) 6285365

POLITICAL ORGANIZATIONS

Democratic Left Alliance

ul. Grunwaldzka 31, 82-300 Elblag, Poland
PHONE: +48 (55) 2339693
FAX: +48 (55) 2337676
NAME: Leszek Miller

Polish Peasant Party

NAME: Jaroslaw Kalinowski

Freedom Union

NAME: Leszek Balcerowicz

Christian National Union

NAME: Marian Pilka

Center Alliance Party

NAME: Jaroslaw Kaczynski

Peaasant Alliance

NAME: Gabriel Janowski

Solidarity Electoral Action Social Movement

NAME: Jerzy Buzek

Union of Labor

NAME: Aleksander Malachowskij

Conservative Party

NAME: Aleksander Hall

Movement for the Reconstruction of Poland

NAME: Jan Olszewski

Confederation for an Independent Poland

NAME: Adam Slomka

German Minority

NAME: Henryk Kroll

Union of Real Politics

NAME: Stanislaw Michalkiewicz

DIPLOMATIC REPRESENTATION

Embassies in Poland

Afghanistan
ul. Staroscinska 1 lok. 20, 02-516 Warsaw, Poland
PHONE: +48 (22) 8491563

Albania
ul. Sloneczna 15, 00-789 Warsaw, Poland
PHONE: +48 (22) 8498427
FAX: +48 (22) 8484004

Algeria
ul. Dabrowiecka 21, 03-932 Warsaw, Poland
PHONE: +48 (22) 6175855; 6175931
FAX: +48 (22) 6160081

Argentina
ul. Styki 17/19, 03-928 Warsaw, Poland
PHONE: +48 (22) 6176028
FAX: +48 (22) 6177162

Australia
ul. Estonska 3/5, 03-903 Warsaw, Poland
PHONE: +48 (22) 6176081
FAX: +48 (22) 6176756

Austria
ul. Gagarina 34, 00748 Warsaw, Poland
PHONE: +48 (22) 8410081
FAX: +48 (22) 8410085

Bangladesh
ul. Rejtana 15 lok.20/21, 02-516 Warsaw, Poland
PHONE: +48 (22) 8483200; 8480637
FAX: +48 (22) 8484974

Belarus
ul. Atenska 67, 03-798 Warsaw, Poland
PHONE: +48 (22) 6173212
FAX: +48 (22) 6178441

Belgium
ul. Senatorska 34, 00-095 Warsaw, Poland
PHONE: +48 (22) 8270233
FAX: +48 (22) 6355711

Brazil
ul. Poselska 11, 03-931 Warsaw, Poland
PHONE: +48 (22) 6174800; 6178689

Bulgaria
al. Ujazdowskie 33/35, 00-540 Warsaw, Poland
PHONE: +48 (22) 6294071
FAX: +48 (22) 6282271

Canada
ul. Matejki 1/5, 00-481 Warsaw, Poland
PHONE: +48 (22) 6298051
FAX: +48 (22) 6296457

Chile
ul. Staroscinska 1b, appt. 2-3, 02-516 Warsaw, Poland
PHONE: +48 (22) 6469962
FAX: +48 (22) 6462610

China
ul. Bonifraterska 1, 00-203 Warsaw, Poland
PHONE: +48 (22) 8313836
FAX: +48 (22) 6354211

Colombia
ul. Zwyciezcow 29, 03-936 Warsaw, Poland
PHONE: +48 (22) 6170973
FAX: +48 (22) 6176684

Congo
ul. Hoza 38 lok. 35, 00-516 Warsaw, Poland
PHONE: +48 (22) 6213736

Costa Rica
ul. Kubickiego 17, appt. 26, 02-954 Warsaw, Poland
PHONE: +48 (22) 6427832

Croatia
ul. Ignacego Krasickiego 10, 02-628 Warsaw, Poland
PHONE: +48 (22) 8441225
FAX: +48 (22) 8440567

Cuba
ul. Rejtana 15, appt.9, 02-516 Warsaw, Poland
PHONE: +48 (22) 6461178
FAX: +48 (22) 8482231

Cyprus
pl. J.H. Dabrowskiego 1, 00-057 Warsaw, Poland
PHONE: +48 (22) 8267318
FAX: +48 (22) 8264759

Czech Republic
ul. Koszykowa 18, 00-555 Warsaw, Poland
PHONE: +48 (22) 6287221
FAX: +48 (22) 6219880

Denmark
ul. Rakowiecka 19, 02-517 Warsaw, Poland
PHONE: +48 (22) 8482600
FAX: +48 (22) 8487580

Ecuador
ul. Rejtana 15, appt.15, 02-516 Warsaw, Poland
PHONE: +48 (22) 8488196

Egypt
ul. Alzacka 18, 03-972 Warsaw, Poland
PHONE: +48 (22) 6176973
FAX: +48 (22) 6179058

Estonia
ul. Karwinska 1, 02-639 Warsaw, Poland
PHONE: +48 (22) 6464480
FAX: +48 (22) 6464481

Finland
ul. Chopina 4/8, 00-559 Warsaw, Poland
PHONE: +48 (22) 6294091
FAX: +48 (22) 6213442

France
ul. Piekna 1, 00-477 Warsaw, Poland
PHONE: +48 (22) 6288401
FAX: +48 (22) 6296480

Germany
ul. Dabrowiecka 30, 03-932 Warsaw, Poland

Great Britain
al. Roz 1, 00-556 Warsaw, Poland
PHONE: +48 (22) 6281001
FAX: +48 (22) 6217161

Greece
ul. Gornoslaska 35, 00-432 Warsaw, Poland
PHONE: +48 (22) 6229460
FAX: +48 (22) 6229464

Guatemala
ul. Genewska 37, 03-940 Warsaw, Poland
PHONE: +48 (22) 6173303

Hungary
ul. Chopina 2, 00-559 Warsaw, Poland
PHONE: +48 (22) 6284451
FAX: +48 (22) 6218561

Iceland
ul. Slowackiego 30, appt.17, 81-872 Sopot, Poland
PHONE: +48 (58) 5515840

India
ul. Rejtana 15, appt. 2/7, 02-516 Warsaw, Poland
PHONE: +48 (22) 8495800
FAX: +48 (22) 8496705

Indonesia
ul. Wachocka 9, 03-934 Warsaw, Poland
PHONE: +48 (22) 6173917

Iran
ul. Krolowej Aldony 22, 03-928 Warsaw, Poland
PHONE: +48 (22) 6174293
FAX: +48 (22) 6178452

Iraq
ul. Dabrowiecka, 9a Warsaw, Poland
PHONE: +48 (22) 6175773
FAX: +48 (22) 6177065

Ireland
ul. Humanska 10, 00-789 Warsaw, Poland
PHONE: +48 (22) 8496655
FAX: +48 (22) 8498431

Israel
ul. Krzywickiego 24, 02-078 Warsaw, Poland
PHONE: +48 (22) 8250028; 8251607

Italy
pl. J. H. Dabrowskiego 6, 00-055 Warsaw, Poland
PHONE: +48 (22) 8263471
FAX: +48 (22) 8278507

Japan
al. Jana Pawla II 23, 00-854 Warsaw, Poland
PHONE: +48 (22) 6539430
FAX: +48 (22) 6539432

Laos
ul. Rejtana 15, appt. 26, 02-516 Warsaw, Poland
PHONE: +48 (22) 8484786
FAX: +48 (22) 8497122

Latvia
ul. Rejtana 15, appt. 19, 02-516 Warsaw, Poland
PHONE: +48 (22) 8481947
FAX: +48 (22) 8480201

Lebanon
ul. Staroscinska, appt.10, 02-516 Warsaw, Poland
PHONE: +48 (22) 8445065
FAX: +48 (22) 6460030

Libya
ul. Kryniczna 2, 03-934 Warsaw, Poland
PHONE: +48 (22) 6174883
FAX: +48 (22) 6175091

Lithuania
al. Szucha 5, 00-580 Warsaw, Poland
PHONE: +48 (22) 6253368
FAX: +48 (22) 6253440

Luxembourg
ul. Zelazna 28/30, 00-806 Warsaw, Poland
PHONE: +48 (22) 6549559
FAX: +48 (22) 6546498

Macedonia
ul. Dominikanska 15, 02-738 Warsaw, Poland
PHONE: +48 (22) 6444672
FAX: +48 (22) 8431326

Malaysia
ul. Gruzinska 3, 03-902 Warsaw, Poland
PHONE: +48 (22) 6174413

United States
al. Ujazdowskie 29/31, 00-540 Warsaw, Poland
PHONE: +48 (22) 6283041
FAX: +48 (22) 6288298

JUDICIAL SYSTEM

Supreme Court

ul. Ogrodowa 6, 00-951 Warsaw, Poland
PHONE: +48 (22) 6200371
FAX: +48 (22) 6203714

Constitutional Tribunal

Al. Szucha 12 A, 00-918 Warsaw, Poland
PHONE: +48 (22) 6216503

BROADCAST MEDIA

Polish Radio Warsaw

PO Box 46, 00-977 Warsaw, Poland
PHONE: +48 (22) 6459305
FAX: +48 (22) 6455917
E-MAIL: radio.polonia@radio.com.pl
WEBSITE: http://www.wrn.org.audio.html
CONTACT: Jerzy Marek Nowakowski

Polskie Radio S.A.

Al. Niepodleglosci 77/85, 00-977 Warsaw, Poland
PHONE: +48 (22) 6459212
FAX: +48 (22) 444119
WEBSITE: http://www.radio.com.pl/
TITLE: President of the Board
CONTACT: Krzysztof Michalski
LANGUAGE: Polish

Polskie Radio 1

Al. Niepodleglosci 77/85, 00-977 Warsaw, Poland
PHONE: +48 (22) 6452266
LANGUAGE: Polish

Polskie Radio 2

Program 2, Al. Niepodleglosci 77/85, 00-977 Warsaw, Poland
E-MAIL: dwojka@radio.com.pl

Radio Aplauz

Ul. Powstaicow S.95, 53-332 Wroclaw, Poland
PHONE: +48 (22) 717878
FAX: +48 (22) 717805
E-MAIL: radio@aplauz.aida.pl; ciesielskam@aplauz.ai
CONTACT: Gosia Ciesielska
LANGUAGE: Polish

Radio Krakow

Al. Juliusza Slowackiego 22, 30-007 Krakow, Poland
PHONE: +48 (12) 2003333
FAX: +48 (12) 6306000
LANGUAGE: Polish

Radio Maks

Nowy Swiat 3, 33-100 Tarnow, Poland
PHONE: +48 (14) 6216621
FAX: +48 (14) 6212929

Radio Maryja

Ul. Zwirki I Wigury 80, 87–100 Torun, Poland
PHONE: +48 (56) 552361
FAX: +48 (56) 552362
E-MAIL: radio@radiomaryja.pl
WEBSITE: http://www.logon.bydgoszcz.pl/goscie/mateusz/rm/
TITLE: Director
CONTACT: Tadeusz Rydzyk
TYPE: Religious

Radio Muzyka Fakty (RMF FM)

Al. Waszyngtona, Kopiec Kosciuszki, 30–204 Krakow, Poland
PHONE: +48 (12) 4270606
FAX: +48 (12) 4270395
E-MAIL: redakcja@rmf.fm

WEBSITE: http://www.rmf.pl/
TITLE: Director
CONTACT: Jolanta Wisniewska

Radio Pogoda

Ul. Migdalowa 91, 02–796 Warsaw, Poland
PHONE: +48 (22) 6483060
FAX: +48 (22) 6493685
E-MAIL: radiopogoda@radiopogoda.com.pl
LANGUAGE: Polish

Radio Rak

Ul. Rostafirskiego 8, 30–073 Krakow, Poland
PHONE: +48 (12) 6367450
FAX: +48 (12) 6367426
E-MAIL: rak@rak.krakow.pl
LANGUAGE: Polish

Radio Zet

Ul. Piekna 66-a, 00–672 Warsaw, Poland
PHONE: +48 (22) 6227676
FAX: +48 (22) 6273300
E-MAIL: radiozet@radiozet.com.pl; weiss@radiozet.com.pl
WEBSITE: http://www.radiozet.com.pl/
TITLE: Secretary
CONTACT: Janusz Weiss

ATV DTH

Krajowa Telewizja Kablowa, Lakowa 29, Lodz, Poland 90 554
PHONE: +48 (42) 375299
FAX: +48 (42) 376838
E-MAIL: atv@atv.com.pl

ATV Kino

Krajowa Telewizja Kablowa, Lakowa 29, Lodz, Poland 90 554
PHONE: +48 (42) 375299
FAX: +48 (42) 376838
E-MAIL: atv@atv.com.pl

Tele-9

Kielce ch R5, Krakow, Poland

Telewizja Polska S.A.

Ul. Woronicza 17, 00–999 Warsaw, Poland
PHONE: +48 (22) 433361
FAX: +48 (22) 447419
WEBSITE: http://www.tvp.com.pl
TITLE: Director
CONTACT: Rajmind Gruszka
TYPE: Government

TV Polonia

Woronicza Street 17, 00–950 Warsaw, Poland
PHONE: +48 (22) 476211
FAX: +48 (22) 437408

TV Polsat

Marchakovska 83, P-00517, Warsaw 84, Poland
PHONE: +48 (22) 295684

COLLEGES AND UNIVERSITIES

Uniwersytet Warszawski

Ul Nowolipki 2 a M 28, 00-160 Warsaw, Poland

Politechnika Warszawska

Pl Politechniki 1, 00-661 Warsaw, Poland
PHONE: +48 (22) 6607211
FAX: +48 (22) 6292962
E-MAIL: jmr@rekt.pw.edu.pl
WEBSITE: http://www.pw.edu.pl

Akademia Medyczna - Warszawa

61, Zwirki I Wigury Str., 03-921 Warsaw, Poland
PHONE: +48 (22) 5720502
FAX: +48 (22) 5720562
E-MAIL: english@akamed.waw.pl
WEBSITE: http://www.amwaw.edu.pl

Szkola Glowna Handlowa-Warszawa

Al Niepodiegloscil 62, 02-544 Warsaw, Poland
PHONE: +48 (22) 8491251
FAX: +48 (22) 8495312
E-MAIL: info@sgh.waw.pl
WEBSITE: http://www.sgh.waw.pl

Katolicki Uniwersytet Lubelski

Ul Prymasa S Wyszynskeigo 6, 20-105 Lublin, Poland

Maria Curie Sklodowskiej University in Lublin

Pl. Marji Curie-Sklodow Skiej 5, 02-031 Lublin, Poland
PHONE: +48 (81) 5375100
FAX: +48 (81) 5333669
WEBSITE: http://www.umcs.lublin.pl

University of Agriculture - Lublin

Ul Akademicka 13, 29-950 Lublin, Poland
PHONE: +48 (81) 4456622
FAX: +48 (81) 5333549

E-MAIL: info@swallow.ar.lublin.pl
WEBSITE: http://www.ar.lublin.pl

Wyzsza Szkola Pedagogiczna - Krakow

Wydzial Humanistyczny, Ul Podchorazych 2, 30-084 Krakow, Poland
PHONE: +48 (12) 6374777
FAX: +48 (12) 6372243
WEBSITE: http://www.wsp.krakow.pl

University of Agriculture - Krakow

Al. Mickiewicza 21, 30-838 Krakow, Poland
PHONE: +48 (12) 6331336
E-MAIL: rector@ar.krakow.pl
WEBSITE: http://www.ar.krakow.pl

Uniwersytet Jagiellonski - Krakow

Collegium Novum, Ul. Golebia 24, 31-007 Krakow, Poland
PHONE: +48 (12) 4226689
FAX: +48 (12) 4226306
E-MAIL: rektor@adm.uj.edu.pl
WEBSITE: http://www.uj.edu.pl

Krakow University of Technology

Warszawska 24, 31-155 Krakow, Poland
PHONE: +48 (12) 6282000
FAX: +48 (12) 6282056
E-MAIL: r-o@admin.pk.edu.pl
WEBSITE: http://www.pk.edu.pl

University of Economics Katowice

Ul Maja 50, 40-226 Katowice, Poland
PHONE: +48 (32) 598421
FAX: +48 (32) 588828
E-MAIL: interrel@ae.katowice.pl
WEBSITE: http://www.ae.katowice.pl

Medical University of Katowice

Ul Szpakow 1, 40-540 Katowice, Poland
PHONE: +48 (32) 2083555
FAX: +48 (32) 2084964
E-MAIL: wmaster@informed.slam.katowice.pl
WEBSITE: http://www.slam.katowice.pl

Pontifical Faculty of Theology

Pl Katedralny 14, 50-329 Wroclaw, Poland
PHONE: +48 (71) 224214
E-MAIL: pft@pft.wroc.pl
WEBSITE: http://www.pft.wroc.pl

Agricultural University of Wroclaw

25/27 C.K. Norwida St., 50-375 Wroclaw, Poland
PHONE: +48 (71) 205000
FAX: +48 (71) 205404
E-MAIL: dss@ozi.ar.wroc.pl
WEBSITE: http://www.ar.wroc.pl

Akademia Ekonomiczna - Wroclaw

Komandorski 118/120, 54-242 Wroclaw, Poland
PHONE: +48 (71) 3680100
FAX: +48 (71) 3672778
E-MAIL: www@alpha.ok.ae.wroc.pl
WEBSITE: http://www.ae.wroc.pl

University of Agriculture - Poznan

Wojska Polskiego 28, 60-637 Poznan, Poland
PHONE: +48 (61) 8487001
FAX: +48 (61) 8487146
E-MAIL: rektorat@au.poznan.pl
WEBSITE: http://www.au.poznan.pl

Poznan University of Technology

Ul Maril Sklodowskiej-Curie 5, 60-965 Poznan, Poland
PHONE: +48 (61) 8334081
FAX: +48 (61) 8330217
E-MAIL: university@put.poznan.pl
WEBSITE: http://www.put.poznan.pl

Medical University of Poznan

Ul Powidzka 19, 61-039 Poznan, Poland
PHONE: +48 (61) 8521161
FAX: +48 (61) 8520455
E-MAIL: info@usoms.poznan.pl
WEBSITE: http://www.usoms.poznan.pl

Uniwersytet Adama Mickiewicza

Ul Wieniawskiego 1, 61-712 Poznan, Poland
PHONE: +48 (61) 8526425
E-MAIL: rectorof@um.aum.edu.pl
WEBSITE: http://www.amu.edu.pl

Politechnika Szczecinska

Al Piastow 17, 70-310 Szczecin, Poland
PHONE: +48 (91) 4494015
FAX: +48 (91) 4494014
E-MAIL: rector@main.tuniv.szczecin.pl
WEBSITE: http://www.tuniv.szczecin.pl

Agricultural University of Szczecinie

Ul Janosika 8, 71-424 Szczecin, Poland

PHONE: +48 (91) 422 0851
FAX: +48 (91) 4232417
E-MAIL: rzw@ns.rektor.ar.szczecin.pl
WEBSITE: http://www.ar.szczecin.pl

Universytet Szczecinski

Al Jednosci Narodowej 22a, 71-658 Szczecin, Poland
PHONE: +48 (91) 4342536
FAX: +48 (91) 4342992
E-MAIL: rektorat@univ.szczecin.pl
WEBSITE: http://www.univ.szczecin.pl

Medical University of Gdansk

Ul Sk Odwskiej Curie 3a, 80-210 Gdansk, Poland
PHONE: +48 (58) 3478222
FAX: +48 (58) 3016115
WEBSITE: http://www.amg.gda.pl

Academy of Fine Arts - Gdansk

Targ Weglowy 6, 80-836 Gdansk, Poland
PHONE: +48 (58) 3012801
FAX: +48 (58) 3012200
E-MAIL: oi@asp.gda.pl
WEBSITE: http://www.asp.gda.pl

Technical University of Gdansk

Ul Narutowicza 11/12, 80-952 Gdansk, Poland
PHONE: +48 (58) 3415791
FAX: +48 (58) 3415821
WEBSITE: http://www.pg.gda.pl

Uniwersytet Gdanski

Bazynskiego 1 A, 90-952 Gdansk, Poland
PHONE: +48 (58) 5525071
FAX: +48 (58) 5525241
WEBSITE: http://www.univ.gda.pl

Polish Naval Academy

Al Marsz J Pilsudskiego 42 M 29, 81-378 Gdynia, Poland
PHONE: +48 (58) 6262514
FAX: +48 (58) 6203091
E-MAIL: akomor@amw.gdynia.pl
WEBSITE: http://www.amw.gdynia.pl

Nicholas Copernicus v Torun

Ul Gagarina 11, 87-100 Torun, Poland
PHONE: +48 (56) 6114010
FAX: +48 (56) 6542948
E-MAIL: rektor@cc.uni.torun.pl
WEBSITE: http://www.cc.uni.torun.pl

University of Lodz

Narutowicza 65, 90-131 Lodz, Poland
PHONE: +48 (42) 6354010
FAX: +48 (42) 6786023
WEBSITE: http://www.lodz.pl

Technical University of Lodz

Ul Skorupki 6/8, 90-431 Lodz, Poland
PHONE: +48 (42) 6367477
FAX: +48 (42) 6368522
E-MAIL: rector@sir-p.lodz.pl

Medical University of Lodz

92-216 Lodz, Poland
E-MAIL: jkk@psk2.am.lodz.pl
WEBSITE: http://www.am.lodz.pl

NEWSPAPERS AND MAGAZINES

Sport

Marquard Press S.A., Sobieskiego 11, skr. Poxzt. 339, 40-082 Katowice, Poland
PHONE: +48 (32) 2539995; 2597271
FAX: +48 (32) 2537138
E-MAIL: sek@sport.com.pl
TITLE: Editor-in-Chief
CONTACT: Adam Barteczko
CIRCULATION: 130,000

Tempo

JMG Sport-Publishing sp z.o.o., Al. Pokoju 3, 30-960 Krakow, Poland
PHONE: +48 (12) 4118801; 4120361
FAX: +48 (12) 4120361
E-MAIL: redakcja@tiempo,krakow.pl
TITLE: Editor-in-Chief
CONTACT: Andrzej Skowronski
CIRCULATION: 52,000 (Tu-Fri); 103,000 (Mon)

Express Wieczorny

"Express Wieczorny" Sp z.o.o., Al. Jerozolimskie 125/127, 00-973 Warsaw, Poland
PHONE: +48 (22) 6285327; 6288502
FAX: +48 (22) 6284929
E-MAIL: express@medianet.com.pl
TITLE: Editor-in-Chief
CONTACT: Katarzyna Nazarewicz
CIRCULATION: 87,000 (Daily); 250,000 (Sat)

Gazeta Wyborcza

Agora-Gazeta sp z.o.o., Czerska 8/10, 00-732 Warsaw, Poland

PHONE: +48 (22) 413010; 415513
FAX: +48 (22) 416920
E-MAIL: listy@gazea.pl
WEBSITE: http://www.gazeta.pl
TITLE: Editor-in-Chief
CONTACT: Adam Michnik
CIRCULATION: 425,000 (Daily); 850,000 (Sat/Sun)

Kurier Polski

Kurier Pokski sp z.o.o., ul. Zgoda 11, 00-018 Warsaw, Poland
PHONE: +48 (22) 8278081
FAX: +48 (22) 8270552
E-MAIL: kp@kurier.ikp.pl
TITLE: Editor-in-Chief
CONTACT: Bozena Skupinska[/Contact
CIRCULATION: 120,000

Polska Zbrojna

Ministerstwo Obrony Narodowej, ul Grzybowska 77, 00-844 Warsaw, Poland
PHONE: +48 (22) 6204293; 6822101
FAX: +48 (22) 6242273
E-MAIL: pzbrojna@pol.pl
TITLE: Editor-in-Chief
CONTACT: Ireneusz Czyewski
CIRCULATION: 47,800

Prawo I Gospodarka

"Infor" sp z.o.o., Miedziana 11, 00-958 Warsaw, Poland
PHONE: +48 (22) 6521840; 6270182
FAX: +48 (22) 6521854
E-MAIL: prawo@pg.com.pl
TITLE: Editor-in-Chief
CONTACT: Zbigniew Maciag
CIRCULATION: 50,000

Przeglad Sportowy

JMG Jerozolimskie 125/127, 00-973 Warsaw, Poland
PHONE: +48 (22) 6289116; 6280231
FAX: +48 (22) 6218697
E-MAIL: ps@polbox.pl
WEBSITE: http://www.przegladsportowy.com.pl
TITLE: Editor-in-Chief
CONTACT: Piotr Gorski
CIRCULATION: 130,000 (Tu-Fri); 265,000 (Mon)

Rzeczpospolita

Presspublica sp z.o.o., Pl. Starynkiewicza 7, 02-015 Warsaw, Poland
PHONE: +48 (22) 6283401
FAX: +48 (22) 6280588
WEBSITE: http://www.rzeczpospolita.pl
TITLE: Editor-in-Chief
CONTACT: Piotr Aleksandrowicz
CIRCULATION: 290,000

Super Express

Media Express sp. z.o.o., Jubilerska 10, 00-939, Warsaw, Poland
PHONE: +48 (22) 5159000; 5159001
FAX: +48 (22) 5159010
E-MAIL: ogloszenia@superexpress.com.pl
WEBSITE: http://www.se.com.pl
TITLE: Editor-in-Chief
CONTACT: Izabella Jablonska
CIRCULATION: 400,000

Trybuna

"Ad Novum" sp. z.o.o., Miedziana 11, 00-835 Warsaw, Poland
PHONE: +48 (22) 6253015; 6151265
FAX: +48 (22) 6204100
E-MAIL: trybuna@it.com.pl
TITLE: Editor-in-Chief
CONTACT: Janusz Rolicki
CIRCULATION: 100,000 (Daily); 145,000 (Sat/Sun)

The Warsaw Voice

Warsaw Voice S.A., Keiecia Janusza 64, 01-452 Warsaw, Poland
PHONE: +48 (22) 366377; 375138; 379145
FAX: +48 (22) 371995; 379962
WEBSITE: http://www.warsawvoice.com.pl
TITLE: Editor
CONTACT: Andrzej Tonas
CIRCULATION: 15,000

Zycie Warszawy

multico Press sp. z.o.o., Armii Ludowej 3/5 00-915 Warsaw, Poland
PHONE: +48 (22) 6256990; 6253873
FAX: +48 (22) 6252426
E-MAIL: zycie@zw.com.pl
WEBSITE: http;//www.zw.com.pl
TITLE: Editor-in-Chief
CONTACT: Andrzej Bober
CIRCULATION: 208,000 (Mon-Fri); 330,000 (Sat)

Dziennuj Zachodni

Mlynska 1, 40-953 Katowice, Poland, Polska Presse sp. z.o.o.
PHONE: +48 (32) 2537241; 2539984
FAX: +48 (32)2539186
E-MAIL: dziennik@mtl.pl
WEBSITE: http://www.dz.com.pl
TITLE: Editor-in-Chief
CONTACT: Marek Chylinski
CIRCULATION: 70,000 (Daily); 450,000 (Sat/Sun)

Gazeta Pomorska

Gazeta Pomorska Media sp. z.o.o., ul. Zamojskiego 2, 85-063 Bydgoszcz, Poland
PHONE: +48 (52) 221928; 229464
FAX: +48 (52) 221542
E-MAIL: gazetpom@logonet.com.pl
WEBSITE: http://www.gpmedia.pl
TITLE: Editor-in-Chief
CONTACT: Maciej Kaminski
CIRCULATION: 85,000 (Daily); 247,000 (Sat/Sun)

Trybuna Slaska

"Gornoslaskie Towarzystwo Prasowe" sp. z.o.o., ul. Mlynska 1, 40-098 Katowice, Poland
PHONE: +48 (32) 2539285; 2539855
FAX: +48 (32) 2537997
E-MAIL: tsl@trybuna-slaska.com.pl
WEBSITE: http://www.trybuna-slaska.com.pl
TITLE: Editor-in-Chief
CONTACT: Tadeusz Biedzki
CIRCULATION: 221,000

Forum

Tygodnik Forum SP, ul. Sniadeckich 10, 00-656, Warsaw, Poland
PHONE: +48 (22) 6256150; 6289503
FAX: +48 (22) 6289503
TITLE: Editor-in-Chief
CONTACT: Bohdan Herbich
CIRCULATION: 30,000
TYPE: General Interest

Nowa Wies

Fundacja Kultury I Rozwoju "Ziemia", ul. Wiejska 17, 00-656 Warsaw, Poland
PHONE: +48 (22)6283292; 6284583
FAX: +48 (22) 62256079
E-MAIL: nova@ikp.atm.com.pl
WEBSITE: http://www.atm.com.pl/nova
TITLE: Editor-in-Chief
CONTACT: Kaimierz Dlugosz
CIRCULATION: 80,000
TYPE: General Interest

Przekroj

Wydawnictwo Przekroj, ul. Reformacka 3, 31-012 Krakow, Poland
PHONE: +48 (12) 4225954; 4221833
FAX: +48 (12) 4214929
E-MAIL: prze_red@przekroj.pl
TITLE: Editor
CONTACT: Mieczyslaw Czuma
CIRCULATION: 80,000
TYPE: General Interest

Reader's Digest Preglad

Lockka 2/4/6, 00-845 Warsaw, Poland
PHONE: +48 (22) 6545544
FAX: +48 (22) 6545533
TITLE: Editor
CONTACT: Andrzej Krajewski
CIRCULATION: 420,000
TYPE: Compilation of articles

Angora

Tygodnik Angora, ul. Piotrowska 94, 90-103 Lodz, Poland
PHONE: +48 (42) 6326179
FAX: +48 (42) 6320767
E-MAIL: angora@lodz.pdi.net
WEBSITE: http://www.angora.pdi.net
TITLE: Editor-in-Chief
CONTACT: Piotr Rizycki
CIRCULATION: 396,000
TYPE: News Magazine

Polityka

Politika, ul. Miedziana 11, 00-835 Warsaw, Poland
PHONE: +48 (22) 6354991; 6351797
FAX: +48 (22) 6354991
E-MAIL: polityka@polityka.com.pl
WEBSITE: http://www.polityka.pol.pl
TITLE: Editor-in-Chief
CONTACT: Jerzy Baczynski
CIRCULATION: 285,000
TYPE: News Magazine

The Warsaw Voice

Warsaw Voice S.A., ul. Ksiecia janusza 64, 01-452 Warsaw, Poland
PHONE: +48 (220 8375138; 8379145

FAX: +48 (22) 8371995
E-MAIL: voice@warsawvoice.com.pl
WEBSITE: http://www.warsawvoice.com.pl
TITLE: Editor-in-Chief
CONTACT: Andrej Jones
CIRCULATION: 15,000
TYPE: News Magazine

Wprost

Agencja Wprost sp z.o.o., Grunwaldzka 104, 60-307 Proznan, Poland
PHONE: +48 (61) 8699371
FAX: +48 (61) 8668097
E-MAIL: wprost@optimus.proznan.pl
WEBSITE: http://www.wprost.pl
TITLE: Editor-in-Chief
CONTACT: Marek Krol
CIRCULATION: 331,000
TYPE: News Magazine

PUBLISHERS

Wydawnictwo Adamantan s.c.

ul. Dobosza 7/7, 02-376 Warsaw, Poland
PHONE: +48 (22) 8225267
FAX: +48 (22) 8225267
E-MAIL: adamantan@adamantan.com.pl
WEBSITE: http://www.adamantan.com.pl
TITLE: Editor-in-Chief
CONTACT: Witold Mizerski
SUBJECTS: Education, Fiction, Geography, History, Mathematics, Science, Children's Books
TOTAL PUBLISHED: 46 print

Dom Wydawniczy Bellona

ul. Grzybowska 77, 00-844 Warsaw, Poland
PHONE: +48 (22) 6202044
FAX: +48 (22) 6522695
E-MAIL: biuro@bellona.pl
WEBSITE: http://www.bellona.pl
SUBJECTS: Economics, Fiction, History, Literature, Mathematics, Medicine, Military History, Science, Sociology

Dom Wydawniczy Rebis

ul. Zmigrodzka 41-49, 60-171 Poznan, Poland
PHONE: +48 (61) 8674708
FAX: +48 (61) 8673774
E-MAIL: rebis@man.poznan.pl
WEBSITE: http://www.rebis.com.pl
TITLE: Founder
CONTACT: Tomasz Szponder
SUBJECTS: Biography, Children's Books, Fantasy, Fiction (General), Literature, Parental Guides, Romance, Science Fiction, Self-Help Books
TOTAL PUBLISHED: 220 titles in 2000

Spoldzielnia Wydawnicza 'Czytelnik'

ul. Wiejska 12a, 00-490 Warsaw, Poland
PHONE: +48 (22) 6281441
FAX: +48 (22) 6283178
E-MAIL: sekretariat@czytelnik.pl
WEBSITE: http://www.czytelnik.pl
TITLE: Managing Director
CONTACT: Zakowski Marek
SUBJECTS: Biography, Fiction, Journalism, Poetry, Social Sciences, Sociology
TOTAL PUBLISHED: 90 titles annually

Instytut Wydawniczy Pax, Inco-Veritas

00-390 Warszawa, Wybrzeze Kosciuszkowskie 21a, Warsaw, Poland
PHONE: +48 (22) 6253398
FAX: +48 (22) 6253398
E-MAIL: iwpax@it.com.pl
WEBSITE: http://www.iwpax.com.pl
TITLE: Chief Editor
CONTACT: Karol Klauza
SUBJECTS: Biblical Studies, Education, History, Literature, Literary Criticism, Essays, Philosophy, Poetry, Religion-Catholic, Theology

Iskry Publishing House Ltd

Smolna 11, Warsaw, Poland
PHONE: +48 (22) 8279424
FAX: +48 (22) 8279415
TITLE: Editor-in-Chief
CONTACT: Krysztaf Obtucki
SUBJECTS: Aeronautics, Aviation, Biography, Cookery, History, Literature, Literary Criticism, Essays, Maritime, Mysteries, Parapsychology, Philosophy, Regional Interests, Science Fiction, Fantasy, Self-Help, Travel

Polskie Wydawnictwo Ekonomiczne

ul. Canaletta 4, 00-098 Warsaw, Poland
PHONE: +48 (22) 8278001
FAX: +48 (22) 8275567
E-MAIL: pwe@pwe.com.pl
WEBSITE: http://www.pwe.com.pl
TITLE: President
CONTACT: Alicja Rutkowska

SUBJECTS: Accounting, Advertising, Business, Economics, Environmental Studies, Finance, Management, Marketing

Ksiazka i Wiedza Spotdzielnia Wydawniczo-Handlowa

ul. Smolna 13, 00-375 Warsaw, Poland
PHONE: +48 (22) 8275401
FAX: +48 (22) 8279416
E-MAIL: publisher@kiw.com.pl
WEBSITE: http://www.kiw.com.pl
TITLE: Director
CONTACT: Marta Stuhr
SUBJECTS: Animals, Pets, Biography, Government, Political Science, History, Philosophy, Social Sciences, Sociology, Travel

Ksiaznica Publishing Ltd

ul. Powstancow 30/401, 40-039 Katowice, Poland
PHONE: +48 (32) 2572216
FAX: +48 (32) 2572217
E-MAIL: ksiaznica@domnet.com.pl
TITLE: President
CONTACT: Mariusz Morga
SUBJECTS: Fiction, Health, Nutrition, Nonfiction (General), Romance

Wydawnictwo Cartall

ul. Rewolucji 1905 r. 4/5, 90-273 Lodz, Poland
PHONE: +48 (42) 6397730
FAX: +48 (42) 6397732
E-MAIL: biuro@cartall.com.pl
WEBSITE: http://www.cartall.com.pl
SUBJECTS: Atlases, Computers, History, Multimedia

Wydawnictwo Literackie

ul. Dluga 1, 31-147 Krakow, Poland
PHONE: +48 (12) 4225423
FAX: +48 (12) 4225423
E-MAIL: redakcja@wl.interkom.pl
TITLE: Director
CONTACT: Barbara Drwota
SUBJECTS: Art, Biography, Drama, Theater, Film, Video, History, Literature, Literary Criticism, Essays

Wydawnictwo Lubelskie

ul. Okopowa, 20-022 Lublin, Poland
PHONE: +48 (81) 7436130
TITLE: Director
CONTACT: Ireneusz Caban
SUBJECTS: Government, Political Science, Human Relations, Poetry, Science (General), Social Sciences, Sociology

Muza SA

ul. Marszalkowska 8, 00-590 Warsaw, Poland
PHONE: +48 (22) 6211775
FAX: +48 (22) 6292349
E-MAIL: muza@muza.com.pl
WEBSITE: http://www.muza.com.pl
TITLE: President
CONTACT: Wlodzimierz Czarzasty
SUBJECTS: Art, Cookery, Education, Fiction, House and Home, Nonfiction (General), Social Sciences, Sociology, Travel

Ossolineum Zaklad Narodowy im Ossolinskich - Wyadawnictwo

Plac Solny 14a, 50-062 Wroclaw, Poland
PHONE: +48 (71) 3436961
FAX: +48 (71) 3448103
E-MAIL: osso_bn@ossolineum.wroc.pl
WEBSITE: http://www.ossolineum.wroc.pl
TITLE: Director
CONTACT: Wojciech Karwacki
SUBJECTS: Architecture and Interior Design, Art, Biography, Biological Sciences, Environmental Studies, History, Language Arts, Linguistics, Literature, Literary Criticism, Essays, Poetry, Social Sciences, Sociology

Panstwowy Instytut Wydawniczy

ul. Foksal 17, 00-372 Warsaw, Poland
PHONE: +48 (22) 8260201
FAX: +48 (22) 8261536
E-MAIL: piw@piw.pl
WEBSITE: http://www.piw.pl
TITLE: Deputy Editor-in-Chief
CONTACT: Tadeus Nowakowski
SUBJECTS: Biography, Drama, Theater, Ethnicity, Fiction, History, Literature, Literary Criticism, Essays, Poetry, Science (General)

Polish Scientific Publishers (PWN)

ul. Miodowa 10, 00-251 Warsaw, Poland
PHONE: +48 (22) 6954180
FAX: +48 (22) 6954288
E-MAIL: international@pwn.com.pl
WEBSITE: http://www.pwn.com.pl
TITLE: Executive Director
CONTACT: Michal Szewielow
SUBJECTS: Agriculture, Art, Business, Chemistry, Dictionaries, Economics, Encyclopedias,

Engineering, Geography, Geology, Journals, Languages, Linguistics, Marketing, Mathematics, Medicine, Philosophy, Physics, Polish Philology, Psychology, Sociology
TOTAL PUBLISHED: 43,000 print; 400 titles annually

Prima Oficyna Wydawnicza

ul. Ewietokrzyska 30/55, 00-116 Warsaw, Poland
PHONE: +48 (22) 6248918
FAX: +48 (22) 6248918
E-MAIL: wydawnictwo@prima.waw.pl
WEBSITE: http://www.prima.waw.pl
TITLE: President
CONTACT: Andrzej Kurylowicz
SUBJECTS: Biography, Fiction, History, Mysteries, Nonfiction (General), Psychology, Psychiatry, Romance, Self-Help
TOTAL PUBLISHED: 240 print; 50 titles annually

PZWL Wydawnictwo Lekarskie Ltd

ul. Dluga 38-40, 00 950 Warsaw, Poland
PHONE: +48 (22) 8314281
FAX: +48 (22) 8310054
E-MAIL: wydawnictwo@pzwl.pl
WEBSITE: http://www.pzwl.pl
TITLE: President
CONTACT: Krystyna Regulska
SUBJECTS: Biological Sciences, Chemistry, Chemical Engineering, Child Care and Development, Health, Nutrition, Medicine, Nursing, Dentistry, Psychology, Psychiatry, Veterinary Science
TOTAL PUBLISHED: 400 print

Slask Ltd.

Al W Korfantego 51, skr poczt 3667, 40-161 Katowice, Poland
PHONE: +48 (32) 580756
FAX: +48 (32) 583229
E-MAIL: biuro@slaskwn.com.pl
TITLE: President
CONTACT: Tadeusz Sierny
SUBJECTS: Advertising, English as a Second Language, History, Literature, Literary Criticism, Essays, Nonfiction (General), Poetry, Regional Interests, Science (General)

Wydawnictwo WAB

ul. Nowolipie 9-11, 00-150 Warsaw, Poland
PHONE: +48 (22) 6357557
FAX: +48 (22) 6351525
E-MAIL: wab@wab.com.pl
WEBSITE: http://www.wab.com.pl
TITLE: Editor
CONTACT: Beata Stasinska
SUBJECTS: Child Care and Development, Fiction, Health, Nutrition, Human Relations, Nonfiction (General), Self-Help
TOTAL PUBLISHED: 220 print; 50 titles annually

Wydawnictwo DiG

Nowy Ewiat 39, 00-029 Warsaw, Poland
PHONE: +48 (22) 8280096
FAX: +48 (22) 8280096
E-MAIL: dig@dig.com.pl
WEBSITE: http://www.dig.com.pl
TITLE: Editor
CONTACT: Slawomir Gorzynski
SUBJECTS: Antiques, Archaeology, Art, Biography, Genealogy, History, Linguistics, Library and Information Sciences, Literature, Literary Criticism, Essays
TOTAL PUBLISHED: 150 print

Znak Spoleczny Instytut Wydawniczy

ul. Kosciuszki 37, 30-105 Krakow, Poland
PHONE: +48 (12) 4291469
FAX: +48 (12) 4219814
E-MAIL: rucinska@znak.com.pl
WEBSITE: http://www.znak.com.pl
TITLE: CEO
CONTACT: Henryk Wozniakowski
SUBJECTS: Autobiography, Fiction, Economics, Essays, Fiction, History, Philosophy, Poetry, Politics, Religion, School Textbooks, Science

RELIGIOUS ORGANIZATIONS

Buddhist

Buddyjska Wspolnota Kannon Sangha
Wandy 10a/1, Warsaw 03-949 Poland
PHONE: +48 (22) 6171292
E-MAIL: lipa@altkom.com.pl
TITLE: Contact
NAME: Slawomir Lipski

Gdansk Zen Center
Grunwaldzka 121/26, Gdansk, Poland

Gdansk Zen Center
Ul. Sienkiewicza 12/1, Gdansk, Poland
E-MAIL: gdansk@underweb.net

Kandzeon Sangha
Husarii 32, Warsaw, 00-714 Poland
PHONE: +48 (22) 427887
TITLE: Contact
NAME: Malgosia Braunek or Andrej Krajewski

Krakow Zen Center
Ul. Bandurskiego 19/4, 31-515 Krakow, Poland
PHONE: +48 (12) 562428
E-MAIL: krakozen@kki.net.pl

Mindfulness Sangha
Czerniakowska 36/80, Warsaw, 00-714 Poland
PHONE: +48 (22) 400658
TITLE: Contact
NAME: Tanna Jakubowica-Mount

Warsaw Zen Center (Head Temple Eastern Europe)
Ul. Malowiejska 24, 04-962 Warszwa- Falencia, Poland
PHONE: +48 (22) 6127223
FAX: +48 (22) 6127223
E-MAIL: kwanumzen@jantar.elektron.pl

Warsaw Zen Group
Ul. Lesna 27, 05-840 Brwinow, Poland
PHONE: +48 (22) 104181
TITLE: Contact
NAME: Anna Golab

ZBZ Sangha
Ul. Filmova 32, Warsaw- Falencia, 04-935 Poland

Zen Center
Husarii 32, Warsaw, 02-951 Poland
TITLE: Contact
NAME: Andrej Krajewski

Zwiazek Buddystow Czan (Ch'an Buddhist Union)
Zlota 64/666 str. Apt. 69, Warsaw, Poland
PHONE: +48 (22) 6208446
FAX: +48 (22) 6208446
E-MAIL: budwod@zigzag.pl

Catholic

Bialystok Archbishop
Plac Jana Pawla II 1, 15-087 Bialystok, Poland
PHONE: +48 (85) 7416473
FAX: +48 (85) 7416473
TITLE: Arcybiskup Metropolita
NAME: Stanislaw Szymecki

Club of Catholic Intelligentsia

Klub Inteligencji Katolickiej
Kopernika St. 34, 00-336 Warsaw, Poland
PHONE: +48 (22) 8273939
FAX: +48 (22) 8272904
E-MAIL: kik@kik.waw.pl
WEBSITE: http://www.kik.waw.pl

Gdansk Archbishop
ul. Cystersow 15, 80-330 Gdansk-Oliwa, Poland
PHONE: +48 (58) 5520053
TITLE: Arcybiskup Metropolita
NAME: Tadeusz Goclowski CM

Krakow Archbishop
Ul. Franciszkarska 3, 31-004 Krakow, Poland
PHONE: +48 (12) 4294340
FAX: +48 (12) 4294405
TITLE: Arcybiskup Metropolita
NAME: Kard. Franciszek Macharski

Lublin Archbishop
Ul. Prymasa Stefana Wyszyiskiego 2, Skr.poczt. 198, 20-950 Lublin, Poland
PHONE: +48 (81) 5323468
FAX: +48 (81) 5346135
E-MAIL: atzycins@nestor.kul.lublin.pl; atzycins@kuria.lublin.pl
TITLE: Arcybiskup Metropolita
NAME: Jozef Zycinski

Poznan Archbishop
Ul. Ostrow Tumski 1, 61-109 Poznan, Poland
PHONE: +48 (61) 8528556
FAX: +48 (61) 8526797
TITLE: Arcybiskup Metropolita
NAME: Juliusz Paetz

Szczecin-Kamien Archbishop
Ul. Ks. Piotra Skargi 30, 71-423 Szczecin, Poland
PHONE: +48 (91) 225157
TITLE: Arcybiskup Metropolita
NAME: Marian Przykucki

Warszawa Archbishop
Ul. Miodowa 17/19, 00-246 Warszawa, Poland
PHONE: +48 (22) 8312157, 6355253
FAX: +48 (22) 6358745
E-MAIL: prymas@perytnet.pl
TITLE: Arcybiskup Metropolita
NAME: Kard. Jozef Glemp, Prymas Polski

Warszawa- Ordynariat Polowy
Ul. Karaszewicza-Tokarzewskiego 4, 00-911 Warszawa, Poland
PHONE: +48 (22) 8269883
FAX: +48 (22) 8269337
TITLE: Ordynariat Polowy
NAME: Wojska Polskiego

Wroclaw Archbishop
Ul. Katedralna 13/15, 50-328 Wroclaw, Poland
PHONE: +48 (71) 3225081
TITLE: Arcybiskup Metropolita
NAME: Kard. Henryk R. Gulbinowicz

Jewish

Mikvah c/o Synagogue
Ul. Miodowa 24, Cracow, Poland
PHONE: +48 62064

Nozyk Synagogue
6, Twarda Str., Warsaw, Poland
PHONE: +48 (22) 6204324
E-MAIL: varshe@kehullah.jewish.org.pl
WEBSITE: http://www.jewish.org.pl
TITLE: Contact
NAME: Robert Pasieczny

Remuh Synagogue
Ul. Miodowa 24, Cracow, Poland
PHONE: +48 62064

Synagogue Vaad Hakehilla
6 Twarda St., Warsaw, Poland
PHONE: +48 (2) 204324
TITLE: Contact
NAME: R. M. Joskowicz

FURTHER READING

Articles

"Blow the Blues." (Obituary for Jerzy Giedroyc, Polish Dissident Writer). *Newsweek International,* September 25, 2000, p. 6.

"Catholics of Poland Apologize to Jews." *New York Times,* August 28, 2000, p. A3.

Erlanger, Steven. "Poland Finds Itself the Border Cop of West Europe." *New York Times,* August 28, 2000, p. A3.

"Hanna Gronkiewicz-Waltz." *Business Week,* June 12, 2000, p. 96.

Kaminiski, Matthew. "Poland Presses to Meet EU Requirements." *Wall Street Journal,* September 7, 2000, p. A21.

"More Potholes on Poland's Road to the EU." *Business Week,* June 12, 2000, p. 32.

Nagorski, Andrew. "The Polish-Russian Gap." *Newsweek International,* July 17, 2000, p. 4.

"Poland: Walesa to Quit, Sort of." *New York Times,* October 17, 2000, p. A8.

Revel, Jean-Francois. "Democracy: If You Can Keep It." *National Review,* January 24, 2000, vol. 52, no. 1, p. 24.

Williamson, Elizabeth. "Exit Polls Point to Victory by Poland's Kwasniewski." *Wall Street Journal,* October 9, 2000, p. A24.

———. "Walesa's Fall: From Revolutionary to Also-Ran." *Wall Street Journal,* September 1, 2000, p. A9.

Books

Biskupski, Mieczyslaw B. *The History of Poland.* Westport, CT: Greenwood Press, 2000.

Friedrich, Karin. *The Other Prussia: Royal Prussia, Poland and Liberty, 1569–1772.* New York: Cambridge University Press, 2000.

Porter, Brian. *When Nationalism Began to Hate: Imagining Modern Politics in Nineteenth Century Poland.* New York: Oxford University Press, 2000.

Samson, Naomi. *Hide: A Child's View of the Holocaust.* Lincoln: University of Nebraska Press, 2000.

POLAND: STATISTICAL DATA

For sources and notes see "Sources of Statistics" at the front of each volume.

GEOGRAPHY

Geography

Area:

Total: 312,685 sq km.

Land: 304,465 sq km.

Land boundaries:

Total: 2,888 km.

Border countries: Belarus 605 km, Czech Republic 658 km, Germany 456 km, Lithuania 91 km, Russia (Kaliningrad Oblast) 206 km, Slovakia 444 km, Ukraine 428 km.

Coastline: 491 km.

Climate: temperate with cold, cloudy, moderately severe winters with frequent precipitation; mild summers with frequent showers and thundershowers.

Terrain: mostly flat plain; mountains along southern border.

Natural resources: coal, sulfur, copper, natural gas, silver, lead, salt, arable land.

Land use:

Arable land: 47%

Permanent crops: 1%

Permanent pastures: 13%

Forests and woodland: 29%

Other: 10% (1993 est.).

HUMAN FACTORS

Demographics (A)

	1990	1995	1998	2000	2010	2020	2030	2040	2050
Population	38,119	38,603	38,664	38,646	38,691	38,455	37,377	35,702	33,780
Life expectancy - males	66.6	67.8	68.8	69.0	71.5	73.6	75.4	76.9	78.1
Life expectancy - females	75.6	76.6	77.3	77.6	79.8	81.6	83.1	84.3	85.2
Birth rate (per 1,000)	14.3	11.2	10.3	10.1	10.9	9.4	8.4	8.8	8.6
Death rate (per 1,000)	10.2	10.0	9.9	10.0	10.3	10.7	11.9	13.9	14.5
Women of reproductive age (15-49 yrs.)	9,398	10,001	10,198	10,251	9,573	8,979	8,027	6,770	6,159
Fertility rate	2.0	1.6	1.4	1.4	1.4	1.5	1.6	1.6	1.7

Except as noted, values for vital statistics are in thousands; life expectancy is in years.

Health Personnel

	National Data	World Data (wtd ave)
Total health expenditure as a percentage of GDP, 1990-1998[a]		
Public sector	4.2	2.5
Private sector	1.7	2.9
Total[b]	5.9	5.5
Health expenditure per capita in U.S. dollars, 1990-1998[a]		
Purchasing power parity	449	561
Total	242	483
Availability of health care facilities per 100,000 people		
Hospital beds 1990-1998[a]	540	330
Doctors 1992-1995[a]	NA	122
Nurses 1992-1995[a]	NA	248

Health Indicators

	National Data	World Data
Life expectancy at birth (years)		
1980	70	61
1998	73	67
Daily per capita supply of calories		
1970	3,445	2,358
1997	3,366	2,791
Daily per capital supply of protein		
1997 (grams)	99	74
Total fertility rate (births per woman)		
1980	2.3	3.7
1998	1.4	2.7
People living with (1997)		
Tuberculosis (cases per 100,000)	36.2	60.4
HIV/AIDS (% aged 15 - 49 years)	0.06	0.99

Infants and Malnutrition

	National Data	World Data (wtd ave)
Under 5 mortality rate (1989)	11	NA
% of infants with low birthweight (1992-98)[1]	9	17
Births attended by skilled health staff (% of total births 1996-98)	98	52
% fully immunized at 1 year of age (1995-98)[1]		
TB	94	82
DPT	95	77
Polio	95	77
Measles	91[2]	74
Prevalence of child malnutrition (1992-98)[1] (based on weight for age, % of children under 5 years)	NA	30

Ethnic Division

Polish 97.6%
German 1.3%
Ukrainian 0.6%
Byelorussian 0.5%

Data for 1990 est.

Religion

Roman Catholic (about 75% practicing) 95%
Eastern Orthodox, Protestant, and other 5%

Major Languages

Polish.

EDUCATION

Public Education Expenditures

	1980	1997
Public expenditures on education as % of GNP	NA	7.5
Expenditures per student as % of GNP per capita		
Primary	8.1	17.1
Secondary	14.8	NA
Tertiary	47.3	40.7
Pupils per teacher at the primary level	NA	15
Duration of primary education in years	NA	8
World data for comparison		
Public expenditures on education as % of GNP (mean)	3.9	4.8
Pupils per teacher at the primary level (wtd ave)	NA	33
Duration of primary education in years (mean)	NA	9

Educational Attainment (A)

Age group (1988) . . . . .25+
Population of this age group 22,986,018

Highest level attained (%)
- No schooling 1.5
- First level
  - Not completed 5.6
  - Completed 37.2
- Entered second level 47.8
- Entered post-secondary 7.9

Literacy Rates (B)

	National Data	World Data
Adult literacy rate		
1980		
Male	99	75
Female	99	58
1995		
Male	100	81
Female	100	65

Libraries

National Libraries **1997**
- Administrative Units 1
- Service Points or Branches 24
- Number of Volumes (000) 2,758
- Registered Users (000) 33
- Loans to Users (000) 121
- Total Library Staff 994

Public Libraries **1997**
- Administrative Units 9,230
- Service Points or Branches 3,565
- Number of Volumes (000) 135,867
- Registered Users (000) 7,222
- Loans to Users (000) 189,035
- Total Library Staff 17,828

GOVERNMENT & LAW

Political Parties

National Assembly (Zgromadzenie Narodowe)	no. of seats
Sejm	
Solidarity Electoral Action (AWS)	201
Democratic Left Alliance (SLD)	164
Freedom Union (UW)	60
Polish Peasant Party (PSL)	27
Movement for the Reconstruction of Poland (ROP)	6
German Minority of Lower Silesia (MNSO)	2
As of January 2000	
Solidarity Electoral Action (AWS)	186
Democratic Left Alliance (SLD)	159
Freedom Union (UW)	60
Polish Peasant Party (PSL)	26
Labor Party (PP)	7
Movement for the Reconstruction of Poland (ROP)	4
German Minority of Lower Silesia (MNSO)	2
Confederation for an Independent Poland-Fatherland (KPN-O)	5
Polish Socialist Party-Movement of Polish Working People (PPS-RLP)	3
Other	8
Senate	
Solidarity Electoral Action (AWS)	51
Democratic Left Alliance (SLD)	28
Freedom Union (UW)	8
Movement for the Reconstruction of Poland (ROP)	5
Polish Peasant Party (PSL)	3
Independents	5

Sejm elections were last held 21 September 1997 (next to be held by September 2001); Senate elections were last held 21 September 1997 (next to be held by September 2001). Two seats in the Senate are assigned to ethnic minorities.

Government Budgets (A)

Year: 1998

Total Expenditures: 207,549 Millions of Zlotys

Expenditures as a percentage of the total by function:
- General public services and public order 8.41
- Defense 4.00
- Education 6.38
- Health 10.01
- Social Security and Welfare 49.88
- Housing and community amenities 1.68
- Recreational, cultural, and religious affairs 1.05
- Fuel and energy 0.48
- Agriculture, forestry, fishing, and hunting 1.85
- Mining, manufacturing, and construction 0.46
- Transportation and communication 2.14
- Other economic affairs and services 0.57

Crime

Crime volume (for 1998)
- Crimes reported 1,073,042
- Total persons convicted 541,886
- Crimes per 100,000 population 2,775

Persons responsible for offenses

Total number suspects 396,055

Total number of female suspects 38,417

Total number of juvenile suspects 58,220

(Continued below.)

LABOR FORCE

Total Labor Force (A)

15.3 million (1998 est.).

Labor Force by Occupation

Industry 25%

Agriculture 25%

Services 50%

Data for 1999 est.

Unemployment Rate

11% (1999 est.)

GOVERNMENT & LAW (cont.)

Military Affairs (A)

	1990	1992	1995	1996	1997
Military expenditures					
Current dollars (mil.)	8,750[e]	3,820	6,060	6,160	5,600
1997 constant dollars (mil.)	10,200[e]	4,230	6,270	6,260	5,600
Armed forces (000)	313	270	250	235	230
Gross national product (GNP)					
Current dollars (bil.)	161	164	209	227	247
1997 constant dollars (bil.)	188	182	216	230	247
Central government expenditures (CGE)					
1997 constant dollars (bil.)	NA	48[e]	93	97	99
People (mil.)	38.1	38.4	38.6	38.6	38.6
Military expenditure as % of GNP	5.4	2.3	2.9	2.7	2.3
World data on military expenditure as % of GNP	4.5	3.4	2.7	2.6	2.6
Military expenditure as % of CGE	NA	8.8	6.7	6.5	5.6
World data on military expenditure as % of CGE	17.0	12.5	10.5	10.3	10.2
Military expenditure per capita (1997 $)	269	110	163	162	145
World data on military expenditure per capita (1997 $)	242	173	146	143	145
Armed forces per 1,000 people (soldiers)	8.2	7.0	6.5	6.1	6.0
World data on armed forces per 1,000 people (soldiers)	5.3	4.5	4.1	3.9	3.8
GNP per capita (1997 $)	4,940	4,740	5,610	5,970	6,390
Arms imports[6]					
Current dollars (mil.)	250	0	70	70	150
1997 constant dollars (mil.)	293	0	72	71	150
Arms exports[6]					
Current dollars (mil.)	230	20	40	70	60
1997 constant dollars (mil.)	269	22	41	71	60
Total imports[7]					
Current dollars (mil.)	8,413	15,700	29,050	37,140	42,310
1997 constant dollars (mil.)	9,852	17,410	30,080	37,760	42,310
Total exports[7]					
Current dollars (mil.)	13,630	13,320	22,890	24,440	25,750
1997 constant dollars (mil.)	15,960	14,770	23,700	24,850	25,750
Arms as percent of total imports[8]	3.0	0	0.2	0.2	0.4
Arms as percent of total exports[8]	1.7	0.2	0.2	0.3	0.2

PRODUCTION SECTOR

Energy Production

Production ....134.879 billion kWh

Production by source

Fossil fuel 96.47%

Hydro 3.18%

Nuclear 0%

Other 0.35%

Exports ....8.1 billion kWh

Data for 1998.

Energy Consumption

Consumption ....121.938 billion kWh

Imports ....4.600 billion kWh

Data for 1998.

Transportation

Highways:

Total: 381,046 km.

Paved: 249,966 km (including 268 km of expressways)

Unpaved: 131,080 km (1998 est.).

Waterways: 3,812 km navigable rivers and canals (1996).

Pipelines: crude oil and petroleum products 2,280 km; natural gas 17,000 km (1996).

Merchant marine:

Total: 57 ships (1,000 GRT or over) totaling 1,120,165 GRT/1,799,569 DWT.

Ships by type: bulk 50, cargo 2, chemical tanker 2, roll-on/roll-off 1, short-sea passenger 2 (1999 est.).

Airports: 123 (1999 est.).

Airports - with paved runways: 85.

Airports - with unpaved runways: 38.

Top Agriculture Products

Potatoes, fruits, vegetables, wheat; poultry, eggs, pork, beef, milk, cheese.

Top Mining Products (A)

	National Production	World Production
Commodities in 1998		
Aluminium (000 mt)	54	22,100
Coal (million mt)	180	4,243
Copper (000 mt)	415	12,200
Gold (000 kg)	0.6	2,460
Lead (000 mt)	60	3,080
Salt (000 mt)	3,900	186,000
Silver (mt)	1,000	16,400

MANUFACTURING SECTOR

GDP & Manufacturing Summary (A)

	1980	1985	1990	1995
GDP ($-1990 mil.)[1]	54,856	54,357	53,290	59,607
Per capita ($-1990)[1]	1,542	1,461	1,398	1,546
Manufacturing share (%) (current prices)[1]	NA	41.2	47.0	NA
Manufacturing				
Value added ($-1990 mil.)[1]	31,971	29,768	25,072	30,102
Industrial production index	128	122	100	122
Value added ($ mil.)	22,833	24,432	23,017	27,149[e]
Gross output ($ mil.)	55,597[e]	54,448[e]	46,092	70,975[e]
Employment (000)	4,063	3,578	3,014	2,193[e]
Profitability (% of gross output)				
Intermediate input (%)	59[e]	55[e]	50	62[e]
Wages and salaries inc. supplements (%)	12[e]	11[e]	8	11[e]
Gross operating surplus	30[e]	34[e]	42	28[e]
Productivity ($)				
Gross output per worker	12,957[e]	13,487[e]	15,293	32,159[e]
Value added per worker	5,321	6,052	7,637	12,305[e]
Average wage (inc. supplements)	1,575	1,627	1,258	3,457[e]
Value added ($ mil.)				
Food products	−889	144	2,595	2,392[e]
Beverages	3,062	3,582	1,838	3,836[e]
Tobacco products	636	74	379	1,132[e]
Textiles	2,795	2,444	1,222	1,112[e]
Wearing apparel	572	801	432	899[e]
Leather and fur products	122	221	120	96[e]
Footwear	403	430	263	225[e]
Wood and wood products	423	434	325	448[e]
Furniture and fixtures	491	500	307	574[e]
Paper and paper products	224	269	348	385[e]
Printing and publishing	154	208	166	238[e]

(Continued on next page.)

GDP & Manufacturing Summary (A) (cont.)

	1980	1985	1990	1995
Industrial chemicals	837	734	1,056	877e
Other chemical products	961	644	649	1,132e
Petroleum refineries	1,058	1,239	1,419	3,089e
Misc. petroleum and coal products	54	60	249	111e
Rubber products	317	341	209	291e
Plastic products	360	296	274	464e
Pottery, china and earthenware	97	146	107	157e
Glass and glass products	269	282	227	312e
Other non-metal mineral products	335	634	602	693e
Iron and steel	868	1,161	1,887	1,411e
Non-ferrous metals	602	336	951	275e
Metal products	1,343	1,347	1,081	1,255e
Non-electrical machinery	3,263	3,360	2,604	2,060e
Electrical machinery	1,558	1,801	1,420	1,214e
Transport equipment	2,436	2,255	1,855	2,148e
Prof. and scientific equipment	244	251	173	200e
Other manufacturing	237	438	258	121e

COMMUNICATIONS

Daily Newspapers

	National Data	World Data for Comparison
Daily Newspapers		
Number of Dailies	55	8,391
Total Circulation (000)	4,351	548,000
Circulation per 1,000 inhabitants	113	96

Telecommunications

Telephones - main lines in use: 8.07 million (1998).

Telephones - mobile cellular: 1.58 million (1998).

Telephone system: underdeveloped and outmoded system; government aims to have 10 million telephones in service by 2000; the process of partial privatization of the state-owned telephone monopoly has begun.

Domestic: cable, open wire, and microwave radio relay; 3 cellular networks; local exchanges 56.6% digital.

International: satellite earth stations - 2 Intelsat, NA Eutelsat, 2 Inmarsat (Atlantic and Indian Ocean regions), and 1 Intersputnik (Atlantic Ocean region).

Radio broadcast stations: AM 14, FM 777, shortwave 1 (1998).

Radios: 20.2 million (1997).

Television broadcast stations: 150 (1997).

Televisions: 13.05 million (1997).

Internet Service Providers (ISPs): 161 (1999).

FINANCE, ECONOMICS, & TRADE

Economic Indicators

National product: GDP—purchasing power parity—$276.5 billion (1999 est.).

National product real growth rate: 3.8% (1999 est.).

National product per capita: $7,200 (1999 est.).

Inflation rate—consumer price index: 8.4% (1999 est.).

Exchange Rates

Exchange rates:

Zlotych (Zl) per US$1

December 1999	4.1696
1999	3.9671
1998	3.4754
1997	3.2793
1996	2.6961
1995	2.4250

Top Import Origins

$40.8 billion (f.o.b., 1999)

Origins (1998)

Germany	25.8%
Italy	9.4%
France	6.5%
Russia	5.1%
United Kingdom	4.9%
United States	3.8%
Netherlands	3.8%

Top Export Destinations

$27.8 billion (f.o.b., 1999)

Destinations (1998)

Germany	36.0%
Italy	5.8%

Russia	5.6%
Netherlands	4.7%
France	4.6%
Ukraine	3.8%
United Kingdom	3.8%

Foreign Aid

Recipient: $4.312 billion (1995).

Import/Export Commodities

Import Commodities	Export Commodities
Manufactured goods and chemicals 43%	Manufactured goods and chemicals 57%
Machinery and equipment 36%	Machinery and equipment 21%
Mineral fuels 9%	Food and live animals 12%
Food and live animals 8%	Mineral fuels 7%

Balance of Payments

	1993	1994	1995	1996	1997
Exports of goods (f.o.b.)	13,582	18,355	25,041	27,557	30,731
Imports of goods (f.o.b.)	−17,087	−18,930	−26,687	−34,844	−40,553
Trade balance	−3,505	−575	−1,646	−7,287	−9,822
Services - debits	−3,631	−3,859	−7,138	−6,429	−5,814
Services - credits	4,201	6,699	10,675	9,833	8,986
Private transfers (net)	5,701	2,046	2,215	2,743	2,580
Government transfers (net)	139	128	244	82	120
Overall balance	−5,788	954	854	−3,264	−5,744

PORTUGAL

CAPITAL: Lisbon (Lisboa).

FLAG: The national flag, adopted in 1911, consists of a green field at the hoist and a larger red field. At the junction of the two, in yellow, red, blue, and white, is the national coat of arms.

ANTHEM: *A Portuguesa (The Portuguese).*

MONETARY UNIT: The escudo (E) is a paper currency of 100 centavos. There are coins of 1, 2.5, 5, 10, 20, 50, 100, and 200 escudos, and notes of 500, 1,000, 2,000, 5,000 and 10,000 escudos. E1 = $0.00654 (or $1 = E153.005).

WEIGHTS AND MEASURES: The metric system is the legal standard.

HOLIDAYS: New Year's Day, 1 January; Carnival Day, 15 February; Anniversary of the Revolution, 25 April; Labor Day, 1 May; National Day, 10 June; Assumption, 15 August; Republic Day, 5 October; All Saints' Day, 1 November; Independence Day, 1 December; Immaculate Conception, 8 December; Christmas, 25 December. Movable religious holidays include Carnival Day, Good Friday, and Corpus Christi.

TIME: GMT.

LOCATION AND SIZE: The westernmost country of Europe, Portugal occupies most of the western coast of the Iberian Peninsula; it shares the peninsula with Spain. Portugal has an area of 92,080 square kilometers (35,552 square miles), including the Azores Archipelago (island chain) and the islands of Madeira and Porto Santo. The area occupied by Portugal is slightly smaller than the state of Indiana. Portugal has a total boundary length of 3,007 kilometers (1,868 miles).

Portugal's capital city, Lisbon, is located on Portugal's west coast.

CLIMATE: The north has cool summers and rainy winters (average annual rainfall 125–150 centimeters/50–60 inches), with occasional snowfall. Central Portugal has hot summers and cool, rainy winters, with 50–75 centimeters (20–30 inches) average annual rainfall. The southern climate is very dry, with rainfall not exceeding 50 centimeters (20 inches) along the coast. In Lisbon, the average temperature is about 21°C (70°F) in July and 4°C (39°F) in January.

Portuguese Republic
República Portuguesa

INTRODUCTORY SURVEY

RECENT HISTORY

During World War II (1939-1945), Portugal supported the Allies, but did not take part in combat. It later became a member of the North Atlantic Treaty Organization (NATO). Portugal attempted to maintain its overseas empire, especially its resource-rich African provinces. The United Nations General Assembly passed a resolution in 1965 calling for a worldwide economic and arms boycott of Portugal in order to force it to grant independence to its African dependencies. Meanwhile, guerrilla movements in Angola, Mozambique, and Guinea-Bissau were met by a steadily increasing commitment of Portuguese troops and supplies.

Salazar, who had served as prime minister of Portugal since 1932, was followed in 1968 by Marcello Caetano. The refusal of the Caetano regime to adopt democratic and economic reforms, coupled with growing discontent over the costly colonial war in Africa, led to a military takeover by the left-wing Armed Forces Movement in April 1974. Democratic liberties were immediately granted and opposition political parties legalized. A decolonization program was also begun, resulting in the independence of all of Portugal's African provinces by November 1975.

Continued differences between right and left-and between communist and socialist factions on the left-led to numerous temporary governments after the 1974 takeover. Political unrest increased in the early 1980s, including urban terrorism. In

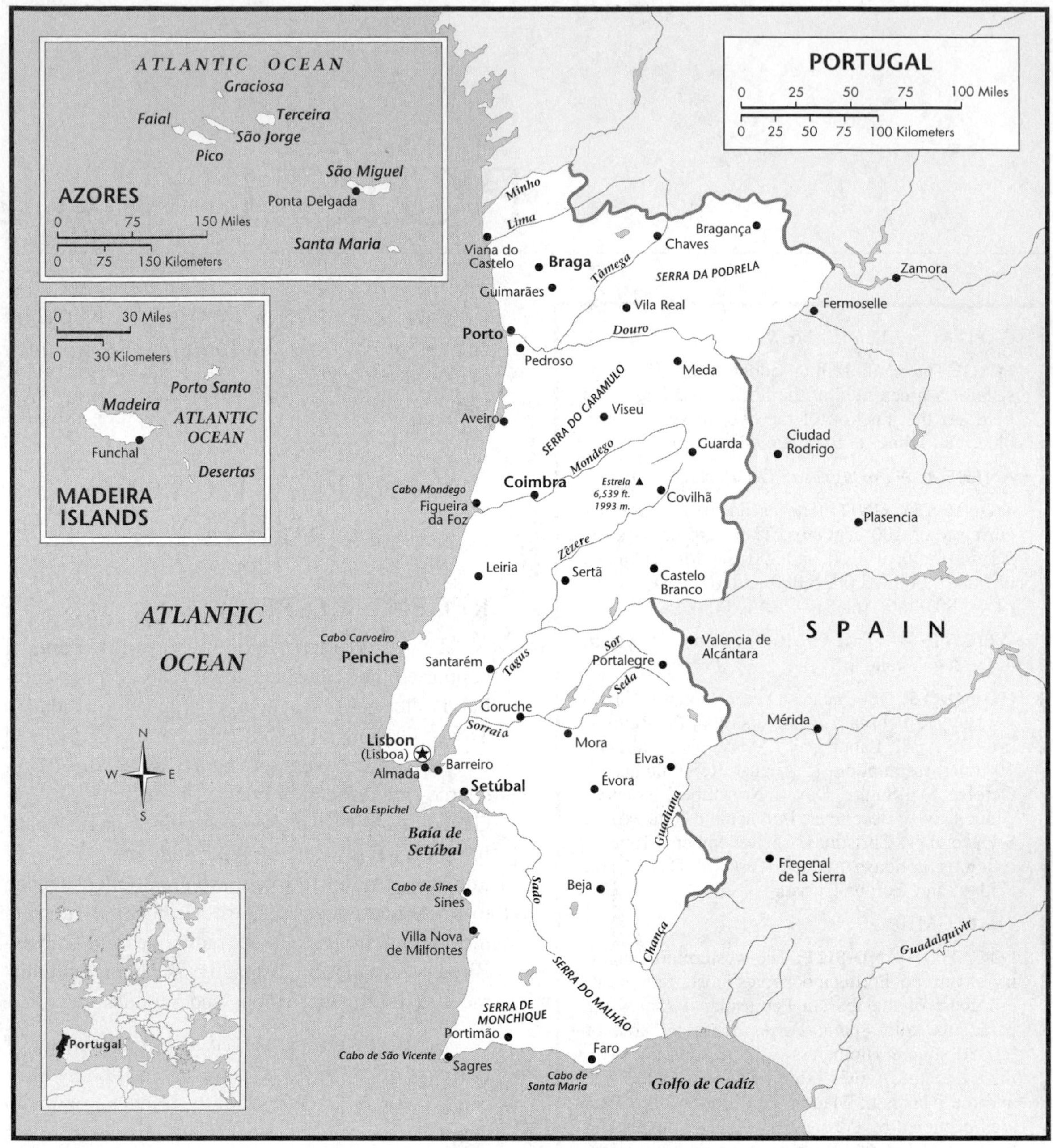

1985, Portugal entered the European Community, boosting its economy.

Economic recession, government deficits, and regional development were major concerns entering the 1990s. Austerity programs and privatization programs contributed to substantial economic gains through the 1990s, leading to acceptance in the European Economic and Monetary Union (EMU) in 1999. As a result, the Socialist Party retained power in the October 1999 Assembly elections. Economic and governmental modernization continued in an effort to attract foreign investment and increase exports.

GOVERNMENT

Portugal has a parliamentary democracy as provided in constitutional revisions in the 1980s. The chief of state is the president, elected by popular vote for a five-year term. The president appoints the prime minister who is normally leader of the legislature's majority party or leader of a majority coalition. The prime minister serves as the head of government. The president, on recommendation of the prime minister, appoints the cabinet, known as Council of Ministers. The 230-seat unicameral Assembly of the Republic composes the legislative branch. Members are elected by popular vote to serve four-year terms. Suffrage is universal at age eighteen.

Portugal is divided into twenty-two districts and two autonomous regions.

Judiciary

Portugal operates under a civil law system, with the Constitutional Tribunal reviewing the constitutionality of legislation. Justice is administered by ordinary and special courts, including the Supreme Court of Justice in Lisbon, four courts of appeal, district courts of first instance, and special courts. Supreme Court judges are appointed for life.

Political Parties

After the 1974 revolution, various left-wing parties that had functioned underground or in exile were recognized. Among these was the Portuguese Communist Party (Partido Comunista Português-PCP), Portugal's oldest political party. It merged with the United Democratic Coalition (CDU). Other active parties in 1999 included the Portuguese Socialist Party (Partido Socialista Português-PSP), the Social Democratic Party (PSD), the Popular Party (PP), and The Left Bloc.

In the October 1999 legislative elections, the PSP won 113 seats; PSD, eighty-three; CDU seventeen; PP, fifteen; and The Left Bloc, two.

DEFENSE

The armed forces are maintained by compulsory service, with terms of four to twelve months for all services. As of 2000, the army had 25,650 personnel (5,500 draftees), the navy 16,600 (including 1,540 marines), and the air force, 7,445 personnel and sixty combat aircraft. The defense budget in 1997 was $2.5 billion comprising 2.6 percent of GDP. The United States maintains an important airbase in the Azores, and the North Atlantic Treaty Organization (NATO) has headquarters at Lisbon. Paramilitary police and republican guards number 40,900.

ECONOMIC AFFAIRS

In the late 1990s, Portugal's upcoming capitalist economy was enjoying great gains. In 1999, the nation saw strong economic growth, decreasing interest rates, and low unemployment. In 1998, Portugal qualified for the European Economic Monetary Union (EMU) and joined ten other European countries in launching the euro. Although a trade deficit continued, stable growth was expected in 2000.

Public Finance

Portugal's budgets have been in deficit since 1974. Major factors contributing to the deficit include spending on health and education programs, funding for major public investment projects, and large state-owned enterprise payrolls. To finance the deficit, the government issues bonds in the domestic market.

The U.S. Central Intelligence Agency (CIA) estimated that, in 1996, government revenues totaled approximately $48 billion and expenditures $52 billion. External debt in 1997 totaled $13.1 billion.

Income

In 1999, Portugal's gross domestic product (GDP) was $151.4 billion, or about $15,300 per capita. The average inflation rate was 2.4 percent, resulting in a real growth rate in GDP of 3.2 percent. The GDP contribution by sector was agriculture 4 percent, industry 36 percent, and services 60 percent.

Industry

The contribution of industry to the national economy grew significantly in the 1990s. In 1998, 36 percent of the labor force was employed in industry. Textiles are the oldest and most important of Portugal's manufactured products. Other principal industries are automotive assembly, electronics, glass and pottery, footwear, cement, cellulose and paper, rubber and chemicals, cork and cork products, and food industries.

Banking and Finance

All twenty-two banks in Portugal, except for three foreign-owned ones (Banco do Brasil, Credit Franco-Portugais, and the Bank of London and South America), were nationalized in 1975. A 1983 law, however, permitted private enterprise to return to the banking industry. The Bank of Portugal, the central bank (founded in 1846), functions as a bank of issue and rediscount, controls gold and foreign exchange movements, and sets the discount rate.

Portugal's banking industry experienced significant restructuring in the late 1990s. Following a series of consolidations, the three largest private banks were Banco Comercial Portuguesês (BCP),

Banco Pinto and Sotto Mayor, and Banco Portuguesês de Investimento.

Portugal's two stock exchanges, located in Lisbon and Porto, were closed after the 1974 coup. The Lisbon exchange reopened in 1976, and the Oporto exchange in 1981. In January 1992, the market included eleven firms whose shares were traded regularly. In the late 1990s, trading outside the stock exchanges was still widespread, as trade on the exchange continued to grow.

Economic Development

In 1975, radical economic transformations occurred through nationalization of major sectors of the national economy including the leading banks, insurance companies, petroleum refineries, the transportation sector, and the steel industry. Large-scale agrarian reform measures led to expropriation of many of the country's privately owned large landholdings; other holdings were seized illegally by peasants. When the nationalization and agrarian reform measures met with only limited success, an emergency austerity plan was approved in October 1975. The program included wage and import controls and the reduction of subsidies on consumer goods.

With Portugal's entry into the EC, the highly protected and inefficient economy was undergoing radical transformation. State intervention was reduced, and infrastructure modernized. Privatization began in 1989, and in 1992, $3.6 billion was raised as banks, insurance companies, and a 25 percent interest in Petrogal-the state oil company-were sold.

In 1996 and 1997, a series of important investments and acquisitions were made by companies such as Sonae and Jernimo Martins, Portugal's leading retail distributors; Cimpor, a cement producer; and Portugal Telecom and Electricidade de Portugal, the last of which was recently privatized. The big banks were developing new overseas operations as well. In recognition of the marked economic progress, Portugal was accepted into the European Monetary Union in 1999.

SOCIAL WELFARE

The government-run social security system provides old age, disability, sickness, and unemployment benefits, family allowances, and health and medical care. The system is funded by payroll contributions from employers and employees. Government subsidizes social pensions for unemployed residents. Maternity benefits are paid for six months.

Healthcare

Portugal adopted a program in the early 1990s to construct twelve hospitals and eight-four health centers. The Santa Maria Hospital in Lisbon is the largest hospital in Portugal. In 1990-1997, there were three doctors for every 1,000 people.

Average life expectancy in 2000 was estimated at seventy-six years. The leading causes of death are circulatory disorders, cancer, and respiratory disorders. Total healthcare expenditures in 1990-1997 were 8.2 percent of GDP.

Housing

In the early 1990s, Portugal built an average of 40,000 housing units annually. In May 1993, the government announced a $2 billion program designed to clear urban slums and construct 20,000 low-income units in Lisbon by 2000.

EDUCATION

In 2000, adult literacy rates were an estimated 87.4 percent. A 1997 law requires nine years of compulsory education. Primary level education is compulsory for six years. Secondary level education is in two stages of three years each. In 1996, primary schools had 867,253 pupils. At the secondary level there were 947,478 pupils. That year, total enrollment in institutions of higher learning was 276,263.

Institutions of higher learning include Coimbra University and universities at Lisbon and Porto. In 1996, 319,525 students were enrolled in institutions of higher learning. Approximately 11.7 percent of Portugal's budget was allocated to education in the late 1990s.

2000 KEY EVENTS TIMELINE

January

- Portugal holds the rotating presidency of the European Union (EU) for the first six-months of the year.

May

- The Vatican discloses the third secret of Fatima, saying that it was the 1981 assassination attempt on the pope.
- U.S. President Bill Clinton visits Portugal.

June

- The Portuguese presidency of the EU announces steps that may lead to the lifting of sanctions against Austria.

July

- The government is designing incentive programs to attract industry, especially high-tech companies, through the Investments, Trade and Tourism of Portugal (ICEP) agency.

November

- The government agrees to assist the fledgling nation of East Timor (formerly a province of Indonesia) in building its military. Portugal is to lend training support while Australia provides the needed funds.

- Bovine spongiform encephalopathy (BSE), or mad cow disease, is detected at an Azores farm; Portugal enforces strict feeding requirements and other measures to control BSE.

ANALYSIS OF EVENTS: 2000

BUSINESS AND THE ECONOMY

In January Portugal took over the rotating presidency of the European Union (E.U.), and made its expansion, economic growth and cutting unemployment the top priorities in its agenda. In accepting the presidency, Portuguese officials said they wanted to turn the European Union into one of the most dynamic economic zones in the world within ten years. That would mean cutting unemployment in the region, which stood at about 10 percent in 2000. With strong ties to its former colonies, the Portuguese also have proposed better relations with Africa, and new trade agreements with nations in that continent. Portuguese officials also called for better e-commerce, echoing the sentiments of other European officials who believe little is being done to match the United States in that economic arena. Portugal called for a common strategy to build an Internet-based economy that would create new jobs. According to some sources, the number of Internet users in Portugal rose 181 percent the first six months of 2000, to 1.3 million, or 13.4 percent of the population.

In July the Portuguese government voted to decriminalize the use of marijuana and heroin, and treat drug addicts instead of sending them to prison. The sale and trafficking of drugs remained a crime. The new law compels police to refer drug users caught with small amounts of marijuana or heroin to special boards that can mandate treatment. In the past, drug users faced up to a year in prison. Portugal became the third European Union member, behind Italy and Spain, to decriminalize drug use. The measure was backed by the ruling Socialist Party, and supported by the Communist Party and other left-of-center parties. The Socialists were one seat short of a parliamentary majority and needed the backing of other parties to approve legislation. The conservative Social Democrat Party sought a referendum on the proposed law, but the Socialist government rejected that proposal.

During the year President Jorge Sampaio became the first Portuguese head of state to visit East Timor since the former colonial power pulled out in 1974. "I bring a message of Portuguese solidarity and, to all of you, my friendship," he told East Timorese on his arrival. Sampaio pledged Portuguese help to help rebuild the island territory, which was preparing for self-rule under the auspices of the United Nations. East Timor officials said Portuguese would become the official language of the new nation. In May U.S. President Bill Clinton visited Portugal and praised that nation for its efforts against AIDS in Africa and peace efforts in East Timor and other places.

CULTURE AND SOCIETY

Pope John Paul II beatified two of three peasant children who reported seeing visions of the Virgin Mary on a hillside near the town of Fátima in Portugal in 1917. During a visit to Portugal in May the Pope blessed Jacinta and Francisco, the first step towards canonization. Both children died from influenza before they reached the age of eleven. The third child, Sister Lucia dos Santos, now a ninety-three-year-old nun, is still alive. The three children claimed to have seen the Virgin Mary in an oak tree in Fátima in central Portugal. The children said the Virgin ordered them to return to the tree on the same day for the next six months. The Virgin, they said, divulged three visions, one that was only revealed by the Vatican in mid-2000. The first revelation was a vision of Hell said to refer to the two world wars. The second vision predicted the fall of Communism and Russia's return to Christianity. The third vision, according to the Vatican, predicted the 1981 assassination attempt on Pope John Paul II, who was joined by hundreds of thousands of pilgrims for the beatification.

Luis Figo is perhaps one of Portugal's greatest soccer players, and in July he became the best paid. Figo signed for $56 million to play for Spain's Real Madrid, one of the world's premier soccer clubs. The contract made him the world's most expensive soccer star. Figo had been playing for Barcelona. During the Euro 2000 championship, he led Portugal into the semifinals.

DIRECTORY

CENTRAL GOVERNMENT

Head of State

President
Jorge Sampaio, Office of the President, Palacio de Belem, R-1300 Lisbon, Portugal
PHONE: +351 (1) 3635768
FAX: +351 (1) 3636603

Prime Minister
Antonio Manuel de Oliveira Guterres, Office of the Prime Minister, Gabinete do Primeiro-Ministro, R-1300 Lisbon, Portugal
E-MAIL: pm@pm.gov.pt

Ministers

Minister of Agriculture and Fisheries
Luis Manuel Capoulas Santos, Ministry of Agriculture and Fisheries, Praça do Comércio, R-1100 Lisbon, Portugal
PHONE: +351 (1) 3463151
FAX: +351 (1) 3473798
E-MAIL: siaza@min-agricultura.pt

Minister of Culture
Jose Sasportes, Ministry of Culture

Minister of Defense
Julio Castro Caldas, Ministry of Defense, Avenida Ilha da Madeira n° 1, P–1400–204 Lisbon, Portugal
PHONE: +351 (1) 3017485
FAX: +351 (1) 3019280

Minister of Economy
Mario Cristina De Sousa, Ministry of Economy, Rua da Horta Seca 15, R-1294 Lisbon, Portugal
PHONE: +351 (1) 3228600
FAX: +351 (1) 3228811
E-MAIL: webmaster@min-economia.pt

Minister of Education
Augusto Santos Silva, Ministry of Education, Av. 5 de Outubro 107, Lisbon, Portugal
PHONE: +351 (1) 7931603
FAX: +351 (1) 7964119
E-MAIL: cirep@min-edu.pt

Minister of the Environment
Jose Socrates, Ministry of the Environment

Minister of Finance
Joaquim Pina Moura, Ministry of Finance, Av. Infante D. Henrique n° 1, R-1194 Lisbon, Portugal

Minister of Foreign Affairs
Jaime José Matos da Gama, Ministry of Foreign Affairs, Palácio das Necessidades, Largo do Rilvas, R-1354 Lisbon, Portugal
PHONE: +351 (1) 3969850
FAX: +351 (1) 609708

Minister of Health
Maria Manuela Arcanjo, Ministry of Health

Minister of Internal Administration
Nuno Severiano Texeira, Ministry of the Internal Administration

Minister of Justice
Antonio Costa, Ministry of Justice

Minister of Planning
Maria Elisa Ferreira, Ministry of Planning, Palacion Penafiel, Rua de S. Mamede ao Caldas 21, R-1149-050 Lisbon, Portugal
PHONE: +351 (1) 8861119
FAX: +351 (1) 8863827

Minister of Science and Technology
Jose Mariano Gago, Ministry of Science and Technology, Praça do Comercio, Ala Oriental, R-1194 Lisbon, Portugal
PHONE: +351 (1) 8812000
FAX: +351 (1) 8882434
E-MAIL: geral@mct.pt

Minister of Social Security and Labor
Eduardo Ferro Rodrigues, Ministry of Social Security and Labor

Minister of Youth and Sports
Armando Vara, Ministry of Youth and Sports

High Commissioner for Immigration and Ethnic Minorities
José Maximiano de Albuquerque Almeida Leitão, Office of the High Commissioner for Immigration and Ethnic Minorities, Av.

CONTACT: Paulo Alves Guerra
TYPE: Commercial

Radio Comercial

Rua Sampaia e Pina 26, 1000 Lisbon, Portugal
PHONE: +351 (1) 3872071
FAX: +351 (1) 689551
E-MAIL: administracao@radiocomercial.pt
WEBSITE: http://www.radiocomercial.pt/
TITLE: Managing Director
CONTACT: Toao David Nunaf
TYPE: Private

Radio Renascenca

Rua Ivens 14, 1294 Lisboa Codex, Portugal
PHONE: +351 (1) 3475270
FAX: +351 (1) 3422658
TYPE: Religious Commercial

Radiodifusao Portuguesa EP (RDP)

Av. Eng. Duarte Pacheco 6, 1070 Lisbon, Portugal
PHONE: +351 (1) 3820000
FAX: +351 (1) 692298
E-MAIL: rdp@telepac.pt
WEBSITE: http://www.rdp.pt

RDP Internacional (Radio Portugal)

Apartado 1011, 1001 Lisbon Codex, Portugal
PHONE: +351 (1) 38201082
FAX: +351 (1) 3474475
E-MAIL: rdpinternacional@rdp.pt
WEBSITE: http://www.rdp.pt
TITLE: Director
CONTACT: Jaime Marques de Almeida

TSF Radio Jornal

Av. Eng. D. Pacheco, Edif. Amoreiras 2-6, 1000 Lisbon, Portugal
PHONE: +351 (1) 3870406
FAX: +351 (1) 3882791
TITLE: Managing Director
CONTACT: D. Borges
TYPE: Commercial

Radiotelevisao Portuguesa (RTP)

Av. 5 de Outubro 197, 1094 Lisbon, Portugal
PHONE: +351 (1) 7931774
FAX: +351 (1) 7931758
TITLE: Station Director
CONTACT: Jose Eduardo Moniz
CHANNEL: 1, 2
TYPE: Commercial

Sociedade Independente de Comunicacao, SA (SIC)

Estrada da Outorela 119, Carnaxide 2795 Linda-e-vehla, Lisbon, Portugal
PHONE: +351 (1) 4173138
FAX: +351 (1) 4187156
TITLE: Chairman
CONTACT: Francisco Pinto Balsemao
TYPE: Private

Televisao Independente, SA (TVI)

Rua 3, Matinha, Edificio Altejo, 6, 1900 Lisbon, Portugal
PHONE: +351 (1) 4347500
FAX: +351 (1) 4355075
E-MAIL: tvi-sa@individual.eunet.pt
WEBSITE: http://www.tvi.pt
TITLE: Chairman
CONTACT: Roberto Carmeiro
TYPE: Private

COLLEGES AND UNIVERSITIES

University of Madeira

Edificio Da Penteade, Penteade, 9000-081 Funchal, Portugal
PHONE: +351 (291) 209400
FAX: +351 (291) 209410
E-MAIL: cdi@dragoeiro.uma.pt
WEBSITE: http://www.uma.pt

New University of Lisbon

Praca do Principe Real 26, 1269-150 Lisbon, Portugal
PHONE: +351 (1) 3242100
FAX: +351 (1) 3461924
E-MAIL: runl.gri@mail.telepac.pt
WEBSITE: http://www.unl.pt

Universidade Autonoma de Lisboa

Rua De Santa Marta 56, 1100 Lisbon, Portugal

Luis de Camoes Autonomous University

Rua Santa Marta 56, 1150 Lisbon, Portugal
PHONE: +351 (1) 3177691
FAX: +351 (1) 3533702
WEBSITE: http://www.universidade-autonoma.pt

Open University Portugal

Rua Do Escola Politecnica 147, 1250 Lisbon, Portugal

PHONE: +351 (1) 3972334
FAX: +351 (1) 3973229
WEBSITE: http://www.univ-ab.pt

University Lusiada Lisbon

Rua Da Junqueira 194, Oporto and Vila Nova De Famalicao, 1300 Lisbon, Portugal
PHONE: +351 (1) 3611500
FAX: +351 (1) 3638307
WEBSITE: http://www.ulusiada.pt

Higher Institute of Labour and Business, Lisbon

Av. Das Forcas Armadas, 1600 Lisbon, Portugal
PHONE: +351 (1) 7935000
FAX: +351 (1) 7964710
E-MAIL: relacoes.exteriores@iscte.pt
WEBSITE: http://www.iscte.pt

Universidade Catolica Portuguesa

Palma De Cima, 1649 023 Lisbon, Portugal
PHONE: +351 (1) 7214000
FAX: +351 (1) 7270256
E-MAIL: info@reitoria.ucp.pt
WEBSITE: http://www.ucp.pt

University of Lisbon

Alameda Da Universidade, Cidade Universtoria Campo Grande, 1649-004 Lisbon, Portugal
PHONE: +351 (1) 7967624
FAX: +351 (1) 7933624
E-MAIL: reitoria@ul.pt
WEBSITE: http://www.ul.pt

Independent University

Av Marechal Gomes Da Costa Lt 9, 1800-255 Lisbon, Portugal
PHONE: +351 (21) 8361900
FAX: +351 (21) 8361922
E-MAIL: uni@uni.pt
WEBSITE: http://www.uni.pt

International University Portela

Rua Vasco Da Gama 8-14, Quinta Da Victoria, 2685-181 Portela, Portugal
PHONE: +351 (1) 9405270
FAX: +351 (1) 9401040
E-MAIL: uinternacional@mail.telepac.pt
WEBSITE: http://www.uinternacional.pt

Universidade de Coimbra

Faculdade De Ciencias, Inst Botanico, Universidade De Coimbra, 3000 Coimbra, Portugal
E-MAIL: webmaster@ci.uc.pt
WEBSITE: http://www.uc.pt

Universidade de Aveiro

R Matio De Sacremento 62, 3800 Aveiro, Portugal

Portucalense University Infante D Henrique

Rua Antonio Bernardino De Almeida 541/619, 4200 Porto, Portugal
PHONE: +351 (2) 5570200
FAX: +351 (2) 5570280
E-MAIL: www-dh@upt.pt
WEBSITE: http://www.uportu.pt

University of Porto

Rua D Manuel Ii, Appartado 211, 4211 Porto Codex, Portugal
PHONE: +351 (22) 6073500
FAX: +351 (22) 6098736
E-MAIL: gri@reit.up.pt
WEBSITE: http://ww.up.pt

Fernando Pessoa University

Praca 9 De Abril 349, 4249-004 Porto, Portugal
PHONE: +351 (22) 5071300
FAX: +351 (22) 5508269
E-MAIL: geral@ufp.pt
WEBSITE: http://www.ufp.pt

University Tecnica de Lisboa

Fonte Da Aldeia 3, Carlavelos, 4415 Lisbon, Portugal

University of Minho

Largo Do Paco, 4700-320 Codex, 4719 Braga, Portugal
PHONE: +351 (53) 601100
FAX: +351 (53) 616936
E-MAIL: coralia@reitoria.uminho.pt
WEBSITE: http://w.um.nho.pt

Instituto Politecnico de Bragnaca

Apdo 172, 5300 Bragnaca, Portugal

Polytechnic Institute of Castelo Branco

Av Pedro Alvares Cabral 12, 6000 Castelo Branco, Portugal
PHONE: +351 (272) 339600
FAX: +351 (272) 339601
E-MAIL: ipcb.pt@mail.ipcb.pt
WEBSITE: http://www.ipcb.pt

Universidade de Beira Interior

Rua Marques De Avila E Bolama, 6200 Covilha, Portugal
PHONE: +351 (75) 319000
FAX: +351 (75) 319057
WEBSITE: http://www.ubi.pt

University of Evora

Apdo. 94 Largo Dos Colegiais 2, 7001 Evora, Portugal
PHONE: +351 (266) 740800
FAX: +351 (266) 744969
WEBSITE: http://www.uevora.pt

Universidade do Algarve

Quinta Da Penha, 8000 Faro, Portugal
PHONE: +351 (289) 800100
E-MAIL: info@ualg.pt
WEBSITE: http://www.ualg.pt

University of the Azores

Rua Da Mae De Deus, Apartacto 1422, 9501-801, Ponta Delgada, Portugal
PHONE: +351 289 96 653 044
FAX: +3512 96 653 070
E-MAIL: info@alf.vac.pt
WEBSITE: http://w.vac.pt

NEWSPAPERS AND MAGAZINES

Expresso

Sojournal S.A., Rua Duque do Palmera 37, 1299 Lisbon, Portugal
PHONE: +351 (1) 31140000
FAX: +351 (1) 3543858
E-MAIL: marketing@mail.expresso.pt
WEBSITE: http://www.expresso.pt
TITLE: Editor
CONTACT: Helena Carneiro
CIRCULATION: 133,054

Correio da Manha

Presse Livre-Imprensa Livre S.A., Av. Joao Crisostoma, 72, 1069-043 Lisbon, Portugal
PHONE: +351 (1) 3185200; 3185222
FAX: +351 (1) 3540382; 3156164; 3540392
E-MAIL: lsantom@mail.telepca.pt
WEBSITE: http://www.correiomanha.pt
TITLE: Editor
CONTACT: Dalmira Viara
CIRCULATION: 73,057

Dario de Noticias

D.N. Publicidade, Avda de Liberdade 266, Apdo 2346, 1250 Lisbon, Portugal
PHONE: +351 (1) 3187500; 3187775
FAX: +351 (1) 3187503; 3187504; 3187508
E-MAIL: publicidade@dn.pt
WEBSITE: http://www.dn.pt
TITLE: Editors
CONTACT: Jose Antonio Santos, Antionio Jose Teixeira
CIRCULATION: 65,000

Correio de Domingo

Impresensa Livre, Av. Joao Crisostomo, 72, 1050 Lisbon, Portugal
PHONE: +351 (1) 3185200
FAX: +351 (1) 3540392
E-MAIL: ondinacm@mail.telepac.pt
WEBSITE: http://www.correiomanha.pt
TITLE: Editor
CONTACT: Agostinho de Azevedo
CIRCULATION: 75,643
TYPE: General Interest

Prestige

Motorpress Lisboa, Rua Sacadura Cabral, 26-3, bgb, 1495-699 Cruz Quebrada/Dafundo, Portugal
PHONE: +351 (1) 4149900
FAX: +351 (1)4140305
E-MAIL: motorpress@mail.telepac.pt
TITLE: Editor-in-Chief
CONTACT: Joao Ferreira
CIRCULATION: 77,548

PUBLISHERS

Editorial Estampa

Rua da Escola do Exercito, 9,R/C-Dto., 1150 Lisbon, Portugal
PHONE: +351 (1) 3555663
FAX: +351 (1) 3141911
E-MAIL: estampa@mail.telepac.pt
WEBSITE: http://www.editorialestampa.pt
CONTACT: Antonio Carlos Pinheiro

SUBJECTS: Anthropology, Antiques, Architecture and Interior Design, Art, Astrology, Occult, Cookery, Drama, Theater, Economics, Education, Fiction, Geography, Geology, Health, Nutrition, History, Law, Literature, Literary Criticism, Essays, Medicine, Nursing, Dentistry, Nonfiction (General), Parapsychology, Philosophy, Psychology, Psychiatry, Religion-Other, Romance, Social Sciences, Sociology, Sports, Athletics

Editorial Presenca

R. Augusto Gil, 35-A, 1064-806 Lisbon, Portugal
PHONE: +351 (1) 7992200
FAX: +351 (1) 7977560
E-MAIL: info@editpresenca.pt
WEBSITE: http://www.editpresenca.pt
TITLE: President
CONTACT: Francisco Espadinha
SUBJECTS: Animals, Pets, Architecture and Interior Design, Art, Astrology, Occult, Biography, Business, Child Care and Development, Computer Science, Cookery, Crafts, Games, Hobbies, Education, Fiction, Gardening, Plants, Government, Political Science, Health, Nutrition, History, How-to, Human Relations, Language Arts, Linguistics, Management, Marketing, Mysteries, Nonfiction (General), Philosophy, Poetry, Psychology, Psychiatry, Religion-Buddhist, Science (General), Self-Help, Social Sciences, Sociology, Sports, Athletics, Travel, Travel Guides, Art Techniques, Esoterics, Leisure Books

Gradiva Publicacoes, Lda.

Rua Almeida e Souse, 21 R/C Esq., 1399-041 Lisbon, Portugal
PHONE: +351 (1) 3974067
FAX: +351 (1) 3953471
E-MAIL: gradiva@ip.pt
WEBSITE: http://www.gradiva.pt
TITLE: Rights Assistant
CONTACT: Joana Goncalves
SUBJECTS: Anthropology, Archaeology, Astronomy, Behavioral Sciences, Biological Sciences, Communications, Computer Science, Crafts, Games, Hobbies, Earth Sciences, Economics, Education, Engineering (General), Environmental Studies, Fiction, Geography, Geology, History, Human Relations, Humor, Literature, Literary Criticism, Essays, Management, Mathematics, Natural History, Philosophy, Physics, Psychology, Psychiatry, Romance, Science Fiction, Fantasy, Science (General), Social Sciences, Sociology

Edicoes Colibri

Apartado 42.001, 1601-801 Lisbon, Portugal
PHONE: +351 (1) 7964038
FAX: +351 (1) 7964038
E-MAIL: colibri@edi-colibri.pt
WEBSITE: http://www.edi-colibri.pt
TITLE: Managing Director
CONTACT: Fernando Mao de Ferro
SUBJECTS: Archaeology, Environmental Studies, Geography, Geology, History, Literature, Literary Criticism, Essays, Philosophy, Social Sciences, Sociology, Political Science
TOTAL PUBLISHED: 400 print; 50 print Titles Annually; 400 online

Dinalivro

Trav Convento de Jesus 15 r/c, 1200 Lisbon, Portugal
PHONE: +351 (1) 670348
FAX: +351 (1) 3908489
E-MAIL: dinalivro@ip.pt
TITLE: President
CONTACT: Silverio Amaro
SUBJECTS: Accounting, Aeronautics, Aviation, Architecture and Interior Design, Art, Astronomy, Biological Sciences, Computer Science, Education, Electronics, Electrical Engineering, Engineering (General), Gardening, Plants, Health, Nutrition, History, Literature, Literary Criticism, Essays, Medicine, Nursing, Dentistry, Photography, Physics, Psychology, Psychiatry, Science (General), Social Sciences, Sociology

RELIGIOUS ORGANIZATIONS

Buddhist

Gyo Fu An
Quinta do, Pombal, S. Romao, Sao Bras De Alportel, 8150 Portugal
PHONE: +351 (89) 842153
TITLE: Contact
NAME: Katja Krabiell

Catholic

Adoradoras Escravas Do Santissmo Sacremento E Da Caridade
Casa De Protecao E Amparo De Santo Antonio, Calcada Das Necessidades 2, 1350-214 Lisboa, Portugal
PHONE: +351 (1) 3902796
FAX: +351 (1) 3954500

Clarissas Do Desagravo (Ordem De Santa Clara)
Mosteiro Do Imaculado Coracao De Maria, Rua Da Estrela 17, 1200-668 Lisboa, Portugal
PHONE: +351 (1) 3974328

Filhas Da Caridade De Sao Vincente De Paulo
Casa De Sao Vicente De Paulo (Casa Provincial), Av. Marechal Craveiro Lopes, 10, 1749-011 Lisboa, Portugal
PHONE: +351 (1) 7575354
FAX: +351 (1) 7593452

Instituto Secular Das Cooperadoras Da Familia
Sede Geral Da Obra, R. ST Antonio A Estrela, 35,1350-043, Lisboa, Portugal
PHONE: +351 (1) 3960300
FAX: +351 (1) 3962502

Missionarias Do Espirito Santo
Casa Provincial E Procuradoria, R.Soc. Cruz Quebradense 19, 1495-708 Cruz Quebrada, Portugal
PHONE: +351 4196310
FAX: +351 4145431

Servas Da Sagrada Familia
Casa Geral, Av. Almirante Gago Coutinho, 72-A, 1700-031 Lisboa, Portugal
PHONE: +351 (1) 8483589
FAX: +351 (1) 8463279

World Apostolate of Fatima (The Blue Army) (WAF)
Avenida Beato Nuno, Caixa Postal 38, 2496 Fatima, Portugal
PHONE: +351 (49) 532931
FAX: +351 (49) 532931
TITLE: President
NAME: Bishop Constantino Luna

Orthodox

Community of the Protecting Veil
C/o Vladimir Reshetilov, Av. Des Communidades Europeias, Torre 8, 6b, Cascais 2750, Portugal
PHONE: +351 (1) 4834063

Protestant

Adventista Viseu
R. Ponte de Pau, 1 3500 Viseu, Portugal
PHONE: +351 (32) 914880183
FAX: +351 (32) 914880183
E-MAIL: ja viseu@mail.pt
WEBSITE: http://www.tagnet.org/viseu

Portuguese Baptist Convention (PBC)

Convencao Baptista Portuguesa (CBP)
Rua Luis Simoes, Numero 7 1st fl., 2745 Queluz, Portugal
PHONE: +351 (1) 4362718
FAX: +351 (1) 4361833
E-MAIL: malexandre@mail.telepac.pt

Seventh-day Adventist Church
Quelez, Portugal
E-MAIL: nop02875@mail.telepac.pt

The Salvation Army
Apartado 50165, Lisboa, Portugal
PHONE: +351 (1) 3528137
FAX: +351 (1) 3160732

Unilao Portugiese dos Adventistas do Setimo Dia
Rua Joaquim Bonifacio, 17, 1150 Lisboa, Portugal
PHONE: +351 (1) 3542169
E-MAIL: dvasco@mail.telpac.pt

FURTHER READING

Articles

"Portugal Rejects Cimpor Takeover Bid." *Wall Street Journal,* August 14, 2000, p. A12.

Howe, Marvine. "Portugal's Dinosaurs Get Their Due at Last." *New York Times,* August 8, 2000, p. D5.

"EU Alleges Currency-charge Price Fixing." *Wall Street Journal,* July 5, 2000, p. A17.

Books

Anderson, James Maxwell. *The History of Portugal.* Westport, CT: Greenwood Press, 2000.

Dun and Bradstreet's Export Guide to Portugal. Parsippany, NJ: Dun & Bradstreet, 1999.

PORTUGAL: STATISTICAL DATA

For sources and notes see "Sources of Statistics" at the front of each volume.

GEOGRAPHY

Geography

Area:

Total: 92,391 sq km.

Land: 91,951 sq km.

Note: includes Azores and Madeira Islands.

Land boundaries:

Total: 1,214 km.

Border countries: Spain 1,214 km.

Coastline: 1,793 km.

Climate: maritime temperate; cool and rainy in north, warmer and drier in south.

Terrain: mountainous north of the Tagus River, rolling plains in south.

Natural resources: fish, forests (cork), tungsten, iron ore, uranium ore, marble, arable land, hydro power.

Land use:

Arable land: 26%

Permanent crops: 9%

Permanent pastures: 9%

Forests and woodland: 36%

Other: 20% (1993 est.).

HUMAN FACTORS

Demographics (A)

	1990	1995	1998	2000	2010	2020	2030	2040	2050
Population	NA	9,969	10,012	10,048	10,183	10,101	9,886	9,551	9,044
Life expectancy - males	NA	71.1	71.7	72.2	74.3	75.9	77.3	78.4	79.3
Life expectancy - females	NA	78.5	78.9	79.5	81.4	82.9	84.1	85.1	85.8
Birth rate (per 1,000)	NA	10.8	11.4	11.5	10.4	9.0	9.0	8.8	8.5
Death rate (per 1,000)	NA	10.4	10.4	10.2	10.6	11.1	11.9	13.3	14.9
Women of reproductive age (15-49 yrs.)	NA	2,566	2,583	2,577	2,458	2,272	1,976	1,793	1,666
Fertility rate	NA	1.4	1.5	1.5	1.5	1.6	1.6	1.6	1.7

Except as noted, values for vital statistics are in thousands; life expectancy is in years.

Health Personnel

	National Data	World Data (wtd ave)
Total health expenditure as a percentage of GDP, 1990-1998[a]		
Public sector	4.7	2.5
Private sector	3.2	2.9
Total[b]	7.9	5.5
Health expenditure per capita in U.S. dollars, 1990-1998[a]		
Purchasing power parity	1,142	561
Total	803	483
Availability of health care facilities per 100,000 people		
Hospital beds 1990-1998[a]	410	330
Doctors 1992-1995[a]	291	122
Nurses 1992-1995[a]	304	248

Health Indicators

	National Data	World Data
Life expectancy at birth (years)		
1980	71	61
1998	75	67
Daily per capita supply of calories		
1970	2,930	2,358
1997	3,667	2,791
Daily per capital supply of protein		
1997 (grams)	113	74
Total fertility rate (births per woman)		
1980	2.2	3.7
1998	1.5	2.7
Population with access (%)		
To safe water (1990-96)	82	NA
To sanitation (1990-96)	100	NA
People living with (1997)		
Tuberculosis (cases per 100,000)	52.1	60.4
HIV/AIDS (% aged 15 - 49 years)	0.69	0.99

Infants and Malnutrition

	National Data	World Data (wtd ave)
Under 5 mortality rate (1989)	9	NA
% of infants with low birthweight (1992-98)[1]	5	17
Births attended by skilled health staff (% of total births 1996-98)	NA	52
% fully immunized at 1 year of age (1995-98)[1]		
TB	88	82
DPT	97	77
Polio	96	77
Measles	96	74
Prevalence of child malnutrition (1992-98)[1] (based on weight for age, % of children under 5 years)	NA	30

Ethnic Division

Homogeneous Mediterranean stock; citizens of black African descent who immigrated to mainland during decolonization number less than 100,000.

Religion

Roman Catholic 94%
Protestant . . . . .NA

Data for 1995.

Roman Catholic 22%
Lutheran 16%
Presbyterian/Methodist/London Missionary Society 8%
Anglican 5%
Evangelical Alliance 4%
Seventh-Day Adventist 1%
Other Protestant 10%
Indigenous beliefs 34%

Major Languages

Portuguese.

EDUCATION

Public Education Expenditures

	1980	1997
Public expenditures on education as % of GNP	3.8	5.8
Expenditures per student as % of GNP per capita		
Primary	13.5[2]	NA

Secondary	NA	20.2
Tertiary	36.3	24.5
Pupils per teacher at the primary level	NA	NA
Duration of primary education in years	NA	9
World data for comparison		
Public expenditures on education as % of GNP (mean)	3.9	4.8
Pupils per teacher at the primary level (wtd ave)	NA	33
Duration of primary education in years (mean)	NA	9

Educational Attainment (A)

Age group (1991) . . . . .25+
Population of this age group 6,280,792
Highest level attained (%)
No schooling 16.1
First level
Not completed 61.5
Completed . . . . .NA
Entered second level 14.8
Entered post-secondary .7.7

Literacy Rates (B)

	National Data	World Data
Adult literacy rate		
1980		
Male	87	75
Female	77	58
1995		
Male	93	81
Female	87	65

Libraries

National Libraries **1997**
Administrative Units 1
Service Points or Branches .1
Number of Volumes (000) 2,387
Registered Users (000) 254
Loans to Users (000) 261
Total Library Staff 250
Public Libraries **1997**
Administrative Units 168
Service Points or Branches 219
Number of Volumes (000) 4,842
Registered Users (000) 49,328
Loans to Users (000) .1,113
Total Library Staff 756

GOVERNMENT & LAW

Political Parties

Assembly of the Republic (Assembleia da Republica)	% of vote	no. of seats
Portuguese Socialist Party (PSP)	43.9%	113
Social Democratic Party (PSD)	32.3%	83
United Democratic Coalition (CDU)	9.0%	17
Popular Party (PP)	8.3%	15
The Left Bloc	2.4%	2

Elections were last held 10 October 1999 (next to be held by October 2003).

Government Budgets (B)

Revenues . . . .$48.0 billion
Expenditures $52.0 billion
Capital expenditures . . . .$7.4 billion

Data for 1996 est.

Crime

Crime volume (for 1998)
Crimes reported 65,035
Total persons convicted 15,543
Crimes per 100,000 population 653
Persons responsible for offenses
Total number suspects 37,172
Total number of female suspects 7,732
Total number of juvenile suspects . . . . .NA

(Continued on next page.)

LABOR FORCE

Total Labor Force (A)

4.75 million (1998 est.).

Labor Force by Occupation

Services 60%
Industry 30%
Agriculture 10%

Data for 1999 est.

Unemployment Rate

4.6% (1999 est.)

PRODUCTION SECTOR

Energy Production

Production . . . . .38.581 billion kWh

Production by source

- Fossil fuel 63.14%
- Hydro 33.46%
- Nuclear 0%
- Other 3.40%

Exports . . . . .3.7 billion kWh

Data for 1998.

Energy Consumption

Consumption . . . . .36.18 billion kWh

Imports . . . . .4.00 billion kWh

Data for 1998.

(Continued on next page.)

GOVERNMENT & LAW (cont.)

Military Affairs (A)

	1990	1992	1995	1996	1997
Military expenditures					
Current dollars (mil.)	2,020	2,210	2,340	2,300	2,390
1997 constant dollars (mil.)	2,360	2,450	2,420	2,340	2,390
Armed forces (000)	87	80	78	73	72
Gross national product (GNP)					
Current dollars (bil.)	74	82	91	96	101
1997 constant dollars (bil.)	86	91	94	97	101
Central government expenditures (CGE)					
1997 constant dollars (bil.)	34	38	41	40	41
People (mil.)	9.9	9.9	9.9	9.9	9.9
Military expenditure as % of GNP	2.7	2.7	2.6	2.4	2.4
World data on military expenditure as % of GNP	4.5	3.4	2.7	2.6	2.6
Military expenditure as % of CGE	7.0	6.4	6.0	5.9	5.9
World data on military expenditure as % of CGE	17.0	12.5	10.5	10.3	10.2
Military expenditure per capita (1997 $)	239	248	244	236	241
World data on military expenditure per capita (1997 $)	242	173	146	143	145
Armed forces per 1,000 people (soldiers)	8.8	8.1	7.9	7.4	7.2
World data on armed forces per 1,000 people (soldiers)	5.3	4.5	4.1	3.9	3.8
GNP per capita (1997 $)	8,740	9,240	9,490	9,790	10,200
Arms imports[6]					
Current dollars (mil.)	390	170	150	90	110
1997 constant dollars (mil.)	457	188	155	92	110
Arms exports[6]					
Current dollars (mil.)	10	20	10	20	10
1997 constant dollars (mil.)	12	22	10	20	10
Total imports[7]					
Current dollars (mil.)	25,260	29,580	32,340	34,100	33,820
1997 constant dollars (mil.)	29,590	32,790	33,490	34,670	33,820
Total exports[7]					
Current dollars (mil.)	16,420	18,350	22,620	23,820	23,400
1997 constant dollars (mil.)	19,230	20,340	23,420	24,220	23,400
Arms as percent of total imports[8]	1.5	0.6	0.5	0.3	0.3
Arms as percent of total exports[8]	0.1	0.1	0	0.1	0

PRODUCTION SECTOR (cont.)

Transportation

Highways:

Total: 68,732 km.

Paved: 59,110 km (including 797 km of expressways).

Unpaved: 9,622 km (1999 est.).

Waterways: 820 km navigable; relatively unimportant to national economy, used by shallow-draft craft limited to 300 metric-ton or less cargo capacity.

Pipelines: crude oil 22 km; petroleum products 58 km; natural gas 700 km.

Note: the secondary lines for the natural gas pipeline that will be 300 km long have not yet been built.

Merchant marine:

Total: 151 ships (1,000 GRT or over) totaling 1,061,202 GRT/1,601,267 DWT.

Ships by type: bulk 13, cargo 80, chemical tanker 14, container 8, liquified gas 8, multi-functional large load carrier 1, petroleum tanker 10, refrigerated cargo 1, roll-on/roll-off 6, short-sea passenger 5, vehicle carrier 5 (1999 est.)

Note: Portugal has created a captive register on Madeira for Portuguese-owned ships; ships on the Madeira Register (MAR) will have taxation and crewing benefits of a flag of convenience (1998 est.).

Airports: 66 (1999 est.).

Airports - with paved runways: 40.

Airports - with unpaved runways: 26.

Top Agriculture Products

Grain, potatoes, olives, grapes; sheep, cattle, goats, poultry, beef, dairy products.

Top Mining Products (B)

Mineral resources include: tungsten, iron ore, uranium ore, marble.

MANUFACTURING SECTOR

GDP & Manufacturing Summary (A)

	1980	1985	1990	1995
GDP ($-1990 mil.)[1]	50,202	52,468	67,271	70,630[e]
Per capita ($-1990)[1]	5,140	5,298	6,816	7,196[e]
Manufacturing share (%) (current prices)[1]	32.5	32.5	32.3	NA
Manufacturing				
Value added ($-1990 mil.)[1]	14,936	14,817	18,765	18,073
Industrial production index	78	83	100	97
Value added ($ mil.)	5,602	4,108	13,609	20,211[e]
Gross output ($ mil.)	17,932	15,534	47,171	61,723
Employment (000)	680	622	489	421[e]
Profitability (% of gross output)				
Intermediate input (%)	69	74	71	67[e]
Wages and salaries inc. supplements (%)	17	14	10[e]	8[e]
Gross operating surplus	14	12	18[e]	25[e]
Productivity ($)				
Gross output per worker	25,887	24,566	46,392	63,026[e]
Value added per worker	8,087	6,497	13,384	20,638[e]
Average wage (inc. supplements)	4,541	3,490	10,129[e]	11,118[e]
Value added ($ mil.)				
Food products	544	475	1,305	1,641[e]
Beverages	135	133	344	503[e]
Tobacco products	64	93	592	952[e]
Textiles	905	679	1,654	1,903[e]
Wearing apparel	186	182	985	1,445[e]
Leather and fur products	41	41	126	150[e]
Footwear	86	86	452	738[e]
Wood and wood products	325	150	532	698[e]
Furniture and fixtures	106	30	233	359[e]
Paper and paper products	274	276	577	701[e]
Printing and publishing	180	140	523	805[e]
Industrial chemicals	147	215	432	601[e]
Other chemical products	224	190	481	682[e]
Petroleum refineries	218[e]	−18[e]	591[e]	2,747[e]
Misc. petroleum and coal products	1[e]	NA	3[e]	11[e]
Rubber products	58	45[e]	54	109[e]

(Continued on next page.)

GDP & Manufacturing Summary (A) (cont.)

	1980	1985	1990	1995
Plastic products	128	87[e]	237	293[e]
Pottery, china and earthenware	80	67	291	447[e]
Glass and glass products	87	53	173	265[e]
Other non-metal mineral products	295	100	724	1,044[e]
Iron and steel	207	98	273	162[e]
Non-ferrous metals	33	26	81	109[e]
Metal products	323	219	826	1,204
Non-electrical machinery	170	143	528	708[e]
Electrical machinery	319	247	834	1,233[e]
Transport equipment	428	222	583	697[e]
Prof. and scientific equipment	15	16	36	106[e]
Other manufacturing	20	11	141	200[e]

COMMUNICATIONS

Daily Newspapers

	National Data	World Data for Comparison
Daily Newspapers		
Number of Dailies	27	8,391
Total Circulation (000)	740	548,000
Circulation per 1,000 inhabitants	75	96

Telecommunications

Telephones - main lines in use: 3.724 million (1996).

Telephones - mobile cellular: 887,216 (1999).

Telephone system:

Domestic: generally adequate integrated network of coaxial cables, open wire, microwave radio relay, and domestic satellite earth stations.

International: 6 submarine cables; satellite earth stations - 3 Intelsat (2 Atlantic Ocean and 1 Indian Ocean), NA Eutelsat; tropospheric scatter to Azores Note: an earth station for Inmarsat (Atlantic Ocean region) is planned.

Radio broadcast stations: AM 47, FM 172 (many are repeaters), shortwave 2 (1998).

Radios: 3.02 million (1997).

Television broadcast stations: 36 (plus 62 repeaters) (1997).

Televisions: 3.31 million (1997).

Internet Service Providers (ISPs): 20 (1999).

FINANCE, ECONOMICS, & TRADE

Economic Indicators

National product: GDP—purchasing power parity—$151.4 billion (1999 est.).

National product real growth rate: 3.2% (1999 est.).

National product per capita: $15,300 (1999 est.).

Inflation rate—consumer price index: 2.4% (1999 est.).

Exchange Rates

Exchange rates:

Euros per US$1

January 2000 .... 0.9867
1999 .... 0.9386

Portuguese escudos (Esc) per US$1

January 1999 .... 172.7800
1998 .... 180.1000
1997 .... 175.3100
1996 .... 154.2400
1995 .... 151.1100

On 1 January 1999, the EU introduced a common currency that is now being used by financial institutions in some member countries at a fixed rate of 200.482 escudos per euro; the euro will replace the local currency in consenting countries for all transactions in 2002.

Top Import Origins

$34.9 billion (f.o.b., 1998)

Origins (1998)

EU 77%
Spain 24%
Germany 15%
France 11%
Italy 8%
United Kingdom 7%
Netherlands 5%
United States .... NA
Japan .... NA

Top Export Destinations

$25 billion (f.o.b., 1998)

Destinations (1998)

EU .82%
- Germany .20%
- Spain .16%
- France .14%
- United Kingdom .12%
- Netherlands .5%
- Benelux .5%
- Italy .NA

United States .5%

Foreign Aid

Donor: ODA, $271 million (1995).

Import/Export Commodities

Import Commodities	Export Commodities
Machinery and transport equipment	Clothing and footwear
Chemicals	Machinery
Petroleum	Chemicals
Textiles	Cork and paper products
Agricultural products	Hides

Balance of Payments

	1994	1995	1996	1997	1998
Exports of goods (f.o.b.)	18,645	24,024	25,519	24,806	26,016
Imports of goods (f.o.b.)	−26,966	−32,934	−34,880	−34,847	−38,293
Trade balance	−8,321	−8,910	−9,360	−10,041	−12,277
Services - debits	−5,486	−6,611	−6,536	−6,306	−7,031
Services - credits	6,755	8,236	7,951	7,605	8,606
Private transfers (net)	3,899	3,874	4,323	3,769	3,804
Government transfers (net)	1,942	3,750	1,002	501	845
Overall balance	−2,196	−132	−4,528	−5,527	−7,250

PUERTO RICO

Commonwealth of Puerto Rico

CAPITAL: San Juan.

FLAG: The flag of Puerto Rico has five equal horizontal bands of red (top and bottom) alternating with white; a blue isosceles triangle based on the hoist side bears a large white five-pointed star in the center; design based on the U.S. flag.

ANTHEM: *La Borinqueña.*

MONETARY UNIT: 1 U.S. dollar (US$) = 100 cents.

WEIGHTS AND MEASURES: The U.S. standard weights and measures are used, but the metric system has been partially adopted.

HOLIDAYS: New Year's Day, 1 January; Three King's Day, 6 January; De Hostos' Birthday, 11 January; Washington's Birthday, 22 February; Emancipation Day, 22 March; Good Friday; Jose de Diego's Birthday, 17 April; Memorial Day, last Monday of May; Independence Day, 4 July; Muñoz Rivera's Birthday, 17 July; Celso Barbosa's Birthday, 27 July; Labor Day, first Monday in September; Columbus Day, 14 October; Veterans Day, 22 October; Discovery Day, 19 November; Thanksgiving Day, last Thursday in November; and Christmas Day, 25 December.

TIME: 8 AM = noon GMT.

LOCATION AND SIZE: Puerto Rico—Total area 8,897 sq. km (3,435 sq. mi.)—is the smallest and most easterly of the Greater Antilles, which screen the Caribbean Sea from the Atlantic proper. The main island of Puerto Rico extends 179 km (111 mi.) E–W and 58 km (36 mi.) N–S. It is crossed from east to west by mountain ranges, the most prominent being the Cordillera Central, rising to nearly 1,338 m (4,390 ft.). Islands off the coast include Mona and Desecheo to the W and Vieques and Culebra to the E.

CLIMATE: The mildly tropical climate is moderated by the surrounding sea, and seasonal variations are slight. The prevailing winds are the northeast trades. In San Juan on the northern coast, mean temperatures range from 24°C (75°F) for January to 27°C (81°F) for July. Mean annual rainfall varies from 74 cm (29 in.) on the south coast to 150 cm (59 in.) in San Juan and may total more than 380 cm (150 in.) on the northern mountain slopes in the interior.

INTRODUCTORY SURVEY

RECENT HISTORY

Puerto Rico was captured by U.S. forces during the Spanish-American War and under the 1898 Treaty of Paris it was ceded outright to the United States. It remained under direct military rule until 1900 when the U.S Congress established an administration with a governor and an executive council appointed by the U.S. president and a popularly elected House of Delegates. In 1917 Puerto Ricans were granted U.S. citizenship.

In 1947 Congress provided for popular election of the governor. In 1948 Luis Munoz Marin was elected to that office. A congressional act of 1950, affirmed by popular vote in the island in June 1951, granted Puerto Rico the right to draft its own constitution. The constitution was ratified by popular referendum on March 3, 1952. Puerto Rico's new status as a free commonwealth voluntarily associated with the United States became effective on July 25. The commonwealth status was upheld in a plebiscite in 1967 with 60.5 percent voting for continuation of the commonwealth and 38.9 percent for Puerto Rican statehood. In 1993 another plebiscite vote drew nearly 1.7 million voters or 73.6 percent of those eligible. The voters choose to keep the commonwealth status 48.4 percent to 46.2 percent for statehood and 4.4 percent for independence.

GOVERNMENT

The Commonwealth of Puerto Rico enjoys almost complete internal autonomy. The chief ex-

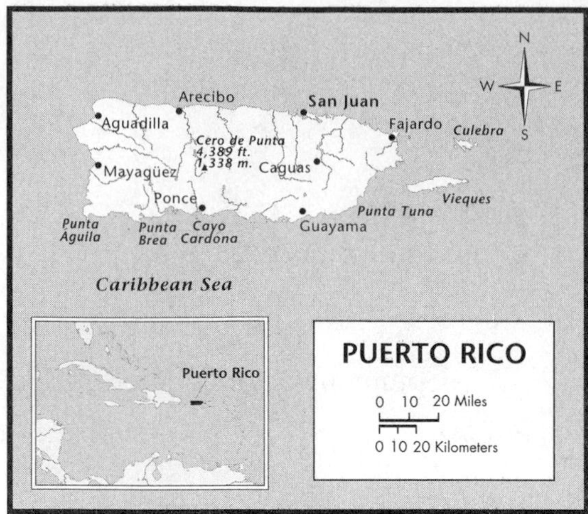

ecutive is the governor, elected by popular vote to a four-year term. The bicameral legislature consists of a 28-member Senate and 54-member House of Representatives elected by popular vote to four-year terms. Puerto Rico elects one non-voting representative to the U.S. House of Representatives.

Judiciary

The Supreme Court and lower courts are tied in with the U.S. federal judiciary and appeals from Puerto Rican courts may be carried as far as the U.S. Supreme Court.

Political Parties

The Popular Democratic Party (PPD) was the dominant political party until 1968 when Luis A. Ferro, a New Progressive Party (PNP) candidate who had supported the statehood position in the 1967 plebiscite, won the governorship. The PNP also won control of the House while the PPD retained the Senate. The PPD returned to power in 1972 but lost to the PNP in 1976 and again by a very narrow margin in 1980. In 1984 it took roughly two-to-one majorities in both houses. The pro-commonwealth PPD remained in control of the government in every election from 1984 to 1992 when Pedro Rossello, a New Progressive and supporter of statehood, was elected governor. Rosello was reelected in 1996. The PNP also took thirty-seven seats in the House, and the PPD took sixteen. There is a small but vocal independence movement, Puerto Rican Independence Party (PIP), divided into two wings: the moderates, favoring social democracy, and the radicals, supporting close ties with the Fidel Castro regime in Cuba. The PIP won one seat in 1996.

ECONOMIC AFFAIRS

For more than 400 years the island's economy was based almost exclusively on sugar. Since 1947 agriculture has been diversified to dairy and livestock, and a thriving manufacturing industry has been established. Since 1956 there has been increasing emphasis on hotel building to encourage the expansion of the tourist industry. A diverse industrial sector has surpassed agriculture as the center of economic activity and income. U.S. firms have heavily invested in Puerto Rico since the 1950s. A chief reason is the duty-free access to the United States. U.S. minimum wage laws apply.

In 1999 five million tourists arrived in Puerto Rico and 2000 again looked favorable for tourism and the related construction sector. By 1998 the gross commonwealth domestic product reached $34.7 billion, up from $15.8 billion in 1985-86.

Public Finance

The U.S. Central Intelligence Agency (CIA) reported Puerto Rico's government took in revenues of $6.7 billion and had expenditures of $9.6 billion in 1999-2000.

Income

The CIA estimated for the 1999 the GDP was $38.1 billion, or $9,800 per capita. The 1999 estimated GDP growth rate was 4.2 percent and inflation 5.2 percent. The 1999 estimated GDP contribution by sector was agriculture 1 percent, industry 45 percent, and services 54 percent.

Industry

The leading industrial products were pharmaceuticals, clothing, electrical machinery, rum, processed foods, and tourism. Sugar processing, once the dominant industry, now plays a lesser role. In 1952 there were only eighty-two labor-intensive plants on the island but by 1990 there were 2,000 plants in Puerto Rico, most of them capital intensive.

Economic Development

Puerto Rico continued to encourage manufacturing and tourism through the 1990s. New or expanding manufacturing and hotel enterprises are granted exemptions of varying lengths and degrees from income taxes and municipal levies. Also San Juan is the busiest commercial center in the Caribbean and more than forty steamship companies provide overseas freight and passenger service.

EDUCATION

In 1995-1996 621,370 students were enrolled in public schools. Fourteen institutions of higher learning had 156,439 students in 1994-1995. The main state-supported university is University of Puerto Rico. Other institutions include Catholic University of Puerto Rico and the Inter-American University.

2000 KEY EVENTS TIMELINE

January

- President Clinton orders the U.S. Navy to resume exercises on the Puerto Rican island of Vieques later in the year, including the explosion of dummy bombs, pursuant to an agreement with Governor Pedro Rossello in exchange for US$40 million.

May

- Pro-life leaders denounce the introduction of the RU-486, after Human Life International (HLI) calls for a ban of the drug in Puerto Rico. The U.S. Food and Drug Administration (FDA) was expected to approve introduction of the drug sometime during 2000.

June

- Despite hundreds of protests from residents, U.S. Navy ships resume military exercises involving shelling the island of Vieques using inert ammunition. Training exercises had not been held since April 1999 when a civilian guard on the military base was killed by practice shelling. Dozens of protestors are arrested.

July

- The United Nations supports Vieque protestors, condemning U.S. military activities in Puerto Rico while calling for the country's self-determination.

October

- The U.S. Navy detains sixty-five demonstrators who may be charged with trespassing on military property on island of Vieques. The move follows a week of protests against U.S. shelling and bombing practice sites on Vieques.
- A Supreme Court ruling upholds Puerto Rico's requirements for registration of new political parties. Members of the Civil Action Party decry the decision, saying overly strict guidelines have prevented any new political party from appearing on election ballots since 1984.
- A federal appeals court hears a lawsuit filed by a group of Puerto Rican citizens who demand the right to vote in November 7 presidential elections. The U.S. Constitution does not allow residents of a territory to select electors.

November

- In November 7 elections, Puerto Rican voters put candidates of the Popular Democratic Party, which supports continuation of the island's commonwealth status, into key mayoral, gubernatorial, and legislative posts. Newly elected lawmakers name party members to head the territory's senate and house of representatives, ousting New Progressive Party leaders who favor Puerto Rican statehood.

ANALYSIS OF EVENTS: 2000

BUSINESS AND THE ECONOMY

Wolverine World Wide, the makers of Hush Puppies shoes, announced in July that it would close several of its factories, including one in Aguadilla, Puerto Rico. About 1,400 workers were expected to lose their jobs companywide, but the number of Puerto Ricans affected was not announced.

The Associated Press and CNN reported that Mattel's Hot Wheels have become one of the best selling products in Puerto Rico, where the little cars have become a cultural phenomenon. One store chain reported that its sales quadrupled during the first six months of 2000, to about 250,000 units. Puerto Ricans gather outside shopping centers and in parking lots to race the cars. They gave away prizes and sometimes even took bets on the winners. Mattel announced it had plans to sell a limited edition of its cars with Puerto Rican license plates.

GOVERNMENT AND POLITICS

In May Federal Bureau of Investigation agents and 100 U.S. Marshals landed in the island of Vieques and arrested more than 200 protesters who had prevented U.S. naval exercises from taking place for more than a year. Several hundred U.S.

Marines landed on the island to stop any other protesters from entering naval property. The arrests ended months of protests by Puerto Rican nationalists who wanted the U.S. Navy to cease bombing exercises on the fifty-two-square-mile island. Among those arrested were two U.S. congressmen of Puerto Rican descent. The year-long siege on Vieques had soured relations between the United States and the territory of Puerto Rico, where some nationalist leaders made impassioned pleas to secede from the United States. The island has been a commonwealth freely associated with the United States since July 25, 1952. The protests were triggered by an accident that occurred during live bombing training on the island of Vieques in April 1999. Two stray bombs killed a security guard and injured four other people. Protesters camped out on the island, effectively stopping naval training exercises. For many Puerto Rican nationalists, the bombing accident became a metaphor for U.S. power and its imposition over the Puerto Rican territory. Vieques represented the divisions that have existed for decades among Puerto Ricans: some citizens want Puerto Rican sovereignty, others want Puerto Rico to become the fifty-first U.S. state, and a third major group that favors the current free association status.

In January U.S. President Bill Clinton and Puerto Rican Governor Pedro Roselló signed an agreement to allow the navy to continue using Vieques as a training facility until 2003. The agreement allowed the navy to use dummy bombs, and gave the island's 9,200 residents the right to decide by referendum on whether to allow the navy to remain in Vieques after 2003. Clinton also pledged $50 million in aid to the island's residents. The agreement did not satisfy nationalist sentiments. In February more than 80,000 Puerto Ricans marched in San Juan to protest naval exercises. A nearly equal number of Puerto Ricans rallied to counter protests against Vieques and to celebrate their U.S. citizenship. Vieques became backdrop to the 2000 elections, even though candidates from the three major parties attempted to draw attention to local political issues.

Governor Roselló and his party, Partido Nuevo Progresista, favored state status. Behind Carlos Ignacio Pesquera, who had led the pro-U.S. rally in March, the party was seeking to remain in power by taking the governorship. Polls in early 2000 gave him a slight lead over Sila Mariá Calderón, the fifty-eight-year-old candidate from the Partido Popular Democratico, which had traditionally favored free status association with the United States. Thanks to Vieques, the pro-independence candidate Ruben Berríos had made some gains, but remained a distant third. In June President Clinton held a historic meeting with the three candidates to discuss the future relation between the island and the United States. Four months later Clinton approved $2.5 million to finance an education campaign in Puerto Rico to help the island's residents decide their future status.

But Calderon had chosen to focus on the perceived shortcomings of the Roselló government instead of talks about Puerto Rico's future. "This is the most corrupt government in our history," the former mayor of San Juan charged in her many speeches. The approach worked. Calderón became the first woman governor of Puerto Rico, winning with 48.6 percent. Pesquera received 46 percent, and Berríos had 4.6 percent. Yet Berríos claimed Calderón's victory represented a clear signal that most Puerto Ricans favored independence and not statehood. Her party wanted to promote a new relationship with the United States that would guarantee the autonomous development of the island with a status that is "not colonial nor territorial." How that would happen remained to be seen, but nationalists continued to press their case on U.S. soil. In November authorities arrested eleven people for hanging flags and peace signs for Vieques on the Statue of Liberty.

CULTURE AND SOCIETY

Puerto Ricans who favor statehood went to a U.S. court in October to press for their rights to vote in U.S. presidential elections. Earlier a lower court found in favor of Puerto Rico's 2.4 million voters, saying they could cast their ballots in a presidential race. But the First U.S. Circuit Court of Appeals said only states can send electors to the Electoral College, even though Puerto Ricans were given U.S. citizenship in 1917. Puerto Ricans are allowed to vote if they reside in any of the fifty states. Chief appellate Judge Juan Torruella did not agree with the decision, saying it denied Puerto Ricans their right to vote as citizens. "The perpetuation of this colonial condition runs against the very principles upon which this nation was founded," Torruella wrote in a dissenting opinion.

The U.S. Justice Department said the issue would have to be resolved by legislation and not the courts. Puerto Rico's Governor Pedro Rosselló said islanders would vote on a U.S. president despite the court's ruling. But shortly before the election, the Puerto Rican Supreme Court said the presidential ballot was unconstitutional and Puerto Ricans could not vote for U.S. president. If Puerto Rico were a state, it would have approximately eight electoral votes.

DIRECTORY

CENTRAL GOVERNMENT

Head of State

President of the United States

George W. Bush, Office of the President, 1600 Pensylvania Avenue, Washington, D.C. 20500
PHONE: +(202) 4561414
FAX: +(202) 4562461
E-MAIL: http://www.whitehouse.gov

Governor of Puerto Rico

Pedro Rossello, Office of the Governor, La Fortzaleza San Juan, Puerto Rico 00901
PHONE: +(787) 7217000
FAX: +(787) 7254569
WEBSITE: http://www.govpr.org

POLITICAL ORGANIZATIONS

Puerto Rican Independence Party

963 F.D. Roosevelt Avenue, Hato Rey, San Juan, Puerto Rico 00918
PHONE: +(787) 7821455
NAME: Ruben Berrios Martinez

Popular Democratic Party

403 Ponce de Leon Avenue, Puerta de Tierra, San Juan, Puerto Rico 00906
PHONE: +(787) 7251992
NAME: Hector Acevedo

New Progressive Party

La Fortalleza, San Juan, Puerto Rico 00901
PHONE: +(787) 7217000
FAX: +(787) 7254569
E-MAIL: webmaster@govpr.org
TITLE: President
NAME: Pedro Rossello

JUDICIAL SYSTEM

Supreme Court of Puerto Rico

P.O. Box 2392, Puerta de Tierra, San Juan, Puerto Rico 00902
PHONE: +(787) 7243551
FAX: +(787) 7254910

The U.S. District Court for the District of Puerto Rico

150 Carlos Chardon Avenue, Clemente Ruiz Nazario Courthouse, Hato Rey, Puerto Rico, 00918

BROADCAST MEDIA

Broadcasters Association of Puerto Rico

Suite 212, Cobians Plaza, 1607 Ave. Ponce de Leon, San Juan, Puerto Rico 00926

New Conscience Network

Marginal Baldorioty de Castro, PO Box 4039, Carolina, Puerto Rico 00984
PHONE: +(787) 7505858
FAX: +(787) 2760870
E-MAIL: ncn@icepr.com
WEBSITE: http://www.icepr.com/ncn
CONTACT: Luis E. Rosado
LANGUAGE: Spanish

NotiUno

Box 363222, San Juan, Puerto Rico 00936
TYPE: News

Super Kadena Noticiosa

117 Calle Eleonor Roosevelt, Hato Rey, Puerto Rico 00918

American Colonial Broadcasting Corporation

Box S-4189, San Juan 00905, Puerto Rico

New Conscience Network

Marginal Baldorioty de Castro, PO Box 4039, Carolina, Puerto Rico 00984
PHONE: +(787) 7505858
FAX: +(787) 2760870
E-MAIL: ncn@icepr.com
WEBSITE: http://www.icepr.com/ncn
CONTACT: Jose Rivera

Ponce TV Corpo

Isabel Esq Montaner, Ponce 00731
TITLE: President
CONTACT: L.T. Muniz

SFN Communications, Inc.

GPO Box 2060, San Juan, Puerto Rico 00938

Siglares Iglesia Catolica Inc.

Buzon C-339, Quebradillas, Puerto Rico 00742

Telemundo of Puerto Rico, Inc.

383 Roosevelt Av., Hato Rey, Puerto Rico 00918
TITLE: General Manager
CONTACT: Jose Ramos

Three Star Telecast Inc.

Box 18, Carolina, Puerto Rico 00628
TITLE: Director General
CONTACT: Bakarat Saleh

Western Broadcasting Corporation of Puerto Rico

Box 1200, Mayaguez, Puerto Rico 00709

COLLEGES AND UNIVERSITIES

Inter-American University of Puerto Rico

PO Box 363255, San Juan, Puerto Rico
PHONE: +(787) 7661912
WEBSITE: http://www.inter.edu

Centro de Estudios Avanzados de Puerto Rico y el Carilse

Apdo. 9023790, San Juan, Puerto Rico 00902-3970
PHONE: +(787) 7238772
FAX: +(787) 7234481
E-MAIL: centro@prtc.net
WEBSITE: http://www.prtc.net/~centro

Pontifical Catholic University of Puerto Rico

2250 Av. Las Americas, Ponce, Puerto Rico 00717-0777
FAX: +(787) 6512000
WEBSITE: http://www.pucpr.edu

Carlos Albizu University

Box 3711 Old San Juan Station, San Juan, Puerto Rico 00902-3711
PHONE: +(787) 7256500
FAX: +(787) 7217187
E-MAIL: webmaster@mip.ccas.edu
WEBSITE: http://www.ccas.edu

University of the Sacred Heart

PO Box 12383, San Juan, Puerto Rico 00914-0383
PHONE: +(787) 7281515
WEBSITE: http://www.usc.clu.edu

Conservatory of Music of Puerto Rico

350 Rafael Lamar St. at Fdr Ave., San Juan, Puerto Rico 00918

University of Puerto Rico

PO Box 364984, San Juan, Puerto Rico 00936-4984
PHONE: +(787) 2500000
WEBSITE: http://www.upr.clu.edu/

Bayamon Central University

PO Box 1725, Bayamon, Puerto Rico 00960
PHONE: +(787) 7863030
FAX: +(787) 7402200
WEBSITE: http://www.worldwide.edu/ci/usa/schools/10509.html

NEWSPAPERS AND MAGAZINES

La Estrella de Puerto Rico

Calle Paris 165, Urb. Floral Park, Halo Rey, Puerto Rico 00917
PHONE: +(787) 7544440
FAX: +(787) 7544452
E-MAIL: anuncios@estrelladepr.com
WEBSITE: http://www.estrelladepr.com
TITLE: Editor
CONTACT: Pete Curras
CIRCULATION: 115,200

El Vocero de Puerto Rico

Caribbean News Corporation, PO Box 3831, San Juan, Puerto Rico 00902-3831
PHONE: +(787) 7212300
FAX: +(787) 7258422
TITLE: Editor
CONTACT: Gaspar Roca
CIRCULATION: 214,000

El Nuevo Dia

El Dia Inc., Lotes 118, 12 Carretera 24/165, Parque Industrial Amelia, Apdo 297, San Juan, Puerto Rico 00507
PHONE: +(787) 6418000 (Ext 2990)
FAX: +(787) 6413959; 7933495
E-MAIL: pastrana@carib.net
WEBSITE: http://www.endi.com
TITLE: Editors
CONTACT: Luis A. Ferre, Maria L, Ferre
CIRCULATION: 233,420 (Daily); 250,449 (Sun)

La Perla Del Sur

Sabanetas Industrial Park, A. St., No. 22, Box 7253, Ponce, Puerto Rico 00732
PHONE: +(787) 8425866
FAX: +(787) 8425823
E-MAIL: perlasur@tld.net
TITLE: Editor
CONTACT: Juan J. Nogueras
CIRCULATION: 75,000

The San Juan Star

The San Juan Star Co., GPO Box 364187, San Juan, Puerto Rico 00936-4187
PHONE: +(787) 7824200; 7814073; 7920933
FAX: +(787) 7835788; 7820310
WEBSITE: http://www.icepr.com/sjmagazine
TITLE: Editor
CONTACT: Andrew Vigluci
CIRCULATION: 54,000

Todo Carolina

PO Box 3558, Valle Arriba Heights Station, Carolina, Puerto Rico 00984-3558
PHONE: +(787) 7544440
FAX: +(787) 7687819
TITLE: Editor
CONTACT: Leroy Camero
CIRCULATION: 52,000

Todo Bayamon

Calle 17 S-5, Flamboyan Gardens, PO Box 1846, Bayamon, Puerto Rico 00960
PHONE: +(787) 7876011
FAX: +(787) 7400022
CIRCULATION: 50,000

El San Juan Star

The San Juan Star Co., PO Box 364187, San Juan, Puerto Rico 00936-4187
PHONE: +(787) 7814073; 7920380
FAX: +(787) 7820310; 7835788
TITLE: Editor
CONTACT: Andrew Viglucci
CIRCULATION: 50,000

la Semana

Editorial Semana Inc., PO Box 6537, Caguas, Puerto Rico 00726
PHONE: +(787) 7433346
FAX: +(787) 7435500
CIRCULATION: 47,000

Todo Norte

Urbanization San Salvador, Apdo 460, Manati, Puerto Rico 00960
PHONE: +(787) 8540555
FAX: +(787) 7687819
CIRCULATION: 43,000

De Moda

El Nuevo Dia, Inc, PO Box 7512, San Juan, Puerto Rico 00906-7512
PHONE: +(787) 6418000
FAX: +(787) 6413921
TITLE: Contact
CONTACT: Maria de la Rosa

Primera Hora

El Dia Inc., PO Box 7512, San Juan, Puerto Rico 0906-7512
PHONE: +(787) 6418000 (Ext. 2990)
FAX: +(787) 6413959
WEBSITE: http://www.endi.com
TITLE: Editor
CONTACT: Hector Olave

Eres

Editorial Televisa, 6355 NW 36th St., Miami FL 33166 USA
PHONE: (305) 8716400
FAX: (305) 8715026
CIRCULATION: 30,000
TYPE: General Interest

Selecciones Del Reader's Digest

RD Latinoamerica, S.A., 2655 Le Jeune Rd., Ste. 301, Coral Gables FL 33134 USA
PHONE: 305 4488233
FAX: 305 4488234
CIRCULATION: 75,000
TYPE: Compilation of articles

PUBLISHERS

Editorial Cordillera

PO Box 192363, San Juan, Puerto Rico 00919-2363
PHONE: +(787) 7676188
FAX: +(787) 7678646
E-MAIL: info@editorialcordillera.com
WEBSITE: http://www.editorialcordillera.com
TITLE: President
CONTACT: Carlos E. Serrano

SUBJECTS: Atlases, Dictionaries, Maps, Literature, Literary Criticism, Essays, Social Sciences, Sociology

Instituto de Cultura Puertorriquena

PO Box 4184, San Juan, Puerto Rico 00905
PHONE: +(787) 7240910
TITLE: Director
CONTACT: Carmelo Degrado Cintron
SUBJECTS: Anthropology, History, Literature, Literary Criticism, Essays, Music, Dance, Poetry

Editorial Cultural Inc.

Calle El Roble #51, Apartado 21056, Piedras, Puerto Rico 00928
PHONE: +(787) 7659767
FAX: +(787) 7659767
E-MAIL: cultural@editorialcultural.com
WEBSITE: http://www.editorialcultural.com
TITLE: Managing Director
CONTACT: Francisco Vazquez
SUBJECTS: Biography, History, Literature, Literary Criticism, Essays

Ediciones Huracan Inc.

Ave. Gonzalez 1002, Rio Piedras, Puerto Rico 00925
PHONE: +(787) 7637404
FAX: +(787) 7637404
TITLE: Director
CONTACT: Carmen Rivera-Izcoa
SUBJECTS: History, Literature, Literary Criticism, Essays, Social Sciences, Sociology

Libros-Ediciones Homines

PO Box 190374, Hato Rey, Puerto Rico 00919
PHONE: +(787) 2501912
E-MAIL: a.frambes@inter.edu
WEBSITE: http://coqui.lce.org/homines/
TITLE: International Rights
CONTACT: Arline Frambes-Buxeda
SUBJECTS: Behavioral Sciences, Government, Political Science, Regional Interests, Social Sciences, Sociology, Women's Studies
TOTAL PUBLISHED: 30 print; 3 CD-ROM

Ediciones Puerto

PO Box 9066272, San Juan, Puerto Rico 00906
PHONE: +(787) 7210844
FAX: +(787) 7250861
E-MAIL: info@edicionespuerto.com
WEBSITE: http://www.edicionespuerto.com
TITLE: President
CONTACT: Jose Carvajal
SUBJECTS: Poetry, Social Sciences, Sociology

University of Puerto Rico Press (EDUPR)

University of Puerto Rico Sta., Rio Piedras, Puerto Rico 00931
PHONE: +(787) 7586932
FAX: +(787) 7539116
TITLE: President
CONTACT: Marta Aponte-Alsina
SUBJECTS: Art, Education, History, Nonfiction (General), Philosophy, Poetry, Psychology, Psychiatry, Social Sciences, Sociology

RELIGIOUS ORGANIZATIONS

Buddhist

El Centro de Puerto Rico
Ave. Emiliano Pol 497, apt. 186, La Cumbre, Rio Piedras, Puerto Rico 00926
PHONE: +(787) 7205578
E-MAIL: moreno@pascal.uprr.pr

Catholic

Arecibo (Diocese)
Obispo de Arecibo, Dr. Salas 205, P.O. Box 616, Arecibo, Puerto Rico 00613
PHONE: +(787) 8783180, 8783110
FAX: +(787) 8802661
E-MAIL: obispado@xsn.net
TITLE: Excmo. Monsenor
NAME: Inaki Mallona Txertudi, C.P.

Conferencia Episcopal De Puerto Rico
P.O. Box 40682, San Juan, Puerto Rico 00940-0682
PHONE: (787) 7281650
FAX: +(787) 7281654

Caguas (Diocese)
Administrador Apostolico "sede plena et ad nutum Sanctae Sedis" de Caguas, P.O. Box 8698, Caguas, Puerto Rico 00626
PHONE: +(787) 7475885, 7475787, 2860075
FAX: +(787) 7475616
E-MAIL: obicag@coqui.net, vicpast@hotmail.com

Instituto De Orientacion Familiar
Estacion 6 Apartado 214, Ponce, Puerto Rico 00732
PHONE: +(787) 8406018
FAX: +(787) 8484523
TITLE: Rvdo. Diacono
NAME: Jesus Maria Pagan

Mayaguez (Diocese)
Obispo de Mayaguez, Calle Obispado, Barrio Miradero, P.O. Box 2272, Mayaguez, Puerto Rico 00709
PHONE: +(787) 8335411, 8335032
E-MAIL: prodima@caribe.net
TITLE: Excmo. Monsenor
NAME: Ulises Aurelio Casiano Vargas

Ponce (Diocese)
Obispado de Ponce, P.O. Box 32205 Estavion, Ponce, Puerto Rico 00732-2205
PHONE: +(787) 8485265, 8403332
FAX: +(787) 8411778
E-MAIL: obispadoponce@pucpr.edu
TITLE: Excmo. Y Rvdmo. Mons.
NAME: Fremiot Torres Oliver

San Juan De Puerto Rico (Arq.)
Arzbispo de San Juan, Calle San Jorge 201, Santurce, P.O. Box S-1967, San Juan, Puerto Rico 00902-1967
PHONE: +(787) 7277373
TITLE: Emmo. Senor Cardenal
NAME: Luis Aponte Martinez

Tribunal Interdiocesano De Puerto Rico
Calle Isabel #31, P.O. Box 32229, Ponce, Puerto Rico 00732-2229
PHONE: +(787) 8484630
FAX: +(787) 8417483

Protestant

Iglesia Adventista Del Septimo Dia Humacao 1
Iglesia Adventista Del Septimo Dia -Humaco 1, Calle Esmeralda #6, Humacao, Puerto Rico 00791
PHONE: +(787) 8524418

Parroquia Bienaventurada Virgen Maria De Lourdes
Apartado Postal 1081, Trujillo Alto, Puerto Rico 00977
PHONE: +(787) 7610571
E-MAIL: mlourdes@tld.net
WEBSITE: http://www.tld.net/users/plrl
TITLE: Padre
NAME: Pedro Luis Reyes Lebron

Parroquia Corazon de Jesus
Parroquia Corazon de Jesus, P.O. Box 577, Mercedita, Puerto Rico 00715
E-MAIL: josgala@caribe.net

Primera Iglesia Adventista del Septimo Dia de Arecibo
P.O. Box 142785, Arecibo, Puerto Rico 00614-2785
PHONE: +(787) 8173017
E-MAIL: ben@xsn.net

FURTHER READING

Articles

Bragg, Rick. "Puerto Ricans Seek Vote for President." *New York Times,* October 8, 2000, p. 16.

"Despite Protests, Navy Resumes Shelling of Puerto Rican Island." *New York Times,* June 26, 2000, p. A10.

Moreno, Sylvia. "Puerto Rican Protestors Await FBI Showdown," *The Washington Post,* May 3, 2000.

Books

Dun and Bradstreet's Guide to Puerto Rico. Parsippany, NJ: Dun & Bradstreet, 1999.

Fuson, Robert Henderson. *Juan Ponce de Leon and the Spanish Discovery of Puerto Rico and Florida.* Blacksburg, VA: McDonald & Woodward, 2000.

Internet

"Puerto Rican Activists Get Big Boost From UN," [Online] Available http://www.thegully.com, July 17, 2000 (accessed July 20, 2000).

Government Publications

United States Congress. *Clemency for the FALN: A Flawed Decision?* Washington, DC: G.P.O., 2000.

———. *Oversight of the 2000 Census: Discussion of the Effects of Including Puerto Rico in the 2000 U.S. population totals.* Washington, DC: G.P.O., 2000.

———. *Puerto Rico Political Status.* Washington, DC: G.P.O., 1999.

PUERTO RICO: STATISTICAL DATA

For sources and notes see "Sources of Statistics" at the front of each volume.

GEOGRAPHY

Geography

Area:

Total: 9,104 sq km.

Land: 8,959 sq km.

Land boundaries: 0 km.

Coastline: 501 km.

Climate: tropical marine, mild; little seasonal temperature variation.

Terrain: mostly mountains, with coastal plain belt in north; mountains precipitous to sea on west coast; sandy beaches along most coastal areas.

Natural resources: some copper and nickel; potential for onshore and offshore oil.

Land use:

Arable land: 4%

Permanent crops: 5%

Permanent pastures: 26%

Forests and woodland: 16%

Other: 49% (1993 est.).

HUMAN FACTORS

Demographics (A)

	1990	1995	1998	2000	2010	2020	2030	2040	2050
Population	3,537	3,731	3,860	3,916	4,089	4,196	4,279	4,297	4,242
Life expectancy - males	70.0	68.9	70.8	71.1	73.3	75.1	76.6	77.8	78.9
Life expectancy - females	78.9	78.8	79.7	80.3	82.0	83.4	84.5	85.4	86.1
Birth rate (per 1,000)	18.8	17.0	15.7	15.5	13.3	12.0	11.4	10.7	10.2
Death rate (per 1,000)	7.4	8.1	7.8	7.7	8.2	9.0	10.1	11.2	12.3
Women of reproductive age (15-49 yrs.)	936	998	1,030	1,038	1,030	991	922	905	869
Fertility rate	2.3	2.1	1.9	1.9	1.9	1.9	1.8	1.8	1.8

Except as noted, values for vital statistics are in thousands; life expectancy is in years.

Health Personnel

	National Data	World Data (wtd ave)
Total health expenditure as a percentage of GDP, 1990-1998[a]		
Public sector	NA	2.5
Private sector	6.5	2.9
Total[b]	NA	5.5
Availability of health care facilities per 100,000 people		
Hospital beds 1990-1998[a]	330	330
Doctors 1992-1995[a]	NA	122
Nurses 1992-1995[a]	NA	248

Health Indicators

	National Data	World Data
Life expectancy at birth (years)		
1980	74	61
1998	76	67
Daily per capita supply of calories		
1970	NA	2,358
1997	NA	2,791
Daily per capital supply of protein		
1997 (grams)	NA	74
Total fertility rate (births per woman)		
1980	2.6	3.7
1998	1.9	2.7
People living with (1997)		
Tuberculosis (cases per 100,000)	NA	60.4
HIV/AIDS (% aged 15 - 49 years)	NA	0.99

Religion

Roman Catholic 85%
Protestant and other 15%

Major Languages

Spanish, English.

EDUCATION

Public Education Expenditures

	1980	1997
Public expenditures on education as % of GNP	NA	NA
Pupils per teacher at the primary level	NA	NA
Duration of primary education in years	NA	10
World data for comparison		
Public expenditures on education as % of GNP (mean)	3.9	4.8
Pupils per teacher at the primary level (wtd ave)	NA	33
Duration of primary education in years (mean)	NA	9

Educational Attainment (B)

	1980	1985
Gross enrollment ratio (%)		
Primary level	93.3	NA
Secondary level	72.7	NA
Tertiary level	41.6	44.3

Literacy Rates (C)

Year	Adult Literacy Rate (Population aged 15 years and older)
1980	88.80%
1985	90.20%
1990	91.50%
1995	92.70%
1997	93.10%

GOVERNMENT & LAW

Political Parties

Legislative Assembly	no. of seats
Senate	
New Progressive Party (PNP)	19
Popular Democratic Party (PPD)	8
Puerto Rican Independence Party (PIP)	1
House of Representatives	
New Progressive Party (PNP)	37
Popular Democratic Party (PPD)	16
Puerto Rican Independence Party (PIP)	1

Elections for the Senate and the House of Representatives were last held 5 November 1996 (next to be held 7 November 2000).

Government Budgets (B)

Revenues . . . .$6.7 billion
Expenditures . . . .$9.6 billion

Data for FY99/00.

Crime

Crime volume (for 1998)

Crimes reported 87,020

Total persons convicted .NA

Crimes per 100,000 population 2,176

LABOR FORCE

Total Labor Force (A)

1.3 million (1996).

Labor Force by Occupation

Agriculture 3%

Industry 20%

Services 77%

Data for 1999 est.

Unemployment Rate

13% (FY97/98 est.)

PRODUCTION SECTOR

Energy Production

Production . . . . .17.765 billion kWh

Production by source

Fossil fuel 98.06%

Hydro 1.94%

Nuclear 0%

Other 0%

Exports . . . . .0 kWh

Data for 1998.

Energy Consumption

Consumption . . . . .16.521 billion kWh

Imports . . . . .0 kWh

Data for 1998.

Transportation

Highways:

Total: 14,400 km.

Paved: 14,400 km.

Unpaved: 0 km (1996 est.).

Merchant marine:

Total: 1 ship (1,000 GRT or over) totaling 17,513 GRT/14,976 DWT.

Ships by type: roll-on/roll-off 1 (1999 est.).

Airports: 30 (1999 est.).

Airports - with paved runways: 21.

Top Agriculture Products

Sugarcane, coffee, pineapples, plantains, bananas; livestock products, chickens.

Top Mining Products (B)

Mineral resources include: some copper and nickel; potential for onshore and offshore oil.

MANUFACTURING SECTOR

GDP & Manufacturing Summary (A)

	1980	1985	1990	1995
GDP: $-1990 mil.)[1]	21,300	24,583	30,604	35,824
Per capita ($-1990)[1]	6,663	7,277	8,675	9,679
Manufacturing share (%) (current prices)[1]	37.2	39.2	39.5	NA
Manufacturing				
Value added ($-1990 mil.)[1]	9,070	10,258	12,126	14,195[e]
Industrial production index	67[e]	76	100	126[e]
Value added ($ mil.)	5,976[e]	7,968	12,126	17,675[e]
Gross output ($ mil.)	18,662[e]	22,901[e]	29,777	37,798[e]
Employment (000)	155	149	129	123[e]
Profitability (% of gross output)				
Intermediate input (%)	68[e]	65[e]	59	53[e]
Wages and salaries inc. supplements (%)	8[e]	9[e]	10[e]	10[e]
Gross operating surplus	25[e]	26[e]	31[e]	37[e]
Productivity ($)				
Gross output per worker	120,663[e]	153,923[e]	193,356	259,883[e]
Value added per worker	38,637[e]	53,554	78,740	121,530[e]
Average wage (inc. supplements)	9,109[e]	13,499	23,196[e]	30,047[e]
Value added ($ mil.)				
Food products	405[e]	485	673	733[e]
Beverages	440[e]	714	1,117	2,167[e]
Tobacco products	122[e]	143	171	200[e]
Textiles	31[e]	34	42	47[e]
Wearing apparel	397[e]	437	486	551[e]
Leather and fur products	15[e]	24[e]	35[e]	57[e]
Footwear	58[e]	64[e]	78[e]	138[e]

(Continued on next page.)

GDP & Manufacturing Summary (A) (cont.)

	1980	1985	1990	1995
Wood and wood products	15[e]	15[e]	19[e]	21[e]
Furniture and fixtures	26[e]	29[e]	40[e]	49[e]
Paper and paper products	51[e]	56	66	80[e]
Printing and publishing	57[e]	86	164	207[e]
Industrial chemicals	55[e]	58	39	33[e]
Other chemical products	1,817[e]	2,849	5,334	9,239[e]
Petroleum refineries	94[e]	146[e]	195[e]	169[e]
Misc. petroleum and coal products	9[e]	19[e]	9[e]	9[e]
Rubber products	27[e]	31[e]	43[e]	51[e]
Plastic products	50[e]	83[e]	120[e]	214[e]
Pottery, china and earthenware	15[e]	18[e]	27[e]	31[e]
Glass and glass products	34[e]	40[e]	62[e]	70[e]
Other non-metal mineral products	48[e]	57[e]	87[e]	98[e]
Iron and steel	3[e]	10[e]	18[e]	14[e]
Non-ferrous metals	6[e]	20[e]	37[e]	29[e]
Metal products	81[e]	93	116	112[e]
Non-electrical machinery	534[e]	502	668	455[e]
Electrical machinery	1,027[e]	1,246	1,409	1,669[e]
Transport equipment	23[e]	29	68	53[e]
Prof. and scientific equipment	438[e]	582	889	1,080[e]
Other manufacturing	98[e]	98	113	101[e]

COMMUNICATIONS

Daily Newspapers

	National Data	World Data for Comparison
Daily Newspapers		
Number of Dailies	3	8,391
Total Circulation (000)	475	548,000
Circulation per 1,000 inhabitants	127	96

Telecommunications

Telephones - main lines in use: 1.196 million (1995).

Telephones - mobile cellular: 171,000 (1995).

Telephone system: modern system, integrated with that of the US by high-capacity submarine cable and Intelsat with high-speed data capability.

Domestic: digital telephone system; cellular telephone service.

International: satellite earth station - 1 Intelsat; submarine cable to US.

Radio broadcast stations: AM 72, FM 17, shortwave 0 (1998).

Radios: 2.7 million (1997).

Television broadcast stations: 18 (plus three stations of the US Armed Forces Radio and Television Service) (1997).

Televisions: 1.021 million (1997).

Internet Service Providers (ISPs): 18 (1999).

FINANCE, ECONOMICS, & TRADE

Economic Indicators

National product: GDP—purchasing power parity—$38.1 billion (1999 est.).

National product real growth rate: 4.2% (1999 est.).

National product per capita: $9,800 (1999 est.).

Inflation rate—consumer price index: 5.2% (1999 est.).

Exchange Rates

Exchange rates: US currency is used.

Top Import Origins

$25.3 billion (c.i.f., 1999)

Origins (1999)

United States 60%

Top Export Destinations

$34.9 billion (f.o.b., 1999)

Destinations (1999)

United States 88%

Import/Export Commodities

Import Commodities	Export Commodities
Chemicals	Pharmaceuticals
Machinery and equipment	Electronics
	Apparel
Clothing	Canned tuna
Food	Rum
Fish	Beverage concentrates
Petroleum products	Medical equipment

QATAR

State of Qatar
Dawlat Qatar

CAPITAL: Doha (Ad-Dawhah).

FLAG: Maroon with white serrated border at the hoist.

ANTHEM: *Qatar National Anthem.*

MONETARY UNIT: The Qatar riyal (QR) of 100 dirhams was introduced on 13 May 1973. There are coins of 1, 5, 10, 25, and 50 dirhams, and notes of 1, 5, 10, 50, 100, and 500 riyals. QR1 = \$0.2747 (or \$1 = QR3.64).

WEIGHTS AND MEASURES: The metric system is the legal standard, although some British measures are still in use.

HOLIDAYS: Emir's Succession Day, 22 February; Independence Day, 3 September. Muslim religious holidays include 'Id al-Fitr, 'Id al-'Adha', and Milad an-Nabi.

TIME: 3 PM = noon GMT.

LOCATION AND SIZE: The State of Qatar, a peninsula projecting northward into the Persian Gulf, has an area of 11,000 square kilometers (4,247 square miles), slightly smaller than the state of Connecticut. Qatar also includes a number of islands.

Qatar's capital city, Doha, is located on the Persian Gulf coast.

CLIMATE: Qatar's summer is extremely hot. Mean temperatures in June are 42°C (108°F), dropping to 15°C (59°F) in winter. Rainfall is minimal.

INTRODUCTORY SURVEY

RECENT HISTORY

At the outbreak of World War I (1914-1918), Qatar established its independence. In 1916, it signed a treaty with the United Kingdom, providing for British protection in exchange for a central role for the United Kingdom in Qatar's foreign affairs. High-quality oil was discovered at Dukhan in 1940, but full-scale use of the discovery did not begin until 1949.

In January 1968, the United Kingdom announced its intention to withdraw its forces from the Persian Gulf states by the end of 1971. On September 3, 1971, the independent State of Qatar was declared. A new treaty of friendship and cooperation was signed with the United Kingdom and Qatar was soon admitted to membership in the twenty-member Arab League (also known as the League of Arab States) and the United Nations.

On February 22, 1972, Sheikh Khalifa bin Hamad al-Thani seized power in a peaceful coup deposing his cousin, Sheikh Ahmad. Sheikh Khalifa pursued a vigorous program of economic and social reforms including the transfer of royal income to the state.

Qatar's boundary disputes with Bahrain disrupted relations between the two countries in the mid-1980s. In December 1992 a minor dispute with Saudi Arabia was resolved with a boundary agreement.

During the late 1980s and early 1990s, Khalifa continuously siphoned off petroleum revenues, crippling the Qatari economy. In February 1995, Sheikh Hamad seized power from his father, Sheikh Khalifa. When Sheikh Hamad took over the government, his father froze the bank accounts further disabling Qatar's treasury.

In 1996, Sheikh Khalifa set up a government in exile in nearby United Arab Emirates. The hostile transfer of power has led to problems among the members of the Gulf Cooperation Council. Budget problems from the lost revenue have caused Sheikh Hamad to cut government spending. However, the

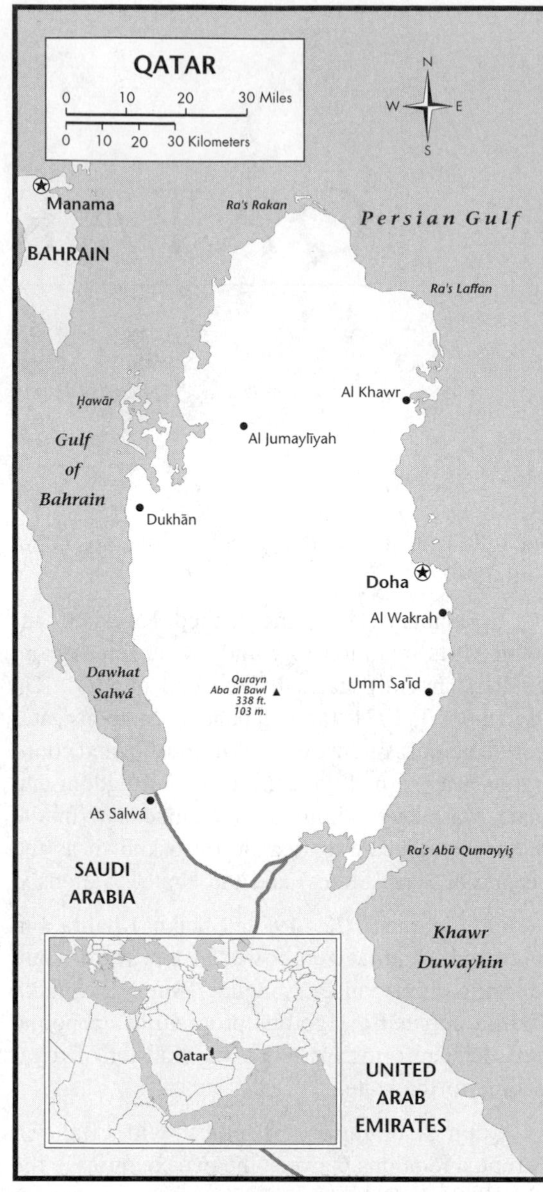

government will need to spend money in order to develop huge offshore natural gas reserves.

In 1999, the former emir still claimed to be the legitimate ruler of Aatar, however, Sheikh Hamad continued to rule and implement change in spite of outside threats. In 1999, Qatar supported the efforts of the Organization of Oil Exporting Countries (OPEC) to increase oil prices by cutting back crude oil production from March 1999 to April 2000. Qatar continued economic reforms and fiscal discipline. Most strikingly, Hamad encouraged political openness. In 1999, women voted and ran for office. A committee was formed to draw-up a permanent constitution and create an elected parliament, and the media was allowed more freedom.

GOVERNMENT

Qatar is a monarchy ruled by an emir (ruler of an Islamic country) who is chief of state. The heads of government are the prime minister and deputy prime minister, both appointed by the monarch, and both, in 2000, are brothers of the monarch. A Basic Law including a bill of rights provides for a nine-member executive Council of Ministers, appointed by the monarch, and a 35-member legislative Advisory Council. No electoral system has been instituted, and no provisions for voting have been established.

Judiciary

The legal system is based on the Shari'ah (canonical Muslim law). The Basic Law of 1970, however, provided for the creation of an independent judiciary including the Court of Appeal which has final jurisdiction in civil and criminal matters; the Higher Criminal Court which judges major criminal cases; the Lower Criminal Court; the Civil Court; and the Labor Court which judges claims involving employees and their employers. The Shari'ah Court has jurisdiction in family and criminal cases, and may also assume jurisdiction in commercial or civil cases if requested by a Muslim litigant.

DEFENSE

The Qatar security force consists of 8,500 army, 1,800 naval, and 1,500 air force personnel. Defense spending was $816 million or 8.1 percent of GDP in 1999-2000.

ECONOMIC AFFAIRS

Until recent decades, the Qatar peninsula was an impoverished area with a scant living provided by pearl diving, fishing, and nomadic herding. In 1940, oil was discovered at Dukhan, and since then it has dominated the Qatari economy. Oil revenues at the turn of the century account for more than 30 percent of GDP, approximately 80 percent of export earnings, and 66 percent of government revenues. A vast field of natural gas promises to add a new dimension to the economy accounting for over 5 percent of the world's total reserves of natural gas, third largest in the world. Production and export of natural gas became a new factor in the Qatari economy.

A temporary drop in oil prices held the GDP to an estimated 1.9 percent in 1999. Declines were predicted for at least three more years.

Public Finance

Revenues from oil and gas constitute about 90 percent of total government income. From 1986 to 1990, the government ran a deficit due to the drop in oil revenues from fallen prices. These deficits often have resulted in the procrastination of payments by the government that creates a financial difficulty for many private companies. The U.S. Central Intelligence Agency (CIA) estimated that in 1999-2000, government revenues totaled approximately $5 billion and expenditures $4 billion.

Income

In 1999, Qatar's gross domestic product (GDP) was estimated at $12.3 billion, or about $17,000 per capita. The 1999 estimated GDP growth rate was 1.5 percent and inflation was 2 percent. The estimated GDP by sector in 1996 was agriculture 1 percent, industry 49 percent, and services 50 percent.

Industry

Other than petroleum and natural gas, industry in Qatar is restricted by the small population and paucity of resources. Major industries include crude oil production and refining, fertilizers, petrochemicals, steel reinforcing bars, and cement.

Banking and Finance

The Qatar Central Bank (QCB) heads Qatar's monetary and banking system. QCB supervises all banks and money exchange companies. In 1993, QCB became independent of the Ministry of Finance and Petroleum and assumed for responsibility for ensuring all banks comply with international standards and auditing procedures. In 1999, fourteen banks operated in Qatar including seven national banks, two Arab banks, and six foreign banks. The largest bank is Qatar National Bank.

There is no stock exchange. Shares in Qatari public companies are traded through banks.

Economic Development

Qatar follows a policy of diversifying and extending its industrial and commercial activities to reduce the current dependence on oil. Infrastructure, heavy and light industry, agriculture, and fishing have all been development targets. The Industrial Development Committee encourages investment and supervises industrial growth. The government also uses surplus oil revenues on the international money market to protect the purchasing power of those revenues. Qatar is currently preparing to launch some major/minor projects worth about $7 billion: LNG plant expansion of the present fertilizer and petrochemical plants, aluminum smelter, Al-Wusail power/water desalination plant, new Doha international airport, and upgrading and expanding the offshore oil fields.

Qatar has extended economic assistance to other Arab states, to other developing nations, and to Palestinian organizations.

SOCIAL WELFARE

Public health services and education are provided free by the state through the Ministry of Labor and Social Affairs that also provides help to orphans, widows, and other Qatari nationals in need of assistance. Both law and Islamic customs closely restrict the activities of Qatari women who are largely limited to roles within the home. Non-Muslims may experience discrimination in employment and education.

Healthcare

Free public health services are extended to all residents of Qatar regardless of nationality. In 1992, there was about one doctor for every 1,000 people. In 1991-1993, 100 percent of the population had access to health care services. In 2000, life expectancy was seventy-two years.

Housing

A "popular housing" scheme provides dwellings through interest-free loans and repayment on easy terms. Qataris are required to pay only 60 percent of the cost of their houses during a period of twenty to thirty-five years. Qataris facing extreme hardship can receive a free house.

EDUCATION

In 2000, adult illiteracy stands at about 18.7 percent and continues to decline. As of 1996, there were 174 schools with 5,864 teachers and 53,631 pupils at the primary level. Secondary level schools had 4,000 teachers and 38,594 pupils. All children receive free books, meals, transport, clothing, and boarding facilities if required.

The leading higher educational institution is the University of Qatar. Enrollment in all higher-level institutions in 1997 was 8,475 pupils with 643 teaching staff.

2000 KEY EVENTS TIMELINE

January

- Qatar and Bahrain establish diplomatic ties. Their agreement to cooperate includes settling a long-standing territorial dispute over the Hawar islands, building a causeway to connect Qatar and Bahrain, and to allow direct flights by Qatar Airways between Doha and Manama.
- Permission to build the Qatar's first Christian church in over 1,000 years is granted to Roman Catholics. Although the population is predominantly Muslim, nearly 7.5 percent of Qatar's population is Christian.

July

- Qatar is making economic reforms aimed at encouraging foreign investment. The Company Law, Foreign Investment Law, and the Agencies Law are simplified along lines of changes already introduced by other members of the Gulf Co-operation Council.

August

- Yemen and Qatar sign eight agreements and protocols encouraging mutual investment, job opportunities, creation of a Supreme Council for businessmen, and in areas of health and culture.
- A firm is set up to oversee the multi-billion dollar Dolphin gas project. The Dolphin gas project aims to bring gas from Qatar's North Field to Abu Dhabi, Dubai, and Oman via an 800-km pipeline.
- The emirs of Bahrain and Qatar continue to discuss their dispute over the Hawar Islands. The territorial dispute over the potently gas- and oil-rich islands is being heard by the World Court.
- Thirty-two Indian workers stranded for nearly a year without money in Doha are repatriated by Qatar's Interior Ministry. This humanitarian gesture is funded the government.

September

- The Gulf Cooperation Council (GCC)—comprised of Qatar, Bahrain, Kuwait, Oman, Saudi Arabia, and the United Arab Emirates (UAE)—meets to study Qatar's suggestion to lift sanctions imposed on Iraq for its 1990 invasion of Kuwait.
- His Highness the Emir Sheikh Hamad bin Khalifa al-Thani visits Cuba to strengthen ties of friendship and cooperation. Qatar's trade with Cuba is limited to tobacco exports. Diplomatic relations are maintained at the ambassadorial level. Qatar is the only Gulf monarchy to do so.
- Qatar and Iraq negotiate to establish a sea link to accept Qatari ships in Iraqi ports.
- Qatar wins a Bronze Medal in the Olympics 2000 in men's heavyweight weightlifting.

November

- Qatari government shuts down its trade mission in Israel. The move is viewed as concession to pressure from Iranian and Saudi leaders and as demonstration of Islamic solidarity.
- The Islamic Conference takes place in the capital city of Doha.
- Sheikh Hamad al-Thani presents Saddam Hussein with the gift of a 747 jumbo jetliner as a show of solidarity between Qatar's royalty and the Iraqi leader, who continues to struggle against U.N. trade sanctions.

ANALYSIS OF EVENTS: 2000

BUSINESS AND THE ECONOMY

High world oil prices led to expectations of about 20 percent economic growth for Qatar in 2000. The main source of growth was the oil and gas sector, constituting 50 percent of gross domestic product (GDP). The expected growth of this sector for 2000 was 33 percent, with the value of overall exports increasing by 25 percent. Qatar's gas reserves remained the third largest in the world.

Economic reforms aimed at simplifying and clarifying Qatari laws were made to attract foreign investors. Changes proposed to the Company Law, Foreign Investment Law and Agencies Law were to be in place by the end of the year. Changes to the Foreign Investment Law permitted 100 percent ownership by foreign investors in agriculture, industry, education, tourism, and to develop natural resources. Banks, insurance companies and real estate ventures were excluded from 100 percent foreign ownership. Company Law was greatly streamlined. The Agencies Law was revised and updated. To promote privatization a new utilities body was created that would eventually replace the Power and Water Ministry.

For the first time in almost three years Qatar sought to raise money as a $500mn syndicated loan on the international money markets. Large-scale borrowing for the massive investment in the development of liquefied natural gas (LNG) and other major petrochemical projects placed a hefty burden of debt repayment a great deal of which short-term. This new loan allowed repayment to be expanded.

GOVERNMENT AND POLITICS

The Gulf Cooperation Council (GCC) consisting of Qatar, Bahrain, Kuwait, Oman, Saudi Arabia and the United Arab Emirates (UAE) condemned Iraq's obstinacy and defiance with legitimate international resolutions and the international community. The GCC further condemned Iraq's antagonistic media campaigns against Kuwait and Saudi Arabia. A call was made for total Palestinian sovereignty over East Jerusalem and Israeli obduracy in peace talks was condemned. Qatar was pressured by other Arab nations to cut its ties with Israeli. It did not do so until November after boycotts to the Islamic summit were made.

Relations between Qatar and Morocco were strained during 2000. Morocco recalled its ambassador to Qatar to protest alleged attempts to worsen the security situation in the Maghreb. Other issues between Qatar and Morocco were Qatar's refusal to support Morocco's bid to host the 2006 football world cup, and the presence in Qatar of the satellite TV channel *Al Jazira*. *Al Jazira* had broadcast a number of programs dealing with the Sahara dispute that Morocco believed were biased in favor of the Polisario Front, an organization seeking independence of the Western Sahara from Morocco. Other nations reacted negatively to these *Al Jazira* broadcasts.

CULTURE AND SOCIETY

A photography museum being built in Qatar by Sheik Saoud Al-Thani and designed by Spanish architect, Santiago Calatrava is expected open in 2003. An avid collector, Sheik Saoud Al-Thani spent over $12 million over the last year.

DIRECTORY

CENTRAL GOVERNMENT

Head of State

Amir
Hamad bin Khalifa al-Thani

Prime Minister
Abdallah bin Khalifa al-Thani

Ministers

Minister of Defense
Hamad bin Khalifa al Thani, Ministry of Defense, P.O. Box 37, Doha, Qatar
PHONE: +974 404111

Minister of the Interior
Abdallah bin Khalifa al Thani, Ministry of the Interior, P.O. Box 2433, Doha, Qatar
PHONE: +974 330000

Minister of Public Health
Hajar bin Ahmad al-Hajar, Ministry of Public Health, P.O. Box 42, Doha, Qatar
PHONE: +974 441555

Minister of Finance, Economy and Commerce
Yusif Husayh al-Kamal, Ministry of Finance, Economy and Commerce, P.O. Box 83, Doha, Qatar
PHONE: +974 461444

Minister of Justice
Hasan bin Abdallah al-Ghanim, Ministry of Justice, P.O. Box 4796, Doha, Qatar
PHONE: +974 427444

Minister of Foreign Affairs
Hamad bin Khalifa al-Thani, Ministry of Foreign Affairs, P.O. Box 250, Doha, Qatar
PHONE: +974 415000

Minister of Endowments and Islamic Affairs
Ahmad Abdallah al-Marri, Ministry of Endowments and Islamic Affairs, P.O. Box 232, Doha, Qatar
PHONE: +974 452222

Minister of Education
Muhammad Abd al-Rahim al-Kafud, Ministry of Education, P.O. Box 80, Doha, Qatar
PHONE: +974 413444

Minister of Electricity and Water
Abdallah bin Hamad al-Altiyah, Ministry of Electricity and Water, P.O. Box 41, Doha, Qatar
PHONE: +974 326622

DIPLOMATIC REPRESENTATION

Embassies in Qatar

Italy
Ali bin Abi Talib Street 41, P.O. Box 4188, Doha, Qatar
PHONE: +974 436842
FAX: +974 446466

United Kingdom
P.O. Box 3, Doha, Qatar
PHONE: +974 421991
FAX: +974 438692

JUDICIAL SYSTEM

Court of Appeal

BROADCAST MEDIA

Ministry of Information and Culture

PO Box 1836, Doha, Qatar
PHONE: +974 831447
TITLE: Minister of Information
CONTACT: Hamad Abdul Aziz Al Kawari

Qatar Broadcasting Service (QBS)

QBS, PO Box 1414, Doha, Qatar
PHONE: +974 894444
FAX: +974 822888
TITLE: Vice-Chairman for Radio and TV Corp.
CONTACT: Abdul Rahman Saif Al Madhadi
TYPE: Government

Qatar Radio Service (QBS)

PO Box 1944, Doha, Qatar
PHONE: +974 894444

Al Jazeera Satellite Channel (JSC)

PO Box 23123, Doha, Qatar
PHONE: +974 885666
FAX: +974 885333
E-MAIL: webmaster@aljazerra.net

Qatar Television Service

Minister of Information and Culture, QTV, PO Box 1944, Doha, Qatar
PHONE: +974 894444
FAX: +974 864511
TITLE: Director of TV
CONTACT: Saad Al-Rumehi

COLLEGES AND UNIVERSITIES

University of Qatar

PO Box 2713, Doha, Qatar
PHONE: + 974 832222; 892055
FAX: +974 835111
E-MAIL: postmaster@qu.edu.qa
WEBSITE: http://www.qu.edu.qa

NEWSPAPERS AND MAGAZINES

Al Arab

Al-Orouba Press & Publishing House, PO Box 3464, Doha, Qatar
PHONE: +974 325874
FAX: +974 325874
E-MAIL: advert@alarab.co.uk
WEBSITE: http://www.alarab.co.uk
TITLE: Editor
CONTACT: Khalid A. Naama
CIRCULATION: 25,000

Gulf Daily Times & Weekly Gulf Times

Gulf Publishing & Printing Organization, PO Box 533, Doha, Qatar
PHONE: +974 466555; 466621
FAX: +974 350474; 418811
E-MAIL: editor@gulf-times.com
WEBSITE: http://www.gult-times.com
TITLE: Editor
CONTACT: Abdul Rahman Saif Al Madhadi
CIRCULATION: 18,000

PUBLISHERS

Dar - Al Shark Printing, Publishing, and Distribution

PO Box 3488, Doha, Qatar
PHONE: +974 4662444
FAX: +974 4662450

Qatar National Printing Press

PO Box 355, Doha, Qatar
PHONE: +974 448451
FAX: +974 449660

University of Qatar

Documentation and Humanities Research Center, PO Box 2713, Doha, Qatar
PHONE: +974 832222
FAX: +974 835111
E-MAIL: postmast@qu.edu.qa
WEBSITE: http://www.qu.edu.qa
SUBJECTS: History, Geography, Language, Literature, Socio-economy

RELIGIOUS ORGANIZATIONS

Protestant

The Diocese of Cyprus and the Gulf
PO Box 3, Doha, Qatar
PHONE: +974 424329

E-MAIL: ianyoung@qatar.net.qa
TITLE: Archdeacon of Cyprus and the Gulf, Diocesan Director of Ordinands
NAME: Ian Young

FURTHER READING

Articles

"Addenda." *National Catholic Reporter*, January 14, 2000, p. 8.

"Bahrain and Qatar Agree to Iron Out Differences." *MEED: Middle East Economic Digest*, January 14, 2000, p. 13.

Books

Dun and Bradstreet's Guide to Qatar. Parsippany, NJ: Dun & Bradstreet, 1999.

Robison, Gordon. *Bahrain, Kuwait & Qatar.* London, Eng.: Lonely Planet, 2000.

QATAR: STATISTICAL DATA

For sources and notes see "Sources of Statistics" at the front of each volume.

GEOGRAPHY

Geography

Area:

Total: 11,437 sq km.

Land: 11,437 sq km.

Land boundaries:

Total: 60 km.

Border countries: Saudi Arabia 60 km.

Coastline: 563 km.

Climate: desert; hot, dry; humid and sultry in summer.

Terrain: mostly flat and barren desert covered with loose sand and gravel.

Natural resources: petroleum, natural gas, fish.

Land use:

Arable land: 1%

Permanent crops: 0%

Permanent pastures: 5%

Forests and woodland: 0%

Other: 94% (1993 est.).

HUMAN FACTORS

Ethnic Division

Arab 40%

Pakistani 18%

Indian 18%

Iranian 10%

Other 14%

Religion

Muslim 95%

Major Languages

Arabic (official), English commonly used as a second language.

Demographics (A)

	1990	1995	1998	2000	2010	2020	2030	2040	2050
Population	482	613	694	745	970	1,116	1,182	1,216	1,239
Life expectancy - males	67.2	68.6	69.4	69.9	72.3	74.3	75.9	77.3	78.4
Life expectancy - females	71.8	73.4	74.3	74.9	77.6	79.8	81.6	83.1	84.3
Birth rate (per 1,000)	22.9	18.0	16.7	16.1	15.5	14.4	13.0	12.8	12.4
Death rate (per 1,000)	4.1	4.0	4.1	4.2	5.2	6.8	9.1	10.7	10.7
Women of reproductive age (15-49 yrs.)	81.5	105.2	121.3	132.4	184.5	226.6	256.1	262.8	264.8
Fertility rate	4.4	3.7	3.4	3.3	2.6	2.2	2.1	2.0	2.0

Except as noted, values for vital statistics are in thousands; life expectancy is in years.

EDUCATION

Educational Attainment (A)

Age group (1986) . . . . .10+
Population of this age group 211,485
Highest level attained (%)
No schooling[2] 53.5
First level
Not completed 9.8
Completed . . . . .NA
Entered second level
Lower Secondary 10.1
Upper Secondary 13.3
Entered post-secondary .13.3

Literacy Rates (A)

In thousands and percent	1990	1995	2000	2010
Illiterate population (15+ yrs.)	80	82	81	74
Literacy rate - total adult pop. (%)	77.2	79.4	81.6	86.0
Literacy rate - males (%)	77.7	79.2	80.8	84.1
Literacy rate - females (%)	75.7	79.9	83.5	89.5

Libraries

National Libraries **1995**
Administrative Units 1
Service Points or Branches .1
Number of Volumes (000) 228
Registered Users (000) 6.5
Loans to Users (000) 12
Total Library Staff 33
Public Libraries **1995**
Administrative Units 5
Service Points or Branches 5
Number of Volumes (000) 138
Registered Users (000) .NA
Loans to Users (000) 466
Total Library Staff 42

GOVERNMENT & LAW

Political Parties

The unicameral Advisory Council or Majlis al-Shura consists of 35 seats. Members are appointed. The constitution calls for elections for part of this consultative body, but no elections have been held since 1970, when there were partial elections to the body; Council members have their terms extended every four years since. There are no political parties.

Government Budgets (B)

Revenues . . . .$5 billion
Expenditures . . . .$4 billion

Data for FY99/00 est.

Crime

Crime volume (for 1998)
Crimes reported 4,897
Total persons convicted 4,343
Crimes per 100,000 population 909
Persons responsible for offenses
Total number suspects 5,617
Total number of female suspects 337
Total number of juvenile suspects 80

(Continued on next page.)

LABOR FORCE

Total Labor Force (A)

233,000 (1993 est.).

PRODUCTION SECTOR

Energy Production

Production .6.715 billion kWh
Production by source
Fossil fuel 100%
Hydro 0%
Nuclear 0%
Other 0%
Exports . . . . .0 kWh

Data for 1998.

Energy Consumption

Consumption . . . . .6.245 billion kWh
Imports . . . . .0 kWh

Data for 1998.

Transportation

Highways:

Total: 1,230 km.

Paved: 1,107 km.

Unpaved: 123 km (1996 est.).

Pipelines: crude oil 235 km; natural gas 400 km.

Merchant marine:

Total: 24 ships (1,000 GRT or over) totaling 721,756 GRT/1,132,510 DWT.

Ships by type: cargo 10, combination ore/oil 2, container 7, petroleum tanker 5 (1999 est.).

Airports: 4 (1999 est.).

Top Agriculture Products

Fruits, vegetables; poultry, dairy products, beef; fish.

GOVERNMENT & LAW (cont.)

Military Affairs (A)

	1990	1992	1995	1996	1997
Military expenditures					
Current dollars (mil.)	NA	806	874	975	NA
1997 constant dollars (mil.)	NA	894	905	992	NA
Armed forces (000)	11	8	10	11	11
Gross national product (GNP)					
Current dollars (mil.)	7,580	7,870	7,410	9,320	10,800
1997 constant dollars (mil.)	8,880	8,720	7,680	9,470	10,800
Central government expenditures (CGE)					
1997 constant dollars (mil.)	NA	3,790[e]	3,640	3,670	4,020[e]
People (mil.)	0.5	0.5	0.6	0.6	0.7
Military expenditure as % of GNP	NA	10.2	11.8	10.5	NA
World data on military expenditure as % of GNP	4.5	3.4	2.7	2.6	2.6
Military expenditure as % of CGE	NA	23.6	24.9	27.0	NA
World data on military expenditure as % of CGE	17.0	12.5	10.5	10.3	10.2
Military expenditure per capita (1997 $)	NA	1,680	1,470	1,540	NA
World data on military expenditure per capita (1997 $)	242	173	146	143	145
Armed forces per 1,000 people (soldiers)	21.8	15.1	16.3	17.1	16.4
World data on armed forces per 1,000 people (soldiers)	5.3	4.5	4.1	3.9	3.8
GNP per capita (1997 $)	15,900	16,400	12,500	14,700	16,200
Arms imports[6]					
Current dollars (mil.)	100	1,400	50	5	625
1997 constant dollars (mil.)	117	1,552	52	5	625
Total imports[7]					
Current dollars (mil.)	1,695	2,015	3,069[e]	2,909[e]	4,373[e]
1997 constant dollars (mil.)	1,985	2,234	3,178[e]	2,958[e]	4,373[e]
Total exports[7]					
Current dollars (mil.)	3,291[e]	3,736	3,651[e]	4,448[e]	5,568[e]
1997 constant dollars (mil.)	3,854[e]	4,142	3,780[e]	4,522[e]	5,568[e]
Arms as percent of total imports[8]	5.9	69.5	1.6	0.2	14.3
Arms as percent of total exports[8]	0	0	0	0	0

MANUFACTURING SECTOR

GDP & Manufacturing Summary (B)

	1980	1985	1990	1993	1994	1995
Gross Domestic Product						
Millions of 1990 dollars	6,006	6,221	7,360	8,012	7,971	8,035
Growth rate in percent	7.10	−2.24	2.67	0.01	−0.50	0.80
Per capita (in 1990 dollars)	26,227	17,377	15,176	15,173	14,817	14,663
Manufacturing Value Added						
Millions of 1990 dollars	462	692	948	984	1,060	1,123[e]
Growth rate in percent	−12.51	2.96	4.17	0.44	7.79	5.88[e]
Manufacturing share in percent of current prices	3.3	7.8	12.7	11.0	11.2[e]	NA

COMMUNICATIONS

Daily Newspapers

	National Data	World Data for Comparison
Daily Newspapers		
Number of Dailies	5	8,391
Total Circulation (000)	90	548,000
Circulation per 1,000 inhabitants	161	96

Telecommunications

Telephones - main lines in use: 146,980 (1995).

Telephones - mobile cellular: 18,469 (1995).

Telephone system: modern system centered in Doha.

Domestic: NA

International: tropospheric scatter to Bahrain; microwave radio relay to Saudi Arabia and UAE; submarine cable to Bahrain and UAE; satellite earth stations - 2 Intelsat (1 Atlantic Ocean and 1 Indian Ocean) and 1 Arabsat.

Radio broadcast stations: AM 6, FM 5, shortwave 1 (1998).

Radios: 256,000 (1997).

Television broadcast stations: 2 (plus three repeaters) (1997).

Televisions: 230,000 (1997).

Internet Service Providers (ISPs): NA

FINANCE, ECONOMICS, & TRADE

Economic Indicators

National product: GDP—purchasing power parity—$12.3 billion (1999 est.).

National product real growth rate: 1.5% (1999 est.).

National product per capita: $17,000 (1999 est.).

Inflation rate—consumer price index: 2% (1999).

Exchange Rates

Exchange rates:

Qatari riyals (QR) per US$1 . . . . .3.6400

Fixed rate.

Top Import Origins

$4.2 billion (f.o.b., 1999 est.)

Origins (1997)

United Kingdom	25%
France	13%
Japan	10%
United States	9%
Italy	6%

Top Export Destinations

$6.7 billion (f.o.b., 1999 est.)

Destinations (1997)

Japan	50%
Singapore	12%
South Korea	9%
United States	NA
UAE	NA

Import/Export Commodities

Import Commodities	Export Commodities
Machinery and transport equipment	Petroleum products 80%
Food	Fertilizers
Chemicals	Steel

GERMANNA COMM COLLEGE LOCUST GROVE VA
3 7218 000 122 924